EDUCATIONAL POLICY
and the LAW

Fourth Edition

EDUCATIONAL POLICY
and the LAW

Fourth Edition

Mark G. Yudof
President, University of Minnesota

David L. Kirp
University of California, Berkeley

Betsy Levin
Nova Southeastern University, Shepard Broad Law Center

Rachel F. Moran
University of California, Berkeley

WEST

™

THOMSON LEARNING

Australia • Canada • Mexico • Singapore • Spain
United Kingdom • United States

WEST

★

™

THOMSON LEARNING

Education Editor: Dan Alpert
Development Editor: Tangelique Williams
Editorial Assistant: Lilah Johnson
Marketing Manager: Becky Tollerson
Project Manager, Editorial Production: Trudy Brown
Print/Media Buyer: Barbara Britton

Permissions Editor: Stephanie Keough-Hedges
Production Service: Carlisle Publishers Services
Copy Editor: Joan Lyon
Compositor: Carlisle Communications
Text and Cover Printer: R.R. Donnelley and Sons, Willard

| For more information about our products, contact us at: |
| Thomson Learning Academic Resource Center |
| 1-800-423-0563 |
| For permission to use material from this text, contact us by: |
| Phone: 1-800-730-2214 |
| Fax: 1-800-730-2215 |
| Web: http://www.thomsonrights.com |

Wadsworth Group/Thomson Learning
10 Davis Drive
Belmont, CA 94002-3098
USA

Asia
Thomson Learning
60 Albert Street, #15-01
Albert Complex
Singapore 189969

Australia
Nelson Thomson Learning
102 Dodds Street
South Melbourne, Victoria 3205
Australia

Canada
Nelson Thomson Learning
1120 Birchmount Road
Toronto, Ontario M1K 5G4
Canada

Europe/Middle East/Africa
Thomson Learning
Berkshire House
168-173 High Holborn
London WC1 V7AA
United Kingdom

Latin America
Thomson Learning
Seneca, 53
Colonia Polanco
11560 Mexico D.F.
Mexico

Spain
Paraninfo Thomson Learning
Calle/Magallanes, 25
28015 Madrid, Spain

Library of Congress Cataloging-in-Publication Data
Educational policy and the law / Mark G. Yudof ... [et al.].–4th ed.
   p. cm.
  Rev. ed of: Educational policy and the law / Mark G. Yudof, David L. Kirp, Betsy Levin. 3rd ed. c1992.
  Includes index.
  ISBN 0-534-57375-4
  1. Educational law and legislation–United States–Cases. I. Yudof, Mark G. II. Yudof, Mark G. Educational policy and the law.
KF4118.K5 2002
344.73'07–dc21

          2001046582

Contents

CHAPTER THREE:

The Disciplinary Process: The Legalization of Dispute Resolution in Public Schools 305

CHAPTER FOUR:

Equal Educational Opportunity and Race 363

CHAPTER FIVE:

Equality and Difference: The Special Challenges of Gender Equity 541

Preface

From the late eighteenth century to the present, law and the legal system have played a major role in the shaping of public education in America. Beginning in the 1860s, the law was used to justify public education, to compel attendance, and to establish a structure for its financing and governance. Toward the close of that century, the structure of state authority became more elaborate, including state superintendents, state boards of education, and standardization of textbooks and the curriculum. Most of the litigation from that period involved finance and governance issues, and existing bodies of private and public law were applied in the school setting.

After World War II, the government played an increasingly important role in administering social services, including education. With the rise of the administrative state came increased legislation and litigation regarding the allocation of authority over educational decision making. During this time, the federal government began to play a significant role in shaping educational policy. Beginning with the United States Supreme Court's declaration that state-mandated racial segregation was unconstitutional in *Brown v. Board of Education*, Congress and the federal courts embarked on efforts to ensure equal educational opportunity not only for racial and ethnic minorities but also for other groups, such as linguistic minorities, women, and students with disabilities.

This newfound activism created tensions because educational policy traditionally had been the purview of state and local governments. Congress created a number of unfunded mandates, so that state legislatures and boards of education had to struggle to pay for programs that satisfied federal requirements. Not surprisingly, state and local officials often chafed at having to implement policies that divested them of their discretion to manage the school system. In the 1980s and 1990s, national policy once again began to shift. Although the federal government today remains an active participant in school policy, state and local legislators, administrators, and judges have begun to reemerge as primary sources of school reform initiatives.

The fourth edition of *Educational Policy and the Law* retains many of the virtues of earlier editions. The new edition continues to stress the interplay of law and policy, legal decision, and educational practice. Among the issues addressed are the relationship between schooling and the state, the nature and scope of students' and teachers' substantive and procedural rights, and the many meanings of equal educational opportunity. The fourth edition also addresses governance issues, highlighting problems of federalism; the distinctive roles of political, professional, and judicial authorities; and the impact of privatization and market-oriented accountability on public schooling.

The book borrows liberally from a range of social science sources as well as from conventional legal materials to describe and analyze how policy problems become legal matters, to canvass alternative solutions, and to specify the effects of legally mandated change. *Educational Policy and the Law* should help the student of education make sense of legal decisions. It offers the law student insight into the political and policy context of legal issues. The abundant notes and references also make the book a useful reference work for lawyers or school administrators working in the field.

The first three chapters of the book take up one of the great themes of educational policy and law: the scope of liberty that students, teachers, and families have with respect to schooling. The book begins with the underlying liberty issues: Can the state compel all children to attend some school? To what extent can it regulate their education? This inquiry, which includes a discussion of alternatives to existing arrangements, identifies tensions among the interests of the state, the family, and the child in education, tensions that recur throughout the text. It also frames the background for a related set of questions, addressed in the second and third chapters. These questions explore the extent to which government can regulate the lives of students and their teachers in order to ensure that public schools serve as an instrument of socialization. In some instances, parents and community leaders want the schools to play an expanded role in reinforcing their values. For example, there are those who believe that religion should feature more prominently in public school life than it currently does. For most of the last fifty years, the Supreme Court has been sensitive to maintaining a sharp divide between religion and public schooling, but in recent years it has shown an increased willingness to accommodate some religious activities on school grounds. The fourth edition chronicles these developments in constitutional law.

In other cases, parents and community leaders ask that the schools play a restricted role in transmitting values to students. Students have pressed for protection of their rights to freedom of speech and association, privacy, and due process. In the 1960s and 1970s, the Court opened the public schools to personal constitutional rights, though limited by context, and it created new procedural protections for students facing suspension and expulsion. Beginning in the 1980s, however, the justices began to reconsider the role of school administrators in creating norms of civility. As a result, it began to accord increased discretion to teachers and principals in managing students' speech and behavior on campus.

In the next three chapters, the book turns to questions of equality and access. Chapter 4 begins by recounting the historic events that led to the demise of state-mandated racial segregation in the public schools. The discussion goes on to explore the dilemmas of implementing this momentous mandate. One particularly vexing challenge has been to untangle the effects of state action from those of private choices about where to live and send one's children to school. As the chapter shows, the federal courts have grown increasingly reluctant to order desegregation when school districts have been subject to judicial oversight for decades, and patterns of residential and school segregation nevertheless persist. As a result, advocates of racial equality have begun to assess alternative strategies, such as choice plans, for improving educational access and opportunity.

Chapters 5 and 6 deal with other groups that pushed for equal educational opportunity by drawing on the lessons of the campaign for racial equality in the schools. These include women, students who are linguistically and culturally different, students with disabilities, and poor and homeless students. For some of these groups, questions of equal opportunity are not clearly linked to patterns of segregation. Women, for instance, have challenged all-male institutions as exclusionary, but at the same time they have recognized the potential benefits of all-female schools and instructional programs. Similarly, students with disabilities have demanded mainstreaming so that they can benefit from academic and social contact with nondisabled peers. Yet, some advocates also have acknowledged the appeal of institutions and classes designed exclusively to serve the special needs of students with disabilities.

As a result, reformers have focused not only on how pupils are assigned to schools and classrooms, but also on how programs and services are delivered. These advocates have challenged traditional curricula as exclusionary and assimilationist, and they have pressed for recognition of diverse backgrounds, circumstances, and learning styles. Students who speak a language other than English have asked for some native-language instruction, and students with a distinctive cultural heritage have requested texts and materials that are sensitive to their background. Some reforms have gone beyond the instructional setting. Homeless children's advocates have asked that rules regarding enrollment be changed to reflect the fact that not all children have a home to which they return when the school day ends. Others have sought full-service schools for poor children, which would provide not only instruction but also basic needs such as food, clothing, and medical care.

The last two chapters of the book turn to questions of school finance and governance. These areas have been among the most prominent in recent efforts to reform the schools. As chapter 7 shows, school finance began as a means to equalize opportunity, but in recent years it has evolved into a way to ensure an adequate education. In some cases, state courts have tied educational adequacy to standards and accountability. As a result, financial resources have been tied explicitly to school management and efficiency. School governance has been a key source of reform initiatives in the 1980s and 1990s, developments which are reviewed in chapter 8. Federal and state policymakers have expressed great interest in testing for promotion, tracking, and graduation. Test scores have been used to allocate resources among schools and determine whether failing schools must be placed in receivership. Reorganizing school administration also has been popular. States and municipalities have experimented with vouchers, charter schools, and site-based management, among other things. Finally, cash-strapped schools have grappled with the impact of commercialization and how to set limits on advertising and merchandising on campus.

The casebook aims to offer a comprehensive picture of a complex and dynamic field. The book can be covered in its entirety in a one-semester course, meeting three hours each week, by an instructor who believes in intellectual jogging. Particular chapters or sets of chapters are rich enough for more focused courses: chapters 1 through 3, for instance, or chapters 4 through 6, or chapters 7 and 8. Instructors' views of the importance of a particular topic or its relationship to the themes being advanced in a given course also will determine how the book is used.

The format of the book deserves brief explanation. The materials have been edited to bring them within reasonable page limitations. Footnote numbers from the original source have been retained, so that readers who want to examine the original texts may easily find their way. Footnotes inserted by editors are noted by asterisks. Each major section is followed by copious notes that offer relevant supplementary information and raise questions both of law and policy.

Much has occurred in the years since 1974 when the first edition of this book appeared—the case law has grown apace, legislative initiatives have blossomed, the social science materials are substantially richer—and all these changes are reflected here. We have also, in particular instances, revised our view of earlier materials. For that reason, the text has changed in substantial ways, and we would like to acknowledge some of the people who helped facilitate that change. Mark G. Yudof extends his appreciation to the following University of Minnesota students and staff: David Zopfi-Jordan, for his prompt and professional retrieval and delivery of legal resources from the Law School Library; Abigail Crouse, Janelle Ibeling, Jennifer L. M. Jacobs, and Anne Troy for their research and editorial assistance; Dianna Gardner and Joyce Wascoe, without whose support and coordination this edition might never have appeared at all. Betsy Levin thanks the following students for their able research assistance on chapters 1, 3, 4, and 7: Matthew Lerner and Linda Naish, Nova Southeastern University; Tanya M. Jones and Neera Parikh, American University; Jennifer Golub, University of Baltimore; and Seth Adam Meinero, Howard University. Rachel F. Moran would like to thank Michelle Fang, Anni Kirkland and Joanna Stromberg for their invaluable help in gathering cases, law review articles, and social science literature for chapters 5, 6, and 8. Professor Moran also owes a huge debt of gratitude to Priscilla Battis, who assisted in the preparation and formatting of these chapters and a portion of chapter 7, as well as the copyediting of these sections. All of these individuals demonstrated the kind of keen mind, good cheer, and attention to detail that made a complex task much easier.

Table of Cases

Main cases are indicated by italicized page numbers

Q

R

EDUCATIONAL POLICY
and the LAW

Fourth Edition

Schooling and the State

I. THE "PIERCE COMPROMISE" AND ITS IMPLICATIONS FOR EDUCATION GOVERNANCE

In every state, American children are legally obliged to attend school or to receive some minimum level of instruction in the home. The first such law was enacted in Massachusetts in 1642. Over two hundred years later Massachusetts adopted the first general compulsory attendance law, requiring children between the ages of eight and fourteen to attend school for twelve weeks each year. T. van Geel, *The Courts and American Education Law* 18 (1987). Today, most children attend publicly run schools whose policies are determined by state and local officials. In many states, private schools also are governmentally regulated and home schooling is permissible in some circumstances. These facts of American schooling are familiar to most citizens. Less generally understood are such matters as how this pattern came to be; its implications for children, parents, educators, and society; the nature and scope of legitimate community and individual interests; and—most significantly for our purposes—the constitutional and statutory bases of the educational structure.

From the perspective of today, the present system of universal, compulsory education, with the overwhelming majority of school-age children attending public schools through high school, may have the appearance of inevitability. But history tells us otherwise. *See* Tyack, "Ways of Seeing: An Essay on the History of Compulsory Schooling," 46 *Harv. Educ. Rev.* 355 (1976). The "common-school cru-

sade" began in the mid-nineteenth century, before schooling was made compulsory by most states, but Americans—or at least white Americans—already "were probably in the vanguard in literacy and mass schooling among the peoples of the world." *Id.* at 359. In the period until 1890 Americans built a vast system of elementary education, one that attracted larger and larger numbers of children. *Id.* But it is important to note that while schooling was increasingly made compulsory, the compulsory education laws were hotly debated on ideological grounds and poorly enforced. *Id.* Professor Tyack describes this phase in the history of compulsory education as the "symbolic" stage, the period in which Americans embraced the necessity of compelling children to go to school. *Id.*

The second stage, beginning near the turn of the twentieth century, involved the bureaucratization of American schooling. School systems grew in size and complexity. In this stage, serious attention was paid to the types of bureaucratic structures necessary to implement universal and compulsory education. *Id.* Even in the South, which largely had resisted compulsory schooling, attitudes toward such schooling became more positive. *Id.* Beginning in the 1930s high school attendance increasingly became the norm, particularly as the effects of the labor surplus of the Great Depression were felt. *Id.* By the 1950s those who failed to complete high school were described as "drop-outs." In the latter half of the twentieth century, the emphasis came to be placed on equality of opportunity for all children and on advancement to higher education.

A third stage now appears to be emerging, involving the rejection of the bureaucratization of the schools, as reflected in the growing school choice movement. *See generally* J. E. Chubb and T. M. Moe, *Politics, Markets, and America's Schools* (1990) (noting that the failure of public schools is due to their unresponsive bureaucratic structure, a result of their direct democratic control, which is "incompatible with effective schooling"). *See also* McConnell, "Governments, Families, and Power: A Defense of Educational Choice," 31 *Conn. L. Rev.* 847, 849 (1999). Alternatives to the traditional public schools range from tuition voucher programs for private schools, to charter schools, to choice within the public school system such as magnet schools, African American male academies, or other kinds of special emphasis alternative public schools, as well as home schooling.

Within the public school system, the emphasis on equality of opportunity has appeared to decrease as dissatisfaction with court-ordered desegregation grew, and studies revealed that American students were falling behind students from other countries, especially in math and science. Instead, the emphasis is on establishing high educational standards, as indicated by the number of states that have adopted standards-based education reforms in recent years. The federal government, through the 1994 Goals 2000: Educate America Act, 20 U.S.C. §5801 *et seq.*, has encouraged the development and implementation of state standards for student learning and achievement tied to promotion and graduation.

Each of these stages was influenced by and in turn influenced the accompanying legal structure of education. *See* T. van Geel, *supra*; D. Tyack, T. James, A. Benavot, *Law and the Shaping of Public Education 1785–1954* (1987).

The impetus for the compulsory schooling movement has been a matter of much discussion and debate. As Professor Tyack has noted, the movement had varied roots:

> Over the long perspective of the last century and a half, both phases of compulsory school attendance may be seen as part of significant shifts in the functions of families and the status of children and youth. Households in American industrial cities became more like units of consumption than of production. . . . Advocates of compulsory schooling often argued that families—or at least some families, like those of the poor and foreign-born—were failing to carry out their traditional functions of moral and vocational training. . . . Much of the drive for compulsory schooling reflected an animus

against parents considered incompetent to train their children. Often combining fear of social unrest with humanitarian zeal, reformers used the powers of the state to intervene in families and to create alternative institutions of socialization.

> * * *

> . . . Most Americans during the early national period apparently felt no need to legitimize citizenship through formal state schooling, although that idea began to take hold by mid-nineteenth century. Until the end of the century there was considerable opposition to centralized state power, both in theory and practice.

Tyack, "Ways of Seeing," at 363, 368.

Tyack goes on to suggest that some religious and ethnic groups may have perceived that compulsory schooling would advance the values of their particular group and that progressive-era efforts to depoliticize education and leave schooling to experts and administrators may have played vital roles. *See generally* C. Glenn, *The Myth of the Common School* (1988). Others, writing from a Marxist perspective, have urged that compulsory education reflects a desire to maintain the dominance of the "ruling class" and to suppress alternatives to capitalism. *See, e.g.,* C. Persell, *Education and Inequality* (1977); S. Bowles and H. Gintis, *Schooling in Capitalist America* (1976); M. Carnoy (ed.), *Schooling in Corporate Society* (1972). *But see* Glenn, *supra.* And, "a powerful recurring argument for compulsion was that taxpayers could realize the full return on their large investment [in education] only if free schooling reached all the children; the presumption was that children who were out of school needed education the most and would become an economic burden to the community if left uneducated." Tyack, "Ways of Seeing," *supra* at 381–82. *See also* M. McCarthy and N. Cambron McCabe, *Public School Law* 44-5 (1988). The latter is known as the human-capital theory of education. *See* T. Schultz, *The Economic Value of Education* (1963).

The following excerpt from the work of philosopher Amy Gutmann explores the normative implications of different conceptions of education and education governance. She explains the range of theoretical choices that a society dedicated to democracy might make, and she articulates and defends her own vision of democratic education. This excerpt is followed by *Pierce v. Society of Sisters*, a landmark Supreme Court decision. *Pierce* establishes the basic constitutional framework within which the states compel and regulate schooling. The power of the state to compel attendance at a school is unquestioned, but, as the case indicates, there are limits on the authority of the state to eliminate or circumscribe educational choices. *Pierce* embodies the tensions among state, family, and child that Professor Gutmann illuminates in her essay.

"Democratic Education"

A. Gutmann, *Democratic Education*, Princeton University Press, Pages 22–26, 28–39, 41–46. Copyright © 1987 by Princeton University Press. Reprinted by permission.

We have inherited not one but several . . . normative theories, which compete for our allegiance and account for many of our social disagreements as well as our personal uncertainties concerning the purposes of education. Three of the most distinct and distinguished of these theories can be drawn from interpretations of Plato, John Locke, and John Stuart Mill. I call them . . . the theories of the *family state*, the *state of families*, and the *state of individuals*. Despite their differences, each treats questions of education (its purposes, distributions, and authorities) as part of a principled *political* theory. . . .

The Family State

Can we speak meaningfully about a good education without knowing what a just society and a virtuous person are? Socrates poses this challenge to the Sophists in the *Protagoras*. Like most of Socrates' questions, it has remained unanswered after twenty-five centuries. But it is still worth re-asking.

In his critique of the Sophists and in the *Republic*, Plato suggests that we cannot speak about a good education without knowing what justice and virtue really are, rather than what a society assumes that they are by virtue of their shared social understandings. Justice, Socrates suggests, is the concurrent realization of individual and social good. Since the good life for individuals entails contributing to the social good, there is no necessary conflict between what is good for us and what is good for our society—provided our society is just. The defining feature of the family state is that it claims exclusive educational authority as a means of establishing a harmony—one might say, a constitutive relation—between individual and social good based on knowledge. Defenders of the family state expect to create a level of like-mindedness and camaraderie among citizens that most of us expect to find only within families (and now perhaps not even there). The purpose of education in the family state is to cultivate that unity by teaching all educable children what the (sole) good life is for them and by inculcating in them a desire to pursue the good life above all inferior ones. Citizens of a well-ordered family state learn that they cannot realize their own good except by contributing to the social good, and they are also educated to desire only what is good for themselves and their society.

One need not accept Plato's view of natural human inequality to take seriously his theoretical defense of the family state. Once we discount this view, we can find in Plato the most cogent defense of the view that state authority over education is necessary for establishing a harmony between individual virtue and social justice. Unless children learn to associate their own good with the social good, a peaceful and prosperous society will be impossible. Unless the social good that they are taught is worthy of pursuit, they will grow to be unfulfilled and dissatisfied with the society that miseducated them. All states that claim less than absolute authority over the education of children will therefore degenerate out of internal disharmony.

. . . Because a family state is at best the *artificial* parent of its citizens, it must create the conditions under which citizens are bound to honor and obey it. The moral force of parental imagery in politics (as suggested by Socrates' subsequent arguments in the *Crito* concerning the freedom available to Athenian citizens) varies either with the degree to which the wisdom of a state exceeds that of its citizens or with the fit between the goods pursued by a state and those valued by its citizens. A state that lacks wisdom or that rules against the moral convictions of most citizens cannot credibly claim parental status. Not even natural parents, moreover, may properly assert an absolute right to educate their children. . . .

The Platonic family state therefore rightly rejects the relativism of the non-Platonic family state, which would ground education on the mere opinions of state authorities, as readily as it rejects the subjectivism of Sophists, which defines a good education as one that simply satisfies the preferences of students. States that assume a parental role to educate according to false opinion are no better than Sophists who assume a professorial role to teach children virtue without knowing what virtue is. Indeed, sophistical states are worse because they wield more power.

But the Platonic family state has its own problems. The most obvious one is the difficulty of determining the best constitution for any society and the correct conception of the good for any person. . . .

The more telling criticism of the family state proceeds by accepting the possibility that someone sufficiently wise and conscientious might discover the good. She would then try to convince the rest of us that she had discovered the good, not just another contestable theory of the good, and the good for us, not just the good appropriate to some other people. It's possible that a few of us—an unusually open-minded or uncommitted few—might be convinced, but most of us (as Plato realized) would not; and we would refuse to relinquish all authority over the education of our children to the philosopher-queen (or the state).

In order to create a just family state, the philosopher therefore must wipe the social slate clean by exiling "all those in the city who happen to be older than ten; and taking over their children, . . . rear them—far away from those dispositions they now have from their parents. . . ." That is an exorbitantly high price to pay for realizing a just society. Socrates himself on behalf of the philosopher recoils from the idea. . . .

This objection to the family state is not a purely practical one—pointing to the impossibility of realizing a just society in an unjust world. Even if the philosopher-queen is right in claiming that a certain kind of life is objectively good, she is wrong in assuming that the objectively good is good for those of us who are too old or too miseducated to identify the objectively good with what is good for our own lives. "That may be the best life to which people—educated from birth in the proper manner—can aspire," we might admit, "but it's not the good life for us. And don't we have a claim to living a life that is good for us?" The objectively good life, defined as the life that is best for people who are rightly educated from birth, need not be the good life, or even the closest approximation of the good life, for people who have been wrongly educated. . . .

. . . As long as we differ not just in our opinions but in our moral convictions about the good life, the state's educational role cannot be defined as realizing the good life, objectively defined, for each of its citizens. Neither can educational authorities simply claim that a good education is whatever in their opinion is best for the state.

The family state attempts to constrain our choices among ways of life and educational purposes in a way that is incompatible with our identity as parents and citizens. In its unsuccessful attempt to do so, it successfully demonstrates that we cannot ground our conception of a good education merely on personal or political preferences. Plato presents a forceful case for resting educational authority exclusively with a centralized state, a case grounded on the principle that knowledge should be translated into political power. But even the Platonic case is not sufficiently strong to override the claims of parents and citizens to share in social reproduction, claims to which I return in defending a democratic state of education.

The State of Families

States that aspire to the moral unity of families underestimate the strength and deny the legitimacy of the parental impulse to pass values on to children. Radically opposed to the family state is the state of families, which places educational authority exclusively in the hands of parents, thereby permitting parents to predispose their children, through education, to choose a way of life consistent with their familial heritage. Theorists of the state of families typically justify placing educational authority in the hands of parents on grounds either of consequences or of rights. John Locke maintained that parents are the best protectors of their children's future interests. Some Catholic theologians, following Thomas Aquinas, claim that parents have a natural right to educational authority. Many modern-day defenders of the state of families maintain both, and add another argument: if the state is committed to the freedom of individuals, then it must cede educational authority to parents whose freedom includes the right to pass their own way of life on to their children.[19] Charles Fried, for example, argues that "the right to form one's child's values, one's child's life plan and the right to lavish attention on the child are extensions of the basic right not to be interfered with

---

[19]For the former justification, see Milton Friedman, *Capitalism and Freedom* (Chicago: University of Chicago Press, 1962), pp. 85–107; and John E. Coons and Stephen Sugarman, *Education by Choice: The Case for Family Control* (Berkeley: University of California Press, 1978). For the latter, see Thomas Aquinas, *Supplement Summa Theologica un Divini Illius Magistri of His Holiness Pope Pius XI*, and the 1936 encyclical of the Catholic Church, where Aquinas is quoted as saying: "The child is naturally something of the father, . . . so by natural right the child before reaching the age of reason, is under the father's care. Hence it would be contrary to natural justice if any disposition were made concerning [the child] against the will of the parents." (Quoted in Francis Schrag, "The Right to Educate," *School Review*, vol. 79, no. 3 [May 1971]: 363.). . .

in doing these things for oneself."[20] Fried bases parental rights over children on "the facts of reproduction" and the absence of a societal right to make choices for children. Fried's denial of a societal right is based on the consequentialist judgment that parents can be relied upon to pursue the best interests of their children.

Although the appeal of the state of families is apparent upon recognizing the defects of a family state, none of these theoretical arguments justifies resting educational authority exclusively—or even primarily—in the hands of parents. It is one thing to recognize the right (and responsibility) of parents to educate their children as members of a family, quite another to claim that this right of familial education extends to a right of parents to insulate their children from exposure to ways of life or thinking that conflict with their own. The consequentialist argument is surely unconvincing: parents cannot be counted upon to equip their children with the intellectual skills necessary for rational deliberation. Some parents, such as the Old Order Amish in America, are morally committed to shielding their children from all knowledge that might lead them to doubt and all worldly influences that might weaken their religious beliefs.[21] Many other parents, less radical in their rejection of modern society, are committed to teaching their children religious and racial intolerance.

To criticize the state of families, however, it is not enough to demonstrate that the perspectives of these parents are *wrong*, for we can never realistically expect any educational authority to be infallible. The strongest argument against the state of families is that neither parents nor a centralized state have a right to exclusive authority over the education of children. Because children are members of both families and states, the educational authority of parents and of policies has to be partial to be justified. We appreciate the danger of permitting a centralized state to monopolize education largely for this reason. The similar danger of placing all authority in the hands of parents may be less widely appreciated, at least in the United States, because support for parental authority over education has been associated historically with Lockean liberalism. Because the Lockean state

cedes adult citizens the freedom to choose their own good, many liberals (like Fried) assume that it must also cede parents the freedom to educate their children without state interference.[22] To the worry that parents might abuse their authority, many liberals invoke a secular variant of Locke's response:

> God hath woven into the Principles of Human Nature such a tenderness for their Off-spring, that there is little fear that Parents should use their power with too much rigour; the excess is seldom on the severe side, the strong byass of Nature drawing the other way.[23]

Other liberals, more critical of the state of families, call Locke's premise into question by citing the prevalence of physical child abuse in this country. But one need not dispute Locke's claim about the direction and force of "Nature's byass" to conclude that parental instincts are an insufficient reason for resting educational authority exclusively in the family. The same principle that requires a state to grant adults personal and political freedom also commits it to assuring children an education that makes those freedoms both possible and meaningful in the future. A state makes choice possible by teaching its future citizens respect for opposing points of view and ways of life. It makes choice meaningful by equipping children with the intellectual skills necessary to evaluate ways of life different from that of their parents. History suggests that without state provision or regulation of education, children will be taught neither mutual respect among persons nor rational deliberation among ways of life. To save their children from future pain, especially the pain of eternal damnation, parents have historically shielded their children from diverse associations, convinced them that all other ways of life are sinful, and implicitly fostered (if not explicitly taught them) disrespect for people who are different. This spirit is inimical to the kind of liberal character that Locke argued that parents should teach their children. The end—moral freedom—that Locke recommends in his *Essay on Education* requires us to question the means— exclusive parental authority—that Locke defends in the *Second Treatise*, once we can assume (as Locke could not) the political possibility of dividing educational authority between families and the state. . . .

---

[20]Charles Fried, *Right and Wrong* (Cambridge, Mass.: Harvard University Press, 1978), p. 152.

[21]*See Wisconsin v. Yoder*, 406 U.S. 210–11.

[22]The Lockean argument, therefore, does not depend for its force, as some critics have maintained, on the claim that children are the property of their parents, a claim that Locke himself rejected.

[23]Locke, "The Second Treatise of Government," in *Two Treatises of Government*, intro. Peter Laslett (New York: Cambridge University Press, 1960), ch. 6, sec. 67, p. 355.

The state of families mistakenly conflates the welfare of children with the freedom of parents when it assumes that the welfare of children is best defined or secured by the freedom of parents. But the state of families rightly recognizes, as the family state does not, the value of parental freedom, at least to the extent that such freedom does not interfere with the interests of children in becoming mutually respectful citizens of a society that sustains family life. There is no simple solution to the tension between the freedom of parents and the welfare of children. The state may not grant parents absolute authority over their children's education in the name of individual freedom, nor may it claim exclusive educational authority in the name of communal solidarity. That there is no simple solution, however, should not deter us from searching for a better solution than that offered by either the family state or the state of families.

The State of Individuals

"It is in the case of children," John Stuart Mill argued, "that misapplied notions of liberty are a real obstacle to the fulfillment by the State of its duties. One would almost think that a man's children were supposed to be literally, and not metaphorically, a part of himself, so jealous is opinion of the smallest interference of law with his absolute and exclusive control over them. . . ."[25] Having exposed the central flaw in the state of families, Mill defended a more liberal conception of education. "All attempts by the State to bias the conclusions of its citizens on disputed subjects are evil," Mill argued. Some contemporary liberals extend the logic of Mill's argument to defend what I call a state of individuals. They criticize all educational authorities that threaten to bias the choices of children toward some disputed or controversial ways of life and away from others. Their ideal educational authority is one that maximizes future choice without prejudicing children towards any controversial conception of the good life. The state of individuals thus responds to the weakness of both the family state and the state of families by championing the dual goals of *opportunity* for choice and *neutrality* among conceptions of the good life. A just educational authority must not bias children's choices among good lives, but it must provide every child with an opportunity to choose freely and rationally among the widest range of lives.

If neutrality is what we value, then a child must be protected from all—or at least all controversial—social prejudices. Neither parents nor states are capable of fulfilling this educational ideal. Parents are unlikely (and unwilling) to resist a strong human impulse: the desire to pass some of their particular prejudices on to their children. And even the most liberal states are bound to subvert the neutrality principle: they will try, quite understandably, to teach children to appreciate the basic (but disputed) values and the dominant (but controversial) cultural prejudices that hold their society together.

* * *

Contemporary liberal theorists often invoke the spirit of Bentham, Kant, or Mill to defend the ideal of neutrality, overlooking both its moral limitations and the substantial qualifications that each of these theorists placed on the ideal. All sophisticated liberals recognize the practical limitation of neutrality as an educational ideal: it is, in its fullest form, unrealizable. But most fail to appreciate the value of our resistance to the ideal of unprejudiced individual freedom: the value of our desire to cultivate, and allow communities to cultivate, only a select range of choice for children, to prune and weed their desires and aspirations so they are likely to choose a worthy life and sustain a flourishing society when they mature and are free to choose for themselves. . . .

[According to Professor Bruce Ackerman,] to have a rational sense of what we want to become, we need to know who we are; otherwise our choices will be endless and meaningless. We learn to speak English rather than Urdu, not by choice, but by cultural determination. And this cultural determination limits the range of our future choices, even if it does not uniquely determine who we become. Ackerman identifies this prior determination with the need for "cultural coherence," which he uses to justify the family and its nonneutral education. The need for cultural coherence, Ackerman argues, does not justify "adult pretensions to moral superiority." Neither parents nor the state may shape the character of children on the grounds that they can distinguish between better and worse moral character, yet they may shape children's character for the sake of cultural coherence, or in order to maximize their future freedom of choice.

Why, one might ask, should parents and states be free to shape children's character and guide their

---

[25]Mill, *On Liberty*, ch. 5, para. 12.

choices for the sake of cultural coherence but not for the sake of their leading morally good lives? Sometimes the claim that we know better than children the difference between morally good and bad lives is not a pretension to moral superiority, but a reflection of our greater moral maturity. Why, then, should adults resist shaping children's character and guiding their choices on *moral* grounds?

The resistance of many contemporary liberals to one of our strongest moral impulses stems, I suspect, from formulating educational purposes and their justifications as a dichotomous choice.[34] Either we must educate children so that they are free to choose among the widest range of lives (given the constraints of cultural coherence) because freedom of choice is the paramount good, or we must educate children so that they will choose *the* life that we believe is best because leading a virtuous life is the paramount good. Let children define their own identity or define it for them. Give children liberty or give them virtue. Neither alternative is acceptable: we legitimately value education not just for the liberty but also for the virtue that it bestows on children; and the virtue that we value includes the ability to deliberate among competing conceptions of the good.

* * *

Because the educational ideal of free choice commands no *special* political legitimacy, the state of individuals poses the same problem as the family state. Even if liberals could establish that, of all disputed aims of education, neutrality is singularly right, they would still have to establish why being right is a necessary or sufficient condition for ruling. The same argument that holds against the family state holds against the state of individuals: being right is not a necessary or sufficient condition because parents and citizens have a legitimate interest (independent of their "rightness") in passing some of their most salient values on to their children.

* * *

Our task therefore is to find a more inclusive ground for justifying nonneutrality in education. We disagree over the relative value of freedom and virtue, the nature of the good life, and the elements of moral character. But our desire to search for a more inclusive ground presupposes a common commitment that is, broadly speaking, political. We are committed to collectively re-creating the society that we share. Al-

though we are not collectively committed to any particular set of educational aims, we are committed to arriving at an agreement on our educational aims (an agreement that could take the form of justifying a diverse set of educational aims and authorities). The substance of this core commitment is conscious social reproduction. As citizens, we aspire to a set of educational practices and authorities of which the following can be said: these are the practices and authorities to which we, acting collectively as a society, have consciously agreed. It follows that a society that supports conscious social reproduction must educate all educable children to be capable of participating in collectively shaping their society.

* * *

A Democratic State of Education

Cultivating character is a legitimate — indeed, an inevitable — function of education. And there are many kinds of moral character — each consistent with conscious social reproduction — that a democratic state may legitimately cultivate. Who should decide what kind of character to cultivate? I have examined and rejected three popular and philosophically forceful answers to this question. . . .

If my criticisms are correct, then these three theories are wrong. None provides an adequate foundation for educational authority. Yet each contains a partial truth. States, parents, and professional educators all have important roles to play in cultivating moral character. A democratic state of education recognizes that educational authority must be shared among parents, citizens, and professional educators even though such sharing does not guarantee that power will be wedded to knowledge, that parents can successfully pass their prejudices on to their children, or that education will be neutral among competing conceptions of the good life.

If a democratic state of education does not guarantee virtue based on knowledge, or the autonomy of families, or neutrality among ways of life, what is the value of its premise of shared educational authority? The broad distribution of educational authority among citizens, parents, and professional educators supports the core value of democracy: conscious social reproduction in its most inclusive

---

[34]The tendency to dichotomize our moral choices is not unique to advocates of liberal neutrality. What I call the "tyranny of dualisms" is also common to communitarian critics of liberalism. See my "Communitarian Critics of Liberalism," *Philosophy and Public Affairs*, vol.14, no. 5 (Summer 1985): 316–20.

form. Unlike a family state, a democratic state recognizes the value of parental education in perpetuating particular conceptions of the good life. Unlike a state of families, a democratic state recognizes the value of professional authority in enabling children to appreciate and to evaluate ways of life other than those favored by their families. Unlike a state of individuals, a democratic state recognizes the value of political education in predisposing children to accept those ways of life that are consistent with sharing the rights and responsibilities of citizenship in a democratic society. A democratic state is therefore committed to allocating educational authority in such a way as to provide its members with an education adequate to participating in democratic politics, to choosing among (a limited range of) good lives, and to sharing in the several subcommunities, such as families, that impart identity to the lives of its citizens.

A democratic state of education constrains choice among good lives not only out of necessity but out of a concern for civic virtue. Democratic states can acknowledge two reasons for permitting communities to use education to predispose children toward some ways of life and away from others. One reason is grounded on the value of moral freedom, a value not uniquely associated with democracy. All societies of self-reflective beings must admit the moral value of enabling their members to discern the difference between good and bad ways of life. Children do not learn to discern this difference on the basis of an education that strives for neutrality among ways of life. Children are not taught that bigotry is bad, for example, by offering it as one among many competing conceptions of the good life, and then subjecting it to criticism on grounds that bigots do not admit that other people's conceptions of the good are "equally" good. Children first become the kind of people who are repelled by bigotry, and then they feel the force of the reasons for their repulsion.

* * *

The second, more specifically democratic, reason for supporting the nonneutral education of states and families is that the good of children includes not just freedom of choice, but also identification with and participation in the good of their family and the politics of their society. The need for cultural coherence does not fully capture this democratic value, because it would not be enough for a centralized state to choose a set of parents and a coherent cultural orientation at random for children. People,

quite naturally, value the specific cultural and political orientations of their society and family more than those of others, even if they cannot provide objective reasons for their preferences. The fact that these cultural orientations are theirs is an adequate (and generalizable) reason. Just as we love our (biological or adopted) children more than those of our friends because they are a part of *our* family, so we differentially value the cultural orientations of our country because it is *ours*. We need not claim moral superiority (or ownership) to say any of this. We need claim only that some ways of life are better than others *for us and our children* because these orientations impart meaning to and enrich the internal life of family and society. To focus exclusively on the value of freedom, or even on the value of moral freedom, neglects the value that parents and citizens may legitimately place on *partially* prejudicing the choices of children by their familial and political heritages.

[A] democratic state must aid children in developing the capacity to understand and to evaluate competing conceptions of the good life and the good society. The value of critical deliberation among good lives and good societies would be neglected by a society that inculcated in children uncritical acceptance of any particular way or ways of (personal and political) life. . . .

To integrate the value of critical deliberation among good lives, we must defend some principled limits on political and parental authority over education, limits that in practice require parents and states to cede some educational authority to professional educators.

One limit is that of *nonrepression*. The principle of nonrepression prevents the state, and any group within it, from using education to restrict rational deliberation of competing conceptions of the good life and the good society. Nonrepression is not a principle of negative freedom. It secures freedom from interference only to the extent that it forbids using education to restrict *rational* deliberation or consideration of different ways of life. Nonrepression is therefore compatible with the use of education to inculcate those character traits, such as honesty, religious toleration, and mutual respect for persons, that serve as foundations for rational deliberation of differing ways of life. . . .

A second principled limit on legitimate democratic authority, which also follows from the primary value of democratic education, is *nondiscrimination*. For democratic education to support conscious *so-*

cial reproduction, all educable children must be educated. Nondiscrimination extends the logic of nonrepression, since states and families can be selectively repressive by excluding entire groups of children from schooling or by denying them an education conducive to deliberation among conceptions of the good life and the good society. . . .

Nondiscrimination can thus be viewed as the distributional complement to nonrepression. In its most general application to education, nondiscrimination prevents the state, and all groups within it, from denying anyone an educational good on grounds irrelevant to the legitimate social purpose of that good. Applied to those forms of education necessary to prepare children for future citizenship (participation in conscious social reproduction), the nondiscrimination principle becomes a principle of nonexclusion. No educable child may be excluded from an education adequate to participating in the political processes that structure choice among good lives.

Why is a theory that accepts these two principled constraints on popular (and parental) sovereignty properly considered democratic?. . .

The principles of nonrepression and nondiscrimination simultaneously support deliberative freedom and communal self-determination. The form of educational relativism acceptable under these principles is therefore democratic in a significant sense: all citizens must be educated so as to have a chance to share in self-consciously shaping the structure of their society. . . .

NOTES AND QUESTIONS

1. State of Families

What is the strongest argument against a "state of families," giving parents full control of the education of their children? May the liberties of parents and children conflict? Professor Peter Shane, for example, has urged that parental choices may "destroy our confidence in the ability of the children as adults to express their genuine preferences without unfair distortion." Shane, "Compulsory Education and the Tension Between Liberty and Equality: A Comment on Dworkin," 73 *Iowa L. Rev.* 97, 103 (1987). What is required to ensure that children are equipped "with the intellectual skills necessary to evaluate ways of life different from that of their parents"? *But see* Gilles, "On Educating Children: A Parentalist Manifesto," 63 *Univ. Chi. L. Rev.* 937 (1996).

2. Cultivating Democratic Character

Professor Gutmann argues against the propositions that the individual choices of children should be determinative in education and that the state should be "neutral" in this process. What are the bases of her objections? Do such rights for children create conflict and adversarial relations between children and adults where there otherwise would be community and shared interest? *See* Minow, "Interpreting Rights: An Essay for Robert Cover," 96 *Yale L.J.* 1860, 1870 (1987). What does Gutmann mean when she says that "we are committed to collectively re-creating the society that we share"? If "neutrality" is not desirable or feasible, on what basis may the state "use education to predispose children toward some ways of life and away from others"? *See* Raz, "Liberalism, Skepticism, and Democracy," 74 *Iowa L. Rev.* 761, 779–86 (1989). Who should define "the difference between good and bad ways of life"?

Is democratic education inherently totalitarian? *See generally* S. Arons, *Compelling Belief* 197 (1983) (Public schooling "not only deprives substantial numbers of families of the ability to participate in culture and public life, it threatens to end the process of growth altogether and to replace it with what Jung called 'the spiritual and moral darkness of state Absolutism.' ").

If "a democratic state must aid children in developing the capacity to understand and to evaluate competing conceptions of the good life and the good society," why must the state choose to embrace nonrepression and nondiscrimination? How does one distinguish between "critical deliberation" and "conscious social reproduction"? Do nonrepression and nondiscrimination flow from "conscious social reproduction" or from democratic principles?

John Dewey spoke of "education as reconstruction" as reflecting an "ideal of growth" involving a process of the "constant reorganizing or reconstructing of experience." J. Dewey, *Democracy and Education* 76 (1966). Is this what Gutmann means by "critical deliberation"?

3. Families and Equality

Are the aspirations of family empowerment, parental liberty, and equality in education consistent with each other? Consider these remarks by Professor James S. Fishkin:

Suppose you were to attempt to equalize life chances while maintaining the system of meritocratic assignment. Given background conditions of inequality, it is the autonomy of families that protects the process by which advantaged families differentially affect the development of talents and other qualifications in their children. Only if this process were interfered with could both the principles of merit and of equal life chances be achieved. In other words, if equality of life chances is to be achieved, through processes consistent with the principle of merit, then conditions for the development of talents and other qualifications must be equalized. Given background conditions of inequality, this can be done only through some mechanism that systematically insulates the development of each new generation from the unequal results achieved by the last. Coercive interferences with the family would be required if advantaged parents were to be prevented, systematically, from passing on cognitive, affective, cultural, and social advantages to their children. Perhaps a massive system of collectivized child-rearing could be devised to achieve such a result. Anything short of such a large-scale alternative to the autonomous nuclear family would probably provide only an imperfect barrier between the inequalities of the parental generation and the developmental processes affecting its children.

From the communal child-rearing in Plato's *Republic* to the test tube nurseries in Huxley's *Brave New World*, the replacement of the family with some alternative strategy of child-rearing has been the centerpiece of any social engineering that required complete manipulation of human development. As long as the private sphere of liberty is in place, crucial developmental factors are entrusted to the autonomous decisions of families and are, by that very fact, insulated from social control. Whether the efforts at social engineering are aimed at equalization or hierarchy, the family constitutes a crucial barrier to the manipulability of the causal factors affecting human development.

. . . The only strategies of intervention that might offer a hope of the required massive effects would amount to such a wholesale change in the child's environment that their obviously prohibitive expense would violate any realistic construction of the budget constraint. Hence, leveling up strategies of intervention—that leave the private sphere intact—are either prohibitive in expense or insufficient in effect. On the other hand, by making many of the children affected worse-off (those who would have been advantaged without the equalization efforts), leveling down strategies clearly violate the autonomy of families if those provisions are to be universally enforced.

J. S. Fishkin, *Justice, Equal Opportunity, and the Family* 64–66 (1983). *See generally* Becker & Murphy, "The Family and the State," 31 *J. of Law & Econ.* 1 (1988); Shane, *supra* at 104.

Pierce v. Society of Sisters
268 U.S. 510, 45 S.Ct. 571, 69 L.Ed. 1070 (1925).

Mr. Justice McReynolds delivered the opinion of the Court.

These appeals are from decrees, based upon undenied allegations, which granted preliminary orders restraining appellants from threatening or attempting to enforce the Compulsory Education Act (Ore. Gen. Laws, ch. 1, p. 9 (1923))[1] adopted November 7, 1922, under the initiative provision of her Constitution by the voters of Oregon. Judicial Code §266 (Comp. St. § 1243). . . .

---

[1] *Be it enacted by the people of the state of Oregon:*

Section 1. That section 5259, Oregon Laws, be and the same is hereby amended so as to read as follows:

Section 5259. Children Between the Ages of Eight and Sixteen Years. Any parent, guardian or other person in the State of Oregon, having control or charge or custody of a child under the age of sixteen years and of the age of eight years or over at the commencement of a term of public school of the district in which said child resides, who shall fail or neglect or refuse to send such child to a public school for the period of time a public school shall be held during the current year in said district, shall be guilty of a misdemeanor and each day's failure to send such child to a public school shall constitute a separate offense; provided, that in the following cases, children shall not be required to attend public schools:

(a) *Children Physically Unable.* Any child who is abnormal, subnormal, or physically unable to attend school.

(b) *Children Who Have Completed the Eighth Grade.* Any child who has completed the eighth grade, in accordance with the provisions of the state course of study.

(c) *Distance from School.* Children between the ages of eight and ten years, inclusive, whose place of residence is more than one and one-half miles, and children over ten years of age whose place of residence is more than three miles, by the nearest traveled road, from a public school; provided, however, that if transportation to and from school is furnished by the school district, this exemption shall not apply.

(d) *Private Instruction.* Any child who is being taught for a like period of time by the parent or private teacher such subjects as are usually taught in the first eight years in the public school; but before such child can be taught by a parent or a private teacher, such parent or private teacher must receive written permission from the county superintendent, and such permission shall not extend longer than the end of the current school year. Such child must report to the county school superintendent or some person designated by him at least once every three months and take an examination in the work covered. If, after such examination, the county superintendent shall determine that such child is not being properly taught then the county superintendent shall order the parent, guardian or other person, to send such child to the public school the remainder of the school year.

If any parent, guardian, or other person having control or charge or custody of any child between the ages of eight and sixteen years, shall fail to comply with any provision of this section, he shall be guilty of a misdemeanor, and shall, on conviction thereof, be subject to a fine of not less than $5, nor more than $100, or to imprisonment in the county jail not less than two nor more than thirty days, or by both such fine and imprisonment in the discretion of the court.

This Act shall take effect and be and remain in force from and after the first day of September, 1926.

The challenged Act, effective September 1, 1926, requires every parent, guardian, or other person having control or charge or custody of a child between eight and sixteen years to send him "to a public school for the period of time a public school shall be held during the current year" in the district where the child resides; and failure to do so is declared a misdemeanor. . . . The manifest purpose is to compel general attendance at public schools by normal children, between eight and sixteen, who have not completed the eighth grade. And without doubt enforcement of the statute would seriously impair, perhaps destroy, the profitable features of appellees' business and greatly diminish the value of their property.

Appellee, the Society of Sisters, is an Oregon corporation, organized in 1880, with power to care for orphans, educate and instruct the youth, establish and maintain academies or schools, and acquire necessary real and personal property. It has long devoted its property and effort to the secular and religious education and care of children, and has acquired the valuable goodwill of many parents and guardians. It conducts interdependent primary and high schools and junior colleges, and maintains orphanages for the custody and control of children between eight and sixteen. In its primary schools many children between those ages are taught the subjects usually pursued in Oregon public schools during the first eight years. Systematic religious instruction and moral training according to the tenets of the Roman Catholic Church are also regularly provided. All courses of study, both temporal and religious, contemplate continuity of training under appellee's charge; the primary schools are essential to the system and the most profitable. It owns valuable buildings, especially constructed and equipped for school purposes. The business is remunerative—the annual income from primary schools exceeds $30,000—and the successful conduct of this requires long-time contracts with teachers and parents. The Compulsory Education Act of 1922 has already caused the withdrawal from its schools of children who would otherwise continue, and their income has steadily declined. The appellants, public officers, have proclaimed their purpose strictly to enforce the statute.

After setting out the above facts, the Society's bill alleges that the enactment conflicts with the right of parents to choose schools where their children will receive appropriate mental and religious training, the right of the child to influence the parents' choice of a school, the right of schools and teachers therein to engage in a useful business or profession, and is accordingly repugnant to the Constitution and void. And, further, that unless enforcement of the measure is enjoined the corporation's business and property will suffer irreparable injury.

Appellee, Hill Military Academy, is a private corporation organized in 1908 under the laws of Oregon, engaged in owning, operating, and conducting for profit an elementary, college preparatory, and military training school for boys between the ages of five and twenty-one years. . . . It owns considerable real and personal property, some useful only for school purposes. The business and incident good will are very valuable. In order to conduct its affairs, long time contracts must be made for supplies, equipment, teachers, and pupils. Appellants, law officers of the State and County, have publicly announced that the act of November 7, 1922, is valid and have declared their intention to enforce it. By reason of the statute and threat of enforcement appellee's business is being destroyed and its property depreciated; parents and guardians are refusing to make contracts for the future instruction of their sons, and some are being withdrawn.

The Academy's bill states the foregoing facts and then alleges that the challenged Act contravenes the corporation's rights guaranteed by the Fourteenth Amendment and that unless appellants are restrained from proclaiming its validity and threatening to enforce it irreparable injury will result. The prayer is for an appropriate injunction.

No answer was interposed in either cause, and after proper notices they were heard by three judges (Judicial Code §266 [Comp. St. §1243]) on motions for preliminary injunctions upon the specifically alleged facts. The court ruled that the Fourteenth Amendment guaranteed appellees against the deprivation of their property without due process of law consequent upon the unlawful interference by appellants with the free choice of patrons, present and prospective. It declared the right to conduct schools was property and that parents and guardians, as a part of their liberty, might direct the education of children by selecting reputable teachers and places. Also, that these schools were not unfit or harmful to the public, and that enforcement of the challenged statute would unlawfully deprive them of patronage and thereby destroy their owners' business and property. Finally, that the threats to enforce the Act would continue to cause irreparable injury; and the suits were not premature.

No question is raised concerning the power of the State reasonably to regulate all schools, to inspect, supervise and examine them, their teachers and pupils; to require that all children of proper age attend some school, that teachers shall be of good moral character and patriotic disposition, that certain studies plainly essential to good citizenship must be taught, and that nothing be taught which is manifestly inimical to the public welfare.

The inevitable practical result of enforcing the Act under consideration would be destruction of appellees' primary schools, and perhaps all other private primary schools for normal children within the State of Oregon. These parties are engaged in a kind of undertaking not inherently harmful, but long regarded as useful and meritorious. Certainly there is nothing in the present records to indicate that they have failed to discharge their obligations to patrons, students, or the State. And there are no peculiar circumstances or present emergencies which demand extraordinary measures relative to primary education. . . .

[W]e think it entirely plain that the Act of 1922 unreasonably interferes with the liberty of parents and guardians to direct the upbringing and education of children under their control. As often heretofore pointed out, rights guaranteed by the Constitution may not be abridged by legislation which has no reasonable relation to some purpose within the competency of the State. The fundamental theory of liberty upon which all governments in this Union repose excludes any general power of the State to standardize its children by forcing them to accept instruction from public teachers only. The child is not the mere creature of the State; those who nurture him and direct his destiny have the right, coupled with the high duty, to recognize and prepare him for additional obligations.

Appellees are corporations, and therefore, it is said, they cannot claim for themselves the liberty which the Fourteenth Amendment guarantees. Accepted in the proper sense, this is true. . . . But they have business and property for which they claim protection. These are threatened with destruction through the unwarranted compulsion which appellants are exercising over present and prospective patrons of their schools. And this court has gone very far to protect against loss threatened by such action. . . .

The courts of the State have not construed the Act, and we must determine its meaning for ourselves. Evidently it was expected to have general application and cannot be construed as though merely intended to amend the charters of certain private corporations, as in *Berea College v. Kentucky*, 211 U.S. 45. No argument in favor of such view has been advanced.

Generally, it is entirely true, as urged by counsel, that no person in any business has such an interest in possible customers as to enable him to restrain exercise of proper power of the State upon the ground that he will be deprived of patronage. But the injunctions here sought are not against the exercise of any proper power. Plaintiffs asked protection against arbitrary, unreasonable, and unlawful interference with their patrons and the consequent destruction of their business and property. Their interest is clear and immediate, within the rule approved in *Truax v. Raich* [239 U.S. 33 (1915)], *Truax v. Corrigan* [257 U.S. 312 (1921)], and *Terrace v. Thompson* [263 U.S. 197 (1923)], and many other cases where injunctions have issued to protect business enterprises against interference with the freedom of patrons or customers. . . .

The suits were not premature. The injury to appellees was present and very real, not a mere possibility in the remote future. If no relief had been possible prior to the effective date of the Act, the injury would have become irreparable. Prevention of impending injury by unlawful action is a well-recognized function of courts of equity.

The decrees below are

Affirmed.

NOTES AND QUESTIONS

1. Historical Background

The requirement that Oregon's children attend public schools was unique among the American states. It had been adopted after a referendum campaign organized and promoted primarily by the Ku Klux Klan and the Oregon Scottish Rite Masons as part of a strategy to "Americanize" the schools: If the campaign was successful, a dozen other states were next in line. Bans on the teaching of Darwinism and foreign languages and requirement of teacher loyalty oaths and inoffensive textbooks were all part of a large assault on pluralism in education and society. As one Klansman noted: "Somehow these mongrel hordes must be Americanized; failing that, deportation is the only remedy." Oregon's public school teachers also supported the bill, apparently fearing that its rejection would be taken as a rejection of public schooling. Parochial schools were the most numerous private schools in the state, and anti-Catholicism—"religious revenge," as the Portland

Telegram put it—helped sway voters' minds. The bill's opponents—among them churchmen who denied that "sectarianism" was "unpatriotic," businessmen fearing increased school taxes, minority groups and civil rights organizations concerned about constitutional and religious liberties—objected to state monopoly over education. But the referendum narrowly carried, splitting political party lines; one Oregon newspaper editor commented that "politics has simply gone mad." How might that background have influenced the *Pierce* decision? For a more extended discussion of the Oregon experience, see Tyack, "The Perils of Pluralism: The Background of the *Pierce Case*," 74 *Amer. Hist. Rev.* 74 (1968). *See also* Carter, "Parents, Religion, and Schools: Reflections on *Pierce*, 70 Years Later," 27 *Seton Hall L. Rev.* 1194, 1196–1202 (1997).

The requirement that children attend some school, public or private, was not new. The common school—locally run and financed and open without tuition to all children—had been energetically and successfully promoted by reformers such as Massachusetts' Horace Mann since the early nineteenth century. *See* C. Glenn, *The Myth of the Common School* (1988). In the view of some school officials, the taxation of property for the support of schools created a "reciprocal obligation" on the part of the state to ensure that all enjoyed the benefits of education. But the uneducated and unassimilated immigrant proletariat resisted this new venture; they badly needed the income their children's labor secured. As the Pennsylvania Board of State Charities saw the issue: "It is precisely those children whose parents or guardians are unable or indisposed to provide them with an education . . . for whom the state is most interested to provide and secure it." Education was simply too important, in the eyes of its promoters, to be left to the caprice of parental choice; it was a good imposed on the benighted by the more "enlightened" members of the community. As historian Michael Katz notes:

> If everyone was taxed for school support, if this was justified by the necessity of schooling for the preservation of urban social order, if the beneficial impact of schooling required the regular and prolonged attendance of all children, and finally, if persuasion and a variety of experiments had failed to bring all the children to school—then, clearly, education had to be compulsory.

M. Katz, *Class, Bureaucracy, and Schools* 48 (1971).

Massachusetts passed the first compulsory education law in 1852, requiring that all children between the ages of eight and fourteen attend school for at least twelve weeks a year, twenty-eight states passed similar legislation in the years following the Civil War. But compulsory education, although legally required, did not immediately become social fact. The resistance of some educators affords one explanation of this phenomenon. In Auburn, New York, School Superintendent B. B. Snow voiced a common sentiment: "The compulsory attendance of the element attempted to be reached by law would be detrimental to the well-being of any respectable school." In many school systems, there was insufficient space to accommodate this class of youngsters: In Illinois, for instance, school buildings could house only one-third of all eligible schoolchildren, while in New York City the average elementary school class enrolled seventy-five pupils. The insatiable demand for cheap labor continued to be satisfied by the hiring of school-age youngsters, and officials—many of whom believed that the education of workers' children was a waste of time—often ignored these violations of the law. An 1884 report drafted by Charles Peck, New York commissioner of statistics of labor, pronounced the compulsory education statute a "dead letter." In the South, compulsory attendance laws were not enforced until well into the twentieth century, and the educational needs of black children were given lowest priority. *See* Walters and James, "Schooling for Some: Child Labor and School Enrollment of Black and White Children in the Early Twentieth-Century South," 57 *Am. Soc. Rev.* 635 (1992).

By the end of the nineteenth century, however, the principle of compulsory schooling was generally accepted, and by the time of the *Pierce* decision, almost every child had at least an elementary education. *See generally* D. Tyack, T. James, and A. Benavot, *Law and the Shaping of Public Education, 1785–1954* (1987). State courts routinely upheld compulsory education laws. *See, e.g., State v. Hoyt*, 84 N.H. 38, 146 A. 170 (1929); *State v. Bailey*, 157 Ind. 324, 61 N.E. 730 (1901). *See also Concerned Citizens for Neighborhood Schools v. Board of Educ.*, 379 F.Supp. 1233 (E.D. Tenn. 1974). For compilations of compulsory attendance laws, *see* "Compulsory Education," in *National Survey of State Laws* 187 (R. Leiter, ed. 1997); L. Kotin and W. Aikman, *Legal Foundations of Compulsory School Attendance* (1980). No thorough history of compulsory schooling in America has been written; for discussion of the phenomenon, see E. Cubberley, *Changing Conceptions of Education* (1909); F. Ensign, *Compulsory School Attendance and Child Labor* (1921); M. S. Katz, *A History of Compulsory Education Laws* (1976); Kotin and Aikman, *supra*; D. Tyack, *The One Best System* (1974); D. Tyack, T. James, and A. Benavot, *supra*; Burgess, "The Goddess, the School Book, and Compulsion," 46 *Harv. Educ. Rev.* 199 (1976); Sugarman and Kirp, "Rethinking Collective Responsibility for Education," 39 *Law & Contemp. Probs.* 144 (1975); Tyack, "Ways of Seeing: An Essay on the History of Compulsory Schooling," 46 *Harv. Educ. Rev.* 355 (1976).

2. *The Constitutional Standard: Family versus State?*

The *Pierce* Court could conceivably have adopted any of three standards. It could have upheld the right of the state to compel public school attendance, or it could have struck down compulsory attendance laws (an issue which was not, however, raised in the litigation), giving complete control of the child's education to the family. The formula it adopted—the third possible choice—was a compromise between these two positions: the state may compel attendance at some school, but it is the parents' right to choose between public and private schools. That result required the Court to balance the claims made by competing interests—the state, the family (speaking, at least nominally, for the child), and the private schools. Is the balance drawn correctly? Does *Pierce* embody the view of democratic education espoused by Professor Gutmann, *supra?*

From this perspective, reread the statute challenged in the *Pierce* case (reprinted in footnote 1, *supra*). Note that the county superintendent must approve of private instruction. Approval is dependent upon the county superintendent determining whether the child is being "properly taught." Given the vagaries of the standard and perhaps the self-interest of the public school officials in promoting public education, might *Pierce* be explained on the basis that the Court feared the result of such a vague delegation of authority (from the legislature) to the officials responsible for overseeing private education? Is it that state legislatures and not state administrative officials should strike the proper balance between family and state in education matters? *Cf.* Linde, "Due Process of Lawmaking," 55 *Neb. L. Rev.* 197 (1976); Tribe, "The Emerging Reconnection of Individual Rights and Institutional Design: Federalism, Bureaucracy, and Due Process of Lawmaking," 10 *Creighton L. Rev.* 433 (1977). In this respect, note that a number of state courts, reviewing statutes under state constitutions, have declared such delegations unconstitutional where the standards for regulating private schools are ambiguous and lodge what

is primarily legislative authority in state educational agencies. *See, e.g., State v. Williams*, 253 N.C. 337, 117 S.E.2d 444 (1960).

Does the actual wording of the statute before the Court in *Pierce* suggest that the Court decided an issue not properly presented to it? Why might the Court have avoided the vagueness and delegation issues? Under what constitutional provision may federal courts police the separation of powers at the state level? Or is it that the Court assumed that the discretion given county superintendents in the statute was simply a facade for abolishing private education? How could the Court know this a year before the effective date of the Act? Might the Court be acting in response to the clear anti-Catholic motivation behind the enactment of the Act?

3. *Option 1: State Monopoly over Education*

What argument might the state make to justify compulsory public schooling? *See generally* Sugarman and Kirp, *supra*; Gutmann, *supra*. For example, might the state claim that all children should be treated equally and thus receive the same education? Might the argument be made that the state has an obligation to instill certain common values, such as love of country and responsibilities of the citizen, and that this function can be performed most successfully through universal public education? *See generally* R. Weissberg, *Political Learning, Political Choice, and Democratic Citizenship* (1974). How are such assertions to be treated by a court? Are they "arbitrary, unreasonable"—the language used in *Pierce?* Consider these remarks by Professor Joseph Tussman:

> The natural right of self-preservation lies behind not only the traditionally asserted powers of war or defense, but also the universally claimed right of the community to shape its children. More fundamental and inalienable than even the war power stands the tutelary power of the state, . . . the teaching power.
>
> The *teaching power* is the inherent constitutional authority of the state to establish and direct the teaching activity and institutions needed to ensure its continuity and further its legitimate, general and special purposes. . . . The teaching power is a peer to the legislative, the executive, and the judicial powers, if it is not, indeed, the first among them.

J. Tussman, *Government and the Mind* 54 (1977). *See also* Sherry, "Responsible Republicanism: Educating for Citizenship," 62 *U. Chi. L. Rev.* 131 (1995). *But see* Gilles, *supra*; Arons, "The Separation of School and State: Pierce Reconsidered," 46 *Harv. Educ. Rev.* 76 (1976).

A century before *Pierce,* Jacksonian Frances Wright proposed that all parents be taxed for the "protective care and guardianship of the state." Their children would be registered at birth and shortly thereafter placed in public nurseries and schools where they would live, work, and study together "in pursuit of the same object—their own and each other's happiness—say! would not such a race, when arrived at manhood and womanhood, work out the reform of society, perfect the free institutions of America?" If adopted, Wright's proposal would have constricted the family's role far more than the Oregon legislation struck down in *Pierce.* Is the proposal unwise, as a matter of policy, or clearly unconstitutional, after *Pierce?* Is it relevant to either question that some societies have adopted a version of Wright's scheme with considerable success? *See, e.g.,* B. Bettelheim, *The Children of the Dream* (1969); M. Spiro, *Children of the Kibbutz* (1975). *But see* Haberman, "Bringing Up Baby: Job for a Kibbutz?" *The New York Times,* Oct. 12, 1994, at A6, indicating that the rearing of children communally in kibbutzim is withering away.

4. *Option 2: The* "Pierce Compromise"

In examining the state's "teaching power," including the power to compel school attendance, Professor Tussman argues that the power may be asserted "in a strong or a weak form":

> The strong claim is that the teaching power is vested fully in the state and is to be exercised exclusively by agencies of government or, in a variation, by licensed, authorized, supervised non-governmental institutions which operate within governmentally determined policy. In the strong view, non-governmental institutions—religious, commercial, private—in the domain of education exist not by inherent right but on tolerance or out of considerations of policy.
>
> In its weak form the assertion is that the state is one of the legitimate claimants to a teaching power; it does not enjoy monopoly or even priority; but it may enter the field. This view would support an extensive proliferation of public education institutions, but governmental exercise of the teaching power would have to accommodate itself to the equal legitimacy and even independence of other teaching institutions. . . .
>
> The strong and weak versions pose . . . the bitter controversy between unitary sovereignty and pluralistic theories of the state. . . . [I]t may well be the weak version which is implied in our theory and practice.

J. Tussman, *Government and the Mind* 55–6 (1977). *See also* Gutmann, *supra* at 115–23.

How does the *Pierce* Court accommodate the state's interest "to the equal legitimacy" of private schools? The Court recognizes the private schools' interest in maintaining their business and property, but how does that interest differ from the claim that any private concern might advance against particular governmental actions that limit or curtail its market? Since *Pierce,* the Court has abandoned aggressive use of the due process clause as a vehicle for overturning social and economic legislation, at least in the economic as opposed to personal liberty sphere. *See generally* McCloskey, "Economic Due Process and the Supreme Court: An Exhumation and Reburial," 1962 *Sup. Ct. Rev.* 34. "[I]f our recent decisions mean anything, they leave debatable issues as respects business, economic, and social affairs to legislative decision." *Day-Brite Lighting v. Missouri,* 342 U.S. 421, 425, 72 S.Ct. 405, 408, 96 L.Ed. 469 (1952). *See also Ferguson v. Skrupa,* 372 U.S. 726 83 S.Ct. 1028, 10 L.Ed.2d 93 (1963). In the light of such statements, do the interests of the private schools seem constitutionally persuasive today?

The *Pierce* decision is most often cited as authority for the proposition that parents have a constitutional right to educate their children in private schools:

> Reading *Pierce* as a First Amendment case and taking account of the nature of schooling suggest that *Pierce* principles reach the basic value choices on which school policy and practice are based. The result of such a reading is that it is the family and not the political majority which the Constitution empowers to make such schooling decisions.

Arons, "The Separation of School and State: *Pierce* Reconsidered," 46 *Harv. Educ. Rev.* 76, 78 (1976). *See* Carter, "Parents, Religion, and Schools: Reflections on *Pierce,* 70 Years Later," 27 *Seton Hall L. Rev.* 1194 (1997).

Is *Pierce* better understood as a First Amendment case? *See also* Yudof, *When Government Speaks* (1982). Why should parents have such a right? As a policy or constitutional matter, should parental values concern us more than the state's values? Does *Pierce* suggest that where the wishes of parent and child with respect to schooling conflict, the parents' view routinely prevails? Do such parental rights survive the demise of substantive due process in the economic sphere? *See Wisconsin v. Yoder, infra,* and subsequent notes for a more detailed discussion of this issue.

The source of this parental right is almost as difficult to fathom as its justification; some Justices have based it on the First Amendment right to freedom of speech (*see, e.g., Griswold v. Connecticut*, 381 U.S. 479, 85 S.Ct. 1678, 14 L.Ed.2d 510 (1965)), whereas others view the due process clause of the Fourteenth Amendment as its proper constitutional basis (*see, e.g., Abington School Dist. v. Schempp*, 374 U.S. 203, 230, 83 S.Ct. 1560, 1575, 10 L.Ed.2d 844 (1963) (Brennan, J., concurring)). Still others regard *Pierce* as a suit upholding the free exercise of religion, thus limiting its scope to issues of religious liberty (*see, e.g., Board of Education v. Allen*, 392 U.S. 236, 88 S.Ct. 1923, 20 L.Ed.2d 1060 (1968)). *See generally* Arons, *supra*. Note that *Pierce* was decided before the First Amendment was made applicable to the states through the Fourteenth Amendment. *See Fiske v. Kansas*, 274 U.S. 380, 47 S.Ct. 655, 71 L.Ed. 1108 (1927); *Whitney v. California*, 274 U.S. 357, 47 S.Ct. 641, 71 L.Ed. 1095 (1927); *Gitlow v. New York*, 268 U.S. 652, 45 S.Ct. 625, 69 L.Ed. 1138 (1925) (assuming, *arguendo*, the applicability to the states of the freedom of expression provision of the First Amendment).

Which textual argument seems most persuasive? What is the nexus between the constitutional right to freedom of speech and the parents' desire to educate their children in private schools? These questions are of more than lawyerly interest; the very scope of the *Pierce* compromise hinges on whether one views religion or speech as critical to the decision. John Stuart Mill's classic essay, *On Liberty*, advances a quite different compromise between state and parental interest:

> Is it not almost a self-evident axiom, that the State should require and compel the education, up to a certain standard, of every human being who is born its citizen? Yet . . . [h]ardly anyone indeed will deny that it is one of the most sacred duties of the parents . . . after summoning a human being into the world, to give to that being an education fitting him to perform his part well in life towards others and towards himself. But while this is unanimously declared to be the father's duty, scarcely anybody, in this country, will bear to hear of obliging him to perform it. . . .
>
> Were the duty of enforcing universal education once admitted there would be an end to the difficulties about what the State should teach, and how it should teach. . . . If the government would make up its

mind to require for every child a good education, it might save itself the trouble of providing one. It might leave to parents to obtain the education where and how they pleased, and content itself with helping to pay the school fees of the poorer classes of children, and defraying the entire school expenses of those who have no one else to pay for them. The objections which are urged with reason against State education do not apply to the enforcement of education by the State, but to the State's taking upon itself to direct that education; which is a totally different thing. . . . A general State education is a mere contrivance for molding people to be exactly like one another. . . . An education established and controlled by the State should exist, if it exists at all, as one among many competing experiments, carried on for the purpose of example and stimulus, to keep the others up to a certain standard of excellence.

J. Mill, "On Liberty," in *The Utilitarians* 586–87 (1961).

Mill attempts to disentangle the question of compulsoriness from the matter of who operates schools, striking a balance of interests differing from both *Pierce* (which presumes that public schooling will be the typical, if not universal, mode of education) and the more radical education critics; his proposal is in many respects similar to the education voucher plan (discussed in chapter 4, *infra*). How would you compare its merits with, for example, Frances Wright's suggested compulsory nursery school for all American youngsters? Is Mill's approach preferable to the *Pierce* Court's alternative? To Professor Gutmann's alternative?

Does the state's interest in compelling children to attend school give rise to any rights on the part of students subject to the compulsion: Are they, for example, entitled to equitable treatment by the public schools? *See Mills v. Board of Education*, 348 F.Supp. 866, 874 (D.D.C. 1972). (For discussion of this concept, see chapters 4–7.) Note that state compulsory education laws generally make no reference to a "right" to education at public expense, albeit many state constitutions do. *See generally* L. Kotin and W. F. Aikman, *Legal Foundations of Compulsory School Attendance* 78–79 (1980). May students exercise their rights of free speech and of expression in the fullest fashion consistent with the constraint of compulsoriness? *See* chapter 2. Can those exempted from the requirement of compulsory attendance—those who, in the words of the Oregon legislation, are "abnormal, subnormal, or physically unable to attend school"—make a legal claim that they are entitled to state-provided educational services (*see* chapter 6), or does the state's interest in compelling "educable" youngsters to attend school carry with it no corollary obligations to those youngsters?

What is the relationship between the decentralization of education in America and the general acceptance of compulsory education laws? *See* R. Healey, *The French Achievement* 19 (1974).

5. *Option 3: Abolishing Compulsory Education*

No litigant in *Pierce* challenged Oregon's compulsory attendance law, and the Court did not seriously entertain the proposition. Indeed, not until the 1960s were any notable objections to compulsory education voiced in this country. A 1959 United Nations General Assembly "Declaration of the Rights of the Child" confirmed what had not been questioned for a century: "The child is entitled to receive education, which shall be free and *compulsory*, at least in the elementary stages." (Emphasis added.)

Leo Tolstoy's claim that "the compulsory structure of the school excludes the possibility of all progress," has been vigorously pressed by some philosophers of education. In *Compulsory Mis-Education* (1964), Paul Goodman declared: "The compulsory system has become a universal trap, and it is no good. Very many of the youth, both poor and middle class, might be better off if the system simply did not exist, even if they then had no formal schooling at all." Ivan Illich has urged that the society be "deschooled" and that "radical alternative[s] . . . the total prohibition of legislative attendance, and the transfer of control over tax funds from benevolent institutions to the individual person" be adopted. "The first article of a bill of rights for a modern, humanist society would correspond to the [F]irst Amendment of the U.S. Constitution: 'The State shall make no law with respect to the establishment of education.' There shall be no ritual obligatory for all." *See, e.g.,* Arons, *supra*; I. Illich, *Deschooling Society* (1971); E. Reiner, *School Is Dead* (1971).

These assaults on compulsory education are not merely criticisms of unhappy experiences in urban schools; these are political criticisms of all required schooling, whether pleasant or oppressive. The critics reject the argument that the state can best provide for the individual's education and point to the historic failure of public schools to alter social-status relations or benefit poor and nonwhite children. *See, e.g.,* C. Greer, *The Great School Legend* (1972);

E. Morgan, *Inequality in Classroom Learning* (1977). They view as illegitimate the state's asserted interest in shaping the political and social attitudes of children through schooling, *see* Arons, *supra.* In short, both as a matter of policy and as a matter of law, these critics prefer a pluralist educational and social system; they stress the interests of the individual and family, discounting the notion of collective or societal interests.

At this point, agreement among the critics of compulsory schooling ends. Paul Goodman's preferred alternatives include " 'no school at all' for a few classes"; "decentraliz[ing] an urban school . . . into small units"; "us[ing] appropriate *unlicensed* adults of the community—the druggist, the storekeeper, the mechanic—as the proper educators . . . [emphasis added]"; and "send[ing] children to economically marginal farms for a couple of months of the year." None of those is necessarily inconsistent with general compulsory education laws. Ivan Illich's views are avowedly more political, directly linked to redistribution of other social resources. Educator John Holt views compulsoriness as but one of many restrictions on children's freedom that should be abolished; his dream is the autonomous child, not the restructured state. *See* J. Holt, *Freedom and Beyond* (1972). Some have suggested that a lowering of the school-leaving age to fourteen would enable schools to better serve students who wish to remain in school. *See, e.g.,* National Commission on the Reform of Secondary Education, *The Reform of Secondary Education: A Report to the Public and Profession* (1973).

These proposals raise questions of both policy and law. Would an end to compulsoriness be desirable in itself? What would be likely to happen if laws requiring school attendance were repealed and no other changes were made either in schools or elsewhere in the society? In other words, would the social functions presently performed by schools disappear if the requirement of school attendance disappeared? *See generally* Katz, "Compulsion and the Discourse on Compulsory Education Attendance," 27 *Educ. Theory* 179 (1977). Would alternative forms of education routinely emerge? If the response to these queries is no, does this suggest that abolishing compulsoriness would have no effect or that it would affect only those who choose—perhaps because of economic necessity—to exercise the option of not attending schools? Might such a pattern of choice actually widen disparities between rich and poor? Professor

Tussman argues that "the faddish vogue of 'de-schooling' would, if anyone listened, merely doom the 'disadvantaged' to permanent hopelessness." *See* J. Tussman, *Government and the Mind* 164 (1977).

6. Pierce *and Government Expression*

In view of the alternative conceptions of *Pierce*, consider the argument by Professor Yudof that *Pierce* is a limitation on government expression, a limitation that circumscribes the ability of governments to indoctrinate a young and captive audience:

> . . . Releasing all or part of a captive audience is one effective way to counter government's persuasive powers. *Pierce v. Society of Sisters* is a superb example in the education context. . . .
>
> *Pierce* is problematic if approached entirely in terms of individual entitlements. Arguably, if the government of a state wills it, private individuals should have no more right to run educational institutions than to organize a private army to defend the nation. The doctrine of academic freedom for teachers would be twisted beyond all recognition if teachers not only had a constitutional right to make reasonable presentational decisions, but had the right to make curricular choices and to force the state to tolerate institutions within which they might make those choices. Parents historically have enjoyed great latitude in making decisions for their children, but apart from the uncertain constitutional derivation of such entitlements, it is not clear why compulsory *public* schooling is an intolerable interference with parental rights. The state frequently, and often more substantially, interferes with parental choice. Compulsory attendance laws interfere more significantly with parental autonomy than the law in *Pierce*, the decision that children must attend *some* school for eight or more years of their lives appears more consequential than the secondary decision that they must attend *public* school. Indeed, even in *Pierce*, the Court did not deny the state extensive authority to regulate the curriculum in private and public schools—presumably by requiring courses in language, history, hygiene, and civics that some parents might find objectionable. Beyond compulsory education, state regulations address intrafamily affairs by terminating parental rights because of child abuse or neglect, or abandonment; by providing compulsory vaccinations and lifesaving medical procedures for children, regard-less of parental choice; by forbidding incest and fornication; by banning the sale of pornography, tobacco, and alcoholic beverages to minors, despite parental consent to their use; by regulating child labor; and by otherwise limiting the public and private rights of minors regardless of the parents' attitude toward those restrictions.[98]

> Thus, *Pierce* becomes intelligible only against the background of a structure limiting the power of government to indoctrinate the young. Although the Justices probably did not intend this construction, *Pierce* may be understood as telling governments that they are free to establish public schools and to make education compulsory for certain age-groups, but they are not free to eliminate competing private sector institutions that promote heterogeneity in education. It is one thing to recognize education as a legitimate enterprise for the state; it is quite another to label private education illegitimate. Similarly, it is one thing for the state to require private schools to offer English, mathematics, or civics courses, and quite another for the state to forbid them from teaching the German language, Bible study, or modern dance.

> A contrary decision in *Pierce* would have fostered a state monopoly in education, a monopoly that would dangerously strengthen the state's ability to mold the young. To be sure, I do not wish to overstate the case. Private schools convey many values and attitudes identical to those conveyed in public schools. Virtually all schools tend to mirror consensual values and to promote accepted norms of social behavior. Further, a requirement that students spend five or six hours a day in school, for roughly half of each year, hardly precludes socialization in the family. Radio and television, films, peer group norms and pressures, clubs, and other institutions and mechanisms for conveying messages and values greatly reduce the danger of compulsory public schooling. But in the face of indeterminacy about how the various actors and institutions contribute to socialization processes and interact with each other,[100] *Pierce* represents a reasonable, if imperfect,[101] accommodation of conflicting pressures. The state may promulgate its messages in the public school, and parents are free to choose private schools with different orientations. The state must tolerate private education, but need not fund it. The state may make some demands of private schools in satisfaction of compulsory schooling laws, but those demands may not be so excessive that they

---

[98]*See generally* R. Mnookin, *Child, Family, and State* (1978) Kleinfeld, "The Balance of Power Among Infants, Their Parents, and the State" (pts. 1 & 2), 4 *Fam. Law Q.* 319, 409 (1970). . . .

[100]*See generally* F. Greenstein, *Children and Politics* (1965); M. K. Jennings & R. Niemi, *The Political Character of Adolescence* (1974); *Political Socialization* (R. Dawson & K. Prewitt eds. 1969); *Socialization and Society* (J. Clausen ed. 1968).

[101]*See* J. Coons & S. Sugarman, *Education by Choice: The Case for Family Control* (1978), in which the authors outline and defend a plan for increasing family autonomy in education. The historic criticism of *Pierce*, as it operates in fact, has been that only the religiously devout (by virtue of numbers) and the affluent (by virtue of their ability to afford expensive private schools for their children) can take advantage of the rights afforded parents by *Pierce*.

19

transform private schools into public schools managed and funded by the private sector. The integrity of the communications and socialization processes in private schools and families remains intact, while the state's interest in producing informed, educated, and productive citizens is preserved. Thus, a structure that limits government speech gives credence to otherwise tenuous individual rights arguments in *Pierce*.

Yudof, "When Governments Speak: Toward a Theory of Government Expression and the First Amendment," 57 *Tex. L. Rev.* 863, 888–91 (1979). *See also* Heyman, "State-Supported Speech," 1999 *Wisc. L. Rev.* 1119.

Consider how Professor Yudof's rationale for *Pierce* differs from the other First Amendment perspectives discussed earlier in this chapter. Do you agree that there is a tenuous relationship between First Amendment freedom of expression and the historically recognized power of parents to direct the education of their children? What difference does it make whether *Pierce* is viewed as affirming the rights of parents or limiting the prerogatives of government to indoctrinate? Would these alternative rationales lead to different concepts of the scope of state and federal power to regulate private schools?

Farrington v. Tokushige
273 U.S. 284, 47 S.Ct. 406, 71 L.Ed. 646 (1927).

Mr. Justice McReynolds delivered the opinion of the Court.

The Circuit Court of Appeals affirmed [11 F.2d 710] an interlocutory decree rendered by the United States District Court of Hawaii July 21, 1925, which granted a temporary injunction forbidding petitioners—Governor, Attorney General and Superintendent of Public Instruction of that Territory—from attempting to enforce the provisions of Act 30, Special Session 1920, Legislature of Hawaii, entitled, "An Act relating to foreign language schools and teachers thereof," as amended by Act 171 of 1923 and Act 152 of 1925, and certain regulations adopted by the Department of Public Instruction June 1, 1925. The interlocutory decree was granted upon the bill and affidavits presented by both sides. No answer has been filed. In these circumstances we only consider whether the judicial discretion of the trial court was improperly exercised.

Respondents claimed below and maintain here that enforcement of the challenged Act would de-

prive them of their liberty and property without due process of law contrary to the Fifth Amendment. Petitioners insist that the entire Act and the regulations adopted thereunder are valid; that they prescribe lawful rules for the conduct of private foreign language schools necessary for the public welfare; also that if any provision of the statute transcends the power of the Legislature it should be disregarded and the remaining ones should be enforced. . . .

There are one hundred and sixty-three foreign language schools in the Territory. Nine are conducted in the Korean language, seven in the Chinese and the remainder in the Japanese. Respondents are members of numerous voluntary unincorporated associations conducting foreign language schools for instruction of Japanese children. These are owned, maintained and conducted by upwards of five thousand persons; the property used in connection therewith is worth two hundred and fifty thousand dollars; the enrolled pupils number twenty thousand; and three hundred teachers are employed. These schools receive no aid from public funds. All children residing within the Territory are required to attend some public or equivalent school; and practically all who go to foreign language schools also attend public or such private schools. It is affirmed by counsel for petitioners that Japanese pupils in the public and equivalent private schools increased from one thousand, three hundred and twenty in 1900 to nineteen thousand, three hundred and fifty-four in 1920, and that out of a total of sixty-five thousand, three hundred and sixty-nine pupils of all races on December 31, 1924, thirty thousand, four hundred and eighty-seven were Japanese.

The challenged enactment declares that the term, "foreign language school," as used therein, "shall be construed to mean any school which is conducted in any language other than the English language or Hawaiian language, except Sabbath schools." And, as stated by the Circuit Court of Appeals, the following are its more prominent and questionable features:

No such school shall be conducted in the territory unless under a written permit therefor from the Department of Public Instruction, nor unless the fee therefor shall have been paid as therein provided, and such permit shall be kept exposed in a prominent place at the school so as to be readily seen and read by visitors thereat.

The fee prescribed is one dollar per pupil on the estimated average attendance of pupils at the school during the period during which such school was conducted during the next preceding school year. . . .

No person shall teach in a foreign language school unless and until he shall have first applied to and obtained a permit so to do from the department and this shall also be construed to include persons exercising or performing administrative powers at any school. No permit to teach in a foreign language school shall be granted unless and until the department is satisfied that the applicant for the same is possessed of the ideals of democracy; knowledge of American history and institutions, and knows how to read, write and speak the English language.

It is the declared object of the Act to fully and effectively regulate the conducting of foreign language schools and the teaching of foreign languages, in order that the Americanism of the pupils may be promoted, and the department is directed to carry out the provisions of the Act in accordance with its spirit and purpose.

Before issuing a permit to conduct a foreign language school or to teach in any such school the department shall require the applicant for such permit to sign a pledge that the applicant will, if granted a permit to teach in such a school, abide by and observe the terms of the Act, and the regulations and orders of the department, and will, to the best of his ability, so direct the minds and studies of pupils in such schools as will tend to make them good and loyal American citizens, and will not permit such students to receive instructions in any way inconsistent therewith.

No foreign language school shall be conducted in the morning before the school hours of the public schools or during the hours while the public schools are in session, nor shall any pupil attend any foreign language school for more than one hour each day, nor exceeding six hours in any one week, nor exceeding thirty-eight weeks in any school year; provided, however, the department may in its discretion and with the approval of the Governor, modify this provision.

The department shall have full power from time to time to prescribe by regulations the subjects and courses of study of all foreign language schools, and the entrance and attendance prerequisites or qualifications of education age, school attainment, demonstrated mental capacity, health and otherwise, and the textbooks used in any foreign language school.

Until otherwise provided by the department, the following regulations are in effect: Up to September 1, 1923, every pupil shall have first satisfactorily completed the American public school first grade, or a course equivalent thereto, before attending or being allowed to attend any foreign language school. Beginning September 1, 1923, and thereafter, every pupil shall have satisfactorily completed the American public school first and second grades, or courses equivalent thereto, before attending or being allowed to attend any foreign language school. Beginning September 1, 1923, and thereafter, for grades one, two and three, and beginning September 1, 1924, and thereafter, for grades four and above, all new textbooks used in elementary foreign language schools shall be based upon the principle that the pupil's normal medium of expression is English and shall contain, as far as practicable, English equivalents for foreign words and idioms.

The department is authorized to prepare, or cause to be prepared, or procure or arrange for procuring suitable textbooks for the teaching of foreign languages in the foreign language schools and to enter into an agreement or agreements for the publishing and sale of the same.

* * *

If the department shall at any time become satisfied that any holder of a permit to conduct a foreign language school or to teach therein does not possess the qualifications required by the Act, or shall have violated or failed to observe any of the provisions of the Act or of the regulations or orders of the department, the department may then and thereupon revoke the permit theretofore granted and the same shall thereupon be and become null and void.

Any person who shall conduct or participate in conducting a foreign language school or who shall teach in a foreign language school contrary to the provisions of the Act, or who shall violate or participate in violating any of the provisions thereof, or any of the regulations or orders of the department, shall be guilty of a misdemeanor, and upon conviction thereof shall be punished by a fine not to exceed twenty-five dollars, and each day's violation shall be deemed a separate offense.

* * *

On June 1, 1925, the Department of Public Instruction adopted, and the Governor approved, certain regulations which undertook to limit the pupils who might attend foreign language schools to those who regularly attended some public school or approved private school, or had completed the eighth grade, or were over fourteen years of age. Also, to designate the textbooks which foreign language schools should use in their primary grades. . . .

[T]he school Act and the measures adopted thereunder go far beyond mere regulation of privately-supported schools where children obtain instruction deemed valuable by their parents and which is not obviously in conflict with any public interest. They give affirmative direction concerning the intimate and essential details of such schools, intrust their control to public officers, and deny both owners and patrons reasonable choice and discretion in respect of teachers, curriculum and textbooks. Enforcement of the Act probably would destroy most, if not all, of them; and, certainly, it would deprive parents of fair opportunity to procure for their children instruction which they think important and we cannot say is harmful. The Japanese parent has the right to direct the education of his own child without unreasonable restrictions; the Constitution protects him as well as those who speak another tongue.

Upon the record and the arguments presented, we cannot undertake to consider the validity of each separate provision of the Act and decide whether, dissociated from the others, its enforcement would violate respondents' constitutional rights. Apparently all are parts of a deliberate plan to bring foreign language schools under a strict governmental control for which the record discloses no adequate reason. Here, the enactment has been defended as a whole. No effort has been made to discuss the validity of the several provisions. In the trial court the cause proceeded upon the theory that petitioners intended to enforce all of them.

The general doctrine touching rights guaranteed by the Fourteenth Amendment to owners, parents and children in respect of attendance upon schools has been announced in recent opinions. [Citing *Pierce v. Society of Sisters*, among other cases]. . . .

We of course appreciate the grave problems incident to the large alien population of the Hawaiian Islands. These should be given due weight whenever the validity of any governmental regulation of private schools is under consideration; but the limitations of the Constitution must not be transcended.

It seems proper to add that when petitioners present their answer the issues may become more specific and permit the cause to be dealt with in greater detail.

We find no abuse of the discretion lodged in the trial court. The decree of the Circuit Court of Appeals must be

Affirmed.

Excerpts from the *Farrington* Briefs, Summarized in the Court's Opinion
273 U.S. 285–87, 288.

Mr. William B. Lymer, Attorney General of the Territory of Hawaii, with whom *Marguerite K. Ashford*, First Deputy Attorney General, was on the brief, for the petitioners.

These laws do not violate the Constitution. *Pierce v. Society of Sisters*, 268 U.S. 510 [1925] . . . concern[s] prohibitory legislation alone, and not purely regulatory measures such as those involved in this case, which attempt rather to supervise and control than to abolish foreign language schools.

It would be a sad commentary on our system of government to hold that the Territory must stand by, impotent, and watch its foreign-born guests conduct a vast system of schools of American pupils, teaching them loyalty to a foreign country and disloyalty to their own country, and hampering them during their tender years in the learning of the home language in the public schools—to hold that the Territory could not by mere regulatory measures even alleviate these evils to a moderate extent while not interfering in the least with the proper maintenance of these schools or the teaching of foreign languages in them, but on the contrary making them more efficient for this their declared object.

The State has authority over such schools for at least two reasons: (1) that as *parens patriae* it has extensive power with respect to infants; and (2) that it is vitally interested in quality of its citizenship. . . .

Private schools are a proper subject of regulation. *State v. Bailey*, 157 Ind. 324, [61 N.E. 730 (1901)]. Compulsory education statutes do not require attendance at public schools alone, but at either public or private schools. Necessarily, in order to meet the requirements in respect of the period of years and the field of knowledge to be covered, it must be within the power of the legislature to regulate within reasonable limits the qualifications of the teachers, the subjects to be covered, the instruction to be given and how and to what extent—within the limits of the power—other instruction should be forbidden. The right to regulate private schools in Hawaii has long been unquestioned. . . .

Mr. Joseph Lightfoot, with whom *Mr. Joseph B. Poindexter* was on the brief, for respondents.

The statute unreasonably interferes with the fundamental right of parents and guardians to direct the upbringing and education of children under their control. . . .

The Hawaiian statute . . . takes from the parent of a child attending a foreign language school, all control and direction of the education of his child. Complete control of these schools is given to the Department of Education. The effect is to make them public schools in all but the name, though the public contributes nothing to their support.

They are prohibited from employing a teacher, teaching a subject, using a book, admitting a pupil, or engaging in any activity of any nature, unless approved by the Department of Education. Nor can such a school be conducted until a permit is granted and an exorbitant fee paid—a condition not imposed on any other private school in the Territory.

In the public schools all are taught the same lessons of Americanism and democratic ideals, which are considered sufficient for a majority of the pupils, yet the minority of the pupils, whose parents desire to fit them for the battle of life by teaching them a language which will be of great benefit to them in their after careers, attend the foreign language schools where they are further regulated, controlled, taxed, and this, too, in the face of the admitted fact that nothing un-American is taught in the foreign language schools, and the Americanism of the pupils is advanced, not retarded in them.

The sole purpose of the law is the Americanization of the pupils of these schools, though it is admitted that nothing un-American is taught in them. . . .

NOTES AND QUESTIONS

1. The Courts and Private School Regulation

The *Pierce* compromise leaves states free "reasonably to regulate all schools, to inspect, supervise and examine them, their teachers and pupils; require . . . that certain studies plainly essential to good citizenship must be taught, and that nothing be taught that is mainfestly inimical to the public welfare." If such regulation were not constitutionally permitted, how would the *Pierce* compromise have been affected? Could the state effectively compel the education of all children at a "school" if any private enterprise could refer to itself by that name? Alternatively, is the *Pierce* compromise too paternalistic? Professor Sacken has suggested "a renegotiation of the '*Pierce* Compromise' that more explicitly restrains state intrusion on private educational alternatives." Sacken, "Regulating Nonpublic Education: A Search for Just Law and Policy," 96 *Amer. J. of Educ.* 394, 395 (1988).

Pierce gives states considerable latitude in the scope of regulation. Might a state exercise that right to adopt regulations so intrusive that they either make all private schools exactly like their pub-

lic counterparts or drive nonpublic education out of business? How should the balance between competing interests be struck in this context?

2. Meyer v. Nebraska

In *Meyer v. Nebraska*, 262 U.S. 390, 43 S.Ct. 625, 67 L.Ed. 1042 (1923), the Supreme Court struck down a Nebraska statute that imposed criminal penalties on public or private schoolteachers who taught in any language except English or who taught languages other than English to students below high school level. The legislation in *Meyer*, as in *Farrington*, was born of the animosity against alien groups aroused by World War I; in Nebraska, the target was Germans generally and the German language in particular. *See generally* M. Janowitz, *The Reconstruction of Patriotism: Education for Civic Consciousness* (1985). The Supreme Court concluded that the legislation interfered with both the language instructor's right to engage in his profession and the parents' right to encourage such instruction. It rejected the state's claim that such legislation was needed to "promote civic development," noting that while the "desire of the legislature to foster a homogeneous people with American ideals" was understandable, the particular measure did "violence to both the letter and spirit of the Constitution." 262 U.S. at 402–03, 43 S.Ct. at 627–28.

Consider these comments by Professor Chafee on *Meyer* and *Pierce*:

In private schools the liberty of teaching is greater, for the state cannot base its interference on its control of its own funds, but only upon the general interest of the community in the training of the young. This reason has been held by the Supreme Court not to justify the total abolition of private schools by legislation. Some governmental regulation of their curriculum will be permitted for the sake of public safety, but teaching a foreign language is not dangerous enough to be constitutionally prohibited. The Lusk Committee sought to bring private schools under strict state control through a system of licenses, but the statute was repealed before its validity was finally adjudicated in the litigation brought by the Rand School. If public school teaching is to be rigorously restricted by officials, the need for free private schools is all the greater. Somebody should be able to experiment. In so far as such schools are regulated, the powers and training of the public officials who supervise them become a matter of great importance.

Z. Chafee, *Free Speech in the United States* 552 (1941).

Does *Meyer* go beyond the rationale of *Pierce*? Would the result in *Meyer* be the same if Latin were forbidden? Is *Meyer* a case about the accommodation of "public safety" and the ability "to experiment"?

3. *Scope of* Farrington *and* Meyer

Farrington v. Tokushige does not indicate which provisions of the Hawaii legislation it finds objectionable. If the Hawaii legislature wished to redraft the bill to render it constitutionally acceptable, which provisions would be stricken and why? Note that by the terms of the Hawaii statute, the foreign language schools can only provide a supplementary education; they are not permitted to provide full instruction. Is that feature of the legislation constitutionally invalid? If Japanese-American students attend public or state-approved private schools during the normal school day, should the state be permitted to impose any regulations on after-school instruction? Could the state, for example, regulate the content of instruction in after-school church-run classes? Could it do so in classes run by the Communist Party? Suppose after-school instruction were structured explicitly to identify and rebut the alleged ideological bias of the public school; could such an enterprise be prohibited or regulated by the state?

Do *Farrington* and *Meyer* ultimately stand for the proposition that state statutes regulating private schools that are motivated primarily by a desire to regulate activities only of particular national origin groups are unconstitutional? Are they more equal protection than First Amendment cases? If so, do they offer much guidance as to the constitutional scope of state regulation of private schools?

Can the state permit voters in local election districts to determine whether a private school may operate in that community? *See Columbia Trust Co. v. Lincoln Institute of Kentucky*, 138 Ky. 804, 129 S.W. 113 (1910).

II. COMPULSORY SCHOOLING, PUBLIC POLICY, AND THE CONSTITUTION

Wisconsin v. Yoder
406 U.S. 205, 92 S.Ct. 1526, 32 L.Ed.2d 15 (1972).

Mr. Chief Justice Burger delivered the opinion of the Court.

On petition of the State of Wisconsin, we granted the writ of certiorari in this case to review a decision of the Wisconsin Supreme Court holding that respondents' convictions of violating the State's compulsory school attendance law were invalid under the Free Exercise Clause of the First Amendment to the United States Constitution made applicable to the States by the Fourteenth Amendment. For the reasons hereafter stated we affirm the judgment of the Supreme Court of Wisconsin.

Respondents Jonas Yoder and Wallace Miller are members of the Old Order Amish religion, and respondent Adin Yutzy is a member of the Conservative Amish Mennonite Church. They and their families are residents of Green County, Wisconsin. Wisconsin's compulsory school-attendance law required them to cause their children to attend public or private school until reaching age 16, but the respondents declined to send their children, ages 14 and 15, to public school after they completed the eighth grade. The children were not enrolled in any private school, or within any recognized exception to the compulsory attendance law, and they are conceded to be subject to the Wisconsin statute.

On complaint of the school district administrator for the public schools, respondents were charged, tried, and convicted of violating the compulsory-attendance law in Green County Court and were fined the sum of $5 each.[3] Respondents defended on the ground that the application of the compulsory-attendance law violated their rights under the First and Fourteenth Amendments. The trial

---

[3]Prior to trial, the attorney for respondents wrote the State Superintendent of Public Instruction in an effort to explore the possibilities for a compromise settlement. Among other possibilities, he suggested that perhaps the State Superintendent could administratively determine that the Amish could satisfy the compulsory attendance law by establishing their own vocational training plan similar to one that has been established in Pennsylvania. . . . Under the Pennsylvania plan, Amish children of high school age are required to attend an Amish vocational school for three hours a week, during which time they are taught such subjects as English, mathematics, health, and social studies by an Amish teacher. For the balance of the week, the children perform farm and household duties under parental supervision, and keep a journal of their daily activities. The major portion of the curriculum is home projects in agriculture and homemaking. *See generally*, J. Hostetler and G. Huntington, *Children in Amish Society* (1971); *Socialization and Community Education* c5 (1971). A similar program has been instituted in Indiana. *Ibid.* See also Iowa Code §299.24; Kansas Stats Ann. §72–1111 (Supp. 1971).

The Superintendent rejected this proposal on the ground that it would not afford Amish children "substantially equivalent education" to that offered in the schools of the area. . . .

testimony showed that respondents believed, in accordance with the tenets of the Old Order Amish communities generally, that their children's attendance at high school, public or private, was contrary to the Amish religion and way of life. They believed that by sending their children to high school, they would not only expose themselves to the danger of the censure of the church community, but, as found by the county court, endanger their own salvation and that of their children. The State stipulated that respondents' religious beliefs were sincere.

In support of their position, respondents presented as expert witnesses scholars on religion and education whose testimony is uncontradicted. They expressed their opinions on the relationship of the Amish belief concerning school attendance to the more general tenets of their religion, and described the impact that compulsory high school attendance could have on the continued survival of Amish communities as they exist in the United States today. The history of the Amish sect was given in some detail, beginning with the Swiss Anabaptists of the 16th century who rejected institutionalized churches and sought to return to the early, simple, Christian life deemphasizing material success, rejecting the competitive spirit, and seeking to insulate themselves from the modern world. As a result of their common heritage, Old Order Amish communities today are characterized by a fundamental belief that salvation requires life in a church community separate and apart from the world and worldly influence. This concept of life aloof from the world and its values is central to their faith.

A related feature of Old Order Amish communities is their devotion to a life in harmony with nature and the soil, as exemplified by the simple life of the early Christian era that continued in America during much of our early national life. Amish beliefs require members of the community to make their living by farming or closely related activities. Broadly speaking, the Old Order Amish religion pervades and determines the entire mode of life of its adherents. Their conduct is regulated in great detail by the *Ordnung*, or rules, of the church community. Adult baptism, which occurs in late adolescence, is the time at which Amish young people voluntarily undertake heavy obligations, not unlike the Bar Mitzvah of the Jews, to abide by the rules of the church community.

Amish objection to formal education beyond the eighth grade is firmly grounded in these central religious concepts. They object to the high school

and higher education generally because the values they teach are in marked variance with Amish values and the Amish way of life; they view secondary school education as an impermissible exposure of their children to a "worldly" influence in conflict with their beliefs. The high school tends to emphasize intellectual and scientific accomplishments, self-distinction, competitiveness, worldly success, and social life with other students. Amish society emphasizes informal learning-through-doing; a life of "goodness," rather than a life of intellect; wisdom, rather than technical knowledge; community welfare, rather than competition; and separation from, rather than integration with, contemporary worldly society.

Formal high school education beyond the eighth grade is contrary to Amish beliefs not only because it places Amish children in an environment hostile to Amish beliefs with increasing emphasis on competition in classwork and sports and with pressure to conform to the styles, manners and ways of the peer group, but because it takes them away from their community, physically and emotionally, during the crucial and formative adolescent period of life. During this period, the children must acquire Amish attitudes favoring manual work and self-reliance and the specific skills needed to perform the adult role of an Amish farmer or housewife. They must learn to enjoy physical labor. Once a child has learned basic reading, writing, and elementary mathematics, these traits, skills, and attitudes admittedly fall within the category of those best learned through example and "doing" rather than in a classroom. And, at this time in life, the Amish child must also grow in his faith and his relationship to the Amish community if he is to be prepared to accept the heavy obligations imposed by adult baptism. In short, high school attendance with teachers who are not of the Amish faith—and may even be hostile to it—interposes a serious barrier to the integration of the Amish child into the Amish religious community. Dr. John Hostetler, one of the experts on Amish society, testified that the modern high school is not equipped, in curriculum or social environment, to impart the values promoted by Amish society.

The Amish do not object to elementary education through the first eight grades as a general proposition because they agree that their children must have basic skills in the "three Rs" in order to read the Bible, to be good farmers and citizens and to be able to deal with non-Amish people when necessary in the course of daily affairs. They view such a basic education as acceptable because it does not significantly expose their children to worldly values or interfere with their development in the Amish community during the crucial adolescent period. While Amish accept compulsory elementary education generally, wherever possible they have established their own elementary schools in many respects like the small local schools of the past. In the Amish belief higher learning tends to develop values they reject as influences that alienate man from God.

On the basis of such considerations, Dr. Hostetler testified that compulsory high school attendance could not only result in great psychological harm to Amish children, because of the conflicts it would produce, but would also, in his opinion, ultimately result in the destruction of the Old Order Amish church community as it exists in the United States today. The testimony of Dr. Donald A. Erickson, an expert witness on education, also showed that the Amish succeed in preparing their high school age children to be productive members of the Amish community. He described their system of learning through doing the skills directly relevant to their adult roles in the Amish community as "ideal" and perhaps superior to ordinary high school education. The evidence also showed that the Amish have an excellent record as law-abiding and generally self-sufficient members of society.

Although the trial court in its careful findings determined that the Wisconsin compulsory school-attendance law "does interfere with the freedom of the Defendants to act in accordance with their sincere religious belief," it also concluded that the requirement of high school attendance until age 16 was a "reasonable and constitutional" exercise of governmental power, and therefore denied the motion to dismiss the charges. The Wisconsin Circuit Court affirmed the convictions. The Wisconsin Supreme Court, however, sustained respondents' claim under the Free Exercise Clause of the First Amendment and reversed the convictions. A majority of the Court was of the opinion that the State had failed to make an adequate showing that its interest in "establishing and maintaining an education system overrides the defendants' right to the free exercise of their religion." 49 Wis2d 430, 447, 182 NW2d 539, 547 (1971).

I

There is no doubt as to the power of a State, having a high responsibility for education of its citizens, to impose reasonable regulations for the control and duration of basic education. *See, e.g., Pierce v. Society of Sisters*, 268 U.S. 510, 534 (1925). Providing public schools ranks at the very apex of the function of a State. Yet even this paramount responsibility was, in *Pierce*, made to yield to the right of parents to provide an equivalent education in a privately operated system. There the Court held that Oregon's statute compelling attendance in a public school from age eight to age 16 unreasonably interfered with the interest of parents in directing the rearing of their offspring, including their education in church-operated schools. . . . Thus, a State's interest in universal education, however highly we rank it, is not totally free from a balancing process when it impinges on fundamental rights and interests, such as those specifically protected by the Free Exercise Clause of the First Amendment, and the traditional interest of parents with respect to the religious upbringing of their children so long as they, in the words of *Pierce*, "prepare [them] for additional obligations." 268 U.S. at 535.

It follows that in order for Wisconsin to compel school attendance beyond the eighth grade against a claim that such attendance interferes with the practice of a legitimate religious belief, it must appear either that the State does not deny the free exercise of religious belief by its requirement, or that there is a state interest of sufficient magnitude to override the interest claiming protection under the Free Exercise Clause. . . .

II

We come then to the quality of the claims of the respondents concerning the alleged encroachment of Wisconsin's compulsory school-attendance statute on their rights and the rights of their children to the free exercise of the religious beliefs they and their forebears have adhered to for almost three centuries. In evaluating those claims we must be careful to determine whether the Amish religious faith and their mode of life are, as they claim, inseparable and interdependent. A way of life, however virtuous and admirable, may not be interposed as a barrier to reasonable state regulation of education if it is based on purely secular considerations; to have the protection of the Religion Clauses, the claims must be rooted in religious belief. Although a determination of what is a "religious" belief or practice entitled to constitutional protection may present a most delicate question, the very concept of ordered liberty precludes allowing every person to make his own standards on matters of conduct in which society as a whole has important interests. Thus, if the Amish asserted their claims because of their subjective evaluation and rejection of the contemporary secular values accepted by the majority, much as Thoreau rejected the social values of his time and isolated himself at Walden Pond, their claim would not rest on a religious basis. Thoreau's choice was philosophical and personal rather than religious, and such belief does not rise to the demands of the Religion Clauses.

Giving no weight to such secular considerations, however, we see that the record in this case abundantly supports the claim that the traditional way of life of the Amish is not merely a matter of personal preference, but one of deep religious conviction, shared by an organized group, and intimately related to daily living. That the Old Order Amish daily life and religious practice stems from their faith is shown by the fact that it is in response to their literal interpretation of the Biblical injunction from the Epistle of Paul to the Romans, "be not conformed to this world. . . ." This command is fundamental to the Amish faith. Moreover, for the Old Order Amish, religion is not simply a matter of theocratic belief. As the expert witnesses explained, the Old Order Amish religion pervades and determines virtually their entire way of life, regulating it with the detail of the Talmudic diet through the strictly enforced rules of the church community.

The record shows that the respondents' religious beliefs and attitude toward life, family, and home have remained constant—perhaps some would say static—in a period of unparalleled progress in human knowledge generally and great changes in education. . . . Their way of life in a church-oriented community, separated from the outside world and "worldly" influences, their attachment to nature and the soil, is a way inherently simple and uncomplicated, albeit difficult to preserve against the pressure to conform. Their rejection of telephones, automobiles, radios, and television, their mode of dress, of speech, their habits of manual work do indeed set them apart from much of contemporary society; these customs are both symbolic and practical.

As the society around the Amish has become more populous, urban, industrialized, and complex, particularly in this century, government regulation of human affairs has correspondingly become more detailed and pervasive. The Amish mode of life has thus come into conflict increasingly with requirements of contemporary society exerting a hydraulic insistence on conformity to majoritarian standards. So long as compulsory education laws were confined to eight grades of elementary basic education imparted in a nearby rural schoolhouse, with a large proportion of students of the Amish faith, the Old Order Amish had little basis to fear that school attendance would expose their children to the worldly influence they reject. But modern compulsory secondary education in rural areas is now largely carried on in a consolidated school, often remote from the student's home and alien to his daily homelife. As the record so strongly shows, the values and programs of the modern secondary school are in sharp conflict with the fundamental mode of life mandated by the Amish religion; modern laws requiring compulsory secondary education have accordingly engendered great concern and conflict. The conclusion is inescapable that secondary schooling, by exposing Amish children to worldly influences in terms of attitudes, goals, and values contrary to beliefs, and by substantially interfering with the religious development of the Amish child and his integration into the way of life of the Amish faith community at the crucial adolescent state of development, contravenes the basic religious tenets and practice of the Amish faith, both as to the parent and the child.

The impact of the compulsory-attendance law on respondents' practice of the Amish religion is not only severe, but inescapable, for the Wisconsin law affirmatively compels them, under threat of criminal sanction, to perform acts undeniably at odds with fundamental tenets of their religious beliefs. *See Braunfeld v. Brown*, 366 U.S. 599, 605 (1961). Nor is the impact of the compulsory-attendance law confined to grave interference with important Amish religious tenets from a subjective point of view. It carries with it precisely the kind of objective danger to the free exercise of religion that the First Amendment was designed to prevent. As the record shows, compulsory school attendance to age 16 for Amish children carries with it a very real threat of undermining the Amish community and religious practice as they exist today; they must either abandon belief and be assimilated into society at large, or be forced to migrate to some other and more tolerant region.[9]

In sum, the unchallenged testimony of acknowledged experts in education and religious history, almost 300 years of consistent practice, and strong evidence of a sustained faith pervading and regulating respondents' entire mode of life support the claim that enforcement of the State's requirement of compulsory formal education after the eighth grade would gravely endanger if not destroy the free exercise of respondents' religious beliefs.

III

Neither the findings of the trial court nor the Amish claims as to the nature of their faith are challenged in this Court by the State of Wisconsin. Its position is that the State's interest in universal compulsory formal secondary education to age 16 is so great that it is paramount to the undisputed claims of respondents that their mode of preparing their youth for Amish life, after the traditional elementary education, is an essential part of their religious belief and practice. Nor does the State undertake to meet the claim that the Amish mode of life and education is inseparable from and a part of the basic tenets of their religion—indeed, as much a part of their religious belief and practices as baptism, the confessional, or a sabbath may be for others.

Wisconsin concedes that under the Religion Clauses religious beliefs are absolutely free from the State's control, but it argues that "actions," even though religiously grounded, are outside the protection of the First Amendment.[10] But our decisions have rejected the idea that religiously grounded conduct is always outside the protection of the Free Exercise Clause. . . .

Nor can this case be disposed of on the grounds that Wisconsin's requirement for school attendance to age 16 applies uniformly to all citizens of the State and does not, on its face, discriminate against religions or a particular religion, or that it is motivated by legitimate secular concerns. A regulation neutral on its face may, in its application, nonetheless offend the constitutional requirement for governmental neutrality if it unduly burdens the free exercise of religion. . . .

We turn, then, to the State's broader contention that its interest in its system of compulsory education is so compelling that even the established religious practices of the Amish must give way. Where fundamental claims of religious freedom are at stake, however, we cannot accept such a sweeping claim; despite its admitted validity in the generality of cases, we must searchingly examine the interests that the State seeks to promote by its requirement for compulsory education to age 16, and the impediment to those objectives that would flow from recognizing the claimed Amish exemption. . . .

The State advances two primary arguments in support of its system of compulsory education. It notes, as Thomas Jefferson pointed out early in our history, that some degree of education is necessary to prepare citizens to participate effectively and intelligently in our open political system if we are to preserve freedom and independence. Further, education prepares individuals to be self-reliant and self-sufficient participants in society. We accept these propositions.

However, the evidence adduced by the Amish in this case is persuasively to the effect that an additional one or two years of formal high school for Amish children in place of their long-established program of informal vocational education would do little to serve those interests. Respondents' experts testified at trial, without challenge, that the value of all education must be assessed in terms of its capacity to prepare the child for life. It is one thing to say that compulsory education for a year or two beyond the eighth grade may be necessary when its goal is the preparation of the child for life in modern society as the majority live, but it is quite another if the goal of education be viewed as the preparation of the child for life in the separated agrarian community that is the keystone of the Amish faith. . . .

The State attacks respondents' position as one fostering "ignorance" from which the child must be

---

[9]Some States have developed working arrangements with the Amish regarding high school attendance. See n. 3. *supra*. However, the danger to the continued existence of an ancient religious faith cannot be ignored simply because of the assumption that its adherents will continue to be able at considerable sacrifice, to relocate ín some more tolerant State or country or work out accommodations under threat of criminal prosecution. Forced migration of religious minorities was an evil that lay at the heart of the Religion Clauses. *See, e.g., Everson v. Board of Education*, 330 U.S. 1, 9–10 (1947); J. Madison, "Memorial and Remonstrance Against Religious Assessments." 2 *Writings of James Madison* 183 (G. Hunt ed. 1901).

[10]That has been the apparent ground for decision in several previous state cases rejecting claims for exemption similar to that here. *See, e.g., State v. Garber*, 197 Kan. 567, 419 P.2d 896 (1966), *cert denied*, 389 U.S. 51 (1967), *State v. Hershberger*, 103 Ohio App. 188, 144 N.E.2d 693 (1955); *Commonwealth v. Beiler*, 168 Pa. Super 462, 79 A.2d 134 (1951).

protected by the State. No one can question the State's duty to protect children from ignorance but this argument does not square with the facts disclosed in the record. Whatever their idiosyncrasies as seen by the majority, this record strongly shows that the Amish community has been a highly successful social unit within our society, even if apart from the conventional "mainstream." Its members are productive and very law-abiding members of society; they reject public welfare in any of its usual modern forms. The Congress itself recognized their self-sufficiency by authorizing exemption of such groups as the Amish from the obligation to pay social security taxes.

It is neither fair nor correct to suggest that the Amish are opposed to education beyond the eighth grade level. What this record shows is that they are opposed to conventional formal education of the type provided by a certified high school because it comes at the child's crucial adolescent period of religious development. Dr. Donald Erickson, for example, testified that their system of learning-by-doing was an "ideal system" of education in terms of preparing Amish children for life as adults in the Amish community. . . . As he put it: "These people aren't purporting to be learned people, and it seems to me the self-sufficiency of the community is the best evidence I can point to—whatever is being done seems to function well."[12]

* * *

The State, however, supports its interest in providing an additional one or two years of compulsory high school education to Amish children because of the possibility that some such children will choose to leave the Amish community, and that if this occurs they will be ill-equipped for life. The State argues that if Amish children leave their church they should not be in the position of making their way in the world without the education available in the one or two additional years the State requires. However, on this record, that argument is highly speculative. There is no specific evidence of the loss of Amish adherents by attrition, nor is there any showing that upon leaving the Amish community Amish children, with their practical agricultural training and habits of industry and self-reliance, would become burdens on society because of educational shortcomings. In-

deed, this argument of the State appears to rest primarily on the State's mistaken assumption, already noted, that the Amish do not provide any education for their children beyond the eighth grade, but allow them to grow in "ignorance." To the contrary, not only do the Amish accept the necessity for formal schooling through the eighth grade level, but continue to provide what has been characterized by the undisputed testimony of expert educators as an "ideal" vocational education for their children in the adolescent years.

There is nothing in this record to suggest that the Amish qualities of reliability, self-reliance, and dedication to work would fail to find ready markets in today's society. Absent some contrary evidence supporting the State's position, we are unwilling to assume that persons possessing such valuable vocational skills and habits are doomed to become burdens on society should they determine to leave the Amish faith, nor is there any basis in the record to warrant a finding that an additional one or two years of formal school education beyond the eighth grade would serve to eliminate any such problem that might exist.

Insofar as the State's claim rests on the view that a brief additional period of formal education is imperative to enable the Amish to participate effectively and intelligently in our democratic process, it must fall. The Amish alternative to formal secondary school education has enabled them to function effectively in their day-to-day life under self-imposed limitations on relations with the world, and to survive and prosper in contemporary society as a separate, sharply identifiable, and highly self-sufficient community for more than 200 years in this country. In itself this is strong evidence that they are capable of fulfilling the social and political responsibilities of citizenship without compelled attendance beyond the eighth grade at the price of jeopardizing their free exercise of religious belief. . . .

The requirement for compulsory education beyond the eighth grade is a relatively recent development in our history. Less than 60 years ago, the educational requirements of almost all of the States were satisfied by completion of the elementary grades, at least where the child was regularly and lawfully em-

---

[12]Dr. Erickson had previously written: "Many public educators would be elated if their programs were as successful in preparing students for productive community life as the Amish system seems to be. In fact, while some public schoolmen strive to outlaw the Amish approach, others are being forced to emulate many of its features." D. Erickson, "Showdown at an Amish Schoolhouse: A Description and Analysis of the Iowa Controversy," in *Public Controls for Nonpublic Schools* 15, 53 (D. Erickson ed. 1969). *And see* F. Littell, "Sectarian Protestantism and the Pursuit of Wisdom: Must Technological Objective Prevail?" *id.* at 61.

ployed.[15] The independence and successful social functioning of the Amish community for a period approaching almost three centuries and more than 200 years in this country are strong evidence that there is at best a speculative gain, in terms of meeting the duties of citizenship, from an additional one or two years of compulsory formal education. Against this background it would require a more particularized showing from the State on this point to justify the severe interference with religious freedom such additional compulsory attendance would entail.

We should also note that compulsory education and child labor laws find their historical origin in common humanitarian instincts, and that the age limits of both laws have been coordinated to achieve their related objectives. In the context of this case, such considerations, if anything, support rather than detract from respondents' position. The origins of the requirement for school attendance to age 16, an age falling after the completion of elementary school but before completion of high school, are not entirely clear. But to some extent such laws reflected the movement to prohibit most child labor under age 16 that culminated in the provisions of the Federal Fair Labor Standards Act of 1938. It is true, then, that the 16 year child labor age limit may to some degree derive from a contemporary impression that children should be in school until that age. But at the same time, it cannot be denied that, conversely, the 16 year education limit reflects, in substantial measure, the concern that children under that age not be employed under conditions hazardous to their health, or in work that should be performed by adults.

The requirement of compulsory schooling to age 16 must therefore be viewed as aimed not merely at providing educational opportunities for children, but as an alternative to the equally undesirable consequence of unhealthful child labor displacing adult workers, or, on the other hand, forced idleness. The

two kinds of statutes—compulsory school attendance and child labor laws—tend to keep children of certain ages off the labor market and in school; this regimen in turn provides opportunity to prepare for a livelihood of a higher order than that which children could pursue without education and protects their health in adolescence.

In these terms, Wisconsin's interest in compelling the school attendance of Amish children to age 16 emerges as somewhat less substantial than requiring such attendance for children generally. For, while agricultural employment is not totally outside the legitimate concerns of the child labor laws, employment of children under parental guidance and on the family farm from age 14 to age 16 is an ancient tradition that lies at the periphery of the objectives of such laws. There is no intimation that the Amish employment of their children on family farms is in any way deleterious to their health or that Amish parents exploit children at tender years. Any such inference would be contrary to the record before us. Moreover, employment of Amish children on the family farm does not present the undesirable economic aspects of eliminating jobs that might otherwise be held by adults.

IV

Finally, the State, on authority of *Prince v. Massachusetts* [321 U.S. 158 (1944)], argues that a decision exempting Amish children from the State's requirement fails to recognize the substantive right of the Amish child to a secondary education, and fails to give due regard to the power of the State as *parens patriae* to extend the benefit of secondary education to children regardless of the wishes of their parents. Taken at its broadest sweep, the Court's language in *Prince* might be read to give support to the State's position. However, the Court was not confronted in *Prince* with a situation comparable to that of the

---

[15]See [U.S.] Dep't of Interior, Bureau of Education, Bulletin No. 47, *Digest of State Laws Relating to Public Education* 527–559 (1916); *Joint Hearings on S 2475 and HR 7200 Before the Senate Committee on Education and the House Committee on Labor*, 75th Cong., 1st Sess., pt. 2, at 416.

Even today, an eighth grade education fully satisfies the educational requirements of at least six States. See Ariz. Rev. Stat. Ann. §15-321 (B)(4) (1956); Ark. Stat. Ann. §80-1504 (1947); Iowa Code §299.2 (1971); S.D. Comp. Laws Ann. §13-27-1 (1967); Wyo. Stat. Ann. §21.1–48 (Supp. 1971). Mississippi has no compulsory education law. A number of other States have flexible provisions permitting children aged 14 or having completed the eighth grade to be excused from school in order to engage in lawful employment. E.g., Colo. Rev. Stat. Ann. §§123-20-5, 80-6-1 to 80-6-12 (1963); Conn. Gen. Stat. Rev. §§10-184, 10-189 (1964); D.C. Code Ann. §§31-202, 36-201 to 36-228 (1967); Ind. Ann. Stat. §§28-505-28-506, 28-519 (1948); Mass. Gen. Laws Ann. c.76, §1 (Supp. 1972) and c. 149, §86 (1971); Mo. Rev. Stat. §§167.031, 294.051 (1969); Nev. Rev. Stat. §392.110 (1968); N.M. Stat. Ann. §77-10-6 (1968).

An eighth grade education satisfied Wisconsin's formal education requirements until 1933. See Wis. Laws 1927, c.425, §97; Laws 1933, c.143. (Prior to 1933, provision was made for attendance at continuation or vocational schools by working children past the eighth grade, but only if one was maintained by the community in question.) For a general discussion of the early development of Wisconsin's compulsory education and child labor laws, see F. Ensign, *Compulsory School Attendance and Child Labor* 203–230 (1921).

Amish as revealed in this record; this is shown by the Court's severe characterization of the evils that it thought the legislature could legitimately associate with child labor, even when performed in the company of an adult. 321 U.S. at 169–170. The Court later took great care to confine *Prince* to a narrow scope in *Sherbert v. Verner*, when it stated:

> On the other hand, the Court has rejected challenges under the Free Exercise Clause to governmental regulation of certain overt acts prompted by religious beliefs or principles, "for even when the action is in accord with one's religious convictions, [it] is not totally free from legislative restrictions." *Braunfeld v. Brown*, 366 U.S. 599, 603 (1961). The conduct or actions so regulated have invariably posed some substantial threat to public safety, peace or order. *See, e.g., Reynolds v. U.S.*, 98 U.S. 145; *Jacobson v. Massachusetts*, 197 U.S. 11; *Prince v. Massachusetts*, 321 U.S. 158. . . . [374 U.S. 398, 402–403 (1963).]

This case, of course, is not one in which any harm to the physical or mental health of the child or to the public safety, peace, order, or welfare has been demonstrated or may be properly inferred. The record is to the contrary, and any reliance on that theory would find no support in the evidence.

Contrary to the suggestion of the dissenting opinion of Mr. Justice Douglas, our holding today in no degree depends on the assertion of the religious interest of the child as contrasted with that of the parents. It is the parents who are subject to prosecution here for failing to cause their children to attend school, and it is their right of free exercise, not that of their children, that must determine Wisconsin's power to impose criminal penalties on the parent. The dissent argues that a child who expresses a desire to attend public high school in conflict with the wishes of his parents should not be prevented from doing so. There is no reason for the Court to consider that point since it is not an issue in the case. The children are not parties to this litigation. The State has at no point tried this case on the theory that respondents were preventing their children from attending school against their expressed desires, and indeed the record is to the contrary. The State's position from the outset has been that it is empowered to apply its compulsory-attendance law to Amish parents in the same manner as to other parents—that is, without regard to the wishes of the child. That is the claim we reject today.

Our holding in no way determines the proper resolution of possible competing interests of parents, children, and the State in an appropriate state court proceeding in which the power of the State is asserted on the theory that Amish parents are preventing their minor children from attending high school despite their expressed desires to the contrary. Recognition of the claim of the State in such a proceeding would, of course, call into question traditional concepts of parental control over the religious upbringing and education of their minor children recognized in this Court's past decisions. It is clear that such an intrusion by a State into family decisions in the area of religious training would give rise to grave questions of religious freedom comparable to those raised here and those presented in *Pierce v. Society of Sisters*, 268 U.S. 510 (1925). On this record we neither reach nor decide those issues.

The State's argument proceeds without reliance on any actual conflict between the wishes of parents and children. It appears to rest on the potential that exemption of Amish parents from the requirements of the compulsory-education law might allow some parents to act contrary to the best interests of their children by foreclosing their opportunity to make an intelligent choice between the Amish way of life and that of the outside world. The same argument could, of course, be made with respect to all church schools short of college. There is nothing in the record or in the ordinary course of human experience to suggest that non-Amish parents generally consult with children up to ages 14–16 if they are placed in a church school of the parents' faith.

Indeed it seems clear that if the State is empowered, as *parens patriae*, to "save" a child from himself or his Amish parents by requiring an additional two years of compulsory formal high school education, the State will in large measure influence, if not determine, the religious future of the child. Even more markedly than in *Prince*, therefore, this case involves the fundamental interest of parents, as contrasted with that of the State, to guide the religious future and education of their children. The history and culture of Western civilization reflect a strong tradition of parental concern for the nurture and upbringing of their children. This primary role of the parents in the upbringing of their children is now established beyond debate as an enduring American tradition. . . .

However read, the Court's holding in *Pierce* stands as a charter of the rights of parents to direct the religious upbringing of their children. And, when the interests of parenthood are combined with a free exercise claim of the nature revealed by this record, more than merely a "reasonable relation to some purpose within the competency of the State" is required to sustain the validity of the State's requirement under the First Amendment. To be sure, the power of the parent, even when linked to a free exercise claim, may be subject to limitation under *Prince* if it appears that parental decisions will jeopardize the health or safety of the child, or have a potential for significant social burdens. But in this case, the Amish have introduced persuasive evidence undermining the arguments the State has advanced to support its claims in terms of the welfare of the child and society as a whole. The record strongly indicates that accommodating the religious objections of the Amish by forgoing one, or at most two, additional years of compulsory education will not impair the physical or mental health of the child, or result in an inability to be self-supporting, or to discharge the duties and responsibilities of citizenship, or in any other way materially detract from the welfare of society.

In the face of our consistent emphasis on the central values underlying the Religion Clauses in our constitutional scheme of government, we cannot accept a *parens patriae* claim of such all-encompassing scope and with such sweeping potential for broad and unforeseeable application as that urged by the State.

V

For the reasons stated we hold, with the Supreme Court of Wisconsin, that the First and Fourteenth Amendments prevent the State from compelling respondents to cause their children to attend formal high school to age 16. Our disposition of this case, however, in no way alters our recognition of the obvious fact that courts are not school boards or legislatures, and are ill-equipped to determine the "necessity" of discrete aspects of a State's program of compulsory education. This should suggest that courts must move with great circumspection in performing the sensitive and delicate task of weighing a State's legitimate social concern when faced with religious claims for exemption from generally applicable educational requirements. It cannot be overemphasized that we are not dealing with a way of life and mode of education by a group claiming to have recently discovered some "progressive" or more enlightened process for rearing children for modern life.

Aided by a history of three centuries as an identifiable religious sect and a long history as a successful and self-sufficient segment of American society, the Amish in this case have convincingly demonstrated the sincerity of their religious beliefs, the interrelationship of belief with their mode of life, the vital role that belief and daily conduct play in the continued survival of Old Order Amish communities and their religious organization, and the hazards presented by the State's enforcement of a statute generally valid as to others. Beyond this, they have carried the even more difficult burden of demonstrating the adequacy of their alternative mode of continuing informal vocational education in terms of precisely those overall interests that the State advances in support of its program of compulsory high school education. In light of this convincing showing, one that probably few other religious groups or sects could make, and weighing the minimal difference between what the State would require and what the Amish already accept, it was incumbent on the State to show with more particularity how its admittedly strong interest in compulsory education would be adversely affected by granting an exemption to the Amish. . . .

Nothing we hold is intended to undermine the general applicability of the State's compulsory school-attendance statutes or to limit the power of the State to promulgate reasonable standards that, while not impairing the free exercise of religion, provide for continuing agricultural vocational education under parental and church guidance by the Old Order Amish or others similarly situated. The States have had a long history of amicable and effective relationships with church-sponsored schools, and there is no basis for assuming that, in this related context, reasonable standards cannot be established concerning the content of the continuing vocational education of Amish children under parental guidance, provided always that state regulations are not inconsistent with what we have said in this opinion.

Affirmed. . . .

[The separate concurring opinion of Mr. Justice Stewart, joined by Mr. Justice Brennan, is omitted.]

Mr. Justice White, with whom Mr. Justice Brennan and Mr. Justice Stewart join, concurring. . . .

In the present case, the State is not concerned with the maintenance of an educational system as an end in itself, it is rather attempting to nurture and develop the human potential of its children, whether Amish or non-Amish: to expand their knowledge, broaden their sensibilities, kindle their imagination, foster a spirit of free inquiry, and increase their human understanding and tolerance. It is possible that most Amish children will wish to continue living the rural life of their parents, in which case their training at home will adequately equip them for their future role. Others, however, may wish to become nuclear physicists, ballet dancers, computer programmers, or historians, and for these occupations, formal training will be necessary. There is evidence in the record that many children desert the Amish faith when they come of age. A State has a legitimate interest not only in seeking to develop the latent talents of its children but also in seeking to prepare them for the life style that they may later choose, or at least to provide them with an option other than the life they have led in the past. In the circumstances of this case, although the question is close, I am unable to say that the State has demonstrated that Amish children who leave school in the eighth grade will be intellectually stultified or unable to acquire new academic skills later. The statutory minimum school attendance age set by the State is, after all, only 16.

Decision in cases such as this and the administration of an exemption for Old Order Amish from the State's compulsory school-attendance laws will inevitably involve the kind of close and perhaps repeated scrutiny of religious practices, as is exemplified in today's opinion, which the Court has heretofore been anxious to avoid. But such entanglement does not create a forbidden establishment of religion where it is essential to implement free exercise values threatened by an otherwise neutral program instituted to foster some permissible, nonreligious state objective. I join the Court because the sincerity of the Amish religious policy here is uncontested, because the potentially adverse impact of the state requirement is great, and because the State's valid interest in education has already been largely satisfied by the eight years the children have already spent in school.

Mr. Justice Douglas, dissenting in part.

I

I agree with the Court that the religious scruples of the Amish are opposed to the education of their children beyond the grade schools, yet I disagree with the Court's conclusion that the matter is within the dispensation of parents alone. The Court's analysis assumes that the only interests at stake in the case are those of the Amish parents on the one hand, and those of the State on the other. The difficulty with this approach is that, despite the Court's claim, the parents are seeking to vindicate not only their own

free exercise claims, but also those of their high-school-age children.

It is argued that the right of the Amish children to religious freedom is not presented by the facts of the case, as the issue before the Court involves only the Amish parents' religious freedom to defy a state criminal statute imposing upon them an affirmative duty to cause their children to attend high school.

First, respondents' motion to dismiss in the trial court expressly asserts, not only the religious liberty of the adults, but also that of the children, as a defense to the prosecutions. It is, of course, beyond question that the parents have standing as defendants in a criminal prosecution to assert the religious interests of their children as a defense. Although the lower courts and the majority of this Court assume an identity of interest between parent and child, it is clear that they have treated the religious interest of the child as a factor in the analysis.

Second, it is essential to reach the question to decide the case, not only because the question was squarely raised in the motion to dismiss, but also because no analysis of religious-liberty claims can take place in a vacuum. If the parents in this case are allowed a religious exemption, the inevitable effect is to impose the parents' notions of religious duty upon their children. Where the child is mature enough to express potentially conflicting desires, it would be an invasion of the child's rights to permit such an imposition without canvassing his views. As in *Prince v. Massachusetts*, 321 U.S. 158 [1944], it is an imposition resulting from this very litigation. As the child has no other effective forum, it is in this litigation that his rights should be considered. And, if an Amish child desires to attend high school, and is mature enough to have that desire respected, the State may well be able to override the parents' religiously motivated objections.

Religion is an individual experience. It is not necessary, nor even appropriate, for every Amish child to express his views on the subject in a prosecution of a single adult. Crucial, however, are the views of the child whose parent is the subject of the suit. Frieda Yoder has in fact testified that her own religious views are opposed to high-school education. I therefore join the judgment of the Court as to respondent Jonas Yoder. But Frieda Yoder's views may not be those of Vernon Yutzy or Barbara Miller. I must dissent, therefore, as to respondents Adin Yutzy and Wallace Miller as their motion to dismiss also raised the question of their children's religious liberty.

II

This issue has never been squarely presented before today. Our opinions are full of talk about the power of the parents over the child's education. . . . And we have in the past analyzed similar conflicts between parent and State with little regard for the views of the child. *See Prince v. Massachusetts, supra.* Recent cases, however, have clearly held that the children themselves have constitutionally protectable interests.

These children are "persons" within the meaning of the Bill of Rights. We have so held over and over again. . . .

On this important and vital matter of education, I think the children should be entitled to be heard. While the parents, absent dissent, normally speak for the entire family, the education of the child is a matter on which the child will often have decided views. He may want to be a pianist or an astronaut or an oceanographer. To do so he will have to break from the Amish tradition.[2]

It is the future of the student, not the future of the parents, that is imperiled by today's decision. If a parent keeps his child out of school beyond the grade school, then the child will be forever barred from entry into the new and amazing world of diversity that we have today. The child may decide that that is the preferred course, or he may rebel. It is the student's judgment, not his parents', that is essential if we are to give full meaning to what we have said about the Bill of Rights and of the right of students to be masters of their own destiny. If he is harnessed to the Amish way of life by those in authority over him and if his education is truncated, his entire life may be stunted and deformed. The child, therefore, should be given an opportunity to be heard before the State gives the exemption which we honor today.

The views of the two children in question were not canvassed by the Wisconsin courts. The matter should be explicitly reserved so that new hearings can be held on remand of the case.

III

I think the emphasis of the Court on the "law and order" record of this Amish group of people is quite irrelevant. A religion is a religion irrespective of what the misdemeanor or felony records of its members might be. I am not at all sure how the Catholics, Episcopalians, the Baptists, Jehovah's Witnesses, the Unitarians, and my own Presbyterians would make out if subjected to such a test. It is, of course, true that if a group or society was organized to perpetuate crime and if that is its motive, we would have rather startling problems akin to those that were raised when some years back a particular sect was challenged here as operating on a fraudulent basis. *United States v. Ballard,* 322 U.S. 78, 64 S.Ct. 822, 88 L.Ed. 1148. But no such factors are present here, and the Amish, whether with a high or low criminal record,[5] certainly qualify by all historic standards as a religion within the meaning of the First Amendment.

The Court rightly rejects the notion that actions, even though religiously grounded, are always outside the protection of the Free Exercise Clause of the First Amendment. . . .

Action, which the Court deemed to be antisocial, could be punished even though it was grounded on deeply held and sincere religious convictions. What we do today, at least in this respect, opens the way to give organized religion a broader base than it has ever enjoyed. . . .

In another way, however, the Court retreats when in reference to Henry Thoreau it says his "choice was philosophical and personal rather than religious, and such belief does not rise to the demands of the Religion Clauses." That is contrary to what we held in *United States v. Seeger,* 380 U.S. 163, where we were concerned with the meaning of the words "religious training and belief" in the Selective Service Act, which were the basis of many conscientious objector claims. We said:

---

[2]A significant number of Amish children do leave the Old Order. Professor Hostetler notes that "[t]he loss of members is very limited in some Amish districts and considerable in others." *Children in Amish Society* 226. In one Pennsylvania church, he observed a defection rate of 30%. *Ibid.* Rates up to 50% have been reported by others. Casad, "Compulsory High School Attendance and the Old Order Amish: A Commentary on *State v. Garber,*" 16 *Kan. L. Rev.* 423, 434 n.51 (1968).

[5]The observation of Justice Heffernan, dissenting below, that the principal opinion in his court portrayed the Amish as leading a life of "idyllic agrarianism," is equally applicable to the majority opinion in this Court. So, too, is his observation that such a portrayal rests on a "mythological basis." Professor Hostetler has noted that "[d]rinking among the youth is common in all the large Amish settlements." *Amish Society* 283. Moreover, "[i]t would appear that among the Amish the rate of suicide is just as high, if not higher, than for the nation." *Id.,* at 300. He also notes an unfortunate Amish "preoccupation with filthy stories," *id.,* at 282, as well as significant "rowdyism and stress." *Id.,* at 281. These are not traits peculiar to the Amish, of course. The point is that the Amish are not people set apart and different.

Within that phrase would come all sincere religious beliefs which are based upon a power or being, or upon a faith, to which all else is subordinate or upon which all else is ultimately dependent. The test might be stated in these words: A sincere and meaningful belief which occupies in the life of its possessor a place parallel to that filled by the God of those admittedly qualifying for the exemption comes within the statutory definition. This construction avoids imputing to Congress an intent to classify different religious beliefs, exempting some and excluding others, and is in accord with the well-established congressional policy of equal treatment for those whose opposition to service is grounded in their religious tenets. [380 U.S. at 176.]

* * *

I adhere to these exalted views of "religion" and see no acceptable alternative to them now that we have become a Nation of many religions and sects, representing all of the diversities of the human race. . . .

NOTES AND QUESTIONS

1. Historical Background

Conflicts between the 30,000 American Amish (the total Amish population is estimated at 134,000, but only adults are counted as full church members) and the government have existed since the Amish arrived in the United States in 1727; in recent years disputes over schooling have predominated. *See generally* J. Hostetler, *Amish Society* (4th ed. (1993); D. Kraybill, ed., *The Amish and the State* (1993); A. Keim, ed., *Compulsory Education and the Amish* (1975); Hostetler, "The Amish and the Law: A Religious Minority and Its Legal Encounters," 40 *Wash. & Lee L. Rev.* 33, 40–44 (1984). The adventures of the Amish in Iowa are the best known and documented. The difficulties of the plain folk began with an effort in 1961 to unify the Hazelton and Olwein school districts. The Amish, who operated two private one-room schools in the Hazelton district, held the swing vote in the unification campaign. After high-echelon school officials promised to provide public schools tailored to their needs, the Amish voted for district reorganization. Many Hazelton residents were upset both by voter approval of the unification plan and by the Amish role in the affair. That, and a more general anti-Amish sentiment, led the school officials to renege on their promise to the Amish and to declare that the Amish schools would stay open no longer than two years and that—after fifteen years of doing

so—no effort would be made to fit school instruction to Amish needs. The Amish retaliated with the announcement that they would no longer permit state-certified teachers to instruct in Amish schools. Already highly irritated, neighbors of the Amish demanded that the Amish be prosecuted for failure to send their children to schools with certified teachers. Amish fathers were accordingly fined and, when they refused to pay, sentenced to three days in jail. Newspaper pictures of Amish women visiting their jailed husbands elicited national sympathy for the plain folk and resulted in volumes of disparaging mail to Iowa officials.

After the routine of Amish fathers driving their buggies to town to appear in court and then faithfully refusing to pay their fines grew tiresome, state and local school officials attempted, without success, to arrange a compromise with the Amish. Then they announced that the Amish children were truants and would be bused to public school. One November morning in 1965, a school bus departed for Amish country, followed by carloads of newspaper reporters. No children were to be found at their homes, but some were discovered at the local school. Before the distraught children filed out of the one-room school, the superintendent announced to the reporters that the children would board the bus and be driven to school. But it was not to be. An unidentified individual yelled "run," and the children scattered through the barbed wire fence and into the cornfields. Cameras clicked and pictures of small, frightened Amish children climbing the cornfield fence found their way into national newspapers. School officials captured one screaming six-year-old girl and a weeping thirteen-year-old boy who had been unable to keep up with their classmates.

The governor then decided to intervene and push for a settlement. In its 1967 session, the state legislature, strongly influenced by outside parties, exempted the Amish from the state's minimum educational standards laws. The state Superintendent of Education was given discretion to fix educational requirements. *See* Erickson, "Showdown in an Amish Schoolhouse," in *Public Controls for Nonpublic Schools* 53 (1969).

Pennsylvania was the first state to attempt to compel the Amish children to attend public school. After initial embarrassments not unlike those suffered by Iowa school officials, the Pennsylvania code was reinterpreted to permit the Amish to manage their own schools. The school day of the Amish school is like that of public schools, and attendance is taken. Beyond these two aspects, however, the Amish school in Pennsylvania is essentially unregulated: Teachers, for example, are not required to be certified. Eighth-grade graduates may enter "vocational high schools" where they perform farm and household chores under parental supervision and attend classes a few hours a week. *See* Hostetler, "The Amish and the Law: A Religious Minority and Its Legal Encounter," 40 *Wash. & Lee L. Rev.* 33, 41 (1984).

In Ohio, Amish schools operate in defiance of the state school code but school officials, perhaps learning from the Iowa and Pennsylvania experiences, have chosen to ignore the situation. *See State Ex. Rel. Nagle v. Olin*, 64 Ohio St.2d 341, 415 N.E.2d 279 (1980). In 1982 a newly formed Amish community left Nebraska in response to a state requirement that teachers in Amish schools must be certified. Hostetler, *supra* at 44.

2. The Constitutional Standard

Yoder raises the question not explicitly posed in *Pierce*: Are there constitutional interests of parents and children that outweigh the state's interest in compelling all youngsters to attend school? The question is one of extreme difficulty; as the *Yoder* decision notes, the contending interests are of the "highest order." Parental direction of the religious upbringing of children has a "high place in our society," the Court declares. The values underlying the constitutional protections of religious freedom have been "zealously protected, sometimes even at the expense of other interests of admittedly high social importance." Compulsory education laws, the Court notes, "demonstrate our recognition of the importance of education to our democratic society." How is the Court meaningfully to evaluate and balance such imponderables? *Cf. United States v. Lee*, 455 U.S. 252, 102 S.Ct. 1051, 71 L.Ed.2d 127 (1982) (Amish employers not exempt from Social Security tax on Amish employees); *United States v. Slabaugh*, 848 F.2d 113 (8th Cir. 1988) (Amish criminal defendant not exempt from photograph requirement despite religious convictions). *See generally* Laycock, "A Survey of Religious Liberty in the United States," 47 *Ohio St. L. J.* 409, 427–31 (1986).

a. The Amish Interest in Religious Freedom. The majority opinion notes that the Amish have "convincingly demonstrated the sincerity of their religious beliefs." What factors does the Court consider in reaching that judgment? Should the Court attempt

to assess religious sincerity? *See generally* Marcus, "The Forum of Conscience: Applying Standards Under the Free Exercise Clause," 1973 *Duke L. J.* 1217.

Would the result in *Yoder* have been the same had the Court not concluded that the Amish faith and mode of life are inseparable and interdependent? *See State v. Patzer*, 382 N.W.2d 631 (N.D. 1986); L. Kotin and W. F. Aikman, *Legal Foundations of Compulsory School Attendance* 252 (1980). In *Duro v. District Attorney, Second Judicial District of North Carolina*, 712 F.2d 96 (4th Cir. 1983), the court denied plaintiff's claim that North Carolina's compulsory school attendance law denied him his right of free exercise of religion. The court distinguished *Yoder* on the following grounds:

> The [parents in this case] . . . , unlike their Amish counterparts [in *Yoder*], are not members of a community which has existed for three centuries and has a long history of being a successful, self-sufficient, segment of American society. Furthermore, in *Yoder*, the Amish children attended public school through the eighth grade and then obtained informal vocational training to enable them to assimilate into the self-contained Amish community. However, in the present case, [plaintiff] . . . refuses to enroll his children in any public or nonpublic school for any length of time, but still expects them to be fully integrated and live normally in the modern world upon reaching the age of 18.

Id. at 98. *See also Burrow v. State*, 282 Ark. 479, 669 S.W.2d 441 (1984); *Delconte v. State*, 65 N.C.App. 262, 308 S.E.2d 898 (App. 1983); *State v. Riddle*, 168 W.Va. 429, 285 S.E.2d 359 (1981). The court disagreed with plaintiff's contention that the state's case was weakened by virtue of North Carolina's "deregulation of nonpublic education." (North Carolina only imposed attendance, disease immunization, and reasonable fire, health, and safety inspection requirements.) *Id.* The court also held that plaintiff had "not demonstrated that home instruction will prepare his children to be self-sufficient participants in our modern society." *Id.* at 99. *See generally* Lines, "Private Education Alternatives and State Regulation," 12 *J. of Law & Educ.* 189 (1983).

Does *Yoder* affect the result of the following cases where any infringement on religious freedom was found to be outweighed by the state's interest in compelling the child to attend public school? *Commonwealth v. Bey*, 166 Pa. Super. 136, 70 A.2d 693 (1950) (Muslim parents refused to send their child to public school on Friday, the sacred day of their religion);

In re Currence, 42 Misc.2d 418, 248 N.Y.S.2d 251 (Fam. Ct., 1963) (parents belonging to the Ancient Divine Order of Melchizedek kept their child out of public school on a Wednesday-through-Thursday sabbath); *Commonwealth v. Renfrew,* 332 Mass. 492, 126 N.E.2d 109 (1955) (Buddhist parents who did not wish their children exposed to the tenets of the Christian faith raised their child at home); *Application of Auster,* 198 Misc. 1055, 100 N.Y.S.2d 60 (Sup. Ct. 1950), *appeal dismissed,* 342 U.S. 884, 72 S.Ct. 178, 96 L.Ed. 663 (1951) (Orthodox Jew sought to send his son to unaccredited yeshiva, believing that secular secondary education was forbidden by his religion). Does *Yoder* overturn cases upholding state laws requiring immunization against diphtheria and other diseases as a condition for attending public schools? *See Zucht v. King,* 260 U.S. 174, 43 S.Ct. 24, 67 L.Ed. 194 (1922); *Hanzel v. Arter,* 625 F. Supp. 1259 (S.D. Ohio 1985); *Itz v. Penick,* 493 S.W.2d 506 (Tex. 1973), *appeal dismissed,* 412 U.S. 925, 93 S.Ct. 2754, 37 L.Ed.2d 152. *See generally* T. van Geel, *The Courts and American Education* 120 (1987).

How credible is the *Yoder* assertion that "compulsory school attendance to age 16 for Amish children carries with it a very real threat of undermining the Amish community and religious practice as it exists today"? Is it critical that "the Amish people are engaged in a social discourse that requires them to build and maintain a redemptive community"? Hostetler, *supra* at 34. Consider the following comment:

> Amish parents have remarkable control over their children, and neither parents nor children, much as they might wish it to be otherwise, live entirely separate from our world. Amish children ride in cars, hear radios, read newspapers and magazines and books, perhaps even sneak off to the movies. Amish children know a great deal more of the outside world than their parents might wish; certainly, even without schools, they are exposed to it frequently. Yet the vast majority of them remain in the faith and join the church. And it may be unrealistic, as well as futile, to argue to the courts that the existence of their religion depends on judicial exemptions for their children from compulsory education laws.

Note, "The Right Not to Be Modern Men: The Amish and Compulsory Education," 53 *Va. L. Rev.* 925, 950 (1967). *See* Rosin, "Modern Vices Test Amish Values," *Washington Post,* June 27, 1998, at A1 (reporting that Amish youth were arrested for buying cocaine, and noting that most Amish teenagers in Lancaster County, Pennsylvania, join youth groups after completing the eighth grade, some of whose members drive cars, smoke, "see movies, bar hop and hold all-night parties," and that teenagers have been taken into custody by the police for underage drinking).

The majority in *Yoder* noted that the state's interest in compulsory schooling to age sixteen, in addition to providing educational opportunities for children, was also to ensure that children below that age would "not be employed under conditions hazardous to their health, or in work that should be performed by adults." The Court noted that the compulsory school attendance statutes and child labor laws operated together to protect children. However, the state's interest was "somewhat less substantial" when it came to the employment of Amish children "under parental guidance and on the family farm." The Court said that "There is no intimation that the Amish employment of their children on family farms is in any way deleterious to their health or that Amish parents exploit children at tender years," nor did employment on the family farm "present the undesirable economic aspects of eliminating jobs that might otherwise be held by adults." In this light, consider H.R. 221, the Amish Youth Employment Bill, passed by the House on March 2, 1999, and intended to amend the Fair Labor Standards Act of 1938 to allow an exemption from the prohibition on the use of child labor under the age of eighteen in occupations considered "hazardous for the employment of children." The exemption would allow minors between the ages of fourteen and eighteen to work in sawmills or in woodworking enterprises, with certain safety precautions, if the minor is a "member of a religious sect whose established teachings do not permit formal education beyond the eighth grade." The bill also requires that the children work under the supervision of someone of the Amish faith, although not necessarily a relative. (The enterprise itself need not be Amish-owned or run.) Does this amendment undermine the Court's rationale for its holding in *Yoder?* Does the amendment violate the Establishment Clause by providing an exemption only for children of the Amish faith? Suppose an Amish child works in the sawmill in order to earn money to see movies, bar hop, and buy a car. Does the amendment encourage displacing adult laborers with child workers? *See* H.R. Report No. 106-31, Committee on Education and Workforce, 106th Cong., 1st Sess. 1999, Minority Views.

How important is it to the *Yoder* decision that the Amish religion countenanced school attendance until the eighth grade? *See State v. Patzer*, 382 N.W.2d 631 (N.D. 1986); *Howell v. State*, 723 S.W.2d 755 (Tex. App. 1986); *State v. Riddle*, 168 W.Va. 429, 285 S.E.2d 359 (1981). What would be the result if only a sixth-grade education were permitted? What would be the result if a particular sect permitted no formal schooling at all, but the good citizenship and economic self-reliance of its members were unquestioned? What if the members of a religious sect, demanding no formal education after the eighth grade, held unimpeachable religious beliefs but were not always "very law abiding"?

b. Parental Rights. "However read," Chief Justice Burger states, "the Court's holding in *Pierce* stands as a charter of the rights of parents to direct the religious upbringing of their children." 406 U.S. at 233. *See generally* Friedman, "The Parental Right to Control the Religious Education of a Child," 29 *Harv. L. Rev.* 485 (1916). Is that the proposition for which *Pierce* stands? *See* Woodhouse, "Who Owns the Child? *Meyer* and *Pierce* and the Child as Property," 33 *William & Mary L. Rev.* 995 (1992).

In *Prince v. Commonwealth of Massachusetts*, 321 U.S. 158, 64 S.Ct. 438, 88 L.Ed. 645 (1944), nine-year-old Betty, under the supervision of her aunt and custodian, Mrs. Prince, sold religious literature on the street in violation of Massachusetts child-labor laws. Both Betty and Mrs. Prince were Jehovah's Witnesses and believed it their religious duty to do this work. The Court held for the state; in its opinion it discussed the "harmful possibilities" that the legislature sought to prevent and then noted: "Parents may be free to become martyrs themselves. But it does not follow they are free . . . to make martyrs of their children before they have reached the age of full and legal discretion when they can make that choice for themselves." 321 U.S. at 170, 64 S.Ct. at 444. *Prince* is characterized in *Yoder* as a case in which the conduct regulated posed a substantial threat to public safety and on that basis is distinguishable from the Amish situation. *See generally* Mangrum, "Family Rights and Compulsory School Laws," 21 *Creighton L. Rev.* 1019, 1039–40 (1988). How satisfactory is that distinction? Should *Prince* have been overruled? Was the danger to the physical or mental health of the child in *Prince* any more than the danger that might be "properly inferred" in *Yoder*?

In the light of *Yoder* and *Prince*, consider these comments:

When viewed with the common law's acceptance of parental control over the child's religious indoctrination, the *Yoder* holding, with its interpretation of the line of cases from *Pierce* through *Prince*, might be read as establishing that the first amendment's free exercise provisions vest in the parents a constitutionally-protected right to direct their child's religious upbringing in the absence of any compelling reason for state interference. Thus the common law standard of "best interest of the child," with its presumption that those interests can best be served without governmental interference, has been incorporated in the first and fourteenth amendments, with the result that the state may not circumscribe parental discretion in religious matters unless some palpable harm would otherwise befall the child.

Note, "Adjudicating What *Yoder* Left Unresolved: Religious Rights for Minor Children after *Danforth* and *Carey*," 126 *U. Pa. L. Rev.* 1135, 1145 (1978). *See also* Arons, "The Separation of School and State: *Pierce* Reconsidered," 46 *Harv. Educ. Rev.* 76 (1976). *But see* Dwyer, "The Children We Abandon: Religious Exemptions to Child Welfare and Education Laws as Denials of Equal Protection to Children of Religious Objectors," 74 *NC L. Rev.* 1321 (1996). What is the source of this constitutional entitlement? What is its scope? In *Troxel v. Granville*, 530 U.S. 57, 120 S.Ct. 2054, 147 L.Ed.2d 49 (2000), involving a broad state nonparental visitation statute, the Supreme Court stated in a plurality opinion that the substantive due process interest at issue in the case—"the interest of parents in the care, custody, and control of their children—is perhaps the oldest of the fundamental liberty interests recognized by this Court," citing *Meyer v. Nebraska, Pierce v. Society of Sisters, Wisconsin v. Yoder*, and numerous subsequent cases. The plurality concluded that "in light of this extensive precedent, it cannot now be doubted that the Due Process Clause of the Fourteenth Amendment protects the fundamental right of parents to make decisions concerning the care, custody, and control of their children." Note that the United Nations General Assembly in *The Universal Declaration of Human Rights* states that "parents have a prior right to choose the kind of education that shall be given to their children." G. A. Res. 217 [III], art. 26 (1948).

c. Interests of the State. Wisconsin suggested two justifications for compulsory education: the preparation of the child for political citizenship and the development of economic self-reliance. *See generally* Project, "Education and the Law: State Interests and Individual Rights," 74 *Mich. L. Rev.* 1373, 1384–85 (1976). Are these concerns satisfied, as the *Yoder* decision suggests, by eight years of schooling?

The answer to that query may turn on whether Amish youngsters remain in the Amish community or choose a quite different lifestyle. As Justice White notes in his concurring opinion: "It is possible that most Amish children will wish to continue living the rural life of their parents, in which case their training at home will adequately equip them for their future role. Others, however, may wish to become nuclear physicists, ballet dancers, computer programmers, or historians, and for these occupations, formal training will be necessary." 406 U.S. at 239. Does the state have a legitimate interest in providing maximum educational opportunities to all youngsters? Does it have the right to do so by protecting a child "against the ignorance of his parents"? *See* K. Alexander and K. F. Jordan, *Legal Aspects of Educational Choice* 5 (1973).

If, in fact, few Amish youngsters deserted their community for the larger society, the interest might be dismissed as of trivial practical significance. But is that the case? Compare the discussions of Justices Burger, White, and Douglas on this point. And consider the conclusion reached by the Wisconsin Supreme Court in *Yoder*: "[T]his harm to the Amish [is not] justified because on speculation some Amish children may after reaching adulthood leave their religion. To force a worldly education on all Amish children, the majority of whom do not want or need it, in order to confer a dubious benefit on the few who might later reject their religion is not a compelling interest." *State v. Yoder*, 49 Wis.2d 430, 440, 182 N.W.2d 539, 543–44 (1971). What does that statement assume with respect to the wishes of Amish children (see d., *infra*)? Compare the position of the dissent in the same case: "The state's interest and obligation runs to each and every child in the state. In the context of the public law of the state, no child's education is below the concern of the law." 49 Wis.2d at 451, 182 N.W.2d at 549.

The state argues that the Amish faith fosters ignorance. The Court's response speaks to the "productive and very law-abiding" nature of the Amish. Does the response confront the question? The Court also notes that the Amish community provides "valuable vocational skills and habits." Just how valuable are these skills likely to be outside of the religious community?

The last paragraph of the majority opinion suggests the state may require Amish children to attend an "Amish vocational school" or at least regulate the content of continuing vocational training provided by Amish parents. One commentator asserts: "It is not simply public school to which [the Amish] object, but all schooling above the eighth grade." Arons, "Compulsory Education: The Plain People Resist," *Saturday Review*, Jan. 15, 1972, at 53. If "the purpose of Amish education is not to get ahead in the world but to get to heaven," what is the likely outcome of a suit by Amish plaintiffs alleging that any type of school at all beyond the eighth grade is inconsistent with their faith? *See* S. Arons, *Compelling Belief* 138 (1983).

d. The Interest of Amish Children. The possibility of a clash between Amish youngsters and their parents is skirted by the Court, which notes that the children were not parties to the litigation. *See generally* Note, "The Interest of the Child in Home Education Question: *Wisconsin v. Yoder* Re-examined," 18 *Ind. L. Rev.* 711 (1985). Since children must be represented in court by an adult (typically but not necessarily by a parent or legal guardian), how might the Amish youngsters make themselves parties to the litigation? *See generally* Guggenheim, "The Right to Be Represented but Not Heard: Reflections on Legal Representation for Children," 59 *N.Y.U. L. Rev.* 76 (1984). The Court also denies the likelihood of a parent-child conflict, noting that "there is nothing in the record or in the ordinary course of human experience to suggest that non-Amish parents generally consult with children up to ages 14 through 16 if they are placed in a church school of their parents' faith." 406 U.S. at 232, 92 S.Ct. at 1541. Is the observation correct? Note that historically American courts sometimes did intervene to thwart "officious intermeddlers" from interfering with parental authority over their children's religious orientation. For example, in *Prieto v. St. Alphonsus Convent of Mercy*, 52 La. Ann. 631, 27 So. 153 (1900), the Louisiana Supreme Court ordered a convent to expel a seventeen-year-old who sought to become a nun without her mother's consent. *See generally* Montana, "The Best Interest of the Child and the Constitutional Rights of Cult Member Parents: Resolution of a Conflict," 5 *N.Y. Law Sch. J. of Human Rts.* 97 (1987).

If the views of the Amish children do bear consideration, how should they be expressed? Should the Court appoint a guardian explicitly to represent the children? Should the children be canvassed, as Justice Douglas's dissent suggests? What impact would such a venture have on the Amish child and on the Amish community? Any device designed to identify the independent interest of Amish youngsters necessarily intrudes into family and community life, imposing both political and legal costs. Is the child's right to be heard of sufficient importance to justify such an intrusion? *See generally* Knudsen, "The Education of the Amish Child," 62 *Calif. L. Rev.* 1506 (1974).

The *Yoder* decision preserves the religious and community interests of the Amish, but in so doing it denies Amish children the opportunity of acquiring sufficient education to choose for themselves whether to stay in the community; a decision compelling these children to attend school would seriously affect the future viability of the Amish religion. Is there a resolution of the issues less far-reaching in its consequences than either of these alternatives? Suppose an Amish child claimed that compelled attendance at a sectarian school violated her constitutional right of free exercise of religion. How should a court treat that claim? Murphy, "Rights and Borderline Cases," 19 *Ariz. L. Rev.* 238 (1978), suggests that in some instances a child has a right to paternalistic treatment. Is this such an instance? Is there a right to compulsory education?

The rights of the child against both his or her parents and the potential role of the state as *parens patriae* have frequently presented perplexing problems to the courts. In *In re Green*, 448 Pa. 338, 292 A.2d 387 (1972), parents refused on religious grounds to permit blood transfusion preparations necessary to proceed with a spinal operation on a sixteen-year-old boy. The Pennsylvania Supreme Court found that where the situation was not one of life-or-death urgency, the state interest in the well-being of the child did not outweigh the interests of the parents in religious freedom. *See also In re Seiferth*, 309 N.Y. 80, 127 N.E.2d 820 (1955) (fourteen-year-old boy with harelip and cleft palate). The court, however, reserved its decision in the light of a possible parent-child conflict and remanded the case for a hearing to determine the child's views.

> [T]he ultimate question . . . is whether a parent's religious beliefs are paramount to the possibly adverse decision of the child. . . . It would be most anomalous to ignore [the child] in this situation when we consider the preference of an intelligent child of sufficient maturity in determining custody. . . . Moreover, we have held that a child of the same age can waive constitu-

tional rights and receive a life sentence. . . . Indeed, minors can now bring a personal injury action in Pennsylvania against their parents.

292 A.2d at 392. The dissent took issue with the majority's disposition of the case.

> I do not believe that sending the case back to allow Ricky to be heard is an adequate solution. We are herein dealing with a young boy who has been crippled most of his life, consequently, he has been under the direct control of his parents for that time. To now presume that he could make an independent decision as to what is best for his welfare and health is not reasonable.

292 A.2d at 395. (The child decided not to have the operation.) In many cases, however, the courts weigh the necessity of medical treatment against the parents' free exercise of religion rights, without ascertaining the wishes of the child. *See, e.g., In the Matter of Elisha McCauley,* 409 Mass. 134, 565 N.E.2d 411 (1991) (blood transfusion ordered for eight-year-old girl with leukemia despite religious objections of parents); *Matter of Hamilton,* 657 S.W.2d 425 (Tenn. App. 1983) (radiation and chemotherapy ordered for twelve-year-old girl with Ewing's Sarcoma, despite religious objection of father); *People in Interest of D.L.E.,* 645 P.2d 271 (Colo. 1982). *See generally* Kessler, "Praying for Relief from *Parens Patriae*: Should a Child Be Allowed to Refuse Life-Saving Medical Treatment on Religious Grounds?" 2 *J. of Law, Ethics & Pub. Policy* 673 (1986). In some cases, courts have held that even when a "mature minor" has clearly indicated a desire to refuse medical treatment on Free Exercise grounds, the state's interests prevail. *See Novak v. Cobb County–Kennestone Hospital Authority,* 849 F. Supp. 1559 (N.D. Ga. 1994) (holding, in case involving sixteen-year-old boy seeking to refuse blood transfusions on religious grounds, that adolescents were "not able to make sound judgments concerning many decisions, including their need for medical care or treatment").

Can *In re Green* be reconciled with *Yoder*? Is the only difference between the two situations one of the foreseeability of serious injury to the child? What if the malady is not literally life threatening but may impede normal psychological development? *See In re Sampson,* 29 N.Y.2d 900, 328 N.Y.S.2d 686, 278 N.E.2d 918 (1972) (despite mother's religious objections, court ordered operation to partially correct severe facial deformity). Is this difference sufficient to justify the conclusion in *Yoder* that the education of the child is for the parents alone to determine? Note in the *Green* case that there was apparently no show-ing of actual conflict between parent and child. Nonetheless, the Pennsylvania court considered the child's opinion essential and thus in essence adopted the approach of Justice Douglas in *Yoder*. But see *In re Sampson*, 29 N.Y.2d 900, 328 N.Y.S.2d 686, 278 N.E.2d 918 (1972) (minor's consent not necessary). Consider in this context the criticism of the dissent in *Green*. Does it apply with equal validity to the opinion of Justice Douglas?

In *Planned Parenthood of Southeastern Pennsylvania v. Casey*, 505 U.S. 833, 112 S.Ct. 2791, 120 L.Ed.2d 674 (1992), the Supreme Court held that it is not unconstitutional for a state to require that a mi-nor seeking an abortion obtain the consent of a par-ent or a guardian, as long as the requirement in-cludes a provision allowing a court, where the parent or guardian has refused to consent, to authorize an abortion upon determining that the minor is mature and capable of giving informed consent and has in fact given her informed consent, or that an abortion would be in her best interests. Is *Casey* distinguish-able from *Green* and *Yoder*? Is the question the com-petence of the minor to make an informed decision in different contexts, or is it the nature of the state's interest that varies? The growing number of in-stances in which juveniles are treated as adults in criminal law is another illustration of the inconsis-tent view the law has of the autonomy of adolescents. *See* Office of Juvenile Justice and Delinquency Pre-vention, *Juvenile Offenders and Victims: A National Report* (1995). Consider these remarks by Professor Martha Minow:

> A persistent argument against rights for children is that children lack the autonomy necessary to engage in adversarial exchange, to protect their own interests. . . . These objections grow out of a more widely accepted conception of rights, which relies on the idea that the rights-bearing person is an autonomous individual ca-pable of exercising choice for personal ends and able to protect personal freedom from the pressure and power of others.
>
> * * *
>
> [But] . . . legal rights are interdependent and mu-tually defining. . . . Rights, in fact, could be under-stood as simply the articulation of legal consequences for particular patterns of human and institutional relationships. . . .
>
> Autonomy, then, is not a precondition for any indi-vidual's exercise of rights. The only precondition is that the community is willing to allow individuals to make claims and to participate in the shifting of boundaries.

Minow, "Interpreting Rights: An Essay for Robert Cover," 96 *Yale L. J.* 1860, 1882, 1884–5 (1987). *See also* Glennon and Schwartz, "Foreword: Looking Back, Looking Ahead: The Evolution of Children's Rights," 68 *Temple L. Rev.* 1557, 1562–65 (1995); Note, "Free Exercise of Religion: The Conflict Be-tween a Parent's Rights and a Minor Child's Right in Determining the Religion of the Child," 34 *Univ. Louisville J. of Fam. Law* 219 (1995–96).

May a child ever assert his own interest in educa-tional liberty? In *In re Mario*, 65 Misc.2d 708, 317 N.Y.S.2d 659 (Fam.Ct. 1971), the New York family court upheld the assignment of a thirteen-year-old boy, "beyond parental control in regard to his school atten-dance," to Warwick State Training School, a residen-tial "rehabilitative" institution. The respondent as-serted that such placement "imposes a restraint on his liberty." The court found the restraint constitutional

> because reasonable rehabilitative measures are justi-fied by respondent's truancy. . . . The State has the power to perform the parental role of insuring the child's education and training, when the parent is un-able to control him sufficiently to perform it. If chil-dren were permitted the same freedom of choice as adults, they might well be unequipped when they at-tain adulthood to exercise any freedom of choice— specifically, without any education or training, they would be unable to choose to work in a job for which they in fact have the potential.

317 N.Y.S.2d at 668.

Is the state's interest more compelling in *Mario* than in *Yoder*? How would the *Yoder* majority (or Jus-tice Douglas) resolve this issue?

3. The Scope of the Yoder Decision

a. A Broad Challenge to Compulsoriness? The *Yo-der* Court notes that the Amish way of life has come "into conflict increasingly with the requirements of contemporary society. . . . There can be no as-sumption that today's majority is 'right,' and that the Amish and others like them are 'wrong.' " 406 U.S. at 223. Are these "others" only religious sects, as the Court's opinion intimates? *See Mason v. General Brown Cent. Sch. District*, 851 F.2d 47 (2d Cir. 1988) (belief in "genetic blueprint" not a religious belief and thus no exemption from immunization requirement for school-age son). Why should the children of a contemporary Thoreau, whose objec-tions to schooling derive not from a religion but from a philosophy of life, be forced to submit to socialization in debatable political and social values? Does freedom of religion have a higher claim to constitutional protection than freedom of expression? One commentator notes:

> The conflict of state-sponsored socialization with private values appears in bold constitutional relief when these private values can be articulated as a religion. *Yoder* holds, therefore, that state-imposed socialization is unconstitutional when it conflicts directly with religious tenets. But none of the value conflicts the Court cited—competitiveness versus cooperation, intellect versus wisdom, or disagreement over the status of manual work, for example—is necessarily religious. Any non-Amish family might be equally committed to such values and see them as threatened by state-sponsored socialization in schools. Religion provided the constitutional nexus between the plaintiff's injury and the state's policy, but the evidence the Court found compelling also supports a broader doctrine: any conflict between public schooling and a family's basic and sincerely held values interferes with the family's First Amendment rights. Thus, even though the opinion was couched in terms of religious beliefs and practices, the Chief Justice's recognition of the various elements of value inculcation, none of which is itself of religious character, has the effect of eroding the meaningfulness of the distinction between secular and religious values upon which the Court has relied so heavily.

Arons, "The Separation of School and State: Pierce Reconsidered," 46 *Harv. Educ. Rev.* 76, 84–85 (1976). *But cf. Mason v. General Brown Cent. Sch. District, supra.*

Does the *Yoder* opinion in fact raise this range of questions, undercutting the *Pierce* premise that the state may compel children to attend some form of school? *See* T. van Geel, *The Courts and American Education* 21 (1987).

b. Compulsoriness and Equal Educational Opportunity. In re Skipwith, 14 Misc.2d 325, 180 N.Y.2d 852 (Dom. Rel. Ct. 1958), poses a quite different constitutional challenge to compulsoriness. In *Skipwith*, parents refused to send their children to ghetto schools, which they alleged were inferior to predominantly white schools. In a suit brought by the Board of Education to compel attendance, the parents introduced testimony of educators and psychologists concerning the harmful impact of racial segregation and evidence that the school in question had unlicensed teachers filling forty-three of eighty-five positions, a proportion substantially greater than the city-wide average (see chapter 4 for a discussion of racial

discrimination and equal educational opportunity). Is it appropriate—as a matter either of policy or constitutional law—to keep children from school as a means of addressing the inequalities asserted by the *Skipwith* parents? Compare *Matter of Baum*, 382 N.Y.S.2d 672 (Fam.Ct. 1976) (allegedly racist remarks by teacher do not justify withdrawing child from public school).

4. *The Demise of the Free Exercise Balancing Test?*

In *Employment Division, Department of Human Resources of Oregon v. Smith*, 494 U.S. 872, 110 S.Ct. 1595, 108 L.Ed. 876 (1990), the Supreme Court addressed the following question:

> [W]hether the Free Exercise Clause of the First Amendment permits the State of Oregon to include religiously inspired peyote use within the reach of its general criminal prohibition on use of that drug, and thus permits the State to deny unemployment benefits to persons dismissed from their jobs because of such religiously inspired use.

494 U.S. at 873, 110 S.Ct. at 1597, 108 L.Ed. at 882. Justice Scalia, writing for the majority, held that Oregon's drug law did not violate the religious freedom of two members of the Native American Church who were fired from their jobs with a private drug rehabilitation organization for ingesting peyote for sacramental purposes at a religious ceremony and subsequently denied unemployment benefits. In a far-reaching decision, Justice Scalia stated that the Court had "never held that an individual's religious beliefs excuse him from compliance with an otherwise valid law prohibiting conduct that the state is free to regulate." 494 U.S. at 878–79, 110 S.Ct. at 1600, 108 L.Ed. at 885. He also specifically declined to embrace a balancing test, holding that "the government's ability to enforce generally applicable prohibitions of socially harmful conduct . . . 'cannot depend on measuring the effects of a governmental action on a religious objector's spiritual development.' " 494 U.S. at 884, 110 S.Ct. at 1603, 108 L.Ed. at 889, citing *Lyng v. Northwest Indian Cemetery Protective Association*, 485 U.S. 439, 451, 108 S.Ct. 1319, 1326, 99 L.Ed.2d 534, 548 (1988).

Is the analysis in *Smith* consistent with the Court's reasoning and result in *Yoder*? Does your answer depend on whether the failure to abide by compulsory education laws is a civil or criminal offense? If it is conceded that a compulsory education law is a legitimate exercise of state authority and if there is no indication that the law was enacted to discriminate against particular religious groups, how can *Smith* and *Yoder* be distinguished? Which test is preferable? Does *Smith* eviscerate the Free Exercise Clause? Is the majority correct in its characterization of the precedents? Does *Yoder* lead to an unprincipled kind of ad hoc balancing by judges?

In the *Smith* decision itself the Court distinguished *Yoder* and a number of other Free Exercise Clause precedents, asserting that those cases involved the Free Exercise Clause "in conjunction with other constitutional protections," or what it called "a hybrid situation," whereas Smith involved "a free exercise claim unconnected with any . . . parental right." Citing *Pierce*, it characterized *Yoder* as also involving "the right of parents . . . to direct the education of their children. . . ." 494 U.S. at 880, 110 S. Ct. at 1601, 108 L. Ed. at 887. Are you persuaded by this distinction? *See* Greenawalt, "Should the Religion Clauses of the Constitution Be Amended?" 32 *Loyola of Los Angeles L. Rev.* 9, 16 (1998) (arguing that the hybrid discussion "seems jerry-built" for the *Yoder* case, and that in many hybrid cases, other constitutional claims could stand on their own); *see also Swanson v. Guthrie Indep. School Dist.,* 135 F.3d 694, 700 (10th Cir. 1998) ("the *Smith* hybrid-rights theory . . . at least requires a colorable showing of some infringement of recognized and specific constitutional rights, rather than the mere invocation of a general right such as the right to control the education of one's child"). Would you advise a legislative committee to create specific exemptions from compulsory attendance for those with religious objections? What of the risk of a violation of the Establishment Clause? See chapter 1, Section VI, and chapter 2, *infra.*

5. Problem: Religious or Cultural Differences and Compulsory Education

A group of Sunni Muslim parents in a rural community refuse to send their daughters to the local public school on the ground that their faith requires that girls be shielded from the skimpy clothes, dating rituals, and foul language that are common in public schools. However, they are sending their sons to school because, they claim, it is important for the boys to learn the skills needed to compete in the job market, since the man will be the provider for the home. The parents intend to teach the girls sewing and cooking skills. Are the parents entitled to an exemption from enforcement of the compulsory attendance laws in

the light of *Yoder?* Is their claim a religious one or a cultural one? In Virginia, state law permits local school boards to decide whether to grant a religious exemption from compulsory school laws. *See* Mack, "Muslim Parents Keep Children Out of School," *Washington Post,* Jan. 16, 1998 at C9. If the state grants the exemption, does it constitute discrimination on the basis of sex? *See* chapter 5, *infra.*

III. STATE REGULATION OF NONPUBLIC SCHOOLS

Notwithstanding the landmark Supreme Court decisions in *Pierce, Meyer,* and *Farrington,* most states regulate private schools and require them to register and seek approval before they can operate. *See, e.g., State v. DeLaBruere,* 154 Vt. 237, 577 A.2d 254 (1990); *New Life Baptist Church Academy v. Town of East Longmeadow,* 885 F.2d 940 (1st Cir. 1989); *State ex. rel. Douglas v. Faith Baptist Church,* 207 Neb. 802, 301 N.W.2d 571 (1981). *See generally* T. van Geel, *Authority to Control the School Program* 153–55 (1976); Bristow, "Private Schools in Vermont: The 'Equivalency Exception' to Compulsory Attendance in *State v. LaBarge*," 2 *Vt. L. Rev.* 205 (1977). State authorities typically have broad powers to set the standards for private schools under statutory mandates. *See, e.g., Wiley House v. Scanlon,* 502 Pa. 228, 465 A.2d 995 (1983). *See generally* L. Furst and C. Russo, *The Legal Aspects of Nonpublic Schools,* chap. 4, 109–165 (1993). Enforcement of the standards within the framework of compulsory attendance laws often is left to local school authorities.

Some state regulation is designed to protect the public only from dangerous business, health, or building practices. *See, e.g., Manley v. Wichita Business College,* 237 Kan. 427, 701 P.2d 893 (1985); *Charton Corp. v. Brockette,* 534 S.W.2d 401 (Tex. Civ. App. 1976). *But see Katharine Gibbs, School, Inc. v. FTC,* 612 F.2d 658 (2d Cir. 1979). *See generally* Sacken, "Regulating Nonpublic Education: A Search for Just Law and Policy," 96 *Amer. J. of Educ.* 394 (1988). But much of it is designed to maintain minimum secular education standards and to promote democratic values in private schools. *See, e.g., New Life Baptist Church Academy, supra. See generally* M. McCarthy and N. Cambron McCabe, *Public School Law* 44–47 (1988); A. Gutmann, *Democratic Education* 115–123 (1987). The excerpt later in this chapter from the work of Professor Lines discusses the modern scope of state regulation of private schools.

Today, only about 13 percent of the school-aged children in the United States attend private schools. National Center for Educational Statistics, *The Condition of Education, 1998* (U.S. Department of Education, 1998) 132. Another 1 percent to 2 percent are home-schooled. *See* Patricia M. Lines, "Home Schoolers: Estimated Numbers and Growth," in *The Condition of Education, 1998, supra.* Of those enrolled in private schools, a substantial majority, 85 percent, attend religiously affiliated schools. In the 1960s, the majority of these schools were Catholic. However, in recent years, Catholic schools have experienced a substantial drop both in students and in the number of schools, while the number of Christian Evangelical schools has increased dramatically. (*Students* attending Catholic schools still comprise nearly 60 percent of those attending religiously affiliated schools, but only about 40 percent of the religiously affiliated *schools* are Catholic.) *See* National Center for Education Statistics, *Digest of Education Statistics, 1997* (U.S. Department of Education, 1997), tables 61 and 59; L. Furst and C. Russo, *supra*, 4.

A much smaller percentage of nonwhite children are enrolled in private schools than in public schools. African American and Hispanic students constituted only 17 percent of those enrolled in private schools compared to 31 percent of those enrolled in all public schools, and 56 percent of those enrolled in central city school district public schools. *See* National Center for Educational Statistics, *The Condition of Education, 1998,* 134 (data are for the 1995 school year). A majority of private schools remain segregated; more than 41 percent have a student enrollment that is less than 5 percent minority and nearly 16 percent have a student enrollment that is more than 50 percent minority. National Center for Education Statistics, *Digest of Education Statistics, 1997, supra*, table 59.

"Private Education Alternatives and State Regulation"

Lines, 12 *J. Law & Education* 189, 194–97 (1983). Reprinted by permission.

State Regulation of Private Education

Traditionally, the mechanism for enforcement of minimum standards for private education has been through a state compulsory attendance law, with punitive action for parents and children, but not for those who run private schools. Typically, the basic requirement is school *attendance*, although some of those laws require education of the child. The law almost always provides for fines and jail sentences for parents who fail to comply, and often truancy charges and possible institutionalization of the child. In almost every state the local superintendent or board, and the local prosecuting attorney are responsible for the identification of truants—that is, children who are not in an approved education program. In most states local officials also have primary responsibility for approving home instruction programs, if allowed by state law. [Today, home instruction, under certain conditions, is allowed in all fifty states.] State boards usually have the responsibility for approving private schools, although in some states, local boards may share in this task.

Acceptable ways of meeting the compulsory schooling requirements vary widely among states. Some states require certification of teachers and schools, some only approval and some only minimal evidence that schooling takes place. States like Alabama, Iowa, Nebraska, North Dakota, West Virginia and Wisconsin are at one end of the spectrum. They have obtained state court approval of at least some aspects of the state's power to regulate private educational alternatives.[21] Ohio provided even more detailed regulation, but its high court has curbed the state's regulatory system as applied to religious schools.[22]

States with more lenient statutory requirements will probably experience less litigation, provided that the state board does not augment the statute with stricter regulations. Such states include, for example, Connecticut, which provides a broad exception to the school attendance requirement. Parents who do not send their children to public school must educate or "cause" their children to be educated in specific subjects.[24] Other states following

---

[21] *See State v. Faith Baptist Church*, 107 Neb. 802, 301 N.W.2d 571 (1981), *appeal dismissed for want of a substantial federal question*, 10 2 S.Ct. 75 (1981); *State v. Shaver*, 294 N.W.2d 883 (N.D. 1980); *State v. Kasuboski*, 87 Wis.2d 407, 275 N.W.2d 101 (Wis. App. 1978); *Hill v. State*, 381 So.2d 91 (Ala. Crim. App. 1979), *reversed on other grounds*, 381 So.2d 94 (Ala. 1980); *Hill v. State*, 410 So.2d 431 (Ala. Crim. App. 1981) (same parties; convictions upheld after procedural defects corrected); *Iowa v. Moorhead*, 308 N.W.2d 60 (Iowa 1981); *State v. Riddle*, 285 S.E.2d 359 (W. Va. 1981).

[22] *State v. Whisner*, 47 Ohio St.2d 181, 351 N.E.2d 750 (1976).

[24] Conn. Gen. Stat. §10-184 (Supp. 1982) ("unless the parent . . . is able to show that the child is elsewhere receiving equivalent instruction in the studies taught in the public schools").

this model include Delaware, Idaho, New Jersey, South Dakota and Vermont. These states do not specify who must be the teacher or where instruction is to take place. Instruction apparently can be by anyone and anywhere, so long as it is equivalent to that taking place in public schools.

Some states, such as Alaska, Arizona, Georgia and Ohio give state and local school officials wide discretionary authority to excuse a child from the compulsory attendance requirement.[26] Virginia and Kentucky expressly permit exemption from compulsory school attendance where the parent has conscientious objections to such attendance.[27] In other states, in certain cases, courts have interpreted federal or state constitutional provisions in a way that permits individuals or churches to operate schools despite the state compulsory attendance law. . . .

Some states have consciously deregulated their private schools. These states expressly limit state administrative authority to promulgate regulations. Tennessee, for example, provides: "The state board of education and local boards of education are prohibited from regulating the selection of faculty or textbooks or the establishment of a curriculum in church related schools."[28] The law contains no hint as to whether the state can impose even minimal reporting requirements. However, private schools in Tennessee still have the option of seeking state approval.

North Carolina presents a somewhat similar option, with two 1979 laws that deregulate all private schools.[29] Prior to passage of the law, the state board had gradually expanded its regulatory framework for private schools until teachers, courses of study and textbooks had to be substantially the same as in the public schools. Under the new law, North Carolina has minimal requirements for recordkeeping (pupil attendance and disease immunization) and requires that the schools select and administer a nationally standardized test to students each year. The schools keep the tests on file and make them available to state inspectors. Eighth graders must be given a competency test. A school must meet fire, health and safety standards established in other laws.

Washington, like Tennessee and North Carolina, has consciously limited the extent to which the state board can regulate private schools.[33] The Washington law provides for stricter requirements for these schools, relative to Tennessee or North Carolina. It sets minimum standards as to school year, length of day and subjects to be taught. It expressly provides that these minimum standards shall not be altered by state agencies. However, the Washington law continues to require teacher certification except for courses in religion and other topics not taught in the public schools.[34] This requirement is a sore point with fundamentalist Christian schools and a stumbling block to many other private education alternatives. However, Washington law allows teaching by a person of "unusual competence," if supervised by a certified teacher. In practice the state may allow more flexibility than would initially appear.

Mississippi,[35] like Tennessee and North Carolina, adopts a laissez faire attitude, but apparently for different reasons. Mississippi abandoned its compulsory attendance law after *Brown v. Board of Education*, apparently not wishing to force children to attend desegregated schools. It has since enacted a new compulsory education law with no sanctions. . . .

Fellowship Baptist Church v. Benton
815 F.2d 485 (8th Cir. 1987).

Before Heaney and Ross, Circuit Judges, and Larson, Senior District Judge.

Larson, Senior District Judge.

In this appeal, the Court is presented with a broad-based attack on Iowa's compulsory school laws. Plaintiffs are two fundamentalist Baptist church

---

[26]Georgia law excuses ". . . children excused from attendance in school by county and/or independent school boards of education in accordance with general policies promulgated by the State Board of Education." Ga. Code Ann. §32-2106(b) (1980). Ohio allows a local board to excuse a child "for good and sufficient reasons. . . ." Ohio Rev. Code Ann. §3321.04(C) (1980). . . .

[27]The Kentucky constitution provides "nor shall any man be compelled to send his child to any school to which he may be conscientiously opposed. . . ." Ky. Const. §5. *See also* Va. Const. Art. VIII §1.

[28]Tenn. Stat. Ann. §§49.5201-5204 (1979).

[29]N.C. Gen. Stat. §§155c-547 *et seq.* (Cum. Supp. 1981) (applies to religious schools); and §§115C-555 *et seq.* (Cum. Supp. 1981) (same; applies to certain nonreligious schools).

[33]Wash. Rev. Code. §§28A.02.201 *et seq.* and 28A.27.010 (1981).

[34]Wash. Rev. Code §§28A.02.201 *et seq.* (1981).

[35]Miss. Code Ann. §37-13-95 (Supp. 1982).

schools, the churches' pastors and principals, and several of the schools' teachers, parents and students. The creation of plaintiffs' church schools is a relatively recent development dating from the 1970s—a part of the growing trend towards the establishment of such schools throughout the country.

Plaintiffs' suit mirrors several previous actions involving fundamentalist groups, including one before the Iowa Supreme Court, which have generally resulted in decisions upholding the states' regulatory schemes. *See, e.g., Johnson v. Charles City Community Schools Board of Education*, 368 N.W.2d 74 (Iowa), [(1985)]. . . .

Although many of the issues are similar to those presented to the *Charles City* Court, we of course have undertaken our own independent review of plaintiffs' challenge to the following specific requirements of Iowa law. First, principals must file annual reports with the local school districts listing their pupils' names, ages and dates of attendance, the texts used, and the names of the teachers. Iowa Code §299.3. Second, parents of children ages 7 to 16 must place their children—until completion of the eighth grade—in either a public school or a school that offers "equivalent instruction by a certified teacher." Iowa Code §299.1. Finally, the state has determined that parents of children in the plaintiff schools are not entitled to the "Amish exemption" to the above requirements, *see* Iowa Code §299.24, and plaintiffs argue this determination is unconstitutional. The district court found the challenged laws and their application to plaintiffs constitutional, except, following the suggestion of the Charles City Court, held that the term "equivalent instruction" was unconstitutionally vague "without further definition." 620 F.Supp. 308, 313–20 (S.D. Iowa 1985). . . .

I. Plaintiffs' Religious Beliefs

An understanding of plaintiffs' religious beliefs and practices is essential to the proper evaluation of plaintiffs' claims. The evidence presented by plaintiffs to the district court unquestionably revealed that their religious beliefs stem from the Bible. They view Christ as the Head of their church and all of its ministries, and adhere to the doctrine of separation of church and state. Their schools were created in response to these beliefs. Neither church has a doctrine which requires members to send their children to the church school, however, and parents are not subject to discipline for removing their children from the church schools. Enrollment in the schools is not limited to those who belong to the church, and both schools have enrolled pupils whose parents are not members of the church. . . .

. . . Each school offers the basic curriculum specified in Iowa statutes with a few minor exceptions, as well as other courses, including a course in computers. Plaintiffs' witnesses admitted that there is nothing in either curriculum which forbids teaching by a certified teacher, and in fact, each school employs a teacher who is certified.

Plaintiffs believe themselves to be "in the world but not of the world," but they do not segregate themselves from modern communities. They live in ordinary residential neighborhoods and they interact with their neighbors and others not of their faith. They believe they are called by God to perform certain occupations in life, but these include ordinary occupations such as nurse, lawyer, engineer and accountant, and there is no evidence that they object to the licensing of these occupations. They own and use radios, televisions, motor vehicles and other modern conveniences and advancements. Their dress and lifestyle, while conservative, is not distinctive.

* * *

II. Reporting Requirements

Iowa's reporting requirements are very straightforward.[2] Each year, the principal of any private school in Iowa must, upon request from the secretary of the local school district, furnish the names, ages and number of days of attendance of each pupil in grades one through eight, the texts used, and the names of the teachers during the preceding year. Iowa Code §299.3. The district court found the reporting requirements did not impinge on plaintiffs' constitutional rights, and we agree.

Administrators from other private schools confirmed that the intrusion by the state under section 299.3 is extremely limited. Once each year, the local school district sends each principal a form, which

---

[2]Iowa does not require private schools to be approved. Private schools may chose [sic] to become approved, as for example the Catholic schools in the Keokuk School District have, or they are free to operate as nonapproved private schools. Parents may satisfy the compulsory school laws by sending their children to nonapproved private schools so long as they provide "equivalent instruction by a certified teacher." Iowa code §299.1. No issue regarding approval of plaintiffs' schools is presented in this case.

can be completed by a secretary under the principal's supervision in less than one day. The forms require nothing more of plaintiffs than that they provide the minimal information requested, and plaintiff principals admitted that the information was readily available to them. Clearly, section 299.3 does not in any way infringe upon the content, approach or structure of plaintiffs' schools.

Plaintiff principals nonetheless argue on appeal, as they did before the district court, that the submission of the form violates their beliefs in the "Headship of Christ" and the separation of church and state. They urge that parental reporting would adequately serve the state's admittedly compelling interest in ensuring its children are receiving an adequate education, and submit that the state should be required to adopt this "least restrictive means." Plaintiff parents and children also assert that the reporting requirements violate their freedom of association, again proposing parental reporting as a "least restrictive means" of obtaining the information sought.

* * *

[W]e have no difficulty upholding the reporting requirements in this case. As the district court determined, the burden on plaintiff principals' religious beliefs—if one exists at all—is very minimal and is clearly outweighed by the state's interest in receiving reliable information about where children are being educated and by whom. . . .

III. Teacher Certification

Plaintiffs also challenge the requirement in Iowa Code §299.1 that parents of children ages 7 to 16 must send their children to public school or to a private school that utilizes certified teachers until the children complete the eighth grade. Plaintiffs allege the certification requirement violates the free exercise clause, the establishment clause, the due process clause and plaintiff teachers' freedom of expression. Plaintiffs allege these violations stem primarily from the certification requirement's interference with a teacher's calling by God to teach, the supervision of certified teachers by the Iowa Professional Teaching Practices Commission, and the "human relations" course required to obtain or maintain certification. The district court upheld the certification requirement, and plaintiffs have emphasized their free exercise objections to it on appeal, arguing

that the administration of achievement tests represents the "least restrictive means" of achieving the state's interest in ensuring a quality education.

A brief outline of the provisions of Iowa law regarding certification may help to place plaintiffs' arguments in their proper context. Because section 299.1 is directed only to parents of compulsory school age children, compliance affects only teachers in grades one through eight. To obtain a certificate to teach, an applicant must have received a bachelor's degree from a recognized institution or must graduate from a nonrecognized institution and have completed not less than three courses in professional education from a recognized institution. Iowa Admin. Code 670-13.1, 13.10 to 13.12. Temporary certificates are available for those who graduate from nonrecognized institutions. *Id.* 670-13.12. In addition, each initial applicant as well as those seeking to renew their certificate must take a human relations course designed to "contribute to the development of sensitivity to and understanding of the values, beliefs, life styles and attitudes of individuals and the diverse groups found in a pluralistic society." *Id.* 670-13.18. The general components of an approved program for an elementary school level teacher include courses in liberal arts, professional education (training in teaching methods), and student teaching. *Id.* 670-15.8, 19.14 to 19.15.

* * *

Plaintiffs argue strenuously on appeal that their religious beliefs cannot be reconciled with the state having any role in the certification or approval of teachers in their schools. They urge that standardized testing be substituted for certification, asserting that many other states do not require certification.

We recognize the sincerity of plaintiffs' beliefs and the burden which they believe the certification requirement imposes upon them. We agree with the Supreme Court of Iowa, however, that plaintiffs' position is "not altogether consistent" on this matter. *Johnson v. Charles City Community Schools Board of Education, supra,* 368 N.W.2d at 78. Plaintiffs believe that licensure wrongfully interferes with a teacher's calling by God to teach, yet they apparently do not object to the licensure of those in their church called by God to other occupations, such as doctor or lawyer, nor do they object to obtaining a driver's license for those serving in their bus ministry, even though Pastor Jaspers testified that none of the churches' ministries could properly be regulated by government.[5]

Moreover, while plaintiffs attempt to analogize their situation to that of the Amish in the *Yoder* case, the burden the certification requirement imposes upon the plaintiffs is not nearly as great as the burden placed upon the plaintiffs in *Yoder*. . . .

Unlike the Old Order Amish in *Yoder*, plaintiffs expect and encourage their children to attend college, and have no objection to college-educated teachers per se. The certification requirement applies only to teachers in grades one through eight, and plaintiff schools in fact each employ a teacher who is certified. Iowa's certification process does not prevent teachers in plaintiff schools from teaching from a Biblical perspective nor does it prevent plaintiff schools from hiring only those teachers who meet their religious criteria. . . .

In evaluating plaintiffs' claims, we must determine whether, in light of the importance of the state's interest in the education of its children and the nature of the burden the certification requirement places on the plaintiffs' religious beliefs, plaintiffs' proposed testing alternative would adequately serve the state's interest. After carefully considering all of the evidence presented, the district court found it would not.

> Plaintiffs object because the certificate requirement relies upon the process (education of the teacher) rather than the product (Is the child learning?). Historically, the emphasis has been on the process. Iowa has required some sort of certificate since 1863. It has been assumed that if the process is followed the children will learn. Recently there has been more interest in attempting to determine if the children are learning. . . . While testing is a valuable tool, it is not sufficient in and of itself to determine whether a student is receiving an adequate education. Tests primarily determine knowledge of content of the subject matter. They do not test other aspects of education necessary to prepare a student for life in today's society.

620 F.Supp. at 316.

The court also approved of the Iowa Supreme Court's observations that

> mere testing would be wholly inadequate to protect the state's rightful interests. A test looks only backward. It can, to a limited extent, measure whether a child has been receiving an education. The state is entitled to the assurance that the child is receiving an education.

368 N.W.2d at 81. . . .

We agree on the basis of the record in this case that the state has met its burden of demonstrating that testing would not adequately serve its interests. Not only do certified teachers receive training in child development and methods of instruction, but they are also mandatory child abuse reporters and take courses on identifying those children with special needs. All of these qualities, as plaintiffs' own expert witnesses conceded, are desirable characteristics for a good teacher. Admittedly, there is a lack of empirical evidence concerning the relationship between certified teachers and a quality education, due to the difficulty of research on this issue, but there is a similar lack of empirical verification concerning plaintiffs' proposed alternative, and we do not believe such evidence is required in this case. For all of these reasons, we agree with the district court that the state's choice of certification as the best means available today to satisfy its interest in the education of its children does not violate plaintiffs' right to the free exercise of their religion.

* * *

As the district court found, . . . nothing in the certification statute or regulations requires agreement or acceptance of the beliefs or values of others. Plaintiffs' objection to the "human relations" course thus appears to be based solely upon the exposure of college-level students to viewpoints other than their own. . . . Nothing prevents a prospective teacher taking Iowa's human relations course from evaluating others' viewpoints from their own religious perspective. . . . We thus conclude the effect of the "human relations" course neither advances nor inhibits religion.

* * *

IV. Equivalent Instruction

Section 299.1 also provides that the instruction children receive from a certified teacher must be "equivalent" to that offered by the public schools. At the time of trial, the term "equivalent instruction" was not specifically defined anywhere in the Iowa Code or regulations, although the state was in the process of promulgating such regulations. Plaintiffs challenged the "equivalent instruction" requirement on vagueness grounds, and the state argued to the district

---

[5]Pastor Jaspers stated, for example, that should the church decide to open a nursing home, it too must be free from licensing or other state requirements: "The only answer I have is that I can't see any point where it will be right for the church to be regulated by the government, period."

court, as it does here, that other statutes sufficiently define the term. The district court rejected the state's contention, based upon statements by the Iowa Supreme Court indicating that Court's rejection of them as well. 602 F.Supp. at 317–18; *Johnson v. Charles City Community Schools Board of Education, supra,* 368 N.W.2d at 79–80. We agree with the district court's conclusion that the other statutes cited by the state do not cure the vagueness problem inherent in the otherwise undefined term "equivalent instruction."

In large measure as a result of the *Charles City* litigation, however, the state has recently promulgated regulations entitled "Equivalent Instruction Standards," which became effective February 6, 1986. Iowa Admin.Code 670-63.1 to 63.4. These standards specify the minimum curriculum to be offered in grades one through eight, including for example courses in English, mathematics and science. *Id.* The state argues that these regulations have effectively rendered its appeal from the district court's decision moot, but we believe the proper course is to remand this portion of the case to the district court for further consideration in light of the newly adopted standards.

V. The Amish Exemption

Plaintiffs' final constitutional challenge involves the state's denial of plaintiff parents' request to be exempted from the above requirements through the "Amish exemption," Iowa Code §299.24.[7] As the district court noted, this exemption has been granted only to parents of children attending Amish schools and one conservative Mennonite school, all of which are located in distinct geographical areas of the state and which follow the style of life and religious tenets described by the Supreme Court in *Yoder.* . . .

Plaintiffs argue before this Court, as they did before the district court and before the Iowa Supreme Court, that this denial violates the equal protection clause. They further contend that granting the exemption to the Amish but not to them violates the establishment clause because the effect is to advance the Amish religion and to inhibit the plaintiffs'.

Because religion is a fundamental right, any classification of religious groups is subject to strict scrutiny. . . . That is, the state must show the classification has been precisely tailored to serve a compelling state interest. . . . Of course, this standard is substantially equivalent to the free exercise standards we have already applied to Iowa's reporting and teacher certification requirements.

* * *

Both the district court and the Iowa Supreme Court recognized that resolving plaintiffs' equal protection challenge required the court to determine whether plaintiffs and the Amish were so similarly situated that the denial of the exemption to the plaintiffs violated the constitution. Both courts analyzed the factors upon which the Supreme Court relied in *Yoder* to create an exemption to Wisconsin's compulsory attendance laws for the Amish who opposed sending their children to high school, and compared plaintiffs' position to that of the Amish. Both courts concluded that plaintiffs were properly denied the exemption. The Iowa Supreme Court stated:

> When the same factors [applied by the Supreme Court in *Yoder*] are placed in balance on this record the opposite conclusion asserts itself. Sincerity of belief is the only factor wholly common to both the Amish and these plaintiffs. The beliefs of the plaintiffs are greatly less interwoven with their daily mode of life. The Amish culture is greatly more isolated from mainstream American life. Plaintiffs' children, for all the distinctive religious convictions they will be given, will live, compete for jobs, work, and move about in a diverse and complex society. Their educational needs are plainly not as circumscribed as those of Amish children. Neither does exposure to the more general American culture pose such an immediate threat to plaintiffs' mode of living as is the case with the Amish.

Johnson v. Charles City Community Schools Board of Education, supra, 368 N.W.2d at 84. After adopting the state court's reasoning and holding, the district court added the following observations:

> The Court is also conscious of the impact that granting these plaintiffs an exception to the compulsory education requirements could have on public education and the courts. Under *Yoder* and *Johnson* a clear line of de-

---

[7]Iowa Code §299.24 provides in relevant part: When members or representatives of a local congregation of a recognized church or religious denomination established for ten years or more within the state of Iowa prior to July 1, 1967, which professes principles or tenets that differ substantially from the objectives, goals, and philosophy of education embodied in standards set forth in section 257.25, and rules adopted in implementation thereof, file with the state superintendent of public instruction proof of the existence of such conflicting tenets or principles, together with a list of the names, ages, and post-office addresses of all persons of compulsory school age desiring to be exempted from the compulsory education law and the educational standards law, whose parents or guardians are members of the congregation or religious denomination, the state superintendent, subject to the approval of the state board of public instruction, may exempt the members of the congregation or religious denomination from compliance with any or all requirements of the compulsory education law and the educational standards law. . . .

marcation is established that offers guidance to parents, school officials and the courts. A blurring of that line by granting an exception here would create an impossible burden upon all persons and agencies involved to decide whether minor variations of fact one way or the other entitled each individual church school to an exception. The Court is convinced that the Supreme Court intended the exception to be a narrow one.

620 F.Supp at 319. We agree with these observations. . . .

We also find no establishment clause violation on the facts of this case. As the *Yoder* Court stated, narrow exemptions such as Iowa has adopted successfully traverse the "tight rope" created by the tension between the free exercise clause and the establishment clause. *Wisconsin v. Yoder, supra,* 406 U.S. at 221, 92 S.Ct. at 1536. This narrowly drawn accommodation to one religious view does not require the state, under the establishment clause, to accommodate all others. . . .

NOTES AND QUESTIONS

1. Yoder Distinguished?

Are you persuaded by Judge Larson that the Fellowship Baptist Church is not entitled to relief under Iowa Code Section 299.24, the "Amish exemption"? In *Johnson v. Charles City Community Schools Bd. of Educ.,* 368 N.W.2d 74 (Iowa 1985), relied upon extensively by Judge Larson, dissenting justices of the Iowa Supreme Court took issue with this conclusion:

> The majority finds that plaintiffs do not fall within the section 299.24 exception because they have not shown "that their children's educational needs are significantly different from those of other children." The statute does not address different educational needs, it is aimed at those with different educational goals. . . . I believe plaintiffs have established different educational goals. Thus, I believe the administrative decision was arbitrary and capricious, requiring reversal.
>
> Plaintiff's ultimate educational goal is the glorification of God. Everything taught in their school must be taught from the perspective of their religious beliefs, emphasizing the role of God and the church in their lives and in every subject taught. The children are taught to make life decisions . . . by resorting directly to God or God's word. Nowhere in section 257.25 do we find reference to a public education goal of teaching facts permeated with religion and teaching children to rely on God or God's word. . . .
>
> The majority suggest that our statute is aimed at a much smaller target than all parochial schools in the

state. Although I would agree with that suggestion, I cannot agree with the implications contained in the majority opinion that places appellants in the same classification as other church groups who choose to provide a religious-oriented education. I perceive from the record that appellants are substantially different in some respects from our other private religious groups. Other parochial schools attempt to cooperate with public regulation of their schools, seeking public financial support and busing as long as the State does not interfere with their teaching of religious doctrines. The appellants, on the other hand, as a part of their ministry, insist that the exclusive right to educate belongs to the church and interpret the Bible to command their educational ministry. They share the conviction that there is no dichotomy between secular truth and sacred truth. Their educational ministry places the minister as the principal teacher. Their religious conviction that any relationship between the church and state is repugnant prevents the minister or any of the teachers from being certified by the state. . . .

Id. at 86 (Justice Schultz, with whom Justice Uhlenhopp joined, dissenting).

Does Judge Larson or Justice Schultz have the more persuasive position? Does the former's view of the case fail to be sufficiently attentive to the institutional autonomy interest of religious groups? *See* Laycock, "Towards a General Theory of the Religion Clauses: The Case of Church Labor Relations and the Right to Church Autonomy," 81 *Colum. L. Rev.* 1373 (1981). If Justice Schultz is correct on the application of the Free Exercise Clause to the Baptist Fellowship Church, is he also correct in arguing that those principles would not exempt all parochial schools from state regulation? *See generally* Johnson, "Concepts and Compromise in First Amendment Doctrine," 72 *Calif. L. Rev.* 817, 842 (1984). Is a non-Amish child attending an Amish school for religious reasons entitled to an exemption? *See State ex rel. Nagle v. Olin,* 64 Ohio St.2d 341, 415 N.E.2d 279 (1980).

2. "Equivalent Instruction"

Is the equivalency of instruction requirement unconstitutionally vague? *See, e.g., Bangor Baptist Church v. Maine,* 549 F.Supp. 1208 (D. Me. 1982); *State v. White,* 109 Wis.2d 64, 325 N.W.2d 76 (App. 1982). *See generally* Lines, *supra* at 211–212. Did Judge Larson err in adopting "a process-oriented approach for assessing educational opportunities rather than a result orientation," i.e., educational testing? Mangrum, "Family Rights and Compulsory School Laws," 21 *Creighton L. Rev.* 1019, 1043 (1988).

3. Reporting Requirements

Do you agree that the reporting requirements for private schools place "a very minimal" burden on the plaintiffs' religious beliefs? *See State v. DeLaBruere*, 154 Vt. 237, 577 A.2d 254 (1990); *New Life Baptist Church Academy v. Town of East Longmeadow*, 885 F.2d 940 (1st Cir. 1989). Is it the impact on beliefs or the impact on church autonomy that ought to be taken into account? *See* Laycock, *supra*. How can the *"Pierce* compromise" be implemented without reporting requirements on who is being educated and where? Are site visits preferable?

4. Teacher Certification

If "there is a lack of empirical evidence concerning the relationship between certified teachers and quality education," how can the certification requirement for private school teachers be upheld in the face of a free exercise challenge? The court argues that "Iowa's certification process does not prevent teachers in plaintiff schools from teaching from a Biblical perspective nor does it prevent plaintiff schools from hiring only those teachers who meet their religious criteria." *See also Sheridan Road Baptist Church v. Department of Education*, 426 Mich. 462, 396 N.W.2d 373 (1986). Do you agree? Consider these remarks by Professor Laycock:

> Church schools . . . are religious institutions, organized to transmit faith and values to succeeding generations. There can be no more important religious function for an institutional church; the very existence of the church depends on its success. And the employees who must carry out this function are the teachers.
>
>   * * *
>
> Not every religious school can or will insist that every teacher actively promote religion. But nearly all will at least require every teacher not to interfere. . . . Thus, even the nonbelieving math teacher has some intrinsically religious responsibilities . . . Churches have strong claims to autonomy with respect to employment of teachers.

Laycock, "Towards a General Theory of the Religion Clauses: The Case of Church Labor Relations and the Right to Church Autonomy," 81 *Colum. L. Rev.* 1373, 1411 (1981). *But see* Foley, "The Regulation of Private Schools," 25 *Cap. U. L. Rev.* 819, 825–26 (1996) (state certification requirement "no more deprives parents of their freedom to choose which, among state-certified teachers, are the best for their children than the medical licensing requirement deprives parents of their free choice among pediatri-

cians"). Does a teacher certification requirement impermissibly interfere with a church school's autonomy in selecting employees? Are there less onerous alternatives? Why does the court reject the standardized testing of students as an alternative? *See also New Life Baptist Church Academy v. Town of East Longmeadow*, 885 F.2d 940 (1st Cir. 1989); *Sheridan Road Baptist Church v. Department of Education, supra. See generally* Foley, *supra*; Mangrum, *supra*.

State of Ohio v. Whisner
47 Ohio St.2d 181, 351 N.E.2d 750 (1976).

Celebrezze, Justice

This cause presents sensitive issues of paramount importance involving the power of the state to impose extensive regulations upon the structure and government of non-public education, and conversely, upon the right of these appellants to freely exercise their professed religious beliefs in the context of providing an education to their children. . . .

At the outset, we recognize that appellants do not facially attack the compulsory school attendance laws of this state as set forth, generally, in R.C. Chapter 3321. . . .

Nor do the appellants maintain that the state is devoid of all power to promulgate and enforce reasonable regulations affecting the operation of non-public schools. Numerous decisions of the Supreme Court of the United States over the years have clearly sounded the death knell with respect to any such assertion.

         * * *

Appellants do contend, however, that application of Ohio's compulsory attendance laws as to them, through the medium of the Minimum Standards for Ohio Elementary Schools, prescribed by the State Board of Education pursuant to the express legislative command contained in R.C. 3321.03, infringes upon their free exercise of religion as guaranteed by the First and Fourteenth Amendments to the Constitution of the United States, and by Section 7, Article I of the Ohio Constitution.

With regard to appellants' assertion that the state's "minimum standards," as applied to them, unconstitutionally interfere with their right to freely exercise their professed religious beliefs, both the Court of Appeals and the Court of Common Pleas committed error in failing to accord the requisite judicial deference to the veracity of those beliefs. . . .

However, at this date and time in the history of our nation, it is crystal clear that neither the validity of what a person believes nor the reasons for so believing may be contested by an arm of the government. As stated in *United States v. Ballard* (1944), 322 U.S. 78, 86, . . . "Men may believe what they cannot prove. They may not be put to the proof of their religious doctrines or beliefs. Religious experiences which are as real as life to some may be incomprehensible to others." The applicable test was enunciated in *United States v. Seeger* (1965), 380 U.S. 163, 185, . . . in these words: " . . . that while the 'truth' of a belief is not open to question, there remains the significant question whether it is 'truly held.' This is the threshold question of sincerity which must be resolved in every case. It is, of course, a question of fact."

Based upon the extensive record before us, there can be no doubt but that appellants' religious beliefs are "truly held." Rev. Whisner's testimony clearly reveals that the religion in which he believes is a historical religion consisting of "born-again" Christians, who adhere to a life of separation from worldliness, and who strictly structure their lives upon a subjective interpretation of Biblical language. The uncontradicted testimony of Rev. Whisner, and that of the other defense witnesses, as documented in the foregoing statement of the case, conclusively establishes that these appellants are God-fearing people with an abiding religious conviction that Biblical training is essential to the proper inculcation of spiritual and moral values into their youth at a time when such precepts are most likely to take root — during the formative years of educational growth and physical development. In this regard, appellants' testimony unmistakenly emphasizes their collective dissatisfaction with the form of the education provided by the public schools of this state, and their total religious compulsion that their offspring be educated in the word of God according to their religious scruples. Moreover, the sincerity of appellants' religious beliefs can best be illustrated by the very fact that they were willing to subject themselves to the criminal process of this state in order to vindicate their position. No more need be said concerning the sincerity of appellants' religious beliefs, for, in our view, it has been established beyond peradventure.

* * *

Through the testimony of Rev. Whisner, appellants voiced religious objections to four of the state's denominated "minimum standards." Those standards, and appellants' objections thereto, are set forth herein as follows:

1. EDb-401-02(E)(6) — "A charter shall be granted after an inspection which determines that all standards have been met." (Appellants do not desire a charter, because acceptance of same would constitute their agreement to comply with all standards, and thereby effectively remove their ability to control the direction of the school by reposing vast powers in the hands of the State.)

2. EDb-401-02(G) — "Based on a minimum five-hour school day or one of greater length, the total instructional time allocation per week shall be:
   "four-fifths — language arts, mathematics, social studies, science, health, citizenship, related directed study and self-help; optional foreign language.
   "one-fifth — directed physical education, music, art, special activities and optional applied arts." (Appellants complain that this standard does not expressly allot time in which Biblical and spiritual training may be given, and, therefore, is inimicable to the fundamental purpose of a religious school in that it severely restricts the ability of the school to incorporate its religious teachings.)

3. EDb-401-02(O) — ". . . All activities shall conform to policies adopted by the Board of Education." (The contention is advanced by appellants that this standard virtually provides a blank check to the public authorities to control the entire operation of their school.)

4. EDb-401-07 — "Efforts toward providing quality education by the school for the community it serves shall be achieved through cooperation and interaction between the school and the community. The understanding of the roles of each and a flow of information are basic to this relationship. . . ." (Appellants maintain that a Christian school cannot seek its direction from the world or from the community it serves.)

In addition, appellants objected, upon religious grounds, to the following statements appearing in the "Interpretation and Explanatory Information" section of the publication containing the "minimum standards":

1. EDb-401-02(J) — "When a pupil transfers, within a school system or moves to a school outside of the school system, pertinent pupil information is

forwarded to the principal of the receiving school. Office records of this nature are not released to parents and guardians. . . ." (Appellants contend that it is very important for a parent to be apprised of everything occurring in school relating to his or her child or children.)

2. EDb-401-03(B) (page 30 of the publication)—

"1. Common problems are solved through the consensus of thinking and action of individuals in the group.

"2. Individuals have a responsibility of authentic citizenship as a member of the school, community, state, nation and world.

"3. Citizens have a responsibility for the welfare of others and for being willing to sacrifice for the common good." (Appellants reject the idea the [sic] common problems are solved solely by the group, because they instead adhere to the belief that problems are solved by the group on their knees. In addition, appellants contend that these comments reflect a philosophy of "secular humanism" on the part of the state—a philosophy to which appellants cannot, consistent with their religious beliefs, ascribe.)

3. EDb-401-03(B) (page 48)—"Organized group life of all types must act in accordance with established rules of social relationships and a system of social controls." (Appellants against object to the "humanism" philosophy allegedly espoused herein.)

4. EDb-401-03(B) (page 60)—"The health of the child is perhaps the greatest single factor in the development of a well-rounded personality. No individual is adequately prepared for effective living unless he has a well-functioning body and can make reasonably successful adjustments to his many problems. Both are essential for facilitating learning, promoting personal efficiency, and developing successful social and family living. For these reasons health education is considered an integral part of the total education program. Its place in the curriculum becomes increasingly important as automation, population growth, changing moral standards and values, mounting pressures, and other changes in our society create new or intensify existing health problems." (Appellants contend that although man's standards may change with respect to moral values, God's does not.)

* * *

[A]s required by *Wisconsin v. Yoder*, . . . 406 U.S. 205, at page 220 . . . , we must . . . determine whether "[a] regulation neutral on its face may, in its application, nonetheless offend the constitutional requirement for governmental neutrality . . . [because] it unduly burdens the free exercise of religion." . . .

To begin with, although admittedly an admirable effort to extol the secular aims of the state in assuring that each child educated in this state obtains a quality education, we believe that these "minimum standards" overstep the boundary of reasonable regulation as applied to a non-public religious school.

* * *

We refer, first, to EDb-401-02(G), which allocates instructional time in the comprehensive curriculum required by R.C. 3313.60,[6] almost to the minute. Since R.C. 3313.48[7] requires a minimum school day of five hours, the requirement of EDb-401-02(G) invariably results in further control of the educational

---

[6]R.C. 3313.60 provided, in pertinent part, at the time of the trial in this cause:

"Boards of education of county, exempted village, and city school districts shall prescribe a graded course of study for all schools under their control subject to the approval of the state board of education. In such graded courses of study there shall be included the study of the following subjects:

"(A) The language arts, including reading, writing, spelling, oral and written English, and literature;

"(B) Geography, the history of the United States and of Ohio, and national, state and local government in the United States;

"(C) Mathematics;

"(D) Natural science, including instruction in the conservation of natural resources;

"(E) Health and physical education, which shall include instruction in the harmful effects, and legal restrictions against the use of drugs of abuse, alcoholic beverages, and tobacco;

"(F) The fine arts including music;

"(G) First aid, safety and fire prevention;

"Every school shall include in the requirements for promotion from the eighth grade to the ninth grade one year's course of study of American history.

* * *

The amendment to R.C. 3313.60, effective November 28, 1975, substantially changed paragraphs (B) and (E) of the foregoing to include additional curriculum requirements, and also added a separate requirement that physical education be taught.

[7]R.C. 3313.48 provides, in pertinent part:

". . . Except as otherwise provided in this section, each day for grades one through six shall consist of not less than five clock hours with pupils in attendance which may include fifteen minute morning and afternoon recess periods, except in such emergency situations, including lack of classroom space, as are approved by the state board of education."

policies of a non-public religious school in a manner that we cannot say is compelled by the enabling legislation pursuant to which the "minimum standards" were adopted. R.C. 3313.48 and 3313.60, although requiring a school day of a defined length, and effectively controlling the courses of study taught non-public school children, do not further impede the ability of a religious school to incorporate the tenets of its particular faith into its required courses. We think that EDb-401-02(G) "unduly burdens the free exercise of religion" and interferes "with the rights of conscience,"[10] by requiring a set amount of time to be devoted to subjects which, by their very nature, may not easily lend themselves to the teaching of religious principles (e.g., mathematics). We do not mean to imply that the subjects contained within EDb-401-02(G), or those contained within R.C. 3313.60, are not helpful in preparing non-public, as well as public, school children for the obligations which will eventually arise in the process of maturing into adulthood. We only emphasize that the reasonableness of the requirements contained within "minimum standard" EDb-401-02(G) wanes in the face of an attack premised upon a violation of the constitutional right of appellants to the free exercise of their chosen religion.

Secondly, in our view, EDb-401-02(O), which requires "all activities" of a non-public school to conform to policies adopted by the board of education, plainly violates appellants' right to the free exercise of their religion. If the state is to discharge its duty of remaining strictly neutral, pursuant to the establishment clause of the First Amendment, with respect to religion, how can the state constitutionally require all activities of a non-public religious school, which, of necessity, must include religious activities, to conform to the policies of a purportedly "neutral" board? . . .

Finally, EDb-401-07(B), which requires a non-public religious school to cooperate with elements of the community in which it exists, infringes upon the rights of these appellants, consistent with their religious beliefs, to engage in complete, or nearly complete, separation from community affairs. As Rev. Whisner testified, these appellants religiously adhere to the literal Biblical command that they "[b]e not conformed to this world. . . ." Upon the face of the record before us, the state may not require the contrary.

[10]Section 7, Article I of the Ohio Constitution. . . .

* * *

There is an additional, independent reason, ignored by the lower courts in this case, that compels upholding appellants' attack upon the state's "minimum standards." In our view, these standards are so pervasive and all-encompassing that total compliance with each and every standard by a non-public school would effectively eradicate the distinction between public and non-public education, and thereby deprive these appellants of their traditional interest as parents to direct the upbringing and education of their children. [Citing *Farrington, Pierce,* and *Meyer.*]

In the opinion of a majority of this court, a "general education of a high quality" can be achieved by means other than the comprehensive regimentation of all academic centers in this state. . . .

Judgment reversed and defendants discharged.

J. J. P. Corrigan, William B. Brown and Paul W. Brown, JJ., concur.

Herbert and Stern, JJ., dissent from the syllabus and opinion, but concur in the judgment. [opinion omitted].

C. William O'Neill, C. J., not participating.

───────────

NOTES AND QUESTIONS

1. Ultra Vires Regulations?

Consider the Ohio statutes quoted in footnotes 6 and 7 in the court's opinion in *Whisner.* The statutes set forth the core curriculum for private schools and require a minimum of five hours of classroom instruction each day. Do the regulations promulgated by the State Board of Education exceed the requirements set forth in the statute? Are they ultra vires? What does the court mean when it states that the regulations set forth policies that are not "compelled by the enabling legislation"? Note that the regulations divide up the day into four-fifths of the day for the traditionally "academic" subjects and one-fifth of the day for physical education, music, art, and so on. Further, the regulations declare that these proportions apply to "a minimum five-hour school day *or one of greater length*" (emphasis added).

Does this suggest that the legislature left private school officials free to teach what they please beyond the minimum of five hours a day of mandated instruction while the State Board of Education did not permit this option? Does this analysis suggest that the court need not have reached the question of whether the minimum standards violate the free exercise of religion clause or that the same decision could have been reached by means of statutory construction? Is this line of analysis implicit in the objection to EDb-401-02(E)(6) in that the vague charter requirement reposes "vast powers in the hands of the state"? *But see* Comment, "Separation of Church and State: Education and Religion in Kentucky," 6 *N. Ky. L. Rev.* 125, 150–51 (1978). After Whisner, the State Board did not alter its regulations, and this led to a second challenge to those regulations. *State ex rel. Nagle v. Olin,* 415 N.E.2d 279 (Ohio 1980) (state minimum standards violate free exercise of religion). *See* Comment, "State Regulation of Private Education: Ohio Law in the Shadow of the United States Supreme Court Decisions," 54 *Cin. L. Rev.* 1003, 1023–24 (1986), suggesting that under *Yoder,* the *Olin* case was wrongly decided. *See generally* Carper, "The *Whisner* Decision: A Case Study in State Regulation of Christian Day Schools," 24 *J. Church & St.* 281 (1982).

2. Interference with Free Exercise of Religion

In what manner do the statutes and regulations relating to private schools in Ohio infringe upon the religious rights of parents who send their children to private religious schools? *See generally* Bainton, "State Regulation of Private Religious Schools and the State's Interest in Education," 25 *Ariz. L. Rev.* 123, 134–139 (1983). Does the conclusion follow only if they are construed so as not to permit substantial religious instruction and activities beyond the minimum five hours a day of mandated instruction? Suppose the religious schools were permitted to offer seven hours of instruction each day and only five hours were stipulated by the state for specific subjects. Would this render the scheme constitutional? Is there a point at which the school day becomes so long to accommodate the minimum state curriculum and the religious orientation of the private school that the minimum itself would violate the free exercise clause?

What of the provision that "all activities shall conform to policies adopted by the board of education"? Is this clearly unconstitutional? Do you think that the provision was addressed to religious instruction and ritual? What saving construction might be given it?

Is the requirement of cooperation and interaction between the school and community anything more than hortatory? Could community be defined as "religious community"? Is the objection to the withholding of student records from parents an objection rooted in plaintiffs' religious beliefs?

Does the court articulate a standard to decide when state regulation of private schools intrudes upon religious belief too deeply? *See generally* Comment, "Regulation of Fundamentalist Christian Schools: Free Exercise of Religion v. The State's Interest in Quality Education," 67 *Ky. L. J.* 415 (1978–79). Is not the objection to "secular humanism" really an objection to the *Pierce* compromise? That is, if the court were to accept this objection (it did not reach it), what demands can the state constitutionally make of private, religious schools? How does *Yoder* resolve this issue? Why does the reasonableness of the state minima wane "in the face of an attack premised upon a violation of the constitutional rights of appellants to the free exercise of their chosen religion"? If Ohio's standards are presently too "pervasive and all-encompassing," what standards would pass constitutional muster? Is *Whisner* a case in which it is clear that the state sought to abolish the distinction "between public and non-public education"? Would the result have been different if the case involved non-religious private schools?

3. Kentucky State Board v. Rudasill

In *Kentucky State Board v. Rudasill,* 589 S.W.2d 877 (Ky. 1979), *cert. denied,* 446 U.S. 938, 100 S.Ct. 2158, 64 L.Ed.2d 792 (1980), plaintiffs successfully attacked the Kentucky rules governing private education under the free exercise clause of the Kentucky constitution. *See* Ky. Const. §5 (1891) ("No human authority shall, in any case whatever, control or interfere with the rights of conscience"). *See generally* S. Arons, *Compelling Belief* ch. 15 (1983); Comment, "Regulation of Fundamentalist Christian Schools: Free Exercise of Religion v. The State's Interest in Quality Education," 67 *Ky. L. J.* 415 (1979); Comment, "Separation of Church and State: Education and Religion in Kentucky," 6 *N. Ky. L. Rev.* 125 (1979). The objections focused, *inter alia,* on the following statutory and regulatory provisions: (1) instruction must be in the English language; (2) instruction must be offered "in the several branches of study required to be taught in the public schools"; (3) private schools may not operate for a term shorter than the public school term; (4) private schoolteachers must have a bachelor's degree in any subject; (5) textbooks must be approved by the state; (6) private and parochial schools must be accredited under state accreditation standards.

The plaintiff schools argued that few teachers who met the religious standards of the school were available and that the schools could not afford to hire teachers with college degrees. 67 *Ky. L. J.* at 422. Further, they asserted that "[S]ome of the approved texts omitted materials which their religion required them to teach, while others included material to which they were religiously opposed." *Id.* at 423. The state responded that the schools need not teach the objectionable material and that omissions could be cured by employing unapproved, supplemental texts (presumably at private and not public expense). With regard to curriculum, the required curriculum, unlike that in *State v. Whisner, supra,* left "plenty of time for religious schools to teach whatever they desire." *Id.* at 424. Plaintiffs then framed their objections in terms of the need to teach religious doctrines in the core curriculum, not limiting themselves to separate classes in religion. In the light of *Whisner,* are these rules governing private schools constitutional? *See 6 N. Ky. L. Rev.* at 144–49. Are rules governing health, fire, and safety in private schools distinguishable? Would a statute requiring that private religious schools administer competency tests and report the results to a state agency be constitutional? *See 6 N. Ky. L. Rev.* at 147–48; 67 *Ky. L. J.* at 427–29. What if students in private schools were required to pass examinations not required of public school students? Could a state requirement that private school students pass proficiency examinations in order to graduate from high school "effectively eradicate the distinction between public and non-public education" even in the case of non-religious schools? *See Ohio Association of Independent Schools v. Goff,* 92 F.3d 419 (6th Cir. 1996), *cert. denied,* 520 U.S. 1104, 117 S.Ct. 1107, 137 L. Ed.2d 309 (1997). *Cf. Rankins v. Louisiana State Board of Elementary and Secondary Education,* 637 So.2d 548 (La. App. 1 Cir. 1994), noting that because the state cannot mandate the content of the curriculum taught in non-public schools and because "graduation exit examinations" (GEE) must test what was in the curriculum, it was not a violation of the equal protection clause to require public school students, but not non-public school students, to pass the GEE as a condition of receiving a state diploma.

4. Application of Health, Safety, and Zoning Rules to Church-Operated Schools

Are rules governing health, fire, and safety in private schools distinguishable from rules governing curriculum, reporting, teacher certification, or testing? *See City of Sumner v. First Baptist Church of Sumner,* 97 Wash.2d 1, 639 P.2d 1358 (1982) (en banc), in which a majority of the Washington State Supreme Court upheld a challenge to zoning and building code regulations by a private, church-operated school. The majority, noting that financial constraints prevented the school, which was housed in the basement of the church building, from meeting the City's building code and zoning ordinance, conceded that the evenhanded application of a regulation concerning a valid governmental interest would "not directly adversely impact religious beliefs or prohibit religious exercise."

It is argued that because the regulation here involved does not impact directly a fundamental tenet of the church, it does not violate a member's First Amendment rights. Direct impact, however, has never been a requirement. It was not against a fundamental tenet of the Amish to send their children to high school; it was the incidental effects of that requirement the Amish believed to be detrimental to their faith and hence violative of their First Amendment rights. *Wisconsin v. Yoder, supra.* It was not a fundamental tenet of the Catholic faith that unionization of teachers be disallowed; yet the Supreme Court indicated that for the National Labor Relations Board to become involved regarding parochial schoolteachers could pose a significant risk of infringement on the free exercise of religion. *NLRB v. Catholic Bishop of Chicago,* 440 U.S. 490 . . . (1979).

It was not a fundamental tenet of "born again" Christians to not allow teaching of basic education 4 hours each day; yet the pernicious though incidental effect of allowing state regulation regarding mandatory subjects and allocation of classroom time has been held to violate the free exercise clause as to that religious group. *State v. Whisner, supra.* Neither is it a fundamental tenet to employ substandard teachers in a parochial school; yet it has been held that a state cannot require nonpublic schoolteachers to have "essentially equivalent" qualifications to those in public schools. *State v. LaBarge,* 134 Vt. 276, 357 A.2d 121 (1976).

So in this case, although there is no fundamental tenet against compliance with building codes or zoning ordinances, the practical effect of their uncompromising enforcement would be to close down the church-operated school. This would deny to church members the right to guide the education of their children by sending them to their church-operated school, a fundamental and constitutionally protected right. . . .

From the record before us, it cannot be determined whether the City used the least restrictive means of achieving its compelling interest. We assume the compelling state interest in this instance is the safety of the children. The City did not develop that issue in the trial record, and the trial court did not require it to do so. The City established only that it had a building code and a zoning ordinance with which the church had not complied.

97 Wash. 2d at 5–7, 9, 639 P.2d at 1361–63.

Do you agree that the inability of the school, which is "an integral and inseparable part of the educational ministry of the Church," to comply with the City's building codes or zoning ordinances for financial reasons, thus forcing it to close, is analogous to *Yoder*? Is compliance with the building code and fire regulations an infringement of the religious beliefs of the parents in this case? The dissenting justice strongly disagreed:

> The position of the majority is that zoning regulations and building codes cannot be enforced against a litigant who claims a First Amendment right of religion unless the governmental agency can demonstrate: (1) a compelling governmental interest; (2) that the governmental interest outweighs appellants' First Amendment rights; (3) that the means chosen to effectuate that interest will accomplish it; and (4) that the end sought cannot be achieved by less restrictive measures.
>
> The sweep of the majority position is breathtaking and as nearly as I have been able to determine utterly without precedent. Certainly none is cited by the majority. . . .
>
> The evidence demonstrates and the trial court found that among the numerous inadequacies of the building for use as a school are: inadequate floor space, inadequate ventilation, no approved fire alarm system, no fire extinguishers, no fire detectors, no sprinkler system, no fire-retardant walls and ceilings, no lighted exit signs, no exit signs at all, stairs that are too narrow, doors that do not open out, and stairs of inconsistent rise and run. In addition to these violations which constitute a safety hazard, there are health code violations such as inadequate restroom facilities.
>
> The attempt by the majority to view this case as analogous to *Wisconsin v. Yoder*, 406 U.S. 205 . . . (1972) . . . is to my mind less than persuasive. In . . . *Yoder* . . ., the plaintiffs were left with no choice. There was no way in which the demands of the state—compulsory education to age 16 . . .—could be met without a violation of a religious tenet. No such violation exists here. No bar of any kind has been raised against defendant establishing and conducting a religious school.

The majority claims "the practical effect of [the] uncompromising enforcement [of the health and safety codes] would be to close down the church-operated school." . . .

It may be that the correction of these deficiencies would cost a substantial sum and would be a burden on the defendants. Rather than attempting to make the appropriate changes in the building, however, or to work with the city authorities to see if there is some "play in the joints," the defendants choose to assert financial inability, raise the banner of the First Amendment, and claim a violation of religious liberty. Children in a school need the protection of fire and safety codes. That they burn and hurt like anybody else and that they need to be protected does not suddenly become less just because a church is operating the school and the protections of the First Amendment are asserted. The great right of freedom of religion should not be mocked.

* * *

Id. at 19–21, 639 P.2d at 1368–69 (Justice Dolliver, dissenting). Can the majority's position be reconciled with the Supreme Court's decision in *Employment Division, Department of Human Resources of Oregon v. Smith, supra?* Is the issue regulations that violate the religious beliefs of the parents or that undermine the institutional autonomy of religious schools? Is it unconstitutional to place a substantial economic burden on religious schools?

Suppose a local zoning ordinance forbids a church from establishing a religious school on its premises in a residential neighborhood not zoned for schools. The city argues that a school in such a neighborhood would disturb the peace of the neighborhood, increasing traffic and noise levels. The church asserts that it has a First Amendment right to establish a religious school on its premises. What result? *See Alpine Christian Fellowship v. County Commissioners of Pitkin*, 870 F.Supp. 991 (D.Colo.1994); *cf. City of Boerne v. Flores*, 521 U.S. 507, 117 S.Ct. 2157 (1997). Would you distinguish between the regulatory burdens of zoning and the cost of compliance with health and safety codes? Do both undermine the institutional autonomy of church schools?

IV. HOME SCHOOLING

The rise of the common school more than a century ago reflected, at least in part, a belief that parentally directed education was too haphazard an enterprise to guarantee educational quality and to ensure that children became productive and literate citizens.

Prior to the 1980s, a number of states did not permit home schooling. Today all fifty states and the District of Columbia permit the child's formal education to take place in the home under certain circumstances. More than two-thirds of the states have enacted statutes (twenty-seven states between 1982 and 1987), while the remaining states either have court decisions that have interpreted their states' compulsory education laws as permitting home schooling, *see, e.g., Texas Education Agency v. Leeper*, 893 S.W.2d 432 (Tex. 1994); *Care and Protection of Charles*, 504 N.E.2d 592 (Mass. 1987); *Sheppard v. Oklahoma*, 306 P.2d 346 (Okla. Crim. App. 1957); *People v. Levisen*, 404 Ill. 574, 90 N.E.2d 213 (1950), or their state departments of education have adopted procedures for approval of home schools. Most states impose specific conditions before allowing a home schooling situation to serve as an alternative means of complying with compulsory education requirements. *See generally* C. J. Klicka, *Home Schooling in the United States: A Legal Analysis* (1995); Mawdsley, "Home Schools and the Law," 137 *Ed. Law Rep.* 1 (1999); Sacken, "Regulating Nonpublic Education: A Search for Just Law and Home Policy," 96 *Amer. J. of Educ.* 394, 397 (1988); Lines, "An Overview of Home Instruction," *Phi Delta Kappan* 510 (March, 1987). Many parents, however, have objected to state regulation of home schooling, and this has resulted in numerous controversies and lawsuits. *See* Mawdsley, "Parental Rights and Home Schooling: Current Home School Litigation," 135 *Ed. Law Rep.* 313 (1999); Henderson, "The Home Schooling Movement: Parents Take Control of Educating Their Children," *1991 Ann. Surv. Am. L.* 985 (1993); Henderson, Golanda, and Lee, "Legal Conflicts Involving Home Instruction of School-Aged Children," 64 *Ed. Law. Rep.* 999 (1991).

Origins and Growth of the Home Schooling Movement

Although home schooling has existed in some form throughout history, most scholars note that the present home schooling movement grew out of the critiques of public education by education reformers in the 1960s and early 1970s, and their views of what education should be and how children learn. *See, e.g.*, Knowles, Marlow, and Muchmore, "From Pedagogy to Ideology: Origins and Phases of Home Education in the United States, 1970–1990," 100 *American Journal of Education* 195 (1992). The size of the

home schooling movement was quite limited until the early 1980s, when it began to grow significantly. For example, Wisconsin reports that in the decade between 1985 and 1995, the number of home-schooled children increased at an annual rate of 20 percent, while in Colorado, the number of home-schooled children quadrupled between 1990 and 1995. Bjorklun, "Home Schooled Students: Access to Public School Extracurricular Activities," 109 *Ed. Law Rep.* 1, 2 (1996). The number of home-schooled students nationally grew from about 15,000 in the 1970s to between 500,000 and 750,000 in 1995. Lines, "Homeschooling: An Overview for Education Policymakers," U.S. Department of Education Working Paper, January 1997 at 4–5. By the 1997–98 school year, the U.S. Department of Education estimated the number as one million (about 1 percent to 2 percent of the school-aged population). *See* Lines, "Home Schoolers: Estimated Numbers and Growth," in National Center for Educational Statistics, *The Condition of Education, 1998*. The Home School Legal Defense Association has reported a somewhat higher number—1.23 million. B. Ray, *Home Education Across the United States* (1997). The number of home schoolers may be significantly underestimated. Not all home schooling parents comply with requirements to notify state or local officials, not all states gather such data, and many parents either refuse to respond to surveys or call their home school a school. *See* Lines, "Homeschooling: An Overview," *supra* at 3–4. Estimating numbers is further complicated by the fact that there is a high turnover rate, with many children being home schooled for a few years and then returning to the public school or a private school. *See* Kohn, "Home Schooling," *The Atlantic* 20, 22 (April 1988), noting that the national average is that home schoolers last one year. Recent years have seen more children being home schooled for longer periods, some of whom are now applying to college.

Reasons for Choosing Home Schooling

Most commentators suggest that parents who choose to home school their children are of two types. One type, sometimes characterized as "the pedagogues," has chosen home schooling based on a child-directed philosophy of education, where education is less structured and more experiential. The early home schoolers were largely of this type, distrustful of bureaucratic educational institutions (whether public or private) as being too rigid and autocratic and inhibiting learning. *See, e.g.,* Knowles, Marlow, and Muchmore, *supra,* at 196–97. The other type, sometimes characterized as "the ideologues," were the predominant home schoolers of the 1980s. For them, schools did not provide a sufficiently structured and formal learning environment for children, as well as failing to teach the values and beliefs these parents considered important. *Id.* Most of these parents had a strong religious orientation and rejected the public school's teaching of evolution, promotion of secular humanism, and denigration of family values by public schools, as well as the lax morality perceived to exist among students, *id. See also* Bjorklun, *supra,* at 2. Although many of these parents are Christian Fundamentalists, a small but growing group of Catholic parents are educating their children at home, rejecting not only the public schools, but also parochial schools, as more liberal and less spiritual than the parochial schools they had attended. *See* Benning, "Home-Schooling's Mass Appeal: More Catholics Turn Away from Public, Parochial Options," *Washington Post,* Jan. 20, 1997, at B1.

However, increasingly, home schoolers include a third type. Although the growth of home schooling in the 1980s is largely attributable to the Christian Fundamentalists, who still constitute a majority of the home schooling families, Knowles, Marlow, and Muchmore, *supra,* at 198, Fig.1, the fastest growing segment today is said to be those who are concerned with the lack of safety and discipline in the public schools, and even in the private schools; those who are dissatisfied with the quality of public school instruction; and those who just want to spend more time with their children uninfluenced by their peers and to strengthen family bonds.

Who Are Home Schoolers?

Surveys show that home schoolers, as a group, are more religious, more politically and socially conservative, white, more likely to be a two-parent family, somewhat more affluent, and have somewhat more years of education than the general population. Typically, the mother does most of the teaching, although sometimes the father participates. Home schooling is more prevalent in the West and the South. In one state survey, one-third of the children being home schooled had previously been enrolled in private schools. Lines,

"Homeschooling: An Overview for Educational Policymakers," U.S. Department of Education Working Paper, January 1997 at 6–7. Almost no data exist regarding numbers of minority children being home schooled, although what little data do exist suggest that the numbers are very small. In one study based on a survey of home schoolers that included a sample of families drawn from all fifty states and the District of Columbia, 96 percent of the parents were white, 1.5 percent were Hispanic, 1 percent were Asian American, and substantially less than 1 percent were African American. *See* B. D. Ray, *Strengths of Their Own: Home Schoolers Across America* (1997).

Change in State Laws

Between 1982 and 1992, thirty-four states adopted home schooling statutes or regulations. Now, all fifty states permit home schooling.

A number of studies have shown that test scores of home schoolers are above average, but the research is inconclusive about the extent to which home schooling is more effective academically than public or private schooling. As one commentator has noted:

> Even the best studies are unable to obtain test scores from a significant portion of homeschooling children. The only data available consists of collections of test scores from selected groups of homeschoolers. Even where state-collected data are available and a state requires testing by law, many homeschoolers simply do not comply with the testing requirements. Moreover, none of the reported research attempts to compare test scores of these children with norming groups by demographic characteristics.

Lines, "Homeschooling: An Overview," *supra* at 9.

Many critics of home schooling argue that even if there are academic benefits, socialization of the child is neglected. There is little evidence, however, indicating whether home schooling hinders or helps a child's social development and ability to work cooperatively with others. As the movement has grown, many do participate in events organized by home school support groups, and increasingly, at the high school level, home schoolers are seeking to participate in extracurricular activities and even specialized academic courses at their public schools. Home schooling parents are less isolated as well. Home school networks, both state and national, have proliferated; the Internet has become a place for obtaining advice and support; commercial enterprises have produced both curricular and "how-to" materials, and home school correspondence courses are widely available, particularly those with Christian orientations. *See, e.g.,* Knowles, Marlow, and Muchmore, *supra* at 217–24; Lines, "Homeschooling: An Overview," *supra* at 12–13.

The three cases that follow examine the major legal issues that have arisen in the context of the national debate over home education.

Care and Protection of Charles
399 Mass. 324, 504 N.E.2d 592 (1987).

Before Hennessey, C. J., and Wilkins, Nolan, Lynch and O'Connor, JJ.

Hennessey, Chief Justice.

This case concerns the education of children at home by their parents. . . . Due to religious convictions, the parents desired to educate their three children, ages eleven, eight, and six, at home during the 1985–1986 school year.[1] Although the parents instructed their children in their "home school," the school committee of Canton, on October 15, 1985, initiated truancy proceedings in Stoughton District Court, asserting a violation of G.L. c. 76, §2. On October 16, 1985, a petition for care and protection of the children under G.L. c. 119, §24, was filed by an attorney for the town, alleging that the three children were "without necessary and proper educational care and discipline" and that their parents were "unwilling and unable or unavailable to provide such care." At a hearing on October 25, the criminal complaints under G.L. c. 76, §2, were dismissed. . . . On May 13, 1986, the judge issued his "findings and order," which determined that the children were in need of care and protection within the meaning of G.L. c. 119 with respect to their educational care only and ordered that the children "commence public or approved school attendance forthwith," although the children were allowed to remain in the physical and legal custody of their parents. The parents appealed this order to the Appeals Court. The judge stayed his order pending appeal. We transferred the case to this court on our own motion.

This case presents us with the question of accommodating the parents' rights under the Constitution of the United States and the Massachusetts Constitution with the governmental interest in the education of its citizens. For reasons which appear in the conclusion to this opinion, we direct that the judge's order be vacated and that the case be remanded to the lower court for further proceedings.

We summarize the relevant facts. . . . On August 21, 1985, the children's mother telephoned Dr. James C. Lynch, assistant superintendent of the Canton public schools, informing him that she and her husband intended to educate their three children at home during the 1985–1986 school year. This telephone call was followed by a letter dated September 1, 1985, which stated that: "[a]s christian parents, we are committed to introducing our children to and nurturing them in the truths of the Bible. . . . Our decision to home-school is based on the conviction that what [our children] need most is exposure to us, their parents, and a family whose foundation is the Word of God."

A meeting was held on September 4 with the parents and Drs. Lynch and Peter S. Capernaros, the superintendent of the Canton schools. At this meeting, the parents explained that they would be using a curriculum, which had yet to arrive, that was customary in "Christian Schools." In addition, they stated that the children would be involved in community activities such as gymnastics and soccer. Doctors Lynch and Capernaros determined that, although neither parent was certified to teach or had a college degree, each parent had a high school education[2] and the children's father had taken courses at the college level.

The parents attended the evening meeting of the Canton school committee on September 19 and were permitted to present their proposal in an executive session. The parents emphasized the superiority of their proposed "tutorial system" compared to the education received in public school classrooms. They stated that, although the curriculum materials still had not arrived, the curriculum would be individualized to meet each child's needs. Furthermore, they stated that they would be their children's only instructors and that the children's mother would be the primary instructor. School committee members

---

[1] Two of the children attended Canton's Kennedy Elementary School during the 1984–1985 school year; however, none of the three children named in this petition attended public school during the 1985–1986 school year. The name assigned to this case is fictitious.

[2] At a subsequent school committee meeting held on September 19, the children's mother admitted that she had not graduated from high school but had only completed the eleventh grade. She subsequently obtained her high school equivalency certificate while this case was pending.

expressed their concern about certain aspects of the parents' proposal, including the parents' objection to school department's testing and evaluation of their children's progress. . . .

On October 2, the children's father met with Drs. Lynch and Capernaros. At this meeting, he refused, for fear of prejudice, to document his educational background and that of his wife. He also stated his unwillingness to provide the administration with the number of hours and days that would be devoted to instruction of his children and his opposition to visits by school department personnel to his home for observation of the program. He did indicate his willingness to provide the administration with copies of the table of contents of the curriculum materials when they arrived and his preference for using a particular standardized test. . . .

Although invited, the parents declined to attend the October 3 meeting of the school committee, stating that they had no additional information for the committee. The committee instructed the school superintendent to send the parents a letter informing them that their consent to the stipulations of a proposed memorandum of agreement would facilitate the committee's consideration of their proposal. On October 16, the parents returned an edited version of the agreement, unsigned, indicating the stipulations that they found unacceptable.

At the November 14 meeting of the school committee, to which the parents were invited but again declined to attend,[3] the members voted to accept the recommendation of the school superintendent to deny the parents permission to educate their children at home. The parents were informed of this vote by letter dated November 19. The letter included a memorandum which outlined the following three major objections to the parents' proposal. First, the superintendent had not been given reason to believe that the parents were competent to teach their children. Second, the parents had indicated that the children would spend less time on formal instruction

than would children in public schools. Third, the parents objected to the school's efforts to monitor or observe the instructional methods used in the home school and periodically to test the children to determine whether they were making reasonable progress in their education. The superintendent indicated that, in his judgment, allowing the parents to educate their children "would be denying those children a proper education, by any reasonable standards."

* * *

The parents . . . argue that G.L. c. 76, §1, is constitutionally deficient due to vagueness because it fails to provide any standards for the approval of a home school proposal or to provide a procedure through which this determination is to be made. The parents couple this argument with a claim that G.L. c. 76, §1, is an unlawful delegation of legislative power to the superintendent and school committee. We have stated that the "constitutional claims of 'void for vagueness' and unlawful delegation of legislative authority are closely related. The principal question posed by both claims is whether the statute is so vague 'that men of common intelligence must necessarily guess at its meaning and differ as to its application.' . . ." *Board of Appeals of Hanover v. Housing Appeals Comm. in the Dep't of Community Affairs*, 363 Mass. 339, 363, 294 N.E.2d 393 (1973). . . . Under this standard, we conclude that G.L. c. 76, §1, is neither void for vagueness nor an unlawful delegation of legislative authority.

. . . The purpose of G.L. c. 76, §1, is to ensure that "all the children shall be educated. . . ." *Commonwealth v. Roberts*, 159 Mass. 372, 374, 34 N.E. 402 (1893) (interpreting a predecessor statute). In order to effectuate this purpose, the Legislature has provided a comprehensive statutory scheme setting the standards for the education of the State's youth. This statutory scheme includes standards under G.L. c. 71, §§1, 2, and 3, concerning the subjects that must be taught in public schools and the requirements for teacher qualification.[7] Further-

---

[3]The parents were represented at the meeting by counsel who addressed the committee.

[7]General Laws c. 71, §1 (1984 ed.), provides in relevant part: "Such schools shall be taught by teachers of competent ability and good morals, and shall give instruction and training in orthography, reading, writing, the English language and grammar, geography, arithmetic, drawing, music, the history and constitution of the United States, the duties of citizenship, health education, physical education and good behavior."

General Laws c. 71, §2 (1984 ed.), provides that: "In all public elementary and high schools American history and civics, including the constitution of the United States, the declaration of independence and the bill of rights, and in all public schools the constitution of the Commonwealth and local history and government, shall be taught as required subjects for the purpose of promoting civic service and a greater knowledge thereof, and of fitting the pupils, morally and intellectually, for the duties of citizenship."

General Laws c. 71, §3 (1984 ed.), provides, in relevant part, that: "Physical education shall be taught as a required subject in all grades for all students in the public schools for the purpose of promoting the physical well-being of such students."

more, G.L. c. 76, §1, specifically provides that: "For the purposes of this section, school committees shall approve a private school when satisfied that the instruction in all the studies required by law equals in thoroughness and efficiency, and in the progress made therein, that in the public schools in the same town; but shall not withhold such approval on account of religious teaching. . . ." Our reading of this statute indicates that the Legislature intended that the approval of a home school proposal fall within the above enunciated standard for the approval of a private school. . . .

General Laws c. 76, §1, also does not fail under the Federal standard of vagueness articulated in *Hoffman Estates v. Flipside, Hoffman Estates, Inc.*, 455 U.S. 489, 498–499, 102 S.Ct. 1186, 1193, 71 L.Ed.2d 362 (1982). . . . Furthermore, the Supreme Court indicated that the most important factor in this determination is whether the law "threatens to inhibit the exercise of constitutionally protected rights." *Id.* at 499, 102 S.Ct. at 1193. General Laws c. 76, §1, specifically forbids the school committee from withholding approval of private schools "on account of religious teaching." Because we conclude that this legislative policy extends to home school proposals, no constitutionally protected right is implicated.

With regard to the claim that G.L. c. 76, §1, constitutes an unlawful delegation of legislative authority, we also note that "[t]he Legislature may delegate to a board or officer the working out of the details of a policy adopted by the Legislature." . . . Although school committees do exercise broad discretion in the performance of their duties, it is not unbridled. Again, the substantial body of statutory law described above sets bounds under which the committees must act. Consequently, G.L. c. 76, §1, does not fail as an unlawful delegation of legislative authority.

We have no doubt that the statute is constitutional. If there were any lingering doubt on this issue, it would be resolved by recognition of the guidelines which we have set out . . . [below] for the assistance of parents and school authorities. These guidelines, like the specific provisions of the statu-

tory scheme, provide particulars through which the reasonableness of parents and public authorities may be measured.

* * *

We now examine the parents' contention that the approval process of G.L. c. 76, § 1, infringes on their right to educate their own children, a right protected by the Fourteenth Amendment to the United States Constitution. General Laws c. 76, § 1, requires that "[e]very child between the minimum and maximum ages established for school attendance by the board of education . . . attend a public day school in [the] town [where the child resides] or some other day school approved by the school committee . . . but such attendance shall not be required . . . of a child who is being otherwise instructed in a manner approved in advance by the superintendent or the school committee. . . ." The Canton school committee does not dispute the parents' right to educate their children at home. . . . However, the school committee does require that the parents submit to them a home schooling proposal, outlining, among other things, the curriculum, materials to be used, and qualifications of the instructors, for its approval as required under G.L. c. 76, § 1. The parents argue that such approval infringes on their rights under the Fourteenth Amendment to control the upbringing and education of their children.[8]

The United States Supreme Court has made it clear that the liberty interests protected by the Fourteenth Amendment extend to activities involving child rearing and education. *Pierce v. Society of Sisters*, 268 U.S. 510, 535, 45 S.Ct. 571, 573, 69 L.Ed. 1070 (1925). . . .

While the parents contend, and we agree, that they possess a basic right in directing the education of their children, such a right is not absolute but must be reconciled with the substantial State interest in the education of its citizenry. . . .

The Massachusetts Constitution itself proclaims the State's interest in ensuring that its citizens are educated. "Wisdom, and knowledge, as well as virtue, diffused generally among the body of the people, being necessary for the preservation of their

---

[8]We recognize that the parents also present arguments based on the First Amendment to the United States Constitution and art. 2 and amended art. 18 of the Declaration of Rights of the Massachusetts Constitution. Because we conclude that the parents have a basic right under the Fourteenth Amendment in directing the educational upbringing of their children subject to reasonable government regulation, we need not address these arguments. We note, however, that under the facts of this case, the free exercise of religion claims under neither the United States nor the Massachusetts Constitution would entitle the parents to any greater protection than we grant them in this opinion. *See Runyon v. McCrary*, 427 U.S. 160, 178 n. 15, 96 S.Ct. 2586, 2598 n. 15, 49 L.Ed.2d 415 (1976); *Duro v. District Attorney, Second Judicial Dist. of N.C.*, 712 F.2d 96, 98 (4th Cir. 1983), *cert. denied*, 465 U.S. 1006, 104 S.Ct. 998, 79 L.Ed.2d 230 (1984).

rights and liberties; and as these depend on spreading the opportunities and advantages of education in the various parts of the country, and among the different orders of the people, it shall be the duty of Legislatures and Magistrates, in all future periods of this Commonwealth, to cherish the interests of literature and the sciences, and all seminaries of them; especially . . . public schools and grammar schools in the towns;. . . ." Mass. Const.Pt. 2, c. 5, §2. . . .

The parents contend that, if the State has a substantial interest in this regard, the interest must be carefully defined as to its true nature. They argue that the extent of the State's interest is not in educating the children but only in knowing that the children are being educated. In the past we have had occasion to consider the State's interest under its compulsory education laws. In *Commonwealth v. Roberts, supra*, 159 Mass. at 374, 34 N.E. 402, we examined the predecessor statute to G.L. c. 76, §1, and stated that "[t]he great object of these provisions of the statutes has been that all children shall be educated, not that they shall be educated in any particular way." Consequently, we agree with the parents that the State interest in this regard lies in ensuring that the children residing within the State receive an education, not that the educational process be dictated in its minutest detail. . . .

However, in order to ensure that "all the children shall be educated," we conclude that the approval process required under G.L. c. 76, §1, is necessary to promote effectively the State's substantial interest. *State v. McDonough*, 468 A.2d 977, 980 (Me.1983). Without such an approval process, the State would be powerless to assert its interest in the case of a child "who is being otherwise instructed." "There is no doubt as to the power of a State, having a high responsibility for education of its citizens, to impose reasonable regulations for the control and duration of basic education." *Wisconsin v. Yoder, supra* at 213, 92 S.Ct. at 1532. Thus, the school committee may enforce, through the approval process under G.L. c. 76, §1, certain reasonable educational requirements similar to those required for public and private schools.

* * *

Having concluded that the approval process under G.L. c. 76, §1, is constitutionally permissible, we caution the superintendent or school committee that the approval of a home school proposal must not be conditioned on requirements that are not essential to the State interest in ensuring that "all the children

shall be educated." We recognize "that courts are not school boards or legislatures, and are ill-equipped to determine the 'necessity' of discrete aspects of a State's program of compulsory education." *Wisconsin v. Yoder, supra* at 235, 92 S.Ct. at 1543. However, because we remand this case to the lower court, we offer some guidance on the extent to which approval of a home school proposal may be conditioned on certain requirements without infringing on the liberty interests of the parents under the Fourteenth Amendment.

We begin by reiterating our holding in *Commonwealth v. Renfrew*, 332 Mass. 492, 494, 126 N.E.2d 109 (1955), that "[h]ome education of their child by the defendants without the prior approval of the superintendent or the [school] committee [does] not show a compliance with the statute and bar the prosecution of the complaints." Thus, as the statute indicates, approval must be obtained in advance, i.e., prior to the removal of the children from the public school and to the commencement of the home schooling program. See *State v. Riddle*, 168 W.Va. 429, 285 S.E.2d 359, 364 (1981). Procedurally, the superintendent or school committee must provide the parents with an opportunity to explain their proposed plan and present witnesses on their behalf. A hearing during a school committee meeting would be sufficient to meet this requirement. In obtaining the superintendent's or the school committee's approval, the parents bear the responsibility of demonstrating that the home school proposal meets the requirements of G.L. c. 76, §1, in that the instruction will equal "in thoroughness and efficiency, and in the progress made therein, that in the public schools in the same town. . . ." See *Matter of Kilroy*, 121 Misc.2d 98, 101, 467 N.Y.S.2d 318 (N.Y.Fam.Ct.1983). If the home school proposal is rejected, the superintendent or the school committee must detail the reasons for the decision. The parents must then be given an opportunity to revise their proposal to remedy its inadequacies. However, if the parents commence the education of their children at home in the face of the school committee's refusal to approve the parents' home school proposal, the burden of proof under G.L. c. 119 or G.L. c. 76, §2, shifts to the school committee to show that the instruction outlined in the home school proposal fails to equal "in thoroughness and efficiency, and in the progress made therein, that in the public schools in the same town. . . ." G.L. c. 76, §1. See *In re Monnig*, 638 S.W.2d 782, 788 (Mo.Ct.App.1982).

The school committee of Canton presented the parents with a memorandum of agreement outlining certain requirements necessary for the parents to obtain approval for their proposal. Although we decline to address the specifics of each requirement, we recognize that certain factors may be considered by the superintendent or school committee in determining whether or not to approve a proposed home school proposal. Primary among these is the proposed curriculum and the number of hours of instruction in each of the proposed subjects. . . . General laws c. 71, §§1, 2, and 3, list the subjects that must be taught in schools maintained by the towns throughout the Commonwealth. Specifically, §1 requires "instruction and training in orthography, reading, writing, the English language and grammar, geography, arithmetic, drawing, music, the history and constitution of the United States, the duties of citizenship, health education, physical education and good behavior." Under §1, the school committee may also require other subjects considered "expedient." Furthermore, G.L. c. 71, §§1 and 4 and 603 Code Mass.Regs. §27.01 (1980), require cities and towns to operate the public schools for a minimum of 180 days. The superintendent or school committee may properly consider the length of the proposed home school year and the hours of instruction in each subject. As we have stated before, "[t]he quality of education can be rendered meaningless if the quantity is subject to manipulation.". . .

The superintendent or school committee may also examine the competency of the parents to teach the children. General Laws c. 71, §1, provides that teachers shall be "of competent ability and good morals." While we recognize that teachers in public schools must be certified, certification would not appropriately be required for parents under a home school proposal. See *State v. Riddle, supra.* 285 S.E.2d at 366 (under a statutory requirement of "persons qualified to give instruction"). But see *Hanson v. Cushman,* 490 F.Supp. 109, 112 (W.D.Mich.1980); *Jernigan v. State,* 412 So.2d 1242, 1245 (Ala.Crim.App.1982); *Grigg v. Commonwealth,* 224 Va. 356, 363–364, 297 S.E.2d 799 (1982). Nor must the parents have college or advanced academic degrees. However, the superintendent or school committee may properly inquire as to the academic credentials or other qualifications of the parent or parents who will be instructing the children.

The superintendent or school committee must also have access to the textbooks, workbooks, and other instructional aids to be used by the children and to the lesson plans and teaching manuals to be used by the parents. This access is necessary only to determine the type of subjects to be taught and the grade level of the instruction for comparison purposes with the curriculum of the public schools. The superintendent or school committee may not use this access to dictate the manner in which the subjects will be taught. This would involve the school authorities in an activity beyond the legitimate scope of the State interest involved.

Finally, the superintendent or school committee may properly require periodic standardized testing of the children to ensure educational progress and the attainment of minimum standards. . . . In consultation with the parents, the school authorities may decide where the testing is to occur and the type of testing instrument to be used. Where practical, a neutral party should administer the test. Other means of evaluating the progress of the children may be substituted for the formal testing process, such as periodic progress reports or dated work samples, subject to the approval of the parents. With appropriate testing procedures or progress reports, there may be no need for periodic on-site visits or observations of the learning environment by school authority personnel. . . .

* * *

The judge properly relied on G.L. c. 76, §1, in determining that the children were, under G.L. c. 119, in need of care and protection with respect to their educational care. We think, also, that the judge's order finding the children in need of care and protection was warranted on the evidence. (For example, the judge found on the evidence that the parents had failed to provide documentation as to their educational qualifications and had refused to permit testing of the children.) Nevertheless, it is apparent that the parties have never confronted the issues before them in light of the legal principles and guidelines set out in this opinion. We conclude that the interests of all will be best served by the following order: the judge's order (presently stayed pending appeal) is vacated; the parties are to proceed expeditiously in a serious effort to resolve the matter by agreement; the case is remanded to the lower court where the trial judge is to have continuing jurisdiction over the case for such further proceedings as he deems necessary.

So ordered.

NOTES AND QUESTIONS

1. A Constitutional Right to Home Education?

Does *Charles* stand for the proposition that there is a constitutional right of parents, apart from their free exercise of religion, to educate children in the home? *See generally* Lupu, "Home Education, Religious Liberty, and the Separation of Powers," 67 *Bost. U. L. Rev.* 971 (1987). Or does the court simply affirm the parents' broad right to direct the education of their children in the course of examining the reasonableness of the conditions placed on home education by Massachusetts? Suppose that the court had not construed Chapter 76, Section 1, as permitting a home education exception to compulsory attendance at a public or private school. Would the statute be unconstitutional as applied to Charles and his parents? *See Peterson v. Minidoka County School Dist.*, 118 F.3d 1351 (9th Cir. 1997); *State v. Edgington*, 99 N.M. 715, 663 P.2d 374 (1983); *cf. State v. Bowman*, 60 Or. App. 184, 653 P.2d 254 (1982).

Note that Chapter 76, Section 1, makes no specific reference to home schooling, home education, or parental instruction. It simply says that compulsory attendance is not required of "a child who is being otherwise instructed in a manner approved in advance by the superintendent or the school committee [of the public school district]." The statute goes on to state that "for the purposes of this section, school committees shall approve a private school when satisfied that the instruction in all the studies required by law equals in thoroughness and efficiency, and in the progress made therein, that in the public schools in the same town; but shall not withhold such approval on account of religious teaching. . . ." It further provides that pupils in private schools "shall be entitled to the same rights and privileges as to transportation to and from school as are provided by law for pupils of public schools. . . . " Does Section 1 allow for home education to satisfy the compulsory attendance law? Has the court misread the statute? Does the court's view of "otherwise instructed" reflect its wish to avoid confronting the underlying constitutional issue? *See Texas Education Agency v. Leeper*, 893 S.W.2d 432 (Tex. 1994).

If *Pierce, Meyer*, and *Farrington* affirm the right of parents to send their children to regulated private schools, does it follow that there necessarily is a constitutional right to opt for home education? *See Clonlara, Inc. v. Runkel*, 722 F.Supp. 1442 (E.D. Mich.

1989). *See generally* T. van Geel, *The Courts and American Education Law* 23 (1987); Mawdsley, "Parental Rights and Home Schooling: Current Home Schooling Litigation," 135 *Ed. Law Rep.* 313 (1999); Note, " Public School Access: The Constitutional Right of Home-Schoolers to 'Opt in' to Public Education on a Part-Time Basis," 82 *Minn. L. Rev.* 1599, 1605–13 (1998); Comment, "*People v. Bennett*: Analytic Approaches to Recognizing a Fundamental Parental Right Under the Ninth Amendment," 1996 *B.Y.U. L. Rev.* 183; Henderson, "The Home Schooling Movement: Parents Take Control of Educating Their Children," *1991 Annual Survey of American Law* (1993); Devins, "A Constitutional Right to Home Instruction?" 62 *Wash. U. L. Q.* 435 (1984). Are there constitutionally relevant distinctions? If, as *Charles* demonstrates, it is more difficult for the state to determine compliance with minimum education standards in the home school setting, would the difficulties of oversight justify the abolition of the home school alternative? *See Delconte v. State*, 65 N.C. App. 262, 308 S.E.2d 898 (1983), *reversed on other grounds*, 313 N.C. 384, 329 S.E.2d 636 (1985). Justify it in individual cases? *See Mazanec v. North Judson-San Pierre School Corp.*, 798 F.2d 230 (7th Cir. 1986). Justify more oversight of home education than private schooling? *See Murphy v. Arkansas*, 852 F.2d 1039, 1043–44 (8th Cir. 1988); *Blount v. Department of Education*, 551 A.2d 1377 (Me. 1988).

Is the constitutional right of parents "to direct the upbringing and education of children under their control" a "fundamental" right, requiring a heightened level of scrutiny by the courts, or merely rational basis scrutiny? *See Troxel v. Granville*, 530 U.S. 57, 120 S. Ct. 2054, 147 L.Ed.2d 49(2000); *Brown v. Hot, Sexy and Safer Productions, Inc.*, 68 F.3d 525, 533 (1st Cir. 1995); *Immediato v. Rye Neck School Dist.*, 73 F.3d 454, 461 (2d Cir. 1996).

2. Vagueness and Unlawful Delegation

Do you agree with the court that Chapter 76, Section 1, is not unconstitutionally vague and does not unlawfully delegate authority to local school officials in the context of home schooling? *See Jeffery v. O'-Donnell*, 702 F.Supp. 516 (M.D.Pa. 1988); *Blackwelder v. Safnauer*, 689 F.Supp. 106 (N.D.N.Y. 1988); *Iowa v. Trucke*, 410 N.W. 2d 242 (Iowa 1987); *State v. Newstrom*, 371 N.W. 2d 525 (Minn. 1985); Lupu, *supra* at 979–82. Is the court correct in using the equality of instruction proviso, applicable on its face only to private schools, to clarify the scope of regulation of home schooling? Do you agree that "the Legislature intended that the approval of a home school proposal fall within the. . . enunciated standard for the approval of a private school"? Suppose that the standards for a private school included a minimum class size or particular grade structure. Would the court approve the application of these standards to home education? Is any impermissible vagueness or unlawful delegation cured by the court's own "guidelines" for regulating home education? *See State v. Popanz*, 332 N.W. 2d 750 (Wis. 1983) (holding Wisconsin's compulsory education statute void for vagueness and dismissing criminal charges against home schooling parents). *See generally* Note, "The Latest Home Education Challenge: The Relationship Between Home Schools and Public Schools," 74 *N.C. L. Rev.* 1913, 1928–29, 1953 (1996).

3. *The State's Interest*

The court quotes with approval the statement in *Commonwealth v. Roberts* that "[t]he great object of these provisions of the statutes has been that all children shall be educated, not that they shall be educated in any particular way." Is this consistent with Chapter 76, Section 1? That section provides for equality in terms of the "progress" made by pupils receiving instruction outside of the public schools and for equality with respect to the "thoroughness and efficiency" of the course of study. Does this language suggest that the legislature is interested in both educational process and outcomes? If the children educated at home do well enough on standardized tests, might the parents successfully argue that the state may not require any course of study or credentials for home instructors? *See* Mangrum, "Family Rights and Compulsory School Laws," 21 *Creighton L. Rev.* 1019 (1988).

4. *Procedural Due Process*

The court is insistent that certain procedural safeguards be observed in the regulation of home schooling. Are such procedures designed to protect the parents or the children or both? Consider these remarks by Professor Lupu:

> The [Massachusetts] statutes create an "entitlement" to education for the children who are the intended beneficiaries of the official and custodial duties thereby established. Children therefore possess a fourteenth amendment "property" interest in education, and a corresponding constitutional interest in a meaningful opportunity to be heard prior to the deprivation of that

interest. Regardless of whether parents or school officials are the moving parties in a decision to remove children from school, the children are constitutionally entitled to some form of hearing at which the lawfulness of any such decision is tested.

Lupu, *supra* at 978. Do you agree? Has the *Charles* court creatively sought to resolve the possible conflict between the rights of parents and children that Justice Douglas noted in his dissent in *Yoder*? Has it succeeded? Are public school officials "biased" in evaluating home schooling? If so, does the absence of impartiality itself constitute a denial of due process? *See State v. Brewer*, 444 N.W.2d 923 (N.D. 1989).

Stephens v. Bongart

15 N.J. Misc. 80, 189 A. 131 (Juv. & Dom. Rel. Ct. 1937).

Siegler, Judge.

Helen Stephens, attendance officer of the school district of the town of West Orange in the county of Essex, filed her complaint against Gertrude R. Bongart and Benno Bongart, the defendants in this action, charging that they reside within the school district of the town of West Orange, and being the parents and having custody and control of William Bongart, aged twelve, and Robert Bongart, aged eleven, their children, have, since the 5th day of April, 1936, failed to cause their said children regularly to attend the public schools of the school district of the said town of West Orange; further charging said defendants having neither caused said children to attend a day school in which there is given instruction equivalent to that provided in the public schools for children of similar grades and attainments, nor have they received equivalent instruction elsewhere than at the school. . . .

The act upon which these proceedings are based, chapter 307 of the Laws of 1931 (N.J. St. Annual 1931, §185-165c), reads as follows:

> Every parent, guardian or other person having custody and control of a child between the ages of seven and sixteen years shall cause such child regularly to attend the public schools of such district or to attend a day school in which there is given instruction equivalent to that provided in the public schools for children of similar grades and attainments or to receive equivalent instruction elsewhere than at school unless such child is above the age of fourteen years. . . . Such regular attendance shall be during all the days and hours that the public schools are in session in said school district, unless it shall be shown

to the satisfaction of the Board of Education of said school district that the mental condition of the child is such that he or she cannot benefit from instruction in the school or that the bodily condition of the child is such as to prevent his or her attendance at school.

* * *

The first point raised by the defendants is that the statute under which these proceedings are brought; to wit, Chapter 307 of the Laws of 1931 is invalid because it invades the Fourteenth Amendment of the United States Constitution. The problem for determination is whether the statute, as construed and applied, unreasonably infringes the liberty guaranteed to the defendants by the Fourteenth Amendment: "No State shall . . . deprive any person of life, liberty, or property, without due process of law." This statute is a legitimate exercise of the police power of the state. The object of the legislation was to create an enlightened American citizenship in sympathy with our principles and ideals, and to prevent children reared in America from remaining ignorant and illiterate. If it is within the police power of the state to regulate wages, to legislate respecting housing conditions in crowded cities, to prohibit dark rooms in tenement houses, to compel landlords to place windows in their tenements which will enable their tenants to enjoy the sunshine, it is within the police power of the state to compel every resident of New Jersey so to educate his children that the light of American ideals will permeate the life of our future citizens. . . .

The defendants rely upon the authority of. . . *Pierce v. Society of Sisters* . . . for support of their contention that the legislation under consideration is unconstitutional. The issue in the *Pierce* case . . . was not that involved here. There the court was considering property rights of the appellees; the right to engage in the business of conducting a school for the instruction of children; but throughout the whole case the question of the right of the state to require children to attend school was not challenged; this right appeared to be conceded.

* * *

The second point for determination is whether or not the defendants provided instruction for their children equivalent to that provided in the public schools for children of similar grades and attainments.

This necessitates an analysis of the testimony. The proof is that the defendants' children, William, twelve, and Robert, eleven, were in the sixth and fifth grades, respectively, in the Washington Street School, West Orange, until April 3, 1936. From that date, these children failed to attend a public or day school, although proper notice was served upon the defendants to return the children to a school. The defendants admit they caused the children's withdrawal from the Washington School.

Since that time, the defendants claim that they instructed their children in their own home in the subjects taught in the fifth and sixth grades. This instruction, they claim, is equivalent to that provided in the public schools for children of similar grades and attainments. The case turns on this factual situation. 2 *Words and Phrases, Second Series* 312, defines the word *equivalent* as follows: "*Equivalent* means 'equal in worth or value, force, power, effect, import and the like.' . . ."

Quite definitely, the term refers to the giving of instruction equal in value and effect to that given in a public school. In determining this question, consideration must be given, first, to the matter of the ability of the parents to provide equivalent instruction, and, secondly, to a comparison of the quality, character, and methods of teaching employed by the defendants and that of the West Orange public school system. Mrs. Bongart was graduated from the Eastern District High School, New York City, in 1911. In 1917 she was a special student at Hunter College, evening course. This required three or four evenings a week, which she carried on for only two years. She studied economics, psychology, art, portrait work, charcoal work and painting; she majored in home economics. Mrs. Bongart had no teaching experience. She was married about fifteen years ago, and her chief employment was that of housewife. Mr. Bongart is a graduate of the University of Strassbourg, in the field of electrical and mechanical engineering. He never trained for teaching, but did have employment as a teacher at the New York Aerial School, Newark Technical School, and the Newark Junior High School until recently. He taught subjects in mechanical drawing and electrical engineering. The teachers in the elementary grades of the public schools, particularly the fifth and sixth grades in the West Orange school system, must have at least a high school education and three years at an approved normal school in the state of New Jersey.

The normal school curriculum includes a type of training and education intended to qualify students to teach in the elementary class in the subjects of English, history, science, sociology, civics, mathematics, hygiene, geography, art, music, and physical education. The major aim is to give the teachers training in techniques of presentation of material to elementary school students. That involves the proper selection of material, knowledge of children, and the organization of their work, so that every teacher should know the results which must be achieved in terms of knowledge, habits, skills, attitudes, and appreciations. Her training should qualify her to develop individuality and the personality of each child under her supervision. One of the major aims of our public school today is to teach the way in which the individual must fit into the social group. The evidence establishes that the teachers in the fifth and sixth grades of Washington School possess this training and qualify in these courses.

It is clear, upon comparison, that there is a substantial variance between the training, qualifications, and experience of the defendants and those obtained in the public school system of West Orange.

Now, what was the instruction given by the defendants at their home? The children assemble, one in the dining room and the other in the front room, each morning at 9 o'clock, and continue until 12; they resume at 1 o'clock, and recess at 3 in the afternoon. They receive instruction in arithmetic, spelling, history, geography, language, and music. In the evening, the father instructs them in science between 7 and 9 o'clock.

In the study of arithmetic a textbook is used by Stone and Millis, dated 1914. There were no textbooks for spelling, language, music, civics, hygiene, and art; while the textbooks used were outmoded and outdated, the latest published in 1921 and the oldest in 1881, and all certainly of questionable value in the instruction of children. Spelling was taught without a book, the mother giving twenty words at random each week, which the children had to learn and place in a notebook. The other subjects were taught by assigning periods of 30 or 35 minutes for each. Language was largely taught through the reading of the newspapers, the Literary Digest and the Saturday Evening Post. Poetry was principally taught by the use of an occasional piece of poetry out of the Sunday Times and the New York Daily News, a tabloid newspaper. No poems were memorized. Music was taught by listening to radio concerts. There were no song books or singing exercises. Mechanical drawing and current events were given by the father in the evening. The Newark Evening News and some other periodicals were sources from which current events were drawn for discussion. The Bible was read once in a while. The flag of the country was exhibited in front of the house on patriotic occasions. The mother spoke to them about hygiene and the danger of alcoholic beverages, but no hygiene textbook was used. There were no instructions in observance of patriotic holidays, and no observance of Arbor Day. There was no physical training except that which they got outside in the ordinary course of their play. They had membership in the YMCA, but failed to attend during September and October. Of this default the parents had no knowledge.

The instruction was interrupted from time to time by the mother's household duties, occasional shopping tours, and house callers. The defendants had no definite schedule for daily instruction. The evidence indicates that the boys obtained from children in school, periodically, information as to the subjects they were studying in school, and transmitted that information to their mother, who guided herself in instructing the children, to some extent, by it. They had no marks for their work. There were no daily work papers, tests, or examinations; at least, there were none presented in evidence. In fact, the mother admits she had no standard by which to determine whether the children were absorbing the instruction she was attempting to give. There was no organized supervision over the teaching the defendants gave; the work of the children, and the results accomplished, were never submitted to any other competent authority for supervision, criticism, or approval.

A summary of the methods of instruction at the Washington School of West Orange will be useful for comparative purposes. The elementary grades are supervised by a specially trained person, who has complete supervision over the courses of study, the textbooks used, and the methods employed by the teachers in transmitting knowledge and the building and developing of the personalities of the children. The school is organized as a miniature community center, a sort of city, where each child considers himself a citizen, with duties toward the community as is required on the outside. The educational structure thus developed is in the nature of a group enterprise, where the children work together for the common good. The teacher creates the atmosphere and becomes the guiding influence. A high discipline is maintained by strict attention to the development of habits, skills and attitudes. There is group discussion. The children bring in articles from the outside. They study the biographies of great men, and discuss their achievements. In the fifth and sixth grades, reading, writing, spelling, arithmetic, English, history, geography, civics, hygiene, safety education, music, art, and penmanship are taught. The children are taught to use the dictionary. The norm for instruction may be found in several monographs on each subject, provided by the state board of education, and strict adherence is required. In the fifth grade, there are seven textbooks in daily use to cover the subjects. In the sixth grade, there are also seven textbooks, supplemented by thirteen reference and reading books used in connection with their courses, and, in addition, the school library is available to them. Every text, reading, and reference book, 26 in number, produced in evidence, is carefully selected in accordance with the regulations of the state board of education and approved by the supervisor of the elementary grades and by the board of education of West Orange. There is a student schedule for the fifth and sixth grades, which provides for instruction from 8:45 a.m. until 3 p.m. from Monday to Friday, inclusive. The curriculum provides for instruction in the development of abilities, habits, and skills. Instruction is also given by way of travel lectures, picture studies, art and music, so that every child has something to talk about. Thus, an audience situation is created for the children, where each child is required to rise and speak to the entire group. This creates self-confidence, and tends to adjust the child to the social group.

One poem a week, and appreciation for the beauties of nature and literature are taught. Besides teaching arithmetic from texts, they instruct in practical matters requiring arithmetic. Geography is taught to meet life situations by creating interest in world travel and training the children to visualize, in their reading, places that they have studied. In music, each child is allowed to develop whatever talent he may possess. In art, each child learns the harmony of color in dress, interior decoration, and everyday life. Every morning the children have a reading from the Bible and recite the Lord's Prayer. They salute the flag and sing patriotic songs. They observe Arbor Day and all patriotic holidays. A course in safety education and fire prevention is pursued. The month of June is devoted to review. They have physical education four periods each week under a special supervisor. In the civics course, the children are on the lookout for all material in current events. There are three school magazines. Washington School has a monthly newspaper, and all children are eligible to participate in its columns.

* * *

From this comparison and analysis of the evidence, I find (1) that the education, training, and equipment of the defendants are substantially inadequate, as compared with those of the public school teacher; (2) that the schedule of study and the program of activities of the defendants are irregular, uncertain, and without form, while the public school curriculum is definite and allots a specified time and, in most cases, a special teacher for every subject studied in the fifth and sixth grades; (3) that the instruction given by the defendants is without proper or modern textbooks, lacks supervision by competent authorities of pupil and teacher, lacks a method, standard, or other means of determining the progress or attainments of the child; none of which deficiencies are present in the public school; (4) that the teaching of discipline and health habits lacks plan and a trained method, fixing responsibility on the child for its execution; while, at the school, it is part of a definite program of character education; (5) that the defendants cannot provide for group or class teaching, and lack the ability to develop attitudes and create a social setting so that the children may be trained to deal with their playmates and friends as a part of a social group; (6) that the public school system provides such social groups and lays emphasis on its development, and stresses the adjustment of the child to group life and group activity and a course of living that he will be required to follow and meet as he goes out into the world.

The primary function of education is to get an understanding and interpretation of modern civilization. In the early days of the Republic, the idea that an educated citizenship lies at the very foundation of a democratic government has defined our philosophy of national development. For these reasons, the maintenance of an adequate system of public education for youth is a fundamental responsibility of any commonwealth. The public school system of New Jersey embodies the highest ideals of American democracy, and has developed a program which offers unusual opportunities to the children of our state. All citizens have a deep interest in our public schools, and should take pride in the high rank which they occupy in the nation. To deny children instruction seems as unnatural as to withhold their necessary subsistence. Education is brought, as it were, to the very door of all classes of society, and ignorance is quite inexcusable. The failure of the parents to provide the child with the benefits of that opportunity should be a matter of great concern when at issue. The education of youth is of such vast importance and of such singular utility in the journey of life that it obviously carries its own recommendation with it, for on it, in a great measure, depends all that we ever hope to be; every perfection that a generous and well-disposed mind would gladly arrive at. It is this that usually renders one man preferable to another. And, as the great end of learning is to teach man to know himself and to fit him for life, so he who knows most is enabled to practice best and to be an example for those who know but little.

The schools, whose function frequently is thought of solely in material terms, have a far more important responsibility. They must aid parents, not simply in the training of their children for the trades and professions, whose criterion of success too often is the amount of money they can make, but, rather, the training and development of men and women of character; men and women whose minds have been trained to the understanding of basic principles and ideals, with the courage and strength of will to live up to and apply them in their daily lives.

I incline to the opinion that education is no longer concerned merely with the acquisition of facts; the instilling of worthy habits, attitudes, appreciations, and skills is far more important than mere imparting of subject matter. A primary objective of education today is the development of character and good citizenship. Education must impart to the child the way to live. This brings me to the belief that, in a cosmopolitan area such as we live in, with all the complexities of life, and our reliance upon others to carry out the functions of education, it is almost impossible for a child to be adequately taught in his home. I cannot conceive how a child can receive in the home instruction and experiences in group activity and in social outlook in any manner or form comparable to that provided in the public school. To give him less than that is depriving the child of the training and development of the most necessary emotions and instincts of life. I cannot accept the theory asserted by Mr. Bongart that, "I am not interested in method, but in results." That theory is archaic, mechanical, and destructive of the finer instincts of the child. It does seem to me, too, quite unlikely that this type of instruction could produce a child with all the attributes that a person of education, refinement, and character should possess.

I have carefully observed the defendants' children in court, their demeanor, their responses under examination, and their reaction to the proceedings while in court, and there is clear evidence that it is their belief that they are on a "grand holiday," free from the restraints, discipline, and responsibility of other children in school attendance. All of this seems to me to be attributable to the course adopted and pursued by the parents. I have also carefully examined all the evidence and exhibits, and it is my opinion that the defendants have failed to give their children instruction equivalent to that provided in the public schools in the fifth and sixth grades, but, rather, have engaged in a haphazard and hit-or-miss kind of instruction, not calculated to conform with the provisions of the statute, and that both defendants actively and independently participated in causing their children not to go to the public school or a day school. I have been satisfied beyond a reasonable doubt by the evidence of the guilt of both defendants as charged. Both defendants are hereby deemed to be disorderly persons.

State v. Massa

95 N.J. Super. 382, 231 A.2d 252 (Morris County Ct. 1967).

Collins, J. C. C.

This is a trial *de novo* on appeal from the Pequannock Township Municipal Court. Defendants were charged and convicted with failing to cause their daughter Barbara, age 12, regularly to attend the public schools of the district and further for failing to either send Barbara to a private school or provide an equivalent education elsewhere than at school, contrary to the provisions of NJSA 18:14-14. The municipal magistrate imposed a fine of $2490 for both defendants.

Mr. and Mrs. Massa appeared *pro se*. Mrs. Massa conducted the case; Mr. Massa concurred.

The State presented two witnesses who testified that Barbara had been registered in the Pequannock Township School but failed to attend the 6th grade class from April 25, 1966, to June 1966 and the following school year from September 8, 1966, to November 16, 1966—a total consecutive absence of 84 days.

Mrs. Massa testified that she had taught Barbara at home for two years before September 1965. Barbara returned to school in September 1965, but began receiving her education at home again on April 25, 1966.

Mrs. Massa said her motive was that she desired the pleasure of seeing her daughter's mind develop. She felt she wanted to be with her child when the child would be more alive and fresh. She also maintained that in school much time was wasted and that at home a student can make better use of her time.

Mrs. Massa is a high school graduate. Her husband is an interior decorator. Neither holds a teacher's certificate. However, the State stipulated that a child may be taught at home and also that Mr. or Mrs. Massa need not be certified by the State of New Jersey to so teach. The sole issue in this case is one of equivalency. Have defendants provided their daughter with an education equivalent to that provided by the Pequannock Township School System?

Mrs. Massa introduced into evidence 19 exhibits. Five of these exhibits, in booklet form, are condensations of basic subjects, are concise and seem to contain all the basic subject material for the respective subjects. Mrs. Massa also introduced textbooks which are used as supplements to her own compilations as well as for test material and written problems.

Mrs. Massa introduced English, spelling and mathematics tests taken by her daughter at the Pequannock School after she had been taught for two years at home. The lowest mark on these tests was a B.

* * *

There is also a report by an independent testing service of Barbara's scores on standard achievement tests. They show that she is considerably higher than the national median except in arithmetic.

Mrs. Massa satisfied this court that she has an established program of teaching and studying. There are definite times each day for the various subjects and recreation. She evaluates Barbara's progress through testing. If Barbara has not learned something which has been taught, Mrs. Massa then reviews that particular area.

Barbara takes violin lessons and attends dancing school. She also is taught art by her father, who has taught this subject in various schools.

Mrs. Massa called Margaret Cordasco as a witness. She had been Barbara's teacher from September 1965 to April 1966. She testified basically that Barbara was bright, well behaved and not different from the average child her age except for some trouble adjusting socially. The State called as a witness David MacMurray, the Assistant Superintendent of Pequannock Schools. He testified that the defendants were not giving Barbara an equivalent education. Most of his testimony dealt with Mrs. Massa's lack of certification and background for teaching and the lack of social development of Barbara because she is being taught alone.

He outlined procedures which Pequannock teachers perform, such as evaluation sheets, lesson plans and use of visual aids. He also stressed specialization since Pequannock schools have qualified teachers for certain specialized subjects. He did not think the defendants had the specialization necessary to teach all basic subjects. He also testified about extracurricular activity, which is available but not required.

The State placed six exhibits in evidence. These included a more recent mathematics book than is being used by defendants, a sample of teacher evaluation, a list of visual aids, sample schedules for the day and lesson plans, and an achievement testing program.

* * *

N.J.S.A. 18:14-14 provides:

> Every parent, guardian or other person having custody and control of a child between the ages of 6 and 16 years shall cause such child regularly to attend the public schools of the district or a day school in which there is given instruction equivalent to that provided in the public schools for children of similar grades and attainments *or to receive equivalent instruction elsewhere than at school.* (Emphasis added.)

State v. Vaughn, 44 N.J. 142, 207 A.2d 537 (1965), interpreted the above statute to permit the parent having charge and control of the child to elect to substitute one of the alternatives for public school. It is then incumbent upon the parent to introduce evidence showing one of the alternatives is being substituted. "If there is such evidence in the case, then the ultimate burden of persuasion remains with the State.". . .

N.J.S.A. 18:14-39 provides for the penalty for violation of N.J.S.A. 18:14-14:

> A parent, guardian or other person having charge or control of a child between the ages of 6 and 16 years, who shall fail to comply with any of the provisions of this article relating to his duties shall be deemed a disorderly person and shall be subject to a fine of not more than $5 for a first offense and not more than $25 for each subsequent offense, in the discretion of the court. . . .

This case presents two questions on the issue of equivalency for determination. What does the word *equivalent* mean in the context of N.J.S.A. 18:14-14? And, has the State carried the required burden of proof to convict defendants?

In *Knox v. O'Brien,* 7 N.J. Super. 608, 72 A.2d 389 (1950), the County Court interpreted the word *equivalent* to include not only academic equivalency but also the equivalency of social development. This interpretation appears untenable in the face of the language of our own statute and also the decisions in other jurisdictions.

If the interpretation in *Knox* were followed, it would not be possible to have children educated outside of school. Under the *Knox* rationale, in order for children to develop socially it would be necessary for them to be educated in a group. A group of students being educated in the same manner and place would constitute a de facto school. Our statute provides that children may receive an equivalent education elsewhere than at school. What could have been intended by the Legislature by adding this alternative?

The Legislature must have contemplated that a child could be educated alone provided the education was equivalent to the public schools. Conditions in today's society illustrate that such situations exist. Examples are the child prodigy whose education is accelerated by private tutoring, or the infant performer whose education is provided by private tutoring. If group education is required by our statute, then these examples as well as all education at home would have to be eliminated.

* * *

Faced with exiguous precedent in New Jersey and having reviewed the above cited cases in other states, this court holds that the language of the New Jersey statute, N.J.S.A. 18:14-14, providing for "equivalent education elsewhere than at school," requires only a showing of academic equivalence. As stated above, to hold that the statute requires equivalent social contact and development as well would emasculate this alternative and allow only group education, thereby eliminating private tutoring or home education. A statute is to be interpreted to uphold its validity in its entirety if possible. . . . This is the only reasonable interpretation available in this case which would accomplish this end.

Having determined the intent of the Legislature as requiring only equivalent academic instruction, the only remaining question is whether the defendants provided their daughter with an education equivalent to that available in the public schools. After reviewing the evidence presented by both the State and the defendants, this court finds that the State has not shown beyond a reasonable doubt that defendants failed to provide their daughter with an equivalent education.

The majority of testimony of the State's witnesses dealt with the lack of social development. The other point pressed by the State was Mrs. Massa's lack of teaching ability and techniques based upon her limited education and experience. However, this court finds this testimony to be inapposite to the actual issue of equivalency under the New Jersey statute and the stipulations of the State. In any case, from my observation of her while testifying and during oral argument, I am satisfied that Mrs. Massa is self-educated and well qualified to teach her daughter the basic subjects from grades one through eight.

* * *

It is the opinion of this court that defendants' daughter has received and is receiving an education equivalent to that available in the Pequannock public schools. There is no indication of bad faith or improper motive on defendants' part. Under a more definite statute with sufficient guidelines or a lesser burden of proof, this might not necessarily be the case. However, within the framework of the existing law and the nature of the stipulations by the State, this court finds the defendant not guilty and reverses the municipal court conviction. . . .

NOTES AND QUESTIONS

1. Contrasting Bongart and Massa

Note the curt treatment the *Bongart* court gives to the argument that New Jersey's compulsory attendance law impinges on *Bongart's* liberty. Is its analysis satisfactory? Does any requirement of prior governmental approval of home schooling violate the parents' rights? *See State v. McDonough*, 468 A.2d 977 (Me. 1983) (requirement upheld); *State v. Schmidt*, 505 N.E.2d 627 (Ohio 1987). What of on-site visits to the home school? Compare *Brunelle v. Lynn Public Schools*, 428 Mass. 512, 702 N.E. 2d 1182 (Mass. 1998) (home visits not essential to state's interest) with *Battles v. Anne Arundel County Board of Education*, 904 F. Supp. 471 (D. Md. 1995), *aff'd*, 95 F.3d 41 (4th Cir. 1996) (monitoring process that included observation of teaching process by state representative upheld over free exercise claim); *Blackwelder v. Safnauer*, 689 F.Supp. 106 (N.D.N.Y. 1988) (on-site visit requirement not unconstitutional); *Matter of Blackwelder*, 139 Misc. 2d 776, 528 N.Y.S. 2d 759 (Sup.Ct. 1988) (on-site visit requirement to determine equivalence of education upheld).

The *Bongart* definition of equivalency renders compulsory education synonymous with compulsory schooling. "[I]n a cosmopolitan area such as we live in . . . it is almost impossible for a child to be adequately taught in his home." Is the conclusion empirically defensible? Is it a justifiable interpretation of a statute that expressly permits equivalent instruction to take place "elsewhere than the school"? At what point do family arrangements for education become "a thinly veiled subterfuge [for] attacking compulsory school attendance"? *See In Interest of Sawyer*, 234 Kan. 436, 672 P.2d 1093 (1983).

Massa defines equivalency in a manner that permits parents to educate their own children at home. *See also Matter of Lash*, 92 Misc.2d 642, 401 N.Y.S.2d 124 (Fam. Ct. 1977); *People v. Levisen*, 404 Ill. 574, 90 N.E.2d 213 (1950). *See generally* F. Kemerer and J. Hairston, *The Educator's Guide to Texas School Law* 30–31 (2d ed. 1990). But is the process by which the court attempts to match fact situation to statutory requirement different in the two cases? How does the court in each case determine whether the parent is qualified to serve as teacher? *See People v. DeJonge*, 442 Mich. 266, 501 N.W. 2d 127 (1993) (teacher certification requirement held unconstitutional in face of free exercise claim); *People v. Bennett*, 442 Mich. 316, 501 N.W. 2d 106 (1993) (teacher certification requirement upheld); *State v. Patzer*, 382 N.W.2d 631 (N.D. 1986) (teacher certification requirement upheld); *State v. Newstrom*, 371 N.W.2d 525 (Minn. 1985) (requirement that home school teacher have "essentially equivalent" qualifications to public school teachers is unconstitutionally vague). How does the court in each case determine whether the curriculum provided at home is adequate? *See Appeal of Pierce*, 122 N.H. 762, 451 A.2d 363 (1982) ("home-education curriculum involved limited and irregular hours of organized instruction"). How does the court in each case decide whether social as well as academic development should be treated as part of the definition of equivalency? *See* Shepherd, "Home Schooling: Dimensions of Controversy, 1970–1984," 31 *J. of Church and State* 101 (1989). In this context, is "equivalency" unconstitutionally vague? *See Ellis v. O'Hara*, 612 F.Supp. 379 (E.D.Mo. 1985) ("substantially equivalent"); *Trucke v. Erlemeier*, 657 F.Supp. 1382 (N.D.Iowa 1987) ("equivalent instruction").

The statutory "equivalency" language appears to compel the same analysis that these questions implicitly criticize. How might one draft legislation to render the task of regulating home instruction more manageable? Are the issues identical to those posed by the task of developing legislation to regulate nonpublic schools? One commentator, citing *Bongart* and *Massa*, has argued that courts frequently sidestep leg-

islative intent in home-instruction cases: "In reaching conflicting conclusions, however, the courts have manipulated canons of statutory construction and selectively read legislative history to achieve an accommodation between state goals and individual interests that they consider appropriate." Project, "Education and the Law: State Interests and Individual Rights," 74 *Mich. L. Rev.* 1373, 1389 (1976).

2. Socialization and Association

At bottom, does *Bongart* rest on the assumption that education involves socialization to values as well as skills training and that this usually can occur only in an institutional environment with children from other families? *See also In re Davis*, 114 N.H. 242, 318 A.2d 151 (1974); *Knox v. O'Brien*, 7 N.J. Super. 608, 72 A.2d 389 (1950). If so, how does this principle conform with the accommodation reached in *Pierce*? *See generally* L. Kotin and W. F. Aikman, *Legal Foundations of Compulsory Attendance* 110–48 (1980); T. van Geel, *Authority to Control the School Program* 159 (1976); Shepherd, *supra*. Home-schooled children spend less time with their peers and more time with adults and children of different ages. Is there a basis for deciding that socialization with one's peers is necessary for "equivalent instruction"?

If a state statute or regulation refers to alternative education at a "private school," the courts may be called upon to define the meaning of school. *See Delconte v. State*, 65 N.C. App. 262, 308 S.E.2d 898 (1983). Is this but another way of raising the association and socialization issues in the context of home instruction or tutoring? *See People v. Levisen*, 404 Ill. 574, 90 N.E.2d 213 (1950). *See generally* Kotin and Aikman, *supra* at 136–42, 157–66; Bumstead, "Educating Your Child at Home: The *Perchenlides* Case," *Phi Delta Kappan* 97 (1979). If the legislature provides little guidance on the meaning of the phrase "private school," is the statute unconstitutionally vague? *See Care and Protection of Charles, supra; Roemhild v. State*, 251 Ga. 569, 308 S.E.2d 154 (1983). *But see Burrow v. State*, 282 Ark. 479, 669 S.W.2d 441 (1984). More cynically, does the requirement of an institutional education environment reflect the "fear that approving one request will lead to an exodus from school"? Bumstead, *supra* at 98–99.

3. Testing Requirements

The *Massa* court appeared to rely heavily on the fact that the home-schooled child performed well both on subject matter tests administered by the public school and on standard achievement tests administered by an independent testing service as evidence that the child was receiving "equivalent instruction." The New Jersey statute did not require testing, however. In *Care and Protection of Charles*, the court noted that school authorities:

> may properly require periodic standardized testing of the children to ensure educational progress and the attainment of minimum standards. . . . In consultation with the parents, the school authorities may decide where the testing is to occur and the type of testing instrument to be used. Where practical, a neutral party should administer the test. Other means of evaluating the progress of the children may be substituted for the formal testing process, such as periodic progress reports or dated work samples, subject to the approval of the parents.

Today, more than half the states mandate testing of home-schooled children, with several permitting the option of an evaluation by a certified teacher or submission of a portfolio in lieu of testing. C.J. Klicka, *Home Schooling in the United States: A Legal Analysis* (1995). Pennsylvania requires both testing and the submission of a portfolio, while two states, Connecticut and Maryland, only require the submission of a portfolio. *Id.* What free exercise or equal protection challenges might be made to these requirements? *See Murphy v. Arkansas*, 852 F.2d 1039 (8th Cir. 1988). What success would a challenge based on parents' Fourteenth Amendment liberty interest in directing the upbringing and education of their child have to a requirement that the child must attain a certain percentile on standardized tests in order to continue home schooling? *See Null v. Board of Education of the County of Jackson*, 815 F.Supp. 937 (S.D. W.Va. 1993). In a number of states, the Home School Legal Defense Association and its members have successfully challenged legislative measures that sought to include home schoolers in state testing requirements to which public school students are subject, and have even mounted attacks against the National Assessment of Educational Progress, which is administered to a sample of public school students. *See* Golden, "Home Schoolers Learn How to Gain Clout Inside the Beltway," *Wall Street Journal*, Apr. 24, 2000, at A-1.

4. *Different Standards of Review for Sectarian and Secular Home Schools?*

Should courts make a distinction between home schools established for religious reasons and those established for secular reasons? What standard of review should courts apply when parents challenge various state regulatory measures as applied to their home schools? *See Murphy v. Arkansas*, 852 F.2d 1039 (8th Cir. 1988) (with regard to requirement for standardized testing for home-schooled children, court suggested home-schooled families "impelled by deep-seated religious convictions" might be entitled to heightened scrutiny, whereas secular individuals who home school their children are not). *See also J.B. v. Washington*, 127 F.3d 919 (10th Cir. 1997) (applying rational basis standard of review to parents home schooling for secular reasons). In two cases decided on the same day, the Michigan Supreme Court held that home schooling parents motivated solely by secular reasons had no constitutional right to object to Michigan's requirement that home school instruction be by a certified teacher, *People v. Bennett*, 442 Mich. 316, 501 N.W.2d 106 (Mich. 1993), but held that the requirement violated the free exercise clause where home schooling parents opposed the teacher certification requirement on religious grounds, *People v. DeJonge*, 442 Mich. 266, 501 N.W.2d 127 (Mich. 1993). In the light of *Employment Division, Department of Human Resources of Oregon v. Smith*, 494 U.S. 872, 110 S.Ct. 1595, 108 L.Ed. 876 (1990), isn't a requirement that all those responsible for the education of children be certified a generally applicable law? Why should the state only be able to ensure that secularly motivated parents are competent teachers? *See* Foley, "The Regulation of Private Schools," 25 *Capital Univ. L. Rev.* 819, 827, n.10 (1996); Comment, "*People v. Bennett*: Analytic Approaches to Recognizing a Fundamental Parental Right Under the Ninth Amendment," 1996 *B.Y.U. L. Rev.* 183 (1996); Note, "*People v. Bennett*: Are Teacher Certification Requirements for Secular Home Educators Constitutional?" 42 *Wayne L. Rev.* 259 (1995); Note, "Home Schooling in Michigan: Is There a Fundamental Right to Teach Your Children at Home?" 71 *U. Det. Mercy L. Rev.* 1053 (1994). Is the right of parents to direct their children's education, guaranteed by the Fourteenth Amendment (*Meyer v. Nebraska*, 262 U.S. 390, 43 S.Ct. 625, 67 L.Ed. 1042 (1923)), not a fundamental right, whereas the right of parents to direct their children's religious education (as part of their own religious beliefs), guaranteed by the First Amendment's Free Exercise Clause, is? Four years after the *Bennett* and *DeJonge* cases, the Michigan legislature suspended the teacher certification requirement for home schooling parents.

5. Right of Home Schoolers to Attend Selected Public School Classes

Does a home-schooled student, who wants to participate in a sports or band program, or study academic courses beyond the teaching skills of the parent, have a right to join the local public school's softball team or enroll in a public school foreign language or chemistry class? In *Swanson v. Guthrie*, 135 F.3d 694 (10th Cir. 1998), plaintiffs sued the school district after their request to allow their home-schooled daughter to take vocal music and science classes at the local public school was denied. The Swansons claimed that this burdened their right to free exercise of religion and discriminated against Christian home-schooled students. The Tenth Circuit found for the school district, stating that the policy was facially neutral and of general applicability, and thus did not violate the Free Exercise Clause. The court agreed that parents had a constitutional right to direct the education of their children, but stated that such a right was limited. In *Bradstreet v. Sobol*, 650 N.Y.S.2d 402 (N.Y. Sup. Ct. 1996), where religion was not an issue, the court dismissed plaintiff's due process and equal protection arguments, finding that participation in varsity sports was not a fundamental right and that requiring that the student be enrolled full-time in a public school in order to participate in the sports program was not irrational. *But see Davis v. Massachusetts Interscholastic Athletic Ass'n*, 3 Mass. L. Rep. 375 (Mass. Super.1995).

Does the fact that home schooling parents seek to broaden their children's education by enrolling them in selected facets of public school education imply that there is an inherent weakness in the home schooling system? *See* Mawdsley, "Parental Rights and Home Schooling: Current Home School Litigation," 135 Ed. Law Rep. 313, 324 (1999). Should public schools serve as "instructional cafeterias" where all students, despite enrollment status, can pick and choose from classes and extracurricular activities? *Id.* Is it unfair for home schoolers to pay taxes and yet not receive the benefits of public school education? *See generally* Dailey, Note, "Home Schooled Children Gaining Limited Access to Public Schools," 28 *Journal of Law & Educ.* 25 (1999); Note, "Public School Access: The Constitutional Right of Home-Schoolers to 'Opt-In' to Public Education on a Part-Time Basis," 82 *Minn. L. Rev.* 1599, 1626–27 (1998); Bjorklun, "Home Schooled Students: Access to Public School Extracurricular Ac-

tivities," 109 *Ed. Law Rep.* 1 (1996) (noting that opposition to home-schooled students participating in extracurricular activities has come not only from local school officials and state interscholastic athletic organizations, but also from national organizations such as the American Association of School Administrators and the National School Boards Association); Comment, "The Latest Home Education Challenge: The Relationship Between Home Schools and Public Schools," 74 *NC L. Rev.* 1913, 1955–1977 (1996).

Thirteen states have enacted statutes that specifically authorize access to public schools for children educated at home. *See* 82 *Minn. L. Rev.*, *supra*, at 1615, n.73. Surveys have shown that 81 percent of home schooling parents want to enroll their children in extracurricular activities and 76 percent want to enroll their children in academic courses at the public schools, 74 *NC L. Rev.*, *supra* at 1954 (citing Mayberry et al., *Home Schooling: Parents as Educators* 77 (1995)). But in those states without statutes, most courts have denied access on a part-time basis to classes or extracurricular activities. 82 *Minn. L. Rev.*, *supra*, at 1615.

6. College Admission of Home-Schooled Children

Maggie Bryson, a high-school-aged student living in Atlanta, has been home schooled since the fifth grade. She wants to apply to the Georgia Institute of Technology. Under a policy adopted by the Georgia Board of Regents, home-schooled students who apply to state colleges are required to submit scores from eight separate standardized tests, tests that applicants from traditional high schools will not be required to take. Does this policy violate the Equal Protection Clause? In addition to the requirements imposed by state officials, Georgia Tech has instituted even stricter requirements for home-schooled applicants—to be considered for admission, they must have a minimum SAT score of 1350, while applicants from Georgia public high schools need a score of only 1100, and those from out-of-state schools 1200. By contrast, North Carolina has adopted a law requiring the university system to adopt a policy that does not arbitrarily treat home-schooled students differently from other students. Tarricone, "States Consider How Colleges Treat Home-Schooled Students," *The Chronicle of Higher Education*, Aug.1, 1997. The National Center for Home Education estimated that at least 200,000 high-school-aged children were being home schooled in 1998, and that over the next decade, as many as one million home schoolers will be applying to college.

7. Other Statutory "Exemptions" from Compulsory Attendance Laws

Strictly speaking, private schooling and home instruction are not so much "exemptions" from compulsory education laws as they are alternative methods of satisfying those laws. See Kotin and Aikman, *supra* at 169–70. But there are other provisions in state statutes which forgive, in whole or in part, the requirement that some children attend a school or receive instruction at home, for example, physically or mentally disabled children, those completing eight grades, expelled students, working children over a specified age, etc. *See* Kotin and Aikman, *supra* at 170–84; K. Alexander and K. F. Jordan, *Legal Aspects of Educational Choice: Compulsory Attendance and Student Assignment* 30–43 (1973). A number of these exceptions have been addressed by federal statutes or been subject to constitutional challenges. See chapter 6, *infra*. *See generally* T. van Geel, *The Courts and American Education* 127–29 (1987).

V. DISCRIMINATION AND PRIVATE EDUCATION

In recent years, there has been a growing concern and debate about the extent to which government, particularly the federal government, should be and is regulating private education. The concern has been expressed not only with regard to elementary and secondary education but also with regard to private institutions of higher learning. *See, e.g.,* D. Bok, *Beyond the Ivory Tower* (1982); W. C. Hobbs (ed.), *Government Regulation of Higher Education* (1978); A.E.D. Howard, *State Aid to Private Higher Education* (1977); Merrill, "The Encroachment of the Federal Government into Private Institutions of Higher Education," 1994 *B.Y.U. Educ. & L.* 63; Dutile, "God and Gays at Georgetown: Observations on *Gay Rights Coalition of Georgetown University Law Center v. Georgetown University*," 15 *J. of Coll. & Univ. L.* 1 (1988); O'Neil, "God and Government at Yale: The Limits of Federal Regulation of Higher Education," 44 *U. Cin. L. Rev.* 525 (1975); O'Neil, "Private Universities and Public Law," 19 *Buffalo L. Rev.* 155 (1970). *See generally* M. A. Olivas, *The Law and Higher Education* (2d ed. 1997); W. A. Kaplin and B. A. Lee, *The Law of Higher Education* (3d ed. 1995).

In the context of private elementary and secondary education, the question of the permissible scope of government regulation can arise in a number of settings. First, as discussed in earlier portions of this chapter, a state may seek to ensure a minimum quality of education and a minimum commitment to democratic principles in private schools. Second, as noted in the following section, the government can seek to condition its assistance to private schools on the meeting of specified criteria. *See Bowen v. Kendrick*, 487 U.S. 589, 108 S.Ct. 2562, 101 L.Ed.2d 520 (1988) (federal grants under Adolescent Family Life Act, 42 U.S.C.A. § 3002 *et seq.* (1982)). The danger is that there is an inevitable temptation for control to follow the dollars. *See, e.g., Roemer v. Maryland Public Works Board*, 426 U.S. 736, 96 S.Ct. 2337, 49 L.Ed.2d 179 (1976) (Justice Stevens, dissenting). *See generally* Capps and Esbeck, "The Use of Government Funding and Taxing Power to Regulate Religious Schools," 14 *J. of Law & Educ.* 553 (1985). Similarly, the tax-exempt status of a private school, and the deductibility of charitable donations, may turn on whether a school meets certain public policy or constitutional norms. *See Virginia Education Fund v. Commissioner*, 799 F.2d 903 (4th Cir. 1986). *Cf. Bob Jones University v. United States*, 461 U.S. 574, 103 S.Ct. 2017, 76 L.Ed.2d 157 (1983) (university practicing racial discrimination does not qualify as a tax-exempt organization under Section 501(c)(3) of the Internal Revenue Code of 1954). *See generally* Shaviro, "From Big Mama Rag to National Geographic: The Controversy Regarding Exemptions for Educational Publications," 41 *Tax. L. Rev.* 693 (1986); Bittker and Kaufman, "Taxes and Civil Rights: 'Constitutionalizing' the Internal Revenue Code," 82 *Yale L. J.* 51 (1972); Note, "The Judicial Role in Attacking Racial Discrimination in Tax-Exempt Private Schools," 93 *Harv. L. Rev.* 378 (1979); Note, "Segregating Schools: The Foreseeable Consequences of Tuition Tax Credits," 89 *Yale L. J.* 168 (1979).

Third, state assistance itself may trigger a finding that the state's largesse may not be used by private schools for unconstitutional or unlawful purposes. *See, e.g., Grove City College v. Bell*, 465 U.S. 555, 104 S.Ct. 1211, 79 L.Ed.2d 516 (1984) (sex discrimination); *Norwood v. Harrison*, 413 U.S. 455, 93 S.Ct. 2804, 37 L.Ed.2d 723 (1973) (state program under which textbooks are loaned to students in public and private schools, without reference to whether any participating private school follows racially discriminatory policies, is unconstitutional). *Cf. Bowen v. Kendrick*, 487 U.S. 589, 108 S.Ct. 2562, 101 L.Ed.2d 520 (1988). *See generally* Note, "Segregation, Academies and State Action," 82 *Yale L. J.* 1436 (1973). *Compare Norwood v. Harrison, supra*, with *Allen v. Wright*, 408 U.S. 737, 104 S.Ct. 3315, 82 L.Ed.2d 556 (1984).

Fourth, to the extent that the activities of private schools are treated as "state action" by the courts, the provisions of the federal constitution will apply to those institutions. This might mean, for example, that private schools would be held to the same standards under the establishment, equal protection, and due process clauses as public institutions. This matter is addressed briefly in chapter 2, *infra*.

Fifth, statutes of general application, for example, state and federal labor relations acts, may be applied to private schools. *See, e.g., Catholic High School Association v. Culvert*, 753 F.2d 1161 (2d Cir. 1985); *South Jersey Catholic School Teachers Ass'n v. St. Teresa*, 150 N.J. 575, 696 A.2d 709 (1997); *Hill-Murray Fed'n of Teachers v. Hill-Murray High School*, 487 N.W.2d 857 (Minn.1992). *See generally* Note, "Requiring Catholic Elementary Schools to Bargain with the Lay Teachers' Collective Bargaining Representative Does Not Violate the Religion Clauses of the First Amendment," 8 *Seton Hall Const. L. J.* 589 (1998); Hartman, "Spitting Distance: Tents Full of Religious Schools in Choice Programs, the Camel's Nose of State Labor-Law Application to Their Relations with Lay Faculty Members, and the First Amendment's Tether," 6 *Cornell J.L. & Pub. Pol'y* 553 (1997); Pushaw, "Labor Relations Board Regulation of Parochial Schools: A Practical Free Exercise Accommodation," 97 *Yale L. J.* 135 (1987); Laycock, "Towards a General Theory of the Religion Clauses: The Case of Church Labor Relations and the Right to Church Autonomy," 81 *Colum. L. Rev.* 1373 (1981).

Finally, government may seek to prevent private elementary and secondary schools, including religious institutions, from engaging in racial, gender, or other forms of illegitimate discrimination. Professor van Geel has well described this development in the law and the tensions that it has created:

> Though in most respects private schools must constitutionally be allowed to set sail on their own course, does that mean they are also constitutionally protected against governmental efforts to prohibit discrimination in admissions (and other student-related matters), and employ-

ment on the basis of race, gender, religion, handicap, age, and national origin? The federal government, as well as state governments, assuming there were no constitutional obstacles, have extended a variety of antidiscrimination provisions to private education. Active governmental pursuit to eliminate private discrimination set the stage for a historical confrontation between the state and its antidiscrimination policy, and private schools claiming that these efforts infringed their rights of privacy, freedom of association and the free exercise of religion.

T. van Geel, *The Courts and American Education Law* 26 (1987). The remainder of this section will focus largely on the application of nondiscrimination laws to private schools, beginning with an excerpt from the work of Professor Laycock on government regulation and church autonomy. *See also* "Developments in the Law: Religion and the State," 100 *Harv. L. Rev.* 1606, 1750–61 (1987).

"Towards a General Theory of the Religion Clauses: The Case of Church Labor Relations and the Right to Church Autonomy"

Douglas Laycock, 81 *Colum. L. Rev.* 1373, 1374–78, 1388–92, 1398–1401 (1981). Copyright (c) 1981 by the Directors of the Columbia Law Review Association, Inc. All rights reserved. Reprinted by permission.

Secular regulation of churches has increased substantially in recent years,[1] and litigation over the constitutionality of such regulation has increased as well. Regulation of church labor relations has been a particularly prolific source of litigation. There have been challenges to the National Labor Relations Act, the Fair Labor Standards Act, the Civil Rights Act of 1964, the Federal Unemployment Tax Act, and other statutes affecting church labor policy. A wide variety of religious groups have become involved in such litigation.

Many of these cases have reached defensible results, but only a few have identified the competing interests with reasonable specificity. Most of the uncertainty results from the Supreme Court's failure to develop any coherent general theory of the religion clauses. This Article offers a start toward such a theory.

The first step is to restore the fundamental distinction between the establishment and free exercise clauses: that government support for religion is an essential element of every claim under the establishment clause. The second step is to distinguish different kinds of rights protected by the free exercise clause. One of

---

[1] Ripple, "The Entanglement Test of the Religion Clauses—A Ten Year Assessment," 27 *U.C.L.A. L. Rev.* 1195, 1230–32 (1980).

these, the right of church autonomy, tends to be over-looked. Quite apart from whether a regulation requires a church or an individual believer to violate religious doctrine or felt moral duty, churches have a constitutionally protected interest in managing their own institutions free of government interference.

This interest, like all others under the religion clauses, may be infringed for sufficiently compelling reasons, and the third step towards a general theory is to examine how this balancing should work. Interests are not arrayed on a single continuum from important to unimportant, and the balance cannot be struck reliably without analyzing the multivariate nature of the interests on each side. Alleged state interests in regulating internal church affairs—e.g., protection of church members and church workers from exploitation—are usually illegitimate and should not count at all.

* * *

The best known series of church labor relations cases resulted from the National Labor Relations Board's decision to assert jurisdiction over religious schools.[9] Two district courts and the Seventh Circuit held the NLRA unconstitutional as applied to teachers' unions in Catholic schools, on grounds of excessive entanglement between church and state,[10] and in the Seventh Circuit case, also on the more persuasive ground that collective bargaining would interfere with ecclesiastical control of church institutions.[11] The Supreme Court affirmed the Seventh Circuit, but on statutory grounds.[12] Finding a serious risk of excessive government entanglement with religion, the Court avoided the constitutional question by requiring " 'the affirmative intention of the Congress clearly expressed' " that the Act extend to such religious schools.[13] Finding no such clear expression, the Court held the Act inapplicable. Four dissenters agreed that the constitutional issue was serious, but argued that it should not be avoided by such a major distortion of the statute.[15] . . .

Similar questions arise under antidiscrimination laws.[17] An exception to title VII of the Civil Rights Act of 1964 permits religious institutions to discriminate on the basis of religion, but not on the basis of race, sex, or national origin.[18] Some courts have criticized this statutory accommodation of religion as clumsy and unconstitutional, too broad in some ways and too narrow in others.[19] . . . But two district courts have concluded that the explicit statutory exception, and rejection of amendments that would have broadened it, clearly express congressional intent to regulate the churches.[21] The Fifth Circuit reached the same conclusion,[22] but implied an exception anyway to avoid a holding of unconstitutionality.[23] The court concluded that sex discrimination against a Salvation Army officer involved "matters of church administration and government and thus, purely of ecclesiastical cognizance," and that the Act would violate the free exercise clause if applied to the case.[24] . . .

---

[9]Henry M. Hald School Ass'n, 213 N.L.R.B. 415 (1974).

[10]*Catholic Bishop v. NLRB*, 559 F.2d 1112 (7th Cir. 1977), aff'd on other grounds, 440 U.S. 490 (1979); *McCormick v. Hirsch*, 460 F.Supp. 1337 (M.D. Pa. 1978); *Caulfield v. Hirsch*, 410 F.Supp. 618 (E.D.Pa. 1976), cert. in advance of judgment denied, 436 U.S. 957 (1978).

[11]559 F.2d at 1124.

[12]*NLRB v. Catholic Bishop*, 440 U.S. 490 (1979). [*See also Universidad de Bayamon v. NLRB*, 793 F.2d 383, 398–99 (1st Cir. 1985) (*en banc*) (equally divided court refused to grant NLRB's request to enforce order against university)].

[13]*Id.* at 500 (quoting *McCulloch v. Sociedad Nacional de Marineros*, 372 U.S. 10, 21–22 (1963) (quoting *Benz v. Compania Naviera Hidalgo*, 353 U.S. 138, 147 (1957))). The opinion emphasized the importance of schools and teachers; the Board will undoubtedly continue to assert jurisdiction over church-owned commercial businesses.

[15]*Id.* at 508. See generally Comment, "NLRB Has No Jurisdiction Over Lay Teachers in Parochial Schools," 58 *Wash. U.L.Q.* 173 (1980).

[17]See generally Bagni, "Discrimination in the Name of the Lord: A Critical Evaluation of Discrimination by Religious Organizations," 79 *Colum. L. Rev.* 1514 (1979).

[18]42 U.S.C. §2000e-1 (1976). [In *Corporation of Presiding Bishop v. Amos*, 483 U.S. 327, 107 S.Ct. 2862, 97 L.Ed.2d 273 (1987), the Supreme Court held that §2000e-1, exempting religious organizations from Title VII's prohibition against discrimination in employment on the basis of religion, did not violate the Establishment or Equal Protection Clauses. The Court found that the provision "is rationally related to the legitimate purpose of alleviating significant governmental interference with the ability of religious organizations to define and carry out their religious missions." 107 S.Ct. at 2870].

[19]*King's Garden, Inc. v. FCC*, 498 F.2d 51, 54–55 (D.C. Cir.), cert. denied, 419 U.S. 996 (1974); *EEOC v. Southwestern Baptist Theological Seminary*, 485 F.Supp. 255, 260 (N.D. Tex. 1980), rev'd in part, 651 F.2d 277 (5th Cir. 1981). *But see EEOC v. Mississippi College*, 626 F.2d 477, 489 (5th Cir. 1980), cert. denied, 101 S.Ct. 3143 (1981).

[21]*Dolter v. Wahlert High School*, 483 F.Supp. 266, 268–69 (N.D. Iowa 1980); *EEOC v. Pacific Press Publ. Ass'n.*, 482 F.Supp. 1291, 1302–07 (N.D. Cal. 1979). Cf. *Ritter v. Mount St. Mary's College*, 495 F.Supp. 724, 726–29 (D. Md. 1980) (relying on absence of similar exceptions in Equal Pay Act and Age Discrimination in Employment Act, and concluding that these acts do not apply to religious institutions).

[22]*McClure v. Salvation Army*, 460 F.2d 553, 558 (5th Cir.), cert. denied as untimely filed, 409 U.S. 896 (1972).

[23]Id. at 560–61.

[24]*Id.* at 560.

Other sex discrimination cases have faced the constitutional issue squarely. A district court held title VII unconstitutional as applied to a Baptist seminary that attempted to maintain what the court variously described as "a pervasively religious environment,"[26] "an atmosphere of intense piety,"[27] and "a virtually cloistral environment."[28] The church . . . said its doctrines might require it to discriminate on the basis of sex under certain circumstances. But this was not the basis of the court's decision that it was totally exempt as to all its employees.[29] Rather, the court held that the seminary was entitled to be left alone—an entitlement I will call the right of church autonomy:

> Its employment decisions, steeped in a perception of divine will and inseparable from its mission, become matters of religious prerogative and warrant the fullest protection from governmental supervision. Enforcement of Title VII claims against a seminary based on race, sex, or national origin, even in the absence of articulated doctrinal compulsion, will lead inevitably to excessive governmental entanglement with religion in the process of dissecting employment functions into religious and secular components and in divining the good faith and legitimacy of religious grounds asserted as a defense to a prima facie case of discrimination.[30]

Similar defenses were rejected in three cases involving Seventh Day Adventists. One complaint alleged sex discrimination against an employee with editorial and secretarial responsibilities in a nonprofit publishing house;[31] one alleged Equal Pay Act[32] violations in the church's schools;[33] and one charged racial discrimination against a typist-receptionist.[34] . . .

There is also a pair of older cases rejecting challenges to key provisions of the Fair Labor Standards Act[48] and its state equivalents. The Supreme Court upheld state child labor laws against a child's claim that it was her religious duty to sell religious tracts, emphasizing the state's interest in protecting children.[49] And the Seventh Circuit upheld the minimum wage and maximum hour provisions of the FLSA as applied to employees in a church-owned printing plant, some of whom swore that they did not consider themselves "mere wage earners," but had come to the plant to help "in the work of the Lord."[50]

. . . The Supreme Court recently found the [Federal Unemployment Tax] Act inapplicable to schools that are not separately incorporated from their sponsoring churches.[52] . . .

These labor law cases illustrate a sufficiently broad range of the constitutional questions raised by regulation of churches to make them a useful tool for analysis. The analysis offered here should be applicable, perhaps with some modifications, to other kinds of regulation, including another set of current issues: regulation of church schools in matters of curriculum,[54] teacher certification,[55] and racial discrimination.[56]

* * *

---

[26]EEOC v. Southwestern Baptist Theological Seminary, 485 F.Supp. 255, 258 (N.D. Tex. 1980), rev'd in part, 651 F.2d 277 (5th Cir. 1981).

[27]Id.

[28]Id. at 261.

[29]Id. at 259.

[30]Id. at 261 (footnote omitted). The Fifth Circuit affirmed with respect to the faculty, but reversed with respect to the administration and staff, 651 F.2d 277 (5th Cir. 1981). The court held that the faculty were ministers and applied its rule that the church-minister relationship is exempt from regulation, see McClure v. Salvation Army, 460 F.2d 553 (5th Cir.), cert. denied as untimely filed, 409 U.S. 896 (1972).

[31]EEOC v. Pacific Press Publ. Ass'n. 482 F.Supp. 1291 (N.D. Cal. 1979). [See also EEOC v. Fremont Christian School, 781 F.2d 1362 (9th Cir. 1986) (application of Title VII and Equal Pay Act to sex discrimination in provision of health insurance to employee does not violate Establishment or Free Exercise Clauses)].

[32]29 U.S.C. §206(d) (1976).

[33]Marshall v. Pacific Union Conf. of Seventh-Day Adventist, 14 Empl. Prac. Dec. 5956 (C.D. Cal. 1977).

[34]Whitney v. Greater N.Y. Corp. of Seventh-Day Adventists, 401 F.Supp. 1363 (S.D.N.Y. 1975).

[48]29 U.S.C. §§201–19 (1976).

[49]Prince v. Massachusetts, 321 U.S. 158, 167–69 (1944). See id. at 164 (making clear that the child's rights were asserted).

[50]Mitchell v. Pilgrim Holiness Church Corp., 210 F.2d 879, 881, 884 (7th Cir.), cert. denied, 347 U.S. 1013 (1954).

[52]St. Martin Evangelical Lutheran Church v. South Dakota, 101 S.Ct. 2142(1981). [See also Baltimore Lutheran High School Assoc. v. Employment Security Administration, 302 Md. 649, 490 A.2d 701 (Md. 1985) (state unemployment insurance law)].

[54]Kentucky State Bd. for Elementary & Secondary Educ. v. Rudasill, 589 S.W.2d 877 (Ky. 1979), cert. denied, 446 U.S. 938 (1980); State v. Whisner, 47 Ohio St.2d 181, 351 N.E.2d 750 (1976); Comment, "Regulation of Fundamentalist Christian Schools: Free Exercise of Religion v. The State's Interest in Quality Education," 67 Ky. L.J. 415, 423–25 (1979).

[55]Kentucky State Bd. for Elementary & Secondary Educ. v. Rudasill, 589 S.W.2d 877 (Ky. 1979), cert. denied, 446 U.S. 938 (1980); Comment, supra note 54, at 422–23.

[56]Bob Jones Univ. v. United States, 639 F.2d 147 (4th Cir. 1980), cert. granted, 50 U.S.L.W. 3278 (U.S. Oct. 13, 1981) (No. 81-3); Fiedler v. Marumsco Christian School, 631 F.2d 1144 (4th Cir. 1980); Brown v. Dade Christian Schools, Inc., 556 F.2d 310 (5th Cir. 1977), cert. denied, 434 U.S. 1063 (1978).

III. Free Exercise and the Right to Church Autonomy

* * *

The free exercise clause protection for religious activity includes at least three rather different kinds of rights. In each category, some claims have been accepted and others rejected; none of these rights is protected absolutely.

One category is the bare freedom to carry on religious activities: to build churches and schools, conduct worship services, pray, proselytize, and teach moral values. This is the exercise of religion in its most obvious sense.

Second, and closely related, is the right of churches to conduct these activities autonomously: to select their own leaders,[129] define their own doctrines,[130] resolve their own disputes,[131] and run their own institutions.[132] Religion includes important communal elements for most believers. They exercise their religion through religious organizations, and these organizations must be protected by the clause.

Third is the right of conscientious objection to government policy. The phrase is most prominently associated with the military draft, but there has also been conscientious objector litigation with respect to war taxes, compulsory education, medical treatment and innoculations, social insurance, Sabbath observance and nonobservance, monogamy, and other requirements that conflict with the moral scruples of certain sects or individual believers. These cases are also within the clause, because one way to exercise one's religion is to follow its moral dictates.

Each of these rights has solid support in the case law, but many courts and commentators think only in terms of conscientious objection. One of the most common errors in free exercise analysis is to try to fit all free exercise claims into the conscientious objector category and reject the ones that do not fit. Under this approach, every free exercise claim requires an elaborate judicial inquiry into the conscience or doctrines of the claimant. If he is not compelled by religion to engage in the disputed conduct, he is not entitled to free exercise protection. Thus, courts have tried to decide whether activities of organized churches were required by church doctrine or were something that the churches did for nonreligious reasons.[142] . . .

This approach reflects a rigid, simplistic, and erroneous view of religion. Many activities that obviously are exercises of religion are not required by conscience or doctrine. Singing in the church choir and saying the Roman Catholic rosary are two common examples. Any activity engaged in by a church as a body is an exercise of religion. This is not to say that all such activities are immune from regulation: there may be a sufficiently strong governmental interest to justify the intrusion. But neither are these activities wholly without constitutional protection. It is not dispositive that an activity is not compelled by the official doctrine of a church or the religious conscience of an individual believer. Indeed, many would say that an emphasis on rules and obligations misconceives the essential nature of some religions.[145]

Moreover, emphasis on doctrine and requirements ignores the fluidity of doctrine and the many factors that can contribute to doctrinal change. A church is a complex and dynamic organization, often including believers with a variety of views on important questions of faith, morals, and spirituality. The dominant view of what is central to the religion, and of what practices are required by the religion, may gradually change. Today's pious custom may be tomorrow's moral obligation, and vice versa.

These characteristics of doctrinal change have two consequences. One is that the officially promulgated church doctrine, on which courts too often rely, is not a reliable indication of what the faithful believe. At best the officially promulgated doctrine of a large denomination represents the dominant or most commonly held view; it cannot safely be imputed to every believer or every affiliated congregation. . . . This gap between official doctrine and rank-and-file belief means that courts are prone to err in deciding whether activities of a local church or small group of believers are compelled by conscience.

The complex and open-ended nature of the processes that lead to doctrinal change has a second consequence that is even more important. When

---

[129]E.g., *Serbian E. Orthodox Diocese v. Milivojevich*, 426 U.S. 696 (1976). . . .

[130]E.g., *Presbyterian Church v. Mary Elizabeth Blue Hull Memorial Presbyterian Church*, 393 U.S. 440, 449 (1969).

[131]E.g., *Jones v. Wolf*, 443 U.S. 595 (1979); *Maryland & Va. Eldership of the Churches of God v. Church of God*, 396 U.S. 367 (1970) (per curiam). . . .

[132]E.g., *NLRB v. Catholic Bishop*, 440 U.S. 490 (1979). . . .

[142]E.g., *Brown v. Dade Christian Schools, Inc.*, 556 F.2d 310, 311–14 (5th Cir. 1977) (en banc) (plurality opinion), cert. denied, 434 U.S. 1063 (1978); *Dolter v. Wahlert High School*, 483 F.Supp. 266, 269–70 (N.D. Iowa 1980).

[145]*See, e.g.*, Galatians 3:13 ("Christ has redeemed us from the curse of the law. . . ."); 2 Corinthians 3:6 ("[T]he letter killeth, but the spirit giveth life.")

the state interferes with the autonomy of a church, and particularly when it interferes with the allocation of authority and influence within a church, it interferes with the very process of forming the religion as it will exist in the future. . . . In the labor relations context, it is impossible to predict the long-term effect of forcing religious leaders to share authority with a secular union, or of substituting one employee for another as a result of a discrimination charge or a union grievance. A number of such substitutions may have a cumulative effect, especially if, as seems likely, there is some bias in the process making them. . . . Thus, any interference with church affairs may disrupt "the free development of religious doctrine."[150]

Such government-induced changes in religion are too unpredictable to be avoided on a case-by-case basis. They can be minimized only by a strong rule of church autonomy. The free exercise clause therefore forbids government interference with church operations unless there is, to use the conventional phrase, a compelling governmental interest to justify the interference. . . .

Church labor relations rather plainly fall within the right of church autonomy. Deciding who will conduct the work of the church and how that work will be conducted is an essential part of the exercise of religion. In the language of the Supreme Court's autonomy cases, labor relations are matters of "church administration"; undoubtedly, they affect "the operation of churches."

. . . [T]he right of church autonomy does not depend on conscientious objection.

* * *

Similarly, antidiscrimination laws initially prevent the church from deciding whether to discriminate among its employees and applicants. Many churches may wish to discriminate on the basis of religion, and some on the basis of race, sex, or national origin. Equally important, churches that do not want to discriminate at all are deprived of the chance to define discrimination. Some may oppose unequal treatment of individuals because of race, sex, or national origin, but want to be free to act on any facially neutral basis even if it has disparate impact on racial, sexual, or ethnic groups.

Even churches that accept the full scope of collective bargaining and the government's definition of discrimination may be seriously alarmed at the prospect of secular enforcement. This requires secular tribunals to review the church's comparisons of the responsibility and difficulty of jobs and of the skills, qualifications, and performance of workers; its motives for personnel decisions and the credibility of its claims to have acted for religious reasons; the religious or other necessity for employment practices that have disparate impact; even the effect on workers of its bishops' prayers and Bible readings. Similar review of church personnel decisions is required under the Federal Unemployment Tax Act.

Some of the lower court decisions and commentary give no weight at all to the loss of autonomy inherent in the enforcement process. They assume that the churches' rights can be protected by determining whether a personnel action was required by church doctrine. But the distinctions required by this approach are difficult, especially for secular courts unversed in theological subtleties, and an error can result in penalizing a church for an act of conscience. More importantly, as argued above, interference in personnel matters interferes with the further development of the religion. And quite aside from these concerns about conscientious objection and the effects of interference with church labor relations, selecting and directing the employees who will carry out the work of the church is an exercise of religion, which the churches are entitled to perform freely.

* * *

NOTES AND QUESTIONS

1. State Regulation of Labor Relations and Church Schools

As Professor Laycock's article has noted, the Supreme Court, in *NLRB v. Catholic Bishop*, 440 U.S. 490 (1979), found the National Labor Relations Act inapplicable to church schools because Congress had not affirmatively expressed its intention to extend the act to religious schools. Since then, however, a number of lower federal courts and state courts have found state labor relations laws applicable to religious schools, and held that their states' labor relations boards did have jurisdiction over labor relations in church schools, despite arguments that requiring these schools to engage in collective bar-

---

[150]*Presbyterian Church v. Mary Elizabeth Blue Hull Memorial Presbyterian Church*, 393 U.S. 440, 449 (1969). . . .

gaining with lay teachers over secular terms and conditions of employment would violate the free exercise and establishment clauses of the First Amendment. *See, e.g., South Jersey Catholic School Teachers Ass'n v. St. Teresa,* 150 N.J. 575, 696 A.2d 709 (1997); *Hill-Murray Federation of Teachers v. Hill-Murray High School,* 487 N.W.2d 857 (Minn. 1992); *Catholic High School Ass'n of Archdiocese of New York v. Culvert,* 753 F.2d 1161 (2d Cir. 1984).

Although the Second Circuit decided *Catholic School Ass'n v. Culvert, supra,* prior to the Supreme Court's decision in *Employment Division, Department of Human Resources of Oregon v. Smith,* 494 U.S. 872 (1990), discussed *supra,* it nevertheless found that neither of the religion clauses were violated by the New York State Labor Relations Board's jurisdiction. (Unlike the National Labor Relations Act, New York law made it clear that the State Labor Relations Board had jurisdiction over church schools.) Applying the balancing test in *Wisconsin v. Yoder,* the court found that the free exercise of religion was not burdened, 753 F.2d at 1170, and that any "indirect and incidental burden on religion" was justified by a "compelling state interest" in "the preservation of industrial peace and a sound economic order" through enforcement of the "duty to bargain collectively and in good faith." *Id.* at 1171.

On the other hand, both *South Jersey Catholic School Teachers Ass'n v. St. Teresa, supra,* and *Hill-Murray Federation of Teachers v. Hill-Murray High School, supra,* relied on the Supreme Court's decision in *Smith, supra.* Although the Minnesota Labor Relations Act did not explicitly include church schools within its coverage, the Minnesota Supreme Court in *Hill-Murray* determined that these schools were meant to be covered. (Note that most of the eighteen state labor relations statutes have been similarly construed to include within their coverage all employers not expressly excluded. Hartman, "Spitting Distance: Tents Full of Religious Schools in Choice Programs, the Camel's Nose of State Labor-Law Application to Their Relations with Lay Faculty Members, and the First Amendment's Tether," 6 *Cornell J.L. & Pub. Pol'y* 553, 570 (1997)). The *Hill-Murray* court, relying on *Smith,* found that the Minnesota Labor Relations Act was "a generally applicable and otherwise valid regulatory law which was not intended to regulate religious conduct or belief and which incidentally burdens the free exercise of religion." 487 N.W.2d at 862 (citing *Employment Divi-*

sion, *Department of Human Resources of Oregon v. Smith,* 494 U.S. 872, 878 (1990)). The court found that there was no such "hybrid" situation as existed in the *Yoder* case, which would have required the application of the compelling interest test. Establishment clause arguments were given even shorter shrift. The reasoning of the New Jersey Supreme Court in *South Jersey Catholic School Teachers Ass'n v. St. Teresa, supra,* was similar. *See* Note, "Requiring Catholic Elementary Schools to Bargain with the Lay Teachers' Collective Bargaining Representative Does Not Violate the Religion Clauses of the First Amendment," 8 *Seton Hall Const. L. J.* 589 (1998); Hartman, *supra.*

2. *Implications of Smith for Church Autonomy*

Following the Supreme Court's decision in *Smith,* Professor Laycock wrote

> If churches must share control of their institutions with administrative agencies, unions, and labor boards; if every church personnel dispute is resolved under secular standards with potential recourse to secular courts; if egalitarian sex roles may be enforced in church employment, or in the church itself as a place of public accommodation; if church schools must conform to secular models of curriculum, student discipline, and academic freedom; if church disciplinary processes are subject to secular standards of due process, or if any church discipline at all risks liability for intentional infliction of emotional distress; if all new ministries require notice to the neighbors and approval from the zoning board; in short, if churches are neutrally subjected to the full range of modern regulation, it is hard to see how they can sustain any distinctive social structure or witness.

Laycock, "Summary and Synthesis: The Crisis in Religious Liberty," 60 *Geo. Wash. L. Rev.* 841, 853 (1992). Does *Smith* lead to this conclusion? What about the argument that *Smith* applies only to generally applicable *criminal* laws? Can *Smith* be limited to its factual situation? *See Hill-Murray Federation of Teachers v. Hill-Murray High School, supra.*

Runyon v. McCrary
427 U.S. 160, 96 S.Ct. 2586, 49 L.Ed.2d 415 (1976).

Mr. Justice Stewart delivered the opinion of the Court.

The principal issue presented by these consolidated cases is whether a federal law, namely 42 U.S.C. §1981, prohibits private schools from excluding qualified children solely because they are Negroes.

I

The respondents in No. 75-62, Michael McCrary and Colin Gonzales, are Negro children. By their parents, they filed a class action against the petitioners in No. 75-62, Russell and Katheryne Runyon, who are the proprietors of Bobbe's Private School in Arlington, Va. Their complaint alleged that they had been prevented from attending the school because of the petitioners' policy of denying admission to Negroes, in violation of 42 U.S.C. §1981[1] and Title II of the Civil Rights Act of 1964, 42 U.S.C. §2000a *et seq.*[2] They sought declaratory and injunctive relief and damages. On the same day Colin Gonzales, the respondent in No. 75-66, filed a similar complaint by his parents against the petitioner in No. 75-66, Fairfax-Brewster School, Inc., located in Fairfax County, Va. The petitioner in No. 75-278, the Southern Independent School Association, sought and was granted permission to intervene as a party defendant in the suit against the Runyons. That organization is a nonprofit association composed of six state private school associations, and represents 395 private schools. It is stipulated that many of these schools deny admission to Negroes.

The suits were consolidated for trial. The findings of the District Court, which were left undisturbed by the Court of Appeals, were as follows. Bobbe's School opened in 1958 and grew from an initial enrollment of five students to 200 in 1972. . . . The Fairfax-Brewster School commenced operations in 1955. . . . A total of 223 students were enrolled at the school during the 1972–1973 academic year. . . . Neither school has ever accepted a Negro child for any of its programs.

In response to a mailed brochure addressed "resident" and an advertisement in the "Yellow Pages" of the telephone directory, Mr. and Mrs. Gonzales telephoned and then visited the Fairfax-Brewster School in May 1969. After the visit, they submitted an application for Colin's admission to the day camp. The school responded with a form letter, which stated that the school was "unable to accommodate [Colin's] application." Mr. Gonzales telephoned the school. Fairfax-Brewster's Chairman of the Board explained that the reason for Colin's rejection was that the School was not integrated. Mr. Gonzales then telephoned Bobbe's School, from which the family had also received in the mail a brochure addressed to "resident." In response to a question concerning that school's admissions policies, he was told that only members of the Caucasian race were accepted. In August 1972, Mrs. McCrary telephoned Bobbe's School in response to an advertisement in the telephone book. She inquired about nursery school facilities for her son, Michael. She also asked if the School was integrated. The answer was no.

Upon these facts, the District Court found that the Fairfax-Brewster School had rejected Colin Gonzales' application on account of his race and that Bobbe's School had denied both children admission on racial grounds. The Court held that 42 U.S.C. §1981 makes illegal the schools' racially discriminatory admissions policies. It therefore enjoined Fairfax-Brewster and Bobbe's School and the member schools of the Southern Independent School Association[3] from discriminating against applicants for admission on the basis of race. The Court awarded compensatory relief to Mr. and Mrs. McCrary, Michael McCrary, and Colin Gonzales.[4] . . .

The Court of Appeals for the Fourth Circuit, sitting en banc, affirmed the District Court's grant of equitable and compensatory relief. . . . *McCrary v. Runyon*, 515 F.2d 1082 (1975). . . .

II

It is worth noting at the outset some of the questions that these cases do not present. They do not present any question of the right of a private social organization to limit its membership on racial or any other grounds. They do not present any question of the

---

[1] 42 U.S.C. §1981 provides:

"All persons within the jurisdiction of the United States shall have the same right in every State and Territory to make and enforce contracts, to sue, be parties, give evidence, and to the full and equal benefit of all laws and proceedings for the security of persons and property as is enjoyed by white citizens, and shall be subject to like punishment, pains, penalties, taxes, licenses, and exactions of every kind, and to no other."

[2] The respondents withdrew their Title II claim before trial.

[3] The District Court determined that the suit could not be maintained as a class action.

[4] For the embarrassment, humiliation, and mental anguish which the parents and children suffered, the Court awarded Colin Gonzales $2,000 against the Fairfax-Brewster School and $500 against Bobbe's School. Michael McCrary was awarded damages of $1,000, and Mr. and Mrs. McCrary $2,000, against Bobbe's School.

right of a private school to limit its student body to boys, to girls, or to adherents of a particular religious faith, since 42 U.S.C. §1981 is in no way addressed to such categories of selectivity. They do not even present the application of §1981 to private sectarian schools that practice racial exclusion on religious grounds.[6] Rather, these cases present only two basic questions: whether §1981 prohibits private, commercially operated, nonsectarian schools from denying admission to prospective students because they are Negroes, and, if so, whether that federal law is constitutional as so applied.

A. Applicability of §1981

It is now well established that §1 of the Civil Rights Act of 1866, 14 Stat. 27, 42 U.S.C. §1981 (1970), prohibits racial discrimination in the making and enforcement of private contracts. See *Johnson v. Railway Express Agency, Inc.*, 421 U.S. 454, 459–460; *Tillman v. Wheaton-Haven Recreation Assn.*, 410 U.S. 431, 439–440. Cf. *Jones v. Alfred H. Mayer Co.*, 392 U.S. 409, 441–443, n. 78.

In *Jones* the Court held that the portion of §1 of the Civil Rights Act of 1866 presently codified as 42 U.S.C. §1982 prohibits private racial discrimination in the sale or rental of real or personal property. Relying on the legislative history of §1, from which both §1981 and §1982 derive, the Court concluded that Congress intended to prohibit "all racial discrimination, private and public, in the sale . . . of property," 392 U.S., at 437, and that this prohibition was within Congress' power under §2 of the Thirteenth Amendment "rationally to determine what are the badges and the incidents of slavery, and . . . to translate that determination into effective legislation." *Id.*, at 440–441.

As the Court indicated in *Jones*, 392 U.S., at 441–443, n. 78, that holding necessarily implied that the portion of §1 of the 1866 Act presently codified as 42 U.S.C. §1981 likewise reaches purely private acts of racial discrimination. The statutory holding in *Jones* was that the "[1866] Act was designed to do just what its terms suggest: to prohibit all racial discrimination, whether or not under color of law, with respect to the rights enumerated therein—including the right to purchase or lease property." 392 U.S., at 436. One of the "rights enumerated" in §1 is "the same right . . . to make and enforce contracts . . . as is enjoyed by white citizens. . . ." 14 Stat. 27. Just as in *Jones* a Negro's §1 right to purchase property on equal terms with whites was violated when a private person refused to sell to the prospective purchaser solely because he was a Negro, so also a Negro's §1 right to "make and enforce contracts" is violated if a private offeror refuses to extend to a Negro, solely because he is a Negro, the same opportunity to enter into contracts as he extends to white offerees.

* * *

It is apparent that the racial exclusion practiced by the Fairfax-Brewster School and Bobbe's Private School amounts to a classic violation of §1981. The parents of Colin Gonzales and Michael McCrary sought to enter into contractual relationships with Bobbe's Private School for educational services. Colin Gonzales' parents sought to enter into a similar relationship with the Fairfax-Brewster School. Under those contractual relationships, the schools would have received payments for services rendered, and the prospective students would have received instruction in return for those payments. The educational services of Bobbe's Private School and the Fairfax-Brewster School were advertised and offered to members of the general public. But neither school offered services on an equal basis to white and nonwhite students. . . .

The petitioning schools and school association argue principally that §1981 does not reach private acts of racial discrimination. That view is wholly inconsistent with *Jones'* interpretation of the legislative history of §1 of the Civil Rights Act of 1866, an interpretation that was reaffirmed in *Sullivan v. Little Hunting Park, Inc.*, 396 U.S. 229, and again in *Tillman v. Wheaton-Haven Recreation Assn., supra.* And this consistent interpretation of the law necessarily requires the conclusion that §1981, like §1982, reaches private conduct. See *Tillman v. Wheaton-Haven Recreation Assn.*, 410 U.S., at 439–440; *Johnson v. Railway Express Agency, Inc.*, 421 U.S., at 459–460.

It is noteworthy that Congress in enacting the Equal Employment Opportunity Act of 1972, 86 Stat. 103, as amended, 42 U.S.C. §2000e *et seq.* (1970 ed. Supp. IV), specifically considered and rejected an amendment that would have repealed the Civil Rights Act of 1866, as interpreted by this Court

---

[6]Nothing in this record suggests that either the Fairfax-Brewster School or Bobbe's Private School excludes applicants on religious grounds, and the Free Exercise Clause of the First Amendment is thus in no way here involved.

in *Jones*, insofar as it affords private sector employees a right of action based on racial discrimination in employment. See *Johnson v. Railway Express Agency, Inc.*, 421 U.S., at 459. There could hardly be a clearer indication of congressional agreement with the view that §1981 does reach private acts of racial discrimination. . . . In these circumstances there is no basis for deviating from the well-settled principles of *stare decisis* applicable to this Court's construction of federal statutes. . . .

B. Constitutionality of §1981 as Applied

The question remains whether §1981, as applied, violates constitutionally protected rights of free association and privacy, or a parent's right to direct the education of his children.[13]

1. Freedom of Association. In *NAACP v. Alabama*, 357 U.S. 449, and similar decisions, the Court has recognized a First Amendment right "to engage in association for the advancement of beliefs and ideas. . . ." *Id.*, at 460. That right is protected because it promotes and may well be essential to the "[e]ffective advocacy of both public and private points of view, particularly controversial ones" that the First Amendment is designed to foster. *Id.*, at 460. . . .

From this principle it may be assumed that parents have a First Amendment right to send their children to educational institutions that promote the belief that racial segregation is desirable, and that the children have an equal right to attend such institutions. But it does not follow that the practice of excluding racial minorities from such institutions is also protected by the same principle. As the Court stated in *Norwood v. Harrison*, 413 U.S. 455, "the Constitution. . . places no value on discrimination," *id.*, at 469, and while "[i]nvidious private discrimination may be characterized as a form of exercising freedom of association protected by the First Amendment. . . it has never been accorded affirmative constitutional protections. And even some private discrimination is subject to special remedial legislation in certain circumstances under §2 of the Thirteenth Amendment; Congress has made such discrimination unlawful in other significant contexts." 413 U.S., at 470. In any event, as the Court of Appeals noted, "there is no showing that discontinu-

ance of [the] discriminatory admission practices would inhibit in any way the teaching in these schools of any ideas or dogma." 515 F.2d, at 1087.

2. Parental Rights. In *Meyer v. Nebraska*, 262 U.S. 390, the Court held that the liberty protected by the Due Process Clause of the Fourteenth Amendment includes the right "to acquire useful knowledge, to marry, establish a home and bring up children," *id.*, at 399, and, concomitantly, the right to send one's children to a private school that offers specialized training—in that case, instruction in the German language. In *Pierce v. Society of Sisters*, 268 U.S. 510, the Court applied "the doctrine of *Meyer v. Nebraska*," *id.*, at 534, to hold unconstitutional an Oregon law requiring the parent, guardian, or other person having custody of a child between eight and 16 years of age to send that child to public school on pain of criminal liability. The Court thought it "entirely plain that the [statute] unreasonably interferes with the liberty of parents and guardians to direct the upbringing and education of children under their control." *Id.*, at 534–535. In *Wisconsin v. Yoder*, 406 U.S. 205, the Court stressed the limited scope of *Pierce*, pointing out that it lent "no support to the contention that parents may replace state educational requirements with their own idiosyncratic views of what knowledge a child needs to be a productive and happy member of society" but rather "held simply that while a State may posit [educational] standards, it may not preempt the educational process by requiring children to attend public schools." *Id.*, at 239. . . .

It is clear that the present application of §1981 infringes no parental right recognized in *Meyer*, *Pierce*, *Yoder*, or *Norwood*. No challenge is made to the petitioners' right to operate their private schools or the right of parents to send their children to a particular private school rather than a public school. Nor do these cases involve a challenge to the subject matter which is taught at any private school. Thus, the Fairfax-Brewster School and Bobbe's Private School and members of the intervenor association remain presumptively free to inculcate whatever values and standards they deem desirable. *Meyer* and its progeny entitle them to no more.

3. The Right of Privacy. The Court has held that in some situations the Constitution confers a right of privacy. *See Roe v. Wade*, 410 U.S. 113, 152–153;

---

[13]It is clear that the schools have standing to assert these arguments on behalf of their patrons. See *Pierce v. Society of Sisters*, 268 U.S. 510, 535–536.

Eisenstadt v. Baird, 405 U.S. 438, 453; *Stanley v. Georgia*, 394 U.S. 557, 564–565; *Griswold v. Connecticut*, 381 U.S. 479, 484–485. See also *Loving v. Virginia*, 388 U.S. 1, 12; *Skinner v. Oklahoma*, 316 U.S. 535, 541.

While the application of §1981 to the conduct at issue here—a private school's adherence to a racially discriminatory admissions policy—does not represent governmental intrusion into the privacy of the home or similarly intimate setting, it does implicate parental interests. These interests are related to the procreative rights protected in *Roe v. Wade, supra,* and *Griswold v. Connecticut, supra.* A person's decision whether to bear a child and a parent's decision concerning the manner in which his child is to be educated may fairly be characterized as exercises of familial rights and responsibilities. But it does not follow that because government is largely or even entirely precluded from regulating the child-bearing decision, it is similarly restricted by the Constitution from regulating the implementation of parental decisions concerning a child's education.

The Court has repeatedly stressed that while parents have a constitutional right to send their children to private schools and a constitutional right to select private schools that offer specialized instruction, they have no constitutional right to provide their children with private school education unfettered by reasonable government regulation. *See Wisconsin v. Yoder,* 406 U.S., at 213; *Pierce v. Society of Sisters,* 268 U.S., at 534; *Meyer v. Nebraska,* 262 U.S., at 402.[15] Indeed, the Court in *Pierce* expressly acknowledged "the power of the State reasonably to regulate all schools, to inspect, supervise and examine them, their teachers and pupils. . . ." 268 U.S., at 534. See also *Prince v. Massachusetts,* 321 U.S. 158, 166.

Section 1981, as applied to the conduct at issue here, constitutes an exercise of federal legislative power under §2 of the Thirteenth Amendment fully consistent with *Meyer, Pierce,* and the cases that followed in their wake. As the Court held in *Jones v. Alfred H. Mayer Co., supra,* "[i]t has never been doubted. . . 'that the power vested in Congress to enforce [the Thirteenth Amendment] by appropriate legislation' . . . includes the power to enact laws 'direct and primary, operating upon the acts of individuals, whether sanctioned by State legislation or

not.' " 392 U.S., at 438 (citation omitted). The prohibition of racial discrimination that interferes with the making and enforcement of contracts for private educational services furthers goals closely analogous to those served by §1981's elimination of racial discrimination in the making of private employment contracts and, more generally, by §1982's guarantee that "a dollar in the hands of a Negro will purchase the same thing as a dollar in the hands of a white man." *Jones v. Alfred H. Mayer Co.,* 392 U.S., at 443.

* * *

For the reasons stated in this opinion, the judgment of the Court of Appeals is in all respects affirmed.

It is so ordered.

Mr. Justice Powell, concurring.

If the slate were clean I might well be inclined to agree with Mr. Justice White that §1981 was not intended to restrict private contractual choices. Much of the review of the history and purpose of this statute set forth in his dissenting opinion is quite persuasive. It seems to me, however, that it comes too late.

The applicability of §1981 to private contracts has been considered maturely and recently, and I do not feel free to disregard these precedents. . . .

Mr. Justice Stevens, concurring.

For me the problem in these cases is whether to follow a line of authority which I firmly believe to have been incorrectly decided.

Jones v. Alfred H. Mayer Co., 392 U.S. 409, and its progeny have unequivocally held that §1 of the Civil Rights Act of 1866 prohibits private racial discrimination. There is no doubt in my mind that construction of the statute would have amazed the legislators who voted for it. Both its language and the historical setting in which it was enacted convince me that Congress intended only to guarantee all citizens the same legal capacity to make and enforce contracts, to obtain, own and convey property, and to litigate and give evidence. Moreover, since the legislative history discloses an intent not to outlaw segregated public schools at that time, it is quite unrealistic to assume that Congress intended the broader result of prohibiting segregated private schools. Were we writing on a clean slate, I would therefore vote to reverse.

But *Jones* has been decided and is now an important part of the fabric of our law. Although I recognize

---

[15]The *Meyer-Pierce-Yoder* "parental" right and the privacy right, while dealt with separately in this opinion, may be no more than verbal variations of a single constitutional right. See *Roe v. Wade,* 410 U.S. 113, 152–153 (*Meyer v. Nebraska, supra* and *Pierce v. Society of Sisters, supra,* cited for the proposition that this Court has recognized a constitutional right of privacy).

the force of Mr. Justice White's argument that the construction of §1982 does not control §1981, it would be most incongruous to give those two sections a fundamentally different construction. The net result of the enactment in 1866, the re-enactment in 1870, and the codification in 1874 produced, I believe, a statute resting on the constitutional foundations provided by both the Thirteenth and Fourteenth Amendments. An attempt to give a fundamentally different meaning to two similar provisions by ascribing one to the Thirteenth and the other to the Fourteenth Amendment cannot succeed. I am persuaded, therefore, that we must either apply the rationale of *Jones* or overrule that decision.

There are two reasons which favor overruling. First, as I have already stated, my conviction that *Jones* was wrongly decided is firm. Second, it is extremely unlikely that reliance upon *Jones* has been so extensive that this Court is foreclosed from overruling it. *Compare Flood v. Kuhn,* 407 U.S. 258, 273–274, 278–279, 283. There are, however, opposing arguments of greater force.

The first is the interest in stability and orderly development of the law. As Justice Cardozo remarked, with respect to the routine work of the judiciary, "the labor of judges would be increased almost to the breaking point if every past decision could be reopened in every case, and one could not lay one's own course of bricks on the secure foundation of the courses laid by others who had gone before him."[2] Turning to the exceptional case, Justice Cardozo noted "that when a rule, after it has been duly tested by experience, has been found to be inconsistent with the sense of justice or with the social welfare, there should be less hesitation in frank disavowal and full abandonment. . . . If judges have woefully misinterpreted the mores of their day, or if the mores of their day are no longer those of ours, they ought not to tie, in helpless submission, the hands of their successors."[3] In this case, those admonitions favor adherence to, rather than departure from, precedent. For even if *Jones* did not accurately reflect the sentiments of the Reconstruction Congress, it surely accords with the prevailing sense of justice today.

The policy of the Nation as formulated by the Congress in recent years has moved constantly in the direction of eliminating racial segregation in all sectors of society.[4] This Court has given a sympathetic and liberal construction to such legislation. For the Court now to overrule *Jones* would be a significant step backwards, with effects that would not have arisen from a correct decision in the first instance. Such a step would be so clearly contrary to my understanding of the mores of today that I think the Court is entirely correct in adhering to *Jones.* With this explanation, I join the opinion of the Court.

Mr. Justice White, with whom Mr. Justice Rehnquist joins, dissenting.

We are urged here to extend the meaning and reach of 42 U.S.C. §1981 so as to establish a general prohibition against a private individual or institution refusing to enter into a contract with another person because of that person's race. Section 1981 has been on the books since 1870 and to so hold for the first time would be contrary to the language of the section, to its legislative history and to the clear dictum of this Court in the Civil Rights cases, 109 U.S. 1, 16–17 (1883), almost contemporaneously with the passage of the statute, that the section reaches only discriminations imposed by state law. The majority's belated discovery of a congressional purpose which escaped this Court only a decade after the statute was passed and which escaped all other federal courts for almost 100 years is singularly unpersuasive.[2] I therefore respectfully dissent.

[Mr. Justice White's lengthy discussion of the legislative history of §1981 is omitted.]

* * *

The majority's holding that 42 U.S.C. §1981 prohibits all racially motivated contractual decisions. . . threatens to embark the judiciary on a treacherous course. Whether such conduct should be condoned or not, whites and blacks will undoubtedly choose to form a variety of associational relationships pursuant to contracts which exclude members of the other race. Social clubs, black and white, and associations designed to further the interests of blacks or whites

---

[2]B. Cardozo, *The Nature of Judicial Process* 149 (1921). [*See also* E. Levi, *An Introduction to Legal Reasoning* 31–33 (1949)].

[3]*Id.*, at 150–152.

[4]*See, e.g.,* The Civil Rights Act of 1964, 78 Stat. 241, as added and as amended, 28 U.S.C. § 1447(d), 42 U.S.C. §§1971, 1975a-1975d, 2000a-2000h-6 (1970 ed. and Supp. IV); The Voting Rights Act of 1965, 79 Stat. 437, as added and as amended, 42 U.S.C. §§1973-1973bb-4; The Civil Rights Act of 1968, Titles VIII, IX, 82 Stat. 81, 89, as amended, 42 U.S.C. §3061-3631 (1970 ed. and Supp. IV).

[2]I do not question at this point the power of Congress or a state legislature to ban racial discrimination in private school admissions decisions. But as I see it Congress has not yet chosen to exercise that power.

are but two examples. Lawsuits by members of the other race attempting to gain admittance to such an association are not pleasant to contemplate. As the associational or contractual relationships become more private, the pressures to hold §1981 inapplicable to them will increase. Imaginative judicial construction of the word "contract" is foreseeable; Thirteenth Amendment limitations on Congress' power to ban "badges and incidents of slavery" may be discovered; the doctrine of the right to association may be bent to cover a given situation. In any event, courts will be called upon to balance sensitive policy considerations against each other—which considerations have never been addressed by any Congress—all under the guise of "construing a statute". This is a task appropriate for the legislature, not for the judiciary.

Such balancing of considerations as has been done by Congress in the area of racially motivated decisions not to contract with a member of the other race has led it to ban private racial discrimination in most of the job market and most of the housing market and to go no further. The judiciary should not undertake the political task of trying to decide what other areas are appropriate ones for a similar rule.

* * *

However, the majority points to language in *Johnson v. REA, Inc.*, 421 U.S. 454, stating with no discussion whatever that 42 U.S.C. §1981 supplies a cause of action for a private racially motivated refusal to contract. . . . [T]he dictum in *Johnson v. REA, Inc.*, is squarely contrary to the dictum in *The Civil Rights Cases, supra.* The issue presented in this case is too important for this Court to let the more recent of two contradictory dicta stand in the way of an objective analysis of legislative history and a correct construction of a statute passed by Congress. *Cf. Jones v. Mayer, supra,* at 420 n. 25.

Accordingly, I would reverse.

NOTES AND QUESTIONS

1. Scope of §1981

What is the nature of the dispute about the meaning of §1981? Section 1981 speaks of blacks having the same rights as whites "to make and enforce" contracts. Does this suggest that African Americans were to have an equal opportunity to enter into contracts? Or does it suggest that African Americans were to have the same contractual capacity as whites and equal access

to the machinery of the state to enforce their contracts? A number of distinguished commentators have viewed the legislative history of §1981 as supporting only the latter point of view. *See, e.g.,* McClellan, "The Foibles and Fables of *Runyon*," 67 *Wash. U.L.Q.* 13 (1989); Casper, "*Jones v. Mayer*: Clio, Bemused and Confused Muse," 1968 *Sup. Ct. Rev.* 89; Henkin, "The Supreme Court, 1967 Term," 82 *Harv. L. Rev.* 63, 96–101 (1968). Others have read the legislative history as inconclusive in itself or at least sufficiently ambiguous so as to encompass racial discrimination in the contracting process. *See, e.g.,* Hilton, "Race, Religion, and Constitutional Restraints on Private Schools," 30 *Rutgers L. Rev.* 329, 360 (1977); Note, "The Desegregation of Private Schools: Is Section 1981 the Answer?" 48 *N.Y.U. L. Rev.* 1147 (1973). One commentator has firmly endorsed the *Runyon* court's reading of the historical record. *See* Kaczorowski, "The Enforcement Provisions of the Civil Rights Act of 1866: A Legislative History in Light of *Runyon v. McCrary*," 98 *Yale L. J.* 565 (1989).

If the legislative history supporting the majority position in *Runyon* is ambiguous at best, why did not the Court construe the statute so as to avoid passing on the constitutionality of §1981 under the First Amendment? Compare *Runyon* with *NLRB v. Catholic Bishop of Chicago,* 440 U.S. 490, 99 S.Ct. 1313, 59 L.Ed.2d 533 (1979). What alternatives did the Court have if it wished to outlaw racial discrimination by private schools? Might the Court have declared that the private schools were so regulated by the state and performed such public functions that their actions should be characterized as "state action"? *But see Moose Lodge No. 107 v. Irvis,* 407 U.S. 163, 92 S.Ct. 1965, 32 L.Ed.2d 627 (1972). *See generally* Note, "Federal Power to Regulate Private Discrimination: The Revival of the Enforcement Clauses of the Reconstruction Era Amendments," 74 *Colum. L. Rev.* 449, 458–59 (1974); Note, "The Desegregation of Private Schools: Is Section 1981 the Answer?," *supra.* What are the dangers of the state action approach? Would §1981 be rendered superfluous if plaintiffs could rely on the Fourteenth Amendment and the more general provisions of §1983? What implications would such an approach have for gender or religious discrimination?

Note that all the justices appear to agree that Congress has the power under the Thirteenth Amendment to outlaw racial discrimination by private schools. Do you agree? If Congress had not enacted §1981, could the Court reach such discrimination by direct judicial enforcement of the Thirteenth Amendment?

2. *Stare Decisis and Statutory Interpretation*

Do you agree with Justice Stevens that the Court should construe §1981 consistent with *Jones v. Mayer* and other recent precedents—even if it is convinced that the earlier statutory constructions were erroneous? Do stability and orderly development of the law outweigh concerns about distorting the judgment of Congress with regard to so important an issue? Should *Brown* and the public policy against racial discrimination allow the Court to reinterpret §1981? *See* Frankel, "*Runyon v. McCrary* Should Not Be Overruled," 67 *Wash. U.L.Q.* 1 (1989). Why? Note that while Justice Stewart considers *Runyon* to involve a "classic" violation of §1981, Justice White chastises the majority for its "belated discovery of a congressional purpose which escaped this Court only a decade after the statute was passed and which escaped all other federal courts for almost 100 years. . . ."

Amidst great controversy, the Supreme Court in *Patterson v. McLean Credit Union*, 485 U.S. 617, 109 S.Ct. 2363, 105 L.Ed.2d 132 (1989) declined to overrule *Runyon* but held that section 1981 does not apply to racial harassment relating to the conditions of employment, which occurs after the formation of a contract and which does not interfere with the right to enforce established contract obligations. *See* Note, "*Patterson v. McLean Credit Union*: New Limitations on an Old Civil Rights Statute," 68 *N.C.L. Rev.* 799 (1990).

With regard to the need for consistency in statutory interpretation, *see* E. Levi, *An Introduction to Legal Reasoning* 23–24 (1949). But even if *Jones v. Mayer* was improperly decided, given the gloss placed on the Reconstruction Civil Rights Act in *Jones*, what is the appropriate resolution of *Runyon*? What is the significance of Congress's failure to overturn *Jones*? *See* Frankel, "*Runyon v. McCrary* Should Not Be Overruled," 67 *Wash. U.L.Q.* 1 1989. Why is not the Court as free to reinterpret §1981 as the equal protection clause of the Fourteenth Amendment? For example, in *Plessy v. Ferguson*, 163 U.S. 537, 16 S.Ct. 1138, 41 L.Ed. 258 (1896), the Court upheld the "separate-but-equal" doctrine, thereby permitting the states to segregate the races. But in *Brown v. Board of Education*, 347 U.S. 483, 74 S.Ct. 686, 98 L.Ed. 873 (1954), the Court repudiated the doctrine in the public school context. Does this suggest that the Court has or should have more flexibility in repudiating constitutional interpretations than in rejecting earlier constructions of federal statutes? *See* E. Levi, *supra*

at 5–6. Compare *id.* with Brest, "The Misconceived Quest for the Original Understanding," 60 *B. U. L. Rev.* 204 (1980). Should the Court have reinterpreted the equal protection clause to apply to racial discrimination in private schools? *See generally* Rotunda, "*Runyon v. McCrary* and the Mosaic of State Action," 67 *Wash. U. L. Q.* 47 (1989).

3. *Freedom of Association, Privacy, and the Rights of Parents*

On what basis does Justice Stewart conclude that the defendants' interests in freedom of association, privacy, and the rights of parents to direct the upbringing of their children are outweighed by the governmental interest in eliminating racial discrimination? *See generally* Note, "*Runyon v. McCrary* and Private School Admission Policies," 16 *J. of Fam. L.* 77 (1977). Does it answer the question to suggest that no affirmative value is attached to racial discrimination and that, indeed, an antidiscrimination principle is embedded in the Fourteenth Amendment? Does not the Constitution, at least as construed in earlier decisions, place an affirmative value on freedom of association and parental rights? *See generally* C. Rice, *Freedom of Association* (1962); Emerson, "Freedom of Association and Freedom of Expression," 74 *Yale L. J.* 1 (1964); Raggi, "An Independent Right to Freedom of Association," 12 *Harv. C. R.-C. L. L. Rev.* 1 (1977). Is a ban on racially discriminatory admissions policies in private schools akin to the reasonable regulation of private schools endorsed in *Pierce?See* Comment "Private School Desegregation Under Section 1981," 124 *U. Pa. L. Rev.* 714, 722 (1976). What is the nature of the associational interest? Is it the right to associate with other persons per se, or is it the right to join together for purposes of political and other expression? If the latter is entitled to greater constitutional protection than the former, on which side of the line does *Runyon* fall? Put somewhat differently, does *Runyon* seek to silence powerful voices advocating racial discrimination? If so, how do you distinguish *Pierce, Meyer*, and *Farrington?* Do the cases turn on the nature of the positions advocated? Is this an acceptable constitutional standard? Or is it that the Court must reconcile the First and Fourteenth Amendments and that it did so in *Runyon* by allowing advocacy of segregation but not the practice of engaging in racially discriminatory admissions? But is not the practice of segregation inextricably tied to the advocacy of that position? Is Justice Stewart persuasive when he argues that permitting the presence of African Americans will not impede the socialization processes of the private schools? Or is it that, despite the unwillingness to rely on the state action doctrine, the Court is treating all education as involving substantial public interests? *See* Hilton, "Race, Religion, and Constitutional Restraints on Private Schools," 30 *Rutgers L. Rev.* 329, 369 (1977). If this is so, does this suggest that *Runyon* will not be extended to private clubs and other relationships of a less public, more intimate, nature? *See generally* Note, "The Expanding Scope of Section 1981: Assault on Private Discrimination and a Cloud on Affirmative Action," 90 *Harv. L. Rev.* 412 (1976).

Is the associational interest of the parents undercut by the fact that the schools hold themselves open to the public at large (by "yellow-page" advertisements and mass mailings) except for African American applicants? Consider this argument:

> Free association has traditionally been deemed to grant only the right to join, not the right to keep others out. Indeed, the recognition of a right to exclude would impair the associational freedom of those individuals who desire to join the group.

Note, 90 *Harv. L. Rev.* at 435. Do you find this argument persuasive?

4. Racial Motivation

Suppose that a student's race is only one factor among several that motivated a private school to deny admission. Would such an admissions policy run afoul of *Runyon? See Riley v. Adirondack Southern School for Girls*, 541 F.2d 1124 (5th Cir. 1976) (en banc). *See generally* Hilton, *supra* at 372–75. What of the fact that "after *McCrary* it is unlikely that any school desiring to remain segregated would be so unsophisticated as to continue to openly rely on racial criteria for refusing to admit black pupils"? *Id.* at 373. *See generally* chapter 4.

5. Cook v. Hudson

In *Cook v. Hudson*, 511 F.2d 744 (5th Cir. 1975) (per curiam), plaintiff public schoolteachers attacked the constitutionality of a county school board policy that prohibited the hiring or rehiring of any teachers whose children were enrolled in racially segregated schools. The school board, prompted by the Department of Justice, successfully defended the rule on the basis that the policy was significantly related to teacher effectiveness; black students were likely to view such teachers as rejecting them and as perceiv-

ing them as inferior. In a concurring opinion, Judge Coleman declared "the general public, who pay taxes, who keep the public school doors open, and who depend on those [public] schools to educate their children, have a right to expect undivided teacher dedication, free of any real or apparent conflict of interest." *Id.* at 749. Judge Roney also concurred separately, arguing that the policy was designed "to strengthen local support for the public schools and to effectively implement the court-ordered requirement to change from a dual segregated school system to a unitary nondiscriminatory system." *Id.* at 750. Judge Clark dissented. He urged that *Pierce* was controlling and that, "whether viewed as a part of a citizen's Fourteenth Amendment liberty or First Amendment freedom of association or a combination of both, the right plaintiffs claim is protected from state intrusion. . . ." *Id.*

The Supreme Court initially granted a writ of certiorari to review the Fifth Circuit decision, but in a per curiam opinion, the Court dismissed the writ as improvidently granted. 429 U.S. 165, 97 S.Ct. 543, 50 L.Ed.2d 373 (1976). Apparently, in the interim, the Mississippi Legislature had enacted legislation forbidding school districts from enacting and enforcing policies such as those in issue in *Cook. See* Miss. Code Ann. §37-9-59 (1974). Chief Justice Burger wrote a cryptic concurring opinion:

> I join in the Court's disposition of this case. In doing so, I emphasize that our decision to dismiss the writ of certiorari as improvidently granted intimates no view on the question of when, if ever, public schoolteachers—or any comparable public employees—may be required, as a condition of their employment, to enroll their children in any particular school or refrain from sending them to a school which they, as parents, in their sole discretion, consider desirable. Few familial decisions are as immune from governmental interference as parents' choice of a school for their children, so long as the school chosen otherwise meets the educational standards imposed by the State. See *Pierce v. Society of Sisters*, 268 U.S. 510 (1925); *Meyer v. Nebraska*, 262 U.S. 390 (1923); *Wisconsin v. Yoder*, 406 U.S. 205 (1972).

Id. at 166.

If Mississippi had not changed its laws, and in the light of *Runyon*, should the Court have affirmed or reversed the Circuit Court decision in *Cook? See Fyfe v. Curlee*, 902 F.2d 401 (5th Cir. 1990); *Stough v. Crenshaw County Bd. of Educ.*, 744 F.2d 1479 (11th Cir. 1984); *Brantley v. Surles*, 718 F.2d 1354 (5th Cir. 1983). *Cf. Peterson v. Minidoka County*

School Dist. No. 331, 118 F.3d 1351 (9th Cir. 1997). *See generally* Johnson, "The Right of Public School Employees to Send Their Children to Private Schools: The Demise of *Cook v. Hudson,*" 68 *Ed.Law Rep.* 21 (1991).

6. *Applicability of* Runyon *to Private Religious Schools*

In *Runyon* the Court explicitly declined to comment on the applicability of its decision to sectarian as opposed to nonsectarian private schools. Should *Runyon* be extended to private religious schools? How should free exercise of religion claims be weighed against the constitutionally based (but still statutory) interest of government in outlawing racial discrimination in private schools? Only a year after *Runyon,* the Fifth Circuit was called upon to pass on this issue.

Brown v. Dade Christian Schools, Inc.

556 F.2d 310 (5th Cir. 1977) (en banc), *cert. denied,* 434 U.S. 1063, 98 S.Ct. 1235, 55 L.Ed.2d 763 (1978).

[African American parents filed suit against the Dade Christian School under 42 U.S.C. §1981 alleging that they and their children had been the victims of racial discrimination in the denial of admission to that school. Dade Christian is a sectarian school which is located on the property of and receives subsidies from the New Testament Baptist Church. "The defendant asserted that its members sincerely held a religious belief that socialization of the races would lead to racial intermarriage, and that this belief, sanctioned by the Free Exercise Clause, should prevail against private interests created by Congress." 556 F.2d at 311 (Plurality opinion of Judge Hill). The parties stipulated that "race was the sole reason" for the refusal of Dade Christian School to enroll the Brown children. *Id.* The plurality declined to reach the question of the constitutionality of §1981 as applied to a religious school, holding that there was substantial evidence to support the findings of the trial judge that "defendant's policy of segregation was not the exercise of religion." 556 F.2d at 312. The plurality stated that

> [t]he absence of references to school segregation in written literature stating the church's beliefs, distributed to members of the church and the public by leaders of the church . . ., is strong evidence that school segregation is not the exercise of religion.
>
> . . . While a religious belief may be of recent vintage or formed instantaneously, the trial judge's conclusion that

school segregation was nothing more than a recent policy developed in response to the growing issue of segregation and integration was amply supported by the evidence.

556 F.2d at 312, 313.

The plurality further held that where the alleged discriminatory action was taken by the institution, it was inappropriate "to scrutinize the individual religious beliefs of the parties. . . ." 556 F.2d at 313.

> In such a situation the only practical course open to a Court is to examine the corporate beliefs of the institution involved, as adopted or promulgated or carried forward as an institutional concept. To do otherwise would allow the institution to pick and choose which of its members' potentially conflicting beliefs it wished to assert at any given time. Thus, an avowedly secular school should not be permitted to interpose a free exercise defense to a §1981 action merely because it can find some of its patrons who have a sincere religiously based belief in racial segregation. Conversely, a school or church which holds racial segregation as a religious tenet should not be barred from asserting a free exercise defense to a §1981 claim merely because some of its patrons or members might individually believe racial segregation is morally wrong.

556 F.2d at 313–14.

The plurality affirmed the decision of the district court, holding the admissions policies of the Dade Christian School in violation of §1981.]

[Concurring opinion of Chief Judge Brown omitted.]

Goldberg, Circuit Judge, specially concurring.

. . . The facts do not support the view that these beliefs were merely "policy" within the plurality's distinction between "policy" and "religion." The plurality seizes upon various instances when school officials—lay persons insensitive to the overtones of their choice of language—spoke loosely of the anti-integration "policy." I believe a more balanced analysis of the record as a whole would indicate that the witnesses also repeatedly referred to the "religious" moorings of the beliefs.

Dr. Arthur E. Kreft, the school's principal, testified at his deposition that enrolling blacks in the Dade Christian school would endanger the practice of his religion. . . . He said the enrollment of blacks would alienate him from God "in the sense that I would be disobedient, according to my beliefs in the Scriptures.". . . Enrollment of blacks would erode Kreft's "religious liberties.". . . Appellees stipulated that they had no basis to impeach these statements by Kreft. . ., and I can conclude only that Kreft's beliefs are sufficiently "religious" to invoke free exercise scrutiny. . . . Kreft's testimony conclusively demonstrates the necessity to address the free exercise claim on its merits.

Similar testimony came from John M. Kalapp, Dade Christian's original vice president, who left the school early in 1973. Kalapp believes that enrollment of blacks at Dade Christian would endanger his "religious beliefs" "[i]f it culminated in an intermarriage situation between the races". . ., which he apparently believes it would. Kalapp derives these views from his "overall concept and understanding of the teaching of the entire Scriptures.". . . Appellees stipulated that they had no basis to impeach these statements. . . .

Also in evidence is a recording of remarks that Dr. Janney made to the New Testament Baptist Church congregation. Dr. Janney is the church pastor and president of Dade Christian Schools, Inc. The tape makes undeniably clear that Dr. Janney entertains religious beliefs that integrating Dade Christian would be wrong. Although he delivered the remarks after this suit was filed and in contemplation of litigation, no one questions their sincerity. The remarks were the message of a pastor to his congregation. Dr. Janney's views, derived from detailed analysis of numerous biblical passages, could hardly be characterized as anything other than "religious," even under the plurality's stringent approach. Dade Christian has standing to assert the free exercise rights of its president and founding church's pastor, and Dr. Janney's views alone should therefore take this court to the merits of the free exercise defense.

* * *

Surely a practice which is based on Biblical interpretation . . . and the contravention of which would constitute disobedience to God . . . is a "religious" practice. . . .[11]

. . . The Dade Christian leadership adopted the rule in response to religious tenets, not transient policy dictates. Knowing that it would one day face the issue, Dade Christian's board of directors undertook a discussion of "what would be the right thing scripturally to do.". . . The directors reached a decision based on "the overall concept of the teachings of the Scriptures, and such things as God's dealing with the nation of Israel, the Tower of Babel, [and] the confusion of tongues in the Book of Acts.". . . The board of directors concluded that "it was God's will that the races were made separate for a purpose.". . . Appellants stip-

ulated that they had no basis to impeach these statements. . . . The plurality characterizes that decision, based on "God's will" as divined from the Bible, as not sufficiently "religious" even to warrant threshold consideration of the free exercise defense. I cannot agree.

* * *

There is of course more to analyzing a free exercise claim than determining whether the belief in question is "religious." We must decide whether sufficient governmental interests justify interfering with the claimant's religious practices. . . .

I now turn to the difficult issues that I believe are unavoidable. The Supreme Court has adopted various formulations in its efforts to reconcile governmental interests with those of free exercise claimants. In *Sherbert v. Verner*, 374 U.S. 398, 403 . . . (1963) the Court said that a religious practice could be infringed only on the basis of a "compelling state interest." In *Wisconsin v. Yoder*, 406 U.S. 205, 215 . . . (1972) the Court announced that free exercise claims could be overbalanced only by "those interests of the highest importance and those not otherwise served." Whatever the precise standard, free exercise analysis requires a careful comparison of the interests on both sides of the issue.

Charting the interests of free exercise claimants requires dispassionate dedication to the principle that courts cannot question the veracity of sincerely held religious beliefs. I therefore proceed on the assumption that desegregating Dade Christian would force the principal and at least some of the teachers, students and parents to be disobedient to God. . . . Rejecting the free exercise claim would impinge upon the religious practice of maintaining racial separation in activities that constitute "socialization."

That religious practice was characterized by Mr. Kalapp as a "very minor" part of the religion. . . . Departure from the practice, although constituting disobedience to God, would not endanger salvation. While these factors do not sap the free exercise defense of vitality, they make clear that overriding that defense will not endanger the church's survival.

Nor can appellant's claim garner appreciable support from the fundamental interests of parents and students in guiding the quality and nature of the education. Allowing blacks into Dade Christian will not affect the substance of the education; the school remains free to teach any doctrine it chooses, including

---

[11]The plurality concludes otherwise, relying on Dade Christian's printed card listing nine items which "we believe." As the plurality notes, the card does not mention racial segregation. The first belief listed, however, is that the Bible is the infallible word of God. If the "we believe" card is to be read with the exacting scrutiny we accord to legal documents, we should treat the segregative beliefs derived from the Bible as incorporated by reference.

the merit and religious requirement of racial segregation. Dade Christian's argument that admission of blacks would itself convey an undesirable message and thereby affect educational content carries little weight. Although the school leadership's voluntary enrollment of blacks might communicate such a message, desegregation in response to a federal court's implementation of the congressional mandate of §1981 would not. Much as merchants were freed by the Civil Rights Act of 1964 from any fear that white customers would react adversely to the acceptance of black business, parents and school leaders are freed by §1981 from any fear that children will interpret acceptance of blacks as an indication of church approval of the practice. The parents' right to direct the upbringing and education of their children remains intact.

Dade Christian is also unable to elicit any support from right of association principles. Here, as in *Runyon v. McCrary*, 427 U.S. 160, 175–79 . . . (1979) (rejecting association defense to §1981 action against private school), the school simply does not operate in a manner implicating associational interests. Dade Christian advertises for students in the yellow pages and concededly exercises no policy of exclusion other than its ban on blacks. . . . Dade Christian therefore can claim no constitutionally cognizable interest in the sanctity of its school community. This case on its facts simply does not implicate the interests of a church in maintaining the intimacy of its activities.

The sole basis of Dade Christian's claim is therefore the "very minor" religious practice of preserving racial segregation in activities that constitute "socialization." . . .

[The school's] . . . grievance extends only to interracial "socialization," which it defines to include children's school attendance. . . . Dade Christian's criterion for distinguishing proscribed "socialization" from other types of interracial contact is apparently the likelihood that interracial marriage will be encouraged. . . . Thus adherents of the New Testament Baptist Church do not seek to overturn the Civil Rights Act of 1964 or to separate themselves from our integrated society; they merely seek to avoid situations that might lead to interracial marriage.

In this respect it is important to note that no one purports to use §1981 as a basis for imposing interracial marriages upon anyone. Dade Christian students, like everyone else, remain free to marry whom they choose. Dade Christian parents remain free to teach their children that interracial marriage violates religious commands. That some students may depart their

parents' commands and that integrating the school might make it infinitesimally easier for them then to effectuate their disobedience are hardly prospects lending weight to Dade Christian's position. The Constitution has never guaranteed parents an opportunity simultaneously to exist in an urban environment and to exclude every possibility that children will hear and adopt ideas at odds with those of the parents.

I do not mean to suggest that the religious beliefs at issue extend only to interracial marriage. Dade Christian advances a sincere belief that integrated education violates divine command. But that belief occupies a minor position in its adherents' religion and is based largely on the prospect of interracial marriage, a prospect that no government proposes to require.

In sum, Dade Christian's interests, while not minimal, do not rise to the level that has characterized numerous free exercise claims. I find that the government's interests, in comparison, are compelling.

Most free exercise cases have involved governmental interests manifested in legislative judgments. . . .

Here, in contrast, the government's interests draw strength not only from the congressional judgment manifested in §1981 but also from the Constitution itself. The Thirteenth Amendment proscribes slavery and involuntary servitude. In ensuring blacks an equal opportunity to enter contracts, §1981 seeks to eradicate some of the badges and incidents of slavery. A more compelling governmental interest has perhaps never been enlisted in opposition to a free exercise claim.

* * *

The claim that Dade Christian advances is not one that we could recognize without inviting numerous additional claims. Opposition to integration does not die easily. Those who turned to white academies in response to public school integration will undoubtedly seek ways to avoid *Runyon v. McCrary*'s mandate to integrate the private schools. We therefore cannot view Dade Christian's claim in isolation. We have three alternatives: recognizing Dade Christian's claim but rejecting a significant number of future claims, recognizing Dade Christian's claim and most others as well, and rejecting Dade Christian's claim.

The first alternative would commit us to a case-by-case effort to distinguish meritorious from meritless future claims. In that way we could minimize the impairment of §1981's goals but we would thrust ourselves into the troublesome course of adjudication that I have described as contrary to more fundamental religion clause values. I believe we should reject this opportunity to set ourselves up as a board of religious arbiters.

The remaining alternatives are to steel ourselves to recognize virtually all of the free exercise claims that a decision for Dade Christian would foster, or to reject Dade Christian's claim. We must choose either to recognize the free exercise defense in this and numerous cases, thus undermining to a large extent the vitality of §1981 in this area, or to override the defense and enforce §1981's constitutionally based mandate.

The appropriate result is clear. The constitutional imperative to eliminate the badges of slavery has not dimmed in the 114 years since President Lincoln issued the Emancipation Proclamation. The compelling governmental interest in moving nearer that noble goal overrides appellant's interest in preserving a "very minor" religious practice. No less restrictive alternative is available; the government cannot afford appellees their right to be free of racial discrimination in contracting without infringing appellant's opposition to such contracts. Although free exercise claims deserve the most careful consideration and the greatest deference, they cannot always prevail. When the government interest is so strong and the impact upon the religion so slight, the religious practice must yield. I concur in the judgment of affirmance.

Roney, Circuit Judge, with whom Gewin, Coleman, Ainsworth, Clark and Tjoflat, Circuit Judges, join, dissenting: [omitted]

Coleman, Circuit Judge, dissenting:

* * *

I do not understand that the church is operating this school as a commercial enterprise. It is a direct, intimate adjunct of church activities, conducted in the house of worship. From the earliest days, when governments were doing absolutely nothing about it, nearly all religious denominations have conducted schools, including colleges, as an integral part of their activities. If the church is to remain absolutely separate and apart from the state, then no court should have the power to compel any church to admit any student to any school operated for religious reasons.

This case may turn out to be the first step of a long, intrusive interference with the exercise of religion. I hope this does not prove to be so.

NOTES AND QUESTIONS

1. Sincerity of Religious Belief

Do you agree with the plurality that the defendant had not demonstrated that its racially exclusionary policy was a manifestation of a sincere religious belief? *See generally* "Developments in the Law: Religion and the State," 100 *Harv. L. Rev.* 1606, 1764–68 (1987) (hereinafter "Religion and the State"). Is it appropriate for the court to examine the religious literature of the church for indications of the roots of the policy? Is this consistent with *Yoder?*

Is a religious belief not reduced to writing to be ignored while the court limits itself to the written religious statements and texts of the group? Or is the plurality simply attempting to distinguish between a Christian "secular" tradition and a nonsecular tradition integrating Christian beliefs and a way of life? *See generally* Galanter, "Religious Freedoms in the United States: A Turning Point?" 1966 *Wis. L. Rev.* 217. Are the issues of religiousness and sincerity simply matters of fact to be proved at trial? If so, who should bear the burden of proof? What are the standards for evaluating those facts? *See generally* Note, "Racial Discrimination in Private Schools, Section 1981, and the Free Exercise of Religion: The Sectarian Loophole of *Runyon v. McCrary*," 48 *Col. L. Rev.* 419, 427–30 (1977). Do both the plurality and Goldberg opinions "threaten a church's right to determine its own religious doctrines"? "Religion and the State," *supra* at 1766.

Did the plurality properly take into consideration the timing of the policy in relation to pending desegregation orders? Does this suggest that recently found doctrine relating to racial separation is more likely to be treated as insincere than doctrine of greater age? Does the lack of specific Biblical references supporting defendant's position indicate that the admissions policy is not a part of a developed theology? What of the references to the Tower of Babel and the "confusion of tongues"? Despite the conventional wisdom that a court may not inquire into the truth or falsity of a religious belief, is there some point at which the logical connections are so attenuated that a court is justified in finding that the beliefs are not sincere? *But see* L. Tribe, *American Constitutional Law* §14-12 (2d ed. 1988) ("[I]nquiry [into sincerity] . . . can be extraordinarily dangerous. The perception of the claimant's sincerity inevitably reflects the fact-finder's view of the reasonableness of the claimant's beliefs.")

Is the plurality on sound ground when it seeks to determine the corporate beliefs of the school rather than the individual beliefs of its members and supporters? *See also Fiedler v. Marumsco Christian School*, 631 F.2d 1144 (4th Cir. 1980). Does the plurality's approach essentially require "virtual unanimity of a church's members before an institutional belief will be recognized"? "Religion and the State," *supra* at 1766. Does the Free Exercise Clause apply to corporate bodies, or do such bodies simply represent the individual beliefs of their members? Does *Yoder* support the plurality's position? Is the plurality simply raising the question of whether the school has standing to raise the interests of parents and students? Was not this issue decided in *Runyon?* In the light of the plurality opinion, are not private nonsecular schools simply encouraged to make sure that their racially discriminatory beliefs and policies are appropriately documented in the charters of their institutions? Might this requirement in itself be a restraint on racial discrimination?

2. Balancing Free Exercise Rights

Is Judge Goldberg correct in concluding that the application of the balancing test articulated in *Yoder* favors the upholding of §1981 as it is applied to private religious schools? *Cf. Goldsboro Christian Schools, Inc. v. United States,* 436 F.Supp. 1314 (E.D. N.C. 1977). Does he ignore a religious "group's right to decide how it will be governed, how issues of religious doctrine and theology will be decided, and who will speak on behalf of the church"? "Religion and the State," *supra* at 1767; Laycock, *supra.* What about the constitutional derivation of the state interest? Is *Yoder* distinguishable in as much as in that case there were less onerous alternatives? What of the notion that the presence of African Americans does not substantially impede religious socialization? Do you agree? What of the relationship between racial intermarriage and school desegregation? Is it attenuated, unreasonable? Does the school have "less onerous" alternatives for seeking to prevent such marriages? Suppose the school expelled a white female for maintaining a romantic relationship with a black male. Would this violate §1981? *See Fiedler v. Marumsco Christian School,* 631 F.2d 1144 (4th Cir. 1980).

Is it appropriate for Judge Goldberg to classify religious beliefs into the categories of major and minor beliefs, or is this simply another way of measuring the degree of intrusion as the court performs its balancing act?

Is the free exercise balancing test so abstract and ill defined that it makes prediction of outcomes in particular cases nearly impossible? Should a strong distinction be drawn between religious beliefs and acts motivated by religious beliefs? *See Employment Division, Department of Human Resources, supra; West Virginia State Board of Education v. Barnette,* 319

U.S. 624, 63 S.Ct. 1178, 87 L.Ed. 1628 (1943) (Justice Frankfurter, dissenting). *See also McDaniel v. Paty,* 435 U.S. 618, 98 S.Ct. 1322, 55 L.Ed.2d 593 (1978); *Cantwell v. Connecticut,* 310 U.S. 296, 60 S.Ct. 900, 84 L.Ed. 1213 (1940); *Hamilton v. Regents of University of California,* 293 U.S. 245, 55 S.Ct. 197, 79 L.Ed. 343 (1934).

When the Congress asserts such a "vital public goal as equality of treatment of blacks and whites," does this in itself constitute an overriding and compelling state interest? *See* Hilton, "Race, Religion, and Constitutional Restraints on Private Schools," 30 *Rutgers L. Rev.* 329, 377 (1977). But does this assertion confuse the issue? If the Thirteenth and Fourteenth Amendments would not reach racially discriminatory practices of private, nonsecular schools, then First Amendment free exercise rights are being balanced against a statutory entitlement. Why should the statutory entitlement prevail? Or is the nature of the state interest such that this is akin to enforcing antipolygamy laws against Mormons? *See United States v. Reynolds,* 98 U.S. 145, 25 L.Ed. 244 (1878). *See also Braunfeld v. Brown,* 366 U.S. 599 (1961) (Sunday closing law).

The *Dade Christian School* case was decided before the Supreme Court's decision in *Employment Division, Department of Human Resources of Oregon v. Smith,* 494 U.S. 872, 110 S.Ct. 1595, 108 L.Ed. 876 (1990), which rejected the balancing test under the Free Exercise Clause for "generally applicable" laws, unless a "hybrid" situation was present as in *Yoder.* Does Judge Goldberg's conclusion that parents "remain free to teach their children that interracial marriage violates religious commands" mean that the Fourteenth Amendment right of parents "to direct the education of their children" is not implicated in this case?

3. Free Exercise and the Bob Jones University Case

In *Bob Jones University v. United States,* 461 U.S. 574, 103 S.Ct. 2017, 76 L.Ed.2d 157 (1983), the Supreme Court upheld the revocation of the tax-exempt status of a religious university and a church-affiliated elementary and secondary school by the Internal Revenue Service (IRS) because of the racially discriminatory practices of those schools. The revocation was based on a revenue ruling issued by the IRS stating that continued exemption of private, racially discriminatory schools was inimical to "public policy." *Id.* at 579. The Court held that the IRS ruling was a fair interpretation of the Internal Revenue Code, *id.* at

585–99, and in accord with the wishes of Congress despite the fact that Congress had not expressly authorized such action, *id.* at 599–603. Although it was conceded that the discriminatory practices of the two schools were based on their religious beliefs, the Court held that eliminating racial discrimination in education was a compelling interest outweighing any Free Exercise or Establishment Clause claims. *Id.* at 602–03, 603 nn. 29–30. If the national interest in nondiscrimination trumps a private school's entitlement to nonprofit tax treatment, as declared in *Bob Jones*, does it follow that *Runyon* prevails over the free exercise claims of private, religious schools practicing racial discrimination? Does *Brown v. Dade Christian Schools* become largely irrelevant, in practical terms, after the later *Bob Jones University* decision?

Ohio Civil Rights Commission v. Dayton Christian Schools, Inc.

477 U.S. 619, 106 S.Ct. 2718, 91 L.Ed.2d 512 (1986).

Justice Rehnquist delivered the opinion of the Court.

Appellee Dayton Christian Schools, Inc. (Dayton) and various individuals brought an action in the United States District Court for the Southern District of Ohio under 42 U.S.C. §1983, seeking to enjoin a pending state administrative proceeding brought against Dayton by appellant Ohio Civil Rights Commission (Commission). Dayton asserted that the Free Exercise and Establishment Clauses of the First Amendment prohibited the Commission from exercising jurisdiction over it or from punishing it for engaging in employment discrimination. The District Court refused to issue the injunction on grounds that any conflict between the First Amendment and the administrative proceedings was not yet ripe, and that in any case the proposed action of the Commission violated neither the Free Exercise nor the Establishment Clause of the First and Fourteenth Amendments. The Court of Appeals for the Sixth Circuit reversed, holding that the exercise of jurisdiction and the enforcement of the statute would impermissibly burden appellees' rights under the Free Exercise Clause and would result in excessive entanglement under the Establishment Clause. . . . We now conclude that we have jurisdiction, and we reverse, holding that the District Court should have abstained under our cases beginning with *Younger v. Harris*, 401 U.S. 37, 91 S.Ct. 746, 27 L.Ed.2d 669 (1971).

* * *

Linda Hoskinson was employed as a teacher at Dayton during the 1978–1979 school year. She subscribed to the Statement of Faith and expressly agreed to resolve disputes internally through the biblical chain of command. In January 1979, she informed her principal, James Rakestraw, that she was pregnant. After consulting with his superiors, Rakestraw informed Hoskinson that her employment contract would not be renewed at the end of the school year because of Dayton's religious doctrine that mothers should stay home with their preschool age children. Instead of appealing this decision internally, Hoskinson contacted an attorney who sent a letter to Dayton's Superintendent, Claude Schindler, threatening litigation based on state and federal sex discrimination laws if Dayton did not agree to rehire Hoskinson for the coming school year.

Upon receipt of this letter, Schindler informed Hoskinson that she was suspended immediately for challenging the nonrenewal decision in a manner inconsistent with the internal dispute resolution doctrine. . . .

Hoskinson filed a complaint with appellant Ohio Civil Rights Commission (Commission), alleging that Dayton's nonrenewal decision constituted sex discrimination, in violation of Ohio Rev. Code Ann. §4112.02(A) (Supp.1985), and that its termination decision penalized her for asserting her rights, in violation of Ohio Rev.Code Ann. §4112.02(I) (Supp.1985). . . .

While these administrative proceedings were pending, Dayton filed this action against the Commission in the United States District Court for the Southern District of Ohio under 42 U.S.C. §1983, seeking a permanent injunction of the state proceedings on the ground that any investigation of Dayton's hiring process or any imposition of sanctions for Dayton's nonrenewal or termination decisions would violate the Religion Clauses of the First Amendment. App. 118–120. The Commission filed a motion to dismiss, arguing, *inter alia*, that the District Court should refrain from enjoining the administrative proceedings based on federal abstention doctrines. . . .

In *Younger v. Harris*, 401 U.S. 37, 91 S.Ct. 746, 27 L.Ed.2d 669 (1971), we held that a federal court should not enjoin a pending state criminal proceeding except in the very unusual situation that an injunction is necessary to prevent great and immediate irreparable injury. We justified our decision both on equitable principles, *id.*, at 43, 91 S.Ct. at 750, and on the "more vital consideration" of the proper respect for the fundamental role of States in our federal system. *Id.*, at 44, 91 S.Ct., at 750. . . .

We have since recognized that our concern for comity and federalism is equally applicable to certain other pending state proceedings. We have applied the *Younger* principle to civil proceedings in which important state interests are involved. . . .

We think the principles enunciated in these [abstention] cases govern the present one. We have no doubt that the elimination of prohibited sex discrimination is a sufficiently important state interest to bring the present case within the ambit of the cited authorities. We also have no reason to doubt that Dayton will receive an adequate opportunity to raise its constitutional claims. Dayton contends that the mere exercise of jurisdiction over it by the state administrative body violates its First Amendment rights. But we have repeatedly rejected the argument that a constitutional attack on state procedures themselves "automatically vitiates the adequacy of those procedures for purposes of the *Younger-Huffman* line of cases.". . .

Even religious schools cannot claim to be wholly free from some state regulation. *Wisconsin v. Yoder,* 406 U.S. 205, 213, 92 S.Ct. 1526, 1532, 32 L.Ed.2d 15 (1972). We therefore think that however Dayton's constitutional claim should be decided on the merits, the Commission violates no constitutional rights by merely investigating the circumstances of Hoskinson's discharge in this case, if only to ascertain whether the ascribed religious-based reason was in fact the reason for the discharge.

Dayton also contends that the administrative proceedings do not afford the opportunity to level constitutional challenges against the potential sanctions for the alleged sex discrimination. In its reply brief in this Court, the Commission cites several rulings to demonstrate that religious justifications for otherwise illegal conduct are considered by it. *See, e.g., In re St. Mary of the Falls,* No. 948 (1975). Dayton in turn relies on a decision of the Supreme Court of Ohio, *Mobil Oil Corp. v. Rocky River,* 38 Ohio St.2d 23, 26, 309 N.E.2d 900, 902 (1974), in which that court held that a local zoning commission could not consider constitutional claims. But even if Ohio law is such that the Commission may not consider the constitutionality of the statute under which it operates, it would seem an unusual doctrine, and one not supported by the cited case, to say that the Commission could not construe its own statutory mandate in the light of fed-

eral constitutional principles. *Cf. NLRB v. Catholic Bishop of Chicago,* 440 U.S. 490, 99 S.Ct. 1313, 59 L.Ed.2d 533 (1979). In any event, it is sufficient . . . that constitutional claims may be raised in state court judicial review of the administrative proceeding. Section 4112.06 of Ohio Rev. Code Ann. (1980) provides that any "respondent claiming to be aggrieved by a final order of the commission . . . may obtain judicial review thereof." Dayton cites us to no Ohio authority indicating that this provision does not authorize judicial review of claims that agency action violates the United States Constitution.

The judgment of the Court of Appeals is therefore reversed and the case remanded for further proceedings consistent with this opinion.

It is so ordered.

Justice Stevens, with whom Justice Brennan, Justice Marshall, and Justice Blackmun join, concurring in the judgment [omitted].

NOTES AND QUESTIONS

1. *The Decision of the Court of Appeals*

The Sixth Circuit Court of Appeals, while reversing the district court's decision in favor of the defendant, affirmed the lower court's finding that the Dayton Christian Schools (DCS) had a dominant religious purpose that permeated all aspects of the educational process including teacher selection. *Dayton Christian Schools, Inc. v. Ohio Civil Rights Commission,* 766 F.2d 932, 936 (6th Cir. 1985), *reversed on other grounds,* 477 U.S. 619, 106 S.Ct. 2718, 91 L.Ed.2d 512 (1986). It quoted with favor the following passage from the district judge's opinion:

> [T]he teachers at DCS are selected because of their ability to blend their avowed religious beliefs into every lesson and school activity. Teachers are required to be born again Christians and to carry with them into their classes the religious fervor and conviction felt necessary to stimulate young minds into accepting Christ as savior. . . [T]he school demands that teachers conform both in thought and conduct to the tenets and principles felt essential to leading a Christian life. The belief system espoused by the members of DCS touches every aspect of their life: work, interpersonal relationships, family and recreational activities. Deviation in any way from what is felt to be the proper religious way of life may cast doubt on a teacher's ability to perform his or her critical role and, may, therefore, be grounds for dismissal.

766 F.2d at 938, quoting 578 F.Supp. at 1018–19. According to the testimony of the DCS superintendent, congregants believe "that the Bible teaches that even though we are equal in the sight of God, our role is different, the role of the female is different than that of the male." Citing various passages of Scriptures, he felt that God's words required that "a woman [be] . . . home with her pre-school age children." 766 F.2d at 934. Further, Ms. Hoskinson's contract with DCS provided that "all differences are to be resolved by utilizing Biblical principles— always presenting a united front." She attested that "[o]bedience to those in authority over you is clearly stated in the Bible. I believe in God's chain of command." 766 F.2d at 939.

Judge Contie, writing for the Court of Appeals, first determined that the Ohio Civil Rights Act covered religious schools, finding that statutory interpretation would not enable the court to avoid the conflict between the Ohio law and the free exercise of religion. *But see NLRB v. Catholic Bishop of Chicago*, 440 U.S. 490, 99 S.Ct. 1313, 59 L.Ed.2d 533 (1979). He also noted that while the Ohio Civil Rights Act was analogous to Title VII of the federal Civil Rights Act (42 U.S.C.A. Section 2000e *et seq.*) in forbidding discrimination on the basis of race, sex, or national origin, the federal law allowed religious educational institutions to discriminate by religion in employment practices. 766 F.2d at 941 n.18, citing 42 U.S.C.A. Sections 2000e-1 and 2000e-2(e)(2). The Ohio law contained no such exemption, and, in any event, he cited a case indicating that the Title VII exemptions for religious institutions may violate the Establishment Clause. *See King's Garden, Inc. v. FCC*, 498 F.2d 51, 55 (D.C. Cir. 1974). Two years later, however, the Supreme Court upheld the Section 2000e-1 exemption. *Corporation of Presiding Bishop v. Amos*, 483 U.S. 327, 107 S.Ct. 2862, 97 L.Ed.2d 273 (1987).

The Sixth Circuit held that the Ohio Civil Rights Act, applied to the Dayton Christian Schools, violated the free exercise of religion rights of the plaintiffs and the "fundamental rights of . . . parents . . . to choose the manner in which their children will be educated, especially with regard to religious values." 766 F.2d at 947. It also found that the very assertion of jurisdiction by the Ohio Civil Rights Commission, including the use of its investigative powers and efforts to cajole a settlement, also violated the First Amendment. In this regard, Judge Contie distinguished *Bob Jones University v. United States*, 461 U.S. 574, 103 S.Ct. 2017, 76 L.Ed.2d 157 (1983):

In *Bob Jones*, the [Supreme] Court upheld denial of tax exempt status to an institution which denied admission to those engaged in interracial dating. In weighing the school's free exercise claim, the Court observed that "[d]enial of tax benefits will inevitably have a substantial impact on the operation of private religious schools, but will not prevent those schools from observing their religious tenets." *Id.* at 603–04, 103 S.Ct. at 2034–35. In the instant case, however, appellants do not have the luxury of simply declining a public benefit. While Bob Jones University is free to continue to practice its religious beliefs free of state intervention, appellants only have the option of either conforming their religiously based employment practices to the secular guidelines promulgated in the Ohio statute or face continued harassing prosecution by the OCRC. . . .

766 F.2d at 952.

The appeals court admitted that the state's interest in eliminating sex discrimination in employment practices was "substantial and compelling," but it noted that "the state is not constitutionally compelled to enact the statute at issue here." 766 F.2d at 954. It also noted that *Runyon v. McCrary*, 427 U.S. 160, 96 S.Ct. 2586, 49 L.Ed.2d 415 (1976), did not reach the question of the constitutionality of applying Section 1981 to private sectarian schools. 766 F.2d at 954 n.40. The court concluded that the state's substantial interest in eliminating sex discrimination "does not justify such a broad and onerous limitation [on free exercise rights]. The state legislation must be 'essential,' and the least drastic means to further the state's interest":

Accommodation of the religious beliefs in this case would not significantly interfere with the state's fulfillment of its goal of eradicating discrimination in employment. The state would still be able to regulate all employment practices of non-religious institutions except where religious belief is implicated. . . . [T]he state might further its interest in eliminating sex discrimination by conditioning receipt of [the benefits of state tax exemptions] . . . on compliance with the Ohio Civil Rights Act.

766 F.2d at 955. Finally, the court held that the assertion of jurisdiction by the Civil Rights Commission violated the entanglement aspect of the Establishment Clause, fostering a continuing and comprehensive state involvement with a religious institution. 766 F.2d at 961.

2. Disposition in the Supreme Court

Chief Justice Rehnquist, writing for the majority, holds that *Younger v. Harris*, 401 U.S. 37, 91 S.Ct. 746, 27 L.Ed.2d 669 (1971), is controlling and that the district court should have abstained from deciding the case during the pendency of the state administrative proceedings. In reaching this conclusion the Court finds that "the Commission violates no constitutional rights by merely investigating the circumstances of Hoskinson's discharge in this case, if only to ascertain whether the ascribed religious-based reason was in fact the reason for the discharge." Is this language consistent with the Sixth Circuit's substantive decision? What of the citation of *Yoder?* Does the majority's reasoning suggest that if the substantive issues were to reach the Supreme Court in a procedurally appropriate posture the Sixth Circuit would be reversed? *Cf. Employment Division, Department of Human Resources v. Smith,* 494 U.S. 872, 110 S.Ct. 1595, 108 L.Ed. 876 (1990).

What of the Chief Justice's remarks about the importance of the state's interest in eliminating prohibited sex discrimination? Is he saying only that there will be adequate opportunity for the Dayton Christian Schools to raise constitutional issues in the state proceeding, or is he suggesting more? Why might *NLRB v. Catholic Bishop of Chicago,* 440 U.S. 490, 99 S.Ct. 1313, 59 L.Ed.2d 533 (1979) be critical to the resolution of the litigation in the state proceedings?

3. *Discrimination and the Free Exercise of Religion*

How should the courts resolve the underlying conflict between the state's interest in banning prohibited sex discrimination or other forms of discrimination in employment (or admissions) and the free exercise of religion in private sectarian schools? Do you agree with Professor Laycock, *supra,* that given the overarching religious mission of church schools such institutions should be largely autonomous with respect to the employment of teachers? Would his reasoning extend to admissions practices? *See Brown v. Dade Christian Schools, Inc.,* 556 F.2d 310, 326 (5th Cir. 1977) (Coleman, J., dissenting). Should the result turn on the type of discrimination? For example, should courts be less deferential to the free exercise of religion and church autonomy where racial discrimination is involved? Is there any principled basis for such a distinction?

What if a church school discriminates in the hiring or retention of teachers on the basis of religion? Should it matter whether the teacher teaches geography, history, theology, or hygiene? *See Maguire v. Marquette University,* 627 F.Supp. 1499 (E.D. Wis. 1986), *aff'd in part on other grounds,* 814 F.2d 1213 (7th Cir. 1987) (court upholds refusal to hire woman

associate professor against a Title VII challenge; plaintiff alleged sex discrimination; defendant argued that she was rejected "because of her perceived hostility to the institutional church and its teachings.") *See* Laycock and Waelbroeck, "Academic Freedom and the Free Exercise of Religion," 66 *Tex. L. Rev.* 1001, 1009 (1988). Are the free exercise concerns more or less important in the university setting?

VI. STATE AID TO PRIVATE SCHOOLS

A. *Pierce* Extended: A Right to a State-Financed Nonpublic Education?

In the preceding sections, discussion focused on the degree to which state and federal governments regulate nonpublic education. That inquiry was necessitated in part by the nature of the *Pierce* compromise. If parents are to have rights to send their children to private schools, private schools subject to reasonable regulation by government, then inevitably courts and legislative bodies must decide what reasonable regulation is. If government remains entirely detached from nonpublic education, taking a strongly libertarian view, there is the danger that the education provided in the private sector will not satisfy the objectives of compulsory attendance laws. If government regulates with a heavy hand, seeking to stamp out any variation from the public school program, then parental choice becomes meaningless. The question of private schools becomes even more acute where parental choices are grounded in religious convictions. As Mark DeWolfe Howe once so elegantly described *Pierce* and *Meyer,*

> In the English language case and in the case of the Society of Sisters, the Court was consciously endeavoring, for one reason or another, to find a ground for what it conceived to be a liberating decision that would do something more than set religion free. This aim seems not unlike that which Mr. Justice Jackson later sought to achieve in his flag-salute opinion [*West Virginia State Board of Education v. Barnette,* 319 U.S. 624 (1943), chapter 2, *infra*]—the aim, that is, of offering to all sincere objectors, not merely to those whose consciences were moved by religious conviction, an assurance that the Constitution provides them protection against senseless tyrannies.

M.D. Howe, *The Garden and the Wilderness* 124 (1965).

But if the goal of the *Pierce* compromise is to promote parental choice, and therefore presumably educational diversity, perhaps more than the absence of unreasonable restrictions on nonpublic education is required. That parents are free of direct regulatory restraints on securing a nonpublic education for their children does not necessarily mean that they, in fact, will have the capacity to choose; private education costs money. And parents who would choose a private school would be required to continue paying school taxes for public schools, while simultaneously absorbing the cost of private school tuition. Many parents will not be sufficiently affluent to bear this double burden; hence, economic circumstances may compel the selection of public schools. As Professor Arons has argued, the present system of public education "confronts the dissenting family with a choice between giving up its basic values and beliefs as the price of gaining a 'free' education in a government school or paying twice in order to preserve its First Amendment rights." S. Arons, *Compelling Belief* 212 (1983). Put somewhat differently, liberty may consist not only of the absence of restrictions on choice (negative liberty) but also the presence of sufficient knowledge and resources to enable the individual to select among alternative courses of action (affirmative liberty). *See generally* I. Berlin, *Four Essays on Liberty* (1969). As Professors Coons and Sugarman have cogently put the argument,

> On grounds of simple fairness children should be guaranteed reasonable access to education whatever their parents' views. . . . The humane response is that the right to education should not be limited by parental resources; parental duty [to educate] means nothing to the child if the family cannot afford to educate him. Therefore, additional collective action is necessary, and unless the child is to be taken from his parents, this requires a subsidy of the parents by the state. Only in that way can the child's hope for education be delivered from the economic limitations of his family.

J. Coons and S. Sugarman, *Education by Choice* 11 (1978).

The question of public support for private education, through subsidies to parents or private schools or otherwise, may be approached as a matter of policy, limited by applicable constitutional principles on the establishment of religion, or as a matter of constitutional entitlement. The former is taken up in the next section. See also the discussion of education vouchers, chapter 8, *infra*. The latter is the focus of attention in the present section.

A number of commentators argue that a broad reading of *Pierce* leads to the conclusion that government, if it is to remain truly neutral with regard to parental education decisions, must subsidize those

decisions. *See, e.g.,* Ball, "Economic Freedom of Parental Choice in Education: The Pennsylvania Constitution," 101 *Dick. L. Rev.* 261 (1997); Arons, *supra*; Arons, "The Separation of School and State: *Pierce* Reconsidered," 46 *Harv. Educ. Rev.* 76, 100–01 (1976); Areen, "Alternative Schools: Better Guardians than Family or State?" 81 *Sch. Rev.* 175 (1973); Areen, "The Judiciary and Education Reform: A Reassessment," 61 *Geo. L. Rev.* 1009 (1973); Areen, "Tuition Vouchers," 6 *Harv. C.R.-C.L. L. Rev.* 446 (1971); Areen, "Public Aid to Nonpublic Schools: A Breach of the Sacred Wall?" 22 *Case West L. Rev.* 230 (1971). The question of constitutionally compelled subsidization of nonpublic education rarely has been adjudicated by the courts, but in those few cases, and in dicta in other cases, the courts have responded negatively to the idea. *See Harris v. McRae,* 448 U.S. 297, 100 S.Ct. 2671, 65 L.Ed.2d 784 (1980) (dicta); *Strout v. Albanese,* 178 F.3d 57 (1st Cir. 1999) (no constitutional violation where cost of religious education must be borne by parents and not the state); *Bagley v. Raymond Sch. Dept.,* 728 A.2d 127 (Me.1999), *cert. denied,* 528 U.S. 947, 120 S.Ct. 364, 145 L.Ed.2d 285 (1999) (statute does not substantially burden free exercise of religion when it merely makes the practice of the individual's religious beliefs more expensive); *Exeter-West Greenwich Regional School District v. Pontarelli,* 460 A.2d 934 (R.I. 1983); *Brusca v. State of Missouri,* 332 F.Supp. 275 (E.D. Mo. 1971), *aff'd,* 405 U.S. 1050, 92 S.Ct. 1493, 31 L.Ed.2d 786 (1972) (per curiam). *See generally* "Developments in the Law: Religion and the State," 100 *Harv. L. Rev.* 1606, 1695–97 (1987).

Suppose parents of students in church schools argue that the failure of the state to subsidize religious schools violates the neutrality that the state is bound to follow under the religion clauses. That is, parents choosing church schools would have to pay twice — property and other taxes to support the public schools that their children did not attend and tuition to the private schools that they did attend. *Cf. Mueller v. Allen,* 463 U.S. 388, 396, 103 S.Ct. 3062, 3068, 77 L.Ed.2d 721 (1983). From this perspective, the forfeiture of the state subsidy "can plausibly be viewed as a penalty on the exercise of a constitutional right." Laycock, "A Survey of Religious Liberty in the United States," 47 *Ohio St. L.J.* 409, 444 (1986). *See Meek v. Pittenger,* 421 U.S. 349, 387, 95 S.Ct. 1753, 1174, 44 L.Ed.2d 217 (1975) (Burger, C.J., dissenting). Might such neutrality, defined in terms of equalizing the burdens for parents of children in church schools, amount to state aid of religion and hence a violation of the Establishment Clause? Which of these positions makes more sense? *See* West, "Constitutional Judgment on Nonpublic School Aid: Fresh Guidelines or New Roadblocks," 35 *Emory L.J.* 795, 815–21 (1986). Is a failure to subsidize church schools a denial of equal treatment to religion or a requirement of the Establishment Clause? *See* M. Perry, *Religion in Politics: Constitutional and Moral Perspectives* 20 (1997); Laycock, *supra* at 444.

Is the state required to subsidize religious alternatives in every sphere in which it provides a state service lest it be accused of favoring its own secular program? If free exercise of religion is a protected liberty like free speech, does it follow that the state must subsidize it? Must the state subsidize private newspapers? Must it open its auditoriums and universities to private speakers? Is the implication of all this that the Free Exercise Clause embodies the concept of negative liberty, whereas the Establishment Clause forbids the state from affirmatively fostering religious liberty? *See generally* Merel, "The Protection of Individual Choice: A Consistent Understanding of Religion Under the First Amendment," 45 *U. Chi. L. Rev.* 805 (1978). Does the Constitution require that all private schools, subject to reasonable regulation, be aided or that none be aided?

Consider these comments by Jesse H. Choper:

> Significant doctrinal questions arise under both the Religion Clauses and the Free Speech Clause in respect to two types of education finance plans. . . . In the first, the state decides only to assist public schools, leaving all private schools (secular and sectarian) without government funding. In the second, under which the state supports nonpublic schools as well, we assume that including parochial schools is constitutionally permissible but that a state implements a system that excludes religious schools from the plan.
>
> * * *
>
> In *Hialeah* [*Church of the Lukumi Babalu Aye, Inc. v. City of Hialeah*, 508 U.S. 520, 113 S.Ct. 2217, 124 L.Ed. 472 (1993)], the Court held that "at a minimum, the protections of the Free Exercise Clause pertain if the law at issue discriminates against some or all religious beliefs or regulates or prohibits conduct because it is undertaken for religious reasons." Does the state discriminate against religion when it funds only public schools?. . . The obvious counterargument is that the state is not discriminating against religion as such but rather against all nonpublic schools. . . . [I]t would likely be concluded that the public-nonpublic distinc-

tion has too loose a fit to be considered discrimination against religion. Rather, the state program would likely be characterized as neutral and generally applicable, such that any incidental burden on religion would not have constitutional significance.

> * * *
>
> While the traditional exclusive funding of public education may survive constitutional challenge . . ., if a state were to craft a voucher program that excluded religious schools but included other nonreligious private schools, the program might well run afoul of both free speech and free exercise precepts. First, such a program would plainly discriminate on its face against "some or all religious beliefs," violating the basic protections of the Free Exercise Clause, unless justified after strict scrutiny. . . . Second, since all schools teach values, the state could be fairly seen as discriminating against religious viewpoints . . ., and would also be subject to strict scrutiny under the Free Speech Clause. Unless Establishment Clause concerns with providing support to parochial schools are found to present a compelling government interest— and I am assuming otherwise in this discussion . . . the inclusion of religious school[s] in any voucher program or other plan of aid to education that included nonreligious private schools [would appear to be compelled].

Choper, "Federal Constitutional Issues," in S.D. Sugarman and F. R. Kemerer (eds.), *School Choice and Social Controversy* 235, 246, 248–49 (1999).

Maine pays grants directly to private schools on behalf of those students who live in districts that do not have public high schools because of their sparse student populations, as long as those private schools are nonsectarian. The parents of several students, otherwise qualified to receive the state-created subsidy, wish to send their children to private sectarian schools. Do the parents have a plausible argument that the statute violates the Establishment Clause because, rather than treating religion neutrally, it demonstrates a hostility toward religion by excluding otherwise eligible sectarian schools from the tuition program based solely on the religious viewpoint presented by these schools? Can parents claim that the statute violates the Equal Protection Clause by discriminating against them on the basis of religion, speech content, and association? *See Strout v. Albanese*, 178 F.3d 57 (1st Cir. 1999); *Bagley v. Raymond Sch. Dept.*, 728 A.2d 127 (Me. 1999); *cert. denied*, 528 U.S. 947, 120 S.Ct. 364 145 L.Ed.2d 285, (1999). *Cf. Rosenberger v. Rector & Visitors of the*

Univ. of Va., 515 U.S. 819, 115 S.Ct. 2510, 132 L.Ed.2d 700 (1995). *See* Note, "See Jane Read the Bible: Does the Establishment Clause Allow School Choice Programs to Include Sectarian Schools After *Agostini v. Felton?*" 56 *Wash. & Lee L. Rev.* 721 (1999); Note, "Educational Vouchers and the Religion Clauses Under *Agostini:* Resurrection, Insurrection, and a New Direction," 49 *Case W. Res. L. Rev.* 747 (1999).

B. State Aid to Private Schools and the Constitution

"School Choice and Public Funding"

S.D. Sugarman, in S.D. Sugarman and F. R. Kemerer (eds.), *School Choice and Social Controversy* 111, 113, 125–27, 130–31 (1999).

In the United States, public funding of elementary and secondary education is largely (but not entirely) reserved for the public schools. More than 90 percent of the money for American public education comes from local and state taxes. . . . Generally speaking, school taxes that are locally assessed and collected (primarily property taxes) are spent by the local school district. (See chapter 7, *infra.*)

* * *

If the children's rights and common good arguments justify taxpayer support for elementary and secondary education, it is yet not clear why this financial support should go only to those who attend public schools. Note that, in a world of subsidized education, choice is not about the abstract right to select a school for one's child. That right is already guaranteed to parents by the U.S. Constitution. [*See Pierce v. Society of Sisters*, 268 U.S. 510, 45 S.Ct. 571, 69 L.Ed. 1070 (1925).] The real issue is whether the family's choice is subsidized.

* * *

If there is a principled defense of the (near) exclusive funding of public education, we should look for it in the underlying reasons for public funding of education at all. Basically, the argument must be that only through public education can society be confident that pupils will be steeped in tolerance and the values of democracy and that the money will be used to bring about their education. By contrast, the strongest fear must be that were nonpublic schools

equally subsidized, they might turn out to be subversive, intolerant, or fraudulent, thereby undermining, instead of achieving, children's rights and common good objectives. A more moderate argument for exclusive funding of public education is that private education too much promotes private, rather than public, goals. This outlook is reflected in one conventional understanding of the religion clauses of the First Amendment—that is, while religious exercise must be ensured, it ought not be subsidized.

Supporters of subsidized private school choice, of course, reject the premises of both the stronger and the milder arguments against the funding of nonpublic education. They see private schools as promoting public objectives in the same way that they see private providers as serving the public good in programs like food stamps, medicaid, and section 8 subsidized housing. But in America the political reality from nearly the beginning of our system of public education has been largely to restrict public funding to public schools.

* * *

In the period between 1875 and World War II, there was widespread political and societal hostility toward private schools, especially Catholic schools. In the late 1800s a majority of states adopted constitutional provisions (generally called Blaine amendments) designed to prevent their legislatures from ever providing any assistance to these schools. Before then, before we had public education in the way we know it today, some states financially supported both Protestant and Catholic schools.[12]

After World War II, this legislative hostility began to thaw, and some states began to pass modest measures especially aimed at assisting pupils enrolled in private schools. Public officials realized that the public schools were getting away with not having to educate pupils who would otherwise be a substantial burden on the public purse; they appreciated the reality that taxpayers had an interest in making sure the private education sector did not collapse financially. Moreover, parents of children attending private schools complained about having to pay twice, and some modest assistance might ameliorate those complaints. The willingness to provide any assistance to private schools also signaled an acknowledgment that these schools were not undermining the collective educational goals for the country's children. But although the U.S. Supreme Court agreed that states could offer religious school users both bus rides and

---

[12]Doyle, "Vouchers for Religious Schools," *Public Interest* 88 (March 1997).

textbooks, in a series of decisions issued during the 1970s, it put substantial roadblocks in the way of further public support of religious schools.[13]

In recent years, the Supreme Court has eased its opposition to certain types of state assistance to pupils attending private schools, including religious schools. Minnesota enacted a law that made a limited amount of private school tuition payment deductible for state tax law purposes, at the same time granting a similar deduction for education costs connected to public schooling. The Supreme Court upheld this measure. The Court also upheld the provision of federal compensatory education services to low-income children attending religious schools.[14]

As a result, in many states private schools benefit from public support in several small ways. The conventional approach remains one of permitting private school students to participate in certain categorical aid programs, most commonly receiving not only free bus rides to school or free textbooks but also a range of targeted, clearly secular, educational services. How much financial aid, if any, is actually provided in any state remains, of course, a matter of state politics, and in some states powerful opposition still exists to assisting private school users. Moreover . . ., some state constitutions are so restrictive that financial support that would be allowed under the federal constitution is nonetheless forbidden.

Although private nonprofit schools also benefit indirectly from the fact that voluntary charitable contributions to them are typically deductible under state and federal tax laws and from the fact that in some states their property is not subject to property taxes,[15] all of this assistance taken together still constitutes a very small amount of financial support of private schools as compared with public schools.

* * *

Some advocates of publicly funded school vouchers valid for use in private schools argue that competition will produce more effective schools. They claim that both children's rights and the common good will be better served by having public and private schools compete for pupils. Public funding of private schools has been seen as the way to bring the power of the market and competition to elementary and secondary education in the way, for example, that Federal Express and United Parcel Service have brought competition to the U.S. Postal Service. . . .

* * *

Other advocates of subsidized private school choice emphasize pluralism. They argue that tolerance would be promoted by trusting parents and by allowing a wide range of family groups with similar values to have their own schools. Rather than undermining our democratic values (as school voucher opponents claim), supporters insist that empowering the ordinary family to take charge of its children's educational goals is fundamental to our democracy. . . .

. . .[In the debate about subsidized private school choice, including religious schools, proponents] emphasize fairness to families with religious beliefs: Why should they have to pay twice to get the schooling they want for their children? Moreover, some pragmatists would argue that the religious-based controversies that now haunt public schools — school prayers, the teaching of evolution and sex education, and so on — would largely disappear if those with strong religious beliefs were enabled to form their own schools with public support.

* * *

Mueller v. Allen
463 U.S. 388, 103 S.Ct. 3062, 77 L.Ed.2d 721 (1983).

Justice Rehnquist delivered the opinion of the Court.

Minnesota allows taxpayers, in computing their state income tax, to deduct certain expenses incurred in providing for the education of their children. Minn.Stat. §290.09(22).[1] The United States Court of

---

[13]*Everson v. Board of Education*, 330 U.S. 1 (1947), and *Board of Education v. Allen*, 392 U.S. 236 (1968); *Lemon v. Kurtzman*, 403 U.S. 602 (1971); and *Committee for Public Education v. Nyquist*, 413 U.S. 756 (1973).

[14]*Mueller v. Allen*, 463 U.S. 388 (1983); *Agostini v. Felton*, 115 S.Ct.2510 (1995).

[15]*Waltz v. Tax Commission*, 397 U.S. 664 (1970).

[1]Minn.Stat. §290.09(22) (1982) permits a taxpayer to deduct from his or her computation of gross income the following:

"*Tuition and transportation expense.* The amount he has paid to others, not to exceed $500 for each dependent in grades K to 6 and $700 for each dependent in grades 7 to 12, for tuition, textbooks and transportation of each dependent in attending an elementary or secondary school situated in Minnesota, North Dakota, South Dakota, Iowa, or Wisconsin, wherein a resident of this state may legally fulfill the state's compulsory attendance laws, which is not operated for profit, and which adheres to the provisions of the Civil Rights Act of 1964 and chapter 363. As used in this subdivision, 'textbooks' shall mean and include books and other instructional materials and equipment used in elementary and secondary schools in teaching only those subjects legally and commonly taught in public elementary and secondary schools in this state and shall not include instructional books and materials used in the teaching of religious tenets, doctrines or worship, the purpose of which is to inculcate such tenets, doctrines or worship, nor shall it include such books or materials for, or transportation to, extracurricular activities including sporting events, musical or dramatic events, speech activities, driver's education, or programs of a similar nature."

Appeals for the Eighth Circuit held that the Establishment Clause of the First and Fourteenth Amendments was not offended by this arrangement. Because this question was reserved in *Committee for Public Education v. Nyquist*, 413 U.S. 756 . . . (1973), and because of a conflict between the decision of the Court of Appeals for the Eighth Circuit and that of the Court of Appeals for the First Circuit in *Rhode Island Federation of Teachers v. Norberg*, 630 F.2d 855 (CA1 1980), we granted certiorari. . . . We now affirm.

Minnesota, like every other state, provides its citizens with free elementary and secondary schooling. Minn.Stat. §§ 120.06, 120.72. . . . [A]bout 820,000 students attended this school system in the most recent school year. During the same year, approximately 91,000 elementary and secondary students attended some 500 privately supported schools located in Minnesota, and about 95 percent of these students attended schools considering themselves to be sectarian.

Minnesota . . . permits state taxpayers to claim a deduction from gross income for certain expenses incurred in educating their children. The deduction is limited to actual expenses incurred for the "tuition, textbooks and transportation" of dependents attending elementary or secondary schools. A deduction may not exceed $500 per dependent in grades K through six and $700 per dependent in grades seven through twelve. Minn.Stat. § 290.09.[2]

Petitioners—certain Minnesota taxpayers—sued in the United States District Court for the District of Minnesota claiming that §290.09(22) violated the Establishment Clause by providing financial assis-

tance to sectarian institutions. They named as respondents the Commissioner of the Department of Revenue of Minnesota and several parents who took advantage of the tax deduction for expenses incurred in sending their children to parochial schools. The District Court granted respondent's motion for summary judgment, holding that the statute was "neutral on its face and in its application and does not have a primary effect of either advancing or inhibiting religion." 514 F.Supp. 998, 1003 (D.Minn.1981). On appeal, the Court of Appeals affirmed, concluding that the Minnesota statute substantially benefited a "broad class of Minnesota citizens."

* * *

One fixed principle in this field is our consistent rejection of the argument that "any program which in some manner aids an institution with a religious affiliation" violates the Establishment Clause. . . . For example, it is now well established that a state may reimburse parents for expenses incurred in transporting their children to school, *Everson v. Board of Education*, 330 U.S. 1 . . . (1947), and that it may loan secular textbooks to all schoolchildren within the state, *Board of Education v. Allen*, 392 U.S. 236 . . . (1968).

Notwithstanding the repeated approval given programs such as those in *Allen* and *Everson*, our decisions also have struck down arrangements resembling, in many respects, these forms of assistance. *See, e.g., Lemon v. Kurtzman*, . . . [403 U.S. 602 (1971)]; *Levitt v. Committee for Public Education*, 413 U.S. 472 . . . (1972); *Meek v. Pittenger*, 421 U.S.

---

[2]Both lower courts found that the statute permits deduction of a range of educational expenses. The District Court found that deductible expenses included:

"1. Tuition in the ordinary sense.

2. Tuition to public school students who attend public schools outside their residence school districts.

3. Certain summer school tuition.

4. Tuition charged by a school for slow learner private tutoring services.

5. Tuition for instruction provided by an elementary or secondary school to students who are physically unable to attend classes at such school.

6. Tuition charged by a private tutor or by a school that is not an elementary or secondary school if the instruction is acceptable for credit in an elementary or secondary school.

7. Montessori School tuition for grades K through 12.

8. Tuition for driver education when it is part of the school curriculum." 514 F.Supp. at 1000.

The Court of Appeals concurred in this finding.

In addition, the District Court found that the statutory deduction for "textbooks" included not only "secular textbooks" but also:

"1. Cost of tennis shoes and sweatsuits for physical education.

2. Camera rental fees paid to the school for photography classes.

3. Ice skates rental fee paid to the school.

4. Rental fee paid to the school for calculators for mathematics classes.

5. Costs of home economics materials needed to meet minimum requirements.

6. Costs of special metal or wood needed to meet minimum requirements of shop classes.

7. Costs of supplies needed to meet minimum requirements of art classes.

8. Rental fees paid to the school for musical instruments.

9. Cost of pencils and special notebooks required for class." *Ibid.*

The Court of Appeals accepted this finding.

349 . . . (1975); *Wolman v. Walter*, 433 U.S. 229, 237–238. . . (1977).[3] In this case we are asked to decide whether Minnesota's tax deduction bears greater resemblance to those types of assistance to parochial schools we have approved, or to those we have struck down. Petitioners place particular reliance on our decision in *Committee for Public Education v. Nyquist, supra*, where we held invalid a New York statute providing public funds for the maintenance and repair of the physical facilities of private schools and granting thinly disguised "tax benefits," actually amounting to tuition grants, to the parents of children attending private schools. As explained below, we conclude that §290.09(22) bears less resemblance to the arrangement struck down in *Nyquist* than it does to assistance programs upheld in our prior decisions and those discussed with approval in *Nyquist*.

The general nature of our inquiry in this area has been guided, since the decision in *Lemon v. Kurtzman*, 403 U.S. 602 . . . (1971), by the "three-part" test laid down in that case: "First, the statute must have a secular legislative purpose; second, its principal or primary effect must be one that neither advances nor inhibits religion . . .; finally, the statute must not foster 'an excessive government entanglement with religion.' " *Id.*, at 612–613. . . . While this principle is well settled, our cases have also emphasized that it provides "no more than [a] helpful signpost" in dealing with Establishment Clause challenges. *Hunt v. McNair, supra*. 413 U.S., at 741. . . . With this caveat in mind, we turn to the specific challenges raised against §290.09(22) under the *Lemon* framework.

Little time need be spent on the question of whether the Minnesota tax deduction has a secular purpose. Under our prior decisions, governmental assistance programs have consistently survived this inquiry even when they have run afoul of other aspects of the *Lemon* framework. . . . This reflects, at least in part, our reluctance to attribute unconstitutional motives to the states, particularly when a plausible secular purpose for the state's program may be discerned from the face of the statute.

A state's decision to defray the cost of educational expenses incurred by parents—regardless of the type of schools their children attend—evidences a purpose that is both secular and understandable. An educated populace is essential to the political and economic health of any community, and a state's efforts to assist parents in meeting the rising cost of educational expenses plainly serves this secular purpose of ensuring that the state's citizenry is well educated. Similarly, Minnesota, like other states, could conclude that there is a strong public interest in assuring the continued financial health of private schools, both sectarian and nonsectarian. By educating a substantial number of students such schools relieve public schools of a correspondingly great burden—to the benefit of all taxpayers. In addition, private schools may serve as a benchmark for public schools, in a manner analogous to the "TVA yardstick" for private power companies. . . .

We turn therefore to the more difficult but related question whether the Minnesota statute has "the primary effect of advancing the sectarian aims of the nonpublic schools." *Committee for Public Education v. Regan*, 444 U.S. 646, 662. . . . In concluding that it does not, we find several features of the Minnesota tax deduction particularly significant. First, an essential feature of Minnesota's arrangement is the fact that §290.09(22) is only one among many deductions—such as those for medical expenses, Minn.Stat. §290.09(10) and charitable contributions, Minn.Stat. §290.21—available under the Minnesota tax laws.[5] Our decisions consistently have recognized that traditionally "[l]egislatures have especially broad latitude in creating classifications and distinctions in tax statutes," *Regan v. Taxation with Representation*, 461 U.S. 540, 547 (1983). . . . Under our prior decisions, the Minnesota legislature's judgment that a deduction for educational expenses fairly equalizes the tax burden of its citizens and en-

---

[3]In *Lemon v. Kurtzman, supra*, the Court concluded that the state's reimbursement of nonpublic schools for the cost of teachers' salaries, textbooks, and instructional materials, and its payment of a salary supplement to teachers in nonpublic schools, resulted in excessive entanglement of church and state. In *Levitt v. Committee for Public Education, supra*, we struck down on Establishment Clause grounds a state program reimbursing nonpublic schools for the cost of teacher-prepared examinations. Finally, in *Meek v. Pittenger, supra*, and *Wolman v. Walter, supra*, we held unconstitutional a direct loan of instructional materials to nonpublic schools, while upholding the loan of textbooks to individual students.

[5]Deductions for charitable contributions, allowed by Minnesota law, Minn.Stat. §290.21, include contributions to religious institutions, and exemptions from property tax for property used for charitable purposes under Minnesota law include property used for wholly religious purposes, Minn.Stat. §272.02. In each case, it may be that religious institutions benefit very substantially from the allowance of such deductions. The Court's holding in *Walz v. Tax Commission*, 397 U.S. 664 . . . (1970), indicates, however, that this does not require the conclusion that such provisions of a state's tax law violate the Establishment Clause.

courages desirable expenditures for educational purposes is entitled to substantial deference.[6]

Other characteristics of §290.09(22) argue equally strongly for the provision's constitutionality. Most importantly, the deduction is available for educational expenses incurred by *all* parents, including those whose children attend public schools and those whose children attend non-sectarian private schools or sectarian private schools. Just as in *Widmar v. Vincent*, 454 U.S. 263 . . . (1981), where we concluded that the state's provision of a forum neutrally "open to a broad class of nonreligious as well as religious speakers" does not "confer any imprimatur of State approval," so here: "the provision of benefits to so broad a spectrum of groups is an important index of secular effect."

In this respect, as well as others, this case is vitally different from the scheme struck down in *Nyquist*. There, public assistance amounting to tuition grants was provided only to parents of children in nonpublic schools. This fact had considerable bearing on our decision striking down the New York statute at issue; we explicitly distinguished both *Allen* and *Everson* on the grounds that "In both cases the class of beneficiaries included *all* schoolchildren, those in public as well as those in private schools," 413 U.S., at 782, n. 38 . . . (emphasis in original). Moreover, we intimated that "public assistance (e.g., scholarships) made available generally without regard to the sectarian-nonsectarian or public-nonpublic nature of the institution benefited," *ibid.*, might not offend the Establishment Clause. We think the tax deduction adopted by Minnesota is more similar to this latter type of program than it is to the arrangement struck down in *Nyquist*. Unlike the assistance at issue in *Nyquist*, §290.09(22) permits all parents — whether their children attend public school or private — to deduct their children's educational expenses. . . . [A] program, like §290.09(22), that neutrally provides state assistance to a broad spectrum of citizens is not readily subject to challenge under the Establishment Clause.

We also agree with the Court of Appeals that, by channeling whatever assistance it may provide to parochial schools through individual parents, Minnesota has reduced the Establishment Clause objections to which its action is subject. It is true, of course, that financial assistance provided to parents ultimately has an economic effect comparable to that of aid given directly to the schools attended by their children. It is also true, however, that under Minnesota's arrangement public funds become available only as a result of numerous, private choices of individual parents of school-age children. For these reasons, we recognized in *Nyquist* that the means by which state assistance flows to private schools is of some importance: we said that "the fact that aid is disbursed to parents rather than to . . . schools" is a material consideration in Establishment Clause analysis, albeit "only one among many to be considered." *Nyquist*, at 781, 93 S.Ct., at 2970. It is noteworthy that all but one of our recent cases invalidating state aid to parochial schools have involved the direct transmission of assistance from the state to the schools themselves. The exception, of course, was *Nyquist*, which, as discussed previously, is distinguishable from this case on other grounds. Where, as here, aid to parochial schools is available only as a result of decisions of individual parents no "imprimatur of State approval," *Widmar*, at 274, 102 S.Ct., at 276, can be deemed to have been conferred on any particular religion, or on religion generally.

We find it useful, in the light of the foregoing characteristics of §290.09(22), to compare the attenuated financial benefits flowing to parochial schools from the section to the evils against which the Establishment Clause was designed to protect. These dangers are well-described by our statement that "what is at stake as a matter of policy [in Establishment Clause cases] is preventing that kind and degree of

---

[6]Our decision in *Nyquist* is not to the contrary on this point. We expressed considerable doubt there that the "tax benefits" provided by New York law properly could be regarded as parts of a genuine system of tax laws. Plainly, the outright grants to low-income parents did not take the form of ordinary tax benefits. As to the benefits provided to middle-income parents, the Court said:

"The amount of the deduction is unrelated to the amount of money actually expended by any parent on tuition, but is calculated on the basis of a formula contained in the statute. The formula is apparently the product of a legislative attempt to assure that each family would receive a carefully estimated net benefit, and that the tax benefit would be comparable to, and compatible with, the tuition grant for lower income families."

Indeed, the question whether a program having the elements of a "genuine tax deduction" would be constitutionally acceptable was expressly reserved in *Nyquist, supra*, 413 U.S. at 790, n. 49. . . . While the economic consequences of the program in *Nyquist* and that in this case may be difficult to distinguish, we have recognized on other occasions that "the form of the [state's assistance to parochial schools must be examined] for the light that it casts on the substance." *Lemon v. Kurtzman, supra*, 403 U.S., at 614. . . . The fact that the Minnesota plan embodies a "genuine tax deduction" is thus of some relevance, especially given the traditional rule of deference accorded legislative classifications in tax statutes.

government involvement in religious life that, as history teaches us, is apt to lead to strife and frequently strain a political system to the breaking point." *Nyquist, supra*, 413 U.S., at 796 . . . quoting, *Walz v. Tax Comm'n*, 397 U.S., at 694 . . . (Harlan, J., concurring). It is important, however, to "keep these issues in perspective":

> "At this point in the 20th century we are quite far removed from the dangers that prompted the Framers to include the Establishment Clause in the Bill of Rights. . . . The risk of significant religious or denominational control over our democratic processes — or even of deep political division along religious lines — is remote, and when viewed against the positive contributions of sectarian schools, and such risk seems entirely tolerable in light of the continuing oversight of this Court."

Wolman, 433 U.S., at 263 . . . (Powell, J., concurring in part, concurring in the judgment in part, and dissenting in part).

The Establishment Clause of course extends beyond prohibition of a state church or payment of state funds to one or more churches. We do not think, however, that its prohibition extends to the type of tax deduction established by Minnesota. The historic purposes of the clause simply do not encompass the sort of attenuated financial benefit, ultimately controlled by the private choices of individual parents, that eventually flows to parochial schools from the neutrally available tax benefit at issue in this case.

Petitioners argue that, notwithstanding the facial neutrality of §290.09(22), in application the statute primarily benefits religious institutions. Petitioners rely, as they did below, on a statistical analysis of the type of persons claiming the tax deduction. They contend that most parents of public school children incur no tuition expenses, *see* Minn.Stat. §120.06, and that other expenses deductible under §290.09(22) are negligible in value; moreover, they claim that 96 percent of the children in private schools in 1978–1979 attended religiously-affiliated institutions. Because of all this, they reason, the bulk of deductions taken under §290.09(22) will be claimed by parents of children in sectarian schools. Respondents reply that petitioners have failed to consider the impact of deductions for items such as transportation, summer school tuition, tuition paid by parents whose children attended schools outside the school districts in which they resided, rental or

purchase costs for a variety of equipment, and tuition for certain types of instruction not ordinarily provided in public schools.

We need not consider these contentions in detail. We would be loath to adopt a rule grounding the constitutionality of a facially neutral law on annual reports reciting the extent to which various classes of private citizens claimed benefits under the law. Such an approach would scarcely provide the certainty that this field stands in need of, nor can we perceive principled standards by which such statistical evidence might be evaluated. Moreover, the fact that private persons fail in a particular year to claim the tax relief to which they are entitled — under a facially neutral statute — should be of little importance in determining the constitutionality of the statute permitting such relief.

. . . If parents of children in private schools choose to take especial advantage of the relief provided by §290.09(22), it is no doubt due to the fact that they bear a particularly great financial burden in educating their children. More fundamentally, whatever unequal effect may be attributed to the statutory classification can fairly be regarded as a rough return for the benefits, discussed above, provided to the state and all taxpayers by parents sending their children to parochial schools. In the light of all this, we believe it wiser to decline to engage in the type of empirical inquiry into those persons benefitted by state law which petitioners urge.

Thus, we hold that the Minnesota tax deduction for educational expenses satisfies the primary effect inquiry of our Establishment Clause cases.

Turning to the third part of the *Lemon* inquiry, we have no difficulty in concluding that the Minnesota statute does not "excessively entangle" the state in religion. The only plausible source of the "comprehensive, discriminating, and continuing state surveillance," 403 U.S., at 619 . . ., necessary to run afoul of this standard would lie in the fact that state officials must determine whether particular textbooks qualify for a deduction. In making this decision, state officials must disallow deductions taken from "instructional books and materials used in the teaching of religious tenets, doctrines, or worship, the purpose of which is to inculcate such tenets, doctrines, or worship." Minn.Stat. §290.09(22). Making decisions such as this does not differ substantially from making the types of decisions approved in earlier opinions of this Court. In *Board of Education v.*

Allen, 392 U.S. 236 . . . (1968), for example, the Court upheld the loan of secular textbooks to parents or children attending nonpublic schools; though state officials were required to determine whether particular books were or were not secular, the system was held not to violate the Establishment Clause. . . . The same result follows in this case.

For the foregoing reasons, the judgment of the Court of Appeals is

Affirmed.

Justice Marshall, with whom Justice Brennan, Justice Blackmun and Justice Stevens join, dissenting.

The Establishment Clause of the First Amendment prohibits a State from subsidizing religious education, whether it does so directly or indirectly. In my view, this principle of neutrality forbids not only the tax benefits struck down in *Committee for Public Education v. Nyquist*, 413 U.S. 756. . . (1973), but any tax benefit, including the tax deduction at issue here, which subsidizes tuition payments to sectarian schools. I also believe that the Establishment Clause prohibits the tax deductions that Minnesota authorizes for the cost of books and other instructional materials used for sectarian purposes.

* * *

NOTES AND QUESTIONS

1. Mueller *and the* Lemon *Test*

In *Committee for Public Education and Religious Liberty v. Nyquist*, 413 U.S. 756, 93 S.Ct. 2955, 37 L.Ed. 2d 948 (1973), the Court held unconstitutional a law that provided (1) direct grants from the state to nonpublic schools that served high concentrations of students from low-income families for maintenance and repair of school facilities; (2) tuition reimbursements to parents of nonpublic school students who had a taxable income of less than $5,000; and (3) tax deductions for parents of nonpublic school students whose income was above $5,000.

a. The "Secular Purpose" Test. The Court, in *Committee for Public Education and Religious Liberty v. Nyquist, supra,* concluded that New York's tuition grant and tax credit legislation reflected a "clearly secular legislative purpose." Similarly, the Court in

Mueller found the Minnesota tax deduction statute had a secular purpose, despite the fact that the statute "contains no express statements of legislative purpose, and its legislative history offers few unambiguous indications of actual intent." Is it likely that the legislators in New York and in Minnesota had both a secular and religious purpose in adopting the legislation in question? Why is it unconstitutional "for legislation to have the purpose or effect of assisting religious practice generally, when the Constitution itself gives a special status to religion"? Johnson, "Concepts and Compromise in First Amendment Religious Doctrine," 72 *Calif. L. Rev.* 817, 827 (1984).

b. The "Primary Effect" Test. In *Nyquist, supra,* the Court noted that "the effect of the [tuition reimbursement and tax relief] aid is unmistakably to provide desired financial support for nonpublic, sectarian institutions." Does that fact alone render it unconstitutional? Is there a clear distinction between the effect of state aid in *Nyquist* and the state provision of transportation and textbooks benefitting "nonpublic, sectarian institutions" upheld in *Everson v. Board of Education,* 330 U.S. 1, 67 S.Ct. 504, 91 L.Ed. 711 (1947) and *Board of Education v. Allen,* 392 U.S. 236, 88 S.Ct. 1923, 20 L.Ed.2d 1060 (1968)?

Does the Rehnquist opinion in *Mueller* indicate "that the Court may be moving toward an effect test that concentrates on the imprimatur concern"? Note, "The Supreme Court, Effect Inquiry, and Aid to Parochial Education," 37 *Stan. L. Rev.* 219, 231–32 (1984). Is this why aid to parents is less objectionable than aid to private schools? In his dissenting opinion in *Nyquist,* Chief Justice Burger noted: "I fear that the Court has in reality followed the insupportable approach of measuring the "effect" of a law by the percentage of the recipients who choose to use the money for religious, rather than secular, education." After *Mueller,* does the amount of the aid no longer matter? Has the effects test been replaced by a balancing test? Note, "The Supreme Court, Effect Inquiry, and Aid to Parochial Education," 37 *Stan. L. Rev.* 219, 232–33 (1984). How should the courts balance secular and religious benefits? Does balancing risk inconsistency and unpredictability of results in specific cases? *Id.* at 235. Does *Mueller* implicitly overrule *Lemon? See generally* Note, "Laws Respecting an Establishment of Religion: An Inquiry into Tuition Tax Benefits," 58 *N.Y.U. L. Rev.* 207 (1983).

c. The "Entanglement" Test. In *Nyquist,* the state of New York, by providing vouchers and tax credits which could be used for any public school activity, had sought to avoid "a comprehensive, discriminating, and continuing state surveillance" of sectarian schools. *Lemon v. Kurtzman,* 403 U.S. 602, 619, 91 S.Ct. 2105, 2114, 29 L.Ed.2d 745 (1971). Can one construct state legislation that avoids the Scylla of entanglement and the Charybdis of financing religion? Professor Choper, in commenting on this aspect of *Lemon,* notes that in that case:

> . . . the Court hung the states (and the recipient parochial schools) on the horns of a dilemma with respect to [the second and third prongs] of the test. The Court began with a critical premise: the mission of church-related elementary and secondary schools is to teach religion, and all subjects either are, or carry the potential of being, permeated with sectarian ideology. Therefore, if the government were to help fund any subjects in these schools, the effect would be to aid religion, unless public officials monitored the situation to see to it that the courses being assisted with public money were not infused with religious doctrine. But if public officials did engage in adequate surveillance— this is the other horn of the dilemma—there would be excessive entanglement between the government and religion, the image being state "spies" regularly or periodically sitting in many or all classes conducted in parochial schools.

Choper, "Federal Constitutional Issues," in S.D. Sugarman and F. R. Kemerer (eds.), *School Choice and Social Controversy* 235, 236–37 (1999).

Note that in *Mueller,* the Court had "no difficulty in concluding that the Minnesota statute does not 'excessively entangle' the state in religion." Although state officials would have to determine whether textbooks and materials for which deductions were taken were used "in the teaching of religious tenets, doctrines, or worship, the purpose of which is to inculcate such tenets, doctrines, or worship," and if so, disallow the deductions, Minn. Stat. §290.09(22), the Court concluded that the decisions state officials would make [were] similar to those of state officials in *Board of Education v. Allen, supra.* The Court quoted the language in *Lemon* that described "excessive entanglement" as "comprehensive, discriminating, and continuing state surveillance, "403 U.S at 619. *See Agostini v. Felton,* 521 U.S. 203, 117 S.Ct. 1997, 138 L.Ed. 2d 391 (1997), *infra,* recharacterizing the nature of the analysis of government entanglement as "an aspect of the inquiry into a statute's

effect," which may mean that the three-pronged test of *Lemon* is now only a two-pronged test.

2. Parental Rights

If parents have a right to send their children to private schools, "how can it be impermissible for a state to make the same option available to all [regardless of wealth] by tuition tax credits, grants, or other forms of aid to private schools?" Johnson, "Concepts and Compromise in First Amendment Doctrine," 72 *Calif. L. Rev.* 817, 822–23 (1984). *But cf. Regan v. Taxation With Representation of Washington,* 461 U.S. 540, 103 S.Ct. 1997, 76 L.Ed.2d 129 (1983); *Harris v. McRae,* 448 U.S. 297, 100 S.Ct. 2671, 65 L.Ed.2d 784 (1980); *Maher v. Roe,* 432 U.S. 464, 97 S.Ct. 2376, 53 L.Ed.2d 484 (1977).

3. Tax Deductions Under State Constitutional Law

In *Opinion of the Justices to the Senate,* 401 Mass. 1201, 514 N.E.2d 353 (1987), the Supreme Judicial Court of Massachusetts was asked to render an advisory opinion on a state senate bill that would have provided for tax deductions for educational expenses incurred in attending public and private elementary and secondary schools. The senate bill was similar to the law upheld in *Mueller.* The Court applied Article 46, §2 of the Amendments to the Massachusetts Constitution:

> No grant, appropriation or use of public money or property or loan of credit shall be made or authorized by the Commonwealth or any political subdivision thereof for the purpose of founding, maintaining, or aiding any infirmary, hospital, institution, primary or secondary school, or charitable or religious undertaking which is not publicly owned and under the exclusive control . . . of public officers or public agents authorized by the Commonwealth or federal authority or both. . . .

The Court held that the proposed bill violated the Massachusetts Constitution, concluding that the legislature had "an intent to aid and to maintain private schools" and that the bill "would provide 'substantial assistance' to private schools." 514 N.E.2d at 356, 357. It also held that "tax subsidies or tax expenditures of this sort are the practical equivalent of direct government grants," and thus the proposed law would violate art. 46, §2 by lessening the financial burden on parents who choose to send their children to private schools. *Id.* at 355, 358. The Massachusetts court specifically noted its unwillingness to adhere to *Mueller,* holding that "the language of our [Massachusetts] anti-aid amendment is 'much more specific' than the First Amendment . . . and its restrictions are 'more stringent.'. . . Its prohibition is 'emphatic and comprehensive,' . . . and it 'marks no difference between "aids," whether religious or secular.' . . ." *Id.* at 354 n. 4. *See generally* Greenawalt, "The Concept of Religion in State Constitutions," 8 *Campbell L. Rev.* 437, 439–441 (1986). Many states have constitutional provisions that appear to be more strict with regard to separation of church and state, and have so been interpreted by their state courts, than the Establishment Clause of the federal constitution. *See* Kemerer, "The Constitutional Dimension of School Vouchers," 3 *Tex. Forum on Civil Liberties & Civil Rights*, 137, 181–82 (1998); Viteritti, "Blaine's Wake: School Choice, the First Amendment, and State Constitutional Law," 21 *Harv. J.L. & Pub. Pol'y*, 657 (1998).

4. Higher versus Lower Education

In *Hunt v. McNair*, 413 U.S. 734, 93 S.Ct. 2868, 37 L.Ed.2d 923 (1973), decided the same day as *Nyquist*, the Supreme Court upheld state legislation that provided financial assistance for higher education construction; secular as well as sectarian institutions are eligible for the assistance. The Court thus reaffirmed a distinction, first advanced in *Tilton v. Richardson*, 403 U.S. 672, 91 S.Ct. 2091, 29 L.Ed.2d 790 (1971), between aid that benefits sectarian primary and secondary schools and aid that benefits sectarian institutions of higher learning. *See generally* Underwood, "Public Funds for Private Schools: The Gap Between Higher and Lower Education Widens," 41 *Educ.L.Rep.* 407 (1987). The Court suggests that the former are likely to promote genuinely secular ends, while the latter seek to indoctrinate their students with religious values. Is the distinction factually correct? Is it a distinction of constitutional dimension?

5. Is the Lemon Test Incoherent?

It has been argued both by some of the justices and by scholars that the *Lemon* test has proved unworkable. Do you agree? *See, e.g.,* J. Choper, *Securing Religious Liberty* 175 (1995) ("It is fair to say that application of the Court's three-part *Lemon* test has produced a conceptual disaster area, generating ad hoc judgments that are incapable of being reconciled on any principled basis"); Laycock, "Survey of Religious Liberty in the United States," 47 *Ohio St. L. J.* 409, 446 (1986) (Establishment Clause cases

have "not produced coherent results" and have "produced distinctions that do not commend themselves to common sense"). *See also* Vaccari, "Public Purpose and the Public Funding of Sectarian Educational Institutions: A More Rational Approach After *Rosenberger* and *Agostini*," 82 *Marq. L. Rev.* 1 (1998); Marks and Bertolini, "*Lemon* Is a Lemon: Toward a Rational Interpretation of the Establishment Clause," 12 *BYU J. Pub. L.* 1 (1997); Garvey, "Another Way of Looking at School Aid," 1985 *Sup. Ct. Rev.* 61; Simson, "The Establishment Clause in the Supreme Court: Rethinking the Court's Approach," 72 *Cornell L. Rev.* 905 (1987). In his dissenting opinion in *Wallace v. Jaffree*, Chief Justice Rehnquist summarized the inconsistent results of the Court's reliance on the *Lemon* test:

> The three-part test has simply not provided adequate standards for deciding Establishment Clause cases, as this Court has slowly come to realize. Even worse, the *Lemon* test has caused this Court to fracture into unworkable plurality opinions, depending upon how each of the three factors applies to a certain state action. The results from our school services cases show the difficulty we have encountered in making the *Lemon* test yield principled results.
>
> For example, a State may lend to parochial school children geography textbooks [*Board of Education v. Allen*, 392 U.S. 236 (1968)] that contain maps of the United States, but the State may not lend maps of the United States for use in geography class [*Meek v. Pittenger*, 421 U.S. 349 (1975)]. A State may lend textbooks on American colonial history, but it may not lend a film on George Washington, or a film projector to show it in history class. A State may lend classroom workbooks, but may not lend workbooks in which the parochial school children write, thus rendering them nonreusable [*Meek, supra*]. A State may pay for bus transportation to religious schools [*Everson v. Board of Education*, 330 U.S. 1 (1947)] but may not pay for bus transportation from the parochial school to the public zoo or natural history museum for a field trip [*Wolman v. Walter*, 433 U.S. 229 (1977)]. A State may pay for diagnostic services conducted in the parochial school but therapeutic services must be given in a different building; speech and hearing "services" conducted by the State inside the sectarian school are forbidden [*Meek, supra*], but the State may conduct speech and hearing diagnostic testing inside the sectarian school [*Wolman, supra*]. Exceptional parochial school students may receive counseling, but it must take place outside of the parochial school [*Wolman, supra; Meek, supra*], such as in a trailer parked down the street. A State may give cash to a parochial school to pay for the administration of state-written tests and state-ordered reporting services

[*Committee for Public Education and Religious Liberty v. Regan*, 444 U.S. 646 (1980)], but it may not provide funds for teacher-prepared tests on secular subjects [*Levitt v. Committee for Public Education and Religious Liberty*, 413 U.S. 472 (1973)]. Religious instruction may not be given in public school [*Illinois ex rel. McCollum v. Board of Education*, 333 U.S. 203 (1948)], but the public school may release students during the day for religion classes elsewhere, and may enforce attendance at those classes with its truancy laws [*Zorach v. Clauson*, 343 U.S. 306 (1952)]. . . . It is not surprising in the light of this record that our most recent opinions have expressed doubt on the usefulness of the *Lemon* test.

Wallace v. Jaffree, 472 U.S. 38, 110–112 (1985) (Rehnquist, J. dissenting). *See* Wood and Petko, "Assessing *Agostini v. Felton* in Light of *Lemon v. Kurtzman*: The Coming of Age in the Debate Between Religious Affiliated Schools and State Aid," 2000 *B.Y.U. Educ. & L.J.* 1, for a review of the Court's decisions from *Lemon* to *Agostini*.

To what extent does the Court, in *Agostini v. Felton*, set out below, vitiate, or at least modify, the *Lemon* test?

Agostini v. Felton
521 U.S. 203, 117 S.Ct. 1997, 138 L.Ed. 2d 391 (1997)

Justice O'Connor delivered the opinion of the Court.

In *Aguilar v. Felton*, 473 U.S. 402, 105 S.Ct. 3232, 87 L.Ed.2d 290 (1985), this Court held that the Establishment Clause of the First Amendment barred the city of New York from sending public school teachers into parochial schools to provide remedial education to disadvantaged children pursuant to a congressionally mandated program. On remand, the District Court for the Eastern District of New York entered a permanent injunction reflecting our ruling. Twelve years later, petitioners—the parties bound by that injunction—seek relief from its operation. Petitioners maintain that *Aguilar* cannot be squared with our intervening Establishment Clause jurisprudence and ask that we explicitly recognize what our more recent cases already dictate: *Aguilar* is no longer good law. We agree with petitioners that *Aguilar* is not consistent with our subsequent Establishment Clause decisions. . . .

I

In 1965, Congress enacted Title I of the Elementary and Secondary Education Act of 1965, 79 Stat. 27, as modified, 20 U.S.C. §6301 *et seq.*, to "provid[e] full educational opportunity to every child regardless of economic background." . . . Toward that end, Title I channels federal funds, through the States, to "local educational agencies" (LEA's). . . . The LEA's spend these funds to provide remedial education, guidance, and job counseling to eligible students. . . . An eligible student is one (i) who resides within the attendance boundaries of a public school located in a low-income area . . . ; and (ii) who is failing, or is at risk of failing, the State's student performance standards. . . . Title I funds must be made available to all eligible children, regardless of whether they attend public schools, . . . and the services provided to children attending private schools must be "equitable in comparison to services and other benefits for public school children."

An LEA providing services to children enrolled in private schools is subject to a number of constraints. . . . Title I services may be provided only to those private school students eligible for aid, and cannot be used to provide services on a "school-wide" basis. . . . In addition, the LEA must retain complete control over Title I funds; retain title to all materials used to provide Title I services; and provide those services through public employees or other persons independent of the private school and any religious institution. . . . The Title I services themselves must be "secular, neutral, and nonideological," and must "supplement, and in no case supplant, the level of services" already provided by the private school. . . .

. . . Approximately 10% of the total number of students eligible for Title I services [in New York City] are private school students. . . . [M]ore than 90% of the private schools within the Board's jurisdiction are sectarian. . . .

[The plan evaluated in *Aguilar v. Felton*] called for the provision of Title I services on private school premises during school hours. . . . [O]nly public employees could serve as Title I instructors and counselors. Assignments to private schools were made on a voluntary basis and without regard to the religious affiliation of the employee or the wishes of the private school. . . . [A] large majority of Title I teachers worked in nonpublic schools with religious affiliations different from their own. The vast majority of Title I teachers also moved among the private schools, spending fewer than five days a week at the same school.

Before any public employee could provide Title I instruction at a private school, she would be given a detailed set of written and oral instructions emphasizing the secular purpose of Title I and setting out the rules to be followed to ensure that this purpose was not compromised. . . . To ensure compliance with these rules, a publicly employed field supervisor was to attempt to make at least one unannounced visit to each teacher's classroom every month.

In 1978, six federal taxpayers . . . sued the Board . . . claiming that the Board's Title I program violated the Establishment Clause. . . . In a 5-4 decision, this Court [held] . . . that the Board's Title I program necessitated an "excessive entanglement of church and state in the administration of [Title I] benefits.". . .

* * *

In October and December of 1995, petitioners—the Board and a new group of parents of parochial school students entitled to Title I services—filed motions in the District Court seeking relief under Federal Rule of Civil Procedure 60(b) from the permanent injunction entered by the District Court on remand from our decision in *Aguilar*. Petitioners argued that relief was proper . . . because the "decisional law [had] changed to make legal what the [injunction] was designed to prevent.". . .

II

. . .[P]etitioners' ability to satisfy the prerequisites of Rule 60(b)(5) hinges on whether our later Establishment Clause cases have so undermined *Aguilar* that it is no longer good law. . .

III

A

* * *

In [*School Dist. of Grand Rapids v. Ball*, 473 U.S. 373, 105 S.Ct. 3216, 87 L.Ed.2d 267 (1985), *Aguilar*'s companion case]. . .[t]he district's Shared Time program, . . . provided remedial and "enrichment" classes, at public expense, to students attending nonpublic schools. The classes were taught during regular school hours by publicly employed teachers, using materials purchased with public funds, on the premises of nonpublic schools. The Shared Time courses were in subjects designed to supplement the "core curriculum" of the nonpublic schools. Of the 41 nonpublic schools eligible for the program, 40 were "pervasively sectarian" in character—that is, "the purpos[e] of [those] schools [was] to advance their particular religions."

The Court conducted its analysis by applying the three-part test set forth in *Lemon v. Kurtzman*, 403 U.S. 602, 91 S.Ct. 2105, 29 L.Ed.2d 745 (1971):

> "First, the statute must have a secular legislative purpose; second, its principal or primary effect must be one that neither advances nor inhibits religion; finally, the statute must not foster an excessive government entanglement with religion.". . .

The Court acknowledged that the Shared Time program served a purely secular purpose, thereby satisfying the first part of the so-called *Lemon* test. Nevertheless, it ultimately concluded that the program had the impermissible effect of advancing religion.

. . . First, . . . "the teachers participating in the programs may become involved in intentionally or inadvertently inculcating particular religious tenets or beliefs.". . .

. . .[C]lasses were conducted on the premises of religious schools. Accordingly, a majority found a "substantial risk" that teachers—even those who were not employed by the private schools—might "subtly (or overtly) conform their instruction to the [pervasively sectarian] environment in which they [taught]." The danger of "state-sponsored indoctrination" was only exacerbated by the school district's failure to monitor the courses for religious content. Notably, the Court disregarded the lack of evidence of any specific incidents of religious indoctrination as largely irrelevant. . . .

The presence of public teachers on parochial school grounds had a second, related impermissible effect: It created a "graphic symbol of the 'concert or union or dependency' of church and state," . . . especially when perceived by "children in their formative years." The Court feared that this perception of a symbolic union between church and state would "conve[y] a message of government endorsement . . . of religion" and thereby violate a "core purpose" of the Establishment Clause.

Third, the Court found that the Shared Time program impermissibly financed religious indoctrination by subsidizing "the primary religious mission of the institutions affected." The Court separated its prior decisions . . . into two categories: those in which it concluded that the aid resulted in an effect that was "indirect, remote, or incidental" (and upheld the aid); and those in which it concluded that the aid resulted in "a direct and substantial advancement of the sectarian enterprise" (and invalidated the aid). . . . Grand Rapids' program fell into the latter category. . . . [In two earlier decisions, *Meek v. Pittenger,* 421 U.S. 349, 95 S.Ct. 1753, 44 L.Ed.2d 217 (1975), and *Wolman v. Walter,* 433 U.S. 229, 97 S.Ct. 2593, 53 L.Ed.2d 714 (1977)], the Court ruled that a state loan of instructional equipment and materials to parochial schools was an impermissible form of "direct aid" because it "advanced the primary, religion-oriented educational function of the sectarian school," . . . by providing "in-kind" aid (e.g., instructional materials) that could be used to teach religion and by freeing up money for religious indoctrination that the school would otherwise have devoted to secular education. Given the holdings in *Meek* and *Wolman,* the Shared Time program—which provided teachers as well as instructional equipment and materials—was surely invalid. The *Ball* Court . . . placed no weight on the fact that the program was provided to the student rather than to the school. Nor was the impermissible effect mitigated by the fact that the program only supplemented the courses offered by the parochial schools.

The New York City Title I program challenged in *Aguilar* closely resembled the Shared Time program struck down in *Ball,* but the Court found fault with an aspect of the Title I program not present in *Ball:* The Board had "adopted a system for monitoring the religious content of publicly funded Title I classes in the religious schools." Even though this monitoring system might prevent the Title I program from being used to inculcate religion, the Court concluded . . . that the level of monitoring necessary to be "certain" that the program had an exclusively secular effect would "inevitably resul[t] in the excessive entanglement of church and state," thereby running afoul of *Lemon's* third prong. . . .

Distilled to essentials, the Court's conclusion that the Shared Time program in *Ball* had the impermissible effect of advancing religion rested on three assumptions: (i) any public employee who works on the premises of a religious school is presumed to inculcate religion in her work; (ii) the presence of public employees on private school premises creates a symbolic union between church and state; and (iii) any and all public aid that directly aids the educational function of religious schools impermissibly finances religious indoctrination, even if the aid reaches such schools as a consequence of private decision making. Additionally, in *Aguilar* there was a fourth assumption: that New York City's Title I program necessitated an excessive government entanglement with religion because public employees who teach on the premises of religious schools must be closely monitored to ensure that they do not inculcate religion.

B

Our more recent cases have undermined the assumptions upon which *Ball* and *Aguilar* relied. To be sure, the general principles we use to evaluate whether government aid violates the Establishment Clause have not changed since *Aguilar* was decided. For example, we continue to ask whether the government acted with the purpose of advancing or inhibiting religion, and the nature of that inquiry has remained largely unchanged. Likewise, we continue to explore whether the aid has the "effect" of advancing or inhibiting religion. What has changed since we decided *Ball* and *Aguilar* is our understanding of the criteria used to assess whether aid to religion has an impermissible effect.

1.

As we have repeatedly recognized, government inculcation of religious beliefs has the impermissible effect of advancing religion. Our cases subsequent to *Aguilar* have, however, modified in two significant respects the approach we use to assess indoctrination. First, we have abandoned the presumption . . . that the placement of public employees on parochial school grounds inevitably results in the impermissible effect of state-sponsored indoctrination or constitutes a symbolic union between government and religion. In *Zobrest v. Catalina Foothills School Dist.,* 509 U.S. 1, 113 S.Ct. 2462, 125 L.Ed.2d 1 (1993), we examined whether the IDEA, 20 U.S.C. §1400 *et seq.,* was constitutional as applied to a deaf student who sought to bring his state-employed sign-language interpreter with him to his Roman Catholic high school. We held that this was permissible. . . . We refused to presume that a publicly employed interpreter would be pressured by the pervasively sectarian surroundings to inculcate religion by "add[ing] to [or] subtract[ing] from" the lectures translated. In the absence of evidence to the contrary, we assumed instead that the interpreter would dutifully discharge her responsibilities as a full-time public employee and comply with the ethical guidelines of her profession by accurately translating what was said. Because the only government aid in *Zobrest* was the interpreter, who was herself not inculcating any religious messages, no government indoctrination took place and we were able to conclude that "the provision of such assistance [was] not barred by the Establishment Clause." *Zobrest* therefore expressly rejected the notion—relied on in *Ball* and *Aguilar*—that, solely because of her presence on private school property, a public employee will be presumed to inculcate religion in the students. *Zobrest* also implicitly repudiated another assumption on which *Ball* and *Aguilar* turned: that the presence of a public employee on private school property creates an impermissible "symbolic link" between government and religion.

* * *

Second, we have departed from the rule relied on in *Ball* that all government aid that directly aids the educational function of religious schools is invalid. In *Witters v. Washington Dept. of Servs. for Blind*, 474 U.S. 481, 106 S.Ct. 748, 88 L.Ed.2d 846 (1986), we held that the Establishment Clause did not bar a State from issuing a vocational tuition grant to a blind person who wished to use the grant to attend a Christian college and become a pastor, missionary, or youth director. Even though the grant recipient clearly would use the money to obtain religious education, we observed that the tuition grants were " 'made available generally without regard to the sectarian-nonsectarian, or public-nonpublic nature of the institution benefited.' " [quoting *Witters*.] The grants were disbursed directly to students, who then used the money to pay for tuition at the educational institution of their choice. . . . [A]ny money that ultimately went to religious institutions did so "only as a result of the genuinely independent and private choices of" individuals. . . .

Zobrest and *Witters* make clear that, under current law, the Shared Time program in *Ball* and New York City's Title I program in *Aguilar* will not, as a matter of law, be deemed to have the effect of advancing religion through indoctrination. . . . First, there is no reason to presume that, simply because she enters a parochial school classroom, a full-time public employee such as a Title I teacher will depart from her assigned duties and instructions and embark on religious indoctrination, any more than there was a reason in *Zobrest* to think an interpreter would inculcate religion by altering her translation of classroom lectures. . . .

. . .*Zobrest* also repudiates *Ball's* assumption that the presence of Title I teachers in parochial school classrooms will, without more, create the impression of a "symbolic union" between church and state. . . .

Nor under current law can we conclude that a program placing full-time public employees on parochial campuses to provide Title I instruction would impermissibly finance religious indoctrination. In all relevant respects, the provision of instructional services under Title I is indistinguisable from the provision of sign-language interpreters under the IDEA. Both programs make aid available only to eligible recipients. That aid is provided to students at whatever school they choose to attend. Although Title I instruction is provided to several students at once, whereas an interpreter provides translation to a single student, this distinction is not constitutionally significant. Moreover, as in *Zobrest*, Title I services are by law supplemental to the regular curricula. . . . These services do not, therefore, "reliev[e] sectarian schools of costs they otherwise would have borne in educating their students."

* * *

2.

. . .[I]t is clear that Title I services are allocated on the basis of criteria that neither favor nor disfavor religion. . . . The services are available to all children who meet the Act's eligibility requirements, no matter what their religious beliefs or where they go to school. . . . The Board's program does not, therefore, give aid recipients any incentive to modify their religious beliefs or practices in order to obtain those services.

3.

We turn now to *Aguilar's* conclusion that New York City's Title I program resulted in an excessive entanglement between church and state. . . . [T]he factors we use to assess whether an entanglement is "excessive" are similar to the factors we use to examine "effect." That is, to assess entanglement, we have looked to "the character and purposes of the institutions that are benefited, the nature of the aid that the State provides, and the resulting relationship between the government and religious authority." Similarly, we have assessed a law's "effect" by examining the character of the institutions benefited (e.g., whether the religious institutions were "predominantly religious"), . . . and the nature of the aid that the State provided (e.g., whether it was neutral and non-ideological). . . . Thus, it is simplest to recognize why entanglement is significant and treat it . . . as an aspect of the inquiry into a statute's effect.

* * *

The pre-*Aguilar* Title I program does not result in an "excessive" entanglement that advances or inhibits religion. As discussed previously, the Court's finding of "excessive" entanglement in *Aguilar* rested on three grounds: (i) the program would require "pervasive monitoring by public authorities" to ensure that Title I employees did not inculcate religion; (ii) the program required "administrative cooperation" between the Board and parochial schools; and (iii) the program might increase the dangers of "political divisiveness." Under our current understanding of the Establishment Clause, the last two considerations are insufficient by themselves to create an "excessive" entanglement. . . . Further, the assumption underlying the first consideration has been undermined. . . . [A]fter *Zobrest* we no longer presume that public employees will inculcate religion simply because they happen to be in a sectarian environment. Since we have abandoned the assumption that properly instructed public employees will fail to discharge their duties faithfully, we must also discard the assumption that pervasive monitoring of Title I teachers is required. There is no suggestion in the record before us that unannounced monthly visits of public supervisors are insufficient to prevent or to detect inculcation of religion by public employees. . . .

To summarize, New York City's Title I program does not run afoul of any of three primary criteria we currently use to evaluate whether government aid has the effect of advancing religion: it does not result in governmental indoctrination; define its recipients by reference to religion; or create an excessive entanglement. We therefore hold that a federally funded program providing supplemental, remedial instruction to disadvantaged children on a neutral basis is not invalid under the Establishment Clause when such instruction is given on the premises of sectarian schools by government employees pursuant to a program containing safeguards such as those present here. The same considerations that justify this holding require us to conclude that this carefully constrained program also cannot reasonably be viewed as an endorsement of religion. . . . Accordingly, we must ac-

knowledge that *Aguilar*, as well as the portion of *Ball* addressing Grand Rapids' Shared Time program, are no longer good law.

* * *

IV

* * *

We do not acknowledge, and we do not hold, that other courts should conclude our more recent cases have, by implication, overruled an earlier precedent. We reaffirm that "if a precedent of this Court has direct application in a case, yet appears to rest on reasons rejected in some other line of decisions, the Court of Appeals should follow the case which directly controls, leaving to this Court the prerogative of overruling its own decisions.". . .

. . .[W]e reverse the judgment of the Court of Appeals and remand to the District Court with instructions to vacate its September 26, 1985, order.

It is so ordered.

Justice Souter, with whom Justice Stevens and Justice Ginsburg join, and with whom Justice Breyer joins as to Part II, dissenting.

* * *

I

* * *

. . . I believe *Aguilar* was a correct and sensible decision. . . . The State is forbidden to subsidize religion directly and is just as surely forbidden to act in any way that could reasonably be viewed as religious endorsement. . . .

. . .[T]he programs at issue in *Aguilar* and *Ball* . . . provided classes on the premises of the religious schools, covering a wide range of subjects including some at the core of primary and secondary education, like reading and mathematics; while their services were termed "supplemental," the programs and their instructors necessarily assumed responsibility for teaching subjects that the religious schools would otherwise have been obligated to provide . . . ; the public employees carrying out the programs had broad responsibilities involving the exercise of considerable discretion . . . ; while the programs offered aid to nonpublic school students generally (and Title I went to public school students as well), participation by religious school students in each program was extensive . . . ; and, finally, aid under Title I and Shared Time flowed directly to the schools in the form of classes and programs, as distinct from indirect aid that reaches schools only as a result of independent private choice. . . .

What, therefore, was significant in *Aguilar* and *Ball* about the placement of state-paid teachers into the physical and social settings of the religious schools . . . was that the schemes in issue assumed a teaching responsibility indistinguishable from the responsibility of the schools themselves. The obligation of primary and secondary schools to teach reading necessarily extends to teaching those who are having a hard time at it, and the same is true of math. Calling some classes remedial does not distinguish their subjects from the schools' basic subjects, however inadequately the schools may have been addressing them.

. . . The off-premises teaching is arguably less likely to open the door to relieving religious schools of their responsibilities for secular subjects simply because these schools are less likely (and presumably legally unable) to dispense with those subjects from their curriculums or to make patently significant cut-backs in basic teaching within the schools to offset the outside instruction; if the aid is delivered outside of the schools, it is less likely to supplant some of what would otherwise go on inside them and to subsidize what remains. On top of that, the difference in the degree of reasonably perceptible endorsement is substantial. Sharing the teaching responsibilities within a school having religious objectives is far more likely to telegraph approval of the school's mission than keeping the State's distance would do. . . . As the Court observed in *Ball*, "[t]he symbolism of a union between church and state [effected by placing the public school teachers into the religious schools] is most likely to influence children of tender years, whose experience is limited and whose beliefs consequently are the function of environment as much as of free and voluntary choice.". . .

II

The Court today . . . claims that recent cases rejected the elemental assumptions underlying *Aguilar* and much of *Ball*. But the Court errs. Its holding that *Aguilar* and the portion of *Ball* addressing the Shared Time program are "no longer good law" rests on mistaken reading.

A

Zobrest held that the Establishment Clause does not prevent a school district from providing a sign-language interpreter to a deaf student enrolled in a sectarian school. The Court today relies solely on *Zobrest* to support its contention that we have "abandoned the presumption erected in . . . *Ball* that the placement of public employees on parochial school grounds inevitably results in the impermissible effect of state-sponsored indoctrination or constitutes a symbolic union between government and religion." *Zobrest*, however, is no such sanction for overruling *Aguilar* or any portion of *Ball*.

In *Zobrest* the Court did indeed recognize that the Establishment Clause lays down no absolute bar to placing public employees in a sectarian school, but the rejection of such a per se rule was hinged expressly on the nature of the employee's job, sign-language interpretation (or signing) and the circumscribed role of the signer. On this point . . . the Court explained itself this way: "[T]he task of a sign-language interpreter seems to us quite different from that of a teacher or guidance counselor. . . . Nothing in this record suggests that a sign-language interpreter would do more than accurately interpret whatever material is presented to the class as a whole. In fact, ethical guidelines require interpreters to 'transmit everything that is said in exactly the same way it was intended.' " The signer could thus be seen as more like a hearing aid than a teacher, and the signing could not be understood as an opportunity to inject religious content in what was supposed to be secular instruction. *Zobrest* accordingly holds only that in these limited circumstances where a public employee simply translates for one student the material presented to the class for the benefit of all students, the employee's presence in the sectarian school does not violate the Establishment Clause.

The Court, however, ignores the careful distinction drawn in *Zobrest* and insists that a full-time public employee such as a Title I teacher is just like the signer, asserting that "there is no reason to presume that, simply because she enters a parochial school classroom, . . . [this] teacher will depart from her assigned duties and instructions and embark on religious indoctrination". . . The Court may disagree with *Ball*'s assertion that a publicly employed teacher working in a sectarian school is apt to reinforce the pervasive inculcation of religious beliefs, but its disagreement is fresh law.

* * *

B

...[The Court in *Ball*] held that the Shared Time program subsidized the religious functions of the parochial schools by taking over a significant portion of their responsibility for teaching secular subjects. The Court noted that it had "never accepted the mere possibility of subsidization ... as sufficient to invalidate an aid program," and instead enquired whether the effect of the proffered aid was "direct and substantial" (and, so, unconstitutional) or merely "indirect and incidental," (and, so, permissible) emphasizing that the question "is one of degree.".... *Witters* and *Zobrest* did nothing to repudiate the principle, emphasizing rather the limited nature of the aid at issue in each case as well as the fact that religious institutions did not receive it directly from the State. In *Witters*, the Court noted that the State would issue the disputed vocational aid directly to one student who would then transmit it to the school of his choice, and that there was no record evidence that "any significant portion of the aid expended under the Washington program as a whole will end up flowing to religious education." *Zobrest* also presented an instance of a single beneficiary, and emphasized that the student (who had previously received the interpretive services in a public school) determined where the aid would be used, that the aid at issue was limited, and that the religious school was "not relieved of an expense that it otherwise would have assumed in educating its students."

It is accordingly puzzling to find the Court insisting that the aid scheme administered under Title I and considered in *Aguilar* was comparable to the programs in *Witters* and *Zobrest*. Instead of aiding isolated individuals within a school system, New York City's Title I program before *Aguilar* served about 22,000 private school students, all but 52 of whom attended religious schools.... Instead of serving individual blind or deaf students, as such, Title I as administered in New York City before *Aguilar* (and as now to be revived) funded instruction in core subjects (remedial reading, reading skills, remedial mathematics, English as a second language) and provided guidance services. Instead of providing a service the school would not otherwise furnish, the Title I services necessarily relieved a religious school of "an expense that it otherwise would have assumed," and freed its funds for other, and sectarian uses.

Finally, instead of aid that comes to the religious school indirectly in the sense that its distribution results from private decision making, a public educational agency distributes Title I aid in the form of programs and services directly to the religious schools. In *Zobrest* and *Witters*, it was fair to say that individual students were themselves applicants for individual benefits on a scale that could not amount to a systemic supplement. But under Title I, a local educational agency ... may receive federal funding by proposing programs approved to serve individual students who meet the criteria of need, which it then uses to provide such programs at the religious schools; ... students eligible for such programs may not apply directly for Title I funds....

In sum, nothing since *Ball* and *Aguilar* and before this case has eroded the distinction between "direct and substantial" and "indirect and incidental.". . .

* * *

[Justice Ginsburg's dissent, joined by Justices Stevens, Souter, and Breyer, on the inappropriateness of using Rule 60(b), is omitted.]

NOTES AND QUESTIONS

1. *Kiryas Joel: Between* Aguilar *and* Agostini

Board of Educ. of Kiryas Joel Village School Dist. v. Grumet, 512 U.S. 687, 114 S.Ct. 2481, 129 L.Ed. 2d 546 (1994), concerned an incorporated village in New York State that was a separate enclave comprised of a group of Satmar Hasidic Jews. "Like all Hasidic Jews, Satmars aspire to follow all of Jewish Laws. Since they believe that failure to comply with all of God's commandments has adverse effects on the Jewish community, they often take on additional obligations of segregation to minimize contact with any influence that might distract them from fulfilling their religious obligations." Failer, "The Draw and Drawbacks of Religious Enclaves in a Constitutional Democracy: Hasidic Public Schools in Kiryas Joel," 72 *Ind. L.J.* 383, 386–387 (1997). This segregation from outside influences included separate private schools for their children. *Id.* at 387. However, the Satmars were unable to provide special education for their disabled children. They established a school for children with disabilities, taught by special education teachers provided by the local public school district. This practice was suspended, however, following the Supreme Court's decision in *Aguilar v. Felton*, 473 U.S. 402 (1985). The Satmar parents then tried to send their children to special education classes in the public schools, but withdrew their children because of "the panic, fear and trauma [the children] suffered in leaving their own community and being with people whose ways were so different." 114 S.Ct. at 2485 (quoting *Board of Educ. of Monroe-Woodbury Central School Dist. v. Wieder,* 531 N.Y.S.2d 889, 892, 527 N.E. 2d 767, 770 (1988)). The state legislature then passed a law making the Village of Kiryas Joel a separate school district. 1989 N.Y. Laws, ch. 748. The Court found that the state, in delegating political power to a religious group, was not neutral with respect to religion and thus violated the Establishment Clause. The law went beyond permissible religious accommodation by "singl[ing] out a particular religious sect for special treatment." 114 S. Ct. at 2493. In its analysis of the statute, the Court did not resort to the *Lemon* framework, but instead focused on the Establishment Clause's requirement of "neutrality." *Cf. Stark v. Independent School District, No. 640,* 123 F.3d 1068 (8th Cir. 1997), *cert. denied,* 118 S. Ct. 1560 (1998).

In concurring and dissenting opinions in *Kiryas Joel,* a number of justices expressed their dissatisfaction with *Aguilar,* as well as the continuing vitality of the *Lemon* test. *See, e.g., id.* at 2498–2500 (O'Connor, J., concurring in part and concurring in the judgment); *id.* at 2505 (Kennedy, J., concurring in the judgment); *id.* at 2515 (Scalia, J., with Rehnquist, C.J., and Thomas, J., dissenting).

For various perspectives on the *Kiryas Joel* case, *see generally* Greene, "*Kiryas Joel* and Two Mistakes About Equality," 96 *Colum. L. Rev.* 1 (1996); Lupu, "Uncovering the Village of Kiryas Joel," 96 *Colum. L. Rev.* 104 (1996); Berg, "Slouching Towards Secularism: A Comment on *Kiryas Joel School District v. Grumet*", 44 *Emory L.J.* 433 (1995).

The New York State Legislature has continued its efforts to create a separate school district for the Satmars, albeit unsuccessfully. *See Grumet v. Cuomo,* 90 N.Y. 2d 57, 659 N.Y.S.2d 173, 681 N.E. 2d 340 (1997) (holding facially neutral statute, enacted four days after the Supreme Court decision, violated Establishment Clause because of its nonneutral effect in limiting its applicability to municipalities "in existence as of the effective date of" the statute); *Grumet v. Pataki,* 93 N.Y. 2d 677, 697 N.Y.S.2d 846, 720 N.E.2d 66, *cert. denied,* 528 U.S. 946, 120 S. Ct. 363, 145 L. Ed. 2d 284 (1999) (holding that new statute's primary effect remains one of nonneutrality, since only 2 of 1,545 municipalities meet statute's qualify-

ing criteria, "consciously drawn to benefit Kiryas Joel"). Some have raised concerns that the attempt to broaden the law to avoid the Establishment Clause would allow communities to create districts divided along lines of wealth and ethnicity. Perez-Pena, "Special School District's Backers Gird for 3d Suit and More," *New York Times* (January 23, 1998).

The New York Court of Appeals, in *Grumet v. Pataki, supra,* noted that *Agostini* "makes clear that the second prong of the *Lemon* test—the requirement that a law's 'primary effect must be one that neither advances nor inhibits religion'—remains a consideration in assessing whether the Establishment Clause has been violated." 93 N.Y.2d at 691. The court concluded by noting that "[t]he genesis of all this legislation and litigation—the seeming insurmountability of *Aguilar v. Felton*—no longer exists," *id.* at 697, and encouraged the parties to end the litigation of more than a decade and take advantage of the opportunity that *Agostini* provided.

2. *Is There Any Juice Left in* Lemon?

Although the Court does not say in *Agostini* that it has abandoned the *Lemon* test, what is the Court's Establishment Clause jurisprudence after *Agostini*? What does O'Connor mean when she says that the "program also cannot reasonably be viewed as an endorsement of religion. . . ."? Justice O'Connor, in her dissenting opinion in *Aguilar v. Felton,* 473 U.S. 402, 105 S.Ct. 3232, 87 L.Ed.2d 290 (1985), indicated that, for her, the critical fact is that "an objective observer of the implementation of the Title I program in New York would hardly view it as endorsing the tenets of the participating parochial schools." This state "endorsement" or "imprimatur" test is one that Justice O'Connor has advocated in a number of Establishment Clause cases. *See Wallace v. Jaffree,* 472 U.S. 38, 105 S.Ct. 2479, 2496–2505, 86 L.Ed. 2d 29 (1985) (O'Connor, J., concurring); *Lynch v. Donnelly,* 465 U.S. 668, 687–94, 104 S.Ct. 1355, 1366–70, 79 L.Ed.2d 604 (1984) (O'Connor, J., concurring). What is the relationship between the "endorsement" test and the *Lemon* formulation? What is the difference between an advancement of religion under the effects test and the endorsement of religion test? *See* Comment, "*Lemon* Reconstituted: Justice O'Connor's Proposed Modifications of the *Lemon* Test for Establishment Clause Violations," 1986 *BYU L. Rev.* 465. Has the wall of separation between church and state that existed under the old *Lemon* test become a permeable membrane under the Court's reformulation?

3. *After* Agostini: *Vouchers for Religiously Affiliated Schools?*

How broadly or narrowly should *Agostini* be read? What implications can be drawn from that case as to whether vouchers for religiously affiliated schools would be upheld in the face of an Establishment Clause claim? To what extent will an aid program be considered valid even if it "directly aids" religion? Consider the comments of Professor Lupu:

> I question the force of the constitutional case against direct state aid to sectarian elementary and secondary schools. The arguments against vouchers-usually characterized as indirect aid to sectarian schools because families are an intervening force between the state and these schools-and the arguments against direct aid rest on precedents and policies whose contemporary relevence has dwindled dramatically.

Lupa, "The Increasingly Anachronistic Case Against School Vouchers," 13 *Notre Dame L.J. Ethics and Pub. Pol'y* 375, 376 (1999). *See also* Hamilton, "Power, The Establishment Clause, and Vouchers," 31 *Conn. L. Rev.* 807 (2000). What criteria has the Court identified for evaluating whether "government aid has the effect of advancing religion"? In *Jackson v. Benson*, 218 Wis. 2d 835, 578 N.W.2d 602; *cert. denied*, 525 U.S. 997,119 S.Ct. 466, 142 L.Ed. 219 (1998), the Wisconsin Supreme Court, guided by *Agostini*, upheld a voucher program that included sectarian schools. *But see Simmons-Harris v. Zelman*, 234 F.3d945 (6th Cir. 2000), holding that a similar program violated the Establishment Clause.

A number of scholars have read *Agostini* as supporting voucher programs that include sectarian schools. *See, e.g.*, McConnell, "Governments, Families, and Power: A Defense of Educational Choice," 31 *Conn. L. Rev.* 847, 855 (1999) ("any well-constructed voucher program should easily be upheld"); Viteritti, "Blaine's Wake: School Choice, the First Amendment, and State Constitutional Law," 21 *Harv. J.L. & Pub. Pol'y* 657, 718 (1998); Morris, "Public Educational Services in Religious Schools: An Opening Wedge for Vouchers?"122 *Ed. Law Rep.* 545 (1998) ("violations of establishment clause may become as rare as findings of intentional discrimination under the Equal Protection Clause"). *See also* Note, "Reinventing the *Lemon: Agostini v. Felton* and the Changing Nature of Establishment Clause Jurisprudence," 1998 *Wis. L. Rev.* 1133; Comment, "Opening the Door to School Choice in Wisconsin: Is *Agostini v. Felton* the Key?" 81 *Marq. L. Rev.* 843 (1998); Note,

"*Agostini v. Felton:* Separating from Separation of Church and State to Allow School Choice," 29 *U. Tol. L. Rev.* 581 (1998); Note, "The Supreme Court's Shifting Tolerance for Public Aid to Parochial Schools and the Implications for Educational Choice," 21 *Harv. J. L. & Pub. Pol'y* 861 (1998); Note, "The Demise of Demarcation: *Agostini v. Felton* Unlocks the Parochial School Gate to State-Sponsored Educational Aid," 33 *Wake Forest L. Rev.* 465 (1998). But not all commentators think the decision can be read so broadly. Consider Professor Choper's analysis:

> In *Agostini v. Felton*, Justice O'Connor emphasized key facts about the Title I program at issue that place extensive limits on the reach of her opinion for the Court. . .
>
> Justice O'Connor . . . stressed that the Title I services were "supplemental to the regular curricula" and did not "relieve sectarian schools of costs they otherwise would have borne in educating their students." Strengthening this point, she added that Title I services are only available to eligible recipients. Second, she underlined that "no Title I funds ever reach the coffers of religious schools." Third, her description of the plan before the Court carefully emphasized that assignment of instructors and counselors to private schools "were made on a voluntary basis and without regard to the religious affiliation of the employer or the wishes of the private school. . . ." [Her description of the plan also emphasized the absence of religious symbols in the rooms used, and the fact that the rules limited instructors to consult with regular classroom teachers only with regard to professional concerns about the student's education.]
>
> Justice O'Connor's highly fact-specific approach supported her characterization of recent rulings . . . and confirmed her exceedingly narrow statement of the holding in the present case. Consequently, it seems that the Court's holding is too narrow and its majority too fragile to support bold claims about a green light for voucher programs or other substantial public aid to parochial schools, as some have suggested.

Choper, "Federal Constitutional Issues," in S.D. Sugarman and F. R. Kemerer (eds.), *School Choice and Social Controversy* 235, 243–44 (1999). *See also* Wood and Petko, "Assessing *Agostini v. Felton* in Light of *Lemon v. Kurtzman:* The Coming of Age in the Debate Between Religious Affiliated Schools and State Aid," 2000 *B.Y.U. Educ. & L.J.* 1, 15; Note, "Educational Vouchers and the Religion Clauses Under *Agostini:* Resurrection, Insurrection and a New Direction," 49 *Case W. Res. L. Rev.* 747, 774–776 (1999).

In *Helms v. Picard*, 151 F.3d 347 (5th Cir. 1998), the Fifth Circuit upheld as constitutional the on-site delivery of special education to children who attended religiously affiliated schools, applying the principles of *Agostini*, but held that a federal program of financial assistance to state and local educational agencies to enable them to implement "innovative assistance programs," 20 U.S.C. §7351(b)(2), and a similar Louisiana program, violated the Establishment Clause. Instructional and educational materials such as library books and materials, projectors, computers and printers, and computer software and hardware, were to be provided to children enrolled in private as well as public schools, although title to all materials and equipment was to remain with the public agency, and any services were to be provided by that agency. The court considered that *Agostini* held only that "the on-premises provision of special education services by state-paid teachers" did not advance religion, but that *Meek v. Pittenger*, 421 U.S. 349 (1975), and *Wolman v. Walter*, 433 U.S. 229 (1977), were still good law and applied to these other programs.

The Supreme Court, by a vote of 6 to 3, with a plurality opinion written by Justice Thomas, reversed, overruling its 1970s cases, *Meek v. Pittenger, supra*, and *Wolman v. Walter, supra*, on which the Fifth Circuit had relied, and applying the "effects" test of *Agostini, supra*. *Mitchell v. Helms*, 530 U.S. 793, 120 S.Ct. 2530, 147 L.Ed. 2d 660 (2000). The plurality opinion concluded that the federal aid program "neither results in religious indoctrination by the government nor defines its recipients by reference to religion." 120 S.Ct. at 2540. Citing *Agostini*, Justice Thomas noted that

> the question whether governmental aid to religious schools results in governmental indoctrination is ultimately a question whether any religious indoctrination that occurs in those schools could reasonably be attributed to governmental action. . . .
>
> In distinguishing between indoctrination that is attributable to the State and indoctrination that is not, we have consistently turned to the principle of neutrality, upholding aid that is offered to a broad range of groups or persons without regard to their religion. If the religious, irreligious, and areligious are all alike eligible for governmental aid, no one would conclude that any indoctrination that any particular recipient conducts has been done at the behest of the government. . . . [I]f the government, seeking to further some legitimate secular purpose, offers aid on the same terms, without regard to religion, to all who adequately further that purpose, . . . then it is fair to say that any aid going to a religious re-

cipient only has the effect of furthering that secular purpose. . . .

> As a way of assuring neutrality, we have repeatedly considered whether any governmental aid that goes to a religious institution does so "only as a result of the genuinely independent and private choices of individuals." *Agostini*. . . . For if numerous private choices, rather than the single choice of a government, determine the distribution of aid pursuant to neutral eligibility criteria, then a government cannot, or at least cannot easily, grant special favors that might lead to a religious establishment. Private choice also helps guarantee neutrality by mitigating the preference for pre-existing recipients that is arguably inherent in any governmental aid program . . . , and that could lead to a program inadvertently favoring one religion or favoring religious private schools in general over nonreligious ones.

* * *

Agostini's second primary criterion for determining the effect of governmental aid . . . requires a court to consider whether an aid program "define[s] its recipients by reference to religion.". . . In *Agostini* we set out the following rule for answering [whether the criteria for allocating the aid "creat[e] a financial incentive to undertake religious indoctrination"]:

> "This incentive is not present, however, where the aid is allocated on the basis of neutral, secular criteria that neither favor nor disfavor religion, and is made available to both religious and secular beneficiaries on a nondiscriminatory basis. Under such circumstances, the aid is less likely to have the effect of advancing religion."

Id. at 2451-43. The plurality saw no distinction between "aid . . . literally placed in the hands of schoolchildren" and aid "given directly to the school for teaching those same children." *Id.* at 2545. The plurality also dismissed the argument that aid in the form of projectors, computers, and computer software and hardware could be readily diverted to religious purposes. *Id.* at 2549.

In sum, the plurality held that "chapter 2 does not result in governmental indoctrination, because it determines eligibility for aid neutrally, allocates that aid based on the private choices of the parents of schoolchildren, and does not provide aid that has an impermissible content. Nor does chapter 2 define its recipients by reference to religion." *Id.* at 2552. In other words, the test that Justice Thomas would apply to governmental aid to religious schools appears to be that unless government aid results in religious indoctrination, defines its recipients by reference to religion, or creates an excessive government entanglement with religion, it is not unconstitutional.

Justice O'Connor, joined by Justice Breyer, concurred in the judgment, agreeing that *Agostini* required the reversal of the Fifth Circuit's decision, and that *Meek v. Pittenger* and *Wolman v. Walter* should be overruled, but refusing to join the plurality opinion's announcement of "a rule of unprecedented breadth for the evaluation of Establishment Clause challenges to government school-aid programs." *Id.* at 2556.

> First, the plurality's treatment of neutrality comes close to assigning that factor singular importance in the future adjudication of Establishment Clause challenges to government school-aid programs. Second, the plurality's approval of actual diversion of government aid to religious indoctrination is in tension with our precedents and, in any event, unnecessary to decide the instant case.

Id. Justice O'Connor would uphold the Chapter 2 program on the same relatively narrow basis as the Title I program upheld in *Agostini.* Her concurrence notes that in addition to the fact that Chapter 2 aid is distributed on the basis of "neutral, secular criteria," designed to assist students regardless of whether they attend public or private religious schools, school districts are required to use Chapter 2 funds only to supplement and not supplant non-Federal funds. Moreover, Chapter 2 requires that the materials and equipment must be "secular, neutral, and nonideological." Finally, in another parallel with *Agostini,* Chapter 2 funds do not go to the religious schools, but are controlled by public agencies—school districts purchase instructional and educational materials with Chapter 2 funds and then lend those materials to public and private schools, retaining title to the materials and equipment allocated to private schools. Justice O'Connor concludes that "[t]ogether with the supplantation restriction, this last provision ensures that religious schools reap no financial benefit by virtue of receiving loans of materials and equipment." *Id.* at 2562.

Although five justices held that government aid to religious schools in the form of instructional and educational materials was not a violation of the Establishment Clause, there does not yet seem to be agreement on the appropriate constitutional standard to apply. For critiques of this decision, *see, e.g.,* Chemerinsky, "Divided Court Grapples with Religion," 36 *Trial* 86 (Sept. 2000) (constitutionality of government programs that allow students to use vouchers to attend parochial schools still open question); Laycock, "The Supreme Court and Religious Liberty," 40 *Catholic Lawyer* 26, 48 (2000) (same); Amar, "Foreword: The Document and the Doctrine," 114 *Harv. L. Rev.* 26, 118 (2000); "The Supreme Court 1999 Term," 114 Harv. L. Rev. 179, 239 (2000), Mead and Underwood, "*Lemon* Distilled with Four Votes for Vouchers: An Examination of *Mitchell v. Helms* and its Implications," 149 *Ed. Law Rep.* 639 (2001).

T W O

Socialization and Student and Teacher Rights

I. INTRODUCTION

A. The Socialization Dilemma

Chapter 1 focused on the legal requirement that children attend some public or private school. That requirement, virtually unchallenged in the case law, is premised on a number of asserted state interests including preparing the individual for citizenship and economic independence, inculcating values, and preserving the security of the state. Indeed, "Americans have thought it easier to instruct the young than to coerce the adult." D. Tyack & L. Cuban, *Tinkering Toward Utopia* 2 (1995). If the American system of government is to survive and if the nation is to be secure, it is necessary to educate—to socialize— each new generation in those values and attitudes essential to the operation of American democracy. The schools inevitably reflect the culture and values of the larger society. But while this governmental interest is strong enough to warrant compulsory education laws and curricular and other requirements for public and private schools, the question may be one of balance. *But see* McConnell, "Why Is Religious Liberty the 'First Freedom'?" 21 *Cardozo L. Rev.* 1243, 1256–7 (2000) ("Government in a liberal society should not attempt to control education any more than it does the content of the press or churches."). The challenge is to maintain continuity, to foster knowledge, and to retain the values of the past while accommodating change, criticism, growth, and individual autonomy. *See generally* Gottlieb, "In the Name of Patriotism: The Constitutionality of 'Bending' History in the Public Secondary

Schools," 62 *N.Y.U. L. Rev.* 497 (1987); Yudof, "Library Book Selection and the Public Schools: The Quest for the Archimedean Point," 59 *Ind. L. J.* 527 (1984); van Geel, "The Search for Constitutional Limits on Governmental Authority to Inculcate Youth," 62 *Tex. L. Rev.* 197 (1983). Basic attitudes, skills, and knowledge must be communicated, while giving the young "ample opportunity of making the decisions upon which these principles are based, and by which they are modified, improved, adapted to changed circumstances, or even abandoned if they become entirely unsuited to a new environment." Hare, "Decisions of Principle," in I. Scheffler, ed., *Philosophy and Education* 72, 85 (1958). *See generally* C. Lindblom, *Inquiry and Change* (1990).

The socialization dilemma is reflected in debates over authority and legal entitlements in public education. *See generally* James, "Totality in Private and Public Schooling," 97 *Am. J. Educ.* 1 (1988); Arons and Lawrence, "The Manipulation of Consciousness: A First Amendment Critique of Schooling," 15 *Harv. C.R.-C.L. L. Rev.* 309 (1980). In the present context, should legislatures, school boards, and administrators have exclusive control of the socialization process within the public schools, or should parents, students, and teachers have rights, and what sort of rights, to shape or resist socialization processes? What are the substantive limits, if any, within which public school systems (and perhaps also parents, students, and teachers) must operate in shaping the educational program? *See, e.g.,* Gottlieb, *supra*; Yudof, *supra*; van Geel, *supra*; Stern, "Challenging Ideological

121

Exclusion of Curricular Material: Rights of Students and Parents," 14 *Harv. C.R.-C.L. L. Rev.* 485 (1979). Put somewhat differently, if the transmission of knowledge cannot be disentangled from socialization to values, who may or must be allowed to shape the content and methods of the education effort, and what sort of limitations, if any, are imposed by our laws and Constitution? Should courts require only "good faith" educational judgments by administrators? *See* Yudof, *"Tinker* Tailored: Good Faith, Civility, and Student Expression," 69 *St. John's L. Rev.* 365 (1995); Yudof, "Personal Speech and Government Expression," 38 *Case W. Res. L. Rev.* 671, 692–97 (1988).

The issues of limitations and the sharing of authority to shape the program of the public schools are intertwined. For example, to the extent that the First Amendment prohibits religious rituals in the public schools as a protection of the rights of parents, students, and taxpayers, parents, students, and taxpayers have a certain degree of authority to shape the content of the school program by insisting upon those rights. To the extent that parents have a right to remove their children from particular classes (e.g., sex education), they have authority to limit the school's program, at least insofar as the program affects their own children. If academic freedom for teachers allows them to make a range of presentational and pedagogical decisions, then the ability of the state to inculcate common values is diminished. Indeed, these issues are closely related to those considered in chapter 8 where the issue of educational governance is taken up more explicitly: Who participates in the general decision-making processes of the public schools? By what political or market mechanisms might public schools be held accountable and accountable to whom? Accountable for what? *See generally* S. Arons, *Compelling Belief* (1983).

From yet another perspective, this chapter deals with the same theme dealt with in chapter 1—the tension among child, family, and state. But in this chapter, these issues are addressed in the context of the public school itself. Section II examines the constitutional limitations directly applicable to state and school board decisions regarding the content and methods of public schooling. Section III turns to the free speech rights of students and teachers and thus their ability to shape the overall socialization process by the exercise of rights to speak within and without the public schools.

B. State Action

With perhaps the exception of the Thirteenth Amendment, the Constitution's guarantees of individual rights generally protect individuals only from governmental action. *See NCAA v. Tarkanian,* 488 U.S. 179, 109 S.Ct. 454, 102 L.Ed.2d 469 (1988); *Runyon v. McCrary,* 427 U.S. 160, 96 S.Ct. 2586, 49 L.Ed.2d 415 (1976); *Sinn v. The Daily Nebraskan,* 829 F.2d 622 (8th Cir. 1987). Thus private schools control student and teacher behavior in ways and for reasons denied to public schools. *See, e.g., Stone v. Dartmouth College,* 682 F.Supp. 106 (D.N.H. 1988). Private schools may suspend students without a hearing to determine whether a school rule has been offended. *See, e.g., Bright v. Isenbarger,* 314 F.Supp. 1382 (N.D. Ind. 1970), *aff'd,* 445 F.2d 412 (7th Cir. 1971); *Blackburn v. Fisk University,* 443 F.2d 121 (6th Cir. 1971). The fact that a private school may be regulated by the state or that it receives governmental financial support or that it uses the name of the state in the name of the school has not been deemed sufficient involvement to conclude that the school's actions were really government action. The courts have tended to accept the position taken by Judge Friendly in *Powe v. Miles,* 407 F.2d 73, 81 (2d Cir. 1968), a case in which students attacked the disciplinary procedures of a private university:

> The contention that [there is state action in this case] overlooks the essential point—that the state must be involved not simply with some activity of the institution alleged to have inflicted injury upon a plaintiff but with the activity that caused the injury. . . . When the state bans a subject from the curriculum of a private school, as in *Meyer v. Nebraska,* 262 U.S. 390, . . . its responsibility needs no elucidation. State action would be similarly present here . . . if New York had undertaken to set policy for the control of demonstrations in all private universities. . . . But the fact that New York has exercised some regulatory powers over the standard of education offered by Alfred University does not implicate it generally in Alfred's policies toward demonstrations and discipline.

407 F.2d at 81. *See also Braden v. University of Pittsburgh,* 552 F.2d 948 (3d Cir. 1977) (en banc). *See generally* H. Friendly, *The Dartmouth College Case and the Public-Private Penumbra* (1968); O'Neill, "Private Universities and Public Law," 19 *Buff. L. Rev.* 155 (1970); Note, "The Supreme Court—1988 Term," 103 *Harv. L. Rev.* 137, 187 (1989).

In the context of this chapter and chapter 1, the state action limitation protects diversity within the educational sector of society. For example, if there were no state action requirement, courts could require private schools to limit teaching about or indoctrination in religion, as the public schools are obliged to do. But to the extent that private schools remain free from the limitations of the Establishment Clause, religious schooling may be largely free of judicial control, and the free exercise of religion may receive broader protection.

Within the context of the public schools, the state action doctrine has been interpreted in such a way that the actions of principals and teachers, even when not expressly authorized by the school board or state legislature, may be viewed as actions of the state. *Cf. Monroe v. Pape*, 365 U.S. 167 (1961).

In *Rendell-Baker v. Kohn*, 457 U.S. 830, 102 S.Ct. 2764, 73 L.Ed.2d 418 (1982), Rendell-Baker, a vocational counselor hired under a grant from the federal Law Enforcement Assistance Administration (LEAA), and five teachers were discharged by the Director of the New Perspectives School, a nonprofit institution located on privately owned property in Brookline, Massachusetts. The school specialized in serving children "who have experienced difficulty completing public high schools," including many with "drug, alcohol, or behavioral problems, or other special needs." Nearly all of the students at the New Perspectives School had been referred to it by public school districts or by the Drug Rehabilitation Division of the Massachusetts Department of Mental Health. Under applicable Massachusetts laws, school districts pay for the education of students referred to the school, and combined with funding from state and federal sources, at least 90 percent of the operating budget of the New Perspectives School came from public funds. Further, as a condition of receiving its LEAA grant, the Massachusetts Committee on Criminal Justice had to approve initial hiring decisions for vocational counselors.

Rendell-Baker and the discharged teachers filed separate suits in federal district court under 42 U.S.C. § 1983, alleging that their rights under the First, Fifth, and Fourteenth Amendments to the Constitution had been violated. In essence, they asserted that they had been fired for protected speech activities and that they had been denied procedural due process. The district judge in the *Rendell-Baker* case held that "the nexus between the school and the State was not sufficiently close so that the action of the

school in discharging *Rendell-Baker* could be considered action of the Commonwealth of Massachusetts," and denied plaintiff any relief. Another judge in the same district, however, ruled in favor of plaintiff teachers, reaching a contrary conclusion on the state action issue. The Court of Appeals for the First Circuit consolidated the two cases, and held that the defendants had not acted under color of state law. The Supreme Court, with two justices dissenting, affirmed the judgment of the Court of Appeals.

Chief Justice Burger, writing for the majority, reasoned that the "core issue in this case is not whether petitioners were discharged because of their speech or without adequate procedural protections, but whether the school's action in discharging them can fairly be seen as state action. If the action of the respondent is not state action, our inquiry ends:"

> The school . . . is not fundamentally different from many private corporations whose business depends primarily on contracts to build roads, bridges, dams, ships, or submarines for the government. Acts of such private contractors do not become acts of the government by reason of their significant or even total engagement in performing public contracts.

* * *

> Here the decisions to discharge the petitioners were not compelled or even influenced by any state regulation. Indeed, in contrast to the extensive regulation of the school generally, the various regulators showed relatively little interest in the school's personnel matters. The most intrusive personnel regulation promulgated by the various government agencies was the requirement that the Committee on Criminal Justice had the power to approve persons hired as vocational counselors. Such a regulation is not sufficient to make a decision to discharge, made by private management, state action. . . .

* * *

> There can be no doubt that the education of maladjusted high school students is a public function, but that is only the beginning of the inquiry. Chapter 766 of the Massachusetts Act of 1972 demonstrates that the State intends to provide services for such students at public expense. That legislative policy choice in no way makes these services the exclusive province of the State. Indeed, the Court of Appeals noted that until recently the State had not undertaken to provide education for students who could not be served by traditional public schools. . . . That a private entity performs a function which serves the public does not make its acts state action.

457 U.S. at 840, 102 S.Ct. at 2771. *See also NCAA v. Tarkanian*, 488 U.S. 179, 109 S.Ct. 454, 102 L.Ed.2d 469 (1988). Does the *Rendell-Baker* decision treat state action more narrowly than the test promulgated in *Powe v. Miles, supra*? *See* W. A. Kaplan and B. A. Lee, *The Law of Higher Education* 45–54 (3d ed. 1995).

II. RELIGIOUS, POLITICAL, AND MORAL SOCIALIZATION

A. Sectarian Socialization

Questions concerning the proper place of religion in the curriculum of the public schools have been with us since the origins of the public school movement. Professor Cremin, reviewing the public school movement generally, notes that from the outset a range of positions were taken on the best way religion could be made part of the school program. The politically dominant position was one worked out as a compromise among various Protestant groups. Under this approach, schools were to instruct pupils in those common values and ideals on which the Protestant sects agreed, but instruction in these values, while rooted in Christianity, would not be taught in a religious context. Instruction in specific doctrine and dogma would be left to the family, the pulpit, and the Sabbath school. The other way of providing a moral base for the teaching of the common school was the introduction of reading from the Bible without comments as part of school exercises. In different places and in different times, prayers were also introduced as part of school exercises. This approach attempted both to respect the religious diversity of the country and avoid an irreligious or non religious morality. L. Cremin, *The American Common School* 66–70 (1951).

Other approaches were also attempted. *See, e.g.,* C. Fairman, *Reconstruction and Reunion 1864–88,* 1310–18 (1971). In New York City, the Public School Society, a quasi-public organization that operated a number of free schools supported by public funds, insisted that its schools must be and were non-sectarian, a claim the Catholic hierarchy vigorously disputed. D. Ravitch, *The Great School Wars, New York City, 1805–1973,* ch. 4 (1974). As the New York City experience suggests, the strategy of trying to avoid at least overt denominationalism met with only partial success. It was attacked as insufficiently religious by some Protestant sects, while Catholics ar-

gued that the public schools were all too sectarian. They pointed with special alarm to the use of the Protestant Bible in the public schools. Dissatisfaction with the Protestant tone of the public schools led to efforts to establish parochial schools. *See* Laycock, "A Survey of Religious Liberty in the United States," 47 *Ohio St. L.J.* 409, 418 (1986). At least in New York City, the drive for parochial schools was also premised on opposition to the notion of common schooling itself.

For much of the twentieth century, religion remained a key part of the curriculum of public schools. The prevailing attitude was aptly described in Professor Beale's classic work, *Are American Teachers Free?* (1936):

> Americans . . . generally are as determined to keep irreligion out of the schools as to exclude sectarianism. An overwhelming majority of citizens believe that teachers with at least a mild interest in religion "have a better influence" on children than those of no religion. . . . Religion makes children "better children." It gives them something that even parents who have discarded it wish them to have. . . . "Christian" in ordinary parlance is an adjective of commendation.
>
> . . . Furthermore, if the purpose of schools is to instill "patriotic" attitudes, correct economic views, and conformity to political, social, and business practices of the community . . . , why should not the community's religious beliefs also be implanted in children: agnostic attitudes where they prevail, and Catholic dogma where Catholics predominate?

Id. at 210, 217. *See* D. Tyack & L. Cuban, *Tinkering Toward Utopia* 16 (1995) ("Protestant Republican Ideology"). But in the post–World War II period, the place of religion in the public schools began to change dramatically. In 1962 the Supreme Court, invoking the prohibition on the establishment of religion in the First Amendment, held that a twenty-two-word prayer used daily in New York classrooms as an invocation at the beginning of the school day was unconstitutional. *Engel v. Vitale,* 370 U.S. 421, 82 S.Ct. 1261, 8 L.Ed.2d 601 (1962). A year later the Supreme Court delivered its landmark decision on school prayer in *Abington School District v. Schempp,* 374 U.S. 203, 83 S.Ct. 1560, 10 L.Ed.2d 844 (1963).

In the *Schempp* case (and a companion case decided in the same opinion), Unitarian and atheist parents mounted a constitutional attack on public school policies requiring readings, without comment, from the Bible at the beginning of each school day. The readings were followed by a recitation of the Lord's Prayer by the students. Students were permitted to absent themselves from participation in the exercises upon a request of the parent. In an opinion by Justice Clark, the Court declared the Bible reading and school prayer to be violative of the Establishment Clause:

> First, this Court has decisively settled that the First Amendment's mandate that "Congress shall make no law respecting an establishment of religion, or prohibiting the free exercise thereof" has been made wholly applicable to the States by the Fourteenth Amendment. . . .
>
> Second, this Court has rejected unequivocally the contention that the Establishment Clause forbids only governmental preference of one religion over another. . . .

                                    * * *

The wholesome "neutrality" of which this Court's [Establishment Clause] cases speak . . . stems from a recognition of the teachings of history that powerful sects or groups might bring about a fusion of governmental and religious functions or a concert or dependency of one upon the other to the end that official support of the State or Federal Government would be placed behind the tenets of one or of all orthodoxies. This the Establishment Clause prohibits. And a further reason for neutrality is found in the Free Exercise Clause, which recognizes the value of religious training, teaching and observance and, more particularly, the right of every person to freely choose his own course with reference thereto, free of any compulsion from the state. This the Free Exercise Clause guarantees. . . . [I]t has been consistently held that the [Establishment] [C]lause withdrew all legislative power respecting religious belief or the expression thereof. The test may be stated as follows: what are the purpose and the primary effect of the enactment? If either is the advancement or inhibition then the enactment exceeds the scope of legislative power as circumscribed by the Constitution. That is to say that to withstand the strictures of the Establishment Clause there must be a secular legislative purpose and a primary effect that neither advances nor inhibits religion. The Free Exercise Clause . . . withdraws from legislative power, state and federal, the exertion of any restraint on the free exercise of religion. Its purpose is to secure religious liberty in the individual by prohibiting any invasions thereof by civil authority. Hence it is necessary in a free exercise case for one to show the coercive effect of the enactment as it operates against him in the practice of his religion. The distinction between the two clauses is apparent—a violation of the Free Exercise Clause is predicated on coercion while the Establishment Clause violation need not be so attended.

                                    * * *

[I]n both cases the laws require religious exercises and such exercises are being conducted in direct violation of the rights of the appellees and petitioners. Nor are these required exercises mitigated by the fact that individual students may absent themselves upon parental request, for that fact furnishes no defense to a claim of unconstitutionality under the Establishment Clause. . . . Further, it is no defense to urge that the religious practices here may be relatively minor encroachments on the First Amendment. The breach of neutrality that is today a trickling stream may all too soon become a raging torrent. . . .

It is insisted that unless these religious exercises are permitted a "religion of secularism" is established in the schools. We agree of course that the State may not establish a "religion of secularism" in the sense of affirmatively opposing or showing hostility to religion, thus "preferring those who believe in no religion over those who do believe." . . . We do not agree, however, that this decision in any sense has that effect. In addition, it might well be said that one's education is not complete without a study of comparative religion or the history of religion and its relationship to the advancement of civilization. It certainly may be said that the Bible is worthy of study for its literary and historic qualities. Nothing we have said here indicates that such study of the Bible or of religion, when presented objectively as part of a secular program of education, may not be effected consistently with the First Amendment. But the exercises here do not fall into those categories. They are religious exercises, required by the States in violation of the command of the First Amendment that the Government maintain strict neutrality, neither aiding nor opposing religion.

Finally, we cannot accept that the concept of neutrality, which does not permit a State to require a religious exercise even with the consent of the majority of those affected, collides with the majority's right to free exercise of religion. While the Free Exercise Clause clearly prohibits the use of state action to deny the rights of free exercise to anyone, it has never meant that a majority could use the machinery of the State to practice his beliefs. . . .

In the early years after the school prayer cases, there was strong resistance to compliance, particularly in the East and South, but gradually the decisions took hold. *See* S. Wasby, *The Impact of the Supreme Court* 129–33 (1970). Subsequently, numerous groups and individuals asserted that irreligion had crept into the public schools, that public schools were hostile to religion, and, in some quarters, even that the public schools were dominated by a religion of secular humanism. *See generally* Dent, "Religious Children, Secular Schools," 61 *So. Cal.*

L. Rev. 864 (1988). For example, by the late 1970s courses on the Bible as religion or literature began to disappear from the curriculum. Association for Supervision and Curriculum Development, *Religion in the Curriculum* ch. 2 (1987) (hereinafter *Religion in the Curriculum*). And a number of studies concluded that references to religion had been excised from textbooks and the curriculum. *See* O. L. Davis et al., *Looking at History: A Review of Major U.S. Textbooks* (1986); P. Vitz, *Censorship: Evidence of Bias in Our Children's Textbooks* (1986). *See* P. E. Johnson, *Reason in the Balance* 155–71 (1995).

Concerns about the diminishing role of religion in the schools manifested themselves in a variety of ways. First, a number of jurisdictions enacted laws mandating "moments of silence" at the beginning of the school day as a substitute for religious exercises. *See Wallace v. Jaffree, infra.* Second, there were numerous calls for constitutional amendments, supported by popular majorities, that would have overturned the school prayer decisions. In 1982 President Reagan proposed the following constitutional amendment: "Nothing in this Constitution shall be construed to prohibit individual or group prayer in public schools or other public institutions. No person shall be required by the United States or by any State to participate in prayer." The proposed amendment was not adopted by the required two-thirds of each house of Congress. Third, lawsuits were filed by religious groups attacking the secular orientation of public education. *See* sections IIA1 and IIA2, *infra.* Fourth, educators began to call for the reintroduction of religion into the public schools in the limited sense of inculcating knowledge of the role of religion in history, literature, and other subjects. They argued that the public schools had overreacted to the school prayer decisions and were willing to allow a distortion of subjects in the curriculum in order to avoid controversy. *Religion in the Curriculum, supra.* As one study urged,

> [T]he quest for religious freedom that fueled the establishment of this nation receives scant treatment at best in many of the textbooks currently in use. The texts have even less to say about the profound part religious belief has played in more recent U.S. history. Students probably won't find out from their textbooks that religious groups were a vital force in the abolitionist and temperance movements of the nineteenth century or the civil rights movement of the twentieth.
>
> Nor is it only texts in American history that are affected. The critical influence of religion in world his-

tory and culture is similarly slighted in texts on political science, sociology, literature, and world history. . . .

> As these few examples suggest, references to religion have been all but excised from the public school curriculum. . . . This filtering of religious influences—intended as such or not . . .—is the result, in part, of concern that the constitutional wall separating church and state might be breached. It also reflects an exaggerated fear of controversy. . . . Despite the absence of teaching about religion in our schools—or perhaps because of it—some parents charge that school officials are scaling that wall by promoting "secular humanism" as a religion itself. Others demand that schools shield their children from ideas that conflict with the family's religious beliefs.

Religion in the Curriculum, supra at 7–8.

In considering the cases and materials that follow on religion and the public schools, the reader should be aware of a number of trends that may have exacerbated tensions. In reaction to the perceived breakdown of traditional values in the 1960s and the school prayer and abortion decisions, evangelical, charismatic, and fundamentalist Christian groups in America greatly gained strength while more liberal Protestant denominations gradually lost membership. The former groups were more sensitive to secular trends in public schooling and objected to the severance of the tie between morality and religion. At the same time, and partially in a misreading or exaggeration of the school prayer decisions, school officials often seemed anxious to avoid any controversy concerning religion, and they reacted by simply avoiding the subject. The latter impulse was strengthened and reinforced by a progressive privatization of religious and moral values:

> [P]ublic schools are cautious to avoid even the possibility of invading individuals' belief systems—a caution that honors the abiding American assumption of religion as private as much as it skirts constitutional issues of church and state. Moreover, distinctions among dogmas, practices, and observances in different religions are not easily drawn. This difficulty leads many schools to back away from teaching about religion to escape the charge that they are teaching the dogma of a particular religion.
>
> In addition, widespread confusion about the relationship of religion and morality makes shaping school policy more difficult. On the one hand, if moral education is held to be religious education, instruction about morality is constitutionally prohibited. (Indeed, many people find the very notion of a body of tenable moral positions inappropriate in a pluralistic society.)

On the other hand, many people reject the assumption . . . that either individual or civic morality rests upon particular religious beliefs. Faced with the prospect of picking their way through a minefield of conflicting opinions, educators generally assert that adherence to moral precepts is essential to a society and then leave it to individuals to decide, in the light of their own religious beliefs, what these precepts are.

Religion in the Curriculum, supra at 15.

1. School Prayer and Moments of Silence

Wallace v. Jaffree

472 U.S. 38, 105 S.Ct. 2479, 86 L.Ed.2d 29 (1985).

Justice Stevens delivered the opinion of the court.

At an early stage of this litigation, the constitutionality of three Alabama statutes was questioned: (1) § 16-1-20, enacted in 1978, which authorized a 1-minute period of silence in all public schools "for meditation";[1] (2) § 16-1-20.1, enacted in 1981, which authorized a period of silence "for meditation or voluntary prayer";[2] and (3) § 16-1-20.2, enacted in 1982, which authorized teachers to lead "willing students" in a prescribed prayer to "Almighty God . . . the Creator and Supreme Judge of the world."[3]

At the preliminary-injunction stage of this case, the District Court distinguished § 16-1-20 from the other two statutes. It then held that there was "nothing wrong" with § 16-1-20,[4] but that §§ 16-1-20.1 and 16-1-20.2 were both invalid because the sole purpose of both was "an effort on the part of the State of Alabama to encourage a religious activity."[5] After the trial on the merits, the District Court did not change its interpretation of these two statutes, but held that they were constitutional because, in its opinion, Alabama has the power to establish a state religion if it chooses to do so.[6]

The Court of Appeals agreed with the District Court's initial interpretation of the purpose of both § 16-1-20.1 and § 16-1-20.2, and held them both unconstitutional.[7] We have already affirmed the Court of Appeals' holding with respect to § 16-1-20.2.[8] Moreover, appellees have not questioned the holding that § 16-1-20 is valid.[9] Thus, the narrow question for decision is whether § 16-1-20.1, which authorizes a period of silence for "meditation or voluntary prayer," is a law respecting the establishment of religion within the meaning of the First Amendment.

I

Appellee Ishmael Jaffree is a resident of Mobile County, Alabama. On May 28, 1982, he filed a complaint on behalf of three of his minor children; two of them were second-grade students and the third was then in kindergarten. The complaint named members of the Mobile County School Board, various

---

[1]Alabama Code § 16-1-20 (Supp. 1984) reads as follows:

"At the commencement of the first class each day in the first through the sixth grades in all public schools, the teacher in charge of the room in which each such class is held shall announce that a period of silence, not to exceed one minute in duration, shall be observed for meditation, and during any such period silence shall be maintained and no activities engaged in."

Appellees have abandoned any claim that § 16-1-20 is unconstitutional.

[2]Alabama Code § 16-1-20.1 (Supp. 1984) provides:

"At the commencement of the first class of each day in all grades in all public schools the teacher in charge of the room in which each class is held may announce that a period of silence not to exceed one minute in duration shall be observed for meditation or voluntary prayer, and during any such period no other activities shall be engaged in."

[3]Alabama Code § 16-1-20.2 (Supp. 1984) provides:

"From henceforth, any teacher or professor in any public educational institution within the state of Alabama, recognizing that the Lord God is one, at the beginning of any homeroom or any class, may pray, may lead willing students in prayer, or may lead the willing students in the following prayer to God:

Almighty God, You alone are our God. We acknowledge You as the Creator and Supreme Judge of the world. May Your justice,
Your truth, and Your peace abound this day in the hearts of our countrymen, in the counsels of our government, in the sanctity of
our homes and in the classrooms of our schools, in the name of our Lord. Amen."

[4]The court stated that it did not find any potential infirmity in § 16-1-20 because "it is a statute which prescribes nothing more than a child in school shall have the right to meditate in silence and there is nothing wrong with a little meditation and quietness." *Jaffree v. James*, 544 F. Supp. 727, 732 (SD Ala. 1982).

[5]*Ibid.*

[6]*Jaffree v. Board of School Comm'rs of Mobile County*, 554 F.Supp. 1104, 1128 (SD Ala. 1983).

[7]705 F.2d 1526, 1535-1536 (11th Cir. 1983).

[8]*Wallace v. Jaffree*, 466 U.S. 924, 104 S.Ct. 1704, 80 L.Ed.2d 178 (1984).

[9]*See* n. 1, *supra*.

school officials, and the minor plaintiffs' three teach- ers as defendants. The complaint alleged that the appellees brought the action "seeking principally a declaratory judgment and an injunction restraining the Defendants and each of them from maintaining or allowing the maintenance of regular religious prayer services or other forms of religious observances in the Mobile County Public Schools in violation of the First Amendment as made applicable to states by the Fourteenth Amendment to the United States Constitution." The complaint further alleged that two of the children had been subjected to various acts of religious indoctrination "from the beginning of the school year in September, 1981"; that the defendant teachers had "on a daily basis" led their classes in say- ing certain prayers in unison; that the minor children were exposed to ostracism from their peer group class members if they did not participate; and that Ishmael Jaffree had repeatedly but unsuccessfully requested that the devotional services be stopped. . . .

* * *

In November 1982, the District Court held a 4-day trial on the merits. The evidence related primarily to the 1981–1982 academic year—the year after the en- actment of § 16-1-20.1 and prior to the enactment of § 16-1-20.2. The District Court found that during that academic year each of the minor plaintiffs' teachers had led classes in prayer activities, even after being in- formed of appellees' objections to these activities.[23]

In its lengthy conclusions of law, the District Court reviewed a number of opinions of this Court interpreting the Establishment Clause of the First Amendment, and then embarked on a fresh exami- nation of the question whether the First Amendment imposes any barrier to the establishment of an offi- cial religion by the State of Alabama. After reviewing at length what it perceived to be newly discovered historical evidence, the District Court concluded that "the establishment clause of the first amend- ment to the United States Constitution does not pro- hibit the state from establishing a religion." In a separate opinion, the District Court dismissed ap- pellees' challenge to the three Alabama statutes be- cause of a failure to state any claim for which relief could be granted. The court's dismissal of this chal- lenge was also based on its conclusion that the Establishment Clause did not bar the States from es- tablishing a religion.[25]

The Court of Appeals consolidated the two cases; not surprisingly, it reversed. The Court of Appeals noted that this Court had considered and had re- jected the historical arguments that the District Court found persuasive, and that the District Court had misapplied the doctrine of stare decisis. The Court of Appeals then held that the teachers' reli- gious activities violated the Establishment Clause of the First Amendment.[27] With respect to § 16-1-20.1 and § 16-1-20.2, the Court of Appeals stated that

---

[23]The District Court wrote:

> "Defendant Boyd, as early as September 16, 1981, led her class at E. R. Dickson in singing the following phrase:
> " 'God is great, God is good,
> " 'Let us thank him for our food,
> " 'bow our heads we all are fed,
> " 'Give us Lord our daily bread.
> " 'Amen!'

"The recitation of this phrase continued on a daily basis through the 1981–82 school year.

> "Defendant Pixie Alexander has led her class at Craighead in reciting the following phrase:
> " 'God is great, God is good,
> " 'Let us thank him for our food.'

"Further, defendant Pixie Alexander had her class recite the following, which is known as the Lord's Prayer:

> " 'Our Father, which art in heaven, hallowed be Thy name. Thy kingdom come. Thy will be done on earth as it is in heaven. Give us this day our daily bread and forgive us our debts as we forgive our debtors. And lead us not into temptation but deliver us from evil, for Thine is the king- dom and the power and the glory forever. Amen.'

"The recitation of these phrases continued on a daily basis throughout the 1981–82 school year.

* * *

"Ms. Green admitted that she frequently leads her class in singing the following song:

> " 'For health and strength and daily food, we praise Thy name, Oh Lord.'

"This activity continued throughout the school year, despite the fact that Ms. Green had knowledge that plaintiff did not want his child exposed to the above-mentioned song." *Jaffree v. Board of School Comm'rs of Mobile County,* 554 F. Supp., at 1107–1108.

[25]*Jaffree v. James,* 554 F. Supp. 1130, 1132 (SD Ala. 1983). The District Court's opinion was announced on January 14, 1983. On February 11, 1983, Jus- tice Powell, in his capacity as Circuit Justice for the Eleventh Circuit, entered a stay which in effect prevented the District Court from dissolving the pre- liminary injunction that had been entered in August 1982. . . .

[27] . . . . This Court has denied a petition for a writ of certiorari that presented the question whether the Establishment Clause prohibited the teachers' re- ligious prayer activities. *Board of School Comm'rs of Mobile County v. Jaffree,* 466 U.S. 926, 104 S.Ct. 1707, 80 L.Ed.2d 181 (1984).

"both statutes advance and encourage religious activities." The Court of Appeals then quoted with approval the District Court's finding that § 16-1-20.1, and § 16-1-20.2, were efforts " 'to encourage a religious activity. Even though these statutes are permissive in form, it is nevertheless state involvement respecting an establishment of religion.' "[30]

* * *

II

Our unanimous affirmance of the Court of Appeals' judgment concerning § 16-1-20.2 makes it unnecessary to comment at length on the District Court's remarkable conclusion that the Federal Constitution imposes no obstacle to Alabama's establishment of a state religion. Before analyzing the precise issue that is presented to us, it is nevertheless appropriate to recall how firmly embedded in our constitutional jurisprudence is the proposition that the several States have no greater power to restrain the individual freedoms protected by the First Amendment than does the Congress of the United States.

As is plain from its text, the First Amendment was adopted to curtail the power of Congress to interfere with the individual's freedom to believe, to worship, and to express himself in accordance with the dictates of his own conscience.[32] Until the Fourteenth Amendment was added to the Constitution, the First Amendment's restraints on the exercise of federal power simply did not apply to the States. But when the Constitution was amended to prohibit any State from depriving any person of liberty without due process of law, that Amendment imposed the same substantive limitations on the States' power to legislate that the First Amendment had always imposed on the Congress' power. This Court has confirmed and endorsed this elementary proposition of law time and time again.

* * *

Just as the right to speak and the right to refrain from speaking are complementary components of a broader concept of individual freedom of mind, so also the individual's freedom to choose his own creed is the counterpart of his right to refrain from accepting the creed established by the majority. At one time it was thought that this right merely proscribed the preference of one Christian sect over another, but would not require equal respect from the conscience of the infidel, the atheist, or the adherent of a non-Christian faith such as Islam or Judaism.[36] But when the underlying principle has been examined in the crucible of litigation, the Court has unambiguously concluded that the individual freedom of conscience protected by the First Amendment embraces the right to select any religious faith or none at all. This conclusion derives support not only from the interest

---

[30]*Ibid.* After noting that the invalidity of § 16-1-20.2 was aggravated by "the existence of a government composed prayer," and that the proponents of the legislation admitted that that section "amounts to the establishment of a state religion," the court added this comment on § 16-1-20.1:

"The objective of the meditation or prayer statute (Ala. Code § 16-1-20.1) was the advancement of religion. This fact was recognized by the district court at the hearing for preliminary relief where it was established that the intent of the statute was to return prayer to the public schools. *James,* 544 F.Supp. at 731. The existence of this fact and the inclusion of prayer obviously involves the state in religious activities. *Beck v. McElrath,* 548 F.Supp. 1161 (MD Tenn.1982). This demonstrates a lack of secular legislative purpose on the part of the Alabama Legislature. Additionally, the statute has the primary effect of advancing religion. We do not imply that simple meditation or silence is barred from the public schools; we hold that the state cannot participate in the advancement of religious activities through any guise, including teacher-led meditation. It is not the activity itself that concerns us; it is the purpose of the activity that we shall scrutinize. Thus, the existence of these elements require that we also hold section 16-1-20.1 in violation of the establishment clause." . . .

[32]The First Amendment provides:

"Congress shall make no law respecting an establishment of religion, or prohibiting the free exercise thereof; or abridging the freedom of speech, or of the press; or the right of the people peaceably to assemble, and to petition the Government for a redress of grievances."

[36]Thus Joseph Story wrote:

"Probably at the time of the adoption of the constitution, and of the amendment to it, now under consideration [First Amendment], the general, if not the universal sentiment in America was, that Christianity ought to receive encouragement from the state, so far as was not incompatible with the private rights of conscience, and the freedom of religious worship. An attempt to level all religions, and to make it a matter of state policy to hold all in utter indifference, would have created universal disapprobation, if not universal indignation." 2 J. Story, Commentaries on the Constitution of the United States § 1874, p. 593 (1851) (footnote omitted).

In the same volume, Story continued:

"The real object of the amendment was, not to countenance, much less to advance, Mahometanism, or Judaism, or infidelity, by prostrating Christianity; *but to exclude all rivalry among Christian sects, and to prevent any national ecclesiastical establishment, which should give to a hierarchy the exclusive patronage of the national government. It thus cut off the means of religious persecution, (the vice and pest of former ages,) and of the subversion of the rights of conscience in matters of religion,* which had been trampled upon almost from the days of the Apostles to the present age. . . . " *Id.,* § 1877, at 594 (emphasis supplied).

in respecting the individual's freedom of conscience, but also from the conviction that religious beliefs worthy of respect are the product of free and voluntary choice by the faithful, and from recognition of the fact that the political interest in forestalling intolerance extends beyond intolerance among Christian sects—or even intolerance among "religions"—to encompass intolerance of the disbeliever and the uncertain. As Justice Jackson eloquently stated in *West Virginia Board of Education v. Barnette*, 319 U.S. 624, 642, 63 S.Ct. 1178, 1187, 87 L.Ed. 1628 (1943):

> "If there is any fixed star in our constitutional constellation, it is that no official, high or petty, can prescribe what shall be orthodox in politics, nationalism, religion, or other matters of opinion or force citizens to confess by word or act their faith therein."

The State of Alabama, no less than the Congress of the United States, must respect that basic truth.

III

When the Court has been called upon to construe the breadth of the Establishment Clause, it has examined the criteria developed over a period of many years. Thus, in *Lemon v. Kurtzman*, 403 U.S. 602, 612-13, 91 S.Ct. 2105, 2111, 29 L.Ed.2d 745 (1971), we wrote:

> "Every analysis in this area must begin with consideration of the cumulative criteria developed by the Court over many years. Three such tests may be gleaned from our cases. First, the statute must have a secular legislative purpose; second, its principal or primary effect must be one that neither advances nor inhibits religion, *Board of Education v. Allen*, 392 U.S. 236, 243 [88 S.Ct. 1923, 1926, 20 L.Ed.2d 1060] (1968); finally the statute must not foster 'an excessive government entanglement with

religion.' *Walz [v. Tax Comm'n*, 397 U.S. 664, 674 [90 S.Ct. 1409, 1414, 25 L.Ed.2d 697] (1970)]."

It is the first of these three criteria that is most plainly implicated by this case. As the District Court correctly recognized, no consideration of the second or third criteria is necessary if a statute does not have a clearly secular purpose. For even though a statute that is motivated in part by a religious purpose may satisfy the first criterion, *see, e.g., Abington School District v. Schempp*, 374 U.S. 203, 296–303, 83 S.Ct. 1560, 1610–1614, 10 L.Ed.2d 844 (1963) (Brennan, J., concurring), the First Amendment requires that a statute must be invalidated if it is entirely motivated by a purpose to advance religion.[41]

In applying the purpose test, it is appropriate to ask "whether government's actual purpose is to endorse or disapprove of religion." In this case, the answer to that question is dispositive. For the record not only provides us with an unambiguous affirmative answer, but it also reveals that the enactment of § 16-1-20.1 was not motivated by any clearly secular purpose—indeed, the statute had no secular purpose.

IV

The sponsor of the bill that became § 16-1-20.1, Senator Donald Holmes, inserted into the legislative record—apparently without dissent—a statement indicating that the legislation was an "effort to return voluntary prayer" to the public schools.[43] Later Senator Holmes confirmed this purpose before the District Court. In response to the question whether he had any purpose for the legislation other than returning voluntary prayer to public schools, he stated: "No, I did not have no other purpose in

---

[41]*See Lynch v. Donnelly*, 465 U.S. 668, 680, 104 S.Ct. 1355, 1362–1363, 79 L.Ed.2d 604 (1984); *id.*, at 690, 104 S.Ct., at 1368 (O'Connor, J., concurring); *id.*, at 697, 104 S.Ct., at 1371–1372 (Brennan, J., joined by Marshall, Blackmun, and Stevens, JJ., dissenting); *Mueller v. Allen*, 463 U.S. 388, 394, 103 S.Ct. 3062, 3066, 77 L.Ed.2d 721 (1983); *Widmar v. Vincent*, 454 U.S., at 271, 102 S.Ct., at 275; *Stone v. Graham*, 449 U.S. 39, 40–41, 101 S.Ct. 192, 193–194, 66 L.Ed.2d 1999 (1980) (per curiam); *Wolman v. Walter*, 433 U.S. 229, 236, 97 S.Ct. 2593, 2599, 53 L.Ed.2d 714 (1977).

[43]The statement indicated, in pertinent part: "Gentlemen, by passage of this bill by the Alabama Legislature our children in this state will have the opportunity of sharing in the spiritual heritage of this state and this country. The United States as well as the State of Alabama was founded by people who believe in God. *I believe this effort to return voluntary prayer* to our public schools for its return to us to the original position of the writers of the Constitution, this local philosophies and beliefs hundreds of Alabamians have urged my continuous support for permitting school prayer. Since coming to the Alabama Senate I *have worked hard on this legislation to accomplish the return of voluntary prayer in our public schools and return to the basic moral fiber.*" App. 50 (emphasis added).

mind." The State did not present evidence of any secular purpose.[45]

The unrebutted evidence of legislative intent contained in the legislative record and in the testimony of the sponsor of § 16-1-20.1 is confirmed by a consideration of the relationship between this statute and the two other measures that were considered in this case. The District Court found that the 1981 statute and its 1982 sequel had a common, nonsecular purpose. The wholly religious character of the later enactment is plainly evident from its text. When the differences between § 16-1-20.1 and its 1978 predecessor, § 16-1-20, are examined, it is equally clear that the 1981 statute has the same wholly religious character.

There are only three textual differences between § 16-1-20.1 and § 16-1-20: (1) the earlier statute applies only to grades one through six, whereas § 16-1-20.1 applies to all grades; (2) the earlier statute uses the word "shall" whereas § 16-1-20.1 uses the word "may"; (3) the earlier statute refers only to "meditation" whereas § 16-1-20.1 refers to "meditation or voluntary prayer." The first difference is of no relevance in this litigation because the minor appellees were in kindergarten or second grade during the 1981–1982 academic year. The second difference would also have no impact on this litigation because the mandatory language of § 16-1-20 continued to apply to grades one through six. Thus, the only significant textual difference is the addition of the words "or voluntary prayer."

The legislative intent to return prayer to the public schools is, of course, quite different from merely protecting every student's right to engage in voluntary prayer during an appropriate moment of silence during the schoolday. The 1978 statute already protected that right, containing nothing that prevented any student from engaging in voluntary prayer during a silent minute of meditation.[47] Appellants have not identified any secular purpose that was not fully served by § 16-1-20 before the enactment of § 16-1-20.1. Thus, only two conclusions are consistent with the text of § 16-1-20.1: (1) the statute was enacted to convey a message of state endorsement and promotion of prayer; or (2) the statute was enacted for no purpose. No one suggests that the statute was nothing but a meaningless or irrational act.

. . . The legislature enacted § 16-1-20.1, despite the existence of § 16-1-20 for the sole purpose of expressing the State's endorsement of prayer activities for one minute at the beginning of each schoolday. The addition of "or voluntary prayer" indicates that the State intended to characterize prayer as a favored practice. Such an endorsement is not consistent with the established principle that the government must pursue a course of complete neutrality toward religion.

* * *

The judgment of the Court of Appeals is affirmed. *It is so ordered.*

Justice Powell, concurring.

I concur in the Court's opinion and judgment that Ala.Code § 16-1-20.1 (Supp. 1984) violates the Establishment Clause of the First Amendment. My concurrence is prompted by Alabama's persistence in attempting to institute state-sponsored prayer in the public schools by enacting three successive statutes. I agree fully with Justice O'Connor's assertion that some moment-of-silence statutes may be constitutional, a suggestion set forth in the Court's opinion as well. . . .

I write separately to express additional views and to respond to criticism of the three-pronged *Lemon*

---

[45]Appellant Governor George C. Wallace now argues that § 16-1-20.1 "is best understood as a permissible accommodation of religion" and that viewed even in terms of the *Lemon* test, the "statute conforms to acceptable constitutional criteria." . . .

These arguments seem to be based on the theory that the free exercise of religion of some of the State's citizens was burdened before the statute was enacted. The United States, appearing as amicus curiae in support of the appellants, candidly acknowledges that "it is unlikely that in most contexts a strong Free Exercise claim could be made that time for personal prayer must be set aside during the school day." . . . There is no basis for the suggestion that § 16-1-20.1 "is a means for accommodating the religious and meditative needs of students without in any way diminishing the school's own neutrality or secular atmosphere." . . . In this case, it is undisputed that at the time of the enactment of § 16-1-20.1 there was no governmental practice impeding students from silently praying for one minute at the beginning of each schoolday; thus, there was no need to "accommodate" or to exempt individuals from any general governmental requirement because of the dictates of our cases interpreting the Free Exercise Clause. . . . What was missing in the appellants' eyes at the time of the enactment of § 16-1-20.1—and therefore what is precisely the aspect that makes the statute unconstitutional—was the State's endorsement and promotion of religion and a particular religious practice.

[47]Indeed, for some persons meditation itself may be a form of prayer. B. Larson, Larson's Book of Cults 62–65 (1982); C. Whittier, Silent Prayer and Meditation in World Religions 1–7 (Congressional Research Service 1982).

test.[3] *Lemon v. Kurtzman*, 403 U.S. 602, 91 S.Ct. 2105, 29 L.Ed.2d 745 (1971), identifies standards that have proved useful in analyzing case after case both in our decisions and in those of other courts. It is the only coherent test a majority of the Court has ever adopted. Only once since our decision in *Lemon*, *supra*, have we addressed an Establishment Clause issue without resort to its three-pronged test. *See Marsh v. Chambers*, 463 U.S. 783, 103 S.Ct. 3330, 77 L.Ed.2d 1019 (1983). *Lemon, supra*, has not been overruled or its test modified. Yet, continued criticism of it could encourage other courts to feel free to decide Establishment Clause cases on an ad hoc basis.

* * *

I join the opinion and judgment of the Court.
Justice O'Connor, concurring in the judgment.

Nothing in the United States Constitution as interpreted by this Court or in the laws of the State of Alabama prohibits public school students from voluntarily praying at any time before, during, or after the schoolday. Alabama has facilitated voluntary silent prayers of students who are so inclined by enacting Ala.Code § 16-1-20 (Supp.1984), which provides a moment of silence in appellees' schools each day. The parties to these proceedings concede the validity of this enactment. At issue in these appeals is the constitutional validity of an additional and subsequent Alabama statute, Ala.Code § 16-1-20.1 (Supp.1984), which both the District Court and the Court of Appeals concluded was enacted solely to officially encourage prayer during the moment of silence. I agree with the judgment of the Court that, in light of the findings of the courts below and the history of its enactment, § 16-1-20.1 of the Alabama Code violates the Establishment Clause of the First Amendment. In my view, there can be little doubt that the purpose and likely effect of this subsequent enactment is to endorse and sponsor voluntary prayer in the public schools. I write separately to identify the peculiar features of the Alabama law that render it invalid, and to explain why moment of silence laws in other States do not necessarily manifest the same infirmity. I also write to explain why neither history nor the Free Exercise Clause of the First Amendment validates the Alabama law struck down by the Court today.

I

* * *

Under the now familiar *Lemon* test, statutes must have both a secular legislative purpose and principal or primary effect that neither advances nor inhibits religion, and in addition they must not foster excessive government entanglement with religion. . . . Despite its initial promise, the *Lemon* test has proved problematic. The required inquiry into "entanglement" has been modified and questioned, *see Mueller v. Allen*, 463 U.S. 388, 403, n. 11, 103 S.Ct. 3062, 3071, n. 11, 77 L.Ed.2d 721 (1983), and in one case we have upheld state action against an Establishment Clause challenge without applying the *Lemon* test at all. *Marsh v. Chambers*, 463 U.S. 783, 103 S.Ct. 3330, 77 L.Ed.2d 1019 (1983). The author of *Lemon* himself apparently questions the test's general applicability. *See Lynch v. Donnelly*, 465 U.S. 668, 679, 104 S.Ct. 1355, 1362, 79 L.Ed.2d 604 (1984). Justice Rehnquist today suggests that we abandon *Lemon* entirely, and in the process limit the reach of the Establishment Clause to state discrimination between sects and government designation of a particular church as a "state" or "national" one . . .

Perhaps because I am new to the struggle, I am not ready to abandon all aspects of the *Lemon* test. I do believe, however, that the standards announced in *Lemon* should be reexamined and refined in order to make them more useful in achieving the underlying purpose of the First Amendment. We must strive to do more than erect a constitutional "signpost," *Hunt v. McNair*, 413 U.S. 734, 741, 93 S.Ct. 2868, 2873, 37 L.Ed.2d 923 (1973), to be followed or ignored in a particular case as our predilections may dictate. Instead, our goal should be "to frame a principle for constitutional adjudication that is not only grounded in the history and language of the first amendment, but one that is also capable of consistent application to the relevant problems." Choper, Religion in the Public Schools: A Proposed Constitutional Standard, 47 Min.L.Rev. 329, 332–33 (1963) (footnotes omitted). Last Term, I proposed a refinement of the *Lemon* test with this goal in mind. *Lynch v. Donnelly*, 465 U.S., at 687–89, 104 S.Ct., at 1366–67 (concurring opinion).

The *Lynch* concurrence suggested that the religious liberty protected by the Establishment Clause

---

[3]Justice O'Connor asserts that the "standards announced in *Lemon* should be reexamined and refined in order to make them more useful in achieving the underlying purpose of the First Amendment." Post, at 2496 (concurring in judgment). Justice Rehnquist would discard the *Lemon* test entirely. Post, at 2518–19 (dissenting).

As I state in the text, the *Lemon* test has been applied consistently in Establishment Clause cases since it was adopted in 1971. In a word, it has been the law. Respect for stare decisis should require us to follow *Lemon*. . . .

is infringed when the government makes adherence to religion relevant to a person's standing in the political community. Direct government action endorsing religion or a particular religious practice is invalid under this approach because it "sends a message to nonadherents that they are outsiders, not full members of the political community, and an accompanying message to adherents that they are insiders, favored members of the political community." *Id.*, at 688, 104 S.Ct., at 1367. Under this view, *Lemon's* inquiry as to the purpose and effect of a statute requires courts to examine whether government's purpose is to endorse religion and whether the statute actually conveys a message of endorsement.

The endorsement test is useful because of the analytic content it gives to the *Lemon*-mandated inquiry into legislative purpose and effect. In this country, church and state must necessarily operate within the same community. Because of this coexistence, it is inevitable that the secular interests of government and the religious interests of various sects and their adherents will frequently intersect, conflict, and combine. A statute that ostensibly promotes a secular interest often has an incidental or even a primary effect of helping or hindering a sectarian belief. Chaos would ensue if every such statute were invalid under the Establishment Clause. For example, the State could not criminalize murder for fear that it would thereby promote the Biblical command against killing. The task for the Court is to sort out those statutes and government practices whose purpose and effect go against the grain of religious liberty protected by the First Amendment.

The endorsement test does not preclude government from acknowledging religion or from taking religion into account in making law and policy. It does preclude government from conveying or attempting to convey a message that religion or a particular religious belief is favored or preferred. Such an endorsement infringes the religious liberty of the nonadherent, for "[w]hen the power, prestige and financial support of government is placed behind a particular religious belief, the indirect coercive pressure upon religious minorities to conform to the prevailing officially approved religion is plain." *Engel v. Vitale, supra,* 370 U.S., at 431, 82 S.Ct., at 1267. At issue today is whether state moment of silence statutes in general, and Alabama's moment of silence statute in particular, embody an impermissible endorsement of prayer in public schools.

Twenty-five states permit or require public school teachers to have students observe a moment of si-lence in their classrooms. A few statutes provide that the moment of silence is for the purpose of meditation alone. *See* Ariz.Rev.Stat.Ann. § 15-522 (1984); Conn.Gen.Stat. § 10-16a (1983); R.I.Gen.Laws § 16-12-3.1 (1981). The typical statute, however, calls for a moment of silence at the beginning of the schoolday during which students may meditate, pray, or reflect on the activities of the day. . . .

The *Engel* and *Abington* decisions are not dispositive on the constitutionality of moment of silence laws. In those cases, public school teachers and students led their classes in devotional exercises. In *Engel*, a New York statute required teachers to lead their classes in a vocal prayer. The Court concluded that "it is no part of the business of government to compose official prayers for any group of the American people to recite as part of a religious program carried on by the government." 370 U.S., at 425, 82 S.Ct., at 1264. In *Abington*, the Court addressed Pennsylvania and Maryland statutes that authorized morning Bible readings in public schools. The Court reviewed the purpose and effect of the statutes, concluded that they required religious exercises, and therefore found them to violate the Establishment Clause. 374 U.S., at 223–24, 83 S.Ct., at 1572. Under all of these statutes, a student who did not share the religious beliefs expressed in the course of the exercise was left with the choice of participating, thereby compromising the nonadherent's beliefs, or withdrawing, thereby calling attention to his or her nonconformity. The decisions acknowledged the coercion implicit under the statutory schemes, *see Engel, supra,* at 431, 82 S.Ct., at 1267, but they expressly turned only on the fact that the government was sponsoring a manifestly religious exercise.

A state-sponsored moment of silence in the public schools is different from state-sponsored vocal prayer or Bible reading. First, a moment of silence is not inherently religious. Silence, unlike prayer or Bible reading, need not be associated with a religious exercise. Second, a pupil who participates in a moment of silence need not compromise his or her beliefs. During a moment of silence, a student who objects to prayer is left to his or her own thoughts, and is not compelled to listen to the prayers or thoughts of others. For these simple reasons, a moment of silence statute does not stand or fall under the Establishment Clause according to how the Court regards vocal prayer or Bible reading. . . .

By mandating a moment of silence, a State does not necessarily endorse any activity that might occur during the period. *Cf. Widmar v. Vincent,* 454 U.S.

263, 272, n. 11, 102 S.Ct. 269, 275, n. 11, 70 L.Ed.2d 440 (1981) ("[B]y creating a forum the [State] does not thereby endorse or promote any of the particular ideas aired there"). Even if a statute specifies that a student may choose to pray silently during a quiet moment, the State has not thereby encouraged prayer over other specified alternatives. Nonetheless, it is also possible that a moment of silence statute, either as drafted or as actually implemented, could effectively favor the child who prays over the child who does not. For example, the message of endorsement would seem inescapable if the teacher exhorts children to use the designated time to pray. Similarly, the face of the statute or its legislative history may clearly establish that it seeks to encourage or promote voluntary prayer over other alternatives, rather than merely provide a quiet moment that may be dedicated to prayer by those so inclined. The crucial question is whether the State has conveyed or attempted to convey the message that children should use the moment of silence for prayer. This question cannot be answered in the abstract, but instead requires courts to examine the history, language, and administration of a particular statute to determine whether it operates as an endorsement of religion. *Lynch*, 465 U.S., at 694, 104 S.Ct., at 1370 (concurring opinion) ("Every government practice must be judged in its unique circumstances to determine whether it constitutes an endorsement or disapproval of religion").

Before reviewing Alabama's moment of silence law to determine whether it endorses prayer, some general observations on the proper scope of the inquiry are in order. First, the inquiry into the purpose of the legislature in enacting a moment of silence law should be deferential and limited. *See Everson v. Board of Education*, 330 U.S. 1, 6, 67 S.Ct. 504, 507, 91 L.Ed. 711 (1947) (courts must exercise "the most extreme caution" in assessing whether a state statute has a proper public purpose). In determining whether the government intends a moment of silence statute to convey a message of endorsement or disapproval of religion, a court has no license to psychoanalyze the legislators. *See McGowan v. Maryland*, 366 U.S. 420, 466 (1961) (opinion of Frankfurter, J.). If a legislature expresses a plausible secular purpose for a moment of silence statute in either the text or the legislative history, or if the statute disclaims an intent to encourage prayer over alternatives during a moment of silence, then courts should generally defer to that stated intent. . . .

Justice Rehnquist suggests that this sort of deferential inquiry into legislative purpose "means little," because "it only requires the legislature to express any secular purpose and omit all sectarian references." . . . It is not a trivial matter, however, to require that the legislature manifest a secular purpose and omit all sectarian endorsements from its laws. That requirement is precisely tailored to the Establishment Clause's purpose of assuring that government not intentionally endorse religion or a religious practice. It is of course possible that a legislature will enunciate a sham secular purpose for a statute. I have little doubt that our courts are capable of distinguishing a sham secular purpose from a sincere one, or that the *Lemon* inquiry into the effect of an enactment would help decide those close cases where the validity of an expressed secular purpose is in doubt. While the secular purpose requirement alone may rarely be determinative in striking down a statute, it nevertheless serves an important function. It reminds government that when it acts it should do so without endorsing a particular religious belief or practice that all citizens do not share. In this sense the secular purpose requirement is squarely based in the text of the Establishment Clause it helps to enforce.

Second, the *Lynch* concurrence suggested that the effect of a moment of silence law is not entirely a question of fact:

> "[W]hether a government activity communicates endorsement of religion is not a question of simple historical fact. Although evidentiary submissions may help answer it, the question is, like the question whether racial or sex-based classifications communicate an invidious message, in large part a legal question to be answered on the basis of judicial interpretation of social facts." 465 U.S., at 693–94, 104 S.Ct., at 1370.

The relevant issue is whether an objective observer, acquainted with the text, legislative history, and implementation of the statute, would perceive it as a state endorsement of prayer in public schools. . . .

A moment of silence law that is clearly drafted and implemented so as to permit prayer, meditation, and reflection within the prescribed period, without endorsing one alternative over the others, should pass this test.

The analysis above suggests that moment of silence laws in many States should pass Establishment Clause scrutiny because they do not favor the child who chooses to pray during a moment of silence over the child who chooses to meditate or reflect. Alabama Code § 16-1-20.1 (Supp.1984) does not stand on the same footing. However deferentially one examines its text and legislative history, however objectively one views the message attempted to be conveyed to the public, the conclusion is unavoidable that the purpose of the statute is to endorse prayer in public schools. I accordingly agree with the Court of Appeals, 705 F.2d 1526, 1535 (1983), that the Alabama statute has a purpose which is in violation of the Establishment Clause, and cannot be upheld. . . .

II

In his dissenting opinion, . . . Justice Rehnquist reviews the text and history of the First Amendment Religion Clauses. His opinion suggests that a long line of this Court's decisions are inconsistent with the intent of the drafters of the Bill of Rights. He urges the Court to correct the historical inaccuracies in its past decisions by embracing a far more restricted interpretation of the Establishment Clause, an interpretation that presumably would permit vocal group prayer in public schools. *See generally* R. Cord, *Separation of Church and State* (1982).

The United States, in an amicus brief, suggests a less sweeping modification of Establishment Clause principles. In the Federal Government's view, a state-sponsored moment of silence is merely an "accommodation" of the desire of some public school children to practice their religion by praying silently. Such an accommodation is contemplated by the First Amendment's guarantee that the Government will not prohibit the free exercise of religion. Because the moment of silence implicates free exercise values, the United States suggests that the *Lemon*-mandated inquiry into purpose and effect should be modified. . . .

* * *

Justice Rehnquist does not assert, however, that the drafters of the First Amendment expressed a preference for prayer in public schools, or that the practice of prayer in public schools enjoyed uninterrupted government endorsement from the time of enactment of the Bill of Rights to the present era. The simple truth is that free public education was virtually nonexistent in the late 18th century. *See Abington*, 374 U.S., at 238, and n. 7, 83 S.Ct., at 1580 and n. 7 (Brennan, J., concurring). Since there then existed few government-run schools, it is un-

likely that the persons who drafted the First Amendment, or the state legislators who ratified it, anticipated the problems of interaction of church and state in the public schools. Sky, "The Establishment Clause, the Congress, and the Schools: An Historical Perspective," 52 *Va. L. Rev.* 1395, 1403–04 (1966). Even at the time of adoption of the Fourteenth Amendment, education in Southern States was still primarily in private hands, and the movement toward free public schools supported by general taxation had not taken hold. . . .

. . . When the intent of the Framers is unclear, I believe we must employ both history and reason in our analysis. The primary issue raised by Justice Rehnquist's dissent is whether the historical fact that our Presidents have long called for public prayers of Thanks should be dispositive on the constitutionality of prayer in public schools.[6] I think not. At the very least, Presidential Proclamations are distinguishable from school prayer in that they are received in a noncoercive setting and are primarily directed at adults, who presumably are not readily susceptible to unwilling religious indoctrination. This Court's decisions have recognized a distinction when government-sponsored religious exercises are directed at impressionable children who are required to attend school, for then government endorsement is much more likely to result in coerced religious beliefs. . . . Although history provides a touchstone for constitutional problems, the Establishment Clause concern for religious liberty is dispositive here.

The element of truth in the United States' arguments, I believe, lies in the suggestion that Establishment Clause analysis must comport with the mandate of the Free Exercise Clause that government make no law prohibiting the free exercise of religion. Our cases have interpreted the Free Exercise Clause to compel the government to exempt persons from some generally applicable government requirements so as to permit those persons to freely exercise their religion. *See, e.g., Thomas v. Review Board of the Indiana Employment Security Division*, 450 U.S. 707, 101 S.Ct. 1425, 67 L.Ed.2d 624 (1981); *Wisconsin v. Yoder*, 406 U.S. 205, 92 S.Ct. 1526, 32 L.Ed.2d 15 (1972); *Sherbert v. Verner*, 374 U.S. 398, 83 S.Ct. 1790, 10 L.Ed.2d 965 (1963). Even where the Free Exercise Clause does not compel the government to

---

[6]Even assuming a taxpayer could establish standing to challenge such a practice, *see Valley Forge Christian College v. Americans United for Separation of Church and State, Inc.*, 454 U.S. 464, 102 S.Ct. 752, 70 L.Ed.2d 700 (1982), these Presidential Proclamations would probably withstand Establishment Clause scrutiny given their long history. *See Marsh v. Chambers*, 463 U.S. 783, 103 S.Ct. 3330, 77 L.Ed.2d 1019 (1983).

grant an exemption, the Court has suggested that the government in some circumstances may voluntarily choose to exempt religious observers without violating the Establishment Clause. *See, e.g., Gillette v. United States*, 401 U.S. 437, 453, 91 S.Ct. 828, 838, 28 L.Ed.2d 168 (1971); *Braunfeld v. Brown*, 366 U.S. 599, 81 S.Ct. 1144, 6 L.Ed.2d 563 (1961). The challenge posed by the United States' argument is how to define the proper Establishment Clause limits on voluntary government efforts to facilitate the free exercise of religion. On the one hand, a rigid application of the *Lemon* test would invalidate legislation exempting religious observers from generally applicable government obligations. By definition, such legislation has a religious purpose and effect in promoting the free exercise of religion. On the other hand, judicial deference to all legislation that purports to facilitate the free exercise of religion would completely vitiate the Establishment Clause. Any statute pertaining to religion can be viewed as an "accommodation" of free exercise rights. Indeed, the statute at issue in *Lemon*, which provided salary supplements, textbooks, and instructional materials to Pennsylvania parochial schools, can be viewed as an accommodation of the religious beliefs of parents who choose to send their children to religious schools.

It is obvious that either of the two Religion Clauses, "if expanded to a logical extreme, would tend to clash with the other." *Walz*, 397 U.S., at 668–69, 90 S.Ct., at 1411. The Court has long exacerbated the conflict by calling for government "neutrality" toward religion. *See, e.g., Committee for Public Education & Religious Liberty v. Nyquist*, 413 U.S. 756, 93 S.Ct. 2955, 37 L.Ed.2d 948 (1973); *Board of Education v. Allen*, 392 U.S. 236, 88 S.Ct. 1923, 20 L.Ed.2d 1060 (1968). It is difficult to square any notion of "complete neutrality," . . . with the mandate of the Free Exercise Clause that government must sometimes exempt a religious observer from an otherwise generally applicable obligation. A government that confers a benefit on an explicitly religious basis is not neutral toward religion. . . .

The solution to the conflict between the Religion Clauses lies not in "neutrality," but rather in identifying workable limits to the government's license to promote the free exercise of religion. The text of the Free Exercise Clause speaks of laws that prohibit the free exercise of religion. On its face, the Clause is directed at government interference with free exercise. Given that concern, one can plausibly assert that government pursues Free Exercise Clause values when

it lifts a government-imposed burden on the free exercise of religion. If a statute falls within this category, then the standard Establishment Clause test should be modified accordingly. It is disingenuous to look for a purely secular purpose when the manifest objective of a statute is to facilitate the free exercise of religion by lifting a government-imposed burden. Instead, the Court should simply acknowledge that the religious purpose of such a statute is legitimated by the Free Exercise Clause. I would also go further. In assessing the effect of such a statute—that is, in determining whether the statute conveys the message of endorsement of religion or a particular religious belief—courts should assume that the "objective observer" . . . is acquainted with the Free Exercise Clause and the values it promotes. Thus individual perceptions, or resentment that a religious observer is exempted from a particular government requirement, would be entitled to little weight if the Free Exercise Clause strongly supported the exemption.

While this "accommodation" analysis would help reconcile our Free Exercise and Establishment Clause standards, it would not save Alabama's moment of silence law. If we assume that the religious activity that Alabama seeks to protect is silent prayer, then it is difficult to discern any state-imposed burden on that activity that is lifted by Alabama Code § 16-1-20.1 (Supp.1984). No law prevents a student who is so inclined from praying silently in public schools. Moreover, state law already provided a moment of silence to these appellees irrespective of § 16-1-20.1. *See* Ala.Code § 16-1-20 (Supp.1984). Of course, the State might argue that § 16-1-20.1 protects not silent prayer, but rather group silent prayer under state sponsorship. Phrased in these terms, the burden lifted by the statute is not one imposed by the State of Alabama, but by the Establishment Clause as interpreted in *Engel* and *Abington*. In my view, it is beyond the authority of the State of Alabama to remove burdens imposed by the Constitution itself. I conclude that the Alabama statute at issue today lifts no state-imposed burden on the free exercise of religion, and accordingly cannot properly be viewed as an accommodation statute.

III

The Court does not hold that the Establishment Clause is so hostile to religion that it precludes the States from affording schoolchildren an opportunity for voluntary silent prayer. To the contrary, the moment of silence statutes of many States should satisfy the Establishment Clause standard we have here applied. The Court holds only that Alabama has intentionally crossed the line between creating a quiet moment during which those so inclined may pray, and affirmatively endorsing the particular religious practice of prayer. This line may be a fine one, but our precedents and the principles of religious liberty require that we draw it. In my view, the judgment of the Court of Appeals must be affirmed.

Chief Justice Burger, dissenting. [omitted]

Justice White, dissenting.

. . . I dissent from the Court's judgment invalidating Ala.Code § 16-1-20.1 (Supp.1984). Because I do, it is apparent that in my view the First Amendment does not proscribe either (1) statutes authorizing or requiring in so many words a moment of silence before classes begin or (2) a statute that provides, when it is initially passed, for a moment of silence for meditation or prayer. As I read the filed opinions, a majority of the Court would approve statutes that provided for a moment of silence but did not mention prayer. But if a student asked whether he could pray during that moment, it is difficult to believe that the teacher could not answer in the affirmative. If that is the case, I would not invalidate a statute that at the outset provided the legislative answer to the question "May I pray?" This is so even if the Alabama statute is infirm, which I do not believe it is, because of its peculiar legislative history.

* * *

Justice Rehnquist, dissenting.

Thirty-eight years ago this Court, in *Everson v. Board of Education*, 330 U.S. 1, 16, 67 S.Ct. 504, 512, 91 L.Ed. 711 (1947), summarized its exegesis of Establishment Clause doctrine thus:

> "In the words of Jefferson, the clause against establishment of religion by law was intended to erect 'a wall of separation between church and State.' *Reynolds v. United States*, [98 U.S. 145, 164, 25 L.Ed. 244 (1879)]."

This language from *Reynolds*, a case involving the Free Exercise Clause of the First Amendment rather than the Establishment Clause, quoted from Thomas Jefferson's letter to the Danbury Baptist Association the phrase "I contemplate with sovereign reverence that act of the whole American people

which declared that their legislature should 'make no law respecting an establishment of religion, or prohibiting the free exercise thereof,' thus building a wall of separation between church and State." 8 Writings of Thomas Jefferson 113 (H. Washington ed. 1861).[1]

It is impossible to build sound constitutional doctrine upon a mistaken understanding of constitutional history, but unfortunately the Establishment Clause has been expressly freighted with Jefferson's misleading metaphor for nearly 40 years. . . .

. . . [W]hen we turn to the record of the proceedings in the First Congress leading up to the adoption of the Establishment Clause of the Constitution, including Madison's significant contributions thereto, we see a far different picture of its purpose than the highly simplified "wall of separation between church and State."

* * *

The language Madison proposed for what ultimately became the Religion Clauses of the First Amendment was this:

> "The civil rights of none shall be abridged on account of religious belief or worship, nor shall any national religion be established, nor shall the full and equal rights of conscience be in any manner, or on any pretext, infringed." . . .

On the same day that Madison proposed them, the amendments which formed the basis for the Bill of Rights were referred by the House to a Committee of the Whole, and after several weeks' delay were then referred to a Select Committee consisting of Madison and 10 others. The Committee revised Madison's proposal regarding the establishment of religion to read:

> "[N]o religion shall be established by law, nor shall the equal rights of conscience be infringed." . . .

The Committee's proposed revisions were debated in the House on August 15, 1789. The entire debate on the Religion Clauses is contained in two full columns of the "Annals," and does not seem particularly illuminating. . . .

Madison . . . spoke, and said that "he apprehended the meaning of the words to be, that Congress should not establish a religion, and enforce the legal observation of it by law, nor compel men to worship God

---

[1] *Reynolds* is the only authority cited as direct precedent for the "wall of separation theory." 330 U.S., at 16, 67 S.Ct., at 512. *Reynolds* is truly inapt; it dealt with a Mormon's Free Exercise Clause challenge to a federal polygamy law.

in any manner contrary to their conscience." . . . He said that some of the state conventions had thought that Congress might rely on the Necessary and Proper Clause to infringe the rights of conscience or to establish a national religion, and "to prevent these effects he presumed the amendment was intended, and he thought it as well expressed as the nature of the language would admit." . . .

* * *

"He believed that the people feared one sect might obtain a pre-eminence, or two combine together, and establish a religion to which they would compel others to conform. . . ."

* * *

The following week, without any apparent debate, the House voted to alter the language of the Religion Clauses to read "Congress shall make no law establishing religion, or to prevent the free exercise thereof, or to infringe the rights of conscience." . . . The floor debates in the Senate were secret, and therefore not reported in the Annals. The Senate on September 3, 1789, considered several different forms of the Religion amendment, and reported this language back to the House:

> "Congress shall make no law establishing articles of faith or a mode of worship, or prohibiting the free exercise of religion." C. Antieau, A. Downey, & E. Roberts, Freedom From Federal Establishment 130 (1964).

The House refused to accept the Senate's changes in the Bill of Rights and asked for a conference; the version which emerged from the conference was that which ultimately found its way into the Constitution as a part of the First Amendment.

> "Congress shall make no law respecting an establishment of religion, or prohibiting the free exercise thereof."

The House and the Senate both accepted this language on successive days, and the Amendment was proposed in this form.

On the basis of the record of these proceedings in the House of Representatives, James Madison was undoubtedly the most important architect among the Members of the House of the Amendments which became the Bill of Rights, but it was James Madison speaking as an advocate of sensible legisla-

tive compromise, not as an advocate of incorporating the Virginia Statute of Religious Liberty into the United States Constitution. During the ratification debate in the Virginia Convention, Madison had actually opposed the idea of any Bill of Rights. His sponsorship of the Amendments in the House was obviously not that of a zealous believer in the necessity of the Religion Clauses, but of one who felt it might do some good, could do no harm, and would satisfy those who had ratified the Constitution on the condition that Congress propose a Bill of Rights.[3] His original language "nor shall any national religion be established" obviously does not conform to the "wall of separation" between church and State idea which latter-day commentators have ascribed to him. His explanation on the floor of the meaning of his language—"that Congress should not establish a religion, and enforce the legal observation of it by law" is of the same ilk. . . .

It seems indisputable from these glimpses of Madison's thinking, as reflected by actions on the floor of the House in 1789, that he saw the Amendment as designed to prohibit the establishment of a national religion, and perhaps to prevent discrimination among sects. He did not see it as requiring neutrality on the part of government between religion and irreligion. Thus the Court's opinion in *Everson*— while correct in bracketing Madison and Jefferson together in their exertions in their home State leading to the enactment of the Virginia Statute of Religious Liberty—is totally incorrect in suggesting that Madison carried these views onto the floor of the United States House of Representatives when he proposed the language which would ultimately become the Bill of Rights.

The repetition of this error in the Court's opinion in *Illinois ex rel. McCollum v. Board of Education*, 333 U.S. 203, 68 S.Ct. 461, 92 L.Ed. 649 (1948), and *inter alia, Engel v. Vitale*, 370 U.S. 421, 82 S.Ct. 1261, 8 L.Ed.2d 601 (1962), does not make it any sounder historically. Finally, in *Abington School District v. Schempp*, 374 U.S. 203, 214, 83 S.Ct. 1560, 1567, 10 L.Ed.2d 844 (1963), the Court made the truly remarkable statement that "the views of Madison and Jefferson, preceded by Roger Williams, came to be incorporated not only in the Federal Constitution but likewise in those of most of our States" (footnote omitted). On the basis of what evi-

---

[3]In a letter he sent to Jefferson in France, Madison stated that he did not see much importance in a Bill of Rights but he planned to support it because it was "anxiously desired by others . . . [and] it might be of use, and if properly executed could not be of disservice." 5 Writings of James Madison 271 (G. Hunt ed. 1904).

dence we have, this statement is demonstrably incorrect as a matter of history.[4] And its repetition in varying forms in succeeding opinions of the Court can give it no more authority than it possesses as a matter of fact; *stare decisis* may bind courts as to matters of law, but it cannot bind them as to matters of history.

None of the other Members of Congress who spoke during the August 15th debate expressed the slightest indication that they thought the language before them from the Select Committee, or the evil to be aimed at, would require that the Government be absolutely neutral as between religion and irreligion. The evil to be aimed at, so far as those who spoke were concerned, appears to have been the establishment of a national church, and perhaps the preference of one religious sect over another; but it was definitely not concerned about whether the Government might aid all religions evenhandedly. . . .

The actions of the First Congress, which reenacted the Northwest Ordinance for the governance of the Northwest Territory in 1789, confirm the view that Congress did not mean that the Government should be neutral between religion and irreligion. . . .

The Northwest Ordinance, 1 Stat. 50, reenacted the Northwest Ordinance of 1787 and provided that "[r]eligion, morality, and knowledge, being necessary to good government and the happiness of mankind, schools and the means of education shall forever be encouraged." . . . Land grants for schools in the Northwest Territory were not limited to public schools. It was not until 1845 that Congress limited land grants in the new States and Territories to nonsectarian schools. . . .

On the day after the House of Representatives voted to adopt the form of the First Amendment Religion Clauses which was ultimately proposed and ratified, Representative Elias Boudinot proposed a resolution asking President George Washington to issue a Thanksgiving Day Proclamation. Boudinot said he "could not think of letting the session pass over without offering an opportunity to all the citizens of the United States of joining with one voice, in returning to Almighty God their sincere thanks for the many blessings he had poured down upon them." . . .

Boudinot's resolution was carried in the affirmative on September 25, 1789. Boudinot and Sherman, who favored the Thanksgiving Proclamation, voted in favor of the adoption of the proposed amendments to the Constitution, including the Religion Clauses; Tucker, who opposed the Thanksgiving Proclamation, voted against the adoption of the amendments which became the Bill of Rights.

* * *

As the United States moved from the 18th into the 19th century, Congress appropriated time and again public moneys in support of sectarian Indian education carried on by religious organizations. Typical of these was Jefferson's treaty with the Kaskaskia Indians, which provided annual cash support for the Tribe's Roman Catholic priest and church. It was not until 1897, when aid to sectarian education for Indians had reached $500,000 annually, that Congress decided thereafter to cease appropriating money for education in sectarian schools. . . . This history shows the fallacy of the notion found in Everson that "no tax in any amount" may be levied for religious activities in any form. . . .

Joseph Story, a Member of this Court from 1811 to 1845, and during much of that time a professor at the Harvard Law School, published by far the most comprehensive treatise on the United States Constitution that had then appeared. Volume 2 of Story's Commentaries on the Constitution of the United States 630–32 (5th ed. 1891) discussed the meaning of the Establishment Clause of the First Amendment this way:

> "Probably at the time of the adoption of the Constitution, and of the amendment to it now under consideration [First Amendment], the general if not the universal sentiment in America was, that Christianity ought to receive encouragement from the State so far as was not incompatible with the private rights of conscience and the freedom of religious worship. An attempt to level all religions, and to make it a matter of state policy to hold all in utter indifference, would have created universal disapprobation, if not universal indignation.
>
> * * *
>
> "The real object of the [First] [A]mendment was not to countenance, much less to advance, Mahometanism, or Judaism, or infidelity, by prostrating Christianity; but to exclude all rivalry among Christian sects, and to prevent any national ecclesiastical establishment which should give to a hierarchy the exclusive patronage of the national government. . . ."

It would seem from this evidence that the Establishment Clause of the First Amendment had acquired a well-accepted meaning: it forbade

---

[4]State establishments were prevalent throughout the late 18th and early 19th centuries. *See* Mass. Const. of 1780, Part 1, Art. III; N.H. Const. of 1784, Art. VI; Md. Declaration of Rights of 1776, Art. XXXIII; R.I. Charter of 1633 (superseded 1842).

establishment of a national religion, and forbade preference among religious sects or denominations. Indeed, the first American dictionary defined the word "establishment" as "the act of establishing, founding, ratifying or ordaining," such as in "[t]he episcopal form of religion, so called, in England." 1 N. Webster, American Dictionary of the English Language (1st ed. 1828). The Establishment Clause did not require government neutrality between religion and irreligion nor did it prohibit the Federal Government from providing nondiscriminatory aid to religion. There is simply no historical foundation for the proposition that the Framers intended to build the "wall of separation" that was constitutionalized in Everson.

Notwithstanding the absence of a historical basis for this theory of rigid separation, the wall idea might well have served as a useful albeit misguided analytical concept, had it led this Court to unified and principled results in Establishment Clause cases. The opposite, unfortunately, has been true; in the 38 years since *Everson* our Establishment Clause cases have been neither principled nor unified. Our recent opinions, many of them hopelessly divided pluralities, have with embarrassing candor conceded that the "wall of separation" is merely a "blurred, indistinct, and variable barrier," which "is not wholly accurate" and can only be "dimly perceived." *Lemon v. Kurtzman,* 403 U.S. 602, 614, 91 S.Ct. 2105, 2112, 29 L.Ed.2d 745 (1971). . . .

Whether due to its lack of historical support or its practical unworkability, the *Everson* "wall" has proved all but useless as a guide to sound constitutional adjudication. . . .

. . . The "wall of separation between church and State" is a metaphor based on bad history, a metaphor which has proved useless as a guide to judging. It should be frankly and explicitly abandoned.

The Court has more recently attempted to add some mortar to Everson's wall through the three-part test of *Lemon v. Kurtzman, supra,* 403 U.S., at 614–15, 91 S.Ct. at 2112, which served at first to offer a more useful test for purposes of the Establishment Clause than did the "wall" metaphor.

Generally stated, the *Lemon* test proscribes state action that has a sectarian purpose or effect, or causes an impermissible governmental entanglement with religion.

* * *

The secular purpose prong has proven mercurial in application because it has never been fully defined, and we have never fully stated how the test is to operate. If the purpose prong is intended to void those aids to sectarian institutions accompanied by a stated legislative purpose to aid religion, the prong will condemn nothing so long as the legislature utters a secular purpose and says nothing about aiding religion. Thus the constitutionality of a statute may depend upon what the legislators put into the legislative history and, more importantly, what they leave out. The purpose prong means little if it only requires the legislature to express any secular purpose and omit all sectarian references, because legislators might do just that. . . .

However, if the purpose prong is aimed to void all statutes enacted with the intent to aid sectarian institutions, whether stated or not, then most statutes providing any aid, such as textbooks or bus rides for sectarian school children, will fail because one of the purposes behind every statute, whether stated or not, is to aid the target of its largesse. In other words, if the purpose prong requires an absence of any intent to aid sectarian institutions, whether or not expressed, few state laws in this area could pass the test, and we would be required to void some state aids to religion which we have already upheld. . . .

The entanglement prong of the *Lemon* test came from *Walz v. Tax Comm'n,* 397 U.S. 664, 674, 90 S.Ct. 1409, 1414, 25 L.Ed.2d 697 (1970). *Walz* involved a constitutional challenge to New York's time-honored practice of providing state property tax exemptions to church property used in worship. The *Walz* opinion . . . upheld the tax exemption. The Court examined the historical relationship between the State and church when church property was in issue, and determined that the challenged tax exemption did not so entangle New York with the church as to cause an intrusion or interference with religion. . . .

We have not always followed *Walz's* reflective inquiry into entanglement, however. . . . One of the difficulties with the entanglement prong is that when divorced from the logic of *Walz,* it creates an "insoluable paradox" in school aid cases: we have required aid to parochial schools to be closely watched lest it be put to sectarian use, yet this close supervision itself will create an entanglement. . . .

The entanglement test . . . also ignores the myriad state administrative regulations properly placed upon sectarian institutions such as curriculum, attendance, and certification requirements for sectarian schools, or fire and safety regulations for churches. Avoiding entanglement between church and State may be an important consideration in a case like *Walz*, but if the entanglement prong were applied to all state and church relations in the automatic manner in which it has been applied to school aid cases, the State could hardly require anything of church-related institutions as a condition for receipt of financial assistance.

These difficulties arise because the *Lemon* test has no more grounding in the history of the First Amendment than does the wall theory upon which it rests. The three-part test represents a determined effort to craft a workable rule from a historically faulty doctrine; but the rule can only be as sound as the doctrine it attempts to service. The three-part test has simply not provided adequate standards for deciding Establishment Clause cases, as this Court has slowly come to realize. Even worse, the *Lemon* test has caused this Court to fracture into unworkable plurality opinions, . . . depending upon how each of the three factors applies to a certain state action. . . .

* * *

The Court strikes down the Alabama statute because the State wished to "characterize prayer as a favored practice." . . . It would come as much of a shock to those who drafted the Bill of Rights as it will to a large number of thoughtful Americans today to learn that the Constitution, as construed by the majority, prohibits the Alabama Legislature from "endorsing" prayer. George Washington himself, at the request of the very Congress which passed the Bill of Rights, proclaimed a day of "public thanksgiving and prayer, to be observed by acknowledging with grateful hearts the many and signal favors of Almighty God." History must judge whether it was the Father of his Country in 1789, or a majority of the Court today, which has strayed from the meaning of the Establishment Clause.

The State surely has a secular interest in regulating the manner in which public schools are conducted. Nothing in the Establishment Clause of the First Amendment, properly understood, prohibits any such generalized "endorsement" of prayer. I would therefore reverse the judgment of the Court of Appeals.

———————

NOTES AND QUESTIONS

1. The Constitutional Standard: The Religious Purpose Test

The majority applies the modern test for constitutionality under the Establishment Clause, asking whether the moment-of-silence statute has the purpose or effect of advancing religion and whether it fosters an excessive entanglement between government and religion. *See Stone v. Graham*, 449 U.S. 39, 101 S.Ct. 192, 66 L.Ed.2d 199 (1980). The majority then cites evidence for the religious motivation behind the Alabama law. Does the purpose test require that the only motivation for the law be the advancement of religion? What if it is only one of a number of reasons for the law? Is a purpose test appropriate where the state claims that it is accommodating religious freedom? Is not any accommodation motivated by a desire to advance religion? *See May v. Cooperman*, 780 F.2d 240 (3d Cir. 1985), *appeal dismissed sub. nom. Karcher v. May*, 484 U.S. 72, 108 S.Ct. 388, 98 L.Ed.2d 327 (1987) (procedural grounds). *See generally* Laycock, *infra* at 62. In this regard, consider these comments by Professor Choper on the purpose test:

> As a matter of logic, the Supreme Court's approach in this area is subject to criticism. The Court's doctrine under the Establishment Clause, that any government action that has a religious purpose is unconstitutional, is in conflict with the Court's doctrine under the other religion clause of the First Amendment, the Free Exercise Clause. Under that provision, the Court has held that not only is government permitted to act for religious purposes, but at least under certain circumstances it must act for religious purposes by granting an exemption from ordinary civil regulation to people because, and only because, they hold a particular religious belief. I think the only fair way to characterize that aspect of the Supreme Court's Free Exercise Clause doctrine is to say that the Court is requiring government to act for a religious purpose. Thus, on the one hand, the Court says that under the Establishment Clause it is unconstitutional for the government to act for a religious purpose, but on the other hand, under the Free Exercise Clause the Court periodically holds that the government must act for a religious purpose.

Choper, "Church, State and the Supreme Court: Current Controversy," 29 *Ariz. L. Rev.* 551, 552 (1987). Has the Court been inconsistent? Or do you agree with Justice Stevens when he says that "the legislative intent to return prayer to the public schools is, of course, quite different from merely protecting every student's right to engage in voluntary prayer during an appropriate moment of silence during the schoolday"?

What is the difference, if any, between an endorsement of religion and a purpose to advance it? *See* Laycock, *infra* at 58–60.

Appellees abandoned their attack on the constitutionality of Alabama Code § 16-1-20. Why did they do so? Does the majority assume that this section is constitutional? *See* Dellinger, "The Sound of Silence: An Epistle on Prayer and the Constitution," 95 *Yale L. J. 1631* (1986). Justice O'Connor, for example, is quite explicit on this point. Professor Choper has remarked that in *Wallace* "the separationists won the battle but lost the war in respect to silent prayer." Choper, *supra* at 555. Do you agree? Consider these comments by Professor Laycock:

> A school that sets aside a moment of silence is creating an open forum for private thought in the midst of the school day. It is not obligated to do so, but it is free to do so. Some students may think religious thoughts, or say a silent prayer. But private religious thought is even less capable of violating the establishment clause than private religious speech. Freedom of thought may be the only constitutional right that is absolutely protected.
>
> Even so, most of the cases that have invalidated moments of silence have reached the right result. Neutral moments of silence are harder to implement than equal access. . . . [I]nescapably, the teacher must introduce a moment of silence. And he must do so in the presence of the whole class. It requires careful preparation for a teacher to introduce a moment of silence without encouraging or discouraging prayer or appearing to do either. The task does not appear unmanageable in theory, but so far, it has exceeded the capacity of the schools in litigated cases. . . .

Laycock, "Equal Access and Moments of Silence: The Equal Status of Religious Speech by Private Speakers," 81 *Nw. V. L. Rev.* 1, 57–58 (1986). *See also* Choper, *supra* at 555. Contrast this perspective with that of Professor Gedicks:

> The most common (and plausible) of the secular purposes advanced for moment of silence laws is that the silence period signals the beginning of the school day and gives students the opportunity mentally to "shift gears" and orient themselves to the business of learning. If this is the purpose of the laws, however, it is not clear why any students should be excused from participating or why special permission should be necessary to participate, nor is it apparent why the moment of silence is prescribed only at the beginning of the school day and not after each recess or change of classrooms. In fact, evidence of a disciplinary or educational purpose rarely is evident in the legislative history of silence laws.
>
> * * *
>
> Most moment of silence statutes . . . evidence an intention that an opportunity for prayer be created (1) on the public school campus, (2) in a school-sanctioned, teacher-monitored classroom setting, and (3) despite the absence of any meaningful impediment to voluntary prayer on an individual basis. The state's insistence on "accommodating" student desire to pray in school notwithstanding the absence of government impediments evidences a governmental purpose not merely to accommodate those who desire to pray but to promote prayer by the use of government influence. In the absence of controverting evidence, the laws should be found unconstitutional.

Gedicks, "Motivation, Rationality, and Secular Purpose in Establishment Clause Review," 1985 *Ariz. St. L.J.* 677, 719, 721–22. *See also* Note, "Daily Moments of Silence in Public Schools: A Constitutional Analysis," 58 *N.Y.U. L. Rev.* 364 (1983). Do you agree with Professor Laycock or Professor Gedicks? Is Professor Laycock looking at effects only and not motivation? Does Professor Gedicks apply a more stringent version of the purpose test than Justice O'Connor? Would any moment-of-silence law survive the scrutiny that Gedicks applies? Is he responding to the suspicion that legislators will articulate secular reasons for a moment-of-silence law, even if their genuine motive is to advance religion? *See* Wilkins, "One Moment Please: Private Devotion in the Public Schools," 2 *B.Y.U. J. Pub. L.* 1, 8 (1988). Is Justice O'Connor simply requiring that prayer not be mentioned in the moment-of-silence law or its legislative history? Is her approach merely cosmetic or does it reflect a reasoned view as to what constitutes government approval of religion? *See* Vieira, "School Prayer and the Principle of Uncoerced Listening," 14 *Hastings Const. L. Q.* 763 (1987). *See also* Laycock, *supra*.

2. *Voluntary Prayer*

Justice O'Connor states that "nothing in the United States Constitution as interpreted by this Court or in the laws of the State of Alabama prohibits public school students from voluntarily praying at any time before, during, or after the school day." *See also* Wilkins, *supra*. The law under review is unconstitutional only because "there can be little doubt that the purpose and likely effect of this subsequent enactment is to endorse and sponsor voluntary prayer in public schools." *See generally* Laycock, *supra*. Consider the relevance of the voluntary nature of moments of silence. Is the emphasis on voluntariness an Establishment Clause formulation or one much more concerned with the free exercise of religion? *See generally* Choper, *supra* at 555–56. In this regard, consider the evidence in *Walter v. West Virginia Bd. of Educ.*, 610 F.Supp. 1169 (S.D. W. Va. 1985):

Q. Okay. And then the next day what happened?

A. [Eleven-year-old Jewish Student] Well, then the next day our principal or guidance counselor read the whole sheet of guidelines to us. Then we had the moment of silence and I read a book during it.

* * *

Q. [Although nothing happened in the home room or in the first period, did anything happen to you in the second period?]

A. Well, in second period, which was science, our teacher left the room . . . and one of the people who was in my home room turned around and asked me why I had been reading a book during the moment of silence. And I told him that I didn't have to pray then and I didn't want to and then he told me that I should be praying all the time and then he said something to the effect that if I prayed all the time, maybe I could go to heaven with all the Christians when Jesus came for the second time instead of, as he put it, going down with all the other Jews.

* * *

Q. Did anyone else participate in the conversation?

A. Yes. There was another person who, this first boy told another boy that the Jews only used the Old Testament and they didn't use the New Testament and this other boy thought that it was really stupid . . . [T]hen the second boy said something to the effect that, why was he even trying to talk to me because the Jews weren't worth saving because they had killed Christ and that was about the end of it.

* * *

Q. Okay. Did you, did you talk with your teacher?

A. No, I didn't.

Q. Any reason that you didn't or—

A. Well, I was afraid that the teacher either wouldn't listen or if the teacher did listen, there would be a big issue made out of it and I would be in the limelight for the wrong reasons and I was afraid that I could have a lot of bad publicity . . .

Id. at 1172–73. Given this evidence, is the moment of silence voluntary? *See* Vieira, *supra* at 765–66. Should the determination of the constitutionality of the moment of silence depend on the specific situation in each school or classroom? *See* Laycock, *supra* at 64–66. Would it be better to have a per se rule? Is the answer to require silence and not to allow reading or other activities for that time span?

Justice O'Connor emphasizes that students in public schools are "impressionable children." Why is this fact relevant to analysis under the Establishment Clause?

3. The Dissent of Chief Justice Rehnquist

Chief Justice Rehnquist disputes the historical basis for interpreting the Establishment Clause to require absolute government neutrality between religion and irreligion or a "wall of separation" between church and state. He succinctly states that "the 'wall of separation between church and State' is a metaphor based on bad history, a metaphor which has proved useless as a guide to judging." Are you persuaded by his arguments? *See* Smith, "Now Is the Time for Reflection: *Wallace v. Jaffree* and its Legislative Aftermath," 37 *Ala. L. Rev.* 345 (1986). If the metaphor were a "useful guide" for judges, should it be retained even if it were historically wrong? What test would the Chief Justice apply in Establishment Clause cases? Note that he concludes that Madison "saw the [First] Amendment as designed to prohibit the establishment of a national religion, and perhaps to prevent discrimination among sects." From this perspective, the Establishment Clause definitely was "not concerned about whether the Government might aid all religions evenhandedly . . ." *See* Kurland, "Of Church and State and the Supreme Court," 29 *U. Chi. L. Rev.* 1 (1961). *But see* Laycock, *supra* at 3.

Lee v. Weisman
505 U.S. 577, 112 S.Ct. 2649 (1992)

JUSTICE KENNEDY delivered the opinion of the Court.

School principals in the public school system of the city of Providence, Rhode Island, are permitted to invite members of the clergy to offer invocation and benediction prayers as part of the formal graduation ceremonies for middle schools and for high schools. The question before us is whether including clerical members who offer prayers as part of the official school graduation ceremony is consistent with the Religion Clauses of the First Amendment, provisions the Fourteenth Amendment makes applicable with full force to the States and their school districts.

Deborah Weisman graduated from Nathan Bishop Middle School, a public school in Providence, at a formal ceremony in June 1989. She was about 14 years old. For many years it has been the policy of the Providence School Committee and the Superintendent of Schools to permit principals to invite members of the clergy to give invocations and benedictions at middle school and high school graduations. Many, but not all, of the principals elected to include prayers as part of the graduation ceremonies. Acting for himself and his daughter, Deborah's father, Daniel Weisman, objected to any prayers at Deborah's middle school graduation, but to no avail. The school principal, petitioner Robert E. Lee, invited a rabbi to deliver prayers at the graduation exercises for Deborah's class. Rabbi Leslie Gutterman, of the Temple Beth El in Providence, accepted.

It has been the custom of Providence school officials to provide invited clergy with a pamphlet entitled "Guidelines for Civic Occasions," prepared by the National Conference of Christians and Jews. The Guidelines recommend that public prayers at nonsectarian civic ceremonies be composed with "inclusiveness and sensitivity," though they acknowledge that "prayer of any kind may be inappropriate on some civic occasions." . . . The principal gave Rabbi Gutterman the pamphlet before the graduation and advised him the invocation and benediction should be nonsectarian. . . .

Rabbi Gutterman's prayers were as follows:

"INVOCATION
"God of the Free, Hope of the Brave:
"For the legacy of America where diversity is celebrated and the rights of minorities are protected, we thank You. May these young men and women grow up to enrich it.
"For the liberty of America, we thank You. May these new graduates grow up to guard it.
"For the political process of America in which all its citizens may participate, for its court system where all may seek justice we thank You. May those we honor this morning always turn to it in trust.
"For the destiny of America we thank You. May the graduates of Nathan Bishop Middle School so live that they might help to share it.
"May our aspirations for our country and for these young people, who are our hope for the future, be richly fulfilled.
AMEN"

"BENEDICTION
"O God, we are grateful to You for having endowed us with the capacity for learning which we have celebrated on this joyous commencement.
"Happy families give thanks for seeing their children achieve an important milestone. Send Your blessings upon the teachers and administrators who helped prepare them.
"The graduates now need strength and guidance for the future, help them to understand that we are not complete with academic knowledge alone. We must each strive to fulfill what You require of us all: To do justly, to love mercy, to walk humbly.
"We give thanks to You, Lord, for keeping us alive, sustaining us and allowing us to reach this special, happy occasion.
AMEN"

Id., at 22–23.

In the Providence school system, most high school graduation ceremonies are conducted away from the school, while most middle school ceremonies are held on school premises. Classical High School, which Deborah now attends, has conducted its graduation ceremonies on school premises. . . . The parties stipulate that attendance at graduation ceremonies is voluntary. . . . The graduating students enter as a group in a processional, subject to the direction of teachers and school officials, and sit together, apart from their families. . . . The school board argued that these short prayers and others like them at graduation exercises are of profound meaning to many students and parents throughout this country who consider that due respect and acknowledgment for divine guidance and for the deepest spiritual aspirations of our people ought to be expressed at an event as important in life as a graduation. We assume this to be so in addressing the difficult case now before us, for the significance of the prayers lies also at the heart of Daniel and Deborah Weisman's case.

Deborah's graduation was held on the premises of Nathan Bishop Middle School on June 29, 1989. Four days before the ceremony, Daniel Weisman, in his individual capacity as a Providence taxpayer and as next friend of Deborah, sought a temporary restraining order in the United States District Court for the District of Rhode Island to prohibit school officials from including an invocation or benediction in the graduation ceremony. The court denied the motion for lack of adequate time to consider it. Deborah and her family attended the graduation, where the prayers were recited. In July 1989, Daniel Weisman filed an amended complaint seeking a permanent injunction barring petitioners, various officials of the Providence public schools, from inviting the clergy to deliver invocations and benedictions at future graduations. We find it unnecessary to address Daniel Weisman's taxpayer standing, for a live and justiciable controversy is before us. Deborah Weisman is enrolled as a student at Classical High School in Providence and from the record it appears likely, if not certain, that an invocation and benediction will be conducted at her high school graduation. . . .

The case was submitted on stipulated facts. The District Court held that petitioners' practice of including invocations and benedictions in public school graduations violated the Establishment Clause of the First Amendment, and it enjoined petitioners from continuing the practice. 728 F. Supp. 68 (R.I. 1990).

* * *

On appeal, the United States Court of Appeals for the First Circuit affirmed.

* * *

The government involvement with religious activity in this case is pervasive, to the point of creating a state-sponsored and state-directed religious exercise in a public school. Conducting this formal religious observance conflicts with settled rules pertaining to prayer exercises for students, and that suffices to determine the question before us.

The principle that government may accommodate the free exercise of religion does not supersede the fundamental limitations imposed by the Establishment Clause.

* * *

That involvement is as troubling as it is undenied. A school official, the principal, decided that an invocation and a benediction should be given; this is a choice attributable to the State, and from a constitutional perspective it is as if a state statute decreed that the prayers must occur. The principal chose the religious participant, here a rabbi, and that choice is also attributable to the State. The reason for the choice of a rabbi is not disclosed by the record, but the potential for divisiveness over the choice of a particular member of the clergy to conduct the ceremony is apparent.

* * *

The State's role did not end with the decision to include a prayer and with the choice of a clergyman. Principal Lee provided Rabbi Gutterman with a copy of the "Guidelines for Civic Occasions," and advised him that his prayers should be nonsectarian. Through these means the principal directed and controlled the content of the prayers. Even if the only sanction for ignoring the instructions were that the rabbi would not be invited back, we think no religious representative who valued his or her continued reputation and effectiveness in the community would incur the State's displeasure in this regard. It is a cornerstone principle of our Establishment Clause jurisprudence that "it is no part of the business of government to compose official prayers for any group of the American people to recite as a part of a religious program carried on by government," *Engel v. Vitale*, 370 U.S. 421, 425, 8 L.Ed.2d 601, 82 S.Ct. 1261 (1962), and that is what the school officials attempted to do.

Petitioners argue, and we find nothing in the case to refute it, that the directions for the content of the prayers were a good-faith attempt by the school to ensure that the sectarianism which is so often the flash-point for religious animosity be removed from the graduation ceremony.

* * *

The question is not the good faith of the school in attempting to make the prayer acceptable to most persons, but the legitimacy of its undertaking that enterprise at all when the object is to produce a prayer to be used in a formal religious exercise which students, for all practical purposes, are obliged to attend.

* * *

The First Amendment protects speech and religion by quite different mechanisms. Speech is protected by ensuring its full expression even when the government participates, for the very object of some of our most important speech is to persuade the government to adopt an idea as its own. *Meese v. Keene*, 481 U.S. 465, 480–481, 95 L. Ed. 2d 415, 107 S.Ct. 1862 (1987); see also *Keller v. State Bar of Calif.*, 496 U.S. 1, 10–11, 110 L. Ed. 2d 1, 110 S.Ct. 2228 (1990); *Abood v. Detroit Bd. of Ed.*, 431 U.S. 209, 52 L. Ed. 2d 261, 97 S.Ct. 1782 (1977). The method for protecting freedom of worship and freedom of conscience in religious matters is quite the reverse. In religious debate or expression the government is not a prime participant, for the Framers deemed religious establishment antithetical to the freedom of all. The Free Exercise Clause embraces a freedom of conscience and worship that has close parallels in the speech provisions of the First Amendment, but the Establishment Clause is a specific prohibition on forms of state intervention in religious affairs with no precise counterpart in the speech provisions. *Buckley v. Valeo*, 424 U.S. 1, 92–93, 96, S. Ct. 612, and n. 127, 46 L. Ed. 2d 659 (1976) (*per curiam*).

* * *

As we have observed before, there are heightened concerns with protecting freedom of conscience from subtle coercive pressure in the elementary and secondary public schools. See *e.g.*, *School Dist. of Abington v. Schempp*, 374 U.S. 203, 307, 83 S.Ct. 1560, 1616, 10 L.Ed. 2d 844 (1963) (Goldberg, J., concurring); *Edwards v. Aguillard*, 482 U.S. 578, 584, 107 S.Ct. 2573, 2578, 96 L.Ed.2d. 510 (1987); *Board of Ed. of Westside Community Schools (Dist. 66) v. Mergens*, 496 U.S. 226, 261-262, 110 S.Ct. 2356, 2377-2378, 110 L.Ed.2d 191 (1990) (Kennedy, J., concurring). Our decisions in *Engel v. Vitale*, 370 U.S. 421, 82 S.Ct. 1261, 8 L.Ed.2d 601 (1962), and *School Dist. of Abington, supra*, recognize, among other things, that prayer exercises in public schools carry a particular risk of indirect coercion. The concern may not be limited to the context of schools, but it is most pronounced there. See *County of Allegheny v. American Civil Liberties Union, Greater Pittsburgh Chapter,* 492 U.S., at 661, 109 S.Ct., at 3717 (Kennedy, J., concurring in judgment in part and dissenting in part). What to most believers may seem nothing more than a reasonable request that the nonbeliever respect their religious practices, in a school context may appear to the nonbeliever or dissenter to be an attempt to employ the machinery of the State to enforce a religous orthodoxy.

* * *

We need not look beyond the circumstances of this case to see the phenomenon at work. The undeniable fact is that the school district's supervision and control of a high school graduation ceremony places public pressure, as well as peer pressure, on attending students to stand as a group or, at least, maintain respectful silence during the invocation and benediction. This pressure, though subtle and indirect, can be as real as any overt compulsion. Of course, in our culture standing or remaining silent can signify adherence to a view or simple respect for the views of others. And no doubt some persons who have no desire to join a prayer have little objection to standing as a sign of respect for those who do. But for the dissenter of high school age, who has a reasonable perception that she is being forced by the State to pray in a manner her conscience will not allow, the injury is no less real. There can be no doubt that for many, if not most, of the students at the graduation, the act of standing or remaining silent was an expression of participation in the rabbi's prayer. That was the very point of the religious exercise. It is of little comfort to a dissenter, then, to be told that for her the act of standing or remaining in silence signifies mere respect, rather than participation. What matters is that, given our social conventions, a reasonable dissenter in this milieu could believe that the group exercise signified her own participation or approval of it.

* * *

Finding no violation under these circumstances would place objectors in the dilemma of participating, with all that implies, or protesting. We do not address whether that choice is acceptable if the affected citizens are mature adults, but we think the State may not, consistent with the Establishment Clause, place primary and secondary school children in this position. Research in psychology supports the common assumption that adolescents are often susceptible to pressure from their peers towards conformity, and that

the influence is strongest in matters of social convention. Brittain, Adolescent Choices and Parent-Peer Cross-Pressures, Am.Sociological Rev. 385 (June 1963); Clasen & Brown, The Multidimensionality of Peer Pressure in Adolescence, 14 J. of Youth and Adolescence 451 (Dec. 1985); Brown, Clasen & Eicher, Perceptions of Peer Pressure, Peer Conformity Dispositions, and Self-Reported Behavior Among Adolescents, 22 Developmental Psychology 521 (July 1986). To recognize that the choice imposed by the State constitutes an unacceptable constraint only acknowledges that the government may no more use social pressure to enforce orthodoxy than it may use more direct means.

* * *

Inherent differences between the public school system and a session of a state legislature distinguish this case from *Marsh v. Chambers,* 463 U.S. 783, 77 L. Ed. 2d 1019, 103 S. Ct. 3330 (1983). The considerations we have raised in objection to the invocation and benediction are in many respects similar to the arguments we considered in *Marsh.* But there are also obvious differences. The atmosphere at the opening of a session of a state legislature where adults are free to enter and leave with little comment and for any number of reasons cannot compare with the constraining potential of the one school event most important for the student to attend. The influence and force of a formal exercise in a school graduation are far greater than the prayer exercise we condoned in *Marsh.*

* * *

No holding by this Court suggests that a school can persuade or compel a student to participate in a religious exercise. That is being done here, and it is forbidden by the Establishment Clause of the First Amendment.

For the reasons we have stated, the judgment of the Court of Appeals is *Affirmed.*

JUSTICE BLACKMUN, with whom JUSTICE STEVENS and JUSTICE O'CONNOR join, concurring.

* * *

I join the Court's opinion today because I find nothing in it inconsistent with the essential precepts of the Establishment Clause developed in our precedents. The Court holds that the graduation prayer is unconstitutional because the State "in effect required participation in a religious exercise." . . . Although our precedents make clear that proof of government coercion is not necessary to prove an Establishment Clause violation, it is sufficient. Government pressure to participate in a religious activity is an obvious indication that the government is endorsing or promoting religion.

But it is not enough that the government restrain from compelling religious practices: It must not engage in them either. See *Schempp*, 374 U.S. at 305 (Goldberg, J., concurring). The Court repeatedly has recognized that a violation of the Establishment Clause is not predicated on coercion.

* * *

We have believed that religious freedom cannot exist in the absence of a free democratic government, and that such a government cannot endure when there is fusion between religion and the political regime. We have believed that religious freedom cannot thrive in the absence of a vibrant religious community and that such a community cannot prosper when it is bound to the secular. And we have believed that these were the animating principles behind the adoption of the Establishment Clause. To that end, our cases have prohibited government endorsement of religion, its sponsorship, and active involvement in religion, whether or not citizens were coerced to conform.

I remain convinced that our jurisprudence is not misguided, and that it requires the decision reached by the Court today. Accordingly, I join the Court in affirming the judgment of the Court of Appeals.

JUSTICE SOUTER, with whom JUSTICE STEVENS and JUSTICE O'CONNOR join, concurring. [Omitted.]

JUSTICE SCALIA, with whom THE CHIEF JUSTICE, JUSTICE WHITE, and JUSTICE THOMAS join, dissenting.

Three Terms ago, I joined an opinion recognizing that the Establishment Clause must be construed in light of the "government policies of accommodation, acknowledgment, and support for religion [that] are an accepted part of our political and cultural heritage." That opinion affirmed that "the meaning of the Clause is to be determined by reference to historical practices and understandings." It said that "[a] test for implementing the protections of the Establishment Clause that, if applied with consistency, would invalidate longstanding traditions cannot be a proper reading of the Clause." *Allegheny County v. Greater Pittsburgh ACLU*, 492 U.S. 573, 657, 670, 109 S. Ct. 3086, 3156, 3142, 106 L. Ed. 2d 472 (1989) (KENNEDY, J., concurring in judgment in part and dissenting in part).

These views of course prevent me from joining today's opinion, which is conspicuously bereft of any

reference to history. In holding that the Establishment Clause prohibits invocations and benedictions at public school graduation ceremonies, the Court—with nary a mention that it is doing so—lays waste a tradition that is as old as public school graduation ceremonies themselves, and that is a component of an even more longstanding American tradition of nonsectarian prayer to God at public celebrations generally. As its instrument of destruction, the bulldozer of its social engineering, the Court invents a boundless, and boundlessly manipulable, test of psychological coercion. . . . Today's opinion shows more forcefully than volumes of argumentation why our Nation's protection, that fortress which is our Constitution, cannot possibly rest upon the changeable philosophical predilections of the Justices of this Court, but must have deep foundations in the historic practices of our people.

* * *

_____

NOTES AND QUESTIONS

1. Coercion and a "Little Bit of Establishment"

What, if any, is the importance of coercion in analyzing the constitutionality of graduation prayers under the Establishment Clause? Do you agree with Justice Kennedy or Justice Blackmun on this issue? In this regard, is it significant that the Court declined to address the particular question of Daniel Weisman's standing as a taxpayer?

Professor Laycock argues that a "little bit of establishment" still violates the Constitution:

> With respect to government speech, my understanding of neutrality is as rigorous as that of the most orthodox secularist. In my view, the establishment clause absolutely disables the government from taking a position for or against religion. . . .
>
> This principle explains the Supreme Court's holdings that teachers cannot lead or encourage prayer in public schools, or post the Ten Commandments on the bulletin board. The Court should have applied the same principle to its other cases. It should not have held that chaplains can open each meeting of a state legislature with prayer, or that municipalities can erect Christmas displays. These decisions are wholly unprincipled and indefensible. A little bit of government support for religion may be only a little bit of establishment, but it is still an establishment. The government should not put "In God We Trust" on coins; it should not open court sessions with "God save the United

States and this honorable Court"; and it should not name a city or a naval vessel for the Body of Christ or the Queen of the Angels. Perhaps religious minorities should not waste political capital on minor violations such as these. But neither should the Supreme Court legitimate such violations.

I mention these views to make clear that my support for the Equal Access Act and my tolerance for properly conducted moments of silence do not stem from any view that the religious right's desire for government support should be modestly indulged. The reason to allow equal access or moments of silence is not that they are acceptably small deviations from neutrality. Rather, they are strictly neutral.

Laycock, "Equal Access and Moments of Silence: The Equal Status of Religious Speech by Private Speakers," 81 N.W. U. L. Rev. 1, 7–9 (1986). Do you agree? Is there no such thing as a de minimus violation of the Establishment Clause? What is the relevance of coercion for Professor Laycock?

2. *Student-Led Prayer*

Is student-led prayer at a graduation ceremony constitutional? At football games? *See Santa Fe Indep. Sch. Dist. v. Doe*, 530 U.S. 290, 120 S.Ct. 2266 (2000) (holding that the school district's policy permitting students to vote on whether to have student-led prayers at high school football games is a violation of the First Amendment's Establishment Clause). If a school prohibits student-initiated religious speech at school-related events, does the school violate students' rights to free expression? *See Chandler v. James*, 180 F.3d. 1254 (11th Cir. 1999) (holding that school district's act of permitting genuinely student-initiated religious speech did not violate the Constitution and that suppression of such speech would violate students' right of free speech).

3. *Religious Songs, Celebrations, and Holidays*

Under *Wallace v. Jaffree* and *Lee v. Weisman*, is it constitutional for a school choir to sing religious songs? Is it constitutional for a school choir to have a religious theme song? *See Doe v. Duncanville Ind. School District*, 70 F.3d 402, 406 (5th Cir. 1995); *Bauchman v. West High School*, 132 F.3d. 542 (10th Cir. 1997) *cert. denied*, 524 U.S. 953, 118 S.Ct. 2370 (June 28, 1998) (No. 97-1764). (D.Utah 1996). Do celebrations of religious holidays in public schools violate the Constitution? *See* Hartenstein, "A Christmas Issue: Christian Holiday Celebration in Public Elementary Schools Is an Establishment of Religion," 80 *Cal. L. Rev.* 981 (1992). Is it unconstitu-

tional to make Good Friday a school holiday? *See* Brookman, Note, "The Constitutionality of the Good Friday Holiday," 73 *N.Y.U. L. Rev.* 193 (1998). During an international awareness week, can a school teach children about the different religions of the world? *See Altman v. Bedford Cent. Sch. Dist.*, 45 F. Supp.2d 368 (S.D. N.Y. 1999).

2. **Evolution and Creationism.**

Though presaged by the work of other scientists, one of the most profound changes in scientific paradigms occurred in 1895 with the publication of Charles Darwin's *Origin of the Species*. The central concept was natural selection, the theory that "the fittest survive and spread their favored traits through populations." S. J. Gould, *Ever Since Darwin* 40 (1977). Darwin concluded that evolution had occurred and that natural selection was the mechanism by which it had occurred. *Id.* at 44. While his earlier work was suggestive, in the early 1870s he extended the theory, often called the theory of evolution, to human beings and the human mind. *Id.* at 25. *See* C. Darwin, *Descent of Man* (1871); C. Darwin, *The Expression of the Emotions in Man and Animals* (1872). By the 1880s some form of the evolution theory was accepted by nearly all American naturalists. *See* Larson, *Trial and Error* 8 (1985).

Darwin himself insisted only that "organic change led only to increasing adaptation between organisms and their own environment," but some scientists and most laypeople equate evolution with biological progress, with descent from a lower, less intelligent order to a higher order. Gould, *supra* at 37. This theory of a continuity with nature—our descent from apes if you will—challenged the uniqueness of human beings and their place in the universe. As Professor Gould has stated, "the differences between adult chimps and people are not trifling, but they do not arise from any difference in kind." *Id.* at 51. *See* M. Ridley, *Genome: The Autobiography of a Species in 23 Chapters* 28 (1999) ("We are, to a ninety-eight percent approximation, chimpanzees. . . ."). Such notions were profoundly disturbing in the nineteenth century, particularly in terms of religious beliefs. They continue to be so today: "[T]he Western world has yet to make its peace with Darwin and the implications of evolutionary theory." *Id.* at 50.

There have been many efforts to reconcile post-Darwinian science with religion. *See, e.g.*, Kass, "Evolution and the Bible," Commentary (Nov. 1988) at 29. But most scholars tend to perceive a fundamental conflict between evolution through natural selection and design by the Creator. *Id.* As Kass has described the conflict:

> . . . [M]ost people tend to see the first chapters of Genesis and the theory of evolution as irreconcilable. On one side, we have scientists and philosophers of science who hold that the teaching of evolution has made "plumb unbelievable" the teachings of the book of Genesis, especially about the special status of man. . . . On the other side, we have Protestant fundamentalists, who, taking the same view of the challenge, declare the teachings of evolution to be false. No longer content just citing chapter and verse, some of them would like to prove it scientifically. In recent decades, they have given birth to a new movement, so-called "creation science" or "scientific creationism," which aims both to embarrass and refute the theory of evolution and to find scientific evidence supporting the account of the origins of the world, life, and man provided by their own particular reading of Scripture.

Id. See Carter, "Evolution, Creationism, and Treating Religion as a Hobby," 1987 *Duke L. J.* 977. Professor Phillip E. Johnson has urged that the orthodox scientific attack on creationism is based on "a theory of naturalistic evolution which means that it absolutely rules out any miraculous or supernatural intervention at any point." Johnson, "Evolution as Dogma: The Establishment of Naturalism," *First Things,* Oct. 1990, at 15, 16. Johnson views this philosophical judgment as highly debatable. He also questions the empirical support for Darwinism, characterizing the "fossil record" as "hostile to a Darwinist interpretation" in "important respects." *Id. See* P. Johnson, *Reason in the Balance* (1995).

The conflict between revelation and reason has manifested itself in controversies and lawsuits over what will be taught in the public schools, for the contestants view the public schools as a primary battleground for the minds of the young. *See generally* Larson, *supra*; D. Nelkin, *Science Textbook Controversies and the Politics of Equal Time* (1977). By the 1920s, the most widely used biology textbook for high school students (Hunter, *A Civic Biology* (1914)) contained sections on heredity and evolution, and science teachers largely embraced Darwinist thinking in their biology courses. *See* Gelfand, "Of Monkeys and Men—An Atheist's Heretical View of the Constitutionality of Teaching the Disproof of a Religion in the Public Schools," 16 *J. L. & Educ.* 271, 277–78 (1987). Perhaps the most famous example is the Tennessee "monkey law," prohibiting the teaching of the the-

ory that human beings evolved from other species. *Scopes v. State,* 154 Tenn. 105, 289 S.W. 363 (1927). *See* Kalven, "A Commemorative Case Note: *Scopes v. State,*" 27 *Chi. L. Rev.* 505 (1960). John Scopes had lectured from the Hunter textbook and he was fined for violating Tennessee law. Gelfand, *supra* at 278–79. The leading protagonists in the eight-day trial—a spectacular media event—were Clarence Darrow and William Jennings Bryan. The Tennessee Supreme Court upheld the anti-evolution law, but reversed Scopes' conviction on the ground that the jury and not the judge should have imposed the $100 fine. Gelfand, *supra* at 280. *See generally* Larson, *supra.* The trial of Scopes was later turned into the widely praised dramatic film, *Inherit the Wind,* starring Spencer Tracy and Frederic March.

In the years after *Scopes,* biology textbooks, particularly in the South, began to play down or omit evolution, prompting one commentator to say that "Darrow had won the battle, but the South had won the war." Gelfand, *supra* at 281. In the post–World War II period, however, textbook publishers again embraced evolution. Gelfand, *supra* at 282; *see generally* Larson, "The Scopes Trial and the Evolving Concept of Freedom," 185 *Va. L. Rev.* 503 (1999). Thus, more than forty years after Scopes, the United States Supreme Court confronted a similar state statute in *Epperson v. Arkansas,* 393 U.S. 97, 89 S.Ct. 266, 21 L.Ed.2d 228 (1968). Relying on the school prayer cases, the Court in *Epperson* declared the Arkansas anti-evolution law unconstitutional under the Establishment Clause:

> The overriding fact is that Arkansas' law selects from the body of knowledge a particular segment which it proscribes for the sole reason that it is deemed to conflict with a particular religious doctrine; that is, with a particular interpretation of the Book of Genesis by a particular religious group. . . .
>
> * * *
>
> No suggestion has been made that Arkansas' law may be justified by considerations of state policy other than the religious views of some of its citizens. It is clear that fundamentalist sectarian conviction was and is the law's reason for existence. . . .

393 U.S. at 107, 89 S.Ct. at 272. The Court declined to reach the question as to whether the teacher's alleged right to pursue his profession or to express himself in the classroom had been violated.

Justice Black concurred in the result in *Epperson* on the ground that the Arkansas law was unconstitutionally vague, but he expressed strong reservations about the majority's approach:

> A . . . question that arises for me is whether this Court's decision forbidding a State to exclude the subject of evolution from its schools infringes the religious freedom of those who consider evolution an antireligious doctrine. If the theory is considered antireligious, as the Court indicates, how can the State be bound by the Federal Constitution to permit its teachers to advocate such an "antireligious" doctrine to school children? The very cases cited by the Court as supporting its conclusion hold that the State must be neutral. . . . [D]oes not the removal of the subject of evolution leave the State in a neutral position . . .
>
> I am also not ready to hold that a person hired to teach school children takes with him into the classroom a constitutional right to teach sociological, economic, political, or religious subjects that the school's managers do not want discussed. . . .
>
> I question whether it is absolutely certain . . . that "academic freedom" permits a teacher to breach his contractual agreement to teach only the subjects designated by the school authorities who hired him.

393 U.S. at 113, 89 S.Ct. at 275.

Justice Stewart also concurred in the *Epperson* result, but he found a violation of the teachers' rights of expression:

> It is one thing for a State to determine that "the subject of higher mathematics, or astronomy, or biology" shall or shall not be included in its public school curriculum. It is quite another thing for a State to make it a criminal offense for a public school teacher so much as to mention the very existence of an entire system of respected human thought.

393 U.S. at 116, 89 S.Ct. at 276. *See generally* Goldstein, "The Asserted Constitutional Right of Public School Teachers to Determine What They Teach," 124 *U. Pa. L. Rev.* 1293 (1976); Van Alstyne, "The Constitutional Rights of Teachers and Professors," 1970 *Duke L.J.* 841.

Four years after *Epperson,* a federal district court confronted the question of whether the teaching of the theory of evolution in public schools, while ignoring the biblical account of human creation, itself evidenced a hostility to religion and the establishment of a religion of secular humanism. The court held that it did not:

> [T]he offending material is peripheral to the matter of religion. Science and religion necessarily deal with many of the same questions, and they may frequently provide conflicting answers. But . . . it is not the business of government to suppress real or imagined attacks upon a particular religious doctrine. . . . Teachers of science in the public schools should not be expected to avoid the discussion of every scientific issue on which some religion claims expertise.

Wright v. Houston Indep. Sch. Dist., 366 F.Supp. 1208, 1211 (S.D. Tex. 1972), *aff'd,* 486 F.2d 137 (5th Cir. 1973), *cert. denied,* 417 U.S. 969, 94 S.Ct. 3173, 41 L.Ed.2d 1140 (1974). *But see* Carter, *supra.*

Edwards v. Aguillard
482 U.S. 578, 107 S.Ct. 2573, 96 L.Ed.2d 510 (1987).

Justice Brennan delivered the opinion of the Court.

The question for decision is whether Louisiana's "Balanced Treatment for Creation-Science and Evolution-Science in Public School Instruction" Act (Creationism Act), La.Rev.Stat.Ann. §§ 17:286.1-17:286.7 (West 1982), is facially invalid as violative of the Establishment Clause of the First Amendment.

I

The Creationism Act forbids the teaching of the theory of evolution in public schools unless accompanied by instruction in "creation science." § 17:286.4A. No school is required to teach evolution or creation science. If either is taught, however, the other must also be taught. *Ibid.* The theories of evolution and creation science are statutorily defined as "the scientific evidences for [creation or evolution] and inferences from those scientific evidences." §§ 17.286.3(2) and (3).

Appellees, who include parents of children attending Louisiana public schools, Louisiana teachers, and religious leaders, challenged the constitutionality of the Act in District Court, seeking an injunction and declaratory relief.[1] Appellants, Louisiana officials charged with implementing the Act, defended on the ground that the purpose of the Act is to protect a legitimate secular interest, namely, academic freedom.

---

[1]Appellants, the Louisiana Governor, the Attorney General, the State Superintendent, the State Department of Education and the St. Tammany Parish School Board, agreed not to implement the Creationism Act pending the final outcome of this litigation. . . .

Appellees attacked the Act as facially invalid because it violated the Establishment Clause. . . .

II

The Establishment Clause forbids the enactment of any law "respecting an establishment of religion." The Court has applied a three-pronged test to determine whether legislation comports with the Establishment Clause. First, the legislature must have adopted the law with a secular purpose. Second, the statute's principal or primary effect must be one that neither advances nor inhibits religion. Third, the statute must not result in an excessive entanglement of government with religion. *Lemon v. Kurtzman,* 403 U.S. 602, 612–13, 91 S.Ct. 2105, 2111, 29 L.Ed.2d 745 (1971). State action violates the Establishment Clause if it fails to satisfy any of these prongs.

* * *

The Court has been particularly vigilant in monitoring compliance with the Establishment Clause in elementary and secondary schools. Families entrust public schools with the education of their children, but condition their trust on the understanding that the classroom will not purposely be used to advance religious views that may conflict with the private beliefs of the student and his or her family. Students in such institutions are impressionable and their attendance is involuntary. . . . The State exerts great authority and coercive power through mandatory attendance requirements, and because of the students' emulation of teachers as role models and the children's susceptibility to peer pressure.[5] . . .

* * *

III

Lemon's first prong focuses on the purpose that animated adoption of the Act. "The purpose prong of the *Lemon* test asks whether government's actual purpose is to endorse or disapprove of religion." *Lynch v. Donnelly,* 465 U.S. 668, 690, 104 S.Ct. 1355, 1368, 79 L.Ed.2d 604 (1984) (O'Connor, J., concurring). A governmental intention to promote religion is clear when the State enacts a law to serve a religious purpose. This intention may be evi-

denced by promotion of religion in general, *see Wallace v. Jaffree, supra,* 472 U.S. at 52–53, 105 S.Ct., at 2488 (Establishment Clause protects individual freedom of conscience "to select any religious faith or none at all"), or by advancement of a particular religious belief, *e.g., Stone v. Graham, supra,* 449 U.S., at 41, 101 S.Ct., at 194 (invalidating requirement to post Ten Commandments, which are "undeniably a sacred text in the Jewish and Christian faiths") (footnote omitted); *Epperson v. Arkansas, supra,* 393 U.S., at 106, 89 S.Ct., at 271 (holding that banning the teaching of evolution in public schools violates the First Amendment since "teaching and learning" must not "be tailored to the principles or prohibitions of any religious sect or dogma"). If the law was enacted for the purpose of endorsing religion, "no consideration of the second or third criteria [of *Lemon*] is necessary." *Wallace v. Jaffree, supra,* 472 U.S., at 56, 105 S.Ct., at 2490. In this case, the petitioners have identified no clear secular purpose for the Louisiana Act. True, the Act's stated purpose is to protect academic freedom. La. Rev. Stat. Ann. § 17:286.2 (West 1982). This phrase might, in common parlance, be understood as referring to enhancing the freedom of teachers to teach what they will. The Court of Appeals, however, correctly concluded that the Act was not designed to further that goal. We find no merit in the State's argument that the "legislature may not [have] use[d] the terms 'academic freedom' in the correct legal sense. They might have [had] in mind, instead, a basic concept of fairness; teaching all of the evidence." . . . Even if "academic freedom" is read to mean "teaching all of the evidence" with respect to the origin of human beings, the Act does not further this purpose. The goal of providing a more comprehensive science curriculum is not furthered either by outlawing the teaching of evolution or by requiring the teaching of creation science.

* * *

It is clear from the legislative history that the purpose of the legislative sponsor, Senator Bill Keith, was to narrow the science curriculum. During the legislative hearings, Senator Keith stated: "My preference would be that neither [creationism nor

---

5The potential for undue influence is far less significant with regard to college students who voluntarily enroll in courses. . . . Thus, for instance, the Court has not questioned the authority of state colleges and universities to offer courses on religion or theology. See Widmar v. Vincent, 454 U.S. 263, 271, 102 S.Ct. 269, 275, 70 L.Ed.2d 440 (1981) (Powell, J.); id., at 281, 102 S.Ct., at 280 (Stevens, J., concurring in judgment).

evolution] be taught." . . . Such a ban on teaching does not promote—indeed, it undermines—the provision of a comprehensive scientific education.

It is equally clear that requiring schools to teach creation science with evolution does not advance academic freedom. The Act does not grant teachers a flexibility that they did not already possess to supplant the present science curriculum with the presentation of theories, besides evolution, about the origin of life. Indeed, the Court of Appeals found that no law prohibited Louisiana public schoolteachers from teaching any scientific theory. 765 F.2d, at 1257. As the president of the Louisiana Science Teachers Association testified, "[a]ny scientific concept that's based on established fact can be included in our curriculum already, and no legislation allowing this is necessary." . . . The Act provides Louisiana schoolteachers with no new authority. Thus the stated purpose is not furthered by it.

The Alabama statute held unconstitutional in *Wallace v. Jaffree, supra,* is analogous. In *Wallace,* the State characterized its new law as one designed to provide a one-minute period for meditation. We rejected that stated purpose as insufficient, because a previously adopted Alabama law already provided for such a one-minute period. Thus, in this case, as in *Wallace,* "[a]ppellants have not identified any secular purpose that was not fully served by [existing state law] before the enactment of [the statute in question]." 472 U.S., at 59, 105 S.Ct., at 2491.

Furthermore, the goal of basic "fairness" is hardly furthered by the Act's discriminatory preference for the teaching of creation science and against the teaching of evolution.[7] While requiring that curriculum guides be developed for creation science, the Act says nothing of comparable guides for evolution. La.Rev.Stat.Ann. § 17:286.7A (West 1982). Similarly, research services are supplied for creation science but not for evolution. § 17:286.7B. Only "creation scientists" can serve on the panel that supplies the resource services. *Ibid.* The Act forbids school

boards to discriminate against anyone who "chooses to be a creation-scientist" or to teach "creationism," but fails to protect those who choose to teach evolution or any other noncreation science theory, or who refuse to teach creation science. § 17:286.4C.

If the Louisiana legislature's purpose was solely to maximize the comprehensiveness and effectiveness of science instruction, it would have encouraged the teaching of all scientific theories about the origins of humankind. But under the Act's requirements, teachers who were once free to teach any and all facets of this subject are now unable to do so. Moreover, the Act fails even to ensure that creation science will be taught, but instead requires the teaching of this theory only when the theory of evolution is taught. Thus we agree with the Court of Appeals' conclusion that the Act does not serve to protect academic freedom, but has the distinctly different purpose of discrediting "evolution by counterbalancing its teaching at every turn with the teaching of creation science. . . ." 765 F.2d, at 1257.

* * *

As in *Stone* and *Abington,* we need not be blind in this case to the legislature's preeminent religious purpose in enacting this statute. There is a historic and contemporaneous link between the teachings of certain religious denominations and the teaching of evolution.[9] It was this link that concerned the Court in *Epperson v. Arkansas,* 393 U.S. 97, 89 S.Ct. 266, 21 L.Ed.2d 228 (1968), which also involved a facial challenge to a statute regulating the teaching of evolution. In that case, the Court reviewed an Arkansas statute that made it unlawful for an instructor to teach evolution or to use a textbook that referred to this scientific theory. Although the Arkansas anti-evolution law did not explicitly state its predominant religious purpose, the Court could not ignore that "[t]he statute was a product of the upsurge of 'fundamentalist' religious fervor" that has long viewed this particular scientific theory as contradicting the literal interpretation of the Bible. . . .[10] After reviewing

---

[7]The Creationism Act's provisions appear among other provisions prescribing the courses of study in Louisiana's public schools. These other provisions, similar to those in other states, prescribe courses of study in such topics as driver training, civics, the Constitution, and free enterprise. None of these other provisions, apart from those associated with the Creationism Act, nominally mandates "equal time" for opposing opinions within a specific area of learning. See, e.g., La.Rev.Stat.Ann. §§ 17:261-17:281 (West 1982 and Supp. 1987).

[9]*See McLean v. Arkansas Bd. of Ed.,* 529 F.Supp. 1255, 1258–64 (ED Ark.1982) (reviewing historical and contemporary antagonisms between the theory of evolution and religious movements).

[10]The Court evaluated the statute in light of a series of anti-evolution statutes adopted by state legislatures dating back to the Tennessee statute that was the focus of the celebrated Scopes trial in 1927. *Epperson v. Arkansas,* 393 U.S., at 98, 101, n. 8, and 109, 89 S.Ct., at 267, 269, n. 8, and 273. The Court found the Arkansas statute comparable to this Tennessee "monkey law," since both gave preference to " 'religious establishments which have as one of their tenets or dogmas the instantaneous creation of man.' " *Id.,* at 103, n. 11, 89 S.Ct., at 270, n. 11 (quoting *Scopes v. State,* 154 Tenn. 105, 126, 289 S.W. 363, 369 (1927) (Chambliss, J., concurring)).

the history of anti-evolution statutes, the Court determined that "there can be no doubt that the motivation for the [Arkansas] law was the same [as other anti-evolution statutes]: to suppress the teaching of a theory which, it was thought, 'denied' the divine creation of man." *Id.*, at 109, 89 S.Ct., at 273. The Court found that there can be no legitimate state interest in protecting particular religions from scientific views "distasteful to them," . . . and concluded "that the First Amendment does not permit the State to require that teaching and learning must be tailored to the principles or prohibitions of any religious sect or dogma," *id.*, at 106, 89 S.Ct., at 271.

These same historic and contemporaneous antagonisms between the teachings of certain religious denominations and the teaching of evolution are present in this case. The preeminent purpose of the Louisiana legislature was clearly to advance the religious viewpoint that a supernatural being created humankind.[11] The term "creation science" was defined as embracing this particular religious doctrine by those responsible for the passage of the Creationism Act. Senator Keith's leading expert on creation science, Edward Boudreaux, testified at the legislative hearings that the theory of creation science included belief in the existence of a supernatural creator. . . . Senator Keith also cited testimony from other experts to support the creation-science view that "a creator [was] responsible for the universe and everything in it."[13] . . .

The legislative history therefore reveals that the term "creation science," as contemplated by the legislature that adopted this Act, embodies the religious belief that a supernatural creator was responsible for the creation of humankind.

Furthermore, it is not happenstance that the legislature required the teaching of a theory that coincided with this religious view. The legislative history documents that the Act's primary purpose was to change the science curriculum of public schools in order to provide persuasive advantage to a particular religious doctrine that rejects the factual basis of evolution in its entirety. The sponsor of the Creationism Act, Senator Keith, explained during the legislative hearings that his disdain for the theory of evolution resulted from the support that evolution supplied to

views contrary to his own religious beliefs. According to Senator Keith, the theory of evolution was consonant with the "cardinal principle[s] of religious humanism, secular humanism, theological liberalism, aetheistism [sic]." . . . The state senator repeatedly stated that scientific evidence supporting his religious views should be included in the public school curriculum to redress the fact that the theory of evolution incidentally coincided with what he characterized as religious beliefs antithetical to his own. The legislation therefore sought to alter the science curriculum to reflect endorsement of a religious view that is antagonistic to the theory of evolution.

In this case, the purpose of the Creationism Act was to restructure the science curriculum to conform with a particular religious viewpoint. Out of many possible science subjects taught in the public schools, the legislature chose to affect the teaching of the one scientific theory that historically has been opposed by certain religious sects. As in *Epperson*, the legislature passed the Act to give preference to those religious groups which have as one of their tenets the creation of humankind by a divine creator. The "overriding fact" that confronted the Court in Epperson was "that Arkansas' law selects from the body of knowledge a particular segment which it proscribes for the sole reason that it is deemed to conflict with . . . a particular interpretation of the Book of Genesis by a particular religious group." 393 U.S., at 103, 89 S.Ct., at 270. Similarly, the Creationism Act is designed *either* to promote the theory of creation science which embodies a particular religious tenet by requiring that creation science be taught whenever evolution is taught or to prohibit the teaching of a scientific theory disfavored by certain religious sects by forbidding the teaching of evolution when creation science is not also taught. The Establishment Clause, however, "forbids *alike* the preference of a religious doctrine or the prohibition of theory which is deemed antagonistic to a particular dogma." *Id.*, at 106–07, 89 S.Ct., at 271 (emphasis added). Because the primary purpose of the Creationism Act is to advance a particular religious belief, the Act endorses religion in violation of the First Amendment.

[11]While the belief in the instantaneous creation of humankind by a supernatural creator may require the rejection of every aspect of the theory of evolution, an individual instead may choose to accept some or all of this scientific theory as compatible with his or her spiritual outlook. . . .

[13]Senator Keith believed that creation science embodied this view: "One concept is that a creator however you define a creator was responsible for everything that is in this world. The other concept is that it just evolved." . . . Besides Senator Keith, several of the most vocal legislators also revealed their religious motives for supporting the bill in the official legislative history. . . .

We do not imply that a legislature could never require that scientific critiques of prevailing scientific theories be taught. Indeed, the Court acknowledged in *Stone* that its decision forbidding the posting of the Ten Commandments did not mean that no use could ever be made of the Ten Commandments, or that the Ten Commandments played an exclusively religious role in the history of Western Civilization. 449 U.S., at 42, 101 S.Ct., at 194. In a similar way, teaching a variety of scientific theories about the origins of humankind to schoolchildren might be validly done with the clear secular intent of enhancing the effectiveness of science instruction. But because the primary purpose of the Creationism Act is to endorse a particular religious doctrine, the Act furthers religion in violation of the Establishment Clause.

IV

Appellants contend that genuine issues of material fact remain in dispute, and therefore the District Court erred in granting summary judgment. . . .

In this case, appellees' motion for summary judgment rested on the plain language of the Creationism Act, the legislative history and historical context of the Act, the specific sequence of events leading to the passage of the act, the State Board's report on a survey of school superintendents, and the correspondence between the Act's legislative sponsor and its key witnesses. Appellants contend that affidavits made by two scientists, two theologians, and an education administrator raise a genuine issue of material fact and that summary judgment was therefore barred. The affidavits define creation science as "origin through abrupt appearance in complex form" and allege that such a viewpoint constitutes a true scientific theory.

* * *

We agree with the lower courts that these affidavits do not raise a genuine issue of material fact. The existence of "uncontroverted affidavits" does not bar summary judgment. Moreover, the postenactment testimony of outside experts is of little use in determining the Louisiana legislature's purpose in enacting this statute. The Louisiana legislature did hear and rely on scientific experts in passing the bill,[17] but none of the persons making the affidavits produced by the appellants participated in or contributed to the enactment of the law or its implementation. The District Court, in its discretion, properly concluded that a Monday-morning "battle of the experts" over possible technical meanings of terms in the statute would not illuminate the contemporaneous purpose of the Louisiana legislature when it made the law. We therefore conclude that the District Court did not err in finding that appellants failed to raise a genuine issue of material fact, and in granting summary judgment.[20]

V

The Louisiana Creationism Act . . . violates the Establishment Clause of the First Amendment because it seeks to employ the symbolic and financial support of government to achieve a religious purpose. The judgment of the Court of Appeals therefore is
Affirmed.

Justice Powell, with whom Justice O'Connor joins, concurring.

I write separately to note certain aspects of the legislative history, and to emphasize that nothing in the Court's opinion diminishes the traditionally broad discretion accorded state and local school officials in the selection of the public school curriculum.

* * *

Even though I find Louisiana's Balanced Treatment Act unconstitutional, I adhere to the view "that the States and locally elected school boards should have the responsibility for determining the educational policy of the public schools." *Board of Education v. Pico*, 457 U.S. 853, 893, 102 S.Ct. 2799, 2822, 73 L.Ed.2d 435 (1982) (Powell, J., dissenting). A decision respecting the subject matter to be taught in public schools does not violate the Establishment Clause simply because the material to be taught " 'happens to coincide or harmonize with the tenets of some or all religions.' " *Harris v. McRae*, 448 U.S. 297, 319, 100 S.Ct. 2671, 2689, 65 L.Ed.2d 784 (1980) (quoting *McGowan v. Maryland*, 366 U.S. 420, 442, 81 S.Ct. 1101, 1113, 6 L.Ed.2d 393 (1961)). . . .

* * *

As a matter of history, school children can and should properly be informed of all aspects of this Nation's religious heritage. I would see no constitu-

---

[17]The experts, who were relied upon by the sponsor of the bill and the legislation's other supporters, testified that creation science embodies the religious view that there is a supernatural creator of the universe. . . .

[20]Numerous other Establishment Clause cases that found state statutes to be unconstitutional have been disposed of without trial. *E.g., Larkin v. Grendel's Den, Inc.*, 459 U.S. 116, 103 S.Ct. 505, 74 L.Ed.2d 297 (1982); *Lemon v. Kurtzman*, 403 U.S. 602, 91 S.Ct. 2105, 29 L.Ed.2d 745 (1971); *Engel v. Vitale*, 370 U.S. 421, 82 S.Ct. 1261, 8 L.Ed.2d 601 (1962).

tional problem if school children were taught the nature of the Founding Fathers' religious beliefs and how these beliefs affected the attitudes of the times and the structure of our government. Courses in comparative religion of course are customary and constitutionally appropriate. In fact, since religion permeates our history, a familiarity with the nature of religious beliefs is necessary to understand many historical as well as contemporary events. In addition, it is worth noting that the Establishment Clause does not prohibit *per se* the educational use of religious documents in public school education. Although this Court has recognized that the Bible is "an instrument of religion," *Abington School District v. Schempp, supra,* 374 U.S., at 224, 83 S.Ct., at 1573, it also has made clear that the Bible "may constitutionally be used in an appropriate study of history, civilization, ethics, comparative religion, or the like." *Stone v. Graham,* 449 U.S., at 42, 101 S.Ct., at 194 (citing *Abington School Dist. v. Schempp, supra,* 374 U.S., at 225, 83 S.Ct., at 1572). The book is, in fact, "the world's all-time best seller" with undoubted literary and historic value apart from its religious content. The Establishment Clause is properly understood to prohibit the use of the Bible and other religious documents in public school education only when the purpose of the use is to advance a particular religious belief.

* * *

In sum, I find that the language and the legislative history of the Balanced Treatment Act unquestionably demonstrate that its purpose is to advance a particular religious belief. Although the discretion of state and local authorities over public school curricula is broad, "the First Amendment does not permit the State to require that teaching and learning must be tailored to the principles or prohibitions of any religious sect or dogma." *Epperson v. Arkansas,* 393 U.S., at 106, 89 S.Ct., at 271. Accordingly, I concur in the opinion of the Court and its judgment that the Balanced Treatment Act violates the Establishment Clause of the Constitution.

Justice White, concurring in the judgment. [Opinion omitted]

Justice Scalia, with whom the Chief Justice joins, dissenting.

Even if I agreed with the questionable premise that legislation can be invalidated under the Establishment Clause on the basis of its motivation alone, without regard to its effects, I would still find no justification for today's decision. The Louisiana legislators who passed the "Balanced Treatment for Creation-Science and Evolution-Science Act" (Balanced Treatment Act), La.Rev.Stat.Ann. §§ 17:286.1–17:286.7 (West 1982), each of whom had sworn to support the Constitution, were well aware of the potential Establishment Clause problems and considered that aspect of the legislation with great care. After seven hearings and several months of study, resulting in substantial revision of the original proposal, they approved the Act overwhelmingly and specifically articulated the secular purpose they meant it to serve. Although the record contains abundant evidence of the sincerity of that purpose (the only issue pertinent to this case), the Court today holds, essentially on the basis of "its visceral knowledge regarding what *must* have motivated the legislators," 778 F.2d 225, 227 (CA5 1985) (Gee, J., dissenting) (emphasis added), that the members of the Louisiana Legislature knowingly violated their oaths and then lied about it. I dissent. Had requirements of the Balanced Treatment Act that are not apparent on its face been clarified by an interpretation of the Louisiana Supreme Court, or by the manner of its implementation, the Act might well be found unconstitutional; but the question of its constitutionality cannot rightly be disposed of on the gallop, by impugning the motives of its supporters.

I

This case arrives here in the following posture: The Louisiana Supreme Court has never been given an opportunity to interpret the Balanced Treatment Act, State officials have never attempted to implement it, and it has never been the subject of a full evidentiary hearing. We can only guess at its meaning. We know that it forbids instruction in either "creation-science" or "evolution-science" without instruction in the other, § 17:286.4A, but the parties are sharply divided over what creation science consists of. Appellants insist that it is a collection of educationally valuable scientific data that has been censored from classrooms by an embarrassed scientific establishment. Appellees insist it is not science at all but thinly veiled religious doctrine. Both interpretations of the intended meaning of that phrase find considerable support in the legislative history.

At least at this stage in the litigation, it is plain to me that we must accept appellants' view of what the statute means. To begin with, the statute itself defines "creation-science" as "the *scientific evidences* for creation and inferences from those *scientific evidences.*" § 17:286.3(2) (emphasis added). If, however, that definition is not thought sufficiently helpful, the means by which the Louisiana Supreme Court will give the term more precise content is quite clear—and again, at this stage in the litigation, favors the appellants' view. "Creation science" is unquestionably a "term of art," . . . and thus, under Louisiana law, is "to be interpreted according to [its] received meaning and acceptation with the learned in the art, trade or profession to which [it] refer[s]." La.Civ. Code Ann., Art. 15 (West 1952). The only evidence in the record of the "received meaning and acceptation" of "creation science" is found in five affidavits filed by appellants. In those affidavits, two scientists, a philosopher, a theologian, and an educator, all of whom claim extensive knowledge of creation science, swear that it is essentially a collection of scientific data supporting the theory that the physical universe and life within it appeared suddenly and have not changed substantially since appearing. . . . These experts insist that creation science is a strictly scientific concept that can be presented without religious reference. . . . At this point, then, we must assume that the Balanced Treatment Act does not require the presentation of religious doctrine.

Nothing in today's opinion is plainly to the contrary, but what the statute means and what it requires are of rather little concern to the Court. Like the Court of Appeals, 765 F.2d 1251, 1253, 1254 (CA5 1985), the Court finds it necessary to consider only the motives of the legislators who supported the Balanced Treatment Act. . . . After examining the statute, its legislative history, and its historical and social context, the Court holds that the Louisiana Legislature acted without "a secular legislative purpose" and that the Act therefore fails the "purpose" prong of the three-part test set forth in *Lemon v. Kurtzman,* 403 U.S. 602, 612, 91 S.Ct. 2105, 2111, 29 L.Ed.2d 2105 (1971). . . . I doubt whether that "purpose" requirement of *Lemon* is a proper interpretation of the Constitution; but even if it were, I could not agree with the Court's assessment that the requirement was not satisfied here.

* * *

Nevertheless, a few principles have emerged from our cases, principles which should, but to an unfortunately large extent do not, guide the Court's application of *Lemon* today. It is clear, first of all, that regardless of what "legislative purpose" may mean in other contexts, for the purpose of the *Lemon* test it means the "actual" motives of those responsible for

the challenged action. The Court recognizes this . . . as it has in the past, *see, e.g., Witters v. Washington Dept. of Services for Blind, supra,* 474 U.S., at 486, 106 S.Ct., at 751; *Wallace v. Jaffree, supra,* 472 U.S., at 56, 105 S.Ct., at 2490. Thus, if those legislators who supported the Balanced Treatment Act in fact acted with a "sincere" secular purpose, . . . the Act survives the first component of the *Lemon* test, regardless of whether that purpose is likely to be achieved by the provisions they enacted.

Our cases have also confirmed that when the *Lemon* Court referred to "a secular . . . purpose," 403 U.S., at 612, 91 S.Ct., at 2111, it meant "a secular purpose." The author of *Lemon,* writing for the Court, has said that invalidation under the purpose prong is appropriate when "there [is] *no question* that the statute or activity was motivated *wholly* by religious considerations." *Lynch v. Donnelly,* 465 U.S. 668, 680, 104 S.Ct. 1355, 1362, 79 L.Ed.2d 604 (1984) (Burger, C. J.) (emphasis added). . . . Thus, the majority's invalidation of the Balanced Treatment Act is defensible only if the record indicates that the Louisiana Legislature had no secular purpose.

It is important to stress that the purpose forbidden by *Lemon* is the purpose to "advance religion." 403 U.S., at 613, 91 S.Ct., at 2111. . . . Our cases in no way imply that the Establishment Clause forbids legislators merely to act upon their religious convictions. We surely would not strike down a law providing money to feed the hungry or shelter the homeless if it could be demonstrated that, but for the religious beliefs of the legislators, the funds would not have been approved. Also, political activism by the religiously motivated is part of our heritage. Notwithstanding the majority's implication to the contrary, . . . we do not presume that the sole purpose of a law is to advance religion merely because it was supported strongly by organized religions or by adherents of particular faiths. . . .

To do so would deprive religious men and women of their right to participate in the political process. Today's religious activism may give us the Balanced Treatment Act, but yesterday's resulted in the abolition of slavery, and tomorrow's may bring relief for famine victims.

Similarly, we will not presume that a law's purpose is to advance religion merely because it " 'happens to coincide or harmonize with the tenets of some or all religions,' " *Harris v. McRae, supra,* at 319, 100 S.Ct., at 2689 (quoting *McGowan v. Maryland,* 366 U.S. 420, 442, 81 S.Ct. 1101, 1113, 6 L.Ed.2d 393 (1961)), or because it benefits religion, even substantially. . . .

Thus, the fact that creation science coincides with the beliefs of certain religions, a fact upon which the majority relies heavily, does not itself justify invalidation of the Act.

Finally, our cases indicate that even certain kinds of governmental actions undertaken with the specific intention of improving the position of religion do not "advance religion" as that term is used in *Lemon*. 403 U.S., at 613, 91 S.Ct., at 2111. Rather, we have said that in at least two circumstances government must act to advance religion, and that in a third it may do so.

First, since we have consistently described the Establishment Clause as forbidding not only state action motivated by the desire to advance religion, but also that intended to "disapprove," "inhibit," or evince "hostility" toward religion. . . .

Thus, if the Louisiana Legislature sincerely believed that the State's science teachers were being hostile to religion, our cases indicate that it could act to eliminate that hostility without running afoul of *Lemon*'s purpose test.

Second, we have held that intentional governmental advancement of religion is sometimes required by the Free Exercise Clause. For example, in *Hobbie v. Unemployment Appeals Comm'n of Fla.*, 480 U.S. 136, 107 S.Ct. 1046, 94 L.Ed.2d 190 (1987); *Thomas v. Review Bd., Indiana Employment Security Div.*, 450 U.S. 707, 101 S.Ct. 1425, 67 L.Ed.2d 624 (1981); *Wisconsin v. Yoder*, 406 U.S. 205, 92 S.Ct. 1526, 32 L.Ed.2d 15 (1972); and *Sherbert v. Verner*, 374 U.S. 398, 83 S.Ct. 1790, 10 L.Ed.2d 965 (1963), we held that in some circumstances States must accommodate the beliefs of religious citizens by exempting them from generally applicable regulations. We have not yet come close to reconciling *Lemon* and our Free Exercise cases, and typically we do not really try. . . .

It is clear, however, that members of the Louisiana Legislature were not impermissibly motivated for purpose of the *Lemon* test if they believed that approval of the Balanced Treatment Act was required by the Free Exercise Clause.

We have also held that in some circumstances government may act to accommodate religion, even if that action is not required by the First Amendment. . . . It is well established that "[t]he limits of permissible state accommodation to religion are by no means co-extensive with the noninterference mandated by the Free Exercise Clause." *Walz v. Tax Comm'n of New York City*, 397 U.S., at 673, 90 S.Ct., at 1413; *see*

also Gillette v. United States, 401 U.S. 437, 453, 91 S.Ct. 828, 838, 28 L.Ed.2d 168 (1971). We have implied that voluntary governmental accommodation of religion is not only permissible, but desirable. . . . Thus, few would contend that Title VII of the Civil Rights Act of 1964, which both forbids religious discrimination by private-sector employers, 78 Stat. 255, 42 U.S.C. § 2000e-2(a)(1), and requires them reasonably to accommodate the religious practices of their employees, t 2000e(j), violates the Establishment Clause, even though its "purpose" is, of course, to advance religion, and even though it is almost certainly not required by the Free Exercise Clause. While we have warned that at some point, accommodation may devolve into "an unlawful fostering of religion," *Hobbie v. Unemployment Appeals Comm'n of Fla.*, *supra*, 480 U.S., at 145, 107 S.Ct., at 1051, we have not suggested precisely (or even roughly) where that point might be. It is possible, then, that even if the sole motive of those voting for the Balanced Treatment Act was to advance religion, and its passage was not actually required, or even believed to be required, by either the Free Exercise or Establishment Clauses, the Act would nonetheless survive scrutiny under *Lemon*'s purpose test.

One final observation about the application of that test: Although the Court's opinion gives no hint of it, in the past we have repeatedly affirmed "our reluctance to attribute unconstitutional motives to the States." . . . We "presume that legislatures act in a constitutional manner."

With the foregoing in mind, I now turn to the purposes underlying adoption of the Balanced Treatment Act.

II

* * *

We have relatively little information upon which to judge the motives of those who supported the Act. About the only direct evidence is the statute itself and transcripts of the seven committee hearings at which it was considered. Unfortunately, several of those hearings were sparsely attended, and the legislators who were present revealed little about their motives. We have no committee reports, no floor debates, no remarks inserted into the legislative history, no statement from the Governor, and no post-enactment statements or testimony from the bill's sponsor or any other legislators. . . . Nevertheless, there is ample evidence that the majority is wrong in holding that the Balanced Treatment Act is without secular purpose.

At the outset, it is important to note that the Balanced Treatment Act did not fly through the

Louisiana Legislature on wings of fundamentalist religious fervor—which would be unlikely, in any event, since only a small minority of the State's citizens belong to fundamentalist religious denominations. . . . The Act had its genesis (so to speak) in legislation introduced by Senator Bill Keith in June 1980. After two hearings before the Senate Committee on Education, Senator Keith asked that his bill be referred to a study commission composed of members of both houses of the Louisiana Legislature. He expressed hope that the joint committee would give the bill careful consideration and determine whether his arguments were "legitimate." . . . The committee met twice during the interim, heard testimony (both for and against the bill) from several witnesses, and received staff reports. Senator Keith introduced his bill again when the legislature reconvened. The Senate Committee on Education held two more hearings and approved the bill after substantially amending it (in part over Senator Keith's objection). After approval by the full Senate, the bill was referred to the House Committee on Education. That committee conducted a lengthy hearing, adopted further amendments, and sent the bill on to the full House, where it received favorable consideration. The Senate concurred in the House amendments and on July 20, 1981, the Governor signed the bill into law.

Senator Keith's statements before the various committees that considered the bill hardly reflect the confidence of a man preaching to the converted. He asked his colleagues to "keep an open mind" and not to be "biased" by misleading characterizations of creation science. . . . He also urged them to "look at this subject on its merits and not on some preconceived idea." . . .

Senator Keith's reception was not especially warm. Over his strenuous objection, the Senate Committee on Education voted 5–1 to amend this bill to deprive it of any force; as amended, the bill merely gave teachers permission to balance the teaching of creation science or evolution with the other. . . . The House Committee restored the "mandatory" language to the bill by a vote of only 6–5, . . . and both the full House (by vote of 52–35) . . . and full Senate (23–15) . . . had to repel further efforts to gut the bill.

The legislators understood that Senator Keith's bill involved a "unique" subject, . . . and they were repeatedly made aware of its potential constitutional problems. . . . Although the Establishment Clause,

including its secular purpose requirement, was of substantial concern to the legislators, they eventually voted overwhelmingly in favor of the Balanced Treatment Act: The House approved it 71–19 (with 15 members absent), . . . the Senate 26–12 (with all members present). . . . The legislators specifically designated the protection of "academic freedom" as the purpose of the Act. La.Rev.Stat. [Ann.] § 17:286.2 (West 1982). We cannot accurately assess whether this purpose is a "sham," . . . until we first examine the evidence presented to the legislature far more carefully than the Court has done.

Before summarizing the testimony of Senator Keith and his supporters, I wish to make clear that I by no means intend to endorse its accuracy. But my views (and the views of this Court) about creation science and evolution are (or should be) beside the point. Our task is not to judge the debate about teaching the origins of life, but to ascertain what the members of the Louisiana Legislature believed. The vast majority of them voted to approve a bill which explicitly stated a secular purpose; what is crucial is not their wisdom in believing that purpose would be achieved by the bill, but their sincerity in believing it would be.

Most of the testimony in support of Senator Keith's bill came from the Senator himself and from scientists and educators he presented, many of whom enjoyed academic credentials that may have been regarded as quite impressive by members of the Louisiana Legislature. To a substantial extent, their testimony was devoted to lengthy, and, to the layman, seemingly expert scientific expositions on the origin of life. . . .

These scientific lectures touched upon, *inter alia*, biology, paleontology, genetics, astronomy, astrophysics, probability analysis, and biochemistry. The witnesses repeatedly assured committee members that "hundreds and hundreds" of highly respected, internationally renowned scientists believed in creation science and would support their testimony. . . .

Senator Keith and his witnesses testified essentially as set forth in the following numbered paragraphs:

(1) There are two and only two scientific explanations for the beginning of life—evolution and creation science. . . . Both are bona fide "sciences." . . .

Both posit a theory of the origin of life and subject that theory to empirical testing. Evolution posits that life arose out of inanimate chemical compounds and has gradually evolved over millions of years. Creation science posits that all life forms now on earth appeared suddenly and relatively recently and have changed little. Since there are only two possible explanations of the origin of life, any evidence that tends to disprove the theory of evolution necessarily tends to prove the theory of creation science, and vice versa. For example, the abrupt appearance in the fossil record of complex life, and the extreme rarity of transitional life forms in that record, are evidence for creation science. . . .

(2) The body of scientific evidence supporting creation science is as strong as that supporting evolution. In fact, it may be stronger. . . .

The evidence for evolution is far less compelling than we have been led to believe. Evolution is not a scientific "fact," since it cannot actually be observed in a laboratory. Rather, evolution is merely a scientific theory or "guess." . . .

It is a very bad guess at that. The scientific problems with evolution are so serious that it could accurately be termed a "myth." . . .

(3) Creation science is educationally valuable. Students exposed to it better understand the current state of scientific evidence about the origin of life. . . . Those students even have a better understanding of evolution. . . . Creation science can and should be presented to children without any religious content. . . .

(4) Although creation science is educationally valuable and strictly scientific, it is now being censored from or misrepresented in the public schools. . . . Evolution, in turn, is misrepresented as an absolute truth. . . . Teachers have been brainwashed by an entrenched scientific establishment composed almost exclusively of scientists to whom evolution is like a "religion." These scientists discriminate against creation scientists so as to prevent evolution's weaknesses from being exposed. . . .

(5) The censorship of creation science has at least two harmful effects. First, it deprives students of knowledge of one of the two scientific explanations for the origin of life and leads them to believe that evolution is proven fact; thus, their education suffers and they are wrongly taught that science has proven their religious beliefs false. Second, it violates the Establishment Clause. The United States Supreme Court has held that secular humanism is a religion. . . . Belief in evolution is a central tenet of that religion. . . . Thus, by censoring creation science and instructing students that evolution is fact, public school teachers are now advancing religion in violation of the Establishment Clause. . . .

Senator Keith repeatedly and vehemently denied that his purpose was to advance a particular religious doctrine. At the outset of the first hearing on the legislation, he testified, "We are not going to say today that you should have some kind of religious instructions in our schools. . . . We are not talking about religion today. . . . I am not proposing that we take the Bible in each science class and read the first chapter of Genesis." . . . At a later hearing, Senator Keith stressed that "to . . . teach religion and disguise it as creationism . . . is not my intent. My intent is to see to it that our textbooks are not censored." . . .

We have no way of knowing, of course, how many legislators believed the testimony of Senator Keith and his witnesses. But in the absence of evidence to the contrary,[4] we have to assume that many of them did. Given that assumption, the Court today plainly errs in holding that the Louisiana Legislature passed the Balanced Treatment Act for exclusively religious purposes.

Even with nothing more than this legislative history to go on, I think it would be extraordinary to invalidate the Balanced Treatment Act for lack of a valid secular purpose. Striking down a law approved by the democratically elected representatives of the people is no minor matter. . . . If history were silent or ambiguous about the existence of a secular purpose—and here it is not—the statute should survive *Lemon*'s purpose test. But even more validation than mere legislative history is present here. The Louisiana Legislature explicitly set forth its secular purpose ("protecting academic freedom") in the very text of the Act. La.Rev.Stat. [Ann.] § 17:286.2 (West 1982). We have in the past repeatedly relied upon or deferred to such expressions. . . .

The Court seeks to evade the force of this expression of purpose by stubbornly misinterpreting it, and then finding that the provisions of the Act do not advance that misinterpreted purpose, thereby showing it to be a sham. . . . Had the Court devoted to this central question of the meaning of the legislatively expressed purpose a small fraction of the research into legislative history that produced its quotations of religiously motivated statements by individual

---

[4]Although appellees and *amici* dismiss the testimony of Senator Keith and his witnesses as pure fantasy, they did not bother to submit evidence of that to the District Court, making it difficult for us to agree with them. The State, by contrast, submitted the affidavits of two scientists, a philosopher, a theologian, and an educator, whose academic credentials are rather impressive. . . .

legislators, it would have discerned quite readily what "academic freedom" meant: students' freedom from indoctrination. The legislature wanted to ensure that students would be free to decide for themselves how life began, based upon a fair and balanced presentation of the scientific evidence—that is, to protect "the right of each [student] voluntarily to determine what to believe (and what not to believe) free of any coercive pressures from the State." *Grand Rapids School District v. Ball*, 473 U.S., at 385, 105 S.Ct., at 3224. The legislature did not care *whether* the topic of origins was taught; it simply wished to ensure that *when* the topic was taught, students would receive " 'all of the evidence.' " . . .

As originally introduced, the "purpose" section of the Balanced Treatment Act read: "This Chapter is enacted for the purposes of protecting academic freedom . . . of students . . . and assisting students in their search for truth." . . . Among the proposed findings of fact contained in the original version of the bill was the following: "Public school instruction in only evolution-science . . . violates the principle of academic freedom because it denies students a choice between scientific models and instead indoctrinates them in evolution science alone." . . .

Senator Keith unquestionably understood "academic freedom" to mean "freedom from indoctrination." . . .

If one adopts the obviously intended meaning of the statutory terms "academic freedom," there is no basis whatever for concluding that the purpose they express is a "sham." . . . To the contrary, the Act pursues that purpose plainly and consistently. . . . The Louisiana legislators had been told repeatedly that creation scientists were scorned by most educators and scientists, who themselves had an almost religious faith in evolution. It is hardly surprising, then, that in seeking to achieve a balanced, "nonindoctrinating" curriculum, the legislators protected from discrimination only those teachers whom they thought were suffering from discrimination. (Also, the legislators were undoubtedly aware of *Epperson v. Arkansas*, 393 U.S. 97, 89 S.Ct. 266, 21 L.Ed.2d 228 (1968), and thus could quite reasonably have concluded that discrimination against evolutionists was already prohibited.) The two provisions respecting the development of curriculum guides are also consistent with "academic freedom" as the Louisiana Legislature understood the term. Witnesses had informed the legislators that, because of the hostility of most scientists and educators to creation science, the topic had been censored from

or badly misrepresented in elementary and secondary school texts. In light of the unavailability of works on creation science suitable for classroom use . . . and the existence of ample materials on evolution, it was entirely reasonable for the Legislature to conclude that science teachers attempting to implement the Act would need a curriculum guide on creation science, but not on evolution, and that those charged with developing the guide would need an easily accessible group of creation scientists. Thus, the provisions of the Act of so much concern to the Court support the conclusion that the Legislature acted to advance "academic freedom."

The legislative history gives ample evidence of the sincerity of the Balanced Treatment Act's articulated purpose. Witness after witness urged the legislators to support the Act so that students would not be "indoctrinated" but would instead be free to decide for themselves, based upon a fair presentation of the scientific evidence, about the origin of life. . . .

* * *

It is undoubtedly true that what prompted the Legislature to direct its attention to the misrepresentation of evolution in the schools (rather than the inaccurate presentation of other topics) was its awareness of the tension between evolution and the religious beliefs of many children. But even appellees concede that a valid secular purpose is not rendered impermissible simply because its pursuit is prompted by concern for religious sensitivities. . . . If a history teacher falsely told her students that the bones of Jesus Christ had been discovered, or a physics teacher that the Shroud of Turin had been conclusively established to be inexplicable on the basis of natural causes, I cannot believe (despite the majority's implication to the contrary . . .) that legislators or school board members would be constitutionally prohibited from taking corrective action, simply because that action was prompted by concern for the religious beliefs of the misinstructed students.

In sum, even if one concedes, for the sake of argument, that a majority of the Louisiana Legislature voted for the Balanced Treatment Act partly in order to foster (rather than merely eliminate discrimination against) Christian fundamentalist beliefs, our cases establish that that alone would not suffice to invalidate the Act, so long as there was a genuine secular purpose as well. We have, moreover, no adequate basis for disbelieving the secular purpose set forth in the Act itself, or for concluding that it is a sham enacted to conceal the legislators' violation of their oaths of office. I am astonished by the Court's unprecedented readiness to reach such a conclusion, which I can only attribute to an intellectual predisposition created by the facts and the legend of *Scopes v. State*, 154 Tenn. 105, 289 S.W. 363 (1927)—an instinctive reaction that any governmentally imposed requirements bearing upon the teaching of evolution must be a manifestation of Christian fundamentalist repression. . . .

Since the existence of secular purpose is so entirely clear, and thus dispositive, I will not go on to discuss the fact that, even if the Louisiana Legislature's purpose were exclusively to advance religion, some of the well established exceptions to the impermissibility of that purpose might be applicable—the validating intent to eliminate a perceived discrimination against a particular religion, to facilitate its free exercise, or to accommodate it. . . . I am not in any case enamored of those amorphous exceptions, since I think them no more than unpredictable correctives to what is . . . a fundamentally unsound rule. It is surprising, however, that the Court does not address these exceptions, since the context of the legislature's action gives some reason to believe they may be applicable.[6]

Because I believe that the Balanced Treatment Act had a secular purpose, which is all the first component of the *Lemon* test requires, I would reverse the judgment of the Court of Appeals and remand for further consideration.

III

I have to this point assumed the validity of the *Lemon* "purpose" test. In fact, however, I think the pessimistic evaluation that the Chief Justice made of the totality of *Lemon* is particularly applicable to the "purpose" prong: it is "a constitutional theory [that] has no basis in the history of the amendment it seeks to interpret, is difficult to apply and yields unprincipled results." *Wallace v. Jaffree*, 472 U.S., at 112, 105 S.Ct., at 2519 (Rehnquist, J., dissenting).

Our cases interpreting and applying the purpose test have made such a maze of the Establishment Clause that even the most conscientious governmental officials can only guess what motives will be held unconstitutional. We have said essentially the following: Government may not act with the purpose of advancing religion, except when forced to do so by the Free Exercise Clause (which is now and then); or when eliminating existing governmental hostility to religion (which exists sometimes); or even when merely accommodating governmentally uninhibited religious practices, except that at some point (it is unclear where) intentional accommodation results in the fostering of religion, which is of course unconstitutional. . . .

But the difficulty of knowing what vitiating purpose one is looking for is as nothing compared with the difficulty of knowing how or where to find it. For while it is possible to discern the objective "purpose" of a statute (i.e., the public good at which its provisions appear to be directed), or even the formal motivation for a statute where that is explicitly set forth (as it was, to no avail, here), discerning the subjective motivation of those enacting the statute is, to be honest, almost always an impossible task. The number of possible motivations, to begin with, is not binary, or indeed even finite. In the present case, for example, a particular legislator need not have voted for the Act either because he wanted to foster religion or because he wanted to improve education. He may have thought the bill would provide jobs for his district, or may have wanted to make amends with a faction of his party he had alienated on another vote, or he may have been a close friend of the bill's sponsor, or he may have been repaying a favor he owed the Majority Leader, or he may have hoped the Governor would appreciate his vote and make a fundraising appearance for him, or he may have been pressured to vote for a bill he disliked by a wealthy contributor or by a flood of constituent mail, or he may have been seeking favorable publicity, or he may have been reluctant to hurt the feelings of a loyal staff member who worked on the bill, or he may have been settling

---

[6]As the majority recognizes, . . . Senator Keith sincerely believed that "secular humanism is a bona fide religion," . . . and that "evolution is the cornerstone of that religion." . . . The Senator even told his colleagues that this Court had "held" that secular humanism was a religion. . . . (In *Torcaso v. Watkins*, 367 U.S. 488, 495, n. 11, 81 S.Ct. 1680, 1684, n. 11, 6 L.Ed.2d 982 (1961), we did indeed refer to "Secular Humanism" as a "religio[n].") Senator Keith and his supporters raised the "religion" of secular humanism not, as the majority suggests, to explain the source of their "disdain for the theory of evolution," . . . but to convince the Legislature that the State of Louisiana was violating the Establishment Clause because its teachers were misrepresenting evolution as fact and depriving students of the information necessary to question that theory. . . . The Senator repeatedly urged his colleagues to pass his bill to remedy this Establishment Clause violation by ensuring state neutrality in religious matters, . . . surely a permissible purpose under *Lemon*. Senator Keith's argument may be questionable, but nothing in the statute or its legislative history gives us reason to doubt his sincerity or that of his supporters.

an old score with a legislator who opposed the bill, or he may have been mad at his wife who opposed the bill, or he may have been intoxicated and utterly unmotivated when the vote was called, or he may have accidentally voted "yes" instead of "no," or, of course, he may have had (and very likely did have) a combination of some of the above and many other motivations. To look for the sole purpose of even a single legislator is probably to look for something that does not exist.

Putting that problem aside, however, where ought we to look for the individual legislator's purpose? We cannot of course assume that every member present (if, as is unlikely, we know who or even how many they were) agreed with the motivation expressed in a particular legislator's pre-enactment floor or committee statement. Quite obviously, "[w]hat motivates one legislator to make a speech about a statute is not necessarily what motivates scores of others to enact it." *United States v. O'Brien*, 391 U.S. 367, 384, 88 S.Ct. 1673, 1683, 20 L.Ed.2d 672 (1968). Can we assume, then, that they all agree with the motivation expressed in the staff-prepared committee reports they might have read—even though we are unwilling to assume that they agreed with the motivation expressed in the very statute that they voted for? Should we consider post-enactment floor statements? Or post-enactment testimony from legislators, obtained expressly for the lawsuit? Should we consider media reports on the realities of the legislative bargaining? All of these sources, of course, are eminently manipulable. Legislative histories can be contrived and sanitized, favorable media coverage orchestrated, and post-enactment recollections conveniently distorted. Perhaps most valuable of all would be more objective indications—for example, evidence regarding the individual legislators' religious affiliations. And if that, why not evidence regarding the fervor or tepidity of their beliefs?

Having achieved, through these simple means, an assessment of what individual legislators intended, we must still confront the question (yet to be addressed in any of our cases) how many of them must have the invalidating intent. If a state senate approves a bill by vote of 26 to 25, and only one of the 26 intended solely to advance religion, is the law unconstitutional? What if 13 of the 26 had that intent? What if 3 of the 26 had the impermissible intent, but 3 of the 25 voting against the bill were motivated by religious hostility or were simply attempting to "balance" the votes of their im-

permissibly motivated colleagues? Or is it possible that the intent of the bill's sponsor is alone enough to invalidate it—on a theory, perhaps, that even though everyone else's intent was pure, what they produced was the fruit of a forbidden tree?

Because there are no good answers to these questions, this Court has recognized from Chief Justice Marshall, *see Fletcher v. Peck*, 6 Cranch 87, 130, 3 L.Ed. 162 (1810), to Chief Justice Warren, *United States v. O'Brien, supra*, 391 U.S. at 383–84, 88 S.Ct. at 1682–83, that determining the subjective intent of legislators is a perilous enterprise. *See also Palmer v. Thompson*, 403 U.S. 217, 224–25, 91 S.Ct. 1940, 1944–45, 29 L.Ed.2d 438 (1971); *Epperson v. Arkansas*, 393 U.S., at 113, 89 S.Ct., at 275 (Black, J., concurring). It is perilous, I might note, not just for the judges who will very likely reach the wrong result, but also for the legislators who find that they must assess the validity of proposed legislation—and risk the condemnation of having voted for an unconstitutional measure—not on the basis of what the legislation contains, nor even on the basis of what they themselves intend, but on the basis of what others have in mind.

Given the many hazards involved in assessing the subjective intent of governmental decision makers, the first prong of *Lemon* is defensible, I think, only if the text of the Establishment Clause demands it. That is surely not the case. The Clause states that "Congress shall make no law respecting an establishment of religion." One could argue, I suppose, that any time Congress acts with the intent of advancing religion, it has enacted a "law respecting an establishment of religion"; but far from being an unavoidable reading, it is quite an unnatural one. . . .

It is, in short, far from an inevitable reading of the Establishment Clause that it forbids all governmental action intended to advance religion; and if not inevitable, any reading with such untoward consequences must be wrong.

* * *

NOTES AND QUESTIONS

1. Religious Purpose

Was the Louisiana law requiring the balanced treatment of creationism and evolution in public schools enacted for the purpose of endorsing religion? Is there a difference between simple suppression of evolution and a requirement that creationism be taught if evolution is taught? In this regard, consider these remarks by Professor Carter:

> These [fundamentalist Christian] parents, very devout and very worried, are trying to protect the core of their own beliefs. It is not that the parents want the public schools to proselytize in their favor; it is rather that they do not want the schools to press their own children to reject what the parents believe by calling into question a central article of their faith. The response of the Christian fundamentalist to evolutionary theory may thus be more consistently viewed as a reaction to a fear of indoctrination: religion demands one intellectual position, and the state seeks to command another. . . . The creationist parents . . . deny the right of the state to tell their children that their worldview is wrong.

Carter, "Evolutionism, Creationism, and Treating Religion as a Hobby," 1987 *Duke L. J.* 977, 981. *See* McConnell, "Why Is Religious Liberty the 'First Freedom'?" cf. p. 121 *Cardozo L.Rev.* 1243, 1258–60 (2000). If Professor Carter is right, is the purpose of the Louisiana law to advance religion or to accommodate it? Does a purpose to accommodate itself render the law constitutional? *See generally* Johnson, "Concepts and Compromise in First Amendment Religious Doctrine," 72 *Calif. L. Rev.* 817 (1984). What does Justice Scalia have to say about this point?

Suppose that in *Wisconsin v. Yoder, supra* at chapter 1, the Amish parents had persuaded the Wisconsin legislature to require a course in public schools with Amish children that emphasized the evils of modern technology and the joys of the simple farm life. Would such a law violate the Establishment Clause? Does the *Yoder* decision suggest that fundamentalist Christians in Louisiana would have had a greater likelihood of success if they had simply challenged the teaching of evolution on free exercise grounds and not sought legislative approval of a balanced curriculum? *But see Mozert v. Hawkins County Board of Education, infra. But cf. Employment Division, Department of Human Resources v. Smith,* 494 U.S. 872, 110 S.Ct. 1595 (1990). Is *Yoder* inconsistent with *Epperson* and *Edwards? See* Gelfand, "Of Monkeys and Men—An Atheist's Heretical View of the Constitutionality of Teaching the Disproof of a Religion in the Public Schools," 16 *J. Law & Educ.* 271 (1987). What if Christian parents simply had sought to exempt their children from classes in which evolution was taught? *But see Smith v. Board of School Commissioners of Mobile County, infra. See generally* Laycock, "The Remnants of Free Exercise," 1990 Sup. Ct. Rev. 1; Gelfand, *supra;*

Lines, "Scientific Creationism in the Classroom: A Constitutional Dilemma," 28 *Loy. L. Rev.* 35 (1982).

Does Justice Scalia, in his dissent, identify a secular purpose for the Louisiana statute? Or does he reject the purpose test in Establishment Clause cases? To take his examples, would laws designed to feed the hungry and house the homeless be unconstitutional if they were motivated, at least in part, by religious convictions? Laws against pornography? *See* Carter, *supra.* Is creationism distinguishable from these examples? Is Justice Scalia actually focusing on effects while the majority is focusing on purpose? Why should a law that does not significantly advance religion be unconstitutional because of the motives behind its enactment? Is the religious purpose itself a violation of the Constitution?

Justice Scalia challenges the notion that legislative motivation can be or should be determined. Is motivation difficult to discern in this case? If courts were limited to examining the face of the law only, would the balanced treatment law be constitutional under the effects test? What of the fact that the law focuses on the scientific evidence for the competing theories and not just the statement of conflicting beliefs? *See* Dhooge, "From *Scopes* to *Edwards:* The Sixty-Year Evolution of Biblical Creationism in the Public School Classroom," 22 *U. Rich. L. Rev.* 187, 210–11 (1988).

2. Science and Religion

Is the problem in *Edwards* that creationism is "bad science"? Carter, *supra* at 980. Is it? *See* Leedes, "Monkeying Around with the Establishment Clause and Bashing Creation-Science," 22 *U. Rich. L. Rev.* 149 (1988). If it is "bad science," does this fact strengthen the majority's conclusion that the Balanced Treatment Act was motivated by a desire to advance religion? *See* Dhooge, *supra* at 222. Or does it suggest that the Court is more concerned with preserving rational discourse, setting aside revelation masquerading as science? *See* Carter, *supra* at 984. Consider these remarks by one commentator:

> This reliance [in creation science] upon supernatural intervention is entirely different from the reliance of modern science upon principles of natural law. Explanations such as those relied upon by creation-scientists which depend upon the whimsical operation and intervention of forces external to the universe which are not guided or explainable by reference to natural law are not scientific.

Dhooge, *supra* at 223–24. Do you agree? *See* Johnson, "Evolution as Dogma: The Establishment of Nationalism," *First Things*, Oct. 1990, at 15. Are creation-scientists suggesting that there are forces beyond the universe? That the order of the universe is whimsical? Is the discourse of creation science irrational? *See* Carter, *supra*; Leedes, *supra*. Must Darwinists deny the possibility of supernatural intervention? Suppose Louisiana teachers were required to subject creationism and evolution to "objective, critical examination." Would that feature of the law render it constitutional? *See* Lines, *supra*. *See also* Choper, "Church, State and the Supreme Court: Current Controversy," 29 *Ariz. L. Rev.* 551, 557 (1987). May Louisiana decide that children should learn revealed truth as well as rational and reflective truth? Or, to qualify as education, must the curriculum foster "an open-minded, rigorous, and precise search for truth"? Morris, "Fundamentalism, Creationism and the First Amendment," 41 *Educ. L. Rep.* [1], [20] (1988).

Is the problem that public schools cannot be neutral as to religion while cultivating science and reason? *See generally* Laycock, "Formal, Substantive, and Disaggregated Neutrality Toward Religion," 39 *DePaul L. Rev.* 993 (1990). Is there an inconsistency between the cultivation of the analytical powers of future citizens and adherence to religious beliefs? *See* Carter, *supra*. A conflict between current conceptions of good citizenship in a democracy and the requirements of religious faith? Consider the provocative comments by Professor McConnell:

> Today there is a widespread sense not only that the government should be neutral, tolerant, and egalitarian, but so should all of us, and so should our private associations. Open-mindedness, not conviction, is the mark of the good liberal citizen. Indeed, there is something suspect in those who are sure that they are right, since it might imply that someone else is wrong. From a religious point of view, however, open-mindedness is principally valuable in the search for Truth, and not as a permanent resting place. Faith and conviction are the hallmarks of a saint. For this and other reasons, the ideal of the liberal citizen thus conflicts with the ideal of belief in religion or in any other comprehensive faith or ideology. To the extent that the state pursues this new vision of the liberal citizen, and enforces its vision by force, religious freedom is gravely endangered. Indeed, liberalism in the old sense is itself endangered, for it becomes not a set of political arrangements by which persons of widely differing views can live

> together in relative harmony, but a narrow and sectarian program enforcing its dogmas by force.

McConnell, *supra*, at 1259. Do you agree that there has been a conceptual transition from "neutral, tolerant, and egalitarian" government to a quest for tolerant and open-minded citizens? If so, is it unconstitutional for the state to pursue this objective in public schools?

3. *Academic Freedom*

What did the Louisiana legislature mean when it said that the balanced treatment law advanced academic freedom? Did it mean academic freedom for the teacher or the student? Does academic freedom mean "freedom from indoctrination"? *See generally* Yudof, "Three Faces of Academic Freedom," 32 *Loy. L. Rev.* 831, 846–50 (1987). May a teacher be dismissed for devoting excessive time to creationism and too little time to evolution? *See Dale v. Board of Education*, 316 N.W.2d 108 (S.D. 1982).

4. *Evolution: Truth in Packaging*

Suppose a state enacted a law requiring that textbooks treating evolution insert a disclaimer that evolution is only a theory and not a scientific fact. Would such a law violate the Establishment Clause? *See Freiler v. Tangipahoo Parish Bd. of Educ.*, 185 F.3d 337 (5th Cir. 2000) (holding that a school policy mandating that a disclaimer be read immediately before the teaching of evolution is an unconstitutional establishment of religion).

3. Secular Humanism. With the successful constitutional attacks on school prayer, moments of silence, and laws designed to prohibit the teaching of evolution or to introduce creationism, some parents perceived a rampant secularism in public schools, a secularism for which the courts were partially responsible, and they initiated lawsuits that focused on the perceived hostility of public schools to their religious beliefs. *See generally* McCarthy, "Secular Humanism and Education," 19 *J. of Law & Educ.* 467 (1990); Dent, "Religious Children, Secular Schools," 61 *So. Cal. L. Rev.* 863 (1988). These plaintiffs relied on the school prayer cases: "[T]he State may not establish a 'religion of secularism' in the sense of affirmatively opposing or showing hostility to religion, thus preferring those who believe in no religion over those who do believe." *School District of Abington v. Schempp*, 374

U.S. 203, 225, 83 S.Ct. 1560, 1573, 10 L.Ed.2d 844 (1963) (quoting *Zorach v. Clauson*, 343 U.S. 306, 314, 72 S.Ct. 679, 683, 96 L.Ed. 954 (1952)). Their arguments took two forms. First, public school authorities had violated the Establishment Clause by establishing a religion of secular humanism, for "nontheistic faiths, including Secular Humanism, can be religious for First Amendment purposes." Dent, *supra* at 867–77. *See* McConnell, *supra* at 1264 ("[S]ecularism is not a neutral stance. It is a partisan stance, no less 'sectarian,' in its way, than religion"). The remedy is to eliminate the texts or practices that create the unlawful establishment—just as school prayers were prohibited. *See* Dent, *supra* at 920.

Second, they argued that the dominant secular humanism in public schools manifested a hostility to religion in violation of the Free Exercise Clause. If this claim succeeded, the children of fundamentalist Christians would be exempted from reading texts or participating in activities that undermined their religious beliefs. *See* Dent, *supra* at 922. This relief would be analogous to the partial exemption granted to Amish children in *Wisconsin v. Yoder*, 406 U.S. 205, 92 S.Ct. 1526, 32 L.Ed.2d 15 (1972) and to state statutes granting exemptions from sex education courses. *See* T. van Geel, *The Courts and American Education Law* 181–185 (1987).

There is no authoritative definition of secular humanism, and many people may hold secular humanist beliefs without so identifying them. Note, "Secular Humanism, the Establishment Clause, and Public Education," 61 *N.Y.U. L. Rev.* 1149, 1153 (1986). The most commonly identified elements are these: regard for the rational individual, ethics based on individual choice, denial of the relevance of a deity, "the determination of truth through free inquiry," religious skepticism, the importance of science and technology, the need for moral education, and the separation of church and state. *Id.* at 1154–56 (1986). The basic conflict between the fundamentalist Christian worldview and modern secularism has been aptly described by Professor Dent in these terms:

> Fundamentalists tend to accept the literal truth of some religious text, to reject theories of evolution in favor of belief in a theistic creation, to insist that morals must derive from religion and that a person cannot be moral without religion, to believe that God dictates

that fathers should be the primary family breadwinners and mothers the primary nurturers of children and that parents must discipline their children and teach them religion; and to oppose, on religious grounds, abortion, homosexuality, divorce, and premarital and extramarital sex. Modernists tend to disagree with fundamentalists on each of these issues.

Id. at 865. The fundamentalists, relying on a number of studies, argue that the hostility to their faith in the modern public school curriculum is systemic and cumulative, not simply trivial and isolated. *But see Grove v. Mead School District No. 354*, 753 F.2d 1528 (9th Cir. 1985); *Jackson v. California*, 460 F.2d 282 (9th Cir. 1972). They assert that the family is treated simply as a "group of people," that marriage and motherhood are not celebrated, that feminist values are propounded, that Protestantism is excluded, and that moral relativism is the dominant philosophy. Dent, *supra* at 867–73. In turn, these claims often have been derided in the mass media, with the fundamentalists accused of a "know-nothing alarmism." Dent, *supra* at 867, citing various articles in the *New York Times* and other national publications. The vitriolic nature of the counterattack on the fundamentalist Christians has led some commentators, even on the left, to claim that much more than the school curriculum is at stake in Establishment Clause cases:

> [A]n incredibly broad cultural spectrum, encompassing the entire center of national self-identity, has constructed creationists as a shared enemy, an "other" through which the American mainstream can identify itself as "not them." From this vantage point, the creationist movement represents ignorance, intolerance, book-burning, religious fanaticism, and similar evils.
>
> * * *
>
> But at a deeper level, the debate . . . is the symbolic face of a broader conflict over the basic terms by which social life is understood. The creationist discourse differs from the evolutionary approach precisely because it reverses the scientific representational norms of objectivity, impersonality, and neutrality. Creationism poses subjectivity, personality and interest as the significant, and legitimate, mode for understanding the world.

Peller, "Creation, Evolution, and the New South," 2 *Tikkun* 72, 75, 76 (1987). Professor McConnell suggests that religious adherents face a "conflation of 'neutrality' and 'secularism.' " McConnell, *supra* at 1262.

Smith v. Board of School Commissioners of Mobile County

827 F.2d 684 (11th Cir. 1987).

Johnson, Circuit Judge:

Appellants, Alabama State Board of Education and Wayne Teague ("Board") and Malcolm Howell, et al. ("Defendant-Intervenors") appeal the district court's order enjoining the use in Alabama public schools of forty-four textbooks approved by the Board for inclusion on the State-Adopted Textbook List, the use of which the district court found to be a violation of the establishment clause of the first amendment. We reverse.

I. Background

A. Procedural History

This case is a continuation of the Alabama school prayer cases. . . . In May 1982, Ishmael Jaffree brought an action on behalf of three of his minor children pursuant to 42 U.S.C.A. § 1983 against the Mobile County School Board, various school officials, and three teachers seeking, *inter alia*, a declaratory judgment that certain classroom prayer activities conducted in the Mobile public school system violated the establishment clause of the first amendment and an injunction against classroom prayer. By his second amended complaint, Jaffree added as defendants the Governor of Alabama and other state officials, including Appellant Board, and challenged three Alabama statutes relevant to the school prayer issue as violative of the establishment clause. Douglas T. Smith and others ("Appellees") filed a motion to intervene in the Jaffree action alleging that an injunction against religious activity in the public schools would violate their right to free exercise of religion, and the district court allowed them to intervene as defendants. Subsequently, Appellees filed a motion entitled "Request for Alternate Relief" in which Appellees requested that, if an injunction were granted in favor of Jaffree, that injunction be enforced "against the religions of secularism, humanism, evolution, materialism, agnosticism, atheism and others" or, alternatively, that

Appellees be allowed to produce additional evidence showing that these religions had been established in the Alabama public schools.

The district court bifurcated the claims against the Mobile County and local defendants and the claims against state officials. The district court granted Jaffree's motion for a preliminary injunction against enforcement of two of the challenged statutes, Ala.Code Ann. §§ 16-1-20.1 and 16-1-20.2, *Jaffree v. James*, 544 F.Supp. 727, 732 (S.D.Ala.1982), but determined after trial on the merits that Jaffree was not entitled to relief in either action because the Supreme Court of the United States had erred in holding that the establishment clause of the first amendment prohibits the states from establishing a religion. . . . The district court therefore dismissed Jaffree's complaint for failure to state a claim upon which relief could be granted. . . .

This Court reversed, finding that both the school room prayer activities and sections 16-1-20.1 and 16-1-20.2 violated the establishment clause. . . . The Supreme Court denied certiorari with regard to the nonstatutory school prayer practices, *Board of School Comm'rs v. Jaffree*, 466 U.S. 926, 104 S.Ct. 1707, 80 L.Ed.2d 181 (1984), and affirmed this Court's decision with regard to the statutory provisions. *Wallace v. Jaffree*, 472 U.S. 38, 105 S.Ct. 2479, 86 L.Ed.2d 29 (1985). . . .

In its opinion denying relief in *Jaffree*, the district court had stated that "[i]f the appellate courts disagree with this Court in its examination of history and conclusion of constitutional interpretation thereof, then this Court will look again at the record in this case and reach conclusions which it is not now forced to reach." *Jaffree*, 554 F.Supp. at 1129. In a footnote, the district court indicated that the issues not reached dealt with (1) the free speech rights of teachers and students who wished to pray in school and (2) the teaching of the religion of secular humanism in the schools. *Id.* at n. 41.[1] On remand, the district court issued an order in response to Jaffree's request for attorney's fees, finding that the relief requested by Appellees had not been fully addressed in the prior decisions in the case and, therefore, remained for consideration by the district court on remand. The district court interpreted the po-

---

[1]With regard to the secular humanism issue, the district court stated:

It was pointed out in the testimony that the curriculum in the public schools of Mobile County is rife with efforts at teaching or encouraging secular humanism—all without opposition from any other ethic—to such an extent that it becomes a brainwashing effort. If this Court is compelled to purge "God is great, God is good, we thank Him for our daily food" from the classroom, then this Court must also purge from the classroom those things that serve to teach that salvation is through one's self rather than through a deity.

sition of the Appellees as that "if Christianity is not a permissible subject of the curriculum of the public schools, then neither is any other religion, and under the evidence introduced it is incumbent upon this Court to strike down those portions of the curriculum demonstrated to contain other religious teachings." For the purpose of considering this issue, the district court *sua sponte* realigned the parties by making Appellees parties plaintiff, consolidated the cases, and invited the parties to submit briefs in support of their positions and to petition the Court to reopen the record for the presentation of additional evidence. The district court stated that the original plaintiffs could withdraw, if they felt their position had been "fully justified," in which case the district court would consider the attorney's fees question, or could remain in the litigation, in which event the motion for attorney's fees would be denied as premature. The original plaintiffs did withdraw, and Appellees filed a position statement in which they asserted, *inter alia*, that the curriculum in the Mobile County School System unconstitutionally advanced the religion of Humanism and unconstitutionally inhibited Christianity, and that the exclusion from the curriculum of "the existence, history, contributions and role of Christianity in the United States and the world" violated their constitutional rights of equal protection, teacher and student free speech, the student's right to receive information, and teacher and student free exercise of religion.

The twelve Defendant-Intervenors, who are parents of children currently enrolled, or soon to be enrolled, in the Mobile County School System, filed a motion to intervene as defendants in the action, which was granted by the district court. The district court certified two plaintiff classes: Class A consisting of "all those persons adhering by belief and practice to a theistic religion, who are or will be teachers in the public schools of Alabama" and Class B consisting of "all those persons adhering by belief and practice to a theistic religion, who are Alabama taxpayers and who are or will be parents of children in the public schools of Alabama." Prior to trial, defendants Governor Wallace and the Mobile County board of School Commissioners agreed to entry of a consent decree in favor of Appellees.

A bench trial was held . . . with regard to Appellees' claims. Appellees' evidence focused on elementary and secondary school textbooks in the areas of history, social studies, and home economics, which were on the Alabama State Approved Textbook List, and which Appellees argued unconstitutionally established the religion of secular humanism. The district court found that use of forty-four of these textbooks violated the establishment clause of the first amendment, and permanently enjoined the use of the textbooks in the Alabama public schools. *Smith v. Board of School Comm'rs*, 655 F.Supp. 939, 988 (S.D.Ala.1987). This appeal followed.

II. Discussion

The first amendment provides in pertinent part that "Congress shall make no law respecting an establishment of religion. . . ." The district court found that secular humanism constitutes a religion within the meaning of the first amendment and that the forty-four textbooks at issue in this case both advanced that religion and inhibited theistic faiths in violation of the establishment clause. The Supreme Court has never established a comprehensive test for determining the "delicate question" of what constitutes a religious belief for purposes of the first amendment, and we need not attempt to do so in this case, for we find that, even assuming that secular humanism is a religion for purposes of the establishment clause, Appellees have failed to prove a violation of the

---

Jaffree, 554 F.Supp. at 1129 n. 41. The district court had expressed similar views on the merits of this issue in its earlier opinion granting a preliminary injunction, which was issued before Appellees had filed their "Request for Alternate Relief":

> The case law, in the opinion of the Court, has overlooked the totality of what is religion in its consideration when deciding issues under the establishment clause of the Constitution. . . . It is apparent from a reading of the decision law that the courts acknowledge that Christianity is the religion to be proscribed. . . . The religions of atheism, materialism, agnosticism, communism and socialism have escaped the scrutiny of the courts throughout the years, and make no mistake these are to the believers religions; they are ardently adhered to and quantitatively advanced in the teachings and literature that is presented to the fertile minds of the students in the various school systems. If the courts are to involve themselves in the proscription of religious activities in the schools, then it appears to this Court that we are going to have to involve ourselves in a whole host of areas, such as censoring, that we have heretofore ignored or overlooked. An example of what the Court heard reflecting on this point is in connection with the claimed use of foul language in literature read by a fourth grader and, though it might seem innocuous to some to condemn the use of the word "Goddamn" as it is used in the writings that are required reading, it can clearly be argued that as to Christianity it is blasphemy and is the establishment of an advancement of humanism, secularism or agnosticism. If the state cannot teach or advance Christianity, how can it teach or advance the Antichrist?

Jaffree, 544 F.Supp. at 732. In that opinion, the district court stated that "[i]t is common knowledge that miscellaneous doctrines such as evolution, socialism, communism, secularism, humanism, and other concepts are advanced in the public schools." *Id.* at n. 2.

establishment clause through the use in the Alabama public schools of the textbooks at issue in this case.

. . . The Supreme Court has developed three criteria to serve as guidelines in determining whether this barrier has been breached by challenged government action:

> First, the statute must have a secular legislative purpose; second, its principal or primary effect must be one that neither advances nor inhibits religion; finally, the statute must not foster "an excessive government entanglement with religion."

Lemon v. Kurtzman, 403 U.S. 602, 612–13, 91 S.Ct. 2105, 2111, 29 L.Ed.2d 745 (1971) (citations omitted). . . .

* * *

The parties agree that there is no question of a religious purpose or excessive government entanglement in this case and our review of the record confirms that conclusion. Our inquiry, therefore, must center on the second *Lemon* criterion: whether use of the challenged textbooks had the primary effect of either advancing or inhibiting religion.

"The effect prong [of the *Lemon* test] asks whether, irrespective of government's actual purpose, the practice under review in fact conveys a message of endorsement or disapproval." *Jaffree*, 472 U.S. at 56 n. 42, 105 S.Ct. at 2490 n. 42 (quoting *Lynch*, 465 U.S. at 690, 104 S.Ct. at 1368 (O'Connor, J., concurring)). If government identification with religion conveys such a message of government endorsement or disapproval of religion, then "a core purpose of the Establishment Clause is violated."

. . . The district court found that the home economics, history, and social studies textbooks both advanced secular humanism and inhibited theistic religion. . . .

A. Home Economics Textbooks

The district court found that the home economics textbooks required students to accept as true certain tenets of humanistic psychology, which the district court found to be "a manifestation of humanism." *Smith*, 655 F.Supp. at 987. In particular, the district court found that the books "imply strongly that a person uses the same process in deciding a moral issue that he uses in choosing one pair of shoes over another,"[5] and teach that "the student must determine right and wrong based only on his own experience, feelings and [internal] values" and that "the validity of a moral choice is only to be decided by the student." *Id.* at 986.[6] The district court stated that "[t]he emphasis and overall approach implies, and would cause any reasonable thinking student to infer, that the book is teaching that moral choices are just a matter of preferences, because, as the books say, 'you are the most important person in your life.' " *Id.* The district court stated that "[t]his highly relativistic and individualistic approach constitutes the promotion of a fundamental faith claim" that "assumes that self-actualization is the goal of every human being, that man has no supernatural attributes or component, that there are only temporal and physical consequences for man's actions, and that these results, alone, determine the morality of an action." *Id.* at 986–87. According to the district court, "[t]his belief strikes at the heart of many theistic religions' beliefs that certain actions are in and of themselves immoral, *whatever the consequences*, and that, in addition, actions will have extra-temporal consequences." *Id.* at 987 (emphasis in original). The district court stated that "some religious beliefs are so fundamental that the act of denying them will completely undermine that religion" and "[i]n addition, denial of *that* belief will result in the affirmance of a contrary belief and result in the establishment of an opposing religion." *Id.* (emphasis in original). It concluded that, while the state may teach certain moral values, such as that lying is wrong, "if, in so doing it advances a reason for the rule, the possible different reasons must be explained even-handedly" and "the state may not promote one particular reason over another in the public schools." . . .

In order to violate the primary effect prong of the *Lemon* test through advancement of religion, it is not

---

[5]In support of this statement, the district court refers to a passage in one of the home economics textbooks in which the author lists the steps in the decision-making process and states that "[a]s you can see, the steps in decision-making can be applied to something as simple as buying a new pair of shoes" and "can also be applied to more complex decisions such as those which involve religious preferences; education and career choices; the use of alcohol, tobacco and drugs; and sexual habits." F. Parnell, *Homemaking Skills for Everyday Living* 26 (1984). The book lists the steps in decision-making as (1) Define the problem; (2) Establish your goals; (3) List your goals in order of importance; (4) Look for resources; (5) Study the alternatives; (6) Make a decision; (7) Carry out the decision; (8) Evaluate the results of your decision. *Id.*

[6]The district court acknowledged that the textbooks do not explicitly state that the validity of a moral choice is only to be decided by the student, but found that this conclusion was implicit in the books' repetition of statements to the effect that decisions are "yours alone," or "purely personal" or that "only you can decide." *Smith*, 655 F.Supp. at 986.

sufficient that the government action merely accommodates religion. The constitution "affirmatively mandates accommodation, not merely tolerance, of all religions, and forbids hostility towards any." *Lynch*, 465 U.S. at 672, 104 S.Ct. at 1358. Nor is it sufficient that government conduct confers an indirect, remote or incidental benefit on a religion . . . or that its effect merely happens to coincide or harmonize with the tenets of a religion:

> [T]he Establishment Clause does not ban federal or state regulation of conduct whose reason or effect merely happens to coincide or harmonize with the tenets of some or all religions. In many instances, the Congress or state legislatures conclude that the general welfare of society, wholly apart from any religious considerations, demands such regulation. Thus, for temporal purposes, murder is illegal. And the fact that this agrees with the dictates of the Judeo-Christian religions while it may disagree with others does not invalidate the regulation. So too with the questions of adultery and polygamy. The same could be said of theft, fraud, etc., because those offenses were also proscribed in the Decalogue.

McGowan v. Maryland, 366 U.S. 420, 442, 81 S.Ct. 1101, 1113–14, 6 L.Ed.2d 393 (1961). . . . In order for government conduct to constitute an impermissible advancement of religion, the government action must amount to an endorsement of religion. . . .

Examination of the contents of these textbooks, including the passages pointed out by Appellees as particularly offensive, in the context of the books as a whole and the undisputedly non religious purpose sought to be achieved by their use, reveals that the message conveyed is not one of endorsement of secular humanism or any religion. Rather, the message conveyed is one of a governmental attempt to instill in Alabama public school children such values as independent thought, tolerance of diverse views, self-respect, maturity, self-reliance and logical decision-making. This is an entirely appropriate secular effect. Indeed, one of the major objectives of public education is the "inculcat[ion of] fundamental values necessary to the maintenance of a democratic

political system." *Bethel School Dist. No. 403 v. Fraser*, 478 U.S. 675, 106 S.Ct. 3159, 3164, 92 L.Ed.2d 549 (1986) (quoting *Ambach v. Norwick*, 441 U.S. 68, 77, 99 S.Ct. 1589, 1594, 60 L.Ed.2d 49 (1979)) (brackets in original). It is true that the textbooks contain ideas that are consistent with secular humanism; the textbooks also contain ideas consistent with theistic religion. However, as discussed above, mere consistency with religious tenets is insufficient to constitute unconstitutional advancement of religion.

Nor do these textbooks evidence an attitude antagonistic to theistic belief. The message conveyed by these textbooks with regard to theistic religion is one of neutrality: the textbooks neither endorse theistic religion as a system of belief, nor discredit it. Indeed, many of the books specifically acknowledge that religion is one source of moral values[8] and none preclude that possibility. While the Supreme Court has recognized that "the State may not establish a 'religion of secularism' in the sense of affirmatively opposing or showing hostility to religion, thus 'preferring those who believe in no religion over those who do believe,' " *Abington [v. Schempp]* . . ., that Court also has made it clear that the neutrality mandated by the establishment clause does not itself equate with hostility towards religion. . . .

It is obvious that Appellees find some of the material in these textbooks offensive. That fact, however, is not sufficient to render use of this material in the public schools a violation of the establishment clause. . . .[10]

B. History and Social Studies Textbooks

The district court's conclusion that the history and social studies textbooks violated the establishment clause was based on its finding that these books failed to include a sufficient discussion of the role of religion in history and culture. The district court found that the history books omit certain historical events with religious significance and "uniformly ignore the religious aspect of most American culture." *Smith*, 655 F.Supp. at 985. The district court found that

---

[8]*See, e.g.*, V. Ryder, *Contemporary Living* 52 (1985); F. Parnell, *Homemaking Skills for Everyday Living* 15 (1984); J. Kelly & E. Eubanks, *Today's Teen* 26 (1981).

[10]Indeed, given the diversity of religious views in this country, if the standard were merely inconsistency with the beliefs of a particular religion there would be very little that could be taught in the public schools. As Justice Jackson has stated:

> Authorities list 256 separate and substantial religious bodies to exist in the . . . United States. . . . If we are to eliminate everything that is objectionable to any of these warring sects or inconsistent with any of their doctrines, we will leave public education in shreds. Nothing but educational confusion and a discrediting of the public school system can result. . . .

McCollum v. Board of Ed., 333 U.S. 203, 235, 68 S.Ct. 461, 477, 92 L.Ed. 649 (1948) (Jackson, J., concurring).

"[r]eligion, where treated at all, is generally represented as a private matter, only influencing American public life at some extraordinary moments," and that "[t]his view of religion is one humanists have been seeking to instill for fifty years." *Id.* The district court concluded that the history books "assist that effort by perpetuating an inaccurate historical picture" and held that the books "lack so many facts as to equal ideological promotion." *Id.* The district court also found that the history books "discriminate against the very concept of religion, and theistic religions in particular, by omissions so serious that a student learning history from them would not be apprised of relevant facts about America's history." *Id.* Use of the social studies books was found unconstitutional because the books failed to integrate religion into the history of American society, ignored the importance of theistic religion as an influence in American society and contained "factual inaccuracies . . . so grave as to rise to a constitutional violation." *Id.* at 985–86.

It is clear on the record of this case that, assuming one tenet of secular humanism is to downplay the importance of religion in history and in American society, any benefit to secular humanism from the failure of the challenged history and social studies books to contain references to the religious aspects of certain historical events or to adequately integrate the place of religion in modern American society is merely incidental. There is no doubt that these textbooks were chosen for the secular purpose of education in the areas of history and social studies, and we find that the primary effect of the use of these textbooks is consistent with that stated purpose. We do not believe that an objective observer could conclude from the mere omission of certain historical facts regarding religion or the absence of a more thorough discussion of its place in modern American society that the State of Alabama was conveying a message of approval of the religion of secular humanism. Indeed, the message that reasonably would be conveyed to students and others is that the education officials, in the exercise of their discretion over school curriculum, chose to use these particular textbooks because they deemed them more relevant to the curriculum, or better written, or for some other non religious reason

found them to be best suited to their needs. *Cf. Board of Ed. v. Pico,* 457 U.S. 853, 880, 102 S.Ct. 2799, 2815, 73 L.Ed.2d 435 (1982) (Blackmun, J., concurring). . . .

Nor can we agree with the district court's conclusion that the omission of these facts causes the books to "discriminate against the very concept of religion." *Smith,* 655 F.Supp. at 985. Just as use of these books does not convey a message of governmental approval of secular humanism, neither does it convey a message of government disapproval of theistic religions merely by omitting certain historical facts concerning them.

The district court's reliance on *Epperson v. Arkansas,* 393 U.S. 97, 89 S.Ct. 266, 21 L.Ed.2d 228 (1968), to support its conclusion that omission of certain material regarding religion in this case constituted a first amendment violation is misplaced. *Epperson* involved an Arkansas statute that made it a crime to teach the theory of evolution in the public schools. *Id.* at 98, 89 S.Ct. at 266. The Supreme Court found that the law violated the establishment clause under the purpose prong of the *Lemon* test: the state forbade the teaching of evolution because it conflicted with a particular religious doctrine. 393 U.S. at 103, 89 S.Ct. at 269. The Court stated that "the First Amendment does not permit the State to require that teaching and learning must be tailored to the principles or prohibitions of any religious sect or dogma." *Id.* at 106, 89 S.Ct. at 271. Thus, "[t]he State's undoubted right to prescribe the curriculum for its public schools does not carry with it the right to prohibit, on pain of criminal penalty, the teaching of a scientific theory or doctrine *where that prohibition is based upon reasons that violate the First Amendment.*" *Id.* at 107, 89 S.Ct. at 272 (emphasis added).

There is no question in this case that the purpose behind using these particular history and social studies books was purely secular. Selecting a textbook that omits a particular topic for non religious reasons is significantly different from requiring the omission of material because it conflicts with a particular religious belief.[11] Further, unlike the situation in *Epperson,* which involved total exclusion of information regarding evolution from the school curriculum, Appellees in this case merely complain that the

---

[11]Indeed, Justice Powell has suggested that, because "the States and locally elected school boards should have the responsibility for determining the educational policy of the public schools," interference with the curriculum decisions of these authorities "is warranted only when the *purpose* for their decisions is clearly religious." *Edwards v. Aguillard,* 482 U.S. 578, 605, 107 S.Ct. 2573, 2589, 96 L.Ed.2d 510 (1987) (Powell, J., concurring) (citations omitted) (emphasis added).

historical treatment of religion in the challenged textbooks is inadequate. Finally, the record indicates that teachers in Alabama were free to supplement the discussion contained in the textbooks in areas they found inadequate. Thus, unlike the situation in *Epperson* where the State of Arkansas had made an attempt to teach the omitted material a criminal offense, there is no active policy on the part of Alabama that prohibits teaching historical facts about religion. There simply is nothing in this record to indicate that omission of certain facts regarding religion from these textbooks of itself constituted an advancement of secular humanism or an active hostility towards theistic religion prohibited by the establishment clause. While these textbooks may be inadequate from an educational standpoint, the wisdom of an educational policy or its efficiency from an educational point of view is not germane to the constitutional issue of whether that policy violates the establishment clause. . . .[12]

III. Conclusion

The home economics, social studies, and history textbooks at issue in this case do not violate the establishment clause of the first amendment. The district court's conclusions to the contrary reflect a misconception of the relationship between church and state mandated by the establishment clause. What is required of the states under the establishment clause is not "comprehensive identification of state with religion," but separation from religion. . . . Yet implicit in the district court's opinion is the assumption that what the establishment clause actually requires is "equal time" for religion.

. . . The district court's opinion in effect turns the establishment clause requirement of "lofty neutrality" on the part of the public schools into an affirmative obligation to speak about religion. Such a result clearly is inconsistent with the requirements of the establishment clause.

The judgment of the district court is reversed and the case is remanded for the sole purpose of entry by the district court of an order dissolving the injunction and terminating this litigation.

NOTES AND QUESTIONS

1. *Is Secular Humanism a Religion?*

Judge Johnson asserts that the Court need not reach the question of whether secular humanism is a religion. Do you agree? If you were representing the plaintiffs, would you have agreed that there was no religious purpose in the adoption of the forty-four textbooks? How can the Court determine whether the primary effect is "neutrality" or the advancement of religion without determining whether secular humanism is a religion? Or is the Court only saying that marginal benefits to a religion do not amount to a violation of the Establishment Clause? If so, is the teaching of creationism, along with evolution, only an incidental benefit? Is there any principled way to make this determination?

Judge Hand, the trial judge in the *Jaffree* and *Smith* cases, treated secular humanism (and atheism, communism, and other ideologies) as religions, urging that they are treated as religions by believers and that they "are ardently adhered to and quantitatively advanced in the teachings and literature." *Jaffree v. James,* 544 F. Supp. 727, 732 (S.D. Ala. 1982). Do you agree? Is a "religion" characterized by a belief in a deity (or more than one)? Must the beliefs "address fundamental questions" about life, death, morality, and the place of humans in the universe? *See Malnak v. Yogi,* 592 F.2d 197, 200 (3d Cir. 1979) (Adams, J., concurring). Must it offer a "comprehensive belief system" that answers those questions? *Id. See* Greenawalt, "Religion as a Concept in Constitutional Law," 72 *Cal. L. Rev.* 753 (1984); Choper, "Defining 'Religion' in the First Amendment," 1982 *U. Ill. L. Rev.* 579.

With regard to whether secular humanism is a religion, consider the analysis of Judge Canby, concurring in *Grove v. Mead School District No. 354,* 753 F.2d 1528, 1535 (9th Cir. 1985):

> The analytical difficulty with plaintiffs' approach is that it tends to divide the universe of value-laden thought into only two categories—the religious and the

---

[12]Appellees assert that the district court also found that the use of the challenged textbooks violated their rights to free exercise of religion and to receive information. While the district court at one point does indicate that some of the history books affected the free exercise of religion, *see Smith,* 655 F.Supp. at 985, it is clear that the district court's holding in this case was based solely on a violation of the establishment clause. Further, we find that Appellees have failed to establish a free exercise violation or impingement upon any constitutional right to receive information.

irreligious. By adopting this dualistic social outlook, and by denominating the anti-religious half of their universe as 'secular,' plaintiffs erect an insurmountable barrier to meaningful application of the establishment clause in controversies like this one. . . .

. . . [P]laintiffs . . . are not dealing in the same linguistic currency as the Supreme Court's establishment decisions. If the establishment clause is to have any meaning, distinctions must be drawn to recognize not simply "religious" and "anti-religious," but "non-religious" governmental activity as well. . . .

Id. at 1537 (Canby, J., concurring), citing *Malnak v. Yogi, supra* at 212 (Adams, J., concurring). *See* Developments in the Law, "Religion and the State," 100 *Harv. L. Rev.* 1606, 1673–74 (1987) (view that secular humanism is a religion leads to "fundamental incoherence"). Do you agree with Judge Canby? If secularism and religion are both religions within the constitutional definition, how can public schools avoid an establishment of religion?

2. *Establishment of Secular Humanism?*

Judge Johnson holds that even if secular humanism is a religion, the adoption of the textbooks and their use in class do not constitute an unconstitutional establishment. *But see* Toscano, "A Dubious Neutrality: The Establishment of Secularism in the Public Schools," 1979 *BYU L. Rev.* 177 (1979). What is his basis for this holding? Is it that the promotion of beliefs that simply coincide with those of a particular religion is not enough to constitute a constitutional violation? *See* Welch, "The State as a Purveyor of Morality," 56 *Geo. Wash. L. Rev.* 540 (1988); Dent, "Religious Children, Secular Schools," 61 *So. Cal. L. Rev.* 863, 878 (1988); Developments in the Law, "Religion and the State," 100 *Harv. L. Rev.* 1606, 1669 n.151 (1987). Is Judge Johnson saying that the public schools have not endorsed secular humanism? That the advocacy of self-reliance, logical decision making, and independence of thought is not the advancement of a particular faith? *See* Developments in the Law, *supra* at 1669 n.152. Are the public schools advancing secular humanism or an "American Civil Religion"? *See* Spiro, *supra* at 3, 55–63; *see also* Carter, *Culture of Disbelief* (1993). Does it matter?

Judge Johnson states that the "textbooks [do not] evidence an attitude antagonistic to theistic belief." *See also Williams v. Board of Educ. of Kanawha County*, 388 F. Supp. 93 (S.D. W. Va. 1975). Do you agree? Is the omission of religion from the books

antagonistic? *See* Nord, *Religion and American Education* 164 (1995) (exiling "religion to irrelevance" is "taking sides"). How can hostility toward religion constitute an establishment of religion? Do you agree that plaintiffs were seeking equal time for religion and not the disestablishment of secular humanism? What is the difference?

What of the claim that the books manifested a preference for the values of some religions over those of others? Should public schools be constitutionally required to expose students to a variety of religious and philosophical views on metaphysical and ethical problems? *See* Spiro, *supra* at 52, 65. In this regard, consider Professor Dent's resolution of this problem:

Preferring certain religious beliefs in the public schools is more troubling than some other governmental actions because of the conflict with freedom of conscience and the need to teach children values. Such a preference may be desirable, however, and in any case, it is inevitable for schools to prefer some values over others, which in turn favors some religions over others. The only solution to this dilemma is to abolish public schools. So long as the public schools neither promote nor disparage any specific religious dogma they should be free to teach values, even if those values conflict with some religious beliefs.

Dent, *supra* at 879–80. Viewed from this perspective, does *Smith* stand for the proposition that some injuries to religious sensitivities must be endured if there are to be public schools? Does this formulation trivialize the concerns of the fundamentalist Christians and ignore the alleged systemic bias in the textbooks and curriculum? *See* Carter, *supra.*

3. *Accommodation or Establishment?*

If a school board, anticipating litigation similar to *Smith,* removed forty-four textbooks because of their bias in favor of secular humanism, would that action be a constitutional accommodation of freedom of religion or an unconstitutional establishment of religion? *See* Dent, *supra* at 919–22.

4. *Good Faith*

Is Judge Johnson, in effect, saying that if school officials make good faith educational judgments with respect to the selection of books and the shaping of the curriculum, their decisions are largely insulated from judicial review? *See Board of Educ. v. Pico*, 457 U.S. 853, 102 S.Ct. 2799, 73 L.Ed.2d 435 (1982), *infra*. *See generally* Yudof, "Library Book Selection and the Public Schools: The Quest for the Archimedean Point," 50 *Ind. L. J.* 527 (1984); *see also* Yudof, "*Tinker* Tailored: Good Faith, Civility, and Student Expression," 69 *St. John's L. Rev.* 365 (1995).

Mozert v. Hawkins County Board of Education
827 F.2d 1058 (6th Cir. 1987).

Lively, Chief Judge.

* * *

I

A

Early in 1983 the Hawkins County, Tennessee Board of Education adopted the Holt, Rinehart and Winston basic reading series (the Holt series) for use in grades 1–8 of the public schools of the county. In grades 1–4, reading is not taught as a separate subject at a designated time in the school day. Instead, the teachers in these grades use the reading texts throughout the day in conjunction with other subjects. In grades 5–8, reading is taught as a separate subject at a designated time in each class. However, the schools maintain an integrated curriculum which requires that ideas appearing in the reading programs reoccur in other courses. By statute public schools in Tennessee are required to include "character education" in their curricula. The purpose of this requirement is "to help each student develop positive values and to improve student conduct as students learn to act in harmony with their positive values and learn to become good citizens in their school, community, and society." Tennessee Code Annotated (TCA) 49-6-1007 (1986 Supp.).

Like many school systems, Hawkins County schools teach "critical reading" as opposed to reading exercises that teach only word and sound recognition. "Critical reading" requires the development of higher order cognitive skills that enable students to evaluate the material they read, to contrast the ideas presented, and to understand complex characters that appear in reading material. Plaintiffs do not dispute that critical reading is an essential skill which their children must develop in order to succeed in

other subjects and to function as effective participants in modern society. Nor do the defendants dispute the fact that any reading book will do more than teach a child how to read, since reading is instrumental in a child's total development as an educated person.

The plaintiff Vicki Frost is the mother of four children, three of whom were students in Hawkins County public schools in 1983. At the beginning of the 1983–84 school year Mrs. Frost read a story in a daughter's sixth grade reader that involved mental telepathy. Mrs. Frost, who describes herself as a "born again Christian," has a religious objection to any teaching about mental telepathy. Reading further, she found additional themes in the reader to which she had religious objections. After discussing her objections with other parents, Mrs. Frost talked with the principal of Church Hill Middle School and obtained an agreement for an alternative reading program for students whose parents objected to the assigned Holt reader. The students who elected the alternative program left their classrooms during the reading sessions and worked on assignments from an older textbook series in available office or library areas. Other students in two elementary schools were excused from reading the Holt books.

B

In November 1983 the Hawkins County School Board voted unanimously to eliminate all alternative reading programs and require every student in the public schools to attend classes using the Holt series. Thereafter the plaintiff students refused to read the Holt series or attend reading classes where the series was being used. The children of several of the plaintiffs were suspended for brief periods for this refusal. Most of the plaintiff students were ultimately taught at home, or attended religious schools, or transferred to public schools outside Hawkins County. One student returned to school because his family was unable to afford alternate schooling. Even after the board's order, two students were allowed some accommodation, in that the teacher either excused them from reading the Holt stories, or specifically noted on worksheets that the student was not required to believe the stories.

. . . [T]he plaintiffs, consisting of seven families—14 parents and 17 children—filed this action pursuant to 42 U.S.C. § 1983. In their complaint the plaintiffs asserted that they have sincere religious beliefs which are contrary to the values taught or inculcated by the reading textbooks and that it is a violation of the religious beliefs and convictions of the plaintiff students to be required to read the books and a violation of the religious beliefs of the plaintiff parents to permit their children to read the books. The plaintiffs sought to hold the defendants liable because "forcing the student-plaintiffs to read school books which teach or inculcate values in violation of their religious beliefs and convictions is a clear violation of their rights to the free exercise of religion protected by the First and Fourteenth Amendments to the United States Constitution."

C

The defendants filed a motion to dismiss or, in the alternative, for summary judgment. The district court granted the defendants' motion for summary judgment, concluding that although passages in the reading textbooks might offend sincere religious beliefs of the plaintiffs, the books appeared neutral on the subject of religion and did not violate the plaintiffs' constitutional rights. *Mozert v. Hawkins County Public Schools*, 582 F.Supp. 201 (E.D.Tenn. 1984). On appeal this court reversed and remanded for further proceedings. *Mozert v. Hawkins County Public Schools*, 765 F.2d 75 (6th Cir.1985). This court concluded that summary judgment was improper because issues of material fact were present. . . .

II

A

Following remand the Commissioner of Education of the State of Tennessee was permitted to intervene as a defendant. At a pretrial hearing the parties made certain stipulations. Counsel for the defendants stipulated that the plaintiffs' religious beliefs are sincere and that certain passages in the reading texts offend those beliefs. However, counsel steadfastly refused to stipulate that the fact that the plaintiffs found the passages offensive made the reading requirement a burden on the plaintiffs' constitutional right to the free exercise of their religion. Similarly, counsel for the plaintiffs stipulated that there was a compelling state interest for the defendants to provide a public education to the children of Hawkins County. However, counsel stipulated only to a narrow definition of the compelling state interest—one that did not involve the exclusive use of a

uniform series of textbooks. These stipulations left for trial the issues of whether the plaintiffs could show a burden on their free exercise right, in a constitutional sense, and whether the defendants could show a compelling interest in requiring all students in grades 1–8 of the Hawkins County public schools to use the Holt, Rinehart and Winston basal reading textbooks. These were questions of law to be determined on the basis of evidence produced at trial.

* * *

B

Vicki Frost was the first witness for the plaintiffs and she presented the most complete explanation of the plaintiffs' position. The plaintiffs do not belong to a single church or denomination, but all consider themselves born again Christians. Mrs. Frost testified that the word of God as found in the Christian Bible "is the totality of my beliefs." . . . There was evidence that other members of their churches, and even their pastors, do not agree with their position in this case.

Mrs. Frost testified that she had spent more than 200 hours reviewing the Holt series and had found numerous passages that offended her religious beliefs. She stated that the offending materials fell into seventeen categories which she listed. These ranged from such familiar concerns of fundamentalist Christians as evolution and "secular humanism" to less familiar themes such as "futuristic supernaturalism," pacifism, magic and false views of death.

In her lengthy testimony Mrs. Frost identified passages from stories and poems used in the Holt series that fell into each category. Illustrative is her first category, futuristic supernaturalism, which she defined as teaching "Man As God." Passages that she found offensive described Leonardo da Vinci as the human with a creative mind that "came closest to the divine touch." Similarly, she felt that a passage entitled "Seeing Beneath the Surface" related to an occult theme, by describing the use of imagination as a vehicle for seeing things not discernible through our physical eyes. She interpreted a poem, "Look at Anything," as presenting the idea that by using imagination a child can become part of anything and thus understand it better. Mrs. Frost testified that it is an "occult practice" for children to use imagination beyond the limitation of scriptural authority. She testified that the story that alerted her to the problem with the reading series fell into the category of futuristic supernaturalism. Entitled "A Visit to Mars," the story portrays thought transfer and telepathy in such a way that "it could be considered a scientific concept," according to this witness. This theme appears in the testimony of several witnesses, i.e., the materials objected to "could" be interpreted in a manner repugnant to their religious beliefs.

Mrs. Frost described objectionable passages from other categories in much the same way. Describing evolution as teaching that there is no God, she identified 24 passages that she considered to have evolution as a theme. She admitted that the textbooks contained a disclaimer that evolution is a theory, not a proven scientific fact. Nevertheless, she felt that references to evolution were so pervasive and presented in such a factual manner as to render the disclaimer meaningless. After describing her objection to passages that encourage children to make moral judgments about whether it is right or wrong to kill animals, the witness stated, "I thought they would be learning to read, to have good English and grammar, and to be able to do other subject work." Asked by plaintiffs' attorney to define her objection to the textbooks, Mrs. Frost replied:

> Very basically, I object to the Holt, Rhinehart [sic] Winston series as a whole, what the message is as a whole. There are some contents which are objectionable by themselves, but my most withstanding [sic] objection would be to the series as a whole.

Another witness for the plaintiffs was Bob Mozert, father of a middle school and an elementary school student in the Hawkins County system. His testimony echoed that of Vicki Frost in large part. . . . He also found objectionable passages in the readers that dealt with magic, role reversal or role elimination, particularly biographical material about women who have been recognized for achievements outside their homes, and emphasis on one world or a planetary society. Both witnesses testified under cross-examination that the plaintiff parents objected to passages that expose their children to other forms of religion and to the feelings, attitudes and values of other students that contradict the plaintiffs' religious views without a statement that the other views are incorrect and that the plaintiffs' views are the correct ones.

C

The district court held that the plaintiffs' free exercise rights have been burdened because their "religious beliefs compel them to refrain from *exposure* to

the Holt series," and the defendant school board "has effectively required that the student plaintiffs either read the offensive texts or give up their free public education." *Mozert v. Hawkins County Public Schools*, 647 F.Supp. 1194, 1200 (E.D.Tenn. 1986), (emphasis added). . . .

* * *

The [district] court entered an injunction prohibiting the defendants "from requiring the student-plaintiffs to read from the Holt series," and ordering the defendants to excuse the student plaintiffs from their classrooms "[d]uring the normal reading period" and to provide them with suitable space in the library or elsewhere for a study hall. 647 F.Supp. at 1203. . . . [T]he court awarded damages to the plaintiffs in the total amount of $51,531, largely to reimburse the plaintiff families for the costs of sending their children to alternate schools and the costs of pursuing this lawsuit.

III

A

The first question to be decided is whether a governmental requirement that a person be exposed to ideas he or she finds objectionable on religious grounds constitutes a burden on the free exercise of that person's religion as forbidden by the First Amendment. This is precisely the way the superintendent of the Hawkins County schools framed the issue in an affidavit filed early in this litigation. . . . "While it is true that these textbooks expose the student to varying values and religious backgrounds, neither the textbooks nor the teachers teach, indoctrinate, oppose or promote any particular value or religion." . . .

It is also clear that exposure to objectionable material is what the plaintiffs objected to albeit they emphasize the repeated nature of the exposure. The complaint mentioned only the textbooks that the students were required to read. It did not seek relief from any method of teaching the material and did not mention the teachers' editions. The plaintiffs did not produce a single student or teacher to testify that any student was ever required to affirm his or her belief or disbelief in any idea or practice mentioned in the various stories and passages contained in the Holt series. However, the plaintiffs appeared to assume that materials clearly presented as poetry, fiction and even "make-believe" in the Holt series were presented as facts which the students were required to believe. Nothing in the record supports this assumption.

. . . Proof that an objecting student was required to participate beyond reading and discussing assigned materials, or was disciplined for disputing assigned materials, might well implicate the Free Exercise Clause because the element of compulsion would then be present. But this was not the case either as pled or proved. . . .

Vicki Frost testified that an occasional reference to role reversal, pacifism, rebellion against parents, one-world government and other objectionable concepts would be acceptable, but she felt it was the repeated references to such subjects that created the burden. The district court suggested that it was a matter of balance, *id.* at 1199, apparently believing that a reading series that presented ideas with which the plaintiffs agree in juxtaposition to those with which they disagree would pass constitutional muster. While balanced textbooks are certainly desirable, there would be serious difficulties with trying to cure the omissions in the Holt series. . . .

However, the plaintiffs' own testimony casts serious doubt on their claim that a more balanced presentation would satisfy their religious views. Mrs. Frost testified that it would be acceptable for the schools to teach her children about other philosophies and religions, but if the practices of other religions were described in detail, or if the philosophy was "profound" in that it expressed a world view that deeply undermined her religious beliefs, then her children "would have to be instructed to [the] error [of the other philosophy]." It is clear that to the plaintiffs there is but one acceptable view—the Biblical view, as they interpret the Bible. Furthermore, the plaintiffs view every human situation and decision, whether related to personal belief and conduct or to public policy and programs, from a theological or religious perspective. Mrs. Frost testified that many political issues have theological roots and that there would be "no way" certain themes could be presented without violating her religious beliefs. She identified such themes as evolution, false supernaturalism, feminism, telepathy and magic as matters that could not be presented in any way without offending her beliefs. The only way to avoid conflict with the plaintiffs' beliefs in these sensitive areas would be to eliminate all references to the subjects so identified. However, the Supreme Court has clearly held that it violates the Establishment Clause to tailor a public school's curriculum to satisfy the principles or prohibitions of any religion. *Epperson v. Arkansas*, 393 U.S. 97, 106, 89 S.Ct. 266, 271, 21 L.Ed.2d 228 (1968).

[Dr. Vitz] found "markedly little reference to religion, particularly Christianity, and also remarkably little to Judaism" in the Holt series. His solution would be to "beef up" the references to these two dominant religions in the United States. However, an adherent to a less widely professed religion might then object to the slighting of his or her faith. Balance in the treatment of religion lies in the eye of the beholder. Efforts to achieve the particular "balance" desired by any individual or group by the addition or deletion of religious material would lead to a forbidden entanglement of the public schools in religious matters, if done with the purpose or primary effect of advancing or inhibiting religion. . . .

B

* * *

C

. . . [T]he plaintiffs, in this court, have relied particularly upon three Supreme Court decisions. We find them all distinguishable.

The issue in *Torcaso v. Watkins*, 367 U.S. 488, 81 S.Ct. 1680, 6 L.Ed.2d 982 (1961), was whether a state could deny public office to a person solely because of the person's refusal to declare a belief in God. Quoting from its earlier decision in *Everson v. Board of Education*, 330 U.S. 1, 15, 67 S.Ct. 504, 511, 91 L.Ed. 711 (1947), the Court stated:

> We repeat and reaffirm that neither a State nor the Federal Government can constitutionally force a person "to profess a belief or disbelief in any religion."

Id. at 495, 81 S.Ct. at 1683. Since there was no evidence that the plaintiff students were ever required to profess or deny a religious belief the issue in *Torcaso* simply is not presented by the instant case.

Board of Education v. Barnette, 319 U.S. 624, 63 S.Ct. 1178, 87 L.Ed. 1628 (1943), grew out of a school board rule that required all schools to make a salute to the flag and a pledge of allegiance a regular part of their daily program. All teachers and students were required to participate in the exercise and refusal to engage in the salute was considered an act of insubordination which could lead to expulsion and possible delinquency charges for being unlawfully absent. The plaintiff was a Jehovah's Witness who considered the flag an "image" which the Bible forbids worshipping in any way. Justice Jackson, writing for the Court, stated:

Here, . . . we are dealing with a compulsion of students to declare a belief. They are not merely made acquainted with the flag salute so that they may be informed as to what it is or even what it means.

Id. at 631, 63 S.Ct. at 1182. . . .

It is abundantly clear that the exposure to materials in the Holt series did not compel the plaintiffs to "declare a belief," "communicate by word and sign [their] acceptance" of the ideas presented, or make an "affirmation of a belief and an attitude of mind." . . .

* * *

The plaintiffs appear to contend that the element of compulsion was supplied by the requirement of class participation in the reading exercises. As we have pointed out earlier, there is no proof in the record that any plaintiff student was required to engage in role play, make up magic chants, read aloud or engage in the activity of haggling. . . . Being exposed to other students performing these acts might be offensive to the plaintiffs, but it does not constitute the compulsion described in the Supreme Court cases. . . .

D

The third Supreme Court decision relied upon by the plaintiffs is the only one that might be read to support the proposition that requiring mere exposure to materials that offend one's religious beliefs creates an unconstitutional burden on the free exercise of religion. *Wisconsin v. Yoder*, 406 U.S. 205, 92 S.Ct. 1526, 32 L.Ed.2d 15 (1972). However, *Yoder* rested on such a singular set of facts that we do not believe it can be held to announce a general rule that exposure without compulsion to act, believe, affirm or deny creates an unconstitutional burden. The plaintiff parents in *Yoder* were Old Order Amish and members of the Conservative Amish Mennonite Church, who objected to their children being required to attend either public or private schools beyond the eighth grade. Wisconsin school attendance law required them to cause their children to attend school until they reached the age of 16. Unlike the plaintiffs in the present case, the parents in *Yoder* did not want their children to attend any high school or be exposed to any part of a high school curriculum. The Old Order Amish and the Conservative Amish Mennonites separate themselves from the world and avoid assimilation into society, and attempt to shield their children from all worldly influences. The Supreme Court found from the record that—

[C]ompulsory school attendance to age 16 for Amish children carries with it a very real threat to undermining the Amish community and religious practice as they exist today; they must either abandon belief and be assimilated into society at large, or be forced to migrate to some other and more tolerant region.

Id. at 218, 92 S.Ct. at 1534 (footnote omitted).

As if to emphasize the narrowness of its holding because of the unique 300 year history of the Old Amish Order, the Court wrote:

It is one thing to say that compulsory education for a year or two beyond the eighth grade may be necessary when its goal is the preparation of the child for life in modern society as the majority live, but it is quite another if the goal of education be viewed as the preparation of the child for life in the separated agrarian community that is the keystone of the Amish faith.

Id. at 222, 92 S.Ct. at 1536 (citation omitted). This statement points up dramatically the difference between *Yoder* and the present case. The parents in *Yoder* were required to send their children to some school that prepared them for life in the outside world, or face official sanctions. The parents in the present case want their children to acquire all the skills required to live in modern society. They also want to have them excused from exposure to some ideas they find offensive. Tennessee offers two options to accommodate this latter desire. The plaintiff parents can either send their children to church schools or private schools, as many of them have done, or teach them at home. . . .

Yoder was decided in large part on the impossibility of reconciling the goals of public education with the religious requirement of the Amish that their children be prepared for life in a separated community. . . . No such threat exists in the present case. . . .

* * *

IV

A

The Supreme Court has recently affirmed that public schools serve the purpose of teaching fundamental values "essential to a democratic society." These values "include tolerance of divergent political and religious views" while taking into account "consideration of the sensibilities of others." *Bethel School Dist. No. 403 v. Fraser*, 478 U.S. 675, 106 S.Ct. 3159, 3164, 92 L.Ed.2d 549 (1986). The Court has noted with apparent approval the view of some educators who see public schools as an "assimilative force" that brings together "diverse and conflicting elements" in our society "on a broad but common ground." *Ambach v. Norwick*, 441 U.S. 68, 77, 99 S.Ct. 1589, 1595, 60 L.Ed.2d 49 (1979). . . . Mrs. Frost stated specifically that she objected to stories that develop "a religious tolerance that all religions are merely different roads to God."

* * *

[In addition,] Mrs. Frost said, "We cannot be tolerant in that we accept other religious views on an equal basis with ours." While probably not an uncommon view of true believers in any religion, this statement graphically illustrates what is lacking in the plaintiffs' case.

The "tolerance of divergent . . . religious views" referred to by the Supreme Court is a civil tolerance, not a religious one. It does not require a person to accept any other religion as the equal of the one to which that person adheres. It merely requires a recognition that in a pluralistic society we must "live and let live." . . .

B

* * *

. . . Since we have found none of the prohibited forms of governmental compulsion in this case, we conclude that the plaintiffs failed to establish the existence of an unconstitutional burden. Having determined that no burden was shown, we do not reach the issue of the defendants' compelling interest in requiring a uniform reading series or the question, raised by the defendant, of whether awarding damages violated the Establishment Clause.

Judge Boggs concludes that the majority reverses the district court because it found the plaintiffs' claims of First Amendment protection so extreme as obviously to violate the Establishment Clause. This is not the holding of the majority. We do point out that under certain circumstances the plaintiffs, by their own testimony, would only accept accommodations that would violate the Establishment Clause. However, this is not the holding. What we do hold is that the requirement that public school students study a basal reader series chosen by the school authorities does not create an unconstitutional burden under the Free Exercise Clause when the students are not required to affirm or deny a belief or engage or refrain from engaging in a practice prohibited or required by their religion. . . .

* * *

The judgment of the district court granting injunctive relief and damages is reversed, and the case is remanded with directions to dismiss the complaint. . . .

Cornelia G. Kennedy, Circuit Judge, concurring.

I agree with Chief Judge Lively's analysis and concur in his opinion. However, even if I were to conclude that requiring the use of the Holt series or another similar series constituted a burden on appellees' free exercise rights, I would find the burden justified by a compelling state interest.

Appellants have stated that a principal educational objective is to teach the students how to think critically about complex and controversial subjects and to develop their own ideas and make judgments about these subjects. Several witnesses testified that the only way to achieve these objectives is to have the children read a basal reader, participate in class discussions, and formulate and express their own ideas and opinions about the materials presented in a basal reader. Thus, appellee students are required to read stories in the Holt series, make personal judgments about the validity of the stories, and to discuss why certain characters in the stories did what they did, or their values and whether those values were proper. . . .

. . . Teaching students about complex and controversial social and moral issues is just as essential for preparing public school students for citizenship and self-government as inculcating in the students the habits and manners of civility.

The evidence at trial demonstrated that mandatory participation in reading classes using the Holt series or some similar readers is essential to accomplish this compelling interest and that this interest could not be achieved any other way. Several witnesses for appellants testified that in order to develop critical reading skills, and therefore achieve appellants' objectives, the students must read and discuss complex, morally and socially difficult issues. Many of these necessarily will be subjects on which appellees believe the Bible states the rule or correct position. Consequently, accommodating appellees' beliefs would unduly interfere with the fulfillment of the appellants' objectives. . . . Additionally, mandatory participation in the reading program is the least restrictive means of achieving appellants' objectives. Appellees' objections would arise even if the School Board selected another basal reading textbook series since the students would be required to engage in critical reading and form their own opinions and judgments on many of the same issues.

The state and the Hawkins County School Board also have a compelling interest in avoiding disruption in the classroom. Hawkins County Schools utilize an integrated curriculum, designed to prepare students for life in a complex, pluralistic society, that reinforces skills and values taught in one subject in other areas. The Director of Elementary Education testified that teachers use every opportunity within the school day to reinforce information taught in the different subject areas. For example, the students may discuss stories in the Holt readers dealing with evolution or conservation of natural resources in the science course. This approach to learning is well-recognized and enables the students to see learning "as part of their total life, not just [as] bits and pieces." . . .

This is particularly true in grades one through four where reading is taught throughout the school day, rather than in a particular period. Appellants would be unable to utilize effectively the critical reading teaching method and accommodate appellees' religious beliefs. If the opt-out remedy were implemented, teachers in all grades would have to either avoid the students discussing objectionable material contained in the Holt readers in non-reading classes or dismiss appellee students from class whenever such material is discussed. To do this the teachers would have to determine what is objectionable to appellees. This would either require that appellees review all teaching materials or that all teachers review appellees' extensive testimony. If the teachers concluded certain material fell in the objectionable classification but nonetheless considered it appropriate to have the students discuss this material, they would have to dismiss appellee students from these classes. The dismissal of appellee students from the classes would result in substantial disruption to the public schools.

Additionally, Hawkins County Public Schools have a compelling interest in avoiding religious divisiveness. . . . The opt-out remedy would permit appellee students to be released from a core subject every day because of their religion. . . .

The divisiveness and disruption caused by the opt-out remedy would be magnified if the schools had to grant other exemptions. Although the District Court found that no other objections to the Hawkins County public school curriculum have been raised and the Hawkins County is homogeneous from a religious perspective, this case would create a precedent for persons from other religions to request exemptions from core subjects because of religious objections. If the school district were required to accommodate exceptions and permit other students to opt-out of the reading program and other core

courses with materials others found objectionable, this would result in a public school system impossible to administer. . . .

* * *

Boggs, Circuit Judge, concurring.

I concur with my colleagues that Hawkins County is not required by the Constitution to allow plaintiffs the latitude they seek in the educational program of these children. However, I reach that result on a somewhat different view of the facts and governing principles here. It seems that the court's opinion rests first on the view that plaintiffs' objection is to any exposure to contrary ideas, and that no one's religious exercise can be burdened simply by compelled exposure. . . . Second, the opinion rests on the view that no burden can exist here because plaintiffs were not compelled to engage in any conduct prohibited by, or refrain from any practice required by, their religious beliefs. . . .

I do not believe these attempted distinctions will survive analysis. If the situation of these children is not a burden on their religious exercise, it must be because of a principle applicable to all religious objectors to public school curricula. Thus, I believe a deeper issue is present here, is implicitly decided in the court's opinion, and should be addressed openly. The school board recognizes no limitation on its power to require any curriculum, no matter how offensive or one-sided, and to expel those who will not study it, so long as it does not violate the Establishment Clause. Our opinion today confirms that right, and I would like to make plain my reasons for taking that position.

. . . For myself, I approach this case with a profound sense of sadness. At the classroom level, the pupils and teachers in these schools had in most cases reached a working accommodation. Only by the decisions of higher levels of political authority, and by more conceptualized presentations of the plaintiffs' positions, have we reached the point where we must decide these harsh questions today. . . .

* * *

Plaintiffs' requests were unusual, but a variety of accommodations in fact were made, with no evidence whatsoever of bad effects. Given the masses of speculative testimony as to the hypothetical future evils of accommodating plaintiffs in any way, had there been any evidence of bad effects from what actually occurred, the board would surely have presented it. As we ultimately decide here, on the present state of constitutional law, the school board is indeed entitled to say, "my way or the highway." But in my view the school board's decision here is certainly not required by the Establishment Clause.

. . . I believe this is a more difficult case than outlined in the court's opinion. I disagree with the first proposition in the court's opinion, that plaintiffs object to any exposure to any contrary idea. I do not believe we can define for plaintiffs their belief as to what is religiously forbidden to be so comprehensive, where both they and the district court have spoken to the contrary. A reasonable reading of plaintiffs' testimony shows they object to the overall effect of the Holt series, not simply to any exposure to any idea opposing theirs. . . .

Ultimately, I think we must address plaintiffs' claims as they actually impact their lives: it is their belief that they should not take a course of study which, on balance, to them, denigrates and opposes their religion, and which the state is compelling them to take on pain of forfeiting all other benefits of public education.

Their view may seem silly or wrong-headed to some, but it is a sincerely held religious belief. By focusing narrowly on references that make plaintiffs appear so extreme that they could never be accommodated, the court simply leaves resolution of the underlying issues here to another case, when we have plaintiffs with a more sophisticated understanding of our own and Supreme Court precedent, and a more careful and articulate presentation of their own beliefs.

Under the court's assessment of the facts, this is a most uninteresting case. It is not the test case sought, or feared, by either side. The court reviews the record and finds that the plaintiffs actually want a school system that affirmatively teaches the correctness of their religion, and prevents other students from mentioning contrary ideas. If that is indeed the case, then it can be very simply resolved. It would obviously violate the Establishment Clause for any school system to agree with such an extravagant view.

It should be noted and emphasized that if such is the holding, this decision is largely irrelevant to the national legal controversy over this case. The extent to which school systems may constitutionally require students to use educational materials that are objectionable, contrary to, or forbidden by their religious beliefs is a serious and important issue.

* * *

I also disagree with the court's view that there can be no burden here because there is no requirement of conduct contrary to religious belief. That view both slights plaintiffs' honest beliefs that studying the full Holt series would be conduct contrary to their religion, and overlooks other Supreme Court Free Exercise cases which view "conduct" that may offend religious exercise at least as broadly as do plaintiffs.

On the question of exposure to, or use of, books as conduct, we may recall the Roman Catholic Church's, "Index Librorum Prohibitorum." This was a list of those books the reading of which was a mortal sin, at least until the second Vatican Council in 1962.[5] I would hardly think it can be contended that a school requirement that a student engage in an act (the reading of the book) which would specifically be a mortal sin under the teaching of a major organized religion would be other than "conduct prohibited by religion," even by the court's fairly restrictive standard. Yet, in what constitutionally important way can the situation here be said to differ from that? Certainly, a religion's size or formality of hierarchy cannot determine the religiosity of beliefs. . . .

* * *

Here, plaintiffs have drawn their line as to what required school activities, what courses of study, do and do not offend their beliefs to the point of prohibition. I would hold that if they are forced over that line, they are "engaging in conduct" forbidden by their religion. The court's excellent summary of its holding on this point . . . appears to concede that what plaintiffs were doing in school was conduct, but that there "was no evidence that the conduct required of the students was forbidden by their religion." I cannot agree. The plaintiffs provided voluminous testimony of the conflict (in their view) between reading the Holt readers and their religious beliefs, including extensive Scriptural references. The district court found that "plaintiffs' religious beliefs *compel* them to refrain from exposure to the Holt series." 647 F.Supp. at 1200 (emphasis supplied). I would think it could hardly be clearer that they believe their religion commands, not merely suggests, their course of action.

If plaintiffs did not use the exact words "reading these books is forbidden by our religion," they certainly seemed to me to make that point clearly. . . .

* * *

---

[5]*New Catholic Encyclopedia*, Vol. 7, pp. 434–35; Vol. 2, pp. 699–701 (McGraw-Hill, 1967).

Thus, I believe the plaintiffs' objection is to the Holt series as a whole, and that being forced to study the books is "conduct" contrary to their beliefs. In the absence of a narrower basis that can withstand scrutiny, we must address the hard issues presented by this case: (1) whether compelling this conduct forbidden by plaintiffs' beliefs places a burden on their free exercise of their religion, in the sense of earlier Supreme Court holdings; and (2) whether within the context of the public schools, teaching material which offends a person's religious beliefs, but does not violate the Establishment Clause, can be a burden on free exercise. . . .

VI

* * *

Running a public school system of today's magnitude is . . . [factually distinguishable from other free exercise cases]. A constitutional challenge to the content of instruction (as opposed to participation in ritual such as magic chants, or prayers) is a challenge to the notion of a politically-controlled school system. Imposing on school boards the delicate task of satisfying the "compelling interest" test to justify failure to accommodate pupils is a significant step.[9] It is a substantial imposition on the schools to require them to justify each instance of not dealing with students' individual, religiously compelled, objections (as opposed to permitting a local, rough and ready, adjustment), and I do not see that the Supreme Court has authorized us to make such a requirement.

* * *

The average public expenditure for a pupil in Hawkins County is about 20% of the income of the average household there. Even the modest tuition in the religious schools which some plaintiffs attended here amounted to about a doubling of the state and local tax burden of the average resident. Had the Founders recognized the possibility of state intervention of this magnitude, they might have written differently. However, it is difficult for me to see that the words "free exercise of religion," at the adoption of the Bill of Rights, implied a freedom from state teaching, even of offensive material, when some alternative was legally permissible.[12]

Therefore, I reluctantly conclude that under the Supreme Court's decisions as we have them, school boards may set curricula bounded only by the Establishment Clause, as the state contends. Thus, contrary to the analogy plaintiffs suggest, pupils may indeed be expelled if they will not read from the King James Bible, so long as it is only used as literature, and not taught as religious truth. . . . Contrary to the position of amicus American Jewish Committee, Jewish students may not assert a burden on their religion if their reading materials overwhelmingly provide a negative view of Jews or factual or historical issues important to Jews, so long as such materials do not assert any propositions as religious truth, or do not otherwise violate the Establishment Clause.

* * *

Schools are very important, and some public schools offend some people deeply. That is one major reason private schools of many denominations—fundamentalist, Lutheran, Jewish—are growing. But a response to that phenomenon is a political decision for the schools to make. . . .

NOTES AND QUESTIONS

1. Burden on Freedom of Religion

Do you agree with Chief Judge Lively that the plaintiffs in *Mozert* have not demonstrated that the use of the Holt, Rinehart & Winston basic reading series in the Hawkins County public schools is an unconstitutional burden on their free exercise of religion? Is this because exposure to views antithetical to fundamentalist Christianity is not the same thing as coercion to act or a compulsion to believe? *See Smith v. Ricci*, 89 N.J. 514, 446 A.2d 501, 505 (1982) and cases cited therein; Strossen, " 'Secular Humanism' and 'Scientific Creationism': Proposed Standards for Reviewing Curricular Decisions Affecting Students' Religious Freedom," 47 *Ohio St. L.J.* 333 (1986). *Cf. Employment Division, Department of Human Resources v. Smith*, 494 U.S. 872, 110 S.Ct. 1595 (1990). Because reading is not conduct? Because some offenses to one's religious beliefs must be endured? Because plaintiffs' legal position is inconsistent with the concept of public schooling?

---

[9]I do not think there is any evidence that actually accommodating pupils in practice need be as difficult as the state contends. Indeed, the state espouses a theory of rigidity (and finds alleged experts to support it) that seems a bit ludicrous in this age of individualized attention to many kinds of student language and interest. There was no evidence of actual confusion or disruption from the accommodation that did take place.

[12]As guaranteed by the Supreme Court's decision in *Pierce v. Society of Sisters*, 268 U.S. 510, 45 S.Ct. 571, 69 L.Ed. 1070 (1925).

Professor Dent has said that "at the least, most would agree that forcibly subjecting citizens to propaganda overtly hostile to their religion would violate free exercise." Dent, "Religious Children, Secular Schools," 61 *S. Cal. L. Rev.* 863, 887 (1988). *See also* Dent, "Of God and Caesar: The Free Exercise Rights of Public School Students," 43 *Case W. Res. L. Rev.* 707 (1993). Do you agree? Professor Dent cites such cases as *Schempp, Epperson,* and *Aguilar.* Do those precedents support his statement? How should courts determine what is "propaganda overtly hostile" to religious beliefs? Does the distinction focus on the difference between readings that convey inconsistent beliefs or fail to affirm one's own beliefs and readings that affirmatively attack one's religious beliefs? For example, the distinction between saying that evolution is right and creation science is a fraud? Does Chief Justice Lively accept the view that exposure to overtly hostile readings would violate the Free Exercise Clause? If he did, how should *Mozert* have been decided? *See* Dent at 888–94.

Wisconsin v. Yoder, supra at chapter 1, is the strongest case in support of the proposition that plaintiffs' free exercise rights have been burdened by the use of the Holt, Rinehart & Winston series. In that case, Amish parents objected to any education for their children beyond the eighth grade. They did not wish their children exposed to the modern world, and they feared that such exposure would lead to the destruction of the Amish community. There is some doubt as to the continuing vitality of *Yoder,* albeit it has not been overruled. *See Employment Division v. Smith, supra. See generally* McConnell, "Free Exercise Revisionism and the *Smith* Decision." 57 *U. Chi. L. Rev.* 1109 (1990); Laycock, "The Remnants of Free Exercise," 1990 *S.Ct. Rev.* 1. In any event, Chief Justice Lively distinguishes *Yoder,* stressing its "singular set of facts" and the "narrowness of the holding." Is this persuasive? Is it dispositive that the Amish lived in a self-contained and homogeneous community? That their religion and way of life could not be separated? That the fundamentalist Christian parents sought a remedy that extended to all grades, whereas the Amish sought relief only from public schooling after the eighth grade? That apparently no private Amish school would be acceptable to Wisconsin authorities under state law, but Tennessee would have allowed the fundamentalist Christians to achieve their objectives in private schools? Do these distinctions go to the question of

burden or to the nature of the state's interest and the means by which it might be vindicated?

Consider these remarks by Professor Dent:

> The objection to exposure was qualitatively different [in *Wisconsin v. Yoder*] than in *Mozert*; in *Yoder* the very presence of the children in school burdened their religious practice. Although *Yoder* could be distinguished on this ground, it should not be. First, the Court's opinion is broad. It states that public high schools contravened the Amish faith "by exposing Amish children to worldly influences in terms of attitudes, goals, and values contrary to their beliefs, and by substantially interfering with the religious development of the Amish child and his integration into the way of life of the Amish faith community." Much the same could be said of the effect of public schools on the plaintiffs in *Mozert* and other fundamentalists.
>
> *Mozert* . . . invites trouble by distinguishing between those whose religion forbids (or requires) a practice or belief and those who consider the practices or belief merely undesirable (or desirable). . . . The Supreme Court has never adopted such a standard and has often reached contrary conclusions. . . .
>
> It does not suffice to argue that the teaching at issue in *Mozert* is not religious because it does not expressly address religion. The religion of individuals and their sects determines what matters are religious to them. . . . To rule otherwise . . . would contravene the principle of neutrality by preferring those who hold modernist or mainstream beliefs . . . over those with more fundamentalist or all-encompassing beliefs.

Dent, *supra* at 890–91.

2. *The Nature of the State's Interest*

Judge Kennedy concurs with Chief Judge Lively, but she argues that any burden on plaintiffs' free exercise rights is justified by the state's compelling interest in education. Is she saying that a basic mission of public education is to teach critical thinking about complex and controversial subjects and that this mission cannot be accomplished without basal readers? If so, does not the mission of public school inevitably require a secular humanism inconsistent with fundamentalist Christianity because critical thinking refers to a way of seeing the world that is inconsistent with the fundamentalist world view? *See* McConnell, "Why Is Religious Liberty the 'First Freedom'?" 21 *Cardozo L. Rev.* 1243 (2000); Carter, "Evolutionism, Creationism, and Teaching Religion as a Hobby," 1987 *Duke L.J.* 977. Is *Yoder* consistent with this approach?

Is Judge Kennedy suggesting that public schools need to teach democratic values and that this goal requires exposure to divergent points of view on controversial subjects? *See generally* Spiro, "The Creation of a Free Marketplace of Religious Ideas: Revisiting the Establishment Clause after the Alabama Secular Humanism Decision," 39 *Ala. L. Rev.* 1 (1987). Which views need to be canvassed and tolerated? Need the schools present the affirmative case for drug addiction or child abuse or communism? If not, does not the mission of the public schools include intolerance of some beliefs and values? *See* Stolzenberg, "He Drew a Circle That Shut Me Out: Assimilation, Indoctrination, and the Paradox of Liberal Education," 106 *Harv. L. Rev.* 581 (1993); Arons & Lawrence, "The Manipulation of Consciousness: A First Amendment Critique of Schooling," 15 *Harv. C.R.-C.L. L.* Rev. 309 (1980). Conversely, if fundamentalist Christian children should be exposed to the idea that women may pursue professional careers outside of the home, should all students be informed that some groups believe that a woman's place is in the home? How should courts distinguish the controversial from core values that public schools may legitimately inculcate? Is religion too "controversial" for inclusion? Is Judge Kennedy confusing secularism with neutrality? Under such circumstances is "liberal neutrality . . . a proxy of majoritarianism and secularism"? McConnell, *supra* at 1262.

Would an "opt-out remedy" protect plaintiff without substantially disrupting public education? Does it depend on how many groups would opt out? What does Judge Boggs have to say about this? If substantial disruption would not occur, does this suggest that there is a less onerous alternative for the state to achieve its objectives? *See Smith v. Ricci*, 89 N.J. 514, 446 A.2d 501 (N.J. 1982).

Consider some reactions to the *Harry Potter* books. In Buffalo, a fifth-grade student whose parents are born-again Christians left the room for the hallway to avoid stories about witchcraft, evil, spells, and magic. *See* Jodi Wilgoren, *"Don't Give Us Little Wizards, The Anti-Potter Parents Cry,"* N.Y. *Times*, November 1, 1999.

3. Judge Boggs' Concurring Opinion

Judge Boggs, while sympathetic to the proposition that plaintiffs' free exercise of religion has been burdened, concurs on the ground that there is "no limi-

tation on . . . [a school board's] power to require any curriculum, no matter how offensive or one-sided, and to expel those who will not study it, so long as it does not violate the Establishment Clause." Is this proposition consistent with *Yoder* and other free exercise cases? *See Employment Division v. Smith, supra.* Or is he saying that any good faith educational judgment with respect to curriculum should not be subject to judicial reexamination? *See Board of Educ. v. Pico*, 457 U.S. 853, 102 S.Ct. 2799, 73 L.Ed.2d 43 (1982), *infra.*

Judge Boggs argues that Chief Justice Lively and Judge Kennedy have misconstrued the facts in a way that renders a "test case" into a "most uninteresting case." That is, the other judges find that "the plaintiffs actually want a school system that affirmatively teaches the correctness of their religion, and prevents other students from mentioning contrary ideas." *See* Wood, "Religion and the Public Schools," 1986 *BYU L. Rev.* 349, 355–56 (1986). Do you agree with Judge Boggs? Have plaintiffs sought judicial intervention to establish their own religion in the public schools?

Recall that the district court in *Mozert* enjoined the defendants from compelling fundamentalist Christian children to read the Holt, Rinehart & Winston series and ordered that they be excused from class during reading periods and that study space elsewhere be made available. *See generally* M. McCarthy & N. Cambron-McCabe, *Public School Law* 39–42 (1988). Presumably, the children would read alternative materials less offensive to their beliefs. If this remedy were satisfactory to the plaintiffs, does this suggest that plaintiffs did not seek to establish their own religion but only to preserve the free exercise of religion? How does the remedy sought in *Mozert* differ from the remedy sought in *Smith*? *See also Rosenberg v. Board of Education*, 196 Misc. 542, 92 N.Y.S.2d 344 (1949).

4. Selective Exemptions

Can tailored exemptions be granted from various aspects of the public school program for religious reasons without significant disruption of the school and frustration of the state's educational goals? *See generally* R. O'Neil, *Classrooms in the Crossfire* ch. 8 (1981); Dent, *supra*; Hirschoff, "Parents and the Public School Curriculum: Is There a Right to Have One's Child Excused from Objectionable Instruction?" 50 *S. Cal. L. Rev.* 871 (1977). Is partial exemption preferable to a "balanced" curriculum? Suppose that the alternative readings emphasized creationism and other beliefs of fundamentalist Christians. *See* Dent, *supra* at 928. Would it be a violation of the Establishment Clause for the school district to allow fundamentalist children the time and space to read such works during school hours? *See McCollum v. Board of Educ.*, 333 U.S. 203, 68 S.Ct. 461, 92 L.Ed. 649 (1948); Dent, *supra* at 915–19, 923–27. What if the school district provided an instructor to teach from the alternative works? *See Parents Ass'n of P.S. 16 v. Quinones*, 803 F.2d 1235 (2d Cir.1986); Dent, *supra* at 927–30. What if the alternative works were read at home and the parents took the responsibility of teaching reading skills at home? *See Zorach v. Clauson*, 343 U.S. 306, 72 S.Ct. 679, 96 L.Ed. 954 (1952); Dent, *supra* at 923–24. Does the answer depend on whether home education under state law is a permissible alternative to public schooling? See Dent, *supra* at 925. Does either alternative, study in another classroom or study at home, constitute state approval of religion? Preference for religion?

Is there a significant distinction between a court compelling a school district to accommodate the views of the fundamentalist Christians and allowing a district to accommodate those views? Between a constitutional right of accommodation and a determination that a voluntary accommodation is not unconstitutional? *See Grove v. Mead School District No. 354*, 753 F.2d 1528 (9th Cir. 1985); *Smith v. Ricci*, 89 N.J. 514, 446 A.2d 501, 505 (1982); *Citizens for Parental Rights v. San Mateo City Bd. of Educ.*, 51 Cal. App. 3d 1, 124 Cal. Rptr. 68 (1975); A. Gutmann, *Democratic Education* 122 (1987). *See generally* McCarthy & Cambron-McCabe, *supra* at 42–44.

5. *Equal Access*

In 1981, under principals of freedom of expression, the Supreme Court held that a campus religious organization could not be denied the same right as other organizations of access to facilities on a university campus. *Widmar v. Vincent*, 454 U.S. 263, 102 S.Ct. 269, 70 L.Ed.2d 440 (1981), *infra; see also Rosenberger v. Regents of the Univ. of Virginia*, 515 U.S 819, 115 S.Ct. 2510 (1995). Three years later, Congress enacted the Equal Access Act, providing that secondary schools receiving federal assistance must not discriminate among extracurricular groups on a basis of religion, politics, or philosophy in terms of access to school facilities if they had established a "limited public forum." 20 U.S.C.A.

§ 4071(a) (Supp.II 1984). See *Lamb's Chapel v. Center Moriches Union Free School*, 508 U.S. 384, 113 S. Ct. 2141, (1993); *Hsu v. Roslyn Union Free School Dist.* No. 3, 85 F.3d 839 (2d Cir. 1996).

6. *Problem*

New York requires that all primary and secondary school students receive instruction concerning the transmission and prevention of AIDS and the avoidance of drug and alcohol abuse. The Plymouth Brethren is a religious order whose members believe that religious doctrine requires that individuals not be exposed to the "details of evil." The law allows for an exemption from classroom instruction on AIDS and substance abuse, but parents must provide assurances that they will provide suitable instruction at home. The Brethren decline to give such an assurance and file suit against the school district, claiming that their religious rights have been violated. What result? *See Ware v. Valley Stream High School Dist.*, 150 A.D.2d 14, 545 N.Y.2d 316 (1989). *Cf. Employment Division, Department of Human Services v. Smith*, 494 U.S. 872, 110 S. Ct. 1595 (1990).

B. Nonsectarian Socialization

"Library Book Selection and the Public Schools: The Quest for the Archimedean Point"
Mark G. Yudof, 59 *Ind. L.J.* 527, 527–37 (1984). Reprinted by permission.

Traditional theories of liberty and autonomy do not fit well when the subjects are children and education. For adults, democratic governments generally seek to abide by the Kantian maxim that each person should be treated as a kingdom of ends—treated with respect for his or her autonomy, rationality, and human worth—and not as a means or an instrument of another person's will. Children, however, are rightfully perceived as both ends in themselves, evolving autonomous beings, and as instruments of larger societal purposes. Those purposes include the assimilation of the child into the larger culture, for the intergenerational, exogenetic transmission of values, knowledge, language, and customs is essential to the preservation of community and to the definition of persons within community. Paradoxically, education both promotes autonomy and, in a sense, denies it by shaping and constraining present and future life choices.

The education of children, in any form, whether compulsory or not, inevitably raises conflict. Children are not born with an appreciation of literature and democratic institutions, and they, including the most precocious among them, certainly are unlikely to discover geometry, computers, or quantum mechanics without the benefit of the accumulated wisdom of the past. Professor Tawney once described children as a "new race of souls" that bursts upon us every year, who stand "on the threshold with the world at their feet, like barbarians gazing upon the time-worn plains of an ancient civilization." But, if one substitutes pejorative words like *propaganda, indoctrination,* and *brainwashing* for an acceptable word like *education,* one gets a sense of the conflict. Children need to be socialized to societal norms, but they also need to grow up to be relatively autonomous beings. . . .

The conflict between acculturation and autonomy inevitably leads to consideration of the concept of justifiable paternalism. Education is a form of affirmative liberty. Children are socialized through subjection to coercive and persuasive measures that enable them to become autonomous as adults—that is, they are socialized for their own good. Education can expand the mind or it can contract it, and mind-expanding education facilitates adult autonomy. Upon reaching adulthood, the subjects of the earlier paternalism would express gratitude, not indignation, for their treatment. But, however justifiable the paternalism for those who have not fully matured into personhood, there remains the problem of balance. If the education is too narrow and all encompassing, then autonomous citizens will not be produced. Words like *domination* and *constraints on choice* creep into the analysis. If autonomy is stressed at the price of education, then there is a justifiable fear of loss of community, alienation, and ignorance.

* * *

The ideal education necessarily requires the location of an Archimedean point, a point positioned somewhere between critical reflection and grounding in the contingent circumstances of society. . . .

How, then, is society to account for and to achieve the Archimedean point in education? Realistically viewed, there may be no optimal, theoretical balance between basic education and an all-pervasive indoctrination. . . .

Children must be integrated into the community but they should not be stifled. The desire to create informed citizens who understand the world in which they were born and live must be tempered by the realization that much of what society achieves depends on individuals who do not or will not conform to the prevailing wisdom. As John Updike . . . expressed the point, "[o]ur artistic heroes tend to be those self-exercisers, like Picasso, and Nabokov, and Wallace Stevens, who rather defiantly kept playing past dark." Children must learn the rules of the game, but that learning must stop short of an orthodoxy that playing after dark is always forbidden.*

* * *

The problem of children and education runs deeper than a reification of the conflict between socialization and autonomy. The question cannot be whether children ought to be socialized, that is, whether their autonomy should be simultaneously constrained and nourished. To paraphrase Professor C. Edwin Baker, to the extent that adults create a reality for children, an acceptable theory must concern itself with questions of who socializes children and how.[14] A world will be created for children, for they are not born with a particular cultural orientation. The relevant question is who will write on the slates, not whether they will be written on at all. If there was no formal education in public institutions, values and beliefs would continue to be instilled by family, church, peers, and life experiences.

* * *

. . . [T]he self in the concept of autonomy is partially defined by the culture; the antithesis between autonomy and indoctrination is an oversimplification because the self has links to and is defined in the context of communicated community norms. The converse is also true. The community and its indoctrination efforts may be shaped by many selves, for there is a mutually affecting relationship between community and individual. . . . An educational system that ignored autonomy and emphasized only indoctrination to communal norms would be thoroughly totalitarian and destructive of human values.

In the context of public schooling and beyond, the key to unraveling the paradoxes of education of the young lies neither in the reification of autonomy nor in the mysticism of transcendental communities.

---

*See Alwin, "From Obedience to Autonomy: Changes in Traits Desired in Children, 1924–1978," *Pub. Opin. Q.* 33 (Spring 1988).

[14]Baker, "The Scope of the First Amendment Freedom of Speech," 25 UCLA L. Rev. 964, 1026 (1978).

Children are autonomous individuals, and they are members of groups. Their selves are in part defined by social relations, but social relations are also in part defined by their personalities. The self and community cannot be completely separated, but they also cannot be completely integrated. The "good" has both particular and universal aspects. Not every cultural influence or imperative constitutes domination. Cultures do and should constrain.

A nagging problem . . . is the need to differentiate between unacceptable constraints on individuality, leading to a loss of autonomy and creativity, and acceptable communitarian constraints that reduce alienation and enhance the cultured definition of self. Unless and until the epistemological millennium is approached, wisdom lies in a pragmatic recognition of the dynamic, uncertain, and complex relationship between cultural authority and individuality. . . .

* * *

Turning from the grand abstractions to life in the trenches, what is the structure of decision making on socialization issues in public schools? Who determines what is to be taught and what books are to be acquired? Who balances autonomy and acculturation? For the most part, elected representatives, school board members, school administrators, librarians, and teachers share responsibility and are, at least in theory, accountable to the citizenry for their performance. There is no necessary reason for arranging affairs this way; many have proposed alternatives that would enhance, for example, either the power of families or the power of professional librarians or teachers to make educational choices. But the basic structural decisions have already been made, and these are reflected in existing legal and institutional arrangements.

* * *

But there are risks. The power of government to make these selections, to control communications, is also the power to destroy the underpinnings of government by consent, since that consent can be manipulated out of or into existence. . . . If the reflective, informed citizen, participating in governance decisions, is a philosophical root of freedom of expression, then government domination of communications networks is potentially as destructive of that concern as government censorship of private speech. Governments, staffed by self-interested politicians and bureaucrats, may aim for self-perpetuation and uncritical acceptance of the status quo and not for the Archimedean point. Because of this danger, letting the government control education may be like letting the fox guard the henhouse. That is why the boundaries of state power need to be probed. But the denial of the power to edit [the curriculum], to determine what shall or shall not be taught and assigned, is inherently incompatible with the public schooling enterprise.

NOTES AND QUESTIONS

1. The Governmental Interest

It is widely believed that it is important for public schools to introduce students to, if not socialize them in, the basic values of the American system of government; to inform students and educate them in the operation of the existing governmental system; and to promote a sense of loyalty and patriotism. See generally M. Janowitz, The Reconstruction of Patriotism: Education for Civic Consciousness (1983). Assuming that this educational effort is legitimate, what are the limits on the methods that the state may employ to socialize students to particular values? See generally chapter 1. Who should decide what is to be communicated and by what criteria? Might socialization to the values of tolerance and free speech be legitimate but not socialization to racial discrimination? A. Gutmann, Democratic Education 41–47 (1987). Are some aspects of the state socialization effort more legitimate than other aspects? See generally Stolzenberg, "He Drew a Circle That Shut Me Out: Assimilation, Indoctrination, and the Paradox of Liberal Education," 106 Harv. L. Rev. 581 (1993).

How does one distinguish between the socialization that takes place in American schools and the propagandizing that occurs in schools in totalitarian countries? Gutmann, supra at 103 ("Democratic communities are not in principle bound to teach the truth . . ., but they must be bound not to teach false doctrines that threaten to undermine the future prospects of a common democratic education"). Is it simply a question of the acceptability of the means employed to accomplish the socialization objective? See F. Wirt and M. Kirst, The Political Web of American Schools 24–26 (1972). Or is it that democracy is superior to totalitarianism and hence that democratic socialization is defensible? See generally Gutmann, supra; J. Dewey, Democracy and Education

(1966). Can socialization expand rather than contract a person's capacity to think critically and to make informed choices? Or does it inhibit inquiry and change? *See* C. Lindblom, *Inquiry and Change* (1990). Can socialization promote individual growth and self-realization? *See* Garvey, "Children and the First Amendment," 57 *Tex. L. Rev.* 321, 345 (1979). Is it true that without agreement on certain matters society would disintegrate? *See generally* C. Lindblom, *Politics and Markets* (1977); P. Wolff, *The Poverty of Liberalism* (1968). Some political scientists argue there is good evidence that shared norms and values are not a necessary condition for political support. R. Rogowski, *Rational Legitimacy* 4–17 (1974). *But see* J. Tussman, *Government and the Mind* (1977). What does one make of the fact that students attending parochial schools do not differ in their political views from students attending public schools? *See* A. M. Greeley and P. H. Rossi, *The Education of Catholic Americans* (1968). Does this evidence suggest (1) that basic American values are communicated by all schools, or (2) that differences in curriculum do not reflect differences over fundamental, underlying values, or (3) the most effective sources of socialization are external to the schools? *See generally* Merelman, "Democratic Politics and the Culture of American Education," 74 *Am. Pol. Sci. Rev.* 319 (1980).

Can it be persuasively argued that the governmental interest in socialization is weak when there are data to show that public schooling does not appear to be a strong influence on the political beliefs of students, compared to parental and peer-group influences? *See* M. K. Jennings and R. G. Niemi, *The Political Character of Adolescence* 217–21 (1974). Is the governmental effort to promote political, social, and other norms simply an insurance policy that society cannot risk doing without? Or might socialization be a cumulative process, with the public schools building incrementally (and immeasurably) on the efforts of others? Is there some reason to believe that private schools would not provide the kind and quality of political education that could be considered a collective good? *See* Sugarman and Kirp, "Rethinking Collective Responsibility for Education," 39 *Law and Contemp. Probs.* 144 (1975).

2. *Constitutional Issues*

If political socialization in some form is generally regarded as legitimate, individual students, parents, teachers, and taxpayers might nonetheless object to the majority's imposition of values. *Cf. Crosby v. Holsinger*, 816 F.2d 162 (4th Cir. 1987) ("Johnny Reb" school logo). Various legal and moral interests may be considered here: interests in personal autonomy, freedom of belief, self-controlled political participation, educational choice, freedom of expression, and noncoercion to support beliefs inimical to one's fundamental beliefs. There are also issues of authority: How does one know when public schools speak for the "majority"? Is socialization controlled by professionals or by the electorate? What of the authority of other institutions that socialize—family, church, private associations, and so on? What of the authority of the individual over his or her own development? These interests may be embedded in legal rights, but what ought to be the scope of such rights? Would judicial or legislative affirmation of rights effectively limit the state's power to socialize? Why should a self-interested state promote these rights and hence pluralism? *See generally* E. Purcell, *Crisis of Democratic Theory* (1973).

Would direct limitations on what governments can communicate in schools be preferable to a theory grounded in vindicating individual entitlements? *See* Yudof, "When Governments Speak: Toward a Theory of Government Expression and the First Amendment," 57 *Tex. L. Rev.* 863, 897–917 (1979). What sorts of rules might one wish to impose: a rule requiring equal treatment of different points of view; a rule that prohibited "indoctrination"; a rule prohibiting an ideologically homogeneous curriculum; a rule requiring good faith educational judgments; a rule requiring affirmative support of important minority viewpoints? *See* Gottlieb, "In the Name of Patriotism: The Constitutionality of 'Bending' History in Public Secondary Schools," 62 *N.Y.U. L. Rev.* 497 (1987). Are these or any of the many other rules one might imagine workable? What would be their constitutional basis? *See* van Geel, "The Search for Constitutional Limits on Governmental Authority to Inculcate Youth," 62 *Tex. L. Rev.* 197 (1983). Might we be better off relying on the traditional adjudication of individual constitutional rights to assure presentation of a wide range of points of view in the schools? *See* M. Yudof, *When Government Speaks* (1983). Consider here Section III, *infra*. What provisions of the Constitution would you rely upon?

3. *Socialization and "Quality Education"*

Is political socialization inconsistent with learning to think for oneself and approaching problems critically?

See C. Lindblom, *Inquiry and Change* (1990); Janowitz, *supra*. Would you, as a matter of policy, limit schools to the task of imparting skills? Consider these comments by Michael B. Katz:

> It must be emphasized that, opinion to the contrary notwithstanding, people ask no more of schools today than they did 125 years ago. Even then the schools were asked to do the impossible. As we have seen, the purpose of the school people has been more the development of attitudes than of intellect, and this continues to be the case. It is true, and this point must be stressed, of radical reformers as well as of advocates of law and order. The latter want the schools to stop crime and check immorality by teaching obedience to authority, respect for the law, and conformity to conventional standards. The former want the schools to reform society by creating a new sense of community through turning out warm, loving, noncompetitive people.
>
> * * *
>
> The moral should be clear. Educational reformers should begin to distinguish between what formal schooling can and cannot do. They must separate the teaching of skills from the teaching of attitudes, and concentrate on the former. In actual fact, it is of course impossible to separate the two; attitudes adhere in any form of practice. But there is a vast difference between leaving the formation of attitudes untended and making them the object of education.

Katz, "The Present Moment in Educational Reform," 41 *Harv. Educ. Rev.* 342, 355 (1971).

4. Meyer v. Nebraska

While most parental challenges to education have been religion-based, the landmark case concerning the rights of parents to control their children's education was not, at least ostensibly, a religion case, although it did take place in the context of a religious school. *Meyer v. Nebraska*, 262 U.S. 390, 43 S.Ct. 625, 67 L.Ed. 1042 (1923), was decided on substantive due process grounds. A teacher of German in Zion Parochial School was convicted under a Nebraska statute that prohibited teaching foreign languages to children before they had passed the eighth grade. The avowed purpose of the legislation was to "promote civic development" by ensuring that students were well-steeped in American ideals and the English language before being exposed to foreign languages and cultures.

The Court struck down the Nebraska statute, holding that it unreasonably infringed the liberty guaranteed by the Due Process Clause of the Fourteenth Amendment:

> While this court has not attempted to define with exactness the liberty thus guaranteed, the term has received much consideration, and some of the included things have been definitely stated. Without doubt, it denotes not merely freedom from bodily restraint, but also the right of the individual to contract, to engage in any of the common occupations of life, to acquire useful knowledge, to marry, establish a home and bring up children, to worship God according to the dictates of his own conscience, and, generally, to enjoy those privileges long recognized at common law as essential to the orderly pursuit of happiness by free men . . . . Mere knowledge of the German language cannot reasonably be regarded as harmful. Heretofore it has been commonly looked upon as helpful and desirable. Plaintiff in error taught this language in school as part of his occupation. His right thus to teach and the right of parents to engage him so to instruct their children, we think, are within the liberty of the Amendment.

262 U.S. at 399, 43 S.Ct. at 626. The court expressly limited this broad holding, however, noting the unquestioned power of the state to impose compulsory education, to regulate all schools (both public and private), to require instruction in the English language, and to "prescribe a curriculum for the institutions which it supports." 262 U.S. at 402, 43 S.Ct. at 628.

The continuing vitality of *Meyer* today is somewhat murky, for the Supreme Court relies infrequently on the Due Process Clause of the Fourteenth Amendment for protecting substantive as opposed to procedural rights. The major exceptions are those cases dealing with rights of privacy and control of procreation. *See Roe v. Wade*, 410 U.S. 113, 93 S.Ct. 705, 35 L.Ed.2d 147 (1973); *Griswold v. Connecticut*, 381 U.S. 479, 85 S.Ct. 1678, 14 L.Ed.2d 510 (1965). *See also Troxel v. Granville*, 530 U.S. 57, 120 S.Ct. 2054, 2060–2061 (2000) (holding a Washington statute which allowed grandparents, or any person, to petition a court for visitation violates the substantive due process rights of the mother to make decisions concerning the care, custody, and control of her children). *See generally* Henkin, "Privacy and Autonomy," 74 *Colum. L. Rev.* 1410 (1974). Substantive due process, at least in the economic sphere, acquired a bad name in the New Deal era, as the Court employed the doctrine to frustrate the political will of state legislatures and Congress. *See* chapter 1. The Court has since retreated from its early heavy reliance on this clause, but it has not overruled *Meyer* and it continues to pay homage to parental rights. *See, e.g., Troxel v. Granville, supra; Smith v. Organization of Foster Families*, 431 U.S.

816, 97 S.Ct. 2094, 53 L.Ed.2d 14 (1977). Some commentators believe that *Meyer* and the procreation and privacy cases rest on traditional (common law, natural law, or constitutional law) notions that adults have a fundamental right to marry, procreate (or not procreate), and rear their children. *See Heymann and Barzelay*, "The Forest and the Trees: *Roe v. Wade* and its Critics," 53 *B.U. L. Rev.* 765 (1973). *But see* Regan, "Rewriting *Roe v. Wade*," 77 *Mich. L. Rev.* 1569 (1979).

It is common for state legislatures to grant parents a right to exempt their children from health and/or sex education courses to which they may object. *See, e.g.,* Mich. Stat. Ann. § 15.41507 (4) (1979). Should the courts recognize a constitutional right of parents to make a reasonable selection from the prescribed studies offered by a public school? Do *Pierce v. Society of Sisters*, discussed in chapter 1, and *Meyer* provide a basis for claiming such a right? Or does the constitutionally required option of private school suggest there is no such right? If such a right were to be established, what would be the origin and scope of the right? Should it apply only to whole courses or might it apply to specific topics, books, or assignments? *See Samuel Benedict Memorial School v. Bradford,* 111 Ga. 801, 36 S.E. 920 (1900), in which a father objected to his daughter's writing a specific composition. Might such a right apply to courses mandated by the state legislature as well as those mandated by the local school board? Should such a right extend to the core curriculum ("basic" courses) or ought it only extend to courses outside the core? How is the core curriculum to be defined? Is a sex-education course not within the core, despite serious public interest in providing students with information about venereal diseases and procreation?

Who should have the burden of proof in these matters? Should the state be forced to justify its educational program? Or should parents be forced to demonstrate how inimical the school's program is to their own values or the adverse impact the school's program will have on their rights as parents to control the upbringing of their child? *See* Moskowitz, "Parental Rights and State Education," 50 *Wash. L. Rev.* 623 (1975).

If some degree of parental control is to be granted, are parents' objections to be recognized, no matter how idiosyncratic they are? Consider *State ex rel. Sheibley v. School District*, 31 Neb. 552, 48 N.W. 393 (1891), in which a parent objected to his daughter's study of grammar on the ground "that said study was not taught in said school as he had been instructed when he went to school." What sorts of objections ought to be honored? Do objections gain more weight the more closely they are tied to the First Amendment? Should only religious objections be given serious consideration? *See generally* S. Arons, *Compelling Belief* (1983).

1. Ritual and Coercion of Beliefs

West Virginia State Board of Education v. Barnette

319 U.S. 624, 63 S.Ct. 1178, 87 L.Ed. 1628 (1943).

Mr. Justice Jackson delivered the opinion of the Court.

Following the decision by this Court on June 3, 1940, in *Minersville School District v. Gobitis*, 310 U.S. 586, the West Virginia legislature amended its statutes to require all schools therein to conduct courses of instruction in history, civics, and in the Constitutions of the United States and of the State "for the purpose of teaching, fostering and perpetuating the ideals, principles and spirit of Americanism, and increasing the knowledge of the organization and machinery of the government." Appellant Board of Education was directed, with advice of the State Superintendent of Schools, to "prescribe the courses of study covering these subjects" for public schools. The Act made it the duty of private, parochial and denominational schools to prescribe courses of study "similar to those required for the public schools."

The Board of Education on January 9, 1942, adopted a resolution containing recitals taken largely from the Court's *Gobitis* opinion and ordering that the salute to the flag become "a regular part of the program of activities in the public schools," that all teachers and pupils "shall be required to participate in the salute honoring the Nation represented by the Flag; provided, however, that refusal to salute the Flag be regarded as an act of insubordination, and shall be dealt with accordingly."

The resolution originally required the "commonly accepted salute to the Flag" which it defined. Objections to the salute as "being too much like Hitler's" were raised by the Parent and Teachers Association, the Boy and Girl Scouts, the Red Cross, and the Federation of Women's Clubs. Some modification appears to have been made in deference to these objections, but no concession was made to Jehovah's Witnesses. What is now required is the "stiff-arm" salute, the saluter to keep the right hand raised with palm turned up while the following is repeated: "I pledge allegiance to the Flag of the United States of America and to the Republic for which it stands; one nation, indivisible, with liberty and justice for all."

Failure to conform is "insubordination" dealt with by expulsion. Readmission is denied by statute until compliance. Meanwhile the expelled child is "unlawfully absent" and may be proceeded against as a delinquent. His parents or guardians are liable to prosecution, and if convicted are subject to fine not exceeding $50 and jail term not exceeding thirty days.

Appellees, citizens of the United States and of West Virginia, brought suit in the United States District Court for themselves and other similarly situated asking its injunction to restrain enforcement of these laws and regulations against Jehovah's Witnesses. The Witnesses are an unincorporated body teaching that the obligation imposed by law of God is superior to that of laws enacted by temporal government. Their religious beliefs include a literal version of Exodus, Chapter 20, verses 4 and 5, which says: "Thou shalt not make unto thee any graven image, or any likeness of anything that is in heaven above, or that is in the earth beneath, or that is in the water under the earth; thou shalt not bow down thyself to them nor serve them." They consider that the flag is an "image" within this command. For this reason they refuse to salute it.

* * *

The freedom asserted by these appellees does not bring them into collision with rights asserted by any other individual. It is such conflicts which most frequently require intervention of the State to determine where the rights of one end and those of another begin. But the refusal of these persons to participate in the ceremony does not interfere with or deny rights of others to do so. Nor is there any question in this case that their behavior is peaceable and orderly. The sole conflict is between authority and rights of the individual. The State asserts power to condition access to public education on making a prescribed sign and profession and at the same time to coerce attendance by punishing both parent and child. The latter stand on a right of self-determination in matters that touch individual opinion and personal attitude.

As the present Chief Justice said in dissent in the *Gobitis* case, the State may "require teaching by instruction and study of all in our history and in the structure and organization of our government, including the guarantees of civil liberty, which tend to inspire patriotism and love of country." 310 U.S. at 604. Here, however, we are dealing with a compulsion of students to declare a belief. They are not merely made acquainted with the flag salute so that they may be informed as to what it is or even what it means. The issue here is whether this slow and easily neglected route to aroused loyalties constitutionally may be short-cut by substituting a compulsory salute and slogan. . . .

* * *

[T]he compulsory flag salute and pledge require affirmation of a belief and an attitude of mind. It is not clear whether the regulation contemplates that pupils forego any contrary convictions of their own and become unwilling converts to the prescribed ceremony or whether it will be acceptable if they simulate assent by words without belief and by a gesture barren of meaning. It is now a commonplace that censorship or suppression of expression of opinion is tolerated by our Constitution only when the expression presents a clear and present danger of action of a kind the State is empowered to prevent and punish. It would seem that involuntary affirmation could be commanded only on even more immediate and urgent grounds than silence. But here the power of compulsion is invoked without any allegation that remaining passive during a flag salute ritual creates a clear and present danger that would justify an effort even to muffle expression. To sustain the compulsory flag salute we are required to say that a Bill of Rights which guards the individual's right to speak his own mind, left it open to public authorities to compel him to utter what is not in his mind.

Whether the First Amendment to the Constitution will permit officials to order observance of [a] ritual of this nature does not depend upon whether as a voluntary exercise we would think it to be good, bad or merely innocuous. Any credo of nationalism is likely to include what some disapprove or to omit what others think essential, and to give off different overtones as it takes on different accents or interpretations. If official power exists to coerce acceptance of any patriotic creed, what it shall contain cannot be decided by courts, but must be largely discretionary with the ordaining authority, whose power to prescribe would no doubt include power to amend. Hence validity of the asserted power to force an American citizen publicly to profess any statement of belief or to engage in any ceremony of assent to one, presents questions of power that must be considered independently of any idea we may have as to the utility of the ceremony in question.

Nor does the issue as we see it turn on one's possession of particular religious views or the sincerity with which they are held. While religion supplies appellees' motive for enduring the discomforts of making the issue in this case, many citizens who do not share these religious views hold such a compulsory rite to infringe constitutional liberty of the individual. It is not necessary to inquire whether nonconformist beliefs will exempt from the duty to salute unless we find power to make the salute a legal duty.

The *Gobitis* decision, however, assumed, as did the argument in that case and in this, that power exists in the State to impose the flag salute discipline upon school children in general. The Court only examined and rejected a claim based on religious beliefs of immunity from an unquestioned general rule. The question which underlies the flag salute controversy is whether such a ceremony so touching matters of opinion and political attitude may be imposed upon the individual by official authority under powers committed to any political organization under our Constitution. . . .

* * *

It was also considered in the *Gobitis* case that functions of educational officers in States, counties and school districts were such that to interfere with their authority "would in effect make us the school board for the country." [310 U.S.] at 598.

The Fourteenth Amendment, as now applied to the States, protects the citizen against the State itself and all of its creatures—Boards of Education not excepted. These have, of course, important, delicate, and highly discretionary functions, but none that they may not perform within the limits of the Bill of Rights. That they are educating the young for citizenship is reason for scrupulous protection of Constitutional freedoms of the individual, if we are not to strangle the free mind at its source and teach youth to discount important principles of our government as mere platitudes.

Such Boards are numerous and their territorial jurisdiction often small. But small and local authority may feel less sense of responsibility to the Constitution, and agencies of publicity may be less vigilant in calling it to account. The action of Congress in making flag observance voluntary and respecting the conscience of the objector in a matter so vital as raising the Army contrasts sharply with these local regulations in matters relatively trivial to the welfare of the nation. There are village tyrants as well as village Hampdens, but none who acts under color of law is beyond reach of the Constitution.

The *Gobitis* opinion reasoned that this is a field "where courts possess no marked and certainly no controlling competence," that it is committed to the legislatures as well as the courts to guard cherished liberties and that it is constitutionally appropriate to "fight out the wise use of legislative authority in the forum of public opinion and before legislative assemblies rather than to transfer such a contest to the judicial arena," since all the "effective means of inducing political changes are left free." [310 U.S.] at 597–98, 600.

The very purpose of a Bill of Rights was to withdraw certain subjects from the vicissitudes of political controversy, to place them beyond the reach of majorities and officials, and to establish them as legal principles to be applied by the courts. One's right to life, liberty, and property, to free speech, a free press, freedom of worship and assembly, and other fundamental rights may not be submitted to vote; they depend on the outcome of no elections.

* * *

Lastly, and this is the very heart of the *Gobitis* opinion, it reasons that "National unity is the basis of national security," that the authorities have "the right to select appropriate means for its attainment," and hence reaches the conclusion that such compulsory measures toward "national unity" are constitutional. [310 U.S.] at 595. Upon the verity of this assumption depends our answer in this case.

National unity as an end which officials may foster by persuasion and example is not in question. The problem is whether under our Constitution compulsion as here employed is a permissible means for its achievement.

Struggles to coerce uniformity of sentiment in support of some end thought essential to their time and country have been waged by many good as well as by evil men. Nationalism is a relatively recent phenomenon but at other times and places the ends have been racial or territorial security, support of a dynasty or regime, and particular plans for saving souls. As first and moderate methods to attain unity have failed, those bent on its accomplishment must resort to an ever-increasing severity. As governmental pressure toward unity becomes greater, so strife becomes more bitter as to whose unity it shall be. Probably no deeper division of our people could proceed from any provocation than from finding it necessary to choose what doctrine and whose program public educational officials shall compel youth to unite in embracing. . . .

The case is made difficult not because the principles of its decision are obscure but because the flag involved is our own. Nevertheless, we apply the limitations of the Constitution with no fear that freedom to be intellectually and spiritually diverse or even contrary will disintegrate the social organization. To believe that patriotism will not flourish if patriotic ceremonies are voluntary and spontaneous instead of a compulsory routine is to make an unflattering estimate of the appeal of our institutions to free minds. . . .

If there is any fixed star in our constitutional constellation, it is that no official, high or petty, can prescribe what shall be orthodox in politics, nationalism, religion, or other matters of opinion or force citizens to confess by word or act their faith therein. If there are any circumstances which permit an exception, they do not now occur to us.

We think the action of the local authorities in compelling the flag salute and pledge transcends constitutional limitations on their power and invades the sphere of intellect and spirit which it is the purpose of the First Amendment to our constitution to reserve from all official control.

Affirmed

Mr. Justice Black and Mr. Justice Douglas, concurring:

We are substantially in agreement with the opinion just read, but since we originally joined with the Court in the *Gobitis* case, it is appropriate that we make a brief statement of reasons for our change of view.

Reluctance to make the Federal Constitution a rigid bar against state regulation of conduct thought inimical to the public welfare was the controlling influence which moved us to consent to the *Gobitis* decision. Long reflection convinced us that although the principle is sound, its application in the particular case was wrong. *Jones v. Opelika*, 316 U.S. 584, 623. We believe that the statute before us fails to accord full scope to the freedom of religion secured to the appellees by the First and Fourteenth Amendments.

The statute requires the appellees to participate in a ceremony aimed at inculcating respect for the flag and for this country. The Jehovah's Witnesses, without any desire to show disrespect for either the flag or the country, interpret the Bible as commanding, at the risk of God's displeasure, that they not go through the form of a pledge of allegiance to any flag. The devoutness of their belief is evidenced by their willingness to suffer persecution and punishment, rather than make the pledge.

No well-ordered society can leave to the individuals an absolute right to make final decisions, unassailable by the State, as to everything they will or will not do. The First Amendment does not go so far. Religious faiths, honestly held, do not free individuals from responsibility to conduct themselves obediently to laws which are either imperatively necessary to protect society as a whole from grave and pressingly imminent dangers or which, without any general prohibition, merely regulate time, place or manner of religious activity. Decision as to the constitutionality of particular laws which strike at the substance of religious tenets and practices must be made by this Court. The duty is a solemn one, and in meeting it we cannot say that a failure, because of religious scruples, to assume a particular physical position and to repeat the words of a patriotic formula creates a grave danger to the nation. Such a statutory exaction is a form of test oath, and the test oath has always been abhorrent in the United States.

Words uttered under coercion are proof of loyalty to nothing but self-interest. Love of country must spring from willing hearts and free minds, inspired by a fair administration of wise laws enacted by the people's elected representatives within the bounds of express constitutional prohibitions. These laws must, to be consistent with the First Amendment, permit the widest toleration of conflicting viewpoints consistent with a society of free men.

Neither our domestic tranquility in peace nor our martial effort in war depend on compelling little children to participate in a ceremony which ends in nothing for them but a fear of spiritual condemnation. If, as we think, their fears are groundless, time and reason are the proper antidotes for their errors. The ceremonial, when enforced against conscientious objectors, more likely to defeat than to serve its high purpose, is a handy implement for disguised religious persecution. As such, it is inconsistent with our Constitution's plan and purpose.

* * *

Mr. Justice Frankfurter, dissenting. . . .

Not so long ago we were admonished that "the only check upon our own exercise of power is our own sense of self-restraint. For the removal of unwise laws from the statute books appeal lies not to the courts but to the ballot and to the processes of democratic government. . . ."

* * *

The reason why from the beginning even the narrow judicial authority to nullify legislation has been viewed with a jealous eye is that it serves to prevent the full play of the democratic process. The fact that it may be an undemocratic aspect of our scheme of government does not call for its rejection or its disuse. But it is the best of reasons, as this Court has frequently recognized, for the greatest caution in its use.

* * *

Under our constitutional system the legislature is charged solely with civil concerns of society. If the avowed or intrinsic legislative purpose is either to promote or to discourage some religious community or creed, it is clearly within the constitutional restrictions imposed on legislatures and cannot stand. But it by no means follows that legislative power is wanting whenever a general nondiscriminatory civil regulation in fact touches conscientious scruples or religious beliefs of an individual or a group. Regard for such scruples or beliefs undoubtedly presents one of the most reasonable claims for the exertion of legislative accommodation. It is, of course, beyond our power to rewrite the State's requirement, by providing exemptions for those who do not wish to participate in the flag salute or by making some other accommodations to meet their scruples. That wisdom might suggest the making of such accommodations and that school administration would not find it too difficult to make them and yet maintain the ceremony for those not refusing to conform, is outside our province to suggest. . . .

This is no dry, technical matter. It cuts deep into one's conception of the democratic process—it concerns no less the practical differences between the means for making these accommodations that are open to courts and to legislatures. A court can only strike down. It can only say "This or that law is void." It cannot modify or qualify, it cannot make exceptions to a general requirement. And it strikes down not merely for a day. . . .

The constitutional protection of religious freedom terminated disabilities, it did not create new privileges. It gave religious equality, not civil immunity. Its essence is freedom from conformity to religious dogma, not freedom from conformity to law because of religious dogma. Religious loyalties may be exercised without hindrance from the state, not the state may not exercise that which except by leave of religious loyalties is within the domain of temporal power. Otherwise each individual could set up his own censor against obedience to laws conscientiously deemed for the public good by those whose business it is to make laws.

* * *

The essence of the religious freedom guaranteed by our Constitution is therefore this: no religion shall either receive the state's support or incur its hostility. Religion is outside the sphere of political government. This does not mean that all matters on which religious organizations or beliefs may pronounce are outside the sphere of government.

Were this so, instead of the separation of church and state, there would be the subordination of the state on any matter deemed within the sovereignty of the religious conscience. Much that is the concern of temporal authority affects the spiritual interests of men. But it is not enough to strike down a nondiscriminatory law that it may hurt or offend some dissident view. It would be too easy to cite numerous prohibitions and injunctions to which laws run counter if the variant interpretations of the Bible were made the tests of obedience to law. The validity of secular laws cannot be measured by their conformity to religious doctrines. It is only in a theocratic state that ecclesiastical doctrines measure legal right or wrong.

An act compelling profession of allegiance to a religion, no matter how subtly or tenuously promoted, is bad. But an act promoting good citizenship and national allegiance is within the domain of governmental authority and is therefore to be judged by the same considerations of power and of constitutionality as those involved in the many claims of immunity from civil obedience because of religious scruples.

* * *

Parents have the privilege of choosing which schools they wish their children to attend. And the question here is whether the state may make certain requirements that seem to it desirable or important for the proper education of those future citizens who go to schools maintained by the states, or whether the pupils in those schools may be relieved from those requirements if they run counter to the consciences of their parents. Not only have parents the right to send children to schools of their own choosing, but the state has no right to bring such schools "under a strict government control" or give "affirmative direction concerning the intimate and essential details of such schools, entrust their control to public officers, and deny both owners and patrons reasonable choice and discretion in respect of teachers, curriculum, and textbooks." *Farrington v. Tokushige,*

273 U.S. 284, 298 (1926). Why should not the state likewise have constitutional power to make reasonable provisions for the proper instruction of children in schools maintained by it?

* * *

We are told that a flag salute is a doubtful substitute for adequate understanding of our institutions. The states that require such a school exercise do not have to justify it as the only means for promoting good citizenship in children, but merely as one of diverse means for accomplishing a worthy end. We may deem it a foolish measure, but the point is that this Court is not the organ of government to resolve doubts as to whether it will fulfill its purpose. Only if there be no doubt that any reasonable mind could entertain can we deny to the states the right to resolve doubts their way and not ours.

* * *

One's conception of the Constitution cannot be severed from one's conception of a judge's function in applying it. The Court has no reason for existence if it merely reflects the pressures of the day. Our system is built on the faith that men set apart for this special function, freed from the influences of immediacy and from the deflections of worldly ambition, will become able to take a view of longer range than the period of responsibility entrusted to Congress and legislatures. We are dealing with matters as to which legislators and voters have conflicting views. Are we as judges to impose our strong convictions on where wisdom lies? That which three years ago had seemed to five successive Courts to lie within permissible areas of legislation is now outlawed by the deciding shift of opinion of two Justices. What reason is there to believe that they or their successors may not have another view a few years hence? Is that which was deemed to be of so fundamental a nature as to be written into the Constitution to endure for all times to be the sport of shifting winds of doctrine? Of course, judicial opinions, even as to questions of constitutionality, are not immutable. As has been true in the past, the Court will from time to time reverse its position. But I believe that never before these Jehovah's Witnesses cases (except for minor deviations subsequently retraced) has this Court overruled decisions so as to restrict the powers of democratic government. Always heretofore, it has withdrawn narrow views of legislative authority so as to authorize what formerly it had denied.

In view of this history it must be plain that what thirteen Justices found to be within the constitu-

tional authority of a state, legislators can not be deemed unreasonable in enacting. Therefore, in denying to the states what heretofore has received such impressive judicial sanction, some other tests of unconstitutionality must surely be guiding the Court than the absence of a rational justification for the legislation. But I know of no other test which this Court is authorized to apply in nullifying legislation.

* * *

The uncontrollable power wielded by this Court brings it very close to the most sensitive areas of public affairs. As appeal from legislation to adjudication becomes more frequent, and its consequences more far-reaching, judicial self-restraint becomes more and not less important, lest we unwarrantably enter social and political domains wholly outside our concern. I think I appreciate fully the objections to the law before us. But to deny that it presents a question upon which men might reasonably differ appears to me to be intolerance. And since men may so reasonably differ, I deem it beyond my constitutional power to assert my view of the wisdom of this law against the view of the State of West Virginia. . . .

NOTES AND QUESTIONS

1. Barnette: A Free Exercise Case?

Is *Barnette* a case about free exercise of religion or freedom of expression? Might the perceived necessity to distinguish *Minersville School District v. Gobitis*, 310 U.S. 586, 60 S.Ct. 1010, 84 L.Ed. 1375 (1940), explain the majority's choice of constitutional doctrine? Do Justices Black and Douglas distinguish or repudiate *Gobitis*? Is Justice Frankfurter responding to the majority or to Black and Douglas? Viewed as a free exercise case, are the arguments in favor of the Jehovah's Witnesses stronger? Is Justice Frankfurter correct in viewing with alarm the granting of exemptions from patriotic rituals on the basis of free exercise claims? *Cf. Employment Division, Department of Human Resources v. Smith*, 494 U.S. 872, 110 S.Ct. 1595 (1990). *See generally* Laycock, "The Remnants of Free Exercise," 1990 *Sup. Ct. Rev.* 1; McConnell, "Free Exercise Revisionism and the *Smith* Decision," 57 *Chi. L. Rev.* 1109 (1990). Is *Wisconsin v. Yoder*, discussed in chapter 1, consistent with Frankfurter's views? *See Sherman v. Community Consol. School Dist.*, 980 F.2d 437 (7th Cir. 1992). Is the state's interest compelling? Does the state have "less onerous" means of inculcating patriotic values?

2. An "Implied Political Establishment Clause"?

Why is a voluntary patriotic ceremony, but not a voluntary religious ceremony, permitted in the public schools? Why is not coercion as much a problem in *Barnette* as in the school prayer cases? Is it that the state's interest in socializing students to patriotic values is more substantial than its interest in sectarian socialization? Or is it that the Constitution bars the establishment of religion but not the establishment of a political "religion"? What of the words in the Pledge of Allegiance about "one nation under God"? Is this an Establishment Clause violation? In *Sherman v. Community Consol. School Dist.*, the court considered the question of whether a state statute requiring daily recitation of the Pledge of Allegiance, which contains the phrase "one nation under God," violates the First Amendment. The court held that as long as students were free not to participate, the state statute was constitutional. The court distinguished patriotism from religion, stating:

> Patriotism is an effort by the state to promote its own survival, and along the way to teach those virtues that *justify* its survival. Public schools help to transmit those virtues and values. Separation of church from state does not imply separation of state from state. Schools are entitled to hold their causes and values out as worthy subjects of approval and adoption, to persuade even though they cannot compel, and even though those who resist persuasion may feel at odds with those who embrace the values they are taught.

980 F.2d at 444.

3. Right Not to Participate in a Political Ceremony?

The majority acknowledges a right on the part of government to attempt to foster patriotism and love of country. *See* T. van Geel, *The Courts and American Education* 189 (1987). Yet it prohibits a compulsory flag salute as a way of achieving this objective. What does this distinction suggest? Might *Barnette* be viewed as forbidding the state from compelling participation in a ceremony that is tantamount to political action? Or can it be viewed as forbidding forced participation in a political demonstration that seeks to foster loyalty through a purely emotional appeal? Thus, might the case be viewed as protecting a right of nonparticipation in a patriotic ritual, or more broadly, might it protect a right not to participate in group political activities or even a right of nonassociation? *Cf. Abood v. De-*troit *Board of Education*, 431 U.S. 209, 97 S.Ct. 1782, 52 L.Ed.2d 261 (1977). If this is the basis of *Barnette*, why is it constitutional for the state to compel attendance in civics courses? *See* S. Arons, *Compelling Belief* 67–68 (1983). As in the school prayer cases, is the Court distinguishing between instruction about religion and patriotism and rituals designed to foster religion and patriotism?

4. Coercion to Speak

Is *Barnette* primarily concerned with a coerced declaration of belief? Does this mean that there is a constitutional right to remain silent? *See generally* Gaebler, "First Amendment Protection Against Government Compelled Expression and Association," 23 *B.C. L. Rev.* 995 (1982).

In *Wooley v. Maynard*, 430 U.S. 705, 97 S.Ct. 1428, 51 L.Ed.2d 752 (1977), a case involving a New Hampshire statute requiring residents' noncommercial motor vehicles to bear license plates embossed with the state motto, "Live Free or Die," the Court struck down the law at the behest of the Jehovah's Witnesses. The Court held that the right to speak and the right not to speak were "complementary components" of the First Amendment. 430 U.S. at 714, 97 S.Ct. at 1435.

What is the constitutional basis of a "right not to speak"? Is it that silence is a form of expression, or is it that a coerced confession of belief is an affront to dignity, an improper *means* of state communication and socialization? *See* T. Emerson, *The System of Freedom of Expression* 30 (1970).

In *Wooley*, Chief Justice Burger, writing for the majority, stated that the issue for decision was "whether the state may constitutionally require an individual to participate in the dissemination of an ideological message by displaying it on his private property in a manner and for the express purpose that it be observed and read by the public." 430 U.S. at 713, 97 S.Ct. at 1434. Was a similar issue involved in *Barnette*? Is it the compulsion to transmit the message that is critical, or is it that observers and listeners may falsely attribute the belief to the speaker? Justice Rehnquist dissented on precisely this ground in *Wooley*, arguing that reasonable people would not construe a message on a license plate as an indication of affirmation of the owner's or driver's beliefs. 430 U.S. at 719, 97 S.Ct. at 1437. Would the other students and the teachers in *Barnette* be likely to think that recital of the flag salute revealed the Jehovah's Witnesses' true beliefs? If not, is not Professor Emerson's interpretation of *Barnette* better supported than Rehnquist's view? Is it correct, then, to assert that the school prayer cases are a substantive limitation on what governments may say, whereas *Barnette* is a limit on how governments may get across a legitimate message? *Cf. Linmark Associates v. Township of Willingboro*, 431 U.S. 85, 97 S.Ct. 1614, 52 L.Ed.2d 155 (1977) (ban on posting of "For Sale" and "Sold" signs in front of residential property declared unconstitutional).

5. Problems

Does *Barnette* prevent public schools from requiring students to stand for the singing of the national anthem? *See Sheldon v. Fannin*, 221 F.Supp. 766 (D. Ariz. 1963). Does *Barnette* require excusing children who object to patriotic exercises that celebrate Memorial Day or Presidents Day?

Schools often close for religious or patriotic holidays. When schools close, could nonattendance be viewed as compelled affirmation of belief in violation of *Barnette* or as compelled "nonassociation" in violation of *Barnette?* Would remaining open but excusing those who wish to celebrate the day provide a solution, or would this policy pose even more problems?

6. Teachers and the Flag Salute

If a teacher refuses to participate in a salute to the flag, does *Barnette* provide the teacher with constitutional protection, or are teachers to be treated differently because they are role models and have been hired to implement the school's curriculum? *See Russo v. Central School District No. 1*, 469 F.2d 623 (2d Cir. 1972), *cert. denied*, 411 U.S. 932, 93 S.Ct. 1899, 36 L.Ed.2d 391 (1973); *see also* Gallancy, "Teachers and the Pledge of Allegiance," 57 *U. of Chi. L. Rev.* 929 (1990).

2. Control of Curricular Materials and Texts

Board of Education, Island Trees Union Free School District No. 26 v. Pico

457 U.S. 853, 102 S.Ct. 2799, 73 L.Ed.2d 435 (1982).

Justice Brennan announced the judgment of the Court, and delivered an opinion in which Justice Marshall and Justice Stevens joined, and in which Justice Blackmun joined except for Part II-A-(1).

The principal question presented is whether the First Amendment imposes limitations upon the exercise by a local school board of its discretion to remove library books from high school and junior high school libraries.

I

Petitioners are the Board of Education of the Island Trees Union Free School District No. 26, in New York, and Richard Ahrens, Frank Martin, Christina Fasulo, Patrick Hughes, Richard Melchers, Richard Michaels, and Louis Nessim. When this suit was brought, Ahrens was the President of the Board, Martin was the Vice-President, and the remaining petitioners were Board members. The Board is a state agency charged with responsibility for the operation and administration of the public schools within the Island Trees School District including the Island Trees High School and Island Trees Memorial Junior High School. Respondents are Steven Pico, Jacqueline Gold, Glenn Yarris, Russell Rieger, and Paul Sochinski. When this suit was brought, Pico, Gold, Yarris, and Rieger were students at the High School, and Sochinski was a student at the Junior High School.

In September 1975, petitioners Ahrens, Martin, and Hughes attended a conference sponsored by Parents of New York United (PONYU), a politically conservative organization of parents concerned about education legislation in the State of New York. At the conference these petitioners obtained lists of books described by Ahrens as "objectionable," . . . and by Martin as "improper fare for school students," . . . .[2] It was later determined that the High School library contained nine of the listed books, and that another listed book was in the Junior High School library.[3] In February 1976, at a meeting with the superintendent

---

[2]The District Court noted, however, that petitioners "concede that the books are not obscene." 474 F.Supp. 387, 392 (1979).

[3]The nine books in the High School library were: *Slaughter House Five*, by Kurt Vonnegut, Jr.; *The Naked Ape*, by Desmond Morris; *Down These Mean Streets*, by Piri Thomas, *Best Short Stories of Negro Writers*, edited by Langston Hughes; *Go Ask Alice*, of anonymous authorship; *Laughing Boy*, by Oliver LaFarge; *Black Boy*, by Richard Wright; *A Hero Ain't Nothin' But a Sandwich*, by Alice Childress; and *Soul on Ice*, by Eldridge Cleaver. The book in the Junior High School library was *A Reader for Writers*, edited by Jerome Archer. Still another listed book, *The Fixer*, by Bernard Malamud, was found to be included in the curriculum of a twelfth grade literature course. 474 F.Supp. 387, 389 and nn. 2–4.

of schools and the principals of the High School and Junior High School, the Board gave an "unofficial direction" that the listed books be removed from the library shelves and delivered to the Board's offices, so that Board members could read them.[4] When this directive was carried out, it became publicized, and the Board issued a press release justifying its action. It characterized the removed books as "anti-American, anti-Christian, anti-Semitic, and just plain filthy," and concluded that "It is our duty, our moral obligation, to protect the children in our schools from this moral danger as surely as from physical and medical dangers." 474 F.Supp. 387, 390.

A short time later, the Board appointed a "Book Review Committee," consisting of four Island Trees parents and four members of the Island Trees schools staff, to read the listed books and to recommend to the Board whether the books should be retained, taking into account the books' "educational suitability," "good taste," "relevance," and "appropriateness to age and grade level." In July, the Committee made its final report to the Board, recommending that five of the listed books be retained[5] and that two others be removed from the school libraries.[6] As for the remaining four books, the Committee could not agree on two,[7] took no position on one,[8] and recommended that the last book be made available to students only with parental approval.[9] The Board substantially rejected the Committee's report later that month, deciding that only one book should be returned to the High School library without restriction,[10] that another should be made available subject to parental approval,[11] but that the remaining nine books should "be removed from elementary and secondary libraries and [from] use in the curriculum." 474 F.Supp., at 391.[12]

The Board gave no reasons for rejecting the recommendations of the Committee that it had appointed.

Respondents reacted to the Board's decision by bringing the present action under 42 U.S.C. § 1983 in the United States District Court for the Eastern District of New York. They alleged that petitioners had "ordered the removal of the books from school libraries and proscribed their use in the curriculum because particular passages in the books offended their social, political and moral tastes and not because the books, taken as a whole, were lacking in educational value." . . . Respondents claimed that the Board's actions denied them their rights under the First Amendment. They asked the court for a declaration that the Board's actions were unconstitutional, and for preliminary and permanent injunctive relief ordering the Board to return the nine books to the school libraries and to refrain from interfering with the use of those books in the schools' curricula. . . .

The District Court granted summary judgment in favor of petitioners. 474 F.Supp. 387 (1979). In the court's view, "the parties substantially agree[d] about the motivation behind the board's actions," id., at 391 — namely, that "the board acted not on religious principles but on its conservative educational philosophy, and on its belief that the nine books removed from the school library and curriculum were irrelevant, vulgar, immoral, and in bad taste, making them educationally unsuitable for the district's junior and senior high school students." Id., at 392. With this factual premise as its background, the court rejected respondents' contention that their First Amendment rights had been infringed by the Board's actions. Noting that statute, history, and precedent had vested local school boards with a broad discretion to formulate educational policy,[13] the court

---

[4]The superintendent of schools objected to the Board's informal directive, noting that: "we already have a policy . . . designed expressly to handle such problems. It calls for the Superintendent, upon receiving an objection to a book or books, to appoint a committee to study them and make recommendations. I feel it is a good policy—and it is Board policy—and that it should be followed in this instance. Further, I think it can be followed quietly and in such a way as to reduce, perhaps avoid, the public furor which has always attended such issues in the past." . . .

The Board responded to the superintendent's objection by repeating its directive "that all copies of the library books in question be removed from the libraries to the Board's office." . . .

[5]The Fixer, Laughing Boy, Black Boy, Go Ask Alice, and Best Short Stories by Negro Writers. . . .

[6]The Naked Ape and Down These Mean Streets. . . .

[7]Soul on Ice and A Hero Ain't Nothin' But a Sandwich. . . .

[8]A Reader for Writers. . . . The reason given for this disposition was that all members of the Committee had not been able to read the book. . . .

[9]Slaughter House Five. . . .

[10]Laughing Boy. . . .

[11]Black Boy. . . .

[12]As a result, the nine removed books could not be assigned or suggested to students in connection with school work. Ibid. However, teachers were not instructed to refrain from discussing the removed books or the ideas and positions expressed in them. . . .

[13]Id., at 396–97, citing Presidents Council, District 25 v. Community School Board #25, 457 F.2d 289 (CA2 1972); James v. Board of Education, 461 F.2d 566, 573 (CA2 1972); East Hartford Educational Assn. v. Board of Education, 562 F.2d 838, 856 (CA2 1977) (en banc).

concluded that it should not intervene in " 'the daily operations of school systems' " unless " 'basic constitutional values' " were " 'sharply implicate[d],' "[14] and determined that the conditions for such intervention did not exist in the present case. Acknowledging that the "removal [of the books] . . . clearly was content-based," the court nevertheless found no constitutional violation of the requisite magnitude: "The board has restricted access only to certain books which the board believed to be, in essence, vulgar. While removal of such books from a school library may . . . reflect a misguided educational philosophy, it does not constitute a sharp and direct infringement of any first amendment right." *Id.*, at 397.

A three-judge panel of the United States Court of Appeals for the Second Circuit reversed the judgment of the District Court, and remanded the action for a trial on respondents' allegations. 638 F.2d 404 (1980). Each judge on the panel filed a separate opinion. Delivering the judgment of the court, Judge Sifton treated the case as involving "an unusual and irregular intervention in the school libraries' operations by persons not routinely concerned with such matters," and concluded that petitioners were obliged to demonstrate a reasonable basis for interfering with respondents' First Amendment rights. *Id.*, at 414–15. He then determined that, at least at the summary judgment stage, petitioners had not offered sufficient justification for their action,[15] and concluded that respondents

"should have . . . been offered an opportunity to persuade a finder of fact that the ostensible justifications for [petitioners'] actions . . . were simply pretexts for the suppression of free speech." *Id.*, at 417.[16] Judge Newman concurred in the result. *Id.*, at 432–38. He viewed the case as turning on the contested factual issue of whether petitioners' removal decision was motivated by a justifiable desire to remove books containing vulgarities and sexual explicitness, or rather by an impermissible desire to suppress ideas. *Id.*, at 436–37.[17] . . .

II

We emphasize at the outset the limited nature of the substantive question represented by the case before us. Our precedents have long recognized certain constitutional limits upon the power of the State to control even the curriculum and classroom. For example, *Meyer v. Nebraska*, 262 U.S. 390 . . . (1923), struck down a state law that forbade the teaching of modern foreign languages in public and private schools, and *Epperson v. Arkansas*, 393 U.S. 97 . . . (1968), declared unconstitutional a state law that prohibited the teaching of the Darwinian theory of evolution in any state-supported school. But the current action does not require us to re-enter this difficult terrain, which *Meyer* and *Epperson* traversed without apparent misgiving. For as this case is presented to us, it does not involve textbooks, or indeed any books that Island Trees students would be required to read.[18] Re-

---

[14]474 F.Supp., at 395–97, quoting *Presidents Council, District 25 v. Community School Board #25, supra,* at 291 (in turn quoting *Epperson v. Arkansas,* 393 U.S. 97 . . . (1968).

[15]After criticizing "the criteria for removal" employed by petitioners as "suffer[ing] from generality and overbreadth," and the procedures used by petitioners as "erratic, arbitrary and free-wheeling," Judge Sifton observed that "precision of regulation and sensitivity to First Amendment concerns" were "hardly established" by such procedures. 638 F.2d, at 41 6.

[16]Judge Sifton stated that it could be inferred from the record that petitioners' "political views and personal taste [were] being asserted not in the interests of the children's well-being, but rather for the purpose of establishing those views as the correct and orthodox ones for all purposes in the particular community." *Id.*, at 417.

[17]Judge Mansfield dissented, 638 F.2d, at 419–32, based upon a distinctly different reading of the record developed in the District Court. According to Judge Mansfield, "the undisputed evidence of the motivation for the Board's action was the perfectly permissible ground that the books were indecent, in bad taste, and unsuitable for educational purposes." *Id.*, at 430. He also asserted that in reaching its decision "the Board [had] acted carefully, conscientiously and responsibly after according due process to all parties concerned." *Id.*, at 422. Judge Mansfield concluded that "the First Amendment entitles students to reasonable freedom of expression but not to freedom from what some may consider to be excessively moralistic or conservative selection by school authorities of library books to be used as educational tools." *Id.*, at 432.

[18]Four of respondents' five causes of action complained of petitioners' "resolutions ordering the removal of certain books from the school libraries of the District and prohibiting the use of those books in the curriculum." . . . The District Court concluded "that respect for the school board's substantial control over educational content . . . precludes any finding of a first amendment violation arising out of removal of any of the books from use in the curriculum." 474 F.Supp., at 397. This holding is not at issue here. Respondents' fifth cause of action complained that petitioners' "resolutions prohibiting the use of certain books in the curriculum of schools in the District" had "imposed upon teachers in the District arbitrary and unreasonable restrictions upon their ability to function as teachers in violation of principles of academic freedom." . . . The District Court held that respondents had not proved this cause of action: "before such a claim may be sustained there must at least be a real, not an imagined controversy." 474 F.Supp., at 397. Respondents have not sought review of that holding in this Court.

spondents do not seek in this Court to impose limitations upon their school board's discretion to prescribe the curricula of the Island Trees schools. On the contrary, the only books at issue in this case are library books, books that by their nature are optional rather than required reading. Our adjudication of the present case thus does not intrude into the classroom, or into the compulsory courses taught there. Furthermore, even as to library books, the action before us does not involve the acquisition of books. Respondents have not sought to compel their school board to add to the school library shelves any books that students desire to read. Rather, the only action challenged in this case is the removal from school libraries of books originally placed there by the school authorities, or without objection from them.

The substantive question before us is still further constrained by the procedural posture of this case. Petitioners were granted summary judgment by the District Court. The Court of Appeals reversed that judgment, and remanded the action for a trial on the merits of respondents' claims. We can reverse the judgment of the Court of Appeals, and grant petitioners' request for reinstatement of the summary judgment in their favor, only if we determine that "there is no genuine issue as to any material fact," and that petitioners are "entitled to a judgment as a matter of law." Fed. Rule Civ. Proc. 56(c). In making our determination, any doubt as to the existence of a genuine issue of material fact must be resolved against petitioners as the moving party. *Adickes v. Kress & Co.*, 398 U.S. 144, 157–59 . . . (1970). Furthermore, "on summary judgment the inferences to be drawn from the underlying facts contained . . . in the affidavits, attached exhibits, and depositions submitted below . . . must be viewed in the light most favorable to the party opposing the motion." *United States v. Diebold*, Inc., 369 U.S. 654, 655 . . . (1962).

In sum, the issue before us in this case is a narrow one, both substantively and procedurally. It may best be restated as two distinct questions. First, does the First Amendment impose any limitations upon the discretion of petitioners to remove library books from the Island Trees High School and Junior High School? Second, if so, do the affidavits and other evidentiary materials before the District Court, construed most favorably to respondents, raise a genuine issue of fact whether petitioners might have exceeded those limitations? . . .

A

(1) We have . . . acknowledged that public schools are vitally important "in the preparation of individuals for participation as citizens," and as vehicles for "inculcating fundamental values necessary to the maintenance of a democratic political system." *Ambach v. Norwick*, 441 U.S. 68, 76–77 . . . (1979). We are therefore in full agreement with petitioners that local school boards must be permitted "to establish and apply their curriculum in such a way as to transmit community values," and that "there is a legitimate and substantial community interest in promoting respect for authority and traditional values be they social, moral, or political." . . .

At the same time, however, we have necessarily recognized that the discretion of the States and local school boards in matters of education must be exercised in a manner that comports with the transcendent imperatives of the First Amendment. . . .

* * *

In short, "First Amendment rights, applied in light of the special characteristics of the school environment, are available to . . . students."

Of course, courts should not "intervene in the resolution of conflicts which arise in the daily operations of school systems" unless "basic constitutional values" are "directly and sharply implicate[d]" in those conflicts. . . . But we think that the First Amendment rights of students may be directly and sharply implicated by the removal of books from the shelves of a school library. Our precedents have focused "not only on the role of the First Amendment in fostering individual self-expression but also on its role in affording the public access to discussion, debate, and the dissemination of information and ideas." *First National Bank of Boston v. Bellotti*, 435 U.S. 765, 783 . . . (1978). And we have recognized that "the State may not, consistently with the spirit of the First Amendment, contract the spectrum of available knowledge." *Griswold v. Connecticut*, 381 U.S. 479, 482 . . . (1965). In keeping with this principle, we have held that in a variety of contexts "the Constitution protects the right to receive information and ideas." *Stanley v. Georgia*, 394 U.S. 557, 564 . . . (1969); *see Kleindienst v. Mandel*, 408 U.S. 753, 762–63 . . . (1972). This right is an inherent corollary of the rights of free speech and press that are explicitly guaranteed by the Constitution, in two senses. First, the right to receive ideas follows ineluctably from the sender's

First Amendment right to send them: "The right of freedom of speech and press . . . embraces the right to distribute literature, . . . and necessarily protects the right to receive it." *Martin v. Struthers*, 318 U.S. 141, 143 . . . (1943) (citation omitted). "The dissemination of ideas can accomplish nothing if otherwise willing addressees are not free to receive and consider them. It would be a barren marketplace of ideas that had only sellers and no buyers." *Lamont v. Postmaster General*, 381 U.S. 301, 308 . . . (1965) (Brennan, J., concurring).

More importantly, the right to receive ideas is a necessary predicate to the recipient's meaningful exercise of his own rights of speech, press, and political freedom. Madison admonished us that "A popular Government, without popular information, or the means of acquiring it, is but a Prologue to a Farce or a Tragedy; or, perhaps both. Knowledge will forever govern ignorance: And a people who mean to be their own Governors, must arm themselves with the power which knowledge gives." 9 *Writings of James Madison* 103 (G. Hunt ed. 1910). . . .

. . . [J]ust as access to ideas makes it possible for citizens generally to exercise their rights of free speech and press in a meaningful manner, such access prepares students for active and effective participation in the pluralistic, often contentious society in which they will soon be adult members. Of course all First Amendment rights accorded to students must be construed "in light of the special characteristics of the school environment." *Tinker v. Des Moines School Dist.*, . . . [393 U.S. 503, 506 (1969)]. But the special characteristics of the school library make that environment especially appropriate for the recognition of the First Amendment rights of students.

. . . *Keyishian v. Board of Regents*, 385 U.S. 589, 87 S.Ct. 675, 17 L.Ed.2d 629 (1967), observed that "students must always remain free to inquire, to study and to evaluate, to gain new maturity and understanding." The school library is the principal locus of such freedom. As one District Court has well put it, in the school library "a student can literally explore the unknown, and discover areas of interest and thought not covered by the prescribed curriculum. . . . Th[e] student learns that a library is a place to test or expand upon ideas presented to him, in or out of the classroom." *Right to Read Defense Comm. v. School Comm.*, 454 F.Supp. 703, 715 (D.Mass. 1978). Petitioners emphasize the inculcative function of secondary education, and argue

that they must be allowed unfettered discretion to "transmit community values" through the Island Trees schools. But that weeping claim overlooks the unique role of the school library. It appears from the record that use of the Island Trees school libraries is completely voluntary on the part of students. Their selection of books from these libraries is entirely a matter of free choice; the libraries afford them an opportunity at self-education and individual enrichment that is wholly optional. Petitioners might well defend their claim of absolute discretion in matters of curriculum by reliance upon their duty to inculcate community values. But we think that petitioners' reliance upon that duty is misplaced where, as here, they attempt to extend their claim of absolute discretion beyond the compulsory environment of the classroom, into the school library and the regime of voluntary inquiry that there holds sway.

(2) In rejecting petitioners' claim of absolute discretion to remove books from their school libraries, we do not deny that local school boards have a substantial legitimate role to play in the determination of school library content. We thus must turn to the question of the extent to which the First Amendment places limitations upon the discretion of petitioners to remove books from their libraries. In this inquiry we enjoy the guidance of several precedents. *West Virginia v. Barnette* . . . stated that "If there be any fixed star in our constitutional constellation, it is that no official, high or petty, can prescribe what shall be orthodox in politics, nationalism, religion, or other matters of opinion. . . . If there are any circumstances which permit an exception, they do not now occur to us." 319 U.S. . . . [624, 642 (1943)]. This doctrine has been reaffirmed in later cases involving education. . . .

With respect to the present case, the message of these precedents is clear. Petitioners rightly possess significant discretion to determine the content of their school libraries. But that discretion may not be exercised in a narrowly partisan or political manner. If a Democratic school board, motivated by party affiliation, ordered the removal of all books written by or in favor of Republicans, few would doubt that the order violated the constitutional rights of the students denied access to those books. The same conclusion would surely apply if an all-white school board, motivated by racial animus, decided to remove all books authored by blacks or advocating racial equality and integration. Our Constitution does not permit the official suppression of ideas. Thus whether petitioners' removal of books from their school libraries denied respondents their First Amendment rights depends upon the motivation behind petitioners' actions. If petitioners intended by their removal decision to deny respondents access to ideas with which petitioners disagreed, and if this intent was the decisive factor in petitioners' decision,[22] then petitioners have exercised their discretion in violation of the Constitution. To permit such intentions to control official actions would be to encourage the precise sort of officially prescribed orthodoxy unequivocally condemned in *Barnette*. On the other hand, respondents implicitly concede that an unconstitutional motivation would not be demonstrated if it were shown that petitioners had decided to remove the books at issue because those books were pervasively vulgar. . . . And again, respondents concede that if it were demonstrated that the removal decision was based solely upon the "educational suitability" of the books in question, then their removal would be "perfectly permissible." . . . In other words, in respondents' view such motivations, if decisive of petitioners' actions, would not carry the danger of an official suppression of ideas, and thus would not violate respondents' First Amendment rights.

* * *

B

We now turn to the remaining question presented by this case: Do the evidentiary materials that were before the District Court, when construed most favorably to respondents, raise a genuine issue of material fact whether petitioners exceeded constitutional limitations in exercising their discretion to remove the books from the school libraries? We conclude that the materials do raise such a question, which forecloses summary judgment in favor of petitioners.

* * *

Standing alone, . . . [the] evidence respecting the substantive motivations behind petitioners' removal decision would not be decisive. This would be a very different case if the record demonstrated that petitioners had employed established, regular, and facially unbiased procedures for the review of controversial materials. But the actual record in the case before us suggests the exact opposite. Petitioners' removal procedures were vigorously challenged below by respondents, and the evidence on this issue sheds further light on the issue of petitioners' motivations. . . .

[W]e cannot conclude that petitioners were "entitled to a judgment as a matter of law." The evidence plainly does not foreclose the possibility that petitioners' decision to remove the books rested decisively upon disagreement with constitutionally protected ideas in those books, or upon a desire on petitioners' part to impose upon the students of the Island Trees High School and Junior High School a political orthodoxy to which petitioners and their constituents adhered. Of course, some of the evidence before the District Court might lead a finder of fact to accept petitioners' claim that their removal decision was based upon constitutionally valid concerns. But that evidence at most creates a genuine issue of material fact on the critical question of the credibility of petitioners' justifications for their decision: On that issue, it simply cannot be said that there is no genuine issue as to any material fact.

The mandate shall issue forthwith.

Affirmed.

Justice Blackmun, concurring in part and concurring in the judgment.

While I agree with much in today's plurality opinion, and while I accept the standard laid down by the plurality to guide proceedings on remand, I write separately because I have a somewhat different perspective on the nature of the First Amendment right involved.

I

To my mind, this case presents a particularly complex problem because it involves two competing principles of constitutional stature. On the one hand, as the dissenting opinions demonstrate, and as we all can agree, the Court has acknowledged the importance of the public schools "in the preparation of individuals for participation as citizens, and in the preservation of values on which our society rests." *Ambach v. Norwick,* 441 U.S. 68, 76 . . . (1979). Because of the essential socializing function of schools, local education officials

---

[22]By "decisive factor" we mean a "substantial factor" in the absence of which the opposite decision would have been reached. *See Mt. Healthy City Board of Ed. v. Doyle,* 429 U.S. . . . [274, 287 (1977)].

may attempt "to promote civic virtues," *Ambach v. Norwick*, 441 U.S., at 80, . . . and to "awake[n] the child to cultural values." *Brown v. Board of Education*, 347 U.S. 483, 493 . . . (1954). Indeed, the Constitution presupposes the existence of an informed citizenry prepared to participate in governmental affairs, and these democratic principles obviously are constitutionally incorporated into the structure of our government. It therefore seems entirely appropriate that the State use "public schools [to] . . . inculcat[e] fundamental values necessary to the maintenance of a democratic political system." *Ambach v. Norwick*, 441 U.S., at 77. . . .

On the other hand, as the plurality demonstrates, it is beyond dispute that schools and school boards must operate within the confines of the First Amendment. In a variety of academic settings the Court therefore has acknowledged the force of the principle that schools, like other enterprises operated by the State, may not be run in such a manner as to "prescribe what shall be orthodox in politics, nationalism, religion, or other matters of opinion." *West Virginia State Board of Education v. Barnette*, 319 U.S. 624, 642 . . . (1943). While none of these cases define the limits of a school board's authority to choose a curriculum and academic materials, they are based on the general proposition that "state-operated schools may not be enclaves of totalitarianism. . . . In our system, students may not be regarded as closed-circuit recipients of only that which the State chooses to communicate." *Tinker v. Des Moines School Dist.*, 393 U.S. 503, 511 . . . (1969).

The Court in *Tinker* thus rejected the view that "a State might so conduct its schools as to 'foster a homogeneous people.' " *Id.*, at 511, . . . quoting *Meyer v. Nebraska*, 262 U.S. 390, 402 . . . (1923). Similarly, *Keyishian v. Board of Regents*, 385 U.S. 589 . . . (1967)—a case that involved the State's attempt to remove "subversives" from academic positions at its universities, but that addressed itself more broadly to public education in general—held that "[t]he classroom is peculiarly the 'marketplace of ideas' "; the First Amend-

ment therefore "does not tolerate laws that cast a pall of orthodoxy over the classroom." *Id.*, at 603. . . . And *Barnette* is most clearly applicable here: its holding was based squarely on the view that "[f]ree public education, if faithful to the ideal of secular instruction and political neutrality, will not be partisan or enemy of any class, creed, party, or faction." The Court therefore made it clear that imposition of "ideological discipline" was not a proper undertaking for school authorities. 319 U.S., at 637. . . .

In combination with more generally applicable First Amendment rules, most particularly the central proscription of content-based regulations of speech, *see Police Department of Chicago v. Mosley*, 408 U.S. 92 . . .(1972), the cases outlined above yield a general principle: the State may not suppress exposure to ideas—for the sole purpose of suppressing exposure to those ideas—absent sufficiently compelling reasons. Because the school board must perform all its functions "within the limits of the Bill of Rights," *Barnette*, 319 U.S., at 637, . . . this principle necessarily applies in at least a limited way to public education. Surely this is true in an extreme case: as the plurality notes, it is difficult to see how a school board, consistent with the First Amendment, could refuse for political reasons to buy books written by Democrats or by Negroes, or books that are "anti-American" in the broadest sense of that term. Indeed, Justice Rehnquist appears "cheerfully [to] concede" this point. . . .

In my view, then, the principle involved here is both narrower and more basic than the "right to receive information" identified by the plurality. I do not suggest that the State has any affirmative obligation to provide students with information or ideas, something that may well be associated with a "right to receive." . . . And I do not believe, as the plurality suggests, that the right at issue here is somehow associated with the peculiar nature of the school library . . . if schools may be used to inculcate ideas, surely libraries may play a role in that process.[1]

---

[1]As a practical matter, however, it is difficult to see the First Amendment right that I believe is at work here playing a role in a school's choice of curriculum. The school's finite resources—as well as the limited number of hours in the day—require that education officials make sensitive choices between subjects to be offered and competing areas of academic emphasis; subjects generally are excluded simply because school officials have chosen to devote their resources to one rather than to another subject. . . . [A] choice of this nature does not run afoul of the First Amendment. In any event, the Court has recognized that students' First Amendment rights in most cases must give way if they interfere "with the schools' work or . . . [with] the rights of other students to be secure and to be let alone," *Tinker v. Des Moines School Dist.*, 393 U.S. 503, 508 . . . (1969), and such interference will rise to intolerable levels if public participation in the management of the curriculum becomes commonplace. In contrast, library books on a shelf intrude not at all on the daily operation of a school.

I also have some doubt that there is a theoretical distinction between removal of a book and failure to acquire a book. But as Judge Newman observed, there is a profound practical and evidentiary distinction between the two actions: "removal, more than failure to acquire, is likely to suggest that an impermissible political motivation may be present. There are many reasons why a book is not acquired, the most obvious being limited resources, but there are few legitimate reasons why a book, once acquired, should be removed from a library not filled to capacity." 638 F.2d 404, 436 (CA2 1980) (Newman, J., concurring in the result).

Instead, I suggest that certain forms of state discrimination between ideas are improper. In particular, our precedents command the conclusion that the State may not act to deny access to an idea simply because state officials disapprove of that idea for partisan or political reasons.[2]

Certainly, the unique environment of the school places substantial limits on the extent to which official decisions may be restrained by First Amendment values. But that environment also makes it particularly important that some limits be imposed. The school is designed to, and inevitably will, inculcate ways of thought and outlooks; if educators intentionally may eliminate all diversity of thought, the school will "strangle the free mind at its source and teach youth to discount important principles of our government as mere platitudes." *Barnette*, 319 U.S., at 637. . . . As I see it, then, the question in this case is how to make the delicate accommodation between the limited constitutional restriction that I think is imposed by the First Amendment, and the necessarily broad state authority to regulate education. In starker terms, we must reconcile the schools' "inculcative" function with the First Amendment's bar on "prescriptions of orthodoxy."

II

In my view, we strike a proper balance here by holding that school officials may not remove books for the purpose of restricting access to the political ideas or social perspectives discussed in them, when that action is motivated simply by the officials' disapproval of the ideas involved. It does not seem radical to suggest that state action calculated to suppress novel ideas or concepts is fundamentally antithetical to the values of the First Amendment. At a minimum, allowing a school board to engage in such conduct hardly teaches children to respect the diversity of ideas that is fundamental to the American system. In this context, then, the school board must "be able to show that its action was caused by something more than a mere desire to avoid the discomfort and unpleasantness that always accompany an unpopular viewpoint," *Tinker v. Des Moines School Dist.*, 393 U.S., at 509, . . . and that the board had something in mind in addition to the suppression of partisan or political views it did not share.

As I view it, this is a narrow principle. School officials must be able to choose one book over another, without outside interference, when the first book is deemed more relevant to the curriculum, or better written, or when one of a host of other politically neutral reasons is present. These decisions obviously will not implicate First Amendment values. And even absent space or financial limitations, First Amendment principles would allow a school board to refuse to make a book available to students because it contains offensive language, *cf. FCC v. Pacifica Foundation*, 438 U.S. 726, 757 . . . (1978) (Powell, J., concurring), or because it is psychologically or intellectually inappropriate for the age group, or even, perhaps, because the ideas it advances are "manifestly inimical to the public welfare." *Pierce v. Society of Sisters*, 268 U.S. 510, 534 . . . (1925). And, of course, school officials may choose one book over another because they believe that one subject is more important, or is more deserving of emphasis.

. . . And I believe that tying the First Amendment right to the purposeful suppression of ideas makes the concept more manageable than Justice Rehnquist acknowledges. Most people would recognize that refusing to allow discussion of current events in Latin class is a policy designed to "inculcate" Latin, not to suppress ideas. Similarly, removing a learned treatise criticizing American foreign policy from an elementary school library because the students would not understand it is an action unrelated to the purpose of suppressing ideas. In my view, however, removing the same treatise because it is "anti-American" raises a far more difficult issue.

* * *

Because I believe that the plurality has derived a standard similar to the one compelled by my analysis, I join all but Part IIA(1) of the plurality opinion. Justice White, concurring in the judgment. [Opinion omitted.]

Chief Justice Burger, with whom Justice Powell, Justice Rehnquist, and Justice O'Connor join, dissenting.

The First Amendment, as with other parts of the Constitution, must deal with new problems in a changing world. In an attempt to deal with a problem in an area traditionally left to the states, a plurality of the Court, in a lavish expansion going beyond any prior holding under the First Amendment, expresses its view that a school board's decision

---

[2] In effect, my view presents the obverse of the plurality's analysis: while the plurality focuses on the failure to provide information, I find crucial the State's decision to single out an idea for disapproval and then deny access to it.

concerning what books are to be in the school library is subject to federal court review. Were this to become the law, this Court would come perilously close to becoming a "super censor" of school board library decisions. Stripped to its essentials, the issue comes down to two important propositions: first, whether local schools are to be administered by elected school boards, or by federal judges and teenage pupils; and second, whether the values of morality, good taste, and relevance to education are valid reasons for school board decisions concerning the contents of a school library. In an attempt to place this case within the protection of the First Amendment, the plurality suggests a new "right" that, when shorn of the plurality's rhetoric, allows this Court to impose its own views about what books must be made available to students.

* * *

Justice Powell, dissenting.

The plurality opinion today rejects a basic concept of public school education in our country: that the States and locally elected school boards should have the responsibility for determining the educational policy of the public schools. After today's decision any junior high school student, by instituting a suit against a school board or teacher, may invite a judge to overrule an educational decision by the official body designated by the people to operate the schools.

* * *

Just this term the Court held, in an opinion I joined, that the children of illegal aliens must be permitted to attend the public schools. *See Plyler v. Doe,* 467 U.S. 202 . . . (1982). Quoting from earlier opinions, the Court noted that "the public school [is] a most vital civic institution for the preservation of a democratic system of government" and that the public schools are "the primary vehicle for transmitting 'the values on which our society rests.'" *Id.,* at 221. . . . By denying to illegal aliens the opportunity "to absorb the values and skills upon which our social order rests" the law under review placed a lifelong disability upon these illegal alien children. *Ibid.*

Today the plurality drains much of the content from these apt phrases. A school board's attempt to instill in its students the ideas and values on which a democratic system depends is viewed as an impermissible suppression of other ideas and values on which other systems of government and other societies thrive. Books may not be removed because they are indecent; extoll violence, intolerance and

racism; or degrade the dignity of the individual. Human history, not the least of the twentieth century, records the power and political life of these very ideas. But they are not our ideas or values. Although I would leave this educational decision to the duly constituted board, I certainly would not require a school board to promote ideas and values repugnant to a democratic society or to teach such values to children.

In different contexts and in different times, the destruction of written materials has been the symbol of despotism and intolerance. But the removal of nine vulgar or racist books from a high school library by a concerned local school board does not raise this specter. For me, today's decision symbolizes a debilitating encroachment upon the institutions of a free people.

Attached as an Appendix hereto is Judge Mansfield's summary of excerpts from the books at issue in this case.

Appendix

The excerpts which led the Board to look into the educational suitability of the books in question are set out (with minor corrections after comparison with the text of the books themselves) below. The pagination and the underlinings are retained from the original report used by the board. In newer editions of some of the books, the quotes appear at different pages.

"1) *SOUL ON ICE* by Eldridge Cleaver

Page quote

157–58 '. . . There are white men who will pay you to fuck their wives.

They approach you and say, 'How would you like to fuck a white woman?'

'What is this?' you ask. 'On the up-and-up,' he assures you. 'It's all right. She's my wife. She needs black rod, is all. She has to have it. It's like a medicine or drug to her. She has to have it. I'll pay you. It's all on the level, no trick involved. Interested?' You go with him and he drives you to their home. The three of you go into the bedroom. There is a certain type who will leave you and his wife alone and tell you to pile her real good. After it is all over, he will pay you and drive you to wherever you want to go. Then there are some who like to peep at you through a keyhole and watch you have his woman, or peep at you through a window, or lie under the bed and listen to the creaking of the bed as you work out. . . .'

"2) *A HERO AIN'T NOTHING BUT A SANDWICH* by Alice Childress

Page quote

10 'Hell, no! *Fuck the society.'*

64–65 'The hell with the junkie, the wino, the capitalist, the welfare checks, the world . . . yeah, and *fuck* you too!'

75–76 'They can have back the spread and curtains, I'm too old for them *fuckin* bunnies anyway.'

"3) *THE FIXER* by Bernard Malamud

Page quote

52 'What do you think goes on in the wagon at night: Are the drivers on their knees *fucking their mothers?'*

90 *'Fuck yourself,* said the blinker, etc.'

92 'Who else would do anything like that but a *motherfucking* Zhid?'

146 'No more noise out of you or I'll shoot your *Jew cock off.'*

189 'Also there's a lot of *fucking in the Old Testament,* so how is that religious?'

192 'You better go *fuck yourself,* Bok, said Kogin, I'm onto your Jew tricks.'

215 'Ding-dong giddyap. A *Jew's cock's* in the devil's hock.'

216 'You *cocksucker* Zhid, I ought make you lick it up off the floor.' "

4) *GO ASK ALICE* by Anonymous

Page quote

31 'I wonder if sex without acid could be so exciting, so wonderful, so indescribable. I always thought it just took a minute, or that it would be like dogs mating.'

47 'Chris and I walked into Richie and Ted's apartment to find the bastards stoned and making love to each other . . . low class queer.'

81 'shitty, goddamned, pissing, ass, goddamned be-Jesus, screwing life's, ass, shit. Doris was ten and had *humped* with who knows how many men in between . . . her current stepfather started having sex with her but good . . . *sonofabitch balling her'*

83 'but now when I face a girl its like facing a boy. I get all excited and turned on. *I want to screw with the girl . . .'*

84 'I'd rather screw with a guy . . . sometimes I want one of the girls to kiss me. I want her to touch me, to have her sleep under me.'

* * *

"5) *SLAUGHTERHOUSE FIVE* by Kurt Vonnegut, Jr.

Page quote

29 'Get out of the road, you dumb *motherfucker.'* The last word was still a novelty in the speech of white

people in 1944. It was fresh and astonishing to Billy, who had never *fucked* anybody . . .'

32 'You stake a guy out on an anthill in the desert—see? He's facing upward, and you put *honey* all over his *balls and pecker,* and you cut off his eyelids so he has to stare at the sun till he dies.'

34 'He had a prophylactic kit containing two tough condoms 'For the prevention of disease only!' . . . He had a dirty picture of a *woman* attempting *sexual intercourse with a shetland pony.'*

94 & 95 'But the Gospels actually taught this: Before you kill somebody, make absolutely sure he isn't well connected . . . The flaw in the Christ stories, said the visitor from outer space, was that Christ who didn't look like much, was actually the son of the Most Powerful Being in the Universe. Readers understood that, so, when they came to the crucifixion, they naturally thought . . . Oh boy—they sure picked the wrong guy to lynch this time! And that thought had a brother: There are right people to lynch. People not well connected. . . . The visitor from outer space made a gift to Earth of a new Gospel. In it, Jesus really WAS a nobody, and a pain in the neck to a lot of people with better connections than he had. . . . So the people amused themselves one day by nailing him to a cross and planting the cross in the ground. There couldn't possibly be any repercussions, the lynchers thought . . . since the new Gospel hammered home again and again what a nobody Jesus was. And then just before the nobody dies . . . the voice of God came crashing down. He told the people that he was adopting the bum as his son . . . God said this: *From this moment on, He will punish horribly anybody who torments a bum who has no connections.'*

* * *

"6) *THE BEST SHORT STORIES BY NEGRO WRITERS* Ed. by Langston Hughes

Page quote

176 'like bat's shit and camel piss,'

228 'that no-count bitch of a daughter of yours is up there up North making a whore of herself.'

237 'they made her get out and stand in front of the headlights of the car and pull down her pants and raise her dress—they said that was the only way they could be sure. And you can imagine what they said and what they did—.'

303 'You need some pussy. Come on, let's go up to the whore house on the hill.' 'Oh, these bastards, these bastards, this God damned Army and the bastards in it. The sons of bitches!'

436 'he produced a brown rag doll, looked at her again, then grabbed the doll by its legs and tore it part way up the middle. Then he jammed his finger into the rip between the doll's legs. The other men laughed. . . .'

444 'The pimps, hustlers, lesbians, and others trying to misuse me.'

* * *

"7) *BLACK BOY* by Richard Wright
Page quote
70–71 'We black children—seven or eight or nine years of age—used to run to the Jew's store and shout:

. . . Bloody Christ Killers
Never trust a Jew
Bloody Christ Killers
What won't a Jew do . . .
Red, white and blue
Your pa was a Jew
Your ma a dirty dago
What the hell is you?'

265 'Crush that nigger's nuts, nigger!' 'Hit that nigger!' 'Aw, fight, you goddam niggers!' 'Sock 'im, in his f-k-g piece!' 'Make 'im bleed!'

"8) *LAUGHING BOY* by Oliver LaFarge
Page quote
38 'I'll tell you, she is all bad; for two bits she will do the worst thing.'

258–59 'I was frightened when he wanted me to lie with him, but he made me feel all right. He knew all about how to make women forget themselves, that man.'

"9) *THE NAKED APE* by Desmond Morris
Page quote
73–74 'Also, the frontal approach provides the maximum possibility for stimulation of the female's clitoris during the pelvic thrusting of the male. It is true that it will be passively stimulated by the pulling effect of the male's thrusts, regardless of his body position in relation to the female, but in a face-to-face mating there will in addition be the direct rhythmic pressure of the male's pubic region on to the clitoral area, and this will considerably heighten the stimulation . . .' 'So it seems plausible to consider that face-to-face copulation is basic to our species. There are, of course, a number of variations that do not eliminate the frontal element: male above, female above, side by side, squatting, standing, and so on, but the most efficient and commonly used one is with both partners horizontal, the male above the female. . . .'

* * *

"10) *READER FOR WRITERS . . .*"
638 F.2d 404, 419–22 n. 1 (Mansfield, J., dissenting).

Justice Rehnquist, with whom The Chief Justice and Justice Powell join, dissenting.

Addressing only those aspects of the constitutional question which must be decided to determine whether or not the District Court was correct in granting summary judgment, I conclude that it was. I agree fully with the views expressed by The Chief Justice, and concur in his opinion. I disagree with Justice Brennan's opinion because it is largely hypothetical in character, failing to take account of the facts as admitted by the parties pursuant to local rules of the District Court for the Eastern District of New York, and because it is analytically unsound and internally inconsistent.

I

A

* * *

Considering only the respondents' description of the factual aspects of petitioners' motivation, Justice Brennan's apparent concern that the Board's action may have been a sinister political plot "to suppress ideas" may be laid to rest. The members of the Board, in deciding to remove these books, were undoubtedly influenced by their own "personal values, morals, and tastes," just as any member of a school board is apt to be so influenced in making decisions as to whether a book is educationally suitable. Respondents essentially conceded that some excerpts of the removed books "contained profanities, some were sexually explicit, some were ungrammatical, some were anti-American, and some were offensive to racial, religious, or ethnic groups."

Respondents also agreed that, "[a]lthough the books themselves were excluded from use in the schools in any way, [petitioners] have not precluded discussion about the themes of the books or the books themselves." . . . Justice Brennan's concern with the "suppression of ideas" thus seems entirely unwarranted on this state of the record, and his creation of constitutional rules to cover such eventualities is entirely gratuitous. Though for reasons stated in part II of this opinion I entirely disagree with Justice Brennan's treatment of the constitutional issue, I also disagree with his opinion for the entirely separate reason that it is not remotely tailored to the facts presented by this case.

In the course of his discussion, Justice Brennan states:

> "Petitioners rightly possess significant discretion to determine the content of their school libraries. But that discretion may not be exercised in a narrowly partisan or political manner. If a Democratic school board, motivated by party affiliation, ordered the removal of all books written by or in favor of Republicans, few would doubt that the order violated the constitutional rights of the students. . . . The same conclusion would surely apply if an all-white school board, motivated by racial animus, decided to remove all books authored by blacks or advocating racial equality and integration. Our Constitution does not permit the official suppression of ideas."

I can cheerfully concede all of this, but as in so many other cases the extreme examples are seldom the ones that arise in the real world of constitutional litigation. In this case the facts taken most favorably to respondents suggest that nothing of this sort happened. The nine books removed undoubtedly did contain "ideas," but in the light of the excerpts from them found in the dissenting opinion of Judge Mansfield in the Court of Appeals, it is apparent that eight of them contained demonstrable amounts of vulgarity and profanity, *see* 638 F.2d, at 419–22 n. 1, and the ninth contained nothing that could be considered partisan or political, *see id.*, at 428 n. 6. As already demonstrated, respondents admitted as much. Petitioners did not, for the reasons stated hereafter, run afoul of the First and Fourteenth Amendments by removing these particular books from the library in the manner in which they did. I would save for another day—feeling quite confident that that day will not arrive—the extreme examples posed in Justice Brennan's opinion.

B

Considerable light is shed on the correct resolution of the constitutional question in this case by examining the role played by petitioners. Had petitioners been the members of a town council, I suppose all would agree that, absent a good deal more than is present in this record, they could not have prohibited the sale of these books by private booksellers within the municipality. But we have also recognized that the government may act in other capacities than as sovereign, and when it does the First Amendment may speak with a different voice. . . . By the same token, expressive conduct which may not be prohibited by the State as sovereign may be proscribed by the State as property owner: "The State, no less than a private owner of property, has power to preserve the property under its control for the use to which it is lawfully dedicated." *Adderley v. Florida*, 385 U.S. 39, 47 . . . (1967) (upholding state prohibition of expressive conduct on certain state property).

With these differentiated roles of government in mind, it is helpful to assess the role of government as educator, as compared with the role of government as sovereign. When it acts as an educator, at least at the elementary and secondary school level, the government is engaged in inculcating social values and knowledge in relatively impressionable young people. Obviously there are innumerable decisions to be made as to what courses should be taught, what books should be purchased, or what teachers should be employed. In every one of these areas the members of a school board will act on the basis of their own personal or moral values, will attempt to mirror those of the community, or will abdicate the making of such decisions to so-called "experts." . . . In the very course of administering the many-faceted operations of a school district, the mere decision to purchase some books will necessarily preclude the possibility of purchasing others. The decision to teach a particular subject may preclude the possibility of teaching another subject. A decision to replace a teacher because of ineffectiveness may by implication be seen as a disparagement of the subject matter taught. In each of these instances, however, the book or the exposure to the subject matter may be acquired elsewhere. The managers of the school district are not proscribing it as to the citizenry in general, but are simply determining that it will not be included in the curriculum or school library. In short, actions by the government as educator do not raise the same First Amendment concerns as actions by the government as sovereign.

II

Justice Brennan would hold that the First Amendment gives high school and junior high school students a "right to receive ideas" in the school. . . . This right is a curious entitlement. It exists only in the library of the school, and only if the idea previously has been acquired by the school in book form. It provides no protection against a school board's decision not to acquire a particular book, even though that decision denies access to ideas as fully as removal of the book from the library, and it prohibits removal of previously acquired books only if the remover "dislike[s] the ideas contained in those books," even though removal for any other reason also denies the students access to the books. . . .

But it is not the limitations which Justice Brennan places on the right with which I disagree; they simply demonstrate his discomfort with the new doctrine which he fashions out of whole cloth. It is the very existence of a right to receive information, in the junior high school and high school setting, which I find wholly unsupported by our past decisions and inconsistent with the necessarily selective process of elementary and secondary education.

A

The right described by Justice Brennan has never been recognized in the decisions of this Court and is not supported by their rationale. . . .

* * *

. . . Justice Brennan correctly characterizes the right of access to ideas as "an inherent corollary of the rights of free speech and press" which "follows ineluctably from the sender's First Amendment right to send them." . . . But he then fails to recognize the predicate right to speak from which the students' right to receive must follow. It would be ludicrous, of course, to contend that all authors have a constitutional right to have their books placed in junior high school and high school libraries. And yet without such a right our prior precedents would not recognize the reciprocal right to receive information. Justice Brennan disregards this inconsistency with our prior cases and fails to explain the constitutional or logical underpinnings of a right to hear ideas in a place where no speaker has the right to express them.

Justice Brennan also correctly notes that the reciprocal nature of the right to receive information derives from the fact that it "is a necessary predicate to the recipient's meaningful exercise of his own rights of speech, press, and political freedom." . . . But the denial of access to ideas inhibits one's own acquisition of knowledge only when that denial is relatively complete. If the denied ideas are readily available from the same source in other accessible locations, the benefits to be gained from exposure to those ideas have not been foreclosed by the State. This fact is inherent in the right-to-receive cases relied on by Justice Brennan, every one of which concerned the complete denial of access to the ideas sought. . . .

B

There are even greater reasons for rejecting Justice Brennan's analysis, however, than the significant fact that we have never adopted it in the past. "The importance of public schools in the preparation of individuals for participation as citizens, and in the preservation of the values on which our society rests, has long been recognized by our decisions." *Ambach v. Norwick*, 441 U.S. 68 . . . (1979). Public schools fulfill the vital role of teaching students the basic skills necessary to function in our society, and of "inculcating fundamental values necessary to the maintenance of a democratic political system." *Id.*, at 77. . . . The idea that such students have a right of access, in the school, to information other than that thought by their educators to be necessary is contrary to the very nature of an inculcative education.

Education consists of the selective presentation and explanation of ideas. The effective acquisition of knowledge depends upon an orderly exposure to relevant information. Nowhere is this more true than in elementary and secondary schools, where, unlike the broad-ranging inquiry available to university students, the courses taught are those thought most relevant to the young students' individual development. Of necessity, elementary and secondary educators must separate the relevant from the irrelevant, the appropriate from the inappropriate. Determining what information not to present to the students is often as important as identifying relevant material. This winnowing process necessarily leaves much information to be discovered by students at another time or in another place, and is fundamentally inconsistent with any constitutionally required eclecticism in public education.

* * *

As already mentioned, elementary and secondary schools are inculcative in nature. The libraries of such schools serve as supplements to this inculcative role. Unlike university or public libraries, elementary and secondary school libraries are not designed for free-wheeling inquiry; they are tailored, as the public school curriculum is tailored, to the teaching of basic skills and ideas. Thus, Justice Brennan cannot rely upon the nature of school libraries to escape the fact that the First Amendment right to receive information simply has no application to the one public institution which, by its very nature, is a place for the selective conveyance of ideas.

After all else is said, however, the most obvious reason that petitioners' removal of the books did not violate respondents' right to receive information is the ready availability of the books elsewhere. Students are not denied books by their removal from a school library. The books may be borrowed from a public library, read at a university library, purchased at a bookstore, or loaned by a friend. The government as educator does not seek to reach beyond the confines of the school. Indeed, following the removal from the school library of the books at issue in this case, the local public library put all nine books on display for public inspection. Their contents were fully accessible to any inquisitive student.

C

Justice Brennan's own discomfort with the idea that students have a right to receive information from their elementary or secondary schools is demonstrated by the artificial limitations which he places upon the right—limitations which are supported neither by logic nor authority and which are inconsistent with the right itself. The attempt to confine the right to the library is one such limitation, the fallacies of which have already been demonstrated.

As a second limitation, Justice Brennan distinguishes the act of removing a previously acquired book from the act of refusing to acquire the book in the first place: "[N]othing in our decision today affects in any way the discretion of a local school board to choose books to add to the libraries of their schools. . . . [O]ur holding today affects only the discretion to remove books." . . . If Justice Brennan truly has found a "right to receive ideas," . . . however, this distinction between acquisition and removal makes little sense. The failure of a library to acquire a book denies access to its contents just as effectively as does the removal of the book from the library's shelf. As a result of either action the book cannot be found in the "principal locus" of freedom discovered by Justice Brennan. . . .

The justification for this limiting distinction is said by Justice Brennan to be his concern in this case with "the suppression of ideas." . . . Whatever may be the analytical usefulness of this appealing sounding phrase, . . . the suppression of ideas surely is not the identical twin of the denial of access to information. Not every official act which denies access to an idea can be characterized as a suppression of the idea.

Thus unless the "right to receive information" and the prohibition against "suppression of ideas" are each a kind of mother-hubbard catch phrase for whatever First Amendment doctrines one wishes to cover, they would not appear to be interchangeable.

* * *

The final limitation placed by Justice Brennan upon his newly discovered right is a motive requirement: the First Amendment is violated only "[i]f petitioners intended by their removal decision to deny respondents access to ideas with which petitioners disagreed." . . . But bad motives and good motives alike deny access to the books removed. If Justice Brennan truly recognizes a constitutional right to receive information, it is difficult to see why the reason for the denial makes any difference. Of course Justice Brennan's view is that intent matters because the First Amendment does not tolerate an officially prescribed orthodoxy. . . . But this reasoning mixes First Amendment apples and oranges. The right to receive information differs from the right to be free from an officially prescribed orthodoxy. Not every educational denial of access to information casts a pall of orthodoxy over the classroom.

It is difficult to tell from Justice Brennan's opinion just what motives he would consider constitutionally impermissible. I had thought that the First Amendment proscribes content-based restrictions on the marketplace of ideas. *See Widmar v. Vincent*, 454 U.S. 263, 269–70 (1981). Justice Brennan concludes, however, that a removal decision based solely upon the "educational suitability" of a book or upon its perceived vulgarity is " 'perfectly permissible.' " . . . But such determinations are based as much on the content of the book as determinations that the book espouses pernicious political views.

* * *

III

Accepting as true respondents' assertion that petitioners acted on the basis of their own "personal values, morals, and tastes," . . . I find the actions taken in this case hard to distinguish from the myriad choices made by school boards in the routine supervision of elementary and secondary schools. "Courts do not and cannot intervene in the resolution of conflicts which arise in the daily operation of school systems and which do not directly and sharply implicate basic constitutional values." *Epperson v. Arkansas*,

393 U.S., at 104. . . . In this case respondents' rights of free speech and expression were not infringed, and by respondents' own admission no ideas were "suppressed." I would leave to another day the harder cases.

* * *

NOTES AND QUESTIONS

1. Right to Receive Information

Justice Brennan, in his plurality opinion, relies upon a right to receive information and ideas to justify the conclusion that the removal of books from a public school library may violate the First Amendment. What is the constitutional basis for such a right? *See generally* Lee, "The Supreme Court and the Right to Receive Expression," 1987 *Sup. Ct. Rev.* 303. Does the right to acquire information and knowledge flow from a right to speak? Suppose there is no willing speaker? For example, might a court require a school library to acquire books that a student wishes to read? If the "right to know" does not encompass the acquisition of books, why should it encompass decisions to remove books? If it does extend to book acquisitions, why should it not include course offerings? *See, e.g., State ex rel. Sheibley v. School Dist.*, 31 Neb. 552, 48 N.W. 393 (1891). For example, might a student seek a court order to require a school district to offer geology if no such course is currently offered? *See generally* Yudof, "Library Book Selection and the Public Schools," 59 *Ind. L. J.* 527, 545–46 (1984) (hereinafter "Library Book Selection"); Note, "State Indoctrination and the Protection of Non-State Voices in the Schools: Justifying a Prohibition of School Library Censorship," 35 *Stan. L. Rev.* 497 (1983).

Do authors, editors, and publishers have a constitutional right to have their books acquired by the state for dissemination in public schools?

Justice Brennan emphasizes the special nature of libraries as a factor in his constitutional analysis. What is so special about the library? *See* "Library Book Selection" at 546–48. Is it that a library can seek a balanced presentation of views through many books, but in the classroom a single text often is required? Or is it that each student can acquire knowledge from library books without interfering with the studies of others? That is, students may read from many books simultaneously in the library (or at home), whereas in class there is conflict if each per-

son chooses what to learn and discuss. In effect, is Justice Brennan saying that the right to know, when exercised in a library, does not disrupt the educational mission of the school? In any event, what is the logical nexus between the right to know and the special characteristics of the school library?

How, if at all, would *Pico* apply to a school district's decision to remove a statue of a Confederate war hero on the ground that the statue conveys repugnant ideas about African Americans?

Would it be unconstitutional for a library only to acquire books that were directly related to the courses that formed the school's curriculum? What does Justice Rehnquist have to say about this?

If compulsory schooling is legitimate and if education inherently involves selection and judgment as to what will be studied, how coherent is a right to know in the public school setting? *See* van Geel, "The Prisoner's Dilemma and Education Policy," 3 *Notre Dame J.L. Ethics & Pub. Pol'y* 301 (1988). If there is such a right, what is the relevance of motive? Why should it matter whether a book was removed for ideological or financial reasons? Or should the Court "have established a principle that would protect students from any effort by public schools to inculcate pupils with political ideas, attitudes, viewpoints, ideologies, values, or beliefs"? van Geel, "The Search for Constitutional Limits on Governmental Authority to Inculcate Youth," 62 *Tex. L. Rev.* 197, 239 (1983). Is this but another way of saying that public schooling is not a legitimate enterprise?

Under *Pico*, may a public school block access to certain World Wide Web sites on the school computers? *See* Harpaz, "Internet Speech and the First Amendment Right of Public School Students," 2000 *BYU Educ. & L.J.* 123. What kind of analysis should courts apply to this issue? *See generally* Mark S. Nadel, "The First Amendment's Limitations on the Use of Internet Filtering in Public and School Libraries: What Content Can Librarians Exclude?" 78 *Tex. L. Rev.* 1117 (2000).

2. Unconstitutional Motivation

Justice Blackmun seeks to balance the inculcative or socialization mission of schools against a constitutional prohibition on the establishment of orthodoxy, and he seeks to achieve this balance through a motivation test: "I suggest that certain forms of state discrimination between ideas are improper. In particular, our precedents command the conclusion that the State may not act to deny access to an idea simply because state officials disapprove of the idea for partisan or political reasons." *See also Zykan v. Warsaw Community School Corp.*, 631 F.2d 1300 (7th Cir. 1980). How many of the justices accept this motivation framework for analysis—even if they disagree as to the application of the principle in *Pico? See* "Library Book Selection" at 549. What is the evidence that the Island Trees school board was motivated by a desire to impose a rigid political orthodoxy? Is it more difficult to justify a deacquisition decision than a decision not to acquire a book in the first place? Can books be too expensive to dust and maintain? Is the annotated list of books dispositive? What of the failure of the board to abide by established policies governing the library? *See* "Library Book Selection" at 551.

What is the difference between an illegitimate "pall of orthodoxy" and a legitimate educational effort, in good faith, to socialize students? Is not the flag salute law challenged in *Barnette* an attempt to create an unconstitutional pall of orthodoxy? Further, why is it unconstitutional to eliminate books written by or about Republicans or minority leaders, but constitutional to remove books that are vulgar or promote promiscuity? Are school officials not closing the minds of students to the pro-vulgarity and libertine positions? Should courts distinguish between consensual values (e.g., opposition to drug abuse and sexual promiscuity, or the fostering of racial tolerance, good spelling, and patriotism) and disputed political and social questions (e.g., advocacy of radical feminism, support of the New Deal, opposition to abortion)? *Cf. Arnold v. Board of Education*, 880 F.2d 305 (11th Cir. 1989) (school counselors may not "coerce" minors to refrain from consulting parents on abortion decision). Is this a principled distinction? Is Justice Blackmun's concurrence "profoundly at odds with itself"? van Geel, *supra* at 326. Or is he attempting to define a constitutional concept of democratic education?

In the light of *Barnette*, should the definition of orthodoxy turn on how ideas are taught or promulgated and not on the content of the ideas? *See* O'Brien, "The Promise of *Pico*: A New Definition of Orthodoxy," 97 *Yale L.J.* 1805 (1988).

Might the constitutionality of a decision hinge entirely on motivation? For example, would a decision not to acquire a Chinese history book on the ground that Chinese history is not part of the curriculum be constitutional, whereas a decision based on objections to the ideas expressed in the book would be unconstitutional? *Cf. McCarthy v. Fletcher*, 207 Cal. App.3d 130, 254 Cal. Rptr. 714, 720 (1989).

What if a particular book is both ideologically objectionable to members of the school board and vulgar? If the board gives the wrong reason, is its action unconstitutional after *Pico*? Is Justice Rehnquist saying that a deacquisition decision is justifiable if the board could have acted on the basis of vulgarity—even if it did not?

Are most of the justices saying "that a school board's removal decision is legitimate if it is based on the educational suitability of the books"? *See Virgil v. School Bd. of Columbia County*, 862 F.2d 1517 (11th Cir. 1989). *See generally* "Library Book Selection" at 549. Is this tantamount to saying that school officials must act in good faith, good faith being tested against the educational mission of public schools? *See* Yudof, "*Tinker* Tailored: Good Faith, Civility, and Student Expression," 69 *St. John's L. Rev.* 365 (1995). Would the removal of religiously oriented books be constitutional? Removal of the Bible? *See Roberts v. Madigan*, 921 F.2d 1047 (10th Cir. 1990). What of the removal of a library book because it is insulting to students of color? Is there a distinction between a library book and a school emblem? *See Crosby v. Holsinger*, 852 F.2d 801 (4th Cir. 1988).

3. *Irrevocable Delegation*

If a school board has delegated decision-making power over school libraries to librarians and other officials, should it be permitted to revoke that delegation in particular cases? *See* "Library Book Selection" at 553–59. If a board is not constitutionally required to delegate authority over book selection, what is the warrant for a holding that it may not revoke a delegation when it disagrees with particular acquisition decisions? Should a board have the authority to remove books on account of their content only if the legislature expressly authorizes such actions? *See Wexner v. Anderson Union High Sch. Dist. Bd. of Trustees*, 209 Cal.App.3d 1438, 258 Cal. Rptr. 26 (1989).

4. *Book Selection and Procedural Due Process*

In *Loewen v. Turnipseed*, 488 F.Supp. 1138 (N.D. Miss. 1980), a "rating committee," appointed by the governor and state superintendent of education in Mississippi, approved a book entitled *Your Mississippi* for purchase by the State Textbook Purchasing Board and disapproved a book entitled *Mississippi: Conflict and Change*. The books were considered for use in ninth grade classes in Mississippi History, and apparently the state would purchase approved books for both public and parochial schools. The controversy arose because *Mississippi: Conflict and Change* allegedly emphasized the mistreatment of African Americans in Mississippi, while the alternative did not. The rating committee split on the issue, with the white majority outvoting the black minority.

The court ultimately held the selection was motivated by racial discrimination, intended to perpetuate segregation, and was therefore unconstitutional. It also concluded that the rating committee's procedure for selecting the textbooks was unconstitutional. Mississippi law did not give "those adversely affected by it a voice in the matter." 488 F.Supp. at 1153. Since the publishers of the books were given an opportunity to present their positions to the committee, presumably the court had in mind the authors, students, faculty, and school districts across the state, and, indeed, they were the plaintiffs.

A governmental body is not constitutionally required to hold an adversary hearing in deciding to award, for example, a construction contract for a public building. On the other hand, governments normally are required to hold a due process hearing where their actions infringe on a protected property right or a liberty interest (see chapter 3). Should a state or local government be required to hold a hearing when it decides to purchase some textbooks and not others?

5. Multiculturalism, Discrimination, and the Public School Curriculum

Crosby v. Holsinger
852 F.2d 801 (4th Cir. 1988).

Ervin, Circuit Judge:

This is the second appearance of "Johnny Reb" in this court. Johnny Reb, the former cartoon symbol of the Fairfax High School Rebels, was eliminated by defendant-appellee Harry Holsinger, the school's principal, after he received complaints from black students and parents. Students protested his decision in a number of ways before filing this action. The district court initially dismissed it as frivolous, but we reversed. 816 F.2d 162 (4th Cir.1987).* At trial, the court granted a directed verdict for Holsinger as to the broad "censorship" claim, and the jury returned a

verdict for him on plaintiff-appellant Cheryl Crosby's narrower "protest restriction" claim. We affirm.

Holsinger acted to remove the symbol based on complaints that it offended black students and a suggestion by the school's Minority Achievement Task Force. He then allowed the students to choose a new symbol which was to be unrelated to the Confederacy.

After the elimination of Johnny Reb, the students protested by holding rallies at school, mounting a petition drive, attending a school board meeting, and displaying blue ribbons. Except for a single incident involving Crosby, Holsinger did nothing to interfere with these protests. In the one instance, he initially stopped Crosby from posting notices on school bulletin boards of the school board meeting before allowing it the next day. . . .

There is a difference between tolerating student speech and affirmatively promoting it. . . .

A school mascot or symbol bears the stamp of approval of the school itself. Therefore, school authorities are free to disassociate the school from such a symbol because of educational concerns. Here, Principal Holsinger received complaints that Johnny Reb offended blacks and limited their participation in school activities, so he eliminated the symbol based on legitimate concerns. Except to make the rough threshold judgment that this decision has an educational component, we will not interfere, and it is clear that educational concerns prompted Holsinger's decision.[2]

＊ ＊ ＊

. . . [S]chool officials have the authority to disassociate the school from controversial speech even if it may limit student expression. Principal Holsinger was within his power to remove a school symbol that blacks found offensive.

Affirmed.

6. Is Crosby Consistent with Pico and Barnette?

The court holds in *Crosby* that the school principal's decision to eliminate the Johnny Reb cartoon symbol for Fairfax High School was prompted by educational concerns and that therefore there was no violation of the freedom of expression of the objecting students. On its face, the court's decision appears to be consistent with the view of most of the justices in *Pico* that good faith educational decisions regarding

---

*Citing *Augustus v. School Board*, 507 F.2d 152, 155–56 (5th Cir. 1975); *Banks v. Muncie Community Schools*, 433 F.2d 292, 298 (7th Cir. 1970).

[2]Appellants argue that Holsinger created a public forum by opening the selection process for a new symbol to outside suggestions. School facilities, however, are deemed a public forum only if opened "for indiscriminate use by the general public," while "permitting limited discourse" does not create such a forum. . . .

library book selections are not constitutionally infirm. But why is not the principal's action an example of attempting to suppress ideas, to impose a pall of orthodoxy? Is it not precisely the symbolism of the Johnny Reb cartoon, rooted in the slavery practiced in the Confederacy, that is objectionable to the Minority Achievement Task Force and Principal Holsinger? Is racial equality a consensual value akin to teaching children not to abuse drugs and alcohol? Suppose that the symbol for Fairfax High School were two clasped hands, one black and one white, and that this symbol agitated segregationists in the student body. If the principal eliminated this symbol, would the result be the same as in *Crosby* if a number of students filed suit on First Amendment grounds? If not, is the relevant distinction between good faith educational judgment and suppression of political ideas or is it between good values and bad values? *Cf. Clarke v. Board of Educ. of Sch. Dist. of Omaha*, 338 N.W.2d 272, 215 Neb. 250 (1983). Is your answer influenced by the fact that the Thirteenth Amendment abolishes slavery and the Fourteenth Amendment affords African Americans the equal protection of the laws? Is *Crosby* an affirmation of democratic education?

7. *Racially Discriminatory Motivation*

More generally, if a book selection, choice of curriculum, or other school decision involving the communication of ideas is motivated by racial discrimination, does the governmental speech violate the First Amendment (or perhaps the Fourteenth Amendment)? Should materials or books that contain racial slurs or stereotypes or that show particular racial groups in an unfavorable light give rise to constitutionally cognizable injuries? What is the nature of the harm? What is the constitutional violation? In short, can a school system violate the Constitution by what it says as well as what it does? *See Loewen v. Turnipseed, infra.*

8. *Equal Protection: Challenges to the Rejection of Materials Proposed for Use*

In *Loewen v. Turnipseed*, 488 F.Supp. 1138 (N.D. Miss. 1980), described in note 4 after the *Pico* case, *supra*, the court's finding of a motive to discriminate in approving a textbook for adoption was based on the following evidence. The committee had split along racial lines, with five white members refusing even to rate *Mississippi: Conflict and Change* while the two African American members of the committee supported its adoption. Two of the white members of the committee had said in their evaluations of the rejected book that it was "too racially oriented" and that it did not present "a true picture of the history of Mississippi." The failure of the other white members of the committee to indicate their reasons for rejection—itself a violation of their statutory duty—was a departure from normal procedure indicative of an improper motive. In the court's view, the history of the whole statewide textbook adoption system revealed a racially discriminatory purpose in the establishment of the system, namely, a desire on the part of the legislature to insure that textbook selection reflected the predominant racial attitudes of the day. The rejected book had received favorable reviews in scholarly publications and in letters to the editors of the book from faculty members at several prominent universities. And the state failed to establish that rejection of the book had been based on alleged violations of the procedural and technical standards promulgated by the state textbook purchasing board. Thus, the court concluded that it was the treatment the book gave to controversial racial issues which led to its rejection and that this was not a justifiable reason for rejection by the committee. The court ordered that both books be eligible for consideration by local school districts. What if the court had ordered the removal of the allegedly biased book from the list of approved books? Is it appropriate or constitutional for courts to ban objectionable books from public schools? What would be the standard? Should the standard include books objectionable on grounds other than race?

9. *"Sanitized" Textbooks*

A number of commentators have suggested that modern American textbooks strive to achieve "neutrality" by eliminating all discussion of controversy, hostility to American values, or cultural differences. *See, e.g.,* J. Nelson & G. Roberts, *The Censors and the Schools*, (1977); H. Kallen, *The Education of Free Men* (1949); Krug, " 'Safe' Textbooks and Citizenship Education," 68 *Sch. Rev.* 463 (1960). *See generally* F. Fitzgerald, *America Revised* (1979). The problem is thought to be not so much that particular groups are offended by the text; rather the problem is that history, in particular, may be distorted in an attempt to please all groups. Professor Stephen E. Gottlieb has ably summarized this perspective. Gottlieb, "In the Name of Patriotism: The Constitutionality of 'Bending' History in Public Secondary Schools," 62 *N.Y.U. L.Rev.* 497, 504–508 (1987):

The effort to pull ideology out of school is evident in battles over history textbooks. Although a few students in the best schools are exposed to better textbooks, most students read carefully censored books. The pursuit of "neutrality" often leads to censorship. The American Textbook Publishers Institute has counseled publishers "to avoid statements that might prove offensive to economic, religious, racial or social groups or any civil, fraternal, patriotic or philanthropic societies in the whole United States." Textbook manufacturers appear to have responded in some cases by deleting materials reflecting cultural differences that might have offended someone. Interest group pressures from diverse ideological camps have resulted in the deletion of materials that would undercut the perception of an American monopoly on decency, as variously defined. Business interests have occasionally attempted to intervene in textbook selection to remove materials considered hostile to the "American system." American policy is sanitized. Books rarely report questionable government action.

Such apparently consistent official wisdom implies that democracy can function without a loyal opposition. Perhaps the most strikingly consistent feature of history textbooks is that they minimize the role of dissent in our history. Government decisions that appear decent or beneficial are often portrayed without any of the political controversy that created them. When opposition from outside government is described, it is frequently not credited with any impact on the eventual government decision. On the issues of Vietnam and McCarthyism, for example, generally only speech by members of the executive and legislative branches is portrayed as effective. Public opinion when it does oppose government is left largely mysterious—springing without leadership or courage from the bowels of an inexplicably well-informed public.

* * *

This portrayal of democracy without disagreement or opposition is consistent in its exclusion of fundamental challenges to the social and economic system. Dissenting voices from the right as well as left are often ignored. Some conservative perspectives are simply omitted from textbooks. For example, though the right-to-work movement played a major role in shaping the Taft-Hartley Act, which continues to govern American labor relations, its activities and ideas are entirely ignored by most textbooks. In another example, the common view that President Franklin Roosevelt was too accommodating towards the Soviet Union at the end of World War II has been omitted from some textbooks.

Most conflict has been edited out of history textbooks in order to avoid affronting any group involved in textbook selection. Racial, ethnic, and sexual roles are distilled to satisfy reigning stereotypes. At one time, publishers were under pressure from the Ku Klux Klan to excise favorable references to Jews and Catholics. More recently, traditional distinctions in sex roles were simply obscured, rather than presented in a balanced light. Textbooks ignored or distorted black history and culture until the 1960s. Even now, the portrayal of the current positions of blacks and women in the textbooks omits a realistic portrayal of the battles that led to their gains. In the newer books, groups are depicted as "struggling," but it is rarely clear against whom. Farm workers, Native Americans, and Blacks are present, but growers, the Bureau of Indian Affairs, and institutionalized racism are mysteriously absent. The early development of the labor movement is similarly portrayed; industrialists are depicted as philanthropic, while skill and ethnic divisions among workers are treated as "natural" with no attempt to explain employer manipulation of such differences.

Do you agree with Professor Gottlieb? What emphasis should textbooks for students in "common schools" have? Should textbooks emphasize dissenting views or the conventional views about political culture? Or should the aspiration be objectivity and accuracy? Is that possible?

10. Nonconstitutional Approaches

In a nonconstitutional challenge, would the following statute, Cal. Educ. Code Ann. § 51501 (1978 Special Pamphlet), provide assistance?

> No textbook or other instructional materials shall be adopted by the state board or any governing board for use in the public schools which contains any matter reflecting adversely upon persons because of their race, sex, color, creed, national origin or ancestry.

What does the phrase "reflecting adversely upon persons because of . . ." mean? *See* Note, "California's 'Social Content' Guidelines for Textbooks," 2 *Const. Comm.* 301 (1985). Would books containing truthful statements that might be viewed adversely by the group referred to be barred by this statute? Whose opinion determines whether or not a book reflects adversely?

11. Gender Bias in the Curriculum

While racial classifications have been declared by the Supreme Court to be "suspect" and subject to strict scrutiny, gender-based classifications, in the Court's most recent cases, have been approached under a standard of review less demanding than strict scrutiny. For a discussion of legal developments in this area, see chapter 7. How should the courts respond, if at all, to books and courses that allegedly cast women in a stereotypical or inferior fashion? May legislatures ban the use of gender-biased materials in public schools? What form should such laws take?

12. *Freedom of Expression, Confederate Symbols, and Multiculturalism*

The decision in *Crosby* deals with the constitutional authority of school officials to remove a school symbol repugnant to African American students, and the court holds that such a decision does not violate the First Amendment rights of students. The focus, however, is on what the school chooses to communicate and its efforts at self-censorship. A related question, addressed generally in Section III of this chapter, is whether school authorities may adopt and implement regulations to ban student expression that is offensive to minority or other students. *See West v. Derby Unified Sch. Dist.*, 206 F.3d 1358 (10th Cir. 2000). Both questions, while presenting different constitutional issues, may be perceived as flowing from a clash of cultures, and such clashes appear to be occurring with greater frequency in recent decades.

Even if *Crosby* is correctly decided, does it follow that public schools may bar individual students from displaying Confederate symbols on campus? Should the result turn on whether the wearing of the symbols results in disruption of school operations? Whether racial tensions are increased? *See* Section III, *infra*. Is a school policy constitutional if it bans "any written material, either printed or in . . . handwriting, that is racially divisive or creates ill will or hatred"? What if the policy prohibits a student from drawing a Confederate flag? *See West v. Derby Unified Sch. Dist.*, *supra*. Equally, or more important, the controversy may reveal a deeper level of conflict over whether public schools are culturally biased. What to many white students may appear as a good faith effort to transmit a common culture may be viewed by minority students as biased and inattentive to the cultural achievements of groups other than the white majority. African American students may view black history month or courses dealing with multiculturalism as much-needed correctives to curricular imbalances, whereas many whites may perceive multiculturalism as a type of interest group, special pleading. The following note attempts to examine briefly the current debate on multiculturalism.

Note on Multicultural Education

The multiculturalism movement has added a new dimension to the debate over the content of school curricula. *See* T. Gitlin, *The Twilight of Common Dreams: Why America Is Wracked by Culture Wars* (1995); D. D'Souza, *Illiberal Education: The Politics of Race and Sex on Campus* (1992) (higher education); A. Schlesinger, *The Disuniting of America* (1991). Proponents of a multicultural education claim that American schools emphasize Western European culture at the expense of other cultures. They differ, however, on the extent of the problem and the remedy to be applied.

Commentators have identified two versions of multiculturalism—a weaker version and a stronger form—both of which depend on the premises that education can reshape students' values and that schools can be something more than a reflection of prevailing mores. Proponents of the weaker form seek equality for cultural groups by ensuring that the school curriculum portrays accurately and fairly the contributions of different cultures to American society. That is, the weaker version attempts to change the way people think about African American, Native American, Latino, and other cultures by teaching all students more about those cultures, thus encouraging the majority to treat non-European traditions and values with dignity and respect. The weaker form of multiculturalism also finds support in sound educational practice: one cannot understand American history without understanding the contributions of African Americans, Asian Americans, Latinos, and women in building the nation. Nor can any humanities curriculum claim to be complete if it ignores Latin American poets, works by African American novelists, the Koran, or Asian art. Proponents of this vision believe that to be a genuine scholar, teacher, or student, one must accept a genuine form of multiculturalism.

The weaker version of multiculturalism is a critique of educational practice, premised largely on normative concepts of democratic education. *See Olneck*, "Terms of Inclusion: Has Multiculturalism Redefined Equality in American Education," 101 *Am. J. of Educ.* 234 (1993) (addressing issues of bilingual education). The stronger version is more a critique of Western European culture in general and American culture in particular. This version depends upon a more controversial set of ideas: (1) mere historical accuracy, inclusion of cultural perspectives that have been overlooked, and tolerance of diverse cultures are inadequate, for education should promote and maintain multiculturalism; (2) the American heritage, at least as taught in universities and public schools, is inherently racist and oppressive; (3) the social, educational, emotional, and economic plight of many members of ethnic and other minority groups is caused, at least in part, by the cultural biases of American education; and (4) the remedy is to gain control of the socialization processes in public schools.

Professor Boateng has advocated the stronger form of multicultural education on the following grounds:

> The comparatively poor performance of African-American children in the public school system has been attributed to a variety of factors. One of the most injurious of these factors . . . is the continuous deculturalization of the African-American child and the neglect of African-American cultural values in the curriculum. . . .
>
> . . . . Culture provides the blueprint that determines the way an individual thinks, feels, and behaves in society. To deculturalize African-American children is, therefore, to deprive them of that which determines the way they think, feel, and behave.
>
> * * *
>
> . . . [M]ulticultural instruction needs to be pervasive rather than supplementary. . . . Since there is a long-standing assumption that only that which is Euro-American is American, and Eurocentric curriculum cannot be changed by simply adding units or lessons here and there about African-American[s] or Chicanos. American history, literature, art, music, and culture should be taught from diverse ethnic and cultural perspectives rather than from only a Euro-American perspective. Multicultural education experts recommend using the conceptual approach in reaching this goal.
>
> In the conceptual curriculum, the understanding of such concepts as racism, acculturation, and assimilation is paramount; the cultural group selected to illustrate the concepts becomes a secondary issue. . . . However, since examples have traditionally been drawn from the Euro-American culture, there is a need to strive for balance by selecting content from other cultures and ethnic groups.

F. Boateng, "Combatting Deculturalization of the African-American Child in the Public School System: A Multicultural Approach," in *Going to School: The African-American Experience* 73, 75 (K. Lomotey, ed. 1990).

Philosopher John Searle has been critical of this stronger version of multiculturalism. While often couched in the language of eliminating elitist practices or promoting excellence and historical accuracy, he believes that this version affirms more radical and contested assumptions:

> [First,] the history of "Western Civilization" is in large part a history of oppression. Internally, Western civilization oppressed women, various slave and serf populations, and ethnic and cultural minorities generally. In foreign affairs, the history of Western civilization is one of imperialism and colonialism. The so-called canon of Western civilization consists in the official publications of this system of oppression, and it is no accident that the authors in the "canon" are almost exclusively Western white males, because the civilization itself is ruled by a caste consisting almost entirely of Western white males. So you cannot reform education by admitting new members to the club, by opening up the canon: the whole idea of "the canon" has to be abolished. It has to be abolished in favor of something that is "multicultural" and "nonhierarchical."
>
> * * *
>
> . . . [Second,] in addition to having political objections to the United States and Europe, many members of the cultural left think that the primary function of teaching the humanities is political: they do not really believe that the humanities are valuable in their own right except as a means of achieving "social transformation." They (apparently) accept that in subjects like physics and mathematics there may be objective and socially independent criteria of excellence (though they do not say much about the sciences at all), but where the humanities are concerned they think that the criteria that matter are essentially political. The argument goes: since any policy in the humanities will inevitably have a political dimension, courses in the humanities might as well be explicitly and beneficially political, instead of being disguised vehicles of oppression.

J. Searle, "The Storm Over the University," *The New York Review*, December 6, 1990 at 34, 35, 36. *See also* T. Wolfe, *Hooking Up* 113–130 (2000).

As Searle suggests, some proponents of the stronger version of multiculturalism believe that the primary value of the humanities lies in their political dimension and that education is and should be treated as a cultural form of politics. Consider the following remarks by Henry Giroux:

> How we read or define a "canonical" work may not be as important as challenging the overall function and social uses the notion of the canon has served. Within this type of discourse, the canon can be analyzed as part of a wider set of relations that connect the academic disciplines, teaching, and power to considerations defined through broader, intersecting political and cultural concerns such as race, class, gender, ethnicity, and nationalism. What is in question here is not merely a defense of a particular canon, but the issue of struggle and

empowerment. In other words, the liberal arts should be defended in the interest of creating critical rather than "good" citizens. The notion of the liberal arts has to be reconstituted around a knowledge-power relationship in which the question of curriculum is seen as a form of cultural and political production grounded in a radical conception of citizenship and public wisdom.

Searle, *supra* at 36 (quoting Giroux). Many proponents of the stronger form of multiculturalism thus reject the notion that it is possible to make curricular choices or to assign readings on the basis of literary or intellectual merit. Calling such determinations elitist and hierarchical, these multiculturalists argue that books and curriculum content should be chosen on the basis of such factors as representativeness, fairness, and whether they give voice to the viewpoints of traditionally underrepresented groups.

The *Baseline Essays*, written in 1982 for schools in Portland, Oregon, have provided a model for several cities incorporating the stronger version of multiculturalism into their school systems. According to the essays, the ancient Egyptians were black, Africa was "the world center of culture and learning in antiquity," and the ancient Greeks borrowed much of their culture from Africa. The *Baseline Essays* assert that Europeans, in an attempt to obscure black achievements, "invented the theory of 'white' Egyptians who were merely browned by the sun."

Similarly, a task force on multiculturalism appointed by the New York State Commissioner of Education issued a 1989 report called *A Curriculum of Inclusion*. The task force was comprised of members from four minority groups: African American, Latinos, Asian American, and Native American. In its report, the task force noted:

> African Americans, Asian Americans, Puerto Ricans/ Latinos, and Native Americans have all been the victims of an intellectual and educational oppression that has characterized the culture and institutions of the United States and the European American world for centuries... [The schools of New York have a] systematic bias toward European culture and its derivatives. . . . . [T]here is something vulgar and revolting in glorifying a process [such as the development of the United States Constitution] that heaped undeserved rewards on a segment of the population while oppressing the majority.

The report also states that including non-European cultures in the curriculum would, in addition to increasing minority children's self-esteem, cause children from European cultures to "have a less arrogant perspective of being part of the group that has 'done it all.' " The report occasioned much debate. For example, Professor Diane Ravitch, *infra*, argued that there is a danger that the strong version of multiculturalism would lead to the teaching of "victim history," thus stirring racial hatred.

Reacting to the more expansive brand of multiculturalism, Professor Ravitch also has described the multiculturalism movement as actually encompassing two movements—the pluralists and the particularists. According to Ravitch:

> . . . Paradoxical though it may seem, the United States has a common culture that is multicultural. . . . In a pluralist curriculum, we expect children to learn a broad and humane culture, to learn about the ideas and art and animating spirit of many cultures. We expect that children, whatever their color, will be inspired by the courage of people like Helen Keller, Vaclav Havel, Harriet Tubman, and Feng Lizhe. We expect that their response to literature will be determined by the ideas and images it evokes, not by the skin color of the writer. But particularists insist that children can learn only from the experiences of people from the same race.
>
> * * *
>
> Particularism can easily be carried to extremes. Students of Fredonian descent must hear that their ancestors were seminal in the development of all human civilization and without the Fredonian contribution, we would all be living in caves or trees, bereft of art, technology, and culture. To explain why Fredonians today are in modest circumstances, given their historic eminence, children are taught that somewhere, long ago, another culture stole the Fredonian's achievements, palmed them off as their own, and then oppressed the Fredonians.

D. Ravitch, "Multiculturalism: E Pluribus Plures," *The American Scholar* 337, 339, 342, 347 (Summer 1990).

Is there, as Professor Ravitch argues, a common American culture in which all ethnic groups share? Or does the "melting pot" simply neutralize the diversity of non-European cultures by assimilating them into the broader American culture? Is Professor Boateng correct in rejecting the existence of a universal American culture? If no common culture exists, does separatism in education necessarily follow? *See* N. Glazer, *We Are All Multiculturalists Now* (1994) (arguing that multiculturalism arises from America's inability to integrate African Americans into society to the same extent as other groups);

M. Asante, *The Afrocentric Idea* (1987) (dismissing the idea of a universal culture and contrasting African culture with European culture); J. Sleeper, *The Closet of Strangers: Liberalism and the Politics of Race in New York* 232–239 (1990) (asserting the existence of a universal culture).

Consider the issue of multiculturalism in the light of *Wallace v. Jaffree, Edwards v. Aguillard,* and *Board of Education v. Pico.* These cases suggest that the Supreme Court has avoided the issue of which viewpoints must be included in the curriculum, focusing instead on the motivation of authorities who mandated a moment of silence, required the teaching of creationism, or removed books from the school library. *See also Smith v. Board of School Commissioners,* 827 F.2d 684 (11th Cir. 1987). That is, if public officials act to suppress a political ideology or to indoctrinate children to religious values, their actions may be held to violate the First Amendment. If, however, the officials make decisions in a good faith attempt to advance educational objectives, the courts have held such decisions to be virtually insulated from judicial review. *See Ambach v. Norwick,* 441 U.S. 68 (1979); *Mozert v. Hawkins County Board of Education,* 827 F.2d 1058 (6th Cir. 1987).

Suppose a group of minority students filed a lawsuit challenging a school system's "Eurocentric" curriculum on free speech and equal protection grounds. What would be the likely result? If one accepts the notions that all or nearly all curricular choices are political and that political transformation is the main purpose of teaching the humanities, could one persuasively argue that school administrators who determine curriculum content are not making good faith decisions to advance educational objectives but are instead designing the curriculum to indoctrinate children to the dominant culture? Would a court be likely to accept such an argument? After all, are not judges—like school board members, administrators, and teachers—part of the "dominant culture"? Are not cultures, by their nature, culturally biased? Is a dominant culture likely to engage in culturally self-destructive behavior? *See generally* C. Lindblom, *Inquiry and Change* (1990).

Should the school curriculum be an instrument of social change? Aspirational? Or should schools simply prepare students to function in American society as it exists—that is, with a decidedly European bent? Many schools, particularly in larger cities, enroll children of a wide variety of ethnic backgrounds. Is it possible to fairly represent in a curriculum all of the cultural back-

grounds present in the particular school? Should school curricula emphasize only the cultures of enrolled students? That is, if a school has no Latinos, should the school be free to de-emphasize teaching on the achievements of the ancient Incans or Mayans?

4. School Rules, Lifestyles, and the Hidden Curriculum. The materials in the previous sections deal with the question of constitutional limitations on the authority of the state and local school boards to shape the content of the courses of instruction. This section turns to a different means of socialization, namely, school rules that prescribe certain patterns of behavior for students and teachers—rules that are backed up with a variety of sanctions. *See generally* M. Janowitz, *The Reconstruction of Patriotism* 163–64 (1985).

These rules touch on a range of behaviors, for example, tardiness, disrespect for teachers, hair and dress styles, marriage and sexual behavior, fighting, and the use of weapons, liquor, or drugs. The rules are instituted for a variety of overlapping reasons. Some of these rules exist simply because schools are ongoing social institutions that, like other such institutions, must establish rules and procedures for carrying out their purposes in an orderly fashion and for ensuring the safety of students and school personnel. In this respect, schools resemble hospitals, prisons, cafeterias, factories, and other public and private institutions that must create an organizational framework within which to carry out their assigned task. Other reasons for some of these rules are simply educative. The rules exist to train students in ways of behaving that will stand them in good stead as they go on to higher education and jobs. *See Felton v. Fayette School District,* 875 F.2d 191 (8th Cir. 1989) ("good citizenship" rule applied to student who stole auto parts; excluded from off-campus vocational program). These rules may be imposed in order to save students from making choices that school officials believe the students will later regret. They also exist to promote desirable behavior or at least to avoid the appearance of endorsing opposing values. *See, e.g., Vernonia Sch. Dist. v. Acton,* 515 U.S. 646, 115 S.Ct. 2386 (1995) (holding that a school rule requiring random drug testing for participation in athletics does not violate the student's constitutional right to freedom from unreasonable searches and seizures); *Steirer v. Bethlehem Area Sch. Dist.,* 987 F.2d 989 (3d Cir. 1993) (finding that school's community service requirement for graduation is constitutionally permissible); *Clayton by Clayton v. Place,* 884 F.2d 376 (8th Cir. 1989) (prohibition of school dances on school premises does not violate Establishment Clause).

Rules governing behavior are a very important part of the life of schools. While grades for academic performance are all-pervasive and affect every student, the imposition of school sanctions for the violation of these quasi-educational and organizational rules is also frequent. Indeed, the penalties of suspension and expulsion are usually limited to enforcing these rules and not to policing academic performance. What students learn by conforming or not conforming to rules for conduct may become more deeply ingrained, become more a part of a person, than what is learned from reading and discussion. They involve learning by doing.

Hair and Dress Codes. A variety of behaviors were associated with student unrest in the 1960s, including the adoption of what were considered to be radical hair and dress styles. One reaction on the part of a significant number of school districts around the country was to adopt hair and dress codes backed up by such sanctions as suspension or exclusion from extracurricular activities. Some of these codes were the focus of constitutional challenges by parents and students. Although the controversy over student dress subsided for a time, dress codes have come back into fashion as a way of promoting school discipline and preventing school violence. In the aftermath of the Columbine shootings, a high school in Georgia, in order to create a school climate where students feel "safe and at ease," ordered a group of students to stop wearing "Goth-like" attire: black clothes, heavy makeup, and "elaborate" hairstyles. *See* "Different Look New Problem," *Fla. Times Union*, September 18, 2000. President Bill Clinton proposed dress codes as a method to reduce school violence. *See* "Uniforms, Curfews in Clinton Plan to Restore School Order," *Minneapolis Star Tribune*, July 21, 1998 at A1. Attention to the rulings and reasoning of the courts on these issues both provides insight into the contemporary controversy and illumines how courts resolve the tensions between the interest of the state in educating pupils in a certain way and what some students and parents believe to be within the sphere of their personal autonomy.

The Supreme Court's views on the constitutionality of hair and dress codes in the public school context remain undetermined. In all school hair and dress cases, whether the lower courts granted or denied students protection from such school regula-

tions, the Supreme Court declined to review the decisions, leaving intact a considerable division of opinion among the circuits. Most of these cases arose prior to the Court's decision in *Kelley v. Johnson*, 425 U.S. 238, 96 S.Ct. 1440, 47 L.Ed.2d 708 (1976), in which the Court upheld the hair length regulation of a police department. In reaching its decision, the Court assumed for purposes of argument that people enjoy some liberty in matters of personal appearance, but the Court only required that the regulation not be irrational. Under this standard, the Court found the hair regulation permissible as part of an effort to make police officers readily recognizable to members of the public and as part of an effort to promote an *esprit de corps*. Whether and to what extent the decision in *Kelley* is applicable to teachers and students in schools remains a matter of speculation. Teachers are not employees in a quasi-military organization, and yet they are role models for the students. And students are analogous neither to police officers nor to teachers.

The circuit courts are split over the regulation of student hair and dress styles. *See Bartlett*, "Hair and Dress Codes Revisited," 33 *Educ. L. Rep.* [7] (1986). The First, Second, Fourth, Seventh, and Eighth Circuits have upheld student objections to hair and dress codes. *See, e.g., Massie v. Henry*, 455 F.2d 779 (4th Cir. 1972); *Holsapple v. Woods*, 500 F.2d 49 (7th Cir. 1974) (per curiam), *cert. denied*, 419 U.S. 901, 95 S.Ct. 185, 42 L.Ed.2d 147 (1974); *Bishop v. Colaw*, 450 F.2d 1069 (8th Cir. 1971); *Richards v. Thurston*, 424 F.2d 1281 (1st Cir. 1970). *But see Olesen v. Board of Educ. of School Dist. No. 228*, 676 F.Supp. 820 (N.D. Ill. 1987) (Seventh Circuit cases protecting students' right to determine hair length distinguishable from school rule forbidding male students from wearing earrings). The Third, Fifth, Sixth, Ninth, Tenth, and Eleventh Circuits have rejected these constitutional claims. *See, e.g., Davenport by Davenport v. Randolph County Bd. of Educ.*, 730 F.2d 1395 (11th Cir. 1984); *Zeller v. Donegel School District*, 517 F.2d 600 (3d Cir. 1975); *Hatch v. Goerke*, 502 F.2d 1189 (10th Cir. 1974); *Karr v. Schmidt*, 460 F.2d 609 (5th Cir. 1972) (en banc), *cert. denied*, 409 U.S. 989, 93 S.Ct. 307, 34 L.Ed.2d 256 (1972); *Gfell v. Rickelman*, 441 F.2d 444 (6th Cir. 1971); *King v. Saddleback Junior College District*, 445 F.2d 932 (9th Cir. 1971), *cert. denied*, 404 U.S. 979, 92 S.Ct. 342, 30 L.Ed.2d 294 (1971).

The circuits that rejected challenges to hair codes held that a right to wear long hair did not lie in the free speech clause of the First Amendment (hair style has insufficient communicative content to warrant protection) or in notions of privacy as developed in cases such as *Griswold v. Connecticut*, 381 U.S. 479, 85 S.Ct. 1678, 14 L.Ed.2d 510 (1965) (protecting the right of married couples to use contraceptives). The more difficult task was to deal with the argument that a right to wear long hair was an element of the concept of "liberty" as protected by the Fourteenth Amendment. These courts responded by holding that the right in question was not sufficiently fundamental to warrant judicial protection. They buttressed this conclusion by noting that this kind of issue was best left to the discretion of school officials. These circuits imposed a *de minimis* standard of review in hair and dress cases. As a consequence, school officials urged successfully that such rules are necessary to prevent disruption of the educational process. This disruption allegedly has been of two sorts. Long hair is associated with disciplinary difficulties, academic failure, injuries in shop; and long hair is distracting to other students, so provocative as to be likely to produce fights.

The Tenth Circuit has also said the American Indian students who wish to wear their hair in a traditional style enjoy no special exemption from the schools' regulations. In these cases the students and their parents argued unsuccessfully that their hair style was based on religious beliefs and that parents had a right to bring up their children according to their own religious, cultural, and moral values. *Hatch v. Goerke*, 502 F.2d 1189 (10th Cir. 1974); *New Rider v. Board of Education*, 480 F.2d 699 (10th Cir. 1973), *cert. denied*, 414 U.S. 1097, 94 S.Ct. 733, 38 L.Ed.2d 556. *See* Doty, "Constitutional Law: The Right to Wear a Traditional Indian Hair Style—Recognition of a Heritage," 4 *Am. Indian L. Rev.* 105 (1976).

Those circuits that have upheld challenges to hair and dress rules in public schools have stressed that the control of one's appearance is a fundamental right within the meaning of the Fourteenth Amendment. Only if school officials have compelling justifications for the rules should they be upheld. These courts concluded that the claims of interference with the education process were not substantiated by the evidence. To the extent that long hair on some students has proved to be provocative to other students, they suggested that the lack of self-control on the part of the student "hecklers" should not result in long-haired students being penalized.

More recently, courts have been asked to decide whether a school dress code prohibiting gang symbols violates students' First Amendment rights. *See Stephenson v. Davenport Community School District*, 110 F.3d 1303 (8th Cir. 1997); *Jeglin v. San Jacinto Unified School District*, 827 F.Supp. 1459 (C.D. Cal.1993). A school can limit students' free expression in order to prevent a substantial disruption or material interference with school purposes, but do gang symbols and clothing lead to such behavior? *See* Murphy, "Restricting Gang Clothing in Public Schools: Does a Dress Code Violate a Student's Right of Expression?" 64 *Cal. L. Rev.* 1321 (1991). What if the school prohibits clothing bearing the insignia of college or professional sports teams because such clothing is popular among gang members? *See Jeglin, supra.* Can a student be prohibited from displaying a symbol if the student has no prior knowledge that the symbol is affiliated with gang activity and without any intent for the symbol to promote gang activity? *See Stephenson, supra.* Is the term "gang symbol" too vague to adequately warn students what they can and cannot wear? *See id.*

Should hair codes and earring bans be struck down as constitutionally invalid because they discriminate on the basis of gender? *See, e.g., Board of Trustees of Bastrop Independent School District v. Toungate*, 958 S.W.2d 365 (S.Ct. Tex. 1998); *Hines v. Caston Sch. Corp.*, 651 N.E.2d 330 (Ind. App. 1995). Most such codes allow girls to wear earrings and long hair but prohibit boys from doing so. One court held that gender-based distinctions in dress codes are constitutionally permissible because a school may impose rules requiring students to follow "community standards" of appearance. *See Hines v. Caston Sch. Corp.*, 651 N.E.2d 330 (Ind. App. 1995). Does the fact that boys have not traditionally worn earrings or long hair pass the intermediate standard of scrutiny the courts employ toward gender-based classifications? How, if at all, do hair and dress codes differ from other gender classifications in terms of deference to community standards? *See United States v. Virginia*, 518 U.S. 515, 116 S.Ct. 2264 (1996); *Mississippi Univ. for Women v. Hogan*, 458 U.S. 718, 723, 102 S.Ct. 3331 (1982).

There have been far fewer federal and state court cases dealing with hair and dress codes for teachers. In *Miller v. School District No. 167*, 495 F.2d 658 (7th Cir. 1974), the court rejected a teacher's constitutional challenge to his dismissal for sporting a Vandyke beard and sideburns. Although the Seventh Circuit had protected students from hair regulations, Judge (later Justice) Stevens concluded that the teacher's liberty interest was not of great importance and that the requirement resulted in a relatively minor deprivation. Conversely, the school board's interest in the appearance of its employees, rooted in education concerns, is strong. *See also Domico v. Rapides Parish School Bd.*, 675 F.2d 100 (5th Cir. 1982); *East Hartford Education Association v. Board of Education*, 562 F.2d 838 (2d Cir. 1977) (en banc). *But see Ramsey v. Hopkins*, 320 F.Supp. 477 (N.D. Ala. 1970); *Lucia v. Duggan*, 303 F.Supp. 112 (D. Mass. 1969); *Braxton v. Board of Public Instruction of Duval Cty.*, 303 F.Supp. 958 (M.D. Fla. 1969). Similarly, courts have upheld a school district's refusal to allow teachers to wear religious attire on campus. *See United States v. Board of Education*, 911 F.2d 882 (3rd Cir. 1990); *Cooper v. Eugene School District No. 45*, 301 Or. 358, 723 P.2d 298 (1986), *appeal dismissed*, 480 U.S. 942, 107 S.Ct. 1597, 94 L.Ed.2d 784 (1987).

Marriage, Pregnancy, and Immorality. Schools have long considered it important not merely to provide courses touching upon teenage marriage and sexual behavior, but also to try to control behavior in this area. For example, they may seek to discourage teenage marriage by excluding married students from extracurricular activities. Students who became pregnant have sometimes received similar treatment whether or not the student was married. Title IX, however, prohibits any penalty for pregnancy. *See infra* chapter 7.

With regard to teachers, there has been a great deal of litigation over the school district's authority to restrict personal lifestyles. *See* M. McCarthy & N. Cambron-McCabe, *Public School Law* 301–04 (1988). Immoral behavior has long been a basis for dismissal, but much depends on the types of behavior encompassed by the term "immorality." *See, e.g., Chicago Board of Educ. v. Payne*, 102 Ill. App.3d 741, 58 Ill. Dec. 368, 430 N.E.2d 310 (1981) (marijuana); *Golden v. Board of Educ.*, 169 W.Va. 63, 285 S.E.2d 665 (1981) (shoplifting). The decision in *Andrews v. Drew Municipal Separate School District*, 507 F.2d 611 (5th Cir. 1975), *cert. granted*, 423 U.S. 820, 96 S.Ct. 33, 46 L.Ed.2d 37, *cert. dismissed as improvidently granted*, 425 U.S. 559, 96 S.Ct. 1752, 48 L.Ed.2d 169 (1976), is instructive. That case considered the constitutionality of a school rule that made unwed parents ineligible to be hired as teachers' aides. The appeals court agreed with the district

court's argument that the status of unwed parenthood did not warrant a presumption of immorality: "A person could live an impeccable life, yet be barred as unfit for employment for an event, whether the result of indiscretion or not, occurring at any time in the past. But human experience refutes the dogmatic attitude inherent in such a policy against unwed parents." *Id.* at 615 (citing 371 F.Supp. at 33–34). As to the school district's point that unwed mothers are poor role models for students, the court said that it did not understand how the students would know of the teacher's marital status. And "the record before us contains no evidence of proselytizing of pupils by the plaintiffs. . . ." *Id.* at 616. The court also opined that it was pure speculation as to whether the hiring of such teachers would contribute to the problem of teenage pregnancies. *Id.* at 617. *See also Ponton v. Newport News Sch. Bd.*, 632 F.Supp. 1056 (E.D. Va. 1986) (compelled leave of absence for unwed, pregnant teacher violates constitutional right to privacy and Title VII of Civil Rights Act of 1964); *Reinhardt v. Board of Education of Alton Community Unit School District*, 19 Ill. App.3d 481, 311 N.E.2d 710 (1974). *See generally* Saken, "The Limits to a Teacher's Privacy Rights: *Ponton v. Newport News School Board*," 42 *Educ. L. Rep.* [19] (1987).

Some courts have overturned the dismissal of a teacher for cohabitation. *See Fisher v. Snyder*, 346 F.Supp. 396 (D. Neb. 1972), *aff'd*, 476 F.2d 375 (8th Cir. 1973). *Contra, Sullivan v. Meade County Independent School District*, 387 F.Supp. 1237 (D.S.D. 1975), *aff'd on other grounds*, 530 F.2d 799 (8th Cir. 1976). They have also upheld the dismissal of teachers for sexual acts in public and semipublic settings. *Wishart v. McDonald*, 500 F.2d 1110 (1st Cir. 1974); *Governing Board of Mountain View School Dist. v. Metcalf*, 36 Cal.App.3d 546, 111 Cal. Rptr. 724 (1974); *Pettit v. State Board of Education*, 10 Cal.3d 29, 109 Cal. Rptr. 665, 513 P.2d 889 (1973). Sexual involvement or related conduct of teachers with pupils almost invariably is a lawful basis for dismissal. *See, e.g., Johnson v. Beaverhead City High School District*, 771 P.2d 137 (Mont. 1989); *Barcheski v. Board of Educ. of Grand Rapids Public Schools*, 162 Mich. App. 388, 412 N.W.2d 296 (Mich. Ct. App. 1987); *Mondragon v. Poudre School Dist. R-1*, 696 P.2d 831 (Colo. App. 1984); *Potter v. Kalama Pub. Sch. Dist., No. 402*, 31 Wash. App. 838, 644 P.2d 1229 (1982); *Lombardo v. Board of Education*, 100 Ill. App.2d 108, 241 N.E.2d 495 (1968). *Compare* Keller, "Consensual Amorous Relationships

Between Faculty and Students: The Constitutional Right to Privacy," 15 *J. of Coll. & Univ. Law* 21 (1988) (college students and faculty). School officials also may fear that the school district will be liable to students when teachers sexually abuse them. *See Gebser v. Lago Vista Ind. Sch. Dist.*, 524 U.S. 274 (1998) (stating that a school district may be liable under Title IX if a teacher sexually harasses a student and the school has notice of the behavior); *Franklin v. Gwinett County Public Schools*, 503 U.S. 60, 112 S.Ct. 1028 (1992) (holding that there is a private cause of action for damages under Title IX). Finally, one court has held that a teacher has a fundamental right "to privacy regarding her marital status," and hence a school board may not refuse to renew the contract of a teacher because she is undergoing a divorce. *Littlejohn v. Rose*, 768 F.2d 765, 769 (6th Cir. 1985).

Does the disciplining of a student or the dismissal of a teacher for pregnancy constitute sex discrimination? Does it matter whether the school district focuses on the behavior—extramarital sex—or the status of being pregnant and unwed? *See Pfeiffer v. Marion Center Area Sch. Dist.*, 917 F.2d 779 (3d. Cir. 1990) (student discipline upheld because based on premarital sexual activity and not pregnancy status); *Wort v. Vierling*, 778 F.2d 1233 (7th Cir. 1985) (dismissal of pregnant student overturned).

Homosexuality. Homosexual teachers have long been the subject of controversy. *See generally* Walden and Culverhouse, "Homosexuality and Public Education," 52 *Educ. Law Rep.* [7] (1989); "Developments in the Law—Sexual Orientation and the Law," 102 *Harv. L. Rev.* 1509, 1595–1603 (1989); Schneider-Vogel, "Gay Teachers in the Classroom: A Continuing Constitutional Debate," 15 *J. L. & Educ.* 285 (1986). As previously noted, actual sexual involvement between a teacher and a student clearly provides a sufficient basis for dismissal, whether the relationship is heterosexual or homosexual. *See, e.g., Korf v. Ball State University*, 726 F.2d 1222 (7th Cir. 1984); *Fisher v. Independent School Dist. No. 622*, 357 N.W.2d 152 (Minn. App. 1984); *Lang v. Lee*, 639 S.W.2d 111 (Mo. App. 1982). *See* Walden and Culverhouse, *supra* at [15]–[16]. Also, a public sexual act by a teacher, whether heterosexual or homosexual, normally will be grounds for dismissal. For example, the Tenth Circuit rejected a facial challenge to an Oklahoma statute providing for dismissal or suspension of teachers who engaged in public homosexual

activity in *National Gay Task Force v. Board of Educ. of City of Okla. City*, 729 F.2d 1270 (10th Cir. 1984), *affirmed by an equally divided court*, 470 U.S. 903, 105 S.Ct. 1858, 84 L.Ed.2d 776 (1985). *But see Board of Educ. v. Jack M.*, 19 Cal.3d 691, 139 Cal. Rptr. 700, 566 P.2d 602 (1977). For a teacher to be disciplined or dismissed, the statute required two findings: (1) the teacher engaged in "public" homosexual activity, construed as oral or anal intercourse in an indiscreet, nonprivate manner; and (2) the teacher had been rendered unfit for teaching by the activity.

Factors in determining unfitness include whether the activity was likely to adversely affect students and its proximity in time and place to the teacher's duties. *See Morrison v. State Bd. of Educ.*, 1 Cal.3d 214, 82 Cal. Rptr. 175, 461 P.2d 375 (1969). For other cases concerning public homosexual acts, *see Corstvet v. Boger*, 757 F.2d 223 (10th Cir. 1985); *Ross v. Springfield Sch. Dist. No. 19*, 56 Or. App. 197, 641 P.2d 600 (1982); *Thompson v. Southwest Sch. Dist.*, 483 F.Supp. 1170 (W.D. Mo. 1980); *Kilpatrick v. Wright*, 437 F.Supp. 397 (M.D. Ala. 1977); *Moser v. State Bd. of Educ.*, 22 Cal. App.3d 988, 101 Cal. Rptr. 86 (1972).

It now appears that no broad constitutional protection exists for homosexual behavior in general, even when conducted in private between consenting adults. *See Bowers v. Hardwick*, 478 U.S. 186, 106 S.Ct. 2841, 92 L.Ed.2d 140 (1986), upholding the Georgia anti-sodomy statute. In *Bowers*, the Supreme Court declined to extend the constitutional right of privacy in marriage and family matters to homosexual behavior, citing its traditionally unprotected status. On the other hand, in *Romer v. Evans*, the Court held that an amendment to Colorado's Constitution violated the equal protection clause because it made it more difficult for homosexuals to seek government aid than it was for others to seek such help. *See Romer v. Evans*, 517 U.S. 620, 116 S.Ct. 1620 (1996). In *Oncale v. Sundowner Offshore Servs. Inc.*, the Court recognized same-sex sexual harassment as a violation of Title VII. 523 U.S. 75 (1998). The federal courts do not presumptively prohibit discrimination on the basis of sexual orientation under the equal protection clause; rather, they consider such claims under a rational basis standard of review. The Supreme Court's most recent decision on homosexuality held that a New Jersey public accommodations statute requiring the Boy Scouts, a private association, to permit an openly homosexual assistant scoutmaster to continue as a member of the organization violated the

Boy Scouts' First Amendment right of association. *Boy Scouts of America and Monmouth Council v. Dale*, 530 U.S. 640, 120 S.Ct. 2446, (2000). Although the Court acknowledged that freedom of association is not an absolute right, the forced inclusion of a homosexual scoutmaster "significantly affect[s] its expression." *Id.* at 2455.

Does the fact that states are free under the Constitution to criminalize homosexual behavior also mean that they may impose employment sanctions against a teacher, without requiring a nexus between the homosexual behavior and the teacher's performance of professional duties? Are homosexual teachers poor role models for students? *See Pryse v. Yakima School Dist. No. 7*, 30 Wash. App. 16, 632 P.2d 60 (1981); *Gaylord v. Tacoma School Dist.*, 88 Wash.2d 286, 559 P.2d 1340 (1977). *But see Developments in the Law, supra* at 1601–02. Should dismissal be permissible if a teacher has violated an anti-sodomy statute? *Bowers* held that community moral disapproval is a rational basis for criminalizing sodomy. Is community moral disapproval also a sufficient basis for finding a homosexual teacher unfit to teach? Several courts have said no, at least implicitly. *See Ross v. Springfield Sch. Dist. No. 19, supra; Burton v. Cascade School District*, 353 F.Supp. 254 (D. Or. 1973), *aff'd*, 512 F.2d 850 (9th Cir. 1975), *cert. denied*, 423 U.S. 839, 96 S.Ct. 69, 46 L.Ed.2d 59 (1975); *Morrison v. State Board of Education*, 1 Cal.3d 214, 82 Cal. Rptr. 175, 461 P.2d 375 (1969). *But see Conway v. Hampshire Cty. Bd. of Educ.*, 352 S.E.2d 739 (W.Va. 1986).

The ultimate question is whether the status of being a homosexual is sufficient reason to terminate the employment of a teacher. *See, e.g., Gaylord v. Tacoma School Dist., supra. See generally* Walden and Culverhouse, *supra*. The Supreme Court has not addressed this issue. *See Webster v. Doe*, 486 U.S. 592, 108 S.Ct. 2047, 100 L.Ed.2d (1988). *See also Padula v. Webster*, 822 F.2d 97 (D.C. Cir. 1987). One commentator has noted that school districts may require applicants for teaching positions to "reveal those associational ties that are relevant to a teacher's effectiveness" and that two courts have "interpreted this requirement to include associations with gay and lesbian organizations." *Developments in the Law, supra* at 1598, citing *Acanfora v. Board of Education*, 491 F.2d 498 (4th Cir. 1974); *McConnell v. Anderson*, 451 F.2d 193 (8th Cir. 1971). In addition, a Sixth Circuit decision may suggest that homosexual status makes a teacher unfit, at

least if she or he makes public her or his sexual orientation. In *Rowland v. Mad River Loc. Sch. Dist., Montgomery Cty.*, 730 F.2d 444 (6th Cir. 1984), *cert. denied*, 470 U.S. 1009, 105 S.Ct. 1373, 84 L.Ed.2d 392 (1985), school officials requested the resignation of a nontenured high school vocational guidance counselor who had told several other employees that she was bisexual and had a female lover. After she refused to resign, she was transferred to a position involving no student contact, and her contract was not renewed. The Sixth Circuit held that her speech was not entitled to First Amendment protection under *Connick v. Myers*, 461 U.S. 138, 103 S.Ct. 1684, 75 L.Ed.2d 708 (1983), because it did not involve a matter of public concern. *But see Developments in the Law, supra* at 1597–98. The court also said that her right to equal protection of the laws was not violated, since there was no evidence that heterosexual school employees who discussed their sexual preference would receive dissimilar treatment. *See generally* Walden and Culverhouse, *supra* at [21]–[24]. When the Supreme Court denied certiorari, Justices Brennan and Marshall joined in a dissent, pointing to jury findings that the employment sanctions against the teacher were imposed solely because she was bisexual and because she revealed her bisexuality. They also argued that her revelation in no way interfered with her job performance or disrupted the regular operation of the school. *See also Developments in the Law, supra* at 1597. The dissenters further suggested that the counselor's speech did involve a matter of public concern and that even private speech deserves constitutional protection when it does not interfere with the business of the employer. *See* Halley, "The Politics of the Closet: Towards Equal Protection for Gay, Lesbian and Bisexual Identity," 36 U.C.L.A. L. Rev. 915, 968–70 (1989).

National Gay Task Force v. Board of Educ. of Okla. City, supra, also addressed the issue of teachers' speech regarding sexual orientation. *See also Aumiller v. University of Delaware*, 434 F.Supp. 1273 (D. Del. 1977). While upholding the section of an Oklahoma statute imposing sanctions for public homosexual acts by teachers, the court struck down as overbroad a section sanctioning public speech about homosexuality. *See* Halley, *supra*. The law punished "advocating, soliciting, imposing, encouraging or promoting public or private homosexual activity in a manner that creates a substantial risk that such conduct will come to the attention of school children or school employees." The court feared that the statute would deter legitimate speech by authorizing dismissal of a teacher who, for example, addressed the state legislature or appeared on television to advocate repeal of a state anti-sodomy statute. The court also said that a state's interest in regulating a teacher's speech does not justify suppression unless the teacher's speech materially or substantially disrupts normal school activities. *See United States v. Coffeeville Consol. School Dist.*, 513 F.2d 244 (5th Cir. 1975) (unauthorized class discussion of homosexuality not just cause for dismissal).

III. OPENING THE SCHOOL TO ALTERNATIVE IDEAS

This section examines the government's authority to socialize students in public schools from a somewhat different perspective than in the previous sections. Sections I and II asked if there were constitutional limits on socialization in public schools, either in terms of the substance of the messages or the methods that the school authorities might use; this section asks whether and to what extent the public schools have a constitutional obligation to tolerate ideas, often conflicting ideas, from the teachers, staff, and students who constitute the school community. *See* T. van Geel, *The Courts and American Education Law* 211–60 (1987). In a sense, the contrast is between limitations on governmental powers and the assertion of rights against government by individuals under the Constitution. But this contrast becomes murky, for it better explains the establishment clause cases than free exercise cases in Sections I and II. The concern here is with rights of freedom of speech and association rather than religious rights. To the extent that nongovernmental voices may be heard, they may counter or diminish the school's effectiveness in communicating its messages. *See* M. Yudof, *When Government Speaks* 224–25 (1983); Bezanson, "The Government Speech Forum: *Forbes* and *Finley* and Government Speech Selection Judgments," 83 *Iowa L. Rev.* 953 (1998); Shiffrin, "Governmental Speech," 27 *U.C.L.A. L. Rev.* 565, 649–51 (1980). *See generally* C. Lindblom, *Inquiry and Change* (1990).

The problem may be posed in a variety of ways. What constitutional rights do students and teachers bring with them when they enter the school environment? Are public schools public forums or limited forums? Yudof, *supra* at 225–27; Garrison, "The Public School as Public Forum," 54 *Tex. L. Rev.* 90 (1975). What are the limits, if any, on the forum? *See Board of Education of Westside Community Schools v. Mergens*, 496 U.S. 226, 110 S.Ct. 2356 (1990). Do children have the same rights of expression as adults? At what point do the private voices exceed the bounds of tolerance and endanger the school's ability to carry out its educational mission? *See* Goldstein, "Reflections on Developing Trends in the Law of Student Rights," 118 *U. Pa. L. Rev.* 612 (1970). What are the limitations on the state's mission? When has the school become impermissibly dominant in drowning out other points of view? How should courts distinguish governmental speech from personal speech? *See* Yudof, "Personal Speech and Government Expression," 38 *Case Wes. Res. L. Rev.* 671 (1988). May the school engage in content regulation of student and teacher speech? What impact do rights-based court decisions have on school governance, discipline, and the student/teacher relationship? What impact do such decisions have on the socialization process itself?

A. Students' Rights of Expression

Students often seek to introduce their own values, beliefs, and opinions into the public schools. They may do so informally with their peers, in classroom discussions, by disseminating materials or wearing insignia, or by other means. These communications may be within the framework of the curriculum, they may be irrelevant to the curriculum, or they may seek to counter the schools' curricular and other objectives. *See generally* Buss, "School Newspapers, Public Forum, and the First Amendment," 74 *Iowa L. Rev.* 505, 516–18 (1989). As such, the students have the capacity, however diminished by their age and maturity, to challenge the values being conveyed by school authorities. And the school authorities themselves are not able to respond with value neutrality or to embrace all student points of view. *See* Shiffrin, "Liberalism, Radicalism, and Legal Scholarship," 30 *U.C.L.A. L. Rev.* 1103, 1131–33, 1165–69 (1983). The inherent tension between school values and personal values raises substantial questions about the degree to which student expression may permissibly interfere with the accomplishment of the school's educational objectives. It also raises significant issues about the scope of freedom of expression in a complex institutional environment.

One historical note is in order. *See* Friedman, "Limited Monarchy: The Rise and Fall of Student Rights," in D. Kirp and D. Jensen (eds.), *School Days, Rule Days* 238 (1986). Many of the student free speech cases discussed and cited in this section arose in the 1960s and early 1970s, when student activism was at its peak. This was the era of the civil rights revolution, protests against the Vietnam War, and draft resistance. Students today may be less concerned with public issues—or at least express their concerns in more conventional ways. *See generally* R. Putnam, *Bowling Alone* (2000). This may explain the decline in the number of student free speech cases in recent years. *See generally* Friedman, *supra*; Marvell, "The Rationales for Federal Question Jurisdiction: An Empirical Examination of Student Rights Litigation," 1984 *Wis. L. Rev.* 1315. Another likely reason for this decline is that school officials may have become more tolerant of student speech and more sophisticated in handling student unrest. Now that the broad constitutional outlines for dealing with student protest have been laid down, school officials are better acquainted with the rules under which they are to operate and are in a better position to make decisions that do not leave them vulnerable to constitutional challenges. Finally, students and their parents may be more reluctant to seek judicial remedies because they perceive the federal courts are more reticent about overturning the decisions of public school officials. *See, e.g., Bethel School District v. Fraser,* 478 U.S. 675, 106 S.Ct. 3159, 92 L.Ed.2d 549 (1986); *West v. Derby Unified Sch. Dist. No. 260,* 206 F.3d 1358 (10th Cir. 2000). As Professor Erwin Chemerinsky has noted,

> Over the three decades of the Burger and Rehnquist Courts, there have been virtually no decisions protecting rights of students in schools. Indeed, there have been remarkably few rulings concerning students' speech, despite hundreds of lower court decisions on the topic. There have been only two Supreme Court cases concerning student speech in elementary, middle schools, and high schools, excluding cases concerning religious expression. . . . In both, the Court rejected the students' First Amendment claims and sided with the schools.

E. Chemerinsky, "Students Do Leave Their First Amendment Rights at the Schoolhouse Gates: What's Left of *Tinker?*" 48 *Drake L. Rev.* 527, 528 (2000).

1. Student Speech

Tinker v. Des Moines Independent Community School District

393 U.S. 503, 89 S.Ct. 733, 21 L.Ed.2d 731 (1969).

Mr. Justice Fortas delivered the opinion of the Court.

Petitioner John F. Tinker, 15 years old, and petitioner Christopher Eckhardt, 16 years old, attended high schools in Des Moines, Iowa. Petitioner Mary Beth Tinker, John's sister, was a 13-year-old student in junior high school.

In December 1965, a group of adults and students in Des Moines held a meeting at the Eckhardt home. The group determined to publicize their objections to the hostilities in Vietnam and their support for a truce by wearing black armbands during the holiday season and by fasting on December 16 and New Year's Eve. Petitioners and their parents had previously engaged in similar activities, and they decided to participate in the program.

The principals of the Des Moines schools became aware of the plan to wear armbands. On December 14, 1965, they met and adopted a policy that any student wearing an armband to school would be asked to remove it and if he refused he would be suspended until he returned without the armband. Petitioners were aware of the regulation that the school authorities adopted.

On December 16, Mary Beth and Christopher wore black armbands to their schools. John Tinker wore his armband the next day. They were all sent home and suspended from school until they would come back without their armbands. They did not return to school until after the planned period for wearing armbands had expired—that is, until after New Year's Day.

This complaint was filed in the United States District Court by petitioners, through their fathers, under § 1983 of Title 42 of the United States Code. It prayed for an injunction restraining the respondent school officials and the respondent members of the board of directors of the school district from disciplining the petitioners, and it sought nominal damages. After an evidentiary hearing the District Court dismissed the complaint. It upheld the constitutionality of the school authorities' action on the ground that it was reasonable in order to prevent disturbance of school discipline. 258 F.Supp. 971 (1966). The court referred to but expressly declined to follow the Fifth Circuit's holding in a similar case that the wearing of symbols like armbands cannot be prohibited unless it "materially and substantially interfere[s] with the requirements of appropriate discipline in the operation of the school." *Burnside v. Byars*, 363 F.2d 744, 749 (1966).[1]

On appeal, the Court of Appeals for the Eighth Circuit considered the case *en banc*. The court was equally divided, and the District Court's decision was accordingly affirmed, without opinion. 383 F.2d 988 (1967). . . .

The District Court recognized that the wearing of an armband for the purpose of expressing certain views is the type of symbolic act that is within the Free Speech Clause of the First Amendment. . . . As we shall discuss, the wearing of armbands in the circumstances of this case was entirely divorced from actually or potentially disruptive conduct by those participating in it. It was closely akin to "pure speech" which, we have repeatedly held, is entitled to comprehensive protection under the First Amendment. *Cf. Cox v. Louisiana*, 379 U.S. 536, 555 (1965); *Adderley v. Florida*, 385 U.S. 39 (1966).

First Amendment rights, applied in light of the special characteristics of the school environment, are available to teachers and students. It can hardly be argued that either students or teachers shed their constitutional rights to freedom of speech or expression at the schoolhouse gate. This has been the unmistakable holding of this Court for almost 50 years. . . . On the other hand, the Court has repeatedly emphasized the need for affirming the comprehensive authority of the States and of school officials, consistent with fundamental constitutional safeguards, to prescribe and control conduct in the schools. *See Epperson v. Arkansas*, [393 U.S. 104 (1968)]; *Meyer v. Nebraska*, [262 U.S. 390, 402 (1923)]. Our problem lies in the area where students in the exercise of First Amendment rights collide with the rules of the school authorities.

The problem posed by the present case does not relate to regulation of the length of skirts or the type of clothing, to hair style, or deportment. *Cf. Ferrell v. Dallas Independent School Dist.*, 392 F.2d 697 (5th Cir. 1968); *Pugsley v. Sellmeyer*, 158 Ark. 247, 250 S.W. 538 (1923). It does not concern aggressive, disruptive action or even group demonstrations. Our problem involves direct, primary First Amendment rights akin to "pure speech."

The school officials banned and sought to punish petitioners for a silent, passive expression of opinion, unaccompanied by any disorder or disturbance on the part of the petitioners. There is here no evidence whatever of petitioners' interference, actual or nascent, with the schools' work or of collision with the rights of other students to be secure and to be let alone. Accordingly, this case does not concern speech or action that intrudes upon the work of the schools or the rights of other students.

Only a few of the 18,000 students in the school system wore the black armbands. Only five students were suspended for wearing them. There is no indication that the work of the schools or any class was disrupted. Outside the classrooms, a few students made hostile remarks to the children wearing armbands, but there were no threats or acts of violence on the school premises.

The District Court concluded that the action of the school authorities was reasonable because it was based upon their fear of a disturbance from the wearing of the armbands. But, in our system, undifferentiated fear or apprehension of disturbance is not enough to overcome the right to freedom of expression. Any departure from absolute regimentation may cause trouble. Any variation from the majority's opinion may inspire fear. Any word spoken in class, in the lunchroom, or on the campus, that deviates from the views of another person may start an argument or cause a disturbance. But our Constitution says we must take this risk, *Terminiello v. Chicago*, 337 U.S. 1 (1949); and our history says that it is this sort of hazardous freedom—this kind of openness—that is the basis of our national strength and of the independence and vigor of Americans who grow up and live in this relatively permissive, often disputatious society.

In order for the State in the person of school officials to justify prohibition of a particular expression of opinion, it must be able to show that its action was caused by something more than a mere desire to avoid the discomfort and unpleasantness that always accompany an unpopular viewpoint. Certainly where there is no finding and no showing that engaging in the forbidden conduct would "materially and substantially interfere with the requirements of appropriate discipline in the operation of the

---

[1] In *Burnside*, the Fifth Circuit ordered that high school authorities be enjoined from enforcing a regulation forbidding students to wear "freedom buttons." It is instructive that in *Blackwell v. Issaquena County Board of Education*, 363 F.2d 749 (1966), the same panel on the same day reached the opposite result on different facts. It declined to enjoin enforcements of such a regulation in another high school where the students wearing freedom buttons harassed students who did not wear them and created much disturbance.

school," the prohibition cannot be sustained. *Burnside v. Byars, supra,* [363 F.2d] at 749.

In the present case, the District Court made no such finding, and our independent examination of the record fails to yield evidence that the school authorities had reason to anticipate that the wearing of the armbands would substantially interfere with the work of the school or impinge upon the rights of other students. Even an official memorandum prepared after the suspension that listed the reasons for the ban on wearing the armbands made no reference to the anticipation of such disruption.[3]

On the contrary, the action of the school authorities appears to have been based upon an urgent wish to avoid the controversy which might result from the expression, even by the silent symbol of armbands, of opposition to this Nation's part in the conflagration in Vietnam.[4] It is revealing, in this respect, that the meeting at which the school principals decided to issue the contested regulation was called in response to a student's statement to the journalism teacher in one of the schools that he wanted to write an article on Vietnam and have it published in the school paper. (The student was dissuaded.)

It is also relevant that the school authorities did not purport to prohibit the wearing of all symbols of political or controversial significance. The record shows that students in some of the schools wore buttons relating to national political campaigns, and some even wore the Iron Cross, traditionally a symbol of Nazism. The order prohibiting the wearing of armbands did not extend to these. Instead, a particular symbol—black armbands worn to exhibit opposition to this Nation's involvement in Vietnam—was singled out for prohibition. Clearly, the prohibition of expression of one particular opinion, at least without evidence that it is necessary to avoid material and substantial interference with schoolwork or discipline, is not constitutionally permissible.

In our system, state-operated schools may not be enclaves of totalitarianism. School officials do not possess absolute authority over their students. Students in school as well as out of school are "persons" under our Constitution. They are possessed of fundamental rights which the State must respect, just as they themselves must respect their obligations to the State. In our system, students may not be regarded as closed-circuit recipients of only that which the State chooses to communicate. They may not be confined to the expression of those sentiments that are officially approved. In the absence of a specific showing of constitutionally valid reasons to regulate their speech, students are entitled to freedom of expression of their views. . . .

In *Keyishian v. Board of Regents,* 385 U.S. 589 . . . Mr. Justice Brennan, speaking for the Court, said:

> "The vigilant protection of constitutional freedoms is nowhere more vital than in the community of American schools." *Shelton v. Tucker,* [364 U.S. 479], at 487. The classroom is peculiarly the "marketplace of ideas." The Nation's future depends upon leaders trained through wide exposure to that robust exchange of ideas which discovers truth "out of a multitude of tongues, [rather] than through any kind of authoritative selection."

The principle of these cases is not confined to the supervised and ordained discussion which takes place in the classroom. The principal use to which the schools are dedicated is to accommodate students during prescribed hours for the purpose of certain types of activities. Among those activities is personal intercommunication among the students.[6] This is not only an inevitable part of the process of attending school; it is also an important part of the educational process. A student's rights, therefore, do not embrace merely the classroom hours. When he is in the cafeteria, or on the playing field, or on the campus during the authorized hours, he may express his opinions, even on controversial subjects like the conflict

---

[3] . . . [T]he testimony of school authorities at trial indicates that it was not fear of disruption that motivated the regulation prohibiting the armbands; the regulation was directed against "the principle of the demonstration" itself. School authorities simply felt that "the schools are no place for demonstrations," and if the students "didn't like the way our elected officials were handling things, it should be handled with the ballot box and not in the halls of our public schools."

[4] The District Court found that the school authorities, in prohibiting black armbands, were influenced by the fact that "the Vietnam War and the involvement of the United States therein has been the subject of a major controversy for some time. When the armband regulation involved herein was promulgated, debate over the Vietnam War had become vehement in many localities. A protest march against the war had been recently held in Washington, D.C. A wave of draft card burning incidents protesting the war had swept the country. At that time two highly publicized draft card burning cases were pending in this Court. Both individuals supporting the war and those opposing it were quite vocal in expressing their views." 258 F.Supp. at 972–73.

[6] In *Hammond v. South Carolina State College,* 272 F.Supp. 947 (D.S.C. 1967), District Judge Hemphill had before him a case involving a meeting on campus of 300 students to express their views on school practices. He pointed out that a school is not like a hospital or a jail enclosure. *Cf. Cox v. Louisiana,* 379 U.S. 536 (1965); *Adderley v. Florida,* 385 U.S. 39 (1966). It is a public place, and its dedication to specific uses does not imply that the constitutional rights of persons entitled to be there are to be gauged as if the premises are purely private property. . .

in Vietnam, if he does so without "materially and substantially interfer[ing] with the requirements of appropriate discipline in the operation of the school" and without colliding with the rights of others. *Burnside v. Byars, supra,* [363 F.2d] at 749. But conduct by the student, in class or out of it, which for any reason — whether it stems from time, place, or type of behavior — materially disrupts classwork or involves substantial disorder or invasion of the rights of others is, of course, not immunized by the constitutional guarantee of freedom of speech. . . .

*   *   *

As we have discussed, the record does not demonstrate any facts which might reasonably have led school authorities to forecast substantial disruption of or material interference with school activities, and no disturbances or disorders on the school premises in fact occurred. These petitioners merely went about their ordained rounds in school. Their deviation consisted only in wearing on their sleeve a band of black cloth, not more than two inches wide. They wore it to exhibit their disapproval of the Vietnam hostilities and their advocacy of a truce, to make their views known, and, by their example, to influence others to adopt them. They neither interrupted school activities nor sought to intrude in the school affairs or the lives of others. They caused discussion outside of the classrooms, but no interference with work and no disorder. In the circumstances, our Constitution does not permit officials of the State to deny their form of expression.

We express no opinion as to the form of relief which should be granted, this being a matter for the lower courts to determine. We reverse and remand for further proceedings consistent with this opinion.

Reversed and remanded.

Mr. Justice Stewart, concurring.

Although I agree with much of what is said in the Court's opinion, and with its judgment in this case, I cannot share the Court's uncritical assumption that, school discipline aside, the First Amendment rights of children are coextensive with those of adults. Indeed, I had thought the Court decided otherwise just last term in *Ginsberg v. New York,* 390 U.S. 629. I continue to hold the view I expressed in that case: "[A] State may permissibly determine that, at least in some precisely delineated areas, a child — like someone in a captive audience — is not possessed of that full capacity for individual choice which is the presupposition of First Amendment guarantees." *Id.,* at 649–50 (concurring in result). *Cf. Prince v. Massachusetts,* 321 U.S. 158.

Mr. Justice White, concurring.

While I join the Court's opinion, I deem it appropriate to note, first, that the Court continues to recognize a distinction between communicating by words and communicating by acts or conduct which sufficiently impinges on some valid state interest; and, second, that I do not subscribe to everything the Court of Appeals said about free speech in its opinion in *Burnside v. Byars,* 363 F.2d 744, 748 (5th Cir. 1966), a case relied upon by the Court in the matter now before us.

Mr. Justice Black, dissenting.

The Court's holding in this case ushers in what I deem to be an entirely new era in which the power to control pupils by the elected "officials of state-supported public schools . . ." in the United States is in ultimate effect transferred to the Supreme Court. The Court brought this particular case here on a petition for certiorari urging that the First and Fourteenth Amendments protect the right of school pupils to express their political views all the way "from kindergarten through high school." Here the constitutional right to "political expression" asserted was a right to wear black armbands during school hours and at classes in order to demonstrate to the other students that the petitioners were mourning because of the death of United States soldiers in Vietnam and to protest that war which they were against. Ordered to refrain from wearing the armbands in school by the elected school officials and the teachers vested with state authority to do so, apparently only seven out of the school system's 18,000 pupils deliberately refused to obey the order. One defying pupil was Paul Tinker, 8 years old, who was in the second grade; another, Hope Tinker, was 11 years old and in the fifth grade; a third member of the Tinker family was 13, in the eighth grade; and a fourth member of the same family was John Tinker, 15 years old, an 11th grade high school pupil. Their father, a Methodist minister without a church, is paid a salary by the American Friends Service Committee. Another student who defied the school order and insisted on wearing an armband in school was Christopher Eckhardt, an 11th grade pupil and a petitioner in this case. His mother is an official in the Women's International League for Peace and Freedom.

As I read the Court's opinion it relies upon the following grounds for holding unconstitutional the judgment of the Des Moines school officials and the two courts below. First, the Court concludes that the wearing of armbands is "symbolic speech" which is "akin to 'pure speech' " and therefore protected by the First and Fourteenth Amendments. Secondly, the Court decides that the public schools are an appropriate place to exercise "symbolic speech" as long as normal school functions are not "unreasonably" disrupted. Finally, the Court arrogates to itself, rather than to the State's elected officials charged with running the schools, the decision as to which school disciplinary regulations are "reasonable."

Assuming that the Court is correct in holding that the conduct of wearing armbands for the purpose of conveying political ideas is protected by the First Amendment, *cf. e.g.*, *Giboney v. Empire Storage & Ice Co.*, 336 U.S. 490 (1949), the crucial remaining questions are whether students and teachers may use the schools at their whim as a platform for the exercise of free speech—"symbolic" or "pure"—and whether the courts will allocate to themselves the function of deciding how the pupils' school day will be spent. While I have always believed that under the First and Fourteenth Amendments neither the State nor the Federal Government has any authority to regulate or censor the content of speech, I have never believed that any person has a right to give speeches or engage in demonstrations where he pleases and when he pleases. . . .

While the record does not show that any of these armband students shouted, used profane language, or were violent in any manner, detailed testimony by some of them shows their armbands caused comments, warnings by other students, the poking of fun at them, and a warning by an older football player that other, nonprotesting students had better let them alone. There is also evidence that a teacher of mathematics had his lesson period practically "wrecked" chiefly by disputes with Mary Beth Tinker, who wore her armband for her "demonstration." Even a casual reading of the record shows that this armband did divert students' minds from their regular lessons, and that talk, comments, etc., made John Tinker "self-conscious" in attending school with his armband. While the absence of obscene remarks or boisterous and loud disorder perhaps justifies the Court's statement that the few armband students did not actually "disrupt" the classwork, I think the record overwhelmingly shows that the armbands did exactly what the elected school officials and principals foresaw they would, that is, took the students' minds off their classwork and diverted them to thoughts about the highly emotional subject of the Vietnam War. And I repeat that if the time has come when pupils of state-supported schools, kindergartens, grammar schools, or high schools, can defy and flout orders of school officials to keep their minds on their own schoolwork, it is the beginning of a new revolutionary era of permissiveness in this country fostered by the judiciary. The next logical step, it appears to me, would be to hold unconstitutional laws that bar pupils under 21 or 18 from voting, or from being elected members of the boards of education.

* * *

I deny, therefore, that it has been the "unmistakable holding of this Court for almost 50 years" that "students" and "teachers" take with them into the "schoolhouse gate" constitutional rights to "freedom of speech or expression." Even *Meyer* did not hold that. It makes no reference to "symbolic speech" at all; what it did was to strike down as "unreasonable" and therefore unconstitutional a Nebraska law barring the teaching of the German language before the children reached the eighth grade. One can well agree with Mr. Justice Holmes and Mr. Justice Sutherland, as I do, that such a law was no more unreasonable than it would be to bar the teaching of Latin and Greek to pupils who have not reached the eighth grade. In fact, I think the majority's reason for invalidating the Nebraska law was that it did not like it or in legal jargon that it "shocked the Court's conscience," "offended its sense of justice," or was "contrary to fundamental concepts of the English-speaking world," as the Court has sometimes said. . . .

In my view, teachers in state-controlled public schools are hired to teach there. Although Mr. Justice McReynolds may have intimated to the contrary in *Meyer v. Nebraska, supra*, certainly a teacher is not paid to go into school and teach subjects the State does not hire him to teach as a part of its selected curriculum. Nor are public school students sent to the schools at public expense to broadcast political or any other views to educate and inform the public. The original idea of schools, which I do not believe is yet abandoned as worthless or out of date, was that children had not yet reached the point of experience and wisdom which enabled them to teach all of their elders. It may be that the Nation has outworn the old-fashioned slogan that "children are to be seen not heard," but one may, I hope, be permitted to harbor the thought that taxpayers send children to school on the premise that at their age they need to learn, not teach. . . .

* * *

But even if the record were silent as to protests against the Vietnam war distracting students from their assigned class work, members of this Court, like all other citizens, know, without being told, that the disputes over the wisdom of the Vietnam war have disrupted and divided this country as few other issues ever have. Of course students, like other people, cannot concentrate on lesser issues when black armbands are being ostentatiously displayed in their presence to call attention to the wounded and dead of the war, some of the wounded and the dead being their friends and neighbors. It was, of course, to distract the attention of other students that some students insisted up to the very point of their own suspension from school that they were determined to sit in school with their symbolic armbands.

Change has been said to be truly the law of life but sometimes the old and the tried and true are worth holding. The schools of this Nation have undoubtedly contributed to giving us tranquility and to making us a more law-abiding people. Uncontrolled and uncontrollable liberty is an enemy to domestic peace. We cannot close our eyes to the fact that some of the country's greatest problems are crimes committed by the youth, too many of school age. School discipline, like parental discipline, is an integral and important part of training our children to be good citizens—to be better citizens. Here a very small number of students have crisply and summarily refused to obey a school order designed to give pupils who want to learn the opportunity to do so. One does not need to be a prophet or the son of a prophet to know that after the Court's holding today some students in Iowa schools and indeed in all schools will be ready, able, and willing to defy their teachers on practically all orders. This is the more unfortunate for the schools since groups of students all over the land are already running loose, conducting break-ins, sit-ins, lie-ins, and smash-ins. Many of these student groups, as is all too familiar to all who read the newspapers and watch the television news programs, have already engaged in rioting, property seizures, and destruction. They have picketed schools to force students not to cross their picket lines and have too often violently attacked earnest but frightened students who wanted an education that the pickets did not want them to get. Students engaged in such activities are apparently confident that they know far more about how to operate public school systems than do their parents, teachers, and elected school officials. It is no answer

to say that the particular students here have not yet reached such high points in their demands to attend classes in order to exercise their political pressures. Turned loose with lawsuits for damages and injunctions against their teachers as they are here, it is nothing but wishful thinking to imagine that young, immature students will not soon believe it is their right to control the schools rather than the right of the States that collect taxes to hire the teachers for the benefit of the pupils. This case, therefore, wholly without constitutional reasons in my judgment, subjects all the public schools in the country to the whims and caprices of their loudest-mouthed, but maybe not their brightest, students. I, for one, am not fully persuaded that school pupils are wise enough, even with this Court's expert help from Washington, to run the 23,390 public school systems in our 50 states. I wish, therefore, wholly to disclaim any purpose on my part to hold that the Federal Constitution compels the teachers, parents, and elected school officials to surrender control of the American public school system to public school students. I dissent.

Mr. Justice Harlan, dissenting.

I certainly agree that state public school authorities in the discharge of their responsibilities are not wholly exempt from the requirements of the Fourteenth Amendment respecting the freedoms of expression and association. At the same time I am reluctant to believe that there is any disagreement between the majority and myself on the proposition that school officials should be accorded the widest authority in maintaining discipline and good order in their institutions. To translate that proposition into a workable constitutional rule, I would, in cases like this, cast upon those complaining the burden of showing that a particular school measure was motivated by other than legitimate school concerns—for example, a desire to prohibit the expression of an unpopular point of view, while permitting expression of the dominant opinion.

Finding nothing in this record which impugns the good faith of respondents in promulgating the armband regulation, I would affirm the judgment below.

NOTES AND QUESTIONS

1. Symbolic Speech

Tinker presumes that the wearing of armbands is a symbolic act, "closely akin to 'pure speech.' " Is that presumption debatable? Is Justice Black arguing that the wearing of armbands is "nonspeech"? *See generally* Ely, "Flag Desecration: A Case Study in the Roles of Categorization and Balancing in First Amendment Analysis," 88 *Harv. L. Rev.* 1482 (1975). Suppose the *Tinker* children had picketed their school. Would such "speech plus" action be entitled to constitutional protection? *See Pickens v. Okolona Mun. Separate School Dist.*, 594 F.2d 433 (5th Cir. 1979); *Karp v. Becker*, 477 F.2d 171 (9th Cir. 1973).

2. Rights of Children

Should children be afforded less extensive rights than mature adults? *See* Garvey, "Children and the First Amendment," 57 *Tex. L.Rev.* 521 (1979). Is the ability to make rational choices essential to the constitutional argument for the protection of expression? If so, should young children be entitled to less constitutional protection of their speech? Should the school's goal be the self-realization of children or their socialization to broad cultural norms? *See* Levin, "Educating Youth for Citizenship: The Conflict Between Authority and Individual Rights in Public Schools," 95 *Yale L. J.* 1647 (1986). Were the *Tinker* children reflecting their own views or those of their parents? If the latter, are the traditional reasons for protecting speech applicable to them? *See* Wright, "Free Speech Values, Public Schools, and the Role of Judicial Deference," 22 *New Eng. L. Rev.* 59, 62 (1987). If the *Tinker* children were in elementary school, would they have been afforded the same rights? *See, e.g., Baxter v. Vigo County Sch. Corp.*, 26 F.3d 728 (7th Cir. 1994).

Do students have a right to resist state socialization processes? What does Justice Black think of this idea? Is recognition of student rights a part of socialization to democracy? *See Hazelwood School District v. Kuhlmeier, infra* (Brennan, J., dissenting). *See generally* A. Gutmann, *Democratic Education* 98 (1987).

3. Rights of Teachers

Consider *Tinker*-like claims pressed by teachers. If teachers are role models and communicators of community values, with access to an audience captured by the government, should their expression receive less protection than that of students? *Cf. Kiluma v. Wayne State University*, 72 *Mich.App.* 446, 250 N.W.2d 81 (1976). Are teachers, as professionals and adults, entitled to more protection of their speech than students? Should teachers be afforded the same rights as students, i.e., their speech should be subject to the sub-

stantial disruption limitation? Which view seems preferable? At least one circuit court has said that when a teacher carries out a nondisruptive protest as in *Tinker*, the teacher's expression is to be protected. In *James v. Board of Education*, 461 F.2d 566 (2d Cir. 1972), *cert. denied*, 409 U.S. 1042, 93 S.Ct. 529, 34 L.Ed.2d 491 (1972), the court overturned a teacher's dismissal for wearing a black armband to class in protest against the Vietnam War. *See also Adamian v. Lombardi*, 608 F.2d 1224 (9th Cir. 1979), *cert. denied*, 446 U.S. 938, 100 S.Ct. 2158, 64 L.Ed.2d 791 (1980).

4. The Constitutional Basis of Tinker

What is the rationale of *Tinker?* Is *Tinker* essentially an equal protection case, in which the constitutional wrong is that the principal discriminated against the content of the message promulgated by the *Tinker* children, singling out their anti-war protest while permitting other forms of expression? Would such an interpretation suggest that it is permissible to suppress all armbands, symbols, and underground newspapers? *See generally* Freeman, "The Supreme Court and First Amendment Rights of Students: A Proposed Model of Analysis," 12 *Hastings Const. L.Q.* 1 (1984).

Alternatively, might *Tinker* be viewed as a case in which the Court upheld the right of students to assert their viewpoint as citizens, despite the fact that they happened to be on public school premises? Does *Tinker* affirm the rights of parents to express themselves through their children? *See* Burt, "Developing Constitutional Rights Of, In, and For Children," 39 *Law & Contemp. Probs.* 118 (1975). Alternatively, one commentator has argued that *Tinker* rests on a particular conception of education, one that emphasizes analysis and intellectual inquiry. Goldstein, "Reflections on Developing Trends in the Law of Student Rights," 118 *U. Pa. L. Rev.* 612, 614–15 (1970). Is this view of the case supportable, and if so, was it proper for the Court to base its decision on its particular conception of educational philosophy? *See* Diamond, "The First Amendment and Public Schools: The Case Against Judicial Intervention," 59 *Tex. L. Rev.* 477 (1981).

Might *Tinker* be seen as resting on the idea of the school as a limited public forum—a marketplace of ideas—where students and teachers with many viewpoints are allowed to express their opinions without being subject to selective regulation on the basis of the content of their messages? *See* Laycock, "Equal Access and Moments of Silence: The Equal Status of

Religious Speech by Private Speakers," 81 *Nw. U. L. Rev.* 1, 47–49 (1986). Is this rationale consistent with *West Virginia State Board of Education v. Barnette*, 319 U.S. 624, 63 S.Ct. 1178, 87 L.Ed. 1628 (1943)? Alternatively, might the idea behind the public forum interpretation of *Tinker* be that it lets voices other than the potentially dominant governmental voice speak to the school's captive audience? The greater the number of voices that are allowed to speak within the school, the less the danger that the government will be able to overwhelm students with its messages. *See* Yudof, *When Government Speaks* 224–25 (1983); Buss, "School Newspapers, Public Forum, and the First Amendment," 74 *Iowa L. Rev.* 505, 515 (1989); Shriffin, "Government Speech," 27 *UCLA L. Rev.* 565, 649–51 (1980). Under the socialization rationale, are *Tinker* and *Pico, supra,* consistent? Is the proper test for curbing speech the good faith of the decision makers or the likelihood that the speech will occasion disruption of the school? Is the dissent of Justice Harlan in *Tinker* now the dominant position in *Pico*? If so, does this theory suggest that if a case such as *Tinker* reached the Supreme Court today, the Court would ask whether school administrators were making a good faith effort to promote educational goals? *See* M. Yudof, "*Tinker* Tailored: Good Faith, Civility, and Student Expression," 69 *St. John's L. Rev.* 365 (1995). Under the facts of *Tinker*, how should the Court answer this question? In effect, has *Tinker* been overruled? *See* E. Chemerinsky, "Students Do Leave Their First Amendment Rights at the Schoolhouse Gates: What's Left of *Tinker*?" 48 *Drake L. Rev.* 527, 528 (2000). *See, e.g., Baxter v. Vigo County Sch. Corp.,* 26 F.3d 728 (7th Cir. 1994)(doubts about continuing vitality of *Tinker*); *Poling v. Murphy,* 872 F.2d 757 (6th Cir. 1989)(applying reasonableness standard); *Gano v. Sch. Dist. No. 411,* 674 F. Supp. 796 (D. Idaho 1987). *But see, e.g., Lovell v. Poway Unified Sch. Dist.,* 90 F.3d 367 (9th Cir. 1996); *Chandler v. McMinnville Sch. Dist.,* 978 F.2d 524 (9th Cir. 1992).

5. *The Substantial Disruption Standard*

If the First Amendment is deemed applicable to student and teacher speech, the critical issue then becomes its appropriate application "in the light of the special characteristics of the school environment." In attempting to reconcile the students' rights with the interest of government in offering a public school program, the Court in *Tinker* suggested several different standards of constitutional review. The central standard is that school officials may prohibit speech activities if they materially and substantially interfere with the operation of the school. The Court also said that speech may be banned if school officials can reasonably forecast substantial disruption or material interference with school activities.

Does the substantial disruption test adequately protect the school's educational mission? *See* Diamond, *supra.* May a school discipline a student for speech not falling within the test? *See Williams v. Spencer,* 622 F.2d 1200, 1206 (4th Cir. 1980). Is the test too restrictive of free expression? Does the importance of *Tinker* lie in its articulation of a rule of law or in its signal to school officials that they do not have unfettered discretion to control student expression? *See* Denno, "Mary Beth Tinker Takes the Constitution to School," 38 *Fordham L. Rev.* 35 (1969). In this respect, is Justice Black correct in his concern about the impact of *Tinker* on authority relationships in public schools? *See also Goss v. Lopez,* 419 U.S. 565, 600 n. 22 (1975) (Powell, J., dissenting).

6. *Defining "Disruption" and "Impairment"*

Does the Court in *Tinker* offer any guidance concerning the meaning of "substantial disruption"? Is noise a form of disruption—disobedience, distraction, inattentiveness? Is a verbal disagreement between students, or between a student and a teacher, a substantial disruption? Is not the purpose of speech to bring the attention of listeners to the speaker's message? *See* Ladd, "Allegedly Disruptive Student Behavior and the Legal Authority of School Officials," 19 *J. Pub. Law* 209, 212–18 (1970). Should the concept of disruption vary depending on whether the institution is an elementary school, high school, or college?

In the light of the disruption standard adopted in *Tinker,* consider these excerpts from the record:

1. "A former student of one of our high schools was killed in Vietnam. Some of his friends are still in school, and it was felt that if any kind of demonstration existed, it might evolve into something which would be difficult to control."
2. "I [John Tinker] felt self-conscious about wearing the armband. . . . some of the other students talked to me about the armband and asked why I was wearing it. I told them why and some of them didn't think I should do this. . . . This discussion took place on and off during the class period."
3. "After gym some students were making fun of me [John Tinker] for wearing it. . . . Two or three boys made remarks in the locker room that were not very

friendly. This lasted for perhaps three or four minutes. They did not threaten me with any physical harm."

4. "[In the lunchroom] there was one student . . . who was making smart remarks for about ten minutes. There were four to five people with him standing milling around. There were quite a few other students standing and milling around the lunchroom. To my knowledge there were no threats to hit me or anything like that. At no time was I in fear that they might attack me or hit me in the student center because there were too many people there. . . . A football player named Joe Thompson told the kids to leave me alone; that everyone had their own opinions."

In addition, plaintiff Chris Eckhardt "was confronted by the captain of the football team who attempted to rip the armband off his jacket," resulting in a "brief scuffle." J. Johnson, "Behind the Scenes in Iowa's Greatest Case: What Is Not in the Official Records of *Tinker v. Des Moines Independent School District,*" 48 *Drake L. Rev.* 473, 478 (2000). Do these facts clarify the majority's concept of disruption? Could the Court have employed the disruption standard and decided the case in favor of the school authorities?

In this regard, is it relevant that the school authorities may not have been aware of the constitutional standard when the protest took place? Consider these remarks made by the school principal to John Tinker at the time of his suspension: ". . . I personally felt that there were appropriate times for us to mourn our dead, including this event [Veteran's Day] and Memorial Day, and it did not seem appropriate or necessary to me to mourn them as he was doing at this time. I told him that I was a veteran of World War II and the Korean War." Brief for petitioner at 8, *Tinker v. Des Moines Independent Community School District,* 393 U.S. 503, 89 S.Ct. 733, 21 L.Ed.2d 731 (1969). With the advantage of hindsight, was this frank admission by the principal a tactical mistake? *Compare Bree v. Kahl,* 296 F.Supp. 702, 705 n. 3 (W.D.Wis. 1969), *aff'd,* 419 F.2d 1034 (7th Cir.), *cert. denied,* 398 U.S. 937, 90 S.Ct. 1836, 26 L.Ed.2d 268 (1970). Does it demonstrate "bad faith" within the meaning of *Pico?* In future student rights cases, how would you advise school officials to defend their actions? Do you have an ethical responsibility to encourage them to be truthful in describing their reasons for the disciplinary measures?

What evidence is necessary to prove a reasonable forecast of substantial disruption? *See Boucher v. School Bd. of Sch. Dist. of Greenfield,* 134 F.3d 821 (7th Cir. 1998). Will the testimony of school officials, standing alone, suffice? Must past instances of material disruption resulting from similar speech or conduct be brought to the attention of the court? Must empirical studies be used? What about the use of expert witnesses? *See Bannister v. Paradis,* 316 F.Supp. 185 (D.N.H. 1970). Which party bears the burden of persuasion? Must the school board prove that the speech did or probably would have resulted in material disruption, or must the student prove that such consequences did not or were unlikely to occur? *See Chandler v. McMinnville Sch. Dist.,* 978 F.2d 524 (9th Cir. 1992) (burden on school district). Does *Tinker* allow trial judges so much discretion that their personal attitudes toward public schools will be decisive? *See* Friedman, "Limited Monarchy: The Rise and Fall of Student Rights," in D. Kirp and D. Jensen (eds.), *School Days, Rule Days* 238, 250–51 (1986).

7. *The Heckler's Veto*

In order to justify limiting student speech, must the disruption arise from the student speaker's conduct? Is it sufficient if others react to the speaker's message in a disruptive fashion? *See generally* Comment, "The Supreme Court and the Decline of Students' Constitutional Rights: A Selective Analysis," 65 *Neb. L. Rev.* 161, 166–67 (1986). In *Ferrell v. Dallas Independent School Dist.,* 392 F.2d 697 (5th Cir. 1968), *cert. denied,* 393 U.S. 856, 89 S.Ct. 98, 21 L.Ed.2d 125 (1968), a case involving the suspension of male students for their failure to abide by school regulations on hair length, Judge Tuttle, in dissenting from the majority's decision in favor of the school district, addressed himself to this issue:

> These boys were not barred from school because of any actions carried out by them which were of themselves a disturbance of the peace. They were barred because it was anticipated, by reason of previous experiences, that their fellow students in some instances would disrupt the serenity or calm of the school. It is these acts which should be prohibited, not the expressions of individuality by the suspended students.

392 F.2d at 706. *See also West v. Derby Unified Sch. Dist. No. 260,* 206 F.3d 1358 (10th Cir. 2000); *Jones v. Board of Regents,* 436 F.2d 618, 621 (9th Cir. 1970). *See generally* Nahmod, "Controversy in the Classroom: The High School Teacher and Freedom of Expression," 39 *Geo. Wash. L. Rev.* 1032, 1039–41 (1971).

Should it ever be permissible to silence the speaker? What if a student wears a "Hinckley should have used a .44"[9] button to a meeting of teenage Republicans in the school building? *See* Comment, *supra* at 166. Should the courts require a showing by school district officials that they attempted to control the disruption or that there were no feasible alternatives to silencing the speaker? *See* Yudof, "Student Discipline in Texas Schools," 3 *J.L. & Educ.* 221 (1974).

8. *Student Demonstrations*

Student demonstrations directed against school policies have a greater potential for disrupting the school and hence are more likely to be punishable. *See Barker v. Hardway*, 394 U.S. 905, 89 S.Ct. 1009, 22 L.Ed.2d 217 (1969) (Justice Fortas concurring in the denial of certiorari). In *Tate v. Board of Education of Jonesboro, Arkansas*, 453 F.2d 975 (8th Cir. 1972), a group of African American students complained of the school policy of playing the song "Dixie" at pep rallies. The school responded by making attendance at the pep assemblies optional; those who did not wish to attend could report to the gymnasium. Some twenty-five black students and five white students chose not to attend the rally. But twenty-nine black students who did attend silently got up and left the rally in protest when "Dixie" was played. The program was not interrupted and apparently continued after the students left, but the students were suspended for five days. When the dispute reached the courts, school officials argued successfully that the protest constituted a disruption to the order and decorum of the school. Hence the protest was not protected by *Tinker*. *See also Pickens v. Okolona Mun. Separate School Dist.*, 594 F.2d 433 (5th Cir. 1979) (student and parent demonstration adjacent to public high school).

9. *Student Criticism of School Officials and Their Policies*

In *Tinker* the students directed their criticism toward the national government and not toward officials in their own school. Would it affect the outcome of the case if the *Tinker* children had been wearing their armbands in protest over, for example, the school's athletic program? *See generally* Buss, *supra* at 517. *But see* Wright, "Free Speech Values, Public Schools, and the Role of Judicial Deference," 22 *New Eng. L. Rev.* 59 (1987). The courts have generally taken the position that criticism of school officials and their policies is to be protected to the same extent as other expression. *See Scoville v. Board of Education of Joliet Township*, 425 F.2d 10 (7th Cir. 1970), *cert. denied*, 400 U.S. 826, 91 S.Ct. 51, 27 L.Ed.2d 55 (1970). *But see Poling v. Murphy*, 872 F.2d 757, 759 (6th Cir. 1989) ("The administration plays tricks on your mind and they hope you won't notice."). In *Sullivan v. Houston Independent School District*, 307 F.Supp. 1328 (S.D.Tex. 1969), the court protected students from suspension for distribution of a paper on school grounds that contained critical remarks on the school's policy regarding the collection of money for various community and charitable projects and contained a satiric article on one school administrator, mocking his manner of speech and attitudes. *See also Thonen v. Jenkins*, 491 F.2d 722 (4th Cir. 1973); *Joyner v. Whiting*, 477 F.2d 456 (4th Cir. 1973).

Bethel School District No. 403 v. Fraser
478 U.S. 675, 106 S.Ct. 3159, 92 L.Ed.2d 549 (1986).

Chief Justice Burger delivered the opinion of the Court.

We granted certiorari to decide whether the First Amendment prevents a school district from disciplining a high school student for giving a lewd speech at a school assembly.

I

A

On April 26, 1983, respondent Matthew N. Fraser, a student at Bethel High School in Bethel, Washington, delivered a speech nominating a fellow student for student elective office. Approximately 600 high school students, many of whom were 14-year-olds, attended the assembly. Students were required to attend the assembly or to report to the study hall. The assembly was part of a school-sponsored educational program in self-government. Students who elected not to attend the assembly were required to report to study hall. During the entire speech, Fraser referred to his candidate in terms of an elaborate, graphic, and explicit sexual metaphor.

Two of Fraser's teachers, with whom he discussed the contents of his speech in advance, informed him that the speech was "inappropriate and that he probably should not deliver it," . . . and that his delivery of the speech might have "severe consequences." . . .

---

[9]John Hinckley, Jr. attempted to assassinate President Reagan in 1981. He was found not guilty by reason of insanity.

During Fraser's delivery of the speech, a school counselor observed the reaction of students to the speech. Some students hooted and yelled; some by gestures graphically simulated the sexual activities pointedly alluded to in respondent's speech. Other students appeared to be bewildered and embarrassed by the speech. One teacher reported that on the day following the speech, she found it necessary to forgo a portion of the scheduled class lesson in order to discuss the speech with the class. . . .

A Bethel High School disciplinary rule prohibiting the use of obscene language in the school provides:

> "Conduct which materially and substantially interferes with the educational process is prohibited, including the use of obscene, profane language or gestures."

The morning after the assembly, the Assistant Principal called Fraser into her office and notified him that the school considered his speech to have been a violation of this rule. Fraser was presented with copies of five letters submitted by teachers, describing his conduct at the assembly; he was given a chance to explain his conduct, and he admitted to having given the speech described and that he deliberately used sexual innuendo in the speech. Fraser was then informed that he would be suspended for three days, and that his name would be removed from the list of candidates for graduation speaker at the school's commencement exercises.

Fraser sought review of this disciplinary action through the School District's grievance procedures. The hearing officer determined that the speech given by respondent was "indecent, lewd, and offensive to the modesty and decency of many of the students and faculty in attendance at the assembly." The examiner determined that the speech fell within the ordinary meaning of "obscene," as used in the disruptive conduct rule, and affirmed the discipline in its entirety. Fraser served two days of his suspension, and was allowed to return to school on the third day.

B

Respondent, by his father as *guardian ad litem*, then brought this action in the United States District Court for the Western District of Washington. Respondent alleged a violation of his First Amendment right to freedom of speech and sought both injunctive relief and monetary damages under 42 U.S.C. § 1983. The District Court held that the school's sanctions violated respondent's right to freedom of speech under the First Amendment to the United States Constitution, that the school's disruptive-conduct rule is unconstitutionally vague and overbroad, and that the removal of respondent's name from the graduation speaker's list violated the Due Process Clause of the Fourteenth Amendment because the disciplinary rule makes no mention of such removal as a possible sanction. The District Court awarded respondent $278 in damages, $12,750 in litigation costs and attorney's fees, and enjoined the School District from preventing respondent from speaking at the commencement ceremonies. Respondent, who had been elected graduation speaker by a write-in vote of his classmates, delivered a speech at the commencement ceremonies on June 8, 1983.

The Court of Appeals for the Ninth Circuit affirmed the judgment of the District Court, 755 F.2d 1356 (1985), holding that respondent's speech was indistinguishable from the protest armband in *Tinker v. Des Moines Independent Community School Dist.*, 393 U.S. 503, 89 S.Ct. 733, 21 L.Ed.2d 731 (1969). . . . We reverse.

II

* * *

The marked distinction between the political "message" of the armbands in *Tinker* and the sexual content of respondent's speech in this case seems to have been given little weight by the Court of Appeals. In upholding the students' right to engage in a nondisruptive, passive expression of a political viewpoint in *Tinker*, this Court was careful to note that the case did "not concern speech or action that intrudes upon the work of the schools or the rights of other students." . . .

* * *

III

The role and purpose of the American public school system was well described by two historians, saying "public education must prepare pupils for citizenship in the Republic. . . . It must inculcate the habits and manners of civility as values in themselves conducive to happiness and as indispensable to the practice of self-government in the community and the nation." C. Beard & M. Beard, *New Basic History of the United States* 228 (1968). In *Ambach v. Norwick*, 441 U.S. 68, 76–77, 99 S.Ct. 1589, 1594, 60 L.Ed.2d 49 (1979), we echoed the essence of this statement of the objectives of public education as the "inculcat[ion of] fundamental values necessary to the maintenance of a democratic political system."

These fundamental values of "habits and manners of civility" essential to a democratic society must, of course, include tolerance of divergent political and religious views, even when the views expressed may be unpopular. But these "fundamental values" must also take into account consideration of the sensibilities of others, and, in the case of a school, the sensibilities of fellow students. The undoubted freedom to advocate unpopular and controversial views in schools and classrooms must be balanced against the society's countervailing interest in teaching students the boundaries of socially appropriate behaviour. Even the most heated political discourse in a democratic society requires consideration for the personal sensibilities of the other participants and audiences.

* * *

The First Amendment guarantees wide freedom in matters of adult public discourse. A sharply divided Court upheld the right to express an antidraft viewpoint in a public place, albeit in terms highly offensive to most citizens. *See Cohen v. California*, 403 U.S. 15, 91 S.Ct. 1780, 29 L.Ed.2d 284 (1971). It does not follow, however, that simply because the use of an offensive form of expression may not be prohibited to adults making what the speaker considers a political point, that the same latitude must be permitted to children in a public school. . . . Surely it is a highly appropriate function of public school education to prohibit the use of vulgar and offensive terms in public discourse. Indeed, the "fundamental values necessary to the maintenance of a democratic political system" disfavor the use of terms of debate highly offensive or highly threatening to others. Nothing in the Constitution prohibits the states from insisting that certain modes of expression are inappropriate and subject to sanctions. The inculcation of these values is truly the "work of the schools." . . . The determination of what manner of speech in the classroom or in school assembly is inappropriate properly rests with the school board.

The process of educating our youth for citizenship in public schools is not confined to books, the curriculum, and the civics class; schools must teach by example the shared values of a civilized social order. Consciously or otherwise, teachers—and indeed the older students—demonstrate the appropriate form of civil discourse and political expression by their conduct and deportment in and out of class. Inescapably, like parents, they are role models. The schools, as instruments of the state, may determine that the essential lessons of civil, mature conduct cannot be conveyed in a school that tolerates lewd, indecent, or offensive speech and conduct such as that indulged in by this confused boy.

The pervasive sexual innuendo in Fraser's speech was plainly offensive to both teachers and students—indeed to any mature person. By glorifying male sexuality, and in its verbal content, the speech was acutely insulting to teenage girl students. . . . The speech could well be seriously damaging to its less mature audience, many of whom were only 14 years old and on the threshold of awareness of human sexuality. Some students were reported as bewildered by the speech and the reaction of mimicry it provoked.

. . . In *Ginsberg v. New York*, 390 U.S. 629, 88 S.Ct. 1274, 20 L.Ed.2d 195 (1968), this Court upheld a New York statute banning the sale of sexually oriented material to minors, even though the material in question was entitled to First Amendment protection with respect to adults.

[A]ll Members of the Court, otherwise sharply divided, acknowledged that the school board has the authority to remove books that are vulgar. *Board of Education v. Pico*, 457 U.S. 853 . . . (1982). . . . These cases recognize the obvious concern on the part of parents, and school authorities acting *in loco parentis* to protect children—especially in a captive audience—from exposure to sexually explicit, indecent, or lewd speech.

* * *

We hold that petitioner School District acted entirely within its permissible authority in imposing sanctions upon Fraser in response to his offensively lewd and indecent speech. Unlike the sanctions imposed on the students wearing armbands in *Tinker*, the penalties imposed in this case were unrelated to any political viewpoint. . . .

* * *

IV

[The Court concludes that respondent's argument that he had no way of knowing that the speech he gave would subject him to disciplinary sanctions is "wholly without merit."]

The judgment of the Court of Appeals for the Ninth Circuit is

Reversed.

Justice Blackmun concurs in the result.

Justice Brennan, concurring in the judgment.

Respondent gave the following speech at a high school assembly in support of a candidate for student government office:

" 'I know a man who is firm—he's firm in his pants, he's firm in his shirt, his character is firm—but most . . . of all, his belief in you, the students of Bethel, is firm.

" 'Jeff Kuhlman is a man who takes his point and pounds it in. If necessary, he'll take an issue and nail it to the wall. He doesn't attack things in spurts—he drives hard, pushing and pushing until finally—he succeeds.

" 'Jeff is a man who will go to the very end—even the climax, for each and every one of you.

" 'So vote for Jeff for A.S.B. vice-president—he'll never come between you and the best our high school can be.' " . . .

The Court, referring to these remarks as "obscene," "vulgar," "lewd," and "offensively lewd," concludes that school officials properly punished respondent for uttering the speech. Having read the full text of respondent's remarks, I find it difficult to believe that it is the same speech the Court describes. To my mind, the most that can be said about respondent's speech—and all that need be said—is that in light of the discretion school officials have to teach high school students how to conduct civil and effective public discourse, and to prevent disruption of school educational activities, it was not unconstitutional for school officials to conclude, under the circumstances of this case, that respondent's remarks exceeded permissible limits. . . .

* * *

Justice Marshall, dissenting.

. . . I dissent from the Court's decision . . . because in my view the school district failed to demonstrate that respondent's remarks were indeed disruptive. . . .

Justice Stevens, dissenting.

"Frankly, my dear, I don't give a damn."

When I was a high school student, the use of those words in a public forum shocked the Nation. Today Clark Gable's four-letter expletive is less offensive than it was then. Nevertheless, I assume that high school administrators may prohibit the use of that word in classroom discussion and even in extracurricular activities that are sponsored by the school and held on school premises. For I believe a school faculty must regulate the content as well as the style of student speech in carrying out its educational mission. It does seem to me, however, that if a student is to be punished for using offensive speech, he is entitled to fair notice of the scope of the prohibition and the consequences of its violation. The interest in free speech protected by the First Amendment[2] and the interest in fair procedure protected by the Due Process Clause of the Fourteenth Amendment combine to require this conclusion.

* * *

NOTES AND QUESTIONS

1. Fraser *and the Substantial Disruption Test*

Is *Fraser* consistent with *Tinker*? *See* E. Chemerinsky, "Students Do Leave Their First Amendment Rights at the School House Gates: What's Left of *Tinker*?" 48 *Drake L. Rev.* 527, 536–7 (2000) (not consistent); Fischer, "From *Tinker* to *TLO*; Are Civil Rights for Students 'Flunking' in School?" 22 *J. of L. & Educ.* 409 (1993); Dienes & Connolly, "When Students Speak: Judicial Review in the Academic Marketplace," 7 *Yale L. & Pol'y Rev.* 343 (1989). Chief Justice Burger emphasizes that Matthew Fraser's speech was greeted by hoots and yells and graphic sexual gestures by some students. Does this indicate that he believes that the *Tinker* substantial disruption test has been satisfied? What of the fact that some students felt "bewildered and embarrassed" by the speech? Is this a substantial disruption? If such a response constitutes substantial disruption, has the Court modified the *Tinker* definition of disruption?

Is *Tinker* distinguishable because Fraser was addressing a school-sponsored assembly? Because the school has a substantial interest in regulating the election of student officers? *Cf. Alabama Student Party v. Student Government Association*, 867 F.2d 1344 (11th Cir. 1989). How is Fraser's speech different than wearing an armband to class? Is there a significant constitutional distinction between a student speaking as part of a school activity (electing student officers) and a student speaking on his or her own behalf apart from regular school activities and curricula? *See Board of Education of Westside Community Schools v. Mergens*, 496 U.S. 226, 110 S.Ct. 2356 (1990); *Hazelwood School District v. Kuhlmeier, infra*.

2. *Lewd Speech*

Is *Tinker* distinguishable because it involved political speech whereas *Fraser* does not? Is this what the Chief Justice means when he says that "unlike . . . *Tinker*, the penalties imposed in this case were unrelated to any political viewpoint. . . ."? Why is a nomination speech for a school office not political speech? Is the Chief Justice suggesting that there is a distinction between the content and context of the message and the manner of presenting the message? *See* Comment, "Students' First Amendment Rights: Gone With the Wind?" 11 *Am. J. Trial Advoc.* 173,

---

[2]As the Court of Appeals noted, there "is no evidence in the record indicating that any students found the speech to be offensive." . . .

182–183 (1987); Note, "*Tinker* Revisited: *Fraser v. Bethel School District* and Regulation of Speech in the Public Schools," 1985 *Duke L. J.* 1164, 1179. If so, how is *Cohen v. California*, 403 U.S. 15, 91 S.Ct. 1780, 29 L.Ed.2d 284 (1971), distinguishable?

Is it that adults have greater latitude in matters of speech than children? That the state can go to greater lengths to protect children from vulgar speech? *See FCC v. Pacifica Foundation*, 438 U.S. 726, 98 S.Ct. 3026, 57 L.Ed.2d 1073 (1978). Would the Court have reached the same result in a case arising in a public university? *See Papish v. Board of Curators of University of Missouri*, 410 U.S. 667, 93 S.Ct. 1197, 35 L.Ed.2d 618 (1973). Is it that a public high school has a different mission than a university? Is this why Chief Justice Burger emphasizes the socialization mission of public schools? *See* Diamond, "The First Amendment and Public Schools: The Case Against Judicial Intervention," 59 *Tex. L. Rev.* 477 (1981). Zirkel, Richardson, and MacKenzie, "Tinkering with the First Amendment Rights of Students," 37 *Educ. L. Rep.* 433, 438–43 (1987); Note, 1985 *Duke L. J. supra* at 1185. Does the *Pico* case, *supra*, support his approach?

With regard to vulgarity or appropriateness for a student audience, should school-sponsored expression be treated identically with the personal expression of students? *See* Yudof, "Personal Speech and Government Expression," 38 *Case W. Res. L. Rev.* 671 (1988). For example, may school officials cancel a student production of a play because of its sexual themes or vulgarity? *See Seyfried v. Walton*, 668 F.2d 214 (3d Cir. 1981) (decision to cancel *Pippin* upheld); *Boring v. Buncombe County Bd. of Education*, 136 F.3d 364 (4th Cir. 1998). *See generally* Faaborg, "High School Play Censorship: Are Students' First Amendment Rights Violated When Officials Cancel Theatrical Productions?" 14 *J. Law & Educ.* 575 (1985). What if a film is removed from the curriculum because of its "exaggerated and undue emphasis on violence and bloodshed"? *See Pratt v. Independent School District*, No. 831, 670 F.2d 771 (8th Cir. 1982). What if a student club, meeting after school, discusses books focusing on sexual themes or the drug culture? May school authorities forbid the club from meeting on campus? *Cf. Board of Education of Westside Community Schools v. Mergens*, 496 U.S. 226, 110 S.Ct. 2356 (1990).

Should school authorities be permitted, as Justice Brennan suggests, to teach students to engage in civilized discourse—either by regulating the curriculum itself or by punishing vulgar speech by students? If so, does this mean that the *Tinker* disruption test simply is not applicable to vulgar speech? *See, e.g., Pyle v. South Hadley Sch. Comm.*, 861 F.Supp. 157 (D. Mass 1994). Or does it mean that such speech, by its nature, substantially interferes with the educational mission of a public school?

What if Fraser's speech contained no sexual metaphors or double entendres but simply was tasteless in the judgment of school officials? For example, what if a candidate for a school office were to use the following joke before a school assembly: "[Y]ou idiots are too darn gullible. For example, what is black and blue and wrapped in plastic? A baby in a trash bag, of course." After *Fraser* may a student be disciplined for such a speech? *See Poling v. Murphy*, 872 F.2d 757 (6th Cir. 1989).

3. *Notice of Violation of the Disciplinary Rule*

Fraser was disciplined for violating a school rule forbidding conduct that "materially and substantially interferes with the educational process . . . , including the use of obscene, profane language or gestures." Does the wording of the rule explain Chief Justice Burger's emphasis on disruption? Did Fraser have notice that his speech would lead to his being charged with a disciplinary offense? Or do you agree with Justice Stevens? Suppose that Fraser had ample advance warning from his teachers, but a court concludes that the rule itself did not extend to a speech with clever sexual innuendos but no profane words. *See* chapter 3, *infra*.

4. *Abusive Speech and Racial Harassment*

Suppose that the Bethel School District adopted a rule that stated that "no person shall upbraid, insult or abuse any teacher of the public schools on the school campus in the presence of students." After *Tinker* and *Fraser*, may a student be disciplined for violating the rule even if he or she does not use profanity? *See Poling v. Murphy*, 872 F.2d 757 (6th Cir. 1989); *Gano v. School District No. 411*, 674 F.Supp. 796 (D.Idaho 1987); *Lovell v. Poway Unified Sch. Dist.*, 90 F.3d 367 (9th Cir. 1996). What if a parent, displeased with a teacher's performance, insults a teacher in front of his child and other students? *See Commonwealth v. Ashcraft*, 691 S.W.2d 229 (Ky.App. 1985) (unconstitutionally overbroad as applied to parent).

What if the Bethel School District made it a disciplinary offense for a student to engage in speech that stigmatizes an individual on the basis of race and that has the purpose or the reasonably foreseeable effect of interfering with an individual's academic efforts or creating a demeaning or intimidating educational environment? Is such a ban on racial harassment by students a violation of the First Amendment? *See Doe v. University of Michigan*, 721 F.Supp. 852 (E.D.Mich. 1989). *See also West v. Derby Unified Sch. Dist. No. 260*, 206 F.3d 1358 (10th Cir. 2000). *See generally* Delgado, "Campus Antiracism Rules: Constitutional Narratives in Collision," 85 *Nw. U. L. Rev.* 343 (1991); Symposium, "Offensive and Libelous Speech," 47 *Wash. & Lee L. Rev.* 1 (1990); Strossen, "Regulating Racist Speech on Campus: A Modest Proposal?" 1990 *Duke L. J.* 484; Post, "The Constitutional Concept of Public Discourse: Outrageous Opinion, Democratic Deliberation and *Hustler Magazine v. Falwell*," 103 *Harv. L. Rev.* 601 (1990); Haviland, "Student Discriminatory Harassment," 16 *J. C. & U. L.* 311 (1989); Delgado, "Words That Wound: A Tort Action for Racial Insults, Epithets, and Name-Calling," 17 *Harv. C.R.–C.L. L. Rev.* 133 (1982).

What of a racial harassment rule based upon the likelihood that particular epithets would cause a fight to occur ("fighting words")? What of a rule treating racial slurs within the framework of intentional infliction of emotional distress? May racial insults create a "hostile" environment for minority students akin to a hostile work environment for employees? Should the limits of expression be the same in these two contexts? *See* Note, "Racist Speech on Campus: A Title VII Solution to a Problem," 64 *S. Cal. L. Rev.* 105 (1990). What of the fact that public school students are compelled to attend school? What of the fact that they are younger and presumedly less mature than college students?

Would the display of confederate symbols by white students constitute racial harassment? If so, may school authorities discipline students for such displays? *See West v. Derby Unified Sch. Dist. No. 260, supra.*

2. Student Newspapers

Hazelwood School District v. Kuhlmeier
484 U.S. 260, 108 S.Ct. 562, 98 L.Ed.2d 592 (1988).

Justice White delivered the opinion of the Court.

This case concerns the extent to which educators may exercise editorial control over the contents of a high school newspaper produced as part of the school's journalism curriculum.

I

Petitioners are the Hazelwood School District in St. Louis County, Missouri; various school officials; Robert Eugene Reynolds, the principal of Hazelwood East High School, and Howard Emerson, a teacher in the school district. Respondents are three former Hazelwood East students who were staff members of Spectrum, the school newspaper. They contend that school officials violated their First Amendment rights by deleting two pages of articles from the May 13, 1983, issue of Spectrum.

Spectrum was written and edited by the Journalism II class at Hazelwood East. The newspaper was published every three weeks or so during the 1982–1983 school year. More than 4,500 copies of the newspaper were distributed during that year to students, school personnel, and members of the community.

The Board of Education allocated funds from its annual budget for the printing of Spectrum. These funds were supplemented by proceeds from sales of the newspaper. The printing expenses during the 1982–1983 school year totaled $4,668.50; revenue from sales was $1,166.84. The other costs associated with the newspaper—such as supplies, textbooks, and a portion of the journalism teacher's salary—were borne entirely by the Board.

The Journalism II course was taught by Robert Stergos for most of the 1982–1983 academic year. Stergos left Hazelwood East to take a job in private industry on April 29, 1983, when the May 13 edition of Spectrum was nearing completion, and petitioner Emerson took his place as newspaper adviser for the remaining weeks of the term.

The practice at Hazelwood East during the spring 1983 semester was for the journalism teacher to submit page proofs of each Spectrum issue to Principal Reynolds for his review prior to publication. On May 10, Emerson delivered the proofs of the May 13 edition to Reynolds, who objected to two of the articles scheduled to appear in that edition. One of the stories described three Hazelwood East students' experiences with pregnancy; the other discussed the impact of divorce on students at the school.

Reynolds was concerned that, although the pregnancy story used false names "to keep the identity of these girls a secret," the pregnant students still might be identifiable from the text. He also believed that the article's references to sexual activity and birth control were inappropriate for some of the younger students at the school. In addition, Reynolds was concerned that a student identified by name in the divorce story had complained that her father "wasn't spending enough time with my mom, my sister and I" prior to the divorce, "was always out of town on business or out late playing cards with the guys," and "always argued about everything" with her mother. . . . Reynolds believed that the student's parents should have been given an opportunity to respond to these remarks or to consent to their publication. He was unaware that Emerson had deleted the student's name from the final version of the article.

Reynolds believed that there was no time to make the necessary changes in the stories before the scheduled press run and that the newspaper would not appear before the end of the school year if printing were delayed to any significant extent. He concluded that his only options under the circumstances were to publish a four-page newspaper instead of the planned six-page newspaper, eliminating the two pages on which the offending stories appeared, or to publish no newspaper at all. Accordingly, he directed Emerson to withhold from publication the two pages containing the stories on pregnancy and divorce.[1] He informed his superiors of the decision, and they concurred.

* * *

II

Students in the public schools do not "shed their constitutional rights to freedom of speech or expression at the schoolhouse gate." *Tinker [v. Des Moines Independent Community School Dist.]*. They cannot be punished merely for expressing their personal views on the school premises—whether "in the cafeteria, or on the playing field, or on the campus during authorized hours," . . . unless school authorities have reason to believe that such expression will "substantially interfere with the work of the school or impinge upon the rights of other students." . . .

We have nonetheless recognized that the First Amendment rights of students in the public schools "are not automatically coextensive with the rights of adults in other settings," *Bethel School District No. 403 v. Fraser.* . . . A school need not tolerate student speech that is inconsistent with its "basic educational mission," . . . even though the government could not censor similar speech outside the school. Accordingly, we held in *Fraser* that a student could be disciplined

for having delivered a speech that was "sexually explicit" but not legally obscene at an official school assembly, because the school was entitled to "disassociate itself" from the speech in a manner that would demonstrate to others that such vulgarity is "wholly inconsistent with the 'fundamental values' of public school education." . . . It is in this context that respondents' First Amendment claims must be considered.

A

We deal first with the question whether Spectrum may appropriately be characterized as a forum for public expression. The public schools do not possess all of the attributes of streets, parks, and other traditional public forums that "time out of mind, have been used for purposes of assembly, communicating thoughts between citizens, and discussing public questions." *Hague v. CIO*, 307 U.S. 496, 515, 59 S.Ct. 954, 964, 83 L.Ed. 1423 (1939). *Cf. Widmar v. Vincent*, 454 U.S. 263, 267–68, n. 5, 102 S.Ct. 269, 273, n. 5, 70 L.Ed.2d 440 (1981). Hence, school facilities may be deemed to be public forums only if school authorities have "by policy or by practice" opened those facilities "for indiscriminate use by the general public," *Perry Education Assn. v. Perry Local Educators' Assn.*, 460 U.S. 37, 47, 103 S.Ct. 948, 956, 74 L.Ed.2d 794 (1983), or by some segment of the public, such as student organizations. . . . If the facilities have instead been reserved for other intended purposes, "communicative or otherwise," then no public forum has been created, and school officials may impose reasonable restrictions on the speech of students, teachers, and other members of the school community. . . . "The government does not create a public forum by inaction or by permitting limited discourse, but only by intentionally opening a nontraditional forum for public discourse." *Cornelius v. NAACP Legal Defense & Educational Fund, Inc.*, 473 U.S. 788, 802, 105 S.Ct. 3439, 3449, 87 L.Ed.2d 567 (1985).

The policy of school officials toward Spectrum was reflected in Hazelwood School Board Policy 348.51 in the Hazelwood East Curriculum Guide. Board Policy 348.51 provided that "[s]chool sponsored publications are developed within the adopted curriculum and its educational implications in regular classroom activities." . . . The Hazelwood East

---

[1]The two pages deleted from the newspaper also contained articles on teenage marriage, runaways, and juvenile delinquents, as well as a general article on teenage pregnancy. Reynolds testified that he had no objection to these articles and that they were deleted only because they appeared on the same pages as the two objectionable articles.

Curriculum Guide described the Journalism II course as a "laboratory situation in which the students publish the school newspaper applying skills they have learned in Journalism I." . . . The lessons that were to be learned from the Journalism II course, according to the Curriculum Guide, included development of journalistic skills under deadline pressure, "the legal, moral, and ethical restrictions imposed upon journalists within the school community," and "responsibility and acceptance of criticism for articles of opinion." . . . Journalism II was taught by a faculty member during regular class hours. Students received grades and academic credit for their performance in the course.

School officials did not deviate in practice from their policy that production of Spectrum was to be part of the educational curriculum and a "regular classroom activit[y]." The District Court found that Robert Stergos, the journalism teacher during most of the 1982–1983 school year, "both had the authority to exercise and in fact exercised a great deal of control over Spectrum." . . . For example, Stergos selected the editors of the newspaper, scheduled publication dates, decided the number of pages for each issue, assigned story ideas to class members, advised students on the development of their stories, reviewed the use of quotations, edited stories, selected and edited the letters to the editor, and dealt with the printing company. Many of these decisions were made without consultation with the Journalism II students. The District Court thus found it "clear that Mr. Stergos was the final authority with respect to almost every aspect of the production and publication of Spectrum, including its content."

. . . Moreover, after each Spectrum issue had been fully approved by Stergos or his successor, the issue still had to be reviewed by Principal Reynolds prior to publication. Respondents' assertion that they had believed that they could publish "practically anything" in Spectrum was therefore dismissed by the District Court as simply "not credible." . . .

The evidence relied upon by the Court of Appeals in finding Spectrum to be a public forum . . . is equivocal at best. For example, Board Policy 348.51, which stated in part that "[s]chool sponsored student publications will not restrict free expression or diverse viewpoints within the rules of responsible journalism," also stated that such publications were "developed within the adopted curriculum and its educational implications." . . . One might reasonably infer from the full text of Policy 348.51 that school officials retained ultimate control over what constituted "responsible journalism" in a school-sponsored newspaper. Although the statement of Policy published in the September 14, 1982, issue of Spectrum declared that "Spectrum, as a student-press publication, accepts all rights implied by the First Amendment," this statement, understood in the context of the paper's role in the school's curriculum, suggests at most that the administration will not interfere with the students' exercise of those First Amendment rights that attend the publication of a school-sponsored newspaper. It does not reflect an intent to expand those rights by converting a curricular newspaper into a public forum.[2] Finally, that students were permitted to exercise some authority over the contents of Spectrum was fully consistent with the Curriculum Guide objective of teaching the Journalism II students "leadership responsibilities as issue and page editors." . . . A decision to teach leadership skills in the context of a classroom activity hardly implies a decision to relinquish school control over that activity. In sum, . . . school officials did not evince either "by policy or by practice," . . . any intent to open the pages of Spectrum to "indiscriminate use," . . . by its student reporters and editors, or by the student body generally. Instead, they "reserve[d] the forum for its intended purpos[e]," . . . a supervised learning experience for journalism students. Accordingly, school officials were entitled to regulate the contents of Spectrum in any reasonable manner. . . . It is this standard, rather than our decision in *Tinker*, that governs in this case.

B

The question whether the First Amendment requires a school to tolerate particular student speech—the question that we addressed in *Tinker*—is different from the question whether the First Amendment

---

[2]The Statement also cited *Tinker v. Des Moines Independent Community School Dist.*, 393 U.S. 503, 89 S.Ct. 733, 21 L.Ed.2d 731 (1969), for the proposition that "[o]nly speech that 'materially and substantially interferes with the requirements of appropriate discipline' can be found unacceptable and therefore be prohibited." . . . This portion of the Statement does not, of course, even accurately reflect our holding in *Tinker*. Furthermore, the statement nowhere expressly extended the *Tinker* standard to the news and feature articles contained in a school-sponsored newspaper. The dissent apparently finds as a fact that the Statement was published annually in Spectrum; however, the District Court was unable to conclude that the Statement appeared on more than one occasion. In any event, even if the Statement says what the dissent believes that it says, the evidence that school officials never intended to designate Spectrum as a public forum remains overwhelming.

requires a school affirmatively to promote particular student speech. The former question addresses educators' ability to silence a student's personal expression that happens to occur on the school premises. The latter question concerns educators' authority over school-sponsored publications, theatrical productions, and other expressive activities that students, parents, and members of the public might reasonably perceive to bear the imprimatur of the school.

These activities may fairly be characterized as part of the school curriculum, whether or not they occur in a traditional classroom setting, so long as they are supervised by faculty members and designed to impart particular knowledge or skills to student participants and audiences.[3]

Educators are entitled to exercise greater control over this second form of student expression to assure that participants learn whatever lessons the activity is designed to teach, that readers or listeners are not exposed to material that may be inappropriate for their level of maturity, and that the views of the individual speaker are not erroneously attributed to the school. Hence, a school may in its capacity as publisher of a school newspaper or producer of a school play "disassociate itself," . . . not only from speech that would "substantially interfere with [its] work . . . or impinge upon the rights of other students," *Tinker*, 393 U.S., at 509, 89 S.Ct., at 738, but also from speech that is, for example, ungrammatical, poorly written, inadequately researched, biased or prejudiced, vulgar or profane, or unsuitable for immature audiences.[4] A school must be able to set high standards for the student speech that is disseminated under its auspices— standards that may be higher than those demanded by some newspaper publishers or theatrical producers in the "real" world—and may refuse to disseminate student speech that does not meet those standards. In addition, a school must be able to take into account the emotional maturity of the intended audience in de-

termining whether to disseminate student speech on potentially sensitive topics, which might range from the existence of Santa Claus in an elementary school setting to the particulars of teenage sexual activity in a high school setting. A school must also retain the authority to refuse to sponsor student speech that might reasonably be perceived to advocate drug or alcohol use, irresponsible sex, or conduct otherwise inconsistent with "the shared values of a civilized social order," . . . or to associate the school with any position other than neutrality on matters of political controversy. . . .

* * *

This standard is consistent with our oft-expressed view that the education of the Nation's youth is primarily the responsibility of parents, teachers, and state and local school officials, and not of federal judges. *See, e.g., Board of Education of Hendrick Hudson Central School Dist. v. Rowley*, 458 U.S. 176, 208, 102 S.Ct. 3034, 3051, 73 L.Ed.2d 690 (1982); *Wood v. Strickland*, 420 U.S. 308, 326, 95 S.Ct. 992, 1003, 43 L.Ed.2d 214 (1975); *Epperson v. Arkansas*, 393 U.S. 97, 104, 89 S.Ct. 266, 270, 21 L.Ed.2d 228 (1968). It is only when the decision to censor a school-sponsored publication, theatrical production, or other vehicle of student expression has no valid educational purpose that the First Amendment is so "directly and sharply implicate[d]," . . . as to require judicial intervention to protect students' constitutional rights.[6]

III

We also conclude that Principal Reynolds acted reasonably in requiring the deletion from the May 13 issue of Spectrum of the pregnancy article, the divorce article, and the remaining articles that were to appear on the same pages of the newspaper.

The initial paragraph of the pregnancy article declared that "[a]ll names have been changed to keep the identity of these girls a secret." The principal con-

---

[3]The distinction that we draw between speech that is sponsored by the school and speech that is not fully consistent with *Papish v. Board of Curators*, 410 U.S. 667, 93 S.Ct. 1197, 35 L.Ed.2d 618 (1973) (per curiam), which involved an off-campus "underground" newspaper that school officials merely had allowed to be sold on a state university campus.

[4]The dissent perceives no difference between the First Amendment analysis applied in *Tinker* and that applied in *Fraser*. We disagree. The decision in *Fraser* rested on the "vulgar," "lewd," and "plainly offensive" character of a speech delivered at an official school assembly rather than on any propensity of the speech to "materially disrupt[] classwork or involve[] substantial disorder or invasion of the rights of others." . . . Indeed, the *Fraser* Court cited as "especially relevant" a portion of Justice Black's dissenting opinion in *Tinker* "disclaim[ing] any purpose . . . to hold that the Federal Constitution compels the teachers, parents and elected school officials to surrender control of the American public school system to public school students." . . . Of course, Justice Black's observations are equally relevant to the instant case.

[6]We reject respondents' suggestion that school officials be permitted to exercise prepublication control over school-sponsored publications only pursuant to specific written regulations. To require such regulations in the context of a curricular activity could unduly constrain the ability of educators to educate. We need not now decide whether such regulations are required before school officials may censor publications not sponsored by the school that students seek to distribute on school grounds. See *Baughman v. Freienmuth*, 478 F.2d 1345 (4th Cir. 1973); *Shanley v. Northwest Independent School Dist.*, *Bexar Cty., Tex.*, 462 F.2d 960 (5th Cir. 1972); *Eisner v. Stamford Board of Education*, 440 F.2d 803 (2d Cir. 1971).

cluded that the students' anonymity was not adequately protected, however, given the other identifying information in the article and the small number of pregnant students at the school. . . . The article did not contain graphic accounts of sexual activity. The girls did comment in the article, however, concerning their sexual histories and their use or nonuse of birth control. It was not unreasonable for the principal to have concluded that such frank talk was inappropriate in a school-sponsored publication distributed to 14-year-old freshmen and presumably taken home to be read by students' even younger brothers and sisters.

The student who was quoted by name in the version of the divorce article seen by Principal Reynolds made comments sharply critical of her father. The principal could reasonably have concluded that an individual publicly identified as an inattentive parent—indeed, as one who chose "playing cards with the guys" over home and family—was entitled to an opportunity to defend himself as a matter of journalistic fairness. . . .

* * *

In sum, we cannot reject as unreasonable Principal Reynolds' conclusion that neither the pregnancy article nor the divorce article was suitable for publication in Spectrum. Reynolds could reasonably have concluded that the students who had written and edited these articles had not sufficiently mastered those portions of the Journalism II curriculum that pertained to the treatment of controversial issues and personal attacks, the need to protect the privacy of individuals whose most intimate concerns are to be revealed in the newspaper, and "the legal, moral, and ethical restrictions imposed upon journalists within [a] school community" that includes adolescent subjects and readers. Finally, we conclude that the principal's decision to delete two pages of Spectrum, rather than to delete only the offending articles or to require that they be modified, was reasonable under the circumstances as he understood them. Accordingly, no violation of First Amendment rights occurred.[9]

The judgment of the Court of Appeals for the Eighth Circuit is therefore *Reversed.*

Justice Brennan, with whom Justice Marshall and Justice Blackmun join, dissenting.

When the young men and women of Hazelwood East High School registered for Journalism II, they expected a civics lesson. Spectrum, the newspaper they were to publish, "was not just a class exercise in which students learned to prepare papers and hone writing skills, it was a . . . forum established to give students an opportunity to express their views while gaining an appreciation of their rights and responsibilities under the First Amendment to the United States Constitution. . . ." 795 F.2d 1368, 1373 (CA8 1986). "[A]t the beginning of each school year," *id.*, at 1372, the student journalists published a Statement of Policy—tacitly approved each year by school authorities—announcing their expectation that "Spectrum, as a student-press publication, accepts all rights implied by the First Amendment. . . . Only speech that 'materially and substantially interferes with the requirements of appropriate discipline' can be found unacceptable and therefore prohibited. . . ." The school board itself affirmatively guaranteed the students of Journalism II an atmosphere conducive to fostering such an appreciation and exercising the full panoply of rights associated with a free student press. "School sponsored student publications," it vowed, "will not restrict free expression or diverse viewpoints within the rules of responsible journalism." . . . (Board Policy § 348.51).

This case arose when the Hazelwood East administration breached its own promise, dashing its students' expectations. The school principal, without prior consultation or explanation, excised six articles—comprising two full pages—of the May 13, 1983, issue of Spectrum. He did so not because any of the articles would "materially and substantially interfere with the requirements of appropriate discipline," but simply because he considered two of the six "inappropriate, personal, sensitive, and unsuitable" for student consumption. 795 F.2d, at 1371.

In my view the principal broke more than just a promise. He violated the First Amendment's prohibitions against censorship of any student expression that neither disrupts classwork nor invades the rights of others, and against any censorship that is not narrowly tailored to serve its purpose.

I

* * *

Free student expression undoubtedly sometimes interferes with the effectiveness of the school's pedagogical functions. Some brands of student expression

---

[9]It is likely that the approach urged by the dissent would as a practical matter have far more deleterious consequences for the student press than does the approach that we adopt today. The dissent correctly acknowledges "[t]he State's prerogative to dissolve the student newspaper entirely." . . . It is likely that many public schools would do just that rather than open their newspapers to all student expression that does not threaten "materia[l] disrup[tion of] classwork" or violation of "rights that are protected by law," . . . regardless of how sexually explicit, racially intemperate, or personally insulting that expression otherwise might be.

do so by directly preventing the school from pursuing its pedagogical mission: The young polemic who stands on a soapbox during calculus class to deliver an eloquent political diatribe interferes with the legitimate teaching of calculus. And the student who delivers a lewd endorsement of a student-government candidate might so extremely distract an impressionable high school audience as to interfere with the orderly operation of the school. *See Bethel School Dist. No. 403 v. Fraser,* . . . Other student speech, however, frustrates the school's legitimate pedagogical purposes merely by expressing a message that conflicts with the school's, without directly interfering with the school's expression of its message: A student who responds to a political science teacher's question with the retort, "Socialism is good," subverts the school's inculcation of the message that capitalism is better. Even the maverick who sits in class passively sporting a symbol of protest against a government policy, *cf. Tinker v. Des Moines Independent School Dist.,* 393 U.S. 503, 89 S.Ct. 733, 21 L.Ed.2d 731 (1969), or the gossip who sits in the student commons swapping stories of sexual escapade could readily muddle a clear official message condoning the government policy or condemning teenage sex. Likewise, the student newspaper that, like Spectrum, conveys a moral position at odds with the school's official stance might subvert the administration's legitimate inculcation of its own perception of community values.

If mere incompatibility with the school's pedagogical message were a constitutionally sufficient justification for the suppression of student speech, school officials could censor each of the students or student organizations in the foregoing hypotheticals, converting our public schools into "enclaves of totalitarianism," . . . that "strangle the free mind at its source," *West Virginia State Board of Education v. Barnette, supra,* 319 U.S., at 637, 63 S.Ct., at 1185. The First Amendment permits no such blanket censorship authority. . . .

In *Tinker,* this Court struck the balance. We held that official censorship of student expression — there the suspension of several students until they removed their armbands protesting the Vietnam War — is unconstitutional unless the speech "materially disrupts classwork or involves substantial disorder or invasion of the rights of others." . . .

This Court applied the *Tinker* test just a Term ago in *Fraser, supra,* upholding an official decision to discipline a student for delivering a lewd speech in support of a student-government candidate. The Court today casts no doubt on *Tinker*'s vitality. Instead it

erects a taxonomy of school censorship, concluding that *Tinker* applies to one category and not another. On the one hand is censorship "to silence a student's personal expression that happens to occur on the school premises." . . . On the other hand is censorship of expression that arises in the context of "school-sponsored . . . expressive activities that students, parents, and members of the public might reasonably perceive to bear the imprimatur of the school." . . .

The Court does not, for it cannot, purport to discern from our precedents the distinction it creates. . . .

Nor has this Court ever intimated a distinction between personal and school-sponsored speech in any other context. Particularly telling is this Court's heavy reliance on *Tinker* in two cases of First Amendment infringement on state college campuses. *See Papish v. University of Missouri Board of Curators,* 410 U.S. 667, 671, n. 6, 93 S.Ct. 1197, 1199, n. 6, 35 L.Ed.2d 618 (1973) (per curiam); *Healy v. James,* 408 U.S. 169, 180, 189, and n. 18, 191, 92 S.Ct. 2338, 2345, 2350, and n. 18, 2351, 33 L.Ed.2d 266 (1972). One involved the expulsion of a student for lewd expression in a newspaper that she sold on campus pursuant to university authorization, *see Papish, supra,* 410 U.S., at 667–68, 93 S.Ct., at 1197–98, and the other involved the denial of university recognition and concomitant benefits to a political student organization, *see Healy, supra,* 408 U.S., at 174, 176, 181–82, 92 S.Ct., at 2342, 2343, 2346–47. Tracking *Tinker*'s analysis, the Court found each act of suppression unconstitutional. In neither case did this Court suggest the distinction, which the Court today finds dispositive, between school-sponsored and incidental student expression.

II

Even if we were writing on a clean slate, I would reject the Court's rationale for abandoning *Tinker* in this case. The Court offers no more than an obscure tangle of three excuses to afford educators "greater control" over school-sponsored speech than the *Tinker* test would permit: the public educator's prerogative to control curriculum; the pedagogical interest in shielding the high school audience from objectionable viewpoints and sensitive topics; and the school's need to dissociate itself from student expression. . . . None of the excuses, once disentangled, supports the distinction that the Court draws. *Tinker* fully addresses the first concern; the second is illegitimate; and the third is readily achievable through less oppressive means.

A

The Court is certainly correct that the First Amendment permits educators "to assure that participants learn whatever lessons the activity is designed to teach." . . . That is, however, the essence of the *Tinker* test, not an excuse to abandon it. Under *Tinker*, school officials may censor only such student speech as would "materially disrup[t]" a legitimate curricular function. Manifestly, student speech is more likely to disrupt a curricular function when it arises in the context of a curricular activity—one that "is designed to teach" something—than when it arises in the context of a noncurricular activity. Thus, under *Tinker*, the school may constitutionally punish the budding political orator if he disrupts calculus class but not if he holds his tongue for the cafeteria. . . . That is not because some more stringent standard applies in the curricular context. (After all, this Court applied the same standard whether the Tinkers wore their armbands to the "classroom" or the "cafeteria." . . .) It is because student speech in the noncurricular context is less likely to disrupt materially any legitimate pedagogical purpose.

I fully agree with the Court that the First Amendment should afford an educator the prerogative not to sponsor the publication of a newspaper article that is "ungrammatical, poorly written, inadequately researched, biased or prejudiced," or that falls short of the "high standards for . . . student speech that is disseminated under [the school's] auspices." . . . But we need not abandon *Tinker* to reach that conclusion; we need only apply it. The enumerated criteria reflect the skills that the curricular newspaper "is designed to teach." The educator may, under *Tinker*, constitutionally "censor" poor grammar, writing, or research because to reward such expression would "materially disrup[t]" the newspaper's curricular purpose.

The same cannot be said of official censorship designed to shield the *audience* or dissociate the sponsor from the expression. Censorship so motivated might well serve . . . some other school purpose. But it in no way furthers the curricular purposes of a student newspaper, unless one believes that the purpose of the school newspaper is to teach students that the press ought never report bad news, express unpopular views, or print a thought that might upset its sponsors. Unsurprisingly, Hazelwood East claims no such pedagogical purpose.

* * *

B

The Court's second excuse for deviating from precedent is the school's interest in shielding an impressionable high school audience from material whose substance is "unsuitable for immature audiences." . . . Specifically, the majority decrees that we must afford educators authority to shield high school students from exposure to "potentially sensitive topics" (like "the particulars of teenage sexual activity") or unacceptable social viewpoints (like the advocacy of "irresponsible se[x] or conduct otherwise inconsistent with 'the shared values of a civilized social order'") through school-sponsored student activities. . . .

Tinker teaches us that the state educator's undeniable, and undeniably vital, mandate to inculcate moral and political values is not a general warrant to act as "thought police" stifling discussion of all but state-approved topics and advocacy of all but the official position. . . .

The mere fact of school sponsorship does not, as the Court suggests, license such thought control in the high school, whether through school suppression of disfavored viewpoints or through official assessment of topic sensitivity.[2] . . . Just as a school board may not purge its state-funded library of all books that " 'offen[d] [its] social, political and moral tastes,' " . . . school officials may not, out of like motivation, discriminatorily excise objectionable ideas from a student publication. The State's prerogative to dissolve the student newspaper entirely (or to limit its subject matter) no more entitles it to dictate which viewpoints students may express on its pages, than the State's prerogative to close down the schoolhouse entitles it to prohibit the non-disruptive expression of antiwar sentiment within its gates.

Official censorship of student speech on the ground that it addresses "potentially sensitive topics" is, for related reasons, equally impermissible. I would not begrudge an educator the authority to limit the substantive scope of a school-sponsored publication to a certain, objectively definable topic, such as literary criticism, school sports, or an overview of the

---

[2]The Court quotes language in *Bethel School Dist. v. Fraser*, 478 U.S. 675, 106 S.Ct. 3159, 92 L.Ed.2d 549 (1986), for the proposition that " '[t]he determination of what manner of speech in the classroom or in school assembly is inappropriate properly rests with the school board.' " *Ante*, at 567 (quoting 478 U.S., at 685, 106 S.Ct., at 3165). As the discussion immediately preceding that quotation makes clear, however, the Court was referring only to the appropriateness of the manner in which the message is conveyed, not of the message's content. . . .

school year. Unlike those determinate limitations, "potential topic sensitivity" is a vaporous nonstandard . . . that invites manipulation to achieve ends that cannot permissibly be achieved through blatant viewpoint discrimination and chills student speech to which school officials might not object. . . .

The case before us aptly illustrates how readily school officials (and courts) can camouflage viewpoint discrimination as the "mere" protection of students from sensitive topics. Among the grounds that the Court advances to uphold the principal's censorship of one of the articles was the potential sensitivity of "teenage sexual activity." . . . Yet the District Court specifically found that the principal "did not, as a matter of principle, oppose discussion of said topi[c] in *Spectrum*." . . . That much is also clear from the same principal's approval of the "squeal law" article on the same page, dealing forthrightly with "teenage sexuality," "the use of contraceptives by teenager," and "teenage pregnancy," . . . If topic sensitivity were the true basis of the principal's decision, the two articles should have been equally objectionable. It is much more likely that the objectionable article was objectionable because of the viewpoint it expressed: It might have been read (as the majority apparently does) to advocate "irresponsible sex." . . .

C

The sole concomitant of school sponsorship that might conceivably justify the distinction that the Court draws between sponsored and nonsponsored student expression is the risk "that the views of the individual speaker [might be] erroneously attributed to the school." . . . Of course, the risk of erroneous attribution inheres in any student expression, including "personal expression" that, like the Tinkers' armbands, "happens to occur on the school premises," . . . . Nevertheless, the majority is certainly correct that indicia of school sponsorship increase the likelihood of such attribution, and that state educators may therefore have a legitimate interest in dissociating themselves from student speech.

. . . Dissociative means short of censorship are available to the school. It could, for example, require the student activity to publish a disclaimer, such as the "Statement of Policy" that *Spectrum* published each school year announcing that "[a]ll . . . editorials appearing in this newspaper reflect the opinions of the *Spectrum* staff, which are not necessarily shared by the administrators or faculty of Hazelwood

East," . . . or it could simply issue its own response clarifying the official position on the matter and explaining why the student position is wrong. Yet, without so much as acknowledging the less oppressive alternatives, the Court approves of brutal censorship.

III

Since the censorship served no legitimate pedagogical purpose, it cannot by any stretch of the imagination have been designed to prevent "materia[l] disrup[tion of] classwork," *Tinker*, 393 U.S., at 513, 89 S.Ct., at 740. Nor did the censorship fall within the category that *Tinker* described as necessary to prevent student expression from "inva[ding] the rights of others," *ibid.* If that term is to have any content, it must be limited to rights that are protected by law. . . .

Finally, even if the majority were correct that the principal could constitutionally have censored the objectionable material, I would emphatically object to the brutal manner in which he did so. . . . [T]he principal used a paper shredder. He objected to some material in two articles, but excised six entire articles. He did not so much as inquire into obvious alternatives, such as precise deletions or additions (one of which had already been made), rearranging the layout, or delaying publication. Such unthinking contempt for individual rights is intolerable from any state official. It is particularly insidious from one to whom the public entrusts the task of inculcating in its youth an appreciation for the cherished democratic liberties that our Constitution guarantees.

IV

. . . The young men and women of Hazelwood East expected a civics lesson, but not the one the Court teaches them today.

I dissent.

NOTES AND QUESTIONS

1. Spectrum: *Government Expression or Personal Expression?*

Professor William G. Buss has written that the First Amendment right of individuals to express their views "has never been understood to create a general right" to use public property or resources for speech purposes. Buss, "School Newspapers, Public Forum, and the First Amendment," 74 *Iowa L. Rev.* 505, 508 (1989). Although the government generally may not curtail individual speech, except in carefully delineated circumstances, it has no obligation to provide or pay for a printing press to allow an individual to reach a broader audience. *See Cornelius v. NAACP Legal Defense and Education Fund, Inc.*, 473 U.S. 788, 800, 105 S.Ct. 3439, 3447, 87 L.Ed.2d 567 (1985). *See generally* Yudof, *When Government Speaks* 235 (1983); A. Greene, "Government of the Good," 53 *Vand. L. Rev.* 1 (2000). This framework for First Amendment analysis is fully applicable in the public school setting:

> [R]ecognition that students retain their first amendment rights when they enter school property does not entail any entitlement of students to use any and all of the school's resources to communicate their views. Consequently, *Tinker* is not affected directly by the *Hazelwood* holding that students did not have a first amendment right to express their views in the official, state-funded and state-sponsored school newspaper.

Buss, *supra* at 508. *See generally* Yudof, "Personal Speech and Government Expression," 38 *Case W. Res. L. Rev.* 671 (1988) (hereinafter "Personal Speech"). If, however, the government does subsidize private communications or provide a forum for private speech, it may be required, depending on the nature of the forum, to be evenhanded in allocating its resources among potential speakers. *See, e.g., Board of Education of Westside Community Schools v. Mergens*, 496 U.S. 226, 110 S.Ct. 2356 (1990) (Equal Access Act); *Healy v. James*, 408 U.S. 169, 92 S.Ct. 2338, 33 L.Ed.2d 266 (1972); *Gay and Lesbian Students Association v. Gohn*, 850 F.2d 361 (8th Cir. 1988). *See generally* Post, "Subsidized Speech," 106 *Yale L.J.* 151 (1996); Redish & Kessler, "Government Subsidies and Free Expression," 80 *Minn. L. Rev.* 543 (1996); Yudof, *When Government Speaks* 234–45 (1983); Karst, "Equality as a Central Principle in the First Amendment," 43 *U. Chi. L. Rev.* 20 (1975). *But see* Greene, "Government of the Good," *supra*.

The distinction between personal and governmental expression focuses on the two ways that students may attempt to counter the socialization that takes place in public schools. They may seek to counter or supplement the school's messages through their own expressive activities, or they may seek to exercise some control over the school's words to dilute or change its messages. "Personal Speech," *supra* at 683. Professor Yudof describes the distinction in these terms:

In the former situation, students have independent constitutional rights. They may decide on what they wish to say and where they wish to say it, subject to the caveat that they have no right to unduly hamper the school's educational mission. Accordingly, they may wear black armbands to protest military activities of the national government or distribute their own newspapers; yet they may not speak on human rights in Nicaragua in the midst of a geometry class.

If the expression is governmental and not personal, students generally may not interfere with the school's articulation of its own educational messages. They do not have a constitutional right to add or delete courses from the curriculum, alter the teacher's lesson plan, or scrutinize the school district's choice of textbooks. Similarly, they do not have final authority over the content of a school newspaper. The primary constitutional limitation . . . is whether the school district is carrying out its legitimate governmental functions or is acting *ultra vires*.

"Personal Speech," *supra* at 683. Does Justice White, writing for the Court in Hazelwood, embrace this distinction? *See Board of Education v. Mergens, supra*. If so, do you agree that there should be two distinct standards of judicial review, one for governmental speech and one for personal speech? Is the distinction itself unreasonable? *See* E. Chemerinsky, "Students Do Leave Their First Amendment Rights at the Schoolhouse Gates: What's Left of *Tinker*?" 48 *Drake L. Rev.* 527, 542 (2000); E. Mineberg, "A Practical Approach to *Tinker* and Its Progeny," 69 *St. John's L. Rev.* 519 (1995); Yudof, "Personal Speech and Government Expression," *supra*.

What does Justice Brennan have to say about this issue? In this regard, consider these comments by Professor Buss:

> Plainly, these reasons [prevention of communications harmful to young students, avoidance of official endorsement of the students' points of view, and prevention of interference with the school's ability to teach its lessons] all point to important school interests. Nevertheless, the Court's discussion falls short of demonstrating how these interests are implicated uniquely by student speech published in the official school newspaper. If certain words or ideas harm other students, the harm would not seem dependent upon the forum in which they are expressed.

Buss, *supra* at 511. Do you agree with Professor Buss? Suppose that Hazelwood employed three students to write articles for *Spectrum*, and its policies were explicit that all editorial decisions were to be made by the principal on the basis of his or her best educational judgment. Would it be unconstitutional to dismiss a student for publishing unapproved views in *Spectrum*—even if there were no material disruption or other cognizable harm?

Should the government be treated differently from private publishers in the context of school newspapers? *See* "Personal Speech," *supra* at 685–86; Gottlieb, "In the Name of Patriotism: The Constitutionality of 'Bending' History in the Public Secondary Schools," 62 *N.Y.U. L. Rev.* 497, 523–24 (1987). What lesson should the students be learning? That a newspaper's owner, whether public or private, has the right to determine the content of the publication? Or have the students learned that government may censor private expression?

Accepting this distinction, how should *Spectrum* be characterized? Clearly it is not a newspaper owned and published by students, an "underground newspaper" distributed on school premises. On the other hand, a school district can choose to delegate editorial and other authority to students, thereby opting to subsidize the students' expression. Which course did the Hazelwood School District select? Is Justice White correct in noting the managerial prerogatives of the faculty and principal? *See also Planned Parenthood v. Clark County School Dist.*, 941 F.2d 817 (9th Cir. 1991); *Burch v. Barker*, 861 F.2d 1149 (9th Cir. 1988). Or did the school district, in reality, create some form of public forum in which the students were granted the authority to express their own views in *Spectrum? See Gambino v. Fairfax*, 429 F.Supp. 731 (W.D. Wis. 1977), aff'd, 564 F.2d 157 (7th Cir.); Buss, *supra* at 509–10. If the record is unclear, should there be a presumption on one side or the other? *See Cornelius v. NAACP Legal Defense & Educ. Fund, Inc.*, 473 U.S. 788, 802, 105 S.Ct. 3439, 3449, 87 L.Ed.2d 567 (1985); *Perry Educ. Ass'n v. Perry Local Educators' Ass'n*, 460 U.S. 37, 103 S.Ct. 948, 74 L.Ed.2d 794 (1983). If the school district did delegate authority to students, is it free to retract that delegation at any time that it becomes unhappy with the students' editorial policies? *See Stanley v. McGrath*, 719 F.2d 279 (8th Cir. 1983); *Joyner v. Whiting*, 477 F.2d 456 (4th Cir. 1973).

How does the majority's emphasis on the fit between *Spectrum* and the curriculum advance the analysis? *See Nicholson v. Board of Education*, 682 F.2d 858 (9th Cir. 1982); *Seyfried v. Walton*, 668 F.2d 214 (3d Cir. 1982); *Associated Students of Western Kentucky University v. Downing*, 475 F.2d 1132 (6th Cir. 1973). Can a school newspaper be both a part of the curriculum and a limited public forum?

See Buss, *supra* at 510. Is the *Hazelwood* majority emphasizing the curriculum-related nature of the speech in *Fraser*, while the dissent focuses on the discussion of disruption in that case? Which view of *Fraser* is more persuasive? What extensions of *Hazelwood*, if any, can you foresee to other areas of the curriculum?

Professor Robert Post asserts that "the state is prohibited from imposing any particular conception of collective identity when it regulates public discourse, but the state must perforce exemplify a particular conception of collective identity when it acts on its own account." Post, "Subsidized Speech," 106 *Yale L.J.* 151, 183 (1996). *See Arkansas Educ. Television Comm. v. Forbes*, 523 U.S. 819 (1995); *Kincaid v. Gibson*, 191 F.3d 719 (6th Cir. 1999); *reh'g granted and opinion vacated*, 197 F.3d 818. Does this distinction explain the *Hazelwood* decision? *Tinker?*

2. Public Forum Analysis

Does it follow that if *Spectrum* is a limited public forum that the student editors should have the final say over editorial policy? One meaning of a limited public forum, in this context, is that *Spectrum* is limited to submissions by Hazelwood students; "outsiders" have no right to publish their views in *Spectrum*. But is the creation of a public forum the same thing as delegating decision-making authority to student editors? *See* Buss, *supra* at 512–13. Consider these remarks by Professor Yudof:

> The question is [not] . . . whether *Spectrum* has been opened by school officials to all [student] contributors, on an equal basis; the question is one of control and authority. Who is running the newspaper, the principal and instructor or the student editors? Presumably, a student editorial board would reject some articles, assign some stories and not others, and develop policies for handling sensitive material on sex, drugs, divorce, and other themes. The very power that Justice Brennan would deny the principal will be exercised by the students; there will be no public forum unless they choose to create one.

"Personal Speech," *supra* at 685. Do you agree? *See Kania v. Fordham*, 702 F.2d 475 (4th Cir. 1983); *Avins v. Rutgers*, 385 F.2d 151 (3d Cir. 1967); *Arrington v. Taylor*, 380 F.Supp. 1348 (M.D.N.C. 1974), *aff'd mem.*, 526 F.2d 587 (4th Cir. 1975). How much depends on the characteristics that may be attributed to a "limited" public forum? *See Planned Parenthood v. Clark County School Dist.*, 941 F.2d 817 (9th Cir. 1991). *Cf. Lehman v. City of Shaker Heights*, 418 U.S. 298, 94 S.Ct. 2714, 41 L.Ed.2d 770 (1974).

3. *Substantial Disruption and the* Hazelwood *Case*

If *Tinker* were applicable in *Hazelwood*, should the Court have upheld the rights of the students? Might the principal have reasonably and foreseeably predicted a material disruption of the school environment? If vulgar student speech may be prohibited, may the principal justifiably delete the noted articles? Is such expression disruptive of the school's mission?

Assuming that a student article was thought to be libelous, may school authorities constitutionally delete it—even if there were no reasonable forecast of a material disruption? *See Gano v. Sch. Dist. No. 411*, 674 F. Supp. 796 (D. Id. 1987); *Shanley v. Northeast Independent School Dist.*, 462 F.2d 960, 971 (5th Cir. 1972); *Fujishima v. Board of Education*, 460 F.2d 1355, 1359 (7th Cir. 1972).

4. *Government Expression and the* Pico *Standard*

What standard of review does the majority apply to the principal's decision to delete articles from *Spectrum*? Is it a reasonableness standard? *See Frasca v. Andrews*, 463 F.Supp. 1043 (E.D.N.Y. 1979). What would be an unreasonable decision? Should the standard be the same as for library book deselection in *Board of Education v. Pico, supra*? That is, must the decision be a good faith educational decision? *See* "Personal Speech," *supra* at 692–96. If so, what would constitute a bad faith decision?

Suppose that an external organization wished to place an advertisement in *Spectrum* that advised students about where to obtain information on birth control and pregnancy. After *Hazelwood*, may the school district decline to print the advertisement? *See Planned Parenthood v. Clark County School Dist., supra*. What about an advertisement for a water pipe that often is used to smoke marijuana? *See Williams v. Spencer*, 622 F.2d 1200 (4th Cir. 1980). Would your answer depend on the district's advertising policies and their implementation? Would it matter if the students and not school officials made decisions on advertising? *See Sinn v. Daily Nebraskan*, 829 F.2d 662 (8th Cir. 1987).

What if a faculty advisor to a school newspaper fails to submit controversial articles to the principal for prior approval pursuant to school policies? May the faculty advisor be fired or removed from his or her advisory responsibilities? *See Nicholson v. Board of Education Torrance Unified School Dist.*, 682 F.2d 858 (9th Cir. 1982).

5. *Advice to School Authorities and Legislative Responses to* Hazelwood

In the light of *Tinker, Bethel, Pico*, and *Hazelwood*, what advice would you give to school authorities planning to set up and sponsor a school newspaper? *See* Buss, *supra* at 522. *See generally* Avery and Simpson, "The Constitution and Student Publications: A Comprehensive Approach," 16 *J. L. & Educ.* 1 (1987). Is there a problem of giving the appearance of a student newspaper or public forum, while editorial authority, in reality, is retained by school officials? *See* Buss, *supra* at 526. If students are given ultimate authority over the content of a school newspaper, what is the district's risk of liability if a particular article is defamatory? *See Mississippi Gay Alliance v. Goudelock*, 536 F.2d 1073 (5th Cir. 1976).

A number of states enacted legislation after *Hazelwood* to guarantee freedom of expression for student editors of school newspapers, subject to limitations for obscenity, libel, encouragement to violate the law or school regulations, and the *Tinker* substantial disruption test. *See, e.g., Iowa Education Code* § 280.22 (1989). The Iowa law specifically provides that school districts will not be subject to civil liability for student expression unless school employees have altered the content of the article in question. *Id.*

6. *Indecency and Underground Newspapers*

In *Papish v. Board of Curators of University of Missouri*, 410 U.S. 667, 93 S.Ct. 1197, 35 L.Ed.2d 618 (1973), the Court held that it was unconstitutional to dismiss a graduate student for on-campus distribution of a newspaper that featured a political cartoon depicting a policeman raping the Statue of Liberty and the Goddess of Justice. The caption of the cartoon read, ". . . With Liberty and Justice for All." The paper also contained an article entitled "M——-F——-Acquitted," which discussed the trial and acquittal of a New York City youth who was a member of an organization known as "UP Against the Wall, M——-F——-." In reaching the decision, the Court said that "mere dissemination of ideas—no matter how offensive to good taste—on a state university campus may not be shut off in the name alone of 'conventions of decency.'" 410 U.S. at 670, 93 S.Ct. at 1199. Does *Papish* apply to high schools? *See Bystrom v. Fridley High Sch.*, 822 F.2d 747 (8th Cir. 1987); *Jacobs v. Board of School Commissioners*, 490 F.2d 601 (7th Cir. 1973), *vacated as moot*, 420 U.S. 128, 95 S.Ct. 848, 43 L.Ed.2d 74 (1975). Is *Fraser* dispositive? *Hazelwood*? Does your answer depend on whether the publication is an underground student newspaper or an official school newspaper? To what extent would *Fraser* be controlling in the former case?

May a school prohibit distribution of an underground newspaper if it does not contain lewd content? What if the paper contained an article about how to hack the school's computers? Does the school have the ability to suspend the author without violating the First Amendment? *See Boucher v. Sch. Bd. of Sch. Dist. of Greenfield,* 134 F.3d 821 (7th Cir. 1998). May a school or university constitutionally adopt a no-solicitation policy to prevent the distribution of non–school–sponsored papers? In *Hays County Guardian v. Supple,* the court held that a no-solicitation policy cannot be used to prevent the distribution of a paper when other papers, not containing advertisements, can be distributed. 969 F.2d 111 (5th Cir. 1992).

B. Changing the School's Message

State and local boards of education are entrusted with the basic authority to shape the content of the school program, subject to the limitation that the program may not establish religion. *See* Section II, *supra.* The state also has an interest in selecting those teachers who are most likely to carry out the school's educational mission and in making sure that they actually do so. Those selected as teachers may seek to supplement the state's messages with their own opinions and beliefs, or they may seek to modify the message that the state and school board wish to convey. This section explores these tensions and related issues.

One way of stating the problem is to ask whether teachers may use public school resources—for example, class time, dollars, and equipment—to introduce their own curriculum materials when school officials disagree with their content. Stated differently, the question is who shall control the content of the school curriculum? The more control given to the individual teacher, the greater the diversity of messages "broadcast" by the schools, and there will be less danger of the school speaking from a single ideological viewpoint. *See* Yudof, "Three Faces of Academic Freedom," 32 *Loy. L. Rev.* 831 (1987). But the more freedom given to teachers, the greater the risk of frustration of the public interest in providing a particular kind of education that the school authorities consider desirable. Teachers are not hired and appointed to proselytize at public expense, disregarding the school board's policies. This danger is

exacerbated by the fact that public elementary and secondary schools have a "captive" audience, an audience that cannot easily escape a teacher's expressed values. Why should a teacher's values or academic freedom prevail over those of school boards responsible to the public? *See* Goldstein, "The Asserted Constitutional Right of Public School Teachers to Determine What They Teach," 124 *U. Pa. L. Rev.* 1293, 1342–43 (1976). But should teachers be compelled to convey only those ideas, beliefs, and opinions that have been officially approved by the school board? *See* Yudof, *supra.*

1. Academic Freedom. With respect to teachers' claim to freedom of expression in the classroom (academic freedom), the cases have not developed a coherent body of constitutional doctrine. *See generally* Byrne, "Academic Freedom: 'A Special Concern of the First Amendment,' " 99 *Yale L.J.* 251 (1989). At least one point seems reasonably well established: Teachers are not free to transform their assigned courses into something other than what the school's administration intended them to be. *Clark v. Holmes,* 474 F.2d 928 (7th Cir. 1972), *cert. denied,* 411 U.S. 972, 93 S.Ct. 2148, 36 L.Ed.2d 695 (1973); *Ahern v. Board of the School District of Grand Island,* 327 F.Supp. 1391 (D. Neb. 1971). Whether the teacher's changes constitute abandonment of the prescribed curriculum may not always be easy to decide. For example, is a change in a college drama course reducing the coverage from twenty-five plays to in-depth coverage of eleven plays an abandonment of the prescribed curriculum? *See Hetrick v. Martin,* 480 F.2d 705 (6th Cir. 1973), *cert. denied,* 414 U.S. 1075, 94 S.Ct. 592, 38 L.Ed.2d 482 (1973).

If there is a right to academic freedom within the public school classroom, that right is not tantamount to granting the teacher a license to do as he or she wishes. Whether a more circumscribed right should exist and what its scope should be raise difficult constitutional questions, especially in the context of elementary and secondary schools. For example, a number of courts have held that "classroom management techniques" and pedagogical methods are not constitutionally protected. *See, e.g., Bradley v. Pittsburgh Board of Education,* 910 F.2d 1172 (3rd Cir. 1990); *Adams v. Campbell County School District,* 511 F.2d 1242 (10th Cir. 1975); *Hetrick v. Martin,* 480 F.2d 705 (6th Cir. 1973).

Cary v. Board of Education

598 F.2d 535 (10th Cir. 1979).

Logan, Circuit Judge.

This is an appeal from summary judgment denying relief in a declaratory judgment action which sought enforcement of claimed rights under the First and Fourteenth Amendments to the United States Constitution. The action was brought by five high school teachers who asserted their rights were violated when the Board of Education for the Adams-Arapahoe School District in Colorado (the board) banned ten books from use in the teachers' language arts classes.

* * *

The relevant facts were stipulated; both sides sought summary judgment. All plaintiffs are tenured teachers who teach high school language arts classes in the defendant school district. The classes involved are elective courses for eleventh and twelfth grade students—Contemporary Literature, Contemporary Poetry, and American Masters—which under the board regulations were designed for elective optional reading materials chosen from classroom libraries or personal sources.

The board first adopted a policy on selection of text material in January 1975. A High School Language Arts Text Evaluation Committee was established to review current and new materials for language arts courses. Membership was composed of representative teachers, administrators, parents and students. The committee reviewed many books which had been used or were recommended for use in these courses. It was instructed to utilize specified criteria: appropriateness to the grade level, value of the material in relation to the course objectives, and fiscal considerations. The guidelines adopted by the board required a written response, including reasons, when suggested materials were rejected.

Only one book was rejected by the majority report of the committee, with apparently 1,285 books approved. A minority report filed by three members listed nine more books they would reject. The recommended texts were on public display for twelve days. Then at a regularly scheduled public meeting of the school board, and following an open discussion, the board voted to approve a list of 1,275 books for use in language arts classes in the high schools. Ten recommended books, all of which had previously been used in those classes, were excluded from the approved list;[1] six of the ten were among those not recommended in the minority report. The majority and minority reports made reference to the specified criteria in discussing titles they rejected, but the board itself set forth no written statement of the reasons for its vote to ban the ten books. Its edict to the teachers issued after the meeting simply referenced the list of books not being approved and made the following declarations:

Books which are not approved for instructional use will not be purchased, nor used for class assignment, nor will an individual be given credit for reading any of these books.

* * *

An unwritten board policy had permitted substitution of materials for assignments offensive to a student or his or her parents. That policy was formally adopted by the board in written form after the meeting above described.

By stipulation the parties agreed the books were not obscene, no systematic effort had been made to exclude any particular system of thought or philosophy, and a "constitutionally proper decision-maker" could decide these books were proper for high school

---

[1]The banned volumes were:

a. Contemporary Literature:

(1) *A Clockwork Orange* by Anthony Burgess;

(2) *The Exorcist* by William P. Blatty;

(3) *The Reincarnation of Peter Proud* by Max Ehrlich.

b. Contemporary Poetry:

(1) *New American Poetry* by Donald Allen;

(2) *Starting from San Francisco* by Lawrence Ferlinghetti;

(3) *The Yage Letters* by William Burroughs and Allen Ginsberg;

(4) *Coney Island of the Mind* by Lawrence Ferlinghetti;

(5) *Kaddish and Other Poems* by Allen Ginsberg;

(6) *Lunch Poems* by Frank O'Hara.

c. American Masters:

Rosemary's Baby by Ira Levin.

language arts classes. It was agreed that the plaintiff teachers were subject to dismissal from their positions for insubordination for any of the following acts:

(a) adding any of the subject textbooks to the reading list of their courses;

(b) assigning the reading of any of the subject textbooks;

(c) giving any student any credit in courses for reading any of the subject textbooks;

(d) reading aloud or causing to be read aloud any of the subject textbooks in the classroom during class time; or

(e) discussing with students in the classroom during class time any of these materials at such length so as to amount to a constructive assignment of the materials.

* * *

We recognize and support the concept that "teachers [do not] shed their constitutional rights to freedom of speech or expression at the schoolhouse gate." *Tinker v. Des Moines Independent Community School Dist.*, 393 U.S. 503, 506 . . . (1969). This general commitment has been stated eloquently on occasion:

> Our Nation is deeply committed to safeguarding academic freedom, which is of transcendent value to all of us and not merely to the teachers concerned. That freedom is therefore a special concern of the First Amendment, which does not tolerate laws that cast a pall of orthodoxy over the classroom. . . . . The classroom is peculiarly the "marketplace of ideas." The Nation's future depends upon leaders trained through wide exposure to that robust exchange of ideas which discovers truth "out of a multitude of tongues, [rather] than through any kind of authoritative selection." *United States v. Associated Press*, [D.C.,] 52 F.Supp. 362, 372.

Keyishian v. Board of Regents, 385 U.S. 589, 603 . . . (1967).

> To regard teachers—in our entire educational system, from the primary grades to the university—as the priests of our democracy is therefore not to indulge in hyperbole. It is the special task of teachers to foster those habits of open-mindedness and critical inquiry which alone make for responsible citizens, who, in turn, make possible an enlightened and effective public opinion. Teachers must fulfill their function by precept and practice, by the very atmosphere which they generate; they must be exemplars of open-mindedness and free inquiry. They cannot carry out their noble task if the conditions for the practice of a responsible and critical mind are denied to them.

Wieman v. Updegraff, 344 U.S. 183, 196 . . . (1952) (Frankfurter J., concurring). Most of the cases, how-

ever, have arisen at the university level, and outside the area of curricular decisions and teaching-related speech in the classroom.

* * *

Quite a number of circuit and district court decisions have involved claims of school board or school authorities' interference with teachers' First Amendment rights to conduct their classes as they see fit in exercise of their professional judgment. Most were discharge cases where the teacher was fired, or a contract not renewed, for allegedly offensive behavior, poor teaching techniques and insubordination. Conflicts over the teachers' use of dirty words in class, or assignment of reading materials containing dirty words, seeming approval of free love, drugs or rebellion against authority, were generally part of a charge of inappropriate conduct alleged to constitute good cause for discharge. The cases which held for the teachers and placed emphasis upon teachers' rights to exercise discretion in the classroom, seemed to be situations where school authorities acted in the absence of a general policy, after the fact, and had little to charge against the teacher other than the assignment with which they were unhappy. *See Sterzing v. Fort Bend Independent School Dist.*, 376 F.Supp. 657 (S.D. Tex. 1972), *vacated on remedial grounds*, 496 F.2d 92 (5th Cir. 1974); *Mailloux v. Kiley*, 436 F.2d 565 (1st Cir. 1971), *on remand*, 323 F.Supp. 1387 (D. Mass.), *aff'd on other grounds*, 448 F.2d 1242 (1st Cir. 1971); *Keefe v. Geanakos*, 418 F.2d 359 (1st Cir. 1969); *Parducci v. Rutland*, 316 F.Supp. 352 (M.D. Ala. 1979). . . . In the cases where the teachers' First Amendment claims were rejected, generally the school authorities had other good grounds supporting their discharge or nonrenewal of the teacher's contract. *Adams v. Campbell County School Dist.*, 511 F.2d 1242 (10th Cir. 1975); *Brubaker v. Board of Educ.*, 502 F.2d 973 (7th Cir. 1974), *cert. denied*, 421 U.S. 965 . . . (1975).

* * *

. . . The teachers acknowledge the right of the school board to prescribe the curriculum and the principal textbooks used in the courses. They agree the school board does not have to offer the three courses at issue here; but they say that once the courses have been approved the teachers' "right of academic freedom includes the right to use non-obscene materials electively in elective courses taught to high school students." They do not ask the board to purchase or endorse certain books; they do not seek to require a student to read materials against the student's will; but they want to be free from restrictions "based upon the personal predilections of members of the school board."

* * *

. . . We have found no law which allows a high school teacher to have the broad latitude which appellants seek.

If the board may decide that Contemporary Poetry may not be offered; if it may select the major text of the course; why may it not go further and exclude certain books from being assigned for instruction in the course? As we understand these language arts courses there is no basic text, or if there is one it is utilized only for a portion of the class study. A large part of the instructional time is review and discussion of items selected by students, with consent of the teacher, from the reading list. As adopted by the board the list contained altogether 1,275 titles approved for the three courses. Thus it can be said with some justification the texts adopted by the school board for these courses is the reading list. That, we believe, is the proper view of the situation before us; and the board was acting within its rights in omitting the books, even though the decision was a political one influenced by the personal views of the members.

We agree with the board characterization of the stipulation that it does not prohibit mention of these books in class, nor treatment by the teacher of the books as examples of contemporary poetry, literature or American masters. The ban is upon such extended reference or use in class as to constitute class assignments which in effect evade the exercise of discretion made by the board in its determination of the parameters of the courses.

[T]he stipulation declares that no systematic effort was made "to exclude any particular type of thinking or book." And no objection was made that the board was not following its own standards in rejecting the books. The approved list is broad, containing 1,275 books for the three courses. No objection is made by the teachers that the exclusions prevent them from studying an entire representative group of writers. Rather the teachers want to be freed from the "personal predilections" of the board. We do not see a basis in the constitution to grant their wish.

The trial court entered judgment in favor of the defendant board and its members. Although we place our holding upon a different basis, we affirm that judgment.

William E. Doyle, Circuit Judge, concurring.

I concur in the result and in most of what appears in the opinion. I would, however, approach it somewhat differently. I would disapprove of any arbitrary selection of books that can be read and those which cannot be on the reading list. One can read the majority as, in effect, making such a ruling.

However, the court does not say it. It recognizes that the School Board has a broad right to select texts and to exclude textbooks. The approach which I prefer would be that the exclusion of books for secondary school students is not to be an arbitrary exclusion. Therefore, reasons have to be given so that there can be court review. If they are excluded because the Board member disapproves for a subjective reason, I would say that this is an unlawful and unconstitutional invasion of the classroom.

So, with the above exceptions, I concur in the submitted opinion.

_____

NOTES AND QUESTIONS

1. Academic Freedom

Teachers' academic freedom is conventionally said to comprise freedom of inquiry and research, freedom of teaching, and freedom of extramural utterance and action. American Association of University Professors, "The 1915 Declaration of Principles," in L. Jouglin, ed., *Academic Freedom and Tenure* (1969). *See generally*, Metzger, "Profession and Constitution: Two Definitions of Academic Freedom in America," 66 *Tex. L. Rev.* 1265 (1988). A basic premise of this right is that truth is discovered through research and inquiry and that there is no such thing as a truth not subject to question and debate. Related to this doctrine is the concept that education ideally ought to liberate students and open their minds to new and provocative ideas. *See generally* C. Lindblom, *Inquiry and Change* (1990); Clarick, "Public School Teachers and the First Amendment: Protecting the Right to Teach," 65 *N.Y.U. L. Rev.* 693 (1990). This concept of academic freedom is clearly applicable to universities, but should it be extended to public elementary and secondary school teachers? *See* Stuller, "High School Academic Freedom: The Evolution of a Fish Out of Water," 77 *Neb. L. Rev.* 301 (1998). If, as earlier portions of this chapter indicate, one constitutionally permissible purpose of public schools is to inculcate values chosen by elected officials or administrators responsible to the community, is there any reason to grant academic freedom to public school teachers, allowing their personal values to be pressed upon a captive audience? Goldstein, "The Asserted Constitutional Right of Public School Teachers to Determine What They Teach," 124 *U. Pa. L. Rev.* 1293, 1343 (1976). On the other hand, academic freedom would promote pluralism within the schools and diminish the danger of governmental indoctrination of students. Does this argument justify academic freedom for public school teachers? Or does the doctrine rest on the notion of the school as a marketplace of ideas?

Is academic freedom a free-standing right protected by the First Amendment or is it an educational policy subsumed within more general First Amendment doctrines? If there is a constitutional right to academic freedom, who holds it—school districts and universities or teachers and professors? In *Urofsky v. Gilmore*, 216 F.3d 401 (4th Cir. 2000), the Fourth Circuit stated:

> The Supreme Court, to the extent it has constitutionalized a right of academic freedom at all, appears to have recognized only an institutional right of self-governance in academic affairs.... [T]he best that can be said for Appellees' claim that the Constitution protects the academic freedom of an individual professor is that teachers were the first public employees to be afforded the now universal protection against dismissal for the exercise of First Amendment rights.... [S]ince declaring that public employees, including teachers, do not forfeit First Amendment rights upon accepting public employment, the Court has focused its discussions of academic freedom solely on issues of institutional autonomy.

216 F.3d at 412, 415. Do you agree with the Fourth Circuit that professors do not have a First Amendment right to academic freedom? May a professor assert a right to academic freedom on behalf of the University or must the University always be the party invoking academic freedom?

The issue before the court in *Urofsky* was whether a Virginia statute prohibiting state employees from using state-owned or leased computers to access sexually explicit materials on the Internet violated the First Amendment rights of professors at public colleges. The court upheld the challenged statute. What if the professors were prohibited from using state-owned computers to access web sites that addressed issues such as gun control, abortion, or homosexuality? Would the Court have reached the same result? Do students and the public have a free speech right to learn from the uncensored research of professors at public colleges? *See generally* 216 F.3d at 426–435 (J. Wilkinson, concurring) (reasoning that Internet research, like all research, by professors relates to a matter of public concern, and therefore the court must use the *Pickering* standard to determine whether the state interest justifies the burden on speech).

The doctrine of academic freedom may be derived from the right of students to learn and to hear.

Do students themselves have rights of free speech derived from academic freedom? *But see* Byrne, "Academic Freedom: A 'Special Concern of the First Amendment,' " 99 *Yale L.J.* 251, 262–63 (1989) (hereinafter "Special Concern"). Is it relevant that many students and parents do not want to hear what the teacher (and other students) wish to say?

What of the need to give special protection to teachers as "priests of our democracy"? *Wieman v. Updegraff*, 344 U.S. 183, 195–96, 73 S.Ct. 215, 221, 97 L.Ed. 216 (1952) (Frankfurter, J., concurring). But who elected these "priests," and how do we know that they will proselytize democratic truths? Is Justice Frankfurter referring to a democratic process involving the free exchange of ideas and opinions? If so, is academic freedom a principle of constitutional law or an education philosophy? *See* Katz, "The First Amendment's Protection of Expressive Activity in the University Classroom: A Constitutional Myth," 16 *U.C. Davis L. Rev.* 857 (1983). Is there a distinction between "academic freedom" and "constitutional academic freedom"? *See* "Special Concern" at 254–55. At bottom, do academic freedom for teachers and rights of expression for students rest on the supposition that public schools must instill democratic values?

What definition of academic freedom would appropriately balance the interest of school officials in overseeing public education with the interest of the teacher in freedom of speech? Does the position adopted by Justice Stewart in *Epperson v. Arkansas, supra*, strike a reasonable balance? That is, should the teacher be able to make reasonable pedagogical judgments within general boundaries set by the state and school board? *See Parate v. Isibor*, 868 F.2d 821 (6th Cir. 1989). *But see Carley v. Arizona Bd. of Regents*, 153 Ariz. 461, 463–65, 737 P.2d 1099, 1101–03 (App. 1987). Does *Cary* affirm this principle? Where does *Cary* draw the line between the extremes of allowing a teacher to substitute one course for another and prohibiting a teacher from deviating in any way from the prescribed materials? *See Clark v. Holmes*, 474 F.2d 928 (7th Cir. 1972).

Does academic freedom protect the teacher's discretion in grading students? *See Keen v. Penson*, 970 F.2d 252 (7th Cir. 1992); *Parate v. Isibor, supra*; *Lovelace v. Southeastern Mass. Univ.*, 793 F.2d 419 (1st Cir. 1986).

The relevant Supreme Court cases do not involve factual situations even remotely parallel to the factual situation in the *Cary* case itself. Should a teacher have standing to attack the constitutionality of the books selected for classroom use? *See Johnson v. Stuart*, 702 F.2d 193 (9th Cir. 1983). If so, is *Hazelwood* controlling? *See Virgil v. School Board of Columbia County*, 677 F.Supp. 1547 (M.D. Fla. 1988).

2. Academic Freedom in Cary

Under what circumstances should the *Cary* court conclude that the academic freedom of the teachers in the language arts courses had been violated by the exclusion of the ten books? Is it relevant that the school board declined to give reasons for the exclusions? What if the board had asserted that the books in question were inappropriate for high school students? *See Board of Education v. Pico*, 457 U.S. 853, 102 S.Ct. 2799, 73 L.Ed.2d 435 (1982). What if it took the position that the books were not good examples of the types of literature to be considered in the language arts courses? What if the board had charged that the books were vulgar, although not legally obscene? Would *Hazelwood, Fraser,* and *Pico* be decisive? *See Virgil v. School Board, supra*. What if the board had argued that some of the books might be psychologically harmful—for example, that *Silence of the Lambs* or *The Exorcist* might frighten impressionable youngsters? Did the plaintiffs concede too much when they stipulated that a constitutionally appropriate decision maker could decide that the excluded books were appropriate?

Is it relevant to the academic freedom issue that the public schools were not being asked to purchase the books, that there was no basic text for each course, and that teachers had over a thousand approved books from which to choose? In conjunction with the admission that there was no systematic effort to exclude any particular type of thinking, is this last point decisive of the academic freedom issue? *See Pico, supra*. Consider the board's policy that allows for the substitution of other assignments when a student or parent objects to a particular book. As a matter of policy, if not constitutional law, would it be preferable to permit teachers to make the initial selections, reserving to families the right to reject specific books? Would this change the result of *Cary?*

3. An Alternative Approach to Academic Freedom: Parducci v. Rutland

The *Cary* court distinguishes *Parducci v. Rutland*, 316 F.Supp. 352 (M.D. Ala. 1970) by stating that "school authorities [there] acted in the absence of a general policy, after the fact, and had little to charge against the teacher other than the assignment with which they were unhappy." Consider these excerpts from Judge Johnson's opinion in *Parducci*:

> On April 21, 1970, plaintiff assigned as outside reading to her junior English classes a story, entitled "Welcome to the Monkey House." The story, a comic satire, was selected by plaintiff to give her students a better understanding of one particular genre of western literature— the short story. The story's author, Kurt Vonnegut, Jr., is a prominent contemporary writer who has published numerous short stories and novels, including *Cat's Cradle* and a recent best seller, *Slaughterhouse-Five*.
>
> The following morning, plaintiff was called to Principal Rutland's office for a conference with him and the Associate Superintendent of the school system. Both men expressed their displeasure with the content of the story, which they described as "literary garbage," and with the "philosophy" of the story, which they construed as condoning, if not encouraging, "the killing off of elderly people and free sex." They also expressed concern over the fact that three of plaintiff's students had asked to be excused from the assignment and that several disgruntled parents had called the school to complain. They then admonished plaintiff not to teach the story in any of her classes.
>
> Plaintiff retorted that she was bewildered by their interpretation and attitude toward the story, that she still considered it to be a good literary work, and that, while not meaning to cause any trouble, she felt that she had a professional obligation to teach the story.... On May 6, the School Board notified the plaintiff that she had been dismissed from her job for assigning materials which had a "disruptive" effect on the school and for refusing "the counseling and advice of the school principal." The School Board also advised the plaintiff that one of the bases for her dismissal was "insubordination" by reason of a statement that she made to the Principal and Associate Superintendent that "regardless of their counseling" she "would continue to teach the eleventh grade English class at the Jeff David High School by the use of whatever material" she wanted "and in whatever manner" she thought best.
>
> * * *
>
> At the outset, it should be made clear that plaintiff's teaching ability is not in issue. The Principal of her school has conceded that plaintiff was a good teacher and that she would have received a favorable evaluation from him at the end of the year but for the single incident which led to her dismissal.
>
> Plaintiff asserts in her complaint that her dismissal for assigning "Welcome to the Monkey House" violated her First Amendment right to academic freedom.
>
> * * *

The right to academic freedom, however, like all other constitutional rights, is not absolute and must be balanced against the competing interests of society. This Court is keenly aware of the state's vital interest in protecting the impressionable minds of its young people from any form of extreme propagandism in the classroom.

* * *

Thus, the first question to be answered is whether "Welcome to the Monkey House" is inappropriate reading for high school juniors. While the story contains several vulgar terms and a reference to an involuntary act of sexual intercourse, the Court, having read the story very carefully, can find nothing that would render it obscene either under the standards of *Roth v. United States* [354 U.S. 476 (1957)] or under the stricter standards for minors as set forth in *Ginsberg v. New York* [390 U.S. 629 (1968)].

The slang words are contained in two short rhymes which are less ribald than those found in many of Shakespeare's plays. The reference in the story to an act of sexual intercourse is no more descriptive than the rape scene in Pope's *Rape of the Lock*. As for the theme of the story, the Court notes that the anthology in which the story was published was reviewed by several of the popular national weekly magazines, none of which found the subject matter of any of the stories to be offensive. It appears to the Court, moreover, that the author, rather than advocating the "killing off of old people," satirizes the practice to symbolize the increasing depersonalization of man in society.

The Court's finding as to the appropriateness of the story for high school students is confirmed by the reaction of the students themselves. Rather than there being a threatened or actual substantial disruption to the educational processes of the school, the evidence reflects that the assigning of the story was greeted with apathy by most of the students. . . .

Since the defendants have failed to show either that the assignment was inappropriate reading for high school juniors, or that it created a significant disruption to the educational process of this school, this Court concludes that plaintiff's dismissal constituted an unwarranted invasion of her First Amendment right to academic freedom.

316 F.Supp. at 352 et seq.

How does Judge Johnson's concept of the nature and scope of academic freedom differ from that of the *Cary* court? *See* Yudof, *supra* at 844–46. Did Judge Logan accurately characterize the *Parducci* decision? Is Judge Johnson saying that teachers enjoy a right to introduce any written materials into a class as long as they are not "inappropriate reading"? Does the *Parducci* standard serve only to exclude materials that are legally obscene for minors, or does it permit a school board to punish a teacher for introduction of other sorts of materials as well? Does this standard provide useful guidance for teachers and school boards, or does the standard amount to a statement that, in effect, if the judge does not object to the book or materials, the teacher will be protected?

Consider these sample passages from "Welcome to the Monkey House" (1970): "The pills were so effective that you could blindfold a man who had taken one, tell him to recite the Gettysburg Address, kick him in the balls while he was doing it, and he wouldn't miss a syllable. . . ." *Id.* at 29. "Virgin hostess, death's recruiter, Life is cute, but you are cuter. Mourn my pecker, purple daughter—all it passed was sky-blue water." *Id.* at 35–36. Do you agree with the court's conclusion that such passages are appropriate for high school juniors? *Compare Parker v. Board of Education*, 348 F.2d 464 (4th Cir. 1965).

A more recent case, *Boring v. Buncombe County Bd. of Education*, 136 F.3d 364 (4th Cir. 1998), provides an interesting contrast to both *Cary* and *Parducci*. Consider these excerpts.

> Margaret Boring was a teacher in the Charles D. Owen High School in Buncombe County, North Carolina. In the fall of 1991, she chose the play *Independence* for four students in her advanced acting class to perform in an annual statewide competition. She stated in her amended complaint that the play "powerfully depicts the dynamics within a dysfunctional, single-parent family—a divorced mother and three daughters; one a lesbian, another pregnant with an illegitimate child." She alleged that after selecting the play, she notified the school principal, as she did every year, that she had chosen *Independence* as the play for the competition. She does not allege that she gave the principal any information about the play other than the name.
>
> The play was performed in a regional competition and won 17 of 21 awards. Prior to the state finals, a scene from the play was performed for an English class in the school. Plaintiff informed the teacher of that class that the play contained mature subject matter and suggested to the teacher that the students bring in parental permission slips to see the play. Following that performance, a parent of one of the students in the English class complained to the school principal, Fred Ivey, who then asked plaintiff for a copy of the script. After reading the play, Ivey informed plaintiff that she and the students would not be permitted to perform the play in the state competition.
>
> Plaintiff and the parents of the actresses performing the play met with Ivey urging him not to cancel the pro-

duction. Ivey then agreed to the production of the play in the state competition, but with certain portions deleted. The complaint states that the students performed the play in the state competition and won second place. The complaint does not state, but we assume, that the play was performed in accordance with Ivey's instructions.

* * *

. . . In June 1992, Ivey requested the transfer of Margaret Boring from Owen High School, citing "personal conflicts resulting from actions she initiated during the course of this school year." Superintendent Yeager approved the transfer stating that she had failed to follow the school system's controversial materials policy in producing the play. Plaintiff . . . alleges that at the time of the production, the controversial materials policy did not cover dramatic presentations, and that the school's policy was amended subsequently to include dramatic presentations.

Plaintiff . . . claims that her transfer was in retaliation for expression of unpopular views through the production of the play and thus in violation of her right to freedom of speech under the First and Fourteenth Amendments. . . .

* * *

Plaintiff's selection of the play *Independence*, and the editing of the play by the principal, . . . does not present a matter of public concern and is nothing more than an ordinary employment dispute. That being so, plaintiff has no First Amendment rights derived from her selection of the play *Independence*.

. . . This principle was illustrated in *Connick v. Myers*, 461 U.S. 138, 103 S.Ct. 1684, 75 L.Ed.2d 708 (1983), in which the Court upheld the firing of an assistant district attorney who had circulated a questionnaire questioning the manner in which the district attorney operated that office. The Court held that "if Myers' questionnaire cannot be fairly characterized as constituting speech on a matter of public concern, it is unnecessary for us to scrutinize the reasons for her discharge." *Connick* at 146, 103 S.Ct. at 1690. Because the questionnaire almost wholly concerned internal office affairs rather than matters of public concern, the court held that, to that extent, it would not upset the decision of the district attorney in discharging Myers. It stated:

"We hold only that when a public employee speaks not as a citizen upon matters of public concern, but instead as an employee upon matters of personal interest, absent the most unusual circumstances, a federal court is not the appropriate forum in which to review the wisdom of a personnel decision taken by a public agency allegedly in reaction to the employee's behavior."
Connick at 147, 103 S.Ct. at 1690.

. . . In a case on facts so near to those in the case at hand as to be indistinguishable, the Fifth Circuit came to the conclusion we have just recited in *Kirkland v. Northside Independent School District*, 890 F.2d 794 (5th Cir.1989), *cert. denied*, 496 U.S. 926, 110 S.Ct. 2620, 110 L.Ed.2d 641 (1990). Kirkland was a case in which the employment contract of a high school history teacher was not renewed. He alleged the nonrenewal was a consequence of, and in retaliation for, his use of an unapproved reading list in his world history class. The high school had provided the teacher with a supplemental reading list for his history class along with a copy of the guidelines used to develop and amend that list. He was aware of the guidelines and understood that if he was dissatisfied, a separate body of reading material could be used in his class if he obtained administrative approval. The teacher, however, used his own substitute list and declined to procure the approval of the school authorities for his substitute list. The authorities at his high school then recommended that his contract not be renewed at the end of the next academic year, which was affirmed by the board of trustees, much like Margaret Boring's transfer was affirmed by the school board in this case after a recommendation by the administrative authorities.

The court held that to establish his constitutional claim, Kirkland must have shown that his supplemental reading list was constitutionally protected speech; not different from Mrs. Boring's selection of the play *Independence* in this case. It went on to hold that under *Connick v. Myers*, 461 U.S. 138, 103 S.Ct. 1684, 75 L.Ed.2d 708 (1983), the question of whether a public employee's speech is constitutionally protected depends upon the public or private nature of such speech. It decided that the selection of the reading list by the teacher was not a matter of public concern and stated that:

"Although, the concept of academic freedom has been recognized in our jurisprudence, the doctrine has never conferred upon teachers the control of public school curricula."
890 F.2d at 800.

. . . Since plaintiff's dispute with the principal, superintendent of schools and the school board is nothing more than an ordinary employment dispute, it does not constitute protected speech and has no First Amendment protection. Her case is indistinguishable from Kirkland's.

* * *

. . . In our opinion, the school administrative authorities had a legitimate pedagogical interest in the makeup of the curriculum of the school, including the inclusion of the play *Independence*.

* * *

. . . We [hold] that the school, not the teacher, has the right to fix the curriculum. Owens being a public school does not give the plaintiff any First Amendment right to fix the curriculum she would not have had if the school were private. *Connick*, 461 U.S. at 147, 103 S.Ct. at 1690.

. . . Someone must fix the curriculum of any school, public or private. In the case of a public school, in our opinion, it is far better public policy, absent a valid statutory directive on the subject, that the makeup of the curriculum be entrusted to the local school authorities who are in some sense responsible, rather than to the teachers, who would be responsible only to the judges, had they a First Amendment right to participate in the makeup of the curriculum.

136 F.3d 364 (4th Cir. 1998).

Does *Boring* hold that high school teachers have no academic freedom at all? Does the court overlook the fact that Boring took steps to seek administrative approval of the play? Is it important that after the principal banned the play, Boring spoke with him, and the students later performed the play with the changes the principal suggested? Did Boring violate a school policy? Was Boring transferred because she violated a school policy or because she disagreed with the principal on a curricular issue? Doesn't a teacher have a First Amendment right to disagree with school administrators on curricular issues as long as she does not violate school policy?

In the light of *Cary, Parducci,* and *Boring,* what right to academic freedom do elementary and secondary school teachers have?

4. Alternative Formulations

Would the following standard be more responsive to the academic freedom problem: Teachers may not introduce materials that effectively frustrate the legitimate interest of the school authorities in regulating the school curriculum? *See James v. Board of Educ.,* 461 F.2d 566 (2d Cir. 1972), *cert. denied,* 409 U.S. 1042, 93 S.Ct. 529, 34 L.Ed.2d 491. Alternatively, teachers have a right to choose a teaching method and/or materials that in the view of the court serve a demonstrated educational purpose as established by the weight of opinion of the teaching profession? *See Mailloux v. Kiley,* 436 F.2d 565 (1st Cir. 1971), *after dismissal,* 323 F.Supp. 1387 (D. Mass.), *aff'd,* 448 F.2d 1242 (1st Cir. 1971) (per curiam). Or should courts examine a broad range of factors in deciding these cases: for example, was the material introduced relevant, did it have educational value, was it appropriate for the age group in question? Is the *Cary* standard preferable? *See Pratt v. Independent School District No. 831,* 670 F.2d 771

(8th Cir. 1982); *Zykan v. Warsaw Community School Corp.,* 631 F.2d 1300 (7th Cir. 1980).

5. Problems

a. Rosebud High School has been the center of controversy. Several students published an issue of the "Purple Albatross" using a series of explicit sexual references. They were suspended. The next morning, faculty and students found a huge sign bearing an "offensive" four-letter word on the front lawn of the school. Everyone in school saw it, and the school is buzzing with conversation over its presence. Mr. Post is teaching a mathematics class, but it is clear that the students are supremely uninterested in what he is saying. Post decides to discuss the presence of the sign and the reasons for the controversy. The incident forms the basis for disciplining Post. How should a court decide a case in which Post challenges his treatment on constitutional grounds? Would your answer be different if Mr. Post were a civics teacher?

b. What constitutional protection, if any, should be afforded Ms. Robinson, a teacher who tells individual students out of class that it is foolish to salute the flag and that Communist China has the best government and America the worst, who distributes to some students a pamphlet on Communism, who disparages Lincoln, who decries religion to other students, and who fails to deny to another student an accusation that she is a member of a Communist club? *See Board of Education of Eureka v. Jewett,* 21 Cal. App.2d 64, 68 P.2d 404 (1937). Would it make a difference if remarks similarly critical of the United States were made in class? *See Joyce v. Board of Education,* 325 Ill.App. 543, 60 N.E.2d 431 (1945).

6. Institutional Academic Freedom

Consider these remarks by Professor Yudof on institutional academic freedom:

> Thus far, I have been speaking only of the rights of teachers in public schools, for all of the cases under consideration involved state action by a public authority against allegedly miscreant instructors. The concept of academic freedom is equally applicable to private institutions, but the violation of academic freedom has a constitutional dimension only in the public sphere.[70] By contract or other arrangements, private institutions may choose to afford the personal autonomy protections of academic freedom to their teachers,[71] but the Constitution cannot plausibly be construed as requiring

---

[70]*See generally . . .* O'Neil, "Private Universities and Public Law," 19 *Buff. L. Rev.* 155 (1970).

[71]*See* Finkin, "Toward a Law of Academic Status," 22 *Buff. L. Rev.* 575 (1973).

them to do so.[72] But there is a third face to academic freedom, a face that is turned toward private schools, that seeks to limit the power of governments to impose their will on such institutions. Consistent with the scholarly work of Professor Matthew Finkin,[73] I describe this as the institutional face of academic freedom.

By way of historical background, the continental tradition of academic freedom as professorial autonomy differed substantially from the pattern of academic freedom, developed over many centuries, in Great Britain and, much later, in the United States. This tradition centered on the "legally autonomous university, chartered by the government or Parliament or the Crown," and it reposed basic institutional authority in internal, academic governing bodies. While this allocation of authority was of great consequence for individual instructors, its basic thrust was the protection of institutional or corporate autonomy and not the protection of the personal autonomy of individual professors. Professor Shils has gone so far as to state that "[l]egislators in Great Britain as on the continent did not regard the universities as falling within their jurisdiction." He hastens to add that "American state legislators did not take quite the same attitude."

In varying forms and degrees, institutional academic freedom was thought to apply to both public and private universities, though the relationship between lay governing boards and academic communities in public universities has sometimes been uneasy and contentious. But it is important to note that through a curious infusion of federal constitutional law, the institutional autonomy face of academic freedom turned toward private elementary and secondary schools in the early years of this century. The leading cases are *Pierce v. Society of Sisters*,[77] and *Meyer v. Nebraska*,[78] 1920s substantive due process decisions of the United States Supreme Court. The Court in *Pierce* held that Oregon could not require all school-age children to attend public schools, and, in effect, that the institutional autonomy of private schools was constitutionally protected. In *Meyer* the justices overturned a law that forbade the teaching of German in private schools. Though the substantive due process underpinnings of *Pierce* and *Meyer* have been thoroughly repudiated over the last sixty years, interestingly enough the results have never been repudiated, and a number of

justices, of varying judicial persuasions, have embraced them on one ground or other.

From a constitutional perspective, *Pierce* and *Meyer* may represent a recognition of the right of parents to direct the education of their children, the right of teachers to affiliate with a private school, the right of individuals to associate with each other, or perhaps the right of religious students, parents and groups to organize their own schools. Each of these justifications is problematic, and many law review pages have been written on this engaging subject. The essential points, however, are that institutional academic freedom protects the private school from an overreaching governmental authority, and that, as in the case of the government expression face of academic freedom, the concept tends to diminish the ability of government to suppress competing ideas and ideologies. From my perspective, institutional academic freedom has less to do with the rights of private schools—and those of their operators, teachers and patrons—than it does with a limitation on the communications powers of government.

The third face of academic freedom does not always smile on individual teachers. The protection of institutional autonomy may require that private school authorities have substantial authority over who teaches and what is taught in their schools.[83] The institution will not be autonomous, a parochial school cannot convey its religious message, if it is required to allow teachers to discuss the pros and cons of abortion or birth control.[84] Indeed, institutional academic freedom does not purport to resolve disputes within a private school; it does not draw a line between the authority of the academicians and that of administrators and governing board members.

Note also that there are limits to institutional autonomy, just as there are limits to personal autonomy, and there are times when governmental regulation is entirely permissible. Private schools may not practice racial discrimination,[85] they may have to abide by building and fire codes, they may be subject to various labor relations, minimum wage, and employment statutes. They also may be required to offer particular courses, to keep attendance records, and to hire qualified teachers if their students are to satisfy compulsory attendance laws.[87] In each case the compelling nature

---

[72]*Cf. Rendell-Baker v. Kohn*, 457 U.S. 830 (1982). *But see* Levinson, "Princeton Versus Free Speech: A Post Mortem," in *Regulating the Intellectuals: Perspectives on Academic Freedom in the 1980s* 189 (C. Kaplan & E. Schrecker eds. 1983).

[73]Finkin, "On 'Institutional' Academic Freedom," 61 *Tex. L. Rev.* 817 (1983). *See generally* R. Hofstadter & W. Metzger, *The Development of Academic Freedom in the United States* ch. 2 (1955).

[77]268 U.S. 510 (1925). . . .

[78]262 U.S. 390 (1923).

[83]*Cf. Widmar v. Vincent*, 454 U.S. 263, 277–78 (1981) (Stevens, J., concurring).

[84]*See* Levinson, *supra* note 72, at 199–200.

[85]*See Runyon v. McCrary*, 427 U.S. 160 (1976); *Brown v. Dade Christian Schools, Inc.*, 556 F.2d 310 (5th Cir. 1977) (en banc), *cert. denied*, 434 U.S. 1063 (1978). *Cf. Bob Jones Univ. v. United States*, 461 U.S. 574 (1983).

[87]*See* T. van Geel, *Authority to Control the School Program* 153–57 (1976); Elson, "State Regulation of Nonpublic Schools: The Legal Framework," in

of the public policy and the limits of tolerance must balance against the specific infringement on institutional autonomy. Not surprisingly, principled results are frequently elusive.

The institutional face of academic freedom is very much in vogue, and a case raising such issues, *Dayton Christian Schools, Inc. v. Ohio Civil Rights Commission*,[88] was recently disposed of by the United States Supreme Court on abstention grounds. Bob Jones University, in a case that brought national attention, unsuccessfully argued that the Internal Revenue Service constitutionally could not require non-discriminatory treatment of minority students as a condition for being granted tax-exempt status.[90] Princeton University also invoked institutional academic freedom a few years ago in unsuccessfully seeking to bar pamphleteers from its campus.[91] Some academicians seem appalled at Princeton's effort to invoke academic freedom because of their belief that the doctrine protects individual teachers and professors and not institutions. But such a view commits the fatal error of confusing the different faces of the concept. Institutional academic freedom may well grant some protections to the managers of private schools, while affording few to faculty members. Put somewhat differently, there is no reason to assume that the personal autonomy model of academic freedom is the only acceptable one or that that model, in its constitutional formulation, should have easy application to private schools.

Yudof, "Three Faces of Academic Freedom," 32 *Loy. L. Rev.* 831, 851–54 (1987). *See also* Byrne, "Academic Freedom: A 'Special Concern' of the First Amendment," 99 *Yale L.J.* 251, 311–39 (1989).

Is institutional academic freedom not so much a free-standing right as an institutional interest to be balanced against individual assertions of right? *See, e.g., University of Pennsylvania v. Equal Employment Opportunity Commission*, 493 U.S. 182, 110 S.Ct. 577, 107 L.Ed.2d 571 (1990); *Regents of University of Michigan v. Ewing*, 474 U.S. 214, 106 S.Ct. 507, 88 L.Ed.2d 523 (1985); *Regents of the University of California v. Bakke*, 438 U.S. 265, 311–19, 98 S.Ct. 2733, 2759–63, 57 L.Ed.2d 750 (1978) (Powell, J.). *See generally* Byrne, *supra* at 317. Does institutional academic freedom extend to public education institutions? *See Urofsky v. Gilmore*, 167 F.3d 191 (4th Cir. 1999). Does institutional academic freedom protect peer evaluations from discovery in a lawsuit alleging racial or sexual discrimination in tenure and promotion decisions?

See University of Pennsylvania, supra. See generally Note, "*University of Pennsylvania v. EEOC* and *Dixon v. Rutgers:* Two Supreme Courts Speak on the Academic Freedom Privilege," 42 *Rutgers L. Rev.* 1089 (1990); Note, "Preventing Unnecessary Intrusions on University Autonomy: A Proposed Academic Freedom Privilege," 69 *Cal. L. Rev.* 1538 (1981).

7. *Academic Freedom and Racial and Sexual Expression*

Can racist or sexist comments by a teacher or professor ever be protected by academic freedom? What if such comments are part of the teaching method? Courts are divided on this issue and the result often turns on the specific facts of the case. In *Cohen v. San Bernardino Valley College*, the court held that a professor's focus on topics of sexual nature, the use of profanity and vulgarity in class, and degrading comments aimed at female students are not protected by academic freedom. 883 F. Supp. 1407 (C.D. Cal. 1995). However, in *Silva v. University of New Hampshire*, the court held that a university violated a professor's right to free expression when it disciplined him for the sexual overtones in classroom examples. 888 F. Supp. 293 (D. N.H. 1994). In that case, the professor had used sex as a metaphor. "I will put focus in terms of sex, so you can better understand it. Focus is like sex. You seek a target. You zero in on your subject. You move in from side to side. You close in on the subject. You bracket the subject and center on it. Focus connects the experience and the language. You and subject become one." *See id.* at 299. Should this speech be protected? If the example makes students uncomfortable, should the professor be allowed to continue to use it? Does it matter whether a college professor or a high-school teacher uses the metaphor?

What if a professor wants to argue through research and writing that African Americans are inferior to whites? *See Levin v. Harleston*, 966 F.2d 85 (2d Cir. 1992). Does a university infringe upon his freedom of expression if it offers an alternative class on the same subject at the same time by another professor so students who disagree with the professor's views are not forced to take his class? Does it matter whether the professor has articulated his racial theories in class? Whether he has actually treated students differently because of their race? In *Levin v.*

---

[88]766 F.2d 932 (6th Cir. 1985), rev'd, 106 S.Ct. 2718 (1986).

[90]*Bob Jones Univ. v. United States*, 461 U.S. 574 (1983).

[91]*State v. Schmid*, 84 N.J. 535, 432 A.2d 615 (1980), *appeal dismissed*, 455 U.S. 100 (1982); *see* Finkin, *supra* note 69; Levinson, *supra* note 72.

Harleston, the Second Circuit held that the offering of such an alternative class did indeed infringe upon the professor's First Amendment rights. *See id.* The court also noted that none of the professor's students had ever complained about unfair treatment on the basis of race. *See id.* Would the result have been different if it were a high school teacher, rather than a college professor, who held the racist views?

Does the theory behind academic freedom determine the outcome for these issues? Under the marketplace of ideas theory, academic freedom protects the search for truth and the process of learning. However, not all speech is protected under this theory. Plagiarism and falsification of research data are two examples of unprotected academic speech — they do nothing to further the search for truth. Should racist and sexist comments be treated similarly? *See* Newman, "At Work in the Marketplace of Ideas: Academic Freedom, The First Amendment, and *Jeffries v. Harleston*," 22 *J.C. & U.L.* 281 (1995). *See generally*, Lawrence, "If He Hollers Let Him Go: Regulating Racist Speech on Campus," 1990 *Duke L.J.* 431. Are such comments protected because, as John Stuart Mill argued, even the discussion of wrong ideas may illuminate the right answer? *See On Liberty*, chapter 2 "Of Liberty of Thought and Discussion" (1859). If the *Cary* rationale were controlling, what should be the result in these cases? If it is legitimate for public schools to teach tolerance and to seek to break down racial and gender stereotypes, should academic freedom for teachers extend to allegedly racist and sexist statements and readings?

Should constitutional protection depend on the form of the speech? Is there a difference between disciplining a professor for spewing racial epithets intended only to appeal to the audience's prejudices — phrases such as "nigger," "ice people," "rich jew" — and disciplining a professor who attempts to use logic and scientific inquiry to support a theory of racial superiority? *Cf. Jeffries v. Harleston*, 21 F.3d 1238 (2d Cir. 1994); *Levin v. Harleston, supra.* Does it matter that more speech and critical inquiry can refute an argument that is supposedly based on logic, whereas appeals to prejudice are difficult to refute through more speech? What if the professor publicly degrades members of a racial group off-campus, but not on-campus? *See Jeffries v. Harleston, supra.* Does it matter if the public and students might attribute discriminatory statements to the educational institution as a whole? *See generally* Newman, *supra.*

2. Access to School Facilities

Board of Education of Westside Community Schools v. Mergens
496 U.S. 226, 110 S.Ct. 2356 (1990).

Justice O'Connor delivered the opinion of the Court, except as to Part III.

This case requires us to decide whether the Equal Access Act, 98 Stat. 1302, 20 U.S.C. §§ 4071–4074, prohibits Westside High School from denying a student religious group permission to meet on school premises during noninstructional time, and if so, whether the Act, so construed, violates the Establishment Clause of the First Amendment.

I

Respondents are current and former students at Westside High School, a public secondary school in Omaha, Nebraska. At the time this suit was filed, the school enrolled about 1,450 students and included grades 10 to 12; in the 1987–1988 school year, ninth graders were added. Westside High School is part of the Westside Community School system, an independent public school district. Petitioners are the Board of Education of Westside Community Schools (District 66); Wayne W. Meier, the president of the school board; James E. Findley, the principal of Westside High School; Kenneth K. Hanson, the superintendent of schools for the school district; and James A. Tangdell, the assistant superintendent of schools for the school district.

Students at Westside High School are permitted to join various student groups and clubs, all of which meet after school hours on school premises. The students may choose from approximately 30 recognized groups on a voluntary basis. A list of student groups, together with a brief description of each provided by the school, appears in the Appendix to this opinion.

School Board Policy 5610 concerning "Student Clubs and Organizations" recognizes these student clubs as a "vital part of the total education program as a means of developing citizenship, wholesome attitudes, good human relations, knowledge and skills." . . . Board Policy 5610 also provides that each club shall have faculty sponsorship and that "clubs and organizations shall not be sponsored by any political or religious organization, or by any organization which denies membership on the basis of race, color, creed, sex or political belief." . . . Board Policy 6180 on "Recognition of Religious Beliefs and Customs" requires that "[s]tudents adhering to a specific set of religious beliefs or holding to little or no belief shall be alike respected." . . . In addition, Board Policy 5450 recognizes its students' "Freedom of Expression," consistent with the authority of the Board. . . .

There is no written school board policy concerning the formation of student clubs. Rather, students wishing to form a club present their request to a school official who determines whether the proposed club's goals and objectives are consistent with school board policies and with the school district's "Mission and Goals"—a broadly worded "blueprint" that expresses the district's commitment to teaching academic, physical, civic, and personal skills and values. . . .

In January 1985, respondent Bridget Mergens met with Westside's principal, Dr. Findley, and requested permission to form a Christian club at the school. The proposed club would have the same privileges and meet on the same terms and conditions as other Westside student groups, except that the proposed club would not have a faculty sponsor. According to the students' testimony at trial, the club's purpose would have been, among other things, to permit the students to read and discuss the Bible, to have fellowship, and to pray together. Membership would have been voluntary and open to all students regardless of religious affiliation.

Findley denied the request, as did associate superintendent Tangdell. In February 1985, Findley and Tangdell informed Mergens that they had discussed the matter with superintendent Hanson and that he had agreed that her request should be denied. The school officials explained that school policy required all student clubs to have a faculty sponsor, which the proposed religious club would not or could not have, and that a religious club at the school would violate the Establishment Clause. In March 1985, Mergens appealed the denial of her request to the Board of Education, but the Board voted to uphold the denial.

Respondents, by and through their parents as next friends, then brought this suit in the United States District Court for the District of Nebraska seeking declaratory and injunctive relief. They alleged that petitioners' refusal to permit the proposed club to meet at Westside violated the Equal Access Act, 20 U.S.C. §§ 4071–4074, which prohibits public secondary schools that receive federal financial assistance and that maintain a "limited open forum" from denying "equal access" to students who wish to meet within the forum on the basis of the content of the speech at such meetings, § 4071(a). Respondents further alleged that petitioners' actions denied them their First and Fourteenth Amendment rights to freedom of speech, association, and the free exercise of religion. Petitioners responded that the Equal Access Act did not apply to Westside and that, if the Act did apply, it violated the Establishment Clause of the First Amendment and was therefore unconstitutional. The United States intervened in the action pursuant to 28 U.S.C. § 2403 to defend the constitutionality of the Act.

The District Court entered judgment for petitioners. The court held that the Act did not apply in this case because Westside did not have a "limited open forum" as defined by the Act—all of Westside's student clubs, the court concluded, were curriculum-related and tied to the educational function of the school. The court rejected respondents' constitutional claims, reasoning that Westside did not have a limited public forum as set forth in *Widmar v. Vincent*, 454 U.S. 263, 102 S.Ct. 269, 70 L.Ed.2d 440 (1981), and that Westside's denial of respondents' request was reasonably related to legitimate pedagogical concerns, *see Hazelwood School Dist. v. Kuhlmeier*, 484 U.S. 260, 273, 108 S.Ct. 562, 571, 98 L.Ed.2d 592 (1988).

The United States Court of Appeals for the Eighth Circuit reversed. 867 F.2d 1076 (1989). The Court of Appeals held that the District Court erred in concluding that all the existing student clubs at Westside were curriculum-related. The Court of Appeals noted that the "broad interpretation" advanced by the Westside school officials "would make the [Equal Access Act] meaningless" and would allow any school to "arbitrarily deny access to school facilities to any unfavored student club on the basis of its speech content," which was "exactly the result that Congress sought to prohibit by enacting the [Act]." *Id.*, at 1078. The Court of Appeals instead found that "[m]any of the student clubs at WHS, including the chess club, are noncurriculum-related." *Id.*, at 1079. Accordingly, because it found that Westside maintained a limited open forum under the Act, the Court of Appeals concluded that the Act applied to "forbi[d] discrimination against [respondents'] proposed club on the basis of its religious content." *Ibid.*

The Court of Appeals then rejected petitioners' contention that the Act violated the Establishment Clause. Noting that the Act extended the decision in *Widmar v. Vincent, supra*, to public secondary schools, the Court of Appeals concluded that "[a]ny constitutional attack on the [Act] must therefore be predicated on the difference between secondary school students and university students." 867 F.2d, at 1080. . . . Because "Congress considered the difference in the maturity level of secondary students and university students before passing the [Act]," the Court of Appeals held, on the basis of Congress' fact-finding, that the Act did not violate the Establishment Clause. *Ibid.*

We granted certiorari . . . and now affirm.

II

A

In *Widmar v. Vincent*, 454 U.S. 263, 102 S.Ct. 269, 70 L.Ed.2d 440 (1981), we invalidated, on free speech grounds, a state university regulation that prohibited student use of school facilities " 'for purposes of religious worship or religious teaching.' " . . . In doing so, we held that an "equal access" policy would not violate the Establishment Clause under our decision in *Lemon v. Kurtzman*, 403 U.S. 602, 612–613, 91 S.Ct. 2105, 2111, 29 L.Ed.2d 745 (1971). In particular, we held that such a policy would have a secular purpose, would not have the primary effect of advancing religion, and would not result in excessive entanglement between government and religion, *Widmar*, 454 U.S., at 271–274, 102 S.Ct., at 275–76. We noted, however, that "[u]niversity students are, of course, young adults. They are less impressionable than younger students and should be able to appreciate that the University's policy is one of neutrality toward religion." . . .

In 1984, Congress extended the reasoning of *Widmar* to public secondary schools. Under the Equal Access Act, a public secondary school with a "limited open forum" is prohibited from discriminating against students who wish to conduct a meeting within that forum on the basis of the "religious, political, philosophical, or other content of the speech at such meetings." 20 U.S.C. §§ 4071(a) and (b). Specifically, the Act provides:

> "It shall be unlawful for any public secondary school which receives Federal financial assistance and which has a limited open forum to deny equal access or a fair opportunity to, or discriminate against, any students who wish to conduct a meeting within that limited open forum on the basis of the religious, political, philosophical, or other content of the speech at such meetings." 20 U.S.C. § 4071(a).

A "limited open forum" exists whenever a public secondary school "grants an offering to or opportunity for one or more noncurriculum related student groups to meet on school premises during noninstructional time." § 4071(b). "Meeting" is defined to include "those activities of student groups which are permitted under a school's limited open forum and are not directly related to the school curriculum." § 4072(3). "Noninstructional time" is defined to mean "time set aside by the school before actual classroom instruction begins or after actual classroom instruction ends." § 4072(4). Thus, even if a public secondary school allows only one "noncurriculum related student group" to meet, the Act's obligations are triggered and the school may not deny other clubs, on the basis of the content of their speech, equal access to meet on school premises during noninstructional time.

The Act further specifies that "[s]chools shall be deemed to offer a fair opportunity to students who wish to conduct a meeting within its limited open forum" if the school uniformly provides that the meetings are voluntary and student-initiated; are not sponsored by the school, the government, or its agents or employees; do not materially and substantially interfere with the orderly conduct of educational activities within the school; and are not directed, controlled, conducted, or regularly attended by "nonschool persons." §§ 4071(c)(1), (2), (4), and (5). "Sponsorship" is defined to mean "the act of promoting, leading, or participating in a meeting. The assignment of a teacher, administrator, or other school employee to a meeting for custodial purposes does not constitute sponsorship of the meeting." § 4072(2). If the meetings are religious, employees or agents of the school or government may attend only in a "nonparticipatory capacity." § 4071(c)(3). Moreover, a State may not influence the form of any religious activity, require any person to participate in such activity, or compel any school agent or employee to attend a meeting if the content of the speech at the meeting is contrary to that person's beliefs. §§ 4071(d)(1), (2), and (3).

Finally, the Act does not "authorize the United States to deny or withhold Federal financial assistance to any school," § 4071(e), or "limit the authority of the school, its agents or employees, to maintain order and discipline on school premises, to protect the well-being of students and faculty, and to assure that attendance of students at the meetings is voluntary," § 4071(f).

B

The parties agree that Westside High School receives federal financial assistance and is a public secondary school within the meaning of the Act. App. 57–58. The Act's obligation to grant equal access to student groups is therefore triggered if Westside maintains a "limited open forum" — i.e., if it permits one or more "noncurriculum related student groups" to meet on campus before or after classes.

Unfortunately, the Act does not define the crucial phrase "noncurriculum related student group." Our immediate task is therefore one of statutory interpretation. We begin, of course, with the language of the statute. . . . The common meaning of the term "curriculum" is "the whole body of courses offered by an educational institution or one of its branches." Webster's Third New International Dictionary 557 (1976); see also Black's Law Dictionary 345 (5th ed. 1979) ("The set of studies or courses for a particular period, designated by a school or branch of a school"). . . . Any sensible interpretation of "noncurriculum related student group" must therefore be anchored in the notion that such student groups are those that are not related to the body of courses offered by the school. The difficult question is the degree of "unrelatedness to the curriculum" required for a group to be considered "noncurriculum related."

The Act's definition of the sort of "meeting[s]" that must be accommodated under the statute, § 4071(a), sheds some light on this question. "[T]he term 'meeting' includes those activities of student groups which are . . . not *directly related* to the school curriculum." § 4072(3) (emphasis added). Congress' use of the phrase "directly related" implies that student groups directly related to the subject matter of courses offered by the school do not fall within the "noncurriculum related" category and would therefore be considered "curriculum related."

The logic of the Act also supports this view, namely, that a curriculum-related student group is one that has more than just a tangential or attenuated relationship to courses offered by the school. Because the purpose of granting equal access is to prohibit discrimination between religious or political clubs on the one hand and other noncurriculum-related student groups on the other, the Act is premised on the notion that a religious or political club is itself likely to be a noncurriculum-related student group. It follows, then, that a student group that is "curriculum related" must at least have a more direct relationship to the curriculum than a religious or political club would have.

Although the phrase "noncurriculum related student group" nevertheless remains sufficiently ambiguous that we might normally resort to legislative history . . . we find the legislative history on this issue

less than helpful. Because the bill that led to the Act was extensively rewritten in a series of multilateral negotiations after it was passed by the House and reported out of committee by the Senate, the committee reports shed no light on the language actually adopted. During congressional debate on the subject, legislators referred to a number of different definitions, and thus both petitioners and respondents can cite to legislative history favoring their interpretation of the phrase. *Compare* 130 Cong.Rec. 19223 (1984) (statement of Sen. Hatfield) (curriculum-related clubs are those that are "really a kind of extension of the classroom"), *with ibid.* (statement of Sen. Hatfield) (in response to question whether school districts would have full authority to decide what was curriculum-related, "[w]e in no way seek to limit that discretion"). *See* Laycock, "Equal Access and Moments of Silence: The Equal Status of Religious Speech by Private Speakers," 81 *Nw. U. L. Rev.* 1, 37–39 (1986).

We think it significant, however, that the Act, which was passed by wide, bipartisan majorities in both the House and the Senate, reflects at least some consensus on a broad legislative purpose. The committee reports indicate that the Act was intended to address perceived widespread discrimination against religious speech in public schools, see H.R.Rep. No. 98-710, p. 4 (1984); S.Rep. No. 98-357, pp. 10–11 (1984), and, as the language of the Act indicates, its sponsors contemplated that the Act would do more than merely validate the status quo. The committee reports also show that the Act was enacted in part in response to two federal appellate court decisions holding that student religious groups could not, consistent with the Establishment Clause, meet on school premises during noninstructional time. See H.R. Rep. No. 98-710, *supra*, at 3–6 (discussing *Lubbock Civil Liberties Union v. Lubbock Independent School Dist.*, 669 F.2d 1038, 1042–1048 (CA5 1982), *cert. denied*, 459 U.S. 1155–1156, 103 S.Ct. 800, 74 L.Ed.2d 1003 (1983), and *Brandon v. Guilderland Bd. of Ed.*, 635 F.2d 971 (CA2 1980), *cert. denied*, 454 U.S. 1123, 102 S.Ct. 970, 71 L.Ed.2d 109 (1981)); S.Rep. No. 98-357, *supra*, at 6–9, 11–14 (same). A broad reading of the Act would be consistent with the views of those who sought to end discrimination by allowing students to meet and discuss religion before and after classes.

In light of this legislative purpose, we think that the term "noncurriculum related student group" is best interpreted broadly to mean any student group

that does not directly relate to the body of courses offered by the school. In our view, a student group directly relates to a school's curriculum if the subject
matter of the group is actually taught, or will soon be
taught, in a regularly offered course; if the subject
matter of the group concerns the body of courses as
a whole; if participation in the group is required for
a particular course; or if participation in the group results in academic credit. . . .

For example, a French club would directly relate
to the curriculum if a school taught French in a regularly offered course or planned to teach the subject
in the near future. A school's student government
would generally relate directly to the curriculum to
the extent that it addresses concerns, solicits opinions, and formulates proposals pertaining to the body
of courses offered by the school. If participation in a
school's band or orchestra were required for the band
or orchestra classes, or resulted in academic credit,
then those groups would also directly relate to the
curriculum. The existence of such groups at a school
would not trigger the Act's obligations.

On the other hand, unless a school could show
that groups such as a chess club, a stamp collecting
club, or a community service club fell within our description of groups that directly relate to the curriculum, such groups would be "noncurriculum related
student groups" for purposes of the Act. The existence of such groups would create a "limited open
forum" under the Act and would prohibit the school
from denying equal access to any other student
group on the basis of the content of that group's
speech. Whether a specific student group is a "noncurriculum related student group" will therefore depend on a particular school's curriculum, but such
determinations would be subject to factual findings
well within the competence of trial courts to make.

* * *

The dissent suggests that "an extracurricular student
organization is 'noncurriculum related' if it has as its
purpose (or as part of its purpose) the advocacy of
partisan theological, political, or ethical views." . . .
This interpretation of the Act, we are told, is mandated by Congress' intention to "track our own Free
Speech Clause jurisprudence," . . . by incorporating
Widmar's notion of a "limited public forum" into the
language of the Act. . . .

This suggestion is flawed for at least two reasons.
First, the Act itself neither uses the phrase "limited
public forum" nor so much as hints that that doctrine
is somehow "incorporated" into the words of the
statute. The operative language of the statute, 20

U.S.C. § 4071(a), of course, refers to a "limited open
forum," a term that is specifically defined in the next
subsection, § 4071(b). Congress was presumably
aware that "limited public forum," as used by the
Court, is a term of art, *see, e.g., Perry Ed. Assn. v. Perry
Local Educators' Assn.*, 460 U.S. 37, 45–49, 103 S.Ct.
948, 954–57, 74 L.Ed.2d 794 (1983), and had it intended to import that concept into the Act, one
would suppose that it would have done so explicitly.
Indeed, Congress' deliberate choice to use a different
term — and to define that term — can only mean that
it intended to establish a standard different from the
one established by our free speech cases. *See* Laycock, *81 Nw. U. L. Rev.*, at 36 ("The statutory 'limited
open forum' is an artificial construct, and comparisons with the constitutional ['limited public forum']
cases can be misleading"). To paraphrase the dissent,
"[i]f Congress really intended to [incorporate] *Widmar* for reasons of administrative clarity, Congress
kept its intent well hidden, both in the statute and in
the debates preceding its passage." . . .

Second, and more significant, the dissent's reliance
on the legislative history to support its interpretation of
the Act shows just how treacherous that task can be.
The dissent appears to agree with our view that the legislative history of the Act, even if relevant, is highly
unreliable, . . . yet the interpretation it suggests rests
solely on a few passing, general references by legislators to our decision in *Widmar* . . . The only thing that
can be said with any confidence is that some Senators
may have thought that the obligations of the Act
would be triggered only when a school permits advocacy groups to meet on school premises during noninstructional time. That conclusion, of course, cannot
bear the weight the dissent places on it.

C

The parties in the case focus their dispute on 10 of
Westside's approximately 30 voluntary student clubs:
Interact (a service club related to Rotary International); Chess; Subsurfers (a club for students interested in scuba diving); National Honor Society; Photography; Welcome to Westside (a club to introduce
new students to the school); Future Business Leaders of America; Zonta (the female counterpart to
Interact); Student Advisory Board (student government); and the Student Forum (student government). . . . Petitioners contend that all of these student activities are curriculum-related because they
further the goals of particular aspects of the school's
curriculum. Welcome to Westside, for example,

helps "further the School's overall goal of developing effective citizens by requiring student members to contribute to their fellow students." . . . The student government clubs "advance the goals of the School's political science classes by providing an understanding and appreciation of government processes." . . . Subsurfers furthers "one of the essential goals of the Physical Education Department—enabling students to develop lifelong recreational interests." . . . Chess "supplement[s] math and science courses because it enhances students' ability to engage in critical thought processes." . . . Participation in Interact and Zonta "promotes effective citizenship, a critical goal of the WHS curriculum, specifically the Social Studies Department." . . .

To the extent that petitioners contend that "curriculum related" means anything remotely related to abstract educational goals, however, we reject that argument. To define "curriculum related" in a way that results in almost no schools having limited open fora, or in a way that permits schools to evade the Act by strategically describing existing student groups, would render the Act merely hortatory. *See* 130 Cong.Rec. 19222 (1984) (statement of Sen. Leahy) ("[A] limited open forum should be triggered by what a school does, not by what it says"). . . .

Rather, we think it clear that Westside's existing student groups include one or more "noncurriculum related student groups." Although Westside's physical education classes apparently include swimming, . . . counsel stated at oral argument that scuba diving is not taught in any regularly offered course at the school. . . . Based on Westside's own description of the group, Subsurfers does not directly relate to the curriculum as a whole in the same way that a student government or similar group might. . . . Moreover, participation in Subsurfers is not required by any course at the school and does not result in extra academic credit. . . . Thus, Subsurfers is a "noncurriculum related student group" for purposes of the Act. Similarly, although math teachers at Westside have encouraged their students to play chess, . . . chess is not taught in any regularly offered course at the school, . . . and participation in the chess club is not required for any class and does not result in extra credit for any class. . . . The chess club is therefore another "noncurriculum related student group" at Westside. Moreover, Westside's principal acknowledged at trial that the Peer Advocates program—a service group that works with special edu-

cation classes—does not directly relate to any courses offered by the school and is not required by any courses offered by the school. . . .

Although our definition of "noncurriculum related student activities" looks to a school's actual practice rather than its stated policy, we note that our conclusion is also supported by the school's own description of its student activities. As reprinted in the Appendix to this opinion, the school states that Band "is included in our regular curriculum"; Choir "is a course offered as part of the curriculum"; Distributive Education "is an extension of the Distributive Education class"; International Club is "developed through our foreign language classes"; Latin Club is "designed for those students who are taking Latin as a foreign language"; Student Publications "includes classes offered in preparation of the yearbook (Shield) and the student newspaper (Lance)"; Dramatics "is an extension of a regular academic class"; and Orchestra "is an extension of our regular curriculum." These descriptions constitute persuasive evidence that these student clubs directly relate to the curriculum. By inference, however, the fact that the descriptions of student activities such as Subsurfers and chess do not include such references strongly suggests that those clubs do not, by the school's own admission, directly relate to the curriculum. . . .

The remaining statutory question is whether petitioners' denial of respondents' request to form a religious group constitutes a denial of "equal access" to the school's limited open forum. Although the school apparently permits respondents to meet informally after school, App. 315–316, respondents seek equal access in the form of official recognition by the school. Official recognition allows student clubs to be part of the student activities program and carries with it access to the school newspaper, bulletin boards, the public address system, and the annual Club Fair. . . . Given that the Act explicitly prohibits denial of "equal access . . . to . . . any students who wish to conduct a meeting within [the school's] limited open forum" on the basis of the religious content of the speech at such meetings, § 4071(a), we hold that Westside's denial of respondents' request to form a Christian club denies them "equal access" under the Act.

Because we rest our conclusion on statutory grounds, we need not decide—and therefore express no opinion on—whether the First Amendment requires the same result.

III

Petitioners contend that even if Westside has created a limited open forum within the meaning of the Act, its denial of official recognition to the proposed Christian club must nevertheless stand because the Act violates the Establishment Clause of the First Amendment, as applied to the States through the Fourteenth Amendment. Specifically, petitioners maintain that because the school's recognized student activities are an integral part of its educational mission, official recognition of respondents' proposed club would effectively incorporate religious activities into the school's official program, endorse participation in the religious club, and provide the club with an official platform to proselytize other students.

We disagree. In *Widmar*, we applied the three-part *Lemon* test to hold that an "equal access" policy, at the university level, does not violate the Establishment Clause. . . . We concluded that "an open-forum policy, including nondiscrimination against religious speech, would have a secular purpose," . . . and would in fact avoid entanglement with religion. . . . We also found that although incidental benefits accrued to religious groups who used university facilities, this result did not amount to an establishment of religion. First, we stated that a university's forum does not "confer any imprimatur of state approval on religious sects or practices." . . . Indeed, the message is one of neutrality rather than endorsement; if a State refused to let religious groups use facilities open to others, then it would demonstrate not neutrality but hostility toward religion. . . . Second, we noted that "[t]he [University's] provision of benefits to [a] broad . . . spectrum of groups"—both non religious and religious speakers—was "an important index of secular effect." . . .

We think the logic of *Widmar* applies with equal force to the Equal Access Act. As an initial matter, the Act's prohibition of discrimination on the basis of "political, philosophical, or other" speech as well as religious speech is a sufficient basis for meeting the secular purpose prong of the *Lemon* test. *See Edwards v. Aguillard*, 482 U.S. 578, 586, 107 S.Ct. 2573, 2579, 96 L.Ed.2d 510 (1987) (Court "is normally deferential to a [legislative] articulation of a secular purpose"). . . . Congress' avowed purpose—to prevent discrimination against religious and other types of speech—is undeniably secular. . . . Even if some legislators were motivated by a conviction that

religious speech in particular was valuable and worthy of protection, that alone would not invalidate the Act, because what is relevant is the legislative purpose of the statute, not the possibly religious motives of the legislators who enacted the law. Because the Act on its face grants equal access to both secular and religious speech, we think it clear that the Act's purpose was not to " 'endorse or disapprove of religion,' " *Wallace v. Jaffree*, 472 U.S. 38, 56, 105 S.Ct. 2479, 2489, 86 L.Ed.2d 29 (1985) (quoting *Lynch v. Donnelly*, 465 U.S. 668, 690, 104 S.Ct. 1355, 1368, 79 L.Ed.2d 604 (1984) (O'Connor, J., concurring)).

Petitioners' principal contention is that the Act has the primary effect of advancing religion. Specifically, petitioners urge that, because the student religious meetings are held under school aegis, and because the state's compulsory attendance laws bring the students together (and thereby provide a ready-made audience for student evangelists), an objective observer in the position of a secondary school student will perceive official school support for such religious meetings. . . .

We disagree. First, although we have invalidated the use of public funds to pay for teaching state-required subjects at parochial schools, in part because of the risk of creating "a crucial symbolic link between government and religion, thereby enlisting—at least in the eyes of impressionable youngsters—the powers of government to the support of the religious denomination operating the school," *Grand Rapids School Dist. v. Ball*, 473 U.S. 373, 385, 105 S.Ct. 3216, 3223, 87 L.Ed.2d 267 (1985), there is a crucial difference between government speech endorsing religion, which the Establishment Clause forbids, and private speech endorsing religion, which the Free Speech and Free Exercise Clauses protect. We think that secondary school students are mature enough and are likely to understand that a school does not endorse or support student speech that it merely permits on a nondiscriminatory basis. *Cf. Tinker v. Des Moines Independent Community School Dist.*, 393 U.S. 503, 89 S.Ct. 733, 21 L.Ed.2d 731 (1969) (no danger that high school students' symbolic speech implied school endorsement); *West Virginia State Bd. of Ed. v. Barnette*, 319 U.S. 624, 63 S.Ct. 1178, 87 L.Ed. 1628 (1943) (same). . . .

Indeed, we note that Congress specifically rejected the argument that high school students are likely to confuse an equal access policy with state sponsorship of religion. See S.Rep. No. 98-357, p. 8 (1984); *id.*, at 35 (''[S]tudents below the college level are capable of distinguishing between State-initiated, school sponsored, or teacher-led religious speech on the one hand and student-initiated, student-led religious speech on the other"). . . .

Second, we note that the Act expressly limits participation by school officials at meetings of student religious groups, §§ 4071(c)(2) and (3), and that any such meetings must be held during "noninstructional time," § 4071(b). The Act therefore avoids the problems of "the students' emulation of teachers as role models" and "mandatory attendance requirement" . . . .

To be sure, the possibility of student peer pressure remains, but there is little if any risk of official state endorsement or coercion where no formal classroom activities are involved and no school officials actively participate. Moreover, petitioners' fear of a mistaken inference of endorsement is largely self-imposed, because the school itself has control over any impressions it gives its students. To the extent a school makes clear that its recognition of respondents' proposed club is not an endorsement of the views of the club's participants, . . . students will reasonably understand that the school's official recognition of the club evinces neutrality toward, rather than endorsement of, religious speech.

Third, the broad spectrum of officially recognized student clubs at Westside, and the fact that Westside students are free to initiate and organize additional student clubs, see App. 221–222, counteract any possible message of official endorsement of or preference for religion or a particular religious belief. . . . Under the Act, a school with a limited open forum may not lawfully deny access to a Jewish students' club, a Young Democrats club, or a philosophy club devoted to the study of Nietzsche. To the extent that a religious club is merely one of many different student-initiated voluntary clubs, students should perceive no message of government endorsement of religion. . . .

Petitioners' final argument is that by complying with the Act's requirement, the school risks excessive entanglement between government and religion. The proposed club, petitioners urge, would be required to have a faculty sponsor who would be charged with actively directing the activities of the group, guiding its leaders, and ensuring balance in the presentation of controversial ideas. Petitioners claim that this influence over the club's religious program would entangle the government in day-to-day surveillance of religion of the type forbidden by the Establishment Clause.

Under the Act, however, faculty monitors may not participate in any religious meetings, and nonschool persons may not direct, control, or regularly attend activities of student groups. §§ 4071(c)(3) and (5). Moreover, the Act prohibits school "sponsorship" of any religious meetings, § 4071(c)(2), which means that school officials may not promote, lead, or participate in any such meeting, § 4072(2). Although the Act permits "[t]he assignment of a teacher, administrator, or other school employee to the meeting for custodial purposes," *ibid.*, such custodial oversight of the student-initiated religious group, merely to ensure order and good behavior, does not impermissibly entangle government in the day-to-day surveillance or administration of religious activities. . . . Indeed, as the Court noted in *Widmar*, a denial of equal access to religious speech might well create greater entanglement problems in the form of invasive monitoring to prevent religious speech at meetings at which such speech might occur. . . .

Accordingly, we hold that the Equal Access Act does not on its face contravene the Establishment Clause. Because we hold that petitioners have violated the Act, we do not decide respondents' claims under the Free Speech and Free Exercise Clauses. For the foregoing reasons, the judgment of the Court of Appeals is affirmed.

It is so ordered.

APPENDIX

Plaintiff's Trial Exhibit 63
Student Activities

August, 1984

BAND—This activity is included in our regular curriculum. Extensions of this activity include Marching Band, Ensembles, Pep Band, and Concert Jazz Band. Performances, presentations, and programs are presented throughout the school year.

CHESS CLUB—This activity is for those interested in playing chess. Opportunities to play are held after school throughout the school year.

CHEERLEADERS—A girls sport cheerleader team is made up of a junior varsity and varsity. The boys sport cheerleaders consist of sophomores, junior varsity, and varsity. Tryouts for these spirit groups are held each spring.

CHOIR—This is a course offered as part of the curriculum. Extensions of this class include Boys and Girls Glee, Warrior Voices, and Concert and Chamber Choirs. Membership in these activities are [sic] determined by enrollment and tryouts.

CLASS OFFICERS—Voting and selection of junior and senior class officers for the following year are held each spring. Students interested in being a class officer will need to secure support, be willing to make a presentation to their class, and serve their class in an officer capacity for the following year.

DISTRIBUTIVE EDUCATION (DECA)—This is an organization that is an extension of the Distributive Education class. Membership in this activity is offered to those students involved in D.E. The club for the current year is formulated at the beginning of school each fall.

SPEECH & DEBATE—This is an activity for students interested in participating on a competitive level in both speech and debate. The season begins the first week in November and continues through March.

DRILL SQUAD & SQUIRES—These are spirit groups primarily concerned with performing at half time at football and basketball games. Selection for these squads is made in the spring of each school year. These marching units are also support groups for other athletic teams.

FUTURE BUSINESS LEADERS OF AMERICA (FBLA)—This is a club designed for students interested in pursuing the field of business. It is open to any student with an interest. Membership begins in the fall of each school year.

FUTURE MEDICAL ASSISTANTS (FMA)—This is a club designed for students with an interest in pursuing any area of medicine. The organization assists in securing blood donations from individuals at Westside High School for the Red Cross. Meetings are held to inform the membership about opportunities in the medical field. Memberships are accepted at the beginning of school each fall.

INTERACT—This is a boys volunteer organization associated with the Rotary Club of America. Its basic function is to do volunteer work within the community. They are also a support and spirit group for our athletic teams. Membership is open to 11th and 12th grade boys; with membership opportunities being available in the fall of each school year.

INTERNATIONAL CLUB—This is a club designed to help students understand people from other countries and is developed through our foreign language classes. French, German, Spanish, and Latin teachers encourage membership in this organization in the fall of each year. Sponsorship of foreign students, who attend Westside, is one of their major activities.

LATIN CLUB (Junior Classical League)—This is a club designed for those students who are taking Latin as a foreign language. This club competes in competitive situations between schools and is involved with state competition as well. Students have the opportunity to join JCL beginning in the fall of each school year.

MATH CLUB—This club is for any student interested in mathematics. Meetings are held periodically during the school year.

STUDENT PUBLICATIONS—This activity includes classes offered in preparation of the yearbook (Shield) and the student newspaper (Lance). Opportunities to learn about journalism are provided for students interested in these areas. Membership in Quill and Scroll is an extension of a student's involvement in school publications.

STUDENT FORUM—Each homeroom elects one representative as a member of the student forum. Their responsibility is to provide ideas, make suggestions, and serve as one informational group to the staff and administration for student government. Selections are made for this membership in the fall of each school year.

DRAMATICS—This activity is an extension of a regular academic class. School plays, one-act plays, and musicals are provided for students with an interest and ability in these areas. Tryouts for these productions are announced prior to the selection of individuals for these activities.

CREATIVE WRITING CLUB—This is an organization that provides students, with the interest and capability, an opportunity to do prose and poetry writing. This club meets periodically throughout the year and publishes the students' work. Any student with an interest is encouraged to become a member.

PHOTOGRAPHY CLUB—This is a club for the student who has the interest and/or ability in photography. Students have an opportunity to take photos of school activities. A dark room is provided for the students' use. Membership in this organization begins in the fall of each school year.

ORCHESTRA—This activity is an extension of our regular curriculum. Performances are given periodically throughout the year. Tryouts are held for some special groups within the orchestra. All students signed up for that class have the opportunity to try out.

* * *

SWIMMING TIMING TEAM—Offers an interested student a chance to be a part of the Timing Team that is used during the competitive swimming season. Regular season meets, invitational meets, and the metro swim meet are swimming activities at which these volunteers will work. Membership in this group is solicited prior to the beginning of the competitive season.

* * *

ZONTA CLUB (Z Club)—Is a volunteer club for girls associated with Zonta International. Approximately one hundred junior and senior girls are involved in this volunteer organization. Eleventh and twelfth grade students are encouraged to join in the fall of each school year.

SUBSURFERS—Is a club designed for students interested in learning about skin and scuba diving and other practical applications of that sport. Opportunities in the classroom and in our pool are made available for students involved in this activity. Membership is solicited in the fall and spring of each year.

WELCOME TO WESTSIDE CLUB—Is an organization for students who are interested in helping students new to District 66 and to Westside High School. Activities are held for them which are geared toward helping them become a part of our school curriculum and activities.

* * *

Justice Kennedy, with whom Justice Scalia joins, concurring in part and concurring in the judgment.

The Court's interpretation of the statutory term "noncurriculum related groups" is proper and correct, in my view, and I join Parts I and II of the Court's opinion. I further agree that the Act does not violate the Establishment Clause, and so I concur in the judgment; but my view of the analytic premise that controls the establishment question differs from that employed by the plurality. I write to explain why I cannot join all that is said in Part III of Justice O'-Connor's opinion.

* * *

I agree with the plurality that a school complying with the statute by satisfying the criteria in § 4071(c) does not violate the Establishment Clause. The accommodation of religion mandated by the Act is a neutral one, and in the context of this case it suffices to inquire whether the Act violates either one of two principles. The first is that the government cannot "give direct benefits to religion in such a degree that it in fact 'establishes a [state] religion or religious faith, or tends to do so.'" *County of Allegheny v. American Civil Liberties Union, Greater Pittsburgh Chapter*, 492 U.S. 537, 109 S.Ct. 3086, 3136, 106 L.Ed.2d 472 (1989) (Kennedy, J., concurring in judgment in part and dissenting in part) (quoting *Lynch v. Donnelly*, 465 U.S. 668, 678, 104 S.Ct. 1355, 1361, 79 L.Ed.2d 604 (1984)). Any incidental benefits that accompany official recognition of a religious club under the criteria set forth in the § 4071(c) do not lead to the establishment of religion under this standard. . . . The second principle controlling the case now before us, in my view, is that the government cannot coerce any student to participate in a religious activity. . . . The Act is consistent with this standard as well. Nothing on the face of the Act or in the facts of the case as here presented demonstrate that enforcement of the statute will result in the coercion of any student to participate in a religious activity. . . .

The plurality uses a different test, one which asks whether school officials, by complying with the Act, have endorsed religion. It is true that when government gives impermissible assistance to a religion it can be said to have "endorsed" religion; but endorsement cannot be the test. The word endorsement has insufficient content to be dispositive. . . . [I]ts literal application may result in neutrality in name but hostility in fact when the question is the government's proper relation to those who express some religious preference.

I should think it inevitable that a public high school "endorses" a religious club, in a common-sense use of the term, if the club happens to be one of many activities that the school permits students to choose in order to further the development of their intellect and character in an extracurricular setting. But no constitutional violation occurs if the school's action is based upon a recognition of the fact that membership in a religious club is one of many permissible ways for a student to further his or her own personal enrichment. The inquiry with respect to coercion must be whether the government imposes pressure upon a student to participate in a religious activity. This inquiry, of course, must be undertaken with sensitivity to the special circumstances that exist in a secondary school where the line between voluntary and coerced participation may be difficult to draw. No such coercion, however, has been shown to exist as a necessary result of this statute, either on its face or as respondents seek to invoke it on the facts of this case.

For these reasons, I join Parts I and II of the Court's opinion, and concur in the judgment.

Justice Marshall, with whom Justice Brennan joins, concurring in the judgment.

I agree with the majority that "noncurriculum" must be construed broadly to "prohibit schools from discriminating on the basis of the content of a student group's speech." . . . As the majority demonstrates, such a construction "is consistent with Congress' intent to provide a low threshold for triggering the Act's requirements." . . . In addition, to the extent that Congress intended the Act to track this Court's free speech jurisprudence, as the dissent argues, . . . the majority's construction is faithful to our commitment to nondiscriminatory access to open fora in public schools. . . . When a school allows student-initiated clubs not directly tied to the school's curriculum to use school facilities, it has "created a forum generally open to student groups" and is therefore constitutionally prohibited from enforcing a "content-based exclusion" of other student speech. . . .

In this respect, the Act as construed by the majority simply codifies in statute what is already constitutionally mandated: schools may not discriminate among student-initiated groups that seek access to school facilities for expressive purposes not directly related to the school's curriculum.

The Act's low threshold for triggering equal access, however, raises serious Establishment Clause concerns where secondary schools with fora that differ substantially from the forum in *Widmar* are required to grant access to student religious groups. Indeed, as applied in the present case, the Act mandates a religious group's access to a forum that is dedicated to promoting fundamental values and citizenship as defined by the school. The Establishment Clause does not forbid the operation of the Act in such circumstances, but it does require schools to change their relationship to their fora so as to disassociate themselves effectively from religious clubs' speech. Thus, although I agree with the plurality that the Act as applied to Westside could withstand Establishment Clause scrutiny, . . . I write separately to emphasize the steps Westside must take to avoid appearing to endorse the Christian Club's goals. . . .

* * *

Westside currently does not recognize any student club that advocates a controversial viewpoint. Indeed, the clubs at Westside that trigger the Act involve scuba diving, chess, and counseling for special education students. . . . As a matter of school policy, Westside encourages student participation in clubs based on a broad conception of its educational mission. . . . That mission comports with the Court's acknowledgment "that public schools are vitally important 'in the preparation of individuals for participation as citizens,' and as vehicles for 'inculcating fundamental values necessary to the maintenance of a democratic political system.' " *Board of Education, Island Trees Union Free School Dist. No. 27 v. Pico,* 457 U.S. 853, 864, 102 S.Ct. 2799, 2806, 73 L.Ed.2d 435 (1982) (plurality) (quoting *Ambach v. Norwick,* 441 U.S. 68, 76–77, 99 S.Ct. 1589, 1594, 60 L.Ed.2d 49 (1979)). Given the nature and function of student clubs at Westside, the school makes no effort to disassociate itself from the activities and goals of its student clubs.

The entry of religious clubs into such a realm poses a real danger that those clubs will be viewed as part of the school's effort to inculcate fundamental values.

The school's message with respect to its existing clubs is not one of toleration but one of endorsement. As the majority concedes, the program is part of the "district's commitment to teaching academic, physical, civic, and personal skills and values." . . . But although a school may permissibly encourage its students to become well-rounded as student-athletes, student-musicians, and student-tutors, the Constitution forbids schools to encourage students to become well-rounded as student-worshippers. Neutrality toward religion, as required by the Constitution, is not advanced by requiring a school that endorses the goals of some noncontroversial secular organizations to endorse the goals of religious organizations as well.

The fact that the Act, when triggered, provides access to political as well as religious speech does not ameliorate the potential threat of endorsement. The breadth of beneficiaries under the Act does suggest that the Act may satisfy the "secular purpose" requirement of the Establishment Clause inquiry we identified in *Lemon.* . . . But the crucial question is how the Act affects each school. If a school already houses numerous ideological organizations, then the addition of a religion club will most likely not violate the Establishment Clause because the risk that students will erroneously attribute the views of the religion club to the schools is minimal. To the extent a school tolerates speech by a wide range of ideological clubs, students cannot reasonably understand the school to endorse all of the groups' divergent and contradictory views. But if the religion club is the sole advocacy-oriented group in the forum, or one of a very limited number, and the school continues to promote its student-club program as instrumental to citizenship, then the school's failure to disassociate itself from the religious activity will reasonably be understood as an endorsement of that activity. That political and other advocacy-oriented groups are permitted to participate in a forum that, through school support and encouragement, is devoted to fostering a student's civic identity does not ameliorate the appearance of school endorsement unless the invitation is accepted and the forum is transformed into a forum like that in *Widmar.*

For this reason, the plurality's reliance on *Widmar* is misplaced. The University of Missouri took concrete steps to ensure "that the University's name will not 'be identified in any way with the aims, policies, programs, products, or opinions of any organization or its members,' " 454 U.S., at 274, n. 14, 102 S.Ct., at 276–77, n. 14 (quoting University of Missouri student handbook). Westside, in contrast, explicitly promotes its student clubs "as a vital part of the total education program [and] as a means of developing citizenship." App. 488. And while the University of Missouri recognized such clubs as the Young Socialist Alliance and the Young Democrats, *Chess v. Widmar,* 635 F.2d 1310, 1312, n. 1 (CA8 1980), Westside has recognized no such political clubs, App. 488.

The different approaches to student clubs embodied in these policies reflect a significant difference, for Establishment Clause purposes, between the respective roles that Westside High School and the University of Missouri attempt to play in their students' lives. To the extent that a school emphasizes the autonomy of its students, as does the University of Missouri, there is a corresponding decrease in the likelihood that student speech will be regarded as school speech. Conversely, where a school such as Westside regards its student clubs as a mechanism for defining and transmitting fundamental values, the inclusion of a religious club in the school's program will almost certainly signal school endorsement of the religious practice.

Thus, the underlying difference between this case and *Widmar* is not that college and high school students have varying capacities to perceive the subtle differences between toleration and endorsement, but rather that the University of Missouri and Westside actually choose to define their respective missions in different ways. That high schools tend to emphasize student autonomy less than universities may suggest that high school administrators tend to perceive a difference in the maturity of secondary and university students. But the school's behavior, not the purported immaturity of high school students, is dispositive. If Westside stood apart from its club program and expressed the view, endorsed by Congress through its passage of the Act, that high school students are capable of engaging in wide-ranging discussion of sensitive and controversial speech, the inclusion of religious groups in Westside's forum would confirm the school's commitment to nondiscrimination. Here, though, the Act requires the school to permit religious speech in a forum explicitly designed to advance the school's interest in shaping the character of its students.

The comprehensiveness of the access afforded by the Act further highlights the Establishment Clause dangers posed by the Act's application to fora such as Westside's. The Court holds that "[o]fficial recognition allows student clubs to be part of the student activities program and carries with it access to the school newspaper, bulletin boards, the public address system, and the annual Club Fair." Ante, at 2370 (citing App.

434–435). Students would be alerted to the meetings of the religion club over the public address system; they would see religion club material posted on the official school bulletin board and club notices in the school newspaper; they would be recruited to join the religion club at the school-sponsored Club Fair. If a school has a variety of ideological clubs, as in *Widmar,* I agree with the plurality that a student is likely to understand that "a school does not endorse or support student speech that it merely permits on a nondiscriminatory basis." Ante, at 2372. When a school has a religion club but no other political or ideological organizations, however, that relatively fine distinction may be lost.

Moreover, in the absence of a truly robust forum that includes the participation of more than one advocacy-oriented group, the presence of a religious club could provide a fertile ground for peer pressure, especially if the club commanded support from a substantial portion of the student body. . . .

. . . When the government, through mandatory attendance laws, brings students together in a highly controlled environment every day for the better part of their waking hours and regulates virtually every aspect of their existence during that time, we should not be so quick to dismiss the problem of peer pressure as if the school environment had nothing to do with creating and fostering it. The State has structured an environment in which students holding mainstream views may be able to coerce adherents of minority religions to attend club meetings or to adhere to club beliefs. Thus, the State cannot disclaim its responsibility for those resulting pressures.

* * *

Given these substantial risks posed by the inclusion of the proposed Christian Club within Westside's present forum, Westside must redefine its relationship to its club program. . . .

Westside thus must do more than merely prohibit faculty members from actively participating in the Christian Club's meetings. It must fully disassociate itself from the Club's religious speech and avoid appearing to sponsor or endorse the Club's goals. It could, for example, entirely discontinue encouraging student participation in clubs and clarify that the clubs are not instrumentally related to the school's overall mission. Or, if the school sought to continue its general endorsement of those student clubs that did not engage in controversial speech, it could do so if it also affirmatively disclaimed any endorsement of the Christian Club.

* * *

Justice Stevens, dissenting.

The dictionary is a necessary, and sometimes sufficient, aid to the judge confronted with the task of construing an opaque act of Congress. In a case like this, however, I believe we must probe more deeply to avoid a patently bizarre result. Can Congress really have intended to issue an order to every public high school in the nation stating, in substance, that if you sponsor a chess club, a scuba diving club, or a French club—without having formal classes in those subjects—you must also open your doors to every religious, political, or social organization, no matter how controversial or distasteful its views may be? I think not. A fair review of the legislative history of the Equal Access Act (Act), 98 Stat. 1302, 20 U.S.C. §§ 4071–4074, discloses that Congress intended to recognize a much narrower forum than the Court has legislated into existence today.

* * *

. . . The Court correctly identifies three useful guides to Congress' intent. First, the text of the statute says that a school creates a limited open forum if it allows meetings on school premises by "noncurriculum related student groups," a concept that is ambiguous at best. . . . Second, because this concept is ambiguous, the statute must be interpreted by reference to its general purpose, as revealed by its overall structure and by the legislative history. . . . Third, the Act's legislative history reveals that Congress intended to guarantee student religious groups access to high school fora comparable to the college forum involved in *Widmar v. Vincent,* 454 U.S. 263, 102 S.Ct. 269, 70 L.Ed.2d 440 (1981). . . .

A fourth [guide] would seem to follow from these three. If "noncurriculum related" is an ambiguous term, and if it must therefore be interpreted in light of Congressional purpose, and if the purpose of Congress was to ensure that the rule of *Widmar* applied to high schools as it did to colleges, then the incidence of the Act in this case should depend upon whether, in light of *Widmar,* Westside would have to permit the Christian student group to meet if Westside were a college.[3] The characteristics of the college forum in *Widmar* should thus provide a useful background for interpreting the meaning of the undefined term "noncurriculum related student groups." But this step the Court does not take, and it is accordingly here that I part company with it.

* * *

To extend *Widmar* to high schools, then, would require us to pose two questions. We would first ask whether a high school had established a forum comparable under our Free Speech Clause jurisprudence to that which existed in *Widmar.* Only if this question were answered affirmatively would we then need to test the constitutionality of the Act by asking whether the Establishment Clause has different consequences when applied to a high school's open forum than when applied to a college's. I believe that in this case the first question must instead be answered in the negative, and that this answer ultimately proves dispositive under the Act just as it would were only constitutional consideration in play.

The forum at Westside is considerably different from that which existed at the University of Missouri. In *Widmar,* we held that the University had created "a generally open forum." . . . Over 100 officially recognized student groups routinely participated in that forum. . . . They included groups whose activities not only were unrelated to any specific courses, but also were of a kind that a state university could not properly sponsor or endorse. Thus, for example, they included such political organizations as the Young Socialist Alliance, the Women's Union, and the Young Democrats. . . . The University permitted use of its facilities for speakers advocating transcendental meditation and humanism. Since the University had allowed such organizations and speakers the use of campus facilities, we concluded that the University could not discriminate against a religious group on the basis of the content of its speech. The forum established by the state university accommodated participating groups that were "noncurriculum related" not only because they did not mirror the school's classroom instruction, but also because they advocated controversial positions that a state university's obligation of neutrality prevented it from endorsing.

The Court's opinion in *Widmar* left open the question whether its holding would apply to a public high school that had established a similar public forum. That question has now been answered in the affirmative by the District Court, the Court of Appeals, and by this Court. I agree with that answer. Before the question was answered judicially, Congress decided to answer it legislatively in order to preclude continued unconstitutional discrimination against high school students interested in religious speech. . . . What the Court of Appeals failed to recognize, however, is the

---

[3] We would, of course, then have to consider, as the Court does now, whether the Establishment Clause permits Congress to apply *Widmar*'s reasoning to secondary schools.

critical difference between the university forum in *Widmar* and the high school forum involved in this case. None of the clubs at the high school is even arguably controversial or partisan.

Nor would it be wise to ignore this difference. High school students may be adult enough to distinguish between those organizations that are sponsored by the school and those which lack school sponsorship even though they participate in a forum that the school does sponsor. See *ante*, at 2372. But high school students are also young enough that open fora may be less suitable for them than for college students. The need to decide whether to risk treating students as adults too soon, or alternatively to risk treating them as children too long, is an enduring problem for all educators. The youth of these students, whether described in terms of "impressionability" or "maturity," may be irrelevant to our application of the constitutional restrictions that limit educational discretion in the public schools, but it surely is not irrelevant to our interpretation of the educational policies that have been adopted. We would do no honor to Westside's administrators or the Congress by assuming that either treated casually the differences between high school and college students when formulating the policy and the statute at issue here.[6]

For these reasons, I believe that the distinctions between Westside's program and the University of Missouri's program suggest what is the best understanding of the Act : an extracurricular student organization is "noncurriculum related" if it has as its purpose (or as part of its purpose) the advocacy of partisan theological, political, or ethical views. A school that admits at least one such club has apparently made the judgment that students are better off if the student community is permitted to, and perhaps even encouraged to, compete along ideological lines. This pedagogical strategy may be defensible or even desirable. But it is wrong to presume that Congress endorsed that strategy—and dictated its nationwide adoption—simply because it approved the application of *Widmar* to high schools. And it seems absurd to presume that Westside has invoked the same strategy by recognizing clubs like Swim Timing Team and Subsurfers which, though they may not correspond directly to anything in Westside's course offerings, are no more controversial than a grilled cheese sandwich.

Accordingly, as I would construe the Act, a high school could properly sponsor a French club, a chess club, or a scuba diving club simply because their activities are fully consistent with the school's curricular mission. It would not matter whether formal courses in any of those subjects—or in directly related subjects—were being offered as long as faculty encouragement of student participation in such groups would be consistent with both the school's obligation of neutrality and its legitimate pedagogical concerns. Nothing in *Widmar* implies that the existence of a French club, for example, would create a constitutional obligation to allow student members of the Ku Klux Klan or the Communist Party to have access to school facilities. More importantly, nothing in that case suggests that the constitutional issue should turn on whether French is being taught in a formal course while the club is functioning.

Conversely, if a high school decides to allow political groups to use its facilities, it plainly cannot discriminate among controversial groups because it agrees with the positions of some and disagrees with the ideas advocated by others. Again, the fact that the history of the Republican party might be taught in a political science course could not justify a decision to allow the young Republicans to form a club while denying Communists, white supremacists, or Christian Scientists the same privilege. In my judgment, the political activities of the young Republicans are "noncurriculum related" for reasons that have nothing to do with the content of the political science course. The statutory definition of what is "noncurriculum related" should depend on the constitutional concern that motivated our decision in *Widmar*.

In this case, the district judge reviewed each of the clubs in the high school program and found that they are all "tied to the educational function of the institution." . . . He correctly concluded that this club system "differs dramatically from those found to create an open forum policy in *Widmar* and *Bender.*" . . . I agree with his conclusion that, under a proper interpretation of the Act, this dramatic difference requires a different result.

                                          * * *

Against all these arguments the Court interposes Noah Webster's famous dictionary. It is a massive tome but no match for the weight the Court would

---

[6]What I have said before of universities is true *a fortiori* with respect to high schools: a school's extracurricular activities constitute a part of the school's teaching mission, and the school accordingly must make "decisions concerning the content of those activities." *Widmar v. Vincent,* 454 U.S., at 278, 102 S.Ct., at 279 (Stevens, J., concurring in judgment). Absent good reason to hold otherwise, these decisions should be left to teachers. . . .

put upon it. The Court relies heavily on the dictionary's definition of "curriculum." . . . That word, of course, is not the Act's; moreover, the word "noncurriculum" is not in the dictionary. Neither Webster nor Congress has authorized us to assume that "noncurriculum" is a precise antonym of the word "curriculum." "Nonplus," for example, does not mean "minus" and it would be incorrect to assume that a "nonentity" is not an "entity" at all. Purely as a matter of defining a newly-coined word, the term "noncurriculum" could fairly be construed to describe either the subjects that are "not a part of the current curriculum" or the subjects that "cannot properly be included in a public school curriculum." Either of those definitions is perfectly "sensible" because both describe subjects "that are not related to the body of courses offered by the school." . . . When one considers the basic purpose of the Act, and its unquestioned linkage to our decision in *Widmar*, the latter definition surely is the more "sensible."

I respectfully dissent.

NOTES AND QUESTIONS

1. Widmar v. Vincent *and the Equal Access Act*

In 1981 the Supreme Court decided *Widmar v. Vincent*, 454 U.S. 263, 102 S.Ct. 269, 70 L.Ed.2d 440 (1981), a case involving whether a state university that makes its facilities generally available to registered student groups may deny the use of its facilities (vacant classrooms and the student center) to a student religious group. The University of Missouri argued that it had a compelling interest in avoiding the establishment of religion, urging that the use of the facilities for religious purposes by an interdenominational group of evangelical Christian students (Cornerstone) would constitute an unconstitutional establishment. The Court held that an equal access policy would not violate *Lemon v. Kurtzman*, 403 U.S. 602, 91 S.Ct. 2105, 29 L.Ed.2d 745 (1971):

[A]n open-forum policy, including nondiscrimination against religious speech, would have a secular purpose and would avoid entanglement with religion. But the District Court concluded, and the University argues here, that allowing religious groups to share the limited public forum would have the "primary effect" of advancing religion.

The University's argument misconceives the nature of this case. The question is not whether the creation of a religious forum would violate the Establishment Clause. The University has opened its facilities for use by student

groups, and the question is whether it can now exclude groups because of the content of their speech. *See Healy v. James*, 408 U.S. 169 (1972). In this context we are unpersuaded that the primary effect of the public forum, open to all forms of discourse, would be to advance religion.

. . . It is possible—perhaps even foreseeable—that religious groups will benefit from access to University facilities. But this Court has explained that a religious organization's enjoyment of merely "incidental" benefits does not violate the prohibition against the "primary advancement" of religion. . . .

[A]n open forum in a public university does not confer any imprimatur of State approval on religious sects or practices.

454 U.S. at 721–74, 102 S.Ct. at 275–76. In the absence of an Establishment Clause justification for the denial of access, the Court held that the exclusion of Cornerstone from university facilities violated the Free Speech Clause. 454 U.S. at 289, 102 S.Ct. at 284. As Professor Laycock summarized the Court's holding:

Regulation of speech must be content-neutral. When the government creates a forum for speech, it cannot pick and choose who can speak or what they can talk about. If students are free to discuss sex, politics, and philosophy, they must be free to discuss religion. The university let Students for a Democratic Society and the Young Socialist alliance use university facilities. It would have let those facilities be used for discussions of agnosticism, Marxism, and other doctrines hostile to religion. There was no doubt that students and faculty enjoyed an open forum in university facilities. The exclusion of religion could not be justified by any policy of neutrality, strict or otherwise. Justice Stevens noted in his concurrence that the university could control its own curriculum, and that a shortage of meeting rooms would require it to choose among voluntary student groups. But neither of those legitimate concerns had any relevance to the facts of *Widmar*. Rather, the university openly discriminated against religious speech.

* * *

With respect to the government's own speech, taking no position on religion is the most neutral practice. But with respect to private speech, protecting religious and antireligious speech equally with secular speech is far more neutral than singling [them] out . . . for special treatment.

Laycock, "Equal Access and Moments of Silence: The Equal Status of Religious Speech by Private Speakers," 81 *Nw. U. L. Rev.* 1, 10, 13–14 (1986).

2. *Cases after* Mergens

Two more recent Supreme Court cases have further clarified the law on equal access to school facilities and programs. In *Lamb's Chapel v. Center Moriches Union Free School District*, all nine justices agreed that the public school district violated the Free Speech Clause when it denied a church access to school facilities after school hours to show a film that contained religious viewpoints on child-rearing and family values. 508 U.S. 384, 113 S.Ct. 2141 (1993). The School District opened school facilities to the public for social, civic, and recreational uses of its schools after school hours. Because the subject matter of child-rearing falls within the purpose of the open forum and had not been placed off-limits to other non religious groups, the Court held that the school district could not discriminate against the religious group. "[T]he First Amendment forbids the government to regulate speech in ways that favor some viewpoints or ideas at the expense of others." *Id.* at 394, 113 S.Ct. at 2147 (quoting *City of Los Angeles v. Taxpayers for Vincent*, 466 U.S. 789, 804 (1994)). Moreover, the Court noted that there was no danger of an establishment of religion. "The showing of this film series would not have been during school hours, would not have been sponsored by the school, and would have been open to the public, not just church members." *Id.* at 395, 113 S.Ct. at 2148.

What would be the result if *Lamb's Chapel* asked to use the school auditorium for worship purposes on Sunday mornings? *See id.* at 387, n.2, 113 S.Ct. at 2144, n.2. Could the school district constitutionally deny the church access to school property for the purpose of worship? Would it matter if the school district did not allow other groups to meet for the purpose of worship? Would a rule prohibiting the use of facilities for worship constitute a lawful subject-matter distinction or unlawful viewpoint discrimination? Does such a rule prefer non religious views to religious views? *Campbell v. St. Tammy's Sch. Bd.*, 206 F.3d 482 (5th Cir. 2000); *Bronx Household of Faith v. Community School District No. 10*, 127 F.3d 207 (2d Cir. 1997).

In *Rosenberger v. Rector and Visitors of the University of Virginia*, the Court considered the question of whether the university could constitutionally deny funding for the publication of a newspaper produced by a student group when that newspaper contained a Christian editorial viewpoint. 515 U.S. 819, 115 S.Ct. 2510 (1995). No other student organizations that produced newspapers were denied publication funding. *See id.* The Court reaffirmed that once the state has opened a limited public forum, it may not discriminate on the basis of view-

point. *Id.* at 829, 115 S.Ct. at 2517. It defined the funding scheme for student groups as "a forum more in a metaphysical than in a spatial or geographic sense" but noted that "the same principles are applicable." *Id.* at 830, 115 S.Ct. at 2517. It reasoned that although a university could make viewpoint-based decisions in the provision of funds to promote its own message, it cannot discriminate on the basis of viewpoint when it expends funds, not to speak for itself, but to "encourage a diversity of views from private speakers." *Id.* at 834, 115 S.Ct. 2519. After holding that the university policy violated the First Amendment right to free speech, the Court then addressed the question of whether the University's actions are excused by the Establishment Clause of the First Amendment. The Court recognized that there are "special Establishment Clause dangers where the government makes direct payments to sectarian institutions," but the Court noted that those precedents were not controlling. The Court emphasized that "the student publication is not a religious institution, at least in the usual sense of that term as used in our case law. . . . It is instead a publication involved in a pure forum for the expression of ideas. . . ." *Id.* at 844, 115 S.Ct. 2524. The Court reasoned that the government usually acts through spending money. By granting religious groups access to a school's physical facilities, the school inevitably expends funds on the upkeep, maintenance, and repair of those facilities as well as expending funds on services such as electricity and computers. *See id.* at 842–43, 115 S.Ct. 2523–24. The Court compared these expenditures to the payment of funds to a third-party publisher for the publication of the religious student newspaper and determined there was no difference between expenditures. *See id.* at 843–44, 115 S.Ct. at 2524. "Any benefit to religion is incidental to the government's provision of secular services for secular purposes on a religion-neutral basis. Printing is a routine, secular, and recurring attribute of student life." *Id.*

Do you agree that public funds can be used to support a religious newspaper? Is the expenditure of public funds for the printing of a religious newspaper really no different than allowing a religious group to use physical facilities at a school or university? Four Justices dissented from the decision, arguing that the Establishment Clause prohibits direct government spending on religion. *See id.* at 868, 115 S.Ct. at 2535 (J. Souter, dissenting) ("Using public funds for the direct subsidization of preaching the word is categorically forbidden under the Establishment Clause, and if the Clause was meant to accomplish nothing else, it was meant to bar this use of public money"). The dissent argued that the majority's analogy between the expenditure of funds on the upkeep and maintenance of classroom facilities and the subsidization of the religious newspaper was flawed. Rather, the dissent argued that government payment for the upkeep of classroom facilities was similar to government financing for the upkeep of city streets. City streets are traditional forums of public expression, and because all speakers are allowed to use the street corner to express their beliefs, religious speakers do gain incidental benefits from state expenditures on street maintenance. However, "[t]here is no street corner printing provided by the government on equal terms to all corners, and the forum cases cannot be [extended] without admitting that new economic benefits are being extended directly to religion in clear violation of the principle barring direct aid."

Do you think *Rosenberger* should be distinguished from *Widmar* and *Mergens* because it involves equal access to government funding, not just equal access to facilities? Does it make a difference that the funds in question here were paid directly to the publisher, not to the religious group?

The funding for publication came out of the University of Virginia's student activities fee, and all students were required to pay this fee. Should the source of the funds be determinative of the outcome of this case? Do fee-paying students have a free speech right not to fund speech with which they disagree? In a subsequent case, the Court held that university students have no such right: "The First Amendment permits a public university to charge its students an activity fee used to fund a program to facilitate extracurricular student speech if the program is view-point neutral." *Board of Regents v. Southworth*, U.S. 120 1346 (2000).

In the light of *Rosenberger*, *Lamb's Chapel*, *Mergens*, and *Widmar*, several questions of equal access remain unsettled. Does the Equal Access Act permit religious student groups to meet during lunchtime, not just after school? *See Ceniceros v. Board of Trustees of San Diego Unified Sch. Dist.*, 106 F.3d 878 (9th Cir. 1997) (holding that lunch period is "noninstructional time" within the meaning of the Equal Access Act, so the student group must be allowed to meet and further holding that such a meeting does not violate the Establishment Clause of the First Amendment). Could a religious student group

meet during study hall if other student groups were allowed to meet at that time?

Can a religious student group that meets on school property require that its president, vice-president, and music leader accept Jesus Christ as their Savior? *See Hsu v. Roslyn Union Free School District No. 3*, 85 F.3d 839 (2d Cir. 1996) (holding that a rule requiring leaders of a student group to be Christians did not violate the Equal Access Act because the roles were religious in nature but also holding that such a rule could not apply to the Club's secretary or activities coordinator because their duties had little to do with religion). If a school has a rule that student groups may not discriminate on the basis of race, gender, national origin, or religion in the selection of its officers or members, may the school apply such a rule to a religious student club? Does the religious student group have a First Amendment right to make religious affiliation a prerequisite regardless of whether the club meets on public or private property? *See* Paulsen, "A Funny Thing Happened on the Way to the Limited Public Forum: Unconstitutional Conditions on 'Equal Access' for Religious Speakers and Groups," 29 *U.C. Davis L. Rev.* 653, 662–668 (1996). Professor Paulsen argues:

> A religious group's acceptance of rights of "equal access" . . . provides no greater justification for government regulation of religious speakers, groups, or institutions than government would possess in any event. . . . [G]overnment may not condition a religious speaker's or group's equal access to a public forum . . . on the . . . group's abandonment of rights of religious autonomy.

See id. at 666–67; *cf.* Choper, "Dangers to Religious Liberty from Governmental Neutral Programs," 29 *U.C. Davis L. Rev.* 719 (1996). Do you agree with Professor Paulsen? Should religious groups retain all their free exercise rights when they use a public forum for religious speech? Can neutral laws or policies applicable to all users of a public forum be applied in the same manner to religious groups? *See City of Boerne v. Flores*, 521 U.S. 507, 117 S.Ct. 2157 (1997); *Employment Division, Department of Human Resources v. Smith*, 494 U.S. 872, 110 S.Ct. 1595 (1990).

3. *Meaning of the Equal Access Act*

In order to trigger the application of the Equal Access Act and to establish a "limited open forum," a public secondary school receiving federal funds

must have given one or more "noncurriculum related student groups" the opportunity to meet on
campus during noninstructional time (before or after classroom instruction). Once a "limited open forum" has been established, then the school may not
discriminate against a student group in the allocation of facilities "on the basis of the religious, political, philosophical, or other content of the speech at
such meetings."

What meaning does Justice O'Connor give to
"noncurriculum related"? What does it mean to say
that the student clubs must have more than a "tangential or attenuated relationship to courses offered
by the school"? Is a chess club curriculum related,
as the *Mergens* Court suggests? Must the group and
its activities be initiated by students to be noncurriculum related? What does the legislative history
of the Equal Access Act show? *See generally*
Strossen, "A Constitutional Analysis of the Equal
Access Act's Standards Governing Public School
Student Religious Meetings," 24 *Harv. J. on Legis.*
117 (1987). Consider the conclusion reached by
Professor Laycock:

> More than one interpretation of "curriculum related" is
> legitimately open to the courts. The best interpretation
> is the one that Senator Hatfield volunteered before he
> got entangled in Senator Gorton's cross-examination:
> curriculum related groups are those that are an exten-
> sion of the classroom. That is what the statutory lan-
> guage seems to say, and that interpretation achieves the
> purposes of the sponsors and avoids the risk of abuse in-
> herent in distinguishing between student-initiated and
> faculty-initiated groups. If a group is sponsored by a
> teacher who teaches a closely related course, and if
> nearly all the members of the group take that course,
> then the group is curriculum related, and its existence
> does not trigger any obligation to recognize other groups.

Laycock, *supra* at 40–41.

Does the majority in *Mergens* adopt the Laycock approach? Under the *Mergens* test, is the meeting of an
athletic team curriculum related? What of the
drama club? A meeting of the cast of a school play?
A meeting of the student government? Board Policy
5610 refers to students clubs as a "vital part of the total education program." Why is this provision not dispositive on the issue of curriculum relatedness?

What is Justice Stevens' definition of curriculum
relatedness? Is he saying that the concept of a limited
open forum is not triggered by a decision to exclude
clubs that engage in or teach partisan theological,
ethical, or political views? Is his view supported by

the legislative history of the Equal Access Act? Is it
supported by the *Widmar* decision?

4. The Constitutionality of the Equal Access Act

Do you agree with Justice O'Connor in *Mergens* that
the Equal Access Act is a constitutional extension of
Widmar? Is *Widmar* distinguishable because high
school students are more easily influenced than college students? What of the fact that high school students may be required to attend school? That high
school teachers may be perceived as authority figures? Do you agree with Justice Marshall that high
school students are more likely to think that the
meetings of religious clubs have received the imprimatur of state approval? Can students distinguish between "accommodation and endorsement"? *See*
Note, "The Constitutional Dimensions of Student-
Initiated Religious Activity in Public High Schools,"
92 *Yale L.J.* 499 (1983); *Clark v. Dallas Independent
School District*, 671 F.Supp. 1119 (N.D. Tex. 1987).
But see Laycock, *supra* at 14–20. Or is the primary issue, as Justice Kennedy urges, whether student participation is coerced?

If a school creates an open forum, is the opening of
the facilities to religious groups better characterized
as an effort to advance religion or one to avoid discrimination against religion? *See Rosenberger v. Rector, supra*. Can a school completely close a limited
public forum in order to prevent religious student
groups from using it? *See Pope v. East Brunswick Bd.
of Educ.*, 12 F.3d 1244, 1254 (3d Cir. 1993).

What if a school district that reluctantly accepted
the prohibition of school-sponsored prayer encourages students to participate in the meetings of religious clubs? Would the practice violate the Establishment Clause? *See* Laycock, *supra* at 53.

Might the need for faculty supervision of student
group activities, under some circumstances, lead to
an unconstitutional entanglement of government
and religion? *See Garnett v. Renton School District
No. 403*, 865 F.2d 1121 (9th Cir. 1989); *Bender v.
Williamsport Area School District*, 741 F.2d 538,
556–57 (3d Cir. 1984), *vacated on other grounds*, 475
U.S. 534, 106 S.Ct. 1326, 89 L.Ed.2d 501 (1986).
See generally Laycock, *supra* at 25–27. Is this a relevant distinction between open forums in universities
and in high schools?

Note that § 4071(c) of the Equal Access Act provides that noncurriculum related religious groups
must be offered "a fair opportunity to meet" on the
same basis as other noncurriculum related groups.
Fairness requires that the meetings must be volun-

tary and student initiated, that nonschool persons may not regularly attend, that the meetings do not materially or substantially interfere with the school's educational mission, and that there be no school sponsorship. *See* Laycock, *supra* at 42–43. While there is some confusion as to whether these requirements apply only to religious groups or to all student groups (Laycock, *supra* at 43–45), are these limitations necessary to preserve the constitutionality of the Equal Access Act? *See* Note, "Student Religious Groups and the Right of Access to Public School Activity Periods," 74 *Geo. L.J.* 205, 215 (1985).

Should a distinction be drawn between student groups that meet to discuss religion and those that meet to engage in ritual prayer and a worship service? *See Campbell v. St. Tammany's Sch. Bd.*, 206 F.3d 482 (5th Cir. 2000); *The Good News Club v. Milford Cent. Sch.*, 202 F.3d 502 (2d Cir. 2000). Is the distinction intelligible? Persuasive? *See generally* Laycock, *supra* at 55–56. Professor Laycock argues that "rules that allow schools to monitor the content of religious meetings and break them up when they become 'too religious' trample the core of the free speech and free exercise clauses. They also violate the establishment clause by giving official sanction to those religious meetings that are allowed to continue." Laycock, *supra* at 57. Conversely, Professor Teitel makes the following argument:

> The Equal Access Act mandates government sponsorship of prayer in the public schools; such state sponsorship never has been given to prayer in the parks. The aegis of the school and required attendance provide state support to those wishing to gather religious adherents. This state support inevitably compromises the religious (or non religious) beliefs of public school students. Governmental assistance to propagation of religious beliefs through equal access . . . legislation constitutes an establishment of religion. . . .

Teitel, "When Separate Is Equal: Why Organized Religious Exercises, Unlike Chess, Do Not Belong in the Public Schools," 81 *Nw. U. L. Rev.* 174, 175–176 (1987). Do you agree with Teitel or Laycock?

5. Access by Secular Student Groups

In *Healy v. James*, 408 U.S. 169, 92 S.Ct. 2338, 33 L.Ed.2d 266 (1972), students at a public university sought to organize a local chapter of the Students for a Democratic Society (SDS) and to obtain official recognition from the university. The university recognized many other student groups, including the Young Americans for Freedom, the Young Democrats, the Young Republicans, and the Liberal Party.

The president of the university denied the application for three reasons: (1) "the organization's philosophy was antithetical to the school's policies"; (2) the group's independence from the national SDS was doubtful; and (3) "approval should not be granted to any group that 'openly repudiates' the College's dedication to academic freedom." The denial of official recognition meant that the SDS chapter could not announce activities and meetings in the student newspaper, it would not have access to campus bulletin boards, and most significantly, it could not use campus facilities in which to hold meetings.

Justice Powell, writing the majority opinion for the Supreme Court, held that "the mere disagreement of the President with the group's philosophy affords no reason to deny it recognition," for the First Amendment guarantees "the right of individuals to associate to further their personal beliefs." The association with the national chapter was not deemed sufficient to deny recognition in the absence of infringement of reasonable campus rules, interruption of classes, or substantial interference "with the opportunity of other students to obtain an education." The appropriate line is that between "permissible speech and impermissible conduct," and there was no "evidential basis to support the conclusion that . . . [the local SDS chapter] posed a substantial threat of material disruption in violation of" campus rules. The Court went on to state that "a college administration may impose a requirement . . . that a group affirm in advance its willingness to adhere to reasonable campus law."

Would the result in *Healy* have been different if the university had not recognized any student groups? Any noncurriculum related student groups? Is *Healy*, considered in the light of *Mergens*, *Rosenberger*, and *Widmar*, a disguised limited public forum case? *See* Wells, "Mandatory Student Fees: First Amendment Concerns and University Discretion," 55 *U. Chi. L. Rev.* 363, 382–85 (1988). *Healy* relies on the *Tinker* disruption test. Does this indicate that *Healy* is applicable to public secondary schools?

While *Healy* is primarily a freedom of association case, it is consistent with the principle, affirmed by *Widmar v. Vincent* and its progeny, that school authorities may not pick and choose among student organizations on the basis of the content of their speech or ideology. *See Board of Regents v. Southworth, supra*; *Rosenberger v. Rector, supra*. This is similar to the constitutional rules governing invitations to outside speakers on university campuses. *See generally* Wright, "The Constitution on Campus,"

22 *Vand. L. Rev.* 1027 (1969). On this basis, courts have overturned denials of recognition of homosexual student groups where other student groups have received recognition. *See Gay, Lesbian Bisexual Alliance v. Pryor*, 110 F.3d 1543 (11th Cir. 1997); *Gay Student Services v. Texas A & M University*, 737 F.2d 1317 (5th Cir. 1984), *cert. denied and appeal dismissed*, 471 U.S. 1001, 105 S.Ct. 1860, 85 L.Ed.2d 155 (1985); *Gay Lib. v. University of Missouri*, 558 F.2d 848 (8th Cir. 1977), *cert. denied*, 434 U.S. 1080, 98 S.Ct. 1276, 55 L.Ed.2d 789 (1978); *Gay Alliance of Students v. Matthews*, 544 F.2d 162 (4th Cir. 1976); *Gay Students Organization of University of New Hampshire v. Bonner*, 509 F.2d 652 (1st Cir. 1974); *Gay Activists Alliance v. Board of Regents*, 638 P.2d 1116 (Okla. 1981). In addition, one appellate court has held that a university may not discriminate against homosexual student organizations in the allocation of university funds. *Gay and Lesbian Students Association v. Gohn*, 850 F.2d 361 (8th Cir. 1988). *Compare Cornelius v. NAACP Legal Defense and Educational Fund*, *supra*; *Regan v. Taxation with Representation*, 461 U.S. 540, 103 S.Ct. 1997, 76 L.Ed.2d 129 (1983). Judge Arnold, writing for the court in *Gohn*, made the following observation:

> It is apparent that the GLSA was denied . . . funds because of the views it espoused. Nor is there a compelling state interest justifying the Senate's denial of funds. The University provides no argument, and we can think of none. True, sodomy is illegal in Arkansas. However, the GLSA does not advocate sodomy, and, even if it did, its speech about an illegal activity would still be protected by the First Amendment. People may extol the virtues of arson or even cannibalism. They simply may not commit the acts. . . . Conduct may be prohibited or regulated, within broad limits. But government may not discriminate against people because it dislikes their ideas, not even when the ideas include advocating that certain conduct now criminal be legalized.

850 F.2d at 367–68.

Is *Gohn* consistent with *Healy*? With *Rosenberger*? Is it consistent with the cases dealing with homosexual teachers, discussed *supra*? Should the result be the same if a gay student organization in a public high school sought recognition? How would the *Mergens* court decide this issue? In the latter case, what is the relevance of *Hazelwood*, *Bethel*, *Pico*, and other cases involving the role of the public schools in socializing students to community norms?

Would the principles of *Healy*, *Widmar*, *Mergens*, and the homosexual student organization cases apply to the recognition of alumni groups by a university or public school? *See Ad-Hoc Committee v. Bernard M. Baruch College*, 835 F.2d 980 (2d Cir. 1987). Would the banning of membership in fraternal organizations or a prohibition on their meeting on campus violate *Mergens* or the First Amendment? *See Waugh v. Board of Trustees*, 237 U.S. 589, 35 S.Ct. 720, 59 L.Ed. 1131 (1915); *Webb v. State University of New York*, 125 F.Supp. 910 (N.D.N.Y. 1954), *appeal dismissed*, 348 U.S. 867, 75 S.Ct. 113, 99 L.Ed. 683. *But see Wright v. Board of Education*, 295 Mo. 466, 246 S.W. 43 (1922). *See generally* Hauser, "Social Fraternities at Public Institutions of Higher Education: Their Rights Under the First and Fourteenth Amendments," 19 *J.L. & Educ.* 433 (1990); Graebner, "Outlawing Teenage Populism: The Campaign Against Secret Societies in the American High School, 1900–1960," 74 *J. Am. Hist.* 411 (1987); Rumsey, "Legal Aspects of the Relationship Between Fraternities and Public Institutions of Higher Education: Freedom of Association and Ability to Prohibit Campus Presence or Student Membership," 11 *J.C. & U.L.* 465 (1985).

After *Mergens*, *Widmar*, *Rosenberger*, and the circuit court cases on homosexual student organizations, do schools have any way to regulate the types of student groups meeting at school? *See generally Pope v. East Brunswick Bd. of Educ.*, 12 F.3d 1244, 1254 (3d Cir. 1993). What if a few students wanted to form a nazi student group, a KKK group, or an anti-homosexual group? Could the school prevent the formation of such student groups? Must the school recognize them? Does the substantial disruption test in *Tinker* empower the schools to prevent the formation of such groups? Does the *Fraser* case allow the school to "disassociate itself" from speech and conduct that is "wholly inconsistent with the 'fundamental values' of public school education"? *See Bethel Sch. Dist. No. 403 v. Fraser*, 478 U.S. 675, 685, 106 S.Ct. 3156, 3159 (1986). Or must the school close the entire limited public forum in order to prevent the formation and official recognition of such groups? *See* Gewirtzman, " 'Make Your Own Kind of Music': Queer Student Groups and the First Amendment," 86 *Cal. L. Rev.* 1131 (1998).

6. *Mandatory Student Fees*

Public universities frequently levy mandatory fees on students to finance student health services, intramural sports, student union activities, student organizations, and other services and activities. The allocation of mandatory fee funds, frequently by student-constituted fees committees that make recommendations to central administration, to registered student organizations has sparked controversy. Students have filed lawsuits alleging that the allocation of a portion of their fees to organizations engaging in political or ideological speech or activities with which they disagree violates their First Amendment rights. Such plaintiffs typically rely on *West Virginia State Board of Education v. Barnette*, 319 U.S. 624, 63 S.Ct. 1178 (1943) and other Supreme Court precedents for this proposition. *See, e.g., Keller v. State Bar of Calif.*, 496 U.S. 1 (1990); *Abood v. Detroit Bd. of Ed.*, 431 U.S. 209 (1977). Appellate courts were divided on whether the students' rights were violated and whether they were entitled to a proportional refund or other remedy. The matter was put to rest in *Board of Regents of the University of Wisconsin System v. Southworth*, 529 U.S. 1346, 120 S.Ct. 217 (2000). Justice Kennedy, writing the majority opinion for the Court, held that mandatory university fees are constitutional if there is viewpoint neutrality:

It is inevitable that government will adopt and pursue programs and policies within its constitutional powers but which nevertheless are contrary to the profound beliefs and sincere convictions of some of its citizens. The government, as a general rule, may support valid programs and policies by taxes or other exactions binding on protesting parties. Within this broader principle it seems inevitable that funds raised by the government will be spent for speech and other expression to advocate and defend its own policies. *See, e.g., Rust v. Sullivan*, 500 U.S. 173 (1991); *Regan v. Taxation with Representation of Wash.*, 461 U.S. 540, 548–549 (1983). The case we decide here, however, does not raise the issue of the government's right, or, to be more specific, the state-controlled University's right, to use its own funds to advance a particular message. The University's whole justification for fostering the challenged expression is that it springs from the initiative of the students, who alone give it purpose and content in the course of their extracurricular endeavors.

The University having disclaimed that the speech is its own, we do not reach the question whether traditional political controls to ensure responsible government action would be sufficient to overcome First Amendment objections and to allow the challenged program under the principle that the government can speak for itself. If the challenged speech here were financed by tuition dollars and the University and its officials were responsible for its content, the case might be evaluated on the premise that the government itself is the speaker. That is not the case before us.

The University of Wisconsin exacts the fee at issue for the sole purpose of facilitating the free and open ex-

change of ideas by, and among, its students. We conclude the objecting students may insist upon certain safeguards with respect to the expressive activities which they are required to support. Our public forum cases are instructive here by close analogy. This is true even though the student activities fund is not a public forum in the traditional sense of the term and despite the circumstance that those cases most often involve a demand for access, not a claim to be exempt from supporting speech. *See, e.g., Lamb's Chapel v. Center Moriches Union Free Sch. Dist.*, 508 U.S. 384 (1993); *Widmar v. Vincent*, 454 U.S. 263 (1981). The standard of viewpoint neutrality found in the public forum cases provides the standard we find controlling. We decide that the viewpoint neutrality requirement of the University program is in general sufficient to protect the rights of the objecting students. The student referendum aspect of the program for funding speech and expressive activities, however, appears to be inconsistent with the viewpoint neutrality requirement.

We must begin by recognizing that the complaining students are being required to pay fees which are subsidies for speech they find objectionable, even offensive. The *Abood* and *Keller* cases, then, provide the beginning point for our analysis. *Abood v. Detroit Bd. of Ed.*, 431 U.S. 209 (1977); *Keller v. State Bar of Cal.*, 496 U.S. 1 (1990). While those precedents identify the interests of the protesting students, the means of implementing First Amendment protections adopted in those decisions are neither applicable nor workable in the context of extracurricular student speech at a university.

In *Abood*, some nonunion public school teachers challenged an agreement requiring them, as a condition of their employment, to pay a service fee equal in amount to union dues. 431 U.S., at 211–212. The objecting teachers alleged that the union's use of their fees to engage in political speech violated their freedom of association guaranteed by the First and Fourteenth Amendments. *Id.*, at 213. The Court agreed and held that any objecting teacher could "prevent the Union's spending a part of their required service fees to contribute to political candidates and to express political views unrelated to its duties as exclusive bargaining representative." *Id.*, at 234. The principles outlined in *Abood* provided the foundation for our later decision in *Keller*. There we held that lawyers admitted to practice in California could be required to join a state bar association and to fund activities "germane" to the association's mission of "regulating the legal profession and improving the quality of legal services." 496 U.S., at 13–14. The lawyers could not, however, be required to fund the bar association's own political expression. *Id.*, at 16. The proposition that students who attend the University cannot be required to pay subsidies for the speech of other students without some First Amendment protection follows from the *Abood* and *Keller* cases. Students enroll in public universities to seek fulfillment of their personal aspirations and of their own potential. If the University conditions the opportunity to receive a college education, an opportunity comparable in importance to joining a labor union or bar association, on an agreement to support objectionable, extracurricular expression by other students, the rights acknowledged in *Abood* and *Keller* become implicated. It infringes on the speech and beliefs of the individual to be required, by this mandatory student activity fee program, to pay subsidies for the objectionable speech of others without any recognition of the State's corresponding duty to him or her. Yet recognition must be given as well to the important and substantial purposes of the University, which seeks to facilitate a wide range of speech.

In *Abood* and *Keller* the constitutional rule took the form of limiting the required subsidy to speech germane to the purposes of the union or bar association. The standard of germane speech as applied to student speech at a university is unworkable, however, and gives insufficient protection both to the objecting students and to the University program itself. Even in the context of a labor union, whose functions are, or so we might have thought, well known and understood by the law and the courts after a long history of government regulation and judicial involvement, we have encountered difficulties in deciding what is germane and what is not. The difficulty manifested itself in our decision in *Lehnert v. Ferris Faculty Ass'n*, 500 U.S. 507 (1991), where different members of the Court reached varying conclusions regarding what expressive activity was or was not germane to the mission of the association. If it is difficult to define germane speech with ease or precision where a union or bar association is the party, the standard becomes all the more unmanageable in the public university setting, particularly where the State undertakes to stimulate the whole universe of speech and ideas.

The speech the University seeks to encourage in the program before us is distinguished not by discernable limits but by its vast, unexplored bounds. To insist upon asking what speech is germane would be contrary to the very goal the University seeks to pursue. It is not for the Court to say what is or is not germane to the ideas to be pursued in an institution of higher learning.

* * *

The University may determine that its mission is well served if students have the means to engage in dynamic discussions of philosophical, religious, scientific, social, and political subjects in their extracurricular campus life outside the lecture hall. If the University reaches this conclusion, it is entitled to impose a mandatory fee to sustain an open dialogue to these ends. The University must provide some protection to its students' First Amendment interests, however. The proper measure, and the principal standard of protection for objecting students, we conclude, is the requirement of viewpoint neutrality in the allocation of funding sup-

port. Viewpoint neutrality was the obligation to which we gave substance in *Rosenberger v. Rector and Visitors of Univ. of Va.*,515 U.S. 819 (1995). There the University of Virginia feared that any association with a student newspaper advancing religious viewpoints would violate the Establishment Clause. We rejected the argument, holding that the school's adherence to a rule of viewpoint neutrality in administering its student fee program would prevent "any mistaken impression that the student newspapers speak for the University." *Id.*, at 841. While *Rosenberger* was concerned with the rights a student has to use an extracurricular speech program already in place, today's case considers the antecedent question, acknowledged but unresolved in *Rosenberger*: whether a public university may require its students to pay a fee which creates the mechanism for the extracurricular speech in the first instance. When a university requires its students to pay fees to support the extracurricular speech of other students, all in the interest of open discussion, it may not prefer some viewpoints to others. There is symmetry then in our holding here and in *Rosenberger*: Viewpoint neutrality is the justification for requiring the student to pay the fee in the first instance and for ensuring the integrity of the program's operation once the funds have been collected.

* * *

We make no distinction between campus activities and the off-campus expressive activities of objectionable RSO's [Registered Student Organizations]. Those activities, respondents tell us, often bear no relationship to the University's reason for imposing the segregated fee in the first instance, to foster vibrant campus debate among students. If the University shares those concerns, it is free to enact viewpoint neutral rules restricting off-campus travel or other expenditures by RSO's, for it may create what is tantamount to a limited public forum if the principles of viewpoint neutrality are respected. We find no principled way, however, to impose upon the University, as a constitutional matter, a requirement to adopt geographic or spatial restrictions as a condition for RSOs' entitlement to reimbursement. Universities possess significant interests in encouraging students to take advantage of the social, civic, cultural, and religious opportunities available in surrounding communities and throughout the country. Universities, like all of society, are finding that traditional conceptions of territorial boundaries are difficult to insist upon in an age marked by revolutionary changes in communications, information transfer, and the means of discourse. If the rule of viewpoint neutrality is respected, our holding affords the University latitude to adjust its extracurricular student speech program to accommodate these advances and opportunities.

Our decision ought not to be taken to imply that in other instances the University, its agents or employees, or—of particular importance—its faculty, are subject to the First Amendment analysis which controls in this case. Where the University speaks, either in its own name through its regents or officers, or in myriad other ways through its diverse faculties, the analysis likely would be altogether different. *See Rust v. Sullivan*, 500 U.S. 173 (1991); *Regan v. Taxation with Representation of Wash.*, 461 U.S. 540 (1983). The Court has not held, or suggested, that when the government speaks the rules we have discussed come into play.

When the government speaks, for instance to promote its own policies or to advance a particular idea, it is, in the end, accountable to the electorate and the political process for its advocacy. If the citizenry objects, newly elected officials later could espouse some different or contrary position. In the instant case, the speech is not that of the University or its agents. It is not, furthermore, speech by an instructor or a professor in the academic context, where principles applicable to government speech would have to be considered. *Cf. Rosenberger, supra*, at 833 (discussing the discretion universities possess in deciding matters relating to their educational mission).

It remains to discuss the referendum aspect of the University's program. While the record is not well developed on the point, it appears that by majority vote of the student body a given RSO may be funded or defunded. It is unclear to us what protection, if any, there is for viewpoint neutrality in this part of the process. To the extent the referendum substitutes majority determinations for viewpoint neutrality it would undermine the constitutional protection the program requires. The whole theory of viewpoint neutrality is that minority views are treated with the same respect as are majority views. Access to a public forum, for instance, does not depend upon majoritarian consent. That principle is controlling here. A remand is necessary and appropriate to resolve this point; and the case in all events must be reexamined in light of the principles we have discussed.

Id. at 1353–57. Is *Southworth* consistent with *West Virginia v. Barnette, supra?* With *Hazelwood?* At what point does subsidized student speech become government speech in a public university? What if a student organization used a portion of its subsidy to engage in an illegal demonstration? What if a university administers a required student fee to pay for student health insurance and that insurance covers off-campus abortions? *See Goehring v. Brophy*, 94 F.3d 37 (9th Cir. 1996) (court holds that payment for abortions did not impose a substantial burden on free exercise of religion and that subsidized health insurance system is the least restrictive means of furthering a compelling government interest); *Erzinger v. Regents of the University of California*, 136 Cal. App. 3d 1, 185 Cal.

Rptr. 791 (1982); *aff'd on reh'g*, 137 Cal. App. 3d 389, 187 Cal. Rptr. 164. *See generally* Antonini, "First Amendment Challenges to the Use of Mandatory Student Fees to Help Fund Student Abortions," 15 *J.C. & U.L.* 61 (1988).

Would it be constitutional for a university to require the student government to refrain from partisan political activities as a condition of funding through a mandatory fee? *See generally* Coté, "The First Amendment and Compulsory Funding of Student Government Political Resolutions at State Universities," 62 *U. Chi. L. Rev.* 825 (1995).

May a university establish a new procedure for student refunds in response to the controversial positions taken by a student organization supported by a mandatory fee? *Compare Southworth v. Grebe*, 151 F.3d 717, 733 (7th Cir. 1998) (rejecting as unconstitutional the use of a refund of the portion of student fees that funds groups engaged in ideological or political activity) *with Smith v. Regents of the Univ. of Cal.*, 844 P.2d 500, 514 (Cal. 1993) (noting that the university could use a refund system). *See also Stanley v. Magrath*, 719 F.2d 279 (8th Cir. 1983).

Does *Southworth* apply with greater or lesser force to elementary and secondary public education?

7. *Outside Groups and the Limited Public Forum*

In *Mergens* the issue was whether a school may deny access to some student groups when it grants access to others. No one contended that public schools were traditional public forums akin to parks and streets, that the schools were required to open the schools to all speakers. *See Perry Educ. Ass'n v. Perry Local Educators Ass'n*, 460 U.S. 37, 103 S.Ct. 948, 74 L.Ed.2d 794 (1983); *Grayned v. Rockford*, 408 U.S. 104, 92 S.Ct. 2294, 33 L.Ed.2d 222 (1972). From this perspective, those cases address the question of content or subject discrimination where the public school already has made a decision not to close the forum to all speakers and groups. *See, e.g., City of Madison Joint School District v. Wisconsin Public Employees Relations Commission*, 429 U.S. 167, 97 S.Ct. 421, 50 L.Ed.2d 376 (1976); *Chicago Police Department v. Mosley*, 408 U.S. 92, 92 S.Ct. 2286, 33 L.Ed.2d 212 (1972). In this sense, the cases have as much to do with notions of equality as with speech and associational rights. *See generally* Karst, "Equality as a Central Principle in the First Amendment," 43 *U. Chi. L. Rev.* 20 (1975).

But it would be incorrect to view *Mergens, Widmar,* and their progeny as involving only equality and content discrimination. First, the forum is restricted by the identity of the speaker. The opening of the forum to student groups does not mean that the forum must be opened to outsiders. *See Cornelius v. NAACP Legal Defense and Educational Fund*, 473 U.S. 788, 806, 105 S.Ct. 3439, 3451, 87 L.Ed.2d 567 (1985); *Perry Educ. Ass'n*, 460 U.S. at 41 n. 4, 103 S.Ct. at 952 n.4. *See Searcey v. Harris*, 888 F.2d 1314 (11th Cir. 1989). In that sense the forum is limited to participants in the schooling enterprise, those who are bound up in the mission of public education. *See Texas State Teachers Association v. Garland Independent School District*, 777 F.2d 1046 (5th Cir. 1985); Yudof, *When Government Speaks* 225 (1983). Second, "there is no general acceptance of the proposition that the state's own communications efforts may allow outsiders to successfully invoke the public-forum doctrine; rather, a right of access by outsiders is granted only when other outsiders have been afforded such a right." Yudof, *supra* at 225–26, citing *Buckel v. Prentice*, 572 F.2d 141 (6th Cir. 1978); *cf. Lamb's Chapel v. Center Moriches Union Free School*, 508 U.S. 384, 384, 113 S.Ct. 2141, 2141 (1993). *But see Bonner-Lyons v. School Committee*, 480 F.2d 442 (1st Cir. 1973). Third, under *Tinker*, students are entitled to express themselves on campus, subject to the substantial disruption rule, and the public schools may not choose to close the school to such speech. *See Tinker v. Des Moines Independent School District*, 393 U.S. 503, 89 S.Ct. 733, 21 L.Ed.2d 731 (1969). In other words, the speech rights of the students follow them into the public school; there is no need to show that the school is a public forum or a limited public forum. *See generally* Farber & Nowak, "The Misleading Nature of the Public Forum Analysis: Content and Context in First Amendment Adjudication," 70 *Va. L. Rev.* 1219 (1984).

Is the notion of the public forum consistent with the state's mission of education and socialization in public schools? *See* Shiffrin, "Government Speech," 27 *UCLA L. Rev.* 565, 579 (1980). Are *Widmar* and *Tinker* inconsistent? Does *Hazelwood* undermine *Tinker*? Is *Mergens* consistent with *Hazelwood*? What is the justification for limiting *Widmar* and *Healy* to student groups? Why did Congress limit the Equal Access Act to student groups? If there is a sense that students "belong" on campus or that they do not lose all of their speech rights at the entrance of the school, does that suggest that public forum analysis is misleading? Is it that ". . . [t]he State, no less than a private owner of property, has power to preserve the property under its control for the use to which it is lawfully dedicated"?

Adderley v. Florida, 385 U.S. 39, 47, 87 S.Ct. 242, 247, 17 L.Ed.2d 149 (1966). *See also Greer v. Spock*, 424 U.S. 828, 96 S.Ct. 1211, 47 L.Ed.2d 505 (1976). If a school may exclude all outsiders, such as civil rights and church organizations, from school premises, why can it not decide to exclude partisan student groups? Is content discrimination between student groups more pernicious than discrimination between inside and outside groups? *See generally* Stone, "Content Regulation and the First Amendment," 25 *Wm. & Mary L. Rev.* 189 (1983). Suppose that some ideologies have no significant student constituency within the school. Is not the closing of the school to outsiders tantamount to content discrimination?

Can a limited public forum be created by accident? *Cf. Mergens, supra.* Or must the government intend, by policy or practice, to open a traditionally closed forum to speakers and groups? *See Cornelius v. NAACP Legal Defense and Educational Fund*, 473 U.S. 788, 802, 105 S.Ct. 3439, 3449, 87 L.Ed.2d 567 (1985); *Planned Parenthood v. Clark County School District*, 941 F.2d 817, 822 (9th Cir. 1991); *Student Coalition for Peace v. Lower Merion School District Board*, 776 F.2d 431 (3rd Cir. 1985).

8. Visitors to School Campuses

Suppose a school board adopts a policy requiring all visitors to a public school to report directly to the principal's office. The principal then has the authority to decide whether to permit the visitation, "keeping in mind the system's obligation is to the safety, welfare, and education of children." Is such a policy constitutional? *See Hall v. Board of School Commissioners of Mobile County*, 681 F.2d 965 (5th Cir. 1982). May a public university declare a former student *persona non grata* with respect to public areas of the campus? If so, under what circumstances? *See People v. Leonard*, 62 N.Y.2d 404, 477 N.Y.S.2d 111, 465 N.E.2d 831 (1984); *Sounders v. Lucero*, 196 F.3d 1040 (9th Cir. 1999). May parents be excluded? *Cf. Commonwealth v. Ashcraft*, 691 S.W.2d 229 (Ky.App. 1985).

The courts have tended to treat commercial speech on campus as less deserving of constitutional protection than other forms of speech, albeit most of the cases involve access to student residence halls and other university facilities. The leading case is *Board of Trustees of State University of New York v. Fox*, 492 U.S. 469, 109 S.Ct. 3028, 106 L.Ed.2d 388 (1989). In that case, American Future Systems, Inc. (AFS) sought to hold "Tupperware parties" in student dormitories in order to demonstrate and sell houseware products. The university excluded AFS under a rule prohibiting

commercial enterprises from operating in campus facilities. The purposes of the rule were to promote "an
educational rather than commercial atmosphere on
[campus], [to promote] . . . safety and security, [to pre-
vent] . . . commercial exploitation of students, and [to
preserve] . . . residential tranquility." 109 S.Ct. at 3032.
The plaintiffs asserted that the rule was more expansive
than necessary to promote the state's interests, i.e., that
it was not the "least-restrictive means" in terms of its
impact on speech. The Court upheld the campus rule,
reasoning that "our decisions require a 'fit' between the
legislature's end and the means chosen to accomplish
those ends . . .—a fit that is not necessarily perfect, but
reasonable. . . ." 109 S.Ct. at 3035. *See also Chapman
v. Thomas*, 743 F.2d 1056 (4th Cir. 1984).

Does the reasoning of *Fox* apply to public elementary and secondary schools? *See Rivers v. Campbell*,
791 F.2d 837 (11th Cir. 1986); *Katz v. McAulay*, 438
F.2d 1058 (2d Cir. 1971), *cert. denied*, 405 U.S. 933, 92
S.Ct. 930, 30 L.Ed.2d 809 (1972). Would the solicitation of donations for a political organization on campus be political or commercial speech? *See Glover v.
Cole*, 762 F.2d 1197 (4th Cir. 1985). *See generally Hef-
fron v. International Society for Krishna Consciousness*,
452 U.S. 640, 101 S.Ct. 2559, 69 L.Ed.2d 298 (1981);
*Village of Schaumburg v. Citizens for a Better Environ-
ment*, 444 U.S. 620, 100 S.Ct. 826, 63 L.Ed.2d 73
(1980). May a public school ban any form of solicitation of students on campus? *See Katz v. McAulay*, 438
F.2d 1058 (2d Cir. 1971), *cert. denied*, 405 U.S. 933, 92
S.Ct. 930, 30 L.Ed.2d 809 (1972).

3. Teacher Selection. To assure that the school's
message is delivered clearly and without distortion (as
well as to assure pedagogical competency), legislatures, school boards, and school officials have historically focused on appropriate criteria for the selection of
teachers. Although there are other ways to control the
message of the school program, selection of teachers
who can be trusted to carry out the job they were hired
to carry out is one important method. As Justice Burton, speaking for the Supreme Court in *Beilan v.*

Board of Education, 357 U.S. 399, 406, 78 S.Ct. 1317,
1322, 2 L.Ed.2d 1414 (1958), stated: "We find no requirement in the federal Constitution that a teacher's
classroom conduct be the sole basis for determining
his fitness. Fitness for teaching depends on a broad
range of factors." These factors can include such matters as college degrees, test scores, teaching certificates,
experience levels, pedagogical skills, and, more con-
troversially, personal lifestyles, attitudes, and beliefs.

Should attitudes and beliefs be relevant to the employment decision? If so, how are they to be determined, and what constitutes an impermissible manifestation of objectionable attitudes and beliefs? *See
generally* H. Beale, *Are American Teachers Free?*
(1936). Are teachers charged with "teaching social
order as a dogma or an article of faith, obfuscating
the question of how much order is desirable"? Do
they emphasize "docility, obedience, authority, inferiority of the lower classes, piety, and faith in providence"? C. Lindblom, *Inquiry and Change* 93
(1990). If so, is the government's purpose in screening teachers a legitimate one?

The following case explores these issues in the
context of state-mandated teacher hiring restrictions
on resident aliens.

Ambach v. Norwick

441 U.S. 68, 99 S.Ct. 1589, 60 L.Ed.2d 49 (1979).

Mr. Justice Powell delivered the opinion of the Court.

This case presents the question whether a State,
consistently with the Equal Protection Clause of the
Fourteenth Amendment, may refuse to employ as
elementary and secondary school teachers aliens
who are eligible for United States citizenship but
who refuse to seek naturalization.

New York Education Law § 3001 (3) (McKinney
1970) forbids certification as a public school teacher
of any person who is not a citizen of the United States,
unless that person has manifested an intention to apply for citizenship.[1] The Commissioner of Education

---

[1]The statute provides:
"No person shall be employed or authorized to teach in the public schools of the state who is:

* * *

"3. Not a citizen. The provisions of this subdivision shall not apply, however, to an alien teacher now or hereafter employed, provided such teacher
shall make due application to become a citizen and thereafter within the time prescribed by law shall become a citizen. The provisions of this subdivision shall not apply after July first, nineteen hundred sixty-seven, to an alien teacher employed pursuant to regulations adopted by the commissioner
of education permitting such employment." N.Y. Educ. Law § 3001 (3) (McKinney 1970).
The statute contains an exception for persons who are ineligible for United States citizenship solely because of an oversubscribed quota. § 3001-a (McKinney 1970). Because this statutory provision is in all respects narrower than the exception provided by regulation, *see* n. 2, *infra*, as a practical matter it has no
effect. The State does not certify the qualifications of teachers in the private schools, although it does require that such teachers be "competent." N.Y. Educ.
Law § 3204 (2) (McKinney Supp. 1978–1979). Accordingly, we are not presented with the question of, and express no view as to, the permissibility of a citizenship requirement pertaining to teachers in private schools.

is authorized to create exemptions from this prohibition, and has done so with respect to aliens who are not yet eligible for citizenship.[2] Unless a teacher obtains certification, he may not work in a public elementary or secondary school in New York.[3]

Appellee Norwick was born in Scotland and is a subject of Great Britain. She has resided in this country since 1965 and is married to a United States citizen. Appellee Dachinger is a Finnish subject who came to this country in 1966 and also is married to a United States citizen. Both Norwick and Dachinger currently meet all of the educational requirements New York has set for certification as a public school teacher, but they consistently have refused to seek citizenship in spite of their eligibility to do so. Norwick applied in 1973 for a teaching certificate covering nursery school through sixth grade, and Dachinger sought a certificate covering the same grades in 1975. Both applications were denied because of appellee's failure to meet the requirements of § 3001 (3). Norwick then filed this suit seeking to enjoin the enforcement of § 3001 (3), and Dachinger obtained leave to intervene as a plaintiff.

* * *

The decisions of this Court regarding the permissibility of statutory classifications involving aliens have not formed an unwavering line over the years. State regulation of the employment of aliens long has been subject to constitutional constraints. In *Yick Wo v. Hopkins*, 118 U.S. 356 (1886), the Court struck down an ordinance which was applied to prevent aliens from running laundries, and in *Truax v. Raich*, 239 U.S. 33 (1915), a law requiring at least 80% of the employees of certain businesses to be citizens was held to be an unconstitutional infringement of an alien's "right to work for a living in the common occupations of the community. . . ." *Id.* at 41. At the same time, however, the Court also has recognized a greater degree of latitude for the States when aliens were sought to be excluded from public employment. At the time *Truax* was decided, the governing doctrine permitted States to exclude aliens from various activities when the restriction pertained to "the regulation or distribution of the public domain, or of the common property or resources of the people of the State. . . ." *Id.*, at 39. . . .

Over time, the Court's decisions gradually have restricted the activities from which States are free to exclude aliens. . . . This process of withdrawal from the former doctrine culminated in *Graham v. Richardson, supra*, which for the first time treated classifications based on alienage as "inherently suspect and subject to close judicial scrutiny." 403 U.S., at 372. Applying *Graham*, this Court has held invalid statutes that prevented aliens from entering a State's classified civil service, *Sugarman v. Dougall*, 413 U.S. 634 (1973), practicing law, *In re Griffiths*, 413 U.S. 717 (1973), working as an engineer, *Examining Board v. Flores de Otero*, 426 U.S. 572 (1976), and receiving state educational benefits, *Nyquist v. Mauclet*, 432 U.S. 1 (1977).

Although our more recent decisions have departed substantially from the public-interest doctrine of *Truax*'s day, they have not abandoned the general principle that some state functions are so bound up with the operation of the State as a governmental entity as to permit the exclusion from those functions of all persons who have not become part of the process of self-government. In *Sugarman*, we recognized that a State could, "in an appropriately defined class of positions, require citizenship as a qualification for office." We went on to observe:

> Such power inheres in the State by virtue of its obligation, already noted above, "to preserve the basic conception of a political community." . . . And this power and responsibility of the State applies, not only to the qualifications of voters, but also to persons holding state elective or important nonelective executive, legislative, and judicial positions, for officers who participate directly in the formulation, execution, or review of broad public policy perform functions that go to the heart of representative government."

413 U.S., at 647 (citation omitted). The exclusion of aliens from such governmental positions would not invite as demanding scrutiny from this Court. *Id.*, at 648. . . .

Applying the rational-basis standard, we held last Term that New York could exclude aliens from the ranks of its police force. *Foley v. Connelie*, 435 U.S. 291 (1978). Because the police function fulfilled "a most fundamental obligation of government to its constituency" and by necessity cloaked policemen with substantial discretionary powers, we viewed the

---

[2] The following regulation governs here:

"Citizenship. A teacher who is not a citizen of the United States or who has not declared intention of becoming a citizen may be issued a provisional certificate providing such teacher has the appropriate educational qualifications as defined in the regulations and (1) possesses skills or competencies not readily available among teachers holding citizenship, or (2) is unable to declare intention of becoming a citizen for valid statutory reasons." 8 N.Y.C.R.R. § 80.2(i) (1978).

[3] Certification by the Commissioner of Education is not required of teachers at state institutions of higher education and the citizenship restriction accordingly does not apply to them. . . .

police force as being one of those appropriately defined classes of positions for which a citizenship requirement could be imposed. *Id.*, at 297. Accordingly, the State was required to justify its classification only "by a showing of some rational relationship between the interest sought to be protected and the limiting classification." *Id.*, at 296.

The rule for governmental functions, which is an exception to the general standards applicable to classifications based on alienage, rests on important principles inherent in the Constitution. The distinction between citizens and aliens, though ordinarily irrelevant to private activity, is fundamental to the definition and government of a State. The Constitution itself refers to the distinction no less than 11 times, *see Sugarman v. Dougall, supra,* at 651–52 (Rehnquist, J., dissenting), indicating that the status of citizenship was meant to have significance in the structure of our government. The assumption of that status, whether by birth or naturalization, denotes an association with the policy which, in a democratic republic, exercises the powers of governance. *See Foley v. Connelie, supra,* at 295. The form of this association is important: an oath of allegiance or similar ceremony cannot substitute for the unequivocal legal bond citizenship represents. It is because of this special significance of citizenship that governmental entities, when exercising the functions of government, have wider latitude in limiting the participation of noncitizens.

In determining whether, for purposes of equal protection analysis, teaching in public schools constitutes a governmental function, we look to the role of public education and to the degree of responsibility and discretion teachers possess in fulfilling that role. *See Foley v. Connelie, supra,* at 297. Each of these considerations supports the conclusion that public

school teachers may be regarded as performing a task "that go[es] to the heart of representative government." *Sugarman v. Dougall, supra,* at 647.[6]

Public education, like the police function, "fulfills a most fundamental obligation of government to its constituency." *Foley, supra,* at 297. The importance of public schools in the preparation of individuals for participation as citizens, and in the preservation of the values on which our society rests, long has been recognized by our decisions. . . .

* * *

. . . Other authorities have perceived public schools as an "assimilative force" by which diverse and conflicting elements in our society are brought together on a broad but common ground. *See, e.g.,* J. Dewey, *Democracy and Education* 26 (1929); N. Edwards & H. Richey, *The School in the American Social Order* 623–24 (2d ed. 1963). These perceptions of the public schools as inculcating fundamental values necessary to the maintenance of a democratic political system have been confirmed by the observations of social scientists. *See* R. Dawson & K. Prewitt, *Political Socialization* 146–67 (1969); R. Hess & J. Torney, *The Development of Political Attitudes in Children* 114, 158–71, 217–20 (1967); V. Key, *Public Opinion and American Democracy* 323–43 (1961).[8]

Within the public school system, teachers play a critical part in developing students' attitude toward government and understanding of the role of citizens in our society. Alone among employees of the system, teachers are in direct, day-to-day contact with students both in the classrooms and in the other varied activities of a modern school. In shaping the student's experience to achieve educational goals, teachers by necessity have wide discretion over the way the course material is communicated to students. They are responsible for presenting and explaining the subject

---

[6]The dissenting opinion of Mr. Justice Blackmun, in reaching an opposite conclusion, appears to apply a different analysis from that employed in our prior decisions. Rather than consider whether public school teachers perform a significant government function, the inquiry mandated by *Foley v. Connelie,* 435 U.S. 291 (1978), and *Sugarman v. Dougall,* the dissent focuses instead on the general societal importance of primary and secondary school teachers both public and private. Thus, the dissent on the one hand depreciates the importance of New York's citizenship requirement because it is not applied to private school teachers, and on the other hand argues that the role teachers perform in our society is no more significant than that filled by attorneys. This misses the point of *Foley* and *Sugarman.* New York's citizenship requirement is limited to a governmental function because it applies only to teachers employed by and acting as agents of the State. The Connecticut statute held unconstitutional in *In re Griffiths,* 413 U.S. 717 (1973), by contrast, applied to all attorneys, most of whom do not work for the government. The exclusion of aliens from access to the bar implicated the right to pursue a chosen occupation, not access to public employment. . . .

[8]The curricular requirements of New York's public school system reflect some of the ways a public school system promotes the development of the understanding that is prerequisite to intelligent participation in the democratic process. The schools are required to provide instruction "to promote a spirit of patriotic and civic service and obligation and to foster in the children of the state moral and intellectual qualities which are essential in preparing to meet the obligations of citizenship in peace or in war. . . ." N.Y. Educ. Law § 801 (1) (McKinney 1969). Flag and other patriotic exercises also are prescribed, as loyalty is a characteristic of citizenship essential to the preservation of a country. § 802 (McKinney 1969 and Supp. 1978–1979). In addition, required courses include classes in civics, United States and New York history, and principles of American government. §§ 3204 (3)(a)(1), (McKinney 1970).

Although private schools also are bound by most of these requirements, the State has a stronger interest in ensuring that the schools it most directly controls, and for which it bears the cost, are as effective as possible in teaching these courses.

matter in a way that is both comprehensible and in-spiring. No amount of standardization of teaching ma-terials or lesson plans can eliminate the personal qual-ities a teacher brings to bear in achieving these goals. Further, a teacher serves as a role model for his stu-dents, exerting a subtle but important influence over their perceptions and values. Thus, through both pre-sentation of course materials and the example he sets, a teacher has an opportunity to influence the attitudes of students toward government, the political process, and a citizen's social responsibilities.[9] This influence is crucial to the continued good health of a democracy.[10]

Furthermore, it is clear that all public school teachers, and not just those responsible for teaching the courses most directly related to government, his-tory, and civic duties, should help fulfill the broader function of the public school system. Teachers, re-gardless of their specialty, may be called upon to teach other subjects, including those expressly dedi-cated to political and social subjects. More impor-tantly, a State property may regard all teachers as having an obligation to promote civic virtues and un-derstanding in their classes, regardless of the subject taught. Certainly a State also may take account of a teacher's function as an example for students, which exists independently of particular classroom sub-jects. In light of the foregoing considerations, we think it clear that public school teachers come well within the "governmental function" principle recog-nized in *Sugarman* and *Foley*. Accordingly, the Con-stitution requires only that a citizenship requirement applicable to teaching in the public schools bear a rational relationship to a legitimate state interest. *See Massachusetts Board of Retirement v. Murgia*, 427 U.S. 307, 314 (1976).

As the legitimacy of the State's interest in furthering the educational goals outlined above is undoubted, it remains only to consider whether § 3001 (3) bears a rational relationship to this interest. The restriction is carefully framed to serve its purpose, as it bars from teaching only those aliens who have demonstrated their unwillingness to obtain United States citizen-ship. Appellees, and aliens similarly situated, in effect have chosen to classify themselves. They prefer to re-tain citizenship in a foreign country with the obliga-tions it entails of primary duty and loyalty.[14] They have rejected the open invitation extended to qualify for eligibility to teach by applying for citizenship in this country. The people of New York, acting through their elected representatives, have made a judgment that citizenship should be a qualification for teaching the young of the State in the public schools, and § 3001 (3) furthers that judgment.[15]

Reversed.

---

[9]Although the findings of scholars who have written on the subject are not conclusive, they generally reinforce the common-sense judgment, and the ex-perience of most of us, that a teacher exerts considerable influence over the development of fundamental social attitudes in students, including those atti-tudes which in the broadest sense of the term may be viewed as political. *See, e.g.,* R. Dawson & K. Prewitt, *Political Socialization* 158–167 (1969); R. Hess & J. Torney, *The Development of Political Attitudes in Children* 162–163, 217–218 (1967). *Cf.,* Note, "Aliens' Right to Teach: Political Socialization and the Public Schools," 85 *Yale L.J.* 90, 99–104 (1975).

[10]Appellees contend that restriction of an alien's freedom to teach in public schools is contrary to principles of diversity of thought and academic freedom embodied in the First Amendment. *See also id.,* at 106–109. We think that the attempt to draw an analogy between choice of citizenship and political ex-pression or freedom of association is wide of the mark, as the argument would bar any effort by the State to promote particular values and attitudes toward government. Section 3001 (3) does not inhibit appellees from expressing freely their political or social views or from associating with whomever they please. *Cf. Givhan v. Western Line Consol. School Dist.,* 439 U.S. 410, 415–416 (1979); *Mt. Healthy City Board of Education v. Doyle,* 429 U.S. 274 (1977); *Pick-ering v. Board of Education,* 391 U.S. 563 (1968). Nor are appellees discouraged from joining with others to advance particular political ends. *Cf. Shelton v. Tucker,* 364 U.S. 479 (1960). The only asserted liberty of appellees withheld by the New York statute is the opportunity to teach in the State's schools so long as they elect not to become citizens of this country. This is not a liberty that is accorded constitutional protection.

[14]As our cases have emphasized, resident aliens pay taxes, serve in the Armed Forces, and have made significant contributions to our country in private and public endeavors. *See In re Griffiths,* 413 U.S., at 722; *Sugarman v. Dougall,* 413 U.S., at 645; *Graham v. Richardson,* 403 U.S. 365, 376 (1971). No doubt many of them, and we do not exclude appellees, would make excellent public school teachers. But the legislature, having in mind the importance of education to state and local governments, *see Brown v. Board of Education,* 347 U.S. 483, 493 (1954), may determine eligibility for the key position in dis-charging that function on the assumption that generally persons who are citizens, or who have not declined the function on the assumption that generally persons who are citizens, or who have not declined the opportunity to seek United States citizenship, are better qualified than are those who have elected to remain aliens. We note in this connection that regulations promulgated pursuant to § 3001 (3) do provide for situations where a particular alien's special qualifications as a teacher outweigh the policy primarily served by the statute. *See* 8 N.Y.C.R.R. § 80.2(i) (1) (1978). The appellants inform us, however, that the authority conferred by this regulation has not been exercised. . . .

[15]Appellees argue that the State cannot rationally exclude aliens from teaching positions and yet permit them to vote for and sit on certain local school boards. We note, first, that the State's legislature has not expressly endorsed this policy. Rather, appellants as an administrative matter have interpreted the statute governing New York City's unique community school boards, N.Y. Educ. Law § 2590-c (4) (McKinney Supp. 1978–1979), to permit aliens who are the parents of public school students to participate in these boards. *See* App. 27, 29. We also may assume, without having to decide, that there is a rational basis for a distinction between teachers and board members based on their respective responsibilities. Although possessing substantial responsibility for the administration of the schools, board members teach no classes, and rarely if ever are known or identified by the students.

Mr. Justice Blackmun, with whom Mr. Justice Brennan, Mr. Justice Marshall, and Mr. Justice Stevens join, dissenting. . . .

As the Court acknowledges, . . . its decisions regarding the permissibility of statutory classifications concerning aliens "have not formed an unwavering line over the years." Thus, just last Term, in *Foley v. Connelie*, 435 U.S. 291 (1978), the Court upheld against equal protection challenge the New York statute limiting appointment of members of the state police force to citizens of the United States. . . .

On the other hand, the Court frequently has invalidated a state provision that denies a resident alien the right to engage in specified occupational activity: . . . *Sugarman v. Dougall, supra,* (New York statute relating to permanent positions in the "competitive class" of the state civil service); *In re Griffiths,* 413 U.S. 717 (1973) (the practice of law). . . .

Indeed, the Court has held more than once that state classifications based on alienage are "inherently suspect and subject to close judicial scrutiny." *Graham v. Richardson,* 403 U.S. 365, 372 (1971). . . .

There is thus a line, most recently recognized in *Foley v. Connelie,* between those employments that a State in its wisdom constitutionally may restrict to United States citizens, on the one hand, and those employments, on the other, that the State may not deny to resident aliens. For me, the present case falls on the *Sugarman-Griffiths-Flores de Otero-Mauclet* side of that line, rather than on the narrowly isolated *Foley* side.

We are concerned here with elementary and secondary education in the public schools of New York State. We are not concerned with teaching at the college or graduate levels. It seems constitutionally absurd, to say the least, that in these lower levels of public education a Frenchman may not teach French or, indeed, an Englishwoman may not teach the grammar of the English language. The appellees, to be sure, are resident "aliens" in the technical sense, but there is not a word in the record that either appellee does not have roots in this country or is unqualified in any way, other than the imposed requirement of citizenship, to teach. Both appellee Norwick and appellee Dachinger have been in this country for over

12 years. Each is married to a United States citizen. Each currently meets all the requirements, other than citizenship, that New York has specified for certification as a public school teacher.[4] Each is willing, if required, to subscribe to an oath to support the Constitutions of the United States and of New York. Each lives in an American community, must obey its laws, and must pay all of the taxes citizens are obligated to pay. Appellees, however, have hesitated to give up their respective British and Finnish citizenships, just as lawyer Fre Le Poole Griffiths, the subject of *In re Griffiths, supra,* hesitated to renounce her Netherlands citizenship, although married to a citizen of the United States and a resident of Connecticut. . . . [T]he Court holds that New York's citizenship requirement is constitutional because it bears a rational relationship to the State's interest in furthering these educational goals.

I perceive a number of difficulties along the easy road the Court takes to this conclusion:

First, the New York statutory structure itself refutes the argument. Section 3001 (3), the very statute at issue here, provides for exceptions with respect to alien teachers "employed pursuant to regulations adopted by the commissioner of education permitting such employment." Section 3001-a (McKinney 1970) provides another exception for persons ineligible for United States citizenship because of oversubscribed quotas. Also, New York is unconcerned with any citizenship qualification for teachers in the private schools of the State, even though the record indicates that about 18% of the pupils at the elementary and secondary levels attend private schools. The education of those pupils seems not to be inculcated with something less than what is desirable for citizenship and what the Court calls an influence "crucial to the continued good health of a democracy." . . . The State apparently, under § 3001 (3), would not hesitate to employ an alien teacher while he waits to attain citizenship, even though he may fail ever to attain it.

Second, the New York statute is all-inclusive in its disqualifying provisions: "No person shall be employed or authorized to teach in the public schools of the state who is . . . [n]ot a citizen." It sweeps indiscriminately. It is "neither narrowly confined nor

---

[4]Appellee Norwick is a *summa cum laude* graduate of a Massachusetts college and received an A average in full-time graduate work in the State University of New York at Albany. She has taught both in this country and in Great Britain.

Appellee Dachinger is a *cum laude* graduate, with a major in German, of Lehman College, a unit of the City University of New York, and possesses a master's degree in Early Childhood Education from that institution. She has taught at a day-care center in the Bronx.

Each appellee thus has received and excelled in educational training the State of New York itself offers.

precise in its application," nor limited to the accomplishment of substantial state interests. *Sugarman v. Dougall*, 413 U.S., at 643. *See* Note, "Alien's Right to Teach: Political Socialization and the Public Schools," 85 *Yale L.J.* 90, 109–11 (1975).

Third, the New York classification is irrational. Is it better to employ a poor citizen teacher than an excellent resident alien teacher? Is it preferable to have a citizen who has never seen Spain or a Latin American country teach Spanish to eighth graders and to deny that opportunity to a resident alien who may have lived for 20 years in the culture of Spain or Latin America? The state will know how to select its teachers responsibly, wholly apart from citizenship, and can do so selectively and intelligently. That is the way to accomplish the desired result. An artificial citizenship bar is not a rational way. It is, instead, a stultifying provision. The route to "diverse and conflicting elements" and their being "brought together on a broad but common ground," which the Court so emphasizes, . . . is hardly to be achieved by disregarding some of the diverse elements that are available, competent, and contributory to the richness of our society and of the education it could provide.

Fourth, it is logically impossible to differentiate between this case concerning teachers and *In re Griffiths* concerning attorneys. If a resident alien may not constitutionally be barred from taking a state bar examination and thereby becoming qualified to practice law in the courts of a State, how is one to comprehend why a resident alien may constitutionally be barred from teaching in the elementary and secondary levels of a State's public schools? . . .

NOTES AND QUESTIONS

1. *Standard of Review*

The Court adopts a stricter standard of review than the rational-basis test if the state has employed a classification approach that employs a "suspect classification," for example, race or religion. The Court has said that when a class of people has been saddled with political and social disabilities and subjected to a history of purposefully unequal treatment, statutes directed "against [such] discrete and insular minorities may be a special condition, which tends seriously to curtail the operation of those political processes ordinarily to be relied upon to protect minorities, and . . . [thus] may call for a correspondingly more searching judicial inquiry." *United States v. Carolene*

Products, Co., 304 U.S. 144, 152 n. 4, 58 S.Ct. 778, 783 n. 4, 82 L.Ed. 1234 (1938).

Do you agree with the Court's decision in *Graham v. Richardson*, 403 U.S. 365, 91 S.Ct. 1848, 29 L.Ed.2d 534 (1971) (cited in *Ambach*), treating classifications based on alienage as inherently suspect? *See also Bernal v. Fainter*, 467 U.S. 216, 104 S.Ct. 2312, 81 L.Ed.2d 175 (1984). Are the reasons for treating alienage as a suspect classification less salient when alienage has been used in conjunction with defining eligibility for public employment? Was the majority correct in not relying upon the strict standard of review in this case? If the majority had adhered to *Graham*, would the result in the case have been different? Is it appropriate to make the character of the classification dependent on the nature of the benefit or privilege that is denied? For example, may a state bar resident aliens from receiving state scholarship awards? *See Nyquist v. Mauclet*, 432 U.S. 1, 97 S.Ct. 2120, 53 L.Ed.2d 63 (1977).

2. *Protective Labor Legislation?*

The majority opinion and the dissent both accept the proposition that the challenged statute is designed to assure that the state's legitimate educational objectives are not frustrated by teachers who are unwilling or unable to achieve those objectives. Is this the sole or primary purpose of the law? Consider the regulation issued by the Commissioner of Education, set forth in note 2 of the opinion. Why does the law permit aliens to be hired when they "possess skills or competencies not readily available among teachers holding citizenship"? What does the availability of citizens as employees have to do with the reliability of aliens as teachers? Is this law best explained as designed to assure priority to the hiring of citizens? If so, should the Court still have ruled that the statute is constitutional? How would you distinguish *Sugarman v. Dougall*, 93 S.Ct. 2842, 37 L.Ed.2d 853, 413 U.S. 634, (1973) (discussed in *Ambach*)?

3. *Narrowing the State's Interest*

Do the majority and dissent quarrel over the teacher's socialization function, or only over whether the New York law is rational in the way it serves that purpose? *See Board of Education v. Pico*, 457 U.S. 853, 102 S.Ct. 2799, 73 L.Ed.2d 435 (1982). Is Justice Blackmun really arguing that the law is "irrational," or is he asserting that a statute could be more narrowly drawn so as to promote the socialization function without unnecessarily impinging on the ability of aliens to secure employment as public schoolteachers? Does

Justice Blackmun oppose any form of exclusion of aliens? Would he accept a more narrowly drawn statute, excluding aliens from teaching only specific subjects or requiring them to sign a loyalty oath or to demonstrate their knowledge of American politics and culture? *See* T. van Geel, *The Courts and American Education Law* 216 (1987).

Why does the majority reject the dissent's argument? Might Justice Powell be concerned with federal judicial intervention in the teacher hiring process? Might he fear that adoption of the minority view could lead to other such judicial forays?

4. Political Status and the Socialization Function

Is the status of being an alien who is eligible to apply for citizenship, but who has not done so, an adequate predictor of what that person will say and do in the classroom? Why are such people not to be trusted to follow the prescribed curriculum? Is it that they lack roots in the polity and hence the necessary knowledge? Might it plausibly be argued that not all aliens are to be distrusted on these grounds and not all citizens are to be trusted? Why cannot the state protect itself by taking action against teachers only after they have taught in such a way as to undermine the state's interest in promoting American values? Or is such an approach too risky? Does it impinge upon the interests of all teachers since constant surveillance of teaching behavior would be required? Do schools routinely do this? If not, does this weaken or strengthen the government's case in *Ambach*?

5. Effectiveness of Teacher Socialization

In note 9, the majority cites social science research for the proposition that teachers have "considerable influence" on the attitudes of students. *See also* Janowitz, *The Reconstruction of Patriotism* (1983). Other research has cast some doubt on the importance of formal schooling for the development of political attitudes. *See, e.g.,* M. Jennings and R. G. Niemi, *The Political Character of Adolescence*, 217–21 (1974). If the second body of research is correct, does this undermine the majority's argument? Should the case turn on the weight of the social science evidence or on "common-sense judgment[s]"?

6. The Legitimacy of the State's Purpose

The alien teachers who brought the suit argued that the New York law sought "to suppress respect for diversity and to compel standardization of ideas." Brief for Appellee at 64, *Ambach v. Norwick*. They argued that the Constitution does not tolerate "laws that cast

a pall of orthodoxy over the classroom." *Keyishian v. Board of Regents*, 385 U.S. 589, 603, 87 S.Ct. 675, 684, 17 L.Ed.2d 629 (1967). *See also Board of Education v. Pico*, 457 U.S. 853, 102 S.Ct. 2799, 73 L.Ed.2d 435 (1982). They also argued that the failure to initiate naturalization is not necessarily a sign of disloyalty to the nation, and aliens may bring to the classroom different perspectives that will benefit the students. In short, they were challenging the governmental purpose of attempting to recruit a group of teachers whose job it would be to voice a set of values and to socialize youngsters in that particular set of values. *See generally* R. Battistoni, *Public Schooling and the Education of Democratic Citizens* (1985); van Geel, "The Search for Constitutional Limits on Government Authority to Inculcate Youth," 62 *Tex. L. Rev.* 197 (1983). Professor Lindblom has gone so far as to urge that teachers close the minds of students to criticism and inquiry, that their job, whether conscious or not, is to use "the school as an instrument for shutting down rather than holding a competition of ideas." C. Lindblom, *Inquiry and Change* 93 (1990). If Lindblom and the others are correct, has the Court missed an opportunity to correct the situation? Are you persuaded by Justice Powell's response, in note 10 of the opinion, that the New York law does not inhibit the plaintiffs from expressing freely their political or social views or from associating with whomever they please? Did the dissent more adequately deal with this challenge? *See* Yudof, *When Government Speaks* 220–24 (1983); Gottlieb, "In the Name of Patriotism: The Constitutionality of 'Bending' History in Public Secondary Schools," 62 *N.Y.U. L. Rev.* 497 (1987). *See generally* C. Lindblom, *Inquiry and Change* (1990).

7. Teacher Loyalty

The majority's opinion in *Ambach* is surprising, when seen against the background of the Court's treatment of the attempts of states to exclude subversives from the teaching profession. The story begins with *Adler v. Board of Education*, 342 U.S. 485, 72 S.Ct. 380, 96 L.Ed. 517 (1952), which upheld a provision of the New York Civil Service Law disqualifying from the civil service and public school system any person who "advocates, advises or teaches" governmental overthrow by force or violence or who organizes or joins any group advocating such doctrine.

In the years following *Adler*, the Court's attitude toward screening out ideologically unfit teachers changed. *Cf. Sweezy v. New Hampshire*, 354 U.S. 234, 77 S.Ct. 1203, 1 L.Ed.2d 1311 (1957);

Slochower v. Board of Higher Education, 350 U.S. 551, 76 S.Ct. 637, 100 L.Ed. 692 (1956). *Cramp v. Board of Public Instruction*, 368 U.S. 278, 82 S.Ct. 275, 7 L.Ed.2d 285 (1961), involved a Florida statute requiring public employees to swear they had never "knowingly lent their aid, support, advice, counsel or influence to the Communist Party." 368 U.S. at 285, 82 S.Ct. at 279. A refusal to take the oath meant immediate discharge. The majority, in striking down the oath requirement, stressed its "extraordinary ambiguity" and found it "completely lacking [in] terms susceptible of objective measurement." 368 U.S. at 286, 82 S.Ct. at 280. Vagueness was also the flaw in the loyalty oath requirements in *Baggett v. Bullitt*, 377 U.S. 360, 84 S.Ct. 1316, 12 L.Ed.2d 377 (1964). *Elfbrandt v. Russell*, 384 U.S. 11, 86 S.Ct. 1238, 16 L.Ed.2d 321 (1966), involved a requirement that state employees swear to support the Constitution, the laws of Arizona, and to defend them against all enemies. Anyone taking the oath who knowingly and willingly became or remained a member of the Communist Party or other organization with a purpose of overthrowing the government was subject to prosecution for perjury and to discharge. The latter provision was declared unconstitutional because it permitted the discharge of those who did not join the subversive organization with the "specific intent" to further illegal action.

In *Keyishian v. Board of Regents*, 385 U.S. 589, 87 S.Ct. 675, 17 L.Ed.2d 629 (1967), faculty members of the State University refused to sign a certificate that required them to declare that they were not Communists, or that if they had been Communists, they had communicated that fact to the President of the State University of New York. Dismissed faculty members challenged a series of related laws that disqualified people from governmental employment for utterance of seditious words, for active or inactive membership in the Communist Party, or for advocating or teaching the doctrine of the forceful overthrow of government. All these provisions were struck down for being overbroad because they imposed sanctions for active or inactive membership unaccompanied by proof of a specific intent to further the unlawful goals of the organization.

In *Connell v. Higgenbotham*, 403 U.S. 207, 91 S.Ct. 1772, 29 L.Ed.2d 418 (1971), the Court upheld an affirmative oath—"That I will support the Constitution of the United States and of the State of Florida." It invalidated a disclaimer oath—"that I do not believe in the overthrow of the Government of the United States or of the State of Florida by force or violence." In *Cole v. Richardson*, 405 U.S. 676, 92 S.Ct. 1332, 31 L.Ed.2d 593 (1972), the Court by a four-to-three vote upheld a two-part loyalty oath required of Massachusetts public employees. The first part required a promise to "uphold and defend" the federal and state constitutions; the second part required a promise to "oppose the overthrow of the government of the United States of America or of this Commonwealth by force, violence or by any illegal or unconstitutional method." Chief Justice Burger found the first part of the oath indistinguishable from the traditionally valid "support" oath. 405 U.S. at 682–83, 92 S.Ct. at 1336–37. As for the second part, the Chief Justice said it did not "require specific action in some hypothetical or actual situation." As he interpreted the "oppose" clause, "it is a commitment not to use illegal and constitutionally unprotected force to change the constitutional system. [It] does not expand the obligation of the first; it simply makes clear the application of the first clause to a particular issue . . . . That the second clause may be redundant is not ground to strike it down; we are not charged with correcting grammar but with enforcing a constitution." 405 U.S. at 684. For discussions of the Court's treatment of academic freedom in the loyalty cases, *see* T. Emerson, *The System of Freedom of Expression* 600–04, 616 (1970); Byrne, "Academic Freedom: A 'Special Concern of the First Amendment,'" 99 *Yale L.J.* 251, 289–98 (1989); Goldstein, "The Asserted Constitutional Right of Public School Teachers to Determine What They Teach," 124 *U. Pa. L. Rev.* 1293, 1295–98 (1976). Why does not *West Virginia State Board of Education v. Barnette*, 319 U.S. 624, 63 S.Ct. 1178, 87 L.Ed. 1628 (1943), render all loyalty oaths unconstitutional?

8. *Freedom of Association*

In *Shelton v. Tucker*, 364 U.S. 479, 81 S.Ct. 247, 5 L.Ed.2d 231 (1960), plaintiff, a public schoolteacher in the Little Rock Schools for twenty-five years, was a member of the National Association for the Advancement of Colored People. He was dismissed from employment when he refused to comply with the requirements of a state law that he file "annually an affidavit listing without limitation every organization to which he has belonged or regularly contributed within the preceding five years." 364 U.S. at 480, 81 S.Ct. at 248. The statute was adopted "to assist in the solution" of problems raised by the Supreme Court's decisions in school desegregation cases. In striking down the provision, Justice Stewart notes that a state may inquire into the fitness and competence of its teachers. Yet to compel a teacher to disclose his every associational tie would undermine his right of free association. "Even if there were no disclosure to the general public, the pressure upon a teacher to avoid any ties which might displease those who control his professional destiny would be constant and heavy. . . ." 364 U.S. at 485–86, 81 S.Ct. at 250–51. Under the circumstances, the Court held that the statute should be tested against the requirement that government use the least drastic means for achieving its purposes and that the unlimited and indiscriminate sweep of the statute went far beyond what might be justified in the exercise of the state's legitimate inquiry into the fitness and competency of its teachers. 364 U.S. at 488, 490, 81 S.Ct. at 252, 253. *See* Byrne, *supra* at 293–98.

Teachers and other public employees also are protected from dismissal for the sole reason of their affiliation with a particular party or candidate for public office. *Branti v. Finkel*, 445 U.S. 507, 100 S.Ct. 1287, 63 L.Ed.2d 574 (1980); *Elrod v. Burns*, 427 U.S. 347, 96 S.Ct. 2673, 49 L.Ed.2d 547 (1976); *Kinsey v. Salado Indep. Sch. Dist.*, 916 F.2d 273 (5th Cir. 1990); *Kercado-Melendez v. Aponte-Roque*, 829 F.2d 255 (1st Cir. 1987). How do the freedom of association and party affiliation cases alter the government's ability to socialize youngsters to particular norms? Do they suggest that the state may not seek to recruit a homogenous faculty for its public schools? If so, is *Ambach* inconsistent with these cases?

4. Teacher Rights of Expression

Pickering v. Board of Education
391 U.S. 563, 88 S.Ct. 1731, 20 L.Ed.2d 811 (1968).

Mr. Justice Marshall delivered the opinion of the Court.

Appellant Marvin L. Pickering, a teacher in Township High School District 205, Will County, Illinois, was dismissed from his position by the appellee Board of Education for sending a letter to a local newspaper in connection with a recently proposed tax increase that was critical of the way in which the Board and the district superintendent of schools had handled past proposals to raise new revenue for the schools. Appellant's dismissal resulted from a deter-mination by the Board, after a full hearing, that the publication of the letter was "detrimental to the efficient operation and administration of the schools of the district" and hence, under the relevant Illinois statute, Ill. Rev.Stat., c. 122, § 10-22.4 (1963), that "interests of the schools require[d] [his dismissal]."

* * *

In May of 1964 a proposed increase in the tax rate to be used for educational purposes was submitted to the voters by the Board and was defeated. Finally, on September 19, 1964, a second proposal to increase the tax rate was submitted by the Board and was likewise defeated. It was in connection with this last proposal of the School Board that appellant wrote the letter to the editor . . . that resulted in his dismissal.

Prior to the vote on the second tax increase proposal a variety of articles attributed to the District 205 Teachers' Organization appeared in the local paper. These articles urged passage of the tax increase and stated that failure to pass the increase would result in a decline in the quality of education afforded children in the district's schools. A letter from the superintendent of schools making the same point was published in the paper two days before the election and submitted to the voters in mimeographed form the following day. It was in response to the foregoing material, together with the failure of the tax increase to pass, that appellant submitted the letter in question to the editor of the local paper.

The letter constituted, basically, an attack on the School Board's handling of the 1961 bond issue proposals and its subsequent allocation of financial resources between the schools' educational and athletic programs. It also charged the superintendent of schools with attempting to prevent teachers in the district from opposing or criticizing the proposed bond issue.

The Board dismissed Pickering for writing and publishing the letter. Pursuant to Illinois law, the Board was then required to hold a hearing on the dismissal. At the hearing the Board charged that numerous statements in the letter were false and that the publication of the statements unjustifiably impugned the "motives, honesty, integrity, truthfulness, responsibility and competence" of both the Board and the school administration. The Board also charged that the false statements damaged the professional reputations of its members and of the school administrators, would be disruptive of faculty discipline, and would tend to foment "controversy, conflict, and dissension" among teachers, administrators, the Board of Education, and the residents of the district.. . .

The Illinois courts reviewed the proceedings solely to determine whether the Board's findings were supported by substantial evidence and whether, on the facts as found, the Board could reasonably conclude that appellant's publication of the letter was "detrimental to the best interests of the schools." Pickering's claim that his letter was protected by the First Amendment was rejected on the ground that his acceptance of a teaching position in the public schools obliged him to refrain from making statements about the operation of the schools "which in the absence of such position he would have an undoubted right to engage in." . . .

To the extent that the Illinois Supreme Court's opinion may be read to suggest that teachers may constitutionally be compelled to relinquish the First Amendment rights they would otherwise enjoy as citizens to comment on matters of public interest in connection with the operation of the public schools in which they work, it proceeds on the premise that has been unequivocally rejected in numerous prior decisions of this Court. *E.g., Wieman v. Updegraff,* 344 U.S. 183 (1952); *Shelton v. Tucker,* 364 U.S. 479 (1960); *Keyishian v. Board of Regents,* 385 U.S. 589 (1967). "[T]he theory that public employment which may be denied altogether may be subjected to any conditions, regardless of how unreasonable, has been uniformly rejected." *Keyishian v. Board of Regents, supra,* at 605–06. At the same time it cannot be gainsaid that the State has interests as an employer in regulating the speech of its employees that differ significantly from those it possesses in connection with regulation of the speech of the citizenry in general. The problem in any case is to arrive at a balance between the interests of the teacher, as a citizen, in commenting upon matters of public concern and the interest of the State, as an employer, in promoting the efficiency of the public services it performs through its employees.

The Board contends that "the teacher by virtue of his public employment has a duty of loyalty to support his superiors in attaining the generally accepted goals of education and that, if he must speak out publicly, he should do so factually and accu-

rately, commensurate with his education and experience." Appellant, on the other hand, argues that the test applicable to defamatory statements directed against public officials by persons having no occupational relationship with them, namely, that statements to be legally actionable must be made "with knowledge that [they were] . . . false or with reckless disregard of whether [they were] . . . false or not," *New York Times Co. v. Sullivan,* 376 U.S. 254, 280 (1964), should also be applied to public statements made by teachers. . . .

An examination of the statements in appellant's letter objected to by the Board reveals that they, like the letter as a whole, consist essentially of criticism of the Board's allocation of school funds between educational and athletic programs, and of both the Board's and the superintendent's methods of informing, or preventing the informing of, the district's taxpayers of the real reasons why additional tax revenues were being sought for the schools. The statements are in no way directed toward any person with whom appellant would normally be in contact in the course of his daily work as a teacher. Thus no question of maintaining either discipline by immediate superiors or harmony among coworkers is presented here. Appellant's employment relationships with the Board and, to a somewhat lesser extent, with the superintendent are not the kind of close working relationships for which it can persuasively be claimed that personal loyalty and confidence are necessary to their proper functioning. Accordingly, to the extent that the Board's position here can be taken to suggest that even comments on matters of public concern that are substantially correct, . . . may furnish grounds for dismissal if they are sufficiently critical in tone, we unequivocally reject it.[3]

We next consider the statements in appellant's letter which we agree to be false. The Board's original charges included allegations that the publication of the letter damaged the professional reputations of the Board and the superintendent and would foment controversy and conflict among the Board, teachers, administrators, and the residents of the district. However, no evidence to support these allegations was introduced at the hearing. So far as the record reveals, Pickering's letter was greeted by everyone but its main tar-

---

[3]It is possible to conceive of some positions in public employment in which the need for confidentiality is so great that even completely correct public statements might furnish a permissible ground for dismissal. Likewise, positions in public employment in which the relationship between superior and subordinate is of such a personal and intimate nature that certain forms of public criticism of the superior by the subordinate would seriously undermine the effectiveness of the working relationship between them can also be imagined. We intimate no views as to how we would resolve any specific instances of such situations, but merely note that significantly different considerations would be involved in such cases.

get, the Board, with massive apathy and total disbelief. The Board must, therefore, have decided, perhaps by analogy with the law of libel, that the statements were *per se* harmful to the operation of the schools.

However, the only way in which the Board could conclude, absent any evidence of the actual effect of the letter, that the statements contained therein were *per se* detrimental to the interest of the schools was to equate the Board members' own interests with that of the schools. Certainly an accusation that too much money is being spent on athletics by the administrators of the school system . . . cannot reasonably be regarded as *per se* detrimental to the district schools . . . .

In addition, the fact that particular illustrations of the Board's claimed undesirable emphasis on athletic programs are false would not normally have any necessary impact on the actual operation of the schools, beyond its tendency to anger the Board. For example, Pickering's letter was written after the defeat at the polls of the second proposed tax increase. It could, therefore, have had no effect on the ability of the school district to raise necessary revenue, since there was no showing that there was any proposal to increase taxes pending when the letter was written.

More importantly, the question whether a school system requires additional funds is a matter of legitimate public concern on which the judgment of the school administration, including the School Board, cannot, in a society that leaves such questions to popular vote, be taken as conclusive. On such a question free and open debate is vital to informed decisionmaking by the electorate. Teachers are, as a class, the members of a community most likely to have informed and definite opinions as to how funds allotted to the operation of the schools should be spent. Accordingly, it is essential that they be able to speak out freely on such questions without fear of retaliatory dismissal.

In addition, the amounts expended on athletics which Pickering reported erroneously were matters of public record on which his position as a teacher in the district did not qualify him to speak with any greater authority than any other taxpayer. The Board could easily have rebutted appellant's errors by publishing the accurate figures itself, either via a letter to the same newspaper or otherwise. We are thus not presented with a situation in which a teacher has carelessly made false statements about matters so closely related to the day-to-day operations of the schools that any harmful impact on the public would be difficult to counter because of the teacher's presumed greater access to the real facts. Accordingly, we have no occasion to consider at this time whether under such circumstances a school board could reasonably require that a teacher make substantial efforts to verify the accuracy of his charges before publishing them.[4]

What we do have before us is a case in which a teacher has made erroneous public statements upon issues then currently the subject of public attention, which are critical of his ultimate employer but which are neither shown nor can be presumed to have in any way either impeded the teacher's proper performance of his daily duties in the classroom[5] or to have interfered with the regular operation of the schools generally. In these circumstances we conclude that the interest of the school administration in limiting teachers' opportunities to contribute to public debate is not significantly greater than its interest in limiting a similar contribution by any member of the general public.

* * *

In sum, we hold that, in a case such as this, absent proof of false statements knowingly or recklessly made by him,[6] a teacher's exercise of his right to speak on issues of public importance may not furnish the basis for his dismissal from public employment. Since no such showing has been made in this case regarding appellant's letter . . . his dismissal for writing it cannot be upheld and the judgment of the Illinois Supreme Court must, accordingly, be reversed and the case remanded for further proceedings not inconsistent with this opinion.

Mr. Justice White, concurring in part and dissenting in part.

The Court holds that truthful statements by a school teacher critical of the school board are within

---

[4]There is likewise no occasion furnished by this case for consideration of the extent to which teachers can be required by narrowly drawn grievance procedures to submit complaints about the operation of the schools to their superiors for action thereon prior to bringing the complaints before the public.

[5]We also note that this case does not present a situation in which a teacher's public statements are so without foundation as to call into question his fitness to perform his duties in the classroom. In such a case, of course, the statements would merely be evidence of the teacher's general competence, or lack thereof, and not an independent basis for dismissal.

[6]Because we conclude that appellant's statements were not knowingly or recklessly false, we have no occasion to pass upon the additional question whether a statement that was knowingly or recklessly false would if it were neither shown nor could reasonably be presumed to have had any harmful effects, still be protected by the First Amendment. *See also* n. 5, *supra*.

the ambit of the First Amendment. So also are false statements innocently or negligently made. The State may not fire the teacher for making either unless, as I gather it, there are special circumstances, not present in this case, demonstrating an overriding state interest, such as the need for confidentiality or the special obligations which a teacher in a particular position may owe to his superiors.[1]

The core of today's decision is the holding that Pickering's discharge must be tested by the standard of *New York Times Co. v. Sullivan*, 376 U.S. 254 (1964). To this extent I am in agreement.

The Court goes on, however, to reopen a question I had thought settled by *New York Times* and the cases that followed it, particularly *Garrison v. Louisiana*, 379 U.S. 64 (1964). The Court devotes several pages to reexamining the facts in order to reject the determination below that Pickering's statements harmed the school system, *ante*, at 570–73, when the question of harm is clearly irrelevant given the Court's determination that Pickering's statements were neither knowingly nor recklessly false and its ruling that in such circumstances a teacher may not be fired even if the statements are injurious. The Court then gratuitously suggests that when statements are found to be knowingly or recklessly false, it is an open question whether the First Amendment still protects them unless they are shown or can be presumed to have caused harm. *Ante*, at 574, n. 6. Deliberate or reckless falsehoods serve no First Amendment ends and deserve no protection under that Amendment. The Court unequivocally recognized this in *Garrison*, where after reargument the Court said that "the knowingly false statement and the false statement made with reckless disregard of the truth, do not enjoy constitutional protection." 379 U.S. at 75. The Court today neither explains nor justifies its withdrawal from the firm stand taken in *Garrison*. As I see it, a teacher may be fired without violation of the First Amendment for knowingly or recklessly making false statements regardless of their harmful impact on the schools. As the Court holds, however, in the absence of special circumstances he may not be fired if his statements were true or only negligently false, even if there is some harm to the school system. . . .

Nor can I join the Court in its findings with regard to whether Pickering knowingly or recklessly published false statements. Neither the State in presenting its evidence nor the state tribunals in arriving at their findings and conclusions of law addressed themselves to the elements of the new standard which the Court holds the First Amendment to require in the circumstances of this case. Indeed, the state courts expressly rejected the applicability of both *New York Times* and *Garrison*. I find it wholly unsatisfactory for this Court to make the initial determination of knowing or reckless falsehood from the cold record now before us. It would be far more appropriate to remand this case to the state courts for further proceedings in light of the constitutional standard which the Court deems applicable to this case, once the relevant facts have been ascertained in appropriate proceedings.

NOTES AND QUESTIONS

1. *The* Pickering *Standard*

Justice Marshall's opinion specifies the circumstances in which an employee is to be protected from dismissal for publicly voicing criticism of the school board's policies. The critical question is whether the school employee has "the kind of close working relationship [with the board and superintendent], which . . . [requires] personal loyalty and confidence" for the employee to carry out his functions. *See Cox v. Dardanelle Public School District*, 790 F.2d 668 (8th Cir. 1986); *Derrickson v. Board of Education*, 738 F.2d 351 (8th Cir. 1984). How does the *Pickering* test differ from the *Tinker* test, discussed earlier in the chapter? Should *Pickering* apply to within-school utterances? May a professor's speech that substantially disrupts the educational process be the basis for dismissal or sanctions? *See, e.g., Adamian v. Jacobsen*, 523 F.2d 929 (9th Cir. 1975), *aff'd after remand sub nom. Adamian v. Lombardi*, 608 F.2d 1224 (9th Cir. 1979); *Franklin v. Leland Stanford Univ.*, 172 Cal.App.3d 322, 218 Cal.Rptr. 228 (Cal.App.1985). When is the former test applicable? Should it matter whether the employee personally criticizes individ-

---

[1]*See ante*, at 569–70, 572 and nn. 3, 4. The Court does not elaborate upon its suggestion that there may be situations in which, with reference to certain areas of public comment, a teacher may have special obligations to his superiors. It simply holds that in this case, with respect to the particular public comment made by *Pickering*, he is more like a member of the general public and, apparently, too remote from the school board to require placing him into any special category. Further, as I read the Court's opinion, it does not foreclose the possibility that under the First Amendment a school system may have an enforceable rule, applicable to teachers, that public statements about school business must first be submitted to the authorities to check for accuracy.

ual superiors or only offers a general critique of school policies? *See Stevenson v. Lower Marion County School District No. 3*, 285 S.C. 62, 327 S.E.2d 656 (1985). Is the emphasis on loyalty a variation of the material-disruption standard of *Tinker*? Does the Court adequately accommodate the public's need for "insider" information and the school authorities' need for confidentiality and loyalty?

What would have been the outcome of the case if Pickering had been the assistant superintendent for academic affairs or the director of the athletic program? What if the case had involved a teacher who played an instrumental role in attempting to dismiss the school superintendent? *See Watts v. Seward School Board*, 395 P.2d 372 (Alaska 1964), *vacated*, 381 U.S. 126, 85 S.Ct. 1321, 14 L.Ed.2d 261 (1965), *on remand*, 421 P.2d 586 (Alaska 1966), *reh'g denied*, 423 P.2d 678 (Alaska 1967), *vacated*, 391 U.S. 592, 88 S.Ct. 1753, 20 L.Ed.2d 842 (1968), *on remand*, 454 P.2d 732 (Alaska 1969).

What would result if an African American teacher criticized school policies regarding black participation in the administrative and instructional process, and was fired on the ground that for philosophical reasons the teacher and school principal could not get along; "one or the other must go"? *See Roberts v. Lake Central School Corp.*, 317 F.Supp. 63 (N.D. Ind. 1970). *See also Jordan v. Cagel*, 474 F.Supp. 1198 (N.D. Miss. 1979), *aff'd mem.*, 620 F.2d 298 (5th Cir. 1980). *See generally Ayoub v. Texas A & M University*, 927 F.2d 834 (5th Cir. 1991).

Does *Pickering* provide protection for a school counselor who, concerned that children were being placed in classes for the mentally retarded because they were tested in English rather than in their native language, advised the parents of affected children to consult the local legal aid society? *See Bernasconi v. Tempe Elementary School District*, 548 F.2d 857 (9th Cir. 1977), *cert. denied*, 434 U.S. 825, 98 S.Ct. 72, 54 L.Ed.2d 82.

2. False Statements

Does the Court's test concerning false statements apply to matters of opinion? What is the difference between a matter of opinion and a matter of fact? *See D'Andrea v. Adams*, 626 F.2d 469, 473 n. 2 (5th Cir. 1980). Should a false statement ever form a constitutionally adequate basis for dismissal, in the absence of interference with working relationships? Does the answer depend on whether the statement was negligently or intentionally made? Whether the speaker uttered the words in reckless disregard of the truth?

The Court leaves open the possibility that a teacher's public statements could be used by a school board as evidence of a lack of fitness to perform his or her duties in the classroom, for example, as when a mathematics teacher publishes a letter filled with computational errors. Might such public expressions be used as evidence that the teacher has character traits undesirable in an employee? *See Garza v. Rodriguez*, 559 F.2d 259 (5th Cir. 1977), *cert. denied*, 439 U.S. 877, 99 S.Ct. 215, 58 L.Ed.2d 191 (1978).

3. Speech Directed to Fellow Teachers and/or the Principal

Might teachers be dismissed for regularly voicing criticism of the principal, superintendent, and/or school board to other teachers? What sort of disruptive impact would warrant dismissal? *See Stroman v. Colleton Cty. Sch. Dist.*, 981 F.2d 152 (4th Cir. 1993); *McGill v. Board of Education of Pekin Elementary School*, 602 F.2d 774 (7th Cir. 1979). May a teacher circulate a questionnaire among other teachers asking their opinion of their "leaders" and their opinion of school decision-making and grievance processes? *See Lindsey v. Board of Regents*, 607 F.2d 672 (5th Cir. 1979).

4. Criticism Expressed in the Classroom or before a Student Audience

Should the *Pickering* doctrine protect teachers who voice their criticisms in the classroom? *See Clark v. Holmes*, 474 F.2d 928 (7th Cir. 1972), *cert. denied*, 411 U.S. 972, 93 S.Ct. 2148, 36 L.Ed.2d 695 (1973); *Moore v. School Board of Gulf County Florida*, 364 F.Supp. 355 (N.D. Fla. 1973). Do the standards of *Pickering*, *Tinker*, or *Cary* control in this situation? Should the frequency of the practice, the age group, the degree of student unrest caused, the relevance of the comments to the course, the kind of language used, and/or the salience of the issue to the lives of the students make a difference?

Cox v. Dardanelle Public School District
790 F.2d 668 (8th Cir. 1986).

Before McMillian, Circuit Judge, Henley, Senior Circuit Judge, and John R. Gibson, Circuit Judge.

John R. Gibson, Circuit Judge.

The Dardanelle Public School District and its officials, as individuals, appeal the judgment of the district court, sitting without a jury, that the school district impermissibly failed to renew the contract of appellee, Nancy Cox, in retaliation for speech and conduct protected by the first amendment, in violation of 42 U.S.C. § 1983 (1982). The appellants contend that the district court improperly concluded that appellee's activities were protected by the first amendment. They further contend that the district court erred in finding that the protected activities in which the appellee engaged were the motivating factor in the decision not to renew her teaching contract, and that but for her protected speech, she would have been rehired. . . . We affirm the judgment of the district court.

Appellee Nancy Cox was first hired by the Dardanelle Public School District to teach eighth grade English at the district's Middle School for the 1976–77 school year. Her employment contract was renewed by the School Board each of the following two years. During the first two years Cox taught at the Middle School, she established a good working relationship with the principal, Ed Bradshaw, who served as her immediate supervisor. Bradshaw gave Cox good evaluations and recommended each year that she be rehired.

At the beginning of the 1979–80 school year, the third year Cox was employed by the School District, appellant John Dillard replaced Ed Bradshaw as principal of the Middle School. During this same school year Cox became more active in the teachers local organization, the Dardanelle Education Association (DEA), and was appointed DEA representative to the Middle School for the 1979–80 school year.

The difficulties between Cox and Dillard were best illustrated by the following factual findings of the district court:

> 4. Defendant Johnny L. Dillard replaced Ed Bradshaw as Principal of the Dardanelle Middle School before the beginning of the 1979–80 school term. Defendant Dillard implemented several changes in the regulations under which the teachers had performed their duties in previous years. Plaintiff, along with a majority of the other members of the faculty of the Dardanelle Middle School, Upper Building, disagreed with some of defendant Dillard's methods.
>
> 5. Plaintiff on numerous occasions spoke out concerning the administration of the educational process at the Dardanelle Middle School, oftentimes in disagreement with defendant Dillard. On November 6, 1979, plaintiff, along with a number of the other faculty members of her school, caused a grievance to be filed with defendant Dillard concerning the educational process in their school. In that grievance, the teachers requested defendant Dillard to meet with them to discuss their dis-

satisfaction with the educational process then existing. Defendant Dillard instructed the teachers to file individual grievances if they wished to have their concerns addressed by him. Three teachers, Richard Johnson, Maxine Kemp and plaintiff, submitted individual grievances reflecting their names thereon to defendant Dillard. All three of the teachers submitting individual grievances were the victims of job-related sanctions from all the defendants herein. Richard Johnson was terminated in February, 1980, plaintiff was dismissed at the conclusion of the 1979–80 school term, and Maxine Kemp was placed on a probationary status for the 1980–81 school term. None of the other members of the Dardanelle Middle School Upper Building faculty suffered any job-related sanctions during or at the conclusion of the 1979–80 school term.

> 7. Plaintiff was informed by defendant Fugatt by letter received on or about February 29, 1980, that he was recommending to the Board of Education that her contract not be renewed for the coming school term. Later, on April 1, 1980, plaintiff received a letter from the President of the School Board specifying eleven (11) grounds for the Superintendent's nonrenewal recommendation. A hearing was held before the School Board on April 16 and 23, 1980, to consider the matter of the nonrenewal recommendation as to plaintiff's employment. After hearing considerable evidence from defendants Fugatt and Dillard, as well as plaintiff and other witnesses, the School Board voted on each of the grounds listed by the Board President in his letter to plaintiff and relied upon by defendant Fugatt. Of those eleven (11) charges, the Board voted that four (4) were false, that four (4) were true but not sufficient grounds for nonrenewal, noted that one (1) had been withdrawn by the Board's attorney, and voted that two (2) were true and constituted sufficient grounds relied upon by the Board in dismissing plaintiff were "(1) on August 30, August 31, September 4, September 7, and September 10, Mrs. Cox refused to follow directions in that she signed in for Mr. Johnson.", and "(2) on February 15, Mrs. Cox refused to follow administrative policy in that she allowed her class to be interrupted by a visitor without permission from the Principal."

Cox v. Dardanelle Public School District, No. LR-C-80-441, . . . (E.D.Ark. April 23, 1984).

The district court found that the appellants had dismissed Cox not for alleged insubordination in failing to comply with administrative directives, but because of her continued expressions of disagreement over the educational policies in force in the Middle School. The district court also found that the grounds advanced by the appellants for Cox's renewal were "pretextual and insignificant," . . . and further, that but for her criticisms, Cox's contract would have been renewed by the School Board. The court also concluded as a matter of law that Cox's expressions were protected by the first amendment. The court thereupon awarded Cox damages for the wrongful dismissal. The appellants filed the instant appeal.

Claims by public employees that they have suffered job-related sanctions as a result of speech are considered in accordance with the now familiar analysis set out by the Supreme Court in *Mt. Healthy City School District Board of Education v. Doyle,* 429 U.S. 274, 97 S.Ct. 568, 50 L.Ed.2d 471 (1977). As a threshold matter, a plaintiff must demonstrate that the speech or conduct, which she alleges as the basis of the adverse employment decision, was entitled to constitutional protection; she must then show that this protected conduct was a substantial or motivating factor in the adverse employment decision; the burden then shifts to the employer to show by a preponderance of the evidence that it would have taken the same action absent the employee's protected conduct. . . .

A

Whether a public employee's expressions are constitutionally protected involves a two-step inquiry. *Connick v. Myers,* 461 U.S. 138, 143–47, 103 S.Ct. 1684, 1688–90, 75 L.Ed.2d 708 (1983). Initially, a court must conclude that the employee's speech can be "fairly characterized as constituting speech on a matter of public concern . . ." *Id.* at 146, 103 S.Ct. at 1689; if the speech falls within this category, the court must then balance "the interest of the [employee] as a citizen, in commenting upon matters of public concern and the interests of the state, as an employer, in promoting the efficiency of the public service it performs through its employees." *Id.* at 142, 103 S.Ct. at 1687 (quoting *Pickering v. Board of Education,* 391 U.S. 563, 568, 88 S.Ct. 1731, 1734, 20 L.Ed.2d 811 (1968)).

The district court concluded that Cox's speech, for the most part, was an "expression of her own ideas concerning the educational process in the Dardanelle Middle School . . . ," . . . and therefore related to a matter of public import. Appellants contend that this conclusion is wrong as a matter of law[4] and that appellant's expressions amounted to no more than her "personal objections to employee work rules," . . . and thus, as expressions of private and not public concern, are not entitled to constitutional protection.

Whether a public employee's expressions relate to a matter of public concern must be considered in light of the "content, form, and context of a given statement, as revealed by the whole record." *Connick,* 461 U.S. at 147–48, 103 S.Ct. at 1690. . . . The question in each case is whether the employee's expressions can be "fairly characterized as relating to any matter of political, social, or other concern to the community . . . ." *Id.* at 146, 103 S.Ct. at 1689. Where a public employee speaks out in public or in private[5] on matters that relate solely to the employee's parochial concerns as an employee, no first amendment interests are at stake. *Id.* at 146, 103 S.Ct. at 1689. The focus is on the role the employee has assumed in advancing the particular expressions: that of a concerned public citizen, informing the public that the state institution is not properly discharging its duties, or engaged in some way in misfeasance, malfeasance or nonfeasance; or merely as an employee, concerned only with internal policies or practices which are of relevance only to the employees of that institution. . . .

Our review of the record convinces us that Cox's speech was composed of more than criticisms of internal personnel policies, but touched on matters of public concern, and was therefore entitled to constitutional protection. To begin with, not all of Cox's speech was directed at Dillard's personnel policies. The very first dispute between Cox and Dillard related to the District's decision to abandon ability grouping of students. The educational theories and practices employed by school administrators is [sic] clearly a question of public concern. The questions how we teach the young, what we teach them, and the environment in which we teach them are of the most central concern to every community in the nation. . . .

---

[4]"The inquiry into the protected status of speech is one of law, not fact." *Connick,* 461 U.S. at 148 n. 7, 103 S.Ct. at 1690 n. 7; *Roberts v. Van Buren Public Schools,* 773 F.2d 949, 954 (8th Cir. 1985).

[5]It is clear that an employee's right to speak out on matters of public concern is not forfeited by the choice of a private forum. *Givhan v. Western Consolidated School District,* 439 U.S. 410, 415–16, 99 S.Ct. 693, of a private forum. *Givhan v. Western Consolidated School District,* 439 U.S. 410, 415–16, 99 S.Ct. 693, 696–97, 58 L.Ed.2d 619 (1979). Although the time, place, and manner of the speech are generally irrelevant to the inquiry into the public import of the speech, they may be relevant in striking the balance between the employee's and employer's interests. *Id.* at 415 n. 4, 99 S.Ct. at 696 n. 4; *see infra* p. 674.

Additionally, we believe that much of Cox's speech directed at the school's personnel policies was not motivated solely by employment concerns, but was legitimate criticism of policies and administration which affected the educational function of the school.[6] Cox was critical in her individual grievance, and by proxy, in the general grievance, of the manner in which Dillard dealt with the faculty, and expressed the view that Dillard's administrative style had discouraged teacher input, inhibited teachers' use of different teaching techniques and classroom methods, significantly affected teacher morale at the school, and affected the students. . . .

Cox's statements on these matters were not the comments of a single employee bearing on issues unique to that employee. . . . Nor were her comments concerned solely with the immediate supervisor-employee relationship between Dillard and the faculty. They obviously touch in great measure upon the ability of Dillard and the faculty to "discharge . . . the public function of education." . . . Cox's comments are clearly attempts to inform Dillard, and ultimately his superiors, that his actions were interfering with the efficient and proper discharge of the crucial responsibilities of the faculty.[7]

We therefore conclude that a significant portion of Cox's speech was of public concern. We must now balance appellee's interest in advancing these expressions with the state's legitimate interest in the "effective and efficient fulfillment of its responsibilities to the public." *Connick*, 461 U.S. at 150, 103 S.Ct. at 1691; *Pickering*, 391 U.S. at 568, 88 S.Ct. at 1734.

An employee's interest in freely commenting on matters of public concern must generally give way to the state's interest in efficiently fulfilling its responsibilities where the employee's speech significantly impairs her ability to perform her duties, disrupts working relationships and harmony among co-workers, or otherwise impedes the normal operations of the institution. *McGee v. South Pemiscot School District R-V*, 712 F.2d 339, 342 (8th Cir. 1983). . . . Where the employee's comments threaten to disrupt or impair close working relationships particularly requiring personal loyalty and confidence, the state must be given an even wider degree of deference. . . . Furthermore, while the fact that an employee's comments are made to superiors in private does not strip them of constitutional protection, . . . the state is entitled to consider whether the time, place and manner of the private expression affected or threatened working relationships and the efficient operations of the institution. . . .

There is no evidence that Cox's criticisms throughout the year introduced discord into otherwise harmonious relations with her colleagues. To the contrary, the evidence indicates that this dispute was between a majority of the teachers at the Middle School and the principal. Moreover, there is no evidence that Cox's speech affected her teaching performance.[8] Nor is there evidence that Cox willfully disobeyed any directive that affected her teaching duties. . . .

Nor do we believe that any statements by Cox can fairly be said to have disrupted her relationship with Dillard. The evidence indicates that the primary source of the disruption in their relationship (indeed, the cause of disruption of the relationship between a majority of the faculty and Dillard), was Dillard's implementation and enforcement of the personnel policies, not Cox's speech. . . . Although we do not intend to minimize the importance of teacher-principal relationship, . . . it is not a "relationship between superior and subordinate . . . of such a personal and intimate nature that certain forms of [] criticism of the superior by the subordinate would seriously undermine the effectiveness of the working relationship between them . . . ." *Pickering*, 391 U.S. at 570 n. 3, 88 S.Ct. at 1735 n. 3. The teacher-principal relationship is not of such a personal and intimate nature that teachers must be precluded from filing responsible grievances. . . .

---

[6]Cox's criticism of the policies requiring teachers to sign in and out and forbidding personal use of the office phones, and her criticism regarding the timing of announcements and messages during the day all bear on internal matters relevant only to the employees of the school, and are not constitutionally protected. *Cf. Knapp v. Whitaker*, 757 F.2d at 827, 840 (7th Cir. 1985) (teacher's remarks on classroom assignments and content of evaluations merely internal, personal matters, not protected speech).

[7]The Court in *Connick* did not hold that criticism of the way in which one's superior administers the office or institution is always solely a question of internal concern. As Justice Brennan noted in dissent, "It is beyond doubt that personnel decisions that adversely affect discipline and morale may ultimately impair an agency's efficient performance of its duties," and comment on these decisions, therefore, is a matter of agency's efficient performance of its duties," and comment on these decisions, therefore, is a matter of public concern as "of interest to persons seeking to develop informed opinions about the manner in which . . . an . . . official charged with managing a vital governmental agency[] discharges his responsibilities." 461 U.S. at 163, 103 S.Ct. at 1698 (Brennan, J., dissenting). The majority did not in principle disagree with Justice Brennan's observations, but only as they applied in the particular context—a questionnaire soliciting employees' views primarily on internal policies relating to transfers and office morale, distributed by an employee transferred against her wishes. . . .

[8]The appellees have not suggested that Cox brought her criticism of Dillard's policies into the classroom. We recognize that a number of the grounds advanced by Dillard and Fugatt for the decision not to renew Cox's contract suggest that Cox's teaching was below acceptable standards. However, there is no suggestion that these putative shortcomings were connected to her protected speech. Furthermore, the School Board found all but one of these charges to be either false or an insufficient ground for nonrenewal, and the district court found these grounds to be pretexts.

Finally, there is no allegation that the time, place or manner of appellee's speech aggravated her relationship with Dillard or impeded the normal operation of the school. Cox did not attempt to circumvent the chain of command . . . nor is there a suggestion that her individual grievance or criticisms throughout the year were intemperate, or antagonistic. . . .

B

The appellants argue that even if Cox's speech, on balance, was constitutionally protected, it was not the motivating factor in the Board's decision not to renew her contract. They contend that the Board's decision was based on Cox's repeated refusal to comply with proper administrative directives, not her criticism of those directives.

A public employee generally can be discharged for refusing to follow administrative policies and directives, even those they contend are misguided. . . . Of the eleven charges listed by the superintendent in his letter to Cox and advanced to the Board, only two were found by the Board to be true and sufficient grounds for nonrenewal: Cox's violation of the sign-in policy on several occasions by signing in for a fellow teacher, Richard Johnson; and her violation of the policy forbidding unauthorized visitors in the classroom.

Whether the protected conduct of the plaintiff was a substantial or motivating factor in the adverse employment decision is question of fact. . . .

We believe that there is sufficient evidence in the record to support the district court's finding that Cox's speech motivated the Board not to renew her contract. Dillard admitted that Cox's individual grievance likely was a factor in subsequent decisions he made regarding her employment. At least three memoranda Dillard placed in Cox's personnel file, describing actions of Cox which he believed violated administrative policies or were improper, made reference to the grievance and suggested in each case that Cox's actions were not consistent with the criticisms she had levied against him in the grievance. . . . Furthermore, the district court took explicit notice of the fact that only the three teachers who filed individual grievances were subject that year to job-related sanctions. . . . The district court's decision is not clearly erroneous.[9]

C

The appellants also argue that the district court erred in finding that the teachers did not successfully discharge the burden of demonstrating by a preponderance of the evidence that the School Board would have reached the same decision but for Cox's protected conduct. *Cf. Mt. Healthy City Board of Education*, 429 U.S. at 287, 97 S.Ct. at 576. As with the previous question of causation, this is a question of fact, and thus subject to review on the clearly erroneous standard. . . .

There is ample evidence to sustain the district court's finding. The appellants offer no reasons other than those advanced by Dillard and Fugatt and considered by the School Board to justify the employment decision. The School Board found only two of the eleven proferred charges sufficient for adverse action, and the district court concluded that these two were mere pretexts and too insignificant to support the allegations. . . .

We also reject appellants' argument that because the School Board members were unaware of Cox's grievance and other criticisms of Dillard's policies, their decision not to renew Cox's contract was not tainted by any impermissible motive. The district court could reasonably conclude that the Board would not have considered an adverse action against Cox had Dillard and Fugatt not advanced these retaliatory charges.

NOTES AND QUESTIONS

1. Matters of Public Concern and Constitutional Theory

The court relies on *Connick v. Myers* for a two-step test for determining whether Nancy Cox's speech is entitled to constitutional protection. *See generally* M. McCarthy & N. Cambion-McCabe, *Public School Law* 272–81 (1988). First, the court must decide whether the speech may be appropriately characterized as addressing "a matter of public concern." Second, if it is a matter of public concern, then the court should apply *Pickering* and determine whether the interest of the teacher in speaking as a citizen is

---

[9]We note, moreover, that neither violation of the administrative policies appears to have been intended as deliberate insubordination. We do not intend to imply that public employees can be sanctioned only for purposeful violations of the rules. However, the rather insignificant nature of the charges here lends support to the district court's finding that the decision not to renew Cox's contract was based not on her performance as a teacher, but upon her conduct and complaints. . . .

outweighed by the state's interest in promoting efficiency in the delivery of educational services in the public schools. Does *Pickering* support this two-part test? Has *Connick* significantly altered the law applicable to public employees? What is the purpose of the "public concern" branch of the test? *See generally* Estlund, "Speech on Matters of Public Concern: The Perils of an Emerging First Amendment Category," 59 *Geo. Wash. L. Rev.* 1 (1990); Allred, "From *Connick* to Confusion: The Struggle to Define Speech on Matters of Public Concern," 64 *Ind. L.J.* 43 (1988); Massaro, "Significant Silences: Freedom of Speech in the Public Sector Workplace," 61 *S. Cal. L. Rev.* 1 (1987). What does the court mean when it says that no First Amendment interests are at stake when the speech relates "solely to the employee's parochial concerns" or criticisms of "internal policies or practices which are of relevance only to the employees of that institution"? *See also Dunn & Bradstreet, Inc. v. Greenmoss Builders, Inc.*, 472 U.S. 749, 105 S.Ct. 2939, 86 L.Ed.2d 593 (1985) (plurality opinion) ("matters of purely private concern" not protected). What if Nancy Cox's speech concerned both public concerns and internal institutional policies? *See Renfroe v. Kirkpatrick*, 722 F.2d 714 (11th Cir. 1984).

How does a court know a public concern when it sees it? *See* Langvardt, "Public Concern Revisited: A New Role for an Old Doctrine in the Constitutional Law of Defamation," 21 *Va. L. Rev.* 241, 259 (1987). Does public concern or discourse refer to speech that is "substantively relevant to the processes of democratic self-governance?" *See* Post, "The Constitutional Concept of Public Discourse: Outrageous Opinion, Democratic Deliberation, and *Hustler Magazine v. Falwell*," 103 *Harv. L. Rev.* 601, 670 (1990). Cannot every issue potentially raise the public's concern? For example, is sexual harassment among employees in the school a matter of public concern or an internal problem? Is an employee who reports alleged sexual harassment protected from discharge by the First Amendment? *See Azzaro v. County of Allegheny*, 110 F.3d 968 (3d Cir. 1997). Is not the purpose of the speech to put the matter under discussion on the public agenda? *Id.* Should the government be able to decide what is a matter of public concern? *Id. See also* Estlund, *supra.* Or does the public-concern test require "speech about issues that happen actually to interest the 'public,' which is to say 'significant number of persons.' "? *Id.* at 672, citing B. Hennessy, *Public Opinion* 8–9 (3d ed.

1975). But is not a major purpose of speech to educate the public as to matters about which it should be concerned? Or does the test require that the speech be publicly disseminated? *Id.* at 675, citing *Hustler Magazine v. Falwell*, 484 U.S. 46, 108 S.Ct. 876, 99 L.Ed.2d 41 (1988). *But see Ferrara v. Mills*, 781 F.2d 1508, 1514 (11th Cir. 1986). Is the burden of proof on the teacher or the public schools? *See Ferrara v. Mills, supra* at 1514 (burden on teacher). Can teachers be fired for speech they are compelled to engage in, such as testimony in a trial or at a deposition? Is testimony before a court of law always on a matter of public concern? *See Padilla v. South Harrison R-II Sch. Dist.*, 181 F.3d 992 (1999) (holding the teacher's testimony at trial did not address a matter of public concern). Do you think the public concern test works? Does it protect speech of public school employees and the school's interest in maintaining a loyal and efficient workforce? Should the public concern test be clarified? *See* Smith, "Beyond 'Public Concern': New Free Speech Standards for Public Employees," 57 *U. Chi. L. Rev.* 249 (1990).

According to Professor Post, "the origin of the phrase 'matters of public concern' in the first amendment doctrine . . . lies in the important 1940 decision of *Thornhill v. Alabama*." *Id.*, citing 310 U.S. 88 (1940). *Thornhill* involved the question of whether labor picketing is constitutionally protected. Does the origin of the doctrine indicate that the purpose is to distinguish between typical employee grievances and larger issues that may concern the public? *See Bradshaw v. Pittsburg Indep. Sch. Dist.*, 207 F.3d 814 (5th Cir. 2000); *Southside Public Schools v. Hill*, 827 F.2d 270 (8th Cir. 1987). To distinguish between speech addressed to the government as employer and speech addressed to government as policymaker? How does one tell the difference? *See* Estlund, *supra.*

Do you agree with Professor Post that the public concern doctrine "lacks internal coherence" and causes courts to examine "a wide array of particular variables inherent in specific communicative contexts"? *Id.* at 679. That "the classification of speech as public discourse" resists "expression in the form of clear, uniform, and helpful doctrinal rules"? *Id.* Consider this effort at a reformulation of the test:

> [T]he first amendment establishes a distinct domain of public discourse in order to implement our common belief in such values as neutrality, diversity, and individualism. It follows that the domain of public discourse will extend only so far as these values override

other competing commitments, such as those . . . necessary [to the] exercise of community authority.

Id. at 680. Do you agree? Does the proposed test abandon *Connick* and return the courts to *Pickering?*

2. *What Is a Matter of Public Concern?*

Judge Gibson asserts that the ability grouping of students, school personnel policies, and the administrative style of the principal are all matters of public concern. How does he reach this conclusion? If questions of "how we teach the young," "what we teach them, and the environment in which we teach them are of the most central concern to every community in the nation," is not virtually all speech by teachers and administrators a matter of public concern? *See Rankin v. Independent School District No. I-3,* 876 F.2d 838 (10th Cir. 1989) (student discipline policies are a matter of public concern); *Anderson v. Central Point School District No. 6,* 746 F.2d 505 (9th Cir. 1984) (criticism of athletic program matter of public concern). *But see Ferrara v. Mills,* 781 F.2d 1508, 1515 (11th Cir. 1986) (rejects the argument that all speech "relating to public education" is "intrinsically" a matter "of vital public concern"); *Daniels v. Quinn,* 801 F.2d 687 (4th Cir. 1986) (criticism of late arrival of remedial reading materials not a public concern); *Saye v. Vrain Valley School District,* 785 F.2d 862 (10th Cir. 1986) (allocation of teacher aide time among teachers not a matter of public concern). On what basis does the court decline to protect criticisms of telephone and announcement policies? Is the court implicitly saying that such trivial matters do not concern the public? Should not concern the public? Has the court implicitly weighed the public's interest against the employer's interest? *See* Estlund, *supra.*

The courts have sharply divided over what constitutes a public concern in the context of speech by teachers and other public school employees. *See, e.g., Kinsey v. Salado Indep. Sch. Dist.,* 916 F. 2d 273 (5th Cir. 1990); *Johnsen v. Independent School District No. 3,* 891 F.2d 1485 (10th Cir. 1989) (criticisms of medication policies by school nurse are matters of public concern, but speech is not protected because of disruptive impact); *Seemuller v. Fairfax County School Board,* 878 F.2d 1578 (4th Cir. 1989) (letters to newspaper, responding to allegations of sexual discrimination against female physical education students, is protected); *Berg v. Hunter,* 854 F.2d 238 (7th Cir. 1988) (unwarranted and misrepresented salary increases are matters of public concern,

but speech had "decidedly adverse impact on the efficient administration of public education"); *Vukadinovich v. Bartels,* 853 F.2d 1387 (7th Cir. 1988) (statements criticizing school board's decision not to rehire plaintiff as basketball coach not protected); *Piver v. Pender County Board of Education,* 835 F.2d 1076 (4th Cir. 1987) (speech favoring retention of principal is matter of public concern); *Southside Public Schools v. Hill,* 827 F.2d 270 (8th Cir. 1987) (letter to state department of education enumerating failures to implement special education program for handicapped pupils is matter of public concern); *Lewis v. Harrison School District No. 1,* 805 F.2d 310 (8th Cir. 1986) (principal's speech to school board criticizing transfer of spouse is matter of public concern); *Ferrara v. Mills,* 781 F.2d 1508 (11th Cir. 1986) (speech on collegiate registration and teacher placement did not relate to a matter of public concern); *Stevenson v. Lower Marion County School District No. 3,* 285 S.C. 62, 327 S.E.2d 656 (1985) (statement accusing superintendent of inciting student disturbances is related to personal employment dispute).

Consider the application of the public concern doctrine in *Knapp v. Whitaker,* 757 F.2d 827, 840–42 (7th Cir. 1985):

d indicates that Knapp contacted the School Board members concerning his classroom assignment; the content of [his] . . . evaluations; the inequitable mileage allowance for . . . coaches; the liability insurance provided by [the district] . . . for coaches and volunteer parents . . . ; and the general ineffectiveness of the grievance procedure within District 150. The issues of Knapp's classroom assignment and the content of his evaluations are clearly personal matters relating solely to Knapp's employment . . . . Knapp's speech on these issues was not an attempt to inform the public that the administrators . . . were failing to discharge their governmental responsibilities. Moreover, Knapp's speech on these subjects was not aimed at uncovering a wrongdoing or breach of the public trust . . . .

The issue of inequitable mileage allowance involves not only Knapp but all of the coaches . . . who travel to area high schools . . . . Knapp's speech to the School Board on the issue of mileage allowance was an attempt to inform the public and the educational policymakers of Peoria that officials in District 150 were failing in their duty to properly administer the allocation of public funds. . . .

The liability insurance coverage . . . is, likewise, a matter of interest and concern to members of the Peoria community . . . .

The functioning of a grievance procedure is generally an internal issue, important only to the teachers and School District employees .... In the present case, however, the grievance procedure was the subject of ongoing collective bargaining negotiations between the teachers' union and the administrators .... [W]e hold that, in the context of this case, such speech is a matter of public concern.

How do you explain the results reached by the *Knapp* court? *See also Hesse v. Board of Education*, 848 F.2d 748 (7th Cir. 1988); *Day v. South Park Independent School District*, 768 F.2d 696 (5th Cir. 1985); *Meyer v. University of Washington*, 105 Wash.2d 847, 719 P. 2d 98 (1986). Is the court balancing personal and public interests and then attaching the appropriate label? *See* Bernheim, "Free Speech for Public Employees: The Supreme Court Strikes a New Balance," 31 *Educ. L. Rep.* [7] (1986). *See generally* Estlund, *supra*. Is the court balancing interests in accordance with *Pickering* in the guise of applying *Connick? See also Bowman v. Pulaski County Special School District*, 723 F.2d 640 (8th Cir. 1983). *See generally Rankin v. McPherson*, 483 U.S. 378, 107 S.Ct. 2891, 97 L.Ed.2d 315 (1987). Does the public concern doctrine lead to predictable results? How would you advise a teacher planning to criticize administrative policies before a public meeting of the school board?

3. *Application of* Connick *to Classroom Speech*

Is the *Connick* public concern doctrine applicable to teacher expression in the classroom? Does it balance the same types of interests that are at issue in academic freedom cases? Is a teacher's unauthorized use of a supplemental reading list for a world history class a matter of public concern? *See Kirkland v. Northside Independent School District*, 890 F.2d 794 (5th Cir. 1989).

4. *Causation*

In teacher speech cases, the teacher has the initial burden of proving that the protected conduct "was a substantial or motivating factor" in the adverse employment or other disciplinary decision. *See Lukan v. North Forest ISD*, 183 F.3d 342, 345 (5th Cir. 1999); *Coats v. Pierce*, 890 F.2d 728 (5th Cir. 1989); *Holley v. Seminole County School District*, 755 F.2d 1492, 1500 (11th Cir. 1985). *See generally Mt. Healthy City School District Board of Education v. Doyle*, 429 U.S. 274, 97 S.Ct. 568, 50 L.Ed.2d 471 (1977). If the plaintiff meets this initial burden, the burden then shifts to the public employer "to show that the same employment decision would have been rendered absent the

protected conduct." *Holley v. Seminole County School District*, *supra* at 1500. *See also Solis v. Rio Grande City Independent School*, 734 F.2d 243 (5th Cir. 1984); *Allen v. Autauga County Board of Education*, 685 F.2d 1302, 1304 (11th Cir. 1982); *Hattisburg Municipal Separate School District v. Gates*, 461 So.2d 730, 737 (Miss. 1984). This standard of causation is generally treated as a "but for" test, i.e., the defendant must show, for example, that the plaintiff would have been dismissed even if the constitutionally protected conduct had not occurred. Do you agree with the standard of causation and the allocation of burdens of proof? Should the dismissed teacher be entitled to remedy if protected expression played any role in the dismissal? What are the perils of such a rule? What are the perils of the *Mt. Healthy* approach?

Causation is a fact question for the trier of fact. *See Copp v. Unified School District*, 882 F.2d 1547 (10th Cir. 1989); *Ratliff v. Wellington Exempted Village Schools Board*, 820 F.2d 792 (6th Cir. 1987); *Solis v. Rio Grande City Independent School*, *supra*; *Wells v. Hico Independent School District*, 736 F.2d 243 (5th Cir. 1984). When is it appropriate to dispose of the issue by summary judgment? *See Holley*, 755 F.2d at 1500–05. What is the standard of appellate review? *See Allen v. Autauga County Board of Education*, *supra* at 1305.

5. *Remedy*

A teacher who is unconstitutionally dismissed from her job because of her exercise of speech rights is entitled to back wages and other provable damages, but she may not recover for the loss of the abstract value of the constitutional right. *See Ratliff v. Wellington Exempted Village Schools Board*, *supra*. *See generally Memphis Community School District v. Stachura*, 477 U.S. 299, 106 S.Ct. 2537, 91 L.Ed.2d 249 (1986). There also is a presumptive rule that reinstatement in the position is appropriate. *See Allen v. Autauga County Board of Education*, *supra* at 1305–06 and cases cited therein.

6. *Profanity*

If a teacher uses profanity in addressing her supervisors and other members of the school community, may the speech still be protected as involving a matter of public concern? Or does the profanity itself provide the school district with an independent reason for dismissal or discipline? *See Ware v. Morgan County School District*, 748 P.2d 1295 (Colo. 1988) (insubordination). *Cf. Martin v. Parrish*, 805 F.2d 583 (5th Cir. 1986).

THREE

The Disciplinary Process:
The Legalization of Dispute Resolution
in Public Schools

I. INTRODUCTION

This chapter focuses on the discipline processes for public school students and teachers as well as the constitutional and statutory constraints that courts and legislatures impose on those processes. It takes up doctrinal issues—issues of law and policy—and questions concerning implementation, institutional competence, and the like, exploring the connection between these nominally disparate matters.

The presentation is essentially sequential, beginning with the requirements for a valid rule and proceeding through the stages of collection, presentation, and evaluation of the evidence in a disciplinary action. The chapter considers such matters as the vagueness and overbreadth doctrines as applied to school rules, limits on the gathering of evidence imposed on public officials by the Fourth Amendment (barring unreasonable searches), and the particulars of procedural due process in the school setting. It concludes with an assessment of the impact of due process decisions on schools and authority relationships within schools, recognizing the difficulties and uncertainties of implementing changes in the decisional processes of complex, bureaucratic public institutions.

A recurrent theme is the degree to which courts, legislatures, and administrative bodies at the federal, state, and local levels have contributed to what could be described as the "legalization" of dispute resolution in the public schools. The term *legalization* refers to the tendency "to discover, construct, and follow rules" as a method for settling disputes and to adhere to prescribed procedures in their formulation and applica-

tion. *See* J. Shklar, *Legalism* 21 (1964). *See also* S. Sitkin and R. Bies, *The Legalistic Organization* (1994); A. Wise, *Legislated Learning* (1979); T. Lowi, *The End of Liberalism* 297–314 (1969); P. Selznick, *Law, Society, and Industrial Justice* 11–12 (1969).

Whatever the etiology of the legalization process, the inevitable result is a diminution or channeling of official discretion to make decisions affecting teachers and students. *See* G. Grant, *The World We Created at Hamilton High* (1988); D. Kirp and D. Jensen, eds., *School Days, Rule Days* (1986). *See generally* K. Davis, *Discretionary Justice* (1969). The formality of decision making is grounded in the supposition that the values of fairness, liberty, dignity, and participation require promulgating general rules and applying them in a uniform fashion. Critics of legalization have focused on the need to maintain authority relationships and a sense of shared community purpose in public schools, and they perceive legalization as a threat to those values. *See* Dupre, "Should Students Have Constitutional Rights? Keeping Order in the Public Schools," 65 *Geo. Wash. L. Rev.* 49 (1996). For courts and policymakers, the ultimate question is one of balance between rule and discretion, formality and informality, trusting and adversarial relationships. *See generally* Manley-Casimir, "Students' Rights," in D. Erickson and T. Reller, *The Principal in Metropolitan Schools* 188 (1978). As Grant Gilmore put the matter,

The better the society, the less law there will be. In Heaven there will be no law, and the lion will lie down with the lamb . . . . The worse the society, the more law

305

there will be. In Hell there will be nothing but law, and due process will be meticulously observed.

G. Gilmore, *The Ages of American Law* 111 (1977).

The legalization of public education drew the fire of William Bennett, Secretary of Education during the Reagan administration. In a 1988 address to the American Bar Association entitled "The Role of Law in Education Reform," Secretary Bennett asserted that

> . . . the excessive legalization of education is inhibiting bold, innovative educators who are willing to shoulder responsibilities and to accept the consequences. Worse still is the effect education law has on school officials who prefer to avoid taking on problems. . . . Stultifying legal restrictions . . . allow them to escape responsibility for their own failings by using the law as an excuse. . . . Let's not perpetuate an environment in which the definition of an effective principal or teacher means having the agility and gall to slip around excessive legal interference. As in the military, let the men and women in the field call the shots.

As you read the materials in this chapter, you should continually ask yourself whether Secretary Bennett is right: whether the balance has been drawn appropriately, whether legalization has advanced or impeded the mission of public schools, whether teachers and students are protected too little or too much from arbitrary decisions by school authorities. *See generally* Levin, "Educating Youth for Citizenship: The Conflict Between Authority and Individual Rights in the Public School," 95 *Yale L. J.* 1647 (1986); Yudof, "Legalization of Dispute Resolution, Distrust of Authority, and Organizational Theory: Implementing Due Process for Students in the Public Schools," 1981 *Wis.L.Rev.* 891; Kirp, "Proceduralism and Bureaucracy: Due Process in the School Setting," 28 *Stan.L.Rev.* 841 (1976). *See* Dupre, *supra*, at 50–51 (attributing the "loss of respect, deference, and trust in the public school" to the Supreme Court's school jurisprudence); Toby, "Everyday School Violence: How Disorder Fuels It," 17 *American Educator* 4, 44 (Winter 1993/1994) (arguing that the extension of civil rights in the school setting contributes to school disorder); Sacken, "The Legalization of Education and the Preparation of School Administrators," 84 *Ed. Law Rep.* 1 (1993); Devins, "Centralization in Education: Why Johnny Can't Spell Bureaucracy," 75 *Calif. L. Rev.* 759 (1987).

Legalization is also related to the socialization issues canvassed in chapter 2. Students learn about accepted norms by observing the actions of others, particularly as those actions have an impact on their day-to-day lives. *See generally* A. Gutmann, *Democratic Education* 88–94 (1987); T. Tapper, *Political Education and Stability* 45 (1976); Levin, *supra*, at 1668–77. *But see* Merelman, "Democratic Politics and the Culture of American Education," 74 *Am. Pol. Sci. Rev.* 319 (1980). Students may develop an understanding of the relative merits of autocracy and democracy from their school experiences:

> Almost from birth people are enmeshed in complex webs of authority relationships. Every type of interpersonal activity—from learning to be a well-behaved child to sports—requires learning a relationship to established authority. In each situation, sets of acceptable behaviors, ways these rules can be modified, and penalties for infractions are acquired. Some of us learn, for example, that all rules must be obeyed regardless of one's own opinion, that authority cannot be challenged, and that disobedience brings inevitable and harsh consequences. Others learn that all regulations are flexible, rules are decided on by common consent, and punishment for wrongdoing can be negotiated. Some scholars argue that exposure to authority patterns in non-political situations creates expectations about the proper use of authority in political situations. . . . The argument suggests that where families, schools, and organizations stress unthinking acceptance of non-negotiable rules handed down by higher authorities, citizens will thus prefer a political system where decisions are similarly made and implemented. The key assumption is that people seek congruence between their personal authority experience and its relationship to broader political authority. Hence, democracy in the larger political system begins with democratic socialization (and autocratic systems similarly begin with autocratic political and non-political learning).

R. Weissberg, *Political Learning, Political Choice, and Democratic Citizenship* 17–18 (1974). *See generally* Gutmann, *supra* at ch. 3.

Do people seek a congruence between their own experiences with authority and their views on political authority generally? Might not students, subjected to undemocratic schools, react by seeking to reform political authority and to make it more democratic? Should policymakers and courts consider the impact of the disciplinary process in public schools on the political orientation of students—irrespective of the empirical answer to the congruence hypothesis?

II. GOVERNMENTAL REGULARITY AND SCHOOL RULES

Must school authorities act on the basis of a preexisting rule before a teacher or student may be punished for violating an institutional norm? The constitutional issue is whether the due process clause of the Fourteenth Amendment requires the prior enactment of such rules in order to assure that those in school have notice of what behavior may be subject to disciplinary sanctions. *See Bethel School District No. 403 v. Fraser*, 478 U.S. 675, 686, 106 S.Ct. 3159, 3166, 92 L.Ed.2d 549 (1986) (Stevens, J., dissenting). Even if the principle were established under the Constitution, it may be applicable only to the most severe sanctions. *Id.* (detailed rules unnecessary for two-day suspension). This is an important matter—important enough that at least one state has legislatively required that all school rules be in writing. Ind. Code Ann. §20-8.1-5-3 (West 1985).

Courts generally have held that some behavior is so plainly disruptive of school life that those engaging in that behavior knew or should have known that they would be subject to sanctions. Moreover, courts have declared that school officials must have flexibility to respond to the unexpected. The prevailing law is that school officials generally may discipline students for conduct disruptive of the educational process or conduct that endangers the health and safety of students and school personnel without having adopted a prior rule forbidding the behavior and specifying the penalties. *See, e.g., Richards v. Thurston*, 424 F.2d 1281 (1st Cir. 1970); *Hasson v. Boothby*, 318 F.Supp. 1183 (D. Mass. 1970). *Cf. Bethel School District No. 403 v. Fraser, supra.*

If a school district promulgates written rules for student and teacher conduct, may those rules be successfully attacked on the ground that they are unconstitutionally vague? The concept of vagueness under the due process clause means that persons "of common intelligence must necessarily guess at its meaning and differ as to its application." *Connally v. General Construction Co.*, 269 U.S. 385, 391, 46 S.Ct. 126, 127, 70 L.Ed. 322 (1926). The concept has been largely limited to the criminal law, and the courts generally have declined to apply it to school rules. *See Wiemerslage v. Maine Township High School Dist. 207*, 29 F.3d 1149, 1151–52 (7th Cir. 1994) ("given the peculiar issues facing school administrators, a school's disciplinary rule need not be drafted as narrowly or with the same precision as criminal statutes"); *Jenkins v. Louisiana State Board of Education*, 506 F.2d 992 (5th Cir. 1975). Thus courts have upheld school disciplinary codes that broadly proscribe "willful disobedience," "intentional disruption," "student walkouts," and "vulgarity." *See, e.g., Williams v. Board of Education*, 274 Ark. 530, 626

S.W.2d 361 (1982); *Murray v. West Baton Rouge Parish School Board*, 472 F.2d 438 (5th Cir. 1973). If there were any doubts on this matter, they were put to rest by Chief Justice Burger in *Bethel School District No. 403 v. Fraser*, 478 U.S. 675, 686, 106 S.Ct. 3159, 3166, 92 L.Ed.2d 549 (1986):

> Respondent contends that the circumstances of his suspension violated due process because he had no way of knowing that the delivery of the speech in question would subject him to disciplinary sanctions. This argument is without merit. . . . Given the school's need to be able to impose disciplinary sanctions for a wide range of unanticipated conduct disruptive of the educational process, the school disciplinary rules need not be as detailed as a criminal code which imposes criminal sanctions . . . . Two days' suspension from school does not rise to the level of a penal sanction calling for the full panoply of procedural due process protections applicable to a criminal prosecution. . . . The school disciplinary rule proscribing "obscene" language and the prespeech admonition of teachers gave adequate warning to Fraser that his lewd speech could subject him to sanctions.

See also Rosa R. v. Connelly, 889 F.2d 435, 439 (2d Cir. 1989). *But see Bethel School District No. 403 v. Fraser, supra* (Stevens, J., dissenting); *Stephenson v. Davenport Community Sch. Dist.*, 110 F.3d 1303 (8th Cir. 1997) (school district regulation banning "gang related activities such as display of . . . symbols" held void for vagueness); *Packer v. Board of Educ. of Town of Thomaston*, 717 A.2d 117 (Conn. 1998) (regulation, as applied to conduct off school grounds, held void for vagueness); *Shamloo v. Mississippi State Board*, 620 F.2d 516, 523 (5th Cir. 1980).

Is the Court implicitly suggesting that Fraser might have been disciplined even if there were no school rule prohibiting obscene language? What if there were prior warnings from teachers but no rule? What if there were neither rules nor prior warnings? Is the standard applicable to students also applicable to teachers? If Fraser had been expelled from school for his infraction, would the vagueness doctrine have been applicable?

The overbreadth doctrine, like the vagueness doctrine, is an attack on a rule or law "on its face" as opposed to "as applied," and it is used primarily to protect expression under the First Amendment. The courts ask whether, irrespective of the plaintiff's conduct, the rule is applicable to some constitutionally protected conduct that may not be prohibited under any rule. That is, the rule may be unconstitutionally overbroad even though the plaintiff's conduct could have been proscribed under a properly drafted rule. While the vagueness doctrine is grounded primarily in the need for governmental regularity, the overbreadth doctrine is premised more on protecting First Amendment interests. If a rule is unconstitutionally broad, the court will strike it down to prevent the "chilling" of protected speech—even at the behest of a party who did not engage in protected activities.

Does *Fraser* close the door on overbreadth attacks on school rules? If a school need not rely on a preexisting rule when disciplining students, why should a court examine a duly enacted school rule for vagueness or overbreadth? Is it that a written rule may be more misleading? May a school district punish a student for behavior that is expressly approved in a school rule?

III. GATHERING THE EVIDENCE TO PROVE THE INFRACTION

What are the limits, if any, on the power of school officials to gather evidence that a teacher or student has violated a school rule? Once schools' concerns may have appeared to be relatively routine—a fugitive copy of *Playboy* or a can of beer in a student's locker—but the increasing presence of (and attention to) drugs and weapons on campus has made this a hotly contested area for both educational policy and law. Among the factors that make the issue legally complex are the institutional characteristics of schools, the age of students, the compulsion to attend school, the potential threat to safety, and the possibility that seized items may be used as evidence in criminal prosecutions as well as for school disciplinary purposes.

New Jersey v. T.L.O.

469 U.S. 325, 105 S.Ct. 733, 83 L.Ed.2d 720 (1985).

Justice White delivered the opinion of the Court.

[A teacher at a New Jersey high school saw T.L.O. and another girl smoking in a lavatory, in violation of a school rule. The two girls were taken to the principal's office where one girl admitted to an assistant vice principal that she had been smoking in the lava-

tory. T.L.O., however, denied the accusation, but in response to his demand, handed her purse to the vice principal. On opening the purse, he found a pack of cigarettes; in removing the pack, he noticed a package of cigarette rolling papers which, in his experience, was associated with the use of marijuana. This prompted him to examine the purse more closely, leading him to find marijuana, drug paraphernalia, and evidence indicating that T.L.O. was selling drugs. These items were turned over to the police, who brought charges against T.L.O. in juvenile court. Although the issue before the Supreme Court was whether evidence seized in an unlawful school search could be excluded from juvenile court proceedings, the Court decided to consider the broader issue of whether the Fourth Amendment applies to searches by school officials.

The Court determined that the Fourth Amendment's prohibition on unreasonable searches and seizures applies to searches conducted by public school officials, and that the search of T.L.O.'s purse did not violate the amendment. The Court expressly declined to determine whether the exclusionary rule applies to the fruits of unlawful searches conducted by school authorities. The Court then discussed the appropriate constitutional standard for searches by school officials.]

* * *

III

. . . Although the underlying command of the Fourth Amendment is always that searches and seizures be reasonable, what is reasonable depends on the context within which a search takes place. The determination of the standard of reasonableness governing any specific class of searches requires "balancing the need to search against the invasion which the search entails.". . . On one side of the balance are arrayed the individual's legitimate expectations of privacy and personal security; on the other, the government's need for effective methods to deal with breaches of public order.

. . . A search of a child's person or of a closed purse or other bag carried on her person,[5] no less than a similar search carried out on an adult, is undoubtedly a severe violation of subjective expectations of privacy.

* * *

---

[5]We do not address the question, not presented by this case, whether a schoolchild has a legitimate expectation of privacy in lockers, desks, or other school property provided for the storage of school supplies. Nor do we express any opinion on the standards (if any) governing school officials. Compare *Zamora v. Pomeroy*, 639 F.2d 662, 670 (CA10 1981) ("Inasmuch as the school had assumed joint control of the locker it cannot be successfully maintained that the school did not have a right to inspect it"), and *People v. Overton*, 24 N.Y.2d 522, 249 N.E.2d 366, 301 N.Y.S.2d 479 (1969) (school administrators have power

Against the child's interest in privacy must be set the substantial interest of teachers and administrators in maintaining discipline in the classroom and on school grounds. Maintaining order in the classroom has never been easy, but in recent years, school disorder has often taken particularly ugly forms: drug use and violent crime in the schools have become major social problems. . . .

. . . [T]he school setting requires some easing of the restrictions to which searches by public authorities are ordinarily subject. The warrant requirement, in particular, is unsuited to the school environment: requiring a teacher to obtain a warrant before searching a child suspected of an infraction of school rules (or of the criminal law) would unduly interfere with the maintenance of the swift and informal disciplinary procedures needed in the schools. . . .

The school setting also requires some modification of the level of suspicion of illicit activity needed to justify a search. Ordinarily, a search—even one that may permissibly be carried out without a warrant—must be based upon "probable cause" to believe that a violation of the law has occurred. . . . However, "probable cause" is not an irreducible requirement of a valid search. The fundamental command of the Fourth Amendment is that searches and seizures be reasonable, and although "both the concept of probable cause and the requirement of a warrant bear on the reasonableness of a search, . . . in certain limited circumstances neither is required." . . . Where a careful balancing of governmental and private interests suggests that the public interest is best served by a Fourth Amendment standard of reasonableness that stops short of probable cause, we have not hesitated to adopt such a standard.

We join the majority of courts that have examined this issue in concluding that the accommodation of the privacy interests of schoolchildren with the substantial need of teachers and administrators for freedom to maintain order in the schools does not require strict adherence to the requirement that searches be based on probable cause to believe that the subject of the search has violated or is violating the law. Rather, the legality of a search of a student should depend simply on the reasonableness, under all the circumstances, of the search. Determining the reasonableness of any search involves a twofold inquiry: first, one must consider "whether the . . . action was justified at its inception," *Terry v. Ohio*, 392 U.S., at 20, 88 S.Ct., at 1879; second, one must determine whether the search as actually conducted "was reasonably related in scope to the circumstances which justified the interference in the first place," *ibid*. Under ordinary circumstances, a search of a student by a teacher or other school official[7] will be "justified at its inception" when there are reasonable grounds for suspecting that the search will turn up evidence that the student has violated or is violating either the law or the rules of the school.[8] Such a search will be permissible in its scope when the measures adopted are reasonably related to the objectives of the search and not excessively intrusive in light of the age and sex of the student and the nature of the infraction.

This standard will, we trust, neither unduly burden the efforts of school authorities to maintain order in their schools nor authorize unrestrained intrusions upon the privacy of schoolchildren. By focusing attention on the question of reasonableness, the standard will spare teachers and school administrators the necessity of schooling themselves in the niceties of probable cause and permit them to regulate their conduct according to the dictates of reason and common sense. At the same time, the reasonableness standard should ensure that the interests of

---

to consent to search of a student's locker), with *State v. Engerud*, 94 N.J. 331, 348, 463 A.2d 934, 943 (1983) ("We are satisfied that in the context of this case the student had an expectation of privacy in the contents of his locker. . . . For the four years of high school, the school locker is a home away from home. In it the student stores the kind of personal 'effects' protected by the Fourth Amendment").

[7]We here consider only searches carried out by school authorities acting alone and on their own authority. This case does not present the question of the appropriate standard for assessing the legality of searches conducted by school officials in conjunction with or at the behest of law enforcement agencies, and we express no opinion on that question. Cf. *Picha v. Wielgos*, 410 F.Supp. 1214, 1219–21 (ND Ill. 1976) (holding probable cause standard applicable to searches involving the police).

[8]We do not decide whether individualized suspicion is an essential element of the reasonableness standard we adopt for searches by school authorities. In other contexts, however, we have held that although "some quantum of individualized suspicion is usually a prerequisite to a constitutional search or seizure[,] . . . the Fourth Amendment imposes no irreducible requirement of such suspicion." *United States v. Martinez-Fuerte*, 428 U.S. 543, 560–61, 96 S.Ct. 3074, 3084, 49 L.Ed.2d 1116 (1976). *See also Camara v. Municipal Court*, 387 U.S. 523, 87 S.Ct. 1727, 18 L.Ed.2d 930 (1967). Exceptions to the requirement of individualized suspicion are generally appropriate only where the privacy interests implicated by a search are minimal and where "other safeguards" are available "to assure that the individual's reasonable expectation of privacy is not 'subject to the discretion of the official in the field.' " *Delaware v. Prouse*, 440 U.S. 648, 654–55, 99 S.Ct. 1391, 1396–97, 59 L.Ed.2d 660 (1979). . . . Because the search of T.L.O.'s purse was based upon an individualized suspicion that she had violated school rules, *see infra*, at 745–46, we need not consider the circumstances that might justify school authorities in conducting searches unsupported by individualized suspicion.

students will be invaded no more than is necessary to achieve the legitimate end of preserving order in the schools.

IV

There remains the question of the legality of the search in this case. . . . Our review of the facts surrounding the search leads us to conclude that the search was in no sense unreasonable for Fourth Amendment purposes.

The incident that gave rise to this case actually involved two separate searches, with the first—the search for cigarettes—providing the suspicion that gave rise to the second—the search for marihuana. Although it is the fruits of the second search that are at issue here, the validity of the search for marihuana must depend on the reasonableness of the initial search for cigarettes, as there would have been no reason to suspect that T.L.O. possessed marihuana had the first search not taken place. Accordingly, it is to the search for cigarettes that we first turn our attention. . . .

. . . The relevance of T.L.O.'s possession of cigarettes to the question whether she had been smoking . . . supplied the necessary "nexus" between the item searched for and the infraction under investigation. . . .

. . . A teacher had reported that T.L.O. was smoking in the lavatory. Certainly this report gave Mr. Choplick reason to suspect that T.L.O. was carrying cigarettes with her; and if she did have cigarettes, her purse was the obvious place in which to find them. Mr. Choplick's suspicion that there were cigarettes in the purse was not an "inchoate and unparticularized suspicion or 'hunch,' " . . . rather, it was the sort of "common-sense conclusio[n] about human behavior" upon which "practical people"— including government officials—are entitled to rely. *United States v. Cortez*, 449 U.S. 411, 418, 101 S.Ct. 690, 695, 66 L.Ed.2d 621 (1981). . . . [T]he requirement of reasonable suspicion is not a requirement of absolute certainty. . . .

Our conclusion that Mr. Choplick's decision to open T.L.O.'s purse was reasonable brings us to the question of the further search for marihuana once the pack of cigarettes was located. The suspicion upon which the search for marihuana was founded was provided when Mr. Choplick observed a package of rolling papers in the purse as he removed the pack of cigarettes. . . . T.L.O. . . . contend[s] that the scope of the search Mr. Choplick conducted ex-

ceeded permissible bounds when he seized and read certain letters that implicated T.L.O. in drug dealing. This argument, too, is unpersuasive. The discovery of the rolling papers concededly gave rise to a reasonable suspicion that T.L.O. was carrying marihuana as well as cigarettes in her purse. This suspicion justified further exploration of T.L.O.'s purse, which turned up more evidence of drug-related activities. . . . Under these circumstances, it was not unreasonable to extend the search to a separate zippered compartment of the purse; and when a search of that compartment revealed an index card containing a list of "people who owe me money" as well as two letters, the inference that T.L.O. was involved in marihuana trafficking was substantial enough to justify Mr. Choplick in examining the letters to determine whether they contained any further evidence. In short, we cannot conclude that the search for marihuana was unreasonable in any respect.

Because the search resulting in the discovery of the evidence of marihuana dealing by T.L.O. was reasonable, the New Jersey Supreme Court's decision to exclude that evidence from T.L.O.'s juvenile delinquency proceedings on Fourth Amendment grounds was erroneous. Accordingly, the judgment of the Supreme Court of New Jersey is

Reversed.

Justice Powell, with whom Justice O'Connor joins, concurring.

I agree with the Court's decision, and generally with its opinion. I would place greater emphasis, however, on the special characteristics of elementary and secondary schools that make it unnecessary to afford students the same constitutional protections granted adults and juveniles in a nonschool setting.

In any realistic sense, students within the school environment have a lesser expectation of privacy than members of the population generally. They spend the school hours in close association with each other, both in the classroom and during recreation periods. The students in a particular class often know each other and their teachers quite well. Of necessity, teachers have a degree of familiarity with, and authority over, their students that is unparalleled except perhaps in the relationship between parent and child. It is simply unrealistic to think that students have the same subjective expectation of privacy as the population generally. . . .

The special relationship between teacher and student also distinguishes the setting within which school children operate. Law enforcement officers function as adversaries of criminal suspects. . . . Rarely does this type of adversarial relationship exist between school authorities and pupils. Instead, there is a commonality of interests between teachers and their pupils. The attitude of the typical teacher is one of personal responsibility for the student's welfare as well as for his education.

The primary duty of school officials and teachers, as the Court states, is the education and training of young people. A state has a compelling interest in assuring that the schools meet this responsibility. Without first establishing discipline and maintaining order, teachers cannot begin to educate their students. And apart from education, the school has the obligation to protect pupils from mistreatment by other children, and also to protect teachers themselves from violence by the few students whose conduct in recent years has prompted national concern. For me, it would be unreasonable and at odds with history to argue that the full panoply of constitutional rules applies with the same force and effect in the schoolhouse as it does in the enforcement of criminal laws.

* * *

Justice Brennan, with whom Justice Marshall joins, concurring in part and dissenting in part.

* * *

I agree that schoolteachers or principals, when not acting as agents of law enforcement authorities, generally may conduct a search of their students' belongings without first obtaining a warrant. To agree with the Court on this point is to say that school searches may justifiably be held to that extent to constitute an exception to the Fourth Amendment's warrant requirement. Such an exception, however, is not to be justified, as the Court apparently holds, by assessing net social value through application of an unguided "balancing test" in which "the individual's legitimate expectations of privacy and personal security" are weighed against "the government's need for effective methods to deal with breaches of public order.". . . Rather, some *special* governmental interest beyond the need merely to apprehend lawbreakers is necessary to justify a categorical exception to the warrant requirement. . . .

* * *

In this case, such extraordinary governmental interests do exist and are sufficient to justify an exception to the warrant requirement. Students are necessarily confined for most of the school day in close proximity to each other and to the school staff. I agree with the Court that we can take judicial notice of the serious problems of drugs and violence that plague our schools. . . . A teacher or principal could neither carry out essential teaching functions nor adequately protect students' safety if required to wait for a warrant before conducting a necessary search.

* * *

I emphatically disagree with the Court's decision to cast aside the constitutional probable-cause standard when assessing the constitutional validity of a schoolhouse search. The Court's decision jettisons the probable-cause standard—the only standard that finds support in the text of the Fourth Amendment—on the basis of its Rohrschach-like "balancing test.". . . This innovation . . . portends a dangerous weakening of the purpose of the Fourth Amendment to protect the privacy and security of our citizens. . . .

* * *

Considerations of the deepest significance for the freedom of our citizens counsel strict adherence to the principle that no search may be conducted where the official is not in possession of probable cause. . . . [T]he Fourth Amendment rests on the principle that a true balance between the individual and society depends on the recognition of "the right to be let alone—the most comprehensive of rights and the right most valued by civilized men." . . .

* * *

A legitimate balancing test whose function was something more substantial than reaching a predetermined conclusion acceptable to this Court's impressions of what authority teachers need would therefore reach rather a different result than that reached by the Court today. On one side of the balance would be the costs of applying traditional Fourth Amendment standards—the "practical" and "flexible" probable-cause standard where a full-scale intrusion is sought, a lesser standard in situations where the intrusion is much less severe and the need for greater authority compelling. Whatever costs were toted up on this side would have to be discounted by the costs of applying an unprecedented and ill-defined "reasonableness under all the circumstances" test that will leave teachers and administrators uncertain as to their authority and will encourage excessive fact-based litigation.

On the other side of the balance would be the serious privacy interests of the student, interests that the Court admirably articulates in its opinion . . . but which the Court's new ambiguous standard places in serious jeopardy. I have no doubt that a fair assessment of the two sides of the balance would necessarily reach the same conclusion that, as I have argued above, the Fourth Amendment's language compels — that school searches like that conducted in this case are valid only if supported by probable cause.

* * *

On my view of the case, we need not decide whether the initial search conducted by Mr. Choplick — the search for evidence of the smoking violation that was completed when Mr. Choplick found the pack of cigarettes — was valid. For Mr. Choplick at that point did not have probable cause to continue to rummage through T.L.O.'s purse. Mr. Choplick's suspicion of marihuana possession at this time was based solely on the presence of the package of cigarette papers. The mere presence without more of such a staple item of commerce is insufficient to warrant a person of reasonable caution in inferring both that T.L.O. had violated the law by possessing marihuana and that evidence of that violation would be found in her purse. . . .

Justice Stevens, with whom Justice Marshall joins, and with whom Justice Brennan joins as to Part I, concurring in part and dissenting in part.

* * *

The majority holds that "a search of a student by a teacher or other school official will be 'justified at its inception' when there are reasonable grounds for suspecting that the search will turn up evidence *that the student has violated or is violating either the law or the rules of the school.*". . . This standard will permit teachers and school administrators to search students when they suspect that the search will reveal evidence of even the most trivial school regulation or precatory guideline for student behavior. The Court's standard for deciding whether a search is justified "at its inception" treats all violations of the rules of the school as though they were fungible. For the Court, a search for curlers and sunglasses in order to enforce the school dress code is apparently just as important as a search for evidence of heroin addiction or violent gang activity.

. . . A [preferable] standard . . . would permit teachers and school administrators to search a student when they have reason to believe that the search will uncover *evidence that the student is violating the law or engaging in conduct that is seriously disruptive of school order, or the educational process.*

NOTES AND QUESTIONS

1. *The Constitutional Standard*

T.L.O. advances a constitutional standard of reasonable suspicion, a standard weaker than the traditional probable cause standard, to determine whether a school search is permissible. Determining reasonableness, according to the Court, involves deciding first whether the search was initially justified — that is, whether there are reasonable grounds for suspecting that it will turn up evidence of a violation of the law or school rules. Second, it means determining whether the conduct of the search is reasonably related in its scope to the circumstances that initially justify the interference — that is, whether the measures taken relate reasonably to the objectives of the search and are not excessively intrusive, taking into account the student's age and sex and the nature of the alleged violation. *See generally* T. van Geel, *The Courts and American Education Law* 327–36 (1987).

Is the reasonable suspicion standard a novel standard, as the dissenters urge, or are there plausible analogies in the existing caselaw? *See* Heder, "The Development of Search and Seizure Law in Public Schools," 1999 *B.Y.U. Educ. & L.J.* 71; Sanchez, "Expelling the Fourth Amendment from American Schools: Students' Rights Six Years after *T.L.O.*," 12 *J.L. & Educ.* 381 (1992); *see also* Comment, "The Supreme Court and the Decline of Students' Constitutional Rights: A Selective Analysis," 65 *Neb. L. Rev.* 161, 178 (1986) ("an unprecedented decision in fourth amendment law"). Is the reasonable suspicion test ambiguous — more ambiguous than the traditional probable cause doctrine? *Compare T.L.O.* with *Illinois v. Gates,* 462 U.S. 213, 103 S.Ct. 2317, 76 L.Ed.2d 527 (1983). *See, e.g.,* Heder, *supra,* 103; van Geel, "Searching of Students After *New Jersey v. T.L.O.*," in T. Jones and D. Semler, eds., *School Law Update 1986* 129 (1986); Note, "School Searches Under the Fourth Amendment: *New Jersey v. T.L.O.*," 72 *Corn.L.Rev.* 368 (1987).

a. Reasonable grounds. What does the requirement of reasonable suspicion or grounds for a search mean? Where is the line between "reasonable suspicion" and an "inchoate and unparticularized suspicion or hunch"? *See Cornfield by Lewis v. Consolidated High School Dist. No. 230,* 991 F.2d 1316 (7th

Cir. 1993). *See also In re Gregory M.*, 627 N.E.2d 500 (N.Y.1993); *Coronado v. State*, 835 S.W. 2d 636 (Tex. Crim. App.1992) . Does reasonable suspicion mean that there must be a suspicion that some specific person has violated the law or a school rule? *See Burnham v. West*, 681 F. Supp. 1160 (E.D. Va. 1987); *Kuehn v. Renton School District No. 403*, 103 Wash.2d 594, 694 P.2d 1078, 1081 (1985). In footnote 8 the Court declines to reach this question, but it notes that the search of T.L.O. "was based upon an individualized suspicion that she had violated school rules." Under what circumstances may school authorities conduct a search where there is no reasonable suspicion of a specific individual? What if suspicion is focused on five or six individuals? *See In re Alexander B.*, 270 Cal.Rptr. 342 (Ct.App. 1990). Or nineteen individuals? *See DesRoches v. Caprio*, 156 F.3d 571 (4th Cir. 1998) (where eighteen of nineteen students consented to search of their backpacks, individualized suspicion arose through process of elimination, and search of unconsenting student's backpack was not unconstitutional). *See generally* McKinney, "The Fourth Amendment and the Public Schools: Reasonable Suspicion in the 1990s," 91 *Ed. Law Rep.* 455 (1994), and Sanchez, "Expelling the Fourth Amendment from American Schools: Students' Rights Six Years After *T.L.O.*," 21 *J. L. & Educ.* 381 (1992), analyzing state and lower federal court cases after *T.L.O.*

In order for a search to be justified, is it sufficient that any violation of the school's rules has occurred — talking back to a teacher, for instance, or engaging in a fist fight with another student — or must the school officials demonstrate the likelihood that evidence of a violation of school rules will be turned up by the search? *See State ex rel. Juvenile Dept. v. Finch*, 925 P.2d 913 (Or.App. 1996); *In re William G.*, 709 P.2d 1287 (Cal. 1985); *State v. Joseph T.*, 336 S.E. 2d 728 (W.Va. 1985).

Is the reasonable grounds test objective or subjective? Does what is reasonable depend on the special knowledge of a school official?

What constitutes a reasonable suspicion — even if the focus is on the conduct of an individual? Professor Tyll van Geel, writing in "Searching of Students After *New Jersey v. T.L.O.*," in T. Jones and D. Semler, eds., *School Law Update 1986* 129, 134 (1986), makes the following point: "A search would be permitted if . . . any one of the following factors were present: the student makes a furtive gesture to his

pocket as the teacher approaches; . . . the student flees as the teacher approaches; . . . the student is present in an area of the school where drug dealing is known to occur; . . . the student is observed placing something in a sock or shoe." Do you agree? *See also In re Alexander B., supra; State v. Michael G.*, 106 N.M. 644, 748 P.2d 17 (App. 1987); *Tarter v. Raybuck*, 742 F.2d 977 (6th Cir. 1984), *cert. denied*, 470 U.S. 1051, 105 S.Ct. 1749, 84 L.Ed.2d 814 (1985); *Bilbrey v. Brown*, 738 F.2d 1462 (9th Cir. 1984). Might such a reading of the law frequently nab the innocent, who just happened to make what looked like a furtive gesture? If so, is that a serious constitutional problem? If the court's standard is in fact more stringent than this, in what way is it? *See generally* Wood and Chestnutt, "Violence in U.S. Schools: The Problems and Some Responses," 97 *Ed. Law Rep.* 619 (1995).

Does information from informants provide reasonable grounds for a search? Should the answer turn on the character or reliability of the informants? *See Commonwealth v. Carey*, 554 N.E.2d 1199 (Mass. 1990). Whether they are anonymous or known? Whether they are students, employees, or others? Whether they have provided accurate information in the past? Whether they purport to be reporting facts or rumors? *Compare In re Alexander B.*, 270 Cal. Rptr. 342 (Cal. Ct. App. 1990); *State v. Michael G.*, 748 P.2d 17 (N.M. App. 1987); *State v. Brooks*, 718 P.2d 837 (Wash. Ct. App. 1986); *State v. Joseph T.*, 336 S.E.2d 728 (W.Va.1985) *with Greenleaf v. Cote*, 77 F.Supp.2d 168 (D.Me. 1999); *Commonwealth v. Carey*, 554 N.E.2d 1199 (Mass. 1990); *State v. Slattery*, 787 P.2d 932 (Wash. 1990). *See Sanchez, supra*, at 389–94, noting that tips supplied by supposedly immature students "are given greater credibility than those of adults in a criminal investigation." *Id.* at 394.

Of what relevance, in assessing reasonableness, is a student's past school record and reputation? *See Coffman v. State*, 782 S.W. 2d 249 (Tex. Ct. App. 1989) (student's "prior propensity to get into trouble," coupled with fact that he was in the hall without a pass and returning from an area where thefts had previously occurred, could reasonably lead principal to suspect student was involved in illegal activity, or had violated school rules); *In re Robert B.*, 218 Cal. Rptr. 337 (Cal. Ct. App. 1985).

Suppose a student, whom school officials have been watching closely for months because of a tip that he had been dealing drugs, is seen entering a restroom twice with a fellow student, leaving ten to fifteen seconds later. Are there grounds to search the student? *See People v. Scott D.*, 34 N.Y.2d 483, 358 N.Y.S.2d 403, 315 N.E.2d 466 (1974).

b. The scope of the search. Do the *T.L.O.* standards govern locker searches? Do students have a "legitimate expectation of privacy" concerning their lockers and desks? *See In Re Patrick Y.*, 358 Md. 50, 746 A.2d 405 (2000) (despite school policy limiting right of school officials to search lockers only in situations where official had probable cause to believe a student possessed contraband, where state law clearly provided that lockers may be searched as part of the physical plant, student has no expectation of privacy); *Commonwealth v. Cass*, 551 Pa. 25, 709 A.2d 350 (1998) (although students possess legitimate expectation of privacy in their lockers, expectation is minimal where lock combinations must be filed in school office, school officials possess a master key, and students are notified lockers are subject to search by school officials without prior warning); *Shoemaker v. State*, 971 S.W.2d 178 (Tex.App.-Beaumont 1998) (student had no legitimate expectation of privacy in her locker inasmuch as written policy made clear lockers are school property remaining under control of school authorities); *In the Interest of Isiah B.*, 176 Wis.2d 639, 500 N.W. 2d 637 (Wis. 1993) (same); *Commonwealth v. Carey*, 554 N.E.2d 1199 (Mass.1990) (student's expectation of privacy in his or her locker may be evaluated in light of school policy governing lockers—e.g., whether school administrators shared custody of lockers with students or lockers are considered school property); *State v. Joseph T.*, 336 S.E.2d 728, 736 (W.Va. 1985) (locker searches must be reasonable where student handbook states that students have privacy rights and lockers will not be searched unless absolutely necessary to protect other students). A number of states have enacted statutes or promulgated regulations which specifically provide that there is no expectation of privacy for a student with regard to his or her locker and that school authorities may search student lockers without prior notice and without reasonable suspicion. *See, e.g.*, Wash. Rev. Code Ann. §§ 28A.600.220 and 28A.600.240 (West 1999); IL ST CH 105 § 5/10-22.6 (West 1999); Ind. Code Ann. § 20-8.1-5.1-25 (West 1999); LA RS. 17:416.3A(1) (West 1999).

The *T.L.O.* majority suggests that "the nature of the infraction," as well as the age and sex of the students involved, affect the permissible scope of the search. How so? Do expectations of privacy vary by age or sex? Would it be appropriate for a school to strip-search second-graders, in response to a classmate's complaint that seven dollars was missing from her purse? Tenth-graders? *Cf. Jenkins v. Talladega City Board of Education*, 115 F.3d 821 (11th Cir.) (*en banc*), *cert. denied sub nom. Jenkins v. Herring*, 522 U.S. 966, 118 S.Ct.412, 139 L.Ed.2d 315 (1997); Goldberg, "Strip Searches of School Children: Legality Depends on Circuit," 14-SPRG *Crim. Just.* 16 (1999); Note, "Students 'Stripped' of Their Constitutional Rights," 23 *So. Ill. U. L. J.* 223 (1998); Note, "Not Your Average School Day—Reading, Writing and Strip Searching: The Eleventh Circuit's Decision in *Jenkins v. Talladega City Board of Education*," 42 *St. Louis U. L. J.*1389 (1998). Or are strip searches inherently degrading and hence impermissible—even where students are suspected of secreting small quantities of hard drugs in body cavities? *Compare Oliver by Hines v. McClung*, 919 F. Supp. 1206 (N.D. Ind. 1995) and *State ex rel. Galford v. Mark Anthony B.*, 189 W. Va. 538, 433 S.E.2d 41 (1993) *with Cornfield v. Consolidated High School District No.230*, 991 F.2d 1316 (7th Cir. 1993) and *Williams v. Ellington*, 936 F.2d 881 (6th Cir. 1991). *See* Stefkovich, "Strip Searching after *Williams*: Reactions to the Concern for School Safety?" 93 *Ed. Law Rep.* 1107 (1994). Should the "nature of the infraction" (illegal drugs versus stolen money or shoes), the intrusiveness of the strip search (removal of all clothing, outer garments only, touching versus looking), and the age and sex of the student be the determinative factors in analyzing the scope requirement? *See* Stefkovich, *supra*, at 1122. What about strip searches where there is no individualized suspicion? Could an entire class be strip searched when a student has reported the theft of her jewelry? When drugs might be present? *See Kennedy v. Dexter Consolidated School*, 124 N.M. 764, 955 P.2d 693 (1998); *Konop v. Northwestern School District*, 26 F.Supp. 2d 1189 (D.S.D. 1998). *See also Sostarecz v. Misko*, 1999 WL 239401 (E.D. Pa.); *cf. Young v. New Haven Board of Education*, 1999 WL 43249 (Conn.Super). *See generally* Blickenstaff, "Strip Searches of Public School Students: Can *New Jersey v. T.L.O.* Solve the Problem?" 99 *Dick. L. Rev.* 1 (1994). Note that some states have enacted laws barring school officials from conducting strip searches, regardless of whether school personnel had reasonable grounds to believe the student had violated a criminal law. *See* NJ ST 18A:37-6.1 (West 1999).

An increasing number of schools are bringing drug-sniffing dogs into schools to combat the use of illegal drugs, with some school districts turning to private companies to provide the service instead of relying on the police department. *See* Davis and Wilgoren, "More Schools Using Dogs to Sniff Out Drugs," *Washington Post*, March 27, 1998. Is the sniffing of student lockers by specially trained dogs, for the purpose of uncovering illegal drugs, a search? *See Horton v. Goose Creek Independent School District*, 690 F.2d 470 (5th Cir. 1982), *cert. denied*, 463 U.S. 1207, 103 S.Ct. 3536, 77 L.Ed.2d 1387 (1983). What about sniffing of students by dogs? *Compare B.C. v. Plumas Unified School District*, 192 F.3d 1003 (9th Cir. 1999) *with Doe v. Renfrow*, 631 F.2d 91 (7th Cir. 1981) (*per curiam*). *See* Comment, "*Vernonia School District 47J v. Acton*: A Step Toward Upholding Suspicionless Dog Sniff Searches in Public Schools?" 68 *U. Colo. L. Rev.* 475 (1997).

Under what circumstances will a court conclude that a student has voluntarily consented to a search? *See State v. Wolfer*, 39 Wash.App. 287, 693 P.2d 154 (1984); *Boynton v. Casey*, 543 F.Supp. 995 (D.Me. 1982). Under what circumstances does the interrogation of a student by a school official constitute an unreasonable seizure or arrest of the student under the Fourth Amendment? *See Edwards v. Rees*, 883 F.2d 882 (10th Cir. 1989) (twenty-minute interrogation of a student by vice principal about bomb threat justified by statements made by two other students); *Coffman v. State*, 782 S.W.2d 249 (Tex.App. 1989). If a student is questioned by school officials about involvement in what may be a violation of criminal law, have the student's Fifth Amendment rights been violated if the student has not been "*Mirandized*"? *Compare In the Matter of the Welfare of G.S.P.*, 610 N.W. 2d 651 (Minn.App.2000) (in juvenile delinquency proceeding, where school official called in police officer assigned as school liaison officer to question student in assistant principal's office, interrogation required *Miranda* warning) with *In Re Harold S.*, 731 A.2d 235 (R.I. 1999) (no constitutional violation where student was not subjected to custodial interrogation nor was principal acting as agent for police, even though student's statement was turned over to the police). *See also State v. Tinkham*, 143 N.H. 73, 719 A.2d 580 (N.H. 1998); *S.A. v. State*, 654 N.E.2d 791 (Ind.App.1995); *State v. Biancamano*, 284 N.J.Super. 654, 666 A.2d 199 (1995); *Commonwealth v. Snyder*, 413 Mass. 521, 597 N.E.2d 1363 (1992). If the student is questioned

by a police official with *Miranda* warnings and his statement is used as the basis for expelling the student in a school disciplinary proceeding? *See Bills v. Homer Consolidated School Dist. No. 33-C*, 967 F.Supp. 1063 (N.D. Ill. 1997).

c. The probable cause standard. How would these questions be answered if Justice Brennan had persuaded his colleagues that the familiar "probable cause" standard, rather than a reasonable suspicion test, should be applied to school-initiated searches? If Justice Stevens' distinction between serious and trivial rules infractions had prevailed?

2. *Remedies: The Exclusionary Rule and T.L.O.*

The relevance of the exclusionary rule (which makes illegally obtained evidence inadmissible in a judicial proceeding, *Mapp v. Ohio*, 367 U.S. 643, 81 S.Ct. 1684, 6 L.Ed.2d 1081 (1961)) to school searches is explicitly left undecided by the *T.L.O.* decision. The purpose of that rule is to deter official police misconduct. Should it follow that the rule also should be applied to deter overzealous school administrators? *See, e.g., Thompson v. Carthage School Dist.*, 87 F.3d 979 (8th Cir. 1996) (exclusionary rule does not apply to school disciplinary hearings); *Juan C. v. Cortines*, 89 N.Y. 2d 659, 679 N.E.2d 1061, 657 N.Y.S.2d 581 (1997) (although gun unlawfully seized from student by school security aide was suppressed in juvenile delinquency proceeding concerning criminal possession of weapon, evidence was admissible in school suspension hearing). *See generally* Comment, "Searching Public Schools: *T.L.O.* and the Exclusionary Rule," 47 *Ohio St. L. J.* 1099 (1986).

The victim of an unreasonable search may file a suit for damages, either for violation of privacy under state law or for a violation of civil rights under the federal statute, 42 U.S.C. §1983. *See, e.g., Doe v. Renfrow*, 635 F.2d 582 (7th Cir. 1980). But §1983 has been read to include a qualified immunity: If officials acted in good faith they are not subject to liability. In this context, what would constitute a bad faith search in violation of the Fourth Amendment?

3. *Police Involvement*

A police-initiated search for purposes of obtaining evidence for a criminal prosecution against a student is typically subject to the traditional Fourth Amendment requirements applicable to police searches of adults. *See State v. McKinnon*, 88 Wash.2d 75, 558 P.2d 781 (1977). Should the Fourth Amendment requirements as applied to the police change if they work together with school officials? *See In the Matter of Josue T.*, 989 P.2d 431 (N.M. 1999) (where school official had reasonable suspicion to initiate search and questioning, but police officer assigned to school as resource officer searched student's pockets at official's request, standard applied to officer's search was reasonable suspicion); *cf. State v. Tywayne H.*, 993 P.2d 251 (N.M. Ct. App.1997) (where search is completely at discretion of police officers, standard is probable cause and not reasonable suspicion). *See also People v. Dilworth*, 661 N.E.2d 310 (Ill. 1996); *Cason v. Cook*, 810 F.2d 188 (8th Cir. 1987); *Commonwealth v. Carey*, 554 N.E.2d 1199 (Mass. 1990). What should be the standard if the police propose a search to school officials in order to obtain evidence for a criminal prosecution, and school officials actually conduct the search either alone or with the police? *See, e.g., In re D.E.M.*, 1999 Pa. Super. 59, 727 A.2d 570 (Pa.Super.1999) ("totality of circumstances" test applied to determine whether school official is acting in an administrative capacity or as an agent for the police); *In re P.E.A.*, 754 P.2d 382 (Colo. 1988) (same); *Picha v. Wielgos*, 410 F.Supp. 1214 (N.D. Ill. 1976); *Piazzola v. Watkins*, 316 F.Supp. 624 (M.D. Ala. 1970), *aff'd*, 442 F.2d 284 (5th Cir. 1971); *People v. Overton*, 24 N.Y.2d 522, 301 N.Y.S.2d 479, 249 N.E.2d 366 (1969).

What standard should apply if the police provide a "tip" to school officials without any express understanding that if the school official finds evidence of criminal violations he or she will turn the evidence over to the police? When is a search instigated by the police? *See People in Interest of P.E.A.*, 754 P.2d 382 (Colo. 1988); *State v. McKinnon, supra*. *See* Comment, "School Searches After *New Jersey v. T.L.O.*: Are There Any Limits?" 34 *U. Louisville J. Fam. L.* 345, 366 (1995–96). What if, without any prior contact with the police, school officials voluntarily turn over incriminating evidence to the police, and a criminal or juvenile prosecution results? *See Coffman v. State*, 782 S.W.2d 249 (Tex.App. 1989). Suppose that the school official has a well-developed working relationship with the police: They meet once a week, exchange information on suspected law violators, and have in the past collaborated in sharing evidence. What would be the result? *Cf. Mercer v. State*, 450 S.W.2d 715, 721 n. 3 (Tex.Civ.App. 1970) (Hughes, J., dissenting). Should school officials be treated as police officers when they conduct a search under the suspicion that criminal misconduct has occurred? *See Piazzola v.*

Watkins, supra; State v. Young, 234 Ga. 488, 510–11, 216 S.E.2d 586, 601 (1975) (Gunter, J., dissenting), *cert. denied*, 423 U.S. 1039, 96 S.Ct. 576, 46 L.Ed.2d 413 (1975). Should juveniles be tried as adults in criminal proceedings based on evidence seized by school officials under the reasonable suspicion standard? *Shamberg v. Alaska*, 762 P.2d 488 (Alaska Ct. App.1988).

If courts allow the police effectively to direct school searches, does that invite the police to carry out investigations that they, burdened with the need to show probable cause, would be unable to accomplish on their own?

An increasing number of school districts have programs where law enforcement officers are placed inside public schools on a full-time basis, partly as a result of the passage of the Safe Schools Act of 1994, 20 U.S.C. § 5961 *et seq.* School districts can obtain federal grants to combat crime and violence, and those funds can be used to purchase metal detectors or hire security guards. *Id.* at § 5965(a)(13). Should these "school resource officers" be considered school employees, and thus permitted to conduct searches based upon the lesser reasonable suspicion standard, or police officers subject to the stricter probable cause standard? *See* Stefkovich and Miller, "Law Enforcement Officers in Public Schools: Student Citizens in Safe Havens?" 1999 *B.Y.U. Educ. & Law Jour.* 25; Note, "Searches and Seizure in Schools: Should Reasonable Suspicion or Probable Cause Apply to School Resource/Liaison Officers?" 67 *UMKC L. Rev.* 543 (1999). *See, e.g., In re F.B.*, 555 Pa. 661, 726 A.2d 1056, *cert. denied sub nom. F.B. v. Pennsylvania*, 528 U.S. 1060, 120 S.Ct. 613, 145 L.Ed.2d 508 (1999); *In the Interest of Angelica B. v. State*, 564 N.W.2d 682 (Wis. 1997); *People v. Dilworth*, 661 N.E.2d 310 (Ill. 1996); *State v. Whorley*, 720 So.2d 282 (Dist. Ct. App. Fla.1998); *State v. Serna*, 860 P.2d 1320 (Ariz. Ct. App. 1993).

4. Violence and Drug Use in the Schools

The *T.L.O.* majority refers to the "particularly ugly forms" of drug use and violent crime that school disorder has taken in recent years. Justice Powell, in his concurrence, also refers to the need for teachers to protect themselves "from violence by the few students whose conduct in recent years has prompted national concern." Even in dissenting from the majority's rejection of a probable cause requirement for school searches, Justice Brennan says that "we can take judicial notice of the serious problems of drugs and violence that plague our schools." To what extent should courts consider these factors in determining the appropriate balance to be struck between the individual's legitimate expectations of privacy and the government's need for effective methods to maintain safety and order? Should judges take judicial notice of increased violence in schools generally or require evidence of increased violence in the particular school in which the search takes place? Is it relevant that several studies have documented a substantial decline in the rate of school violence, with some researchers noting that the extent of the violence in American public schools has been "hyped" by the media. *See* Brener, *et al.*, "Recent Trends in Violence-Related Behaviors Among High School Students in the United States," 282 *Jour. Am. Med. Ass'n* 440 (1999) (between 1991 and 1997, the number of students in a physical fight decreased 14 percent; the number of students injured in a physical fight decreased 20 percent; and the number of students who carried a weapon on school property decreased 30 percent). *See also* National Center for Education Statistics, *The Condition of Education, 1999* (U.S. Department of Education, 1999) (reporting that drug and alcohol use by high school seniors declined substantially between 1976 and 1998). *See also* Dodd, "Can We Create Violence-Free Schools That Are Still Free?" 34 *New Eng. L. Rev.* 623, 624–26 (2000). Serious violent crime affecting young people is substantially greater in society at large than it is in school. In 1997, twenty-four of every one thousand students were victims of serious violent crimes away from school compared to only eight of every one thousand students at school or going to or from school. U.S. Department of Education and U.S. Department of Justice, *1999 Annual Report on School Safety* (1999), at 4. Nevertheless, despite the downward trend in violence and drug use, a number of reports indicate that the availability of drugs in schools is high (65 percent of the students surveyed in 1995 reported that drugs were available in their schools) and that students were more likely to report that gangs were present in their schools in 1995 than in 1989. National Center for Education Statistics, *Students' Reports of School Crime: 1989 and 1995* (U.S. Department of Education, 1998).

5. *T.L.O. and the School Culture*

Justice Powell argues in his concurrence that, because of "the special characteristics of elementary and secondary schools," students should have "a lesser expectation of privacy than members of the population generally. . . . Without first establishing discipline and maintaining order, teachers cannot begin to educate their students."

Justice Stevens holds a very different view: "Schools are places where we inculcate the values essential to the meaningful exercise of rights and responsibilities by self-governing citizenry. If the nation's students can be convicted through the use of arbitrary methods destructive of personal liberty, they cannot help but feel that they have been dealt with unfairly." Who has the better argument? *See* Levin, "Educating Youth for Citizenship: The Conflict Between Authority and Individual Rights in the Public School," 95 *Yale L. J.* 1647 (1986).

Vernonia School District 47J v. Acton
515 U.S. 646, 115 S.Ct. 2386, 132 L.Ed. 2d 564 (1995)

Justice Scalia delivered the opinion of the Court.

The Student Athlete Drug Policy adopted by School District 47J in the town of Vernonia, Oregon, authorizes random urinalysis drug testing of students who participate in the District's school athletics programs. We granted certiorari to decide whether this violates the Fourth and Fourteenth Amendments to the United States Constitution.

I

A

Petitioner Vernonia School District 47J (District) operates one high school and three grade schools in the logging community of Vernonia, Oregon. As elsewhere in small-town America, school sports play a prominent role in the town's life, and student athletes are admired in their schools and in the community.

Drugs had not been a major problem in Vernonia schools. In the mid-to-late 1980's, however, teachers and administrators observed a sharp increase in drug use. Students began to speak out about their attraction to the drug culture, and to boast that there was nothing the school could do about it. Along with more drugs came more disciplinary problems. Between 1988 and 1989 the number of disciplinary referrals in Vernonia schools rose to more than twice the number reported in the early 1980's, and several students were suspended. Students became increasingly rude during class; outbursts of profane language became common.

. . . [A]thletes were the leaders of the drug culture. This caused the District's administrators particular concern, since drug use increases the risk of sports-related injury. Expert testimony at the trial confirmed the deleterious effects of drugs on motivation, memory, judgment, reaction, coordination, and performance. . . .

* * *

B

The Policy applies to all students participating in interscholastic athletics. Students wishing to play sports must sign a form consenting to the testing and must obtain the written consent of their parents. Athletes are tested at the beginning of the season for their sport. In addition, once each week of the season the names of the athletes are placed in a "pool" from which a student, with the supervision of two adults, blindly draws the names of 10% of the athletes for random testing. Those selected are notified and tested that same day, if possible.

The student to be tested completes a specimen control form which bears an assigned number. Prescription medications that the student is taking must be identified by providing a copy of the prescription or a doctor's authorization. The student then enters an empty locker room accompanied by an adult monitor of the same sex. Each boy selected produces a sample at a urinal, remaining fully clothed with his back to the monitor, who stands approximately 12 to 15 feet behind the student. Monitors may (though do not always) watch the student while he produces the sample, and they listen for normal sounds of urination. Girls produce samples in an enclosed bathroom stall, so that they can be heard but not observed. After the sample is produced, it is given to the monitor, who checks it for temperature and tampering and then transfers it to a vial.

* * *

. . . If the . . . test is positive, the athlete's parents are notified, and the school principal convenes a meeting with the student and his parents, at which the student is given the option of (1) participating for six weeks in an assistance program that includes weekly urinalysis, or (2) suffering suspension from athletics for the remainder of the current season and the next athletic season. . . .

C

In the fall of 1991, respondent James Acton, then a seventh-grader, signed up to play football at one of the District's grade schools. He was denied participation, however, because he and his parents refused to sign the testing consent forms. . . .

II

* * *

In *Skinner v. Railway Labor Executives' Assn.*, 489 U.S. 602 (1989), we held that state-compelled collection and testing of urine, such as that required by the Student Athlete Drug Policy, constitutes a "search" subject to the demands of the Fourth Amendment. . . .

. . . [W]hether a particular search meets the reasonableness standard "is judged by balancing its intrusion on the individual's Fourth Amendment interests against its promotion of legitimate governmental interests." *Skinner*, supra. . . . A search unsupported by probable cause can be constitutional, we have said, "when special needs, beyond the normal need for law enforcement, make the warrant and probable-cause requirement impracticable." . . .

We have found such "special needs" to exist in the public-school context. There, the warrant requirement "would unduly interfere with the maintenance of the swift and informal disciplinary procedures [that are] needed," and "strict adherence to the requirement that searches be based upon probable cause" would undercut "the substantial need of teachers and administrators for freedom to maintain order in the schools." *T.L.O.* The school search we approved in *T.L.O.*, while not based on probable cause, was based on individualized suspicion of wrongdoing. As we explicitly acknowledged, however, "the Fourth Amendment imposes no irreducible requirement of such suspicion," . . . .

III

The first factor to be considered is the nature of the privacy interest upon which the search here at issue intrudes. The Fourth Amendment does not protect all subjective expectations of privacy, but only those that society recognizes as "legitimate." *T.L.O.* What expectations are legitimate varies, of course, with context. . . . In addition, the legitimacy of certain privacy expectations vis-a-vis the State may depend upon the individual's legal relationship with the State. . . . Central, in our view, to the present case is the fact that the subjects of the Policy are (1) children, who (2) have been committed to the temporary custody of the State as schoolmaster.

* * *

. . . *T.L.O.* . . . emphasized that the nature of [the State's power over schoolchildren] is custodial and tutelary, permitting a degree of supervision and control that could not be exercised over free adults. . . .

. . . For their own good and that of their classmates, public school children are routinely required to submit to various physical examinations, and to be vaccinated against various diseases. . . . Particularly with regard to medical examinations and procedures, therefore, "students within the school environment have a lesser expectation of privacy than members of the population generally." *T.L.O.* (Powell, J., concurring).

Legitimate privacy expectations are even less with regard to student athletes. School sports are not for the bashful. They require "suiting up" before each practice or event, and showering and changing afterwards. Public school locker rooms, the usual sites for these activities, are not notable for the privacy they afford. The locker rooms in Vernonia are typical: no individual dressing rooms are provided; shower heads are lined up along a wall, unseparated by any sort of partition or curtain; not even all the toilet stalls have doors. . . .

There is an additional respect in which school athletes have a reduced expectation of privacy. By choosing to "go out for the team," they voluntarily subject themselves to a degree of regulation even higher than that imposed on students generally. In Vernonia's public schools, they must submit to a preseason physical exam . . . , they must acquire adequate insurance coverage or sign an insurance waiver, maintain a minimum grade point average, and comply with any "rules of conduct, dress, training hours and related matters as may be established for each sport by the head coach and athletic director with the principal's approval." . . . [S]tudents who voluntarily participate in school athletics have reason to expect intrusions upon normal rights and privileges, including privacy.

<h2 style="text-align:center">IV</h2>

Having considered the scope of the legitimate expectation of privacy at issue here, we turn next to the character of the intrusion that is complained of. We recognized in *Skinner* that collecting the samples for urinalysis intrudes upon "an excretory function traditionally shielded by great privacy." We noted, however, that the degree of intrusion depends upon the manner in which production of the urine sample is monitored. Under the District's Policy, male students produce samples at a urinal along a wall. They remain fully clothed and are only observed from behind, if at all. Female students produce samples in an enclosed stall, with a female monitor standing outside listening only for sounds of tampering. These conditions are nearly identical to those typically encountered in public restrooms, which men, women, and especially school children use daily. Under such conditions, the privacy interests compromised by the process of obtaining the urine sample are in our view negligible.

. . . [T]he results of the tests are disclosed only to a limited class of school personnel who have a need to know; and they are not turned over to law enforcement authorities or used for any internal disciplinary function. . . .

Respondents argue, however, that the District's Policy is in fact more intrusive than this suggests, because it requires the students, if they are to avoid sanctions for a falsely positive test, to identify in advance prescription medications they are taking. We agree that this raises some cause for concern. . . . On the other hand, we have never indicated that requiring advance disclosure of medications is per se unreasonable. Indeed, in *Skinner* we held that it was not "a significant invasion of privacy.". . .

<h2 style="text-align:center">V</h2>

Finally, we turn to consider the nature and immediacy of the governmental concern at issue here, and the efficacy of this means for meeting it. . . .

That the nature of the concern is important—indeed, perhaps compelling—can hardly be doubted. . . . School years are the time when the physical, psychological, and addictive effects of drugs are most severe. . . . And of course the effects of a drug-infested school are visited not just upon the users, but upon the entire student body and faculty, as the educational process is disrupted. In the present case, moreover, the necessity for the State to act is magnified by the fact that this evil is being visited not just upon individuals at large, but upon children for whom it has undertaken a special responsibility of care and direction.

Finally, it must not be lost sight of that this program is directed more narrowly to drug use by school athletes, where the risk of immediate physical harm to the drug user or those with whom he is playing his sport is particularly high. Apart from psychological effects, which include impairment of judgment, slow reaction time, and a lessening of the perception of pain, the particular drugs screened by the District's Policy have been demonstrated to pose substantial physical risks to athletes. . . .

* * *

As to the efficacy of this means for addressing the problem: It seems to us self-evident that a drug problem largely fueled by the "role model" effect of athletes' drug use, and of particular danger to athletes, is effectively addressed by making sure that athletes do not use drugs. Respondents argue that a "less intrusive means to the same end" was available, namely, "drug testing on suspicion of drug use." We have repeatedly refused to declare that only the "least intrusive" search practicable can be reasonable under the Fourth Amendment. . . .

. . . The record shows no objection to this districtwide program by any parents other than the couple before us here—even though, as we have described, a public meeting was held to obtain parents' views. We find insufficient basis to contradict the judgment of Vernonia's parents, its school board, and the District Court, as to what was reasonably in the interest of these children under the circumstances.

* * *

[The concurring opinion of Justice Ginsburg is omitted.]

Justice O'Connor, with whom Justice Stevens and Justice Souter join, dissenting.

The population of our Nation's public schools, grades 7 through 12, numbers around 18 million. By the reasoning of today's decision, the millions of these students who participate in interscholastic sports, an overwhelming majority of whom have given school officials no reason whatsoever to suspect they use drugs at school, are open to an intrusive bodily search.

In justifying this result, the Court dispenses with a requirement of individualized suspicion on considered policy grounds. First, it explains that precisely because every student athlete is being tested, there is no concern that school officials might act arbitrarily in choosing who to test. Second, a broad-based search regime, the Court reasons, dilutes the accu-

satory nature of the search. In making these policy arguments, of course, the Court sidesteps powerful, countervailing privacy concerns. Blanket searches, because they can involve "thousands or millions" of searches, "pos[e] a greater threat to liberty" than do suspicion-based ones, which "affec[t] one person at a time." Searches based on individualized suspicion also afford potential targets considerable control over whether they will, in fact, be searched because a person can avoid such a search by not acting in an objectively suspicious way. . . .

But whether a blanket search is "better" than a regime based on individualized suspicion is not a debate in which we should engage. In my view, it is not open to judges or government officials to decide on policy grounds which is better and which is worse. For most of our constitutional history, mass, suspicionless searches have been generally considered per se unreasonable within the meaning of the Fourth Amendment. And we have allowed exceptions in recent years only where it has been clear that a suspicion-based regime would be ineffectual. Because that is not the case here, I dissent.

I

A

* * *

The view that mass, suspicionless searches, however evenhanded, are generally unreasonable remains inviolate in the criminal law enforcement context. . . . It is worth noting in this regard that state-compelled, state-monitored collection and testing of urine, while perhaps not the most intrusive of searches, is still "particularly destructive of privacy and offensive to personal dignity.". . . See Fried, "Privacy," 77 *Yale L.J.* 475, 487 (1968) ("[I]n our culture the excretory functions are shielded by more or less absolute privacy"). . . .

Outside the criminal context, however, in response to the exigencies of modern life, our cases have upheld several evenhanded blanket searches, including some that are more than minimally intrusive, after balancing the invasion of privacy against the government's strong need. Most of these cases, of course, are distinguishable insofar as they involved searches either not of a personally intrusive nature, such as searches of closely regulated businesses, . . . or arising in unique contexts such as prisons . . . .

In any event, . . . we upheld the suspicionless search only after first recognizing the Fourth Amendment's longstanding preference for a suspicion-based search regime, and then pointing to sound reasons why such a regime would likely be ineffectual under the unusual circumstances presented. . . .

* * *

Moreover, an individualized suspicion requirement was often impractical in these cases because they involved situations in which even one undetected instance of wrongdoing could have injurious consequences for a great number of people. *Camara* [*v. Municipal Court of City and County of San Francisco*, 387 U.S. 523, 87 S.Ct. 1727, 18 L.Ed.2d 930 (1967)] (even one safety code violation can cause "fires and epidemics [that] ravage large urban areas"); *Skinner* [*v. Railway Labor Executives' Ass'n*, 109 S.Ct. 1402, 103 L.Ed.2d 639 (1989)] (even one drug- or alcohol-impaired train operator can lead to the "disastrous consequences" of a train wreck, such as "great human loss") . . . .

B

The instant case stands in marked contrast. . . . Far from acknowledging anything special about individualized suspicion, the Court treats a suspicion-based regime as if it were just any run-of-the-mill, less intrusive alternative—that is, an alternative that officials may bypass if the lesser intrusion, in their reasonable estimation, is outweighed by policy concerns unrelated to practicability.

As an initial matter, I have serious doubts whether the Court is right that the District reasonably found that the lesser intrusion of a suspicion-based testing program outweighed its genuine concerns for the adversarial nature of such a program, and for its abuses. For one thing, there are significant safeguards against abuses. The fear that a suspicion-based regime will lead to the testing of "troublesome but not drug-likely" students, for example, ignores that the required level of suspicion in the school context is objectively reasonable suspicion. In this respect, the facts of our decision in *New Jersey v. T.L.O.* should be reassuring. . . . Moreover, any distress arising from what turns out to be a false accusation can be minimized by keeping the entire process confidential.

For another thing, the District's concern for the adversarial nature of a suspicion-based regime (which appears to extend even to those who are rightly accused) seems to ignore the fact that such a regime would not exist in a vacuum. Schools already have adversarial, disciplinary schemes that require teachers and administrators in many areas besides drug use to investigate student wrongdoing (often by means of accusatory searches); to make determinations about whether the wrongdoing occurred; and to impose punishment. To such a scheme, suspicion-based drug testing would be only a minor addition. The District's own elaborate disciplinary scheme is reflected in its handbook, which, among other things, lists the following disciplinary "problem areas" carrying serious sanctions: "DEFIANCE OF AUTHORITY," "DISORDERLY OR DISRUPTIVE CONDUCT INCLUDING FOUL LANGUAGE," "AUTOMOBILE USE OR MISUSE," "FORGERY OR LYING," "GAMBLING," "THEFT," "TOBACCO," "MISCHIEF," "VANDALISM," "RECKLESSLY ENDANGERING," "MENACING OR HARASSMENT," "ASSAULT," "FIGHTING," "WEAPONS," "EXTORTION," "EXPLOSIVE DEVICES," and "ARSON." . . .

In addition to overstating its concerns with a suspicion-based program, the District seems to have understated the extent to which such a program is less intrusive of students' privacy. By invading the privacy of a few students rather than many (nationwide, of thousands rather than millions), and by giving potential search targets substantial control over whether they will, in fact, be searched, a suspicion-based scheme is significantly less intrusive.

* * *

. . . [N]owhere is it less clear that an individualized suspicion requirement would be ineffectual than in the school context. In most schools, the entire pool of potential search targets—students—is under constant supervision by teachers and administrators and coaches, be it in classrooms, hallways, or locker rooms. *See T.L.O.*

. . . The great irony of this case is that most (though not all) of the evidence the District introduced to justify its suspicionless drug-testing program consisted of first- or second-hand stories of particular, identifiable students acting in ways that plainly gave rise to reasonable suspicion of in-school drug use—and thus that would have justified a drug-related search under our *T.L.O.* decision. Small groups of students, for example, were observed by a teacher "passing joints back and forth" across the street at a restaurant before school and during school hours. Another group was caught skipping school and using drugs at one of the students' houses. Several students actually admitted their drug use to school officials (some of them being caught with marijuana pipes). One student presented himself to his teacher as "clearly obviously inebriated" and had to be sent home. Still another was observed dancing and singing at the top of his voice in the back of the classroom; when the teacher asked what was going on, he replied, "Well, I'm just high on life." To take a final example, on a certain road trip, the school wrestling coach smelled marijuana smoke in a hotel room occupied by four wrestlers, an observation that (after some questioning) would probably have given him reasonable suspicion to test one or all of them.

In light of all this evidence of drug use by particular students, there is a substantial basis for concluding that a vigorous regime of suspicion-based testing (for which the District appears already to have rules in place) would have gone a long way toward solving Vernonia's school drug problem while preserving the Fourth Amendment rights of James Acton and others like him. . . .

* * *

. . . [I]ntrusive, blanket searches of school children, most of whom are innocent, for evidence of serious wrongdoing are not part of any traditional school function of which I am aware. Indeed, many schools, like many parents, prefer to trust their children unless given reason to do otherwise. As James Acton's father said on the witness stand, "[suspicionless testing] sends a message to children that are trying to be responsible citizens . . . that they have to prove that they're innocent . . . , and I think that kind of sets a bad tone for citizenship."

I find unpersuasive the Court's reliance on the widespread practice of physical examinations and vaccinations, which are both blanket searches of a sort. Of course, for these practices to have any Fourth Amendment significance, the Court has to assume that these physical exams and vaccinations are typically "required" to a similar extent that urine testing and collection is required in the instant case, i.e., that they are required regardless of parental objection and that some meaningful sanction attaches to the failure to submit. In any event, without forming any particular view of such searches, it is worth noting that a suspicion requirement for vaccinations is not merely impractical; it is nonsensical, for vaccinations are not searches for anything in particular and so there is nothing about which to be suspicious. . . .

It might also be noted that physical exams (and of course vaccinations) are not searches for conditions that reflect wrongdoing on the part of the student, and so are wholly nonaccusatory and have no consequences that can be regarded as punitive. These facts may explain the absence of Fourth Amendment challenges to such searches. . . . .

II

I do not believe that suspicionless drug testing is justified on these facts. But even if I agreed that some such testing were reasonable here, I see two other Fourth Amendment flaws in the District's program. First, and most serious, there is virtually no evidence in the record of a drug problem at the Washington Grade School, which includes the 7th and 8th grades, and which Acton attended when this litigation began. . . .

Second, even as to the high school, I find unreasonable the school's choice of student athletes as the class to subject to suspicionless testing—a choice that appears to have been driven more by a belief in what would pass constitutional muster (indicating that the original program was targeted at students involved in any extracurricular activity), than by a belief in what was required to meet the District's principal disciplinary concern. . . . [T]he record in this case surely demonstrates there was a drug-related discipline problem in Vernonia of "epidemic proportions." The evidence of a drug-related sports injury problem at Vernonia, by contrast, was considerably weaker.

* * *

NOTES AND QUESTIONS

1. The Constitutional Standard for Suspicionless Searches

Acton addresses an issue not present in *T.L.O.*: the appropriate standard to apply to searches where there is no individualized suspicion. However, in *T.L.O.* the Court emphasized that it had previously noted in nonschool cases that "the Fourth Amendment imposes no irreducible requirement of [individualized] suspicion." To determine when a suspicionless search is reasonable, the Court applies a balancing test based on an examination of three factors: (1) the nature of the privacy interest being invaded, (2) the intrusiveness of the search, and (3) the nature and immediacy of the governmental concern, and the efficacy of the practice involved in addressing that concern.

The majority concludes its analysis with the fact that the record showed no opposition to the school district's policy by any parents other than James Acton's. 515 U.S. at 665, 115 S.Ct. at 2397. Is that fact constitutionally relevant?

a. Legitimate expectation of privacy. The Court, citing *T.L.O.*, finds that students have a lesser expectation of privacy than the population at large (including students in a nonschool setting). Is it that compulsory education significantly intrudes on liberty and privacy, and thus searches are not much of a further imposition? Do you find the Court's arguments as to why student athletes have even less expectation of privacy than students generally convincing?

b. The intrusiveness of the search. The Court finds that the monitoring process for the collection of samples for urinalysis used by the school district does not compromise privacy interests (conditions, according to the Court, are nearly indistinguishable from those experienced in any public restroom). Moreover, the fact that students have to identify to school authorities the prescription medications they are taking for various medical conditions in advance of the drug-testing program does not, according to the Court, significantly increase the intrusiveness of the search. Do you agree? Should it make a difference to the majority in determining reasonableness if the results of the tests were used in disciplinary proceedings (other than suspending the student from participation in athletics) or were turned over to the police? Why or why not? Would the *Acton* Court permit schools to install surveillance cameras in the bathrooms and locker rooms used by student athletes? Used by all students taking physical education?

c. The nature and immediacy of the governmental concern. The Court finds that deterring drug use by students is an important, if not compelling, concern. Are you convinced by the Court that there is an "epidemic" of drug use in the school district and that an effective way to address the problem is to randomly test student athletes?

See generally Stefkovich and O'Brien, "Drug Testing of Students in Public Schools: Implications of *Vernonia School District v. Acton* for Other Types of School-Related Drug Searches," 113 *Ed. Law Rep.* 521 (1996); Pittman and Slough, "Drug Testing of High School Student Athletes after *Vernonia*," 104 *Ed.Law Rep.* 15 (1995); Note, "Random, Suspicionless Drug Testing of High School Athletes," 86 *J. Crim. L. & Criminology* 1265 (1996); Note, "The 4 R's of Drug Testing in Public Schools: Random Is Reasonable and Rights Are Reduced," 80 *Minn. L. Rev.* 1221 (1996); Note, "A Casualty of the 'War on Drugs': Suspicionless Drug Testing of Student Athletes in *Vernonia School District 47J v. Acton*," 74 *N.C.L. Rev.* 833 (1996); Note, "Suspicionless Drug Testing and the Fourth Amendment: *Vernonia School District 47J v. Acton*," 19 *Harv. J. L & Pub. Pol'y* 209 (1996); Note, "The Constitution Expelled: What Remains of Students' Fourth Amendment Rights?" 28 *Ariz. St. L. J.* 673 (1996).

2. *Applying Acton's Three-Pronged Test to Determine Reasonableness*

a. Random drug testing. Which factor caused the majority to conclude that student athletes in *Acton* have a lower expectation of privacy—the fact that extracurricular activities are voluntary or that student athletes are used to undressing in front of fellow students and coaches? What significance, if any, should it have on the determination of reasonableness that the Vernonia school district's policy was limited to illegal drugs? Two high school students, one of whom is a member of the Library Club and the other a member of the Future Farmers of America at Rushville Consolidated High School, challenge their school district's policy barring high school students from participating in *any* extracurricular activities or driving to and from school unless the student and parent consent to a test for drugs, alcohol, or tobacco in random, unannounced urinalysis examinations. A positive test result will not be used in school discipline proceedings. What result? *See Todd v. Rush County Schools*, 133 F.3d 984 (7th Cir.), *cert. denied*, 525 U.S. 824, 119 S.Ct 68, 142 L.Ed.2d 53 (1998); *Miller v. Wilkes*, 172 F.3d 574, 579, *vacated as moot*, 172 F.3d 582 (8th Cir. 1999) ("students who elect to be involved in school activities have a legitimate expectation of privacy that is diminished to a level below that of the already lowered expectation of non-participating students"). *But see Earls v. Board of Educ. of Tecumseh Public Sch. Dist.*, 242 F. 3d 1264 (2001) (random suspicionless urinalysis drug testing policy for all students participating in competitive extracurricular activities violates Fourth Amendment); *Trinidad School District No. 1 v. Lopez*, 963 P.2d 1095 (Colo. 1998). What about a school district policy that requires all students who have been suspended for three days or more (for fighting, smoking, computer tampering, leaving campus without permission, or profanity directed at faculty or staff, among other offenses) to undergo a drug and alcohol test prior to returning to school? *See Willis by Willis v. Anderson Community School Corp.*, 158 F.3d 415 (7th Cir. 1998), *cert. denied*, 526 U.S. 1019, 119 S.Ct 1254, 143 L. Ed.2d 351 (1999). *But see Vernonia School District 47J v. Acton*, 515 U.S. 646, 685–86, 115 S.Ct.2386, 2406 (1995) (O'Connor, J. dissenting).

A rural school district in West Texas has adopted a policy requiring mandatory drug testing of all teachers and of its students in grades six through twelve. Refusal by a student to consent to testing is treated as a positive test. The policy was adopted after an incident in which thirteen adults in the town were indicted on charges of distributing cocaine. A twelve-year-old student who refused to comply with the policy and acquiesce in the testing, was suspended from school as if he had tested positive for drugs. Each refusal is considered a repeat offense, so that if he continues to refuse to be tested, he can be suspended indefinitely. Is the policy likely to be upheld in the face of a challenge by his parents? *See Tannahill v. Lockney Independent Sch. Dist.*, 133 F. Supp. 2d 919 (2001). Suppose the school district had required medical examinations for many years, including a urinalysis, and it simply had added drug screening to the list of tests. *See Odenheim v. Carlstadt-East Rutherford Regional School Dist.*, 211 N.J. Super. 54, 510 A.2d 709 (1985). In the light of the incidence of alcohol abuse among the young nationally, is it constitutional for school districts to require all students to submit to Breathalyzer tests as they enter school each day? *See generally* Colwell, "Beyond *Vernonia*: When Has a School District Drug Testing Policy Gone Too Far?" 131 *Ed. Law Rep.* 547 (1999); Note, "High School Students, You're in Trouble: How the Seventh Circuit Has Expanded the Scope of Permissible Suspicionless Searches in Public Schools," 1999 *Wis. L. Rev.* 851; Note, "Reclaiming Our Public Schools: A Proposal for School-wide Drug Testing," 21 *Cardozo L. Rev.* 999 (1999).

b. *Random searches for guns and other weapons.* After advising students and their parents at the beginning of the school year of the policy, a high school randomly selects days on which all students, as a condition of entering the school that day, must stand in line before a table and empty their pockets while their backpacks, coats, and other possessions are searched by police officers detailed to the school system. Students are also scanned by a handheld metal detector. A student was found to have a Swiss army knife in his pocket and was arrested for possession of a weapon on school property. Applying the three factors in *Acton*, was the search reasonable? Can the search be characterized as an "administrative search" comparable to searches in airports and government buildings, or does the fact that students are compelled to attend school differentiate this search? Suppose there had been no notice at the beginning of the school year. Were the police acting as agents of school authorities or in their own right? *See In re F.B.*, 555 Pa. 661, 726 A.2d 1056, *cert. denied sub nom. F.B. v. Pennsylvania*, 528 U.S. 1060, 120 S.Ct. 613, 145 L.Ed.2d 508 (1999). *See also In the Interest of S.S.*, 452 Pa.Super. 15, 680 A.2d 1172 (1996). Suppose that a student sees other students being searched as he arrives at school and turns to walk away, and a police officer notices this, apprehends him, and finds a knife. Did the fact that the student turned away give rise to individualized suspicion? *See People v. Parker*, 284 Ill.App.3d 860, 672 N.E.2d 813 (1996).

The use of handheld metal detectors and magnetometers through which students pass has become widespread. Because of the compulsory school laws, students have to comply with these searches. Although they are of limited intrusiveness, the searches are not based on individualized suspicion. What factors would support such searches? *See Thompson v. Carthage School Dist.*, 87 F.3d 979 (8th Cir. 1996); *State v. J.A.*, 679 So.2d 316 (Fla.App. 3 Dist.1996); *People v. Pruitt*, 278 Ill.App.3d 194, 662 N.E. 2d 540, *appeal denied*, 167 Ill.2d 564, 667 N.E.2d 1061 (1996); *People v. Dukes*, 151 Misc.2d 295, 580 N.Y.S.2d 850 (N.Y.Crim.Ct.1992). *Compare* Ferraraccio, "Metal Detectors in the Public Schools: Fourth Amendment Concerns," 28 *J. L. & Educ.* 209 (1999) *with* Johnson, "Metal Detector Searches: An Effective Means to Help Keep Weapons Out of Schools," 29 *J.L. & Educ.* 197 (2000). *See also* Daniel, "Violence and the Public Schools: Student Rights Have Been Weighed in the Balance and Found Wanting," 27 *J. L. & Educ.* 573, 594–95 (1998); Bjorklun, "Using Metal Detectors in the Public Schools: Some Legal Issues," 111 *Ed.Law Rep* 1 (1996).

c. *Drug testing and school employees.* Is mandatory drug testing of school employees—based on concern about a perceived "drug culture"—permissible? What if the fear is that employees are selling illegal drugs to students? Is the policy more likely to be upheld if the testing regime is confined to school bus drivers? Probationary teachers? New hires? *See Knox County Educ. Ass'n v. Knox County Board of Educ.*,58 F.3d 361 (6th Cir. 1998), *cert. denied*, 528 U.S. 812, 120 S.Ct. 46, 145 L.Ed.2d 41 (1999) (despite lack of evidence of a drug or alcohol abuse problem among Knox County's teachers or other professional employees, mandatory suspicionless drug testing of all teachers held constitutional); *Jones v. McKenzie*, 833 F.2d 335 (D.C. Cir. 1987); *Patchoque-Medford Congress of Teachers v. Board of Education*, 119 A.D.2d 35, 505 N.Y.S.2d 888 (1986); *cf. Chandler v. Miller*, 520 U.S. 305, 117 S.Ct. 1295, 137 L.Ed.2d 513 (1997).

3. *Constitutional Duty to Protect Students from Violence and Drugs*

While at school, a student is shot and killed by a fellow student who had previously threatened violence against the deceased. Although these threats were known to school authorities, they failed to take measures to protect the student. Do school officials have a constitutional duty to protect students by virtue of the fact that children are required to attend school in accordance with the compulsory school laws? Is it relevant that school officials have a "custodial and tutelary" relationship with students, as the relationship is characterized by the majority in *Acton? See, e.g., Hasenfus v. LaJeunesse*, 175 F.3d 68, 71–72 (1st Cir. 1999); *Armijo v. Wagon Mound Public Schools*; 159 F.3d 1253, 1261 (10th Cir. 1998); *Graham v. Independent School Dist. No. I-89*, 22 F.3d 991 (10th Cir. 1994) (holding that compulsory school attendance laws do not create an affirmative duty to protect students because there is no custodial relationship equivalent to that when the state has restrained the individual's freedom to act on his own behalf through incarceration or institutionalization). *See also Dorothy J. v. Little Rock School District*, 7 F.3d 729 (8th Cir. 1993); *D.R. v. Middle Bucks Area Vocational Technical School*, 972 F.2d 1364 (3d Cir. 1992). In dicta, the *Acton* Court noted that school officials, despite the "custodial and tutelary" relationship, do not have a constitutional duty to protect students, citing *DeShaney v. Winnebago County Dept. of Social Services*, 489 U.S. 189, 109 S.Ct. 998, 103 L.Ed.2d 249 (1989). *See* Schulze and Martinez, "Into the Snakepit: Section 1983 Liability Under the State-Created Danger Theory for Acts of Private Violence at School," 104 *Ed.Law Rep.* 539 (1995); Note, "Affirmative Duties in the Public Schools After *DeShaney*," 90 *Colum. L. Rev.* 1940 (1990).

IV. PROCEDURAL DUE PROCESS

A. The Allure of Due Process

The issue of liberty within the school has partly to do with the substantive entitlements of students and teachers, their freedom to speak and act without state interference. But even where the substantive standard is clearly fixed, the rights of students and teachers also turn on the degree of assurance that the state will not act arbitrarily in particular instances. Procedural protections are intended to secure the individual against arbitrary governmental action.

Any number of devices might be designed to minimize the risk of arbitrariness. Internal monitoring of administrative behavior within the school that renders school officials bureaucratically accountable for their lapses; reliance on school-based ombudsmen, empowered to investigate student and teacher complaints; inquisitorial inquiries, in which the dispute-resolver draws on whatever information is available: these are all among the conceivable alternatives. *See, e.g.,* Boyer, "Alternatives to Administrative Trial-Type Hearings for Resolving Complex Scientific, Economic, and Social Issues," 71 *Mich. L.Rev.* 111 (1972); Mashaw, "The Management Side of Due Process: Some Theoretical and Litigation Notes on the Assurance of Accuracy, Fairness, and Timeliness in the Adjudication of Social Welfare Claims," 59 *Cornell L.Rev.* 772 (1974); Tribe, "Policy Science: Analysis or Ideology?" 2 *Philos. & Pub. Aff.* 66 (1972).

In American jurisprudence, procedural protections are routinely bound up in the notion of due process of law entailing some sort of hearing conducted by a neutral fact-finder. The equation of the hearing with procedural justice also shapes social policy. As the discussion of the rights of children with disabilities to an appropriate education in chapter 6, *infra*, suggests, the hearing is increasingly regarded as an instrument for vindicating substantive rights. The idea that government is appropriately restrained from acting arbitrarily is not a new one. In *R. v. University of Cambridge*, (1723) 1 Str. 557, the first English case to shape the terms of what in that country is called "natural justice," the court retells the Adam and Eve story as a tale of due process:

> Even God himself did not pass sentence upon Adam, before he was called upon to make his defense. "Adam," says God, "where art thou? Hast thou not eaten of the tree, whereof I commanded thee that thou shouldst not eat?" And the same question was put to Eve also.

The allure of procedural protection—specifically, some sort of hearing—has grown considerably in the intervening centuries. In the late 1950s, Warren Seavey decried the unwillingness of schools to hedge their disciplinary regimes with even rudimentary procedural safeguards. "It is shocking," he argued, "that the officials of a state educational institution . . . should not understand the elementary principles of fair play. It is equally shocking to find that a court supports them in denying to a student the protection given to a pickpocket." Seavey, "Dismissal of Students: 'Due Process,'" 70 *Harv. L.Rev.* 1406, 1407 (1957). As the following excerpt indicates, significant changes occurred in the decades following Professor Seavey's article:

"Proceduralism and Bureaucracy: Due Process in the School Setting"

D. Kirp, 28 *Stan.L.Rev.* 841, 843–47 (1976). Reprinted by permission.

The history of public law during the past decade has been, in no small part, a history of the expansion of procedural protection. Relationships between citizens and government, traditionally shaped by administrative prerogative or legislative rule, are increasingly constrained by the command of the due process clause. Judicial decisions have dramatically altered the legal status of citizens dependent upon government largesse for such services as welfare benefits, housing, employment, and education. While these recipients were traditionally viewed as mere supplicants with few defenses against even admittedly arbitrary government actions, . . . they may now advance claims based on legally cognizable rights. This constitutional claim does not guarantee some minimally adequate level of goods or services. Rather it embodies the right to impartial review of governmental actions which threaten most statutorily created substantive entitlements.

The demand for such rights is partly attributable to the vastly greater goods- and service-providing activities of government, and the resulting increased reliance upon government assistance. Coupled with this new dependency is a growing, albeit difficult to measure, distrust of the ways in which public officials exercise their delegated discretion. . . .

Skepticism about the supposedly enlightened nature of governmental behavior has prompted critics of government programs to equate the discretion exercised by the housing authority or school principal with arbitrariness, to treat the substantial freedom delegated to welfare caseworkers as an instrument of coercion, and to perceive deviations from a norm of uniformity as favoritism. Particular individuals serving in these roles have, without doubt, abused the prerogatives of their offices. But the new perception maintains that discretionary official decisionmaking, in the context of benefits programs, not only works individual injustices but also promotes patterns of disadvantage: black children are suspended from school proportionately more frequently than whites, unwed mothers are denied access to public housing, and outspoken civil servants lose their jobs. The causes of these phenomena are said to inhere in corrupted decisionmaking devices. Given that view, the utility of due process is obvious. Constitutionally guaranteed hearings secure at least a measure of protection against governmental arbitrariness as it affects both individuals and groups, and so encourage the emergence of fair official behavior. . . .

The enduring appeal of due process justice is evident at several levels. Most obviously, it is a basic tenet of American constitutional law. Moreover, fair process has been treated as synonymous with justice, while one *particular* process—the due process hearing—is popularly thought more fair than any alternative mode of decisionmaking. . . .

These general considerations apply with particular force to the schools. For teachers, the right to a hearing has been viewed as a way of curbing the schools' capacity to dismiss them without reason. For students, the hearing has been seen as a device to combat the dramatic rise in student suspensions. . . .

Those who urged that schools be made to conform to a regime of due process envisioned presuspension and pretermination hearings as essential in preserving the student's and teacher's rights as individuals. They hoped that such hearings would produce fairer outcomes and outcomes accepted as fair by those affected. They also anticipated that the constraint of a hearing might have salutary effects: With respect to teachers, it would encourage early evaluation and assessment of performance designed to improve practice; for students, it would reduce reliance on suspensions as a disciplinary tool, encouraging educators to seek less punitive ways of restoring authority and respect.

These aspirations treat due process as important in two distinct respects: as important in and of itself and as important for the outcomes that it generates.

Compare Professor Kirp's analysis with that of Professor Tribe:

> [As an *intrinsic* good,] the hearing may be considered both as a "mode of politics" and as an expression of the rule of law. . . . Whatever its outcome, such a hearing represents a valued human interaction in which the affected person experiences at least the satisfaction of participating in the decision . . . and perhaps the separate satisfaction of receiving an explanation of why the decision is being made in a certain way. . . . [T]hese rights to interchange express the elementary idea that to be a *person*, rather than a *thing*, is at least to be *consulted* about what is done with one. . . . A second, more *instrumental* approach . . . views the requirements of due process as constitutionally . . . valued . . . for their anticipated consequences as means of assuring that the society's agreed-upon rules of conduct, and its rules for distributing various benefits, are in fact accurately and consistently followed. . . . From this "instrumental" perspective, due process . . . ensures that a challenged action accurately reflects the substantive rules applicable to such action; its point is less to assure *participation* than to *use* participation to assure *accuracy*.

L. Tribe, *American Constitutional Law* 666–67 (2d ed. 1988) (emphasis in original).

Which view do you find more persuasive as a matter of legal theory? As a description of how individuals perceive due process? Does a student threatened with suspension or a teacher faced with dismissal care about participation? Is it the rightness of the decision process that matters or whether he or she wins? *See* M. Tushnet, *Red, White and Blue* 241 (1988). *See also* McGuinness, "Procedural Due Process Rights of Public Employees: Basic Rules and a Rationale for a Return to Rule-Oriented Process," 33 *New Eng. L. Rev.* 931, 937 (1999), suggesting both the intrinsic and instrumental rationales for procedural due process:

> Public employers, employees, and the public are well served by meaningful procedural due process protections before adverse action. Procedural due process protections safeguard against errors, retaliation, and other conduct which can deprive a public employee of his or her career and deprive the employer of a valuable employee. Procedural due process also promotes a sense of fairness in the workplace which in turn promotes employee confidence and a positive morale, leading to benefits for all concerned. A positively motivated workforce breeds an environment of collegiality, efficiency, and esprit de corps. Without procedural due process, erroneous

personnel decisions go unchecked. Denials of due process frustrate the entire system by demoralizing valuable employees and rewarding abusive management officials for their own misconduct.

The introduction of due process norms into the life of the school has two other implications that bear noting. It affects the process of student socialization discussed in chapter 2. The student who perceives herself or himself as the passive recipient of whatever measure of justice school authorities make available may develop one view of citizenship rights and relationships with authority; a student who is listened to before discipline is meted out may form a different perception. Due process, in short, can take sides in the dispute between hierarchical and democratic norms of education. *See generally* J. Dewey, *Democracy and Education* (1966); Biber and Minuchin, "The Impact of School Philosophy and Practice on Child Development," in M. Silberman, ed., *The Experience of Schooling* 39 (1971). It also may influence the internal governance structure of the school. Teachers' due process rights, for example, supplement the rights that teachers may acquire through collective bargaining. More generally, reliance on due process legalizes dispute resolution in the school.

The next section charts the development of doctrine. While the focus is on the due process clause—specifically, on whether process is due, and if so, what process is due—the broader concern of the section is with procedural protections against allegedly arbitrary official action.

B. The Development of Constitutional Doctrine

Board of Regents v. Roth
408 U.S. 564, 92 S.Ct. 2701, 33 L.Ed.2d 548 (1972).

Mr. Justice Stewart delivered the opinion of the Court.

In 1968 the respondent, David Roth, was hired for his first teaching job as assistant professor of political science at Wisconsin State University-Oshkosh. He was hired for a fixed term of one academic year. The notice of his faculty appointment specified that his employment would begin on September 1, 1968, and would end on June 30, 1969.[1] The respondent completed that term. But he was informed that he would not be rehired for the next academic year.

---

[1] The respondent had no contract of employment. Rather, his formal notice of appointment was the equivalent of an employment contract. . . .

The respondent had no tenure rights to continued employment. Under Wisconsin statutory law a state university teacher can acquire tenure as a "permanent" employee only after four years of year-to-year employment. Having acquired tenure, a teacher is entitled to continued employment "during efficiency and good behavior." A relatively new teacher without tenure, however, is under Wisconsin law entitled to nothing beyond his one-year appointment.[2] There are no statutory or administrative standards defining eligibility for re-employment. State law thus clearly leaves the decision whether to rehire a nontenured teacher for another year to the unfettered discretion of university officials.

The procedural protection afforded a Wisconsin State University teacher before he is separated from the University corresponds to his job security. As a matter of statutory law, a tenured teacher cannot be "discharged except for cause upon written charges" and pursuant to certain procedures.[3] A nontenured teacher, similarly, is protected to some extent during his one-year term. Rules promulgated by the Board of Regents provide that a nontenured teacher "dismissed" before the end of the year may have some opportunity for review of the "dismissal." But the Rules provide no real protection for a nontenured teacher who simply is not re-employed for the next year. He must be informed by February 1 "concerning retention or nonretention for the ensuing year." But "no reason for non-retention need be given. No review or appeal is provided in such case."[4]

In conformance with these Rules, the President of Wisconsin State University-Oshkosh informed the respondent before February 1, 1969, that he would not be rehired for the 1969–1970 academic year. He gave the respondent no reason for the decision and no opportunity to challenge it at any sort of hearing.

The respondent then brought this action in Federal District Court alleging that the decision not to rehire him for the next year infringed his Fourteenth Amendment rights. . . . First, he alleged that the true reason for the decision was to punish him for certain statements critical of the University administration, and that it therefore violated his right to freedom of speech.[5] Second, he alleged that the failure of University officials to give him notice of any reason for nonretention and an opportunity for a hearing violated his right to procedural due process of law.

. . . The only question presented to us at this stage in the case is whether the respondent had a constitutional right to a statement of reasons and a hearing on the University's decision not to rehire him for another year. We hold that he did not.

I

The requirements of procedural due process apply only to the deprivation of interests encompassed by the Fourteenth Amendment's protection of liberty and property. When protected interests are implicated, the right to some kind of prior hearing is paramount. But the range of interests protected by procedural due process is not infinite.

The District Court decided that procedural due process guarantees apply in this case by assessing and balancing the weights of the particular interests involved. It concluded that the respondent's interest in reemployment at the Wisconsin State University-

---

[2]Wis. Stat. 1967, § 37.31(1), in force at the time, provided in pertinent part that: "All teachers in any state university shall initially be employed on probation. The employment shall be permanent, during efficiency and good behavior, after 4 years of continuous service in the state university system as a teacher."

[3]Wis. Stat. § 37.31(1) further provided that:

"No teacher who has become permanently employed as herein provided shall be discharged except for cause upon written charges. Within 30 days of receiving the written charges, such teacher may appeal the discharge by a written notice to the president of the board of regents of state colleges. The board shall cause the charges to be investigated, hear the case and provide such teacher with a written statement as to their decision."

[4]The Rules, promulgated by the Board of Regents in 1967, provide:

"RULE I—February 1st is established throughout the State University system as the deadline for written notification of non-tenured faculty concerning retention or nonretention for the ensuing year. The President of each University shall give such notice each year on or before this date.

"RULE II—During the time a faculty member is on probation, no reason for nonretention need be given. No review or appeal is provided in such case.

"RULE III— 'Dismissal' as opposed to 'Nonretention' means termination of responsibilities during an academic year. When a nontenure faculty member is dismissed he has no right under Wisconsin Statutes to a review of his case or to appeal. The President may, however, in his discretion, grant a request for a review within the institution, either by a faculty committee or by the President, or both. Any such review would be informal in nature and would be advisory only.

"RULE IV—When a non-tenure faculty member is dismissed he may request a review by or hearing before the Board of Regents. Each such request will be considered separately and the board will, in its discretion, grant or deny same in each individual case."

[5]While the respondent alleged that he was not rehired because of his exercise of free speech, the petitioners insisted that the nonretention decision was based on other, constitutionally valid grounds. The District Court came to no conclusion whatever regarding the true reason for the University President's decision. . . .

Oshkosh outweighed the University's interest in denying him reemployment summarily. 310 F. Supp., at 977–79. Undeniably, the respondent's reemployment prospects were of major concern to him—concern that we surely cannot say was insignificant. And a weighing process has long been a part of any determination of the *form* of hearing required in particular situations by procedural due process.[8] But, to determine whether due process requirements apply in the first place, we must look not to the "weight" but to the *nature* of the interest at stake. . . . We must look to see if the interest is within the Fourteenth Amendment's protection of liberty and property.

"Liberty" and "property" are broad and majestic terms. They are among the "great [constitutional] concepts . . . purposely left to gather meaning from experience. . . . [T]hey relate to the whole domain of social and economic fact, and the statesmen who founded this Nation knew too well that only a stagnant society remains unchanged." *National Ins. Co. v. Tidewater Co.*, 337 U.S. 582, 646 (Frankfurter, J., dissenting). For that reason, the Court has fully and finally rejected the wooden distinction between "rights" and "privileges" that once seemed to govern the applicability of procedural due process rights.[9] The Court has also made clear that the property interests protected by procedural due process extend well beyond actual ownership of real estate, chattels, or money.[10] By the same token, the Court has required due process protection for deprivations of liberty beyond the sort of formal constraints imposed by the criminal process.[11]

Yet, while the Court has eschewed rigid or formalistic limitations on the protection of procedural due process, it has at the same time observed certain boundaries. For the words "liberty" and "property" in the Due Process of the Fourteenth Amendment must be given some meaning.

II

"While this Court has not attempted to define with exactness the liberty . . . guaranteed [by the Fourteenth Amendment], the term has received much consideration, and some of the included things have been definitely stated. Without doubt, it denotes not merely freedom from bodily restraint but also the right of the individual to contract, to engage in any of the common occupations of life, to acquire useful knowledge, to marry, establish a home and bring up children, to worship God according to the dictates of his own conscience, and generally to enjoy those privileges long recognized . . . as essential to the orderly pursuit of happiness by free men." *Meyer v. Nebraska*, 262 U.S. 390, 399 [1923]. In a Constitution for a free people, there can be no doubt that the meaning of "liberty" must be broad indeed. *See, e.g., Bolling v. Sharpe*, 347 U.S. 397, 499–500 [1954]; *Stanley v. Illinois*, 405 U.S. 645.

There might be cases in which a State refused to reemploy a person under such circumstances that interests in liberty would be implicated. But this is not such a case.

The State, in declining to rehire the respondent, did not make any charge against him that might seriously damage his standing and associations in his community. It did not base the nonrenewal of his contract on a charge, for example, that he had been guilty of dishonesty, or immorality. Had it done so, this would be a different case. For "[w]here a person's good name, reputation, honor or integrity is at stake because of what the government is doing to him, notice and an opportunity to be heard are essential." *Wisconsin v. Constantineau*, 400 U.S. 433, 437. . . . *See Cafeteria Workers v. McElroy*, 367 U.S. 886, 898. In such a case, due process would accord an opportunity to refute the charge before University officials.[12] In the

---

[8]"The formality and procedural requisites for the hearing can vary, depending upon the importance of the interest involved and the nature of the subsequent proceedings." *Boddie v. Connecticut*, [401 U.S. 371], 378. *See, e.g., Goldberg v. Kelly*, 397 U.S. 254, 263; *Hannah v. Larche*, 363 U.S. 420. The constitutional requirement of opportunity for some form of hearing before deprivation of a protected interest, of course, does not depend upon such a narrow balancing process. . . .

[9]In a leading case decided many years ago, the Court of Appeals for the District of Columbia Circuit held that public employment in general was a "privilege," not a "right," and that procedural due process guarantees therefore were inapplicable. *Bailey v. Richardson*, 182 F.2d 46 (D.C. Cir. 1950), *aff'd by an equally divided Court*, 341 U.S. 918 [1951]. The basis of this holding has been thoroughly undermined in the ensuing years. For, as Mr. Justice Blackmun wrote for the Court . . . , "this Court now has rejected the concept that constitutional rights turn upon whether a governmental benefit is characterized as a 'right' or a 'privilege.' " *Graham v. Richardson*, 403 U.S. 365, 374. *See, e.g., Morrissey v. Brewer*, [408 U.S. 471], 482 [1972]; *Bell v. Burson*, [402 U.S. 535], 539; *Goldberg V v. Kelly*, [397 U.S. 254], 262; *Shapiro v. Thompson*, 394 U.S. 618, 627 n6; *Piekering v. Board of Educ.*, 391 U.S. 563, 568; *Sherbert v. Verner*, 374 U.S. 398, 404.

[10]*See, e.g., Connell v. Higgenbotham*, 403 U.S. 207, 208; *Bell v. Burson*, [402 U.S. 535]; *Goldberg v. Kelly*, [397 U.S. 254].

[11]"Although the Court has not assumed to define 'liberty' [in the Fifth Amendment's Due Process Clause] with any great precision, that term is not confined to mere freedom from bodily restraint." *Bolling v. Sharpe*, 347 U.S. 497, 499. *See, e.g., Stanley v. Illinois*, 405 U.S. 645.

[12]The purpose of such notice and hearing is to provide the person an opportunity to clear his name. Once a person has cleared his name at a hearing, his employer, of course, may remain free to deny him future employment for other reasons.

present case, however, there is no suggestion whatever that the respondent's interest in his "good name, reputation, honor or integrity" is at stake.

Similarly, there is no suggestion that the State, in declining to reemploy the respondent, imposed on him a stigma or other disability that foreclosed his freedom to take advantage of other employment opportunities. The State, for example, did not invoke any regulations to bar the respondent from all other public employment in state universities. Had it done so, this, again, would be a different case. For "to be deprived not only of present government employment but of future opportunity for it certainly is no small injury. . . ." *Joint Anti-Fascist Refugee Comm. v. McGrath,* [341 U.S.] 185 (Jackson, J., concurring). *See Truax v. Raich,* 239 U.S. 33, 41.[13]

To be sure, the respondent has alleged that the nonrenewal of his contract was based on his exercise of his right to freedom of speech. But this allegation is not now before us. The District Court stayed proceedings on this issue, and the respondent has yet to prove that the decision not to rehire him was, in fact, based on his free speech activities.[14]

Hence, on the record before us, all that clearly appears is that the respondent was not rehired for one year at one university. It stretches the concept too far to suggest that a person is deprived of "liberty" when he simply is not rehired in one job but remains as free as before to seek another. *Cafeteria Workers v. McElroy,* . . . .

III

The Fourteenth Amendment's procedural protection of property is a safeguard of the security of interests that a person has already acquired in specific benefits. These interests—property interests—may take many forms.

Thus the Court has held that a person receiving welfare benefits under statutory and administrative standards defining eligibility for them has an interest in continued receipt of those benefits that is safeguarded by procedural due process. *Goldberg v. Kelly,* 397 U.S. 254. *See Flemming v. Nestor,* 363 U.S. 603, 611. Similarly, in the area of public employment, the Court has held that a public college professor dismissed from an office held under tenure provisions, *Slochower v. Board of Education,* 350 U.S. 551 [1956], and college professors and staff members dismissed during the terms of their contracts, *Wieman v. Updegraff,* 344 U.S. 183 [1952], have interests in continued employment that are safeguarded by due process. Only last year, the Court held that this principle "proscribing summary dismissal from public employment without hearing or inquiry required by due process" also applied to a teacher recently hired without tenure or a formal contract, but nonetheless with a clearly implied promise of continued employment. *Connell v. Higgenbotham,* 403 U.S. 207, 208.

Certain attributes of "property" interests protected by procedural due process emerge from these decisions. To have a property interest in a benefit, a per-

---

[13]The District Court made an assumption "that nonretention by one university or college creates concrete and practical difficulties for a professor in his subsequent academic career." 310 F.Supp., at 979. And the Court of Appeals based its affirmance of the summary judgment largely on the premise that "the substantial adverse effect nonretention is likely to have upon the career interests of an individual professor" amounts to a limitation on future employment opportunities sufficient to invoke procedural due process guarantees. 446 F.2d at 809. But even assuming arguendo, that such a "substantial adverse effect" under these circumstances would constitute a state-imposed restriction on liberty, the record contains no support for these assumptions. There is no suggestion of how nonretention might affect the respondent's future employment prospects. Mere proof, for example, that his record of nonretention in one job, taken alone, might make him somewhat less attractive to some other employers would hardly establish the kind of foreclosure of opportunities amounting to a deprivation of "liberty. . . ."

[14]. . . The Court of Appeals, nonetheless, argued that opportunity for a hearing and a statement of reasons were required here "as a *prophylactic* against nonretention decisions improperly motivated by exercise of protected rights." 446 F.2d at 810 (emphasis supplied). While the Court of Appeals recognized the lack of a finding that the respondent's nonretention was based on exercise of the right of free speech, it felt that the respondent's interest in liberty was sufficiently implicated here because the decision not to rehire him was made "with a background of controversy and unwelcome expressions of opinion." *Ibid.*

When a State would directly impinge upon interests in free speech or free press, this Court has on occasion held that opportunity for a fair adversary hearing must precede the action, whether or not the speech or press interest is clearly protected under substantive First Amendment standards. Thus, we have required fair notice and opportunity for an adversary hearing before an injunction is issued against the holding of rallies and public meetings. *Carroll v. Princess Anne,* 393 U.S. 175. Similarly, we have indicated the necessity of procedural safeguards before a State makes a large-scale seizure of a person's allegedly obscene books, magazines, and so forth. *A Quantity of Books v. Kansas,* 378 U.S. 205; *Marcus v. Search Warrant,* 367 U.S. 717. *See Freedman v. Maryland,* 380 U.S. 51; *Bantam Books v. Sullivan,* 372 U.S. 58. *See generally* Monaghan, "First Amendment Due Process," 83 *Harv.L.Rev.* 518.

In the respondent's case, however, the State has not directly impinged upon interests in free speech or free press in any way comparable to a seizure of books or an injunction against meetings. Whatever may be a teacher's rights of free speech, the interest in holding a teaching job at a state university, *simpliciter,* is not itself a free speech interest.

son clearly must have more than an abstract need or desire for it. He must have more than a unilateral expectation of it. He must, instead, have a legitimate claim of entitlement to it. It is a purpose of the ancient institution of property to protect those claims upon which people rely in their daily lives, reliance that must not be arbitrarily undermined. It is a purpose of the constitutional right to a hearing to provide an opportunity for a person to vindicate those claims.

Property interests, of course, are not created by the Constitution. Rather, they are created and their dimensions are defined by existing rules or understandings that stem from an independent source such as state laws—rules or understandings that secure certain benefits and that support claims of entitlement to those benefits. Thus the welfare recipients in *Goldberg v. Kelly*, 397 U.S. 254 (1970), had a claim of entitlement to welfare payments that was grounded in the statute defining eligibility for them. The recipients had not yet shown that they were, in fact, within the statutory terms of eligibility. But we held that they had a right to a hearing at which they might attempt to do so.

Just as the welfare recipients' "property" interest in welfare payments was created and defined by statutory terms, so the respondent's "property" interest in employment at the Wisconsin State University-Oshkosh was created and defined by the terms of his appointment. Those terms secured his interest in employment up to June 30, 1969. But the important fact in this case is that they specifically provided that the respondent's employment was to terminate on June 30. They did not provide for contract renewal absent "sufficient cause." Indeed, they made no provision for renewal whatsoever.

Thus the terms of the respondent's appointment secured absolutely no interest in reemployment for the next year. They supported absolutely no possible claim of entitlement to reemployment. Nor, significantly, was there any state statute or University rule or policy that secured his interest in reemployment or that created any legitimate claim to it.[16] In these circumstances, the respondent surely had an abstract concern in being rehired, but he did not have a property interest sufficient to require the University authorities to give him a hearing when they declined to renew his contract of employment.

IV

* * *

We must conclude that the summary judgment for the respondent should not have been granted, since the respondent has not shown that he was deprived of liberty or property protected by the Fourteenth Amendment. The judgment of the Court of Appeals, accordingly, is reversed and the case is remanded for further proceedings consistent with this opinion.

It is so ordered.

Mr. Justice Powell took no part in the decision of this case.

Mr. Justice Douglas, dissenting.

Respondent Roth, like Sindermann in the companion case, had no tenure under Wisconsin law and, unlike Sindermann, he had had only one year of teaching at Wisconsin State University-Oshkosh—where during 1968–69 he had been Assistant Professor of Political Science and International Studies. Though Roth was rated by the faculty as an excellent teacher, he had publicly criticized the administration for suspending an entire group of 94 black students without determining individual guilt. He also criticized the university's regime as being authoritarian and autocratic. He used his classroom to discuss what was being done about the black episode; and one day, instead of meeting his class, he went to the meeting of the Board of Regents.

* * *

No more direct assault on academic freedom can be imagined than for the school authorities to be allowed to discharge a teacher because of his or her philosophical, political, or ideological beliefs. The same may well be true of private schools, if through the device of financing or other umbilical cords they become instrumentalities of the State. . . .

When a violation of First Amendment rights is alleged, the reasons for dismissal or for nonrenewal of an employment contract must be examined to see if the reasons given are only a cloak for activity or attitudes protected by the Constitution. . . .

In the case of teachers whose contracts are not renewed, tenure is not the critical issue. In the *Sweezy* case, the teacher, whose First Amendment rights

---

[16]To be sure, the respondent does suggest that most teachers hired on a year-to-year basis by the Wisconsin State University-Oshkosh are, in fact, rehired. But the District Court has not found that there is anything approaching a "common law" of reemployment (*see Perry v. Sindermann*, 408 U.S. 602) so strong as to require University officials to give the respondent a statement of reasons and a hearing on their decision not to rehire him.

were honored, had no tenure but was only a guest lecturer. In the *Keyishian* case, one of the petitioners (Keyishian himself) had only a "one-year-term contract" that was not renewed. 385 U.S. at 592. In *Shelton v. Tucker*, 364 U.S. 479, one of the petitioners was a teacher whose "contract for the ensuing school year was not renewed" ([364 U.S.] at 483) and two others who refused to comply were advised that it made "impossible their reemployment as teachers for the following school year." [364 U.S.] at 484. The oath required in *Keyishian* and the affidavit listing memberships required in *Shelton* were both, in our view, in violation of the First Amendment rights. Those cases mean that conditioning renewal of a teacher's contract upon surrender of First Amendment rights is beyond the power of a State.

There is sometimes a conflict between a claim for First Amendment protection and the need for orderly administration of the school system, as we noted in *Pickering v. Board of Education*, 391 U.S. 563, 569. That is one reason why summary judgments in this class of cases are seldom appropriate. Another reason is that careful factfinding is often necessary to know whether the given reason for nonrenewal of a teacher's contract is the real reason or a feigned one.

* * *

If this nonrenewal implicated the First Amendment, then Roth was deprived of constitutional rights because his employment was conditioned on a surrender of First Amendment rights; and, apart from the First Amendment, he was denied due process when he received no notice and hearing of the adverse action contemplated against him. Without a statement of the reasons for the discharge and an opportunity to rebut those reasons—both of which were refused by petitioners—there is no means short of a lawsuit to safeguard the right not to be discharged for the exercise of First Amendment guarantees. . . . .

* * *

Mr. Justice Marshall, dissenting.

* * *

In my view, every citizen who applies for a government job is entitled to it unless the government can establish some reason for denying the employment. This is the "property" right that I believe is protected by the Fourteenth Amendment and that

cannot be denied "without due process of law." And it is also liberty—liberty to work—which is the "very essence of the personal freedom and opportunity" secured by the Fourteenth Amendment. . . .

Employment is one of the greatest, if not the greatest, benefits that governments offer in modern-day life. When something as valuable as the opportunity to work is at stake, the government may not reward some citizens and not others without demonstrating that its actions are fair and equitable. And it is procedural due process that is our fundamental guarantee of fairness, our protection against arbitrary, capricious, and unreasonable government action.

* * *

We have often noted that procedural due process means many different things in the numerous contexts in which it applies. *See, e.g., Goldberg v. Kelly*, 397 U.S. 254 (1970); *Bell v. Burson*, 402 U.S. 535 (1971). Prior decisions have held that an applicant for admission to practice as an attorney before the United States Board of Tax Appeals may not be rejected without a statement of reasons and a chance for a hearing on disputed issues of fact;[4] that a tenured teacher could not be summarily dismissed without notice of the reasons and a hearing;[5] that an applicant for admission to a state bar could not be denied the opportunity to practice law without notice of the reasons for the rejection of his application and a hearing;[6] and even that a substitute teacher who had been employed only two months could not be dismissed merely because she refused to take a loyalty oath without an inquiry into the specific facts of her case and a hearing on those in dispute.[7] I would follow these cases and hold that respondent was denied due process when his contract was not renewed and he was not informed of the reasons and given an opportunity to respond.

It may be argued that to provide procedural due process to all public employees or prospective employees would place an intolerable burden on the machinery of government. *Cf. Goldberg v. Kelly, supra.* The short answer to that argument is that it is not burdensome to give reasons when reasons exist. Whenever an application for employment is denied, an employee is discharged, or a decision not to rehire an employee is made, there should be some reason

---

[4]*Goldsmith v. Board of Tax Appeals*, 270 U.S. 117 (1926).

[5]*Slochower v. Board of Higher Educ.*, 350 U.S. 551 (1956).

[6]*Willner v. Committee on Character*, 373 U.S. 96 (1963).

[7]*Connell v. Higgenbotham*, 403 U.S. 207 (1971).

for the decision. It can scarcely be argued that government would be crippled by a requirement that the reason be communicated to the person most directly affected by the government's action.

* * *

It might also be argued that to require a hearing and a statement of reasons is to require a useless act, because a government bent on denying employment to one or more persons will do so regardless of the procedural hurdles that are placed in its path. Perhaps this is so, but a requirement of procedural regularity at least renders arbitrary action more difficult. Moreover, proper procedures will surely eliminate some of the arbitrariness that results, not from malice, but from innocent error. "Experience teaches . . . that the affording of procedural safeguards, which by their nature serve to illuminate the underlying facts, in itself often operates to prevent erroneous decisions on the merits from occurring." *Silver v. New York Stock Exchange*, 373 U.S. 341, 366 (1963). When the government knows it may have to justify its decisions with sound reasons, its conduct is likely to be more cautious, careful, and correct. . . .

Accordingly, I dissent.

NOTES AND QUESTIONS

1. Roth: *Scope of the Decision*

To what sources does the Court look in determining whether there exists an interest in liberty or property that would necessitate holding a hearing? Does the Court look to the Constitution itself for the proposition that "government may not adjudicate the claims of individuals by unreliable means"? *See* Van Alstyne, "Cracks in 'The New Property': Adjudicative Due Process in the Administrative State," 62 *Corn.L.Rev.* 445, 483 (1977). Or does the Court insist upon finding some source in state law to buttress each of these interests? *See* McGuinness, "Procedural Due Process Rights of Public Employees: Basic Rules and a Rationale for a Return to Rule-Oriented Process," 33 *New Eng. L. Rev.* 931, 944–45 (1999), describing the various bases on which courts have found property interests protected by the due process clause.

Is the problem, as Justice Stewart suggests, largely definitional rather than one of balancing institutional and individual interests? Did Roth lose because his claim did not fall within acceptable defini-

tions of *property* or *liberty?* How did Justice Douglas define those terms? How should they be defined? Does not the term *property* convey a myriad of legal meanings depending on the context of litigation? Might it mean a right to exclusive enjoyment over competing private interests or a right to compensation or some legal process when governmental deprivation takes place? If the latter meaning is appropriate to *Roth*, is Justice Stewart's formulation of the problem defensible? *See generally* Reich, "The New Property," 73 *Yale L. J..* 733 (1964).

With regard to what constitutes a property interest, *see Geddes v. Northwest Missouri State University*, 49 F.3d 426 (8th Cir. 1995)(even assuming university president had orally promised lifetime employment to untenured professor on annual contracts each limited to one year, in light of contracts and university's written policies providing that oral employment contracts are not binding, professor could not establish the existence of a legitimate expectation of continued employment and thus had no property right); *Huang v. Board of Governors of University of North Carolina*, 902 F.2d 1134 (4th Cir. 1990) (transfer of tenured professor from one department to another, without loss of rank or pay, does not implicate any property interest protected by the due process clause).

2. *The* Sindermann *Case*

In *Perry v. Sindermann*, 408 U.S. 593, 92 S.Ct. 2694, 33 L.Ed.2d 570 (1972), decided the same day as *Roth*, the Supreme Court held that a professor, teaching at an institution lacking a tenure system, might nonetheless have a legitimate claim of entitlement to job tenure, entitling him to procedural due process protection. Sindermann, a professor of government at Odessa Junior College for four years, alleged that his property interest in continued employment, though not secured by a formal contractual tenure provision, was secured by a no less binding understanding fostered by the college administration. The Court declared: "the respondent has alleged the existence of rules and understandings, promulgated and fostered by state officials, that may justify his legitimate claim of entitlement to continued employment absent 'sufficient cause.' We disagree with the Court of Appeals insofar as it held that a mere subjective 'expectancy' is protected by procedural due process, but we agree that the respondent must be given an opportunity to prove the legitimacy of his claim of such entitlement in light of 'the policies and practices of the institution.' "

3. *Distinguishing* Roth *and* Sindermann

What might distinguish the *Roth* and *Sindermann* cases? Was Sindermann's dismissal more stigmatizing than Roth's? Did Sindermann have a more reasonable expectancy of reemployment than Roth? Why was the university's practice with respect to other teachers irrelevant to Roth but relevant to Sindermann? What is the difference between a contract for continued employment implied from the conduct of the parties and a reasonable expectancy of reemployment? *See Bunger v. University of Oklahoma Bd. of Regents*, 95 F.3d 987 (10th Cir. 1996) (failure to follow procedural guidelines for reappointment in university faculty handbook did not create a property interest in reappointment of untenured professors). If property interests are created by reasonable expectations of continued employment or receipt of a benefit, can a state defeat those expectations by explicitly stating that the government may terminate employment or benefits at any time at its discretion?

4. *Interest-Balancing*

Applying a functional approach to the problem of hearings for nontenured teachers, what interests of the school would you take into account? A school district is not required to make public its reasons for dismissal, and the absence of reasons, by itself, does not implicate a liberty interest. *See, e.g., Hayes v. Phoenix-Talent School District*, 893 F.2d 235 (9th Cir. 1990). Does the school have an interest in secrecy? If a school dismisses a teacher for personal reasons, for example, the teacher is contentious or discourteous, are these legitimate reasons that should not be publicized? Is it adequate to argue that the teacher should have an option to demand reasons and a hearing and should bear the consequences of his or her choice? Might the formality of providing reasons and a hearing discourage educational institutions from making hard personnel decisions? Does a hearing subtly shift the burden of persuasion to the school? What of the expenses of a hearing? Should the dismissed teacher be required to pay part of the costs?

What are the interests of the dismissed teacher that you would take into account? Might the absence of reasons for dismissal lead prospective employers to think that he or she was fired for academic incompetence or immorality, even if the firing had no such cause? Will required formalities of hearing and reasons alter substantive decisions or correct arbitrary or erroneous behavior? Might a hearing requirement make schools less likely to dismiss a teacher for the exercise of First Amendment rights?

5. *What Are Property Interests: Subsequent Developments*

A . . . reluctance to look beyond positive state law as a source of rights protected by due process guarantees was evident in Bishop v. Wood, where a three and a half year veteran of the police force, classified as a "permanent employee" by a city ordinance which also provided that he could be dismissed if certain grounds were present, was fired for failure to discharge his duties properly, "without affording him a hearing to determine the sufficiency of the cause for his discharge."[8] Justice Stevens, writing for a closely divided Court, reasoned that "the sufficiency of the claim of entitlement must be decided by reference to state law," which in this case was governed by Still v. Lance,[10] where the North Carolina Supreme Court had held "that an enforceable expectation of continued employment in that state can exist only if the employer by statute or contract has actually granted some form of guarantee." . . .

This exclusively positivist analysis of entitlements undertaken in . . . *Bishop* presents a profoundly novel vision of procedural due process. . . . By failing to conduct "an analysis of the common practices utilized and the expectations generated by [the city], and the manner in which the local ordinance would reasonably be read" by members of the police force, the Court in *Bishop* . . . significantly retreated from its position in *Perry v. Sindermann*, where its finding that a professor arguably had a property interest in his job was based on "an unwritten common law." The practical impact of the Court's adoption of a positivist approach to the definition of "property" in *Bishop v. Wood* is that a public employee can count on procedural due process protection only if the law or contract defining the employee's job expressly provides that the employee can be discharged *only* for cause. . . .

L. Tribe, *American Constitutional Law* 695–697 (2d ed. 1988).

6. *What Are Liberty Interests: Subsequent Developments*

. . . [I]n *Wisconsin v. Constantineau*, the Court found that an individual's liberty was denied when the chief of police posted a notice in all local retail liquor stores forbidding sales of liquor to the person.[110] The

---

[8]426 U.S. 341, 344, 342, 96 S.Ct. 2074, 2076, 48 L.Ed.2d 684 (1976).

[10]279 N.C. 254, 182 S.E.2d 403 (1971).

individual objected that the posting was done without any notice or a hearing. The Court agreed and stated: "Where a person's good name, reputation, honor, or integrity is at stake because of what the government is doing to him, notice and an opportunity to be heard are essential."[111]

However, just a few years later, in *Paul v. Davis*, the Court held that harm to reputation, by itself, is not a deprivation of liberty.[112] In *Paul*, the Louisville, Kentucky chief of police circulated a flyer of those "known" to have committed shoplifting. The individual whose picture and name was included objected saying that his reputation, a liberty interest, was denied without any due process. The Supreme Court, however, disagreed and held that an "interest in reputation alone . . . is neither liberty nor property guaranteed against state deprivation without due process of law."[113]

The Court emphasized that liberty interests are created either by the Bill of Rights or by state law. The Court explained that in addition to the provisions of the Fourteenth Amendment, liberty and property "interests attain this constitutional status by virtue of the fact that they have been initially recognized and protected by state law."[114] In other words, in deciding if there is a liberty interest, the Court is to look at the positive law and not base its decision on a conclusion about the importance of the interest to the individual.

The Court reaffirmed *Paul v. Davis* in *Siegert v. Gilley*.[115] In *Siegert*, an unfavorable recommendation letter was the basis for a civil rights suit. The Supreme Court held that there was not a claim for a denial of liberty because harm to reputation, by itself, is not a loss of liberty.

The issue of whether a person has a liberty interest in his or her reputation is important. On the one hand, recognizing a liberty interest makes sense in light of the obvious importance of a person's reputation within a community and the fact that this is recognized by state laws, such as those creating liability for defamation. On the other hand, the Court in *Paul* clearly was struggling to limit the meaning of liberty and sought to do this by recognizing only liberty interests that are expressly mentioned in the Constitution or created by statute. The Court found that reputation met neither of these requirements.

The Court has indicated, however, that due process is required when there is harm to reputation if it is accompanied by a tangible detriment, such as loss of employment. In *Owen v. City of Independence*, the Supreme Court explained that "[d]ue process requires a hearing on the discharge of a government employee 'if the employer creates and disseminates a false and defamatory impression about the employee in connection with his termination.' "[116] The question, of course, is why reputation matters only if it is accompanied by a loss of a job. Harm to reputation might prevent a person from getting a job in the future and it might be difficult, if not impossible, for a person to prove that effect.

E. Chemerinsky, *Constitutional Law* 446–47 (1997).

See Allen v. Denver Public School Bd., 928 F.2d 978 (10th Cir. 1991) (liberty interest not implicated where dismissed teacher alleged loss of reputation and esteem in her community, but could not show stigmatization resulted in inability to obtain other employment); *Hayes v. Phoenix-Talent School Dist. No. 4*, 893 F.2d 235 (9th Cir. 1990) (even if dismissal of principal for incompetence, inability to relate well with others, and lack of tact amounted to stigmatizing charges, no liberty interest was implicated since reasons were not disclosed to public and plaintiff remained free to seek another job). *But see Winegar v. Des Moines Indep. Community School Dist.*, 20 F.3d 895 (8th Cir. 1994) (allegations of physical abuse of a student by a teacher "are sufficiently stigmatizing to a teacher's reputation, honor and good name in the community to implicate liberty interests").

7. Due Process as an Intrinsic or Instrumental Good

Consider again the distinction between due process as an intrinsic good, important because it protects the interest in participation, and due process as an instrumental good whose significance inheres in the reliability of outcome that it assures. In sharply delimiting the circumstances when due process protections are required, has the Court opted for the latter position? What do you make of the argument that the Court's insistence on identifying a state-created property interest assures that there is a sufficient moral force behind the individual's entitlement claim to assure that a meaningful—that is, fully participatory—hearing is in fact held? *See*

---

[110]400 U.S. 433 (1971).

[111]*Id.* at 437.

[112]424 U.S. 693 (1976).

[113]*Id.* at 712.

[114]*Id.* at 710.

[115]500 U.S. 226 (1991).

[116]445 U.S. 622, 661 (1980), quoting *Codd v. Velger*, 429 U.S. 624 (1977).

Michelman, "Formal and Associational Aims in Procedural Due Process," XVIII *Nomos* 148–53 (1977). *Compare* Tribe, "The Puzzling Persistence of Process-Based Constitutional Theories," 89 *Yale L.J.* 1063 (1980).

8. *Applying the Constitutional Standard*

In the light of *Roth*, *Sindermann*, and the subsequent decisions, how ought the following problems be analyzed:

a. A school district employee stated on his employment application that he had never been convicted of a felony. When a later school board review disclosed that he had been convicted of grand larceny, the employee was dismissed by letter. Is some type of hearing required before the discharge? *See Coleman v. Reed*, 147 F.3d 751,754 (8th Cir. 1998), citing *Cleveland Board of Education v. Loudermill*, 470 U.S. 532, 105 S.Ct. 1487, 84 L.Ed.2d 494 (1985) (pretermination hearing not required, as long as notice and opportunity to respond in order to determine whether reasonable grounds for action).

b. The state of Uncertainty does not formally grant tenure. State law declares: "By May 30th of each school year, the school board shall renew the contracts of its teachers unless it is of the opinion that a teacher's contract shall not be renewed because the teacher has demonstrated a lack of professional competence, has engaged in immoral or insubordinate behavior, or has otherwise demonstrated that he or she is unfit to teach or will have an adverse impact upon the educational program of the school." Should a teacher who was not rehired in an Uncertainty school district be entitled to some kind of hearing? *Compare Greenholtz v. Nebraska Penal Inmates*, 442 U.S. 1 (1979); *Aggarwal v. Ponce School of Medicine*, 837 F.2d 17 (1st Cir. 1988); *Robertson v. Rogers*, 679 F.2d 1090 (4th Cir. 1982); *Grounds v. Tolar Indep. School Dist.*, 856 S.W.2d 417 (Tex. 1993).

c. At a school board meeting, a teacher is accused by one parent of being a "sexpot" and by a student of having lent the student a salacious book. A board member adds, "I know enough about the teacher to make me sick." The school board fails to renew the teacher's contract without making any charge or introducing findings concerning the basis of the board's actions. Should a court require a hearing? *Compare Harden v. Adams*, 841 F.2d 1091

(11th Cir. 1988); *Brandt v. Board of Co-operative Education Services*, 820 F.2d 41 (2d Cir. 1987); *Hardiman v. Jefferson County Board of Education*, 709 F.2d 635 (11th Cir. 1983); *Dennis v. S & S Consolidated Rural High School District*, 577 F.2d 338 (5th Cir. 1978); *McGhee v. Draper*, 564 F.2d 902 (10th Cir. 1977). *See also Seibert v. University of Oklahoma Health Sciences Center*, 867 F.2d 591 (10th Cir. 1989).

d. Should the demotion of a department head to the status of classroom teacher require a hearing if department heads serve at the pleasure of the principal and if the principal had indicated that he thought the teacher incompetent as department head? *Compare Moore v. Otero*, 557 F.2d 435 (5th Cir. 1977); *Levitt v. University of Texas at El Paso*, 759 F.2d 1224 (5th Cir. 1985); *Skehan v. Board of Trustees*, 669 F.2d 142 (3d Cir. 1982); *Smith v. Ouachita Parish School Board*, 702 So.2d 727 (La.App.2 Cir. 1997). Would the transfer of a teacher to another school, under circumstances that hinted at reprimand but without reduced compensation, require a hearing? *See Thomas v. Smith,* 897 F.2d 154 (5th Cir. 1989); *Sullivan v. Brown*, 544 F.2d 279 (6th Cir. 1976). What about a teacher who is removed from his position as head football coach, although retaining his position as a teacher? *See Hill v. Silsbee Indep. School Dist.*, 933 F.Supp. 616 (E.D.Texas 1996); *Brewer v. Purvis*, 816 F.Supp. 1560 (M.D. Ga. 1993); *Lagos v. Modesto City Schools Dist.*, 843 F.2d 347 (9th Cir.), *cert. denied*, 488 U.S. 926, 109 S.Ct. 309, 102 L.Ed.2d 328 (1988). *But see Lowder v. Minidoka County Joint School Dist. No. 331*, 132 Idaho 834, 979 P.2d 1192 (Idaho 1999) (property interest in extra day assignments, which by statute were part of the automatically renewable terms of employment, mandated notice and hearing prior to elimination of extra day assignments and reduction in salary to base 190 days).

e. The contract of an untenured university lecturer is not renewed, the university stating publicly that he lacks a sufficient number of scholarly publications. Should he have a due process claim? Suppose the statement was made in a private meeting involving only the lecturer and the responsible administrator. *See Weinstein v. University of Illinois*, 811 F.2d 1091, 1096 (7th Cir. 1987).

f. A teacher is ordered, without explanation, to take a psychiatric examination. He refuses and is transferred from the classroom to the library. Is he entitled to a hearing? *See Newman v. Board of Edu-*

cation, 594 F.2d 299 (2d Cir. 1979); *Stewart v. Pearce*, 484 F.2d 1031 (9th Cir. 1973). Does placement of a teacher on medical leave without a hearing violate due process? *Palmer v. Independent School Dist. No. 917*, 547 N.W. 2d 899 (Minn.1996).

g. A psychologist, informed by a student that he feels guilty about "something sexual" which occurred with a teacher, directs the student to see a therapist. Only later, in consultation with the student and the therapist, is the incident reported to school authorities. The teacher is suspended for five days. Is he entitled to a hearing? *See Pesce v. J. Sterling Morton High School District 201*, 830 F.2d 789 (7th Cir. 1987).

h. A teacher is arrested on charges of endangering the welfare of children, selling/furnishing liquor to minors, and corruption of minors. A statute requires the state Commission on Professional Standards to suspend the license of teachers arrested on charges involving crimes of moral turpitude. The teacher has not yet been convicted. Is the teacher entitled to a hearing prior to the suspension of her teaching certificate? *See Slater v. Pennsylvania Dept. of Educ.* 725 A.2d 1248 (Pa. 1999); *Petron v. Dept. of Educ.*, 726 A.2d 1091 (Pa.1999).

i. Would the invalidation of permanent teaching certificates for all teachers in a state violate procedural or substantive due process? *See Connecticut Education Association v. Tirozzi*, 210 Conn. 286, 554 A.2d 1065 (Conn. 1989).

j. If a school dismisses tenured teachers due to financial exigency, do the dismissed teachers have a constitutional right to a hearing, at which they can challenge the existence of the alleged financial exigency? *See Johnston-Taylor v. Gannon*, 974 F.2d 1338 (6th Cir. 1992); *Goldberg v. Board of Educ. of the Hempstead School Dist.*, 777 F. Supp. 1109 (E.D. N.Y.1991). Is an elementary school principal reassigned to a teaching position because of budgetary constraints or a principal displaced because her school is closed and reassigned to a lesser administrative position, entitled to a hearing before nonrenewal of the contract for position of principal? *See Cole v. Ruidoso Municipal Schools*, 947 F.2d 903 (10th Cir. 1991); *Hatcher v. Board of Public Education*, 809 F.2d 1546 (11th Cir. 1987). *See* Seaquist and Kelly, "Faculty Dismissal Because of Enrollment Declines," 28 *J. L. & Educ.* 193 (1999).

9. *Statutory Dismissal Procedures*

With few exceptions, most statutes require lengthy and detailed procedures before dismissal. Alabama's statutory provisions are typical. AL ST §§ 16-24-1 *et seq.* (West 1999). A dismissed teacher must be notified of his or her dismissal in writing and is entitled to a detailed statement of the reasons for the dismissal. If the dismissed teacher indicates a desire for a hearing, the school administration is required to conduct one. The hearing may be public or private at the teacher's discretion; the teacher has the right to counsel, to present evidence and witnesses, to cross-examine witnesses, and to subpoena witnesses. The hearing is held before the board of education, and a majority of the board must vote to dismiss the teacher for the removal to be effective. Provision is made for appeal to the state tenure commission, which reviews the record made before the board of education, with the board and the teacher each being given an opportunity to be heard. The decision of the state commission is final.

In Colorado, if the teacher requests a hearing it shall be conducted by an impartial hearing officer selected jointly by the teacher and the superintendent. If they fail to agree on the selection of a hearing officer, they are to request the department of personnel to assign an administrative law judge. The board of education reviews the hearing officer's findings of fact and recommendation, and enters its written order. If the teacher is dismissed, he or she can appeal to the court of appeals, which bases its review on the record before the hearing officer. C.R.S.A. § 22-63-602.

Is the majority in *Roth* and *Sindermann* open to the charge that they have chosen to protect only those who do not need protection?

---

g
419 U.S. 565, 95 S.Ct. 729, 42 L.Ed.2d 725 (1975).

Mr. Justice White delivered the opinion of the Court.

This appeal by various administrators of the Columbus, Ohio, Public School system (CPSS) challenges the judgment of a three-judge federal court, declaring that appellees—various high school students in the CPSS—were denied due process of law contrary to the command of the Fourteenth Amendment in that they were temporarily suspended from their high schools without a hearing either prior to suspension or within a reasonable time thereafter, and enjoining the administrators to remove all references to such suspensions from the students' records.

I

Ohio law, Rev. Code Ann. § 3313.64 (1972), provides for free education to all children between the ages of six and 21. Section 3313.66 of the Code empowers the principal of an Ohio public school to suspend a pupil for misconduct for up to 10 days or to expel him. In either case, he must notify the student's parents within 24 hours and state the reasons for his action. A pupil who is expelled, or his parents, may appeal the decision to the Board of Education and in connection therewith shall be permitted to be heard at the board meeting. The Board may reinstate the pupil following the hearing. No similar procedure is provided in § 3313.66 or any other provision of state law for a suspended student. Aside from a regulation tracking the statute, at the time of the imposition of the suspensions in this case the CPSS itself had not issued any written procedure applicable to suspensions. Nor, so far as the record reflects, had any of the individual high schools involved in this case. Each, however, had formally or informally described the conduct for which suspension could be imposed.

The nine named appellees, each of whom alleged that he or she had been suspended from public high school in Columbus for up to 10 days without a hearing pursuant to § 3313.66, filed an action under 42 U.S.C. § 1983 against the Columbus Board of Education and various administrators of the CPSS. The complaint sought a declaration that § 3313.66 was unconstitutional in that it permitted public school administrators to deprive plaintiffs of their rights to an education without a hearing of any kind, in violation of the procedural due process component of the Fourteenth Amendment. It also sought to enjoin the public school officials from issuing future suspensions pursuant to § 3313.66 and to require them to remove references to the past suspensions from the records of the students in question.

* * *

II

At the outset, appellants contend that because there is no constitutional right to an education at public expense, the Due Process Clause does not protect against expulsions from the public school system. This position misconceives the nature of the issue and is refuted by prior decisions. The Fourteenth Amendment forbids the State to deprive any person of life, liberty, or property without due process of law.

Protected interests in property are normally "not created by the Constitution. Rather, they are created and their dimensions are defined" by an independent source such as state statutes or rules entitling the citizen to certain benefits. *Board of Regents v. Roth*, 408 U.S. 564, 577 (1972).

* * *

Here, on the basis of state law, appellees plainly had legitimate claims of entitlement to a public education. Ohio Rev. Code Ann. §§ 3313.48 and 3313.64 (1972 and Supp. 1973) direct local authorities to provide a free education to all residents between five and 21 years of age, and a compulsory-attendance law requires attendance for a school year of not less than 32 weeks. Ohio Rev. Code Ann. § 3321.04 (1972). It is true that § 3313.66 of the Code permits school principals to suspend students for up to 10 days; but suspensions may not be imposed without any grounds whatsoever. All of the schools had their own rules specifying the grounds for expulsion or suspension. Having chosen to extend the right to an education to people of appellees' class generally, Ohio may not withdraw that right on grounds of misconduct, absent fundamentally fair procedures to determine whether the misconduct has occurred. . . .

. . . The authority possessed by the State to prescribe and enforce standards of conduct in its schools, although concededly very broad, must be exercised consistently with constitutional safeguards. Among other things, the State is constrained to recognize a student's legitimate entitlement to a public education as a property interest which is protected by the Due Process Clause and which may not be taken away for misconduct without adherence to the minimum procedures required by that Clause.

The Due Process Clause also forbids arbitrary deprivations of liberty. "Where a person's good name, reputation, honor, or integrity is at stake because of what the government is doing to him," the minimal requirements of the Clause must be satisfied. *Wisconsin v. Constantineau*, 400 U.S. 433, 437 (1971); *Board of Regents v. Roth, supra*, at 573. School authorities here suspended appellees from school for periods of up to 10 days based on charges of misconduct. If sustained and recorded, those charges could seriously damage the students' standing with their fellow pupils and their teachers as well as interfere with later opportunities for higher education and employment. It is apparent that the claimed right of the State to determine unilaterally and without process whether that misconduct has occurred immediately collides with the requirements of the Constitution.

Appellants proceed to argue that even if there is a right to a public education protected by the Due Process Clause generally, the Clause comes into play only when the State subjects a student to a "severe detriment or grievous loss." The loss of 10 days, it is said, is neither severe nor grievous and the Due Process Clause is therefore of no relevance. Appellants' argument is again refuted by our prior decisions; for in determining "whether due process requirements apply in the first place, we must look not to the 'weight' but to the *nature* of the interest at stake." *Board of Regents v. Roth, supra*, at 570–71. Appellees were excluded from school only temporarily, it is true, but the length and consequent severity of a deprivation, while another factor to weigh in determining the appropriate form of hearing, "is not decisive of the basic right" to a hearing of some kind. *Fuentes v. Shevin*, 407 U.S. 67, 86 (1972). . . .

A short suspension is, of course, a far milder deprivation than expulsion. But, "education is perhaps the most important function of state and local governments," *Brown v. Board of Education*, 347 U.S. 483, 493 (1954), and the total exclusion from the educational process for more than a trivial period, and certainly if the suspension is for 10 days, is a serious event in the life of the suspended child. Neither the property interest in educational benefits temporarily denied nor the liberty interest in reputation, which is also implicated, is so insubstantial that suspensions may constitutionally be imposed by any procedure the school chooses, no matter how arbitrary.

III

"Once it is determined that due process applies, the question remains what process is due." *Morrissey v. Brewer*, 408 U.S. at 481. We turn to that question, fully realizing as our cases regularly do that the interpretation and application of the Due Process Clause are intensely practical matters and that "[t]he very nature of due process negates any concept of inflexible procedures universally applicable to every imaginable situation." *Cafeteria Workers v. McElroy*, 367 U.S. 886, 895 (1961). We are also mindful of our own admonition:

> "Judicial interposition in the operation of the public school system of the Nation raises problems requiring care and restraint. . . . By and large, public education

in our Nation is committed to the control of state and local authorities." *Epperson v. Arkansas*, 393 U.S. 97, 104 (1968).

There are certain bench marks to guide us, however. *Mullane v. Central Hanover Trust Co.*, 339 U.S. 306 (1950), a case often invoked by later opinions, said that "[m]any controversies have raged about the cryptic and abstract words of the Due Process Clause but there can be no doubt that at a minimum they require that deprivation of life, liberty or property by adjudication be preceded by notice and opportunity for hearing appropriate to the nature of the case." *Id.* at 313. . . . At the very minimum, therefore, students facing suspension and the consequent interference with a protected property interest must be given *some* kind of notice and afforded some kind of hearing. . . .

It also appears from our cases that the timing and content of the notice and the nature of the hearing will depend on appropriate accommodation of the competing interests involved. . . . The student's interest is to avoid unfair or mistaken exclusion from the educational process, with all of its unfortunate consequences. The Due Process Clause will not shield him from suspensions properly imposed, but it disserves both his interest and the interest of the State if his suspension is in fact unwarranted. The concern would be mostly academic if the disciplinary process were a totally accurate, unerring process, never mistaken and never unfair. Unfortunately, that is not the case, and no one suggests that it is. Disciplinarians, although proceeding in utmost good faith, frequently act on the reports and advice of others; and the controlling facts and the nature of the conduct under challenge are often disputed. The risk of error is not at all trivial, and it should be guarded against if that may be done without prohibitive cost or interference with the educational process.

The difficulty is that our schools are vast and complex. Some modicum of discipline and order is essential if the educational function is to be performed. Events calling for discipline are frequent occurrences and sometimes require immediate, effective action. Suspension is considered not only to be a necessary tool to maintain order but a valuable educational device. The prospect of imposing elaborate hearing requirements in every suspension case is viewed with great concern, and many school authorities may well prefer the untrammeled power to act unilaterally, unhampered by rules about notice and hearing. But it would be a strange disciplinary system in an educational institution if no communication was sought by the disciplinarian with the student in an effort to inform him of his dereliction and to let him tell his side of the story in order to make sure that an injustice is not done. . . .[9]

We do not believe that school authorities must be totally free from notice and hearing requirements if their schools are to operate with acceptable efficiency. Students facing temporary suspension have interests qualifying for protection of the Due Process Clause, and due process requires, in connection with a suspension of 10 days or less that the student be given oral or written notice of the charges against him and, if he denies them, an explanation of the evidence the authorities have and an opportunity to present his side of the story. The Clause requires at least these rudimentary precautions against unfair or mistaken findings of misconduct and arbitrary exclusion from school.

There need be no delay between the time "notice" is given and the time of hearing. In the great majority of cases the disciplinarian may informally discuss the alleged misconduct with the student minutes after it has occurred. We hold only that, in being given an opportunity to explain his version of the facts at this discussion, the student first be told what he is accused of doing and what the basis of the accusation is. . . . Since the hearing may occur almost immediately following the misconduct, it follows that as a general rule notice and hearing should precede removal of the student from school. We agree with the District Court, however, that there are recurring situations in which prior notice and hearing cannot be insisted upon. Students whose presence poses a continuing danger to persons or property or an ongoing threat of disrupting the academic process may be immediately removed from school. In such cases, the necessary notice and rudimentary hearing should follow as soon as practicable, as the District Court indicated.

In holding as we do, we do not believe that we have imposed procedures on school disciplinarians which are inappropriate in a classroom setting. Instead we have imposed requirements which are, if anything, less than a fair-minded school principal would impose upon himself in order to avoid unfair suspensions. Indeed, according to the testimony of the principal of Marion-Franklin High School, that school had an informal procedure, remarkably similar to that which we now require, applicable to suspensions generally but which was not followed in this case. Similarly, . . . school principals in the CPSS are now required by local rule to provide at least as much as the constitutional minimum which we have described.

We stop short of construing the Due Process Clause to require, countrywide, that hearings in connection with short suspensions must afford the student the opportunity to secure counsel, to confront and cross-examine witnesses supporting the charge, or to call his own witnesses to verify his version of the incident. Brief disciplinary suspensions are almost countless. To impose in each such case even truncated trial-type procedures might well overwhelm administrative facilities in many places and, by diverting resources, cost more than it would save in educational effectiveness. Moreover, further formalizing the suspension process and escalating its formality and adversary nature may not only make it too costly as a regular disciplinary tool but also destroy its effectiveness as part of the teaching process.

On the other hand, requiring effective notice and informal hearing permitting the student to give his version of the events will provide a meaningful hedge against erroneous action. At least the disciplinarian will be alerted to the existence of disputes about facts and arguments about cause and effect. He may then determine himself to summon the accuser, permit cross-examination, and allow the student to present his own witnesses. In more difficult

---

[9]The facts involved in this case illustrate the point. Betty Crome was suspended for conduct which did not occur on school grounds, and for which mass arrests were made—hardly guaranteeing careful individualized factfinding by the police or by the school principal. She claims to have been involved in no misconduct. However, she was suspended for 10 days without ever being told what she was accused of doing or being given an opportunity to explain her presence among those arrested. Similarly, Dwight Lopez was suspended, along with many others, in connection with a disturbance in the lunchroom. Lopez says he was not one of those in the lunchroom who was involved. However, he was never told the basis for the principal's belief that he was involved, nor was he ever given an opportunity to explain his presence in the lunchroom. The school principals who suspended Crome and Lopez may have been correct on the merits, but it is inconsistent with the Due Process Clause to have made the decision that misconduct had occurred without at some meaningful time giving Crome or Lopez an opportunity to persuade the principals otherwise.

We recognize that both suspensions were imposed during a time of great difficulty for the school administrations involved. At least in Lopez' case there may have been an immediate need to send home everyone in the lunchroom in order to preserve school order and property; and the administrative burden of providing 75 "hearings" of any kind is considerable. However, neither factor justifies a disciplinary suspension without at any time gathering facts relating to Lopez specifically, confronting him with them, and giving him an opportunity to explain.

cases, he may permit counsel. In any event, his discretion will be more informed and we think the risk of error substantially reduced.

Requiring that there be at least an informal give-and-take between student and disciplinarian, preferably prior to the suspension, will add little to the factfinding function where the disciplinarian himself has witnessed the conduct forming the basis for the charge. But things are not always as they seem to be, and the student will at least have the opportunity to characterize his conduct and put it in what he deems the proper context.

We should also make it clear that we have addressed ourselves solely to the short suspension, not exceeding 10 days. Longer suspensions or expulsions for the remainder of the school term, or permanently, may require more formal procedures. Nor do we put aside the possibility that in unusual situations, although involving only a short suspension, something more than the rudimentary procedures will be required.

IV

The District Court found each of the suspensions involved here to have occurred without a hearing, either before or after the suspension, and that each suspension was therefore invalid and the statute unconstitutional insofar as it permits such suspensions without notice or hearing. Accordingly, the judgment is
Affirmed.

Mr. Justice Powell, with whom The Chief Justice, Mr. Justice Blackmun, and Mr. Justice Rehnquist join, dissenting.

The Court today invalidates an Ohio statute that permits student suspensions from school without a hearing "for not more than ten days." The decision unnecessarily opens avenues for judicial intervention in the operation of our public schools that may affect adversely the quality of education. The Court holds for the first time that the federal courts, rather than educational officials and state legislatures, have the authority to determine the rules applicable to routine classroom discipline of children and teenagers in the public schools. It justifies this unprecedented intrusion into the process of elementary and secondary education by identifying a new constitutional right: the right of a student not to be suspended for as much as a single day without notice and a due process hearing either before or promptly following the suspension.

The Court's decision rests on the premise that, under Ohio law, education is a property interest protected by the Fourteenth Amendment's Due Process Clause and therefore that any suspension requires notice and a hearing. In my view, a student's interest in education is not infringed by a suspension within a limited period prescribed by Ohio law. Moreover, to the extent that there may be some arguable infringement, it is too speculative, transitory, and insubstantial to justify imposition of a constitutional rule.

I

In identifying property interests subject to due process protections, the Court's past opinions make clear that these interests "are created and their *dimensions are defined* by existing rules or understandings that stem from an independent source such as state law." *Board of Regents v. Roth, supra,* at 577 (emphasis supplied). The Ohio statute that creates the right to a "free" education also explicitly authorizes a principal to suspend a student for as much as 10 days. Ohio Rev. Code Ann. §§ 3313.48, 3313.64, 3313.66 (1972 and Supp. 1973). Thus the very legislation which "defines" the "dimension" of the student's entitlement, while providing a right to education generally, does not establish this right free of discipline imposed in accord with Ohio law. Rather, the right is encompassed in the entire package of statutory provisions governing education in Ohio—of which the power to suspend is one. . . .

But however one may define the entitlement to education provided by Ohio law, I would conclude that a deprivation of not more than 10 days' suspension from school, imposed as a routine disciplinary measure, does not assume constitutional dimensions. Contrary to the Court's assertion, our cases support rather than "refute" appellants' argument that "the Due Process Clause . . . comes into play only when the State subjects a student to a 'severe detriment or grievous loss.' " . . .

The Ohio suspension statute allows no serious or significant infringement of education. It authorizes only a maximum suspension of eight school days, less than 5% of the normal 180-day school year. Absences of such limited duration will rarely affect a pupil's opportunity to learn or his scholastic performance. Indeed, the record in this case reflects no educational injury to appellees. . . .

The Court also relies on a perceived deprivation of "liberty" resulting from any suspension, arguing— again without factual support in the record pertaining to these appellees—that a suspension harms a student's reputation. In view of the Court's decision in *Board of Regents v. Roth, supra,* I would have thought that this argument was plainly untenable. Underscoring the need for "serious damage" to reputation, the Roth Court held that a nontenured teacher who is not rehired by a public university could not claim to suffer sufficient reputational injury to require constitutional protections. Surely a brief suspension is of less serious consequence to the reputation of a teenage student.

II

In prior decisions, this Court has explicitly recognized that school authorities must have broad discretionary authority in the daily operation of public schools. This includes wide latitude with respect to maintaining discipline and good order. . . .

The Court today turns its back on these precedents. It can hardly seriously be claimed that a school principal's decision to suspend a pupil for a single day would "directly and sharply implicate basic constitutional values." . . .

A

I turn now to some of the considerations which support the Court's former view regarding the comprehensive authority of the States and school officials "to prescribe and control conduct in the schools." . . . Unlike the divergent and even sharp conflict of interests usually present where due process rights are asserted, the interests here implicated—of the State through its schools and of the pupils—are essentially congruent.

The State's interest, broadly put, is in the proper functioning of its public school system for the benefit of all pupils and the public generally. Few rulings would interfere more extensively in the daily functioning of schools than subjecting routine discipline to the formalities and judicial oversight of due process. Suspensions are one of the traditional means—ranging from keeping a student after class to permanent expulsion—used to maintain discipline

in the schools. It is common knowledge that maintaining order and reasonable decorum in school buildings and classrooms is a major educational problem, and one which has increased significantly in magnitude in recent years. Often the teacher, in protecting the rights of other children to an education (if not his or their safety), is compelled to rely on the power to suspend.

The facts set forth in the margin[10] leave little room for doubt as to the magnitude of the disciplinary problem in the public schools, or as to the extent of reliance upon the right to suspend. They also demonstrate that if hearings were required for a substantial percentage of short-term suspensions, school authorities would have time to do little else.

B

The State's generalized interest in maintaining an orderly school system is not incompatible with the individual interest of the student. Education in any meaningful sense includes the inculcation of an understanding in each pupil of the necessity of rules and obedience thereto. This understanding is no less important than learning to read and write. One who does not comprehend the meaning and necessity of discipline is handicapped not merely in his education but throughout his subsequent life. In an age when the home and church play a diminishing role in shaping the character and value judgments of the young, a heavier responsibility falls upon the schools. When an immature student merits censure for his conduct, he is rendered a disservice if appropriate sanctions are not applied or if procedures for their application are so formalized as to invite a challenge to the teacher's authority—an invitation which rebellious or even merely spirited teenagers are likely to accept.

The lesson of discipline is not merely a matter of the student's self-interest in the shaping of his own character and personality; it provides an early understanding of the relevance to the social compact of respect for the rights of others. The classroom is the laboratory in which this lesson of life is best learned. . . .

In assessing in constitutional terms the need to protect pupils from unfair minor discipline by school authorities, the Court ignores the commonality of inter-

---

[10]. . . . [A]n amicus brief submitted by several school associations in Ohio indicates that the number of suspensions is significant: in 1972–1973, 4,054 students out of a school enrollment of 81,007 were suspended in Cincinnati; 7,352 of 57,000 students were suspended in Akron; and 14,598 of 142,053 students were suspended in Cleveland. . . .

est of the State and pupils in the public school system. Rather, it thinks in traditional judicial terms of an adversary situation. To be sure, there will be the occasional pupil, innocent of any rule infringement who is mistakenly suspended or whose infraction is too minor to justify suspension. But, while there is no evidence indicating the frequency of unjust suspensions, common sense suggests that they will not be numerous in relation to the total number, and that mistakes or injustices will usually be righted by informal means.

C

One of the more disturbing aspects of today's decision is its indiscriminate reliance upon the judiciary, and the adversary process, as the means of resolving many of the most routine problems arising in the classroom. In mandating due process procedures the Court misapprehends the reality of the normal teacher-pupil relationship. There is an ongoing relationship, one in which the teacher must occupy many roles—educator, adviser, friend, and, at times, parent-substitute. It is rarely adversary in nature except with respect to the chronically disruptive or insubordinate pupil whom the teacher must be free to discipline without frustrating formalities.

* * *

III

No one can foresee the ultimate frontiers of the new "thicket" the Court now enters. Today's ruling appears to sweep within the protected interest in education a multitude of discretionary decisions in the educational process. Teachers and other school authorities are required to make many decisions that may have serious consequences for the pupil. They must decide, for example, how to grade the student's work, whether a student passes or fails a course, whether he is to be promoted, whether he is required to take certain subjects, whether he may be excluded from interscholastic athletics or other extracurricular activities, whether he may be removed from one school and sent to another, whether he may be bused long distances when available schools are nearby, and whether he should be placed in a "general," "vocational," or "college-preparatory" track.

In these and many similar situations claims of impairment of one's educational entitlement identical in principle to those before the Court today can be asserted with equal or greater justification. Likewise, in many of these situations, the pupil can advance the same types of speculative and subjective injury given critical weight in this case. The District Court, relying upon generalized opinion evidence, concluded that a suspended student may suffer psychological injury. . . . The Court appears to adopt this rationale.

It hardly need be said that if a student, as a result of a day's suspension, suffers "a blow" to his "self esteem," "feels powerless," views "teachers with resentment," or feels "stigmatized by his teachers," identical psychological harms will flow from many other routine and necessary school decisions. The student who is given a failing grade, who is not promoted, who is excluded from certain extracurricular activities, who is assigned to a school reserved for children of less than average ability, or who is placed in the "vocational" rather than the "college preparatory" track, is unlikely to suffer any less psychological injury than if he were suspended for a day for a relatively minor infraction.

If, as seems apparent, the Court will now require due process procedures whenever such routine school decisions are challenged, the impact upon public education will be serious indeed. . . .

NOTES AND QUESTIONS

1. Is Goss *Still Good Law?*

Goss was decided prior to the *Bishop* opinion, discussed in the excerpt from Tribe, *American Constitutional Law, supra*. Does *Goss* look beyond the terms of state law in determining the nature of the student's property interest in a manner inconsistent with *Bishop*? *Goss* rejects the argument that the statutorily created right to an education, on which the property claim rests, is properly qualified by the possibility of short suspensions as expressly permitted in the same statute. Can that position be reconciled with the subsequent decisions? Is the nature of the interest—access to education in *Goss* and employment in *Bishop*—constitutionally relevant here? If so, how?

What of the interest in liberty identified in *Goss*? Does it survive the *Paul v. Davis* and *Siegert v. Gilley* decisions, discussed in Chemerinsky, *Constitutional Law, supra*?

2. Goss: *Scope of the Opinion*

What is the nature of the property interest, and the liberty interest, which leads the *Goss* Court to conclude that some sort of hearing must precede short-term suspensions? In *Cleveland Board of Education v. Loudermill*, 470 U.S. 532, 105 S.Ct. 1487, 84 L.Ed.2d 494 (1985), decided nine years later, the Court held that a postdetermination hearing met the requirements of due process for teachers. Is *Loudermill* now controlling?

How do the majority and dissent differ with respect to the intrinsic importance of a due process hearing; the instrumental importance of a due process hearing, that is, the possibility that such hearings will uncover errors of fact and hence prevent injustices; the impact of the decision on the governance of schools; and the appropriate role of the judiciary in setting educational policy? In this light, how do you reconcile the majority's assertion that the required procedures "are, if anything, less than a fair-minded school principal would impose upon himself" with the minority's claim that "few rulings would interfere more extensively in the daily functioning of the schools"? Do the two opinions have in mind different understandings of school governance?

3. *What Kind of Hearing?*

Goss speaks both to the appropriateness of providing some sort of process and to the specifics of the process that is due. The two are treated as analytically distinct, the "what" process calculus being premised on essentially utilitarian considerations. In *Mathews v. Eldridge*, 424 U.S. 319, 335, 96 S.Ct. 893, 903, 47 L.Ed.2d 18 (1976), the Court summarizes these factors: "First, the private interest that will be affected by the official action; second, the risk of an erroneous deprivation of such interest through the procedures used, and the probable value, if any, of additional substitute procedural safeguards; and finally, the Government's interest, including the function involved and the fiscal and administrative burdens that the additional or substitute procedural requirement would entail."

How well does the Court apply this utilitarian calculus to the circumstances of short-term suspensions? What do you make of the following assessment of the aspiration of the opinion?

> By the very device of imposing minimal procedural safeguards, premised on a formal (but thin) statutory entitlement, the decision aspires to increase reliance on nonformal nonadversarial procedures, to encourage a kind of collegiality—actual exchange and even negotiation, leading to mutually acceptable outcomes or at least shared understandings—in a system which has treated fiat as an administratively convenient rule of thumb....

More than . . . "*rituals and ceremonies*" designed to foster "courtesy and respect" are at issue here. Inherent in the creation of opportunities for colloquy is the *possibility* that both students and disciplinarians will hear each other out with something other than the patience born of legal necessity, that there exists what Kenneth Clark speaks of as the "possibility of empathy." . . . [Conversation] enables students to feel that they are being listened to and may encourage them to raise underlying grievances. It provides administrators with a relatively inexpensive vehicle for monitoring, and hence a basis for reshaping institutional relationships. The outcome of these "orderly, thoughtful" conversations may well be decisions different in their particulars from what might otherwise have been anticipated; repeated conversations which touch upon similar student grievances may ultimately lead disciplinarians to reassess whether control is so vital, and collaboration so improbable, as a means of assuring institutional order.

Kirp, "Proceduralism and Bureaucracy: Due Process in the School Setting," 28 *Stan. L. Rev.* 841, 864–66 (1976) (emphasis in original).

Does this analysis fairly reflect *Goss*? Does it speak to the relevance of the intrinsic value of due process in the *Goss* opinions? Does it suggest a way of distinguishing the post-*Goss* cases? *See* Wald, "*Goss v. Lopez*: Not the Devil; Nor the Panacea," 1 *Mich. L. & Pol'y Rev.* 331, 332 (1996) (suggesting that the value of *Goss* may be that "it tells students that they are real people, that they are participants in the democratic process").

What of longer suspensions: do the same considerations pertain? What procedural protections should be provided when a student is faced with an eleven-day suspension, a semester-long suspension, or an expulsion? At what point does it become appropriate to design the hearing to approximate a traditional due process hearing, with legal representation, a written record, a formal appeals process, and the like? *See Nash v. Auburn University*, 812 F.2d 655 (11th Cir. 1987); *Lamb v. Panhandle Community Unit School District No. 2*, 826 F.2d 526 (7th Cir. 1987); *Brewer v. Austin Indep. School Dist.*, 779 F.2d 260 (5th Cir. 1985); *Fuller v. Decatur Public School Bd. of Educ. School Dist. 61*, 78 F.Supp.2d 812, 822–23 (C.D. Ill. 2000); *Craig v. Selma City School Bd.*, 801 F.Supp. 585 (S.D. Ala. 1992); *Draper v. Columbus Public Schools*, 760 F.Supp.131 (S.D. Ohio 1991); *Cole v. Newton Special Mun. Separate School District*, 676 F.Supp. 749 (S.D. Miss. 1987). *See* Cooper and Strope, "Long-Term Suspensions and Expulsions after *Goss*," 57 *Ed. Law Rep.* 29 (1990); Daniel and Coriell, "Suspension and Expulsion in America's Public Schools: Has Unfairness Resulted from a Narrowing of Due Process?" 13 *Hamline L. Pub. L. & Pol'y* 1, 18–21, 28–30 (1992); Daniel, "Violence and the Public Schools: Student Rights Have Been Weighed in the Balance and Found Wanting," 27 *J. Law & Educ.* 573, 599 (1998).

4. Applications: When Is Process Due?

Should students who are suspended from a particular class and are required to spend a certain amount of time in a detention area be provided with *Goss* protections? *See Casey v. Newport School Committee*, 13 F.Supp.2d 242 (D.R.I. 1998); *Cole v. Newton Special Mun. Separate School Dist.*, 676 F.Supp. 749, 752 (S.D. Miss. 1987), *aff'd*, 853 F.2d 924 (5th Cir. 1988); *Warren County Board of Education v. Wilkinson*, 500 So.2d 455 (Miss. 1986); *Jordan v. School District of City of Erie, Pennsylvania*, 583 F.2d 91 (3d Cir. 1978).

Is participation in extracurricular activities a protectable property interest, deprivation of which—by keeping the star quarterback from playing (and perhaps frustrating his opportunities for an athletic scholarship to college), for example—should trigger due process procedures? *See Jordan v. O'Fallon Township High School Dist. No. 203 Board of Educ.*, 302 Ill.App.3d 1070, 706 N.E.2d 137 (Ill.App 5 Dist. 1999); *Palmer v. Merluzzi*, 868 F.2d 90, 96–99 (3d Cir. 1989) (Cowen, J., dissenting); *Hardy v. University Interscholastic League*, 759 F.2d 1233 (5th Cir. 1985); *Davenport v. Randolph County Bd. of Educ.*, 730 F.2d 1395, 1397 (11th Cir. 1984); *Hebert v. Ventetuolo*, 638 F.2d 5 (1st Cir. 1981); *Piwonka v. Tidehaven Indep. School Dist.*, 961 F.Supp. 169 (S.D. Tex. 1997); *McFarlin v. Newport Special School Dist.*, 784 F.Supp. 589 (E.D. Ark.1992); *Boyd v. Board of Directors of McGehee School Dist.*, 612 F.Supp. 86, 93 (E.D. Ark.1985); *Dallam v. Cumberland Valley School District*, 391 F.Supp. 358 (M.D. Pa. 1975); *Braesch v. DePasquale*, 200 Neb. 726, 265 N.W.2d 842 (1978), *cert. denied*, 439 U.S. 1068, 99 S.Ct. 836, 59 L.Ed.2d 34 (1979).

Is the transfer of a student from a regular school to a disciplinary school for disciplinary reasons an infringement of protected interests that should require a prior hearing? *See Nevares v. San Marcos Consolidated Indep. School Dist.*, 111 F.3d 25, 26–27 (5th Cir. 1997); *Buchanan v. City of Bolivar, Tennessee*, 99 F.3d 1352, 1359 (6th Cir. 1996); *Riggan v. Mid-land Indep. School Dist.*, 86 F.Supp.2d 647 (W.D. Tex. 2000). *See* Note, "Procedural Due Process for Texas Public School Students Receiving Disciplinary Transfers to Alternative Education Programs," 3 *Tex. Wesleyan L. Rev.* 209 (1996). *See generally* Bartlett and McCullagh, "Exclusion from the Educational Process in the Public Schools: What Process Is Now Due," 1993 *B.Y.U. Educ. & L. J.* 1.

5. Double Jeopardy

Police and school officials, acting on an anonymous tip, searched a student's car in the parking lot of the high school he attended, and found a loaded semiautomatic pistol. Following a hearing, the student was expelled for one year. Should the state be barred from bringing juvenile delinquency proceedings on double jeopardy grounds? *See In the Matter of C.M.J.*, 915 P.2d 62 (Kan. 1996); *Clark v. State*, 220 Ga.App. 251, 469 S.E. 2d 250 (Ga.App.1996); *In the Matter of the Welfare of E.R.D.*, 551 N.W.2d 238 (Minn.App.1996); Baker, "Criminal Sanctions for Student Misconduct: Double Jeopardy Litigation in the 1990s," 130 *Ed.Law Rep.* 1 (1998).

6. Due Process and Children with Disabilities

The Individuals with Disabilities Education Act (IDEA), 20 U.S.C. §§ 1401 *et seq.*, entitles disabled students to a hearing before any change in placement—even when the proposed change is premised on misconduct. *See Honig v. Doe*, 484 U.S. 305, 108 S.Ct. 592, 98 L.Ed.2d 686 (1988), discussed in chapter 6, *infra*. A student subject to IDEA cannot be expelled without a hearing to determine whether the misconduct was attributable to his or her disability. Even if the hearing results in a determination that the behavior is not a manifestation of the student's disability, the student must be provided with an alternative education. 20 U.S.C. § 1415(k)(5)(A). *See* chapter 6, *infra*. *See generally* Bryant, "The Death Knell for School Expulsion: The 1997 Amendments to the Individuals with Disabilities Education Act," 47 *Am. U. L. Rev.* 487 (1998); Comment, "Discipline and the Disabled Student: The IDEA Reauthorization Responds," 1998 *Wis. L. Rev.* 1085; McKinney, "Disciplining Children With(out) Disabilities: Schools Behind the Eight Ball," 130 *Ed. Law Rep.* 365 (1999). Do children with disabilities have greater protection under the federal statute than nondisabled children have under the Constitution even though they may be involved in the same misconduct?

7. Racial Disparities in Student Discipline

There is increasing evidence of racial disparity in student discipline, particularly in the use of suspension and expulsion. *See, e.g.,* The Civil Rights Project, Harvard University, *Opportunities Suspended: The Devastating Consequences of Zero Tolerance and School Discipline Policies,* http://www.law.harvard.edu/groups/civilrights/conferences/zero/zt_report.html, at 5–7 (2000); Pauken and Daniel, "Race Discrimination and Disability Discrimination in School Discipline: A Legal and Statistical Analysis," 139 *Ed. Law Rep.* 759 (2000); Adams, "The Status of School Discipline and Violence," 567 *Annals Am. Acad. Pol. & Soc. Sci.* 140, 149–50 (2000); Stone, "Crime & Punishment in Public Schools: An Empirical Study of Disciplinary Proceedings," 17 *Am. Jour. Trial Advoc.* 351, 366 (1993); Daniel and Coriell, "Suspension and Expulsion in America's Public Schools: Has Unfairness Resulted from a Narrowing of Due Process?" 13 *Hamline J. Pub. L. & Pol'y* 1, 32–34 (1992); U.S. Department of Education Office for Civil Rights, *1994 Elementary and Secondary School Civil Rights Survey*; Cooper, "Group Finds Racial Disparity in Schools' 'Zero Tolerance,'" *The Washington Post,* June 15, 2000, at 8A. Creek, "Report Says Zero Tolerance May Mean No School," *The Tennessean,* Mar. 5, 1998, at 7B. This issue is explored in greater detail in chapter 4, *infra.*

Ingraham v. Wright

430 U.S. 651, 97 S.Ct. 1401, 51 L.Ed.2d 711 (1977).

Mr. Justice Powell delivered the opinion of the Court.

This case presents questions concerning the use of corporal punishment in public schools: First, whether the paddling of students as a means of maintaining school discipline constitutes cruel and unusual punishment in violation of the Eighth Amendment; and second, to the extent that paddling is constitutionally permissible, whether the Due Process Clause of the Fourteenth Amendment requires prior notice and an opportunity to be heard.

I

* * *

Petitioners' evidence may be summarized briefly. In the 1970–1971 school year many of the 237 schools in Dade County used corporal punishment as a means of maintaining discipline pursuant to Florida legislation and a local school board regulation. The statute then in effect authorized limited corporal punishment by negative inference, proscribing punishment which was "degrading or unduly severe" or which was inflicted without prior consultation with the principal or the teacher in charge of the school. . . . The regulation, Dade County School Board Policy 5144, contained explicit directions and limitations. The authorized punishment consisted of paddling the recalcitrant student on the buttocks with a flat wooden paddle measuring less than two feet long, three or four inches wide, and about one-half inch thick. The normal punishment was limited to one to five "licks" or blows with the paddle and resulted in no apparent physical injury to the student. School authorities viewed corporal punishment as a less drastic means of discipline than suspension or expulsion. . . .

Petitioners focused on Drew Junior High School, the school in which both Ingraham and Andrews were enrolled in the fall of 1970. In an apparent reference to Drew, the District Court found that "[t]he instances of punishment which could be characterized as severe, accepting the students' testimony as credible, took place in one junior high school." . . . The evidence, consisting mainly of the testimony of 16 students, suggests that the regime at Drew was exceptionally harsh. The testimony of Ingraham and Andrews, in support of their individual claims for damages, is illustrative. Because he was slow to respond to his teacher's instructions, Ingraham was subjected to more than 20 licks with a paddle while being held over a table in the principal's office. The paddling was so severe that he suffered a hematoma requiring medical attention and keeping him out of school for 11 days. Andrews was paddled several times for minor infractions. On two occasions he was struck on his arms, once depriving him of the full use of his arm for a week.

* * *

We granted certiorari, limited to the questions of cruel and unusual punishment and procedural due process. . . .

* * *

The use of corporal punishment in this country as a means of disciplining school children dates back to the colonial period. It has survived the transformation of primary and secondary education from the colonials' reliance on optional private arrangements to our present system of compulsory education and dependence on public schools. Despite the general abandonment of corporal punishment as a means of punishing criminal offenders, the practice continues to play a role in the public education of school children in most parts of the country. Professional and public opinion is sharply divided on the practice, and has been for more than a century. Yet we can discern no trend toward its elimination. . . .

Although the early cases viewed the authority of the teacher as deriving from the parents, the concept of parental delegation has been replaced by the view—more consonant with compulsory education laws—that the State itself may impose such corporal punishment as is reasonably necessary "for the proper education of the child and for the maintenance of group discipline." I. F. Harper & F. James, *The Law of Torts* 292. All of the circumstances are to be taken into account in determining whether the punishment is reasonable in a particular case. . . .

Against this background of historical and contemporary approval of reasonable corporal punishment, we turn to the constitutional questions before us.

III

. . . An examination of the history of the amendment and the decisions of this Court construing the proscription against cruel and unusual punishment confirms that it was designed to protect those convicted of crimes. We adhere to this longstanding limitation and hold that the Eighth Amendment does not apply to the paddling of children as a means of maintaining discipline in public schools.

* * *

IV

The Fourteenth Amendment prohibits any State deprivation of life, liberty or property without due process of law. Application of this prohibition requires the familiar two-stage analysis: we must first ask whether the asserted individual interests are encompassed within the Fourteenth Amendment's protection of "life, liberty or property"; if protected interests are implicated, we then must decide what procedures constitute "due process of law." . . . Following that analysis here, we find that corporal punishment in public school implicates a constitutionally protected liberty interest, but we hold that the traditional common law remedies are fully adequate to afford due process.

A

. . . Due process is required only when a decision of the State implicates an interest within the protection of the Fourteenth Amendment. And "to determine whether due process requirements apply in the first place, we must look not to the 'weight' but to the nature of the interest at stake."

* * *

While the contours of this historic liberty interest in the context of our federal system of government have not been defined precisely, they always have been thought to encompass freedom from bodily restraint and punishment. *See Rochin v. California*, 342 U.S. 165 (1952). It is fundamental that the state cannot hold and physically punish an individual except in accordance with due process of law.

This constitutionally protected liberty interest is at stake in this case. There is, of course a *de minimis* level of imposition with which the Constitution is not concerned. But at least where school authorities, acting under color of state law, deliberately decided to punish a child for misconduct by restraining the child and inflicting appreciable physical pain, we hold that Fourteenth Amendment liberty interests are implicated.

B

"[T]he question remains what process is due." *Morrissey v. Brewer*, 408 U.S., at 481. Were it not for the common law privilege permitting teachers to inflict reasonable corporal punishment on children in their care, and the availability of the traditional remedies for abuse, the case for requiring advance procedural safeguards would be strong indeed. But here we deal with a punishment—paddling—within that tradition, and the question is whether the common law remedies are adequate to afford due process.

* * *

1. Because it is rooted in history, the child's liberty interest in avoiding corporal punishment while in the care of public school authorities is subject to historical limitations. . . . The concept that reasonable corporal punishment in school is justifiable continues to be recognized in the laws of most States. . . . It represents "the balance struck by this country," *Poe v. Ullman*, 367 U.S. 497, 542 (1961) (Harlan, J., dissenting), between the child's interest in personal security and the traditional view that some limited corporal punishment may be necessary in the course of

a child's education. Under that longstanding accommodation of interests, there can be no deprivation of substantive rights as long as disciplinary corporal punishment is within the limits of the common law privilege.

This is not to say that the child's interest in procedural safeguards is insubstantial. The school disciplinary process is not "a totally accurate, unerring process, never mistaken and never unfair. . . ." *Goss v. Lopez*, 419 U.S. 565, 579–80 (1975). In any deliberate infliction of corporal punishment on a child who is restrained for that purpose, there is some risk that the intrusion on the child's liberty will be unjustified and therefore unlawful. In these circumstances the child has a strong interest in procedural safeguards that minimize the risk of wrongful punishment and provide for the resolution of disputed questions of justification.

We turn now to a consideration of the safeguards that are available under applicable Florida law.

2. Florida has continued to recognize, and indeed has strengthened by statute, the common law right of a child not to be subjected to excessive corporal punishment in school. Under Florida law the teacher and principal of the school decide in the first instance whether corporal punishment is reasonably necessary under the circumstances in order to discipline a child who has misbehaved. But they must exercise prudence and restraint. For Florida has preserved the traditional judicial proceedings for determining whether the punishment was justified. If the punishment inflicted is later found to have been excessive—not reasonably believed at the time to be necessary for the child's discipline or training—the school authorities inflicting it may be held liable in damages to the child and, if malice is shown, they may be subject to criminal penalties.

Although students have testified in this case to specific instances of abuse, there is every reason to believe that such mistreatment is an aberration. The uncontradicted evidence suggests that corporal punishment in the Dade County schools was, "[w]ith the exception of a few cases, . . . unremarkable in physical severity." . . .

In those cases where severe punishment is contemplated, the available civil and criminal sanctions for abuse—considered in light of the openness of the school environment—afford significant protection against unjustified corporal punishment. . . . Teachers and school authorities are unlikely to inflict corporal punishment unnecessarily or excessively when a possible consequence of doing so is the institution of civil or criminal proceedings against them.

It still may be argued, of course, that the child's liberty interest would be better protected if the common law remedies were supplemented by the administrative safeguards of prior notice and a hearing. We have found frequently that some kind of prior hearing is necessary to guard against arbitrary impositions on interests protected by the Fourteenth Amendment. *See, e.g., Board of Regents v. Roth*, 408 U.S., at 569–70; *Wolff v. McDonnell*, 418 U.S. 539, 557–58 (1974). . . . but where the State has preserved what "has always been the law of the land," *United States v. Barnett, supra*, the case for administrative safeguards is significantly less compelling.

* * *

3. But even if the need for advance procedural safeguards were clear, the question would remain whether the incremental benefit could justify the cost. Acceptance of petitioners' claims would work a transformation in the law governing corporal punishment in Florida and most other States. Given the impracticability of formulating a rule of procedural due process that varies with the severity of the particular imposition, the prior hearing petitioners seek would have to precede *any* paddling, however moderate or trivial.

Such a universal constitutional requirement would significantly burden the use of corporal punishment as a disciplinary measure. Hearings—even informal hearings—require time, personnel, and a diversion of attention from normal school pursuits. School authorities may well choose to abandon corporal punishment rather than incur the burdens of complying with the procedural requirements. Teachers, properly concerned with maintaining authority in the classroom, may well prefer to rely on other disciplinary measures—which they may view as less effective—rather than confront the possible disruption that prior notice and a hearing may entail. Paradoxically, such an alteration of disciplinary policy is most likely to occur in the ordinary case where the contemplated punishment is well within the common law privilege. . . . In view of the low incidence of abuse, the openness of our schools, and the common law safeguards that already exist, the risk of error that may result in violation of a schoolchild's substantive rights can only be regarded as minimal. Imposing additional administrative safeguards as a constitutional requirement might reduce that risk marginally, but would also entail a significant intrusion into an area of primary educational responsibility. We conclude that the Due Process Clause does not require notice and a hearing prior to the imposition of corporal punishment in the public schools, as that practice is authorized and limited by the common law.

* * *

Mr. Justice White, with whom Mr. Justice Brennan, Mr. Justice Marshall, and Mr. Justice Stevens join, dissenting.

Today the Court holds that corporal punishment in public schools, no matter how severe, can never be the subject of the protections afforded by the Eighth Amendment. It also holds that students in the public school systems are not constitutionally entitled to a hearing of any sort before beatings can be inflicted on them. Because I believe that these holdings are inconsistent with the prior decisions of this Court and are contrary to a reasoned analysis of the constitutional provisions involved, I respectfully dissent.

I

[The discussion of the Eighth Amendment claim is omitted.]

II

The majority concedes that corporal punishment in the public schools implicates an interest protected by the Due Process Clause—the liberty interest of the student to be free from "bodily restraint and punishment" involving "appreciable physical pain" inflicted by persons acting under color of state law. . . . The question remaining, as the majority recognizes, is what process is due.

The reason that the Constitution requires a State to provide "due process of law" when it punishes an individual for misconduct is to protect the individual from erroneous or mistaken punishment that the State would not have inflicted had it found the facts in a more reliable way. . . . In *Goss v. Lopez*, 419 U.S. 565 (1975), the Court applied this principle to the school disciplinary process, holding that a student must be given an informal opportunity to be heard before he is finally suspended from public school. . . .

The Court now holds that these "rudimentary precautions against unfair or mistaken findings of misconduct," . . . are not required if the student is punished with "appreciable physical pain" rather than with a suspension, even though both punishments deprive the student of a constitutionally protected in-

terest. Although the respondent school authorities provide absolutely no process to the student before the punishment is finally inflicted, the majority concludes that the student is nonetheless given due process because he can later sue the teacher and recover damages if the punishment was "excessive."

This tort action is utterly inadequate to protect against erroneous infliction of punishment for two reasons. First, under Florida law, a student punished for an act he did not commit cannot recover damages from a teacher "proceeding in utmost good faith . . . on the reports and advice of others," p. 1423, *supra*; the student has no remedy at all for punishment imposed on the basis of mistaken facts, at least as long as the punishment was reasonable from the point of view of the disciplinarian, uninformed by any prior hearing. The "traditional common law remedies" on which the majority relies, *ante*, at 1413, thus do nothing to protect the student from the danger that concerned the Court in *Goss*—the risk of reasonable, good faith mistake in the school disciplinary process.

Second, and more important, even if the student could sue for good faith error in the infliction of punishment, the lawsuit occurs after the punishment has been finally imposed. The infliction of physical pain is final and irreparable; it cannot be undone in a subsequent proceeding. There is every reason to require, as the Court did in *Goss*, a few minutes of "informal give-and-take between student and disciplinarian" as a "meaningful hedge" against the erroneous infliction of irreparable injury. . . .

The majority's conclusion that a damage remedy for excessive corporal punishment affords adequate process rests on the novel theory that the State may punish an individual without giving him any opportunity to present his side of the story, as long as he can later recover damages from a state official if he is innocent. The logic of this theory would permit a State that punished speeding with a one-day jail sentence to make a driver serve his sentence first without a trial and then sue to recover damages for wrongful imprisonment. Similarly, the State could finally take away a prisoner's good time credits for alleged disciplinary infractions and require him to bring a damage suit after he was eventually released. There is no authority for this theory, nor does the majority purport to find any, in the procedural due process decisions of this Court. Those cases have "consistently held that *some kind of hearing is required at some time before a person is finally* deprived of his property interests . . . [and that] a person's liberty is equally protected. . . ."

[Mr. Justice Stevens' dissenting opinion has been omitted.]

NOTES AND QUESTIONS

1. Scope of the Opinion: Cruel and Unusual Punishment

The majority argues that protection against cruel and unusual punishment is properly confined to those convicted of crimes. How relevant is the fact that all of the cases in which the Court has found punishment to be cruel and unusual involved the treatment of criminals? How would the majority respond to the hypothetical case of a student who was seriously injured for being late to class? *See generally* Rosenberg, "*Ingraham v. Wright*: The Supreme Court's Whipping Boy," 78 *Colum. L. Rev.* 75 (1978).

2. Scope of the Opinion: Due Process

The majority and dissent agree that some process is due to students subject to corporal punishment; the disagreement concerns the nature of the process. How would you characterize that disagreement? Is it a dispute over the weight to be attached to the interests of student and school in determining the most efficacious course of action? Does it speak to the circumstances in which it is appropriate not to afford a right of prior review? Does it address the utility of the process that is in fact provided?

3. Models of Governance Revisited

Is the disagreement between the majority and the dissenters—in *Ingraham* as in *Goss v. Lopez*—at heart a disagreement about models of school governance and the role of courts in choosing among those models? What do you make of the discussion, in the majority opinion in *Ingraham*, of the "openness of the public school and its supervision by the community"? Is this a factually accurate portrayal? *See* Comment, "Due Process, Due Politics, and Due Respect: Three Models of Legitimate School Governance," 94 *Harv. L. Rev.* 1106 (1981). What is the constitutional relevance of the point? How does it relate to the facts of the case? One commentator describes the differing views on the Court as follows:

[T]he *Goss* and *Ingraham* opinions represent two starkly different premises regarding the public school as an institution. On one side were the Justices who essentially viewed the institution as the adversary of the child, whom the Court must protect as the child attempts to rebut the values that the school attempts to inculcate. On the other side were the Justices who viewed the institution, and its students as sharing in a common enterprise that consisted, at least in part, of teaching children how to be responsible citizens. . . . [T]he Court has tottered from one model to the other in its attempt to resolve the school power question.

Dupre, "Should Students Have Constitutional Rights? Keeping Order in the Public Schools," 65 *Geo. Wash. L. Rev.* 49, 64 (1996).

The majority notes that "the practice [of corporal punishment] continues to play a role in the public education of school children in most parts of the country," and "we can discern no trend toward its elimination." At the time of *Ingraham*, only six states prohibited corporal punishment. Today, at least one-half of the states prohibit the use of corporal punishment, as well as many individual school districts within states that otherwise permit its use. Should this trend toward eliminating the use of corporal punishment affect its constitutionality?

4. Challenges to the Punishment Itself

Goss does not address the constitutionality of suspension and expulsion per se, but only the procedural safeguards required before the student is suspended or expelled. However, *Ingraham* deals not only with whether some procedural protections are required before a student is corporally punished, but also with the permissibility of the discipline itself.

a. Is the punishment excessive? Might a court conclude that certain acts of corporal punishment are so excessive that they violate a student's substantive due process interest in liberty? *See Jefferson v. Ysleta Indep. School Dist.*, 817 F.2d 303 (5th Cir. 1987) (second grader tied to a chair for an entire school day and part of the next; school district asserted that an instructional technique was being employed); *Garcia v. Miera*, 817 F.2d 650 (10th Cir. 1987) (one teacher held nine-year-old female student upside down by her ankles, while a second teacher struck her on the front of her leg with a split wooden paddle five times); *Turley v. School District of Kansas City, Missouri*, 713 F.Supp. 331 (W.D.Mo. 1989) (without warning and in violation of school district policy, teacher hit students on the face, neck, shoulders, and legs with a plastic baseball bat). *Compare Saylor v. Board of Educ. of Harlan County, Ky*, 118 F.3d 507 (6th Cir. 1996); *Wise v. Pea Ridge School Dist.*, 855 F.2d 560 (8th Cir. 1988).

The standard for determining whether the administration of corporal punishment violates substantive due process is set very high. The majority of circuits that have addressed the issue follow the Fourth Circuit in *Hall v. Tawney*, 621 F.2d 607, 613 (4th Cir. 1980): "whether the force applied caused injury so severe, was so disproportionate to the need presented, and was so inspired by malice or sadism rather than a merely careless or unwise excess of zeal that it amounted to a brutal and inhumane abuse of official power literally shocking to the conscience." The Fifth Circuit, however, has held that corporal punishment can never be a substantive due process violation as long as there are adequate criminal and tort remedies for excessive punishment. *See Cunningham v. Beavers*, 858 F.2d 269 (5th Cir. 1988); *cert. denied*, 489 U.S. 1067, 109 S.Ct.1343, 103 L.Ed.2d 812 (1989). *See generally* Parkinson, "Federal Court Treatment of Corporal Punishment in Public Schools: Jurisprudence That Is Literally Shocking to the Conscience," 39 *S.D. L. Rev.* 276 (1994); Dayton, "Corporal Punishment in the Public Schools: The Legal and Political Battle Continues," 89 *Ed. Law Rep.* 729 (1994); Benz, "Corporal Punishment in Today's Public Schools: Child Discipline or Legal Abuse?" 13 *J. Juv. L.* 13 (1992); Rosenberg, "Study in Irrationality: Refusal to Grant Substantive Due Process Protection Against Excessive Corporal Punishment in Public Schools," 27 *Hous. L. Rev.* 399 (1990); Edwards, "Corporal Punishment and the Legal System," 36 *Santa Clara L. Rev.* 983 (1996); Henderson, "Constitutional Implications Involving the Use of Corporal Punishment in the Public Schools: A Comprehensive Review," 15 *J. Law and Educ.* 255 (1986). Teachers may be disciplined or dismissed for inflicting excessive force with respect to corporal punishment. *See, e.g., Burton v. Kirby*, 775 S.W.2d 834 (Tex.App. 1989).

For a discussion of the efficacy of corporal punishment in changing student behavior, *see* I. Hyman, *Reading, Writing, and the Hickory Stick: The Appalling Story of Physical and Psychological Abuse in American Schools* (1990); Bongiovanni, "A Review of Research on the Effects of Punishment: Implications for Corporal Punishment in the Schools," in *Proceedings: Conference on Corporal Punishment in the Schools: A National Debate* 35 (The National Institute of Education, February 18–20, 1977); Note, "Curbing Violence or Teaching It: Criminal Immunity for Teachers Who Inflict Corporal Punishment," 74 *Wash. U. L. Q.* 1251 (1996).

Corporal punishment is barred in nearly every other developed country with the exception of one state in Australia and parts of Canada. *See* Hyman, *supra*, at 227–28. The United Nations Convention on the Rights of the Child requires States Parties to "take all appropriate measures to ensure that school discipline is administered in a manner consistent with the child's human dignity and in conformity with the present Convention." U.N. Convention on the Rights of the Child, Jan. 26, 1990, art. 28.2.

b. Parental rights and corporal punishment. Should parents be permitted to determine whether the school may administer corporal punishment to their child? *See Baker v. Owen*, 395 F.Supp. 294 (M.D.N.C. 1975), *aff'd mem.*, 423 U.S. 907, 96 S.Ct. 210, 46 L.Ed.2d 137.

c. Disproportionate punishment. Does the penalty fit the deed? *See Cunningham v. Beavers*, 858 F.2d 269 (5th Cir. 1988); *cert. denied*, 489 U.S. 1067, 109 S.Ct.1343, 103 L.Ed.2d 812 (1989) (two six-year-old children struck with a paddle three times for snickering in the halls, creating black and blue bruises, causing them to miss six days of school, and characterized by two social workers as "child abuse" was neither disproportionate nor violated substantive due process); *Gaither v. Barron*, 924 F. Supp, 134 (M.D. Ala. 1996) (ninth-grade hearing-impaired student butted in head by teacher when he turned to help another student with a computer assignment and failed to hear command to turn around did not violate Constitution because punishment was neither arbitrary nor excessive). *See Restatement of the Law of Torts, Second,* §150, Comment c.

d. "Zero tolerance" policies. When is expulsion or suspension disproportionate? The Gun-Free Schools Act of 1994 requires school districts, as a condition for the receipt of federal funds under the Elementary and Secondary Education Act of 1965, to provide for the mandatory expulsion for at least one year of students who bring firearms to school, 20 U.S.C. § 8921 (West 2000). In response, many states and localities adopted broader "zero tolerance" laws and regulations that cover weapons in addition to firearms (e.g., knives, cutting instruments, cutting tools, nunchaku, or look-alike weapons), alcohol, and drugs. *See, e.g.,*

Dodd, "Can We Create Violence-Free Schools that Are Still Free?" 34 *New Eng. L. Rev.* 623, 626–28 (2000). The National Center for Education Statistics reports that three-fourths of all schools have zero tolerance policies, with 94 percent of those reporting policies for firearms and 91 percent for weapons other than firearms. Slightly less than 90 percent have zero tolerance policies for drugs and alcohol, while 79 percent have such policies for violence and 79 percent for the use of tobacco. National Center for Education Statistics, *Violence and Discipline Problems in U.S. Public Schools: 1996–97* (1998), Fig. 8. While some states require school districts to provide alternative education programs for those students who have been expelled, a number of states do not. *See* Bogos, *supra*, at 376–77.

Challenging the constitutionality of "zero tolerance" policies on substantive grounds, assuming the appropriate procedural safeguards have been accorded prior to the expulsion of the students who have engaged in misconduct, is difficult. On what constitutional grounds might yearlong expulsions under a school district's "zero tolerance" policies for weapons, drugs, alcohol, or for threatening behavior, be challenged in the following cases? A fourteen-year-old student is found to be carrying a semiautomatic gun at school. A thirteen-year-old student threatens another student with a fake gun while they are waiting for the school bus, putting the look-alike weapon to her head and saying, "Give me your money or I'll blow your brains out." A middle school student brings a knife to school to cut the brownies she baked for her friend's birthday. A seven-year-old student brings a Boy Scout knife to school for "show and tell" in his second-grade class to show classmates the corkscrew, scissors, magnifying glass, and other accessories on the knife. A twelve-year-old student finds a miniature Swiss Army knife in a school hallway, where a teacher sees him filing his fingernails with it. A high school student attends a party off school grounds where three other students test positive for alcohol, although the student in question does not. A junior high school student takes diet pills away from a friend who threatened to use them to commit suicide and puts the pills in his locker until he can find a teacher. An eighth-grade student creates a web site at home on his computer threatening his math teacher. A middle school student makes an obscene phone call to a classmate on the weekend. A high school student writes an essay involving a nuclear bomb. A senior sips wine during a toast by her employers at her school-sponsored work internship. *See, e.g., James v. Unified School Dist. No. 512, Johnson County, Kansas*, 899 F.Supp. 530, 534 (D. Kans. 1995); *Lyons v. Penn Hills School Dist.*, 723 A.2d 1073 (Pa. 1999); *Kolesnick v. Omaha Public School Dist.*, 251 Neb. 575, 582–83, 558 N.W.2d 807, 813–14 (1997) (only if "shocking disparity" between expulsion sentence and the offense); *In the Matter of the Expulsion of Daniel Polonia from Indep. School Dist. No. 709*, 1996 WL 45169 (Minn. App. Feb. 6, 1996) (No. C7-95-1523) (unpublished op.); *Doe v. Board of Educ. of Oak Park & River Forest High School Dist. 200*, 1995 WL 608534, 12 A.D.D. 680 (N.D. Ill. Oct. 12, 1995) (No.94-C-6449) ("although such a punishment might appear to be harsh under the given circumstances the decision properly remained within the province of the Board"). *See also* Bogos, " 'Expelled. No Excuses. No Exceptions.' — Michigan's Zero-Tolerance Policy in Response to School Violence," 74 *U. Det. Mercy L. Rev.* 357 (1997); Shepherd and DeMarco, "Weapons in Schools and Zero Tolerance," 11-Sum *Crim. Just.* 46 (1996); Comment, "Beyond Sticks & Stones: A First Amendment Framework for Educators Who Seek to Punish Student Threats," 30 *Seton Hall L. Rev.* 635 (2000); "Florence Second-Grader Expelled Over Knife," *Associated Press Newswires*, Thurs. Dec. 9, 1999; Seymour, "Getting Too Tough? Schools Are Expanding Their Zero-Tolerance Policies, Disciplining and Even Kicking Out Students Who Misbehave Off-Campus," *Los Angeles Times*, Feb. 24, 1999, at B2; Smith, "Court Casts Doubt on 'Zero-Tolerance' Policy," *St. Petersburg Times*, Nov. 14, 1998, at B1; Breckenridge, "Schools' Zero-Tolerance Challenged in Recent Cases," *South Bend Tribune*, Nov. 23, 1997, at D1; Milloy, "Watch Jack and Jill Get Handcuffed," *Washington Post*, May 1, 1994, at B1.

A recent analysis of the application of zero tolerance policies found that an increasingly broad range of student actions completely unrelated to violence and drugs has been subjected to mandatory suspension and expulsion policies, that students are frequently diverted by school officials into the criminal justice system for nonviolent behavior, that excluded students are generally not provided with alternative education, that more incidents are occurring of younger children being suspended or expelled (as early as kindergarten and first grade) for trivial misconduct, and that zero tolerance policies are applied more frequently in predominantly black and Latino school districts. The Civil Rights Project, Harvard

University, *Opportunities Suspended: The Devastating Consequences of Zero Tolerance and School Discipline Policies,* http://www.law.harvard.edu/groups/civillights/conferences/zero/zt_report.html, 2000. *See also* Adams, "The Status of School Discipline and Violence," 567 *Annals Am. Acad. Pol. & Soc. Sci.* 140, 147–48 (2000); Noguera, "Preventing and Producing Violence: A Critical Analysis of Responses to School Violence," 65 *Harv. Educ. Rev.* 189 (1995), discussing concerns raised by zero tolerance policies.

In an increasing number of states, statutes or regulations apply to student conduct off school grounds. *See, e.g.,* Conn. G.S. § 10-233d; *Packer v. Board of Educ. of Town of Thomaston,* 246 Conn. 89, 717 A.2d 117 (1998) (statute held unconstitutionally vague as applied); *Pirschel v. Sorrell,* 2 F.Supp.2d 930 (E.D. Ky. 1998) (student's disposing of beer in parking lot of school in another county during basketball tournament in which student's school was participating arose at a "school-sponsored activity," thus constituting a violation of student's own school's disciplinary policy).

e. First Amendment issues. A growing number of students are being suspended and expelled for spoken or written comments, including comments made outside of school in e-mails, chat rooms, and other Internet outlets, *see, e.g., J.S. v. Bethlehem Area School District,* 757 A.2d 412 (Pa. 2000), or for having "unusual" hair colors or wearing "disruptive" clothing to school, particularly in the wake of the incident at Columbine High School in Littleton, Colorado. *See* Murray, "Are We on the Right Track?" 34 *New Eng. L. Rev.* 635 (2000); Martinez, "School Dress Code Outlined: New State Law Bans 'Disruptive' Clothing Items," *The Denver Post,* Aug. 3, 2000, at 5B. *See* chapter 2, *infra.*

5. Grade Reductions as Punishment

Should it be permissible for schools to reduce students' grades or deny course credit as a punishment for unauthorized absences or misconduct? *Compare Smith v. School City of Hobart,* 811 F.Supp. 391 (N.D. Ind. 1993) (substantive due process violation), *with Dunn v. Fairfield Community High School Dist.,* 158 F.3d 962 (7th Cir. 1998). *See also Gutierrez v. School Dist. R-1,* 41 Colo. App. 411, 585 P.2d 935 (1978) (practice violated state statute); *Dorsey v. Bale,* 521 S.W.2d 76 (Ky. 1975); Bartlett, "Academic Evaluation and Student Discipline Don't Mix," 16 *J. Law & Educ.* 155 (1987); Pepe, "Student Grades and School Discipline—A Philosophical and Legal Question," 7 *NOLPE School L. J.* 126 (1977);

Liggett, "Discipline by Grade Reduction and Grade Denial Based on Attendance," in M. McGhehy, ed., *School Law in Changing Times* 40 (1982).

6. Other Forms of Behavior Control

Drugs such as Ritalin have been prescribed for students to curb excessively aggressive behavior. Studies show that 10 percent to 12 percent of all male schoolchildren in the United States are taking the drug Ritalin, far more than any other country in the world. Livingston, "Ritalin: Miracle Drug or Cop-Out?" 127 *The Public Interest* 3, 5 (1997). ADD (attention deficit disorder) and ADHD (attention deficit hyperactivity disorder) is now the most commonly diagnosed behavioral disorder among children. One study reports that prescriptions for Ritalin increased 390 percent between 1995 and 2000. *See* ABC News, "A Lawsuit Alleges Attention Deficit Disorder Is Over-Diagnosed," http://abcnews.go.com/sections/living/DailyNews/ritalin_lawsuit0808.html, August 10, 2000. Teachers or other school authorities are asked to identify such ADD behaviors on a diagnostic form as "often fails to give close attention to details or makes careless mistakes in schoolwork," "often avoids, dislikes, or is reluctant to engage in tasks that require mental effort (such as schoolwork or homework)"; while symptoms for ADHD include "often fidgets with hands or feet or squirms in seat." ABC News, *supra.*

The use of Ritalin by school systems has been viewed by some critics as an illegitimate form of control. Do you agree? Does your answer depend on the effectiveness of the drug? The side effects? Whether the parents have consented? Whether the student has consented? *See* Note, "A Spoonful of Sugar Won't Help this Medicine Go Down; Psychotropic Drugs for Abused and Neglected Children," 72 *S. Cal. L. Rev.* 1151 (1999); Livingston, *supra,* at 16 (suggesting that pressure to get students to perform at high levels on exit exams or competency tests may be leading teachers to promote diagnosis of ADHD and subsequent treatment controlling student behavior); Diller, *Running on Ritalin* (1998), at 339-40 (similarly arguing that parents and teachers both are pressured by demands for higher performance in school); Powers, "Race for Perfection: Children's Rights and Enhancement Drugs," 13 *J. L. & Health* 141 (1998–99); Adams, "The Status of School Discipline and Violence," 567 *Annals Am. Acad. Pol. & Soc. Sci.* 140, 148-149 (2000); O'Leary, "An Analysis of the Legal Issues Surrounding the Forced Use of

Ritalin: Protecting a Child's Legal Right to 'Just Say No,'" 27 *New Eng. L. Rev.* 1173 (1993). What about the stigma for children who are pulled out of class each day and sent to the school nurse for their dose of Ritalin?

Can parents require school health personnel or other school employees to administer the dosage prescribed by the family physician for their child, even if it is beyond the generally recommended dose? See *Davis v. Francis Howell School Dist.*, 138 F.3d 754 (8th Cir. 1998); *DeBord v. Board of Educ. of the Ferguson-Florissant School Dist.*, 126 F.3d 1102 (8th Cir. 1997); Schultze, "Reading, Writing and Ritalin: The Responsibility of Public School Districts to Administer Medications to Students," 32 *Creighton L. Rev.* 793 (1999).

May schools use behavioral profiling, based on newly developed "threat assessment" software, to identify potentially violent students? See Cooper, "Riley Rejects Schools' Profiling of Potentially Violent Students," *Washington Post*, Apr. 29, 2000, at A11; "Software Gauges Students for Violence," *Columbus Dispatch*, Apr. 28, 2000, at A1. Does your answer depend upon how the schools use the information?

Board of Curators of the University of Missouri v. Horowitz

435 U.S. 78, 98 S.Ct. 948, 55 L.Ed.2d 124 (1978).

Mr. Justice Rehnquist delivered the opinion of the Court.

* * *

I

Respondent was admitted with advanced standing to the Medical School in the fall of 1971. During the final years of a student's education at the school, the student is required to pursue in "rotational units" academic and clinical studies pertaining to various medical disciplines such as obstetrics-gynecology, pediatrics, and surgery. Each student's academic performance at the School is evaluated on a periodic basis by the Council on Evaluation, a body composed of both faculty and students, which can recommend various actions including probation and dismissal. The recommendations of the Council are reviewed by the Coordinating Committee, a body composed solely of faculty members, and must ultimately be approved by the Dean. Students are not typically al-

lowed to appear before either the Council or the Coordinating Committee on the occasion of their review of the student's academic performance.

In the spring of respondent's first year of study, several faculty members expressed dissatisfaction with her clinical performance during a pediatrics rotation. The faculty members noted that respondent's "performance was below that of her peers in all clinical patient-oriented settings," that she was erratic in her attendance at clinical sessions, and that she lacked a critical concern for personal hygiene. Upon the recommendation of the Council on Evaluation, respondent was advanced to her second and final year on a probationary basis.

Faculty dissatisfaction with respondent's clinical performance continued during the following year. For example, respondent's docent, or faculty adviser, rated her clinical skills as "unsatisfactory." In the middle of the year, the Council again reviewed respondent's academic progress and concluded that respondent should not be considered for graduation in June of that year; furthermore, the Council recommended that, absent "radical improvement," respondent be dropped from the School.

Respondent was permitted to take a set of oral and practical examinations as an "appeal" of the decision not to permit her to graduate. Pursuant to this "appeal," respondent spent a substantial portion of time with seven practicing physicians in the area who enjoyed a good reputation among their peers. The physicians were asked to recommend whether respondent should be allowed to graduate on schedule and, if not, whether she should be dropped immediately or allowed to remain on probation. Only two of the doctors recommended that respondent be graduated on schedule. Of the other five, two recommended that she be immediately dropped from the school. The remaining three recommended that she not be allowed to graduate in June and be continued on probation pending further reports on her clinical progress. Upon receipt of these recommendations, the Council on Evaluation reaffirmed its prior position.

The Council met again in mid-May to consider whether respondent should be allowed to remain in school beyond June of that year. Noting that the report on respondent's recent surgery rotation rated her performance as "low-satisfactory," the Council unanimously recommended that "barring receipt of any reports that Miss Horowitz has improved radically, [she] not be allowed to re-enroll in the . . . School of Medicine." The Council delayed making its recommendation official until receiving reports on other rotations; when a report on respondent's emergency rotation also turned out to be negative, the Council unanimously reaffirmed its recommendation that respondent be dropped from the School. The Coordinating Committee and the Dean approved the recommendation and notified respondent, who appealed the decision in writing to the University's Provost for Health Sciences. The Provost sustained the School's actions after reviewing the record compiled during the earlier proceedings.

II

A

. . . [R]espondent argued that her dismissal deprived her of "liberty" by substantially impairing her opportunities to continue her medical education or return to employment in a medically related field.

* * *

B

We need not decide, however, whether respondent's dismissal deprived her of a liberty interest in pursuing a medical career. . . . Assuming the existence of a liberty or property interest, respondent has been awarded at least as much due process as the Fourteenth Amendment requires. The School fully informed respondent of the faculty's dissatisfaction with her clinical progress and the danger that this posed to timely graduation and continued enrollment. The ultimate decision to dismiss respondent was careful and deliberate. These procedures were sufficient under the Due Process Clause of the Fourteenth Amendment. . . .

In *Goss v. Lopez*, 419 U.S. 565 (1975), we held that due process requires, in connection with the suspension of a student from public school for disciplinary reasons, "that the student be given oral or written notice of the charges against him and, if he denies them, an explanation of the evidence the authorities have and an opportunity to present his side of the story." . . . The Court of Appeals apparently read *Goss* as requiring some type of formal hearing at which respondent could defend her academic ability and performance. All that *Goss* required was an "informal give-and-take" between the student and the administrative body dismissing him that would, at least, give the student "the opportunity to charac-

terize his conduct and put it in what he deems the proper context." . . . But we have frequently emphasized that "[t]he very nature of due process negates any concept of inflexible procedures universally applicable to every imaginable situation." *Cafeteria Workers v. McElroy*, 367 U.S. 886, 895 (1961). The need for flexibility is well illustrated by the significant difference between the failure of a student to meet academic standards and the violation by a student of valid rules of conduct. This difference calls for far less stringent procedural requirements in the case of an academic dismissal.

* * *

Academic evaluations of a student, in contrast to disciplinary determinations, bear little resemblance to the judicial and administrative fact-finding proceedings to which we have traditionally attached a full hearing requirement. In *Goss*, the school's decision to suspend the students rested on factual conclusions that the individual students have participated in demonstrations that had disrupted classes, attacked a police officer, or caused physical damage to school property. The requirement of a hearing, where the student could present his side of the factual issue, could under such circumstances "provide a meaningful hedge against erroneous action." The decision to dismiss respondent, by comparison, rested on the academic judgment of school officials that she did not have the necessary clinical ability to perform adequately as a medical doctor and was making insufficient progress toward that goal. Such a judgment is by its nature more subjective and evaluative than the typical factual questions presented in the average disciplinary decision. Like the decision of an individual professor as to the proper grade for a student in his course, the determination whether to dismiss a student for academic reasons requires an expert evaluation of cumulative information and is not readily adapted to the procedural tools of judicial or administrative decisionmaking.

Under such circumstances, we decline to ignore the historic judgment of educators and thereby formalize the academic dismissal process by requiring a hearing. The educational process is not by nature adversarial: instead it centers around a continuing relationship between faculty and students, "one in which the teacher must occupy many roles—educator, adviser, friend, and, at times, parent-substitute." *Goss v. Lopez*, 419 U.S. 565, 594 (1975) (Powell, J., dissenting). This is especially true as one advances through the varying regimes of the educational system, and the instruction becomes both more individualized and more specialized. In *Goss*, this Court concluded that the value of some form of hearing in a disciplinary context outweighs any resulting harm to the academic environment. Influencing this conclusion was clearly the belief that disciplinary proceedings, in which the teacher must decide whether to punish a student for disruptive or insubordinate behavior, may automatically bring an adversarial flavor to the normal student-teacher relationship. The same conclusion does not follow in the academic context. We decline to further enlarge the judicial presence in the academic community and thereby risk deterioration of many beneficial aspects of the faculty-student relationship. . . . "Judicial interposition in the operation of the public school system of the Nation raises problems requiring care and restraint. . . . By and large, public education in our Nation is committed to the control of state and local authorities." *Epperson v. Arkansas*, 393 U.S. 97, 104 (1968). We see no reason to intrude on that historic control in this case.[6]

[Concurring and dissenting opinions have been omitted.]

NOTES AND QUESTIONS

1. Horowitz: Scope of the Decision

The determination of how much process is due, even assuming that a liberty or property interest is at stake in *Horowitz*, turns on the majority's classification of the interest as "academic" and not "disciplinary." How persuasive do you find the distinction? What factors are relevant to making the distinction: the degree of subjectivity of the required judgment, the inaptness of a *Goss*-type exchange, the degree and type of expertise required to make the decision, the nonadversarial nature of the process? Is it the characterization of the interest or the fact and extent of the deprivation that merits attention in determining what process is due? Does the Court's standard give judges too much leeway? Precisely what sort of hearing, if any, is required after *Horowitz*, where the

dispute is academic in nature? *See Board of Regents v. Tomanio*, 446 U.S. 478, 493, 100 S.Ct. 1790, 1799, 64 L.Ed.2d 440 (1980).

Was the dispute in *Horowitz* in fact academic? What is the relevance to academic performance of Ms. Horowitz's allegedly unsatisfactory personal hygiene, discussed in footnote 6 of the opinion? Is good hygiene part of "clinical competence," the articulated basis for the school's action? *Compare Alcorn v. Vaksman*, 877 S.W.2d 390 (Tex.App.-Hous.(1st Dist.) 1994).

Is the loss of a semester of high school credit because of excessive absences a disciplinary or an academic sanction? *Compare State ex rel. Yarber v. McHenry*, 915 S.W.2d 325 (Mo.1995) (en banc) with *Campbell v. Board of Educ. of New Milford*, 193 Conn. 93, 475 A.2d 289 (1984) and *Slocum v. Holton Board of Educ.*, 171 Mich.App.92, 429 N.W.2d 607 (1988).

The conceptual basis for the *Horowitz* decision was later elaborated upon by the Supreme Court. In *Regents of the University of Michigan v. Ewing*, 474 U.S. 214, 106 S.Ct. 507, 88 L.Ed.2d 523 (1985), a university student challenged the constitutionality of his dismissal from a six-year program of study leading to an undergraduate and medical degree. Scott Ewing was dismissed after failing five of the seven sections of a test administered by the National Board of Medical Examiners. The dismissal decision was made by a faculty Promotion and Review Board after individual review of the student's file. Upon petition by Ewing to reconsider the matter, he was allowed to appear personally before the Board, and he argued that the test did not fairly represent his academic progress or potential. The Board then reaffirmed its decision. The Court assumed, without so holding, that Ewing had a constitutionally protected property interest, but nonetheless it held that he had not been denied due process:

The record unmistakably demonstrates . . . that the faculty's decision was made conscientiously and with careful deliberation, based on an evaluation of the entirety of Ewing's academic career. When judges are asked to review the substance of a genuinely academic decision, such as this one, they should show great respect for the faculty's professional judgment. Plainly, they may not

---

[6]Respondent contends in passing that she was not dismissed because of "clinical incompetence," an academic inquiry, but for disciplinary reasons similar to those involved in *Goss*. Thus, as in *Goss*, a hearing must be conducted. In this regard, respondent notes that the school warned her that significant improvement was needed not only in the area of clinical performance but also in her personal hygiene and in keeping to her clinical schedules. The record, however, leaves no doubt that respondent was dismissed for pure academic reasons, a fact assumed without discussion by the lower courts. Personal hygiene and timeliness may be as important . . . in a school's determination of whether a student will make a good medical doctor as the student's ability to take a case history or diagnose an illness. . . .

override it unless it is such a substantial departure from accepted academic norms as to demonstrate that the person or committee responsible did not actually exercise professional judgment.

. . . Added to our concern for lack of standards is a reluctance to trench on the prerogatives of state and local educational institutions and our responsibility to safeguard their academic freedom, "a special concern of the First Amendment." . . . If a "federal court is not the appropriate forum in which to review the multitude of personnel decisions that are made daily by public agencies," . . . far less is it suited to evaluate the substance of the multitude of academic decisions that are made daily by faculty members of public educational institutions—decisions that require "an expert evaluation of cumulative information and [are] not readily adapted to the procedural tools of judicial or administrative decision making." . . .

. . . [T]he Regents "had good reason to dismiss Ewing from the program." . . . Before failing the [test] . . ., Ewing accumulated an unenviable record characterized by low grades, seven incompletes, and several terms during which he was on an irregular or reduced course load. Ewing's failure of his medical boards, in the words of one of his professors, "merely culminate[d] a series of deficiencies. . . . In many ways, it's the straw that broke the camel's back." . . .

474 U.S. at 224–27, 106 S.Ct. at 513–14. *See also Wheeler v. Miller*, 168 F.3d 251 (5th Cir. 1999); *Megenity v. Stenger*, 27 F.3d 1120 (6th Cir. 1994); *Akins v. Board of Governors*, 840 F.2d 1371 (7th Cir. 1988); *Clements v. County of Nassau*, 835 F.2d 1000 (2d Cir. 1987); *Harris v. Blake*, 798 F.2d 419 (10th Cir. 1986); *Mauriello v. University of Medicine and Dentistry of New Jersey*, 781 F.2d 46 (3d Cir. 1986); *Lewin v. Medical College of Hampton Roads*, 910 F.Supp. 1161 (E.D. Va. 1996); *In the Matter of Susan M. v. New York Law School*, 76 N.Y.2d 241, 556 N.E. 2d 1104 (N.Y.1990); *Perez v. Hastings College of the Law*, 45 Cal. App.4th 453, 53 Cal. Rptr.2d 1 (1996); *Sage v. CUNY Law School*, 617 N.Y.S.2d 825, 208 A.D.2d 751 (1994). *See generally* Berger and Berger, "Academic Discipline: A Guide to Fair Process for the University Student," 99 *Colum. L. Rev.* 289, 302–05 (1999); Ford and Strope, "Judicial Responses to Adverse Academic Decisions Affecting Public Postsecondary Institution Students Since 'Horowitz' and 'Ewing' "; Schweitzer, " 'Academic Challenge' Cases: Should Judicial Review Extend to Academic Evaluations of Students?" 41 *Am. U. L. Rev.* 267 (1992); Buss, "Easy Cases Make Bad Law: Academic Expulsion and the Uncertain Law of Procedural Due Process," 65 *Iowa L. Rev.* 1 (1979).

In the light of *Ewing*, is *Horowitz* an institutional academic freedom case? Does *Ewing* indicate that nearly all cases will be characterized as involving academic rather than disciplinary dismissals? If a student is dismissed from veterinary school for cheating on examinations, is that an academic or disciplinary decision? *See University of Texas Medical School at Houston v. Than*, 874 S.W.2d 839 (Tex.App.-Hous. (1st Dist.) 1994), *aff'd as modified*, 901 S.W.2d 926 (Texas 1995); *Nash v. Auburn University*, 812 F.2d 655 (11th Cir. 1987).

2. Horowitz *and Stigma*

To be dismissed from one university . . . means the student can never again be a candidate for any degree. . . . The employee may find a new job; the student cannot find a new university. . . . The economic wound inflicted by dismissal remains with the student for the rest of his life, but often the wound goes deeper. In notorious cases, universities are wont to publicize apprehensions of offending students in order to placate the university community, irrespective of the emotional distress to the student or the irreparable harm to the student's reputation. When one tallies the potential harm to a student . . . the penalty for dismissal from a university for disciplinary reasons resembles the suspended sentence a felon might receive in a criminal court.

Picozzi, "University Disciplinary Process: What's Fair, What's Due, and What You Don't Get," 96 *Yale L. J.* 2132, 2138–40 (1987). Do you agree with Professor Picozzi? Is it enough that the harms are similar—even if the underlying offenses are not? If you accept the suspended sentence analogy, what should be the constitutional consequences?

3. *What Process Is Due?*

As *Goss, Ingraham*, and *Horowitz* reveal, the nature of the process that is due is of critical importance.

a. Notice. What constitutes adequate advance notice of the charges and the date of the hearing? Must the notice be in writing? Must the notice actually be communicated to the student or teacher? *See University of Texas Medical School at Houston v. Than*, 874 S.W.2d 839 (Tex.App.-Hous. (1st Dist.) 1994), *aff'd as modified*, 901 S.W.2d 926 (Texas 1995); *Mueller v. University of Minnesota*, 855 F.2d 555 (8th Cir. 1988); *Nash v. Auburn University*, 812 F.2d 655 (11th Cir. 1987); *Strickland v. Inlow*, 519 F.2d 744 (8th Cir. 1975).

b. Impartial hearing. What constitutes impartiality? Can a racially charged atmosphere for a hearing render it unfair? *See The Dartmouth Review v. Dartmouth College*, 889 F.2d 13 (1st Cir. 1989). Does prior knowledge of the case disqualify a hearing officer? *See Nash v. Auburn University*, 812 F.2d 655 (5th Cir. 1987). May the trier of fact commingle the decision-making and prosecutorial functions? Does a prior history of friendship or animosity toward the accused disqualify a trier of fact? *See Newsome v. Batavia Local School Dist.*, 842 F.2d 920 (6th Cir. 1988); *Gorman v. University of Rhode Island*, 837 F.2d 7 (1st Cir. 1988); *Sullivan v. Houston Indep. School Dist.*, 475 F.2d 1071 (5th Cir. 1973), *cert. denied*, 414 U.S. 1032, 1077, 94 S.Ct. 461, 38 L.Ed.2d 323; *Duke v. North Texas State University*, 469 F.2d 829 (5th Cir. 1972), *cert. denied*, 412 U.S. 932, 93 S.Ct. 2760, 37 L.Ed.2d 160 (1973); Buss, "Procedural Due Process for School Discipline: Probing the Constitutional Outline," 119 *U. Pa. L. Rev.* 545, 618–30 (1971).

c. Cross-examination. Should examination and cross-examination of witnesses be required in school cases? Consider *Newsome v. Batavia Local School Dist.*, 842 F.2d 920, 924–25 (6th Cir. 1988). A student was accused by an anonymous tipster of selling marijuana cigarettes on school grounds. Denying the student's claim that he was entitled to cross-examine his accusers, or at least to know their identities, the court declared:

> In this turbulent, sometimes violent, school atmosphere, it is critically important that we protect the anonymity of students who "blow the whistle" on their classmates who engage in drug trafficking and other serious offenses. Without the cloak of anonymity, students who witness criminal activity on school property will be much less likely to notify school authorities. . . . [T]he necessity of protecting student witnesses from ostracism and reprisal outweighs the value to the truth-determining process of allowing the accused student to cross-examine his accusers.

Do you agree? *Compare John A. v. San Bernardino City Unified School District*, 187 Cal. Rptr. 472, 654 P.2d 242 (1982) (under state statute, it was improper to expel student without testimony of witnesses to altercation). *See also Nash v. Auburn University*, 812 F.2d 655 (11th Cir. 1987); *Brands v. Sheldon Community School*, 671 F.Supp. 627 (N.D. Iowa 1987). Are the circumstances of the case decisive? Should it, for instance, be permissible to discipline a student accused of assaulting fe-

male students if the alleged victims are afraid of retaliation if they testify and will only offer unsigned written statements? *See Tibbs v. Board of Education*, 114 N.J. Super. 287, 276 A.2d 165 (1971), *aff'd*, 59 N.J. 506, 284 A.2d 179. *See* Comment, "The Admissibility of Hearsay in Public Secondary School Disciplinary Hearings," 1991 *U. Chi. Legal Forum* 375.

d. Counsel. Should the due process clause be read to permit students and teachers to be represented by legal counsel, to require counsel, or to allow school districts to insist that no counsel be present? Does your answer depend on the severity of the potential sanction? Would your answer differ if the school case were factually intertwined with a pending criminal case? Would your answer be affected by whether or not the school district employed a lawyer to represent it? *See, e.g., Osteen v. Henley*, 13 F.3d 221 (7th Cir. 1993); *Gorman v. University of Rhode Island*, 837 F.2d 7 (1st Cir. 1988); *Gabrilowitz v. Newman*, 582 F.2d 100 (1st Cir. 1978); *Black Coalition v. Portland School District No. 1*, 484 F.2d 1040 (9th Cir. 1973). *See generally* Blaskey, "University Students' Right to Retain Counsel for Disciplinary Proceedings," 24 *Cal. W. L. Rev.* 65 (1988).

e. Evidence. Should the technical rules of evidence be followed in school proceedings? For example, should the rules regarding the exclusion of hearsay evidence apply in these proceedings? *See Brewer v. Austin Indep. School Dist.*, 779 F.2d 260 (5th Cir. 1985). What should constitute sufficient evidence to warrant action by a school board? *See Jones v. Board of Trustees*, 524 So.2d 968 (Miss. 1988). Is this a constitutional question? Is it a denial of due process if there is no relevant evidence as to a critical element of the alleged infraction? *Cf. Vachon v. New Hampshire*, 414 U.S. 478, 94 S.Ct. 664, 38 L.Ed.2d 666 (1974).

f. Transcript. Should a school be required to provide a transcript of the hearing when the student or teacher requests one? *Compare Mills v. Board of Education*, 348 F.Supp. 866 (D.D.C. 1972) *with Wasson v. Trowbridge*, 382 F.2d 807 (2d Cir. 1967).

4. Federal Legislation: The Family Educational Rights and Privacy Act and the Hatch Amendment

In the early 1970s, a number of organizations, including the American Civil Liberties Union and the Russell Sage Foundation, began to identify abuses in the keeping of public records by public educational institutions. Public elementary and secondary school officials sometimes released student records to law enforcement agencies, creditors, prospective employers, credit card companies, and so on without obtaining students' or parents' permission. There was also grave concern about the nature and educational relevance of the information being kept in the files. *See Merriken v. Cressman*, 364 F.Supp. 913 (E.D. Pa. 1973). Horror stories were cited in which records identified parents of students as radicals, described high school students as bedwetters in their preteenage years, and presented unverified personal opinions of teachers about the psychological health of students. Concern was also expressed that parents and students might not know what was in the educational records, might be denied access to those records, and might have no opportunity to challenge harmful statements contained in the records. *Cf. Van Allen v. McCleary*, 27 Misc.2d 81, 211 N.Y.S.2d 501 (1961). *See* Divoky, "Cumulative Records: Assault on Privacy," *Learning*, Sept. 1973. These pressures and others led to the passage of the Federal Educational Rights and Privacy Act (20 U.S.C.A. §§ 1232g-1232i). *See generally* Daggett, "Bucking Up Buckley I: Making the Federal Student Records Statute Work," 46 *Cath. U. L. Rev.* 617 (1997); Johnson, "Managing Student Records: The Courts and the Family Educational Rights and Privacy Act of 1974," 79 *Ed. Law Rep.* 1 (1993).

The Act provides that parents (or students, for those over age eighteen or in postsecondary school) have a right of access to school records and a right to request that the record be amended or altered if they believe that statements in the record are false or misleading, violate the right to privacy, or are violative of other rights. School authorities generally must permit access to the records within forty-five days of a request and must consider the parents' request for alteration. If parents and school authorities are unable to agree, the student and his parents are entitled to a hearing within a reasonable period of time. If the student does not prevail at the hearing, no corrective action need be taken by school officials. If the student does prevail, the appropriate changes in the record must be made. Even in the event of an adverse decision by the hearing officer or body, the student is entitled to append a statement to the record explaining his or her side of the story. Appeals from an adverse decision are administrative in nature, and no private right of action to sue in federal court is

provided in the Act. *See Smith v. Duquesne University*, 612 F. Supp. 72 (W.D. Pa.1985), *aff'd*, 787 F.2d 583 (3d Cir. 1986); *Girardier v. Webster College*, 563 F.2d 1267 (8th Cir. 1977); *Maynard v. Greater Hoyt School Dist. No. 61-4*, 876 F.Supp. 1104, 1107 (D. S.D. 1995). But the statute contemplates withholding all federal funds to districts that violate the Act; and a school district may be liable, under 42 U.S.C. § 1983, for a FERPA violation. *Tarka v. Cunningham*, 917 F.2d 890 (5th Cir. 1990); *Fay v. South Colonie Central School District*, 802 F.2d 21 (2d Cir. 1986); *Maynard v. Greater Hoyt School Dist. No. 61-4, supra.*

The Act requires a "full and fair" hearing, including notice; the right to present evidence and to cross-examine witnesses; and the right to have an attorney or other person represent the student at the hearing. The hearing officer may be a school person or anyone who has no direct involvement in the case. A decision must be rendered within a reasonable period of time, be in writing, and summarize the evidence and the reasons for the decision. The decision may be based only upon the evidence actually received at the hearing. *See Lewin v. Medical College of Hampton Roads*, 910 F.Supp. 1161 and 931 F.Supp.443 (E.D.Va. 1996), *aff'd*, 131 F.3d 135 (4th Cir. 1997). *See generally* Regulations for the Family Educational Rights and Privacy Act of 1974, 34 C.F.R. §§ 99.1-99.67 (1999).

Consider to what extent the Family Educational Rights and Privacy Act supplements or supplants judicially imposed due process procedures. On the face of the Act, the student and his parents may contest anything contained in the record. The only clear exception from the limited legislative history is that grades may not be challenged unless the contention is that the grade was improperly recorded. A student may not challenge the accuracy of the grade itself. *See Tarka v. Cunningham*, 917 F.2d 890 (5th Cir. 1990). *See generally* Baker, "Inaccurate and Misleading: Student Hearing Rights Under FERPA," 114 *Ed. Law Rep.* 721 (1997); Johnson, "Managing Student Records: The Courts and the Family Educational Rights and Privacy Act of 1974," 79 *Ed. Law Rep.* 1 (1993).

See Mawdsley, "Litigation Involving FERPA," 110 *Ed.Law Rep.* 897, 914 (1996), noting that FERPA has generated a considerable amount of litigation, often "enmeshed with state freedom of information or open records laws, as well as constitutional questions about student or parent privacy."

The Hatch Amendment to FERPA, adopted in 1978, and substantially revised in 1994, gives parents the right to examine instructional materials "used in connection with any survey, analysis, or evaluation" and also requires parental consent before students participate in federally funded programs that involve surveys or evaluations that reveal information concerning political affiliations, personal beliefs and behaviors, mental and psychological problems "potentially embarrassing to the student or his family," family relationships, and income. 20 U.S.C.A. § 1232(h) (West Supp. 2000).

The Act was also amended to provide that the term *education records* did not include "records maintained by a law enforcement unit of the educational agency or institution that were created by that law enforcement unit for the purpose of law enforcement." 20 U.S.C. §1232g(a)(4)(B)(ii). This amendment was enacted after several universities had relied upon FERPA as the basis for refusing to make public campus crime reports that contained personally identifiable information about students. *See* Johnson, *supra*, at 16–17.

5. *State Statutes*

The procedures to be followed in teacher and student discipline cases are controlled not only by constitutional requirements but also by state statutes. Student discipline is often governed by state statutes that show the influence of *Goss*. For example, the New York State Education Code permits a school principal to suspend a student for up to five school days. The student and his or her parents must, if they so request, be provided an opportunity for an informal conference with the principal, during which the parents may question complaining witnesses. If a student is suspended for more than five days, he or she must be given an opportunity for a fair hearing, after reasonable notice, at which the student has the right to be represented by counsel, and the right to question witnesses against the student and to present witnesses and other evidence on the student's behalf. Where a student is suspended by the board of education, the board may either hear the case itself or may appoint a hearing officer, who is authorized to administer oaths and to issue subpoenas in conjunction with the proceeding. A record of the hearing must be made. The hearing officer makes findings of fact and recommendations as to the appropriate measure of discipline. The report of the hearing officer is advisory only, subject to any final action by the board, which may reject, confirm, or modify the conclusions of the hearing officer. Each member of the board, before voting, is required to review the testimony and become acquainted with the evidence in the case. The statute further provides that where a student has been suspended as insubordinate or disorderly and is of compulsory attendance age, immediate steps must be taken to provide the student with alternative instruction. McKinney's (New York) Educ. Law Ann. § 3214, 3b,c,e (West 2000).

C. Implementing Due Process Protections

Constitutional rights are not just declarations about doctrine. They also are shaped by efforts to put those declarations into practice. School officials who implement constitutional decisions or who ignore those decisions are thus, in a vital sense, making law. The ways in which constitutional rights are implemented have already been noted (see chapter 2); the subject is more fully treated in chapters 5 and 7.

This section looks at implementation in two contexts. It begins with damage suits brought against school officials who violate students' (or teachers') constitutional rights, and then takes up the implementation of those rights.

1. The Threat of Damage Suits as a Goad to Implementation. 42 U.S.C. § 1983, a Civil War–era statute, has been used to prod officials—including school officials—into enforcing constitutional rights. That law authorizes suits for damages against anyone who, acting under color of state law, deprives an individual of federal constitutional or statutory rights.

The theory was that fear of pocketbook loss through a § 1983 lawsuit might make prompt effectuation of substantive rights a reality. *See, e.g.,* Wilkinson, "*Goss v. Lopez*: The Supreme Court as School Superintendent," 1975 *Sup. Ct. Rev.* 25; Note, "Procedural Due Process in Public Schools: The 'Thicket' of *Goss v. Lopez*," 1976 *Wis. L. Rev.* 934. Compare "Symposium on Medical Malpractice," 1975 *Duke L. J.* 1177. The reality, however, has proved to be more complex.

In *Wood v. Strickland*, 420 U.S. 308, 95 S.Ct. 992, 43 L.Ed.2d 214 (1975), the Supreme Court declared that school officials were not absolutely liable if they denied students or teachers their constitutional rights. Good faith is the test, and only violations of "the basic, unquestioned constitutional rights of [an official's] charges" would lead to liability. Even that formulation worried Justice Powell, who wondered in his dissent "whether qualified persons will continue in the desired numbers to volunteer for service in public education," knowing they might be financially liable if they failed to divine the law.

The restrictive standard set out in *Wood* was subsequently refined in *Harlow v. Fitzgerald*, 457 U.S. 800, 818, 102 S.Ct. 272, 2738, 73 L.Ed.2d 396 (1982), which held that the test of liability is whether officials' conduct "violates clearly established statutory or constitutional rights of which a reasonable person would have known." *See also Davis v. Scherer*, 468 U.S. 183, 104 S.Ct. 3012, 82 L.Ed.2d 139 (1984); *Anderson v. Creighton*, 483 U.S. 635, 107 S.Ct. 3034, 97 L.Ed.2d 523 (1987). The impact of this judicial grant of limited immunity has been to eliminate the subjective test of good faith in favor of an objective test, thereby limiting the role of juries in such cases. *See generally* Kinports, "Qualified Immunity in Section 1983 Cases: The Unanswered Questions," 23 *Ga. L. Rev.* 597 (1989).

One frequently litigated issue is just what are "clearly established constitutional rights" of which a reasonable school official should have known, an issue the Supreme Court expressly declined to address in *Harlow*. Must there have been a Supreme Court decision in a case with similar facts? How similar must the facts be? If there is no Supreme Court case on point, must there have been a case in the same circuit before school officials can be held liable in damages? A decision by a district court within the circuit? State court decisions? An opinion by the state attorney general? Suppose there is a conflict among circuits. *See P.B. v. Koch*, 96 F.3d 1298 (9th Cir. 1996); *Price v. Akaka*, 3 F.3d 1220, 1225 (9th Cir. 1993); *Anderson v. Romero*, 72 F.3d 518, 525 (7th Cir. 1995); *Jenkins v. Talledega City Board of Educ.*, 115 F.3d 821, 827 n.4 (11th Cir.) (en banc), *cert. denied sub nom. Jenkins v. Herring*, 522 U.S. 966, 118 S.Ct. 412, 139 L.Ed.2d 315 (1997); *Wilson v. Strong*, 156 F.3d 1131, 1135 (11th Cir. 1998); *Garcia v. Miera*, 817 F.2d 650, 656–58 (10th Cir. 1987). Although the Supreme Court attempted to clarify some of these questions in its decisions in *Anderson v. Creighton*, 483 U.S. 635 (1987) and *United States v. Lanier*, 520 U.S. 259, 268–71, 117 S.Ct.1219, 1226–28,137 L.Ed.2d 432 (1997), lower courts are still in disagreement as to the appropriate standard. *Compare Jenkins v. Talledega City Board of Educ.*, 115 F.3d 821 (11th Cir.) (en banc), *cert. denied sub*

nom. Jenkins v. Herring, 522 U.S. 966, 118 S.Ct. 412, 139 L.Ed.2d 315 (1997) *with Sostarecz v. Misko*, 1999 WL 239401 (E.D. Pa., Mar.26, 1999). *See* Goldberg, "Strip Searches of School Children: Legality Depends on Circuit," 14-SPRG *Crim. Just.* 16 (1999); Note, "Eleventh Circuit Finds Students' Fourth Amendment Rights Not 'Clearly Established,'" 111 *Harv. L. Rev.* 1341 (1998).

Federal judges also have imposed restrictions on damage awards under § 1983. In a suit brought by students who were suspended without a hearing, the justices held that only compensatory damages for proven actual injury could be awarded under this section. *Carey v. Piphus*, 435 U.S. 247, 98 S.Ct. 1042, 55 L.Ed.2d 252 (1978). Subsequently, in *Memphis Community School District v. Stachura*, 477 U.S. 299, 106 S.Ct. 2537, 91 L.Ed.2d 249 (1986), a case involving a tenured junior-high science teacher suspended without a hearing for showing his class films on human sexuality, the Court denied a claim for damages based on the "value" of the constitutional rights at stake. Compensatory or actual damages, said the justices, suffice to vindicate the rights protected by § 1983 and to discourage constitutional violations. The Court, however, also noted in *Carey* that "the denial of procedural due process should be actionable for nominal damages without proof of actual injury," pointing out that the awarding of nominal damages for the right of procedural due process "recognizes the importance to organized society that [this] righ[t] be scrupulously observed" while "remain[ing] true to the principle that substantial damages should be awarded only to compensate actual injury." 435 U.S. at 266, 98 S.Ct. at 1054. *See also Farrar v. Hobby*, 506 U.S. 103, 112, 113 S.Ct. 566,573, 121 L.Ed.2d 494 (1992); *Grounds v. Tolar Indep. School Dist.*, 872 S.W.2d 823 (Tex.App.–Fort Worth 1994).

Section 1983 is complex—some would say less than coherent—judicial terrain. For discussion of these issues and other related questions, including the immunity standard and damage test to be applied in § 1983 suits against governmental units (rather than officials), *see generally*, S. Nahmod, *Civil Rights and Civil Liberties Litigation*, Vol. 2, "The Law of Section 1983" (4th ed. 1999); I. Bodensteiner and R. Levinson, *State and Local Government Civil Rights Liability*, Chap. 1, "Protecting Federal Rights Under § 1983" (1999); M. Schwartz & J. Kirklin, *Section 1983 Litigation: Claims, Defenses and Fees* (2d ed.1991); Wright, "Qualified and

Civic Immunity in Section 1983 Actions: What Do Justice and Efficiency Require?" 49 *Syracuse L. Rev.* 1 (1998); Chen, "The Ultimate Standard: Qualified Immunity in the Age of Constitutional Balancing Tests," 81 *Iowa L. Rev.* 261 (1965); Kinports, *supra*; Yudof, "Liability for Constitutional Torts and the Risk-Averse Public School Official," 49 *So. Cal. L. Rev.* 1322 (1976).

2. Implementation and Due Process: Goss Revisited. Following the *Goss* decision, such issues as whether the authority of teachers and administrators would be undermined by the introduction into the schools of a formal mode of dispute resolution, whether few students would demand hearings, whether schools would ignore the decision, or whether the right to notice and hearing would be so watered down as to be meaningless, were intensely debated by educators and scholars. *Compare* Kirp, "Proceduralism and Bureaucracy: Due Process in the School Setting" 28 *Stan. L. Rev.* 841, 859 (1976), *with* Yudof, "Legalization of Dispute Resolutions, Distrust of Authority, and Organizational Theory: Implementing Due Process for Students in the Public Schools," 1981 *Wisc. L. Rev.* 891. Since *Goss* was decided, courts have had occasion to determine what process is required in the case of longer term suspensions or expulsions, and generally have held that school officials need not follow all of the procedures required in a judicial proceeding. *See, e.g.,* Cooper and Strope, "Long-Term Suspensions and Expulsions after *Goss,*" 57 *Ed. Law. Rep.* 29 (1990). One commentator has noted that "although the authority to discipline and protect students carries some possible liability to school administrators, by and large, student perpetrators or victims of school violence face almost insurmountable obstacles to constitutional or statutory redress in the courts" and that "courts have been highly deferential to school personnel relative to the disciplining or the care of students." Daniel, "Violence and the Public Schools: Student Rights Have Been Weighed in the Balance and Found Wanting," 27 *J. L. & Educ.* 573, 613 (1998). It has also been noted that courts have not been consistent in determining how much or what kind of process is due, in part because of "court efforts to weigh student protected interests against additional procedural burdens on school officials." Bartlett and McCullagh, "Exclusions from the Educational Process in the Public Schools: What Process Is Now Due," 1993 *B.Y.U. Educ. & Law Jour.* 1, 54. *See also* Daniel and Coriell, "Suspension and Expulsion in America's Public Schools: Has Unfairness Resulted from a Narrowing of Due Process?" 13 *Hamline L. Pub. L. & Pol'y* 1, 18–21, 28–30 (1992). But as the use of long-term suspensions and expulsions increases (*see, e.g.,* Shear and Wilgoren, "Expulsions Rise as Schools Get Tough on Violence," *Washington Post,* July 10, 1994), the burden on school boards of disciplinary hearings has also increased. *See* Benning, "School Boards Seek Relief from Burden of Disciplinary Hearings," *Washington Post,* Dec. 22, 1996. One commentator has suggested that *Goss* has proven to be neither as disruptive of the schools as its critics feared nor as protective of students' rights as its proponents hoped. *See* Wald, "*Goss v. Lopez:* Not the Devil; Nor the Panacea," 1 *Mich. L. & Pol'y Rev.* 331, 332 (1996).

Equal Educational Opportunity and Race

I. INTRODUCTION

This chapter and the two chapters that follow focus on what educational opportunities the individual student is entitled to receive from the state. These entitlements are embodied in federal and state constitutions and laws, and they function as constraints on the ways in which public schools operate. Typically they are defined and vindicated through the judicial process. Demands upon public schools can be affirmative, asserting an entitlement to equal access to the schooling process, an adequate education or a specified educational outcome; or they may be framed negatively, asserting a right to be free of race, sex, or class discrimination in the operation of the public schools.

This chapter deals with the fully matured and litigated definition of equal educational opportunity: the rights of students to be free of racial discrimination. The chapter is organized primarily along historical lines. The complex issues presented by segregation in both the North and the South, the scope of unlawful racial segregation, the Civil Rights Act of 1964, and the controversy over racial balance remedies can be understood best against the backdrop of historical changes in social attitudes and governmental policy. In addition, the materials examine the ethical and policy implications of racial discrimination. Why is state-created segregation unconstitutional? What is the impact of segregation on the educational achievement of students? What ethical, social, and economic costs attach to the alternative means of undoing racial segregation in the schools?

Is the goal desegregation or racially integrated schools? How are such concepts defined and implemented?

Finally, this chapter raises sensitive issues of federalism and democracy. It examines the relationship among the federal courts, Congress, and the president in the context of school desegregation, as well as the relationship among the federal courts, the U.S. Department of Education, and local school districts. More importantly, it seeks to assess the role of the judiciary in carrying out what now appears to have been a social revolution of mammoth proportions. Other groups have sought, either through litigation or legislation, to use the approach taken by racial minorities defining equal educational opportunity. Thus this chapter provides the necessary background for understanding the developments described in chapters 5–7.

II. THE JUDICIAL RESPONSE TO SCHOOL SEGREGATION: THE *BROWN* DECISION

A. *Brown I*: Legal and Policy Implications

Brown v. Board of Education
347 U.S. 483, 74 S.Ct. 686, 98 L.Ed. 873 (1954).

Chief Justice Warren delivered the opinion of the Court.

These cases come to us from the states of Kansas, South Carolina, Virginia, and Delaware. They are premised on different facts and different local conditions, but a common legal question justifies their consideration together in this consolidated opinion.[1]

In each of the cases, minors of the Negro race, through their legal representatives, seek the aid of the courts in obtaining admission to the public schools of their community on a nonsegregated basis. In each instance, they have been denied admission to schools attended by white children under laws requiring or permitting segregation according to race. This segregation was alleged to deprive the plaintiffs of the equal protection of the laws under the Fourteenth Amendment. In each of the cases other than the Delaware case, a three-judge federal district court denied relief to the plaintiffs on the so-called "separate but equal doctrine" announced by this court in *Plessy v. Ferguson*, 163 U.S. 537. Under that doctrine, equality of treatment is accorded when the races are provided substantially equal facilities, even though these facilities be separate. In the Delaware case, the Supreme Court of Delaware adhered to that doctrine, but ordered that the plaintiffs be admitted to the white schools because of their superiority to the Negro schools.

The plaintiffs contend that segregated public schools are not "equal" and cannot be made "equal," and that hence they are deprived of the equal protection of the laws. Because of the obvious importance of the question presented, the Court took jurisdiction. Argument was heard in the 1952 Term, and reargument was heard this term on certain questions propounded by the Court.

Reargument was largely devoted to the circumstances surrounding the adoption of the Fourteenth Amendment in 1868. It covered exhaustively consideration of the Amendment in Congress, ratification by the states, then existing practices in racial segregation, and the views of proponents and opponents of the Amendment. This discussion and our own investigation convince us that, although these sources cast some light, it is not enough to resolve the problem with which we are faced. At best, they are inconclusive. The most avid proponents of the post-War Amendments undoubtedly intended them to remove all legal distinctions among "all persons born or naturalized in the United States." Their opponents, just as certainly, were antagonistic to both the letter and the spirit of the Amendments and wished

---

[1]In the Kansas case, *Brown v. Board of Education*, the plaintiffs are Negro children of elementary school age residing in Topeka. They brought this action in the United States District Court for the District of Kansas to enjoin enforcement of a Kansas statute which permits, but does not require, cities of more than 15,000 population to maintain separate school facilities for Negro and white students. Kan. Gen. Stat. § 72-1724 (1949). Pursuant to that authority, the Topeka Board of Education elected to establish segregated elementary schools. Other public schools in the community, however, are operated on a non-segregated basis. The three-judge District Court, convened under 28 U.S.C. §§ 2281 and 2284, found that segregation in public education has a detrimental effect upon Negro children, but denied relief on the ground that the Negro and white schools were substantially equal with respect to buildings, transportation, curricula, and educational qualifications of teachers. 93 F.Supp. 797. The case is here on direct appeal under 28 U.S.C. t 1253.

In the South Carolina case, *Briggs v. Elliott*, the plaintiffs are Negro children of both elementary and high school age residing in Clarendon County. They brought this action in the United States District Court for the Eastern District of South Carolina to enjoin enforcement of provisions in the state constitution and statutory code which require the segregation of Negroes and whites in public schools. S.C. Const. Art XI, § 7; S.C. Code § 5377 (1942). The three-judge District Court . . . denied the requested relief. The court found that Negro schools were inferior to the white schools and ordered the defendants to begin immediately to equalize the facilities. But the court sustained the validity of the contested provisions and denied the plaintiffs admission to the white schools during the equalization program. 98 F.Supp. 529. This Court vacated the District Court's judgment and remanded the case for the purpose of obtaining the court's views on a report filed by the defendants concerning the progress made in the equalization program. 342 U.S. 350. On remand, the District Court found that substantial equality had been achieved except for buildings and that the defendants were proceeding to rectify this inequality as well. 103 F.Supp. 920. The case is again here on direct appeal under 28 U.S.C. 1253. . . .

In the Virginia case, *Davis v. County School Board*, the plaintiffs are Negro children of high school age residing in Prince Edward County. They brought this action in the United States District Court for the Eastern District of Virginia to enjoin enforcement of provisions in the state constitution and statutory code which require the segregation of Negroes and whites in public schools. Va. Const. § 140, Va. Code § 22-221 (1950). The three-judge District Court . . . denied the requested relief. The court found the Negro school inferior in physical plant, curricula, and transportation, and ordered the defendants forthwith to provide substantially equal curricula and transportation and to "proceed with all reasonable diligence and dispatch to remove" the inequality in physical plant. But, as in the South Carolina case, the court sustained the validity of the contested provisions and denied the plaintiffs admission to the white schools during the equalization program. 103 F.Supp. 337. The case is here on direct appeal under 28 U.S.C. §1253.

In the Delaware case, *Gebhart v. Belton*, the plaintiffs are Negro children of both elementary and high school age residing in New Castle County. They brought this action in the Delaware Court of Chancery to enjoin enforcement of provisions in the state constitution and statutory code which require the segregation of Negroes and whites in public schools. Del. Const., Art. X, § 2; Del. Rev. Code § 2631 (1935). The Chancellor gave judgment for the plaintiffs and ordered their immediate admission to schools previously attended only by white children, on the ground that the Negro schools were inferior with respect to teacher training, pupil-teacher ratio, extracurricular activities, physical plant, and time and distance involved in travel. 87 A.2d 862. The Chancellor also found that segregation itself results in inferior education for Negro children . . ., but did not rest his decision on that ground. *Id.*, at 865. The Chancellor's decree was affirmed by the Supreme Court of Delaware, which intimated, however, that the defendants might be able to obtain a modification of the decree after equalization of the Negro and white schools had been accomplished. 91 A.2d 137, 152. The defendants, contending only that the Delaware courts had erred in ordering the immediate admission of the Negro plaintiffs to the white schools, applied to this court for certiorari. The writ was granted, 344 U.S. 891. . . .

them to have the most limited effect. What others in Congress and the state legislatures had in mind cannot be determined with any degree of certainty.

An additional reason for the inconclusive nature of the Amendment's history, with respect to segregated schools, is the status of public education at that time. In the South, the movement toward free common schools, supported by general taxation, had not yet taken hold. Education of white children was largely in the hands of private groups. Education of Negroes was almost nonexistent, and practically all of the race were illiterate. In fact, any education of Negroes was forbidden by law in some states. Today, in contrast, many Negroes have achieved outstanding success in the arts and sciences as well as in the business and professional worlds. It is true that public school education at the time of the Amendment had advanced further in the North, but the effect of the Amendment on Northern States was generally ignored in the congressional debates. Even in the North, the conditions of public education did not approximate those existing today. The curriculum was usually rudimentary; ungraded schools were common in rural areas; the school term was but three months a year in many states; and compulsory school attendance was virtually unknown. As a consequence, it is not surprising that there should be so little in the history of the Fourteenth Amendment relating to its intended effect on public education.

In the first cases in this Court construing the Fourteenth Amendment, decided shortly after its adoption, the Court interpreted it as proscribing all state-imposed discriminations against the Negro race. The doctrine of "separate but equal" did not make its appearance in this Court until 1896 in the case of *Plessy v. Ferguson, supra* involving not education but transportation[6]. American courts have since labored with the doctrine for over half a century. In this Court, there have been six cases involving the "separate but equal" doctrine in the field of public education. In *Cumming v. County Board of Education*, 175 U.S. 528, and *Gong Lum v. Rice*, 275 U.S. 78, the validity of the doctrine itself was not challenged. In more recent cases, all on the graduate school level, inequality was found in that specific benefits enjoyed by white students were denied to Negro students of the same educational qualifications. *Missouri ex rel. Gaines v.*

Canada, 305 U.S. 337; *Sipuel v. Oklahoma*, 332 U.S. 631; *Sweatt v. Painter*, 339 U.S. 629; *McLaurin v. Oklahoma State Regents*, 339 U.S. 637. In none of these cases was it necessary to re-examine the doctrine to grant relief to the Negro plaintiff. And in *Sweatt v. Painter, supra*, the Court expressly reserved decision on the question whether *Plessy v. Ferguson* should be held inapplicable to public education.

In the instant cases, that question is directly presented. Here, unlike *Sweatt v. Painter*, there are findings below that the Negro and white schools involved have been equalized, or are being equalized, with respect to buildings, curricula, qualifications and salaries of teachers, and other "tangible" factors. Our decision, therefore, cannot turn on merely a comparison of these tangible factors in the Negro and white schools involved in each of the cases. We must look instead to the effect of segregation itself on public education.

In approaching this problem, we cannot turn the clock back to 1868 when the Amendment was adopted, or even to 1896 when *Plessy v. Ferguson* was written. We must consider public education in the light of its full development and its present place in American life throughout the Nation. Only in this way can it be determined if segregation in public schools deprives these plaintiffs of the equal protection of the laws.

Today, education is perhaps the most important function of state and local governments. Compulsory school attendance laws and the great expenditures for education both demonstrate our recognition of the importance of education to our democratic society. It is required in the performance of our most basic public responsibilities, even service in the armed forces. It is the very foundation of good citizenship. Today it is a principal instrument in awakening the child to cultural values, in preparing him for later professional training, and in helping him to adjust normally to his environment. In these days, it is doubtful that any child may reasonably be expected to succeed in life if he is denied the opportunity of an education. Such an opportunity, where the state has undertaken to provide it, is a right which must be made available to all on equal terms.

We come then to the question presented: Does segregation of children in public schools solely on

---

[6]The doctrine apparently originated in *Roberts v. City of Boston*, [5 Cush. 198,] 59 Mass. 198, 206 (1850), upholding school segregation against attack as being violative of a state constitutional guarantee of equality. Segregation in Boston public schools was eliminated in 1855. Mass. Acts 1855, c. 256. But elsewhere in the North segregation in public education has persisted in some communities until recent years. It is apparent that such segregation has long been a nationwide problem, not merely one of sectional concern.

the basis of race, even though the physical facilities and other "tangible" factors may be equal, deprive the children of the minority group of equal educational opportunities? We believe that it does.

In *Sweatt v. Painter, supra,* in finding that a segregated law school for Negroes could not provide them equal educational opportunities, this Court relied in large part on "those qualities which are incapable of objective measurement but which make for greatness in a law school." In *McLaurin v. Oklahoma State Regents, supra,* the Court, in requiring that a Negro admitted to a white graduate school be treated like all other students, again resorted to intangible considerations: ". . . his ability to study, to engage in discussions and exchange views with other students, and, in general, to learn his profession." Such considerations apply with added force to children in grade and high schools. To separate them from others of similar age and qualifications solely because of their race generates a feeling of inferiority as to their status in the community that may affect their hearts and minds in a way unlikely ever to be undone. The effect of this separation on their educational opportunities was well stated by a finding in the Kansas case by a court which nevertheless felt compelled to rule against the Negro plaintiffs:

> Segregation of white and colored children in public schools has a detrimental effect upon the colored children. The impact is greater when it has the sanction of the law; for the policy of separating the races is usually interpreted as denoting the inferiority of the Negro group. A sense of inferiority affects the motivation of a child to learn. Segregation with the sanction of law, therefore, has a tendency to retard the educational and mental development of Negro children and to deprive them of some of the benefits they would receive in a racial[ly] integrated school system.

Whatever may have been the extent of psychological knowledge at the time of *Plessy v. Ferguson,* this finding is amply supported by modern authority.[11] Any language in *Plessy v. Ferguson* contrary to this finding is rejected.

We conclude that in the field of public education the doctrine of "separate but equal" has no place. Separate educational facilities are inherently unequal. Therefore we hold that the plaintiffs and others similarly situated for whom the actions have been brought are, by reason of the segregation complained of, deprived of the equal protection of the laws guaranteed by the Fourteenth Amendment. This disposition makes unnecessary any discussion whether such segregation also violates the Due Process Clause of the Fourteenth Amendment.

Because these are class actions, because of the wide applicability of this decision, and because of the great variety of local conditions, the formulation of decrees in these cases presents problems of considerable complexity. On reargument, the consideration of appropriate relief was necessarily subordinated to the primary question—the constitutionality of segregation in public education. We have now announced that such segregation is a denial of the equal protection of the laws. In order that we may have the full assistance of the parties in formulating decrees, the cases will be restored to the docket, and the parties are requested to present further argument on Questions 4 and 5 previously propounded by the Court for the reargument this term.[13] The Attorney General of the United States is again invited to participate. The Attorneys General of the states requiring or permitting segregation in public education will also be permitted to appear as amici curiae upon request to do so. . . .

It is so ordered.

---

[11] K. B. Clark, *Effect of Prejudice and Discrimination on Personality Development* (Mid-century White House Conference on Children and Youth, 1950); Witmer and Kotinsky, *Personality in the Making,* c. 6 (1952); Deutscher and Chein, "The Psychological Effects of Enforced Segregation: A Survey of Social Science Opinion," 26 J. *Psychol.* 259 (1948); Chein, "What Are the Psychological Effects of Segregation under Conditions of Equal Facilities?" 3 *Int. J. Opinion and Attitude Res.* 229 (1949); Brameld, "Educational Costs," in *Discrimination and National Welfare,* 44–48 (MacIver ed. 1949); Frazier, *The Negro in the United States,* 674–81 (1949). And see generally Myrdal, *An American Dilemma* (1944).

[13] "4. Assuming it is decided that segregation in public schools violates the Fourteenth Amendment

"(a) would a decree necessarily follow providing that, within the limits set by normal geographic school districting, Negro children should forthwith be admitted to schools of their choice, or

"(b) may this Court, in the exercise of its equity powers, permit an effective gradual adjustment to be brought about from existing segregated systems to a system not based on color distinctions?

"5. On the assumption on which questions 4(a) and (b) are based, and assuming further that this Court will exercise its equity powers to the end described in question 4(b),

"(a) should this Court formulate detailed decrees in these cases;

"(b) if so, what specific issues should the decrees reach;

"(c) should this Court appoint a special master to hear evidence with a view to recommending specific terms for such decrees;

"(d) should this Court remand to the courts of first instance with directions to frame decrees in these cases, and if so what general directions should the decrees of this Court include and what procedures should the courts of first instance follow in arriving at the specific terms of more detailed decrees?"

NOTES AND QUESTIONS

1. Brown I *and the "Separate But Equal" Doctrine*

Brown I must be understood in light of the Court's prior decision in *Plessy v. Ferguson*, 163 U.S. 537, 16 S.Ct. 1138, 41 L.Ed. 256 (1896), which established that "separate but equal" accommodations do not violate the Fourteenth Amendment. In *Plessy*, the Court upheld a Louisiana statute that provided that "all railway companies . . . shall provide equal but separate accommodations for the white, and colored races. . . ." The Court wrote:

> The object of the [fourteenth] amendment was undoubtedly to enforce the absolute equality of the two races before the law, but in the nature of things it could not have been intended to abolish distinctions based upon color, or to enforce social, as distinguished from political equality, or a commingling of the two races upon terms unsatisfactory to either. Laws permitting, and even requiring, their separation in places where they are liable to be brought into contact do not necessarily imply the inferiority of either race to the other, and have been generally, if not universally, recognized as within the competency of the state legislatures in the exercise of their police power. The most common instance of this is connected with the establishment of separate schools for white and colored children, which has been held to be a valid exercise of the legislative power even by courts of States where the political rights of the colored race have been longest and most earnestly enforced.

Plessy, 163 U.S. at 544, 16 S.Ct. at 1140. Justice Harlan, in dissent, stated:

> Our Constitution is color-blind, and neither knows nor tolerates classes among citizens. In respect of civil rights, all citizens are equal before the law. . . . The law regards man as man, and takes no account of his surroundings or of his color when his civil rights as guaranteed by the supreme law of the land are involved. It is, therefore, to be regretted that this high tribunal, the final expositor of the fundamental law of the land, has reached the conclusion that it is competent for a state to regulate the enjoyment by citizens of their civil rights solely upon the basis of race. . . .

Id. at 560, 16 S.Ct. 1146.

The *Plessy* standard subsequently was extended to public schooling. In *Gong Lum v. Rice*, 275 U.S. 78, 85–86, 48 S.Ct. 91, 93, 72 L.Ed. 172 (1927), the Supreme Court, almost without analysis, treated the separate but equal rule as an orthodox constitutional principle applicable to public education. *See also Cumming v. Richmond County Board of Education*, 175 U.S. 528, 20 S.Ct. 197, 44 L.Ed. 262 (1899).

Did *Brown* explicitly repudiate *Plessy* when it held that "in the field of public education the doctrine of separate but equal has no place"? *See generally* Kauper, "Segregation in Public Education: The Decline of *Plessy v. Ferguson*," 53 *Mich. L. Rev.* 1137 (1954); McKay, "Segregation and Public Recreation," 40 *Va. L. Rev.* 697 (1954). Or is it more accurate to say that *Brown* was decided within the ambit of the *Plessy* rule but that the Court simply found that in the context of public education, "separate educational facilities are inherently unequal"? Why did the Court choose not to overrule *Plessy* directly?

Professor Hutchinson observes:

> Warren made his opinion acceptable to Reed, and perhaps also to Clark, by appearing to do no more than rest the decision on prior precedents and at least superficially analogous language from those precedents. The elements producing unanimity in Brown included not only the refinement of the issues over time, but also the appeal to a slowly growing body of case law that, by its very existence, rebutted the claim by the states . . . that history was on the side of segregation.

Hutchinson, *infra* at 43–44. *Plessy* was subsequently overruled in *Gayle v. Browder*, 352 U.S. 903, 77 S.Ct. 145, 1 L.Ed.2d 114 (1956) (per curiam), a case concerned with segregated seating on buses.

2. *Legal Developments from* Plessy *to* Brown

The National Association for the Advancement of Colored People (NAACP) initiated its attack on *Plessy* in *Missouri ex rel. Gaines v. Canada*, 305 U.S. 337, 59 S.Ct. 232, 83 L.Ed. 208 (1938). Gaines, a black law school applicant, was obliged by Missouri to attend a law school outside the state because Missouri had not yet established a separate law school for blacks. Missouri would have defrayed Gaines's out-of-state tuition fees. The Court held that the "separate but equal doctrine" required Missouri to provide its black citizens with an educational opportunity equal to that of its white citizens and that the availability of services in adjacent states did not meet this obligation. This was the first time the Court "provided content to the 'equal' branch of the 'separate but equal' doctrine." Hutchinson, "Unanimity and Desegregation: Decisionmaking in the Supreme Court, 1948–1958," 68 *Geo.L.J.* 1, 5 (1979).

Three more education cases were litigated before the Supreme Court by the NAACP: *Sipuel v. Board of Regents of the University of Oklahoma*, 332 U.S. 631, 68 S.Ct. 299, 92 L.Ed. 247 (1948), *Sweatt v. Painter*, 339 U.S. 629, 70 S.Ct. 848, 94 L.Ed. 1114 (1950), both of which concerned law school admissions, and *McLaurin v. Oklahoma State Regents*, 339 U.S. 637, 70 S.Ct. 851, 94 L.Ed. 1149 (1950), which applied to graduate programs other than law.

The opinion in *Sweatt* recognized the need to compare both the tangible factors of Texas's separate law schools, and the intangible factors such as prestige, faculty reputation, and experience of the administration as integral parts of the equality determination. "Moreover," said the Court,

> the law school, the proving ground for legal learning and practice, cannot be effective in isolation from the individuals and institutions with which the law interacts. Few students and no one who has practiced law would choose to study in an academic vacuum, removed from the interplay of ideas and the exchange of views with which the law is concerned. The law school to which Texas is willing to admit petitioner excludes from its student body members of the racial groups which number 85% of the population of the State and include most of the lawyers, witnesses, jurors, judges and other officials with whom petitioner will inevitably be dealing when he becomes a member of the Texas Bar.

Sweatt, 339 U.S. at 634, 70 S.Ct. at 850.

Two features of this historical sketch stand out: the Supreme Court increasingly recognized that interaction with others was part of the learning process itself rather than merely a social by-product; and the NAACP strategy obliged the Court to focus on the "equal" provision of the *Plessy* rule, compelling it to determine whether separateness might carry with it subtle and unquantifiable inequalities. *See generally* Hutchinson, *supra*; Ransmeier, "The Fourteenth Amendment and the 'Separate But Equal' Doctrine," 50 *Mich.L.Rev.* 203 (1951); Roche, "Education, Segregation and the Supreme Court—A Political Analysis," 99 *U.Pa.L.Rev.* 949 (1951). The next logical step was to extend such reasoning to the primary and secondary schools. *See* R. Kluger, *Simple Justice* (1975), for an excellent and very readable account of the NAACP's strategy in these pre-*Brown* cases and the planning that led to the Supreme Court's decision in *Brown*.

3. *Debate About the "Original Meaning" of the Fourteenth Amendment*

One of the fundamental debates in *Brown* concerned the intended scope of the Fourteenth Amendment. A number of justices had been greatly troubled by a perceived lack of legislative or judicial history to support a holding that school segregation was unconstitutional. *See* R. Kluger, *Simple Justice* 590–609 (1975); Hutchinson, "Unanimity and Desegregation: Decision-making in the Supreme Court, 1948–1958," 68 *Geo. L.J.* 1, 40 (1979). The NAACP attorneys representing the plaintiffs contended that congressional debates from the era in which the amendment was enacted demonstrate that it was designed to operate "as a prohibition against the imposition of any racial classification in respect to civil rights." Counsel for the southern school districts argued that such a reading misread and distorted the words and history of the amendment. In their eyes, the abolitionist movement's sole target had been slavery, and banning slavery does not reach the question of mixed or segregated schools. The Court concluded that the legislative history is ambiguous on the issue raised by the parties. How important should legislative history be in constitutional interpretation and application? *See generally* Brest, "The Misconceived Quest for the Original Understanding," 60 *B.U.L. Rev.* 204 (1980); Bickel, "The Original Understanding and the Segregation Decision," 69 *Harv.L.Rev.* 1 (1955); Frank and Munro, "The Original Understanding of 'Equal Protection of the Laws,'" 1972 *Wash. U. L. Q.* 421. *But see* R. Berger, *Government by Judiciary* (1977).

4. **Brown I:** *A Case About Education or a Case About Race?*

a. Education. Is *Brown* most appropriately described as a case about education? In other words, is the central thrust of *Brown* the idea that all children must be afforded equal educational opportunities and that segregated schooling is antithetical to that policy, just as inferior textbooks or teachers might be? Certainly, the encomium to education in the *Brown* opinion gives support to this view. Does treating *Brown* as a case primarily concerned with educational equality imply that all school segregation—adventitious as well as deliberate—is constitutionally defective? Does it imply that the Court is treating the student peer group as an educational resource? *See generally* Cohen, "Defining Racial Equality in Education," 16 *U.C.L.A. L. Rev.* 255 (1969). Should the focus of relief be "on obtaining real educational effectiveness which may entail the improvement of presently desegregated schools as well as the creation or preservation of model black schools"? Bell, "*Brown v. Board of Education* and the Interest-Convergence Dilemma," 93 *Harv. L. Rev.* 518, 532 (1980).

Bolling v. Sharpe, 347 U.S. 497, 74 S.Ct. 693, 98 L.Ed. 884 (1954), the companion case to *Brown*, applied that decision to the District of Columbia (not a "state" under the Fourteenth Amendment). The Court stated that "The Fifth Amendment [does] not contain an equal protection clause. . . . But, as this Court has recognized, discrimination may be so unjustifiable as to be violative of [Fifth Amendment] due process. Classifications based solely upon race must be scrutinized with particular care, since they are contrary to our traditions and hence constitutionally suspect." 347 U.S. at 499, 74 S.Ct. at 694. But in Chief Justice Warren's original proposed opinion for the Court, he took a very different tack:

> This Court has applied similar reasoning to analogous situations in the field of education, the very subject now before us. Thus children and parents are deprived of the liberty protected by the Due Process Clause when the children are prohibited from pursuing certain courses, or from attending private schools and foreign-language schools. Such prohibitions were found to be unreasonable, and unrelated to any legitimate governmental objective. Just as a government may not impose arbitrary restrictions on the parent's right to educate his child, the government must not impose arbitrary restraints on access to the education which the government itself provides.

"Memorandum on the *District of Columbia Case* from the Chief Justice to the Conference" (May 7, 1954), *reprinted in* Hutchinson, *supra* at 93–94 App.

In effect, Warren proposed that education be treated as a "fundamental" interest under the Fifth Amendment's due process clause, and the first sentence of the quoted excerpt specifically was grounded in *Meyer v. Nebraska, Pierce v. Society of Sisters,* and *Farrington v. Tokushige. See* chapter 1. In response to objections by Justice Frankfurter and perhaps other justices, Warren abandoned the "fundamental" interest approach. "With a flick of the wrist he changed *Bolling v. Sharpe* from an education case into a race case, and the equal protection component of the fifth amendment was born." Hutchinson, *supra* at 46. The birth has not been well received by some. *See, e.g.,* Linde, "Judges, Critics, and the Realist Tradition," 82 *Yale L.J.* 227, 233–34 (1972).

b. Race. Is *Brown* more aptly described as a case primarily concerned with racial constraints and freedom of association? If so, does the holding in *Brown* become applicable to any situation in which racial segregation occurs, provided, of course, that the requisite governmental involvement can be demonstrated? Historic judicial hostility to state-imposed racial classification and the numerous per curiam extensions of *Brown* striking down racial separation in noneducation areas suggest that race may have been the critical factor. *See, e.g., Watson v. Memphis,* 373 U.S. 526, 83 S.Ct. 1314, 10 L.Ed.2d 529 (1963); *New Orleans City Park Improvement Ass'n v. Detiege,* 358 U.S. 54, 79 S.Ct. 99, 3 L.Ed.2d 46 (1958) (per curiam).

c. Race and Education. Is *Brown* best treated as both an education and a race case; that is, one that posits a relationship between unconstrained racial association, equality of educational resources, and equality of opportunity, with the benefits of equality seen as following from school desegregation?

d. Unanimity. Why is *Brown* so difficult to interpret? Professor Hutchinson posits that the quest for unanimity ultimately led to obfuscation:

> [U]nanimity both masked the uncertainty within the Court over how to police Brown and contained what otherwise could have erupted into severe and debilitating division over the precise meaning of the revolutionary decision. . . . Indeed, the Court's continuing desire to be united outweighed its responsibility to be persuasive on enough occasions that it has been recently asked if, on balance, unanimity was worth the price. The question, which is now compelling in hindsight, is anachronistic: to the judges faced with Brown and its aftermath, the costs of disunity were much too high to accept.

Hutchinson, *supra* at 87. Why was unanimity thought to be so important?

5. Ethical Principles and Social Science Evidence

a. Quality of Social Science Evidence in Brown. The social science evidence that *Brown* relied on to assess the effects of segregation has been attacked on methodological and interpretive grounds. *See, e.g.,* Cahn, "Jurisprudence," 30 *N.Y.U.L. Rev.* 150 (1955); Garfinkel, "Social Science Evidence and the School Desegregation Cases," 21 *J. Pol.* 37 (1959); Van Den Haag, "Social Science Testimony in the Desegregation Cases—A Reply to Professor Kenneth Clark," 6 *Vill. L. Rev.* 69 (1960). In this regard, consider the following excerpts from the social scientists' amicus brief in *Brown,* which illustrates the type of empirical data before the Supreme Court:

> [T]he opinion stated by a large majority (90 percent) of social scientists who replied to a questionnaire concerning the probable effects of enforced segregation under conditions of equal facilities [is] . . . that, regardless of the facilities which are provided, enforced segregation is psychologically detrimental to the members of the segregated group [here, the blacks].
>
> * * *
>
> The available scientific evidence indicates that much, perhaps all, of the observable differences among various racial and national groups may be adequately explained in terms of environmental differences.
>
> * * *
>
> Comprehensive reviews of . . . instances [of desegregation] clearly establish the fact that desegregation has been carried out successfully in a variety of situations although outbreaks of violence had been commonly predicted.

Is this survey really evidence at all? *See* Arkes, "The Problem of Kenneth Clark," 58 *Commentary* 37 (1974). Dr. Kenneth B. Clark, one of the moving forces behind the introduction of empirical data in the *Brown* case, has commented: "By providing such evidence, the social scientists made it possible to avoid the need to obtain proof of individual damage and to avoid assessment of the equality of facilities in each individual school situation. The assumption of inequality could now be made wherever segregation existed." Clark, "The Social Scientists, the *Brown* Decision, and Contemporary Confusion," in L. Friedman, ed., *Argument* xxxvii (1969). Might the appellants have submitted empirical evidence of greater probative force without resorting to a school-by-school survey of each district involved in the litigation? Do you agree with Clark's conclusion?

Should the lawyers for appellants in *Brown* be faulted for relying on such inconclusive data? *See* Greenberg, "Social Scientists Take the Stand," 54 *Mich. L. Rev.* 953 (1956).

If the school districts had submitted evidence indicating that segregated schooling has little effect on variations in school performance and that differences in family background or home environment were critical, *see, e.g.,* J. Coleman et al., *Equal Educational Opportunity* (1966) (The Coleman Report), or differences in heredity, *see* Jensen, "How Much Can We Boost IQ and Scholastic Achievement," 39 *Harv. Ed. Rev.* 1 (1969), what weight should the trial court or the Supreme Court have given such evidence in determining the nature and scope of the constitutional right? *See generally* B. Levin and W. Hawley, eds., "School Desegregation: Lessons of the First Twenty-Five Years," 42 *Law & Contemp. Probs.* 1 (1978) (pt. 1). What if the evidence indicated that following desegregation the achievement levels of black students remained unchanged or declined? *See, e.g.,* H. Gerard and N. Miller, *School Desegregation: A Long-Term Study* (1975). What if the evidence showed that racial attitudes worsened rather than improved after desegregation? *See, e.g.,* Armor, "The Evidence on Busing," 28 *Pub. Interest* 90 (1972). *See,* respectively, Crain and Mahard, "Desegregation and Black Achievement: A Review of the Research," 42 *Law & Contemp. Probs.* 17 (1978) (pt. 2), and Epps, "The Impact of School Desegregation on the Self-Evaluation and Achievement Orientation of Minority Children," *id.* at 57, for contrasting evidence. Would long-term versus short-term effects be more relevant? *See* Braddock, Crain, and McPartland, "A Long-Term View of School Desegregation: Some Recent Studies of Graduates as Adults," 66 *Phi Delta Kappan* 259 (1984).

Did the decision in *Plessy,* which rejected the argument that segregation might be stigmatizing or otherwise injurious, invite reliance on psychological and sociological data by the Court and appellants in *Brown? See* R. Kluger, *Simple Justice* 705–7 (1975); J. Peltason, 58 *Lonely Men* 49 (1961). Might this reliance be explained by the necessity of giving a controversial decision an aura of legitimacy by demonstrating that it was consistent with both a constitutional and empirical calculus? *See* Cohen and Weiss, "Social Science and Social Policy: Schools and Race," in *Education, Social Science, and the Judicial Process* 72, 79 (R. Rist and R. Anson, eds., 1977).

b. The Controversy. To what extent does the *Brown* opinion rest upon the social science evidence cited in footnote 11 rather than upon principles of law? Legal scholars have addressed both the significance of the social science evidence to the result and the propriety of the Court's reliance on social science research to justify the desegregation decisions. Professor Frank Goodman, for example, has observed that "Constitutional scholars, whatever their views as to the correctness of the decision, have been reluctant to believe that the Court relied to any great extent on the 'modern authorities' cited in its opinion." Goodman, "De Facto School Segregation: A Constitutional and Empirical Analysis," 60 *Calif. L. Rev.* 275, 279 (1972). *See also* Black, "The Lawfulness of the Segregation Decisions," 69 *Yale L.J.* 421 (1960); Cahn, "Jurisprudence," 30 *N.Y.U. L. Rev.* 150 (1955); Heyman, "The Chief Justice, Racial Segregation, and the Friendly Critics," 49 *Calif. L. Rev.* 104 (1961); Yudof, "School Desegregation: Legal Realism, Reasoned Elaboration, and Social Science Research in the Supreme Court," 42 *Law & Contemp. Probs.* 57 (1978) (pt. 2).

For additional insight into the significance of the evidence of footnote 11 to some members of the Court, *see* Justice Jackson's memorandum of February 15, 1954, on the school desegregation decision, quoted in part in R. Kluger, *Simple Justice* at 689 (1975). For the views of Chief Justice Warren and several other members of the Court, *see* Kluger, *supra* at 705–07.

B. *Brown II*: The Scope of Relief

Brown v. Board of Education
349 U.S. 294, 75 S.Ct. 753, 99 L.Ed. 1083 (1955).

Chief Justice Warren delivered the opinion of the Court.

These cases were decided on May 17, 1954. The opinions of that date, declaring the fundamental principle that racial discrimination in public education is unconstitutional, are incorporated herein by reference. All provisions of federal, state, or local law requiring or permitting such discrimination must yield to this principle. There remains for consideration the manner in which relief is to be accorded.

Because these cases arose under different local conditions and their disposition will involve a variety of local problems, we requested further argument on the question of relief. . . .

These presentations were informative and helpful to the Court in its consideration of the complexities arising from the transition to a system of public education freed of racial discrimination. The presentations also demonstrated that substantial steps to eliminate racial discrimination in public schools have already been taken, not only in some of the communities in which these cases arose, but in some of the states appearing as *amici curiae*, and in other states as well. . . .

Full implementation of these constitutional principles may require solution of varied local school problems. School authorities have the primary responsibility for elucidating, assessing, and solving these problems; courts will have to consider whether the action of school authorities constitutes good faith implementation of the governing constitutional principles. Because of their proximity to local conditions and the possible need for further hearings, the courts which originally heard these cases can best perform this judicial appraisal. Accordingly, we believe it appropriate to remand the cases to those courts.

In fashioning and effectuating the decrees, the courts will be guided by equitable principles. Traditionally, equity has been characterized by a practical flexibility in shaping its remedies and by a facility for adjusting and reconciling public and private needs. These cases call for the exercise of these traditional attributes of equity power. At stake is the personal interest of the plaintiffs in admission to public schools as soon as practicable on a nondiscriminatory basis. To effectuate this interest may call for elimination of a variety of obstacles in making the transition to school systems operated in accordance with the constitutional principles set forth in our May 17, 1954, decision. Courts of equity may properly take into account the public interest in the elimination of such obstacles in a systematic and effective manner. But it should go without saying that the vitality of these constitutional principles cannot be allowed to yield simply because of disagreement with them.

While giving weight to these public and private considerations, the courts will require that the defendants make a prompt and reasonable start toward full compliance with our May 17, 1954, ruling. Once such a start has been made, the courts may find that additional time is necessary to carry out the ruling in an effective manner. The burden rests upon the defendants to establish that such time is necessary in the public interest and is consistent with good faith compliance at the earliest practicable date. To that end, the courts may consider problems related to administration, arising from the physical condition of the school plant, the school transportation system, personnel, revision of school districts and attendance areas into compact units to achieve a system of determining admission to the public schools on a nonracial basis, and revision of local laws and regulations which may be necessary in solving the foregoing problems. They will also consider the adequacy of any plans the defendants may propose to meet these problems and to effectuate a transition to a racially nondiscriminatory school system. During this period of transition, the courts will retain jurisdiction of these cases.

The judgments below, except that in the Delaware case, are accordingly reversed and the cases are remanded to the District Courts to take such proceedings and enter such orders and decrees consistent with this opinion as are necessary and proper to admit to public schools on a racially nondiscriminatory basis with all deliberate speed the parties to these cases. The judgment in the Delaware case—ordering the immediate admission of the plaintiffs to schools previously attended only by white children—is affirmed on the basis of the principles stated in our May 17, 1954, opinion, but the case is remanded to the Supreme Court of Delaware for such further proceedings as that court may deem necessary in light of this opinion.

It is so ordered.

NOTES AND QUESTIONS

1. "All Deliberate Speed": An Unusual Remedy?

The "all deliberate speed" standard describes an unspecified remedy that would take effect in an undefined interval of time. That standard differs from the typically precise formulations of relief that usually require immediate implementation. As Professor Bickel points out:

> In the vast majority of cases—barring those that are dismissed outright as not suitable for adjudication—the normal and expected judgment of the court is a crisp and specific writing which tells one of the parties exactly what he must do, such as pay a judgment, deliver certain real estate, cease from doing something, or, in-

deed, go to jail. The equivalent in these cases would have been a decree ordering the named children, and perhaps, since these were class actions, all children in the five school districts affected who were similarly situated, to be admitted forthwith to the white schools of their choice.

A. Bickel, *The Least Dangerous Branch* 247 (1962). *See also* McKay, " 'With All Deliberate Speed'—A Study of School Desegregation," 31 *N.Y.U. L. Rev.* 991 (1956).

Does the Court's approach minimize the legal significance of the injury suffered by the actual plaintiffs who initiated *Brown I*? Did the Court, in characterizing *Brown* as a test case of broad dimensions, submerge the claims of the individual plaintiffs into the hypothesized claims of all African Americans—with the consequence that an eventual remedy ("with all deliberate speed") for all blacks would ultimately benefit the particular parties who had brought the suit? *See* Hartman, "The Right to Equal Educational Opportunities as a Personal and Present Right," 9 *Wayne L. Rev.* 424 (1963); Lusky, "The Stereotype: Hard Core of Racism," 13 *Buff. L. Rev.* 450, 458 (1964). *See generally* Fiss, "Groups and the Equal Protection Clause," 5 *J. Philosophy & Pub. Aff.* 107 (1976). In this sense, is "all deliberate speed" analogous to "prospective overruling"? Typically a prospective decree is one that overrules a prior decision but does not apply the new rule to the case before it, leaving the parties without relief. *See* Comment, "Prospective Overruling and Retroactive Application in the Federal Courts," 71 *Yale L.J.* 907 (1962). Does the "all deliberate speed" standard spring from practical problems in implementation rather than from considerations of more abstract principles of justice? *See* E. Warren, *The Memoirs of Earl Warren* 288–89 (1977). *See generally* Yudof, "Implementation Theories and Desegregation Realities," 32 *Ala. L. Rev.* 441 (1981).

If a more straightforward and forceful standard, as urged by the NAACP, had been embraced by the Court's decree, would actual desegregation have occurred more quickly? Justice Black once stated that the "deliberate speed" formula "delayed the process of outlawing segregation" and that "the Court should have forced its judgment on the counties it affected that minute." "Justice Black and the Bill of Rights," 9 *Sw. U. L. Rev.* 937, 941 (1977) (transcript of interview with Justice Black). *See also* Carter, "The Warren Court and Desegregation," 67 *Mich. L. Rev.* 237

(1968). Might such a decree have engendered even more hostile resistance than that which greeted the "all deliberate speed" mandate?

2. Brown II *and the Lower Federal Courts*

Because the Court placed responsibility for school desegregation in the hands of federal district courts and local school boards, delay in the implementation of *Brown* was inevitable. *See generally* H. Rodgers and C. Bullock, *Law and Social Change*, ch. 4 (1972); G. Orfield, *The Reconstruction of Southern Education* 15–18 (1969). The Court had not developed adequate guidelines for school desegregation, and thus much time was to be wasted in lower courts converting nebulous doctrine into understandable and administrable constitutional law. *See* Carter, "Equal Educational Opportunities for Negroes—Abstraction or Reality," 1968 *U. Ill. L.F.* 160, 177–80. *See* Crump, "From *Freeman* to *Brown* and Back Again: Principle, Pragmatism, and Proximate Cause in the School Desegregation Decisions," 68 *Wash. L. Rev.* 753, 765 (1993), arguing that *Brown II* was a decision with "pragmatic flexibility" but without principle. By putting "the defendants in charge of the remedy," the Court was "plac[ing] the fox in charge of bringing the hen house into compliance with law," while at the same time, the failure to provide clear rules "disadvantaged the honest politician who sincerely desired to achieve compliance."

For an excellent analysis of *Brown*, its history, the efforts to implement the dismantling of "separate but equal" schools, and the current trend toward resegregation, see J. T. Patterson, Brown v. Board of Education: *A Civil Rights Milestone and Its Troubled Legacy* (2001).

III. THE PROGRESS OF SCHOOL DESEGREGATION: 1954–1968

A. Southern Resistance

From 1955 until *Cooper v. Aaron*, 358 U.S. 1, 78 S.Ct. 1401, 3 L.Ed.2d 5 (1958), the Supreme Court failed to grant "plenary consideration to any case involving racial segregation in education." Hutchinson, "Unanimity and Desegregation: Decisionmaking in the Supreme Court, 1948–1958," 68 *Geo. L.J.* 1 (1979). The Court's policy was apparently to dispose summarily of race cases by per curiam orders in order "to maximize the effect of *Brown* and to minimize controversy and resistance." Hutchinson, *supra*

at 61. *See also* S. Wasby, A. D'Amato, and R. Metrailer, *Desegregation from* Brown *to* Alexander (1977); Bickel and Wellington, "Legislative Purpose and the Judicial Process: The *Lincoln Mills* Case," 71 *Harv. L. Rev.* 1, 3–4 (1957).

From 1954 until 1964, progress in the desegregation of southern school districts was minuscule. In 1964, in seven of the eleven states, only 2.14 percent of black students attended desegregated schools. H. Horowitz and K. Karst, *Law, Lawyers, and Social Change* 239 (1969). As Professors Horowitz and Karst have noted, in the decade after *Brown* "the desegregation of southern school districts was not characterized by speed, deliberate or otherwise. . . . The fact is that most of the putative beneficiaries of the legal principle declared in *Brown* [were] frustrated in the vindication of their rights." *Id.* at 239–40 (1969).

The modes of southern resistance were varied. On March 12, 1956, ninety-six congressmen from the South issued a manifesto in which they promised to use "all lawful means" to maintain segregation and "commended those states which have declared the intention to resist." Popular opposition to school desegregation, supported by political leaders playing on the race issue, often resulted in massive resistance to the enforcement of *Brown*. *See Bush v. Orleans Parish School Board*, 187 F.Supp. 42 (S.D. La. 1960), *aff'd*, 365 U.S. 569, 81 S.Ct. 754, 5 L.Ed.2d 806. The myriad new pupil assignment laws, "interposition" plans, and other ingenious schemes demonstrated the truth of the popular saying, "as long as we can legislate, we can segregate." *See generally* Meador, "The Constitution and the Assignment of Pupils to Public Schools," 45 *Va. L. Rev.* 517 (1959); Bickel, "The Decade of School Desegregation: Progress and Prospects," 64 *Colum. L. Rev.* 193 (1964); B. Muse, *Ten Years of Prelude: The Story of Integration Since the Supreme Court's 1954 Decision* (1964).

The most important of these devices was the pupil assignment law, which purported to assign pupils to schools on the basis of considerations and characteristics other than race. In practice such laws perpetuated one-race schools. On one occasion, the Supreme Court affirmed a three-judge court decision upholding a pupil placement act. *Shuttlesworth v. Birmingham Board of Education*, 358 U.S. 101, 79 S.Ct. 221, 3 L.Ed.2d 145 (1958). *See* Johnson, "School Desegregation Problems in the South: An Historical Perspective," 54 *Minn. L. Rev.* 1157 (1970). A popular variation of pupil assignment laws was the "minority to majority transfer" arrangement. After formally desegregating, a Southern school district would grant to any students who constituted a racial minority in their new school the option of transferring back to their old school in which their race was a majority. In *Goss v. Board of Education*, 373 U.S. 683, 83 S.Ct. 1405, 10 L.Ed.2d 632 (1963), the Supreme Court struck down such plans as in violation of *Brown:* "Here the right of transfer, which operates solely on the basis of a racial classification, is a one-way ticket leading to but one destination, i.e., the majority race of the transferee and continued segregation." 373 U.S. at 687, 83 S.Ct. at 1408.

B. Measuring the Impact of *Brown*

In the light of the early history of noncompliance, some commentators questioned whether *Brown* was wisely decided. Although empirical proof of the proposition is lacking and likely to remain so, the symbolic consequences of *Brown,* transcending the immediate difficulties in securing compliance, contributed significantly to the creation of a political and social environment in which progress toward racial justice became possible. *See, e.g.,* W. Murphy and J. Tanenhaus, *The Study of Public Law* 38 (1972); Frantz, "Is the First Amendment Law?—A Reply to Professor Mendelson," in L. Levy, ed., *Judicial Review and the Supreme Court* 161 (1967). The costs of *Brown* in terms of social dislocation, controversy, delay, and judicial energy were great. Yet there has been significant progress toward achieving racial equality since *Brown. See generally* G. Orfield, *Must We Bus?* (1978); C.V. Woodward, *The Strange Career of Jim Crow* (3d ed. 1974); H. Commager, ed., *The Struggle for Racial Equality* (1967). This progress has manifested itself not only in the integration of the public schools, but also in voting, employment, public accommodations, and housing.

Too often judges and lawyers ignore a fundamental truth that is obvious to laypeople and politicians: Regardless of the formal rules of constitutional adjudication, a judicial declaration that a state law is constitutional is likely to enshrine it as the recommended solution of a difficult question of public policy. *Plessy v. Ferguson* serves as a constant reminder of this proposition. Although certainly not a golden age of race relations, the early post-Reconstruction years saw a clumsy search for accommodation between the "old heritage of slavery and the new and insecure heritage of legal equality." It was a time of experimentation and testing in which blacks found a place in society they had never before enjoyed. Yet as the twentieth century approached, the trend reversed, heralded by widespread adoption of Jim Crow legislation and the Supreme Court's refusal to uphold the civil rights of blacks. *See* Woodward, *supra* at 67–109.

In *Plessy v. Ferguson,* the Supreme Court legitimated the abandonment of black rights, placing the judicial seal of approval on a racial ostracism that reached all phases of life. The Court not only created a doctrinal justification for racist policies, but also symbolically affirmed the Social Darwinists' theory that whites were superior to blacks. This judicial coup de grace certainly accounts, at least in part, for the lack of progress toward racial justice in the decades after *Plessy.* A reaffirmation of *Plessy* in *Brown* might well have portended a similar blow to racial equality and the civil rights movement—not only in the courts, but also in the legislatures, the voting booths, the universities, and the job and housing markets.

The judicial declaration that discrimination by race in pupil assignment was unconstitutional undoubtedly helped to mold public opinion and prod the legislative and executive branches of government into action. Certainly federal governmental hopes for racial justice preceded the *Brown* decision. Under the "separate but equal doctrine," the Supreme Court had struck down a number of racially discriminatory practices in the late post-*Plessy* period, and in 1948 President Truman had courageously declared: "We shall not . . . finally achieve the ideals for which this nation was founded so long as any American suffers discrimination as a result of his race, or religion, or color, or the land of origin of his forefathers." Numerous private groups, including the NAACP, worked forcefully for the protection of Negro rights, and the political consciousness of blacks rose dramatically. The combination of private and public movement toward racial justice might well have enabled the Supreme Court to do in 1954 what it was apparently incapable of doing in 1896. But cause and effect merge; whatever the forces that brought *Brown* into being, those forces were strengthened by the decision itself. In the early years after *Brown,* reform proposals that would have allowed the Attorney General to sue local school boards that engaged in segregation were seriously considered. Proposals for federal aid to education that would have strengthened the dual school system were defeated. Nondiscrimination clauses were inserted by the U.S. Department of Health, Education, and Welfare in contracts with colleges participating in National Defense Education Act programs. Federal funds were denied to local school districts that forced children living on military bases to attend segregated schools.

Perhaps the most immediate result of *Brown* was to arouse black organizations and their white liberal allies: "*Brown* . . . awakened a new consciousness of group identity among blacks and a fresh awareness of the possibilities of removing the discrepancy between their supposed and actual rights." W. Murphy and J. Tanenhaus, *The Study of Public Law* 38 (1972). This awakening probably led to the confrontations between civil rights groups and southern political leadership. The impact of those confrontations on American public opinion and on the federal leadership was profound, leading to the 1964 Civil Rights Act, the greatest blow to southern resistance to desegregation. G. Orfield, *The Reconstruction of Southern Education* 2–3, 33–46 (1969).

C. The Administrative-Judicial Era

During the post–*Brown II* period, the Supreme Court appeared reluctant to intervene, letting the standards by which desegregation litigation was to be decided evolve in the lower courts. Ambiguity in *Brown I* and *II*, the Court's post–*Brown II* silence, and the reluctance of lower federal courts and school boards contributed to the delay in implementing *Brown*. However, the failure of the Congress and the president to support the Court was also significant. *See* G. Orfield, *The Reconstruction of Southern Education* 15–22 (1969); J. Vander Zanden, *Race Relations in Transition* 88–94 (1966). The awesome political ramifications of *Brown* required the active assistance of the other branches of government, but this support did not materialize in the early post–*Brown* years.

Significant progress toward desegregation in the South came only with what has been characterized as the "administrative-judicial era" (H. Rodgers and C. Bullock, *Law and Social Change* 18 (1972)), which began with passage of the Civil Rights Act of 1964, 42 U.S.C.A. §§ 2000c, d (1970). *See generally* G. Orfield, *The Reconstruction of Southern Educa-*

tion (1969). This legislation empowered the Department of Health, Education, and Welfare to withhold federal funds from school districts that discriminated against blacks and gave the Attorney General authority to file desegregation suits on the complaint of private citizens. 42 U.S.C.A. §§ 2000c-6, d-1 (1970). *See generally* Note, "The Courts, HEW, and Southern School Desegregation," 77 *Yale L.J.* 321, 356–64 (1967). Under the Civil Rights Act of 1964, HEW promulgated guidelines requiring school districts to make a good faith start toward desegregation. U.S. Office of Education, HEW, *General Statement of Policies under Title VI of the Civil Rights Act of 1964 Respecting Desegregation of Elementary and Secondary Schools* (1965), *reprinted in Price v. Denison Independent School District Board of Education*, 348 F.2d 1010, 1015 (5th Cir. 1965). *See also* U.S. Office of Education, HEW, *Revised Statement of Policies for School Desegregation Plans under Title VI of the Civil Rights Act of 1964*, 45 C.F.R. §181 (1967). The relationship between the HEW guidelines and developing constitutional standards has been explored by Professor Read, "Judicial Evolution of the Law of School Integration Since *Brown v. Board of Education*," 39 *Law & Contemp. Probs.* 7, 20–26 (1975).

Judge Wisdom once noted that "a national effort, bringing together Congress, the executive, and the judiciary may be able to make meaningful the right of Negro children to equal educational opportunities. *The courts acting alone have failed.*" *United States v. Jefferson County Board of Education*, 372 F.2d 836, 847 (5th Cir. 1966) (emphasis added), *aff'd*, 380 F.2d 385, *cert. denied*, 389 U.S. 840, 88 S.Ct. 67, 19 L.Ed.2d 103. Is this an assessment of the relative competency of the courts? Does it imply that the Congress, the executive branch, and the courts will succeed where the courts alone have failed? *See* Comment, "The Courts, HEW, and Southern School Desegregation," 77 *Yale L.J.* 321, 339–56 (1967).

IV. DESEGREGATION: EVOLUTION OF A CONSTITUTIONAL STANDARD

A. Introduction

One of the persistent and complex themes in the school desegregation cases is what standard should be used to determine whether the Constitution has been violated; that is, when has a violation of the equal protection clause occurred, giving rise to the duty of the school board to desegregate? *See generally* J. H. Wilkinson, *Serving Justice* 133–34 (1974). *See also* T. van Geel, "Racial Discrimination from Little Rock to Harvard," 49 *Cin.L.Rev.* 49 (1980); Sedler, "The Constitution and School Desegregation: An Inquiry into the Nature of the Substantive Right," 68 *Ky.L.J.* 879 (1979–80). Is the constitutional violation the use of a racial classification, the constitutional wrong being the school board's deliberate exclusion of black students from white schools, or is the constitutional wrong the maintenance of racially identifiable schools? If the latter is the violation, is it still a violation if the racially identifiable schools arose not as a result of deliberate and intentionally discriminatory policies adopted by the school authorities but rather as a result of racially neutral policies superimposed on existing demographic segregation? *See, e.g.,* W. Stephan and J. Feagin, eds., *School Desegregation: Past, Present, and Future* 69–131 (1980); Goodman, "De Facto School Segregation: A Constitutional and Empirical Analysis," 60 *Calif.L.Rev.* 275 (1972).

The other persistent issue is concerned with remedy: that is, once it has been determined that the equal protection clause has been violated, what is the scope of the remedy that should be imposed on school boards by the courts? Is a policy of race-neutral student assignment a sufficient remedy? These two issues — violation and remedy — obviously overlap. The nature and scope of the remedy might vary according to the conception of the violation. Commentators have long argued over whether active integration or merely passive nondiscrimination is the appropriate remedy, and the view that is taken depends partly on what one conceives is the scope of the constitutional violation. *See, e.g.,* Dworkin, "Social Sciences and Constitutional Rights — The Consequences of Uncertainty," in R. Rist and R. Anson, eds., *Education, Social Science, and the Judicial Process* 20 (1977); Graglia, "From Prohibiting Segregation to Requiring Integration: Developments in the Law of Race and the Schools Since *Brown*," in Stephan and Feagin, *supra* at 69; Brest, "The Supreme Court, 1975 Term — Foreword: In Defense of the Antidiscrimination Principle," 90 *Harv.L.Rev.* 1 (1976); Kanner, "From Denver to Dayton: The Development of a Theory of Equal Protection Remedies," 72 *Nw.U.L.Rev.* 382 (1977); Wolf, "Northern School Desegregation and Residential

Choice," 1977 *Sup.Ct.Rev.* 63. The differing positions are discussed in Yudof, "School Desegregation: Legal Realism, Reasoned Elaboration, and Social Science Research in the Supreme Court," 42 *Law & Contemp. Probs.* 57 (1978) (pt. 2).

B. *Green:* Divining the Constitutional Violation from the Court's Remedial Requirements

Green v. County School Board arose in a rural district in Virginia that had maintained a racially dual school system by law. The New Kent County school district had made no attempts to desegregate its schools until 1965 when it adopted a freedom-of-choice plan. *Green* has a historic place in the evolution of constitutional standards, and it triggered a major change in the nature and pace of desegregation in the South.

Green v. County School Board
391 U.S. 430, 88 S.Ct. 1689, 20 L.Ed.2d 716 (1968).

Justice Brennan delivered the opinion of the Court.

The question for decision is whether, under all the circumstances here, respondent School Board's adoption of a "freedom-of-choice" plan which allows a pupil to choose his own public school constitutes adequate compliance with the Board's responsibility "to achieve a system of determining admission to the public schools on a nonracial basis. . . ." *Brown v. Board of Education*, 349 U.S. 294, 300–01 *(Brown II)*.

Petitioners brought this action in March 1965 seeking injunctive relief against respondent's continued maintenance of an alleged racially segregated school system. New Kent County is a rural county in Eastern Virginia. About one-half of its population of some 4,500 are Negroes. There is no residential segregation in the county; persons of both races reside throughout. The school system has only two schools, the New Kent school on the east side of the county and the George W. Watkins school on the west side. In a memorandum filed May 17, 1966, the District Court found that the "school system serves approximately 1,300 pupils, of which 740 are Negro and 550 are White. The School Board operates one white combined elementary and high school [New Kent], and one Negro combined elementary and high school [George

W. Watkins]. There are no attendance zones. Each school serves the entire county." The record indicates that twenty-one school buses—eleven serving the Watkins school and ten serving the New Kent school—travel overlapping routes throughout the county to transport pupils to and from the two schools.

The segregated system was initially established and maintained under the compulsion of Virginia constitutional and statutory provisions mandating racial segregation in public education, Va. Const. Art. IX, § 140 (1902); Va. Code § 22-221 (1950). These provisions were held to violate the Federal Constitution in *Davis v. County School Board of Prince Edward County*, decided with *Brown v. Board of Education*, 347 U.S. 483, 487 (*Brown I*). The respondent School Board continued the segregated operation of the system after the *Brown* decisions, presumably on the authority of several statutes enacted by Virginia in resistance to those decisions. Some of these statutes were held to be unconstitutional on their face or as applied. One statute, the Pupil Placement Act, Va. Code § 22-232.1 *et seq.* (1964), not repealed until 1966, divested local boards of authority to assign children to particular schools and placed that authority in a State Pupil Placement Board. Under that Act children were each year automatically reassigned to the school previously attended unless upon their application the State Board assigned them to another school; students seeking enrollment for the first time were also assigned at the discretion of the State Board. To September 1964, no Negro pupil had applied for admission to the New Kent school under this statute and no white pupil had applied for admission to the Watkins school.

The School Board initially sought dismissal of this suit on the ground that petitioners had failed to apply to the State Board for assignment to New Kent school. However on August 2, 1965, five months after the suit was brought, respondent School Board, in order to remain eligible for federal financial aid, adopted a "freedom-of-choice" plan for desegregating the schools. Under that plan, each pupil, except those entering the first and eighth grades, may annually choose between the New Kent and Watkins schools and pupils not making a choice are assigned to the school previously attended; first- and eighth-grade pupils must affirmatively choose a school. After the plan was filed the District Court denied petitioners' prayer for an injunction and granted respondent leave to submit an amendment to the plan with respect to employment and assignment of teachers and staff on a racially nondiscriminatory basis. The amendment was duly filed and on June 28, 1966, the District Court approved the "freedom-of-choice" plan as so amended. The Court of Appeals for the Fourth Circuit, *en banc*, 382 F.2d 338, affirmed the District Court's approval of the "freedom-of-choice" provisions of the plan. . . . We granted certiorari, 389 U.S. 1003.

The pattern of separate "white" and "Negro" schools in the New Kent County school system established under compulsion of state laws is precisely the pattern of segregation to which *Brown I* and *Brown II* were particularly addressed, and which *Brown I* declared unconstitutionally denied Negro school children equal protection of the laws. Racial identification of the system's schools was complete, extending not just to the composition of student bodies at the two schools but to every facet of school operations—faculty, staff, transportation, extracurricular activities and facilities. In short, the State, acting through the local school board and school officials, organized and operated a dual system, part "white" and part "Negro."

It was such dual systems that fourteen years ago *Brown I* held unconstitutional and a year later *Brown II* held must be abolished; school boards operating such school systems were required by *Brown II* "to effectuate a transition to a racially nondiscriminatory school system." 349 U.S. at 301. It is of course true that for the time immediately after *Brown II* the concern was with making an initial break in a long-established pattern of excluding Negro children from schools attended by white children. The principal focus was on obtaining for those Negro children courageous enough to break with tradition a place in the "white" schools. *See, e.g., Cooper v. Aaron*, 358 U.S. 1. Under *Brown II* that immediate goal was only the first step, however. The transition to a unitary, nonracial system of public education was and is the ultimate end to be brought about; it was because of the "complexities arising from the transition to a system of public education freed of racial discrimination" that we provided for "all deliberate speed" in the implementation of the principles of *Brown I*, 349 U.S. at 299–301.

It is against this background that 13 years after *Brown II* commanded the abolition of dual systems we must measure the effectiveness of respondent School Board's "freedom-of-choice" plan to achieve that end. The School Board contends that it has fully discharged its obligation by adopting a plan by which every student, regardless of race, may "freely" choose the school he will attend. The Board attempts to cast the issue in its broadest form by arguing that its "freedom-of-choice" plan may be faulted only by reading the Fourteenth Amendment as universally requiring "compulsory integration," a reading it insists the wording of the Amendment will not support. But that argument ignores the thrust of *Brown II*. In the light of the command of that case, what is involved here is the question whether the Board has achieved the "racially nondiscriminatory school system" *Brown II* held must be effectuated in order to remedy the established unconstitutional deficiencies of its segregated system. In the context of the state-imposed segregated pattern of long standing, the fact that in 1965 the Board opened the doors of the former "white" school to Negro children and of the "Negro" school to white children merely begins, not ends, our inquiry whether the Board has taken steps adequate to abolish its dual, segregated system. *Brown II* was a call for the dismantling of well-entrenched dual systems tempered by an awareness that complex and multifaceted problems would arise which would require time and flexibility for a successful resolution. School boards such as the respondent then operating state-compelled dual systems were nevertheless clearly charged with the affirmative duty to take whatever steps might be necessary to convert to a unitary system in which racial discrimination would be eliminated root and branch. *See Cooper v. Aaron, supra,* at 7; *Bradley v. School Board,* 382 U.S. 103; *cf. Watson v. City of Memphis,* 373 U.S. 526. The constitutional rights of Negro school children articulated in *Brown I* permit no less than this; and it was to this end that *Brown II* commanded school boards to bend their efforts.

In determining whether respondent School Board met that command by adopting its "freedom-of-choice" plan, it is relevant that this first step did not come until some eleven years after *Brown I* was decided and ten years after *Brown II* directed the making of a "prompt and reasonable start." This deliberate perpetuation of the unconstitutional dual system can only have compounded the harm of such a system. Such delays are no longer tolerable, for "the

governing constitutional principles no longer bear the imprint of newly enunciated doctrine." . . . The burden on a school board today is to come forward with a plan that promises realistically to work, and promises realistically to work now.

. . . It is incumbent upon the school board to establish that its proposed plan promises meaningful and immediate progress toward disestablishing state-imposed segregation. It is incumbent upon the district court to weigh that claim in light of the facts at hand and in light of any alternatives which may be shown as feasible and more promising in their effectiveness. Where the court finds the board to be acting in good faith and the proposed plan to have real prospects for dismantling the state-imposed dual system "at the earliest practicable date," then the plan may be said to provide effective relief. Of course, the availability to the board of other more promising courses of action may indicate a lack of good faith; and at least it places a heavy burden upon the board to explain its preference for an apparently less effective method. Moreover, whatever plan is adopted will require evaluation in practice, and the court should retain jurisdiction until it is clear that state-imposed segregation has been completely removed. . . .

We do not hold that "freedom of choice" can have no place in such a plan. We do not hold that a "freedom-of-choice" plan might of itself be unconstitutional, although that argument has been urged upon us. Rather, all we decide today is that in desegregating a dual system a plan utilizing "freedom of choice" is not an end in itself. As Judge Sobeloff has put it,

> "Freedom of choice" is not a sacred talisman; it is only a means to a constitutionally required end—the abolition of the system of segregation and its effects. If the means prove effective, it is acceptable, but if it fails to undo segregation, other means must be used to achieve this end. The school officials have the continuing duty to take whatever action may be necessary to create a "unitary, nonracial system."

Bowman v. County School Board, 382 F.2d 326, 333 (4th Cir. 1967) (concurring opinion). *Accord, Kemp v. Beasley,* 389 F.2d 178 (8th Cir. 1968); *United States v. Jefferson County Board of Education, supra.* Although the general experience under "freedom of choice" to date has been such as to indicate its ineffectiveness as a tool of desegregation,[5] there may well be instances in which it can serve as an effective device. Where it offers real promise of aiding a desegregation program to effectuate conversion of a state-imposed dual system to a unitary, nonracial system there might be no objection to allowing such a device to prove itself in operation. On the other hand, if there are reasonably available other ways, such for illustration as zoning, promising speedier and more effective conversion to a unitary, nonracial school system, "freedom of choice" must be held unacceptable.

The New Kent School Board's "freedom-of-choice" plan cannot be accepted as a sufficient step to "effectuate a transition" to a unitary system. In three years of operation not a single white child has chosen to attend Watkins school and although 115 Negro children enrolled in New Kent school in 1967 (up from 35 in 1965 and 111 in 1966) 85 percent of the Negro children in the system still attend the all-Negro Watkins school. In other words, the school system remains a dual system. Rather than further the dismantling of the dual system, the plan has operated simply to burden children and their parents with a responsibility which *Brown II* placed squarely on the School Board. The Board must be required to formulate a new plan and, in light of other courses which appear open to the Board, such as zoning, fashion steps which promise realistically to convert promptly to a system without a "white" school and a "Negro" school, but just schools.

The judgment of the Court of Appeals is vacated insofar as it affirmed the District Court and the case is remanded to the District Court for further proceedings consistent with this opinion.

It is so ordered.

NOTES AND QUESTIONS

1. Green *and* Brown

Is *Green* concerned with determining when the Constitution has been violated or with what the appropriate remedy is once a constitutional violation has been established? To what extent has the Court made clear what the violation is? In the first line of the *Green* opinion, Justice Brennan states that the question for decision is whether the school board has complied with *Brown v. Board of Education* by "determining admission to the public schools on a nonracial basis." If this is the issue, how can the result in the case be defended? Did the defendants assign students according to their race? Were the assignments not made on the basis of racially neutral choices made by black and white parents?

Justice Brennan attempts to deal with these problems by contending that although the initial concern after *Brown II* was the assignment of African American youngsters to white schools from which they were excluded solely because of their race, that was only a first step toward the ultimate goal: the "transition to a unitary, nonracial system of public education." What is a unitary school system?

a. Racial Classification Ethic and Remedies. If prohibition of racial classifications underlies the desegregation cases and if the constitutional wrong identified in those cases is the exclusion of blacks from white schools, isn't the logical remedy the admission of black students to the schools from which they were excluded because of their race? *See* Bickel, "The Decade of School Desegregation: Progress and

---

[5]The views of the United States Commission on Civil Rights, which we neither adopt nor refuse to adopt, are as follows:

"Freedom-of-choice plans, which have tended to perpetuate racially identifiable schools in the Southern and border States, require affirmative action by both Negro and white parents and pupils before such disestablishment can be achieved. There are a number of factors which have prevented such affirmative action by substantial numbers of parents and pupils of both races:

"(a) Fear of retaliation and hostility from the white community continue to deter many Negro families from choosing formerly all-white schools;

"(b) During the past school year [1966–67], as in the previous year, in some areas of the South, Negro families with children attending previously all-white schools under free choice plans were targets of violence, threats of violence and economic reprisal by white persons and Negro children were subjected to harassment by white classmates notwithstanding conscientious efforts by many teachers and principals to prevent such misconduct.

"(c) During the past school year, in some areas of the South public officials improperly influenced Negro families to keep their children in Negro schools and excluded Negro children attending formerly all-white schools from official functions;

"(d) Poverty deters many Negro families in the South from choosing formerly all-white schools. Some Negro parents are embarrassed to permit their children to attend such schools without suitable clothing. In some districts special fees are assessed for courses which are available only in the white schools;

"(e) Improvements in facilities and equipment . . . have been instituted in all-Negro schools in some districts in a manner that tends to discourage Negroes from selecting white schools." *Southern School Desegregation, 1966–1967*, 88 (1967). *See id.* at 45–69; *Survey of School Desegregation in the Southern and Border States., 1965–1966.* 30–44, 51–52 (U.S. Comm'n on Civil Rights 1966).

Prospects," 64 *Colum.L.Rev.* 193, 212 (1964). Yet in *Green* the Court emphasized the abolition of racially identifiable schools. Can that be done other than by integrating black and white students throughout the system? Of what significance is the Court's comment that the school board relied on children and their parents to dismantle the dual system rather than undertaking the responsibility itself?

b. The "Bad Faith" Argument. Proponents of the racial neutrality principle have attempted to explain the integration remedy by focusing on the bad faith of many school boards in implementing *Brown.* In *Green,* for example, the school board had not taken any steps to eliminate segregation until 1965, eleven years after *Brown I.* According to this theory, the duty to integrate "might be justified as a prophylactic, a way of making certain that a school board's policy of racial segregation has in fact been discarded." Goodman, "De Facto Segregation: A Constitutional and Empirical Analysis," 60 *Calif.L.Rev.* 275, 293 (1972). If only racial classifications are forbidden, and a school board has abandoned its policy of making such classifications, of what relevance is its good or bad faith?

Does the harm to blacks in *Green* lie in the self-evident proposition that the school board took race into account in adopting its freedom-of-choice plan? Does this justify the remedy of integration? *See* Simon, "Racially Prejudiced Governmental Actions: A Motivation Theory of the Constitutional Ban Against Racial Discrimination," 15 *San Diego L.Rev.* 1041, 1122–27 (1978); Yudof, "School Desegregation: Legal Realism, Reasoned Elaboration, and Social Science Research in the Supreme Court," 42 *Law & Contemp. Probs.* 57, 58 (1978) (pt. 2). What remedy would you propose? *See, e.g., Crawford v. Board of Education,* 17 Cal. 3d 280, 305–06, 130 Cal. Rptr. 724, 741, 551 P.2d 28, 45 (1976), *aff'd,* 458 U.S. 527, 102 S.Ct. 3211, 73 L.Ed.2d 948.

c. Elimination of Discriminatory Effects of Past Segregation. Another explanation of the integration remedy in *Green* is that integration is necessary to eliminate the discriminatory effects of past practices. *See Hearings on School Busing Before Subcomm. No. 5 of the House Comm. on the Judiciary,* 92d Cong., 2d. Sess., ser. 32, pt. 3, at 1631–32 (1972) (statement of Professor Wright); Cox, "The Role of Congress in Constitutional Determinations," 40 *U. Cin.L.Rev.* 199, 258 (1971). Integration is thus not a substantive

entitlement; rather it stands as a remedy to cure past instances of racial discrimination in the public schools. What is the relationship between the past discrimination in *Green* and the unacceptability of the freedom-of-choice plan? Can it be persuasively argued that the prior dual school system has influenced the current assignment choices of black and white parents?

Was *Green* premised on the view that the choices of blacks were dictated by economic and physical threats made against them? Why did the Court include footnote 5? Might the difficulties of the case-by-case search for coercion have led the Court to adopt a per se rule against freedom-of-choice plans? Is there any language in the opinion to support this position?

Might *Green* rest on the principle that any form of segregation is particularly injurious in previously de jure school districts because the past discrimination could have "helped to shape the attitudes of the community, both black and white, toward Negroes and Negro schools"? Goodman, "De Facto Segregation: A Constitutional and Empirical Analysis," 60 *Calif.L.Rev.* 275, 295 (1972). Is this approach realistic? Is the stigma of assignment to an all-black school limited to previously de jure systems? Will integration necessarily change these perceptions?

2. A Plan That "Promises Realistically to Work Now"

The Supreme Court did not further define what it meant when it said a plan had to "work" and what "effects" had to be undone and how, nor what it meant by a "unitary system." The Court did, however, make clear what it meant by "now" in *Alexander v. Holmes County Board of Education,* 396 U.S. 19, 90 S.Ct. 29, 24 L.Ed.2d 19 (1969) and *Carter v. West Feliciana Parish School Board,* 396 U.S. 290, 90 S.Ct. 608, 24 L.Ed.2d 530 (1970), in which it held that a few months' delay in desegregation to avoid disruption during the school year was impermissible and peremptorily ordered immediate desegregation. It was these decisions, even more than *Green,* that moved the South from minimal desegregation to significant levels of integration.

3. The Green Factors

The Court noted that a dual system is one that is racially identifiable and ordered the defendants to "convert promptly" to a "unitary, nonracial school system," that is, "a system without a 'white' school and a 'Negro' school, but just schools." What factors might make a school racially identifiable? The Court suggests that, in addition to the composition of the student bodies, the schools were racially identifiable with regard to faculty, staff, transportation, extracurricular activities, and physical facilities. These factors became known as "the six *Green* factors," and lower courts began to require desegregation plans that not only addressed pupil assignments, but also the other five areas. *See, e.g., Board of Education of Oklahoma City Public Schools v. Dowell*, 498 U.S. 237, 111 S.Ct. 630, 112 L.Ed.2d 715 (1991); *Freeman v. Pitts*, 503 U.S. 467, 112 S.Ct. 1430, 118 L.Ed. 2d 108 (1992).

C. Establishing the Constitutional Violation in the South: *Swann* and the Connection Between Past *De Jure* Conduct and Present Segregative Effects

Swann v. Charlotte-Mecklenburg Board of Education, 402 U.S. 1, 91 S.Ct. 1267, 28 L.Ed.2d 554 (1971), raises questions about the extent to which past constitutional violations have causal connections to present segregation, thus creating a continuing violation that must be overcome. *Swann* arose in a state "having a long history of maintaining two sets of schools in a single school system deliberately operated to carry out a governmental policy to separate pupils in schools solely on the basis of race. That was what *Brown v. Board of Education* was all about." But the school board argued that the present segregated pattern of school attendance was not due to deliberate assignment by race on the part of school officials but rather to the nature of residential patterns. What is a "continuing violation," and what may a district court compel the school district to do in such a case?

Swann v. Charlotte-Mecklenburg Board of Education
402 U.S. 1, 91 S.Ct. 1267, 28 L.Ed.2d 554 (1971).

Chief Justice Burger delivered the opinion of the Court:

We granted certiorari in this case to review important issues as to the duties of school authorities and the scope of powers of federal courts under this Court's mandates to eliminate racially separate public schools established and maintained by state action. . . .

This case and those argued with it arose in States having a long history of maintaining two sets of schools in a single school system deliberately operated to carry out a governmental policy to separate pupils in schools solely on the basis of race. That was what *Brown v. Board of Education* was all about. These cases present us with the problem of defining in more precise terms than heretofore the scope of the duty of school authorities and district courts in implementing *Brown I* and the mandate to eliminate dual systems and establish unitary systems at once. Meanwhile district courts and courts of appeals have struggled in hundreds of cases with a multitude and variety of problems under this Court's general directive. Understandably, in an area of evolving remedies, those courts had to improvise and experiment without detailed or specific guidelines. This Court, in *Brown I*, appropriately dealt with the large constitutional principles; other federal courts had to grapple with the flinty, intractable realities of day-to-day implementation of those constitutional commands. Their efforts, of necessity, embraced a process of "trial and error," and our effort to formulate guidelines must take into account their experience. . . .

I

The Charlotte-Mecklenburg school system, the 43rd largest in the Nation, encompasses the city of Charlotte and surrounding Mecklenburg County, North Carolina. The area is large—550 square miles— spanning roughly 22 miles east-west and 36 miles north-south. During the 1968–69 school year the system served more than 84,000 pupils in 107 schools. Approximately 71% of the pupils were found to be white and 29% Negro. As of June 1969 there were approximately 24,000 Negro students in the system, of whom 21,000 attended schools within the city of Charlotte. Two-thirds of those 21,000—approximately 14,000 Negro students—attended twenty-one schools which were either totally Negro or more than 99% Negro.

This situation came about under a desegregation plan approved by the District Court at the commencement of the present litigation in 1965, 243 F.Supp. 667 (W.D.N.C.), *aff'd*, 369 F.2d 29 (4th Cir. 1966), based upon geographic zoning with a free-transfer provision. The present proceedings were initiated in September 1968 by petitioner Swann's motion for further relief based on *Green v. County*

School Board, 391 U.S. 430 (1968), and its companion cases. All parties now agree that in 1969 the system fell short of achieving the unitary school system that those cases require. . . .

In April 1969 the District Court ordered the school board to come forward with a plan for both faculty and student desegregation. . . . [I]n February 1970, the District Court was presented with two alternative pupil assignment plans—the finalized "board plan" and the "Finger plan" [a plan submitted by the court-appointed expert, Dr. Finger]. . . .

[The Finger plan modified the board's plan for senior and junior high schools by increasing the amount of desegregation. The Finger plan included satellite zones for the junior high schools, under which "inner-city Negro students were assigned by attendance zones to nine outlying predominately white junior high schools, thereby substantially desegregating every junior high school in the system." With regard to elementary schools, under the board plan, "more than half of the Negro elementary pupils were left in nine schools that were 86% to 100% Negro; approximately half of the white elementary pupils were assigned to schools 86% to 100% white." By contrast, the Finger plan used "zoning, pairing, and grouping techniques, with the result that student bodies throughout the system would range from 9% to 38% Negro." The District Court adopted the Finger plan.]

On appeal the Court of Appeals affirmed the District Court's order as to faculty desegregation and the secondary school plans, but vacated the order respecting elementary schools. While agreeing that the District Court properly disapproved the board plan concerning these schools, the Court of Appeals feared that the pairing and grouping of elementary schools would place an unreasonable burden on the board and the system's pupils. The case was remanded to the District Court for reconsideration and submission of further plans. . . .

II

Nearly 17 years ago this Court held, in explicit terms, that state-imposed segregation by race in public schools denies equal protection of the laws. At no time has the Court deviated in the slightest degree from that holding or its constitutional underpinnings. None of the parties before us challenges the Court's decision [in *Brown I* and *II*].

Over the 16 years since *Brown II*, many difficulties were encountered in implementation of the basic constitutional requirement that the State not discriminate between public school children on the basis of their race. Nothing in our national experience prior to 1955 prepared anyone for dealing with changes and adjustments of the magnitude and complexity encountered since then. Deliberate resistance of some to the Court's mandates has impeded the good-faith efforts of others to bring school systems into compliance. The detail and nature of these dilatory tactics have been noted frequently by this Court and other courts.

By the time the Court considered *Green v. County School Board*, 391 U.S. 430, in 1968, very little progress had been made in many areas where dual school systems had historically been maintained by operation of state laws. In *Green*, the Court was confronted with a record of a freedom-of-choice program that the District Court had found to operate in fact to preserve a dual system more than a decade after *Brown II*. While acknowledging that a freedom-of-choice concept could be a valid remedial measure in some circumstances, its failure to be effective in *Green* required that: "The burden on a school board today is to come forward with a plan that promises realistically to work . . . now . . . until it is clear that state-imposed segregation has been completely removed." *Green, supra*, at 439.

This was plain language, yet the 1969 Term of Court brought fresh evidence of the dilatory tactics of many school authorities. *Alexander v. Holmes County Board of Education*, 396 U.S. 19, restated the basic obligation asserted in *Griffin v. School Board*, 377 U.S. 218, 234 (1964), and *Green, supra*, that the remedy must be implemented *forthwith*.

The problems encountered by the district courts and courts of appeals make plain that we should now try to amplify guidelines, however incomplete and imperfect, for the assistance of school authorities and courts. The failure of local authorities to meet their constitutional obligations aggravated the massive problem of converting from the state-enforced discrimination of racially separate school systems. This process has been rendered more difficult by changes since 1954 in the structure and patterns of communities, the growth of student population, movement of families, and other changes, some of which had marked impact on school planning, sometimes neutralizing or negating remedial action before it was fully implemented. Rural areas accustomed for half a century to the consolidated school systems implemented by bus transportation could make adjustments more readily than metropolitan areas with dense and shifting population, numerous schools, congested and complex traffic patterns.

III

The objective today remains to eliminate from the public schools all vestiges of state-imposed segregation. Segregation was the evil struck down by *Brown I* as contrary to the equal protection guarantees of the Constitution. That was the violation sought to be corrected by the remedial measures of *Brown II.* That was the basis for the holding in *Green* that school authorities are "clearly charged with the affirmative duty to take whatever steps might be necessary to convert to a unitary system in which racial discrimination would be eliminated root and branch." . . .

If school authorities fail in their affirmative obligations under these holdings, judicial authority may be invoked. Once a right and a violation have been shown, the scope of a district court's equitable powers to remedy past wrongs is broad, for breadth and flexibility are inherent in equitable remedies.

* * *

In seeking to define even in broad and general terms how far this remedial power extends it is important to remember that judicial powers may be exercised only on the basis of a constitutional violation. Remedial judicial authority does not put judges automatically in the shoes of school authorities whose powers are plenary. Judicial authority enters only when local authority defaults.

School authorities are traditionally charged with broad power to formulate and implement educational policy and might well conclude, for example, that in order to prepare students to live in a pluralistic society each school should have a prescribed ratio of Negro to white students reflecting the proportion for the district as a whole. To do this as an educational policy is within the broad discretionary powers of school authorities; absent a finding of a constitutional violation, however, that would not be within the authority of a federal court. As with any equity case, the nature of the violation determines the scope of the remedy. In default by the school authorities of their obligation to proffer acceptable

remedies, a district court has broad power to fashion a remedy that will assure a unitary school system.

* * *

IV

* * *

We turn now to the problem of defining with more particularity the responsibilities of school authorities in desegregating a state-enforced dual school system in light of the Equal Protection Clause. . . .

In *Green*, we pointed out that existing policy and practice with regard to faculty, staff, transportation, extracurricular activities, and facilities were among the most important indicia of a segregated system. 391 U.S. at 435. Independent of student assignment, where it is possible to identify a "white school" or a "Negro school" simply by reference to the racial composition of teachers and staff, the quality of school buildings and equipment, or the organization of sports activities, a *prima facie* case of violation of substantive constitutional rights under the Equal Protection Clause is shown.

When a system has been dual in these respects, the first remedial responsibility of school authorities is to eliminate invidious racial distinctions. With respect to such matters as transportation, supporting personnel, and extracurricular activities, no more than this may be necessary. Similar corrective action must be taken with regard to the maintenance of buildings and the distribution of equipment. In these areas, normal administrative practice should produce schools of like quality, facilities, and staffs. Something more must be said, however, as to faculty assignment and new school construction.

In the companion *Davis* case [402 U.S. 33], the Mobile school board has argued that the Constitution requires that teachers be assigned on a "color-blind" basis. It also argues that the Constitution prohibits district courts from using their equity power to order assignment of teachers to achieve a particular degree of faculty desegregation. We reject that contention.

* * *

[The Court noted that in *United States v. Montgomery County Board of Education*, 395 U.S. 225 (1969), it had upheld the order of the district judge setting an initial ratio for the school system of "at least two Negro teachers out of each 12 in any given school" as within the "spirit" of *Green*, inasmuch as the plan would "expedite . . . the day when a completely unified, unitary nondiscriminatory school system becomes a reality instead of a hope." 395 U.S. at 235–236.]

The principles of *Montgomery* have been properly followed by the District Court and the Court of Appeals in this case.

The construction of new schools and the closing of old ones are two of the most important functions of local school authorities and also two of the most complex. They must decide questions of location and capacity in light of population growth, finances, land values, site availability, through an almost endless list of factors to be considered. The result of this will be a decision which, when combined with one technique or another of student assignment, will determine the racial composition of the student body in each school in the system. Over the long run, the consequences of the choices will be far reaching. People gravitate toward school facilities, just as schools are located in response to the needs of people. The location of schools may thus influence the patterns of residential development of a metropolitan area and have important impact on composition of inner-city neighborhoods.

In the past, choices in this respect have been used as a potent weapon for creating or maintaining a state-segregated school system. In addition to the classic pattern of building schools specifically intended for Negro or white students, school authorities have sometimes, since *Brown*, closed schools which appeared likely to become racially mixed through changes in neighborhood residential patterns. This was sometimes accompanied by building new schools in the areas of white suburban expansion farthest from Negro population centers in order to maintain the separation of the races with a minimum departure from the formal principles of "neighborhood zoning." Such a policy does more than simply influence the short-run composition of the student body of a new school. It may well promote segregated residential patterns which, when combined with "neighborhood zoning," further lock the school system into the mold of separation of the races. . . .

In ascertaining the existence of legally imposed school segregation, the existence of a pattern of school construction and abandonment is thus a factor of great weight. In devising remedies where legally imposed segregation has been established, it is the responsibility of local authorities and district

courts to see to it that future school construction and abandonment are not used and do not serve to perpetuate or reestablish the dual system. . . .

V

The central issue in this case is that of student assignment, and there are essentially four problem areas:

(1) to what extent racial balance or racial quotas may be used as an implement in a remedial order to correct a previously segregated system;

(2) whether every all-Negro and all-white school must be eliminated as an indispensable part of a remedial process of desegregation;

(3) what the limits are, if any, on the rearrangement of school districts and attendance zones, as a remedial measure; and

(4) what the limits are, if any, on the use of transportation facilities to correct state-enforced racial school segregation.

(1) Racial Balances or Racial Quotas. . . . We do not reach in this case the question whether a showing that school segregation is a consequence of other types of state action, without any discriminatory action by the school authorities, is a constitutional violation requiring remedial action by a school desegregation decree. This case does not present that question and we therefore do not decide it.

Our objective in dealing with the issues presented by these cases is to see that school authorities exclude no pupil of a racial minority from any school, directly or indirectly, on account of race; it does not and cannot embrace all the problems of racial prejudice, even when those problems contribute to disproportionate racial concentrations in some schools.

In this case it is urged that the District Court has imposed a racial balance requirement of 71% to 29% on individual schools. . . .

. . . If we were to read the holding of the District Court to require, as a matter of substantive constitutional right, any particular degree of racial balance or mixing, that approach would be disapproved and we would be obliged to reverse. The constitutional command to desegregate schools does not mean that every school in every community must always reflect the racial composition of the school system as a whole.

As the voluminous record in this case shows, the predicate for the District Court's use of 71% to 29%

ratio was twofold: first, its express finding, approved by the Court of Appeals and not challenged here, that a dual school system had been maintained by the school authorities at least until 1969; second, its finding, also approved by the Court of Appeals, that the school board had totally defaulted in its acknowledged duty to come forward with an acceptable plan of its own. . . .

We see therefore that the use made of the mathematical ratios was no more than a starting point in the process of shaping a remedy, rather than an inflexible requirement. From that starting point the District Court proceeded to frame a decree that was within its discretionary powers, as an equitable remedy for the particular circumstances. As we said in *Green*, a school authority's remedial plan or a district court's remedial decree is to be judged by its effectiveness. Awareness of the racial composition of the whole school system is likely to be a useful starting point in shaping a remedy to correct past constitutional violations. In sum, the very limited use made of mathematical ratios was within the equitable remedial discretion of the District Court.

(2) **One-Race Schools.** The record in this case reveals the familiar phenomenon that in metropolitan areas minority groups are often found concentrated in one part of the city. In some circumstances certain schools may remain all or largely of one race until new schools can be provided or neighborhood patterns change. Schools all or predominantly of one race in a district of mixed population will require close scrutiny to determine that school assignments are not part of state-enforced segregation.

In light of the above, it should be clear that the existence of some small number of one-race, or virtually one-race, schools within a district is not in and of itself the mark of a system that still practices segregation by law. The district judge or school authorities should make every effort to achieve the greatest possible degree of actual desegregation and will thus necessarily be concerned with the elimination of one-race schools. No *per se* rule can adequately embrace all the difficulties of reconciling the competing interests involved; but in a system with a history of segregation the need for remedial criteria of sufficient specificity to assure a school authority's compliance with its constitutional duty warrants a presumption against schools that are substantially disproportionate in their racial composition. Where the school authority's proposed plan for conversion from a dual to a unitary system contemplates the

continued existence of some schools that are all or predominately of one race, they have the burden of showing that such school assignments are genuinely nondiscriminatory. The court should scrutinize such schools, and the burden upon the school authorities will be to satisfy the court that their racial composition is not the result of present or past discriminatory action on their part. . . .

(3) **Remedial Altering of Attendance Zones.** . . . [O]ne of the principal tools employed by school planners and by courts to break up the dual school system has been a frank—and sometimes drastic—gerrymandering of school districts and attendance zones. An additional step was pairing, "clustering," or "grouping" of schools with attendance assignments made deliberately to accomplish the transfer of Negro students out of formerly segregated Negro schools and transfer of white students to formerly all-Negro schools. More often than not, these zones are neither compact or contiguous; indeed they may be on opposite ends of the city. As an interim corrective measure, this cannot be said to be beyond the broad remedial powers of a court.

Absent a constitutional violation there would be no basis for judicially ordering assignments of students on a racial basis. All things being equal, with no history of discrimination, it might well be desirable to assign pupils to schools nearest their homes. But all things are not equal in a system that has been deliberately constructed and maintained to enforce racial segregation. The remedy for such segregation may be administratively awkward, inconvenient, and even bizarre in some situations and may impose burdens on some; but all awkwardness and inconvenience cannot be avoided in the interim period when remedial adjustments are being made to eliminate the dual school systems.

No fixed or even substantially fixed guidelines can be established as to how far a court can go, but it must be recognized that there are limits. The objective is to dismantle the dual school system. "Racially neutral" assignment plans proposed by school authorities to a district court may be inadequate; such plans may fail to counteract the continuing effects of past school segregation resulting from discriminatory location of school sites or distortion of school size in order to achieve or maintain an artificial racial separation. When school authorities present a district court with a "loaded game board," affirmative action in the form of remedial altering of attendance zones is proper to achieve truly nondiscriminatory assignments. In short, an assignment plan is not acceptable simply because it appears to be neutral.

In this area, we must of necessity rely to a large extent, as this court has for more than 16 years, on the informed judgment of the district courts in the first instance and on courts of appeals.

We hold that the pairing and grouping of noncontiguous school zones is a permissible tool and such action is to be considered in light of the objectives sought. . . .

(4) Transportation of Students. The scope of permissible transportation of students as an implement of a remedial decree has never been defined by this Court and by the very nature of the problem it cannot be defined with precision. No rigid guidelines as to student transportation can be given for application to the infinite variety of problems presented in thousands of situations. Bus transportation has been an integral part of the public education system for years, and was perhaps the single most important factor in the transition from the one-room schoolhouse to the consolidated school. Eighteen million of the nation's public school children, approximately 39%, were transported to their schools by bus in 1969–70 in all parts of the country.

The importance of bus transportation as a normal and accepted tool of educational policy is readily discernible in this and the companion case, *Davis, supra.* The Charlotte school authorities did not purport to assign students on the basis of geographically drawn zones until 1965 and then they allowed almost unlimited transfer privileges. The District Court's conclusion that assignments of children to the school nearest their home serving their grade would not produce an effective dismantling of the dual system is supported by the record.

Thus the remedial techniques used in the District Court's order were within that court's power to provide equitable relief; implementation of the decree is well within the capacity of the school authority.

The decree provided that the buses used to implement the plan would operate on direct routes. Students would be picked up at schools near their homes and transported to the schools they were to attend. The trips for elementary school pupils average about seven miles and the District Court found that they would take "not over 35 minutes at the most." This system compares favorably with the transportation plan previously operated in Charlotte under which each day 23,600 students on all grade levels

were transported an average of 15 miles one way for an average trip requiring over an hour. In these circumstances, we find no basis for holding that the local school authorities may not be required to employ bus transportation as one tool of school desegregation. Desegregation plans cannot be limited to the walk-in school.

An objection to transportation of students may have validity when the time or distance of travel is so great as to either risk the health of the children or significantly impinge on the educational process. District courts must weigh the soundness of any transportation plan in light of what is said in subdivisions (1), (2), and (3) above. It hardly needs stating that the limits on time of travel will vary with many factors, but probably with none more than the age of the students. The reconciliation of competing values in a desegregation case is, of course, a difficult task with many sensitive facets but fundamentally no more so than remedial measures courts of equity have traditionally employed.

VI

The Court of Appeals, searching for a term to define the equitable remedial power of the district courts, used the term "reasonableness." In *Green, supra,* this Court used the term "feasible" and by implication, "workable," "effective," and "realistic" in the mandate to develop "a plan that promises realistically to work, and . . . to work *now.*" On the facts of this case, we are unable to conclude that the order to the District Court is not reasonable, feasible and workable. However, in seeking to define the scope of remedial power or the limits on remedial power of courts in an area as sensitive as we deal with here, words are poor instruments to convey the sense of basic fairness inherent in equity. Substance, not semantics, must govern, and we have sought to suggest the nature of limitations without frustrating the appropriate scope of equity.

At some point, these school authorities and others like them should have achieved full compliance with this Court's decision in *Brown I.* The systems would then be "unitary" in the sense required by our decisions in *Green* and *Alexander.*

It does not follow that the communities served by such systems will remain demographically stable, for in a growing, mobile society, few will do so. Neither school authorities nor district courts are constitutionally required to make year-by-year adjustments of the racial composition of student bodies once the affirmative duty to desegregate has been accomplished and racial discrimination through official action is eliminated from the system. This does not mean that federal courts are without power to deal with future problems; but in the absence of a showing that either the school authorities or some other agency of the State has deliberately attempted to fix or alter demographic patterns to affect the racial composition of the schools, further intervention by a district court should not be necessary.

For the reasons herein set forth, the judgment of the Court of Appeals is affirmed as to those parts in which it affirmed the judgment of the District Court. The order of the District Court, dated August 7, 1970, is also affirmed.

It is so ordered.

NOTES AND QUESTIONS

1. Per se Violation or Rebuttable Presumption?

Does the Court suggest that there is a causal connection between the school district's past discriminatory actions and the present pattern of segregated schools? Does this mean that in a system formerly segregated by law, plaintiffs can invoke a presumption that the current segregated patterns are "vestiges" of past state-imposed segregation? What must defendants show to rebut this presumption? Are southern school districts, unlike some northern districts, under a duty to racially balance all schools regardless of the degree to which the current segregated pattern could arise from fortuitous residential segregation rather than deliberate state policy? Is the presumed causal relationship empirically defensible? *Compare* Farley, "Residential Segregation and Its Implications for School Integration," 39 *Law & Contemp. Probs.* 164 (1975), *with* Wolf, "Northern School Desegregation and Residential Choice," 1977 *Sup.Ct.Rev.* 63.

2. Relevance of the Length of Time Between Past Segregative Acts and Present Segregation

At what point in time might the relationship between a system's past segregative acts and present segregation have become so attenuated as to be incapable of supporting a finding of *de jure* segregation warranting judicial intervention? *See Brown v. Board of Education of Topeka*, 978 F.2d 585 (10th Cir. 1992);

cert. denied sub nom. Unified School Dist. No. 501, Shawnee County, Kan. v. Smith, 509 U.S. 903, 113 S.Ct. 2994, 125 L.Ed.2d 688 (1993).

If a school board complies with a court order to desegregate, but resegregation occurs almost immediately, may a district court order further desegregation? In *Pasadena City Board of Education v. Spangler*, 427 U.S. 424, 96 S.Ct. 2697, 49 L.Ed.2d 599 (1976), the Court ruled that it may not. It held that a district court could not require pupil reassignments to maintain a racial balance some four or five years after the original decree was implemented unless the original decree had been violated or further deliberate segregative practices had occurred. Is *Spangler* consistent with *Green*? Does *Spangler* permit a form of freedom-of-choice plan wherein parents can "vote with their feet" once the formality of a unitary system is implemented?

3. Swann *and the Discretion of District Courts*

Once plaintiffs have established that a constitutional violation exists, the district court must formulate a decree that will provide a remedy for the constitutional wrong. The *Brown II* Court, in remanding the cases consolidated in *Brown I* to the federal district courts in which they originated, told the lower courts that they were to be guided by traditional principles of equity in fashioning remedial decrees. "Traditionally, equity has been characterized by a practical flexibility in shaping its remedies and by a facility for adjusting and reconciling public and private needs." *Brown v. Board of Education*, 349 U.S. 294, 300, 75 S.Ct. 753, 756, 99 L.Ed.2d 1083 (1955).

While *Swann* alone might be read as merely upholding the broad discretionary powers of an equity court, the Supreme Court's decision in a companion case, *Davis v. Board of School Commissioners*, 402 U.S. 33, 91 S.Ct. 1289, 28 L.Ed.2d 577 (1971), casts doubt on this interpretation. Chief Justice Burger, who wrote the *Davis* opinion on behalf of a unanimous Court, saw the fundamental issue in *Davis* as the failure of the court of appeals to consider the possible use of busing and split zoning in its desegregation order for Mobile. Citing *Swann*, Burger pointed out that

> "neighborhood school zoning," whether based directly on home-to-school distance or on "unified geographic zones," is not the only constitutionally permissible remedy; nor is it *per se* adequate to meet the remedial responsibilities of local boards. Having once found a violation, the district judge or school authorities

should make every effort to achieve the greatest possible degree of actual desegregation, taking into account the practicalities of the situation. A district court may and should consider the use of all available techniques including restructuring of attendance zones and both contiguous and noncontiguous attendance zones. . . . The measure of any desegregation plan is its effectiveness.

402 U.S. at 37, 91 S.Ct. at 1291.

Is Chief Justice Burger's reference to the "effectiveness" standard consistent with his assertion that busing is a remedy that the lower courts have the discretionary power to order? Consider these remarks by Professor Powe:

> The . . . language [of *Davis*] is ambiguous. What is meant by "inadequate consideration" of busing and split zoning? Who gave the "inadequate consideration"? The Court observed that a "district court may and should consider the use of all available techniques" of desegregation. Yet that was just what Judge Thomas [the district court judge] did. . . . His order . . . was explicit; since the Supreme Court had not mandated racial balance, he was not going to order busing across [an interstate highway]. . . .
>
> . . . The Supreme Court in effect underscored the following language first used in the *Green* trilogy: "The measure of any desegregation plan is its effectiveness." District judges may well have large discretion in choosing a remedy, as *Swann* suggests, but it is a one-way discretion and must be used to facilitate integration. . . . Judge Thomas erred not by failing to consider busing, but by rejecting it. . . .

Powe, "The Road to *Swann:* Mobile County Crawls to the Bus," 51 *Tex.L.Rev.* 505, 523–25 (1973). To what extent is it relevant that interstate highways were sometimes located with the intent to separate black and white neighborhoods? Can a busing order perpetuate segregative effects of decisions by non-school officials?

4. Swann: *Permissible Remedial Techniques and Their Limits*

a. Racial Quotas. In *Green v. County School Board,* the Court struck down a freedom-of-choice plan as ineffective because only 15 percent of the black students attended a previously all-white school and none of the whites attended the black school. Thus the Court began to focus on the percentage of the races in each school. With *Swann,* the Supreme

Court turned its attention to how the unitary system required by *Green* was to be achieved in the context of a large urban school district.

Swann recognizes the appropriateness of racial quotas as a "starting point" for judicial analysis. But what weight should this "starting point" be given? If the measure of a desegregation plan is its effectiveness, may quotas be used to calculate that effectiveness?

b. One-Race Schools. While not requiring the elimination of all one-race schools, the *Swann* opinion places the burden of demonstrating that they are "genuinely nondiscriminatory" on the school board. *Davis* suggests that the burden is a heavy one. Under what circumstances would one-race schools be permissible?

c. Limits on the Use of Busing. Although the Supreme Court explicitly approved intradistrict transportation ("busing") to achieve a unitary school system, it noted that there were limits to the use of that remedy. Busing, according to the Court, may be used where "feasible," but its use is limited by regard for times and distances that would "either risk the health of the children or significantly impinge on the educational process." How long a bus ride would this be? Should the maximum permissible length of time or the distance traveled vary according to the age of the child? What kind of evidence should a court consider to determine whether the educational process will be impinged upon or if a child's health will be impaired? By what standards should a court determine that convenience, health, and other costs of busing do or do not outweigh the advantages of a particular remedy? Lacking more detailed guidance from the Supreme Court, lower courts have taken varied approaches to these questions. *See* Levin, "School Desegregation Remedies and the Role of Social Science Research," 42 *Law & Contemp. Probs.* 1 (1978) (pt. 2).

V. DESEGREGATION: AN EMERGING NATIONAL STANDARD

A. Introduction

Racial segregation in the public schools has not been a phenomenon limited to the South. In 1967, the

United States Commission on Civil Rights found that in fifteen major northern cities, roughly three in four African American students attended majority black schools. In nine of those fifteen cities, more than half of the African American students attended 90 to 100 percent black schools. United States Commission on Civil Rights, *Racial Isolation in the Public Schools* (1967). In 1970, the Department of Health, Education, and Welfare reported that 57.6 percent of all black students in thirty-two northern and western states attended 80 to 100 percent minority schools. Dimond, "School Segregation in the North: There Is But One Constitution," 7 *Harv.C.R.–C.L. L.Rev.* 1 (1972). One study showed that in 1976 nearly one-third of all minority students in six northern industrial states (Illinois, Indiana, Michigan, New York, Ohio, and Pennsylvania) were attending segregated schools. Institute for Southern Studies, *Just Schools* (1979). *See also* G. Orfield, *Must We Bus?* (1978).

The causes of northern racial segregation are complex, interrelated, and often debated. In some school districts in the North, purposeful segregation of the southern variety was apparent:

> [I]n some places in the North . . . laws and policies explicitly authorized segregation by race. State statutes authorizing separate but equal public schools were on the books in Indiana until 1959, in New Mexico and Wyoming until 1954, and in New York until 1938. Other northern states authorized such segregation after the Civil War and did not repeal their authorizing statutes until early in the twentieth century.

United States Commission on Civil Rights, *Racial Isolation in the Public Schools* (1967). *See also Beckett v. School Board*, 308 F.Supp. 1274, 1311–15 (E.D. Va. 1969), *rev'd*, 434 F.2d 408 (4th Cir.), *cert. denied*, 399 U.S. 929, 90 S.Ct. 2247, 26 L.Ed.2d 796.

The division of many metropolitan areas into a large number of school districts, each serving distinct racial and socioeconomic groups, has contributed to the phenomenon. Demographic trends (with African Americans concentrated in inner cities and whites divided between inner cities and suburbs), disparities in personal income between the races, segregation in housing (sometimes encouraged by federal, state, and local policies), and the availability of nearly all-white private schools have reinforced racial segregation resulting from

school district organization and neighborhood school assignment policies. *See also* K. Tauber, *Negroes in Cities* (1965); Wolf, "Northern School Desegregation and Residential Choice," 1977 *Sup. Ct. Rev.* 63.

Early constitutional attacks on school desegregation in the North met with varied judicial responses. *Compare Bell v. School City of Gary*, 324 F.2d 209 (7th Cir. 1963), *cert. denied*, 377 U.S. 924, 84 S.Ct. 1223, 12 L.Ed.2d 216 (1964) and *Deal v. Cincinnati Board of Education*, 369 F.2d 55 (6th Cir. 1966), *cert. denied*, 389 U.S. 847, 88 S.Ct. 39, 19 L.Ed.2d 114 (1965) *with Kelly v. Guinn*, 456 F.2d 100 (9th Cir. 1972), *cert. denied*, 413 U.S. 919, 93 S.Ct. 3048, 37 L.Ed.2d 1041 and *Johnson v. San Francisco Unified School District*, 339 F.Supp. 1315 (N.D.Cal.1971), *vacated and remanded*, 500 F.2d 349 (9th Cir. 1974).

In *Bell v. School City of Gary*, the plaintiffs argued that segregation, whatever its cause, is inherently harmful and therefore unconstitutional. They did not attempt to prove specific harm. Is this argument constitutionally sound under *Brown*? Is an African American child who finds himself or herself in a segregated school likely to care whether the racial isolation is purposeful or not? *See* A. Bickel, *The Supreme Court and the Idea of Progress* 119 (1970). In the *Bell* decision, the Seventh Circuit sharply distinguished fortuitous or de facto segregation and de jure segregation that was a result of deliberate board policies. In *Kelly*, on the other hand, the Ninth Circuit ruled that northern school segregation violates the Fourteenth Amendment, but it did not do so by repudiating the *de jure/de facto* distinction; rather, it expanded the scope of de jure segregation.

B. Northern School Desegregation and the Supreme Court

Keyes v. School District No. 1

413 U.S. 189, 93 S.Ct. 2686, 37 L.Ed.2d 548, *rehearing denied*, 414 U.S. 883, 94 S.Ct. 27, 38 L.Ed.2d 131 (1973).

Justice Brennan delivered the opinion of the Court.

This school desegregation case concerns the Denver, Colorado, school system. That system has never been operated under a constitutional or statutory provision that mandated or permitted racial segregation in public education. Rather, the gravamen of this action, brought in June 1969 in the District Court for the District of Colorado by parents of Denver school children, is that respondent School Board alone, by use of various techniques such as the manipulation of student attendance zones, schoolsite selection and a neighborhood school policy, created or maintained racially or ethnically (or both racially and ethnically) segregated schools throughout the school district, entitling petitioners to a decree directing desegregation of the entire school district.

The boundaries of the school district are coterminous with the boundaries of the city and county of Denver. There were in 1969, 119 schools with 96,580 pupils in the school system. In early 1969, the respondent School Board adopted three resolutions, Resolutions 1520, 1524, and 1531, designed to desegregate the schools in the Park Hill area in the northeast portion of the city. Following an election which produced a Board majority opposed to the resolutions, the resolutions were rescinded and replaced with a voluntary student transfer program. Petitioners then filed this action, requesting an injunction against the rescission of the resolutions and an order directing that the respondent School Board desegregate and afford equal educational opportunity "for the School District as a whole." The District Court found that by the construction of a new, relatively small elementary school, Barrett, in the middle of the Negro community west of Park Hill, by the gerrymandering of student attendance zones, by the use of so-called "optional zones," and by the excessive use of mobile classroom units, among other things, the respondent School Board had engaged over almost a decade after 1960 in an unconstitutional policy of deliberate racial segregation with respect to the Park Hill schools. The court therefore ordered the Board to desegregate those schools through the implementation of the three rescinded resolutions. 303 F.Supp. 279 and 289 (1969).

Segregation in Denver schools is not limited, however, to the schools in the Park Hill area, and not satisfied with their success in obtaining relief for Park Hill, petitioners pressed their prayer that the District Court order desegregation of all segregated schools in the city of Denver, particularly the heavily segregated schools in the core city area. But that court concluded that its finding of a purposeful and systematic program of racial segregation affecting thousands of students in the Park Hill area did not, in itself, impose on the School Board an affirmative duty to eliminate segregation throughout the school district. Instead, the court fractionated the district and held that petitioners must make a fresh showing of *de jure* segregation in each area of the city for which they seek relief. Moreover, the District Court held that its finding of intentional segregation in Park Hill was not in any sense material to the question of segregative intent in other areas of the city. Under this restrictive approach, the District Court concluded that petitioners' evidence of intentionally discriminatory School Board action in areas of the district other than Park Hill was insufficient to "dictate the conclusion that this is *de jure* segregation which calls for an all-out effort to desegregate. It is more like *de facto* segregation, with respect to which the rule is that the court cannot order desegregation in order to provide a better balance." 313 F.Supp. 61, 73 (1970).

Nevertheless, the District Court went on to hold that the proofs established that the segregated core city schools were educationally inferior to the predominantly "white" or "Anglo" schools in other parts of the district—that is, "separate facilities . . . unequal in the quality of education provided." *Id.*, at 83. Thus, the court held that, under the doctrine of *Plessy v. Ferguson*, 163 U.S. 537 (1896), respondent School Board constitutionally "must at a minimum . . . offer an equal educational opportunity," . . . and, therefore, although all-out desegregation "could not be decreed, . . . the only feasible and constitutionally acceptable program—the only program which furnishes anything approaching substantial equality—is a system of desegregation and integration which provides compensatory education in an integrated environment." 313 F.Supp. 90, 96 (1970). The District Court then formulated a varied remedial plan to that end which was incorporated in the Final Decree.

Respondent School Board appealed, and petitioners cross-appealed, to the Court of Appeals for the Tenth Circuit. That court sustained the District Court's finding that the Board had engaged in an unconstitutional policy of deliberate racial segregation with respect to the Park Hill schools and affirmed the Final Decree in that respect. As to the core city schools, however, the Court of Appeals reversed the legal determination of the District Court that those schools were maintained in violation of the Fourteenth Amendment because of the unequal educational opportunity afforded, and therefore set aside so much of the Final Decree as required desegregation and educational improvement programs for those schools. 445 F.2d at 990. . . .

II

In our view, the only other question that requires our decision at this time is . . . whether the District Court and the Court of Appeals applied an incorrect legal standard in addressing petitioners' contention that respondent School Board engaged in an unconstitutional policy of deliberate segregation in the core city schools. Our conclusion is that those courts did not apply the correct standard in addressing that contention.

Petitioners apparently concede for the purposes of this case that in the case of a school system like Denver's, where no statutory dual system has ever existed, plaintiffs must prove not only that segregated schooling exists but also that it was brought about or maintained by intentional state action. Petitioners proved that for almost a decade after 1960 respondent School Board had engaged in an unconstitutional policy of deliberate racial segregation in the Park Hill schools. Indeed, the District Court found that "[b]etween 1960 and 1969 the Board's policies with respect to these northeast Denver schools show an undeviating purpose to isolate Negro students" in segregated schools "while preserving the Anglo character of [other] schools." 303 F.Supp F. Supp. at 294. This finding did not relate to an insubstantial or trivial fragment of the school system. On the contrary, respondent School Board was found guilty of following a deliberate segregation policy at schools attended, in 1969, by 37.69 percent of Denver's total Negro school population, including one-fourth of the Negro elementary pupils, over two-thirds of the Negro junior high pupils, and over two-fifths of the Negro high school pupils. In addition, there was un-

controverted evidence that teachers and staff had for years been assigned on a minority teacher to minority school basis throughout the school system. Respondent argues, however, that a finding of state-imposed segregation as to a substantial portion of the school system can be viewed in isolation from the rest of the district, and that even if state-imposed segregation does exist in a substantial part of the Denver school system, it does not follow that the District Court could predicate on that fact a finding that the entire school system is a dual system. We do not agree. We have never suggested that plaintiffs in school desegregation cases must bear the burden of proving the elements of de jure segregation as to each and every school or each and every student within the school system. Rather, we have held that where plaintiffs prove that a current condition of segregated schooling exists within a school district where a dual system was compelled or authorized by statute at the time of our decision in *Brown v. Board of Education*, 347 U.S. 483 (1954) *(Brown I)*, the State automatically assumes an affirmative duty "to effectuate a transition to a racially nondiscriminatory school system," *Brown v. Board of Education*, 349 U.S. 294, 301 (1955) *(Brown II)*, see also *Green v. County School Board*, 391 U.S. 430, 437–38 (1968), that is, to eliminate from the public schools within their school system "all vestiges of state-imposed segregation." *Swann v. Charlotte-Mecklenburg Board of Education*, 402 U.S. 1, 15 (1971).[11]

This is not a case, however, where a statutory dual system has ever existed. Nevertheless, where plaintiffs prove that the school authorities have carried out a systematic program of segregation affecting a substantial portion of the students, schools, teachers and facilities within the school system, it is only common sense to conclude that there exists a predicate for a finding of the existence of a dual school system. Several considerations support this conclusion. First, it is obvious that a practice of concentrating Negroes in certain schools by structuring attendance zones or

[11]Our Brother Rehnquist argues in dissent that *Brown v. Board of Education* did not impose an "affirmative duty to integrate" the schools of a dual school system but was only a "prohibition against discrimination" "in the sense that the assignment to a child of a particular school is not made to depend on his race. . . ."

That is the interpretation of *Brown* expressed 18 years ago by a three-judge court in *Briggs v. Elliott*, 132 F.Supp. 776, 777 (1955): "The Constitution, in other words, does not require integration. It merely forbids discrimination." But *Green v. County School Board*, 391 U.S. 430, 438 (1968), rejected that interpretation insofar as Green expressly held that "School boards . . . operating state-compelled dual systems were nevertheless clearly charged [by Brown II] with the affirmative duty to take whatever steps might be necessary to convert to a unitary system in which racial discrimination would be eliminated root and branch." *Green* remains the governing principle, *Alexander v. Holmes County Board of Education*, 396 U.S. 19 (1969); *Swann v. Charlotte-Mecklenburg Board of Education*, 402 U.S. I, 15 (1971). See also *Kelley v. Metropolitan County Board of Education*, 317 F.Supp. 980, 984 (1970).

designating "feeder" schools on the basis of race has the reciprocal effect of keeping other nearby schools predominantly white.[12] Similarly, the practice of building a school—such as the Barrett Elementary School in this case—to a certain size and in a certain location, "with conscious knowledge that it would be a segregated school," 303 F.Supp. at 285, has a substantial reciprocal effect on the racial composition of other nearby schools. So also, the use of mobile classrooms, the drafting of student transfer policies, the transportation of students, and the assignment of faculty and staff, on racially identifiable bases, have the clear effect of earmarking schools according to their racial composition, and this, in turn, together with the elements of student assignment, and school construction, may have a profound reciprocal effect on the racial composition of residential neighborhoods within a metropolitan area, thereby causing further racial concentration within the schools. We recognized this in *Swann*. . . .

In short, common sense dictates the conclusion that racially inspired school board actions have an impact beyond the particular schools that are the subjects of those actions. This is not to say, of course, that there can never be a case in which the geographical structure of or the natural boundaries within a school district may have the effect of dividing the district into separate, identifiable and unrelated units. Such a determination is essentially a question of fact to be resolved by the trial court in the first instance, but such cases must be rare. In the absence of such a determination, proof of state-imposed segregation in a substantial portion of the district will suffice to support a finding by the trial court of the existence of a dual system. . . .

III

Although petitioners had already proved the existence of intentional school segregation in the Park Hill schools, this crucial finding was totally ignored when attention turned to the core city schools. Plainly, a finding of intentional segregation as to a portion of a school system is not devoid of probative value in assessing the school authorities' intent with respect to other parts of the same school system. On

the contrary, where, as here, the case involves one school board, a finding of intentional segregation on its part in one portion of a school system is highly relevant to the issue of the board's intent with respect to other segregated schools in the system. This is merely an application of the well-settled evidentiary principle that "the prior doing of other similar acts, whether clearly a part of a scheme or not, is useful as reducing the possibility that the act in question was done with innocent intent." 2 J. Wigmore, *Evidence* 200 (3d ed. 1940). . . .

Applying these principles in the special context of school desegregation cases, we hold that a finding of intentionally segregative school board actions in a meaningful portion of a school system, as in this case, creates a presumption that other segregated schooling within the system is not adventitious. It establishes, in other words, a prima facie case of unlawful segregative design on the part of school authorities, and shifts to those authorities the burden of proving that other segregated schools within the system are not also the result of intentionally segregative actions. . . . We emphasize that the differentiating factor between *de jure* segregation and so-called *de facto* segregation to which we referred in *Swann* is *purpose* or *intent* to segregate. . . . [W]here an intentionally segregative policy is practiced in a meaningful or significant segment of a school system, as in this case, the school authorities cannot be heard to argue that plaintiffs have proved only "isolated and individual" unlawfully segregative actions. In that circumstance, it is both fair and reasonable to require that the school authorities bear the burden of showing that their actions as to other segregated schools within the system were not also motivated by segregative intent.

* * *

In discharging that burden, it is not enough, of course, that the school authorities rely upon some allegedly logical, racially neutral explanation for their actions. Their burden is to adduce proof sufficient to support a finding that segregative intent was not among the factors that motivated their actions. The courts below attributed much significance to the fact that many of the Board's actions in the core city area antedated our decision in *Brown*. We reject

---

[12] . . .Judge Wisdom has recently stated: "Infection at one school infects all schools. To take the most simple example, in a two-school system, all blacks at one school means all or almost all whites at the other." *United States v. Texas Education Agency*, 467 F.2d 848, 888 (5th Cir. 1972).

any suggestion that remoteness in time has any relevance to the issue of intent. If the actions of school authorities were to any degree motivated by segregative intent and the segregation resulting from those actions continues to exist, the fact of remoteness in time certainly does not make those actions any less "intentional."

This is not to say, however, that the prima facie case may not be met by evidence supporting a finding that a lesser degree of segregated schooling in the core city area would not have resulted even if the Board had not acted as it did. In *Swann*, we suggested that at some point in time the relationship between past segregative acts and present segregation may become so attenuated as to be incapable of supporting a finding of *de jure* segregation warranting judicial intervention. 402 U.S., at 31–32. . . . We made it clear, however, that a connection between past segregative acts and present segregation may be present even when not apparent and that close examination is required before concluding that the connection does not exist. Intentional school segregation in the past may have been a factor in creating a natural environment for the growth of further segregation. Thus, if respondent School Board cannot disprove segregative intent, it can rebut the prima facie case only by showing that its past segregative acts did not create or contribute to the current segregated condition of the core city schools.

The respondent School board invoked at trial its "neighborhood school policy" as explaining racial and ethnic concentrations within the core city schools, arguing that since the core city area population had long been Negro and Hispano, the concentrations were necessarily the result of residential patterns and not of purposefully segregative policies. We have no occasion to consider in this case whether a "neighborhood school policy" of itself will justify racial or ethnic concentrations in the absence of a finding that school authorities have committed acts constituting *de jure* segregation. It is enough that we hold that the mere assertion of such a policy is not dispositive where, as in this case, the school authorities have been found to have practiced *de jure* segregation in a meaningful portion of the school system by techniques that indicate that the "neighborhood school" concept has not been maintained free of manipulation. . . .

The judgment of the Court of Appeals is modified to vacate instead of reverse the parts of the Final Decree that concern the core city schools, and the case is remanded to the District Court for further proceedings consistent with this opinion.

It is so ordered.

Chief Justice Burger concurs in the result.

Justice White took no part in the decision of this case.

[The concurring opinion of Justice Douglas is omitted.]

Justice Powell, concurring in part and dissenting in part.

I concur in the remand of this case for further proceedings in the District Court, but on grounds that differ from those relied upon by the Court.

This is the first school desegregation case to reach this Court which involves a major city outside the South. It comes from Denver, Colorado, a city and a State which have not operated public schools under constitutional or statutory provisions which mandated or permitted racial segregation. . . .

The situation in Denver is generally comparable to that in other large cities across the country in which there is a substantial minority population and where desegregation has not been ordered by the federal courts. There is segregation in the schools of many of these cities fully as pervasive as that in southern cities prior to the desegregation decrees of the past decade and a half. The focus of the school desegregation problem has now shifted from the South to the country as a whole. Unwilling and footdragging as the process was in most places, substantial progress toward achieving integration has been made in Southern States. No comparable progress has been made in many nonsouthern cities with large minority populations primarily because of the *de facto/de jure* distinction nurtured by the courts and accepted complacently by many of the same voices which denounced the evils of segregated schools in the South. But if our national concern is for those who attend such schools, rather than for perpetuating a legalism rooted in history rather than present reality, we must recognize that the evil of operating separate schools is no less in Denver than in Atlanta.

I

In my view we should abandon a distinction which long since has outlived its time, and formulate constitutional principles of national rather than merely regional application. When *Brown v. Board of Education*, 347 U.S. 483 (1954) (*Brown I*), was decided, the distinction between *de jure* and *de facto* segregation was consistent with the limited constitutional rationale of that case. The situation confronting the Court, largely confined to the Southern States, was officially imposed racial segregation in the schools extending back for many years and usually embodied in constitutional and statutory provisions.

The great contribution of *Brown I* was its holding in unmistakable terms that the Fourteenth Amendment forbids state-compelled or authorized segregation of public schools. 347 U.S. at 488, 493–95. Although some of the language was more expansive, the holding in *Brown I* was essentially negative: It was impermissible under the Constitution for the States, or their instrumentalities, to force children to attend segregated schools. . . .

But the doctrine of *Brown I*, as amplified by *Brown II*, 349 U.S. 294 (1955), did not retain its original meaning. In a series of decisions extending from 1954 to 1971 the concept of state neutrality was transformed into the present constitutional doctrine requiring affirmative state action to desegregate school systems. The keystone case was *Green v. County School Board*, 391 U.S. 430, 437–438 (1968), where school boards were declared to have "the affirmative duty to take whatever steps might be necessary to convert to a unitary system in which racial discrimination would be eliminated root and branch." . . .

Whereas *Brown I* rightly decreed the elimination of state-imposed segregation in that particular section of the country where it did exist, *Swann* imposed obligations on southern school districts to eliminate conditions which are not regionally unique but are similar both in origin and effect to conditions in the rest of the country. As the remedial obligations of *Swann* extend far beyond the elimination of the outgrowths of the state-imposed segregation outlawed in *Brown*, the rationale of *Swann* points inevitably towards a uniform, constitutional approach to our national problem of school segregation.

II

The Court's decision today, while adhering to the *de jure/de facto* distinction, will require the application of the *Green/Swann* doctrine of "affirmative duty" to the Denver School Board despite the absence of any history of state-mandated school segregation. The only evidence of a constitutional violation was found in various decisions of the School Board. I concur in

the Court's position that the public school authorities are the responsible agency of the state, and that if the affirmative duty doctrine is sound constitutional law for Charlotte, it is equally so for Denver. I would not, however, perpetuate the *de jure/de facto* distinction nor would I leave to petitioners the initial tortuous effort of identifying "segregative acts" and deducing "segregative intent." I would hold, quite simply, that where segregated public schools exist within a school district to a substantial degree, there is a *prima facie* case that the duly constituted public authorities (I will usually refer to them collectively as the "school board") are sufficiently responsible to impose upon them a nationally applicable burden to demonstrate they nevertheless are operating a genuinely integrated school system.

A

The principal reason for abandonment of the *de jure/de facto* distinction is that, in view of the evolution of the holding in *Brown I* into the affirmative duty doctrine, the distinction no longer can be justified on a principled basis. . . .

* * *

Having school boards operate an integrated school system provides the best assurance of meeting the constitutional requirement that racial discrimination, subtle or otherwise, will find no place in the decisions of public school officials. Courts judging past school board actions with a view to their general integrative effect will be best able to assure an absence of such discrimination while avoiding the murky, subjective judgments inherent in the Court's search for "segregative intent." Any test resting on so nebulous and elusive an element as a school board's segregative "intent" provides inadequate assurance that minority children will not be short-changed in the decisions of those entrusted with the nondiscriminatory operation of our public schools.

Public schools are creatures of the State, and whether the segregation is state-created or state-assisted or merely state-perpetuated should be irrelevant to constitutional principle. . . .

The Court today does move for the first time toward breaking down past sectional disparities, but it clings tenuously to its distinction. It searches for *de jure* action in what the Denver School Board has done or failed to do, and even here the Court does not rely upon the results or effects of the Board's conduct but feels compelled to find segregative intent. . . . I can discern no basis in law or logic for holding that the motivation of school board action is irrelevant in Virginia and controlling in Colorado. . . .

B

There is thus no reason as a matter of constitutional principle to adhere to the *de jure/de facto* distinction in school desegregation cases. In addition, there are reasons of policy and prudent judicial administration which point strongly toward the adoption of a uniform national rule. . . .

Mr. Justice Rehnquist, dissenting.

. . . . Underlying the Court's entire opinion is its apparent thesis that a district judge is at least permitted to find that if a single attendance zone between two individual schools in the large metropolitan district is found by him to have been "gerrymandered," the school district is guilty of operating a "dual" school system, and is apparently a candidate for what is in practice a federal receivership. Not only the language of the Court in the opinion, but its reliance on the case of *Green v. County School Board*, 391 U.S. 430, 437–38 (1968), indicates that such would be the case. It would therefore presumably be open to the District Court to require, *inter alia*, that pupils be transported great distances throughout the district to and from schools whose attendance zones have not been gerrymandered. Yet unless the Equal Protection Clause of the Fourteenth Amendment now be held to embody a principle of "taint," found in some primitive legal systems but discarded centuries ago in ours, such a result can only be described as the product of judicial fiat.

* * *

NOTES AND QUESTIONS

1. The De Jure/De Facto Distinction

The Court retains the distinction between *de facto* segregation, which is unintentional, and *de jure* segregation, which is purposeful or intentional.

a. What Is Intentional Segregation? Why did the Court quote from the district court's opinion, saying that often a school location and size decision is made "with conscious knowledge that the result would be

a segregated school . . ."? Is "conscious knowledge" the same as "discriminatory intent"? *See generally* Brest, "The Supreme Court, 1975 Term-Foreword: In Defense of the Antidiscrimination Principle," 90 *Harv. L. Rev.* 1 (1976). What of the Court's reference to student transfer, student transportation, and faculty assignment policies that have the "effect" of creating a dual school system? Is the meaning of the reference changed by the notation that these decisions were made on "racially identifiable bases"? What evidence does the Court cite for this proposition?

b. Proving Intentional Segregation. How should a court determine whether school segregation was racially motivated? Suppose some members of the board of education admitted that they voted to close a school to avoid integration, but others joined in the vote for unrelated reasons. Is it enough that any single member of a decision-making body was improperly motivated? What if a board member was influenced only in part by racial considerations? What impact will the *Keyes* decision have on the willingness of board members to reveal their motivations? Will courts imply motive from the segregatory decisions themselves? If so, what is left of the *de facto/de jure* distinction?

Is the Court, in reality, addressing itself to "institutional" intent or prejudice? How may it be proven? *See* Note, "Reading the Mind of the School Board: Segregative Intent and the De Facto/De Jure Distinction," 86 *Yale L.J.* 317 (1976). Is the relevant question whether the board would have acted as it did "but for" racial prejudice? *See* Simon, "Racially Prejudiced Governmental Actions: A Motivation Theory of the Constitutional Ban Against Racial Discrimination," 15 *San Diego L. Rev.* 1041, 1059 (1978). Suppose a decision (for example, maintenance of neighborhood attendance zones) is influenced by racial prejudice, but there is substantial reason to believe that the same decision would have been made even in the absence of a concern for race?

c. Proving Intentional Segregation in Keyes. What proof did the plaintiffs offer in *Keyes* to demonstrate unlawful intent to segregate? Are there any references in the Court's opinion to specific racial pronouncements by board members? Does the decision to build a small elementary school in the middle of the black community necessarily indicate a discriminatory intent? If parents in some areas were given a choice of more than one school, and black parents chose predominantly black schools and white parents chose predominantly white schools, is this proof that school authorities had adopted the policy with the purpose of fostering segregation? Does the "excessive" use of mobile classrooms reveal segregatory intent?

d. Relevance of Intention to Discriminate. Why is intentional segregation unconstitutional while other forms of segregation are not? If segregation is stigmatizing, harmful, or otherwise undesirable as a matter of public policy, how do the good or bad motivations of governmental decision makers alter the equation? Is Justice Powell correct when he asserts: "Public schools are creatures of the state, and whether the segregation is state-created or state-assisted or merely state-perpetuated should be irrelevant to constitutional principle"?

e. Burden of Proof. In the Court's view, which party must prove intentional segregation? Does the burden shift once some intentional discrimination has been proven?

f. De Jure Segregation: North and South. Justice Powell stated in *Keyes* that he could discern "no basis in law or logic for holding that the motivation of school board action is irrelevant in Virginia and controlling in Colorado." Is this a fair statement of the majority's position? Is not the enactment of compulsory segregation laws in the South the clearest example of an intention to discriminate? Is intention to discriminate simply more difficult to prove in the North?

2. What Is a Segregated School?

Is a school segregated when it has more than 70 to 75 percent blacks? Is it segregated when the ratio of blacks to whites is greater than the ratio in the entire student population of the school district? *See Capacchione v. Charlotte-Mecklenburg Schools*, 57 F.Supp. 2d 228, 244–45 (W.D. N.C. 1999). The regulations implementing the federal Magnet Schools Assistance Program, 20 U.S.C. §§ 7201 *et seq.* (West 2000), consider a school "minority-isolated" if minority group students constitute more than 50 percent of the school's enrollment. 34 C.F.R. Part 280.4(b). If desegregation is premised on the denial of equal educational opportunity to blacks, should the courts determine at what point the school becomes sufficiently segregated to injure black students? Is there an underlying assumption "that

whites are better [educational] resources than blacks"? Dimond, "School Segregation in the North: There Is But One Constitution," 7 *Harv. C.R.–C.L. Rev.* 1, 16 (1972).

3. Relationship Between Racially Motivated Acts and Obligation to Desegregate

a. Past Discrimination and Present Segregation. The Court notes that "if the actions of school authorities were to any degree motivated by segregative intent and the segregation resulting from those actions continues to exist, the fact of remoteness does not make those actions any less 'intentional.' " Does this statement mean that a district which was previously *de jure* segregated must first have racially balanced all of its schools before it can argue that resegregation is the result of changing residential patterns? If so, then in the absence of the implementation of a complete racial balance remedy, is not the presumption that the segregated pattern is still a "vestige" of previous state-imposed segregation an irrebuttable presumption?

What does this suggest with regard to the question of a "continuing" violation and attributing "intent" to a school board in 1999 for actions taken by a school board in 1954, which had an entirely different membership? Is the "board" a single, continuous entity over time? *See generally* Note, "Reading the Mind of the School Board: Segregative Intent and the De Facto/De Jure Distinction," 86 *Yale L. J.* 317 (1976). In *Columbus Board of Education v. Penick*, 443 U.S. 449, 99 S.Ct. 2941, 61 L.Ed.2d 666 (1979) *(Columbus II)*, Justice White, writing for the majority, noted that since the decision in *Brown II*, the Columbus, Ohio, school board was under "a continuous constitutional obligation to disestablish its dual school system." Justice White explained that

> . . . each instance of a failure or refusal to fulfill this affirmative duty continues the violation of the Fourteenth Amendment. . . .
>
> * * *
>
> The Board's continuing "affirmative duty to disestablish the dual school system" is therefore beyond question, . . . and it has pointed to nothing in the record persuading us that at the time of trial the dual school system and its effects had been disestablished. . . . [A]t the time of trial most blacks were still going to black schools and most whites to white schools. Whatever the Board's current purpose with respect to racially sepa-

rate education might be, it knowingly continued its failure to eliminate the consequences of its past intentionally segregative policies. The board "never actively set out to dismantle this dual system." . . .

Id. at 459–61, 99 S.Ct. at 2947–48. Justice Rehnquist (joined by Justice Powell) dissented.

. . . As a matter of history, case law, or logic, there is nothing to support the novel proposition that the primary inquiry in school desegregation cases involving systems without a history of statutorily mandated racial assignment is what happened in those systems before 1954. As a matter of history, 1954 makes no more sense as a benchmark—indeed it makes less sense—than 1968, 1971 or 1973. Perhaps the latter year has the most to commend it, if one insists on a benchmark, because in *Keyes* this Court first confronted the problem of school segregation in the context of systems without a history of statutorily mandated segregation of the races.

. . . It is sophistry to suggest that a school board in *Columbus* in 1954 could have read *Brown* and gleaned from it a constitutional duty "to diffuse black students throughout the system" or take whatever other action the Court today thinks it should have taken. . . .

443 U.S. at 501–02, 99 S.Ct. at 2958–59 (Rehnquist, J. and Powell, J., dissenting).

The nature of the "continuing violation" was further elaborated in the companion case of *Dayton Board of Education v. Brinkman*, 443 U.S. 526, 535, 99 S.Ct. 2971, 2977, 61 L.Ed.2d 720 (1979) (*Dayton II*).

Part of the affirmative duty imposed by our cases . . . is the obligation not to take any action that would impede the process of disestablishing the dual system and its effects. . . . The Dayton Board, however, had engaged in many post-*Brown* actions that had the effect of increasing or perpetuating segregation. . . . [T]he measure of the post-*Brown* conduct of a school board under an unsatisfied duty to liquidate a dual system is the effectiveness, not the purpose, of the actions in decreasing or increasing the segregation caused by the dual system. . . . As was clearly established in *Keyes* and *Swann*, the Board had to do more than abandon its prior discriminatory purpose. . . . The Board has had an affirmative responsibility to see that pupil assignment policies and school construction and abandonment practices "are not used and do not serve to perpetuate or re-establish the dual school system," *Columbus* [443 U.S.], at 460, and the Board has a 'heavy burden' of showing that actions that increased or continued the effects of the dual system serve important and legitimate ends . . . .

Dayton II, 443 U.S. at 537–38, 99 S.Ct. at 2978–80.

b. De Jure *Segregation in Part of the System. The issue:* The Court frames the issue narrowly: When substantial segregation exists in part of a school system, is the entire system a dual school system that must be wholly desegregated?

Resolving the issue: The Court treats the issue of substantial segregation in a part of the system as relevant in two ways to a systemwide determination of *de jure* segregation. First, the Court notes that *de jure* segregation in part of the system may determine the racial composition of other neighborhoods within a metropolitan area, thereby causing the segregation of schools outside the tainted area of the city. This is particularly true since the decision to maintain segregated schools in one area necessarily limits the possibilities for integration in other areas. The Court admits that sometimes this will not be the case but intimates that such occasions are rare. Second, the Court holds that intentional segregation in a portion of a school system creates a presumption that segregation elsewhere in the system is racially motivated, shifting the burden of proof to the defendants.

Result: Can the Court's treatment of less than systemwide discrimination be accurately described as a sort of "Catch 22"? If substantial racially motivated segregation is found, lower courts will usually find that the entire system has been tainted. If the school district does convince the court that the *de jure* practices are isolated episodes, there is still a presumption that any other segregation in the system is racially motivated. Consider also the burden of proof borne by the district. It must prove that "segregative intent was not among the factors that motivated their actions." Does the Court's elaboration of evidentiary rules largely obliterate the *de facto/de jure* distinction?

4. *"The Essential Element of De Jure Segregation" Further Defined:* Washington v. Davis and Arlington Heights

In *Washington v. Davis*, 426 U.S. 229, 96 S.Ct. 2040, 48 L.Ed.2d 597 (1976), two unsuccessful black applicants for the Washington, D.C., police force challenged the department's use of a standardized test measuring verbal ability, vocabulary, and reading comprehension on the ground that it violated the Equal Protection Clause of the Fourteenth Amendment. They demonstrated that the test, which had not been validated to establish its reliability for measuring job performance, disqualified a disproportionate number of minority applicants.

The Court of Appeals held that the evidence of discriminatory impact was sufficient to shift the burden of proving the test's efficacy and racial neutrality to defendants. The Supreme Court reversed. Justice White, writing for the majority, noted that

> The central purpose of the Equal Protection Clause of the Fourteenth Amendment is the prevention of official conduct discriminating on the basis of race. . . . But our cases have not embraced the proposition that a law or other official act, without regard to whether it reflects a racially discriminatory purpose, is unconstitutional *solely* because it has a racially disproportionate impact.

> * * *

> The school desegregation cases have . . . adhered to the basic equal protection principle that the invidious quality of a law claimed to be racially discriminatory must ultimately be traced to a racially discriminatory purpose. That there are both predominantly black and predominantly white schools in a community is not alone violative of the Equal Protection Clause. The essential element of de jure segregation is a "current condition of segregation resulting from intentional state action." [citing *Keyes*] . . .

> * * *

> This is not to say that the necessary discriminatory racial purpose must be express or appear on the face of the statute, or that a law's disproportionate impact is irrelevant in cases involving Constitution-based claims of racial discrimination. A statute, otherwise neutral on its face, must not be applied so as invidiously to discriminate on the basis of race. . . .

> Necessarily, an invidious discriminatory purpose may often be inferred from the totality of the relevant facts, including the fact, if it is true, that the law bears more heavily on one race than another. It is also not infrequently true that the discriminatory impact—in the jury cases for example, the total or seriously disproportionate exclusion of Negroes from jury venires—may for all practical purposes demonstrate unconstitutionality because in various circumstances the discrimination is very difficult to explain on nonracial grounds. Nevertheless, we have not held that a law, neutral on its face and serving ends otherwise within the power of government to pursue, is invalid under the Equal Protection Clause simply because it may affect a greater proportion of one race than of another. Disproportionate impact is not irrelevant, but it is not the sole touchstone of an invidious racial discrimination forbidden by the Constitution. Standing alone, it does not trigger the rule, that racial classifications are to be subjected to the strictest scrutiny and are justifiable only by the weightiest of considerations. . . .

426 U.S. at 239–242.

Village of Arlington Heights v. Metropolitan Housing Development Corporation, 429 U.S. 252, 97 S.Ct. 555, 50 L.Ed.2d 450 (1977), involved a challenge by a nonprofit developer to the refusal of housing authorities to rezone land for the building of racially integrated low and moderate income housing, arguing that the refusal was racially discriminatory. The Supreme Court, citing *Washington v. Davis* and *Keyes*, said that proof of racially discriminatory purpose is necessary. The Court noted that determining whether "invidious discriminatory purpose" was a motivating factor would include an examination of both circumstantial and direct evidence of intent to discriminate. Although a racially disproportionate impact of the official action "may provide an important starting point . . ., impact alone is not the determinative." The Court suggested that the historical background of the official action, the specific sequence of events leading up to the official action, departures from the normal procedural sequence, and the legislative or administrative history "might afford evidence that improper purposes are playing a role." Thus, as applied to school desegregation cases, *Washington v. Davis* and *Arlington Heights* suggest that mere racial imbalance would not be enough to trigger a presumption of discriminatory intent; there must be some independent evidence of that intent.

5. *School Board Liability for Intentionally Discriminatory Actions by Other Governmental Agencies*

Should school boards be liable for correcting segregation that is the result of intentionally discriminatory action of other governmental agencies? *Swann* expressly reserved that issue for future decision. 402 U.S. at 23. *See also Delaware State Board of Education v. Evans*, 446 U.S. 923, 100 S.Ct. 1862, 64 L.Ed.2d 278 (1980) (Justice Rehnquist, dissenting). Several lower court cases, however, have focused on the actions of other governmental agencies that might have contributed to residential segregation in order to find that the pattern of segregated schooling resulting from neighborhood assignment plans constitutes *de jure* segregation. *See United States v. Board of School Commissioners*, 573 F.2d 400 (7th Cir. 1978), *cert. denied*, 439 U.S. 824, 99 S.Ct. 93, 58 L.Ed.2d 116; *Evans v. Buchanan*, 393 F.Supp. 428 (D. Del. 1975), *cert. denied sub nom. Delaware State Board of Education v. Evans*, 446 U.S. 923, 100 S.Ct. 1862, 64 L.Ed.2d 278; *Bradley v. Milliken*, 338

F.Supp. 582, 587 (E.D. Mich. 1971), *rev'd on other grounds*, 418 U.S. 717, 94 S.Ct. 3112, 41 L.Ed.2d 1069. Cases repudiating school board liability for nonboard actions include *Higgins v. Board of Education*, 508 F.2d 779, 788–89 (6th Cir. 1974) and *Alvarado v. El Paso Independent School District*, 426 F.Supp. 575, 595 (W.D. Tex. 1976), *aff'd*, 593 F.2d 577 (5th Cir. 1979).

Why should school boards be responsible for the constitutional violations of other governmental agencies? *See* Feagin, "School Desegregation: A Political-Economic Perspective," in *School Desegregation* 25 (W. Stephan and J. Feagin, eds., 1980). Should these other agencies at least be parties to the school desegregation suit? *See Hart v. Community School Board*, 383 F.Supp. 699 (E.D. N.Y. 1974), *aff'd*, 512 F.2d 37 (2d Cir. 1975), in which the school board impleaded city, state, and federal housing and urban development agencies on the theory that they had fostered residential segregation which resulted in school segregation. *See also Bell v. Board of Education, Akron Public Schools*, 683 F.2d 963 (6th Cir. 1982). In that case, the plaintiffs argued that the school board was liable for intentionally segregative actions of other governmental agencies that caused residential segregation, which, together with geographic attendance zoning as the primary method of school assignment, produced racially segregated schools. Their contention was that the obligation to remedy the constitutional violation fell on the school authorities as they were the only parties that could remedy the school segregation. The court declined to hold the school board "otherwise innocent of segregative intent" liable for "discriminatory conduct of the FHA in making housing loans and local housing authorities in the construction and rental of public housing." 683 F.2d at 968. *See* Levin & Moise, "School Desegregation Litigation in the Seventies and the Use of Social Science Evidence: An Annotated Guide," 39 *Law & Contemp. Prob.* 50 (1975).

In *United States v. Yonkers Board of Education*, the city, its public housing agency, and the school board were sued and the court found all defendants liable. Although the court suggested the evidence justified holding both the city and the school board liable independently for intentional segregative acts, it concluded that the most important factors indicated a joint effort to create and maintain a racially segregated school system. 624 F.Supp. 1276 (S.D.N.Y. 1985). Thus both the school board and the city were ordered to remedy the segregation in

the schools. *United States v. Yonkers Board of Education*, 635 F.Supp. 1538 (S.D.N.Y. 1986), and 635 F.Supp.1577 (S.D.N.Y. 1986), *aff'd*, 837 F.2d 1181 (2d Cir. 1987), *cert. denied*, 486 U.S. 1055, 108 S.Ct. 2821, 100 L.Ed. 2d 922 (1988). *See* Note, "Residential Segregation: Where Do We Draw the Lines? A View of *United States v. Yonkers Board of Education* and Democratic Theory," 23 *Colum. J.L. & Soc. Probs.* 467 (1990).

C. School District Boundaries: Does the Bus Stop Here?

Milliken v. Bradley
418 U.S. 717, 94 S.Ct. 3112, 41 L.Ed.2d 1069 (1974).

Mr. Chief Justice Burger delivered the opinion of the Court.

We granted certiorari in these consolidated cases to determine whether a federal court may impose a multidistrict, areawide remedy to a single-district *de jure* segregation problem absent any finding that the other included school districts have failed to operate unitary school systems within their districts, absent any claim or finding that the boundary lines of any affected school district were established with the purpose of fostering racial segregation in public schools, absent any finding that the included districts committed acts which effected segregation within the other districts, and absent a meaningful opportunity for the included neighboring school districts to present evidence or be heard on the propriety of a multidistrict remedy or on the question of constitutional violations by those neighboring districts.

I

The action was commenced in August 1970 by the respondents . . . on behalf of . . . "all school children in the City of Detroit, Michigan, and all Detroit resident parents who have children of school age." The named defendants in the District Court included the Governor of Michigan, the Attorney General, the State Board of Education, the State Superintendent of Public Instruction, the Board of Education of the city of Detroit, its members, and the city's former superintendent of schools. . . .

The trial of the issue of segregation in the Detroit school system began on April 6, 1971, and continued through July 22, 1971, consuming some 41 trial days. On September 27, 1971, the District Court issued its findings and conclusions on the issue of segregation, finding that "Governmental actions and inaction at all levels, federal, state and local, have combined, with those of private organizations, such as loaning institutions and real estate associations and brokerage firms, to establish and to maintain the pattern of residential segregation throughout the Detroit metropolitan area." 338 F.Supp. 582, 587 (E.D. Mich.1971). While still addressing a Detroit-only violation, the District Court reasoned:

> While it would be unfair to charge the present defendants with what other governmental officers or agencies have done, it can be said that the actions or the failure to act by the responsible school authorities, both city and state, were linked to that of these other governmental units. When we speak of governmental action we should not view the different agencies as a collection of unrelated units. Perhaps the most that can be said is that all of them, including the school authorities, are, in part, responsible for the segregated condition which exists. And we note that just as there is an interaction between residential patterns and the racial composition of the schools, so there is a corresponding effect on the residential pattern by the racial composition of the schools.

Ibid.

* * *

[The Court then discussed the findings of the District Court with regard to intentional segregative actions taken by the Detroit Board of Education. The District Court's ultimate finding that the Detroit school district was *de jure* segregated by actions of Detroit officials was not questioned by the Supreme Court, 418 U.S. at 738 n. 18, and the Court assumed, *arguendo,* that the state was also responsible for the segregated schools within Detroit. 418 U.S. at 748. *See also Milliken v. Bradley (Milliken II),* 433 U.S. 267–70 n.1 (1977).]

. . . Accordingly, the District Court proceeded to order the Detroit Board of Education to submit desegregation plans limited to the segregation problems found to be existing within the city of Detroit. At the same time, however, the state defendants were directed to submit desegregation plans encompassing the three-county metropolitan area[10] despite the fact that the 85 outlying school districts of these three counties were not parties to the action and despite the fact that there had been no claim that these outlying districts had committed constitutional violations. . . .

. . . [The] District Court issued its findings and conclusions on the three Detroit-only plans submitted by the city Board and the respondents. It found that the best of the three plans "would make the Detroit school system more identifiably Black . . . thereby increasing the flight of Whites from the city and the system." . . . From this the court concluded that the plan "would not accomplish desegregation . . . within the corporate geographical limits of the city." . . . Accordingly, the District Court held that it "must look beyond the limits of the Detroit school district for a solution to the problem," and that "[s]chool district lines are simply matters of political convenience and may not be used to deny constitutional rights." . . .

. . . The court acknowledged at the outset that it had "taken no proofs with respect to the establishment of the boundaries of the 86 public school districts in the counties [in the Detroit area], nor on the issue of whether, with the exclusion of the city of Detroit school district, such school districts have committed acts of de jure segregation." Nevertheless, the court designated 53 of the 85 suburban school districts plus Detroit as the "desegregation area" and appointed a panel to prepare and submit "an effective desegregation plan" for the Detroit schools that would encompass the entire desegregation area. The plan was to be based on 15 clusters, each containing part of the Detroit system and two or more suburban districts, and was to "achieve the greatest degree of actual desegregation to the end that, upon implementation, no school, grade or classroom [would be] substantially disproportionate to the overall pupil racial composition." . . .

---

[10]These counties cover 1,952 square miles, Michigan Statistical Abstract (9th ed. 1972), and the area is approximately the size of the State of Delaware (2,057 square miles). . . . The populations of Wayne, Oakland, and Macomb Counties were 2,666,751; 907,871; and 625,309, respectively, in 1970. Detroit, the State's largest city, is located in Wayne County.

In the 1970–1971 school year, there were 2,157,449 children enrolled in school districts in Michigan. There are 86 independent, legally distinct school districts within the tri-county area, having a total enrollment of approximately 1,000,000 children. In 1970, the Detroit Board of Education operated 319 schools with approximately 276,000 students.

The Court of Appeals also agreed with the District Court that "any less comprehensive a solution than a metropolitan area plan would result in an all black school system immediately surrounded by practically all white suburban school systems, with an overwhelmingly white majority population in the total metropolitan area."

. . . [The Court of Appeals] reasoned that such a plan would be appropriate because of the State's violations, and could be implemented because of the State's authority to control local school districts. . . . An interdistrict remedy was thus held to be "within the equity powers of the District Court." . . .

II

* * *

Viewing the record as a whole, it seems clear that the District Court and the Court of Appeals shifted the primary focus from a Detroit remedy to the metropolitan area only because of their conclusion that total desegregation of Detroit would not produce the racial balance which they perceived as desirable. . . .

Here the District Court's approach to what constituted "actual desegregation" raises the fundamental question, not presented in *Swann*, as to the circumstances in which a federal court may order desegregation relief that embraces more than a single school district. The court's analytical starting point was its conclusion that school district lines are no more than arbitrary lines on a map drawn "for political convenience." Boundary lines may be bridged where there has been a constitutional violation calling for interdistrict relief, but the notion that school district lines may be casually ignored or treated as a mere administrative convenience is contrary to the history of public education in our country. No single tradition in public education is more deeply rooted than local control over the operation of schools; local autonomy has long been thought essential both to the maintenance of community concern and support for public schools and to quality of the educational process. *See Wright v. Council of the City of Emporia*, 407 U.S., at 469. Thus, in *San Antonio School District v. Rodriguez*, 411 U.S. 1, 50 (1973), we observed that local control over the educational process affords citizens an opportunity to participate in decisionmaking, permits the structuring of school programs to fit local needs, and encourages "experimentation, innovation, and a healthy competition for educational excellence."

The Michigan educational structure involved in this case, in common with most States, provides for a large measure of local control, and a review of the scope and character of these local powers indicates the extent to which the interdistrict remedy approved by the two courts could disrupt and alter the structure of public education in Michigan. The metropolitan remedy would require, in effect, consolidation of 54 independent school districts historically administered as separate units into a vast new super school district. . . . Entirely apart from the logistical and other serious problems attending large-scale transportation of students, the consolidation would give rise to an array of other problems in financing and operating this new school system. Some of the more obvious questions would be: What would be the status and authority of the present popularly elected school boards? Would the children of Detroit be within the jurisdiction and operating control of a school board elected by the parents and residents of other districts? What board or boards would levy taxes for school operations in these 54 districts constituting the consolidated metropolitan area? What provisions could be made for assuring substantial equality in tax levies among the 54 districts, if this were deemed requisite? What provisions would be made for financing? Would the validity of long-term bonds be jeopardized unless approved by all of the component districts as well as the State? What body would determine that portion of the curricula now left to the discretion of local school boards? Who would establish attendance zones, purchase school equipment, locate and construct new schools, and indeed attend to all the myriad day-to-day decisions that are necessary to school operations affecting potentially more than three-quarters of a million pupils? . . .

. . . [I]t is obvious from the scope of the interdistrict remedy itself that absent a complete restructuring of the laws of Michigan relating to school districts the District Court will become first, a de facto "legislative authority" to resolve these complex questions, and then the "school superintendent" for the entire area. This is a task which few, if any, judges are qualified to perform and one which would deprive the people of control of schools through their elected representatives.

* * *

The controlling principle consistently expounded in our holdings is that the scope of the remedy is determined by the nature and extent of the constitutional violation. *Swann*, 402 U.S., at 16. Before the boundaries of separate and autonomous school districts may be set aside by consolidating the separate units for remedial purposes or by imposing a cross-district remedy, it must first be shown that there has been a constitutional violation within one district that produces a significant segregative effect in another district. Specifically, it must be shown that racially discriminatory acts of the state or local school districts, or of a single school district have been a substantial cause of interdistrict segregation. Thus an interdistrict remedy might be in order where the racially discriminatory acts of one or more school districts caused racial segregation in an adjacent district, or where district lines have been deliberately drawn on the basis of race. . . .

The record before us, voluminous as it is, contains evidence of *de jure* segregated conditions only in the Detroit schools; indeed, that was the theory on which the litigation was initially based and on which the District Court took evidence. . . . With no showing of significant violation by the 53 outlying school districts and no evidence of any interdistrict violation or effect, the court went beyond the original theory of the case as framed by the pleadings and mandated a metropolitan area remedy. . . .

. . . [T]he remedy [in desegregation cases] is necessarily designed, as all remedies are, to restore the victims of discriminatory conduct to the position they would have occupied in the absence of such conduct. Disparate treatment of white and Negro students occurred within the Detroit school system, and not elsewhere, and on this record the remedy must be limited to that system. . . .

The constitutional right of the Negro respondents residing in Detroit is to attend a unitary school system in that district. Unless petitioners drew the district lines in a discriminatory fashion, or arranged for white students residing in the Detroit District to attend schools in Oakland and Macomb Counties, they were under no constitutional duty to make provisions for Negro students to do so. . . .

III

We recognize that the six-volume record presently under consideration contains language and some specific incidental findings thought by the District Court to afford a basis for interdistrict relief. However, these comparatively isolated findings and brief comments concern only one possible interdistrict vi-

olation and are found in the context of a proceeding that, as the District Court conceded, included no proof of segregation practiced by any of the 85 suburban school districts surrounding Detroit. . . .

. . . [The Court of Appeals] held the State derivatively responsible for the Detroit Board's violations on the theory that actions of Detroit as a political subdivision of the State were attributable to the State. Accepting, *arguendo*, the correctness of this finding of state responsibility for the segregated conditions within the city of Detroit, it does not follow that an interdistrict remedy is constitutionally justified or required. With a single exception, discussed later, there has been no showing that either the State or any of the 85 outlying districts engaged in activity that had a cross-district effect. . . .

. . . There was evidence introduced at trial that, during the late 1950's, Carver School District, a predominantly Negro suburban district, contracted to have Negro high school students sent to a predominantly Negro school in Detroit. At the time, Carver was an independent school district that had no high school because, according to the trial evidence, "Carver District . . . did not have a place for adequate high school facilities." 484 F.2d, at 231. Accordingly, arrangements were made with Northern High School in the abutting Detroit School District so that the Carver high school students could obtain a secondary school education. . . .

According to the Court of Appeals, the arrangement during the late 1950's which allowed Carver students to be educated within the Detroit District was dependent upon the "tacit or express" approval of the State Board of Education and was the result of the refusal of the white suburban districts to accept the Carver students. Although there is nothing in the record supporting the Court of Appeals' supposition that suburban white schools refused to accept the Carver students, it appears that this situation, whether with or without the State's consent, may have had a segregative effect on the school populations of the two districts involved. However, since "the nature of the violation determines the scope of the remedy," *Swann*, 402 U.S., at 16, this isolated instance affecting two of the school districts would not justify the broad metropolitanwide remedy contemplated by the District Court and approved by the Court of Appeals, particularly since it embraced potentially 52 districts having no responsibility for the arrangement and involved 503,000 pupils in addition to Detroit's 276,000 students.

* * *

Reversed and remanded.

Justice Stewart, concurring.

* * *

The [lower] courts were in error for the simple reason that the remedy they thought necessary was not commensurate with the constitutional violation found. Within a single school district whose officials have been shown to have engaged in unconstitutional racial segregation, a remedial decree that affects every individual school may be dictated by "common sense," see *Keyes v. School District No. 1, Denver, Colorado*, 413 U.S. 189, 203, and indeed may provide the only effective means to eliminate segregation "root and branch," *Green v. County School Board of New Kent County*, 391 U.S. 430, 438, and to "effectuate a transition to a racially nondiscriminatory school system." *Brown v. Board of Education*, 349 U.S. 294, 301. See *Keyes, supra,* at 198–205. But in this case the Court of Appeals approved the concept of a remedial decree that would go beyond the boundaries of the district where the constitutional violation was found, and include schools and schoolchildren in many other school districts that have presumptively been administered in complete accord with the Constitution.

* * *

This is not to say, however, that an interdistrict remedy of the sort approved by the Court of Appeals would not be proper, or even necessary, in other factual situations. Were it to be shown, for example, that state officials had contributed to the separation of the races by drawing or redrawing school district lines, see *Haney v. County Board of Education of Sevier County*, 429 F.2d 364; *cf. Wright v. Council of the City of Emporia*, 407 U.S. 451; *United States v. Scotland Neck Board of Education*, 407 U.S. 484; by transfer of school units between districts, *United States v. Texas*, 321 F.Supp. 1043, *aff'd*, 447 F.2d

441; *Turner v. Warren County Board of Education*, 313 F.Supp. 380; or by purposeful, racially discriminatory use of state housing or zoning laws, then a decree calling for transfer of pupils across district lines or for restructuring of district lines might well be appropriate.

In this case, however, no such interdistrict violation was shown. Indeed, no evidence at all concerning the administration of schools outside the city of Detroit was presented other than the fact that these schools contained a higher proportion of white pupils than did the schools within the city. Since the mere fact of different racial compositions in contiguous districts does not itself imply or constitute a violation of the Equal Protection Clause in the absence of a showing that such disparity was imposed, fostered, or encouraged by the State or its political subdivisions, it follows that no interdistrict violation was shown in this case.[2] The formulation of an interdistrict remedy was thus simply not responsive to the factual record before the District Court and was an abuse of that court's equitable powers.

* * *

[The dissenting opinion of Justice Douglas is omitted.]

Justice White, with whom Justice Douglas, Justice Brennan, and Justice Marshall join, dissenting.

* * *

Regretfully, and for several reasons, I can join neither the Court's judgment nor its opinion. The core of my disagreement is that deliberate acts of segregation and their consequences will go unremedied, not because a remedy would be infeasible or unreasonable in terms of the usual criteria governing school desegregation cases, but because an effective remedy would cause what the Court considers to be undue administrative inconvenience to the State. The result is that the State of Michigan, the entity at which the Fourteenth Amendment is directed, has successfully insulated itself from its duty to provide effective

---

[2]My Brother Marshall seems to ignore this fundamental fact when he states, . . . that "the most essential finding [made by the District Court] was that Negro children in Detroit had been confined by intentional acts of segregation to a growing core of Negro schools surrounded by a receding ring of white schools." This conclusion is simply not substantiated by the record presented in this case. The record here does support the claim made by the respondents that white and Negro students within Detroit who otherwise would have attended school together were separated by acts of the State or its subdivision. However, segregative acts within the city alone cannot be presumed to have produced—and no factual showing was made that they did produce—an increase in the number of Negro students in the city as a whole. It is this essential fact of a predominantly Negro school population in Detroit—caused by unknown and perhaps unknowable factors such as in-migration, birth rates, economic changes, or cumulative acts of private racial fears—that accounts for the "growing core of Negro schools," a "core" that has grown to include virtually the entire city. The Constitution simply does not allow federal courts to attempt to change that situation unless and until it is shown that the State, or its political subdivisions, have contributed to cause the situation to exist. No record has been made in this case showing that the racial composition of the Detroit school population or that residential patterns within Detroit and in the surrounding areas were in any significant measure caused by governmental activity, and it follows that the situation over which my dissenting Brothers express concern cannot serve as the predicate for the remedy adopted by the District Court and approved by the Court of Appeals.

desegregation remedies by vesting sufficient power over its public schools in its local school districts. If this is the case in Michigan, it will be the case in most States.

. . . [The] proposed intracity remedies were beset with practical problems. . . . The most promising proposal, submitted by respondents, who were the plaintiffs in the District Court, would "leave many of its schools 75 to 90 percent Black." 484 F.2d 215, 244 (CA6 1973). Transportation on a "vast scale" would be required; 900 buses would have to be purchased for the transportation of pupils who are not now bused. *Id.*, at 243. The District Court also found that the plan "would change a school system which is now Black and White to one that would be perceived as Black, thereby increasing the flight of Whites from the city and the system, thereby increasing the Black student population." *Id.*, at 244. For the District Court, "[t]he conclusion, under the evidence in this case, is inescapable that relief of segregation in the public schools of the City of Detroit cannot be accomplished within the corporate geographical limits of the city." *Ibid.*

The District Court therefore considered extending its remedy to the suburbs. After hearings, it concluded that a much more effective desegregation plan could be implemented if the suburban districts were included. In proceeding to design its plan on the basis that student bus rides to and from school should not exceed 40 minutes each way as a general matter, the court's express finding was that "[f]or all the reasons stated heretofore—including time, distance, and transportation factors—desegregation within the area described is physically easier and more practicable and feasible, than desegregation efforts limited to the corporate geographic limits of the city of Detroit." 345 F.Supp. 914, 930 (E.D. Mich.1972).

* * *

This Court . . . does not question the District Court's findings that *any* feasible Detroit-only plan would leave many schools 75 to 90 percent black and that the district would become progressively more black as whites left the city. Neither does the Court suggest that including the suburbs in a desegregation plan would be impractical or infeasible because of educational considerations, because of the number of children requiring transportation, or because of the length of their rides. Indeed, the Court leaves unchallenged the District Court's conclusion that a plan including the suburbs would be physically eas-

ier and more practical and feasible than a Detroit-only plan. Whereas the most promising Detroit-only plan, for example, would have entailed the purchase of 900 buses, the metropolitan plan would involve the acquisition of no more than 350 new vehicles.

Despite the fact that a metropolitan remedy, if the findings of the District Court accepted by the Court of Appeals are to be credited, would more effectively desegregate the Detroit schools, would prevent resegregation, and would be easier and more feasible from many standpoints, the Court fashions out of whole cloth an arbitrary rule that remedies for constitutional violations occurring in a single Michigan school district must stop at the school district line. Apparently, no matter how much less burdensome or more effective and efficient in many respects, such as transportation, the metropolitan plan might be, the school district line may not be crossed. Otherwise, it seems, there would be too much disruption of the Michigan scheme for managing its educational system, too much confusion, and too much administrative burden.

* * *

I am even more mystified as to how the Court can ignore the legal reality that the constitutional violations, even if occurring locally, were committed by governmental entities for which the State is responsible and that it is the State that must respond to the command of the Fourteenth Amendment. An interdistrict remedy for the infringements that occurred in this case is well within the confines and powers of the State, which is the governmental entity ultimately responsible for desegregating its schools. The Michigan Supreme Court has observed that "[t]he school district is a State agency," *Attorney General ex rel. Kies v. Lowrey*, 131 Mich. 639, 644, 92 N. W. 289, 290 (1902), and that " '[e]ducation in Michigan belongs to the State. It is no part of the local self-government inherent in the township or municipality, except so far as the legislature may choose to make it such. The Constitution has turned the whole subject over to the legislature. . . .' " *Attorney General ex rel. Zacharias v. Detroit Board of Education*, 154 Mich. 584, 590, 118 N. W. 606, 609 (1908).

* * *

Until today, the permissible contours of the equitable authority of the district courts to remedy the unlawful establishment of a dual school system have been extensive, adaptable, and fully responsive to the ultimate goal of achieving "the greatest possible degree of actual desegregation." There are indeed limitations on the equity powers of the federal judiciary, but until now the Court has not accepted the proposition that effective enforcement of the Fourteenth Amendment could be limited by political or administrative boundary lines demarcated by the very State responsible for the constitutional violation and for the disestablishment of the dual system. Until now the Court has instead looked to practical considerations in effectuating a desegregation decree such as excessive distance, transportation time, and hazards to the safety of the schoolchildren involved in a proposed plan. . . .

Justice Marshall, with whom Justice Douglas, Justice Brennan, and Justice White join, dissenting.

In *Brown v. Board of Education*, 347 U.S. 483 (1954), this Court held that segregation of children in public schools on the basis of race deprives minority group children of equal educational opportunities and therefore denies them the equal protection of the laws under the Fourteenth Amendment. . . .

After 20 years of small, often difficult steps toward that great end, the Court today takes a giant step backwards. Notwithstanding a record showing widespread and pervasive racial segregation in the educational system provided by the State of Michigan for children in Detroit, this Court holds that the District Court was powerless to require the State to remedy its constitutional violation in any meaningful fashion. Ironically purporting to base its result on the principle that the scope of the remedy in a desegregation case should be determined by the nature and the extent of the constitutional violation, the Court's answer is to provide no remedy at all for the violation proved in this case, thereby guaranteeing that Negro children in Detroit will receive the same separate and inherently unequal education in the future as they have been unconstitutionally afforded in the past.

* * *

The rights at issue in this case are too fundamental to be abridged on grounds as superficial as those relied on by the majority today. We deal here with the right of all of our children, whatever their race, to an equal start in life and to an equal opportunity to reach their full potential as citizens. Those children who have been denied that right in the past deserve better than to see fences thrown up to deny them that right in the future. Our Nation, I fear, will be ill served by the Court's refusal to remedy separate and unequal education, for unless our children begin to learn together, there is little hope that our people will ever learn to live together.

* * *

II

. . . [T]he District Court's decision to expand its desegregation decree beyond the geographical limits of the city of Detroit rested in large part on its conclusions (A) that the State of Michigan was ultimately responsible for curing the condition of segregation within the Detroit city schools, and (B) that a Detroit-only remedy would not accomplish this task. In my view, both of these conclusions are well supported by the facts of this case and by this Court's precedents.

A

To begin with, the record amply supports the District Court's findings that the State of Michigan, through state officers and state agencies, had engaged in purposeful acts which created or aggravated segregation in the Detroit schools. The State Board of Education, for example, prior to 1962, exercised its authority to supervise local schoolsite selection in a manner which contributed to segregation. 484 F.2d 215, 238 (CA6 1973). Furthermore, the State's continuing authority, after 1962 to approve school building construction plans had intertwined the State with site-selection decisions of the Detroit Board of Education which had the purpose and effect of maintaining segregation.

The State had also stood in the way of past efforts to desegregate the Detroit city schools. In 1970, for example, the Detroit School Board had begun implementation of its own desegregation plan for its high schools, despite considerable public and official resistance. The State Legislature intervened by enacting Act 48 of the Public Acts of 1970, specifically prohibiting implementation of the desegregation plan and thereby continuing the growing segregation of the Detroit school system. Adequate desegregation of the Detroit system was also hampered by discriminatory restrictions placed by the State on the use of transportation within Detroit. . . .

Also significant was the State's involvement during the 1950's in the transportation of Negro high school students from the Carver School District past a closer white high school in the Oak Park District to a more distant Negro high school in the Detroit system. . . .

* * *

Under Michigan law a "school district is an agency of the State government." *School District of the City of Lansing v. State Board of Education,* 367 Mich. 591, 600, 116 N.W.2d 866, 870 (1962). It is "a legal division of territory, created by the State for educational purposes, to which the State has granted such powers as are deemed necessary to permit the district to function as a State agency." *Detroit Board of Education v. Superintendent of Public Instruction,* 319 Mich. 436, 450, 29 N.W.2d 902, 908 (1947). Racial discrimination by the school district, an agency of the State, is therefore racial discrimination by the State itself, forbidden by the Fourteenth Amendment. . . .

* * *

Vesting responsibility with the State of Michigan for Detroit's segregated schools is particularly appropriate as Michigan, unlike some other States, operates a single statewide system of education rather than several separate and independent local school systems. The majority's emphasis on local governmental control and local autonomy of school districts in Michigan will come as a surprise to those with any familiarity with that State's system of education. School districts are not separate and distinct sovereign entities under Michigan law, but rather are "'auxiliaries of the State,'" subject to its "absolute power." *Attorney General of Michigan ex rel. Kies v. Lowrey,* 199 U.S. 233, 240 (1905). The courts of the State have repeatedly emphasized that education in Michigan is not a local governmental concern, but a state function.

* * *

The State's control over education is reflected in the fact that, contrary to the Court's implication, there is little or no relationship between school districts and local political units. To take the 85 outlying local school districts in the Detroit metropolitan area as examples, 17 districts lie in two counties, two in three counties. One district serves five municipalities; other suburban municipalities are fragmented into as many as six school districts. Nor is there any apparent state policy with regard to the size of school districts, as they now range from 2,000 to 285,000 students.

Centralized state control manifests itself in practice as well as in theory. The State controls the financing of education in several ways. The legislature contributes a substantial portion of most school districts' operating budgets with funds appropriated from the State's General Fund revenues raised through statewide taxation. The State's power over the purse can be and is in fact used to enforce the State's powers over local districts. In addition, although local districts obtain funds through local property taxation, the State has assumed the responsibility to ensure equalized property valuations throughout the State. The State also establishes standards for teacher certification and teacher tenure; determines part of the required curriculum; sets the minimum school term; approves bus routes, equipment, and drivers; approves textbooks; and establishes procedures for student discipline. The State Superintendent of Public Instruction and the State Board of Education have the power to remove local school board members from office for neglect of their duties.

Most significantly for present purposes, the State has wide-ranging powers to consolidate and merge school districts, even without the consent of the districts themselves or of the local citizenry. *See, e.g., Attorney General ex rel. Kies v. Lowrey,* 131 Mich. 639, 92 N.W. 289 (1902), *aff'd,* 199 U.S. 233 (1905). Indeed, recent years have witnessed an accelerated program of school district consolidations, mergers, and annexations, many of which were state imposed. . . .

Whatever may be the history of public education in other parts of our Nation, it simply flies in the face of reality to say, as does the majority, that in Michigan, "[n]o single tradition in public education is more deeply rooted than local control over the operation of schools. . . ."

* * *

Under a Detroit-only decree, Detroit's schools will clearly remain racially identifiable in comparison with neighboring schools in the metropolitan community. Schools with 65% and more Negro students will stand in sharp and obvious contrast to schools in neighboring districts with less than 2% Negro enrollment. Negro students will continue to perceive their schools as segregated educational facilities and this perception will only be increased when whites react to a Detroit-only decree by fleeing to the suburbs to avoid integration. School district lines, however innocently drawn, will surely be perceived as fences to separate the races when, under a Detroit-only decree, white parents withdraw their children from the Detroit city schools and move to the suburbs in order to continue them in all-white schools. The message of this action will not escape the Negro children in the city of Detroit. See *Wright*, 407 U.S., at 466. It will be of scant significance to Negro children who have for years been confined by *de jure* acts of segregation to a growing core of all-Negro schools surrounded by a ring of all-white schools that the new dividing line between the races is the school district boundary.

Nor can it be said that the State is free from any responsibility for the disparity between the racial makeup of Detroit and its surrounding suburbs. The State's creation, through *de jure* acts of segregation, of a growing core of all-Negro schools inevitably acted as a magnet to attract Negroes to the areas served by such schools and to deter them from settling either in other areas of the city or in the suburbs. By the same token, the growing core of all-Negro schools inevitably helped drive whites to other areas of the city or to the suburbs. . . .

. . . The rippling effects on residential patterns caused by purposeful acts of segregation do not automatically subside at the school district border. With rare exceptions, these effects naturally spread through all the residential neighborhoods within a metropolitan area. . . .

The State must also bear part of the blame for the white flight to the suburbs which would be forthcoming from a Detroit-only decree and would render such a remedy ineffective. Having created a system where whites and Negroes were intentionally kept apart so that they could not become accustomed to learning together, the State is responsible for the fact that many whites will react to the dismantling of that segregated system by attempting to flee to the suburbs. . . .

The majority asserts, however, that involvement of outlying districts would do violence to the accepted principle that "the nature of the violation determines the scope of the remedy." *Swann, supra*, at 16. . . . Not only is the majority's attempt to find in this single phrase the answer to the complex and difficult questions presented in this case hopelessly simplistic, but more important, the Court reads these words in a manner which perverts their obvious meaning. The nature of a violation determines the scope of the remedy simply because the function of any remedy is to cure the violation to which it is addressed. In school segregation cases . . . a remedy which effectively cures the violation is what is required. . . . To read this principle as banning a district court from imposing the only effective remedy for past segregation . . . is, in my view, to turn a simple common-

sense rule into a cruel and meaningless paradox. Ironically, by ruling out an interdistrict remedy, the only relief which promises to cure segregation in the Detroit public schools, the majority flouts the very principle on which it purports to rely.

Nor should it be of any significance that the suburban school districts were not shown to have themselves taken any direct action to promote segregation of the races. Given the State's broad powers over local school districts, it was well within the State's powers to require those districts surrounding the Detroit school district to participate in a metropolitan remedy. . . .

* * *

Desegregation is not and was never expected to be an easy task. Racial attitudes ingrained in our Nation's childhood and adolescence are not quickly thrown aside in its middle years. But just as the inconvenience of some cannot be allowed to stand in the way of the rights of others, so public opposition, no matter how strident, cannot be permitted to divert this Court from the enforcement of the constitutional principles at issue in this case. Today's holding, I fear, is more a reflection of a perceived public mood that we have gone far enough in enforcing the Constitution's guarantee of equal justice than it is the product of neutral principles of law. In the short run, it may seem to be the easier course to allow our great metropolitan areas to be divided up each into two cities—one white, the other black—but it is a course, I predict, our people will ultimately regret. I dissent.

NOTES AND QUESTIONS

1. Milliken I: *Of Wrongs and Remedies*

Milliken was the first case in which a majority of the Supreme Court overturned a lower court order that had sought to bring about greater integration. Indeed, it marked the first time in more than thirty-five years that the Court had rejected the position of the NAACP on desegregation in a written opinion. The decision was greeted with widespread criticism among scholars to the effect that the Court was turning back on its previous decisions. *See, e.g.,* Lawrence, "Segregation 'Misunderstood': The *Milliken* Decision Revisited," 12 *U.S.F.L. Rev.* 15 (1977); Taylor, "The Supreme Court and Urban Reality: A Tactical Analysis of *Milliken v. Bradley*," 21

Wayne L. Rev. 751 (1975). *But see* L. Graglia, *Disaster by Decree* (1976); Wolf, "Northern Desegregation and Residential Choice," 1977 *Sup. Ct. Rev.* 63. Recently, two commentators, looking back on the quarter of a century since *Milliken*, have concluded that the effect of that decision was not only to foreclose significant northern urban desegregation, but also to contribute to the rapidly increasing segregation of urban schools. *See* G. Orfield and S. Eaton, *Dismantling Desegregation: The Quiet Reversal of* Brown v. Board of Education (1996).

Was the Supreme Court's decision inconsistent with its earlier cases? In *Keyes*, the Court said that *de jure* segregation in a substantial or meaningful portion of a school district triggered the presumption that the segregation in the remaining part of the school district was also *de jure*, thus requiring a systemwide racial balance remedy unless the defendants can rebut the presumption. Why then should not a finding of *de jure* segregation in the central city, attributable in part to the actions of the state, trigger a presumption of a reciprocal segregative effect in the suburbs? Is the connection between constitutional wrong and proposed remedy any more speculative in *Milliken* than in *Swann* or *Keyes*? Did the majority chastise the lower courts for doing precisely what it had presaged in its decisions in those cases? *See* Yudof, "School Desegregation: Legal Realism, Reasoned Elaboration, and Social Science Research in the Supreme Court," 42 *Law & Contemp. Prob.* 57, 93–97 (1978) (pt. 2).

2. Milliken I: *A Case about Desegregation or Federalism?*

Chief Justice Burger, in discussing the reasons that a metropolitan remedy was impermissible in *Milliken*, noted that the consolidation of fifty-four independent school districts would not only create logistical and administrative problems, but would also alter the status of the presently *popularly elected* school boards and would necessitate turning the district court into a legislature to resolve such complex issues as the financing of the new units, the drawing of attendance zones, and the construction of new schools. The court would then have to function as a school superintendent in order to make the day-to-day operational decisions. If the "condition that offends the Constitution" is limited to the boundaries of the Detroit school district, then such major dislocations of the separate and autonomous suburban school districts were unwarranted. *But see Delaware*

State Board of Education v. Evans, 446 U.S. 923, 100 S.Ct. 1862, 64 L.Ed.2d 278 (1980).

3. *Local Control of Schools*

Are there considerations that might militate against an interdistrict remedy even if intentional segregative acts occurred on an interdistrict basis? What weight should the concern for preserving "local control" be given in the desegregation context? *See* Shane, "School Desegregation Remedies and the Fair Governance of Schools," 132 *U.Pa.L.Rev.* 1041, 1097–1104 (1984). In several cases prior to the statement in *Milliken* that "no single tradition in public education is more deeply rooted than local control over the operation of schools . . .," the Supreme Court has suggested that local autonomy in public education is a very substantial interest. *See San Antonio Independent School District v. Rodriguez*, 411 U.S. 1, 49–50, 93 S.Ct. 1278, 1304–05, 36 L.Ed.2d 16 (1973); *Wright v. Council of the City of Emporia*, 407 U.S. 451, 469, 92 S.Ct. 2196, 2206, 33 L.Ed.2d 51 (1972). The Sixth Circuit, however, had devoted nearly four pages of its opinion to a review of the evidence of state control over education in Michigan, noting that "under the Constitution and laws of Michigan . . . the public school system is a State function and that local school districts are instrumentalities of the State created for administrative convenience." 484 F.2d 215, 246 (6th Cir. 1973). *See* Gewirtz, "Remedies and Resistance," 92 *Yale L.J.* 585, 647–49 (1983).

4. *When Are Interdistrict Remedies Permissible?*

After *Milliken*, what must plaintiffs be able to demonstrate in order to obtain a metropolitan remedy? *See Little Rock School District v. Pulaski County Special School District No. 1*, 778 F.2d 404 (8th Cir. 1985), *cert. denied*, 476 U.S. 1186, 106 S.Ct. 2926, 91 L.Ed.2d 554 (1986); *Newburg Area Council v. Board of Education*, 510 F.2d 1358 (6th Cir. 1974), *cert. denied*, 429 U.S. 1074, 97 S.Ct. 812, 50 L.Ed.2d 792 (1977); *United States v. Board of School Commissioners*, 456 F.Supp. 183 (S.D. Ind. 1978), *vacated and remanded*, 429 U.S. 1068, 97 S.Ct. 800, 50 L.Ed.2d 786 (1977); *Evans v. Buchanan*, 393 F.Supp. 428 (D. Del. 1975), *aff'd mem.*, 423 U.S. 963, 96 S.Ct. 381, 46 L.Ed.2d 293. *See also Delaware State Board of Education v. Evans*, 446 U.S. 923, 100 S.Ct. 1862, 64 L.Ed.2d 278 (1980).

In *Liddell v. Missouri*, 731 F.2d 1294 (8th cir. 1984), *cert. denied*, 469 U.S. 816, 105 S.Ct. 82, 83

L.Ed.2d 30, the Court of Appeals approved a settlement agreement that called for an interdistrict remedy despite the fact that there was no finding of an interdistrict violation. The agreement included a provision that required the state to fund the voluntary transfer of students between the city and sixteen suburban school districts. The court indicated that because the state had been found to be a "primary constitutional wrongdoer," it could be required to take "those actions which will further the desegregation of the city schools even if the actions required will occur outside the boundaries of the city school district." *Liddell v. Board of Education*, 677 F.2d 626, 630 (8th Cir. 1982), *cert. denied*, 459 U.S. 877, 103 S.Ct. 172, 74 L.Ed.2d 142. Under the settlement agreement, the largest voluntary school transfer program in the country developed, with 12,000 children attending schools outside of their designated districts each day. The sixteen suburban districts agreed to accept the voluntary transfer of black city students (and white suburban students were to be attracted to city schools with special programs) out of fear that if the case went to trial, the suburban districts might be found to have contributed to the constitutional violation and be merged into a single metropolitan district. The court distinguished *Milliken I* on the ground that, considering the "breadth, gravity and duration of the state's violation," it was appropriate for the district court to mandate an equally comprehensive remedy. 731 F.2d at 1308. Moreover, the court noted that the remedy does not "threaten the autonomy of local school districts" because they are neither coerced nor reorganized and "retain the rights and powers accorded them by state and federal laws." *Id. See* Gewirtz, "Choice in Transition: School Desegregation and the Corrective Ideal," 86 *Colum L.Rev.* 728, 779–82 (1986).

5. The Role of "White Flight" in Determining the Extent of the Remedy

Was the approach taken by the district court in *Milliken* a response to white flight? Much of the testimony before the district judge stressed that a "city-only" remedy would result in the rapid departure of most of the remaining whites, leaving behind a nearly all-black school district. Does the majority's decision in *Milliken* ensure that there will be white flight by indicating that the suburbs will be a "safe haven" for those who otherwise would be caught up in a desegregation decree? Is it constitutionally appropriate for federal courts to seek to prevent such

demographic shifts? *See Pasadena City Board of Education v. Spangler*, 427 U.S. 424, 96 S.Ct. 2697, 49 L.Ed.2d 599 (1976); *Spencer v. Kugler*, 404 U.S. 1027, 92 S.Ct. 707, 30 L.Ed.2d 723 (1972). *But see Delaware State Board of Education v. Evans*, 446 U.S. 923, 100 S.Ct. 1862, 64 L.Ed.2d 278 (1980).

To what extent may a court take white flight into account in devising a school desegregation remedy? The fear of white flight to the suburbs (or private schools) has been used by some courts to limit a systemwide remedy. Mr. Justice Powell, in his dissenting opinion in *Columbus II*, argued against a remedy requiring school boards to racially balance every school because "parents, unlike school officials, are not bound by these decrees and may frustrate them through the simple expedient of withdrawing their children from a public school system in which they have lost confidence." 433 U.S. at 484. *See also Estes v. Metropolitan Branches of Dallas NAACP*, 444 U.S. 437, 100 S.Ct. 716, 62 L.Ed.2d 626 (1980) (Powell, J., with whom Stewart and Rehnquist, J.J., join, dissenting). Justice Powell attributes this white flight not to "a racist response to integration *per se*" but to "a natural reaction to the displacement of professional and local control that occurs when courts go into the business of restructuring and operating school systems." *Columbus II*, 443 U.S. at 485. What are the reasons for the exodus of white students from the central city schools? Consider this summary of the evidence by Professor David Armor:

> First, the *fact* that white loss is associated with desegregation in some instances is not in dispute. Second, it is a conditional relationship: it occurs under some conditions but not others. Third, the effect is seen most clearly in the year that desegregation takes place. . . .
>
> First, the effect appears to depend upon a substantial proportion of Black (or minority) students, perhaps on the order of 20–25%. Second, the effect appears strongest for central-city districts surrounded by accessible white suburbs (e.g., Boston) and weakest for large metropolitan school districts surrounded by minimally developed rural areas (e.g., Charlotte, North Carolina). Finally, the effect appears strongest when there is a significant shift in the racial balance of schools, and primarily when white reassignment is involved in the shift.

Armor, "White Flight and the Future of School Desegregation," in W. Stephan and J. Feagin, eds., *School Desegregation* 187, 196–97 (1980).

Might some white families seek to escape from central cities for reasons other than those given by

Powell, for example, lower taxes, better housing, less crime, or superior municipal services? *See* Farley, "Racial Integration in the Public Schools, 1967–1972: Assessing the Effects of Governmental Policies," 8 *Soc. Focus* 3 (1975). Consider also to what extent white flight is really a reflection of the more rapidly declining birth rates among whites. In assessing the relative weight of these factors in causing "white flight," why is it that the most significant exodus of middle class whites usually occurs in the first year of implementation of a school desegregation decree? *See* Armor, *supra.* Note also that many cities with no school busing orders have also experienced sharp declines in the percentage of whites during the past thirty years. G. Orfield and S. Eaton, *Dismantling Desegregation: The Quiet Reversal of Brown v. Board of Education* 93–96 (1996).

If a judge believes that a systemwide desegregation remedy will result in white flight and the resegregation of the entire school district, what is the judge to do? Does it make sense to order a "fruit-basket turnover [of the school population] through busing to create [uniform racial balance] throughout the system" if it was clear that within a few months' time the school district population would be all-minority as a result of white flight? *See Calhoun v. Cook*, 332 F.Supp. 804, 806, 808 (N.D. Ga.), *vacated in part and remanded*, 451 F.2d 583 (5th Cir. 1971). A number of courts have limited the scope of desegregation because of evidence of potential white flight. *See, e.g., Mapp v. Board of Education*, 325 F.2d 169 (6th Cir. 1975), *cert. denied*, 427 U.S. 911 (1976). *See* Levin, "School Desegregation Remedies and the Role of Social Science Research," 42 *Law & Contemp. Probs.* 1, 8–25 (1978) (pt.2). On the other hand, what did the Court in *Brown II* mean when it said that "the vitality of these constitutional principles cannot be allowed to yield simply because of disagreement with them"? *See* Gewirtz, "Remedies and Resistance," 92 *Yale L.J.* 585, 632–43 (1983).

6. The Role of Social Science Evidence in Determining the Extent of the Remedy

In *Brown v. Board of Education*, the Court referred to segregation as generating "a feeling of inferiority [among blacks] as to their status in the community that may affect their hearts and minds in a way unlikely ever to be undone." It quoted with favor the finding of the lower court that "segregation with the sanction of law . . . has a tendency to [retard] the ed-

ucational and mental development of Negro children. . . ." And in the now-famous footnote 11, the Court cited what it called modern authority on the effects of segregation on black children. These references have given support to a sociological interpretation of the desegregation cases. Among the arguments that have been made are that segregated schools harm African American children in a number of ways: There is a "lessening of motivation, alienation of the child from the educational institution, distortion of personal relationships, and various forms of antisocial behavior." Fiss, "Racial Imbalance in the Public Schools: The Constitutional Concepts," 78 *Harv.L.Rev.* 564, 569 (1965).

It has also been argued that segregated schools are academically inferior and thus African American children who attend such schools are impaired in their ability to compete in society. *Id.* at 570. *See generally Hart v. Community School Board*, 383 F.Supp. 699, 739 (E.D.N.Y.1974); N. St. John, *School Desegregation: Outcomes for Children* (1975). The converse argument is that integrated schools will lessen the achievement gap between black and white students and, ultimately, the gap in educational and economic attainment between white and black adults. *See, e.g.,* Crain and Mahard, "School Racial Composition and Black College Attendance and Achievement Test Performance," 51 *Soc. of Educ.* 81 (1978); R.Crain et al., *Finding Niches: Desegregated Students Sixteen Years Later* (1989). Further, the hope is that desegregation of the schools will improve relations between the races. *See generally* National Opinion Research Center, *Southern Schools: An Evaluation of the Effects of the Emergency School Assistance Program and of School Desegregation* (1973).

Extensive debates among social scientists have centered on the impact of mandatory desegregation, particularly through the use of busing,; on minority achievement, aspirations, self-concept, college attendance, and race relations. The classic debate on the effects of busing on minorities is that between David Armor in "The Evidence on Busing," 28 *Pub. Interest* 90 (1972) and Thomas Pettigrew and his colleagues in Pettigrew, Useem, Normand, and Smith, "Busing: A Review of the 'Evidence,' " 30 *Pub. Interest* 88 (1973), and Armor's response to Pettigrew, et al. This debate is summarized by Krol, "Desegregation and Academic Achievement," in D. Bartz and M. Maehr, *Advances in Motivation and Achievement*, Vol. 1 (1984), at 81–82, as follows:

... In his original articles and in his reply to Pettigrew et al...., Armor seriously questioned the effectiveness of busing and other strategies as techniques for improving minority achievement. He presented evidence that busing in six different locations had not had a positive effect on minority student performance. Much of Armor's review of the literature concentrated on a comparison of the academic gains of bused and non-bused siblings. Armor concluded that there were not significant differences in academic gains between the bused group and the non-bused brothers and sisters.

Armor's conclusion was quickly challenged by Pettigrew et al.... Pettigrew contended that Armor's review of the literature was incomplete, biased, misleading, and that it lacked a thorough analysis of the studies selected. He singled out a study conducted by Armor ... in Boston as being unrepresentative and inadequately discussed and noted that a great deal of the evidence used by Armor to make his point came from the study. Pettigrew then went on to present a list of eight studies which had not been reviewed by Armor that were purported to support the success of various desegregation programs. Pettigrew limited his discussion and analysis to these eight studies even though he had chastised Armor for performing an incomplete and inadequate review of the literature....

Armor replied to Pettigrew's reply by accusing Pettigrew, et al.... of applying a "double double standard" to the research literature. He said the first double standard related to the burden of proof.... The second double standard related to the appropriateness of scientific evidence in arguing the question of busing: "One willingly applies social science findings to public policy if they are in accordance with one's values but declares them irrelevant if they contradict one's values." ... In addition to these accusations, Armor responded to Pettigrew's criticism of the ... [Boston] research and pointed out that many of the studies cited by Pettigrew were biased and inadequate.

a. Controversy over Evidence. It may well be that many of the issues discussed in the Armor-Pettigrew debate cannot be definitively answered unless a carefully controlled social experiment is undertaken. Such experimentation is rare in education, largely because parents resist the coercion (and possible educational injury) that experimentation implies.

The debate has continued. *See, e.g.,* N. St. John, *School Desegregation Outcomes for Children* (1975); Braddock, Crain, and McPartland, "A Long-Term View of School Desegregation: Some Recent Studies of Graduates as Adults," *Phi Delta Kappan,* Dec. 1984, at 259; Coleman, "New In-centives for Desegregation," 7 *Human Rights* 10 (1978); Crain and Mahard, "Desegregation and Black Achievement: A Review of the Research," 42 *Law & Contemp. Probs.* 17 (1978) (pt. 1); Epps, "The Impact of School Desegregation on the Self-Evaluation and Achievement Orientation of Minority Children," *Id.* at 57; McConahay, "The Effects of School Desegregation Upon Students' Racial Attitudes and Behavior: A Critical Review of the Literature and a Prolegomenon to Future Research," *Id.* at 77. *See Columbus Board of Education v. Penick,* 443 U.S. 449, 485 n.5, 99 S.Ct. 2941, 2952, n. 5, 61 L.Ed.2d 666 (1977) (Powell, J., dissenting); *Capacchione v. Charlotte-Mecklenburg Schools,* 57 F.Supp. 2d 228, 272 (W.D. N.C. 1999) ("the maintenance of racially balanced schools appears to have no effect on test score disparities and seems to make little difference in the level of black achievement").

Mahard and Crain, "Research on Minority Achievement in Desegregated Schools," in *The Consequences of School Desegregation* 103 (C. Rossell & W. Hawley, eds., 1983) found that desegregation has had a positive effect on achievement levels for minority children with no detrimental effect on the achievement of white students, and this study's findings are supported by more recent research. *See* Joondeph, "Review Essay: A Second Redemption?" 56 *Wash. & Lee L. Rev.* 169, 191–194 (1999).

Some critics argue for more policy-relevant research on desegregated schools. Instead of simply documenting achievement outcomes, researchers should investigate factors that lead to more effective desegregated schools. The question should not be whether desegregation works, but rather under what conditions it operates most effectively. For a summary of some components of effective desegregation, *see* Henderson, von Euler, and Schneider, "Remedies for Segregation: Some Lessons from Research," 3 *Educ. Evaluation and Pol'y Analysis* 4 (1981) at 67.

b. The Burden of Proving Harm. In the light of the controversy over the effects of desegregation, where should the legal burden of proof of injury rest? Is it necessary for black litigants to prove that integration favorably affects academic performance, racial attitudes, or psychological well-being before a court may order integration?

c. Social Science Evidence and Constitutional Decisions. What weight should the courts attach to social science studies of the effects of desegregation? *See generally* Yudof, "School Desegregation: Legal Realism, Reasoned Elaboration, and Social Science Research in the Supreme Court," 42 *Law & Contemp. Probs.* 57 (1978).

In view of the fact that there is considerable disagreement among social scientists as to the research findings and the conclusions to be drawn from those findings, is the adversary process the appropriate way of dealing with controversial social science issues? *See* P. Ellsworth and J. Getman, *Law and the Social Sciences* (1986), at 620–21, describing some of the difficulties of using social science evidence at the appellate level:

> How is the court to choose in an argument involving the adequacy of the data base, the significance of regression co-efficients, and the choice of appropriate control analyses? In a situation like this, one party may, in fact, have the stronger arguments, but the court can only conclude . . . that experts disagree. But disagreement among experts should not be grounds for disregarding the empirical issues entirely. Instances of complete unanimity among the social science community are extremely rare, and it would be unfortunate if the Court were to insist on a standard of absolute agreement before accepting social science data. . . .

Ellsworth and Getman discuss the problem of the "battle of the experts" at the trial court level as follows:

> . . . [T]here is no reason to believe that the skill of effective courtroom testimony is highly correlated with the skill of scientific expertise, and there is every reason to believe that a trial attorney, if forced to choose, will prefer the better witness to the better scientist. Even an excellent scientist is likely to be less than perfectly coherent, and perhaps less than perfectly honest, on the witness stand. Unable to anticipate questions, to prepare answers in advance, or to offer full explanations; threatened by contemptuous attacks with no opportunity for rebuttal; restricted by a good cross-examiner to yes and no answers—the scientists are not apt to appear at their best. A facile dogmatism may sound better—and read better in the record—than a more hesitant and more accurate response. The mode of presentation and the kinds of questions asked are often so foreign to the professional experience of most research scientists that it is difficult to believe that the answers given in this context could possibly be the best account of the re-

search or that the interchange could provide a valid test for deciding what is scientifically true and what is not.

Id. at 623.

Courts rarely rely on social science research in determining whether segregation is unconstitutional, and when they have done so, they have been preemptorily reversed. *See Stell v. Savannah-Chatham County Board of Education*, 220 F.Supp. 667 (S.D. Ga. 1963), *rev'd*, 333 F.2d 55 (5th Cir.), *cert. denied*, 379 U.S. 933, 85 S.Ct. 332, 13 L.Ed.2d 344. *See also Evers v. Jackson Municipal Separate School District*, 232 F.Supp. 241 (S.D. Miss. 1964), *aff'd*, 357 F.2d 653 (5th Cir.), *cert. denied*, 384 U.S. 961, 86, S.Ct. 1586, 16 L.Ed.2d 673. Courts have continued, however, to refer to social science research with regard to questions concerning the nature and extent of the remedies to be applied. *See* Levin, "School Desegregation Remedies and the Role of Social Science Research," 42 *Law & Contemp. Probs.* 1 (1978) (pt. 2). Professor Levin examines the extent to which courts rely on social science evidence in deciding on the ages of the children to be bused and the distances, whether magnet schools can be used, whether the potential for white flight mandates a lesser remedy, and whether compensatory educational programs may be included in a desegregation decree.

d. Other Studies of the Effects of Desegregation. The social science literature on the effects of desegregation is immense. For the interested reader, the following books and articles afford a useful starting place: Coleman, et al., *Equality of Educational Opportunity* (1966); F. Mosteller and P. Moynihan, *On Equality of Educational Opportunity* (1970); R. O'Reilly, *Racial and Social Class Isolation in the Schools* (1970); N. St. John, *School Desegregation Outcomes for Children* (1975); Clark, "Desegregation: An Appraisal of the Evidence," 9 *J. Social Issues* 2 (1953); Crain, "School Integration and Occupational Achievement of Negroes," 75 *Am. J. Soc.* 593 (1971); Frary and Goolsby, "Achievement of Integrated and Segregated Negroes and White First Graders in a Southern City," 8 *Integrated Educ.* 48 (1970); Katz, "Review of Evidence Relating to Effects of Desegregation on the Intellectual Performance of Negroes," 19 *Am. Psych.* 381 (1964); Katz, "The Socialization of Academic Motivation in Minority Group Children," in D. Levine, ed., *Nebraska Symposium on Motivation* (1967); Kiesling, "The Value to Society of Integrated Education and Compensatory Education," 61 *Geo. L.J.* 857 (1973); Symposium,"The Courts, Social Science, and School Desegregation," Symposium, "School Desegregation: Lessons of the First Twenty-five Years," 42 *Law & Contemp. Probs.* (B. Levin and W. Hawley, eds., 1978); 39 *Law & Contemp. Probs.* (B. Levin and W. Hawley, eds., 1975); Braddock, Crain, and McPartland, "A Long-Term View of Desegregation: Some Recent Studies of Graduates as Adults," 66 *Phi Delta Kappan*, 259 (1984).

D. Court-Ordered Remedies Other than Pupil Reassignment

"School Desegregation Remedies and the Role of Social Science Research"

B. Levin, 42 *Law & Contemp. Probs.* 1, 30–33 (1978) (pt.2). Reprinted with permission.

In *Milliken II*,[185] the Supreme Court was faced with the question of whether it was within the scope of a district court's remedial powers to require compensatory education programs, in-service training programs for teachers, and guidance and counseling programs as part of the desegregation plan. The inclusion of these and similar educational components was challenged on the ground that such remedies exceeded the scope of the constitutional violation.[187] Since the constitutional violation was racially discriminatory pupil assignments, it was argued, the desegregation plan must be limited to reassignment of the pupils.

The district court had heard extensive testimony from both academic experts and school officials on each of the four major components. With regard to the first component, remedial reading, the court declared that "[t]here is no educational component more directly associated with the process of desegregation than reading." The remedial reading program was to redress the lower reading ability of black students compared to that of white students. In-service training for teachers was also supported by substantial testimony, primarily from state and local school officials. The third component related to testing. There was evidence that prior testing had been racially and culturally biased, and thus the court ordered bias-free testing programs to be instituted. The fourth component on which there was extensive testimony with regard to its importance in the desegregation process was a counseling and guidance program.[194]

. . . The State Board of Education was unable to refute the testimony of expert witnesses provided by the plaintiffs or by the Detroit School Board. Indeed, the State's own expert witness confirmed the need for educational components.[197]

The Supreme Court's decision in *Milliken II* held that since the purpose of a remedy was to restore the victims of discriminatory conduct to the position they would have occupied in the absence of discrimination, a desegregation plan might have to include programs to undo the inequalities caused by a dual system. The Court concluded that the compensatory programs and other educational components mandated by the district court were "aptly tailored to remedy the consequences of the constitutional violation."

---

[185]*Milliken v. Bradley*, 433 U.S. 267, 97 S.Ct. 2749, 53 L.Ed.2d 745 (1977).

[187]It should be noted that it was not the Detroit city school board, in *Milliken II*, that challenged the remedial programs ordered by the district court. These programs were under attack from the state defendants. The trial court had ordered the state to pay half the cost of the programs, a sum estimated at $5.8 million. Brief of Petitioners at 13. The state argued that (1) the district court had no authority to order the ancillary relief, but was restricted to ordering pupil reassignment, *id.* at 21, and (2) even if the special relief was needed, the state could not be compelled to pay for it under the eleventh amendment. Brief of Petitioners at 34. The Court denied both claims. 433 U.S. at 288, 290, 97 S.Ct. at 2761, 2762.

[194]. . . Charles Wells, Assistant Superintendent of the Detroit Public Schools, testified that the counseling and guidance component was needed: "Because we feel that this counseling support is necessary to relate educationally to the adjustments required in desegregation." Brief of Respondent, *supra*, Appendix at 51. Mr. Wells also testified that a revised counseling and guidance component was needed to eradicate previous counseling practices that stereotyped black children. Brief of Respondent at 26 & Appendix at 52.

Professor Ashworth described the need for a guidance and counseling program to eliminate the effects of past segregation:

[W]hat we are saying is that in order to correct the inequalities for the students and right the wrongs of students that the person has to be retrained and that program has to be revamped . . . students have been counseled in or out of certain programs based on their race. If this had not been so the Aero Mechanics would not be 84 percent white in a school system that is more than 70 percent black.

Brief of Respondent, *supra*, at 26 & Appendix at 34.

[197]. . . the State Board of Education, in its critique of the Detroit Board's plan, conceded that "the in-service training [and] guidance and counseling . . . components appear to deserve special emphasis" in effecting desegregation. Record, vol. 4, doc. 591, at 38–39, *quoted in Milliken v. Bradley*, 433 U.S. at 273.

Children who have been . . . educationally and culturally set apart from the larger community will inevitably
acquire habits of speech, conduct, and attitudes reflecting their cultural isolation. They are likely to acquire speech habits, for example, which vary from the
environment in which they must ultimately function
and compete, if they are to enter and be a part of that
community. This is not peculiar to race; in this setting,
it can affect any children who, as a group, are isolated
by force of law from the mainstream. . . .

Pupil assignment alone does not automatically remedy the impact of previous, unlawful educational isolation; the consequences linger and can be dealt with
only by independent measures. In short, speech habits
acquired in a segregated system do not vanish simply by
moving the child to a desegregated school. The root
condition shown by this record must be treated directly
by special training at the hands of teachers prepared for
that task.

The Court noted that there was "abundant evidence" that the specific educational remedies ordered by the district court were essential to correct
the unconstitutional condition.

NOTES AND QUESTIONS

1. The Standard for Ancillary Relief

Under what circumstances may a court prescribe the
educational programming to be provided by the
school system? How can the courts decide which
programs will cure the "condition that offends the
Constitution" and will restore the victims of discrimination to the position they would have occupied in
the absence of discrimination? *Milliken v. Bradley*,
433 U.S. 267, 282, 97 S.Ct. 2749, 2758, 53 L.Ed.2d
745 (1977). How is it possible to determine what that
position is? What role might expert testimony play?
See Jenkins v. Missouri, 639 F.Supp. 19, 24 (W.D.
Mo. 1985); *Berry v. School District of Benton Harbor*,
515 F.Supp. 344, 369 (W.D. Mich. 1981).

2. The Role of District Courts

Does the standard articulated in *Milliken II* require
district courts to substitute themselves for school officials and determine which compensatory reading
program is most likely to restore the victim to the position he or she would have occupied except for the
unconstitutional conduct? See Justice Powell's comment that the district court had "virtually assumed
the role of school superintendent and school board."

Milliken v. Bradley, 433 U.S. 267, 297, 97 S.Ct.
2749, 2765, 53 L.Ed.2d 745 (1977) (Powell, J.,
concurring in the judgment). How significant is it
that local school officials joined plaintiffs in *Milliken
II* in pressing for the remedial programs? What are
the financial implications of such court-ordered
programming?

3. Compensatory Programs as a Substitute for Pupil Reassignment Remedies

In the light of the facts that Detroit had a minority
student population that exceeded 80 percent, and
that the Court had earlier struck down a metropolitan desegregation plan, does *Milliken II* suggest that
a remedy involving remedial education programming may be substituted for a remedy that involves
busing? *Cf. Calhoun v. Cook*, 522 F.2d 717 (5th Cir.
1975), *rehearing denied*, 525 F.2d 1203. *But see
Bradley v. Milliken*, 620 F.2d 1143 (6th Cir. 1980);
Jenkins v. Missouri, 639 F.Supp. 19 (W.D. Mo.
1985). Or are compensatory programs only ancillary
to the desegregation of a school system?

4. The Use of Magnet Schools to Desegregate

Some courts have used the concept of "magnet
schools" as an incentive to promote desegregation
without extensive mandatory busing, and as a way of
limiting white flight. *See, e.g., Jenkins v. Missouri*,
639 F.Supp.19 (W.D. Mo.1985), *aff'd as modified*,
807 F.2d 657 (8th Cir. 1986); *Liddell v. Missouri*, 731
F.2d 1294 (8th Cir. 1984); *Tasby v. Estes*, 412
F.Supp. 1192 (N.D. Tex.1975), *remanded*, 572 F.2d
1010 (5th Cir. 1978). Magnet schools are those that
offer a specialized school curriculum organized
around a particular subject matter (e.g., mathematics, science, or the arts) or theme, or that use a distinctive teaching methodology, and seek to attract
both white and minority students from all parts of the
city, and away from their neighborhood schools or
private schools. *See, e.g.,* Price and Stern, "Magnet
Schools as a Strategy for Integration and School Reform," 5 *Yale Law & Pol'y Rev.* 291 (1987); Gewirtz,
"Choice in Transition: School Desegregation and
the Corrective Ideal," 86 *Colum. L. Rev.* 728,
767–68 (1986); Levin, "School Desegregation
Remedies and the Role of Social Science Research,"
42 *Law & Contemp. Probs.* 1, 25–30 (1978) (pt.2).
The number of magnet schools more than doubled
between 1983 and 1992, and the number of students
enrolled in magnet schools or programs increased
more than threefold during this period, to 1.2 mil-

lion. L. Steele and M. Eaton, *Reducing, Eliminating, and Preventing Minority Isolation in American Schools: The Impact of the Magnet Schools Assistance Program* 1–2 (1996). Over half of the magnet schools had waiting lists, comprising nearly 123,000 students nationwide. L. Steele and R. Levine, *Educational Innovation in Multiracial Contexts: The Growth of Magnet Schools in American Education* vii (1994).

The circumstances under which magnet schools are most likely to promote desegregation were delineated in a 1983 national study of magnet programs commissioned by the U.S. Department of Education, *Survey of Magnet Schools: Analyzing a Model for Quality Integrated Education*, and summarized in Price and Stern, *supra*:

> Larger districts, districts experiencing population growth due to new economic opportunities, and districts that were multiracial and multiethnic had the most success desegregating with magnets. The study also indicated that districts had a better chance for successful desegregation if they used magnets as one aspect of a total plan, which also included a variety of voluntary and involuntary desegregation methods such as pairing, rezoning, two-way busing, and mandatory assignment.

Price and Stern, *supra*, at 295. *See also* Report of the Citizens' Commission on Civil Rights, *Difficult Choices: Do Magnet Schools Serve Children in Need?* (C. Yu and W. Taylor, eds., 1997), which found that in three urban school districts using magnet schools as a key element of court-ordered desegregation plans, those schools were successful in creating desegregated schools and in improving educational opportunities for minority students. However, this study also found that lower socioeconomic status children remained more highly concentrated in nonmagnet schools.

Magnet schools, particularly those that are "schools within schools," often result in classroom segregation, and thus have been criticized for failing to promote desegregation. *See* Note, "A Desegregation Tool That Backfired: Magnet School and Classroom Segregation," 103 *Yale L. J.* 2567 (1994). *See Stell v. Savannah-Chatham County Board of Education*, 888 F.2d 82 (11th Cir. 1989) (voluntary magnet programs within schools, with 50% white and 50% black students, upheld in face of plaintiffs' challenge that the nonmagnet programs in each of the schools would consist of predominantly black students).

Some of the ways in which magnet schools may obstruct, rather than advance, desegregation, found by the *Survey of Magnet Schools*, are also summarized in Price and Stern, *supra*:

> Although the National Magnet Study found that magnets have been used successfully to promote integration, it also offered instructive examples of how magnets can be utilized to obstruct, not advance, integration. Some magnets serve as "shell games" to create the mere appearance of desegregation. Some serve to relieve pressure from courts and state agencies to desegregate. Some use "elitist" selection criteria to reduce minority access to the best available learning opportunities. Others admit minority students but then fail them and remand them to inferior schools. Even in desegregated magnets the danger remains that tracking within the school will have resegregative effects.
>
> Equitable access to magnet schools depends not only on fair selection methods, but also on adequate information about the available options. Poor, non-English speaking, and illiterate families are severely disadvantaged under traditional information systems. . . .
>
>   * * *
>
> While the National Magnet Study found relatively few magnets were selective, it did discover that 89% of magnets had some method for weeding out students with severe academic or behavioral problems. Elite student bodies, in practice, if not intent, can also result from student self-selection, school marketing strategies directed at middle-class neighborhoods or higher achieving feeder schools, and guidance practices that steer children to different schools on the basis of their perceived abilities. . . .

Id. at 299, 300. The debate over the merits of magnet schools continues. Among those who contend that they contribute to school desegregation and to improving the quality of education are Blank, "Analyzing Educational Effects of Magnet Schools Using Local District Data," 1 *Sociological Practice Rev.* 40 (1990); C. Rossell, *The Carrot or the Stick for School Desegregation Policy: Magnet Schools vs. Forced Busing* (1990); and Witte and Walsh, "A Systematic Test of the Effective Schools Model," 12 *Educational Eval. & Pol'y Analysis* 188 (1990). Critics of magnet programs have been concerned about the potential for elitism and inequity, or that they fail to contribute significantly to desegregation. *See, e.g.,* Hendrie, "Magnets' Value in Desegregating Schools Is Found to Be Limited," *Education Week*, Nov. 13, 1996, p.1. The federal government, under the Magnet Schools Assistance Program, makes grants to eligible school districts for magnet schools that are part of a court-ordered desegregation plan, or part of a plan approved by the Department of Education as adequate under Title VI of the Civil Rights Act of 1964 for the desegregation of minority children or faculty in such schools. 20 U.S.C. §§ 7201 *et seq.* (West 2000).

In *Capacchione v. Charlotte-Mecklenburg Schools,* 57 F.Supp. 2d 228, 285 (W.D.N.C. 1999), the school district's expanded magnet schools program was held to have exceeded the scope of its requirements under earlier desegregation orders, and under a strict scrutiny analysis, the district court found the program's race-conscious admissions policy unconstitutional. The Fourth Circuit reversed, finding that the expanded magnet schools program was designed to remedy the effects of past racial discrimination, and noting that magnet school programs generally include an assignment policy that takes race into account in order to ensure that these voluntary programs do not undermine progress toward desegregation. *Belk v. Charlotte-Mecklenburg Board of Educ.,* 233 F.3d 232, 267–269, 273 (4th Cir. 2000).

5. Who Pays for Court-Ordered Educational and Related Programs?

A number of courts, relying on *Milliken II,* have ordered the state or other governmental units to share the costs of implementing and maintaining desegregation and compensatory education programs with the local school board. *See Jenkins v. Missouri,* 807 F.2d 657, 683 (8th Cir. 1986) (en banc), *aff'd in part and remanded,* 495 U.S. 33, 110 S.Ct. 1651, 109 L.Ed. 2d 31 (1990); *Liddell v. State of Missouri,* 731 F.2d 1294 (8th Cir. 1984); *Little Rock School District v. Pulaski County Special School District No. 1,* 778 F.2d 404 (8th Cir. 1985); *Reed v. Rhodes,* 662 F.2d 1219 (6th Cir. 1981), *cert. denied,* 455 U.S. 1018, 102 S.Ct. 1713, 72 L.Ed.2d 135 (1982); *Brinkman v. Gilligan,* 610 F.Supp. 1288 (S.D. Ohio 1985); *Arthur v. Nyquist,* 547 F.Supp. 468 (W.D.N.Y. 1982). In each case, the state has been found liable to some degree for the segregation. *See Kelley v. Board of Education of Nashville and Davidson County,* 836 F.2d 986 (6th Cir. 1987); and *United States v. Texas Education Agency,* 790 F.2d 1262 (5th Cir. 1986), both holding that the state did not have to share in the costs as there was no finding that the state was liable for the segregation. Generally, state funding is ordered only when it is necessary to the continuance of a program that materially aids desegregation and not for programs that merely improve

the educational quality of the school district. *See Arthur v. Nyquist, supra.* However, the state may not force a school district to pay for desegregation out of general education funds. *Id.*

After a district court found that the Kansas City, Missouri School District (KCMSD) and the state of Missouri had operated an unconstitutionally segregated school system, the court ordered a detailed desegregation remedy and allocated the cost of the remedy between the state and the city school district.

The *Milliken II*–type remedy provided for improvements in the quality of the curriculum, tutoring programs, child development programs, and magnet schools—including a 25-acre farm and a 25-acre wild land area for science study, and extensive (and expensive) capital improvements. *Missouri v. Jenkins,* 495 U.S.33, 110 S.Ct. 1651, 109 L.Ed.2d 31(1990). However, Missouri's constitution and state laws placed limits on the local property tax rate that a district can levy, thus preventing KCMSD from raising the revenues necessary to fund its share of the desegregation remedy. The district court ordered KCMSD to impose a property tax levy that would be sufficient to raise the necessary funds. The Supreme Court held that in the circumstances of this case, the tax increase ordered by the district court violated principles of federal/state comity. However, Justice White, writing for the majority, did not completely rule out the imposition of a tax rate increase by a federal court, but noted that "before taking such a drastic step the district court was obliged to assure itself that no permissible alternative would have accomplished the required task." *Id.* at 51. The Court found that there was an alternative route the district court could have followed that would have been less intrusive: "it could have authorized or required KCMSD to levy property taxes at a rate adequate to fund the desegregation remedy and could have enjoined the operation of state laws that would have prevented KCMSD from exercising this power." *Id.* The majority distinguished the court's imposing its own tax increase on the school district from the court's ordering the school district to levy a tax increase, as follows:

> Authorizing and directing local government institutions to devise and implement remedies not only protects the function of those institutions but, to the extent possible, also places the responsibility for solutions to the problems of segregation upon those who have themselves created the problems. . . .

... Whatever the merits of this argument [that an order to increase taxes violates Article III of the Constitution] when applied to the district court's own order increasing taxes, a point we have not reached ..., a court order directing a local government body to levy its own taxes is plainly a judicial act within the power of the federal court. ...

Id. at 51, 55. The majority stated that federal judicial power can go further and set aside state-imposed limitations on local taxing authority "where there is reason based in the Constitution for not observing the statutory limitation." *Id.* at 57.

Here the KCMSD may be ordered to levy taxes despite the statutory limitations on its authority in order to compel the discharge of an obligation imposed on KCMSD by the Fourteenth Amendment. To hold otherwise would fail to take account of the obligations of local governments, under the Supremacy Clause, to fulfill the requirements that the Constitution imposes on them. ... Even though a particular remedy may not be required in every case to vindicate constitutional guarantees, where (as here) it has been found that a particular remedy is required, the State cannot hinder the process by preventing a local government from implementing that remedy.

Id.

Do you agree that federal courts should order states or their political subdivisions to levy taxes, despite state statutory or constitutional restrictions? See Chapter 7's discussion of both federal and state court cases challenging state school finance laws.

E. Desegregation in Multiethnic Districts

Although most of the case law in the school desegregation area was the result of lawsuits brought by African Americans, the benefits of the equal protection clause have been sought by other minorities, the largest group being Latinos. Should Latinos be treated as an identifiable class for purposes of determining whether a school or school system is segregated? *See Cisneros v. Corpus Christi Independent School District*, 467 F.2d 142 (5th Cir. 1972), *cert. denied*, 413 U.S. 920, 93 S.Ct. 3053, 37 L.Ed.2d 1041; *United States v. Texas Educ. Agency*, 467 F.2d 848 (5th Cir. 1972), *vacated sub nom. Austin Independent School District v. United States*, 429 U.S. 990, 97 S.Ct. 517, 50 L.Ed.2d 603.

The Supreme Court in *Keyes* dealt with this issue as follows:

[A] word must be said about the district court's method of defining a "segregated" school. Denver is a triethnic, as distinguished from a biracial, community. The overall racial and ethnic composition of the Denver public schools is 66% Anglo, 14% Negro and 20% Hispano. The District Court, in assessing the question of *de jure* segregation in the core city schools, preliminarily resolved that Negroes and Hispanos should not be placed in the same category to establish the segregated character of a school. 313 F.Supp. at 69. ...

We conclude, however, that the District Court erred in separating Negroes and Hispanos for purposes of defining a "segregated" school. We have held that Hispanos constitute an identifiable class for purposes of the Fourteenth Amendment. *Hernandez v. Texas*, 347 U.S. 475 (1954). ... [T]here is ... much evidence that in the Southwest Hispanos and Negroes have a great many things in common. The United States Commission on Civil Rights has recently published two reports on Hispano education in the Southwest. Focusing on students in the states of Arizona, California, Colorado, New Mexico, and Texas, the Commission concluded that Hispanos suffer from the same educational inequities as Negroes and American Indians. In fact, the District Court itself recognized that "one of the things which the Hispano has in common with the Negro is economic and cultural deprivation and discrimination." 313 F.Supp. at 69. This is agreement that, though of different origins, Negroes and Hispanos in Denver suffer identical discrimination in treatment when compared with the treatment afforded Anglo students. In that circumstance, we think petitioners are entitled to have schools with a combined predominance of Negroes and Hispanos included in the category of "segregated" schools.

Keyes v. School District No. 1, 413 U.S. 189, 195–98, 93 S.Ct. 2686, 2690–92, 37 L.Ed.2d 548 (1973).

NOTES AND QUESTIONS

1. Which Minorities Constitute an Identifiable Class?

The *Keyes* Court notes that Hispanics in the Southwest have suffered "economic and cultural deprivation and discrimination" identical to that of African Americans. If this is the necessary and sufficient test, would all Spanish-speaking students fit into that category, for example, the Puerto Ricans or

Colombians in New York? Does *Keyes* indicate that *Brown* should be extended to other minorities—such as Asian American students?

Is the finding that Latinos (or other minorities) have suffered "educational inequities" sufficient, or must there be evidence of intentional segregative action? *See Zamora v. New Braunfels Independent School District*, 519 F.2d 1084 (5th Cir. 1975); *United States v. Texas Education Agency*, 467 F.2d 848 (5th Cir. 1972).

2. Multiethnic Remedies

Do *Keyes* and *Swann*, read together, mean that schools must be ethnically as well as racially balanced? Many advocates of bilingual education for Latinos have opposed the dispersal of Latino students on the ground that the bilingual programs will be jeopardized. May a court order pupil reassignment for African American and white students to end racially segregated schools at the same time that Latino students are permitted to remain in ethnically isolated schools or classrooms in order to permit bilingual-bicultural instruction? *See Tasby v. Estes*, 412 F.Supp F. Supp. 1192 (N.D. Tex. 1976), *remanded on other grounds, aff'd in part*, 572 F.2d 1010 (5th Cir. 1978); *Keyes v. School District No. 1*, 380 F.Supp F. Supp. 673, 692 (D. Colo. 1974), *rev'd on this point*, 521 F.2d 465, 480 (10th Cir. 1972), *cert. denied*, 423 U.S. 1066, 96 S.Ct. 806, 46 L.Ed.2d 657 (1976). The district court in the Boston school desegregation case ordered the assignment of Hispanic students before the assignment of black and white students in order to prevent their dispersal. *Morgan v. Kerrigan*, 401 F.Supp. 216, 242, 252 (D. Mass. 1975), *aff'd*, 530 F.2d 401 (1st Cir.), *cert. denied*, 426 U.S. 935, 96 S.Ct. 2648, 49 L.Ed.2d 386 (1976). *See* Roos, "Bilingual Education: The Hispanic Response to Unequal Educational Opportunity," 42 *Law & Contemp. Probs.* 111, 136–37 (1978) (pt. 2), for a description of the court's order.

Latinos, who in many cases have not entered a school desegregation case until the remedy phase, have at times successfully argued for a bilingual component in a remedial plan. *See, e.g., United States v. Texas Education Agency*, 342 F.Supp. 24 (E.D. Tex. 1971), *rev'd on other grounds*, 467 F.2d 848 (5th Cir. (1972)). *But see Keyes v. School District No. 1*, 521 F.2d 465 (10th Cir. 1975), *cert. denied*, 432 U.S. 1066, 96 S.Ct. 806, 46 L.Ed.2d 657 (1976). Might *Milliken II* provide a constitutional basis for this argument? *Bradley v. Milliken*, 402 F.Supp.

1096, 1118 (E.D. Mich. 1975), *aff'd in part, rev'd on other grounds*, 540 F.2d 229 (6th Cir. (1976)), *aff'd*, 443 U.S. 267, 97 S.Ct. 2749, 53 L.Ed.2d 745 (1977). Is there a plausible causal relationship between segregation and limited English-speaking ability?

Concern has been expressed that treating African Americans and Latinos as indistinguishable "minorities" in desegregation orders disadvantages the latter group. *See, e.g.,* Orfield, "The Growth of Segregation: African Americans, Latinos, and Unequal Education," in *Dismantling Desegregation: The Quiet Reversal of* Brown v. Board of Education (G. Orfield and S. Eaton, eds., 1996); Bowman, Note, "The New Face of School Desegregation," 50 *Duke L.J.* ___ (forthcoming 2001). Bowman argues that the black-white binary that was the legacy of *Brown*, the white-nonwhite paradigm that was the legacy of *Keyes*, and the minority-nonminority approach taken in *Missouri v. Jenkins* have marginalized Latinos or even made them invisible at a time when they comprise a larger share of the school-age population nationally than African Americans and in an increasing number of school districts constitute the majority of the student population. *Id.*

VI. END OF AN ERA?

A. The Legal Significance of Achieving Unitary Status: *Board of Education of Oklahoma City Public Schools v. Dowell*

In *Board of Education of Oklahoma City Public Schools v. Dowell*, 498 U.S. 237, 111 S.Ct. 630, 112 L.Ed.2d 715 (1991), a district court dissolved a 1972 school desegregation decree on the ground that the school board had complied in good faith for a sufficient period of time. The plaintiffs argued, and the Tenth Circuit agreed, that prior Supreme Court decisions required "a clear showing of grievous wrong evoked by new and unforeseen conditions" before a decree could be lifted. The plaintiffs also argued that the board's recent student assignment plan had increased the number of segregated schools. The Supreme Court reversed the Tenth Circuit on the ground that school desegregation decrees, unlike other kinds of decrees, "are not intended to operate in perpetuity."

> . . . Local control over the education of children allows citizens to participate in decisionmaking, and allows innovation so that school programs can fit local needs [citing *Milliken I*]. The legal justification for displace-

ment of local authority by an injunctive decree in a school desegregation case is a violation of the constitution by the local authorities. Dissolving a desegregation decree after the local authorities have operated in compliance with it for a reasonable period of time properly recognizes that "necessary concern for the important values of local control of public school systems dictates that a federal court's regulatory control of such systems not extend beyond the time required to remedy the effects of past intentional discrimination. . . ."

Id. at 247.

The Court, while declining to define precisely what is meant by a unitary system, indicated that district courts should engage in a two-part test in determining unitariness: (1) "whether the Board had complied in good faith with the desegregation decree since it was entered," and (2) "whether the vestiges of past discrimination had been eliminated to the extent practicable." *Id.* at 249–50. On the latter point, the Court said that "[i]n considering whether the vestiges of *de jure* segregation had been eliminated as far as practicable, the District Court should look not only at student assignments, but 'to every facet of school operations—faculty, staff, transportation, extra-curricular activities and facilities,' " citing *Green. Id.* at 250.

Finally, once the district court has determined that the system is unitary, then the plaintiffs have the burden of showing that any increase in segregated schools is due to intentional actions taken by the school board subsequent to its having been found unitary, citing *Washington v. Davis* and *Arlington Heights.*

Justice Marshall, joined by Justices Blackmun and Stevens, vigorously dissented, noting that for sixty-five years after Oklahoma had gained statehood, the board had

> maintained segregated schools—initially relying on laws requiring dual school systems; thereafter, by exploiting residential segregation that had been created by legally enforced restrictive covenants. In 1972 . . . a federal court finally interrupted this cycle. . . .
>
> The practical question now before us is whether, 13 years after that injunction was imposed, the same School Board should have been allowed to return many of its elementary schools to their former one-race status. . . .

Id. at 251. The dissenters pointed to the prolonged "recalcitrance" of the board, leading the district court, when the board failed to come forward with its

own plan, to impose the plaintiffs' plan. After only three years of operation, the board moved to close the case on the ground that it had eliminated all vestiges of the *de jure* system. The district court granted the board's motion and issued an order terminating the case. Eight years later, the board implemented a new plan that resegregated a considerable number of schools. The dissenters argued that the board's obligation should not cease because "residential segregation is now perpetuated by 'private decisionmaking,' " in light of the fact that the state, local officials, and the board had been involved "in creating what are now self-perpetuating patterns of residential segregation."

Justice Marshall also rejected the majority's suggestion that the length of federal court supervision should be a factor in determining whether the decree should be dissolved. "Our jurisprudence requires . . . that the job of school desegregation be fully completed and maintained so that the stigmatic harm identified in *Brown I* will not recur upon lifting the decree." *Id.* at 266.

NOTES AND QUESTIONS

1. When Does the District Court's Jurisdiction Cease?

Is the real debate over what is a unitary system and when court supervision should end a debate over the ultimate objective of *Brown*, i.e., whether it was the elimination of state-imposed segregation or integration of the public schools? Whether integration is a substantive constitutional entitlement or a remedy to correct prior *de jure* segregation?

After *Dowell*, does the determination of unitariness by a district court mean that its jurisdiction thereby ceases? Inasmuch as the *Dowell* majority expressly declined to define "unitary," has it made clear to lower courts what the standard is by which unitariness is to be determined? To what extent is the lapse of a number of years during which the school board has complied with a school desegregation decree sufficient to permit the court to end its jurisdiction? What is a "reasonable period of time" for the school board to have acted in compliance with a desegregation decree? Has the *Dowell* Court provided adequate guidelines to enable district courts to determine whether the vestiges of past discrimination have been eliminated "to the extent practicable"?

2. *The Burden of Proof*

In challenging subsequent school board actions that may lead to resegregation, must the plaintiff prove discriminatory intent or is a showing of segregative effects sufficient? The circuits are also split on this issue. The Tenth Circuit concluded that a school board that has established unitariness but that has not convinced the district court to dissolve an injunction "bears a 'heavy burden' to show that its implementation of [new programs] does not 'serve to perpetuate or re-establish the dual school system.' " *Dowell*, 890 F.2d at 1493 (quoting *Dayton Board of Education v. Brinkman*, 443 U.S. 526, 538, 99 S.Ct. 2971, 2979, 61 L.Ed.2d 720 (1979)). Those challenging board actions may bear an initial burden to show that the original decree has been violated, but the burden then shifts "to defendants to produce evidence of changed circumstances or oppressive hardship." *Id*. The Fourth Circuit, however, concluded that a finding of unitariness not only requires the termination of jurisdiction but also shifts the burden to plaintiffs to prove that later actions by the board are motivated by discriminatory intent. *Riddick v. School Bd. of City of Norfolk*, 784 F.2d 521, 534 (4th Cir.1986). Similarly, the Fifth Circuit reasoned that a finding of unitariness means that only intentional discrimination constitutes a new constitutional violation and that a challenged school board should no longer bear the "burden of proving that its decisions are free of segregative purpose." *United States v. Overton*, 834 F.2d 1171, 1171 (5th Cir. 1987).

Where does the Supreme Court decision leave the burden of proof? The dissenting opinion in *Dowell* notes that:

> The majority does not discuss the burden of proof under its test for dissolution of a school desegregation decree. However, every presumption we have established in our school desegregation cases has been against the school district found to have engaged in *de jure* segregation. *See Dayton Bd. of Education v. Brinkman*, 443 U.S. 526, 537 (1979) (conduct resulting in increased segregation was presumed to be caused by past intentional discrimination where dual system was never affirmatively remedied); *Keyes v. School Dist. No. 1, Denver, Colo.*, 413 U.S. 189, 208 (1973) (proof of state-imposed segregation in a substantial portion of a school district will support a prima facie finding of a system-wide violation, thereby shifting the burden to school authorities to show that current segregation is not caused by past intentional discrimination); *Swann v. Charlotte-Mecklenburg Bd. of Education*, 402 U.S. 1, 26 (1971) (establishing a presumption against racially

identifiable schools once past state discrimination has been shown, thereby shifting the burden to the school district to show that current segregation was not caused by past intentional discrimination). Moreover, in addition to the "affirmative duty" placed upon school districts to eliminate vestiges of their past discrimination, *Green*, 391 U.S., at 437–438, school districts initially have the burden of coming forward with desegregation plans and establishing that such plans promise to be effective. *Id*., at 439. And, while operating under a decree, a school board has a "heavy burden" to justify use of less effective or resegregative methods. *Ibid. Accord, Dayton, supra*, at 538; *Wright v. Council of City of Emporia*, 407 U.S. 451, 467 (1972).

> Given the original obligation placed on formerly *de jure* segregated school districts to provide an effective remedy that will eliminate all vestiges of its segregated past, a school district seeking dissolution of an injunctive decree should also bear the burden of proving that this obligation has been fulfilled. *Cf. Keyes, supra*, at 211, n. 17 (noting that the plaintiffs should not bear the burden of proving "non-attenuation").

Dowell, 498 U.S. at 266, 111 S.Ct. at 647, n. 10 (Marshall, J., joined by Blackmun, J. and Stevens, J., dissenting). *See* Note, "Allocating the Burden of Proof After a Finding of Unitariness in School Desegregation Litigation," 100 *Harv.L.Rev.* 653, 667 (1987). Has the Supreme Court in *Dowell* in effect abandoned the presumption of *Green* and *Swann* that the existence of one-race schools was a vestige of the formerly dual school system? *See also Freeman v. Pitts*, 503 U.S. 467, 112 S.Ct. 1430, 118 L.Ed.2d 108 (1992).

B. The Legal Significance of Achieving Partial Unitary Status

The significance of achieving partial unitary status was not addressed in *Dowell*, and lower courts had held different positions on the issue. The Eleventh Circuit held that in order to achieve unitary status, a school system formerly declared segregated must achieve desegregation for a period of at least three years, as measured simultaneously by all six *Green* factors (student assignment, faculty, staff, transportation, extracurricular activities, and facilities). *Pitts v. Freeman*, 887 F.2d 1438, 1445–46 (11th Cir. 1989) (citing *Green v. County School Bd.*, 391 U.S. 430, 435, 88 S.Ct. 1689, 1692, 20 L.Ed.2d 716 (1968)). The First Circuit, however, concluded that a school system's failure to achieve unitariness in some of the *Green* factors does not preclude a finding of unitariness in others and that remedies should be limited to the factors not yet found to be unitary. *Morgan v. Nucci*, 831 F.2d 313, 318 (1st Cir. 1987). The Supreme Court resolved this issue in the case below.

Freeman v. Pitts
503 U.S. 467, 112 S.Ct. 1430, 118 L.Ed.2d 108 (1992)

Justice Kennedy delivered the opinion of the Court.

DeKalb County, Georgia, is a major suburban area of Atlanta. This case involves a court-ordered desegregation decree for the DeKalb County School System (DCSS). DCSS now serves some 73,000 students in kindergarten through high school and is the 32d largest elementary and secondary school system in the Nation.

DCSS has been subject to the supervision and jurisdiction of the United States District Court for the Northern District of Georgia since 1969, when it was ordered to dismantle its dual school system. In 1986, [DCSS] filed a motion for final dismissal. The District Court ruled that DCSS had not achieved unitary status in all respects but had done so in student attendance and three other categories. In its order the District Court relinquished remedial control as to those aspects of the system in which unitary status had been achieved, and retained supervisory authority only for those aspects of the school system in which the district was not in full compliance. The Court of Appeals for the Eleventh Circuit reversed, 887 F.2d 1438 (1989), holding that a district court should retain full remedial authority over a school system until it achieves unitary status in six categories at the same time for several years.

We now reverse the judgment of the Court of Appeals and remand, holding that a district court is permitted to withdraw judicial supervision with respect to discrete categories in which the school district has achieved compliance with a court-ordered desegregation plan. A district court need not retain active control over every aspect of school administration until a school district has demonstrated unitary status in all facets of its system.

I

A

For decades before our decision in *Brown v. Board of Education*, . . . DCSS was segregated by law. DCSS'

initial response to the mandate of *Brown II* was an all too familiar one. Interpreting "all deliberate speed" as giving latitude to delay steps to desegregate, DCSS took no positive action toward desegregation until the 1966–1967 school year, when it did nothing more than adopt a freedom of choice transfer plan. . . .

* * *

Within two months of our ruling in *Green*, respondents, who are black schoolchildren and their parents, instituted this class action. . . . The District Court, in June 1969, entered a consent order approving . . . a neighborhood school attendance plan. . . . Under the plan all of the former *de jure* black schools were closed, and their students were reassigned among the remaining neighborhood schools. The District Court retained jurisdiction.

* * *

In 1986, [DCSS] . . . sought a declaration that DCSS had satisfied its duty to eliminate the dual education system, that is to say a declaration that the school system had achieved unitary status. . . . The District Court approached the question whether DCSS had achieved unitary status by asking whether DCSS was unitary with respect to each of the factors identified in *Green*. The court considered an additional factor that is not named in *Green*: the quality of education being offered to the white and black student populations.

The District Court found DCSS to be . . . a unitary system with regard to student assignments, transportation, physical facilities, and extracurricular activities, and ruled that it would order no further relief in those areas. The District Court stopped short of dismissing the case, however, because it found that DCSS was not unitary in every respect. The court said that vestiges of the dual system remain in the areas of teacher and principal assignments, resource allocation, and quality of education. DCSS was ordered to take measures to address the remaining problems.

B

. . . Here, as in most cases where the issue is the degree of compliance with a school desegregation decree, a critical beginning point is the degree of racial imbalance in the school district, that is to say a comparison of the proportion of majority to minority students in individual schools with the proportions of the races in the district as a whole. . . .

... Remarkable changes in the racial composition of the county presented DCSS and the District Court with a student population in 1986 far different from the one they set out to integrate in 1969. ... The school system that the District Court ordered desegregated in 1969 had 5.6% black students; by 1986 the percentage of black students was 47%.

To compound the difficulty of working with these radical demographic changes, the northern and southern parts of the county experienced much different growth patterns. The District Court found that "[a]s the result of these demographic shifts, the population of the northern half of DeKalb County is now predominantly white and the southern half of DeKalb County is predominantly black." ... Most of the growth in the nonwhite population in the southern portion of the county was due to the migration of black persons from the city of Atlanta. Between 1975 and 1980 alone, approximately 64,000 black citizens moved into southern DeKalb County, most of them coming from Atlanta. During the same period, approximately 37,000 white citizens moved out of southern DeKalb County to the surrounding counties.

* * *

[Respondents presented evidence of substantial racial imbalance, and argued that it was a vestige of the formerly *de jure* system.]

In determining whether DCSS has achieved unitary status with respect to student assignment, the District Court saw its task as one of deciding if petitioners "have accomplished maximum practical desegregation of the DCSS or if the DCSS must still do more to fulfill their affirmative constitutional duty." ...

Having found no constitutional violation with respect to student assignment, the District Court next considered the other *Green* factors, beginning with faculty and staff assignments. The District Court first found that DCSS had fulfilled its constitutional obligation with respect to hiring and retaining minority teachers and administrators. DCSS has taken active steps to recruit qualified black applicants and has hired them in significant numbers, employing a greater percentage of black teachers than the statewide average. The District Court also noted that DCSS has an "equally exemplary record" in retention of black teachers and administrators. ... Nevertheless, the District Court found that . . . a racial imbalance existed in the assignment of minority teachers and ad-

ministrators. ... [B]lack principals and administrators were overrepresented in schools with high percentages of black students and underrepresented in schools with low percentages of black students.

* * *

Addressing the more ineffable category of quality of education, the District Court ... found that DCSS had not achieved unitary status with respect to quality of education because teachers in schools with disproportionately high percentages of white students tended to be better educated and have more experience than their counterparts in schools with disproportionately high percentages of black students, and because per-pupil expenditures in majority white schools exceeded per-pupil expenditures in majority black schools. From these findings, the District Court ordered DCSS to equalize spending and remedy the other problems.

In accordance with its factfinding, the District Court held that it would order no further relief in the areas of student assignment, transportation, physical facilities, and extracurricular activities. ...

... The Court of Appeals affirmed the District Court's ultimate conclusion that DCSS has not yet achieved unitary status, but reversed the District Court's ruling that DCSS has no further duties in the area of student assignment. 887 F.2d 1438 (1989). The Court of Appeals held that the District Court erred by considering the six *Green* factors as separate categories. The Court of Appeals rejected the District Court's incremental approach, an approach that has also been adopted by the Court of Appeals for the First Circuit, *Morgan v. Nucci*, 831 F.2d 313, 318–319 (1987), and held that a school system achieves unitary status only after it has satisfied all six factors at the same time for several years. 887 F.2d, at 1446. Because, under this test, DCSS had not achieved unitary status at any time, the Court of Appeals held that DCSS could "not shirk its constitutional duties by pointing to demographic shifts occurring prior to unitary status." *Id.*, at 1448. The Court of Appeals held that petitioners bore the responsibility for the racial imbalance, and in order to correct that imbalance would have to take actions that "may be administratively awkward, inconvenient, and even bizarre in some situations," *Swann v. Charlotte-Mecklenburg Bd. of Education*, such as pairing and clustering of schools, drastic gerrymandering of school zones, grade reorganization, and busing. We granted certiorari. ...

II

* * *

Today, we make explicit the rationale that was central in *Spangler* [*Pasadena Bd. of Education v. Spangler*, 427 U.S. 424, 96 S.Ct. 2697, 49 L.Ed.2d 599 (1976)]. A federal court in a school desegregation case has the discretion to order an incremental or partial withdrawal of its supervision and control. This discretion derives both from the constitutional authority which justified its intervention in the first instance and its ultimate objectives in formulating the decree. The authority of the court is invoked at the outset to remedy particular constitutional violations. . . . A remedy is justifiable only insofar as it advances the ultimate objective of alleviating the initial constitutional violation.

We have said that the court's end purpose must be to remedy the violation and, in addition, to restore state and local authorities to the control of a school system that is operating in compliance with the Constitution. [*Milliken II*]. . . . Partial relinquishment of judicial control, where justified by the facts of the case, can be an important and significant step in fulfilling the district court's duty to return the operations and control of schools to local authorities. In *Dowell*, we emphasized that federal judicial supervision of local school systems was intended as a "temporary measure." Although this temporary measure has lasted decades, the ultimate objective has not changed—to return school districts to the control of local authorities. . . . [A] court [must] provide an orderly means for withdrawing from control when it is shown that the school district has attained the requisite degree of compliance. A transition phase in which control is relinquished in a gradual way is an appropriate means to this end.

As we have long observed, "local autonomy of school districts is a vital national tradition." *Dayton Bd. of Education v. Brinkman*, 433 U.S. 406, 410, 97 S.Ct. 2766, 2770, 53 L.Ed.2d 851 (1977) *(Dayton I)*. Returning schools to the control of local authorities at the earliest practicable date is essential to restore their true accountability in our governmental system. When the school district and all state entities participating with it in operating the schools make decisions in the absence of judicial supervision, they can be held accountable to the citizenry, to the political process, and to the courts in the ordinary course. . . .

We hold that, in the course of supervising desegregation plans, federal courts have the authority to relinquish supervision and control of school districts in incremental stages, before full compliance has been achieved in every area of school operations. While retaining jurisdiction over the case, the court may determine that it will not order further remedies in areas where the school district is in compliance with the decree. That is to say, upon a finding that a school system subject to a court-supervised desegregation plan is in compliance in some but not all areas, the court in appropriate cases may return control to the school system in those areas where compliance has been achieved, limiting further judicial supervision to operations that are not yet in full compliance with the court decree. In particular, the district court may determine that it will not order further remedies in the area of student assignments where racial imbalance is not traceable, in a proximate way, to constitutional violations.

. . . [A] court should give particular attention to the school system's record of compliance. A school system is better positioned to demonstrate its good-faith commitment to a constitutional course of action when its policies form a consistent pattern of lawful conduct directed to eliminating earlier violations. And, with the passage of time, the degree to which racial imbalances continue to represent vestiges of a constitutional violation may diminish, and the practicability and efficacy of various remedies can be evaluated with more precision.

These are the premises that guided our formulation in *Dowell* of the duties of a district court during the final phases of a desegregation case: "The District Court should address itself to whether the Board had complied in good faith with the desegregation decree since it was entered, and whether the vestiges of past discrimination had been eliminated to the extent practicable."

B

* * *

The Court of Appeals was mistaken in ruling that our opinion in *Swann* requires "awkward," "inconvenient," and "even bizarre" measures to achieve racial balance in student assignments in the late phases of carrying out a decree, when the imbalance is attributable neither to the prior *de jure* system nor to a later violation by the school district but rather to independent demographic forces. . . . In the case before us the District Court designed a comprehensive plan for desegregation of DCSS in 1969, one that included racial balance in student assignments. The desegregation decree was designed to achieve maximum practicable desegregation. Its central remedy was the closing of black schools and the reassignment of pupils to neighborhood schools, with attendance zones that achieved racial balance. The plan accomplished its objective in the first year of operation, before dramatic demographic changes altered residential patterns. . . .

The effect of changing residential patterns on the racial composition of schools, though not always fortunate, is somewhat predictable. Studies show a high correlation between residential segregation and school segregation. . . . The District Court in this case heard evidence tending to show that racially stable neighborhoods are not likely to emerge because whites prefer a racial mix of 80% white and 20% black, while blacks prefer a 50-50 mix.

Where resegregation is a product not of state action but of private choices, it does not have constitutional implications. It is beyond the authority and beyond the practical ability of the federal courts to try to counteract these kinds of continuous and massive demographic shifts. To attempt such results would require ongoing and never-ending supervision by the courts of school districts simply because they were once *de jure* segregated. Residential housing choices, and their attendant effects on the racial composition of schools, present an ever-changing pattern, one difficult to address through judicial remedies.

* * *

As the *de jure* violation becomes more remote in time and these demographic changes intervene, it becomes less likely that a current racial imbalance in a school district is a vestige of the prior *de jure* system. The causal link between current conditions and the prior violation is even more attenuated if the school district has demonstrated its good faith. . . .

We next consider whether retention of judicial control over student attendance is necessary or practicable to achieve compliance in other facets of the school system. Racial balancing in elementary and secondary school student assignments may be a legitimate remedial device to correct other fundamental inequities that were themselves caused by the constitutional violation. We have long

recognized that the *Green* factors may be related or interdependent. . . .

There was no showing that racial balancing was an appropriate mechanism to cure other deficiencies in this case. It is true that the school district was not in compliance with respect to faculty assignments, but the record does not show that student reassignments would be a feasible or practicable way to remedy this defect. . . .

* * *

Justice Thomas took no part in the consideration or decision of this case.

Justice Scalia, concurring.

* * *

Our decision will be of great assistance to the citizens of DeKalb County, who for the first time since 1969 will be able to run their own public schools, at least so far as student assignments are concerned. It will have little effect, however, upon the many other school districts throughout the country that are still being supervised by federal judges, since it turns upon the extraordinarily rare circumstance of a finding that no portion of the current racial imbalance is a remnant of prior *de jure* discrimination. . . . [W]e must resolve—if not today, then soon—what is to be done in the vast majority of other districts, where, though our cases continue to profess that judicial oversight of school operations is a temporary expedient, democratic processes remain suspended, with no prospect of restoration, 38 years after *Brown v. Board of Education.* . . .

Identifying and undoing the effects of some violations of the law is easy. . . . That is not so with respect to the effects of unconstitutionally operating a legally segregated school system; they are uncommonly difficult to identify and to separate from the effects of other causes. But one would not know that from our instructions to the lower courts on this subject, which tend to be at a level of generality that assumes facile reduction to specifics. " '[Desegregation] decrees,' " we have said, " 'exceed appropriate limits if they are aimed at eliminating a condition that does not violate the Constitution or does not flow from such a violation,' " [citing *Dowell* and *Milliken II*]. . . . We have never sought to describe how one identifies a condition as the effluent of a violation, or how a "vestige" or a "remnant" of past discrimination is to be recognized. . . .

Racially imbalanced schools are . . . the product of a blend of public and private actions, and any assessment that they would not be segregated, or would not be as segregated, in the absence of a particular one of those factors is guesswork. It is similarly guesswork, of course, to say that they would be segregated, or would be as segregated, in the absence of one of those factors. Only in rare cases such as this one and *Spangler*, . . . where the racial imbalance had been temporarily corrected after the abandonment of *de jure* segregation, can it be asserted with any degree of confidence that the past discrimination is no longer playing a proximate role. Thus, allocation of the burden of proof foreordains the result in almost all of the "vestige of past discrimination" cases. If, as is normally the case under our equal protection jurisprudence (and in the law generally), we require the plaintiffs to establish the asserted facts entitling them to relief—that the racial imbalance they wish corrected is at least in part the vestige of an old *de jure* system—the plaintiffs will almost always lose. Conversely, if we alter our normal approach and require the school authorities to establish the negative—that the imbalance is not attributable to their past discrimination—the plaintiffs will almost always win. . . .

. . . Our post-*Green* cases provide that, once state-enforced school segregation is shown to have existed in a jurisdiction in 1954, there arises a presumption, effectively irrebuttable (because the school district cannot prove the negative), that any current racial imbalance is the product of that violation, at least if the imbalance has continuously existed [citing *Swann* and *Keyes*]. . . .

But granting the merits of this approach at the time of *Green*, it is now 25 years later. "From the very first, federal supervision of local school systems was intended as a *temporary* measure to remedy past discrimination." *Dowell* . . . (emphasis added). We envisioned it as temporary partly because "[n]o single tradition in public education is more deeply rooted than local control over the operation of schools," . . . *Milliken I* . . . But we also envisioned it as temporary, I think, because the rational basis for the extraordinary presumption of causation simply must dissipate as the *de jure* system and the school boards who produced it recede further into the past. Since a multitude of private factors has shaped school systems in the years after abandonment of *de jure* segregation— normal migration, population growth (as in this case), "white flight" from the inner cities, increases in the costs of new facilities—the percentage of the current makeup of school systems attributable to the prior, government-enforced discrimination has di-

minished with each passing year, to the point where it cannot realistically be assumed to be a significant factor.

* * *

Justice Souter, concurring.

* * *

We recognize that although demographic changes influencing the composition of a school's student population may well have no causal link to prior *de jure* segregation, judicial control of student assignments may still be necessary to remedy persisting vestiges of the unconstitutional dual system, such as remaining imbalance in faculty assignments. . . . This is, however, only one of several possible causal relationships between or among unconstitutional acts of school segregation and various *Green*-type factors. I think it is worth mentioning at least two others: the dual school system itself as a cause of the demographic shifts with which the district court is faced when considering a partial relinquishment of supervision, and a *Green*-type factor other than student assignments as a possible cause of imbalanced student assignment patterns in the future.

The first would occur when demographic change toward segregated residential patterns is itself caused by past school segregation and the patterns of thinking that segregation creates. Such demographic change is not an independent, supervening cause of racial imbalance in the student body, and we have said before that when demographic change is not independent of efforts to segregate, the causal relationship may be considered in fashioning a school desegregation remedy. . . .

The second and related causal relationship would occur after the district court has relinquished supervision over a remedied aspect of the school system, when future imbalance in that remedied *Green*-type factor (here, student assignments) would be caused by remaining vestiges of the dual system. Even after attaining compliance as to student composition, other factors such as racial composition of the faculty, quality of the physical plant, or per-pupil expenditures may leave schools racially identifiable. . . . If such other factors leave a school identifiable as "black," as soon as the district court stops supervising student assignments, nearby white parents may move in the direction of racially identifiable "white" schools, or may simply move their children into these schools. In such a case, the vestige of discrimination in one factor will act as an incubator for resegregation in others. Before a district court ends its supervision of student assignments, then, it should make a finding that there is no immediate threat of unremedied *Green*-type factors causing population or student enrollment changes that in turn may imbalance student composition in this way. And, because the district court retains jurisdiction over the case, it should of course reassert control over student assignments if it finds that this does happen.

Justice Blackmun, with whom Justice Stevens and Justice O'Connor join, concurring in the judgment.

It is almost 38 years since this Court decided *Brown v. Board of Education.* . . . In those 38 years the students in DeKalb County, Ga., never have attended a desegregated school system even for one day. The majority of "black" students never have attended a school that was not disproportionately black. Ignoring this glaring dual character of the DeKalb County School System (DCSS), part "white" and part "black," the District Court relinquished control over student assignments, finding that the school district had achieved "unitary status" in that aspect of the system. No doubt frustrated by the continued existence of duality, the Court of Appeals ordered the school district to take extraordinary measures to correct all manifestations of this racial imbalance. Both decisions, in my view, were in error, and I therefore concur in the Court's decision to vacate the judgment and remand the case.

. . . I agree that in some circumstances the District Court need not interfere with a particular portion of the school system, even while, in my view, it must retain jurisdiction over the entire system until all vestiges of state-imposed segregation have been eliminated. . . . I also agree that whether the District Court must order DCSS to balance student assignments depends on whether the current imbalance is traceable to unlawful state policy and on whether such an order is necessary to fashion an effective remedy. . . . Finally, I agree that the good faith of the school board is relevant to these inquiries. . . .

I

* * *

That the District Court's jurisdiction should continue until the school board demonstrates full compliance with the Constitution follows from the reasonable skepticism that underlies judicial supervision in the first instance. . . . It makes little sense, it seems to me, for the court to disarm itself by renouncing jurisdiction in one aspect of a school system, while violations of the Equal Protection Clause persist in other aspects of the same system. . . . It would seem especially misguided to place unqualified reliance on the school board's promises in this case, because the two areas of the school system the District Court found still in violation of the Constitution—expenditures and teacher assignments—are two of the *Green* factors over which DCSS exercises the greatest control.

* * *

II

A

DCSS claims that it need not remedy the segregation in DeKalb County schools because it was caused by demographic changes for which DCSS has no responsibility. It is not enough, however, for DCSS to establish that demographics exacerbated the problem; it must prove that its own policies did not contribute. Such contribution can occur in at least two ways: DCSS may have contributed to the demographic changes themselves, or it may have contributed directly to the racial imbalance in the schools.

To determine DCSS' possible role in encouraging the residential segregation, the court must examine the situation with special care. . . . [W]hat might seem to be purely private preferences in housing may in fact have been created, in part, by actions of the school district. . . .

This interactive effect between schools and housing choices may occur because many families are concerned about the racial composition of a prospective school and will make residential decisions accordingly. Thus, schools that are demonstrably black or white provide a signal to these families, perpetuating and intensifying the residential movement. . . .

In addition to exploring the school district's influence on residential segregation, the District Court here should examine whether school-board actions might have contributed to school segregation. . . .

B

The District Court's opinion suggests that it did not examine DCSS' actions in light of the foregoing principles. The court did note that the migration farther into the suburbs was accelerated by "white flight" from black schools and the "blockbusting" of former white neighborhoods. It did not examine, however, whether DCSS might have encouraged that flight by assigning faculty and principals so as to identify some schools as intended respectively for black students or white students. . . . Nor did the court consider how the placement of schools, the attendance zone boundaries, or the use of mobile classrooms might have affected residential movement. The court, in my view, failed to consider the many ways DCSS may have contributed to the demographic shifts.

Nor did the District Court correctly analyze whether DCSS' past actions had contributed to the school segregation independent of residential segregation. . . .

As the Court describes, the District Court placed great emphasis on its conclusion that DCSS, in response to the court order, had desegregated student assignment in 1969. DCSS' very first action taken in response to the court decree, however, was to shape attendance zones to result in two schools that were more than 50% black, despite a district-wide black student population of less than 6%. . . . Within a year, another school became majority black, followed by four others within the next two years. . . . Despite the existence of these schools, the District Court found that DCSS effectively had desegregated for a short period of time with respect to student assignment. . . . The District Court justified this finding by linking the school segregation exclusively to residential segregation existing prior to the court order. . . .

But residential segregation that existed prior to the desegregation decree cannot provide an excuse. It is not enough that DCSS adopt race-neutral policies in response to a court desegregation decree. Instead, DCSS is obligated to "counteract the continuing effects of past school segregation." *Swann* . . . Accordingly, the school district did not meet its affirmative duty simply by adopting a neighborhood-school plan, when already existing residential segregation inevitably perpetuated the dual system. . . .

Virtually all the demographic changes that DCSS claims caused the school segregation occurred after 1975. . . . Of particular relevance to the causation inquiry, then, are DCSS' actions prior to 1975; failures during that period to implement the 1969 decree render the school district's contentions that its noncompliance is due simply to demographic changes less plausible.

A review of the record suggests that from 1969 until 1975, DCSS failed to desegregate its schools. During that period, the number of students attending racially identifiable schools actually increased, and increased more quickly than the increase in black students. By 1975, 73% of black elementary students and 56% of black high school students were attending majority black schools, although the percentages of black students in the district population were just 20% and 13%, respectively. . . .

Of the 13 new elementary schools DCSS opened between 1969 and 1975, 6 had a total of four black students in 1975. . . . One of the two high schools DCSS opened had no black students at all. . . .

[I]n 1976, before most of the demographic changes, the District Court found that DCSS had not complied with the 1969 order to eliminate the vestiges of its former *de jure* school system. Indeed, the 1976 order found that DCSS had contributed to the growing racial imbalance of its schools. Given these determinations in 1976, the District Court, at a minimum, should have required DCSS to prove that, but for the demographic changes between 1976 and 1985, its actions would have been sufficient to "convert promptly to a system without a 'white' school and a 'Negro' school, but just schools." *Green.* . . . The available evidence suggests that this would be a difficult burden for DCSS to meet.

* * *

_____

NOTES AND QUESTIONS

1. Piecemeal Unitariness

Has the piecemeal approach to unitariness taken by the Court, meaning that lower courts may relinquish jurisdiction over one factor although vestiges of *de jure* segregation have not been dismantled with regard to other factors, ignore the command in *Green* that racial discrimination must be eliminated "root and branch," so that schools are no longer racially identifiable? *See* Orfield and Thronson, "Dismantling Desegregation: Uncertain Gains, Unexpected Costs," 42 *Emory L.J.* 759, 765 (1993), noting that in DeKalb County, "the various components of a desegregated school system established by *Green* were never present simultaneously in the district for even a single school year." *See Freeman v. Pitts* at 509 (Blackmun, J., concurring in the judgment) (noting that in the 38 years since *Brown*, "the students in

DeKalb County, Ga., never have attended a desegregated school system even for one day"). Although the Court in *Freeman* found that the racial identifiability of the schools in the northern (primarily white) and southern (primarily black) sections of DeKalb County resulted from "demographic shifts," the school district had never used the usual mechanisms for reducing segregation, such as pairing or clustering of schools, gerrymandering school assignment zones, or busing students. *See Swann v. Charlotte-Mecklenburg Board of Education*, 402 U.S. 1 (1971). Instead, the district relied on a majority-to-minority voluntary transfer program to bring about desegregation, without providing transportation for those African American students in the southern part of the county who might want to transfer to the predominantly white schools in the north.

2. Further Defining Standards for Determining Unitariness

Has the Court in *Freeman* further clarified the standards articulated in *Dowell* for determining when a school system has achieved unitariness? Inasmuch as the Court appears to endorse the addition of "quality of education" to the list of factors district courts may consider in determining unitariness, hasn't the Court made it more difficult for school districts to demonstrate that they have achieved a unitary system? What is the meaning of "quality of education"? If there are gaps in achievement scores on standardized tests between white students and African American students, has the school district failed to achieve unitary status with regard to this factor? *See, e.g., School Board v. Baliles*, 829 F.2d 1308, 1312 (4th Cir. 1987) (holding that "comparative dropout rates, graduation rates, and scores on standardized tests" could be considered in making the determination of whether a system is unitary). Has it left it to the discretion of district judges to determine both what a "quality education" is and whether the school district has met the requirements of unitariness regarding the quality of education? *See* Orfield and Thronson, *supra*, at 764. In *Belk v. Charlotte-Mecklenburg Board of Education*, the Fourth Circuit concluded that an analysis of disparities in student achievement may only be appropriate once the school system has achieved unitary status in other respects, inasmuch as it is inextricably intertwined with the other *Green* factors, particularly student assignment. 233 F.3d 232, 264 (4th Cir. 2000). The court quoted from the district court's opinion in *Swann:* "Until unlawful

segregation is eliminated, it is idle to speculate whether some of this [achievement] gap can be charged to racial differences or to 'socio-economic-cultural' lag." 306 F.Supp. 1299, 1309 (W.D. N.C. 1969). *But see United States v. City of Yonkers*, 197 F.3d 41, 54 (2d Cir. 1999) ("using achievement test scores as a measure, either direct or indirect, of a school system's movement away from segregation is deeply problematic"); *People Who Care v. Rockford Board of Educ.*, 111 F.3d 528, 537 (7th Cir. 1997) (noting that a number of variables, other than discrimination, account for the achievement gap).

3. The Problem of Determining Causation

May a school board return to a neighborhood school assignment plan once it shows that it has complied with the decree with regard to student assignments for a period of years, and has completely eliminated segregation in its schools, even though the schools will resegregate because of segregated housing patterns? Or do the Supreme Court decisions in *Dowell* and *Freeman* require that district courts first determine whether segregated housing patterns are themselves "vestiges" of *de jure* school segregation? If the latter, how does a district court determine whether, and how much, of the housing segregation is the result of past school desegregation rather than the result of "private decisionmaking and economics"? Does Justice Blackmun's concurring opinion bring any greater clarity to what it is a district court must do? In a large, highly residentially segregated urban area, just how does a district court determine the extent to which the segregated schools are (1) vestiges of the prior dual system, (2) due to actions of other officials that have intentionally segregated housing, (3) the result of the formerly dual school system's contribution to residential segregation, or (4) attributable to private decisions? For a discussion of the difficulty of determining causation, and separating official actions from private decisions during a period in which the metropolitan area has been undergoing a myriad of other changes, *see* Crump, "From *Freeman* to *Brown* and Back Again: Principle, Pragmatism, and Proximate Cause in the School Desegregation Decisions," 68 *Wash. L. Rev.* 753, 765 (1993).

4. Swann and Unitary Status

In most cases, either the school district has initiated the action seeking a declaration of unitary status in order to get the district court to relinquish its jurisdiction, or the school system claims that it has achieved unitary status as a defense when plaintiffs have returned to court seeking further desegregation. However, in a case decided nearly three decades after the Supreme Court's decision in *Swann v. Charlotte-Mecklenburg Bd. of Education,* 402 U.S. 1, 91 S.Ct. 1267, 28 L.Ed.2d 554 (1971), the school district reversed its position, and argued that the district court should not relinquish jurisdiction. *Capacchione v. Charlotte-Mecklenburg Schools,* 57 F.Supp. 2d 228 (W.D. N.C. 1999). The judge commented as follows:

> CMS [Charlotte-Mecklenburg Schools] takes a bizarre posture in this late phase of the case, arguing that it has not complied with the Court's orders. In 1965, when the *Swann* litigation began, CMS strongly resisted federal supervision, but today, the school system is equally fervent in resisting the removal of the desegregation order because it now wishes to use that order as a pretext to pursue race-conscious, diversity-enhancing policies in perpetuity. Consequently, CMS, the defendants, are now allied with the original class action plaintiffs who represent parents of black children in the district. . . .

57 F.Supp. 2d at 232. The district judge found that "CMS, to the extent reasonably practicable, has complied with the thirty-year-old desegregation order in good faith; that racial imbalances existing in schools today are no longer vestiges of the dual system; and that it is unlikely that the school board will return to an intentionally-segregative system," and ordered the school system to refrain from adopting any race-based policies promoting further racial balance. One study of the Charlotte-Mecklenburg district "found that if busing ended, more than half of the district's students would attend schools with little or no racial diversity because of housing patterns. The number of children attending mostly single-race schools would triple, to almost 50,000, from 17,000. . . ." Yellin, "By Court Order, Busing Ends Where It Began," *New York Times,* Sept. 11, 1999. *See* Boger, "Willful Colorblindness: The New Racial Piety and the Resegregation of Public Schools," 78 *N.C. L. Rev.* 1719 (2000) for a detailed analysis of *Capacchione v. Charlotte-Mecklenburg Schools.*

The Fourth Circuit reversed on the ground that the district court's findings did not support its conclusion that CMS had attained unitary status in all respects. *Belk v. Charlotte-Mecklenburg Board of Educ.,* 233 F.3d 232 (4th Cir. 2000). According to the inquiry courts are required to make under *Free-*man v. Pitts with respect to each of the *Green* factors, the circuit court found that the record was deficient with regard to whether CMS had achieved unitary status in the areas of student assignment, facilities, transportation, and student achievement. The court further noted that if the school system has not achieved unitary status in its entirety, *Freeman* requires that the "degree of interrelatedness existing between the various *Green* factors" be weighed, which the district court failed to do. *Id.* at 251. In particular, the court noted that, in accordance with *Swann,* the burden was on the plaintiffs to prove that the present racial isolation was not a vestige of past discrimination or that nothing can practically be done to remedy the vestiges of prior discrimination. *Id.* at 257.

5. Vestiges of De Jure Segregation and Stigma

Despite Justice Scalia's concern that the Court has never been able "to describe how one identifies a condition as the effluent of a violation, or how a 'vestige' or a 'remnant' of past discrimination is to be recognized," the *Freeman* majority still requires that the lower courts carefully assess the extent to which the vestiges of a dual system might still be present before a determination of unitariness. The Court suggests that the reason for ensuring that vestiges of the dual system are eliminated is "to insure that the principal wrong of the *de jure* system, the injuries and stigma inflicted upon the race disfavored by the violation, is no longer present," quoting *Brown I:* "To separate [black students] from others of similar age and qualifications solely because of their race generates a feeling of inferiority as to their status in the community that may affect their hearts and minds in a way unlikely ever to be undone." *Freeman v. Pitts,* 503 U.S. at 485, 112 S. Ct. at 1443. However, the Court does not consider that the racial identifiability of schools alone will cause stigmatic injury. *But see* Justice Marshall's dissenting opinion in *Dowell,* noting that because "state-sponsored segregation conveys a message of 'inferiority' . . ., formerly *de jure* segregated school districts [must] take all feasible steps to eliminate racially identifiable schools." 498 U.S. 237 at 251. Thus, "a desegregation decree cannot be lifted so long as conditions likely to inflict the stigmatic injury condemned in *Brown I* persist and there remain feasible methods of eliminating such conditions." *Id. See* Landsberg, "Equal Educational Opportunity: The Rehnquist Court Revisits *Green* and *Swann*," 42 *Emory L.J.* 821, 834–39 (1993), criticizing the Court's apparent focus on stigma as undercutting the logic of *Green* and *Brown*. "If students do not experience stigma by attending a *de facto* one-race school [in a formerly *de jure* system], then the fact that twenty years ago the school had been *de jure* segregated would hardly seem to affect the perception of this generation of elementary school students." *Id.* at 843.

C. Limits on Court-Ordered Remedies Other Than Pupil Reassignment

---

Missouri v. Jenkins
515 U.S. 70, 115 S. Ct. 2038, 132 L.Ed. 2d 63 (1995)

Chief Justice Rehnquist delivered the opinion of the Court.

As this school desegregation litigation enters its 18th year, we are called upon again to review the decisions of the lower courts. In this case, the State of Missouri has challenged the District Court's order of salary increases for virtually all instructional and noninstructional staff within the Kansas City, Missouri, School District (KCMSD) and the District Court's order requiring the State to continue to fund remedial "quality education" programs because student achievement levels were still "at or below national norms at many grade levels."

I

A general overview of this litigation is necessary for proper resolution of the issues upon which we granted certiorari. This case has been before the same United States District Judge since 1977. . . . Plaintiffs alleged that the State, the surrounding suburban school districts (SSD's), and various federal agencies had caused and perpetuated a system of racial segregation in the schools of the Kansas City metropolitan area. The District Court realigned the KCMSD as a nominal defendant. . . . The KCMSD brought a cross-claim against the State for its failure to eliminate the vestiges of its prior dual school system.

After a trial that lasted 7 1/2 months, the District Court dismissed the case against the federal defendants and the SSD's, but determined that the State

and the KCMSD were liable for an intradistrict violation, i. e., they had operated a segregated school system within the KCMSD. . . . Furthermore, the KCMSD and the State had failed in their affirmative obligations to eliminate the vestiges of the State's dual school system within the KCMSD. . . .

In June 1985, the District Court issued its first remedial order and established as its goal the "elimination of all vestiges of state imposed segregation." . . . The District Court determined that "segregation had caused a system wide reduction in student achievement in the schools of the KCMSD.". . . The District Court made no particularized findings regarding the extent that student achievement had been reduced or what portion of that reduction was attributable to segregation. The District Court also identified 25 schools within the KCMSD that had enrollments of 90% or more black students. . . .

The District Court, pursuant to plans submitted by the KCMSD and the State, ordered a wide range of quality education programs for all students attending the KCMSD. First, the District Court ordered that the KCMSD be restored to an AAA classification, the highest classification awarded by the State Board of Education. . . . Second, it ordered that the number of students per class be reduced so that the student-to-teacher ratio was below the level required for AAA standing. . . . The District Court justified its reduction in class size as

> "an essential part of any plan to remedy the vestiges of segregation in the KCMSD. Reducing class size will serve to remedy the vestiges of past segregation by increasing individual attention and instruction, as well as increasing the potential for desegregative educational experiences for KCMSD students by maintaining and attracting non-minority enrollment."

The District Court also ordered programs to expand educational opportunities for all KCMSD students: full-day kindergarten; expanded summer school; before- and after-school tutoring; and an early childhood development program. . . . Finally, the District Court implemented a state-funded "effective schools" program that consisted of substantial yearly cash grants to each of the schools within the KCMSD. . . . Under the "effective schools" program, the State was required to fund programs at both the 25 racially identifiable schools as well as the 43 other schools within the KCMSD. . . .

* * *

The District Court also set out to desegregate the KCMSD but believed that "to accomplish desegregation within the boundary lines of a school district whose enrollment remains 68.3% black is a difficult task." . . . Because it had found no interdistrict violation, the District Court could not order mandatory interdistrict redistribution of students between the KCMSD and the surrounding SSD's [*Milliken I*]. The District Court refused to order additional mandatory student reassignments because they would "increase the instability of the KCMSD and reduce the potential for desegregation." . . . [T]he District Court determined that "achievement of AAA status, improvement of the quality of education being offered at the KCMSD schools, magnet schools, as well as other components of this desegregation plan can serve to maintain and hopefully attract non-minority student enrollment." . . .

In November 1986, the District Court approved a comprehensive magnet school and capital improvements plan and held the State and the KCMSD jointly and severally liable for its funding. . . . The District Court adopted the magnet-school program to "provide a greater educational opportunity to all KCMSD students" . . . .

In June 1985, the District Court ordered substantial capital improvements to combat the deterioration of the KCMSD's facilities. In formulating its capital-improvements plan, the District Court dismissed as "irrelevant" the "State's argument that the present condition of the facilities [was] not traceable to unlawful segregation.". . . Instead, the District Court focused on its responsibility to "remedy the vestiges of segregation" and to "implement a desegregation plan which would maintain and attract non-minority enrollment." . . .

. . . The District Court rejected what it referred to as the "'patch and repair' approach proposed by the State" because it "would not achieve suburban comparability or the visual attractiveness sought by the Court as it would result in floor coverings with unsightly sections of mismatched carpeting and tile, and individual walls possessing different shades of paint." . . . The District Court reasoned that "if the KCMSD schools underwent the limited renovation proposed by the State, the schools would continue to be unattractive and substandard, and would certainly serve as a deterrent to parents considering enrolling their children in KCMSD schools." . . .

As part of its desegregation plan, the District Court has ordered salary assistance to the KCMSD. . . .

The District Court's desegregation plan has been described as the most ambitious and expensive remedial program in the history of school desegregation. . . . The annual cost per pupil at the KCMSD far exceeds that of the neighboring SSD's or of any school district in Missouri. Nevertheless, the KCMSD, which has pursued a "friendly adversary" relationship with the plaintiffs, has continued to propose ever more expensive programs. As a result, the desegregation costs have escalated and now are approaching an annual cost of $200 million. These massive expenditures have financed

> "high schools in which every classroom will have air conditioning, an alarm system, and 15 microcomputers; a 2,000-square-foot planetarium; green houses and vivariums; a 25-acre farm with an air-conditioned meeting room for 104 people; a Model United Nations wired for language translation; broadcast capable radio and television studios with an editing and animation lab; a temperature controlled art gallery; movie editing and screening rooms; a 3,500-square-foot dust-free diesel mechanics room; 1,875-square-foot elementary school animal rooms for use in a zoo project; swimming pools; and numerous other facilities."

Jenkins II, 495 U.S. at 77 (Kennedy, J., concurring in part and concurring in judgment).

Not surprisingly, the cost of this remedial plan has "far exceeded KCMSD's budget, or for that matter, its authority to tax." *Id.*, at 60. The State, through the operation of joint-and-several liability, has borne the brunt of these costs. . . .

II

With this background, we turn to the present controversy. First, the State has challenged the District Court's requirement that it fund salary increases for KCMSD instructional and noninstructional staff. . . . The State claimed that funding for salaries was beyond the scope of the District Court's remedial authority. . . . Second, the State has challenged the District Court's order requiring it to continue to fund the remedial quality education programs for the 1992–1993 school year. . . . The State contended that under *Freeman v. Pitts*, 503 U.S. 467, 118 L. Ed. 2d 108, 112 S. Ct. 1430 (1992), it had achieved partial unitary status with respect to the quality education programs already in place. As a result, the State argued that the District Court should have relieved it of responsibility for funding those programs.

The District Court rejected the State's arguments. It first determined that the salary increases were warranted because "high quality personnel are necessary not only to implement specialized desegregation programs intended to 'improve educational opportunities and reduce racial isolation,' but also to 'ensure that there is no diminution in the quality of its regular academic program.'"... Its "ruling [was] grounded in remedying the vestiges of segregation by improving the desegregative attractiveness of the KCMSD."...

The Court of Appeals for the Eighth Circuit affirmed....

* * *

Because of the importance of the issues, we granted certiorari to consider the following: (1) whether the District Court exceeded its constitutional authority when it granted salary increases to virtually all instructional and noninstructional employees of the KCMSD, and (2) whether the District Court properly relied upon the fact that student achievement test scores had failed to rise to some unspecified level when it declined to find that the State had achieved partial unitary status as to the quality education programs....

III

Respondents argue that the State may no longer challenge the District Court's remedy, and in any event, the propriety of the remedy is not before the Court....

... We conclude that a challenge to the scope of the District Court's remedy is fairly included in the question presented....

* * *

The ultimate inquiry is " 'whether the [constitutional violator] has complied in good faith with the desegregation decree since it was entered, and whether the vestiges of past discrimination have been eliminated to the extent practicable' " [Freeman v. Pitts].

Proper analysis of the District Court's orders challenged here, then, must rest upon their serving as proper means to the end of restoring the victims of discriminatory conduct to the position they would have occupied in the absence of that conduct and their eventual restoration of "state and local authori-

ties to the control of a school system that is operating in compliance with the Constitution."... We turn to that analysis.

The State argues that the order approving salary increases is beyond the District Court's authority because it was crafted to serve an "interdistrict goal," in spite of the fact that the constitutional violation in this case is "intradistrict" in nature.... The proper response to an intradistrict violation is an intradistrict remedy... that serves to eliminate the racial identity of the schools within the affected school district by eliminating, as far as practicable, the vestiges of *de jure* segregation in all facets of their operations....

Here, the District Court has found, and the Court of Appeals has affirmed, that this case involved no interdistrict constitutional violation that would support interdistrict relief.... Thus, the proper response by the District Court should have been to eliminate to the extent practicable the vestiges of prior *de jure* segregation within the KCMSD: a systemwide reduction in student achievement and the existence of 25 racially identifiable schools with a population of over 90% black students....

The District Court and Court of Appeals, however, have felt that because the KCMSD's enrollment remained 68.3% black, a purely intradistrict remedy would be insufficient.... But, as noted in *Milliken I*, ... we have rejected the suggestion "that schools which have a majority of Negro students are not 'desegregated' whatever the racial makeup of the school district's population and however neutrally the district lines have been drawn and administered."...

Instead of seeking to remove the racial identity of the various schools within the KCMSD, the District Court has set out on a program to create a school district that was equal to or superior to the surrounding SSD's. Its remedy has focused on "desegregative attractiveness," coupled with "suburban comparability."...

The purpose of desegregative attractiveness has been not only to remedy the systemwide reduction in student achievement, but also to attract nonminority students not presently enrolled in the KCMSD. This remedy has included an elaborate program of capital improvements, course enrichment, and extracurricular enhancement not simply in the formerly identifiable black schools, but in schools throughout the district....

We previously have approved of intradistrict desegregation remedies involving magnet schools. See,

e. g., *Milliken II*. . . . Magnet schools have the advantage of encouraging voluntary movement of students within a school district in a pattern that aids desegregation on a voluntary basis, without requiring extensive busing and redrawing of district boundary lines. . . . As a component in an intradistrict remedy, magnet schools also are attractive because they promote desegregation while limiting the withdrawal of white student enrollment that may result from mandatory student reassignment. . . .

The District Court's remedial plan in this case, however, is not designed solely to redistribute the students within the KCMSD in order to eliminate racially identifiable schools within the KCMSD. Instead, its purpose is to attract non-minority students from outside the KCMSD schools. But this interdistrict goal is beyond the scope of the intradistrict violation identified by the District Court. In effect, the District Court has devised a remedy to accomplish indirectly what it admittedly lacks the remedial authority to mandate directly: the interdistrict transfer of students. . . .

* * *

What we meant in *Milliken I* by an interdistrict violation was a violation that caused segregation between adjoining districts. Nothing in *Milliken I* suggests that the District Court in that case could have circumvented the limits on its remedial authority by requiring the State of Michigan, a constitutional violator, to implement a magnet program designed to achieve the same interdistrict transfer of students that we held was beyond its remedial authority. Here, the District Court has done just that: created a magnet district of the KCMSD in order to serve the interdistrict goal of attracting nonminority students from the surrounding SSD's and redistributing them within the KCMSD. The District Court's pursuit of "desegregative attractiveness" is beyond the scope of its broad remedial authority. . . .

. . . It is certainly theoretically possible that the greater the expenditure per pupil within the KCMSD, the more likely it is that some unknowable number of nonminority students not presently attending schools in the KCMSD will choose to enroll in those schools. Under this reasoning, however, every increased expenditure, whether it be for teachers, noninstructional employees, books, or buildings, will make the KCMSD in some way more attractive, and thereby perhaps induce nonminority students to enroll in its schools. But this rationale is not susceptible to any objective limitation. . . .

. . . [W]e conclude that the District Court's order of salary increases, which was "grounded in remedying the vestiges of segregation by improving the desegregative attractiveness of the KCMSD," . . . is simply too far removed from an acceptable implementation of a permissible means to remedy previous legally mandated segregation. . . .

Similar considerations lead us to conclude that the District Court's order requiring the State to continue to fund the quality education programs because student achievement levels were still "at or below national norms at many grade levels" cannot be sustained. The State does not seek from this Court a declaration of partial unitary status with respect to the quality education programs. . . . It challenges the requirement of indefinite funding of a quality education program until national norms are met, based on the assumption that while a mandate for significant educational improvement, both in teaching and in facilities, may have been justified originally, its indefinite extension is not.

. . . The basic task of the District Court is to decide whether the reduction in achievement by minority students attributable to prior *de jure* segregation has been remedied to the extent practicable. Under our precedents, the State and the KCMSD are "entitled to a rather precise statement of [their] obligations under a desegregation decree." [*Dowell*] Although the District Court has determined that "segregation has caused a system wide reduction in achievement in the schools of the KCMSD," . . . it never has identified the incremental effect that segregation has had on minority student achievement or the specific goals of the quality education programs. . . .

In reconsidering this order, the District Court should apply our three-part test from *Freeman v. Pitts*. The District Court should consider that the State's role with respect to the quality education programs has been limited to the funding, not the implementation, of those programs. As all the parties agree that improved achievement on test scores is not necessarily required for the State to achieve partial unitary status as to the quality education programs, the District Court should sharply limit, if not dispense with, its reliance on this factor. . . . Just as demographic changes independent of *de jure* segregation will affect the racial composition of student assignments, *Freeman*, so too will numerous external factors beyond the control of the KCMSD and the State affect minority student achievement. So long as these external factors are not the result of segregation, they do not figure in the remedial calculus.... Insistence upon academic goals unrelated to the effects of legal segregation unwarrantably postpones the day when the KCMSD will be able to operate on its own.

* * *

On remand, the District Court must bear in mind that its end purpose is not only "to remedy the violation" to the extent practicable, but also "to restore state and local authorities to the control of a school system that is operating in compliance with the Constitution." *Freeman.*

The judgment of the Court of Appeals is reversed.

It is so ordered.

Justice O'Connor, concurring.

... In the paradigmatic case of an interdistrict violation, where district boundaries are drawn on the basis of race, a regional remedy is appropriate to ensure integration across district lines. So, too, where surrounding districts contribute to the constitutional violation by affirmative acts intended to segregate the races.... Beyond that, interdistrict remedies are also proper where "there has been a constitutional violation within one district that produces a significant segregative effect in another district." ... Such segregative effect may be present where a predominantly black district accepts black children from adjacent districts, ... or perhaps even where the fact of intradistrict segregation actually causes whites to flee the district ..., for example, to avoid discriminatorily underfunded schools—and such actions produce regional segregation along district lines. In those cases, where a purely intradistrict violation has caused a significant interdistrict segregative effect, certain interdistrict remedies may be appropriate. Where, however, the segregative effects of a district's constitutional violation are contained within that district's boundaries, there is no justification for a remedy that is interdistrict in nature and scope.

Here, where the District Court found that KCMSD students attended schools separated by their race and that facilities have "literally rotted," ... it of course should order restorations and remedies that would place previously segregated black KCMSD students at par with their white KCMSD counterparts. The District Court went further, however, and ordered certain improvements to KCMSD as a whole, including schools that were not previously segregated; these district-wide remedies may also be justified (the State does not argue the point here) in light of the finding that segregation caused

"a system wide reduction in student achievement in the schools of the KCMSD,".... Such remedies obviously may benefit some who did not suffer under—and, indeed, may have even profited from—past segregation. There is no categorical constitutional prohibition on nonvictims enjoying the collateral, incidental benefits of a remedial plan designed "to restore the victims of discriminatory conduct to the position they would have occupied in the absence of such conduct." *Milliken I.* Thus, if restoring KCMSD to unitary status would attract whites into the school district, such a reversal of the white exodus would be of no legal consequence.

What the District Court did in this case, however, and how it transgressed the constitutional bounds of its remedial powers, was to make desegregative attractiveness the underlying goal of its remedy for the specific purpose of reversing the trend of white flight. However troubling that trend may be, remedying it is within the District Court's authority only if it is "directly caused by the constitutional violation." ...

This case, like other school desegregation litigation, is concerned with "the elimination of the discrimination inherent in the dual school systems, not with myriad factors of human existence which can cause discrimination in a multitude of ways on racial, religious, or ethnic grounds." *Swann v. Charlotte-Mecklenburg Bd. of Ed.,* 402 U.S. at 22. Those myriad factors are not readily corrected by judicial intervention, but are best addressed by the representative branches; time and again, we have recognized the ample authority legislatures possess to combat racial injustice. ...

In this case, it may be the "myriad factors of human existence" ... that have prompted the white exodus from KCMSD. ... The Court today discusses desegregative attractiveness only insofar as it supports the salary increase order under review, ... and properly refrains from addressing the propriety of all the remedies that the District Court has ordered, revised, and extended in the 18-year history of this case. These remedies may also be improper to the extent that they serve the same goals of desegregative attractiveness and suburban comparability that we hold today to be impermissible, and, conversely, the District Court may be able to justify some remedies without reliance on these goals. But these are questions that the Court rightly leaves to be answered on remand. ...

Justice Thomas, concurring.

It never ceases to amaze me that the courts are so willing to assume that anything that is predominantly black must be inferior. Instead of focusing on remedying the harm done to those black schoolchildren injured by segregation, the District Court here sought to convert the Kansas City, Missouri, School District (KCMSD) into a "magnet district" that would reverse the "white flight" caused by desegregation. In this respect, I join the Court's decision concerning the two remedial issues presented for review. I write separately, however, to add a few thoughts with respect to the overall course of this litigation. In order to evaluate the scope of the remedy, we must understand the scope of the constitutional violation and the nature of the remedial powers of the federal courts.

Two threads in our jurisprudence have produced this unfortunate situation, in which a District Court has taken it upon itself to experiment with the education of the KCMSD's black youth. First, the court has read our cases to support the theory that black students suffer an unspecified psychological harm from segregation that retards their mental and educational development. This approach not only relies upon questionable social science research rather than constitutional principle, but it also rests on an assumption of black inferiority. Second, we have permitted the federal courts to exercise virtually unlimited equitable powers to remedy this alleged constitutional violation. The exercise of this authority has trampled upon principles of federalism and the separation of powers and has freed courts to pursue other agendas unrelated to the narrow purpose of precisely remedying a constitutional harm.

I

A

The mere fact that a school is black does not mean that it is the product of a constitutional violation. A "racial imbalance does not itself establish a violation of the Constitution.". . . Instead, in order to find unconstitutional segregation, we require that plaintiffs "prove all of the essential elements of *de jure* segregation—that is, stated simply, a current condition of segregation resulting from intentional state action directed specifically to the [allegedly segregated] schools." *Keyes.* . . .

In the present case, the District Court inferred a continuing constitutional violation from two pri-

mary facts: the existence of *de jure* segregation in the KCMSD prior to 1954, and the existence of *de facto* segregation today. . . . The District Court also concluded that because of the KCMSD's failure to "become integrated on a system-wide basis," the dual system still exerted "lingering effects" upon KCMSD black students, whose "general attitude of inferiority" produced "low achievement . . . which ultimately limits employment opportunities and causes poverty." . . .

Without more, the District Court's findings could not have supported a finding of liability against the State. It should by now be clear that the existence of one-race schools is not by itself an indication that the State is practicing segregation. . . . The continuing "racial isolation" of schools after *de jure* segregation has ended may well reflect voluntary housing choices or other private decisions. Here, for instance, the demography of the entire KCMSD has changed considerably since 1954. . . . That certain schools are overwhelmingly black in a district that is now more than two-thirds black is hardly a sure sign of intentional state action.

. . . The District Court therefore rested the State's liability on the simple fact that the State had intentionally created the dual school system before 1954, and had failed to fulfill "its affirmative duty of disestablishing a dual school system subsequent to 1954." . . .

In order for a "vestige" to supply the ground for an exercise of remedial authority, it must be clearly traceable to the dual school system. . . . District courts must not confuse the consequences of *de jure* segregation with the results of larger social forces or of private decisions. . . . As state-enforced segregation recedes further into the past, it is more likely that "these kinds of continuous and massive demographic shifts," *Freeman*, will be the real source of racial imbalance or of poor educational performance in a school district. And as we have emphasized, "it is beyond the authority and beyond the practical ability of the federal courts to try to counteract" these social changes. . . .

When a district court holds the State liable for discrimination almost 30 years after the last official state action, it must do more than show that there are schools with high black populations or low test scores. . . . I do not doubt that Missouri maintained the despicable system of segregation until 1954. But I question the District Court's conclusion that because the State had enforced segregation until 1954, its actions, or lack thereof, proximately caused the "racial isolation" of the predominantly black schools in 1984. . . .

B

Without a basis in any real finding of intentional government action, the District Court's imposition of liability upon the State of Missouri improperly rests upon a theory that racial imbalances are unconstitutional. . . . This position appears to rest upon the idea that any school that is black is inferior, and that blacks cannot succeed without the benefit of the company of whites.

The District Court's willingness to adopt such stereotypes stemmed from a misreading of our earliest school desegregation case. In *Brown I*, the Court noted several psychological and sociological studies purporting to show that *de jure* segregation harmed black students by generating "a feeling of inferiority" in them. Seizing upon this passage in *Brown I*, the District Court asserted that "forced segregation ruins attitudes and is inherently unequal." . . . The District Court suggested that this inequality continues in full force even after the end of *de jure* segregation. . . . As the District Court later concluded, compensatory educational programs were necessary "as a means of remedying many of the educational problems which go hand in hand with racially isolated minority student populations." . . . Such assumptions and any social science research upon which they rely certainly cannot form the basis upon which we decide matters of constitutional principle.[2]

. . . *Brown I* did not say that "racially isolated" schools were inherently inferior; the harm that it identified was tied purely to *de jure* segregation, not *de facto* segregation. Indeed, *Brown I* itself did not need to rely upon any psychological or social-science research in order to announce the simple, yet fundamental, truth that the government cannot discriminate among its citizens on the basis of race. . . .

Segregation was not unconstitutional because it might have caused psychological feelings of inferiority. Public school systems that separated blacks and provided them with superior educational resources—making blacks "feel" superior to whites sent to lesser schools—would violate the Fourteenth Amendment, whether or not the white students felt stigmatized, just as do school systems in which the positions of the races are reversed. Psychological injury or benefit is irrelevant to the question whether state actors have engaged in intentional discrimination—the critical inquiry for ascertaining violations of the Equal Protection Clause. . . .

Regardless of the relative quality of the schools, segregation violated the Constitution because the State classified students based on their race. Of course, segregation additionally harmed black students by relegating them to schools with substandard facilities and resources. But neutral policies, such as local school assignments, do not offend the Constitution when individual private choices concerning work or residence produce schools with high black populations. . . . The Constitution does not prevent individuals from choosing to live together, to work together, or to send their children to school together, so long as the State does not interfere with their choices on the basis of race.

Given that desegregation has not produced the predicted leaps forward in black educational achievement, there is no reason to think that black students cannot learn as well when surrounded by members of their own race as when they are in an integrated environment. . . .

II

* * *

Two clear restraints on the use of the equity power—federalism and the separation of powers—derive from the very form of our Government. Federal courts should pause before using their inherent eq-

---

[2]The studies cited in *Brown I* have received harsh criticism. See, e.g., Yudof, "School Desegregation: Legal Realism, Reasoned Elaboration, and Social Science Research in the Supreme Court," 42 *Law & Contemp. Prob.* 57, 70 (1978); L. Graglia, *Disaster by Decree: The Supreme Court Decisions on Race and the Schools* 27–28 (1976). Moreover, there simply is no conclusive evidence that desegregation either has sparked a permanent jump in the achievement scores of black children, or has remedied any psychological feelings of inferiority black schoolchildren might have had. See, e.g., Bradley & Bradley, "The Academic Achievement of Black Students in Desegregated Schools," 47 *Rev. Educational Research* 399 (1977); N. St. John, *School Desegregation: Outcomes for Children* (1975); Epps, "The Impact of School Desegregation on Aspirations, Self-Concepts and Other Aspects of Personality," 39 *Law & Contemp. Prob.* 300 (1975). *Contra*, Crain & Mahard, "Desegregation and Black Achievement: A Review of the Research," 42 *Law & Contemp. Prob.* 17 (1978); Crain & Mahard, "The Effect of Research Methodology on Desegregation-Achievement Studies: A Meta-Analysis," 88 *Am. J. of Sociology* 839 (1983). Although the gap between black and white test scores has narrowed over the past two decades, it appears that this has resulted more from gains in the socioeconomic status of black families than from desegregation. See Armor, "Why Is Black Educational Achievement Rising?," 108 *The Public Interest* 65, 77–79 (1992).

uitable powers to intrude into the proper sphere of the States. We have long recognized that education is primarily a concern of local authorities. . . . A structural reform decree eviscerates a State's discretionary authority over its own program and budgets and forces state officials to reallocate state resources and funds to the desegregation plan at the expense of other citizens, other government programs, and other institutions not represented in court. . . .

. . . [T]he District Court failed to target its equitable remedies in this case specifically to cure the harm suffered by the victims of segregation. Of course, the initial and most important aspect of any remedy will be to eliminate any invidious racial distinctions in matters such as student assignments, transportation, staff, resource allocation, and activities. This element of most desegregation decrees is fairly straightforward and has not produced many examples of overreaching by the district courts. It is the "compensatory" ingredient in many desegregation plans that has produced many of the difficulties in the case before us.

* * *

Of course, a district court may see fit to order necessary remedies that have the side effect of benefiting those who were not victims of segregation. But the court cannot order broad remedies that indiscriminately benefit a school district as a whole, rather than the individual students who suffered from discrimination. . . .

To ensure that district courts do not embark on such broad initiatives in the future, we should demand that remedial decrees be more precisely designed to benefit only those who have been victims of segregation. . . . In the absence of special circumstances, the remedy for *de jure* segregation ordinarily should not include educational programs for students who were not in school (or were even alive) during the period of segregation. . . .

* * *

Justice Souter, with whom Justice Stevens, Justice Ginsburg and Justice Breyer join, dissenting.

The Court's process of orderly adjudication has broken down in this case. The Court disposes of challenges to only two of the District Court's many discrete remedial orders by declaring that the District Court erroneously provided an interdistrict remedy for an intradistrict violation. In doing so, it resolves a foundational issue going to one element of the District Court's decree that we did not accept for review in this case, that we need not reach in order

to answer the questions that we did accept for review, and that we specifically refused to consider when it was presented in a prior petition for certiorari. Since, under these circumstances, the respondent school district and pupils naturally came to this Court without expecting that a fundamental premise of a portion of the District Court's remedial order would become the focus of the case, the essence of the Court's misjudgment in reviewing and repudiating that central premise lies in its failure to have warned the respondents of what was really at stake. This failure lulled the respondents into addressing the case without sufficient attention to the foundational issue, and their lack of attention has now infected the Court's decision.

No one on the Court has had the benefit of briefing and argument informed by an appreciation of the potential breadth of the ruling. The deficiencies from which we suffer have led the Court effectively to overrule a unanimous constitutional precedent of 20 years standing, which was not even addressed in argument, was mentioned merely in passing by one of the parties, and discussed by another of them only in a misleading way.

The Court's departures from the practices that produce informed adjudication would call for dissent even in a simple case. But in this one, with a trial history of more than 10 years of litigation, the Court's failure to provide adequate notice of the issue to be decided (or to limit the decision to issues on which certiorari was clearly granted) rules out any confidence that today's result is sound, either in fact or in law.

I

* * *

. . . [T]he State presented, and we agreed to review, these two questions:

"1. Whether a remedial educational desegregation program providing greater educational opportunities to victims of past *de jure* segregation than provided anywhere else in the country nonetheless fails to satisfy the Fourteenth Amendment (thus precluding a finding of partial unitary status) solely because student achievement in the District, as measured by results on standardized test scores, has not risen to some unspecified level?

"2. Whether a federal court order granting salary increases to virtually every employee of a school district—including non-instructional personnel—as a part of a school desegregation remedy conflicts with applicable decisions of this court which require that remedial components must directly address and relate to the constitutional violation and be tailored to cure the condition that offends the Constitution?" . . .

These questions focus on two discrete issues: the extent to which a district court may look at students' test scores in determining whether a school district has attained partial unitary status as to its *Milliken II* educational programs, and whether the particular salary increases ordered by the District Court constitute a permissible component of its remedy.

The State did not go beyond these discrete issues, and it framed no broader, foundational question about the validity of the District Court's magnet concept. The Court decides, however, that it can reach that question of its own initiative. . . .

II

A

The test score question as it comes to us is one of word play, not substance. While the Court insists that the District Court's Order of June 17, 1992 (the only order relevant to the test score question on review here), "required the State to continue to fund the quality education programs because student achievement levels [in the KCMSD] were still 'at or below national norms at many grade levels' . . .," that order contains no discussion at all of student achievement levels in the KCMSD in comparison to national norms, and in fact does not explicitly address the subject of partial unitary status. . . . The reference to test scores "at or below national norms" comes from an entirely different and subsequent order of the District Court (dated Apr. 16, 1993) which is not under review. . . . In any event, what is important here is that none of the District Court's or Court of Appeals's opinions or orders requires a certain level of test scores before unitary status can be found, or indicates that test scores are the only thing standing between the State and a finding of unitary status as to the KCMSD's *Milliken II* programs. . . .

If, then, test scores do not explain why there was no finding of unitary status as to the *Milliken II* programs, one may ask what does explain it. The answer is quite straightforward. The Court of Appeals refused to order the District Court to enter a finding of partial unitary status as to the KCMSD's *Milliken II* programs . . . simply because the State did not attempt to make the showing required for that re-

lief. . . . [W]e have established a clear set of procedures to be followed by governmental entities seeking the partial termination of a desegregation decree. In *Freeman v. Pitts*, we held that "the duty and responsibility of a school district once segregated by law is to take all steps necessary to eliminate the vestiges of the unconstitutional *de jure* system." . . . Accordingly, before a district court may grant a school district (or other governmental entity) partial release from a desegregation decree, it must first consider "whether there has been full and satisfactory compliance with the decree in those aspects of the system where supervision is to be withdrawn. . . ." Full and satisfactory compliance, we emphasized in *Freeman*, is to be measured by " ' whether the vestiges of past discrimination have been eliminated to the extent practicable.' " . . . The district court must then consider "whether retention of judicial control is necessary or practicable to achieve compliance with the decree in other facets of the school system; and whether the school district [or other governmental entity] has demonstrated, to the public and to the parents and students of the once disfavored race, its good-faith commitment to the whole of the court's decree and to those provisions of the law and the Constitution that were the predicate for judicial intervention in the first instance." . . . The burden of showing that these conditions to finding partial unitary status have been met rests (as one would expect) squarely on the constitutional violator who seeks relief from the existing remedial order. . . .

While the Court recognizes the three-part showing that the State must make under *Freeman* in order to get a finding of partial unitary status, it fails to acknowledge that the State did not even try to make a *Freeman* showing in the litigation leading up to the District Court's Order of June 17, 1992. . . .

The State did not claim that implementation of the *Milliken II* component of the decree had remedied the reduction in student achievement in the KCMSD to the extent practicable; it simply argued that various *Milliken II* programs had been implemented. . . . [T]he State's expert witness . . . said nothing about the effects of those programs on student achievement, and in fact admitted on cross-examination that he did not have an opinion as to whether the programs had remedied to the extent practicable the reduction in student achievement caused by the segregation in the KCMSD. . . .

Nor did the State focus on its own good faith in complying with the District Court's decree; it emphasized instead the district's commitment to the decree and to the constitutional provisions on which the decree rested. . . . The State, indeed, said nothing to contradict the very findings made elsewhere by the District Court that have called the State's own commitment to the success of the decree into question. . . .

Thus, it was the State's failure to meet or even to recognize its burden under *Freeman* that led the Court of Appeals to reject the suggestion that it make a finding of partial unitary status as to the district's *Milliken II* education programs. . . .

Examining only the first *Freeman* prong, there can be no doubt that the Court of Appeals was correct. *Freeman* and *Dowell* make it entirely clear that the central focus of this prong of the unitary status enquiry is on effects: to the extent reasonably possible, a constitutional violator must remedy the ills caused by its actions before it can be freed of the court-ordered obligations it has brought upon itself. . . .

Looking ahead, if indeed the State believes itself entitled to a finding of partial unitary status on the subject of educational programs, there is an orderly procedural course for it to follow. It may frame a proper motion for partial unitary status, and prepare to make a record sufficient to allow the District Court and the Court of Appeals to address the continued need for and efficacy of the *Milliken II* programs.

In the development of a proper unitary status record, test scores will undoubtedly play a role. It is true, as the Court recognizes, that all parties to this case agree that it would be error to require that the students in a school district attain the national average test score as a prerequisite to a finding of partial unitary status, if only because all sorts of causes independent of the vestiges of past school segregation might stand in the way of the goal. That said, test scores will clearly be relevant in determining whether the improvement programs have cured a deficiency in student achievement to the practicable extent. . . . While the significance of scores is thus open to judgment, the judgment is not likely to be very sound unless it is informed by more of a record than we have in front of us, and the Court's admonition that the District Court should "sharply limit" its reliance on test scores, should be viewed in this light.

B

The other question properly before us has to do with the propriety of the District Court's recent salary orders. While the Court suggests otherwise, the District Court did not ground its orders of salary increases solely on the goal of attracting students back to the KCMSD. From the start, the District Court has consistently treated salary increases as an important element in remedying the systemwide reduction in student achievement resulting from segregation in the KCMSD. . . . The only issue, then, is whether the salary increases ordered by the District Court have been reasonably related to achieving that goal, keeping in mind the broad discretion enjoyed by the District Court in exercising its equitable powers.

The District Court first ordered KCMSD salary increases, limited to teachers, in 1987, basing its decision on the need to raise the level of student achievement. "It is essential that the KCMSD have sufficient revenues to fund an operating budget which can provide quality education, including a high quality faculty." . . . The State raised no objection to the District Court's order. . . .

When the District Court's 1987 order expired in 1990, all parties, including the State, agreed to a further order increasing salaries for both instructional and noninstructional personnel through the 1991–1992 school year. . . . In 1992 the District Court merely ordered that salaries in the KCMSD be maintained at the same level for the following year, rejecting the State's argument that desegregation funding for salaries should be discontinued. . . .

It is the District Court's 1992 and 1993 orders that are before us, and it is difficult to see how the District Court abused its discretion in either instance. The District Court had evidence in front of it that adopting the State's position and discontinuing desegregation funding for salary levels would result in their abrupt drop to 1986–1987 levels, with the resulting disparity between teacher pay in the district and the nationwide level increasing to as much as 40 to 45 percent, and a mass exodus of competent employees likely taking place. . . .

Indeed, the Court does not question the District Court's salary orders insofar as they relate to the objective of raising the level of student achievement in the KCMSD, but rather overlooks that basis for the orders altogether. The Court suggests that the District Court rested its approval of salary increases only on the object of drawing students into the district's schools, and rejects the increases for that reason. It seems clear, however, that the District Court and the Court of Appeals both viewed the salary orders as serving two complementary but distinct purposes, and to the extent that the District Court concludes on remand that its salary orders are justified by reference to the quality of education alone, nothing in the Court's opinion precludes those orders from remaining in effect.

III

The two discrete questions that we actually accepted for review are, then, answerable on their own terms without any need to consider whether the District Court's use of the magnet school concept in its remedial plan is itself constitutionally vulnerable. The capacity to deal thus with the questions raised, coupled with the unfairness of doing otherwise without warning, are enough to demand a dissent.

But there is more to fuel dissent. On its face, the Court's opinion projects an appealing pragmatism in seeming to cut through the details of many facts by applying a rule of law that can claim both precedential support and intuitive sense, that there is error in imposing an interdistrict remedy to cure a merely intradistrict violation. Since the District Court has consistently described the violation here as solely intradistrict, and since the object of the magnet schools under its plan includes attracting students into the district from other districts, the Court's result seems to follow with the necessity of logic, against which arguments about detail or calls for fair warning may not carry great weight.

The attractiveness of the Court's analysis disappears, however, as soon as we recognize two things. First, the District Court did not mean by an "intradistrict violation" what the Court apparently means by it today. The District Court meant that the violation within the KCMSD had not led to segregation outside of it, and that no other school districts had played a part in the violation. It did not mean that the violation had not produced effects of any sort beyond the district. Indeed, the record that we have indicates that the District Court understood that the violation here did produce effects spanning district borders and leading to greater segregation within the KCMSD, the reversal of which the District Court

sought to accomplish by establishing magnet schools.[4] Insofar as the Court assumes that this was not so in fact, there is at least enough in the record to cast serious doubt on its assumption. Second, the Court violates existing case law even on its own apparent view of the facts, that the segregation violation within the KCMSD produced no proven effects, segregative or otherwise, outside it. Assuming this to be true, the Court's decision that the rule against interdistrict remedies for intradistrict violations applies to this case, solely because the remedy here is meant to produce effects outside the district in which the violation occurred, is flatly contrary to established precedent.

A

* * *

The Court . . . rejects the findings of the District Court, endorsed by the Court of Appeals, that segregation led to white flight from the KCMSD, and does so at the expense of another accepted norm of our appellate procedure. We have long adhered to the view that "[a] court of law, such as this Court is, rather than a court for correction of errors in factfinding, cannot undertake to review concurrent findings of fact by two courts below in the absence of a very obvious and exceptional showing of error." . . . The Court fails to show any exceptional circumstance present here, however: it relies on a "contradiction" that is not an obvious contradiction at all, and on an arbitrary "supposition" that " 'white flight' may result from desegregation, not *de jure* segregation," a supposition said to be bolstered by the District Court's statement that there was "an abundance of evidence that many residents of the KCMSD left the district and moved to the suburbs because of the district's efforts to integrate its schools." . . .

The doubtful contradiction is said to exist between the District Court's findings, on the one hand, that segregation caused white flight to the SSD's, and the Court of Appeals's conclusion, on the other, that the District Court " 'made specific findings that

---

[4]This was not the only, or even the principal, purpose of the magnet schools. The District Court found that magnet schools would assist in remedying the deficiencies in student achievement in the KCMSD. Moreover, while the Court repeatedly describes the magnet school program as looking beyond the boundaries of the district, the program is primarily aimed not at drawing back white children whose parents have moved to another district, but rather at drawing back children who attend private schools while living within the geographical confines of the KCMSD, whose population remains majority white, *Jenkins v. Missouri*, 855 F.2d 1295, 1302–1303 (CA8 1988). . . . ("Most importantly, the Court believes that the proposed magnet plan is so attractive that it would draw non-minority students from the private schools who have abandoned or avoided the KCMSD, and draw in additional non-minority students from the suburbs"). As such, a substantial impetus for the District Court's remedy does not consider the world beyond district boundaries at all, and much of the Court's opinion is of little significance to the case before it.

negate current significant interdistrict effects. . . . ' "
Any impression of contradiction quickly disappears,
however, when the Court of Appeals's statement is
read in context. . . .

Without the contradiction, the Court has nothing
to justify its rejection of the District Court's finding
that segregation caused white flight but its supposition that flight results from integration, not segregation. The supposition, and the distinction on which
it rests, are untenable. At the more obvious level,
there is in fact no break in the chain of causation
linking the effects of desegregation with those of segregation. There would be no desegregation orders
and no remedial plans without prior unconstitutional segregation as the occasion for issuing and
adopting them, and an adverse reaction to a desegregation order is traceable in fact to the segregation
that is subject to the remedy. When the Court quotes
the District Court's reference to abundant evidence
that integration caused flight to the suburbs, then, it
quotes nothing inconsistent with the District Court's
other findings that segregation had caused the flight.
The only difference between the statements lies in
the point to which the District Court happened to
trace the causal sequence.

The unreality of the Court's categorical distinction can be illustrated by some examples. There is no
dispute that before the District Court's remedial plan
was placed into effect the schools in the unreformed
segregated system were physically a shambles. . . .
The cost of turning this shambles into habitable
schools was enormous, as anyone would have seen
long before the District Court ordered repairs. . . .
Property tax-paying parents of white children, seeing
the handwriting on the wall in 1985, could well have
decided that the inevitable cost of cleanup would
produce an intolerable tax rate and could have
moved to escape it. The District Court's remedial orders had not yet been put in place. Was the white
flight caused by segregation or desegregation? The
distinction has no significance.

Another example makes the same point. After
Brown, white parents likely came to understand that
the practice of spending more on white schools than
on black ones would be stopped at some point. If
they were unwilling to raise all expenditures to
match the customary white school level, they must
have expected the expenditures on white schools to
drop to the level of those for the segregated black
schools or to some level in between. . . . If they thus
believed that the white schools would deteriorate

they might then have taken steps to establish private
white schools, starting a practice of local private education that has endured. Again, what sense does it
make to say of this example that the cause of white
private education was desegregation (not yet underway), rather than the segregation that led to it?

I do not claim that either of these possible explanations would ultimately turn out to be correct, for
any such claim would head me down the same road
the Court is taking, of resolving factual issues independently of the trial court without warning the respondents that the full evidentiary record bearing on
the issue should be identified for us. My point is only
that the Court is on shaky grounds when it assumes
that prior segregation and later desegregation are
separable in fact as causes of "white flight," that the
flight can plausibly be said to result from desegregation alone, and that therefore as a matter of fact the
"intradistrict" segregation violation lacked the relevant consequences outside the district required to
justify the District Court's magnet concept. With the
arguable plausibility of each of these assumptions seriously in question, it is simply rash to reverse the
concurrent factual findings of the District Court and
the Court of Appeals. . . .

The reality is that the Court today overturns the
concurrent factual findings of the District Court and
the Court of Appeals without having identified any
circumstance in the record sufficient to warrant such
an extraordinary course of action.

* * *

Justice Ginsburg, dissenting.

I join Justice Souter's illuminating dissent and emphasize a consideration key to this controversy.

The Court stresses that the present remedial programs have been in place for seven years. But compared to more than two centuries of firmly entrenched official discrimination, the experience with
the desegregation remedies ordered by the District
Court has been evanescent.

In 1724, Louis XV of France issued the Code Noir,
the first slave code for the Colony of Louisiana, an
area that included Missouri. . . . When Missouri entered the Union in 1821, it entered as a slave State.

Before the Civil War, Missouri law prohibited the
creation or maintenance of schools for educating
blacks: "No person shall keep or teach any school for
the instruction of negroes or mulattoes, in reading or
writing, in this State." . . .

Beginning in 1865, Missouri passed a series of
laws requiring separate public schools for blacks. . . .

The Missouri Constitution first permitted, then required, separate schools. . . .

After this Court announced its decision in *Brown v. Board of Education,*. . . . Missouri's Attorney General declared these provisions mandating segregated schools unenforceable. . . . The statutes were repealed in 1957 and the constitutional provision was rescinded in 1976. Nonetheless, 30 years after *Brown,* the District Court found that "the inferior education indigenous of the state-compelled dual school system has lingering effects in the Kansas City, Missouri School District." . . . . The District Court concluded that "the State . . . cannot defend its failure to affirmatively act to eliminate the structure and effects of its past dual system on the basis of restrictive state law." Just ten years ago, in June 1985, the District Court issued its first remedial order. . . .

Today, the Court declares illegitimate the goal of attracting nonminority students to the Kansas City, Missouri, School District, and thus stops the District Court's efforts to integrate a school district that was, in the 1984/1985 school year, sorely in need and 68.3% black. . . . Given the deep, inglorious history of segregation in Missouri, to curtail desegregation at this time and in this manner is an action at once too swift and too soon. . . .

NOTES AND QUESTIONS

1. Remedies with Interdistrict Effects After Jenkins

The Court notes that it has approved magnet schools as part of an intradistrict desegregation remedy because they "encourage voluntary movement of students . . . that aids desegregation on a voluntary basis, without requiring extensive busing and redrawing of district boundary lines," citing *Milliken II.* Why, then, does the majority find the KCMSD magnet school program, which might attract nonminority students from the surrounding suburban school districts or from private schools within KCMSD voluntarily, without involving mandatory student assignment across district lines, to be beyond the scope of the district court's remedial authority? Should lower courts have been able to anticipate this from the decision in *Milliken I* barring mandatory desegregation involving the "large-scale transportation of students" and "consolidation of 54 independent school districts historically administered as separate units into a vast new super school district," with

the attendant "problems in financing and operating this new school system," the creation of new attendance zones, and so on?

Should it make a difference in determining whether an intradistrict violation had interdistrict effects, if the effects were caused by *de jure* segregation (as suggested by the dissent, white flight may have resulted from the anticipation or fear of the fiscal or other impacts of desegregation) or were caused by court-ordered desegregation of KCMSD? Is the dissent correct that there is "no break in the chain of causation linking the effects of desegregation with those of segregation"?

2. Who Has the Burden Regarding a Claim of Unitariness?

Justice Souter, in his dissenting opinion, suggests that the state failed to make the requisite showing for a district court to grant partial release from a desegregation decree, that is, "whether the vestiges of past discrimination" as evidenced by student achievement had been "eliminated to the extent practicable," and whether the state had demonstrated "its good-faith commitment to the whole of the court's decree," citing *Freeman v. Pitts.* Has the majority shifted the burden to the plaintiffs to show the need for continued judicial supervision?

3. The Future of Milliken II–type Remedies after Jenkins

The majority implies that before ordering educational programming designed to restore the victims of discrimination to the position they would have occupied in the absence of discrimination, as in *Milliken II,* the district court would have to show that the programs would remedy only the effects that *de jure* segregation may have had on achievement, separating out those effects from the effects of poverty, parental education and other social background factors, English language deficiencies, and even *de facto* segregation. What evidence could plaintiffs introduce to enable such a determination to be made? Do plaintiffs now have the burden of showing both how much of the gap in student achievement is a vestige of the dual system, and what kinds of programs would address only that increment?

4. The Court's View of Court-Enforced Desegregation Forty-Five Years After Brown

In reflecting on the Court's position in *Dowell, Freeman v. Pitts,* and *Jenkins,* do you think that the Court has decided that judicial efforts to end school segregation in the nearly forty-five years since *Brown* have been a failure? Consider these comments by Professor Chemerinsky:

> During the Vietnam War, Vermont Senator George Aiken said the United States should declare victory in Vietnam and withdraw. The Rehnquist Court is saying something very similar; it is declaring victory over the problem of school segregation and having the federal courts withdraw. They are saying this even though public schools in the United States are more segregated today than any other time since 1954 and even though today much less is spent, on average, on a black child's elementary and secondary education than on a white child's education in the United States.

Chemerinsky, "The Rehnquist Court & Justice: An Oxymoron?" 1 *Wash. U. J. L. & Pol'y* 37, 49 (1999). *See* Joondeph, "Review Essay: A Second Redemption?" 56 *Wash & Lee L. Rev.* 169, 197–201 (1999), arguing that although these three cases did not alter any of the "basic doctrinal principles in the area," they signaled a shift in the Court's emphasis from eliminating all vestiges of prior *de jure* segregation and ending the racial identifiability of the formerly dual system, to "the importance of returning public school systems to the control of local, politically accountable officials as soon as practicable." *See also* Boger, "Willful Colorblindness: The New Racial Piety and the Resegregation of Public Schools," 78 *N.C. L. Rev.*1719 (2000).

5. The Current Status of Desegregation

By the end of 1999, approximately forty-five school districts, including Oklahoma City, Oklahoma (*Dowell v. Board of Education*, 606 F.Supp. 1548 (W.D. Okla. 1985), *rev'd*, 890 F.2d 1483 (10th Cir. 1989), *rev'd*, 498 U.S. 237 (1991)), Denver, Colorado (*Keyes v. Congress of Hispanic Educators*, 902 F.Supp. 1274 (D. Colo. 1995)), Austin, Texas (*United States v. Overton*, 834 F.2d 1179 (5th Cir. 1987)), Buffalo, New York (*Arthur v. Nyquist*, 904 F. Supp. 112 (W.D.N.Y. 1995)), Wilmington, Delaware (*Coalition to Save Our Children v. State Board of Education*, 901 F. Supp. 784 (D. Del. 1995)), and Norfolk, Virginia (*Riddick v. School Board*, 627 F. Supp. 814 (E.D. Va. 1984), *aff'd*, 784 F.2d 521 (4th Cir. 1986)), DeKalb County, Georgia (*Freeman v. Pitts*, 503 U.S. 467 (1992); *Mills v. Freeman*, 942 F. Supp. 1449 (N.D. Ga. 1996)), Cleveland, Ohio (*Reed v. Rhodes*, 1 F.Supp. 2d 705 (N.D. Ohio, 1998)), had been released from court supervision. Pressley, "New Ways to Assign Students Sought After Order to End Busing," *Washington Post*, Nov. 8, 1999. *See also* Joondeph, "Review Essay: A Second Redemption?" 56 *Wash & Lee L. Rev.* 169 & n.1 (1999).

The vast majority of large urban school districts are now predominantly minority—whether due to white flight as a result of court-ordered desegregation, middle-class flight due to crime or deteriorating municipal services, demographic changes, economic changes, segregative housing practices, or a combination of these or other reasons. *See* Orfield and Yun, "Resegregation in American Schools," Table 4, http://www.law.harvard.edu/groups/civil-rights/publications/resegregation99.html, p.8. By the late 1980s, only 3.3 percent of white students attended schools in central city school districts. G. Orfield and F. Monfort, *Racial Change and Desegregation in Large School Districts* (1988). *See also* F. Welch and A. Light, *New Evidence on School Desegregation* (1987).

By 1970, court orders and the enforcement of the Civil Rights Act of 1964 had made the South the nation's most integrated region for both blacks and whites. Integration increased during the 1970s and 1980s, reaching a peak in 1988 with 43.5 percent of black students in majority white schools, followed by "an accelerating process of resegregation since the late 1980s." *See* Orfield and Yun, *supra*, at 12–13, and Figure 1 at 34. Indeed, between 1991 and 1996, the southern and border states became the regions with the largest increases in segregation. *Id.* at 19. Nationally, school segregation has followed a similar pattern. "The percent of African American students in majority white schools peaked in the early 1980s and declined to the levels of the 1960s by the 1996–97 school year." *Id.* at 13. The segregation of Latino students, on the other hand, has consistently increased since the 1960s. The most segregated states for black students today, in addition to four states of the old South (Mississippi, Alabama, Louisiana, and Texas), are Michigan, Illinois, New York, New Jersey, and California. The Northeast is the most segregated region for Latinos, followed by the South and the West. *Id.* at 22–26 and accompanying tables. While the average white student attends schools where the overwhelming majority of students are white, the racial composition of schools that nonwhite students attend are more likely to be multiracial. *Id.* at 13–16 and accompanying tables.

The Orfield and Yun study has also documented the strong relationship between segregation and poverty. Their analysis of data from the National Center for Educational Statistics indicates that "black and Latino students, on average, attend schools with more than twice as many poor classmates as white students and Asians and American Indian students are about halfway in-between. Latinos have the highest average percentage of impoverished classmates (46%), compared to 19% for whites." *Id.* at 16–19 and accompanying tables. Several studies measuring changes in segregation in large urban districts have found that African Americans enrolled in school systems with metropolitan-wide desegregation orders have remained very much more integrated than other school systems, except in a few cases where court-ordered desegregation plans began to be phased out. *See* Orfield and Yun, *supra*, at 20; G. Orfield and F. Monfort, *Racial Change and Desegregation in Large School Districts* (1988).

D. Limits on Voluntary Actions by School Boards to Reduce Segregation

1. Constitutionality of State Limits on Voluntary Actions by School Boards.

Washington v. Seattle School District No. 1
458 U.S. 457, 102 S.Ct. 3187, 73 L.Ed.2d 896 (1982).

Justice Blackmun delivered the opinion of the Court.

* * *

Seattle School District No. 1 (District), which is largely coterminous with the city of Seattle, Wash., is charged by state law with administering 112 schools and educating approximately 54,000 public school students. About 37% of these children are of Negro, Asian, American Indian, or Hispanic ancestry. Because segregated housing patterns in Seattle have created racially imbalanced schools, the District historically has taken steps to alleviate the isolation of minority students; since 1963, it has permitted students to transfer from their neighborhood schools to help cure the District's racial imbalance.

Despite these efforts, the District in 1977 came under increasing pressure to accelerate its program of desegregation. In response, the District's Board of Directors (School Board) enacted a resolution defining "racial imbalance" as "the situation that exists

when the combined minority student enrollment in a school exceeds the districtwide combined average by 20 percentage points, provided that the single minority enrollment . . . of no school will exceed 50 percent of the student body." 473 F.Supp. 996, 1006 (W.D. Wash. 1979). The District resolved to eliminate all such imbalance from the Seattle public schools by the beginning of the 1979–1980 academic year.

. . . The District . . . concluded that mandatory reassignment of students was necessary if racial isolation in its schools was to be eliminated. Accordingly, in March 1978, the School Board enacted the so-called "Seattle Plan" for desegregation. The plan, which makes extensive use of busing and mandatory reassignments, desegregates elementary schools by "pairing" and "triading" predominately minority with predominately white attendance areas, and by basing student assignments on attendance zones rather than on race. . . . The District represents that the plan results in the reassignment of roughly equal numbers of white and minority students, and allows most students to spend roughly half of their academic careers attending a school near their homes. . . .

The desegregation program, implemented in the 1978–1979 academic year, apparently was effective: the District Court found that the Seattle Plan "has substantially reduced the number of racially imbalanced schools in the district and has substantially reduced the percentage of minority students in those schools which remain racially imbalanced." 473 F.Supp., at 1007.

* * *

In late 1977, shortly before the Seattle Plan was formally adopted by the District, a number of Seattle residents who opposed the desegregation strategies being discussed by the School Board formed an organization called the Citizens for Voluntary Integration Committee (CiVIC). . . . CiVIC drafted a statewide initiative designed to terminate the use of mandatory busing for purposes of racial integration. This proposal, known as Initiative 350, provided that "no school board . . . shall directly or indirectly require any student to attend a school other than the school which is geographically nearest or next nearest the student's place of residence . . . and which offers the course of study pursued by such student. . . ." *See* Wash.Rev. Code §28A.26.010 (1981). The initiative then set out, however, a number of broad exceptions to this requirement: a student may be assigned beyond his neighborhood school if he "requires special education, care, or guidance," or if "there are health or safety hazards, either natural or man made, or physical barriers or obstacles . . . between the student's place of residence and the nearest or next nearest school," or if "the school nearest or next nearest to his place of residence is unfit or inadequate because of overcrowding, unsafe conditions or lack of physical facilities." *See ibid.* Initiative 350 also specifically proscribed use of seven enumerated methods of "indirec[t]" student assignment—among them the redefinition of attendance zones, the pairing of schools, and the use of "feeder" schools—that are a part of the Seattle Plan. *See* §28A.26.030. The initiative envisioned busing for racial purposes in only one circumstance: it did not purport to "prevent any court of competent jurisdiction from adjudicating constitutional issues relating to the public schools." *See* §28A.26.060.

. . . Initiative 350 passed by a substantial margin, drawing almost 66% of the vote statewide. The initiative failed to attract majority support in two state legislative districts, both in Seattle. In the city as a whole, however, the initiative passed with some 61% of the vote. Within the month, the District, together with the Tacoma and Pasco school districts, initiated this suit against the State in United States District Court for the Western District of Washington, challenging the constitutionality of Initiative 350 under the Equal Protection Clause of the Fourteenth Amendment. The United States and several community organizations intervened in support of the District; CiVIC intervened on behalf of the defendants.

. . . In our view, Initiative 350 must fall because it does "not attemp[t] to allocate governmental power on the basis of any general principle." *Hunter v. Erickson*, 393 U.S.[385 (1969)], at 395, 89 S.Ct., at 563 (Harlan, J., concurring). Instead, it uses the racial nature of an issue to define the governmental decision-making structure, and thus imposes substantial and unique burdens on racial minorities.

* * *

Noting that Initiative 350 nowhere mentions "race" or "integration," appellants suggest that the legislation has no racial overtones; they maintain that *Hunter* is inapposite because the initiative simply permits busing for certain enumerated purposes while neutrally forbidding it for all other reasons. We find it difficult to believe that appellants' analysis is seriously advanced, however, for despite its facial neutrality there is little doubt that the initiative was effectively drawn for racial purposes. Neither the initiative's sponsors, nor the District Court, nor the Court of Appeals had any difficulty perceiving the racial nature of the issue settled by Initiative 350. . . .

* * *

We are . . . satisfied that the practical effect of Initiative 350 is to work a reallocation of power of the kind condemned in *Hunter*. The initiative removes the authority to address a racial problem—and only a racial problem—from the existing decision-making body, in such a way as to burden minority interests. Those favoring the elimination of *de facto* school segregation now must seek relief from the state legislature, or from the statewide electorate. Yet authority over all other student assignment decisions, as well as over most other areas of educational policy, remains vested in the local school board. Indeed, by specifically exempting from Initiative 350's proscriptions most non-racial reasons for assigning students away from their neighborhood schools, the initiative expressly requires those championing school integration to surmount a considerably higher hurdle than persons seeking comparable legislative - action. . . .

. . . The issue here, after all, is not whether Washington has the authority to intervene in the affairs of local school boards; it is, rather, whether the State has exercised that authority in a manner consistent with the Equal Protection Clause. . . .

At the outset, it is irrelevant that the State might have vested all decision-making authority in itself, so long as the political structure it in fact erected imposes comparative burdens on minority interests; that much is settled by *Hunter*. . . . And until the passage of Initiative 350, Washington law in fact had established the local school board, rather than the State, as the entity charged with making decisions of the type at issue here. Like all 50 States, . . . Washington of course is ultimately responsible for providing education within its borders. . . . But Washington has chosen to meet its educational responsibilities primarily through "state and local officials, boards, and committees," §28A.02.020, and the responsibility to devise and tailor educational programs to suit local needs has emphatically been vested in the local school boards.

* * *

Given this statutory structure, we have little difficulty concluding that Initiative 350 worked a major reordering of the State's educational decision-making process. Before adoption of the initiative, the power to determine what programs would most appropriately fill a school district's educational needs—including programs involving student assignment and desegregation—was firmly committed to the local board's discretion. The question whether to provide an integrated learning environment rather than a system of neighborhood schools surely involved a decision of that sort. . . . After passage of Initiative 350, authority over all but one of those areas remained in the hands of the local board. By placing power over desegregative busing at the state level, then, Initiative 350 plainly "differentiates between the treatment of problems involving racial matters and that afforded other problems in the same area." . . .

To be sure, "the simple repeal or modification of desegregation or anti-discrimination laws, without more, never has been viewed as embodying a presumptively invalid racial classification." *Crawford v. Los Angeles Board of Education*, 458 U.S. 527, 539. . . .

Initiative 350, however, works something more than the "mere repeal" of a desegregation law by the political entity that created it. It burdens all future attempts to integrate Washington schools in districts throughout the State, by lodging decision-making authority over the question at a new and remote level of government. . . .

Accordingly, the judgment of the Court of Appeals is

Affirmed.

Justice Powell, with whom The Chief Justice, Justice Rehnquist, and Justice O'Connor join, dissenting.

The people of the State of Washington, by a two to one vote, have adopted a neighborhood school policy. The policy is binding on local school districts but in no way affects the authority of state or federal courts to order school transportation to remedy violations of the Fourteenth Amendment. Nor does the policy affect the power of local school districts to establish voluntary transfer programs for racial integration or for any other purpose.

In the absence of a constitutional violation, no decision of this Court compels a school district to adopt or maintain a mandatory busing program for racial integration. Accordingly, the Court does not hold that the adoption of a neighborhood school policy by local school districts would be unconstitutional. Rather, it holds that the adoption of such a policy at the *State* level—rather than at the local level—violates the Equal Protection Clause of the Fourteenth Amendment.

I dissent from the Court's unprecedented intrusion into the structure of a state government. The School Districts in this case were under no Federal Constitutional obligation to adopt mandatory busing programs. The State of Washington, the governmental body ultimately responsible for the provision of public education, has determined that certain mandatory busing programs are detrimental to the education of its children. . . .

* * *

The principles that should guide us in reviewing the constitutionality of Initiative 350 are well established. To begin with, we have never held, or even intimated, that absent a federal constitutional violation, a State must choose to treat persons differently on the basis of race. In the absence of a federal constitutional violation requiring race-specific remedies, a policy of strict racial neutrality by a State would violate no federal constitutional principle. . . .

In particular, a neighborhood school policy and a decision not to assign students on the basis of their race, does not offend the Fourteenth Amendment. The Court has never held that there is an affirmative duty to integrate the schools in the absence of a finding of unconstitutional segregation. . . . Indeed, even where desegregation is ordered because of a constitutional violation, the Court has never held that racial balance itself is a constitutional requirement. . . . And even where there have been segregated schools, once desegregation has been accomplished no further constitutional duty exists upon school boards or States to maintain integration. See *Pasadena City Board of Education v. Spangler*, 427 U.S. 424 . . . (1976).

Moreover, it is a well-established principle that the States have "extraordinarily wide latitude . . . in creating various types of political subdivisions and conferring authority upon them." *Holt Civic Club v. Tuscaloosa*, 439 U.S. 60, 71 . . . (1978). The Constitution does not dictate to the States a particular division of authority between legislature and judiciary or between state and local governing bodies. It does not define institutions of local government.

* * *

Application of these settled principles demonstrates the serious error of today's decision—an error that cuts deeply into the heretofore unquestioned right of a State to structure the decision-making authority of its government. In this case, by Initiative 350, the State has adopted a policy of racial neutrality in student assignments. The policy in no way interferes with the power of State or Federal Courts to remedy constitutional violations. And if such a policy had been adopted by any of the school districts in this litigation there could have been no question that the policy was constitutional.

The issue here arises only because the Seattle School District—in the absence of a then established State policy—chose to adopt race specific school assignments with extensive busing. It is not questioned that the District itself, at any time thereafter, could have changed its mind and cancelled its integration program without violating the Federal Constitution. Yet this Court holds that neither the legislature nor the people of the State of Washington could alter what the District had decided.

The Court argues that the people of Washington by Initiative 350 created a racial classification, and yet must agree that identical action by the Seattle School District itself would have created no such classification. This is not an easy argument to answer because it seems to make no sense. School boards are the creation of supreme State authority, whether in a State Constitution or by legislative enactment. Until today's decision no one would have questioned the authority of a State to abolish school boards altogether, or to require that they conform to any lawful State policy. And in the State of Washington, a neighborhood school policy would have been lawful.

Under today's decision this heretofore undoubted supreme authority of a State's electorate is to be curtailed whenever a school board—or indeed any other state board or local instrumentality—adopts a race specific program that arguably benefits racial minorities. Once such a program is adopted, *only* the local or subordinate entity that approved it will have authority to change it. The Court offers no authority or relevant explanation for this extraordinary subordination of the ultimate sovereign power of a State to act with respect to racial matters by subordinate bodies. It is a strange notion—alien to our system—that local governmental bodies can forever preempt the ability of a State—the sovereign power—to address a matter of compelling concern to the State. The Constitution of the United States does not require such a bizarre result.

* * *

NOTES AND QUESTIONS

1. Education as a State Function

The states have plenary power with regard to education, although most states have delegated considerable educational policy-making authority to local school districts. In doing so, however, states have "not surrendered their prerogatives, but have merely determined the machinery by which the state function shall be performed." E. Bolmeier, *The School in the Legal Structure* 63 (1968). Thus in most states the local school district is merely a subordinate arm of the state agency. The state legislature at any time can consolidate, merge, or eliminate school districts at will, without the consent of the districts. The powers of local boards may be changed at any time. Why then does the majority in *Seattle* hold that the state, through its voters, cannot decide that a neighborhood school assignment policy is the most appropriate educational policy and require local districts to carry out that policy?

2. Crawford *and Restrictions on Court-Ordered Busing*

Crawford v. Board of Education of Los Angeles, 458 U.S. 527, 102 S.Ct. 3211, 73 L.Ed.2d 948 (1982), was decided the same day as *Seattle*. *Crawford* involved a state constitutional amendment approved by California voters in a referendum that prevented state courts from using mandatory pupil reassignment and busing except where there was a violation of the Equal Protection Clause of the Fourteenth Amendment to the U.S. Constitution and where federal courts would be permitted to impose such a remedy. In other words, the amendment prevents the state courts from using busing to remedy state-created rights, a remedial technique previously upheld by the California courts where there was a finding of racial imbalance, regardless of its cause. *Jackson v. Pasadena City School District*, 59 Cal.2d 876, 31 Cal.Rptr. 606, 382 P.2d 878 (1963) (en banc). The Court upheld the California amendment. How can the *Seattle* and *Los Angeles* cases be distinguished? Why is the action of the California voters treated differently from that of the Washington voters? *See* Thro, "The Constitutionality of Eliminating De Facto Segregation in the Public Schools," 120 *Ed. Law Rep.* 895 (1997), arguing that the Court, in subsequent decisions, has effectively limited the scope of *Seattle*.

2. Federal Constitutional Limits on Voluntary Actions by School Boards. In *Regents of the University of California v. Bakke*, 438 U.S. 265, 98 S.Ct. 2733, 57 L.Ed.2d 750 (1978), the Court sharply divided over the constitutionality of an admissions

program at the University of California at Davis medical school designed to increase minority enrollment. Under this program, sixteen seats were set aside for members of minority groups, and applicants for those slots were considered separately from other applicants. Four justices would have upheld the program as constitutional, under an intermediate level of scrutiny, requiring that the classification have an important, articulated purpose, and that no individual or group be stigmatized by the program. Four other justices viewed the program as in violation of Title VI of the Civil Rights Act of 1964, and thus did not reach the issue of its constitutionality. The judgment of the Court striking down the program was controlled by Justice Powell, who alone among the justices determined that the program violated the Equal Protection Clause because it failed the strict scrutiny level of review. He argued that all racial classifications, even those that purported to benefit racial minorities, were suspect, and thus required a compelling justification. Absent findings by a judicial, legislative, or administrative body of specific instances of racial discrimination, the school could not adopt a program that remedied the effects of "societal discrimination" by imposing burdens on "other innocent individuals." 438 U.S. at 307. Justice Powell acknowledged that attainment of a diverse student body was a constitutionally permissible goal for an institution of higher education, based on those principles of academic freedom protected by the First Amendment that allow a university to make its own educational judgments, including selection of its student body. *Id*. at 311–12. Justice Powell concluded, however, that although university admissions programs may "take race into account in achieving the educational diversity valued by the First Amendment, . . . the assignment of a fixed number of places to a minority group is not a necessary means toward that end." Race or ethnic background may be treated as a "plus" in considering a particular applicant as long as it "does not insulate the individual from comparison with all other candidates for the available seats" and is not the decisive factor when compared with other qualities that are likely to enhance educational diversity. *Id*. at 316.

Subsequent to the *Bakke* decision, a majority of the Supreme Court, in several cases involving racial set-aside programs, applied the strict scrutiny standard of review to strike down the programs on the ground that such racial preferences were designed solely to remedy past societal discrimination, rather than being based on any specific findings of discrimination with regard to the particular governmental body involved. Moreover, even if there had been a compelling justification for these race-conscious remedies, they failed because they were not sufficiently narrowly tailored to remedy prior discrimination. *See Adarand Constructors, Inc. v. Pena*, 515 U.S. 200, 115 S.Ct. 2097, 132 L.Ed.2d 158 (1995); *City of Richmond v. J.A. Croson Co.*, 488 U.S. 469,109 S.Ct. 706, 102 L.Ed.2d 854 (1989). These cases involved minority business enterprises, rather than educational institutions concerned with educational diversity.

Several lower courts, however, have applied strict scrutiny to invalidate race-conscious admissions programs. In *Hopwood v. Texas*, 78 F.3d 932 (5th Cir.), *cert. denied*, 116 S.Ct. 2581 (1996), the circuit court explicitly rejected Justice Powell's position that the goal of educational diversity, under certain circumstances, may be a compelling justification for the use of race as a "plus" factor, arguing that subsequent Supreme Court decisions have indicated that the only compelling justification for the use of a racial classification is the need to remedy the present effects of specific prior unconstitutional discrimination. *See generally* Siegel, "The Racial Rhetorics of Colorblind Constitutionalism: The Case of *Hopwood v. Texas*," in *Race and Representation: Affirmative Action* 29 (R. Post & M. Rogin, eds., 1998); Levinson, "*Hopwood*: Some Reflections on Constitutional Interpretation by an Inferior Court," 2 *Tex. F. on Civ. Liberties & Civ. Rts.* 113 (1996). *See also* Professor Levinson's essay on "Diversity," 2 *Journal of Const. Law* 573 (2000).

Following *Hopwood*, several courts have had occasion to address the constitutionality of race-conscious admissions to magnet or academically elite or "examination" schools, both with regard to whether there is a "strong basis in evidence" for present effects of past discrimination to justify remedial measures and whether the goal of diversity either is a compelling interest or there is sufficient evidence that the race-conscious program in question will contribute to diversity. *See generally* Lewin, "Public Schools Confronting Issue of Racial Preferences," *New York Times*, Nov. 29, 1998, at 1.

Wessmann v. Gittens
160 F.3d 790 (1st Cir. 1998)

Before Selya, Boudin and Lipez, Circuit Judges.

Selya, Circuit Judge.

The City of Boston operates three renowned "examination schools," the most prestigious of which is Boston Latin School (BLS). The entrance points for admission to BLS occur principally at the seventh- and ninth-grade levels. In this litigation, plaintiff-appellant Henry Robert Wessmann, on behalf of his minor child, Sarah P. Wessmann, challenges the constitutionality of BLS's admissions policy (the Policy). . . .

I. Background

* * *

Over two decades ago, a federal district court adjudged the City of Boston (through its School Committee) to have violated the constitutional rights of African-American children by promoting and maintaining a dual public school system. . . . [T]he court conclude[d] that the City's examination schools (BLS included) were complicit in promoting and maintaining the dual system. . . .

The remedy adopted by the district court . . . obligated BLS to ensure that at least 35% of each entering class would be composed of African-American and Hispanic students. . . .

. . . By 1987, systemic progress permitted us to conclude that, for all practical purposes, the School Committee had achieved unitariness in the area of student assignments. . . .

After 1987, the City's three examination schools— BLS, Boston Latin Academy, and the O'Bryant School—were no longer under a federal court mandate to maintain a 35% set-aside. Nevertheless, the School Committee remained committed to the policy until 1995, when a disappointed applicant challenged the set-aside's constitutionality. . . . The School Committee then discontinued the 35% set-aside.

Concerned that the number of African-American and Hispanic students admitted to the examination schools might drop precipitously without a predetermined set-aside, school officials began researching alternative admissions policies in hopes of finding one that might prevent that result without offending the Constitution. . . .

[The Policy adopted was as follows:] To gain admission to one of Boston's three examination schools, a student must take a standardized test. Based on a mathematical formula that purports to predict academic performance, school hierarchs combine each applicant's test score with his or her grade point average, derive a composite score, rank all applicants accordingly, and proceed to assign individuals to the applicant pool for the examination school(s) in which they have indicated an interest. To be eligible for admission to any of the examination schools, an applicant must be in the qualified applicant pool (QAP), a group composed of those who rank in the top 50% of the overall applicant pool for that particular school.

Half of the available seats for an examination school's entering class are allocated in strict accordance with composite score rank order. The other half are allocated on the basis of "flexible racial/ethnic guidelines" promulgated as part of the Policy. To apply these guidelines, school officials first determine the relative proportions of five different racial/ethnic categories—white, black, Hispanic, Asian, and Native American—in the remaining pool of qualified applicants (RQAP). . . . They then fill the open seats in rank order, but the number of students taken from each racial/ethnic category must match the proportion of that category in the RQAP. Because the racial/ethnic distribution of the second group of successful applicants must mirror that of the RQAP, a member of a designated racial/ethnic group may be passed over in favor of a lower-ranking applicant from another group if the seats allotted for the former's racial/ethnic group have been filled.

Sarah Wessmann encountered such a fate. BLS had 90 available seats for the 1997 ninth-grade entering class. Based on her composite score, Sarah ranked 91st (out of 705) in the QAP. To fill the first 45 seats, the school exhausted the top 47 persons on the list (two aspirants declined in order to accept invitations from another examination school). Had composite scores alone dictated the selection of the remainder of the ninth-grade entering class, Sarah would have been admitted. But the racial/ethnic composition of the RQAP was 27.83% black, 40.41% white, 19.21% Asian, 11.64% Hispanic, and 0.31% Native American. Consequently, the Policy required school officials to allocate the final 45 seats to 13 blacks, 18 whites, 9 Asians, and 5 Hispanics. As a result, black and Hispanic students whose composite score rankings ranged from 95th to 150th displaced Sarah and ten other white students who had higher composite scores and ranks.

* * *

II. Analysis

* * *

A. Standards of Review

. . . [S]trict scrutiny is the proper standard for evaluating the Policy. Hence, the Policy must be both justified by a compelling governmental interest and narrowly tailored to serve that interest in order to stand.

* * *

B. Compelling Interests: An Overview

The question of precisely what interests government may legitimately invoke to justify race-based classifications is largely unsettled. Of course, we know that such state action is acceptable upon a showing, inter alia, that it is needed to undo the continuing legacy of an institution's past discrimination. . . .

In considering whether other governmental interests, beyond the need to heal the vestiges of past discrimination, may be sufficiently compelling to justify race-based initiatives, courts occasionally mention "diversity". . . .

. . . In the education context, *Hopwood* is the only appellate court to have rejected diversity as a compelling interest, and it did so only in the face of vigorous dissent from a substantial minority of the active judges in the Fifth Circuit. *See Hopwood v. State of Texas* (5th Cir.), *cert. denied*, 116 S.Ct. 2581 (1996). The question that divided the Fifth Circuit centered on the precedential value of Justice Powell's controlling opinion in *Bakke*. . . .

. . . [W]e assume arguendo—but we do not decide—that *Bakke* remains good law and that some iterations of "diversity" might be sufficiently compelling, in specific circumstances, to justify race-conscious actions. . . . [W]e address the School Committee's asserted "diversity" justification for the Policy. Thereafter, we turn to its alternate justification: that the Policy is an appropriate means of remediating the vestiges of past discrimination.

C. Diversity

. . . [I]n order to persuade us that diversity may serve as a justification for the use of a particular racial classification, the School Committee must . . . give substance to the word.

The School Committee endeavors to meet this challenge primarily by lauding benefits that it ascribes to diversity. Drawing on the testimony of various witnesses (school administrators, experts, and alumni), the Committee asserts that, because our society is racially and ethnically heterogeneous, future leaders must learn to converse with and persuade those who do not share their outlook or experience. . . . For these reasons, the School Committee exhorts us to find that diversity is essential to the modern learning experience.

Stated at this level of abstraction, few would gainsay the attractiveness of diversity. Encounters between students of varied backgrounds facilitate a vigorous exchange of ideas that not only nourishes the intellect, but also furthers mutual understanding and respect, thereby eroding prejudice and acting as a catalyst for social harmony. Indeed, Justice Powell's opinion in *Bakke* acknowledges that these very attributes may render an educational institution's interest in promoting diversity compelling. . . . [W]e must look beyond the School Committee's recital of the theoretical benefits of diversity and inquire whether the concrete workings of the Policy merit constitutional sanction. . . .

By its terms, the Policy focuses exclusively on racial and ethnic diversity. Its scope is narrowed further in that it takes into account only five groups—blacks, whites, Hispanics, Asians, and Native Americans—without recognizing that none is monolithic. No more is needed to demonstrate that the School Committee already has run afoul of the guidance provided by the principal authority on which it relies: "The diversity that furthers a compelling state interest encompasses a far broader array of qualifications and characteristics of which racial or ethnic origin is but a single though important element." A single-minded focus on ethnic diversity "hinder[s] rather than further[s] attainment of genuine diversity." . . . [*Bakke*].

. . . [T]he School Committee's able counsel responded that it is unnecessary for the Policy to consider other indicia of diversity because BLS historically has been diverse with respect to everything but race and ethnicity. For empirical confirmation of this assertion, the School Committee points to [its expert's] handiwork. Having analyzed various admissions options, [the expert] suggested that all the options would result in substantial gender, neighborhood, and socioeconomic diversity, but that, unless race and ethnicity were explicitly factored into the admissions calculus, attainment of racial and ethnic diversity might be jeopardized. This attempted confirmation does not pass constitutional muster.

. . . Statistics compiled for the last ten years show that under a strict merit-selection approach, black and Hispanic students together would comprise between 15% and 20% of each entering class, and minorities, in toto, would comprise a substantially greater percentage. Even on the assumption that the need for racial and ethnic diversity alone might sometimes constitute a compelling interest sufficient to warrant some type of corrective governmental action, it is perfectly clear that the need would have to be acute—much more acute than the relatively modest deviations that attend the instant case. In short, the School Committee's flexible racial/ethnic guidelines appear to be less a means of attaining diversity in any constitutionally relevant sense and more a means for racial balancing. . . .

It cannot be said that racial balancing is either a legitimate or necessary means of advancing the lofty principles recited in the Policy. The closest the School Committee comes to linking racial balancing to these ideals is by introducing the concept of "racial isolation." The idea is that unless there is a certain representation of any given racial or ethnic group in a particular institution, members of that racial or ethnic group will find it difficult, if not impossible, to express themselves. Thus, the School Committee says, some minimum number of black and Hispanic students—precisely how many, we do not know—is required to prevent racial isolation.

. . . [T]he "racial isolation" justification is extremely suspect because it assumes that students cannot function or express themselves unless they are surrounded by a sufficient number of persons of like race or ethnicity. Insofar as the Policy promotes groups over individuals, it is starkly at variance with Justice Powell's understanding of the proper manner in which a diverse student body may be gathered. . . . Furthermore, if justified in terms of group identity, the Policy suggests that race or ethnic background determines how individuals think or behave— although the School Committee resists this conclusion by arguing that the greater the number of a particular group, the more others will realize that the group is not monolithic. Either way, the School Committee tells us that a minimum number of persons of a given race (or ethnic background) is essential to facilitate individual expression. This very position concedes that the Policy's racial/ethnic guidelines treat "individuals as the product of their race," a practice that the Court consistently has denounced as impermissible stereotyping.

In the second place, the School Committee has failed to give us a plausible reason why we should believe that racial balancing of any type is necessary to promote the expression of ideas or any of the other ideals referenced in the Policy. . . . The School Committee has provided absolutely no competent evidence that the proportional representation promoted by the Policy is in any way tied to the vigorous exchange of ideas, let alone that, in such respects, it differs significantly in consequence from, say, a strict merit-selection process. . . .

. . . The Policy does precisely what Justice Powell deemed anathematic: at a certain point, it effectively forecloses some candidates from all consideration for a seat at an examination school simply because of the racial or ethnic category in which they fall. That happened to Sarah Wessmann. . . .

D. Vestiges of Past Discrimination

. . . The School Committee endeavors, in the alternative, to uphold the Policy as a means of redressing the vestiges of past discrimination. . . .

. . . [H]owever, government actors must be able to muster a "strong basis in evidence" showing that a current social ill in fact has been caused by such conduct. . . .

. . . [T]he School Committee disclaims the necessity for such evidence. Its disclaimer rests on the premise that a decree issued in the quarter-century-old desegregation litigation mandates local authorities to remedy any racial imbalance occurring in the school system and thereby obviates the need for an independent showing of causation. . . .

The decree in question was entered in 1994. . . . It enjoins the School Committee "from discriminating on the basis of race in the operation of the public schools of the City of Boston and from creating, promoting or maintaining racial segregation in any school or other facility in the Boston public school system." Nothing in the plain language of this provision requires school officials to undertake any affirmative action, let alone to adopt a race-based classification (such as is contained in the Policy).... [T]he cited provision ... operates as a negative injunction, forbidding the defendants from engaging in the acts that supported the original cause of action....

... Once there is a finding of unitariness and the "affirmative duty to desegregate has been accomplished," school authorities are not expected to make "year-by-year adjustments of the racial composition of student bodies" absent a "showing that either the school authorities or some other agency of the State has deliberately attempted to fix or alter demographic patterns to affect the racial composition of the schools." [Swann; Freeman]....

Because the 1994 decree turns out to be a blind alley, the School Committee must identify a vestige of bygone discrimination and provide convincing evidence that ties this vestige to the de jure segregation of the benighted past.... [T]he School Committee cites an "achievement gap" between black and Hispanic students, on the one hand, and white and Asian students, on the other, and claims that this gap's roots can be traced to the discriminatory regime of the 1970s and before.

... [W]e accept arguendo the School Committee's position that, in principle, a documented achievement gap may act as an indicator of a diminution in the quality of education. Even so, whether an achievement gap is a vestige of past discrimination depends on whether there is satisfactory evidence of a causal connection.

... The mere fact that an institution once was found to have practiced discrimination is insufficient, in and of itself, to satisfy a state actor's burden of producing the reliable evidence required to uphold race-based action.[7]

* * *

The centerpiece of the School Committee's showing consists of statistical evidence addressed to a persistent achievement gap at the primary school level between white and Asian students, on the one hand, and black and Hispanic students, on the other.... The School Committee theorizes that, because of this achievement gap, BLS receives fewer African-

American and Hispanic applicants than otherwise might be the case, and even in comparison to this modest universe, an abnormally small number of black and Hispanic students qualify for admission. Accordingly, the Committee concludes that the statistics documenting the achievement gap, on their own, satisfy the "strong basis in evidence" requirement.

* * *

In this case, the "barrier to entry" comparable to those in the employment discrimination cases is BLS's requirement of an entrance examination and the resultant composite score—and no one (least of all, the School Committee) claims that the examination or any component thereof is discriminatory in operation or effect, or that it would be discriminatory if it were used as the sole criterion for admission....

With the admissions process eliminated as an illegitimate barrier to entry, the achievement gap statistics, by themselves, must specifically point to other allegedly discriminatory conduct in order to suggest a causal link between those discriminatory acts and the achievement gap. Unlike the focused inquiry characteristic of the employment discrimination cases, however, the raw achievement gap statistics presented in this case do not by themselves isolate any particular locus of discrimination for measurement. Without such a focus, the achievement gap statistics cannot possibly be said to measure the causal effect of any particular phenomenon, whether it be discrimination or anything else. As such, the achievement gap statistics, by themselves, do not even eliminate the possibility that they are caused by what the Court terms "societal discrimination."...

The School Committee ... point[s] to certain alleged phenomena that it claims constitute substantial causes of the achievement gap. Chief among these is "low teacher expectations" vis-a-vis African-American and Hispanic students, a condition which the School Committee argues is an attitudinal remnant of the segregation era.... Dr. Trent, a sociologist, identified teachers' low expectations of African-American and Hispanic students as a significant factor underlying the achievement gap in the Boston public schools. He based his conclusion on an anal-

---

[7]The situation at BLS illustrates why no such knee-jerk inference can be drawn. In 1987, we ruled that the Boston public schools had achieved unitariness with respect to student assignments. Thereafter, though not obligated to do so, BLS continued its policy of setting aside 35% of the seats in its incoming classes for black and Hispanic pupils and jettisoned the set-aside only after a court challenge. Nothing in the record suggests that BLS has in the past ten years been discriminating against minorities. Under such circumstances, a conclusion that a previous finding of discrimination in and of itself establishes that current disparities are due to that discrimination would be little more than an ipse dixit. See Freeman (warning that "[t]he causal link between current conditions and the prior violation is even more attenuated if the school district has demonstrated its good faith").

ogy that he drew from studies he had performed in the Kansas City school system, including a "climate survey" of teacher attitudes and a multiple regression analysis designed to determine whether the low expectations reflected in teachers' answers to the questions posed in the climate survey might partially explain the achievement gap. . . . Dr. Trent had concluded that, in Kansas City, teacher "efficacy" — a term of art referring to a teacher's success in encouraging pupils to succeed — correlated with higher achievement test scores.

* * *

Dr. Trent, however, never conducted a "climate survey" for the Boston school system. His conclusions for Boston were based only on a review of statistical data documenting the achievement gap . . ., statistics concerning teacher seniority, and anecdotal evidence about teacher attitudes supplied by school officials. . . .

. . . [Dr. Trent] could not validly establish whether Boston teachers' attitudes in fact were discriminatory, let alone show that they caused (or even significantly contributed to) the achievement gap. . . . [W]ith no methodological support, he could not produce a meaningful analysis of causation. . . .

. . . Even if the School Committee had proven the requisite connection between the Policy and the vestiges of past discrimination, the Policy could not endure. When authorized by the Constitution, race-conscious remedies not only must respond to a compelling governmental interest, but also must be narrowly tailored to rectify the specific harms in question. Under this test, the Policy sweeps too broadly.

. . . First, since there is no discrimination at entry to BLS, we fail to see how the adoption of an admissions policy that espouses a brand of proportional representation is designed to ameliorate the harm that allegedly has occurred (a system-wide achievement gap at the primary school level). . . .

Second, the increased admission of black and Hispanic students cannot be viewed as partial compensation for injustices done at the primary school level. This is so because the victims of the achievement gap are public school students, and they are the ones who ought to be the focus of the remedy. The Policy does not focus in this direction, for many of the black and Hispanic students admitted under it come from private or parochial schools. Thus, the Policy is not sufficiently particularized toward curing the harm done to the class of actual victims. . . .

Third, if palliating the effects of past discrimination is the ostensible justification for the Policy, then the Policy, on its face, has been crafted in puzzling ways. Suppose that in a particular year a group of Hispanic students does very well, such that they cluster between ranks 45 and 90, but that the Hispanic student population in the RQAP is sparse. Suppose further that whites and Asians form a significant majority of the RQAP. There is then a likelihood that, by reason of the Policy, a number of the Hispanic students — archetypal victims of discrimination — will be displaced by white and Asian students. . . .

* * *

Boudin, Circuit Judge, concurring. [omitted]

Lipez, Circuit Judge, dissenting.

. . . The Boston School Committee argues that the Boston Latin admissions program serves two compelling interests: promoting diversity in the public schools and remedying the vestiges of past discrimination. The majority rejects both arguments. Although I have reservations about the Committee's diversity argument on the facts of this case, I have none about its remedial argument. . . .

I. Some Relevant History

. . . I wish to offer some additional background which more fully reveals the antecedents of the Boston Latin admissions program in the long history of court supervised desegregation of the Boston school system. That court-supervised desegregation began in 1974, when the district court found that the Boston School Committee had engaged in "affirmative acts [which] intentionally created or maintained racial segregation." The Committee's acts included the manipulation of facilities utilization, new school construction, and redistricting to preserve distinctively white or minority districts. The district court noted that the Committee was particularly successful in maintaining a segregated school system through the establishment and use of "feeder patterns" for students going from primary schools into the high schools. The primary schools were segregated in part because their districts were geographically drawn and based on residentially-segregated neighborhoods. As the high schools were far fewer in number than the primary schools, and each high school drew on several geographic primary school districts, the high schools might naturally have been more racially balanced than the primary schools. However, under the

Committee's skewed feeder patterns, students were assigned from white "junior high" schools into predominantly white high schools beginning with the tenth grade, and from African-American "middle" schools into predominantly African-American high schools beginning with the ninth grade. . . .

. . . [T]he district court concluded that pervasive *de jure* segregation throughout the Boston public school system established a "prima facie case of unlawful segregative design" in the examination schools. This presumption was not rebutted. Although little evidence was presented on the causes of the exam schools' imbalanced racial composition, the court attributed part of the disparity to the tying of admission to achievement (as opposed to aptitude) test scores. The court also noted that the "advanced work classes" that prepared public school fifth and sixth graders for the examination schools were segregated. On appeal, we summarized the situation as follows: "The examination schools are segregated because black children fare worse on the entrance examinations than whites. These children are products of the segregated elementary classes which constituted 'tracks' to the examination schools and were more than 80% white. . . . Thus, the segregation of the lower schools had inevitable consequences for the examination . . . schools. . . ." *Morgan v. Kerrigan,* 509 F.2d 580 (1st Cir.1974).

* * *

As a remedy for its finding of discrimination by the Boston School Committee, the court ultimately mandated that "[a]t least 35% of each of the entering classes at Boston Latin School, Boston Latin Academy and Boston Technical High in September 1975 shall be composed of black and Hispanic students." . . . In reviewing the district court ruling, we concluded that the 35% floor was not an impermissible racial quota because "overall racial composition [of the system was ordered] to be used as a starting point in designing a school desegregation plan." This approach is specifically approved in *Swann*.

* * *

In 1987, some twelve years after the initial court desegregation orders, we held that court supervision of student assignments in the Boston schools should end in light of the Committee's good faith, the State Board's findings of compliance, and the general notion that the maximum practicable level of desegre-

gation had been achieved (given the impact of factors exoteric to School Committee control, such as white flight). . . . [C]ontrol over the student assignment process was returned to the Boston School Committee, with the express reservation that " 'unitariness' . . . in all aspects of the Boston schools has not yet been achieved."[15] Finally, in 1994 the district court . . . "permanently enjoined" the Committee "from creating, promoting or maintaining racial segregation in any school or other facility in the Boston Public school system."

The School Committee voluntarily continued the 35% African-American/Hispanic set-aside at the exam schools even after this policy ceased in 1987 to be a court mandate. In 1996, however, the set-aside effectively ended with *McLaughlin v. Boston School Committee*, when the district court issued a preliminary injunction ordering the admission to Boston Latin of a student who challenged the set-aside's constitutionality. In making that ruling, the court acknowledged that

> the set aside had its origins in a court-ordered desegregation plan; that it had already played a crucial and successful role in desegregating the once virtually all-white examination schools; that the First Circuit had in no way called its validity into question in returning to the [Boston School Committee] control over student assignments; and that the appeals court had, if anything, strongly hinted that in-place corrective measures ought to be continued. Indeed, it may not be too much of a stretch to say that, without the set aside, there would not have been a finding of unitariness with respect to student assignments at all.

The court then warned that "abandonment of the 35% set aside at the present time without adopting other remedial measures would, within the next six years or sooner, convert BLS into an overwhelmingly white and Asian-American school with a black and Hispanic enrollment of about 15%."

Nonetheless, the district court found a likelihood of success for the disappointed white applicant Julia McLaughlin on the narrow tailoring aspect of her challenge to the admissions program. . . . The court offered as one possible alternative to the rigid 35% set-aside a periodically updated target for minority enrollment, with "percentages [tailored] to the relevant qualified applicant populations." In light of the preliminary injunction, the Committee replaced the

---

[15]Faculty and staff desegregation, along with the failure to develop a plan to address poor upkeep of facilities, were the primary continuing concerns of the court, not student assignments.

set-aside, and the district court's suggestion of a float-ing target was influential in molding . . . the current admissions program.

II. The Legal Framework for an Analysis of the Evidence

. . . [T]he majority asserts that the School Commit-tee failed to present satisfactory evidence of a causal connection between the achievement gap docu-mented by the Committee and the prior *de jure* seg-regation of the Boston schools. . . . In my view, the majority . . . misperceives the Committee's eviden-tiary burden in defending its affirmative action program. . . .

The law is clear that a public entity adopting an af-firmative action program to remedy the lingering ef-fects of past discrimination must have a "strong basis in evidence" for concluding that the lingering effects it identifies are causally linked to past discrimina-tion. . . . I conclude that this "strong basis" require-ment is met preliminarily if the public entity whose affirmative action program is challenged in court demonstrates that the entity adopted the program on the basis of evidence sufficient to establish a prima facie case of a causal link between past discrimina-tion and the current outcomes addressed by the re-medial program. . . .

In the instant case, where there is a long history of court findings of discriminatory acts by the School Committee, there is no dispute about the public en-tity's responsibility for prior discrimination. Instead, given the time lapse between those court findings of discrimination and the claim that this discrimination still disadvantages minorities, the issue in dispute here is whether the vestiges of that prior discrimina-tion now affect minorities. This showing necessarily requires evidence of the existence of vestiges of the prior discrimination and of a present harm to mi-norities. It also requires evidence of causal connec-tions between the past discrimination and the claimed vestiges, and between the vestiges and the present harm.

. . .[T]he Committee had to show that the evi-dence before it would constitute a prima facie case of a constitutional or statutory violation if brought by a putative minority plaintiff. If this prima facie case was not effectively rebutted by Wessmann, who al-ways retains the burden of persuasion, the School Committee prevails.

. . . Precisely as in the employment cases, there is an identifiable barrier to entry that could be chal-lenged by minority applicants in the event the race-conscious aspects of the Boston Latin admissions program were elided. Amicus curiae NAACP makes this claim on appeal; it tried doggedly to intervene below; and its position explains why the School Committee could not, in the context of litigation both current and anticipated, freely admit that com-posite score ranking may have had a discriminatory impact if used alone.[21] Despite this constraint, the School Committee did allude to the notion of dis-criminatory impact, . . . and there was evidence pre-sented at trial that, for African-Americans and His-panics, composite score was not reliably correlated with future performance at BLS. . . .

Although the admissions program challenged here was "voluntary," in the sense of not being im-pelled by the 1994 order . . . the mere act of making a selection among students seeking admission to Boston Latin exposed the Committee to legal action by minority students . . . based on the disparate im-pact of the selection criteria used. Here, the relevant provision of federal law is Title VI of the Civil Rights Act of 1964. . . .

There was evidence produced at trial that any ex-clusive focus on composite score in admissions had a disparate impact on African-Americans and His-panics. Although the ability of minority plaintiffs to make colorable claims of Title VI violations would not be sufficient to justify a race-conscious affirma-tive action program (such claims would only be suf-ficient to force the Committee to find some alterna-tive to composite score rank order admissions), the presence of the disparate impact underlying such claims, when causally related to the history of *de jure* segregation in the system, imposed on the School Committee a duty to ensure that it did not violate the Constitution by using selection criteria that perpetuated the effects of past governmental discrimination. . . . The Committee chose a reme-dial measure for admission to the Boston Latin School in the wake of a long history of desegregation orders and under the threat of Title VI suits by dis-appointed minority applicants if no affirmative ac-tion were taken.

---

[21]The NAACP's amicus brief states that its motion to intervene was motivated by the belief that "it was contrary to the [School Committee's] interests to present evidence of [the School Committee's] potential liability to African-American and Hispanic students for discriminatory admissions practices."

. . . A government entity need not admit conclusive guilt for past discrimination's current effects before going forward with a remedial plan. Instead, it must satisfy the court that the evidence before it established a prima facie case of a causal link between past discrimination and the current outcomes addressed by the remedial program. If this prima facie case is not effectively rebutted by a reverse discrimination plaintiff, who always retains the burden of proving the illegality of the affirmative action program, the government has met its burden of establishing a compelling remedial interest under strict scrutiny analysis. With this legal framework in mind, I turn to an analysis of the evidence on the vestiges of discrimination.

III. The Evidence on the Vestiges of Discrimination

* *

1. The Achievement Gap

The evidence at trial revealed large gaps between African-Americans and Hispanics, on the one hand, and whites and Asians, on the other, in admissions to the exam schools, and in achievement and allocation of resources throughout the system. . . . Expert witness analysis of the test results over a several year period showed a persistent and relatively unchanging gap in achievement in all subject matters which correlated with race: African-American and Hispanic students fared much worse on the tests than whites. The tests also revealed that, in general, Asians fared worse than whites on language skills achievement.

The evidence also demonstrated that African-Americans and Hispanics from the public schools apply to the examination schools at half the application rate of other students in the public schools. . . . Finally, there was evidence that African-American and Hispanic applicants to Boston Latin from private elementary schools do much better in the admissions process than their Boston public school counterparts. . . .

2. The Relationship of the Achievement Gap to Prior Discrimination

The Committee presented evidence of a connection between low teacher expectations for minority stu-

dents and low minority performance on achievement tests. The Committee presented further evidence that these low teacher expectations for minority students . . . is a vestige of the long years of segregation in the Boston school system. Given these connections between student achievement, teacher expectations for students, and the impact of years of segregation on these teacher expectations, the achievement gap itself is a current and lingering effect of discrimination. I will now summarize the evidence on these connections.

(a) **The connection generally between teacher expectations and student performance** Both Dr. William Trent and Deputy Superintendent Janice Jackson testified that teacher expectations affected student performance. Dr. Trent gave extensive testimony concerning the research he performed for the Kansas City School District in connection with the district's efforts to determine whether it had remedied the vestiges of prior segregation in compliance with a court order. In this study, Dr. Trent relied upon "climate surveys" — comprehensive questionnaires distributed to teachers, students and parents — to evaluate and score teacher efficacy. . . . A higher efficacy score indicated that the teachers considered themselves able to make a difference in their teaching activities and that they held their students in high regard. The Kansas City study showed that there was a correlation between high teacher efficacy scores and higher student test performance, while low teacher efficacy scores were associated with low student test performance.

Deputy Superintendent Jackson also testified that teacher expectations affect student performance. Early in Jackson's career she was specifically trained in TESA (Teacher Expectations and Student Achievement) techniques. . . . Specifically, the techniques attempt to focus the teachers on their unconscious biases about low and high achievers, including how their racial attitudes influence their expectations of the students. For many years, Jackson instructed teachers on these techniques and conducted countless training sessions to demonstrate how teachers' interactions with students, even at an unconscious level, can have a significant impact on student performance.

* * *

(b) Low expectations for minority students in the Boston School System Deputy Superintendent Jackson described her numerous opportunities to observe the interactions among students, teachers and administrators in the Boston public schools. In fact, Jackson testified that she observed between thirty and forty Boston public schools in her first year as Deputy Superintendent and at least another forty schools in the system her second year. During these classroom visits, she observed that teachers had different expectations for the African-American and Hispanic children versus the Asian and white children. She saw incidents of unjustified disciplinary action directed at minority students, and noted a frequent failure of teachers to call upon African-American and Hispanic students in class. She also saw recurring instances of teachers withholding praise for minorities and treating them with condescending laxity when calling upon them in class.

. . . Dr. Trent connected these low expectations for minority students described by Jackson to the minority students' low test performance and low admissions rate at the examination schools. Dr. Trent explained that "[t]o the extent teachers play a central role in encouraging and preparing students to apply for one of the more valued resources in the Boston Public Schools, [the difference in application rates] reflects a very different rate of success with encouraging or facilitating black and Hispanic students applying, in contrast to the rate at which white and Asian students do." . . .

(c) Low expectations for minority students as a vestige of prior discrimination Dr. Trent provided the primary evidence on the causal link between prior discrimination and low teacher expectations for minority students and the effect of these low expectations on the achievement gap. Dr. Trent tied these low expectations to the lingering effects of a segregated school system. He explained: "It appears that in the seniority ranks, as many as 28.4 percent of the teachers currently employed in the district have been with the district since prior to 1973, and about 47 percent have been with the district from 1980 and prior." These numbers indicated to Dr. Trent that many of the teachers' attitudes towards their students and expectations of them were shaped in a segregated school system. Dr. Trent explained the difficulty of changing such

teacher attitudes following a desegregation order. . . .

. . . Dr. Trent did not conduct a specific study of the Boston school system, as he had done for the Kansas City School District. . . . In lieu of such a study, Trent relied on the seniority statistics discussed above as well as statistics relating to the different student application rates to the exam schools, indicating a substantial disparity between the application rates of African-Americans and Hispanics compared to whites and Asians. He also relied on statistics that show that African-American and Hispanic students attending the Boston public schools receive invitations to attend Boston Latin at a much lower rate than do African-Americans and Hispanics attending private schools, whereas the invitation rates for white and Asian private school and white and Asian public school students were comparable. Finally, he relied on interviews with headmasters, principals and other personnel, as well as an interview with Deputy Superintendent Janice Jackson, who, as noted, had special training in observing teacher interactions with students, and had made a personal survey of over seventy schools in the Boston school system over the course of two years. Based on this information, he offered his expert opinion that low teacher expectations for minorities, shaped in the segregation era, are a cause of the current achievement gap, and thus the achievement gap itself is a vestige of discrimination.

* * *

3. A Prima Facie Case of Causation

* * *

The majority asserts that Dr. Trent's failure to conduct a survey of the type conducted in Kansas City disabled him from validly establishing that teachers had different expectations for minority students. . . . We should be wary of dismissing as "anecdotal" the extensive observational accounts of experienced school administrators testifying about the prevalence of different teacher expectations in their school systems, particularly when, as in the case of Deputy Superintendent Jackson, the administrator is trained to make such observations.

. . . Dr. Trent's expertise in identifying patterns of vestigal effects of discrimination necessarily was acquired through his prior studies of other school systems, including Kansas City. He did not attempt to use national statistics or statistics from other localities to infer the existence of similar local conditions, as was done by the city council in *Croson*.

. . . Dr. Trent . . . testified that his conclusions were based on a reasonable methodology in his profession. . . . Seeing statistics and patterns in Boston that he had observed in other school systems where he had found a link between student achievement gaps and prior discrimination, he testified to the probability of such a link in the Boston school system. He had an adequate basis for making that judgment.

. . . In the majority's view, the Committee's evidence had to account for other variables that might explain all or part of the achievement gap in terms of societal discrimination. This insistence reflects a misconception of the School Committee's evidentiary burden, and would elevate the Committee's evidentiary burden far beyond the prima facie standard contemplated in the Title VII cases. The Committee did not have to present proof that would permit the court to make an independent finding of causation. The Committee had to satisfy the court that the Committee had before it a strong basis in evidence for its judgment that the achievement gap is linked to past discrimination in the Boston school system. . . . By setting the bar of proof for the School Committee unrealistically high, the majority has ignored precedents that impose only a prima facie burden on the School Committee.

* * *

I am concerned that the majority's evidentiary requirements in this case will force school systems contemplating affirmative action programs designed to address the effects of past discrimination to establish, through the collection of quantifiable social science data, that past discrimination is the sole or primary cause of variable achievement. . . .

The evidence presented by the School Committee established a prima facie case that differential teacher expectations, grounded in the long history of segregation in the Boston school system, were a substantial causal factor in the undeniable achievement gap found in the Boston school system. In the face of this evidence, Wessmann had the burden of challenging the Committee's prima facie case by disproving the alleged causal linkages between prior discrimination, teacher expectations, and the achievement gap.

* * *

[The remainder of the dissenting opinion addressed the issue of narrow tailoring, arguing that the

Policy met the standards with regard to flexibility, limited duration, impact on the rights of third parties, and the efficacy of race neutral alternatives.]

———

NOTES AND QUESTIONS

1. *Remedying the Present Effects of Prior Discrimination*

As both the majority and dissent recognize in *Wessmann*, the Supreme Court has indicated that remedying the present effects of prior discrimination can be a compelling interest, but only if the governmental entity has a "strong basis in evidence" for its conclusion that remedial action is necessary. Inasmuch as the Boston school district had been judicially determined to be unitary, however, Boston school authorities could no longer rely solely on the fact that the school district had been under court order to desegregate as the basis for its remedial action. What is the nature of the evidence and the level of proof that the *Wessmann* majority appears to require before the school district can take remedial action? Must school authorities prove that achievement gaps were caused entirely by prior *de jure* segregation, eliminating all other potentially contributing factors, including "societal discrimination," before they can take remedial action? Is this position analogous to the position the majority appears to have taken in *Missouri v. Jenkins* with regard to *Milliken II*–type remedies? Do you agree that a school system must prove that disparities in achievement are the sole result of its past discriminatory acts, rather than societal discrimination, before it can undertake voluntary efforts to address those disparities?

2. *The Goal of Diversity*

Although the Fifth Circuit in *Hopwood v. Texas* rejected the goal of diversity as a compelling interest, the Supreme Court has not yet rejected Justice Powell's position in *Bakke* that "the attainment of a diverse student body . . . clearly is a constitutionally permissible goal." *See Smith v. University of Washington Law School*, 233 F.3d 1188 (9th Cir. 2000) (until Supreme Court declares rationale in *Bakke* "moribund," "educational diversity is a compelling governmental interest that meets the demands of strict scrutiny of race-conscious measures"). *See also Gratz v. Bollinger*, 122 F. Supp. 2d 811 (E.D. Mich. 2000); *contra, Grutter v.*

Bollinger, 137 F. Supp.2d 821 (E.D. Mich.), *stay granted by* 247 F.3d 631 (6th Cir. 2001).

The *Wessmann* court assumes that "some iterations of 'diversity' might be sufficiently compelling, in specific circumstances, to justify race-conscious actions," but finds that the Boston School Committee's Policy appears "to be less a means of attaining diversity in any constitutionally relevant sense and more a means for racial balancing." What evidence would the First Circuit require before holding that a school district's policy would contribute to educational diversity? *See Eisenberg v. Montgomery County Public Schools*, 197 F.3d 123 (4th Cir. 1999), *cert. den.*, 529 U.S. 1019, 120 S.Ct. 1420, 146 L.Ed. 312 (2000) (in barring denial of student's request to transfer from his neighborhood school to a magnet school because it would leave his school racially imbalanced, court refused to decide whether diversity is a compelling interest, holding instead that "mere racial balancing in a pure form" is not "narrowly tailored to the interest of obtaining diversity"). *See also Tuttle v. Arlington County School Board*, 195 F.3d 698 (4th Cir. 1999), *cert. dismissed*, 529 U.S. 1050, 120 S.Ct. 1552, 146 L.Ed.2d 364 (2000).

Although a court may not engage in racial balancing, the Supreme Court, in *dicta*, has indicated that school authorities, acting for pedagogical reasons, might have more leeway. In *Swann v. Charlotte-Mecklenburg Board of Education*, 402 U.S. 1, 91 S.Ct. 1267, 28 L.Ed.2d 544 (1971), the Supreme Court distinguished between the role of school authorities and the role of the federal court as follows:

> School authorities are traditionally charged with broad power to formulate and implement educational policy and might well conclude, for example, that in order to prepare students to live in a pluralistic society each school should have a prescribed ratio of Negro to white students reflecting the proportion for the district as a whole. To do this as an educational policy is within the broad discretionary powers of school authorities; absent a finding of a constitutional violation, however, that would not be within the authority of a federal court.

402 U.S. at 16. *See Brewer v. West Irondequoit Central School District*, 212 F.3d 738, 750–51 (2d Cir. 2000), noting that this passage in *Swann*, as well as *Washington v. Seattle School Dist. No. 1*, *supra*, established the principle that "local school authorities have the power to voluntarily remedy *de facto* segregation existing in schools." *See* Boger, *supra*, at 1740, 1776. Has the *Wessmann* majority rejected this posi-

tion? On what grounds, if any, should school districts be allowed latitude to take actions to achieve diversity? Is the argument for diversity greater in the case of elementary and secondary education than it is in the case of higher education? *See* Note, "The Constitutionality of Race-Conscious Admissions Programs in Public Elementary and Secondary Schools," 112 *Harv. L. Rev.* 940 (1999); Note, "Lessons in Humanity: Diversity as a Compelling State Interest in Public Education," 40 *B.C. L. Rev.* 995 (1999). Is there a distinction between the goal of diversity and reducing racial isolation? *See Brewer v. West Irondequoit Central School District*, 212 F.3d at 752. Should there be?

Although the First Circuit, in *Wessmann*, did not hold that diversity can never be a compelling justification for race-conscious admissions policies, several courts have applied the Fifth Circuit's decision in *Hopwood* involving the University of Texas law school to elementary and secondary schools. In *Tito v. Arlington County School Board*, 1997 U.S. Dist. LEXIS 7932 (E.D. Va., 1997), the district court, citing *Hopwood*, rejected diversity arguments on behalf of the method of selecting kindergarten-age students for an alternative or magnet school. Since the applicant pool for the Arlington Traditional School was predominantly white, the school considered race "to the extent necessary to compensate for the disproportionality of the applicant pool." The admission system involved a lottery, adjusted by race. The court found that once the white "cap" was met through random selection, race was the "sole decisive factor" in admission, and stated that, as a result, students were denied a benefit they otherwise would have received if a truly random lottery was used solely because of their race. The court dismissed the school board's argument that passed-over students were not denied a benefit because they were still offered a free education at another school within the system, in contrast to the denial of admission to a graduate or professional program, as was the case in *Bakke*. Following this decision, the school board adopted a new policy that used three equally weighted factors: (1) whether the applicant was from a low-income family, (2) whether English was the applicant's second language, and (3) race/ethnicity. The district court found that the first language factor was "nothing more than a proxy for a national origin classification," and the family income factor did not alter the impermissibility of the race/ethnicity factor. *Tuttle v. Arlington County School Board*, 1998 U.S. Dist. LEXIS 19788

(E.D. Va., 1998). On appeal, the Fourth Circuit found that the race/ethnicity factor was independent of the other factors, and held that it was not narrowly tailored because it relied on "nonremedial racial balancing," 195 F.3d 698, 705 (4th Cir. 1999), *cert. dismissed*, 529 U.S. 1050, 120 S.Ct. 1552, 146 L.Ed.2d 364 (2000).

3. *Urban-Suburban Transfers*

Several actions have challenged policies that permit minority students to transfer out of racially isolated schools within city school districts to suburban schools, but have barred white students in city schools from similarly transferring to adjacent suburban school districts. Some policies are concerned with limiting state "open enrollment" laws which would further increase segregation in city districts; other policies are concerned directly with promoting desegregation. Courts have been divided as to the constitutionality of these policies. *Compare Brewer v. West Irondequoit Central School Dist.*, 212 F.3d 738 (2d Cir. 2000) *with Equal Open Enrollment Association v. Board of Education of the Akron City School Dist.*, 937 F.Supp. 700 (N.D. Ohio, 1996). *See generally* Hawke, "The 'Choice' for Urban School Districts: Open Enrollment or Desegregation?" 115 *Ed. Law Rep.* 609 (1997); Rinas, "A Constitutional Analysis of Race-Based Limitations on Open Enrollment in Public Schools," 82 *Iowa L. Rev.* 1501 (1997).

4. *The Aftermath of* Wessmann *and Alternatives to Race-Conscious Admissions Policies*

Following the decision in *Wessmann* and the rejection of the Boston School Committee's admissions policy, minority admissions dropped. *See* Pressley, "Fewer Minorities Invited to Boston Latin," *Boston Herald*, Mar. 23, 1999, at 10; Daley, "Troubling Admissions Statistics at Latin; Chances for Blacks Attending Remain Poor," *Boston Globe*, Mar. 23, 1999, at B1. The same effect has been observed in other districts when race has been eliminated as a factor in admissions. *See* "Magnet Schools See Dip in Minority Enrollment," Markley, *The Houston Chronicle*, May 14, 1998, at A25.

What alternative factors other than examination scores or lotteries might be used to increase diversity in admission to magnet schools or academically elite schools? Would class-based preferences be constitutional? Would such preferences be as effective in producing diverse student bodies?

E. State Innovation in the Face of a Declining Federal Commitment

Although recent Supreme Court cases suggest that it is becoming increasingly difficult to address racially isolated schools under the federal Equal Protection Clause, state courts have at times turned to provisions in their state constitutions to find support for educational equity claims. The principal area of state constitutional development over the past several decades has been the financing of education, addressed in Chapter 7. However, at least one state supreme court has addressed claims of severe educational disadvantages arising from racial and ethnic isolation, combined with socioeconomic deprivation, under its state constitution.

Sheff v. O'Neill

238 Conn. 1, 678 A.2d 1267 (Conn.1996).

Peters, Chief Justice.

The public elementary and high school students in Hartford suffer daily from the devastating effects that racial and ethnic isolation, as well as poverty, have had on their education. Federal constitutional law provides no remedy for their plight. The principal issue in this appeal is whether, under the unique provisions of our state constitution, the state, which already plays an active role in managing public schools, must take further measures to relieve the severe handicaps that burden these children's education. The issue is as controversial as the stakes are high. We hold today that the needy schoolchildren of Hartford have waited long enough. The constitutional imperatives contained in article eighth, § 1,[22] and article first, §§ 1 and 20,[23] of our state constitu-

---

[22]The constitution of Connecticut, article eighth, § 1, provides: "There shall always be free public elementary and secondary schools in the state. The general assembly shall implement this principle by appropriate legislation."

[23]The constitution of Connecticut, article first, § 1, provides: "All men when they form a social compact, are equal in rights; and no man or set of men are entitled to exclusive public emoluments or privileges from the community."

The constitution of Connecticut, article first, § 20 . . . provides: "No person shall be denied the equal protection of the law nor be subjected to segregation or discrimination in the exercise or enjoyment of his or her civil or political rights because of religion, race, color, ancestry, national origin, sex or physical or mental disability."

tion entitle the plaintiffs to relief. At the same time, the constitutional imperative of separation of powers persuades us to afford the legislature, with the assistance of the executive branch, the opportunity, in the first instance, to fashion the remedy that will most appropriately respond to the constitutional violations that we have identified. . . .

. . . Statewide, in the 1991–92 school year, children from minority groups constituted 25.7 percent of the public school population. In the Hartford public school system in that same period, 92.4 percent of the students were members of minority groups, including, predominantly, students who were either African-American or Latino. Fourteen of Hartford's twenty-five elementary schools had a white student enrollment of less than 2 percent. The Hartford public school system currently enrolls the highest percentage of minority students in the state. In the future, if current conditions continue, the percentage of minority students in the Hartford public school system is likely to increase rather than decrease. . . . Although enrollment of African-American students in the twenty-one surrounding suburban towns has increased . . ., only seven of these school districts had a minority student enrollment in excess of 10 percent in 1992. Because of the negative consequences of racial and ethnic isolation, a more integrated public school system would likely be beneficial to all schoolchildren.

A majority of the children who constitute the public school population in Hartford come from homes that are economically disadvantaged, that are headed by a single parent and in which a language other than English is spoken. The percentage of Hartford schoolchildren at the elementary level who return to the same school that they attended the previous year is the lowest such percentage in the state. Such socioeconomic factors impair a child's orientation toward and skill in learning and adversely affect a child's performance on standardized tests. The gap in the socioeconomic status between Hartford schoolchildren and schoolchildren from the surrounding twenty-one suburban towns has been increasing. The performance of Hartford schoolchildren on standardized tests falls significantly below that of schoolchildren from the twenty-one surrounding suburban towns.

Directly or indirectly, the state has always controlled public elementary and secondary education in Connecticut. . . . Since 1941, as a result of a state statute . . . the public school district boundaries in Hartford have been coterminous with the boundaries of the city of Hartford. Since at least 1909, as a result of another state statute . . . schoolchildren have been assigned to the public school district in which they reside.

* * *

The state has not intentionally segregated racial and ethnic minorities in the Hartford public school system. . . . There has never been any other manifestation of de jure segregation either at the state or the local level. . . . Since 1970, the state has supported and encouraged voluntary plans for increasing interdistrict diversity.

The state has nonetheless played a significant role in the present concentration of racial and ethnic minorities in the Hartford public school system. Although intended to improve the quality of education and not racially or ethnically motivated, the districting statute that the legislature enacted in 1909 . . . is the *single most important factor* contributing to the present concentration of racial and ethnic minorities in the Hartford public school system. The districting statute and the resultant school district boundaries have remained virtually unchanged since 1909. The districting statute is of critical importance because it establishes town boundaries as the dividing line between all school districts in the state.

* * *

. . . The plaintiffs claim that the state bears responsibility to correct the constitutional violations alleged in their complaint because of the state's failure to "take corrective measures to [e]nsure that its Hartford public schoolchildren receive an equal educational opportunity." That failure is actionable, according to the plaintiffs, because of the state's knowledge of the racial and ethnic isolation in the Hartford schools, combined with the state's extensive involvement in the operations of Connecticut's public schools and the impact of state statutes mandating school attendance within statutorily defined school districts. . . . The defendants maintain, to the contrary, that the state's constitutional duty to provide for the elementary and secondary education of Connecticut schoolchildren is triggered only by state action that is alleged to be intentional state misconduct. . . .

The defendants' argument, derived largely from principles of federal constitutional law, founders on the fact that article eighth, § 1, and article first, §§ 1 and 20, impose on the legislature an *affirmative* constitutional obligation to provide schoolchild-ren throughout the state with a substantially equal educational opportunity. . . . It follows that, if the legislature fails, for whatever reason, to take action to remedy substantial inequalities in the educa-tional opportunities that such children are being afforded, its actions and its omissions constitute state action.

The affirmative constitutional obligation . . . was not premised on a showing that the legislature had played an active role in *creating* the inequalities that the constitution requires it to redress. . . .

The claims now before us likewise implicate the legislature's affirmative constitutional obligation to provide a substantially equal educational opportu-nity to all of the state's schoolchildren. . . .

[D]efendants urge us to follow federal precedents that concededly require, as a matter of federal con-stitutional law, that claimants seeking judicial relief for educational disparities pursuant to the equal pro-tection clause of the fourteenth amendment to the United States constitution must prove intentional governmental discrimination against a suspect class. See, e.g., *Freeman v. Pitts*, 503 U.S. 467, 494, 112 S.Ct. 1430, 1447, 118 L.Ed.2d 108 (1992) [and re-lated Supreme Court cases]. . . . According to the de-fendants, because the plaintiffs raise claims of unconstitutional disparities in educational opportu-nities on the basis of severe racial and ethnic imbal-ances among school districts, the plaintiffs, too, must prove intentional state action.

For two reasons, we are not persuaded that we should adopt these precedents as a matter of state constitutional law. First and foremost, the federal cases start from the premise that there is no right to education under the United States constitution. *San Antonio Independent School District v. Rodriguez*, 411 U.S. 1, 35, 93 S.Ct. 1278, 1297–98, 36 L.Ed.2d 16 (1973). Our Connecticut constitution, by con-trast, contains a fundamental right to education and a corresponding affirmative state obligation to im-plement and maintain that right. . . . Second, the federal cases are guided by principles of federalism as "a foremost consideration in interpreting any of the pertinent constitutional provisions under which [a court] examines state action." *San Antonio Inde-pendent School District v. Rodriguez*. . . . Principles of federalism, however, do not restrict *our* constitu-tional authority to enforce the constitutional man-dates contained in article eighth, § 1, and article first, §§ 1 and 20.

* * *

In summary, under our law, which imposes an af-firmative constitutional obligation on the legislature to provide a substantially equal educational opportu-nity for all public schoolchildren, the state action doctrine is not a defense to the plaintiffs' claims of constitutional deprivation. The state had ample no-tice of ongoing trends toward racial and ethnic isola-tion in its public schools, and indeed undertook a number of laudable remedial efforts that unfortu-nately have not achieved their desired end. The fact that the legislature did not affirmatively create or in-tend to create the conditions that have led to the racial and ethnic isolation in the Hartford public school system does not, in and of itself, relieve the defendants of their affirmative obligation to provide the plaintiffs with a more effective remedy for their constitutional grievances.

* * *

We turn now to the merits of the plaintiffs' claims. No statute, no common law precedent, no federal constitutional principle provides this state's school-children with a right to a public education that is not burdened by de facto racial and ethnic segregation. The plaintiffs make no such claim. The issue that they raise is whether they have stated a case for relief under our state constitution, which was amended in 1965 to provide both a right to a free public elemen-tary and secondary education; Conn. Const., art. VIII, § 1; and a right to protection from segregation. Conn. Const., art. I, § 20. This issue raises questions that are difficult; the answers that we give are con-troversial. We are, however, persuaded that a fair reading of the text and the history of these amend-ments demonstrates a deep and abiding constitu-tional commitment to a public school system that, in fact and in law, provides Connecticut schoolchild-ren with a substantially equal educational opportu-nity. A significant component of that substantially equal educational opportunity is access to a public school education that is not substantially impaired by racial and ethnic isolation.

. . . [The plaintiffs] argue that the combination of "racial segregation, the concentration of poor chil-dren in the schools, and disparities in educational re-sources . . . deprive [Hartford schoolchildren] of sub-stantially equal educational opportunities." We agree with the plaintiffs in part. We need not decide, in this case, the extent to which substantial socio-economic disparities or disparities in educational re-sources would themselves be sufficient to require the state to intervene in order to equalize educational opportunities. For the purposes of the present litigation, we decide only that the scope of the constitutional obligation expressly imposed on the state by article eighth, § 1, is informed by the constitutional prohibition against segregation contained in article first, § 20. Reading these constitutional provisions conjointly, we conclude that the existence of extreme racial and ethnic isolation in the public school system deprives schoolchildren of a substantially equal educational opportunity and requires the state to take further remedial measures.

Two factors persuade us that it is appropriate to undertake a conjoint reading of these provisions of our state constitution. One is the special nature of the affirmative constitutional right embodied in article eighth, § 1. The other is the explicit prohibition of segregation contained in article first, § 20.

* * *

For Connecticut schoolchildren, the scope of the state's constitutional obligation to provide a substantially equal educational opportunity is informed and amplified by the highly unusual provision in article first, § 20, that prohibits segregation not only indirectly, by forbidding discrimination, but directly, by the use of the term "segregation." The section provides in relevant part: "No person shall be denied the equal protection of the law *nor be subjected to segregation* or discrimination . . . because of . . . race [or] . . . ancestry. . . ." (Emphasis added.)

The express inclusion of the term "segregation" in article first, § 20, has independent constitutional significance. The addition of this term to the text of our equal protection clause distinguishes this case from others in which we have found a substantial equivalence between our equal protection clause and that contained in the United States constitution. . . .

The issue before us, therefore, is what specific meaning to attach to the protection against segregation contained in article first, § 20, in a case in which that protection is invoked as part of the plaintiff schoolchildren's fundamental affirmative right to a substantially equal educational opportunity under article eighth, § 1. In concrete terms, this issue devolves into the question of whether the state has a constitutional duty to remedy the educational impairment that results from segregation in the Hartford public schools, even though the conditions of segregation that contribute to such impairment neither were caused nor are perpetuated by invidious intentional conduct on the part of the state.

Linguistically, the term "segregation" in article first, § 20, which denotes "separation," is neutral about segregative intent. The section prohibits segregation that occurs "*because of* religion, race, color, ancestry, national origin, sex or physical or mental disability"; (emphasis added); without specifying the manner in which such a causal relationship must be established.

. . . [W]e are persuaded that, in the context of public education, in which the state has an affirmative obligation to monitor and to equalize educational opportunity, the state's awareness of existing and increasing severe racial and ethnic isolation imposes upon the state the responsibility to remedy "segregation . . . because of race [or] . . . ancestry. . . ." We therefore hold that, textually, article eighth, § 1, as informed by article first, § 20, requires the legislature to take affirmative responsibility to remedy segregation in our public schools, regardless of whether that segregation has occurred de jure or de facto.

The history of the promulgation of article eighth, § 1, and article first, § 20, supports our conclusion that these constitutional provisions include protection from de facto segregation, at least in public schools. That history includes not only the contemporaneous addition, in 1965, of these two provisions to our constitution, but also the strong commitment to ending discrimination and segregation that is evident in the remarks of the delegates to the 1965 constitutional convention.

* * *

Sound principles of public policy support our conclusion that the legislature's affirmative constitutional responsibility for the education of all public schoolchildren encompasses responsibility for segregation to which the legislature has contributed, even unintentionally. The parties agree, as the trial court expressly found, that racial and ethnic segregation is harmful, and that integration would likely have positive benefits for all children and for society as a whole. Further, as the trial court also expressly found, the racial and ethnic isolation of children in the Hartford schools is likely to worsen in the future.

Racial and ethnic segregation has a pervasive and invidious impact on schools, whether the segregation results from intentional conduct or from unorchestrated demographic factors. "[S]chools are an important socializing institution, imparting those shared values through which social order and stability are maintained." . . . Schools bear central responsibility for "inculcating [the] fundamental values necessary to the maintenance of a democratic political system. . . ." When children attend racially and ethnically isolated schools, these "shared values" are jeopardized: "If children of different races and economic and social groups have no opportunity to know each other and to live together in school, they cannot be expected to gain the understanding and mutual respect necessary for the cohesion of our society." . . .

* * *

The final issue before us is whether, in light of the findings of the trial court, . . . the plaintiffs have proven a violation of their fundamental right, under the state constitution, to a substantially equal educational opportunity that is free from substantial racial and ethnic isolation. We conclude that they have done so.

"[I]n Connecticut the right to education is so basic and fundamental that any infringement of that right must be strictly scrutinized." [citing Connecticut cases]. . . . Proper evaluation of the plaintiffs' claims . . . requires us to balance the legislature's affirmative constitutional obligation to provide all of the state's schoolchildren with a substantially equal educational opportunity against the legislature's recognized significant discretion in matters of public elementary and secondary education.

The analysis . . . requires a three-step process: "First, the plaintiffs must make a prima facie showing that the disparities . . . are more than de minimis in that the disparities continue to jeopardize the plaintiffs' fundamental right to education. If they make that showing, the burden then shifts to the state to justify these disparities as incident to the advancement of a legitimate state policy. If the state's justification is acceptable, the state must further demonstrate that the continuing disparities are nevertheless not so great as to be unconstitutional." . . . [W]e are persuaded that the current school assignment scheme . . . violates the plaintiffs' fundamental right to a substantially equal educational opportunity.

The plaintiffs have shown, and the defendants do not contest, that the disparities in the racial and ethnic composition of public schools in Hartford and the surrounding communities are more than de minimis. . . . These disparities jeopardize the plaintiffs' fundamental right to education.

The defendants stress that the trial court also made extensive findings about the significant role that adverse socioeconomic conditions play in the difficulties encountered by Hartford schoolchildren. Although the findings of the trial court are supported

by credible evidence, they do not undermine the plaintiffs' claim. It is well established, under prevailing principles governing the law of equal protection, that poverty is not a suspect classification. . . . The plaintiffs have not brought an equal protection claim challenging these principles.

The trial court's findings simply demonstrate that Hartford's schoolchildren labor under a dual burden: their poverty *and* their racial and ethnic isolation. These findings regarding the causal relationship between the poverty suffered by Hartford schoolchildren and their poor academic performance cannot be read in isolation. They do not diminish the significance of the stipulations and undisputed findings that the Hartford public school system suffers from severe and increasing racial and ethnic isolation, that such isolation is harmful to students of all races, and that the districting statute . . . is the single most important factor contributing to the concentration of racial and ethnic minorities in the Hartford public school system. The fact that, as pleaded, the plaintiffs' complaint does not provide them a constitutional remedy for one of their afflictions, namely, their poverty, is not a ground for depriving them of a remedy for the other.

The uncontested evidence of the severe racial and ethnic isolation of Hartford's schoolchildren demonstrates that the state has failed to fulfill its affirmative constitutional obligation to provide all of the state's schoolchildren with a substantially equal educational opportunity. . . . [T]he disparity in access to an unsegregated educational environment in this case arises out of state action and inaction that, prima facie, violates the plaintiffs' constitutional rights, although that segregation has occurred de facto rather than de jure. Thus, because the plaintiffs have made the requisite prima facie showing that their fundamental right to a substantially equal educational opportunity has been jeopardized, the burden of justification shifts to the state.

* * *

The statutes enacted by the legislature and the educational strategies adopted by the state demonstrate that the state has acted to further policies that are both legitimate and facially neutral with respect to racial and ethnic isolation. The General Assembly has enacted no legislation that was intended to cause either de jure or de facto segregation. It enacted the districting statute, not to impose or to foster racial or ethnic isolation, but to improve educational quality for all Connecticut schoolchildren by increasing state involvement in all aspects of public elementary and secondary education. Moreover, the districting scheme presently furthers the legitimate nonracial interests of permitting considerable local control and accountability in educational matters. Furthermore, in recognition of its moral obligation to address the adverse consequences of racial and ethnic discrimination, the state reorganized the board of education, during the 1980s, to concentrate on the needs of urban schoolchildren and to promote diversity in the public schools. Under [a state statute] which the legislature enacted to remedy racial imbalances *within* public school districts, all schools within a district must maintain, within specified tolerances, a student population that reflects the student population in the district as a whole. In addition, the state has supported and encouraged voluntary plans for increasing interdistrict diversity. It has provided financial support to interdistrict magnet programs and has enacted legislation to promote *voluntary* interdistrict solutions to racial and ethnic isolation. . . . In all these respects, the state has furthered agendas that are legitimate. Accordingly, the defendants have sustained their initial burden of justifying the legitimacy of the state's actions.

. . . In the context of the present claims, the state must demonstrate that, in light of its recognized discretion in matters of public elementary and secondary education, and taking into account the measures that it has taken to remedy racial and ethnic disparities in the public schools, the disparities are not so significant as to rise to the level of a constitutional deprivation. . . .

We conclude that the defendants have failed to satisfy their difficult burden. Despite the initiatives undertaken by the defendants to alleviate the severe racial and ethnic disparities among school districts, and despite the fact that the defendants did not intend to create or maintain these disparities, the disparities that continue to burden the education of the plaintiffs infringe upon their fundamental state constitutional right to a substantially equal educational opportunity.

Our conclusion finds uncontested factual support in the stipulations of the parties, which provide dramatic documentation of the wide disparities in the racial and ethnic composition of the student populations in the public schools in Hartford and those in the twenty-one surrounding communities. . . .

Because the parties have not had the opportunity to present evidence directed to the remedial consequences that follow from our decision on the merits of the plaintiffs' complaint, we could remand this case to the trial court for further proceedings to address remedies. Alternatively, if no further evidentiary inquiries would be required, we could invite further briefing in this court and attempt to resolve the issues ourselves.

We have decided not to follow either of these avenues. . . . In light of the complexities of developing a legislative program that would respond to the constitutional deprivation that the plaintiffs had established, . . . further judicial intervention should be stayed "to afford the General Assembly an opportunity to take appropriate legislative action." . . .

In staying our hand, we do not wish to be misunderstood about the urgency of finding an appropriate remedy for the plight of Hartford's public schoolchildren. Every passing day denies these children their constitutional right to a substantially equal educational opportunity. Every passing day shortchanges these children in their ability to learn to contribute to their own well-being and to that of this state and nation. We direct the legislature and the executive branch to put the search for appropriate remedial measures at the top of their respective agendas. We are confident that with energy and good will, appropriate remedies can be found and implemented in time to make a difference before another generation of children suffers the consequences of a segregated public school education.

* * *

NOTES AND QUESTIONS

1. An Alternative Constitutional Approach to Achieving Desegregation

In light of the substantial likelihood of rapid resegregation in most urban school districts following federal court withdrawal of judicial supervision of school desegregation, how likely are state courts to follow the example of the Connecticut Supreme Court and require desegregation based on state constitutional provisions? *See* Moran, "Milo's Miracle," 29 *Conn. L. Rev.* 1079 (1997) (state inertia in the area of desegregation remedies likely to persist despite *Sheff* decision).

Note that the *Sheff* court found only two other state constitutions that explicitly prohibit segregation, those of Hawaii and New Jersey. And the provision in Hawaii's constitution, Art.I, § 9, is addressed only to segregation "in any military organization" of the state. Although the New Jersey constitution prohibits discrimination and segregation "in the public schools, because of religious principles, race, color, ancestry or national origin," Art.I, paragraph 5, the courts of New Jersey have not held that this provision requires the state to prevent de facto segregation within its public school system. In several cases in the 1960s and early 1970s, however, the New Jersey Supreme Court held that the state commissioner of education and local boards of education have broad statutory authority, in light of the constitutional provision against segregation in schools, to prevent local actions that would increase racial imbalance. With regard to whether the segregation clause in the Connecticut constitution was essential to the decision or whether the court could have used the education clause alone to remedy de facto racial and ethnic segregation, *see* Ryan, "*Sheff*, Segregation, and School Finance Litigation," 74 *NYU L. Rev.* 529, 550–553 (1999) (segregation clause "an unnecessary prop in the court's decision").

The General Assembly's response to the Connecticut Supreme Court's mandate, "An Act Enhancing Educational Choices and Opportunities," 1997 Conn. Acts 290 (Reg.Sess.), has been criticized for failing to meet the principles outlined in *Sheff. See, e.g.*, Note, "How *Sheff* Revives *Brown*: Reconsidering Desegregation's Role in Creating Equal Educational Opportunity," 74 *NYU L. Rev.* 485 (1999).

2. An Adequate Education

In a concurring opinion, Justice Berdon wrote that in addition to his agreement with the rationale provided in the majority opinion, he believed that "a racially and ethnically segregated educational environment also deprives schoolchildren of an adequate education as required by the state constitution." 678 A.2d at 1292. He argued that inasmuch as the state constitution "provides that *education is a fundamental right* of every child regardless of his or her race or ethnicity," *id.* at 1292, the education

guaranteed in the state constitution must be an "adequate" education, and that "in order to provide an adequate or 'proper' education, our children must be educated in a nonsegregated environment." *Id.* at 1293. Does this mean that white children who may live in parts of the state where there are no racial or ethnic minority students in the geographic area are receiving an inadequate education? How might either a legislature or a court address this inadequacy?

3. "Appropriate Legislative Action"

The majority expresses confidence that the legislature will enact appropriate remedial measures in a timely fashion. Has the majority articulated sufficiently clear guidelines to enable the legislature to meet the constitutional mandate? The dissent strongly disagreed:

> [T]he majority sends to the legislature and the executive branch a mandate to fashion a remedy for de facto racial and ethnic concentration in our public schools, a task that those branches of government will inevitably find to be extraordinarily difficult or perhaps even impossible, because the majority articulates no principle upon which to structure such a remedy. The necessary implication of the majority's reasoning is that virtually every school district in the state is now either unconstitutional or constitutionally suspect. Without explicitly saying so, the majority has effectively struck down, not just for the greater Hartford area but for the entire state, the municipality based school system that has been in effect in this state since 1909.
>
> * * *
>
> . . . [I]f I were a member of either the executive or legislative branch of our government, I would have but the slightest glimmering of what kind of legislation would comport with the majority's mandate, because the opinion articulates no principle or standard upon which to base such legislation. Confining my discussion here to the Hartford metropolitan area, I can find no principle or standard in the majority opinion by which to measure the level of racial and ethnic integration of the African-American and Hispanic schoolchildren that will be constitutional. The closest thing to such a principle are three statements by the majority. The first is that "the existence of *extreme racial and ethnic isolation*" in the public schools violates the constitution. (Emphasis added.) The second is that if "*significant* racial and ethnic isolation continues to occur," no intent to bring about or maintain that isolation is required in order to establish a constitu-

tional violation. (Emphasis added.) The third is that a "significant component of [a] substantially equal educational opportunity is access to a public school education that is not substantially impaired by racial and ethnic isolation."

. . . Does significant isolation or "substantially impaired" mean that, with respect to the Hartford metropolitan area, the legislature must start with the last census figures, and redraw the district lines so that each municipality has a substantially equal percentage of African-American and Hispanic schoolchildren? Or does the reference to "extreme racial and ethnic isolation" mean that, so long as the concentration is not massive—something less than the current 92 or 95 percent figure, for example—the constitution will not be violated? Or is the measure a statewide, rather than a district-wide figure? . . .

Further, why is the municipality the appropriate measuring unit, rather than the individual school? After all, if a student's constitutional right to an integrated education is violated by being required to be educated in a racially or ethnically concentrated setting, thereby, according to the majority, missing out on the social benefits of an integrated education and incurring the social burdens of a segregated education upon which the majority's analysis rests, then is it not appropriate that we look at the actual setting in which each child's education takes place? After all, a student who attends a racially and ethnically concentrated school, albeit in a racially and ethnically integrated school district, will not have those benefits and will carry those burdens. If so, then it seems that each school must, constitutionally, have the appropriate racial and ethnic makeup. These are just some of the questions that are raised, but not addressed, by the majority opinion.

678 A.2d at 1295–96, 1329–1330 (Justice Borden, dissenting). *See* Rebell and Hughes, "Efficacy and Engagement: The Remedies Problem Posed by *Sheff v. O'Neill*—and a Proposed Solution," 29 *Conn. L. Rev.* 1115 (1997), suggesting an effective remedy that the court could have ordered.

4. Poverty or Race

Justice Borden's dissenting opinion also emphasizes that the educational disadvantage experienced by "black and Hispanic youngsters" is attributable to the "social and economic conditions under which they and their families live." 678 A.2d at 1304. The dissent quotes extensively from the trial court's findings:

. . . "It is poverty and not race that is a principal causal factor in lower educational achievement." The prob-

lems of the Hartford schools are compounded by the fact that minorities in the inner cities are disproportionately poor, and the "real correlation with academic achievement is socioeconomic class rather than race. . . ." The fact that the students come from poor families "in and of itself is a significant problem in the schools. . . . The reason that children who live in poverty do not do well in statewide academic testing is because they are poor and disadvantaged and not because they are an ethnic or racial minority, because poor minority children exhibit the same patterns as those of their poor white counterparts, and poverty is the strongest predictor of poor academic achievement." Moreover, the concentration of poverty may adversely affect academic achievement over and above the effect of family poverty. The socioeconomic status of schoolchildren dictates their academic performance. Thus, the improvement in the socioeconomic status of blacks explains the reduction by almost one half of the achievement gap between black and white students nationally between 1970 and 1990. The trial court also specifically found that "[v]irtually all of the differences in performance between Hartford students and those in other towns, as well as differences in college attendance, can be explained by differences in socioeconomic status and the background factors that socioeconomic status represents."

* * *

The trial court also found that Hartford students and those in the surrounding towns are scoring at the level to be expected if the dramatic differences between them in poverty levels are taken into account. The disparity in test scores does not indicate that Hartford is doing an inadequate job of educating its students or that its schools are failing, because the test scores, based on the relevant socioeconomic factors, are at the approximate projected level when adjustments are made for those factors.

Id. at 1304, 1305. Can the effects of racial and ethnic isolation be separated from the effects of poverty? Should the inability to determine how much of the educational disadvantage is attributable to poverty and how much to racial isolation affect the state constitutional claim? *See* Moran, *supra*, at 1106–09.

5. The Sheff Decision and the Federal Equal Protection Clause

In light of the Supreme Court's current position on the use of race by government officials to achieve greater minority participation, unless it constitutes a narrowly drawn remedy for prior intentional segregation, *see, e.g., Adarand Contractors, Inc. v. Pena*, 515 U.S. 200, 115 S.Ct. 2097, 132 L.Ed.2d 158 (1995), will the state's efforts to eliminate or reduce racial isolation in Hartford in response to the Connecticut Supreme Court's mandate in *Sheff v. O'Neill* be found to violate the federal Equal Protection Clause? The affirmative obligation to end de facto racial and ethnic isolation, which the *Sheff* majority determined was grounded in the Connecticut constitution, is clearly distinguishable from the desegregation remedies federal courts order to undo prior intentional segregation of public schools. *See Hopwood v. Texas*, 78 F.3d 932 (5th Cir.), *cert. denied*, 116 S.Ct. 2581 (1996). Does the evidence of educational harm attributable to racial and ethnic isolation by the majority establish a compelling justification? If so, what remedies would be sufficiently narrowly tailored to meet the requirements of the strict scrutiny standard of review? *See* Brown, "The Implications of the Equal Protection Clause for the Mandatory Integration of Public School Students," 29 *Conn. L. Rev.* 999 (1997)(contending that Connecticut has a compelling interest in the proper socialization of public school students as part of its responsibility to inculcate fundamental values necessary to maintain a democratic system).

VII. SCHOOL DESEGREGATION: THE ROLE OF THE POLITICAL BRANCHES

A. Federal Legislation Prohibiting Discrimination on the Basis of Race

The passage of the Civil Rights Act of 1964, 42 U.S.C. § 2000c,d, shifted the burden of litigation from minority litigants to the federal government. This legislation empowered the Department of Health, Education, and Welfare (now the Department of Education) to withhold federal funds from school districts that continued to discriminate against blacks and gave the Attorney General authority to file desegregation suits on the complaint of private citizens. 42 U.S.C. §§ 2000c-6, d-1 (2000). *See generally* Note, "The Courts, HEW, and Southern School Desegregation," 77 *Yale L.J.* 321, 356–64 (1967). Under the Civil Rights Act of 1964, HEW promulgated guidelines requiring school districts to make a good faith start toward desegregation. U.S.

Office of Education, HEW, "General Statement of Policies under Title VI of the Civil Rights Act of 1964 Respecting Desegregation of Elementary and Secondary Schools (1965)," *reprinted in Price v. Denison Independent School District*, 348 F.2d 1010, 1015 (5th Cir. 1965). *See also* U.S. Office of Education, HEW, "Revised Statement of Policies for School Desegregation Plans under Title VI of the Civil Rights Act of 1964," 45 C.F.R. § 181 (1967).

Title IV

42 U.S.C. § 2000c (2000); Pub. L. 88-352, Title IV, §§ 407, 409–10, July 2, 1964, 78 Stat.248–49.

§ 2000c-6. Civil actions by the Attorney General

(a) . . . Whenever the Attorney General receives a complaint in writing—

(1) signed by a parent or group of parents to the effect that his or their minor children, as members of a class of persons similarly situated, are being deprived by a school board of the equal protection of the laws, or

(2) signed by an individual, or his parent, to the effect that he has been denied admission to or not permitted to continue in attendance at a public college by reason of race, color, religion, or national origin, and the Attorney General believes the complaint is meritorious and certifies that the signer or signers of such complaint are unable in his judgment, to initiate and maintain appropriate legal proceedings for relief and that the institution of an action will materially further the orderly achievement of desegregation in public education, the Attorney General is authorized, after giving notice of such complaint to the appropriate school board or college authority and after certifying that he is satisfied that such board or authority has had a reasonable time to adjust the conditions alleged in such complaint, to institute for or in the name of the United States a civil action in any appropriate district court of the United States against such parties and for such relief as may be appropriate, and such court shall have and shall exercise jurisdiction of proceedings instituted pursuant to this section, provided that nothing herein shall empower any official or court of the United States to issue any order seeking to achieve a racial balance in any school by requiring the transportation of pupils or students from one school to another or one school district to another in order to achieve such racial balance, or otherwise enlarge the existing power of the

court to insure compliance with constitutional standards. The Attorney General may implead as defendants such additional parties as are or become necessary to the grant of effective relief hereunder.

(b) . . . The Attorney General may deem a person or persons unable to initiate and maintain appropriate legal proceedings within the meaning of subsection (a) of this section when such person or persons are unable, either directly or through other interested persons or organizations, to bear the expense of the litigation or to obtain effective legal representation; or whenever he is satisfied that the institution of such litigation would jeopardize the personal safety, employment, or economic standing of such person or persons, their families, or their property. . . .

§ 2000c-8. Personal suits for relief against discrimination in public education

Nothing in this subchapter shall affect adversely the right of any person to sue for or obtain relief in any court against discrimination in public education.

§ 2000c-9. Classification and assignment

Nothing in this subchapter shall prohibit classification and assignment for reasons other than race, color, religion, or national origin.

Title VI

42 U.S.C. § 2000d (2000); Pub. L. 88-352, Title VI, §§ 601–02, July 2, 1964, 78 Stat. 252.

§ 2000d. Prohibition against exclusion from participation in, denial of benefits of, and discrimination under federally assisted programs on ground of race, color, or national origin

No person in the United States shall, on the ground of race, color, or national origin, be excluded from participation in, be denied the benefits of, or be subjected to discrimination under any program or activity receiving Federal financial assistance.

§ 2000d-1. Federal authority and financial assistance to programs or activities by way of grant, loan, or contract other than contract of insurance or guaranty; rules and regulations; approval by President; compliance with requirements; reports to Congressional committees; effective date of administrative action

Each Federal department and agency which is empowered to extend Federal financial assistance to any program or activity, by way of grant, loan, or contract other than a contract of insurance or guaranty, is authorized and directed to effectuate the provisions of section 2000d of this title with respect to such program or activity by issuing rules, regulations, or orders of general applicability which shall be consistent with achievement of the objectives of the statute authorizing the financial assistance in connection with which the action is taken. No such rule, regulation, or order shall become effective unless and until approved by the President. Compliance with any requirement adopted pursuant to this section may be effected (1) by the termination of or refusal to grant or to continue assistance under such program or activity to any recipient as to whom there has been an express finding on the record, after opportunity for hearing, of a failure to comply with such requirement, but such termination or refusal shall be limited to the particular political entity, or part thereof, or other recipient as to whom such a finding has been made and, shall be limited in its effect to the particular program, or part thereof, in which such noncompliance has been so found, or (2) by any other means authorized by law: Provided, however, that no such action shall be taken until the department or agency concerned has advised the appropriate person or persons of the failure to comply with the requirement and has determined that compliance cannot be secured by voluntary means. In the case of any action terminating, or refusing to grant or continue, assistance because of failure to comply with a requirement imposed pursuant to this section, the head of the Federal department or agency shall file with the committees of the House and Senate having legislative jurisdiction over the program or activity involved a full written report of the circumstances and the grounds for such action. No such action shall become effective until thirty days have elapsed after the filing of such report.

* * *

§ 2000d-6 (1970). [Pub. L. 91-230, § 2, April 13, 1970, 84 Stat. 121; Pub. L. 96-88, Title III, §301, Title V, §507, Oct. 17, 1979, 93 Stat.677,692] Policy of United States as to application of nondiscrimination provisions in schools of local educational agencies

(a) . . . It is the policy of the United States that guidelines and criteria established pursuant to title VI of the Civil Rights Act of 1964 and section 182 of the Elementary and Secondary Education Amendments of 1966 dealing with conditions of segregation by race, whether de jure or de facto, in the schools of the local educational agencies of any State shall be applied uniformly in all regions of the United States whatever the origin or cause of such segregation.

(b) . . . Such uniformity refers to one policy applied uniformly to *de jure* segregation wherever found and such other policy as may be provided pursuant to law applied uniformly to *de facto* segregation wherever found.

(c) . . . Nothing in this section shall be construed to diminish the obligation of responsible officials to enforce or comply with such guidelines and criteria in order to eliminate discrimination in federally-assisted programs and activities as required by Title VI of the Civil Rights Act of 1964.

(d) . . . It is the sense of the Congress that the Department of Justice and the Secretary of Education should request such additional funds as may be necessary to apply the policy set forth in this section throughout the United States.

NOTES AND QUESTIONS

1. Section 2000c-6 of Title IV

a. Purpose and Significance. What is the purpose of § 2000c-6, which authorizes civil rights actions by the Attorney General? Is it to reduce the financial burdens imposed on individuals and civil rights groups, or is it to place the power and prestige of the federal government behind the desegregation movement? Is the Attorney General likely to be more successful than private litigants in particular litigation? If so, for what reasons—greater resources, greater judicial sympathy?

b. Relationship to Private Litigants. What role does § 2000c-6 envision for private litigants? *See also* § 2000c-8. Would it permit both private parties and the Attorney General to participate in the same litigation, even if the Attorney General and the private parties disagree on the theory of the suit or the appropriateness of a particular remedy? What difficulties might this pose for courts? Should the Attorney General be permitted to intervene in private suits? *See* 42 U.S.C. § 2000h-2.

c. Complaint Procedures. What is the difference between paragraphs (a)(1) and (a)(2) of §2000c-6 with respect to complaint procedures? Does (a)(1) apply to all denials of equal protection, whether or not segregation is involved? If so, how does the complaint procedure embodied in this section differ from that in (a)(2), which explicitly applies to denials of admissions based on race? Under both sec-

tions, the Attorney General must determine whether a complaint is "meritorious" before he or she acts.

d. Enforcement of Brown. What impact might § 2000c-6 have on the course of desegregation in the South? If the issue is one of securing compliance with court decrees, overcoming the recalcitrance of federal district courts, and resolving the ambiguity of Supreme Court decisions, how would the addition of the United States as a party resolve any of these difficulties?

e. Racial Balance. How should the language in § 2000c-6, stating that "nothing herein shall empower any official or court . . . to issue any order seeking to achieve a racial balance in any school," be construed? *Compare United States v. Jefferson County Board of Education,* 372 F.2d 836 (5th Cir. 1966), *aff'd,* 380 F.2d 385 (1967) (en banc), *cert. denied,* 389 U.S. 840, 88 S.Ct. 77, 19 L.Ed.2d 104, *with* L. Graglia, *Disaster by Decree* 46–52, 58–66 (1976). Would the limitation, if construed to prohibit racial balance remedies where de jure segregation had occurred, be constitutional? Would it be a limit only on the Department of Justice or would it also extend to private litigants in desegregation suits?

2. Section 2000d of Title VI

Does § 2000d restate the principle embodied in *Brown I* and *II?* What is the difference between discrimination and the denial of benefits? Why did Congress limit governmental review under this section to programs receiving federal financial assistance?

3. Section 2000d-1

a. Administration of § 2000d-1. The process of identifying a violation of § 2000d is left to existing federal agencies, but their regulations must be approved by the president. Why might Congress have adopted this approach?

b. Fund Cutoffs. Why did Congress limit the fund cutoff for noncompliance with § 2000d "to the particular program, or part thereof, in which such noncompliance has been so found . . ."? *See Board of Public Instruction v. Finch,* 414 F.2d 1068 (5th Cir. 1969).

Although funding cutoffs have been rare, the threat of such cutoffs has been thought to be the strongest weapon against local officials in the effort to desegregate public schools. *See generally*, G. Orfield, *The Reconstruction of Southern Education*, 252–58 (1969). *Compare* Badger and Browning, "Title I and Comparability: Recent Developments," 7 *Clearinghouse Rev.* 263 (1973); *Natonabah v. Board of Education*, 355 F.Supp. 716 (D.N.M. 1973). Would this be true in all districts? Suppose a district were composed largely of African American students, most of whom qualified for assistance to disadvantaged children under Title I of the Elementary and Secondary Education Act, 20 U.S.C. § 6301 (2000). Who would be the greater loser as a result of a fund cutoff? Does this particular weapon run the risk of dividing private litigants and the federal government, with the former opposing a fund cutoff and the latter advocating it?

c. Alternatives to Fund Cutoffs. In addition to allowing the administering agency to achieve compliance by terminating or refusing aid to recipients who refuse to comply with desegregation requirements, Title VI also empowers the agency to proceed "by any other means authorized by law." This represents an effort to provide an alternative to the severe step of denying federal aid. One such alternative, which would entail reliance on the courts, is suggested by the standard paragraph in the form all recipients must sign which states that the appropriate assurance of compliance "is given in consideration of and for the purpose of obtaining any and all federal grants, loans, contracts, property, discounts or other federal financial assistance. . . . The applicant recognizes and agrees that such federal financial assistance will be extended in reliance on the representations and agreements made in the assurance and that the United States or the state agency . . . jointly or severally shall have the right to seek enforcement of this assurance."

HEW included this wording with the specific intent of making assurances enforceable in a court action asking for specific performance. Does this approach seem preferable to cutoffs?

4. Enforcement of the Civil Rights Act

The primary responsibility for enforcing Title VI of the Civil Rights Act was given to the Office of Education within the Department of Health, Education, and Welfare (HEW). Historically, the United States Office of Education had been a powerless agency without any policymaking functions whose sole responsibility was to collect educational statistics and publish reports. The impotency of the Office of Education derived from traditional American adherence to localism in educational matters, the office's small staff, and its total dependence on local and state education officials. Orfield, *supra* at 9. Needless to say, the Office of Education was not prepared for the monumental task that confronted it after the enactment of the Civil Rights Act of 1964. Vast institutional and staffing changes were required. Chaos in the early months of the "administrative-judicial era" was not uncommon, but despite these problems, substantial progress was made in desegregating southern schools. *See* Orfield, *id.* at 147–50. *See generally* B. Radin, *Implementation, Change, and the Federal Bureaucracy* (1977).

Subsequently, the Office for Civil Rights (OCR) was moved out of the Office of Education directly to the Office of the Secretary of HEW. Under the Department of Education Organization Act, Pub. L. No. 96–88, 93 Stat. 669 (1979), which established the Department of Education (leaving what remained of the former HEW as the new Department of Health and Human Services), the position of OCR director was elevated to the level of an assistant secretary, appointed by the president, with authority not previously accorded that position. OCR investigates complaints of discrimination filed by individuals and groups, and it conducts OCR-initiated compliance reviews of selected institutions triggered by its analysis of statistical reports. When school districts or universities are found to have violated Title VI, they are given an opportunity to achieve compliance voluntarily. If, after negotiations, voluntary compliance is not obtained, OCR initiates an administrative hearing or refers the matter to the Department of Justice for initiation of court proceedings. If OCR prevails in the administrative hearing, the Secretary of Education may terminate federal funds. The termination order can then be appealed to the appropriate U.S. Circuit Court of Appeals.

The current regulations state that school systems receiving federal funds may not:

(i) Deny an individual any service, financial aid, or other benefit provided under the program;

(ii) Provide any service, financial aid, or other benefit to an individual which is different, or is provided in a different manner, from that provided to others under the program;

(iii) Subject an individual to segregation or separate treatment in any matter related to his receipt of any service, financial aid, or other benefit under the program;

(iv) Restrict an individual in any way in the enjoyment of any advantage or privilege enjoyed by others receiving any service, financial aid, or other benefit under the program;

(v) Treat an individual differently from others in determining whether he satisfies any admission, enrollment, quota, eligibility, membership or other requirement or condition which individuals must meet in order to be provided any service, financial aid, or other benefit provided under the program;

(vi) Deny an individual an opportunity to participate in the program through the provision of services or otherwise or afford him an opportunity to do so which is different from that afforded others under the program (including the opportunity to participate in the program as an employee but only to the extent set forth in paragraph (c) of this section);

(vii) Deny a person the opportunity to participate as a member of a planning or advisory body which is an integral part of the program.

The regulations further provide that:

(2) A recipient, in determining the types of services, financial aid, or other benefits, or facilities which will be provided under any such program, or the class of individuals to whom, or the situations in which, such services, financial aid, other benefits, or facilities will be provided under any such program, or the class of individuals to be afforded an opportunity to participate in any such program, may not directly or through contractual or other arrangements, utilize criteria or methods of administration which have the effect of subjecting individuals to discrimination because of their race, color, or national origin, or have the effect of defeating or substantially impairing accomplishment of the objectives of the program as respect individuals of a particular race, color, or national origin.

* * *

(6)(i) In administering a program regarding which the recipient has previously discriminated against persons on the ground of race, color, or national origin, the recipient must take affirmative action to overcome the effects of prior discrimination.

(6)(ii) Even in the absence of such prior discrimination, a recipient in administering a program may take affirmative action to overcome the effects of conditions which resulted in limiting participation by persons of a particular race, color, or national origin.

34 C.F.R. § 100.3(b)(1). This section also includes provisions that apply to faculty and staff. *See* 34 C.F.R. §100.3(c).

5. *"Under Any Program or Activity"*

Title VI, § 2000d, provides that no person may "be excluded from participation in, be denied the benefits of, or be subjected to discrimination under *any program or activity* receiving federal financial assistance." (Emphasis added.) Section 2000d-1 provides that compliance with any of the regulations implementing Title VI may be affected by a cutoff of funds "under such program or activity . . . but . . . shall be limited in its effect to the particular program or part thereof, in which such noncompliance has been so found." What might "program or activity" mean? Should the Department of Education and the courts interpret the language broadly or narrowly? Up until 1984, the Department construed Title VI and Title IX, which parallels Title VI in the area of sex discrimination, broadly. Thus, for example, the Department and courts had considered athletics sponsored by educational institutions to be an integral part of the educational program or activity provided by the institution and therefore covered by Title VI and Title IX, if the school system received federal assistance under various federal programs, even though athletics received no direct federal funds. In 1984, however, in a case involving Title IX, the Supreme Court construed "program or activity" narrowly. In *Grove City College v. Bell*, 465 U.S. 555, 104 S.Ct. 1211, 79 L.Ed.2d 516 (1984), Justice White, writing for the majority, determined that Grove City College, which accepted no direct federal assistance but enrolled students who received federal financial aid, is subject to Title IX of the Educational Amendments, and having so determined, found it necessary to identify the "education program or activity" at the college that was "receiving federal financial assistance." The majority concluded that "[a]lthough the legislative history contains isolated suggestions that entire institutions are subject to the nondiscrimination provision whenever one of their programs receives federal assistance, . . . we cannot accept the Court of Appeals' conclusion that in the circumstances present here Grove City itself is a 'program or activity' that may be regulated in its entirety." 465 U.S. at 570–71, 104 S.Ct. at 1220. Receipt of federal financial assistance by some of Grove City's students did not trigger institution-wide coverage under Title IX. Only the College's own financial aid program could be regulated under Title IX.

Justices Brennan and Marshall, concurring in part and dissenting in part, looked to the history of Title VI to argue that the majority's narrow definition of "program or activity" was "directly contrary to congressional intent." Justice Brennan noted that

> [t]he absurdity of the Court's decision is further demonstrated by examining its practical effect. According to the Court, the "financial aid program" at Grove City College may not discriminate on the basis of sex because it is covered by Title IX, but the College is not prohibited from discriminating in its admissions, its athletic programs, or even its various academic departments. The Court thus sanctions practices that Congress clearly could not have intended: for example, after today's decision, Grove City College would be free to segregate male and female students in classes run by its mathematics department. This would be so even though the affected students are attending the College with the financial assistance provided by federal funds. If anything about Title IX were ever certain, it is that discriminatory practices like the one just described were meant to be prohibited by the statute.

465 U.S. at 601–02, 104 S.Ct. at 1236.

What was the likely effect of *Grove City College* on the application of Title VI to a school district that discriminated in its athletics program by having separate African American and white teams and that received no federal funds, although the school system as a whole received federal assistance under various federal statutes? Could the Office for Civil Rights have proceeded against a school district's ability-grouping system that was found to discriminate against African American students if the district received federal funds for students with disabilities under the Individuals with Disabilities Education Act, funds for the disadvantaged under Title I of the Elementary and Secondary Education Act, and Vocational Education Act funds?

Following pronouncements by the Reagan administration that Title VI (as well as the Age Discrimination Act of 1975, 42 U.S.C. 6101, *et seq.*, and Section 504 of the Rehabilitation Act of 1973, 29 U.S.C. 794) would be interpreted in the same way as Title IX had been in the *Grove City* decision, a bipartisan coalition brought about the adoption of the Civil Rights Restoration Act which defines "program or activity" to mean "a college, university" or "a local educational agency," "any part of which is extended federal financial assistance." Pub. L. 88-352, Title VI, § 606, as added Pub. L. 100-259, § 6, Mar. 22, 1988, 107 Stat. 31 provides as follows:

SEC. 2. The Congress finds that—

(1) certain aspects of recent decisions and opinions of the Supreme Court have unduly narrowed or cast doubt upon the broad application of Title IX of the Education Amendments of 1972, section 504 of the Rehabilitation Act of 1973, the Age Discrimination Act of 1975, and Title VI of the Civil Rights Act of 1964; and

(2) legislative action is necessary to restore the prior consistent and long-standing executive branch interpretation and broad, institution-wide application of those laws as previously administered.

* * *

SEC. 6. Title VI of the Civil Rights Act of 1964 is amended by adding at the end the following new section:

SEC. 606. [42 U.S.C. § 2000d-4a] For the purposes of this title, the term 'program or activity' and the term 'program' mean all of the operations of—

(1)(A) a department, agency, special purpose district, or other instrumentality of a State or of a local government; or
(B) the entity of such State or local government that distributes such assistance and each such department or agency (and each other State or local government entity) to which the assistance is extended, in the case of assistance to a State or local government;

(2)(A) a college, university, or other postsecondary institution, or a public system of higher education; or
(B) a local educational agency (as defined in section 198(a)(10) of the Elementary and Secondary Education Act of 1965), system of vocational education, or other school system; . . .

See *Ass'n of Mexican-American Educators v. State of California*, 195 F.3d 465 (9th Cir. 1999) (analyzing legislative history of Civil Rights Restoration Act of 1987 to determine that fact that all schools in state derive from state power does not make all schools and school districts a single "public school system" for purposes of Title VI).

In *Cureton v. NCAA*, 198 F.3d 107 (3d Cir. 1999), the court held that because the Department of Education had failed to amend its Title VI regulations following the enactment of the Civil Rights Restoration Act, its application of the regulations to disparate impact discrimination claims must be program-specific, rather than institution-wide. Disagreeing with this interpretation on the ground that it was contrary to congressional intent, the Department nevertheless, to avoid confusion and to eliminate the concerns raised by the Third Circuit, has issued a Notice of Proposed Rulemaking (NPRM) in which the regulations would track the statutory language and apply both to disparate impact discrimination and "different treatment" (intentional) discrimination. *See* 65 *Fed. Reg.* 26464 (May 5, 2000).

B. Intent versus Effect Standard for Title VI Regulations and Private Rights of Action

Title VI, 42 U.S.C. § 2000d, prohibits discrimination on the basis of race, color, or national origin in federally aided programs. The regulations implementing this requirement provide that: "A recipient . . . may not . . . utilize criteria or methods of administration which have the *effect* of subjecting individuals to discrimination because of their race, color, or national origin. . . ." 34 C.F.R. §100.3(2). (Emphasis added.)

In *Lau v. Nichols*, 414 U.S. 563, 94 S.Ct. 786, 39 L.Ed.2d 1 (1974) (discussed in chapter 6), the Supreme Court held that a school system's failure to provide English language instruction to Chinese-speaking students denied them a meaningful opportunity to participate in the educational program offered by the school district and thus was a violation of Title VI. The Court, specifically citing the HEW guidelines, declared that "[d]iscrimination is barred which has the *effect* even though no purposeful design is present." *Id.* at 568, 94 S.Ct. at 789. Subsequently, in *Regents of the University of California v. Bakke*, 438 U.S. 265, 98 S.Ct. 2733, 57 L.Ed.2d 750 (1978), five members of the Supreme Court took the position that the standard for a Title VI violation ought to be the same as the standard for an equal protection clause violation. Inasmuch as Justice Powell applied the strict scrutiny standard of review to the equal protection clause, he applied the same standard to Title VI. The four other justices viewed Title VI as not barring preferential treatment of racial minorities to remedy past societal discrimination, citing *Lau*, but expressing concern that the *Bakke* decision had now cast doubt on the *Lau* "effects-only" standard. 438 U.S. at 351–52 (Brennan, White, Marshall, and Blackmun, J.J., concurring and dissenting). The four remaining justices refused to consider whether the statute and the Constitution required similar or different standards, but were of the view that Title VI barred race-conscious admissions policies to overcome the effects of societal discrimination.

In *Guardians Association v. Civil Service Commission*, 463 U.S. 582, 103 S.Ct. 322, 77 L.Ed.2d 866 (1983), which also cast some doubt on *Lau v. Nichols*, the Supreme Court confronted the question of "whether the private plaintiffs in this case need to prove discriminatory intent to establish a violation of Title VI of the Civil Rights Act of 1964, 42 U.S.C. § 2000d, *et seq.*, and administrative implementing regulations promulgated thereunder." The case involved "a challenge by black and Hispanic police officers . . . to several written examinations administered by New York City between 1968 and 1970 that were used to make entry-level appointments to the city's police department . . . through October 1974." Appointments were made in the order of test scores, and plaintiff black and Hispanic officers were hired later than otherwise similarly situated whites. When police officers were laid off in 1975 in accordance with a "last-hired, first-fired," policy, the result was that minority officers were disproportionately affected by the layoffs.

The Court split badly in the case, with the judgment of the Court announced by Justice White in an opinion joined only by Justice Rehnquist (except for Part II). Five justices (White and dissenters Stevens, Brennan, Blackmun, and Marshall) held that proof of discriminatory intent was not required by Title VI, although they reached this conclusion by a variety of routes. Two justices (White and Rehnquist), however, would not allow compensatory relief in a private Title VI action in the absence of proof of discriminatory intent (only declaratory or injunctive relief would be permitted). Two justices (Powell and Burger) would never allow private relief under Title VI, and one justice (O'Connor) would deny all relief unless discriminatory intent were proven.

Three justices (Stevens, Brennan, and Blackmun) reasoned that although, as a result of the *Bakke* decision, Title VI required proof of discriminatory intent, if the regulations promulgated by the agency to effectuate provisions of Title VI incorporated an "effects" standard, it would be valid. Justices White and Marshall would go further, arguing that even under Title VI itself, only disparate impact is needed, although Justice White emphasized that even if Title VI by itself did require proof of discriminatory intent, he agreed with Justice Stevens that federal agencies may promulgate regulations barring the use of criteria that have a disparate impact. Justice White also noted his disagreement with the lower court which thought that the *Bakke* decision had undermined *Lau v. Nichols*.

In light of the holding in *Guardians Association* that Title VI regulations may prohibit recipients of federal funds from "utiliz[ing] criteria or methods of administration which have the effect of subjecting individuals to discrimination because of their race, color, or national origin," even where there is no discriminatory intent, the issue is what are the appropriate legal standards for establishing liability for an action that has a disparate impact. The Eleventh Circuit, in *Elston v. Talladega County Board of Educ.*, 997 F.2d 1394, 1407 (11th Cir. 1993), outlined the standards as follows:

> [A] plaintiff must first demonstrate by a preponderance of the evidence that a facially neutral practice has a disproportionate adverse effect on a group protected by Title VI. . . . If the plaintiff makes such a prima facie showing, the defendant then must prove that there exists a substantial legitimate justification for the challenged practice in order to avoid liability. If the defendant carries this rebuttal burden, the plaintiff will still prevail if able to show that there exists a comparably effective alternative practice which would result in less disproportionality, or that the defendant's proffered justification is a pretext for discrimination.
>
> The plaintiff's duty to show that a practice has a disproportionate effect by definition requires the plaintiff to demonstrate a causal link between the defendant's challenged practice and the disparate impact identified. Thus, the plaintiff cannot make out a prima facie disparate impact claim if the evidence tends to show that even had the defendant not engaged in the challenged practice, the same disparate impact would nonetheless have existed.

See also Powell v. Ridge, 189 F.3d 387, 393-94 (3d Cir.), *cert. denied*, 528 U.S. 1046, 120 S. Ct. 579, 145 L.Ed. 2d 482 (1999). Other circuit courts, confronted with the issue, have concluded that a private right of action exists to enforce Title VI regulations. *See, e.g., Villanueva v. Carere*, 85 F.3d 481, 486 (10th Cir., 1996); *Larry P. v. Riles*, 793 F.2d 969, 981–982 (9th Cir. 1986); *Castaneda v. Pickard*, 781 F.2d 456, 465, n.11 (5th Cir. 1986).

In a recent 5-4 decision, however, the Supreme Court held that there was no private right of action to enforce disparate impact regulations promulgated under Title VI.

Alexander v. Sandoval
__U.S.__, 121 S.Ct. 1511, 149 L.Ed.2d 517 (2001).

Justice Scalia delivered the opinion of the Court.

[The case was brought by an applicant for a driver's license, challenging the Alabama Department of Public Safety's policy of administering the driver's license examination only in English. The plaintiff challenged this policy as in violation of Title VI regulations promulgated by the Department of Justice prohibiting recipients of federal funding from "utiliz[ing] criteria or methods of administration which have the effect of subjecting individuals to discrimination because of their race, color, or national origin. . . ." Both the district court and the Eleventh Circuit enjoined the English-only policy on the ground that it had the effect of subjecting non-English speakers to discrimination based on national origin.]

* * *

Although Title VI has often come to this Court, it is fair to say (indeed, perhaps an understatement) that our opinions have not eliminated all uncertainty regarding its commands. For purposes of the present case, however, it is clear from our decisions, from Congress's amendments of Title VI, and from the parties' concessions that three aspects of Title VI must be taken as given. First, private individuals may sue to enforce § 601 of Title VI and obtain both injunctive relief and damages. . . .

Second, it is similarly beyond dispute—and no party disagrees—that § 601 prohibits only intentional discrimination. In *Regents of Univ. of Cal. v. Bakke*, 438 U.S. 265, 98 S.Ct. 2733, 57 L.Ed.2d 750 (1978), the Court reviewed a decision of the California Supreme Court that had enjoined the University of California Medical School from "according any consideration to race in its admissions process." *Id.*, at 272, 98 S.Ct. 2733. Essential to the Court's holding reversing the aspect of the California court's decision was the determination that § 601 "proscribe[s] only those racial classifications that would violate the Equal Protection Clause or the Fifth Amendment." *Id.*, at 287, 98 S.Ct. 2733 (opinion of Powell, J.). . . . In *Guardians Assn. v. Civil Serv. Comm'n of New York City*, 463 U.S. 582, 102 S.Ct. 3221, 77 L.Ed.2d 866 (1963), the Court made clear that under *Bakke* only intentional discrimination was forbidden by § 601. . . . What we said in *Alexander v. Choate*, 469 U.S. 287, 293, 105 S.Ct. 712, 83 L.Ed.2d 661 (1985), is true today: "Title VI itself directly reach[es] only instances of intentional discrimination."

Third, we must assume for purposes of deciding this case that regulations promulgated under § 602 of Title VI may validly proscribe activities that have a disparate impact on racial groups, even though such activities are permissible under § 601. Though no opinion of this Court has held that, five Justices in *Guardians* voiced that view of the law at least as `alternative grounds for their decisions. . . . These statements are in considerable tension with the rule of *Bakke* and *Guardians* that § 601 forbids only intentional discrimination, . . . but petitioners have not challenged the regulations here. We therefore assume for the purposes of deciding this case that the . . . regulations proscribing activities that have a disparate impact on the basis of race are valid.

. . . In *Guardians*, the Court held that private individuals could not recover compensatory damages under Title VI except for intentional discrimination. Five Justices in addition voted to uphold the disparate-impact regulations . . ., but of those five, three expressly reserved the question of a direct private right of action to enforce the regulations, saying that "[w]hether a cause of action against private parties exists directly under the regulations . . . [is a] questio[n] that [is] not presented by this case." . . . Neither that case, nor any other in this Court, has held that the private right of action exists.

Nor does it follow straightaway from the three points we have taken as given that Congress must have intended a private right of action to enforce disparate-impact regulations. We do not doubt that regulations applying § 601's ban on intentional discrimination are covered by the cause of action to enforce that section. Such regulations, if valid and reasonable, authoritatively construe the statute itself . . ., and it is therefore meaningless to talk about a separate cause of action to enforce the regulations apart from the statute. A Congress that intends the statute to be enforced through a private cause of action intends the authoritative interpretation of the statute to be so enforced as well. . . .

We must face now the question avoided by *Lau* [*v. Nichols*, 414 U.S. 563, 94 S.Ct. 786, 39 L.Ed.2d 1 (1974)], because we have since rejected *Lau's* interpretation of § 601 as reaching beyond intentional discrimination. It is clear now that the disparate-impact regulations do not simply apply § 601—since they indeed forbid conduct that § 601 permits—and therefore clear that the private right of action to enforce § 601 does not include a private right to enforce these regulations. . . . That right must come, if at all, from the independent force of § 602. As stated earlier, we assume for purposes of this decision that § 602 confers the authority to promulgate disparate-impact regulations; the question remains whether it confers a private right of action to enforce them. If not, we must conclude that a failure to comply with regulations promulgated under § 602 that is not also a failure to comply with § 601 is not actionable.

* * *

We therefore begin (and find that we can end) our search for Congress's intent with the text and structure of Title VI. Section 602 authorizes federal agencies "to effectuate the provisions of [§ 601] . . . by issuing rules, regulations, or orders of general applicability." 42 U.S.C. § 200d-1. . . . Far from displaying congressional intent to create new rights, § 602 limits agencies to "effectuat[ing]" rights already created by § 601. And the focus of § 602 is twice removed from the individuals who will ultimately benefit from Title VI's protection. . . . Section 602 is yet a step further removed: it focuses neither on the individuals protected nor even on the funding recipients being regulated, but on the agencies that will do the regulating. . . . So far as we can tell, this authorizing portion of § 602 reveals no congressional intent to create a private right of action.

Nor do the methods that § 602 goes on to provide for enforcing its authorized regulations manifest an intent to create a private remedy; if anything, they suggest the opposite. Section 602 empowers agencies to enforce their regulations either by terminating funding to the "particular program, or part thereof," that has violated the regulation or "by any other means authorized by law," 42 U.S.C. § 2000d-1. No enforcement action may be taken, however, "until the department or agency concerned has advised the appropriate person of the failure to comply with the requirement and has determined that compliance cannot be secured by voluntary means." And every agency enforcement action is subject to judicial review. § 2000d-2. If an agency attempts to terminate program funding, still more restrictions apply. The agency head must "file with the committees of the House and Senate having legislative jurisdiction over the program or activity involved a full written report of the circumstances and the grounds for such action." § 2000d-1. And the termination of funding does not "become effective until thirty days have elapsed after the filing of such report." Whatever these elaborate restrictions on agency enforcement may imply for the private enforcement of rights created outside of § 602, . . . they tend to contradict a congressional intent to create privately enforceable rights through § 602 itself. The express provision of one method of enforcing a substantive rule suggests that Congress intended to preclude others. . . .

Neither as originally enacted nor as later amended does Title VI display an intent to create a freestanding private right of action to enforce regulations promulgated under § 602. We therefore hold that no such right of action exists. . . .

The judgment of the Court of Appeals is reversed. *It is so ordered.*

Justice Stevens, with whom Justices Souter, Ginsburg, and Breyer join, dissenting.

In 1964, as part of a groundbreaking and comprehensive civil rights Act, Congress prohibited recipients of federal funds from discriminating on the basis of race, ethnicity, or national origin. Title VI of the Civil Rights Act of 1964, 78 Stat. 252, 42 U.S.C. §§ 2000d to 2000d-7. Pursuant to powers expressly delegated by that Act, the federal agencies and departments responsible for awarding and administering federal contracts immediately adopted regulations prohibiting federal contractees from adopting policies that have the "effect" of discriminating on those bases. At the time of the promulgation of these regulations, prevailing principles of statutory construction assumed that Congress intended a private right of action whenever such a cause of action was necessary to protect individual rights granted by valid federal law. Relying both on this presumption and on independent analysis of Title VI, this Court has repeatedly and consistently affirmed the right of private individuals to bring civil suits to enforce rights guaranteed by Title VI. A fair reading of those cases, and coherent implementation of the statutory scheme, required the same result under Title VI's implementing regulations.

In separate lawsuits spanning several decades, we have endorsed an action identical in substance to the one brought in this case, see *Lau v. Nichols* . . .; demonstrated that Congress intended a private right of action to protect the rights guaranteed by Title VI, see *Cannon v. University of Chicago*, 441 U.S. 677, 99 S.Ct. 1946, 60 L.Ed.2d 560 (1979); and concluded that private individuals may seek declaratory and injunctive relief against state officials for violations of regulations promulgated pursuant to Title VI, see *Guardians Assn. v. Civil Serv. Comm'n of New York City.* . . . Giving fair import to our language and our holdings, every Court of Appeals to address the question has concluded that a private right of action exists to enforce the rights guaranteed both by the text of Title VI and by any regulations validly promulgated pursuant to that Title, and Congress had adopted several statutes that appear to ratify the status quo.

Today, in a decision unfounded in our precedent and hostile to decades of settled expectations, a majority of this Court carves out an important exception to the right of private action long recognized under Title VI. In so doing, the Court makes three distinct, albeit interrelated, errors. First, the Court provides a muddled account of both the reasoning and the breadth of our prior decisions endorsing a private right of action under Title VI, thereby obscuring the conflict between those opinions and today's decision. Second, the Court offers a flawed and unconvincing analysis of the relationship between §§ 601 and 602 of the Civil Rights Act of 1964, ignoring more plausible and persuasive explanations detailed in our prior opinions. Finally, the Court badly misconstrues the theoretical linchpin of our decision in *Cannon v. University of Chicago* . . ., mistaking that decision's careful contextual analysis for judicial fiat.

* * *

Our fractured decision in *Guardians Assn. v. Civil Serv. Comm'n of New York City* reinforces the conclusion that this issue is effectively settled. While the various opinions in that case took different views as to the spectrum of relief available to plaintiffs in Title VI cases, a clear majority of the Court expressly stated that private parties may seek injunctive relief against governmental practices that have the effect of discriminating against racial and ethnic minorities. . . .

As I read today's opinion, the majority declines to accord precedential value to *Guardians* because the five Justices in the majority were arguably divided over the mechanism through which private parties might seek such injunctive relief. . . .

. . . As *Guardians* involved an action against a governmental entity, making § 1983 relief available, the Court might have discussed the availability of judicial relief without addressing the scope of the implied private right of action available directly under Title VI. . . . However, the analysis in each of the relevant opinions did not do so. Rather than focusing on considerations specific to § 1983, each of these opinions looked instead to our opinion in *Cannon*, to the intent of the Congress that adopted Title VI and the contemporaneous executive decisionmakers who crafted the disparate-impact regulations, and to general principles of remediation.

* * *

Underlying the majority's dismissive treatment of our prior cases is a flawed understanding of the structure of Title VI and, more particularly, of the relationship between §§ 601 and 602. To some extent, confusion as to the relationship between the provisions is understandable, as Title VI is a deceptively simple statute. Section 601 of the Act lays out its straightforward commitment: "No person in the United States shall, on the ground of race, color, or national origin, be excluded from participation in, be denied the benefits of, or be subjected to discrimination under any program or activity receiving Federal financial assistance." 42 U.S.C. § 2000d. Section 602 "authorize[s] and direct[s]" all federal departments and agencies empowered to extend federal financial assistance to issue "rules, regulations, or orders of general applicability" in order to "effectuate" § 601's antidiscrimination mandate, 42 U.S.C. § 2000d-1.

* * *

The majority's statutory analysis does violence to both the text and the structure of Title VI. Section 601 does not stand in isolation, but rather as part of an integrated remedial scheme. Section 602 exists for the sole purpose of forwarding the antidiscrimination ideals laid out in § 601. The majority's persistent belief that the two sections somehow forward different agendas finds no support in the statute. Nor does Title VI anywhere suggest, let alone state, that for the purpose of determining their legal effect, the "rules, regulations, [and] orders of general applicability" adopted by the agencies are to be bifurcated by the judiciary into two categories based on how closely the courts believe the regulations track the text of § 601.

What makes the Court's analysis even more troubling is that our cases have already adopted a simpler and more sensible model for understanding the relationship between the two sections. For three decades, we have treated § 602 as granting the responsible agencies the power to issue broad prophylactic rules aimed at realizing the vision laid out in § 601, even if the conduct captured by these rules is at times broader than that which would otherwise be prohibited.

* * *

This understanding is firmly rooted in the text of Title VI. As § 602 explicitly states, the agencies are authorized to adopt regulations to "effectuate" § 601's antidiscrimination mandate. 42 U.S.C. § 2000d-1. The plain meaning of the text reveals Congress' intent to provide the relevant agencies with sufficient authority to transform the statute's broad aspiration into social reality. So too does a lengthy, consistent, and impassioned legislative history.

. . . On its own terms, the statute supports an action challenging policies of federal grantees that explicitly or unambiguously violate antidiscrimination norms (such as policies that on their face limit benefits or services to certain races). With regard to more subtle forms of discrimination (such as schemes that limit benefits or services on ostensibly race-neutral grounds but have the predictable and perhaps intended consequence of materially benefiting some races at the expense of others), the statute does not establish a static approach but instead empowers the relevant agencies to evaluate social circumstances to determine whether there is a need for stronger measures.[13] Such an approach builds into the law flexibility, an ability to make nuanced assessments of complex social realities, and an admirable willingness to credit the possibility of progress.

The "effects" regulations at issue in this case represent the considered judgment of the relevant agencies that discrimination on the basis of race, ethnicity, and national origin by federal contractees are significant social problems that might be remedied, or at least ameliorated, by the application of a broad prophylactic rule. Given the judgment underlying them, the regulations are inspired by, at the service of, and inseparably intertwined with § 601's antidiscrimination mandate. Contrary to the majority's suggestion, they "appl[y]" § 601's prohibition on discrimination just as surely as the intentional discrimination regulations the majority concedes are privately enforceable.

. . . If the regulations promulgated pursuant to § 602 are either an authoritative construction of § 601's meaning or prophylactic rules necessary to actualize the goals enunciated in § 601, then it makes no sense to differentiate between private actions to enforce § 601 and private actions to enforce § 602.

---

[13]It is important, in this context, to note that regulations prohibiting policies that have a disparate impact are not necessarily aimed only—or even primarily—at unintentional discrimination. Many policies whose very intent is to discriminate are framed in a race-neutral manner. It is often difficult to obtain direct evidence of this motivating animus. Therefore, an agency decision to adopt disparate-impact regulations may very well reflect a determination by that agency that substantial intentional discrimination pervades the industry it is charged with regulating but that such discrimination is difficult to prove directly. As I have stated before: "Frequently the most probative evidence of intent will be objective evidence of what actually happened rather than evidence describing the subjective state of mind of the actor." *Washington v. Davis*, 426 U.S. 229, 253, 96 S.Ct. 2040, 48 L.Ed.2d 597 (1976)(concurring opinion). On this reading, Title VI simply accords the agencies the power to decide whether or not to credit such evidence.

There is but one private action to enforce Title VI, and we already know that such an action exists.

* * *

Underlying today's opinion is the conviction that *Cannon* must be cabined because it exemplifies an "expansive rights-creating approach." . . . But . . . it was Congress, not the Court, that created the cause of action, and it was the Congress that later ratified the *Cannon* holding in 1986 and again in 1988.

In order to impose its own preferences as to the availability of judicial remedies, the Court today adopts a methodology that blinds itself to important evidence of congressional intent. . . .

. . . [I]f the majority is genuinely committed to deciphering congressional intent, its unwillingness to even consider evidence as to the context in which Congress legislated is perplexing. Congress does not legislate in a vacuum. . . . [T]he objective manifestations of congressional intent to create a private right of action must be measured in light of the enacting Congress' expectations as to how the judiciary might evaluate the question. . . .

At the time Congress was considering Title VI, it was normal practice for the courts to infer that Congress intended a private right of action whenever it passed a statute designed to protect a particular class that did not contain enforcement mechanisms which would be thwarted by a private remedy. . . .

. . . Today, the Court coins a new rule, holding that a private cause of action to enforce a statute does not encompass a substantive regulation issued to effectuate that statute unless the regulation does nothing more than "authoritatively construe the statute itself." . . . But . . . the distinction is untenable. There is simply no reason to assume that Congress contemplated, desired, or adopted a distinction between regulations that merely parrot statutory text and broader regulations that are authorized by statutory text.

Beyond its flawed structural analysis of Title VI and an evident antipathy toward implied rights of action, the majority offers little affirmative support for its conclusion that Congress did not intend to create a private remedy for violations of the Title VI regulations. The Court offers essentially two reasons for its position. First, it attaches significance to the fact that the "rights-creating" language in § 601 that defines the classes protected by the statute is not repeated in § 602. But, of course, there was no reason to put that language in § 602 because it is perfectly obvious that the regulations authorized by § 602

must be designed to protect precisely the same people protected by § 601. . . .

Second, the Court repeated the argument advanced and rejected in *Cannon* that the express provision of a fund cut-off remedy "suggests that Congress intended to preclude others." In *Cannon*, we carefully explained why the presence of an explicit mechanism to achieve one of the statute's objectives (ensuring that federal funds are not used "to support discriminatory practices") does not preclude a conclusion that a private right of action was intended to achieve the statute's other principal objective ("to provide individual citizens effective protection against those practices"). In support of our analysis, we offered policy arguments, cited evidence from the legislative history, and noted the active support of the relevant agencies. . . .

Like much else in its opinion, the present majority's unwillingness to explain its refusal to find the reasoning in *Cannon* persuasive suggests that today's decision is the unconscious product of the majority's profound distaste for implied causes of action rather than an attempt to discern the intent of the Congress that enacted Title VI of the Civil Rights Act of 1964. . . .

* * *

I respectfully dissent.

NOTES AND QUESTIONS

1. *The* Sandoval *Holding*

The decision in *Alexander v. Sandoval*, that there is no private right of action to enforce disparate-impact regulations promulgated under Title VI, also applies to Title IX with regard to discrimination on the basis of sex. In the absence of a private right of action, if the federal government fails to enforce the disparate-impact regulations through the procedures specified in § 2000d-1, can private individuals sue to compel the agency to administer the law and its regulations diligently? *See Women's Equity Action League v. Cavazos*, 906 F.2d 472 (D.C. Cir. 1990).

2. *The* Sandoval *Dicta*

Justice Scalia casts some doubt on whether Title VI authorizes federal agencies to promulgate *any* regulations that prohibit activities that have a disproportionate impact on the basis of race (and of sex under Title IX). He notes that no opinion of the Supreme Court has clearly held that "regulations promulgated under § 602 of Title VI may validly proscribe activities that have a disparate impact on racial groups even though such activities are permissible under § 601." He points out that statements by some justices to that effect "are in considerable tension with the rule of *Bakke* and *Guardians* that § 601 forbids only intentional discrimination." He notes, however, that inasmuch as the defendants did not challenge the regulations themselves, for purposes of deciding the case the Court will assume that a regulation prohibiting recipients of federal funds from using "criteria or methods of administration which have the effect of subjecting individuals to discrimination because of their race, color, or national origin" is valid.

C. Efforts to Compel Administrative Enforcement

After the election of President Nixon, significant changes were made in the federal role in civil rights enforcement. In *Alexander v. Holmes County Board of Education*, 396 U.S. 19, 90 S.Ct. 29, 24 L.Ed.2d 19 (1969), the Supreme Court rejected the administration's request for a one-year delay of school integration in southern school districts and ordered the immediate integration of previously *de jure* school districts. That case marked the first split between the government and the NAACP since they joined forces in supporting the passage of the Civil Rights Act. Subsequently, a joint HEW and Department of Justice statement on school desegregation was issued that, while noteworthy for its lack of clarity, was widely interpreted as signifying a slowdown in the integration process. H. Rogers and C. Bullock, *Law and Social Change* 89–90 (1972). *See generally* G. Orfield, *Must We Bus?* (1978).

President Nixon's opposition to school busing was further evidenced in the administration of Title VI of the Civil Rights Act of 1964 by HEW. Civil rights groups charged that the Nixon administration had relaxed its standards with respect to school desegregation by refusing to threaten or employ the ultimate sanction of a cutoff of federal funds in noncomplying districts. Suit was filed against the Secretary of Health, Education, and Welfare, and, in an extraordinary decision, the United States Court of Appeals for the District of Columbia ordered HEW to take "appropriate action to end segregation in public educational institutions receiving federal funds." *Adams v. Richardson*, 480 F.2d 1159 (D.C. Cir. 1973). In that case, the court affirmed an order re-

quiring HEW to commence enforcement proceedings against school districts found to be in violation of Title VI and the Supreme Court's ruling in *Swann*, request explanations of disproportionate racial distributions from school districts, and monitor all school districts under court desegregation orders. The court found that:

> HEW is actively supplying segregated institutions with federal funds, contrary to the expressed purposes of Congress. It is one thing to say the Justice Department lacks the resources necessary to locate and prosecute every civil rights violator; it is quite another to say HEW may affirmatively continue to channel federal funds to defaulting schools. The anomaly of this latter assertion fully supports the conclusion that Congress's clear statement of an affirmative enforcement duty should not be discounted.
>
> Appellants attempt to avoid the force of this argument by saying that, although enforcement is required, the means of enforcement is a matter of absolute agency discretion, and that they have chosen to seek voluntary compliance in most cases. This position is untenable in light of the plain language of the statute. . . .
>
> Although the Act does not provide a specific limit to the time period within which voluntary compliance may be sought, it is clear that a request for voluntary compliance, if not followed by responsive action on the part of the institution within a reasonable time, does not relieve the agency of the responsibility to enforce Title VI by one of the two alternative means contemplated by the statute. A consistent failure to do so is a dereliction of duty reviewable in the courts. . . .

480 F.2d at 1162–63.

In a subsequent case, HEW was found to have "over-relied" on "voluntary negotiations over protracted time periods" and demonstrated its reluctance to bring enforcement proceedings to bear in southern school districts with substantial segregation. *Adams v. Weinberger*, 391 F.Supp. 269 (D.D.C. 1975). In *Brown v. Weinberger*, 417 F.Supp. 1215 (D.D.C. 1976), a suit brought on behalf of public school students in thirty-three northern and western states, the court held that HEW had failed to fulfill its duties under Title VI. In *Adams v. Califano*, 430 F.Supp. 118 (D.D.C. 1977), HEW was found to be in violation of Title VI in continuing to provide federal aid to public institutions of higher education in six southern states that had failed to desegregate. Additional classes of plaintiffs as well as other statutory civil rights guarantees were included in the litigation. *Adams v. Mathews*, 536 F.2d 417 (D.C. Cir. 1976). In 1977, a consent order was entered into that established time frames governing the processing of complaints and a schedule for compliance reviews under Title VI, Title IX, and Section 504 of the Rehabilitation Act. In 1982, the Department of Education, then under a new administration, moved to vacate the 1977 order.

Twenty years after the case was first brought challenging the federal government's dilatory enforcement of federal civil rights statutes, the District of Columbia Circuit, in *Women's Equity Action League v. Cavazos*, 906 F.2d 742 (D.C. Cir. 1990), denied the plaintiff's claim of a generalized private right of action against federal executive agencies in the absence of clear legislative authorization, and removed all prior court-imposed obligations on the executive branch. In doing so, the court noted that the litigation, which began in 1970 when black students attending racially segregated public schools in seventeen states complained of the failure of HEW to enforce Title VI, had

> expanded to colossal proportions: the litigation came to encompass enforcement by units of the Department of Education and the Department of Labor of four civil rights measures as they pertain to the education systems of all fifty states—Title VI, forbidding discrimination on account of race or national origin in any federally-assisted program; Title IX of the Education Amendments of 1972, 20 U.S.C. §§ 1681–86, prohibiting discrimination on the basis of sex or visual impairment in educational institutions receiving federal funds; Executive Order 11246, . . . proscribing discrimination by government contractors; and Section 504 of the Rehabilitation Act of 1972, 29 U.S.C. §794, barring federal fund recipients from discriminating against the handicapped.

As the litigation swelled in scope, it shifted in focus. Plaintiffs at first demanded relief from executive defiance of congressional commands, in the form of a deliberate policy of nonenforcement. At the end of 1987, however, the district court observed: "[P]laintiffs [no longer] claim that defendants have abrogated their statutory responsibilities, but rather that, in carrying them out, they do not always process complaints, conduct investigations, issue letters of findings, or conduct compliance reviews as promptly or expeditiously as plaintiffs would like." See *Adams v. Bennett*, 675 F.Supp. 668, 680 (D.D.C. 1987).

* * *

The government had argued in *Adams v. Richardson* that plaintiffs possessed no right of action under the Administrative Procedure Act (APA), . . . because en-forcement of Title VI was committed to agency discretion by law. Rejecting that argument, we pointed to plaintiffs' allegation that HEW had "consciously and expressly adopted a general policy which is in effect an abdiction of its statutory duty." 480 F.2d at 1162. Under the statute, this court held, a federal agency lacks discretion to desist when its request to a state or school district for voluntary compliance is not met by responsive action within a reasonable time. *Id.* at 1163. . . .

The expansion of this litigation coincided with doctrinal shifts that curtailed the availability of suits directly against federal enforcement authorities for tardigrade administration of antidiscrimination prescriptions. . . .

As *Cannon* [*v. University of Chicago*, 441 U.S. 677, 99 S.Ct. 1946, 60 L.Ed. 560 (1979)] made clear, to hold that an enactment provides an implied right of action of the sort plaintiffs plead, the court must be satisfied that the enactor intended to create such a right. . . . [W]e discern no legislative intent to authorize the grand scale, long term rights of action plaintiffs claim here.

* * *

Plaintiffs urge, however, that individual actions against discriminators cannot redress the systematic lags and lapses by federal monitors about which they complain. . . . But under our precedent, situation-specific litigation affords an adequate, even if imperfect, remedy. . . . [T]he suit targeting specific discriminatory acts of fund recipients is the only court remedy Congress has authorized for private parties, situated as plaintiffs currently are.

* * *

In sum, instructed by currently controlling precedent, we hold that the generalized action plaintiffs pursue against federal executive agencies lacks the requisite green light from the legislative branch. We do not suggest that such an action could not be authorized. . . . The courts, however, may not on their own initiative create the claim for relief. That authority resides in Congress. . . .

906 F.2d at 744–48, 751.

NOTES AND QUESTIONS

1. *Private Suits/Public Agencies*

Should private parties be permitted to file lawsuits to compel an administrative agency to comply with its own guidelines and regulations? Can a court order an administrative agency to be diligent and to act in good faith in administering a law? To what effect? Does this case raise a separation of powers issue?

2. *Impact of* Adams v. Richardson *on other Statutory Guarantees*

The Office for Civil Rights of the Department of Health, Education, and Welfare claimed that the district court's order to enforce Title VI within certain time frames meant that there would be no resources available to review Title IX and Section 504 complaints. Can a court determine what resources should be allocated to the enforcement of each statute?

3. *The Consent Agreement Settling* Adams

In the December, 1977, consent agreement, the plaintiffs in *Adams v. Richardson* (involving school districts in seventeen southern states), *Brown v. Weinberger* (involving school districts in thirty-three northern and western states), and *Women's Equity Action League* (seeking resources for the enforcement of Title IX) agreed to drop their cases in exchange for the agency's promise to eliminate the backlog of three thousand complaints by September 30, 1979, and to double the staff by immediately hiring 898 new personnel. The consent agreement also established timetables for civil rights complaints for all fifty states for all three civil rights statutes—Title VI, Title IX, and Section 504. By 1981, the backlog of complaints in the Department of Education had increased in size. What recourse would plaintiffs have? If the Department responds that it was unable to hire additional staff because the Office of Management and Budget disapproved, or Congress refused to appropriate the funds, what action can the court take?

D. Congressional Reactions to Federal Enforcement by Courts and Administrative Agencies

In 1972, following the Supreme Court's decision in *Swann,* at least fifty-nine constitutional amendments addressed to school desegregation and busing were proposed in Congress. *See Hearings on School Busing Before Subcomm. No. 5 of the House Comm. on the Judiciary,* 92d Cong.,2d Sess., Ser.32, pt. 3, at xii–xiii (1972). Congress, rejecting an administration proposal that would have effectively banned busing for integration below the seventh grade, enacted a busing moratorium as part of the Education Amendments of 1972.

Title VIII—General Provisions Relating to the Assignment or Transportation of Students

Prohibition Against Assignment or Transportation of Students to Overcome Racial Imbalance

Section 801. No provision of this act shall be construed to require the assignment or transportation of students or teachers in order to overcome racial imbalance.

Prohibition Against Use of Appropriated Funds for Busing

Section 802(a). No funds appropriated for the purpose of carrying out any applicable program may be used for the transportation of students or teachers (or for the purchase of equipment for such transportation) in order to overcome racial imbalance in any school or school system, or for the transportation of students or teachers (or for the purchase of equipment for such transportation) in order to carry out a plan of racial desegregation of any school or school system, except on the express written voluntary request of appropriate local school officials. No such funds shall be made available for transportation when the time or distance of travel is so great as to risk the health of the children or significantly impinge on the educational process of such children, or where the educational opportunities available at the school to which it is proposed that any such student be transported will be substantially inferior to those opportunities offered at the school to which such student would otherwise be assigned under a nondiscriminatory system of school assignments based on geographic zones established without discrimination on account of race, religion, color, or national origin.

(b) No officer, agent, or employee of the Department of Health, Education, and Welfare (including the Office of Education), the Department of Justice, or any other federal agency shall, by rule, regulation, order, guideline, or otherwise (1) urge, persuade, induce, or require any local education agency, or any private non-profit agency, institution, or organization to use any funds derived from any state or local sources for any purpose, unless constitutionally required, for which federal funds appropriated to carry out any applicable program may not be used, as provided in this section, or (2) condition the receipt of federal funds under any federal program upon any action by any state or local public officer or employee which would be prohibited by clause (1) on the part of a federal officer or employee. . . .

NOTES AND QUESTIONS

1. Statutory Interpretation

In light of the *Swann* decision, was the 1972 busing moratorium law intended to prevent the integration of public schools in previously *de jure* school systems? The Supreme Court interpreted the law as limited to *de facto* segregation, rendering it consistent with *Swann. See Drummond v. Acree*, 409 U.S. 1228, 93 S.Ct. 18, 34 L.Ed.2d 33 (1972).

2. The Equal Educational Opportunities Act of 1974

Congress again limited busing in the Equal Educational Opportunities Act of 1974, 20 U.S.C. §§ 1701 *et seq.* (the Esch Amendment). Section 1713 establishes a priority for remedies: the assignment to neighborhood schools, taking into account school capacity and natural barriers; the assignment to neighborhood schools but considering school capacity only; the transfer of students from schools where their racial group is a majority to schools where their group is a minority; the creation or revision of attendance zones with minimum transportation; the building of new schools or the closing of old ones; the creation of magnet schools; and finally, "any other plan." Section 1755 then provides that "notwithstanding any other provision of law, . . . no court of the United States shall order the implementation of any plan to remedy a finding of *de jure* segregation which involves the transportation of students, unless the court first finds that all alternative remedies are inadequate." Moreover, when busing is ordered, no student may be bused beyond the school next closest to his or her home, unless the courts determine that more extensive busing is needed to ensure the protection of constitutional rights. 20 U.S.C. §§ 1714 and 1718.

If the courts interpreted these restrictions on the use of busing as a limitation on the power of federal courts to remedy unconstitutional segregation, would these laws be constitutional? In other words, to what extent can Congress define the scope of the Equal Protection Clause by limiting the range of judicial remedies? *See generally* Cox, "The Role of Congress in Constitutional Determinations," 40 *U. Cin.L.Rev.* 199, 253, 257–61 (1971); Cox, "The Supreme Court, 1965 Term, Foreword: Constitutional Adjudication and the Promotion of Human Rights," 80 *Harv.L.Rev.* 91 (1966); *Hearings on School Busing Before Subcomm. No. 5 of the House Committee on the Judiciary*, 92d Cong., 2d Sess., Ser. 32, pt. 3, at 1631–32 (1972) (statement of Professor Wright).

The First Circuit Court of Appeals construed the 1974 amendments as follows: "By explicitly leaving the district court the power to determine the adequacy of remedies, the Act necessarily does not restrict the breadth of discretion of that court to determine what scope of remedy is judicially required. Thus the Act manifests a purpose not to limit judicial power but to guide and channel its exercise." *Morgan v. Kerrigan*, 530 F.2d 401, 412 (1st Cir. 1976), *cert. denied*, 426 U.S. 935, 96 S.Ct. 2648, 49 L.Ed.2d 386. *See also Brinkman v. Gilligan*, 518 F.2d 853, 856 (6th Cir. 1975), *cert. denied*, 423 U.S. 1000, 96 S.Ct. 433, 46 L.Ed.2d 376.

3. Restrictions on the Agency

An amendment to the Labor-HEW appropriations bill for fiscal 1976 (the Byrd Amendment) prohibited HEW (now the Department of Education) from using funds, either directly or indirectly, to force a school district to transport a student beyond the school nearest his or her home for reasons of race. Appropriations acts in subsequent years also carried this restriction. In 1977, the Eagelton-Biden Amendment, modifying the Byrd Amendment, prohibited the use of federal funds by HEW to require busing to implement desegregation plans that involve the pairing or clustering of schools or other methods of reorganizing the grade structure of schools.

Has Congress acted unconstitutionally by restricting the agency's ability to require busing remedies? In a case challenging these amendments, the Court of Appeals for the District of Columbia Circuit held that since HEW could still encourage school districts found to be in noncompliance with Title VI to adopt a voluntary busing plan and could refer cases to the Justice Department to initiate court action, the amendments were not unconstitutional on their face. *Brown v. Califano*, 627 F.2d 1221 (D.C. Cir. 1980).

VIII. "SECOND GENERATION" PROBLEMS

A. Introduction

School systems can remain segregated even after a court-ordered school desegregation plan has been implemented. Through practices such as ability grouping and the use of exclusionary disciplinary measures, minority children may continue to be isolated from white children. These practices can bring about resegregation among schools, within a school, or even within a classroom. One difficulty is determining whether these practices are intentionally used to segregate or whether they are educationally motivated and racially neutral but have the effect of segregating students. If the latter is the case, do such practices still violate the Fourteenth Amendment? *See Washington v. Davis*, 426 U.S. 229, 96 S.Ct. 2040, 48 L.Ed.2d 597 (1976); *Village of Arlington Heights v. Metropolitan Housing Corporation*, 429 U.S. 252, 97 S.Ct. 555, 50 L.Ed.2d 450 (1977). Do they violate Title VI of the Civil Rights Act of 1964? (*See* discussion *supra*.)

Many of the legal and policy problems raised in this section clearly extend beyond the question of racial discrimination, particularly with regard to student classification practices, but since most of the litigation has focused on the effects of these practices on minority students, these issues will be dealt with here. Similar questions are raised in chapter 6, particularly with respect to students with mental and physical disabilities.

B. Student Classification Practices

Until recently, the focus for both policymakers and lawyers was primarily on educational issues at the national, state, or district level rather than on what happens within the schools. While courts have struggled to define equality of educational opportunity and to demarcate the liberties that students retain while attending public school, they generally have been unwilling to review pedagogical judgments, such as the classification or sorting of students—that is, differentiations made among students, ostensibly based solely on intellectual performance or potential.

Ability grouping (or tracking) and assignment to special classes for children with disabilities, as well as the devices that facilitate classification—testing, grading, and counseling—have been heavily criticized. Among the chief criticisms leveled at present classification practices are (1) that they misidentify or misclassify significant numbers of students; (2) that they are racially discriminatory; and (3) that they deny some students an equal educational opportunity.

Perhaps more than almost any other issue, student classification presses at the limits of judicial competence to affect educational policy. The minuteness of many within-school and within-class decisions makes it difficult to conceive of them as posing legally manageable problems. Such decisions are complex, interrelated, and numerous. For that reason, a court that undertook routinely to review them might well find itself acting as schoolmaster in an uncomfortably literal sense. Furthermore, these practices are at the heart of the school official's claim to professional competence; any challenge could be perceived as a threat to that competence and for that reason strenuously resisted. Whether such resistance is indeed proper—whether, for some or all of the questions considered in this section, judicial involvement is inappropriate—is a critical and unresolved issue.

1. The Nature and Purpose of Classification.

"Tracking," in *High Stakes: Testing for Tracking, Promotion, and Graduation*

Chap. 5, 89 (J.P. Heubert and R.M. Hauser, eds., Committee on Appropriate Test Use, National Academy of Sciences, 1999). Reprinted with permission.

In a typical American elementary or secondary school, the curriculum serves two purposes that often exist in tension with each other. One is to have all students master a common core of knowledge, an objective reflected in the current emphasis on "high standards for all." The other is to provide curricular differentiation—differentiated instruction suited to students' varied needs, interests, and achievement levels. . . . This second purpose is pursued in many schools through practices variously known as "tracking," "ability grouping," and "homogeneous grouping." Put differently, educators "organize school systems so that students who appear to vary in their educational needs and abilities can be taught separately, either in specialized schools or in the same school in distinct programs, classes, or instructional groups within classrooms" [Oakes, Gamoran, and

Page, "Curriculum Differentiation: Opportunities, Outcomes, and Meanings," in *Handbook of Research on Curriculum* 570 (P. Jackson, ed., 1992)].

Limitations of Terminology

Although many terms are used to describe practices of curricular differentiation, each has its limitations.

Tracking . . . suggests the classic, rigid form of curricular differentiation in which a student's program or "track"—academic, general, or vocational—determines virtually every course that the student will take and at what level of difficulty. In recent decades, formal grouping systems this rigid have become less common in schools. . . .

Ability grouping . . . implies—incorrectly, in our view—that students are being grouped on the basis of "ability," a quality that some view as innate and immutable. . . . [S]chools that group students usually do so on the basis of classroom performance and other measures of achievement that reflect acquired knowledge—something that can and does change over time—rather than ability. It is therefore misleading to use the term "ability grouping." Moreover, given the degree of racial and socioeconomic stratification that is often associated with grouping, it may reinforce false stereotypes to imply incorrectly that students in different groups are distinguished by ability. We find it more accurate to say that schools that group students typically try to do so by "skill level" or "achievement level". . . .

Homogeneous grouping is also a misnomer, based on studies of actual practice. The term "homogeneous" suggests that all the students in a given group are alike, or at least similar, in their achievement levels. Empirical studies cast doubt on this assumption, however. "Grouping's effect on reducing even cognitive diversity may be very small" . . . [Oakes *et al.*, *supra* at 594]. "Other studies document considerable overlap of students' skills and abilities among groups. . . . Thus the degree to which tracking reduces heterogeneity may be far less than we typically assume." [*Ibid.*] . . . [I]t appears that factors other than student achievement—scheduling constraints, parental interventions, and student choice, in particular—often help to determine who takes which classes. Although these other factors may be

entirely legitimate, they often produce groupings that are not very homogeneous. In some circumstances, "it is unclear whether it is possible to organize classes that contain a narrow range of student ability" . . . [Gamoran and Weinstein, "Differentiation and Opportunity in Restructured Schools," 106 *American Jour. of Educ.* 385, 387 (1998)]. At the same time, there is evidence of considerable homogeneity in secondary mathematics classes. . . .

The committee has decided to use in this report the term . . . tracking [which it defines] as forms of placement whereby individual students are assigned, usually on the basis of perceived achievement or skill level, to separate schools or programs, classes within grade levels, groups within classes (at the elementary level), and courses within subject areas (at the secondary level).

Nature and Extent of Tracking

Tracking takes many forms in American schools. Among them are "exam" schools and "gifted and talented" programs or classes, to which only certain students are admitted usually on the basis of their perceived achievement levels or talents.[2] Some scholars and practitioners also see programs for students with mild mental disabilities (mild mental retardation, learning disabilities, and emotional problems) as a form of tracking . . . because students are often referred for possible placement in such programs on the basis of their perceived abilities or achievement levels. . . .

. . . "[D]ifferentiation begins early, with most elementary schools employing between-class . . . grouping for the entire day, between-class grouping for specific subjects, and/or within-class grouping for specific subjects" [Oakes *et al.*, *supra* at 571]. In the last decade, however, there has been an increase in heterogeneous grouping within elementary schools, and new techniques, such as cooperative learning, offer promising ways of grouping children heterogeneously within classrooms. . . .

Tracking also remains typical in American secondary schools . . ., despite opposition from many middle school educators . . . and despite the demise of formal tracking, under which a student's program of study (college preparatory, general, or vocational) largely determined the courses he or she would

---

[2]An exam school is a public school to which students apply and are accepted based on exemplary test performance and academic record. A gifted and talented class or program provides an accelerated curriculum and requires students to demonstrate advanced achievement and/or test performance to participate.

take. . . . Within-school grouping continues, although less rigidly than in the past. . . .

The secondary school schedule also tends to promote tracking. "Because students assigned to a high-level class for one subject tended to be assigned to a similar level in other subjects, the end result was a set of curricular tracks as distinct as in the past. Sometimes students were actually assigned to sets of classes at the same ability level all at once" . . . [Oakes *et al.*, *supra* at 575].

Parental intervention also operates to preserve curricular differentiation in public secondary schools. "Middle-class parents intervene to obtain advantageous positions for their children even over and against school personnel. . . . Middle-class parents are the protectors of the existing in-school stratification system" . . . [S. Lucas, *Tracking Inequality: Stratification and Mobility in American Schools* 206 (in press)].

The secondary curriculum is differentiated by subject . . . as well as by track. The degree of differentiation in secondary mathematics, for example, is considerable. It is common to find within a single high school courses ranging from remedial and "business" math to calculus and statistics, arrayed in as many as four distinct tracks. . . . [R]esults from the Second International Mathematics Study show that the variation in student math performance associated with tracking is far greater in the United States than in most other countries[4]. . . .

Role of Tests in Tracking Decisions

. . . Although practice varies considerably, even from school to school, educators consistently report that [tracking] decisions are based on multiple sources of information: test scores, teacher and counselor recommendations, grades, and (at secondary levels) student choice. . . . Also, . . . parents often play a powerful role.

On the other hand, standardized tests are routinely used in making tracking decisions. . . . Moreover, they may play an important, even dominant, role in selecting children for exam schools and gifted and talented programs.[5] IQ tests play an important part in the special education evaluation process, and their use contributes to the disproportionate placement of minority students into classes for students with mild mental retardation. . . . Even when test scores are just one factor among several that influence tracking decisions, they may carry undue weight by appearing to provide a scientific justification and legitimacy for tracking decisions that such decisions would not otherwise have.

. . . [S]chools improperly use norm-referenced multiple-choice tests for tracking purposes; . . . such tests are designed to rank students and not to support instruction, and . . . linking such test scores to student tracking can seriously limit students' learning [Darling-Hammond, "The Implications of Testing Policy for Quality and Equality," 73 *Phi Delta Kappan* 220 (1991)]. . . . [A] recent report . . . calls attention to a troubling use of tests to track young children [*Principles and Recommendations for Early Childhood Assessments* 4 (L. Shepard, S. Kagan, and E. Wurtz, eds., 1998)]:

> Recently . . . there has been an increase in formal assessments and testing [of children up through age 8], the results of which are used to . . . [track] youngsters into high- and low-ability groups. . . . In many cases, the instruments developed for one purpose or even one age group of children have been misapplied to other groups. As a result, schools [sic] have often identified as "not yet ready" for kindergarten, or "too immature" for group settings, large proportions of youngsters (often boys and non-English speakers) who would benefit enormously from the learning opportunities provided in these settings. In particular, because the alternative treatment is often inadequate, screening out has fostered inequities.

There is some evidence that students' race or socioeconomic status (SES) may influence the weight that educators accord to their test scores, leading to differential treatment in the tracking process. For example, one case study found "that school counselors and teachers respond to comparable achievement scores of Asian and Hispanic students quite differ-

---

[4]"The class component of variance accounted for almost half of the total variability in performance in the U.S., whereas the class component accounted for a much smaller fraction of the total variability in most other countries" . . . [Linn, "Assessments and Accountability," Paper presented at annual meeting of American Educational Research Association 3 (1998)].

[5]The use of traditional IQ tests for such purposes has been criticized, and when IQ test scores are the sole criterion for selection, such use is plainly inconsistent with professional standards. Even when such placement decisions are based on IQ test scores and other criteria, traditional IQ tests have been criticized, both because they measure a fairly narrow range of human qualities . . . and because they often serve to exclude minority applicants at significantly higher rates than other available selection standards and procedures for gifted programs. . . .

ently, with Asians far more likely to be placed in advanced classes than Hispanics with similar scores" [Oakes *et al.*, *supra* at 577]. Similarly, more than one court decision has established that some school officials assign low-scoring white students to high tracks and high-scoring minority students to low tracks. . . . [There is] powerful evidence that middle- and higher-income parents intervene in tracking decisions, effectively overriding test scores (and other factors that schools may use in tracking decisions) to produce tracks that are highly stratified by SES and race. The importance of social class in tracking decisions is suggested by a study that controlled for prior achievement, social class, and school. . . . [The study] concluded that white students were 10 percent more likely than comparable black students to be placed in high-track classes.

* * *

Effects of Low-Track Placement

* * *

. . . As tracking is currently practiced, students assigned to typical low-track classes are worse off than they would be in other placements. The most common reasons for this disadvantage are the failure to provide students in low-track classes with high-quality curriculum and instruction and the failure to convey high expectations for such students' academic performance. . . .

This is not to say that grouping students by achievement or skill level is in general a bad practice. Some forms of tracking, such as proficiency-based placement in foreign language classes or other classes for which there is a demonstrated need for prerequisites, may be beneficial. . . . [Moreover, there are] some schools and programs in which students in low-track classes received beneficial, high-quality instruction. These, however, involved not typical public schools but Catholic schools . . ., alternative schools, dropout programs . . ., magnet programs . . ., and a school that had recently undergone a thorough restructuring of staff and curriculum. . . . And what made some of these low-track classes educationally beneficial appears to have been such factors as high teacher expectations, small class size, extra resources that permitted individualized instruction, strong intellectual leadership, a rigorous academic curriculum, extra efforts by teachers to promote extensive class discussion, the capacity to

choose students and teachers, and "no system of assigning inexperienced or weak teachers to the low-track classes" [Gamoran and Weinstein, "Differentiation and Opportunity in Restructured Schools," 106 *Amer. Jour. of Sociology* 385 (1998); Gamoran, "Alternative Uses of Ability Grouping in Secondary Schools: Can We Bring High-Quality Instruction to Low-Ability Classrooms?" 102 *Amer. Jour. of Educ.* 1 (1993)].

Unfortunately, however, empirical research demonstrates that there is a very different reality in typical low-track classes. Moreover, there are serious structural and attitudinal barriers to change: "[Trying] to improve the quality of instruction in low tracks . . . fails to address the problem that tracking and ability grouping constitute not merely differentiation but stratification—that is, an unequal distribution of status—which typically leads to an unequal allocation of resources such as curricular materials [and] teaching competencies" [Gamoran and Weinstein, *supra*, at 387]. That minority students and low-SES students are disproportionately assigned to low-track classes is further cause for concern. . . .

Teacher Distribution

. . . [S]tudents in most low-track classes have less access to well-qualified, highly motivated teachers than do their peers in other tracks. "[T]eachers often prefer instructing high-ability classes" and principals commonly "use class assignments as a reward for teachers judged more powerful or successful and as a sanction against those deemed weaker or undeserving". . . . "This process may result in a vicious circle for low tracks: Repeated assignment to the bottom of the school's status hierarchy may demoralize teachers, hindering their improvement and perhaps even reducing their competency over time". . . . For example, "[t]eachers of low-ability secondary science and mathematics classes are consistently less experienced, less likely to be certified in math and science, hold fewer degrees in those subjects, have less training in the use of computers, and less often report themselves to be 'master teachers' " [Oakes *et al.*, *supra*, at 583].

Access to Knowledge

In elementary school, students in low tracks proceed by design at a slower pace than do students in higher tracks. Consequently, students who have been in high-track classes "are likely to have covered considerably more material by the end of elementary school" [*Ibid.*]. The type of material they have covered is also different; "low reading groups spend relatively more time on decoding activities, whereas more emphasis is placed on the meanings of stories in high groups" [*Ibid.*].

"In secondary schools, low-track classes consistently offer greater exposure to less demanding topics and skills, whereas high-track classes typically include more complex material and more difficult thinking and problem-solving tasks" [*Ibid.*]. . . . [L]ow-track classes are characterized by "a dull, isolating curriculum of passive drill and practice with trivial bits of information, whereas the upper-track curriculum encompass[es] imaginative, engaging assignments with 'high-status knowledge' such as Shakespeare or calculus" [*Ibid.*].

In sum, the research suggests that instruction in low-track classes is far less demanding than in high-track classes . . . and far less oriented to the higher-order knowledge and thinking skills that are strongly associated with future success. . . .

Equally important, low-track placements do not serve a remedial function, in that they do not help low-track students catch up with students in other tracks. Instead, "numerous studies provide evidence of the increasing disparity between high- and low-track students over time" [*Id.* at 591]. Track effects are large, moreover; . . . [it has been] estimated that "the academic track advantage was larger than the gap between students in school and dropouts" [*Ibid.*]. Not surprisingly, therefore, mobility between low tracks and higher tracks is limited. . . .

Finally, students in low-track classes would learn more if they received high-quality teaching and a demanding curriculum, as research demonstrates. . . .

Disproportions Based on Race, National Origin, Language, and SES

Research on patterns of student stratification has found disproportionate percentages of low-SES students and minority students in curricula designed for low-ability and noncollege-bound students. . . .

Minority students in racially mixed schools are disproportionately placed in low-track classes. . . and consistently underrepresented in programs for the gifted and talented. . . . The same holds true for advanced placement classes; in Milwaukee for example, whites make up 24 percent of the total student population but 54 percent of those enrolled in advanced placement courses, whereas black students constitute 61 percent of the student population but only 17 percent of those in advanced placement courses. . . .

There is evidence that tests used for tracking contribute to these disproportions: lower test scores by minority students and low-SES students undergird these patterns. . . .

---

2. Racial Discrimination and Ability Grouping.

Few schools, if any, sort students explicitly on the basis of race. The grounds on which school administrators defend sorting—its alleged benefits to both students and teachers—reveal no apparent racial motivation. Yet, as the previous excerpt indicated, school sorting does have significant racial consequences. It tends to concentrate minority children in less-advanced school programs. The proportion of minority students assigned to special programs for the educable mentally retarded and placed in slow learners' classes and nonacademic high school programs is typically two or three times greater than their proportion of the school-age population. Racial disproportionality does not, however, characterize programs for students with readily identifiable disabilities, such as classes for the trainable mentally retarded or blind, for example.

The policy implications of racial overrepresentation in less-advanced school programs are difficult to assess. If African American students are proportionately in greater need of special educational services, then there appears to be nothing illegitimate in providing those services, even if some degree of racial isolation becomes inevitable. But if the mechanisms of classification are racially biased, if the special programs do not meet the special needs of African American children, or if the classification scheme is a disguised effort to segregate the races, racial overrepresentation in less-advanced programs could give rise to legitimate policy concerns. Legal challenges to classification schemes that allegedly discriminate on the basis of race have arisen from two situations: (1) efforts by formerly dual school systems to adopt new classification schemes; and (2) use of particular classifications—notably, special classes for the mildly (or educable) mentally retarded—in districts that lack a history of *de jure* segregation.

Lemon v. Bossier Parish School Board
444 F.2d 1400 (5th Cir. 1971).

Before Gewin, Goldberg, and Dyer, Circuit Judges.

Per Curiam:

This is an appeal from an order of the district court approving a school board plan for the operation of the public schools in Plain Dealing, Louisiana. The plan in question provides that students in grades 4–12 will be assigned to one of two schools in the system on the basis of scores made on the California Achievement Test. Plaintiffs appeal, contesting the validity of the board's plan.

We think it obvious that the plan approved by the district court, insofar as it provides for the assignment of students on the basis of achievement test scores, is not in compliance with previous orders of this court in school desegregation cases. In *Singleton v. Jackson Municipal Separate School District*, 419 F.2d 1211 (5th Cir. 1969), *rev'd in part on other grounds*, 396 U.S. 290, this court sitting en banc said: "This suit seeks to desegregate two school districts, Marshall County and Holly Springs, Mississippi. The district court approved plans which would assign students to schools on the basis of achievement test scores. We pretermit a discussion of the validity per se of a plan based on testing except to hold that testing cannot be employed in any event until unitary school systems have been established." 419 F.2d at 1219.

Since *Singleton* we have repeatedly rejected testing as a basis for student assignments, *United States v. Sunflower County School District*, 430 F.2d 839 (5th Cir. 1970); *United States v. Tunica County School District*, 421 F.2d 1236 (5th Cir. 1970), and we see no occasion to depart from this rule in the present case. The Plain Dealing School System has been a unitary system for only one semester. This is insufficient to even raise the issue of the validity of testing itself. In *Singleton* we made it clear that regardless of the innate validity of testing, it could not be used until a school district had been established as a unitary system. We think at a minimum this means that the district in question must have for several years operated as a unitary system. . . .

Vacated and remanded with direction.

NOTES AND QUESTIONS

1. Basis of Decision

What is the constitutional basis for the *Lemon* decision? If the court is simply asserting that a formerly dual school system has an obligation to remedy all vestiges of *de jure* segregation, why is an ability-grouping plan necessarily inconsistent with that objective? *See also Reed v. Rhodes*, 455 F.Supp. 569 (N.D. Ohio 1978); *Moses v. Washington Parish School Board*, 330 F.Supp. 1340 (E.D.La. 1971), *aff'd*, 456 F.2d 1285 (5th Cir. 1972) (per curiam), *cert. denied*, 409 U.S. 1013, 93 S.Ct. 431, 34 L.Ed.2d 307. Is the court suggesting that the prior discrimination might cause or perpetuate lower black achievement and thus, despite its neutral gloss, assignment according to ability is discriminatory? *See McNeal v. Tate County School District*, 508 F.2d 1017 (5th Cir. 1975).

Is the court assuming that black students will predominate in the lower track, whites in the upper track? If so, why is that of constitutional concern? Is the court suggesting that the motive for adopting ability grouping is racial prejudice? In this regard, would the district's past grouping practices be relevant? *See* Simon, "Racially Prejudiced Governmental Actions: A Motivation Theory of the Constitutional Ban Against Racial Discrimination," 15 *San Diego L. Rev.* 1041 (1978). What if the lower tracks offered well-designed and implemented remedial programs? *Cf. Copeland v. School Bd.*, 464 F.2d 932 (4th Cir. 1972).

Is the use of testing as a basis for student assignments in a district that has not operated as a unitary system for more than a few years *per se* invalid? If not, how might defendant school officials demonstrate that the assignment scheme is legitimate? Several cases have implied that school officials would have to show that the assignment scheme is not based on the present result of past segregation, and that the assignment scheme will remedy past segregation through better educational opportunities. *See, e.g., Georgia State Conference of Branches of NAACP v. Georgia*, 775 F.2d 1403 (11th Cir. 1985); *United States v. Gadsden County School District*, 572 F.2d 1049 (5th Cir. 1978); *Montgomery v. Starkville Municipal Separate School District*, 665 F.Supp. 487 (N.D. Mass. 1987); *Bond v. Keck*, 616 F.Supp. 581 (D.C. Mo. 1985).

2. *Testing*

The *Lemon* court views the constitutionality of "testing *per se*" as a "complex and troubling question." What might be legally troubling about testing: the use of tests, the reliability of tests identifying student ability, the likelihood that test use will yield racial overrepresentation in less advanced school programs, or the competency of courts to pass on such educational issues? *See Moses v. Washington Parish School Board*, 330 F.Supp. 1340 (E.D. La. 1971).

3. *Intraschool Grouping and Unitary School Systems*

Would the result in the *Lemon* case have changed if defendants had proposed grouping within schools rather than between them? *See Moses v. Washington Parish School Board, supra.* Should there be any difference in legal standards between intraschool and interschool grouping? In *Morales v. Shannon*, 516 F.2d 411 (5th Cir. 1975), *cert. denied*, 423 U.S. 1034, 96 S.Ct. 566, 46 L.Ed.2d 408, the Fifth Circuit found that the concentration of Mexican-American students in the lower tracks of the junior and senior high schools of Uvalde, Texas, was the result of test scores, grades, and teacher recommendations. The court was led to conclude:

> Given that ability groupings are not unconstitutional per se, the statistical results of the groupings here are not so abnormal or unusual in any instance as to justify an inference of discrimination. The record shows no more than the use of a non-discriminatory teaching practice or technique, a matter which is reserved to educators under our system of government.

516 F.2d at 414. Are *Morales* and *Lemon* distinguishable?

3. **Ability Grouping and Equal Educational Opportunities.**

The basic premise of school classification is that treating children differently who have identifiably different needs will increase the educational opportunities available to all. That premise has been questioned by critics who assert that particular classifications diminish, rather than enhance, educational opportunity.

Alleged diminution of educational opportunity may rest on three quite different grounds: (1) students assigned to certain programs receive fewer tangible resources than students assigned to other programs; (2) certain programs, because of their structural rigidity or inefficacy, restrict the educational potential of students assigned to them; and (3) certain programs unnecessarily stigmatize students.

Outside the racial discrimination context, no court has assessed whether particular classifications deny equal educational opportunity. *Hobson v. Hansen*, the most famous of the classification cases, focuses primarily on the race and class discrimination that tracking assertedly fosters. *See generally* Bersoff, "Regarding Psychologists Testily: Legal Regulation of Psychological Assessment in the Public Schools," 39 *Md. L. Rev.* 27, 44–58 (1979). Yet *Hobson* raises questions broader than race and class discrimination; it suggests that other nonracial aspects of classification might be the subject of constitutional challenge.

Hobson v. Hansen

269 F.Supp. 401 (D.D.C. 1967), *aff'd sub. nom. Smuck v. Hobson*, 408 F.2d 175 (D.C. Cir. 1969) (en banc).

Judge Wright:

* * *

IV. The Track System

The District of Columbia school system employs a form of ability grouping commonly known as the track system, by which students at the elementary and secondary level are placed in tracks or curriculum levels according to the school's assessment of each student's ability to learn. . . . As the evidence in this case makes painfully clear, ability grouping as presently practiced in the District of Columbia school system is a denial of equal educational opportunity to the poor and a majority of the Negroes attending school in the nation's capital, a denial that contravenes not only the guarantees of the Fifth Amendment but also the fundamental premise of the track system itself. What follows, then, is a discussion of that evidence—an examination of the track system: in theory and in reality. . . .

Purpose and Philosophy. Dr. Hansen [Superintendent of Schools] believes that the comprehensive high school (and the school system generally) must be systematically organized and structured to provide differing levels of education for students with widely differing levels of academic ability. This is the purpose of the track system. In expressing the track system's philosophy Dr. Hansen has said, "Every pupil in the school system must have the maximum opportunity for self-development and this can best be brought about by adjusting curriculum offerings to different levels of need and ability as the pupil moves through the stages of education and growth in our schools." . . .

Student Types. Within the student body Dr. Hansen sees generally four types of students: the intellectually gifted, the above-average, the average, and the retarded. He assumes that each of these types of students has a maximum level of academic capability and, most importantly, that that level of ability can be accurately ascertained. The duty of the school is to identify these students and provide a curriculum commensurate with their respective abilities. Dr. Hansen contends that the traditional school curriculum . . . does a disservice to those at either end of the ability spectrum.

The gifted student is not challenged, so that he becomes bored, lazy, and perhaps performs far below his academic potential; his intellectual talents are a wasted resource. The remedy lies in discovering the gifted student, placing him with others of his own kind, thereby stimulating him through this select association as well as a rigorous, demanding curriculum to develop his intellectual talent. . . .

On the other hand, continues Dr. Hansen, the retarded or "stupid" student typically has been forced to struggle through a curriculum he cannot possibly master and only imperfectly comprehends. Typically he is slow to learn and soon falls behind in class; he repeatedly fails, sometimes repeating a grade again and again; he becomes isolated, frustrated, depressed, and—if he does not drop out before graduation—graduates with a virtually useless education. Here the remedy is seen as separating out the retarded student, directing him into a special curriculum geared to his limited abilities and designed to give him a useful "basic" education—one which makes no pretense of equalling traditionally taught curricula.

In short, Hansen views the traditional school curriculum as doing too little for some students and expecting too much of others. As for the latter type,

whom Dr. Hansen characterizes as "the blue-collar student," going to school—a "white-collar occupation"—can be an artificial experience. "Twelve years of white-collar experience is unrealistic preparation for the young man or woman who will suddenly make the change into work clothes for jobs in kitchens, stockrooms, street maintenance or building construction. . . ."

Tracking. In order to tailor the educational process to the level appropriate to each student, Dr. Hansen adopted the track system. Each track is intended to be a separate and self-contained curriculum, with the educational content ranging from the very basic to the very advanced according to the track level. In the elementary and junior high schools three levels are used: Basic or Special Academic (retarded students), General (average and above-average), and Honors (gifted). In the senior high school a fourth level is added: the Regular Track, a college-preparatory track intended to accommodate the above-average student.

The significant feature of the track system in this regard is its emphasis on the ability of the student. A student's course of instruction depends upon what the school system decides he is capable of handling. . . .

Flexibility. Dr. Hansen, while assuming that some students can be educated to their maximum potential in one of the four curricula, also anticipates that not all students will neatly or permanently fit into a track. Thus a second important assumption underlying the track system is that tracking will be a flexible process. Flexibility encompasses two things: First, although a student today may demonstrate an ability level which calls, for example, for placement in the General Track, a constant and continuing effort must be made to assure that he is at his true ability level. This calls for instruction directed toward correcting any remediable educational problems which account for the student's present poor performance; and it calls for close analysis and counseling to determine whether these remediable deficiencies exist and when they have been sufficiently corrected. When the latter is determined, the student is to be upgraded to the next higher track. Second, even though a student may not be in a position to make an across-the-board move from one track to another, his ability level may be such that he needs to take courses in two track levels on a subject-by-subject basis. This process, known as crosstracking, is critical: it is the mechanism the system relies upon to assure that students whose ability levels vary according to particular subjects are not thwarted in developing their strong areas because their weak areas result in their being placed in a lower curriculum level. . . .

Fundamental Assumptions. . . .

The express assumptions of this approach are three: First, a child's maximum educational potential can and will be accurately ascertained. Second, tracking will enhance the prospects for correcting a child's remediable educational deficiencies. Third, tracking must be flexible so as to provide an individually tailored education for students who cannot be pigeonholed in a single curriculum. . . .

. . . Flexibility in Pupil Programming.

The importance of flexibility to the proper operation of the track system has been adverted to earlier in this opinion. . . .

. . . [However] flexibility in pupil programming in the District of Columbia school system is an unkept promise.

1. Movement Between Tracks: Upgrading. . . . [A]t least 85% of those assigned to the special academic track—and it appears that something over 90% is more typical—remain at the lowest achievement level. Although it cannot be said that an assignment to the Special Academic Track inevitably is permanent, neither can it be said that the chances of progressing into a more challenging curriculum are very high.

Plaintiffs have charged that this lack of movement is attributable to a complex of causes: the simplified curriculum, coupled with the absence of variety in the students' levels of ability, does not stimulate the Special Academic student; remedial training is inadequate; Special Academic teachers are not formally trained for special educational problems; teachers underestimate the potential of their students and therefore undereducate them. None of these reasons can be either isolated or proved with absolute certainty. Nonetheless, there is substantial evidence . . . that the cause of limited upgrading in the Special Academic Track lies more with faults to be found in the system than with the innate disabilities of the students. And certainly the results . . . do not support the thesis that tracking is flexible. . . .

. . . [T]he pattern observed with respect to upgrading from the Special Academic Track is repeated in all track levels. Movement between tracks borders on the nonexistent. . . .

Viewed as a whole, the evidence of overall movement between tracks conclusively demonstrates the defendants' failure to translate into practice one of the most critical tenets of the track system: "Pupil placement in a curriculum must never be static or unchangeable. Otherwise, the four-track system will degenerate into a four-rut system." The tragedy has occurred.

2. Movement Between Tracks: Cross-Tracking. . . . In practice cross-tracking of the sort described is confined to the senior high level, there being structural reasons why elementary and junior high pupils do not really "cross-track." And . . . even at the senior high school level cross-tracking proves to be the exception, not the rule. . . .

. . . [T]here is substantial evidence, some of it already discussed in relation to upgrading, pointing to several reasons.

The first is that students are being denied permission to cross-track—or discouraged from seeking that permission—on the assumption that they cannot handle a more difficult assignment. . . .

Another reason, related to the first, is . . . that many students do not obtain effective, individual counseling on programs, counseling that is obviously necessary if a student is to be directed to a curricular program fitted to his needs and abilities. . . .

A third reason for limited cross-tracking, . . . is the inability to qualify for the more advanced courses either for lack of the prerequisite fundamental courses or because of continuing academic deficiencies. . . .

A fourth reason . . . is the substantial possibility that some school principals, or their staffs, take a very restrictive view of cross-tracking. . . .

Causes of Discrimination and the
Collapse of Track Theory. . . .

Here the focus will be on the major institutional shortcomings that not only thrust the disadvantaged student into the lower tracks but tend to keep him there once placed. The first area of concern is the lack of kindergartens and Honors programs in certain [predominantly black] schools; the second relates to remedial and compensatory programs for the disadvantaged and educationally handicapped student; and the third, and most important, involves the whole of the placement and testing process by which the school system decides who gets what kind of education. . . .

[The court finds that disadvantaged students have less access to kindergarten programs (which, the court asserts, may be "indispensable to their success in the whole of their academic career") and to honors track instruction.]

. . . Remedial and Compensatory Education.

One purpose of the track system is to facilitate remedial education for students who are temporarily handicapped in basic academic skills. In addition, the school system has recognized that it must provide a substantial number of its students with special compensatory education programs for there to be any real hope of their becoming qualified for the more advanced tracks. There is substantial evidence, however, that neither the remedial nor the compensatory education programs presently in existence are adequate; rather the disadvantaged student consigned to the lower track tends simply to get the lesser education, not the push to a higher level of achievement.

[The court reviews the lack of remedial programs in each track. Judge Wright notes that "[w]hat has not been made clear, however, is how a student given a steady diet of simplified materials can keep up, let alone catch up, with children his own age who are proceeding in a higher curriculum at a faster pace and with a more complex subject-matter content. While much has been made of the 'enriched' Honors curriculum . . . nothing has been said to indicate that the slower learner—who almost certainly is in some degree slow due to a disadvantaged background—is also given an enriched curriculum to stimulate him to higher achievement. . . ." 269 F.Supp. at 470.]

* * *

. . . Special Remedial and Compensatory Education Programs.

It is because of the high proportion of disadvantaged children in the District school system that it is imperative that special programs outside the regular school curriculum be adopted so that the disadvantaged child has a real opportunity to achieve at his maximum level of ability. . . .

. . . It is true that the schools alone cannot compensate for all the handicaps that are characteristic of the disadvantaged child; but it is the schools that must—as defendants admit—lead the attack on the verbal handicaps which are the major barrier to academic achievement. . . .

The track system adds to that obligation, however, because tracking translates ability into educational opportunity. When a student is placed in a lower track, in a very real sense his future is being decided for him; the kind of education he gets there shapes his future progress not only in school but in society in general. Certainly, when the school system undertakes this responsibility it incurs the obligation of living up to its promise to the student that placement in a lower track will not simply be a shunting off from the mainstream of education, but rather will be an effective mechanism for bringing the student up to his true potential. Yet in the District the limited scope of remedial and compensatory programs, the miniscule number of students upgraded, and the relatively few students cross-tracking make inescapable the conclusion that existing programs do not fulfill that promise. . . .

[The court then examines what it terms "the most important single aspect of the track system . . . the process by which the school system goes about sorting students into the different tracks. This importance stems from the fact that the fundamental premise of the sorting process is the keystone of the whole track system: that school personnel can with reasonable accuracy ascertain the maximum potential of each student and fix the content and pace of his education accordingly." 269 F.Supp. at 473–4.]

* * *

a. Fundamentals of track placement.

. . . [T]he tripartite division of the curriculum at the elementary school level takes place midway through the fourth grade. . . .

. . . [T]he burden of the placement decision rests with the teacher. The teacher is the one who, through daily contact with the student, presumably knows him best. Equally important, it is the teacher who gives the grades and records the comments that go into making up the student's 'paper image,' which follows him through school as a part of his file; and it is the teacher who, in the day-to-day teacher-pupil relationship, greatly influences how the student acts and how well he succeeds in school.

. . . The court does accept the general proposition that tests are but one factor in programming students; but it also finds that testing looms as a most important consideration in making track assignments. There are several reasons for this finding.

First, as a review of the official criteria makes obvious, there is a heavy emphasis on achievement and aptitude test scores, including IQ levels.

Second, and more importantly, the proper operation of the track system practically demands reliance on test scores. For one thing, classes are designed to serve students of similar achievement or ability levels, and this requires uniformity in the standards by which students are selected for placement in particular classes. . . .

b. *Frequency of testing.*

* * *

A student tested only according to the mandatory schedule will take a total of six aptitude tests of various kinds and five achievement tests of various kinds. Four of the six aptitude tests and three of the five achievement tests are given in elementary school, and one of each at both the junior and the senior high levels. Under such a program a student may go as many as three years without undergoing new tests (sixth grade to ninth grade; ninth grade to 11th grade), so that his most recent test scores may be as much as three years old.

There is a distinct possibility that students are not seriously reevaluated for upgrading except when the time for mandatory testing comes around. . . . This would tend to account for the relatively limited amount of upgrading and cross-tracking found to exist. . . .

c. *The use and misuse of tests.*

The court now turns to the crucial issue posed by plaintiffs' attack on defendants' use of tests: whether it is possible to ascertain with at least reasonable accuracy the maximum educational potential of certain kinds of schoolchildren. This question goes to the very foundation of the track system since . . . one of the fundamental premises of track theory is that students' potential can be determined. On this premise rests the practice of separating students into homogeneous ability groups; and most importantly, on this premise rests the sole justification for a student's being *permanently* assigned to lower track classes where the instructional pace and content have been scaled down to serve students of supposedly limited abilities. That is, according to track theory, those who remain in a lower curriculum remain *because they are achieving at their maximum level of ability.* They are not admitted to—or are at least discouraged from seeking admission to—a higher instructional level because the school system has determined that they cannot 'usefully' and 'successfully' rise above their present level. . . .

(1) *Test structure.*

(a) *The nature of scholastic aptitude tests.*

There are essentially two types of tests used in educational evaluation, achievement tests and scholastic aptitude tests. An *achievement* test is designed primarily to measure a student's level of attainment in a given subject, such as history, science, literature, and so on. The test presumes the student has been instructed in the subject matter; it seeks to find out how well he has learned that subject. . . .

A *scholastic aptitude* test is specifically designed to predict how a student will achieve in the future in an academic curriculum. It does this by testing certain skills which have come to be identified as having a high correlation with scholastic achievement. Once a student's present proficiency in these skills is ascertained, an inference is drawn as to how well he can be expected to do in the future.

The skills measured by scholastic aptitude tests are verbal. More precisely, an aptitude test is essentially a test of the student's command of standard English and grammar. The emphasis on these skills is due to the nature of the academic curriculum, which is highly verbal; without such skills a student cannot be successful. Therefore, by measuring the student's present verbal ability the test makes it possible to estimate the student's likelihood of success in the future.

. . . [T]he skills being measured are *not* innate or inherited traits. They are learned, acquired through experience. . . . [A]ptitude tests can only test a student's present level of learning in certain skills and from that infer his capability to learn further.

Of utmost importance is the fact that, to demonstrate the ability to learn, a student must have had the opportunity to learn those skills relied upon for prediction. In other words, an aptitude test is necessarily measuring a student's background, his environment. It is a test of his cumulative experiences in his home, his community and his school. Each of these social institutions has a separate influence on his development. . . .

(b) *Causes of low test scores.*

A low aptitude test score may mean that a student is innately limited in intellectual ability. On the other hand, there may be other explanations possible that have nothing to do with native intelligence. . . .

. . . [O]ne of the important factors that could account for a low test score is the student's *environment.* If a student has had little or no opportunity to acquire and develop the requisite verbal or nonverbal skills, he obviously cannot score well on the tests.

Another source of variation is the student's *emotional or psychological condition* when he takes the test. He may have a poor attitude toward the test or the testing situation, generally characterized as apathy. This may be due to lack of motivation; or it may be a defensive reaction caused by worry or fear— what has been called 'test anxiety.' Anxiety can also cause extremely nervous reactions. All of these behavior patterns will cause the student to perform poorly on a test, either because he panics and forgets what he knows or rushes through the test skipping questions, guessing at answers, or otherwise acting carelessly.

* * *

(c) Test standardization.

A standardized test is one for which a norm or average score has been established so that subsequently obtained scores can be comparatively evaluated. A test is standardized on a selected group of students whose scores are distributed to obtain a median; the median then becomes the norm for that test. Usually the standard is a national one, in the sense that the test publisher seeks to recreate in the norming group a representative cross-section of American schools. . . .

The norming group of students is selected according to certain factors. The principal ones are socio-economic and cultural status, as defined by the median annual income and average amount of schooling of the adults in the students' community. Other factors considered are region and school size. Race is not a controlled factor. Given the demography of the total population, the standardizing group will be predominantly white and middle class. . . .

(2) Testing the Disadvantaged Child.

. . . The issue plaintiffs have raised is whether standard aptitude tests are appropriate for making inferences about the innate intellectual capabilities of [disadvantaged]children.

. . . [T]he term "disadvantaged" . . . is commonly based on two factors: the child's socio-economic status, as measured by the family's annual income; and his cultural status, as measured by the number of years of schooling attained by his parents. Both of these factors have been identified as having a high correlation with achievement both in school and in society generally, since they tend to reflect the kinds of background more or less conducive to developing scholastic-type skills. There are also indications that racial factors may well have some separate bearing on whether a child can be considered disadvantaged.

. . . [A] substantial portion of the District's Negro schoolchildren can be characterized as disadvantaged. . . . As far as educational attainment is concerned, the pattern is the same. . . . At least one-third of the [black] elementary school pupils live in tracts where the educational level is under 10 years. Almost eight out of 10 [black] elementary school pupils live in areas where the majority of the adults have not completed high school.

(a) Handicaps to learning.

Disadvantaged children typically are saddled with tremendous handicaps when it comes to competing in the ethnocentric academic society of public schools. That society, mirroring American society generally, is strongly influenced by white and middle class experiences and values. While there is nothing necessarily wrong about this orientation, it does raise certain barriers for lower class and Negro children— barriers that are to be found in most aptitude tests as well.

1. Environmental factors. The chief handicap of the disadvantaged child where verbal tests are concerned is in his limited exposure to people having command of standard English. Communication within the lower class environment, although it may rise to a very complex and sophisticated level, typically assumes a language form alien to that tested by aptitude tests. . . .

Other circumstances interact with and reinforce the language handicap. Verbalization tends to occur less frequently and often less intensively. Because of crowded living conditions, the noise level in the home may be quite high with the result that the child's auditory perception—his ability to discriminate among word sounds—can be retarded. There tends to be less exposure to books or other serious reading material—either for lack of interest or for lack of money.

The disadvantaged child has little or no opportunity to range beyond the boundaries of his immediate neighborhood. He is unfamiliar, therefore, with concepts that will expand both his range of experiences and his vocabulary. He has less exposure to new things that he can reduce to verbal terms. For example, one defense witness, a principal of a low-income Negro elementary school, told of how most of the children had never been more than a few blocks from home; they had never been downtown, although some had been to a Sears department store; they did not know what an escalator was, had not seen a department-store Santa Claus, had not been to a zoo. These experiences, common in the subject matter of tests and textbooks, were alien to the lives of these children.

* * *

2. Psychological factors. . . . [T]here is a good deal of evidence that disadvantaged children and Negro children are more likely than others to suffer from influences that have a depressing effect on test scores. The problem can generally be described as one of low self-esteem, or lack of self-confidence.

i. Socio-economic causes. There is evidence that disadvantaged children, black or white, are those most likely to lack self-confidence in the school situation. This is due to a complex of causes, many of them directly related to the environmental factors already discussed. The disadvantaged child is made profoundly aware of this academic shortcoming as soon as he enters school. There is a great risk of his losing confidence in his ability to compete in school with children who are 'better off'. A frequent manifestation of this is for the child to become a discipline problem, as he goes through the process of rejecting a situation in which he feels inadequate. All of this can have a direct and significant effect on test performance as much as on scholastic performance.

ii. Racial causes. Apart from factors related to socio-economic status, there is striking evidence that Negro children undergo a special kind of psychological stress that can have a debilitating effect on academic and test performance. Because of their race and the ever present reminders of being "different," Negro children generally are subject to very serious problems of self-identification. By the time the Negro child is about to enter school he has become very much racially self-conscious, which causes considerable psychological turmoil as he attempts to come to terms with his status as a Negro. He tends to be imbued with a sense of worthlessness, of inferiority, of fear and despair which is transmitted to him primarily through his parents.

In this state of turmoil, many Negro children approach school with the feeling they are entering a strange and alien place that is the property of a white school system or of white society, even though the school may be all-Negro. And when the school *is* all-Negro or predominantly so, this simply reinforces the impressions implanted in the child's mind by his parents, for the school experience is then but a perpetuation of the segregation he has come to expect in life generally. . . .

When economically based deprivation is combined with the traumas suffered simply because of being Negro, the psychological impact can be crushing.

iii. Manifestations of low self-esteem: anxiety and apathy. When a child lacks confidence in himself or is self-degrading, he is likely to manifest this during the test-taking experience. One reaction that has been identified has been called "test anxiety." The child, apprehensive about his ability to score well and fearful about what others—especially his teacher or principal—might see in the test score, reacts in a self-defeating manner: He becomes highly nervous, even "wildly rampant"; or he withdraws. Either reaction lowers his test score. . . .

Aside from anxiety-caused withdrawal, a child may be apathetic about a test simply because he does not see it as important. Children who come from backgrounds lacking in parental and environmental support for academic achievement will be more prone to be apathetic about testing; and disadvantaged children are those most likely to have nonsupportive backgrounds. . . .

(3) Empirical confirmation.

Empirical confirmation of the disadvantaged child's handicaps on aptitude tests can be found in the remarkably high degree of correlation between test scores on standard aptitude tests and the socio-economic status of the child. The more disadvantaged the child, the lower his test score will be. . . .

Defendants, while acknowledging the handicaps of the disadvantaged child, have steadfastly maintained that the cause of low test scores is strictly a matter of socio-economic status, not race. In their view, the fact that a child is Negro is irrelevant to test performance. The evidence, however, does not support such a definitive conclusion. . . .

* * *

(4) The influence of school.

For the disadvantaged child, handicapped as he is by home and community circumstances, the school remains as the last hope for overcoming academic deficiencies. In recognition of this fact the urban schools, including the District school system, are giving more and more attention to providing compensatory education for these children, for it is the school that by definition is best suited to providing students with the opportunity to acquire and perfect the academic skills which the school itself demands. And if the school fails in this task, the disadvantaged child will remain handicapped both in class and in taking tests.

But the influence of the school is not confined to how well it can teach the disadvantaged child; it also has a significant role to play in shaping the student's emotional and psychological make-up. The formula for reaching a student who comes to school academically ill-equipped from the start, who is disposed to reject the whole educational complex because of feelings of fear, frustration and an abiding sense of futility, is still one of the unsolved problems in American education. . . .

. . . [O]ne of the most important influences on both academic achievement and aptitude test scores inheres in the teacher-pupil relationship, ... "teacher expectation." Studies have found that a teacher will commonly tend to underestimate the abilities of disadvantaged children and will treat them accordingly—in the daily classroom routine, in grading, and in evaluating these students' likelihood of achieving in the future. The horrible consequence of a teacher's low expectation is that it tends to be a self-fulfilling prophecy. The unfortunate students, treated as if they were subnormal, come to accept as a fact that they *are* subnormal. They act out in their school behavior and in the testing situation what they have been conditioned to believe is their true status in life; and in conforming to expectations, they 'confirm' the original judgment. . . .

d. Accuracy of test measurements.

Plaintiffs charge that the disadvantaged child's handicaps—both environmental and psychological— are such that standard aptitude tests cannot serve as accurate measurements of innate ability to learn. . . . The evidence that this is so is persuasive.

It will be recalled that a scholastic aptitude test is constructed to test present facility in verbal—and, sometimes, nonverbal—skills so as to make possible an inference about an individual's innate ability to succeed in school. The inference is expressed in the form of a test score which is a statement of how the individual student compares with the median score of the norming group. The median reflects an 'average' ability to learn, a score above or below that average indicating superior or inferior ability. A crucial assumption in this comparative statement, however, is that the individual is fairly comparable with the norming group in terms of environmental background and psychological make-up; to the extent the individual is not

comparable, the test score may reflect those differences rather than innate differences. . . .

. . . [T]he best circumstance for making accurate estimates of ability is when the tested student is most like the typical norming student: white and middle class. Because the white middle class student predominates in the norming sample, it is possible to say the average student in that group will have had roughly the same opportunities to develop standard verbal and nonverbal skills as the rest of the group and will probably be psychologically similar as well. Thus the national median or norm is a reasonably accurate statistical statement of what the average American student ought to have learned in the way of verbal and nonverbal skills by a certain age and what can therefore be considered average intelligence or ability to learn. For this reason, standard aptitude tests are most precise and accurate in their measurements of innate ability when given to white middle class students.

When standard aptitude tests are given to low income Negro children, or disadvantaged children, however, the tests are less precise and less accurate— so much so that test scores become practically meaningless. Because of the impoverished circumstances that characterize the disadvantaged child, it is virtually impossible to tell whether the test score reflects lack of ability—or simply lack of opportunity. Moreover, the probability that test scores of the Negro child or the disadvantaged child will be depressed because of somewhat unique psychological influences further compounds the risk of inaccuracy.

* * *

The Self-Fulfilling Prophecy. The real tragedy of misjudgments about the disadvantaged student's abilities is . . . the likelihood that the student will act out that judgment and confirm it by achieving only at the expected level. . . . [W]hile the tragedy of misjudgments can occur even under the best of circumstances, there is reason to believe the track system compounds the risk.

First, . . . [b]y assuming the responsibility of deciding who gets what kind of educational opportunity, the school system places a dear price on teacher misjudgments. Thus, when a misjudgment does occur, the result will be institutionally to shunt the student into a curriculum paced to his presumed abilities, where he is likely to progress only at the speed at which he is taught.[146] A sixth-grade

---

[146]. . . [A]nother risk of reinforcing a child's present disabilities [is] the lack of contact with students having a command of standard English. The homogeneous class, by grouping students similarly handicapped, removes a source of stimulation available in a mixed ability setting.

student nourished on third-grade instruction is apt to finish the year with a third-grade education; yet the haunting question: could he have done better?

Another aspect of . . . the track system is its tendency to reinforce the psychological impact of being adjudged of low ability. By consigning students to specifically designated curricula, the track system makes highly visible the student's status within the school structure. . . .

None of this is to suggest either that a student should be sheltered from the truth about his academic deficiencies or that instruction cannot take account of varying levels of ability. It is to say that a system that presumes to tell a student what his ability is and what he can successfully learn incurs an obligation to take account of the psychological damage that can come from such an encounter between the student and the school; and to be certain that it is in a position to decide whether the student's deficiencies are true, or only apparent. The District of Columbia school system has not shown that it is in such a position.

Opinion of Law

* * *

The sum result of . . . [t]he infirmities [of the track system], when tested by the principles of equal protection and due process, is to deprive the poor and a majority of the Negro students in the District of Columbia of their constitutional right to equal educational opportunities.

At the outset it should be made clear that what is at issue here is not whether defendants are entitled to provide different kinds of students with different kinds of education. Although the equal protection clause is, of course, concerned with classifications which result in disparity of treatment, not all classifications resulting in disparity are unconstitutional. If classification is reasonably related to the purposes of the governmental activity involved and is rationally carried out, the fact that persons are thereby treated differently does not necessarily offend.

. . . Whatever may be said of the concept of ability grouping in general, it has been assumed here that such grouping can be reasonably related to the purposes of public education. Plaintiffs have eschewed taking any position to the contrary. Rather the substance of plaintiffs' complaint is that in practice, if not by design, the track system — as administered in the District of Columbia public schools —

has become a system of discrimination founded on socioeconomic and racial status rather than ability, resulting in the undereducation of many District students. . . .

* * *

Remedy

* * *

As to the remedy with respect to the track system, the track system simply must be abolished. In practice, if not in concept, it discriminates against the disadvantaged child, particularly the Negro. Designed in 1955 as a means of protecting the school system against the ill effects of integrating with white children the Negro victims of *de jure* separate but unequal education, it has survived to stigmatize the disadvantaged child of whatever race relegated to its lower tracks — from which tracks the possibility of switching upward, because of the absence of compensatory education, is remote.

Even in concept the track system is undemocratic and discriminatory. Its creator admits it is designed to prepare some children for white-collar, and other children for blue-collar, jobs. Considering the tests used to determine which children should receive the blue-collar special, and which the white, the danger of children completing their education wearing the wrong collar is far too great for this democracy to tolerate. Moreover, any system of ability grouping which, through failure to include and implement the concept of compensatory education for the disadvantaged child or otherwise, fails in fact to bring the great majority of children into the mainstream of public education denies the children excluded equal educational opportunity and thus encounters the constitutional bar. . . .

* * *

It is further ordered, adjudged and decreed that the defendants be, and they are hereby, permanently enjoined from operating the track system in the District of Columbia public schools. . . .

NOTES AND QUESTIONS

1. Scope of the Decision

Hobson declares that the tracking system "simply must be abolished." What is the basis for that conclusion? Is it the fact that black and poor students are assigned in disproportionate numbers to the lowest tracks? *See Johnson v. San Francisco Unified School District*, 339 F.Supp. 1315 (N.D.Cal. 1971), *vacated and remanded*, 500 F.2d 349 (9th Cir. 1974). *But see Berkelman v. San Francisco Unified School District*, 501 F.2d 1264 (9th Cir. 1974) (assignment to college preparatory high school based on previous academic achievement is constitutional). Is the decision based on the inadequacy of aptitude tests as a means of assigning these students to tracks? Does the inadequacy lie in the failure to measure innate ability for all students or only for poor and black students? *See* Bersoff, "Regarding Psychologists Testily: Legal Regulation of Psychological Assessment in the Public Schools," 39 *Md. L. Rev.* 27, 51–58 (1979); Shea, "An Educational Perspective of the Legality of Intelligence Testing and Ability Grouping," 6 *J. of Law & Educ.* 137, 147–48 (1977). Is the inflexibility of the classification system or the inadequacy of education provided for lower-track students the basis for the decision? *See Berkelman v. San Francisco Unified School District, supra.* Should a distinction be drawn between tracking in the elementary grades and tracking in the high schools? *See* Orfield, "How to Make Desegregation Work: The Adaptation of Schools to Their Newly-Integrated Student Bodies," 39 *Law & Contemp. Probs.* 314, 326–27 (1975).

There was no express finding of intentional segregation in *Hobson*, although Judge Wright notes that the track system was "[d]esigned in 1955 [following the decision in *Bolling v. Sharpe*, 347 U.S.497, 74 S.Ct. 693, 98 L.Ed.884 (1954), the companion case to *Brown*] as a means of protecting the school system against the ill effects of integrating with white children the Negro victims of *de jure* separate but unequal education." After the Supreme Court's decision in *Washington v. Davis*, 426 U.S. 229, 96 S.Ct. 2040, 48 L.Ed. 2d 597 (1976) and subsequent cases, plaintiffs would have had to show racially discriminatory purpose for an equal protection violation. If this case arose today, would the plaintiffs be able to make a Title VI disparate impact claim against the tracking system? *See Georgia State of Branches of NAACP v. Georgia*, 775 F.2d 1403, 1418 (11th Cir. 1985) (ability grouping did not violate Title VI because it was necessary to meet the needs of the student population and was an "accepted pedagogical practice"). *But see* Losen, "Silent Segregation in Our Nation's Schools," 34 *Harv. C.R.–C.L. L. Rev.* 517 (1999); Note, "Teaching Inequality: The Problem of Public School Tracking," 102 *Harv. L. Rev.* 1318

(1989). *But see Alexander v. Sandoval, supra*, holding that there is no private right of action to enforce Title VI disparate-impact regulations.

Judge Wright also states that the tracking system "stigmatize[s] the disadvantaged child of whatever race relegated to its lower tracks." If *Hobson* is not primarily a race case, then what is the constitutional warrant for the decision—that education is a "fundamental" constitutional interest, or that (even unintentional) classifications by socioeconomic status are suspect? *But see San Antonio Independent School District v. Rodriguez*, chapter 7.

The *Hobson* decision was affirmed on appeal. *Smuck v. Hobson*, 408 F.2d 175 (D.C. Cir. 1969) (en banc). The court held:

> The district court's decree must be taken to refer to the "track system" as it existed at the time of the decree . . . [Neither] the school board nor Superintendent Hansen were satisfied with the track system as it was or desired a freeze in its features. . . .
>
> Therefore, the provision of the decree below directing abolition of the track system will not be modified. We conclude that this directive does not limit the discretion of the school board with full recognition of the need to permit the school board latitude in fashioning and effectuating the remedies for the ills of the District school system. . . . The simple decree enjoining the "track system" does not interpose any realistic barrier to flexible school administration by a school board genuinely committed to attainment of more quality and equality of educational opportunity.

408 F.2d at 189–90.

Does the appellate court's interpretation undercut the force of Judge Wright's conclusion? Does it allow the school district to implement a different type of track system? Compare *id.* with *Spangler v. Pasadena City Board of Education*, 311 F.Supp. 501, 504 (C.D. Cal. 1970), *aff'd*, 427 F.2d 1352 (9th Cir.), *cert. denied*, 402 U.S. 943, 91 S.Ct. 1607, 29 L.Ed.2d 111 (1971)(intraschool grouping of students violates equal protection clause but, given "delicate educational nature of decisions," only reexamination of grouping policies is required). Or is the appellate decision consistent with Judge Wright's statement that: "What is at issue here is not whether defendants are entitled to provide different kinds of students with different kinds of education. . . . [I]t has been assumed here that [ability] grouping can be reasonably related to the purposes of public education [and thus be found constitutionally valid]." *See* Shea, *supra* at 153–54; Orfield, *supra* at 324–28.

Challenges to tracking and ability grouping since the *Hobson* case, unless clearly shown to be a vestige of prior unlawful segregation, as in *Simmons v. Hooks*, 843 F.Supp. 1296, 1299 (E.D. Ark. 1994), have been unsuccessful, with courts deferring to educational authorities. *See, e.g., People Who Care v. Rockford Board of Educ., School Dist. No. 205* (7th Cir. 1997), reversing a lower court order forbidding grouping students by ability, and establishing racial quotas for permitted classes for gifted students. Chief Judge Posner commented as follows with regard to tracking:

> Tracking is a controversial educational policy, although just grouping students by age, something no one questions, is a form of "tracking." Lawyers and judges are not competent to resolve the controversy. The conceit that they are belongs to a myth of the legal profession's omnicompetence that was exploded long ago. To abolish tracking is to say to bright kids, whether white or black, that they have to go at a slower pace than they're capable of; it is to say to the parents of the brighter kids that their children don't really belong in the public school system; and it is to say to the slower kids, of whatever race, that they may have difficulty keeping up, because the brighter kids may force the pace of the class. . . . [A]s the consensus of the nation's educational authorities, [tracking] deserves some consideration by a federal court.

Id. at 536. *See also Quarles v. Oxford Municipal Separate School Dist.*, 868 F.2d 750 (5th Cir. 1989).

2. Rigidity of the System

Hobson notes that the assignments of relatively few students are changed. This phenomenon is not unique to Washington, D.C. A study of urban school systems found that fewer than 10 percent of all students assigned to special education classes ever returned to the regular program. Gallagher, "The Special Education Contract for Mildly Handicapped Children," 38 *J. Exceptional Children* 527, 529 (1972). The court of appeals opinion in *Hobson* observes: "In some cases statistics are ineluctably ambiguous in their import—the fact that only a small percentage of pupils are reassigned may indicate either general adequacy of initial assignments or inadequacy of review." *Smuck v. Hobson*, 408 F.2d 175, 187 (D.C. Cir. 1969). Does any of the evidence reviewed by the trial court suggest which of these hypotheses might in fact be correct? Might the small percentage simply reflect the accuracy of the school district's assignments—that most students belong where they are originally placed?

One study showed that 63 percent of all teachers in the United States find tracking useful, and it is clear that the practice is deeply ingrained. It is found in almost all secondary schools and in most elementary schools. *Academic Tracking*, Report of the NEA Subcommittee on Academic Tracking (1990). This study concluded that, as practiced in most schools, academic tracking does more harm than good. The way tracking operates in most schools is that the students are segregated all or most of the day based on general achievement or behavior rather than on skill in a particular subject. In addition, the groupings are rigid and likely to create racially identifiable classes. At some point, virtually all students are ability grouped, with minority students (African Americans, Latinos, Native Americans) disproportionately placed in low ability and special education classes. In most cases, students are in these tracks for their entire school careers. Another major finding in the study was that minority students are significantly underrepresented in what are called "gatekeeper classes"—courses such as eighth grade algebra or ninth grade geometry—which are prerequisites to higher level courses. The report noted that often these "gatekeeper classes" are not even offered in low socioeconomic status schools. Without these foundation courses, students are prevented from pursuing careers in certain fields such as science or engineering.

A study by the Rand Corporation found that disproportionately high numbers of African American and Latino students are assigned to low-ability mathematics and science classes, while very few minorities gain access to high-ability classes. In addition, low-ability classes are taught by less qualified teachers and receive fewer resources, including science laboratories and equipment. Even in elementary schools, 65 percent of math and science classes are tracked and the tracking is strongly correlated with race, although tracking in these earlier years is less based on an academic record than in high school. The study determined that high-ability students in the least advantaged and predominantly minority schools may actually have fewer opportunities and less qualified teachers than low-ability students in schools that are more than 90 percent white. The report concludes that although tracking is "commonly viewed as a neutral, educationally sound response to wide ranges of student aptitude and achievement . . . such groupings are easily and commonly confounded with race and social class. Moreover, the differences in opportunities they provide actually limit instruction rather than fine-tune it." J. Oakes, *Multiplying Inequalities: The Effects of Race, Social Class, and Tracking on Opportunities to Learn Mathematics and Science* (Rand Corp. 1990). "Because schools judge so many low-income and minority students to have low ability, many of these students suffer from being in classrooms that offer less, even if their schools, as a whole, do not." *Id.* at x–xi. The implications the study draws from the findings are that "although schools may think that they ration good teaching to those students who can most profit from it, *we find no empirical evidence to justify unequal access to valued science and mathematics curriculum, instruction, and teachers.*" (Emphasis in original.) *Id.* at xi.

3. Educational Outcomes: Social Science Evidence

Hobson notes that classification can affect student achievement: "A sixth-grade student nourished on third-grade instruction is apt to finish the year with a third-grade education; yet the haunting question: could he have done better?" There have been numerous studies of the educational efficacy of ability grouping and special education. These studies attempt to answer a question slightly different from the one posed in *Hobson*: Is a given student likely to learn more in an ability-grouped system than he would in a heterogeneously grouped system? In general the evidence suggests that grouping is most efficacious for children with profound problems (below 25 IQ, autistic) and least efficacious for children in the normal range of intelligence. *See generally* Kirp, "Schools as Sorters: The Constitutional and Policy Implications of Student Classification," 121 *U. Pa. L. Rev.* 905 (1973).

One study undertook a comprehensive review of the research published on ability grouping of *elementary* school students dating back to 1932. This study examines the effects of between- and within-class ability grouping on achievement. The study found as follows: Assigning students to self-contained classes according to ability does not enhance student achievement; the research is unclear on the achievement outcomes of schemes in which students remain in heterogeneous classes most of the day, but are regrouped by ability within grade levels for reading and/or mathematics; research on within-class ability grouping, although limited to mathematics and upper elementary schools, supports the use of within-class grouping if the number of groups is kept small—achievement effects were found to be slightly larger for low than for higher average achiev-

ers. R. Slavin, *Ability Grouping and Student Achievement in Elementary Schools: A Best-Evidence Synthesis* (1986). Another study reviewing the research literature on ability-grouped class assignments led to the conclusion that ability grouping in self-contained classes does not increase either achievement or self-esteem of students of any ability level, and negatively affects low-ability students. Dawson, "Beyond Ability Grouping: A Review of the Effectiveness of Ability Grouping and its Alternatives," 16 *School Psychology Review* 348 (1987).

A study that summarizes the findings of over fifty research studies on ability grouping of *secondary* school students found that grouping had a very small, positive overall effect on student achievement, with the effect being strongest for high-ability students in special honors classes. Those research studies which included students of all ability levels showed virtually no difference in achievement between grouping arrangements for students of high, middle, or low ability. No difference was found on student self-concept or attitude toward school, although students in grouped classes did have somewhat more positive attitudes toward the subject they were studying than ungrouped students. Kulik and Kulik, "Effects of Ability Grouping on Secondary School Students: A Meta-Analysis of Evaluation Findings," 19 *Am. Educ. Res. J.* 415 (1982). *But see* Marsh, "Self-Concept, Social Comparison, and Ability Grouping: A Reply to Kulik and Kulik," 21 *Am. Educ. Res. J.* 799 (1984) (suggesting that ability grouping may have a negative effect on academic self-concept). *See generally* Slavin, "Achievement Effects of Ability Grouping in Secondary Schools: A Best-Evidence Synthesis," 60 *Rev. of Educ. Res.* 471 (1990) (no clear indication that ability-grouping practices help students in the highest ability classes and clear evidence that these practices are harmful to students in the lower levels);W. Findley and M. Bryan, *Ability Grouping: 1970 Status, Impact and Alternatives* 54 (1970) (finding that "[a]mong those studies showing significant effects the slight preponderance of evidence show the practice favorable for the learning of high-ability students is more than offset by evidence of unfavorable effects on the learning of average and low-ability groups, particularly the latter"). With regard to minority students, most studies show that tracking does not benefit them. D Levine and R. Levine, *Society and Education* 38-41 (9th ed. 1996). *But see* Gamoran and Mare, "Secondary School Tracking and Educational Inequality: Compensation, Reinforcement, or Neutrality?"

94 *Am. J. Sociology* 1146, 1177 (1989) (evidence that at least some minority students benefit from tracking).

An increasing number of education experts argue that the practice of grouping by ability is psychologically damaging to children and of little or no value educationally. *See, e.g.,* J. Oakes, *Keeping Track, How Schools Structure Inequality* (Rand Corp. 1985); Welsh, "Fast-Track Trap: How 'Ability Grouping' Hurts Our Schools, Kids and Families," *Washington Post*, Sept. 16, 1990. Others argue that the problem is not tracking but how it is used. One study, based on research in seven school districts in California, outlines the sorting process, examining how students are assigned at all grade levels to schools, teachers, and courses, and how initial assignments are changed, if they are. The authors argue that disclosure to parents of how the school district's sorting process works is important, and they weigh the cost and benefits of disclosure. Friedman & Sugarman, "School Sorting and Disclosure: Disclosure to Families as a School Reform Strategy, Part I: Existing Practices and the Social Interests in School Information Disclosure," 17 *Jour. Law & Educ.* 53 (1988). The authors subsequently argue the possibility of relying on the Fourteenth Amendment Due Process Clause as a doctrinal basis for compelling disclosure, at least "where the sorting decisions are readily subject to discretionary abuse or neglect and where the consequences of the wrong decision are potentially severe." Sugarman & Friedman, "School Sorting and Disclosure: Disclosure to Families as a School Reform Strategy, Part II: Policy and Legal Analysis," 17 *Jour. Law & Educ.* 147, 200 (1988).

4. Stigma

Hobson notes the stigma that attaches to placement in a slow track or special education class. "By consigning students to specifically designated curricula, the track system makes the student's status highly visible within the school structure. To the unlearned, tracks can become pejorative labels, symptomatic of which is the recent abandonment of the suggestive 'Basic' for the more euphemistic 'Special Academic' as the nomenclature of the lowest track."

The following excerpt describes in greater detail the process of stigmatization:

> Many of the classifications that schools impose on students are stigmatizing. However well-motivated the decision or complex the factual bases leading to a particular classification, the classification lends itself to simplified labels. . . .

These adverse school classifications [e.g., placement in slow learner tracks or special education classes] reduce both the individual's sense of self-worth and his value in the eyes of others. For many children, this process is particularly painful because it is novel. It represents the first formal revelation of differentness. The school's inclination to cope with a particular learning or social problem by isolating those who share that problem reinforces the child's sense of stigma. . . .

The stigmatized child, who "tends to hold the same beliefs about identity that [others] do," comes to learn, through contact with the school, that he has in effect been devalued by both the school and the society.

Children perceive all too well what the school's label means. Jane Mercer observes that those assigned to special education classes "were ashamed to be seen entering the MR room because they were often teased by other children about being MR . . . [and] dreaded receiving mail that might bear compromising identification." . . .

Students assigned to the general or slow learner track described similar feelings: "General teachers make kids feel dumb. Their attitude is, 'Well, nobody's been able to do anything with you, and I can't do better.'"

Differences among school children clearly exist, and it would be folly to ignore them: to treat everyone in exactly the same fashion typically benefits no one. Yet even with that qualification, the consequentiality of the school's classification is an awesome fact with which the child must cope. Its psychological ramifications extend beyond the child; they reach his family, and those with whom the child has contact. . . .

The stigma is further exacerbated, at least in part, by the school's curriculum. The curriculum offered to the "slow" or "special" child is less demanding than that provided for "normal" children; even if the child assigned to the special class does creditable work, he falls further behind the school norm. The initial assignment becomes a self-fulfilling prophesy; the child's belief in his inferiority is reinforced by the knowledge that he is increasingly unable to return to the regular school program. In addition, because his classmates and teachers make fewer demands on him (for by definition less can be expected of the handicapped than the normal), he comes to accept their judgment of acceptable progress as his own. . . .

D. Kirp, "Schools as Sorters: The Constitutional and Policy Implications of Student Classification," 121 *U. Pa. L. Rev.* 705, 733–37 (1973). *See* Welsh, "Fast-Track Trap: How 'Ability Grouping' Hurts Our Schools, Kids and Families," *Washington Post*, Sept. 16, 1990, at B1 (observing that "there is hardly any kid who isn't bright enough to understand that he isn't very bright"). Welsh notes that "for minority students the implied label of 'ungifted' is especially pernicious," quoting an African American student who has bitter memories of the days in fourth grade when her 'gifted' peers would be pulled out of class.

> They got to do the interesting things that would stimulate any kid to learn. They had the plays, the fun projects; they cooked Chinese food. The rest of us would sit in the classroom and do 50 of the same problems over and over again. That would make anyone feel inferior. But when you're black and almost all the 'gifted' kids who are pulled out are white, it makes you feel even worse.

Ibid.

Stigma is not a phenomenon that admits of ready empirical confirmation. While some studies of student self-perception suggest that students in less advanced school programs typically refer to themselves as "dumb" or "lazy," other studies reach inconclusive or inconsistent results. A summary of this research suggests that "the impact of ability grouping on the affective development of children is to build (inflate?) the egos of the high groups and reduce the self-esteem of average and low groups in the total student population." W. Findley and M. Bryan, *Ability Grouping: 1970*, 40 (1971). *See also* Jones, "Labels and Stigma in Special Education," 38 J. *Exceptional Children* 553 (1972). Few of these studies attempt to relate stigma to student achievement.

What is the legal significance of governmentally imposed stigma? Is the problem one of appropriate process before labeling takes place?

5. *Equal Educational Opportunity*

Does the discussion of student achievement and stigma suggest that classification does in fact deny some students—those placed in slower tracks and special classes for the mildly retarded—equal educational opportunity? In the absence of racial discrimination, what is the constitutional basis for such a claim? *See San Antonio Independent School District v. Rodriguez*, 411 U.S. 1, 93 S.Ct. 1278, 36 L.Ed.2d 16 (1973). Is a constitutional challenge to particular school classifications on the ground that they do not benefit (and might in fact harm) students just another way of stating that particular programs do not meet the educational needs of children assigned to them? Is it constitutionally relevant that the needs argument requires the creation of additional classifica-

tions with special school programs for each, while the no-benefit argument would probably restrict the number of permissible classifications?

6. *Racially Specific Harm*

Assignment to a less-advanced program might give rise to a claimed denial of equal educational opportunity, premised on the assertion that such placement secures no educational benefit—and may even cause injury. But assuming that the motivation for placement is not discriminatory, what does the fact of racial overrepresentation add to the constitutional argument? Are minority students more likely to be harmed by such placement than their white peers are? *See Simmons v. Hooks*, 843 F.Supp. 1296, 1299 (E.D. Ark. 1994), discussing testimony indicating that "ability grouping [entire classes] is not beneficial for any group and is harmful to the low group, as it stigmatizes those children, and would be particularly harmful to the low group if it were overwhelmingly black and the other groups were not."

Fragmentary evidence suggests a positive answer to the question whether minority students are harmed to a greater extent than white students. Although few studies have examined the racially specific harm of sorting, one reanalysis of the Coleman Report did attempt to assess the impact of intraschool segregation on the verbal achievement of black students. It concluded that while school integration does not benefit blacks, classroom integration does improve black students' test scores. Since proportionately more whites than blacks are assigned to higher tracks, advanced track placement does influence student success. But the differences in verbal achievement between black students in mostly white classes and those in mostly black classes cannot simply be explained by selection processes that operate within the school. Classroom segregation itself causes harm for black students in fast as well as slow classes; classroom desegregation has racially specific benefits. *See* McPartland, "The Relative Influences of School and of Classroom Desegregation in the Academic Achievement of Ninth Grade Negro Students," 25 J. *Social Issues* 93 (1969). *Compare* Zito and Bardon, "Achievement Motivation among Negro Adolescents in Regular and Special Education Programs," 74 *Am. J. Mental Deficiency* 20 (1969).

The United States Civil Rights Commission's reexamination of the Coleman data noted a subtler (and difficult to document) effect of intraschool segregation: Black students in nominally integrated schools, "accorded separate treatment, with others of their race, in a way which is obvious to them as they travel through their classes, felt inferior and stigmatized." 2 *United States Commission on Civil Rights, Racial Isolation in the Public Schools* 86–87 (1967). The harm caused by interschool segregation appeared to the Commission far less substantial than the harm caused by intraschool segregation; while interschool segregation resulted from the relatively impersonal criterion of neighborhood residence, intraschool segregation was clearly caused by personal and pejorative judgments of ability. *See also* Jones, Erickson, and Crowell, "Increasing the Gap between Whites and Blacks: Tracking as a Contributory Source," 4 *Educ. & Urban Soc'y* 339 (1972).

7. Race and Intelligence

Some researchers have sought to explain minority overrepresentation in less advanced programs on the ground that blacks are genetically inferior to whites. One recent, widely publicized, and highly controversial analysis is that by R. Hernstein and C. Murray, *The Bell Curve: Intelligence and Class Structure in American Life* (1994).

a. Empirical Evidence: Pro and Con. Since the publication of Professor Arthur Jensen's article, "How Much Can We Boost IQ and Scholastic Achievement?" in the Winter 1969 issue of the *Harvard Education Review*, a controversy has raged over the degree to which intelligence is genetically determined. *See generally* R. Herrnstein and C. Murray, *supra,* and its many critics, e,g, C. Fischer *et al., Inequality by Design: Cracking the Bell Curve Myth* (1996); *The Bell Curve Wars: Race, Intelligence, & the Future of America* (S. Fraser, ed., 1995); *See also* Lehmann, "The Bell Curve Flattened," http://slate.msn.com/Features/BellCurve/Bell Curve.asp (posted Jan. 17, 1997) (summarizing research undercutting *The Bell Curve*). The focus of the debate is whether inherited elements of intelligence are responsible for the substantially lower IQ scores of lower social class groups and whether these differences provide pedagogical justification for elaborate classification schemes in the public schools. Not surprisingly, the debate has often been more acrimonious than scholarly.

Professor Jensen asserted that IQ tests, while measuring more than innate ability, for example, acquisition of information, reflect a general ability that underlies surface skills. *See also* H. J. Eysenck, *The Inequality of Man* 55–56 (1975). This quality, com-

monly referred to as g, Jensen asserted, is largely inherited. *See* A. Jensen, *Bias in Mental Testing* (1980). Since IQ highly correlates with social class and race, he concluded that these IQ differences between populations reflect real genetic variation between social strata. This is true for Jensen even after steps are taken to eliminate cultural bias in testing. Thus, Jensen argued, much of the disparity in IQ scores between blacks and whites must be attributed to inherited differences in intelligence. He later argued that because intelligence is "more biological than psychological or behavioral in nature, educational interventions may have a relatively small effect on IQ or scholastic achievement." Jensen, "Compensatory Education and the Theory of Intelligence," 66 *Phi Delta Kappan* 554, 558 (1985). *See also* R. Herrnstein and C. Murray, *supra*. *But see* H. Gardner, *Intelligence Reframed* (1999); H. Gardner, M. Kornhaber, and W. Wake, *Intelligence: Multiple Perspectives* (1996); S. Gould, "The Real Error of Cyril Burt: Factor Analysis and the Reification of Intelligence," in *The Mismeasure of Man* (1981); Fields, "Heredity and Environment, but Not Race, Found to Influence Intelligence," *The Chronicle of Higher Education,* Sept. 12, 1977 at 5.

Critics of Professor Jensen and of Professors Herrnstein and Murray do not deny that an individual's intelligence is highly influenced by his genetic background. Nor do the critics deny the undeniable: that the IQ test scores of children from low socioeconomic backgrounds, including most blacks, are substantially lower than those of middle-class white children. Rather the critics challenge the interpretation of the evidence, which asserts that the differences in IQ scores between racial and socioeconomic groups are largely genetic and not environmental in origin. *See, e.g.,* C. Fischer *et al., supra; The Bell Curve Wars, supra;* S. Gould, "The Hereditarian Theory of IQ," in *The Mismeasure of Man* (1981); Green, "In Defense of Measurement," 33 *Am. Psych.* 664 (1978). The critics frequently contend that tests, "rather than reflecting cultural inferiority, are indicative of the educational—not genetic—deficiencies of minority children and . . . perhaps the inadequacy of public schools in their present state." Bersoff, "Regarding Psychologists Testily: Legal Regulation of Psychological Assessment in the Public Schools," 39 *Md. L. Rev.* 27, 52–53 (1979).

Cole and Bruner argue that standard intelligence tests, adapted to use in schools, are effective for certain well-established organizational purposes and are fairly effective measures of the performance of certain subcultural groups, particularly the white upper-middle class. It is questionable, in their view, whether they give accurate indications of the abilities of poor and minority children because the demands of their lives are so different from those of middle-class children. These children score poorly on IQ tests because they have not developed many of the skills demanded by schools and tests. Cole and Bruner, "Cultural Differences and Inferences about Psychological Processes," 57 *Am. Psych.* 10, 874 (1971).

Theories about intelligence are changing. Many researchers now view intelligence more as a collection of developed rather than innate abilities. *See* H. Gardner, *Intelligence Reframed* (1999), arguing that there is not a single "intelligence" (as in the general ability or g discussed by A. Jensen, *supra*), but that there are seven intelligences: visual/spatial intelligence, musical intelligence, verbal intelligence, logical/mathematical intelligence, interpersonal intelligence, intrapersonal intelligence, and bodily/kinesthetic intelligence. *See also* H. Gardner, M. Kornhaber, and W. Wake, *supra*; H. Gardner, "Reflections on Multiple Intelligences: Myths and Messages," 77 *Phi Delta Kappan* 200 (1995). The emphasis is shifting from selection or classification to collecting information that will improve understanding of the way individual students learn. *See* Curtis and Glaser, "Changing Conceptions of Intelligence," in *Review of Research in Education* 111(D. Berliner ed. 1981). For a recent symposium on many of these issues, *see* "Ranking Ourselves: Perspectives on Intelligence Testing, Affirmative Action, and Educational Policy," 6 *Psychol. Pub. Pol'y & L.* 1 (2000). Note also that recent research on the sequencing of the human genome has cast considerable doubt on theories of racial differences in intelligence. *See, e.g.,* M. Ridley, *The Autobiography of a Species in 23 Chapters* (1999).

b. Constitutional Implications. How might courts employ data suggesting that the inherited intelligence of blacks is less than that of whites in deciding a case in which a classificatory scheme is attacked because of the overrepresentation of blacks in less advanced educational programs? Is the evidence clear enough to permit any such conclusions to be drawn from it? Might a court decide that the racial isolation attributable to classification decisions is unconstitutional notwithstanding the lower test scores of blacks—whether those scores are genetically or environmentally determined? *Cf.* Reynolds, "Why Is Psychometric Research on Bias in Mental Testing So Often Ignored?" 6 *Psychol. Pub. Pol'y & L.* 144 (2000); Hunter and Schmidt, "Racial and Gender Bias in Ability and Achievement Tests: Resolving the Apparent Paradox," 6 *Psychol. Pub. Pol'y & L.* 151 (2000); Reschly, "Nonbiased Assessment," in *School Psychology: Perspectives and Issues* (G. Phye and D. Reschly, eds., 1979); Hunter and Schmidt, "Critical Analysis of the Statistical and Ethical Implications of Various Definitions of Test Bias," 83 *Psych. Bull.* 1053 (1976).

4. Misclassification and Test Bias.

Any sorting decision—for example, assignment to an advanced track or to a class for the mildly retarded—is typically based both on certain nominally objective criteria, such as aptitude tests, and on more subtle judgments of ability and potential, such as teacher evaluations.

Misclassification can mean several quite different things. It may denote the misapplication of approved criteria. If the criteria are objective, the issue may be relatively simple to resolve, but if the criteria are judgmental, resolution becomes more difficult.

Misclassification might also denote disputes over the criteria themselves. For example, those who assert that IQ tests are incapable of measuring intellectual potential contend that those tests should not be used to assign students to tracks. One study of 378 educable mentally retarded (EMR) students from thirty-six school districts in the Philadelphia area notes such misclassification. The researchers tested mildly retarded students with a battery of tests, rather than the single IQ test typically used by school systems; they found the diagnosis for 25 percent of the youngsters to be clearly erroneous, while, for an additional 43 percent, the diagnosis was questionable. Garrison and Hammill, "Who Are the Retarded?" 38 *J. Exceptional Children* 13 (1971). The judgment of system-made error is premised on the assumption that the researchers' multiple criteria are better classifying instruments than using a single criterion.

In *Hobson v. Hansen,* 269 F.Supp. 401, 490 (D.D.C. 1967), the district court noted an instance of this type of misclassification:

> In 1965 Dr. Hansen announced a change in official policy: thenceforth, no student was to be assigned to

the Special Academic Track without first being evaluated by a clinical psychologist and, if necessary, undergoing an individual test of ability. In September of that year 1,272 students, either already in the Special Academic Track or about to be enrolled in it on the recommendations of their teachers and principals, were reevaluated by the psychologists under the new order. As a result of this reevaluation approximately 820, almost two-thirds, were discovered to have been improperly judged as requiring assignment to the Special Academic curriculum. . . .

Does either type of misclassification pose issues of constitutional dimension? Would a parent have a constitutional right to have his child reclassified (1) on the basis that the school had incorrectly scored the aptitude test which was administered; (2) on the basis that the retesting of the child by an independent psychologist yielded a score considerably higher than that recorded by the school; or (3) on the basis that the aptitude test did not in fact measure the child's aptitude because it was not administered in the child's primary language? *See, e.g., Guadalupe Organization, Inc. v. Tempe School District No. 3*, Civ. No. 71-435 (D. Ariz., filed August 9, 1971) (settled by consent decree, Jan. 24, 1972); *Covarrubias v. San Diego Unified School District*, Civ. No. 70-394-S (S.D. Cal., filed Feb. 1971) (settled by consent decree, July 31, 1972); *Diana v. State Board of Education*, C.A. No. C-70-37 R.F.P. (N.D. Cal., filed Jan., 1970) (settled by stipulation of the parties, Feb. 3, 1970).

Aptitude or IQ tests are the primary basis for determining in which educational program a given student should be placed. But are IQ tests in fact appropriate classifying instruments? *See generally* R. Subotnik and K. Arnold, eds., *Beyond Terman* (1994); J. Salvia and J. Ysseldyke, *Assessment in Special and Remedial Education* (1978); Cronbach, "Five Decades of Public Controversy Over Mental Testing," 30 *Am. Psych.* 1 (1975). Do IQ tests predict educational success? Do they accurately measure ability? Do they distinguish between students in need of different types of education? As Judge Irving Goldberg has noted, "[a] sorting device would be invalid to the extent that it does not measure aptitude for a group of students . . . the basis for separation is simply irrational." *Allen v. City of Mobile*, 466 F.2d 122, 127 (5th Cir. 1972) (Goldberg, J., dissenting), *cert. denied*, 412 U.S. 909, 93 S.Ct. 2292; 36 L.Ed.2d 975 (1973). *See* discussion of IQ and other aptitude tests in *Hobson v. Hansen, supra. See generally* Bersoff, "Regarding Psy-

chologists Testily: Legal Regulation of Psychological Assessment in the Public Schools," 39 *Md. L. Rev.* 27 (1979); Shea, "An Educational Perspective of the Legality of Intelligence Testing and Ability Grouping," 6 *J. of Law & Educ.* 137 (1977); Note, "The Legal Implications of Cultural Bias in the Intelligence Testing of Disadvantaged School Children." 61 *Geo. L. Rev.* 1027 (1973).

While the predictive power of IQ tests is far from perfect, might the IQ test be better able to estimate future academic performance than school grades or teacher recommendations—the other plausible criteria for school classifications which may be limited in their utility by their subjectivity and the likelihood that teacher biases and prejudices will be reflected in the results? *See* Sowell, "Race and Intelligence," in *Black Education: Myths and Tragedies* (1972):

> It is easy enough to criticize IQ, college entrance examinations, and other such tests and to show that they need much improvement. But the practical question at any given point in time is, what are the alternatives? Other selection devices and criteria have ranged from ineffective to disastrous. Moreover, it is precisely the black students who need IQ tests most of all, for it is precisely with black students that alternative methods of spotting intellectual ability have failed. Dr. Martin Jenkins, who has conducted more studies of high-IQ black children than anyone else, has commented on how frequently even children with IQ's of 150 have not been spotted as outstanding by their teachers.

Critics have asserted that IQ tests have many shortcomings:

1. Their questions are ambiguous, a trap for the overly thoughtful who rightly recognize that more than one answer may be correct.
2. They treat intelligence (or more accurately, school intelligence) in aggregate terms, failing to recognize that a given student is likely to be competent at some things but not at others, and that combining those strengths and weaknesses into a single score necessarily misdescribes and oversimplifies the notion of intelligence.
3. They fail to measure "adaptive behavior," the capacity to survive in society, and place too high a premium on school intelligence.
4. The tests do not indicate why a given student did poorly in a particular subject. That a child scores in the fortieth percentile in mathematics aptitude, for example, does not tell the teacher what

he did not understand or why he did not understand it. It provides no basis for educational intervention to improve performance.

5. The intelligence tests treat a highly mutable phenomenon—aptitude—as a given with which the school can work. They identify intelligence as static and not dynamic, and fail to account for the uneven growth patterns of individual children.

See, e.g., R. Canero, ed., *Intelligence: Genetic and Environmental Influences* (1971); C. Senna, ed., *The Fallacy of I.Q.* (1973).

Many of the asserted shortcomings of IQ tests relate more to the use made of test results than to the basic construction of the test instrument. Often school officials and teachers view test scores punitively rather than remedially: they are used to label students as "smart" or "dumb" or to distinguish "college material" from future blue-collar workers. In that sense, IQ test results become self-fulfilling prophecies. *See Hobson v. Hansen, supra.*

Criticism of aptitude tests as a basis for student classification acquires particular force when these tests lead to the overrepresentation of minorities in classes for the educable mentally retarded (EMR) or other low-ability groupings. *See, e.g.,* Bersoff, *supra;* Bernal, "A Response to 'Educational Uses of Tests with Disadvantaged Subjects,' 30 *Am. Psych.* 93 (1975); Cleary, Humphreys, Kendrick, and Wesman, "Educational Uses of Tests with Disadvantaged Students," 30 *Am. Psych.* 15 (1975); Jackson, "On the Report of the Ad Hoc Committee on Educational Uses of Tests with Disadvantaged Students: Another Psychological View from the Association of Black Psychologists," 30 *Am. Psych.* 88 (1975). Aptitude tests and their use by schools are condemned on several grounds: (1) aptitude tests reward white and middle-class values and skills, especially the ability to speak standard English, and thus penalize minority children because of their backgrounds; (2) the impersonal environment in which aptitude tests are given depresses the scores of minority students, who become anxious or apathetic in such situations; (3) aptitude tests, standardized (or "normed") for white, middle-class children, cannot determine the intelligence of minority children whose backgrounds differ notably from those of the normed population. *See Hobson v. Hansen, supra. See generally* Note, "Test Validation in the Schools," 58 *Tex.L.Rev.* 1123 (1980).

Larry P. v. Riles

793 F.2d 969 (9th Cir. 1984), as amended on denial of rehearing and rehearing en banc (1986).

Before Skopil and Poole, Circuit Judges, and Enright, District Judge.

Poole, Circuit Judge:

The State Superintendent of Public Instruction appeals a decision holding that IQ tests used by the California school system to place children into special classes for the educable mentally retarded (E.M.R.) violated federal statutes and the equal protection clauses of the United States and California Constitutions. The district court enjoined the use of non-validated IQ tests, and ordered the state to develop plans to eliminate the disproportionate enrollment of black children in E.M.R. classes. We affirm on the statutory grounds and reverse on the federal and state constitutional issues.

* * *

The district court permanently enjoined the defendants from utilizing any standardized IQ test for the identification of black E.M.R. children or their placement into E.M.R. classes, without securing prior approval of the court. *Id.* at 989. The court ordered the defendants to direct each school district to re-evaluate every black child currently identified as an E.M.R. pupil without using standardized intelligence tests.

Further, the defendants were "ordered to monitor and eliminate disproportionate placement of black children in California's E.M.R. classes." . . .

II. Facts

* * *

In the mid-60's California created programs for several categories of students with educational problems. The "educable mentally retarded" (E.M.R.) program was for schoolchildren of retarded intellectual development who are considered incapable of being educated through the regular educational program, but who could benefit from special educational facilities to make them economically useful and socially adjusted. The "trainable mentally retarded" (T.M.R.) category was for children with more severe retardation than educable mentally retarded. Cal.Educ.Code § 56515 (West 1978) (repealed 1980). . . .

The E.M.R. classes are for children who are considered "*incapable* of learning in the regular classes," and the E.M.R. curriculum "is not designed to help students learn the skills necessary to return to the regular instructional program." *Id.* at 941 (emphasis in original). The E.M.R. classes are designed only to teach social adjustment and economic usefulness. *Id.*

"The [E.M.R.] classes are conceived of as 'dead-end classes,'" and a misplacement in E.M.R. causes a stigma and irreparable injury to the student. *Id.* at 941–42.

. . . [B]lack children have been significantly overrepresented in E.M.R. classes. For example, in 1968–69, black children were about 9% of the state school population, yet accounted for 27% of the E.M.R. population. *Id.* at 938.

"These apparent overenrollments could not be the result of chance. For example, there is less than a one in a million chance that the overenrollment of black children and the underenrollment of non-black children in the E.M.R. classes in 1976–77 would have resulted under a color-blind system." *Id.* at 944. To explain this overenrollment, the defendants proffered a theory that there is a higher incidence of mental retardation among the black population. The district court found that this theory fails to account for the problem, because even "if it is assumed that black children have a 50 percent greater incidence of this type of mental retardation, there is still less than a one in 100,000 chance that the enrollment could be so skewed towards black children. . . . [Further,] the disproportionate E.M.R. enrollment of black children is not duplicated in the classes for the so-called 'trainable mentally retarded' children." . . .

. . . In 1969 "the [State] Department [of Education (SDE)] proposed and the State Board of Education adopted, an addition to the California Administrative Code requiring that approved IQ tests be used as part of the E.M.R. placement process." *Larry P.*, 495 F.Supp. at 946. The district court found that the SDE moved extremely quickly and unsystematically to select those IQ tests for the mandatory list. The district court further found that the person who oversaw this selection was not an expert in IQ testing, and that the SDE did not expressly consider or investigate the problems concerning the disproportionate enrollment of minorities or the cultural bias of IQ tests despite its awareness of these problems. In addition, the SDE contacted no independent testing experts regarding the compilation of the

list, and ignored requests from field personnel to take more time to select tests.

* * *

The district court found that the requirement of parental consent for E.M.R. placement does not overcome any deficiencies caused by bias in the placement process, because "that consent is rarely withheld, particularly by minorities, since the mystique of teacher authority and IQ scores tends to overwhelm parents." *Id.* at 950 n. 51.

* * *

On the average, black children score fifteen points, or one standard deviation, below white children on standardized intelligence tests. . . .

The court found that "the tests were never designed to eliminate cultural biases against black children; it was assumed in effect that black children were less 'intelligent' than whites. . . . The tests were standardized and developed on an all-white population, and naturally their scientific validity is questionable for culturally different groups." *Id.* at 956–57. Since the 1920's it has been generally known that black persons perform less well than white persons on the standardized intelligence tests. IQ tests had been standardized so that they yielded no bias because of sex. For example, when sample tests yielded different scores for boys and girls, the testing experts assumed such differences were unacceptable and modified the tests so that the curve in the standardization sample for boys and girls was identical. No such modifications on racial grounds has ever been tried by the testing companies. The district court noted that "the experts have from the beginning been willing to tolerate or even encourage tests that portray minorities, especially blacks, as intellectually inferior." *Id.* at 955.

The district court analyzed and rejected the defendants' arguments advanced at trial that would explain the test score differences, which theorized that the lower scores for blacks were the result of actual, relevant differences between black and white children. The first argument is the genetic argument, which states that natural selection has resulted in black persons having a "gene pool" with lower intelligence than whites. . . .

The second theory is the socioeconomic argument, which theorizes that because of blacks' lower socioeconomic status, they are at a greater risk for all kinds of diseases due to malnutrition and poor medical attention. The district court found that the facts did not support this theory, since it did not explain why more severe mental retardation, *e.g.* that consistent with placement into classes for the trainable mentally retarded children, does not occur in greater proportions among blacks and poorer sections of the population. *Id.* at 956.

The district court found that the appellants failed to show that the IQ tests were validated for blacks with respect to the characteristics consistent with E.M.R. status and placement in E.M.R. classes, *i.e.*, that the defendants failed to establish that the IQ tests were accurate predictors that black elementary schoolchildren who scored less than 70 were indeed mentally retarded. *Id.* at 971–73.

The district court found that alternatives to IQ testing for E.M.R. placement have been in effect since the state moratorium on IQ testing in 1975. These procedures, in which schools take more time and care with their assessments for E.M.R. classification and rely more on observational data, are less discriminatory than under the IQ-centered standard. *Id.* at 973–74.

The district court found that defendants were guilty of intentional discrimination in the use of the IQ tests for E.M.R. placement. The court based this determination on the facts that the historical background of the IQ tests shows cultural bias; the adoption of the mandatory IQ testing requirement in 1969 was riddled with procedural and substantive irregularities, in which no outside sources were consulted by the State Board and the question of bias was never considered, even though the officials were well aware of the bias and disproportionate placement problems caused by the IQ tests (this problem having been addressed in a legislative resolution); the defendants' "complete failure to ascertain or attempt to ascertain the validity of the tests for minority children"; and the failure of the state to investigate and act on legal requirements to report significant variances in racial and ethnic composition in E.M.R. classes. *Id.* at 980–82. The court noted that "the SDE's actions revealed a complacent acceptance of those disproportions, and that complacency was evidently built on easy but unsubstantiated assumptions about the incidence of retardation or at least low intelligence among black children." *Id.* at 983.

* * *

VI. Rehabilitation Act

* * *

In summary, the Education For All Handicapped Children Act specifically requires that tests and evaluation procedures be free of racial and cultural bias. Both the EAHCA and the Rehabilitation Act require that the tests used for evaluation be validated for the specific purpose for which they are used, and that placement not be based upon a single criterion but on a variety of sources. . . .

Appellant argues that the IQ tests were validated for the specific purposes for which they are used. Appellant analogizes to Title VII cases, notably *Washington v. Davis*, 426 U.S. 229, 96 S.Ct. 2040, 48 L.Ed.2d 597 (1976), for the proposition that tests that are valid predictors of future performance can be utilized even if they have a discriminatory impact. There are two problems with appellant's proposition. First, the employment context is quite different from the educational situation. As the district court stated, "[i]f tests can predict that a person is going to be a poor employee, the employer can legitimately deny that person a job, but if tests suggest that a young child is probably going to be a poor student, the school cannot on that basis alone deny that child the opportunity to improve and develop the academic skills necessary to success in our society." *Larry P.*, 495 F.Supp. at 969. Assigning a student to an E.M.R. class denies that child the opportunity to develop the necessary academic skills, since E.M.R. classes do not teach academic subjects and are essentially a dead-end academic track. Second, and more important, the question for predictive validity in schools is not whether the standardized intelligence tests predict future school performance generally, as appellant argues, but whether the tests predict specifically that black elementary schoolchildren (as opposed to white elementary schoolchildren) who score at or below 70 on the IQ tests are mentally retarded and incapable of learning the regular school curriculum. In this case, the appellant would have to have shown that the tests are a proven tool to determine which students have characteristics consistent with E.M.R. status and placement in E.M.R. classes, *i.e.*, "whose mental capabilities make it impossible for them to profit from the regular educational programs" even with remedial instruction. The regulations place the burden of showing such validation on the defendants.

The district court found that defendants failed to show that the tests were validated for placing black students with scores of 70 or less in E.M.R. classes. The district court noted that very few studies had examined the difference of IQ predictability for black as compared to white populations, and that those studies which had examined this problem found the tests much less valid for blacks than for whites. Further, the district court found that, even assuming the tests were validated for placement of white schoolchildren in E.M.R. classes, such validation for blacks had been generally assumed but not established. For example, the tests had been adjusted to eliminate differences in the average scores between the sexes, but such adjustment was never made to adjust the scores to be equal for black and white children. *Id.* at 971. The court found that the reason for this was a basic assumption of a lower level of intelligence in blacks than in whites. The fact that early test developers indeed made this assumption is borne out by the literature and testimony at trial. *See id.* at 954–60. In addition, no studies have been made, either by the defendants or the testing companies, to investigate the reasons for the one standard deviation difference in test scores between the races or to determine whether test redesign could eliminate any bias. *Id.* at 971. There was expert testimony that a much larger percentage of black than white children had been misplaced in E.M.R. classes. Based on the evidence in the record, the district court finding that the appellant had not established validation of the test is not clearly erroneous.

The district court also found that the appellant did not utilize the variety of information required by statute and regulation to make E.M.R. placements, but relied primarily on the IQ test. This finding also is not clearly erroneous. Testimony showed that school records lacked sufficient evidence of educational history, adaptive behavior, social and cultural background or health history for these factors to have been utilized in placement. . . .

* * *

VII. Title VI

. . . Regulations issued under [Title VI] require that recipients of federal funding may not

> utilize criteria or methods of administration which have the effect of subjecting individuals to discrimina-

tion because of their race, color, or national origin, or have the effect of defeating or substantially impairing accomplishment of the objectives of the program as respect individuals of a particular race, color, or national origin.

34 C.F.R. § 100.3(b)(2) . . .

In *Guardians Association v. Civil Service Commission of City of New York,* 463 U.S. 582, 103 S.Ct. 3221, 77 L.Ed.2d 866 (1983), a majority of the Court held that a violation of Title VI required proof of discriminatory intent.[7] A different majority held, however, that proof of discriminatory effect suffices to establish liability when the suit is brought to enforce regulations issued pursuant to the statute rather than the statute itself.

The appellees relied on the regulations issued pursuant to Title VI. *Larry P.,* 495 F.Supp. at 965. The lower court held that the placement mechanisms for E.M.R. classes operated with a discriminatory effect in violation of the regulations and HEW's "interpretative guidelines". *Id.* In light of appellees' reliance on the regulations, we find it appropriate to apply a discriminatory effect analysis.

A prima facie case is demonstrated by showing that the tests have a discriminatory impact on black schoolchildren. . . . Once a plaintiff has established a prima facie case, the burden then shifts to the defendant to demonstrate that the requirement which caused the disproportionate impact was required by educational necessity.

Appellees clearly demonstrated the discriminatory impact of the challenged tests. It is undisputed that black children as a whole scored ten points lower than white children on the tests, and that the percentage of black children in E.M.R. classes was much higher than for whites. As discussed previously, these test scores were used to place black schoolchildren in E.M.R. classes and to remove them from the regular educational program. The burden therefore shifted to the defendants to demonstrate that the IQ tests which resulted in the disproportionate placement of black children were required by educational necessity.

---

[7]The Court previously held that no discriminatory intent must be proved to show a violation of the statute. *Lau v. Nichols,* 414 U.S. 563, 568, 94 S.Ct. 786, 789, 39 L.Ed.2d 1 (1974). This circuit has expressly followed *Lau.* . . . The district court applied *Lau* while recognizing that subsequent dicta in Supreme Court opinions questioned that conclusion. E.g., . . . *Regents of the University of California v. Bakke,* 438 U.S. 265, 284–87, 98 S.Ct. 2733, 2745–46, 57 L.Ed.2d 750 (1978). Nevertheless, even after *Bakke,* the Supreme Court reaffirmed an "effects" standard. *Fullilove v. Klutznick,* 448 U.S. 448, 479–80, 100 S.Ct. 2758, 2775–76, 65 L.Ed.2d 902 (1980). Despite these conflicting signals, a majority of Justices now agree that discriminatory intent is required. *Guardians Association.* . . .

Appellant argues first that E.M.R. classes are a benefit for, rather than adverse discrimination against, black children, implying that appellees did not even establish a prima facie case. However, the district court found that improper placement in E.M.R. classes has a definite adverse effect, in that E.M.R. classes are dead-end classes which de-emphasize academic skills and stigmatize children improperly placed in them. *Larry P.*, 495 F.Supp. at 941–42. Even appellant's witnesses testified that it would be extremely improper for a non-mentally retarded child to be placed in an E.M.R. classroom. Though the E.M.R. class might be a benefit for those students who are educable mentally retarded, it is clearly damaging to a non-retarded student to be placed in those classes. The district court's finding is not clearly erroneous, and thus appellees established a prima facie case of a Title VI violation based upon discriminatory effect.

Appellant next argues that even if the impact is adverse, it is not caused by discriminatory criteria (the IQ tests), but by other nondiscriminatory factors: (1) placement is based on a variety of information and evaluation tools that are non-discriminatory, and not solely on the IQ tests; (2) the tests are validated for black schoolchildren, and therefore accurately reflect mental retardation in black children; and (3) blacks have a higher percentage of mental retardation than whites.

Appellant's first two arguments have been discussed in VI, *supra*, and are unavailing. Appellant's third argument is that the disproportionate number of black children in E.M.R. classes is based on a higher incidence of mental retardation in blacks than in whites that is due to poor nutrition and poor medical care brought on by the lower socioeconomic status of blacks. This argument also fails. Appellees showed, and the district court made a finding, that "the overrepresentation of black children in E.M.R. classes cannot be explained away solely on the grounds of the generally lower socio-economic status of black children and their parents." *Id.* at 956. The district court specifically found the testimony of appellant's experts in support of this argument failed to explain why more severe mental retardation does not occur in greater proportions among the poorer sections of the population. In addition, there was testimony from other experts that poor nutrition or medical care during early life does not affect later performance on IQ scores, unless it is a severe malnutrition of a type that is rare in this country. This finding of the district court has not been shown to be clearly erroneous.

* * *

VIII. Equal Protection Violation

* * *

We cannot, however, sustain the finding of a violation by Superintendent Riles of the equal protection clause of the fourteenth amendment on the theory that the pervasiveness of discriminatory effect can, without more, be equated with the discriminatory intent required by *Washington v. Davis*. Accordingly, we reject these facts of the trial court and reverse the conclusions that the Superintendent was guilty of intentional discrimination under the fourteenth amendment.

* * *

X. Remedy

The district court, in addition to enjoining the use of nonvalidated intelligence tests and requiring re-evaluation of every current black E.M.R. pupil, ordered the defendants to require every school district that had a racial disproportion in E.M.R. classes to devise a three-year remedial plan, and to bring to the court's attention any disparities that persist at the end of this period. *Larry P.*, 495 F.Supp. at 989–90.

* * *

Appellant . . . contends that the court's order to eliminate the disproportionate enrollment requires an impermissible quota. The district court's order, though, does not impose any quota on future E.M.R. placements. Even with respect to eliminating present disproportionate enrollment, the district court allowed an error leeway of one standard deviation. Further, the district court does not require that students properly placed in an E.M.R. class be removed. The court only required that any disproportion in excess of one standard deviation after three years be brought to the court's attention. If the school district can show, utilizing properly validated procedures complying with applicable statutes, that the black students in the E.M.R. classes properly belong there, there would be no need to eliminate the remaining disproportion. Since there are no fixed numerical requirements, the district court's order is not an impermissible quota. *See Regents of the University of California v. Bakke*, 438 U.S. 265, 98 S.Ct. 2733, 57 L.Ed.2d 750 (1978).

* * *

Enright, District Judge, dissenting in part and concurring in part:

* * *

In the instant case, the appellees have shown only that a higher percentage of blacks were placed in the E.M.R. classes. As I interpret those cases applying a discriminatory effects analysis, the appellees should have been required to show that a disproportionate number of minority students were improperly placed by virtue of their IQ test scores.

Proper placement in the E.M.R. classes is a benefit, not a stigmatic dead-end assignment. As discussed in the majority opinion, these classes were established to assist students incapable of satisfactory achievement in the regular school curriculum. The program was thought to be extremely helpful to enrollees in that it permitted those individuals to acquire skills within their capabilities that in turn would permit them to have useful and productive lives and thus reach their full potential. It is, and always has been, a completely voluntary program, requiring two fully informed parental consents, one for permission to initially test and one to place a child in such a program. Placement in the program requires testing, evaluation and observation by trained personnel, as well as the objective measure of IQ testing procedures. Once enrolled, parents had the option *at any time* to withdraw their child from the program.

Yet, solely because of the disproportionate number of black children within the E.M.R. program, the district court struck down the heretofore accepted IQ tests and required the composition of the class to mirror the racial percentages of the school district. That holding ignores the beneficial aspect of proper placement and misstates the appellees' burden of proof. Before the tests in question can be labeled as discriminatory, there must be a showing that they produced improper placement into the E.M.R. program. No such showing was made. The only arguable finding of specific misplacement is the conclusory observation of the district court that

> while we see no reason to enter into the cases of the named plaintiffs, we can observe that the only relevant evidence on their cases indicated that they were not retarded.

* * *

That analysis assumes that the statistical disparity in the composition of the classes is caused by improper placement of black children. Upon that unsubstan-

tiated premise rests the district court's finding that the appellees made an initial showing of discriminatory impact. The burden then shifted to the defendants to justify the use of IQ tests in the E.M.R. placement process, despite the fact that none of the named appellees were shown to have been improperly placed in the classes. In so doing, the district court and the majority invert the allocation of proof on the critical issue presented in the case; namely, did the appellants' testing procedures place black children in the E.M.R. program who did not belong there.

Though regrettable, it is not surprising the district court neglected to ascertain the validity of the specific E.M.R. placements. It would seem difficult, if not impossible, to identify an individual as a proper candidate for the E.M.R. program without employing some form of standardized IQ testing. Faced with the unenviable task of pinpointing educably retarded children on the basis of subjective data independent of the challenged IQ tests, the district court elected to base its conclusions on the supposition detailed above. Yet, the school districts are left in the same difficult position of proving that certain black students belong in the E.M.R. program in those districts where statistical disparity remains.

It is clear that the causes of racially disparate placement are complex, as well as controversial. Experts in the area have disagreed in the past and continue to disagree. The particular methodology chosen and the understandable failure to account for the universe of potential explanatory variables opens every purported finding to criticism. The record in this case shows that widely recognized IQ tests employed by defendants have long been hailed for their ability to correct the exact abuse complained of in this case—misevaluations and misplacement. Educators recognize that subjective evaluation, uncorroborated by objective criteria, carries enormous potential for abuse and misplacement based on the personal or cultural values of the evaluator. Here we strike the only objective criteria.

* * *

NOTES AND QUESTIONS

1. *Title VI Disparate Impact Standard*

What is the majority's view of the disparate impact standard triggered by Title VI regulations that bar recipients of federal funding from "utiliz[ing] criteria or methods of administration which have the effect of subjecting individuals to discrimination because of their race, color, or national origin"? How does the standard that Judge Enright would apply differ? Other circuits appear to be more strict with regard to plaintiff's initial burden than the majority in *Larry P. See, e.g., Elston v. Talladega County Board of Educ.,* 997 F.2d 1394, 1407 (11th Cir. 1993); *Powell v. Ridge,* 189 F.3d 387, 393–94 (3d Cir.), *cert. denied,* 528 U.S. 1046, 120 S. Ct. 579, 145 L.Ed. 2d 482 (1999). In light of *Alexander v. Sandoval, supra,* would *Larry P. v. Riles* be decided the same way today? Although the *Larry P.* majority noted that Supreme Court precedent required proof of discriminatory intent for a violation of the Title VI statute, it also cited *Guardians Association* as authority for the position that proof of disproportionate effect is sufficient to establish liability when a suit is brought to enforce Title VI regulations. *Sandoval,* however, suggests that a disparate impact claim cannot be brought by private litigants.

Recall that the *Larry P. v. Riles* plaintiffs also challenged the use of IQ tests for determining placement in E.M.R. classes under the Education for All Handicapped Children Act (now the Individuals with Disabilities Education Act), and the Rehabilitation Act (Part VI of the opinion). Would these statutes be sufficient to support the result in *Larry P.* even without reliance on a disparate impact analysis under Title VI regulations? *See* Chapter 6, *infra.*

2. Cultural Bias

How does the *Larry P.* court deal with the question of cultural bias in IQ testing given the evidence that IQ tests are no worse predictors for minorities than for whites? Does the existence of differential scores between blacks and whites prove cultural bias? Is the problem that blacks in EMR classes (as well as whites) receive an inadequate education and that the tests are unacceptable because they are used to reach the judgment that a class of children cannot profit from regular classes? *See* Note, "Test Validation in the Schools," 58 *Tex.L.Rev.* 1123, 1139, 1151–53 (1980).

In *Parents in Action on Special Education v. Hannon,* 506 F.Supp. 831 (N.D. Ill. 1980), the court was confronted with the same issue as in *Larry P.* but reached a different result. After a thorough examination of the Wechsler Intelligence Scale for Children (WISC), the WISC Revised (WISC-R), and the

Stanford-Binet, the tests used to help determine educable mentally handicapped (EMH) status in the Chicago school system, the court concluded that these tests, when used in conjunction with other criteria that are statutorily mandated for determining EMH status, do not discriminate against African American children. *Id.* at 883. Although the court found several questions on these tests were culturally biased, it concluded that the possibility of these questions causing an improper EMH placement was "practically nonexistent." *Id.* at 876. (*But see* Weiss, "It's Time to Examine the Examiners," 38 *Negro Educ. Rev.* 107 (1987), discussing the impact of the WISC-R IQ test on minority students.) The court relied on the fact that these tests required that a child had to have a certain number of consecutive misses on the test, which becomes increasingly more difficult, before the child's educational status is determined. Thus, even if a child missed a question because it was culturally biased, this would not prejudice the child as he or she would have to miss several more questions in a row before a determination of the child's IQ is made. *Id.* at 875. The court also pointed out that most of the racially biased questions occur at a level of difficulty that is beyond the level which EMH students could reach. *Id.* at 875–76. Finally, and most important, the court emphasized the fact that there is an extensive assessment process involved in making the determination of EMH status that goes far beyond reliance on these tests. *Id.* at 879–80. *See* Heaston, "Chicago Public Schools Experience with Alternatives to IQ Testing: The Color of Rubies," 38 *Negro Educ. Rev.* 163 (1987).

What evidence shows that IQ tests are culturally biased? Would minority students perform better on so-called culture-free tests? *See* Weiss, *supra;* Taylor and Lee, "Standardized Tests and African Americans: Communication and Language Issues," 38 *Negro Educ. Rev.* 67 (1987). So far, efforts to create culture-free tests have been unavailing. *See, e.g.,* Reschly, "Nonbiased Assessment," in *School Psychology: Perspectives and Issues* 215 (G. Phye and D. Reschly, eds., 1979); Chase and Pugh, "Social Class and Performance on an Intelligence Test," 8 *J. Educ. Measurement* 197 (1971); Ebel, "The Social Consequences of Educational Testing," in *Testing Problems in Perspective* 18 (A. Anastasi, ed., 1966). What is a culture-free test? For example, would the language in which the test is given be considered part of the cultural bias? Should IQ tests be administered in one's primary language? Would this include minority dialects? *Cf. Martin Luther King Jr. Elementary School Children v. Michigan Board of Education,* 451 F.Supp. 1324 (E.D. Mich. 1978). Does the definition of cultural bias depend upon the purposes to which the test results will be put? That is, is an English language test appropriate for placement in a remedial English class but not appropriate for classification as a retarded student?

Whatever the shortcomings of aptitude tests, do they not merely confirm that nonmiddle-class and minority children do poorly in schools as presently organized? If tests are culturally biased, are school curricula and employer expectations also biased? *See* Glennon, "Race, Education, and the Construction of a Disabled Class," 1995 *Wisc. L. Rev.* 1237. Does this suggest that using a culturally neutral (or culturally relevant) test for minority students might well be an academic exercise unless such tests were accompanied by drastic alterations in schooling and hiring practices? *See* Green, "In Defense of Measurement," 33 *Am. Psych.* 664, 669 (1978).

3. Larry P. *and* Hobson

In the *Hobson* case, Judge Wright made the following comment:

> When standard aptitude tests are given to low income Negro children, or disadvantaged children, . . . the tests are less precise and less accurate—so much so that test scores become practically meaningless. Because of the impoverished circumstances that characterize the disadvantaged child, it is virtually impossible to tell whether the test score reflects lack of ability—or simply lack of opportunity. Moreover, the probability that test scores of the Negro child or the disadvantaged child will be depressed because of somewhat unique psychological influences further compounds the risk of inaccuracy.

269 F.Supp. at 485.

Is this consistent with the position taken in *Larry P.?* Is it fair to say that *Larry P.* questions the efficacy of using IQ tests to make EMR placements for all students, whereas *Hobson* focused only on their alleged inadequacies for minority students? If so, why then is *Larry P.* a race case? Is it that the harm of IQ tests is greater for minority students?

Professor Bersoff has questioned the assumption that IQ tests are less accurate for blacks than for others. Bersoff, "Regarding Psychologists Testily: Legal Regulation of Psychological Assessments in the Public Schools," 39 *Md. L.Rev.* 27, 52, 56 (1979). *See* Cleary, Humphreys, Kendrick, and Wesman, "Educational Uses of Tests with Disadvantaged Students," 30 *Am. Psych.* 15, 24 (1975). Is this another way of saying that the education system and not the tests is the "villain"? Professor Bersoff notes that "from the psychometric point of view the [*Hobson*] court's gravest error was its insistence that grouping can only be based on tests that measure innate ability. No psychologist who has written on the subject believes that tests measure hereditary endowment solely." Bersoff, *supra*, at 51, citing, *inter alia*, A. Jensen, *Bias in Mental Testing* (1980).

In the *Hobson* case, Judge Wright notes that the standard aptitude tests are less accurate in the case of low-income black children "because of the impoverished circumstances that characterize the disadvantaged child." In *Larry P.*, the school district had argued that "because of blacks' lower socioeconomic status, they are at a greater risk for all kinds of diseases due to malnutrition and poor medical attention." On what basis did the court dismiss this argument? The *Hannon* court concluded, however, that the socioeconomic argument was a valid one. The court found that the lack of cognitive stimulation, which is essential for intellectual development, is often associated with economic poverty in the home. Thus, the fact that blacks score lower on the tests used to determine educable mentally retarded status than whites is a result of their lower economic status. *Hannon, supra,* at 877–88. Even though both *Larry P.* and *Hannon* label the argument as one based on socioeconomic status, is the theory explaining the discrepancies in test scores between whites and blacks in *Hannon* the same as that put forward in *Larry P.?* Assuming the *Hannon* court was correct that the discrepancy in test scores is due to lack of intellectual stimulation because of poverty, does it follow that these children belong in classes for the educable mentally retarded? *See* Glennon, *supra.*

For a useful analysis and discussion of the disproportionate assignment of minority students to special education classes, the placement procedures used, and the effects of such placements, *see* K. Heller, W. Holtzman, and S. Messick, *Placing Children in Special Education: A Strategy for Equity* (1982).

> [T]he main purpose of assessment in education is to improve instruction and learning. Children are or should be assessed in order to identify strengths and weaknesses that necessitate specific forms of remediation or educational practice. . . .

. . . A concern with disproportion per se dictates a focus on bias in assessment instruments and a search for instruments that will reduce disproportion. A concern with instructional utility leads to a search for assessment procedures and instruments that will aid in selecting or designing effective programs for all children. We believe that better assessment and a closer link between assessment and instruction will in fact reduce disproportion, because minority children have been the victims of poor instruction. We also believe the problem should be attacked at its roots, which lie in the presumption that learning problems must imply deficiencies in the child and in consequent inattention to the role of education itself in creating and ameliorating these problems.

This viewpoint has led us to urge a greater emphasis on systematic intervention before a child is referred for individual assessment. When poor instruction has been ruled out as a cause of learning failure, it becomes appropriate to look for problems within the child or in the child's environment outside the school, again with an eye toward problems that can be corrected; this is the purpose of individual assessment.

Id. at 72. The authors also pose the following question:

Rather than inquiring about the causes of disproportion and how to remedy the problem of disproportion in special education and in EMR classes in particular, a different and more constructive perspective is to ask: Under what circumstances does disproportion constitute a problem? While remedies to disproportion per se are based on an assumption that the disproportions in themselves constitute an inequity, the educational and social conditions under which such an assumption is true should be examined explicitly. Three aspects of the regular and special education programs and placement procedures are most salient in this regard: Disproportion is a problem (1) if children are invalidly placed in programs for mentally retarded students; (2) if they are unduly exposed to the likelihood of such placement by virtue of having received poor-quality regular instruction; or (3) if the quality and academic relevance of the special instruction programs block students' educational progress, including decreasing the likelihood of their return to the regular classroom.

Id. at 17–18.

Several recent studies indicate that African American students (and to a lesser extent, other racial and ethnic minorities) are significantly overidentified as mentally retarded and emotionally disturbed when compared with white students, and the likelihood of being identified as in these categories increases in states where the minority group constitutes a relatively large proportion of the state's population. In 38 states, black students are more than twice as likely to be classified as mentally retarded as white students. Parrish, "Disparities in the Identification, Funding, and Provision of Special Education," (draft), http://www.law.harvard.edu/civilrights/conferences/SpecEd/parrishpaper2.html (March 2001). *See also* Oswald, Coutinho, and Best, "Community and School Predictors of Over Representation of Minority Children in Special Education," (draft), http://www.law.harvard.edu/civilrights/conferences/SpecEd/oswaldpaper2.html (March 2001), noting that living in a largely white community substantially *increases* the odds of African American students being identified as mentally retarded, but only slightly for white students; as poverty increases, the disproportionate number of black males classified as mentally retarded *decreases*. The authors suggest that "a significant portion of the over representation problem may be a function of inappropriate interpretation of ethnic and cultural differences as disabilities." *Id. See* Glennon, *supra.*

4. Postscript to Larry P.

The district court's original injunction in 1979 barred the use of IQ tests to evaluate African American children for placement in EMR classes, 495 F.Supp. 926 (N.D.Cal.1979), *aff'd in part, rev'd in part,* 793 F.2d 969 (9th Cir. 1986). However, in 1986, following a settlement in which the state abolished the EMR category, the court modified its 1979 injunction to ban the use of IQ tests to evaluate African American children referred to for any special education assessment. As a result, a suit was filed by African American students, who had been diagnosed as learning disabled, seeking IQ testing. In *Crawford v. Honig,* 37 F.3d 485 (9th Cir. 1995), the circuit court affirmed the district court's summary judgment vacating the 1986 modification. The circuit court agreed that the factual findings in the 1979 proceedings did not support the 1986 modification extending its ban on IQ tests for all special education assessments. The court noted that the district court had been concerned with the "potentially racist nature of I.Q. testing," including "the racial and cultural biases in I.Q. tests and the lack of scientific validation of the tests for culturally and racially different groups," but that the focus of the inquiry was the disproportionate enrollment of African American children in EMR classes, not the use of IQ tests generally, and, in particular, the usefulness of IQ tests to identify learning disabilities other than EMR.

C. Impact of "High-Stakes Testing" on Racial and Ethnic Minorities

I.Q. tests are not the only tests to have been challenged in the courts. The standards-based reform movement (see chapter 8) has led to increased use of achievement tests for decisions that have significant consequences for individual students. *See* Note, "Now Pinch Hitting for Educational Reform: Delaware's Minimum Competency Test and the Diploma Sanction," 18 *Jour. L. & Commerce* 373, 377 (1999) (criticizing testing programs that hold students, but not teachers and administrators, accountable). These "high-stakes" decisions include tracking, promotion, and graduation from high school. To ensure that tests used to evaluate student performance were not used discriminatorily, Congress asked the National Research Council of the National Academy of Sciences to undertake a study and to make recommendations on appropriate safeguards. Among other things, the National Research Council's report addresses some of the legal problems with the use of high-stakes tests and the role that courts have played in ensuring that testing is done fairly. The findings are summarized as follows.

"High Stakes"

National Research Council, *High Stakes: Testing for Tracking, Promotion, and Graduation* 52–65 (1999). Reprinted with permission.

* * *

Defining Discrimination in the Context of High-Stakes Testing

The legal literature reveals several distinct arguments that courts have considered in determining whether the use of a test to make high-stakes decisions about individual students is illegally discriminatory. The outcomes of some cases depend on whether the decision to administer a high-stakes test is based on a present intent to discriminate. Other cases depend on whether a test carries forward or preserves the effects of prior illegal discrimination. A third claim, grounded in federal civil rights statutes and accompanying regulations, employs an "effects test" that considers whether a high-stakes test has a disproportionate, adverse impact; whether the use of a test having such an impact can be adequately justified on educational grounds; and whether there are equally feasible alternative tests that have less disproportionate impact. These legal claims bear directly on whether tests are used in a discriminatory manner for tracking, promotion, or graduation. Each type of claim is therefore considered separately below.

Claims of Intentional Discrimination

The equal protection clause of the Fourteenth Amendment forbids public employees and entities—including state and local school officials—from engaging in acts of intentional discrimination on the basis of race, color, national origin, or sex. . . . Findings of current intentional discrimination have been rare, especially in recent decades; the applicable legal standard is a stringent one, and few courts have been prepared to find that educators are acting out of invidious motives. The plaintiffs' burden cannot be met merely by showing that a policy or practice has a disproportionate, adverse impact on some group, or even by demonstrating that the disproportionate impact was foreseeable or actually foreseen (*Washington v. Davis*, 1976). Thus, for example, lower courts have refused to find intentional discrimination solely on the basis of evidence showing that high-stakes graduation tests had a disproportionate, adverse impact by race or national origin. . . .

According to the Supreme Court, those who allege intentional discrimination must show not only foreseeable, disproportionate adverse impact but also that "the decisionmaker selected or reaffirmed a particular course of action *at least in part 'because of,'* not merely 'in spite of,' its adverse effects" on the group disproportionately affected. . . .[2]

---

[2] Recognizing that each situation "demands a sensitive inquiry into such circumstantial and direct evidence of intent as may be available," the Supreme Court has identified criteria to aid courts in determining whether a decision maker has acted "because of" the disproportionate adverse effects its policy or practice will have (*Village of Arlington Heights v. Metropolitan Housing Development Corp.*, 1977 . . .). As applied in the testing context, these criteria include (1) whether the test produces a disproportionate, adverse impact on the group that alleges discrimination; (2) whether the test's disproportionate impact was reasonably foreseeable or actually foreseen; (3) whether adoption or administration of the test can be explained on grounds other than an intent to discriminate; (4) whether the historical background of the decision supports a claim of intentional discrimination; (5) whether adoption or use of the test represents a departure from the decision maker's normal policies or procedures; and (6) whether there is direct evidence of intent to discriminate, such as statements evincing discriminatory intent.

[3] Current standards for proving intentional discrimination evolved nearly a decade after *Hobson v. Hansen*, beginning with *Washington v. Davis* (1976) and other Supreme Court decisions noted above.

Where high-stakes testing programs are concerned, courts have almost uniformly dismissed claims of intentional discrimination. Most often courts have found that there are legitimate, nondiscriminatory educational reasons for adopting such programs. In sustaining high-stakes graduation tests, for example, lower courts have found "no present intent to discriminate" . . ., accepting the defendants' view that such tests can help to improve students' educational performance, to identify students who need remedial assistance, and to evaluate the attainment of state educational objectives. . . . This is true even when decisions to deny high school diplomas have been made automatically on the basis of one or more test scores. Similarly, despite legal challenges to tracking, whether based on tests or on other information, there are only a few reported decisions in which courts found that tracking, or student classification more generally, constituted intentional racial segregation. . . . One of these is an older case (*Hobson v. Hansen*, 1967),[3] and one is a decision that an appellate court later reversed in pertinent part (*People Who Care v. Rockford Board of Education*, 1997).

A third such case is *Larry P. v. Riles*. . . . A federal district court, affirmed by the U.S. court of appeals, found California's use of the IQ test for EMR placements to be intentionally discriminatory, based on a number of factors. [*Eds.* The circuit court rejected the district court's conclusion that the facts showed the discriminatory intent required by *Washington v. Davis* for a violation of the equal protection clause, but upheld the lower court's findings that Title VI disparate-impact regulations and the Education for All Handicapped Children Act were violated.]

First, state department of education officials had foreseen that the test would have a significant disproportionate impact by race. Second, they had failed "to ascertain or attempt to ascertain the validity of the tests for minority children." Third, "the adoption of [a] mandatory IQ testing requirement was riddled with procedural and substantive irregularities, in which no outside sources were consulted . . . and . . . the person who oversaw [test] selection was not an expert in IQ testing." Fourth, the state had failed to use alternative tests that were "less discriminatory than the IQ-centered standard." Fifth, "the [state department of education's] actions revealed a complacent acceptance of [racial differences in intelligence] that was built on easy assumptions about the incidence of retardation or at least low intelligence among black children". . . . Sixth, the court regarded EMR classes "as 'dead-end' classes. . . . [A]

misplacement in E.M.R. causes a stigma and irreparable injury to the student". . . .

An Illinois district court, however, reached opposite conclusions when faced with facts similar in many respects to those in *Larry P.* . . . (*Parents in Action on Special Education (PASE) v. Hannon*, 1980 . . .).

Although they reach different conclusions, these decisions are consistent in several important respects. First, even under a stringent intent standard, liability findings may turn in part on the extent to which courts believe that educators have complied with generally accepted standards and procedures governing proper test use. In *Larry P.* and *PASE*, for example, the outcomes depended in part on such measurement issues as test validity, item bias, and whether educators were relying on single test scores in making student placement decisions. The outcome in *Larry P.* also turned on an issue of proper attribution of cause, with the court questioning the defendants' claim that black students' IQ scores were an accurate reflection of mental retardation among blacks. Third, the decisions in *Larry P.* and *PASE* both rest partly on the courts' views of whether the resulting placements were beneficial or dead ends; both courts were interested in the educational consequences of test use for students. . . . More generally, the courts' concern with tracking, remediation, and special education is plainly focused on whether or not students will receive enhanced and effective educational opportunities as a result of the educational intervention. Furthermore, complying with relevant professional testing standards reduces the risk of legal liability for high-stakes assessments.

Claims That Tests Preserve the Effects of Prior Discrimination

The Supreme Court has long held that the Constitution forbids practices that, although seemingly neutral, serve to preserve, or carry forward, the effects of prior illegal school segregation. This suggests that it would be unlawful for school officials to use tests to track minority students, deny them high school diplomas, or retain them in grade if those students' low test scores are traceable to their having attended illegally segregated schools.

* * *

The leading court decision on competency testing illustrates a "preserve the effects" approach. In the mid-1970s, Florida had adopted a minimum competency test that students needed to pass in order to receive high school diplomas. The failure rate among black students, 20 percent, was 10 times that for white students. Black high school juniors who had attended illegally segregated schools for the first five grades argued that the test results reflected the discrimination they had suffered and claimed that the diploma sanction served to preserve the effects of the prior illegal segregation. The appeals court agreed, ruling that Florida could begin to withhold diplomas from black students only four years later, when the students taking the test would not have attended illegally segregated schools [*Debra P. v. Turlington*, 664 F.2d 397 (5th Cir. 1981)]. Courts in several judicial circuits have applied the same principle to many cases involving tracking, particularly in the years after initial school desegregation.

If a state or school district has had a recent history of segregation or intentional discrimination, judges will scrutinize more closely test-use policies that produce disproportionate adverse impact. Even in formerly segregated school districts, however, there are several arguments that educators may invoke to defend the use of high-stakes tests that have racially disproportionate impact. . . . First, it is permissible to use such a test if the state or school district can demonstrate that enough time has passed that the racially disproportionate impact no longer results from prior illegal segregation. . . .

Second, lower courts have ruled that it is permissible to use a classification mechanism that has disproportionate impact if the classes that are disproportionately minority provide bona fide remedial instruction—that is, if the consequences of tracking decisions are beneficial rather than adverse. Thus the *Debra P.* court approved remedial education programs for students who had failed Florida's competency test, even though most of the students needing remedial help were black, because it believed that the programs would help remedy the effects of prior illegal segregation. Although the court did not ask whether remedial classes constituted the most effective available placements, it mattered to the *Debra P.* court whether tracking decisions produced beneficial educational consequences for the students placed.

[C]laims of this nature are increasingly rare, if only because there are fewer children each year who can show that they themselves attended illegally segregated schools. Nonetheless, recent court decisions, such as *Simmons on Behalf of Simmons v. Hooks* [843 F.Supp. 1296 (E.D. Ark. 1994)],[9] and the fact that school desegregation cases remain active in many other jurisdictions, suggest that such claims remain viable in some communities.

Claims of Disparate Impact

Several federal civil rights statutes prohibit recipients of federal funds, including state education agencies and public school districts, from discriminating against students. Title VI of the Civil Rights Act of 1964 prohibits discrimination on the basis of race, color, or national origin, including limited English proficiency. . . . Title IX of the Education Amendments of 1972 forbids sex discrimination, and two federal civil rights statutes . . . prohibit discrimination against students with disabilities.

These statutes forbid intentional discrimination against students, as does the Constitution's equal protection clause, but federal regulations go further: they provide that a federal fund recipient may not "utilize criteria or methods of administration which have the *effect* of subjecting individuals to discrimination." In interpreting this Title VI regulation and similar regulations under Title IX, courts have drawn on interpretations of a federal employment discrimination statute, Title VII.

This method of proving a legal violation is known as a disparate impact claim, and lower courts in many jurisdictions have recognized a three-part legal test for judging such claims. . . .

First, plaintiffs must show by a preponderance of the evidence that some policy or practice, such as the use of a test, has disproportionate adverse impact on a protected group. Whether a test's impact is disproportionate is not always easy to determine;[13] generally, it depends on a comparison of the entire pool of test takers with those the test identifies for some educational placement or treatment. If statistical analysis shows that the success rate for members of a

---

[9]In *Simmons*, the district court rejected the arguments of school officials who claimed that low-track placements were educationally beneficial for black children. The court also found no educational justification for grouping classes of children for all subjects. . . .

[13]In some cases, the relevant question is whether the mean score for one group was lower than that for another group, or whether members of one group were *misclassified* at a significantly higher rate than members of another group. . . . In other cases, courts have had to decide how to account for individuals who were discouraged from taking a test that they alleged was discriminatory. . . . If it is impossible to determine the pool precisely, courts typically make informed estimates.

protected class is significantly lower (or the failure rate is significantly higher) than what would be expected from a random distribution, then the test has disproportionate *adverse* impact.

Even if the plaintiffs can establish disparate impact, the case is not over; rather, the burden of proof shifts to the defendant to justify its policy or practice; according to the Supreme Court, the legal standard of justification is one of educational necessity. . . . Federal regulations do not define the term "educational necessity"; some lower courts interpret it to mean that defendants must show "a substantial legitimate justification" for the challenged policy or practice . . ., whereas others require proof of a "manifest relationship" between the policy or practice and the defendants' educational objectives. . . .

In the testing context, defendants can usually meet their burden of proof by showing that the test in question meets professional standards that apply given the purpose for which the test is being used. Thus, psychometric standards—those that apply generally and those that apply to particular test uses . . .—are also relevant in the legal context.

* * *

Thus, under a disparate impact standard, legal liability may depend in part on whether the test raises problems of measurement, which may be the case if the test has not been validated for the particular purpose for which it is being used or has not been validated for all parts of the test-taking population. . . . It may also depend in part on whether test users make high-stakes decisions about students based on one test score or on multiple factors; in *United States v. Fordice* [505 U.S. 717 (1992)], for example, the Supreme Court rejected Mississippi's exclusive reliance on ACT composite scores in making college admissions decisions because the *ACT User's Manual* called instead for admissions standards based on ACT subtest scores, self-reported high school grades, and other factors. . . .

Similarly, whether a particular test use is proper depends in part on making attributions of cause: "It is imperative to account for various 'plausible rival interpretations of low test performance [such as] anxiety, inattention, low motivation, fatigue, limited English proficiency, or certain sensory handicaps' other than low ability". . . . Thus, for example, "if students with limited English proficiency are tested in English—in areas other than language arts—and then classified on the basis of their test scores . . . [t]his constitutes discrimination under Title VI". . . .

Finally, the likelihood of an adverse court ruling increases if the consequence of test use is a low-quality program or placement rather than one that is "educationally necessary." For example, using a Title VI disparate impact analysis in *Larry P.*, the district court ruled that, although tests having predictive validity may be the basis for denying a job, "if tests suggest that a young child is probably going to be a poor student, the school cannot on that basis alone deny the child the ability to improve and develop the academic skills necessary to success in our society". . . . Whether a particular educational placement or treatment is beneficial or harmful depends on empirical evidence about that program and, in court, on a judge's interpretation of that evidence.

Even if a state or school district can establish that its use of a test is educationally necessary, plaintiffs may nonetheless prevail by showing that there exists "an equally effective alternative that would result in less disproportionality". . . . In the testing context, such showings have been infrequent.

* * *

Due Process Challenges to High-Stakes Tests

High-stakes tests may be illegal even if they are not discriminatory. For example, high school graduation tests have been challenged successfully under the due process provisions of the U.S. Constitution (Fifth and Fourteenth Amendments). Such claims usually hinge either on whether students have received sufficient advance notice of high-stakes test requirements or on whether they have been taught the knowledge and skills that a high-stakes test measures. These claims rest on the proposition that students have a constitutionally protected property interest in receiving diplomas (*Debra P. v. Turlington*, 1981).

Adequate Notice

One concern, first raised in the context of high-stakes graduation tests, is that school officials must ensure fairness by giving students prior notice of a new high-stakes assessment requirement. In *Debra P. v. Turlington* (1981), the court found that four years constituted sufficient notice; courts in Georgia and New York have found that two years did *not* constitute adequate notice. . . . As to the content of such notice . . . :

[S]tudents and school personnel should be provided with clear indications of the specific content . . . and performance for which they will be held accountable. General scoring guidelines and examples that demonstrate attainment of the standards should also be disseminated. Curricular frameworks, assessment specifications, sample tasks, and model answers may also be helpful in communicating expectations.

And although the issue has not been litigated to date, similar notice may be called for when states or school districts are adopting new high-stakes tests for promotion.

Curricular Validity

A second due process requirement concerns what the *Debra P.* court referred to as "curricular validity": "a state may condition the receipt of a public school diploma on the passing of a test so long as it is a fair test of that which was taught". . . .[23]

There have been disagreements over how educational entities can demonstrate that a test measures what students have been taught. Some argue that it is sufficient for a state or school district to show that the formal written curriculum mentions the knowledge and skills that the test is designed to measure. Others assert that what matters most is not the formal written curriculum but the actual curriculum and instruction in each classroom . . . —that instructional rather than curricular validity is required. The *Debra P.* court accepted something in between: evidence that the test measured skills included in the official curriculum coupled with a showing that most teachers considered the skills to be ones they should teach. . . . Similar evidence may be called for when a high-stakes test for promotion is involved.

The matter of curricular or instructional validity has several important implications for high-stakes testing of individual students. First, to the extent that new assessments designed to induce changes in curriculum and instruction are used for high-stakes purposes, there is a danger that the new instruments will lack the curricular or instructional validity that the Constitution requires. . . .

Policymakers who wish to use tests for high-stakes purposes must therefore allow enough time for [alignment of their curricula and their teaching with the requirements of the tests]. The time needed, probably several years, would in practice depend on several factors, including the extent of the initial discrepancy and the availability of resources needed to bring curriculum and instruction into alignment with the new standards.

* * *

NOTES AND QUESTIONS

1. *Federalism Issues and High-Stakes Testing*

Although the Clinton Administration sought to encourage the development of national education standards, and national tests that would assess attainment of those standards, Congress prohibited the U.S. Department of Education from using funds to develop such tests. Department of Education Appropriations Act of 1998, Pub. L. No. 105-277, §447, 112 Stat. 2681 (1998). *See* Moran, "Sorting and Reforming: High-Stakes Testing in the Public Schools," 34 *Akron L. Rev.* 107, 112 (2000). Congressional concerns that state and local authority over curriculum would be superceded by the federal government are not new. *See* the General Provisions Concerning Education Act, applicable to all federal programs and first enacted in 1970, which bars the federal government from "exercis[ing] any direction, supervision, or control over the curriculum, program of instruction, administration, or personnel of any educational institution, school or school system. . . ." 20 U.S.C. §1232a (West 1999). Thus states have taken the major role in standards-based reform and testing. According to Moran, *supra* at 113, nineteen states condition the receipt of a high school diploma on a standardized examination, and seven more states plan to enact such a requirement. Many of the states requiring a high school exit exam are in the South.

2. *Relationship Between Past De Jure Segregation and Present Minority Failure Rates*

Is the Florida competency testing scheme addressed in *Debra P. v. Turlington*, and described in the National Research Council's report as an example of a test that preserves the effects of prior illegal discrimination, unconstitutional as applied to African American students? The court found that African American students encountered numerous problems following formal desegregation of the schools in

---

[23]Conceptually, a claim that students have not been taught what the test measures is similar to a claim that students have been denied a fair opportunity to learn.

Florida, which occurred beginning with the 1971–72 school year:

> Although children of all races suffered in the initial years of integration, black children suffered to a greater degree. The most significant burden which accompanied black children into the integrated schools was the existence of years of inferior education. . . . Other problems presented to black children were disparate busing schedules, lingering racial stereotypes, disproportionate terminations of black principals and administrators, and a high incidence of suspensions. . . . Additionally, the state during part of this period did not offer the leadership or the funding to mount a wide-scale attack on the educational deficits created during segregation. Remediation with specifically delineated objectives and programs did not commence until 1977.

Debra P. v. Turlington, 474 F.Supp. 244, 252 (M.D. Fla.1979), *aff'd in part*, 644 F.2d 397 (5th Cir. 1981). The district court concluded as follows:

> In the Court's opinion, punishing the victims of past discrimination for deficits created by an inferior educational environment neither constitutes a remedy nor creates better educational opportunities. When students regardless of race are permitted to commence and pursue their education in a unitary school system without the taint of the dual school system, then a graduation requirement based on a neutral test will be permitted. The Court must conclude that utilization of the SSAT II in the present context . . . is a violation of the equal protection clause of the Fourteenth Amendment . . .

Debra P. v. Turlington, 474 F.Supp. at 257. Does it follow from the proposition that African American students are not responsible for their high rate of failure on the competency test in Florida that the test is unconstitutional or that there is no substantial state interest in determining competencies, irrespective of the reasons for failure?

Is the district court persuasive that there is a cause-and-effect relationship between past *de jure* segregation practices in Florida and present black failure rates on the State Student Assessment Test? The court of appeals, in affirming the lower court's decision, states that the defendants had "failed to demonstrate either that the disproportionate failure of blacks was not due to the present effects of past intentional segregation or, that, as presently used, the diploma sanction was necessary to remedy those effects." *Debra P. v. Turlington*, 644 F.2d 397, 407 (5th Cir. 1981), *on remand*, 564 F.Supp. 177 (M.D. Fla. 1983), *aff'd*, 730 F.2d 1405 (11th Cir. 1984). Under

what circumstances might a state that has previously engaged in racial discrimination successfully carry its burden of proof?

At what point in time would it become constitutional for Florida to impose competency tests on its black students? In *Debra P.* the state was required to wait until students who had attended dual school systems had graduated before the new testing requirement could take effect. *Debra P.*, 730 F.2d at 1414. This was done so that residual effects of early inferior schooling could not be a factor in the way blacks scored on the test. The court also found that the testing requirement may actually help to compensate for past inequities, since it sets standards that will help to motivate both students and staff. *Id.* at 1416. *See also Johnson v. Sikes*, 540 F.Supp. 761 (S.D. Ga. 1982), holding that plaintiffs prevailed on their claim that the competency test required for graduation discriminated on the basis of race, and ordered defendants not to impose the diploma sanction until the class of 1983, since that would be the first group of graduating students who began their education after the abolition of the segregated school system. The court also held that the school district could reinstate the diploma sanction only if it could show that the increased educational opportunities of the test outweighed any lingering causal connection between the past discriminatory tracking system and the imposition of the diploma sanction. The circuit court dismissed the appeal on procedural grounds. 730 F.2d 644 (11th Cir. 1984). In *GI Forum v. Texas Education Agency*, 87 F.Supp. 2d 667 (W.D.Tex. 2000), plaintiffs relied on *Debra P.* to argue that the use of the Texas Assessment of Academic Skills (TAAS) as a graduation requirement, resulting in a disproportionate number of African Americans and Latinos being denied high school diplomas, perpetuated vestiges of prior discrimination. The court, however, agreed with state officials that past violations had been sufficiently cured. *See also Erik V. v. Causby*, 977 F.Supp. 834 (E.D.N.C. 1997) (use of test for promotion to the next grade). *See* Moran, *supra*, for a critique of the court's decision in *GI Forum*, in particular the shifting of the burden from defendants to plaintiffs on a number of critical issues; Gomez, "The Texas Assessment of Academic Skills Exit Test—'Driver of Equity' or 'Ticket to Nowhere,' " 2 *Scholar: St. Mary's L. Rev. Minority Issues* 187 (2000).

See Love v. Turlington, 733 F.2d 1562 (11th Cir. 1984), in which an 11th grade aptitude test that more blacks than whites failed was upheld because the test was designed only to target students who needed remedial work, and was not used as a basis for granting or denying a diploma. *See also Bester v. Tuscaloosa City Board of Education*, 722 F.2d 1514 (11th Cir. 1984).

3. *Disparate Impact Claims and "High Stakes" Testing*

The preceding excerpt from the National Research Council's report suggests that even if it cannot be shown that a racially disproportionate impact is a "vestige" of the prior segregated system, a prima facie case of disproportionate impact might be made under Title VI regulations that bar a recipient of federal funds from "utiliz[ing] criteria or methods of administration which have the effect of subjecting individuals to discrimination." 34 C.F.R. § 100.3(b)(2). However, after the recent Supreme Court decision in *Alexander v. Sandoval, supra*, private litigants could not make such a claim. Presumably, the Office for Civil Rights may still seek to enforce the Title VI disparate impact regulations and, if pursuing the case in court, would have to be able to meet the three-part test that lower courts have used in the past to evaluate claims brought by private plaintiffs.

4. *Educational Failure*

Can a test truly separate the competent from the incompetent? Are students just above a passing score likely to be very different in ability or in mastery of specific knowledge or skills for purposes either of promotion to the next grade or award of a high school diploma from those just below the cutoff score? Those who argue against standardized tests with high-stakes consequences presumably believe that teachers are thought to be better able to make judgments as to whether a student failed a course or should be promoted to the next grade. What evidence is there to support this proposition? Or is it that, in such a sensitive area, policymakers should prefer decentralized decision making, eschewing standardized written tests as the sole measures of competence? Might teacher-created examinations suffer from the same flaws as standardized tests (lack of instructional verification, cultural bias)? Might teachers sometimes be less objective? The National Council on Measurement in Education's Code of Professional Responsibilities in Educational Measurement provides that "multiple sources and types of relevant information" should be used whenever possible in making educational decisions. Should a single score on a standardized test determine whether or not a student receives a high school diploma or is promoted to the next grade? *See GI Forum, Image de Tejas v. Texas Education Agency*, 87 F.Supp. 2d 667, 680–681 (W.D. Tex. 2000); *Tyler v. Vickery*, 517 F.2d 1089 (5th Cir. 1975). Studies have shown that automatic retention policies based on student test scores have produced lower achievement, lower self-esteem, and higher dropout rates than students of equal achievement levels who were promoted. Darling-Hammond, "The Implications of Testing Policy for Quality and Equality," 73 *Phi Delta Kappan* 220, 222–223 (1991). Some commentators have expressed concern about racial bias in retention decisions. *See, e.g.*, Note, "Making the Grade, Public Education Reform: The Use of Standardized Testing to Retain Students and Deny Diplomas," 30 *Colum. Hum. Rts. L.Rev.* 495, 532 (1999).

Are critics of high-stakes testing implicitly suggesting that children should not fail, that they are stigmatized by failure? Or is it that critics believe that these tests create failures that would not otherwise exist? Do standardized or competency-based tests and traditional classroom tests attempt to measure the same thing? *See* Coleman, "Excellence and Equity in Education: High Standards for High-Stakes Tests," 6 *Va. J. Soc. Pol'y & Law* 81, 86 (1998), noting that there is a risk that schools may maintain lower educational standards to avoid potential civil rights issues.

5. *Unequal Access to Educational Resources*

A disproportionate number of African American and Latino students are being denied high school diplomas in Texas because they have not passed the high school graduation exit test that purports to measure mastery of the state-mandated curriculum. *See* Gomez, "The Texas Assessment of Academic Skills Exit Test—'Driver of Equity' or 'Ticket to Nowhere,'" 2 *Scholar: St. Mary's L. Rev. Minority Issues* 187, 188 (2000) (of the 7,000 high school seniors denied a diploma in 1998 because they failed the exit examination, but who were otherwise qualified to graduate, 85 percent were Hispanic or African American). The plaintiffs in *GI Forum v. Texas Education Agency*, 87 F.Supp.2d 667 (W.D. Tex. 2000) argue that in Texas, many minority students are the victims of educational inequality—they are underrepresented in advanced placement courses, and in gifted and talented programs, and are much more likely than nonminority students to be taught by noncertified teachers. Is this a sufficient basis to find that the test, as applied to those students, violates the due process clause?

The National Research Council report notes that "low-SES children, blacks, Hispanics, and English-language learners are more likely than other students to attend the schools in which high-stakes tests are given, and they are therefore likelier to be subject to high-stakes test policies and their consequences. . . . The same groups are also more likely to attend schools that do not provide high-quality curriculum and instruction." National Research Council, *supra*, at 175–76. *See also* Heubert, "Nondiscriminatory Use of High-Stakes Tests: Combining Professional Test-Use Standards with Federal Civil-Rights Enforcement," 133 *Ed. Law Rep.* 17, 22 (1999) ("standards of appropriate test use require test users to determine whether students' poor performance is due to shortcomings in school curriculum and pedagogy, which is more often likely to be the case for low-SES students and minority students"); Moran, *supra* at 116–117 (high-stakes testing is concentrated in states and districts with substantial low-income and minority populations, often in underfunded districts, and who thus have not had an equal opportunity to meet the standards).

6. *Constitutionality of the Test for Any Group*

If a competency or standardized achievement test is unconstitutional as applied to African Americans who receive an inferior educational experience, does it follow that the tests are unconstitutional for any group that receives an inferior education? Consider the alternative holding of the court of appeals in *Debra P.*:

> . . . It is clear that in establishing a system of free public education and in making school attendance mandatory, the state has created an expectation in the students. From the students' point of view, the expectation is that if a student attends school during those required years, and indeed more, and if he takes and passes the required courses, he will receive a diploma. This is a property interest as that term is used constitutionally. *See Goss v. Lopez*, 419 U.S. 565, 579 . . . (1975). . . .
>
> Based upon this implied property right, we find that the trial court was correct in holding that the implementation schedule for the test violated due process of law. . . .

> The due process violation potentially goes deeper than deprivation of property rights without adequate notice. When it encroaches upon concepts of justice lying at the basis of our civil and political institutions, the state is obligated to avoid action which is arbitrary and capricious, does not achieve or even frustrates a legitimate state interest, or is fundamentally unfair. . . . We believe that the state administered a test that was, at least on the record before us, fundamentally unfair in that it may have covered matters not taught in the schools of the state.

644 F.2d 397, 403–404 (5th Cir. 1981). *See* Note, "Testing the Test: The Due Process Implications of Minimum Competency Testing," 59 *N.Y.U. L.Rev.* 577 (1984).

Would language minorities (for example, Latinos) who are not given high-stakes tests in their primary language have a constitutional claim similar to that of African Americans in *Debra P.? See* National Research Council, *supra*, at 62–63, noting that Title VI applies to situations in which educational tests have a disproportionate adverse effect on English-language learners. The Equal Educational Opportunities Act of 1974, 20 U.S.C. § 1703(f), may also be relevant. (*See* chapter 6.)

The Office for Civil Rights has established principles for the use of high-stakes tests to minimize the risk of noncompliance with federal nondiscrimination laws. U.S. Department of Education Office for Civil Rights, *The Use of Tests When Making High-Stakes Decisions for Students: A Resource Guide for Educators and Policymakers* (December 2000). *See also* Heubert, "Nondiscriminatory Use of High-Stakes Tests: Combining Professional Test-Use Standards with Federal Civil-Rights Enforcement," 133 *Ed. Law Rep.* 17 (1999).

7. *Rights and Duties Created by Standards-Based Requirements*

Might the existence of state standards, with tests that purport to test the extent to which students have attained the necessary skills and competencies mandated by the state for promotion and graduation establish a duty on the part of the state to provide remedial education adequate to enable students to pass these tests? *See* Liebman, "Implementing Brown in the 90's: Political Reconstruction, Liberal Recollection, and Litigatively Enforced Legislative Reform," 76 *Va. L. Rev.* 349 (1990), in which Professor Liebman argues that educational performance standards mandated by the state could establish a judicially enforceable right to a minimally adequate education. This position has been more fully developed by Michael Rebell as follows:

> The extensive educational reform initiatives most states adopted . . . provided the courts with workable criteria for defining a minimally adequate education and for developing the "judicially manageable standards" they had long sought in dealing with potential remedies in complex educational litigations.
>
> * * *
>
> Standards-based reform is built around substantive content standards in English, mathematics, social studies and other major subject areas. These content standards are usually set at sufficiently high cognitive levels to meet the competitive standards of the global economy, and they are premised on the assumption that virtually all students can meet these high expectations if given sufficient opportunities and resources. . . .
>
> Standards-based reform substantially enhanced the fledgling educational adequacy notions alluded to in *Rodriguez* and others of the early fiscal equity cases. "Adequate education" was no longer a vague notion. . . . The concept now had substantive content, and its underlying message was that most state education systems—and certainly many school districts that served predominantly poor and minority students—could probably be assumed to be below, and not above, the level of substantive expectations.

Rebell, "Education Adequacy Litigation and the Quest for Equal Educational Opportunity," in 2 *Studies in Judicial Remedies and Public Engagement* at 8, 11–12 (Nov.1999). *See also* Comment, "Beyond School Financing: Defining the Constitutional Right to an Adequate Education," 78 *N.C. L. Rev.* 399, 462–465 (2000). *Cf. Peter W. v. San Francisco Unified School District*, 60 Cal. App.3d 814, 131 Cal. Rptr. 854 (1976).

D. Exclusionary Disciplinary Measures

Although the disciplinary process and the due process requirements for sanctions are discussed generally in chapter 3, this section addresses the issue of racial disparity in suspensions and expulsions. A recent study by the Civil Rights Project at Harvard University indicates that the increasing use of "zero tolerance" policies throughout the country is excluding substantial numbers of children from educational opportunities, and that minority students frequently receive harsher discipline than white students receive for similar, or less serious, offenses. Report by the Advancement Project and the Civil Rights Project, *Opportu-*

nities Suspended: The Devastating Consequences of Zero Tolerance and School Discipline Policies, http://www.law.harvard.edu/groups/civilrights/conferences/zero/zt_report.html (June 23, 2000). In many cases, the zero tolerance policies are employed for minor infractions that do not threaten the safety of anyone, or involve the possession of weapons or drugs. Minority students are more likely than whites to be referred for such subjective infractions as "defiance of authority." *See* Civil Rights Project, *supra* at 29. Moreover, students subjected to zero tolerance policies are often diverted into the criminal justice system, relying on law enforcement officials rather than school officials to punish them.

U.S. Department of Education data show that nationally, African American students constitute 16.9 percent of the nation's public school population, but 32 percent of all suspensions. Latinos make up 14 percent of students and 13.5 percent of those suspended, whereas whites account for 66 percent of students and just under 50 percent of those suspended. Civil Rights Project, *supra*. In many large urban school districts, the racial disparity is even more pronounced. For example in San Francisco, African American students are 56 percent of those expelled, although they constitute only 18 percent of the school population. Applied Research Center, *Facing the Consequences: An Examination of Racial Discrimination in U.S. Public Schools* at 9 (March 1, 2000). Chicago instituted a zero tolerance policy in the middle of the 1995–96 school year, and within three years, the number of expulsions had jumped from 81 to 1,000, a disproportionate number of those expelled being African American. *Id.* at 12. *See also* Civil Rights Project, *supra* at 3. In Durham, North Carolina, nearly 70 percent of all suspended or expelled students were African American, although they comprised 58 percent of the student population. By contrast, white students in that district were only 16 percent of those suspended. *Id.* at 26 (table at Appendix A). Other studies have also noted that minority students are consistently suspended at much higher rates than white students. *See, e.g.,* Pauken and Daniel, "Race Discrimination and Disability Discrimination in School Discipline: A Legal and Statistical Analysis," 139 *Ed. Law Rep.* 759, 766 (2000); Skiba and Peterson, "The Dark Side of Zero Tolerance: Can Punishment Lead to Safe Schools?" 80 *Phi Delta Kappan* 372 (1999); Note, "Education and the State Constitutions: Alternatives for Suspended and Expelled Students," 81 *Cornell L. Rev.*

582, 607 (1996); Rochester, "IPS Suspension Rate Soars," *Indianapolis Star* (May 10, 1995), at A01 (nearly a third of the enrollment in Indianapolis Public Schools was suspended, and blacks were suspended at twice the rate of whites). One study found that African Americans were overrepresented in suspensions by 54 percent and in expulsions by 161 percent. The results for Hispanic students were also disproportionate, but not as pronounced. Pauken and Daniel, *supra*, at 767, citing a study by England, Meier, and Fraga, "Barriers to Equal Opportunity: Educational Practices and Minority Students," 23 *Urban Affairs Quarterly* 635 (1988), analyzing data collected by the U.S. Department of Education's Office for Civil Rights.

Racially disproportionate use of exclusion policies predates the widespread adoption of zero tolerance policies, beginning in the 1970s with court-ordered desegregation. *See Hawkins v. Coleman*, 376 F.Supp. 1330 (N.D. Tex. 1974); Pauken and Daniel, *supra* at 773. However, zero tolerance policies are said to have exacerbated the disparity. *See* Applied Research Center, *supra* at 2. Several studies note that African American students are disproportionately excluded for nonviolent conduct, such as being disrespectful or insubordinate, rather than for drugs or weapons. Some states have laws permitting expulsion for habitual profanity. *See, e.g.,* Civil Rights Project, *supra*; Adams, "The Status of School Discipline and Violence," 567 *Annals Am. Acad. Pol. & Soc. Sci.* 140, 148 (2000)(noting that zero tolerance policies often remove students from the educational process for such minor offenses as tardiness, class cutting, and tobacco use, as well as insubordination).

Courts disagree as to the appropriate standard for a successful challenge to racial disparities in discipline. The following case discusses the weight to be given to statistical evidence.

Fuller v. Decatur Public School Board of Education School District 61
78 F.Supp.2d 812 (C.D. Ill. 2000).

McCuskey, District Judge.

* * *

The students in this case argue that they were expelled by the School Board for a period of two years because of a "zero tolerance" policy which punished them as a group, denied their constitutional rights

and was racially motivated. The students additionally argue that they were stereotyped as gang members and racially profiled by the actions of the School Board. The students claim that, because the fight was of a short duration and that no guns, no knives, and no drugs were involved, no expulsion was warranted for their actions in the fight.

After reviewing the evidence presented at trial, this court finds that the students have failed to meet their burden of proof on all issues presented. . . .

At the outset, this court wants to emphasize that the students in this case were involved in a violent fight in the stands at a high school football game. None of the students testified at trial and they have never denied their involvement in the fight. This court observed from the videotape presented at trial that the fight involved many individuals raising havoc in the midst of a captive audience of football fans, which included parents, grandparents, teachers and children. Because of the violent nature of the fight, a portion of which was captured on videotape, approximately one-half of the spectators in the bleachers scattered and left the stands to avoid confrontation and possible injury. It is undisputed that seven spectators, six students and one adult, filed accident reports at MacArthur High School following the incident. . . .

. . . [T]his court concludes that the students did not present any evidence which established that the School Board's decision to expel them for engaging in violent behavior was in any way based upon race. The students' evidence consisted solely of statistics which were compiled during the course of trial. . . . These statistics failed to establish that any similarly situated Caucasian students were treated less harshly. . . .

Facts

. . . [The plaintiff students attended three high schools] located in Decatur, Illinois. . . . On Friday, September 17, 1999, a football game was held at Eisenhower High School between Eisenhower and MacArthur High School. Approximately six minutes into the third quarter of the game, a fight broke out in the bleachers on the east end of the football field, the bleachers where fans of MacArthur were sitting. . . .

. . . [A] videotape showed a violent fight where the participants were punching and kicking at each other, with no regard for the safety of individuals seated in the stands watching the game. The video-tape also showed that spectators in the bleachers were scrambling to get away from the fight.

The following Monday, September 20, 1999, an investigation was begun by the administration at each high school to determine who was involved in the fight. During the investigation, evidence was gathered which showed that each of the students was involved in the fight. . . . [The principals of the high schools attended by the plaintiffs recommended that they be expelled for two years.]

* * *

At the outset, it is important to note that a federal court's role in school disciplinary matters is very limited. School discipline is an area which courts are reluctant to enter. . . .

The Seventh Circuit recently noted that the Supreme Court " 'has repeatedly emphasized the need for affirming the comprehensive authority of the States and of school officials, consistent with fundamental constitutional safeguards, to prescribe and control conduct in the schools.' " *Boucher* [*v. School Bd. of School Dist. of Greenfield*], 134 F.3d at 827 (quoting *Tinker v. Des Moines Indep. Community School Dist.*, 393 U.S. 503, 507, 89 S.Ct. 733, 21 L.Ed.2d 731 (1969)). In *Boucher*, the Seventh Circuit reversed an injunction granted by a district court which enjoined the school board from enforcing a one-year expulsion. The court stated, "[w]hile the district court's statement that a year's expulsion is extreme is understandable, we cannot accept the conclusion that the harm the injunction imposes on the Board is insignificant." *Boucher*, 134 F.3d at 826. The court determined in that case, where the expelled student did not engage in any kind of violent activity, that the district court did not adequately consider the potential harm to the Board's authority to take disciplinary action for what it believed to be a serious threat to school property. *Boucher*, 134 F.3d at 826–27.

Moreover, the "right to an education [is] not guaranteed, either explicitly or implicitly, by the Constitution, and therefore could not constitute a fundamental right." *Smith v. Severn*, 129 F.3d 419, 429 (7th Cir.1997) (citing *San Antonio Indep. School Dist. v. Rodriguez*, 411 U.S. 1, 35–37, 93 S.Ct. 1278, 36 L.Ed.2d 16 (1973)). . . . Accordingly, a challenge to a school disciplinary policy fails unless the policy is "wholly arbitrary." . . . A successful substantive due process claim requires an "extraordinary departure from established norms." . . . Because the right to an

education is not a fundamental constitutional right, this court reviews the School Board's action to determine if it is an "exercise of governmental power without any reasonable justification.". . . A court must look for an abuse of power that "shocks the conscience.". . .

* * *

The students have also alleged racial discrimination and a violation of their equal protection rights. The students alleged that the District has maintained a policy and practice of arbitrary and disparate expulsions with regard to African-American students.

. . . [An analysis of all expulsions in the school district from the beginning of the 1996–1997 school year through October 5, 1999] showed that the majority of students expelled were African American. In fact, the Summary indicated that 82% of students expelled from the beginning of the 1996–1997 school year through December 1999, were African American. The remaining 18% of students expelled were Caucasian. The evidence at trial showed that African American students comprise approximately 46–48% of the student body in the District.

This court notes that the statistics produced during trial could lead a reasonable person to speculate that the School Board's expulsion action was based upon the race of the students. However, this court cannot make its decision solely upon statistical speculation. The court's finding must be based upon the solid foundation of evidence and the law that applies to this case.

* * *

The students assert that a "valid inference can be raised by large statistical disparities in racial situations including discipline that a given School District and/or School Board has discriminated intentionally." However, the cases cited by the students do not support this proposition. In fact, the law is clear that a claim of racial discrimination and violation of equal protection cannot be based upon mere statistics standing alone. . . . In *United States v. Armstrong*, 517 U.S. 456, 116 S.Ct. 1480, 134 L.Ed.2d 687 (1996), the United States Supreme Court concluded that a study which showed that most persons prosecuted for crack cocaine trafficking were black did *not* constitute some evidence tending to show the existence of the essential elements of a selective prosecution claim (a violation of equal protection). *Armstrong*, 517 U.S. at 470, 116 S.Ct. 1480. The Supreme Court held that, to "establish a discriminatory effect in a race case, the claimant must show that similarly situated individuals of a different race were not prosecuted." *Armstrong*, 517 U.S. at 465, 116 S.Ct. 1480. Accordingly, the claim in *Armstrong* failed because the "study failed to identify individuals who were not black and could have been prosecuted for the offenses for which respondents were charged, but were not so prosecuted." *Armstrong*, 517 U.S. at 470, 116 S.Ct. 1480. The decision in *Armstrong* is applicable to civil cases where plaintiffs claim discrimination on the basis of race. . . . In a race case, "plaintiffs must show that similarly situated individuals of a different race were not subjected to the challenged conduct." . . .

Here, in this case, the students have not even attempted to show that Caucasian students who engaged in similar conduct were not subjected to the same discipline. . . . [The court noted that the school board had expelled some Caucasian students for fighting in the past.]

Moreover, none of the Caucasian students who were expelled for physical confrontations or fighting can be considered "similarly situated" to the students involved in this case. [One of the principals] testified that no other fight . . . even came close to the magnitude of the September 17, 1999, fight. [Another principal] testified that it was the only fight of this magnitude he had seen in 27 years in education. Accordingly, because the students failed to show that any similarly situated Caucasian students were treated less harshly, they failed to establish that race played any role in the School Board's expulsion decision.

* * *

NOTES AND QUESTIONS

1. Statistical Evidence of Racial Disparity in Exclusionary Policies

The *Fuller* court suggests that data showing substantial racial disparities in the use of suspension and expulsion are insufficient for an inference of intentional discrimination under an equal protection claim, and presumably the same would be true for a claim under the civil rights statute, Title VI, which has been held to require proof of intent to discriminate. *See Guardians Association v. Civil Service Commission of City of New York*, 463 U.S. 582, 103 S.Ct. 3221, 77 L.Ed.2d 866 (1983). In *Parker v. Trin-*

ity High School, 823 F.Supp. 511, 519 (N.D.Ill. 1993), the court said that "discriminatory intent or motive may be inferred from statistical or other evidence showing that minority students are disciplined more severely than white students for similar conduct," but found that the evidence submitted by plaintiffs was insufficient to demonstrate this. Although statistical disparities alone might be insufficient to show intentional discrimination under the standard required for a violation of the statute, would statistical disparities be sufficient evidence for a disparate impact claim under regulations promulgated to implement Title VI?

> A recipient, in determining the types of services . . . or other benefits, or facilities which will be provided under any such program, or the class of individuals to whom, or the situations in which, such services . . ., other benefits, or facilities will be provided under any such program, or the class of individuals to be afforded an opportunity to participate in any such program, may not . . . utilize criteria or methods of administration which have the effect of subjecting individuals to discrimination because of their race, color, or national origin, or have the effect of defeating or substantially impairing accomplishment of the objectives of the program as respect individuals of a particular race, color, or national origin.

34 C.F.R. §100.3(2). *See Elston v. Talladega County Board of Educ.*, 997 F.2d 1394, 1407 (11th Cir. 1993). *But see Alexander v. Sandoval, supra*, barring a private right of action for disparate impact claims under Title VI regulations. *Sandoval* does not, however, necessarily bar enforcement of 34 C.F.R. § 100.3 (2) by the Office for Civil Rights.

However, if racial and ethnic minority students are more likely to be identified as misbehaving, particularly for such subjective infractions as defiance of authority or insubordination, proving that minorities are treated differently than similarly situated white students would be impossible inasmuch as those white students were never referred for disciplinary action. Civil Rights Project, *supra* at 29.

2. Causes of Racial Disparity in Discipline

Some commentators have suggested cultural differences between black students and white school officials as an explanation for the increased suspension and expulsion of African American students, particularly when minority students of a lower socioeconomic status come into conflict with the middle-class public school system. *See* Pauken and Daniel, *supra* at 764. However, other studies have indicated that even after controlling for socioeconomic background, African Americans are overrepresented in suspensions and expulsions. Skiba and Peterson, *supra*.

Other researchers have suggested that because of poorly specified expectations and the lack of consistency in disciplining students when they fail to meet these expectations, school administrators and teachers are able to discipline racial and ethnic minority students for conduct that would not be punished if engaged in by white students. Pauken and Daniel, *supra* at 765.

Although school officials and others often contend that there is a higher rate of misbehavior on the part of minorities, several studies have shown that disproportionate behavior does not explain why African American students are disciplined more frequently and more harshly. *See* Pauken and Daniel, *supra* at 766, summarizing the findings of a study of five major city school districts. *See also* Skiba and Peterson, *supra*.

3. *Effects of Exclusionary Practices*

The dropout rate for racial and ethnic minority students is substantially greater than that for whites, particularly in large urban school districts. Studies show that suspension is one of the major factors affecting the decision to drop out of school. The impact on the individual student and on society is substantial. *See, e.g.,* Pauken and Daniel, *supra*, at 771–772; Adams, "The Status of School Discipline and Violence," 567 *Annals Am. Acad. Pol. & Soc. Sci.* 140, 145 (2000); Note, "Education and the State Constitutions: Alternatives for Suspended and Expelled Students," 81 *Cornell L. Rev.* 582, 606–607 (1996). One study notes that some schools implement suspensions as early as kindergarten, often initiating a downward spiral that results in dropping out. Applied Research Center, *supra*, at 5. Schools with limited resources in central city districts, serving predominantly minority students of lower socioeconomic status, are more likely than other schools to exclude students entirely rather than use in-school suspensions or provide alternative education programs. Adams, *supra* at 149. Although excluded students are unlikely to be able to claim a right to an alternative education program under the federal equal protection clause, could they claim such a right under their state constitutions? *See State in Interest of G.S.*, 330 N.J. Super. 383, 749 A.2d 902 (N.J. Super. Ct. Ch. Div. 2000)

(state has constitutional obligation to provide alternative education in another setting to expelled student); *see also* Note, "Education and the State Constitutions: Alternatives for Suspended and Expelled Students," 81 *Cornell L. Rev.* 582 (1996).

E. Impact of School Choice on Racial and Ethnic Minorities

In light of the expanding movement for school choice, issues have been raised about the potential impact of such a movement on racial and ethnic minorities and the economically disadvantaged. Will choice enhance or limit educational opportunities for these students? The history of the use of choice in preserving segregation has colored the perceptions among some as to whether these students are likely to benefit from the growing choice movement. Some of the questions that have been raised are explored in the following article.

"Race and School Choice"

B. Levin, in S.D. Sugarman and F. R. Kemerer (eds.), *School Choice and Social Controversy* 266, 267–68, 273–89 (1999). Reprinted with permission.

* * *

Among the issues raised [with regard to the impact of school choice on racial and ethnic minorities] are . . . whether choice is likely to increase racial and economic isolation; whether admissions criteria or other factors will limit access for racial and ethnic minorities; whether the supply of choice opportunities will grow to meet the demands of racial and ethnic minorities at the same pace as for nonminorities; whether there are likely to be inequalities in the information available to racial minorities or the poor; whether educational opportunities are likely to be enhanced, including whether choice schools available for racial minorities will be staffed by teachers of appropriate quality and experience; and whether adequate resources will be available to allow equality of opportunity for choice for minority and poor parents.

A Historic Perspective on School Choice

For at least a decade and a half after the Supreme Court's decision in *Brown v. Board of Education* black students remained almost completely segregated in the South as school boards and state legislatures tried various measures to evade the command of *Brown*. . . . When those measures were struck down by the courts, states enacted laws providing for the closure of public schools while subsidizing private school attendance with tuition grants, and assisting private segregated academies in school districts that were required to desegregate.[3]

The massive withdrawal of white students to these private segregation academies was initially funded by state tuition grants.[4] After court decisions holding such funding unconstitutional, the schools relied on tuition fees, with the burden on parents being relieved by state and federal tax exemptions, free transportation, state-owned textbooks and supplies donated by various governmental entities (often transferred from the public school system), the use of public facilities, and so on.[5] The establishment of these segregated academies resulted not only in the withdrawal of white students from the public schools but also the withdrawal of substantial financial support from public schools, resulting in the public schools being stigmatized as inferior.[6] One case study of a county in Alabama found that these segregation academies drew their enrollment disproportionately from whites at the higher socioeconomic levels, meaning that the public schools were not only increasingly racially isolated, but economically isolated as well.[7] Many choice opponents today express the fear that school choice will similarly lead to the racial and economic isolation of students remaining in the traditional public schools.

. . . In the 1980s and 1990s, not only has racial and ethnic school segregation increased substantially, but central city school districts have also become increasingly economically segregated.[14] By 1986, only 3 percent of the nation's white school-aged children were enrolled in the twenty-five largest urban districts.[15] Even in the remaining integrated schools in the large urban districts, gifted and talented within-school programs that are predominantly white and middle class have proliferated.[16]

Racial and Ethnic Minorities and School Choice

* * *

. . . [S]chool choice plans may include a wide variety of programs: tuition vouchers that can be used in either private or public schools (Cleveland); charter school programs that permit private schools to convert to public school status (Arizona); charter schools limited to new or existing public schools (California); magnet schools within the public school system, either as separate schools or schools-within-schools, generally in urban areas and often part of a court-ordered desegregation plan; interdistrict transfers (St. Louis and its suburbs); and controlled-choice districts (Cambridge, Mass.). By design, some of these may encourage a higher percentage of minorities than private schools generally (Cleveland). . . .

While data are sketchy with regard to the number of minority students in private schools of choice, there are some indications from existing studies as to who takes advantage of what kinds of choice opportunities. . . . Although the percentage of blacks and Hispanics enrolling in private schools has increased between 1972 and 1995, the percentage of racial and ethnic minorities relative to non-minorities is still

---

[3]*Griffin v. County School Board*, 377 U.S. 218 (1964); *Hall v. St. Helena Parish School Board*, 197 F.Supp. 649 (E.D. La. 1961); aff'd mem., 368 U.S. 515 (1962); *Norwood v. Harrison*, 413 U.S. 455 (1973).

[4]Seven southern states enacted tuition grant laws. See Helen Hershkoff and Adam S. Cohen, "School Choice and the Lessons of Choctaw County," *Yale Law and Policy Review*, vol. 10 (1992), pp. 1, 6.

[5]Note, "Segregation Academies and State Action," *Yale Law Journal*, vol. 82 (1973), pp. 1436, 1446–47; Hershkoff and Cohen, "School Choice and the Lessons of Choctaw County," pp. 3, 8.

[6]"Segregation Academies and State Action," pp. 1452–53; Hershkoff and Cohen, "School Choice and the Lessons of Choctaw County," pp. 8, 13.

[7]Hershkoff and Cohen, "School Choice and the Lessons of Choctaw County," p. 13.

[14]This has been well documented by Gary Orfield over the last decade. See generally Gary Orfield and Susan E. Eaton, *Dismantling Desegregation* (New Press, 1996), pp. 53–71. See also Gary Orfield, *The Growth of Segregation in American Schools* (Alexandria, Va.: National School Boards Association, 1993); Gary Orfield, Franklin Monfort, and Melissa Aaron, *Status of School Desegregation 1968–1986* (Alexandria, Va.: National School Boards Association Council of Urban Boards of Education, 1989); Gary Orfield, Franklin Monfort, and Rosemary George, "School Segregation in the 1980s," *IDRA Newsletter* (November 1987), pp. 3–5, 9.

[15]Orfield and Eaton, *Dismantling Desegregation*, pp. 62–63.

[16]Patrick Welsh, "Fast-Track Trap: How Ability Grouping Hurts Our Schools, Kids and Families," *Washington Post*, September 16, 1990; Jeannie Oakes, *Keeping Track: How Schools Structure Inequality* (Yale University Press, 1985).

much greater in public schools than in private schools.[35] In 1995 blacks and Hispanics comprised only 17.1 percent of students enrolled in private schools compared to 31.1 percent of students enrolled in public schools. About 41.2 percent of private schools have a student enrollment of less than 5 percent minority students; 15.6 percent have a student enrollment of 50 percent or more minority.[36] . . . Blacks and Hispanics constitute 56.1 percent of those enrolled in public schools in central city school districts.[38] The high correlation of poverty and race in central cities means that the racial isolation of many central city schools is compounded by socioeconomic class isolation.

. . . To what extent are racial and ethnic minorities electing choice plans today?

. . . [A] higher proportion of racial and ethnic minorities attend charter schools than attend private schools: a study of charter schools in ten states shows that 14 percent of the students enrolled were African American and 25 percent were Hispanic. However, those data do not tell us the proportion of whites and nonwhites in individual alternative schools in those states. Perhaps a more important factor for predicting not only whether minorities will take advantage of an expanded choice movement but also whether choice is likely to increase or decrease racial and economic stratification is *why* parents choose a school other than the one assigned. . . .

* * *

Most studies of minority parental and student satisfaction with school choice programs, particularly tuition voucher experiments and charter schools, cite as positive factors the small size of the school.[40] Size of classroom, sense of community, especially in the first year of a start-up school (and the sense of greater ownership that choosing a school gives to par-

ents and students), more involved and caring teachers, the belief that the individual needs of the particular child are given greater attention, and the adaptation of the curriculum to ethnic and cultural considerations are also factors. In addition, many minority and low-income parents report that they sought alternative schools because they felt their child's previous school was unsafe.[41] Advocates of school choice also point to the increased parent involvement in their child's education, which is likely to occur in many school choice programs, and to the advantage to many working-class families of schools that operate well past the hours that public schools operate.[42] Some students and parents like the fact that choice schools often have a single, clear mission and hence a greater focus than do schools in the public school system. In general, parent and student satisfaction with choice schools appears to be substantial.

One of the major arguments for expanding school choice is that it will improve student achievement. However, . . . it is difficult at this point to draw firm conclusions of improved academic achievement. Many programs have been in existence for only a short time, so that gains are not yet measurable. And since not all of the choice schools administer the same achievement tests given by the public schools in the district or state in which the choice school is located, it is not easy to make comparisons. There is such a diversity of choice schools, with diverse missions, and designed to appeal to students with different needs, that one cannot generalize as to the appropriate outcomes to measure. . . . However, several studies have found preliminary indications of achievement gains in students attending choice schools, and others show that at least attendance and retention have improved for disadvantaged children—certainly a necessary, if

---

[35]National Center for Education Statistics, *The Condition of Education*, 1998, p. 134.

[36]National Center for Education Statistics, *Digest of Education Statistics*, 1997, Table 59.

[38]The data are for 1995; National Center for Education Statistics, *The Condition of Education*, 1998.

[40]In 1995, the average enrollment in charter schools was 287 students, and most of them were elementary schools. Linda Jacobson, "Under the Microscope; As Charter Schools Flourish, the Big Question for Researchers Is: Do They Work?" *Education Week*, November 6, 1996. The U.S. Department of Education's report on charter schools in ten states notes that 62 percent of the charter schools enroll fewer than 200 students. *A Study of Charter Schools: First Year Report* (U.S. Department of Education, 1997).

[41]Gregg Vanourek and others, *Charter Schools in Action Project: Final Report*, pt.5 (New York: Hudson Institute, 1997).

[42]Bruno V. Manno and others, "How Charter Schools Are Different: Lessons and Implications from a National Study," *Phi Delta Kappan* (1998), p. 488.

not sufficient, condition for improving academic achievement.[44]

* * *

One of the major issues in the debate about school choice is whether certain school choice options will lead to increased racial and economic isolation. Although the statistics indicate increasing enrollment of minorities in private schools . . ., as well as in public school choice plans (especially magnet school programs), that does not necessarily mean that the individual schools are less racially or economically stratified than the public schools these students previously attended. . . .

. . . [A]lthough some studies suggest that some school choice plans (particularly those that require some racial balance) may not necessarily increase racial stratification, the evidence is mixed. . . .

The evidence of increased economic isolation resulting from school choice programs is more uniform, however. For example, the study of magnet school programs in Cincinnati, Nashville, and St. Louis finds that poor children remain more highly concentrated in nonmagnet than in magnet schools, even with special efforts to inform and attract students from poor families.[52] In the communities studied, researchers found that families of children in magnet schools have higher income and educational levels than those in the assigned public schools, and that children in magnet schools are more likely to live in two-parent households with at least one parent employed. Even when the comparison is limited to minority parents, "positive correlations between magnet school attendance and higher socioeconomic status hold true." In other words, when minority parents are given a choice, those of higher socioeconomic status are more likely to choose magnets than those who are poorer and less educated. The study concludes that magnets, by and large, "have contributed to a new phenomenon — schools that have achieved a measure of desegrega-

tion by race but that remain largely segregated on the basis of income."[53]

* * *

An evaluation of Milwaukee's voucher experiment, which was designed solely for low-income students, found that even among the poor, "parents seeking to get into the program are more educated, more involved, and have higher educational expectations than the average parent."[57] They also have smaller families than those who do not want to participate in the program. Choice parents were significantly more likely to have done volunteer work for the public school their child had previously attended than nonchoice parents, suggesting that, as in other studies, the parents are more likely to believe in the importance of education and to feel less alienated and powerless.[58] The result, of course, is that this cadre of public school volunteers is removed from the traditional public schools.

These and other studies suggest that even when choice options are designed specifically for low-income students, those students who remain behind in their traditional public schools are more likely to be at the bottom economically, with significant numbers of them from the most alienated and powerless families. . . .

Much of the research is in agreement not only with regard to the difference in amount and quality of information available across socioeconomic groups, but also with regard to the difference in sources and types of information used by parents of different socioeconomic groups. The authors of one article note that research shows that members of "dominant status groups," defined as white and wealthy, "will have greater market resources, including time, money, information, educational backgrounds, political clout, and personal connections and far fewer market constraints," which will give them an "advantage in the competition against members of subordinate status groups for seats in the

---

[44]Vanourek and others, *Charter Schools in Action*; Peter W. Cookson Jr. and Sonali M. Shroff, *Recent Experience with Urban School Choice Plans*, Digest 127 (ERIC/Clearinghouse on Urban Education, 1997).

[52][Corrine M.] Yu and [William L.] Taylor, [eds.,] *Difficult Choices [:Do Magnet Schools Serve Children in Need?* (Washington, DC: Citizens Commission on Civil Rights, 1997)], p. 2.

[53]Ibid., p. 27. See also R. Kenneth Godwin, Frank R. Kemerer, and Valerie J. Martinez, "Comparing Public Choice and Private Voucher Programs in San Antonio," in Peterson and Hassel, *Learning From School Choice*, pp. 296–297, which notes a similar sorting by race and socioeconomic status in a districtwide thematic choice program operated by the San Antonio public school district.

[57]John Witte, "The Milwaukee Parental Choice Program," in Rasell and Rothstein, *School Choice*.

[58]Ibid., pp. 83–84.

most demanded schools."[60] Even among nonwhite and low-income parents, those with less disadvantaged backgrounds will have better sources of information. . . .

* * *

Advocates of the market-driven approach to school choice programs, who believe that educational improvements will result through competitive market forces, and that bad schools will be driven out of business, assume that parents act rationally and choose schools based on "the quality of the academic program offered and the match between teaching styles and their child's individual needs."[65] Two researchers challenge the rational choice theory on the ground that it is distorted by racial and class bias. They review research showing that "race- and class-based views of image and status affect parents' perceptions of 'good' and 'bad' schools," noting that alienated parents with the least education are "inhibited from gathering information that would allow them to make decisions based on school-quality factors as opposed to school location and convenience." An upwardly mobile family, they argue, might rationally choose a school because of its social clout, while an isolated and alienated black family might equally rationally choose to remain in a predominantly black school because of its familiarity and comfort level. It is unlikely, they suggest, that choices based on these nonacademic factors will lead to any significant educational improvement.

Other studies of the reasons for attending private schools also show that the perceptions of the academic quality of public schools have little or no apparent impact on private school enrollment, but that race and class do affect choice. The percentage of minority students enrolled in the public schools has a significant effect on the decision of white parents to enroll their children in private schools.[66] And studies show that the percentage of minorities in choice schools similarly affects decisions, with white parents

choosing schools with low percentages of minority students, and minority parents seeking schools with high percentages of minority students.[67] Even those minority parents who choose schools where there are few children of their own race do so because of the perceived quality of predominantly white and middle-class schools. In the public school transfer program in St. Louis, transfer parents were found not to have any more factual information than nontransfer parents regarding the academic quality of the transfer school. Decisions were based on impressions, rather than objective information, with the decision to send a child to a suburban school apparently based on the assumption that a school in a wealthier, higher-status (white) neighborhood would be better and have more resources than the inner-city assigned school (whether this was actually true or not). Assessments of school quality appeared to be based primarily on the race of the students enrolled.[68]

* * *

Apart from race or class concerns, which appear to be a major factor in choosing a school, . . . the studies suggest that parents probably look less to curricular or other educational innovations and academic quality of the educational program than they do to the size of the school and the classes, and the fact that their child gets more individual attention from the teacher (which is in part related to size).

A number of commentators suggest that the use of a first-come, first-served selection criterion disadvantages those who do not obtain as much information as early as others—who are more likely to be those of higher socioeconomic status.[74] Many charter school laws provide that preference should be given to siblings of students currently enrolled in the school, potentially disadvantaging those parents who do not get as much information as early as others. The application process and forms themselves may deter economically disadvantaged families from applying.[75]

---

[60][Amy Stuart] Wells and [Robert L.] Crain, "Do Parents Choose School Quality or School Status? [A Sociological Theory of Free Market Education," in Cookson, *The Choice Controversy*], p. 76.

[65]Wells and Crain, "Do Parents Choose School Quality or School Status?" pp. 65, 66, 69, 70.

[66]Kevin B. Smith and Kenneth J. Meier, "School Choice, Panacea or Pandora's Box," *Phi Delta Kappan* (1995), p. 312.

[67]Jeffrey R. Henig, "The Local Dynamics of Choice: Ethnic Preferences and Institutional Responses," in Fuller and Elmore, *Who Chooses? Who Loses?*, p. 105. See also Wells, "The Sociology of Choice," p. 35.

[68]Wells, "The Sociology of Choice," pp. 40–43.

[74]Peterson, "School Choice," [in Peterson and Hassel, *Learning from School Choice*] p. 17. See also *Villanueva v. Carere*, 85 F.3d 481, 488 n.3 (10th Cir. 1996).

[75]*Villanueva v. Carere*, 873 F.Supp. 434, 449 (D. Colo. 1994); aff'd, 85 F.3d 481 (10th Cir. 1996).

Clearly, schools that use academic achievement test scores or other measures of academic achievement will disproportionately exclude minorities and low income students.[76] Some choice school plans allow students to be excluded on the basis of their record of behavior at their prior school, which would limit choice at those schools to those who had been able to conform to the standards of the traditional public school to which they were assigned.[77] Behavior potentially could include the student's prior attendance record.

Some charter schools expect parents to contribute a certain number of hours of volunteer work on behalf of the school, sometimes known as sweat equity, both to increase the involvement of parents in the school their child attends, and to provide in-kind support for the school.[78] If this is made a condition of admission, it may act as a substantial barrier for single-parent families, or for those families in which both parents work in jobs that do not allow the flexibility that some professional positions might permit. The buy-out option offered by some schools whereby parents who do not have the time to volunteer either would pay others to do their share of volunteer work or contribute financial support directly to the school, obviously would also not be a feasible option for low-income parents. An admission criterion requiring parents to commit to volunteer time on behalf of the school thus may limit access for children from low-income, single-parent families.

With regard to tuition voucher programs, if the amount of the voucher does not cover the entire cost of tuition, it will be difficult for low-income students to take advantage of those programs unless schools were required to take a certain number of students without charging them the difference between the voucher and full tuition. Most private schools would be likely, at best, to accept only a limited number of such scholarship students. Larger families would be particularly disadvantaged in these circumstances. . . .

[A] number of studies of voucher experiments, even those designed solely for low-income students, found that parents seeking to participate had smaller families than those who did not, even without the barrier created by having to supplement the voucher.[79] Charter schools and choice within the public school system do not present the same problem as voucher programs, because they are not tuition dependent. . . .

[An] important issue . . . is whether the state or school district will ensure transportation for all who want to choose schools, regardless of where they are located within the district or even within another district. The lack of transportation clearly will affect student and parent choice of schools.[80] Those families that can afford transportation or who have both the time and the means to provide their own transportation for their children will be favored. Since few programs involve complete subsidy of the transportation needs to maximize choice for low-income families, poor families and those isolated within the inner city may not have equal access to choice opportunities.

Some studies show that the lack of start-up money and the difficulty in obtaining funding for a building may also impact adversely on charter school organizers in states in which private entities are allowed to organize charter schools.[81] This lack of capital may affect low-income communities wanting to establish a charter school more than it will affect better-off communities.

School choice will have a substantial impact on the traditional public schools in central city districts by exacerbating the economic isolation and, in some circumstances, the racial isolation of those schools. Most studies show that many school choice programs leave the traditional public schools increasingly economically isolated. . . . One commentator, analyzing New York City's magnet schools—even though choice is controlled and the schools are quite limited in opportunities for selectivity—found that the remaining schools became "pockets of concentrated

---

[76]Some charter school laws, but not all, prohibit charter schools from discriminating on the basis of academic achievement. See Mass. Gen. Laws, chap. 71, section 89 (1997). However, the Massachusetts law also includes a provision that a charter school may establish reasonable academic standards as a condition for eligibility for applicants.

[77]The Texas open-enrollment charter school law allows charter schools to exclude students who have a documented history of discipline problems. Texas Education Code Ann., section 12.111(6) (West 1998).

[78]Manno and others, "How Charter Schools Are Different," p. 488. See also *Villanueva v. Carere*, 85 F.3d 481, 484 (10th Cir. 1996).

[79]See the analysis of the Milwaukee voucher experiment, Witte, "The Milwaukee Parental Choice Program," p. 70.

[80]Stuart Biegel, "School Choice Policy and Title VI: Maximizing Equal Access for K-12 Students in a Substantially Deregulated Educational Environment," *Hastings Law Journal*, vol. 46, (1995), p. 1533.

[81]Jacobson, "Under the Microscope," [*Education Week*, November 6, 1996], p. 21.

disadvantage."[82] The impact on the education of children where race and poverty are concentrated is well documented.

A second, and related, concern is the impact of school choice on the improvement of education in the traditional public schools. Parents whose children remain in the assigned schools have been shown to be alienated and to feel powerless. Since several studies have found that parents who participate in choice programs are likely to have been more involved in their children's education at their prior school, and are the more assertive parents who believe in the importance of education, the traditional schools lose not only those parents who have volunteered to work in the schools, but also those parents most likely to press for reform.[83]

Another concern is the impact school choice may have on the resources available to the traditional public schools. . . . Studies even of choice within public school systems suggest that there is some adverse impact on resources available to the remaining public schools. Even within the limited public choice involved with magnet schools, researchers find that magnet schools have higher costs—including transportation, new equipment, teacher retraining, and smaller class size—than the traditional public schools.[84] Some have argued that magnet school programs thus drain resources and also the best teachers from other schools.

. . . Are teachers who bring energy and commitment to their jobs likely to remain in public schools with already limited resources, as more upwardly mobile, motivated, and active parents exit, leaving behind children impacted by poverty and the sense that education is less relevant to their lives? Central city school districts are already experiencing severe shortages of qualified teachers and teachers with experience in the fields they are assigned to teach. One potential effect of an expansion of the school choice movement may be to exacerbate the problem.

* * *

The expansion of the school choice movement poses several risks to equality of educational opportunity for racial and ethnic minorities and the poor. . . . Some choice programs clearly offer educational and other opportunities for minority children that they are not able to get in some of the traditional public schools to which they are assigned, at least as those schools are now organized and financed.[87] It is also clear . . . that school choice programs must include certain safeguards if minority and poor children are to have equal access to these opportunities. On the other hand, excessive regulation may frustrate the promise of school choice to improve education, so the safeguards should be no more than are necessary to ensure equality of access and opportunity.

Ensuring that Choice Does Not Increase Racial and Economic Stratification

Many school choice programs appear to increase racial and ethnic stratification, at least in certain circumstances, and are even more likely to increase economic segregation. Obviously, some choice schools will remain predominantly one race because of the mission of those schools and the type of curriculum (for example, a school that emphasizes an Afrocentric curriculum). . . . The effort should be to minimize factors that lessen diversity on bases other than choice grounded in personal preferences, values, interests, and perceived needs.

Several state charter school laws expressly prohibit discrimination on the basis of race or national origin (as well as on other grounds) in the admission of students. Such provisions, alone, are not likely to have much effect on the diversity of the student body. Other states, in order to ensure that school choice does not lead to increased segregation, include racial balance provisions in legislation providing for school choice. Some statutes require that the charter school's racial and ethnic balance reflect that of the school district as a whole. Others provide that the school's balance not deviate more than 10 percent from that of the district in which it is located.[89] . . . [The ability to achieve diversity under these laws

---

[82]Robert L. Crain, "New York City's Career Magnet High School," in Rasell and Rothstein, *School Choice*, p. 265.

[83]Jeanne M. Powers and Peter W. Cookson, Jr., "The Politics of School Choice Research: Fact, Fiction, and Statistics," *Educational Policy*, vol.13 (1999), pp. 104, 115.

[84]Yu and Taylor, *Difficult Choices*, p. 9, note that Houston spends $400 to $1,300 more per student on its magnet school program. See also Orfield and Eaton, *Dismantling Desegregation*, p. 103; Blank and others, "After Fifteen Years," pp. 164–65.

[87]See Yu and Taylor, *Difficult Choices*, p. 1; Vanourek and others, *Charter Schools in Action Project*.

[89]South Carolina Code Ann., section 59-40-50 (B)(6) (Law Co-Op 1998); Nevada Revised Statutes, 386.580(2)(1997).

may be limited when the charter school is] located in a predominantly white suburban school district or a predominantly minority central city district. In addition to the fact that the requirement may be ineffective, there are substantial legal barriers to a school's selecting students to maintain a racially balanced student body.

There have been a number of challenges to the use of racial preferences in admissions to magnet schools or other specialized choice schools within the public school system. One recent case was brought by white parents who sued when their children were denied admission to a magnet school on the basis of their race. School officials, to ensure that the school's enrollment reflected the racial composition of the school district as a whole, had used a lottery system weighted by race to compensate for a disproportionately white applicant pool. The district court held that the school could not use race-conscious admissions policies, finding that under the strict scrutiny standard of review, the school system did not meet its burden of demonstrating that a compelling interest was served.[90] Other cases challenging the use of race-conscious admissions policies to ensure racial balance in alternative or choice schools reached similar results or were settled.[91] Nevertheless, an argument can be made that admissions programs that consider race as one factor among a number of criteria might survive constitutional scrutiny.[92] . . .

Laws requiring that racial and ethnic balance in choice schools reflect that of the school district as a whole also present problems for schools that may offer programs that appeal primarily to minority students and their families. For example, North Carolina's charter school law includes a requirement that the charter schools established under the act reasonably reflect the racial composition of the school district in which they are located. However, recent estimates are that twenty-two of the sixty charter schools in North Carolina may violate this requirement because they are more than 85 percent African American. This has led to an alliance between the state teachers' union and members of the state legislature's Black Caucus, who are calling for the law to be enforced or that the charter schools be closed, while in the other camp are minority parents whose children attend these charter schools, Republican members of the state legislature, and such conservative organizations as the North Carolina Foundation for Individual Rights (which has challenged affirmative action at the university level).[93] . . .

If the means states have used to ensure racial diversity in choice schools are constitutionally questionable, can measures to ensure diversity of socioeconomic background be taken? The Supreme Court has held that classifications based on wealth, unlike race, are not strictly scrutinized by the courts, so that such measures are much more likely to be found constitutional.[94] One suggestion is to require that the proportion of students eligible for the free or reduced-price lunch program reflect the proportion in the school district as a whole.[95] The Kansas charter school law has adopted this approach, requiring that a charter school be reasonably reflective of the socioeconomic composition of the school district in which it is located.[96] . . . The only decision to date that has questioned the use of

---

[90]Tito v. Arlington County School Board, 1997 U.S. Dist. LEXIS 7932 (E.D. Va). The Supreme Court has held that all racial classifications are subject to strict scrutiny by the courts, requiring the government to demonstrate that the classification serves a compelling state interest, and that the use of the classification is narrowly tailored to achieve that goal for it to be found constitutional. Adarand Constructors, Inc. v. Pena, 515 U.S. 200 (1995).

[91]*Wessman v. Gittens*, 160 F.3d 790 (1st Cir. 1998) (admission to academically elite school based on standardized test scores plus racial/ethnic guidelines held unconstitutional); *Ho v. San Francisco Unified School District*, 965 F.Supp. 1316 (N.D. Cal. 1997) (court denied motion for summary judgment in case brought by Chinese Americans challenging racial-ethnic guidelines for admission to academically elite school; case recently settled with school officials being directed to develop new assignment plan in which no student could be assigned to a particular school on basis of race or ethnicity, ending priority given to African American and Latino students in school assignments); *Equal Open Enrollment Ass'n v. Akron City School District*, 937 F.Supp.700 (N.D. Ohio 1996) (court enjoined school district's policy of barring white students from transferring to nearby suburban districts while allowing black students to do so in order to prevent white flight). But see *Eisenberg v. Montgomery County Public Schools*, 19 F.Supp. 2d 449 (D. Md. 1998) (court denied preliminary injunction in challenge to district policy denying transfer from assigned school to magnet school on grounds of racial balance).

[92]Note, "The Constitutionality of Race-Conscious Admissions Programs in Public Elementary and Secondary Schools," *Harvard Law Review*, vol. 112 (1999), p. 940. But see *Hopwood v. Texas*, 78 F.3d 932 (5th Cir. 1996).

[93]Dent, "Diversity Rules Threaten North Carolina Charter Schools," [*New York Times*, December 23, 1998, p. B8].

[94]But see *Tuttle v. Arlington County School Board*, 1998 U.S. Dist. LEXIS 19788 (E.D. Va), in which the court held that a magnet school's use of a lottery weighted by family income, together with using first language, violated both the Due Process and Equal Protection Clauses.

[95]Yu and Taylor, *Difficult Choices*.

[96]Kansas Statutes Ann., section 72-1906(d)(2) (1997).

socioeconomic preferences for admission is one in which the district court had previously struck down a lottery weighted by race and ethnicity in order to have a magnet school whose enrollment approximated that of the general school population. The judge found that changing the weighted lottery to use first- language and family income classifications was attempting to achieve the same end that had earlier been ruled unconstitutional. The judge viewed the first-language criterion as a proxy for a national origin classification, and said that the family income classification, which he characterized as creating "a rigid dichotomy between students who qualify for free or reduced lunch and all other students," did not make the weighted system constitutional.[97]

Some state statutes have specified that a certain percentage of at-risk students must be served. The Colorado Charter School Act defines an at-risk student as a pupil who because of physical, emotional, and socioeconomic or cultural factors, is less likely to succeed in a conventional educational environment. The law, however, mandates only that a percentage of the charter schools that are established under the act serve at-risk children, rather than requiring each choice school to take a certain percentage of at-risk children.[98]

NOTES AND QUESTIONS

1. State Action and Charter Schools

While most tuition voucher programs are designed to provide tuition grants or scholarships to students to use at either existing or newly established private schools, charter schools fall somewhere between private and traditional public schools. In many states, charters may be provided to new schools as well as existing public schools (sometimes termed *conversion schools*). State laws vary as to whether schools are granted charters by the school district in which they are located, a state agency, or an independent board. Unlike public schools, charter schools have much more independence from state and school district regulation. In effect, they are publicly funded but privately managed schools. Charter schools generally receive the same amount per pupil as the districtwide or statewide average per pupil expenditure, but often are given much more flexibility to raise funds privately.Are privately. Are charter schools sufficiently public to characterize them as state actors for purposes of the Equal Protection Clause? *Compare Burton v. Wilmington Parking Authority*, 365 U.S. 715, 81 S.Ct. 856, 6 L.Ed 2d 45 (1961) *with Rendell-Baker v. Kohn*, 457 U.S. 830, 102 S.Ct. 2764, 73 L.Ed.2d 418 (1982). *See* Brown-Nagin, "Toward a Pragmatic Understanding of Status-Consciousness: The Case of Deregulated Education," 50 *Duke L. J.* 753, 851 (2000) (contending that although charter schools are state actors, they should not be "treated precisely the same as conventional public schools for purposes of equal protection analysis"); *see also* Parker, "The Color of Choice: Race and Charter Schools," 75 *Tulane L. Rev.* 563, 604 (2001).

Consider the following:

> . . . [S]ome deregulated schools may be deemed to occupy a distinct "quasi-public" status. In the event of equal protection litigation relating to such schools, courts should generally give deference to schools that are considered quasi-public by subjecting their practices to rational relation review. The exception to this rule would be cases in which affirmative acts by the state or school authorities result in the exclusion of status-identifiable groups from enrollment in charter schools, or where evidence shows that particular charter schools would undermine existing court orders.

Id. Do you agree that the rational relation review would be appropriate for predominantly minority schools? Is this approach consistent with the use of the strict scrutiny standard of review in *Wessmann v. Gittens*, 160 F.3d 790 (1st Cir. 1998); *Tuttle v. Arlington County School Board*, 195 F.3d 698 (4th Cir. 1999), *cert. dismissed*, 529 U.S. 1050, 120 S.Ct. 1552, 146 L.Ed.2d 364 (2000)? Are racial preferences in public school magnet programs, or other public school alternatives distinguishable from charter schools whose mission is to serve a particular racial or ethnic group?

2. Choice Schools and Desegregation Decrees

In light of the history of the use of tuition vouchers to fund private "segregation" academies, to what ex-

---

[97]*Tuttle v. Arlington County School Board.*

[98]Colorado Revised Statutes, sections 22-30.5-109 (2)(a) (1999); 22-30.5-103 (1999).

tent should tuition voucher programs be permitted in school districts under school desegregation decrees? Approximately 500 school districts are currently subject to court-ordered desegregation, Brown-Nagin, *supra* at 779, n.103. Should charter schools be established without considering their impact on school districts under court order? *See Berry v. School District of City of Benton Harbor*, 56 F.Supp.2d 866 (W.D. Mich. 1999); *Beaufort County Board of Educ. v. Lighthouse Charter School Committee*, 516 S.E.2d 655 (S.C. 1999). Or are such schools, even if predominantly one-race, merely the product of individual, private choices? *See Freeman v. Pitts*, 503 U.S. 467, 112 S.Ct. 1430, 118 L.Ed.2d 108 (1992); *Board of Education of Oklahoma City Public Schools v. Dowell*, 498 U.S. 237, 111 S.Ct. 360, 112 L.Ed.2d 715 (1991). *See* Parker, "The Color of Choice: Race and Charter Schools," 75 *Tulane L. Rev.* 563, 615-624 (2001).

3. Racial Balance Provisions

As noted in Professor Levin's article, a number of states have included racial balance requirements in their charter school legislation. Are these provisions unconstitutional or is the state's objective of diversity sufficiently compelling to withstand a constitutional challenge? *See* Parker, *supra*. Does the requirement of racial balance defeat the purpose of allowing charter schools the flexibility to design their own curriculum to attract students who feel that the public school curriculum is not responsive to their needs or interests? Should it make a difference on either constitutional or policy grounds whether the school serves predominantly African American or Hispanic students or has attracted a student body that is predominantly white? *Compare Berry v. School District of City of Benton Harbor*, 56 F.Supp.2d 866 (W.D. Mich. 1999) with *Beaufort County Board of Educ. v. Lighthouse Charter School Committee*, 516 S.E.2d 655 (S.C. 1999). *See* Brown-Nagin, *supra* at 834–836, arguing for an "asymmetrical and fact-intensive analysis" in applying the Equal Protection Clause to both racial balance provisions and to schools attended predominantly by racial minorities. In other words, under her approach, rational relation review would apply to "historically disfavored' groups, but heightened scrutiny would apply to "charter schools whose student bodies are overwhelmingly white." Do you agree? Are the courts likely to adopt this approach? *See Adarand Constructors, Inc. v. Pena*, 515 U.S.

200, 115 S.Ct.2097, 132 L.Ed.2d 158 (1995), *overruling Metro Broadcasting, Inc. v. Federal Communications Commission*, 497 U.S. 547, 110 S.Ct. 2997, 111 L.Ed.2d 445 (1990).

The Office for Civil Rights of the U.S. Department of Education has issued a document noting that "the civil rights principles that apply to charter schools are the same principles that apply to all public schools." U.S. Department of Education, Office for Civil Rights, *Applying Federal Civil Rights Law to Public Charter Schools* (May, 2000). This publication includes issues relating to recruitment and admissions, schools affected by desegregation plans or court orders, students with disabilities, and students who are limited-English proficient. Furthermore, according to OCR, a charter school may take race into account in making decisions if used for such compelling interests as remedying discrimination, promoting the educational benefits of diversity, or reducing minority-group isolation. OCR adds a caveat, however: "the state of the law in this area is undergoing close examination by the courts" and the legal standard may vary depending upon state law and the particular federal circuit. *Id.* at 7.

4. The Case of African American Academies

A number of urban school districts, including Detroit, Baltimore, Chicago, Milwaukee, Minneapolis, Cleveland, and Seattle, have established African American schools or classes, most of them focusing on male students who are at risk of dropping out of school. These schools, sometimes called immersion schools, often feature an African-centered curriculum, including the Swahili language, black history, literature by black authors, and even in science and math, an emphasis on the contributions of blacks. They may also include "rites of passage" ceremonies and self-esteem classes. The schools stress positive behavior and strict discipline, foster high expectations for achievement, and emphasize racial pride. Most, if not all, of the teachers are African American, with a substantially higher proportion of males than at most schools, who can serve as positive role models to students, many of whom are from female-headed households. Numerous articles have been written about the educational and legal implications of these schools and classes. *See, e.g.,* Cummings, "All-Male Black Schools: Equal Protection, The New Separatism and *Brown v. Board of Education*,"

20 *Hastings Const. L. Q.* 725 (1993); Brown, "After the Desegregation Era: The Legal Dilemma Posed by Race and Education," 37 *St. Louis U. L. J.* 897 (1993); Comment, "Black Male Academies: Re-Examining the Strategy of Integration," 42 *Buff. L. Rev.* 829 (1994); Note, "Immersed in an Educational Crisis: Alternative Programs for African-American Males," 45 *Stan. L. Rev.* 1099 (1993); Note, "All Things Not Being Equal: The Case for Race Separate Schools," 43 *Case W. Res. L. Rev.* 591 (1993); Note, "The Constitutionality of African-American Male Schools and Programs," 24 *Colum. Hum. Rts. L. Rev.* 239 (1993); Comment, "All-Male Black Schools and the Equal Protection Clause: A Step Forward Toward Education," 66 *Tul. L. Rev.* 2003 (1992); Note, "Creating Space for Racial Difference: The Case for African-American Schools," 27 *Harv. Civ. Rts–Civ. Lib. L. Rev.* 187 (1992); Green, "The Academy: All-Male Education a Successful Experiment in City Schools," *The Hartford Courant*, June 16, 1996, at A1; Jones, "A Place All Their Own: Detroit Uses Special Academies to Help Black Boys Overcome Challenges," *The Plain Dealer*, April 23, 1996, at 1A.

a. Application of the Equal Protection Clause. These schools are "choice" alternatives, created by public school districts as a voluntary alternative to the assigned public school, but do not fall under provisions of charter school legislation. Such schools are more like magnet schools than charter schools. Although most of these schools or classes have been located in predominantly black areas, to what extent would these schools survive a constitutional challenge if admission is restricted to African American students who apply to the school? Is it relevant that research has shown that African Americans "suffer when schools teach only the accomplishments of white civilization, while neglecting the accomplishments of both Africans and African Americans"? Note, "Creating Space for Racial Difference: The Case for African-American Schools," 27 *Harv. Civ. Rts–Civ. Lib. L. Rev.* 187, 213 (1992).

A school limited to African-Americans is a response to a dominant culture that both defines African-American culture as deviant and presumes its own neutrality. African-Americans can remedy their cultural victimization by defining their own cultural identity: "We must recapture our heritage and our identity if we are ever to liberate ourselves from the bonds of white supremacy" [quoting Malcolm X, *By Any Means Neces-*

sary (1970)]. To restore and preserve the specificity of black culture, African-Americans may need to create their own institutions and exclude those who do not share their specificity. Separate institutions strengthen group bonds and insulate individuals from those who assert the dominance of their culture.

Id. at 214–215. Proponents of these schools and classes, in which enrollment is completely voluntary, argue that they are necessary to respond to the crisis facing African American males in terms of the disproportionate numbers in the criminal or juvenile justice systems, and the high homicide, unemployment, and dropout rates. Is this a compelling justification and are the means sufficiently narrowly tailored to meet the strict scrutiny standard of equal protection review? Compare some of the arguments made on behalf of the constitutionality of African American academies in Comment, "All-Male Black Schools and the Equal Protection Clause: A Step Forward Toward Education," 66 *Tul. L. Rev.* 2003 (1992); Note, "Creating Space for Racial Difference: The Case for African-American Schools," 27 *Harv. Civ. Rts–Civ. Lib. L. Rev.* 187 (1992) with the arguments against the constitutionality of such racially separate schools in Cummings, "All-Male Black Schools: Equal Protection, The New Separatism and *Brown v. Board of Education*," 20 *Hastings Const. L. Q.* 725 (1993). *See also* Parker, *supra.* Even if attendance of the students at these schools is deemed constitutional, is it constitutional for school authorities to assign an all–African American teaching and administrative staff to those schools?

b. A Milliken II *Remedy?* Could such schools or programs, in districts undergoing court-ordered desegregation, be justified under *Milliken II* as remedial programs designed to enhance the academic performance of the victims of prior unlawful segregation? *Milliken v. Bradley*, 433 U.S. 267, 97 S.Ct. 2749, 53 L.Ed.2d 745 (1977). Would this justification apply to those not previously subjected to intentional segregation?

c. Constitutional Right to a Curriculum Reflecting African American or Other Minority Group Culture. On what basis might African American or other minority groups claim a constitutional right to an alternative school on the ground that the curriculum offered in the public schools is systematically biased against them, in that it "distorts and demeans the role of African Americans and excludes the existence, contributions, and participation of African Americans in the various aspects of world and American culture, sciences, history, arts and other areas of human endeavor"? In *Grimes v. Sobol*, 832 F.Supp. 704 (S.D.N.Y. 1993), African American plaintiffs argued that such a public school curriculum resulted in emotional and psychological harm, affecting their self-esteem and ability to learn, and thus denied them an equal educational opportunity in violation of the Equal Protection Clause and Title VI of the Civil Rights Act. With regard to the Title VI claim, defendants responded that 34 C.F.R. §100.3(b)(2), implementing Title VI, which prohibits the use of "criteria or methods of administration" that have a racially discriminatory effect does not extend to the content of the curriculum. Do you agree? *See also Guadalupe Organization, Inc. v. Tempe Elementary School Dist.*, 587 F.2d 1022 (9th Cir. 1978) (denying claim of students of Mexican-American and Yaqui Indian origin that the failure to reflect their language, culture, and historical contributions violated the Equal Protection Clause and Title VI and its regulations). *See* Neely, "Pedagogy of Culturally Biased Curriculum in Public Education: An Emancipatory Paradigm for Afrocentric Educational Initiatives," 23 *Cap. U. L. Rev.* 131, 146–147, 149 (1994) (plaintiffs in *Grimes* should have argued that New York's failure to remove culturally biased curriculum content violated First Amendment rights of all children in the city's public schools, and not just African American children).

d. Problem. The Jefferson Davis Middle School was established as an alternative school within a predominantly African American school district that emphasizes an Afrocentric curriculum. The Davis school, by contrast, emphasizes Anglo-Saxon history and culture, and Western European literature and philosophy. What arguments could you make as to why a court should find this school unconstitutional, and yet find constitutional the establishment of the Malcolm X African-American Academy as an alternative school of choice in a school district with a curriculum that is primarily Eurocentric?

e. The Single-Sex Aspect. Most of the African American academies have been all-male schools. In *Garrett v. Board of Education of the School District of the City of Detroit*, 775 F.Supp. 1004 (E.D. Mich. 1991), a district court found that the African American male academies established by the Detroit Board of Education violated the Equal Protection Clause, under the intermediate scrutiny applied to gender classifications. Although the objective of combating unemployment, dropout, and homicide rates among urban males was an important governmental interest, the exclusion of females was not substantially related to that interest. The court found no evidence "that the educational system is failing urban males because females attend schools with males." *Id.* at 1008. The court also found that the all-male schools violated Title IX of the Education Act Amendments of 1972. *See* Truely and Davis, "Public Education Programs for African-American Males: A Gender Equity Perspective," 21 *N.Y.U. Rev. L. & Soc. Change* 725 (1995); Note, " 'Separate But Equal' Revisited: The Detroit Male Academies Case," 1992/92 *Ann. Surv. Am. L.* 85; Comment, " Public Education: An Inner-City Crisis! Single-Sex Schools: An Inner-City Answer?" 42 *Emory L. J.* 591 (1993). As a result of *Garrett*, Detroit school authorities opened the schools to girls. However, few girls have applied. *See* Jones, "A Place All Their Own: Detroit Uses Special Academies to Help Black Boys Overcome Challenges," *The Plain Dealer*, April 23, 1996, at 1A.

Equality and Difference: The Special Challenges of Gender Equity

I. INTRODUCTION

Although American public schools are for the most part coeducational institutions, differences in the treatment of male and female students have long been commonplace. Some differences such as the exclusion of women from school sports teams are obvious. Others are more subtle—textbooks that define male and female roles differently and teachers who treat boys and girls differently. M. Sadker and D. Sadker, *Failing at Fairness: How America's Schools Cheat Girls* (1994); American Association of University Women, *How Schools Shortchange Girls* (1992).

During the 1970s, gender-based differentiation in education, like gender-based differentiation generally, became the subject of litigation. Differentiation in the treatment of married or pregnant students, gender-specific curricular restrictions, and sex-differentiated rules for athletic participation have each been said to deny equal opportunity to women; the permissibility of "separate but equal" educational opportunity afforded in single-sex schools and programs has also been questioned.

Many of these issues were addressed by Congress in Title IX of the 1972 Education Amendments. Since the passage of that Act, the nonjudicial branches have become primary definers and enforcers of equal educational opportunity with respect to gender. Yet, as one might anticipate, the implementation effort has hardly been unproblematic. At the outset, particularly in the realm of athletics, opposition was substantial and enforcement consequently vacillating. In addition, the development of protections against sexual harassment has been highly controversial. Title IX also leaves unresolved (or, from the viewpoint of the advocate, it unsatisfactorily resolves) many of the central educational policy issues concerning gender and schooling. Sexism in texts, for instance, goes deliberately unaddressed in the federal law. Moreover, it is unclear whether antidiscrimination provisions offer any protection to students who face hostile treatment in schools based on sexual orientation. Even after the passage of Title IX, these issues have been raised in constitutional litigation.

Just as race raises complicated questions about the meaning of equality, gender differences pose troubling questions about assimilation to male norms and respect for the unique history and perspectives of women. These issues are made even more difficult by ongoing uncertainty about the role of biology and socialization in the development of gender differences.

"Reconstructing Sexual Equality"
C. Littleton, 75 *California Law Review* 1279, 1287–1304 (1987).© 1987 by California Law Review, Inc.

* * *

A. Legal Equality

Legal concern with sexual equality is very recent. It developed primarily in response to powerful analogies between the situation of racial minorities, especially Blacks as a class, and the situation of women.

Those analogies were and are highly problematic, both theoretically and historically, but they supported the claim that women must necessarily be included within the equality-of-persons norm embedded in the political and social framework of this society, and specifically articulated in the equal protection clause of the fourteenth amendment.

Although enacted with the specific situation of Black people—actually of Black men—in mind, the equal protection clause meant very little to its purported beneficiaries until the notion of "separate spheres" was jettisoned. The paradigm example of separate spheres in the racial context is the 1896 decision of *Plessy v. Ferguson*,[50] where the Supreme Court upheld a state statute requiring segregation of Blacks and whites on railroad carriages. This notion was expressed in the opinion as "separate but equal"; theoretically at least, segregation was unsupportable where the facilities were not the same. However, this theoretical point did not gain practical significance until 1950, when, in *Sweatt v. Painter*,[51] the Supreme Court ordered a Black student admitted to an all-white law school on the ground that the Black law schools offered by the state did not have similar facilities.

The idea that Blacks and whites "naturally" inhabited separate social spheres was finally rejected in 1954 in the justly famous case of *Brown v. Board of Education*.[53] However controversial the various means of implementing that decision have been, its underlying rejection of separate spheres in the racial context remains surprisingly resilient. At the core of that rejection is the powerful notion that Black men are fundamentally the same as white men, and that it is irrational for such surface differences of skin color and physiognomy to carry any significant meaning, except perhaps an esthetic one (similar to, say, eye color or foot size).

The consistent message of racial equality analysis since *Brown* is that any disadvantages Black men face in participating equally with white men in this society are traceable to either irrational prejudice or socially imposed burdens growing out of previous prejudice. In other words, they face no natural handicaps and possess no natural significant differences.

Whether in fact this message has had a sufficient impact on the conditions of Black life in America is open to question, especially given the Supreme Court's unwillingness to match remedies to its brave ideals. Nevertheless, this message's significance for the legal recognition of other equality-based claims is indisputable.

The notion that women naturally inhabit a separate sphere lasted longer. As late as 1961, the Supreme Court was still using the "fact" that "woman is still regarded as the center of home and family life" as a rationale for legal decisions. Not until ten years later, in *Reed v. Reed*,[63] did the Court finally start to break down separate sexual spheres ideology. It has still never fully adopted the idea that women have *no* important natural differences from men. Thus, while the Court has held that a state may *not* automatically prefer men over women as estate administrators, because women are not naturally different from men with regard to estate administration, it has held that a state may automatically prefer men over women as prison guards, because women are naturally different from men with regard to prison guarding.

While separate spheres ideology has historically disadvantaged both Blacks and women, the nature of the disadvantage and the method of its imposition have differed substantially. It kept Blacks out of white law schools and white railway cars, while keeping white women at home and Black women invisible. Blacks were kept out of white society as a class; women were kept out of male society in public, but lived in intimate association with men in private. In this sense, then, Blacks were segregated together, while women were segregated individually.

Similarly, the breakdown of separate spheres has proceeded differently for the two classes. At least in theory, it has meant a rejection of *any* natural differences between races, but it has meant a rejection of only *some* natural differences between sexes. The difference between *Lochner v. New York*,[71] in which the Supreme Court struck down protective legislation for workers on "freedom of contract" grounds, and *Muller v. Oregon*,[72] in which the Court upheld similar legislation for women, was the perceived inca-

---

[50]163 U.S. 537 (1896).

[51]339 U.S. 629 (1950).

[53]347 U.S. 483 (1954).

[63]404 U.S. 71 (1971) (striking down a statutory preference for male estate administrators).

[71]198 U.S. 45 (1905).

[72]208 U.S. 412 (1908).

pacity of women—a perception that even today continues to justify the exclusion of women from some areas of social life. It is little wonder, then, that the spectre of a return to separate spheres ideology looms so large in any discussion of what feminists should do on behalf of women.

B. Feminist Responses

Feminist legal theory has been primarily reactive, responding to the development of legal racial equality theory. The form of response, however, has varied. One response has been to attempt to equate legal treatment of sex with that of race and deny that there are in fact any significant natural differences between women and men; in other words, to consider the two sexes symmetrically located with regard to *any* issue, norm, or rule. This response, which I term the "symmetrical" approach, classifies asymmetries as illusions, "overbroad generalizations," or temporary glitches that will disappear with a little behavior modification. A competing response rejects this analogy, accepting that women and men are or may be "different," and that women and men are often asymmetrically located in society. This response, which I term the "asymmetrical" approach, rejects the notion that all gender differences are likely to disappear, or even that they should.

1. Symmetrical Models of Sexual Equality.

Feminist theorists frequently take the symmetrical approach to sexual equality, not as an ideal, but as the only way to avoid returning to separate spheres ideology. For example, in her highly compelling defense of symmetry in the law, Wendy Williams warns that "we can't have it both ways, we need to think carefully about which way we want to have it."[78]

There are two models of the symmetrical vision—referred to here as "assimilation" and "androgyny." Assimilation, the model most often accepted by the courts, is based on the notion that women, given the chance, really are or could be just like men. Therefore, the argument runs, the law should require social institutions to treat women as they already treat men—requiring, for example, that the professions admit women to the extent they are "qualified," but also insisting that women who enter time-demanding professions such as the practice of law sacrifice relationships (especially with their children) to the same extent that male lawyers have been forced to do.

Androgyny, the second symmetrical model, also posits that women and men are, or at least could be, very much like each other, but argues that equality requires institutions to pick some golden mean between the two and treat both sexes as androgynous persons would be treated. However, given that all of our institutions, work habits, and pay scales were formulated without the benefit of substantial numbers of androgynous persons, androgynous symmetry is difficult to conceptualize, and might require very substantial restructuring of many public and private institutions. In order to be truly androgynous within a symmetrical framework, social institutions must find a single norm that works equally well for all gendered characteristics. Part of my discomfort with androgynous models is that they depend on "meeting in the middle," while I distrust the ability of any person, and especially any court, to value women enough to find the "middle." Moreover, the problems involved in determining such a norm for even one institution are staggering. At what height should a conveyor belt be set in order to satisfy a symmetrical androgynous ideal?

Symmetry appears to have great appeal for the legal system, and this is not surprising. The hornbook definition of equal protection is "that those who are similarly situated be similarly treated," and many courts, following the Supreme Court's lead, have held that absent a showing of similarity, strict scrutiny is simply inapplicable. Symmetrical analysis also has great appeal for liberal men, to whom it appears to offer a share in the feminist enterprise. If perceived difference between the sexes is only the result of overly rigid sex roles, then men's liberty is at stake too. Ending this form of sexual inequality could free men to express their "feminine" side, just as it frees women to express their "masculine" side.

2. Asymmetrical Models of Sexual Equality.

Asymmetrical approaches to sexual equality take the position that difference should not be ignored or eradicated. Rather, they argue that any sexually equal society must somehow deal with difference, problematic as that may be. Asymmetrical approaches include "special rights," "accommodation," "acceptance," and "empowerment."

---

[78]Williams, "The Equality Crisis," *supra* note 27 [Williams, "The Equality Crisis: Some Reflections on Culture, Courts and Feminism," 7 *Women's Rts. L. Rep.* 175 (1982)], at 196. . . .

The special rights model affirms that women and men *are* different, and asserts that cultural differences, such as childrearing roles, are rooted in biological ones, such as reproduction. Therefore, it states, society must take account of these differences and ensure that women are not punished for them. This approach, sometimes referred to as a "bivalent" model, is closest to the "special treatment" pole of the asymmetrical/symmetrical equality debate. Elizabeth Wolgast, a major proponent of special rights, argues that women cannot be men's "equals" because equality by definition requires sameness. Instead of equality, she suggests seeking justice, claiming special rights for women based on their special needs.

The second asymmetrical model, accommodation, agrees that differential treatment of biological differences (such as pregnancy, and perhaps breastfeeding) is necessary, but argues that cultural or hard-to-classify differences (such as career interests and skills) should be treated under an equal treatment or androgynous model. Examples of accommodation models include Sylvia Law's approach to issues of reproductive biology[96] and Herma Hill Kay's "episodic" approach to the condition of pregnancy.[97] These approaches could also be characterized as "symmetry, with concessions to asymmetry where necessary." The accommodationists limit the asymmetry in their models to biological differences because, like Williams, they fear a return to separate spheres ideology should asymmetrical theory go too far.

My own attempt to grapple with difference, which I call an "acceptance" model, is essentially asymmetrical. While not endorsing the notion that cultural differences between the sexes are biologically determined, it does recognize and attempt to deal with both biological and social differences. Acceptance does not view sex differences as problematic per se, but rather focuses on the ways in which differences are permitted to justify inequality. It asserts that eliminating the unequal consequences of sex differences is more important than debating whether such differences are "real," or even trying to eliminate them altogether.

Unlike the accommodationists, who would limit asymmetrical analysis to purely biological differences, my proposal also requires equal acceptance of cultural differences. The reasons for this are twofold. First, the distinction between biological and cultural, while useful analytically, is itself culturally based. Second, the inequality experienced by women is often presented as a necessary consequence of cultural rather than of biological difference. If, for instance, women do in fact "choose" to become nurses rather than real estate appraisers, it is not because of any biological imperative. Yet, regardless of the reasons for the choice, they certainly do not choose to be paid less. It is the *consequences* of gendered difference, and not its sources, that equal acceptance addresses.

If, as it appears from [Carol] Gilligan's studies [of the moral development of boys and girls],[101] women and men tend to develop somewhat differently in terms of their values and inclinations, *each* of these modes of development must be equally valid and valuable. In our desire for equality, we should not be forced to jettison either; rather, we should find some way to value both. That such different modes do not perfectly correspond to biological sex does not prevent them from being typed socially as "male" and "female," and neither should it prevent us from demanding that they be equally valued. Thus, if women currently tend to assume primary responsibility for childrearing, we should not ignore that fact in an attempt to prefigure the rosy day when parenting is fully shared. We should instead figure out how to assure that equal resources, status, and access to social decisionmaking flow to those women (and few men) who engage in this socially female behavior.

The focus of equality as acceptance, therefore, is not on the question of whether *women* are different, but rather on the question of how the social fact of gender asymmetry can be dealt with so as to create some symmetry in the lived-out experience of all members of the community. I do not think it matters so much whether differences are "natural" or not; they are built into our structures and selves in either event. As social facts, differences are created by the interaction of person with person or person with institution; they inhere in the relationship, not in the person. On this view, the function of equality is to make gender differences, perceived or actual, cost-

---

[96]Law, "Rethinking Sex and the Constitution," 132 *U. Pa. L. Rev.* 955, 1007–13 (1984) (calling for equal treatment in all areas except reproduction, where an analysis based on empowerment approach . . . should be adopted).

[97]Kay, "Equality and Difference: The Case of Pregnancy," 1 *Berkeley Women's L.J.* 1, 27–37 (1985) (sex differences should be ignored, except during the time a female is actually pregnant).

[101]*See* C. Gilligan, *supra* note 11 [C. Gilligan, *In a Different Voice* (1982)].

less relative to each other, so that anyone may follow a male, female, or androgynous lifestyle according to their natural inclination or choice without being punished for following a female lifestyle or rewarded for following a male one.

* * *

The foregoing asymmetrical models, including my own, share the notion that, regardless of their differences, women and men must be treated as full members of society. Each model acknowledges that women may need treatment different than that accorded to men in order to effectuate their membership in important spheres of social life; all would allow at least some such claims, although on very different bases, and probably in very different circumstances.

A final asymmetrical approach, "empowerment," rejects difference altogether as a relevant subject of inquiry. In its strongest form, empowerment claims that the subordination of women to men has itself constructed the sexes, and their differences. For example, Catherine MacKinnon argues:

> [I]t makes a lot of sense that women might have a somewhat distinctive perspective on social life. We may or may not speak in a different voice—I think that the voice that we have been said to speak in is in fact in large part the 'feminine' voice, the voice of the victim speaking without consciousness. But when we understand that women are *forced* into this situation of inequality, it makes a lot of sense that we should want to negotiate, since we lose conflicts. It makes a lot of sense that we should want to urge values of care, because it is what we have been valued for. We have had little choice but to be valued this way.[118]

A somewhat weaker version of the claim is that we simply do not and cannot know whether there are any important differences between the sexes that have not been created by the dynamic of domination and subordination. In either event, the argument runs, we should forget about the question of differences and focus directly on subordination and domination. If a law, practice, or policy contributes to the subordination of women or their domination by men, it violates equality. If it empowers women or contributes to the breakdown of male domination, it enhances equality.

The reconceptualization of equality as antidomination, like the model of equality as acceptance, at-

tempts to respond directly to the concrete and lived-out experience of women. Like other asymmetrical models, it allows different treatment of women and men when necessary to effectuate its overall goal of ending women's subordination. However, it differs substantially from the acceptance model in its rejection of the membership, belonging, and participatory aspects of equality.

3. The Difference that Difference Makes.

Each of the several models of equality discussed above, if adopted, would have a quite different impact on the structure of society. If this society wholeheartedly embraced the symmetrical approach of assimilation—the point of view that "women are just like men"—little would need to be changed in our economic or political institutions except to get rid of lingering traces of irrational prejudice, such as an occasional employer's preference for male employees. In contrast, if society adopted the androgyny model, which views both women and men as bent out of shape by current sex roles and requires both to conform to an androgynous model, it would have to alter radically its methods of resource distribution. In the employment context, this might mean wholesale revamping of methods for determining the "best person for the job." Thus, while assimilation would merely require law firms to hire women who have managed to get the same credentials as the men they have traditionally hired, androgyny might insist that the firm hire only those persons with credentials that would be possessed by someone neither "socially male" nor "socially female."

If society adopted an asymmetrical approach such as the accommodation model, no radical restructuring would be necessary. Government would need only insist that women be given what they need to resemble men, such as time off to have babies and the freedom to return to work on the same rung of the ladder as their male counterparts. If, however, society adopted the model of equality as acceptance, which seeks to make difference costless, it might additionally insist that women and men who opt for socially female occupations, such as child-rearing, be compensated at a rate similar to those women and men who opt for socially male occupations, such as legal practice. Alternatively, such occupations might be restructured to

---

[118]"Feminist Discourse," *supra* note 13 [DuBois, Dunlap Gilligan, MacKinnon & Menkel-Meadow, "Feminist Discourse, Moral Values, and the Law—A Conversation," 34 *Buffalo L. Rev.* 11, 40–41 (1985)], at 27 . . . .

make them equally accessible to those whose behavior is culturally coded "male" or "female."

* * *

There must be choices beyond those of ignoring difference or accepting inequality. So long as difference itself is so expensive in the coin of equality, we approach the variety of human experience with blinders on. Perhaps if difference were not so costly, we, as feminists, could think about it more clearly. Perhaps if equality did not require uniformity, we, as women, could demand it less ambivalently.

* * *

NOTES AND QUESTIONS

1. Race and Gender Compared

Is the law obligated to be gender-blind as it is color-blind? Are there differences between men and women that policymakers need to acknowledge? If so, what are they, and can courts, legislatures, and government administrators be trusted to recognize them? Can the law at most make minor accommodations of these differences under an equality principle? Why or why not?

2. Biological and Social Differences

Are there reasons to distinguish between differences that are biological and those that are cultural? Is Littleton correct that the distinction is theoretically useful but practically impossible to apply in a consistent and coherent way? Are there dangers of reifying gender that come with legal recognition of both biological and social differences?

II. THE SEARCH FOR A CONSTITUTIONAL STANDARD

Sex-distinguishing legislation is historically pervasive. *See* J. Hoff, *Law, Gender, and Injustice: A Legal History of U.S. Women* (1991). Numerous state and federal laws have treated women and men differently with respect to social conduct, familial responsibility, obligations of citizenship (for example, service in the armed forces), access to jobs and public accommodations, labor regulations, and criminal sentencing. *See* D. Rhode, *Speaking of Sex: The Denial of Gender Inequality* (1997). This body of legislation was premised either on the presumed need to protect women or on assumed es-

sential gender-specific differences in ability. *See* Case, "Disaggregating Gender from Sex and Sexual Orientation: The Effeminate Man in the Law and Feminist Jurisprudence," 105 *Yale L.J.* 1, 38 (1995) (first-generation sex stereotyping relied on blanket assumptions about men and women and brooked no special treatment for exceptional cases).

A. From Deference to Heightened Scrutiny

Historically, judicial review of challenges to such sex distinctions was characterized "by two prominent features: a vague but strong substantive belief in women's separate place, and an extraordinary methodological casualness in reviewing state legislation based on such stereotypical views of women." Brown, et al., "The Equal Rights Amendment: A Constitutional Basis for Equal Rights for Women," 80 *Yale L.J.* 871, 876 (1971). In *Goesaert v. Cleary*, 335 U.S. 464, 69 S.Ct. 198, 93 L.Ed. 163 (1948), for example, the Supreme Court upheld a Michigan statute that barred a woman from being licensed as a bartender unless she was "the wife or daughter of the male owner of a licensed liquor establishment." The *Goesaert* Court, finding that the subject "need not detain us long," applied the "reasonable classification" test and virtually ignored the obvious effect of the statute—monopolization of the bartending profession for men. In *Hoyt v. Florida*, 368 U.S. 57, 82 S.Ct. 159, 7 L.Ed.2d 118 (1961) (overruled in *Taylor v. Louisiana*, 419 U.S. 522, 95 S.Ct. 692, 42 L.Ed.2d 690 [1975]), the Court adopted the same approach in upholding legislation that excluded women from jury service unless they voluntarily applied. "We cannot say that it is constitutionally impermissible for a state, acting in pursuit of the general welfare, to conclude that a woman should be relieved from the civic duty of jury service unless she herself determines that such service is consistent with her own special responsibilities." 368 U.S. at 62, 82 S.Ct. at 162.

Beginning with its decision in *Reed v. Reed*, 404 U.S. 71, 92 S.Ct. 251, 30 L.Ed.2d 225 (1971), the Supreme Court looked more carefully at claims of gender discrimination. In *Reed*, the Court purported to apply the traditional equal protection test, concluding that a state probate code provision which gave preference to men as administrators of the estates of those dying intestate served no rational purpose. But the Court tacitly rejected the state's assertion that "men are as a rule more conversant with business affairs than . . . women," and in doing so actually applied a standard of review less deferential to the state than mere rationality. *See generally* Note, "Legislative Purpose, Rationality, and Equal Protection," 82 *Yale L.J.* 123, 150–51 (1972). In *Frontiero v. Richardson*, 411 U.S. 677, 93 S.Ct. 1764, 36 L.Ed.2d 583 (1973), a plurality of the Court was willing to equate gender with race for purposes of equal protection, defining both as constitutionally suspect classifications that require a "compelling" state justification. But the other four justices who concurred in the result would not go so far, and all of the justices have subsequently retreated from this position.

The standard that the Court presently applies in most gender cases was first announced in *Craig v. Boren*, 429 U.S. 190, 97 S.Ct. 451, 50 L.Ed.2d 397 (1976), in which the Court struck down an Oklahoma statute prohibiting the sale of 3.2% beer to males but not to females between the ages of eighteen and twenty-one: "Classifications by gender must serve *important* governmental objectives and must be *substantially* related to achievement of those objectives." 429 U.S. at 197, 97 S.Ct. at 456 (emphasis added). This standard is far more demanding than the conventional equal protection standard but less rigorous than that applied in the race cases. Its use has generally but not universally resulted in judicial rejection of legislation differentiating on the basis of sex. *Compare Califano v. Goldfarb*, 430 U.S. 199, 97 S.Ct. 1021, 51 L.Ed.2d 270 (1977) (widowers could not receive less protection than widows under the Federal Old-Age, Survivors, and Disability Benefits program), with *Califano v. Webster*, 430 U.S. 313, 97 S.Ct. 1192, 51 L.Ed.2d 360 (1977) (women could receive higher old-age insurance benefits than men). "Important" and "substantial" are, of course, judicial terms of art, that acquire meaning from a series of decisions over time. Other standards have, from time to time, contended for attention. *See, e.g., Rostker v. Goldberg*, 453 U.S. 57, 101 S.Ct. 2646, 69 L.Ed.2d 478 (1981) and *Michael M. v. Superior Court of Sonoma County*, 450 U.S. 464, 101 S.Ct. 1200, 67 L.Ed.2d 437 (1981) (are men and women "similarly situated" with respect to the aim of the law?); *Mississippi University for Women v. Hogan*, 458 U.S. 718, 102 S.Ct. 3331, 73 L.Ed.2d 1090 (1982) (an "exceedingly persuasive justification" for sex-based distinctions required). *See* Williams, "The Equality Crisis: Some Reflections on Culture, Courts and Feminism," 7 *Women's Rights Law Reporter* 175 (1982).

The Supreme Court's opinions left several central issues open. Although the Court in *Boren* speaks of classifications based on gender and thus suggests that laws disadvantaging women or men are equally problematic, the extent to which women can be provided with special benefits, either to offset or compensate for past sex-based discrimination, has remained unclear. *See Johnson v. Transportation Agency*, 480 U.S. 616, 107 S.Ct. 1442, 94 L.Ed.2d 615 (1987); *Califano v. Webster*, 430 U.S. 313, 97 S.Ct. 1192, 51 L.Ed.2d 360 (1977); *Schlesinger v. Ballard*, 419 U.S. 498, 95 S.Ct. 572, 42 L.Ed.2d 610 (1975); *Kahn v. Shevin*, 416 U.S. 351, 94 S.Ct. 1734, 40 L.Ed.2d 189 (1974). Although this issue posed concerns comparable to affirmative action on behalf of racial minorities, the Court did not seriously try to reconcile its positions in the two spheres. *See* Berkeley, "Gender Based Affirmative Action: A Journey That Has Only Just Begun," 50 *Wash.U.J.Urb. & Contemp.L.* 353 (1996) (arguing that the Court has taken a strict view of race-based affirmative action but has left the treatment of gender-based affirmative action ambiguous).

The cases also failed to clarify how ostensibly gender-neutral actions that markedly disadvantage one sex—either because they are based on a sex-specific trait such as childbearing or because they provide special treatment to a predominantly single-sex group—were to be decided. *See Personnel Administrator of Massachusetts v. Feeney*, 442 U.S. 256, 99 S.Ct. 2282, 60 L.Ed.2d 870 (1979) (veterans); Kirp and Robyn, "Pregnancy, Justice, and the Justices," 57 *Tex.L.Rev.* 947 (1979). In 1994, Congress passed the Pregnancy Discrimination Act to clarify protections for pregnant employees under Title VII. 42 U.S.C. § 2000e(k) (1994). The Family and Medical Leave Act, passed the same year, also affords limited protection to women who take unpaid leave to care for young children. 29 U.S.C. § 2612(a)(1)(A) (1994).

The analogy between race and sex deserves some attention. Even though the analogy is not fully embraced in *Boren*, that opinion indicates that sex-based classifications are offensive nonetheless. Consider the plurality opinion in *Frontiero*, which argues that the two should be legally indistinguishable:

> There can be no doubt that our nation has had a long and unfortunate history of sex discrimination. Traditionally, such discrimination was rationalized by an attitude of "romantic paternalism" which, in practical effect, put women not on a pedestal, but in a cage. . . .
>
> As a result of notions such as these, our statute books gradually became laden with gross, stereotypical

distinctions between the sexes and, indeed, throughout much of the nineteenth century the position of women in our society was, in many respects, comparable to that of blacks under the pre–Civil War slave codes. Neither slaves nor women could hold office, serve on juries, or bring suit in their own names, and married women traditionally were denied the legal capacity to hold or convey property or to serve as legal guardians of their own children. . . . And although blacks were guaranteed the right to vote in 1870, women were denied even that right—which is itself "preservative of other basic civil and political rights"—until adoption [of] the Nineteenth Amendment half a century later.

It is true, of course, that the position of women in America has improved markedly in recent decades. Nevertheless, it can hardly be doubted that, in part because of the high visibility of the sex characteristic, women still face pervasive, although at times more subtle, discrimination in our educational institutions, on the job market and, perhaps most conspicuously, in the political arena. . . .

Moreover, since sex, like race and national origin, is an immutable characteristic determined solely by the accident of birth, the imposition of special disabilities upon the members of a particular sex because of their sex would seem to violate "the basic concept of our system that legal burdens should bear some relationship to individual responsibility. . . ." *Weber v. Aetna Casualty and Surety Co.*, 406 U.S. 164, 175, 92 S.Ct. 1400, 1406, 31 L.Ed.2d 768 (1972). And what differentiates sex from such nonsuspect statuses as intelligence or physical disability, and aligns it with the recognized suspect criteria, is that the sex characteristic frequently bears no relation to ability to perform or contribute to society. As a result, statutory distinctions between the sexes often have the effect of invidiously relegating the entire class of females to inferior legal status without regard to the actual capabilities of its individual members.

We might also note that, over the past decade, Congress has itself manifested an increasing sensitivity to sex-based classifications. In Title VII of the Civil Rights Act of 1964, for example, Congress expressly declared that no employer, labor union, or other organization subject to the provisions of the act shall discriminate against any individual on the basis of "race, color, religion, sex, or national origin." Similarly, the Equal Pay Act of 1963 provides that no employer covered by the act "shall discriminate . . . between employees on the basis of sex." And § 1 of the Equal Rights Amendment, passed by Congress on March 22, 1972, and submitted to the legislatures of the states for ratification, declares that "equality of rights under the law shall not be denied or abridged by the United States or by any state on account of sex." Thus, Congress has itself concluded that classifications based upon sex are inherently invidious, and this conclusion of a coequal branch of government

is not without significance to the question presently under consideration. . . .

411 U.S. 677, 684–88 (1973).

How persuasive is this reasoning? Consider the following observations in Rossi, "Sex Equality: The Beginning of Ideology," 29 *Humanist* 3, 4–5 (1969):

. . . [T]here are also fundamental differences between sex as a category of social inequality and the categories of race, religion, or ethnicity. . . .

In the case of race, religion, and ethnicity, we are literally dealing with minority groups in the American population, whether Mexican, Indian, Jewish, Catholic, or black. This is not the case for sex, since women are actually a numerical majority in the population.

While the potential is present for numerical strength to press for the removal of inequalities, this is counterbalanced by other ways in which women are prevented from effectively utilizing their numerical strength. . . . [Because] women are for the most part *evenly distributed throughout the population* [, they] can exert political pressure in segmental roles as consumers, workers, New Yorkers, or the aged; but not as a cohesive political group based on sex solidarity.

Age and sex are the earliest social categories an individual learns. The differentiation between mother and father, or parent and child, is learned at a tender, formative stage of life; and consequently, we carry into adulthood a set of age and sex-role expectations that are extremely resistant to change.

As a result of early sex-role socialization, there is bound to be a lag between political and economic emancipation of women and the inner adjustment to equality of both men and women. Even in radical political movements, women have often had to caucus and fight for their acceptance as equal peers to men. Without such efforts on their own behalf, women are as likely to be "girl Friday" assistants in a radical movement espousing class and racial equality as they are in a business corporation, a labor union, or a conservative political party. . . .

Racial, ethnic, and religious conflict can reach an acute stage of political strife in the movement for equality, without affecting the solidarity of the families of blacks, whites, Jews, or Gentiles. Such strife may, in fact, increase the solidarity of these family units. A "we versus them" dichotomy does not cut into family units in the case of race, religion, or ethnicity as it does in the case of sex. Since women typically live in greater intimacy with men than they do with other women, there is potential conflict within family units when women press hard for sex equality. Their demands are on predominantly male legislators and employers in the public domain—husbands and fathers in the private sector. A married black woman can affiliate with an activist civil rights group with no implicit threat to her marriage. For a married woman to affiliate with an activist women's rights group might very well trigger tension in her marriage. . . . A large proportion of married women [who] have not combated sex discrimination . . . fear conflict with men, or benefit in terms of a comfortable high status in exchange for economic dependence upon their husbands. There are many more women in the middle class who benefit from sex inequality than there are blacks in the middle class who benefit from racial inequality.

Do Professor Rossi's observations suggest that sex and race discrimination should be treated as constitutionally different phenomena or that they are politically different phenomena? How should the Court have resolved this question—and with what implications for educational policy and law? *See also* D. Kirp, M. Yudof, and M. Franks, *Gender Justice* (1986); B. Barber, *Liberating Feminism* (1976); Wasserstrom, "Racism, Sexism, and Preferential Treatment: An Approach to the Topics," 24 *U.C.L.A.L.Rev.* 581 (1977); Wildman and Grillo, "Obscuring the Importance of Race: The Implications of Making Comparisons Between Racism and Sexism (or Other-Isms)," 1991 *Duke L.J.* 397 (later version appears in S. Wildman et al., *Privilege Revealed: How Invisible Preference Undermines America* (1996)). *See generally* J. Ely, *Democracy and Distrust: A Theory of Judicial Review* 166–69 (1980).

B. The Limits of the Analogy Between Race and Sex: Sex-Segregated Programs and Institutions

Although educators cannot make student assignments based solely on race, some scholars and policymakers believe that assignments based on gender can be pedagogically beneficial. For a thorough discussion of the rise of coeducation in the United States and the second thoughts about its benefits that many feminists expressed, *see* D. Tyack and E. Hansot, *Learning Together: A History of Coeducation in American Schools* (1990). Indeed, when enacting a principle of nondiscrimination based on sex, Congress expressly exempted single-sex educational institutions from the statute's coverage. In some instances, teachers and administrators have expressed a desire to shelter women from male classmates so that they can excel. Policymakers have also claimed that limiting admissions only to women can compensate for past discrimination. The Court has proved unreceptive to these claims.

Mississippi University for Women v. Hogan
458 U.S. 718, 102 S.Ct. 3331, 73 L.Ed.2d 1090 (1982).

Justice O'Connor delivered the opinion of the Court.

This case presents the narrow issue of whether a state statute that excludes males from enrolling in a state-supported professional nursing school violates the Equal Protection Clause of the Fourteenth Amendment.

I

The facts are not in dispute. In 1884, the Mississippi legislature created the Mississippi Industrial Institute and College for the Education of White Girls of the State of Mississippi, now the oldest state-supported all-female college in the United States. 1884 Miss.Gen.Laws, Ch. XXX, § 6. The school, known today as Mississippi University for Women (MUW), has from its inception limited its enrollment to women.[1]

In 1971, MUW established a School of Nursing, initially offering a two-year associate degree. Three years later, the school instituted a four-year baccalaureate program in nursing and today also offers a graduate program. The School of Nursing has its own faculty and administrative officers and establishes its own criteria for admission.

Respondent, Joe Hogan, is a registered nurse but does not hold a baccalaureate degree in nursing. Since 1974, he has worked as a nursing supervisor in a medical center in Columbus, the city in which MUW is located. In 1979, Hogan applied for admission to the MUW School of Nursing's baccalaureate program. Although he was otherwise qualified, he was denied admission to the School of Nursing solely because of his sex. School officials informed him that he could audit the courses in which he was interested, but could not enroll for credit. . . .

Hogan filed an action in the United States District Court for the Northern District of Mississippi, claiming the single-sex admissions policy of MUW's School of Nursing violated the Equal Protection Clause of the Fourteenth Amendment. Hogan sought injunctive and declaratory relief, as well as compensatory damages.

---

[1] Mississippi maintains no other single-sex public university or college. Thus, we are not faced with the question of whether States can provide "separate but equal" undergraduate institutions for males and females. *Cf. Vorchheimer v. School District of Philadelphia*, 532 F.2d 880 (CA3 1975), aff'd by an equally divided court, 430 U.S. 703 (1977). . . .

Following a hearing, the District Court denied preliminary injunctive relief. . . . The court concluded that maintenance of MUW as a single-sex school bears a rational relationship to the state's legitimate interest "of providing the greatest practical range of educational opportunities for its female student population." . . . Furthermore, the court stated, the admissions policy is not arbitrary because providing single-sex schools is consistent with a respected, though by no means universally accepted, educational theory that single-sex education affords unique benefits to students. . . . Stating that the case presented no issue of fact, the court informed Hogan that it would enter summary judgment dismissing his claim unless he tendered a factual issue. When Hogan offered no further evidence, the District Court entered summary judgment in favor of the State. . . .

The Court of Appeals for the Fifth Circuit reversed, holding that, because the admissions policy discriminates on the basis of gender, the District Court improperly used a "rational relationship" test to judge the constitutionality of the policy. 646 F.2d 1116, 1118. Instead, the Court of Appeals stated, the proper test is whether the State has carried the heavier burden of showing that the gender-based classification is substantially related to an important governmental objective. . . .

On rehearing, the State contended that Congress, in enacting § 901(a)(5) of Title IX of the Education Amendments of 1972, Pub.L. 92-318, 86 Stat. 373, 20 U.S.C. § 1681 *et seq.*, expressly had authorized MUW to continue its single-sex admissions policy by exempting public undergraduate institutions that traditionally have used single-sex

admissions policies from the gender discrimination prohibition of Title IX.[5] Through that provision, the State argued, Congress limited the reach of the Fourteenth Amendment by exercising its power under § 5 of the Amendment.[6] The Court of Appeals rejected the argument, holding that § 5 of the Fourteenth Amendment does not grant Congress power to authorize States to maintain practices otherwise violative of the Amendment. 653 F.2d 223.

We granted certiorari, . . . and now affirm the judgment of the Court of Appeals.[7]

II

We begin our analysis aided by several firmly established principles. Because the challenged policy expressly discriminates among applicants on the basis of gender, it is subject to scrutiny under the Equal Protection Clause of the Fourteenth Amendment. *Reed v. Reed*, 404 U.S. 71, 75 . . . (1971). That this statute discriminates against males rather than against females does not exempt it from scrutiny or reduce the standard of review.[8] *Caban v. Mohammed*, 441 U.S. 380, 394 . . . (1979); *Orr v. Orr*, 440 U.S. 268, 279 . . . (1979). Our decisions also establish that the party seeking to uphold a statute that classifies individuals on the basis of their gender must carry the burden of showing an "exceedingly persuasive justification" for the classification. *Kirchberg v. Feenstra*, 450 U.S. 455, 461 . . . (1981); *Personnel Administrator of Massachusetts v. Feeney*, 442 U.S. 256, 273 . . . (1979). The burden is met only by showing at least that the classification serves "impor-

[5]Section 901(a) of Title IX, Education Amendments of 1972, Pub. L. 92-318, 86 Stat. 373, 20 U.S.C. § 1681(a)(§ 1681), provides in part:

"(a) No person in the United States shall, on the basis of sex, be excluded from participation in, be denied the benefits of, or be subjected to discrimination under any education program or activity receiving Federal financial assistance, except that:

"(1) in regard to admissions to educational institutions, this section shall apply only to institutions of vocational education, professional education, and graduate higher education, and to public institutions of undergraduate higher education;

* * *

"(5) in regard to admissions this section shall not apply to any public institution of undergraduate higher education which is an institution that traditionally and continually from its establishment has had a policy of admitting only students of one sex. . . ."

[6]Section 5 of the Fourteenth Amendment provides:

"The Congress shall have power to enforce, by appropriate legislation, the provisions of this article."

[7]Although some statements in the Court of Appeals' decision refer to all schools within MUW, see 646 F.2d, at 1119, the factual underpinning of Hogan's claim for relief involved only his exclusion from the nursing program. Complaint ¶ 8-10, and the Court of Appeals' holding applies only to Hogan's individual claim for relief. 646 F.2d, at 1119-20. . . . [W]e decline to address the question of whether MUW's admissions policy, as applied to males seeking admission to schools other than the School of Nursing, violates the Fourteenth Amendment.

[8]Without question, MUW's admissions policy worked to Hogan's disadvantage. Although Hogan could have attended classes and received credit in one of Mississippi's state-supported coeducational nursing programs, none of which was located in Columbus, he could attend only by driving a considerable distance from his home. . . . A similarly situated female would not have been required to choose between foregoing credit and bearing that inconvenience. Moreover, since many students enrolled in the School of Nursing hold full-time jobs. . . . Hogan's female colleagues had available an opportunity, not open to Hogan, to obtain credit for additional training. The policy of denying males the right to obtain credit towards a baccalaureate degree thus imposed upon Hogan "a burden he would not bear were he female." *Orr v. Orr*, 440 U.S. 268, 273 . . . (1979).

tant governmental objectives and that the discriminatory means employed" are "substantially related to the achievement of those objectives." . . .[9]

Although the test for determining the validity of a gender-based classification is straightforward, it must be applied free of fixed notions concerning the roles and abilities of males and females. Care must be taken in ascertaining whether the statutory objective itself reflects archaic and stereotypic notions. Thus, if the statutory objective is to exclude or "protect" members of one gender because they are presumed to suffer from an inherent handicap or to be innately inferior, the objective itself is illegitimate. *See Frontiero v. Richardson*, 411 U.S. 677, 684, 685 . . .(1973) (plurality opinion).[10]

If the State's objective is legitimate and important, we next determine whether the requisite direct, substantial relationship between objective and means is present. The purpose of requiring that close relationship is to assure that the validity of a classification is determined through reasoned analysis rather than through the mechanical application of traditional, often inaccurate, assumptions about the proper roles of men and women. The need for the requirement is amply revealed by reference to the broad range of statutes already invalidated by this Court, statutes that relied upon the simplistic, outdated assumption that gender could be used as a "proxy for other, more germane bases of classification," *Craig v. Boren*, 429 U.S. 190 . . . (1976), to establish a link between objective and classification.

Applying this framework, we now analyze the arguments advanced by the State to justify its refusal to allow males to enroll for credit in MUW's School of Nursing.

III

A

The State's primary justification for maintaining the single-sex admissions policy of MUW's School of Nursing is that it compensates for discrimination against women and, therefore, constitutes educational affirmative action. Pet. Brief.[13] As applied to

---

[9]In his dissenting opinion, Justice Powell argues that a less rigorous test should apply because Hogan does not advance a "serious equal protection claim. . . ." Justice Blackmun, without proposing an alternative test, labels the test applicable to gender-based discrimination as "rigid" and productive of "needless conformity." . . . Our past decisions establish, however, that when a classification expressly discriminates on the basis of gender, the analysis and level of scrutiny applied to determine the validity of the classification do not vary simply because the objective appears acceptable to individual members of the Court. While the validity and importance of the objective may affect the outcome of the analysis, the analysis itself does not change.

Thus, we apply the test previously relied upon by the Court to measure the constitutionality of gender-based discrimination. Because we conclude that the challenged statutory classification is not substantially related to an important objective, we need not decide whether classifications based upon gender are inherently suspect. *See Stanton v. Stanton*, 421 U.S. 7, 13 . . . (1975).

[10]History provides numerous examples of legislative attempts to exclude women from particular areas simply because legislators believed women were less able than men to perform a particular function. In 1872, this Court remained unmoved by Myra Bradwell's argument that the Fourteenth Amendment prohibited a State from classifying her as unfit to practice law simply because she was a female. *Bradwell v. Illinois*, 16 Wall. 130 . . . (1872). In his concurring opinion, Justice Bradley described the reasons underlying the State's decision to determine which positions only men could fill:

"It is the prerogative of the legislator to prescribe regulations founded on nature, reason, and experience for the due admission of qualified persons to professions and callings demanding special skill and confidence. This fairly belongs to the police power of the State; and, in my opinion, in view of the peculiar characteristics, destiny, and mission of woman, it is within the province of the legislature to ordain what offices, positions, and callings shall be filled and discharged by men, and shall receive the benefit of those energies and responsibilities, and that decision and firmness which are presumed to predominate in the sterner sex."

Id., 16 Wall., at 142.

In a similar vein, the Court in *Goesaert v. Cleary*, 335 U.S. 464, 466 . . . (1948), upheld a legislature's right to preclude women from bartending, except under limited circumstances, on the ground that the legislature could devise preventive measures against "moral and social problems" that result when women, but apparently not men, bartend. Similarly, the many protective labor laws enacted in the late nineteenth and early twentieth centuries often had as their objective the protection of weaker workers, which the laws assumed meant females. *See generally*, B. Brown, A. Freedman, H. Katz, & A. Price, *Women's Rights and the Law* 209–10 (1977).

[13]In its Reply Brief, the State understandably retreated from its contention that MUW was founded to provide opportunities for women which were not available to men. Reply Brief 4. Apparently, the impetus for founding MUW came not from a desire to provide women with advantages superior to those offered men, but rather from a desire to provide white women in Mississippi access to state-supported higher learning. In 1856, Sally Reneau began agitating for a college for white women. Those initial efforts were unsuccessful, and, by 1870, Mississippi provided higher education only for white men and black men and women. E. Mayes, *History of Education in Mississippi* 178, 228, 245, 259, 266, 270 (1899)(hereinafter Mayes). *See also* S. Neilson, *The History of Mississippi State College for Women* 4–5 (unpublished manuscript, 1952)(hereinafter Neilson). In 1882, two years before MUW was chartered, the University of Mississippi opened its doors to women. However, the institution was in those early years not "extensively patronized by females: most of those who come being such as desire to qualify themselves to teach." Mayes, at 178. By 1890, the largest number of women in any class at the University had been 23, while nearly 350 women enrolled in the first session of MUW. Mayes, at 178, 253. Because the University did not solicit the attendance of women until after 1920, and did not accept women at all for a time between 1907 and 1920, most Mississippi women who attended college attended MUW. Neilson, at 86. Thus, in Mississippi, as elsewhere in the country, women's colleges were founded to provide some form of higher education for the academically disenfranchised. *See generally* 2 T. Woody, *A History of Women's Education in the United States* 137–223 (1929); L. Baker, *I'm Radcliffe! Fly Me! The Seven Sisters and the Failure of Women's Education* 22, 136–41 (1976).

the School of Nursing, we find the State's argument unpersuasive.

In limited circumstances, a gender-based classification favoring one sex can be justified if it intentionally and directly assists members of the sex that is disproportionately burdened. *See Schlesinger v. Ballard,* 419 U.S. 498 . . . (1975). However, we consistently have emphasized that "the mere recitation of a benign, compensatory purpose is not an automatic shield which protects against any inquiry into the actual purposes underlying a statutory scheme." *Weinberger v. Wisenfeld,* 420 U.S. 636, 648 . . . (1975). The same searching analysis must be made, regardless of whether the State's objective is to eliminate family controversy, *Reed v. Reed, supra,* to achieve administrative efficiency, *Frontiero v. Richardson, supra,* or to balance the burdens borne by males and females.

It is readily apparent that a State can evoke a compensatory purpose to justify an otherwise discriminatory classification only if members of the gender benefited by the classification actually suffer a disadvantage related to the classification. We considered such a situation in *Califano v. Webster,* 430 U.S. 313 . . . (1977), which involved a challenge to a statutory classification that allowed women to eliminate more low-earning years than men for purposes of computing Social Security retirement benefits. Although the effect of the classification was to allow women higher monthly benefits than were available to men with the same earning history, we upheld the statutory scheme, noting that it took into account that women "as such have been unfairly hindered from earning as much as men" and "work[ed] directly to remedy" the resulting economic disparity. *Id.,* at 318. . . .

* * *

In sharp contrast, Mississippi has made no showing that women lacked opportunities to obtain training in the field of nursing or to attain positions of leadership in that field when the MUW School of Nursing opened its door or that women currently are deprived of such opportunities. In fact, in 1970, the year before the School of Nursing's first class enrolled, women earned 94 percent of the nursing baccalaureate degrees conferred in Mississippi and 98.6 percent of the degrees earned nationwide. . . . As one would expect, the labor force reflects the same predominance of women in nursing. When MUW's School of Nursing began operation, nearly 98 percent of all employed registered nurses were female. . . .

Rather than compensate for discriminatory barriers faced by women, MUW's policy of excluding males from admission to the School of Nursing tends to perpetuate the stereotyped view of nursing as an exclusively woman's job.[15] By assuring that Mississippi allots more openings in its state-supported nursing schools to women than it does to men, MUW's admissions policy lends credibility to the old view that women, not men, should become nurses, and makes the assumption that nursing is a field for women a self-fulfilling prophecy. *See Stanton v. Stanton,* 421 U.S. 7, 95 S.Ct. 1373, 43 L.Ed.2d 688 (1975). Thus, we conclude that, although the State recited a "benign, compensatory purpose," it failed to establish that the alleged objective is the actual purpose underlying the discriminatory classification.

The policy is invalid also because it fails the second part of the equal protection test, for the State has made no showing that the gender-based classification is substantially and directly related to its proposed compensatory objective. To the contrary, MUW's policy of permitting men to attend classes as auditors fatally undermines its claim that women, at least those in the School of Nursing, are adversely affected by the presence of men.

. . . The uncontroverted record reveals that admitting men to nursing classes does not affect teaching style, . . . that the presence of men in the classroom would not affect the performance of the female nursing students, . . . and that men in co-educational nursing schools do not dominate the classroom. . . . In sum, the record in this case is flatly inconsistent with the claim that excluding men from the School of Nursing is necessary to reach any of MUW's educational goals.

Thus, considering both the asserted interest and the relationship between the interest and the methods used by the State, we conclude that the State has fallen far short of establishing the "exceedingly persuasive justification" needed to sustain the gender-based classification. Accordingly, we hold that MUW's policy of denying males the right to enroll for credit in its School of Nursing vi-

---

[15]Officials of the American Nurses Association have suggested that excluding men from the field has depressed nurses' wages. Hearings Before the United States Equal Employment Opportunity Commission on Job Segregation and Wage Discrimination 510–11, 517–18, 523 (April 1980). To the extent the exclusion of men has that effect, MUW's admissions policy actually penalizes the very class the State purports to benefit. *Cf. Weinberger v. Wisenfeld, supra.*

olates the Equal Protection Clause of the Fourteenth Amendment.[17]

B

In an additional attempt to justify its exclusion of men from MUW's School of Nursing, the State contends that MUW is the direct beneficiary "of specific congressional legislation which, on its face, permits the institution to exist as it has in the past." . . . The argument is based upon the language of § 901(a) in Title IX of the Education Amendments of 1972, 20 U.S.C. § 1681(a). Although § 901(a) prohibits gender discrimination in education programs that receive federal financial assistance, subsection 5 exempts the admissions policies of undergraduate institutions "that traditionally and continually from [their] establishment [have] had a policy of admitting only students of one sex" from the general prohibition. *See* n. 5, *supra.* Arguing that Congress enacted Title IX in furtherance of its power to enforce the Fourteenth Amendment, a power granted by § 5 of that Amendment, the State would have us conclude that § 1681(a)(5) is but "a congressional limitation upon the broad prohibitions of the Equal Protection Clause of the Fourteenth Amendment." . . .

The argument requires little comment. Initially, it is far from clear that Congress intended, through § 1681(a)(5), to exempt MUW from any constitutional obligation. Rather, Congress apparently intended, at most, to exempt MUW from the requirements of Title IX.

Even if Congress envisioned a constitutional exemption, the State's argument would fail. Section 5 of the Fourteenth Amendment gives Congress broad power indeed to enforce the command of the Amendment and "to secure to all persons the enjoyment of perfect equality of civil rights and the equal protection of the laws against State denial or invasion. . . ." *Ex parte Virginia*, 100 U.S. (10 Otto) 339, 346 . . . (1879). Congress' power under § 5, however, "is limited to adopting measures to enforce the guarantees of the Amendment; § 5 grants Congress no power to restrict, abrogate, or dilute these guarantees." *Katzenbach v. Morgan*, 384 U.S. 641, 651 n. 10 . . . (1966). Although we give deference to congressional decisions and classifications, neither Congress nor a State can validate a law that denies the rights guaranteed by the Fourteenth Amendment. . . .

* * *

IV

Because we conclude that the State's policy of excluding males from MUW's School of Nursing violates the Equal Protection Clause of the Fourteenth Amendment, we affirm the judgment of the Court of Appeals.

Chief Justice Burger, dissenting.

I agree generally with Justice Powell's dissenting opinion. I write separately, however, to emphasize that the Court's holding today is limited to the context of a professional nursing school. . . . Since the Court's opinion relies heavily on its finding that women have traditionally dominated the nursing profession, . . . it suggests that a State might well be justified in maintaining, for example, the option of an all-women's business school or liberal arts program.

Justice Blackmun, dissenting.

* * *

While the Court purports to write narrowly, declaring that it does not decide the same issue with respect to "separate but equal" undergraduate institutions for females and males, . . . or with respect to units of MUW other than its School of Nursing, . . . there is inevitable spillover from the Court's ruling today. That ruling, it seems to me, places in constitutional jeopardy any state-supported educational institution that confines its student body in any area to members of one sex, even though the State elsewhere provides an equivalent program to the complaining applicant. The Court's reasoning does not stop with the School of Nursing of the Mississippi University for Women.

I hope that we do not lose all values that some think are worthwhile (and are not based on differences of race or religion) and relegate ourselves to needless conformity. The ringing words of the Equal Protection Clause of the Fourteenth Amendment—what Justice Powell aptly describes as its "liberating spirit," *post*, at 3345,—do not demand that price.

Justice Powell, with whom Justice Rehnquist joins, dissenting.

---

[17]Justice Powell's dissent suggests that a second objective is served by the gender-based classification in that Mississippi has elected to provide women a choice of educational environments. . . . Since any gender-based classification provides one class a benefit or choice not available to the other class, however, that argument begs the question. The issue is not whether the benefited class profits from the classification, but whether the State's decision to confer a benefit only upon one class by means of a discriminatory classification is substantially related to achieving a legitimate and substantial goal.

The Court's opinion bows deeply to conformity. Left without honor—indeed, held unconstitutional—is an element of diversity that has characterized much of American education and enriched much of American life. The Court in effect holds today that no State now may provide even a single institution of higher learning open only to women students. It gives no heed to the efforts of the State of Mississippi to provide abundant opportunities for young men and young women to attend coeducational institutions, and none to the preferences of the more than 40,000 young women who over the years have evidenced their approval of an all-women's college by choosing Mississippi University for Women (MUW) over seven coeducational universities within the State. The Court decides today that the Equal Protection Clause makes it unlawful for the State to provide women with a traditionally popular and respected choice of educational environment. It does so in a case instituted by one man, who represents no class, and whose primary concern is personal convenience.

It is undisputed that women enjoy complete equality of opportunity in Mississippi's public system of higher education. Of the State's eight universities and sixteen junior colleges, all except MUW are coeducational. At least two other Mississippi universities would have provided respondent with the nursing curriculum that he wishes to pursue.[1] No other male has joined in his complaint. The only groups with any personal acquaintance with MUW to file *amicus* briefs are female students and alumnae of MUW. And they have emphatically rejected respondent's arguments, urging that the State of Mississippi be allowed to continue offering the choice from which they have benefited.

Nor is respondent significantly disadvantaged by MUW's all-female tradition. His constitutional complaint is based upon a single asserted harm: that he must *travel* to attend the state-supported nursing schools that concededly are available to him. The Court characterizes this injury as one of "inconvenience." . . . This description is fair and accurate, though somewhat embarrassed by the fact that there is, of course, no constitutional right to attend a state-supported university in one's hometown. Thus the

Court, to redress respondent's injury of inconvenience, must rest its invalidation of MUW's single-sex program on a mode of "sexual stereotype" reasoning that has no application whatever to the respondent or to the "wrong" of which he complains. . . .

* * *

II

The issue in this case is whether a State transgresses the Constitution when—within the context of a public system that offers a diverse range of campuses, curricula, and educational alternatives—it seeks to accommodate the legitimate personal preferences of those desiring the advantages of an all-women's college. In my view, the Court errs seriously by assuming—without argument or discussion—that the equal protection standard generally applicable to sex discrimination is appropriate here. That standard was designed to free women from "archaic and overbroad generalizations. . . ." *Schlesinger v. Ballard*, 419 U.S. 498, 508 . . . (1975). In no previous case have we applied it to invalidate state efforts to expand women's choices. Nor are there prior sex discrimination decisions by this Court in which a male plaintiff, as in this case, had the choice of an equal benefit.

The cases cited by the Court therefore do not control the issue now before us. In most of them women were given no opportunity for the same benefit as men. Cases involving male plaintiffs are equally inapplicable. . . .

By applying heightened equal protection analysis to this case,[9] the Court frustrates the liberating spirit of the Equal Protection Clause. It forbids the States from providing women with an opportunity to choose the type of university they prefer. And yet it is these women whom the Court regards as the *victims* of an illegal, stereotyped perception of the role of women in our society. The Court reasons this way in a case in which no woman has complained, and the only complainant is a man who advances no claims on behalf of anyone else. His claim, it should be recalled, is not that he is being denied a substantive educational opportunity, or even the right to attend an all-male or a coeducational college. *See* Brief for

---

[1]"[T]wo other Mississippi universities offered coeducational programs leading to a Bachelor of Science in Nursing—the University of Southern Mississippi in Hattiesburg, 178 miles from Columbus and the University of Mississippi in Jackson, 147 miles from Columbus. . . ." Brief for Respondent 3. . . .

[9]Even the Court does not argue that the appropriate standard here is "strict scrutiny"—a standard that none of our "sex discrimination" cases ever has adopted. Sexual segregation in education differs from the tradition, typified by the decision in *Plessy v. Ferguson*, 163 U.S. 537 . . . (1896), of "separate but equal" racial segregation. It was characteristic of racial segregation that segregated facilities were offered, not as alternatives to increase the choices available to blacks, but as the sole alternative. MUW stands in sharp contrast. Of Mississippi's eight public universities and sixteen public junior colleges, only MUW considers sex as a criterion for admission. Women consequently are free to select a coeducational education environment for themselves if they so desire; their attendance of MUW is not a matter of coercion.

Respondent 24.[10] It is *only* that the colleges open to him are located at inconvenient distances.

III

The Court views this case as presenting a serious equal protection claim of sex discrimination. I do not, and I would sustain Mississippi's right to continue MUW on a rational basis analysis. But I need not apply this "lowest tier" of scrutiny. I can accept for present purposes the standard applied by the Court: that there is a gender-based distinction that must serve an important governmental objective by means that are substantially related to its achievement. *E.g., Wengler v. Druggists Mutual Ins. Co.,* 446 U.S. 142, 150 . . . (1980). The record in this case reflects that MUW has a historical position in the State's educational system dating back to 1884. More than 2,000 women presently evidence their preference for MUW by having enrolled there. The choice is one that discriminates invidiously against no one. . . .

In arguing to the contrary, the Court suggests that the MUW is so operated as to "perpetuate the stereotyped view of nursing as an exclusively women's job." . . . [But] [t]he School of Nursing makes up only one part—a relatively small part—of MUW's diverse modern university campus and curriculum. The other departments on the MUW campus offer a typical range of degrees and a typical range of subjects. There is no indication that women suffer fewer opportunities at other Mississippi state campuses because of MUW's admission policy.

In sum, the practice of voluntarily chosen single-sex education is an honored tradition in our country, even if it now rarely exists in state colleges and universities. Mississippi's accommodation of such student choices is legitimate because it is completely consensual and is important because it permits students to decide for themselves the type of college education they think will benefit them most. Finally, Mississippi's policy is substantially related to its long-respected objective.

IV

A distinctive feature of America's tradition has been respect for diversity. This has been characteristic of the peoples from numerous lands who have built our country. It is the essence of our democratic system. At stake in this case as I see it is the preservation of a small aspect of this diversity. But that aspect is by no means insignificant, given our heritage of available choice between single-sex and coeducational institutions of higher learning. The Court answers that there is discrimination—not just that which may be tolerable, as for example between those candidates for admission able to contribute most to an educational institution and those able to contribute less—but discrimination of constitutional dimensions. But, having found "discrimination," the Court finds it difficult to identify the victims. It hardly can claim that women are discriminated against. A constitutional case is held to exist solely because one man found it inconvenient to travel to any of the other institutions made available to him by the State of Mississippi. In essence he insists that he has a right to attend a college in his home community. This simply is not a sex discrimination case. The Equal Protection Clause was never intended to be applied to this kind of case.[18]

NOTES AND QUESTIONS

1. Scope of the Decision

What standard of review does the Court use in *Hogan?* Does the dissent suggest a different standard in cases where males are the victims of discrimination? What does Justice Powell mean in asserting that a less rigorous standard should be applied because *Hogan* does not advance a "serious equal protection claim"? Is he saying that no one is guaranteed

---

[10]The Court says that "any gender-based classification provides one class a benefit or choice not available to the other class. . . ." It then states that the issue "is not whether the benefited class profits from the classification, but whether the state's decision to confer a benefit *only* upon *one* class by means of a discriminatory classification is substantially related to achieving a legitimate and substantial goal." . . . This is *not* the issue in this case. Hogan is not complaining about any benefit conferred upon women. Nor is he claiming discrimination because Mississippi offers no all-male college. As his brief states, at p. 24: "Joe Hogan does not ask to attend an all-male college which offers a Bachelor of Science in nursing; he asks only to attend MUW." And he asks this only for his personal convenience.

[18]. . .The Court . . . purports to decide this case "narrow[ly]." Normally and properly we decide only the question presented. It seems to me that in fact the issue properly before us is the single-sex policy of the University, and it is this issue that I have addressed in this dissent. The Court of Appeals so viewed this case, and unambiguously held that a single-sex state institution of higher education no longer is permitted by the Constitution. I see no principled way—in light of the Court's rationale—to reach a different result with respect to other MUW schools and departments. But given the Court's insistence that its decision applies only to the School of Nursing, it is my view that the Board and officials of MUW may continue to operate the remainder of the University on a single-sex basis without fear of personal liability. . . .

an equal right to attend a professional school in his or her hometown? Is that the issue?

2. *Equality and Choice: The Puzzle Not Considered*

For Joe Hogan, the practical consequence of the MUW admissions standard was to compel him to choose between his home and his vocation. But, while limiting his choices, the admissions policy also expanded the educational options of women, who were enabled to select a coeducational or single-sex course of instruction. Is it one thing to free men and women from gender-based rules premised on "archaic and overbroad generalizations" and something quite different to allow women to choose between two very different educational environments? Is that difference constitutionally relevant? Does it require, at a minimum, that there be a defensible educational rationale for the separation?

In this regard, does it matter that nursing, the field in question, is historically dominated by women? Would a similar challenge to, say, an all-female engineering school raise different questions? What about an all-female women's studies department? Single-sex social institutions? *See* Note, "Discrimination on Campus: A Critical Examination of Single-Sex College Social Organizations," 75 *Calif.L.Rev.* 2117 (1987).

3. *Single-Sex Mathematics and Science Instruction*

In *Hogan*, the Court rejects single-sex education for women in nursing, a field that they traditionally have dominated. In some instances, however, public schools have created single-sex academies or classes to help girls excel in areas, such as mathematics and science, in which they have lagged behind boys. *See* Ramsey, "Subtracting Sexism from the Classroom: Law and Policy in the Debate Over All-Female Math and Science Classes in Public Schools," 8 *Tex.J.Women & L.* 1 (1998). In 1996, California enacted the Single-Gender Academies Pilot Program, Cal.Educ.Code §§ 58520–58524 (1996), to enhance educational opportunity and quality through diverse program offerings. As one justification, Governor Pete Wilson cited evidence that single-sex academies could help girls improve their performance in stereotypically male-dominated disciplines. Reiter, "California Single-Gender Academies Pilot Program: Separate but Really Equal," 72 *S.Cal.L.Rev.* 1401, 1402–03 (1999). Are such academies defensible in a way that the nursing program at MUW was not?

Title IX regulations provide that a school "may take affirmative action to overcome the effects of conditions which resulted in limited participation

therein by persons of a particular sex." 34 C.F.R. § 106.3 (2000). This regulation does not require a finding of past discrimination and would seem to permit compensatory programs based on gender. Even so, in 1993, Stanford University discontinued a popular class on self-defense for women out of concern that it violated Title IX. von Lohmann, "Single-Sex Courses, Title IX, and Equal Protection: The Case for Self-Defense for Women," 48 *Stan.L.Rev.* 177, 179–80 (1995). That year, Stanford offered a companion course for men on "Men Understanding Issues in Self-Defense for Women." Cancelled because of low enrollment, this class did not offer self-defense instruction to men, but instead focused on problems of violence against women. The Office for Civil Rights (OCR), when asked to evaluate the legality of the self-defense program, apparently did not believe the availability of the men's class was an adequate response to Title IX concerns. *Id.* at 179 n.16. One year later, OCR held that Santa Rosa Junior College's single-sex computer bulletin boards were impermissible under Title IX. The bulletin boards had been created in response to female students' complaints about harassment. Lewin, "Dispute Over Computer Messages: Free Speech or Sex Harassment?" *N.Y.Times*, Sept. 22, 1994, at A1, A16.

C. Single-Sex Education Revisited

Despite continuing interest in single-sex education, many public elementary and secondary schools retreated from offering it, as Stanford and Santa Rosa College did. Then, in 1996, the Court revisited the constitutionality of same-sex education in a case that captivated the nation.

U.S. v. Virginia
518 U.S. 515, 116 S.Ct. 2264, 135 L.Ed.2d 735 (1996).

Justice Ginsburg delivered the opinion of the Court.

Virginia's public institutions of higher learning include an incomparable military college, Virginia Military Institute (VMI). The United States maintains that the Constitution's equal protection guarantee precludes Virginia from reserving exclusively to men the unique educational opportunities VMI affords. We agree.

I

Founded in 1839, VMI is today the sole single-sex school among Virginia's 15 public institutions of higher learning. VMI's distinctive mission is to produce "citizen-soldiers," men prepared for leadership in civilian life and in military service. VMI pursues this mission through pervasive training of a kind not available anywhere else in Virginia. Assigning prime place to character development, VMI uses an "adversative method" modeled on English public schools and once characteristic of military instruction. VMI constantly endeavors to instill physical and mental discipline in its cadets and impart to them a strong moral code. The school's graduates leave VMI with heightened comprehension of their capacity to deal with duress and stress, and a large sense of accomplishment for completing the hazardous course.

VMI has notably succeeded in its mission to produce leaders; among its alumni are military generals, Members of Congress, and business executives. The school's alumni overwhelmingly perceive that their VMI training helped them to realize their personal goals. VMI's endowment reflects the loyalty of its graduates; VMI has the largest per-student endowment of all public undergraduate institutions in the Nation.

Neither the goal of producing citizen-soldiers nor VMI's implementing methodology is inherently unsuitable to women. And the school's impressive record in producing leaders has made admission desirable to some women. Nevertheless, Virginia has elected to preserve exclusively for men the advantages and opportunities a VMI education affords.

II

A

From its establishment in 1839 as one of the Nation's first state military colleges, see 1839 Va. Acts, ch. 20, VMI has remained financially supported by Virginia and "subject to the control of the [Virginia] General Assembly," Va.Code Ann. § 23-92 (1993). . . .

VMI today enrolls about 1,300 men as cadets.[2] Its academic offerings in the liberal arts, sciences, and engineering are also available at other public colleges and universities in Virginia. But VMI's mission is special. It is the mission of the school

" 'to produce educated and honorable men, prepared for the varied work of civil life, imbued with love of

learning, confident in the functions and attitudes of leadership, possessing a high sense of public service, advocates of the American democracy and free enterprise system, and ready as citizen-soldiers to defend their country in time of national peril.' " 766 F.Supp. 1407, 1425 (W.D.Va.1991) (quoting Mission Study Committee of the VMI Board of Visitors, Report, May 16, 1986).

In contrast to the federal service academies, institutions maintained "to prepare cadets for career service in the armed forces," VMI's program "is directed at preparation for both military and civilian life"; "[o]nly about 15% of VMI cadets enter career military service." 766 F.Supp., at 1432.

VMI produces its "citizen-soldiers" through "an adversative, or doubting, model of education" which features "[p]hysical rigor, mental stress, absolute equality of treatment, absence of privacy, minute regulation of behavior, and indoctrination in desirable values." Id., at 1421. As one Commandant of Cadets described it, the adversative method " 'dissects the young student,' " and makes him aware of his " 'limits and capabilities,' " so that he knows " 'how far he can go with his anger, . . . how much he can take under stress, . . . exactly what he can do when he is physically exhausted.' " Id., at 1421–1422 (quoting Col. N. Bissell).

VMI cadets live in spartan barracks where surveillance is constant and privacy nonexistent; they wear uniforms, eat together in the mess hall, and regularly participate in drills. Id., at 1424, 1432. Entering students are incessantly exposed to the rat line, "an extreme form of the adversative model," comparable in intensity to Marine Corps boot camp. Id., at 1422. Tormenting and punishing, the rat line bonds new cadets to their fellow sufferers and, when they have completed the 7-month experience, to their former tormentors. Ibid.

VMI's "adversative model" is further characterized by a hierarchical "class system" of privileges and responsibilities, a "dyke system" for assigning a senior class mentor to each entering class "rat," and a stringently enforced "honor code," which prescribes that a cadet " 'does not lie, cheat, steal nor tolerate those who do.' " Id., at 1422–1423.

VMI attracts some applicants because of its reputation as an extraordinarily challenging military school, and "because its alumni are exceptionally close to the school." Id., at 1421. "[W]omen have no opportunity anywhere to gain the benefits of [the system of education at VMI]." Ibid.

---

[2]Historically, most of Virginia's public colleges and universities were single sex; by the mid-1970's, however, all except VMI had become coeducational. 766 F.Supp. 1407, 1418–1419 (W.D.Va.1991). . . .

B

In 1990, prompted by a complaint filed with the Attorney General by a female high-school student seeking admission to VMI, the United States sued the Commonwealth of Virginia and VMI, alleging that VMI's exclusively male admission policy violated the Equal Protection Clause of the Fourteenth Amendment. *Id.*, at 1408.[3] . . . .

In the two years preceding the lawsuit, the District Court noted, VMI had received inquiries from 347 women, but had responded to none of them. *Id.*, at 1436. "[S]ome women, at least," the court said, "would want to attend the school if they had the opportunity." *Id.*, at 1414. The court further recognized that, with recruitment, VMI could "achieve at least 10% female enrollment"—"a sufficient 'critical mass' to provide the female cadets with a positive educational experience." *Id.*, at 1437–1438. And it was also established that "some women are capable of all of the individual activities required of VMI cadets." *Id.*, at 1412. In addition, experts agreed that if VMI admitted women, "the VMI ROTC experience would become a better training program from the perspective of the armed forces, because it would provide training in dealing with a mixed-gender army." *Id.*, at 1441.

* * *

[The district court nevertheless ruled in favor of VMI because its single-sex program brought diversity to an otherwise coeducational system of public education. 766 F.Supp. at 1415. The Fourth Circuit court of appeals disagreed, concluding that "[a] policy of diversity . . . must do more than favor one gender." 976 F.2d 890, 892 (1992). The court of appeals did acknowledge that three aspects of VMI's program would be materially affected by coeducation: physical training, the absence of privacy, and the adversative approach. *Id.* at 896–97. The court offered three remedial options to Virginia on remand: admitting women to VMI; establishing parallel programs or institutions; and abandoning state support by becoming a private institution. *Id.* at 900.]

C

In response to the Fourth Circuit's ruling, Virginia proposed a parallel program for women: Virginia Women's Institute for Leadership (VWIL). The 4-year, state-sponsored undergraduate program would be located at Mary Baldwin College, a private liberal arts school for women, and would be open, initially, to about 25 to 30 students. Although VWIL would share VMI's mission—to produce "citizen-soldiers"—the VWIL program would differ, as does Mary Baldwin College, from VMI in academic offerings, methods of education, and financial resources. See 852 F.Supp. 471, 476–477 (W.D.Va.1994).

The average combined SAT score of entrants at Mary Baldwin is about 100 points lower than the score for VMI freshmen. See *id.*, at 501. Mary Baldwin's faculty holds "significantly fewer Ph.D.'s than the faculty at VMI," *id.*, at 502, and receives significantly lower salaries, see Tr. 158 (testimony of James Lott, Dean of Mary Baldwin College), reprinted in 2 App. in Nos. 94-1667 and 94-1717(CA4) (hereinafter Tr.). While VMI offers degrees in liberal arts, the sciences, and engineering, Mary Baldwin, at the time of trial, offered only bachelor of arts degrees. See 852 F.Supp., at 503. A VWIL student seeking to earn an engineering degree could gain one, without public support, by attending Washington University in St. Louis, Missouri, for two years, paying the required private tuition. See *ibid.*

Experts in educating women at the college level composed the Task Force charged with designing the VWIL program; Task Force members were drawn from Mary Baldwin's own faculty and staff. *Id.*, at 476. Training its attention on methods of instruction appropriate for "most women," the Task Force determined that a military model would be "wholly inappropriate" for VWIL. *Ibid.*; see 44 F.3d 1229, 1233 (C.A.4 1995).

VWIL students would participate in ROTC programs and a newly established, "largely ceremonial" Virginia Corps of Cadets, *id.*, at 1234, but the VWIL House would not have a military format, 852 F.Supp., at 477, and VWIL would not require its students to eat meals together or to wear uniforms during the schoolday, *id.*, at 495. In lieu of VMI's adversative method, the VWIL Task Force favored "a cooperative method which reinforces self-esteem." *Id.*, at 476. In addition to the standard bachelor of arts program offered at Mary Baldwin, VWIL students would take courses in leadership, complete an off-campus leadership externship, participate in community service projects, and assist in arranging a speaker series. See 44 F.3d, at 1234.

---

[3]The District Court allowed the VMI Foundation and the VMI Alumni Association to intervene as defendants. 766 F.Supp., at 1408.

Virginia represented that it will provide equal financial support for in-state VWIL students and VMI cadets, 852 F.Supp., at 483, and the VMI Foundation agreed to supply a $5.4625 million endowment for the VWIL program, *id.*, at 499. Mary Baldwin's own endowment is about $19 million; VMI's is $131 million. *Id.*, at 503. Mary Baldwin will add $35 million to its endowment based on future commitments; VMI will add $220 million. *Ibid.* The VMI Alumni Association has developed a network of employers interested in hiring VMI graduates. The Association has agreed to open its network to VWIL graduates, *id.*, at 499, but those graduates will not have the advantage afforded by a VMI degree.

* * *

[The district court subsequently approved the proposed remedial plan, 852 F.Supp. at 473, and a divided court of appeals affirmed. 44 F.3d 1229 (4th Cir. 1995).]

III

The cross-petitions in this suit present two ultimate issues. First, does Virginia's exclusion of women from the educational opportunities provided by VMI — extraordinary opportunities for military training and civilian leadership development — deny to women "capable of all of the individual activities required of VMI cadets," 766 F.Supp., at 1412, the equal protection of the laws guaranteed by the Fourteenth Amendment? Second, if VMI's "unique" situation, *id.*, at 1413 — as Virginia's sole single-sex public institution of higher education — offends the Constitution's equal protection principle, what is the remedial requirement?

IV

We note, once again, the core instruction of this Court's pathmarking decisions in *J.E.B. v. Alabama ex rel. T. B.*, 511 U.S. 127, 136–137, and n. 6, 114 S.Ct. 1419, 1425–1426, and n. 6, 128 L.Ed.2d 89 (1994), and *Mississippi Univ. for Women*, 458 U.S., at 724, 102 S.Ct., at 3336 (internal quotation marks omitted): Parties who seek to defend gender-based government action must demonstrate an "exceedingly persuasive justification" for that action.

* * *

In 1971, for the first time in our Nation's history, this Court ruled in favor of a woman who complained that her State had denied her the equal protection of its laws. *Reed v. Reed*, 404 U.S. 71, 73 (holding unconstitutional Idaho Code prescription that, among " 'several persons claiming and equally entitled to administer [a decedent's estate], males must be preferred to females' "). . . .

Without equating gender classifications, for all purposes, to classifications based on race or national origin,[6] the Court, in post-*Reed* decisions, has carefully inspected official action that closes a door or denies opportunity to women (or to men). See *J.E.B.*, 511 U.S., at 152 (Kennedy, J., concurring in judgment) (case law evolving since 1971 "reveal[s] a strong presumption that gender classifications are invalid"). To summarize the Court's current directions for cases of official classification based on gender: Focusing on the differential treatment or denial of opportunity for which relief is sought, the reviewing court must determine whether the proffered justification is "exceedingly persuasive." The burden of justification is demanding and it rests entirely on the State. See *Mississippi Univ. for Women*, 458 U.S., at 724. The State must show "at least that the [challenged] classification serves 'important governmental objectives and that the discriminatory means employed' are substantially related to the achievement of those objectives." *Ibid.* (quoting *Wengler v. Druggists Mut. Ins. Co.*, 446 U.S. 142, 150 (1980)). The justification must be genuine, not hypothesized or invented *post hoc* in response to litigation. And it must not rely on overbroad generalizations about the different talents, capacities, or preferences of males and females. See *Weinberger v. Wiesenfeld*, 420 U.S. 636, 643, 648 (1975); *Califano v. Goldfarb*, 430 U.S. 199, 223–224 (1977) (Stevens, J., concurring in judgment).

The heightened review standard our precedent establishes does not make sex a proscribed classification. Supposed "inherent differences" are no longer accepted as a ground for race or national origin classifications. See *Loving v. Virginia*, 388 U.S. 1 (1967). Physical differences between men and women, however, are enduring: "[T]he two sexes are not fungible; a community made up exclusively of one [sex] is different from a community composed of both." *Ballard v. United States*, 329 U.S. 187, 193 (1946).

---

[6]The Court has thus far reserved most stringent judicial scrutiny for classifications based on race or national origin, but last Term observed that strict scrutiny of such classifications is not inevitably "fatal in fact." *Adarand Constructors, Inc. v. Peña*, 515 U.S. 200, 237 (1995)(internal quotation marks omitted).

"Inherent differences" between men and women, we have come to appreciate, remain cause for celebration, but not for denigration of the members of either sex or for artificial constraints on an individual's opportunity. Sex classifications may be used to compensate women "for particular economic disabilities [they have] suffered," *Califano v. Webster*, 430 U.S. 313, 320 (1977) (*per curiam*), to "promot[e] equal employment opportunity," see *California Fed. Sav. & Loan Assn. v. Guerra*, 479 U.S. 272, 289 (1987), to advance full development of the talent and capacities of our Nation's people.[7] But such classifications may not be used, as they once were, *see Goesaert*, 335 U.S., at 467, to create or perpetuate the legal, social, and economic inferiority of women.

Measuring the record in this case against the review standard just described, we conclude that Virginia has shown no "exceedingly persuasive justification" for excluding all women from the citizen-soldier training afforded by VMI. We therefore affirm the Fourth Circuit's initial judgment, which held that Virginia had violated the Fourteenth Amendment's Equal Protection Clause. Because the remedy proffered by Virginia—the Mary Baldwin VWIL program—does not cure the constitutional violation, *i.e.*, it does not provide equal opportunity, we reverse the Fourth Circuit's final judgment in this case.

V

The Fourth Circuit initially held that Virginia had advanced no state policy by which it could justify, under equal protection principles, its determination "to afford VMI's unique type of program to men and not to women." 976 F.2d, at 892. Virginia challenges that "liability" ruling and asserts two justifications in defense of VMI's exclusion of women. First, the Commonwealth contends, "single-sex education

provides important educational benefits," Brief for Cross-Petitioners 20, and the option of single-sex education contributes to "diversity in educational approaches," *id.*, at 25. Second, the Commonwealth argues, "the unique VMI method of character development and leadership training," the school's adversative approach, would have to be modified were VMI to admit women. *Id.*, at 33–36 (internal quotation marks omitted). We consider these two justifications in turn.

A

Single-sex education affords pedagogical benefits to at least some students, Virginia emphasizes, and that reality is uncontested in this litigation.[8] Similarly, it is not disputed that diversity among public educational institutions can serve the public good. But Virginia has not shown that VMI was established, or has been maintained, with a view to diversifying, by its categorical exclusion of women, educational opportunities within the Commonwealth. In cases of this genre, our precedent instructs that "benign" justifications proffered in defense of categorical exclusions will not be accepted automatically; a tenable justification must describe actual state purposes, not rationalizations for actions in fact differently grounded. . . .

Mississippi Univ. for Women is immediately in point. There the State asserted, in justification of its exclusion of men from a nursing school, that it was engaging in "educational affirmative action" by "compensat[ing] for discrimination against women." 458 U.S., at 727, 102 S.Ct., at 3337. Undertaking a "searching analysis," *id.*, at 728, 102 S.Ct., at 3338, the Court found no close resemblance between "the alleged objective" and "the actual purpose underlying the discriminatory classification," *id.*, at 730, 102

---

[7]Several *amici* have urged that diversity in educational opportunities is an altogether appropriate governmental pursuit and that single-sex schools can contribute importantly to such diversity. Indeed, it is the mission of some single-sex schools "to dissipate, rather than perpetuate, traditional gender classifications." See Brief for Twenty-six Private Women's Colleges as *Amici Curiae* 5. We do not question the Commonwealth's prerogative evenhandedly to support diverse educational opportunities. We address specifically and only an educational opportunity recognized by the District Court and the Court of Appeals as "unique," see 766 F.Supp., at 1413, 1432; 976 F.2d, at 892, an opportunity available only at Virginia's premier military institute, the Commonwealth's sole single-sex public university or college. Cf. *Mississippi Univ. for Women v. Hogan*, 458 U.S. 718, 720, n.1 (1982)("Mississippi maintains no other single-sex public university or college. Thus, we are not faced with the question of whether States can provide 'separate but equal' undergraduate institutions for male and females.").

[8]On this point, the dissent sees fire where there is no flame. See *post*, at 2305–2306, 2306–2307. "Both men and women can benefit from a single-sex education," the District Court recognized, although "the beneficial effects" of such education, the court added, apparently "are stronger among women than among men." 766 F.Supp., at 1414. The United States does not challenge that recognition. Cf. C. Jencks & D. Riesman, The Academic Revolution 297–298 (1968):

"The pluralistic argument for preserving all-male colleges is uncomfortably similar to the pluralistic argument for preserving all-white colleges. . . . The all-male college would be relatively easy to defend if it emerged from a world in which women were established as fully equal to men. But it does not. It is therefore likely to be a witting or unwitting device for preserving tacit assumptions of male superiority—assumptions for which women must eventually pay."

S.Ct., at 3339. Pursuing a similar inquiry here, we reach the same conclusion.

Neither recent nor distant history bears out Virginia's alleged pursuit of diversity through single-sex educational options. . . .

* * *

[The Court then recounts the historical struggle for women to gain access to public institutions of higher education in Virginia. After being completely barred from the state's colleges and universities, women were allowed to attend several all-women's seminaries and colleges. These separate schools for women had all become coeducational by the mid-1970s. Only in 1970 did women gain access to the state's flagship campus, the University of Virginia.]

Virginia describes the current absence of public single-sex higher education for women as "an historical anomaly." Brief for Cross-Petitioners 30. But the historical record indicates action more deliberate than anomalous: First, protection of women against higher education; next, schools for women far from equal in resources and stature to schools for men; finally, conversion of the separate schools to coeducation. The state legislature, prior to the advent of this controversy, had repealed "[a]ll Virginia statutes requiring individual institutions to admit only men or women." 766 F.Supp., at 1419. And in 1990, an official commission, "legislatively established to chart the future goals of higher education in Virginia," reaffirmed the policy " 'of affording broad access' " while maintaining " 'autonomy and diversity.' " 976 F.2d, at 898–899 (quoting Report of the Virginia Commission on the University of the 21st Century). Significantly, the commission reported:

> " 'Because colleges and universities provide opportunities for students to develop values and learn from role models, it is extremely important that they deal with faculty, staff, and students without regard to sex, race, or ethnic origin.' " Id., at 899 (emphasis supplied by Court of Appeals deleted).

This statement, the Court of Appeals observed, "is the only explicit one that we have found in the record in which the Commonwealth has expressed itself with respect to gender distinctions." Ibid.

Our 1982 decision in Mississippi Univ. for Women prompted VMI to reexamine its male-only admission policy. See 766 F.Supp., at 1427–1428. Virginia relies on that reexamination as a legitimate basis for maintaining VMI's single-sex character. See Reply Brief for Cross-Petitioners 6. A Mission Study Committee, appointed by the VMI Board of Visitors, studied the problem from October 1983 until May 1986, and in that month counseled against "change of VMI status as a single-sex college." See 766 F.Supp., at 1429 (internal quotation marks omitted). Whatever internal purpose the Mission Study Committee served—and however well meaning the framers of the report—we can hardly extract from that effort any Commonwealth policy evenhandedly to advance diverse educational options. As the District Court observed, the Committee's analysis "primarily focuse[d] on anticipated difficulties in attracting females to VMI," and the report, overall, supplied "very little indication of how th[e] conclusion was reached." Ibid.

In sum, we find no persuasive evidence in this record that VMI's male-only admission policy "is in furtherance of a state policy of 'diversity.' " See 976 F.2d, at 899. No such policy, the Fourth Circuit observed, can be discerned from the movement of all other public colleges and universities in Virginia away from single-sex education. See ibid. That court also questioned "how one institution with autonomy, but with no authority over any other state institution, can give effect to a state policy of diversity among institutions." Ibid. A purpose genuinely to advance an array of educational options, as the Court of Appeals recognized, is not served by VMI's historic and constant plan—a plan to "affor[d] a unique educational benefit only to males." Ibid. However "liberally" this plan serves the Commonwealth's sons, it makes no provision whatever for her daughters. That is not equal protection.

B

Virginia next argues that VMI's adversative method of training provides educational benefits that cannot be made available, unmodified, to women. Alterations to accommodate women would necessarily be "radical," so "drastic," Virginia asserts, as to transform, indeed "destroy," VMI's program. See Brief for Cross-Petitioners 34–36. Neither sex would be favored by the transformation, Virginia maintains: Men would be deprived of the unique opportunity currently available to them; women would not gain that opportunity because their participation would "eliminat[e] the very aspects of [the] program that distinguish [VMI] from . . . other institutions of higher education in Virginia." Id., at 34.

The District Court forecast from expert witness testimony, and the Court of Appeals accepted, that coeducation would materially affect "at least these three aspects of VMI's program—physical training, the absence of privacy, and the adversative approach." 976 F.2d, at 896–897. And it is uncontested that women's admission would require accommodations, primarily in arranging housing assignments and physical training programs for female cadets. See Brief for Cross-Respondent 11, 29–30. It is also undisputed, however, that "the VMI methodology could be used to educate women." 852 F.Supp., at 481. The District Court even allowed that some women may prefer it to the methodology a women's college might pursue. See *ibid.* "[S]ome women, at least, would want to attend [VMI] if they had the opportunity," the District Court recognized, 766 F.Supp., at 1414, and "some women," the expert testimony established, "are capable of all of the individual activities required of VMI cadets," *id.*, at 1412. The parties, furthermore, agree that "*some* women can meet the physical standards [VMI] now impose[s] on men." 976 F.2d, at 896. In sum, as the Court of Appeals stated, "neither the goal of producing citizen soldiers," VMI's *raison d'etre*, "nor VMI's implementing methodology is inherently unsuitable to women." *Id.*, at 899.

* * *

The United States does not challenge any expert witness estimation on average capacities or preferences of men and women. Instead, the United States emphasizes that time and again since this Court's turning point decision in *Reed v. Reed*, 404 U.S. 71, 92 S.Ct. 251, 30 L.Ed.2d 225 (1971), we have cautioned reviewing courts to take a "hard look" at generalizations or "tendencies" of the kind pressed by Virginia, and relied upon by the District Court. See O'Connor, Portia's Progress, 66 N.Y.U.L.Rev. 1546, 1551 (1991). State actors controlling gates to opportunity, we have instructed, may not exclude qualified individuals based on "fixed notions concerning the roles and abilities of

males and females." *Mississippi Univ. for Women*, 458 U.S., at 725, 102 S.Ct., at 3336; see *J.E.B.*, 511 U.S., at 139, n. 11, 114 S.Ct., at 1427, n. 11 (equal protection principles, as applied to gender classifications, mean state actors may not rely on "overbroad" generalizations to make "judgments about people that are likely to . . . perpetuate historical patterns of discrimination").

It may be assumed, for purposes of this decision, that most women would not choose VMI's adversative method. . . . [H]owever, . . . it is also probable that "many men would not want to be educated in such an environment." . . . Education, to be sure, is not a "one size fits all" business. The issue, however, is not whether "women—or men— should be forced to attend VMI"; rather, the question is whether the Commonwealth can constitutionally deny to women who have the will and capacity, the training and attendant opportunities that VMI uniquely affords.

The notion that admission of women would downgrade VMI's stature, destroy the adversative system and, with it, even the school, is a judgment hardly proved, a prediction hardly different from other "self-fulfilling prophec[ies]," see *Mississippi Univ. for Women*, 458 U.S., at 730, 102 S.Ct., at 3339, once routinely used to deny rights or opportunities. . . .

* * *

Women's successful entry into the federal military academies,[13] and their participation in the Nation's military forces,[14] indicate that Virginia's fears for the future of VMI may not be solidly grounded.[15] The Commonwealth's justification for excluding all women from "citizen-soldier" training for which some are qualified, in any event, cannot rank as "exceedingly persuasive," as we have explained and applied that standard.

* * *

. . . . [T]he Commonwealth's great goal [of producing "citizen-soldiers"] is not substantially advanced by women's categorical exclusion, in total disregard of their individual merit, from the Commonwealth's pre-

---

[13]Women cadets have graduated at the top of their class at every federal military academy. See Brief for Lieutenant Colonel Rhonda Cornum et al. as *Amici Curiae* 11, n. 25; cf. Defense Advisory Committee on Women in the Services, Report on the Integration and Performance of Women at West Point 64 (1992).

[14]Brief for Lieutenant Colonel Rhonda Cornum, *supra*, at 5–9 (reporting the vital contributions and courageous performance of women in the military); see Mintz, "President Nominates 1st Woman to Rank of Three-Star General," *Washington Post*, Mar. 27, 1996, p. A19, col. 1 (announcing President's nomination of Marine Corps Major General Carol Mutter to rank of Lieutenant General; Mutter will head corps manpower and planning); M. Tousignant, "A New Era for the Old Guard," *Washington Post*, Mar. 23, 1996, p. C1, col. 2 (reporting admission of Sergeant Heather Johnsen to elite Infantry unit that keeps round-the-clock vigil at Tomb of the Unknowns in Arlington National Cemetery).

[15]Inclusion of women in settings where, traditionally, they were not wanted inevitably entails a period of adjustment. As one West Point cadet squad leader recounted: "[T]he classes of '78 and '79 see the women as women, but the classes of '80 and '81 see them as classmates." U.S. Military Academy, A. Vitters, Report of Admission of Women (Project Athena II) 84 (1978) (internal quotation marks omitted).

mier "citizen-soldier" corps.[16] Virginia, in sum, "has fallen far short of establishing the 'exceedingly persuasive justification,' " *Mississippi Univ. for Women*, 458 U.S., at 731, 102 S.Ct., at 3340, that must be the solid base for any gender-defined classification.

VI

In the second phase of the litigation, Virginia presented its remedial plan—maintain VMI as a male-only college and create VWIL as a separate program for women. . . .

A

A remedial decree, this Court has said, must closely fit the constitutional violation; it must be shaped to place persons unconstitutionally denied an opportunity or advantage in "the position they would have occupied in the absence of [discrimination]." See *Milliken v. Bradley*, 433 U.S. 267, 280, 97 S.Ct. 2749, 2757, 53 L.Ed.2d 745 (1977) (internal quotation marks omitted). The constitutional violation in this suit is the categorical exclusion of women from an extraordinary educational opportunity afforded men. A proper remedy for an unconstitutional exclusion, we have explained, aims to "eliminate [so far as possible] the discriminatory effects of the past" and to "bar like discrimination in the future." *Louisiana v. United States*, 380 U.S. 145, 154, 85 S.Ct. 817, 822, 13 L.Ed.2d 709 (1965).

Virginia chose not to eliminate, but to leave untouched, VMI's exclusionary policy. For women only, however, Virginia proposed a separate program, different in kind from VMI and unequal in tangible and intangible facilities. . . .

VWIL affords women no opportunity to experience the rigorous military training for which VMI is famed. See 766 F.Supp., at 1413–1414 ("No other school in Virginia or in the United States, public or private, offers the same kind of rigorous military training as is available at VMI."); *id.*, at 1421 (VMI "is known to be the most challenging military school in the United States"). Instead, the VWIL program "deemphasize[s]" military education, 44 F.3d, at 1234, and uses a "cooperative method" of education "which reinforces self-esteem," 852 F.Supp., at 476.

VWIL students participate in ROTC and a "largely ceremonial" Virginia Corps of Cadets, see 44 F.3d, at 1234, but Virginia deliberately did not make VWIL a military institute. The VWIL House is not a military-style residence and VWIL students need not live together throughout the 4-year program, eat meals together, or wear uniforms during the schoolday. See 852 F.Supp., at 477, 495. VWIL students thus do not experience the "barracks" life "crucial to the VMI experience," the spartan living arrangements designed to foster an "egalitarian ethic." See 766 F.Supp., at 1423–1424. "[T]he most important aspects of the VMI educational experience occur in the barracks," the District Court found, *id.*, at 1423, yet Virginia deemed that core experience nonessential, indeed inappropriate, for training its female citizen-soldiers.

VWIL students receive their "leadership training" in seminars, externships, and speaker series, see 852 F.Supp., at 477, episodes and encounters lacking the "[p]hysical rigor, mental stress, . . . minute regulation of behavior, and indoctrination in desirable values" made hallmarks of VMI's citizen-soldier training, see 766 F.Supp., at 1421. Kept away from the pressures, hazards, and psychological bonding characteristic of VMI's adversative training, see *id.*, at 1422, VWIL students will not know the "feeling of tremendous accomplishment" commonly experienced by VMI's successful cadets, *id.*, at 1426.

Virginia maintains that these methodological differences are "justified pedagogically," based on "important differences between men and women in learning and developmental needs," "psychological and sociological differences" Virginia describes as "real" and "not stereotypes." . . . .

As earlier stated, see *supra*, at 2280, generalizations about "the way women are," estimates of what is appropriate for *most women*, no longer justify denying opportunity to women whose talent and capacity place them outside the average description. Notably, Virginia never asserted that VMI's method of education suits *most men*. It is also revealing that Virginia accounted for its failure to make the VWIL experience "the entirely militaristic experience of VMI" on the ground that VWIL "is planned for women who do not necessarily expect to pursue military careers." 852

---

[16]VMI has successfully managed another notable change. The school admitted its first African-American cadets in 1968. See *The VMI Story* 347–349 (students no longer sing "Dixie," salute the Confederate flag or the tomb of General Robert E. Lee at ceremonies and sports events). As the District Court noted, VMI established a program on "retention of black cadets" designed to offer academic and social-cultural support to "minority members of a dominantly white and tradition-oriented student body." 766 F.Supp., at 1436–1437. The school maintains a "special recruitment program for blacks" which, the District Court found, "has had little, if any, effect on VMI's method of accomplishing its mission." *Id.*, at 1437.

F.Supp., at 478. By that reasoning, VMI's "entirely militaristic" program would be inappropriate for men in general or *as a group*, for "[o]nly about 15% of VMI cadets enter career military service." See 766 F.Supp., at 1432.

In contrast to the generalizations about women on which Virginia rests, we note again these dispositive realities: VMI's "implementing methodology" is not "inherently unsuitable to women," 976 F.2d, at 899; "some women . . . do well under [the] adversative model," 766 F.Supp., at 1434 (internal quotation marks omitted); "some women, at least, would want to attend [VMI] if they had the opportunity," *id.*, at 1414; "some women are capable of all of the individual activities required of VMI cadets," *id.*, at 1412, and "can meet the physical standards [VMI] now impose[s] on men," 976 F.2d, at 896. It is on behalf of these women that the United States has instituted this suit, and it is for them that a remedy must be crafted,[19] a remedy that will end their exclusion from a state-supplied educational opportunity for which they are fit, a decree that will "bar like discrimination in the future." *Louisiana,* 380 U.S., at 154, 85 S.Ct., at 822.

B

In myriad respects other than military training, VWIL does not qualify as VMI's equal. VWIL's student body, faculty, course offerings, and facilities hardly match VMI's. Nor can the VWIL graduate anticipate the benefits associated with VMI's 157-year history, the school's prestige, and its influential alumni network.

Mary Baldwin College, whose degree VWIL students will gain, enrolls first-year women with an average combined SAT score about 100 points lower than the average score for VMI freshmen. 852 F.Supp., at 501. The Mary Baldwin faculty holds "significantly fewer Ph.D.'s," *id.*, at 502, and receives substantially lower salaries, see Tr. 158 (testimony of James Lott, Dean of Mary Baldwin College), than the faculty at VMI.

Mary Baldwin does not offer a VWIL student the range of curricular choices available to a VMI cadet. VMI awards baccalaureate degrees in liberal arts, biology, chemistry, civil engineering, electrical and computer engineering, and mechanical engineering. See 852 F.Supp., at 503; Virginia Military Institute: More than an Education 11 (Govt. exh. 75, lodged with Clerk of this Court). VWIL students attend a school that "does not have a math and science focus," 852 F.Supp., at 503; they cannot take at Mary Baldwin any courses in engineering or the advanced math and physics courses VMI offers, see *id.*, at 477.

For physical training, Mary Baldwin has "two multi-purpose fields" and "[o]ne gymnasium." *Id.*, at 503. VMI has "an NCAA competition level indoor track and field facility; a number of multi-purpose fields; baseball, soccer and lacrosse fields; an obstacle course; large boxing, wrestling and martial arts facilities; an 11-laps-to-the-mile indoor running course; an indoor pool; indoor and outdoor rifle ranges; and a football stadium that also contains a practice field and outdoor track." *Ibid.*

Although Virginia has represented that it will provide equal financial support for in-state VWIL students and VMI cadets, *id.*, at 483, and the VMI Foundation has agreed to endow VWIL with $5.4625 million, *id.*, at 499, the difference between the two schools' financial reserves is pronounced. Mary Baldwin's endowment, currently about $19 million, will gain an additional $35 million based on future commitments; VMI's current endowment, $131 million—the largest public college per-student endowment in the Nation—will gain $220 million. *Id.*, at 503.

The VWIL student does not graduate with the advantage of a VMI degree. Her diploma does not unite her with the legions of VMI "graduates [who] have distinguished themselves" in military and civilian life. See 976 F.2d, at 892–893. "[VMI] alumni are exceptionally close to the school," and that closeness accounts, in part, for VMI's success in attracting applicants. See 766 F.Supp., at 1421. A VWIL graduate cannot assume that the "network of business owners, corporations, VMI graduates and non-graduate employers . . . interested in hiring VMI graduates," 852 F.Supp., at 499, will be equally responsive to her search for employment, see 44 F.3d, at 1250 (Phillips, J., dissenting) ("the

---

[19]Admitting women to VMI would undoubtedly require alterations necessary to afford members of each sex privacy from the other sex in living arrangements, and to adjust aspects of the physical training programs. See Brief for Petitioner 27–29; cf. note following 10 U.S.C. § 4342 (academic and other standards for women admitted to the Military, Naval, and Air Force Academies "shall be the same as those required for male individuals, except for those minimum essential adjustments in such standards required because of physiological differences between male and female individuals"). Experience shows such adjustments are manageable. See U.S. Military Academy, A. Vitters, N. Kinzer, & J. Adams, Report of Admission of Women (Project Athena I-IV) (1977–1980) (4-year longitudinal study of the admission of women to West Point); Defense Advisory Committee on Women in the Services, Report on the Integration and Performance of Women at West Point 17–18 (1992).

powerful political and economic ties of the VMI alumni network cannot be expected to open" for graduates of the fledgling VWIL program).

Virginia, in sum, while maintaining VMI for men only, has failed to provide any "comparable single-gender women's institution." *Id.*, at 1241. Instead, the Commonwealth has created a VWIL program fairly appraised as a "pale shadow" of VMI in terms of the range of curricular choices and faculty stature, funding, prestige, alumni support and influence. See *id.*, at 1250 (Phillips, J., dissenting).

Virginia's VWIL solution is reminiscent of the remedy Texas proposed 50 years ago, in response to a state trial court's 1946 ruling that, given the equal protection guarantee, African-Americans could not be denied a legal education at a state facility. See *Sweatt v. Painter*, 339 U.S. 629, 70 S.Ct. 848, 94 L.Ed. 1114 (1950). Reluctant to admit African-Americans to its flagship University of Texas Law School, the State set up a separate school for Heman Sweatt and other black law students. *Id.*, at 632, 70 S.Ct., at 849. As originally opened, the new school had no independent faculty or library, and it lacked accreditation. *Id.*, at 633, 70 S.Ct., at 849–850. Nevertheless, the state trial and appellate courts were satisfied that the new school offered Sweatt opportunities for the study of law "substantially equivalent to those offered by the State to white students at the University of Texas." *Id.*, at 632, 70 S.Ct., at 849 (internal quotation marks omitted).

* * *

. . . . Facing the marked differences reported in the *Sweatt* opinion, the Court unanimously ruled that Texas had not shown "substantial equality in the [separate] educational opportunities" the State offered. Id., at 633, 70 S.Ct., at 850. Accordingly, the Court held, the Equal Protection Clause required Texas to admit African-Americans to the University of Texas Law School. *Id.*, at 636, 70 S.Ct., at 851. In line with *Sweatt*, we rule here that Virginia has not shown substantial equality in the separate educational opportunities the Commonwealth supports at VWIL and VMI.

C

* * *

. . . Valuable as VWIL may prove for students who seek the program offered, Virginia's remedy affords no cure at all for the opportunities and advantages withheld from women who want a VMI education and can make the grade. . . . In sum,

Virginia's remedy does not match the constitutional violation; the Commonwealth has shown no "exceedingly persuasive justification" for withholding from women qualified for the experience premier training of the kind VMI affords.

VII

* * *

VMI . . . offers an educational opportunity no other Virginia institution provides, and the school's "prestige"—associated with its success in developing "citizen-soldiers"—is unequaled. Virginia has closed this facility to its daughters and, instead, has devised for them a "parallel program," with a faculty less impressively credentialed and less well paid, more limited course offerings, fewer opportunities for military training and for scientific specialization. Cf. *Sweatt*, 339 U.S., at 633, 70 S.Ct., at 849–850. VMI, beyond question, "possesses to a far greater degree" than the VWIL program "those qualities which are incapable of objective measurement but which make for greatness in a . . . school," including "position and influence of the alumni, standing in the community, traditions and prestige." *Id.*, at 634, 70 S.Ct., at 850. Women seeking and fit for a VMI-quality education cannot be offered anything less, under the Commonwealth's obligation to afford them genuinely equal protection.

A prime part of the history of our Constitution, historian Richard Morris recounted, is the story of the extension of constitutional rights and protections to people once ignored or excluded. VMI's story continued as our comprehension of "We the People" expanded. See *supra*, at 2275, n. 6. There is no reason to believe that the admission of women capable of all the activities required of VMI cadets would destroy the Institute rather than enhance its capacity to serve the "more perfect Union."

* * *

Justice THOMAS took no part in the consideration or decision of these cases.

Chief Justice REHNQUIST, concurring in the judgment.

The Court holds first that Virginia violates the Equal Protection Clause by maintaining the Virginia Military Institute's (VMI's) all-male admissions policy, and second that establishing the Virginia Women's Institute for Leadership (VWIL) program does not remedy that violation. While I agree with these conclusions, I disagree with the Court's analysis and so I write separately.

I

Two decades ago in *Craig v. Boren*, 429 U.S. 190, 197, 97 S.Ct. 451, 456–457, 50 L.Ed.2d 397 (1976), we announced that "[t]o withstand constitutional challenge, . . . classifications by gender must serve important governmental objectives and must be substantially related to achievement of those objectives." We have adhered to that standard of scrutiny ever since. . . . While the majority adheres to this test today, . . . it also says that the Commonwealth must demonstrate an " 'exceedingly persuasive justification' " to support a gender-based classification. . . . It is unfortunate that the Court thereby introduces an element of uncertainty respecting the appropriate test.

While terms like "important governmental objective" and "substantially related" are hardly models of precision, they have more content and specificity than does the phrase "exceedingly persuasive justification." That phrase is best confined, as it was first used, as an observation on the difficulty of meeting the applicable test, not as a formulation of the test itself. See, *e.g.*, *Feeney, supra*, at 273, 99 S.Ct., at 2293 ("[T]hese precedents dictate that any state law overtly or covertly designed to prefer males over females in public employment require an exceedingly persuasive justification"). To avoid introducing potential confusion, I would have adhered more closely to our traditional, "firmly established," *Hogan, supra*, at 723, 102 S.Ct., at 3335; *Heckler, supra*, at 744, 104 S.Ct., at 1397–1398, standard that a gender-based classification "must bear a close and substantial relationship to important governmental objectives." *Feeney, supra*, at 273, 99 S.Ct., at 2293.

Our cases dealing with gender discrimination also require that the proffered purpose for the challenged law be the actual purpose. . . . It is on this ground that the Court rejects the first of two justifications Virginia offers for VMI's single-sex admissions policy, namely, the goal of diversity among its public educational institutions. While I ultimately agree that the Commonwealth has not carried the day with this justification, I disagree with the Court's method of analyzing the issue.

* * *

Before this Court, Virginia has sought to justify VMI's single-sex admissions policy primarily on the basis that diversity in education is desirable, and that while most of the public institutions of higher learning in the Commonwealth are coeducational, there should also be room for single-sex institutions. I agree with the Court that there is scant evidence in the record that this was the real reason that Virginia decided to maintain VMI as men only.* But, unlike the majority, I would consider only evidence that postdates our decision in *Hogan*, and would draw no negative inferences from the Commonwealth's actions before that time. I think that after *Hogan*, the Commonwealth was entitled to reconsider its policy with respect to VMI, and not to have earlier justifications, or lack thereof, held against it.

Even if diversity in educational opportunity were the Commonwealth's actual objective, the Commonwealth's position would still be problematic. The difficulty with its position is that the diversity benefited only one sex; there was single-sex public education available for men at VMI, but no corresponding single-sex public education available for women. When *Hogan* placed Virginia on notice that VMI's admissions policy possibly was unconstitutional, VMI could have dealt with the problem by admitting women; but its governing body felt strongly that the admission of women would have seriously harmed the institution's educational approach. Was there something else the Commonwealth could have done to avoid an equal protection violation? Since the Commonwealth did nothing, we do not have to definitively answer that question.

I do not think, however, that the Commonwealth's options were as limited as the majority may imply. The Court cites, without expressly approving it, a statement from the opinion of the dissenting judge in the Court of Appeals, to the effect that the Commonwealth could have "simultaneously opened single-gender undergraduate institutions having substantially comparable curricular and extracurricular programs, funding, physical plant, administration and support services, and faculty and library resources." . . . (internal quotation marks omitted). If this statement is thought to exclude

---

*The dissent equates our conclusion that VMI's "asserted interest in promoting diversity" is not " 'genuine,' " with a "charge" that the diversity rationale is "a pretext for discriminating against women." . . . Of course, those are not the same thing. I do not read the Court as saying that the diversity rationale is a pretext for discrimination, and I would not endorse such a proposition. We may find that diversity was not the Commonwealth's real reason without suggesting, or having to show, that the real reason was "antifeminism," . . . . Our cases simply require that the proffered purpose for the challenged gender classification be the actual purpose, although not necessarily recorded. . . . The dissent also says that the interest in diversity is so transparent that having to articulate it is "absurd on its face." . . . Apparently, that rationale was not obvious to the Mission Study Committee which failed to list it among its reasons for maintaining VMI's all-men admission policy.

other possibilities, it is too stringent a requirement. VMI had been in operation for over a century and a half, and had an established, successful, and devoted group of alumni. No legislative wand could instantly call into existence a similar institution for women; and it would be a tremendous loss to scrap VMI's history and tradition. In the words of Grover Cleveland's second inaugural address, the Commonwealth faced a condition, not a theory. And it was a condition that had been brought about, not through defiance of decisions construing gender bias under the Equal Protection Clause, but, until the decision in *Hogan*, a condition that had not appeared to offend the Constitution. Had Virginia made a genuine effort to devote comparable public resources to a facility for women, and followed through on such a plan, it might well have avoided an equal protection violation. I do not believe the Commonwealth was faced with the stark choice of either admitting women to VMI, on the one hand, or abandoning VMI and starting from scratch for both men and women, on the other.

* * *

Virginia offers a second justification for the single-sex admissions policy: maintenance of the adversative method. I agree with the Court that this justification does not serve an important governmental objective. A State does not have substantial interest in the adversative methodology unless it is pedagogically beneficial. While considerable evidence shows that a single-sex education is pedagogically beneficial for some students, see 766 F.Supp., at 1414, and hence a State may have a valid interest in promoting that methodology, there is no similar evidence in the record that an adversative method is pedagogically beneficial or is any more likely to produce character traits than other methodologies.

II

The Court defines the constitutional violation in these cases as "the categorical exclusion of women from an extraordinary educational opportunity afforded to men." . . . By defining the violation in this way, and by emphasizing that a remedy for a constitutional violation must place the victims of discrimination in " 'the position they would have occupied in the absence of [discrimination],' " *ibid.*, the Court necessarily implies that the only adequate remedy would be the admission of women to the all-male institution. As the foregoing discussion suggests, I

would not define the violation in this way; it is not the "exclusion of women" that violates the Equal Protection Clause, but the maintenance of an all-men school without providing any—much less a comparable—institution for women.

Accordingly, the remedy should not necessarily require either the admission of women to VMI or the creation of a VMI clone for women. An adequate remedy in my opinion might be a demonstration by Virginia that its interest in educating men in a single-sex environment is matched by its interest in educating women in a single-sex institution. To demonstrate such, the Commonwealth does not need to create two institutions with the same number of faculty Ph.D.'s, similar SAT scores, or comparable athletic fields. . . . Nor would it necessarily require that the women's institution offer the same curriculum as the men's; one could be strong in computer science, the other could be strong in liberal arts. It would be a sufficient remedy, I think, if the two institutions offered the same quality of education and were of the same overall caliber.

If a State decides to create single-sex programs, the State would, I expect, consider the public's interest and demand in designing curricula. And rightfully so. But the State should avoid assuming demand based on stereotypes; it must not assume *a priori*, without evidence, that there would be no interest in a women's school of civil engineering, or in a men's school of nursing.

In the end, the women's institution Virginia proposes, VWIL, fails as a remedy, because it is distinctly inferior to the existing men's institution and will continue to be for the foreseeable future. VWIL simply is not, in any sense, the institution that VMI is. In particular, VWIL is a program appended to a private college, not a self-standing institution; and VWIL is substantially underfunded as compared to VMI. I therefore ultimately agree with the Court that Virginia has not provided an adequate remedy.

Justice SCALIA, dissenting.

Today the Court shuts down an institution that has served the people of the Commonwealth of Virginia with pride and distinction for over a century and a half. To achieve that desired result, it rejects (contrary to our established practice) the factual findings of two courts below, sweeps aside the precedents of this Court, and ignores the history of our people. As to facts: It explicitly rejects the finding that there exist "gender-based developmental differences" supporting Virginia's restriction of the "adversative" method to only a men's institution, and the finding that the all-male composition of the Virginia Military Institute (VMI) is essential to that institution's character. As to precedent: It drastically revises our established standards for reviewing sex-based classifications. And as to history: It counts for nothing the long tradition, enduring down to the present, of men's military colleges supported by both States and the Federal Government.

* * *

I

* * *

. . . [I]n my view the function of this Court is to *preserve* our society's values regarding (among other things) equal protection, not to *revise* them; to prevent backsliding from the degree of restriction the Constitution imposed upon democratic government, not to prescribe, on our own authority, progressively higher degrees. For that reason it is my view that, whatever abstract tests we may choose to devise, they cannot supersede—and indeed ought to be crafted so as to *reflect*—those constant and unbroken national traditions that embody the people's understanding of ambiguous constitutional texts. More specifically, it is my view that "when a practice not expressly prohibited by the text of the Bill of Rights bears the endorsement of a long tradition of open, widespread, and unchallenged use that dates back to the beginning of the Republic, we have no proper basis for striking it down." *Rutan v. Republican Party of Ill.*, 497 U.S. 62, 95, 110 S.Ct. 2729, 2748, 111 L.Ed.2d 52 (1990) (SCALIA, J., dissenting). . . .

The all-male constitution of VMI comes within such a governing tradition. . . .

And the same applies, more broadly, to single-sex education in general, which, as I shall discuss, is threatened by today's decision with the cutoff of all state and federal support. Government-run *non*military educational institutions for the two sexes have until very recently also been part of our national tradition. "[It is] [c]oeducation, historically, [that] is a novel educational theory. From grade school through high school, college, and graduate and professional training, much of the Nation's population during much of our history has been educated in sexually segregated classrooms." *Mississippi Univ. for Women v. Hogan*, 458 U.S. 718, 736, 102 S.Ct. 3331, 3342, 73 L.Ed.2d 1090 (1982) (Powell, J., dissent-

ing); see *id.*, at 736–739, 102 S.Ct., at 3342–3344. These traditions may of course be changed by the democratic decisions of the people, as they largely have been.

Today, however, change is forced upon Virginia, and reversion to single-sex education is prohibited nationwide, not by democratic processes but by order of this Court. Even while bemoaning the sorry, bygone days of "fixed notions" concerning women's education, see *ante*, at 2277–2278, and n. 10, 2277–2278, 2280–2282, the Court favors current notions so fixedly that it is willing to write them into the Constitution of the United States by application of custom-built "tests." This is not the interpretation of a Constitution, but the creation of one.

II

* * *

Although the Court in two places recites the test as stated in *Hogan*, see *ante*, at 2271, 2275, which asks whether the State has demonstrated "that the classification serves important governmental objectives and that the discriminatory means employed are substantially related to the achievement of those objectives," 458 U.S., at 724, 102 S.Ct., at 3336 (internal quotation marks omitted), the Court never answers the question presented in anything resembling that form. When it engages in analysis, the Court instead prefers the phrase "exceedingly persuasive justification" from *Hogan*. The Court's nine invocations of that phrase, . . . and even its fanciful description of that imponderable as "the core instruction" of the Court's decisions in *J.E.B. v. Alabama ex rel. T. B.*, *supra*, and *Hogan*, *supra*, . . . would be unobjectionable if the Court acknowledged that *whether* a "justification" is "exceedingly persuasive" must be assessed by asking "[whether] the classification serves important governmental objectives and [whether] the discriminatory means employed are substantially related to the achievement of those objectives." Instead, however, the Court proceeds to interpret "exceedingly persuasive justification" in a fashion that contradicts the reasoning of *Hogan* and our other precedents.

That is essential to the Court's result, which can only be achieved by establishing that intermediate scrutiny is not survived if there are *some* women interested in attending VMI, capable of undertaking its activities, and able to meet its physical demands. . . .

* * *

Only the amorphous "exceedingly persuasive justification" phrase, and not the standard elaboration of intermediate scrutiny, can be made to yield this conclusion that VMI's single-sex composition is unconstitutional because there exist several women (or, one would have to conclude under the Court's reasoning, a single woman) willing and able to undertake VMI's program. Intermediate scrutiny has never required a least-restrictive-means analysis, but only a "substantial relation" between the classification and the state interests that it serves. . . .

Not content to execute a *de facto* abandonment of the intermediate scrutiny that has been our standard for sex-based classifications for some two decades, the Court purports to reserve the question whether, even in principle, a higher standard (*i.e.*, strict scrutiny) should apply. . . .

The Court's intimations are particularly out of place because it is perfectly clear that, if the question of the applicable standard of review for sex-based classifications were to be regarded as an appropriate subject for reconsideration, the stronger argument would be not for elevating the standard to strict scrutiny, but for reducing it to rational-basis review. The latter certainly has a firmer foundation in our past jurisprudence: Whereas no majority of the Court has ever applied strict scrutiny in a case involving sex-based classifications, we routinely applied rational-basis review until the 1970's. . . . It is hard to consider women a "discrete and insular minorit[y]" unable to employ the "political processes ordinarily to be relied upon," when they constitute a majority of the electorate. And the suggestion that they are incapable of exerting that political power smacks of the same paternalism that the Court so roundly condemns. . . . Moreover, a long list of legislation proves the proposition false. See, *e.g.*, Equal Pay Act of 1963, 29 U.S.C. § 206(d); Title VII of the Civil Rights Act of 1964, 42 U.S.C. § 2000e-2; Title IX of the Education Amendments of 1972, 20 U.S.C. § 1681; Women's Business Ownership Act of 1988, Pub.L. 100-533, 102 Stat. 2689; Violence Against Women Act of 1994, Pub.L. 103-322, Title IV, 108 Stat. 1902.

III

With this explanation of how the Court has succeeded in making its analysis seem orthodox—and indeed, if intimations are to be believed, even overly generous to VMI—I now proceed to describe how

the analysis should have been conducted. The question to be answered, I repeat, is whether the exclusion of women from VMI is "substantially related to an important governmental objective."

A

It is beyond question that Virginia has an important state interest in providing effective college education for its citizens. That single-sex instruction is an approach substantially related to that interest should be evident enough from the long and continuing history in this country of men's and women's colleges. But beyond that, as the Court of Appeals here stated: "That single-gender education at the college level is beneficial to both sexes is a *fact established in this case.*" 44 F.3d 1229, 1238 (C.A.4 1995) (emphasis added).

* * *

But besides its single-sex constitution, VMI is different from other colleges in another way. It employs a "distinctive educational method," sometimes referred to as the "adversative, or doubting, model of education." 766 F.Supp., at 1413, 1421. "Physical rigor, mental stress, absolute equality of treatment, absence of privacy, minute regulation of behavior, and indoctrination in desirable values are the salient attributes of the VMI educational experience." *Id.*, at 1421. No one contends that this method is appropriate for all individuals; education is not a "one size fits all" business. Just as a State may wish to support junior colleges, vocational institutes, or a law school that emphasizes case practice instead of classroom study, so too a State's decision to maintain within its system one school that provides the adversative method is "substantially related" to its goal of good education. Moreover, it was uncontested that "if the state were to establish a women's VMI-type [*i.e.*, adversative] program, the program would attract an insufficient number of participants to make the program work," 44 F.3d, at 1241; and it was found by the District Court that if Virginia were to include women in VMI, the school "would eventually find it necessary to drop the adversative system altogether," 766 F.Supp., at 1413. Thus, Virginia's options were an adversative method that excludes women or no adversative method at all.

There can be no serious dispute that, as the District Court found, single-sex education and a distinctive educational method "represent legitimate contributions to diversity in the Virginia higher education system." . . .

Virginia did not make this determination regarding the make-up of its public college system on the unrealistic assumption that no other colleges exist. Substantial evidence in the District Court demonstrated that the Commonwealth has long proceeded on the principle that " '[h]igher education resources should be viewed as a whole—public and private' "—because such an approach enhances diversity and because " 'it is academic and economic waste to permit unwarranted duplication.' " *Id.*, at 1420–1421 (quoting 1974 Report of the General Assembly Commission on Higher Education to the General Assembly of Virginia). It is thus significant that, whereas there are "four all-female private [colleges] in Virginia," there is only "one private all-male college," which "indicates that the private sector is providing for th[e] [former] form of education to a much greater extent that it provides for all-male education." 766 F.Supp., at 1420–1421. In these circumstances, Virginia's election to fund one public all-male institution and one on the adversative model—and to concentrate its resources in a single entity that serves both these interests in diversity—is substantially related to the Commonwealth's important educational interests.

* * *

IV

As is frequently true, the Court's decision today will have consequences that extend far beyond the parties to the litigation. What I take to be the Court's unease with these consequences, and its resulting unwillingness to acknowledge them, cannot alter the reality.

A

Under the constitutional principles announced and applied today, single-sex public education is unconstitutional. By going through the motions of applying a balancing test—asking whether the State has adduced an "exceedingly persuasive justification" for its sex-based classification—the Court creates the illusion that government officials in some future case will have a clear shot at justifying some sort of single-sex public education. Indeed, the Court seeks to create even a greater illusion than that: It purports to have said nothing of rele-

vance to *other* public schools at all. "We address specifically and only an educational opportunity recognized . . . as 'unique'." . . .

* * *

. . . [T]he rationale of today's decision is sweeping: for sex-based classifications, a redefinition of intermediate scrutiny that makes it indistinguishable from strict scrutiny. . . . Indeed, the Court indicates that if any program restricted to one sex is "uniqu[e]," it must be opened to members of the opposite sex "who have the will and capacity" to participate in it. . . . I suggest that the single-sex program that will not be capable of being characterized as "unique" is not only unique but nonexistent.[8]

In any event, regardless of whether the Court's rationale leaves some small amount of room for lawyers to argue, it ensures that single-sex public education is functionally dead. The costs of litigating the constitutionality of a single-sex education program, and the risks of ultimately losing that litigation, are simply too high to be embraced by public officials. . . .

This is especially regrettable because, as the District Court here determined, educational experts in recent years have increasingly come to "suppor[t] [the] view that substantial educational benefits flow from a single-gender environment, be it male or female, *that cannot be replicated in a coeducational setting.*" 766 F.Supp., at 1415 (emphasis added). "The evidence in th[is] case," for example, "is virtually uncontradicted" to that effect. *Ibid.* Until quite recently, some public officials have attempted to institute new single-sex programs, at least as experiments. In 1991, for example, the Detroit Board of Education announced a program to establish three boys-only schools for inner-city youth; it was met with a lawsuit, a preliminary injunction was swiftly entered by a District Court that purported to rely on *Hogan*, see *Garrett v. Board of Ed. of School Dist. of Detroit*, 775 F.Supp. 1004, 1006 (E.D.Mich.1991), and the Detroit Board of Education voted to abandon the litigation and thus abandon the plan, see "Detroit Plan to Aid Blacks with All-Boy Schools Abandoned," *Los Angeles Times*, Nov. 8, 1991, p. A4, col. 1. Today's opinion assures that no such experiment will be tried again.

---

[8]In this regard, I note that the Court—which I concede is under no obligation to do so—provides no example of a program that *would* pass muster under its reasoning today: not even, for example, a football or wrestling program. On the Court's theory, any woman ready, willing, and physically able to participate in such a program would, *as a constitutional matter*, be entitled to do so.

B

There are few extant single-sex public educational programs. The potential of today's decision for widespread disruption of existing institutions lies in its application to *private* single-sex education. Government support is immensely important to private educational institutions. Mary Baldwin College—which designed and runs VWIL—notes that private institutions of higher education in the 1990–1991 school year derived approximately 19 percent of their budgets from federal, state, and local government funds, *not including financial aid to students.* See Brief for Mary Baldwin College as *Amicus Curiae* 22, n. 13 (citing U.S. Dept. of Education, National Center for Education Statistics, Digest of Education Statistics, p. 38 and Note (1993)). Charitable status under the tax laws is also highly significant for private educational institutions, and it is certainly not beyond the Court that rendered today's decision to hold that a donation to a single-sex college should be deemed contrary to public policy and therefore not deductible if the college discriminates on the basis of sex. See Note, The Independent Sector and the Tax Laws: Defining Charity in an Ideal Democracy, 64 S. Cal. L.Rev. 461, 476 (1991). See also *Bob Jones Univ. v. United States,* 461 U.S. 574, 103 S.Ct. 2017, 76 L.Ed.2d 157 (1983).

* * *

NOTES AND QUESTIONS

1. The Future of Single-Sex Public Education After VMI

The VMI case clearly pitted different visions of sexual equality against one another. Various commentators concluded that the decision sounded the death knell for single-sex education, but others countered that school districts could provide such programs so long as they offered a sufficiently compelling justification. The case divided the feminist community, and in the lower courts, leading women's advocates offered opinions on both sides. Those who testified for the state wished to preserve a constitutional space for single-sex education, whereas their opponents viewed the practice as a vestige of past discrimination and stereotyping. Avery, "Institutional Myths, Historical Narratives and Social Science Evidence: Reading the 'Record' in the Virginia Military Institute Case," 5 *S. Cal.Rev.L. & Women's Stud.* 189, 277–318 (1996). After *VMI,* some commentators have wondered whether there is any legal way to operate single-sex public schools. Corcoran, "Single-Sex Education After *VMI:* Equal Protection and East Harlem's Young Women's Leadership School," 145 *U.Pa.L.Rev.* 987 (1997); Morgan, "Anti-Subordination Analysis After *United States v. Virginia:* Evaluating the Constitutionality of K-12 Single-Sex Public Schools," 1999 *U.Chi.L.Forum* 381; Peter, "What Remains of Public Choice and Parental Rights: Does the *VMI* Decision Preclude Exclusive Schools or Classes Based on Gender?" 33 *Cal.W.L.Rev.* 249 (1997); Reiter, "California Single-Gender Academies Pilot Program: Separate But *Really* Equal," 72 U.S.C.L.Rev. 1401 (1999). What do you think about the constitutional viability of an all-male or all-female school?

2. Single-Sex Education: The Vorchheimer Decision

VMI was not the first case to raise concerns about the constitutionality of single-sex education. In *Vorchheimer v. School District of Philadelphia,* 532 F.2d 880 (3d Cir. 1976), *aff'd by an equally divided court,* 430 U.S. 703, 97 S.Ct. 1671, 51 L.Ed.2d 750 (1977), the Court affirmed, without opinion, a lower court ruling that neither Title IX nor the Constitution forbids a public school system from maintaining a limited number of single-sex high schools in which enrollment is voluntary and educational opportunities are "essentially equal." As the court of appeals had explained, "We are not unsympathetic with [plaintiff's] desire to have an expanded freedom of choice, but its cost should not be overlooked. If she were to prevail, then all public single-sex schools would have to be abolished. The absence of these schools would stifle the ability of the local school board to continue with a respected education methodology." 532 F.2d at 888. Does the *VMI* decision cast doubt on the outcome in *Vorchheimer?* What justifications for single-sex education remain available to school districts after *VMI?*

3. Can Separate Be Equal?

Like *VMI,* the *Vorchheimer* case triggered a debate about whether schools segregated by sex are inherently unequal. One commentator noted that "the problem with the *Vorchheimer* majority's theory of equal benefit is analogous to the problem with *Plessy v. Ferguson*'s concept of 'separate but equal.' " Note, "Single Sex Public Schools: The Last Bastion of 'Separate but Equal'?" 1977 *Duke L. J.* 259, 268. Is this analogy between race and gender correct? Are all-female schools generally perceived as inferior? Shortly before *Vorchheimer* was decided, a leading scholar argued that sex-separate schools are legally and pedagogically defensible. He considered challenges to separate schools a quest for "a single standard of sameness . . . a doctrinaire equality," and he explicitly rejected any simple analogy between race and sex:

> It is sometimes said that a rigid requirement of equality is no less proper for the sexes than for the races, and no less workable. But the moral dimensions of the concept of equality are clearly not the same in the two cases. . . . A school system offering a triple option based on race — all white, all-black, and mixed schools — would elevate freedom of choice over equal protection in an impermissible way. Are we prepared to pass that judgment as readily on a school system that offers a choice of boys', girls', and coeducational schools?

Freund, "The Equal Rights Amendment Is Not the Way," 6 *Harv.C.R.-C.L.Rev.* 234, 238, 240 (1971).

Do race and gender raise comparable fears of a stigmatizing "separate but equal" education? Or does this analogy obscure more than it clarifies? Did *VMI* embrace the analogy, or did it treat concerns about gender discrimination as unique and independently deserving of special protection?

4. Single-Sex Schools as a Remedy for Racial Disadvantage

For advocates of single-sex education, the analogy between race and gender has proven particularly ironic. In Detroit, the school district wanted to establish all-male black academies in the inner city to battle low academic achievement, high dropout rates, and delinquency. *See* Weber, "Immersed in an Educational Crisis: Alternative Programs for African-American Males," 45 *Stan.L.Rev.* 1099 (1993); Truely and Davis, "Public Education Programs for African-American Males: A Gender Equity Perspective," 21 *NYU Rev.L. & Soc. Change* 725 (1994–95); "Note: Inner-City Single-Sex Schools: Educational Reform or Invidious Discrimination?" 105 *Harv.L.Rev.* 17–41 (1992). However, a federal court held that assignment to the academies based on sex violated Title IX and the Equal Protection Clause. *Garrett v. Board of Education*, 775 F. Supp. 1004 (E.D. Mich. 1991). In striking down the program, the judge noted that the Detroit school district offered no similar opportunities for girls, and that it had not shown that the presence of girls in the classroom bore a substantial relationship to

boys' academic problems. As a result, the district did not show that the all-male academies were a constitutionally permissible way to advance the admittedly important goal of improving young black males' achievement. Because no girls' academy existed, the court noted that it was "not presented with the question of whether the [Detroit School] Board can provide separate but equal public school institutions for boys and girls." *Id.* at 1006 n.4.

The Young Women's Leadership School in East Harlem, New York, which was designed to boost mathematics and science performance and promote leadership skills, also prompted a legal challenge. When the ACLU filed a complaint with the New York Office for Civil Rights of the Department of Education, the school district announced that it was considering plans for a comparable all-male school. Steinberg, "All-Girls Public School to Open Despite Objections," *N.Y. Times*, Aug. 14, 1996, at B1; Steinberg, "Central Board Backs All-Girls School," *N.Y. Times*, Aug. 22, 1996, at B3; Henry, "A New Push for Girls–Only Public Schools," *USA Today*, Sept. 18, 1996, at 1D; Meyers, "Schools Dodge the Law," *USA Today*, Oct. 16, 1996, at 14A; Goodman and Kornblut, "New School Agenda: Boy's HS," *Daily News* (N.Y.), Dec. 11, 1996, at 2. Does creation of an all-male school insulate the district from legal challenges?

5. The Intersection of Race and Gender Stereotypes

Should efforts to compensate for racial disadvantage and poverty outweigh concerns about sexual stereotyping? These concerns are quite real, as demonstrated by Michelle Fine's research on black and Latina adolescents in New York City's low-income school districts. She found that these women often effaced themselves, subordinating their ambitions and offering comfort to males perceived as more fragile and vulnerable to the pressures of inner-city life, Fine, "Sexuality, Schooling, and Adolescent Females: The Missing Discourse of Desire," 58 *Harv.Educ.Rev.* 29 (1988). Are there other ways for educators to address low academic achievement and self-esteem that do not reinforce gender differences?

III. THE LEGISLATIVE FRAMEWORK: TITLE IX OF THE EDUCATION AMENDMENTS OF 1972

Although the 1964 Civil Rights Act proscribes some types of discrimination on the basis of sex, that provision has not been directly applied to the schools.

During the 1970 congressional hearings, Daisy Shaw, the Director of Educational and Vocational Guidance for the New York Schools, urged that some federal action be taken: "A special commission or task force [should] be appointed . . . looking into the educational practices starting with Headstart and kindergarten to see what practices we engage in that brainwash girls from an early age to see themselves in a subservient role. . . ." Representative Edith Green was skeptical: "I don't think [Congress] would be receptive. I think the majority of our colleagues see that as the woman's role and why have a commission to study it. I suspect, from public opinion polls, that that sentiment is shared by the American people." *Hearings on Sec. 805 of H.R. 16098 Before the Special Subcomm. on Education of the Comm. on Education and Labor*, 91st Cong., 2d Sess., (June 17, 1970). *See generally* H. Graham, *The Civil Rights Era: Origins and Development of National Policy* 393–420 (1990). Despite the perception that Congress would be unreceptive, it enacted Title IX, which establishes a general principle of nondiscrimination on the basis of sex. However, this principle has been riddled with exceptions. How do the exceptions relate to a congressional vision of equality?

A. The Statutory Framework

Title IX—Prohibition of Sex Discrimination Sex Discrimination Prohibited
20 U.S.C. §§ 1681–86 (1972 Education Amendments).

Sec. 1681. (a) No person in the United States shall, on the basis of sex, be excluded from participation in, be denied the benefits of, or be subjected to discrimination under any education program or activity receiving federal financial assistance, except that:

(1) in regard to admissions to educational institutions, this section shall apply only to institutions of vocational education, professional education, and graduate higher education, and to public institutions of undergraduate higher education;

(2) in regard to admissions of educational institutions, this section shall not apply (A) for one year from June 23, 1972, nor for six years after June 23, 1972 in the case of an educational institution which has begun the process of changing from being an institution which admits only students of one sex to being an institution which admits students of both sexes, but only if it is carrying out a plan for such a change which is approved by the commissioner of education or (B) for seven years from the date an educational institution begins the process of changing from being an institution which admits only students of only one sex to being an institution which admits students of both sexes, but only if it is carrying out a plan for such a change which is approved by the Secretary of Education, whichever is the later;

(3) this section shall not apply to an educational institution which is controlled by a religious organization if the application of this subsection would not be consistent with the religious tenets of such organization;

(4) this section shall not apply to an educational institution whose primary purpose is the training of individuals for the military services of the United States, or the merchant marine;

(5) in regard to admissions this section shall not apply to any public institution of undergraduate higher education which is an institution that traditionally and continually from its establishment has had a policy of admitting only students of one sex.

(b) Nothing contained in subsection (a) of this section shall be interpreted to require any educational institution to grant preferential or disparate treatment to the members of one sex on account of an imbalance which may exist with respect to the total number or percentage of persons of that sex participating in or receiving the benefits of any federally supported program or activity, in comparison with the total number or percentage of persons of that sex in any community, State, section, or other area: *Provided,* That this subsection shall not be construed to prevent the consideration in any hearing or proceeding under this chapter of statistical evidence tending to show that such an imbalance exists with respect to the participation in, or receipt of the benefits of, any such program or activity by the members of one sex.

(c) For purposes of this chapter an educational institution means any public or private preschool, elementary, or secondary school, or any institution of vocational, professional, or higher education, except that in the case of an educational institution composed of more than one school, college, or department which are administratively separate units, such term means each such school, college, or department.

Federal Administrative Enforcement

Sec. 1682. Each federal department and agency which is empowered to extend Federal financial assistance to any education program or activity, by way of grant, loan, or contract other than a contract of insurance or guaranty, is authorized and directed to effectuate the provisions of section 1681 with respect to such program or activity by issuing rules, regulations, or orders of general applicability which shall be consistent with achievement of the objectives of the statute authorizing the financial assistance in connection with which the action is taken. No such rule, regulation, or order shall become effective unless and until approved by the President. Compliance with any requirement adopted pursuant to this section may be effected (1) by the termination of or refusal to grant or to continue assistance under such program or activity to any recipient as to whom there has been an express finding on the record, after opportunity for hearing, of a failure to comply with such requirement, but such termination or refusal shall be limited to the particular political entity, or part thereof, or other recipient as to whom such a finding has been made, and shall be limited in its effect to the particular program, or part thereof, in which such noncompliance has been so found, or (2) by any other means authorized by law: *Provided, however,* That no such action shall be taken until the department or agency concerned has advised the appropriate person or persons of the failure to comply with the requirement and has determined that compliance cannot be secured by voluntary means. In the case of any action terminating, or refusing to grant or continue, assistance because of failure to comply with a requirement imposed pursuant to this section, the head of the Federal department or agency shall file with the committees of the House and Senate having legislative jurisdiction over the program or activity involved a full written report of the circumstances and the grounds for such action. No such action shall become effective until thirty days have elapsed after the filing of such report.

* * *

Interpretation with Respect to Living Facilities

Sec. 1686. Notwithstanding anything to the contrary contained in this chapter, nothing contained herein shall be construed to prohibit any educational institution receiving funds under this Act, from maintaining separate living facilities for the different sexes.

To supplement the statute itself, the Department of Education's Office for Civil Rights promulgated regulations to assist school districts in complying with Title IX's mandate of nondiscrimination. Some of these regulations follow:

"Nondiscrimination on the Basis of Sex in Education Programs and Activities, Receiving or Benefiting from Federal Financial Assistance"

Department of Education Regulations, 34 C.F.R. § 106.1-106.71.

Subpart C — Discrimination on the Basis of Sex in Admission and Recruitment Prohibited

§ 106.21 Admission

(a) *General.* No person shall, on the basis of sex, be denied admission, or be subjected to discrimination in admission, by any recipient to which this subpart applies, except as provided in §§ 106.16 and 106.17 [relating to transition plans for single-sex institutions converting to a coeducational program].

(b) *Specific prohibitions.* (1) In determining whether a person satisfies any policy or criterion for admission, or in making any offer of admission, a recipient to which this subpart applies shall not:

(i) Give preference to one person over another on the basis of sex, by ranking applicants separately on such basis, or otherwise;

(ii) Apply numerical limitations upon the number or proportion of persons of either sex who may be admitted; or

(iii) Otherwise treat one individual differently from another on the basis of sex.

(2) A recipient shall not administer or operate any test or other criterion for admission which has a disproportionately adverse effect on persons on the basis of sex unless the use of such test or criterion is shown to predict validly success in the education program or activity in question and alternative tests or criteria which do not have such a disproportionately adverse effect are shown to be unavailable.

(c) *Prohibitions relating to marital or parental status.* In determining whether a person satisfies any policy or criterion for admission, or in making any offer of admission, a recipient to which this subpart applies:

(1) Shall not apply any rule concerning the actual or potential parental, family, or marital status of a

student or applicant which treats persons differently on the basis of sex;

(2) Shall not discriminate against or exclude any person on the basis of pregnancy, childbirth, termination of pregnancy, or recovery therefrom, or establish or follow any rule or practice which so discriminates or excludes;

(3) Shall treat disabilities related to pregnancy, childbirth, termination of pregnancy, or recovery therefrom in the same manner and under the same policies as any other temporary disability or physical condition; and

(4) Shall not make pre-admission inquiry as to the marital status of an applicant for admission, including whether such applicant is "Miss" or "Mrs." A recipient may make pre-admission inquiry as to the sex of an applicant for admission, but only if such inquiry is made equally of such applicants of both sexes and if the results of such inquiry are not used in connection with discrimination prohibited by this part.

§ 106.22 Preference in admission

A recipient to which this subpart applies shall not give preference to applicants for admission, on the basis of attendance at any educational institution or other school or entity which admits as students or predominantly members of one sex, if the giving of such preference has the effect of discriminating on the basis of sex in violation of this subpart.

Subpart D—Discrimination on the Basis of Sex in Education Programs and Activities Prohibited

§ 106.31 Education programs and activities

(a) *General.* Except as provided elsewhere in this part, no person shall, on the basis of sex, be excluded from participation in, be denied the benefits of, or be subjected to discrimination under any academic, extracurricular, research, occupational training, or other education program or activity operated by a recipient which receives or benefits from Federal financial assistance. This subpart does not apply to actions of a recipient in connection with admission of its students to an education program or activity of (1) a recipient to which Subpart C does not apply, or (2) an entity, not a recipient, to which Subpart C would not apply if the entity were a recipient. [These are institutions

controlled by certain religious organizations, military and merchant marine educational institutions, social fraternities and sororities, YMCA, YWCA, Girl Scouts, Boy Scouts, Camp Fire Girls, traditionally single-sex voluntary youth organizations, and traditionally single-sex institutions.]

(b) *Specific prohibitions.* Except as provided in this subpart, in providing any aid, benefit, or service to a student, a recipient shall not, on the basis of sex:

(1) Treat one person differently from another in determining whether such person satisfies any requirement or condition for the provision of such aid, benefit, or service;

(2) Provide different aid, benefits, or services or provide aid, benefits, or services in a different manner;

(3) Deny any person any such aid, benefit, or service;

(4) Subject any person to separate or different rules of behavior, sanctions, or other treatment;

(5) Apply any rule concerning the domicile or residence of a student or applicant, including eligibility for in-state fees and tuition;

(6) Aid or perpetuate discrimination against any person by providing significant assistance to any agency, organization, or person which discriminates on the basis of sex in providing any aid, benefit or service to students or employees;

(7) Otherwise limit any person in the enjoyment of any right, privilege, advantage, or opportunity.

§ 106.34 Access to course offerings

A recipient shall not provide any course or otherwise carry out any of its education program or activity separately on the basis of sex, or require or refuse participation therein by any of its students on such basis, including health, physical education, industrial, business, vocational, technical, home economics, music, and adult education courses.

(a) With respect to classes and activities in physical education at the elementary school level, the recipient shall comply fully with this section as expeditiously as possible but in no event later than one year from the effective date of this regulation. With respect to physical education classes and activities at the secondary and post-secondary levels, the recipient shall comply fully with this section as expeditiously as possible but in no event later than three years from the effective date of this regulation.

(b) This section does not prohibit grouping of students in physical education classes and activities by ability as assessed by objective standards of individual performance developed and applied without regard to sex.

(c) This section does not prohibit separation of students by sex within physical education classes or activities during participation in wrestling, boxing, rugby, ice hockey, football, basketball and other sports the purpose or major activity of which involves bodily contact.

(d) Where use of a single standard of measuring skill or progress in a physical education class has an adverse effect on members of one sex, the recipient shall use appropriate standards which do not have such effect.

(e) Portions of classes in elementary and secondary schools which deal exclusively with human sexuality may be conducted in separate sessions for boys and girls.

(f) Recipients may make requirements based on vocal range or quality which may result in a chorus or choruses of one or predominantly one sex.

§ 106.35 Access to schools operated by L.E.A.s

A recipient which is a local educational agency shall not, on the basis of sex, exclude any person from admission to:

(a) Any institution of vocational education operated by such recipient; or

(b) Any other school or educational unit operated by such recipient, unless such recipient otherwise makes available to such person, pursuant to the same policies and criteria of admission, courses, services, and facilities comparable to each course, service and facility offered in or through such schools.

§ 106.36 Counseling and use of appraisal and counseling materials

(a) *Counseling.* A recipient shall not discriminate against any person on the basis of sex in the counseling or guidance of students or applicants for admission.

(b) *Use of appraisal and counseling materials.* A recipient which uses testing or other materials for appraising or counseling students shall not use different materials for students on the basis of their sex or use materials which permit or require different treatment of students on such basis unless such different materials cover the same occupations and interest areas and the use of such different materials is shown to be essential to eliminate sex bias. Recipients shall develop and use internal procedures for ensuring

that such materials do not discriminate on the basis of sex. Where the use of a counseling test or other instrument results in a substantially disproportionate number of members of one sex in any particular course of study or classification, the recipient shall take such action as is necessary to assure itself that such disproportion is not the result of discrimination in the instrument or its application.

(c) *Disproportion in classes.* Where a recipient finds that a particular class contains a substantially disproportionate number of individuals of one sex, the recipient shall take such action as is necessary to assure itself that such disproportion is not the result of discrimination on the basis of sex in counseling or appraisal materials or by counselors.

§ 106.40 Marital or parental status

(a) *Status generally.* A recipient shall not apply any rule concerning a student's actual or potential parental, family, or marital status which treats students differently on the basis of sex.

(b) *Pregnancy and related conditions.*

(1) A recipient shall not discriminate against any student, or exclude any student from its education program or activity, including any class or extracurricular activity, on the basis of such student's pregnancy, childbirth, false pregnancy, termination of pregnancy or recovery therefrom, unless the student requests voluntarily to participate in a separate portion of the program or activity of the recipient.

(2) A recipient may require such a student to obtain the certification of a physician that the student is physically and emotionally able to continue participation in the normal education program or activity so long as such a certification is required of all students for other physical or emotional conditions requiring the attention of a physician.

(3) A recipient which operates a portion of its education program or activity separately for pregnant students, admittance to which is completely voluntary on the part of the student as provided in paragraph (b)(1) of this section shall ensure that the instructional program in the separate program is comparable to that offered to non-pregnant students.

(4) A recipient shall treat pregnancy, childbirth, false pregnancy, termination of pregnancy and recovery therefrom in the same manner and under the same policies as any other temporary disability with respect to any medical or hospital benefit, service, plan or policy which such recipient administers, op-

erates, offers or participates in with respect to students admitted to the recipient's educational program or activity.

(5) In the case of a recipient which does not maintain a leave policy for its students, or in the case of a student who does not otherwise qualify for leave under such a policy, a recipient shall treat pregnancy, childbirth, false pregnancy, termination of pregnancy and recovery therefrom as a justification for a leave of absence for so long a period of time as is deemed medically necessary by the student's physician, at the conclusion of which the student shall be reinstated to the status which she held when the leave began.

§ 106.41 Athletics

(a) *General.* No person shall, on the basis of sex, be excluded from participation in, be denied the benefits of, be treated differently from another person or otherwise be discriminated against in any interscholastic, intercollegiate, club or intramural athletics offered by recipient, and no recipient shall provide any such athletics separately on such basis.

(b) *Separate teams.* Notwithstanding the requirements of paragraph (a) of this section, a recipient may operate or sponsor separate teams for members of each sex where selection for such teams is based upon competitive skill or the activity involved is a contact sport. However, where a recipient operates or sponsors a team in a particular sport for members of one sex but operates or sponsors no such team for members of the other sex, and athletic opportunities for members of that sex have previously been limited, members of the excluded sex must be allowed to try out for the team offered unless the sport involved is a contact sport. For the purposes of this part, contact sports include boxing, wrestling, rugby, ice hockey, football, basketball and other sports the purpose or major activity of which involves bodily contact.

(c) *Equal opportunity.* A recipient which operates or sponsors interscholastic, intercollegiate, club or intramural athletics shall provide equal athletic opportunity for members of both sexes. In determining whether equal opportunities are available the Director will consider, among other factors:

(1) Whether the selection of sports and levels of competition effectively accommodate the interests and abilities of members of both sexes;

(2) The provision of equipment and supplies;

(3) Scheduling of games and practice time;

(4) Travel and per diem allowance;

(5) Opportunity to receive coaching and academic tutoring;

(6) Assignment and compensation of coaches and tutors;

(7) Provision of locker rooms, practice and competitive facilities;

(8) Provision of medical and training facilities and services;

(9) Provision of housing and dining facilities and services;

(10) Publicity.

Unequal aggregate expenditures for members of each sex or unequal expenditures for male and female teams if a recipient operates or sponsors separate teams will not constitute noncompliance with this section, but the Assistant Secretary may consider the failure to provide necessary funds for teams for one sex in assessing equality of opportunity for members of each sex.

* * *

§ 106.42 Textbooks and curricular material

Nothing in this regulation shall be interpreted as requiring or prohibiting or abridging in any way the use of particular textbooks or curricular materials.

NOTES AND QUESTIONS

1. Scope of Coverage

How does the congressional understanding of sex discrimination in Title IX differ from its treatment of racial discrimination in Title VI (*see* chapter 5, *supra*)? Note each of the practices deemed not to constitute sex discrimination or otherwise excluded from the scope of the legislation and regulations, paying particular attention to the treatment of athletes. Do these, taken together, constitute a coherent governmental policy with respect to sex discrimination?

The language of § 1681(a) of the legislation, barring exclusion, denial of benefits, or discrimination on the basis of sex, mirrors the language of the 1964 Civil Rights Act (42 U.S.C. § 2000d). Does this suggest that—with the exceptions enumerated in §§ 1681(1)–(5) and 1686—Congress views race and sex discrimination as similar, or do the exceptions indicate a very different perception?

2. *Textbooks and Curriculum*

The regulations exclude textbook or curricular content from the scope of administrative purview (34 C.F.R. § 106.42). That exclusion was premised on a concern that federal intervention in such matters would "thrust the Department into the role of Federal censor" and possibly violate the First Amendment (40 Fed. Reg. 24135). Do you find this a plausible contention? Is federal nonintervention a sound policy determination? How does the existence of textbook review and adoption procedures at the state and local levels or the existence of state statutes mandating curricula that positively demonstrate the achievements of women, for example, affect your response? *See, e.g.,* Ala. Code 516-36-60 (2000) (State Textbook Committee shall reflect gender diversity of the state); Fla. Stat. § 233.061 (1999) (mandating study of women's contribution to the United States); 105 Ill. Comp. Stat. Ann. Ch. 5, § 27-20.5 (2000) (requiring a unit of instruction on the history of women in America); Tenn. Code Ann. § 49-6-1006 (1999) (mandating that the curriculum include the "history, heritage, culture, experience and ultimate destiny of all . . . gender . . . groups").

B. Judicial Application of the Statutory Framework

1. Denial or Restriction of Educational Opportunities for Women. In several areas, women have either been excluded from or provided with less of a given educational opportunity than men. Athletic competition has been restricted to male students. Pregnant women, but not their impregnators, have been barred from high school. Admission criteria for selective academic high schools have been set higher for women than for men. Each of these practices presents the following questions:

(1) How might a school district justify a policy restricting the educational opportunities of women? Would such justifications pass judicial muster?

(2) Assuming that the school's policy does discriminate against female students, what remedy is legally appropriate (or mandated)? For example, if females have historically been excluded from athletic teams, would the school district meet its legal obligation by opening these teams to them on a freedom-of-choice basis? Should significant deviations from the school's male/female ratio in shop classes be

treated as indicating sex-based discrimination? Does the response depend on whether the claim is based on Title IX or the Equal Protection Clause?

(3) In each case, a "separate-but-equal" remedy is theoretically plausible. These diverse situations should provoke consideration of when, if at all, such a solution might be valid in the sex discrimination context.

(a) Athletics.

Force v. Pierce City R-VI School District
570 F.Supp. 1020 (W.D. Mo. 1983).

Ross T. Roberts, District Judge:

Nichole Force, a thirteen year old female student enrolled in the eighth grade at the Pierce City, Missouri, Junior High School, seeks an injunction which would allow her to compete for a place on the school's eighth grade football team. Her claims are relatively simple and straightforward: that defendants' refusal to accord her that opportunity is based—and based solely—upon the fact that she is a female rather than a male, and that a sex-based determination of that sort violates her right to the equal protection of the laws under the Fourteenth Amendment, and in turn 42 U.S.C. § 1983.

* * *

Sometime during the spring of 1982, Nichole Force mentioned to her mother that she was greatly looking forward, that coming fall, to trying out for the seventh grade football team. Since Nichole had already been involved to a considerable extent in athletics (swimming, diving, organized softball, organized basketball and elementary school football), and since she had grown up with two brothers who excelled at football and who encouraged and helped her in her own athletic endeavors, her mother was perhaps less startled than some mothers might have been. Family debate ensued, nonetheless. After an apparently frank and thorough discussion on the matter, Mrs. Force decided to approach the school authorities to see what might be done.

Mrs. Force spoke first with the boys' athletics coach for the school. He stated that so long as the school administration approved, he would let Nichole participate. Mrs. Force then sought out the appropriate school administrative officials. They advised her that the matter would have to be presented to the Board for its decision.

* * *

. . . [T]he Board voted unanimously to deny the request. According to Mrs. Force, defendant [Superintendent] John Williams explained the decision to her by stating that while "they all agreed" Nichole would be a good football player and would have no problems playing, if she were permitted to play the same allowance would have to be made for all other girls as well.

* * *

The record makes clear, and I find, that defendants' refusal to grant plaintiff's request is the product of a gender-based classification. Stated simply, only males are permitted to compete for a place on the Pierce City Junior High School eighth grade football team. Since Nichole is a female, that opportunity is denied to her.

The principles which must govern in this situation are summarized in . . . the Supreme Court's recent decision in *Mississippi University for Women v. Hogan*, 458 U.S. 718, 102 S.Ct. 3331, 73 L.Ed.2d 1090 (1982). . . .

> Because the challenged policy expressly discriminates among applicants on the basis of gender, it is subject to scrutiny under the Equal Protection Clause of the Fourteenth Amendment. 404 U.S. 71, 75. . . . Our decisions also establish that the party seeking to uphold a statute that classifies individuals on the basis of their gender must carry the burden of showing an "exceedingly persuasive justification" for the classification. . . .
>
> The burden is met only by showing at least that the classification serves "important governmental objectives and that the discriminatory means employed" are "substantially related to the achievement of those objectives." . . .
>
> Although the test for determining the validity of a gender based classification is straightforward, it must be applied free of fixed notions concerning the roles and abilities of males and females. Care must be taken in ascertaining whether . . . the objective itself reflects archaic and stereotypic notions. Thus if the . . . objective is to exclude or "protect" members of one gender because they are presumed to suffer from an inherent handicap or to be innately inferior, the objective itself is illegitimate. . . .
>
> If the State's objective is legitimate and important, we next determine whether the requisite direct, sub-

stantial relationship between objective and means is present. The purpose of requiring that close relationship is to assure that the validity of the classification is determined through reasoned analysis rather than through the mechanical application of traditional, often inaccurate, assumptions about the proper roles of men and women. The need for the requirement is amply revealed by reference to the broad range of statutes already invalidated by this Court, statutes that relied upon the simplistic, outdated assumption that gender could be used as a "proxy for other, more germane bases of classification," . . . to establish a link between objective and classification.

Defendants do not quarrel with the fact that the present case must be governed by these principles; indeed they candidly acknowledge that fact. They argue, rather, that in the circumstances shown here a gender-based classification fully satisfies those principles. To that end, they identify four "important governmental objectives" which are said to be at stake: (a) maximization of equal athletic educational opportunities for all students, regardless of gender; (b) maintenance of athletic educational programs which are as safe for participants as possible; (c) compliance with Title IX of the Educational Amendments of 1972 and the regulations thereunder; and (d) compliance with the constitution and by-laws of MSHSAA [Missouri State High School Athletic Association]. . . .

Defendants' suggestion with respect to the necessity of compliance with Title IX can, I think, be dealt with in relatively short order. There is in fact nothing whatsoever in Title IX, or in its implementing regulations (34 C.F.R. § 106.41(b)), which would mandate the action defendants have taken here.[3] To the contrary, Title IX's regulations leave each school free to choose whether co-educational participation in a contact sport will be permitted. *Yellow Springs Exempted Village School District Board of Education v. Ohio High School Athletic Association*, 647 F.2d 651, 655–56 (6th Cir. 1981). Allowing Nichole Force to compete with males for a place on the Pierce City Junior High School eighth grade football team would no more violate those regulations than would refusing her that opportunity. Title IX simply takes a neutral stand on the subject.

---

[3]34 C.F.R. § 106.41(b) reads as follows:

"(b) *Separate teams.* Notwithstanding the requirements of paragraphs (a) of this section, a recipient may operate or sponsor separate teams for members of each sex where selection for such teams is based upon competitive skill or the activity involved is a contact sport. However, where a recipient operates or sponsors a team in a particular sport for members of one sex but operates or sponsors no such team for members of the other sex, and athletic opportunities for members of that sex have previously been limited, members of the excluded sex must be allowed to try-out for the team offered unless the sport involved is a contact sport. For the purposes of this part, contact sports include boxing, wrestling, rugby, ice hockey, football, basketball and other sports the purpose or major activity of which involves bodily contact."

Nor in my judgment can defendants' point regarding compliance with MSHSAA rules withstand scrutiny. A school can hardly validate an otherwise unconstitutional act (assuming for the moment that there is one here) by noting that it has agreed with other schools to commit that act. . . .

. . . Defendants' first two points, however, have more meat to their bones, and are deserving of more detailed treatment. Each will be examined separately below.

* * *

One might wonder, at first blush, how denying all females the right to participate in a sport—which is the case here, since Pierce City eighth grade girls are not allowed to compete for a place on the only football team which might be available to them—will result in maximizing the participation of both sexes in athletics. And the short answer is that it probably does not. Defendants' argument in this regard, however, is sufficiently sophisticated to merit more than first blush treatment.

That argument proceeds on three interrelated theories. Defendants suggest, first, that males (as a class) will outperform females (as a class) in most athletic endeavors, given male size, speed and greater ratio of lean body mass. That being so, the argument proceeds, the best way in which to encourage and maximize female participation in athletics is by providing separate male and female teams, where males compete only against males and females only against females, since otherwise males will dominate the competition and ultimately discourage female participation. Pursuant to this idea, defendants have established separate interscholastic athletic programs for the two sexes in the Pierce City secondary schools, with the fall season sport being football for males and volleyball for females. But if (second) Nichole Force is permitted to compete for a place on

the football team, then other girls must be accorded the same privilege, and boys must be allowed to compete for positions on the volleyball team. When (third) that happens, the girls will lose their best athletes, the boys will come to dominate volleyball, and overall female participation will ultimately wither.

Based upon the expert testimony presented in this case I am willing to accept the proposition that the average male, even at age 13, will to some extent outperform the average female of that age in most athletic events, although the matter may be open to some dispute.[6] And I note, without being called upon to decide the issue, that a number of courts have held that the establishment of separate male/female teams in a sport is a constitutionally permissible way of dealing with the problem of potential male athletic dominance. *See Ritacco v. Norwin School District*, 361 F.Supp. 930 (W.D.Pa. 1973); *Bucha v. Illinois High School Association*, 351 F.Supp. 69 (N.D.Ill. 1972); *Ruman v. Eskew*, 168 Ind.App. 428, 343 N.E.2d 806 (1976), and *cf. O'Connor v. Board of Education of School District No. 23*, 645 F.2d 578, 581 (7th Cir.), *cert. den.* 454 U.S. 1084, 102 S.Ct. 641, 70 L.Ed.2d 619 (1981); *on remand* 545 F.Supp. 376 (1981); *Hoover v. Meiklejohn*, 430 F.Supp. 164, 170 (D.Colo. 1977); *Gilpin v. Kansas State Activities Ass'n., Inc.*, 377 F.Supp. 1233, 1243 (D.Kan. 1973); *Attorney General v. Massachusetts Interscholastic Athletic Association, Inc.*, 378 Mass. 342, 393 N.E.2d 284, 296 (1979). Beyond these two points, however, I am unable to accept defendants' argument.

The principal difficulty with the remaining portions of that argument, it seems to me, is that the various hypotheses used to bind it together are just that—hypotheses, and nothing more. There is, for example, no factual indication that the girls' eighth grade volleyball team will be blighted by the defec-

---

[6]The various studies and statistics relied upon by both defendants' expert, Dr. Harold Falls (a professor in Health, Physical Education and Biology at Southwest Missouri State College and the Director of the Human Performance Laboratory there), and plaintiff's expert, Dr. N. Peggy Burke (Chairman of the Department of Physical Education at the University of Iowa), suggest that at age 13 the average female tends to be slightly taller and heavier than the average male of that age, although there is a wide range of variance amongst all the members in both sexes. It would appear, on the other hand, that the average boy at that age has a very slightly higher ratio of lean body mass (muscle and bone mass) to fat mass, and a somewhat higher ratio of lean body mass to heighth, has heavier bones, may have somewhat more speed and upper body strength, and has somewhat better motor coordination. Some of these characteristics, particularly lean body mass ratios, relate to achievement of sexual maturity (which in girls averages between the 12th and 13th years), since girls begin to develop more fat mass at sexual maturity. But in any event there is some overlap with respect to these characteristics as between males and females at age 13, although the extent of that overlap was disputed by Dr. Falls and Dr. Burke. After age 13 these differences begin to widen appreciably as between the "average" boy and the "average" girl, and by the time the later teens are reached the "average" male has not only greatly widened the gap in terms of lean body mass ratio, but has also considerably surpassed the "average" female in terms of heighth and total body weight.

All of the above physiological factors are said to have a bearing on one's physical ability to compete in a sport. There are, obviously, other factors involved as well, including conditioning, desire and intelligence. And according to Dr. Burke, the statistics may also be skewed to some extent by the fact that conditioning can have a bearing on lean body mass ratios, and the fact that females have in the past been less physically active than males, by virtue of the roles society has assigned them, although there are no studies to support this.

tion of its best players to the football field, if Nichole Force is allowed to play football. To the contrary, defendants' own testimony is that Nichole Force is the first and only girl, at any grade level, who has ever made a request to play football. And for that matter, if defendants are correct in their position that females are unable to compete successfully with males in athletics, particularly in contact sports, it is to be expected that such defections would be short-lived in any event, and that the situation would prove to be self-regulating. *See Fortin v. Darlington Little League,* 514 F.2d 344, 350 (1st Cir. 1975).

Nor is there any factual indication that eighth grade boys at Pierce City Junior High School are waiting eagerly for volleyball to be desegregated. Again to the contrary, there is no indication that any boy has ever expressed a desire to play on the volleyball team. Indeed, there may be something of a false premise involved in the idea that volleyball in the Pierce City R-VI School District is in fact segregated, since nothing in the MSHSAA rules would prevent boys from competing with girls on a volleyball team, and since defendants themselves have never articulated any such rule.[7] Instead, it would seem, the question has simply never arisen. And in any event, it is by no means clear that the District would be constitutionally required to permit boys to participate in girls' volleyball, even if girls were allowed to participate in football. *See Clark v. Arizona Interscholastic Association,* 695 F.2d 1126, 1131–32 (9th Cir. 1982); *Petrie v. Illinois High School Association,* 75 Ill.App.3d 980, 31 Ill.Dec. 653, 394 N.E.2d 855 (1979) (both holding, on a theory similar to that utilized in *Regents of the University of California v. Bakke,* 438 U.S. 265, 98 S.Ct. 2733, 57 L.Ed.2d 750 (1978), that the governmental interest in redressing past discrimination against women in athletics is sufficient to justify a regulation which excludes boys from participating on girls' teams, even though girls are allowed to compete on boys' teams).[8]

Finally, even if by some chance defendants' worst case scenario should be realized, there might still be no need for the general breakdown which defendants postulate. For example, if a sufficient number of girls wish to play football, one obvious solution

would be to organize a girls' football team; or if so many boys wish to play volleyball that they would dominate the girls' competition in that sport, to form a boy's volleyball team. . . . Such solutions would of course presumably involve added expense to the District, but there is no evidence on how troublesome that factor might be, and I cannot decide this case by adding speculation on that subject to an already lengthy list of other speculative items.

* * *

. . . There is, however, a further point implicit in defendants' argument on this subject which should be addressed before passing on: the apparent assumption that if, in the interest of maximizing equal athletic opportunities, it is constitutionally permissible to establish separate male and female teams in a given sport and to exclude each sex from the other's team . . . then it is equally permissible, in that same interest, to designate separate male and female sports and to exclude each sex from participation in the other's sport. That is a proposition I am unwilling to accept, at least as a general matter. . . .

Each sport has its own relatively unique blend of requirements in terms of skills and necessary physical attributes, and each person, male or female, will for a variety of reasons probably find one or another sport more enjoyable and rewarding than others. In point of fact, volleyball is *not* football; and baseball is *not* hockey; and swimming is *not* tennis. Accordingly, if the idea is to "maximize educational athletic opportunities for all students, regardless of gender," it makes no sense, absent some substantial reason, to deny all persons of one sex the opportunity to test their skills at a particular sport. Of course there may be certain exceptional instances in which there is a "substantial reason" for such an exclusion, as for example where peculiar safety and equipment requirements demand it, *see Lafler v. Athletic Board of Control,* 536 F.Supp. 104 (W.D.Mich. 1982) (boxing), or perhaps where excluding males is necessary to redress past inequality and to foster female participation.

* * *

I [do not] . . . question the fact that the "maintenance of athletic educational programs which are as safe for participants as possible" is an "important

---

[7]In fact, according to one construction which has been given the regulations under Title IX, the School District might already be required to let boys participate on the volleyball team, regardless whether girls play football. *See Gomes v. Rhode Island Interscholastic League,* 469 F.Supp. 659 (D.R.I. 1979), *vacated as moot,* 604 F.2d 733 (1st Cir. 1979). *Contra, Mularadelis v. Haldane Central School Board,* 74 App.Div.2d 248, 427 N.Y.S.2d 458 (1980).

[8]But see *Gomes v. Rhode Island Interscholastic League, supra* n. 7, and *Attorney General v. Massachusetts Interscholastic Athletic Association, supra* (both holding that such "reverse" disparate treatment is impermissible).

governmental objective." Indeed, that would seem obvious. Again, however, the facts of this case do not demonstrate a sufficiently "substantial" relationship between that objective and a blanket rule which prohibits all eighth grade females from competing for a place on the Pierce City Junior High School eighth grade football team.

There is no evidence, or even any suggestion, that Nichole Force herself could not safely participate in that football program. And while I do find, from the expert testimony presented, that a "typical" (i.e., average) 13 year old female would in fact, to some degree, have a higher potential for injury in mixed-sex football than would a "typical" (i.e., average) 13 year old male, this does not in my judgment greatly assist the defendants' argument.[12] The problem, of course, is that not all 13 year old females are "typical," any more than all 13 year old males are "typical." Indeed, as defendants' own expert candidly admitted, some 13 year old females could safely play eighth grade football in mixed sex competition, and some 13 year old males could not. And yet I note that the Pierce City R-VI School District permits *any* male to compete in football, regardless of his size, speed, body type, lean body mass, fat body mass, bone structure, "Q" angle measurement or any other factor which might have a bearing on his potential for injury.

In short, the "safety" factor which defendants would utilize to prevent any female from playing eighth grade football—including those who could play safely—is not applied to males at all, even to those who could not play safely. . . .

It is of course true, as defendants point out, that the Supreme Court has recognized that governmental bodies are free to take into account *actual* differences between the sexes, including physical ones, with the result that a statute or policy which employs a gender based classification will be upheld where that classification merely reflects the fact that the sexes are not "similarly situated" in certain circumstances. *See Michael M. v. Superior Court of Sonoma County*, 450 U.S. 464, 469, 101 S.Ct. 1200, 1204, 67 L.Ed.2d 437 (1981) (noting, in reference to a statutory rape law which penalized males only, that "only women may become pregnant," *id*. at 471, 101 S.Ct. at 1205). I do not, however, read such observations to be an endorsement of the use of broad generalizations which—while perhaps empirically supported *as generalizations*—do not hold true for all members of a sex. In fact the Supreme Court has rather consistently rejected that idea, . . . since a gender based classification which results from ascribing a particular trait or quality to one sex, when not all share that trait or quality, is not only inherently unfair but generally tends only to perpetuate "stereotypic notions" regarding the proper roles of men and women.

This is not to say that reliance upon a factually established generalization concerning a particular male or female trait might never be appropriate. But there must obviously be a substantial justification . . . for using such an imprecise and potentially mischievous tool for these purposes; and the only justification which might even arguably be applied in such circumstances would be that of "administrative ease" to the governmental body. That, in turn, is an argument, which has never fared well at the hands of the Supreme Court, . . . and I reject it here for the simple reason that it is sophistry to suggest a concern with the "administrative burden" of weeding out physically unfit 13 year old females in connection with a football program when there is no concern at all with weeding out physically unfit 13 year old males involved in the same program. In fact, I think, it might be rather difficult to sustain a requirement that females competing for a place on a particular athletic team be subjected to a fitness screening program, when males competing for a place on the same team are subjected to none at all.

I conclude, accordingly, that there is an insufficient relationship between defendants' announced goal of "safety" and a rule which automatically excludes all eighth grade females from competing with eighth grade males for a place on a football team. That holding, I note, is consistent with the result reached by virtually every other court which has considered this same sort of "safety" argument in

---

[12]There are apparently no studies which have compared the incidence of injuries as between males and females playing football, or any other contact sport at age 13, either on segregated teams or co-educational teams. The potential for injury, however, at least in contact sports, is said to be related to the physical characteristics mentioned in footnote 5, particularly lean body mass ratios. If that is so, to that extent perhaps the "average" boy at age 13 will have somewhat less potential for injury in football than the "average" girl at age 13. In addition, girls who have reached sexual maturity (on the average between 12 and 13 years, although in some instances much later) begin to develop a wider hip structure, and the angle between the hip and the knee (called the "Q" angle") increases, with resulting potential for increased knee injury. How significant that increased "Q" angle is, and just what its real potential for increased knee injury in football might be, was a subject disputed by Dr. Falls and Dr. Burke.

connection with male/female competition in contact sports. . . .[14]

* * *

Nichole Force obviously has no legal entitlement to a starting position on the Pierce City Junior High School eighth grade football team, since the extent to which she plays must be governed solely by her abilities, as judged by those who coach her. But she seeks no such entitlement here.

Instead she seeks simply a chance, like her male counterparts, to display those abilities. She asks, in short, only the right to try.

I do not suggest there is any such thing as a constitutional "right to try." But the idea that one should be allowed to try—to succeed or to fail as one's abilities and fortunes may dictate, but in the process at least to profit by those things which are learned in the trying—is a concept deeply engrained in our way of thinking; and it should indeed require a "substantial" justification to deny that privilege to someone simply because she is a female rather than a male. I find no such justification here.[16] . . .

NOTES AND QUESTIONS

1. The Constitutional Standard

In cases alleging discrimination in athletic programs, courts have applied a variety of constitutional standards. Moreover, each standard—the "middle tier" scrutiny test of *Boren* and the "exceedingly persuasive justification" standard of *Hogan* and *VMI*—is applied in diverse ways. Does the *Force* court apply the prevailing standard correctly? Is it too flexible to be a "standard" at all?

2. The Availability of Separate Programs for Women

The *Force* court suggests that a separate women's football team would be a satisfactory solution. Do you agree? Would the casual observer, noting the existence of a girls' and boys' tennis team, assume that the two were of equal caliber? What

of the able female athlete who—if not for the separation—could successfully compete for a place on the all-boys team? If she is not "stigmatized," are her opportunities nevertheless limited on the basis of her sex?

What if separate but different programs are provided for women athletes? In some states, women's basketball teams consist of six players, impose half-court restrictions, and permit only forwards to shoot. Suppose female athletes allege that the restrictions on shooting and dribbling limit their possibilities of being awarded a college basketball scholarship. How should such challenges be resolved? *See Dodson v. Arkansas Activities Association*, 468 F.Supp. 394 (E.D.Ark. 1979) (school district must extend benefits of similar rules to male and female students); *Cape v. Tennessee Secondary School Athletic Association*, 563 F. 2d 793 (6th Cir. 1977) (finding that different rules for girls' and boys' basketball were permissible).

3. Contact Versus Noncontact Sports

The *Force* court considers the argument that female athletes are more likely to suffer injury. Is it a failure of proof or a failure of argument that persuades the court? Other courts, upholding the right of women to participate in noncontact sports, have distinguished those sports from their rougher cousins. *See, e.g., Magill v. Avonworth Baseball Conference*, 364 F.Supp. 1212 (W.D.Pa. 1973), *aff'd on other grounds*, 516 F.2d 1328 (3d Cir. 1975). Is the distinction a valid one? To what sports should it be applied—soccer, baseball, wrestling? Is it physical violence or the possibility of physical intimacy that really is at issue in these cases? In recent years, courts have become increasingly receptive to allowing girls to try out for contact sports that would involve competition with boys. *See, e.g., Barnett v. Texas Wrestling Association*, 16 F.Supp.2d 690 (N.D.Tex. 1998) (allowing plaintiff to sue for equal protection violation but noting that constitutional issue was not settled); *Adams v. Baker*, 919 F.Supp. 1496 (D.Kan. 1996) (finding that a policy of excluding girls from the high school wrestling team was unlikely to be substantially related

---

[14]I do not consider the holding in *Lafler v. Athletic Board of Control, supra*, to be inconsistent with the reasoning expressed here and in those cases cited above. As the court there noted, the necessity that plaintiff (a female) wear a protective chest covering would violate Amateur Boxing Federation rules, and I gather would give her something of an unfair advantage in any event. The court expressly noted the difference between the case before it and cases involving football, soccer and baseball. . . .

[16]For those interested, or merely curious, there would appear to be five other reported cases, involving football in whole or in part, which reach the same result reached here: *Leffel v. Wisconsin Interscholastic Athletic Ass'n, supra* (all sports); *Clinton v. Nagy, supra* (football); *Attorney General v. Massachusetts Interscholastic Athletic Association, Inc., supra* (all sports); *Darrin v. Gold, supra* (football); and *Commonwealth v. Pennsylvania Interscholastic Association, supra* (all sports). I find no cases involving football which reach a contrary result. . . .

to the school's goals of ensuring student safety, avoiding sexual harassment litigation, and preventing disruption of the school setting); *see also Saint v. Nebraska School Activities Association*, 684 F.Supp. 626 (D.Neb. 1988) (noting overwhelming authority in support of plaintiff's equal protection claim); *Lantz v. Ambach*, 620 F.Supp. 663 (S.D.N.Y. 1985) (noting uniform precedent in favor of allowing female student to try out for varsity football team); *Leffel v. Wisconsin Interscholastic Athletic Association*, 444 F.Supp. 117 (E.D.Wisc. 1978) (Title IX regulations that exclude qualified female students from male contact sports are unconstitutional).

4. Discrimination Against Male Athletes?

May a school field only a female volleyball team, thereby denying a male volleyball enthusiast the chance to compete? Is it relevant that volleyball has been introduced to the school in order to foster female interest in sports or that some females might not compete on a team if males were also eligible? May a school permit females to try out for the men's team while barring males from trying out for the women's team in order to preserve the emergent female sports program? *See Clark v. Arizona Interscholastic Association*, 695 F.2d 1126 (9th Cir. 1982) (boys can be excluded to avoid displacing females); *Petrie v. Illinois High School Association*, 394 N.E.2d 855 (Ill. 1979) (exclusion of boys from girls' sports teams is permissible because it does not stigmatize them as unworthy); *Williams v. School District of Bethlehem*, 799 F. Supp. 513 (E.D.Pa. 1992), *rev'd on other grounds*, 998 F.2d 168 (3d Cir. 1993) (boy's exclusion from girls' team violated equal protection when girls could try out for twenty-two teams and boys could try out for only twelve teams).

5. Title IX and Athletics

As the *Force* opinion notes, Title IX leaves schools free to determine whether to allow coeducational participation in contact sports. 34 C.F.R. § 106.41(b). Could the relative weakness of the statutory standard stem from the political controversy that underlies the issue of female participation in school-sponsored athletics?

At the college level, funding women's athletics has proved to be a continuing concern. The decision in *NCAA v. Board of Regents of Oklahoma*, 468 U.S. 85, 104 S.Ct. 2948, 82 L.Ed.2d 70 (1984), voiding the National Collegiate Athletic Association's control of television contracts, has reduced available revenues at some schools. *See* "Big TV Revenues Now Tougher to Get, Most College Football Powers Discover," *Chron.Higher Educ.*, Jan. 9, 1985, at 37. But the nation's 105 major universities have committed themselves to sponsor at least seven women's and eight men's sports programs. Throughout the late 1980s and 1990s, colleges and universities regularly faced tight fiscal times. Ross, Kahrs, and Heinrich, "Rededication Panel Discussion on Gender Equity and Inter-Collegiate Athletics," 1995 *U.Ill.L.Rev.* 133. In general, however, courts have been reluctant to accept limited resources as a justification for shutting down women's teams. *See, e.g. Cohen v. Brown University*, 809 F.Supp. 978 (D.R.I. 1992), *aff'd and remanded*, 991 F.2d 888 (1st Cir. 1993), *on remand*, 879 F.Supp. 185 (1995), *aff'd and remanded*, 101 F.3d 155 (1996), *cert. denied*, 520 U.S. 1186 (1997); *Favia v. Indiana University of Pennsylvania*, 812 F.Supp. 578 (W.D.Pa. 1992); *Roberts v. Colorado State Board of Agriculture*, 998 F.2d 824 (10th Cir. 1993); *see also Cook v. Colgate University*, 802 F.Supp. 737 (N.D.N.Y. 1992), *vacated as moot*, 992 F.2d 17 (2d Cir. 1993). However, a federal court has allowed a men's team to be terminated under these circumstances. *Kelley v. Board of Trustees*, 35 F.3d 265 (7th Cir. 1994).

As a result, some have expressed concern that vigorous enforcement of Title IX would harm minority male athletes, particularly African Americans. Connolly and Adelman, "A University's Defense to a Title IX Gender Equity in Athletics Lawsuit: Congress Never Intended Gender Equity Based on Student Body Ratios," 71 *U.Det.Mercy L.Rev.* 845, 847 (1994); George, "Who Plays and Who Pays: Defining Equality in Intercollegiate Athletics," 1995 *Wis.L.Rev.* 647, 652–53. Critics of recent decisions have argued that the quest for parity in college sports has led to the imposition of quotas and that a nondiscrimination principle has been converted into an affirmative action program. Gavora, "You're in Trouble Again, Johnny," 14 *Women's Quarterly* 4 (Winter 1998). For a full review of these cases and the attendant controversy, *see* Heckman, "The Explosion of Title IX Legal Activity in Intercollegiate Athletics During 1992–93: Defining the Equal Opportunity Standard," 1994 *Det.C.L.Rev.* 953.

After twenty-five years of Title IX enforcement, the operating expenses of men's and women's sports programs remain dramatically different. At Division I schools, men's teams received an average of $1,165,100 (or 77 percent of the operating budget), while women's teams received $388,600 (or 23 percent). NCAA Gender Equity Study at Table 3 (April 1997). Similarly, the Women's Sports Foundation reported that overall, women receive 27 percent of operating expenses. Women's Sports Foundation, Gender Equity Report Card 4 (June 18, 1997). At least some of this difference is due to the high cost of football programs for which there are no female sports equivalents. Very often, this gap is attributed to the differential revenue that men's teams generate. Equalizing resources therefore would require a substantial redistribution of the profits that a few teams generate to the many sports that break even or lose money. See Kelman, "(Why) Does Gender Equity in College Athletics Entail Gender Equality?" 7 *S.Cal.Rev.L. & Women's Stud.* 63 (1997). So far, revenues from men's sports programs do not appear to subsidize women's sports programs. In Division I schools, men's teams generated $3,857,000 in revenues but cost $3,398,000 to sponsor. Women's teams generated $300,000 in revenues but cost $1,525,000 to operate. In Division I-A schools, men's sports were highly profitable, generating an average of $9,561,000 and costing an average of $6,388,000. For most schools, though, sports programs are quite expensive and not particularly lucrative ventures. NCAA Gender Equity Study, *supra*, at Table 8. If revenues are not redistributed, women's sports must be subsidized in other ways. At public institutions, however, legislatures may be reluctant to fund sports programs when academic priorities seem more urgent.

Does it violate Title IX to have separate athletic directors for men's and women's athletics? A number of women's coaches at colleges and universities have filed suit, alleging employment discrimination and retaliation under Title IX. *See, e.g., Lowrey v. Texas A & M University System*, 117 F.3d 242 (5th Cir. 1997); *Stanley v. University of Southern California*, 13 F.3d 1313 (9th Cir. 1994), *summary judgment granted*, 1995 U.S.Dist.LEXIS 5026 (C.D.Cal. 1995), *aff'd in part and remanded in part*, 178 F.3d 1069 (1999). *O'Connor v. Peru State College*, 781 F.2d 632 (8th Cir. 1986); *Clay v. Board of Trustees of Neosho Community College*, 905 F.Supp. 1488 (D.Kan. 1995); *Harker v. Utica College of Syracuse University*, 885 F.Supp. 378 (N.D.N.Y. 1995); *Bartges v. University of North Carolina at Charlotte*, 908 F.Supp. 1312 (W.D.N.C. 1994), *aff'd*, 94 F.3d 641 (4th Cir. 1996); *Deli v. University of Minnesota*, 863 F.Supp. 958 (D.Minn. 1994); *Bowens v. University of Baylor*, 862 F.Supp. 142 (W.D.Tex. 1994).

According to a 1997 study by the National Collegiate Athletic Association, coaches of men's teams on average earned more than coaches of women's teams. Once again, these disparities have been attributed to differences in the teams' potential to generate revenue.

Yet, the earnings gap applies to both high-profile and low-profile sports. Men's basketball coaches earned an average of $99,283, while women's basketball coaches earned $60,603. Men's ice hockey coaches received an average of $64,214, while women's ice hockey coaches received $25,478. (Football coaches earned the highest average salary at $103,382.) Pay disparities also persisted in lacrosse, rowing, soccer, and squash as well. Pay equity was being achieved in fencing, golf, gymnastics, rifle, swimming and diving, track, field and cross country, tennis, and volleyball. NCAA Gender Equity Study at Table 6 (April 1997). According to the Women's Sports Foundation, only 1.9 percent of the head coaches for men's teams were women, while 45 percent of those for women's teams were men. Women's Sports Foundation, Gender Equity Report Card, *supra*, at 12–13.

6.   Further Reading

The issues raised in *Force* are canvassed in K. Tokarz, *Women, Sports and the Law: A Comprehensive Research Guide to Sex Discrimination in Sports* (1986); Johnson, "Throwing Like a Girl: Constitutional Implications of Title IX Regarding Gender Discrimination in High School Athletic Programs," 18 *N. Ill.U.L.Rev.* 575 (1998); Heckman, "Women and Athletics: A Twenty Years Perspective on Title IX," 9 *U.Miami Ent. & Sports L.Rev.* 1 (1992); Woods, "Comment: Boys Muscling in on Girls' Sports," 53 *Ohio St.L.J.* 891 (1992); Wong and Ensor, "Sex Discrimination in Athletics: A Review of Two Decades of Accomplishments and Defeats," 21 *Gonzaga L.Rev.* 345 (1985–86); Tokarz, "Separate But Unequal Educational Sports Programs: The Need for a New Theory of Equality," 1 *Berkeley Women's L.J.* 1 (1985); Note, "Sex Discrimination in High School Athletics: An Examination of Applicable Legal Doctrines," 66 *Minn.L.Rev.* 1185 (1985); Note, "Where the Boys Are: Can 'Separate' Be Equal in Sports?" 58 *U.S.C.L.Rev.* 1425 (1985).

7.   The Equal Rights Amendment and Equal Opportunities in Athletics

Would passage of the Equal Rights Amendment to the United States Constitution have affected the outcome of any of these cases? Decisions reached under state equal rights amendments suggest an answer. A rule barring girls from competing against boys in any athletic contest was struck down in one state, *Commonwealth by Packel v. Pennsylvania Interscholastic Athletic Association*, 18 Pa.Cmwlth.Ct. 45, 334 A.2d 839 (1975), as was a rule denying young women the opportunity to compete in interscholastic high school football. *Darrin v. Gould*, 85 Wash.2d 859, 540 P.2d 882 (1975) (*en banc*). In *Darrin*, the Washington Supreme Court held that the state would need to demonstrate a compelling justification for following the athletic association rule. Since males as well as females are prone to football injury, fear of injury would not suffice as a reason. *See* Comment, "*Blair v. Washington State University*: Making State ERA's a Potent Remedy for Sex Discrimination in Athletics," 14 *J.of Coll. & Univ.Law* 575 (1988).

8. *Implementing Equal Opportunity with Respect to Athletics*

No issue arising under Title IX has aroused so much interest, and so much controversy, as athletic opportunities. Observed former Health, Education and Welfare Department Secretary Caspar Weinberger, "I had not realized until the comment period [on HEW's proposed Title IX regulations] that athletics is the single most important thing in the United States." N.Y.*Times*, June 27, 1975, § 1 at 16.

Sports programs for women expanded substantially after the passage of Title IX. During the period from 1971 to 1978, for example, the number of female participants in organized high school sports increased from 294,000 to 2,038,000—an increase of over 600 percent. In contrast, between fall 1971 and fall 1977, the enrollment of females in high school decreased from approximately 7,600,000 to approximately 7,150,000—a decrease of over 5 percent.

The growth in athletic participation by high school women has been reflected on the campuses of the nation's colleges and universities. During the period from 1971 to 1976 the enrollment of women in the nation's institutions of higher education rose 52 percent, from 3,400,000 to 5,201,000. During this same period, the number of women participants in sports increased from 16,386 to 25,541, or 55 percent. In intercollegiate sports, women's participation increased 102 percent, from 31,852 to 64,375. These developments reflect the growing interest of women in competitive athletics, as well as the efforts of colleges and universities to accommodate those interests. 44 Fed.Reg. 71419 (1979).

These changes did not occur painlessly. Equalization of athletic opportunities at the collegiate level has been of special concern. The Title IX regulations promulgated in 1975 note ten factors—among them the selection of sports, the provision of equipment and supplies, coaching and tutoring opportunities, and practice and competitive facilities—relevant in determining whether equality exists. Just how these factors would be weighted remained unclear. Three years later, HEW undertook to draft a "Policy Interpretation" of the regulation. A December 1978 draft proposed that compliance be established by a showing that "average per capita" expenditures for male and female athletes were substantially equal in the area of "readily financially measurable" benefits and opportunities and that benefits and opportunities in areas not financially measurable "were comparable." Universities, faced with the specter of "equalizing" expenditures on big-time football and women's field hockey, reacted sharply. Confronted with over 700 comments on the proposal, HEW modified its stance, abandoning financial equality measures in favor of a "governing principle . . . that male and female athletes should receive equivalent treatment, benefits, and opportunities." 44 Fed.Reg. 71414 (1979).

The quest for equal opportunity for female athletes has been an ongoing struggle. Women challenged Temple University's athletic program as a violation of Title IX and equal protection. *Haffer v. Temple University*, 678 F.Supp. 517 (E.D.Pa. 1987). In 1992, the NCAA released its first gender equity study and began to require that Division I member schools craft plans to promote greater equity in men's and women's sports programs as a condition of certification. NCAA Gender Equity Study (1992); NCAA 1996–97 Division I Athletics Certification Handbook (Revised June 1996). In *Cohen v. Brown University*, 991 F.2d 888, 897–900 (1st Cir. 1993), a federal court of appeals described a three-pronged test for measuring equality of athletic opportunity: (1) whether opportunities to participate in intercollegiate sports are provided in numbers "substantially proportionate to their respective enrollments"; (2) whether the college or university can show "a history and continuing practice of program expansion which is demonstrably responsive to the developing interest and abilities of the members of [a previously underrepresented] sex"; or (3) whether "the interests and abilities of the members of [an underrepresented] sex have been fully and effectively accommodated" by the college's or university's present program. This test has been highly controversial but also highly influential. Brake and Catlin, "The Path of Most Resistance: The Long Road Toward Gender Equity in Intercollegiate Athletics," 3 *Duke J.Gender L. & Pol'y* 51 (1996); Stellmach, "Title IX: The Mandate for Equality in Collegiate Athletics," 41 *Wayne*

L.Rev. 203 (1994); Cheesebrough, *"Cohen v. Brown: I Am Woman, Hear Me Score,"* 5 *Vill.Sports & Ent.L.Forum* 295 (1998).

In 1994, Congress passed the Equity in Athletics Disclosure Act as part of the Improving America's Schools Act. Pub. L. No. 103-382, 108 Stat. 3969 (1994). The Act requires schools to prepare and disseminate reports on participation rates and financial support for men's and women's intercollegiate sports programs. In 1997, Senator Carol Mosely-Braun and Representative Nita M. Lowey sought to expand these protections by introducing the Fair Play Act to expand disclosure of these reports. S. 933, 105th Cong., 1st Sess. (1997); *see* Heckman, "Scoreboard: A Concise Chronological Twenty-Five Year History of Title IX Involving Interscholastic and Intercollegiate Athletics," 7 *Seton Hall Sports L.* 391 (1997); Wilson, "Title IX's Collegiate Sports Application Raises Serious Questions Regarding the Role of the NCAA," 31 *J.Marshall L.Rev.* 1303, 1309 n. 46 (1998).

The number of female athletes in NCAA member schools has grown substantially since Title IX's enactment from 80,040 in 1982–83 to 110,524 in 1994–96. NCAA Participation Statistics Report 1982–95, at 4; National Federation of State High School Associations Summary: 1995–96 Athletics Participation Survey. Despite these gains, in 1997, *USA Today* reported that female college athletes received only 38 percent of scholarship money and 27 percent of recruiting money. Governmental Affairs Report, NCAA Register, May 5, 1997, at 3. That same year, the National Women's Law Center filed administrative complaints against twenty-five institutions of higher education, the largest mass filing of its kind. The complaints alleged an inequitable distribution of athletic scholarships. Samuels, "Title IX Complaints Filed on 25 Schools," *Newsday*, June 3, 1997, at A55.

(b) Pregnancy and Marriage. At least until the early 1970s, most school districts excluded pregnant students from regular classes at some time during their pregnancy, Knowles, "High School, Marriage and the Fourteenth Amendment," 11 *J.Fam.L.* 711, 732 (1972), a practice that may have contributed to the "feminization" of poverty. *See* Fox-Genovese, "Women's Rights, Affirmative Action and the Myth of Individualism," 54 *Geo.Wash.L.Rev.* 338 (1986). The Title IX regulations specifically prohibit discrimination on the basis of pregnancy. If, however, the school maintains a separate program for mothers

and expectant mothers, the student may ask to participate in that program. Participation must be entirely voluntary, and the program's instructional component must be comparable to what is generally offered by the school.

In *Perry v. Grenada Municipal Separate School District,* 300 F.Supp. 748 (N.D.Miss. 1969), the court enjoined the school district from excluding unwed mothers from its schools. But the opinion suggested that under some circumstances a school might bar a pregnant student because of the corrupting effect she might have on other students. Recent cases have tested the limits of the distinction between discrimination based on pregnancy and standards predicated on good moral character. In each case, a female student who bore a child out of wedlock was excluded from the National Honor Society for failure to meet the character requirements. Courts have split on whether these practices violate Title IX.

Pfeiffer v. Marion Center Area School District
917 F.2d 779 (3rd Cir. 1990).

Before Higginbotham, C.J., Scirica, J., and Aldisert, J. Aldisert, J.:

* * *

The appellant, Arlene Pfeiffer, was a member of the class of 1984 at the Marion Center Area High School in Marion, Indiana County, Pennsylvania. She was a good student who earned high grades and participated in a wide variety of school organizations, including serving as president of the student council. Based on her record, she was elected to her high school's chapter of the National Honor Society (NHS) in 1981. The society had a local chapter in existence at the school from approximately 1975 until 1986. The local chapter was governed by a faculty council composed of . . . the principal of the high school and . . . [four] teachers at the Marion Center Area High School.

During the spring of 1983, Pfeiffer, who was unmarried, discovered that she was pregnant. She informed her school guidance counselor and principal and indicated that she wanted to rear her child but that she also wanted to finish high school. Principal [Robert L.] Stewart told her that he saw no problem in her plan to continue school and graduate.

The handbook for the National Honor Society requires that students be selected for membership on the basis of scholarship, service, leadership and character.

The constitution of the local chapter followed that of the national organization, requiring admission and maintenance be based on the same qualities. The high school had a selection procedure which followed the national organization's instructions, in which these qualities were assessed by teachers. To be admitted into the NHS, a student was rated by at least five teachers. In the instructions under the heading "Leadership" one of the qualities to be assessed was whether the student exerted the type of leadership which directly influences others for good conduct. Another quality to be assessed under the heading "Character" was whether the student upholds principles of morality and ethics.

Upon learning of Pfeiffer's pregnancy, Judith Skubis, a teacher and member of the faculty council, brought the matter to the attention of the other council members in the spring of 1983. That fall, when school resumed, the council scheduled a meeting for November 4, 1983, and Pfeiffer was invited to attend. The council members explained to her that her NHS membership was in question because premarital sex appeared to be contrary to the qualities of leadership and character essential for membership. When asked if her sexual activity leading to her pregnancy had been voluntary, the plaintiff answered in the affirmative. The council deferred further action.

On November 8, 1983, Pfeiffer's father, Delmont Pfeiffer, telephoned Principal Stewart requesting a prompt decision because an induction ceremony for seniors was scheduled for the next day and Arlene wanted to attend. The council met on the morning of November 9, 1983, and by secret ballot unanimously voted to dismiss her from the NHS chapter. By letter the council advised her:

> By action of the faculty council, you have been dismissed from the National Honor Society for the following reason:
>
> Failure to uphold the high standards of leadership and character required for admission and maintenance of membership.
>
> It is the opinion of the faculty council that a member must consistently set a positive example for others and, as outlined in the selection guidelines, always uphold all of the high standards of moral conduct.

App. at 27.

On November 30, 1983, the council met with her parents, who requested that the subject be placed on the agenda of the school board meeting scheduled for December 12, 1983. Pfeiffer and her parents appeared at the meeting with counsel. The board requested that the matter be discussed privately, but

Pfeiffer and her parents insisted that the issue be discussed publicly.

At the discussion, the board was asked to review the decision of the faculty council. On December 19, 1983, the board and the council met to consider the matter further and on January 16, 1984, the school board adopted a resolution unanimously affirming the action of the faculty council.

After graduation from high school, with honors, Pfeiffer elected not to go to college and began working with the Holiday Inn of Indiana, where she is presently a sales manager. She is married, but not to the father of the child conceived while she was in school.

III

Arlene Pfeiffer filed suit alleging discrimination in her dismissal from the local chapter of the NHS, seeking an injunction that she be reinstated in the chapter, that the records of the school district be corrected to show that she remains in good standing in the society, that a procedure for dismissal be ordered that is not discriminatory, that the NHS be prohibited from disseminating information about her dismissal and that she be awarded compensatory and punitive damages.

Injunctive relief and damages were requested under Title IX of the Education Amendments of 1972, 20 U.S.C. §§ 1681, *et seq.*, and its implementing regulations. The complaint included claims of gender discrimination pursuant to 42 U.S.C. §§ 1983 and 1985 and included state law claims under the Pennsylvania Human Relations Act (PHRA), 43 P.S. 955(i)(1) (Purdon's Supp.1988), and the Pennsylvania Equal Rights Amendment, Commonwealth Constitution art. 1, § 28.

In addition to the Marion Center Area School District, the appellant named in her complaint the Board of School Directors and the individual members of the Board in their individual capacities. She also named members of the Faculty Council of the NHS chapter and John Mallino, Superintendent of the School District.

IV

At the onset of the case, the question arose whether Title IX applied because the School District did not receive federal funds for the operation of its chapter of the NHS, while it did receive federal funds for its school lunch program. Under the holding of *Grove City College v. Bell*, 465 U.S. 555, 104 S.Ct. 1211, 79 L.Ed.2d 516 (1984), the district court denied Pfeiffer her Title IX claim. While the case was pending, Congress passed the Civil Rights Restoration Act of 1987, part of which amended Title IX to circumvent the Supreme Court's decision in *Grove City*. By an Opinion and Order of August 17, 1989, the district court ruled that the Restoration Act made the School District subject to Title IX, but that Pfeiffer's constitutional claims were subsumed within the Title IX claim. In addition, the court held that the state law claims would be considered during trial.

During a bench trial, the court heard testimony that the school district keeps no records of a student's extracurricular activities and that there are no records therefore concerning Pfeiffer's induction or absence thereof, or of her membership in the NHS. The NHS no longer exists at Marion Center Area High School and the national organization is no longer a party to this suit.

Testimony was presented that a pregnant female student had resigned from the NHS chapter after an admission of engaging in premarital sex 10 to 12 years earlier. She apparently had been given the choice of resignation or dismissal by the faculty council. No male member of the chapter has ever been dismissed for premarital sexual activity. The appellant offered to introduce testimony by a former student who was a male member of the chapter, that two years after Pfeiffer's dismissal, while a senior at the high school he impregnated his girlfriend and that he was not dismissed from the chapter. The district court excluded the evidence.

After considering the admitted evidence, the district court made a factual finding that the plaintiff was not dismissed for her pregnancy but because the faculty council concluded that she had failed to uphold the standards of the National Honor Society by engaging in premarital sexual intercourse.

* * *

VI

[2] In *Wort v. Vierling*, No. 82-3169, slip op. (C.D.Ill. Sept. 4, 1984), *aff'd on other grounds*, 778 F.2d 1233 (7th Cir.1985), the court held that a school district's dismissal of a pregnant student from the National Honor Society was a violation both of Title IX and the equal protection clause of the fourteenth amendment. In *Wort*, the court concluded that "[p]laintiff was dismissed from the NHS because of her pregnancy or the acts leading up to her pregnancy." *Id.*, slip. op. at 4.

In reaching that decision, the court in *Wort* declined to distinguish the sexual conduct from the resulting pregnancy. But the district court here did make this distinction. It specifically found that Pfeiffer was dismissed not because she was pregnant but because she had engaged in premarital sexual activity. This is an important distinction between the two cases. Regulation of conduct of unmarried high school student members is within the realm of authority of the National Honor Society given its emphasis on leadership and character.

In any event, the appellant's entire argument before us rests upon her allegation that she was dismissed from the chapter because of her condition of pregnancy. Unfortunately for her theory, however, the district court found that

> The plaintiff was not dismissed for her pregnancy but because the council thought she had failed to uphold the standards already discussed as evidenced by Plaintiff's Exhibit 1 (the letter directed to her) and Plaintiff's Exhibit 3 (the resolution of the School Board dated January 16, 1984.)

Memorandum Opinion at 8–9; App. at 603–04. As a finding of fact, this holding may not be disturbed unless clearly erroneous. We do not believe that it is erroneous. Supporting this finding is the stated reason given by the council for her dismissal: Failure to uphold the standards of leadership and character required for admission and maintenance of membership. App. at 27. Moreover, the finding is supported by the testimony of the faculty council members before the district court, each of whom testified at trial. . . . Each faculty council member specifically denied that his or her dismissal vote was based anywhere on Pfeiffer's sex, on her pregnancy, or on her failure to marry after she had engaged in premarital sexual activity.

> This factual finding is bolstered by the district court's reasoning that
> [f]aced with the task of educating hundreds of young people, and with constant demand by the public that the schools instill attributes of good character as part of the educational process, the Council and the Board can scarcely be criticized for taking the action which was taken.

Memorandum Opinion at 9; App. at 604. Indeed, the Supreme Court has given us express guidance in matters relating to student conduct in public schools:

The process of educating our youth for citizenship in public schools is not confined to books, the curriculum, and the civics class; schools must teach by example the shared values of a civilized social order. Consciously or otherwise, teachers—and indeed the older students—demonstrate the appropriate form of . . . conduct and deportment in and out of class. Inescapably, like parents, they are role models. The schools, as instruments of the state, may determine that the essential lessons of civil, mature conduct cannot be conveyed in a school that tolerates lewd, indecent, or offensive speech and conduct. . . .

Bethel School Dist. No. 403 v. Fraser, 478 U.S. 675, 683, 106 S.Ct. 3159, 3164, 92 L.Ed.2d 549 (1986).

VII

More difficult, however, is appellant's contention that the district court abused its discretion in excluding the proffered testimony of a former student, a male member of the Marion Center Area High School chapter of the NHS. At trial, the following colloquy took place:

THE COURT: Do you want to make an offer?

MR. RUBIN: Yes, your Honor. What we intend to prove with [the proffered testimony] is that he was in fact a student in the Marion Center Area High School and was a member of the National Honor Society in the same year that Arlene was a senior.

He was a sophomore and was also a member during that year and was knowledgeable as to the events regarding Arlene's dismissal. Further we would like to offer that, during his senior year two years later, with the same faculty council sitting on the National Honor Society, that he in fact got married, had a child, shortly thereafter getting married, and he had informed his teacher and other members of the Marion Center community that he was the father and that he got married because his fiance had gotten pregnant.

Additionally, we would be able to show through evidence that a document of the Marion Center Area School District called biographies has two entries into it showing that this boy was known generally in the high school community by the nickname daddy, and that he made the comment at his 15th year reunion he will be able to celebrate his wedding anniversary and child's birth.

The point of putting this individual on is that he can testify that nobody ever approached him about his conduct with regard to premarital sexual activity, that nobody ever approached him from the National Honor Society concerning this. There is evidence through depositions that they have stated on numerous occasions if they were aware of any situation dealing with a

male, that they would in fact consider that in the same light that they had considered Arlene.

Trial Transcript at 87–88; App. at 346–47.

We find this evidence can possibly be relevant to the state of mind of the faculty council on November 3, 1983, and whether the council and the board's explanation for their actions was pretextual when they dismissed Pfeiffer. The proffered testimony is relevant to the issue of intentional discrimination at the time Pfeiffer was dismissed. We, therefore, disagree with the district court's exclusion of it on the grounds that the events in the proffer post-dated by some years the November 1983 action of the council.

Although the proffer was not as precise as it could have been, and recognizing that Pfeiffer's counsel did not indicate with specificity how the later events were relevant to the activities of November 1983, we believe that the evidence has the potential of being relevant to whether the council members followed a double standard in evaluating premarital sexual activities of NHS chapter members. Under these circumstances, to exclude it was not consistent with sound exercise of discretion.

However, in directing that this testimony be considered, we are not saying that the proffer was sufficient. For example, all the proffer said was that the male student "had informed his teacher and other members of the Marion Center community that he was the father and that he had got married because his fiance had gotten pregnant." App. at 346–47. There is nothing in the proffer declaring that any member of the council had any knowledge of this situation.

What is important to the ultimate determination is what information was communicated to the council members. Lacking such communication, the testimony may not even be relevant. Moreover, even if the district court finds that the council did know of the male student's premarital sexual activity and did nothing about it, this by itself does not require the district court to make automatic findings one way or another. By remanding, we only instruct the district court to consider the proffered testimony for what it may be worth.

* * *

The judgment of the district court will be affirmed in part and vacated and remanded in part.

———————

Using a disparate impact analysis, a federal district judge in Kentucky analyzed the situation somewhat differently and issued a preliminary injunction enjoining the district from excluding unwed mothers from the National Honor Society.

Chipman v. Grant County School District
30 F. Supp. 2d 975 (1998).

William O. Bertelsman, District Judge:

* * *

The plaintiffs have met their burden of proving that the challenged practices of the defendants in screening students for admission to the NHS has caused a significant adverse effect on the protected group, i.e., young women who have become pregnant from premarital sex and have become visibly pregnant.

Statistically, 100% of such young women are not admitted to the GCNHS [Grant County National Honor Society]. Although the defendants argue that they are not basing their decision on pregnancy, but rather on non-marital sexual relations, the disparate impact on young women such as the plaintiffs is apparent.

Although 100% of young women who are visibly pregnant or who have had a child out of wedlock are denied membership, as far as the record reflects, defendants' policy excludes 0% of young men who have had premarital sexual relations and 0% of young women who have had such relations but have not become pregnant or have elected to have an early abortion.

The defendants claim that they would also exclude such students from the NHS membership but none have ever come to their attention. It may be that the discriminatory impact resulting from this policy is unintentional but, as stated above, proof of intentional discrimination is not required under a disparate impact theory.

The plaintiffs having met their initial burden of showing the significant adverse impact of defendants' policy, the burden now shifts to the defendants to show that the challenged practice is a reasonable necessity.

The defendants have not met such burden on the record now before the court. There are many alternate means to assess the character of candidates for membership in the NHS by non-discriminatory criteria.

Therefore the court holds that plaintiffs' probability of success herein is very high using a disparate impact theory.

* * *

[The district court also concluded that the students were likely to succeed on a disparate treatment claim based on intentional discrimination.]

* * *

Considering solely the evidence in the present record, the court must find that the defendants here have failed to articulate a legitimate credible non-discriminatory reason for their NHS pregnancy policy. The reasons articulated for the exclusion of the plaintiffs are vague, conclusory and undocumented. In the face of the admitted fact that plaintiffs were the only students surpassing the grade cutoff who were excluded, the court on the present record finds these proffered non-discriminatory reasons insufficient and not credible. Therefore, an adverse inference of intentional discrimination arises.

* * *

NOTES AND QUESTIONS

1. Unwed Mothers and Moral Character
Should having a child out of wedlock be a bar to identification as a leader with good moral character? How can such judgments be separated from discrimination based on pregnancy? Would it be relevant that students who had premarital sex but did not become pregnant or did not carry the pregnancy to term were admitted to the National Honor Society? What if married students who were pregnant were admitted? Would this be relevant to defining the nature of the discrimination? For an article reviewing cases in which pregnant students were denied admission to or expelled from the National Honor Society, *see* Schweitzer, " 'A' Students Go to Court: Is Membership in the National Honor Society a Cognizable Legal Right?" 50 *Syracuse L.Rev.* 63 (2000).

2. Pregnancy and Gender Discrimination
Should courts strike down policies that penalize unmarried students who bear children because the exclusion necessarily burdens women more than men? Is this because even if the policy is formally neutral, enforcement is stricter for women than for men precisely because only women become pregnant? Would it make any difference if men identified as fathering children out of wedlock were also barred from membership in the National Honor Society? Why or why not?

3. Separate Schools for Pregnant Students
Many school districts have established alternative schools for pregnant students. Although these are in fact single-sex institutions, they have largely escaped

judicial scrutiny because the assignment is based on pregnancy rather than gender. Title IX permits schools to create such programs so long as participation is voluntary and comparable education is provided. 34 C.F.R. § 106.40 (b)(1), (3). Are these alternative schools a permissible way to address increased dropout rates among pregnant teenagers? Or does a practice of segregation reinforce invidious stereotypes? *See* Stamm, "A Skeleton in the Closet: Single-Sex Schools for Pregnant Girls," 98 *Colum.L.Rev.* 1203 (1998); "Bias Against Pregnant Students Alleged in N.Y.," *Washington Post*, Dec. 3, 2000, at A7.

4. *Discrimination Based on Marital Status*

Many school districts historically restricted the educational opportunities available to married students. The exclusion of married students, premised on a desire to deter teenage marriage or to protect innocent teenagers from the company of young marrieds, has generally been overturned on nonconstitutional grounds. In *McLeod v. State ex rel. Colmer*, 154 Miss. 468, 475, 122 So. 737, 738 (1929), for example, the Mississippi Supreme Court noted: "Marriage is a domestic relation highly favored by the law. When the relation is entered into with correct motives, the effect on the husband and wife is refining and elevating, rather than demoralizing. Pupils associating in school with a child occupying such a relation, it seems, would be benefited instead of harmed." *See also Anderson v. Canyon Independent School District*, 412 S.W.2d 387 (Tex.Civ.App. 1967); *Alvin Independent School District v. Cooper*, 404 S.W.2d 76 (Tex.Civ.App. 1966).

School districts have more frequently barred married students from participating in extracurricular activities. The rationales for such rules include discouraging early marriage, preventing fraternization that might cause undue interest in sex among unmarrieds, freeing the individual student's time for marital responsibilities, and keeping schools free of jealousy between spouses. Although in the past courts have upheld such practices, *see Kissick v. Garland Independent School District*, 330 S.W.2d 708 (Tex.Civ.App. 1959), more recent decisions have struck down these rules, either as denials of equal protection, as impermissible invasions of students' rights to privacy, or as an infringement on the "fundamental right of marriage." *Moran v. School District No. 7, Yellowstone County*, 350 F.Supp. 1180 (D.Mont. 1972), for example, recognized that the right to attend school includes the right to participate in extracurricular activities. The court found a violation of the Equal Protection Clause in

that the board discriminated against married students without showing it to be a reasonable action within statutory authority for a legitimate purpose. *Indiana High School Athletic Association v. Raike*, 164 Ind.App. 169, 329 N.E.2d 66 (1975), held that rules barring married students from interscholastic competition do not bear a fair and substantial relation to the objective of promoting wholesomeness in competition.

The Title IX regulations bar differential treatment of married students based on gender in classes or extracurricular activities. *See* 34 C.F.R. § 106.40(a).

C. Scholarships and School Admission Standards

Title IX and its accompanying regulations address the potentially discriminatory impact of testing on women. Although most of the debate has focused on racial differences, some empirical studies suggest that women's scores on standardized tests systematically underpredict their performance. *See* Cook, "Standardized Tests—Cop Out for Schools, Women Students," 6 *Women in Higher Education* 9–10 (Nov. 1997); "Gender Bias in SATs Reduces the Number of Women Admitted to Colleges," 5 *About Women on Campus* 1 (Winter 1996); Hirsch, "Standardized Tests: Whose Standard Is It?" 4 *Women in Higher Education* 12–13 (Mar. 1995). The following case examines whether these types of gender differences provide the basis for a legal action.

Sharif by Salahuddin v. New York State Education Department
709 F.Supp. 345 (S.D.N.Y. 1989).

John M. Walker, District Judge:

This case raises the important questions of whether New York State denies female students an equal opportunity to receive prestigious state merit college scholarships by its sole reliance upon the Scholastic Aptitude Test ("SAT") to determine eligibility. To the Court's knowledge, this is the first case where female students are seeking to use the federal civil rights statute prohibiting sex discrimination in federally-funded educational programs to challenge a state's reliance on standardized tests. This case also presents a legal issue of first impressions: whether discrimination under Title IX can be established by proof of disparate impact without proof of intent to discriminate.

After careful consideration, this Court finds that defendants are discriminating against female plaintiffs and their putative class in violation of Title IX and the equal protection clause of the U.S. Constitution. For the reasons set forth below, this Court enjoins the State Education Department and its Commissioner from awarding the merit scholarships at issue solely on the basis of the SAT.

* * *

New York State, in one of the most expensive merit scholarship programs in the country, each year makes 26,000 academic achievement awards to New York's high school graduates.

In 1974, . . . the legislature restructured its awards, creating two types of awards: first, "general awards" which provide substantial monetary assistance, and second, "academic performance awards" which recognize achievement. Classifying Regents Scholarships as "academic performance awards," the legislature reduced the awards to a stipend of $250, and increased the number of awards to 25,000 to be allocated by county of residence.

* * *

In the "general awards" category, the legislature created a Tuition Assistance Program ("TAP") to fund college students based upon financial need. The legislature made TAP awards available to all students enrolled in approved programs and are given to those who demonstrate the ability to complete such program's courses, and who satisfy financial need requirements established by the Commissioner of Education. . . .

* * *

In 1977, the legislature directed that the scholarships be awarded on the basis of "nationally established competitive examinations. . . . [T]he SED [State Education Department] chose the SAT, the test taken by the greatest number of students." [T]he entire SAT is labeled an "aptitude" test, and the SAT's only purpose is to test two subjects—Math and English.

In response to allegations that the SED's practice of relying solely upon the SAT in awarding Regents and Empire State Scholarships discriminated against females who consistently scored below males, the Board of Regents asked the Governor and legislature for $100,000 to develop a new scholarship achievement examination. The legislature declined to fund a special examination but, instead, amended the Education Law to require that the awards be based . . . in part upon the student's grade point average ("GPA") as a measure of high school achievement. Senator Kenneth Lavalle, introducing the legislation, explained that the "statute

intended to correct a gross inequity that pervaded the New York educational system caused by awarding of Regents College Scholarships and Empire State Scholarships of Excellence based solely on the results of a nationally administered standardized examination." . . . The SED specified in its announcement of the new legislation to high school principals that the law was changed "[i]n order to provide for a better balance of male and female winners," . . .

The new legislation, for the first time, expressly stated that awards are to be based on a measure of "high school performance." . . . In doing so, the legislature altered the criteria for scholarship eligibility—on a one-year, experimental basis—to require the SED Commissioner to base awards on a formula which at least includes a measure of high school performance, and which may include nationally established examinations.

* * *

Despite comparability difficulties, the SED chose to use GPAs [grade point averages] as the best available measure of high school achievement. In awarding the Regents and Empire Scholarships for the 1988 graduates, the SED gave equal weight to students' SAT scores and GPAs, as the measure of high school performance.

* * *

In 1988, under the procedure using a combination of grades and SATs weighted equally women received substantially more Regents and Empire Scholarships than in all prior years in which the SAT had been the sole criterion. In both 1987 and 1988, young women comprised approximately 54% of the applicant pool for the scholarship, yet the results in 1988 when grades and SATs were used were markedly different. The results are summarized as follows:

When GPAs were used in 1988, the mean GPAs were: 85 for females and 84.4 for males.

* * *

In September, 1989, the SED determined that it would award Regents and Empire Scholarships to 1989 high school graduates on the basis of SAT scores alone. It is the SED's sole reliance on SAT

	Winners of Empire State Scholarships of Excellence		Winners of Regents College Scholarships	
	Males	Females	Males	Females
1988	62	38	51	49
1987	72	28	57	43

scores for 1989 graduates that plaintiffs complain denies them equal protection under the fourteenth amendment to the U.S. Constitution and violates Title IX of the Education Amendments of 1972.

* * *

The Educational Testing Service ("ETS") developed the SAT in order to predict academic performance in college. . . . It is undisputed, however, that the SAT predicts the success of students differently for males and females. In other words, while the SAT will predict college success as well for males within the universe of males as for females within the universe of females, when predictions are within the combined universe of males and females, the SAT *underpredicts* academic performance of females in their freshman year of college, and *overpredicts* such academic performance for males. The SAT has never been validated as a measure of past high school performance.

Both the ETS and the College Board, which administers the SAT, specifically advise against exclusive reliance upon the SAT, even for the purpose for which the SAT has been validated—predicting future college performance. Instead, ETS researchers recommend that college admissions counselors use a combination of high school grades and test scores because this combination provides the highest median correlation with freshman grades.

* * *

Both the Empire and Regents Scholarships are intended to reward past academic achievement of high school students, and to encourage those students who have demonstrated such achievement to pursue their education in New York State . . . .It is undisputed, however, that the SAT was developed and validated to serve a different purpose–predicting performance in college

. . . . [I]t is teh SED's current position that the SAT provides a good measure of high school performance because it "measures skills and knowledge primarily developed in school." . . .

* * *

Plaintiffs invoke the protections provided by Title IX, which prohibits sex discrimination in federally-funded educational programs. Plaintiffs do not claim that defendants have intentionally discriminated against them based on their sex. Rather, they claim that defendants' practice of sole reliance upon SAT scores to award prestigious state scholarships disparately impacts female students. To this Court's

knowledge, this is the first disparate impact case challenging educational testing practices under Title IX.

Neither the Supreme Court nor any court in the Second Circuit has determined whether intent must be shown in Title IX cases. This Court, however, is not without substantial guidance. Recognizing that "Title IX was patterned after Title VI of the Civil Rights Act of 1964," *Grove City College v. Bell*, 465 U.S. 555, 566, . . . (1984) courts examining Title IX questions have looked to the substantial body of law developed under Title VI, 42 U.S.C. § 2000d, which prohibits race discrimination in federally-funded programs, and Title VII, 42 U.S.C. § 2000e, which prohibits discrimination in employment. *See, e.g., Mabry v. State Board of Community Colleges and Occupational Education*, 813 F.2d 311, 317 (10th Cir.), *cert. denied*, 484 U.S. 849, 108 S.Ct. 148, 98 L.Ed.2d 104 (1987); *Haffer v. Temple University*, 678 F.Supp. 517, 539 (E.D.Pa. 1987).

In *Guardians Association v. Civil Service Commission*, 463 U.S. 582 . . . (1983), the Supreme Court held that a violation of Title VI itself requires proof of discriminatory intent. However, a majority also agreed that proof of discriminatory effect suffices to establish liability when a suit is brought to enforce the regulations promulgated under Title VI, rather than statute itself. *See also Alexander v. Choots*, 469 U.S. 287, 293–294, 105 S.Ct. 712, 716, 83 L.Ed.2d 661 (1985); *Latinos Unidos de Chelsea v. Secretary of Housing*, 799 F.2d 774, 785 n. 20 (1st Cir. 1986).

Plaintiffs' amended complaint explicitly alleges both violations of Title IX and its implementing regulations. This Court finds no persuasive reason not to apply Title VI's substantive standards to the present Title IX suit. . . .

The Title IX implementing regulations, like the regulations promulgated under Title VI, to which Title IX is frequently compared, are consistent with the interpretation of the comprehensive reach of the statute. Several Title IX regulations specifically prohibit facially neutral policies. For example, the provision governing admissions procedures, 34 C.F.R. § 106.21(b)(2), prohibits a recipient from

> administer[ing] or operat[ing] any test or other criteria for admission which has a disproportionately adverse effect on persons on the basis of sex unless the use of such test or criterion is shown to predict validly success in the education program or activity in question and alternative tests or criteria which do not have such a disproportionate adverse effect are shown to be unavailable.

See also 34 C.F.R. §§ 106.22, 106.23(b), 106.34(d), 106.37(b), 106.52, and 106.53(b).

Based upon a reading of the Title IX regulations, as well as the decisions that apply them, the Court finds that Title IX regulations, like the Title VI regulations at issue in *Guardians*, prohibit testing practices with a discriminatory *effect* on one sex. Consequently, plaintiffs need not prove intentional discrimination. . . .

In educational testing cases, courts have required defendants to show an "educational necessity." For example, the Eleventh Circuit, in *Georgia State Conf. of Branches of NAACP v. State of Georgia*, 775 F.2d 1403 (11th Cir. 1985), held that defendants had a burden of proving that their practices in question bore "a manifest demonstrable relationship to classroom education." *Id.* at 1413. *See also Board of Education v. Harris*, 444 U.S. 130, 151 . . . (1979) ("educational necessity" analogous to "business necessity").

Applying the Title VII formulations to this Title IX case as modified to take into account "educational necessity," this Court finds that plaintiffs have demonstrated a likelihood of success on the merits. Plaintiffs have met their burden of establishing a *prima facie* case through persuasive statistical evidence and credible expert testimony that the composition of scholarship winners tilted decidedly toward males and could not have occurred by a random distribution.

Plaintiffs, moreover, have established that the probability, absent discriminatory causes, that women would consistently score 60 points less on the SAT than men is nearly zero. . . . [T]his court finds that plaintiffs have demonstrated that the State's practice of sole reliance upon the SAT disparately impacts young women.

Thus, to prevail, defendants must show a manifest relationship between use of the SAT and recognition and award of academic achievement in high school. The Court finds that defendants have failed to show even a reasonable relationship between their practice and their conceded purpose. The SAT was not designed to measure achievement in high school and was never validated for that purpose. Instead, in arguing that the SAT somehow measures high school performances, defendants rely upon anecdotal evidence that the SAT partially tracks what is generally learned in high school Math and English courses. This argument is meritless.

Plaintiffs have offered substantial evidence that the SATs do not mirror high school Math and English classes.

Moreover, even if SATs provided a partial measurement of what is learned in high school Math and English, these two courses constitute only 2% of a high school student's studies.

Plaintiffs have offered an alternative to sole reliance upon the SAT: a combination of GPAs and SATs. The SED's use of this alternative in 1988 sharply reduced the disparate impact against females caused by the use of the SAT alone. A significantly greater number of female students received scholarships in 1988 than in each prior year in which the SED relied solely upon the SAT. Defendants concede that females had a greater opportunity to receive scholarships under the combination system. Defendants also concede that grades are the best measure of high school achievement within the walls of a single school. Instead, they argue that since there is a disparity among schools and their grading systems it is both unfair and impossible to use grades as part of the scholarship eligibility determination. Defendants plan instead to develop a statewide achievement test. While this Court does not dispute the apparent advantages of a statewide achievement test—if indeed a valid test can be developed—it does not agree that pending the implication of such a test, use of grades would be either unfair or infeasible.

While a combination system—using both GPAs and SATs—is not a perfect alternative, it is the best alternative presently available.

* * *

The SED cannot justify its discriminatory practice because any alternative would be more difficult to administer. All states giving merit scholarships awards, with the exception of New York and Massachusetts, use GPAs, without concern for either administrative difficulties, grade inflation or the comparability of grades. . . .

[P]laintiffs also have established a likelihood that they will succeed on their equal protection claim. The classification of scholarship applicants solely on the basis of SAT scores violates the equal protection clause of the Fourteenth Amendment because this method is not rationally related to the state's goal of rewarding students who have demonstrated academic achievement.

Under the lowest standard of equal protection review—the "rational relationship standard"—"[t]he

State may not rely on a classification whose relationship to an asserted goal is so attenuated as to render the distinction arbitrary or irrational." *City of Cleburne v. Cleburne Living Center*, 473 U.S. 432, 446, . . . (1985). Although considerable deference is given to the decisions of legislators and state administrators under the rational basis test, the test "is not a toothless one." *Baccus v. Karger*, 692 F.Supp. 290, 298 (S.D.N.Y. 1988) (invalidating New York bar rule that required applicants for bar admission to have commenced the study of law after their 18th birthday). . . .

For the reasons stated above, the SED's use of the SAT as a proxy for high school achievement is too unrelated to the legislative purpose of awarding academic achievement in high school to survive even the most minimal scrutiny. The evidence is clear that females score significantly below males on the SAT while they perform equally or slightly better than males in high school. Therefore, the SED's use of the SAT as the sole criterion for awarding Regents and Empire Scholarships discriminates against females and, since such a practice is not rationally related to the legislative purpose, it unconstitutionally denies young women equal protection of the laws and must be enjoined on that ground as well.

* * *

Defendants' practice of relying solely upon SAT scores in awarding Regents and Empire Scholarships deprives young women of the opportunity to compete equally for these prestigious scholarships in violation of both Title IX and the Constitution's equal protection clause. Defendants are hereby ordered to discontinue such discriminatory practices and, instead, to award Regents and Empire Scholarships in a manner that more accurately measures students' high school achievement. For the present year, the best available alternative is a combination of grades and SATs. The SAT component is justified, not as a measure of achievement, but to weight the GPA component. The Court, however, does not limit the SED's discretion to develop other alternatives in the future, including a statewide achievement test.

NOTES AND QUESTIONS

1. Disparate Impact

Is the court in *Sharif* correct in allowing, under Title IX, a showing of disparate impact—that is, a showing that women fare less well than men—rather than requiring evidence that discrimination is the motivating factor behind the use of the test?

Had plaintiffs been required to show discriminatory intent, could they have prevailed? How does your appraisal of this question bear on the treatment of the same issue in the context of race, as discussed in chapter 4?

2. Grades and Scholarships

Most states, as the *Sharif* opinion notes, rely partly on students' grades in awarding state scholarships. But would reliance on grades be preferable to using the SAT scores, as New York State does? Are grades a reliable indicator of school performance? Are they comparable across subjects? Across schools? Would the development of a state exam be a preferable alternative?

3. The Gender Gap in Standardized Testing

In 1997, the Educational Testing Service released the results of a four-year study of gender differences in performance on standardized tests. N. Cole, *The ETS Gender Study: How Females and Males Perform in Educational Settings* (May 1997). The study found that overall the gender differences are quite small for most subjects, that females have significantly closed the gap in mathematics and science, and that males continue to lag behind in writing and language skills. *Id.* at 10. The study did acknowledge that girls consistently earn higher grades than boys, despite generally symmetric outcomes on standardized tests. Moreover, SAT scores alone did systematically although slightly underpredict female students' first-year college performance. Using both grades and SAT scores improved the overall accuracy in predicting performance and narrowed the gender gap. *Id.* at 18–20.

According to the author, not every difference in scores between boys and girls should be equated with bias. In some instances, the differences are real ones, "found in many types of measures, by many different approaches, and in many samples." *Id.* at 23. Moreover, she contended that test content should not be changed to narrow the gender gap if the content is educationally important. *Id.* at 23–24. How can researchers reliably distinguish between real differences and gender bias? Even if test scores are equalized for men and women, is it discriminatory to rely on them exclusively when women's grades are systematically higher than men's? Is it necessary to demonstrate that test scores alone underpredict female performance? Or is it enough that test scores alone fail to reward women for the record of achievement represented by their grade point average?

4. Admission

May an academically selective high school set different admission standards for male and female applicants? Does the fact that the academic high school for boys has a larger capacity for students than the academic high school for girls provide a justification? *See Bray v. Lee*, 337 F.Supp. 934 (D.Mass. 1972). Suppose a district chose to admit equal numbers of young men and women to maintain "a balanced community representation of the population." *See Berkelman v. San Francisco Unified School District*, 501 F.2d 1264 (9th Cir. 1974). What if a balance could be achieved only by setting a higher standard for one sex? How does Title IX affect differential admissions? Which of the following factors are relevant: the level of the institution, the historical practices of the institution, or the rationale proferred? *See* 20 U.S.C.A. § 1681(a)(1).

2. A Private Right of Action Under Title IX: The Special Case of Sexual Harassment. In 1979, the United States Supreme Court held that Title IX implicitly authorizes a private right of action. *Cannon v. University of Chicago*, 441 U.S. 677 (1970). According to the Court:

> Title IX explicitly confers a benefit on persons discriminated against on the basis of sex, and petitioner is clearly a member of that class for whose special benefit the statute was enacted. . . .
>
> [T]he history of Title IX rather plainly indicates that Congress intended to create such a remedy [noting that the statute was patterned after Title VI, which had already been construed as creating a private remedy]. . . . Finally, the very persistence . . . of the assumption that both Title VI and Title IX created a private right of action for the victims of illegal discrimination and the absence of legislative action to change that assumption provide further evidence that Congress at least acquiesces in, and apparently affirms, that assumption.

441 U.S. at 694, 702–703, 99 S.Ct. at 1961.

The Court dismissed the University of Chicago's argument that "it is unwise to subject admissions decisions . . . to judicial scrutiny at the behest of disappointed applicants on a case-by-case basis." This contention "is not a legal argument at all; it addresses a policy issue that Congress had already resolved." And "the fact that other provisions of a complex statutory scheme create express remedies has not been accepted as a sufficient reason for refusing to imply an otherwise appropriate remedy under a separate section. . . . Rather, the Court has generally

avoided this type of 'excursion into extrapolation of legislative intent,' . . . unless there is other, more convincing evidence that Congress meant to exclude the remedy. . . ."

Having recognized a private right of action, the Court then had to address the scope of Title IX's coverage in subsequent litigation. In *North Haven Board of Education v. Bell*, 456 U.S. 512, 102 S.Ct. 1912, 72 L.Ed.2d 299 (1982), the Supreme Court ruled that Title IX applies to discrimination in employment, not just discrimination against students. Lower courts had earlier read the statutory language "no person" restrictively, as not including employees. But the Court declared that, since the language and legislative history did not explicitly or implicitly exclude employment discrimination, employees were covered.

Congress could have used the word "students" instead of "persons," said the Court, if that was its intention. And there was relevant legislative history: The sponsor of the measure, Indiana Senator Birch Bayh, had described the legislation as reaching "discrimination in employment within an institution, as a member of a faculty or whatever." *See* Brower, "Now You See It, Now You Don't: Title IX As an Alternate Remedy for Sex Discrimination in Educational Employment," 31 N.Y.L.Sch.L.Rev. 657 (1986).

In *Grove City College v. Bell*, 465 U.S. 555, 104 S.Ct. 1211, 79 L.Ed.2d 516 (1984), the Justices limited the reach of Title IX. The issue was whether the federal government could cut off all federal assistance to an entire institution when only a particular program was discriminating in violation of Title IX. The Court, relying on the legislative history, declared that the federal government could terminate only those funds earmarked specifically for the discriminatory program. Title VI and Section 504 of the Rehabilitation Act were implicated since the relevant statutory language is virtually identical. *See Consolidated Rail Corp. v. Darrone*, 465 U.S. 624, 104 S.Ct. 1248, 79 L.Ed.2d 568 (1984) (§ 504).

The impact of *Grove City* on Title IX enforcement was significant. The Court's ruling allowed a university (or any other institution subject to Title IX) to discriminate in particular program areas (*e.g.*, the engineering school or the athletic program)—indeed, any place except in a program where it received federal aid. On the other hand, a single instance of discrimination in one limited program would not trigger a university-wide sanction.

Within months of ruling, the *Grove City* decision prompted the Department of Education's Office of

Civil Rights to close twenty-three civil rights investigations and to narrow the scope of eighteen others. A compliance action against the University of Maryland was dropped, for example, even though instances of discrimination by the athletic department had allegedly been documented. Since the only federal aid to that department was loan money received by athletes, and since there had been no discrimination in the disbursement of the loan funds, OCR declared that it could not proceed. *See* Griffin, "*Grove City College v. Bell*: Restricting the Scope of Title IX," 8 *Harv.Women's L.J.* 179 (1985); Mezey, "Gender Equality in Education: A Study of Policy-Making by the Burger Court," 20 *Wake Forest L.Rev.* 793 (1984).

In 1988 the Supreme Court's ruling was overturned by Congress. The Civil Rights Restoration Act of 1988, 20 U.S.C.A. § 1687, redefines "program or activity" in Title VI and Title IX: as "a college, university, or other postsecondary institution, or a public system of higher education; or a local educational agency . . . any part of which is extended Federal financial assistance (constitutes a program or activity under the Act), except that such term does not include any operation of an entity which is controlled by a religious organization if the application of [Title IX] would not be consistent with the religious tenets of such organization." Section 1688 clarifies that the provision does not speak to the issue of abortion, neither requiring nor prohibiting its provision or financing.

With these inclusive interpretations of Title IX in place, the Court turned to one of the most vexing areas of private litigation under Title IX: sexual harassment. In 1992, the Justices held that a student could sue for money damages based on sexual coercion and abuse inflicted on her by a male teacher. These intentional acts, if proven at trial, could provide the basis for a monetary award because the student's remedies were not limited to back pay and prospective relief. Such remedies would be meaningless here because the plaintiff was not an employee receiving wages and because neither she nor the male teacher remained at the school. *Franklin v. Gwinnett County Public Schools*, 503 U.S. 60, 112 S.Ct. 1028, 117 L.Ed.2d 208 (1992).

(a) The Scope of Liability for the Acts of Employees.
Although the Court had made clear that a range of relief was available under Title IX, its decision did not provide guidance on the scope of a district's liability for acts of harassment by teachers and students. The Court addressed a district's responsibility under Title IX for the acts of employees in 1998.

Gebser v. Lago Vista Independent School District
524 U.S. 274, 118 S.Ct. 1989, 141 L.Ed.2d 277 (1998).

* * *

Justice O'Connor delivered the opinion of the Court.

The question in this case is when a school district may be held liable in damages in an implied right of action under Title IX of the Education Amendments of 1972, 86 Stat. 373, as amended, 20 U.S.C. § 1681 *et seq.* (Title IX), for the sexual harassment of a student by one of the district's teachers. We conclude that damages may not be recovered in those circumstances unless an official of the school district who at a minimum has authority to institute corrective measures on the district's behalf has actual notice of, and is deliberately indifferent to, the teacher's misconduct.

I

In the spring of 1991, when petitioner Alida Star Gebser was an eighth-grade student at a middle school in respondent Lago Vista Independent School District (Lago Vista), she joined a high school book discussion group led by Frank Waldrop, a teacher at Lago Vista's high school. Lago Vista received federal funds at all pertinent times. During the book discussion sessions, Waldrop often made sexually suggestive comments to the students. Gebser entered high school in the fall and was assigned to classes taught by Waldrop in both semesters. Waldrop continued to make inappropriate remarks to the students, and he began to direct more of his suggestive comments toward Gebser, including during the substantial amount of time that the two were alone in his classroom. He initiated sexual contact with Gebser in the spring, when, while visiting her home ostensibly to give her a book, he kissed and fondled her. The two had sexual intercourse on a number of occasions during the remainder of the school year. Their relationship continued through the summer and into the following school year, and they often had intercourse during class time, although never on school property.

Gebser did not report the relationship to school officials, testifying that while she realized Waldrop's conduct was improper, she was uncertain how to react and she wanted to continue having him as a teacher. In October 1992, the parents of two other students complained to the high school principal about Waldrop's comments in class. The principal arranged a meeting, at which, according to the principal, Waldrop indicated that he did not believe he had made offensive remarks but apologized to the parents and said it would not happen again. The principal also advised Waldrop to be careful about his classroom comments and told the school guidance counselor about the meeting, but he did not report the parents' complaint to Lago Vista's superintendent, who was the district's Title IX coordinator. A couple of months later, in January 1993, a police officer discovered Waldrop and Gebser engaging in sexual intercourse and arrested Waldrop. Lago Vista terminated his employment, and subsequently, the Texas Education Agency revoked his teaching license. During this time, the district had not promulgated or distributed an official grievance procedure for lodging sexual harassment complaints; nor had it issued a formal anti-harassment policy.

Gebser and her mother filed suit against Lago Vista and Waldrop in state court in November 1993, raising claims against the school district under Title IX, Rev. Stat. § 1979, 42 U.S.C. § 1983, and state negligence law, and claims against Waldrop primarily under state law. They sought compensatory and punitive damages from both defendants. After the case was removed, the United States District Court for the Western District of Texas granted summary judgment in favor of Lago Vista on all claims, and remanded the allegations against Waldrop to state court. In rejecting the Title IX claim against the school district, the court reasoned that the statute "was enacted to counter *policies* of discrimination . . . in federally funded education programs," and that "[o]nly if school administrators have some type of notice of the gender discrimination and fail to respond in good faith can the discrimination be interpreted as a *policy* of the school district." App. to Pet. for Cert. 6a-7a. Here, the court determined, the parents' complaint to the principal concerning Waldrop's comments in class was the only one Lago Vista had received about Waldrop, and that evidence was inadequate to raise a genuine issue on whether the school district had actual or constructive notice that Waldrop was involved in a sexual relationship with a student.

Petitioners appealed only on the Title IX claim. The Court of Appeals for the Fifth Circuit affirmed, *Doe v. Lago Vista Independent School Dist.*, 106 F. 3d 1223 (1997), relying in large part on two of its recent decisions, *Rosa H. v. San Elizario Independent School Dist.*, 106 F.3d 648 (1997), and *Canutillo Independent School Dist. v. Leija*, 101 F.3d 393 (1996), cert. denied, 520 U.S. 1265 (1997). The court first declined to impose strict liability on school districts

for a teacher's sexual harassment of a student, reiterating its conclusion in *Leija* that strict liability is inconsistent with "the Title IX contract." 106 F. 3d, at 1225 (internal quotation marks omitted). The court then determined that Lago Vista could not be liable on the basis of constructive notice, finding that there was insufficient evidence to suggest that a school official should have known about Waldrop's relationship with Gebser. *Ibid.* Finally, the court refused to invoke the common law principle that holds an employer vicariously liable when an employee is "aided in accomplishing [a] tort by the existence of the agency relation," Restatement (Second) of Agency § 219(2)(d) (1957) (hereinafter Restatement), explaining that application of that principle would result in school district liability in essentially every case of teacher-student harassment. 106 F. 3d, at 1225–1226.

The court concluded its analysis by reaffirming its holding in *Rosa H.* that, "school districts are not liable in tort for teacher-student [sexual] harassment under Title IX unless an employee who has been invested by the school board with supervisory power over the offending employee actually knew of the abuse, had the power to end the abuse, and failed to do so," 106 F. 3d, at 1226, and ruling that petitioners could not satisfy that standard. The Fifth Circuit's analysis represents one of the varying approaches adopted by the Courts of Appeals in assessing a school district's liability under Title IX for a teacher's sexual harassment of a student. See *Smith v. Metropolitan School Dist. Perry Twp.*, 128 F. 3d 1014 (1997); *Kracunas v. Iona College*, 119 F. 3d 80 (1997); *Doe v. Claiborne County*, 103 F. 3d 495, 513–515 (1996); *Kinman v. Omaha Public School Dist.*, 94 F. 3d 463, 469 (1996). We granted certiorari to address the issue, 522 U.S. 1101 (1997), and we now affirm.

II

* * *

. . . Petitioners, joined by the United States as *amicus curiae*, would invoke standards used by the Courts of Appeals in Title VII cases involving a supervisor's sexual harassment of an employee in the workplace. . . .

Specifically, they advance two possible standards under which Lago Vista would be liable for Waldrop's conduct. First, relying on a 1997 "Policy Guidance" issued by the Department of Education, they would hold a school district liable in damages under Title IX where a teacher is " 'aided in carrying out the sexual harassment of students by his or her position of authority with the institution,' " irrespective of whether school district officials had any knowledge of the harassment and irrespective of their response upon becoming aware. Brief for Petitioners 36 (quoting Dept. of Education, Office of Civil Rights, Sexual Harassment Policy Guidance, 62 Fed.Reg. 12034, 12039 (1997) (1997 Policy Guidance)); Brief for United States as *Amicus Curiae* 14. That rule is an expression of *respondeat superior* liability, i.e., vicarious or imputed liability, see Restatement § 219(2)(d), under which recovery in damages against a school district would generally follow whenever a teacher's authority over a student facilitates the harassment. Second, petitioners and the United States submit that a school district should at a minimum be liable for damages based on a theory of constructive notice, *i.e.*, where the district knew or "should have known" about harassment but failed to uncover and eliminate it. Brief for Petitioners 28; Brief for United States as *Amicus Curiae* 15–16; see Restatement § 219(2)(b). Both standards would allow a damages recovery in a broader range of situations than the rule adopted by the Court of Appeals, which hinges on actual knowledge by a school official with authority to end the harassment.

* * *

In this case . . . petitioners seek not just to establish a Title IX violation but to recover *damages* based on theories of *respondeat superior* and constructive notice. It is that aspect of their action, in our view, which is most critical to resolving the case. Unlike Title IX, Title VII contains an express cause of action, § 2000e-5(f), and specifically provides for relief in the form of monetary damages, § 1981a. Congress therefore has directly addressed the subject of damages relief under Title VII and has set out the particular situations in which damages are available as well as the maximum amounts recoverable. § 1981a(b). With respect to Title IX, however, the private right of action is judicially implied, see *Cannon*, 441 U.S., at 717, 99 S.Ct., at 1968, and there is thus no legislative expression of the scope of available remedies, including when it is appropriate to award monetary damages. In addition, although the general presumption that courts can award any appropriate relief in an established cause of action, *e.g., Bell v. Hood*, 327 U.S. 678, 684, 66 S.Ct. 773, 776–777, 90 L.Ed. 939 (1946), coupled with Congress' abrogation of the States' Eleventh Amendment immunity under Title IX, see 42 U.S.C. § 2000d-7, led us to conclude in

Franklin that Title IX recognizes a damages remedy, 503 U.S., at 68–73, 112 S.Ct., at 1033–1037; see *id.*, at 78, 112 S.Ct., at 1039 (SCALIA, J., concurring in judgment), we did so in response to lower court decisions holding that Title IX does not support damages relief at all. We made no effort in *Franklin* to delimit the circumstances in which a damages remedy should lie.

III

Because the private right of action under Title IX is judicially implied, we have a measure of latitude to shape a sensible remedial scheme that best comports with the statute. See, *e.g., Musick, Peeler & Garrett v. Employers Ins. of Wausau*, 508 U.S. 286, 292–293, 113 S.Ct. 2085, 2089–2090, 124 L.Ed.2d 194 (1993); *Virginia Bankshares, Inc. v. Sandberg*, 501 U.S. 1083, 1104, 111 S.Ct. 2749, 2764, 115 L.Ed.2d 929 (1991). That endeavor inherently entails a degree of speculation, since it addresses an issue on which Congress has not specifically spoken. See, *e.g., Lampf, Pleva, Lipkind, Prupis & Petigrow v. Gilbertson*, 501 U.S. 350, 359, 111 S.Ct. 2773, 2780, 115 L.Ed.2d 321 (1991). To guide the analysis, we generally examine the relevant statute to ensure that we do not fashion the parameters of an implied right in a manner at odds with the statutory structure and purpose. See *Musick, Peeler*, 508 U.S., at 294–297, 113 S.Ct., at 2089–2091; *id.*, at 300, 113 S.Ct., at 2092–2093 (THOMAS, J., dissenting); *Virginia Bankshares, supra*, at 1102, 111 S.Ct., at 2763.

Those considerations, we think, are pertinent not only to the scope of the implied right, but also to the scope of the available remedies. See *Transamerica Mortgage Advisors, Inc. v. Lewis*, 444 U.S. 11, 100 S.Ct. 242, 62 L.Ed.2d 146 (1979); see also *Franklin, supra*, at 77–78, 112 S.Ct., at 1038–1039 (SCALIA, J., concurring in judgment). We suggested as much in *Franklin*, where we recognized "the general rule that all appropriate relief is available in an action brought to vindicate a federal right," but indicated that the rule must be reconciled with congressional purpose. 503 U.S., at 68, 112 S.Ct., at 1033–1034. The "general rule," that is, "yields where necessary to carry out the intent of Congress or to avoid frustrating the purposes of the statute involved." *Guardians Assn. v. Civil Serv. Comm'n of New York City*, 463 U.S. 582, 595, 103 S.Ct. 3221, 3228–3229, 77 L.Ed.2d 866 (1983) (opinion of White, J.); cf., *Cannon*, 441 U.S., at 703, 99 S.Ct., at 1960–1961 ("[A] private remedy should not be implied if it would frustrate the underlying purpose of the legislative scheme").

Applying those principles here, we conclude that it would "frustrate the purposes" of Title IX to permit a damages recovery against a school district for a teacher's sexual harassment of a student based on principles of *respondeat superior* or constructive notice, *i.e.*, without actual notice to a school district official. Because Congress did not expressly create a private right of action under Title IX, the statutory text does not shed light on Congress' intent with respect to the scope of available remedies. *Franklin*, 503 U.S., at 71, 112 S.Ct., at 1035–1036; *id.*, at 76, 112 S.Ct., at 1038 (SCALIA, J., concurring in judgment). Instead, "we attempt to infer how the [1972] Congress would have addressed the issue had the . . . action been included as an express provision in the" statute. *Central Bank of Denver, N.A. v. First Interstate Bank of Denver, N. A.*, 511 U.S. 164, 178, 114 S.Ct. 1439, 1448, 128 L.Ed.2d 119 (1994); see *Musick, Peeler, supra*, at 294–295, 113 S.Ct., at 2089–2090; *North Haven Bd. of Ed. v. Bell*, 456 U.S. 512, 529, 102 S.Ct. 1912, 1922, 72 L.Ed.2d 299 (1982).

As a general matter, it does not appear that Congress contemplated unlimited recovery in damages against a funding recipient where the recipient is unaware of discrimination in its programs. When Title IX was enacted in 1972, the principal civil rights statutes containing an express right of action did not provide for recovery of monetary damages at all, instead allowing only injunctive and equitable relief. See 42 U.S.C. § 2000a-3(a) (1970 ed.); § 2000e-5(e), (g) (1970 ed., Supp. II). It was not until 1991 that Congress made damages available under Title VII, and even then, Congress carefully limited the amount recoverable in any individual case, calibrating the maximum recovery to the size of the employer. See 42 U.S.C. § 1981a(b)(3). Adopting petitioners' position would amount, then, to allowing unlimited recovery of damages under Title IX where Congress has not spoken on the subject of either the right or the remedy, and in the face of evidence that when Congress expressly considered both in Title VII it restricted the amount of damages available.

Congress enacted Title IX in 1972 with two principal objectives in mind: "to avoid the use of federal resources to support discriminatory practices" and "to provide individual citizens effective protection against those practices." *Cannon, supra*, at 704, 99 S.Ct., at 1961–1962. The statute was modeled after

Title VI of the Civil Rights Act of 1964, see 441 U.S., at 694–696, 99 S.Ct., at 1956–1958; *Grove City College v. Bell*, 465 U.S. 555, 566, 104 S.Ct. 1211, 1217–1218, 79 L.Ed.2d 516 (1984), which is parallel to Title IX except that it prohibits race discrimination, not sex discrimination, and applies in all programs receiving federal funds, not only in education programs. See 42 U.S.C. § 2000d *et seq.* The two statutes operate in the same manner, conditioning an offer of federal funding on a promise by the recipient not to discriminate, in what amounts essentially to a contract between the Government and the recipient of funds. See *Guardians*, 463 U.S., at 599, 103 S.Ct., at 3231 (opinion of White, J.); *id.*, at 609, 103 S.Ct., at 3236 (Powell, J., concurring in judgment); cf., *Pennhurst State School and Hospital v. Halderman*, 451 U.S. 1, 17, 101 S.Ct. 1531, 1539–1540, 67 L.Ed.2d 694 (1981).

That contractual framework distinguishes Title IX from Title VII, which is framed in terms not of a condition but of an outright prohibition. Title VII applies to all employers without regard to federal funding and aims broadly to "eradicat[e] discrimination throughout the economy." *Landgraf v. USI Film Products*, 511 U.S. 244, 254, 114 S.Ct. 1483, 1491, 128 L.Ed.2d 229 (1994) (internal quotation marks omitted). Title VII, moreover, seeks to "make persons whole for injuries suffered through past discrimination." *Ibid.* (internal quotation marks omitted). Thus, whereas Title VII aims centrally to compensate victims of discrimination, Title IX focuses more on "protecting" individuals from discriminatory practices carried out by recipients of federal funds. *Cannon, supra*, at 704, 99 S.Ct., at 1961–1962. That might explain why, when the Court first recognized the implied right under Title IX in *Cannon*, the opinion referred to injunctive or equitable relief in a private action, see 441 U.S., at 705, and n. 38, 710, n. 44, 711, 99 S.Ct., at 1962, and n. 38, 1964, n. 44, 1965, but not to a damages remedy.

Title IX's contractual nature has implications for our construction of the scope of available remedies. When Congress attaches conditions to the award of federal funds under its spending power, U.S. Const., Art. I, § 8, cl. 1, as it has in Title IX and Title VI, we examine closely the propriety of private actions holding the recipient liable in monetary damages for noncompliance with the condition. See *Franklin*, 503 U.S., at 74–75, 112 S.Ct., at 1037; *Guardians, supra*, at 596–603, 103 S.Ct., at 3229–3230 (White, J.); see generally *Pennhurst, supra*, at 28–29, 101 S.Ct., at 1545–1546. Our central concern in that regard is with ensuring "that the receiving entity of federal funds [has] notice that it will be liable for a monetary award." *Franklin, supra,* at 74, 112 S.Ct., at 1037. Justice White's opinion announcing the Court's judgment in *Guardians Assn. v. Civil Serv. Comm'n of New York City,* for instance, concluded that the relief in an action under Title VI alleging unintentional discrimination should be prospective only, because where discrimination is unintentional, "it is surely not obvious that the grantee was aware that it was administering the program in violation of the [condition]." 463 U.S., at 598, 103 S.Ct., at 3230. We confront similar concerns here. If a school district's liability for a teacher's sexual harassment rests on principles of constructive notice or *respondeat superior,* it will likewise be the case that the recipient of funds was unaware of the discrimination. It is sensible to assume that Congress did not envision a recipient's liability in damages in that situation. See *Rosa H.,* 106 F.3d, at 654 ("When the school board accepted federal funds, it agreed not to discriminate on the basis of sex. We think it unlikely that it further agreed to suffer liability whenever its employees discriminate on the basis of sex").

Most significantly, Title IX contains important clues that Congress did not intend to allow recovery in damages where liability rests solely on principles of vicarious liability or constructive notice. Title IX's express means of enforcement—by administrative agencies—operates on an assumption of actual notice to officials of the funding recipient. The statute entitles agencies who disburse education funding to enforce their rules implementing the non-discrimination mandate through proceedings to suspend or terminate funding or through "other means authorized by law." 20 U.S.C. § 1682. Significantly, however, an agency may not initiate enforcement proceedings until it "has advised the appropriate person or persons of the failure to comply with the requirement and has determined that compliance cannot be secured by voluntary means." *Ibid.* The administrative regulations implement that obligation, requiring resolution of compliance issues "by informal means whenever possible," 34 CFR § 100.7(d) (1997), and prohibiting commencement of enforcement proceedings until the agency has determined that voluntary compliance is unobtainable and "the recipient . . . has been notified of its failure to comply and of the action to be taken to effect compliance," § 100.8(d); see § 100.8(c).

In the event of a violation, a funding recipient may be required to take "such remedial action as [is]

deem[ed] necessary to overcome the effects of [the] discrimination." § 106.3. While agencies have conditioned continued funding on providing equitable relief to the victim, see, *e.g., North Haven,* 456 U.S., at 518, 102 S.Ct., at 1916 (reinstatement of employee), the regulations do not appear to contemplate a condition ordering payment of monetary damages, and there is no indication that payment of damages has been demanded as a condition of finding a recipient to be in compliance with the statute. See Brief for United States as *Amicus Curiae* in *Franklin v. Gwinnett County School District,* O.T.1991, No. 918, p. 24. In *Franklin,* for instance, the Department of Education found a violation of Title IX but determined that the school district came into compliance by virtue of the offending teacher's resignation and the district's institution of a grievance procedure for sexual harassment complaints. 503 U.S., at 64, n. 3, 112 S.Ct., at 1032, n. 3.

Presumably, a central purpose of requiring notice of the violation "to the appropriate person" and an opportunity for voluntary compliance before administrative enforcement proceedings can commence is to avoid diverting education funding from beneficial uses where a recipient was unaware of discrimination in its programs and is willing to institute prompt corrective measures. The scope of private damages relief proposed by petitioners is at odds with that basic objective. When a teacher's sexual harassment is imputed to a school district or when a school district is deemed to have "constructively" known of the teacher's harassment, by assumption the district had no actual knowledge of the teacher's conduct. Nor, of course, did the district have an opportunity to take action to end the harassment or to limit further harassment.

It would be unsound, we think, for a statute's *express* system of enforcement to require notice to the recipient and an opportunity to come into voluntary compliance while a judicially *implied* system of enforcement permits substantial liability without regard to the recipient's knowledge or its corrective actions upon receiving notice. Cf., *Central Bank of Denver, N.A. v. First Interstate Bank of Denver, N. A.,* 511 U.S., at 180, 114 S.Ct., at 1449 ("[I]t would be 'anomalous to impute to Congress an intention to expand the plaintiff class for a judicially implied cause of action beyond the bounds it delineated for comparable express causes of action' "), quoting *Blue Chip Stamps v. Manor Drug Stores,* 421 U.S. 723, 736, 95 S.Ct. 1917, 1925–1926, 44 L.Ed.2d 539 (1975).

Moreover, an award of damages in a particular case might well exceed a recipient's level of federal funding. See Tr. of Oral Arg. 35 (Lago Vista's federal funding for 1992–1993 was roughly $120,000). Where a statute's express enforcement scheme hinges its most severe sanction on notice and unsuccessful efforts to obtain compliance, we cannot attribute to Congress the intention to have implied an enforcement scheme that allows imposition of greater liability without comparable conditions.

IV

Because the express remedial scheme under Title IX is predicated upon notice to an "appropriate person" and an opportunity to rectify any violation, 20 U.S.C. § 1682, we conclude, in the absence of further direction from Congress, that the implied damages remedy should be fashioned along the same lines. An "appropriate person" under § 1682 is, at a minimum, an official of the recipient entity with authority to take corrective action to end the discrimination. Consequently, in cases like this one that do not involve official policy of the recipient entity, we hold that a damages remedy will not lie under Title IX unless an official who at a minimum has authority to address the alleged discrimination and to institute corrective measures on the recipient's behalf has actual knowledge of discrimination in the recipient's programs and fails adequately to respond.

We think, moreover, that the response must amount to deliberate indifference to discrimination. The administrative enforcement scheme presupposes that an official who is advised of a Title IX violation refuses to take action to bring the recipient into compliance. The premise, in other words, is an official decision by the recipient not to remedy the violation. That framework finds a rough parallel in the standard of deliberate indifference. Under a lower standard, there would be a risk that the recipient would be liable in damages not for its own official decision but instead for its employees' independent actions. Comparable considerations led to our adoption of a deliberate indifference standard for claims under § 1983 alleging that a municipality's actions in failing to prevent a deprivation of federal rights was the cause of the violation. See *Board of Comm'rs of Bryan Cty. v. Brown*, 520 U.S. 397, 117 S.Ct. 1382, 137 L.Ed.2d 626 (1997); *Canton v. Harris*, 489 U.S. 378, 388–392, 109 S.Ct.

1197, 1204–1207, 103 L.Ed.2d 412 (1989); see also *Collins v. Harker Heights*, 503 U.S. 115, 123–124, 112 S.Ct. 1061, 1067–1068, 117 L.Ed.2d 261 (1992).

Applying the framework to this case is fairly straightforward, as petitioners do not contend they can prevail under an actual notice standard. The only official alleged to have had information about Waldrop's misconduct is the high school principal. That information, however, consisted of a complaint from parents of other students charging only that Waldrop had made inappropriate comments during class, which was plainly insufficient to alert the principal to the possibility that Waldrop was involved in a sexual relationship with a student. Lago Vista, moreover, terminated Waldrop's employment upon learning of his relationship with Gebser. Justice STEVENS points out in his dissenting opinion that Waldrop of course had knowledge of his own actions. See *post*, at 2003, n. 8. Where a school district's liability rests on actual notice principles, however, the knowledge of the wrongdoer himself is not pertinent to the analysis. See Restatement § 280.

Petitioners focus primarily on Lago Vista's asserted failure to promulgate and publicize an effective policy and grievance procedure for sexual harassment claims. They point to Department of Education regulations requiring each funding recipient to "adopt and publish grievance procedures providing for prompt and equitable resolution" of discrimination complaints, 34 C.F.R. § 106.8(b) (1997), and to notify students and others "that it does not discriminate on the basis of sex in the educational programs or activities which it operates," § 106.9(a). Lago Vista's alleged failure to comply with the regulations, however, does not establish the requisite actual notice and deliberate indifference. And in any event, the failure to promulgate a grievance procedure does not itself constitute "discrimination" under Title IX. Of course, the Department of Education could enforce the requirement administratively: Agencies generally have authority to promulgate and enforce requirements that effectuate the statute's non-discrimination mandate, 20 U.S.C. § 1682, even if those requirements do not purport to represent a definition of discrimination under the statute. *E.g., Grove City*, 465 U.S., at 574–575, 104 S.Ct., at 1221–1222 (permitting administrative enforcement of regulation requiring college to execute an "Assurance of Compliance" with

Title IX). We have never held, however, that the implied private right of action under Title IX allows recovery in damages for violation of those sorts of administrative requirements.

V

The number of reported cases involving sexual harassment of students in schools confirms that harassment unfortunately is an all too common aspect of the educational experience. No one questions that a student suffers extraordinary harm when subjected to sexual harassment and abuse by a teacher, and that the teacher's conduct is reprehensible and undermines the basic purposes of the educational system. The issue in this case, however, is whether the independent misconduct of a teacher is attributable to the school district that employs him under a specific federal statute designed primarily to prevent recipients of federal financial assistance from using the funds in a discriminatory manner. Our decision does not affect any right of recovery that an individual may have against a school district as a matter of state law or against the teacher in his individual capacity under state law or under 42 U.S.C. § 1983. Until Congress speaks directly on the subject, however, we will not hold a school district liable in damages under Title IX for a teacher's sexual harassment of a student absent actual notice and deliberate indifference. We therefore affirm the judgment of the Court of Appeals.

Justice STEVENS, with whom Justice SOUTER, Justice GINSBURG, and Justice BREYER join, dissenting.

* * *

Although the opinion the Court announces today is not entirely clear, it does not purport to overrule *Franklin*. See *ante*, at 1994–1996 ("*Franklin* thereby establishes that a school district can be held liable in damages in cases involving a teacher's sexual harassment of a student"). Moreover, I do not understand the Court to question the conclusion that an intentional violation of Title IX, of the type we recognized in *Franklin*, has been alleged in this case. During her freshman and sophomore years of high school, petitioner Alida Star Gebser was repeatedly subjected to sexual abuse by her teacher, Frank Waldrop, whom she had met in the eighth grade when she joined his high school book discussion group. Waldrop's conduct was surely intentional and it occurred during, and as a part of, a curriculum activity in which he wielded authority over Gebser that had been delegated to him by respondent. Moreover, it is undisputed that the activity was subsidized, in part, with federal moneys.

The Court nevertheless holds that the law does not provide a damages remedy for the Title IX violation alleged in this case because no official of the school district with "authority to institute corrective measures on the district's behalf" had actual notice of Waldrop's misconduct. *Ante*, at 1993. That holding is at odds with settled principles of agency law,[8] under which the district is responsible for Waldrop's misconduct because "he was aided in accomplishing the tort by the existence of the agency relation." Restatement (Second) of Agency, § 219(2)(d) (1957)[9]. This case presents a paradigmatic example of a tort that was made possible, that was effected, and that was repeated over a prolonged period because of the powerful influence that Waldrop had over Gebser by reason of the authority that his employer, the school district, had delegated to him. As a secondary school teacher, Waldrop exercised even greater authority and control over his students than employers and supervisors exercise over their employees. His gross misuse of that authority allowed him to abuse his young student's trust.[10]

---

[8]The Court's holding is also questionable as a factual matter. Waldrop himself surely had ample authority to maintain order in the classes that he conducted. Indeed, that is a routine part of every teacher's responsibilities. If petitioner had been the victim of sexually harassing conduct by other students during those classes, surely the teacher would have had ample authority to take corrective measures. The fact that he did not prevent his own harassment of petitioner is the consequence of his lack of will, not his lack of authority.

[9]The Court suggests that agency principles are inapplicable to this case because Title IX does not expressly refer to an "agent," as Title VII does. See *ante*, at 1995–1996 (citing 42 U.S.C. § 2000e(b)). Title IX's focus on the protected class rather than the fund recipient fully explains the statute's failure to mention "agents" of the recipient, however. See n. 5, *supra*. Moreover, in *Meritor Savings Bank, FSB v. Vinson*, 477 U.S. 57, 106 S.Ct,. 2399, 91 L.Ed.2d 49 (1986), we viewed Title VII's reference to an "agent" as a *limitation* on the liability of the employer: "Congress' decision to define 'employer' to include any 'agent' of an employer, 42 U.S.C. § 2000e(b), surely evinces an intent to place some limits on the acts of employees for which employers under Title VII are to be help responsible." *Id.*, at 72, 106 S.Ct., at 2408 (citations omitted).

[10]For example, Waldrop first sexually abused Gebser when he visited her house on the pretense of giving her a book that she needed for a school project. See App. 54a (deposition of Star Gebser). Gebser, then a high school freshman, stated that she "was terrified": "He was the main teacher at the school with whom I had discussions, and I didn't know what to do." *Id.*, at 56a. Gebser was the only student to attend Waldrop's summer advanced placement course, and the two often had sexual intercourse during the time allotted for the class. See *Id.*, at 60a. Gebser stated that she declined to report the sexual relationship because "if I was to blow the whistle on that, then I wouldn't be able to have this person as a teacher anymore." *Id.*, at 62a. She also stated that Waldrop "was the person in Lago administration . . . who I most trusted, and he was the one that I would have been making the complaint against." *Id.*, at 63a.

Reliance on the principle set out in § 219(2)(b) of the Restatement comports with the relevant agency's interpretation of Title IX. The United States Department of Education, through its Office for Civil Rights, recently issued a policy "Guidance" stating that a school district is liable under Title IX if one of its teachers "was aided in carrying out the sexual harassment of students by his or her position of authority with the institution." Dept. of Ed., Office for Civil Rights, Sexual Harassment Guidance: Harassment of Students by School Employees, Other Students, or Third Parties, 62 Fed.Reg. 12034, 12039 (1997). As the agency charged with administering and enforcing Title IX, see 20 U.S.C. § 1682, the Department of Education has a special interest in ensuring that federal funds are not used in contravention of Title IX's mandate. It is therefore significant that the Department's interpretation of the statute wholly supports the conclusion that respondent is liable in damages for Waldrop's sexual abuse of his student, which was made possible only by Waldrop's affirmative misuse of his authority as her teacher.

The reason why the common law imposes liability on the principal in such circumstances is the same as the reason why Congress included the prohibition against discrimination on the basis of sex in Title IX: to induce school boards to adopt and enforce practices that will minimize the danger that vulnerable students will be exposed to such odious behavior. The rule that the Court has crafted creates the opposite incentive. As long as school boards can insulate themselves from knowledge about this sort of conduct, they can claim immunity from damages liability.[11] Indeed, the rule that the Court adopts would preclude a damages remedy even if every teacher at the school knew about the harassment but did not have "authority to institute corrective measures on the district's behalf." *Ante*, at 1993. It is not my function to determine whether this newly fashioned rule is wiser than the established common-law rule. It is proper, however, to suggest that the Court bears the burden of justifying its rather dramatic departure from settled law, and to explain why its opinion fails to shoulder that burden.

III

The Court advances several reasons why it would "frustrate the purposes" of Title IX to allow recovery against a school district that does not have actual notice of a teacher's sexual harassment of a student. *Ante*, at 1996–1997. As the Court acknowledges, however, the two principal purposes that motivated the enactment of Title IX were: (1) " 'to avoid the use of federal resources to support discriminatory practices' "; and (2) " 'to provide individual citizens effective protection against those practices.' " *Ante*, at 1997 (quoting *Cannon*, 441 U.S., at 704, 99 S.Ct., at 1961). It seems quite obvious that both of those purposes would be served—not frustrated—by providing a damages remedy in a case of this kind. To the extent that the Court's reasons for its policy choice have any merit, they suggest that no damages should ever be awarded in a Title IX case—in other words, that our unanimous holding in *Franklin* should be repudiated.

First, the Court observes that at the time Title IX was enacted, "the principal civil rights statutes containing an express right of action did not provide for recovery of monetary damages at all." *Ante*, at 1997. *Franklin*, however, forecloses this reevaluation of legislative intent; in that case, we "evaluate[d] the state of the law when the Legislature passed Title IX," 503 U.S., at 71, 112 S.Ct., at 1036, and concluded that "the same contextual approach used to justify an implied right of action more than amply demonstrates the lack of any legislative intent to abandon the traditional presumption in favor of all available remedies," *id.*, at 72, 112 S.Ct., at 1036. The Court also suggests that the fact that Congress has imposed a ceiling on the amount of damages that may be recovered in Title VII cases, see 42 U.S.C. § 1981a, is somehow relevant to the question whether any damages at all may be awarded in a Title IX case. *Ante*, at 1997. The short answer to this creative argument is that the Title VII ceiling does not have any bearing on when damages may be recovered from a defendant in a Title IX case. Moreover, this case does not present any issue concerning the amount of any possible damages award.

---

[11] The Court concludes that its holding "does not affect any right of recovery that an individual may have against a school district as a matter of state law or against the teacher in his individual capacity under state law or under 42 U.S.C. § 1983." *Ante*, at 2000. In this case, of course, the District Court denied petitioner's § 1983 claim on summary judgment, and it is undisputed that the Texas Tort Claims Act, Tex. Civ. Prac. & Rem.Code Ann. § 101.051 (1997), immunizes school districts from tort liability in cases like this one.

Second, the Court suggests that the school district did not have fair notice when it accepted federal funding that it might be held liable " 'for a monetary award' " under Title IX. *Ante,* at 1998 (quoting *Franklin,* 503 U.S., at 74, 112 S.Ct., at 1037). The Court cannot mean, however, that respondent was not on notice that sexual harassment of a student by a teacher constitutes an "intentional" violation of Title IX for which damages are available, because we so held shortly before Waldrop began abusing Gebser. See *id.,* at 74–75, 112 S.Ct., at 1037–1038. Given the fact that our holding in *Franklin* was unanimous, it is not unreasonable to assume that it could have been foreseen by counsel for the recipients of Title IX funds. Moreover, the nondiscrimination requirement set out in Title IX is clear, and this Court held that sexual harassment constitutes intentional sex discrimination long before the sexual abuse in this case began. See *Meritor,* 477 U.S., at 64, 106 S.Ct., at 2404. Normally, of course, we presume that the citizen has knowledge of the law.

The majority nevertheless takes the position that a school district that accepts federal funds under Title IX should not be held liable in damages for an intentional violation of that statute if the district itself "was unaware of the discrimination." *Ante,* at 1998. The Court reasons that because administrative proceedings to terminate funding cannot be commenced until after the grant recipient has received notice of its noncompliance and the agency determines that voluntary compliance is not possible, see 20 U.S.C. § 1682, there should be no damages liability unless the grant recipient has actual notice of the violation (and thus an opportunity to end the harassment). See *ante,* at 1998–1999.

The fact that Congress has specified a particular administrative procedure to be followed when a subsidy is to be terminated, however, does not illuminate the question of what the victim of discrimination on the basis of sex must prove in order to recover damages in an implied private right of action. Indeed, in *Franklin,* 503 U.S., at 64, n. 3, 112 S.Ct., at 1031, n. 3, we noted that the Department of Education's Office of Civil Rights had declined to terminate federal funding of the school district at issue — despite its finding that a Title IX violation had occurred — because "the district had come into compliance with Title IX" after the harassment at issue.

See *ante,* at 1998–1999. That fact did not affect the Court's analysis, much less persuade the Court that a damages remedy was unavailable. Cf. *Cannon,* 441 U.S., at 711, 99 S.Ct., at 1965 ("The fact that other provisions of a complex statutory scheme create express remedies has not been accepted as a sufficient reason for refusing to imply an otherwise appropriate remedy under a separate section").

The majority's inappropriate reliance on Title IX's administrative enforcement scheme to limit the availability of a damages remedy leads the Court to require not only actual knowledge on the part of "an official who at a minimum has authority to address the alleged discrimination and to institute corrective measures on the recipient's behalf," but also that official's "refus[al] to take action," or "deliberate indifference" toward the harassment. *Ante,* at 1999–2000. Presumably, few Title IX plaintiffs who have been victims of intentional discrimination will be able to recover damages under this exceedingly high standard. The Court fails to recognize that its holding will virtually "render inutile causes of action authorized by Congress through a decision that *no* remedy is available." *Franklin,* 503 U.S., at 74, 112 S.Ct., at 1037.

IV

We are not presented with any question concerning the affirmative defenses that might eliminate or mitigate the recovery of damages for a Title IX violation. It has been argued, for example, that a school district that has adopted and vigorously enforced a policy that is designed to prevent sexual harassment and redress the harms that such conduct may produce should be exonerated from damages liability. The Secretary of Education has promulgated regulations directing grant recipients to adopt such policies and disseminate them to students. A rule providing an affirmative defense for districts that adopt and publish such policies pursuant to the regulations would not likely be helpful to respondent, however, because it is not at all clear whether respondent adopted any such policy, and there is no evidence that such a policy was made available to students, as required by regulation.[17]

A theme that seems to underlie the Court's opinion is a concern that holding a school district liable in damages might deprive it of the benefit of the federal subsidy — that the damages remedy is somehow moroner-

---

[17]The district's superintendent stated that she did not remember if any handbook altering students to grievance procedures was disseminated to students. App. 72a–73a (Collier deposition). Moreover, Gebser herself stated: "If I had known at the beginning what I was supposed to do when a teacher starts making sexual advances towards me, I probably would have reported it. I was bewildered and terrified and I had no idea where to go from where I was." *Id.,* at 64a.

ous than a possible termination of the federal grant. See, *e.g., ante,* at 1999 (stating that "an award of damages in a particular case might well exceed a recipient's level of federal funding"). It is possible, of course, that in some cases the recoverable damages, in either a Title IX action or a state-law tort action, would exceed the amount of a federal grant. That is surely not relevant to the question whether the school district or the injured student should bear the risk of harm—a risk against which the district, but not the student, can insure. It is not clear to me why the well-settled rules of law that impose responsibility on the principal for the misconduct of its agents should not apply in this case. As a matter of policy, the Court ranks protection of the school district's purse above the protection of immature high school students that those rules would provide. Because those students are members of the class for whose special benefit Congress enacted Title IX, that policy choice is not faithful to the intent of the policymaking branch of our Government. . . .

Justice GINSBURG, with whom Justice SOUTER and Justice BREYER join, dissenting.

Justice STEVENS' opinion focuses on the standard of school district liability for teacher-on-student harassment in secondary schools. I join that opinion, which reserves the question whether a district should be relieved from damages liability if it has in place, and effectively publicizes and enforces, a policy to curtail and redress injuries caused by sexual harassment. *Ante,* at 2006. I think it appropriate to answer that question for these reasons: (1) the dimensions of a claim are determined not only by the plaintiff's allegations, but by the allowable defenses; (2) this Court's pathmarkers are needed to afford guidance to lower courts and school officials responsible for the implementation of Title IX.

In line with the tort law doctrine of avoidable consequences, see generally C. McCormick, Law of Damages 127–159 (1935), I would recognize as an affirmative defense to a Title IX charge of sexual harassment, an effective policy for reporting and redressing such misconduct. School districts subject to Title IX's governance have been instructed by the Secretary of Education to install procedures for "prompt and equitable resolution" of complaints, 34 CFR § 106.8(b) (1997), and the Department of Education's Office of Civil Rights has detailed elements of an effective grievance process, with specific reference to sexual harassment, 62 Fed.Reg. 12034, 12044–12045 (1997).

The burden would be the school district's to show that its internal remedies were adequately publicized

and likely would have provided redress without exposing the complainant to undue risk, effort, or expense. Under such a regime, to the extent that a plaintiff unreasonably failed to avail herself of the school district's preventive and remedial measures, and consequently suffered avoidable harm, she would not qualify for Title IX relief.

NOTES AND QUESTIONS

1. The Standard of Liability: The "Actual Notice" Requirement

Did the majority properly require victims of sexual harassment to show that school officials had actual notice of an employee's misconduct? Or does the dissent correctly surmise that this standard gives districts an incentive to learn as little as possible about teachers who make sexual overtures to students? *See Massey v. Akron City Board of Education,* 82 F.Supp.2d 735 (N.D.Ohio 2000) (district failed to screen prospective teacher and therefore did not learn of history of inappropriate sexual contacts with students). Does the actual notice requirement discourage districts from devising and publicizing grievance procedures that would bring harassment to their attention? Or are there incentives other than liability to develop such procedures and investigate wrongdoing? Should a district be deemed to have actual notice when it learns that a teacher has had inappropriate sexual contact with a minor student, even if the plaintiff's classmates had not yet reported the teacher's misconduct with them? *See Doe v. School Administrative District No. 19,* 66 F.Supp.2d 57 (D.Me. 1999) (finding that actual notice requirement is satisfied).

2. The "Deliberate Indifference" Requirement

Once school officials have actual notice of harassment, they are liable only if they respond with "deliberate indifference" to the complaint. Federal courts have interpreted this standard differently. In *Kinman v. Omaha Public School District,* 171 F.3d 607, 610 (8th Cir. 1999), the court of appeals found that a district was deliberately indifferent only if it "turn[ed] a blind eye and d[id] nothing." Another court warned that "[a]ctions and decisions by officials that are merely inept, erroneous, ineffective, or negligent do not amount to deliberate indifference." *Doe v. Dallas Independent School District,* 153 F.3d 211, 219 (5th Cir. 1998). But the First Circuit has held that a district is deliberately indifferent if it fails to take "timely and reasonable measures to end the harassment" or fails to take further steps once it realizes its intervention has been ineffective. *Wills v. Brown University*, 184 F.3d 20 (1st Cir. 1999); *Canty v. Old Rochester Regional School District*, 66 F.Supp.2d 114 (D.Mass. 1999). Should the "deliberate indifference" standard be tantamount to recklessness? Or is it enough to demonstrate a knowing failure to respond adequately to the complaint?

Subsequently, the Court applied a similar approach to sexual harassment by students.

Davis v. Monroe County Board of Education
526 U.S. 629, 119 S.Ct. 1661, 143 L.Ed.2d 839 (1999).

Justice O'Connor delivered the opinion of the Court.

* * *

Petitioner's minor daughter, LaShonda, was allegedly the victim of a prolonged pattern of sexual harassment by one of her fifth-grade classmates at Hubbard Elementary School, a public school in Monroe County, Georgia. According to petitioner's complaint, the harassment began in December 1992, when the classmate, G. F., attempted to touch LaShonda's breasts and genital area and made vulgar statements such as " 'I want to get in bed with you' " and " 'I want to feel your boobs.' " Similar conduct allegedly occurred on or about January 4 and January 20, 1993. LaShonda reported each of these incidents to her mother and to her classroom teacher, Diane Fort. Petitioner, in turn, also contacted Fort, who allegedly assured petitioner that the school principal, Bill Querry, had been informed of the incidents. Petitioner contends that, notwithstanding these reports, no disciplinary action was taken against G. F.

G. F.'s conduct allegedly continued for many months. In early February, G. F. purportedly placed a door stop in his pants and proceeded to act in a sexually suggestive manner toward LaShonda during physical education class. LaShonda reported G. F.'s behavior to her physical education teacher, Whit Maples. Approximately one week later, G. F. again allegedly engaged in harassing behavior, this time while under the supervision of another classroom teacher, Joyce Pippin. Again, LaShonda allegedly reported the incident to the teacher, and again petitioner contacted the teacher to follow up.

Petitioner alleges that G. F. once more directed sexually harassing conduct toward LaShonda in physical education class in early March, and that LaShonda reported the incident to both Maples and Pippen. In mid-April 1993, G. F. allegedly rubbed his body against LaShonda in the school hallway in what LaShonda considered a sexually suggestive manner, and LaShonda again reported the matter to Fort.

The string of incidents finally ended in mid-May, when G. F. was charged with, and pleaded guilty to, sexual battery for his misconduct. The complaint alleges that LaShonda had suffered during the months of harassment, however; specifically, her previously high grades allegedly dropped as she became unable to concentrate on her studies, and, in April 1993, her father discovered that she had written a suicide note. The complaint further alleges that, at one point, LaShonda told petitioner that she " 'didn't know how much longer she could keep [G. F.] off her.' "

Nor was LaShonda G. F.'s only victim; it is alleged that other girls in the class fell prey to G. F.'s conduct. At one point, in fact, a group composed of LaShonda and other female students tried to speak with Principal Querry about G. F.'s behavior. According to the complaint, however, a teacher denied the students' request with the statement, " 'If [Querry] wants you, he'll call you.' "

Petitioner alleges that no disciplinary action was taken in response to G. F.'s behavior toward LaShonda. In addition to her conversations with Fort and Pippen, petitioner alleges that she spoke with Principal Querry in mid-May 1993. When petitioner inquired as to what action the school intended to take against G. F., Querry simply stated, " 'I guess I'll have to threaten him a little bit harder.' " Yet, petitioner alleges, at no point during the many months of his reported misconduct was G. F. disciplined for harassment. Indeed, Querry allegedly asked petitioner why LaShonda " 'was the only one complaining.' "

Nor, according to the complaint, was any effort made to separate G. F. and LaShonda. On the contrary, notwithstanding LaShonda's frequent complaints, only after more than three months of reported harassment was she even permitted to change her classroom seat so that she was no longer seated next to G. F. Moreover, petitioner alleges that, at the time of the events in question, the Monroe County Board of Education (Board) had not instructed its personnel on how to respond to peer sexual harassment and had not established a policy on the issue.

* * *

[The district court dismissed the complaint because Title IX did not create a cause of action for student-on-student harassment. The Eleventh Circuit court of appeals reversed, but sitting en banc, it concluded that the district had properly ruled that the plaintiff had no cause of action because Title IX did not provide school districts with unambiguous notice that acceptance of federal funds would subject them to liability for this type of misconduct.]

* * *

We granted certiorari, in order to resolve a conflict in the Circuits over whether, and under what circumstances, a recipient of federal educational funds can be liable in a private damages action arising from student-on-student sexual harassment. . . .

We now reverse.

II

* * *

There is no dispute here that the Board is a recipient of federal education funding for Title IX purposes. 74 F.3d, at 1189. Nor do respondents support an argument that student-on-student harassment cannot rise to the level of "discrimination" for purposes of Title IX. Rather, at issue here is the question whether a recipient of federal education funding may be liable for damages under Title IX under any circumstances for discrimination in the form of student-on-student sexual harassment.

A

* * *

Here, . . . we are asked to do more than define the scope of the behavior that Title IX proscribes. We must determine whether a district's failure to respond to student-on-student harassment in its schools can support a private suit for money damages. See *Gebser v. Lago Vista Independent School Dist.*, 524 U.S. 274, 283, 118 S.Ct. 1989, 141 L.Ed.2d 277 (1998) ("In this case, . . . petitioners seek not just to establish a Title IX violation but to recover *damages* . . ."). This Court has indeed recognized an implied private right of action under Title IX, see *Cannon v. University of Chicago, supra*, and we have held that money damages are available in

such suits, *Franklin v. Gwinnett County Public Schools*, 503 U.S. 60, 112 S.Ct. 1028, 117 L.Ed.2d 208 (1992). Because we have repeatedly treated Title IX as legislation enacted pursuant to Congress' authority under the Spending Clause, however, see, *e.g., Gebser v. Lago Vista Independent School Dist., supra*, at 287, 118 S.Ct. 1989 (Title IX); *Franklin v. Gwinnett County Public Schools, supra*, at 74–75, and n. 8, 112 S.Ct. 1028 (Title IX); see also *Guardians Assn. v. Civil Serv. Comm'n of New York City*, 463 U.S. 582, 598–599, 103 S.Ct. 3221, 77 L.Ed.2d 866 (1983) (opinion of White, J.) (Title VI), private damages actions are available only where recipients of federal funding had adequate notice that they could be liable for the conduct at issue. . . .

* * *

We agree with respondents that a recipient of federal funds may be liable in damages under Title IX only for its own misconduct. The recipient itself must "exclud[e] [persons] from participation in, . . . den[y] [persons] the benefits of, or . . . subjec[t] [persons] to discrimination under" its "program[s] or activit[ies]" in order to be liable under Title IX. The Government's enforcement power may only be exercised against the funding recipient, see § 1682, and we have not extended damages liability under Title IX to parties outside the scope of this power. See *National Collegiate Athletic Assn. v. Smith*, 525 U.S. 459, 467 n. 5 (1999) (rejecting suggestion "that the private right of action available under . . . § 1681(a) is potentially broader than the Government's enforcement authority"); cf. *Gebser v. Lago Vista Independent School Dist., supra*, at 289, 118 S.Ct. 1989 ("It would be unsound, we think, for a statute's *express* system of enforcement to require notice to the recipient and an opportunity to come into voluntary compliance while a judicially *implied* system of enforcement permits substantial liability without regard to the recipient's knowledge or its corrective actions upon receiving notice").

We disagree with respondents' assertion, however, that petitioner seeks to hold the Board liable for G. F.'s actions instead of its own. Here, petitioner attempts to hold the Board liable for its *own* decision to remain idle in the face of known student-on-student harassment in its schools. In *Gebser*, we concluded that a recipient of federal education funds may be liable in damages under Title IX where it is deliberately indifferent to known acts of sexual harassment by a teacher. . . .

* * *

We consider here whether the misconduct identified in *Gebser*—deliberate indifference to known acts of harassment—amounts to an intentional violation of Title IX, capable of supporting a private damages action, when the harasser is a student rather than a teacher. We conclude that, in certain limited circumstances, it does. . . .

* * *

This is not to say that the identity of the harasser is irrelevant. On the contrary, both the "deliberate indifference" standard and the language of Title IX narrowly circumscribe the set of parties whose known acts of sexual harassment can trigger some duty to respond on the part of funding recipients. Deliberate indifference makes sense as a theory of direct liability under Title IX only where the funding recipient has some control over the alleged harassment. A recipient cannot be directly liable for its indifference where it lacks the authority to take remedial action.

The language of Title IX itself—particularly when viewed in conjunction with the requirement that the recipient have notice of Title IX's prohibitions to be liable for damages—also cabins the range of misconduct that the statute proscribes. The statute's plain language confines the scope of prohibited conduct based on the recipient's degree of control over the harasser and the environment in which the harassment occurs. If a funding recipient does not engage in harassment directly, it may not be liable for damages unless its deliberate indifference "subject[s]" its students to harassment. That is, the deliberate indifference must, at a minimum, "cause [students] to undergo" harassment or "make them liable or vulnerable" to it. . . . Moreover, because the harassment must occur "under" "the operations of" a funding recipient, see 20 U.S.C. § 1681(a); § 1687 (defining "program or activity"), the harassment must take place in a context subject to the school district's control . . . .

These factors combine to limit a recipient's damages liability to circumstances wherein the recipient exercises substantial control over both the harasser and the context in which the known harassment occurs. Only then can the recipient be said to "expose" its students to harassment or "cause" them to undergo it "under" the recipient's programs. We agree with the dissent that these conditions are satisfied most easily and most obviously when the offender is an agent of the recipient. *Post*, at 1680. We rejected the use of agency analysis in *Gebser*, however, and

we disagree that the term "under" somehow imports an agency requirement into Title IX. See *ibid*. . . . [T]he theory in *Gebser* was that the recipient was *directly* liable for its deliberate indifference to discrimination. See *supra*, at 1671. Liability in that case did not arise because the "teacher's actions [were] treated" as those of the funding recipient, *post*, at 1680; the district was directly liable for its *own* failure to act. The terms "subjec[t]" and "under" impose limits, but nothing about these terms requires the use of agency principles.

Where, as here, the misconduct occurs during school hours and on school grounds—the bulk of G. F.'s misconduct, in fact, took place in the classroom—the misconduct is taking place "under" an "operation" of the funding recipient. See *Doe v. University of Illinois*, 138 F.3d, at 661 (finding liability where school fails to respond properly to "student-on-student sexual harassment that takes place while the students are involved in school activities or otherwise under the supervision of school employees"). In these circumstances, the recipient retains substantial control over the context in which the harassment occurs. More importantly, however, in this setting the Board exercises significant control over the harasser. . . . We thus conclude that recipients of federal funding may be liable for "subject[ing]" their students to discrimination where the recipient is deliberately indifferent to known acts of student-on-student sexual harassment and the harasser is under the school's disciplinary authority.

* * *

We stress that our conclusion here—that recipients may be liable for their deliberate indifference to known acts of peer sexual harassment—does not mean that recipients can avoid liability only by purging their schools of actionable peer harassment or that administrators must engage in particular disciplinary action. We thus disagree with respondents' contention that, if Title IX provides a cause of action for student-on-student harassment, "nothing short of expulsion of every student accused of misconduct involving sexual overtones would protect school systems from liability or damages." See Brief for Respondents 16; see also 120 F.3d, at 1402 (Tjoflat, J.) ("[A] school must immediately suspend or expel a student accused of sexual harassment"). Likewise, the dissent erroneously imagines that victims of peer harassment now have a Title IX right to make particular remedial demands. See *post*, at 1691 (contemplating that victim could demand new desk assignment). In fact, as we have previously noted, courts should refrain from second guessing the disciplinary decisions made by school administrators. *New Jersey v. T. L. O., supra*, at 342–343, n. 9, 105 S.Ct. 733.

School administrators will continue to enjoy the flexibility they require so long as funding recipients are deemed "deliberately indifferent" to acts of student-on-student harassment only where the recipient's response to the harassment or lack thereof is clearly unreasonable in light of the known circumstances. . . .

Like the dissent, see *post*, at 1681–1683, we acknowledge that school administrators shoulder substantial burdens as a result of legal constraints on their disciplinary authority. To the extent that these restrictions arise from federal statutes, Congress can review these burdens with attention to the difficult position in which such legislation may place our Nation's schools. We believe, however, that the standard set out here is sufficiently flexible to account both for the level of disciplinary authority available to the school and for the potential liability arising from certain forms of disciplinary action. . . .

While it remains to be seen whether petitioner can show that the Board's response to reports of G. F.'s misconduct was clearly unreasonable in light of the known circumstances, petitioner may be able to show that the Board "subject[ed]" LaShonda to discrimination by failing to respond in any way over a period of five months to complaints of G. F.'s in-school misconduct from LaShonda and other female students.

B

The requirement that recipients receive adequate notice of Title IX's proscriptions also bears on the proper definition of "discrimination" in the context of a private damages action. We have elsewhere concluded that sexual harassment is a form of discrimination for Title IX purposes and that Title IX proscribes harassment with sufficient clarity to satisfy *Pennhurst*'s notice requirement and serve as a basis for a damages action. See *Gebser v. Lago Vista Independent School Dist.*, 524 U.S., at 281, 118 S.Ct. 1989; *Franklin v. Gwinnett County Public Schools, supra*, at 74–75, 112 S.Ct. 1028. Having previously determined that "sexual harassment" is "discrimination" in the school context under Title IX, we are constrained to conclude that student-on-student sexual harassment, if sufficiently severe, can likewise rise to the level of discrimination actionable under

the statute. See *Bennett v. Kentucky Dept. of Ed.*, 470 U.S. 656, 665–666, 105 S.Ct. 1544, 84 L.Ed.2d 590 (1985) (rejecting claim of insufficient notice under *Pennhurst* where statute made clear that there were some conditions placed on receipt of federal funds, and noting that Congress need not "specifically identif[y] and proscrib[e]" each condition in the legislation). The statute's other prohibitions, moreover, help give content to the term "discrimination" in this context. Students are not only protected from discrimination, but also specifically shielded from being "excluded from participation in" or "denied the benefits of" any "education program or activity receiving Federal financial assistance." § 1681(a). The statute makes clear that, whatever else it prohibits, students must not be denied access to educational benefits and opportunities on the basis of gender. We thus conclude that funding recipients are properly held liable in damages only where they are deliberately indifferent to sexual harassment, of which they have actual knowledge, that is so severe, pervasive, and objectively offensive that it can be said to deprive the victims of access to the educational opportunities or benefits provided by the school.

The most obvious example of student-on-student sexual harassment capable of triggering a damages claim would thus involve the overt, physical deprivation of access to school resources. Consider, for example, a case in which male students physically threaten their female peers every day, successfully preventing the female students from using a particular school resource—an athletic field or a computer lab, for instance. District administrators are well aware of the daily ritual, yet they deliberately ignore requests for aid from the female students wishing to use the resource. The district's knowing refusal to take any action in response to such behavior would fly in the face of Title IX's core principles, and such deliberate indifference may appropriately be subject to claims for monetary damages. It is not necessary, however, to show physical exclusion to demonstrate that students have been deprived by the actions of another student or students of an educational opportunity on the basis of sex. Rather, a plaintiff must establish sexual harassment of students that is so severe, pervasive, and objectively offensive, and that so undermines and detracts from the victims' educational experience, that the victim-students are effectively denied equal access to an institution's resources and opportunities. Cf. *Meritor Savings Bank, FSB v. Vinson*, 477 U.S., at 67, 106 S.Ct. 2399.

Whether gender-oriented conduct rises to the level of actionable "harassment" thus "depends on a constellation of surrounding circumstances, expectations, and relationships," *Oncale v. Sundowner Offshore Services, Inc.*, 523 U.S. 75, 82, 118 S.Ct. 998, 140 L.Ed.2d 201 (1998), including, but not limited to, the ages of the harasser and the victim and the number of individuals involved, see OCR Title IX Guidelines 12041–12042. Courts, moreover, must bear in mind that schools are unlike the adult workplace and that children may regularly interact in a manner that would be unacceptable among adults. See, *e.g.*, Brief for National School Boards Association et al. as *Amici Curiae* 11 (describing "dizzying array of immature . . . behaviors by students"). Indeed, at least early on, students are still learning how to interact appropriately with their peers. It is thus understandable that, in the school setting, students often engage in insults, banter, teasing, shoving, pushing, and gender-specific conduct that is upsetting to the students subjected to it. Damages are not available for simple acts of teasing and name-calling among school children, however, even where these comments target differences in gender. Rather, in the context of student-on-student harassment, damages are available only where the behavior is so severe, pervasive, and objectively offensive that it denies its victims the equal access to education that Title IX is designed to protect.

* * *

Moreover, the provision that the discrimination occur "under any education program or activity" suggests that the behavior be serious enough to have the systemic effect of denying the victim equal access to an educational program or activity. Although, in theory, a single instance of sufficiently severe one-on-one peer harassment could be said to have such an effect, we think it unlikely that Congress would have thought such behavior sufficient to rise to this level in light of the inevitability of student misconduct and the amount of litigation that would be invited by entertaining claims of official indifference to a single instance of one-on-one peer harassment. By limiting private damages actions to cases having a systemic effect on educational programs or activities, we reconcile the general principle that Title IX prohibits official indifference to known peer sexual harassment with the practical realities of responding to student behavior, realities that Congress could not have meant to be ignored. . . .

The fact that it was a teacher who engaged in harassment in *Franklin* and *Gebser* is relevant. The relationship between the harasser and the victim necessarily affects the extent to which the misconduct can be said to breach Title IX's guarantee of equal access to educational benefits and to have a systemic effect on a program or activity. Peer harassment, in particular, is less likely to satisfy these requirements than is teacher-student harassment.

C

Applying this standard to the facts at issue here, we conclude that the Eleventh Circuit erred in dismissing petitioner's complaint. Petitioner alleges that her daughter was the victim of repeated acts of sexual harassment by G. F. over a 5-month period, and there are allegations in support of the conclusion that G. F.'s misconduct was severe, pervasive, and objectively offensive. The harassment was not only verbal; it included numerous acts of objectively offensive touching, and, indeed, G. F. ultimately pleaded guilty to criminal sexual misconduct. Moreover, the complaint alleges that there were multiple victims who were sufficiently disturbed by G. F.'s misconduct to seek an audience with the school principal. Further, petitioner contends that the harassment had a concrete, negative effect on her daughter's ability to receive an education. The complaint also suggests that petitioner may be able to show both actual knowledge and deliberate indifference on the part of the Board, which made no effort whatsoever either to investigate or to put an end to the harassment.

On this complaint, we cannot say "beyond doubt that [petitioner] can prove no set of facts in support of [her] claim which would entitle [her] to relief." *Conley v. Gibson*, 355 U.S. 41, 45–46, 78 S.Ct. 99, 2 L.Ed.2d 80 (1957). See also *Scheuer v. Rhodes*, 416 U.S. 232, 236, 94 S.Ct. 1683, 40 L.Ed.2d 90 (1974) ("The issue is not whether a plaintiff will ultimately prevail but whether the claimant is entitled to offer evidence to support the claims"). Accordingly, the judgment of the United States Court of Appeals for the Eleventh Circuit is reversed, and the case is remanded for further proceedings consistent with this opinion.

Justice KENNEDY, with whom THE CHIEF JUSTICE, Justice SCALIA, and Justice THOMAS join, dissenting.

* * *

A vital safeguard for the federal balance is the requirement that, when Congress imposes a condition on the States' receipt of federal funds, it "must do so unambiguously." *Pennhurst State School and Hospital v. Halderman*, 451 U.S. 1, 17, 101 S.Ct. 1531, 67 L.Ed.2d 694 (1981). . . .

* * *

. . . Title IX does not by its terms create any private cause of action whatsoever, much less define the circumstances in which money damages are available. The only private cause of action under Title IX is judicially implied. See *Cannon v. University of Chicago*, 441 U.S. 677, 99 S.Ct. 1946, 60 L.Ed.2d 560 (1979).

The Court has encountered great difficulty in establishing standards for deciding when to imply a private cause of action under a federal statute which is silent on the subject. We try to conform the judicial judgment to the bounds of likely congressional purpose but, as we observed in *Gebser v. Lago Vista Independent School District*, 524 U.S. 274, 118 S.Ct. 1989, 141 L.Ed.2d 277 (1998), defining the scope of the private cause of action in general, and the damages remedy in particular, "inherently entails a degree of speculation, since it addresses an issue on which Congress has not specifically spoken." *Id.*, at 284, 118 S.Ct. 1989.

When the statute at issue is a Spending Clause statute, this element of speculation is particularly troubling because it is in significant tension with the requirement that Spending Clause legislation give States clear notice of the consequences of their acceptance of federal funds. Without doubt, the scope of potential damages liability is one of the most significant factors a school would consider in deciding whether to receive federal funds. Accordingly, the Court must not imply a private cause of action for damages unless it can demonstrate that the congressional purpose to create the implied cause of action is so manifest that the State, when accepting federal funds, had clear notice of the terms and conditions of its monetary liability.

* * *

I

I turn to the first difficulty with the majority's decision. Schools cannot be held liable for peer sexual harassment because Title IX does not give them clear and unambiguous notice that they are liable in damages for failure to remedy discrimination by their students. As the majority acknowledges, Title IX prohibits only misconduct by grant recipients, not misconduct by third parties. *Ante*, at 1670. . . . The majority argues, nevertheless, that a school "subjects" its students to discrimination when it knows of peer harassment and fails to respond appropriately.

The mere word "subjected" cannot bear the weight of the majority's argument. As we recognized in *Gebser*, the primary purpose of Title IX is "to prevent recipients of federal financial assistance from using the funds in a discriminatory manner." *Gebser*, 524 U. S, at 292, 118 S.Ct. 1989. We stressed in *Gebser* that Title IX prevents discrimination by the grant recipient, whether through the acts of its principals or the acts of its agents. . . . The majority does not even attempt to argue that the school's failure to respond to discriminatory acts by students is discrimination by the school itself.

A

In any event, a plaintiff cannot establish a Title IX violation merely by showing that she has been "subjected to discrimination." Rather, a violation of Title IX occurs only if she is "subjected to discrimination under any education program or activity," 20 U.S.C. § 1681(a), where "program or activity" is defined as "all of the operations of" a grant recipient, § 1687.

Under the most natural reading of this provision, discrimination violates Title IX only if it is authorized by, or in accordance with, the actions, activities, or policies of the grant recipient. . . . This reading reflects the common legal usage of the term "under" to mean pursuant to, in accordance with, or as authorized or provided by. . . .

It is not enough, then, that the alleged discrimination occur in a "context subject to the school district's control." *Ante*, at 1672. The discrimination must actually be "controlled by"—that is, be authorized by, pursuant to, or in accordance with, school policy or actions. Compare *ante*, at 1672 (defining "under" as "*in* or into *a condition of* subjection, regulation, or subordination") (emphasis added) with *ibid.* (defining "under" as "*subject to* the guidance and instruction of") (emphasis added).

This reading is also consistent with the fact that the discrimination must be "under" the "operations" of the grant recipient. The term "operations" connotes active and affirmative participation by the grant recipient, not merely inaction or failure to respond. . . .

Teacher sexual harassment of students is "under" the school's program or activity in certain circumstances, but student harassment is not. . . .

* * *

I am aware of no basis in law or fact . . . for attributing the acts of a student to a school and, indeed, the majority does not argue that the school acts through its students. See *ante*, at 1670 ("We disagree with respondents' assertion . . . that petitioner seeks to hold the Board liable for G. F.'s actions instead of its own. Here, petitioner attempts to hold the Board liable for its *own* decision to remain idle in the face of known student-on-student harassment in its schools"). Discrimination by one student against another therefore cannot be "under" the school's program or activity as required by Title IX. The majority's imposition of liability for peer sexual harassment thus conflicts with the most natural interpretation of Title IX's "under a program or activity" limitation on school liability. At the very least, my reading undermines the majority's implicit claim that Title IX imposes an unambiguous duty on schools to remedy peer sexual harassment.

B

1. Quite aside from its disregard for the "under the program" limitation of Title IX, the majority's reading is flawed in other respects. The majority contends that a school's deliberate indifference to known student harassment "subjects" students to harassment—that is, "cause[s] [students] to undergo" harassment. *Ante*, at 1672. The majority recognizes, however, that there must be some limitation on the third-party conduct that the school can fairly be said to cause. In search of a principle, the majority asserts, without much elaboration, that one causes discrimination when one has some "degree of control" over the discrimination and fails to remedy it. *Ante*, at 1672.

To state the majority's test is to understand that it is little more than an exercise in arbitrary line-drawing. The majority does not explain how we are to determine what degree of control is sufficient—or, more to the point, how the States were on clear notice that the Court would draw the line to encompass students.

* * *

2. The majority nonetheless appears to see no need to justify drawing the "enough control" line to encompass students. In truth, however, a school's control

over its students is much more complicated and limited than the majority acknowledges. A public school does not control its students in the way it controls its teachers or those with whom it contracts. Most public schools do not screen or select students, and their power to discipline students is far from unfettered.

* * *

The practical obstacles schools encounter in ensuring that thousands of immature students conform their conduct to acceptable norms may be even more significant than the legal obstacles. School districts cannot exercise the same measure of control over thousands of students that they do over a few hundred adult employees. The limited resources of our schools must be conserved for basic educational services. Some schools lack the resources even to deal with serious problems of violence and are already overwhelmed with disciplinary problems of all kinds.

* * *

* * *

3. Our decision in *Gebser* did not . . . recognize some ill-defined, free-standing legal duty on schools to remedy discrimination by third parties. In particular, *Gebser* gave schools no notice whatsoever that they might be liable on the majority's novel theory that a school "subjects" a student to third-party discrimination if it exercises some measure of control over the third party. We quoted the "subjected to discrimination" language only once in *Gebser*, when we quoted the text of Title IX in full, and we did not use the word "control." Instead, we affirmed that Title IX prohibits discrimination by the grant recipient. See *Gebser*, 524 U.S., at 286, 118 S.Ct. 1989; *id.*, at 291–292, 118 S.Ct. 1989; *supra*, at 1668.

Neither the DOE's Title IX regulations nor state tort law, moreover, could or did provide States the notice required by our Spending Clause principles. . . .

* * *

II

* * *

Title IX, . . . gives schools neither notice that the conduct the majority labels peer "sexual harassment" is gender discrimination within the meaning of the Act nor any guidance in distinguishing in individual cases between actionable discrimination and the immature behavior of children and adolescents. The majority thus imposes on schools potentially crushing financial liability for student conduct that is not prohibited in clear terms by Title IX and that cannot, even after today's opinion, be identified by either schools or courts with any precision.

* * *

The majority, nevertheless, has no problem labeling the conduct of fifth graders "sexual harassment" and "gender discrimination." Indeed, the majority sidesteps the difficult issue entirely, first by asserting without analysis that respondents do not "support an argument that student-on-student harassment cannot rise to the level of 'discrimination' for purposes of Title IX," *ante*, at 1669, and then by citing *Gebser* and *Franklin v. Gwinnett County Public Schools*, 503 U.S. 60, 112 S.Ct. 1028, 117 L.Ed.2d 208 (1992), for the proposition that "[w]e have elsewhere concluded that sexual harassment is a form of discrimination for Title IX purposes and that Title IX proscribes harassment with sufficient clarity to satisfy *Pennhurst*'s notice requirement and serve as a basis for a damages action," *ante*, at 1674.

Contrary to the majority's assertion, however, respondents have made a cogent and persuasive argument that the type of student conduct alleged by petitioner should not be considered "sexual harassment," much less gender discrimination actionable under Title IX:

> "[A]t the time Petitioner filed her complaint, no court, including this Court had recognized the concept of sexual harassment in any context other than the employment context. Nor had any Court extended the concept of sexual harassment to the misconduct of emotionally and socially immature children. The type of conduct alleged by Petitioner in her complaint is not new. However, in past years it was properly identified as misconduct which was addressed within the context of student discipline. The Petitioner now asks this Court to create out of whole cloth a cause of action by labeling childish misconduct as 'sexual harassment,' to stigmatize children as sexual harassers, and have the federal court system take on the additional burden of second guessing the disciplinary actions taken by school administrators in addressing misconduct, something this Court has consistently refused to do." Brief for Respondents 12–13 (citation omitted).

See also Brief for Independent Women's Forum as *Amicus Curiae* 19 (questioning whether "at the primary and secondary school level" it is proper to label "sexual misconduct by students" as "sexual harassment" because there is no power relationship between the harasser and the victim).

* * *

The majority admits that, under its approach, "[w]hether gender-oriented conduct rises to the level of actionable 'harassment' . . . 'depends on a constellation of surrounding circumstances, expectations, and relationships, including, but not limited to, the ages of the harasser and the victim and the number of individuals involved.' " *Ante*, at 1675 (citations omitted). The majority does not explain how a school is supposed to discern from this mishmash of factors what is actionable discrimination. Its multi-factored balancing test is a far cry from the clarity we demand of Spending Clause legislation.

The difficulties schools will encounter in identifying peer sexual harassment are already evident in teachers' manuals designed to give guidance on the subject. For example, one teachers' manual on peer sexual harassment suggests that sexual harassment in kindergarten through third grade includes a boy being "put down" on the playground "because he wants to play house with the girls" or a girl being "put down because she shoots baskets better than the boys." Minnesota Dept. of Education, Girls and Boys Getting Along: Teaching Sexual Harassment Prevention in the Elementary Classroom 65 (1993). Yet another manual suggests that one student saying to another, "You look nice" could be sexual harassment, depending on the "tone of voice," how the student looks at the other, and "who else is around." N. Stein & L. Sjostrom, Flirting or Hurting? A Teacher's Guide on Student-to-Student Sexual Harassment in Schools (Grades 6 through 12) 14 (1994). Blowing a kiss is also suspect. *Ibid.* This confusion will likely be compounded once the sexual-harassment label is invested with the force of federal law, backed up by private damages suits.

The only guidance the majority gives schools in distinguishing between the "simple acts of teasing and name-calling among school children," said not to be a basis for suit even when they "target differences in gender," *ante* at 1675, and actionable peer sexual harassment is, in reality, no guidance at all. The majority proclaims that "in the context of student-on-student harassment, damages are available only in the situation where the behavior is so serious, pervasive, and objectively offensive that it denies its victims the equal access to education that Title IX is designed to protect." *Ante*, at 1675. The majority does not even purport to explain, however, what constitutes an actionable denial of "equal access to education." Is equal access denied when a girl who tires of being chased by the boys at recess refuses to go outside? When she cannot concentrate during class because she is worried about the recess activities? When she pretends to be sick one day so she can stay home from school? It appears the majority is content to let juries decide.

The majority's reference to a "systemic effect," *ante* at 1676, does nothing to clarify the content of its standard. The majority appears to intend that requirement to do no more than exclude the possibility that a single act of harassment perpetrated by one student on one other student can form the basis for an actionable claim. That is a small concession indeed.

The only real clue the majority gives schools about the dividing line between actionable harassment that denies a victim equal access to education and mere inappropriate teasing is a profoundly unsettling one: On the facts of this case, petitioner has stated a claim because she alleged, in the majority's words, "that the harassment had a concrete, negative effect on her daughter's ability to receive an education." *Ante*, at 1676. In petitioner's words, the effects that might have been visible to the school were that her daughter's grades "dropped" and her "ability to concentrate on her school work [was] affected." App. to Pet. for Cert. 97a. Almost all adolescents experience these problems at one time or another as they mature.

III

* * *

The majority's limitations on peer sexual harassment suits cannot hope to contain the flood of liability the Court today begins. The elements of the Title IX claim created by the majority will be easy not only to allege but also to prove. A female plaintiff who pleads only that a boy called her offensive names, that she told a teacher, that the teacher's response was unreasonable, and that her school performance suffered as a result, appears to state a successful claim.

There will be no shortage of plaintiffs to bring such complaints. Our schools are charged each day with educating millions of children. Of those millions of students, a large percentage will, at some point during their school careers, experience something they consider sexual harassment. A 1993 Study by the American Association of University Women Educational Foundation, for instance, found that "fully 4 out of 5 students (81%) report that they have been the target of some form of sexual harassment during their school lives." Hostile Hallways: The AAUW Survey on Sexual Harassment in America's

Schools 7 (1993). The number of potential lawsuits against our schools is staggering.

The cost of defending against peer sexual harassment suits alone could overwhelm many school districts, particularly since the majority's liability standards will allow almost any plaintiff to get to summary judgment, if not to a jury. In addition, there are no damages caps on the judicially implied private cause of action under Title IX. As a result, school liability in one peer sexual harassment suit could approach, or even exceed, the total federal funding of many school districts. . . .

* * *

The prospect of unlimited Title IX liability will, in all likelihood, breed a climate of fear that encourages school administrators to label even the most innocuous of childish conduct sexual harassment. . . .

* * *

Even schools that resist overzealous enforcement may find that the most careful and reasoned response to a sexual harassment complaint nonetheless provokes litigation. . . .

* * *

The majority's holding in this case appears to be driven by the image of the school administration sitting idle every day while male students commandeer a school's athletic field or computer lab and prevent female students from using it through physical threats. See *ante*, at 1675. Title IX might provide a remedy in such a situation, however, without resort to the majority's unprecedented theory of school liability for student harassment. If the school usually disciplines students for threatening each other and prevents them from blocking others' access to school facilities, then the school's failure to enforce its rules when the boys target the girls on a widespread level, day after day, may support an inference that the school's decision not to respond is itself based on gender. That pattern of discriminatory response could form the basis of a Title IX action.

* * *

Even more important, in most egregious cases the student will have state-law remedies available to her. The student will often have recourse against the offending student (or his parents) under state tort law. In some cases, like this one, the perpetrator may also be subject to criminal sanctions. And, as the majority notes, the student may, in some circumstances, have recourse against the school under state law. *Ante*, at 1672.

Disregarding these state-law remedies for student misbehavior and the incentives that our schools already have to provide the best possible education to all of their students, the majority seeks, in effect, to put an end to student misbehavior by transforming Title IX into a Federal Student Civility Code. See Brief for Independent Women's Forum as *Amicus Curiae* 2 (urging the Court to avoid that result). . . .

* * *

NOTES AND QUESTIONS

1. *Scope of the Problem*

In 1993, the American Association of University Women conducted a survey of 1,632 public school students in grades eight through eleven in seventy-nine different schools in the United States. According to the survey, 85 percent of girls and 76 percent of boys reported experiencing unwanted and unwelcome sexual behavior. In addition, 31 percent of girls and 18 percent of boys reported that such experiences occurred "often." The students typically first encountered these problems during middle school or junior high. The most commonly reported conduct involved sexual comments, jokes, gestures, or looks. However, 13 percent of girls and 9 percent of boys indicated that they had been forced to do something sexual other than kissing. American Association of University Women, *Hostile Hallways: The AAUW Survey on Sexual Harassment in America's Schools* (1993). How does this study affect your views about the *Davis* case? Does it matter to you whether some states protect school districts from tort liability under a doctrine of governmental immunity? *See, e.g., Doe v. Park Center High School*, 592 N.W.2d 131 (Minn.App. 1999) (school district could not be held vicariously liable based on a teacher's sexual relationship with a student under Minnesota tort law).

2. *School District Responses to* Davis *and the AAUW Survey*

In the wake of the AAUW survey, several instances of school discipline for peer harassment received national attention. In one case, dubbed the "kiss that shook the nation," a six-year-old boy in the first grade in a North Carolina school reportedly was suspended for kissing a female classmate on the cheek. Harrell, "Kiss May Be a Kiss, But Teen Sex Harassment No Joke," *San Diego Union-Tribune*, Oct. 12, 1996, at E5; Phillips, "Kissing and Correctness," *MacLean's*, Oct. 14, 1996, at 49. A month later, in a New York school, a second-grade boy faced similar sanctions for kissing a girl in his class and tearing a button off of her skirt. "Seven-Year-Old Suspended 5 Days for Kissing Classmate," *Buffalo News*, Oct. 2, 1996, at A16. Some commentators charged that the public schools had succumbed to the AAUW's demands for political correctness and were being "held hostage by a litigious society." Maxwell, "Pity the Schools in These Litigious Times," *St. Petersburg Times*, Oct. 6. 1996, at 1D. Despite these highly publicized examples of alleged "hypercompliance" by school districts, advocates of the law have responded that the most serious problem continues to be noncompliance and underenforcement of protections for girls. N. Stein, *Secrets in Public: Sexual Harassment in Public (and Private) Schools* (rev. ed 1993); Goodman, "The Truth Behind 'the Kiss,'" *Boston Globe*, Oct. 13, 1996, at D7. Does *Davis* help to clarify the scope of school districts' legal obligations, or as Justice Kennedy argues, does it reinforce a fear of crushing liability that in turn leads to overcompliance? Kennedy has cited cases like those in North Carolina and New York as evidence of the lengths to which litigation-averse districts will go to avoid a lawsuit. Was he right to offer them as proof of the dangers of imposing liability for peer harassment?

3. *The Legal Standard*

Given widespread reports of unwanted sexual overtures by peers, is the dissent right to be concerned about the prospect of crushing and unpredictable liability? Does the majority's requirement of "deliberate indifference" on the part of school officials address this concern adequately? Will there be line-drawing problems in defining sexual harassment and gender discrimination? *See Carroll K. v. Fayette County Board of Education*, 19 F.Supp.2d 618 (4th Cir. 1998) (allowing harassment claim to proceed but warning that "not every unwanted interaction of a physical or sexual nature between adolescents states a Title IX claim against a school district") (quoting *Collier v. William Penn School District*, 956 F.Supp. 1209, 1214 (E.D.Pa. 1997)). Are these line-drawing problems substantially mitigated by the majority's requirement that the harassment be "so severe, pervasive, and objectively offensive that it can be said to deprive the victims of access to the educational opportunities or benefits provided by the school"? *See Murrell v. School District No. 1*, 186 F.3d 1238 (10th Cir. 1999) (finding that severe and pervasive harassment by a classmate deprived a special education student of access to the instructional program).

Is the dissent correct in asserting that state remedies are sufficient and that Title IX should not be used to police school districts in this way? Or do the statistics on the commonplace nature of unwelcome sexual conduct indicate that state remedies have failed to rectify the problem? Should the analysis in *Davis* be extended to other situations, such as racial harassment? *See Gant v. Wallingford Board of Education*, 195 F.3d 134 (2d Cir. 1999) (applying standards to complaint of harassment against lone black first-grade student).

4. Gender Equality and Punishment for Sexual Misconduct

Justice Kennedy's dissent notes that a school district can be liable for meting out unequal discipline to boys and girls when sexual misconduct occurs at school. How can the equality of punishments be measured? *See Priddy v. Hardin County Board of Education*, 1998 U.S.Dist.LEXIS 12968 (W.D.Ky 1998) (equivalent penalties of expulsion for sexual activity on the school bus despite the female student's claim that she was coerced to participate and that the male student was carrying a knife).

(b) Same-Sex Harassment and Title IX. Although the Supreme Court has focused on male-on-female harassment in its cases, Title IX protects males from harassment as well. In addition, the statute seems to apply to same-sex harassment. *H. M. v. Jefferson County Board of Education*, 719 S.2d 793 (Ala. 1998). Even before the *Davis* decision, at least one federal court of appeals had extended protection to a gay male student by finding that a district failed to respond to his reports of harassment when it would have done so for a female student.

Nabozny v. Podlesny
92 F. 3d 446 (7th Cir. 1996).

Before Bauer, J., Eschbach, J., and Flaum, J.
Eschbach, J.:

* * *

II

From his birth in 1975, Nabozny lived in Ashland, Wisconsin. Throughout his childhood, adolescence, and teenaged years he attended schools owned and

operated by the Ashland Public School District. In elementary school, Nabozny proved to be a good student and enjoyed a positive educational experience.

When Nabozny graduated to the Ashland Middle School in 1988, his life changed. Around the time that Nabozny entered the seventh grade, Nabozny realized that he is gay. Many of Nabozny's fellow classmates soon realized it too. Nabozny decided not to "closet" his sexuality, and considerable harassment from his fellow students ensued. Nabozny's classmates regularly referred to him as "faggot," and subjected him to various forms of physical abuse, including striking and spitting on him. Nabozny spoke to the school's guidance counselor, Ms. Peterson, about the abuse, informing Peterson that he is gay. Peterson took action, ordering the offending students to stop the harassment and placing two of them in detention. However, the students' abusive behavior toward Nabozny stopped only briefly. Meanwhile, Peterson was replaced as guidance counselor by Mr. Nowakowski. Nabozny similarly informed Nowakowski that he is gay, and asked for protection from the student harassment. Nowakowski, in turn, referred the matter to school Principal Mary Podlesny; Podlesny was responsible for school discipline.

Just before the 1988 Winter holiday, Nabozny met with Nowakowski and Podlesny to discuss the harassment. During the meeting, Nabozny explained the nature of the harassment and again revealed his homosexuality. Podlesny promised to protect Nabozny, but took no action. Following the holiday season, student harassment of Nabozny worsened, especially at the hands of students Jason Welty and Roy Grande. Nabozny complained to Nowakowski, and school administrators spoke to the students. The harassment, however, only intensified. A short time later, in a science classroom, Welty grabbed Nabozny and pushed him to the floor. Welty and Grande held Nabozny down and performed a mock rape on Nabozny, exclaiming that Nabozny should enjoy it. The boys carried out the mock rape as twenty other students looked on and laughed. Nabozny escaped and fled to Podlesny's office. Podlesny's alleged response is somewhat astonishing; she said that "boys will be boys" and told Nabozny that if he was "going to be so openly gay," he should "expect" such behavior from his fellow students. In the wake of Podlesny's comments, Nabozny ran home. The next day Nabozny was forced to speak with a counselor, not because he was subjected to a mock rape in a classroom, but because he left the school without obtaining the proper permission. No action was taken against the students involved. Nabozny was forced to return to his regular schedule. Understandably, Nabozny was "petrified" to attend school; he was subjected to abuse throughout the duration of the school year.

The situation hardly improved when Nabozny entered the eighth grade. Shortly after the school year began, several boys attacked Nabozny in a school bathroom, hitting him and pushing his books from his hands. This time Nabozny's parents met with Podlesny and the alleged perpetrators. The offending boys denied that the incident occurred, and no action was taken. Podlesny told both Nabozny and his parents that Nabozny should expect such incidents because he is "openly" gay. Several similar meetings between Nabozny's parents and Podlesny followed subsequent incidents involving Nabozny. Each time perpetrators were identified to Podlesny. Each time Podlesny pledged to take action. And, each time nothing was done. Toward the end of the school year, the harassment against Nabozny intensified to the point that a district attorney purportedly advised Nabozny to take time off from school. Nabozny took one and a half weeks off from school. When he returned, the harassment resumed, driving Nabozny to attempt suicide. After a stint in a hospital, Nabozny finished his eighth grade year in a Catholic school.

The Catholic school attended by Nabozny did not offer classes beyond the eighth grade. Therefore, to attend the ninth grade, Nabozny enrolled in Ashland High School. Almost immediately Nabozny's fellow students sang an all too familiar tune. Early in the year, while Nabozny was using a urinal in the restroom, Nabozny was assaulted. Student Stephen Huntley struck Nabozny in the back of the knee, forcing him to fall into the urinal. Roy Grande then urinated on Nabozny. Nabozny immediately reported the incident to the principal's office. Nabozny recounted the incident to the office secretary, who in turn relayed the story to Principal William Davis. Davis ordered Nabozny to go home and change clothes. Nabozny's parents scheduled a meeting with Davis and Assistant Principal Thomas Blauert. At the meeting, the parties discussed numerous instances of harassment against Nabozny, including the restroom incident.

Rather than taking action against the perpetrators, Davis and Blauert referred Nabozny to Mr. Reeder, a school guidance counselor. Reeder was supposed to change Nabozny's schedule so as to minimize Nabozny's exposure to the offending students. Eventually the school placed Nabozny in a special education class; Stephen Huntley and Roy Grande were special education students. Nabozny's parents continued to insist that the school take action, repeatedly meeting with Davis and Blauert among others. Nabozny's parents' efforts were futile; no action was taken. In the middle of his ninth grade year, Nabozny again attempted suicide. Following another hospital stay and a period living with relatives, Nabozny ran away to Minneapolis. His parents convinced him to return to Ashland by promising that Nabozny would not have to attend Ashland High. Because Nabozny's parents were unable to afford private schooling, however, the Department of Social Services ordered Nabozny to return to Ashland High.

In tenth grade, Nabozny fared no better. Nabozny's parents moved, forcing Nabozny to rely on the school bus to take him to school. Students on the bus regularly used epithets, such as "fag" and "queer," to refer to Nabozny. Some students even pelted Nabozny with dangerous objects such as steel nuts and bolts. When Nabozny's parents complained to the school, school officials changed Nabozny's assigned seat and moved him to the front of the bus. The harassment continued. Ms. Hanson, a school guidance counselor, lobbied the school's administration to take more aggressive action to no avail. The worst was yet to come, however. One morning when Nabozny arrived early to school, he went to the library to study. The library was not yet open, so Nabozny sat down in the hallway. Minutes later he was met by a group of eight boys led by Stephen Huntley. Huntley began kicking Nabozny in the stomach, and continued to do so for five to ten minutes while the other students looked on laughing. Nabozny reported the incident to Hanson, who referred him to the school's "police liaison" Dan Crawford. Nabozny told Crawford that he wanted to press charges, but Crawford dissuaded him. Crawford promised to speak to the offending boys instead. Meanwhile, at Crawford's behest, Nabozny reported the incident to Blauert. Blauert, the school official supposedly in charge of disciplining, laughed and told Nabozny that Nabozny deserved such treatment because he is gay. Weeks later Nabozny collapsed from internal bleeding that resulted from Huntley's beating. Nabozny's parents and counselor Hanson repeatedly urged Davis and Blauert to take action to protect Nabozny. Each time aggressive action was promised. And, each time nothing was done.

Finally, in his eleventh grade year, Nabozny withdrew from Ashland High School. Hanson told Nabozny and his parents that school administrators were unwilling to help him and that he should seek educational opportunities elsewhere. Nabozny left Ashland and moved to Minneapolis where he was diagnosed with Post Traumatic Stress Disorder. In addition to seeking medical help, Nabozny sought legal advice.

On February 6, 1995, Nabozny filed the instant suit pursuant to 42 U.S.C. § 1983 . . . alleging, among other things, that the defendants violated his Fourteenth Amendment rights to equal protection . . . . The . . . defendants moved for summary judgment.

The district court ruled in favor of the defendants. The court dispensed with Nabozny's gender equal protection claim, holding that Nabozny failed to produce evidence to establish that the defendants discriminated against him based on his gender. . . . Nabozny now brings this timely appeal. . . .

III

. . . Wisconsin has elected to protect the students in its schools from discrimination. Wisconsin statute section 118.13(1), regulating general school operations, provides that:

> No person may be denied . . . participation in, be denied the benefits of or be discriminated against in any curricular, extracurricular, pupil services, recreational or other program or activity because of the person's sex, race, religion, national origin, ancestry, creed, pregnancy, marital or parental status, sexual orientation or physical, mental, emotional or learning disability.

Since at least 1988, in compliance with the state statute, the Ashland Public School District has had a policy of prohibiting discrimination against students on the basis of gender or sexual orientation. The District's policy and practice includes protecting students from student-on-student sexual harassment and battery. Nabozny maintains that the defendants denied him the equal protection of the law by denying him the protection extended to other students, based on his gender and sexual orientation.

The Equal Protection Clause grants to all Americans "the right to be free from invidious discrimination in statutory classifications and other governmental activity." *Harris v. McRae*, 448 U.S. 297, 322, 100 S.Ct. 2671, 2691, 65 L.Ed.2d 784 (1980). When

a state actor turns a blind eye to the Clause's command, aggrieved parties such as Nabozny can seek relief pursuant to 42 U.S.C. § 1983. . . . In order to establish liability under § 1983, Nabozny must show that the defendants acted with a nefarious discriminatory purpose, *Personnel Adm'r of Massachusetts v. Feeney*, 442 U.S. 256, 279, 99 S.Ct. 2282, 2296, 60 L.Ed.2d 870 (1979), and discriminated against him based on his membership in a definable class. *Albright v. Oliver*, 975 F.2d 343, 348 (7th Cir.1992), *aff'd*, 510 U.S. 266, 114 S.Ct. 807, 127 L.Ed.2d 114 (1994); *Falls v. Town of Dyer*, 875 F.2d 146, 148 (7th Cir.1989). As we explained in *Shango v. Jurich*, 681 F.2d 1091 (7th Cir.1982):

> The gravamen of equal protection lies not in the fact of deprivation of a right but in the invidious classification of persons aggrieved by the state's action. A plaintiff must demonstrate intentional or purposeful discrimination to show an equal protection violation. Discriminatory purpose, however, implies more than intent as volition or intent as awareness of consequences. It implies that a decisionmaker singled out a particular group for disparate treatment and selected his course of action at least in part for the purpose of causing its adverse effects on the identifiable group.

Id. at 1104 (citations and internal quotations omitted). A showing that the defendants were negligent will not suffice. Nabozny must show that the defendants acted either intentionally or with deliberate indifference. *Archie v. City of Racine*, 847 F.2d 1211, 1219 (7th Cir.1988), *cert. denied*, 489 U.S. 1065, 109 S.Ct. 1338, 103 L.Ed.2d 809 (1989); *Jackson v. City of Joliet*, 715 F.2d 1200, 1203 (7th Cir.1983), *cert. denied*, 465 U.S. 1049, 104 S.Ct. 1325, 79 L.Ed.2d 720 (1984); *Shango*, 681 F.2d at 1104; *Cf. Muckway*, 789 F.2d at 522 (holding that a violation of a state law does not establish an equal protection violation absent proof that the defendant intentionally discriminated against otherwise similarly situated persons). To escape liability, the defendants either must prove that they did not discriminate against Nabozny, or at a bare minimum, the defendants' discriminatory conduct must satisfy . . . heightened scrutiny in the case of gender discrimination . . . .

* * *

The district court disposed of Nabozny's equal protection claims in two brief paragraphs. Regarding the merits of Nabozny's gender claim, the court concluded that "[t]here is absolutely nothing in the record to indicate that plaintiff was treated differently because of his gender." The district court's conclusion affords two interpretations: 1) there is no evidence that the defendants treated Nabozny differently from other students; or, 2) there is no evidence that the discriminatory treatment was based on Nabozny's gender. We will examine each in turn.

The record viewed in the light most favorable to Nabozny, combined with the defendants' own admissions, suggests that Nabozny was treated differently from other students. The defendants stipulate that they had a commendable record of enforcing their anti-harassment policies. Yet Nabozny has presented evidence that his classmates harassed and battered him for years and that school administrators failed to enforce their anti-harassment policies, despite his repeated pleas for them to do so. If the defendants otherwise enforced their anti-harassment policies, as they contend, then Nabozny's evidence strongly suggests that they made an exception to their normal practice in Nabozny's case.

Therefore, the question becomes whether Nabozny can show that he received different treatment because of his gender. Nabozny's evidence regarding the defendants' punishment of male-on-female battery and harassment is not overwhelming. Nabozny contends that a male student that struck his girlfriend was immediately expelled, that males were reprimanded for striking girls, and that when pregnant girls were called "slut" or "whore," the school took action. Nabozny's evidence does not include specific facts, such as the names and dates of the individuals involved. Nabozny does allege, however, that when he was subjected to a mock rape Podlesny responded by saying "boys will be boys," apparently dismissing the incident because both the perpetrators and the victim were males. We find it impossible to believe that a female lodging a similar complaint would have received the same response.

More important, the defendants do not deny that they aggressively punished male-on-female battery and harassment. The defendants argue that they investigated and punished all complaints of battery and harassment, regardless of the victim's gender. According to the defendants, contrary to the evidence presented by Nabozny, they aggressively pursued each of Nabozny's complaints and punished the alleged perpetrators whenever possi-

ble. Like Nabozny, the defendants presented evidence to support their claim. Whether to believe the defendants or Nabozny is, of course, a question of credibility for the fact-finder. In the context of considering the defendants' summary judgment motion, we must assume that Nabozny's version is the credible one. If Nabozny's evidence is considered credible, the record taken in conjunction with the defendants' admissions demonstrates that the defendants treated male and female victims differently.

The defendants also argue that there is no evidence that they either intentionally discriminated against Nabozny, or were deliberately indifferent to his complaints. The defendants concede that they had a policy and practice of punishing perpetrators of battery and harassment. It is well settled law that departures from established practices may evince discriminatory intent. *Village of Arlington Heights v. Metropolitan Housing Dev. Corp.*, 429 U.S. 252, 267, 97 S.Ct. 555, 564–65, 50 L.Ed.2d 450 (1977). Moreover, Nabozny introduced evidence to suggest that the defendants literally laughed at Nabozny's pleas for help. The defendants' argument, considered against Nabozny's evidence, is simply indefensible.

* * *

NOTES AND QUESTIONS

1. Equal Protection and the Standard of Review for Same-Sex Harassment

One question that arises is whether a student like Nabozny is entitled to any heightened protection under the Equal Protection Clause based on his sexual orientation. The district court found that even under the weakest standard of review, one of mere rationality, there was no rational basis for a school district to allow students to harass a peer based on sexual orientation. *Id.* at 458. The district reportedly settled the lawsuit with Nabozny for $900,000 on remand. "Gay Man Wins $900,000 in School-District Case," *Wall St.J.*, Nov. 21, 1996, at A6. For a discussion of peer harassment based on sexual orientation, *see* Lovell, "Other Students Always Used to Say, 'Look at the Dykes': Protecting Students from Peer Sexual Orientation Harassment," 86 *Calif.L.Rev.* 617 (1998).

2. Sexual Orientation and Title IX's Scope of Coverage

Although Title IX's nondiscrimination principle may protect gay and lesbian students from hostile conduct at school in some instances, the statute does not address many other concerns that these students have, such as the lack of inclusion of issues related to sexual orientation in the curriculum, the absence of role models, and the unavailability of counseling services. Fontaine, "The Sound of Silence: Public School Response to the Needs of Gay and Lesbian Youth," 7 *J.Gay & Lesbian Social Services* 101 (1997); Edwards, "Let's Stop Ignoring Our Gay and Lesbian Youth," 54 *Educ.Leadership* 68 (1997). *But cf.* Jordan, Vaughan, and Woodworth, "I Will Survive: Lesbian, Gay, and Bisexual Youth's Experience of High School," 7 *J.Gay and Lesbian Social Services* 17 (1997) (73.5 percent of gay, lesbian, and bisexual students surveyed at thirty-four high schools reported getting support about sexual orientation concerns from someone at school, and 41.2 percent stated that information on these issues was available from school staff).

(c) Beyond Title IX: Does the Statute Reach the Roots of Gender Discrimination? Title IX is the principal means by which the federal government seeks to promote gender equity. However, some critics fear that it does not reach key aspects of educational practice that put girls in educational jeopardy. In a 1992 report, the American Association of University Women reported on how some schools create an unsupportive climate for female students through curricular choices and teaching techniques.

"How Schools Shortchange Girls"

AAUW Educational Foundation and National Education Association, *The AAUW Report* 106–112, 114–127 (paperback ed. 1995).

Part 4
Chapter One
The Formal Curriculum

* * *

Research on Curriculum

Since the early 1970s, many studies have surveyed instructional materials for sex bias. Published in 1975, *Dick and Jane As Victims: Sex Stereotyping in Children's Readers* set a pattern for line-by-line examination of the messages about girls and boys delivered by texts, examples, illustrations, and thematic organization of material in everything from basal readers to science textbooks. In 1971 a study of thirteen popular U.S. history textbooks revealed that material on women comprised no more than 1 percent of any text, and that women's lives were trivialized, distorted, or omitted altogether.[6] Studies from the late 1980s reveal that although sexism has decreased in some elementary school texts and basal readers, the problems persist, especially at the secondary school level, in terms of what is considered important enough to study.[7]

A 1989 study of book-length works taught in high school English courses reports that, in a national sample of public, independent, and Catholic schools, the ten books assigned most frequently included only one written by a woman and none by members of minority groups.[8] This research, which used studies from 1963 and 1907 as a base line, concludes that "the lists of most frequently required books and authors are dominated by white males, with little change in overall balance from similar lists 25 or 80 years ago."

During the late 1970s and '80s, experiments with more inclusive school curricula were aided by the rapid development of scholarly work and courses in black studies, ethnic studies, and women's studies in colleges and universities. . . .

What effects did the revised curricula have on students? A 1980 review of research on how books influence children cited twenty-three studies that

---

[6]J. Trecker, "Women in U.S. History High School Textbooks," *Social Education* 35, no. 3 (1971):249–60, 338.

[7]O. Davis et al., "A Review of U.S. History Textbooks," *The Education Digest* 52, no. 3 (November 1986):50–53; M. Hitchcock and G. Tompkins, "Basal Readers: Are They Still Sexist?" *The Reading Teacher* 41, no. 3 (December 1987):288–92; M. Tetreault, "Integrating Women's History: The Case of United States History High School Textbooks," *The History Teacher* 19 (February 1986):211–62; M. Tetreault, "The Journey from Male-Defined to Gender-Balanced Education," *Theory into Practice* 25, no. 4 (Autumn 1986):227–34; A. Nilsen, "Three Decades of Sexism in School Science Materials," *School Library Journal* 34, no. 1 (September 1987):117–22; E. Hall, "One Week for Women? The Structure of Inclusion of Gender Issues in Introductory Textbooks," *Teaching Sociology* 16, no. 4 (October 1988):431–42; P. Purcell and L. Stewart, "Dick and Jane in 1989," *Sex Roles* 22, nos. 3 and 4 (February 1990):177–85.

[8]A. Applebee, *A Study of Book-Length Works Taught in High School English Courses* (Albany, NY: Center for the Learning and Teaching of Literature, State University of New York School of Education, 1989).

demonstrated that books do transmit values to young readers, that multicultural readings produce markedly more favorable attitudes toward non-dominant groups than do all-white curricula, that academic achievement for all students was positively correlated with use of nonsexist and multicultural curriculum materials, and that sex-role stereotyping was reduced in those students whose curriculum portrayed females and males in nonstereotypical roles.[9]

During the 1980s, federal support for research and action on sex equity and race equity dropped sharply. But many individual teachers, librarians, authors, and local or state school authorities continued a variety of efforts to lessen stereotyping and omission, or expand and democratize the curriculum.

Virtually all textbook publishers now have guidelines for nonsexist language. Unfortunately, not all insist that authors follow them. Change in textbooks is observable but not striking. Research on high school social studies texts reveals that while women are more often included, they are likely to be the usual "famous women," or women in protest movements. Rarely is there dual and balanced treatment of women and men, and seldom are women's perspectives and cultures presented on their own terms.[14]

Researchers at a 1990 conference reported that even texts designed to fit within the current California guidelines on gender and race equity for textbook adoption showed subtle language bias, neglect of scholarship on women, omission of women as developers of history and initiators of events, and absence of women from accounts of technological developments.[15] An informal survey of twenty U.S. history textbooks compiled each year from 1984 to 1989 found a gradual but steady shift away from an overwhelming emphasis on laws, wars, and control over territory and public policy, toward an emphasis on people's daily lives in many kinds of circumstances.

The books, however, continued to maintain the abstract, disengaged tone that was characteristic of the earlier texts. The recommended assignments still relied heavily on debate techniques in which stu-

dents were asked to develop an argument defending a single point of view. Few assignments offered students an opportunity to reflect on a genuine variety of perspectives or to consider feelings as well as actions.

Conceptualizations of Equity in the Curriculum

Side by side with research on gender and the curriculum came various ways of conceptualizing and categorizing what is meant by gender and race equity in curriculum content. Recognizing elements of bias was an important first step. Building on earlier efforts, including work by Martha Matthews and Shirley McCune at the National Foundation for the Improvement of Education, leaders of workshops sponsored by the National Council of Teachers of Foreign Languages in 1984 listed six common forms of sex bias in instructional materials: *exclusion* of girls, *stereotyping* of members of both sexes, *subordination* or *degradation* of girls, *isolation* of materials on women, *superficiality* of attention to contemporary issues or social problems, and *cultural inaccuracy*, through which most of the people active in a culture are excluded from view. . . .[18]

In 1990, after a review of more than 100 sex- and race-equity programs identified further markers of bias in the classroom, the National Education Association developed a checklist specifying eleven kinds of sex bias. The "overt and subtle behaviors" it listed include: double standards for males and females, condescension, tokenism, denial of achieved status or authority, backlash against women who succeed in improving their status, and divide-and-conquer strategies that praise individuals as better than others in their ethnic or gender group.[20]

Unfortunately, checklists on bias, prejudice, and discrimination can sometimes hurt the very groups they are meant to help by assigning them the status of "victims." In a provocative essay, "Curriculum As Window and Mirror," Emily Style compares the curriculum to an architectural structure that schools build around students.[21] Ideally, the curriculum provides each student with both windows

[9]P. Campbell and J. Wirtenberg, "How Books Influence Children: What the Research Shows," *Interracial Books for Children Bulletin* 11, no. 6 (1980):3–6.

[14]M. Tetreault, "Integrating Women's History: The Case of U.S. History High School Textbooks," *The History Teacher* 19 (February 1986):211–62; "Women in the Curriculum," *Comment on Conferences and Research on Women* (February 1986):1–2; "Rethinking Women, Gender, and the Social Studies," *Social Education* 51 (March 1987):171–78.

[15]Newsletter of the Special Interest Group on Gender and Social Justice, National Council for Social Studies, December 1990.

[18]See B. Wright, "What's in a Noun? A Feminist Perspective on Foreign Language Instruction," *Women's Studies Quarterly* 12, no. 3 (Fall 1984):2–6; B. Schmitz, "Guidelines for Reviewing Foreign Language Textbooks for Sex Bias," *Women's Studies Quarterly* 12, no. 3 (Fall 1984):7–9.

[20]Bogart, *Solutions That Work*, vol. 3, pp. 107–108.

[21]E. Style, "Curriculum As Window and Mirror," in *Listening for All Voices: Gender Balancing the School Curriculum* (Summit, NJ: Oak Knoll School,

out onto the experiences of others and mirrors of her or his own reality and validity. But for most students, the present curriculum provides many windows and few mirrors.

Teachers themselves may recall few mirrors. For the last eleven years, teachers joining a large faculty-development project have been asked, "What did you study about women in high school?" More than half initially respond, "Nothing." Some recall a heroine, one or two historical figures, a few goddesses or saints. Marie Curie is the only female scientist who has been mentioned in ten years of this survey. Many women as well as men are surprised at their answers, and surprised to realize how little they themselves are teaching about women and girls. Questions about cultural diversity draw similar responses. Virtually all teachers polled recall feeling a distance between their own lives and what was portrayed in the formal curriculum.

Curriculum researcher Gretchen Wilbur states that gender-fair curriculum has six attributes. It acknowledges and affirms variation, i.e., similarities and differences among and within groups of people. It is *inclusive*, allowing both females and males to find and identify positively with messages about themselves. It is accurate, presenting information that is data-based, verifiable, and able to withstand critical analysis. It is affirmative, acknowledging and valuing the worth of individuals and groups. It is *representative*, balancing multiple perspectives. And, finally, it is *integrated*, weaving together the experiences, needs, and interests of both males and females.[23]

Wilbur maintains that so far no major curriculum-reform efforts have used explicitly gender-fair approaches....

* * *

Wilbur categorizes many attempts to design gender-fair courses as pullout curricula, which target a "problem" population (for example, pregnant teenagers or persons with disabilities), or *fragmented* curricula, which add units on "women's issues" to the main curriculum. Such approaches, she maintains, fall short of genuinely gender-fair integration of women into central course content.

* * *

Over the last forty years, most educators have assumed that the existing subject areas of the curriculum serve a useful purpose. They are in such universal use that consideration of alternatives is difficult. They are viewed as providing a rational educational grounding, especially in preparation for standardized tests such as College Board or Regents' Exams in individual subject areas. Increasingly, however, educational organizations, colleges, and testing agencies themselves are acknowledging the importance of students' gaining the ability not only to describe concepts but to apply them in new situations. Traditional discipline-based courses, while providing factual information, may not be the best way to do this.

Changing the curriculum in any substantial way is bound to result in some initial resistance. A recent study commissioned by the National Education Association identified several key barriers to gender equity in the curriculum. The report cited students' reluctance to be singled out as having cultural or gender experience that does not fit the assumed norms; parents' suspicions about unfamiliar curricula; teachers' lack of training on multicultural and gender-neutral goals and techniques; unwillingness to commit funds for teachers to participate in curriculum-change efforts.[32]

School systems often lack in-service funds and energy to provide new opportunities for teachers. Tracy Kidder's noted study of a year in the life of a fourth-grade teacher, *Among School Children*, notes that the teacher uses twenty-year-old curriculum guides.[33]

Arthur Applebee, author of the noted *Study of Book-Length Works Taught in High School English Courses*, says that twenty years of consciousness raising and resource development have not changed the basic curriculum because teachers have not had the time and support to familiarize themselves with new materials. He recommends preservice course work in schools of education, in-service workshops, and departmental discussion groups to give teachers enough familiarity with alternative materials so that they will be comfortable in finding their own ways to introduce new works into their classes.[34] The restructuring of schools should acknowledge that curricular design and revision are central—not peripheral—to teachers' work with students.

* * *

---

[23]G. Wilbur, "Gender-fair Curriculum," research report prepared for Wellesley College Research on Women, August 1991.

[32]Bogart, *Solutions That Work*, vol. 1, pp. 97–98.

[33]T. Kidder, *Among Schoolchildren* (New York: Avon Books, 1989), p. 27.

[34]A. Applebee, *A Study of Book-Length Works*, p. 18. For an example of a product that came out of a school-based departmental discussion, see *New Voices for the English Classroom*, C. Peter, ed., (Providence, RI: Lincoln School, 1986). For similar strategies, see E. Style, *Multicultural Education and Me*, and the school-based, teacher-led seminars established through the National SEED Project on Inclusive Curriculum, Wellesley College Center for Research on Women.

Girls, Self-Esteem, and the Curriculum

Researchers have puzzled over the drop in girls' self-esteem as they go through school, even though they do as well as boys on many standardized measures and get better grades. Teacher trainer Cathy Nelson attributes this drop in self-esteem to the negative messages delivered to girls by school curricula.[36] Students sit in classes that, day in and day out, deliver the message that women's lives count for less than men's. Historian Linda Kerber suggests a plausible connection between falling self-esteem and curricular omission and bias. "Lowered self-esteem is a perfectly reasonable conclusion if one has been subtly instructed that what people like oneself have done in the world has not been important and is not worth studying."[37] There is no social science research to document cause and effect in this matter, but educators must take more responsibility for understanding that the curriculum is the central message-giving instrument of the school.

Chapter Two
The Classroom as Curriculum

Students can learn as much from what they experience in school as they can from the formal content of classroom assignments. Classroom interactions, both with the teacher and other students, are critical components of education. These interactions shape a school. They determine in large measure whether or not a school becomes a community: a place where girls and boys can learn to value themselves and others, where both the rights and the responsibilities of citizens are fostered.

Teacher-Student Interactions

Whether one looks at preschool classrooms or university lecture halls, at female teachers or male teachers, research spanning the past twenty years consistently reveals that males receive more teacher attention than do females. In preschool classrooms boys receive more instructional time, more hugs, and more teacher attention. The pattern persists through elementary school and high school. One reason is that boys demand more attention. Researchers David and Myra Sadker have studied these patterns for many years. They report that boys in one study of elementary and middle school students called out answers eight times more often than girls did. When boys called out, the typical teacher reaction was to listen to the comment. When girls called out, they were usually corrected with comments such as, "Please raise your hand if you want to speak."[3]

It is not only the attention demanded by male students that explains their greater involvement in teacher-student exchanges. Studies have found that even when boys do not volunteer, the teacher is more likely to solicit their responses.

The issue is broader than the inequitable distribution of teacher contacts with male and female students; it also includes the inequitable *content* of teacher comments. Teacher remarks can be vague and superficial or precise and penetrating. Helpful teacher comments provide students with insights into the strengths and weaknesses of their answers. Careful and comprehensive teacher reactions not only affect student learning, they can also influence student self-esteem.

The Sadkers conducted a three-year study of more than 100 fourth-, sixth- and eighth-grade classrooms. They identified four types of teacher comments: praise, acceptance, remediation, and criticism.

They found that while males received more of all four types of teacher comments, the difference favoring boys was greatest in the more useful teacher reactions of praise, criticism, and remediation. When teachers took the time and made the effort to specifically evaluate a student's performance, the student receiving the comment was more likely to be male.[5] These findings are echoed in other investigations, indicating that boys receive more precise teacher comments than females in terms of both scholarship and conduct.

The differences in teacher evaluations of male and female students have been cited by some researchers as a cause of "learned helplessness," or lack of academic perseverance, in females. Initially investigated

---

[36]C. Nelson, "Gender and the Social Studies: Training Preservice Secondary Social Studies Teachers" (Ph.D. diss., University of Minnesota, 1990), pp. 8, 38–39.

[37]L. Kerber, " 'Opinionative Assurance' ": The Challenge of Women's History," address to the Organization of History Teachers, American Historical Association, New York, NY, 28 December 1990, p. 11.

[3]M. Sadker and D. Sadker, "Sexism in the Classroom: From Grade School to Graduate School," *Phi Delta Kappan* 68 (1986):513; M. Sadker and D. Sadker, "Is the OK Classroom OK?" *Phi Delta Kappan* 55 (1985):361.

[5]M. Sadker and D. Sadker, *Year 3: Final Report, Promoting Effectiveness in Classroom Instruction* (Washington, DC: National Institute of Education, 1984).

in animal experiments, "learned helplessness" refers to a lack of perseverance, a debilitating loss of self-confidence. This concept has been used to explain why girls sometimes abandon while boys persistently pursue academic challenges for which both groups are equally qualified.

One school of thought links learned helplessness with attribution theory. While girls are more likely to attribute their success to luck, boys are more likely to attribute their success to ability. As a result of these different causal attributions, boys are more likely to feel mastery and control over academic challenges, while girls are more likely to feel powerless in academic situations.

* * *

The majority of studies on teacher-student interaction do not differentiate among subject areas. However, there is some indication that the teaching of certain subjects may encourage gender-biased teacher behavior while others may foster more equitable interactions. Sex differences in attributing success to luck versus effort are more likely in subject areas where teacher responses are less frequent and where single precise student responses are less common.

Two recent studies find teacher-student interactions in science classes particularly biased in favor of boys.[14] Some mathematics classes have less biased patterns of interaction overall when compared to science classes, but there is evidence that despite the more equitable overall pattern, a few male students in each mathematics class receive particular attention to the exclusion of all other students, male and female.[15]

Research on teacher-student interaction patterns has rarely looked at the interaction of gender with race, ethnicity, and/or social class. The limited data available indicate that while males receive more teacher attention than females, white boys receive more attention than boys from various racial and ethnic minority groups.[16]

Evidence also suggests that the attention minority students receive from teachers may be different in nature from that given to white children. In elementary school, black boys tend to have fewer interactions overall with teachers than other students and yet they are the recipients of four to ten times the amount of qualified praise ("That's good, but...") as other students.[17] Black boys tend to be perceived less favorably by their teachers and seen as less able than other students.[18] The data are more complex for girls. Black girls have less interaction with teachers than white girls, but they attempt to initiate interaction much more often than white girls or than boys of either race. Research indicates that teachers may unconsciously rebuff these black girls, who eventually turn to peers for interaction, often becoming the class enforcer or go-between for other students.[19] Black females also receive less reinforcement from teachers than do other students, although their academic performance is often better than boys.[20]

In fact, when black girls do as well as white boys in school, teachers attribute their success to hard work but assume that the white boys are not working up to their full potential.[21] This, coupled with the evidence that blacks are more often reinforced for their social behavior while whites are likely to be reinforced for their academic accomplishments, may contribute to low academic self-esteem in black girls.[22] Researchers have found that black females value their academic achievements less than black males in spite of their better performance.[23] Another study found that black

[14]J. Kahle, "Why Girls Don't Know," in *What Research Says to the Science Teacher—The Process of Knowing*, M. Rowe, ed. (Washington, DC: National Science Testing Association, 1990), pp. 55–67; V. Lee, "Sexism in Single-Sex and Coeducational Secondary School Classrooms, paper presented at the annual meeting of the American Sociological Association, Cincinnati, OH, August 8, 1991.

[15]J. Eccles, "Bringing Young Women to Math and Science," in *Gender and Thought: Psychological Perspectives*, M. Crawford and M. Gentry, eds. (New York: Springer-Verlag, 1989), pp. 36–58; Licht et al., "Children's Achievement Related Beliefs."

[16]Sadker and Sadker, *Year 3*; L. Grant, "Race-Gender Status, Classroom Interaction and Children's Socialization in Elementary School," in *Gender Influences in Classroom Interaction*, L. Wilkinson and C. Marrett, eds. (Orlando, FL: Academic Press, 1985), pp.57–75.

[17]Grant, "Race-Gender Status," p. 66.

[18]C. Cornbleth and W. Korth, "Teacher Perceptions and Teacher-Student Interaction in Integrated Classrooms," *Journal of Experimental Education* 48 (Summer 1980):259–63; B. Hare, *Black Girls: A Comparative Analysis of Self-Perception and Achievement by Race, Sex and Socioeconomic Background*, Report No. 271 (Baltimore, MD: John Hopkins University, Center for Social Organization of Schools, [1979]).

[19]S. Damico and E. Scott, "Behavior Differences Between Black and White Females in Desegregated Schools," *Equity and Excellence* 23 (1987):63–66; Grant, "Race-Gender Status." See also J. Irvine, "Teacher-Student Interactions: Effects of Student Race, Sex, and Grade Level," *Journal of Educational Psychology* 78 (1986):14–21.

[20]Damico and Scott, "Behavior Differences"; Hare, "Black Girls: A Comparative Analysis."

[21]L'amico and Scott, "Behavior Differences"; L. Grant, "Black Females 'Place' in Integrated Classrooms," *Sociology of Education* 57 (1984):98–111.

[22]Damico and Scott, "Behavior Differences."

[23]D. Scott-Jones and M. Clark, "The School Experience of Black Girls: The Interaction of Gender, Race and Socioeconomic Status," *Phi Delta Kappan* 67 (March 1986):20–526.

boys have a higher science self-concept than black girls although there were no differences in achievement.[24]

The Design of Classroom Activities

Research studies reveal a tendency beginning at the preschool level for schools to choose classroom activities that will appeal to boys' interests and to select presentation formats in which boys excel or are encouraged more than are girls.[25] For example, when researchers looked at lecture versus laboratory classes, they found that in lecture classes teachers asked males academically related questions about 80 percent more often than they questioned females; the patterns were mixed in laboratory classes.[26] However, in science courses lecture classes remain more common than laboratory classes.

Research indicates that if pupils begin working on an activity with little introduction from the teacher, everyone has access to the same experience. Discussion that follows after all students have completed an activity encourages more participation by girls.[27] In an extensive multistate study, researchers found that in geometry classes where the structure was changed so that students read the book and did problems *first* and *then* had classroom discussion of the topic, girls outperformed boys in two of five tests and scored equally in the other three. Girls in the experimental class reversed the general trend of boys' dominance on applications, coordinates, and proof taking, while they remained on par with boys on visualizations in three dimensions and transformations. In traditional classes where topics were introduced by lecture first and then students read the book and did the problems, small gender differences favoring boys remained.

Successful Teaching Strategies

There are a number of teaching strategies that can promote more gender-equitable learning environments. Research indicates that science teachers who are successful in encouraging girls share several strategies. These included using more than one textbook, eliminating sexist language, and showing fairness in their treatment and expectations of both girls and boys.

Other research indicates that classrooms where there are no gender differences in math are "girl friendly," with less social comparison and competition and an atmosphere students find warmer and fairer.

In their 1986 study, *Women's Ways of Knowing*, Belenky, Clinchy, Goldberger, and Tarule point out that for many girls and women, successful learning takes place in an atmosphere that enables students to empathetically enter into the subject they are studying, an approach the authors term "connected knowing." The authors suggest that an acceptance of each individual's personal experiences and perspectives facilitates students' learning. They argue for classrooms that emphasize collaboration and provide space for exploring diversity of opinion.[31]

Few classrooms foster "connected learning," nor are the majority of classrooms designed to encourage cooperative behaviors and collaborative efforts. The need to evaluate, rank, and judge students can undermine collaborative approaches. One recent study that sampled third-, fifth-, and seventh-grade students found that successful students reported fewer cooperative attitudes than did unsuccessful students. In this study the effects of gender varied as a function of grade level. Third-grade girls were more cooperative than their male peers, but by fifth grade the gender difference had disappeared.[32] Other studies do not report this grade level–gender interaction, but rather indicate that girls tend to be more cooperative than boys but that cooperative attitudes decline for all students as they mature.

Some educators view the arrival of new classroom organizational structures as a harbinger of more effective and more equitable learning environments.

[24]V. Washington and J. Newman, "Setting Our Own Agenda: Exploring the Meaning of Gender Disparities Among Blacks in Higher Education," *Journal of Negro Education* 60 (1991):19–35.

[25]E. Fennema and P. Peterson, "Effective Teaching for Girls and Boys: The Same or Different?" in *Talks to Teachers*, D. Berliner and B. Rosenshine, eds. (New York: Random House, 1987), pp. 111–25; J. Stallings, "School Classroom and Home Influences on Women's Decisions to Enroll in Advanced Mathematics Courses," in *Women and Mathematics: Balancing the Equation*, S. Chipman, L. Brush, and D. Wilson, eds. (Hillsdale, NJ: Erlbaum, 1985), pp. 199–224; S. Greenberg, "Educational Equity in Early Education Environments," in *Handbook for Achieving Sex Equity Through Education*, S. Klein, ed. (Baltimore, MD: John Hopkins University Press, 1985), pp. 457–69.

[26]D. Baker, "Sex Differences in Classroom Interactions in Secondary Science," *Journal of Classroom Interaction* 22 (1986):212–18.

[27]D. Jorde and A. Lea, "The Primary Science Project in Norway," in *Proceedings of Growth GSAT Conference*, J. Kahle, J. Daniels, and J. Harding, eds. (West Lafayette, IN: Purdue University, 1987), pp. 66–72.

[31]M. Belenky et al., *Women's Ways of Knowing: The Development of Self, Body, and Mind* (New York: Basic Books, Inc., 1986).

[32]G. Engelhard and J. Monsaas, "Academic Performance, Gender and the Cooperative Attitudes of Third, Fifth and Seventh Graders," *Journal of Research and Development in Education* 22 (1989):13–17.

"Cooperative learning" has been viewed as one of these potentially more successful educational strategies. Cooperative learning is designed to eliminate the negative effects of classroom competition while promoting a cooperative spirit and increasing heterogeneous and cross-race relationships. . . . A number of positive results have been attributed to cooperative learning groups, including increasing cross-race friendships, boosting academic achievement, mainstreaming students with disabilities, and developing mutual student concerns.

However, positive cross-sex relationships may be more difficult to achieve than cross-race friendships or positive relationships among students with and without disabilities. First, as reported earlier in this report, there is a high degree of sex-segregation and same-sex friendships in elementary and middle school years. Researchers have found that the majority of elementary students preferred single-sex work groups. Second, different communication patterns of males and females can be an obstacle to effective cross-gender relationships. Females are more indirect in speech, relying often on questioning, while more direct males are more likely to make declarative statements or even to interrupt. Research indicates that boys in small groups are more likely to receive requested help from girls; girls' requests, on the other hand, are more likely to be ignored by the boys. In fact, the male sex may be seen as a status position within the group. As a result, male students may choose to show their social dominance by not readily talking with females.

Not only are the challenges to cross-gender cooperation significant, but cooperative learning as currently implemented may not be powerful enough to overcome these obstacles. Some research indicates that the infrequent use of small, unstructured work groups is not effective in reducing gender stereotypes, and, in fact, increases stereotyping. Groups often provide boys with leadership opportunities that increase their self-esteem. Females are often seen as followers and are less likely to want to work in mixed-sex groups in the future. Another study indicates a decrease in female achievement when females are placed in mixed-sex groups. Other research on cooperative education programs have reported more positive results. However, it is clear that merely providing an occasional group learning experience is not the answer to sex and gender differences in classrooms.

The report by the American Association of University Women as well as the work of researchers like the Sadkers proved highly influential. More recent studies, however, have found that females consistently perform as well as or better than boys except in math and science. On April 25, 2000, the National Center for Education Statistics released "without fanfare" a report requested by Congress that compared the educational experiences of girls and boys. Bowman, "Federal Study Finds Gains in Gender Equity," *Educ.Week*, May 3, 2000, at 1. The study found that female students experience fewer problems than males in the early grades, consistently outperform males in reading and writing, have higher educational goals than males as high school seniors, and are more likely than males to enroll in and complete college. The only areas in which boys have a significant advantage over girls are in mathematics and science. National Center for Education Statistics, *Trends in Educational Equity of Girls and Women* 3–5, 7–9, 18–21, 42–45, 60–69 (NCES2000-03, Mar. 2000).

The gender gap between males and females in education has led some commentators to wonder who is really being shortchanged and why.

"The War Against Boys"

C. Sommers, *The Atlantic Monthly*, May 2000, at 59–60, 62–74.

It's a bad time to be a boy in America. The triumphant victory of the U.S. women's soccer team at the World Cup last summer has come to symbolize the spirit of American girls. The shooting at Columbine High last spring might be said to symbolize the spirit of American boys.

That boys are in disrepute is not accidental. For many years women's groups have complained that boys benefit from a school system that favors them and is biased against girls. "Schools shortchange girls," declares the American Association of University Women. Girls are "undergoing a kind of psychological foot-binding," two prominent educational psychologists say. A stream of books and pamphlets cite research showing not only that boys are classroom favorites but also that they are given to schoolyard violence and sexual harassment.

In the view that has prevailed in American education over the past decade, boys are resented, both as the unfairly privileged sex and as obstacles on the path to gender justice for girls. This perspective is promoted in schools of education, and many a teacher now feels that girls need and deserve special indemnifying consideration. "It is really clear that boys are Number One in this society and in most of the world," says Patricia O'Reilly, a professor of education and the director of the Gender Equity Center, at the University of Cincinnati.

The idea that schools and society grind girls down has given rise to an array of laws and policies intended to curtail the advantage boys have and to redress the harm done to girls. That girls are treated as the second sex in school and consequently suffer, that boys are accorded privileges and consequently benefit—these are things everyone is presumed to know. But they are not true.

The research commonly cited to support claims of male privilege and male sinfulness is riddled with errors. Almost none of it has been published in peer-reviewed professional journals. Some of the data turn out to be mysteriously missing. A review of the facts shows boys, not girls, on the weak side of an education gender gap. The typical boy is a year and a half behind the typical girl in reading and writing; he is less committed to school and less likely to go to college. In 1997 college full-time enrollments were 45 percent male and 55 percent female. The Department of Education predicts that the proportion of boys in college classes will continue to shrink.

Data from the U.S. Department of Education and from several recent university studies show that far from being shy and demoralized, today's girls outshine boys. They get better grades. They have higher educational aspirations. They follow more-rigorous academic programs and participate in advanced-placement classes at higher rates. According to the National Center for Education Statistics, slightly more girls than boys enroll in high-level math and science courses. Girls, allegedly timorous and lacking in confidence, now outnumber boys in student government, in honor societies, on school newspapers, and in debating clubs. Only in sports are boys ahead, and women's groups are targeting the sports gap with a vengeance. Girls read more books. They outperform boys on tests for artistic and musical ability. More girls than boys study abroad. More join the Peace Corps. At the same time, more boys than girls are suspended from school. More are held back and more drop out. Boys are three times as likely to receive a diagnosis of attention-deficit hyperactivity disorder. More boys than girls are involved in crime, alcohol, and drugs. Girls attempt suicide more often than boys, but it is boys who more often succeed. In 1997, a typical year, 4,483 young people aged five to twenty-four committed suicide: 701 females and 3,782 males.

In the technical language of education experts, girls are academically more "engaged." Last year an article in *The CQ Researcher* about male and female academic achievement described a common parental observation: "Daughters want to please their teachers by spending extra time on projects, doing extra credit, making homework as neat as possible. Sons rush through homework assignments and run outside to play, unconcerned about how the teacher will regard the sloppy work."

School engagement is a critical measure of student success. The U.S. Department of Education gauges student commitment by the following criteria: "How much time do students devote to homework each night?" and "Do students come to class prepared and ready to learn? (Do they bring books and pencils? Have they completed their homework?)" According to surveys of fourth, eighth, and twelfth graders, girls consistently do more homework than boys. By the twelfth grade boys are four times as likely as girls not to do homework. Similarly, more boys than girls report that they "usually" or "often" come to school without supplies or without having done their homework.

The performance gap between boys and girls in high school leads directly to the growing gap between male and female admissions to college. The Department of Education reports that in 1996 there were 8.4 million women but only 6.7 million men enrolled in college. It predicts that women will hold on to and increase their lead well into the next decade, and that by 2007 the numbers will be 9.2 million women and 6.9 million men.

* * *

The Incredible Shrinking Girl

How did we get to this odd place? How did we come to believe in a picture of American boys and girls that is the opposite of the truth? And why has that belief persisted, enshrined in law, encoded in governmental and school policies, despite overwhelming evidence against it? The answer has much to do with one of the American academy's most celebrated women—Carol Gilligan, Harvard University's first professor of gender studies.

Gilligan first came to widespread attention in 1982, with the publication of *In a Different Voice*, which this article will discuss shortly. In 1990 Gilligan announced that America's adolescent girls were in crisis. In her words, "As the river of a girl's life flows into the sea of Western culture, she is in danger of drowning or disappearing." Gilligan offered little in the way of conventional evidence to support this alarming finding. Indeed, it is hard to imagine what sort of empirical research could establish such a large claim. But she quickly attracted powerful allies. Within a very short time the allegedly vulnerable and demoralized state of adolescent girls achieved the status of a national emergency.

Popular writers, electrified by Gilligan's discovery, began to see evidence of the crisis everywhere. Anna Quindlen, who was then a *New York Times* columnist, recounted in a 1990 column how Gilligan's research had cast an ominous shadow on the celebration of her daughter's second birthday: "My daughter is ready to leap into the world, as though life were chicken soup and she a delighted noodle. The work of Professor Carol Gilligan of Harvard suggests that some time after the age of 11 this will change, that even this lively little girl will pull back [and] shrink."

A number of popular books soon materialized, including Myra and David Sadker's *Failing at Fairness* [1994] and Peggy Orenstein's *Schoolgirls: Young Women, Self-Esteem, and the Confidence Gap* (1994). Elizabeth Gleick wrote in *Time* in 1996 on a new trend in literary victimology: "Dozens of troubled teenage girls troop across [the] pages: composite sketches of Charlottes, Whitneys and Danielles who were raped, who have bulimia, who have pierced bodies or shaved heads, who are coping with strict religious families or are felled by their parents' bitter divorce."

* * *

The description of America's teenage girls as silenced, tortured, and otherwise personally diminished was (and is) indeed dismaying. But no real evidence has ever been offered to support it. Certainly neither Gilligan nor the popular writers who followed her lead produced anything like solid empirical evidence, gathered according to the conventional protocols of social-science research.

Scholars who do abide by those protocols describe adolescent girls in far more optimistic terms. Anne Petersen, a former professor of adolescent development and pediatrics at the University of Minnesota and now a senior vice-president of the W. K. Kellogg Foundation, reports the consensus of researchers working in adolescent psychology: "It is now known that the majority of adolescents of both genders successfully negotiate this developmental period without any major psychological or emotional disorder, develop a positive sense of personal identity, and manage to forge adaptive peer relationships with

their families." Daniel Offer, a professor of psychiatry at Northwestern, concurs. He refers to a "new generation of studies" that find 80 percent of adolescents to be normal and well adjusted.

At the time that Gilligan was declaring her crisis, a study conducted by the University of Michigan asked a scientifically selected sample of 3,000 high school seniors, "Taking all things together, how would you say things are these days—would you say you're very happy, pretty happy, or not too happy these days?" Nearly 86 percent of the girls and 88 percent of the boys responded that they were "pretty happy" or "very happy." If the girls polled were caught in "an accelerating downward spiral," they were unaware of it.

Contrary to the story told by Gilligan and her followers, American girls were flourishing in unprecedented ways by the early 1990s. To be sure, some—including many who found themselves in the offices of clinical psychologists—felt they were crashing and drowning in the sea of Western culture. But the vast majority were occupied in more-constructive ways, moving ahead of boys in the primary and secondary grades, applying to college in record numbers, filling challenging academic classes, joining sports teams, and generally enjoying more freedom and opportunities than any other young women in history.

The great discrepancy between what Gilligan says she discovered about adolescent girls and what numerous other scientists say they have learned raises obvious questions about the quality of Gilligan's research. And these questions loom larger the more one examines Gilligan's methods. . . .

In a Different Voice offered the provocative thesis that men and women have distinctly different ways of dealing with moral quandaries. Relying on data from three studies she had conducted, Gilligan found that women tend to be more caring, less competitive, and less abstract than men; they speak "in a different voice." Women approach moral questions by applying an "ethic of care." In contrast, men approach moral issues by applying rules and abstract principles; theirs is an "ethic of justice." Gilligan argued further that women's moral style had been insufficiently studied by professional psychologists. She complained that the entire fields of psychology and moral philosophy had been built on studies that excluded women.

In a Different Voice was an instant success. It sold more than 600,000 copies and was translated into nine languages. A reviewer at *Vogue* explained its appeal: "[Gilligan] flips old prejudices against women on their ears. She reframes qualities regarded as women's weaknesses and shows them to be human strengths. It is impossible to consider [her] ideas without having your estimation of women rise."

The book received a mixed reaction from feminists. Some—such as the philosophers Virginia Held and Sara Ruddick, and those in various fields who would come to be known as "difference feminists"—were tantalized by the idea that women were different from, and quite probably better than, men. But other academic feminists attacked Gilligan for reinforcing stereotypes about women as nurturers and caretakers.

Many academic psychologists, feminist and non-feminist alike, found Gilligan's specific claims about distinct male and female moral orientations unpersuasive and ungrounded in empirical data. Lawrence Walker, of the University of British Columbia, has reviewed 108 studies of sex differences in solving moral problems. He concluded in a 1984 review article in *Child Development* that "sex differences in moral reasoning in late adolescence and youth are rare." In 1987 three psychologists at Oberlin College attempted to test Gilligan's hypothesis: they administered a moral-reasoning test to 101 male and female students and concluded, "There were no reliable sex differences . . . in the directions predicted by Gilligan." Concurring with Walker, the Oberlin researchers pointed out that "Gilligan failed to provide acceptable empirical support for her model."

* * *

"Politics Dressed Up as Science"

Gilligan's ideas about demoralized teenage girls had a special resonance with women's groups that were already committed to the proposition that our society is unsympathetic to women. The interest of the venerable and politically influential American Association of University Women, in particular, was piqued. Its officers were reported to be "intrigued and alarmed" by Gilligan's research. They wanted to know more.

In 1990 *The New York Times Sunday Magazine* published an admiring profile of Gilligan that heralded the discovery of a hidden crisis among the nation's girls. Soon after, the AAUW commissioned a study from the polling firm Greenberg-Lake. The pollsters asked 3,000 children (2,400 girls and 600 boys in grades four through ten) about their self-perceptions. In 1991 the association announced the

disturbing results, in a report titled *Shortchanging Girls, Shortchanging America*: "Girls aged eight and nine are confident, assertive, and feel authoritative about themselves. Yet most emerge from adolescence with a poor self-image, constrained views of their future and their place in society, and much less confidence about themselves and their abilities." Anne Bryant, the executive director of the AAUW and an expert in public relations, organized a media campaign to spread the word that "an unacknowledged American tragedy" had been uncovered. Newspapers and magazines around the country carried reports that girls were being adversely affected by gender bias that eroded their self-esteem. Sharon Schuster, at the time the president of the AAUW, candidly explained to *The New York Times* why the association had undertaken the research in the first place: "We wanted to put some factual data behind our belief that girls are getting shortchanged in the classroom."

As the AAUW's self-esteem study was making headlines, a little-known magazine called *Science News*, which has been supplying information on scientific and technical developments to interested newspapers since 1922, reported the skeptical reaction of leading specialists on adolescent development. The late Roberta Simmons, a professor of sociology at the University of Pittsburgh (described by *Science News* as "director of the most ambitious longitudinal study of adolescent self-esteem to date"), said that her research showed nothing like the substantial gender gap described by the AAUW. According to Simmons, "Most kids come through the years from 10 to 20 without major problems and with an increasing sense of self-esteem." But the doubts of Simmons and several other prominent experts were not reported in the hundreds of news stories that the Greenberg-Lake study generated.

The AAUW quickly commissioned a second study, *How Schools Shortchange Girls*. This one, conducted by the Wellesley College Center for Research on Women and released in 1992, focused on the alleged effects of sexism on girls' school performance. It asserted that schools deflate girls' self-esteem by "systematically cheating girls of classroom attention." Such bias leads to lower aspirations and impaired academic achievement. Carol Gilligan's crisis was being transformed into a civil-rights issue: girls were the victims of widespread sex discrimination. "The implications are clear," the AAUW said. "The system must change."

With great fanfare *How Schools Shortchange Girls* was released to the remarkably uncritical media. A 1992 article for *The New York Times* by Susan Chira was typical of coverage throughout the country. The headline read "BIAS AGAINST GIRLS IS FOUND RIFE IN SCHOOLS, WITH LASTING DAMAGE." The piece was later reproduced by the AAUW and sent out as part of a fundraising package. Chira had not interviewed a single critic of the study.

*　＊　＊*

Six years after the release of *How Schools Shortchange Girls*, *The New York Times* ran a story that raised questions about its validity. . . . [According to former U.S. Assistant Secretary of Education] Diane Ravitch . . ., "That [1992] AAUW report was just completely wrong. What was so bizarre is that it came out right at the time that girls had just overtaken boys in almost every area. It might have been the right story twenty years earlier, but coming out when it did, it was like calling a wedding a funeral. . . . There were all these special programs put in place for girls, and no one paid any attention to boys."

One of the many things about which the report was wrong was the famous "call-out" gap. According to the AAUW, "In a study conducted by the Sadkers, boys in elementary and middle school called out answers eight times more often than girls. When boys called out, teachers listened. But when girls called out, they were told 'raise your hand if you want to speak.' "

But the Sadker study turns out to be missing—and meaningless, to boot. In 1994 Amy Saltzman, of *U.S. News & World Report*, asked David Sadker for a copy of the research backing up the eight-to-one call-out claim. Sadker said that he had presented the findings in an unpublished paper at a symposium sponsored by the American Educational Research Association; neither he nor the AERA had a copy. Sadker conceded to Saltzman that the ratio may have been inaccurate. Indeed, Saltzman cited an independent study by Gail Jones, an associate professor of education at the University of North Carolina at Chapel Hill, which found that boys called out only twice as often as girls. Whatever the accurate number is, no one has shown that permitting a student to call out answers in the classroom confers any kind of academic advantage. What does confer advantage is a student's attentiveness. Boys are less attentive—which could explain why some teachers might call on them more or be more tolerant of call-outs.

Despite the errors, the campaign to persuade the public that girls were being diminished personally and academically was a spectacular success. The Sadkers described an exultant Anne Bryant, of the AAUW, telling her friends, "I remember going to bed the night our report was issued, totally exhilarated. When I woke up the next morning, the first thought in my mind was, 'Oh, my God, what do we do next?' " Political action came next, and here, too, girls' advocates were successful.

Categorizing girls as an "under-served population" on a par with other discriminated-against minorities, Congress passed the Gender Equity in Education Act in 1994. Millions of dollars in grants were awarded to study the plight of girls and to learn how to counter bias against them. At the United Nations Fourth World Conference on Women, in Beijing in 1995, U.S. delegates presented the educational and psychological deficits of American girls as a human-rights issue.

The Myth Unraveling

By the late 1990s the myth of the downtrodden girl was showing some signs of unraveling, and concern over boys was growing. In 1997 the Public Education Network (PEN) announced at its annual conference the results of a new teacher-student survey titled *The American Teacher 1997: Examining Gender Issues in Public Schools*. The survey was funded by the Metropolitan Life Insurance Company and conducted by Louis Harris and Associates.

During a three-month period in 1997 various questions about gender equity were asked of 1,306 students and 1,035 teachers in grades seven through twelve. The MetLife study had no doctrinal ax to grind. What it found contradicted most of the findings of the AAUW, the Sadkers, and the Wellesley College Center for Research on Women: "Contrary to the commonly held view that boys are at an advantage over girls in school, girls appear to have an advantage over boys in terms of their future plans, teachers' expectations, everyday experiences at school and interactions in the classroom."

Some other conclusions from the MetLife study: Girls are more likely than boys to see themselves as college-bound and more likely to want a good education. Furthermore, more boys (31 percent) than girls (19 percent) feel that teachers do not listen to what they have to say.

At the PEN conference, Nancy Leffert, a child psychologist then at the Search Institute, in Minneapolis, reported the results of a survey that she and colleagues had recently completed of more than 99,000 children in grades six through twelve. The children were asked about what the researchers call "developmental assets." The Search Institute has identified forty critical assets—"building blocks for healthy development." Half of these are external, such as a supportive family and adult role models, and half are internal, such as motivation to achieve, a sense of purpose in life, and interpersonal confidence. Leffert explained, somewhat apologetically, that girls were ahead of boys with respect to thirty-seven out of forty assets. By almost every significant measure of well-being girls had the better of boys: they felt closer to their families; they had higher aspirations, stronger connections to school, and even superior assertiveness skills. Leffert concluded her talk by saying that in the past she had referred to girls as fragile or vulnerable, but that the survey "tells me that girls have very powerful assets."

The Horatio Alger Association, a fifty-year-old organization devoted to promoting and affirming individual initiative and "the American dream," releases annual back-to-school surveys. Its survey for 1998 contrasted two groups of students: the "highly successful" (approximately 18 percent of American students) and the "disillusioned" (approximately 15 percent). The successful students work hard, choose challenging classes, make schoolwork a top priority, get good grades, participate in extracurricular activities, and feel that teachers and administrators care about them and listen to them. According to the association, the successful group in the 1998 survey is 63 percent female and 37 percent male. The disillusioned students are pessimistic about their future, get low grades, and have little contact with teachers. The disillusioned group could accurately be characterized as demoralized. According to the Alger Association, "Nearly seven out of ten are male."

In the spring of 1998 Judith Kleinfeld, a psychologist at the University of Alaska, published a thorough critique of the research on schoolgirls titled "The Myth That Schools Shortchange Girls: Social Science in the Service of Deception." Kleinfeld exposed a number of errors in the AAUW/Wellesley Center study, concluding that it was "politics dressed up as science." Kleinfeld's report prompted several publications, including *The New York Times* and *Education Week*, to take a second look at claims that girls were in a tragic state.

The AAUW did not adequately respond to any of Kleinfeld's substantive objections; instead its current president, Maggie Ford, complained in the *New York Times* letters column that Kleinfeld was "reducing the problems of our children to this petty 'who is worse off, boys or girls?' [which] gets us nowhere." From the leader of an organization that spent nearly a decade ceaselessly promoting the proposition that American girls are being "shortchanged," this comment is rather remarkable.

* * *

NOTES AND QUESTIONS

1. The Research Debate

Is the debate over research on the educational experience of boys and girls similar to that over bilingual and multicultural education described in chapter 6? Are both controversies motivated by political as well as pedagogical agendas? How should courts and legislatures respond to such conflicting evidence? Should intense disagreement among researchers put a stop to legal reform initiatives? If the empirical evidence is contested, how can educators exercise their discretion to ensure that all students enjoy an equal educational opportunity?

2. Title IX's Limits Revisited

Does the argument about gender equity reveal the dangers of trying to micromanage the classroom experience in the name of fairness? Are Title IX's limits appropriate because educators should decide how to structure the curriculum and classroom participation? Does it matter to your answer that the teaching force in elementary and secondary schools is overwhelmingly female?

3. Nondiscrimination and Equity

Can a norm of nondiscrimination be enforced without resolving the questions of gender equity raised by the research debate over male and female educational attainment? Is there any way to determine whether boys or girls are being shortchanged by the schools? Should one expect equal outcomes for males and females in all areas?

IV. CONCLUSION

The dilemma of gender equity demonstrates the complex and contested norms that can lie behind a principle of nondiscrimination. Schools are at the center of these conflicts because of their important role in the socialization process. At times, educators are caught between judicial and legal mandates on the one hand and inconsistent empirical evidence on the other. The politics of fairness and equality can leave teachers and administrators searching for formal rules and procedures to protect themselves in an uncertain and shifting political and judicial climate. Still, like it or not, educators will continue to participate in the challenge of forging equal educational opportunity for all students.

Equal Educational Opportunity and the Dilemma of Difference: Beyond Race and Gender

I. INTRODUCTION

In the wake of *Brown*, other groups began to organize around claims of disadvantage and exclusion. Moving beyond race, these constituencies demanded that the law recognize and enforce principles of nondiscrimination based on ethnicity and national origin, gender, and disability. As discussed in chapter 5, women have made substantial gains using this approach, although doubts about the analogy between race and gender persist. Just as women grappled with the definition of equality, advocates for those who are linguistically or culturally different and for those with disabilities sometimes have rejected a model of assimilation, instead insisting that equality requires special attention to their unique needs. In this new political climate, some disadvantaged children, such as the poor and homeless, have received sparse attention because they lack a coherent organizing principle rooted in an "alternative identity." Moreover, the proliferation of groups demanding recognition of their differences can lead to fears of a divisive and destructive identity politics. *See* A. Schlesinger, Jr., *The Disuniting of America* (1992). According to Professor Martha Minow, this range of claims about equality has created a "dilemma of difference," a newfound uncertainty about whether groups should conform to a single norm or preserve their differences in a pluralistic society. Compounding these doubts is a concern that the law, while trying to eradicate inequality, will simply entrench our differences.

"The Dilemma of Difference"
M. Minow, in *Making All the Difference* 19–23 (1990).

All the teachers in the San Francisco public schools during the 1960s taught their classes in English, just as they always had. But by the end of the decade a group of parents sought out a lawyer to object that this instruction deprived their children of the chance for an equal education. Their children, who spoke primarily Chinese, were falling far behind in classes taught only in English. The parents pushed the courts to consider whether according the same treatment to people who differ—to the students who speak English and those who speak Chinese—violates commitments to equality.

Ultimately, the Supreme Court of the United States heard the case. In 1974 the Court concluded that "the Chinese-speaking minority receives less benefits than the English-speaking majority" from the schools and that therefore the school system "denies them a meaningful opportunity to participate in the educational program." The Court directed the school system to take affirmative steps to rectify the language deficiency. "Special," not similar, treatment was the legal solution to the question of equality. The decision encouraged bilingual education programs that separated the students lacking English proficiency from their peers for part of the school day or provided months or even years of specialized schooling.

Also during the 1970s, parents and lawyers challenged traditional educational practices for children with physical or mental disabilities, claiming that those children were being denied equal treatment. Here, though, the challengers objected to the exclusion of disabled children from the public school classrooms attended by their peers. Borrowing rhetoric and legal analysis from the crusade for racial desegregation, advocates for the rights of handicapped students urged their integration into mainstream classrooms, along with services to facilitate such programs.

Perhaps ironically, then, educational policymakers and law reformers during the 1970s and 1980s switched allegiance to bilingual programs that pull students at least part time from the mainstream classroom, while simultaneously sponsoring special education programs that integrate handicapped students into either the mainstream classroom or the "least restrictive alternative." The apparent contrast between these two responses to students who differ from their peers, however, suggests a deeper similarity. Schools, parents, and legal officials confront in both contexts the difficult task of remedying inequality. With both bilingual and special education, schools struggle to deal with children defined as "different" without stigmatizing them. Both programs raise the same question: when does treating people differently emphasize their differences and stigmatize or hinder them on *that* basis? and when does treating people the same become insensitive to their difference and likely to stigmatize or hinder them on *that* basis?

I call this question "the dilemma of difference." The stigma of difference may be recreated both by ignoring and by focusing on it. Decisions about education, employment, benefits, and other opportunities in society should not turn on an individual's ethnicity, disability, race, gender, religion, or membership in any other group about which some have deprecating or hostile attitudes. Yet refusing to acknowledge these differences may make them continue to matter in a world constructed with some groups, but not others, in mind. The problems of inequality can be exacerbated both by treating members of minority groups the same as members of the majority and by treating the two groups differently.

The dilemma of difference may be posed as a choice between integration and separation, as a choice between similar treatment and special treatment, or as a choice between neutrality and accommodation. Governmental neutrality may be the best way to assure equality, yet governmental neutrality may also freeze in place the past consequences of differences. Do the public schools fulfill their obligation to provide equal opportunities by including all

students in the same integrated classroom, or by offering some students special programs tailored to their needs? Special needs arise from "differences" beyond language proficiency and physical or mental disability. Religious differences also raise questions of same versus different treatment. Students who belong to religious minorities may seek exemption from courses in sex education or other subjects that conflict with their religious teachings. Religiously observant students may ask to use school time and facilities to engage in religious activities, just as other students engage in other extracurricular activities. But the legal obligation of neutrality is explicit here, in a polity committed to separating church and state. Do the schools remain neutral toward religion by balancing the teaching of evolution with the teaching of scientific arguments about creation? Or does this accommodation of a religious viewpoint depart from the requisite neutrality?

* * *

I suggest that the dilemma of difference is not an accidental problem in this society. The dilemma of difference grows from the ways in which this society assigns individuals to categories and, on that basis, determines whom to include in and whom to exclude from political, social, and economic activities. Because the activities are designed, in turn, with only the included participants in mind, the excluded seem not to fit because of something in their own nature. Thus, people have used categories based on age, race, gender, ethnicity, religion, and disability to decide formally and informally who is eligible to enroll in a given school, who is excluded from a particular sports activity, who may join a particular club, who may adopt a given child, and a variety of other questions.

An organization that holds its meetings in a club that excludes women, non-Christians, or nonwhites, for example, reflects the assumptions held by its conveners about who will be members. Yet if the organization tries to remedy the historical exclusion by heralding that the former blackballing category is now a basis for inclusion, the dilemma of difference becomes palpable. This solution still focuses on a category rather than treating persons as unique individuals, each one an intersection of countless categories; moreover, this solution reemphasizes the particular category that has mattered in the past. Racially segregated schools thus are changed by a focus on the racial identity of the individual students and an enrollment design to balance the composition of the school on this, and only this, basis. Similarly, when an organization that has excluded women in the past seeks to change by soliciting women members, it runs the risk of treating such new members as eligible and welcome only because they are women. Besides reducing people to one trait, this solution risks new harms if the category itself still carries stigmatizing or exclusionary consequences in other contexts.

The dilemma persists when legal reasoning itself not only typically deploys categorical approaches that reduce a complex situation, and a multifaceted person, to a place in or out of a category but also treats those categories as natural and inevitable. A complex legal dispute becomes focused on a narrow question: for example, does an employer's refusal to hire a woman fall within the statutory exemption from the antidiscrimination statute as a business necessity? Both the social and legal constructions of difference have the effect of hiding from view the relationships among people, relationships marked by power and hierarchy. Within these relationships, we each become who we are and make order out of our own lives. Yet, by sorting people and problems into categories, we each cede power to social definitions that we individually no longer control.

Difference, after all, is a comparative term. It implies a reference: different from whom? I am no more different from you than you are from me. A short person is different only in relation to a tall one; a Spanish-speaking student is different in relation to an English-speaking one. But the point of comparison is often unstated. Women are compared with the unstated norm of men, "minority" races with whites, handicapped persons with the able-bodied, and "minority" religions and ethnicities with majorities. If we identify the unstated points of comparison necessary to the idea of difference, we will then examine the relationships between people who have and people who lack the power to assign the label of difference. If we explore the environmental context that makes some trait stand out and some people seem not to fit in, we will have the opportunity to reconsider how and for what ends we construct and manage the environment. Then difference will no longer seem empirically discoverable, consisting of traits inherent in the "different person." Instead, perceptions of difference can become clues to broader problems of social policy and human responsibility.

* * *

Having examined the challenges that race and gender pose in defining equal educational opportunity in chapters 4 and 5, the analysis now turns to the dilemma of difference in three other contexts: ethnicity and national origin; disability; and class. In each instance, you should consider whether nondiscrimination means giving individuals the opportunity to assimilate or accommodating their differences through special programs. How do the legal remedies for each group address this tension between assimilation and pluralism? Why have distinct remedies evolved for different constituencies? How have the remedies affected the definition of the affected class? Why have groups enjoyed disparate degrees of success in demanding legislative and judicial recognition of their needs?

II. ETHNICITY AND NATIONAL ORIGIN

When *Brown v. Board of Education*, 347 U.S. 483 (1954), was decided, the nonwhite population in the United States was almost entirely black. According to 1960 census data, one in ten Americans identified themselves as nonwhite, and of these, 90 percent reported that they were black. Ramirez, "Multicultural Empowerment: It's Not Just Black and White Anymore," 47 *Stan.L.Rev.* 957, 958–59 (1995). Beginning in the 1970s, however, the Latino and Asian American populations in the United States grew dramatically. *Id.* at 959–62. In fact, early in the twenty-first century, Latinos will overtake blacks as the single largest minority group. In contrast to blacks, Latinos and Asians have high rates of immigration. As a result, they face special barriers based on language, culture, and lack of citizenship. While Asian Americans often have been held up as the model minority based on high academic achievement, Latinos experience educational problems similar to blacks. Moreover, some Asian American subgroups, such as Cambodians, Laotians, and Hmong, have faced bleak prospects in school and in the workforce.

A. Language, Identity, and Equality

One of the first areas of concern to Latino and Asian American newcomers that received legislative attention was language difference. In 1968, Congress enacted the Bilingual Education Act, a grant-in-aid program designed to promote research and experimentation on how best to meet the needs of non-English-proficient (NEP) and limited-English-proficient (LEP) students. Bilingual Education Act of 1968, Pub.L.No. 90–247, 81 Stat. 783, 816–19 (codified as amended at 20 U.S.C. §§7401–7491). Although funding under the Act was extremely modest, the legislation did put bilingual education on the national agenda.

The Bilingual Education Act, 20 U.S.C. § 880b, is a grants program, providing support for school districts enrolling sizable numbers of limited-English-proficient students. Due to limited federal funding, however, fewer than 10 percent of the estimated four million eligible children received benefits under the act, even before cutbacks in the 1980s and 1990s.

The Reagan Administration tried unsuccessfully to eliminate this program by proposing to consolidate it into a block grant to the states. In 1984, Congress weakened the bilingual requirements, giving the Department of Education permission to distribute up to 4 percent of bilingual funds to districts providing English-only instruction. For a detailed history, *see* Moran, "The Politics of Discretion: Federal Intervention in Bilingual Education," 76 *Cal.L.Rev.* 1249 (1988).

The Bilingual Education Act created a discretionary grant-in-aid program, but advocates wanted the federal government to recognize an entitlement to special assistance. In 1970, the Office for Civil Rights (OCR) issued a memorandum that extended the nondiscrimination provisions of Title VI of the Civil Rights Act of 1964 to NEP and LEP students. OCR did not aggressively enforce its interpretation in the early 1970s, but the memorandum afforded private litigants the chance to challenge local educational practices. One such lawsuit reached the United States Supreme Court.

1. The Rise of a Statutory Entitlement.

Lau v. Nichols
414 U.S. 563, 94 S.Ct. 786, 39 L.Ed.2d 1 (1974).

Mr. Justice Douglas delivered the opinion of the Court.
* * *

This class suit brought by non-English speaking Chinese students against officials responsible for the operation of the San Francisco Unified School District seeks relief against the unequal educational opportunities which are alleged to violate the Fourteenth Amendment. No specific remedy is urged upon us. Teaching English to the students of Chinese ancestry who do not speak the language is one

choice. Giving instructions to this group in Chinese is another. There may be others. Petitioner asks only that the Board of Education be directed to apply its expertise to the problem and rectify the situation.

The District Court denied relief. The Court of Appeals affirmed, holding that there was no violation of the Equal Protection Clause of the Fourteenth Amendment nor of § 601 of the Civil Rights Act of 1964, which excludes from participation in federal financial assistance, recipients of aid which discriminate against racial groups. . . .

The Court of Appeals reasoned that "every student brings to the starting line of his educational career different advantages and disadvantages caused in part by social, economic and cultural background, created and continued completely apart from any contribution by the school system." 483 F.2d, at 797. Yet in our view the case may not be so easily decided. . . .

We do not reach the Equal Protection Clause argument which has been advanced but rely solely on § 601 of the Civil Rights Act of 1964, 42 U.S.C. § 2000d, to reverse the Court of Appeals.

That section bans discrimination based "on the ground of race, color, or national origin," in "any program or activity receiving Federal financial assistance." The school district involved in this litigation receives large amounts of federal financial assistance. HEW, which has authority to promulgate regulations prohibiting discrimination in federally assisted school systems, 42 U.S.C. § 2000d, in 1968 issued one guideline that "school systems are responsible for assuring that students of a particular race, color, or national origin are not denied the opportunity to obtain the education generally obtained by other students in the system." 33 CFR § 4955. In 1970 HEW made the guidelines more specific, requiring school districts that were federally funded "to rectify the language deficiency in order to open" the instruction to students who had "linguistic deficiencies," 35 Fed. Reg. 11595.

By § 602 of the act HEW is authorized to issue rules, regulations, and orders to make sure that recipients of federal aid under its jurisdiction conduct any federally financed projects consistently with § 601. HEW's regulations specify, 45 CFR § 80.3(b)(1), that the recipients may not:

> "Provide any service, financial aid, or other benefit to an individual which is different, or is provided in a different manner, from that provided to others under the program;
>
> * * *

"Restrict an individual in any way in the enjoyment of any advantage or privilege enjoyed by others receiving any service, financial aid, or other benefit under the program;"

Discrimination among students on account of race or national origin that is prohibited includes "discrimination in the availability or use of any academic . . . or other facilities of the grantee or other recipient."

Discrimination is barred which has that *effect* even though no purposeful design is present: a recipient "may not . . . utilize criteria or methods of administration which have the effect of subjecting individuals to discrimination" or has "the effect of defeating or substantially impairing accomplishment of the objectives of the program as respects individuals of a particular race, color, or national origin." *Id.*, 80.3(b)(2).

It seems obvious that the Chinese-speaking minority receives less benefits than the English-speaking majority from respondents' school system which denies them a meaningful opportunity to participate in the educational program—all earmarks of the discrimination banned by the Regulations. In 1970 HEW issued clarifying guidelines (35 Fed. Reg. 11595) which include the following:

"Where inability to speak and understand the English language excludes national origin-minority group children from effective participation in the educational program offered by a school district, the district must take affirmative steps to rectify the language deficiency in order to open its instructional program to these students." . . .

Respondent school district contractually agreed to "comply with title VI of the Civil Rights Act of 1964 . . . and all requirements imposed by or pursuant to the Regulations" of HEW (45 CFR Pt. 80) which are "issued pursuant to that title . . ." and also immediately to "take any measures necessary to effectuate this agreement." The Federal Government has power to fix the terms on which its money allotments to the States shall be disbursed. . . .

We accordingly reverse the judgment of the Court of Appeals and remand the case for the fashioning of appropriate relief.

Reversed. . . .

Mr. Justice Blackmun, with whom the Chief Justice joins, concurring in the result. . . .

. . . I stress the fact that the children with whom we are concerned here number about 1800. This is a very substantial group that is being deprived of any meaningful schooling because they cannot understand the language of the classroom. We may only guess as to why they have had no exposure to English in their preschool years. Earlier generations of American ethnic groups have overcome the language barrier by earnest parental endeavor or by the hard fact of being pushed out of the family or community nest and into the realities of broader experience.

I merely wish to make plain that when, in another case, we are concerned with a very few youngsters, or with just a single child who speaks only German or Polish or Spanish or any language other than English, I would not regard today's decision, or the separate concurrence, as conclusive upon the issue whether the statute and the guideline require the funded school district to provide special instruction. For me, numbers are at the heart of this case and my concurrence is to be understood accordingly.

NOTES AND QUESTIONS

1. The Constitutional and Statutory Issues

The Ninth Circuit had decided *Lau* on Fourteenth Amendment grounds, ruling that there was no constitutional basis for requiring the defendant school district to remedy disadvantages for which the state was not responsible. Moreover, both parties stressed constitutional, not statutory, issues in their arguments before the Supreme Court. Why did the Court choose to decide the case on statutory grounds? What are the relevant doctrinal differences between the basis for a Title VI suit, on the one hand, and an Equal Protection Clause suit on the other? Recall in this context the discussion in chapter 4 of the need to prove "intentional" discrimination under Title VI and the Fourteenth Amendment. *See Regents of the University of California v. Bakke*, 438 U.S. 265 (1978). Of what doctrinal or practical moment are these distinctions?

2. Language and National Origin

Title VI bans, in pertinent part, discrimination based on "national origin." In what sense is the claim of the *Lau* plaintiffs based on race or national origin rather than linguistic disability (which is not specifically covered by the Act)? Is it relevant, in appraising the Court's reliance on Title VI, that in basing the decision on Title VI the Court is upholding the standards of a coordinate branch of government rather than acting on its own? Is it relevant that Title VI is subject to congressional revision?

2. The Scope of the Entitlement. Because Title VI treats language as a proxy for race, ethnicity, and national origin, questions arise about what kinds of "language deficiency" trigger its protections. One of the most controversial areas has been whether speakers of "Black English" can seek relief under this statute.

Martin Luther King Jr. Elementary School Children v. Michigan Board of Education
451 F.Supp. 1324 (E.D.Mich. 1978).

Charles W. Joiner, District Judge:

Plaintiffs are fifteen black preschool or elementary school children residing at the Green Road Housing Project in Ann Arbor, Michigan, who previously attended, are currently attending, or will be eligible to attend the Martin Luther King, Jr., Elementary School. . . .

In this lawsuit the plaintiffs allege that in the process of determining the eligibility of all students for special education services . . . the defendants have failed to determine whether plaintiffs' learning difficulties stem from cultural, social, and economic deprivation and to establish a program which would enable plaintiffs to overcome the cultural, social, and economic deprivations which allegedly prevent them, in varying degrees, from making normal progress in school. Plaintiffs assert that these omissions constitute violations of . . . (III) their right to equal educational opportunity protected by 20 U.S.C. §§ 1703(f) and 1706. . . . [Other claims, based on federal and state constitutional arguments, are rejected by the court and not excerpted.]

. . . Plaintiffs are alleged to be culturally, socially, and economically deprived. . . . Five of the fifteen named plaintiffs have been found eligible to receive special education services for the handicapped as hereinafter explained. Four of these children have actually received services. Two children have been classified as "Learning Disabled." Two children have been classified as "Emotionally Impaired." The mother of the fifth child, who is also the mother of one of the learning disabled children, refused any further special services for her other child. There is no separate category or discrete assistance in the program for handicapped for learning difficulties arising from cultural, social, and economic deprivation. Several other plaintiffs have been referred for an evaluation of their eligibility but these referrals have not resulted in any classification or access to services. . . .

In count III of the complaint plaintiffs allege that the defendants' previously described acts and omissions constitute a failure to take appropriate action to overcome language barriers in violation of 20 U.S.C. §§ 1703(f) . . . Section 1703(f) of Title 20 of the United States Code states:

> No State shall deny equal educational opportunity to an individual on account of his or her race, color, sex, or national origin, by—(f) the failure by an educational agency to take appropriate action to overcome language barriers that impede equal participation by its students in its instructional programs.

Plaintiffs assert that as a class of black economically disadvantaged children living in the social isolation of a housing project they speak a vernacular of English, referred to as "Black English," which is so different from the English commonly spoken in the public school as to constitute a language barrier which impedes their equal participation in King School's instructional programs.

In their attack on the legal sufficiency of this claim defendants present [as an issue for] resolution, . . . whether the term "language barrier" can be interpreted to include a child's inability to use standard English effectively because that child's native language is what plaintiffs have termed "Black English" as opposed to a foreign language such as Spanish. . . .

Federal Courts have not explicitly addressed the issue of whether the language barrier specified in § 1703(f) must be a foreign language barrier or may also include the barrier standard English presents to a black child with a "Black English" background. . . .

This section (f) requires a showing of two things. (1) The denial of educational opportunity must be on "account of" race, color, sex or national origin and, (2) the educational agency must fail to take action to overcome language barriers that are sufficiently severe so as to impede a student's equal participation in instructional programs. So the allegations in this case must be examined to determine the seriousness of the language barriers and the cause of the alleged denial of educational opportunities that results from the failure to take action to overcome the language barriers.

The statutory language places no limitations on the character or source of the language barrier except that it must be serious enough to "impede equal participation by . . . students in . . . instructional programs." Barring any more explicit legislative guidance to the contrary § 1703(f) applies to language barriers of appropriate severity encountered by students who speak "Black English" as well as to language barriers encountered by students who speak German.

The legislative history of this section does not provide a meaning more specific or limited in scope than the language of the statute. In his message to Congress President Nixon stated:

> School authorities must take appropriate action to overcome *whatever* language barriers might exist, in order to enable all students to participate equally in educational programs. This would establish, in effect, an educational bill of rights for Mexican-Americans, Puerto Ricans, Indians and others who start under language handicaps, and ensure at last that they too would have equal opportunity. [Emphasis added].

118 Cong. Rec. 8931 (1972). The President's list of persons covered by his proposal is not only merely illustrative but could well include students whose "language barrier" results from the use of some type of nonstandard English. The report of the House Committee on Education and Labor simply paraphrases the statutory language and commends HEW for having initiated a compliance review of school districts throughout the country to ascertain whether they have fulfilled their obligation to remove language and cultural barriers under Title VI of the Civil Rights Act of 1964.

Paragraph 120 of the complaint contains an allegation that plaintiffs are all Black and economically disadvantaged and that the defendants have failed to take appropriate action to overcome language barriers. There is enough stated implicitly in this allegation as to causation to prevent this court from granting a motion to dismiss. In keeping with the terms of the statute this court holds that allegations of failure by an educational agency to take appropriate action to overcome language barriers of students which impede their equal participation in instructional programs when tied, as alleged, to race allege a violation of 20 U.S.C. § 1703(f). . . .

NOTES AND QUESTIONS

1. Martin Luther King Jr. Elementary School Children: *Scope of the Decision*

How does the court determine what constitutes "language barriers that impede equal participation"? Are you persuaded by the court's treatment of the language of the statute and its legislative history that the statute was meant to encompass the "language barrier" of Black English? Does one speak Black English

on "account of" race? *See* Smith, "Our Children's Burden: The Many-Headed Hydra of the Educational Disenfranchisement of Black Children," 42 *How.L.J.* 133 (1999); van Geel, "Law, Politics, and the Right to Be Taught English," 83 *Sch.Rev.* 245 (1975). *See also* Gaulding, "Against Common Sense: Why Title VII Should Protect Speakers of Black English," *U.Mich.J.L.Ref.* 637 (1998).

In a subsequent opinion, 473 F.Supp. 1371 (E.D. Mich. 1979), the court concluded that Black English was indeed a distinct dialect that impedes equal participation and ordered the school district to prepare a plan to teach standard English to Black English speakers. The district committed $42,000 to a teacher training course designed to steer students away from "she be gone" to "she is gone."

2. Who Is Entitled to Special Language Assistance?

Under what circumstances should students be assigned to bilingual programs? Can a student with limited English skills be placed in such a program, even if his skills in his native language are just as poor or even worse? One bilingual education proponent argues that "any child, irrespective of the language in which he is most proficient, is entitled to special language assistance if he can show that some language 'impediment' stemming from his linguistic background is causing '[in]effective' or '[un]equal' participation in a school district's educational program." Roos, "Bilingual Education: The Hispanic Response to Unequal Educational Opportunity," 42 *Law & Contemp.Probs.* 111, 119 (1978). If this reading of the law is correct, how might such a nexus be identified? A disproportionate number of students who come from homes in which English is not the primary language are also poor, have parents with limited educational backgrounds, and so on. How does one disentangle linguistic background from these other impediments to academic success? *See Otero v. Mesa County Valley School District No. 51*, 408 F.Supp. 162 (D. Colo. 1975), *vacated and remanded on other grounds*, 568 F.2d 1312 (10th Cir. 1977). Is it also appropriate to require a showing that some special language assistance will aid in overcoming the impediment? How likely is it that this can be established?

3. Beyond *Lau*: The Development of Federal Bilingual Education Law.

Despite some ambiguities about its scope, the *Lau* decision prompted new efforts to address the needs of NEP and LEP students. In 1975, OCR issued a memorandum expanding upon the *Lau* entitlement. That memo, "Task Force Findings Specifying Remedies for Eliminating Past Educational Practices Ruled Unlawful Under *Lau v. Nichols*," outlined the procedures to be followed by school districts that enroll twenty or more limited-English-proficient students. In determining a student's primary language, the memo called for an analysis of the child's first acquired language, the language most often spoken by the child, and the language most often spoken in the child's home. If in any of these circumstances a language other than English was used, then the child would be treated as having a non-English primary language. Such students were then classified as monolingual speakers of a language other than English, predominant speakers of a language other than English, bilingual (equally fluent), predominantly English-speaking, and monolingual English-speaking.

These classifications were supposed to determine the program that a school district adopted. For example, the monolingual (non-English-speaking) elementary or intermediate school student might be offered programs that relied on the native language, such as transitional bilingual education, bilingual-bicultural education, or multilingual-multicultural education. According to the OCR "*Lau* remedies," that child could not be enrolled in an English-as-a-second-language (ESL) course, which focused on English-acquisition and did not employ the child's native tongue. More curricular flexibility was permitted at the secondary than the primary level and with respect to children who had a greater command of English. The OCR memorandum also addressed issues of curriculum, personnel, ethnic isolation, and the like. Instructional personnel, for instance, had to be linguistically and culturally familiar with the background of students in the program. The OCR expectation was that "voluntary compliance plans . . . will be equally effective in ensuring equal educational opportunity." Neither the meaning of "equally effective" nor the mechanisms for enforcement were specified. These guidelines were withdrawn in 1980.

In 1974, Congress solidified protections for linguistic minority students by passing the Equal Educational Opportunity Act, § 204. The act provides that: "No State shall deny equal educational opportunity to an individual on account of his or her race, color, sex, or national origin, by . . . (f) the failure by an educational agency to take appropriate action to overcome language barriers that impede equal par-

ticipation by its students in the instructional program." 20 U.S.C. § 1703 (1976). Of critical importance, the Act's protections are triggered when the school's program has the effect of excluding linguistic minority students, regardless of whether officials acted with discriminatory intent. However, the Act gives districts considerable leeway to define appropriate action to overcome language barriers. What this provision requires—what groups are reached, what kinds of programs are called for, whether "equal participation" and "effective participation" are synonymous—has been the subject of policy debate. It has also been the subject of litigation. One of the most prominent cases involved Spanish-speaking students in Texas.

Castaneda v. Pickard
648 F.2d 989 (5th Cir. 1981).

Before Thornberry, J., Randall, J., and Tate, J.
Randall, J.:

Plaintiffs, Mexican-American children and their parents who represent a class of others similarly situated, instituted this action against the Raymondville, Texas Independent School District (RISD) alleging that the district engaged in policies and practices of racial discrimination against Mexican-Americans which deprived the plaintiffs and their class of rights secured to them by the fourteenth amendment and 42 U.S.C. § 1983 (1976), Title VI of the Civil Rights Act of 1964, 42 U.S.C. § 2000d *et seq.* (1976), and the Equal Educational Opportunities Act of 1974, 20 U.S.C. § 1701 *et seq.* (1976). Specifically, plaintiffs charged that the school district unlawfully discriminated against them by using an ability grouping system for classroom assignments which was based on racially and ethnically discriminatory criteria and resulted in impermissible classroom segregation, by discriminating against Mexican-Americans in the hiring and promotion of faculty and administrators, and by failing to implement adequate bilingual education to overcome the linguistic barriers that impede the plaintiffs' equal participation in the educational program of the district. . . .

[T]he district court entered judgment in favor of the defendants based upon its determination that the policies and practices of the RISD, in the areas of hiring and promotion of faculty and administrators, ability grouping of students, and bilingual education did not violate any constitutional or statutory rights of the plaintiff class. From that judgment, the plaintiffs have brought this appeal. . . .

* * *

[W]e think it helpful to outline some of the basic demographic characteristics of the Raymondville school district. Raymondville is located in Willacy County, Texas. Willacy County is in the Rio Grande Valley; by conservative estimate based on census data, 77% of the population of the county is Mexican-American and almost all of the remaining 23% is "Anglo." The student population of RISD is about 85% Mexican-American.

Willacy County ranks 248th out of the 254 Texas counties in average family income. Approximately one-third of the population of Raymondville is composed of migrant farm workers. Three-quarters of the students in the Raymondville schools qualify for the federally funded free school lunch program. The district's assessed property valuation places it among the lowest 10% of all Texas counties in its per capita student expenditures. . . .

* * *

RISD currently operates a bilingual education program for all students in kindergarten through third grade. The language ability of each student entering the Raymondville program is assessed when he or she enters school. The language dominance test currently employed by the district is approved for this purpose by the TEA. The program of bilingual instruction offered students in the Raymondville schools has been developed with the assistance of expert consultants retained by the TEA and employs a group of materials developed by a regional educational center operated by the TEA. The articulated goal of the program is to teach students fundamental reading and writing skills in both Spanish and English by the end of the third grade.

Although the program's emphasis is on the development of language skills in the two languages, other cognitive and substantive areas are addressed, *e.g.*, mathematics skills are taught and tested in Spanish as well as English during these years. All of the teachers employed in the bilingual education program of the district have met the minimum state requirements to teach bilingual classes. However, only about half of these teachers are Mexican-American and native-Spanish speakers; the other teachers in the program have been certified to teach bilingual classes following a 100 hour course designed by TEA to give them a limited Spanish vocabulary (700

words) and an understanding of the theory and methods employed in bilingual programs. Teachers in the bilingual program are assisted by classroom aides, most of whom are fluent in Spanish.

RISD does not offer a program of bilingual education after the third grade. In grades 4 and 5, although classroom instruction is only in English, Spanish-speaking teacher aides are used to assist students having language difficulties which may impair their ability to participate in classroom activities. For students in grades 4–12 having limited English proficiency or academic deficiencies in other areas, the RISD provides assistance in the form of a learning center operated at each school. This center provides a diagnostic/prescriptive program in which students' particular academic deficiencies, whether in language or other areas, are identified and addressed by special remedial programs. Approximately 1,000 of the district's students, almost one-third of the total enrollment, receive special assistance through small classes provided by these learning centers. The district also makes English as a Second Language classes and special tutoring in English available to all students in all grades; this program is especially designed to meet the needs of limited-English-speaking students who move into the district in grades above 3.

Plaintiffs claim that the bilingual education and language remediation programs offered by the Raymondville schools are educationally deficient and unsound and that RISD's failure to alter and improve these programs places the district in violation of Title VI and the Equal Educational Opportunities Act. The plaintiffs claim that the RISD programs fail to comport with the requirements of the "Lau Guidelines" promulgated in 1975 by the Department of Health, Education and Welfare. Specifically, plaintiffs contend that the articulated goal of the Raymondville program—to teach limited-English-speaking children to read and write in both English and Spanish at grade level—is improper because it overemphasizes the development of English language skills to the detriment of the child's overall cognitive development. Under the Lau Guidelines, plaintiffs argue, "pressing English on the child is not the first goal of language remediation." Plaintiffs criticize not only the premise and purpose of the RISD language programs but also particular aspects of the implementation of the program. Specifically, plaintiffs take issue with the tests the district employs to identify and assess limited-English-speaking children and the qualifications of the teachers and staff involved in the district's language remediation program. Plaintiffs contend that in both of these areas RISD falls short of standards established by the Lau Guidelines and thus has fallen out of compliance with Title VI and the EEOA.

We agree with the district court that RISD's program does not violate Title VI. Much of the plaintiffs' argument with regard to Title VI is based upon the premise that the Lau Guidelines are administrative regulations applicable to the RISD and thus should be given great weight by us in assessing the legal sufficiency of the district's programs. This premise is, however, flawed. . . .

* * *

Following the Supreme Court's decision in *Lau,* HEW developed the "Lau Guidelines" as a suggested compliance plan for school districts which, as a result of *Lau,* were in violation of Title VI because they failed to provide any English language assistance to students having limited English proficiency. Clearly, Raymondville is not culpable of such a failure. Under these circumstances, the fact that Raymondville provides (and long has provided) a program of language remediation which differs in some respects from these guidelines is, as the opinion of the Reviewing Authority for the OCR noted, "not in itself sufficient to rule that program unlawful in the first instance."

* * *

We must confess to serious doubts not only about the relevance of the Lau Guidelines to this case but also about the continuing vitality of the rationale of the Supreme Court's opinion in *Lau v. Nichols* which gave rise to those guidelines. *Lau* was written prior to *Washington v. Davis,* . . . in which the Court held that a discriminatory purpose, and not simply a disparate impact, must be shown to establish a violation of the Equal Protection Clause, and *University of California Regents v. Bakke,* . . . in which . . . a majority of the court interpreted Title VI to be coextensive with the Equal Protection Clause. Justice Brennan's opinion (in which Justices White, Marshall and Blackmun joined) in *Bakke* explicitly acknowledged that these developments raised serious questions about the vitality of *Lau.*

. . . Although the Supreme Court in *Bakke* did not expressly overrule *Lau,* as we noted above, we understand the clear import of *Bakke* to be that Title VI, like the Equal Protection Clause, is violated only by conduct animated by an intent to discriminate and not by conduct which, although benignly moti-

vated, has a differential impact on persons of different races. Whatever the deficiencies of the RISD's program of language remediation may be, we do not think it can seriously be asserted that this program was intended or designed to discriminate against Mexican-American students in the district. . . .

Plaintiffs, however, do not base their legal challenge to the district's language program solely on Title VI. They also claim that the district's current program is unlawful under § 1703(f) of the EEOA which makes it unlawful for an educational agency to fail to take "appropriate action to overcome language barriers that impede equal participation by its students in its instructional programs." . . . [W]e have very little legislative history from which to glean the Congressional intent behind the EEOA's provisions. Thus, . . . we shall adhere closely to the plain language of § 1703(f) in defining the meaning of this provision. . . . [Section] 1703(f) does not contain language that explicitly incorporates an intent requirement nor . . . does this subsection employ words such as "discrimination" whose legal definition has been understood to incorporate an intent requirement. . . . [I]n *Morales v. Shannon,* . . . we assumed that the failure of an educational agency to undertake appropriate efforts to remedy the language deficiencies of its students, regardless of whether such a failure is motivated by an intent to discriminate against those students, would violate § 1703(f) and we think that such a construction of that subsection is most consistent with the plain meaning of the language employed in § 1703(f). Thus, although serious doubts exist about the continuing vitality of *Lau v. Nichols* as a judicial interpretation of the requirements of Title VI or the fourteenth amendment, the essential holding of *Lau, i.e.,* that schools are not free to ignore the need of limited-English-speaking children for language assistance to enable them to participate in the instructional program of the district, has now been legislated by Congress, acting pursuant to its power to enforce the fourteenth amendment, in § 1703(f). The difficult question presented by plaintiffs' challenge to the current language remediation programs in RISD is really whether Congress in enacting § 1703(f) intended to go beyond the essential requirement of *Lau,* that the schools do something, and impose, through the use of the term "appropriate action" a more specific obligation on state and local educational authorities.

* * *

We note that . . . Congress, in describing the remedial obligation it sought to impose on the states in the EEOA, did not specify that a state must provide a program of "bilingual education" to all limited-English-speaking students. We think Congress' use of the less specific term, "appropriate action," rather than "bilingual education," indicates that Congress intended to leave state and local educational authorities a substantial amount of latitude in choosing the programs and techniques they would use to meet their obligations under the EEOA. However, by including an obligation to address the problem of language barriers in the EEOA and granting limited-English-speaking students a private right of action to enforce that obligation in § 1706, Congress also must have intended to insure that schools made a genuine and good faith effort, consistent with local circumstances and resources, to remedy the language deficiencies of their students and deliberately placed on federal courts the difficult responsibility of determining whether that obligation had been met.

. . . Confronted, reluctantly, with this type of task in this case, we have attempted to devise a mode of analysis which will permit ourselves and the lower courts to fulfill the responsibility Congress has assigned to us without unduly substituting our educational values and theories for the educational and political decisions reserved to state or local school authorities or the expert knowledge of educators.

In a case such as this one . . ., we believe that the responsibility of the federal court is threefold. First, the court must examine carefully the evidence the record contains concerning the soundness of the educational theory or principles upon which the challenged program is based. This, of course, is not to be done with any eye toward discerning the relative merits of sound but competing bodies of expert educational opinion, for choosing between sound but competing theories is properly left to the educators and public officials charged with responsibility for directing the educational policy of a school system. The state of the art in the area of language remediation may well be such that respected authorities legitimately differ as to the best type of educational program for limited-English-speaking students and we do not believe that Congress in enacting § 1703(f) intended to make the resolutions of these differences the province of federal courts. The court's responsibility, insofar as educational theory is concerned, is only to ascertain that a school system is pursuing a program informed by an educational theory recognized as sound by some experts in the field or, at least, deemed a legitimate experimental strategy.

The court's second inquiry would be whether the programs and practices actually used by a school system are reasonably calculated to implement effectively the educational theory adopted by the school. We do not believe that it may fairly be said that a school system is taking appropriate action to remedy language barriers if, despite the adoption of a promising theory, the system fails to follow through with practices, resources and personnel necessary to transform the theory into reality.

Finally, a determination that a school system has adopted a sound program for alleviating the language barriers impeding the educational progress of some of its students and made bona fide efforts to make the program work does not necessarily end the court's inquiry into the appropriateness of the system's actions. If a school's program, although premised on a legitimate educational theory and implemented through the use of adequate techniques, fails, after being employed for a period of time sufficient to give the plan a legitimate trial, to produce results indicating that the language barriers confronting students are actually being overcome, that program may, at that point, no longer constitute appropriate action as far as that school is concerned. We do not believe Congress intended that under § 1703(f) a school would be free to persist in a policy which, although it may have been "appropriate" when adopted, in the sense that there were sound expectations for success and bona fide efforts to make the program work, has, in practice, proved a failure.

* * *

In this case, the plaintiffs' challenge . . . does not rest on an argument over the soundness of the educational policy being pursued by the district, but rather on the alleged inadequacy of the program actually implemented by the district. Plaintiffs contend that in three areas essential to the adequacy of a bilingual program—curriculum, staff and testing—Raymondville falls short. Plaintiffs contend that although RISD purports to offer a bilingual education program in grades K–3, the district's curriculum actually overemphasizes the development of reading and writing skills in English to the detriment of education in other areas such as mathematics and science, and that, as a result, children whose first language was Spanish emerge from the bilingual education program behind their classmates in these other areas. . . .

Even if we accept this allegation as true, however, we do not think that a school system which provides limited-English-speaking students with a curriculum, during the early part of their school career, which has, as its primary objective, the development of literacy in English, has failed to fulfill its obligations under § 1703(f), even if the result of such a program is an interim sacrifice of learning in other areas during this period. The language of § 1703(f) speaks in terms of taking action "to overcome language barriers" which impede the "equal participation" of limited-English-speaking children in the regular instructional program. We believe the statute clearly contemplates that provision of a program placing primary emphasis on the development of English language skills would constitute "appropriate action."

Limited-English-speaking students entering school face a task not encountered by students who are already proficient in English. Since the number of hours in any school day is limited, some of the time which limited-English-speaking children will spend learning English may be devoted to other subjects by students who entered school already proficient in English. In order to be able ultimately to participate equally with the students who entered school with an English language background, the limited-English-speaking students will have to acquire both English language proficiency comparable to that of the average native speakers and to recoup any deficits which they may incur in other areas of the curriculum as a result of this extra expenditure of time on English language development. We understand § 1703(f) to impose on educational agencies not only an obligation to overcome the direct obstacle to learning which the language barrier itself poses, but also a duty to provide limited-English-speaking-ability students with assistance in other areas of the curriculum where their equal participation may be impaired because of deficits incurred during participation in an agency's language remediation program. If no remedial action is taken to overcome the academic deficits that limited-English-speaking students may incur during a period of intensive language training, then the language barrier, although itself remedied, might, nevertheless, pose a lingering and indirect impediment to these students' equal participation in the regular instructional program. We also believe, however, that § 1703(f) leaves schools free to determine whether they wish to discharge these obligations simultaneously, by implementing a program designed to keep limited-English-speaking students at grade level in other areas of the curriculum by providing instruction in their native language at the same time that an English language development effort is pursued, or to address these problems in sequence, by focusing first on the development of English language skills and then later providing students with compensatory and supplemental education to remedy deficiencies in other areas which they may develop during this period. . . . Therefore, we disagree with plaintiffs' assertion that a school system which chooses to focus first on English language development and later provides students with an intensive remedial program to help them catch up in other areas of the curriculum has failed to fulfill its statutory obligation under § 1703(f).

. . . [W]e are more troubled by the plaintiffs' allegations that the district's implementation of the program has been severely deficient in the area of preparing its teachers for bilingual education. . . . We begin by noting that any school district that chooses to fulfill its obligations under § 1703 by means of a bilingual education program has undertaken a responsibility to provide teachers who are able competently to teach in such a program. The record in this case indicates that some of the teachers employed in the RISD bilingual program have a very limited command of Spanish, despite completion of the TEA course. . . .

The record in this case thus raises serious doubts about the actual language competency of the teachers employed in bilingual classrooms by RISD and about the degree to which the district is making a genuine effort to assess and improve the qualifications of its bilingual teachers. As in any educational program, qualified teachers are a critical component of the success of a language remediation program. A bilingual education program, however sound in theory, is clearly unlikely to have a significant impact on the language barriers confronting limited-English-speaking school children, if the teachers charged with day-to-day responsibility for educating these children are termed "qualified" despite the fact that they operate in the classroom under their own unremedied language disability. The use of Spanish-speaking aides may be an appropriate interim measure, but such aides cannot, RISD acknowledges, take the place of qualified bilingual teachers. The record in this case strongly suggests that the efforts RISD has made to overcome the language barriers confronting many of the teachers assigned to the bilingual education program are inadequate. On this record, we think a finding to the contrary would be clearly erroneous. Nor can there be any question that deficiencies in the in-service training of teachers for bilingual classrooms seriously undermine the promise of the district's bilingual education program. Until deficiencies in this aspect of the program's implementation are remedied, we do not think RISD can be deemed to be taking "appropriate action" to overcome the language disabilities of its students. Although we certainly hope and expect that RISD will attempt to hire teachers who are already qualified to teach in a bilingual classroom as positions become available, we are by no means suggesting that teachers already employed by the district should be replaced or that the district is limited to hiring only teachers who are already qualified to teach in a bilingual program. We are requiring only that RISD undertake further measures to improve the ability of any teacher, whether now or hereafter employed, to teach effectively in a bilingual classroom.

* * *

The third specific area in which plaintiffs claim that RISD programs are seriously deficient is in the testing and evaluation of students having limited English proficiency. . . .

. . . Plaintiffs contend, RISD apparently does not deny, and we agree that proper testing and evaluation is essential in determining the progress of students involved in a bilingual program and ultimately, in evaluating the program itself. In their brief, plaintiffs contend that RISD's testing program is inadequate because the limited-English-speaking students in the bilingual program are not tested in their own language to determine their progress in areas of the curriculum other than English language literacy skills. Although during the bilingual program Spanish-speaking students receive much of their instruction in these other areas in the Spanish language, the achievement level of these students is tested, in part, by the use of standardized English language achievement tests. No standardized Spanish language tests are used. Plaintiffs contend that testing the achievement levels of children, who are admittedly not yet literate in English and are receiving instruction in another language, through the use of an English language achievement test, does not meaningfully assess their achievement, any more than it does their ability, a contention with which we can scarcely disagree.

Valid testing of students' progress in these areas is, we believe, essential to measure the adequacy of a language remediation program. The progress of limited-English-speaking students in these other areas of the curriculum must be measured by means of a standardized test in their own language because no other device is adequate to determine their progress vis-a-vis that of their English-speaking counterparts. . . . [T]hese students cannot be permitted to incur irreparable academic deficits during this period. Only by measuring the actual progress of students in these areas during the language remediation program can it be determined that such irremediable deficiencies are not being incurred. . . .

Finally plaintiffs contend that test results indicate that the limited-English-speaking students who participate in the district's bilingual education program do not reach a parity of achievement with students who entered school already proficient in English at any time throughout the elementary grades and that since the district's language program has failed to establish such parity, it cannot be deemed "appropriate action" under § 1703(f). Although this question was raised at the district court level, no findings were made on this claim. While under some circumstances it may be proper for a court to examine the achievement scores of students involved in a language remediation program in order to determine whether this group appears on the whole to attain parity of participation with other students, we do not think that such an inquiry is, as yet, appropriate with regard to RISD. Such an inquiry may become proper after the inadequacies in the implementation of the RISD's program, which we have identified, have been corrected and the program has operated with the benefit of these improvements for a period of time sufficient to expect meaningful results.

To summarize, we affirm the district court's conclusion that RISD's bilingual education program is not violative of Title VI; however, we reverse the district court's judgment with respect to the other issues presented on appeal and we remand these issues for further proceedings not inconsistent with this opinion. . . .

NOTES AND QUESTIONS

1. Castaneda: *Scope of the Decision*

Is the court correct to question the continuing vitality of *Lau* — to insist that Title VI, like the Fourteenth Amendment, requires a showing of intentional discrimination and not just discriminatory impact? *See Guardians Association v. Civil Service Commission*, chapter 4, *supra.*

How does the court read the statutory language that requires school districts to take "appropriate action to overcome language barriers"? Does the legislation require the court to become the arbiter of educational effectiveness—to assess "the soundness of educational theory," the relationship between theory and practice, and the success of the venture? Is this an appropriate judicial role?

The court notes that "[l]ow test scores may well reflect many obstacles to learning other than language" and acknowledges, with becoming understatement, that "the process of delineating the causes . . . may well be a complicated one." Suppose the test scores of limited-English-proficient students start out, and remain, well below those of the native-language population. What remedy would then be appropriate? Part II, Section B, *infra*, discusses these policy questions in greater detail.

2. Monolingual Teachers and Limited-English-Proficient Students

In *Teresa P. v. Berkeley Unified School District*, 724 F.Supp. 698 (N.D.Cal. 1989), a law reform group, the Multicultural Education Training and Advocacy Project (META), challenged the school district's approach to teaching limited-English-proficient students. The district offered transitional bilingual instruction for Spanish- and Cantonese-speaking elementary school children, and English as a Second Language (ESL) instruction to other language groups in elementary school and to all secondary school students. The ESL teachers were not bilingual. The California Education Department interprets federal law as mandating "equality of educational achievement," when limited-English-proficient and native English speakers are compared.

META argued that without any instruction in their native tongues, students would not develop their academic skills while learning English. The district court, following *Castaneda*, held that federal law "does not require school districts to adopt a specific educational theory or implement an ideal academic program"; instead, it leaves local officials "substantial latitude. . . ." *See also Gomez v. Illinois State Board of Education*, 811 F.2d 1030 (7th Cir. 1987). What is required is that the program be supported by a plausible pedagogical theory—of which, given the uncertain state of the art, there are many—and that it actually teach English to limited-English-proficient children. If the students do not suffer "permanent or irreparable" academic harm while

learning English, courts will not intervene. Moreover, the court declared that specialized credentials for teachers are not required, for "good teachers are good teachers no matter what the educational challenge may be."

Berkeley enrolled 571 limited-English-proficient students, out of a total enrollment of approximately 8,000, and they were spread through the district's schools. No fewer than thirty-eight languages—among them Farsi, Samoan, and Armenian—are represented among the 571 students. What bearing, if any, should these facts have had on the nature of the school district's legal obligation to provide bilingual instruction? *Compare Zambrano v. Oakland Unified School District*, No. 584503-9 (Alameda Superior Court, May 1, 1985), discussed in Moran, "Bilingual Education as a Status Conflict," 75 *Calif.L.Rev.* 321, 335–38 (1984).

3. Language and Community

The Hutterite community, which emigrated to the United States a century ago, still speaks Tyrolean German (a combination of sixteenth-century German and twentieth-century anglicizations); only the Hutterites speak this language. This language is retained for religious reasons, for reasons of cultural tradition, and to foster a separate sense of identity. Hutterite children growing up in the community speak only Tyrolean German.

To what remedy, if any, are the Hutterites entitled under federal law: a bilingual program, a bilingual-bicultural program, a publicly run school operated by the community to preserve the children's sense of cultural identity? How, if at all, is *Wisconsin v. Yoder*, discussed in chapter 1, relevant? *See Deerfield Hutterian Association v. Ipswich Board of Education*, 468 F.Supp. 1219 (D.S.D. 1979).

4. The Conflict with Desegregation

Because special assistance for the limited-English-proficient requires some separation, such programs potentially conflict with desegregation decrees. For a discussion of the fit between bilingual instruction and desegregation, *see United States v. Texas*, 680 F.2d 356 (5th Cir. 1982); *Morgan v. Kerrigan*, 401 F.Supp. 216 (D.Mass. 1975), *aff'd*, 530 F.2d 401 (1st Cir. 1976); Moran, "Milo's Miracle," 29 *Conn.L.Rev.* 1079 (1997); Roos, "Bilingual Education: The Hispanic Response to Unequal Educational Opportunity," 42 *Law & Contemp.Probs.* 111 (1978). *Compare Cintron v. Brentwood Union Free*

School District, 455 F.Supp. 57 (E.D.N.Y. 1978). *See also* the discussion in chapter 4 of desegregation in tri-ethnic school districts.

B. Policy and Politics

1. Introduction: The Persisting Controversy. There is apparently very little about the education of limited-English-proficient students that could be described as uncontroversial. Should bilingual education be transitional? Should students be placed as quickly as possible in English-language classes? Should the goal of English-acquisition be balanced against maintaining full academic competency in other subjects, such as mathematics, social studies, and science? Is the goal to maintain (or in some instances to foster) competency in the students' native language and/or native culture? Debated too, as the cases suggest, are the techniques, which range from native language instruction to classes conducted entirely in English. The following excerpt speaks to the passions aroused by bilingualism:

"Bye-bye to Bilingual Ed?"

Jorge Amselle, 15 *World & I*, March 1, 2000.

* * *

Throughout the country's past, the notion of bilingual education was essentially at odds with the prevailing U.S. "melting-pot" culture. Assimilation, not separation, has historically been the key to America's nation-building success, and a common, standardized language has been, many argue, indispensable. This ideology has played a key role in America's domestic policies toward immigrants, particularly in the area of education.

At the start of the twentieth century, schools were placed in the forefront of new "Americanization" efforts, which the arrival of large numbers of newcomers had fostered. Schools focused on immersing their students in English and teaching American history, customs, and traditions. Native language and cultures had no place in the public schools and were to be left at home. This policy dominated American education until the civil rights upheavals of the 1960s.

Until that time, the notion of bilingual education had been rejected out of hand. Comments by Arturo Vargas, current chairman of the National Hispanic Leadership Agenda, illustrate the mindset of the era. "History has proven that English-only instruction harms Hispanic students in several ways," he says. "It makes their acquisition of English more difficult and frustrating, it unnecessarily delays their academic subject matter learning, it prevents parents with limited English skills from actively participating in their children's schooling, and it sharply increases the rate at which Hispanic students drop out of school."

These dropout rates motivated Congress to pass the bilingual education act in 1968, providing federal funding for programs that taught part of the day in a child's native language. Sen. Ralph Yarborough (D-Texas), sponsor of the act, stressed that the purpose of his bill was "not to try to make the mother tongue the dominant language, but just to try to make those children fully literate in English."

In 1974, the Supreme Court held in *Lau v. Nichols* that Chinese students in sink-or-swim programs in San Francisco had a civil right to receive specialized assistance services. The court did not, however, mandate any particular approach.

According to NABE, "Bilingual education is an instructional approach that uses a child's native language to make instruction meaningful. Bilingual education programs build upon the knowledge that all children bring to school." In essence, bilingual programs were meant to offer academic instruction in the native language until English was mastered so that students would not fall behind.

Clash of the Scholars

Stephen Krashen, a professor of education at the University of Southern California and a leading advocate of bilingual education, explains his educational theory in the book *Condemned Without a Trial: Bogus Arguments Against Bilingual Education.*

"The knowledge that children get through their first language helps make the English they hear and read more comprehensible," Krashen says. "Literacy developed in the primary language transfers to the second language."

A principal aspect of bilingual theory is that students must spend five to seven years mastering their native language before they can learn English. But, according to Rosalie Pedalino Porter, a researcher and former director of bilingual education programs in Lowell, Massachusetts, "Bilingual education is a classic example of an experiment that was begun with the best of humanitarian intentions but has turned out to be terribly wrongheaded."

Educators who are critical of bilingual education instead support alternative programs that focus more on English instruction. Christine Rossell, a professor at Boston University, found that a structured, intensive program of English acquisition is exactly what most children who speak less-common languages receive. English as a Second Language programs provide instruction to students in English acquisition for a portion of their school day from a teacher specially trained in improving language skills.

"The research evidence suggests that all-English instruction holds the least risk and usually has the greatest benefit for limited-English-proficient children," Rossell declares.

This contrasts sharply with the views of Jim Cummins of the University of Toronto, who is widely viewed as the developer of bilingual education theory. Cummins, speaking before a gathering of the American Association on Higher Education in Washington, D.C., last March, said that "the academic debate lines up virtually all North American applied linguists who have carried out research on language learning as advocates of bilingual programs against only a handful of academics who oppose bilingual education."

Cummins often denounces the "coercive relations of power" that he discerns in the traditional American multiethnic classroom. He sees this coercion stemming from a "curriculum that reflects only the experience and values of white middle-class English-speaking students." Those who disagree with him are branded "intellectual xenophobes" and "cultural hegemonists."

Such belligerence and arrogance, critics of bilingual education say, help keep this form of schooling among the dominant movements on the education front today. Although bilingual education has been thrown on the defensive nationwide and rolled back in a few localities, it is still a fixture in most school districts and will likely remain so for years to come.

* * *

This debate has been carried out on the federal level, most notably by former Education Secretary William Bennett. In a 1985 address to the Association for a Better New York, published in *La Raza Law Journal* (1 *La Raza L.J.* 213 (1986)), Bennett argues that "we expect our schools to help teach all of our students English, the common language that will enable them to participate fully in our political, economic, and social life." While "pride in one's heritage is natural and commendable . . . the responsibility of the federal government must be to help ensure that local schools succeed in teaching non-English students English." That was the original purpose of the Bilingual Education Act, says Bennett, claiming that it has become so " 'perverted and politicized' that . . . English has been sort of thinned out and stretched out and in many cases banished into the mists and all of the courses tended to be taught in Spanish." Methods of instruction may well vary, Bennett declares, "but the goal of any method should be clear: Fluency in English." *See also* R. Porter, *Forked Tongue* (1990).

Not surprisingly, many scholars who support bilingual education took strong exception. Replying in the same issue of *La Raza Law Journal* (1 *La Raza L. J.* 225 (1986)), Lori Orum and Raul Yzaguirre argue that Bennett is too narrow in his focus on English language instruction for those who don't speak the language—that the "total educational well-being of limited-English proficient children" is the government's responsibility. It is not entirely clear that Bennett would disagree with this assessment; the real difference may be the fear, on the part of Orum and Yzaguirre, that Bennett is upsetting a delicate bipartisan consensus and would "substantially reduce the amount of federal support available for bilingual education." *See generally* Moran, "Bilingual Education as a Status Conflict," 75 *Calif.L.Rev.* 321 (1987). Of concern, too, is the perception that Bennett's position may give aid and comfort to those who promote the English-only cause, in schools as well as in the society generally. *See, e.g.*, Chavez, "Language Policy and Language Rights in the United States," in T. Kangas and J. Cummins, eds., *From Shame to Struggle: Language Policy and Language Rights* 42 (1989); K. Hakuta, *Mirror of Language: The Debate on Bilingualism* (1986); R. Lamm and G. Imhoff, *The Immigration Time Bomb: The Fragmenting of America* (1985); N. Glazer, *Ethnic Dilemmas* (1983); Tanton, "Bilingual Education: Is It Threatening to Divide the United States Along Language Lines?" *Vital Issues* 1 (Nov. 1984).

This longstanding controversy has not abated. Recently, Secretary of Education Richard Riley expressed his support for dual-language instruction as a way to capitalize on the assets that immigrant students, particularly Latinos, bring to the public schools. Hardi, "Riley Promotes Bilingual Instruction in Speech on Latino Education," *Chronicle of Higher Education*, Mar. 24, 2000, at A35. His speech was immediately attacked by bilingual education foe Linda Chavez, who insisted that Riley review the track record for native-language instruction and endorse English-immersion programs instead. Chavez, "Reviving Bi-lingual With Dual-Immersion," *Wash. Times*, Mar. 26, 2000, at B3.

2. The Contribution of Research. Both Bennett and Chavez on the one hand, and Riley, Orum, and Yzaguirre on the other, call upon educational research to support their respective positions. This is familiar news. Three years after the Office of Civil Rights issued its memorandum specifying remedies that a school district might adopt to comply with *Lau*—the so-called Lau Guidelines—a study prepared for HEW by the American Institutes for Research (AIR), *Education of the Impact of ESEA Title VII Spanish/English Bilingual Education Program* (1978), sharply criticized the program. It concluded: (1) in English, participation in a bilingual education project did not produce gains in achievement above what would be expected had the students been assigned to a traditional classroom; indeed, in several grades the nonparticipating students made slightly greater gains; (2) in mathematics, students participating in an ESEA Title VII project had achievement gains approximately equal to those of non–Title VII students; and (3) while Hispanic students showed improvement in Spanish reading, the extent to which such gains should be attributed to the program was not clear.

The AIR report in turn produced substantial critical reaction, mostly leveled at its methodology. The Center for Applied Linguistics, for example, notes: (1) the report aggregates very different programs and populations, thus canceling out the positive effects of good programs; (2) the short (five-month) period between pretest and posttest makes findings concerning the lack of achievement gains unreliable; (3) the "comparison groups" were never tested for comparability at the outset of the study, and they may have started with substantial differences in achievement.

Over two decades after the AIR Report, there is no consensus on the efficacy of bilingual instruction.

"The Educational Effectiveness of Bilingual Education"

C. Rossell and K. Baker, 30 *Research in the Teaching of English* 9–12, 19–26 (Feb. 1996).*

* * *

The ill-considered and thoughtless treatment of linguistic minorities during the first half of this century (e.g., mislabeling LEP children as mentally retarded and punishing LEP children who used their native tongue in school), combined with the continuing problem of a high dropout rate and low achievement, has influenced many social scientists, practitioners, civil rights attorneys, and reviewers of the research to believe that any policy which ignores the mother tongue in favor of English is racist, and any policy which maintains the mother tongue, however inadequately, is equitable. This has created an atmosphere in which it is difficult for anyone to criticize current policy in this field, and all too easy for both supporters and critics of bilingual education to interpret flawed studies as support for, or refutation of, bilingual education.

To assess the educational effectiveness of transitional bilingual education, it must be compared to three other educational programs for LEP children. The first instructional alternative we call *submersion*, commonly known as "sink-or-swim." In this model, the LEP child is placed in a regular English classroom with English-speaking children and given no more special help than any child with educational problems.

A second alternative is *English as a Second Language* (ESL) instruction for one or two periods a day, or in some districts two or three periods a week, and participation in the regular classroom for the rest of the time. ESL is a pull-out program usually based on a special curriculum for teaching English to LEP children, but the instructors do not have to speak the child's native language.

A third alternative is *structured immersion* where instruction is in the language being learned (L2), but the teacher speaks the students' native tongue (L1). The second language used in these programs is always geared to the children's language proficiency at each stage so that it is comprehensible. The native tongue is used only in the rare instances when the student cannot complete a task without it. The student thus learns the second language and subject matter content simultaneously. Immersion programs in which the second language is not the dominant language of the country typically include at least 30–60 minutes a day of native tongue language arts beginning sometime in the early elementary years. In fact, most of the Canadian "immersion" programs become bilingual programs after the first grade and,

---

*Editor's Note: citations to scholarly works have been inserted as footnotes and identified with small letters *a*, *b*, etc. When other footnotes appear, they are numbered as they appear in the original text.

as a result, serve as a laboratory for assessing the effect of "time-on-task" in second language learning.

In transitional bilingual education (TBE), the student is taught to read and write in the native tongue, and subject matter is also taught in the native tongue. The second language (English) is initially taught for only a small portion of the day. As the child progresses in English, the amount of instructional time in the native tongue is reduced and English increased, until the student is proficient enough in English to join the regular instructional program. The rationale underlying TBE differs depending on the age of the child. For very young children, learning to read in the native tongue first is considered a necessary condition for optimal reading ability in the second language. For all children, it is argued that learning a second language takes time and children should not lose ground in other subject matters, particularly math, during that time period.

A variation on transitional bilingual education is bilingual maintenance. These programs resemble TBE in their early years, but they differ in that the goal of a bilingual maintenance program is to produce bilingual children and thus students are not exited when they master English. Although bilingual maintenance programs enjoy a great deal of support from the intellectual community, they are not implemented widely because they do not enjoy political support from the state and federal legislatures that fund bilingual education.

The majority of elementary school programs have as their goal exiting a student after three years. But these programs also allow students to stay in the program longer than three years if they are judged to be below par in English language skills. Indeed, many children stay in a bilingual program throughout their elementary school career. Transitional bilingual education is less common once a child reaches the grade where departmentalization occurs and different subjects are taught by different teachers. Because teachers have to be certified in both a subject matter and in a foreign language to teach in a bilingual program in junior high or high school, few school districts are able to staff bilingual programs at these grade levels. Thus the typical LEP child enters a regular English program at junior high school. It is only in large school districts with large numbers of LEP students of a single language group that native tongue instruction in a subject might occur at the secondary level.

According to Young and his colleagues[a] at least 40% of all LEP children nationwide are in TBE programs, and only 26% are in English instruction classrooms. The other 34% are divided among bilingual maintenance, Spanish instruction, and ESL classes. However, Okada's study found *no* projects which reported *English only* as a literacy goal for LEP students. The American Legislative Exchange Council[b] recently reported that 60% of the state and locally funded programs were labeled bilingual education in 1991–92. Thus, at least nominally, TBE appears to be the dominant special language instructional program in the United States. We use the word "nominally" in a deliberate sense, however, because it is quite clear from visiting classrooms and reading evaluation reports that virtually the only children receiving native tongue instruction in the United States according to the theory—learning to read and write in the native tongue and learning subject matter in the native tongue—are Spanish-speaking children and Creole-speaking Haitian children. Other bilingual education programs are generally closer to what we call structured immersion, even though for political, legal, or funding reasons they may describe themselves as "bilingual education." This phenomenon, of course, only complicates the issue of evaluating and analyzing the effects of bilingual education programs.

While ethnographic studies can tell us a great deal about what goes on in a bilingual classroom, they cannot tell us whether bilingual education is more or less effective than some other instructional approach. The typical ethnographic study is limited to one classroom and cannot tell us how the pedagogical approach varies across classrooms and ethnic groups. The first author, for example, visited more than a hundred bilingual education classrooms in Massachusetts and California over the last 15 years, discovering that Spanish-speaking elementary school children are the only LEP students in true bilingual education programs in those states, a situation we did not learn from the dozens of ethnographic studies of bilingual classrooms that we have read. Conclusions about the effectiveness of bilingual education as a pedagogical approach

---

[a]M. Young et al., *LEP Student Characteristics and School Services* (1984).

[b]American Legislative Exchange Council, *The Cost of Bilingual Education in the United States: 1991–1992* (1994).

cannot be drawn from these ethnographic studies, although they often are, because there are no comparisons to similar students in a different kind of classroom and no attempt to systematically link classroom processes to outcomes.

* * *

Results

If we consider only the 72 methodologically acceptable studies which assess alternative second language programs, . . . there is as yet . . . no consistent research support for transitional bilingual education as a superior instructional practice for improving the English language achievement of limited English proficient children.

* * *

TBE v. Submersion. . . . [F]or second language reading,[8] 22% of the studies show transitional bilingual education to be superior, 33% show it to be inferior, and 45% show it to be no different from submersion—that is, doing nothing. Altogether, 78% of the studies show TBE to be no different from or worse than the supposedly discredited submersion technique.[9]

In a standardized achievement test of language (a test of a student's understanding of grammatical rules), transitional bilingual education ranks more poorly than it does in reading. Seven percent of the studies show transitional bilingual education to be superior, 64% show it to be inferior, and 29% show it to be no different from submersion—doing nothing. Altogether, 93% of the studies show TBE to be no different from or worse than doing nothing at all.[10]

These more negative findings for language than for reading suggest that a child is less dependent on school for many of the skills learned in reading—

decoding, vocabulary, and understanding concepts—than they are for grammar. The fine rules of grammar, it appears, are learned mostly in school, and because they are more complex, they are more influenced by school time-on-task. Thus, these results suggest there is a risk that bilingual education students will incur a deficit in English grammatical rules because they have spent less time on them than have LEP children in an all-English environment.

In *math*, 9% of the studies show TBE to be superior, 35% show it to be inferior, and 56% show it to be no different from TBE. Altogether 91% of the studies show it to be no different from or worse than the supposedly discredited submersion technique in developing math proficiency.[11]

TBE v. ESL. Although many so-called submersion situations probably have an English-as-a-Second-Language (ESL) program where the students are pulled out of the regular classroom and taught English in small groups for one period each day or a few times a week, it is generally not specified in the evaluations. Nevertheless, we suspect that many of the studies classified . . . as submersion may in fact include an ESL pullout component. In 7 studies, transitional bilingual education is specifically compared to reading achievement in the regular classroom with ESL pullout. None of these studies show TBE to be better than ESL pullout in reading. . . . Of the 3 studies that examined language achievement, none showed TBE to be superior, 2 showed no difference between TBE and ESL, and 1 showed TBE to be worse. Of the 4 studies that examined mathematics, 1 showed TBE to be superior, 2 showed no difference, and 1 showed TBE to be worse.

TBE v. Structured Immersion. . . . Most of the studies [comparing TBE to structured immersion] come from the Canadian immersion programs which

---

[8]We included oral progress in preschool or kindergarten in this category because a reading test for these grades is obviously inappropriate.

[9]This is slightly more negative than Baker and de Kanter's 1981 findings [K. Baker and A. de Kanter, *Effectiveness of Bilingual Education: A Review of the Literature*. Final draft report for Office of Technical and Analytic Systems, U.S. Dept. of Ed. (1981)] that 33% of the studies found TBE to be superior, 17% found it to be inferior, and 50% found it to be no different from submersion. Altogether, 67% of their studies found TBE to be no different from or worse than submersion. It is also slightly more negative than Rossell and Ross's 1986 findings [C. Rossell and J. Ross, "The Social Science Evidence on Bilingual Education," 15 *J. of Law and Ed.* 385 (1986)] that in second language learning 29% of the studies show transitional bilingual education to be superior, 21% show it to be inferior, and 50% show it to be no different from submersion—doing nothing. Altogether, 71% found TBE to be no different or worse than the supposedly discredited submersion approach.

[10]Neither Baker and de Kanter nor Rossell and Ross examined language because at that time there were too few studies that examined this outcome.

[11]This is also slightly more negative than Baker and de Kanter [K. Baker and A. de Kanter, *Effectiveness of Bilingual Education: A Review of the Literature*. Final draft report for Office of Technical and Analytic Systems, U.S. Dept. of Ed. (1981); K. Baker and A. de Kanter, "An Answer from Research on Bilingual Education," 56 *Am.Ed* 157 (1983); K. Baker and A. de Kanter, "Federal Policy and the Effectiveness of Bilingual Education," in K. Baker and A. de Kanter, eds., *Bilingual Education* (1983)]. They concluded that 14% of the studies found TBE to be superior, 21% found it to be inferior, and 64% of the studies found TBE to be no different from submersion. Altogether, 85% of their studies found TBE to be no different from or worse than submersion. These findings are pretty much the same as Rossell and Ross [C. Rossell and J. Ross, "The Social Science Evidence on Bilingual Education," 15 *J.of Law and Ed.* 385 (1986)] however. They found that in mathematics, 7% of the studies showed TBE to be superior, 27% showed it to be inferior, and 67% showed it to be no different from TBE. Altogether 93% of the studies showed it to be no different or worse than the supposedly discredited submersion approach in developing math proficiency.

come in several carefully documented types—early immersion (which means late bilingual), delayed immersion (which means early bilingual), dual immersion, and so forth. In many cases we had to "translate" the programs into United States terminology. Twelve studies had reading outcomes, 1 study had language outcomes, and 8 studies had mathematics outcomes. No studies showed TBE to be superior to structured immersion in reading, language, or math. In reading, 83% of the studies showed TBE to be worse than structured immersion and 17% showed no difference. In language, the 1 study showed no difference. In mathematics, studies showed no difference and 3 studies showed TBE to be worse than immersion.

All but 4 of the studies of structured immersion compared to TBE or ESL were conducted in Canada. Most bilingual education advocates do not see the applicability of these studies to the United States. First, they argue that the studies are not relevant to the United States immigrant experience because the immersion and bilingual education students in Canada are middle class. In fact, however, the experiments were conducted with working class children as well and produced the same or better results. Both the middle class and working class English-speaking students who were immersed in French in kindergarten and grade one were almost the equal of native French-speaking students until the curriculum became bilingual in grade two, at which point their French ability declined and continued to decline as English was increased. The "time-on-task" principle—that is, the notion that the amount of time spent learning a subject is the greatest predictor of achievement in that subject—holds across classes in the Canadian programs.

A second argument made to dismiss the Canadian French immersion experiments as applicable to the United States is that the Canadian students were self-selected and their mother tongue was the dominant language of the country. The fact that the students were self-selected means that they were probably better language learners than other students, all other things being equal. Self-selected English language students taught bilingually after grade one were sometimes, but not always, the equal of the English controls because they heard English at home and in the rest of the non-school environment. Superior language learners hearing a language most of the time could sometimes, although not always, equal other students hearing it all of the time. Once the curriculum became bilingual, however, these students were never the equal of the French native speakers or of those English language students immersed completely in French. Thus, if self-selected, "elite" language learners have these problems, it is hard to imagine that ordinary LEP children in the United States would not encounter any of them. Accordingly, contrary to many interpretations of the Canadian experiments, we think there is much we can learn about second language learning from these experiments that is applicable to the United States experience, although clearly it is not a program that can be imported without major adaptation to the United States situation where immigrant children arrive at public school every day of the year, including the last day, and must be admitted regardless of their academic preparation.

TBE v. Maintenance Bilingual Education. The final category . . . compares transitional bilingual education to maintenance bilingual education. This study showed that transitional bilingual education produced significantly higher English reading achievement than maintenance bilingual education.[12]

TBE v. Submersion ESL. Because we suspect that many, if not most, of the so-called submersion alternatives had an ESL component, we show . . . the outcomes for a category that combines submersion and ESL studies. Because of the small number of studies that specifically examine ESL pullout, there is virtually no difference in the findings—81% of the studies show TBE to be no different from or worse than submersion/ESL in reading, 94% show TBE to be no different from or worse than submersion/ESL in language, and 89% show TBE to be no different from or worse than submersion/ESL in math.

. . . .Confronted with th[is] kind of evidence . . . , the advocates of bilingual education have sometimes contended that the issue is learning *in* a language, not learning a language. These data, however, do not show it to be superior in either learning a language or learning *in* a language—in this case, math. Moreover, there is no research evidence on the effects of TBE on learning other subjects such as geography,

---

[12]Ramirez and his colleagues [J. Ramirez et al., *Final Report: Longitudinal Study of Structured English Immersion Strategy, Early-Exit and Late-Exit Transitional Bilingual Education Programs for Language-Minority Children*, Vol. 1 and Vol. 2 (1991)] also examined maintenance bilingual education (late-exit bilingual education), but did not directly compare it to transitional bilingual education (contrary to media reports and his own conclusions). Although his graphs appear to show that the students in late-exit bilingual education were doing worse than the students in transitional bilingual education, no statistical analysis was performed to verify that.

social studies, and history because standardized achievement tests are not given in these content areas.[13] Thus, any assertion regarding the superiority of TBE in these areas is anecdotal. Moreover, the math findings for TBE suggest an important problem: Subject matter is taught in the native tongue, but the student is tested on his or her understanding of that subject in *English*. It is possible that for many students the difficulty of having to translate what was learned in another language may be great enough that the subject matter lost in the translation may equal or surpass what is lost in submersion before the second language is mastered enough to understand subject content. On the other hand, . . . the solution is not to test LEP children in their native tongue because the goal of TBE is that students reach their potentially highest level in a subject in English.

* * *

Other Research Reviews

This review of the research is not the first to show a lack of superiority for transitional bilingual education. Baker and de Kanter,[c] Engle,[d] Epstein,[e] Holland,[f] Rossell and Ross, and Rotberg[g] have also concluded that there is no research support for transitional bilingual education.

Given this evidence, on what basis have some reviewers of bilingual education research claimed superiority for the program? One strategy, used by Zappert and Cruz,[h] is to simply redefine the word. As they argue:

> No significant difference should not be interpreted as a negative finding for bilingual education . . . When one adds the fact that students in bilingual education classrooms learn two languages, their native language and a second language, one can conclude that a statistically non-significant finding demonstrates the positive advantages of bilingual education. (p. 8)

The problem with this argument is that the court decisions, the federal regulations, and state laws are based on the assumption that TBE produces *greater* English language achievement and content area mastery, not the same achievement. Doing nothing is assumed to be a violation of a child's equal educational opportunity that transitional bilingual education will *remedy*, rather than a violation whose outcome TBE does not alter.

Another strategy used in some research reviews to make transitional bilingual education appear to be superior is to include performance in Spanish language arts. Zappert and Cruz also do this. Again, while we agree Spanish language arts are important, it is not the goal of government policy nor the stated object of the court decisions. If we examine the findings of the 12 studies reviewed by Zappert and Cruz for their effect on *English* language achievement, 63% of the findings show no difference between transitional bilingual education and doing nothing.

Willig[i] conducted a meta-analysis of studies of bilingual education and concluded that transitional bilingual education was superior to all other alternatives. However, in order to do this, she excluded a large number of studies whose outcome measure could not be converted into an effect size. In addition, she excluded all studies conducted in foreign countries, leaving only 16 studies for analysis. . . . Finally, a careful reading of her results actually shows transitional bilingual education to be inferior to all-English instruction. It was only when she controlled for other variables, which partly eliminated the actual treatment effect, that TBE became superior.

There are similar problems with the conclusions of many of the research evaluations. A study by Leyba and his colleagues[j] of Santa Fe, New Mexico exemplifies this. It begins by criticizing the AIR national study by Danoff and his associates[k] because it

---

[13]Qualitative studies do not address the effectiveness of bilingual education on achievement in these areas because they never have a comparison group of students receiving an alternative treatment.

[c]K. Baker and A. de Kanter, *Effectiveness of Bilingual Education: A Review of the Literature*, Final draft report for Office of Technical and Analytic Systems, U.S. Dept. of Ed. (1981); Baker, "An Answer"; Baker, "Federal Policy."

[d]P. Engle, "The Use of the Vernacular Language in Education," in *Bilingual Education*, Center for Applied Linguistics Series No. 2 (1975).

[e]N. Epstein, *Language, Ethnicity and the Schools: Policy Alternatives for Bilingual-Bicultural Education* (1977).

[f]R. Holland, *Bilingual Education: Recent Evaluations of Local School District Programs and Related Research on Second-Language Learning* (1986).

[g]I. Rotberg, "Federal Policy in Bilingual Education," 52 *Am.Ed.* 30 (1982).

[h]L. Zappert and B. Cruz, *Bilingual Education: An Appraisal of Empirical Research* (1977).

[i]A. Willig, "A Meta-Analysis of Selected Studies on the Effectiveness of Bilingual Education," 55 *Rev. of Ed. Res.* 269 (1985).

[j]C. Leyba et al., *Longitudinal Study of the Title VII Bilingual Program in the Santa Fe Public Schools* (1978).

[k]M. Danoff, B. Arias and G. Coles, *Evaluation of the Impact of ESEA Title VII Spanish/English Bilingual Education Programs, Volume I and II* (1977); M. Danoff et al., *Evaluation of the Impact of ESEA Title VII Spanish/English Bilingual Education Program, Volume III and IV* (1978).

failed to study their "successful" program and concluded that, contrary to the findings of AIR, Title VII bilingual education students in Santa Fe "showed over time increasing capability in English language skills, [and] . . . in the majority of cases outperformed the non–Title VII students in Reading and Mathematics" (p. ii). The study could be rejected simply because it failed to control for the lower pre-program achievement of several comparison groups of non–Title VII students. But even disregarding this problem, the data presented in the report show virtually no difference after four and five years of bilingual education between those students in the program and similar students not in the program, contrary to the author's conclusions.[14]

This study exemplifies a problem with studies of bilingual education. One cannottrust an author's conclusion to be an accurate representation of the data on which it is supposedly based. Moreover, this is as true of the studies done by supporters of bilingual education as it is of those done by its critics. This field is so ideologically charged that no one is immune from ideological bias or preconceived notions. As a result, those attempting to make policy recommendations from the research must carefully read each study and draw their own conclusions. This does not guarantee that such conclusions will be free from bias, only that they will be free from someone else's bias.

* * *

Consider now a reply to Rossell and Baker's review of the research on bilingual education by Professor Jay P. Greene. He agrees that Rossell and Baker have adopted appropriate criteria for deciding which studies are methodologically sound. However, Greene contends that Rossell and Baker have themselves succumbed to a lack of rigor and consistency in applying these criteria.

"A Meta-Analysis of the Effectiveness of Bilingual Education"

J. Greene, Tomas Rivera Policy Institute (1998).

* * *

Method for Selecting Studies and Computing Results

The eleven studies included in this meta-analysis [of the effectiveness of bilingual education] are drawn from a list of 75 "methodologically acceptable" studies compiled by Christine Rossell and Keith Baker, two vocal critics of bilingual education, in a 1996 literature review. The Rossell and Baker list is used as the pool of studies examined for this meta-analysis for a few reasons despite the potential for bias in their selections. First, Rossell and Baker claim to have selected their methodologically acceptable studies based on criteria that I believe are reasonable. To be acceptable the studies had to:

1) compare students in a bilingual program to a control group of similar students
2) differences between the treatment and control groups had to be controlled statistically or assignment to treatment and control groups had to be random
3) results had to be based on standardized test scores in English, and
4) differences between the scores of treatment and control groups had to be determined by applying appropriate statistical tests.

In addition to these requirements this meta-analysis only included studies that measured the effects of bilingual programs after at least one academic year. Bilingual programs were defined as ones in which students with limited English proficiency are taught using at least some of their native language. An appropriate control group was one in which students were taught only in English. If students were not assigned to treatment and control groups randomly, adequate statistical controls for this non-random assignment was defined as requiring controls for individual previous test scores as well as at least some of the individual demographic factors that influence test scores (e.g. family income, parental education, etc.). Rossell and Baker identify 72 studies that they say meet these standards (although there are

---

[14]Powers and Rossman [S. Powers and M. Rossman, "Evidence of the Impact of Bilingual Education: A Meta Analysis" (paper presented at the annual Arizona Bilingual Education Conference, Tucson, AZ, 1983)] did a statistical analysis of the effects found in Leyba's study because they also were perplexed as to how it could call the TBE program successful when only 21% of its comparisons of the students in bilingual education with those not in bilingual education yielded statistically significant results. Its analysis, which also had no control for pre-treatment group differences, found no positive effect for reading, but one for mathematics. Because the treatment group showed a large pre-treatment advantage in mathematics, this effect would have disappeared if Leyba had controlled for it.

actually 75 citations listed under their heading for acceptable studies in a mimeo provided by Rossell).

Second, critics of Rossell and Baker's literature review have not offered additional studies that meet the above criteria. Stephen Krashen, a vocal proponent of bilingual education for example, has instead suggested that the standards are too strict and has proposed that Rossell and Baker include additional studies favorable to bilingual education even though they do not meet the criteria. Here I have to agree with Rossell and Baker that their standards are reasonable and reject considering Krashen's additional studies. The inability of others to advance the names of more studies that meet Rossell and Baker's criteria lends credence to the assumption that their list is a comprehensive pool from which to select acceptable studies for a meta-analysis.

Unfortunately, only 11 of the 75 studies identified as acceptable by Rossell and Baker actually meet their own criteria for an acceptable study. Fifteen of the studies duplicate the evaluations found in some of the remaining 60 studies. That is, 15 of the 75 are separately released reports of the same programs by the same authors that are already included in Rossell and Baker's list. Where appropriate I combine results so that each remaining observation represents an independent evaluation of a program. Despite our best efforts, an additional 5 studies in Rossell and Baker's list could not be found. . . .

Of the remaining 55 studies, 3 are excluded because they are not evaluations of bilingual programs. One is about "direct instruction" and makes no mention of foreign language learning. Another is a list of exemplary bilingual programs, not an evaluation of programs. And yet another is primarily about the effects of retention (being held back a grade).

An additional 14 studies are excluded because they do not have adequate control groups. In most of these studies both the treatment and control groups receive bilingual instruction, meaning that all students are taught in both their native language and in the target language in varying amounts. I only include in the meta-analysis studies that compare bilingual instruction (meaning the use of at least some native language in instruction) to "English-only" instruction. There are several reasons for this choice. First, comparing the use of some native language to English-only instruction is the clearest division possible in the literature. Program labels, such as transitional bilingual education, English as a second language, immersion, submersion, and maintenance bilingual education,

have no consistent meaning in the evaluations, nor are the detailed features of many programs fully described. The only division of programs that can accurately and consistently be applied is whether native languages are used in instruction or not.

Second, the most policy-relevant question . . . is whether it is desirable to ban the use of native language instruction in the education of younger students with limited English proficiency. The question is not whether it is better to use a modest amount of native language versus a large amount, nor is the issue whether it is better to have children in bilingual programs for a short versus long time. Thus only studies that speak to the policy-relevant issue of comparing bilingual to English-only instruction are included in this meta-analysis. In addition, it is not possible to extrapolate results from studies that compare different amounts or lengths of bilingual instruction to whether bilingual instruction is desirable at all. . . . The only way to evaluate whether the use of any native language instruction is harmful or helpful is to compare students who receive any bilingual instruction to those who are taught only in English.

Of the remaining 38 studies, 2 are excluded because they measure the effects of bilingual programs after an unreasonably short period of time. One study evaluates a program after 7 weeks of bilingual instruction for 35 minutes a day. The other evaluates a program after 10 weeks. Every study included in the meta-analysis measures effects after at least one academic year (about 40 weeks). While the requirement that studies evaluate the effects of bilingual programs after at least one academic year was not one of Rossell and Baker's original criteria for identifying acceptable studies, this is a reasonable standard to add. . . .

An additional 25 studies are excluded because they inadequately control for the differences between students assigned to bilingual programs and students assigned to English-only control groups. If students are randomly assigned to these two groups, then no controls are necessary and one can place high confidence in the results. But when students are not randomly assigned, it is necessary to control statistically for the differences between the groups that may affect their future performance. . . .

* * *

The remaining 11 studies that are included in the meta-analysis consist of 5 studies in which students are randomly assigned and 6 in which there is non-random assignment but some effort to control for the individual background characteristics. . . .

* * *

[Using this smaller set of studies, Greene concludes that the available evidence supports the positive effects of native language instruction.]

While it would be desirable to have a meta-analysis based on a greater number of studies, the unfortunate reality is that the vast majority of evaluations of bilingual programs are so methodologically flawed in their design that their results offer more noise than signal. Adding seriously flawed studies would bias the results of this meta-analysis in ways that are nearly impossible to predict or correct. In addition, including studies that do not meet minimal criteria would require identifying the entire universe of inadequate studies and including all or a random sample of those studies in a meta-analysis. The incredible amount of effort that would require is not justified given the low amount of information that could be gained. Focusing on studies that meet certain "bright-line" criteria, such as all studies that control for individual background characteristics as well as pretest scores or on the smaller group of studies based on random assignment, provides an unbiased sample of studies that can offer useful information on the effects of bilingual education. Despite the relatively small number of studies, the strength and consistency of these results, especially from the highest quality randomized experiments, increases confidence in the conclusion that bilingual programs are effective at increasing standardized test scores measured in English.

The limited number of useful studies, however, makes it difficult to address other important issues, such as the ideal length of time students should be in bilingual programs, the ideal amount of native language that should be used in instruction, and the age groups in which these techniques are most appropriate. It is possible that the individual needs of students are so varied that there may be no simple set of ideal policies. But if we want to learn more about how to develop public policy that is most effective at addressing the needs of students with limited English proficiency, we need to conduct a series of experiments in which students are randomly assigned to different types of programs. These randomized experiments yield the clearest and most precise information to help guide policymaking. The results from the 5 randomized experiments examined here clearly suggest that native language instruction is useful. We need additional randomized experiments to determine how best to design those bilingual programs.

* * *

NOTES AND QUESTIONS

1. *The Meaning of Equal Opportunity for Limited-English-Proficient Children*

Consider again, in the light of the discussion of the research, the issue posed at the beginning of this section: What is the meaning of equal opportunity for children whose native language is not English? Bilingualism? Fluency in English? Pride in native culture? Acculturation? Suppose, as Rossell and Baker suggest, that there are trade-offs among these goals—that, for instance, a student who has maintained his or her native language through in-school instruction may be weaker in English than one instructed entirely in that language. But what if bilingualism brings an economic advantage? A cultural advantage? Which is the correct policy goal? Which is the goal set by the legislation?

2. *The Research and the Judges*

How, if at all, should judges make use of conflicting and ambiguous research? Should judges defer to educators when the experts cannot agree among themselves? How can a principle of nondiscrimination be enforced in the face of such uncertainty? For an effort to address these issues, *see* Moran, "The Politics of Discretion: Federal Intervention in Bilingual Education," 76 *Calif.L.Rev.* 1249 (1988).

3. **The Impact of the "New Federalism."** Because of continuing debate over the efficacy and propriety of bilingual education, federal officials have been reluctant to impose programmatic mandates. Instead, for nearly two decades, they have been delegating increasing discretion to state and local educational agencies to fashion instructional programs for NEP and LEP students. It is appropriate to assess this strategy's success, particularly in jurisdictions with large immigrant populations like California and New York.

"Bilingual Education, Immigration, and the Culture of Disinvestment"
R. Moran, 2 *J.Gender, Race and Justice* 163–211 (1999).

There is no reason to presume that under all circumstances, the new federalism [which delegates discretion to the state and local level] leads inexorably to the deterioration of classroom instruction for NEP and LEP students. Indeed, local districts may be better able than the federal government to assess parents' values about English acquisition, native language fluency, and cultural instruction so that appropriate programs can be designed. Freed of federal oversight, state and local educational agencies should be able to experiment with instructional alternatives to find those that work best for their students. In fact, however, the experiences in two states, California and New York, suggest that the new federalism has neither mitigated ideological conflict over the role of English nor enhanced experimentation to resolve pedagogical uncertainty.

A. California

When federal support for bilingual education was at its apex, California enacted the Chacon-Moscone Bilingual-Bicultural Education Act in 1976. The Act endorsed programs that rely on native language instruction to meet NEP and LEP students' needs. By 1980, when federal leadership was beginning to wane, California adopted the Bilingual Education Improvement and Reform Act. This new legislation emphasized the singular importance of learning English and allowed a larger role for intensive English instruction in serving NEP and LEP students. In the mid-1980s, the state's Board of Education, a policymaking body consisting of political appointees chosen by the Governor, became concerned about the warehousing of NEP and LEP children in bilingual programs. The Board required that children in the programs be promptly reclassified and placed in English-speaking classrooms at the earliest opportunity.

Despite these changes, bilingual education programs remained highly controversial. In November 1986, California voters passed an initiative that amended the state's constitution to make English the official language of the state. This constitutional amendment did not render native language instruction improper so long as it was designed to foster the acquisition of English. Still, the intensity of opposition to anything that sounded bilingual had hit home. When an expert panel recommended that the California legislature enact a new bilingual education law to replace the act when it sunset in 1987, lawmakers did so. However, Governor Deukmejian rejected the bill, and the state legislature was unable to muster sufficient votes to override his veto. With the largest population of linguistic minority students in the country, California no longer had any state bilingual education act.

To fill the gap, the State Department of Education continued to monitor and enforce programmatic requirements as part of its oversight role in dispensing state funds to local educational authorities. In contrast to the Board of Education, the Department of Education is staffed by career professionals in education under the stewardship of a state-wide elected official, the Superintendent of Public Instruction. After California's bilingual education act sunset, the Department successfully preserved many of its requirements, although districts probably had more leeway than previously to use intensive English instruction. The Department's role sparked new controversy. In 1993, the Little Hoover Commission, a panel of experts appointed by the Governor, issued a scathing report that gave bilingual education a failing grade in the state. The panel attributed the programs' shortcomings to the overly prescriptive role of the State Department of Education. The Commission therefore recommended that local officials be given greater flexibility to experiment with alternative instructional approaches, most particularly intensive English instruction.

With the Commission's report in hand, the State Board of Education announced in 1995 that it would grant waivers to local districts that sought to use ESL or structured immersion rather than programs that rely more heavily on native language instruction. An Orange County school district took the Board up on its invitation and successfully obtained a waiver from the Department of Education's guidelines. Subsequently, bilingual education advocates challenged the waiver's validity, insisting that a state-wide consent decree provided that only the Department itself could exempt districts from its programmatic regulations. Nevertheless, other districts in Orange County sought and received similar waivers from the Board. A federal district court refused to nullify the waivers because they did not violate federal requirements regarding the instruction of NEP and LEP students. A state superior court judge later held that the waivers were not even necessary because state officials could no longer enforce the provisions of a bilingual education act that had sunset over a decade ago. The court concluded that local districts should be free to choose programs without state interference. Shortly thereafter, the Board adopted a policy that accorded local educators flexibility in selecting among instructional methods. The legislature passed a bill providing for local control of programmatic choices, but then-Governor Wilson vetoed it.

Those concerned that native language instruction is not only ineffective but sometimes harmful to children were not satisfied with cumbersome waivers or untrammeled local control. Silicon Valley millionaire Ron Unz, once a Republican gubernatorial hopeful, successfully campaigned for an initiative that amends the California Education Code to establish a preference for intensive English instruction. The law generally requires schools to teach English to NEP and LEP children during one year of intensive instruction so that students can quickly enter English-speaking classrooms. Parents can seek waivers from the mandated instruction under the following circumstances: if their children already know English; if they are ten years or older and would benefit from an alternate course of study that promotes rapid acquisition of English; or if they have special physical, emotional, psychological, or educational needs that make another instructional approach desirable. The initiative passed by a wide margin despite opposition from Democratic and Republican gubernatorial candidates and President Clinton. Endorsed by 61% of the voters, the measure was opposed by nearly two-thirds of Latino voters and by a majority of Black voters. Although 57% of Asian Americans voted for the initiative, exit polls showed that in immigrant enclaves, Asian Americans registered strong opposition to it.

Far from resolving the questions surrounding bilingual education, the initiative's passage has prompted new controversies. A lawsuit that sought to block implementation of the initiative on the ground that it violates federal law did not succeed. However, many other legal issues remain unanswered. School districts are currently challenging the State Board of Education's claim that it has no authority to exempt them from the statute's requirements, even though the Education Code's general provisions allow local school officials to apply for district-wide waivers. The Board has insisted that only individual parental waivers are permitted, but a superior court judge in California disagreed. Despite the ruling, the Board continues to refuse to grant waivers to districts pending the outcome of an appeal. [The California courts eventually endorsed the Board's position on waivers.]

The Board has put together emergency regulations for districts to use as guidance in complying with the new law. However, the regulations do not specify the proportion of native language instruction that is now permissible, so districts vary dramatically in their definitions of how much English is an "over-whelming" amount in the curriculum. Some have mandated that a little over half of the instruction be in English, while others have demanded over 90%. Moreover, because local districts have considerable discretion in administering parental requests for waivers, there have been substantial disparities in rates of application and approval of these requests. In some schools, almost no parents have sought a waiver, while in others, as many as 99% have. Some districts have granted nearly all waiver requests, while at least one superintendent has rejected every application for a waiver. Despite all of these uncertainties, the initiative allows individual administrators and teachers to be sued in their personal capacities if they fail to implement the law. Because Unz and his supporters have repeatedly threatened to sue recalcitrant school personnel, the California Teachers Association has filed suit to enjoin such actions as a violation of the free speech rights of educators. [A federal district judge dismissed the lawsuit in September 1999.]

The ongoing debate over the bilingual education initiative in California occurs against the backdrop of a fiscal crisis in the California public schools. The public school population has grown dramatically, partly due to the heavy influx of immigrants into the state. Many of these children have special language needs, but schools lack qualified teachers and other resources to meet those needs. Indeed, [as discussed later in this chapter,] the increased demands on the school system led California voters to endorse a measure that would bar undocumented immigrant children from receiving a public education. In supporting the measure, Governor Wilson pointed out that with the money saved by excluding the undocumented, the state could buy computers for every fourth-grader in public school. Although the initiative to cut services to undocumented immigrants passed by an overwhelming margin in 1994, a federal court judge struck down most of its provisions as an unconstitutional interference with congressional power to make immigration policy.

The concern over scarce resources in California schools reflects a larger decline in the state's commitment to public education, one that predates the controversies over language and immigration. During the early 1970s, [as discussed in chapter 7,] the California Supreme Court was in the vanguard of school finance reform, . . . [but its efforts were thwarted when] voters chose to cap . . . [property] taxes [for schools] rather than subsidize less affluent districts. The tax limits have greatly eroded overall fiscal support for the public schools, and the state is now among the least generous in funding its instructional programs. Efforts to supplement property taxes with other revenue sources like the state lottery have not staved off the decline.

Urban schools with rapid immigrant population growth have been hit especially hard. In a school finance case in Los Angeles, for example, the proceedings did little more than demonstrate that if funding of the district's schools were equalized, all students would receive a comparably inadequate education. Faced with tight budgets, districts may find intensive English instruction attractive because it is a cheaper instructional method than programs that utilize native language instruction. Before passage of the Unz initiative, the schools that were most aggressive in pursuing waivers came from Orange County, an area that had to accommodate a substantial number of new immigrants while addressing a municipal funding crisis. Even if immigrants believe that their children are being shortchanged in a time of scarcity, they have few avenues of political redress: non-citizens in California are ineligible to vote in any state or local election.

In short, California has been unable to develop any consensus about how best to educate NEP and LEP students. Ongoing conflict over the use of native language instruction has led to unstable policy outcomes. Local educators have been forced to grapple with legal and pedagogical uncertainty against a backdrop of persistent financial need. The result has been a political process that seems increasingly fragmented and polarized.

B. New York

On its face, the status of bilingual education seems better in New York than in California. In 1972, Aspira, a group of middle-class Puerto Rican professionals concerned about access to education, filed suit against the New York City Board of Education, alleging that it was not meeting the needs of Puerto Rican students, particularly those who did not speak English. Shortly after the *Lau* decision and just as the federal government was fashioning guidelines for bilingual education, the Board entered into a consent agreement with Aspira. The decree provided standards for identifying students in need of bilingual services and regulated the programs that the Board could offer. The Puerto Rican Legal Defense and Education Fund (PRLDEF), which represented Aspira in the lawsuit, took primary responsibility for working with the Board to implement the decree. After an initial period of bickering and conflict, the Board adopted comprehensive procedures to identify students with limited fluency in English and committed itself to native language instruction to meet their needs.

The Board's increasingly cooperative stance derived in part from the deteriorating fiscal condition of New York City schools. New York's state constitution does not require that schools be funded equally, and state funding formulas produce less generous allotments for students in the city than for those in the rest of the state. In the mid-1970s, the city's fiscal crisis left the public schools unable to maintain facilities. With an influx of immigrant students in the 1980s, the schools were ill-prepared to meet their needs. Indeed, the situation has become so dire that in a recent lawsuit, a New York state court found that underfunding of some public schools may have created such deficient conditions that children are being unconstitutionally denied minimum access to education. [For a fuller discussion of school finance issues, see chapter 7.] In the midst of this pressing need, one potential source of money for New York City schools has been federal and state aid for bilingual education. As federal funding has declined, state aid has grown in importance. New York's bilingual education act, passed the same year that *Lau* was decided, appropriates money on a per capita basis for children in bilingual programs. As a result, inclusive methods of identifying eligible students maximize revenues for city schools.

The state's bilingual education act continues to endorse native language instruction. There has been little impetus for the New York legislature to revise this programmatic preference to expand the role of intensive English instruction because most NEP and LEP children reside in New York City and are covered by the *Aspira* consent decree. In 1993, for example, approximately 90% of the children eligible for state aid under the bilingual education act were in New York City schools. Under the *Aspira* decree, the Board must, where possible, use native language instruction to meet those students' needs. So long as the decree is in effect, state funding for NEP and LEP children will be invested primarily in programs that have a native language component, no matter what the legislature does.

Opponents of the programs have cited the deleterious effects of the city's cash-starved approach to linguistic minority education. They contend that the push to maximize supplemental revenues has led to the warehousing of students in bilingual programs, regardless of whether instruction is effective and whether children are ready to enter an English-speaking classroom. In 1994, the New York City Board of Education issued a report indicating that whatever their original level of English proficiency, children in intensive English programs exited more quickly than those in transitional bilingual education programs that used a child's native language as a bridge to learning English. The more quickly the children exited the program, the better they performed in English-speaking classrooms. Most of the children in native language instructional programs were Spanish-speakers, while those in intensive English instruction tended to be Korean, Russian, or Chinese students, whose small numbers did not support a full-scale bilingual program. Despite their small numbers, Haitian students also tended to be placed in transitional bilingual education programs. Faced with these findings, the Board nevertheless reiterated its support for programs that rely on native language instruction in a supplementary report the following year.

In 1995, the New York Board of Regents also issued a report on services for NEP and LEP children. The Regents found that students in New York City remained in bilingual programs substantially longer than children elsewhere in the state. In 1992–93, within three years after receiving special instruction, 95% of students outside the city had successfully met the criteria for entering English-speaking classrooms, but only 42% of students in the city had done so. Students in New York City programs systematically lagged behind those outside the city in making gains on English and mathematics tests.

Moreover, only 43.2% of NEP and LEP students finished high school compared to 52.9% of English-proficient students. Of NEP and LEP students who graduated from high school, only 3.9% obtained a diploma by passing the Regents' examination. The prestigious Regents' diploma qualifies a student to compete for state-provided financial aid for higher education. Of the remaining NEP and LEP students who completed high school, 91% received a local diploma, and 5.1% got a high school equivalency diploma. The equivalency degree is the least marketable way of completing high school, adding at

best marginal value to the job opportunities available to high school dropouts. Recently, the Regents decided to require that all students successfully complete standardized testing to obtain a high school diploma. As a result, high schools will no longer be able to award local diplomas to students who attend but fail to meet minimum competency requirements. Implementation of the new policy has been delayed, in part because of concerns about the lack of tests in languages other than English.

Confronted with this dismaying evidence about bilingual programs, particularly in New York City, an activist Catholic nun mobilized the Bushwick Parents Organization (BPO) to protest the local school district's treatment of their children. Comprised of mainly Dominican parents, BPO reflected the changing face of the Latino population in New York City. When the *Aspira* case was filed, Puerto Ricans dominated the city's Latino population; however, by the mid-1990s, Puerto Ricans represented slightly less than half of the population due to an influx of Dominican, Mexican, and South American immigrants. These new constituents did not particularly identify with the bilingual education establishment that the Puerto Rican community had fought so hard to put in place.

BPO went to the community school board to demand improved educational opportunities for immigrant children. In particular, BPO expressed concern that the board was keeping NEP and LEP students in bilingual programs that did not enable them to acquire English and other academic skills. BPO's initial strategy was designed to capitalize on the decentralized system of educational governance in New York City. Under this system, each district elects its own officials to oversee day-to-day operations of the school. Instituted in the 1970s, community control is supposed to give racial and ethnic constituencies a voice in the governance of their own schools. To maximize representativeness, noncitizens can vote in community board elections, although turnouts are low and many immigrants are unaware that they can exercise the franchise. Despite the purportedly greater accessibility of community representatives, BPO's efforts to gain the local board's ear failed. Fearful of the group's confrontational tactics, community board members broke off all relations with BPO. In fact, local control revealed the schisms in the rapidly changing Latino population. More established Latinos, such as school board chairman Tito Velez, rebuffed the emerging constituency of immigrant parents in Bushwick.

As a result, BPO turned to the state court system for relief. Although the parents had been interested in quality education, Robert Smith, the partner from Paul, Weiss, Rifkind, Wharton & Garrison who offered his services on a pro bono basis, converted the lawsuit into a referendum on bilingual education. In the litigation, he contended that the State Commissioner of Education had abused his discretion by routinely granting waivers to New York City school districts. These waivers allowed students to remain in the programs for longer than the presumptive three years set forth in the state's bilingual education act. According to the complaint, the Commissioner made no effort to determine whether the programs were effective in promoting acquisition of English and other skills before awarding the waivers. Relying on the recent reports of the New York City Board of Education and the New York Board of Regents, Smith argued on behalf of BPO that the programs were merely warehousing students and that the waivers therefore were inappropriate under state law.

Along with the State Attorney General's Office, the Puerto Rican Legal Defense and Education Fund assumed a leading role in defending the city's system of bilingual education services under the consent decree in *Aspira*. Like the skirmish between BPO and the community board, the lawsuit pitted "old guard" Latino organizations, PRLDEF and Aspira, against an upstart Latino newcomer, BPO. The established bilingual regime easily prevailed in the contest. PRLDEF and the Attorney General successfully argued that New York law permitted the Commissioner to extend a child's stay in bilingual programs for up to five years if a student did not meet the criteria for entering an English-speaking classroom. The legislature therefore expressly recognized that even in a well-run program, not all children would be prepared to exit in three years. Consequently, the Commissioner's grant of the waivers was entirely justified. Despite BPO's lack of success, a group of Haitian parents subsequently filed another lawsuit challenging the adequacy of bilingual education programs in their district.

In contrast to California, New York has adopted a relatively stable educational policy for NEP and LEP students. At both the state and local level, officials have expressed an ongoing commitment to native language instruction as a bridge to learning English. Most conflicts over program quality have been localized, community disputes. Even when dissatisfied parents have challenged the programs' structure, implementation, and philosophy on a statewide basis, courts have readily contained the controversy because of the clear normative consensus under the *Aspira* consent decree and the state bilingual education law.

C. The Culture of Disinvestment and the Failure of the New Federalism

The California and New York experiences represent different faces of the failed experiment with the new federalism. In California, efforts to enforce state-wide regulations and to legislate by initiative have generated high-profile conflict. State agencies have battled over the appropriate approach to use, and the legislature has been so paralyzed by indecision, controversy, and gubernatorial opposition that California remained without a bilingual education act for over a decade. With this highly visible breakdown of state decisionmaking processes, voters have taken matters into their own hands by using the state's initiative process to legislate by popular vote. Precisely because state politics have been central in the bilingual education conflict, racial and ethnic tensions have been highlighted as a predominantly White electorate mandates policies for newly arrived, predominantly Latino and Asian immigrants.

Even at the local level, bilingual education controversies in California have taken on strong racial and ethnic overtones. With rapid immigration, many urban neighborhoods have undergone a turnover in their racial and ethnic composition. Yet immigrants, whether lawfully present or not, can not vote in school board elections until they become citizens, even if their children attend public schools. Consequently, school boards seldom reflect the immigrant makeup of their student bodies. In Orange County, for example, White school board members sought waivers from requirements to use native language instruction over the protests of many Latino immigrant parents. In Oakland, bilingual education programs have sparked intense disputes, in part because Black board members resent the fact that special treatment is given to immigrants' linguistic needs, while Black English (or Ebonics) is treated as an object of ridicule.

In New York, there has been little state-wide conflict over bilingual education because the bilingual education act is mainly a vehicle for appropriating money to help students in New York City. These students are already subject to a consent decree that limits flexibility in setting criteria for student identification, program choice, and reclassification and exit. As a result, there is much less conflict over bilingual education at the state level, and racial and ethnic polarization is therefore not as salient as in California. In New York City itself, the appearance of racial and ethnic conflict is further deflected by the role of the Puerto Rican Legal Defense and Education Fund in defending current programs from challenges by immigrant parents who are likely to be Dominican, Mexican, or South American. Whites may play a role in handling the immigrant parents' cases and they may even set the agenda in these cases, but nominally at least, the battle seems to be one among Latinos over the best system of education for their children.

Community school boards in New York City provide an additional buffer against the emergence of racial and ethnic polarization. Community boards often oversee racially homogeneous communities because of pervasive residential segregation in the city. In contrast to California, non-citizens can vote in school board elections. Even if turnouts are low, at least some community school board members are apt to be Latino. As a result, when school boards rebuff challenges to bilingual education, as in Bushwick, the conflict is apt to seem like a power struggle among Latinos, rather than a battle between Whites and emerging non-White populations.

Although California's approach to bilingual education has accentuated conflict while New York's has contained it, the two states share significant commonalities that overshadow these differences. In both places, large numbers of immigrants have overwhelmed available state and local services, including the schools. There has been little commitment to investing substantial resources in the education of immigrant children in either state. For the NEP or LEP child, the symbolism of the state and local political processes is undoubtedly less important than the day-to-day experience in the classroom. Whether in California or New York, this student is likely to be in an overcrowded, underfunded school with a teacher who is not certified to offer special instruction and who lacks the necessary resources and materials to implement a high-quality program.

The failure of the new federalism in California and New York is a result not only of the federal government's retreat from leadership in the field of bilingual education, but also its unwillingness to al-

leviate the fiscal impact of immigration in states with large numbers of newcomers [like California and New York]. . . .

* * *

The failure of the new federalism to promote responsive, innovative bilingual education programs can only be understood in relation to immigration. Had the population of NEP and LEP students been relatively stable, state and local educational agencies might have been able to generate resources to design at least some model programs, particularly if the federal government had continued to fund research and experimentation. However, the decline in federal funding and leadership, coupled with the explosive growth in linguistic minority, immigrant student populations, made the grant of discretion to state and local officials under the new federalism an illusory one. State and local educators have been forced to rely on triage to address the needs of a growing number of students with a shrinking amount of resources.

The failure of bilingual programs in California and New York has no easy solutions at the state level. Whatever programmatic choice is made, it is unlikely to succeed in overcrowded, underfunded classrooms with teachers who lack sufficient training and must use outdated textbooks and inadequate materials. Ultimately, the problem is one that requires federal intervention to assist states in coping with the impact of high levels of immigration, including increased demands on the public educational system. Despite recent modest increases in federal funding for bilingual education, these programs have suffered from more than a decade of fiscal neglect. Moreover, opponents in Congress perennially renew efforts to cut program support. Without a significant change in the culture of disinvestment that has driven federal policy, states like California and New York will continue to struggle to manage the ongoing educational crisis in their schools.

_____

NOTES AND QUESTIONS

1. Bilingual Education and Federalism

In light of the ongoing polarization and uncertainty surrounding bilingual education, should the federal government increase or decrease its presence in this area? If national policymakers were to pursue a more interventionist role, what approaches should they employ? Would these efforts succumb to ideological and pedagogical conflict as the *Lau* regime did? If the federal government continues to opt for a deregulatory approach, is it abdicating its responsibility to NEP and LEP students? Can Congress or the Department of Education effectively protect linguistic minorities from state and local politics? These issues are discussed at length in L. McDonnell and P. Hill, *Newcomers in American Schools: Meeting the Educational Needs of Immigrant Youth* (1993).

2. Bilingual Education and Immigration

Why did the bilingual education debate evolve as a research debate over pedagogical practices and a civil rights debate over the scope of protections under equal protection, Title VI, and the EEOA? Why did the analysis of bilingual education develop without strong connections to immigration policy? Are bilingual education and immigration issues likely to converge in future policymaking efforts?

3. The Impact of California's English Immersion Policy

The impact of California's new English immersion policy has been hotly contested. In the summer of 2000, the state of California released the results of its statewide Stanford 9 standardized test. According to the report, limited-English-proficient (LEP) students posted gains in reading and mathematics similar to those for their English-speaking counterparts. However, the LEP students' scores continued to lag substantially behind those of other students. The initiative's supporters also contended that LEP students made the greatest progress in districts that granted the fewest waivers from the English-immersion program. Steinberg, "Increase in Test Scores Counters Dire Forecasts for Bilingual Ban," *N.Y.Times*, Aug. 20, 2000, at §1, p. 1, col. 4; Groves, "English Skills Still the Key in Test Scores; Stanford 9: Results Show Vast Divide in Achievement Between Students Who Have Language Fluency and Those Who Don't," *L.A.Times*, Aug. 15, 2000, pt. A1, p.3.

Some scholars have sounded a cautionary note, saying that it is too early to tell what the test scores mean. Wilson, "California Students' Test Scores Show Moderate Gains," *Ventura County Star*, Aug. 15, 2000, at A1; Gorman, "English Learners Post Gains in State Test; Stanford 9: Nonfluent Students Still Badly Lag Their Proficient Classmates in County and State," *L.A.Times*, Aug. 15, 2000, at B1. Efforts are under way to devise a statewide test for English-language learners that evaluates progress in

oral, reading, and writing skills. Tapia and Sacchetti, "Prop. 227's Effect on Fluency Remains Unclear," *Orange County Register*, Nov. 1, 2000, at K2631. *See generally* Zehr, "Cause of Higher Calif. Test Scores Sore Point in Bilingual Ed. Debate," *Educ. Week*, Sept. 6, 2000, at 1.

Meanwhile, the Office for Civil Rights (OCR) has been investigating complaints against California school districts operating under the new English immersion policy. OCR found that the Pittsburg school system, located near Oakland, California, failed to provide adequate programs for limited-English-proficient students to learn English or other academic subjects. "District's LEP Services Faulted," *Educ. Week*, May 17, 2000, at 4. Later, OCR concluded that the Oceanside school district did not provide students with limited English proficiency full access to the curriculum, that the district did not have sound criteria for placing students in programs and transitioning them out, and that the district did not properly monitor the students' progress in English and other subjects. Ironically, supporters of English immersion praised Oceanside's strict implementation of the new policy and cited improvement in test scores there as evidence that the policy was working. "Calif. District Found to Violate LEP Rights," *Educ. Week*, Oct. 11, 2000, at 4.

4. The Political Consequences of California's Initiative in Other States

The successful drive to adopt an English-immersion policy in California has prompted similar efforts in other states. Arizona recently became the second state to approve such a policy. Gonzales, "Bilingual Education Gets Rebuke from State Voters," *Arizona Republic*, Nov. 8, 2000, at EX 1. Ron Unz, the most prominent backer of the California initiative, predicts that other states, such as Colorado, Texas, Massachusetts, and New York, will follow suit. Gonzales, "Bilingual-Ed Supporter: Defy Prop. 203," *Arizona Republic*, Nov. 9, 2000, at A20. Yet, commentators in Texas and New York, both states that have no initiative process, disagree with Unz's predictions. Hughes, "Language 'Immersion' Not Likely in Texas, Officials Say," *Dallas Morning News*, Nov. 16, 2000, at 1L; Steinberg, "Answers to an English Question; Instead of Ending Program, New York May Offer a Choice," *N.Y.Times*, Oct. 22, 2000, at §1, p. 37, col. 2. The New York City board of education recently released yet another report on bilingual education and English as a Second Language (ESL) programs. New York City Board of Education,

ELL Subcommittee Research Studies Progress Report (2000) (http://www.nycenet.edu/). Commentators accused the board of systematically downplaying evidence that ESL students exited programs more quickly than students in bilingual education programs and outperformed them at reading and mathematics. Zehr, "N.Y.C. Study Adds Fuel to Bilingual Ed. Debate," *Educ.Week*, Sept. 13, 2000, at 3. Critics alleged that the board was trying to avoid controversy and preserve bilingual programs.

5. Further Reading

Proposition 227, the initiative that mandated intensive English instruction in California, prompted considerable commentary. Among the articles are Farquharson, "Proposition 227: A Burning Issue for California's Bilingual Students," 8 *B.U.Pub.Int.L.J.* 333 (1999); Felton, "Sink or Swim? The State of Bilingual Education in the Wake of California Proposition 227," 48 *Catholic U.L.Rev.* 843 (1999); Gullixson, "California Proposition 227: An Examination of the Legal, Educational and Practical Issues Surrounding the New Law," 17 *Law & Ineq.J.* 505 (1999); Johnson, "The California Backlash Against Bilingual Education: *Valeria G. v. Wilson* and Proposition 227," 34 *U.S.F.L.Rev.* 169 (1999); Rodriguez, "Discretion and Destruction: The Debate Over Language in California's Schools," 4 *Tex.Forum on Civ.Lib. & Civ.Rts.* 189 (1999).

C. Culture and the Classroom

In the bilingual education debate, language often is linked to culture. Still, federal policy has focused almost exclusively on exclusion based on language and has left decisions about the role of culture in the curriculum to state and local educators, as discussed in chapter 2. Just as blacks have demanded Afrocentric schools, Latinos have asserted that their problems in school reflect more than a mere language difference. Instead, they insist that the school environment is often rife with cultural insensitivity and destructive stereotypes. These barriers can affect students, regardless of their ability to speak English.

"Educational Rights and Latinos: Tracking as a Form of Second Generation Discrimination"
P. Noguera, 8 *La Raza L.J.* 25, 35, 36–39, 41 (1995). ©1995 by La Raza Law Journal, Inc.

* * *

In our interviews with students at the secondary level [in Lockwood Unified School District, a relatively small district in northern California], we found widely shared perceptions that the schools were hostile toward Latino students and their culture. [Latinos were the most rapidly growing ethnic group in the district and accounted for 10% of the district's student population.] This hostility was described in several ways. First, Chicano and Latino students consistently reported that they had experienced overt racism, discrimination and stereotyping within the classroom and the school. Examples of biased treatment included being ignored or neglected by teachers (e.g., not being called upon during class discussions, little eye contact, minimal attention except in the form of punishment, etc.) and being unfairly targeted for punishment and ostracism. Students also reported feeling as though their teachers looked down upon them and were not willing to give them needed assistance. The students we interviewed felt that some teachers stereotyped them as being less capable of succeeding in school and thus expected less of them due to their ethnic background.

* * *

The feelings of estrangement and alienation described by Latino students in Lockwood's secondary schools are reinforced by the lack of Latinos in professional roles at the school sites. Latino students report that they are disturbed by the fact that they do not have equal representation on campus or in the school district. Students see few Chicanos or Latinos on the school board, in parent and student organizations, or on the school staff. There is one Chicana faculty member at Northside Junior High School, none at Southside Junior High, and three Latino teachers and one Latino guidance counselor at the high school. Most of the adults the students encounter, even in the bilingual, ESL and sheltered classes, are not Latino, and the vast majority do not speak Spanish.

Commenting on the lack of representation of Latinos on the school faculty, one twelfth grade, upper tracked student said the following:

> [One] of the main things that needs to change is the representation in the staff and . . . in the classes. The school needs to hire more Chicano and Latino teachers so that students feel included and more like they are a part of the school. A lot of us don't feel comfortable in the school because there are no role models around. We need people that we can talk to and identify with.

Another ninth grade student made a similar point regarding the need for Latino role models:

> I think that teachers should be mentors and role models to the students, and that's what I look for in a teacher. Someone who cares and reaches out to me and who I can talk to. Someone who is interested, who is interested in my culture and who will let me bring my culture into class . . . I like it when we learn about Chicano/Latino writers, African American writers, Asian American writers, European writers, and writers from all over, you know, the world. People have so much to offer us through their writing, we learn about their culture and then we're not ignorant or bored because we learn about everyone . . . Do you understand?

The lack of representation at the school sites exacerbates the students' feelings of exclusion. Students feel that this problem is further compounded by a curriculum that largely omits any mention of their history or culture. Many believe that their teachers are uninterested or hostile to covering material that is relevant to their socioeconomic and cultural reality. One student expressed his frustration with the curriculum in the following way:

> [I]t [bothers] me that all the discussions seem to focus on black and white issues . . . it's important but I don't see my people represented at all. I think during class discussion, everyone should be included. When you learn about your people you feel more motivated to do the work.

Many students expressed a desire to learn more about their history and culture in school, and regarded its absence from the curriculum as a sign of discrimination. The students we interviewed said they want classes in Chicano/Latino studies which focus on history, culture and contemporary issues relevant to the experience of Latinos in the United States. The students also want to see literature and material written by Latino scholars included in their traditional classes, especially English and History. An eighth grade student at Northside Junior High School made the following argument for the inclusion of Latino issues in the school curriculum:

> If kids have to wait until they get out of school to find out about all the bad things that white people have done to us it just makes them madder. Then they might end up hating white people and hurting the wrong ones. It's better if you give us a chance to learn these things in school so that we can think about it in an intelligent way. Maybe then so many of us won't be so angry.

Many of the students that we interviewed connected the cultural bias of the curriculum to their placement in low ability classes. In addition to what they regarded as "straight up racism," many of the students said that they were unmotivated to take on the more challenging work offered in the college prep courses since it was not made relevant to their experience. In addition, many said that they did not want to be the only Latinos in those classes and would prefer to be in less challenging classes than to feel alienated and isolated. . . .

* * *

This student and many of the others that we interviewed seemed to have resigned themselves to accept a marginalized position within the school. Acceptance of placement in lower track classes in order to avoid being isolated from other Latino students has been widely embraced as an effective coping strategy. Although students recognize the implications of their placement—that their high school preparation will prevent them from being accepted by one of the better universities—they willingly make the trade-off because they find the hostility and alienation in the upper-tracked classes unbearable.

* * *

. . . In light of the current xenophobic climate evidenced, in part, by growing hostility to providing services to immigrants, efforts to improve the education of Latinos generally, must not become marginalized or treated as an exclusively Latino issue. Most Latino students will continue [to] attend schools where the majority of teachers and administrators are not Latino. Even without the leverage of the courts, we must find ways to make those responsible for educating Latino students accountable and responsive to the needs of our children.

NOTES AND QUESTIONS

1. The Historical Experience of Immigrants in the Public Schools

In recent decades, the United States has experienced high rates of immigration, particularly from Asia and Latin America. At the turn of the century, however, the United States had to absorb an even larger proportion of immigrants, mostly from southern and eastern Europe. During this period, the public schools were called upon to play a central role in the process of "Americanizing" the newcomers. School administration became increasingly centralized, standardized, and professionalized in urban areas serving large numbers of immigrant students. *See* D. Tyack, *The One Best System: A History of American Urban Education* (1974). The results for pupils were hardly uniform, however. While some thrived, others felt the pain of assimilation deeply. Leonard Covello wrote about the estrangement from his parents that Americanization entailed and how he "soon got the idea that 'Italian' meant something inferior." L. Covello, *The Heart Is the Teacher* (1958). Covello went on to become a teacher and principal, and he worked to develop a community school that would enable students to feel proud of their heritage and empower parents and neighborhood leaders to participate in the educational process. *Id.* at 197–98; Covello, "A High School and Its Immigrant Community—A Challenge and an Opportunity," 9 *J.Educ.Soc.* 331, 332 (1936); Covello, "The School as the Center of Community Life in an Immigrant Area," in *The Community School* 125–63 (S. Everett ed. 1938).

2. *Assimilation, Pluralism, and Cultural Sensitivity*

Should civil rights reformers attempt to redress pervasive claims of injustice based on ethnicity, language, and culture through the courts? Or are these issues best left to the local political process? How is your answer affected by the demographics of the Latino population? To what extent can schools assimilate students without being culturally insensitive? Should schools embrace pluralistic programs of education?

3. *The Question of Remedies*

If reforms are necessary, what strategies are likely to prove effective? Should school districts adopt new curricula that are culturally sensitive, should they use training programs to sensitize teachers to problems of bias, or should they hire a more diverse teaching force? Are all of these steps needed? Or are other measures more likely to succeed? If so, what are they? How does the debate over culture in the classroom parallel the bilingual education debate? How are the two controversies different?

D. Immigrant Status and Access to School

The rapid growth in Latino and Asian immigrant populations has sometimes strained the public schools' limited resources. As in the late 1800s and early 1900s, educators today play a critical role in helping newcomers adjust to life in the United States. Immigrant students understand that schooling is a key avenue to upward mobility and successful participation in American life. Still, the process of "Americanization" poses some serious challenges in the late 1990s and early 2000s. In particular, immigrants may learn lessons of equality and inclusion in the formal curriculum, while the informal curriculum reveals the realities of stratification and exclusion.

1. The Dilemmas of Americanization.

"Made in America"
L. Olsen, 239–243 (1997).

* * *

Madison High, one multicultural high school campus in one of many communities being changed by immigration, demonstrates how a community can both "celebrate its diversity," yet continue to reproduce a stratified and inequitable racial and language hierarchy and a narrow version of what it means to be "American." [Madison High is a pseudonym for a school in Northern California.] It illustrates the efforts and heartbreaks of those engaged in activity to provide more educational opportunity and equal access to schooling for immigrants, as well as the confusions, blindnesses, and concerns of those who resist changing their ways "for them." In the lives of the students—immigrant and U.S. born—we have witnessed a social life among the young people on the campus in which their very desires to affirm who they are meet headlong with American racial systems, and where students abandon the fullness of their human identities as part of the process of becoming and being American. Madison High has offered a hard look at the ways in which our schools still sort and consign students to very different futures based on their skin colors, class, and language. . . .

* * *

The Americanization Project of Schools

There are three pieces to the process of Americanization that newcomers to these United States undergo in our high schools: academic marginalization and separation; the requirements to become English-speaking (despite many odds) and to drop one's native language in order to participate in the academic and social life of the high school; and insistent pressures to find and take one's place in the racial hierarchy of the United States.

Exclusion and Separation of Immigrant Students Academically

As we saw at Madison High, because of a lack of capacity and will to serve newcomers, immigrant students are either placed in inadequately supported classes where they do not have access to English-speaking peers or friends or placed in "mainstream" classes taught by unprepared teachers who do not address their needs and they cannot fully comprehend, hence dooming them to academic failure and loss of access to the academic program. With insufficient English language development and insufficient access to the curriculum in a language they can understand, most immigrant students are (through the forces of schooling) denied equal access to an education. Some manage to achieve, but many drop out of school or become stuck in the category of "ESL lifers."

Pressure to Give Up One's National Identity and Language

Immigrants learn that to become English speaking is not sufficient for membership in this new society. They must cease using their mother tongue in public places and must give up their national identities as a condition of being accepted as "American." Immigrants face what feels to them to be polar choices between being accepted by becoming as American as possible (which includes becoming racialized into the lower echelons of an American hierarchy and giving up their own national and language identities) and remaining marginalized and holding on to their traditional cultural forms (national identity, home language, and home culture). The middle ground of multicultural identities is intensely uncomfortable, for they find little support either in their home or school worlds for simultaneously embracing both. Their experiences examining and then determining their relationship to nationality and mother tongue occupies center stage during the early years of the immigrant experience.

Taking One's Place in the Racial Hierarchy of the United States

Newcomers group together with others of their same religion and language in what becomes social shelter from the exclusion and hostility of U.S.-born peers who laugh at their accents and foreign ways. The journey immigrants understand they must make as a condition of acceptance in this new land is to become English speakers. They assume at first that the language is synonymous with becoming American. But they discover a different reality. As they become more English speaking, they participate more and more in the social world of the high school and discover that they have to learn and find a place in the racialized structures of the school. What they do not yet understand is that these racialized places also have implications for the paths that are open to them academically. As students become Americanized, they begin to group more like their American peers, racially.

In all three of these elements of the Americanization process, the slots waiting for newcomers are positions of only partial acceptance. As they adopt the English language as their sole language, they are not given sufficient tools or access to develop the levels of English really required for full academic participation and inclusion. They become English speakers, but seldom proficient readers and writers of the language, grappling with academic content in English. And as they learn English, they also learn to abandon their mother tongue. Giving up one's native language for the sake of learning English and being accepted has a high price in loss of strong family connection and access to one's history. Furthermore, giving up one's national identity to become American is a one-way journey. The places they are to take in the racial hierarchy are largely at the bottom. There is no going back for immigrant youth, although their new nation makes the message clear that it is not at all sure it wants them here. This is the racialized Americanization of the 1990s.

* * *

All of these transitions are painful, for they involve giving up a significant aspect of one's identity and accepting a place in a system that not only will not acknowledge or prize the cultures and languages of the newcomer, but which offers them only marginalized and subordinated places in the hierarchy of their new land. Whether a result of policies and leadership that do not recognize or respond to the academic needs of immigrant students, or the result of prejudices and exclusionary attitudes of their teachers and fellow American students, the impact is the same. The process for immigrants of participation in American high schools is one of loss.

And the teachers? As we saw, they too are immersed in an effort to make sense of the new realities of diversity. But they remain largely oblivious to the day-to-day intense maneuvering of their students over issues of racial identity. Their world is one defined by academic programs and tracks. "American" students and teachers collude in establishing the criteria of English fluency for participation in their school world. And so English becomes the measure of denationalization and the explicitly acknowledged path to citizenship and participation. To the degree people hold on to this notion, it denies the reality that American students see so clearly, that taking one's place in the racial order is the measure of arrival on the American map. But the racializing process of the school becomes obscured behind an ideology of pride in diversity, an insistent color-blindness, and a belief that learning English is the only barrier to participation.

It is a seamless web of Americanization and racialization. While immigrants are engaged in trying to understand the racialization and Americanization processes, they also become instructed in practices of getting along. They learn silence and denial. Students learn a way of moving through their social world, where what they experience and what they are safe in articulating are quite different. This mirrors the experience of the adults, who learn a similar silence. To name inequality in an "eggshell" atmosphere is dangerous, viewed as divisive, and leads to marginalization for teachers.

* * *

NOTES AND QUESTIONS

1. Intergenerational Status and Schooling

Are the problems of culturally appropriate instruction the same for first-generation immigrants as for ethnic minorities who are second- and third-generation Americans? Are the imperatives of assimilation greatest for newcomers? Are the pressures of adopting new customs and traditions necessarily intense for the newly arrived, regardless of race or ethnicity?

2. Segregation of Immigrant Students

Is segregation of immigrants in a "Newcomer High" program pedagogically appropriate? Does this segregation lead to social stigma and stratification? Can students subsequently be mainstreamed into traditional classes without being categorized based on their race and immigration status?

2. Constitutional Protections for the Undocumented: *Plyler v. Doe.* Although schools are still the gatekeepers to the American dream, access to a free, public education for undocumented immigrant students has been highly controversial. Periodically, states like Texas and California, which have been heavily impacted by immigration, have tried to bar the undocumented from the public schools. So far, the federal courts have stood in the way of these efforts. In 1982, the United States Supreme Court declared such policies an unconstitutional violation of equal protection.

Plyler v. Doe
457 U.S. 202, 1025 S.Ct. 2382, 72 L.Ed.2d 786 (1982).

* * *

Justice Brennan delivered the opinion of the Court.

The question presented by these cases is whether, consistent with the Equal Protection Clause of the Fourteenth Amendment, Texas may deny to undocumented school-age children the free public education that it provides to children who are citizens of the United States or legally admitted aliens.

I

Since the late 19th century, the United States has restricted immigration into this country. Unsanctioned entry into the United States is a crime, 8 U.S.C. § 1325, and those who have entered unlawfully are subject to deportation, 8 U.S.C. §§ 1251, 1252 (1976 ed. and Supp.IV). But despite the existence of these legal restrictions, a substantial number of persons have succeeded in unlawfully entering the United States, and now live within various States, including the State of Texas.

In May 1975, the Texas Legislature revised its education laws to withhold from local school districts any state funds for the education of children who were not "legally admitted" into the United States.

The 1975 revision also authorized local school districts to deny enrollment in their public schools to children not "legally admitted" to the country. Tex. Educ. Code Ann. § 21.031 (Vernon Supp.1981). These cases involve constitutional challenges to those provisions.

No. 80-1538
Plyler v. Doe

This is a class action, filed in the United States District Court for the Eastern District of Texas in September 1977, on behalf of certain school-age children of Mexican origin residing in Smith County, Tex., who could not establish that they had been legally admitted into the United States. The action complained of the exclusion of plaintiff children from the public schools of the Tyler Independent School District. The Superintendent and members of the Board of Trustees of the School District were named as defendants; the State of Texas intervened as a party-defendant. . . .

* * *

The District Court held that illegal aliens were entitled to the protection of the Equal Protection Clause of the Fourteenth Amendment, and that § 21.031 violated that Clause. Suggesting that "the state's exclusion of undocumented children from its public schools . . . may well be the type of invidiously motivated state action for which the suspect classification doctrine was designed," the court held that it was unnecessary to decide whether the statute would survive a "strict scrutiny" analysis because, in any event, the discrimination embodied in the statute was not supported by a rational basis. *Id.*, at 585. The District Court also concluded that the Texas statute violated the Supremacy Clause.[15] *Id.*, at 590–592.

The Court of Appeals for the Fifth Circuit upheld the District Court's injunction. 628 F.2d 448 (1980). The Court of Appeals held that the District Court had erred in finding the Texas statute pre-empted by fed-

eral law.[16] With respect to equal protection, however, the Court of Appeals affirmed in all essential respects the analysis of the District Court, *id.*, at 454–458, concluding that § 21.031 was "constitutionally infirm regardless of whether it was tested using the mere rational basis standard or some more stringent test," *id.*, at 458. We noted probable jurisdiction. . . .

No. 80-1934
In re Alien Children Education Litigation

During 1978 and 1979, suits challenging the constitutionality of § 21.031 and various local practices undertaken on the authority of that provision were filed in the United States District Courts for the Southern, Western, and Northern Districts of Texas. Each suit named the State of Texas and the Texas Education Agency as defendants, along with local officials. In November 1979, the Judicial Panel on Multidistrict Litigation, on motion of the State, consolidated the claims against the state officials into a single action to be heard in the District Court for the Southern District of Texas. A hearing was conducted in February and March 1980. In July 1980, the court entered an opinion and order holding that § 21.031 violated the Equal Protection Clause of the Fourteenth Amendment. *In re Alien Children Education Litigation*, 501 F.Supp. 544.[7] . . . While appeal of the District Court's decision was pending, the Court of Appeals rendered its decision in No. 80-1538. Apparently on the strength of that opinion, the Court of Appeals, on February 23, 1981, summarily affirmed the decision of the Southern District. We noted probable jurisdiction, . . . and consolidated this case with No. 80-1538 for briefing and argument.[8]

II

The Fourteenth Amendment provides that "[n]o State shall . . . deprive any person of life, liberty, or property, without due process of law; nor deny to *any*

---

[15]The court found § 21.031 inconsistent with the scheme of national regulation under the Immigration and Nationality Act, and with federal laws pertaining to funding and discrimination in education. The court distinguished *DeCanas v. Bica*, 424 U.S. 351, 96 S.Ct. 933, 47 L.Ed.2d 43 (1976), by emphasizing that the state bar on employment of illegal aliens involved in that case mirrored precisely the federal policy, of protecting the domestic labor market, underlying the immigration laws. The court discerned no express federal policy to bar illegal immigrants from education. 458 F.Supp., at 590–592.

[16]The Court of Appeals noted that *DeCanas v. Bica, supra*, had not foreclosed all state regulation with respect to illegal aliens, and found no express or implied congressional policy favoring the education of illegal aliens. The court therefore concluded that there was no pre-emptive conflict between state and federal law. 628 F.2d, at 451–454.

[7]The court concluded that § 21.031 was not pre-empted by federal laws or international agreements. 501 F.Supp., at 584–596.

[8]Appellees in both cases continue to press the argument that § 21.031 is pre-empted by federal law and policy. In light of our disposition of the Fourteenth Amendment issue, we have no occasion to reach this claim.

person within its jurisdiction the equal protection of the laws." (Emphasis added.) Appellants argue at the outset that undocumented aliens, because of their immigration status, are not "persons within the jurisdiction" of the State of Texas, and that they therefore have no right to the equal protection of Texas law. We reject this argument. Whatever his status under the immigration laws, an alien is surely a "person" in any ordinary sense of that term. Aliens, even aliens whose presence in this country is unlawful, have long been recognized as "persons" guaranteed due process of law by the Fifth and Fourteenth Amendments. *Shaughnessy v. Mezei*, 345 U.S. 206, 212, . . . (1953); *Wong Wing v. United States*, 163 U.S. 228, 238, . . . (1896); *Yick Wo v. Hopkins*, 118 U.S. 356, 369, . . . (1886). Indeed, we have clearly held that the Fifth Amendment protects aliens whose presence in this country is unlawful from invidious discrimination by the Federal Government. *Mathews v. Diaz*, 426 U.S. 67, 77, . . . (1976).[9]

Appellants seek to distinguish our prior cases, emphasizing that the Equal Protection Clause directs a State to afford its protection to persons *within its jurisdiction* while the Due Process Clauses of the Fifth and Fourteenth Amendments contain no such assertedly limiting phrase. In appellants' view, persons who have entered the United States illegally are not "within the jurisdiction" of a State even if they are present within a State's boundaries and subject to its laws. Neither our cases nor the logic of the Fourteenth Amendment supports that constricting construction of the phrase "within its jurisdiction." We have never suggested that the class of persons who might avail themselves of the equal protection guarantee is less than coextensive with that entitled to due process. To the contrary, we have recognized that both provisions were fashioned to protect an identical class of persons, and to reach every exercise of state authority.

> "The Fourteenth Amendment to the Constitution is not confined to the protection of citizens. It says: 'Nor shall any state deprive any person of life, liberty, or property without due process of law; nor deny to any person within its jurisdiction the equal protection of the laws.' *These provisions are universal in their application, to all persons within the territorial jurisdiction,* without regard to any differences of race, of color, or of nationality; and the protection of the laws is a pledge of the protection of equal laws." *Yick Wo, supra,* at 369, . . . (emphasis added).

In concluding that "all persons within the territory of the United States," including aliens unlawfully present, may invoke the Fifth and Sixth Amendments to challenge actions of the Federal Government, we reasoned from the understanding that the Fourteenth Amendment was designed to afford its protection to all within the boundaries of a State. . . .

* * *

There is simply no support for appellants' suggestion that "due process" is somehow of greater stature than "equal protection" and therefore available to a larger class of persons. To the contrary, each aspect of the Fourteenth Amendment reflects an elementary limitation on state power. To permit a State to employ the phrase "within its jurisdiction" in order to identify subclasses of persons whom it would define as beyond its jurisdiction, thereby relieving itself of the obligation to assure that its laws are designed and applied equally to those persons, would undermine the principal purpose for which the Equal Protection Clause was incorporated in the Fourteenth Amendment. The Equal Protection Clause was intended to work nothing less than the abolition of all caste-based and invidious class-based legislation. That objective is fundamentally at odds with the power the State asserts here to classify persons subject to its laws as nonetheless excepted from its protection.

* * *

Our conclusion that the illegal aliens who are plaintiffs in these cases may claim the benefit of the Fourteenth Amendment's guarantee of equal protection only begins the inquiry. The more difficult question is whether the Equal Protection Clause has been violated by the refusal of the State of Texas to reimburse local school boards for the education of children who cannot demonstrate that their presence within the United States is lawful, or by the imposition by those school boards of the burden of tuition on those children. It is to this question that we now turn.

III

* * *

. . . The Equal Protection Clause was intended as a restriction on state legislative action inconsistent with elemental constitutional premises. Thus we have treated as presumptively invidious those classifications that disadvantage a "suspect class," or that

---

[9]It would be incongruous to hold that the United States, to which the Constitution assigns a broad authority over both naturalization and foreign affairs, is barred from invidious discrimination with respect to unlawful aliens, while exempting the States from a similar limitation. . . .

impinge upon the exercise of a "fundamental right." With respect to such classifications, it is appropriate to enforce the mandate of equal protection by requiring the State to demonstrate that its classification has been precisely tailored to serve a compelling governmental interest. . . .

A

Sheer incapability or lax enforcement of the laws barring entry into this country, coupled with the failure to establish an effective bar to the employment of undocumented aliens, has resulted in the creation of a substantial "shadow population" of illegal migrants—numbering in the millions—within our borders.[15] This situation raises the specter of a permanent caste of undocumented resident aliens, encouraged by some to remain here as a source of cheap labor, but nevertheless denied the benefits that our society makes available to citizens and lawful residents. The existence of such an underclass presents most difficult problems for a Nation that prides itself on adherence to principles of equality under law.[19]

The children who are plaintiffs in these cases are special members of this underclass. Persuasive arguments support the view that a State may withhold its beneficence from those whose very presence within the United States is the product of their own unlawful conduct. These arguments do not apply with the same force to classifications imposing disabilities on the minor *children* of such illegal entrants. At the least, those who elect to enter our territory by stealth and in violation of our law should be prepared to bear the consequences, including, but not limited to, deportation. But the children of those illegal entrants are not comparably situated. Their "parents have the ability to conform their conduct to societal norms," and presumably the ability to remove themselves from the State's jurisdiction; but the children who are plaintiffs in these cases "can affect neither their parents' conduct nor their own status." *Trimble v. Gordon*, 430 U.S. 762, 770, 97 S.Ct. 1459, 1465, 52 L.Ed.2d 31 (1977). Even if the State found it expedient to control the conduct of adults by acting against their children, legislation directing the onus of a parent's misconduct against his children does not comport with fundamental conceptions of justice.

> "[V]isiting . . . condemnation on the head of an infant is illogical and unjust. Moreover, imposing disabilities on the . . . child is contrary to the basic concept of our system that legal burdens should bear some relationship to individual responsibility or wrongdoing. Obviously, no child is responsible for his birth and penalizing the . . . child is an ineffectual—as well as unjust—way of deterring the parent." *Weber v. Aetna Casualty & Surety Co.*, 406 U.S. 164, 175, . . . (1972) (footnote omitted).

Of course, undocumented status is not irrelevant to any proper legislative goal. Nor is undocumented status an absolutely immutable characteristic since it is the product of conscious, indeed unlawful, action. But § 21.031 is directed against children, and imposes its discriminatory burden on the basis of a legal characteristic over which children can have little control. It is thus difficult to conceive of a rational justification for penalizing these children for their presence within the United States. Yet that appears to be precisely the effect of § 21.031.

Public education is not a "right" granted to individuals by the Constitution. *San Antonio Independent School Dist. v. Rodriguez*, 411 U.S. 1, . . . (1973). But neither is it merely some governmental

---

[15]The Attorney General recently estimated the number of illegal aliens within the United States at between 3 and 6 million. In presenting to both the Senate and House of Representatives several Presidential proposals for reform of the immigration laws—including one to "legalize" many of the illegal entrants currently residing in the United States by creating for them a special status under the immigration laws—the Attorney General noted that this subclass is largely composed of persons with a permanent attachment to the Nation, and that they are unlikely to be displaced from our territory: "We have neither the resources, the capability, nor the motivation to uproot and deport millions of illegal aliens, many of whom have become, in effect, members of the community. By granting limited legal status to the productive and law-abiding members of this shadow population, we will recognize reality and devote our enforcement resources to deterring future illegal arrivals." Joint Hearing before the Subcommittee on Immigration, Refugees, and International Law of the House Committee on the Judiciary and the Subcommittee on Immigration and Refugee Policy of the Senate Committee on the Judiciary, 97th Cong., 1st Sess., 9 (1981) (testimony of William French Smith, Attorney General).

[19]We reject the claim that "illegal aliens" are a "suspect class." No case in which we have attempted to define a suspect class . . . has addressed the status of persons unlawfully in our country. Unlike most of the classifications that we have recognized as suspect, entry into this class, by virtue of entry into this country, is the product of voluntary action. Indeed, entry into the class is itself a crime. In addition, it could hardly be suggested that undocumented status is a "constitutional irrelevancy." With respect to the actions of the Federal Government, alienage classifications may be intimately related to the conduct of foreign policy, to the federal prerogative to control access to the United States, and to the plenary federal power to determine who has sufficiently manifested his allegiance to become a citizen of the Nation. No State may independently exercise a like power. But if the Federal Government has by uniform rule prescribed what it believes to be appropriate standards for the treatment of an alien subclass, the States may, of course, follow the federal direction. See *DeCanas v. Bica*, 424 U.S. 351, 96 S.Ct. 933, 47 L.Ed.2d 43 (1976).

"benefit" indistinguishable from other forms of social welfare legislation. Both the importance of education in maintaining our basic institutions, and the lasting impact of its deprivation on the life of the child, mark the distinction. The "American people have always regarded education and [the] acquisition of knowledge as matters of supreme importance." *Meyer v. Nebraska*, 262 U.S. 390, 400, . . . (1923). . . . [E]ducation has a fundamental role in maintaining the fabric of our society. We cannot ignore the significant social costs borne by our Nation when select groups are denied the means to absorb the values and skills upon which our social order rests.

In addition to the pivotal role of education in sustaining our political and cultural heritage, denial of education to some isolated group of children poses an affront to one of the goals of the Equal Protection Clause: the abolition of governmental barriers presenting unreasonable obstacles to advancement on the basis of individual merit. Paradoxically, by depriving the children of any disfavored group of an education, we foreclose the means by which that group might raise the level of esteem in which it is held by the majority. But more directly, "education prepares individuals to be self-reliant and self-sufficient participants in society." *Wisconsin v. Yoder, supra*, 406 U.S., at 221. . . . Illiteracy is an enduring disability. The inability to read and write will handicap the individual deprived of a basic education each and every day of his life. The inestimable toll of that deprivation on the social economic, intellectual, and psychological well-being of the individual, and the obstacle it poses to individual achievement, make it most difficult to reconcile the cost or the principle of a status-based denial of basic education with the framework of equality embodied in the Equal Protection Clause. . . .

B

These well-settled principles allow us to determine the proper level of deference to be afforded § 21.031. Undocumented aliens cannot be treated as a suspect class because their presence in this country in violation of federal law is not a "constitutional irrelevancy." Nor is education a fundamental right; a State need not justify by compelling necessity every variation in the manner in which education is provided to its population. See *San Antonio Independent School Dist. v. Rodriguez, supra*, at 28–39. . . . But more is involved in these cases than the abstract question

whether § 21.031 discriminates against a suspect class, or whether education is a fundamental right. Section 21.031 imposes a lifetime hardship on a discrete class of children not accountable for their disabling status. The stigma of illiteracy will mark them for the rest of their lives. By denying these children a basic education, we deny them the ability to live within the structure of our civic institutions, and foreclose any realistic possibility that they will contribute in even the smallest way to the progress of our Nation. In determining the rationality of § 21.031, we may appropriately take into account its costs to the Nation and to the innocent children who are its victims. In light of these countervailing costs, the discrimination contained in § 21.031 can hardly be considered rational unless it furthers some substantial goal of the State.

IV

It is the State's principal argument, and apparently the view of the dissenting Justices, that the undocumented status of these children *vel non* establishes a sufficient rational basis for denying them benefits that a State might choose to afford other residents. The State notes that while other aliens are admitted "on an equality of legal privileges with all citizens under non-discriminatory laws," *Takahashi v. Fish & Game Comm'n*, 334 U.S. 410, 420, . . . (1948), the asserted right of these children to an education can claim no implicit congressional imprimatur. Indeed, in the State's view, Congress' apparent disapproval of the presence of these children within the United States, and the evasion of the federal regulatory program that is the mark of undocumented status, provides authority for its decision to impose upon them special disabilities. . . .

* * *

As we recognized in *DeCanas v. Bica*, 424 U.S. 351, . . . (1976), the States do have some authority to act with respect to illegal aliens, at least where such action mirrors federal objectives and furthers a legitimate state goal. In *DeCanas*, the State's program reflected Congress' intention to bar from employment all aliens except those possessing a grant of permission to work in this country. *Id.*, at 361. . . . In contrast, there is no indication that the disability imposed by § 21.031 corresponds to any identifiable congressional policy. The State does not claim that the conservation of state educational resources was ever a congressional concern in restricting immigration. More importantly, the classification reflected in § 21.031 does not operate harmoniously within the federal program.

To be sure, like all persons who have entered the United States unlawfully, these children are subject to deportation. 8 U.S.C. §§ 1251, 1252. . . . But there is no assurance that a child subject to deportation will ever be deported. An illegal entrant might be granted federal permission to continue to reside in this country, or even to become a citizen. *See, e.g.,* 8 U.S.C. §§ 1252, 1253(h), 1254 (1976 ed. and Supp.IV). In light of the discretionary federal power to grant relief from deportation, a State cannot realistically determine that any particular undocumented child will in fact be deported until after deportation proceedings have been completed. It would of course be most difficult for the State to justify a denial of education to a child enjoying an inchoate federal permission to remain.

We are reluctant to impute to Congress the intention to withhold from these children, for so long as they are present in this country through no fault of their own, access to a basic education. In other contexts, undocumented status, coupled with some articulable federal policy, might enhance state authority with respect to the treatment of undocumented aliens. But in the area of special constitutional sensitivity presented by these cases, and in the absence of any contrary indication fairly discernible in the present legislative record, we perceive no national policy that supports the State in denying these children an elementary education. The State may borrow the federal classification. But to justify its use as a criterion for its own discriminatory policy, the State must demonstrate that the classification is reasonably adapted to *"the purposes for which the state desires to use it."* Oyama v. California, 332 U.S. 633, 664–665, . . . (1948) (Murphy, J., concurring) (emphasis added). We therefore turn to the state objectives that are said to support § 21.031.

V

Appellants argue that the classification at issue furthers an interest in the "preservation of the state's limited resources for the education of its lawful residents." . . . Of course, a concern for the preservation of resources standing alone can hardly justify the clas-

sification used in allocating those resources. . . . The State must do more than justify its classification with a concise expression of an intention to discriminate. *Examining Board v. Flores de Otero,* 426 U.S. 572, 605, . . . (1976). Apart from the asserted state prerogative to act against undocumented children solely on the basis of their undocumented status—an asserted prerogative that carries only minimal force in the circumstances of these cases—we discern three colorable state interests that might support § 21.031.

First, appellants appear to suggest that the State may seek to protect itself from an influx of illegal immigrants. While a State might have an interest in mitigating the potentially harsh economic effects of sudden shifts in population, § 21.031 hardly offers an effective method of dealing with an urgent demographic or economic problem. There is no evidence in the record suggesting that illegal entrants impose any significant burden on the State's economy. To the contrary, the available evidence suggests that illegal aliens underutilize public services, while contributing their labor to the local economy and tax money to the state fisc. 458 F.Supp., at 578; 501 F.Supp., at 570–571. The dominant incentive for illegal entry into the State of Texas is the availability of employment; few if any illegal immigrants come to this country, or presumably to the State of Texas, in order to avail themselves of a free education. Thus, even making the doubtful assumption that the net impact of illegal aliens on the economy of the State is negative, we think it clear that "[c]harging tuition to undocumented children constitutes a ludicrously ineffectual attempt to stem the tide of illegal immigration," at least when compared with the alternative of prohibiting the employment of illegal aliens. . . .

Second, while it is apparent that a State may "not . . . reduce expenditures for education by barring [some arbitrarily chosen class of] children from its schools," *Shapiro v. Thompson,* 394 U.S. 618, 633, . . . (1969), appellants suggest that undocumented children are appropriately singled out for exclusion because of the special burdens they impose on the State's ability to provide high-quality public education. But the record in no way supports the claim that exclusion of undocumented children is likely to improve the overall quality of education in the State.[25] . . . Of course, even if improvement in the quality of education were a likely result of barring

---

[25]Nor does the record support the claim that the educational resources of the State are so direly limited that some form of "educational *triage*" might be deemed a reasonable (assuming that it were a permissible) response to the State's problems. *Id.,* at 579–581.

some *number* of children from the schools of the State, the State must support its selection of *this* group as the appropriate target for exclusion. In terms of educational cost and need, however, undocumented children are "basically indistinguishable" from legally resident alien children. . . .

Finally, appellants suggest that undocumented children are appropriately singled out because their unlawful presence within the United States renders them less likely than other children to remain within the boundaries of the State, and to put their education to productive social or political use within the State. Even assuming that such an interest is legitimate, it is an interest that is most difficult to quantify. The State has no assurance that any child, citizen or not, will employ the education provided by the State within the confines of the State's borders. In any event, the record is clear that many of the undocumented children disabled by this classification will remain in this country indefinitely, and that some will become lawful residents or citizens of the United States. . . .

VI

If the State is to deny a discrete group of innocent children the free public education that it offers to other children residing within its borders, that denial must be justified by a showing that it furthers some substantial state interest. No such showing was made here. Accordingly, the judgment of the Court of Appeals in each of these cases is

Affirmed.

Justice Marshall, concurring.

While I join the Court's opinion, I do so without in any way retreating from my opinion in *San Antonio Independent School District v. Rodriguez*, 411 U.S. 1, 70–133, . . . (dissenting opinion). I continue to believe that an individual's interest in education is fundamental, and that this view is amply supported "by the unique status accorded public education by our society, and by the close relationship between education and some of our most basic constitutional values." *Id.*, at 111. . . . Furthermore, I believe that the facts of these cases demonstrate the wisdom of rejecting a rigidified approach to equal protection analysis, and of employing an approach that allows for varying levels of scrutiny depending upon "the constitutional and societal importance of the interest adversely affected and the recognized invidiousness of the basis upon which the particular classification is drawn." *Id.*, at 99. . . .

Justice Blackmun, concurring.

I join the opinion and judgment of the Court.

Like Justice Powell, I believe that the children involved in this litigation "should not be left on the streets uneducated." . . . I write separately, however, because in my view the nature of the interest at stake is crucial to the proper resolution of these cases.

* * *

In my view, when the State provides an education to some and denies it to others, it immediately and inevitably creates class distinctions of a type fundamentally inconsistent with . . . the Equal Protection Clause. Children denied an education are placed at a permanent and insurmountable competitive disadvantage, for an uneducated child is denied even the opportunity to achieve. And when those children are members of an identifiable group, that group—through the State's action—will have been converted into a discrete underclass. Other benefits provided by the State, such as housing and public assistance, are of course important; to an individual in immediate need, they may be more desirable than the right to be educated. But classifications involving the complete denial of education are in a sense unique, for they strike at the heart of equal protection values by involving the State in the creation of permanent class distinctions. Cf. Rodriguez, 411 U.S., at 115, n. 74, . . . (Marshall, J., dissenting). In a sense, then, denial of an education is the analogue of denial of the right to vote: the former relegates the individual to second-class social status; the latter places him at a permanent political disadvantage.

This conclusion is fully consistent with [the view in] *Rodriguez* [that the Constitution does not create a fundamental right to education]. The Court there reserved judgment on the constitutionality of a state system that "occasioned an absolute denial of educational opportunities to any of its children," noting that "no charge fairly could be made that the system [at issue in *Rodriguez*] fails to provide each child with an opportunity to acquire . . . basic minimal skills." *Id.*, at 37, 93 S.Ct., at 1299. . . . Here, however, the State has undertaken to provide an education to most of the children residing within its borders. And, in contrast to the situation in *Rodriguez*, it does not take an advanced degree to predict the effects of a complete denial of education upon those children targeted by the State's classification. In such circumstances, the voting decisions suggest that the State must offer something more than a rational basis for its classification.

* * *

Because I believe that the Court's carefully worded analysis recognizes the importance of the equal protection and preemption interests I consider crucial, I join its opinion as well as its judgment.

Justice Powell, concurring.

I join the opinion of the Court, and write separately to emphasize the unique character of the cases before us.

The classification in question severely disadvantages children who are the victims of a combination of circumstances. Access from Mexico into this country, across our 2,000-mile border, is readily available and virtually uncontrollable. Illegal aliens are attracted by our employment opportunities, and perhaps by other benefits as well. This is a problem of serious national proportions, as the Attorney General recently has recognized. See *ante*, at 2395, n. 17. . . . It therefore is certain that illegal aliens will continue to enter the United States and, as the record makes clear, an unknown percentage of them will remain here. I agree with the Court that their children should not be left on the streets uneducated.

Although the analogy is not perfect, our holding today does find support in decisions of this Court with respect to the status of illegitimates. In *Weber v. Aetna Casualty & Surety Co.*, 406 U.S. 164, 175, . . . (1972), we said: "[V]isiting . . . condemnation on the head of an infant" for the misdeeds of the parents is illogical, unjust, and "contrary to the basic concept of our system that legal burdens should bear some relationship to individual responsibility or wrongdoing."

In these cases, the State of Texas effectively denies to the school-age children of illegal aliens the opportunity to attend the free public schools that the State makes available to all residents. They are excluded only because of a status resulting from the violation by parents or guardians of our immigration laws and the fact that they remain in our country unlawfully. The appellee children are innocent in this respect. They can "affect neither their parents' conduct nor their own status." *Trimble v. Gordon*, 430 U.S. 762, 770, . . . (1977).

Our review in a case such as these is properly heightened. See *id.*, at 767,. . . . Cf. *Craig v. Boren*, 429 U.S. 190, . . . (1976). The classification at issue deprives a group of children of the opportunity for education afforded all other children simply because they have been assigned a legal status due to a violation of law by their parents. These children thus have been singled out for a lifelong penalty and stigma. A legislative classification that threatens the creation of an underclass of future citizens and residents cannot be reconciled with one of the fundamental purposes of the Fourteenth Amendment. In these unique circumstances, the Court properly may require that the State's interests be substantial and that the means bear a "fair and substantial relation" to these interests.[3] . . .

In my view, the State's denial of education to these children bears no substantial relation to any substantial state interest. Both of the District Courts found that an uncertain but significant percentage of illegal alien children will remain in Texas as residents and many eventually will become citizens. The discussion by the Court, *ante*, at Part V, of the State's purported interests demonstrates that they are poorly served by the educational exclusion. Indeed, the interests relied upon by the State would seem to be insubstantial in view of the consequences to the State itself of wholly uneducated persons living indefinitely within its borders. By contrast, access to the public schools is made available to the children of lawful residents without regard to the temporary nature of their residency in the particular Texas school district. The Court of Appeals and the District Courts that addressed these cases concluded that the classification could not satisfy even the bare requirements of rationality. One need not go so far to conclude that the exclusion of appellees' class of children from state-provided education is a type of punitive discrimination based on status that is impermissible under the Equal Protection Clause.

In reaching this conclusion, I am not unmindful of what must be the exasperation of responsible citizens and government authorities in Texas and other States similarly situated. Their responsibility, if any, for the influx of aliens is slight compared to that imposed by the Constitution on the Federal Government. . . . But it hardly can be argued rationally that anyone benefits from the creation within our borders of a subclass of illiterate persons many of whom will

---

[3]The Chief Justice argues in his dissenting opinion that this heightened standard of review is inconsistent with the Court's decision in *San Antonio Independent School District v. Rodriguez*, 411 U.S. 1, 93 S.Ct. 1278, 36 L.Ed.2d 16 (1973). But in *Rodriguez* no group of children was singled out by the State and then penalized because of their parents' status. Rather, funding for education varied across the State because of the tradition of local control. Nor, in that case, was any group of children totally deprived of all education as in these cases. If the resident children of illegal aliens were denied welfare assistance, made available by government to all other children who qualify, this also — in my opinion — would be an impermissible penalizing of children because of their parents' status.

remain in the State, adding to the problems and costs of both State and National Governments attendant upon unemployment, welfare, and crime.

Chief Justice Burger, with whom Justice White, Justice Rehnquist, and Justice O'Connor join, dissenting.

Were it our business to set the Nation's social policy, I would agree without hesitation that it is senseless for an enlightened society to deprive any children—including illegal aliens—of an elementary education. I fully agree that it would be folly—and wrong—to tolerate creation of a segment of society made up of illiterate persons, many having a limited or no command of our language.[15] However, the Constitution does not constitute us as "Platonic Guardians" nor does it vest in this Court the authority to strike down laws because they do not meet our standards of desirable social policy, "wisdom," or "common sense." . . .

. . . The failure of enforcement of the immigration laws over more than a decade and the inherent difficulty and expense of sealing our vast borders have combined to create a grave socioeconomic dilemma. It is a dilemma that has not yet even been fully assessed, let alone addressed. However, it is not the function of the Judiciary to provide "effective leadership" simply because the political branches of government fail to do so.

* * *

I

* * *

[B]y patching together bits and pieces of what might be termed quasi-suspect-class and quasi-fundamental-rights analysis, the Court spins out a theory custom-tailored to the facts of these cases.

In the end, we are told little more than that the level of scrutiny employed to strike down the Texas law applies only when illegal alien children are deprived of a public education. . . . If ever a court was guilty of an unabashedly result-oriented approach, this case is a prime example.

* * *

The Court first suggests that these illegal alien children, although not a suspect class, are entitled to special solicitude under the Equal Protection Clause because they lack "control" over or "responsibility" for their unlawful entry into this country. . . . Similarly, the Court appears to take the position that § 21.031 is presumptively "irrational" because it has the effect of imposing "penalties" on "innocent" children. . . . However, the Equal Protection Clause does not preclude legislators from classifying among persons on the basis of factors and characteristics over which individuals may be said to lack "control." Indeed, in some circumstances persons generally, and children in particular, may have little control over or responsibility for such things as their ill health, need for public assistance, or place of residence. Yet a state legislature is not barred from considering, for example, relevant differences between the mentally healthy and the mentally ill, or between the residents of different counties,[5] simply because these may be factors unrelated to individual choice or to any "wrongdoing." . . .

The Court does not presume to suggest that appellees' purported lack of culpability for their illegal status prevents them from being deported or otherwise "penalized" under federal law. Yet would deportation be any less a "penalty" than denial of privileges provided to legal residents? Illegality of presence in the United States does not—and need not—depend on some amorphous concept of "guilt" or "innocence" concerning an alien's entry. Similarly, a state's use of federal immigration status as a basis for legislative classification is not necessarily rendered suspect for its failure to take such factors into account.

The Court's analogy to cases involving discrimination against illegitimate children—see *ante*, at 2396; *ante*, at 2406–2407 (Powell, J., concurring)—is grossly misleading. The State has not thrust any disabilities upon appellees due to their "status of birth." Cf. *Weber v. Aetna Casualty & Surety Co.*, 406 U.S. 164, 176, 92 S.Ct. 1400, 1407, 31 L.Ed.2d 768 (1972). Rather, appellees' status is predicated upon the circumstances of their concededly illegal pres-

---

[15]It does not follow, however, that a state should bear the costs of educating children whose illegal presence in this country results from the default of the political branches of the Federal Government. A state has no power to prevent unlawful immigration, and no power to deport illegal aliens; those powers are reserved exclusively to Congress and the Executive. If the Federal Government, properly chargeable with deporting illegal aliens, fails to do so, it should bear the burdens of their presence here. Surely if illegal alien children can be identified for purposes of this litigation, their parents can be identified for purposes of prompt deportation.

[5]Appellees "lack control" over their illegal residence in this country in the same sense as lawfully resident children lack control over the school district in which their parents reside. Yet in *San Antonio Independent School Dist. v. Rodriguez*, 411 U.S. 1, 93 S.Ct. 1278, 36 L.Ed.2d 16 (1973), we declined to review under "heightened scrutiny" a claim that a State discriminated against residents of less wealthy school districts in its provision of educational benefits. There was no suggestion in that case that a child's "lack of responsibility" for his residence in a particular school district had any relevance to the proper standard of review of his claims. The result was that children lawfully here but residing in different counties received different treatment.

ence in this country, and is a direct result of Congress' obviously valid exercise of its "broad constitutional powers" in the field of immigration and naturalization. U.S. Const., Art. I, § 8, cl. 4; see *Takahashi v. Fish & Game Comm'n*, 334 U.S. 410, 419, 68 S.Ct. 1138, 1142,92 L.Ed. 1478 (1948). This Court has recognized that in allocating governmental benefits to a given class of aliens, one "may take into account the character of the relationship between the alien and this country." *Mathews v. Diaz*, 426 U.S. 67, 80, 96 S.Ct. 1883, 1891, 48 L.Ed.2d 478 (1976). When that "relationship" is a federally prohibited one, there can, of course, be no presumption that a state has a constitutional duty to include illegal aliens among the recipients of its governmental benefits.

* * *

The second strand of the Court's analysis rests on the premise that, although public education is not a constitutionally guaranteed right, "neither is it merely some governmental 'benefit' indistinguishable from other forms of social welfare legislation." . . .

The importance of education is beyond dispute. Yet we have held repeatedly that the importance of a governmental service does not elevate it to the status of a "fundamental right" for purposes of equal protection analysis. *San Antonio Independent School Dist. v. Rodriguez*, 411 U.S. 1, 30–31, . . . (1973); *Lindsey v. Normet*, 405 U.S. 56, 73–74, . . . (1972). In *San Antonio Independent School Dist., supra*, Justice Powell, speaking for the Court, expressly rejected the proposition that state laws dealing with public education are subject to special scrutiny under the Equal Protection Clause. Moreover, the Court points to no meaningful way to distinguish between education and other governmental benefits in this context. Is the Court suggesting that education is more "fundamental" than food, shelter, or medical care?

* * *

Once it is conceded—as the Court does—that illegal aliens are not a suspect class, and that education is not a fundamental right, our inquiry should focus on and be limited to whether the legislative classification at issue bears a rational relationship to a legitimate state purpose. . . .

The State contends primarily that § 21.031 serves to prevent undue depletion of its limited revenues available for education, and to preserve the fiscal integrity of the State's school-financing system against an ever-increasing flood of illegal aliens—aliens over whose entry or continued presence it has no control. Of course such fiscal concerns alone could not justify discrimination against a suspect class or an arbitrary and irrational denial of benefits to a particular group of persons. Yet I assume no Member of this Court would argue that prudent conservation of finite state revenues is *per se* an illegitimate goal. . . . The significant question here is whether the requirement of tuition from illegal aliens who attend the public schools—as well as from residents of other states, for example—is a rational and reasonable means of furthering the State's legitimate fiscal ends.[10]

* * *

Without laboring what will undoubtedly seem obvious to many, it simply is not "irrational" for a state to conclude that it does not have the same responsibility to provide benefits for persons whose very presence in the state and this country is illegal as it does to provide for persons lawfully present. By definition, illegal aliens have no right whatever to be here, and the state may reasonably, and constitutionally, elect not to provide them with governmental services at the expense of those who are lawfully in the state. . . .

* * *

The Court maintains—as if this were the issue—that "barring undocumented children from local schools would not necessarily improve the quality of education provided in those schools." *Ante*, at 2401. See 458 F.Supp. 569, 577 (ED Tex.1978). However, the legitimacy of barring illegal aliens from programs such as Medicare or Medicaid does not depend on a showing that the barrier would "improve the quality" of medical care given to persons lawfully entitled to participate in such programs. Modern education, like medical care, is enormously expensive, and there can

---

[10]The Texas law might also be justified as a means of deterring unlawful immigration. While regulation of immigration is an exclusively federal function, a state may take steps, consistent with federal immigration policy, to protect its economy and ability to provide governmental services from the "deleterious effects" of a massive influx of illegal immigrants. . . . The Court maintains that denying illegal aliens a free public education is an "ineffectual" means of deterring unlawful immigration, at least when compared to a prohibition against the employment of illegal aliens. . . . Perhaps that is correct, but it is not dispositive; the Equal Protection Clause does not mandate that a state choose either the most effective and all-encompassing means of addressing a problem or none at all. . . . Texas might rationally conclude that more significant "demographic or economic problem[s]," *ante*, at 2401, are engendered by the illegal entry into the State of entire families of aliens for indefinite periods than by the periodic sojourns of single adults who intend to leave the State after short-term or seasonal employment. It blinks reality to maintain that availability of governmental services such as education plays no role in an alien family's decision to enter, or remain in, this country; certainly, the availability of a free bilingual public education might well influence an alien to bring his children rather than travel alone for better job opportunities.

be no doubt that very large added costs will fall on the State or its local school districts as a result of the inclusion of illegal aliens in the tuition-free public schools. The State may, in its discretion, use any savings resulting from its tuition requirement to "improve the quality of education" in the public school system, or to enhance the funds available for other social programs, or to reduce the tax burden placed on its residents; each of these ends is "legitimate." The State need not show, as the Court implies, that the incremental cost of educating illegal aliens will send it into bankruptcy, or have a " 'grave impact on the quality of education,' " *ante*, at 2401; that is not dispositive under a "rational basis" scrutiny. . . .

Denying a free education to illegal alien children is not a choice I would make were I a legislator. Apart from compassionate considerations, the long-range costs of excluding any children from the public schools may well outweigh the costs of educating them. But that is not the issue; the fact that there are sound *policy* arguments against the Texas Legislature's choice does not render that choice an unconstitutional one.

II

The Constitution does not provide a cure for every social ill, nor does it vest judges with a mandate to try to remedy every social problem. . . .

Congress, "vested by the Constitution with the responsibility of protecting our borders and legislating with respect to aliens," . . . bears primary responsibility for addressing the problems occasioned by the millions of illegal aliens flooding across our southern border. Similarly, it is for Congress, and not this Court, to assess the "social costs borne by our Nation when select groups are denied the means to absorb the values and skills upon which our social order rests." . . .

The solution to this seemingly intractable problem is to defer to the political processes, unpalatable as that may be to some.

NOTES AND QUESTIONS

1. The Constitutional Underpinning of Plyler

Is *Plyler* a case that successfully circumvents the fact that alienage is not always a suspect classification and education is not a fundamental interest? The Court has treated alienage as suspect for most purposes, except when the state seeks to exclude non-

citizens from activities that are central to democratic self-governance. Aliens can be barred from voting, as discussed in chapter 8, and from teaching in public schools, which prepare students for citizenship, as discussed in chapter 2. As described at greater length in the analysis of school finance in chapter 7, education is one of the most important activities that the state undertakes, but it is not one that the United States Constitution recognizes as fundamental. With the possible exception of an absolute deprivation of education, the Court applies only a rational relation test to policies that affect access to education. Should the Court be able to cumulate a sometimes suspect status and an important interest to apply heightened scrutiny to a legislative classification? Does such an approach lead to the kind of trade-offs that more closely resemble policymaking than constitutional analysis?

2. The Role of the Court and the Political Process

Is it appropriate for the Court to consider whether the undocumented are likely to remain in the United States and become a permanent underclass? Is it unconstitutional for the state of Texas to create an underclass by denying some children access to public education? Or, as the dissent argues, is it merely a misguided policy judgment that should be corrected through the political process? Is judicial protection essential because the undocumented cannot participate effectively in the political arena? Does it matter that the legislation targets children, who cannot vote and who are largely unable to countermand their parents' decisions to enter the United States?

3. The Future of Plyler

Because of its slim 5–4 majority, its weaving together of alienage and education to invoke heightened scrutiny, and changes in membership on the Court, scholars have speculated that *Plyler* might not survive if the issue came before the justices again. Carter, "Intermediate Scrutiny Under Fire: Will *Plyler* Survive State Legislation to Exclude Undocumented Children from School?" 31 *U.S.F.L.Rev.* 345 (1997); Cooper, "*Plyler* at the Core: Understanding the Proposition 187 Challenge," 17 *Chicano-Latino L.Rev.* 64 (1995).

3. Plyler Revisited: Ongoing Efforts to Bar the Undocumented from Public Schools. California voters gave the federal courts an opportunity to reconsider *Plyler* when they adopted Proposition 187

in 1994. The initiative provides in relevant part the following:

Proposition 187
Text of Proposed Law, 1994.

* * *

SECTION 7. Exclusion of Illegal Aliens from Public Elementary and Secondary Schools.

Section 48215 is added to the Education Code, to read:

48215. (a) No public elementary or secondary school shall admit, or permit the attendance of, any child who is not a citizen of the United States, an alien lawfully admitted as a permanent resident, or a person who is otherwise authorized under federal law to be present in the United States.

(b) Commencing January 1, 1995, each school district shall verify the legal status of each child enrolling in the school district for the first time in order to ensure the enrollment or attendance only of citizens, aliens lawfully admitted as permanent residents, or persons who are otherwise authorized to be present in the United States.

(c) By January 1, 1996, each school district shall have verified the legal status of each child already enrolled and in attendance in the school district in order to ensure the enrollment or attendance only of citizens, aliens lawfully admitted as permanent residents, or persons who are otherwise authorized under federal law to be present in the United States.

(d) By January 1, 1996, each school district shall also have verified the legal status of each parent or guardian of each child referred to in subdivisions (b) and (c), to determine whether such parent or guardian is one of the following:

(1) A citizen of the United States.
(2) An alien lawfully admitted as a permanent resident.
(3) An alien admitted lawfully for a temporary period of time.

(e) Each school district shall provide information to the State Superintendent of Public Instruction, the Attorney General of California, and the United States Immigration and Naturalization Service regarding any enrollee or pupil, or parent or guardian, attending a public elementary or secondary school in the school district determined or reasonably suspected to be in violation of federal immigration laws within forty-five days after becoming aware of an apparent violation. The notice shall also be provided to the parent or legal guardian of the enrollee or pupil, and shall state that an existing pupil may not continue to attend the school after ninety calendar days from the date of the notice, unless legal status is established.

(f) For each child who cannot establish legal status in the United States, each school district shall continue to provide education for a period of ninety days from the date of the notice. Such ninety day period shall be utilized to accomplish an orderly transition to a school in the child's country of origin. Each school district shall fully cooperate in this transition effort to ensure that the educational needs of the child are best served for that period of time.

* * *

The initiative also barred undocumented students from public colleges and universities. Proposition 187, § 8.

Approximately one year after its passage, a federal district court held that Proposition 187 impermissibly preempted federal law when it attempted to bar the undocumented from public elementary and secondary schools. However, the state could bar the undocumented from access to public higher education.

League of United Latin American Citizens (LULAC) v. Wilson
908 F.Supp. 755 (C.D.Cal. 1995).

Mariana R. Pfaelzer, District Judge:

* * *

The question of whether provisions of Proposition 187 are preempted by federal law is governed by the Supreme Court's decision in *De Canas v. Bica*, 424 U.S. 351, 96 S.Ct. 933, 47 L.Ed.2d 43 (1976) (California statute prohibiting an employer from knowingly employing an alien who is not entitled to lawful residence in the United States held not preempted under federal law). In *De Canas*, the Supreme Court set forth three tests to be used in determining whether a state statute related to immigration is preempted. Pursuant to *De Canas*, if a statute fails any one of the three tests, it is preempted by federal law.

Under the first test, the Court must determine whether a state statute is a "regulation of immigration." Since the "[p]ower to regulate immigration is unquestionably exclusively a federal power," *id.* at 354, 96 S.Ct. at 936, any state statute which regulates immigration is "constitutionally proscribed." *Id.* at 356, 96 S.Ct. at 936.

Under the second test, even if the state law is not an impermissible regulation of immigration, it may still be preempted if there is a showing that it was the "clear and manifest purpose of Congress" to effect a "complete ouster of state power—including state power to promulgate laws not in conflict with federal laws" with respect to the subject matter which the statute attempts to regulate. *Id.* at 357, 96 S.Ct. at 937. In other words, under the second test, a statute is preempted where Congress intended to "occupy the field" which the statute attempts to regulate.

Under the third test, a state law is preempted if it "stands as an obstacle to the accomplishment and execution of the full purposes and objectives of Congress." *Id.* at 363, 96 S.Ct. at 940 (*citing Hines v. Davidowitz*, 312 U.S. 52, 67, 61 S.Ct. 399, 404, 85 L.Ed. 581 (1941)). Stated differently, a statute is preempted under the third test if it conflicts with federal law making compliance with both state and federal law impossible. *Michigan Canners & Freezers v. Agricultural Marketing and Bargaining Board*, 467 U.S. 461, 469, 104 S.Ct. 2518, 2523, 81 L.Ed.2d 399 (1984); *Florida Lime & Avocado Growers v. Paul*, 373 U.S. 132, 142–43, 83 S.Ct. 1210, 1217–18, 10 L.Ed.2d 248 (1963).

A. Whether Proposition 187 Constitutes an Impermissible Regulation of Immigration.

The federal government possesses the exclusive power to regulate immigration. *De Canas*, 424 U.S. at 354–355, 96 S.Ct. at 936 ("Power to regulate immigration is unquestionably exclusively a federal power.") That power derives from the Constitution's grant to the federal government of the power to "establish a uniform Rule of Naturalization," U.S. Const. art. I, § 8, cl. 4., and to "regulate Commerce with foreign Nations." *Id.*, cl. 3. In addition, the Supreme Court has held that the federal government's power to control immigration is inherent in the nation's sovereignty. . . .

Congress has exercised its power over immigration in the Immigration and Nationality Act, 8 U.S.C. § 1101 *et seq.* (the "INA"). The INA is a comprehensive regulatory scheme which regulates the authorized entry, length of stay, residence status and deportation of aliens. *See Gonzales v. City of Peoria*, 722 F.2d 468, 474–75 (9th Cir.1983) (recognizing that the regulatory scheme created by the INA is so pervasive as to be consistent with the exclusive federal power over immigration). The INA delegates en-

forcement duties to the Immigration and Naturalization Service ("INS").

Because the federal government bears the exclusive responsibility for immigration matters, the states "can neither add to nor take from the conditions lawfully imposed by Congress upon admission, naturalization and residence of aliens in the United States or the several states." *Takahashi v. Fish & Game Comm'n*, 334 U.S. 410, 419, 68 S.Ct. 1138, 1142, 92 L.Ed. 1478 (1948). *See also Plyler v. Doe*, 457 U.S. 202 at 225, 102 S.Ct. 2382 at 2399, 72 L.Ed.2d 786 (1982) ("The States enjoy no power with respect to the classification of aliens." (*citing Hines v. Davidowitz*, 312 U.S. 52, 61 S.Ct. 399, 85 L.Ed. 581 (1941))).

* * *

In this case, plaintiffs urge that the entirety of Proposition 187 constitutes a scheme to regulate immigration and is therefore preempted. . . .

In *De Canas*, the statute at issue provided that "[n]o employer shall knowingly employ an alien who is not entitled to lawful residence in the United States if such employment would have an adverse effect on lawful resident workers." *Id.* at 352 n. 1, 96 S.Ct. at 935; Cal.Lab.Code § 2805. Noting that in that case, California had "sought to strengthen its economy by adopting federal standards in imposing criminal sanctions against state employers who knowingly employ aliens who have no federal right to employment within the country," the Supreme Court found that the statute did not constitute an immigration regulation, but rather, had only "some purely speculative and indirect impact on immigration." *Id.* at 355, 96 S.Ct. at 936.

Unlike the statute at issue in *De Canas*, various of Proposition 187's provisions have much more than a "purely speculative and indirect impact on immigration." Indeed, Proposition 187's verification, notification and cooperation/reporting requirements [including those mandating that school districts verify the legal status of students and their parents] directly regulate immigration by creating a comprehensive scheme to detect and report the presence and effect the removal of illegal aliens. The scheme requires state agents to question all arrestees, applicants for medical and social services, students, and parents of students about their immigration status; to obtain and examine documents relating to the immigration status of such persons; to identify "suspected" "illegal" immigrants present in California; to report suspected "illegal" immigrants to state and federal authorities; and to instruct people suspected of being in the United States illegally to obtain "legal status" or "leave the country." Thus, Proposition 187's scheme has a direct and substantial impact on immigration.

Further, certain of Proposition 187's provisions require state agents to make *independent* determinations of who is subject to the initiative's benefits denial, notification and cooperation/reporting provisions and who may lawfully remain in the United States. Unlike the statute at issue in *De Canas*, which adopted *federal standards* to determine whether an individual's immigration status subjected an employer to liability, Proposition 187's classification provisions create an entirely *independent* set of criteria by which to classify individuals based on immigration status. *See, e.g.*, Prop. 187 §§ 5(b); 6(b); 7(d).

On the other hand, the benefits denial provisions of sections 5 through 8 [including those related to public education] may be likened to the statute at issue in *De Canas*. While the denial of benefits to persons not lawfully present in the United States may indirectly or incidentally affect immigration by causing such persons to leave the state or deterring them from entering California in the first place, such a denial does not amount to a "determination of who should or should not be admitted into the country." *De Canas*, 424 U.S. at 355, 96 S.Ct. at 936. Accordingly, the benefits denials provisions are not impermissible regulations of immigration and thus are not preempted under the first *De Canas* test.

* * *

Accordingly, the classification, notification and cooperation/reporting provisions of the initiative, contained in sections 4 through 9 and in the preamble, which are aimed solely at regulating immigration, are preempted. The provisions which have the permissible purpose and effect of denying state-funded benefits to persons who are unlawfully present in the United States are not a regulation of immigration and therefore survive the first *De Canas* test.

* * *

[The district court then went on to determine whether the denial of benefits, including public education, was impermissible on other grounds.]

3. *Section 7*

Section 7 is entitled "Exclusion of Illegal Aliens From Public Elementary and Secondary Schools."

. . . [S]ection 7 contains classification, notification and cooperation/reporting requirements that, taken together, serve only to further the scheme to regulate immigration and are unnecessary to the denial of public education.

In section 7, subsections (a) through (c) require schools to verify the immigration status of children for the purposes of denying access to public elementary and secondary education. Subsection (d) requires verification of the immigration status of *parents* of school children. Subsection (e) requires school districts to report the "illegal" status of any parent, guardian, enrollee or pupil to state agencies and the INS. Subsection (f) requires school districts to "fully cooperate" in "accomplish[ing] an orderly transition to a school in the child's country of origin."

Subsections (a), (b) and (c), together, assure that undocumented children will be denied access to public education. Subsection (d) is wholly unnecessary to implementing the denial of education mandated by section 7, because the state has no need to know the immigration status of *parents* in order to deny benefits to *children*. . . . [T]he only purpose and effect of subsections (d), (e), and (f) is to ensure that persons determined by the state to be in the United States unlawfully are "transitioned" to the "country of their origin." Subsections (d), (e) and (f) are part of an impermissible scheme to regulate immigration and are therefore preempted under the first *De Canas* test.

In any event, an analysis of section 7 under the rigors of the first *De Canas* test is not necessary to sustain the Court's ruling on these motions. In light of the United States Supreme Court's decision in *Plyler v. Doe*, 457 U.S. 202, 102 S.Ct. 2382, 72 L.Ed.2d 786 (1982), in which the Court held that the Equal Protection Clause of the Fourteenth Amendment prohibits states from excluding undocumented alien children from public schools, section 7 in its entirety conflicts with and is therefore preempted by federal law.

* * *

NOTES AND QUESTIONS

1. *Public Postsecondary Education and Proposition 187*

In the *LULAC* case, the district court went on to hold that the state could deny public postsecondary education to undocumented students, but it could not employ a reporting and verification system different from that used by the INS. 908 F.Supp. at 1255–56. Afterwards, Congress passed the Personal Responsibility and Work Opportunity Reconciliation Act ("PRA") of 1996, Pub.L.No. 104–193, 110 Stat. 2105 (1996). The PRA expressly deferred to *Plyler*'s conclusion that the Constitution did not permit undocumented children to be barred from public elementary and secondary schools. The PRA also denied federal postsecondary education benefits to any alien who was not qualified under the immigration laws. In assessing the PRA's impact on Proposition 187, the district court once again found that Proposition 187 could not bar access to public elementary and secondary schools; however, the new federal law preempted Proposition 187's provisions regarding public postsecondary education so they were struck down. *League of United Latin American Citizens (LULAC) v. Wilson*, 997 F.Supp. 1244 (C.D.Cal. 1997).

2. *The Aftermath of Proposition 187*

After the *LULAC* decision, Governor Pete Wilson appealed to the Ninth Circuit. His successor, Gray Davis, sought mediation to resolve the dispute and announced that he would not seek to bar undocumented students from public schools. "Davis to Oppose Part of Prop. 187; He Won't Help 'Kick Kids out of School,' " *San Diego Union-Tribune*, May 22, 1999, at A3; Lesher, "Davis Won't Follow Prop. 187 on Schools," *L.A.Times*, May 21, 1999, at A1. A taxpayers' association filed suit in state court challenging the governor's authority to pursue mediation. Smith, "Davis Sued Over Mediation Proposal for Prop. 187," *Sacramento Bee*, June 2, 1999, at A3. Eventually, the appeal initiated by Wilson was dropped, and most of Proposition 187's provisions, including those related to elementary and secondary education, were nullified. McDonnell, "Davis Won't Appeal Prop. 187 Ruling, Ending Court Battles," *L.A.Times*, July 29, 1999, at A1; McDermott, "Some Are Embittered by Fate of Prop. 187," *L.A.Times*, Aug. 2, 1999, at A1.

3. *New Battles Over Undocumented Immigration*

In 2000, one year after Proposition 187 was largely nullified, its proponents mobilized to put a new initiative on the California ballot relating to undocumented immigration. However, it would not include any provisions on access to public education. Fernandez, "Prop. 187 Backers Pushing New Initiative," *L.A. Times*, Dec. 3, 1999, at B1. Despite this modification, the proposition's backers could not get enough signatures to qualify for the ballot. Mena, "New Effort to Deny Services to Illegal Immigrants Fizzles," *L.A.Times*, Apr. 22, 2000, at B7. Even so, the battle over public education for the undocumented is unlikely to end anytime soon. Do courts play a unique role in this debate because of the politically disempowered status of children and immigrants? Does it make any difference whether immigrants can vote in school board elections (a matter discussed in chapter 8)? Why or why not?

III. DISABILITY: FROM "INCAPABLE OF BENEFITING" FROM AN EDUCATION TO THE RIGHT TO AN "APPROPRIATE" EDUCATION

A. Introduction

As with ethnicity and national origin, disability creates a dilemma of difference. Once again, questions arise about the extent to which students with disabilities should be assimilated through mainstreaming and accommodation or should be given different treatment because of their special educational needs. For instance, the "Deaf Pride" movement has emphasized the beauty and utility of sign language as an alternative to oral speech. Advocates have demanded equivalent respect for deaf culture and have even questioned technological advances, such as cochlear implants, that would enable children, even those with severe hearing impairments, to communicate orally. Manning, "The Changing Deaf Culture," *USA Today*, May 2, 2000, at 1D. The following excerpt describes the struggle for recognition of deaf culture and traditions. At times, these issues are framed in terms of pluralism and respect for distinct cultures, as the "Deaf Pride" movement makes clear.

"The Making of the Deaf"

J. Rée, *I See a Voice: Deafness, Language and the Senses—A Philosophical History* 230–233 (1999).

* * *

In the second half of the nineteenth century, the oralist movement spread through Europe and North America, inspiring politicians, philanthropists and teachers with the dream of converting all deaf children, however poor, into happy and active citizens. Hard-won skills in speech and lip-reading would allow the deaf to merge imperceptibly into hearing society, no longer condemned to a solitary life as sullen outcasts confined to the language of signs. Following the Milan Congress of 1880, the remaining sign-language residential institutions were reformed, and hundreds of new oralist schools were founded—day schools, on the whole, because their aim was to integrate the deaf into the hearing world, rather than allow them to form silent sign-language communities separated from the rest of society.

A hundred years later, however, the old oralist schools would themselves be almost universally condemned, on the grounds that they were paternalistic and violent, catering to the prejudices of hearing adults rather than the needs of deaf children. But still, the oral method had achieved some undeniable successes, especially with pupils who had a little vestigial hearing. In the past, such children would have been classified as totally deaf, but with the help of devices like Alexander Graham Bell's 'audiometer,' the 'semi-deaf' could now be identified at an early age and equipped with mechanical (or, later, electronic) hearing aids to help them learn speech directly. Even those with very severe hearing loss sometimes benefited from strict oralist regimes, especially if they were 'post-lingually' deaf, and many of them grew up to be grateful to the exacting teachers who, by forbidding them to use signs as children, had forced them to cultivate lip-reading and articulation to the point where their handicap was almost undetectable in much of the everyday business of their lives.

In other ways, however, the new deaf schools did not work out as their founders had hoped. In practice, the deaf would never be able to participate as full equals in the activities of those who could hear; and meantime the schools were encouraging the very tendencies that the oralists most feared—they were allowing the deaf to create a whole new social world for themselves, an exclusive society of the deaf. Local networks of deaf mutual aid, like those which had occasionally established themselves in the past (in Paris, for example, or on Martha's Vineyard), became the rule rather than the exception, and they linked up with each other to form extensive deaf communities—regional, national and even international. For the first time, the deaf came to constitute a conspicuous social group, robust, permanent and sometimes a little defiant. From now on, deaf people were as likely as the rest of the population to marry and have children; and what is more they nearly all chose a deaf partner, usually someone encountered at or through their school. Ironically, then, the oral-

ist opponents of sign language were helping to bring about exactly the kind of separate deaf society they had always wanted to prevent.

Although medical and educational opinion was beginning to regard deafness as a multidimensional disability and a matter of degree, for social purposes it was still defined in simple and absolute terms: culturally, everyone had to be one thing or the other, either deaf or hearing. To be truly deaf—or Deaf with a capital D, to follow a convention introduced in the 1970s—you needed to be brought up in a Deaf community, rather than simply unable to hear. The sociologist Paul Higgins, for instance, is a child of deaf parents, and though his hearing is normal, he can still be accepted as Deaf: 'to be a member of a deaf community,' as he puts it, 'one need not actually be deaf.' The American Deaf world may be riven by deep social divisions—between rich and poor, or black and white, or between those using an elaborate and cosmopolitan version of sign language and those whose repertoire is restricted to a dialect of supposedly rustic and inelegant gestures, or between those who freely use sign language in public and those who regard such conduct as vulgar or obscene—but still it is bound together by a shared sense of unity in opposition to an alien Hearing world. As with sex and sexuality, people who do not fit in with such dichotomies cause embarrassment, anxiety, and even hostility: Higgins explains that the semi-deaf, and those who have lost their hearing 'post-vocationally' or after adolescence, cause 'both ill feelings and amusement', because 'their behaviour does not respect the identity of the deaf community.'

Nevertheless, the utopian aspirations of deaf nationalists like John James Flournoy proved as mistaken as the apocalyptic fears of oralists like Alexander Graham Bell. However much they might want to, the Deaf could never generate the kind of self-reproducing internal structure characteristic of a 'nation,' a 'people,' or a 'race.' Congenital prelingual deafness may be largely hereditary, but that does not mean that it runs in families—that deaf parents have deaf children, and hearing parents do not. So Bell's eugenicist forebodings about marriages between deaf partners turned out to be unfounded. According to a study carried out in the 1970s, in fact, nine out of ten deaf children are born to hearing parents. And even in marriages where both partners are deaf (which account for nine deaf marriages out of ten), more than eight out of ten children have normal hearing.

Deaf communities are therefore a very peculiar hybrid from the point of view of social theory: they are unable to perpetuate themselves by family tradition. The collective life of the Deaf is passed from generation to generation not by the family but by the school; in fact deaf school, in some respects, is the Deaf child's family.

* * *

NOTES AND QUESTIONS

1. Assimilation, Pluralism, and Disability

The push to recognize deaf traditions illustrates the problems of defining equality for the disabled. Even the term "disability" has come under attack because it suggests a deficiency. Some have argued that they are differently abled, rather than disabled. How should equality be defined, and does the definition depend on the nature or severity of an individual's disability? Is assimilation a more realistic goal for a person with a discrete or less profound disability than for one with multiple, severe disabilities? Are the former also better able to forge vibrant, alternative cultures than the latter?

2. The Role of Schools

In defining equal educational opportunity, should it matter that separate schools have played a critical role in the formation of the deaf community and perpetuation of deaf culture? Should such schools be continued, or is it better to assign hearing-impaired children to regular classrooms to the greatest extent possible?

3. The Role of Parents

Should parents be able to choose separate schools or regular classrooms for their hearing-impaired children? Can hearing parents decide that they want their children to be part of the hearing community rather than the deaf community? Can parents enforce this choice by insisting that their children learn to read lips rather than sign? Should parents be permitted to obtain cochlear implants that enable their deaf child to resemble a hearing child?

B. Establishing a Legal Conception of Equality for the Disabled

Although programs for the disabled have been urged since the mid-nineteenth century, the education received by disabled children was historically viewed as a matter of discretionary governmental largess. That situation has changed dramatically. Judicial decisions in the early 1970s asserted that disabled children enjoyed constitutional entitlements to an "appropriate" education, the meaning of which would vary with the nature of the disability, and to procedural protections against arbitrary treatment. These constitutional entitlements, never passed upon by the Supreme Court, have been given a federal statutory basis, as Congress—through Section 504 of the Rehabilitation Act and the Education for All Handicapped Children Act (EAHCA), later renamed the Individuals with Disabilities Education Act (IDEA)—has specified a broad set of rights, both substantive and procedural in nature, for disabled students. Subsequent court decisions have elaborated on the meaning of those statutorily based rights and have reassessed constitutionally rooted claims.

As part of its effort to reduce Washington's role in education, the Reagan Administration sought to repeal EAHCA, consolidating it, along with other categorical programs, in a block grant that states could spend as they wished. Congress rejected that proposal. In 1990, the EAHCA was incorporated into the Individuals with Disabilities Education Act. Pub.L.No. 105–476, 104 Stat. 1103 (1990) (codified as amended at 20 U.S.C. §§1400–1491). In 1997, Congress reauthorized the IDEA. Pub. L. No. 105–17, 111 Stat. 37 (1997).

This section traces the early constitutionalization of the rights of the disabled through the development of federal legislation and its subsequent interpretation in the courts. It examines the interplay between substantive and procedural entitlements, focusing specifically on the feasibility of giving meaning to "appropriate" education through due process hearings. As one might expect from the earlier treatment of implementation issues, changes in policy of this magnitude are not effortlessly achieved. Court decisions and legislation do not, by themselves, guarantee differences in educational practice. These issues are also explored.

The following excerpt briefly describes the education that was typically provided to the disabled as recently as 1970 and the criticisms it provoked.

***

"Legal Reform of Special Education: Empirical Studies and Procedural Proposals"

D. Kirp, W. Buss, and P. Kuriloff, 62 *California Law Review* 40, 41–45 (1974).©1974 by California Law Review, Inc.

Education of the Handicapped

Handicapped, or "exceptional" or "special" children form an extraordinarily diverse group, estimated to include between 8.7 and 35% of the entire student population.[2] From the viewpoint of the general educator, all that the handicapped have in common is that they differ from normal students. Some have problems so severe that their need for special educational attention is self-evident; they literally cannot survive without almost constant assistance.[3] The learning deficiency of most exceptional children, however, is slight and hard to detect.[4] Children who systematically write letters backwards, write in mirror fashion, or seem not to read some letters are common phenomena in lower elementary grades. In many cases, children who have physical disabilities which might interfere with learning cannot be distinguished by school officials from their supposedly normal classmates. Children with slight loss of hearing or sight can often compensate for their difficulty and thus go undetected until a systematic screening program is introduced, as can children with psycholinguistic learning disabilities. Typically, state law denies the most severely handicapped youngsters any right to publicly supported schooling. For the rest, a bewildering variety of special categories distinguishing both type of handicap (*e.g.*, between blindness and retardation) and severity of handicap (*e.g.*, between educable and trainable retardates) have been adopted.

A. Criticisms and Suggested Reforms of Classification Schemes

1. The Severely Handicapped. Most severely handicapped children are classified as ineducable and are denied access to publicly supported instruction. But this practice is inconsistent with the research findings that all children are educable, that is, able through instruction to move from relative dependence to relative independence. Many of these children—estimated to number between 450,000 and 4,000,000—spend their entire lives in state-run institutions, which, while providing minimal care,

lack the resources to undertake any training in self-help. Private schools licensed by the states do train children with specific handicaps. But because these schools are self-supporting, they generally enroll only children from well-to-do homes. While a few states have sought to alleviate this fiscal inequity by providing vouchers for handicapped youngsters, the burden of caring for the severely handicapped falls most heavily upon the poor, the group least able to sacrifice the time and energy needed to ensure adequate educational help.

Even when public schools provide some instruction for the severely handicapped, they do not do enough. Autistic children, for example, require costly, highly structured, professionally staffed programs. Placing autistic children in any other type of program is viewed as the functional equivalent of excluding them from school.

These criticisms of the education of severely handicapped children view the public schools as doing nothing, or too little, for this group. The suggested remedy is to create additional special programs or make available additional resources for existing programs for hard-to-educate children. The criticisms provoked by the schools' treatment of the mildly handicapped, however, are quite different.

2. The Mildly Handicapped. Special programs for the mildly handicapped have been faulted for a host of reasons: they misclassify students, enroll a disproportionate share of minority children, appear educationally inefficacious, and too readily become permanent assignments.

a. Misclassification. "Misclassification," as the critics use that term, means two quite different phenomena. First, it may denote the misapplication of agreed-upon criteria. When, for example, the school violates state law by assigning a student with a 100 I.Q., to a class for the mildly retarded, misclassification is evident. . . .

Misclassification also may denote a dispute over how data are gathered so that established criteria can

---

[2]N.Y. *State Comm'n, Report on the Quality, Cost and Financing of Elementary and Secondary Educ.* 9B.2 (1972). The spread in the figures is almost wholly accounted for by disparities in estimating the percentage of brain-injured and learning-disabled children.

[3]*See generally* Kirk, "Research in Education," in *Mental Retardation* 57 (H. Stevens and R. Heber eds. 1964).

[4]*See* E. Rubin, C. Simson & M. Betwee, *Emotionally Handicapped Children and the Elementary School* 3132, 3134 (1966). *See also* Dunn, "Special Education for the Mildly Retarded: Is Much of It Justifiable?" in *Problems and Issues in the Education of Exceptional Children* 382 (R. Jones ed. 1971).

be applied. Even if a school consistently distinguishes between handicapped and normal students on the basis of a particular test, the test itself may be inadequate or susceptible to multiple interpretations. Many documented instances of misclassification are of this variety. In Washington, D.C., for example, the school system concluded that up to two-thirds of its mildly handicapped students were in fact normal. This reversal in judgment resulted from the substitution of individually administered I.Q. tests for group aptitude tests.[10] . . .

b. Differential Vulnerability.
That certain types of students are particularly vulnerable to special classification makes the critics uneasy. Not all children are even considered for special programs, and those who are do not represent a random sample of the student population. Students who make life difficult for the regular classroom teacher are most apt to have their normal status questioned: more boys than girls[12] and more aggressive than quiescent students are identified as possibly handicapped. White students typically must display both intellectual and behavioral quirks to be considered for special classification, while intellectual difficulties alone are sufficient to render black or Mexican-American students suspect.[13] Non-white students are overrepresented in programs for the mildly handicapped by as much as 250 percent relative to their proportion of the school-age population,[14] a fact which evokes considerable political concern. Overrepresentation diminishes the possibility of school integration, may diminish the educational opportunities of minority students, and calls into question the legitimacy of the entire system of special education classification. Differential vulnerability may lead the school both to ignore the special needs of students who do not disrupt the classroom and to underestimate the educational potential of minority students.

c. Efficacy.
The efficacy of programs for the mildly handicapped frequently has been questioned. Studies comparing the performance of matched groups of students in regular and special programs generally conclude that, despite the additional resources in spe-cial programs, special classes generally have either no effect or a slightly adverse effect on both the motivation and achievement of students assigned to them. Furthermore, these programs may impose a stigma of "differentness" without securing offsetting benefits.

d. Permanent Placement.
Special program assignment for the mildly handicapped is supposed to be temporary, enabling the student ultimately to return to the regular class. In fact, special placements often prove to be permanent assignments: one survey of urban school systems found that fewer than ten percent of the students identified as mildly handicapped ever returned to regular classes. Regular review of special class placement coupled with a commitment to return students to regular programs as soon as possible, might well resolve this problem.

C. The Constitution and Education for the Disabled

The struggle to recognize that all children are educable began in the federal courts. The plaintiffs argued that the total exclusion of disabled children from public education violated their constitutional rights. What follows is a landmark case vindicating this position.

Mills v. Board of Education
348 F.Supp. 866 (D.D.C. 1972).

Joseph C. Waddy, District Judge:

This is a civil action brought on behalf of seven children of school age by their next friends in which they seek a declaration of rights and to enjoin the defendants from excluding them from the District of Columbia Public Schools and/or denying them publicly supported education and to compel the defendants to provide them with immediate and adequate education and educational facilities in the public schools or alternative placement at public expense. They also seek additional and ancillary relief to effectuate the primary relief. They allege that although they can profit from an education either in regular classrooms with supportive services or in spe-

---

[10]*Hobson v. Hansen*, 269 F.Supp. 401, 490–91 (D.D.C. 1967), *appeal dismissed*, 393 U.S. 801, 89 S.Ct. 40, 21 L.Ed.2d 85 (1968), *aff'd en banc sub nom. Smuck v. Hobson*, 408 F.2d 175, 187 (D.C. Cir. 1969).

[12]*See* N. Frazier & M. Sadker, *Sexism in School and Society* 86–94 (1973).

[13]*See* J. Mercer, *Labeling the Mentally Retarded* 67–82 (1973); *cf.* Jensen, "A Theory of Primary and Secondary Familial Mental Retardation," in 4 *Int'l. Rev. of Research in Mental Retardation* 33 (N. Ellis ed. 1970).

[14]*See* Kirp, "Schools as Sorters: The Constitutional and Policy Implications of Student Classification," 121 *U.Pa.L.Rev.* 705, 759–62 (1973).

cial classes adopted to their needs, they have been labeled as behavioral problems, mentally retarded, emotionally disturbed or hyperactive, and denied admission to the public schools or excluded therefrom after admission, with no provision for alternative educational placement or periodical review. . . .

The Problem

The genesis of this case is found (1) in the failure of the District of Columbia to provide publicly supported education and training to plaintiffs and other "exceptional" children, members of their class, and (2) the excluding, suspending, expelling, reassigning and transferring of "exceptional" children from regular public school classes without affording them due process of law.

The problem of providing special education for "exceptional" children (mentally retarded, emotionally disturbed, physically handicapped, hyperactive and other children with behavioral problems) is one of major proportions in the District of Columbia. The precise number of such children cannot be stated because the District has continuously failed to comply with § 31-208 of the District of Columbia Code which requires a census of all children aged 3 to 18 in the District to be taken. Plaintiffs estimate that there are "22,000 retarded, emotionally disturbed, blind, deaf, and speech or learning disabled children, and perhaps as many as 18,000 of these children are not being furnished with programs of specialized education." According to data prepared by the Board of Education, Division of Planning, Research and Evaluation, the District of Columbia provides publicly supported special education programs of various descriptions to at least 3,880 school age children. However, in a 1971 report to the Department of Health, Education and Welfare, the District of Columbia Public Schools admitted that an estimated 12,340 handicapped children were not to be served in the 1971–72 school year.

Each of the minor plaintiffs in this case qualifies as an "exceptional" child. . . .

Although all of the named minor plaintiffs are identified as Negroes the class they represent is not limited by their race. They sue on behalf of and represent all other District of Columbia residents of school age who are eligible for a free public education and who have been, or may be, excluded from such education or otherwise deprived by defendants of access to publicly supported education.

* * *

Plaintiffs Are Entitled to Relief

Plaintiffs' entitlement to relief in this case is clear. The applicable statutes and regulations and the Constitution of the United States require it.

Statutes and Regulations

Section 31-201 of the District of Columbia Code requires that:

> Every parent, guardian, or other person residing . . . in the District of Columbia who has custody or control of a child between the ages of seven and sixteen years shall cause said child to be regularly instructed in a public school or in a private or parochial school or instructed privately during the period of each year in which the public schools of the District of Columbia are in session. . . .

Under § 31-203, a child may be "excused" from attendance only when ". . . upon examination ordered by . . . [the Board of Education], [the child] is found to be unable mentally or physically to profit from attendance at school: Provided, however, that if such examination shows that such child may benefit from specialized instruction adapted to his needs, he shall attend upon such instruction."

Failure of a parent to comply with § 31-201 constitutes a criminal offense. DC Code § 31-207. The Court need not belabor the fact that requiring parents to see that their children attend school under pain of criminal penalties presupposes that an educational opportunity will be made available to the children. The Board of Education is required to make such opportunity available. . . .

The Constitution—Equal Protection and Due Process

* * *

In *Hobson v. Hansen*, 269 F.Supp. 401 (D.C. Cir. 1967), Circuit Judge J. Skelly Wright . . . stated that "the Court has found the due process clause of the Fourteenth Amendment elastic enough to embrace not only the First and Fourth Amendments, but the self-incrimination clause of the Fifth, the speedy trial, confrontation and assistance of counsel clauses of the Sixth and the cruel and unusual clause of the Eighth." (269 F.Supp. 401, 493, citations omitted.) Judge Wright concluded "from these considerations the court draws the conclusion that the doctrine of equal educational opportunity—the equal protection clause in its application to public school education—is in its full sweep a component of due process binding on the District under the due process clause of the Fifth Amendment."

In *Hobson v. Hansen*, supra, Judge Wright found that denying poor public school children educational opportunities equal to that available to more affluent public school children was violative of the Due Process Clause of the Fifth Amendment. A *fortiori*, the defendants' conduct here, denying plaintiffs and their class not just an equal publicly supported education but all publicly supported education while providing such education to other children, is violative of the Due Process Clause.

* * *

The Defense

The Answer of the defendants to the Complaint contains the following:

> These defendants say that it is impossible to afford plaintiffs the relief they request unless:
> (a) The Congress of the United States appropriates millions of dollars to improve special education services in the District of Columbia; or
> (b) These defendants divert millions of dollars from funds already specifically appropriated for other educational services in order to improve special educational services. These defendants suggest that to do so would violate an Act of Congress and would be inequitable to children outside the alleged plaintiff class.

This Court is not persuaded by that contention.

The defendants are required by the Constitution of the United States, the District of Columbia Code, and their own regulations to provide a publicly-supported education for these "exceptional" children. Their failure to fulfill this clear duty to include and retain these children in the public school system, or otherwise provide them with publicly-supported education, and their failure to afford them due process hearing and periodical review, cannot be excused by the claim that there are insufficient funds. In *Goldberg v. Kelly*, 397 U.S. 254 (1969) the Supreme Court, in a case that involved the right of a welfare recipient to a hearing before termination of his benefits, held that Constitutional rights must be afforded citizens despite the greater expense involved. The Court stated . . . that "the State's interest that his [welfare recipient] payments not be erroneously terminated, clearly outweighs the State's competing concern to prevent any increase in its fis-

cal and administrative burdens." Similarly the District of Columbia's interest in educating the excluded children clearly must outweigh its interest in preserving its financial resources. If sufficient funds are not available to finance all of the services and programs that are needed and desirable in the system, then the available funds must be expended equitably in such a manner that no child is entirely excluded from a publicly supported education consistent with his needs and ability to benefit therefrom. The inadequacies of the District of Columbia Public School System, whether occasioned by insufficient funding or administrative inefficiency, certainly cannot be permitted to bear more heavily on the "exceptional" or handicapped child than on the normal child.

Implementation of Judgment

* * *

Inasmuch as the Board of Education has presented for adoption by the Court a proposed "Order and Decree" embodying its present plans for the identification of "exceptional" children and providing for their publicly supported education, including a time table, and further requiring the Board to formulate and file with the Court a more comprehensive plan, the Court will not now appoint a special master as was requested by plaintiffs. . . .

Judgment and Decree . . .

[I]t is hereby ordered, adjudged and decreed that summary judgment in favor of plaintiffs and against defendants be, and hereby is, granted, and judgment is entered in this action as follows:

1. That no child eligible for a publicly supported education in the District of Columbia public schools shall be excluded from a regular public school assignment by a Rule, policy, or practice of the Board of Education of the District of Columbia or its agents unless such child is provided (a) adequate alternative educational services suited to the child's needs, which may include special education or tuition grants, and (b) a constitutionally adequate prior hearing and periodic review of the child's status, progress, and the adequacy of any educational alternative. . . .

3. The District of Columbia shall provide to each child of school age a free and suitable publicly-supported education regardless of the degree of the child's mental, physical or emotional disability or impairment. Furthermore, defendants shall not ex-

clude any child resident in the District of Columbia from such publicly-supported education on the basis of a claim of insufficient resources. . . .

5. Defendants shall provide each identified member of plaintiff class with a publicly-supported education suited to his needs within thirty days of the entry of this order.

* * *

9.a. Defendants shall utilize public or private agencies to evaluate the educational needs of all identified "exceptional" children and, within twenty days of the entry of this order, shall file with the Clerk of this Court their proposal for each individual placement in a suitable educational program, including the provision of compensatory educational services where required. . . .

10.a. Within forty-five days of the entry of this order, defendants shall file with the Clerk of the Court, with copy to plaintiffs' counsel, a comprehensive plan which provides for the identification, notification, assessment, and placement of class members. Such plan shall state the nature and extent of efforts which defendants have undertaken or propose to undertake to

(1) describe the curriculum, educational objectives, teacher qualifications, and ancillary services for the publicly supported educational programs to be provided to class members; and

(2) formulate general plans of compensatory education suitable to class members in order to overcome the present effects of prior educational deprivations. . . .

11. The defendants shall make an interim report to this Court on their performance within forty-five days of the entry of this order. Such report shall show:

(1) The adequacy of Defendants' implementation of plans to identify, locate, evaluate and give notice to all members of the class.

(2) The number of class members who have been placed, and the nature of their placements.

(3) The number of contested hearings before the Hearing Officers, if any, and the findings and determinations resulting therefrom.

12. Within forty-five days of the entry of this order, defendants shall file with this Court a report showing the expunction from or correction of all official records of any plaintiff with regard to past expulsions, suspensions, or exclusions effected in violation of [plaintiff's] procedural rights . . . together with a plan for procedures pursuant to which par-

ents, guardians, or their counsel may attach to such students' records any clarifying or explanatory information which the parent, guardian or counsel may deem appropriate. . . .

13. Hearing Procedures.

a. Each member of the plaintiff class is to be provided with a publicly supported educational program suited to his needs, within the context of a presumption that among the alternative programs of education, placement in a regular public school class with appropriate ancillary services is preferable to placement in a special school class.

b. Before placing a member of the class in such a program, defendants shall notify his parent or guardian of the proposed educational placement, the reasons therefore, and the right to a hearing before a Hearing Officer if there is an objection to the placement proposed. Any such hearing shall be held in accordance with the provision of Paragraph 13.e., below.

c. Hereinafter, children who are residents of the District of Columbia and are thought by any of the defendants, or by officials, parents or guardians, to be in need of a program of special education, shall neither be placed in, transferred from or to, nor denied placement in such a program unless defendants shall have first notified their parents or guardians of such proposed placement, transfer or denial, the reasons therefore, and of the right to a hearing before a Hearing Officer if there is an objection to the placement, transfer or denial of placement. Any such hearings shall be held in accordance with the provisions of Paragraph 13.e., below. . . .

e. Whenever defendants take action regarding a child's placement, denial of placement, or transfer, as described in Paragraphs 13.b. or 13.c., above, the following procedures shall be followed.

(1) Notice required hereinbefore shall be given in writing by registered mail to the parent or guardian of the child.

(2) Such notice shall:

(a) describe the proposed action in detail;

(b) clearly state the specific and complete reasons for the proposed action, including the specification of any tests or reports upon which such action is proposed;

(c) describe any alternative educational opportunities available on a permanent or temporary basis;

(d) inform the parent or guardian of the right to object to the proposed action at a hearing before the Hearing Officer;

(e) inform the parent or guardian that the child is eligible to receive, at no charge, the services of a federally or locally funded diagnostic center for an independent medical, psychological and educational evaluation and shall specify the name, address and telephone number of an appropriate local diagnostic center;

(f) inform the parent or guardian of the right to be represented at the hearing by legal counsel; to examine the child's school records before the hearing, including any tests or reports upon which the proposed action may be based, to present evidence, including expert medical, psychological and educational testimony; and, to confront and cross-examine any school official, employee, or agent of the school district or public department who may have evidence upon which the proposed action was based.

(3) The hearing shall be at a time and place reasonably convenient to such parent or guardian.

(4) The hearing shall be scheduled not sooner than twenty (20) days waivable by parent or child, nor later than forty-five (45) days after receipt of a request from the parent or guardian.

(5) The hearing shall be a closed hearing unless the parent or guardian requests an open hearing.

(6) The child shall have the right to a representative of his own choosing, including legal counsel. If a child is unable, through financial inability, to retain counsel, defendants shall advise child's parents or guardians of available voluntary legal assistance including the Neighborhood Legal Services Organization, the Legal Aid Society, the Young Lawyers Section of the D. C. Bar Association, or from some other organization.

NOTES AND QUESTIONS

1. Pennsylvania Association for Retarded Children (PARC) v. Commonwealth

A consent order in *PARC*, 334 F.Supp. 1257 (E.D.Pa. 1971), 343 F.Supp. 279 (E.D.Pa. 1972), issued prior to *Mills*, required Pennsylvania to provide a "free, public program of education and training appropriate to the child's capacity, within the context of a presumption that, among the alternative programs of education and training required by statute to be available, placement in a regular public school class is preferable to placement in a special public school class [that is, a class for disabled children] and place-

ment in a special public school class is preferable to placement in any other type of program of education and training." 334 F.Supp. at 1260. The basis for that requirement was the stipulation that "Having undertaken to provide a free public education to all of its children, including its exceptional children, the Commonwealth of Pennsylvania may not deny any mentally retarded child access to a free public program of education and training." 334 F.Supp. at 1259. Although it is a consent order, *PARC* is generally regarded as the first "right to education" case concerning the disabled.

2. Mills v. Board of Education: *The Substantive Entitlement*

The class of plaintiffs in *Mills* is considerably broader than in *PARC*. It includes not only retarded children but all children excluded from publicly supported instruction. By holding such exclusions unconstitutional, does *Mills* suggest that all children have a right to attend public schools or a right to publicly supported instruction? Would the outcome in *Mills* differ if a school district sought to cut off all public funds for schooling?

In *Mills* one fairly typical plaintiff, Janice King, is described by the court as "brain-damaged and retarded, with right hemiplegia." 348 F.Supp. at 870. Suppose the cost of providing her a "suitable" education is five times the cost of providing the "normal" student an education. Assuming that no additional money is forthcoming from nonlocal sources, must the district reduce its expenditures for other students in order to provide King a "suitable" education? How would a court respond to the argument that such reductions deny "suitable" instruction to students without disabilities?

PARC and *Mills* assert that all children are capable of benefiting from education. What does this mean? For certain children, notably the profoundly retarded (those with IQ scores below 30), "education" may mean learning to use the bathroom and tie one's shoes. Is that the sort of education that publicly supported instruction should provide? If not, on whom should the burden of providing such instruction fall?

Concerning the scope of *Mills* and *PARC*, *see* Kirp, "Schools as Sorters: The Constitutional and Policy Implications of Student Classification," 121 *Pa.L.Rev.* 705 (1973); Haggerty and Sacks, "Education of the Handicapped: Towards a Definition of an Appropriate Education," 50 *Temple L.Q.* 961, 967–75 (1977); Krass, "The Right to Public Education for Handi-

capped Children: A Primer for the New Advocate,"
1976 *Univ.of Ill.L.Forum* 1016, 1044–47.

3. Mills v. Board of Education: *The Procedural Entitlement*

Traditionally, procedural protection under the Due Process Clause of the Fourteenth Amendment is provided to assure that official action is not arbitrary but rather consistent with general guidelines for ensuring fairness in governmental decisions. As Professor Fuller has noted:

> [A]djudication must take place within the framework of accepted or imposed standards of decision before the litigant's participation in the decision can be meaningful. If the litigant has no idea on what basis the tribunal will decide the case, his . . . opportunity to present proofs and arguments becomes useless. . . . [T]here must be an extralegal community, existent or in the process of coming into existence, from which principles of decision may be derived.

Fuller, "Adjudication and the Rule of Law," *1960 Proceedings of the American Society of International Law*, 1, 5–7.

Does *Mills* provide the parents of disabled children with such "standards of decision"? Just how is the hearing officer to determine whether a proposed education is "suitable"? What is the nexus between procedural protection and substantive rights in *Mills*? What purpose is served by such procedural safeguards as an independent hearing officer, access to records, and the right to an independent evaluation? Should similar procedures be used in disputes over grading? How do these procedures differ from those that courts have required in student discipline cases? Should they differ? *See* chapter 3.

4. *Impact of Procedural Safeguards*

Sociologist Michael Young notes: "Castes or classes are universal, and the measure of harmony that prevails within a society is everywhere dependent upon the degree to which stratification is sanctioned by its code of morality." M. Young, *The Rise of the Meritocracy* 152 (1961). Does proceduralization in fact render differential treatment of the disabled more legitimate? If so, is this a good or bad consequence?

D. The Federal Statutory Framework

The judicial successes in *Mills* and *PARC* spawned substantial popular and scholarly attention and similar lawsuits in more than thirty states. This litigation campaign was designed to demonstrate that the disabled have a constitutional entitlement to an appropriate education; it was also meant to persuade a broader public that the disabled deserved to be more equitably treated. In the Rehabilitation Act (Section 504), 29 U.S.C. §§ 701–796.1, and the Education for All Handicapped Children Act, now known as the Individuals with Disabilities in Education Act, 20 U.S.C. §§ 1400–1490, Congress attended to these claims. That legislation codifies *Mills* and *PARC* in several respects; it is also substantially more detailed in its specification of rights than the prior case law. *See generally* L. Rothstein, *Disabilities and the Law* §§ 2.01–2.05 (2d ed. 1997).

1. The Definition of a Disability. One issue of critical importance in determining the scope of federal protections is deciding what constitutes a disability. While some conditions such as blindness or deafness clearly qualify, others have raised serious concerns. For example, since Congress first passed the Education for All Handicapped Children Act in 1975, the population of students with learning disabilities has grown dramatically. In 1975–76, only 1.2 percent of the school-age population reportedly had learning disabilities. In 1976–77, about one in four students with disabilities were classified as learning disabled, while in 1989–90, just over half of them were classified this way. M. Kelman and G. Lester, *Jumping the Queue: An Inquiry into the Legal Treatment of Students with Learning Disabilities* 1–2 (1977).

The Individuals with Disabilities Education Act defines a learning disability as "a disorder in one or more of the basic psychological processes involved in understanding or in using language, spoken or written, which disorder may manifest itself in imperfect ability to listen, think, speak, read, write, spell, or do mathematical calculations. Such disorders include such conditions as perceptual handicaps, brain injury, minimal brain dysfunction, dyslexia, and developmental aphasia. Such term does not include children who have learning problems which are primarily the result of visual, hearing, or motor disabilities, of mental retardation, of emotional disturbance, or of environmental, cultural, or economic disadvantage." U.S.C. § 1401 (a) (15). Critics have argued that this definition is vague and does not clearly identify a set of disabilities.

"Technical Controversies"

* * *

. . . [T]he federal definition [of a learning disability]
is essentially "negative," or exclusionary, rather than affirmative. A student is said to have a learning disability
not when we observe any particular set of neurological
traits, but when we decide that we *cannot* explain poor
academic performance on the basis of either low IQ or
a set menu of excluded nonneurological factors. Of
course, even if excluded "adverse" factors are present
(for example, socioeconomic disadvantage, physical
handicap), we cannot readily discern whether those
forces actually caused the achievement deficiencies.

Initially, some states set "expectations" on the basis simply of age and grade, rather than individual IQ
scores, mandating that districts find a discrepancy
between achievement and potential when a
child's achievement lagged substantially behind age-
appropriate levels. Thus if a student were performing, say, two grade levels below the grade he was in,
he would meet the discrepancy (inclusionary) aspect
of the test for learning disabilities. He might well still
have been excluded by the district's observation team
if his IQ were low, because the team might have attributed the discrepancy to "mild" mental retardation or because his IQ fell below some explicit eligibility cut-off point. Nonetheless, such systems
included low-IQ children and excluded high-IQ
children more often than the IQ-achievement discrepancy models more typically employed today.

The use of grade-expectation inclusionary definitions are decidedly on the wane: only two states defined discrepancies in this fashion in 1989–90,[7]
while seven states so defined them in 1980. Meanwhile, in 1989–90, thirty-seven states directed that
districts should pay attention to the discrepancy between achievement- and IQ-based expectations (federal law prohibits districts from relying exclusively on
test scores in identifying pupils with learning disabilities) rather than chronological age-based expecta-

tions in making diagnostic judgments, compared
with only sixteen in 1981–82.[9]

There are different ways to measure discrepancy
between IQ and achievement. The simplest and
most prevalent technique is simply to label a child as
having a substantial discrepancy between IQ and
achievement if her IQ score is more than some number of standard deviations (SD) above her achievement score. Twenty states used such a system in 1990
and another eleven used "expectancy" formulas that
had much the same effects and difficulties.

What magnitude of discrepancy will qualify a child
for LD [learning disabled] diagnosis varies across
states. Distinct discrepancy score formulas generate
dramatically different numbers of pupils "eligible" to
be treated as having a learning disability. In a study by
Sinclair and Axelson,[13] the authors sampled 137 children and assessed whether they would be classified as
having a learning disability according to distinct formulas used by five researchers: the percentages classed
as having an LD were 4, 9, 9, 14, and 28 percent of the
same sample. Moreover, growth in the population
classified as learning disabled in the late 1980s was
lower in states demanding higher discrepancy levels
than in those demanding lower discrepancies.

High-IQ children will be overdiagnosed as LD/
discrepant in any system which simply compares IQ
and achievement scores, given the tendency of all test
scores to regress toward the mean. Since the concurrent validity coefficients of achievement and IQ tests
are roughly .7, we would expect students with an IQ
of 130 to have an achievement score from 121 to 123,
not 130, even if achievement and "intelligence" were
perfectly correlated, while a student with an IQ of 85
should be expected to have an achievement score of
89. Thus, the hypothetical high IQ child is not truly
discrepant unless his achievement score is 1.5 SD below 121–123, while the hypothetical low-IQ student
is truly discrepant when his score is less than 1.5 SD
below an 89 score. Given that the general correlation
between ability and achievement is only .6, the problem worsens; achievement will be substantially lower
than "ability" for most high-IQ children and above it
for lower-IQ children. To respond to this problem, 12
states (as of 1989–90) required that the student perform less well on achievement tests than would be

---

[7]William Frankenberger and Kathryn Fronzaglio, "A Review of States' Criteria and Procedures for Identifying Children with Learning Disabilities," 24 *J. of Learning Disabilities* 495, 497 (1991).

[9][*Id.*] at 499.

[13]See Esther Sinclair and Joyce Axelson, "Learning Disability Discrepancy Formulas: Similarities and Differences Among Them," *Learning Disabilities Research* 112 (1986).

predicted *given his IQ* (asking, in essence, whether he's done considerably worse than the average child with his IQ has done).

There are also disputes about which form of the Wechsler IQ test that psychometricians generally employ one should use in diagnosing children as having learning disabilities. The basic choice is between using the verbally loaded WISC-R (Verbal), the WISC-R (Performance), or the WISC-R (Full Scale, combining both verbal and performance scores). Once again, the point is not just of theoretical interest: changes in the characteristics of the IQ test used result in the identification of a somewhat different subgroup of "discrepant" children. . . .

* * *

Strong opponents of defining learning disabilities in terms of disparities between IQ and achievement argue that these problems are insoluble regardless of the sort of IQ test one administers. They believe, among other things . . ., some combination of the following propositions: (a) the IQ test itself is essentially an achievement test anyway so that most low-achieving students will have suppressed IQs; (b) though the IQ test may measure potential as distinct from current achievement in non-LD students, students with LDs will not be able to cope with the IQ test as generally administered so that *their* IQ scores will be suppressed by their reading deficits; (c) reading itself causes further development in related cognitive abilities so that older dyslexics will have increasingly suppressed IQs as their reading disabilities impair development, even if the IQ test is designed in such a way as to deemphasize direct reading skills. Some opponents believe that attempting to measure "potential" is simply beside the point—that we should seek to remedy students' current deficits, without regard to what will inevitably be imperfect hypotheses about their capacity to overcome them. It is more relevant to the question about "proper" diagnostic method, though, to note that others believe we can identify students with learning disabilities more accurately by measuring potential through non-IQ measurement modes. Stanovich, for instance, argues that students ordinarily score similarly on listening comprehension and reading tests, and that a student who exhibits a substantial discrepancy between scores on these two tests has revealed the particular

problem we are trying to diagnose: phonological processing difficulties that give rise to reading deficits.[26]

It is important to recall that the LD diagnosis is not very exacting. Many believe that it is unlikely that the proportion of children who are actually learning disabled in any particular state varies widely, but the proportion of children each state *diagnoses* as having LDs ranges rather substantially. In 1989–90, it varied from a low of 1.69 percent (in Georgia) to a high of 5.8 percent (in Rhode Island); the mean was 3.617, the standard deviation .926. These disparities persist even taking into account the degree to which some states may label children with more severe cognitive disabilities as LD to avoid stigma.

* * *

Skepticism about Diagnosis

It is plausible that there truly are children with learning disabilities out in the world, but that our diagnostic techniques are so poor that a high proportion of children labeled as having LDs do not "really" have them, while a significant number of those who actually have LDs are not so identified.

Researchers who doubt that students with LDs are accurately identified make use of two basic methods to convince others of the prevalence of misdiagnosis. Some independently review case records of students who are classified either as having an LD or as not having one to assess the accuracy of the identifications. Others run controlled experiments, in which people ordinarily asked to make diagnoses are given the opportunity to diagnose a group of students whose "true" traits are somehow known by the experimenters. There is a good deal of evidence that misclassification is rampant.

Thus, for instance, Ysseldyke, Algozzine, and Epps[52] contrasted a group of fourth graders who had been labeled as having learning disabilities with a group of fourth graders with parallel academic achievement levels who had not been so labeled. They found that there were considerable similarities between the two groups; in fact, an average of 96 percent of the scores were within a common range, and the performance of LD and underachieving children on many subtests was identical. Comparing characteristics of these children with the federal

[26]Stanovich, "Discrepancy Definitions" [Keith Stanovich, "Discrepancy Definitions of Reading Disability: Has Intelligence Led Us Astray?" 26 *Reading Research Quarterly* 7 (1991)] 19–21.

[52]J. Ysseldyke, B. Algozzine, and S. Epps, "A Logical and Empirical Analysis of Current Practices in Classifying Students as Handicapped," 50 *Exceptional Children* 160 (1983).

definition showed that as many as 40 percent of the students may have been misclassified. Similarly, Shepard, Smith, and Vojir found that fewer than half of the sample of all children labeled LD in Colorado in the early 1980s "had characteristics that are associated in federal law and professional literature with the definitions of learning disabilities . . . Though most . . . have learning problems, they are incorrectly called learning disabled."[53]

It is possible, though, that some "misdiagnosis" is, in essence, deliberate. Since both students classified as EMR (educable mentally retarded) and those classified as having LDs receive individualized educational programs (IEPs) entitling them to appropriate special educational services in the least restrictive environment, there is no real consequence to mislabeling a child one believes is EMR as LD, so long as one develops an appropriate IEP for the student so mislabeled. The evaluation team members may believe it is a poor idea to use the EMR diagnosis. The child himself may be harmed by the stigmatic label, potential employers may view the label as signaling more extreme inability than is appropriate, or parents may resent or resist the label.

Controlled experiments may be considerably more disheartening to those who believe that we can tailor a workable public policy to help those with genuine LDs without considerable leakage, since such investigations tend to find not only that students with other sorts of learning problems are called LD, but that pupils with no learning difficulties at all are simply "overdiagnosed."

For instance, Algozzine and Ysseldyke assembled a group of 224 professionals from public and private schools in Minnesota, all of whom had previously participated in at least two placement team meetings in which placement decisions were made about real pupils. (Many of the participants, though, were not school psychologists, who are most prone to be making these sorts of placement decisions, and the study seems vulnerable to the accusation that the authors tested too many "nonprofessionals" in the field.) The researchers gave each subject a referral folder in

which a student's sex, SES (socioeconomic status), age, grade, parents' occupation, medical history, and physical attractiveness (based on a previously judged photograph of the student) were listed, alongside an explanation of "reasons for the referral." "None of the issues listed under the statement of the referral problem was unusual for a fifth grader." The subjects were then given access to a computer terminal which allowed them to view the results supposedly obtained on forty-nine different assessment devices in seven domains (including intelligence, achievement, perceptual motor abilities, and behavior ratings). Subjects could also request technical information on the available devices as well as "qualitative information" about the child's performance on any device. The key to the experiment was that regardless of the device selected, the subject was always provided with data indicating that the test performance and behavior were within the average range.[54]

Approximately 51 percent of the participants nonetheless identified the child they were asked to assess as eligible for special education services: 8 indicated the child was likely to be mentally retarded, 103 felt the child was likely to be LD, and 48 felt the child was likely to be emotionally disturbed. Our view is that the LD diagnosis is inevitably expectationally driven; that is, a student is viewed as LD when the observer finds it *surprising* that he or she is performing rather poorly. Thus we were not surprised to find that 90 percent of the subjects who reviewed the file of a female student judged physically attractive with a high socioeconomic status felt that special education would be appropriate for her, though of course all the test scores the subjects could examine were in the average range.[55]

In four articles authored or coauthored by Heubner, however, diagnosticians proved more capable of categorizing pupils in the fashion that they were directed to by relevant regulation, at least when presented with data that were more readily manipulable mathematically. Thus Heubner in 1985 re-created Algozzine and Ysseldyke's 1983 study, but provided test scores in "standardized" rather than grade-equivalent form. He

---

[53]L. Shepard, M. Smith, and C. Vojir, "Characteristics of Pupils Identified as Learning Disabled," 20 *American Educational Research Journal* 309, 328 (1983).

[54]Bob Algozzine and James Ysseldyke, "Special Education Services for Normal Children: Better Safe than Sorry?" 48 *Exceptional Children* 238, 241 (1981). . . .

[55]E. Scott Heubner, "The Effects of Type of Referral Information and Test Data on Psychoeducational Decisions," 16 *School Psychology Review* 382 (1987); E. Scott Heubner, "Errors in Decision-Making: A Comparison of School Psychologists' Interpretations of Grade Equivalents, Percentiles, and Deviation IQs," 18 *School Psychology Review* 51 (1989); E. Scott Heubner and Jack Cummings, "The Impact of Sociocultural Background and Assessment Data upon School Psychologists' Decisions," 23 *Journal of School Psychology* 157 (1985); Jack Cummings, E. Scott Heubner, and James McLeskey, "Psychoeducational Decision-Making: Reason for Referral vs. Test Data," 1 *Professional School Psychology* 249 (1986).

presented researchers with a sample, half of whom should have been diagnosed as having an LD and half of whom should not have. Only 4 of 28 non-LD children were diagnosed as having an LD and only 6 of 27 children with LDs were misdiagnosed as non-LD, results which, while hardly a ringing endorsement of diagnostic practices, are less disheartening than those in the Algozzine and Ysseldyke study. . . . In later studies, Heubner found that psychologists made ample use of test data, rather than reaching conclusions based solely on the referral report and that a large (150-person) sample of school psychologists was better able to reach "appropriate" conclusions when given either direct IQ-achievement discrepancy scores or grade equivalent achievement scores than when they were given percentile achievement scores. . . .

We do not pretend that we can resolve issues about the frequency of "misclassification" according to existing criteria. We want to emphasize a narrower policy point. While we recognize that classification errors inevitably exist in any setting, radical distinctions in the treatment of students ought not to be based on the presence or absence of a diagnostic label in which we have little confidence.

It may well be the case that the number of classification errors is so high as to make the use of the classification system completely counterproductive. But assuming diagnosis remains far better than random, we can make a more tailored inquiry about the propriety of using an imperfect diagnostic system. Presumably, we would feel more comfortable with an inaccurate classification system when the consequences of misdiagnosis are less extreme. A medical diagnostic test with false positives is less acceptable if the proffered treatment is harmful; a medical diagnostic test with false negatives is less tolerable if delay in treatment significantly affects mortality or morbidity.

In the field of special education, we can control how extreme the consequences of mislabeling are. Essentially, every salient increase in the disparity in treatment of labeled and nonlabeled children renders any level of misdiagnosis less tolerable. If getting diagnosed as eligible for special education at one point in time significantly affects the probability of diagnosis at a later point in time *and* diagnosis is non-neutral, either because it is a benefit (entitling the student to extra resources) or a burden (suppressing performance by lowering academic expectations or by placing students in "dead end" school settings), then mislabeling becomes a more serious issue.

* * *

NOTES AND QUESTIONS

1. *Further Reading*

See also Note, "Toward Reasonable Equality: Accommodating Learning Disabilities Under the Americans with Disabilities Act," 111 *Harv.L.Rev.* 1560 (1998); Smith and Runyon, "How Private Secondary Schools Can Meet Their Obligations to Accommodate Students with Specific Learning Disabilities," 17 *New Eng.L.Rev.* 77 (1995).

2. *Asymptomatic HIV Infection as a Disability*

In addition to skepticism about learning disabilities, there have been some doubts about whether children with asymptomatic HIV infection qualify as having a disability. The United States Supreme Court held that such infections constitute a disability under the Americans with Disabilities Act because they limit the major life activity of reproduction. *Bragdon v. Abbott*, 524 U.S. 624, 118 S.Ct. 2196 118 S.Ct. 2196 (1998). At least one commentator has argued that this approach does not extend the ADA's protection to asymptomatic, HIV-infected children because sex and reproduction are not part of their everyday existence. Chambers, "Asymptomatic HIV as a Disability Under the Americans with Disabilities Act," 73 *Wash.L.Rev.* 403 (1998). So far, the reported cases have involved children with AIDS. In general, the courts have found that so long as the illness does not limit the child's ability to learn, the child is "otherwise qualified" to participate and should be admitted to the classroom. The courts have protected children from discrimination under the Rehabilitation Act but often have concluded that a child does not require special accommodations under IDEA. *See, e.g., District 27 Community School Board v. Board of Education*, 502 N.Y.S. 2d 325 (N.Y.Sup.Ct. 1986); *Ray v. School District of DeSoto County*, 666 F.Supp. 1524 (M.D.Fla. 1987); *but cf. Martinez v. School Board of Hillsborough County, Florida*, 711 F.Supp. 1066 (M.D.Fla. 1989) (allowing a district court to consider whether a mentally handicapped student with AIDS required special accommodation in an isolated setting with an aide).

For a discussion of cases involving students with AIDS, see D. Kirp, *Learning by Heart: AIDS and Schoolchildren in America's Communities* I (1989); Note, "AIDS in the Classroom: A New Perspective on Educating School-Age Children Inflicted with HIV," 9 *Rev.of Lit.* 149 (1990); Note, "Public

Schools and Public Health: Exclusion of Children with AIDS," 5 *J. of Law and Politics* 605 (1989); Note, "Undoing a Lesson of Fear in the Classroom: The Legal Recourse of AIDS-Linked Children," 135 *U.Pa.L.Rev.* 193 (1986); Note, "Protecting Children with AIDS against Arbitrary Exclusion from School," 74 *Calif.L.Rev.* 1373 (1986).

3. *The Scope of Disability Protection*

The United States Supreme Court has been addressing the definition of a disability under the Americans with Disabilities Act. Although these cases have arisen in an employment context, they are suggestive of how courts will deal with the question in an educational setting. In *Sutton v. United Airlines*, 527 U.S. 471, 119 S.Ct. 2139, 144 L.Ed. 2d 450 (1999), the Court refused to find that poor vision that could be corrected with glasses or contact lenses qualified as a disability. Had the Court found otherwise, the ADA would have extended to far more Americans than Congress intended to cover. In reaching its result, the Court defined a disability as: (1) a physical or mental impairment that substantially limits one or more of the individual's major life activities; (2) a record of such an impairment; or (3) being regarded as having such an impairment. The Court disagreed with the Equal Employment Opportunity Commission and Department of Justice that the degree of impairment should be evaluated based on an individual's uncorrected condition. Because the plaintiffs' condition was correctable, they were not impaired in a major life activity. Moreover, the Court concluded that the plaintiffs were not regarded as having a disability simply because United Airlines refused to hire them as global airline pilots based on their uncorrected visual impairment. The Court found that the plaintiffs still could serve as copilots or courier pilots, despite the policy. The dissenters expressed concern that the Court's approach would allow employers to discriminate arbitrarily on the basis of correctable conditions.

In companion cases, the Court concluded that hypertension that could be controlled with medication was not a disability, *Murphy v. United Parcel Service*, 527 U.S. 516, 119 S.Ct. 2133, 144 L.Ed. 2d 484 (1999) and that monocular vision was not invariably a disability but had to be judged on a case-by-case basis to determine whether it interfered with a major life activity. *Albertson's, Inc. v. Kirkingburg*, 527 U.S. 555, 119 S.Ct. 2162, 144 L.Ed.2d 518 (1999).

Although these cases were decided under the ADA, its language is drawn almost verbatim from the Rehabilitation Act of 1973, which applies to educational institutions. How is the Court's treatment of correctable conditions apt to affect the definition of disabilities in elementary and secondary education? Should the same analysis apply when children are involved and their chances to correct a condition may depend heavily on the assistance they receive at school? Does your answer differ depending on the student's age? As the next section shows, the Rehabilitation Act protects college and graduate students as well as those in elementary and secondary school.

2. The Rehabilitation Act (Section 504). The Rehabilitation Act expresses a congressional commitment to nondiscrimination based on disability. The following case explores how far an educational institution must go in accommodating a disability to avoid a claim of discrimination.

Southeastern Community College v. Davis

442 U.S. 397, 99 S.Ct. 2361, 60 L.Ed.2d 980 (1979).

Mr. Justice Powell delivered the opinion of the Court.

This case presents a matter of first impression for this Court: Whether § 504 of the Rehabilitation Act of 1973, which prohibits discrimination against an "otherwise qualified handicapped individual" in federally funded programs "solely by reason of his handicap," forbids professional schools from imposing physical qualifications for admission to their clinical training programs.

I

Respondent, who suffers from a serious hearing disability, seeks to be trained as a registered nurse. During the 1973–1974 academic year she was enrolled in the College Parallel program of Southeastern Community College, a state institution that receives federal funds. Respondent hoped to progress to Southeastern's Associate Degree Nursing program, completion of which would make her eligible for state certification as a registered nurse. In the course of her application to the nursing program, she was interviewed by a member of the nursing faculty. It became apparent that respondent had difficulty understanding questions asked, and on inquiry she acknowledged a history of hearing problems and dependence on a hearing aid. She was advised to consult an audiologist.

On the basis of an examination at Duke University Medical Center, respondent was diagnosed as having a "bilateral, sensori-neural hearing loss." . . . A change in her hearing aid was recommended, as a result of which it was expected that she would be able to detect sounds "almost as well as a person would who has normal hearing," . . . But this improvement would not mean that she could discriminate among sounds sufficiently to understand normal spoken speech. Her lipreading skills would remain necessary for effective communication. . . .

Southeastern next consulted Mary McRee, Executive Director of the North Carolina Board of Nursing. On the basis of the audiologist's report, McRee recommended that respondent not be admitted to the nursing program. In McRee's view, respondent's hearing disability made it unsafe for her to practice as a nurse. In addition, it would be impossible for respondent to participate safely in the normal clinical training program, and those modifications that would be necessary to enable safe participation would prevent her from realizing the benefits of the program. . . .

After respondent was notified that she was not qualified for nursing study because of her hearing disability, she requested reconsideration of the decision. The entire nursing staff of Southeastern was assembled, and McRee again was consulted. . . . [T]he staff voted to deny respondent admission.

Respondent then filed suit in the United States District Court for the Eastern District of North Carolina, alleging . . . a violation of § 504 of the Rehabilitation Act of 1973. . . .

II

. . . Section 504 by its terms does not compel educational institutions to disregard the disabilities of handicapped individuals or to make substantial modifications in their programs to allow disabled persons to participate. Instead, it requires only that an "otherwise qualified handicapped individual" not be excluded from participation in a federally funded program "solely by reason of his handicap," indicating only that mere possession of a handicap is not a permissible ground for assuming an inability to function in a particular context.[6]

The court below, however, believed that the "otherwise qualified" persons protected by § 504 include those who would be able to meet the requirements of a particular program in every respect except as to limitations imposed by their handicap. . . . Taken literally, this holding would prevent an institution from taking into account any limitation resulting from the handicap, however disabling. It assumes, in effect, that a person need not meet legitimate physical requirements in order to be "otherwise qualified." We think the understanding of the District Court is closer to the plain meaning of the statutory language. An otherwise qualified person is one who is able to meet all of a program's requirements in spite of his handicap.

The regulations promulgated by the Department of HEW to interpret § 504 reinforce, rather than contradict, this conclusion. According to these regulations, a "[q]ualified handicapped person" is, "[w]ith respect to postsecondary and vocational education services, a handicapped person who meets the academic and technical standards requisite to admission or participation in the [school's] education program or activity. . . ." 45 CFR § 84.3(k)(3) (1978). An explanatory note states:

> "The term 'technical standards' refers to all nonacademic admissions criteria that are essential to participation in the program in question." 45 CFR pt. 84, App. A, p. 405 (1978) (emphasis supplied).

A further note emphasizes that legitimate physical qualifications may be essential to participation in

---

[6]The Act defines "handicapped individual" as follows: "The term 'handicapped individual' means any individual who (A) has a physical or mental disability which for such individual constitutes or results in a substantial handicap to employment and (B) can reasonably be expected to benefit in terms of employability from vocational rehabilitation services provided pursuant to subchapters I and III of this chapter. For the purposes of subchapters IV and V of this chapter, such term means any person who (A) has a physical or mental impairment which substantially limits one or more of such person's major life activities, (B) has a record of such an impairment, or (C) is regarded as having such an impairment." [Section 7(6) of the Rehabilitation Act of 1973, 87 Stat. 361 as amended, 88 Stat. 1619, 89 Stat. 2–5, 29 U.S.C. § 706(6). . . .

This definition comports with our understanding of § 504. A person who has a record of, or is regarded as having, an impairment may at present have no actual incapacity at all. Such a person would be exactly the kind of individual who could be "otherwise qualified" to participate in covered programs. And a person who suffers from a limiting physical or mental impairment still may possess other abilities that permit him to meet the requirements of various programs. Thus, it is clear that Congress included among the class of "handicapped" persons covered by § 504 a range of individuals who could be "otherwise qualified." See S. Rep. No. 93-1297, pp. 38–39(1974).

particular programs.[15] We think it clear, therefore, that HEW interprets the "other" qualifications which a handicapped person may be required to meet as including necessary physical qualifications.

III

The remaining question is whether the physical qualifications Southeastern demanded of respondent might not be necessary for participation in its nursing program. It is not open to dispute that, as Southeastern's Associate Degree Nursing program currently is constituted, the ability to understand speech without reliance on lipreading is necessary for patient safety during the clinical phase of the program. As the District Court found, this ability also is indispensable for many of the functions that a registered nurse performs.

Respondent contends nevertheless that § 504, properly interpreted, compels Southeastern to undertake affirmative action that would dispense with the need for effective oral communication. First, it is suggested that respondent can be given individual supervision by faculty members whenever she attends patients directly. Moreover, certain required courses might be dispensed with altogether for respondent. It is not necessary, she argues, that Southeastern train her to undertake all the tasks a registered nurse is licensed to perform. Rather, it is sufficient to make § 504 applicable if respondent might be able to perform satisfactorily some of the duties of a registered nurse or to hold some of the positions available to a registered nurse.

Respondent finds support for this argument in portions of the HEW regulations discussed above. In particular, a provision applicable to postsecondary educational programs requires covered institutions to make "modifications" in their programs to accommodate handicapped persons, and to provide "auxiliary aids" such as sign-language interpreters. Respondent argues that this regulation imposes an obligation to ensure full participation in covered programs by handicapped individuals and, in particular, requires Southeastern to make the kind of adjustments that would be necessary to permit her safe participation in the nursing program.

We note first that on the present record it appears unlikely respondent could benefit from any affirmative action that the regulation reasonably could be interpreted as requiring. Section 84.44(d)(2), for example, explicitly excludes "devices or services of a personal nature" from the kinds of auxiliary aids a school must provide a handicapped individual. Yet the only evidence in the record indicates that nothing less than close, individual attention by a nursing instructor would be sufficient to ensure patient safety if respondent took part in the clinical phase of the nursing program. . . . Furthermore, it also is reasonably clear that § 84.44(a) does not encompass the kind of curricular changes that would be necessary to accommodate respondent in the nursing program. In light of respondent's inability to function in clinical courses without close supervision, Southeastern, with prudence, could allow her to take only academic classes. Whatever benefits respondent might realize from such a course of study, she would not receive even a rough equivalent of the training a nursing program normally gives. Such a fundamental alteration in the nature of a program is far more than the "modification" the regulation requires.

Moreover, an interpretation of the regulations that required the extensive modifications necessary to include respondent in the nursing program would raise grave doubts about their validity. If these regulations were to require substantial adjustments in existing programs beyond those necessary to eliminate discrimination against otherwise qualified individuals, they would do more than clarify the meaning of § 504. Instead, they would constitute an unauthorized extension of the obligations imposed by that statute.

The language and structure of the Rehabilitation Act of 1973 reflect a recognition by Congress of the distinction between the evenhanded treatment of qualified handicapped persons and affirmative efforts to overcome the disabilities caused by handicaps. Section 501(b), governing the employment of handicapped individuals by the Federal Government, requires each federal agency to submit "an affirmative action program plan for the hiring, placement, and advancement of handicapped indi-

---

[15]The note states: "Paragraph (k) of § 84.3 defines the term 'qualified handicapped person.' Throughout the regulation, this term is used instead of the statutory term 'otherwise qualified handicapped person.' The Department believes that the omission of the word 'otherwise' is necessary in order to comport with the intent of the statute because, read literally, 'otherwise' qualified handicapped persons include persons who are qualified except for their handicap, rather than in spite of their handicap. Under such a literal reading, a blind person possessing all the qualifications for driving a bus except sight could be said to be 'otherwise qualified' for the job of driving. Clearly, such a result was not intended by Congress. In all other respects, the terms 'qualified' and 'otherwise qualified' are intended to be interchangeable." 45 CFR pt. 84, App. A, p. 405.

viduals. . . ." These plans "shall include a description of the extent to which and methods whereby the special needs of handicapped employees are being met." Similarly, § 503(a), governing hiring by federal contractors, requires employers to "take affirmative action to employ and advance in employment qualified handicapped individuals. . . ." The President is required to promulgate regulations to enforce this section.

Under § 501(c) of the Act, by contrast, state agencies such as Southeastern are only "encourage[d] . . . to adopt . . . such policies and procedures." Section 504 does not refer at all to affirmative action, and except as it applies to federal employers it does not provide for implementation by administrative action. A comparison of these provisions demonstrates that Congress understood accommodation of the needs of handicapped individuals may require affirmative action and knew how to provide for it in those instances where it wished to do so. . . . [E]ven if HEW has attempted to create such an obligation itself, it lacks the authority to do so.

IV

We do not suggest that the line between a lawful refusal to extend affirmative action and illegal discrimination against handicapped persons always will be clear. It is possible to envision situations where an insistence on continuing past requirements and practices might arbitrarily deprive genuinely qualified handicapped persons of the opportunity to participate in a covered program. Technological advances can be expected to enhance opportunities to rehabilitate the handicapped or otherwise to qualify them for some useful employment. Such advances also may enable attainment of these goals without imposing undue financial and administrative burdens upon a State. Thus, situations may arise where a refusal to modify an existing program might become unreasonable and discriminatory. Identification of those instances where a refusal to accommodate the needs of a disabled person amounts to discrimination against the handicapped continues to be an important responsibility of HEW.

In this case, however, it is clear that Southeastern's unwillingness to make major adjustments in its nursing program does not constitute such discrimination.

The uncontroverted testimony of several members of Southeastern's staff and faculty established that the purpose of its program was to train persons who could serve the nursing profession in all customary ways. . . . This type of purpose, far from reflecting any animus against handicapped individuals, is shared by many if not most of the institutions that train persons to render professional service. It is undisputed that respondent could not participate in Southeastern's nursing program unless the standards were substantially lowered. Section 504 imposes no requirement upon an educational institution to lower or to effect substantial modifications of standards to accommodate a handicapped person.[12]

One may admire respondent's desire and determination to overcome her handicap, and there well may be various other types of service for which she can qualify. In this case, however, we hold that there was no violation of § 504 when Southeastern concluded that respondent did not qualify for admission to its program. Nothing in the language or history of § 504 reflects an intention to limit the freedom of an educational institution to require reasonable physical qualifications for admission to a clinical training program. Nor has there been any showing in this case that any action short of a substantial change in Southeastern's program would render unreasonable the qualifications it imposed.

V

Accordingly, we reverse the judgment of the court below, and remand for proceedings consistent with this opinion.

NOTES AND QUESTIONS

1. Rehabilitation Act, Section 504: Scope of the Act
Section 504 is the analog for the disabled of the 1964 Civil Rights Act. *See generally* L. Rothstein, *Disabilities and the Law* § 2.02 (2d ed., 1997). Like that act, it protects against discrimination "solely by reason of . . . handicap." How do the guarantees of due process bear on the entitlement to nondiscrimination? What about the entitlement to an "appropriate education"?

---

[12]. . . Southeastern's program, structured to train persons who will be able to perform all normal roles of a registered nurse, represents a legitimate academic policy, and is accepted by the State. In effect, it seeks to ensure that no graduate will pose a danger to the public in any professional role in which he or she might be cast. Even if the licensing requirements of North Carolina or some other State are less demanding, nothing in the Act requires an educational institution to lower its standards.

34 C.F.R. § 104.33(b)(1)(i) defines an "appropriate education," which the school district must provide, as one "designed to meet individual education needs of handicapped persons as adequately as the needs of nonhandicapped persons. . . ." What does this provision mean? Must all disabled children perform as well as those without disabilities? Must they show the same academic progress? May the school district satisfy the requirement by treating the disabled in the same fashion as those without disabilities, or does "adequacy" require that the disabled receive something more? *See* L. Rothstein, *supra* at § 2.02. Does adequacy turn on the treatment of children without disabilities in a particular school district? For example, would a wealthy district be expected to do more for its disabled pupils than a poor district? How does *Davis* affect your reading of this regulation?

Is discrimination the appropriate framework for analyzing the claims of the disabled? Consider Rebell, "Structural Discrimination and the Rights of the Disabled," 74 *Geo.L.J.* 1435, 1437–41 (1986):

> . . . [D]espite the history and continuing vestiges of invidious discrimination against the handicapped, their situation clearly is not the same as that of victims of racial discrimination. The very notion of "disability" or "handicap" implies inherent limitations which, in many situations, do justify differential treatment of a disabled person. In addition, some of the "stereotyping" that results in the exclusion of disabled persons from jobs or activities they could adequately perform stems from . . . a well-intentioned, though often misplaced, concern that certain activities would be detrimental to the particular disabled person. . . . [I]n contrast with the brutal history of racism in America, the treatment of the disabled has reflected a complex mixture of stereotyping and sympathy, apprehension and accommodation.
>
> Legal attempts to deal with problems of discrimination against the disabled are complicated by two other distinguishing features. First is the difficulty of defining precisely who are "the handicapped". . . .
>
> The second distinguishing feature is that "handicapping" conditions are, to a large extent, relative and socially defined characteristics, not absolute criteria. . . .
>
> To date, no principled legal standard geared to the conceptual differences between race discrimination and discrimination against the disabled has been articulated by the courts. . . . The lack of coherent doctrine in this area allows for virtually unbridled judicial discretion. . . .

See also Yudof, "Education for the Handicapped: *Rowley* in Perspective," 92 *Amer.J.Educ.* 163 (1984).

2. Southeastern Community College v. Davis: *Scope of the Decision*

Is the Court correct in interpreting "otherwise qualified" as "one who is able to meet all of a program's requirements in spite of his handicap" and not as including "those who would be able to meet the requirements of a particular program in every respect except as to limitations imposed by their handicap"? What are the practical consequences of this reading of the Act?

The Court distinguishes between "affirmative action" and "discrimination," suggesting that under the Act a government agency is not obliged to do more than afford "evenhanded treatment." What does this distinction mean? Could a school, for example, refuse to install the ramp that an "otherwise qualified" individual requires to gain access to the building and on that basis deny him or her admission to the school (assuming no other legislation speaks explicitly to this issue)? Would the Court require some but not "extensive modifications" in a program in order to accommodate the disabled? *See* L. Rothstein, *supra* at § 3.03. What financial and administrative burdens are permissibly imposed? What of other burdens that the disabled assertedly impose? Could a professor who conducts his or her classes as platonic dialogues refuse to admit a mute student on the ground that such a student could not fully participate in, and hence was not qualified for, the course? What if an applicant to a professional school has a mental disorder? Can the application be denied if he or she is emotionally unstable? *See* L. Rothstein, *supra* at § 3.03.

Does the *Davis* Court suggest that discrimination, as developed in the racial context, is an appropriate framework to apply in the context of disability? Is there an alternative judicially cognizable framework?

3. *Subsequent Developments in Section 504*

In *Alexander v. Choate*, 469 U.S. 287, 105 S.Ct. 712, 83 L.Ed.2d 661 (1985), the Supreme Court unanimously approved a decision by the state of Tennessee to reduce inpatient hospital days to each eligible recipient, a change that had a disproportionate detrimental impact on disabled patients. The Court did not insist on a showing that the rule was motivated by discriminatory animus to warrant § 504 review. But they rejected a claimed entitlement to equal results, holding that so long as the disabled were given equal access to the benefit at issue, and so long as the access was "meaningful," further judicial inquiry was not justified. As in *Davis*, the alternative seemed too open-ended to the Court, but *Alexander* adopts a more expansive interpretation of § 504. It builds on the *Davis* discussion of exceptions to the absence of an affirmative action requirement to conclude: "while a . . . [recipient of federal funds] need not be required to make 'fundamental' or 'substantial' modifications to accommodate the handicapped, it may be required to make 'reasonable' ones." 469 U.S. at 300, 105 S.Ct. at 719.

4. *Primary and Secondary Schools: The Implications of Section 504*

Under § 504, how should the following cases be decided:

a. A disabled student demands full tuition reimbursement for private instruction; the state provides only partial tuition support and concedes that no "appropriate" public instruction is provided. Is it relevant that the disabled student is indigent? *See Burlington School Committee v. Department of Education*, 471 U.S. 359, 105 S.Ct. 1996, 85 L.Ed.2d 385 (1985); *Doe v. Brookline School Committee*, 722 F.2d 910 (1st Cir. 1983); *Kruse v. Campbell*, 431 F.Supp. 180 (E.D.Va. 1977), *vacated and remanded*, 434 U.S. 808, 98 S.Ct. 38, 54 L.Ed.2d 65 (1977). The question of whether damage recoveries are available to private plaintiffs under Section 504 has divided federal courts. *See* L. Rothstein, *supra*, at § 1.14.

b. A student with vision in only one eye seeks to participate in contact sports, with the attendant risk of injury to the functioning eye. *See Kampmeier v. Nyquist*, 553 F.2d 296 (2d Cir. 1977); L. Rothstein, *supra* at § 3.11.

c. A student under psychiatric care is moved from his parents' to his grandparents' home because of "deep hostilities." He now seeks to play football for his newly adopted school. State regulations, passed to eliminate recruiting of athletes by high school coaches, bar unmarried students not living with their natural parents or guardians from playing interscholastic athletics for one year. *See Doe v. Marshall*, 459 F.Supp. 1190 (S.D.Tex. 1978).

d. Black students allege that the educable mentally retarded program is racially discriminatory because there are disproportionate numbers of blacks in those classes and because of allegations of misclassification. *See Georgia State Conference of Branches of NAACP v. State of Georgia*, 775 F.2d 1403 (11th Cir. 1985). *See generally* L. Rothstein, *supra* at § 2.32; J. Wegner, "Educational Rights of Handicapped Children: Three Federal Statutes and an Evolving Jurisprudence: Part I—The Statutory Maze," 17 *J.of Law and Educ.* 387 (1988).

3. The Individuals with Disabilities in Education Act (IDEA).

The Individuals with Disabilities in Education Act (IDEA), formerly titled the Education for All Handicapped Children Act (EAHCA), was enacted in 1975, codifies *Mills* and *PARC*, and moves well beyond those cases in the rights it affords to disabled children. The legislation combines a civil rights and an entitlement approach. *See* Yudof, "Education for the Handicapped: *Rowley* in Perspective," 92 *Amer.J.of Educ.* 163 (1984). It both outlaws discrimination and guarantees educational services. "Full educational opportunity" and a "free appropriate public education" are the substantive standards; it also requires an "individualized educational program" (IEP), a plan for "specifically designed instruction to meet the unique needs of handicapped children." The legislation states a preference for mainstreaming, requiring the placement of handicapped children in regular classrooms "to the maximum extent appropriate." Section 1412(5). Parental participation is part of the panoply of rights, with parents guaranteed notice of any changes in the educational placement of their child and an opportunity to contest changes through a due process hearing, an administrative appeal, and the right to sue in state or federal district court. *See generally* L. Rothstein, *Disabilities and the Law* § 2.07 *et seq.* (2d ed. 1997). According to a 1997 law review note, a search of an on-line legal database revealed that nearly 1,000 cases had been brought under the IDEA since it was first enacted. Approximately three-fourths were filed in federal court. Dannenberg, "A Derivative Right to Education: How Standards-Based Education Reform Redefines the Individuals with Disabilities Education Act," 15 *Yale L. & Pol'y Rev.* 629, 631 n. 10 (1997). This is likely to be an undercount if cases were settled without a judicial decision or otherwise resolved informally outside the courts.

a. The Substantive Entitlement. The IDEA requires that students with disabilities receive a free, appropriate public education. Even when a child is mainstreamed in a regular classroom, questions arise as to whether the education received there is appropriate. In the following case, the United States Supreme Court provided guidance about when an instructional program can be characterized as appropriate.

Board of Education v. Rowley

458 U.S. 176, 102 S.Ct. 3034, 73 L.Ed.2d 690 (1982).

Justice Rehnquist delivered the opinion of the Court.

This case arose in connection with the education of Amy Rowley, a deaf student at the Furnace Woods School in the Hendrick Hudson Central School District, Peekskill, New York. Amy has minimal residual hearing and is an excellent lipreader. During the year before she began attending Furnace Woods, a meeting between her parents and school administrators resulted in a decision to place her in a regular kindergarten class in order to determine what supplemental services would be necessary to her education. Several members of the school administration prepared for Amy's arrival by attending a course in sign-language interpretation, and a teletype machine was installed in the principal's office to facilitate communication with her parents who are also deaf. At the end of the trial period it was determined that Amy should remain in the kindergarten class, but that she should be provided with an FM hearing aid which would amplify words spoken into a wireless receiver by the teacher or fellow students during certain classroom activities. Amy successfully completed her kindergarten year.

As required by the Act, an IEP [individual educational plan] was prepared for Amy during the fall of her first-grade year. The IEP provided that Amy should be educated in a regular classroom at Furnace Woods, should continue to use the FM hearing aid, and should receive instruction from a tutor for the deaf for one hour each day and from a speech therapist for three hours each week. The Rowleys agreed with the IEP but insisted that Amy also be provided a qualified sign-language interpreter in all of her academic classes. Such an interpreter had been placed in Amy's kindergarten class for a two-week experimental period, but the interpreter had reported that Amy did not need his services at that time. The school administrators likewise concluded that Amy did not need such an interpreter in her first-grade classroom. They reached this conclusion after consulting the school district's Committee on the Handicapped, which had received expert evidence from Amy's parents on the importance of a sign-language interpreter, received testimony from Amy's teacher and other persons familiar with her academic and social progress, and visited a class for the deaf.

When their request for an interpreter was denied, the Rowleys demanded and received a hearing before an independent examiner. After receiving evidence from both sides, the examiner agreed with the administrators' determination that an interpreter was not necessary because "Amy was achieving educationally, academically, and socially" without such assistance. . . .

The District Court found that Amy "is a remarkably well-adjusted child" who interacts and communicates well with her classmates and has "developed an extraordinary rapport" with her teachers. It also found that "she performs better than the average child in her class and is advancing easily from grade to grade," but "that she understands considerably less of what goes on in class than she would if she were not deaf" and thus "is not learning as much, or performing as well academically, as she would without her handicap." This disparity between Amy's achievement and her potential led the court to decide that she was not receiving a "free appropriate public education," which the court defined as "an opportunity to achieve [her] full potential commensurate with the opportunity provided to other children." According to the District Court, such a standard "requires that the potential of the handicapped child be measured and compared to his or her performance, and that the remaining differential or 'shortfall' be compared to the shortfall experienced by nonhandicapped children."

* * *

A divided panel of the United States Court of Appeals for the Second Circuit affirmed. . . . This is the first case in which this Court has been called upon to interpret any provision of the [Education for All Handicapped Children] Act.

. . . The Act does expressly define "free appropriate public education":

> The term "free appropriate public education" means *special education and related services* which (A) have been provided at public expense, under public supervision and direction, and without charge, (B) meet the standards of the State educational agency, (C) include an appropriate preschool, elementary, or secondary school education in the State involved, and (D) are provided in conformity with the individualized education program. . . .

* * *

According to the definitions contained in the Act, a "free appropriate public education" consists of educational instruction specially designed to meet the unique needs of the handicapped child, supported by such services as are necessary to permit the child "to benefit" from the instruction. Almost as a checklist for adequacy under the Act, the definition also requires that such instruction and services be provided at public expense and under public supervision, meet the State's educational standards, approximate the grade levels used in the State's regular education, and comport with the child's IEP. Thus, if personalized instruction is being provided with sufficient supportive services to permit the child to benefit from the instruction, and the other items on the definitional checklist are satisfied, the child is receiving a "free appropriate public education" as defined by the Act.

* * *

Noticeably absent from the language of the statute is any substantive standard prescribing the level of education to be accorded handicapped children. Certainly the language of the statute contains no requirement like the one imposed by the lower courts — that States maximize the potential of handicapped children "commensurate with the opportunity provided to other children."

. . . By passing the Act, Congress sought primarily to make public education available to handicapped children. But in seeking to provide such access to public education, Congress did not impose upon the States any greater substantive educational standard than would be necessary to make such access meaningful. Indeed, Congress expressly "recognize[d] that in many instances the process of providing special education and related services to handicapped children is not guaranteed to produce any particular outcome." . . .

Thus, the intent of the Act was more to open the door of public education to handicapped children on appropriate terms than to guarantee any particular level of education once inside.

* * *

That the Act imposes no clear obligation upon recipient States beyond the requirement that handicapped children receive some form of specialized education is perhaps best demonstrated by the fact that Congress, in explaining the need for the Act, equated an "appropriate education" to the receipt of some specialized educational services. The Senate Report states: "[T]he most recent statistics provided by the Bureau of Education for the Handicapped estimate that of the more than 8 million children . . . with handicapping conditions requiring special education and related services, only 3.9 million such children are receiving an appropriate education." . . .

It is evident from the legislative history that the characterization of handicapped children as "served" referred to children who were receiving some form of specialized educational services from the States, and that the characterization of children as "unserved" referred to those who were receiving no specialized educational services. . . .

Respondents contend that "the goal of the Act is to provide each handicapped child with an equal educational opportunity." . . . We think, however, that the requirement that a State provide specialized educational services to handicapped children generates no additional requirement that the services so provided be sufficient to maximize each child's potential "commensurate with the opportunity provided other children." . . .

The educational opportunities provided by our public school systems undoubtedly differ from student to student, depending upon a myriad of factors that might affect a particular student's ability to assimilate information presented in the classroom. The requirement that States provide "equal" educational opportunities would thus seem to present an entirely unworkable standard requiring impossible measurements and comparisons. Similarly, furnishing handicapped children with only such services as are available to nonhandicapped children would in all probability fall short of the statutory requirement of "free appropriate public education"; to require, on the other hand, the furnishing of every special service necessary to maximize each handicapped child's potential is, we think, further than Congress intended to go. Thus to speak in terms of "equal" services in one instance gives less than what is required by the Act and in another instance more. The theme of the Act is "free appropriate public education," a phrase which is too complex to be captured by the word "equal" whether one is speaking of opportunities or services.

The District Court and the Court of Appeals thus erred when they held that the Act requires New York to maximize the potential of each handicapped child commensurate with the opportunity provided nonhandicapped children. Desirable though that goal might be, it is not the standard that Congress imposed upon States which receive funding under the Act. Rather, Congress sought primarily to identify and evaluate handicapped children, and to provide them with access to a free public education.

* * *

Implicit in the congressional purpose of providing access to a "free appropriate public education" is the requirement that the education to which access is provided be sufficient to confer some educational benefit upon the handicapped child. . . .

The determination of when handicapped children are receiving sufficient educational benefits to satisfy the requirements of the Act presents a more difficult problem. The Act requires participating States to educate a wide spectrum of handicapped children, from the marginally hearing-impaired to the profoundly retarded and palsied. It is clear that the benefits obtainable by children at one end of the spectrum will differ dramatically from those obtainable by children at the other end, with infinite variations in between. One child may have little difficulty competing successfully in an academic setting with nonhandicapped children while another child may encounter great difficulty in acquiring even the most basic of self-maintenance skills. We do not attempt today to establish any one test for determining the adequacy of educational benefits conferred upon all children covered by the Act. Because in this case we are presented with a handicapped child who is receiving substantial specialized instruction and related services, and who is performing above average in the regular classrooms of a public school system, we confine our analysis to that situation.

The Act requires participating States to educate handicapped children with nonhandicapped children whenever possible. When that "mainstreaming" preference of the Act has been met and a child is being educated in the regular classrooms of a public school system, the system itself monitors the educational progress of the child. Regular examinations are administered, grades are awarded, and yearly advancement to higher grade levels is permitted for those children who attain an adequate knowledge of the course material. The grading and advancement system thus constitutes an important factor in determining educational benefit. Children who graduate from our public school systems are considered by our society to have been "educated" at least to the grade level they have completed, and access to an "education" for handicapped children is precisely what Congress sought to provide in the Act.

* * *

When the language of the Act and its legislative history are considered together, the requirements imposed by Congress become tolerably clear. Insofar as a State is required to provide a handicapped child with a "free appropriate public education," we hold that it satisfies this requirement by providing personalized instruction with sufficient support services to permit the child to benefit educationally from that instruction. Such instruction and services must be provided at public expense, must meet the State's educational standards, must approximate the grade levels used in the State's regular education, and must comport with the child's IEP. In addition, the IEP, and therefore the personalized instruction, should be formulated in accordance with the requirements of the Act and, if the child is being educated in the regular classrooms of the public education system, should be reasonably calculated to enable the child to achieve passing marks and advance from grade to grade. . . .

When the elaborate and highly specific procedural safeguards contrasted with the general and somewhat imprecise substantive admonitions contained in the Act, we think that the importance Congress attached to these procedural safeguards cannot be gainsaid. It seems to us no exaggeration to say that Congress placed every bit as much emphasis upon compliance with procedures giving parents and guardians a large measure of participation at every stage of the administrative process . . . as it did upon the measurement of the resulting IEP against a substantive standard. We think that the Congressional emphasis upon full participation of concerned parties throughout the development of the IEP, as well as the requirements that state and local plans be submitted to the Commissioner for approval, demonstrate the legislative conviction that adequate compliance with the procedures prescribed would in most cases assure much if not all of what Congress wished in the way of substantive content in an IEP.

Thus the provision that a reviewing court base its decision on the "preponderance of the evidence" is by no means an invitation to the courts to substitute their own notions of sound educational policy for those of the school authorities which they review. . . .

A court's inquiry in suits . . . is twofold. First, has the State complied with the procedures set forth in the Act? And second, is the individualized educational program developed through the Act's procedures reasonably calculated to enable the child to receive educational benefits? If these requirements are met, the State has complied with the obligations imposed by Congress and the courts can require no more.

In assuring that the requirements of the Act have been met, courts must be careful to avoid imposing their view of preferable educational methods upon the States. The primary responsibility for formulating the education to be accorded a handicapped child, and for choosing the educational method most suitable to the child's needs, was left by the Act to state and local educational agencies in cooperation with the parents or guardian of the child.

* * *

Applying these principles to the facts of this case, we conclude that the Court of Appeals erred in affirming the decision of the District Court. Neither the District Court nor the Court of Appeals found that petitioners had failed to comply with the procedures of the Act, and the findings of neither court would support a conclusion that Amy's educational program failed to comply with the substantive requirements of the Act. On the contrary, the District Court found that the "evidence firmly establishes that Amy is receiving an 'adequate' education, since she performs better than the average child in her class and is advancing easily from grade to grade." In light of this finding, and of the fact that Amy was receiving personalized instruction and related services calculated by the Furnace Woods school administrators to meet her educational needs, the lower courts should not have concluded that the Act requires the provision of a sign-language interpreter. Accordingly, the decision of the Court of Appeals is reversed and the case is remanded for further proceedings consistent with this opinion.

* * *

Justice White, with whom Justice Brennan and Justice Marshall join, dissenting. In order to reach its result in this case, the majority opinion contradicts itself, the language of the statute, and the legislative history. Both the majority's standard for a "free appropriate education" and its standard for judicial review disregard congressional intent.

The majority first turns its attention to the meaning of a "free appropriate public education." The Act provides:

The term "free appropriate public education" means special education and related services which (A) have been provided at public expense, under public supervision and direction, and without charge, (B) meet the standards of the State educational agency, (C) include

an appropriate preschool, elementary, or secondary school education in the State involved, and (D) are provided in conformity with the individualized education program required. . . .

The majority reads this statutory language as establishing a congressional intent limited to bringing "previously excluded handicapped children into the public education systems of the States and requiring the States to adopt *procedures* which would result in individualized consideration of and instruction for each child." . . . In its attempt to constrict the definition of "appropriate" and the thrust of the Act, the majority opinion states, "Noticeably absent from the language of the statute is any substantive standard prescribing the level of education to be accorded handicapped children. Certainly the language of the statute contains no requirement like the one imposed by the lower courts—that States maximize the potential of handicapped children commensurate with the opportunity provided to other children." . . .

* * *

The majority opinion announces a different substantive standard, that "Congress did not impose upon the States any greater substantive standard than would be necessary to make such access meaningful." While "meaningful" is no more enlightening than "appropriate," the Court purports to clarify itself. Because Amy was provided with *some* specialized instruction from which she obtained *some* benefit and because she passed from grade to grade, she was receiving a meaningful and therefore appropriate education.[2]

This falls far short of what the Act intended. The Act details as specifically as possible the kind of specialized education each handicapped child must receive. It would apparently satisfy the Court's standard of "access to specialized instruction and related services which are individually designed to provide educational benefit to the handicapped child," for a deaf child such as Amy to be given a teacher with a loud voice, for she would benefit from that service. The Act requires more. It defines "special education" to

---

[2]As further support for its conclusions, the majority opinion turns to *Pennsylvania Association for Retarded Children v. Commonwealth of Pennsylvania (PARC)*, 334 F.Supp. 1257 (1971), 343 F.Supp. 279 (E.D.Pa. 1972) and *Mills v. Board of Education of the District of Columbia*, 348 F.Supp. 866 (D.D.C. 1972). That these decisions served as an impetus for the Act does not, however, establish them as the limits of the majority quotes from *Mills* . . . sets a standard not of some education, but of educational opportunity equal to that of non-handicapped children. Indeed, *Mills*, relying on decisions since called into question by this Court's opinion in *San Antonio School District v. Rodriguez*, 411 U.S. 1, 93 S.Ct. 1278, 36 L.Ed.2d 16 (1973), states, "In *Hobson v. Hansen* [269 F.Supp. 401 (D.D.C.).] Judge Wright found that denying poor public school children educational opportunity equal to that available to more affluent public school children was violative of the Due Process Clause of the Fifth Amendment. A fortiori, the defendants' conduct here, denying plaintiffs and their class not just an equal publicly supported education but all publicly supported education while providing such education to other children, is violative of the Due Process Clause." 348 F.Supp., at 875.

Whatever the effect of *Rodriguez* on the validity of this reasoning, the statement exposes the majority's mischaracterization of the opinion and thus of the assumptions of the legislature that passed the act.

mean "specifically designed instruction, at no cost to parents or guardians, to *meet the unique needs* of a handicapped child. . . ." § 1401(16) (emphasis added). Providing a teacher with a loud voice would not meet Amy's needs and would not satisfy the Act. The basic floor of opportunity is instead, as the courts below recognized, intended to eliminate the effects of the handicap, at least to the extent that the child will be given an equal opportunity to learn if that is reasonably possible. Amy Rowley, without a sign language interpreter, comprehends less than half of what is said in the classroom—less than half of what normal children comprehend. This is hardly an equal opportunity to learn, even if Amy makes passing grades.

* * *

I agree that the language of the Act does not contain a substantive standard beyond requiring that the education offered must be "appropriate." However, if there are limits not evident from the face of the statute on what may be considered an "appropriate education," they must be found in the purpose of the statute or its legislative history. The Act itself announces it will provide a *"full* educational opportunity to all handicapped children" (emphasis added). This goal is repeated throughout the legislative history . . . in statements too frequent to be " 'passing references and isolated phrases.' " Indeed, at times the purpose of the Act was described as tailoring each handicapped child's educational plan to enable the child "to achieve his or her maximum potential."

* * *

The Court's discussion of the standard for judicial review is as flawed as its discussion of a "free appropriate public education." According to the Court, a court can ask only whether the State has "complied with the procedures set forth in the Act" and whether the individualized education program is "reasonably calculated to enable the child to receive educational benefit." Both the language of the Act and the legislative history, however, demonstrate that Congress intended the courts to conduct a far more searching inquiry.

* * *

The legislative history shows that judicial review is not limited to procedural matters and that the state educational agencies are given first, but not final, responsibility for the content of a handicapped child's education. The Conference Committee directs courts to make an "independent decision." The deliberate change in the review provision is an unusu-

ally clear indication that Congress intended courts to undertake substantive review instead of relying on the conclusions of the state agency.

* * *

Thus, the Court's limitations on judicial review have no support in either the language of the Act or the legislative history. Congress did not envision that inquiry would end if a showing is made that the child is receiving passing marks and is advancing from grade to grade. Instead, it intended to permit a full and searching inquiry into any aspect of a handicapped child's education. The Court's standard, for example, would not permit a challenge to part of the IEP; the legislative history demonstrates beyond doubt that Congress intended such challenges to be possible, even if the plan as developed is reasonably calculated to give the child some benefits.

* * *

NOTES AND QUESTIONS

1. Board of Education v. Rowley: *Scope of the Decision*

a. The Substantive Standard. In *Rowley*, the first Supreme Court appraisal of the EAHCA, the Court attempted to give meaning to its vaguely worded core mandate: the right to a "free appropriate public education." " '[F]ree appropriate public education' [is] a phrase too complex to be captured by the word 'equal,' " says Justice Rehnquist. Do you agree? *See generally* L. Rothstein, *Disabilities and the Law* § 2.17 (2d ed. 1997).

Is the standard the majority embraces—the "educational benefit" standard—consistent with congressional intent? Does it provide useful guidance to administrators or judges, or does it invite purely ad hoc decisions? How different is it from the "commensurate opportunity" standard proposed by the lower court and adopted by most circuits before *Rowley? See, e.g., Springdale School Dist. No. 50 v. Grace*, 656 F.2d 300 (8th Cir. 1981); *Battle v. Commonwealth of Pennsylvania*, 629 F.2d 269 (3d Cir. 1980). How different is it from "minimal access," on the one side and "full potential," on the other? In *Grace*, the appeals court reconsidered its decision—keeping a deaf child in a regular class with a certified specialist rather than sending her on to a special school for the deaf—after *Rowley*, but found no reason to alter either its conclusion or its reasoning. Does this suggest a defiant lower court—or a Supreme Court distinction without a difference? *See* Gallegos, "Beyond *Board of Education v. Rowley*," 97 *Amer.J.Educ.* 258 (1989).

Among the commentaries on *Rowley*'s "appropriateness" standard, *see* Babin, "Adequate Special Education: Do California Schools Meet the Test?" 37 *San Diego L.Rev.* 211 (2000); Goldman, "Promises Made, Promises Broken by the Individuals with Disabilities Education Act," 20 *U.Dayton L.Rev.* 243 (1994); Weber, "The Transformation of the Education of the Handicapped Act: A Study in the Interpretation of Radical Statutes," 24 *U.C.Davis L.Rev.* 349 (1990); Broadwell and Walden, " 'Free Appropriate Public Education' After *Rowley*: An Analysis of Recent Court Decisions," 17 *J.of Law and Educ.* 35 (1988); Gallegos, *supra*; Wegner, "Variations on a Theme—The Concept of Equal Educational Opportunity and Programming Decisions Under the Education for All Handicapped Children Act of 1975," 48 *Law and Contemp.Probs.* 169 (1985); Hill, "Legal Conflicts in Special Education: How Competing Paradigms in the Education for All Handicapped Children Act Create Litigation," 64 *U.Detroit L.Rev.* 129 (1986); Myers and Jenson, "The Meaning of 'Appropriate' Educational Programming Under the Education for All Handicapped Children Act," 1984 *So.Ill.U.L.J.* 401; Yudof, "Education for the Handicapped: *Rowley* in Perspective," 92 *Amer.J.Educ.* 163 (1984).

Is educational benefit a useful standard when applied, not to an obviously bright, hearing-impaired child like Amy Rowley, but to severely mentally retarded or emotionally disturbed children who often cannot function in the regular classroom? *See* Rebell, "Structural Discrimination and the Rights of the Disabled," 74 *Geo.L.J.* 1435, 1475 (1986): "[I]n many cases the educational benefits standard becomes almost synonymous with the maximum benefits standard: a school district might need to expend virtually unlimited resources if it is required to teach severely handicapped and profoundly retarded children certain minimal self-help skills." *See also* Yudof, *supra*.

In applying *Rowley*, may a court take into account the resources of a school district, making comparisons with existing levels of service for the nonhandicapped? *See* Collins and Zirkel, "To What Extent, If Any, May Cost Be a Factor in Special Education Cases?" 71 *Ed.L.Rep.* 11 (1992); Bartlett, "The Role of Cost in Educational Decisionmaking for the Handicapped Child," 48 *Law and Contemp.Probs.* 7 (1985). *See generally* Rothstein, *supra* at § 2.21.

b. The Procedural Standard. The *Rowley* Court stresses that "courts lack the specialized knowledge and experience necessary to resolve persistent and difficult questions of educational policy." For that reason, the decision emphasizes procedural regularity over substantive standards. *See also Doe by and through Doe v. Defendant J*, 898 F.2d 1186 (6th Cir. 1990). Is that an appropriate allocation of authority based on institutional competence? Will lower courts abide by that allocation? *See* Gallegos, *supra*.

2. Applying the Rowley Standard

How should the following issues be resolved?

a. The school district proposes regular classroom placement while the parents argue for a private school placement. *See Gonzalez v. Puerto Rico Department of Education*, 969 F.Supp. 801 (D.P.R. 1997); *Manuel R. v. Ambach*, 635 F.Supp. 791 (E.D.N.Y. 1986).

Does it matter that state and local officials disagree about which program is appropriate? *See Heather S. v. Wisconsin*, 125 F.3d 1045 (7th Cir. 1997); *Board of Education v. Illinois State Board of Education*, 938 F.2d 712 (7th Cir. 1991); *Karl v. Board of Education*, 736 F.2d 873 (2d Cir. 1984). May a court rely on additional evidence of appropriateness, not considered by school administrators, in determining appropriate placement? *See Fuhrmann v. East Hanover Bd. of Educ.*, 993 F.2d 1031 (3d Cir. 1993) (concurring opinion of Mansmann, J.); *Russell by and through Russell v. Jefferson School District*, 609 F.Supp. 605 (N.D.Cal. 1985). How relevant is a child's failing school performance in a court's evaluation of appropriate placement? *See Sylvie M. v. Board of Education* (W.D.Tex. 1999).

How relevant is it that a child, though able to cope in school, presents major behavior problems at home? So long as some educational benefit is secured, is the *Rowley* standard satisfied? *Compare McKenzie v. Smith*, 771 F.2d 1527, 1533 (D.C. Cir. 1985) (" 'potentially explosive emotional situation' ") with *Sanger v. Montgomery Board of Education*, 916 F.Supp. 518 (D.Md. 1996) ("Allowing that Ross's suicide crisis had been dealt with and given his highly charged family situation, [the school district's placement supervisor] reasoned that any residential placement would have been dictated primarily by family concerns"); *Ahern v. Keene*, 593 F.Supp. 902, 906, 907 (D.Del. 1984) (at home, the child "talked loudly to herself and to imaginary friends, withdrew into a fantasy world . . . wandered away from home, talked to strangers, occasionally related in a bizarre and inappropriate manner" but at school the child's emotional problems did not " 'present a problem in the classroom' and did not interfere with her learning").

If the state establishes a higher standard for the education of the disabled than the *Rowley* standard—for instance, a "best achieve success" standard or "maximum possible development" standard—how does this affect the court's reviewing role? *See O'Toole v. Olathe District Schools Unified School District No. 233*, 144 F.3d 692 (10th Cir. 1998); *Kathleen H. v. Massachusetts Department of Education*, 154 F.3d 9 (1st Cir. 1998); *D.B.V. Ocean Township Board of Education*, 985 F.Supp. 457 (D.N.J. 1997).

b. Parents claim that, without summer school, their handicapped children will regress and so lose skills acquired during the school year. *See Chagnon v. Town of Shrewsbury*, 901 F.Supp. 32 (D.Md. 1995); *Reusch v. Fountain*, 872 F.Supp. 1421 (D.Md. 1994); *Johnson v. Bismarck*, 949 F.2d 100 (8th Cir. 1991); *Johnson v. Independent School District*, 921 F.2d 1022 (10th Cir. 1990). *See generally* Gallegos, *supra* at 281–82.

Does it matter that prohibition of summer school is a statewide policy, not an individual determination about educational benefit? *See Hoeft v. Tucson Unified School District*, 967 F.2d 1298 (9th Cir. 1992); *Crawford v. Pittman*, 708 F.2d 1028 (5th Cir. 1983).

c. A disabled child seeks more than twelve years of publicly supported education. *See Wekler v. Westfield Board of Education*, 784 F.2d 176 (3rd Cir. 1986); *Helms v. Independent Sch. Dist. No. 3*, 750 F.2d 820 (10th Cir. 1984); *Evans v. Tuttle*, 613 N.E.2d 854 (Ind.App. 1993); *Natrona County School District v. McKnight*, 764 P.2d 1039 (Wyo. 1988).

d. Timothy W., a multiply disabled and profoundly mentally retarded child, suffers from complex developmental disabilities, spastic quadriplegia, cerebral palsy, seizure disorder, and cortical blindness. The boy's pediatrician, noting that the youngster responds to sounds, recommends that the district institute a regime emphasizing physical therapy and stimulation; another developmental pediatrician reports that the child has no educational potential. The district proposes to offer no education on the grounds that Timothy is incapable of benefiting from one. *Timothy W. v. Rochester, N.H. School Dist.*, 875 F.2d 954 (1st Cir. 1989), *cert. denied sub nom. Rochester, N.H. School Dist. v. Timothy W.*, U.S. , 110 S.Ct. 519, 107 L.Ed.2d 520, 58 U.S.L.W.

3351 (1989). For later cases adopting a broad definition of "education" under the IDEA, *see Lenn v. Portland School Commission*, 998 F.2d 1083 (1st Cir. 1993); *Christopher M. v. Corpus Christi Independent School District*, 933 F.2d 1285 (5th Cir. 1991); *Brown v. Wilson County School Board*, 747 F.Supp. 436 (M.D. Tenn. 1990).

3. *"Related Services" and the IDEA*

All the services for disabled children discussed to this point—summer school, tutoring and the like—are educational in nature. What is the standard to be applied when school authorities refuse to provide services that relate to the health of a disabled student? *See* Gallegos, *supra* at 282.

In *Irving Independent School District v. Tatro*, 466 U.S. 923, 104 S.Ct. 1703, 80 L.Ed.2d 176 (1984), the Supreme Court took up the issue. Eight-year-old Amber Tatro was born with spina bifida. To maintain her health, she required clean intermittent catheterization services. But the school district refused to provide catheterization, arguing that this was a "medical service" which, under the Act, need not be offered.

In upholding Amber's claim, the Supreme Court purported to apply the *Rowley* standard. "[O]nly those services necessary to aid a handicapped child to benefit from special education must be provided, regardless [of] how easily a school nurse or lay person could furnish them." But "without having services available during the school day, Amber cannot attend school and thereby 'benefit from special education.' " The Court rejected the argument that three hours of schooling, with no catheterization provided, offers some educational benefit (rather as hearing half the words spoken in a classroom, according to the justices in *Rowley*, offers some benefit).

In *Cedar Rapids Community School District v. Garret F.*, 526 U.S. 66, 119 S.Ct. 992, 143 L.Ed. 2d 154 (1999), the Court upheld a Department of Education regulation that read the "medical services" exception narrowly, to exclude only services that a doctor, rather than a nurse or layperson, must provide. The Court refused to credit the school district's concerns about the cost of providing continuous assistance to a student who was dependent on a ventilator to breathe. Justices Thomas and Kennedy dissented, insisting that the IDEA focuses on the nature of the services, not the identity of the provider.

Just how different are *Tatro* and *Rowley*? *See* Gallegos, *supra* at 271. Both children needed specialized personnel to benefit from the school program.

Is the difference that Tatro sought help under the related services section, whereas the Rowleys relied on the free appropriate public education section of the IDEA? If so, is this a sensible distinction to draw?

4. Process and Substance Entwined: The Fiscal Responsibility Question

In *Burlington School Committee v. Massachusetts Department of Education*, 471 U.S. 359, 105 S.Ct. 1996, 85 L.Ed.2d 385 (1985), the Supreme Court addressed one of the most common disputes arising under the EAHCA: whether parents who send their disabled child to private school can obtain reimbursement from the responsible public agency. The justices did not pass on the appropriateness, under the act, of the private placement but only on the scope of the reviewing court's authority once the court finds such placement to be appropriate:

> . . . In a case where a court determines that a private placement desired by the parents was proper under the Act and that an IEP calling for placement in a public school was inappropriate, it seems clear beyond cavil that "appropriate" relief would include a prospective injunction directing the school officials to develop and implement at public expense an IEP placing the child in a private school.
>
> If the administrative and judicial review under the Act could be completed in a matter of weeks, rather than years, it would be difficult to imagine a case in which such prospective injunctive relief would not be sufficient. As this case so vividly demonstrates, however, the review process is ponderous. A final judicial decision on the merits of an IEP will in most instances come a year or more after the school term covered by that IEP has passed. In the meantime, the parents who disagree with the proposed IEP are faced with a choice: go along with the IEP to the detriment of their child if it turns out to be inappropriate or pay for what they consider to be the appropriate placement. If they choose the latter course, which conscientious parents who have adequate means and who are reasonably confident of their assessment normally would, it would be an empty victory to have a court tell them several years later that they were right but that these expenditures could not in a proper case be reimbursed by the school officials. If that were the case, the child's right to a *free* appropriate public education, the parents' right to participate fully in developing a proper IEP, and all of the procedural safeguards would be less than complete. Because Congress undoubtedly did not intend this result, we are confident that by empowering the court to grant "appropriate" relief Congress meant to include retroactive reimbursement to parents as an available remedy in a proper case.

In this Court, the Town repeatedly characterizes reimbursement as "damages," but that simply is not the case. Reimbursement merely requires the Town to belatedly pay expenses that it should have paid all along and would have borne in the first instance had it developed a proper IEP. Such a *post-hoc* determination of financial responsibility was contemplated in the legislative history:

> "If a parent contends that he or she has been forced, at that parent's own expense, to seek private schooling for the child because an appropriate program does not exist within the local educational agency responsible for the child's education and the local educational agency disagrees, that disagreement and the question of who remains financially responsible is a matter to which the due process procedures established under [the predecessor to § 1415] appl[y]." . . .

See 34 CFR § 300.403(b) (1984) (disagreements and question of financial responsibility subject to the due process procedures).

Regardless of the availability of reimbursement as a form of relief in a proper case, the Town maintains that the [parents of the handicapped child] have waived any right they otherwise might have to reimbursement because they violated § 1415(e)(3), which provides:

> "During the pendency of any proceedings conducted pursuant to [§ 1415], unless the State or local educational agency and the parents or guardian otherwise agree, the child shall remain in the then current educational placement of such child. . . ."

We do not agree with the Town that a parental violation of §1415(e)(3) constitutes a waiver of reimbursement. The provision says nothing about financial responsibility, waiver, or parental right to reimbursement at the conclusion of judicial proceedings. Moreover, if the provision is interpreted to cut off parental rights to reimbursement, the principal purpose of the Act will in many cases be defeated in the same way as if reimbursement were never available. As in this case, parents will often notice a child's learning difficulties while the child is in a regular public school program. If the school officials disagree with the need for special education or the adequacy of the public school's program to meet the child's needs, it is unlikely they will agree to an interim private school placement while the review process runs its course. Thus, under the Town's reading of § 1415(e)(3), the parents are forced to leave the child in what may turn out to be an inappropriate educational placement or to obtain the appropriate placement only by sacrificing any claim for reimbursement. The Act was intended to give handicapped children both an appropriate education and a free one; it should not be interpreted to defeat one or the other of those objectives. We think at least one purpose of § 1415(e)(3) was to prevent school officials from removing a child from the regular public school classroom over the parents' objection pending completion of the review proceedings.

This is not to say that § 1415(e)(3) has no effect on parents. While we doubt that this provision would authorize a court to order parents to leave their child in a particular placement, we think it operates in such a way that parents who unilaterally change their child's placement during the pendency of review proceedings, without the consent of state or local school officials, do so at their own financial risk. If the courts ultimately determine that the IEP proposed by the school officials was appropriate, the parents would be barred from obtaining reimbursement for any interim period in which their child's placement violated § 1415(e)(3).

In *Florence County School District Four v. Carter*, 510 U.S. 7, 114 S.Ct. 361, 126 L.Ed. 2d 284, (1993), the parents of a learning disabled student placed her in a private academy when public school officials refused to change her IEP. The private school specialized in education for children with disabilities, but it did not comply with all of the IDEA's procedures. When the district's IEP was found inadequate, school officials argued that they could not be forced to reimburse the costs of a school that did not satisfy IDEA and was not approved by the state. The Court held that the parents could be reimbursed so long as the private school provides an education that is otherwise proper under the Act. Because the district objected to placement in the academy, it was not made under public supervision and direction, so the institution did not have to be approved by the state. Parents were unlikely to know whether a private school complied with IDEA procedures or was approved by the state. As a result, adopting the district's position would defeat the IDEA's purpose of ensuring that "children with disabilities receive an education that is both appropriate and free." The Court rejected the district's concerns about the expense of reimbursing parents for private academies because school officials could avoid this burden by putting together an appropriate IEP.

Parents' unilateral decisions to withdraw children from public schools and enroll them in private institutions are nevertheless financially risky. In *Board of Education of the Avon Lake School District v. Patrick M.*, 9 F.Supp. 2d 811 (E.D.Ohio 1998), the parents of a seventeen-year-old teenager with multiple disabilities placed him in Elan School, a residential school in Maine, without school district approval. They subsequently sought reimbursement of $71,971.04 in costs associated with their son's placement there. Because the court concluded that the school district had offered an appropriate IEP, the parents had to absorb the expenses of removing their child from the public school system.

5. *The Interplay Between IDEA and Section 504*

In *Smith v. Robinson*, 468 U.S. 992, 104 S.Ct. 3457, 82 L.Ed.2d 746 (1984), the Supreme Court held that Congress intended the Education for All Handicapped Children Act (now the IDEA) to be the exclusive avenue for raising legal claims about the provision of "free appropriate public education" for disabled children. The decision meant such claims could not be brought under Section 504 of the Rehabilitation Act of 1973 or under 42 U.S.C. § 1983, the statute most commonly relied on for raising constitutional claims. The 1986 Handicapped Children's Protection Act reversed *Smith* and reestablished the rights of disabled students under these statutes. *See* Gallegos, "Beyond *Board of Education v. Rowley:* Educational Benefit for the Handicapped," 97 *Amer.J.Educ.* 258, 270 (1989).

In *Sellers v. School Board of the City of Manassas*, 141 F.3d 524 (4th Cir.), *cert. denied*, 525 U.S. 871 (1998), a high school student and his parents sued the school board, alleging that it had violated the IDEA, the Rehabilitation Act, 42 U.S.C. § 1983, and Virginia state law. According to the complaint, the school district had failed to diagnose the student's learning disability until he was eighteen years old. As a result, he received no special services, even though his test scores should have alerted the school to his needs as early as the fourth grade. Both a hearing officer and district court judge refused to award the plaintiffs compensatory or punitive damages. The Fourth Circuit affirmed, concluding that the IDEA allowed tuition reimbursement but did not authorize compensatory or punitive damages. Although damages could be recovered under the Rehabilitation Act, a claim could not be based solely on a failure to comply with the IDEA. Rather, the plaintiffs had to show bad faith or gross misjudgment to recover. Here, the school district's failure to recognize a student's disability at most amounted to negligence, not discrimination.

Citing *Smith v. Robinson*, the court of appeals also rejected the plaintiff's § 1983 claim. The court concluded that the 1986 amendments that Congress enacted in response to the decision did not alter *Smith's* holding that the IDEA offered the exclusive remedies for violations of that statute. To prevail under

§ 1983, the plaintiffs would have to demonstrate a constitutional violation. Under equal protection law, they would need to show that the school board's decision had no rational basis. The plaintiffs could not satisfy this standard. The Supreme Court declined to review the decision, and the issues continue to generate controversy in the courts. *See, e.g., Ridgewood Board of Education v. N.E. for M.E.*, 172 F.3d 238 252–53 (3d Cir. 1999) (claims under IDEA are actionable under § 1983); *Padilla v. School District No. 1*, 35 F.Supp.2d, 1260, 1266–69 (D.Colo. 1999) (compensatory damage awards to individuals are available under § 1983 for IDEA violations).

b. Mainstreaming and the Least Restrictive Environment: The Uncertain Legal Standard. The IDEA contains a preference for mainstreaming, but the Supreme Court has yet to address when a child must be integrated into a regular classroom and when the child can be placed in separate classes for special instruction. In the absence of such guidance, lower courts have struggled to find the proper criteria to decide when mainstreaming is beneficial and when it is so detrimental that any congressional preference for it is overridden. Some jurisdictions have emphasized the central importance of full inclusion, often noting social as well as academic benefits, in favoring mainstreaming.

Roncker v. Walter

700 F. 2d 1058 (6th Cir. 1983).

Before Kennedy, J., Contie, J., and Gordon, J.

Contie, J.:

[The plaintiff's son Neill Roncker, was a nine-year-old who was severely mentally retarded. Classified as Trainable Mentally Retarded, Neill had an IQ below 50 and functioned in most respects at a mental age of two or three. Neill was not a danger to others but did need constant supervision because he could not recognize dangerous situations. When the school district recommended that Neill be placed in a county school exclusively for mentally retarded children, his mother challenged the decision on the ground that Neill should be placed in a special education class in the regular school setting. Neill's mother believed that he would benefit from contact with children who did not have disabilities, but the school district claimed that mainstreaming would not afford him any significant benefits. The district court agreed with the school district.

On appeal, the court of appeals explained why it was overturning the district court's ruling:]

* * *

The Act does not require mainstreaming in every case but its requirement that mainstreaming be provided to the *maximum* extent appropriate indicates a very strong congressional preference.[22] The proper inquiry is whether a proposed placement is appropriate under the Act. In some cases, a placement which may be considered better for academic reasons may not be appropriate because of the failure to provide for mainstreaming. The perception that a segregated institution is academically superior for a handicapped child may reflect no more than a basic disagreement with the mainstreaming concept. Such a disagreement is not, of course, any basis for not following the Act's mandate. *Campbell v. Talladega City Bd. of Education*, 518 F.Supp. 47, 55 (N.D.Ala.1981). In a case where the segregated facility is considered superior, the court should determine whether the services which make that placement superior could be feasibly provided in a non-segregated setting. If they can, the placement in the segregated school would be inappropriate under the Act. Framing the issue in this manner accords the proper respect for the strong preference in favor of mainstreaming while still realizing the possibility that some handicapped children simply must be educated in segregated facilities either because the handicapped child would not benefit from mainstreaming, because any marginal benefits received from mainstreaming are far outweighed by the benefits gained from services which could not feasibly be provided in the non-segregated setting, or because the handicapped child is a disruptive force in the non-segregated setting. Cost is a proper factor to consider since excessive spending on one handicapped child deprives other handicapped children. *See Age v. Bullitt County Schools*, 673 F.2d 141, 145 (6th Cir.1982). Cost is no defense, however, if the school district has failed to use its funds to provide a proper continuum of alternative placements for handicapped children. The provision of such alternative placements benefits all handicapped children.

---

[22]The Act's mainstreaming requirement applies to non-academic activities such as lunch, gym, recess and transportation to and from school. *See* 34 C.F.R. § 300.553.

In the present case, the district court must determine whether Neill's educational, physical or emotional needs require some service which could not feasibly be provided in a class for handicapped children within a regular school or in the type of split program advocated by the State Board of Education. [In the split program, Neill would go to the county school but have some contact with non-handicapped children.] Although Neill's progress, or lack thereof, at Pleasant Ridge [a regular school where Neill attended special education classes] is a relevant factor in determining the maximum appropriate extent to which he can be mainstreamed, it is not dispositive since the district court must determine whether Neill could have been provided with additional services, such as those provided at the county schools, which would have improved his performance at Pleasant Ridge.

We recognize that the mainstreaming issue imposes a difficult burden on the district court. Since Congress has chosen to impose that burden, however, the courts must do their best to fulfill their duty. . . .

* * *

See also *Sacramento City Unified School District v. Rachel H.*, 14 F.3d 1398 (9th Cir. 1994); *Roland M. v. Concord School Committee*, 910 F.2d 983 (1st Cir. 1990); *A. W. v. Northwest R-I School District*, 813 F.2d 158 (8th Cir. 1987).

On the other hand, some courts have focused primarily on the disabled child's academic achievement in separate and regular classes, treating other benefits as secondary considerations. These courts have concluded that the preference for mainstreaming cannot trump the child's interest in an appropriate education. The following case addresses the difficult task of balancing factors that define an "educational benefit" in separate and regular classrooms.

Hartmann v. Loudoun County Board of Education
118 F.3d 996 (4th Cir. 1997).

Before Wilkinson, C.J., Luttig, J., and Copenhaver, J. Wilkinson, Chief Judge:

Roxanna and Joseph Hartmann brought suit on behalf of their disabled son Mark against the Loudoun County Board of Education under the Individuals With Disabilities Education Act (IDEA), 20 U.S.C. § 1400 et seq. The Hartmanns alleged that the

Board had failed to ensure that Mark was educated with non-handicapped children "to the maximum extent appropriate" as required by the IDEA's mainstreaming provision, 20 U.S.C. § 1412(5)(B). The district court agreed, rejecting the findings of both the local hearing officer and the state review officer. The Board appeals, contending that the court's decision is contrary to the law and the evidence in the record. We agree. As Supreme Court precedent makes clear, the IDEA does not grant federal courts a license to substitute their own notions of sound educational policy for those of local school authorities, or to disregard the findings developed in state administrative proceedings. Upon careful review of the record, however, we are forced to conclude that this is precisely what has occurred in this case. Accordingly, we reverse and remand with directions to dismiss.

I

Mark Hartmann is an eleven-year-old autistic child. Autism is a developmental disorder characterized by significant deficiencies in communication skills, social interaction, and motor control. Mark is unable to speak and suffers severe problems with fine motor coordination. Mark's writing ability is extremely limited; he does not write by hand and can consistently type only a few words such as "is" and "at" by himself on a keyboard device known as a Canon communicator. The parties agree that Mark's greatest need is to develop communication skills.

Mark spent his pre-school years in various programs for disabled children. In kindergarten, he spent half his time in a self-contained program for autistic children and half in a regular education classroom at Butterfield Elementary in Lombard, Illinois. Upon entering first grade, Mark received speech and occupational therapy one-on-one, but was otherwise included in the regular classroom at Butterfield full-time with an aide to assist him.

After Mark's first-grade year, the Hartmanns moved to Loudoun County, Virginia, where they enrolled Mark at Ashburn Elementary for the 1993–1994 school year. Based on Mark's individualized education program (IEP) from Illinois, the school placed Mark in a regular education classroom. To facilitate Mark's inclusion, Loudoun officials carefully selected his teacher, hired a full-time aide to assist him, and put him in a smaller class with more independent children. Mark's teacher, Diane Johnson, read extensively about autism, and both

Johnson and Mark's aide, Suz Leitner, received training in facilitated communication, a special communication technique used with autistic children. Mark received five hours per week of speech and language therapy with a qualified specialist, Carolyn Clement. Halfway through the year, Virginia McCullough, a special education teacher, was assigned to provide Mark with three hours of instruction a week and to advise Mark's teacher and aide.

Mary Kearney, the Loudoun County Director of Special Education, personally worked with Mark's IEP team, which consisted of Johnson, Leitner, Clement, and Laurie McDonald, the principal of Ashburn. Kearney provided in-service training for the Ashburn staff on autism and inclusion of disabled children in the regular classroom. Johnson, Leitner, Clement, and McDonald also attended a seminar on inclusion held by the Virginia Council for Administrators of Special Education. Mark's IEP team also received assistance from educational consultants Jamie Ruppmann and Gail Mayfield, and Johnson conferred with additional specialists whose names were provided to her by the Hartmanns and the school. Mark's curriculum was continually modified to ensure that it was properly adapted to his needs and abilities.

Frank Johnson, supervisor of the county's program for autistic children, formally joined the IEP team in January, but provided assistance throughout the year in managing Mark's behavior. Mark engaged in daily episodes of loud screeching and other disruptive conduct such as hitting, pinching, kicking, biting, and removing his clothing. These outbursts not only required Diane Johnson and Leitner to calm Mark and redirect him, but also consumed the additional time necessary to get the rest of the children back on task after the distraction.

Despite these efforts, by the end of the year Mark's IEP team concluded that he was making no academic progress in the regular classroom. In Mark's May 1994 IEP, the team therefore proposed to place Mark in a class specifically structured for autistic children at Leesburg Elementary. Leesburg is a regular elementary school which houses the autism class in order to facilitate interaction between the autistic children and students who are not handicapped. The Leesburg class would have included five autistic students working with a special education teacher and at least one full-time aide. Under the May IEP, Mark would have received only academic instruction and speech in the self-contained classroom, while joining a regular class for art, music, physical education, library, and recess. The Leesburg program also would have permitted Mark to increase the portion of his instruction received in a regular education setting as he demonstrated an improved ability to handle it.

The Hartmanns refused to approve the IEP, claiming that it failed to comply with the mainstreaming provision of the IDEA, which states that "to the maximum extent appropriate," disabled children should be educated with children who are not handicapped. 20 U.S.C. § 1412(5)(B). The county initiated due process proceedings, see 20 U.S.C. § 1415(b), and on December 14, 1994, the local hearing officer upheld the May 1994 IEP. She found that Mark's behavior was disruptive and that despite the "enthusiastic" efforts of the county, he had obtained no academic benefit from the regular education classroom. On May 3, 1995, the state review officer affirmed the decision, adopting both the hearing officer's findings and her legal analysis. The Hartmanns then challenged the hearing officer's decision in federal court.

* * *

The district court reversed the hearing officer's decision. The court rejected the administrative findings and concluded that Mark could receive significant educational benefit in a regular classroom and that "the Board simply did not take enough appropriate steps to try to include Mark in a regular class." The court made little of the testimony of Mark's Loudoun County instructors, and instead relied heavily on its reading of Mark's experience in Illinois and Montgomery County. While the hearing officer had addressed Mark's conduct in detail, the court stated that "[g]iven the strong presumption for inclusion under the IDEA, disruptive behavior should not be a significant factor in determining the appropriate educational placement for a disabled child." Loudoun County now appeals.

II

The IDEA embodies important principles governing the relationship between local school authorities and a reviewing district court. Although section 1415(e)(2) provides district courts with authority to grant "appropriate" relief based on a preponderance of the evidence, 20 U.S.C. § 1415(e)(2), that section "is by no means an invitation to the courts to substitute their own notions of sound educational policy for those of the school authorities which they review." *Board of Education of Hendrick Hudson Central Sch. Dist. v. Rowley,* 458 U.S. 176, 206, 102 S.Ct. 3034, 3050, 73 L.Ed.2d 690 (1982). Absent some statutory infraction, the task of education belongs to the educators who have been charged by society with that critical task. Likewise, federal courts must accord "due weight" to state administrative proceedings. *Id.* Administrative findings in an IDEA case "are entitled to be considered prima facie correct," and "the district court, if it is not going to follow them, is required to explain why it does not." *Doyle v. Arlington County Sch. Bd.,* 953 F.2d 100, 105 (4th Cir.1991).

These principles reflect the IDEA's recognition that federal courts cannot run local schools. Local educators deserve latitude in determining the individualized education program most appropriate for a disabled child. The IDEA does not deprive these educators of the right to apply their professional judgment. Rather it establishes a "basic floor of opportunity" for every handicapped child. *Rowley,* 458 U.S. at 201, 102 S.Ct. at 3047. States must provide specialized instruction and related services "sufficient to confer some educational benefit upon the handicapped child," *id.* at 200, 102 S.Ct. at 3047 but the Act does not require "the furnishing of every special service necessary to maximize each handicapped child's potential," *id.* at 199, 102 S.Ct. at 3047.

In this same vein, the IDEA's mainstreaming provision establishes a presumption, not an inflexible federal mandate. Under its terms, disabled children are to be educated with children who are not handicapped only "to the maximum extent appropriate." 20 U.S.C. § 1412(5)(B). Section 1412(5)(B) explicitly states that mainstreaming is not appropriate "when the nature or severity of the disability is such that education in regular classes with the use of supplementary aids and services cannot be achieved satisfactorily." 20 U.S.C. § 1412(5)(B); *see also Rowley,* 458 U.S. at 181 n. 4, 102 S.Ct. at 3038 n. 4.

III

The district court's ruling strayed generally from the aforementioned principles. It diverged in particular from our decision in *DeVries v. Fairfax County Sch. Bd.,* 882 F.2d 876 (4th Cir.1989). In *DeVries,* we held that mainstreaming is not required where (1) the disabled child would not receive an educational benefit from mainstreaming into a regular class; (2) any mar-

ginal benefit from mainstreaming would be significantly outweighed by benefits which could feasibly be obtained only in a separate instructional setting; or, (3) the disabled child is a disruptive force in a regular classroom setting. *Id.* at 879. . . .

A

In finding that Mark could receive an educational benefit in a regular classroom, the district court disregarded both the hearing officer's finding and the overwhelming evidence that Mark made no academic progress in the regular second grade classroom at Ashburn. Mark's teacher testified, for example, that he was unable to retain skills: "once we thought he mastered [a math skill] and we left it alone and went onto another concept, if we went back to review, it seemed that he had forgotten." She confessed, "I felt like he lost a year in my classroom." Other Loudoun County personnel testified to the same effect. His speech therapist, for instance, stated that "[t]he only gain that I saw him make was in the one to one setting." The supervisor for the county's program for autistic students likewise concluded, "I think there has been no progress academically in the inclusive settings;" "I think we're wasting his time." The hearing officer accordingly found that "Mark made no measurable academic progress attributable to his placement in the regular classroom."

Mark's situation is similar to the one we faced in *DeVries,* 882 F.2d 876. In upholding Fairfax County's decision not to place Michael DeVries in Annandale High School, the court observed not only that Michael would derive virtually no academic benefit from the regular classroom, but also that his work would be at a much lower level than his classmates and that he would in effect "simply be monitoring classes." *Id.* at 879. Here the hearing officer made an identical finding, concluding that Mark "did not participate in the regular curriculum, but was provided his own curriculum." Mark's special education teacher in Loudoun County explained, "Mark needs a completely different program. . . . His skills have to be taught in a different way, in a different sequence, and even a different group of skills . . . from what his typical functioning peers are learning."

The district court acknowledged the testimony of Mark's second grade teacher regarding his lack of progress, but asserted that the hearing officer's conclusions were erroneous because the officer failed to give due weight to the testimony of Cathy Thornton, Mark's private tutor during second grade, and to Mark's first grade experience in Illinois. To the contrary, the administrative decisions took careful note of both. The hearing officer fully credited Thornton's testimony, finding that Mark made progress with both her and his speech therapist. The officer went further, however, and observed that both the tutoring and speech instruction occurred in a one-to-one setting outside of the regular class. In light of Mark's failure to progress in the regular classroom, the officer drew the only reasonable inference from this evidence, namely that separate instruction was precisely what Mark needed to make educational progress. As to Mark's experience in Illinois, the state review officer explained that the Illinois assessment of Mark's capabilities was flawed:

> It became clear during the course of the second grade that Mark's academic skills were not as advanced as the Illinois school system thought. Mark cannot read and cannot add, yet the Illinois teachers thought he was reading at first grade level and progressing in the first grade math workbook. . . . Mark apparently did not make the academic progress in first grade the records forwarded to Loudoun County from Illinois indicated. . . .

While the district court opinion references the hearing officer's decision, its failure to address the administrative findings noted above simply does not reflect the teachings of *Rowley* and *Doyle* that state proceedings must command considerable deference in federal courts.

* * *

Finally, the district court pointed to perceived improvement in Mark's social skills due to interaction with his non-disabled peers. Any such benefits, however, cannot outweigh his failure to progress academically in the regular classroom. The mainstreaming provision represents recognition of the value of having disabled children interact with non-handicapped students. The fact that the provision only creates a presumption, however, reflects a congressional judgment that receipt of such social benefits is ultimately a goal subordinate to the requirement that disabled children receive educational benefit. Here the evidence clearly supports the judgment of the local education officials and the admin-

istrative hearing officers that Mark's educational progress required significant instruction outside of the regular classroom setting.

B

The district court attributed Mark's lack of progress in Loudoun County to the county's alleged failure to make reasonable efforts to accommodate him in the regular classroom. We interpret this as a ruling that the county failed to provide the supplementary aids and services contemplated by the IDEA's mainstreaming provision. 20 U.S.C. § 1412(5)(B).

The district court's conclusion is remarkable in light of the extensive measures taken on Mark's behalf. The hearing officer found that Loudoun personnel were "enthusiastic" about including Mark at Ashburn, a description fully supported by the record. The Ashburn principal deliberately reduced the size of Mark's class and ensured that it was composed of students who were more independent and had higher level skills. Mark's teacher was selected because of her excellent teaching abilities, and the county hired a full-time, one-on-one aide for Mark. Mark received a full hour of speech and language instruction daily. Frank Johnson, the supervisor of the county's program for autistic children, provided assistance in behavior management throughout the year. Halfway through the year, the school's efforts increased when Virginia McCullough began providing special education services directly to Mark as well as advising Mark's teacher and aide. Inclusion specialists Gail Mayfield and Jamie Ruppmann consulted with the school during the fall, and Mark's teacher sought advice from other experts whose names were provided to her by the school or the Hartmanns. The teacher testified that she met constantly with Mark's aide, his speech therapist, the IEP team, and others to work on Mark's program—daily at the beginning of the year and at least twice a week throughout.

The district court nonetheless found the county's efforts insufficient. The court relied primarily on its conclusion that the Loudoun educators involved with Mark had inadequate training and experience to work with an autistic child.[2] The court found the credentials of two groups to be lacking. Neither the special

---

[2]The court also concluded that Loudoun County's commitment to mainstreaming Mark lapsed at mid-year. Such a conclusion again does not take proper account of the administrative record as required by *Rowley* and *Doyle*. The hearing officer pointed out, for example, that the county actually added services for Mark in the second half of the year, when McCullough began providing special education instruction to Mark. Moreover, the hearing officer noted that the IEP prepared by Mark's team in March—three months after the county allegedly gave up on mainstreaming him—called for retaining him in the regular classroom.

education professionals nor the regular education instructors were deemed properly qualified. The conclusion that Mark had inadequately trained personnel developing and implementing his program, however, is irreconcilable with either the law or the record.

As to special education personnel, the district court concedes that the individuals working with Mark during the first half of the year, Mary Kearney and Jamie Ruppmann, were fully competent to assist him. Kearney led Mark's IEP team, while Ruppmann provided consultation services. In addition to serving as the county Director of Special Education, Kearney had participated in the Virginia Systems Change Project, a two-year state program on mainstreaming which involved selected schools from across the state. Ruppmann is an experienced, highly qualified consultant.

During the second half of the year, Frank Johnson led the IEP team, and Virginia McCullough provided Mark with special education services. The district court rejected their qualifications, asserting, for example, that Johnson's credentials were clearly inadequate because they were inferior to those of Kearney and Ruppmann. However, in addition to serving as the supervisor of Loudoun County's program for autistic children, Johnson had a special education masters degree, did graduate work with an autistic child, worked directly with approximately ten autistic children as a teacher, and had attended special education courses and seminars relating to autism throughout his professional career. Both McCullough's early childhood degree program and her work in Loudoun County focused specifically on integrating children with disabilities into the regular classroom.

To dismiss Johnson's and McCullough's qualifications is to adopt exactly the sort of potential-maximizing standard rejected by the Supreme Court in *Rowley*. We think the Court's admonition that the IDEA does not require "the furnishing of every special service necessary to maximize each handicapped child's potential," *Rowley*, 458 U.S. at 199, 102 S.Ct. at 3047 encompasses the notion that the IDEA likewise does not require special education service providers to have every conceivable credential relevant to every child's disability. Not all school systems will have the resources to hire top-notch consultants, nor will every school have the good fortune to have personnel who were involved in a major state program related to the needs of every disabled child. We note that in Virginia, there is no

certification for autism. Furthermore, at the time of the trial, Loudoun County had eleven autistic children in a total school population of approximately 20,000 students. In this light, Johnson's experience teaching ten autistic children was substantial. Johnson and McCullough were clearly qualified to work with Mark as special educators, even accepting the district court's assertion that Ruppmann and Kearney had better credentials.

The suggestion that the regular education instructors, Mark's teacher and aide, were not adequately qualified also does not survive close scrutiny. Diane Johnson was an experienced professional properly certified under state law, and Virginia law does not require teaching assistants to be certified. Furthermore, Johnson and Leitner both obtained special training to work with Mark. Both received in-service instruction and attended an outside seminar on inclusion of disabled children in the regular classroom. They also were trained in facilitated communication, a special communication method used with Mark in Illinois.

To demand more than this from regular education personnel would essentially require them to become special education teachers trained in the full panoply of disabilities that their students might have. Virginia law does not require this, nor does the IDEA. First, such a requirement would fall afoul of *Rowley*'s admonition that the IDEA does not guarantee the ideal educational opportunity for every disabled child. Furthermore, when the IDEA was passed, "Congress' intention was not that the Act displace the primacy of States in the field of education, but that States receive funds to assist them in extending their educational systems to the handicapped." *Rowley*, 458 U.S. at 208, 102 S.Ct. at 3051. The IDEA "expressly incorporates State educational standards." *Schimmel v. Spillane*, 819 F.2d 477, 484 (4th Cir.1987). We can think of few steps that would do more to usurp state educational standards and policy than to have federal courts re-write state teaching certification requirements in the guise of applying the IDEA.

In sum, we conclude that Loudoun County's efforts on behalf of Mark were sufficient to satisfy the IDEA's mainstreaming directive.

C

The district court also gave little or no weight to the disruptive effects of Mark's behavior in the classroom, stating that "[g]iven the strong presumption for inclusion under the IDEA, disruptive behavior should not be a significant factor in determining the appropriate educational placement for a disabled child." This statement simply ignores *DeVries*, where we specifically held that mainstreaming is inappropriate when "the handicapped child is a disruptive force in the non-segregated setting." 882 F.2d at 879 (quoting *Roncker v. Walter*, 700 F.2d 1058, 1063 (6th Cir.1983)). In this case, disruptive behavior was clearly an issue. The hearing officer summarized:

> [Mark's] misbehaviors include continual vocalization, especially whining, screeching and crying when unhappy or frustrated, hitting, pinching, kicking, biting, sucking the leg of a chair, rolling on the floor, and removing his shoes and clothing. Mark is a big strong child who cannot be easily restrained when he engages in injurious behaviors such as hitting, kicking, pinching and biting. His continual vocalizations are distracting and make it difficult for other children to stay on task. When Jamie Ruppmann observed Mark in his classroom, she observed two instances of significant disruption, in which he threw himself on the floor. She noted that in each instance it took about five to eight minutes to get Mark settled down. His loud screeching outbursts, which occur daily, take the attention of the teacher and the aide to redirect him; these outbursts also take the other children off task and they then have to be redirected. Mark hits and pinches others several times a day.

While the hearing officer did not find Mark's disruptive behavior by itself to be dispositive, the attention she gave to Mark's conduct was entirely appropriate, indeed required, under *DeVries*.

* * *

The IDEA encourages mainstreaming, but only to the extent that it does not prevent a child from receiving educational benefit. The evidence in this case demonstrates that Mark Hartmann was not making academic progress in a regular education classroom despite the provision of adequate supplementary aids and services. Loudoun County properly proposed to place Mark in a partially mainstreamed program which would have addressed the academic deficiencies of his full inclusion program while permitting him to interact with nonhandicapped students to the greatest extent possible. This professional judgment by local educators was deserving of respect. The approval of this educational approach by the local and state administrative officers likewise deserved a deference from the district court which it failed to receive. In rejecting reasonable pedagogical choices and dis-

regarding well-supported administrative findings, the district court assumed an educational mantle which the IDEA did not confer. Accordingly, the judgment must be reversed, and the case remanded with directions to dismiss it.

See also Oberti v. Board of Education, 995 F.2d 1204 (3d Cir. 1993); *Greer v. Rome City School District*, 950 F.2d 688 (11th Cir. 1991).

NOTES AND QUESTIONS

1. Factors to Be Weighed

How should district courts weigh measurable academic gains against more diffuse, social benefits? Can judges consider the cost of accommodating disabled children in regular classrooms? Are these costs purely monetary or do they include intangible burdens, such as distraction from lessons, placed on other students? What about the benefits to classmates of increased tolerance of those with disabilities? Can this benefit be measured and weighed in court?

2. Standards and Deference

Should courts generally defer to educators when evidence about the benefit of a placement is contested? Does the IDEA order courts to defer to decisions to mainstream but to scrutinize closely decisions to segregate? If so, is this asymmetrical standard appropriate? Why shouldn't courts apply the same level of review whenever parents and educators are in sufficient disagreement to litigate? Why should it matter what the parents' or districts' preferred remedy is?

c. Mainstreaming, Segregation, and Equality. Underlying the congressional preference for mainstreaming is a belief that it can safeguard children against the harms of misclassification and segregation in dead-end classes. Some scholars have argued that this fear of segregation is rooted in a false analogy to race.

Disability and the Public Schools: The Case Against "Inclusion"
A. Dupre, 22 *Wash.L.Rev.* 775 (1997).

* * *

The movement to achieve rights for the disabled has often been compared to the civil rights movement for racial equality. Inclusion advocates claim that the exclusion of disabled children from all educational services is similar to the exclusion of African American children from white schools. Some have compared special education to apartheid, and even to slavery. But, as explained below, although some parallels exist when assessing the harm of exclusion, the analogy fails when it comes to the remedy of inclusion. Moreover, the forty-odd years since *Brown* was decided have allowed time for reflection regarding some of the underlying beliefs that fueled the racial integration movement in schools. Scholars have begun to examine the premises of the racial integration model in the public schools and to analyze its effects on African American children and on African American institutions. Some commentators and judges—with the acute vision of hindsight—have sharply criticized the path that the courts took in the racial integration cases, and groups that have fought for inclusion in the past are now waging a fight for separate classrooms in the hope of achieving greater academic success. Some African American leaders stress that there is no evidence that blacks must attend school with whites to learn, and both "African American advocates and parents have indicated a willingness to forego racial balance in favor of effective education when the two seem incompatible."

Racial desegregation, similar to disability inclusion, was thought to enhance academic achievement, raise self-esteem for African American students, improve race relations, and produce other long-term benefits for all students in desegregated schools. Yet some scholars have concluded that these standard justifications for desegregation lack any verifiable support. The evolution of racial integration and the criticisms of the direction it has taken have been largely ignored by the full inclusion advocates and the courts that have accepted their strikingly similar justifications. Before careening toward full disability inclusion, its advocates should pause and reconsider whether inclusion actually advances the beneficial values it purports to advance for disabled students and whether the cost to the important functions of the public school is worth the benefit obtained. In this section, I begin this inquiry by examining the premises that sustain the disability inclusion movement through the prism of the racial integration model, a critical perspective that adds rich insight to the disability inclusion issue.

Although . . . there are significant distinctions between school segregation because of race and school segregation because of disability, there are also un-

deniable similarities. Both African American children and disabled children were excluded by law from many public schools. African American children were excluded by law from white schools in some states because they were viewed as different and inferior. Similarly, disabled children were also excluded from educational opportunity because they were viewed as different and inferior. The difference that excluded the African American child was the color of his skin. The difference that excluded the disabled child was his disability. In deciding that excluding African American children by law was unconstitutional, the U.S. Supreme Court in *Brown v. Board of Education* underscored the importance of education. Education is "the very foundation of good citizenship." As a "principal instrument in awakening the child to cultural values, in preparing him for later professional training, and in helping him to adjust normally to his environment," the court understood that "education is necessary for individuals to function in a democratic society." Thus, according to the Court, educational opportunity "must be made available to all on equal terms."

The *Brown* Court's emphasis on the importance of education explains why disabled children should not be excluded from all educational opportunities because of their disabilities, but it does not support inclusion in the regular classroom for a disabled child if the disabled child would achieve better elsewhere. Indeed, the opinion's emphasis on the importance of education seems to point in the opposite direction. *Brown* is limited to irrational line-drawing based on race. At least for some mental and physical disabilities, there is a rational reason for differential treatment.

The "difference" that is a result of some kinds of disability—while it most certainly does not warrant excluding the child by law from all educational services—is a difference that may have at least some relevance to academic achievement if the child were included in the general education classroom. With race there is no question of degree—no child of whatever shade or hue should be excluded from a classroom because of color, because color is not related to any relevant educational consideration. But children have a wide range of disabilities; where few would argue that a child missing a leg should be excluded from the general education classroom because she is in a wheelchair, a child with no brain stem who cannot walk, talk or control bodily functions should be placed in a special segregated classroom. A child with certain kinds of severe cognitive disabilities simply may not be able to achieve academically in the regular classroom. Because of the varied manifestations and limitations of the many cognitive, behavioral, and physical disabilities that can affect a child, segregation by disability, unlike by race, involves line drawing between those whose disability allows them to be included in the regular classroom and those whose disability is too severe for satisfactory inclusion. Indeed, some children with severe cognitive disabilities may become defeated and frustrated if they are placed in regular classrooms where they are unable to perform with their nondisabled peers.

Thus, although the *result* of racial and disability discrimination was the same—outright exclusion from certain schools by law—this does not necessarily mean that the *remedy* for the wrong—full inclusion—should be the same in each and every disability case. It is true that the civil rights issue for racial minorities and for disabled students is one of access. But in the former case the issue is one of access to the same services provided to others, regardless of skin color; in the latter case, however, the issue is one of "access to a differentiated education designed specifically to accommodate [the special needs of the disabled child] even if accommodation requires separation." In addition, as examined below, some commentators and judges have debated whether the integration remedy, even as conceived for racial exclusion, has itself exacerbated the "feelings of inferiority" that it was supposed to cure.

Despite these differences between disability and racial segregation, the full inclusion advocates have insinuated much of the analytical framework used by the courts in the race cases into the disability inclusion rhetoric. Full inclusionists argue that the stigma that results from segregation either by race or by disability is an overarching evil—a plague that only inclusion will cure. This cry for total inclusion has emotional appeal and fosters the image of the full inclusion advocate as taking the moral high ground.

As H. L. Mencken once said, "For every complex issue there is a simple answer, and it is wrong." Inclusion for all disabled students is viewed as the "simple answer"—the therapy necessary to cure a serious pathology—and, as such, it takes on a force of its own. In short, inclusion must be achieved, even at great cost. It must subjugate other values, even—in the case of the disabled child—the value of academic training. Yet after considering the arguments of some of the critics of the legal process of racial de-

segregation, it may well be that the path forged in the racial integration movement would best be left untraveled by children with disabilities.

The *Brown* Court established the premise that segregation inherently constitutes nonequality, a premise that advocates of full inclusion use to press their claim for including all students in general education classrooms in their neighborhood schools. The Court described the harm caused by de jure racial segregation in very much the way inclusion advocates describe the harm caused by placing a disabled child in a separate special education classroom: "To separate [these black students] from others of similar age and qualifications solely because of their race generates a feeling of inferiority as to their status in the community that may affect their hearts and minds in a way unlikely ever to be undone." Moreover, the Court stated:

> Segregation of white and colored children in public school has a detrimental effect upon the colored children. . . . [F]or the policy of separating the races is usually interpreted as denoting the inferiority of the negro group. A sense of inferiority affects the motivation of a child to learn. Segregation with the sanction of law, therefore, has a tendency to [retard] the educational and mental development of negro children.

Ever since the *Brown* Court made this pronouncement, "[r]emedying and avoiding the recurrence of this stigmatizing injury"—promoting integration—have been the "guiding objectives of [the U.S. Supreme] Court's desegregation jurisprudence."

* * *

The problem with the stigmatic injury theory may be its failure to distinguish for future cases—like disability inclusion—the difference between separation and the meaning behind the separation. De jure segregation was wrong—not simply because African American children were being educated in all-black schools, although that was a part of the problem. It was wrong because the meaning behind that forced segregation was the belief that African American children were inferior and did not belong in a classroom with Caucasian children. It was wrong because no child should be excluded by law from any public school classroom because of skin color. Unless the separation and the meaning behind that separation are analyzed separately, however, it can appear that the stigma occurs because of the separation itself, that is, because African American children were attending all-black schools.

Critics of the racial integration model claim that its implicit message—that going to an all-black school somehow stigmatized black children—was "just as harmful to their self-esteem as the idea of forced segregation." Thus, Professor Kevin Brown claims that "[a]t the same time that the country was dismantling de jure segregation and its concomitant message of African American inferiority, it was also constructing a policy of integration which carried its own message of African American inferiority."[347] He asserts that "[t]he very remedies that were undertaken in an attempt to eliminate a belief in African-American inferiority were also—like segregation that had preceded it—standing as symbols for it."

The stigmatic injury theory is a part of the ideological foundation that has supported the racial integration remedy, and the Supreme Court has continued to accept it. Despite criticism of the theory, it has taken on a power of its own, with a force field that has reached into the disability arena. But the criticism of Professor Brown and others should give pause to the full inclusion advocates. By failing to analyze separately the meaning behind separation and by failing to acknowledge that—unlike race—there may be legitimate pedagogical reasons for placing a disabled child in a special class, the full inclusion advocates have implied that there is something inferior about a classroom that contains only disabled students. To avoid the inevitable stigma that taints a "disabled-only" class, full inclusion advocates would include these children with the nondisabled in the general education classroom. Full inclusion advocates should consider whether, by enshrining the idea that an all-disabled class somehow stigmatizes the disabled, their "cure" for stigma—inclusion—has in reality injected more of the disease.

In addition to curing the stigma that occurs from separation, there has been some suggestion that the racial integration model will also give African American students other students to model. For instance, the Court in *Milliken v. Bradley* ("*Milliken II*"), "in reference to the African-American school children who would continue to attend segregated schools, stated that '[c]hildren who have been . . . educationally and culturally set apart from the larger community will inevitably acquire habits of speech, conduct and attitudes reflecting their cultural isolation. . . .' " . . . .This notion fueled the belief "that 'white'

schools had 'better' students whose achievement-oriented, achievement-ready backgrounds created a powerful environmental press for academic attainment." Thus—much like the modeling rationale that underlies the inclusion movement—racial integration was viewed as a way to "provide social modeling of higher aspirations, skills and motivation to minority students whose segregated school environments produced a defeating climate of failure and hopelessness." The "intimation that black children can only achieve academically when educated with white children" reverberates with the assumption by full inclusion advocates that disabled children can improve themselves—and work to "cure" their disability—by modeling their nondisabled peers. This assumption brushes aside themes of independence, pride, and competence and fails to recognize that close association among minority groups may actually enhance self-esteem by promoting the "acceptance of group difference as positive."

Education reform movements—like the disability inclusion movement—that have arisen in the wake of school desegregation have been profoundly affected by the Court's jurisprudence. Some educators, specifically inclusion advocates, have referred to language in *Brown* when discussing the need for educational reform. This reliance on *Brown* is not surprising. Certainly the "public discourse of judges is given a preferred meaning and assumed to reflect accurately reality." Indeed, court opinions on racial desegregation operate "to validate particular conceptions of society. . . ." Yet by relying on *Brown*, inclusion advocates have also imported into the disability area some of the same troubling assumptions that critics claim have plagued racial integration. By "[c]onfusing the social *goal* of equal opportunity with *place* of opportunity," they have distracted attention and effort from the primary academic mission of the school. In so doing, inclusion advocates have also failed to recognize "the complexity of achieving equal educational opportunity for children to whom it so long has been denied." Those who would set inclusion as the primary goal for disabled students—a goal that would supersede academic performance—should carefully study the racial integration model and reconsider whether they wish to follow that road to its ultimate destination.

---

[347]Brown, *supra*, note 320 [Kevin Brown, "The Legal Rhetorical Structure for the Conversion of Desegregation Lawsuits to Quality Education Lawsuits," 42 *Emory L.J.* 791 (1993) (describing historical debate over separate versus integrated education in African American community)], at 817.

In their concern over placement, stigma, and de facto segregation, the full inclusionists ignore "the overriding fact" that many children have "overwhelming learning problems" that will not simply disappear when the children are included in the regular classroom communities. Children are seldom identified as candidates for placement in special education classes before they enter school. Differences become apparent as the disabled child fails to make expected progress in the regular kindergarten or first grade classrooms. Indeed, the primary reason that a child is referred for placement in special classes is the failure of the child to learn in the regular class. Inclusion in that very same regular classroom will hardly resolve the child's serious learning problems — without a massive effort in additional individualized special aids and services.

* * *

See also Bryant, "Drowning in the Mainstream: Integration of Children with Disabilities After *Obertie v. Clementon School District*," 22 *Ohio N.U.L.Rev.* 83 (1995). At least one author has cautioned against funding formulas for special education that discourage mainstreaming. Willard, "Economics and the Individuals with Disabilities Education Act: The Influence of Funding Formulas on the Identification and Placement of Disabled Students," 31 *Indiana L.Rev.* 1167, 1181–84 (1998).

On the other hand, supporters of an inclusionary approach embrace both its philosophical and pedagogical implications. They believe that mainstreaming will help to reconceive the notion of disability as a spectrum of differences, rather than a bright-line distinction.

"Beyond Special Education: Toward a Quality System for All Students"

A. Gartner and D. Lipsky, 57 *Harv.Educ.Rev.* 367 (1987).

[I]n special education . . . the child and family are considered impaired, instruction is disability-focused, professional personnel are often trained and certified to work with specific disabilities, and attention to societal issues is often considered too political and not the business of educational institutions. The assumptions underlying such beliefs can be tersely summarized: "(1) Disability is a condition that individuals have; (2) disabled/typical is a useful and objective distinction; and (3) special education is a rationally conceived and coordinated system of ser-

vices that help children labeled disabled. . . ." This view of students labeled as handicapped, however, adversely affects expectations regarding their academic achievement. It causes them to be separated from other students; to be exposed to a watered-down curriculum; to be excused from standards and tests routinely applied to other students; to be allowed grades that they have not earned; and, in some states, to be permitted special diplomas.

The rationale given for such watered-down expectations is that they are in the best interest of the child. Professionals often suggest that a child be placed in an environment where he or she will be "safe . . . because he would never be asked to do things there 'we know he cannot do.' "

Not only do "small expectations" excuse students from academic performance; they have also led state education departments, school systems, and the courts to excuse them from the social and behavioral expectations and standards set for other students. The medical or clinical model that undergirds special education inextricably leads to the belief that persons with a handicap, especially the severely disabled, are not capable of making choices or decisions. . . . Having denied individuals with disabilities autonomy and decisionmaking authority — in effect denying them the respect given to people whom society respects — we then excuse their behavior, ascribing it to the disability. . . .

An alternative way to serve students with mild and moderate handicaps is to integrate them into general education programs at the building level.

* * *

While clearly an improvement over the present special education practice, this broad proposal nonetheless continues a dual system approach for a smaller (more severely impaired) population. As described a decade ago, such students will continue to be faced with consequences of negative attitudes and lowered expectations, with teachers making comparisons between them "in relation to degrees of handicap rather than comparing [their] skill levels to the criteria of nonhandicapped skill performance." . . .

How then does one shape an educational system to include students with disabilities, one which is both consonant with and builds toward an inclusive society? Clearly, it is not done by taking students from the general education setting and labeling them as "deficient," nor is it done, as in special education, by focusing on the setting in which instruction takes place. Rather, research indicates that we must focus on the features of instruction that can produce improved learning for students.

An important step toward a restructured unitary system is expressed in a concept called "Rights without Labels": namely, the provision of needed services for students without the deleterious consequences of classification and labeling.

Regardless of the conceptual undergirding or the organizational arrangements of education for students with handicapping conditions, special education practice needs substantial improvement. In maintaining a separate special education system, however, no matter how refined or improved, education will continue to operate based on a set of organizational and individual assumptions that disabled and nondisabled youngsters require two distinct sets of services, which in turn require distinct funding, service delivery, and organization. While PL 94-142 [the Education for All Handicapped Children Act, now the IDEA] requires educational services for students with handicapping conditions, it does not require a special education system.

There is an alternative to separate systems: a merged or unitary system. The conception of a unitary system requires a "paradigm shift," a fundamental change in the way we think about differences among people, in the ways we choose to organize schools for their education, and in how we view the purpose of that education. It rejects the bimodal division of handicapped and nonhandicapped students, and recognizes that individuals vary—that single-characteristic definitions fail to capture the complexity of people. Moreover, it rejects the belief, common to all human services work that incorporates a medical or deviancy model, that the problem lies in the individual and the resolution lies in one or another treatment modality. The unitary system, in contrast, requires adaptations in society and in education, not solely in the individual. . . .

In the United States, there is a body of "adaptive education" approaches and specific educational practice attuned to individual differences that have been shown to be effective for students with handicapping conditions. Asserting the legal duty to provide effective schooling, lawyers at the Public Interest Law Center of Philadelphia put it succinctly: "Play school is out. Schooling is a profession. The law requires that practice in the schools measure up to the art of what has been demonstrated by the professional to be possible. What is done must be calculated to be effective." . . .

The ultimate rationale for quality education of students in an integrated setting is based not only on law or pedagogy, but also on values. What kinds of people are we? What kind of society do we wish to develop? What values do we honor? The current failure to provide a quality education to all students and the perpetuation of segregated settings expresses one set of answers to these questions. To change the outcome, we need to develop another set of values. . . .

NOTES AND QUESTIONS

1. Segregation and Equality

Does the integrationist approach advanced by Gartner and Lipsky make educational sense? Or is Dupre correct that fears of segregation are rooted in histories of racial discrimination that are not instructive in making policy for students with disabilities? Should a distinction be drawn between the mild or moderately disabled on the one hand and the severely disabled on the other? Did Congress intend mainstreaming as a protection for students with mild to moderate disabilities? Is inclusion in public education sufficient, even if disabled children are in separate classrooms? Did Congress adopt a flexible preference for mainstreaming that permits special classroom instruction for severely disabled children? If so, did Congress then reject the notion that such separation is inherently stigmatizing? Does this undercut the claim that the IDEA rests on an overly simplistic analogy to race? Why or why not?

In a 1996 follow-up to their highly influential discussion of quality programs in special education, Gartner and Lipsky note that the principle of a least restrictive environment has a number of important consequences. They conclude that this approach is "inherently flawed" because it "legitimates restrictive environments . . .; confuses segregation and integration on the one hand with the intensity of services on the other . . .; is based on a 'readiness' model . . . [that requires students to] prove their readiness for an integrated setting, rather than presuming such a setting as the norm . . .; and directs attention to the physical setting rather than to the services and supports people need to be integrated into the community." Gartner and Lipsky, "Inclusion, School Restructuring, and the Remaking of American Society," 66 Harv.Educ.Rev. 762, 769-780 (1996) [hereinafter Gartner and Lipsky, "Inclusion."].

2. *Mainstreaming and Institutional Change*

How might Gartner's and Lipsky's approach be implemented? Do schools have the capacity or the will to make the "paradigm shift" that Gartner and Lipsky say is demanded? Should advocates for the disabled fear that, under the guise of offering special treatment in a common setting, school administrators would provide little for their clientele? For a discussion of teachers' views of mainstreaming, *see* Scruggs and Mastropieri, "Teacher Perceptions of Mainstreaming/Inclusion, 1958–1995: A Research Synthesis," 63 *Exceptional Children* 59 (1996). According to Gartner and Lipsky, "The attention to students with disabilities in the Goals 2000: Educate America Act (PL 103-227) represents a significant breakthrough." Unlike other national reform efforts, it includes students with disabilities in establishing national standards. The authors argue that by excluding half of the country's students with disabilities, the National Assessment of Educational Progress had previously sent "two pernicious messages: first, that their education is not a matter of concern, and second, more fundamentally that they cannot achieve." Gartner and Lipsky, "Inclusion," at 778.

3. *Disability and the Common School*

Gartner and Lipsky suggest that integration is not just a claim rooted in pedagogy or values but also based on law—that truly common schooling is tantamount to effective education, and that such education is a legal right. Elaborating on this argument, they contend that: "For students with disabilities, the critical challenge will be how we view and treat difference–as an abnormality or as an aspect of the human condition." Gartner and Lipsky, "Inclusion," at 788. Gartner and Lipsky believe that reformulating disability as difference rather than deviance is an advance, yet they also recognize that this approach "moves the discussion from one of epistemology to that of the distribution of power." That is, institutions must avoid creating norms such as "mainstreaming" and "readiness" that place the burden on the disabled to show their worth. *Id.* at 790. Dupre, of course, does not believe that common schooling requires full integration of all students, regardless of their unique, individualized needs. This debate continues among researchers, administrators, and teachers. For further discussion of the arguments about mainstreaming, *see* Hallahan and Kauffman, "Toward a Culture of Disability in the Aftermath of *Deno* and *Dunn*," 27 *J.Special Education* 496 (1994).

d. The Procedural Entitlement. The IDEA is weak on substance, strong on procedure. It "guarantees procedures whereby parents may challenge the appropriateness of their child's educational program, but provides only the most general guidelines for resolving the substantive questions such challenges may present." Note, "Enforcing the Right to an 'Appropriate' Education: The Education for All Handicapped Children Act of 1975," 92 *Harv.L.Rev.* 1103 (1979). Both in evaluation procedures and in due process hearings, which may be requested in instances of disagreement between parents and school officials, the IDEA seeks to protect against discrimination. *See Doe v. Defendant I*, 898 F.2d 1186 (6th Cir. 1990).

The IDEA does not specifically speak to the authority of school officials to discipline disabled students. But the extensive procedural protections built into the act, primarily intended as safeguards against reclassification of disabled children for pedagogical reasons, have been read to create procedural rights in disciplinary situations. *See generally* Comment, "The Legal Limits of School Discipline for Children with Handicaps," 69 *Ore.L.Rev.* 117 (1990).

Honig v. Doe
484 U.S. 305, 108 S.Ct. 592, 98 L.Ed.2d 686 (1988).

Justice Brennan delivered the opinion of the Court.

As a condition of federal financial assistance, the Education of the Handicapped Act requires States to ensure a "free appropriate public education" for all disabled children within their jurisdictions. In aid of this goal, the Act establishes a comprehensive system of procedural safeguards designed to ensure parental participation in decisions concerning the education of their disabled children and to provide administrative and judicial review of any decisions with which those parents disagree. Among these safeguards is the so-called "stay-put" provision, which directs that a disabled child "shall remain in [his or her] then current educational placement" pending completion of any review proceedings, unless the parents and state or local educational agencies otherwise agree. 20 U.S.C. § 1415(e)(3). Today we must decide whether, in the face of this statutory proscription, state or local school authorities may nevertheless unilaterally exclude disabled children from the classroom for dangerous or disruptive conduct growing out of their disabilities. . . .

I

In the Education of the Handicapped Act . . . Congress sought "to assure that all handicapped children have available to them . . . a free appropriate public education which emphasizes special education and related services designed to meet their unique needs, [and] to assure that the rights of handicapped children and their parents or guardians are protected." § 1400(c). . . .

* * *

. . . In responding to these problems, Congress did not content itself with passage of a simple funding statute. Rather, the EHA confers upon disabled students an enforceable substantive right to public education in participating States, see *Board of Education of Hendrick Hudson Central School Dist. v. Rowley*, 458 U.S. 176, 102 S.Ct. 3034, 73 L.Ed.2d 690 (1982),[1] and conditions federal financial assistance upon a State's compliance with the substantive and procedural goals of the Act. Accordingly, States seeking to qualify for federal funds must develop policies assuring all disabled children the "right to a free appropriate public education," and must file with the Secretary of Education formal plans mapping out in detail the programs, procedures and timetables under which they will effectuate these policies. 20 U.S.C. §§ 1412(1), 1413(a). Such plans must assure that, "to the maximum extent appropriate," States will "mainstream" disabled children. . . .

The primary vehicle for implementing these congressional goals is the "individualized educational program" (IEP), which the EHA mandates for each disabled child. Prepared at meetings between a representative of the local school district, the child's teacher, the parents or guardians, and, whenever appropriate, the disabled child, the IEP sets out the child's present educational performance, establishes annual and short-term objectives for improvements in that performance, and describes the specially designed instruction and services that will enable the child to meet those objectives. § 1401(19). The IEP must be reviewed and, where necessary, revised at least once a year in order to ensure that local agencies tailor the statutorily required "free appro-

priate public education" to each child's unique needs. § 1414(a)(5).

Envisioning the IEP as the centerpiece of the statute's education delivery system for disabled children, and aware that schools had all too often denied such children appropriate educations without in any way consulting their parents, Congress repeatedly emphasized throughout the Act the importance and indeed the necessity of parental participation in both the development of the IEP and any subsequent assessments of its effectiveness. See §§ 1400(c), 1401(19), 1412(7), 1415(b)(1)(A), (C), (D), (E), and 1415(b)(2). Accordingly, the Act establishes various procedural safeguards that guarantee parents both an opportunity for meaningful input into all decisions affecting their child's education and the right to seek review of any decisions they think inappropriate. These safeguards include the right to examine all relevant records pertaining to the identification, evaluation, and educational placement of their child; prior written notice whenever the responsible educational agency proposes (or refuses) to change the child's placement or program; an opportunity to present complaints concerning any aspect of the local agency's provision of a free appropriate public education; and an opportunity for "an impartial due process hearing" with respect to any such complaints. § 1415(b)(1), (2).

At the conclusion of any such hearing, both the parents and the local educational agency may seek further administrative review and, where that proves unsatisfactory, may file a civil action in any state or federal court. § 1415(c), (e)(2). In addition to reviewing the administrative record, courts are empowered to take additional evidence at the request of either party and to "grant such relief as [they] determine[ ] is appropriate." § 1415(e)(2). The "stay-put" provision at issue in this case governs the placement of a child while these often lengthy review procedures run their course. It directs that:

> "During the pendency of any proceedings conducted pursuant to [§ 1415], unless the State or local educational agency and the parents or guardian otherwise agree, the child shall remain in the then current educational placement of such child. . . ." § 1415(e)(3).

---

[1]Congress' earlier efforts to ensure that disabled students received adequate public education, had failed in part because the measures it adopted were largely hortatory. In the 1966 amendments to the Elementary and Secondary Education Act of 1965, Congress established a grant program "for the purpose of assisting the States in the initiation, expansion, and improvement of programs and projects . . . for the education of handicapped children." Pub.L. 89-750, § 161, 80 Stat. 1204. It repealed that program four years later and replaced it with the original version of the Education of the Handicapped Act, Pub.L., 91-230, 84 Stat. 175, Part B of which contained a similar grant program. Neither statute, however, provided specific guidance as to how States were to use the funds, nor did they condition the availability of the grants on compliance with any procedural or substantive safeguards. In amending the EHA to its present form, Congress rejected its earlier policy of "merely establish[ing] an unenforceable goal requiring all children to be in school." 121 Cong.Rec. 37417 (1975) (remarks of Sen. Schweiker). Today, all 50 states and the District of Columbia receive funding assistance under the EHA. U.S. Dept. of Education, Ninth Annual Report to Congress on Implementation of Education of the Handicapped Act (1987).

The present dispute grows out of the efforts of certain officials of the San Francisco Unified School District (SFUSD) to expel two emotionally disturbed children from school indefinitely for violent and disruptive conduct related to their disabilities. In November 1980, respondent John Doe assaulted another student at the Louise Lombard School, a developmental center for disabled children. Doe's April 1980 IEP identified him as a socially and physically awkward 17 year old who experienced considerable difficulty controlling his impulses and anger. . . .

On November 6, 1980, Doe responded to the taunts of a fellow student in precisely the explosive manner anticipated by his IEP: he choked the student with sufficient force to leave abrasions on the child's neck, and kicked out a school window while being escorted to the principal's office afterwards. . . . Doe admitted his misconduct and the school subsequently suspended him for five days. Thereafter, his principal referred the matter to the SFUSD Student Placement Committee (SPC or Committee) with the recommendation that Doe be expelled. On the day the suspension was to end, the SPC notified Doe's mother that it was proposing to exclude her child permanently from SFUSD and was therefore extending his suspension until such time as the expulsion proceedings were completed. The Committee further advised her that she was entitled to attend the November 25 hearing at which it planned to discuss the proposed expulsion.

After unsuccessfully protesting these actions by letter, Doe brought this suit against a host of local school officials and the state superintendent of public education. Alleging that the suspension and proposed expulsion violated the EHA, he sought a temporary restraining order cancelling the SPC hearing and requiring school officials to convene an IEP meeting. The District Judge granted the requested injunctive relief and further ordered defendants to provide home tutoring for Doe on an interim basis; shortly thereafter, she issued a preliminary injunction directing defendants to return Doe to his then current educational placement at Louise Lombard School pending completion of the IEP review process. Doe re-entered school on December 15, 5 1/2 weeks, and 24 school days, after his initial suspension.

Respondent Jack Smith was identified as an emotionally disturbed child by the time he entered the second grade in 1976. School records prepared that year indicated that he was unable "to control verbal or physical outburst[s]" and exhibited a "[s]evere disturbance in relationships with peers and adults." . . . Further evaluations subsequently revealed that he had been physically and emotionally abused as an infant and young child and that, despite above average intelligence, he experienced academic and social difficulties as a result of extreme hyperactivity and low self-esteem. . . .

Based on these evaluations, SFUSD placed Smith in a learning center for emotionally disturbed children. His grandparents, however, believed that his needs would be better served in the public school setting and, in September 1979, the school district acceded to their requests and enrolled him at A. P. Giannini Middle School. His February 1980 IEP recommended placement in a Learning Disability Group, . . . [and] noted that Smith was easily distracted, impulsive, and anxious; it therefore proposed a half-day schedule and suggested that the placement be undertaken on a trial basis.

At the beginning of the next school year, Smith was assigned to a full-day program; almost immediately thereafter he began misbehaving. School officials met twice with his grandparents in October 1980 to discuss returning him to a half-day program; although the grandparents agreed to the reduction, they apparently were never apprised of their right to challenge the decision through EHA procedures. The school officials also warned them that if the child continued his disruptive behavior—which included stealing, extorting money from fellow students, and making sexual comments to female classmates—they would seek to expel him. On November 14, they made good on this threat, suspending Smith for five days after he made further lewd comments. His principal referred the matter to the SPC, which recommended exclusion from SFUSD. As it did in John Doe's case, the Committee scheduled a hearing and extended the suspension indefinitely pending a final disposition in the matter. On November 28, Smith's counsel protested these actions on grounds essentially identical to those raised by Doe, and the SPC agreed to cancel the hearing and to return Smith to a half-day program at A. P. Giannini or to provide home tutoring. Smith's grandparents chose the latter option and the school began home instruction on December 10; on January 6, 1981, an IEP team convened to discuss alternative placements.

After learning of Doe's action, Smith sought and obtained leave to intervene in the suit. . . .

* * *

II

At the outset, we address the suggestion, raised for the first time during oral argument, that this case is moot. Under Article III of the Constitution this Court may only adjudicate actual, ongoing controversies. . . .

In the present case, we have jurisdiction if there is a reasonable likelihood that respondents will again suffer the deprivation of EHA-mandated rights that gave rise to this suit. We believe that, at least with respect to respondent Smith, such a possibility does in fact exist and that the case therefore remains justiciable.

Respondent John Doe is now 24 years old and, accordingly, is no longer entitled to the protections and benefits of the EHA, which limits eligibility to disabled children between the ages of three and 21. See 20 U.S.C. § 1412(2)(B). . . .

Respondent Jack Smith, however, is currently 20 and has not yet completed high school. Although at present he is not faced with any proposed expulsion or suspension proceedings, and indeed no longer even resides within the SFUSD, he remains a resident of California and is entitled to a "free appropriate public education" within that State. His claims under the EHA, therefore, are not moot if the conduct he originally complained of is " 'capable of repetition, yet evading review.' " *Murphy v. Hunt,* 455 U.S. 478, 482, 102 S.Ct. 1181, 1183, 71 L.Ed.2d 353 (1982). Given Smith's continued eligibility for educational services under the EHA, the nature of his disability, and petitioner's insistence that all local school districts retain residual authority to exclude disabled children for dangerous conduct, we have little difficulty concluding that there is a "reasonable expectation," . . . that Smith would once again be subjected to a unilateral "change in placement" for conduct growing out of his disabilities were it not for the state-wide injunctive relief issued below. . . .

* * *

III

The language of § 1415(e)(3) is unequivocal. It states plainly that during the pendency of any proceedings initiated under the Act, unless the state or local educational agency and the parents or guardian of a disabled child otherwise agree, "the child *shall* remain in the then current educational placement." § 1415(e)(3) (emphasis added). Faced with this clear directive, petitioner asks us to read a "dangerousness" exception into the stay-put provision on the basis of either of two essentially inconsistent assumptions: first, that Congress thought the residual authority of school officials to exclude dangerous students from the classroom too obvious for comment; or second, that Congress inadvertently failed to provide such authority and this Court must therefore remedy the oversight. Because we cannot accept either premise, we decline petitioner's invitation to rewrite the statute.

Petitioner's arguments proceed, he suggests, from a simple, common-sense proposition: Congress could not have intended the stay-put provision to be read literally, for such a construction leads to the clearly unintended, and untenable, result that school districts must return violent or dangerous students to school while the often lengthy EHA proceedings run their course. We think it clear, however, that Congress very much meant to strip schools of the *unilateral* authority they had traditionally employed to exclude disabled students, particularly emotionally disturbed students, from school. In so doing, Congress did not leave school administrators powerless to deal with dangerous students; it did, however, deny school officials their former right to "self-help," and directed that in the future the removal of disabled students could be accomplished only with the permission of the parents or, as a last resort, the courts.

. . . Congress passed the EHA after finding that school systems across the country had excluded one out of every eight disabled children from classes. In drafting the law, Congress was largely guided by the recent decisions in *Mills v. Board of Education of District of Columbia,* 348 F.Supp. 866 (1972), and *PARC,* 343 F.Supp. 279 (1972), both of which involved the exclusion of hard-to-handle disabled students. *Mills* in particular demonstrated the extent to which schools used disciplinary measures to bar children from the classroom. There, school officials had labeled four of the seven minor plaintiffs "behavioral problems," and had excluded them from classes without providing any alternative education to them or any notice to their parents. . . . After finding that this practice was not limited to the named plaintiffs but affected in one way or another an estimated class of 12,000 to 18,000 disabled students, . . . [*Mills,* 348 F.Supp.] at 868–869, 875, the District Court enjoined future exclusions, suspensions, or expulsions "on grounds of discipline." . . .

Congress attacked such exclusionary practices in a variety of ways. It required participating States to educate *all* disabled children, regardless of the severity of their disabilities, 20 U.S.C. § 1412(2)(C), and included within the definition of "handicapped" those children with serious emotional disturbances. § 1401(1). It further provided for meaningful parental participation in all aspects of a child's educational placement, and barred schools, through the stay-put provision, from changing that placement over the parent's objection until all review proceedings were completed. Recognizing that those proceedings might prove long and tedious, the Act's drafters did not intend § 1415(e)(3) to operate inflexibly, see 121 Cong.Rec. 37412 (1975) (remarks of Sen. Stafford), and they therefore allowed for interim placements where parents and school officials are able to agree on one. Conspicuously absent from § 1415(e)(3), however, is any emergency exception for dangerous students. This absence is all the more telling in light of the injunctive decree issued in *PARC*, which permitted school officials unilaterally to remove students in " 'extraordinary circumstances.' " . . . 343 F.Supp., at 301. Given the lack of any similar exception in *Mills*, and the close attention Congress devoted to these "landmark" decisions . . . we can only conclude that the omission was intentional; we are therefore not at liberty to engraft onto the statute an exception Congress chose not to create.

. . . Our conclusion that § 1415(e)(3) means what it says does not leave educators hamstrung. The Department of Education has observed that, "[w]hile the [child's] placement may not be changed [during any complaint proceeding], this does not preclude the agency from using its normal procedures for dealing with children who are endangering themselves or others." Comment following 34 CFR § 300.513 (1987). Such procedures may include the use of study carrels, timeouts, detention, or the restriction of privileges. More drastically, where a student poses an immediate threat to the safety of others, officials may temporarily suspend him or her for up to 10 school days.[8] This authority, which respondent in no way disputes, not only ensures that school administrators can protect the safety of others by promptly removing the most dangerous of students, it also provides a "cooling down" period during which officials can initiate IEP review and seek to persuade the child's parents to agree to an interim placement. And in those cases in which the parents of a truly dangerous child adamantly refuse to permit any change in placement, the 10-day respite gives school officials an opportunity to invoke the aid of the courts under §1415(e)(2), which empowers courts to grant any appropriate relief.

. . . Petitioner contends, however, that the availability of judicial relief is more illusory than real, because a party seeking review under § 1415(e)(2) must exhaust time-consuming administrative remedies, and because under the Court of Appeals' construction of § 1415(e)(3), courts are as bound by the stay-put provision's "automatic injunction," 793 F.2d, at 1486, as are schools. It is true that judicial review is normally not available under § 1415(e)(2) until all administrative proceedings are completed, but as we have previously noted, parents may by-pass the administrative process where exhaustion would be futile or inadequate. . . . While many of the EHA's procedural safeguards protect the rights of parents and children, schools can and do seek redress through the administrative review process, and we have no reason to believe that Congress meant to require schools alone to exhaust in all cases, no matter how exigent the circumstances. The burden in such cases, of course, rests with the school to demonstrate the futility or inadequacy of administrative review, but nothing in § 1415(e)(2) suggests that schools are completely barred from attempting to make such a showing. Nor do we think that § 1415(e)(3) operates to limit the equitable powers of district courts such that they cannot, in appropriate cases, temporarily enjoin a dangerous disabled child from attending school. As the EHA's

---

[8]The Department of Education has adopted the position first espoused in 1980 by its Office of Civil Rights that a suspension of up to 10 school days does not amount to a "change in placement" prohibited by § 1415(c)(3). U.S. Dept. of Education, Office of Special Education Programs, Policy Letter (Feb. 26, 1987). Ed. for Handicapped L. Rep. 211:437 (1987). The EHA nowhere defines the phrase "change in placement," nor does the statute's structure or legislative history provide any guidance as to how the term applies to fixed suspensions. Given this ambiguity, we defer to the construction adopted by the agency charged with monitoring and enforcing the statute. See *INS v. Cardoza-Fonseca*, 480 U.S. 421, 428, 107 S.Ct. 1207, 1211, 94 L.Ed.2d 434 (1987). Moreover, the agency's position comports fully with the purposes of the statute: Congress sought to prevent schools from permanently and unilaterally excluding disabled children by means of indefinite suspensions and expulsions; the power to impose fixed suspensions of short duration does not carry the potential for total exclusion that Congress found so objectionable. Indeed, despite its broad injunction, the District Court in *Mills v. Board of Education of District of Columbia*, 348 F.Supp. 866 (DC 1972), recognized that school officials could suspend disabled children on a short-term, temporary basis. See *id*, at 880. *Cf. Goss v. Lopez*, 419 U.S. 565, 574–576, 95 S.Ct. 729, 736–737, 42 L.Ed.2d 725 (1975) (suspension of 10 school days or more works a sufficient deprivation of property and liberty interests to trigger the protections of the Due Process Clause). Because we believe the agency correctly determined that a suspension in excess of 10 days does constitute a prohibited "change in placement," we conclude that the Court of Appeals erred to the extent it approved suspensions of 20 and 30 days' duration.

legislative history makes clear, one of the evils Congress sought to remedy was the unilateral exclusion of disabled children by *schools*, not courts. . . .

In short, then, we believe that school officials are entitled to seek injunctive relief under § 1415(e)(2) in appropriate cases. In any such action, § 1415(e)(3) effectively creates a presumption in favor of the child's current educational placement which school officials can overcome only by showing that maintaining the child in his or her current placement is substantially likely to result in injury either to himself or herself, or to others. In the present case, we are satisfied that the District Court, in enjoining the state and local defendants from indefinitely suspending respondent or otherwise unilaterally altering his then current placement, properly balanced respondent's interest in receiving a free appropriate public education in accordance with the procedures and requirements of the EHA against the interests of the state and local school officials in maintaining a safe learning environment for all their students. . . . [The opinions of Justice Rehnquist, concurring, and Justice Scalia, dissenting, on the mootness issue are deleted.]

NOTES AND QUESTIONS

1. Honig v. Doe: *Scope of the Decision*

In holding that a dangerous disabled student may not be expelled from school, does the Court fairly read the Act's procedural requirements?

How does the Act's standard differ from the constitutional due process protections that, under *Goss v. Lopez*, chapter 3, *supra*, all students enjoy? Is that difference in treatment appropriate? Does it suggest that the disabled are less responsible individuals? More in need of protection?

After the Court's holding that a disabled student's assignment can be changed only with the permission of the parents or the court, how can a school system maintain order? *See* Comment, "The Legal Limits of School Discipline for Children with Handicaps," 69 *Ore.L.Rev.* 117, 128 (1990). Are in-school punishments—detention and restricted privileges or short-term suspension in the case of immediate danger—permitted? *See Hayes through Hayes v. Unified School District No. 377*, 669 F.Supp. 1519 (D.Kan. 1987). Are such "cooling down" approaches sufficient to meet the threat of a student

like Doe, who choked a fellow student hard enough to leave bruises, then kicked out a school window? May a school impose a series of ten-day suspensions on such a student?

Should it matter that the student's misconduct is directly related to his or her disability—as in *Honig*, where the student was emotionally disturbed? Or is it always possible to establish some tie between misconduct and handicap? *See, e.g., School Board of Prince William County, Va. v. Malone*, 762 F.2d 1210 (4th Cir. 1985) (student cannot be disciplined for minor role in drug dealing because it is a manifestation of his learning disability); *Kaelin v. Grubbs*, 682 F.2d 595 (6th Cir. 1982) (student can be expelled for conduct unrelated to disability but educational services cannot be terminated); *S-1 v. Turlington*, 635 F.3d 342 (5th Cir. 1981) (same); *Magyar v. Tucson Unified School District*, 958 F.Supp. 1423 (D.Ariz. 1997) (same). *See generally* Osborne, "Making the Manifestation Determination When Disciplining a Special Education Student," 119 *Ed.Law.Rep.* 323 (1997).

Virginia included a provision in its state plan that would subject disabled students and students without disabilities to the same disciplinary action for conduct unrelated to a disability. The Department of Education then sought to block the state's receipt of federal funds on the ground that the plan failed to comply with IDEA's requirement to provide alternative schooling following expulsion. That is, even disabled students who were suspended or expelled were entitled to a free, appropriate public education. *Virginia Department of Education v. Riley*, 23 F.3d 80 (4th Cir. 1994). The Fourth Circuit ultimately rejected the Department of Education's interpretation of the IDEA. *Virginia Department of Education v. Riley*, 106 F.3d 559 (4th Cir. 1997). The Seventh Circuit also faced challenges to the Department's position. *Metropolitan School District v. Davila*, 969 F.2d 485 (7th Cir. 1992) (upholding validity of interpretation as a matter of procedure); *Doe v. Oak Park & River Forest High School District Zoo*, 115 F.3d 1273 (7th Cir.), *cert. denied*, 522 U.S. 998, 118 S.Ct. 564, 139 L.Ed.2d 404 (1997) (rejecting the substance of the policy interpretation). To resolve the uncertainty, Congress amended the statute to make clear that the Department of Education's interpretation was correct. 20 U.S.C. §§ 1412(a)(1), 1415(k)(5)(A). For a general discussion of school discipline under the IDEA, *see* Sorensen, "Special Education Discipline in the 1990s," 62 *Ed.Law Rep.* 387 (1990); Sorensen, "Update on Legal Issues in Special Education Discipline," 81 *Ed.Law Rep.* 399 (1993); E.

Hartwig and G. Ruesch, *Discipline in the School* (1st ed. 1994).

2. *Congressional Responses to* Honig v. Doe

Concerned about the schools' ability to protect students, Congress enacted the Gun-Free School Zones Act of 1994, 20 U.S.C. §§ 8921–8926. The Act allows schools to expel for at least one year any student who brings a gun to school. To reconcile this provision with the IDEA, Congress passed the Jeffords Amendment that same year. It authorized schools to place a disabled student who engaged in this misconduct in an interim alternative educational setting for up to forty-five days. Pub. L. No. 103-382, tit. II, § 314(a)(1)(1994). The amendment was a stopgap measure rather than a long-term solution. Rachelson, "Expelling Students Who Claim to Be Disabled: Escaping the Individuals with Disabilities Education Act's 'Stay-Put' Provision," 2 *Mich.L. & Pol'y Rev.* 127 (1997).

In 1997, the IDEA Reauthorization Act once again addressed the question of student discipline. The Act authorizes districts unilaterally to suspend students for up to ten days. Alternatively, the district can place the student in an interim alternative educational setting or another setting. 20 U.S.C. § 1415(k)(1)(A). An interim alternative educational setting is one that places students in an environment other than the one specified in their IEP but gives them access to the general curriculum and educational services included in the IEP. § 1415(K)(3)(B). The school can petition a hearing officer to keep the child in the interim placement for up to forty-five days if the child's conduct appears "substantially likely to result in injury to the child or others." § 1415(K)(2)(AA). A school cannot unilaterally remove a disabled student to an interim alternative educational placement unless the student brings a dangerous weapon to school or knowingly possesses illegal drugs in school. § 1415(K)(1)(A)(ii).

A hearing officer can extend the placement for forty-five days beyond the initial period of punishment. § 1415(K)(7)(B). If a child's parents request a due process hearing, the child is to remain in the interim placement for the period of unilateral suspension or until the hearing officer decides. If the hearing officer has not reached a decision by the time the period of unilateral suspension has expired, the student is returned to the original placement. If school officials conclude that it would be dangerous to the student or others to reinstate the original placement, then the school can seek an expedited hearing.

§ 1415(K)(7). The IDEA Reauthorization Act also authorizes schools to contact law enforcement officials if a disabled student commits a crime. The school must provide the enforcement agency with the child's special education and disciplinary records. § 1415(K)(0).

The 1997 amendments to the IDEA leave some issues unaddressed. First, it is not clear whether schools must provide a free, appropriate public education during ten-day suspensions and whether the ten-day period refers to ten consecutive days or ten days cumulated throughout the school year. The Department of Education's regulations indicate that a child is entitled to a free appropriate public education only after more than ten days of suspension and that a change in placement occurs only after a student is removed for more than ten consecutive days or when the series of removals constitutes a pattern. 34 C.F.R. § 300.519 (1999). For a discussion of these issues, *see* Groeschal, "Discipline and the Disabled Student: The IDEA Reauthorization Responds," 1998 *Wis.L.Rev.* 1085, 1102–1111.

The IDEA Reauthorization Act also does not define the "general curriculum" in conjunction with an interim alternative educational placement. The Department of Education has interpreted the term to mean "the same curriculum as for nondisabled children." 34 C.F.R. 300.347 (1999). Finally, the Act creates new controversy about a key issue that has vexed the courts. That is, can a student who has previously not been classified as disabled seek that classification after committing a disciplinary infraction and gain the IDEA's protections against suspension and expulsion? *See, e.g., Rodiriecus v. Waukegan School District*, 90 F.3d 249 (7th Cir. 1996); *Hacienda LaPuente Unified School District of Los Angeles v. Honig*, 976 F.2d 487 (9th Cir. 1992); *M.P. v. Governing Board of the Grossmont Union High School District*, 858 F.Supp. 1044 (S.D. Cal. 1994). *See generally* McKinney, "Disciplining Children With(out) Disabilities: Schools Behind the Eight Ball," 130 *Ed.Law Rep.* 365 (1999); Rachelson, *supra* (collecting cases and urging measures to deter nondisabled students from abusing the IDEA's protections).

The 1997 amendments say that a child can benefit from the IDEA's protections if the school has "knowledge" of the child's disability. A school is deemed to know if any of the following can be shown: (1) the parents wrote to express their concern that a child might need special education; (2) the parents requested an evaluation; (3) the the teacher expressed concern about the child's performance or behavior to appropriate personnel; or (4) the child's behavior indicated that he might need special education. Even so, the amendments leave considerable room for debate in a particular case about whether a district had "knowledge." Groeschal, *supra*, at 1125–32 (describing ambiguities in the congressional standard and recommending appropriate interpretations of the "knowledge" test); Bryant, "The Death Knell for School Expulsion: The 1997 Amendments to the Individuals with Disabilities Education Act," 47 *Am.U.L.Rev.* 487, 534–49 (1998) (contending that the 1997 amendments, including the provisions related to previously unidentified disabilities, substantially limit a district's ability to discipline students).

3. Other Due Process Issues

a. Budgets. A state, acting for budgetary reasons, closes a day-treatment facility for emotionally disabled students; the students are transferred to a program that is not comparable. They assert that this is a change of placement, requiring a prior hearing. How should a court respond? *See Tilton by Richardson v. Jefferson County Bd. of Educ.*, 705 F.2d 800 (6th Cir. 1983); *Concerned Parents v. New York City Board of Education*, 629 F.2d 751 (2d Cir. 1980); *Brookline School Committee v. Golden*, 628 F.Supp. 113 (D.Mass. 1986).

b. Transcripts. Are disabled students entitled to free written transcripts of their administrative hearings under a provision of the IDEA that assures parties "the right to a written or electronic verbatim record"? *See Caroline T. v. Hudson School District*, 915 F.2d 752 (1st Cir. 1990); *Edward B. v. Paul*, 814 F.2d 52 (1st Cir. 1987); *Militello v. Board of Education*, 803 F.Supp. 974 (D.N.J. 1992).

c. Whose Rights? May a child's mother agree to the child's withdrawal from school, or does the right to an education under the IDEA belong to the child, not the mother? *See Jackson v. Franklin County School Board*, 806 F.2d 623 (5th Cir. 1986); *Woods v. New Jersey Department of Education*, 796 F.Supp. 767 (D.N.J. 1992).

d. Impartial Panels. May officers and employees of local school boards constitute the administrative appeal panel under the IDEA or are they too closely aligned with the state to be impartial? *See Mayson by Mayson v. Teague*, 749 F.2d 652 (11th Cir. 1984); *Kotowicz v. Mississippi State Board of Education*, 630 F.Supp. 925 (S.D.Miss. 1986).

e. Mediation. In 1997, Congress provided expressly for mediation of disputes that arise under the IDEA. § 1415(e). The mediation must be voluntary, cannot be used to deny or delay a parent's right to a due process hearing, and has to be conducted by a qualified and impartial mediator. § 1415(e)(2)(A). Local or state educational agencies may make information available to parents to encourage the use of mediation. § 1415(e)(2)(B). The state must bear the cost of mediation, § 1415(e)(2)(D), and any agreement that results must be put in writing. § 1415(e)(2)(F). The mediation proceedings are confidential and cannot be used as evidence in a later due process hearing. § 1415(e)(2)(G). (These requirements are in the Department of Education's regulations. 34 C.F.R. § 303.419).

A recent study of the benefits of mediation under the IDEA concluded that parties who enter mediation may be "angry and firmly fixed on their positions." Kuriloff and Goldberg, "Is Mediation a Fair Way to Resolve Special Education Disputes? First Empirical Findings," 2 *Harv.Negotiation L.Rev.* 35, 63 (1997). As a result, one-shot mediation may not temper these strongly felt differences. Instead, "[e]arly mediation, required and implemented at the very first signs of a dispute, might be more effective than the current practice of offering mediation only as an alternative to litigation." *Id.* at 66. Do you agree that mediation can help parties to develop a cooperative, rather than an adversarial relationship? Or does conflict arise because of intensely held beliefs and values, differences that cannot be entirely mitigated by an alternative process? For an argument that systematic power differences between parents and school districts are likely to render mediation inherently unworkable, *see* Sternberg, "Mediation as an Alternative Method of Dispute Resolution for the Individuals with Disabilities Education Act: A Just Proposal?" 12 *Ohio St.J.on Disp.Resol.* 739 (1997).

f. Evaluation. The IDEA proscribes racial or cultural bias in evaluation procedures, requires administration of tests in the child's native language, and assures that no single procedure be the basis for placement.

How is the thoroughness of evaluation procedures to be determined? Are cost considerations relevant here? 34 C.F.R. § 300.502(b)(1) provides that "a parent has the right to an independent educational evaluation at public expense if the parent disagrees with an evaluation obtained by the public agency." However, the public agency may initiate a hearing to show that its evaluation is appropriate. If the final decision is that the evaluation is appropriate, "the parent still has the right to an independent educational evaluation, but not at public expense." What does this provision mean? May the district demand a hearing prior to authorizing an independent evaluation? If so, on what basis does the hearing officer determine whether the evaluation is "appropriate"? How can parents effectively challenge that appraisal unless their child has been independently evaluated?

Racial bias in testing procedures typically refers to treatment of racial or ethnic groups, not individuals. See the discussion of this issue in chapter 4, *supra*. Moreover, the expense of data gathering effectively limits such claims to class suits. *See Griggs v. Duke Power Company*, 401 U.S. 424, 91 U.S. 849, 28 L.Ed.2d 158 (1971). Does the Act create any effective mechanism for testing assertions of group bias? *Cf. Georgia State Conf. of Branches of NAACP v. State of Georgia*, 775 F.2d 1403 (11th Cir. 1985) (challenge to assignment of disproportionate number of black children to special education classes, based partly on § 504 of the Rehabilitation Act). *See generally* Glennon, "Race, Education, and the Construction of a Disabled Class," 1995 *Wis.L.Rev.* 1237 (critiquing the IDEA's individualistic focus, which obscures structural inequalities that harm African Americans).

Minimum competency tests pose a different type of evaluation problem. During the 1980s and 1990s, a number of states adopted such tests as a prerequisite for graduation. Are disabled students entitled to additional time to prepare for the test? Does denying them diplomas for failing the test deprive them of a free appropriate public education? *See Brookhart v. Illinois State Board of Educ.*, 697 F.2d 179 (7th Cir. 1983). *See generally* National Research Council, *High Stakes: Testing for Tracking, Promotion, and Graduation* 188–210 (1999); Dannenberg, "A Derivative Right to Education: How Standards-Based Education Reform Redefines the Individuals with Disabilities Education Act," 15 *Yale L. & Pol'y Rev.* 629 (1997) (arguing that children with disabilities can claim a right to receive a standards-based education in a regular classroom). Disabled students in Indiana recently filed suit, alleging that the state's high school exit examination violated the IDEA because of a failure to accommodate their special needs. *Rene v. Reed*, 726 N.E. 2d 808 (Ind.App. 2000).

E. Implementing the Right to an "Appropriate" Education

The changes in educational practice with respect to disabled children worked by federal statute and court decisions are truly massive. Substantial numbers of children previously denied any schooling are to be brought into the system; an appropriate education is to be provided for all young people with disabilities; efforts are to be made to integrate disabled and normal children to the greatest extent possible; procedural protections and safeguards concerning incorrect or biased evaluations hedge a process previously left to professional discretion.

Imagine yourself a lawyer, educator, or policymaker charged with implementation responsibilities in this domain. What problems are you likely to confront?

"The Allure of Legalization Reconsidered: The Case of Special Education"

D. Neal and D. Kirp in D. Kirp and D. Jensen, eds., *School Days, Rule Days: The Legalization and Regulation of Education* (1986).

The evolutionary nature of legalization in special education policy (through PARC, Mills, and EAHCA) precluded any detailed consideration of the appropriateness of a legalized model in the education setting, at least in the policy formulation stage. Now that some of the major abuses that led to the court decisions and ultimately the legislation have been corrected, questions are being raised about the appropriateness of legalization in the education setting.

This reappraisal poses serious issues of policy. Does it make sense to impose on education a policy mold which does not place much faith in the professional discretion of the service provider? The implications of this shift are not lost on educators who may understandably resent the implicit loss of confidence. More generally, does legalization fit the needs and demands of schools—or of children? The imposition of legalization onto ongoing complex organizations, such as schools, also creates particular problems. Studies of the implementation history speak less of the promise of legalization and more of its pathology: compliance with the letter rather than the spirit of the law; preparation of standard form IEPs, resentment that handicapped children have gained a priority that does or may gain them more than their fair share of the education dollar; and defensive strategies, such as the tape recording of IEP meetings, to protect the interests of the school district and teachers.

Yet the story is more complex than this. While implementation studies view the due process procedures as a separate and severable part of the federal legislation, these procedures are an integral part of a legislative scheme which adopts a legalized policy style. The appropriateness of this policy style must be judged with reference to the place of special education in the school system, not by focusing only on the due process hearings ignoring this overall context. To be sure, the benefits to special education flowing from the federal presence—more money, more initiatives, and the like—must be offset by the costs of the due process hearings. Yet the question is whether these gains could have been achieved without the legalized policy style of PL 94-142.

A radical reorientation of priorities in special education was needed in the American context and those who shaped PL 94-142 judged that legalization was the only way to bring it about. That view has much to recommend it. In certain situations shock treatment is called for to convince service deliverers in an ongoing institution that established patterns and values must be changed. Legalization was not the first but the last in a series of approaches taken by educators of the handicapped. Years of campaigning had not convinced the education community of the justice of the claims made on behalf of the handicapped.

Legalization was a plausible approach. While law may not be the only way to reorder priorities or legitimate claims—the availability of a great deal of new money for special education or the operation of a competitive market, for example, might have brought about the same result—law and legal sanctions offered a surer and more direct means of institutionalizing the values promoted by the proponents of change. The embodiment of values in law and the possibility of sanctions offer powerful reference points to those implementing a reform, serving as a rallying point for claims on the system and a powerful mechanism for responding to arguments from competing value positions. The law also provides a frame in which values can be translated into services and new values and services can emerge, for it requires the adjustment of power positions of the various groups with a system. Proponents of the new values gain power in the institution and can introduce still further changes on behalf of their interests.

In short, legalization is neither so cost-free as its proponents suggested nor so defective as subsequent analyses contend. In what follows we explore the effects of legalization by examining the implementation of PL 94-142 and the due process mechanisms in particular.

* * *

The studies of the implementation of the due process aspects of PL 94-142 are the best available indicators of the effects of legalization but they need to be evaluated with caution. For one thing, they report a fairly short experience of the legislation and necessarily do not deal with the possibility that implementation improves over time. For another, they are flawed in a variety of ways. The research typically relies on small, non-random samples of individuals involved in the hearings. While valid as a guide to the experience of those who undertake a hearing, these cases focus on the deficiencies of the process. They do not speak to the appropriateness of the due process procedures generally, or to the level of satisfaction in general of parents of handicapped children with the new law. This research approach shortchanges the systemic effect of the procedural reforms. Moreover, since the studies only report the cost-legislation experience, the ill-effects attributed to the due process procedures may simply be old problems transferred from other forms or made more visible by the existence of the hearings.

* * *

The notification and procedures required to draw up the IEP and hold the meeting are generally in place. After some early hearings where schools failed to comply with notice deadlines, and the like, the mechanics of the IEP procedures seem to be operating.

The qualitative picture is not as clear. Two types of IEP meetings have been identified: a legalistic form in which half the time is devoted to narrow procedural requirements, and a child-oriented form, faithful to the spirit of the law. IEP sessions in which the parents are overwhelmed with professional jargon and other strategies used by schools to minimize the portion of their resources devoted to meetings have been reported in two states. There are also hearsay accounts of IEPs prepared in advance where the parent is pressured to sign on the dotted line, but little evidence to indicate how widespread this practice is.

Reactions of the IEP process are mixed. Parents generally seem satisfied, even enthusiastic, about the development of the IEP, but in the districts characterized as legalistic, one third of the parents describe the meetings as formalistic. Teachers generally regard the IEP as useful but reports differ as to whether there is a high degree of actual use of the IEP as an instructional tool or such use is the exception rather than the rule.

Even this more pessimistic accounting acknowledges that the IEP has the force of law and serves as new found leverage both within the school and the district and provides a basis for a due process hearing.

* * *

The total number of due process hearings held pursuant to the Education for All Handicapped Children Act is not known. Scattered reports suggest wide variations from state to state. In California, 278 hearings were held in 1978–79, the first year of uniform state regulations, and one-third of these were held in two school districts. That number represents just 0.08 percent of California's special education population. A nationwide study of twenty-two sites found half had experienced hearings; seven had only one hearing. Massachusetts had 350 hearings between 1974 and 1979.

As with litigation generally, it is difficult to say whether those figures represent a large percentage of hearings relative to the number of people who had grievances. Data from other comparable contexts—welfare, for instance—suggest that hearings are highly unusual phenomena in relation to the number of people or even the number of complaints in a given area. Right to education hearings are not a typical in this regard.

The impact of hearings, however, cannot be measured simply in terms of the number of hearings held. The prospect of a hearing and estimations of its likely outcome shape the behavior of participants, both in the formulation of their basic relationships and in the way they handle their disputes. The shadow of the law extends well beyond the formally affected parties.

* * *

Middle class parents bring the majority of hearings—the proportion of middle class users was as high as 82 percent in one study—leading one commentator to observe that (d)ue process and appeal procedures are used to advantage by the well-to-do and almost not at all by the poor.

The middle class are usually best able to press their claims. Factors similar to those identified in other contexts seem to be at work in relation to reliance on hearings in the special education context. People in ongoing relationships are unlikely to resort to legal sanctions. Parents who know that their children will have to deal with the local school district personnel for twelve years are understandably reluctant to resort to legal action, with the anxieties that such undertakings generate, in all but the most serious cases. The opportunities for reprisal even after an outcome favorable to the parents, and the difficulties of enforcing such a de-

cision in the face of an intransigent school district pose too great a risk.

Middle and upper class parents do not face such high odds, for they have an exit strategy. Their complaints typically assert the inability of the local school district to provide appropriate education and claim reimbursement for tuition in private schools. If this proves unsuccessful, these parents can pay for the private schooling themselves. Lower class parents do not have this option, when they are involved in hearings at all, it is most often to resist changes proposed by the school, rather than to initiate change. The ongoing nature of their relationship with the school system means that circumspection is probably in the best interests of these parents. This pattern points up an important limitation on the capacity of due process to bring about change in professionally-run bureaucracies. It also raises questions about the wisdom of placing primary reliance on due process to effect policy change.

Adversariness and legalism seem to characterize the conduct of hearings, rather than adopting an informal negotiating format, the due process hearings tend to provide a forum for culmination of long-term bad relations between the school and the parents involved. Involving lawyers aggravates the situation, rendering proceedings more legalistic. Emphasis on compliance with procedural matters such as notices, signatures, and time deadlines offers an easy substitute for harder substantive questions, such as the meaning to be given to the word "appropriate" in the phrase "free, appropriate, public education" in a given case. This legalistic pattern seems particularly evident in the earlier stages of implementation. As schools have learned to comply with the forms of the law opportunities for evasion have diminished, and there is some evidence of reduced formalism as in reliance on pre-hearing hearings and negotiations among the participants.

Parents generally reported both considerable expense and psychological cost in the hearing process. They often felt themselves blamed either for being bad parents or for being troublemakers.

School districts regarded the hearings as expensive, time-consuming and a threat to their professional judgment and skill. The private school placements which parents often sought are enormously costly and also carry an implied criticism of the public school program. Directors of special education programs often regarded parents seeking these placements as "ripping off" the school system, depriving other children of the benefits that would otherwise accrue to the public school program. They complained about inconsistency in interpreting the appropriateness criterion from one hearing to the next and difficulties in accounting to the school board for expensive new services endorsed in hearings. Special education administrators see themselves as caught in a cross-fire between parents and hearings officers who charge them with denying entitlements and school boards who blame them for failing to hold the line on expensive new services.

Some school districts which have experienced a number of hearings have developed an array of defensive strategies. There are reports of districts tape-recording IEP meetings, retaining lawyers, tightening up on procedures and interpreting education and related services narrowly; all ways of sticking to the letter of the law. Other districts negotiated extra services with parents who promised not to pursue a hearing or threatened to demand a hearing in order to coerce parents into accepting an IEP.

While a few participants in due process hearings regarded them as positive experiences, allowing some sort of catharsis and a forum in which an independent party could suggest a solution, most held a negative view. In many instances, hearings have become an additional weapon with which the disputants can bludgeon one another. Parents see themselves as pursuing the best interests of their child while the school district is anxious to preserve limited resources.

* * *

The negative effects of the due process hearings should not be exaggerated. Even though they impose a high economic and psychological cost on all involved, their incidence is concentrated on relatively few school districts. Furthermore, these are districts where parents have a long history of dissatisfaction with the school system. The hearings provide an arena in which old conflicts are played out, and sometimes escalated. In view of this the assertion that the introduction of due process procedures has caused relations between schools and parents to deteriorate must be treated with extreme caution.

* * *

The implementation studies discussed in the previous section assess the appropriateness of legalization in special education without either attending to the wider context of the education system or proposing plausible alternative means of rectifying the indisputable abuses of the past. To focus exclusively on the due process procedures in isolation and to identify the undesirable effects associated with them misses the broader institutional changes associated with the legislation, of which the due process procedures form an integral component.

Passage of PL 94-142 has had an enormous effect on special education. More than 230,000 children were identified and provided with education within the first two years after passage of the law and the rate of increase is steady.

There has been an enormous increase in special education expenditure which has produced not only cash benefits, but also augmented the prestige and attractiveness of special education as a field of endeavor. The formal procedures mandated by the Education for All Handicapped Children Act are in place and many new programs are being developed in school districts.

Much of this change might have been achieved without reliance on such a legalized policy style. Implicit in the criticisms of due process procedures is the suggestion that the policy-makers were wrong in believing that the legalized model was essential to achieve their purposes, and that legalization is inappropriate in the context of education. Even if we remain skeptical about the causal links between the due process hearings and the effect attributed to them by the studies canvassed in the previous section, there is reason enough to raise concerns about the appropriateness of the due process procedures in the school setting. . . .

* * *

Leaving substantive determinations to due process hearings had both the virtues and the vices of legalization. It contemplates principled arguments about the amount and type of services due to a given child. This may be preferable to such alternatives as centralized bureaucratic decision-making, with its attendant problems of distance and rigid categorizations or professional judgments which are often paternalistic and give undue weight to the needs of the professionals at the expense of the handicapped student. The legalized model also creates problems. Handicapped children are accorded formal rights not made available to other children in the education system. There is for instance, a tendency for rights to know no dollar limitations. Yet the reality that school administrators face is that they have limited budgets and must make difficult decisions about the just distribution of those funds among competing sectors of the school system.

Ambiguity surrounding the word "appropriate" also produces tension between schools and parents. School officials complain about parents looting the public treasury to obtain private school placements and express frustration that they feel unable to put these sorts of arguments to the hearings officers. This limitation may be attributable to the tendency of due process hearings to individualize problems but it is not a necessary interpretation of the legislation. Acting on this perception, school administrators are resorting to indirect means of protecting funds, adopting defensive or delaying tactics, and attempting to translate arguments based on the needs of the school system in general into arguments about a particular child. For their part, parents' expectations may have been raised to unrealistic levels by the law. Their concern is likely to reside exclusively with their child, in their eyes the word "appropriate" may have come to mean whatever is appropriate regardless of the cost. This would explain parental frustration with school districts, and their perception concerning the lack of candor in the school officials with whom they deal.

While this dispute over the relevance of costs is partly attributable to the fact that entitlements of handicapped children, but not those of nonhandicapped children, are clearly spelled out, it is also partly a function of the adjudicative process itself. The hearing mechanism is, in its ideal form, a case-by-case process: it formally assumes that two parties are disputing in a contextual vacuum. That fiction alone is enough to give rise to considerable frustrations. Moreover, different hearing officers will render different decisions on similar cases. There is no consistent interpretation of "appropriate" and there does not appear to be much communication among hearing officers about their decisions. While this may change as precedents develop, several factors—the variegated nature of appropriateness, the fact that hearings officers lack either the legal or educational expertise to render consistent judgments, and the variability of schools and handicapping conditions—make consistency unlikely. . . .

The broadest concerns relate to the effects of legalization of special education on the school as a bureaucratic/professional organization. Schools face serious problems of coordination, confronting acutely complex questions of distributive justice among different elements of their program, of management vis-a-vis their own professional staff, and of accountability to the community, especially to the parents of currently enrolled students. The meaning of a good education is controversial, and limited in any case by funding realities. Potential lines of conflict run in every direction: between school board and teachers, teacher and principal, teacher and student, and teacher and parents.

The effect of legalization on special education entails a radical reorientation of this complex network. It empowers what was previously an out group: the handicapped must now be included in policy decisions. No one in the school system can maintain that handicapped children should be excluded from school, at least not publicly. The force of the state and the moral authority of the law is available to the handicapped.

Legalization has also improved the status of the special education professional. In an era of shrinking education budgets, special education has received an infusion of new money. It has become an attractive area for new teachers and a way for existing teachers to earn additional salary and avoid retrenchment. Special education teachers are assuming places in school administrations which, hitherto, they had not held, and this too will affect the organizational goals of schools and strengthen the perceived legitimacy of the claims of the handicapped.

The pathologies of legalization must also be owned. There is some evidence that the values promoted by the legislation are provoking resistance from the education community. Despite increased funding there are too few resources to treat all handicapped children individually. By distinguishing the handicapped children from the regular school network and granting them rights not enjoyed by other school children, the law potentially distorts the allocation of resources. This potential is aggravated by the legal model which treats the parties to a dispute as discrete from the system in which they are located.

Finally, legalization betrays a mistrust of schools. It may inhibit the discretion of professionals whose judgment should be exercised creatively on behalf of the child. In the past that distrust may have been deserved. But legalization can be a blunt instrument, undermining healthy as well as malevolent exercise of discretion. Special education teachers now find themselves as "defendants" in due process hearings. This represents a marked change from their self-perception, prior to passage of PL 94-142, as lone advocates for the handicapped child. From the viewpoint of the handicapped it would be disastrous to alienate this group, particularly in view of their role as primary service providers and their new status in the school hierarchy. Encouraging mediation and negotiation, rather than due process hearings, should diminish this danger. . . . In this way, parents and teachers could be reunited in the task of providing the best education, within budget constraints, for handicapped children.

Finally, the utility of the due process hearing as a compliance device is dubious. Individualization, lack of coordination and the settlement of strategic cases to avoid hearings suggest systemic problems which may be missed by the individualized nature of the hearings. Hearings alone are ill-suited for the task of precipitating systemic review and reform. Agency-wide review, litigation, and political change remain key parts of appraising and modifying any program.

Only in the context of those wider considerations may the appropriateness of legalization be assessed. Legalization jolted the education system into according handicapped children a fair share of the education pie. As the system comes to accept the presence of handicapped children and recognizes the legitimacy of their claims and, as special education teachers acquire new status in school hierarchies, there are sound reasons to diminish reliance on some aspects of the legalized structure of special education. . . .

* * *

NOTES AND QUESTIONS

1. Legalization as a Policy Strategy

a. Appraising the Evidence. At about the time Neal and Kirp expressed their doubts about the legalization of special education, a survey of five diverse school districts found considerable variation in implementation of the law, depending on the capacity of the district (its wealth and willingness to respond) and the participation of parents. Singer and Butler, "The Education for All Handicapped Children Act: Schools as Agents of Social Reform," 57 *Harv.Educ.Rev.* 125 (1987). Concerns about variable implementation of the IDEA persist. When the law was amended in 1997, Congress commissioned research to assess the efficacy of state and local efforts to apply the law with a particular focus on student performance, curricular access, behavioral supports, parental inclusion, and assistance during key transitions from home to school and from school to adult life. U.S. Department of Education, *Twenty-second Annual Report to Congress on the Implementation of the Individuals with Disabilities Education Act* (1998) (http://www.ed.gov/offices/OSERS/OSEP/OSEP2000An/Rept.html). The results of these studies will begin to be released in fall 2001. Office of Special Education, U.S. Department of Education, *The Study of State and Local Implementation and Impact of the Individuals with Disabilities Education Act* (http://www.abt.sliidea.org/study.htm).

In January 2000, the National Council on Disability, an independent federal agency, released a report that concluded that all states fail to comply with at least some of the IDEA's provisions. The long-term study cited continuing segregation and inadequate services as key barriers to educational participation for the disabled. The report urged the Department of Education and the Department of Justice to collaborate on national compliance standards to ensure vigorous enforcement of the IDEA's requirements. National Council on Disability, *Back to School on Civil Rights* (2000) (http://www.ncd.gov/newsroom/publication/backtoschool1.html). For a general discussion of implementation concerns, *see* P. First and J. Curcio, *Implementing the Disabilities Acts: Implications for Educators* (1993).

b. Rights as Trumps. The IDEA provides benefits to the disabled that are not afforded to other groups: guarantees of an appropriate education, procedural safeguards, and protection against sanctions. Is it appropriate to treat the claim of the disabled to an education as a civil right?

Consider the position of the Heritage Foundation, which criticizes the federal legislation for resting "on the questionable assumption that the responsibility for disabled individuals is primarily society's as a civil right," and argues that "public schools should not be required to educate those children who cannot, without damaging the main purposes of public education, function in a normal classroom setting." Heritage Foundation, "The Crisis: Washington Shares the Blame," *The Heritage Foundation Backgrounder* 1, 12 (1984).

What are the consequences of assigning rights to some but not all children—in terms of equity, political clout, and formal claims on resources? *Compare* Kirp, "Professionalization as a Policy Choice: British Special Education in Comparative Perspective," 44 *World Politics* 137 (1982), reprinted in J. Chambers and W. Hartman, eds., *Special Education Policies: Their History, Implementation and Finance* (1983).

c. Changing the Law. Imagine that you are a staffer on the House Education Subcommittee, which once again is considering the policy approach taken by IDEA. Does the Neal and Kirp analysis suggest any changes in its structure that would make sense? For instance, would it be possible—and desirable—to rely less on formal procedures and more on professional judgment? *See generally* Engel, "Law, Culture, and Children with Disabilities: Educational Rights and the Construction of Difference," 1991

Duke L.J. 166; Pittenger and Kuriloff, "Educating the Handicapped: Reforming a Radical Law," 66 *Public Interest* 72 (Winter 1982); Benveniste, "Implementation and Intervention Strategies: The Case of PL 94-142," in D. Kirp and D. Jensen, eds., *School Days, Rule Days: The Legalization and Regulation of Education* 146 (1986).

IV. POVERTY AND HOMELESSNESS

A. The Concept of Poverty

In contrast to ethnicity, national origin, gender, and disability, poverty has not become the basis for identity politics. Perhaps this is because the poor lack the resources to organize effectively and lobby for reform. *See generally* F. Piven and R. Cloward, *Poor People's Movements: Why They Succeed, How They Fail* (1977). Alternatively, poverty may be viewed as a dysfunctional and undesirable condition, one that can be changed through personal effort or structural reform. *See* W. Wilson, *The Truly Disadvantaged: The Inner City, the Underclass, and Public Policy* 6–19 (paperback ed. 1987) (describing liberal and conservative perspectives on the culture of poverty). Indeed, during the 1960s, the Office of Economic Opportunity declared "War on Poverty" as part of the federal government's efforts to build the Great Society. J. Dryfoos, *Full-Service Schools: A Revolution in Health and Social Services for Children, Youth, and Families* 35 (1994).

Although the schools traditionally have been viewed as key avenues of upward mobility for the disadvantaged, relatively few reforms have been targeted directly at the needs of low-income children. Instead, benefits to poor children have often been merely incidental consequences of other reform movements, whether to promote racial equality, access for the disabled, or fairness in the financing of schools. Unfortunately, relegating poverty to secondary importance can obscure pressing needs of the economically disadvantaged.

"The Limited Visions of Race Relations and the War on Poverty"

* * *

In the mid-1960s a series of insightful articles were written by black and white intellectuals that raised questions about the direction and goals of the black protest movement. Basically, the authors of these articles made it clear that from 1955 to 1965 the chief objectives of the civil rights movement were to integrate public accommodations and to eliminate black disfranchisement. These were matters of constitutional rights and basic human dignity, matters that affected blacks and other minorities exclusively and therefore could be defined and addressed simply as problems of civil rights. However, these authors noted that despite the spectacular victories in the area of civil rights, by the latter half of the 1960s a more complex and fundamental set of problems had yet to be attacked—problems of jobs, education, and housing that affected not only blacks but other minorities and whites as well.

A consistent theme running throughout these articles is that in the period from 1955 to 1963, all blacks, regardless of their station in life, were concerned about the banning of discrimination in public accommodations and in voting. As Bayard Rustin observed, "Ralph Bunche was as likely to be refused service in a restaurant or a hotel as any illiterate sharecropper. This common bond prevented the latent class differences and resentments from being openly expressed." However, it did not take long to realize that the group that had profited the most from the civil rights legislation up to 1965 was middle-class blacks—blacks who had competitive resources such as steady incomes, education, and special talents. As Kenneth Clark argued in 1967, "The masses of Negroes are now starkly aware of the fact that recent civil rights victories benefited a very small percentage of middle-class Negroes while their predicament remained the same or worsened."

What these observers were telling us in the mid-1960s is that a close examination of ghetto black discontent, most dramatically seen in the riots of that period, reveals issues that transcend the creation and implementation of civil rights laws. "To the segregation by race," Bayard Rustin observed, "was now added segregation by class, and all the problems created by segregation and poverty—inadequate schooling, substandard and overcrowded housing, lack of access to jobs and job training, narcotics and crime—were greatly aggravated." In short, for ghetto blacks the problems move beyond the issue of civil rights. The late Martin Luther King, Jr., recognized this point in 1968 when shortly before his death he asked, "What good is it to be allowed to eat in a restaurant if you can't afford a hamburger?" It would not be unfair to suggest that he was probably influenced by the thoughts of Bayard Rustin, who, four years earlier in his now-classic article "From Protest to Politics," phrased the matter in much the same way: "What is the value of winning access to public accommodations for those who lack money to use them?"

Thus, these perceptive civil rights advocates recognized in the 1960s that removing artificial racial barriers would not enable poor blacks to compete equally with other groups in society for valued resources because of an accumulation of disadvantages flowing from previous periods of prejudice and discrimination, disadvantages that have been passed on from generation to generation. Basic structural changes in our modern industrial economy have compounded the problems of poor blacks because education and training have become more important for entry into the more desirable and higher-paying jobs and because increased reliance on labor-saving devices has contributed to a surplus of untrained black workers. In short, once the movement faced these more fundamental issues, argued Rustin in 1965, "it was compelled to expand its vision beyond race relations to economic relations, including the role of education in society."

The Problem of the Race Relations Vision

During the same period in which problems of structural inequality were being raised, scholars such as Kenneth Clark, Lee Rainwater, and Elliot Liebow were also raising important issues about the experiences of inequality. . . . [W]hat was both unique and important about these studies in the 1960s was that discussions of the experiences of inequality were inextricably tied to discussions of the structure of inequality. Thus, in reading these works one received a clear understanding of how the economic and social situations into which so many poor blacks are born produce modes of adaptation and create subcultural patterns that take the form of a "self-perpetuating pathology." In other words, and in sharp contrast to approaches that simply "blame the victim" or that use a "culture-of-poverty" thesis to explain group disadvantages, the works of scholars such as Clark, Rainwater, and Liebow not only presented a sensitive portrayal of the destructive features of ghetto life, they also provided a comprehensive analysis of the deleterious structural conditions that produce these features.

However, arguments stressing economic relations in determining the structure of inequality and in significantly influencing the experiences of inequality

began to compete with a new definition, description, and explanation of the black condition. This new approach, proclaimed as the "black perspective," revealed an ideological shift from interracialism, to racial solidarity. It first gained currency among militant black spokespersons in the late 1960s and became a theme in the writings of young black academics and intellectuals by the early 1970s. . . . Although the "black perspective" represented a variety of views and arguments on issues of race, the trumpeting of racial pride and self-affirmation was common to all the writings and speeches on the subject. Thus interracial cooperation and integration were being challenged by the ideology of racial solidarity, and the rhetoric of black militancy, symbolized by the cry of Black Power, gradually moved from expressions of selective to generalized hostility toward whites.

* * *

Consistent with the dominant focus on racial solidarity in the late sixties was an emphasis on we versus they and black versus white. Since the accent was on race, little attention was paid to the social-economic differences within the black community and the implications they had for different public policy options, and little discussion was devoted to problems with the economy and the need for economic reform. Thus, the promising move in the early and mid-1960s to pursue programs of economic reform by defining the problems of American economic organization and outlining their effect on the minority community was offset by slogans calling for "reparations," or "black control of institutions serving the black community." This is why Orlando Patterson was led to proclaim in a later analysis that black ethnicity had become "a form of mystification, diverting attention from the correct kinds of solutions to the terrible economic conditions of the group," thereby making it difficult for blacks to see the inextricable connection between their own fate and the structure of the modern American economy.

* * *

However, because the government not only adopted and resolutely implemented antidiscrimination legislation to enhance minority individual rights but also mandated and purposefully enforced affirmation and related programs to promote minority group rights, it was clear that by 1980 many thoughtful American citizens, including civil rights supporters, were puzzled by recent developments in the black community. Despite the passage of antidiscrimination legislation and the creation of affirmative action programs, they sensed that conditions were getting worse, not better, for a significant segment of black Americans. This perception had emerged because of the constant flow of pessimistic reports concerning the sharp rise in black unemployment, the substantial decline of blacks in the labor force, the steady drop in the black-white family income ratio, the consistent increase in the percentage of blacks on the welfare rolls, the remarkable growth of single-parent households, and the persistent problems of black crime and black victims of crime. The perception was reinforced by the almost uniform cry among black leaders that conditions were deteriorating and white Americans had abandoned the cause of blacks as well. In the face of these developments, there were noticeable signs (even before Ronald Reagan was elected president and well before his administration adopted a conspicuously laissez-faire attitude toward civil rights) that demoralization had set in among many blacks who had come to believe that "nothing really works" and among many whites who were otherwise committed to social reform.

These recent developments in the black community will remain puzzling, and the feeling that "nothing really works" will likely become more widespread if advocates of minority rights fail in significant numbers to understand that many contemporary problems of race cannot be satisfactorily addressed . . . solely by race-specific programs to eliminate racial discrimination and eradicate racial prejudices.

A Parallel Development: The Problem of the War on Poverty Vision

The War on Poverty emerged paradoxically during an era of general economic prosperity and economic growth. In the early 1960s a budget surplus existed, and economists, optimistic about continued economic growth, predicted that this surplus would continue to rise throughout the latter half of the decade. As Daniel Patrick Moynihan argued, federal revenues were growing so rapidly that many economists (not foreseeing the Vietnam War buildup) were concerned that if new expenditures could not be generated to reduce the growing tax surplus, it would ultimately slow economic growth. Accordingly, despite high levels of unemployment in the inner city and in other low-income areas, it was not difficult for the key advisers in the Kennedy and Johnson administrations to see minority poverty as a problem unrelated to the national economy. As Weir, Orloff, and Skocpol have argued, when the United States started to face the problems associated with the concentration of minorities in large urban ghettos, members of the Council of Economic Advisers discussed these problems not within the realm of central economic concerns but as "marginal issues of 'poverty' to be addressed by much less academically prestigious groups of labor economists and sociologists."[13]

Accordingly, increasing black joblessness was viewed as a problem of poverty and discrimination, not of American economic organization, and therefore could be addressed by antipoverty measures (such as compensatory job training, compensatory schooling, income redistribution) and antidiscrimination legislation. In the succinct words of Lawrence Mead, "the main impetus of Great Society policy, therefore, was to give the disadvantaged the income and skills they needed to function in the free market, not change the economic rules in their favor."[14]

The separation of antipoverty measures from national economic policy was respected by the newly created and expanding network of "poverty researchers" who, throughout the 1960s and 1970s, tended to ignore the effects of fundamental economic processes on the work histories of the poor while paying considerable attention to the question of individual work incentives and the association between the work efforts of the poor and income maintenance programs. As Walter Korpi has pointed out, in his perceptive critique of approaches to the study of poverty in this country from a European perspective, "efforts to explain poverty and inequality in the United States . . . appear primarily to have been sought in terms of the characteristics of the poor." Whereas American poverty analysts have produced volumes of research on the work motivation of the poor, problems of human capital (whereby poverty is

---

[13]Margaret Weir, Ann S. Orloff, and Theda Skocpol, "The Future of Social Policy in the United States," in *The Politics of Social Policy in the United States*, ed. Margaret Weir, Ann S. Orloff, and Theda Skocpol (Princeton, N.J.: Princeton University Press, forthcoming [1988]). For a good discussion of the Council of Economic Advisers approach to the problem of poverty, see Lawrence M. Mead, *Beyond Entitlement: The Social Obligations of Citizenship* (New York: Free Press, 1986), chap. 3.

[14][L.] Mead, *Beyond Entitlement* [:*The Social Obligations of Citizenship* (New York: Free Press, 1986)], p. 35.

seen as a reflection of insufficient education and occupational skills), and the effects of income maintenance programs on the labor supply, they have
largely neglected the impact of the extremely high
levels of postwar unemployment on the poor. "In
Europe, where unemployment has been considerably lower," states Korpi, "the concerns of politicians
as well as researchers have been keyed much more
strongly to the question of unemployment. It is an intellectual paradox that living in a society that has
been a sea of unemployment, American poverty researchers have concentrated their research interests
on the work motivation of the poor."[16]

Since changes in the rate of poverty in the United
States are very closely related to changes in overall
economic performance, this research orientation
presents a problem for those seeking a comprehensive
explanation of minority poverty. Recent research by
the economists Rebecca Blank and Alan Blinder of
Princeton reveals that a downturn in the economy,
measured in this case by a 1 percent increase in the
baselevel unemployment (unemployment rate for
white males), results in an additional increase in unemployment among black males that is 2 percent to
2.5 percent greater than an additional increase in unemployment among white males.[17] Low-income
groups, particularly black males, are especially hard
hit when unemployment rises and real wages decline.

It was only a short step to move from an analysis
that segregates the economic woes of underem-
ployed or unemployed minorities in the category of
poverty-related programs to one that associates the
crystallization of a ghetto underclass or the explosion
of minority female-headed households not with the
"more inclusive economic or institutional insuffi-
ciencies in American life" but with ghetto-specific
values or family background. Thus, . . . research on
the relationship between the growth of income transfers and in-kind benefits and the increase of black female-headed families has dwarfed research on the
relationship between joblessness and black female-
headed families in recent years.

In the final analysis, the policy agenda set by the
architects of the Great Society, that is, the labor
economists and sociologists who fashioned the War
on Poverty in the 1960s, established the vision for the

subsequent research and analysis of minority
poverty. Although this vision attributed the behavioral problems of the poor to adverse social conditions, the emphasis was mainly on the environments
of the poor, "the disarray at the bottom of society"
where ignorance is widespread, crime is rampant,
positive role models are lacking, and apathy is en-
demic. Since this vision did not consider poverty as
a problem of American economic organization, efforts to alter the characteristics of individuals
through employment and training programs were
seen as the most efficacious way to fight poverty. "After 1960," states Lawrence Mead,

> poverty and disadvantaged seemed rooted mostly in the
> limited skills of the poor themselves, yet government
> could do little to raise skills simply with benefits. Polit-
> ically, that left unpalatable alternatives. Either equality
> must be achieved by a leveling of income or status with-
> out regard to the capacities of the poor, the prescription
> of the far left, or the poor themselves must be seen as
> malingerers or congenitally incompetent. Sociological
> analysis offered a way out. It defined a set of less obvi-
> ous social barriers permitting further reformism. By
> providing further benefits and services, it was argued
> government could push back the barriers of "disadvan-
> tage" without either embracing revolutionary change
> or blaming the poor for their condition.[pp. 55–56]

However, just as the rate of poverty is in large measure
determined by the state of the economy, particularly
the levels of wages and unemployment, so too does
the effectiveness of training, education, and employment programs depend on a favorable economic climate. If gainful employment is problematic because
of a stagnant economy, as was frequently the case
throughout the 1970s, participants in these programs
understandably lose interest. Indeed, it would be surprising if program participants took training seriously
when there is little or no chance for placement.

Given the most comprehensive civil rights legislation and the most comprehensive antipoverty
program in the nation's history, it becomes difficult
for liberals (who have adopted either the race relations vision in addressing the problems of the minority poor or the vision of the War on Poverty) to
explain the sharp increase in inner-city poverty,
joblessness, female-headed families, and welfare

---

[16]W. Korpi, "Approaches to the Study of Poverty in the United States: Critical Notes from a European Perspective," in Poverty and Public Policy: An Evaluation of Social Research, ed. V. T. Covello (Boston: G. K. Hall, 1980), pp. 305, 306.

[17]Rebecca M. Blank and Alan A. Blinder, "Macroeconomics, Income Distribution, and Poverty," in Fighting Poverty: What Works and What Doesn't, ed.
Sheldon Danziger and Daniel H. Weinberg (Cambridge, Mass.: Harvard University Press, 1986).

dependency since 1970 without reference to individual or group deficiencies. By the end of the 1970s these liberals were on the defensive, and their position made it easy for the more conservative policy analysts, such as Charles Murray, to argue that liberal programs have been ineffective and misdirected and that emphasis should now be placed on forcing value and behavior changes, particularly among ghetto residents.

Just as the architects of the War on Poverty failed to relate the problems of the poor to the broader processes of American economic organization, so too have the advocates for minority rights failed in significant numbers to understand that many contemporary problems of race, especially those that engulfed the minority poor, emanate from the broader problems of societal organization and therefore cannot be satisfactorily addressed by race-specific programs to eliminate racial discrimination and eradicate racial prejudices. What is presently lacking is a comprehensive and integrated framework—in other words, a holistic approach—that shows how contemporary racial problems in America, or issues perceived to be racial problems, are often part of a more general or complex set of problems whose origin and/or development may have little or no direct or indirect connection with race.

* * *

NOTES AND QUESTIONS

1. *Individual and Structural Accounts of Poverty*

Wilson argues that conceptualizing poverty as a product of individual and family traits or cultural deficiencies masks the structural, economic conditions that systematically generate an underclass. Should inadequate schools be characterized as one structural factor in the perpetuation of poverty? Or are inner-city schools less influential than parents, peers, or urban blight?

2. *Structural Reform and the Schools*

How should Wilson's observations be used in shaping educational reform? Do programs need to target schoolwide policies and practices rather than the problems of particular students? Do schoolwide reforms dilute the impact on the neediest students, or do these reforms indirectly benefit them by enhancing their peers' performance and influence?

B. Title I: Equity and the "Educationally Disadvantaged"

The educationally disadvantaged—students primarily from poor families who perform far below grade level in school—were the first major beneficiaries of the new federal largess in education. The benefits program for this group was developed as an integral part of President Lyndon Johnson's War on Poverty. By looking at Title I of the Elementary and Secondary Education Act, first enacted in 1965, one can trace the course of federal involvement through its several stages: policy inception, program adoption, early implementation failures, and subsequent program modifications.

From the outset, this program exhibited the difficulties as well as the potential of federal involvement in education. Its very purpose was uncertain: Was the Act designed primarily to provide special educational services for the educationally disadvantaged, or was it to benefit school systems, using the number of educationally deprived merely as the basis for funding? The confusion over means led to problems of implementation. These problems in turn spawned a variety of compliance devices—maximizing local discretion, compliance through litigation, administrative accountability, encouraging the politicization of the program through parental involvement—designed to secure one or another objective.

The size and scope of the program, as well as its detailed requirements, made it a prime target for the Reagan Administration, which hoped to eliminate the program entirely, giving local districts authority to spend all federal education funds as they wished. Though that effort was resisted by Congress, the legislation was amended to reduce mandates to the states out of deference to the "new federalism." In 1994, the law was amended again, this time to emphasize the need for low-income students to meet the same high educational standards as other students. Pub.L.No. 103-382, 108 Stat. 3519 (codified at 20 U.S.C. § 6301-6514); Dougherty, "Getting Beyond Policy: School Reform in Practice," 6 *Va.J.Soc.Pol'y & L.* 127 (1998).

"Improving America's Schools for Children in Greatest Need"

T. Payzant and J. Levin in J. Jennings ed., *National Issues in Education: Elementary and Secondary Education Act* 55–72 (1995).

Three decades after its creation by the historic Elementary and Secondary Education Act of 1965, the

Title I program remains the centerpiece of the federal commitment to elementary and secondary education. In 1965, Title I symbolized a new era of federal involvement in education, with federal assistance focusing on students who needed it most: poor and disadvantaged children. In 1994, the reauthorization of Chapter 1 in the Improving America's Schools Act of 1994 (IASA) signals an important new era in the history of federal education programs.

The reauthorization of Chapter 1 (returning to its original name, Title I) reaffirms the values that have undergirded Title I since its inception: a commitment to equity and to meeting the educational needs of disadvantaged children. However, it adopts dramatically different strategies for addressing those needs.

The new Title I calls for high standards for all children and comprehensive schoolwide reform strategies to enable all children to achieve these standards. It rejects the program's decades-long reliance on isolated, add-on services, as well as the lower expectations for the children it serves. Instead, the new Title I embraces a fundamentally different approach—one that seeks every opportunity to focus Title I dollars on leveraging overall improvement of teaching and learning in schools with the highest levels of poverty.

* * *

3. *Chapter 1 Evaluation Under the Hawkins-Stafford Amendments of 1988.* The reauthorization of the former Chapter 1 law benefited . . . from the findings of several rigorous evaluations on the effectiveness of the Chapter 1 program. These Chapter 1 evaluations, many of them spearheaded by the U.S. Department of Education, demonstrated that despite some real successes throughout the years, the Chapter 1 program was still far from realizing its full potential.

In the 1970s and most of the 1980s, Chapter 1 helped to reduce inequities in public education and to support a national effort to improve the basic skills of all children. During this period, for example, the gap in mathematics achievement between students in disadvantaged urban communities and more advantaged students narrowed substantially, according to the National Assessment of Educational Progress (NAEP).

In more recent years, progress has stalled. Performance data from *Prospects*, a longitudinal assessment of Chapter 1 students' progress, suggested that the Chapter 1 program was no longer closing the gap between disadvantaged children and others. Over a one-year period, for example, Chapter 1 participants did not improve their relative standing in reading or math in the fourth grade or in math in the eighth

grade; only eighth-grade reading participants showed improvement relative to their peers. Chapter 1 participants did no better on norm-referenced or criterion-referenced tests than nonparticipants with similar background and prior achievement.

However, these data merely confirmed the lessons derived from our collective experience. Despite the best efforts of policy makers, administrators, and school staff, Chapter 1 programs seldom have triggered the broad changes that are needed in schools to enable all students to meet the high standards demanded in these challenging times. Nor have they met the overall purpose of the 1988 Chapter 1 law, "to improve the educational opportunities of educationally deprived children by helping such children succeed in the regular program of the LEA [local educational agency], attain grade-level proficiency, and improve achievement in basic and more advanced skills."

4. *The Operation of the Former Chapter 1 Program.* Of course, a summary of these findings can mask the important role that Chapter 1 has played in the education of many disadvantaged children. Perhaps most critically, the former Chapter 1 helped to focus the nation's attention on the education needs of disadvantaged children. Until the late 1980s, it also significantly helped to close the gap in basic skills achievement between disadvantaged students and their more advantaged peers. Moreover, Chapter 1 has been at the forefront of efforts to involve parents in all aspects of their children's education and has laid the groundwork for broader parent involvement in education generally.

Many Chapter 1 programs, and those who have worked tirelessly in them, also have made important differences in the education and lives of individual students through such strategies as innovative extended-time opportunities, effective individualized attention, increased professional development opportunities for teachers, and effective coordination of Chapter 1 services with other health and social services.

However, under the former Chapter 1 law, these examples remained isolated success stories, rather than the norm. Key features of the program sometimes worked against success, thereby preventing effective practices from going to scale.

School districts have played the largest role in designing and operating the former Chapter 1 program. The 1988 Chapter 1 law required districts to use their Chapter 1 resources "to meet the special needs of . . . educationally deprived children at the pre-school, elementary and secondary levels." According to the law, this included conducting an "assessment of educational needs" to determine both the grades and children to receive Chapter 1 services and the design of those services to address those children's needs.

However, too often the Chapter 1 program decisions have not reflected the specific needs of either individual schools or students. Typically, districts have decided to conduct a Chapter 1 program in the same grades and subject areas in every school served by Chapter 1. Then they have assigned additional Chapter 1 staff to each school based on its total number of children who score below an established cut-off point on a districtwide test. For example, every 40 Chapter 1 children below this cut-off point may generate one additional Title I teacher and 1.5 Title I teacher aides.

The result has been a district-directed "one-size-fits-all" Chapter 1 program. That "one-size" in 70% of Chapter 1 schools has been the Chapter 1 "pull-out" program. These pull-out programs, by and large, have taken children identified for Chapter 1 out of their regular classrooms during prime class time for instruction in a separate location. Chapter 1 staff have provided this instruction, often through "drill and practice" on basic reading and math skills. Although pull-out programs have replaced a student's regular class period, research shows that, on average, they have added only 10 minutes of extra instruction a day. Therefore, participation in pull-out programs has come with a high price tag for children—missing the regular instructional program. Moreover, even the best Chapter 1 pull-out programs have had little effect on the regular program of instruction, where the children served by Chapter 1 still spend most of their school day.

To address this latter problem, the 1988 reauthorization of Chapter 1 expanded the opportunities for schools to develop schoolwide projects—permitting any school with more than 75% poverty to use Chapter 1 funds to serve all children in a school and "to upgrade the entire educational program," rather than to provide "add-on" services for identified children. But even where schoolwide projects have reduced class size, they rarely have stimulated the additional instructional reforms needed to enable all students to improve achievement.

The jobs of teachers, administrators, and parents also have been complicated by the absence of an overall framework and clear goals to guide their efforts. Rather, the program has been driven by federally mandated, norm-referenced tests and the watered-down goal of minimum achievement gains on these tests. This has reinforced Chapter 1's low expectations and heavy reliance on drill and practice.

Despite codifying these low expectations, the program improvement provisions of the former Chapter 1 law did significantly advance Chapter 1 accountability by beginning to focus on achievement gains, rather than just on compliance with prescribed procedures. For the first time, the law outlined a consequence for schools failing to make progress: identification for "program improvement." Nonetheless, schools did not receive the professional development and support they needed to significantly improve their programs.

Although Chapter 1 is the largest federal education program (funded at $6.7 billion in the 1994–95 school year), it is still only one of many federal, state, and local programs serving the nation's students. In fact, the typical high-poverty urban elementary school may have as many as 15 or 20 unconnected programs, each with its own staff, plan, evaluation, and reporting requirements. These programs, taken together, are extraordinarily difficult to administer and absorb considerable energy from all involved. They also inhibit a sense of ownership and responsibility among school staff for the education of each child. It is all too common to hear, "Chapter 1 children are not my responsibility; they are the responsibility of the Chapter 1 teacher." "Limited-English-proficient children? They belong in that other classroom, not mine."

These conclusions do not negate Chapter 1's successes. Nor are they meant to cast any blame on those who have been working hard to achieve what they thought would be in the best interest of children. But the implications are clear: the former Chapter 1 program cannot adequately address the needs of children in the changing context of the 1990s.

Converting Title I into an Important Tool to Enable All Children to Achieve High Standards

Early in the reauthorization, there was widespread agreement about the need for a significant overhaul of the former Chapter 1 law and the importance of converting the program into a more effective tool for those working in Title I schools to help students reach high standards. There also was remarkable consensus on the major new strategies that the new Title I should embrace: 1) a focus on teaching and learning, 2) comprehensive schoolwide reform strategies, 3) greater program flexibility, 4) targeting of resources, and 5) new partnerships to address the full range of children's needs affecting their ability to learn.

* * *

New Goal—Helping All Children Reach High Standards. The emphasis on high standards for all children provides a clearly defined goal for the new Title I law: enabling children served by the program to achieve to the challenging standards established by the state. In fact, the new Title I makes a powerful break with past practice by replacing minimum standards for some children with challenging standards for all. Challenging state content standards become the centerpiece of the new Title I law.

But asking for high standards will not guarantee getting them. The history of the Title I/Chapter 1 program offers a different lesson. Any separate system of standards and assessments for Title I is likely to be a system with lower standards. Therefore, the standards and assessments used for Title I purposes must be the same as those used by the state for all its other students, either under Goals 2000 or any other statewide process. Only in the absence of overall standards and assessments for all children will states develop standards and assessments just for Title I.

In addition to supporting higher expectations for children in Title I schools, challenging content standards—defining what all children should know and be able to do—can provide a substantive framework so sorely needed in the Title I program. Under this framework, all aspects of the education system—high-quality assessments, curriculum and instruction, professional development, school leadership, and school improvement—can work together to ensure that all children served by Title I achieve high standards. Moreover, the standards can support a stronger results-based accountability system, in which the success of the system is measured according to how well all its parts help students meet the standards. As a result, under the new Title I, high standards replace federally mandated, low-level, norm-referenced tests as the driving force behind education change.

Focusing on Teaching and Learning. Research suggests that for all students to achieve to high standards, states, districts, and schools must maintain a constant focus on improving teaching and learning. For far too long, teaching and learning played a subordinate role to administration, process, and compliance with rules and regulations in the Chapter 1 program.

Thus the first major reform strategy in the new Title I is moving teaching and learning to center stage. Everything we do ought to be guided by this fundamental question: What difference do what I decide and what I do make for teaching and learning? If this question cannot be answered for a particular Title I decision—whether about priorities, allocation of resources, or institutional practices—that decision is unlikely to make a positive difference for children.

Asking this question will lead to a new focus on what children are taught and how they are taught. This will likely mean replacing remediation with an accelerated curriculum and replacing drill and practice with more enriched instruction. It also will require a greater reliance on proven practices, rather than the latest fads. And it means that schools that continue to target resources on their lowest-achieving children must explore ways other than traditional pull-out programs, such as extended time strategies (extended day or extended year programs) that build on a challenging regular program for all children.

A focus on teaching and learning also necessitates a new investment and approach to professional development, recognizing that teachers, like the students they teach, are continuous learners. This new professional development—intensive, sustained, and embedded in the daily lives of teachers—will prove critical to helping teachers understand and teach to high standards. Therefore, Title I and Title II of the Improving America's Schools Act strongly reinforce each other through this new focus on teaching and learning.

Promoting Comprehensive, Schoolwide Reform to Improve Teaching and Learning. Evaluations of the former Chapter 1 program, as well as three decades of experience with pull-out programs, have demonstrated that the program's structure prevented it from sufficiently supporting improvements in teaching and learning. The development, under the former law, of "in-class" Chapter 1 programs—where Chapter 1 staff provide additional help to Chapter 1 students within the regular classroom—was one response to the widespread criticism of pull-out programs. However, unless in-class programs also are carefully structured to minimize the segregation of Chapter 1 children in the classroom, they can perpetuate the tracking, stigmatization, and fragmentation commonly found in pull-out programs.

Therefore the new Title I law embraces a radically different strategy: comprehensive school reform through schoolwide programs. It embodies the adage that "a rising tide lifts all boats." This reflects the belief that a strategy for total school improvement can more effectively lift the achievement levels of all children, including those who are farthest behind, as long as schools understand their responsibility to serve every child and to expect every child to learn. Moreover, schoolwide approaches can help bring entire school staffs together to develop and implement comprehensive plans for improving teaching and learning for all students, eliminating the isolation that characterizes working conditions for so many educators.

In support of this new approach, the new Title I significantly expands the ability of schools to develop schoolwide programs by lowering the minimum poverty level eligibility from 75% to 60% poor children in school year 1995–1996, and to 50% poverty in subsequent years. While there still will be some schools—called targeted assistance schools—that must continue to direct their Title I resources to their lowest achieving students, there will be 12,000 more schools (for a total of 20,000 schools nationwide) that will be able to use Title I funds to "upgrade the entire educational program" in the school.

We emphasize that this shift in Title I diminishes neither the program's continuing commitment to equity nor its central purpose of meeting the educational needs of disadvantaged children. Indeed, it is the strength of this commitment that has led to a dramatically new program approach for addressing those needs.

Freeing Schools, Districts, and States to Better Enable Reforms. Launching comprehensive reform efforts to support schoolwide improvements in teaching and learning will require far more time, energy, and latitude than currently are available to most Title I schools. Differing requirements, conflicting planning provisions, and separate accountability mechanisms associated with different program funds can further complicate their best efforts to launch and sustain comprehensive reforms.

Recognizing this, Title I strives to give schoolwide programs greater flexibility and more opportunities than they had under the former law. Under the new law, a schoolwide program will not have to draw solely on its Title I funds. Instead, a school may use the vast majority of all of its federal funds, as well as its state and local funds, to support the schoolwide program. In addition, schoolwide programs no longer will have to conform to the specific statutory and regulatory provisions of each separate federal program as long as the intent and purposes of those programs, as well as certain requirements relating to such critical areas as civil rights and health and safety, are met. No longer should there be "Title I schoolwides" or even "IASA schoolwides," but simply a single schoolwide program, supported by a school's resources.

Other new vehicles to support increased flexibility in Title I include: greater school-level decision making for all schoolwide and targeted assistance schools; the opportunity for states and districts to develop a single consolidated plan, rather than separate plans, for all of their IASA programs; and the unprecedented ability of states, districts, and schools to seek waivers of provisions in the Title I law that impede their efforts to support higher student achievement.

Channeling More Title I Resources to High-Poverty Schools. Greater concentration of Title I funds can better leverage comprehensive reforms in schoolwide programs and support higher quality programs in all Title I schools. For this reason and on grounds of fundamental fairness, the Clinton Administration sought to better channel Title I resources to areas where the needs were greatest.

While this overall goal was only partially achieved by the reauthorization, several new Title I provisions promise to channel more funds to high-poverty schools in every school district. First, districts will allocate funds to every Title I school based on its total number of poor children, rather than the number of low-achieving children. This not only will bring more funds to the highest poverty schools but also will eliminate existing penalties for success. Second, districts that serve any school below 35% poverty must allocate a minimum number of dollars per child to all schools that it serves. Third, tightened eligibility rules will allow districts to serve schools below the district poverty average only if the school has a poverty rate of 35% or more. Finally, in order to ensure that Title I resources flow to the most needy middle and high schools, districts must serve *all* schools with poverty rates above 75% before serving any other school.

The new Title I ensures more effective use of Title I funds, not only through a greater concentration of those funds in high-poverty schools, but also by establishing clear strategic priorities for their use throughout the education system.

Bringing Schools, Families, and Communities Together to Address Other Needs that Affect Learning. The final, major Title I strategy involves bringing schools, families, and communities together to address the wide array of other needs that affect a child's learning. We all know that other factors in the lives of children—poor health, inadequate nutrition, family problems, violence—significantly affect their ability to learn.

Schools cannot do everything alone, particularly as they redouble their efforts to improve teaching and learning. Therefore, the new Title I calls on parents to take advantage of a wide range of new opportunities to support their children's learning. Moreover, schools and their districts are called on to engage parents, community members, business people, and other agencies that serve children and families as partners in supporting the success of children. The entire IASA, in fact, is built on the premise that broad partnerships are necessary to provide comprehensive support for children so that good teaching and learning *can* take place in all schools.

Forging an Integrated Education System. To accomplish its goal of enabling all children to achieve high standards, the new Title I law attempts to convert the program from a separate set of services into a critical support for schools, districts, and states as they implement overall reforms. In fact, all other IASA resources—including professional development resources under Title II, grants for technology to improve teaching and learning under Title III, and additional programs under Title IV to ensure that schools will be safe and drug free—are designed to work with the Title I program to play this important supporting role.

Through its investment in such critical areas as professional development, high-quality instruction, parent involvement, and stronger, results-based reforms, the new Title I law strives to leverage comprehensive new reforms as well as to ensure that reforms already under way become reality. In this context, we no longer can view the Title I program apart from other education programs. Indeed, its success depends on connecting with and supporting all efforts that are designed to enable all children to reach high standards.

New Roles to Take Advantage of New Opportunities

Taken together, all these strategies offer dramatically expanded opportunities to help ensure that all children—whether poor, low-achieving, migrant, LEP, disabled, or gifted—receive the education they need to achieve the high state standards. To take advantage of these strategies, those involved in education—schools, districts, states, the federal government, parents, and children—will have to play fundamentally new roles and work together in new ways to improve teaching and learning.

The School Level—the New Centerpiece of Title I. At the heart of these strategies is a new focus on schools as active and central participants in all aspects of the Title I program. All Title I schools will

have far greater authority to make program decisions. This includes deciding whether to develop a schoolwide program, determining how to use the Title I funds to best address the needs of their students, and participating in the selection of the children to be served by a targeted assistance program.

* * *

To be successful, these efforts will require not only unprecedented collaboration but also very different approaches to planning. Too often, school planning has amounted to little more than a compilation of subcommittee reports, each filed behind a separator in a three-ring binder, to be pulled off the shelf when the district requires its resubmission. To free schools to concentrate their planning on their own needs, Title I no longer requires schools to develop plans on a pre-determined cycle nor to submit them to their district or state in order to receive program funds. Instead, schools are encouraged to convert their plans into evolving strategic documents that can be used to marshal a school's resources.

Effective collaboration in support of improved teaching and learning depends on more than just good planning. It also requires every member of the school community to share a sense of responsibility for the success of every student. Moreover, because creativity and personal commitment is so critical to Title I reform, each individual in the school community also will need to explore ways to best tap his or her unique contributions to promote the well-being and the achievement of children. For example, a principal who feels responsible for all students in the school will serve not only as a final arbiter and administrator but also as a facilitator, coach, and advocate who is willing to work closely with all staff and parents to improve the entire school. Teachers and other staff who feel responsible for the success of the school's students will work continually to expand their knowledge about teaching and learning, update their teaching skills, and employ a variety of approaches to actively engage all students in learning. They also will seek new approaches to coordinating instruction with other teachers throughout the school and new ways of effectively involving parents in the education of their children.

Finally, parents have new responsibilities or, more accurately, shared responsibilities with teachers and other school staff. They will be encouraged to join the educators in new Title I compacts, identifying their mutual responsibilities and sustaining an ongoing dialogue about their children's achievement. Many parents also may choose to become involved in the development of overall school policies, including the development of strategies to involve other parents effectively in their children's education. Schools and communities must ensure that parents have the information, training, and other supports they may need to effectively play these roles.

Districts as Facilitators of Title I Change. In order for schools to move successfully to the center stage of Title I reform, they must receive far greater training and technical assistance. The new law calls on school districts to forgo making some of their traditional decisions and instead take on this support role in at least four critical ways.

First, school districts will be called on to work with schools as they develop their Title I programs and to ensure that schools receive any technical assistance needed for effective program implementation. This support could involve drawing on the district's own expertise for school planning efforts or providing schools with an opportunity to learn about what works in other schools. A major source of support also may include connecting schools to other technical assistance providers, such as universities, regional labs, and the new IASA technical assistance centers.

Second, a district will work with school-level staff to develop a strategy for improved professional development, equipping all teachers and other staff who are involved in the education of the children served by the Title I program to teach to high standards. A one-hour presentation on "everything you need to know about the new math curriculum" at the end of a full day of teaching is no longer enough. Instead, ongoing, high-quality professional development funded by Title I should be connected to overall school improvement strategies and classroom practice and, where possible, integrated into teachers' daily work. This can include significant regular planning time and ongoing opportunities for teachers to learn from their successful colleagues.

Third, under the new Title I law, school districts will play a critical role in helping to forge greater connections among schools and between schools, communities, and other social agencies. Although schools, particularly high-poverty ones, can benefit greatly from such connections, they often have trouble creating them. Therefore, the new Title I asks each district to coordinate the Title I program with other education programs and, to the extent feasible, with services provided by other agencies that serve children and families. This includes providing for the sufficient transition of young children from Head Start and other preschool programs to schools,

coordinating family literacy programs and other districtwide parental involvement activities, and, where desired, using up to 5% of its IASA funds for coordination/collaboration activities.

Finally, while it will be critical for districts to support schools as they engage in reforms, districts also will be responsible for holding schools accountable for results. This includes recognizing and rewarding schools that are making satisfactory progress on a regular basis and identifying for "school improvement" those schools that do not make such progress for two consecutive years. It also requires districts to ensure that schools failing to make adequate progress first receive the technical assistance they need but, ultimately, face corrective actions for persistently low performance.

Taking these responsibilities seriously will require the district to shift its focus from compliance to quality and from "command and control" to "suggest and support." It will call on district staff members to draw heavily on their own knowledge of teaching, learning, and organizational change. Whether schools succeed in their new Title I roles will depend in part on how well districts carry out their own new Title I responsibilities.

Anchoring the Program: State Standards and Assessments. Each state also has a new, critical role to play under the new Title I law. That is providing an anchor and framework to support the new Title I program. At the core of this framework will be high-quality, challenging standards and assessments that are created by the states, not mandated by the federal government. States will be able to develop their own content and performance standards and high-quality, carefully aligned assessments to determine how well children are meeting those standards. States also can approve the use of district-adopted standards and aligned assessments for Title I purposes—but only if those standards and assessments are at least as challenging as the state's and meet the other requirements of the law.

* * *

The Federal Role—Forging a New Partnership for Title I Change. Because the federal government plays such a critical role in shaping the Title I program at all other levels, the federal government also must play a dramatically new Title I role. The federal government has long been the source of Title I's command-and-control approach, supplying plenty of mandates about the operation of Title I programs but little extra support to enhance program effectiveness. The new Title I is designed to promote a different federal approach that relies on assistance, rather than solely on enforcement, and program support, rather than program control.

For example, the federal government no longer will require federally mandated tests for the Title I program. Schools will be more able to draw on their federal funds to support comprehensive reforms that meet their needs. Fifteen comprehensive technical centers also will bring the expertise of the former categorical program centers together to make it easier for states, districts, and schools to benefit from these sources of expertise. This "one-stop shopping" will be particularly helpful to the growing number of schools, districts, and states engaged in comprehensive reform.

Meanwhile, the Department of Education's implementation strategies are designed to further revamp the federal role in Title I. The department is working to enable states, districts, and schools to take full advantage of the new flexibility in the law. Regulations will be avoided wherever possible and, when used, will seek to expand rather than curtail options. The department's plan to integrate its monitoring across programs and to focus increasingly on quality and results will further redefine how it relates to states, districts, and schools.

This new federal approach under the IASA is part of the Clinton Administration's broad education reform strategy of moving programmatic decisions to states, districts, and schools, with far less prescription from Washington; redirecting the energies of entire school systems from compliance and enforcement to support, technical assistance, peer review, and continuous improvement; and forging a new federal, state, and local partnership that reflects education as a national priority and a state and local responsibility.

* * *

_____

NOTES AND QUESTIONS

1. Litigation Under Title I

Surprisingly little private litigation has been brought to enforce Title I. Generally courts have accepted plaintiffs' claims but provided only limited relief. *See, e.g., Nicholson v. Pittenger,* 364 F.Supp. 669 (E.D.Pa. 1973); *Alexander v. Califano,* 432 F.Supp. 1182 (N.D.Cal. 1977); *Natonabah v. Board of Education,* 355 F.Supp. 716 (D.N.M. 1973); *Community School Board, District 3 v. Board of Education,* 66 Misc.2d 739, 321 N.Y.S.2d 949 (Sup.Ct. 1971). Do those results

speak to the limitations of securing reform through litigation? Are low-income children likely to have access to counsel who can frame their claims for relief?

1. Parent Participation. Participation and litigation were viewed as complementary means to the same end: the creation of a political base, at the local level, responsive to the concerns of the eligible community, able to act as a countervailing power to state officials and local education. Indeed, one of the objectives of litigation was to secure effective parent participation. *See* Breezer, "Title I Parent Advisory Councils: To What Extent Must They Be Involved?" 7 *J.Law & Educ.* 151 (1978).

Through Parent Advisory Councils (PACs), parents were given formal responsibilities for program management. Under Title I, parents were entitled to select the PAC; a majority of its members were parents of children to be served by Title I projects; representatives of children attending schools that were eligible for, but not receiving, Title I funds, were included on the PAC. The PAC was entitled to information relating to legal requirements of Title I and to any state or federal audit reports. Parents generally were entitled to "participate in the establishment of [Title I] programs, and . . . to make recommendations with respect to the instructional goals of the program. . . ."

Congress eliminated the PAC requirement in the 1981 legislation. This was perhaps the biggest change in the law, and the issue remained controversial. Those who opposed a federal PAC mandate argued that a uniform requirement failed to distinguish significant differences between urban and rural districts; that states and school districts should choose their own form of parent involvement, not have one imposed on them; and that, historically, PACs promoted political activity that had little to do with educating children. Those who would reinstate PACs argued that, in the 1970s, they were effective instruments of parental involvement, and that eliminating them simply led districts to diminish the role of parents. Half the states did report significantly less organized parental involvement than before. *See* Plunkett, "From Title I to Chapter 1: The Evolution of Compensatory Education," 66 *Phi Delta Kappan* 533 (April 1985). They also urged that limiting parental involvement affects the education of Title I children (*see* A. Henderson, ed., *Parent Participation–Student Achievement: The Evidence Grows, An Annotated Bibliography* (1981)) and that political mobilization of parents was a good, not a bad, thing—that it invited more democratic decision making on the local level and, nationally, encouraged organized political resistance to cuts in Title I funding.

In 1988, PACs were reinstated as an optional way to involve parents, but many other methods were recognized as well. These included support for parents to help children with homework, training for teachers to work effectively with low-income parents, and development of home-school partnerships. Augustus F. Hawkin–Robert T. Stafford Elementary and Secondary School Improvement Amendments of 1988, Pub. L. No. 100-297, 102 Stat. 140.

The 1994 amendments strengthened parental involvement requirements. Although the new law does not mandate PACs, it does impose extensive requirements for schools and districts to consult with parents in developing and implementing plans and programs. The law also mandates that schools create compacts with Title I parents to ensure shared responsibility for high student performance. Schools must provide parents with information about laws and standards related to their children's academic progress. Schools may use Title I funds for other forms of training and support that develop a school's or district's capacity to involve parents. 20 U.S.C. § 6319. At least one author has argued that the 1994 amendments wrongly emphasize parental participation in general policymaking when they should focus on ways to enlist parents in helping their children to learn. Johnson, "Putting the Cart Before the Horse: Parent Involvement in the Improving America's Schools Act," 85 *Calif.L.Rev.* 1757 (1997).

2. Federal Monitoring and Enforcement Activities. With varying degrees of vigilance, the federal government has sought to enforce Title I mandates and, more ambitiously, to prod districts into strengthening the quality of their educational programs. Lawsuits to recover misspent funds have been the chief compliance-promoting instrument. During the 1980s, the federal government audited and sought reimbursement from a number of state departments of education. Typically, federal officials claimed that states had used the funds to cover general educational costs, rather than to meet the special needs of low-income children. *See, e.g., Bennett v. Kentucky Department of Education*, 470 U.S. 656 (1985).

States regularly—and often unsuccessfully—challenged demands for reimbursement of misspent federal education funds. California in particular was at loggerheads with the Department of Education. *See, e.g., State of California, Department of Education v. Bennett*, 849 F.2d 1227 (9th Cir. 1988) (disallowing conference expenses but allowing recovery for the cost of field trips which included non-Chapter 1 as well as Chapter 1 pupils); *State of California, Department of Education v. Bennett*, 843 F.2d 333 (9th Cir. 1988) (upholding disallowance of expenditures for graduate training of migrant student counselors). *See also Virginia Department of Education v. Secretary of Education*, 806 F.2d 78 (4th Cir. 1986); *State of Indiana, Department of Public Instruction v. Bell*, 728 F.2d 938 (7th Cir. 1984). As a result of the audits, local school officials "interpreted the [Title I] rules in the most conservative and restrictive way. . . . As a consequence, creativity and imagination in program planning . . . suffered. . . ." as educators adopted an increasingly formalistic and legalistic stance. Burnes, "A Case Study of Federal Involvement in Education," 33 *Proceedings of the Academy of Political Science* 87 (1978). *Compare* M. McLaughlin, P. Shields, and D. Rezasbek, "State and Local Response to Chapter 1 of the Education Consolidation and Improvement Act, 1981," *National Institute of Education*, Grant No. OB-NIE-G-83-0003 (1985). Do the 1994 changes restore discretion to state and local educators and minimize the dangers of intrusive, embarrassing audits? Does the new emphasis on comprehensive schoolwide reform mean that resources will be diverted from the children in greatest need and leave them without meaningful federal protection from state and local abuses?

C. Homeless Children and Educational Access

1. The New Poor: Families Without Homes. In the late 1980s, Congress turned its attention to a new kind of poverty: homelessness. Although homelessness is not new, most policymakers associated it with single men on skid row. Stronge, "History and Problems of Schooling for the Homeless," in J. Stronge, ed., *Educating Homeless Children and Adolescents: Evaluating Policy and Practice* 3, 6 (1992). Beginning in the 1970s, the demographics of the homeless began to change, and by 1993, the U.S. Conference of Mayors estimated that families made up 43 percent of the homeless based on usage of shelters and city services. Hopper and Hamburg, "The Making of America's Homeless: From Skid Row to New Poor, 1945–1984," in R. Bratt, C. Hartman, and A. Meyerson, eds., *Critical Perspectives on Housing* 12 (1986);

U.S. Conference of Mayors, A *Status Report on Hunger and Homelessness in America's Cities: 1993* (1994); Shinn and Waitzman, "Homeless Families Are Different," in J. Baumohl, ed., *Homelessness in America* 109, 109–10 (1996) (noting that 43 percent estimate could be inflated because families are more likely than single men to make use of shelters and services). In the late 1980s, Jonathan Kozol brought the new face of homelessness to America's attention in an award-winning book. In it, he chronicled the obstacles that homeless children faced in getting an education in New York.

"Concealment"

From *Rachel and Her Children* by Jonathan Kozol, copyright © 1988 by Jonathan Kozol. Used by permission of Crown Publishers, a division of Random House, Inc.

* * *

What of the children who do not become entangled in the legal system but remain to do their best in the hotels and public schools? Many do not get to school at all. Transient existence cuts them from the rolls. If readmitted to their former schools, they may face a long ride on a bus or subway twice a day. If the bus or train is late, they arrive at school too late for breakfast and must struggle through their lessons on an empty stomach. If transferred to another school close to their temporary residence, they still face the other obstacles that we have seen. Just getting up and getting out may be a daunting task.

At P.S. 64, on New York's Lower East Side, 125 children from the Martinique [a hotel for the homeless] were registered in February 1987. Only about 85 arrived on any given day. This estimate indicates that almost one third aren't in regular attendance but does not include those who, because of bureaucratic complications or parental disarray, have never been enrolled. I would guess, based on a head count of the school-age children in the ballroom of the Martinique at lunch, that *more* than a third of the children in this building do not usually get to school.

What of those who do make it to school? Teachers speak of kids who fall into a deep sleep at their desks because conditions in their hotel rooms denied them a night's rest. How much can such children learn? Stanley Goldstein, principal of P.S. 64, estimates that a quarter of the hotel children are between two and three grades behind their peers in academic skills. This, he observes, makes them still more re-

luctant to appear at all. "They feel like idiots . . .," he says. "Can you blame them?"

A reporter describes a nine-year-old in the third grade, already a year behind his proper grade, who cannot read, cannot tell time, and has a hard time adding and subtracting numbers of two digits. He has been classified "learning disabled" and "emotionally disturbed." Many of the hotel children, school officials say, are becoming "deeply troubled" and exhibiting the symptoms of withdrawal. Others are becoming hyperactive.

Mr. Goldstein notes that it is difficult to reach the parents of a child. (Families in the Martinique seldom have phones.) He adds that, even when attendance officers attempt to visit parents at the Martinique, they are often unsuccessful. He says that sometimes no one answers—"Or sometimes there's no one there." What does the attendance officer do? He can leave a message at the desk, but parents tell me there is a good chance that it will never be received.

"You're not dealing with the Pierre [an upscale hotel], you know . . .," says Mr. Goldstein. "We have children who just disappear from the face of the earth."

The New York Board of Education does not know how often children of the homeless lose out on an education; nor does it keep records of how well those who are registered in school perform. Nor has it any central policy to dictate to the schools how homeless children should be treated.

For children in the barracks shelters, pedagogic damage may be worse. In these situations, rudimentary classrooms are provided as a substitute for school. In some of these shelters, according to the *New York Times*, "the one-room schoolhouse—a fond bit of Americana—has been revised and updated to serve the city's dispossessed." There is nothing fond, and little of Americana, in the setup that the city has contrived to fill the days, if not the minds, of these unlucky children. One courageous teacher, given few supplies, does the best she can with a forty-year-old encyclopedia, donated desks, and storybooks on loan. "I've had three children and I've had forty-five . . . I never know, from one morning to the next, who will be here or how many." Sometimes her biggest job, she says, is calming the kids down.

The problem is not limited to the five boroughs of New York. Homeless children in Westchester County undertake extraordinary journeys to get to their schools: Of 860 dislocated children living in motels, half or more must travel up to forty miles twice a day. Many travel longer distances. Because of shortages of space in Westchester motels and (according to one press report) because motels in other counties offer cheaper rooms, 454 children have been sheltered in motels in four different counties.

Each morning, they are put on buses—or, where there are not enough of them to justify a bus, in taxis—and they ride from town to town, county to county, in their search for education. Often these taxis take a number of different children to a number of different schools. "This results in children arriving at school either very early or late," reports a school psychologist in Peekskill. Many of these children rise so early that they don't eat breakfast and arrive at school carsick and hungry. "In our school," he says, "we have children as young as four years old traveling over thirty miles. . . ."

There is unintended irony in this. A society that vocally rejects the "busing" of poor children over distances of two to seven miles to achieve desegregation finds it acceptable to ship a child forty miles to be sure she goes to school where she originally lived. One homeless twelve-year-old at school in Peekskill says that she has been commuting from Poughkeepsie since the age of ten. A ten-year-old at school in Yonkers rides sixty miles *twice a day* from a motel in Newburgh. Because the system lacks coordination, schools in Mt. Vernon have children who commute from Yonkers, while Yonkers schools have children who commute from Brewster. Westchester County, according to the *New York Times*, is trying to devise "a computer program" that would "keep track" of the children and their parents, "cross-referencing the homeless. . . ."

In provision of transportation, as of basic shelter, money may be made out of despair. A long taxi ride costs $10 a day per child: $1,800 for the academic year. A bus ride, priced at $1 per child per mile, costs up to $80 a day. In one extreme case, a homeless child relocated in Poughkeepsie has to commute to school in Yonkers at a state expense of $180 a day—$32,000 if projected for the academic year. For one-third this sum, the child could be sent to private school. For a great deal less, she could be sent to school with children from Poughkeepsie. Is there a reason she must ride to Yonkers every day?

The owner of a motel housing thirty homeless children sees an opportunity for profit. He recently bought four buses and obtained a contract with Westchester County to transport the kids to school. He gets a dollar a mile for each child. "I would anticipate we will be picking up from more motels . . .," he says. "I don't think homelessness is going to disappear."

* * *

2. The Congressional Response: The McKinney Act. Barriers to enrollment were so substantial that the U.S. Department of Education estimated that 30 percent of 220,000 school-age children were not attending school in the mid-1980s. Rafferty, "Developmental and Educational Consequences of Homelessness on Children and Youth," in J. Kryder-Coe, L. Salamon and J. Molnar, eds., *Homeless Children and Youth: A New American Dilemma* (1991). Problems like these prompted some lawsuits to force schools to enroll homeless children. The results were mixed. Stronge and Helm, "Legal Barriers to the Education of Homeless Children and Youth: Residency and Guardianship Issues," 20 *J.L. & Educ.* 201, 211–13 (1991). To help homeless children overcome bureaucratic obstacles to getting an education, Congress passed the Stewart B. McKinney Homeless Assistance Act of 1987, Pub.L.No. 100-77, 101 Stat. 482 (codified as amended at 42 U.S.C. §§ 11431–11435. The Act provides the following:

"Statement of Policy"
Pub.L.No. 100-77, 101 Stat. 482 (42 U.S.C. §§ 11431).

It is the policy of the Congress that—

(1) each State educational agency shall ensure that each child of a homeless individual and each homeless youth has equal access to the same free, appropriate public education, including a public preschool education, as provided to other children and youth;

(2) in any State that has a compulsory residency requirement as a component of the State's compulsory school attendance laws or other laws, regulations, practices, or policies that may act as a barrier to the enrollment, attendance, or success in school of homeless children and youth, the State will review and undertake steps to revise such laws, regulations, practices, or policies to ensure that homeless children and youth are afforded the same free, appropriate public education as provided to other children and youth;

(3) homelessness alone should not be sufficient reason to separate students from the mainstream school environment; and

(4) homeless children and youth should have access to the education and other services that such children and youth need to ensure that such children and youth have an opportunity to meet the same challenging State student performance standards to which all students are held.

Despite limited funding, the Act has played a critical role in ensuring access to public education. In 1990, over half of homeless children were not enrolled in school. By 1997, only 12 percent of identified homeless children were out of school. National Law Center on Homelessness and Poverty, *Separate and Unequal: A Report on Educational Barriers for Homeless Children and Youth* 2 (Jan. 2000). *But cf.* Thompson, "Breaking the Cycle of Poverty: Models of Legal Advocacy to Implement the Educational Promise of the McKinney Act for Homeless Children and Youth," 31 *Creighton L.Rev.* 1209, 1213–14 (1998) (noting that underfunding and underenforcement have compromised the Act's effectiveness). Despite these gains, homeless children continued to find their educations disrupted by frequent moves and high levels of absenteeism. Even if these children make it to school, they are unlikely to find the special services they need. R. da Costa Nunez, *The New Poverty: Homeless Families in America* 85–92 (1996). Moreover, as more homeless children enroll, school districts are increasingly relying on separate schools to insulate them from other children and meet their special needs. Advocates contend that the schools are stigmatizing and unequal. National Law Center on Homelessness and Poverty, *supra*, at 17–61.

3. Litigation Under the McKinney Act. Much of the progress under the Act has occurred without litigation. In fact, it was initially unclear whether the Act authorized a private right of action. Nearly a decade after the Act was passed, one federal court of appeals permitted a lawsuit seeking prompt placement, appropriate services, and transportation to go forward.

Lampkin v. District of Columbia

27 F.3d 605 (D.C.Cir. 1994)

Before Edwards, J., Buckley, J., and Sentelle, J.
  Buckley, J.:

* * *

C. Private Enforcement of the McKinney Act

In . . . [determining whether there is a private right of action under] the McKinney Act, the first question to ask is whether the statute was intended to benefit persons such as appellants' children. *See Wilder*, 496 U.S. at 509, 110 S.Ct. at 2517; *Suter*, 503 U.S. at —, 112 S.Ct. at 1367. This point is not in dispute here: The parties all agree that the McKinney Act was

enacted to benefit homeless children. *See* 42 U.S.C. § 11431. That said, we must hold that the Act "creates an enforceable right *unless* it reflects merely a congressional preference for a certain kind of conduct rather than a binding obligation on the governmental unit." *Wilder*, 496 U.S. at 509, 110 S.Ct. at 2517 (citation and internal quotation marks omitted; emphasis added). Mindful of the need "to analyze the statutory provisions in detail, in light of the entire legislative enactment, to determine whether the language in question create[s] enforceable rights, privileges, or immunities within the meaning of § 1983," *Suter*,— U.S. at —, 112 S.Ct. at 1367 (internal quotation marks omitted), we must determine whether the Act creates rights that are substantively enforceable under section 1983.

Section 11432(f) of the McKinney Act provides:

> No State may receive a grant under this section unless the state educational agency submits an application to the Secretary at such time, in such manner, and containing or accompanied by such information as the Secretary may reasonably require.

42 U.S.C. § 11432(f) (1988). The regulations issued by the Secretary stipulate that a State may not begin to obligate funds received pursuant to a federal grant until the later of the two following dates: "[t]he date that the State plan is mailed or hand delivered to the Secretary in substantially approvable form" and "[t]he date that the funds are first available for obligation by the Secretary." 34 C.F.R. § 76.703(a)(1) & (2). The regulations further stipulate that a State

> shall comply with the State plan and applicable statutes, regulations, and approved applications, and shall use Federal funds in accordance with those statutes, regulations, plan, and applications.

Id. at § 76.700. Here, of course, the "applicable statute[ ]" is the McKinney Act, and the obligations it imposes on participating States are clear. The Act requires that grants provided by the Secretary be used, *inter alia*, "to prepare and carry out the State plan," 42 U.S.C. § 11432(c)(4), and that "[e]ach plan . . . assure . . . that local educational agencies within the State will comply with the requirements of paragraphs (3) through (9)," *id.* at § 11432(e)(2). Paragraphs (3) through (9) in turn provide highly specific instructions for meeting a variety of needs of homeless children and youths. This structure markedly contrasts with that of the Child Welfare Act, with which the *Suter* Court was concerned. Although both Acts describe in detail the contents of the plan a participating State must adopt, only the McKinney Act provides specific directions for the plan's execution. *Compare* 42 U.S.C. § 671(a) *with* 42 U.S.C. § 11432(e). It is this distinction that is ignored by our dissenting colleague, who concludes that "the genuine statutory duty of a recipient state under the McKinney Act is to prepare and carry out a plan, *designed* to achieve nine designated goals." Dissent at 2 (internal quotation marks omitted, emphasis in original). While we agree that the McKinney Act requires the State to submit such a plan, it also differs significantly from the Adoption Act in that paragraphs (3) through (9) of subsection 11432(e) of the McKinney Act not only inform the State in great detail on how its plan is to be implemented, they impose obligations that are independent of the plan. These are set forth in specific, mandatory terms; and it is these that appellants seek to enforce. Thus, paragraph (3) requires that

> [t]he local educational agency of each homeless child and each homeless youth *shall* [assign the child or youth to a school which] is in the child's best interest or the youth's best interest. . . . In determining the best interests of the child or youth . . . consideration *shall* be given to a request made by a parent regarding school selection.

Id. § 11432(e)(3) (emphasis added). Succeeding paragraphs stipulate that "[e]ach homeless child *shall* be provided services comparable to services offered to other students in the school . . . ," *id.* § 11432(e)(5) (emphasis added), and that records ordinarily kept by the school "*shall* be maintained" so as to be available when the child enters a new school district. *Id.* § 11432(e)(6) (emphasis added). Furthermore, they provide that

> [e]ach local educational agency serving homeless children or youth that receives assistance under this subchapter *shall* coordinate with local social services agencies, and other agencies or programs providing services to such children or youth and their families[,]

id. § 11432(e)(7) (emphasis added), and "*shall* designate a homelessness liaison." *Id.* § 11432(e)(8) (emphasis added). We read this language as "mandatory rather than hortatory." This interpretation is supported by paragraph (2), which describes paragraphs (3) through (9) as "requirements" rather than options. *Id.* § 11432(e)(2).

In addition to the mandatory obligations listed in those seven paragraphs, the McKinney Act also provides that

> [t]he Coordinator of Education of Homeless Children and Youth established in each State *shall* . . . once every 2 years, gather data on the number and location of homeless children and youth in the State . . . develop

and carry out the State plan . . . [and] facilitate coordination between the State education agency, the State social services agency, and other agencies providing services to homeless children and youth and their families.

Id. § 11432(d). The language of these provisions is sufficiently clear to put the States on notice of the obligations they assume when they choose to accept grants made under the Act. *Pennhurst State School and Hospital v. Halderman*, 451 U.S. 1, 17, 101 S.Ct. 1531, 1539, 67 L.Ed.2d 694 (1981) ("if Congress intends to impose a condition on the grant of federal moneys, it must do so unambiguously" (footnote omitted)).

Moreover, as we noted earlier, the Secretary has promulgated regulations stipulating that for state-administered programs like the McKinney Act, "[a] State . . . shall comply with the State plan and applicable statutes, regulations, and approved applications, and shall use Federal funds in accordance with those statutes, regulations, plan, and applications." 34 C.F.R. § 76.700. *Contrast Suter,—* U.S. at —, 112 S.Ct. at 1369 (noting that the regulations accompanying the Child Welfare Act "do not evidence a view that [the statute] places any requirement for state receipt of federal funds other than the requirement that the State submit a plan to be approved by the Secretary" (footnote omitted)). Here, the regulations merely reinforce our conclusion that States undertake well-defined obligations when they elect to accept funds under the McKinney Act.

Finally, the McKinney Act contains no statutory mechanisms for the administrative enforcement of the beneficiaries' rights, suggesting that Congress did not intend to foreclose a private cause of action that is enforceable under section 1983. *See, Suter,* 112 S.Ct. at 1368–69 (citing alternative enforcement mechanisms provided by sections 671(b) and 672(a)(1) of the Child Welfare Act as showing that "the absence of a remedy to private plaintiffs under § 1983 does not make the reasonable efforts clause a dead letter" (footnote omitted)). Thus there is nothing in the structure of the McKinney Act to suggest that its beneficiaries may not invoke section 1983 to enforce their rights under the Act.

One hurdle remains before we can declare that the rights conferred on homeless children by the Act are enforceable in federal court. Even if a statute confers rights on a beneficiary, their judicial enforcement requires that they not be overly "vague and amorphous." *Wilder,* 496 U.S. at 519, 110 S.Ct. at 2522 (internal quotation marks omitted). The District argues that the statutory requirement that a school be selected in accordance with the "best interests" of a homeless child is at least as vague as the "reasonable efforts" clause that the Court found too amorphous in *Suter*. *See New York v. United States,* — U.S. 144, —, 112 S.Ct. 2408, 2445, 120 L.Ed.2d 120 (1992) (Justice White, concurring in part, dissenting in part, describing *Suter* as "not permitting a § 1983 suit under a Spending Clause statute when the ostensible federal right created was too vague and amorphous").

This argument asserts, in essence, that the judiciary is incapable of determining the "best interests" of children, just as the plaintiffs in *Wilder* argued that the judiciary was incapable of determining what constitutes "reasonable and adequate" hospital rates. *See Wilder*, 496 U.S. at 519, 110 S.Ct. at 2522. In response, the Court observed:

> That the [Boren] [A]mendment gives the States substantial discretion in choosing among reasonable methods of calculating rates may affect the standard under which a court reviews whether the rates comply with the amendment, but it does not render the amendment unenforceable by a court. While there may be a range of reasonable rates, there certainly are *some* rates outside that range that no State could ever find to be reasonable and adequate under the Act. Although some knowledge of the hospital industry might be required to evaluate a State's findings with respect to the reasonableness of its rates, such an inquiry is well within the competence of the Judiciary.

Id. at 519–20, 110 S.Ct. at 2522–23 (footnote omitted) (emphasis in original).

The obligations imposed by the McKinney Act involve, for the most part, the exercise of judgment by a local educational agency. A court, however, may discern whether the criteria or procedures adopted by the agency are reasonably designed to aid it in making the school placement decision. Moreover, we have little doubt that the court would also have the competence to determine whether the District had complied with its obligation to assign a particular homeless child to a school that was in his best interests.

In recent years, the courts of this circuit have frequently been called upon to determine whether the District of Columbia public school system had met a comparable obligation under the Education for the Handicapped Act, 20 U.S.C. §§ 1400 *et seq.* (1988), which requires participating States to assure handicapped children of an "appropriate education." *See, e.g., Kerkam v. Superintendent, D.C. Public Schools,* 931 F.2d 84 (D.C.Cir.1991); *Knight by Knight v.*

District of Columbia, 877 F.2d 1025 (D.C.Cir. 1989). Although the criteria and procedures set forth in the Education for the Handicapped Act are more detailed than those in the McKinney Act, the ultimate determination made under that Act—that the handicapped child's education is "appropriate" to his needs—is no less vague or amorphous than the one at issue here. As in *Kerkam* and *Knight*, should a dispute arise between the educational agency and the parents of the homeless child as to whether the school to which the child has been assigned is in his best interest, a court is clearly competent to consider the testimony of opposing witnesses and to decide whether the agency's determination of the child's best interest was reasonable.

We conclude, from the foregoing, that section 11432(e)(3) of the McKinney Act confers enforceable rights on its beneficiaries and that appellants may invoke section 1983 to enforce those rights.

* * *

Sentelle, Circuit Judge, dissenting:

I respectfully dissent from the court's conclusion that the McKinney Homeless Assistance Act, 42 U.S.C. § 11301 *et seq.* (1988), creates a federal right enforceable under 42 U.S.C. § 1983. I do so recognizing that the question is a close one, though in my mind it should not be. That is, I agree with Justice Powell that the Supreme Court in *Maine v. Thiboutot,* 448 U.S. 1, 100 S.Ct. 2502, 65 L.Ed.2d 555 (1980), by holding "almost casually, that 42 U.S.C. § 1983 creates a cause of action for deprivations . . . of any federal statutory right" distorted the Civil Rights Act far beyond any support in its then already lengthy history. 448 U.S. at 11, 100 S.Ct. at 2508 (Powell, J., dissenting, for himself, Chief Justice Burger and then-Justice Rehnquist). . . .

Although the Supreme Court has counseled us that in the post-*Thiboutot* framework of § 1983 interpretation "each statute must be interpreted by its own terms," *Suter v. Artist M.,* — U.S. —, — n. 8, 112 S.Ct. 1360, 1367 n. 8, 118 L.Ed.2d 1 (1992), obviously, the high court's prior interpretations of other statutes instructs our interpretation of the present one. In *Suter*, as the majority points out today, the Supreme Court found no right enforceable under § 1983 in the Child Welfare Act. In *Wilder v. Virginia Hospital Association,* 496 U.S. 498, 110 S.Ct. 2510, 110 L.Ed.2d 455 (1990), the Supreme Court did find such a right in the Boren Amendment to the Medicaid Act. The majority opinion today does a commendable job of cataloging the similarities and differences between the two cases and I will not re-hash them. I do not disagree with the majority's summary of either case, only with its conclusion as to the side upon which the McKinney Act falls.

As the majority notes, the *Suter* decision was based at least in part upon the conclusion "that the [statutory] directive to use reasonable efforts was so open-ended, and the resulting state discretion so broad, that judicial enforcement was an impossibility." Maj. op. at 159. That is to say, whatever other grounds may exist for denying judicial enforcement to statutorily-created federal "rights" under § 1983, the "judicial enforcement" of such rights "requires that they not be overly 'vague and amorphous.' " Maj. op. at 612 (quoting *Wilder*, 496 U.S. at 519, 110 S.Ct. at 2522). Therefore, for us to undertake judicial enforcement of rights under the McKinney Act presupposes an ability by the federal courts to carry out for the recalcitrant state the duty of determining school assignments in the "best interests" of children and youths. To me this is no less vague and amorphous than the "reasonable efforts" language which the Supreme Court in *Suter* held insufficient to create such an enforceable right.

Certainly the majority is correct that in other circumstances courts must determine the "best interests" of particular children. However, the usual exercise of judicial wisdom in pursuit of the "best interests" of a particular child is just that—a particularized one. Here, the courts would be called upon to make programmatic decisions not as to the best interest of a particular child, but as to how a grant-augmented state program should be designed to meet the needs of *groups* of particularized children. The programmatic operation of a state agency is not within the judicial competence.

Finally, it appears to me that the genuine statutory duty of a recipient state under the McKinney Act is to "prepare and carry out" a plan, "*designed to*" achieve nine designated goals. 42 U.S.C. §§ 11432(c)(4) & 11432(e)(1). Given the amorphousness of the "designed to" mandate, I do not see how this differs in a controlling way from the Adoption Act construed in *Suter*. There the Court held that statute did not create a right enforceable under § 1983 because it did not "place[ ] any requirement for state receipt of federal funds other than the requirement that the State submit a plan to be approved by the Secretary." *Suter*, — U.S. at —, 112 S.Ct. at 1369. The mandating paragraphs of the McKinney Act listed by the majority do not change this. The Adoption Act also contained de-

scriptions of the relevant plan. Indeed, 42 U.S.C. § 671 provided a description of the required plan approximately as detailed, and with as many uses of mandatory words such as "shall" and "will," as does the McKinney Act outlined in the majority opinion. Nonetheless, the Supreme Court held that the statute did not create a civil right enforceable under § 1983.

* * *

NOTES AND QUESTIONS

1. The Aftermath of Lampkin

On remand, the district court granted the plaintiffs' request for declaratory and injunctive relief. The District of Columbia was ordered to identify homeless children at the time they first arrive at intake shelters and to refer them within seventy-two hours for educational services, including transportation, while they were on waiting lists for shelters. For families already on waiting lists, children were to be identified and referred within two weeks. The district also was ordered to provide students and their adult escorts with bus tokens to get to school, and to avoid delays due to once-a-week distribution of the tokens at shelters. *Lampkin v. District of Columbia*, 879 F. Supp. 116 (D.D.C. 1995). This victory proved hollow, however. Only two months later, the school district reported that the costs of compliance were so burdensome that it would have to opt out of the McKinney grant program altogether. Federal funds were simply insufficient to cover the costs of educating the homeless in the District of Columbia. Without federal grant money, the McKinney Act no longer applied, and *Lampkin* was dismissed. After the dismissal, the school district reapplied for funds under the Act. Goedert, "The Education of Homeless Children: The McKinney Act and Its Implications," 140 *Ed.L.Rep.* 9 (2000).

2. Other Litigation Under the McKinney Act

After *Lampkin*, only one other lawsuit was filed, this time to enforce the McKinney Act in Chicago. After four years, the parties in *Salazar v. Edwards* settled the case, and the plaintiffs were able to eliminate barriers to enrollment and shut down a segregated shelter program. The litigation apparently heightened the district's commitment to homeless education. Goedert, *supra*, at 17. In light of this experience under the McKinney Act, how likely is it that private lawsuits will be an effective means to secure educational services for homeless students? If so, what other resources can be mobilized to secure the act's enforcement?

D. Full-Service Schools: Reconsidering the Role of Educational Institutions in a Stratified Society

The discussion of homeless children suggests that for highly disadvantaged children, comprehensive services may be needed to make the educational process meaningful. A child who is hungry, tired, sick, anxious, or depressed is unlikely to be an effective learner. Because of increasing disparities in wealth and income in the United States, some reformers want to develop full-service schools, schools that could offer comprehensive services to children and their families. Dupper and Evans, "From Band-Aids and Putting Out Fires to Prevention: School Social Work Practice Approaches for the New Century," 18 *Soc.Work in Educ.* 187 (1996). Although these demands may seem novel and even radical, they harken back to Progressive-era reforms designed to address the problems of urbanization and immigration in turn-of-the-century America.

"Health and Social Services in Public Schools: Historical Perspectives"

D. Tyack, 2 *The Future of Children* 19–31 (Spring 1992). Reprinted with the permission of the David and Lucille Packard Foundation.

"The time has come for a new conception of the responsibilities of the school," the reformer writes. The lives of youth in cities are desperate, parents "bring up their children in surroundings which make them in large numbers vicious and criminally dangerous," and some agency must take charge of "the entire problem of child life and master it." It is clear who should do so: "If the school does not assume this responsibility, how shall the work be done?" An urban superintendent agrees: The school should "serve as a clearinghouse for children's activities so that all child welfare agencies may be working simultaneously and efficiently, thus creating a child world within the city wherein all children may have a wholesome environment all of the day and every day." A sociologist echoes this idea: All agencies dealing with "neglected or behavior-problem children" should "be closely coordinated" under the aegis of the school, including "medical inspection, school nursing, attendance control, vocational guidance and placement, psychological testing, visiting teachers and special schools and classes."

The reformer was the muckraker Robert Hunter, writing in 1904. The superintendent was William Wirt, of Gary, Indiana, speaking in 1923. The sociologist was Thomas D. Eliot, who, in 1928, urged a blending of education and other forms of child welfare.

The "forgotten half" in today's reform movement has its precursor in Jacob Riis's *How the Other Half Lives.*[4] For a century reformers have called for school-based social services to prevent or remedy ill health, crime, child neglect, poverty, dropping out, addiction, hunger, pain, and unemployment.

During the years from 1890 to World War I, in the Progressive Era, activist writers like Jacob Riis, Robert Hunter, and John Spargo cast a bright light on the suffering of children—the wasting of the next generation—and cried out for action. Reformers pressed for school lunches, medical and dental inspections and clinics, classes for handicapped and sick children, vocational guidance and placement, school social workers to counsel wayward youth and to assist their parents, summer schools to provide recreation and learning for urban children in the long hot summers, and child welfare officers to deal with truant and delinquent youth. Some reformers created schools that were social centers, community-based institutions that provided counseling about welfare services, job training, English classes, recreation, crafts, sports, and civic instruction for all members of immigrant families in city ghettos. These ideas have been periodically rediscovered, as in the war on poverty of the 1960s.

Today, once again, reformers mount a concerted campaign to provide more and better-coordinated health and social services for children and their families. Current services are too skimpy and fragmented, they argue, and it is essential to create collaboration among different agencies that deal with health, delinquency, mental health, welfare, recreation, before- and after-school child care, nutrition, and various kinds of counseling.

What perspectives does the history of health and social services offer to policymakers today? Who pro-

---

[4]William T. Grant Foundation Commission on Work, Family, and Citizenship. *The forgotten half: Non-college youth in America.* Washington, D.C.: William T. Grant Foundation, 1988; Riis, J. *How the other half lives.* New York: Scribner, 1902.

posed such services in the past and why? Who were the targets for these reforms? How did the "clients" react? How did public school employees respond to the new social services? To what degree did the new programs become embedded in the everyday operation of schools? Under what circumstances did the reforms succeed, and when and why were they abandoned or so transformed that they lost their original purposes? This essay suggests some answers to these questions and explores implications for reform in school-linked health and social services today.

Who Proposed Health and Social Services in the Progressive Era and Why?

Initially, the impetus for health and social services in education came mostly from outside the schools. Through vivid articles in popular magazines and books, muckrakers aroused public concern about children, especially the immigrant poor in city slums. Different groups of activists took the lead in different reforms, often beginning a service on a volunteer basis and then persuading school boards to adopt it as part of the school structure. Public health doctors; local, state, and national medical groups; and dentists interested in preventive medicine and dentistry, for example, were the pioneers in providing free inspections and clinics. Women's clubs took the initiative in many reforms, including free or inexpensive school meals, transportation and special classes for sickly or handicapped children, playgrounds, and vacation schools. In many cities park and recreation programs collaborated with school districts in planning sites and sharing facilities. Settlement-house workers developed model programs for social work and vocational counseling and placement—models that the public schools adopted. Foundations and the federal government publicized and sometimes financed the new health and social services.

Schools were attractive targets for reformers seeking to improve the health and welfare of children, for schools provided sustained contact with children and a captive audience. Often, voluntary groups and school authorities collaborated for an extended period and cofunded activities. The voluntary groups usually saw their favored service as a cause rather than job they intended to perform for pay. When the new reforms became incorporated as part of the school bureaucracy, with specialists paid by public funds, the character and clientele of the innovative program sometimes changed.

* * *

. . . [E]lite reformers usually thought they knew what was best for immigrants; the elite seldom asked their clients' opinions about new social and health programs. Many of the reformers used a deficit model to characterize the people they sought to help: Immigrants did not know about proper health care, dental care, or nutrition; they did not possess acceptable civic values; and they did not know how to raise children. The reformers had a utopian faith, however, that their services could fix people: Clean mouths could produce clean minds; proper playgrounds could eliminate juvenile delinquency; adenoidectomies could prevent academic failure; and vocational counselors could mesh youth with jobs through a smooth process of social engineering.

The elite reformers' clients were often on better terms with reality than the reformers. They found some programs helpful though they were not cure-alls. Parents were eager to place their children in the supervised vacation schools or to use school facilities for evening adult classes in sewing or English. Families struggling to make ends meet probably welcomed free or subsidized breakfasts and lunches in the schools. Some women who sponsored these meals recognized that the children had different food preferences (in one community school, for example, thick soups for Italians, thin for Irish). Visiting teachers were often able to counsel parents and children and help them adjust to a strange new country.

But many immigrant parents fought the more intrusive activities of those who would "improve" them and their children. This was especially true of their reaction to medical interventions. In New York in 1906, Jewish parents rioted outside a school when a rumor spread that school officials were "slitting the throats" of their children; without parents' permission, doctors were excising students' enlarged adenoids. "During the same year," Reese reported, "1,500 angry Italian mothers in Brooklyn fought police, pelted the local school with stones and other objects, and prevented any medical treatments." A mother complained to a teacher when she received a note from a medical inspector saying that her son smelled bad: "Teacher, Johnny ain't no rose. Learn him; don't smell him."

* * *

Who Received Services and Who Did Not?

Health and social services were originally designed as compensatory treatment for urban immigrants: Middle-class parents were supposed to be able to provide what was needed for their children. Intended for the poor, school services may in fact have gone disproportionately to the well-to-do to the degree that they became institutionalized from 1920 to 1960. One reason is that services cost money. In an educational system based primarily on taxes on local property, as the system was at that time, the result was often more services to the rich and less to the poor.

Whole sectors of the American public had no school services. The worst off were southern rural blacks. African-Americans in the Dine Hollow School in the deep South had no desks or books, not to mention such luxuries as health care. By contrast, rich suburban high schools like the one in Shaker Heights, Ohio, often had large libraries, elaborate lunchrooms, doctors and nurses, and counselors with time to attend to the bruises of upper-middle-class adolescence. New Deal reformers focused their own health and social service efforts directly on poor children rather than putting money into general support for the schools. They did not trust the educational establishment to spend funds on those who needed help the most.

In hard times, like the 1930s, educational leaders have often targeted social services for retrenchment or elimination, in part because they were on the periphery of the system. Meanwhile, the basic academic subjects were the last to feel the knife. Here again, rich communities were often able to preserve services when needy communities were not. Prosperous Evanston, Illinois, kept its health and social services intact during the Great Depression while Chicago cut its social services to the bone. In the present fiscal crisis in Los Angeles, where one in five children is poor and one in three lacks medical insurance, layoff notices went in April 1991 to 276 of the district's 526 nurses and to hundreds of other health workers; relatively few teachers of regular academic subjects received pink slips. . . .

What Are the Developments Since World War II?

Michael W. Sedlak and Robert L. Church noted that during the 1950s educators attempted "to develop and apply social service universally to virtually all students," believing that "even conscientious parents and well-organized families could not guarantee that the delicate task of child rearing would be carried out effectively."[12] Professionals provided health and social services in prosperous suburbs as well as in inner cities, confident that their training and official positions certified their expertise.

During the 1960s, as during the Progressive Era, reformers targeted "particularly disadvantaged populations," especially the poor and minorities in cities, as the recipients of services. Reformers were also concerned with assisting whole families, not only children. A time of vigorous social movements for African Americans, Hispanics, women, and the handicapped, among others, the decade of the 1960s was also a period when education was a vanguard institution in the war on poverty. The federal government passed the Head Start legislation and the Elementary and Secondary Education Act of 1965 (whose Title I focused on the poor) and developed programs to improve nutrition, job training and placement, and health.

As money flowed to schools from these federal and state programs, educators expanded services for the poor. This balanced—somewhat—the uneven distribution of social and health services between the haves and the have-nots, a situation that resulted from the highly uneven tax base of states and individual school districts. But, at the same time, many of the federal sponsors of such programs as well as the poor and minorities themselves questioned the top-down model of the professional caregiver and the passive client.

Like their predecessors in the New Deal,[21] federal poverty warriors of the 1960s often lacked faith in the ability of public educators to understand or assist the poor. Sometimes these reformers bypassed the schools entirely and funneled money for services through community-action agencies of various kinds. When program planners included schools, they often required the participation of client families on advisory boards and as employed aides and other workers. Sedlak and Church observed that reformers sought to "demystify expertise and to undermine professional hegemony . . . by placing racial minorities and the poor in positions of autonomy and authority in the administration of federally-funded programs." Not surprisingly, this produced,

---

[12]Sedlak, M., and Church, R. *A history of social services delivered to youth, 1880–1977*. Final report to the National Institute of Education (Contract No. 400-79-0017). Washington, DC:NIE, 1982.

[21]Tyack, D., Lowe, R., and Hansot, E. *Public schools in hard times: The Great Depression and recent years*. Cambridge, MA: Harvard University Press, 1984.

in schools and other public agencies, conflict with existing authorities, who were accustomed to running health and social services without consulting their clients.

Another source of conflict was the habit federal and state governments had of mandating new services without allocating sufficient new funds to pay for them. A prominent example was the legislation requiring expensive new programs in special education. "As a result," Sedlak and Church noted in 1982, "many educational administrators have begun to withdraw as a constituency vocally committed to preserving non-academic social services."

During the late 1970s and 1980s, talk about education policy began to shift from concern about poverty and equality—and related health and social services—to worries about academic standards and international economic competitiveness. This back-to-basics ideology triggered legislation in almost every state. The new laws were designed to stiffen graduation requirements, improve the performance of teachers, and test students' academic achievement. Nonetheless, as demonstrated by the increasing proportion of school staff who were not teachers . . . schools were increasingly becoming multipurpose agencies—even when the antipoverty fervor of the 1960s diminished.

Today, discussions of education seem to be debates about restoring an imagined golden age of academic rigor. Lost in these debates and ignored even in discussions of school-linked services is an important fact: In the years from World War II to 1991, school administrators, willy-nilly, have become managers of schools that deliver complex social and health services as well as academic instruction. The dimensions of the change are striking. In 1950 teachers constituted 70% of all school employees. In 1986 only 52% of school employees were teachers. In that same period the ratio of pupils to support staff (that is, noninstructional employees) fell from 83 to 30; the absolute number of support staff rose from 303,280 to 1,348,813, not counting the nonteachers who were members of the instructional staff.

* * *

Busing, feeding, counseling, making medical inspections, nursing, supervising play—these became an increasing part of everyday work in school systems from 1950 to 1986. Health and social services were not a new idea advanced by lay reformers, as in the Progressive Era; they were established programs provided by a diverse set of public agencies, including

the schools. Some reformers in the 1990s are asking how to coordinate these services and make them effective where they are most needed.

How Do Current Reform Proposals Relate to History?

Schools have become major agencies of broad social welfare, not just academic institutions. Some see these noninstructional services not as a virtue, but as a diversion from the main task of schools; others would like to see still more school-linked health and social services. To see policy choices today in broad perspective, it may be useful to sketch in broad brush two current conceptions of reform.

The first sketch might be called a vision of a *nation* at risk. According to this view, schools should be lean and mean. Education should radically improve the academic performance of the next generation so that the nation can be viable in international competition. Reacting to reports of lackluster scholastic performance, reformers who share this vision argue that schools should shuck off what they regard as extraneous functions, trim "bureaucracy," and concentrate on strict instruction in the "basics." School administrators are already overburdened and ineffective, these critics say; professionals in education are struggling to reconcile federal and state programs with conflicting mandates, are beset by regulations and legal rulings that tie their hands, and are failing to educate ghetto children. Adding to their burdens by asking them to collaborate with other agencies in providing services would simply make them even less effective in their main task. Some people of this persuasion point to parochial schools as models of lean and effective institutions that attend to academic business while, generally, not performing or coordinating a host of other services.

This vision of a nation at risk has spawned a myriad of proposals for reform. The proposals incorporate ideas from curriculum change to new testing requirements to giving parents a choice of schools by giving them vouchers. This latter strategy would replace the present system of public governance of schools by a regulated market.

The second vision focuses instead on children at risk. According to this view, the key problem in American schooling is that it vastly underserves the poor, especially immigrants and people of color. Child advocates who hold this view would not take away the safety net of health and social services already provided to poor children and their families; instead, they would greatly expand it by coordinating and intensifying existing services that are presently meager and fragmented. Public schools, they contend, should collaborate with other agencies to bring these social and health services to the downtrodden.

In theory, there need be no conflict between seeking higher academic standards and providing school-based services. In practice, however, the two approaches may well collide. . . .

* * *

See also J. Dryfoos, *Full-Service Schools: A Revolution in Health and Human Services for Children, Youth, and Families* 19–43 (1994) (discussing historical precedents for comprehensive school services).

Despite the historical antecedents, full-service schools may seem like a distant prospect. Even so, some cities have begun to experiment with collaborative services. Very often, these new programs are aimed at the "children at risk" described in Tyack's essay.

"A Look at Current School-linked Service Efforts"

J. Levy and W. Shepardson, 2 *The Future of Children* 44–56 (Spring 1992). Reprinted with the permission of the David and Lucille Packard Foundation.

Millions of America's children and families face a combination of circumstances that not only threaten their immediate well-being, but put them at risk of long-term disadvantage. Of the children entering school this year, one in five is living in poverty, many in households with an income far below the official poverty level. Half a million in the incoming class were born to teenage mothers, often at low birth weight, with attendant risks to physical and intellectual development. A significant number were exposed to drugs in utero or carry HIV infection. More than half of these new students are expected at some point during their childhood to live with only one parent, usually the mother, in households that are particularly prone to poverty and stress.

Traditionally, education has been viewed as the means of escape from poverty and disadvantage. Yet today, when a high school education is barely sufficient to secure work that can provide economic stability, one of every four youngsters entering ninth grade will not graduate. In urban areas and areas of concentrated poverty, the outlook is even more dismal.

Although poverty and the other cited conditions cannot always be equated with school failure—many of those "at risk" do succeed. . . .

* * *

Why School-linked Services?

Within the swirl of interest in better connections among the institutions serving children and families, the school is rapidly becoming a central focus. Fundamental to this focus is the continuing popular belief, challenged as it may be by the statistics cited previously, that education is an escape route from whatever problems a child or family may confront. In the domain of social policy, where broad-reaching consensus is rarely found, there is virtually undisputed agreement that education is a good thing, indeed an irreplaceable element in achieving success in the current and future marketplace. A not illogical leap leads to the conclusion that, if supportive services can help ensure educational success and self-sufficiency, then the institution responsible for education should have a part in the provision of those services.

This philosophical basis of interest in school-linked services is complemented by a number of practical reasons. The most important and obvious is that the school is where children can be found and, in fact, is the only institution with which virtually every child and family has contact. The school also offers a cadre of skilled staff that regularly comes into contact with children and families. The quality of these relationships and the extent to which these interactions are fully exploited as opportunities to identify and respond to need are potentially of great significance in constructing an effective system of support. Finally, the school building is an easily accessible physical plant—often one of the few reasonably maintained facilities in a hard-pressed community—that can be used as a center of positive community activity.

A Cautionary Word About Models

The growing interest in cross-sector collaboration as a strategy to secure successful outcomes for children and families, and the specific interest in schools as a focal point in that collaboration, is manifesting itself in a rich base of experimentation with school-linked services.

As more communities begin exploring the idea of a school-linked service strategy, they understandably are eager to extract from this experimentation "models" that can be replicated. Yet, from our perspective, a distillation and promotion of models seems premature. The very diversity of efforts in itself defies categorization into a limited number of structures and approaches. Moreover, because the movement is still so young, there is a lack of hard evidence that what is being tried is indeed effective. Drew Altman, president of the Henry Kaiser Family Foundation and creator of the New Jersey School-Based Youth Service Program when he was that state's human services commissioner, has observed that he hopes "someday soon what we know will catch up with what we believe." With a longer history and the structured evaluation of efforts that is now beginning, in time that should be the case. At this point, however, measures of effect on which to base a solid judgment of "best practice" and "model" are rarely to be found.

A final concern with respect to the idea of models is that, even when the experience and knowledge base is more mature, it is unlikely that there will ever be one or two models that could or should be reproduced "cookie-cutter" style throughout the country. To succeed, a community must develop an approach and tailor program design to capitalize on its particular strengths and opportunities and to respond to its citizens' unique combination of needs and expectations.

Some Current Efforts at School-linked Services

Nonetheless, communities clearly can learn a great deal from one another, and those who have yet to develop their own school-linked service strategy can benefit from the experience of early leaders on this agenda. In the following sections, we describe some promising and informative early efforts, with a particular eye to how they have addressed key elements that go into a school-linked service strategy, such as what the goals of the effort are, who is served, what services are offered, where services are located, and who is responsible for actual service provision.

Reaching Youth at the School Site: The School-Based Youth Services Program — New Jersey

The idea of bringing nonacademic services to the school site is not a new one. The school-based health clinic movement, for example, began in 1970, when the first comprehensive health center offering a range of health and social services was opened on a Dallas campus. But today's widespread activity really dates from 1987, when the New Jersey School-Based Youth

Services Program (SBYSP) was enacted. This was the first substantial effort by a state to link schools and social services to help ensure youngsters' success.

Seeking to assist New Jersey's youth in making the often difficult transition from adolescence to adulthood, the New Jersey Department of Human Services (DHS) initiated this program to place comprehensive services in or very near high schools. There are 30 program sites, at least one in each county and most in low-income urban or rural areas. Managing agencies of local sites include schools, hospitals, social services agencies, and community-based organizations.

The state does not impose a single statewide design, but requires each of the sites to offer at least a core set of services and to operate not only during school hours, but also after school, on weekends, and during vacations. Core services include mental health and family counseling, primary and preventive health services (on-site or by referral), substance-abuse counseling, employment counseling, summer and part-time job development, academic counseling, and referral to other health and social services not available onsite. Recreation is offered by the sites as a way to attract youngsters. Some sites also offer other services, such as day care, services for teen parents, special vocational programs, family planning, transportation, and hotlines.

* * *

SBYSP is one of the few school-linked service programs that is open to any student in a participating school. There are no limiting eligibility criteria, nor does a student have to have an identified problem. This open approach is intended to avoid stigma and encourage students to use the center before small concerns become big problems; the high volume of student participation in the centers suggests that this strategy is working. Parental consent is required for all SBYSP services and some family services are available, but generally speaking the target for services is the youngster, not the family.

Preventing "Risk" From Becoming Reality: Project Pride — Illinois

The objective of Illinois's Project Pride was similar to that of New Jersey's SBYSP — to provide school-based support to high school students to keep them on a successful track. In Illinois, however, both the target population and services provided were narrower in scope. This program, which began in 1986 as a federal demonstration project, closed at the end of the 1990–91 school year because funding was no longer available. Its reported results and its truly preventive orientation are notable enough, however, that the program merits continued attention.

Project Pride, located in Joliet West High School, sought to improve future prospects for girls whose families were receiving Aid to Families with Dependent Children (AFDC). Program participants had not necessarily manifested any problems, but research suggests that family circumstances such as theirs put them at risk for too-early childbearing and future welfare dependency. Many of the participants came from families who had been welfare recipients for several generations; Project Pride aimed to break the "cycle of dependence" by helping these girls gain the skills, knowledge, and personal confidence to achieve economic self-sufficiency as adults.

In its first year, with $150,000 in federal funds and $60,000 in state funds, Project Pride enrolled 59 students; additional students were added each year. After the federal demonstration period ended, funding was provided entirely by the Illinois Department of Public Aid and the school in which the program was housed.

The program focused on enhancing the participants' employability, educational achievement, and personal relationships. Staff located in the school provided individualized case management, as needed. Tutoring, homework assistance, and advice on study skills and test taking helped participants maintain or improve their grades. Through group and individual counseling, Project Pride students learned to develop and sustain mutually supportive relationships with boyfriends, family members, and friends. Volunteer mentors from the business community taught participants the qualities employers value and what is expected in the work world; coached them in interview techniques; and, in some instances, helped them find part-time jobs.

The program reported an 80% high school graduation rate among participants, a remarkable achievement among this high-risk population when compared with the overall national graduation rate of 70% in the same period. Further, the reported number of pregnancies among Project Pride participants has been about half that of Joliet's city-wide average for adolescents since 1986.

Making Connections for Families: Probtsfield Elementary School—Moorhead, Minnesota

At the middle school and high school levels, youngsters are old enough to seek and receive services themselves, although many would argue that the family continues to be important and should be a part of any intervention if at all possible. But at the elementary school level, the family's role and responsibility is undeniably central, and service efforts for children at this age must actively engage the family. Serving the family also means that siblings of a child experiencing difficulties may be reached before they themselves begin to experience problems. The value of a family focus is clearly recognized by teachers and school administrators at Probtsfield Elementary School, who are seeking to help their students by helping the families.

Among Probtsfield's students are youngsters from two nearby housing projects. School personnel were concerned that many of these children were performing poorly on schoolwork, that they and their families had needs that were not being met, and that there was little trust between the families and the school. School officials reasoned that trust could be built and the children's achievement improved if parents saw the school as a source of help in solving problems.

In contrast to the New Jersey and Illinois programs, Probtsfield tackled this objective by developing an effective information and referral capacity in the school, rather than by bringing services to the school site itself. The school began by asking all the human services agencies in the community to contribute information about their services to a resource manual for teachers. A copy of the manual was given to each teacher—making it much easier to use than if there were a copy in the library only—and teachers received in-service training in how to identify problems and make referrals. With the help of the manual and training, teachers now are expected to explore family needs in parent-teacher conferences and to make referrals as appropriate.

To increase the likelihood that the referrals will result in a connection between the family and an agency that can help, agencies have representatives in the school building on the days parent-teacher conferences are held. Even though services beyond the initial conversation are provided off-site, through this arrangement a parent need only walk across the hall, rather than travel across town, to take the first step to act on the teacher's suggestion. Although no formal evaluation has been conducted, members of the school staff believe that many of the concerns that underlie this initiative are now being addressed and that the circumstances of the children who were of priority interest are improving.

* * *

Revitalizing a Community: The Walbridge Caring Communities Program — St. Louis

The preceding examples distinguished between school-linked programs that target only students and those programs that reach beyond the school building to serve the students' families as well. The Walbridge Caring Communities Program (WCCP) goes even further, to address the needs of the community surrounding Walbridge School in St. Louis, where the program is based. Most community residents have low incomes, and the neighborhood is struggling with drug dealing, unemployment, and crime. WCCP is guided by an African proverb — "It takes a village to rear a child" — and seeks to re-create in this extremely challenged community a "village" that can nurture its children and help them succeed.

Caring Communities is a pilot project of four Missouri state agencies — the Departments of Elementary and Secondary Education, Mental Health, Health, and Social Services — and the Danforth Foundation. Its objectives are to keep high-risk children performing successfully in school; to help those children and their families avoid family dysfunction and separation; and to help the children stay out of trouble with the law.

WCCP is co-located with Walbridge School (preschool through grade 5) and a "community school" offering adult education and after-school programs for neighborhood youth. The school principal and the directors of the two co-located programs work as a team to operate a facility that is open more than 15 hours a day.

Referrals to WCCP come mostly from school personnel, although some families living in the community are referred by the courts and the Division of Family Services. WCCP services are both school- and home-based. They include case management, an intensive crisis-intervention program for families at risk of having children removed from their homes, a daytime in-school treatment program for troubled youth who need individual and group therapy, before- and after-school child care, substance-abuse counseling, school nursing services, pre-employ-

ment training and job placement for parents, academic tutoring, and a food bank. Classroom presentations using an Afrocentric curriculum reinforce students' self-esteem as a way to prevent drug abuse, and monthly parent meetings keep families posted on what their children are learning.

Community empowerment is as important a part of WCCP's mission as service delivery. The Substance Abuse Task Force, for example, is organizing anti-drug-dealing marches in which parents, students, and police participate. Empowering the community also means giving the residents a say in how best to use the resources of the participating state agencies in that community. Most of WCCP's $570,000 budget comes from redirected state agency dollars that would have been spent serving children and families in the area. The Advisory Council — drawn in equal parts from parents, community representatives, agency representatives, and school personnel — guides WCCP in deciding how those funds should be used and the services the program should offer.

Outcome data are limited at this point, pending completion of a formal evaluation now under way, but there already is evidence of improved school attendance and achievement and a reduction in problem behavior.

* * *

Rethinking How a City Serves Its Youth: New Beginnings — San Diego

Like WCCP, New Beginnings reaches well beyond the boundaries of a school building and its students. In fact, this initiative did not begin with a school focus; school-linked services are only one component in a multifaceted, citywide effort to ensure the well-being of children and families.

A partnership that spans jurisdictional as well as sector lines and includes both political and professional leadership, New Beginnings involves top executives from the county Departments of Social Services and Health and Probation, the San Diego City Schools, the Community College District, and the city Housing Commission, Parks and Recreation Department, library system, and police force. The county's chief administrative officer and the city manager participate as well.

In mid 1988 these officials began a series of informal but penetrating conversations about the condition of and outlook for San Diego's children and families. As unmet needs and fragmentation of services became focal points of discussion among the executives, they turned to school-linked services as a key strategy in an overall effort to improve the way the city deals with concerns such as the growing number of children in poverty.

For New Beginnings, the concept of school-linked services has already taken multiple forms. A parent-school communication curriculum has been included in the training provided to San Diego welfare recipients participating in California's welfare-reform effort, Greater Avenues to Independence (GAIN). Special procedures have been adopted so that school nurses and the Department of Social Services, working together, can expedite access to benefits and services for pregnant and parenting teens, to help them fulfill the dual roles of student and parent. The Department of Social Services was also an active participant with the school system in designing a new middle school, where the staff now includes a family advocate at the school site to counsel students and staff and coordinate with other agencies.

To explore the potential of using the school site as a locus of more comprehensive service delivery, New Beginnings recently opened a demonstration center at Hamilton Elementary School. Like Walbridge School, Hamilton is in an extremely challenged community. Families in the community and staff in the school and service agencies participated in determining the kind of services the center would provide. Initially, the center has been charged with serving Hamilton's 1,300 students, grades K–5, and their families; future plans include expansion to pre-school-age children. In an innovative twist that helps introduce all families to the center and its resources, basic registration for school now takes place at the center rather than in the school's administrative offices. The center offers parent education classes, adult education classes, and health care services such as immunizations and basic physicals. A team of family services advocates provides service planning, counseling, and some direct services. Complementing the school-based staff is an "extended team." Team members remain in their own agencies but are trained and ready to take referrals from the Hamilton center.

The center opened in the fall of 1991; as yet there are no outcome data available. However, because the New Beginnings leadership itself regards the center as an experiment from which they intend to draw lessons for wider implementation of school-linked services, this endeavor may well eventually provide some of the most useful data about the efficacy of this strategy.

* * *

NOTES AND QUESTIONS

1. *Measuring Success*

How can the success of these varied initiatives be measured? Given the complex objectives, how can priorities be set? For example, if an initiative improves parent involvement but has little impact on academic achievement, is it more or less successful than one that leaves parents largely disengaged but boosts students' test scores? Does the theory behind full-service schools preclude consideration of such trade-offs because it presumes that academic gains can only be achieved through comprehensive change?

2. *The Role of Schools*

Does the full-service school movement transform schools into panaceas for all of the ills that afflict children? Will teachers and administrators in inner-city schools feel even more under siege than they currently do if they are expected to compensate for the general failure of America's social safety net? Are schools the appropriate locus of reformist zeal, or should advocates be demanding comprehensive support for families and communities in crisis as well as for at-risk students?

V. CONCLUSION

Having explored the legal treatment of ethnicity and national origin, disability, and poverty, how do you think the dilemma of difference should be resolved? Is the danger of entrenching difference while trying to eradicate it the same for each of these categories? Are all of these differences equally susceptible of being overcome through a strategy of assimilation? Are the differences equally likely to be reconstructed as positive attributes in a pluralistic society? Has the law wrongly tried to use a paradigm based on race to address other forms of difference? Is the law evolving in ways that are sensitive to the unique issues associated with ethnicity and national origin, disability, and poverty? Has the law been successful in transforming school cultures to promote equal educational opportunity? Or do federal protections remain a formal promise for most children, rather than a real chance to learn?

Equal Educational Opportunity
and School Finance

I. INTRODUCTION

The denial of equal educational opportunity is, as shown in previous chapters, one doctrinal source for objection to discrimination based on race or gender. But for policymakers and courts, the concept has other meanings and uses as well. Historically, educational opportunity has been defined primarily in resource (or input) terms; its elements included a universally available and free education, a common curriculum, and equality of resources—teachers, texts, and the like—within a given school district. *See* Coleman, "The Concept of Equality of Educational Opportunity," 38 *Harv. Educ. Rev.* 7 (1968). In the last thirty years, however, the contending definitions of equal opportunity have multiplied, with increasing sensitivity to spending variations across and among school districts. Others have perceived this critical issue as one of adequacy and not equity.

"Concepts of School Finance Equity: 1970 to the Present"

Robert Berne and Leanna Stiefel, in National Research Council, *Equity and Adequacy in Education Finance* 7-24 (1999). Reprinted by permission.

* * *

The idea of providing opportunity by using education as a vehicle has occupied social scientists and educational policy makers throughout the twentieth century. . . . Early school finance work focused on the resources available to children (inputs), although the authors of this work implicitly assumed that equalizing resources would also equalize performance and life outcomes. We now know that the linkages between inputs and outputs are complicated. While a common statement among experts in education is that changing resource allocation can lead to improvements in outputs if schools use their funds productively, the enormous literature on education production functions is not conclusive about which specific resources, under which particular circumstances, will affect outputs and outcomes. . . .

In addition to conceptual issues about the extent to which finance inputs are related to improving performance, fairness in financing also runs headlong into the particular American way of funding and delivering public primary and secondary education. All 50 states [with the exception of Hawaii] create public school systems that are generally organized into local school districts and rely heavily on financing from local property taxes. Property taxes in turn are based on property values that are unequally distributed across school districts and across states. Beginning at the turn of the century, the traditional policy response to inequities caused by unequal property tax bases has been to restructure state financing systems to mitigate the disequalizing effects within states while still maintaining the 50-state system.

* * *

The 1970s mark the beginning of a significant period to examine school finance equity. . . . The early 1970s were watershed years, most dramatically marked by the California Supreme Court's decision against the state in *Serrano v. Priest I*. This landmark case declared that "the quality of education may not be a function of wealth other than the wealth of the state as a whole" and ushered in a series of court cases, academic studies, and legislative changes focused on the equity of state school financing systems. . . .

Distinctions Implicit in Analyzing School Finance Equity

. . . A school finance system is a set of formulas and rules for using publicly collected revenues to pay for K–12 education. In the United States, each state is responsible for K–12 education within its borders and thus the school finance system is established in state law, often supplemented by state department of education regulations. Revenues to finance K–12 education come almost equally from state and local sources (about 93 percent of the total) and only in a small percentage from federal sources (about 7 percent of the total). State revenues are derived from each state's general tax and other revenues, consisting in most states primarily of sales and income taxes. Local revenues are derived mostly from property taxes and, to a lesser extent, from local sales and income taxes. States usually delegate responsibility for provision of K–12 education to local school districts and then design complex formulas to govern how state funds will be distributed to those districts. A general formula often applies to all students, with varying numbers of special formulas for different types of students (e.g., at-risk, gifted, handicapped), for specific types of spending (e.g., transportation, buildings), and for differences among districts in costs and size. In addition, state legislators often design some of the formulas to provide more money to poorer districts and/or to match local spending more generously for poorer districts. The federal government's aid to states and local school districts is almost entirely for special needs students such as economically disadvantaged or at-risk (Title I) or disabled (P.L. 94-142).

Once the formulas are in place, school districts "respond" to them by deciding how much to spend per pupil. Increasingly over the last 30 years, voters in states have placed limits on how much can be spent from local sources and sometimes state sources as well. . . .

Child Versus Taxpayer Perspectives

When equity is approached out of a concern for opportunity, in many people's minds the child or student perspective is paramount. Thus, school-age children are most often the subject of an equity definition in school finance. Because we are discussing the financing of education with public funds, however, taxpayers are sometimes brought into definitions along with the children. Occasionally, the interests of both groups are served simultaneously in the same definition.

When children are the subject of equity definitions, differences among the children, such as whether they speak English as a second language, are mildly or severely handicapped, have learning disabilities, or are poor or minority, become important. Resources made available to different groups of children are often the principal concern of equity discussions, sometimes with the emphasis on fairness of access, but increasingly with an eye toward how differing resources relate to the costs of bringing each group of children to an acceptable (or adequate) performance level.

The school finance and public finance conceptions of taxpayer equity do not always conform to one another. From a school finance perspective, a system would be judged fair to taxpayers if every taxpayer was assured that a given tax rate would translate into the same amount of spending per pupil regardless of where the taxpayer lived. From a public finance perspective, on the other hand, a system would be judged fair to taxpayers on the basis of either the ability to pay or the benefit principle. The ability to pay principle enables one to judge how fairly tax burdens change as ability to pay changes. Tax burdens are defined as reductions in welfare, usually measured by changes in income, and ability to pay is usually measured by annual or average lifetime income. Thus, while school finance taxpayer equity compares tax rates to spending per child, public finance taxpayer equity compares tax burdens to ability to pay.

The benefit principle states that, where possible, taxation should relate to the value of the services that the tax provides. This idea can only apply when a direct relationship exists between a particular tax and a service (e.g., tolls and highway maintenance) and when the service does not involve a significant public goods aspect. While some have tried to link local property taxation and K–12 education in this way, it is difficult to do in states that finance large shares of K–12 education through general state taxes.

In general, neither the courts nor advocates nor researchers in school finance have focused on the public finance concepts of equity; rather, they have based taxpayer equity on the idea of fairness of tax rates faced by or effort exerted by districts. Some exceptions to this are the occasional discussion of whether commercial or utility property should be made a statewide asset for school finance purposes or whether a major change in the school finance system will result in such large changes in residential property values as to undo the intended direction of equity (i.e., will changes be capitalized into property values in ways that make unclear the direction of change for taxpayers' real tax burdens?). But aside from these occasional discussions of commercial property or capitalization, the vast majority of school finance work on taxpayer equity has not used public finance ideas.

The Unit of Analysis

States, districts, schools, and students grouped by socioeconomic or other characteristics have all been used as units of analysis in school finance equity analyses. The federal government and analysts have often compared and ranked states according to their school finance equity. Common questions using the state as the unit of analysis are (1) Is state A more equitable than state B? and (2) Has equity improved in state C? For any given state, the unit in most instances is the district because the financing and provision of public education are carried out largely through local school districts. Within districts, schools have been important in two court cases and, in urban districts with large numbers of schools, researchers and policy makers are increasingly interested in intra-district equity. In addition, the school reform movement that emphasizes school-based decision making, including budgetary decisions, potentially elevates the school to a position of particular interest. Although the individual student is rarely the unit of analysis, groups of students (e.g., poor versus rich, minority versus non-minority, handicapped versus non-handicapped) have been used in some analyses. . . .

Inputs, Processes, Outputs, and Outcomes

One way to understand different approaches to school finance equity is to examine the varying emphases on different stages in the "production" of education. Some definitions of equity focus on inputs—labor, equipment, capital—in their dollar or raw unit forms. That is, the ideal is to have these inputs distributed equitably, which is not necessarily equally. Sometimes the discussion ends here with an assertion that it is inputs, measured in dollars, that should be the focus of school finance equity. In other cases the idea of equity goes beyond inputs to something further along in the education production process. For example, concern about issues such as what occurs in the classroom, what courses students take, or educational tracking can be seen as a focus on equitable processes.

More recently, attention is turning to outputs (e.g., what schools produce, such as types of achievement and graduates) and outcomes (e.g., lifetime accomplishments, such as earnings or health status) that are variously related to what schools do. This output focus is consistent with the attention paid over the past 15 years to the quality of the U.S. education system in general and in comparison with other nations. Focusing on output equity invariably leads to questions about what levels and uses of inputs and processes are required to achieve desired distributions or levels of outputs. . . . [T]hese distinctions begin to hint at how the concepts of equity and adequacy interact. Of course, specifying how processes relate to outputs within a school is very difficult, both because of variations in factors outside the school environment as well as uncertainties about the ways in which dollars and resources are currently used or could be used more effectively within schools. . . .

Alternative Groups of Special Interest

The connections between education equity and opportunity have oriented the discourse around those who are most in need of enhanced opportunities. Low-income, minority, and disabled students are often the most targeted groups in this context, and the same general focus has been applied to low-wealth or low-income taxpayers. Many court cases since the 1970s have focused on property poor school districts. This latter emphasis has proved problematic in some instances because the correlation between poor districts and poor children is not high. . . .

Ex Ante Versus Ex Post Concepts

Ex ante concepts outline the conditions for equity in the statutory formulas of K–12 financing systems. Ex ante concepts analyze the equity of statutory design elements such as the way a formula provides aid for poor versus rich districts or the way a formula is designed to provide additional funding for at-risk students. Ex post concepts are used to analyze actual outcomes that result from behavioral changes of school districts as they respond to the design elements of a school finance system. These observed outcomes may or may not differ from the intended, ex ante ones. For example, legislators might design a school finance formula that matches spending in a property-poor local school district at some multiple of the matching rate of a property-rich local district. Such a formula would have elements of ex ante equity with respect to property-poor and -rich districts. Ex post, however, as property-poor school districts respond to the matching rate, they might or might not spend equally per child compared to property-rich districts. For example, property poor districts might spend less per child for any number of reasons, including that the matching rate was not high enough or that other factors (e.g., tastes or income levels of residents) were working in the direction of lower per pupil spending.

* * *

Equal Opportunity

The idea that public policy can be designed to improve or equalize the opportunity for some Americans, coupled with the belief in education as one of the most effective institutions in this regard, makes the concept of equal opportunity the logical place to start a discussion of equity concepts. But while it may be the right starting point and the most widely held value, our review of the history of concepts of school finance equity since 1970 suggests that it is perhaps among the more ambiguous concepts of equity.

In positive terms, the general idea of equal opportunity is that all students should have an equal chance to succeed, with actual observed success dependent on certain personal characteristics, such as motivation, desire, effort, and to some extent ability. In negative terms, the idea of equal opportunity is that success should not depend on circumstances outside the control of the child, such as the financial position of the family, geographic location, ethnic or racial identity, gender, and disability. "Success" has been defined in many different ways, including ability to obtain resources (often measured in dollars) while in school, access to high-level curricular offerings, achievement on tests, and accomplishments in life.

Equal opportunity is defined both ex ante and ex post. The ex ante idea is that education should provide access to opportunity or a fair starting line, especially for students who are poor, minority, female, or disabled. An ex ante question to be answered in order for equal opportunity to be achieved is: Are the conditions set up to allow the possibility for all to "succeed"?

* * *

Part of the ambiguity in the concept of equal opportunity is the intermingling of educational and legal concepts within the courts. Equal educational opportunity is an educational concept, while the similar idea of equal protection is a legal concept that extends to a wide array of public services. It is possible that efforts to move the legal concepts of equal protection, and now adequacy, further into educational outcomes and processes (as opposed to just inputs) will encourage the courts to address, with more specificity, the types of curriculum, program, teacher quality, or technology that constitute "equal educational opportunity" or "an adequate education."

The equal opportunity concept is much broader in application to education than in school finance issues per se. School finance equity has stressed one particular formulation of equal opportunity—wealth neutrality . . . . Nevertheless, some of the more general thinking about equal opportunity in education has been influential in the school finance area. One court case and three early books have been particularly influential. *Brown v. Board of Education* (1954) riveted the nation's attention to inequality in educational opportunity, focusing on inequalities due to differences in racial composition of schools. Although the Supreme Court did not tie its findings in the *Brown* case to financing of schools, the subsequent remedies to the findings involved additional financial resources, which quickly affected school finance. . . .

Equality of Educational Opportunity (Coleman et al., 1966), written for the U.S. Office of Education to fulfill a legislative mandate of the 1964 Civil Rights Act, surveyed principals and teachers about students and schools in an effort to understand variations in school resources as well as their effects on student achievement. Its conclusions, the most controversial of which indicated that students' family and other background characteristics were more important than school resources in determining school achievement, set off an academic and public debate that continues today.[15] Production functions relating inputs to outputs have been reestimated using alternative units of analysis, measures of inputs, outputs, controls, and functional forms. The continuing lack of consensus among social science researchers about "whether money matters" has influenced the development of concepts of school finance equity. With the controversy over how outputs are influenced by increasing resources for schools, litigators appear to be reluctant to argue too strenuously for output or outcome equity and perhaps, until recently, academics are also reluctant to try harder to measure output equity. The area of school finance equity is truly one where the major actors (courts, legislators, academics, and the public) are influenced by one another's work.

Christopher Jencks and co-authors followed Coleman et al. with a major collaborative study, culminating in the publication of *Inequality* (1972). *Inequality*'s most broad finding was that reducing disparity in income among adults was most effectively brought about by attacking the problem head-on rather than by trying to change personal characteristics, such as education levels. Income redistribution programs (including more progressive taxation systems) would work better than changing inequality in education services. . . .[16]

The work of Coleman et al. and of Jencks et al. occurred at the beginning of a long line of research on education production functions and in the middle of a body of work on investment in human capital. . . . These works of the 1960s and 1970s that questioned the link between resources and effects in education may have had a very particular influence on the development of school finance equity concepts by convincing those working with school finance equity to stick more closely to inputs and processes, waiting for more definitive, less controversial findings on the link to outputs before using output concepts. More recent work is indeed beginning to challenge the findings of the 1960s. . . .

* * *

Wealth Neutrality

Wealth neutrality as a school finance equity concept specifies that no relationship should exist between the education of children and the property wealth (or other fiscal capacity) that supports the public funding of that education. Alternatively, it specifies that taxpayers should be taxed at equal rates to fund equal education per child (generally defined as equal spending per child).

Wealth neutrality has been formulated both ex ante and ex post. The idea argued in the *Serrano* court cases, that no child's education should depend on the wealth of his neighbors, can be thought of as an ex ante idea. It led to the formulation of the guaranteed tax base (GTB) formula for distributing state aid to school districts, which, in its pure form, is constructed so that districts that levy the same tax rates will spend the same amount of money per pupil. GTB has also been used as a way to achieve ex ante taxpayer equity based on the idea that potential tax rate equity is a good measure of taxpayer equity.

A large amount of school finance research as well as legislative and court activity has focused on the ex post definitions of wealth neutrality. Ex post analysts look for statistical relationships (associations) between education, usually measured in dollars, and school district wealth. They ask whether or not there is an actual association between educational inputs and ability to pay. Much of the earlier work focused on district-level inputs (per-pupil dollars or per-pupil resources, such as staff or teachers) and per-pupil property wealth.

The unit of analysis for wealth neutrality has been the state and its districts. It is not a relevant concept at the school level because schools do not have the authority to levy taxes, but rather districts and/or states levy taxes for the schools within them. At the beginning of the period, the focus was on inputs; now, in addition, users are interested in outputs and outcomes.

In *Private Wealth and Public Education* (1970), Coons et al. set the stage for court and legislative activity in the 1970s in three ways: by establishing an ex ante principle that could be used to argue for

---

[15]One of the most famous and controversial findings of the report was ". . . that schools bring little influence to bear on a child's achievement that is independent of his background and general social context; and that this very lack of an independent effect means that the inequalities imposed on children by their home, neighborhood, and peer environment are carried along to become the inequalities with which they confront adult life at the end of school." [J.S. Coleman et al., *Equality of Educational Opportunity* 325 (1966).]

[16]Christopher Jencks, in a personal communication, now believes there is evidence to support the view that education can change outcomes for disadvantaged students. *See also* [C. Jencks and M. Phillips, *The Black-White Test Score Gap*, 1998].

judicial intervention on the basis of the Fourteenth Amendment (or its state constitutional versions), by demonstrating that the specifics of current state financing systems violated the principle both ex ante and ex post, and by proposing a new system that would remedy the problem. Their ex ante principle was that a child's education should not depend on his neighbor's wealth, and their analyses showed that current financing systems did not prevent such dependence. They proposed the district power equalizing finance formula (DPE, also known as guaranteed tax base or GTB) as a way to make a child's education depend on local effort not wealth. Explicit in their work was an emphasis on inputs and a remedy that preserved local choice.

Trite but true, the rest is history. *Private Wealth and Public Education* wrote the script for *Serrano* and many cases that followed. . . . It also stimulated analytical, legislative, and legal work. Martin Feldstein ["Wealth Neutrality and Local Choice in Public Education," 61 *Econ. Rev.* 75 (1975)] showed that the power-equalizing formula does not in theory sever the relationship between a community's expenditures per pupil and its wealth per pupil. School districts make decisions about spending per pupil based on their local tax price, income levels of residents, and other taste and socioeconomic factors. Feldstein demonstrated that district power equalizing does not correctly offset the effects of DPE's tax price and other wealth related factors and, therefore, districts do not respond in ways that break the positive wealth-spending relationship.

. . . Some state legislatures did change their systems to a form of power equalizing, although none moved to a fully implemented system. In 1986–87, six states used some form of this system, although by 1993–94 the number had dropped to two. . . .

Research using the wealth neutrality concept continues to this day. Using 1991–92 data, the U.S. General Accounting Office [*School Finance: State Efforts to Reduce Funding Gaps Between Poor and Wealthy Districts* (1997)] recently completed a study that concluded that fiscal neutrality has not been achieved in most states: "Although most states pursued strategies to supplement the local funding of poor school districts, wealthier districts in 37 states had more total (state and local combined) funding than poor districts in the 1991–92 school year. This disparity existed even after adjusting for differences in geographic and student need-related education costs. . . ."

Some economists advocate the use of broader tax bases to fund education in order to make it more fiscally neutral and more acceptable to taxpayers. . . .

Horizontal Equity

Horizontal equity, as a children's concept, specifies that equally situated children should be treated equally. A challenge to users of the concept is how to identify students who are "equally situated." When analyzing inputs, researchers have usually defined general education, at-risk (or educationally disadvantaged), and special education students as separate groups. Intra-group equality of inputs is a reasonable criteria to apply to these groups. When the focus moves to outputs, however, horizontal equity is more difficult to apply. Nobody argues that outputs (such as achievement scores or graduation rates) should be the same (perfectly horizontally equitable) for all students. On the other hand, we do not use distinctions such as at-risk or disabled students to justify differences in outputs. Perhaps the idea of a sufficiently high level of achievement for all (one possible version of the adequacy idea) is a more meaningful concept for outputs than is horizontal equity.

* * *

Interestingly, the courts, even in the early 1980s when defendants were using the wealth neutrality concept, often heard testimony about the degree of ex post horizontal equity. States, including California, made arguments that their systems were improving in equity on the basis of measures of horizontal equity. Horizontal equity is a useful concept if it is measured correctly, as intra-group equality, with equally situated groups identified and separated in an analysis. On the other hand, the concept is less useful when analysts apply horizontal equity with no distinctions to all students and all funding streams, as has often been the case in legal analyses.

* * *

The staying power of the concept of horizontal equity is unusual, especially since it could not reasonably be applied to outputs or outcomes. It is most useful as a concept for inputs that involve equally situated students. Such application requires that funding streams meant for compensatory or other purposes (such as gifted programs) be separated from streams meant for all students so that intragroup equality can be measured.

Vertical Equity

Vertical equity, a children's concept that has been used both ex ante and ex post, specifies that differently situated children should be treated differently. Analogous to the challenge for users of horizontal equity, users of vertical equity must identify "differently situated" students. This identification is usually done, implicitly or explicitly, by identifying groups of students who differ in their needs for quality or use of inputs to achieve defined levels of outputs. Thus, in concept, vertical equity ties input equity to output equity. When inputs are "adjusted" for the costs of educating various groups of children, as is often done when vertical equity is measured, the adjustment is meant to indicate the amount of additional resources that are needed (higher costs that are incurred) to bring some students to given output levels. Such adjustments are empirically difficult to execute. For example, many might agree that learning disabled students need more resources, but how much more is not clear. One must define the outputs that are the goal (e.g., minimum competency, maximum potential, sufficient level, the point where the value of the marginal gain in output equals the marginal cost of resources), and all require knowledge of the quantitative relationship between inputs and outputs. Often we do not know enough about these quantitative relationships to know how to adjust resources.

The state and its districts have been the traditional units of analysis for vertical equity analyses. Now, as with horizontal equity, school-level data that allow students and funds to be separated into general education, special education, and other streams are resulting in an application of the concept at the school level, where the separate streams can be linked to the "differently situated" students.

* * *

Vertical equity is an appealing concept to many analysts because it takes into account differences among pupils and (implicitly) outputs. Federal legislation, such as Title I and the Individuals with Disabilities Education Act, is based on a vertical equity idea. [See chapter 6.] Beyond some basic agreements that some children need more resources, however, there is little agreement on how much more. This absence of agreement goes back to the research findings on production functions, which have not been able to pinpoint exactly where and how more resources will result in more achievement.

Adequacy

A Nation at Risk (National Commission on Excellence in Education, 1983) changed the nature of the debate about the goals of public education, shifting it for several years from its preoccupation with equity to concern about achievement, especially achievement of U.S. students compared to those in other countries with developed economies. Later in the 1980s a more balanced public concern emerged, with both equity and excellence as goals. The increased focus on outcomes, the continued appeal of equal opportunity, and the shift in legal strategies . . . have increased the use of the concept of adequacy in educational analyses.

Adequacy could be defined in a number of ways. One definition specifies a level of resources that is sufficient to meet defined or absolute, rather than relative, output standards. In the words of William Clune "adequacy refers to resources which are sufficient (or adequate) to achieve some educational result, such as a minimum passing grade on a state achievement test." ["Accelerated Education as a Remedy for High-Poverty Schools," 28 *Mich. L. Rev.* 481 (1995).]

Lawyers generally make a distinction between adequacy and equity. To us the most useful distinction between adequacy and equity concepts is the focus on sufficient and absolute levels in adequacy and on relative levels or distributions in equity.

There is an ex ante definition of adequacy that involves specifying the kinds of outputs that must be achieved and even how they will be measured. . . . [A]dequacy is also an ex post idea, lending itself to quantification of results on various kinds of outcomes, such as test scores, graduation rates, attendance rates, college enrollment rates, etc. . . .

Adequacy is a child-based concept. Conceptually, the unit could be the individual child, but litigators in state school finance cases have thus far used it as a district-level concept. The concept's unit would probably follow the funding patterns, so if funding were to go to schools, then the schools would be assessed for their adequacy on the basis of levels of achievement of students in those schools.

A distinction between adequacy and the way some equity concepts have been conceived historically is adequacy's emphasis on outputs. The definition of adequacy begins with the idea of adequate performance by students, which requires specifications of performance in various kinds of output dimensions.

But we believe that it is conceptually most useful to maintain the distinction between absolute levels (adequacy) and relative distributions of levels (equity). It is entirely possible for inputs, outputs, and outcomes to be equitable or inequitable, and it is possible for inputs, outputs, and outcomes to be adequate and inadequate.*

* * *

Legislators have also begun to use the concept of adequacy as they consider remedies, even in cases where the court's decision involved equity. . . .

Clune and others say that adequacy is a different concept from equity because it changes the focus from inputs to outputs and because it leaves behind the idea of equal resources for all. As we note above, in a broader view of equity, neither of these distinctions is essential, since outputs and outcomes can be accommodated in equity concepts and because fiscal neutrality, vertical equity, and equal opportunity concepts of school finance equity do not require equal inputs or resources per pupil. The use of minimum, albeit high levels of outputs, rather than the use of the idea of relative levels (distributions) of outputs, does help distinguish adequacy from equity. Whether people would be content to see vast disparities in educational outcomes, once adequacy was achieved, is a matter of speculation. And certainly one can think of equitable situations (condensed distributions) that are inadequate. Perhaps California or some of the low-spending and low-achieving Southern states fall into this latter category.

School Finance Equity As We Enter the Twenty-First Century

Equity is a concept that is steeped in values and requires conceptual clarity to avoid spinning conceptual and empirical wheels and talking past one another. Our review of school finance equity concepts since 1970 suggests that several ideas seem to be reasonably well accepted among researchers, lawyers, and policymakers. First, there are alternative concepts of equity, and no single concept serves the purposes of all users, in part because people have different values and in part because people use the concepts for different purposes (to argue court cases, to design school finance systems, etc.). Second, children and taxpayers each have a legitimate perspec-

tive from which to view equity. Third, we should continue to examine inputs even as we move to using concepts of output equity because many users (e.g., lawyers, the public) find input equity meaningful. And, fourth, given the American structure of primary and secondary education, states and school districts are important units of analysis.

* * *

NOTES AND QUESTIONS

1. Expenditures and Achievement

Professors Berne and Stiefel raise the issue of how to determine what levels of inputs and what processes are required to achieve certain outputs. The relationship of expenditures to student achievement has been the subject of many studies, often with conflicting results and conclusions. Consider the following summary of some of these studies by Lawrence Picus:

Resource Effectiveness Questions

A large body of literature, both in economics and school finance, has focused on production function analyses that attempt to relate inputs to outputs. Studies of this type are useful for answering questions on the effectiveness of resource use and the cost-effectiveness of different programs. To date, production function analyses that attempt to relate the student outcomes to resources have not clearly identified a link between spending and student achievement. Eric Hanushek's work in this field led him to conclude that there does not appear to be a systematic link between student achievement and the level of spending. . . . . He does not suggest that such a link does not exist, only that at the present time schools need to spend the resources they have more efficiently if they are to improve student learning with more money. . . . [See, e.g., E. A. Hanushek, *Making Schools Work: Improving Performance and Controlling Costs* (1994).]

In recent years, a number of authors have challenged Hanushek's findings, arguing that more money does relate to higher levels of student achievement. Hedges, Laine, and Greenwald have argued extensively that if different statistical methods are used to conduct meta-analyses of production function studies, there is a clear link between spending and student achievement. . . . [L.V. Hedges, R.D. Laine, and R. Greenwald, "Does Money Matter? A Meta-analysis of Studies of the Effects of Differential School Inputs on Student Outcomes," 23 *Educational Researcher* 5 (1994).] Ferguson . . . found that 'hiring teachers with

*See Buzuvis, "Education Reform in Response to Judicial Demands for Equity and Adequacy," 86 *Corn. L. Rev.* 644 (2001).

stronger literacy skills, hiring more teachers (when students-per-teacher exceed eighteen), retaining experienced teachers, and attracting more teachers with advanced training are all measures that produce higher test scores in exchange for more money. . . ." [R. F. Ferguson, "Paying for Public Education: New Evidence on How and Why Money Matters," 28 *Harvard Journal on Legislation* 465, 485 (1991).] Other work by Ladd and Ferguson . . . in Alabama found similar links between spending and student achievement. [H. Ladd and R. Ferguson, "How and Why Money Matters: An Analysis of Alabama Schools." In H. F. Ladd (ed.), *Holding Schools Accountable* 299 (1996).]

Cost-effectiveness studies are less common in the educational literature. In part this is due to the difficulty in measuring educational outcomes consistently across children. Cost-benefit analysis, of which cost-effectiveness is a derivative . . . relies on the ability to value both costs and benefits in dollar terms. The difficulty in education is that to compare student achievement we need to rely on various test scores and measures of gain. Because tests in different subjects use different scales, as do different tests of the same subjects, it is virtually impossible to compare the cost-effectiveness of different programs with district- and state-level aggregate cost data.

* * *

Resources Available to Children from Other Sources

An important component of resource availability for students is the services that they, and their families, receive from other government and nonprofit agencies, including religious institutions, food banks, and social service agencies. To fully understand the resources available for each child, some knowledge of these services is also important. The most likely place to get this kind of information is through the parent survey and interview. McCroskey and Meezan . . . show that there is a very high correlation between parent self-reports on social services received and social worker reports on family receipt of these services. [J. McCroskey and W. Meezan, *Family Preservation and Family Functioning* (1997).]Thus it might be possible to develop reasonable data on what other services are available to children through the addition of items to the parent survey.

In addition to public or quasi-public services, the time parents spend helping their children with homework after school is an important educational resource, as is knowledge of the parents' income and educational attainment. In addition, some measure of the number of books in the home, and whether the child's family has a computer, may provide information on resources available to each child that might help in linking educational resources to student outcomes—even if those resources are found outside the traditional school.

In summary, although no studies to date have looked systematically at student-level resource allocation patterns, it is clear that much of the school finance community would benefit from such knowledge. . . .

Picus, "Student-Level Finance Data: Wave of the Future," *The Clearing House*, Nov./Dec. 2000 at 75, 76–77.

Do these studies suggest that approaches to school finance reform that emphasize fiscal equalization or inputs to schooling are not likely to have any impact on the quality of education? Do they suggest a different remedy for inequities in resources than in outcomes? How might a remedy be devised to affect outcomes? Can courts only address problems in the process that have led to inequities in funding, rather than requiring new funds into areas that will make a difference?

2. Non-School Factors that Affect Achievement

How, if at all, should courts and policymakers take account of resources available to students outside of public education? What if the resources come from personal family wealth or from corporate contributions to particular schools or districts?

3. Adequacy

How should an adequate education be defined? What is the difference between a minimum education entitlement and an entitlement to an adequate education? What impact does the research literature on student achievement have on the adequacy approach?

II. INTERDISTRICT INEQUALITIES

A. Introduction

As the materials in the previous section emphasize, there exists in all states (except perhaps Hawaii which constitutes a single school district) a wide range of per-pupil expenditures among local school districts. Whether this difference constitutes a "problem" depends upon the standard one chooses for assessing the system. One of the first efforts to define the problem and seek a solution through the courts is represented by the decision in *McInnis v. Shapiro*, 293 F.Supp. 327 (N.D. Ill. 1968), *aff'd sub nom.*, *McInnis v. Ogilvie*, 394 U.S. 322, 89 S.Ct. 1197, 22 L.Ed.2d 308 (1969). The data in the case showed that per-pupil expenditures among school districts varied between $480 and $1,000 despite some effort on the part of the state through its state aid formula to equalize differences. The plaintiffs in the case argued that these differences were unconstitutional but seemed to suggest different and conflicting reasons for this conclusion. On the one hand, the plaintiffs argued that only a financing scheme that apportioned funds according to the needs of the students would satisfy the Fourteenth Amendment. However, they also suggested that a system that allocated funds on the basis of flat dollar equality or assured that equal tax rates yielded equal dollars would be constitutionally permissible. The district court did not dwell on this confusion but denied relief on a variety of grounds: a lack of judicially manageable standards, the rationality of the system insofar as it promoted local control, the fact that the allocation of public revenues was a basic policy decision more appropriately handled by a legislature than a court, and the fact that the Constitution did not require allocation either on the basis of need or on the basis of equal dollars per pupil.

Although the *McInnis* case was a setback to those seeking to reform educational finance, it did not signal the end of attempts to use the courts for that purpose. The reform effort was set in motion again with the publication of two books: A. Wise, *Rich Schools, Poor Schools: The Promise of Equal Educational Opportunity* (1968) and J. Coons, W. Clune, and S. Sugarman, *Private Wealth and Public Education* (1970), noted in the previous section. Of these, the latter was destined to become the moving force behind two of the most notable school finance cases, *Serrano v. Priest, infra*, and *San Antonio Independent School District v. Rodriguez, infra*.

Coons and his colleagues argued that Supreme Court precedent could be read to support the following proposition: The quality of public education may not be a function of wealth other than the total wealth of the state. Coons, Clune, and Sugarman, *supra* at 304. They called this proposition the *principle of fiscal neutrality*, in that it is designed to sever the correlation between local district property wealth per pupil and the amount of money spent per pupil. Fully implemented, the proposition would achieve the result that equal tax rates produced equal yields. It would not require that districts choose the same tax rates, however, thus preserving local control over how much money was to be raised locally. Inequalities in expenditures could persist under this standard, but they would not be caused by inequalities in property wealth per pupil. An important assumption

was that the principle of fiscal neutrality would achieve not just taxpayer equity but also educational equity, because equal fiscal capacity—it was hoped and predicted—would mean that educational offerings would be equalized among districts. As just noted, however, the equalization of educational offerings is not a necessary result of the application of the fiscal neutrality principle.

Coons, Clune, and Sugarman fastened on the principle of fiscal neutrality for a number of legal, tactical, and policy reasons. First, they believed that the Supreme Court's own precedents seemed to be moving toward the notion that government may not discriminate on the basis of wealth. For example, in *Griffin v. Illinois*, 351 U.S. 12, 76 S.Ct. 585, 100 L.Ed. 891 (1956), and *Douglas v. California*, 372 U.S. 353, 83 S.Ct. 814, 9 L.Ed.2d 811 (1963), the Supreme Court ordered that a state must provide indigent criminal defendants appealing their convictions with a free trial transcript and a lawyer, respectively. These cases, it was argued, established the proposition that the "poor" constituted a "suspect" class entitled to special judicial protection and that governmental differences in treatment between rich and poor could only be sustained under the Fourteenth Amendment's equal protection clause if the government had a compelling interest and the differences in treatment were necessary to the achievement of that interest. It was thus an easy step to say that it was discrimination on the basis of wealth when the amount of money spent on a child (the quality of a child's education) differed depending upon the property wealth of the district in which the child resided. This was discrimination on the basis of school district wealth, equally as obnoxious as the discrimination on the basis of personal wealth that occurred in the cases of *Griffin* and *Douglas*.

Second, it was argued that education was a "fundamental interest," as that term was understood by the Supreme Court in the context of the equal protection clause; hence, since the finance system affected a fundamental interest, the courts had to examine the system in light of the strict scrutiny standard of review. Coons and his colleagues contended that the finance system could not survive strict scrutiny; that is, it did not serve a compelling state interest, and that even if local control were a compelling interest, the existing system was not "necessary" to the achievement of local control. Other finance systems would serve the interest of local control and yet not make the quality of a child's education a function of local district wealth.

Third, Coons and his coauthors also believed that the fiscal neutrality principle would be acceptable to the courts because it was judicially manageable and did not involve the courts in usurping the prerogative of the state legislatures to design their own system of school finance. The principle could be complied with in a number of different ways, and the choice among these ways was to be left to the legislature.

NOTES AND QUESTIONS

1. Alternative Revenue Sources

What are alternatives to the local property tax as sources of revenue that a legislature might choose? An increase in state taxes, particularly the sales or income taxes, or the imposition of a statewide property tax for education, would offer more flexibility in raising funds for education than a local property tax because they would not be subject to annual local voter approval. Statewide taxes would also break the connection between per-pupil spending and local district wealth. If either the state sales tax or the state income tax were used alone as the substitute revenue producer for revenues raised from local property taxes, the impact on taxpayers in many states would be significant. One study showed that California would have had to increase its state sales tax by 5 cents on the dollar to replace revenues generated by all local school property taxes; using the state income tax to replace revenues generated by all local school property taxes would have necessitated an increase of 125 percent. B. Levin, M. Cohen, T. Muller, and W. Scanlon, *Paying for Public Schools: Issues of School Finance in California* 31 (1972). Thus, use of either the state sales tax or the state income tax as the sole substitute for revenues raised by the local property tax may not be politically feasible. The use of a statewide property tax, however, also creates problems. A statewide property tax that would generate the same amount of revenue produced by the local property tax in a state would mean that large cities in particular would have a heavy tax burden. Generally, in major urban areas there are comparatively low property taxes for education but high property taxes for other public services. Increasing the property tax might hasten the deterioration of some cities. A statewide property tax would also mean substantial increases in the tax rates of rural areas. Levin, "Alternatives to the Present System of School Finance: Their Problems and Prospects," 61 *Georgetown L.J.* 879, 911–12 (1973).

2. Alternative Methods of Distributing Resources

Alternative distribution criteria can be grouped into several categories: (1) full state funding alternatives with state aid distribution formulas that require no local contribution on the part of districts; (2) partial state funding alternatives with state aid distribution formulas that permit some local contribution and therefore allow the local school district to retain some measure of fiscal autonomy; (3) redrawing the district boundaries to ensure districts of approximately equal wealth, thus giving each district equal fiscal capacity but allowing individual district choice as to the amount to be raised for education; (4) full state funding with the state providing funds directly to the individual school rather than to the school district; and (5) some variety of family voucher system under which funds are provided by the government to parents to be used for their child's education at any public or private school in which the parent elects to enroll his or her child. Each one of these, of course, raises both fiscal and political problems.

B. Fiscal Neutrality in the Courts

As described in the preceding section, the principle of fiscal neutrality was developed as a way of giving judges judicially manageable standards for determining whether a state's school financing system violated the equal protection clause. The case that follows was the first to apply that principle.

1. Fiscal Neutrality and Federal Equal Protection

Serrano v. Priest
5 Cal. 3d 584, 96 Cal.Rptr. 601, 487 P.2d 1241 (1971).

Sullivan, Justice:
[Plaintiffs' complaint set forth basically two causes of action. First, plaintiff children alleged that the California system of finance relied heavily on local property taxes which caused substantial disparities among the school districts in the amount of money spent per pupil and that this arrangement violated the equal protection clauses of the U.S. and California constitutions because it constituted discrimination

on the basis of wealth. Second, plaintiff taxpayers alleged that, as a direct result of the finance scheme, they were required to pay a higher tax rate than taxpayers in other school districts in order to obtain for their children the same or lesser educational opportunities afforded children in those other districts. Defendants demurred, asserting that none of the claims stated facts sufficient to constitute a cause of action. The trial court sustained the demurrers and dismissed the complaints, and the plaintiffs appealed.

The court examined the California public school financing system, assuming the facts as alleged by the plaintiffs to be correct for purposes of ruling on the legal sufficiency of the complaint. The court noted that the plaintiffs alleged that the heavy reliance of the existing system on local property taxation resulted in differences in the amount of money spent per pupil among the districts, differences which state aid did not equalize. State aid was provided in the form of both a flat grant and in the form of "equalization aid" distributed in inverse proportion to the wealth of the districts. Additional "supplemental aid" was available to subsidize particular poor school districts that were willing to make an extra local tax effort. Nevertheless great disparities remained; for example, Baldwin Park spent $577.49 per pupil in 1968–69, Pasadena, $840.19, and Beverly Hills, $1,231.72.]

. . . [W]e take up the chief contention underlying plaintiffs' complaint, namely that the California public school financing scheme violates the equal protection clause of the Fourteenth Amendment to the United States Constitution.[11]

As recent decisions of this court have pointed out, the United States Supreme Court has employed a two-level test for measuring legislative classifications against the equal protection clause. "In the area of economic regulation, the high court has exercised restraint, investing legislation with a presumption of constitutionality and requiring merely that distinctions drawn by a challenged statute bear some rational relationship to a conceivable legitimate state purpose." . . .

On the other hand, in cases involving 'suspect classifications' or touching on 'fundamental interests,' . . . the Court has adopted an attitude of active and critical analysis, subjecting the classification to strict scrutiny. . . . Under the strict standard applied in such cases, the state bears the burden of establishing not only that it has a *compelling* interest which justifies the law but that the distinctions drawn by the law are *necessary* to further its purpose.

* * *

A.
Wealth as a Suspect Classification

* * *

Plaintiffs contend that the school financing system classifies on the basis of wealth. We find this proposition irrefutable. As we have already discussed, over half of all educational revenue is raised locally by levying taxes on real property in the individual school districts. Above the foundation program minimum ($355 per elementary student and $488 per high school student), the wealth of a school district, as measured by its assessed valuation, is the major determinant of educational expenditures. Although the amount of money raised locally is also a function of the rate at which the residents of a district are willing to tax themselves, as a practical matter districts with small tax bases simply cannot levy taxes at a rate sufficient to produce the revenue that more affluent districts reap with minimal tax efforts. For example, Baldwin Park citizens, who paid a school tax of $5.48 per $100 of assessed valuation in 1968–1969, were able to spend less than half as much on education as Beverly Hills residents, who were taxed only $2.38 per $100. . . .

More basically, however, we reject defendants' underlying thesis that classification by wealth is constitutional so long as the wealth is that of the district, not the individual. We think that discrimination on the basis of district wealth is equally invalid. The commercial and industrial property which augments a district's tax base is distributed unevenly throughout the state. To allot more educational dollars to the children of one district than to those of another merely because of the fortuitous presence of such property is to make the quality of a child's education

---

[11]The complaint also alleges that the financing system violates article I, sections 11 and 21, of the California Constitution. Section 11 provides: "All laws of a general nature shall have a uniform operation." Section 21 states: "No special privileges or immunities shall ever be granted which may not be altered, revoked, or repealed by the Legislature; nor shall any citizen, or class of citizens, be granted privileges or immunities which, upon the same terms, shall not be granted to all citizens." We have construed these provisions as "substantially the equivalent" of the equal protection clause of the Fourteenth Amendment to the federal Constitution. . . . Consequently, our analysis of plaintiffs' federal equal protection contention is also applicable to their claim under these state constitutional provisions.

dependent upon the location of private commercial and industrial establishments. Surely, this is to rely on the most irrelevant of factors as the basis for educational financing. . . .

B.
Education as a Fundamental Right

But plaintiffs' equal protection attack on the fiscal system has an additional dimension. They assert that the system not only draws lines on the basis of wealth but that it "touches upon," indeed has a direct and significant impact upon, a "fundamental interest," namely education. It is urged that these two grounds, particularly in combination, establish a demonstrable denial of equal protection of the laws. To this phase of the argument we now turn our attention.

Until the present time wealth classifications have been invalidated only in conjunction with a limited number of fundamental interests—rights of defendants in criminal cases . . . and voting rights . . . . Plaintiffs' contention—that education is a fundamental interest which may not be conditioned on wealth—is not supported by any direct authority.

We, therefore, begin by examining the indispensable role which education plays in the modern industrial state. This role, we believe, has two significant aspects: first, education is a major determinant of an individual's chances for economic and social success in our competitive society; second, education is a unique influence on a child's development as a citizen and his participation in political and community life. "[T]he pivotal position of education to success in American society and its essential role in opening up to the individual the central experiences of our culture lend it an importance that is undeniable." (Note, "Developments in the Law-Equal Protections" (1969) 82 *Harv.L.Rev.* 1065, 1129.) Thus, education is the lifeline of both the individual and society.

* * *

We are convinced that the distinctive and priceless function of education in our society warrants, indeed compels, our treating it as a "fundamental interest."

First, education is essential in maintaining what several commentators have termed "free enterprise democracy"—that is, preserving an individual's opportunity to compete successfully in the economic marketplace, despite a disadvantaged background. Accordingly, the public schools of this state are the bright hope for entry of the poor and oppressed into the mainstream of American society.

Second, education is universally relevant. "Not every person finds it necessary to call upon the fire department or even the police in an entire lifetime. Relatively few are on welfare. Every person, however, benefits from education . . . ." (Coons, Clune, & Sugarman, *supra*, 57 *Cal.L.Rev.* at p. 388.)

Third, public education continues over a lengthy period of life—between 10 and 13 years. Few other government services have such sustained, intensive contact with the recipient.

Fourth, education is unmatched in the extent to which it molds the personality of the youth of society. While police and fire protection, garbage collection and street lights are essentially neutral in their effect on the individual psyche, public education actively attempts to shape a child's personal development in a manner chosen not by the child or his parents but by the state. (Coons, Clune, & Sugarman, *supra*, 57 *Cal.L.Rev.* at p. 389.) . . .

Finally, education is so important that the state has made it compulsory—not only in the requirement of attendance but also by assignment to a particular district and school. Although a child of wealthy parents has the opportunity to attend a private school, this freedom is seldom available to the indigent. In this context, it has been suggested that "a child of the poor assigned willy-nilly to an inferior state school takes on the complexion of a prisoner, complete with a minimum sentence of 12 years." (Coons, Clune & Sugarman, *supra*, 57 *Cal.L.Rev.* at p. 388.)

C.
The Financing System Is Not Necessary to Accomplish a Compelling State Interest

We now reach the final step in the application of the "strict scrutiny" equal protection standard—the determination of whether the California school financing system, as presently structured, is necessary to achieve a compelling state interest.

The state interest which defendants advance in support of the current fiscal scheme is California's policy "to strengthen and encourage local responsibility for control of public education." (Ed.Code, §17300.) We treat separately the two possible aspects of this goal: first, the granting to local districts of effective decision-making power over the administration of their schools; and second, the promotion of local fiscal control over the amount of money to be spent on education.

The individual district may well be in the best position to decide whom to hire, how to schedule its educational offerings, and a host of other matters which are either of significant local impact or of such a detailed nature as to require decentralized determination. But even assuming arguendo that local administrative control may be a compelling state interest, the present financial system cannot be considered necessary to further this interest. No matter how the state decides to finance its system of public education, it can still leave this decision-making power in the hands of local districts.

The other asserted policy interest is that of allowing a local district to choose how much it wishes to spend on the education of its children. Defendants argue: "[I]f one district raises a lesser amount per pupil than another district, this is a matter of choice and preference of the individual district and reflects the individual desire for lower taxes rather than an expanded educational program, or may reflect a greater interest within that district in such other services that are supported by local property taxes as, for example, police and fire protection or hospital services."

We need not decide whether such decentralized financial decision-making is a compelling state interest, since under the present financing system, such fiscal freewill is a cruel illusion for the poor school districts. We cannot agree that Baldwin Park residents care less about education than those in Beverly Hills solely because Baldwin Park spends less than $600 per child while Beverly Hills spends over $1,200. As defendants themselves recognize, perhaps the most accurate reflection of a community's commitment to education is the rate at which its citizens are willing to tax themselves to support their schools. Yet by that standard, Baldwin Park should be deemed far more devoted to learning than Beverly Hills, for Baldwin Park citizens levied a school tax of well over $5 per $100 of assessed valuation, while residents of Beverly Hills paid only slightly more than $2.

In summary, so long as the assessed valuation within a district's boundaries is a major determinant of how much it can spend for its schools, only a district with a large tax base will be truly able to decide how much it really cares about education. The poor

district cannot freely choose to tax itself into an excellence which its tax rolls cannot provide. Far from being necessary to promote local fiscal choice, the present financing system actually deprives the less wealthy districts of that option. . . .

The judgment is reversed and the cause remanded to the trial court with directions to overrule the demurrers and to allow defendants a reasonable time within which to answer.

Wright, C. J., and Peters, Tobriner, Mosk and Burke, JJ., concur.

[The dissenting opinion of Justice McComb is omitted.]

NOTES AND QUESTIONS

1. California Legislature's Initial Response to Serrano

After the California Supreme Court's decision in *Serrano I*, the California legislature passed an act (SB 90) that altered, in some important respects, the educational finance system of California. While primarily intended to provide property tax relief, SB 90 did attempt to respond to the constitutional challenge of *Serrano I*. Most significantly, the law placed a ceiling on how quickly districts increase their revenues. High-spending districts were limited to a smaller increase than low-spending districts. Thus, over time, low-spending districts could catch up with high-spending districts, assuming the high-spending districts did not exercise their prerogative under SB 90 to vote a tax override that would lift the ceiling on expenditure increases. One study has shown that this assumption was not a valid one. Voters approved approximately 40 percent of 580 referenda to override the ceiling on expenditure increases. Fischel, "Did *Serrano* Cause Proposition 13?" 42 *National Tax J.* 465 (1989).

2. Reaction to Serrano

Serrano articulated the principle that the quality of a child's education cannot be a function of the wealth of his or her parents and neighbors. This was translated into a principle of fiscal neutrality that stated that the level of expenditures per pupil may not be a function of wealth, other than the wealth of the state as a whole. This principle was argued to federal and state courts around the country. Within eighteen months of the *Serrano* decision, fifty-three suits were filed in thirty-eight states challenging those states' systems of financing education. One of those suits was brought in Texas where a three-judge federal district court adopted the approach taken by the *Serrano* court and ordered the state to bring the system of financing education into compliance with the principle of fiscal neutrality. *Rodriguez v. San Antonio Independent School District*, 337 F.Supp. 280 (W.D. Tex. 1971). The State of Texas appealed to the Supreme Court.

San Antonio Independent School District v. Rodriguez

411 U.S. 1, 93 S.Ct. 1278, 36 L.Ed.2d 16 (1973).

Mr. Justice Powell delivered the opinion of the Court.

This suit attacking the Texas system of financing public education was initiated by Mexican-American parents whose children attended the elementary and secondary schools in the Edgewood Independent School District, an urban school district in San Antonio, Texas. They brought a class action on behalf of school children throughout the State who are members of minority groups or who are poor and reside in school districts having a low property tax base. Named as defendants were the State Board of Education, the Commissioner of Education, the State Attorney General, and the Bexar County (San Antonio) Board of Trustees. . . . For the reasons stated in this opinion we reverse the decision of the District Court [holding the Texas school finance system unconstitutional under the Equal Protection Clause of the Fourteenth Amendment]. . . .

Recognizing the need for increased state funding to help offset disparities in local spending and to meet Texas' changing educational requirements, the state legislature in the late 1940's undertook a thorough evaluation of public education with an eye toward major reform. In 1947, an 18 member committee, composed of educators and legislators, was appointed to explore alternative systems in other States and to propose a funding scheme that would guarantee a minimum or basic educational offering to each child and that would help overcome interdistrict disparities in taxable resources. The Committee's efforts led to the [establishment of] . . . the Texas Minimum Foundation School Program. Today this Program accounts for approximately half of the total educational expenditures in Texas. . . .

The design of [the new] complex system was twofold. First, it was an attempt to assure that the Foundation Program would have an equalizing influence on expenditure levels between school districts by placing the heaviest burden on the school districts most capable of paying. Second, the Program's architects sought to establish a Local Fund Assignment that would force every school district to contribute to the education of its children but that would not by itself exhaust any district's resources. . . .

The school district in which appellees reside, the Edgewood Independent School District, has been compared throughout this litigation with the Alamo Heights Independent School District. This comparison between the least and most affluent districts in the San Antonio area serves to illustrate the manner in which the dual system of finance operates and to indicate the extent to which substantial disparities exist despite the state's impressive progress in recent years. Edgewood is one of seven public school districts in the metropolitan area. Approximately 22,000 students are enrolled in its 25 elementary and secondary schools. The district is situated in the core-city sector of San Antonio in a residential neighborhood that has little commercial or industrial property. The residents are predominately of Mexican-American descent: approximately 90% of the student population is Mexican-American and over 6% is Negro. The average assessed property value per pupil is $5,960 — the lowest in the metropolitan area — and the median family income ($4,686) is also the lowest. At an equalized tax rate of $1.05 per $100 of assessed property — the highest in the metropolitan area — the district contributed $26 to the education of each child for the 1967–1968 school year above its Local Fund Assignment for the Minimum Foundation Program. The Foundation Program contributed $222 per pupil for a state-local total of $248. Federal funds added another $108 for a total of $356 per pupil.

Alamo Heights is the most affluent school district in San Antonio. Its six schools, housing approximately 5,000 students, are situated in a residential community quite unlike the Edgewood District. The school population is predominantly "Anglo," having only 18% Mexican-Americans and less than 1% Negroes. The assessed property value per pupil exceeds $49,000 and the median family income is $8,001. In 1967–68 the local tax rate of $.85 per $100 of valuation yielded $333 per pupil over and above its contribution to the Foundation Program. Coupled with the $225 provided from that Program, the district was able to supply $558 per student. Supplemented by a $36 per-pupil grant from federal sources, Alamo Heights spent $594 per pupil. . . .

. . . For the 1970–1971 school year, the Foundation School Program allotment for Edgewood was $356 per pupil, a 62% increase over the 1967–1968 school year. Indeed, state aid alone in 1970–1971 equaled Edgewood's entire 1967–1968 school budget from local, state, and federal sources. Alamo Heights enjoyed a similar increase under the Foundation Program, netting $491 per pupil in 1970–71. . . .[35]

Despite these recent increases, substantial interdistrict disparities in school expenditures found by the District Court to prevail in San Antonio and in varying degrees throughout the State still exist. And it was these disparities, largely attributable to differences in the amounts of money collected through local property taxation, that led the District Court to conclude that Texas' dual system of public school financing violated the Equal Protection Clause. . . .

. . . We must decide, first, whether the Texas system of financing public education operates to the disadvantage of some suspect class or impinges upon a fundamental right explicitly or implicitly protected by the Constitution, thereby requiring strict judicial scrutiny. If so, the judgment of the District Court should be affirmed. If not, the Texas scheme must still be examined to determine whether it rationally furthers some legitimate, articulated state purpose and therefore does not constitute an invidious discrimination in violation of the Equal Protection Clause of the Fourteenth Amendment.

II

The District Court's opinion does not reflect the novelty and complexity of the constitutional questions posed by appellees' challenge to Texas' system of school financing. In concluding that strict judicial scrutiny was required, that court relied on decisions dealing with the rights of indigents to equal treatment in the criminal trial and appellate processes,[45] and on cases disapproving wealth restrictions on the right to vote.[46] Those cases, the District Court concluded, established wealth as a suspect classification. Finding that the local property tax system discriminated on the basis of wealth, it regarded those precedents as controlling. It then reasoned, based on decisions of this Court affirming the undeniable importance of education, that there is a fundamental right to education and that, absent some compelling state justification, the Texas system could not stand.

We are unable to agree that this case, which in significant aspects is *sui generis*, may be so neatly fitted into the conventional mosaic of constitutional analysis under the Equal Protection Clause. Indeed, for the several reasons that follow, we find neither the suspect classification nor the fundamental interest analysis persuasive.

A

The wealth discrimination discovered by the District Court in this case, and by several other courts that have recently struck down school financing laws in other States,[48] is quite unlike any of the forms of wealth discrimination heretofore reviewed by this Court. . . .

The case comes to us with no definitive description of the classifying facts or delineation of the disfavored class. . . . The Texas system of school financing might be regarded as discriminating (1) against "poor" persons whose incomes fall below some identifiable level of poverty or who might be characterized as functionally "indigent," or (2) against those who are relatively poorer than others, or (3) against all those who, irrespective of their personal incomes, happen to reside in relatively poorer school districts. Our task must be to ascertain whether, in fact, the Texas system has been shown to discriminate on any of these possible bases and, if so, whether the resulting classification may be regarded as suspect.

---

[35]Although the Foundation Program has made significantly greater contributions to both school districts over the last several years, it is apparent that Alamo Heights has enjoyed a larger gain. The sizable difference between the Alamo Heights and Edgewood grants is due to the emphasis in the State's allocation formula on the guaranteed minimum salaries for teachers. Higher salaries are guaranteed to teachers having more years of experience and possessing more advanced degrees. Therefore, Alamo Heights, which has a greater percentage of experienced personnel with advanced degrees, receives more state support. In this regard the Texas Program is not unlike that presently in existence in a number of other States. . . .

[45]E.g., *Griffin v. Illinois,* 351 U.S. 12 (1956); *Douglas v. California,* 372 U.S. 353 (1963).

[46]*Harper v. Virginia Bd. of Elections,* 383 U.S. 663 (1966) . . . .

[48]*Serrano v. Priest,* 5 Cal.3d 584, 487 P.2d 1241 (1971); *Van Dusartz v. Hatfield,* 334 F.Supp. 870 (Minn. 1971); *Robinson v. Cahill,* 118 N.J. Super. 223, 287 A.2d 187 (1972); *Milliken v. Green,* 389 Mich. 1, 203 N.W.2d 457 (1972), rehearing granted, Jan. 1973.

The precedents of this Court provide the proper starting point. The individuals or groups of individuals who constituted the class discriminated against in our prior cases shared two distinguishing characteristics: because of their impecunity they were completely unable to pay for some desired benefit, and as a consequence, they sustained an absolute deprivation of a meaningful opportunity to enjoy that benefit. In *Griffin v. Illinois*, 351 U.S. 12 (1956), and its progeny, the Court invalidated state laws that prevented an indigent criminal defendant from acquiring a transcript, or an adequate substitute for a transcript, for use at several stages of the trial and appeal process. The payment requirements in each case were found to occasion *de facto* discrimination against those who, because of their indigency, were totally unable to pay for transcripts. . . .

Williams v. Illinois, 399 U.S. 235 (1970), and *Tate v. Short*, 401 U.S. 395 (1971), struck down criminal penalties that subjected indigents to incarceration simply because of their inability to pay a fine. Again, the disadvantaged class was composed only of persons who were totally unable to pay the demanded sum. Those cases do not touch on the question whether equal protection is denied to persons with relatively less money on whom designated fines impose heavier burdens. . . .

Only appellees' first possible basis for describing the class disadvantaged by the Texas school finance system—discrimination against a class of definably "poor" persons—might arguably meet the criteria established in these prior cases. Even a cursory examination, however, demonstrates that neither of the two distinguishing characteristics of wealth classifications can be found here. First, in support of their charge that the system discriminates against the "poor," appellees have made no effort to demonstrate that it operates to the peculiar disadvantage of any class fairly definable as indigent, or as composed of persons whose incomes are beneath any designated poverty level. Indeed, there is reason to believe that the poorest families are not necessarily clustered in the poorest property districts. A recent and exhaustive study of school districts in Connecticut concluded that "it is clearly incorrect . . . to contend that the 'poor' live in 'poor' districts. . . . Thus, the major factual assumption of *Serrano*—that the educational financing system discriminates against the 'poor'—is simply false in Connecticut."[53] Defining "poor" families as those below the Bureau of the Census "poverty level," the Connecticut study found, not surprisingly, that the poor were clustered around commercial and industrial areas—those same areas that provide the most attractive sources of property tax income for school districts. . . .

Second, neither appellees nor the District Court addressed the fact that, unlike each of the foregoing cases, lack of personal resources has not occasioned an absolute deprivation of the desired benefit. The argument here is not that the children in districts having relatively low assessable property values are receiving no public education; rather, it is that they are receiving a poorer quality education than that available to children in districts having more assessable wealth. Apart from the unsettled and disputed question whether the quality of education may be determined by the amount of money expended for it, a sufficient answer to appellees' argument is that at least where wealth is involved the Equal Protection Clause does not require absolute equality or precisely equal advantages. . . .

For these two reasons—the absence of any evidence that the financing system discriminates against any definable category of "poor" people or that it results in the absolute deprivation of education—the disadvantaged class is not susceptible of identification in traditional terms.[60]

As suggested above, appellees and the District Court may have embraced a second or third approach, the second of which might be characterized as a theory of relative or comparative discrimination based on family income. Appellees sought to prove that a direct correlation exists between the wealth of families within each district and the expenditures therein for education. That is, along a continuum, the poorer the family the lower the dollar amount of education received by the family's children. . . .

[A] survey of approximately 10% of the school districts in Texas . . . [shows] only that the wealthiest few

[53]Note, "A Statistical Analysis of the School Finance Decisions: On Winning Battles and Losing Wars," 81 *Yale L.J.* 1303, 1328–29 (1972).

[60]An educational financing system might be hypothesized, however, in which the analogy to the wealth discrimination cases would be considerably closer. If elementary and secondary education were made available by the State only to those able to pay a tuition assessed against each pupil, there would be a clearly defined class of "poor" people—definable in terms of their inability to pay the prescribed sum—who would be absolutely precluded from receiving an education. That case would present a far more compelling set of circumstances for judicial assistance than the case before us today. After all, Texas has undertaken to do a good deal more than provide an education to those who can afford it. It has provided what it considers to be an adequate base education for all children and has attempted, though imperfectly, to ameliorate by state funding and by the local assessment program the disparities in local tax resources.

districts in the sample have the highest median family incomes and spend the most on education, and that the several poorest districts have the lowest family incomes and devote the least amount of money to education. For the remainder of the districts—96 districts composing almost 90% of the sample—the correlation is inverted, i.e., the districts that spend next to the most money on education are populated by families having next to the lowest median family incomes while the districts spending the least have the highest median family incomes. It is evident that, even if the conceptual questions are answered favorably to appellees, no factual basis exists upon which to found a claim of comparative wealth discrimination.

This brings us, then, to the third way in which the classification scheme might be defined—district wealth discrimination. Since the only correlation indicated by the evidence is between district property wealth and expenditures, it may be argued that discrimination might be found without regard to the individual income characteristics of district residents. . . .

However described, it is clear that appellees' suit asks this Court to extend its most exacting scrutiny to review a system that allegedly discriminates against a large, diverse, and amorphous class, unified only by the common factor of residence in districts that happen to have less taxable wealth than other districts. The system of alleged discrimination and the class it defines have none of the traditional indicia of suspectness: the class is not saddled with such disabilities, or subjected to such a history of purposeful unequal treatment, or relegated to such a position of political powerlessness as to command extraordinary protection from the majoritarian political process.

We thus conclude that the Texas system does not operate to the peculiar disadvantage of any suspect class. But in recognition of the fact that this Court has never heretofore held that wealth discrimination alone provides an adequate basis for invoking strict scrutiny, appellees have not relied solely on this contention. They also assert that the State's system impermissibly interferes with the exercise of a "fundamental" right and that accordingly the prior decisions of this Court require the application of the strict standard of judicial review. . . .

B

In *Brown v. Board of Education*, 347 U.S. 483 (1954), a unanimous Court recognized that "educa-

tion is perhaps the most important function of state and local governments. . . ." This theme, expressing an abiding respect for the vital role of education in a free society, may be found in numerous opinions of Justices of this Court writing both before and after *Brown* was decided. . . .

Nothing this Court holds today in any way detracts from our historic dedication to public education. We are in complete agreement with the conclusion of the three-judge panel below that "the grave significance of education both to the individual and to our society" cannot be doubted. But the importance of a service performed by the State does not determine whether it must be regarded as fundamental for purposes of examination under the Equal Protection Clause. . . .

. . . It is not the province of this Court to create substantive constitutional rights in the name of guaranteeing equal protection of the laws. Thus the key to discovering whether education is "fundamental" is not to be found in comparisons of the relative societal significance of education as opposed to subsistence or housing. Nor is it to be found by weighing whether education is as important as the right to travel. Rather, the answer lies in assessing whether there is a right to education explicitly or implicitly guaranteed by the Constitution. . . .

Education, of course, is not among the rights afforded explicit protection under our Federal Constitution. Nor do we find any basis for saying it is implicitly so protected: As we have said, the undisputed importance of education will not alone cause this Court to depart from the usual standard for reviewing a State's social and economic legislation. It is appellees' contention, however, that education is distinguishable from other services and benefits provided by the State because it bears a peculiarly close relationship to other rights and liberties accorded protection under the Constitution. Specifically, they insist that education is itself a fundamental personal right because it is essential to the effective exercise of First Amendment freedoms and to intelligent utilization of the right to vote. In asserting a nexus between speech and education, appellees urge that the right to speak is meaningless unless the speaker is capable of articulating his thoughts intelligently and persuasively. The "marketplace of ideas" is an empty forum for those lacking basic communicative tools. Likewise, they argue that the corollary right to receive information becomes little more than a hollow privilege when the recipient has not been taught to read, assimilate, and utilize available knowledge.

A similar line of reasoning is pursued with respect to the right to vote. Exercise of the franchise, it is contended, cannot be divorced from the educational foundation of the voter. The electoral process, if reality is to conform to the democratic ideal, depends on an informed electorate: a voter cannot cast his ballot intelligently unless his reading skills and thought processes have been adequately developed.

We need not dispute any of these propositions. The Court has long afforded zealous protection against unjustifiable governmental interference with the individual's rights to speak and to vote. Yet we have never presumed to possess either the ability or the authority to guarantee to the citizenry the most *effective* speech or the most *informed* electoral choice. That these may be desirable goals of a system of freedom of expression and of a representative form of government is not to be doubted. These are indeed goals to be pursued by a people whose thoughts and beliefs are freed from governmental interference. But they are not values to be implemented by judicial intrusion into otherwise legitimate state activities.

Even if it were conceded that some identifiable quantum of education is a constitutionally protected prerequisite to the meaningful exercise of either right, we have no indication that the present levels of educational expenditure in Texas provide an education that falls short . . . [N]o charge fairly could be made that the system fails to provide each child with an opportunity to acquire the basic minimal skills necessary for the enjoyment of the rights of speech and of full participation in the political process.

Furthermore, the logical limitations on appellees' nexus theory are difficult to perceive. How, for instance, is education to be distinguished from the significant personal interests in the basics of decent food and shelter? Empirical examination might well buttress an assumption that the ill-fed, ill-clothed, and ill-housed are among the most ineffective participants in the political process and that they derive the least enjoyment from the benefits of the First Amendment. If so, appellees' thesis would cast serious doubt on the authority of *Dandridge v. Williams* . . . and *Lindsey v. Normet.* . . .

C

We need not rest our decision, however, solely on the inappropriateness of the strict scrutiny test. A century of Supreme Court adjudication under the Equal Protection Clause affirmatively supports the application of the traditional standard of review, which requires only that the State's system be shown to bear some rational relationship to legitimate state purposes. This case represents far more than a challenge to the manner in which Texas provides for the education of its children. We have here nothing less than a direct attack on the way in which Texas has chosen to raise and disburse state and local tax revenues. We are asked to condemn the State's judgment in conferring on political subdivisions the power to tax local property to supply revenues for local interests. In so doing, appellees would have the Court intrude in an area in which it has traditionally deferred to state legislatures. . . .

[T]he Justices of this Court lack both the expertise and the familiarity with local problems so necessary to the making of wise decisions with respect to the raising and disposition of public revenues. Yet we are urged to direct the States either to alter drastically the present system or to throw out the property tax altogether in favor of some other form of taxation. No scheme of taxation, whether the tax is imposed on property, income, or purchases of goods and services, has yet been devised which is free of all discriminatory impact. In such a complex arena in which no perfect alternatives exist, the Court does well not to impose too rigorous a standard of scrutiny lest all local fiscal schemes become subjects of criticism under the Equal Protection Clause.[85]

---

[85]Those who urge that the present system be invalidated offer little guidance as to what type of school financing should replace it. The most likely result of rejection of the existing system would be statewide financing of all public education with funds derived from taxation of property or from the adoption or expansion of sales and income taxes. See Simon, ["The School Finance Decisions: Collective Bargaining and Future Finance Systems," 82 *Yale L.J.* 409, 439-40 (1973).] The authors of *Private Wealth and Public Education, supra,* n13, at 201-242, suggest an alternative scheme, known as "district power equalizing." In simplest terms, the State would guarantee that at any particular rate of property taxation the district would receive a stated number of dollars regardless of the district's tax base. To finance the subsidies to "poorer" districts, funds would be taken away from the "wealthier" districts that, because of their higher property values, collect more than the stated amount at any given rate. This is not the place to weigh the arguments for and against "district power equalizing," beyond noting that commentators are in disagreement as to whether it is feasible, how it would work, and indeed whether it would violate the equal protection theory underlying appellees' case. President's Commission on School Finance, *Schools, People & Money* 32-33 (1972); Bateman and Brown, "Some Reflections on Serrano v. Priest," 49 *J. Urban L.* 701, 706-8 (1972); Brest, Book Review, 23 *Stan. L.Rev.* 591, 594-96 (1971); Goldstein, *supra,* [n.68], at 542-43; Wise, "School Finance Equalization Lawsuits: A Model Legislative Response," 2 *Yale Rev. L. & Soc. Action* 123, 125 (1971); Silard and White, "Intrastate Inequalities in Public Education: The Case for Judicial Relief Under the Equal Protection Clause," 1970 *Wis.L.Rev.* 7, 29–30.

In addition to matters of fiscal policy, this case also involves the most persistent and difficult questions of educational policy, another area in which this Court's lack of specialized knowledge and experience counsels against premature interference with the informed judgments made at the state and local levels. . . . On even the most basic questions in this area the scholars and educational experts are divided. Indeed, one of the major sources of controversy concerns the extent to which there is a demonstrable correlation between educational expenditures and the quality of education[86]—an assumed correlation underlying virtually every legal conclusion drawn by the District Court in this case. Related to the questioned relationship between cost and quality is the equally unsettled controversy as to the proper goals of a system of public education. . . . In such circumstances the judiciary is well advised to refrain from imposing on the States inflexible constitutional restraints that could circumscribe or handicap the continued research and experimentation so vital to finding even partial solutions to educational problems and to keeping abreast of ever changing conditions.

It must be remembered also that every claim arising under the Equal Protection Clause has implications for the relationship between national and state power under our federal system. . . . [I]t would be difficult to imagine a case having a greater potential impact on our federal system than the one now before us, in which we are urged to abrogate systems of financing public education presently in existence in virtually every State.

The foregoing considerations buttress our conclusion that Texas' system of public school finance is an inappropriate candidate for strict judicial scrutiny. These same considerations are relevant to the determination whether that system, with its conceded imperfections, nevertheless bears some rational relationship to a legitimate state purpose. It is to this question that we next turn our attention. . . .

The Texas system of school finance . . . , [w]hile assuring a basic education for every child in the State, . . . permits and encourages a large measure of participation in and control of each district's schools at the local level. . . .

The persistence of attachment to government at the lowest level where education is concerned reflects the depth of commitment of its supporters. In part, local control means, as Professor Coleman suggests, the freedom to devote more money to the education of one's children. Equally important, however, is the opportunity it offers for participation in the decision-making process that determines how those local tax dollars will be spent. . . .

Appellees do not question the propriety of Texas' dedication to local control of education. To the contrary, they attack the school financing system precisely because, in their view, it does not provide the same level of local control and fiscal flexibility in all districts. Appellees suggest that local control could be preserved and promoted under other financing systems that resulted in more equality in educational expenditures. While it is no doubt true that reliance on local property taxation for school revenues provides less freedom of choice with respect to expenditures for some districts than for others,[107] the existence of "some inequality" in the manner in which the State's rationale is achieved is not alone a sufficient basis for striking down the entire system. . . . The people of Texas may be justified in believing that other systems of school financing, which place more of the financial responsibility in the hands of the State, will result in a comparable lessening of desired local autonomy. That is, they may believe that along with increased control of the purse strings at

---

[86]The quality-cost controversy has received considerable attention. Among the notable authorities on both sides are the following: C. Jencks, *Inequality* (1972); C. Silberman, *Crisis in the Classroom* (1970); Office of Education, *Equality of Educational Opportunity* (1966) (The Coleman Report); *On Equality of Educational Opportunity* (Moynihan and Mosteller eds., 1972); J. Guthrie, G. Kleindorfer, H. Levin, and R. Stout, *Schools and Inequality* (1971); President's Comm'n on School Finance, *supra*, n85; Swanson, "The Cost-Quality Relationship, in The Challenge of Change in School Finance," *10th Nat'l Educational Ass'n Conf. on School Finance* 151 (1967).

[107]Mr. Justice White suggests in his dissent that the Texas system violates the Equal Protection Clause because the means it has selected to effectuate its interest in local autonomy fail to guarantee complete freedom of choice to every district. He places special emphasis on the statutory provision that establishes a maximum rate of $1.50 per $100 valuation at which a local school district may tax for school maintenance. Tex. Educ. Code 20.04(d) (1972). The maintenance rate in Edgewood when this case was litigated in the District Court was $.55 per $100, barely one-third of the allowable rate. [The tax rate of $1.05 per $100, see *supra* at 658, is the equalized rate for maintenance and for the retirement of bonds.] Appellees do not claim that the ceiling presently bars desired tax increases in Edgewood or in any other Texas district. Therefore, the constitutionality of that statutory provision is not before us and must await litigation in a case in which it is properly presented. Cf. *Hargrave v. Kirk*, 313 F.Supp. 944 (M.D. Fla. 1970), *vacated*, 401 U.S. 476 (1971).

the state level will go increased control over local policies.[109]

Appellees further urge that the Texas system is unconstitutionally arbitrary because it allows the availability of local taxable resources to turn on "happenstance." They see no justification for a system that allows, as they contend, the quality of education to fluctuate on the basis of the fortuitous positioning of the boundary lines of political subdivisions and the location of valuable commercial and industrial property. But any scheme of local taxation—indeed the very existence of identifiable local governmental units—requires the establishment of jurisdictional boundaries that are inevitably arbitrary. . . .

Moreover, if local taxation for local expenditures were an unconstitutional method of providing for education then it might be an equally impermissible means of providing other necessary services customarily financed largely from local property taxes, including local police and fire protection, public health and hospitals and public utility facilities of various kinds. We perceive no justification for such a severe denigration of local property taxation and control as would follow from appellees' contentions. . . .

In sum, to the extent that the Texas system of school financing results in unequal expenditures between children who happen to reside in different districts, we cannot say that such disparities are the product of a system that is so irrational as to be invidiously discriminatory. Texas has acknowledged its shortcomings and has persistently endeavored—not without some success—to ameliorate the differences in levels of expenditures without sacrificing the benefits of local participation. The Texas plan is not the result of hurried, ill-conceived legislation. It certainly is not the product of purposeful discrimination against any group or class. . . .

IV

The complexity of these [school finance] problems is demonstrated by the lack of consensus with respect to whether it may be said with any assurance that the poor, the racial minorities, or the children in over-burdened core-city school districts would be benefitted by abrogation of traditional modes of financing education. Unless there is to be a substantial increase in state expenditures on education across the board—an event the likelihood of which is open to considerable question—these groups stand to realize gains in terms of increased per-pupil expenditures only if they reside in districts that presently spend at relatively low levels, i.e., in those districts that would benefit from the redistribution of existing resources. Yet recent studies have indicated that the poorest families are not invariably clustered in the most impecunious school districts. Nor does it now appear that there is any more than a random chance that racial minorities are concentrated in property-poor districts. Additionally, several research projects have concluded that any financing alternative designed to achieve a greater equality of expenditures is likely to lead to higher taxation and lower educational expenditures in the major urban centers, a result that would exacerbate rather than ameliorate existing conditions in those areas.

These practical considerations, of course, play no role in the adjudication of the constitutional issues presented here. But they serve to highlight the wisdom of the traditional limitations on this Court's function. . . . We hardly need add that this Court's action today is not to be viewed as placing its judicial imprimatur on the status quo. The need is apparent for reform in tax systems which may well have relied too long and too heavily on the local property tax. And certainly innovative thinking as to public education, its methods and its funding, is necessary to assure both a higher level of quality and greater uniformity of opportunity. These matters merit the continued attention of the scholars who already have contributed much by their challenges. But the ultimate solutions must come from the lawmakers and from the democratic pressures of those who elect them.

Reversed.

Mr. Justice Stewart, concurring.

The method of financing public schools in Texas, as in almost every other State, has resulted in a system of public education that can fairly be described as chaotic and unjust. It does not follow, however, and I

---

[109]This theme—that greater state control over funding will lead to greater state power with respect to local educational programs and policies—is a recurrent one in the literature on financing public education. Professor Simon, in his thoughtful analysis of the political ramifications of this case, states that one of the most likely consequences of the District Court's decision would be an increase in the centralization of school finance and an increase in the extent of collective bargaining by teacher unions at the state level. He suggests that the subjects for bargaining may include many "nonsalary" items, such as teaching loads, class size, curricular and program choices, questions of student discipline, and selection of administrative personnel—matters traditionally decided heretofore at the local level. Simon, ["The School Finance Decisions: Collective Bargaining and Future Systems," 82 *Yale L.J.* 409, 434–36 (1973)]. . . .

cannot find, that this system violates the Constitution of the United States. I join the opinion and judgment of the Court because I am convinced that any other course would mark an extraordinary departure from principled adjudication under the Equal Protection Clause of the Fourteenth Amendment. . . .

Mr. Justice White, with whom Mr. Justice Douglas and Mr. Justice Brennan join, dissenting. . . .

I cannot disagree with the proposition that local control and local decision making play an important part in our democratic system of government. . . . Much may be left to local option, and this case would be quite different if it were true that the Texas system, while insuring minimum educational expenditures in every district through state funding, extended a meaningful option to all local districts to increase their per-pupil expenditures and so to improve their children's education to the extent that increased funding would achieve that goal. The system would then arguably provide a rational and sensible method of achieving the stated aim of preserving an area for local initiative and decision.

The difficulty with the Texas system, however, is that it provides a meaningful option to Alamo Heights and like school districts but almost none to Edgewood and those other districts with a low per-pupil real estate tax base. In these latter districts, no matter how desirous parents are of supporting their schools with greater revenues, it is impossible to do so through the use of the real estate property tax. In these districts the Texas system utterly fails to extend a realistic choice to parents, because the property tax, which is the only revenue-raising mechanism extended to school districts, is practically and legally unavailable. . . .

. . . If the State aims at maximizing local initiative and local choice, by permitting school districts to resort to the real property tax if they choose to do so, it utterly fails in achieving its purpose in districts with property tax bases so low that there is little if any opportunity for interested parents, rich or poor, to augment school district revenues. Requiring the State to establish only that unequal treatment is in furtherance of a permissible goal, without also requiring the State to show that the means chosen to effectuate that goal are rationally related to its achievement, makes equal protection analysis no more than an empty gesture. In my view, the parents and children, in Edgewood, and in like districts, suffer from an invidious discrimination violative of the Equal Protection Clause. . . .

There is no difficulty in identifying the class that is subject to the alleged discrimination and that is entitled to the benefits of the Equal Protection Clause. I need go no farther than the parents and children in the Edgewood district, who are plaintiffs here and who assert that they are entitled to the same choice as Alamo Heights to augment local expenditures for schools but are denied that choice by state law. This group constitutes a class sufficiently definite to invoke the protection of the Constitution . . . [I]n the present case we would blink reality to ignore the fact that school districts, and students in the end, are differentially affected by the Texas school financing scheme with respect to their capability to supplement the Minimum Foundation School Program. At the very least, the law discriminates against those children and their parents who live in districts where the per-pupil tax base is sufficiently low to make impossible the provision of comparable school revenues by resort to the real property tax which is the only device the State extends for this purpose.

Mr. Justice Marshall, with whom Mr. Justice Douglas concurs, dissenting.

The Court today decides, in effect, that a State may constitutionally vary the quality of education which it offers its children in accordance with the amount of taxable wealth located in the school districts within which they reside. The majority's decision represents an abrupt departure from the mainstream of recent state and federal court decisions concerning the unconstitutionality of state educational financing schemes dependent upon taxable local wealth. More unfortunately, though, the majority's holding can only be seen as a retreat from our historic commitment to equality of educational opportunity and as unsupportable acquiescence in a system which deprives children in their earliest years of the chance to reach their full potential as citizens. The Court does this despite the absence of any substantial justification for a scheme which arbitrarily channels educational resources in accordance with the fortuity of the amount of taxable wealth within each district. . . .

I

The Court acknowledges that "substantial interdistrict disparities in school expenditures" exist in Texas . . . and that these disparities are "largely attributable to differences in the amounts of money collected through local property taxation". . . . But instead of closely examining the seriousness of these disparities and the invidiousness of the Texas financing scheme, the Court undertakes an elaborate exploration of the efforts Texas has purportedly made to close the gaps between its districts in terms of levels of district wealth and resulting educational funding. Yet, however praiseworthy Texas' equalizing efforts, the issue in this case is not whether Texas is doing its best to ameliorate the worst features of a discriminatory scheme, but rather whether the scheme itself is in fact unconstitutionally discriminatory in the face of the Fourteenth Amendment's guarantee of equal protection of the laws. When the Texas financing scheme is taken as a whole, I do not think it can be doubted that it produces a discriminatory impact on substantial numbers of the school-age children of the State of Texas. . . .

* * *

B

The appellants do not deny the disparities in educational funding caused by variations in taxable district property wealth. They do contend, however, that whatever the differences in per-pupil spending among Texas districts, there are no discriminatory consequences for the children of disadvantaged districts. . . .

In my view, though, even an unadorned restatement of this contention is sufficient to reveal its absurdity. Authorities concerned with educational quality no doubt disagree as to the significance of variations in per-pupil spending. . . . We sit, however, not to resolve disputes over educational theory but to enforce our Constitution. It is an inescapable fact that if one district has more funds available per pupil than another district, the former will have greater choice in educational planning than will the latter. In this regard, I believe the question of discrimination in educational quality must be deemed to be an objective one that looks to what the State provides its children, not to what the children are able to do with what they receive. . . .

. . . [I]t is difficult to believe that if the children of Texas had a free choice, they would choose to be educated in districts with fewer resources, and hence with more-antiquated plants, less-experienced teachers, and a less-diversified curriculum. In fact, if financing variations are so insignificant to educational quality, it is difficult to understand why a number of our country's wealthiest school districts, which have no legal obligation to argue in support of the constitutionality of the Texas legislation, have nevertheless zealously pursued its cause before this Court. . . .

At the very least, in view of the substantial interdistrict disparities in funding and in resulting educational inputs shown by appellees to exist under the Texas financing scheme, the burden of proving that these disparities do not in fact affect the quality of children's education must fall upon the appellants. . . . Yet appellants made no effort in the District Court to demonstrate that educational quality is not affected by variations in funding and in resulting inputs. . . .

Nor can I accept the appellants' apparent suggestion that the Texas Minimum Foundation School Program effectively eradicates any discriminatory effects otherwise resulting from the local property tax element of the Texas financing scheme. Appellants assert that, despite its imperfections, the Program "does guarantee an adequate education to every child." The majority, in considering the constitutionality of the Texas financing scheme, seems to find substantial merit in this contention. . . . But I fail to understand how the constitutional problems inherent in the financing scheme are eased by the Foundation Program. . . .

The suggestion may be that the state aid received via the Foundation Program sufficiently improves the position of property poor districts *vis-a-vis* property rich districts—in terms of educational funds—to eliminate any claim of interdistrict discrimination in available educational resources which might otherwise exist if educational funding were dependent solely upon local property taxation. . . . But as has already been seen, we are hardly presented here with some *de minimis* claim of discrimination resulting from the play necessary in any functioning system; to the contrary, it is clear that the Foundation Program utterly fails to ameliorate the seriously discriminatory effects of the local property tax.

Alternatively, the appellants and the majority may believe that the Equal Protection Clause cannot be offended by substantially unequal state treatment of persons who are similarly situated so long as the State provides everyone with some unspecified amount of education which evidently is "enough." The basis for such a novel view is far from clear. . . . The Equal Protection Clause is not addressed to the minimal sufficiency but rather to the unjustifiable inequalities of state action. It mandates nothing less than that "all persons similarly circumstanced shall be treated alike." *F. S. Royster Guano Co. v. Virginia,* 253 U.S. 412, 415 (1920).

Even if the Equal Protection Clause encompassed some theory of constitutional adequacy, discrimination in the provision of educational opportunity would certainly seem to be a poor candidate for its application. Neither the majority nor appellants inform us how judicially manageable standards are to be derived for determining how much education is "enough" to excuse constitutional discrimination. . . .

C

Despite the evident discriminatory effect of the Texas financing scheme, both the appellants and the majority raise substantial questions concerning the precise character of the disadvantaged class in this case. . . .

[W]hile on its face the Texas scheme may merely discriminate between local districts, the impact of that discrimination falls directly upon the children whose educational opportunity is dependent upon where they happen to live. Consequently, the District Court correctly concluded that the Texas financing scheme discriminates, from a constitutional perspective, between school children on the basis of the amount of taxable property located within their local districts. . . .

A number of theories of discrimination have, to be sure, been considered in the course of this litigation. Thus, the District Court found that in Texas the poor and minority group members tend to live in property poor districts, suggesting discrimination on the basis of both personal wealth and race. . . . Although I have serious doubts as to the correctness of the Court's analysis in rejecting the data submitted below,[56] I have no need to join issue on these factual disputes.

I believe it is sufficient that the overarching form of discrimination in this case is between the school children of Texas on the basis of the taxable property wealth of the districts in which they happen to live. . . . In their complaint appellees asserted that the Constitution does not permit local district wealth to be determinative of educational opportunity. This is simply another way of saying, as the District Court concluded, that consistent with the guarantee of equal protection of the laws, "the quality of public education may not be a function of wealth, other than the wealth of the state as a whole."

. . . Whether this discrimination, against the school children of property poor districts, inherent in the Texas financing scheme is violative of the Equal Protection Clause is the question to which we must now turn.

II

* * *

A

To begin, I must once more voice my disagreement with the Court's rigidified approach to equal protection analysis. *See Dandridge v. Williams*, 397 U.S. 471, 519–21 (1970) (dissenting opinion); *Richardson v. Belcher*, 404 U.S. 78, 90 (1971) (dissenting opinion). The Court apparently seeks to establish today that equal protection cases fall into one of two neat categories which dictate the appropriate standard of review—strict scrutiny or mere rationality. But this Court's decisions in the field of equal protection defy such easy categorization. A principled reading of what this Court has done reveals that it has applied a spectrum of standards in reviewing discrimination allegedly violative of the Equal Protection Clause. This spectrum clearly comprehends variations in the degree of care with which the Court will scrutinize particular classifications, depending, I believe, on the constitutional and societal importance of the interest adversely affected and the recognized invidiousness of the basis upon which the particular classification is drawn. . . .

I therefore cannot accept the majority's labored efforts to demonstrate that fundamental interests, which call for strict scrutiny of the challenged classification, encompass only established rights which we are somehow bound to recognize from the text of the Constitution itself. To be sure, some interests which the Court has deemed to be fundamental for

---

[56]The Court rejects the District Court's finding of a correlation between poor people and poor districts with the assertion that "there is reason to believe that the poorest families are not necessarily clustered in the poorest property districts" in Texas. . . . In support of its conclusion the Court offers absolutely no data—which it cannot on this record—concerning the distribution of poor people in Texas to refute the data introduced below by appellees; it relies instead on a recent law review note concerned solely with the State of Connecticut, Note, "A Statistical Analysis of the School Finance Decisions: On Winning Battles and Losing Wars," 81 *Yale L.J.* 1303 (1972). Common sense suggests that the basis for drawing a demographic conclusion with respect to a geographically large, urban-rural, industrial-agricultural State such as Texas from a geographically small, densely populated, highly industrialized State such as Connecticut is doubtful at best.

Furthermore, the article upon which the Court relies to discredit the statistical procedures employed by Professor Berke to establish the correlation between poor people and poor districts based its criticism primarily on the fact that only 4 of the 110 districts studied were in the lowest of the five categories, which were determined by relative taxable property per pupil, and most districts clustered in the middle three groups. See Goldstein, "Interdistrict Inequalities in School Financing: A Critical Analysis of Serrano v. Priest and Its Progeny," 120 *U. Pa. L.Rev.* 504, 524 n 67 (1972). But the Court fails to note that the four poorest districts in the sample had over 50,000 students which constituted 10% of the students in the entire sample. It appears, moreover, that even when the richest and the poorest categories are enlarged to include in each category 20% of the students in the sample, the correlation between district and individual wealth holds true.

Finally, it cannot be ignored that the data introduced by appellees went unchallenged in the District Court. The majority's willingness to permit appellants to litigate the correctness of those data for the first time before this tribunal—where effective response by appellees is impossible—is both unfair and judicially unsound.

purposes of equal protection analysis are themselves constitutionally protected rights. . . .

[But] I would like to know where the Constitution guarantees the right to procreate, *Skinner v. Oklahoma*, 316 U.S. 535, 541 (1942), or the right to vote in state elections, *e.g.*, *Reynolds v. Sims*, 377 U.S. 533 (1964), or the right to an appeal from a criminal conviction, *e.g.*, *Griffin v. Illinois*, 351 U.S. 12 (1956). These are instances in which, due to the importance of the interests at stake, the Court has displayed a strong concern with the existence of discriminatory state treatment. But the Court has never said or indicated that these are interests which independently enjoy full-blown constitutional protection. . . .

The majority is, of course, correct when it suggests that the process of determining which interests are fundamental is a difficult one. But I do not think the problem is insurmountable. . . . The task in every case should be to determine the extent to which constitutionally guaranteed rights are dependent on interests not mentioned in the Constitution. As the nexus between the specific constitutional guarantee and the nonconstitutional interest draws closer, the nonconstitutional interest becomes more fundamental and the degree of judicial scrutiny applied when the interest is infringed on a discriminatory basis must be adjusted accordingly. . . .

[Justice Marshall next discusses several cases which, while assertedly testing the constitutionality of legislation against the traditional equal protection "rationality" standard, in fact reject the "two tier" review approach.]

In summary, it seems to me inescapably clear that this Court has consistently adjusted the care with which it will review state discrimination in light of the constitutional significance of the interests affected and the invidiousness of the particular classification. . . . The majority suggests, however, that a variable standard of review would give this Court the appearance of a "superlegislature." . . . I cannot agree. . . .

. . . [T]he majority today attempts to force this case into the same category for purposes of equal protection analysis as decisions involving discrimination affecting commercial interests. By so doing, the majority singles this case out for analytic treatment at odds with what seems to me to be the clear trend of recent decisions in this Court, and thereby ignores the constitutional importance of the interest at stake and the invidiousness of the particular classification, factors that call for far more than the lenient scrutiny

of the Texas financing scheme which the majority pursues. . . .

B

. . . [T]he fundamental importance of education is amply indicated by the prior decisions of this Court, by the unique status accorded public education by our society, and by the close relationship between education and some of our most basic constitutional values.

The special concern of this Court with the educational process of our country is a matter of common knowledge [citing *Brown v. Board of Educ.*, 347 U.S. 483, 493 (1954): "Today, education is perhaps the most important function of state and local governments"; *Wisconsin v. Yoder*, 406 U.S. 205, 213 (1972): "Providing public schools ranks at the very apex of the function of a State."] . . .

Education directly affects the ability of a child to exercise his First Amendment interest both as a source and as a receiver of information and ideas, whatever interests he may pursue in life. . . .

Of particular importance is the relationship between education and the political process. . . . Education serves the essential function of instilling in our young an understanding of and appreciation for the principles and operation of our governmental processes. Education may instill the interest and provide the tools necessary for political discourse and debate. Indeed, it has frequently been suggested that education is the dominant factor affecting political consciousness and participation. . . . But of most immediate and direct concern must be the demonstrated effect of education on the exercise of the franchise by the electorate. The right to vote in federal elections is conferred by Art. I, §2, and the Seventeenth Amendment of the Constitution, and access to the state franchise has been afforded special protection because it is "preservative of other basic civil and political rights," *Reynolds v. Sims*, 377 U.S. 533, 562 (1964). Data from the Presidential Election of 1968 clearly demonstrates a direct relationship between participation in the electoral process and level of educational attainment; and, as this Court recognized in *Gaston County v. United States*, 395 U.S. 285, 296 (1969), the quality of education offered may influence a child's decision to "enter or remain in school." It is this very sort of intimate relationship between a particular personal interest and specific constitutional guarantees that has heretofore caused the Court to attach special significance, for purposes of equal protection analysis, to individual interests such as procreation and the exercise of the state franchise.[74]

While ultimately disputing little of this, the majority seeks refuge in the fact that the Court has "never presumed to possess either the ability or the authority to guarantee to the citizenry the most *effective* speech or the most *informed* electoral choice." ... This serves only to blur what is in fact at stake. With due respect, the issue is neither provision of the most *effective* speech nor of the most *informed* vote. Appellees do not now seek the best education Texas might provide. ... The issue is ... one of discrimination that affects the quality of the education which Texas has chosen to provide its children; and, the precise question here is what importance should attach to education for purposes of equal protection analysis of that discrimination. ...

C

... This Court has frequently recognized that discrimination on the basis of wealth may create a classification of a suspect character and thereby call for exacting judicial scrutiny. ... The majority, however, considers any wealth classification in this case to lack certain essential characteristics which it contends are common to the instances of wealth discrimination that this Court has heretofore recognized. We are told that in every prior case involving a wealth classification, the members of the disadvantaged class have "shared two distinguishing characteristics: because of their impecunity they were completely unable to pay for some desired benefit, and as a consequence, they sustained an absolute deprivation of a meaningful opportunity to enjoy that benefit." ... I cannot agree.

In *Harper,* the Court struck down as violative of the Equal Protection Clause an annual Virginia poll tax of $1.50, payment of which by persons over the age of 21 was a prerequisite to voting in Virginia elections. In part, the Court relied on the fact that the poll tax interfered with a fundamental interest—the exercise of the state franchise. In addition, though, the Court emphasized that "[l]ines drawn on the ba-

sis of wealth or property . . . are traditionally disfavored." 383 U.S. at 668. . . . [T]he Equal Protection Clause "bars a system which excludes [from the franchise] those unable to pay a fee to vote or who *fail to pay.*" . . . So far as the Court was concerned, the "degree of the discrimination [was] irrelevant." . . . Thus, the Court struck down the poll tax *in toto*; it did not order merely that those too poor to pay the tax be exempted; complete impecunity clearly was not determinative of the limits of the disadvantaged class, nor was it essential to make an equal protection claim.

Similarly, *Griffin* and *Douglas* refute the majority's contention that we have in the past required an absolute deprivation before subjecting wealth classifications to strict scrutiny. The Court characterizes *Griffin* as a case concerned simply with the denial of a transcript or an adequate substitute therefore, and *Douglas* was involving the denial of counsel. But in both cases the question was in fact whether "a State that [grants] appellate review can do so in a way that discriminates against some convicted defendants on account of their poverty." *Griffin v. Illinois,* [351 U.S.] at 18. . . . In that regard, the Court concluded that inability to purchase a transcript denies "the poor an adequate appellate review accorded to all who have money enough to pay the costs in advance," . . . and that "the type of an appeal a person is afforded . . . hinges upon whether or not he can pay for the assistance of counsel," *Douglas v. California,* [372 U.S.] at 355–56. . . . The right of appeal itself was not absolutely denied to those too poor to pay; but because of the cost of a transcript and of counsel, the appeal was a substantially less meaningful right for the poor than for the rich. It was on these terms that the Court found a denial of equal protection, and those terms clearly encompassed degrees of discrimination on the basis of wealth which do not amount to outright denial of the affected right or interest.

This is not to say that the form of wealth classification in this case does not differ significantly from those recognized in the previous decisions of this Court. Our prior cases have dealt essentially with discrimination on the basis of personal wealth. Here, by

---

[74]I believe that the close nexus between education and our established constitutional values with respect to freedom of speech and participation in the political process makes this a different case from our prior decisions concerning discrimination affecting public welfare, see, *e.g., Dandridge v. Williams,* 397 U.S. 471 (1970), or housing, see, *e.g., Lindsey v. Normet,* 405 U.S. 56 (1972). There can be no question that, as the majority suggests, constitutional rights may be less meaningful for someone without enough to eat or without decent housing. . . . But the crucial difference lies in the closeness of the relationship. Whatever the severity of the impact of insufficient food or inadequate housing on a person's life, they have never been considered to bear the same direct and immediate relationship to constitutional concerns for free speech and for our political processes as education has long been recognized to bear. Perhaps, the best evidence of this fact is the unique status which has been accorded public education as the single public service nearly unanimously guaranteed in the constitution of our States. . . . Education, in terms of constitutional values, is much more analogous in my judgment, to the right to vote in state elections than to public welfare or public housing. . . .

contrast, the children of the disadvantaged Texas school districts are being discriminated against not necessarily because of their personal wealth, or the wealth of their families, but because of the taxable property wealth of the residents of the district in which they happen to live. The appropriate question, then, is whether the same degree of judicial solicitude and scrutiny that has previously been afforded wealth classifications is warranted here. . . .

. . . [D]iscrimination on the basis of group wealth in this case likewise calls for careful judicial scrutiny. First, it must be recognized that while local district wealth may serve other interests, it bears no relationship whatsoever to the interest of Texas school children in the educational opportunity afforded them by the State of Texas. Given the importance of that interest, we must be particularly sensitive to the invidious characteristics of any form of discrimination that is not clearly intended to serve it, as opposed to some other distinct state interest. Discrimination on the basis of group wealth may not, to be sure, reflect the social stigma frequently attached to personal poverty. Nevertheless, insofar as group wealth discrimination involves wealth over which the disadvantaged individual has no significant control, it represents in fact a more serious basis of discrimination than does personal wealth. For such discrimination is no reflection of the individual's characteristics or his abilities. . . .

The disability of the disadvantaged class in this case extends as well into the political processes upon which we ordinarily rely as adequate for the protection and promotion of all interests. Here legislative reallocation of the State's property wealth must be sought in the face of inevitable opposition from significantly advantaged districts that have a strong vested interest in the preservation of the status quo, a problem not completely dissimilar to that faced by underrepresented districts prior to the Court's intervention in the process of reapportionment, see *Baker v. Carr*, 369 U.S. 186, 191–92 (1962).

Nor can we ignore the extent to which, in contrast to our prior decisions, the State is responsible for the wealth discrimination in this instance. . . . The means for financing public education in Texas are selected and specified by the State. It is the State that has created local school districts, and tied educational funding to the local property tax and thereby to local district wealth. . . . In short, this case, in contrast to the Court's previous wealth discrimination decisions, can only be seen as "unusual in the extent to which governmental action is the cause of the wealth classifications."

D

The only justification offered by appellants to sustain the discrimination in educational opportunity caused by the Texas financing scheme is local educational control. . . .

. . . I do not question that local control of public education, as an abstract matter, constitutes a very substantial state interest. . . . The State's interest in local educational control—which certainly includes questions of educational funding—has deep roots in the inherent benefits of community support for public education. Consequently, true state dedication to local control would present, I think, a substantial justification to weigh against simply interdistrict variations in the treatment of a State's school children. But I need not now decide how I might ultimately strike the balance were we confronted with a situation where the State's sincere concern for local control inevitably produced educational inequality. For on this record, it is apparent that the State's purported concern with local control is offered primarily as an excuse rather than as a justification for interdistrict inequality.

In Texas, statewide laws regulate in fact the most minute details of local public education. For example, the State prescribes required courses. All textbooks must be submitted for state approval, and only approved textbooks may be used. The State has established the qualifications necessary for teaching in Texas public schools and the procedures for obtaining certification. The State has even legislated on the length of the school day.

Moreover even if we accept Texas' general dedication to local control in educational matters, it is difficult to find any evidence of such dedication with respect to fiscal matters. It ignores reality to suggest . . . that the local property tax element of the Texas financing scheme reflects a conscious legislative effort to provide school districts with local fiscal control. If Texas had a system truly dedicated to local fiscal control one would expect the quality of the educational opportunity provided in each district to vary with the decision of the voters in that district as to the level of sacrifice they wish to make for public education. In fact, the Texas scheme produces precisely the opposite result. Local school districts cannot choose to have the best education in the State by imposing the highest tax rate. Instead, the quality of the educational opportunity offered by any particular district is largely determined by the amount of taxable property located in the district—a factor over which local voters can exercise no control. . . .

III

In conclusion, it is essential to recognize that an end to the wide variations in taxable district property wealth inherent in the Texas financing scheme would entail none of the untoward consequences suggested by the Court or by the appellants.

First, affirmance of the District Court's decisions would hardly sound the death knell for local control of education. It would mean neither centralized decision-making nor federal court intervention in the operation of public schools. Clearly, this suit has nothing to do with local decision making with respect to educational policy or even educational spending. It involves only a narrow aspect of local control—namely, local control over the raising of educational funds. In fact, in striking down interdistrict disparities in taxable local wealth, the District Court took the course which is most likely to make true local control over educational decision-making a reality for all Texas school districts.

Nor does the District Court's decision even necessarily eliminate local control of educational funding. The District Court struck down nothing more than the continued interdistrict wealth discrimination inherent in the present property tax. Both centralized and decentralized plans for educational funding not involving such interdistrict discrimination have been put forward.[98] The choice among these or other alternatives would remain with the State, not with the federal courts. . . .

The District Court's decision, at most, restricts the power of the State to make educational funding dependent exclusively upon local property taxation so long as there exists interdistrict disparities in taxable property wealth. But it hardly eliminates the local property tax as a source of educational funding or as a means of providing local fiscal control.

* * *

[Justice Brennan's dissenting opinion is omitted.]

NOTES AND QUESTIONS

1. Poverty as a Suspect Classification

The majority opinion first wrestles with whether the so-called "new equal protection" test is to be used. This test requires the state to demonstrate that its differential treatment is justified because it serves a compelling state interest that cannot be satisfied by some less onerous alternative; that is, the means chosen is necessary to the achievement of a compelling end. The use of this test is triggered when the state has either afforded inferior treatment to a "suspect class" or has detrimentally affected a "fundamental interest." Justice Powell turns first to the question of whether the state system of finance afforded inferior treatment of a suspect class. How was it argued that a suspect class was involved in this case? In discussing the concept of a suspect class in terms of poor persons, the majority concludes that in its earlier poverty discrimination cases, the disadvantaged class "shared two distinguishing characteristics: because of their impecunity they were completely unable to pay for some desired benefit, and as a consequence, they sustained an absolute deprivation of a meaningful opportunity to enjoy that benefit." Were the criminal defendants who could not afford a trial transcript or a lawyer absolutely deprived of an opportunity to appeal their cases? Might the standard of judicial review of asserted discrimination against the poor vary with (1) the nature of the burden placed on them by the state of their poverty and (2) the nature of the state's justification for imposing that burden? See Brest, Book Review, 23 Stan.L.Rev. 591 (1971).

The data convinced the majority that equating a suspect class with relative poverty was not sustained by the facts in the case. See footnote 56 of Justice

---

[98]Centralized educational financing is, to be sure, one alternative. . . . Central financing would leave in local hands the entire gamut of local educational policy making—teachers, curriculum, school sites, the whole process of allocating resources among alternative educational objectives.

A second possibility is the much discussed theory of district power equalization put forth by Professors Coons, Clune, and Sugarman in their seminal work, *Private Wealth and Public Education* 201-42 (1970). Such a scheme would truly reflect a dedication to local fiscal control. Under their system, each school district would receive a fixed amount of revenue per pupil for any particular level of tax effort regardless of the level of local property tax base. Appellants criticize this scheme on the rather extraordinary ground that it would encourage poorer districts to overtax themselves in order to obtain substantial revenues for education. But under the present discriminatory scheme, it is the poor districts that are already taxing themselves at the highest rates, yet are receiving the lowest returns.

District wealth reapportionment is yet another alternative which would accomplish directly essentially what district power equalization would seek to do artificially. . . .

A fourth possibility would be to remove commercial, industrial, and mineral property from local tax rolls, to tax this property on a statewide basis, and to return the resulting revenues to the local districts in a fashion that would compensate for remaining variations in the local tax bases.

None of these particular alternatives are necessarily constitutionally compelled; rather, they indicate the breadth of choice which would remain to the State if the present inter-district disparities were eliminated.

Marshall's opinion. Is it important that despite the overall trend, the bulk of the districts fall in the middle range where the relationship of family income to expenditures is reversed? Should the Court have rested so heavily on this point given the possibility that in other states the inverse relationship of family income to expenditures is likely to be stronger? *See* Grubb and Michelson, "Public School Finance in a Post-*Serrano* World," 8 *Harv.C.R.-C.L.L.Rev.* 550 (1973). Was it relevant to the decision in this case that there might be a strong negative relationship between family income and expenditures per pupil in other states? What does this tell us about the role of the Court as policymaker? Could the decision in this case have been written to leave open the possibility of federal challenges in other states based on the association of family income and school expenditures? Should the Court, as a matter of constitutional law, recognize the existence of wealth discrimination when there is a negative correlation between family wealth and school expenditures? How strong as a constitutional matter must the correlation be to warrant the finding of wealth discrimination? Would this approach open the door to challenges to the financing of all local government, and if so, should the Court open this possibility? *Cf. Hawkins v. Town of Shaw*, 437 F.2d 1286 (5th Cir. 1971), *aff'd on rehearing*, 461 F.2d 1171 (5th Cir. 1972) (*en banc*).

The Court dismisses the third wealth discrimination argument on the ground that its own precedents should not be read to permit defining wealth discrimination as concerned with discrimination against residents of poor districts. Does the majority adequately answer the argument of Justice Marshall in his dissent? Why does the majority want to limit its special protection to those groups that have the "traditional indicia of suspectness"? Is the real issue dividing Justice Powell and Justice Marshall the proper role of the federal courts in our system of government? *See* Levin, "The Courts, Congress, and Educational Adequacy: The Equal Protection Predicament," 39 *Md.L.Rev.* 187, 198–202 (1979), for a discussion of the criticisms of the *Rodriguez* majority's treatment of the suspect class issue. *See also* Coons, "Recent Trends in Science Fiction: *Serrano* Among the People of Number," 6 *J. of Law and Educ.* 23 (1977).

In the abortion funding case, *Harris v. McRae*, 448 U.S. 297, 100 S.Ct.2671, 65 L.Ed.2d 784 (1980), the Supreme Court categorically stated "this Court has held repeatedly that poverty, standing alone is not a suspect classification."

2. Education as a Fundamental Interest

Justices Powell and Marshall both concede the importance of education as a basic social good. Yet the majority declines to treat education as a "fundamental" interest whose unequal provision requires "strict judicial scrutiny." The Court equates fundamental interests with rights "explicitly or implicitly guaranteed in the Constitution." Is that standard consistent with prior opinions? What might an implicit constitutional guarantee be? Is Justice Marshall's nexus approach preferable? Does it provide any stopping place for continued expansion of judicial power?

Plaintiffs sought to limit the use of the principle of fiscal neutrality to education by arguing that its relationship to constitutionally guaranteed rights was unique among state-supported goods. The majority, however, was not persuaded: "Empirical examination might well buttress an assumption that the ill-fed, ill-clothed, and ill-housed are among the most ineffective participants in the political process and that they derive the least enjoyment from the benefits of the First Amendment." Is education constitutionally distinguishable from other public goods? If fiscal neutrality were to apply to education, why should it not also apply to other public services? How can fiscal neutrality be limited?

3. Absolute Versus Relative Deprivation of Education

The Supreme Court's opinion in *Rodriguez* distinguishes interdistrict financing inequities from a state "financing system [that] occasioned an absolute denial of educational opportunities to any of its children." The Court also notes that a tuition assessment plan that "absolutely precluded [poor children] from receiving an education . . . would present a far more compelling set of circumstances for judicial assistance than the case before us today." *See Plyler v. Doe*, 457 U.S. 202, 1025 S.Ct.2382, 72 L.Ed.2d 786 (1982). Yet consider the following passage from the Brief of the Appellees to the Supreme Court:

> To be sure complete denial of all educational opportunity is more compelling than a relative denial. But in view of the magnitude of the differences in the capacity of state-created school districts in Texas to raise education dollars, and in light of the vast disparities in educational expenditures between districts, plaintiffs have surely been injured in a comparable way. A complete denial of all educational opportunity is not necessary to demonstrate an unconstitutional deprivation.

Brief of Appellees at 38. One commentator notes that the disparity in per-pupil expenditures, if recomputed based on present-day dollars, would be as if the Edgewood district spent $3,600, while the Alamo Heights district spent $6,000, a difference that would amount to $960,000 per year for a school with 400 students, enough to hire many additional teachers. Foley, "*Rodriguez* Revisited: Constitutional Theory and School Finance," 32 *Ga. L. Rev.* 475, 482 (1998).

4. When Might Education Be a Fundamental Interest?

The Court did leave open the possibility that some minimally adequate level of education might be found to be a constitutionally protected interest (whether or not characterized as "fundamental"):

> Even if it were conceded that some identifiable quantum of education is a constitutionally protected prerequisite to the meaningful exercise of either [the right to speak or the right to vote], we have no indication that the present levels of educational expenditure in Texas provide an education that falls short . . . [N]o charge fairly could be made that the system fails to provide each child with an opportunity to acquire the basic minimal skills necessary for the enjoyment of the rights of speech and of full participation in the political process.

In *Papasan v. Allain*, 478 U.S. 265, 283, 106 S.Ct. 2932, 2943, 92 L.Ed.2d 209 (1986), Justice White described *Rodriguez* as not foreclosing this possibility.

> As *Rodriguez* and *Plyler* indicate, this Court has not yet definitively settled the questions whether a minimally adequate education is a fundamental right and whether a statute alleged to discriminatorily infringe that right should be accorded heightened equal protection review. . . .
>
> This case is therefore very different from *Rodriguez*, where the differential financing available to school districts was traceable to school district funds available from local real estate taxation, not to a state decision to divide state resources unequally among school districts. The rationality of the disparity in *Rodriguez*, therefore, which rested on the fact that funding disparities based on differing local wealth were a necessary adjunct of allowing meaningful local control over school funding, does not settle the constitutionality of disparities alleged in this case. . . .

Id. at 285–90, 106 S.Ct. at 2944–46.

What are the boundaries that define the extent to which the federal Equal Protection Clause addresses disparities in the provision of education, and to what extent will differential treatment rise to the level of unconstitutionality in light of *Papasan* as read against *Rodriguez*? *See also Kadrmas v. Dickinson Public Schools*, 487 U.S. 450, 108 S.Ct. 2481, 101 L.Ed.2d 399 (1988), *infra*, where the dissenting opinion emphasized that ". . . the Court therefore does not address the question whether a state constitutionally could deny a child access to a minimally adequate education. In prior cases, this Court explicitly has left open the question whether such a deprivation of access would violate a fundamental constitutional right. That question remains open today." *Id.* at 466 n.1, 108 S.Ct. at 2491 n.1. What situation might lead the Court to find that education is a fundamental right? What might the Court mean by a minimally adequate education? Doesn't the opinion imply that what the Court would deem a minimally adequate level of education would indeed be quite minimal? What is needed "to provide each child with an opportunity to acquire the basic minimum skills necessary for the enjoyment of the rights of speech and of full participation in the political process"? 411 U.S. at 38, 93 S.Ct. at 1299. Might a "basic education" or minimally adequate education be one that ended at the eighth grade? *Cf. Wisconsin v. Yoder*, 406 U.S. 205, 92 S.Ct. 1526, 32 L.Ed.2d 15 (1972). How could plaintiffs, in light of conflicting social science research, relate the level of resources to such outcomes as the ability to fully participate in the political process? What factors relating resource disparity to classifications other than district wealth might also trigger heightened scrutiny?

5. Money and Quality

Justice Powell's opinion notes the "considerable dispute among educators" about the relationship between school resources and outcomes. Is the Court suggesting that existing inequalities are invulnerable to constitutional attack unless such a relationship is established? Does this viewpoint adequately deal with Justice Marshall's argument that inequalities in what is actually delivered to students by way of services is what counts?

Who should have the burden of proof in the money-quality debate? Consider the following argument: (1) The state should not be allowed to deny that money determines quality since the whole system of educational finance in every state is predicated on the proposition that money does make a difference. (2) Hence, the burden of proof should be on the state to prove that spending above a certain minimum is wasteful. (3) If it is doubtful that spending above a minimum is less efficacious, it is unfair that only children of rich districts are insured against the unknown. (4) The social science dispute on this point is based on educational quality measured only in terms of reading scores—a measure much too narrow since it excludes such effects of money as whether or not a child learns to play the violin or swim.

The *Rodriguez* decision raises the problem of the use of social science data by the courts. When should the courts rely on common sense—on what everybody "knows"—and when should they defer to social science? Here, for example, common sense suggests that money can and does make a difference as to what services and programs are available to children, yet Justice Powell cites social science research to support the notion that we know little about the effects of money. When should a court defer to social science "not for its wisdom but for its very ignorance"? *See* Coons, "Recent Trends in Science Fiction: *Serrano* Among the People of Number," 6 *J. of Law & Educ.* 23, 31 (1977). In *Abbott v. Burke*, 119 N.J. 287, 575 A.2d 359 (1990), the New Jersey Supreme Court noted as follows:

> If the claim is that additional funding will not enable the poorer urban districts to satisfy the thorough and efficient test, the constitutional answer is that they are entitled to pass or fail with at least the same amount of money as their competitors.
>
> * * *
>
> The State's claim that the statistical evidence fails to prove a significant relationship between education expenditures and property wealth is joined with a more fundamental objection: money is not a critical factor in the quality of education in the first place. . . . The conclusion is that since all districts in the state have much more than whatever the minimum amount may be, the excess and the differences in the excess, are irrelevant to the quality of education.
>
> . . . [W]hile we are unable to conclude from this record that the State is clearly wrong, we would not strip all notions of equal and adequate funding from the constitutional obligation unless we were convinced that the State was clearly right. . . .

575 A.2d at 375–77. Which court, the *Rodriguez* Court or the *Abbott* court, took the correct approach in the face of inconclusive social science research?

6. *The Rational Basis Standard*

The majority finds that since the finance system neither discriminates on the basis of a suspect class nor touches on a fundamental interest, the scheme must be assessed in terms of the rational basis standard of review. Does the Court make a case for the idea that the existing system is rationally related to the purpose of promoting local control? Does Justice Powell adequately answer the dissents of Justices White and Marshall? Could not the state promote local control even more effectively if it adopted the district power equalizing concept? Does local autonomy require local control of the funding of public education? Is local control consistent with the fact that education is a state-delegated function? *See* Briffault, "Our Localism: Part I—The Structure of Local Government Law," 90 *Colum.L.Rev.* 1 (1990).

7. *The Role of the Supreme Court*

At numerous places in the *Rodriguez* opinion, Justice Powell reflects on problems faced by a court in dealing with public school financing. He expresses concern for maintaining the federal system, for not shifting too much power to the judicial branch of the central government. How strong a consideration is this factor? Why does it play a role in this case but not in *Brown v. Board of Education*, discussed in chapter 4? When should a concern for maintaining the federal system enter into the calculus of deciding a case? For a recent critique of the *Rodriguez* decision, *see* Foley, "*Rodriguez* Revisited: Constitutional Theory and School Finance," 32 *Ga. L. Rev.* 475 (1998). Critics of the *Rodriguez* Court's emphasis on local control have argued that the Court has privileged private power by protecting wealthy suburbs. *See, e.g.,* Briffault, "Part II–Localism and Legal Theory," 90 *Colum. L. Rev.* 346, 411–417, 441 (1990); Briffault, "The Role of Local Control in School Finance Reform," 24 *Conn. L. Rev.* 773 (1992); Williams, "The Constitutional Vulnerability of American Local Government: The Politics of City Status in American Law," 1986 *Wis. L. Rev.* 83, 100–120. *But see* Barron, "The Promise of Cooley's City: Traces of Local Constitutionalism," 147 *U. Pa. L. Rev.* 487, 554–560 (1999), critiquing the critics.

2. Equity Litigation Under State Constitutional Provisions: Return to *Serrano*

The *Rodriguez* decision appeared to have eliminated the *federal* Equal Protection Clause as a basis for holding California's financing system unconstitutional. When *Serrano* was remanded for trial, the trial judge noted that *Serrano I* had relied on the state's equivalent of the Equal Protection Clause as well as on the Fourteenth Amendment (see footnote 11 of that opinion), and thus held that education was a fundamental right under the state constitution, requiring the state to show a compelling interest in order to permit this right to be conditioned on district wealth. This was affirmed by the California Supreme Court in *Serrano II*. 18 Cal. 3d 728, 135 Cal.Rptr. 345, 557 P.2d 929 (1976). The state supreme court noted that although California's equal protection provisions are "substantially the equivalent of" the Equal Protection Clause of the Fourteenth Amendment to the United States Constitution, they "are possessed of an independent vitality which, in a given case, may demand an analysis different from that which would obtain if only the federal standards were applicable." *Id.* at 764, 135 Cal.Rptr. at 366, 557 P.2d at 950. The court also pointed out that while considerations of federalism may have been one basis for the Supreme Court's decision in *Rodriguez*, "[t]he constraints of federalism, so necessary to the proper functioning of our unique system of national government, are not applicable to this Court in its determination of whether our own state's public school financing system runs afoul of state constitutional provisions." *Id.* at 766–67, 135 Cal. Rptr. at 368, 557 P.2d at 952. Thus, *Serrano* became purely a state constitutional decision.

SB 90, which had been enacted by the California legislature following *Serrano I*, was reviewed by the trial judge, who found that California's system of financing education still did not meet the fiscal neutrality principle adopted by the California Supreme Court in *Serrano I* inasmuch as SB 90 failed to reduce expenditure disparities in any meaningful way. In deciding whether the wealth-determined disparities in expenditures affected the quality of the education provided, Judge Jefferson rejected an outcome measure of quality and instead adopted an input measure. Using this measure, he found that the higher-spending districts were able to purchase services, programs, materials, and equipment that low-spending districts could not. The major factual premises of the plaintiff's case having been established, the judge then proceeded to the remedy. Most significantly, the court ordered that whatever the financial scheme adopted by the state legislature, it must reduce per pupil expenditure disparities to less than $100 per pupil and reduce variations in tax rates to nonsubstantial variations, and that this must be accomplished within six years.

NOTES AND QUESTIONS

1. Legislative Response to Serrano II

In September 1977, the California legislature responded to *Serrano II* by adopting yet another amendment to its school finance system, AB 65. This was an intricate bill that significantly increased the foundation level, continued the flat grant, and imposed a revenue limit with voter override, but power equalized the tax override the districts could vote. This bill took the state a step closer to meeting the fiscal neutrality standard, but it still left large expenditure differences correlated with property wealth in place. *See* A. Frentz and R. Marshall, Jr., *AB 65: California's Reply to* Serrano (1978). Then, in 1978, California voters adopted Proposition 13, an amendment to the California Constitution. The proposition provided four things: (1) No property should be taxed at more than 1 percent of 1975 fair market value; (2) municipalities may impose "special taxes" by a two-thirds vote of the electors; (3) assessments may not grow more than 2 percent annually from their 1975–76 levels, to which they were rolled back, except for property sold after 1975–76; and (4) no increase in state taxes may be enacted without a two-thirds vote of each legislature. Provision 1 rolled back property taxes in California and in effect imposed a statewide local property tax of 1 percent. Most districts in the state were unable to support their educational programs on the basis of this 1 percent property tax, requiring the state to bail them out by using $2.2 billion of the $3 billion state surplus to make up the difference. Proposition 13 turned California toward full state funding. Thus, differences in spending among school districts are now most importantly determined by how state aid is distributed—a very different source of inequalities than was the target of *Serrano I* and *II*.

2. Serrano III

The legislature subsequently adopted AB 8 which was designed over time to bring the high-spending and low-spending districts together by imposing strict revenue limits on high-spending districts and providing state aid to low-spending districts. However, the failure to achieve this by the court's 1980 deadline resulted in the plaintiffs returning to court to seek an order requiring compliance with *Serrano II*. In *Serrano v. Priest*, 200 Cal.App.3d 897, 226 Cal.Rptr. 584 (1986) (*Serrano III*), the appellate court affirmed the decision of the trial judge, who found that the state had complied with the "*Serrano* mandate" by overcoming disparities in educational spending to the point that "remaining differences in spending are not significant, either mathematically or educationally." *Id.* at 620. Although *Serrano II* had said that spending differences had to be reduced to no greater than $100, the *Serrano III* court rejected rigid reliance on the $100 figure, although it also held that the state had met that standard once the $100 figure was adjusted for inflation. "Thus, in 1982–83, 93.2% of the state's ADA [were] in districts within a hundred dollar band adjusted for inflation. The comparable figure for 1974 was 56%." *Id.* at 614. The court further held that remaining disparities were "justified by legitimate state interests." *Id.* at 616. These interests included "the need for an orderly transition from the old wealth-related system to the new state funded system," *id.*, and cost differences due to climate and other factors. *Id.* at 617. Although the new funding system had largely succeeded in "level[ing] up low revenue limit districts, high revenue districts had suffered by the combined impact of the equalization formulas, declining enrollment, and inflation." *Id.* at 618. Such "leveling down" had had especially great impact on districts with high proportions of poor and minority students and "further leveling down would produce far more harm than good." *Id.* at 621.

One commentator has argued that *Serrano* "caused" the adoption of the statewide ballot initiative known as Proposition 13, which "has continued to starve the public sector in California, and school funding has been its major victim." Fischel, "How *Serrano* Caused Proposition 13," 12 *J.L. & Pol.* 607 (1996). As a result of *Serrano* and Proposition 13, California fell to last or nearly last in the country in terms of the percent of personal income spent on public education. *Id.* at 613. Professor Fischel argues that centralizing school finance reduces the incentive to support public school spending. For a review of the *Serrano* litigation and legislative responses, *see* Minorini and Sugarman, "School Finance Litigation in the Name of Educational Equity: Its Evolution, Impact, and Future," in *Equity and Adequacy in Education Finance* 34, 48–50 (H. Ladd, R.Chalk, and J. Hansen, eds., 1999).

3. *The Fiscal Neutrality Principle*

Is the principle of fiscal neutrality concerned with the level of educational expenditures for children, or is it primarily a principle of taxpayer equity with little attention to the educational program children receive? Is the principle of fiscal neutrality a proper response to a finding that education is a fundamental interest? Is it plausible to assume that equalizing fiscal capacity to raise money will result in greater equality in the provision of education services?

Is the trial court's remedy, affirmed by the California Supreme Court in *Serrano II*, consistent with the principle of fiscal neutrality? Does it logically follow from the principle of fiscal neutrality that expenditures per pupil may not vary among districts by more than $100? Does the principle require that tax rates be equal? Would "district power equalizing" (state guarantee of equal revenues per pupil for equal tax rates, regardless of the district's property wealth) be an acceptable response to *Serrano II* even if it resulted in different levels of per-pupil expenditure?

If the principle of fiscal neutrality is primarily directed toward achieving taxpayer equity, is it even an adequate notion of taxpayer equity? Is not the real problem from the taxpayer's perspective the proportion of one's income that must be paid out for schooling? As a matter of taxpayer equity, should not the aim of reformers be to move away from the property tax to a proportional or progressive tax system? *See* Goldstein, "Interdistrict Inequalities in School Financing: A Critical Analysis of *Serrano v. Priest* and its Progeny," 120 *U.Pa.L.Rev.* 504 (1972). What differences does it make to the individual taxpayer that equal tax rates produce an equal yield if the tax system itself is regressive?

Current economic theory and evidence suggest that variations in tax rates and public services across communities may cause property values to vary. Thus, tax rates and services could determine property wealth more than property wealth determines tax rates and expenditures. A useful nontechnical summary of this "capitalization" literature is to be found in Wendling, *Expenditures and Tax Capitalization: Its Relation to School Finance and Tax Reform* (Report No. F79-11, Education Commission of the States, December 1979).

One possible implication of this body of research is that the system of financing education is already "wealth neutral." That is, the real cost of purchasing educational services might be the same in all districts. The real cost is the tax bill plus the cost of housing. There is some evidence indicating that for the individual living in a district filled with highly valued industrial property which increases per-pupil property wealth and reduces the tax liability, the cost of housing will be higher because of the lower tax liability. The individual residing in a purely residential district, however, will have a higher tax liability but lower housing costs for a comparable house since the higher tax liability on those houses dampens demand. The total (housing cost plus tax liability) works out to be the same for both. *Id.* at 25–26.

In these circumstances, judicial imposition of the fiscal neutrality principle coupled with legislative adoption of a district power equalizing (DPE) formula could result in a number of unanticipated consequences. Depending on the district power equalizing formula (with or without "recapture" provisions), the real cost of schooling in the property-poor district could increase (DPE would, in effect, drive up the cost of housing), and decrease in the property-rich district for individuals who buy or sell a house after DPE has been implemented. Similarly, if full state funding were adopted, other equally surprising results could occur, for example, windfall gains and losses in property values.

In light of the complexities involved in implementing fiscal neutrality, is it a principle the courts should adopt as a matter of constitutional law?

The principle of fiscal neutrality also permits expenditure variations to be a function of the voters' taste for education in each of the various school districts of the state. Should the quality of a child's education be a function of the stinginess of the residents in a particular school district? Should the quality of a child's education be only a function of the desires of the state legislature? Or should it be a function of the desires and wealth of a child's family or only a function of the desires of the family and not of its wealth? *See* Coons and Sugarman, "Family Choice in Education: A Model State System for Vouchers," 59 *Calif.L.Rev.* 321 (1971). Is it, however, fair to leave a child at the mercy of the educational tastes of his or her parents? The problem is now brought full circle: Who should determine the quality of a child's education?

The principle of fiscal neutrality met with a mixed reception in other state courts. Only a few courts followed the path taken by *Serrano II*, and held that their state systems of financing education violated their state equal protection clauses. *See, e.g., Washakie County School District No. 1 v. Herschler*, 606 P.2d 310 (Wyo. 1980); *Horton v. Meskill*, 172 Conn. 615, 376 A.2d 359 (1977). In these states, the courts ruled that wealth was a suspect class and that education was a fundamental right.

Courts in many other states during the 1970s and early 1980s specifically concluded that wealth was not a suspect classification. These include Colorado, *Lujan v. Colorado State Board of Education*, 649 P.2d 1005 (Colo. 1982); Maryland, *Hornbeck v. Somerset County Board of Education*, 295 Md. 597, 458 A.2d 758 (1983); and Oklahoma, *Fair School Finance Council Inc. v. State of Oklahoma*, 746 P.2d 1135 (Okl. 1987). *See also Shofstall v. Hollins*, 110 Ariz. 88, 515 P.2d 590 (1973), *Thompson v. Engelking*, 96 Idaho 793, 537 P.2d 635 (1976), *Northshore School District No. 417 v. Kinnear*, 84 Wash. 2d 685, 530 P.2d 178 (1974), which found that under the state equal protection clause, education was not a fundamental right. Inasmuch as education is explicitly mentioned in every state constitution, what might the reasoning be for finding that it is not fundamental?

3. Equity Litigation in the 1990s

During the late 1970s and1980s, more states found their state school financing systems did *not* violate their state's equal protection clause than did find them in violation. *See* Minorini and Sugarman, *supra*, at 53–55. The school finance litigation movement seemed to be grinding to a halt. However, in 1989, three state supreme courts struck down their school finance systems. One of the cases was based on a newly emerging adequacy theory, discussed in the next section. The notion of equity persisted, however, and the school finance systems of Montana, *Helena v. Elementary School District No. 1 v. State*, 236 Mont. 44, 769 P.2d 684 (1989), and Texas, *Edgewood Independent School District v. Kirby*, 777 S.W.2d 391 (Tex. 1989), were found unconstitutional on the basis of some variant of the fiscal neutrality principle. In the Texas case, the court relied on the constitutional mandate requiring an efficient system of public schools, rather than on a general equal protection clause. In Montana, the court looked to the constitutional guarantee of "equality of educational opportunity." *See* Enrich, "Leaving Equality Behind: New Directions in School Finance Reform," 48 *Vand. L. Rev.* 101, 139–140 (1995), discussing some of the more recent cases that, although relying on their state education clauses instead of the equal protection clause, remained grounded in notions of equality.

The Texas case was in the state supreme court four times, and illustrates some of the issues that arise from application of the fiscal neutrality principle.

a. Edgewood I. The Texas Supreme Court noted that over 50 percent of the total cost of education was provided by the local school districts from the local property tax, and that the disparity in taxable property wealth per student between the wealthiest district and poorest district amounted to a 700 to 1 ratio. The average property wealth in the 100 wealthiest districts was more than twenty times that of the average property wealth in the 100 poorest districts. The court illustrated the disparities with the two school districts within the same county that had figured so prominently in *Rodriguez:* Edgewood Independent School District had $38,854 in property wealth per student while Alamo Heights Independent School District had $570,109 in property wealth per student.

The *Edgewood* court noted that although the state's foundation program was supposed to ensure that each school district had sufficient funds to provide its students with at least a basic education, the program did "not cover even the cost of meeting the state-mandated minimum requirements." *Id.* at 392. Because of disparities in district property wealth, variations in spending per pupil ranged from $2,112 to $19,333 and, in general, the lower expenditures in the property-poor districts were not the result of lack of tax effort. "[P]roperty-poor districts are trapped in a cycle of poverty from which there is no opportunity to free themselves. Because of their inadequate tax base, they must tax at significantly higher rates in order to meet minimum requirements for accreditation; yet their educational programs are typically inferior." *Id.* at 393.

The court also found that the amount of money spent per student was significantly related to the educational opportunity available to that student.

> High-wealth districts are able to provide for their students broader educational experiences including more extensive curricula, more up-to-date technological equipment, better libraries and library personnel, teacher aides, counseling services, lower student-teacher ratios, better facilities, parental involvement programs, and drop-out prevention programs. They are also better able to attract and retain experienced teachers and administrators.

Id. The court concluded that the inequalities in per-pupil expenditures produced by the present system

were "directly contrary" to the constitutional requirement that the legislature "establish and make suitable provision for the support and maintenance of an efficient system of public free schools." *Id.* The constitution demanded that there "be a direct and close correlation between a district's tax effort and the educational resources available to it; in other words, districts must have substantially equal access to similar revenues per pupil at similar levels of tax effort." *Id.* at 397.

Has the Texas Supreme Court mandated a district power equalizing system of school finance? What courses of action are left to the legislature in providing an efficient system? If the state does not provide for recapture of revenues from wealthy districts, will the state subsidies needed to ensure "substantially equal access to similar revenues per pupil at similar levels of tax effort" be politically and economically feasible? What does the court mean by "substantially equal?" Does it mean that the state need not guarantee the same yield for the same tax rate in the wealthiest districts? *See* Yudof, "School Finance Reform in Texas," 28 *Harv. J. on Legis.* 499 (1991).

b. Edgewood II—A More Stringent Standard? Following the decision in *Edgewood I,* the state legislature enacted Senate Bill 1. In *Edgewood Independent School District v. Kirby,* 804 S.W.2d 491 (Tex. 1991) (*Edgewood II*), the state supreme court found that the school finance system of the State of Texas was still unconstitutional, noting that Senate Bill 1 maintained the foundation program that was viewed as inadequate in *Edgewood I.*

The state argued that as more funds are shifted to lower wealth districts, there would be substantial equity among those districts educating 95 percent of the students in the state. The court noted, however, that by limiting the Senate Bill 1 funding formula to districts in which 95 percent of the students attend school, "the 170,000 students in the wealthiest districts are still supported by local revenues drawn from the same tax base as the 1 million students in the poorest districts." *Id.* at 495.

> The fundamental flaw of Senate Bill 1 lies not in any particular provisions but in its overall failure to restructure the system. Most property owners must bear a heavier tax burden to provide a less expensive education for students in their districts, while property owners in a few districts bear a much lighter burden to provide more funds for their students. Thus, Senate Bill 1 fails to provide "a direct and close correlation between

a district's tax effort and the educational resources available to it." 777 S.W.2d at 397.

Id. at 496.

The court then suggested that the legislature consider consolidation of school districts or tax base consolidation as possible ways of achieving an "efficient" system. Has the court stepped into the role of the legislature when it proposes that the legislature consider these remedies? Is the court, by holding that the state must include all school districts, requiring the legislature to "recapture" funds that the wealthiest districts can raise through local property taxes in order to subsidize other districts? Does *Edgewood II* require either consolidation of school districts so that property values per pupil are equal or district power equalizing with complete recapture, or might other financing alternatives satisfy the Edgewood II court? *See* Yudof, *supra.*

The state had argued that the annual cost of equalizing all districts to the revenue levels that the richest districts can attain under Senate Bill 1 would be approximately four times the annual cost of operating the entire state government. *Id.* at 495–96. Does the court suggest that the state constitution compels that the wealthiest 5 percent of districts be included in the equalization formulas, regardless of cost to the state?

c. Edgewood IIa—A Retreat? The plaintiffs filed a motion for rehearing on the specific question of whether a 1931 precedent would prevent recapture and redistribution of local property taxes for purposes of equalization. *Edgewood Independent School District v. Kirby*, 804 S.W.2d 499 (Tex. 1991) (on motion for rehearing) (*Edgewood IIa*). The court held that funds raised in one school district could not be redistributed to other school districts under the specific wording of the state's education clause. In addition, the court decided that the plaintiffs' motion raised the question whether the legislature may authorize school districts to determine whether unequalized local enrichment is permissible. The court found that "because the constitution does permit such enrichment, without equalization, local taxes cannot be considered 'state taxes subject to state-wide recapture.' " *Id.* The court went on to comment, beyond what the plaintiffs were seeking in their motion for rehearing, that the school financing system is unconstitutional "not because any unequalized local supplementation is employed, but

because the State relies so heavily on unequalized local funding in attempting to discharge its duty to 'make suitable provision for the support and maintenance of an efficient system of public free schools.' " *Id.* at 500. Although the first two decisions had been unanimous, there were four justices who dissented from the opinion on motion for rehearing in *Edgewood IIa*, arguing that the court had exceeded its jurisdiction under the motion for rehearing and was backing off its bolder position in *Edgewood II* because of political pressure.

Has the court's opinion in *Edgewood IIa*, by barring recapture and permitting unequalized local enrichment, weakened its rulings in *Edgewood I* and *Edgewood II*? Was *Edgewood II* wrongly decided? Does *Edgewood IIa* return to the standard of *Edgewood I*? Note that in *Edgewood I*, the court had stated that local school districts would not be "precluded from supplementing an efficient system established by the legislature; however any local enrichment must derive solely from local tax effort." *Id.* at 398. In a footnote in *Edgewood II*, the court noted that "the question of local enrichment continues to be controlled by this court's opinion in *Edgewood I*." *Id.* at 495, n. 11. Are the political realities such that complete fiscal neutrality is unlikely ever to be achieved? *See* Yudof, "School Finance Reform: Don't Worry, Be Happy," 10 *Rev. Litig.* 585 (1991). Should courts consider political realities in deciding constitutional issues?

d. Edgewood III. After yet another legislative attempt (Senate Bill 351), several groups of wealthy school districts challenged the newly enacted law. This law, too, was overturned by a bitterly divided supreme court. *Carrollton-Farmers Branch Independent School District v. Edgewood Independent School District*, 826 S.W.2d 489 (Tex. 1992) (*Edgewood III*). The opinion did not clarify what *Edgewood I* meant by "substantially equal access to similar revenues per pupil at similar levels of tax effort." The court's opinion focused primarily on what it considered to be a statewide property tax levied under Senate Bill 351, holding that both the tax and the failure of the legislature to provide for voter authorization violated the Texas constitution.

Under a threat by the trial court that the school system would be closed down if the legislature failed to come up with a new plan by June 1, 1993, and with the inability to achieve any kind of consensus, the legislature proposed a constitutional amendment that would address some of the problems Senate Bill 351 encountered in *Edgewood III*. After a heated campaign for its passage, the voters of Texas rejected it. *See* Farr and Trachtenberg, "The *Edgewood* Drama: An Epic Quest for Education Equity," 17 *Yale L. & Pol'y Rev.* 607, 674–676 (1999). The legislature had to return to the drawing board. A bill was finally adopted (Senate Bill 7) that gave 100 of the wealthiest districts five different options for sharing their property wealth over a certain amount per pupil with poorer districts, plus some "hold harmless" provisions for three years. It was signed by the governor on the day before the trial court had said it would close down the school system. *See* Graves, "Governor Signs School Bill, Sends It to Judge," *Austin American-Statesman*, June 1, 1993, at A7; Stutz, "Richards Signs School Funding Bill, Measure May Face Court Challenges from Some Poor, Rich Districts," *Dallas Morning News*, June 1, 1993, at 10A; Rugeley, "Richards Signs Bill on Schools, Court's Deadline Beaten by a Day," *Houston Chronicle*, June 1, 1993, at 11.

e. Edgewood IV. Both wealthy and poor districts returned to the trial court arguing that Senate Bill 7 was unconstitutional — the rich districts primarily because of the recapture provision, and the poor districts because the disparities were still too great. The trial judge held that the school financing system established by Senate Bill 7 was constitutional, and the decision was promptly appealed. The state supreme court, in a five to four decision, upheld the law as constitutional, *Edgewood Independent School District v. Meno*, 917 S.W.2d 717 (Tex. 1995) (*Edgewood IV*), but redefined what was meant by the constitutional requirement that the legislature establish "an efficient system of public free schools", Tex. Const. art. VII, § 1. The court interpreted an "efficient system" as *not* requiring "equality of access to revenue at all levels." 917 S.W.2d at 729. Efficiency, therefore, is not synonymous with equity. *Id.* at 730.

> The effect of this "equity at all levels" theory of efficiency is to "level-down" the quality of our public school system, a consequence which is universally regarded as undesirable from an educational perspective. Under this theory, it would be constitutional for the Legislature to limit all districts to a funding level of $500 per student as long as there was equal access to this $500 per student, *even if* $3,500 per student were required for a general diffusion of knowledge. Neither

the Constitution nor our previous *Edgewood* decisions warrant such an interpretation.

Id. The court thus responded to the challenge brought by property-poor districts by noting that "[t]he State's duty to provide districts with substantially equal access to revenue applies *only* to the provision of funding necessary for a general diffusion of knowledge," permitting unequalized supplementation beyond that level. *Id.* at 731. Only one justice dissented on this aspect of the decision, arguing that the majority had completely distorted the holdings in the earlier cases.

With regard to the argument made by the property-rich districts that the new finance system, viewed as a whole, was in effect a statewide property tax in violation of the state constitution, the majority held that it was a state-encouraged local tax, without sufficient state control to be a statewide property tax. *Id.* at 737–738. In response to the argument that "recapture" of revenues was prohibited by an earlier case, the court said that the districts could avoid "recapture" of their revenues for use by poorer districts by selecting one of the nonrecapture options that the law provided, such as consolidating with another district, detaching a portion of its territory, or consolidating its tax base with that of another district. *Id.* at 738–739.

For a detailed legal, political, and economic analysis of the decade-long saga to reform Texas's school finance system, *see* Farr and Trachtenberg, "The *Edgewood* Drama: An Epic Quest for Education Equity," 17 *Yale L. & Pol'y Rev.* 607(1999). Farr and Trachtenberg note that this tortuous history of reform did result in a more equitable system. When the case was first brought, the ratio between property values per student of the richest and poorest districts was 700 to 1, while full implementation of Senate Bill 7 lowered it to 28 to 1. Moreover, the link between local property values and access to revenues was diminished: "in 1989, wealth explained 56% of the variation in revenue for local districts, while tax effort explained only 13.5%. By 1994, wealth only explained 18% of the variation, while tax effort accounted for 65%." *Id.* at 703–704. The amount of overall funding for education has also increased. *Id.* at 705.

Is there an *Edgewood V* in the future? Several of Texas's wealthiest school districts have recently challenged the 1993 law on the ground that because they must now tax at the state-set maximum rate to support their current programs, the districts no longer have discretion over the tax rate, creating in effect a state property tax in violation of the constitution. About 20 percent of the state's school districts have now reached the tax cap. Reston, "School Finance System Facing a New Lawsuit," *Austin American-Statesman*, Apr. 10, 2001, at A1. The district judge recently dismissed the lawsuit on the ground that the issue was decided by the state supreme court in 1995 in *Edgewood IV, supra.* Plaintiffs have vowed to appeal the dismissal. *See e.g.*, Sutton, "'Robin Hood' Has Worn Out Its Welcome," *Daily Texan*, July 18, 2001; Zethraus, "Defeat May Lead to Quick Appeal," *Dallas Morning Herald*, July 18, 2001.

A number of challenges to state school financing systems based on equity or fiscal neutrality principles continued to be brought throughout the decade of the 1990s. Some state supreme courts found that equalization was not mandated by the state constitution, while other courts interpreted their state constitutional provision providing for education, often read together with the state constitution's equivalent of the equal protection clause, as requiring equalization. The following challenge to Vermont's school finance system is illustrative of the latter.

Brigham v. State

166 Vt. 246, 692 A.2d 384 (Vt. 1997)

Before Allen, C.J., and Gibson, Dooley, Morse and Johnson, JJ.

Per Curiam.

In this appeal, we decide that the current system for funding public education in Vermont, with its substantial dependence on local property taxes and resultant wide disparities in revenues available to local school districts, deprives children of an equal educational opportunity in violation of the Vermont Constitution. . . .

When we consider the evidence in the record before us, and apply the Education and Common Benefits Clauses of the Vermont Constitution to that evidence, . . . the conclusion becomes inescapable that the present system has fallen short of providing every school-age child in Vermont an equal educational opportunity. . . .

I. Procedural History

This declaratory judgment action against the State of Vermont was filed . . . by . . . students . . . who

claimed that the State's method of financing public education deprived them of their right under the Vermont and federal constitutions to the same educational opportunities as students who reside in wealthier school districts . . . .

. . . [T]he trial court ruled that plaintiffs' claims predicated on the federal constitution were barred by the United States Supreme Court decision in *San Antonio Independent School District v. Rodriguez*, 411 U.S. 1, 93 S.Ct. 1278, 36 L.Ed.2d 16 (1973), which held that there is no fundamental right to an education under the United States Constitution, that state education-funding schemes are therefore subject only to "rational basis" scrutiny under the Equal Protection Clause of the Fourteenth Amendment, and that interdistrict funding disparities are rationally related to the legitimate state purpose of fostering local control over education funding and programs. . . . Although the *Rodriguez* Court conceded that "some identifiable quantum of education" might deserve constitutional protection to ensure the "basic minimal skills necessary" for the exercise of free speech rights and participation in the political process, . . . plaintiffs here have not alleged that public education in Vermont is fundamentally inadequate or fails to impart minimal basic skills.

* * *

Plaintiffs alleged that the constitutional language, the case law, and the history of Vermont establish that [the Education Clause of the Vermont constitution] guarantees a fundamental right to education, and by extension a right to equal educational opportunities, and that the current funding disparities must, therefore, be strictly scrutinized under the Common Benefits Clause of the Vermont Constitution. The State must demonstrate, in other words, that the current financing scheme advances a compelling governmental interest and is narrowly tailored to serve that interest. . . . The trial court rejected this argument . . . .

The court denied summary judgment as to plaintiffs' remaining claims that (1) the current educational financing system was not rationally related to a legitimate governmental purpose, and therefore violated the right to equal protection of the laws under [the state constitution] . . . . In explaining its decision to deny summary judgment on these claims, the court stated that it was "unclear" whether the parties agreed on precisely what constitutes equal educational opportunities, or how the relative wealth of a district affects those opportunities. It consequently set the case for trial to develop a factual record.

The parties moved jointly for permission to appeal the judgment except for that portion disposing of plaintiffs' federal equal protection claims. . . . The trial court denied the motion. The parties thereupon renewed their motion with this Court, and we granted the motion. . . .

II. Facts

In our view the material facts are not in dispute. Public schools in Vermont are financed principally by two means: funds raised by cities and towns solely through assessments on property within them, . . . and funds distributed by the state under a complex aid formula, currently known as the Foundation Plan. . . . The purpose of a foundation formula is to enable each school district to spend an amount per pupil that will provide at least a minimum-quality education program, known as the foundation cost. . . .

From an equity standpoint, the major weakness of a foundation formula distribution system is that it equalizes capacity only to a level of a minimally adequate education program. . . . School districts with greater property wealth, however, can more easily spend above foundation costs to improve education, and the record before us shows that they usually make these expenditures. Thus, a foundation-formula, state-aid program can boost the capacity of the poorest districts, but still leave substantial deficiencies in overall equity. . . .

. . . The object of the Plan is not equality of educational opportunity generally, or even equality of local capacity to facilitate opportunity. It is only to equalize capacity to produce a minimally adequate education, assuming the voters can sustain the state-selected tax rate.

That the foundation formula does not eliminate wealth disparities is shown dramatically by the record before us. Notwithstanding the fact that state aid has increased substantially in recent years, the percentage of the local contribution to education revenues has remained exceptionally high. In fiscal year 1994, public education revenues raised through local property taxes represented over 60% of the total cost of public education, one of the highest local shares in the nation. Furthermore, . . . there remain wide differences among school districts in per-pupil spending. At the extremes, in fiscal year 1995 the Town of Eden spent $2979 per student, compared with the Town of Winhall, which spent $7726, or 160% more than Eden. In December 1994, the top 5% of school districts spent from $5812 to $7803 per student, while the bottom 5% spent from $2720 to $3608. Thus, some school districts in Vermont commonly spend twice as much or more per student as other districts.

The correlation between spending disparities and taxable property wealth within the districts is also well established. . . . The data dramatically bear this out. In fiscal year 1995, for example, the Town of Richford's property tax base was approximately $140,000 per student, second lowest in the state, and its average student expenditure was also among the lowest at $3743. By contrast, the Town of Peru enjoyed a tax base of approximately $2.2 *million* per student, and its per-pupil expenditure was $6476. Of course, property wealth does not invariably correlate with student expenditures. Stannard's property tax base in fiscal year 1995 was somewhat over $118,000 per student, compared with Sherburne's of $2.5 million. Notwithstanding the vast disparity in property wealth, Stannard's average expenditure per pupil, $5684, was nearly equal to Sherburne's of $5731. Not surprisingly, however, there was a huge disparity in their effective tax rates: on an $85,000 home, the tax in Sherburne was $247; in Stannard, it was $2040. It is thus readily apparent . . . "that spending per pupil . . . tends to be highest in resource-rich districts who benefit further with low school tax rates . . . [while] [c]onversely, towns with limited resources spend less per student [and] pay higher tax rates."

The undisputed evidence thus amply supports plaintiffs' claim that wide disparities in student expenditures exist among Vermont school districts and that these disparities correlate generally with taxable property wealth within the districts. The record is relatively less developed with respect to plaintiffs' further assertion that funding disparities result in unequal educational opportunities, and specifically that "[c]omparatively low expenditures for education cause comparatively diminished educational opportunities for the students attending the affected schools." The essential point, however, is undisputed. The trial court noted the State had "concede[d] that the present funding scheme denies children residing in comparatively property-poor school districts the same 'educational opportunities' that are available to students residing in wealthier districts."

. . . [T]he parties assumed that unequal funding yields, at a minimum, unequal curricular, technological, and human resources. School districts of equal size but unequal funding would not have the capacity, for example, to offer equivalent foreign language training, purchase equivalent computer technology, hire teachers and other professional personnel of equivalent training and experience, or provide equivalent salaries and benefits.

In this respect the State concedes the obvious. While we recognize that equal dollar resources do not necessarily translate equally in effect, there is no reasonable doubt that substantial funding differences significantly affect opportunities to learn. To be sure, some school districts may manage their money better than others, and circumstances extraneous to the educational system may substantially affect a child's performance. Money is clearly not the only variable affecting educational opportunity, but it is one that government can effectively equalize.

III. Discussion

We now turn to the chief contention of this dispute, namely whether the disparities in educational opportunities outlined above violate Vermont law. We find the law to be unambiguous on this point. Whether we apply the "strict scrutiny" test urged by plaintiffs, the "rational basis" standard advocated by the State, or some intermediate level of review, the conclusion remains the same; in Vermont the right to education is so integral to our constitutional form of government, and its guarantees of political and civil rights, that any statutory framework that infringes upon the equal enjoyment of that right bears a commensurate heavy burden of justification. The State has not provided a persuasive rationale for the undisputed inequities in the current educational funding system. Accordingly, we conclude that the current system, which concededly denies equal educational opportunities, is constitutionally deficient.

* * *

A. The Right to Education in Vermont

From its earliest days, Vermont has recognized the obligation to provide for the education of its youth. That obligation begins with the Education Clause in the Vermont Constitution. A provision for the establishment of public schools was contained in the first Vermont Constitution of 1777. That section, in part, provided: "A school or schools shall be established in each town, by the legislature, for the convenient instruction of youth." . . .

The important point is not simply that public education was mentioned in the first Constitution. It is, rather, that education was the *only* governmental service considered worthy of constitutional status. The framers were not unaware of other public needs. . . .

. . . Indeed, many essential governmental services such as welfare, police and fire protection, transportation, and sanitation receive no mention whatsoever in our Constitution. Only one governmental service—public education—has ever been accorded constitutional status in Vermont.

. . . The Legislature has implemented the education clause by authorizing school districts to raise revenue through local property taxes. But neither this method, nor any other means of financing public education, is constitutionally mandated. Public education is a constitutional obligation of the state; funding of education through locally-imposed property taxes is not.

* * *

Apart from its prominence in the Constitution, the importance of education to self-government and the state's duty to ensure its proper dissemination have been enduring themes in the political history of Vermont. . . .

The courts of this state have been no less forthright in declaring education to be a fundamental obligation of the state. . . .

. . . [T]he State contends that the primary constitutional responsibility for education rests with the *towns* of Vermont, that its funding must be derived from whatever sources are available locally, that the only substantial tax available to towns is the property tax, and therefore that funding inequities are an inevitable—but nevertheless constitutional—consequence of local disparities in property wealth. . . .

This argument fundamentally misunderstands the state's constitutional responsibility—outlined above—for public education. The state may delegate to local towns and cities the authority to finance and administer the schools within their borders; it cannot, however, abdicate the basic responsibility for education by passing it on to local governments, which are themselves creations of the state.

The State's position confuses constitutional ends—the obligation to maintain a "competent number of schools . . . in each town,". . . with legislative means, that is, the methods it has employed to fulfill its obligation. As noted, our Constitution *nowhere* states that the revenue for education must be raised locally, that the source of the revenue must be property taxes, or that such revenues must be distributed unequally in conformity with local wealth. To be sure, these are longstanding and traditional components of the educational financing system in Vermont, but none of these represents a constitutional imperative. They are choices made by the government of the State of Vermont, and choices for which it bears ultimate responsibility.

The wisdom of the original constitutional structure becomes most apparent when considered in a modern context. Chapter II, § 68 states in general terms the state's responsibility to provide for education, but is silent on the means to carry it out. What the State characterizes as the basic constitutional structure of the system is really the legislative means of implementing it, which can and should be modified if it no longer fulfills its purpose. Means and methods that were effective in a rural society with limited development of property resources and largely local industries may become ineffective with the advent of major ski resorts and sizable industrial developments. The towns where the employees of these businesses actually live and educate their children bear the financial burden of development, while reaping none of the tax advantages.

Whether this dysfunction between means and ends ultimately denies the citizens of Vermont the "common benefit," Vt. Const. ch. I, art. 7, of the education constitutionally guaranteed is the question to which we now turn.

B. The Right to Equal Educational Opportunities

. . . We have held that the Common Benefits Clause in the Vermont Constitution . . . is generally coextensive with the equivalent guarantee in the United States Constitution, and imports similar methods of analysis. . . . As a general rule, challenges under the Equal Protection Clause are reviewed by the rational basis test, whereby "distinctions will be found unconstitutional only if similar persons are treated differently on 'wholly arbitrary and capricious grounds.'" . . . Where a statutory scheme affects fundamental constitutional rights or involves suspect classifications, both federal and state decisions have recognized that proper equal protection analysis necessitates a more searching scrutiny; the State must demonstrate that any discrimination occasioned by the law serves a compelling governmental interest, and is narrowly tailored to serve that objective. *Rodriguez*, 411 U.S. at 16–17, 93 S.Ct. at 1287–88 . . .

This is not a case, however, that turns on the particular constitutional test to be employed. Labels aside, we are simply unable to fathom a legitimate governmental purpose to justify the gross inequities in educational opportunities evident from the record. The distribution of a resource as precious as

educational opportunity may not have as its determining force the mere *fortuity* of a child's residence. It requires no particular constitutional expertise to recognize the capriciousness of such a system.

The principal rationale offered by the State in support of the current financing system is the laudable goal of local control. Individual school districts may well be in the best position to decide whom to hire, how to structure their educational offerings, and how to resolve other issues of a local nature. The State has not explained, however, why the current funding system is necessary to foster local control. Regardless of how the state finances public education, it may still leave the basic decision-making power with the local districts. Moreover, insofar as "local control" means the ability to decide that more money should be devoted to the education of children within a district, we have seen—as another court once wrote—that for poorer districts "such fiscal freewill is a cruel illusion." *Serrano v. Priest*, 5 Cal.3d 584, 96 Cal.Rptr. 601, 620, 487 P.2d 1241, 1260 (1971). We do not believe that the voters of Londonderry necessarily care more about education than their counterparts in Lowell simply because they spend nearly twice as much per student ($6005 as compared to $3207 in fiscal year 1995). On the contrary, if commitment to learning is measured by the rate at which residents are willing to *tax* themselves, then Lowell, with a property base of less than one-third per student than that of Londonderry, and a property tax nearly *twice* as high, should be considered the more devoted to education.

In short, poorer districts cannot realistically choose to spend more for educational excellence than their property wealth will allow, no matter how much sacrifice their voters are willing to make. The current system plainly does not enhance fiscal choice for poorer school districts.

The State also appears to argue that the current system must be upheld because, even conceding the Constitution provides a basic right to education, there is no evidence the framers intended that the right be distributed equally. The answer to this argument is twofold. First, although the documentary evidence of the framers' particular intentions in this regard is negligible, as early as 1828 the scope of the state's duty to educate was defined in terms of fundamental equality. . . .

The second response to the State's argument is simply that equal protection of the laws cannot be limited by eighteenth-century standards. While history must inform our constitutional analysis, it cannot bind it. Yesterday's bare essentials are no longer sufficient to prepare a student to live in today's global marketplace. To keep a democracy competitive and thriving, students must be afforded equal access to all that our educational system has to offer. In the funding of what our Constitution places at the core of a successful democracy, the children of Vermont are entitled to a reasonably equal share.

* * *

Finally, the State contends that the Common Benefits Clause is simply not offended by the unequal treatment of public schoolchildren residing in different districts so long as all are provided a minimally "adequate" education. The basis for such an argument is not entirely clear. We find no authority for the proposition that discrimination in the distribution of a constitutionally mandated right such as education may be excused merely because a "minimal" level of opportunity is provided to all. As Justice Marshall observed, "The Equal Protection Clause is not addressed to . . . minimal sufficiency but rather to the unjustifiable inequalities of state action." *Rodriguez*, 411 U.S. at 89, 93 S.Ct. at 1325 (Marshall, J., dissenting).

The evidence demonstrates, in sum, that the system falls well short of achieving reasonable educational equality of opportunity. Therefore, we hold that the student and school district plaintiffs are entitled to judgment as a matter of law that the current educational financing system in Vermont violates the right to equal educational opportunities under Chapter II, § 68 and Chapter I, Article 7 of the Vermont Constitution.

In so holding we emphasize that *absolute* equality of funding is neither a necessary nor a practical requirement to satisfy the constitutional command of equal educational opportunity. As plaintiffs readily concede, differences among school districts in terms of size, special educational needs, transportation costs, and other factors will invariably create unavoidable differences in per-pupil expenditures. Equal opportunity does not necessarily require precisely equal per-capita expenditures, nor does it necessarily prohibit cities and towns from spending more on education if they choose, but it does not allow a system in which educational opportunity is necessarily a function of district wealth. Equal educational opportunity cannot be achieved when property-rich school districts may tax low and property-poor districts must tax high to achieve even minimum standards. Children who live in property-poor districts and children who live in property-rich

districts should be afforded a substantially equal opportunity to have access to similar educational revenues. Thus, as other state courts have done, we hold only that to fulfill its constitutional obligation the state must ensure *substantial* equality of educational opportunity throughout Vermont. See *Rose v. Council for Better Educ.*, 790 S.W.2d 186, 211 (Ky.1989) (state constitution requires that educational opportunities be "substantially uniform throughout the state"); *McWherter*, 851 S.W.2d at 156 [Tenn. 1993](state education financing system must provide "substantially equal educational opportunities"); *Edgewood*, 777 S.W.2d at 397 [Tex. 1989](state constitution requires "substantially equal access to similar revenues per pupil").

* * *

NOTES AND QUESTIONS

1. *The Decision in Brigham v. Vermont*

Has the state supreme court provided sufficient guidance to the Vermont legislature with regard to devising a school financing scheme that would comply with the mandates of the state constitution? Has the court ruled out unenriched local supplementation when it states that the constitution does not "necessarily prohibit cities and towns from spending more on education if they choose, but it does not allow a system in which educational opportunity is necessarily a function of district wealth?" What does the court mean when it says that "to fulfill its constitutional obligation the state must ensure *substantial* equality of educational opportunity throughout Vermont?" (Emphasis in original.) Note that the Vermont court quotes *Edgewood I* with regard to Texas's constitutional requirement of "substantially equal access to similar revenues per pupil." Will this lead to a debate similar to that in Texas as to whether only 95 percent of the districts or the districts containing 95 percent of the students will have to be equalized? What is the standard of review employed by the court–strict scrutiny, rational basis, or something in between? Is the court correct when it assumes that local control is unrelated to local revenue raising? Or is it simply adopting a fiscal neutrality principle where districts are guaranteed equal revenues per pupil for equal tax effort (a district power equalizing principle)? But if the quality of education is a function of the level of per-pupil expenditures, isn't the court requiring substantially equal spending levels rather than tax equity? *See* Teachout, "'No Simple Disposition': The *Brigham* Case and the Future of Local Control over School Spending in Vermont," 22 *Vt. L. Rev.* 21 (1997).

2. *The Legislative Response*

The legislature adopted the Equal Educational Opportunity Act of 1997 (Act 60) in response to the *Brigham* decision. It interpreted the decision as mandating equalized fiscal capacity rather than equal spending, but did not restrict how much local communities could spend. Education is funded by a statewide property tax. All Vermont homeowners pay $1.10 per $100 of assessed property valuation, for which each school district receives $5,100 (to be adjusted for inflation in future years) per-pupil. School districts may levy additional taxes to raise the level of per pupil expenditures, but property-rich districts will have some of their funds "recaptured" for distribution to property-poor districts. The reform has meant that about 90 percent of Vermont homeowners have had their taxes reduced or, at worst, raised slightly. In addition, in many property-poor districts, expenditures for education have increased. However, property-rich districts (such as the ski resort towns with high-priced vacation condominiums noted in the *Brigham* opinion, with relatively few students but very high-quality schools where per-pupil expenditures exceeded 260 percent of some poor districts) find that a substantial amount of their taxes goes to poor districts. *See* Green, "Is Vermont's Funding Experiment a Lesson for Connecticut Schools?" *Hartford Courant*, June 28, 1998, at A1. Not surprisingly, the act has generated much political heat, and it is likely to be revised in the near future, particularly the "tax-sharing" or recapture provisions. Some wealthy towns have sought private contributions to support their schools, allowing them to opt out of the tax-sharing pool, forcing the state to replenish it with other tax revenues. Last year $7.3 million that otherwise would have been included in the pool was made up from private donations. *See* Kilborn, "Vermont Spending Plan Seems to Help Schools," *New York Times*, Jan. 31, 2001. A number of legal challenges were also initiated by some of the so-called "gold towns". *See Stowe Citizens for Responsible Governments v. State*, 730 A.2d 573 (Vt.1999) (court rejected claim that Act 60 was unconstitutional). *See* Note, "'A' for Effort: Evaluating Recent State Education Reform in Response to

Judicial Demands for Equity and Adequacy," 86 *Cornell L. Rev.* 644, 679 (2001), discussing the reaction of property-rich districts in Vermont to Act 60.

3. *Equity Claims That Have Been Unsuccessful*

Although a number of courts during the last decade found their state school finance systems unconstitutional under some theory of equity or fiscal neutrality, along lines similar to those relied upon by the Texas and Vermont courts, *see, e.g., Roosevelt Elementary School Dist. No. 66 v. Bishop*, 179 Ariz. 233, 877 P.2d 806 (1994) (applied to capital budget); *Tennessee Small School Systems v. McWherter*, 851 S.W.2d 139 (Tenn. 1993), other state supreme courts rejected such claims. *See, e.g., Vincent v. Voight*, 236 Wis.2d 588, 614 N.W.2d 388 (Wis. 2000); *Scott v. Commonwealth*, 443 S.E. 2d 138 (Va. 1994); *Skeen v. State*, 505 N.W.2d 299 (Minn.1993).

In *Vincent v. Voight*, 236 Wis.2d 588, 614 N.W.2d 388 (Wis. 2000), plaintiffs alleged that the state's school finance system, by failing to equalize access to financial resources among school districts, violated the uniformity clause of the education article of the Wisconsin constitution (which provides that school districts "shall be as nearly uniform as practicable"), and the constitution's equal protection clause. Plaintiffs sought an order that would require the legislature to "eliminate the tax base disparities from the system so districts that tax the same (at whatever level they choose) spend the same." *Id.* at 408. With regard to the uniformity clause, the court reviewed the plain meaning of the text, the practices at the time of the constitutional convention, early statutes, and precedents, and concluded that the uniformity clause referred only to the "character of the instruction" provided in the public schools, meaning that the clause guaranteed students a basic education but not equal allocation of resources. The court defined a basic education as follows:

> An equal opportunity for a sound basic education is one that will equip students for their roles as citizens and enable them to succeed economically and personally. The legislature has articulated a standard for equal opportunity for a sound basic education in Wis. Stat. §§ 118.30(1g)(a) and 121.02(L). Section 118.30(1g)(a) states that "each school board shall adopt pupil academic standards in mathematics, science, reading and writing, geography and history." Section 121.02(L) requires that "each school board shall . . . provide instruction" in several subjects, according to school grades.

By grounding the standard in statutes, we . . .defer to the legislature because it "is uniquely equipped to evaluate and respond to such questions of public policy. . . ." As such, we defer here to the legislature's wisdom in choosing which core subjects should be involved in providing an equal opportunity for a sound basic education.

* * *

The state adequately funds each school district to provide for a basic education, and any disparity between districts is a result of district revenue-raising capacity above the state's guaranteed tax base. The right to an equal opportunity for a sound basic education has not been shown to be violated by the present school finance system.

Id. at 407–408. The court concluded that disparity in the revenue-raising capacity of a school district does not constitute a violation of the uniformity clause, and that "a school finance system that uniformly funds school districts to provide a basic level of education is constitutional." *Id.* at 411.

The court noted that the plaintiffs had failed to demonstrate that any children lacked a basic education in any school district. "Merely showing disparity of the financial resources among school districts is not enough in this state to prove a lack of equal opportunity for a sound basic education. . . . Wisconsin requires districts to fulfil a constitutional minimum educational offering, not a maximum." *Id.* Evidence of "deteriorating school facilities, limited curricula, and lack of computer technology of some 'property poor' school districts, . . . [and] the elimination or reduction of certain advanced or elective courses from some districts does not mean that those school districts fail to offer a basic education." *Id.*

With regard to plaintiffs' contention that the school finance system violated Wisconsin's equal protection clause, the court noted that while there is a fundamental right to an equal opportunity for a sound basic education under the uniformity clause, it does not rest on any classification based on wealth. Applying the rational basis test, the court found the legislative classifications rationally related to the purpose of educating Wisconsin's children.

Note the different approaches to interpreting the state constitution adopted by the Vermont and Wisconsin courts. Was the Vermont court right in saying that the court cannot be "limited by eighteenth century standards", and looking to the role of education today, or should it have been governed more closely

by what the framers intended? To what extent, if at all, do the different outcomes to constitutional challenges in the various states turn on differences in the text of each state constitution's education clause? Eight states have education clauses that mandate "a thorough and efficient" system of free public schools: Maryland, Minnesota, New Jersey, Ohio, Pennsylvania, South Dakota, West Virginia, and Wyoming. Another seven states use either "thorough" or "efficient": Arkansas, Colorado, Delaware, Idaho, Illinois, Kentucky, and Texas. Others use "general" or "uniform," and some use a combination, such as mandating the state to establish and maintain "a general, uniform and thorough system of public, free schools." *See, e.g.,* Idaho const. art. IX, §1. Some states have education clauses that simply mandate a "system of common schools" or "a public educational system," such as California, Iowa, Louisiana, and New York. Washington State's constitution mandated the legislature to make "ample provision for the education of all children." Wash. const. art. IX, §1. Recall that Vermont's constitutional provision said only that "a competent number of schools ought to be maintained in each town." *See* Jensen, "Advancing Education Through Education Clauses of State Constitutions," 1997 *BYU Educ. & L. J.* 1, 3–8; Thro, "The Role of Language of the State Education Clauses in School Finance Litigation," 79 *Ed. Law Rep.* 19 (1993).

4. Backlash Litigation

A number of states included a "district power equalizing" formula (equal revenues for equal tax rates) in legislation enacted in response to court decisions finding the disparities in per-pupil expenditures resulting from tax base inequities to be unconstitutional. Under a "pure" district power equalizing formula, the state "recaptures" revenues raised in excess of the predetermined expenditure level for a particular tax rate, and distributes the excess (together with additional state funds, if necessary) to poorer school districts where, because of low property values, the selected tax rates cannot generate sufficient revenues to meet the predetermined level. These so-called "Robin Hood" schemes, *see* Verhovek, "Texans Reject Sharing School Wealth," *New York Times,* May 3, 1993, at A12, have often come under legal attack, as described in Levin, "Equal Educational Opportunity in School Finance Reform: What Went Wrong? Can (Should) It Be Fixed?" in *Quality Education for All in the 21st Century: Can We Get There*

From Here? 129, 156 (Lovell, ed., 1994). *See, e.g., Buse v. Smith*, 74 Wis.2d 550, 247 N.W.2d 141 (1976), discussed in *Vincent v. Voight, supra* (taxpayers and parents in "negative-aid" districts successfully challenged Wisconsin's recapture provision). Texas and Vermont also illustrate the strong political reaction of high property wealth districts to tax equalization that includes recapture provisions or that limits local supplementation.

5. *The Inadequacy of the Equity Approach*

As noted earlier, many state courts rejected equity-based arguments during the 1970s and 1980s. Although a few cases in the 1990s, such as *Brigham v. Vermont*, were successfully argued on equity grounds, an increasing number of school finance reformers were becoming dissatisfied with equity-based theories. Plaintiffs have not always been clear about what it is that they are asking courts to equalize: (1) equal funding for education (eliminating spending disparities), (2) equal education, (3) equal educational attainment, or (4) equal capacity to raise education revenues (taxpayer equity). Moreover, even when successful, equity cases often did not adequately address the improvements in educational opportunity many advocates were seeking for children most disadvantaged by the current system.

For example, if the equity-based goal was eliminating per-pupil expenditure disparities among districts, the fiscal neutrality principle offered no solution if all districts were equally inadequately funded, the situation that existed in California after *Serrano* and Proposition 13. Equalizing funding does not necessarily equalize the education that is delivered, let alone educational attainment, which may be affected by how the dollars are allocated, how the school system is administered, and in particular, the needs of different students. Many were concerned that if the legislative response were strict equality of expenditures, the greater needs of disadvantaged children concentrated in certain districts, and differences among districts in costs for the same educational services, would actually result in substantial inequalities. *See, e.g.,* McUsic, "The Law's Role in the Distribution of Education: The Promises and Pitfalls of School Finance Litigation," in *Law and School Reform* 88, 106 (J. Heubert, ed., 1999). Another concern was the weakening of local control or choice over the level of spending for education over other public services or tax relief that equalizing educational expenditures across districts might entail.

The cost of "leveling up" the lowest spending districts to the state average, let alone to the level of per-pupil expenditures in the highest spending districts, often proved economically infeasible and the alternative, attaining equal spending by lowering the level of expenditures in the high spending districts to the state average, was politically infeasible.

"Taxpayer equity", defined as freeing the tie between capacity (the district's per-pupil property value) and effort (the district's tax rate), triggered some similar concerns as well as concerns related specifically to this approach to equalization. The advantage of equalizing the capacity to raise funds for education was seen as retaining local control over spending, by leaving decisions about the tax rate to individual districts, but ensuring, as the *Edgewood I* court noted, that districts had equal access to similar spending at similar levels of tax effort. This would give property-poor districts real choice, which they did not have under an unequalized system, often taxing themselves at much higher rates but generating less revenue per student than districts with greater property wealth. A primary concern, however, was that under this approach, "the level of expenditures for a child's education would still be dependent upon where he lives–the difference being that disparities in expenditures are related to the preference of local voters rather than district wealth." Levin, "Current Trends in School Finance Reform Litigation: A Commentary," 1977 *Duke L. J.* 1099, 1113. A particular concern was the possibility that voters in a district where a majority did not have school-aged children or who could afford to send their children to private schools might refuse to vote for higher tax rates. *See, e.g.,* Pressley, "School Fight in a Gray Area: Retirees in Phoenix Suburb Resist Taxation for Education," *Washington Post*, Jan. 13, 1998. In noting a recent study that found that increases in the percentage of elderly residents in a jurisdiction is associated with a significant reduction in spending per pupil, it was observed that this was "a result with ominous overtones in a society whose average age is rapidly increasing as the baby boom generation approaches retirement age." National Research Council, *Making Money Matter: Financing America's Schools* 97 (H. Ladd and J. Hansen, eds., 1999).

Questions were also raised regarding whether property-poor local governments, under a scheme that equalized capacity to raise education revenues (but not other public services) might attempt to shift some of their other functions to the school budget. On the other hand, might not property-rich local governments attempt to shift some functions out of the school budget to those budgets not subject to tax capacity equalizing? *See* Kurtz, "Eanes Weighs Idea to Dodge Financing Law: Plan Would Call for Other Taxing Entities to Assume School Services," *Austin American-Statesman*, July 9, 2000.

Yet another substantial concern was that urban districts, with high concentrations of students with extraordinary educational need would be among the losers regardless of whether spending or revenue-raising capacity was equalized. *See* Janssen, "Public School Finance, School Choice, and Equal Educational Opportunity in Texas: The Enduring Importance of Background Conditions," 19 *Rev. Litig.* 1 (2000), arguing that equalization of resources will not address the root causes of educational inequities, particularly for poor children. Janssen argues that fiscal neutrality "may prove more costly to school districts with many poor students than a non-neutral system. Districts with greater property wealth per student may have concentrations of poorer families and children. In the equalization process, districts with such concentrations may actually have their funding reduced." *Id.* at 7. Similarly, urban school districts, although often with higher tax bases than the state average, also experience higher costs for educational services, and thus would be disadvantaged by some applications of the fiscal neutrality principle. *See, e.g.,* B. Levin, T. Muller, and C. Sandoval, *The High Cost of Education in Cities* (1973).

The focus on input measures has also been criticized as failing to address the quality of educational services or to address the growing emphasis on standards-based educational reforms.

These and other arguments against equity-based approaches to school finance reform are detailed in Minorini and Sugarman, *supra,* at 183–187. For other critiques of fiscal neutrality principles, *see, e.g.,* McUsic, *supra;* Heise, "Equal Educational Opportunity, Hollow Victories, and the Demise of School Finance Equity Theory: An Empirical Perspective and Alternative Explanation," 32 *Ga. L. Rev.* 543 (1998); Enrich, "Leaving Equality Behind: New Directions in School Finance Reform," 48 *Vand. L. Rev.* 101 (1995); Heise, "State Constitutions, School Finance Litigation, and the 'Third Wave': From Equity to Adequacy," 68 *Temp. L. Rev.* 1151, 1168–1174 (1995).

6. *Impact of Equity-Based Reforms*

Despite all of the problems with equity-based reforms, research indicates that expenditure disparities were reduced over a 20-year period (1972–1992) in states in which courts mandated school finance reform. *See* National Research Council, *Making Money Matter: Financing America's Schools* 90–91 (H. Ladd and J. Hansen, eds., 1999), summarizing the research findings. In addition, as a result of court-ordered reform, spending rose by 11 percent in the poorest school districts, by 7 percent in the median district, and remained roughly constant in the wealthiest districts. *But see* Joondeph, "The Good, the Bad, and the Ugly: An Empirical Analysis of Litigation-Prompted School Finance Reform," 35 *Santa Clara L. Rev.* 763 (1995), which, in a study of six school districts, found that disparities decreased, but that the overall rate of increase in expenditures was lowered. The 20-year study reported by the National Research Council, *supra,* also found that the states' share of total educational spending rose. Nevertheless, district spending levels are still related to district wealth and tax levels. *Id.* at 96.

A recent study compared several states where school finance litigation was successful with comparable states where courts refused to overturn their states' financing schemes (states that were predominantly urban, relatively affluent, with racially identified urban poverty were compared, as were states that were more rural with significant rural poverty). Reed, "Twenty-Five Years After *Rodriguez*: School Finance Litigation and the Impact of the New Judicial Federalism," 32 *Law and Soc'y Rev.* 175 (1998). In the states where finance reform litigation was successful there was an increase in spending in the lowest spending districts (with the exception of Texas), compared with a decrease or no increase in the lowest spending districts in states where litigation was unsuccessful. In those states where equity suits were successful, the level of disparities in expenditures decreased, while in those states where litigation was unsuccessful, disparities either were significantly worse or remained unchanged. *Id.* at 190–191, 197, 201.

A study of the impact of the Texas legislation adopted following the *Edgewood* decisions shows that the link between a school district's property wealth and educational attainment, as measured by the Texas Assessment of Academic Skills, has been eliminated. "Study Says Law Erases Link Between Schools' Wealth, TAAS Results," *Dallas Morning*

News, May 19, 1999, at 23A. The study showed that in 1996–97, students in lower wealth school districts—white, black, and Hispanic—performed just as well on the TAAS as did similar students in higher wealth districts. In previous years, those students did better on the TAAS when enrolled in higher wealth districts.

C. From Equity to Adequacy

As the problems with relying on an equity theory became apparent, litigators searched for an alternative way to frame school finance cases. One of the most promising appeared to be an adequacy approach, one which insisted that state constitutions guarantee children the right to a minimum level of public education. The adequacy approach seemed to avoid the political pitfalls of restructuring the traditional property tax system to equalize education. Moreover, it shifted the focus from defining equality to determining what constitutes a sound basic education. As a result, courts did not need to conclude that there is any precise, linear relationship between money and achievement but simply could ascertain whether current programs satisfy a minimum standard. The question of adequacy returns the focus to pedagogical concerns, and state legislative adoption of minimum competency testing can aid the courts in giving content to the concept. Enrich, "Leaving Equality Behind: New Directions in School Finance Reform," 48 *Vand.L.Rev.* 101, 166–83 (1995); Heise, "State Constitutions, School Finance Litigation, and the 'Third Wave': From Equity to Adequacy," 68 *Temple L.Rev.* 1151, 1174–76 (1995); McUsic, "The Law's Role in the Distribution of Education: The Promises and Pitfalls of School Finance Litigation," in *Law and School Reform: Six Strategies for Promoting Educational Equity* 88, 90–91 (J.Heubert, ed., 1999); Morgan, Cohen, and Hershkoff, "Establishing Education Program Inadequacy: The Alabama Example," 28 *U.Mich.J.L.Ref.* 559, 586–94 (1995).

1. Defining an Adequate Education.

Although the adequacy approach sidesteps some of the difficulties inherent in enforcing a principle of strict equity, the notion of adequacy presents complicated problems of its own. These challenges are summed up by a leading attorney in the field of school finance:

"Judicial Analysis During the Third Wave of School Finance Litigation: The Massachusetts Decision as a Model"
William E. Thro, 35 *B.C.L.Rev.* 597, 605–08 (1994).

* * *

First, before a court can properly analyze any school finance suit, it must ascertain, preferably explicitly, whether the litigation before it is primarily an equality suit or a quality suit. Obviously, if the case is primarily an equality suit, application of quality suit analysis, which is detailed below, is totally inappropriate. In such a case, the court should utilize the equal protection analysis that was common to first and second wave cases. Consequently, such questions as whether education is a fundamental right or whether the school finance system is irrational will dominate the analysis.

Second, if the court finds that it has a quality suit, it must begin its analysis by determining if the education clause imposes a specific standard of quality or is "merely hortatory or aspirational."[51] In making this assessment, the court should recognize that the mere fact that a state constitution has an education clause does not mean that a particular standard of quality is necessarily mandated. After all, forty-nine states have education clauses of some form. Yet, the clauses have a variety of different wordings. Given the differences in wording, courts should not assume that all of them mandate the same or nearly the same quality standard. Instead, the court should focus on the actual language of the education clause and the way it compares to the educational provisions of other states.

As Professors Grubb and Ratner have independently observed, the state education clauses can be divided into four categories based upon the duty imposed on the state legislature.[54] In some states, "Category I" clauses impose a legislative duty which is met by simply establishing a public school system.[55] In other states,[56] "Category II" clauses require that the

---

[51]*McDuffy* [v. *Secretary of the Exec. Office of Educ.*], 615 N.E.2d [516,] at 519 [(Ma. 1993)].

[54]Grubb, *Breaking The Language Barrier: The Right To Bilingual Education*, 9 Harv.C.R.-C.L.L.Rev. 52, 66–70 (1974); Gershon M. Ratner, *A New Legal Duty For Urban Public Schools: Effective Education In Basic Skills*, 63 Tex.L.Rev. 777, 814–16, n.143–46 (1985). . . .

[55]*See* Ala. Const. art. 14, § 256; Alaska Const. art. VII, § 1; Ariz. Const. art. XI, § 1; Conn. Const. art. VIII, § 1; Hawaii Const. art. IX, § 1; Kan. Const. art. VI, § 1; La. Const. art. VIII, § 1; Mass. Const. Ch 5, § 2; Neb. Const. art. VII, § 1; N.M. Const. art. XII, § 1; N.Y. Const. art. XI, § 1; N.C. Const. art. IX, § 2; Okla. Const. art. XIII, § 1; S.C. Const. art. XI, § 3; Tenn. Const. art. XI, § 12; Utah Const. art. X, § 1; Vt. Const. ch. 2, § 68.

system be of a specific quality or have some characteristic such as "uniformity."[57] The "Category III" education clauses go beyond the specific quality level of Category II and set up the school system for a specific purpose.[58] Finally, in the few states with "Category IV" clauses, education is the "primary," "fundamental" or "paramount" duty of the state legislature.[59] If this language is taken literally, the needs of the public school system must be addressed *before* the state's needs for roads, parks and other social services.

It is quite easy to see how these differences could manifest themselves in judicial analysis. For example, because Category I clauses do not specify any level of quality, courts would not find such a mandate; to find a quality mandate with a Category I education clause is to ignore the plain language of the provision.[61] Similarly, because Category III and IV clauses appear to impose either a greater quality standard or a greater duty than Category II clauses, a plaintiffs' victory, theoretically, should be easier in states with these clauses.

Third, if the court answers the second question by determining that the education clause does impose a standard of quality, it must move to the next question and define exactly what that quality standard means. The answer to this inquiry effectively determines the outcome of the litigation. If the court sets an extremely high standard, then it will be virtually impossible for school districts to measure up. In contrast, if the court sets a low standard, such as the minimum standards for accreditation required by the State Board of Education, the system will almost always pass muster.

Fourth, having answered the third question and determined what the quality standard means, the court then must apply that standard to the particular school districts and determine if there has been a violation. Although, as noted above, the exact definition of quality will effectively determine whether school districts fall below the standard, arguably there remains an issue as to how widespread the failure must be in order for there to be a violation. If only one school district fails to measure up, does that mean that the entire system is in violation? What if ten, twenty, or even fifty percent fail to meet the constitutionally mandated standard? Does the size of those districts which fail to meet the standard matter?

Fifth, if the court determines that the failure to meet the constitutional standard is extensive enough to warrant a finding of a system-wide violation, there remains the question of the significance of funding in the failure of the system to meet the constitutionally mandated standard. The mere fact that all school districts do not measure up does not necessarily mean that this failure is caused by a lack of money. There are a wide variety of other factors, including mismanagement, excessive administration, too many incompetent teachers, misplaced spending priorities, outright corruption, nepotism, an improper emphasis on some programs, the need to bus to achieve racial desegregation and the necessity of complying with other federal laws such as the Individuals With Disabilities Education Act or Title IX, which might cause a school district to fall below the constitutional standard. Even if lack of money is a cause, or even the primary cause, of the district's inadequacy, it is almost inevitable that there will be other non-financial causes. Thus, in order to correct the inadequacy, it may be necessary to do more than restructure the finance system. Indeed, it may be necessary for a district to undergo fundamental reform of its entire educational system rather than simply to distribute more money.

* * *

NOTES AND QUESTIONS

1. Strict Textualism and State Constitutional Interpretation

Is Thro correct in suggesting that the principal consideration in determining whether students have a right to a minimally adequate education is the lan-

---

[56]*See* Ark. Const. art. XIV, § 1; Colo. Const. art. IX, § 2; Del. Const. art. X, § 1; Fla. Const. art. IX, § 1; Idaho Const. art. IX, § 1; Ky. Const. § 183; Md. Const. art. VIII, § 1; Minn. Const. art. XIII, § 1; Mont. Const. art. X, § 1; N.D. Const. art. VIII, § 1; Ohio Const. art. VI, § 3; Or. Const. art. VIII, § 3; Pa. Const. art. III, § 14; Tex. Const. art. VII, § 1; Va. Const. art. VIII, § 1; W. Va. Const. art. XII, § 1; Wis. Const. art. X, § 3.

[57]Generally, the specific quality is "thorough and/or efficient." As the West Virginia Supreme Court observed, Maryland, Minnesota, New Jersey, Ohio and Pennsylvania have thorough and efficient clauses; Colorado, Idaho and Montana require thorough systems; and Arkansas, Delaware, Illinois, Kentucky and Texas require efficient systems. Pauley v. Kelly, 255 S.E.2d 859, 865 (W. Va. 1979).

[58]*See* Cal. Const. art. IX, § 1; Ind. Const. art. VIII, § 1; Iowa Const. art. 9; § 2; Nev. Const. art. XI, § 2, R.I. Const. art. XII, § 1; S.D. Const. art. VIII, § 1; Wyo. Const. art. VII, § 1. Ratner, *supra* note 54, at 815 & n. 145; Grubb, *supra* note 54, at 68.

[59]*See* Gal. Const. art. VIII, § 1, ¶ 1; Ill. Const. art. X, § 1; Me. Const. art. 8, § 1; Mich. Const. art. VIII, § 2; Mo. Const. art. 9, § 1(a); N.H. Const. Pt 2, art. 83; Wash. Const. art. IX, § 1.

[61]Only two Category I clauses, those in Massachusetts and Tennessee, have ever been interpreted as imposing a quality standard. *See McDuffy*, 6154 N.E.2d 516, 548 (Ma. 1993); [*Tennessee Small Sch. Sysm. V.*] *McWherter*, 851 S.W.2d 139, 150–51 (Tenn. 1993).

guage of the state's education clause? Should courts attach substantial significance to the use of the term "uniformity" rather than "paramount duty"? Is it likely that those who crafted this language had specific implications for school finance in mind?

2. *Deference or Activism?*

Once a court determines that the state constitution imposes a quality standard, how should it decide whether to defer to accreditation requirements set by the board of education or to create an independent judicial test of adequacy? Can the language of the state constitution answer this question? If not, what other factors may be relevant? For a discussion of these issues, *see* Dietz, "Manageable Adequacy Standards in Education Reform Litigation," 74 *Wash.U.L.Q.* 1193, 1204–12 (1996).

3. *Pedagogical Questions and the Judicial Role*

Should the courts generally presume that a school system meets a standard of adequacy? Should the plaintiffs bear the burden of offering extensive, detailed evidence about the school's systemic deficiencies? If the plaintiffs offer evidence that a substantial number of schools fall short, should the burden shift to the state board to show that the system is adequate? When a state court finds a system wide violation, how should it go about remedying it? The remainder of this section examines how different courts have answered these questions.

2. The Historical Underpinnings of the Adequacy Claim: *Robinson v. Cahill.*

The adequacy movement has its roots in a New Jersey case that included this type of claim in addition to an equity argument. The February 1970 complaint contained not only a prayer for relief based on equal protection but also an argument "that the New Jersey constitution's 'thorough and efficient' education clause required the state to afford each child 'at least such instruction as is necessary to fit it for the ordinary duties of citizenship' and 'to provide the minimum education to all children . . . so that they may be able to read, write and function in a political environment.'" Tractenberg, "*Robinson v. Cahill:* The 'Thorough and Efficient' Clause," 38 *Law & Contemp.Probs.* 312, 315 (1974). With the filing of this complaint, a new line of litigation based on the education clauses of state constitutions began.

The trial court in *Robinson v. Cahill* concluded that the system of school finance in New Jersey vio-

lated the federal and state equal protection rights of taxpayers and students of poor districts and that the low level of funding of the existing finance law did not ensure all students of the "thorough and efficient system of free public schools" guaranteed by the state constitution. *Robinson v. Cahill*, 118 N.J. Super. 223, 287 A.2d 187 (1972). The state obtained a stay of the court's order and appealed.

Robinson v. Cahill
62 N.J. 473, 303 A.2d 273 (1973).

The opinion of the Court was delivered by Weintraub, CJ.

[The opinion begins by describing the New Jersey education finance system, similar in pertinent respects to the Texas legislation reviewed in the *Rodriguez* decision.]

* * *

The question whether the equal protection demand of our State Constitution is offended remains for us to decide. Conceivably a State Constitution could be more demanding. For one thing, there is absent the principle of federalism which cautions against too expansive a view of a federal constitutional limitation upon the power and opportunity of the several States to cope with their own problems in the light of their own circumstances. . . .

* * *

We hesitate to turn this case upon the State equal protection clause. The reason is that the equal protection clause may be unmanageable if it is called upon to supply categorical answers in the vast area of human needs, choosing those which must be met and a single basis upon which the State must act. The difficulties become apparent in the argument in the case at hand. [The court rejects constitutional arguments premised either on wealth being a suspect classification, or education meriting treatment as a fundamental interest.]

* * *

The remaining question is whether certain provisions of our State Constitution . . . [are violated by the current system of financing public education in New Jersey].

The provisions relating to public education were added to the Constitution of 1844 by amendments adopted in 1875. Art. IV, §7, ¶6, was amended by adding this sentence: 'The legislature shall provide for the maintenance and support of a thorough and efficient system of free public schools for the instruction of all the children in this State between the ages of five and eighteen years.' This provision is now Art. VIII, §4, ¶1, of the 1947 Constitution. The other amendment in 1875 added Art. IV, §7, ¶11, which prohibits "private, local or special laws" in "enumerated cases," among which appears: 'Providing for the management and support of free public schools.' The quoted provision is item (7) in Art. IV, §7, ¶9, of the 1947 Constitution, with the word "control" substituted for the word "support." . . .

* * *

It seems clear that the 1875 amendment has not been understood to prohibit the State's use of local government with local tax responsibility in the discharge of the constitutional mandate. . . .

. . . [I]t cannot be said the 1875 amendments were intended to ensure statewide equality among taxpayers. But we do not doubt that an equal educational opportunity for children was precisely in mind. The mandate that there be maintained and supported 'a thorough and efficient system of free public schools for the instruction of all the children in the State between the ages of five and eighteen years' can have no other import. Whether the State acts directly or imposes the role upon local government, the end product must be what the Constitution commands. A system of instruction in any district of the state which is not thorough and efficient falls short of the constitutional command. Whatever the reason for the violation, the obligation is the State's to rectify it. If local government fails, the state government must compel it to act, and if the local government cannot carry the burden, the State must itself meet its continuing obligation. . . .

. . . Today, a system of public education which did not offer high school education would hardly be thorough and efficient. The Constitution's guarantee must be understood to embrace that educational opportunity which is needed in the contemporary setting to equip a child for his role as a citizen and as a competitor in the labor market.

We are brought then to the question whether the State has fulfilled its obligation to afford all pupils that level of instructional opportunity which is comprehended by a thorough and efficient system of education for students between the ages of five and eighteen. . . .

The trial court found the constitutional demand had not been met and did so on the basis of discrepancies in dollar input per pupil. We agree. We deal with the problem in those terms because dollar input is plainly relevant and because we have been shown no other viable criterion for measuring compliance

with the constitutional mandate. The constitutional mandate could not be said to be satisfied unless we were to suppose the unlikely proposition that the lowest level of dollar performance happens to coincide with the constitutional mandate and that all efforts beyond the lowest level are attributable to local decisions to do more than the State was obliged to do.

Surely the existing statutory system is not visibly geared to the mandate that there be 'a thorough and efficient system of free public schools for the instruction of all the children in this state between the ages of five and eighteen years.' Indeed the State has never spelled out the content of the educational opportunity the Constitution requires. Without some such prescription, it is even more difficult to understand how the tax burden can be left to local initiative with any hope that statewide equality of educational opportunity will emerge. . . .

On its face the [1970] statutory scheme has no apparent relation to the mandate for equal educational opportunity. . . .

We have outlined the formula of the 1970 act to show . . . it is not demonstrably designed to guarantee that local effort plus the State aid will yield to all the pupils in the State that level of educational opportunity which the 1875 amendment mandates. We see no basis for a finding that the 1970 Act, even if fully funded, would satisfy the constitutional obligation of the State. . . .

. . . [I]f the State chooses to assign its obligation under the 1875 amendment to local government, the State must do so by a plan which will fulfill the State's continuing obligation. To that end the State must define in some discernible way the educational obligation and must compel the local school districts to raise the money necessary to provide that opportunity. The State has never spelled out the content of the constitutionally mandated educational opportunity. Nor has the State required the school districts to raise moneys needed to achieve that unstated standard. Nor is the State aid program designed to compensate for local failures to reach that level. It must be evident that our present scheme is a patchy product reflecting provincial contests rather than a plan sensitive only to the constitutional mandate.

* * *

Upon the record before us, it may be doubted that the thorough and efficient system of schools required by the 1875 amendment can realistically be met by reliance upon local taxation. The discordant correlations between the educational needs of the school districts and their respective tax bases suggest any such effort would likely fail. . . .

Although we have dealt with the constitutional problem in terms of dollar input per pupil, we should not be understood to mean that the State may not recognize differences in area costs, or a need for additional dollar input to equip classes of disadvantaged children for the educational opportunity. Nor do we say that if the State assumes the cost of providing the constitutionally mandated education, it may not authorize local government to go further and to tax to that further end, provided that such authorization does not become a device for diluting the State's mandated responsibility.

The present system being unconstitutional, we come to the subject of remedies. We agree with the trial court that relief must be prospective. The judiciary cannot unravel the fiscal skein. Obligations incurred must not be impaired. And since government must go on, and some period of time will be needed to establish another statutory system, obligations hereafter incurred pursuant to existing statutes will be valid in accordance with the terms of the statutes. . . .

Subject to the modifications expressed in this opinion and the matters reserved in the preceding paragraph, the judgment of the trial court is affirmed.

NOTES AND QUESTIONS

1. *The Standard of* Robinson I

Robinson I concludes that Art. IV, §7 was not intended to provide taxpayer equity but to protect children. From this perspective, the court finds that New Jersey's financing scheme is not a "thorough and efficient" system because it does not provide for equal educational opportunity for children. Does "efficient" mean equitable? Does "thorough"? What is the court's conception of equal educational opportunity? Is it an input or output theory of equal educational opportunity? Does the court require equal expenditures per pupil, no wealth discrimination, minimal adequacy? What does the court mean when it says that "The constitutional mandate could not be said to be satisfied unless we were to suppose the unlikely proposition that the lowest level of dollar performance happens to coincide with the constitutional mandate and that all efforts beyond the lowest

level are attributable to local decisions to do more than the state was obliged to do"? Might it be argued that the court in *Robinson I* has no standard of its own but is merely troubled by the state's creation of a system of finance without itself first spelling out "the content of the educational opportunity the constitution requires"? Is the court asking the legislature to develop its own definition of what the constitution requires and then redesign the state system to meet that standard? Or does the court have its own notion of what the state constitution requires? Considering *Robinson I* alone, what is it that the legislature must do to comply with the state's constitution? How does the court's approach differ from that in *Serrano*?

2. Robinson II *through* Robinson VII

One month after *Robinson I*, the New Jersey Supreme Court took up the issue of the remedial timetable and held that it would not disturb the existing statutory scheme unless the legislature failed to enact, by December 31, 1974, legislation compatible with *Robinson I*. *Robinson II*, 63 N.J. 196, 306 A.2d 65 (1973). In November 1973, the state chose a new governor whose task it became to develop proposed legislation in response to *Robinson I* and *II*. The case forced the governor to consider new criteria for governing local educational programs, a new system of state aid, and a new way of raising sufficient money to pay for the new state aid system. He made his proposals for change to the legislature on May 15, 1974, but the legislature was unable to reach agreement, particularly on a new tax plan. Thus the court's December 31, 1974, deadline came and went. The court therefore ordered oral argument to be held on the relief to be granted for the coming school year, commencing July 1, 1975. *Robinson III*, 67 N.J. 35, 335 A.2d 6 (1975). In May of that year *Robinson IV* was issued. In order to give the legislature yet more time to work on the complex problem that the court had handed it, the court limited its remedy to the 1976–77 school year. The provisional remedy ordered redistribution of two kinds of existing state aid in such a way as to benefit property-poor school districts. *Robinson IV*, 67 N.J. 333, 339 A.2d 193 (1975). The state legislature finally adopted a new system of school finance on September 29, 1975.

The 1975 Act contained the following provisions: It established a goal that the public schools prepare all students, regardless of social class, so that they could function politically, economically, and socially in a democratic society; the creation of an elaborate monitoring system involving the use of state-administered standardized tests of basic skill areas; the formulation of plans by local districts for achieving the legislatively mandated goal noted above; a delegation of power to the state commissioner to rectify local defects in providing an adequate education, including forcing an increase in the amount of the local budget; and a modified system for allocating state aid. The modified plan still provided minimum aid on a per-pupil basis, limited annual budget increases, and took steps to equalize per-pupil tax resources by establishing a guaranteed property valuation per pupil. The court, on January 30, 1976, said that if the system were fully funded, the new law would be constitutional despite the fact that its basic financial provisions were similar to those in the law struck down in *Robinson I*. The court gave the legislature until April 6, 1976, to fund the law. *Robinson V,* 69 N.J. 449, 355 A.2d 129 (1976). But the legislature deadlocked on a new tax bill, the law went unfunded, and *Robinson* was back in the court. On May 13, 1976, its patience having run out, the court enjoined every public officer—state, county, or municipal—from expending any funds for the support of the public school system. New Jersey schools were shut down by court order. *Robinson VI,* 70 N.J. 155, 358 A.2d 457 (1976). The immediate effect of the shutdown was to shift sufficient votes in the state senate to enable the passage of New Jersey's first state income tax on July 9, 1976. That same day the court dissolved its order closing the schools. *Robinson VII,* 70 N.J. 464, 360 A.2d 400 (1976). These dramatic events did not put an end to school finance litigation in New Jersey however. Five years later, students from four urban school districts brought suit, alleging that their needs were not adequately addressed by the state's education act. *See Abbott v. Burke,* 710 A.2d 450, 455 (N.J. 1998) (*Abbott V*). This litigation has continued and is discussed in Section II. D. of this chapter.

3. Robinson *and the Policymaking Process*

In a detailed historical account of the litigation of the *Robinson* case, Professor Richard Lehne concludes that *Robinson* had few positive effects and a number of negative ones. He believes that *Robinson* did shift somewhat the allocation of state aid within the state to the benefit of property-poor districts but to the disadvantage of districts with large numbers of poor families—districts that had benefited from the old formula replaced by the 1975 Act. R. Lehne, *The Quest for Justice* 173 (1978). Lehne sees *Robinson* as

an agenda-setting case—a case that forced the other branches of government to move an issue already in the public realm higher on their political agenda. It was not a decision-making case in which the court itself settled an issue.

Is it a proper use of judicial power merely to set an agenda rather than decide specific issues? Do *Robinson I* through *Robinson VII* represent a better approach than *Serrano I* and *II* or *Rodriguez? See* Kirp, "Law, Politics, and Equal Educational Opportunity," 47 *Harv.Educ.Rev.* 117 (1977). More recently, however, Professor James E. Ryan has contended that spending disparities were reduced in New Jersey. He reports that "the twenty-eight urban minority districts are currently funded at the same level as the wealthiest suburban districts—and this in the state that has the highest average per-pupil expenditure." Ryan, "The Influence of Race in School Finance Reform," 98 *Mich.L.Rev.* 432, 472 (1999). However, he notes that in New Jersey, the legislature continues to chafe at court-ordered reform. *Id.* Does the evolution of the *Robinson* case suggest that it is sometimes difficult to distinguish between an adequacy and an equity case?

3. Approaches to Adequacy After *Robinson v. Cahill.*

The political fallout of the *Robinson v. Cahill* litigation did not deter advocates from pursuing adequacy claims. Courts, however, may have been influenced by the New Jersey example when they considered how to define adequacy and how to remedy inadequacy.

a. A Deferential Judicial Stance. Some states like Rhode Island and Arizona have adopted a deferential approach. In *City of Pawtucket v. Sundlun,* 662 A.2d 40 (R.I. 1995), the high court held that the legislature, not the judiciary, was responsible for defining standards of adequacy when they were not set forth explicitly in the state constitution's education clause. A concurring opinion in the Arizona Supreme Court adopted a similar view. *Roosevelt Elementary School No. 66 v. Bishop,* 877 P.2d 806 (Ariz. 1994). *See generally* Dietz, *supra,* at 1204–06. In addition to the Rhode Island and Arizona examples, Dietz contends that the Tennessee high court made "a conscious decision to dodge the adequacy issue" in *Tennessee Small School Systems v. McWherter,* 851 S.W.2d 139 (Tenn. 1993). *See* Dietz, *supra,* at 1205.

b. An Activist Judicial Stance.   Other courts have continued to provide independent judicial review of educational adequacy. Some have pursued vigorous intervention that has built on but modified the New Jersey court's approach. Perhaps the most notable of these is the Kentucky Supreme Court's decision.

Rose v. Council for Better Education, Inc.
790 S.W.2d 186 (Ky. 1989).

Stephens, Chief Justice.

The issue we decide on this appeal is whether the Kentucky General Assembly has complied with its constitutional mandate to "provide an efficient system of common schools throughout the state."[1]

In deciding that it has not, we intend no criticism of the substantial efforts made by the present General Assembly and by its predecessors, nor do we intend to substitute our judicial authority for the authority and discretion of the General Assembly. We are, rather, exercising our constitutional duty in declaring that, when we consider the evidence in the record, and when we apply the constitutional requirement of Section 183 to that evidence, it is crystal clear that the General Assembly has fallen short of its duty to enact legislation to provide for an efficient system of common schools throughout the state. In a word, the present system of common schools in Kentucky is not an "efficient" one in our view of the clear mandate of Section 183. The common school system in Kentucky is constitutionally deficient.

In reaching this decision, we are ever mindful of the immeasurable worth of education to our state and its citizens, especially to its young people. The framers of our constitution intended that each and every child in this state should receive a proper and an adequate education, *to be provided for by the General Assembly.* This opinion dutifully applies the constitutional test of Section 183 to the existing system of common schools. We do no more, nor may we do any less.

The goal of the framers of our constitution, and the polestar of this opinion, is eloquently and movingly stated in the landmark case of *Brown v. Board of Education:*

> "*education is perhaps the most important function of state and local governments.* Compulsory school attendance laws and the great expenditures for education

both demonstrate our recognition of the importance of education to our democratic society. It is required in the performance of our most basic public responsibilities, even service in the armed forces. It is the very foundation of good citizenship. Today it is a principal instrument in awakening the child to cultural values, in preparing him for later professional training, and in helping him to adjust normally to his environment. In these days, it is doubtful that any child may reasonably be expected to succeed in life if he is denied the opportunity of an education. *Such an opportunity, where the state has undertaken to provide it, is a right which must be made available to all on equal terms.*" Id., 347 U.S. 483, 493, 74 S.Ct. 686, 691, 98 L.Ed. 873 (1954) (emphasis added).

These thoughts were as applicable in 1891 when Section 183 was adopted as they are today and the goals they express reflect the goals set out by the framers of our Kentucky Constitution.

* * *

Definition of "Efficient"

We now hone in on the heart of this litigation. In defining "efficient," we use all the tools that are made available to us. In spite of any protestations to the contrary, we do not engage in judicial legislating. We do not make policy. We do not substitute our judgment for that of the General Assembly. We simply take the plain directive of the Constitution, and, armed with its purpose, we decide what our General Assembly must achieve in complying with its solemn constitutional duty.

Any system of common schools must be created and maintained with the premise that education is absolutely vital to the present and to the future of our Commonwealth. As Herbert Spencer observed, "Education has for its object the formation of character." H. Spencer, *Social Studies* pt. 1, ch. 2, p. 17 (1851). No tax proceeds have a more important position or purpose than those for education in the grand scheme of our government. The importance of common schools and the education they provide Kentucky's children cannot be overemphasized or overstated.

The sole responsibility for providing the system of common schools is that of our General Assembly. It is a duty—it is a constitutional mandate placed by the people on the 138 members of that body who represent those selfsame people.

The General Assembly must not only establish the system, but it must monitor it on a continuing basis so that it will always be maintained in a constitutional

---

[1] Ky. Const. Sec. 183.

manner. The General Assembly must carefully supervise it, so that there is no waste, no duplication, no mismanagement, at any level.

The system of common schools must be adequately funded to achieve its goals. The system of common schools must be substantially uniform throughout the state. Each child, *every child*, in this Commonwealth must be provided with an equal opportunity to have an adequate education. Equality is the key word here. The children of the poor and the children of the rich, the children who live in the poor districts and the children who live in the rich districts must be given the same opportunity and access to an adequate education. This obligation cannot be shifted to local counties and local school districts.

As we have indicated, Section 183 requires the General Assembly to establish a system of common schools that provides an equal opportunity for children to have an adequate education. In no way does this constitutional requirement act as a limitation on the General Assembly's power to create local school entities and to grant to those entities the authority to supplement the state system. Therefore, if the General Assembly decides to establish local school entities, it may also empower them to enact local revenue initiatives to supplement the uniform, equal educational effort that the General Assembly must provide. This includes not only revenue measures similar to the special taxes previously discussed, but also the power to assess local ad valorem taxes on real property and personal property at a rate over and above that set by the General Assembly to fund the statewide system of common schools. Such local efforts may not be used by the General Assembly as a substitute for providing an adequate, equal and substantially uniform educational system throughout this state.

Having declared the system of common schools to be constitutionally deficient, we have directed the General Assembly to recreate and redesign a new system that will comply with the standards we have set out. Such system will guarantee to all children the opportunity for an adequate education, through a *state* system. To allow local citizens and taxpayers to make a supplementary effort in no way reduces or negates the minimum quality of education required in the statewide system.

We do not instruct the General Assembly to enact any specific legislation. We do not direct the members of the General Assembly to raise taxes. It is their decision how best to achieve efficiency. We only decide the nature of the constitutional mandate. We only determine the intent of the framers. Carrying-out that intent is the duty of the General Assembly.

A child's right to an adequate education is a fundamental one under our Constitution. The General Assembly must protect and advance that right. We concur with the trial court that an efficient system of education must have as its goal to provide each and every child with at least the seven following capacities: (i) sufficient oral and written communication skills to enable students to function in a complex and rapidly changing civilization; (ii) sufficient knowledge of economic, social, and political systems to enable the student to make informed choices; (iii) sufficient understanding of governmental processes to enable the student to understand the issues that affect his or her community, state, and nation; (iv) sufficient self-knowledge and knowledge of his or her mental and physical wellness; (v) sufficient grounding in the arts to enable each student to appreciate his or her cultural and historical heritage; (vi) sufficient training or preparation for advanced training in either academic or vocational fields so as to enable each child to choose and pursue life work intelligently; and (vii) sufficient levels of academic or vocational skills to enable public school students to compete favorably with their counterparts in surrounding states, in academics or in the job market.[22]

The essential, and minimal, characteristics of an "efficient" system of common schools, may be summarized as follows:

1) The establishment, maintenance and funding of common schools in Kentucky is the sole responsibility of the General Assembly.

2) Common schools shall be free to all.

3) Common schools shall be available to all Kentucky children.

4) Common schools shall be substantially uniform throughout the state.

5) Common schools shall provide equal educational opportunities to all Kentucky children, re-

---

[22]In recreating and redesigning the Kentucky system of common schools, these seven characteristics should be considered as minimum goals in providing an adequate education. Certainly, there is no prohibition against higher goals—whether such are implemented statewide by the General Assembly or through the efforts of any local education entities that the General Assembly may establish—so long as the General Assembly meets the standards set out in this Opinion.

gardless of place of residence or economic circumstances.

6) Common schools shall be monitored by the General Assembly to assure that they are operated with no waste, no duplication, no mismanagement, and with no political influence.

7) The premise for the existence of common schools is that all children in Kentucky have a constitutional right to an adequate education.

8) The General Assembly shall provide funding which is sufficient to provide each child in Kentucky an adequate education.

9) An adequate education is one which has as its goal the development of the seven capacities recited previously.

XI. Is the Present System "Efficient"?

We have described . . . in some detail, the present system of common schools. We have noted the overall inadequacy of our system of education, when compared to national standards and to the standards of our adjacent states. We have recognized the great disparity that exists in educational opportunities throughout the state. We have noted the great disparity and inadequacy, of financial effort throughout the state.

In spite of the past and present efforts of the General Assembly, Kentucky's present system of common schools falls short of the mark of the constitutional mandate of "efficient." When one juxtaposes the standards of efficiency as derived from our Constitution, the cases decided thereunder, the persuasive authority from our sister states and the opinion of experts, with the virtually unchallenged evidence in the record, no other decision is possible.

XII. Did the Trial Court's Judgment Violate the Separation of Powers Provision of the Kentucky Constitution?

Appellants assert that the trial court's judgment violates the separation of powers doctrine in that it exceeded the authority of the court in "dictating" to the General Assembly, and it exceeded the authority of the court by creating a type of open-ended judgment which required legislator-defendants to report their progress to the trial court.

* * *

It is argued that the trial court directed the General Assembly to enact specific legislation and to raise taxes and that such is a violation of the separation of powers. We do not agree that that is what the judgment of the trial court does. The trial judge did define "efficient," he did declare that a common school education is a fundamental constitutional right in this state, and he did say that any educational system to be "efficient," must have certain characteristics. He commented on the possible methods of financing the system of common schools in Kentucky and did, of course, opine that additional money would be required. This later conclusion was based on an abundance of virtually uncontested and unchallenged evidence in this record.

Moreover, the trial judge specifically denied that he was directing the General Assembly to enact any *specific legislation*, including raising taxes. His mandate to the General Assembly was to bring the system of common schools into compliance with Section 183 of our Constitution. He did as we have done, established certain criteria, standards and goals which must be met to so comply. It is clear that the specifics of the legislation will be left up to the wisdom of the General Assembly. Clearly, no "legislating" is present in the decision of the trial court, and more importantly, as we have previously said, there is none present in the decision of this Court. . . .

* * *

Our job is to determine the constitutional validity of the system of common schools within the meaning of the Kentucky Constitution, Section 183. We have done so. We have declared the system of common schools to be unconstitutional. It is now up to the General Assembly to re-create, and re-establish a system of common schools within this state which will be in compliance with the Constitution. We have no doubt they will proceed with their duty.

* * *

Summary/Conclusion

* * *

Lest there be any doubt, the result of our decision is that Kentucky's *entire system* of common schools is unconstitutional. There is no allegation that only part of the common school system is invalid, and we find no such circumstance. This decision applies to the entire sweep of the system—all its parts and parcels. This decision applies to the statutes creating, implementing and financing the *system* and to all regulations, etc., pertaining thereto. This decision covers the creation of local school districts, school boards, and the Kentucky Department of Education to the Minimum Foundation Program and Power Equalization Program. It covers school construction and maintenance, teacher certification—the whole gamut of the common school system in Kentucky.

While individual statutes are not herein addressed specifically or considered and declared to be facially unconstitutional, the statutory system as a whole and the interrelationship of the parts therein are hereby declared to be in violation of Section 183 of the Kentucky Constitution. Just as the bricks and mortar used in the construction of a schoolhouse, while contributing to the building's facade, do not ensure the overall structural adequacy of the schoolhouse, particular statutes drafted by the legislature in crafting and designing the current school system are not unconstitutional in and of themselves. Like the crumbling schoolhouse which must be redesigned and revitalized for more efficient use, with some component parts found to be adequate, some found to be less than adequate, statutes relating to education may be reenacted as components of a constitutional system if they combine with other component statutes to form an efficient and thereby constitutional system.

Since we have, by this decision, declared the system of common schools in Kentucky to be unconstitutional, Section 183 places an absolute duty on the General Assembly to re-create, re-establish a new system of common schools in the Commonwealth. As we have said, the premise of this opinion is that education is a basic, fundamental constitutional right that is available to all children within this Commonwealth. The General Assembly should begin with the same premise as it goes about its duty. The system, as we have said, must be efficient, and the criteria we have set out are binding on the General Assembly as it develops Kentucky's new system of common schools.

As we have previously emphasized, the *sole responsibility* for providing the system of common schools lies with the General Assembly. If they choose to delegate any of this duty to institutions such as the local boards of education, the General Assembly must provide a mechanism to assure that the ultimate control remains with the General Assembly, and assure that those local school districts also exercise the delegated duties in an efficient manner.

The General Assembly must provide adequate funding for the system. How they do this is their de-

cision. However, if ad valorem taxes on real and personal property are used by the General Assembly as part of the financing of the redesigned state system of common schools, the General Assembly has the obligation to see that *all such property* is assessed at 100% of its fair market value. *Russman v. Luckett*, Ky., 391 S.W.2d 694 (1965). Moreover, because of the great disparity of local tax efforts in the present system of common schools, the General Assembly must establish a uniform *tax rate* for such property. In this way, all owners of real and personal property throughout the *state* will make a comparable effort in the financing of the state system of common schools.

This decision has not been reached without much thought and consideration. We do not take our responsibilities lightly, and we have decided this case based on our perception and interpretation of the Kentucky Constitution. We intend no criticism of any person, persons or institutions. We view this decision as an opportunity for the General Assembly to launch the Commonwealth into a new era of educational opportunity which will ensure a strong economic, cultural and political future.

Because of the enormity of the task before the General Assembly to re-create a new statutory system of common schools in the Commonwealth, and because we realize that the educational process must continue, we withhold the finality of this decision until 90 days after the adjournment of the General Assembly, *sine die*, at its regular session in 1990.

* * *

NOTES AND QUESTIONS

1. The Significance of Rose

The *Rose* decision has been heralded as "one of the most dramatic and significant constitutional law decisions in the history of Kentucky." Combs, "Creative Constitutional Law: The Kentucky School Reform Law," 28 *Harv.J.on Legis.* 367, 369 (1991). The case was the first to find an entire state school system unconstitutional because it did not provide an adequate education to its students. The case also offered a new definition of adequacy that focused on students' capacities and made the legislature accountable for ensuring that students mastered these skills. Trimble and Forsaith, "Achieving Equity and Excellence in Kentucky Education," 28 *U.Mich.J.L.Ref.* 599, 608 (1995).

2. *The Legislative Response to* Rose

In the wake of the *Rose* decision, the Kentucky legislature enacted the Kentucky Education Reform Act (KERA) of 1990. KERA represented a comprehensive reform effort arguably unprecedented in the nation. Not only was school funding increased but the legislature also mandated school-based decision-making, statewide curricular standards, and a rigorous accountability system. These initiatives are described at greater length in chapter 8. For an informative account of the Kentucky experience with school reform, *see* Trimble and Forsaith, *supra*, at 599.

3. *The Impact of* Rose *on Other Courts*

Four years later, the high court in Massachusetts adopted the definition of adequacy in *Rose*. *McDuffy v. Secretary of the Executive Office of Education*, 615 N.E.2d 516, 554 (Mass. 1993). Unlike *Rose*, however, the holding in *McDuffy* was limited to funding issues and did not deal with the restructuring of the school system. New Hampshire also embraced the *Rose* standards as a measure of adequacy. *Claremont School Dist. v. Governor*, 703 A.2d 1353, 1359 (N.H. 1997). South Carolina's supreme court established its own constitutional standards of adequacy and held the legislature directly accountable to meet them. *Abbeville County School Dist. v. State*, 515 S.E.2d 535, 540–41 (1999). For further discussion of the *Abbeville* case, *see* Fogle, "*Abbeville County School District v. State*: The Right to a Minimally Adequate Education in South Carolina," 51 *S.C.L.Rev.* 420 (2000).

c. Reliance on Existing State Standards.

Some courts have chosen a middle way between deference and activism by relying on existing state standards without specifying a constitutional minimum for educational services. In Kansas, the state supreme court looked to legislative standards that had been based on comprehensive study of expert evidence. The court concluded that the school finance system satisfied these standards. *Unified School District No. 229 v. State*, 885 P.2d 1170, 1186–87 (Kan. 1994), *cert. denied*, 515 U.S. 1144 (1995). For an account of the events leading up to the Kansas decision, *see* Berger, "Equity Without Adjudication: Kansas School Finance Reform and the 1992 School District Finance and Quality Performance Act," 27 *J.L. & Educ.* 1 (1998). Berger notes that after the high court's disposition of the case, "Kansas still has not had a binding, affirmative definition of the state's duty to provide adequate or equal education or a child's corresponding right to education. The 1994 litigation merely established that the [state's school finance act] was permissible, not that any of its provisions were required. . . ." *Id.* at 39–40.

In Alabama, the state supreme court relied on standards promulgated by the legislature and state department of education, including accreditation standards, as well as output measures such as dropout rates, readiness for work, and need for remedial instruction in college. *Opinion of the Justices*, 624 So.2d 107, 128–29, 136–38 (Ala. 1993) (advisory opinion for the state senate), *appeal dismissed, motion denied, and remanded sub nom. Pinto v. Alabama Coalition for Equity*, 662 So.2d 894 (Ala. 1995). Applying these standards, the high court found that the state's system of public education was constitutionally inadequate. 624 So.2d at 126–44. For a discussion of how the Alabama decision offered a model for defining inadequacy, *see* Morgan, Cohen, and Hershkoff, "Establishing Education Program Inadequacy: The Alabama Example," 28 *U.Mich.J.L.Ref.* 559 (1995). In a somewhat similar vein, North Carolina's supreme court used legislative goals and standards, students' test scores, and general and per-pupil expenditures to determine adequacy. *Leandro v. State*, 488 S.E.2d 249, 254–60 (1997). *See also* Packard, "A Sound, Basic Education: North Carolina Adopts an Adequacy Standard in *Leandro v. State*," 76 *N.C.L.Rev.* 1481, 1506–07 (1998).

One challenge that comes with relying on existing state standards involves gathering appropriate evidence of available legislative and administrative guidelines. In Montana, for instance, the plaintiffs introduced state accreditation standards, and the court held that they were a necessary but insufficient measure of adequacy. Because there were no other guidelines in evidence, the justices could not elaborate further on the meaning of adequacy. *Helena Elementary School District No. 1 v. State*, 769 P.2d 684, 691–92 (Mont. 1989). Conversely, in *Campaign for Fiscal Equity, Inc. v. State*, 655 N.E.2d 661, 666 (N.Y. 1995), the New York high court found that standards set by the Board of Regents and the Commissioner of Education were more rigorous than those required to deliver a constitutionally sound, basic education. *See* Anker, "Differences and Dialogue: School Finance in New York State," 24 *N.Y.U.Rev.L. & Soc.Change* 345, 371–75 (1998);

Dyson, "A Covenant Broken: The Crisis of Educational Remedy for New York City's Failing Schools," 44 *How.L.J.* 107, 142–49 (2000). For a general discussion of the use of existing standards to define adequacy, *see* Dietz, *supra*, at 1212–22.

4. The Matter of Remedy.

Adequacy litigation raises questions about the appropriate remedy for a constitutional violation. The most modest remedy arguably would be to enhance resources available to failing schools so that they can afford their students a minimum level of educational opportunity. However, Professor William Clune argues that "At its heart, adequacy refers to a shift in the emphasis of school finance from inputs to outcomes, e.g. from dollars to student achievement as measured by standardized tests and avoidance of dropping out." Clune, "Educational Adequacy: A Theory and Its Remedies," 28 *U.Mich.J.L.Ref.* 481, 485 (1995). Consequently, he believes that the Kentucky court properly prompted changes that included not only fiscal improvements but also systems of accountability and revised structures for school governance. *Id.* at 487–489. Yet, the broader the remedy, the greater the concern about the propriety of judicial intervention and the administrability of court-ordered relief. In the following excerpt, Professor Peter Enrich considers these questions of institutional competency.

"Leaving Equality Behind: New Directions in School Finance Reform"

Peter Enrich, 48 *Vanderbilt L.Rev.* 101, 175–182 (1995).

* * *

To gain a fuller understanding of where . . . courts have found the courage to overcome the hurdle of institutional competence, we have to look behind the words of their opinions to the political contexts in which they wrote. In a number of these states, particularly Washington, Kentucky, and Massachusetts, a common pattern emerges. In each, at the time that the court issued its decision, the state legislature had recently taken significant steps to transform the educational system challenged in the case. In Washington, a major reform package had been enacted while the appeal was pending. In Kentucky, education reform and school finance were high on the political agenda, although the legislature and governor had reached an impasse over the costs of the proposed legislative reforms. In Massachusetts, legislation re-

forming school finances and governance was on the Governor's desk awaiting his signature.

Thus, while the courts were surely acting boldly, they were not acting alone. Indeed, in both Washington and Massachusetts, the legislative measures, like the courts' opinions, expressly addressed the need to spell out the content of an adequate education. So, the courts' efforts at definition must be understood as part of a broader political effort pointing in the same general direction. In large measure, the court's role, at least in these states, was not to displace the legislative function of identifying realistic parameters for the state's ambitions, but rather to serve as a goad or as a backstop to the legislature's accomplishment of that task.

Seen in light of this political context, the insistence by these courts that they were not attempting to usurp the proper responsibilities of the legislative branch but were simply insisting that the political branches do their job turns out to be far more than a ritualistic incantation of judicial passivity. Their role truly was limited, if critical. The knowledge that the legislature was ready to take up the challenge of defining and endeavoring to meet standards of educational quality largely mooted concerns about the judicial role. It both spared the courts from the awkward task of attempting a comprehensive judicial definition of adequacy, and it afforded them some confidence that their directives would be heeded without unseemly conflict among the branches.

Shifting the onus of standard-setting back to the legislative branch may seem to accomplish little for poor school districts and their underserved students, but, in fact, as the Kentucky, Washington, and Massachusetts examples suggest, the political dynamics stimulated by such limited judicial intervention are likely to be quite productive.

Whatever the misgivings about the current functioning of our schools and about the financial costs of reform, free public education remains a vital and popular element in our vision of state and local governmental responsibilities. When a legislature is called upon to define standards for the state's school system, it is unlikely to set its sights too low. Particularly after a decade of well-publicized expressions of concern about the mediocrity of American education, the pressures of both politics and policy are apt to produce legislative standards that aim at excellence, not at minimal sufficiency.

There is, of course, no guarantee that the measures the political process produces in response to judicial prompting will provide acceptable standards of adequacy. The need may remain for a judicial determination that the legislature or executive has not satisfied its responsibilities. The suggestion here is not that courts can simply defer to legislative choices in seeking standards for adequacy, but rather that courts can best address the difficult issues of educational adequacy, and of institutional competence, by engaging the legislative branch in a constructive collaboration.

Even when a legislature has adopted appropriate standards, questions will commonly remain about whether it has done enough, and particularly whether it has committed sufficient resources, to meet the standards it has set. As the history of foundation funding approaches reminds us, good intentions to support education adequately can rapidly erode, as other demands compete for limited tax resources.

Inevitably, these questions about whether the concrete efforts live up to the articulated standards will come back to the courts. But they will present the judicial branch with a far more tractable, and more institutionally familiar, problem than the prior question of how to define educational adequacy. For, while these new challenges will still focus on whether the legislature has satisfied a broadly phrased constitutional mandate, the court will nonetheless be able to turn to the legislative articulation of standards as a reasonable and appropriate yardstick for measuring the actual results.

In sum, the examples of Kentucky, Washington, and Massachusetts suggest a strategy by which courts can play an activist and effective role in pursuing educational adequacy without stepping outside of conventional institutional roles. But the prospect of continuing political and judicial struggles over whether appropriate standards of adequacy have been identified and whether the standards have been met points out a second major obstacle to reliance on adequacy arguments.

Like equality, the norm of adequacy is unassailably attractive when considered in the abstract. But when its practical implications—primarily its implications for resource allocations but secondarily its impact on the division of power between state and local authorities as well—are considered, adequacy quickly loses some of its luster. The question, then, is whether we, and particularly our courts and legislatures, are any more prepared to commit to the norm of adequacy than to the norm of equality, when that commitment is understood to have substantial practical ramifications.

Concerns about the costs—both financial and institutional—of implementing adequacy norms may discourage courts, or legislatures, from assuming the initial burden of a commitment to educational adequacy. A court, after all, can easily sidestep adequacy claims as inherently political or as delegated to legislative discretion. And legislatures can, unless courts intervene, confine their attention to particularized issues of funding and regulation, without addressing the underlying standards or goals to be achieved.

Even when a court or legislature has taken up the challenge of mandating educational adequacy, the inherent indefiniteness of the concept of adequacy leaves ample opportunity to abandon the substance, while retaining the formal commitment. A legislature can simply fail to provide the resources required to achieve its stated goals. And courts can put the best face on even the most inadequate of legislative efforts.

Only time will tell whether adequacy arguments can fare better than equality arguments in overcoming the powerful resistance aroused by recognition of the very real costs that both ideals entail. But, . . . there seems reason to hope that the resistance to adequacy claims will be less intense than the resistance to equality demands.

This is due, in no small part, to the fact that the costs of adequacy are far less than the costs of equality, especially for the elites who derive the greatest benefits from the existing inequalities, because adequacy does not threaten their ability to retain a superior position. At the same time, adequacy arguments can draw powerful support from our natural sympathies for the appalling condition of schooling in the poorest communities, and they can make compelling appeals to societal self-interest, both in providing an adequately skilled workforce to support the economy and in affording a meaningful opportunity for self-advancement to society's most disadvantaged elements.

Moreover, even if adequacy arguments cannot ultimately overcome these resistances, they are more apt than equality arguments to achieve at least partial successes. As noted earlier, adequacy, unlike equality, is essentially a matter of degree. Hence, mandates for adequacy are less likely to encounter legislative stonewalling and brinksmanship of the sort engendered, . . . by equality mandates . . . than to invite incremental responses, which offer at least some additional support to the worst off districts. And courts, in turn, recognizing the greater flexibility that adequacy claims offer to policymakers, may be less troubled by concerns about proper institutional roles when presented with adequacy arguments than when faced with equality claims.

Because its goals are less radical and because it is more receptive to compromise solutions and partial measures, adequacy seems better suited than equality to overcome the incessant resistance that confronts efforts to redirect substantial resources to poorer school districts. But these same aspects of adequacy arguments also expose a third, and final, set of difficulties that challenge the wisdom of reliance on such arguments. In short, is adequacy too modest, and too manipulable, a standard to warrant advocates, litigants, courts, or policymakers in placing reliance upon it?

While I am convinced that the persistent tendency to conceptualize the school funding problem as an issue of inequality has created unnecessary obstacles for funding reform, and while I believe that reframing the debate as an issue of inadequacy holds the promise of generating greater assistance for our poorer schools, I remain troubled by this last difficulty—the question of whether aiming at adequacy is simply aiming too low.

After all, the notion of adequacy limits the state's responsibility to the assurance of a minimum level of educational opportunities for all children. Regardless of how high or low the minimum level in a state turns out to be, adequacy arguments accept that districts with the resources and the will can choose to provide something better for their children. One practical result is that those with the option of living in such more-than-adequate districts—a group that is likely to include a disproportionate share of those who shape state law and policy—have little direct stake in the content of the standard of adequacy at the same time that they are sure to bear a substantial part of its costs.

Thus, when we give up appeals to equality in favor of appeals to adequacy, we in all likelihood relegate vast groups of children to mediocre educational opportunities (or worse), and we ensure that they will face significant competitive disadvantages relative to their peers from privileged communities. It is perhaps little wonder, then, that litigants and advocates representing the interests of poorer communities have been reluctant to cast their arguments in the language of adequacy, rather than equality. These

are high prices to pay in exchange for improved chances of progress.

Moreover, when we turn away from appeals to equality, we run the risk of surrendering the moral high ground of absolute standards and falling back onto the slippery slopes of relative judgments of adequacy. The norm of equality, for all its difficulties, lies near the core of our notions of justice and fairness; it is recognized as a fundamental constitutional value. Educational adequacy, by contrast, is the sort of thing we expect bureaucrats and academicians to squabble over; it has no self-evident core. Especially once it is conceded that adequacy allows for disparities, even quite substantial disparities, between the schooling provided in rich and poor districts, it is unclear whether adequacy is capable of eliciting the commitment and momentum necessary to achieve significant and lasting reform.

In short, adequacy arguments promise results that look relatively meager, and they rest on principles that lack the clarity and force of calls for equality. Hence, advocates of education finance reform face a difficult, if familiar, strategic choice. Do they take the high road of continuing to demand equal educational opportunities for all children, recognizing that the legal and political obstacles that have hampered equality arguments for the last quarter-century will likely continue to frustrate them? Or do they opt to pursue the more achievable, but more modest, goals of adequacy?

* * *

NOTES AND QUESTIONS

1. Judicial Mandates and School Reform

Enrich notes that court-ordered reform, whether based on equity or adequacy, can be stymied by the political process. Echoing this concern, Professor Michael Heise has observed that an "assumption common to equity and adequacy court decisions . . . is that such decisions can influence educational spending. This assumption rests on empirical questions that remain largely unaddressed. Legal impact research on the relation between courts and educational policy is scant, qualitative data are thin, and helpful quantitative data are all but nonexistent." Heise, "State Constitutions, School Finance Litigation, and the 'Third Wave': From Equity to Adequacy," 68 Temple L.Rev. 1151, 1167

(1995). Should courts proceed even when the benefits of school reform remain highly uncertain? Why or why not?

2. *Adequacy and Distributive Justice*

As Enrich points out, the shift to adequacy relinquishes the normative power of a vision of equal education for all. At the same time, adequacy claims may not escape the limited interest of political elites in the fate of poor, often nonWhite students. Professor Mildred Wigfall Robinson has noted that reform works best where it is needed least. As she explains, "Ironically, erosion of political support is likely to be most pronounced where the quality of education is already perceived to be most troubling—in urban centers and in poor rural districts. These are areas also most likely to be beset by difficulties stemming from inadequate revenue generated by levying against a stagnant or declining property base." Robinson, "School Finance Reform: Financing Adequate Educational Opportunity," 14 *J.L.&Pol.* 483, 511 (1998). As a result, she argues that "school districts most in need of financial help are likely to be those in which the relevant interest group proves least able to use political clout locally to force a reallocation of available resources, a reallocation that may be a critical component for the future success of the educational system." *Id.* at 511–12. Can adequacy claims be framed in ways that have broad political appeal? If so, can this broad support be sustained when some redistribution of resources is necessary to meet standards of adequacy?

D. The Special Problems of Large Urban Districts

Particularly in equity or fiscal neutrality suits, but also in adequacy suits, large urban school districts have argued that despite the fact that in some cases they may have higher than average property wealth, their special problems have the effect of sharply reducing their fiscal capacity. In a 1974 fiscal neutrality case in New York, the four major cities—New York, Rochester, Buffalo, and Syracuse–intervened to argue that their special financial burdens included the following:

> (1) demands on municipal budgets (from which local funds for education are secured) for noneducation needs peculiar to cities ("municipal overburden"), (2) diminished purchasing power of the municipal education dollar, (3) significantly greater student ab-

senteeism (with a resulting adverse effect both because of added operational costs and because State aid is largely allocated on the basis of average daily attendance), and (4) larger concentrations in cities of pupils with special educational needs, all four of which may be comprehended within the term "metropolitan overburden." These factors are said to result in greatly disparate educational opportunities available to children in the cities' public schools when compared to the offerings of some of the school districts not located within cities.

Board of Education, Levittown v. Nyquist, 57 N.Y.2d 27, 36, 453 N.Y.S.2d 643, 646, 439 N.E.2d 359 (1982). The *Levittown* court rejected the intervenors' claims, however, interpreting the education clause in New York State's constitution merely to require the provision of a "sound basic education."

The principal burdens that cities are said uniquely to bear are sometimes characterized as (1) municipal overburden, (2) education overburden, and (3) cost differentials.

1. Municipal Overburden. Central city fiscal problems are said to stem in part from the higher noneducational public services that central cities must support out of the property tax, such as police and fire protection or health and welfare services. The comparatively high percentage of the property tax allocated for those noneducation services acts as a constraint on the tax rate levied for education. Most suburban and rural school districts are not so heavily burdened by these noneducational expenses, permitting most of their property tax revenues to be allocated to the schools.

In providing state aid to equalize the varying capabilities of the state's school districts to finance public education, must a state system of financing take into account the noneducational services that cities must provide from property tax revenues? If the purpose of the fiscal neutrality principle is to equalize fiscal capacity, why would not the extent to which property tax revenues must be used to support other public services affect the capacity of the district to raise funds for education? Professor Coons and his colleagues, however, argue that the principle of fiscal neutrality is aimed at the fact that existing systems of finance are "designed to create differences in school quality; it may not and does not follow that there is a constitutional objection to . . . every act of the state with a similar effect. An area may be 'city poor' . . . and the condition may affect school spending, but the cause of this relative poverty is by definition outside the system of public finance." J. Coons, W. Clune, and S. Sugarman, *Private Wealth and Public Education* 311 (1970).

2. *Education Overburden.* Large urban districts also argue that they have a higher proportion than other types of districts of those students who require greater than average educational resources—such as students with disabilities, children in poverty, the educationally disadvantaged, and students with limited English language ability. These translate into such "education overburdens" as impaired learning readiness; impaired mental, emotional, and physical health; mental retardation and other learning disabilities; and English-language difficulties. Because of inadequate resources, programs to address these "overburdens" cannot be adequately provided.

3. *Cost Differentials.* The third "unique burden" argued by large city districts is that state finance formulas fail to take into account "cost differentials," that is, the fact that higher prices or wage rates mean that urban districts have to spend more per pupil than rural or suburban school districts to provide a comparable educational program. This price-wage differential reflects area "labor market" differences and the fact that cities generally have a higher proportion of professional staff with advanced degrees and years of experience. Site acquisition costs and the costs per square foot of constructing school facilities are also substantially higher in cities than in suburban and rural areas, as are the costs of plant maintenance and security. *See generally* B. Levin, T. Muller, and C. Sandoval, *The High Cost of Education in Cities* (1973).

In New Jersey, urban school districts have property values below the state average and also suffer from the unique burdens described above. *Robinson v. Cahill,* discussed *supra,* was initiated by city districts, and in the New Jersey supreme court's decision in *Robinson I,* it noted that municipal overburden was a problem in many urban districts in the state, *Robinson v. Cahill (Robinson I),* 62 N. J. 473, 519, 303 A.2d 273, 297 (1973), and that the state, in revising its school finance system, could recognize "differences in area costs, or a need for additional dollar input to equip classes of disadvantaged children." 303 A.2d at 298. Following the long saga of *Robinson,* plaintiffs representing school children from Camden, East Orange, Jersey City, and Irvington in poor urban districts challenged the Public School Education Act of 1975, as applied, violated the state constitution's thorough and efficient clause. *See* Tractenberg, "The Evolution and Implementation of Educational Rights Under the New Jersey Constitution of 1947," 29 *Rutgers L. J.* 827 (1998). The resulting decision in *Abbott v. Burke,* which follows, was focused solely on poor urban districts and addresses some of the unique burdens of city school districts.

Abbott v. Burke
119 N.J. 287, 575 A.2d 359 (1990).

Wilentz, J.

. . . We find that under the present system the evidence compels but one conclusion: the poorer the district and the greater its need, the less the money available, and the worse the education. That system is neither thorough nor efficient. We hold the Act unconstitutional as applied to poorer urban school districts. Education has failed there, for both the students and the State. We hold that the Act must be amended to assure funding of education in poorer urban districts at the level of property-rich districts; that such funding cannot be allowed to depend on the ability of local school districts to tax; that such funding must be guaranteed and mandated by the State; and that the level of funding must also be adequate to provide for the special educational needs of these poorer urban districts in order to redress their extreme disadvantages.

We note . . . that funding alone will not achieve the constitutional mandate of an equal education in these poorer urban districts; that without educational reform, the money may accomplish nothing, and that in these districts, substantial, far-reaching change in education is absolutely essential to success.

* * *

On this record we find a constitutional deficiency only in the poorer urban districts, and our remedy is limited to those districts. We leave unaffected the disparity in substantive education and funding found in other districts throughout the state, although that disparity too may some day become a matter of constitutional dimension. . . .

* * *

II. The Constitutional Provision

* * *

. . . [O]ur holding in *Robinson I* was clear and formed the basis for our holding in *Robinson V*: a thorough and efficient education requires a certain level of educational opportunity, a minimum level, that will equip the student to become "a citizen and . . . a competitor in the labor market." *Robinson I*. . . .

The change of focus from the dollar disparity in *Robinson I* to substantive educational content in *Robinson V* is clear; it was the main theme underlying the Court's determination that the Act was constitutional. Noting at the outset that for the first time we had before us a statute that defined the constitutional obligation, provided for its implementation through both state and local administration, required that implementation to be monitored, directed the State to compel compliance where that monitoring revealed deficiencies, and provided a funding mechanism to achieve the constitutional goal, we observed that the state's school-aid provisions "must be considered not in comparative isolation, but as part of the whole proposal formulated by the Legislature." *Robinson V*. . . . The only question about financing was not whether it provided equal dollars per pupil—indeed, we noted that "there may be and probably are legitimate differences between and among districts and students" . . . , but whether it was sufficient to support the entire system and its goal of achieving a thorough and efficient education throughout the state.

. . . [T]he requirement of a thorough and efficient education to provide "that educational opportunity which is needed in the contemporary setting to equip a child for his role as a citizen and as a competitor in the labor market," *Robinson I* . . . meant that poorer disadvantaged students must be given a chance to be able to compete with relatively advantaged students. The Act and its system of education have failed in that respect, and it is that failure that we address in this case.

* * *

A. The Funding Scheme

* * *

The Act gives poorer districts—poor in terms of property valuation per pupil—taxing power to raise more money for school purposes than what a school district with the average property valuation and no

equalization aid could raise. Putting aside for the moment the impact of "municipal overburden" (a condition in many poorer districts where the cost of local government—police, firefighters, other municipal employees, road maintenance, garbage collection, etc.—is so high that the municipality and the school district are reluctant to increase taxes for any purpose, including education), equalization aid attempts to obliterate the enormous disparity between rich and poor for school tax purposes; it creates, instead of rich and poor districts, two different classes: those districts with a guaranteed tax base—almost two-thirds of the districts in the state—and those with a tax base in excess of the guaranteed tax base of $233,100, running from $223,667 to $7.8 million and clustering at $300,000 (1984–85 figures). . . .

B. Educational Funding Disparities

. . . [T]he funding and spending disparities referred to in *Robinson I* are worse now than they were before adoption of the Act. . . . Prior to the Act, in 1971–72, the spread between the lowest and highest spending districts was $700 per pupil to $1,500 per pupil, a difference of $800. *Robinson V* . . . . This difference of $800 per pupil reflects the range between the absolute highest spending districts and the absolute lowest. . . . For a few years after the Act was funded, the disparity diminished, but thereafter it generally increased to the point where in 1984–85 districts at the fifth percentile spent $2,687, while districts at the ninety-fifth percentile spent $4,755, a disparity of $2,068 per pupil. The disparity in expenditures is significant even when adjusted for inflation—in 1975-dollars, the disparity grew from $898 per pupil in 1975–76 to $1,135 per pupil in 1984–85.

The impact of this disparity, solely in dollar terms, is that on the average, in 1984–85, a group of richer districts with 189,484 students spend 40% more per pupil than a group of poorer districts with 355,612 students; one provides an education worth $4,029 per pupil, the other $2,861. . . .

That disadvantage in expenditures per pupil is clearly related to all of the other aspects of poverty that define poorer urban districts and their youth. Although the statistical relationships are the subject of considerable dispute, we conclude that generally they show that the poorer the district—measured by equalized valuation per pupil, or by other indicators of poverty—the less the per pupil expenditure; the poorer and more urban the district, the heavier its municipal property tax, the greater the school tax burden; whatever the measure of disadvantage, need, and poverty—the greater it is, the less there is to spend.

. . . [E]xpenditure disparity does play a role, an important one, in our conclusion that the constitutional level has not been achieved in the poorer urban districts. This disparity has multiple relevance: to the extent educational quality is deemed related to dollar expenditures, it tends to prove inadequate quality of education in the poorer districts, unless we were to assume that the substantial differential in expenditures is attributable to an education in the richer districts far beyond anything that thorough and efficient demands; it indicates even more strongly the probability that the poorer districts' students will be unable to compete in the society entered by the richer districts' students; and by its consistency over the years, it suggests that the system as it now operates is unable to correct this.

. . . [W]e do not believe a thorough and efficient education in the poorer urban districts "can realistically be met" by reliance on the system now in place. While local taxation no longer has the same impact, it is still significant. More than that, however, we believe that because of the complex factors leading to a failure of thorough and efficient in the poorer urban districts, including disparity of expenditures, we are no more likely ever to achieve thorough and efficient than we believed we could by relying on local taxation in *Robinson I*. Combined with these disparities of wealth and expenditure are the much more serious disparities of educational need, students in the poorer urban districts dramatically disadvantaged compared to their peers in the affluent suburbs. These intractable differences of wealth and need between the poorer and the richer, and the "discordant correlations" within a poorer district between its students' educational needs and its ability to spend, are more than the present funding system can overcome. The failure has gone on too long; the factors are ingrained; the remedy must be systemic. The present scheme cannot cure it.

. . . [T]he State may be correct in its contention that measured against the entire spectrum of districts in the state, the disparities and their relationships are not sufficient to condemn the system, because they exist significantly only when the extremes are compared. That gives little comfort to those students confined to the poorest districts, and they number in the

hundreds of thousands (in 1984–85 there were 280,081 resident students in the twenty-nine poorer urban districts, about 25% of the entire public school population). Their deprivation is real, of constitutional magnitude, and not blunted in the least by the State's statistical analysis.

C. Substantive Educational Opportunity: The Administration of the Act by the Commissioner and the Board

. . . Before this Court voids the statute, overrules the Board and the Commissioner, and orders the Legislature to provide a new system, the constitutional failure must be clear. As to most districts of the state, it is not. But as to some—the poorer urban districts—it is glaringly clear.

. . . "Municipal overburden" is the excessive tax levy some municipalities must impose to meet governmental needs other than education. It is a common characteristic in poorer urban districts, a product of their relatively low property values against which the local tax is assessed and their high level of governmental need. The governmental need includes the entire range of goods and services made available to citizens: police and fire protection, road maintenance, social services, water, sewer, garbage disposal, and similar services. Although the condition is not precisely defined, it is usually thought of as a tax rate well above the average.

The underlying causes of municipal overburden are many and complex. Its consequences in this case, however, are clear and simple. The poorer urban school districts, sharing the same tax base with the municipality, suffer from severe municipal overburden; they are extremely reluctant to increase taxes for school purposes. Not only is their local tax levy well above average, so is their school tax rate. The oppressiveness of the tax burden on their citizens by itself would be sufficient to give them pause before raising taxes. Additionally, the rates in some cases are so high that further taxation may actually decrease tax revenues by diminishing total property values, either directly because of the tax-value relationship, or indirectly by causing business and industry to relocate to another municipality.

Plaintiffs argue that municipal overburden restricts these poorer urban districts' ability to raise more money through increased school taxes to achieve a thorough and efficient education. . . .

The Commissioner's position is that municipal overburden is irrelevant to the constitutional issue. He maintains that the school board is obliged as a matter of statutory and constitutional duty to raise as much money as is needed for a thorough and efficient education no matter what the tax consequences, no matter how much the tax increase, no matter how high the present tax, and no matter how high the present local municipal tax. If tax inequity exists, that may be a concern for the Legislature but it must not be for the school district. . . .

We respectfully disagree. The social and economic pressures on municipalities, school districts, public officials, and citizens of these disaster areas—many poorer urban districts—are so severe that tax increases in any substantial amount are almost unthinkable. . . .

. . . Our conclusion concerning municipal overburden is that it effectively prevents districts from raising substantially more money for education. It is a factual conclusion. . . . That factual finding is one of the bases for our conclusion that the funding mechanism of the Act will never achieve a thorough and efficient education because it relies so heavily on a local property base already over-taxed to exhaustion.

D. The Quality of Education in the Poorer Urban Districts

The primary basis for our decision is the constitutional failure of education in poorer urban districts. . . . Our conclusion that the constitutional mandate has not been satisfied is based both on the absolute level of education in those districts and the comparison with education in affluent suburban districts.

. . . [T]he level of education offered to students in some of the poorer urban districts is tragically inadequate. Many opportunities offered to students in richer suburban districts are denied to them. For instance, exposure to computers is necessary to acquire skills to compete in the workplace. In South Orange/ Maplewood school district, kindergartners are introduced to computers; children learn word processing in elementary school; middle school students are offered beginning computer programming; and high school students are offered advanced courses in several programming languages or projectoriented independent studies. Each South Orange/Maplewood school has a computer lab.

By contrast, many poorer urban districts cannot offer such variety of computer science courses. While Princeton has one computer per eight children, East Orange has one computer per forty-three children, and Camden has one computer per fifty-eight children. Camden can offer formal computer instruction to only 3.4% of its students. . . . Paterson offers no computer education other than computer-assisted basic skills programs. Further, many of these districts do not have sufficient space to accommodate computer labs. In Jersey City, computer classes are being taught in storage closets.

Science education is deficient in some poorer urban districts. Princeton has seven laboratories in its high school, each with built-in equipment. South Brunswick elementary and middle schools stress hands-on, investigative science programs. However, many poorer urban districts offer science classes in labs built in the 1920's and 1930's, where sinks do not work, equipment such as microscopes is not available, supplies for chemistry or biology classes are insufficient, and hands-on investigative techniques cannot be taught. In Jersey City and Irvington, middle school science classes are taught without provision for laboratory experience. In East Orange middle schools, teachers wheel a science cart into a three-foot-by-six-foot science area for instruction. The area contains a sink, but no water, gas, or electrical lines.

The disparity in foreign-language programs is dramatic. Montclair's students begin instruction in French or Spanish at the pre-school level. In Princeton's middle school, fifth grade students must take a half-year of French and a half-year of Spanish. Most sixth graders continue with one of these languages. Many begin a second language in the ninth grade, where four-year programs in German, Italian, Russian, and Latin are offered. French and Spanish are offered on two tracks, one for students who began instruction in middle school and the other for those who begin in the ninth grade. Advanced placement courses are available. In contrast, many of the poorer urban schools do not offer upper level foreign language courses, and only begin instruction in high school. . . .

Music programs are vastly superior in some richer suburban districts. South Brunswick offers music classes starting in kindergarten; Montclair begins with preschoolers. Millburn and South Brunswick offer their middle school students a music curriculum that includes courses such as guitar, electronic-piano laboratory, and music composition on synthesizers. Princeton offers several performing groups, including bands, choruses, and small ensembles. However, Camden and Paterson do not offer a music course until the fourth grade; only introductory level music courses are offered in high school. In 1981, Camden eliminated all its elementary school music teachers and provided "helpers" to assist in teaching music. Many poorer urban school districts have inadequate space for instrumental music lessons, bands, and choruses. In one elementary school in Jersey City, instrumental music lessons are provided in the back of the lunchroom. At lunchtime, the class moves to an area in the school's basement.

Art programs in some poorer urban districts suffer compared to programs in richer suburban districts. In Montclair, the art program begins at the preschool level; there is an art teacher in every elementary school; every school has at least one art room; and the district has purchased a variety of art equipment, such as a kiln for ceramic artwork. In contrast, art programs in some poorer urban districts are sparse. There are no art classrooms in East Orange elementary schools, and art teachers, who must travel from class to class, are limited in the forms of art they can teach. . . .

In South Brunswick school district, the industrial-arts program includes an automotive shop, a woodworking shop, a metal shop, a graphics shop, and a greenhouse for a horticultural course. The vocational education program has a computer drafting laboratory and a graphics laboratory with a darkroom. In Camden, state-of-the-art equipment is not purchased; the old equipment in the classrooms is not maintained or repaired. There have even been problems heating the industrial-arts wing of the school.

Physical education programs in some poorer urban districts are deficient. While many richer suburban school districts have flourishing gymnastics, swimming, basketball, baseball, soccer, lacrosse, field hockey, tennis, and golf teams, with fields, courts, pools, lockers, showers, and gymnasiums, some poorer urban districts cannot offer students such activities. In East Orange High School there are no such sports facilities; the track team practices in the second floor hallway. All of Irvington's elementary schools have no outdoor play space; some of the playgrounds had been converted to faculty parking lots. In a middle school in Paterson, fifth- and sixth-graders play basketball in a room with such a

low ceiling that the net is placed at the level appropriate for third-graders.

Many of these poorer urban districts are burdened with teaching basic skills to an overwhelming number of students. They are essentially "basic skills districts." In 1985, 53% of Camden's children received remedial education; in East Orange, 41%; in Irvington, 30%. By contrast, only 4% of the students in Millburn school district received remedial education.

A thorough and efficient education also requires adequate physical facilities. . . . Many poorer urban districts operate schools that, due to their age and lack of maintenance, are crumbling. These facilities do not provide an environment in which children can learn; indeed, the safety of children in these schools is threatened. For example, in 1986 in Paterson a gymnasium floor collapsed in one school, and in another school the entire building was sinking. According to East Orange's long-range facility plan there are ten schools in immediate need of roof repair, fifteen schools with heating, ventilation or air conditioning problems; two schools that need total roof replacement; nine with electrical system problems; eight with plumbing system problems; thirteen needing structural repairs; seventeen needing patching, plastering or painting; and thirteen needing asbestos removal or containment.

In an elementary school in Paterson, the children eat lunch in a small area in the boiler room area of the basement; remedial classes are taught in a former bathroom. In one Irvington school, children attend music classes in a storage room and remedial classes in converted closets. At another school in Irvington a coal bin was converted into a classroom. In one elementary school in East Orange, there is no cafeteria, and the children eat lunch in shifts in the first floor corridor. In one school in Jersey City, built in 1900, the library is a converted cloakroom; the nurse's office has no bathroom or waiting room; the lighting is inadequate; the bathrooms have no hot water (only the custodial office and nurse's office have hot water); there is water damage inside the building because of cracks in the facade; and the heating system is inadequate.

In contrast, most schools in richer suburban districts are newer, cleaner, and safer. They provide an environment conducive to learning. They have sufficient space to accommodate the childrens' needs now and in the future. While it is possible that the richest of educations can be conferred in the rudest

of surroundings, the record in this case demonstrates that deficient facilities are conducive to a deficient education.

Thorough and efficient means more than teaching the skills needed to compete in the labor market, as critically important as that may be. It means being able to fulfill one's role as a citizen, a role that encompasses far more than merely registering to vote. It means the ability to participate fully in society, in the life of one's community, the ability to appreciate music, art, and literature, and the ability to share all of that with friends. As plaintiffs point out in so many ways, and tellingly, if these courses are not integral to a thorough and efficient education, why do the richer districts invariably offer them? . . .

The State contends that the education currently offered in these poorer urban districts is tailored to the students' present need, that these students simply cannot now benefit from the kind of vastly superior course offerings found in the richer districts. . . . The State's conclusion is that basic skills are what they need first, intensive training in basic skills. We note, however, that these poorer districts offer curricula denuded not only of advanced academic courses but of virtually every subject that ties a child, particularly a child with academic problems, to school—of art, music, drama, athletics, even, to a very substantial degree, of science and social studies. . . .

. . . [C]onstitutionally, these districts should not be limited to such choices. However desperately a child may need remediation in basic skills, he or she also needs at least a modicum of variety and a chance to excel.

Equally, if not more important, the State's argument ignores the substantial number of children in these districts, from the average to the gifted, who can benefit from more advanced academic offerings. Since little else is available in these districts, they too are limited to basic skills.

. . . [With regard to teacher ratios (the number of teachers per 1,000 pupils), the average experience of instructional staff, their average level of education], the poorer urban districts suffer by comparison to the rich. Indeed, although the incremental showing is far from dramatic, teacher ratios, experience, and education consistently improve as the districts' property wealth, per pupil expenditure, socioeconomic status or other similar factor improves. . . .

In summary, . . . [the evidence] is more than sufficient to prove the constitutional deficiency in a limited number of districts. . . . Disparity exists . . . between education in these poorer urban districts and that in the affluent suburban districts; it is severe and forms an independent basis for our finding of a lack of a thorough and efficient education in these poorer urban districts—these students simply cannot possibly enter the same market or the same society as their peers educated in wealthier districts.

E. The Quality of Students' Needs in the Poorer Urban Districts

This record shows that the educational needs of students in poorer urban districts vastly exceed those of others, especially those from richer districts. The difference is monumental, no matter how it is measured. Those needs go beyond educational needs, they include food, clothing and shelter, and extend to lack of close family and community ties and support, and lack of helpful role models. They include the needs that arise from a life led in an environment of violence, poverty, and despair. Urban youth are often isolated from the mainstream of society. Education forms only a small part of their home life, sometimes no part of their school life, and the dropout is almost the norm. There are exceptions, fortunately, but substantial numbers of urban students fit this pattern. The goal is to motivate them, to wipe out their disadvantages as much as a school district can, and to give them an educational opportunity that will enable them to use their innate ability.

* * *

The dropout rate in these poorer urban districts is further testimony both to their failure and to the students' needs. The "unofficial" dropout rate (1984–85) for some urban high schools can be as high as 47%. A district cannot deliver a thorough and efficient education to a dropout. For a multitude of tragic reasons, these students lack the most basic requirement for achieving a thorough and efficient education—the will to learn. That characteristic is assumed, accepted, a given, in richer suburban districts.

* * *

Obviously, we are no more able to identify what these disadvantaged students need in concrete educational terms than are the experts. What they don't need is more disadvantage, in the form of a school district that does not even approach the funding level that supports advantaged students. They need more, and the law entitles them to more.

* * *

In *Robinson I* we observed that the State may "recognize . . . a need for additional dollar input to equip classes of disadvantaged [students] for the educational opportunity." . . .

It is clear to us that in order to achieve the constitutional standard for the student from these poorer urban districts—the ability to function in that society entered by their relatively advantaged peers—the totality of the district's educational offering must contain elements over and above those found in the affluent suburban district. If the educational fare of the seriously disadvantaged student is the same as the "regular education" given to the advantaged student, those serious disadvantages will not be addressed, and students in the poorer urban districts will simply not be able to compete. A thorough and efficient education requires such level of education as will enable all students to function as citizens and workers in the same society, and that necessarily means that in poorer urban districts something more must be added to the regular education in order to achieve the command of the Constitution. . . .

. . . We realize that perhaps nothing short of substantial social and economic change affecting housing, employment, child care, taxation, welfare will make the difference for these students; and that this kind of change is far beyond the power or responsibility of school districts. We have concluded, however, that even if not a cure, money will help, and that these students are constitutionally entitled to that help.

If the claim is that additional funding will not enable the poorer urban districts to satisfy the thorough and efficient test, the constitutional answer is that they are entitled to pass or fail with at least the same amount of money as their competitors.

If the claim is that these students simply cannot make it, the constitutional answer is, give them a chance. The Constitution does not tell them that since more money will not help, we will give them less; that because their needs cannot be fully met, they will not be met at all. It does not tell them they will get the minimum because that is all they can benefit from. Like other states, we undoubtedly have some "uneducable" students, but in New Jersey there is no such thing as an uneducable district, not under our Constitution.

All of the money that supports education is public money, local money no less than state money. It is authorized and controlled, in terms of source, amount, distribution, and use, by the State. The students of Newark and Trenton are no less citizens than their friends in Millburn and Princeton. They are entitled to be treated equally, to begin at the same starting line. Today the disadvantaged are doubly mistreated: first, by the accident of their environment and, second, by the disadvantage added by an inadequate education. The State has compounded the wrong and must right it.

F. Impact of the Level of Funding on the Quality of Education

The State's claim that the statistical evidence fails to prove a significant relationship between education expenditures and property wealth is joined with a more fundamental objection: money is not a critical factor in the quality of education in the first place. The position is not quite that extreme, of course—obviously, a certain minimum amount is needed to operate an effective school system, as the Commissioner notes. But beyond that minimum amount, not clearly defined in the record, the difference, the excess, is characterized as an unreliable indicator of the quality of education, and what the money buys—better staff ratios, more experienced teachers, equipment, more varied course offerings—is not determinative either. The conclusion is that since all districts in the state have much more than whatever the minimum amount may be, the excess and the differences in the excess, are irrelevant to the quality of education.

* * *

We deal here with questions of educational theory debated over the years, and now debated by experts of the very highest order. These issues have come to the fore not just in this case but throughout the nation, with states struggling as we are here in New Jersey to find an answer to urban problems, especially urban education. . . . The only thing universally agreed on is that those schools are failing. After that, controversy abounds. Our observation, simplistic perhaps, that "money is only one of a number of elements [involved in education]," *Robinson V* . . . still represents most of what one can profitably glean from this controversy for the purposes of this litigation. More concretely, while we are unable to conclude from this record that the State is clearly wrong, we would not strip all notions of equal and adequate funding from the constitutional obligation unless we were convinced that the State was clearly right.

The results of all of this research . . . shows beyond doubt that money alone has not worked. . . . But it

does not show that money makes no difference. What it strongly suggests is that money can be used more effectively than it is being used today. The inconclusiveness of the research is conceded, at least to the extent of admitting that although money is not the main determinant of the quality of education no one is quite convinced what is, nor totally confident about what works. . . .

* * *

We find that in order to provide a thorough and efficient education in these poorer urban districts, the State must assure that their educational expenditures per pupil are substantially equivalent to those of the more affluent suburban districts, and that, in addition, their special disadvantages must be addressed.

* * *

Whatever the legislative remedy, . . . it must assure that these poorer urban districts have a budget per pupil that is approximately equal to the average of the richer suburban districts, whatever that average may be, and be sufficient to address their special needs.

* * *

We have not attempted to address disparity of spending as such. To the extent that the State allows the richer suburban districts to continue to increase that disparity, it will, by our remedy, be required to increase the funding of the poorer urban districts. We limit our remedy at this point to increasing funding where we find a deficiency. We do not require equalized funding statewide. . . .

NOTES AND QUESTIONS

1. The Abbott v. Burke Decision

Approximately 300,000 students are in the thirty poor urban districts covered by the *Abbott* ruling, attending 450 schools staffed by 21,000 teachers. These students constitute 22 percent of New Jersey's public school students, but 49 percent of the state's minority students. Seventy-three percent of the students are eligible for free or reduced price lunches under the federal guidelines. "The *Abbott* Schools Initiative," http//:www.edlawcenter.org/abschproj.htm.

Is the court's decision in *Abbott v. Burke* a much stronger mandate for equal educational opportunity than what was required in *Robinson I*? Note that while the court did not mandate any controls on lo-

cal spending by affluent districts, the court did specify that to the extent that high-property-wealth districts increased their spending, the state must "increase the funding of the poorer urban districts." *Id.* at 410. Is the *Abbott* court applying an adequacy standard? A positive outcomes standard? Is the court requiring the state to ensure — or make its best efforts to do so — that all students are able to compete for the same kind of jobs? Must everyone be a computer programmer or brain surgeon? In light of what is presently known about the resource-outcome relationship, is an outcomes standard implementable? For a discussion of whether *Abbott* adopts an equity or an adequacy standard, *see* Enrich, *supra*, at 133–135.

To what extent does the *Abbott* court take into account municipal overburden? *See* Trachtenberg, "The Evolution and Implementation of Education Rights Under the New Jersey Constitution of 1947," 29 *Rutgers L. J.* 827, 895 (1998). Can the different approaches of *Board of Education, Levittown v. Nyquist, supra,* and *Abbott* concerning municipal overburden be attributed to the fact that in New Jersey urban school districts have both low property values and high "municipal overburden" while in New York the four largest cities have high property values, although substantial property tax revenues are still needed for other governmental services?

With regard to "education overburden," is the *Abbott* court arguing that expenditures must be on the basis of pupils' educational needs without regard to the fiscal capacity of local school districts? If so, are there judicially manageable standards for determining how much is needed? Who is to determine what a student's needs are? Even if it were possible for a court to determine the issue of need, how can the court decide if a particular program is in fact suited to whatever the need is? Does that mean that the program must guarantee that a particular skill or level of understanding will be achieved? Does this suggest a needs standard is really an outcomes standard in disguise? Or does a needs standard only require that the program be reasonably designed to address the student's needs in light of existing educational knowledge? How does the *Abbott* court treat these issues?

To what extent does the *Abbott* decision address "cost differentials?" Is a financing system that fails to take cost differentials into account unconstitutionally discriminatory? This issue was confronted in *Seattle School District No. 1 v. State*, 90 Wash.2d 476, 585 P.2d 71 (1978). The trial court implicitly accepted a "cost differentials" principle that would take into account the wage-price differences central cities often have to pay to provide the same educational offering that the typical student receives in a suburban or rural school district. *See* Levin, "Current Trends in School Finance Reform Litigation: A Commentary," 1977 *Duke L.J.* 1099, 1115–16, for a discussion of the three possible methods for determining the "basic education" that the state constitutionally is required to provide, each of which would take into account cost differences.

Should the *Abbott* court have given greater consideration to the state's argument that poor urban districts had sufficient funds, but had poorly administered and mismanaged them?

A recent urban district case is *Campaign for Fiscal Equity v. New York*, 719 N.Y.S.2d 475 (2001), which was based on an adequacy theory. In that case, following a lengthy trial, the judge found that New York City students—nearly 84 percent of whom are minority, 40 percent of whom are from welfare homes, more than 70 percent of whom are eligible for the federal free or reduced price lunch program, 16 percent of whom are "limited English proficient"—attend schools that are not providing a "sound basic education." *Id.* at 489–491. The court found that the school district has a high proportion of teachers who are uncertified and inexperienced, *id.* at 492–500; overcrowded, unsafe buildings with inadequate wiring and lacking science labs, *id.* at 501–509; a higher class size than the state average, *id.* at 513; and inadequate textbooks, library books, classroom supplies and equipment, and instructional technology, *id.* at 513–515. The case is being appealed.

2. Legislative Responses and Subsequent Litigation

Shortly after the opinion in *Abbott* (known as *Abbott II* because it was preceded by a procedural decision, *Abbott I*, 100 N.J. 269, 495 A.2d 376 (1985)), the New Jersey legislature enacted the Quality Education Act of 1990. To fund the act, an income tax was adopted, which led to a political backlash against the governor and the legislature. *See* Trachtenberg, *supra*, at 911. In 1991, the Quality Education Act was amended to divert $360 million to property relief, primarily benefitting wealthy suburban school districts. *Id.* at 912.

Plaintiffs returned to court seeking to have the Quality Education Act declared unconstitutional, which the state supreme court did in 1994, *Abbott*

III, 136 N.J. 444, 643 A.2d 575 (1994), on the ground that it failed "to assure parity of regular education expenditures between the special needs districts and the more affluent districts," 643 A.2d at 576, and failed to address "the 'special educational needs' of poorer urban districts for which *Abbott* required funding in addition to that necessary to achieve parity with the richer districts." 643 A.2d at 578. The court explained that "students in the special needs districts have distinct and specific requirements for supplemental educational and educationally-related programs and services that are unique to those students, not required in wealthier districts, and that represent an educational cost not included within the amounts expended for regular education." *Id.* at 580.

The court concluded by reaffirming its holding in *Abbott II*:

> For these special needs districts, a thorough and efficient education—one that will enable their students to function effectively in the same society with their richer peers both as citizens and as competitors in the labor market—is an education that is the substantial equivalent of that afforded in the richer districts. Those students in the special needs districts, given their educational disadvantages and the circumstances of their environment, will not be able to function effectively as citizens in that society, will not be able to fairly compete as workers. They are entitled at least to the chance of doing so, and without an equal educational opportunity, they will not have that chance. Their situation in society is one of extreme disadvantage; the State must not compound it by providing an inferior education. It is the State and only the State that is responsible for this educational disparity, and only the State can correct it.

Id. at 581.

The legislature then passed yet another statute, the Comprehensive Educational Improvement and Financing Act of 1996 (CEIFA), which was a standards-based approach, with achievement goals in specific academic areas. Plaintiffs went back to court and in *Abbott IV*, 149 N.J. 145, 693 A.2d 417 (1997), it was found to be unconstitutional because it again failed to achieve parity with regard to regular education, or adequately provide for supplemental programs. The court noted that CEIFA "does not in any concrete way attempt to link the content standards to the actual funding needed to deliver the content." 693 A.2d at 429. *Cf. DeRolphe v. Ohio*, 89 Ohio St.3d 1, 32–34, 728 N.E.2d 993, 1017–1019 (2000), finding that although the state had established academic standards that students were required to meet, and holding school districts accountable, it failed to provide adequate funding, particularly for "students and schools who start out furthest from the goal line."

Abbott IV was remanded for a determination of appropriate remedies for supplemental programs and facilities needs. On remand, the judge ordered the implementation of specific programs which the state supreme court, in *Abbott V*, 153 N.J. 480, 710 A.2d 450 (1998), endorsed and required them to be implemented immediately in the special needs districts. In addition to parity of regular funding, the programs included the following:

- Whole school reform
- Full-day kindergarten
- At least half-day preschool for three- and four-year-olds
- School-based coordination and referral of students to off-site health and social services, and, if necessary, school-based services
- Enhanced security
- Enhanced technology
- Alternative schools
- School-to-work and college-transition programs
- Safe, sanitary, and sufficient facilities

Trachtenberg, "Using Law to Advance the Public Interest: Rutgers Law School and Me," 51 *Rutgers L. Rev.* 1001, 1013 (1999), citing *Abbott V*.

Not surprisingly, considering the past history of this case and the state's responses, plaintiffs returned to court to complain that the preschool programs for disadvantaged children being implemented by the state were inadequate. The court, in *Abbott VI*, 163 N.J. 95, 748 A.2d 82 (2000), agreed that the programs were in violation of the standards it established in *Abbott V*.

3. Comparing Abbott *to Other Equity and Adequacy Cases*

How does the approach the court took in the *Abbott* case compare with that taken in *Serrano* or *Edgewood*, two equity cases calling either for equalizing spending or tax bases? How does it compare to *Rose v. Council for Better Education*, an adequacy case? Professor Trachtenberg argues that *Abbott* is far more prescriptive than any of the other decisions. Trachtenberg, "The Evolution and Implementation of Educational Rights Under the New Jersey Constitution of 1947," 29 *Rutgers L. J.* 827, 931 (1998).

Do you agree? Consider these comments by Professor Trachtenberg:

> [T]he *Abbott* litigation was the only one not to end with court approval of a legislative solution. Instead, the *Abbott* court itself dictated the precise terms of constitutional compliance, with the input of the plaintiffs and the state commissioner of education. The final product was an extensively detailed, comprehensive plan encompassing funding, educational standards and methods . . . , supplemental school and community programs and facilities improvement, all firmly embedded within a constitutional order.

Id. For a detailed comparison of each of the above-mentioned cases with *Abbott* and a discussion of the reasons for the differences, *see id.* at 932–935.

III. INTRADISTRICT INEQUALITIES

A. Introduction

Most reform efforts have been directed toward reforming differences among districts within a state in the distribution of educational resources per pupil, rather than toward intradistrict or even intraschool inequalities in the distribution of resources. Yet in a number of urban school districts, the level of spending per pupil may be considerably higher in those schools serving children from middle-class backgrounds than in schools where the student body is predominantly poor and minority. *See, e.g.,* J. Kozol, "The Savage Inequalities of Public Education in New York," in *Savage Inequalities: Children in America's Schools* 83 (1991), contrasting schools in Riverdale and South Bronx, within the same school district. With respect to intraschool inequalities, *see* Kirp, "The Educational Equities in Historical Perspective," in *Historical Perspectives on the Current Education Reforms* 173 (D. Ravitch and M. Vinovskis, eds., 1993), *available at* ERIC, ED359623, noting that "the most significant differences in treatment of students may well be found *within* schools, in the dollars spent on, and the quality of teachers assigned to, different classes." (Emphasis in original.) *See also* J. Kozol, *supra,* 92–98.

As noted in the preceding section, the principal source of inequalities in interdistrict per-pupil expenditures is the heavy reliance on the local property tax to fund education and the underlying inequalities in revenues generated by the use of this tax. These inequalities are due to differences among districts in property values per pupil, differences in tax rates, and inequitable property assessment practices. These factors, of course, cannot explain differences within a school district in expenditures per pupil. Moreover, arguments regarding the value of local control, which prevailed in *San Antonio School District v. Rodriguez* and a number of state cases, have no relevance when one is concerned with how a school board distributes resources among the buildings within a school system or how the principal distributes resources within his or her school.

B. Inequality in Washington, D.C.

One of the few cases that has addressed disparities within a school district arose in Washington, D.C. In an earlier phase of this same case, *Hobson v. Hansen*, 269 F.Supp. 401 (D.D.C. 1967), *aff'd en banc sub nom.*, *Smuck v. Hobson*, 408 F.2d 175 (D.C. Cir. 1969), the court considered three related constitutional problems: the segregation of students in the District of Columbia school system; the tracking system by which students were assigned to different educational programs on the basis of tested aptitude (the portion of the opinion concerning student classification appears in chapter 4); and inequities in the distribution of resources within the District. This last issue is addressed in the following case.

Hobson v. Hansen
327 F.Supp. 844 (D.D.C. 1971).

J. Skelly Wright, Circuit Judge.

[In its earlier opinion, the court sought to determine (1) whether the distribution of educational resources favored white over black and poor students, and (2) if so, whether such discrimination was legally justifiable. The court found that there was systematic discrimination in the distribution of educational inputs: the age, physical condition, and educational adequacy of school buildings; quality of the textbooks; library books and facilities; school congestion; such factors assertedly relevant to assessing faculty quality as teacher experience, faculty education, and reliance on temporary (noncertified) teachers; curricula and special programs; and per-pupil expenditures. In each area, the court identified inequities which favored white students. Predominantly black schools, for example, were filled to 115 percent of capacity, while predominantly white schools had 23 percent of their space unfilled; teachers at white

schools were better educated, more experienced, and were more typically certified than their counterparts at black schools. Financial disparities were notable, with the median per-pupil expenditure for schools with 85 to 100 percent black students being $292 and the median per-pupil expenditure for schools with 0 to 15 percent black students being $392.

Plaintiffs sought further relief several years after the 1967 decree "in view of the fact that the spread in total expenditures per pupil at various district elementary schools had increased by over 100% since 1964." The court focused not on total expenditure differences, but on the substantial differences between elementary schools west of the Park (the predominantly white and middle class area of the city) and elementary schools in Anacostia (one of the poorest sections among the predominantly black and poor east of the Park area) in pupil-teacher ratios—18.1:1 to 22.6:1, as well as in teacher expenditures per pupil—$669 to $478, or 40 percent greater in the schools west of the Park.]

* * *

[T]he court has considered and rejected defendants' argument that the observed wide discrepancies in teacher expenditures per pupil favoring schools west of the Park are random and do not favor any particular racial group or economic class of children. The court has also rejected defendants' position that, even if an objective pattern of discrimination exists, it does so solely or primarily for technological reasons (i.e., economics of scale) which are beyond defendants' control and which cannot be remedied by a court order. Now the court comes to defendants' ultimate defense: that even if a pattern of unequal expenditures does exist, and even if the differential expenditures per pupil are within defendants' control, the resulting real resource differentials are nonetheless inconsequential as they relate to equal educational opportunity.

Teacher expenditure per pupil is a sum, of course, which reflects both the size of the class in which a given student finds himself and the salary paid his teacher. With regard to the average teacher salary component of teacher expenditures per pupil, defendants take the position that the different salaries paid teachers are primarily rewards for experience, and that experience has not been shown to have a significant correlation with a teacher's productivity measured by student achievement tests. . . .

It is almost an affront to common sense to say, as do defendants, that a pattern of spending so discriminatory on its face as the one which exists in the District reflects no discrimination in "educational opportunity." . . . [A]s the court reads them, the rather inconclusive educational studies tell us only that teachers seem to be overcompensated for experience relative to their productivity. That is, researchers consistently find some relationship between experience and achievement, though not so great as is traditionally paid for. In the absence of more conclusive studies, large differentials such as exist in the District of Columbia cannot be condoned.

Moreover, the Board cannot be allowed in one breath to justify budget requests to the Congress and to the District of Columbia City Council by stressing the connection between longevity and quality teaching, and then in the next breath to disavow any such connection before the court. Speaking before the City Council on the subject of teacher salary legislation, the chairman of the school board said:

> The Board recognizes that to achieve quality education in the District of Columbia public schools it is imperative that students must be housed in educational facilities conducive to learning and be taught by a highly motivated and well-trained teaching staff. It believes that in order to accomplish this objective, it must begin to offer a salary schedule attractive enough to retain its experienced master teachers. . . .

Under these circumstances, where teacher experience has not been proved to be unrelated to educational opportunity, where the administration itself has chosen to reward experience, and where a pattern of racial and socioeconomic discrimination in expenditures continues in the District, the law requires either that experienced teachers be distributed uniformly among the schools in the system or that some offsetting benefit be given to those schools which are denied their fair complement of experienced teachers.[22]

Defendants have also alleged that the observed variations in pupil-teacher ratios—the second and larger component of the widely disparate teacher expenditures per pupil—are of no consequence in terms of educational performance or opportunity. Without here going into this contention exhaustively, the court rejects it for much the same reasons as those given in the discussion of the value of teacher experience. The outside studies referred to . . . [by expert witnesses for plaintiffs and defendants] are themselves inconclusive. There are so many other variables to be controlled in a study of the relationship between teacher-pupil ratio and educational product that the indefiniteness of the studies made to date is not the least bit surprising. . . .

In the end the court finds itself most persuaded, once again, by defendants' own words, uttered before the lawyerly rationalization process began in earnest. . . . [I]n the program justification for the 1972 fiscal budget we read that "class size is one of the most important factors in maximizing education achievement." . . . Thus do defendants put themselves in the awkward position of asking to be applauded for their expensive efforts to reduce class sizes generally and of requesting funds for further reduction of class sizes under the rationale of productivity, while inconsistently maintaining for purposes of this litigation that no discrimination results when class sizes remain significantly smaller in west of the Park schools as compared with those in the rest of the city.

Plaintiffs' *prima facie* case of discrimination in the provision of educational opportunity, based upon the pattern of unequal expenditures which favors the schools west of the Park, is strongly buttressed by further evidence in the record concerning the results of citywide sixth grade reading achievement tests. The record shows that the west of the Park elementary

---

[22]At the same time they argue that the longevity component of teachers' salaries is unrelated to the effectiveness of their performance—an argument which I reject for the reasons outlined above—defendants seek to justify the current spending pattern and to prove themselves innocent of discriminatory intent by giving several alternative reasons why a policy which rewards longevity might be employed. In this regard, defendants seek first to "explain" the presence of the most experienced and most educated teachers in the schools west of the park as being merely "historical. . . ."

[Defendants [also] maintain that there are at least three sound theoretical economic reasons why length of service might be compensated in excess of its associated productivity increases. According to defendants:

"(1) Turnover costs supply a rationale for an age-earnings profile that starts with earnings below productivity and, as experience accumulates, begins to pay wages in excess of productivity. . . .

"(2) The market for teachers services has a supply side as well as a demand side. Union pressures are another possible explanation for salary patterns. If more experienced teachers control the union, they will use negotiations to get high salaries for themselves relative to new teachers. . . .

"(3) A third reason why the relative pay of experienced teachers may be higher than their relative productivity has to do with costs which are the same for all teachers, regardless of experience. Examples of such costs are hiring costs and the cost of providing a classroom for the teacher. . . .

Any worry that shifts in teaching personnel necessitated by an equalization order "would breach the contract which has been effected with the Washington Teachers Union" (Benjamin Henley, Acting Superintendent of Schools, Supplemental Affidavit of August 12, 1970) is quickly allayed by reference to the contract itself which provides that "the fundamental transfer policy shall take into consideration the following factors: . . . legal requirements as ordered by the courts or Congress. . . ." The other alternative reasons offered by defendants for rewarding experience without regard to productivity smack of post hoc rationalization, are extremely speculative, and are essentially makeweights. Without pursuing them in detail in this opinion, the court rejects them. . . .

schools produced an average reading achievement test score that was significantly higher—indeed 2.4 grades higher—than the average for the rest of the city. Obviously, these results tend to corroborate the presumption created by the pattern of expenditures that the city provides a better educational opportunity to its richer, white students. . . .

These achievement test results suggest that not only are the children in schools east of the Park being denied an educational opportunity equal to those west of the Park, but also they in fact are not being as well educated. Thus these test scores reflect the result of the discrimination against the east of the Park children in per-pupil expenditure. The burden of establishing that these test results reflect something other than the proven discriminatory distribution of educational opportunity falls upon defendants. And once again defendants have failed to meet their burden.

. . . Although defendants have argued strenuously that there is no proven connection between the showing that black students have unequal access to dollars [for teachers' salaries and benefits] and the crucial constitutional showing that black students are denied equal educational opportunity, the court has found otherwise. . . .

. . . For reasons already discussed, the court finds that plaintiffs' initially requested relief requiring equalization of total expenditures per pupil across the system would sweep too broadly and would require the school administration to equalize some inputs which have little or nothing to do with educational opportunity. But upon careful consideration, the court does find that the equalization order approach is a good one, provided it is focused upon expenditures per pupil for teachers' salaries and benefits, so as to cover only inputs which do have a direct bearing on the quality of a child's education.

Having found continuing substantial discrimination, the court cannot agree with defendants' expert that an equalization order would amount to "much ado about nothing." Defendants stress that implementation of the proposed order would result merely in an increase of $3.39 per black child across the city. . . . Defendants' figure of $3.39 per child masks the fact that some individual black schools are shockingly far below the citywide average expenditure per pupil level. Thus, to take one of many possible examples, if teacher expenditures per pupil in fiscal 1971 at the Draper School (actually $362) had been at the citywide average ($497), they would have increased by $135 per pupil. The increase in total

teacher expenditures would then have been approximately $147,000. Under salary scales currently in effect, this would have permitted the addition of perhaps fifteen new teachers at Draper. This addition would have reduced the pupil-teacher ratio from the present 25 to 1 to 18 to 1. Even defendants' expert seems to concede that such a reduction has a beneficial effect on school outcomes when measured by achievement test scores.

* * *

Wherefore it is ordered, adjudged and decreed that

1. On and after October 1, 1971, per-pupil expenditures for all teachers' salaries and benefits from the regular District of Columbia budget (excluding . . . all funds not from the regular congressional appropriation) in any single elementary school (not "administrative unit") shall not deviate by more than 5 percent from the mean per-pupil expenditure for all teachers' salaries and benefits at all elementary schools in the District of Columbia school system as that mean is defined in this paragraph. The 5 percent limit may be exceeded only for adequate justification on an individual school basis shown to this court in advance. "Adequate justification" shall include provision of compensatory education for educationally deprived pupils at certain schools or provision of special educational services for the mentally retarded or physically handicapped at certain schools or for other "exceptional" students. It shall also include a showing that variance above or below the 5 percent limit is accounted for solely on the basis of economies or diseconomies of scale. For purposes of this order, the "mean" shall be computed after excluding from the computation total expenditures for all teachers' salaries and benefits and total average daily membership at all schools for which permission to exceed the 5 percent limitation because of compensatory education or education of "exceptional" students is sought and granted. . . .

NOTES AND QUESTIONS

1. Politics of Educational Budget Making

The allocation of the education budget is the most crucial issue to confront the school board. The budget is prepared by the superintendent and his or her staff and presented to the board; it is a document that reflects internal bureaucratic bargaining. Teachers and noncertificated service personnel present their demands—either through union representatives or informally—to the superintendent before formal submission. When the budget is presented, the administrative staff "has in mind a definite dollar amount, or percentage figure, which they believe the board will accept." James, Kelly, and Garms, "The School Budget Process in Large Cities," in *The Politics of Education* 74, 82 (M. Kirst, ed., 1970). In large cities, the power of the school bureaucracy over the budget is countered to some extent by various interest groups—unions, taxpayers' groups, and the like—who rely on their own professional research staffs to prepare "counterbudgets." As a consequence, the school board typically finds itself balancing a variety of conflicting pressures: middle-class parents seeking better (and more costly) educational programs; school personnel seeking more money for higher salaries and better working conditions; and taxpayers' groups anxious to keep costs and taxes as low as possible.

While specifics may vary, the bargaining that characterizes education budget making is a general organizational phenomenon. *See* A. Wildavsky, *The Politics of the Budgetary Process* (1964). Two effects of the process are worth noting: (1) the give and take that characterizes decisions over dollars makes dramatic change unlikely from one year to the next, for budgetary increases or cutbacks are likely to arouse strong political opposition; (2) individuals and groups who are both outside the system and unable to wield considerable political pressure are in essence shut out of the budgetary bargaining. The historic powerlessness of these groups—notably poor and minority communities—has meant that their educational needs, translated into budget terms, are considered last, although that political pattern has changed noticeably in recent years.

Does this discussion suggest a possible explanation for the black-white resource disparities noted in the *Hobson* opinions? Does it indicate what difficulties might beset the implementation of the second *Hobson* decision?

2. The Court's Analysis

Why did the *Hobson* court choose to examine some but not all inputs in assessing whether black and poor students receive fewer educational resources than do white and better off students? Is the court tacitly assuming that these inputs affect educational outcomes even though the research is inconclusive,

that they are perceived as important by the black community, or that taken together, they constitute the bulk of the district's school budget? An estimate of the breakdown of per pupil expenditures nationally for 1994–95 indicates that 60.8 percent goes to instruction, 10.4 percent to school operation and maintenance, 8.7 percent to administration, 8.5 percent to student services, 7.4 percent to food services, and 4.2 percent to transportation. "Where the Money Goes," 13 *State Education Leader* 25 (1994). Should the court distinguish between such factors as age of school buildings and teacher experience? If so, on what constitutional basis? Can any of the disparities in resources examined in *Hobson* be justified on demographic or other nondiscriminatory grounds? Would assignment of teachers by seniority constitute such a ground?

After discussing "the range of inequities" in resources provided to black and white students in its earlier decision, the court ignores all of them except teacher inequalities. If the court had chosen to equalize distribution of each of the factors it had discussed earlier (e.g., physical plant, textbooks, under- or overutilization of facilities), how would it have gone about the task?

The *Hobson II* opinion focuses exclusively on black-white inequities in teacher expenditure. Professor Horowitz explains this focus as partially the result of the tactics of plaintiff's counsel. Of all the inputs that could have been focused upon, for example, equalization of test scores of teachers' verbal abilities, equalization of years of experience, and so forth, Horowitz writes that in the end it was decided to focus on per-pupil expenditures as a whole because they were identified in *Hobson I* and because it was an objective measure that could be judicially enforced. D. Horowitz, *The Courts and Social Policy* 121–22 (1977). The court itself on its own initiative further narrowed the issue to the equalization of inequities in expenditures for teachers. The question then becomes, why? Is the court suggesting that money spent on teachers is somehow "most important"? Does educational research support this contention? Is the court's attention focused on teachers' salaries and benefits (as opposed to salaries for librarians and counselors, books, and so on) because these are the biggest items in the school budget? Horowitz reports that counsel for the school district did not object. Why do you suppose there was no objection?

Once disparities in teacher salaries and pupil-staff ratios between "white" and "black" schools were demonstrated, the court placed the burden on the school district either to rebut the inference of discrimination or to offer "compelling" justification for the disparities. Given the state of knowledge about the effectiveness of various school inputs, does the placement of the burden decide the outcome? If so, is the approach constitutionally justifiable? Are there policy reasons that support the standard of review adopted by the court? *See* Hornby and Holmes, "Equalization of Resources within School Districts," 58 *Va.L.Rev.* 1119, 1143–55 (1972).

3. *Race and Class*

The plaintiffs had emphasized the fact that poor students had fewer teacher-dollars spent on them than did middle-class students. The *Hobson* opinion, however, emphasizes the racial discrimination issue, even though over 95 percent of the Washington, D.C., student population was black at the time of the litigation. Is the court suggesting that discrimination against the poor does not raise constitutional questions analogous to those presented by discrimination against minorities? *See Dandridge v. Williams*, 397 U.S. 471, 90 S.Ct. 1153, 25 L.Ed.2d 491 (1970) (per-household ceilings on welfare grants); *San Antonio Independent School District v. Rodriguez*, 411 U.S. 1, 93 S.Ct. 1278, 36 L.Ed.2d 16 (1973); *Harris v. McRae*, 448 U.S. 297, 100 S.Ct. 2671, 65 L.Ed.2d 784 (1980). As the foregoing cases make clear, wealth classifications do not receive heightened judicial scrutiny. After *Washington v. Davis*, discussed in chapter 4, is it likely that resource differentials adversely affecting minority students would be sufficient to trigger heightened scrutiny?

4. *The Remedy*

The *Hobson* remedy requires expenditure equalization within 5 percent of mean expenditure. The court permits expenditure deviations greater than 5 percent with "adequate justification." Is justification limited to instances where additional help is provided on a "catch-up" basis to students with disabilities or who are educationally disadvantaged? Could a program for the gifted be justified to the court? Is the court converting into constitutional doctrine what philosopher John Rawls has termed "the difference principle": "All social primary goods—liberty and opportunity, income and wealth, and the bases of self-respect—are to be distributed equally unless an unequal distribution of any or all of these goods is to the advantage of the least favored." J. Rawls, *A Theory of Justice* 303 (1971).

Is it easier—as a matter of either law or policy—for a court to remedy disparities within a given school district than to remedy interdistrict disparities? Consider the following comment:

> Since partition of the municipal budget has already occurred, the court [assessing intradistrict inequalities] need not consider the entire budgetary process. . . . Moreover, action by the court will not entail substantial interference with the political process. Most intradistrict allocation decisions are administrative in character and therefore somewhat isolated from electoral control. Finally, the protection of students from excessive discrimination would seem to be a function for which the courts have peculiar institutional competence.

Schoettle, "The Equal Protection Clause in Public Education," 71 *Colum.L.Rev.* 1355, 1412 (1971).

Professor Horowitz notes that not only was the equalization issue in the case narrowed from equalizing all resources to equalizing only per-pupil expenditures on teachers' salaries, but also the options for implementing the decree. The decree was to be implemented "by one method only—transferring teachers—and later almost entirely by transferring special-subject or resource teachers." D. Horowitz, *The Courts and Social Policy* 146 (1977). This tactic was hit upon as the only available alternative after rejecting the idea of moving students (by mandatory busing) and deciding to move as few teachers as possible. The most easily moved teachers were the special subject teachers because of union rules, less resistance from principals, and the ease of finding funds to compensate losses in special programs. *Id.* at 148–49. The result of the school's policy of transferring special subject teachers was to break the significant negative correlation between school size and the ratio of resource teachers to pupils: now resource teachers were distributed more equitably. The additional effect was to increase the ratio in schools attended predominantly by disadvantaged pupils. Thus, the implementation of *Hobson II* had the perverse effect of hurting the schools of the disadvantaged. *Id.* at 152–53. The apparent reason was that in order to maintain compliance with *Hobson II* as enrollments dropped in many schools, the district shifted away resource teachers.

C. Other Intradistrict Disparity Litigation

There has been only one intradistrict disparity decision since *Hobson*. In *Brown v. Board of Education*,

Chicago, 386 F.Supp. 110 (N.D. Ill. 1974), inequalities in the distribution of resources within the city of Chicago were challenged on wealth and race discrimination grounds. As to the wealth discrimination claim, the court concluded that *Rodriguez* required the plaintiffs to establish—in order to trigger the use of strict scrutiny—that a group of poor persons whose incomes fell below some identifiable level of poverty were absolutely deprived of a minimally adequate education. Since the plaintiffs had failed to establish these two points, inequalities in per-pupil staffing expenditures had to be assessed in light of the rational basis standard of review pursuant to which the court concluded the existing inequalities were justifiable. ". . . [A]dministrative convenience, sudden unexpected demographic changes, and response to the special educational need of certain neighborhoods serve as sufficient justification for the Board's policies." 386 F.Supp. at 123. With regard to the racial discrimination claim, the court concluded that the plaintiff's data were sufficient to establish a prima facie case of discrimination (the decision predated *Washington v. Davis*), but did not issue an injunction inasmuch as the school board convinced the court that it had undertaken a series of programs to correct the funding disparities between black and white schools.

NOTES AND QUESTIONS

1. *Dearth of Additional Intradistrict Disparity Cases*

As noted, the only other intradistrict disparity case was *Brown v. Board of Education, Chicago,* 386 F.Supp. 110 (N.D. Ill. 1974). Why are so few intradistrict disparity suits brought while interdistrict disparity decisions continue to be handed down with some frequency? Consider whether Title I of the Elementary and Secondary Education Act, 20 USC §6301 *et seq.* (West 2000), has helped to equalize expenditures within school districts since the early 1970s. Title I requires school districts to provide services to its Title I schools that are "at least comparable" to the services being provided in non-Title I schools within the district. Initially, regulations established five tests of comparability: pupils per certified teacher; pupils per certified instructional staff other than teachers; pupils per noncertified instructional staff; instructional salaries per pupil; and other

instructional costs per pupil, with allowable differences on these measures between Title I and non-Title I schools being no more than 5 percent. Later amendments, however, reduced the measures of comparability and indicated that differences of 10 percent were acceptable. Currently, the statute specifically precludes a school district from including staff salary differentials for longevity in calculating comparability; there are no current regulations. Whether the more relaxed standards for comparability will mean that disparities in resources among schools within districts may begin to widen again remains to be seen.

Some commentators have predicted that as adequacy theories are further developed, they may be applied to intradistrict disparities.

> In the past, [within-district disparities have] not been viewed as a fruitful litigation target because of the absence of an obvious structural objection to the way districts distribute their money to schools. This is in contrast to the ready objection that has been mounted against the local property tax-based system for getting money to districts. Moreover, the schools with the most children from low-income families and the highest proportion of educationally-least-successful children often spend more dollars per pupil than the district average when state and federal categorical aid are counted. But as judicial concerns about need and outcomes come more to the fore, there are sure to be those whose objections may be couched in terms of how poor children in some schools within urban districts fare compared with other children in the district. Indeed, litigation of this sort is ongoing now in Los Angeles.

Minorini and Sugarman, "School Finance Litigation in the Name of Educational Equity: Its Evolution, Impact, and Future," in *Equity and Adequacy in Education Finance* 34, 65 (H. Ladd, R. Chalk, and J. Hansen, eds., 1999).

A suit was recently filed in California, *Williams v. State*, alleging that schools in poor and predominantly minority areas in eighteen California school districts, subsequently expanded to schools in forty-six school districts, are providing an inadequate education because of large numbers of uncredentialed teachers, shortages of textbooks, overcrowded and rat-infested classrooms, and so on. Rather than suing the districts, however, the suit contends that the state is liable for failing to oversee and manage the public school system to ensure that schools are providing an adequate education. *See* Sahagun and Helfand, "ACLU Sues State Over Conditions in Poor

Schools," *Los Angeles Times*, May 18, 2000, at A1; "ACLU Sues States Over 'Substandard' Schools," *San Francisco Examiner*, Aug. 16, 2000, at A7; Egelko, "ACLU School Suit is Approved," *San Francisco Examiner*, Nov. 17, 2000, at B14. The state countersued the school districts, claiming that substandard conditions in schools in those districts were the responsibility of the local district, not the state; that suit, however, has been put on hold by the judge. Egelko, "Davis' Schools Lawsuit Stalled," *San Francisco Chronicle*, Apr.12, 2001, at A2.

Another California lawsuit is taking a somewhat different approach to resource inequalities. In 1999, an action was brought against the Inglewood Unified School District and the state education department, *Daniels v. State*, charging that in violation of both the state equal protection clause and the state education clause, they were denying equal educational opportunity to minority and low-income students by offering few, if any, advanced placement courses in their schools, while offering a wide array of such courses in schools attended by predominantly white, middle-class students. Advanced placement courses figure prominently in admission to California's universities. With the end of affirmative action, university officials are relying more heavily on grade point averages, and give extra weight to advanced placement courses. Sahagun and Weiss, "Bias Suit Targets Schools Without Advanced Classes," *Los Angeles Times*, July 28, 1999, at A1. The case was settled after legislation was adopted addressing the disparity in advanced placement courses.

2. *Intradistrict Disparities in Private Resources*

PTAs no longer are relying on bake sales to pay for band uniforms or similar supplemental school needs. Private donations to public schools are assuming a larger role, raising the concern that inequities between rich and poor schools will increase. PTAs in wealthy schools are beginning to subsidize essential classroom activities, including teachers' salaries. In Washington, D.C., an elementary school in a middle-class area of the city raises over $100,000 annually, using the funds to hire a full-time art teacher and school nurse. By contrast, an elementary school that primarily serves students whose families are on public assistance raised less than $1,000. Stecklow, "Education: Parents' Largess to Schools Splits Communities,"*Wall Street Journal*, Jan. 26, 1995, at B1. *See also* Blum, "PTAs Give Some D.C. Schools an Edge: Affluent Northwest Parents Providing Extras that

Poorer Neighbors Can't," *Washington Post*, April 17, 2000, at B-1 (one affluent D.C. elementary school hired seven teaching assistants to reduce class size and a part-time vocal instructor with funds raised by parents while an elementary school in a poor neighborhood had trouble raising money for an awards ceremony). Some of the more elite public schools are engaged in substantial fund-raising campaigns. Boston Latin School, which already has an endowment portfolio of more than $14 million, has launched a $60 million campaign among its alumni to build a new library and media center. The Harry A. Burke High School in Omaha is raising $32 million for an information technology center, athletic complex, and new classrooms. Walnut Hills High School in Cincinnati, Brookline High School in Massachusetts, and the Bronx High School of Science in New York, are all examples of schools that are raising $10 million or more with the help of their alumni. These private funds are being used for enhancing teacher training, hiring consultants to develop curricula and a technology plan, integrating technology into classrooms, upgrading computer equipment and science laboratories, and providing supplemental course materials. Ferdinand, "True to Their Public High Schools: Powerful Alumni Aid Major Fund-Raising," *Washington Post*, Mar. 1, 2000, at A3.

Should private donations be prohibited when they exacerbate inequalities among schools, or should such private, individual choices by parents and alumni be unrestricted? Should equity concerns prevent schools in more affluent areas from improving themselves, meaning that instead of some students having enhanced opportunities, none can have them? If middle-class parents are prevented from improving the quality of their children's education, might they remove their children to private schools? On the other hand, if PTAs and alumni of schools in more affluent neighborhoods raise money for additional staff, technology, modernizing science labs, and so on, will it be more difficult to get taxpayers to support all schools within the district? Would middle-class parents themselves, if permitted to fund the schools their children attend, be less likely to press for improvements in the rest of the schools within the district? *See* Schomberg, "Equity v. Autonomy: The Problems of Private Donations to Public Schools," 1998 *Ann. Surv. Am. L.* 143, 163–164 (1998). How should the tension between equal educational opportunity for all and the desire of parents to provide the best possible education for their children that they can afford be resolved? If the state provided a fully adequate education for all children, would this concern about inequity arise?

Should private funding be permitted for enrichment but not for the core educational program? PTAs of two elementary schools in New York City, concerned about the loss of a teacher due to lack of district funds, and the increase in class size that would result, raised money to cover the salaries and benefits for the teachers. The New York City chancellor, however, barred the use of privately raised dollars for full-time classroom teachers, because of concern for "the implications it would have on the core issue of equity for all children throughout the system." Schomberg, *supra*, at 144. *See also* Steinberg, "Fair or Not, Rules Are Bent to Bankroll Public Schools," *New York Times*, Sept. 24, 1997, at A1.The Montgomery County, Maryland school district has also banned PTAs from paying for classroom instruction. Stecklow, *supra*. Should school districts restrict private expenditures for teaching the core curriculum, but permit private funds to be used for science equipment or textbooks? What should be deemed to be core and what enrichment? Can a school system distinguish between contributions of money and contributions of time? What about the contributions that affluent parents provide their children, such as having a computer and books in the home, or taking them to the theater or museums, or sending them to nursery school or to summer camp, that better prepare them for school than children of poor parents?

What about corporate and foundation dollars? One commentator has pointed out that rural schools that are far removed from corporate headquarters are likely to be left out, and that "also neglected are the urban school districts whose dangerous neighborhoods keep corporations away for fear of associating their names with violence. Thus, many of the neediest schools are cut off from the corporate dollar." Schomberg, *supra*, at 160.

In a system that permits substantial private contributions, what should be done about schools in poorer neighborhoods? Low-income parents not only cannot afford to contribute funds, but also often cannot afford to contribute time. One proposal is similar to the "recapture" proposal for property taxes raised by wealthy districts:

> [B]eyond a certain level of fund-raising, a portion of all dollars raised would go to a state or district fund for distribution to poorer schools (e.g., for every dollar a school

raised over $1500, fifty cents would go to the state fund; for every dollar raised over $10,000, seventy cents would go to a state fund; etc.). Parents would still be able to see and control the direct results of their contributions without creating more glaring disparities between their children's school and its poorer counterparts.

Schomberg, *supra*, at 173. Would this be any more acceptable to affluent parents than recapture has been to property-rich school districts? What legal challenges might parents make to such a system?

IV. THE RIGHT TO A "FREE" PUBLIC EDUCATION

A. Introduction

School districts increasingly rely on student fees to help keep their programs intact. This increased need to charge student fees for various activities in part reflects not only inadequate budgets, but also changes in the classroom. Students rely less on textbooks and more on original source material that can be costly to photocopy for the entire class; science classes involve more hands-on, experiential learning; and computers are increasingly part of the regular program. *See* Beyers, "Student Fees Stretch School Budgets, but Many Families Feel the Strain," *Washington Post*, Mar. 3, 1996. As noted earlier in this chapter, almost every state constitution has an express provision guaranteeing a free public education, although the specific constitutional language varies among the states. Moreover, education is compulsory up to a certain age in every state. (See chapter 1.) What does it mean to have a right to a free public education? Can school districts charge tuition, or fees for textbooks, supplies and materials, particular courses, lab equipment, towels and lockers, transcripts, and so on? What about transportation fees for children who are compelled to attend school but who are too far from any school to be able to get there on their own? Are these user fees permissible under the "free" public education mandated by state constitutions? Even if such fees are not part of the constitutionally mandated free public education, is it a violation of the Equal Protection Clause if indigent children are unable to participate either wholly or less beneficially because of inability to pay the fees? This section will explore some of these issues, which raise questions not only concerning what is a "free" education, but also what is integral to that education that must be provided free of charge, and whether the state can make education compulsory without providing equality of access to that education.

B. School Fees

The issue of school fees has been addressed by state courts for over a century. *See Irvin v. Gregory*, 86 Ga. 605, 13 S.E. 120 (1891) (incidental fees of $5 to $10 per year were unconstitutional if children could be excluded from attending public school if unwilling as well as unable to pay the fee). The majority of older cases invalidated tuition fees, relying on the state constitutional provisions providing for free schools. *See, e.g., Special School District v. Bangs*, 144 Ark. 34, 221 S.W. 1060 (1920); *State ex rel. Roberts v. Wilson*, 221 Mo.App. 9, 297 S.W. 419 (1927); *Batty v. Board of Education*, 67 N.D. 6, 269 N.W. 49 (1936), *cf. Plyler v. Doe*, 457 U.S. 202, 102 S.Ct. 2382, 72 L.Ed.2d 786 (1982).

More recent cases fall into four categories: textbook fees, fees for particular materials or courses, fees for extracurricular activities, and transportation fees. *See* Schomberg, *supra*; Note, "Education Fees in Public Schools: A Practitioner's Guide," 73 *B. U. L. Rev.* 71 (1993); Note, "Student Fees in Public Schools: Defining the Scope of Education," 72 *Iowa L. Rev.* 1401 (1987).

1. Textbook Fees. More than half the recent cases challenging textbook fees have been unsuccessful. *See, e.g., Marshall v. School District No. 3, Morgan Co.*, 191 Colo. 451, 553 P.2d 784 (1976); *Carpio v. Tucson High School District*, 111 Ariz. 127, 524 P.2d 948 (1974), *cert. den.*, 420 U.S. 982, 95 S.Ct. 1412, 43 L.Ed.2d 664 (1975). But, with the exception of Arizona, *see Carpio*, *supra*, all of the states where textbook fees were upheld had some procedure for providing texts free of charge to children of indigent parents. In *Carpio*, however, the Arizona Supreme Court held that the failure of the state to provide free textbooks to high school children had a rational basis. "It is within the Legislature's discretion to say what the limits of a free education should be beyond the minimum set forth in the Arizona Constitution." 111 Ariz. at 130, 513 P.2d at 951.

In a substantial number of cases, however, textbook fees have been invalidated. *See, e.g., Paulson v. Minidoka County School District*, 93 Idaho 469, 463 P.2d 935 (1970) (books are necessary and therefore must be free, although fees for extracur-

ricular activities are permitted); *Bond v. Public Schools of Ann Arbor School District*, 383 Mich. 693, 178 N.W.2d 484 (1970) (books must be free either under the "necessary element of any school's activity" or the "integral fundamental part of the elementary and secondary education" test); *Cardiff v. Bismarck Public School District*, 263 N.W.2d 105 (N.D. 1978) (constitutional provision mandating "free public schools" does not mean merely "free from tuition" but also includes textbooks). As of 1991, only eight states allowed school districts to charge fees for required textbooks. Schomberg, "Equity v. Autonomy: The Problems of Private Donations to Public Schools," 1998 *Ann. Surv. Am. L.* 143, 155 (1998).

In *Paulson v. Minidoka County School District*, *supra*, the court found that textbooks were necessary elements of education and thus within the scope of the guarantee of a free public education. Other courts have followed a similar approach on school fees for a variety of purposes, determining whether a fee is a necessary element or integral part of a district's educational program, and therefore impermissible, or is not a necessary element. *See* Note, "Student Fees in Public Schools: Defining the Scope of Education," 72 *Iowa L. Rev.* 1401 (1987).

2. Fees for Materials, Courses, and Extracurricular Activities. These cases fall into three categories: (1) "reasonable" fees are upheld, even for required courses; (2) fees for required courses or necessary items are barred, but fees for supplemental or extracurricular courses or activities are upheld; and (3) even fees for extracurricular activities violate the free public education guarantee of the state constitution. Many of these cases, at least those in the latter two categories, turn on whether the particular course or activity is deemed part of the "education" that is guaranteed or is supplemental. Other cases turn on what is meant by "free" education.

In many of the cases that upheld instructional and course fees for required as well as elective courses, the courts ruled that the constitutional mandate to provide "free public schools" meant "without tuition," which is satisfied as long as public funds are used to provide the school building and staff salaries necessary for a basic system of public education. *See, e.g., Sneed v. Greensboro City Board of Education*, 299 N.C. 609, 264 S.E.2d 106 (1980).

Those cases that struck down fees for required courses or "necessary" items, but permitted the charging of fees for supplemental courses or extracurricular activities, viewed the constitutional requirement of free public schools as including "necessary" elements of a school's activity, *Paulson v. Minidoka County School District*, 93 Idaho 469, 463 P.2d 935 (1970), or even including any fees in connection with courses for which academic credit is given, *Concerned Parents v. Caruthersville School District*, 548 S.W.2d 554 (Mo. 1977). Some courts state that no fees may be charged for any course or activity reasonably related to the academic and educational goals of a particular system. Thus, a New Jersey court has held that driver's education is an essential part of the constitutionally mandated "thorough and efficient" education but that "behind-wheel training" was not essential and therefore could be subject to a fee. *Parsippany-Troy Hills Education Association v. Board of Education*, 188 N.J. Super. 161, 457 A.2d 15 (1983).

Those courts that have struck down fees for extracurricular activities have extended the guarantee of free schooling to cover even interscholastic athletics when thought to be an integral part of the total education process. *Hartzell v. Connell*, 35 Cal.3d 899, 679 P.2d 35, 201 Cal.Rptr. 601 (Cal. 1984) (en banc) (extracurricular activities "constitute an integral component of public education"); *Bond v. Public Schools of Ann Arbor School District*, 383 Mich. 693, 178 N.W.2d 484 (1970).

The policy arguments on both sides of the issue have been stated as follows:

> The use of fees relieves the burden on taxpayers and allows the school to purchase and uniformly provide items so all students have the proper type of material at the time it is needed. Fees allow schools to offer specialized activities to those who are interested when they might not feel justified in expenditures for a small number of students. Fees may give individual parents a sense of responsibility by providing certain incidental needs for their children rather than depending upon the community.
>
> But fees cause a hardship, especially on poorer families. They are a problem for teachers, sponsors, and school secretaries to collect and handle. They result in less participation in activities.

Note, "Student Fees in Public School: New Statutory Authority," 16 *Washburn L.J.* 439, 440 n. 8 (1977). It has been noted that the stigma of seeking a fee waiver may discourage students from applying and thus diminish participation. *Hartzell v. Connell*, 679 P.2d at 44; Schomberg, *supra*, at 157.

3. Transportation. Some courts that have held that a "free" public education includes books and supplies, and even extracurricular activities, have nevertheless held that fees may be charged for transportation. *See, e.g., Sutton v. Cadillac Area Public Sch.*, 323 N.E.2d 582 (Mich. Ct. App.1982) (transportation is important but not a "necessary element" of education); *Arcadia Unified Sch. Dist. v. State Department of Educ.*, 2 Cal.4th 251, 825 P.2d 438, 5 Cal. Rptr.2d 545 (Cal. 1992). Under California law, transportation fees are waived for indigent parents. In New York, transportation is an "ordinary contingent expense" and thus is covered by taxes. Note, "Education Fees in Public Schools: A Practitioner's Guide," 73 *B. U. L. Rev.* 71, 88 (1993).

The Supreme Court, in the following case, addressed the issue of charging user fees for transportation. In *San Antonio Independent School District v. Rodriguez*, 411 U.S. 1, 93 S.Ct. 1278, 36 L.Ed.2d 16 (1973), the majority indicated that some minimal level of adequate education might be required under the Fourteenth Amendment. *Id.* at 36–37. *Plyler v. Doe*, 457 U.S. 202, 102 S.Ct. 2382, 72 L.Ed.2d 786 (1982), gave heightened equal protection scrutiny to the "important" interest in education when the class denied access to an education by being singled out for tuition charges was comprised of undocumented alien children. For children who live too far from their school to get there on their own, should the failure to provide transportation or the charging of user fees for transportation, effectively denying access to education for those unwilling or unable to pay the fee, be similarly treated?

Kadrmas v. Dickinson Public Schools
487 U.S. 450, 108 S.Ct. 2481, 101 L.Ed.2d 399 (1988).

O'Connor, J.

[Under North Dakota law, the school board of any school district that had not been reorganized could charge a fee for bus service. Reorganized school districts, however, may not permit a charge for bus transportation, so that in those districts, all students who ride the bus do so for free. Of the 310 school districts in North Dakota, only eight—primarily the larger school districts—had not reorganized. The Dickinson School District was one of those eight. Thus, only those eight districts are permitted to charge a fee for busing.

Sarita Kadrmas lived with her family about sixteen miles from the elementary school she attended. The

Kadrmas family is at or near "the officially defined poverty level." Unable to pay the fee, as well as their other bills, the family refused to sign a contract obligating them to pay the user fee for school bus service—$97—for the 1985 school year. Since the school bus no longer picked up Sarita, the family arranged to transport her to school privately. The North Dakota Supreme Court concluded that the fees authorized by statute are "rationally related to the legitimate governmental objective of allocating limited resources and that the statute does not discriminate on the basis of wealth so as to violate federal or state equal protection rights." 402 N.W.2d 897, 903 (N.D. 1987).]

* * *

. . . Appellants contend that Dickinson's user fee for bus service unconstitutionally deprives those who cannot afford to pay it of "minimum access to education." . . . Sarita Kadrmas, however, continued to attend school during the time that she was denied access to the school bus. Appellants must therefore mean to argue that the busing fee unconstitutionally places a greater obstacle to education in the path of the poor than it does in the path of wealthier families. Alternatively, appellants may mean to suggest that the Equal Protection Clause affirmatively requires government to provide free transportation to school, at least for some class of students that would include Sarita Kadrmas. Under either interpretation of appellants' position, we are evidently being urged to apply a form of strict or "heightened" scrutiny to the North Dakota statute. Doing so would require us to extend the requirements of the Equal Protection Clause beyond the limits recognized in our cases, a step we decline to take.

We have previously rejected the suggestion that statutes having different effects on the wealthy and the poor should on that account alone be subjected to strict equal protection scrutiny. . . . Nor have we accepted the proposition that education is a "fundamental right," like equality of the franchise, which should trigger strict scrutiny when government interferes with an individual's access to it. . . .

Relying primarily on *Plyler v. Doe*, . . . appellants suggest that North Dakota's 1979 statute should be subjected to "heightened" scrutiny. . . . In *Plyler*, . . . the State of Texas had denied to the children of illegal aliens the free public education that it made available to other residents. Applying a heightened level of equal protection scrutiny, the Court concluded that the State had failed to show that its clas-

sification advanced a substantial state interest. 457 U.S., at 217–218, and n. 16, 224, 230, 102 S.Ct., at 2395, and n. 16, 2398, 2401–02. . . . [We do not] think that the case before us today is governed by the holding in *Plyler*. Unlike the children in that case, Sarita Kadrmas has not been penalized by the government for illegal conduct by her parents. . . . On the contrary, Sarita was denied access to the school bus only because her parents would not agree to pay the same user fee charged to all other families that took advantage of the service. Nor do we see any reason to suppose that this user fee will "promot[e] the creation and perpetuation of a sub-class of illiterates within our boundaries, surely adding to the problems and costs of unemployment, welfare, and crime." *Id.* at 230 . . . . The case before us does not resemble *Plyler*, and we decline to extend the rationale of that decision to cover this case.

Appellants contend, finally, that whatever label is placed on the standard of review, this case is analogous to decisions in which we have held that government may not withhold certain especially important services from those who are unable to pay for them. . . .

[Cases such as *Griffin v. Illinois*, 351 U.S. 12 (1956) (right to appellate review of a criminal conviction conditioned on the purchase of a trial transcript) are distinguishable as] each involved a rule that barred indigent litigants from using the judicial process in circumstances where they had no alternative to that process. Decisions invalidating such rules are inapposite here. . . . North Dakota does not maintain a legal or a practical monopoly on the means of transporting children to school. Thus, unlike the complaining parties in all the cases cited by appellants, the Kadrmas family could and did find a private alternative to the public school bus service for which Dickinson charged a fee. That alternative was more expensive, to be sure, and we have no reason to doubt that genuine hardships were endured by the Kadrmas family when Sarita was denied access to the bus. Such facts, however, do not imply that the Equal Protection Clause has been violated. . . .

Applying the appropriate test—under which a statute is upheld if it bears a rational relation to a legitimate government objective—we think it is quite clear that a State's decision to allow local school boards the option of charging patrons a user fee for bus service is constitutionally permissible. The Constitution does not require that such service be provided at all, and it is difficult to imagine why choosing to offer the service should entail a constitutional obligation to offer it for free. No one denies that encouraging local school districts to provide school bus service is a legitimate state purpose or that such encouragement would be undermined by a rule requiring that general revenues be used to subsidize an optional service that will benefit a minority of the district's families. It is manifestly rational for the State to refrain from undermining its legitimate objective with such a rule.

* * *

In sum, the statute challenged in this case discriminates against no suspect class and interferes with no fundamental right. Appellants have failed to carry the heavy burden of demonstrating that the statute is arbitrary and irrational. The Supreme Court of North Dakota correctly concluded that the statute does not violate the Equal Protection Clause of the Fourteenth Amendment, and its judgment is

Affirmed.

Justice Marshall, with whom Justice Brennan joins, dissenting.

In *San Antonio Independent School Dist. v. Rodriguez,* 411 U.S. 1, 93 S.Ct. 1278, 36 L.Ed.2d 16 (1973), I wrote that the Court's holding was a "retreat from our historic commitment to equality of educational opportunity and [an] unsupportable acquiescence in a system which deprives children in their earliest years of the chance to reach their full potential." *Id.,* at 71, 93 S.Ct., at 1316 (Marshall, J., dissenting). Today, the Court continues the retreat from the promise of equal educational opportunity by holding that a school district's refusal to allow an indigent child who lives 16 miles from the nearest school to use a schoolbus service without paying a fee does not violate the Fourteenth Amendment's Equal Protection Clause. Because I do not believe that this Court should sanction discrimination against the poor with respect to "perhaps the most important function of state and local governments," *Brown v. Board of Education,* 347 U.S. 483, 493, 74 S.Ct. 686, 691, 98 L.Ed. 873 (1954), I dissent.

The Court's opinion suggests that this case does not concern state action that discriminates against the poor with regard to the provision of a basic education. The Court notes that the particular governmental action challenged in this case involves the provision of transportation, rather than the provision of educational services. Moreover, the Court stresses that the denial of transportation to Sarita Kadrmas did not in fact prevent her from receiving an education; notwithstanding the denial of bus service, Sarita's family ensured that she attended school each day.[1] . . . This case involves state action that places a special burden on poor families in their pursuit of education. Children living far from school can receive a public education only if they have access to transportation; as the state court noted in this case, "a child must reach the schoolhouse door as a prerequisite to receiving the educational opportunity offered therein." 402 N.W.2d 897, 901 (N.D. 1987). Indeed, for children in Sarita's position, imposing a fee for transportation is no different in practical effect from imposing a fee directly for education. Moreover, the fee involved in this case discriminated against Sarita's family because it necessarily fell more heavily upon the poor than upon wealthier members of the community. . . .

. . . The intent of the Fourteenth Amendment was to abolish caste legislation. See *Plyler v. Doe,* 457 U.S. 202, 213, 102 S.Ct. 2382, 2392, 72 L.Ed.2d 786 (1982). When state action has the predictable tendency to entrap the poor and create a permanent underclass, that intent is frustrated. See *id.,* at 234, 102 S.Ct., at 2403 (Blackmun, J., concurring). Thus, to the extent that a law places discriminatory barriers between indigents and the basic tools and opportunities that might enable them to rise, exacting scrutiny should be applied.

The statute at issue here burdens a poor person's interest in an education. The extraordinary nature of this interest cannot be denied. . . . A statute that erects special obstacles to education in the path of the poor naturally tends to consign such persons to their current disadvantaged status. By denying equal opportunity to exactly those who need it most, the law not only militates against the ability of each poor child to advance herself, but also increases the likelihood of the creation of a discrete and permanent underclass. Such a statute is difficult to reconcile with the framework of equality embodied in the Equal Protection Clause.

* * *

The State's rationale for this policy is based entirely on fiscal considerations. The State has allowed

---

[1]The Court therefore does not address the question whether a State constitutionally could deny a child access to a minimally adequate education. In prior cases, this Court explicitly has left open the question whether such a deprivation of access would violate a fundamental constitutional right. See *Papasan v. Allain,* 478 U.S. 265, 289, 106 S.Ct. 2932, 2946, 92 L.Ed.2d 209 (1986); *San Antonio Independent School Dist. v. Rodriguez,* 411 U.S. 1, 25, n. 60, 36–37, 93 S.Ct. 1278, 1292, n. 60, 1298–99, 36 L.Ed.2d 16 (1973). That question remains open today.

Dickinson and certain other school districts to charge a nonwaivable flat fee for bus service so that these districts may recoup part of the costs of the service. The money that Dickinson collects from applying the busing fee to indigent families, however, represents a minuscule proportion of the costs of the bus service. As the Court notes, ante, at 2485, all of the fees collected by Dickinson amount to only 11% of the cost of providing the bus service, and the fees collected from poor families represent a small fraction of the total fees. Exempting indigent families from the busing fee therefore would not require Dickinson to make any significant adjustments in either the operation or the funding of the bus service. Indeed, as the Court states, most school districts in the State provide full bus service without charging any fees at all. The state interest involved in this case is therefore insubstantial; it does not begin to justify the discrimination challenged here.

. . . For the poor, education is often the only route by which to become full participants in our society. In allowing a State to burden the access of poor persons to an education, the Court denies equal opportunity and discourages hope. I do not believe the Equal Protection Clause countenances such a result. I therefore dissent.

[Dissenting opinion by Stevens, J., in which Blackmun, J. joined, omitted]

NOTES AND QUESTIONS

1. *The* Kadrmas *Decision*

The Supreme Court in *Plyler v. Doe* stated that although "public education is not a 'right' granted to individuals by the constitution . . . neither is it merely some governmental 'benefit' indistinguishable from other forms of social welfare legislation." 457 U.S. 202, 221, 102 S.Ct. 2382, 2396, 72 L.Ed.2d 786 (1982). In that case, the Court applied a heightened level of scrutiny, because education is an important, albeit not fundamental, interest. Are not indigent children who cannot pay for transportation to school deprived of minimum access to education just as much as were the undocumented alien children in *Plyler?* Was the plaintiffs' argument that free transportation is part of the obligation to provide free public schooling—that is, is getting *to* the school an integral part of the education the state is mandated to provide for free? Or are the plaintiffs making an

equal access to education claim—that is, a case involving discrimination on the basis of wealth? Would the result have been different if Sarita Kadrmas had not had alternate means of transportation and thus have been denied access to an education because of inability to pay the busing fee? Or is it that the Court interpreted that the interest was in busing rather than in education and thus not sufficiently important to trigger heightened judicial review?

Are children of indigent parents any more responsible for their status than the undocumented alien children in *Plyler*, or illegitimate children, to whom the heightened level of scrutiny has also been applied? *See, e.g., Trimble v. Gordon*, 430 U.S. 762, 97 S.Ct. 1459, 52 L.Ed.2d 31 (1977). In the cases involving illegitimate children, the identification of a burdened class alone, with the presence of an important interest, has been sufficient to trigger heightened scrutiny. *See* Biegel, "Reassessing the Applicability of Fundamental Rights Analysis: The Fourteenth Amendment and the Shaping of Educational Policy after *Kadrmas v. Dickinson Public Schools*," 74 *Corn. L. Rev.* 1078 (1989), arguing that the Court should have applied the intermediate level of scrutiny in *Kadrmas*.

The Court determined that the rational basis test was the appropriate test. Is conditioning access to a basic public education on the payment of user fees a rational nondiscriminatory means of conserving resources? Does it make the user fee more or less rational that schooling is compulsory and the parents of Sarita, if they did not find alternative means of transportation to get her to the school, could have been prosecuted for violating the compulsory school law?

2. *Claim Under State Constitutional Provisions*

Education has been held to be a fundamental right under the North Dakota state constitution. *In the Interest of G.H.*, 218 N.W.2d 441 (N.D.1974). Should that have produced a different result in the North Dakota state supreme court under a state equal protection clause analysis?

V. RACE AND SCHOOL FINANCE

A. Introduction

One theory about school finance litigation is that it arose out of disillusionment with the progress of desegregation. Professor Ryan has described this view as follows:

School finance litigation is . . . often depicted both as a means of moving beyond race as the salient issue in education reform and as an effective way to achieve educational equity and adequacy for disadvantaged students from all racial and ethnic backgrounds. Concomitantly, from its inception thirty years ago to the present, such litigation has been seen as either a supplement to or a substitute for desegregation litigation.

   School finance litigation began in the late 1960s, at a time when civil rights advocates were growing disillusioned with the pace and progress of desegregation.

Ryan, "Schools, Race, and Money," 100 *Yale L. J.* 249, 252–253 (1999). Professor Ryan notes that racially isolated schools and school districts are also isolated by poverty. His thesis is that "although it is possible that school finance reform could have been a helpful supplement to desegregation, it is a poor substitute," and that "the needs of racially and socioeconomically isolated schools may exceed the reach of school finance reform." *Id.* at 256–257. In another article, he argues that urban minority districts are more likely to lose school finance cases than white districts, and that in the few cases where minority districts have been successful in the courts, the legislative resistance to school finance reform has been much stronger than when white districts have succeeded in their lawsuits. Ryan, "The Influence of Race in School Finance Reform," 98 *Mich. L. Rev.* 432 (1999). *See also* Reed, "Twenty-Five Years After *Rodriguez:* School Finance Litigation and the Impact of the New Judicial Federalism," 32 *Law & Soc'y Rev.* 175, 211 (1998) (studies show racial attitudes affect attitudes toward school finance equalization).

   Sheff v. O'Neill, 678 A.2d 1267 (Conn. 1996), discussed in chapter 4, is one school case that has linked poverty and race. Plaintiffs, students in the Hartford school district, alleged that they were "burdened by severe educational disadvantages arising out of their racial and ethnic isolation and their socioeconomic deprivation." 678 A.2d at 1271. Relying on both the state constitution's education clause and its clause prohibiting segregation, the plaintiffs argued that the state was obligated to remedy the educational disparities. The Connecticut Supreme Court concluded that it did not need to decide "the extent to which substantial socioeconomic disparities or disparities in educational resources would themselves be sufficient to require the state to intervene in order to equalize educational opportunities." *Id.* at 1281. Instead, it agreed with the plaintiffs that the two constitutional provisions, when read to-

gether, required the state to address the unequal educational opportunity experienced by Hartford school children. *See* Ryan, "*Sheff*, Segregation, and School Finance Litigation," 74 *N.Y.U. L. Rev.* 529 (1999). Professor Ryan has suggested that this case may initiate a "fourth wave" of litigation that focuses on racially and socioeconomically isolated districts disadvantaged by the state's failure to address educational disparities. Ryan, "Schools, Race, and Money," 100 *Yale L. J.* 249, 307–308 (1999). *See also* Note, "The Turning Tide: The Emerging Fourth Wave of School Finance Reform Litigation and the Courts' Lingering Institutional Concerns," 58 *Ohio St. L. J.* 1867 (1998); Morgan, "The Less Polite Questions: Race, Place, Poverty and Public Education," 1998 *Ann. Surv. Am. L.* 267. *See Paynter v. State,* 720 N.Y.S.2d 712, 2001 N.Y. Slip Op. 21067 (N.Y. Sup. Nov. 14, 2000).

B. Title VI Disparate Impact and Resource Equity

Several school finance suits have proceeded on a theory that the state's underfunding of predominantly minority districts has a disparate impact on minority children in violation of Title VI of the Civil Rights Act of 1964. The Third Circuit, in reversing a lower court's dismissal of a complaint, held that the allegation that the state's system of financing education had a racially discriminatory impact stated a claim under Title VI regulations.

Powell v. Ridge
189 F.3d 387 (3d Cir.), *cert. denied,* 528 U.S. 1046 (1999)

Before Sloviter and Mansmann, Circuit Judges and Ward, District Judge.

Sloviter, Circuit Judge.

   [The plaintiffs included parents of children who attended public schools in Philadelphia. They alleged that state officials, "through their funding policies and practices, discriminate against African-American, Hispanic, Asian and other minority students in the School District." The complaint was based on the Title VI regulation prohibiting a funding recipient from "utiliz[ing] criteria or methods of administration which have the effect of subjecting individuals to discrimination because of their race, color, or national origin, or have the effect of defeating or substantially impairing accomplishment of the program as respects individuals of a particular race, color, or national origin." 34 C.F.R. §100.3(b)(2).]

* * *

. . . To survive a motion to dismiss, all that [a Title VI] plaintiff must do is plead that a facially neutral practice's adverse effects fall disproportionately on a group protected by Title VI. . . .

The complaint in this case states, *inter alia*:

> The Commonwealth Defendants' funding system for education gives school districts with high proportions of white students on average more Commonwealth treasury revenues than school districts with high proportions of non-white students, where the levels of student poverty are the same.
>
> When Commonwealth treasury revenues per pupil are analyzed by the amount of poverty in school districts across the Commonwealth . . . school districts with higher proportions of non-white students receive less Commonwealth treasury revenues than districts with higher proportions of white students.
>
> On average, for 1995–96, for two school districts with the same level of poverty . . . the school districts with higher non-white enrollment received $52.88 *less* per pupil for each increase of 1% in non-white enrollment.
>
> The Commonwealth's funding policies and practices disadvantage . . . students in [underfunded] districts. . . . The foreseeable result [of the funding policies] has been serious impairment of the educational opportunities of the students in the School District, including the Student Plaintiffs. Lack of sufficient resources in the School District results, *inter alia*, in larger class sizes and higher pupil-to-teacher ratios than in surrounding school districts; reduced curricula; cuts in and elimination of programs and electives and advanced placement courses, shortages of textbooks and use of outdated textbooks; shortages of equipment, supplies and technology; spartan physical education and extracurricular programs; lack of librarians and library services; insufficient numbers of counselors and psychologists; and many inadequate and crumbling physical facilities.

These allegations are sufficient to put the defendants on notice that the plaintiffs will attempt to prove (1) that less educational funding is provided by the Commonwealth to school districts attended by most non-white students in Pennsylvania than to school districts attended by most white students, (2) that the school districts attended by most non-white students in Pennsylvania receive less total educational funding than do the school districts attended by most white students, (3) that these disparities in funding are produced by the Commonwealth's funding formula, and (4) that the funding disparities injure nonwhite students by limiting their educational opportunities. Although the language of the complaint may not always be precise or its thrust clear, we nonetheless believe that plaintiffs' allegations provide more than sufficient notice to meet the pleading standard. We therefore hold that the plaintiffs should be given the opportunity to offer evidence in support of their claims. Whether they will ultimately be entitled to prevail is a very different question on which we express no opinion.

. . . The District Court described the complaint as alleging that "the uniformly applied state formula for allocating basic education funds among the 501 school districts does not bring about the same results in Philadelphia as it might in another, more affluent district. . . ." This characterization suggests that the disparity the plaintiffs have pled is one based on economic circumstances rather than race. However, the complaint specifically alleges that the disparity in funding cannot be explained by reference to relative wealth or poverty because the disparities are present when districts of the same poverty level are compared.

* * *

Defendants argue that the complaint fails to state a claim because it compares the effect of the funding formula on school districts rather than its effect on individuals. Unquestionably, under Title VI and 34 C.F.R. § 100.3(b)(2), the disparate impact complained of must fall on an individual rather than on a school district. Plaintiffs, cognizant of that requirement, have alleged that the Commonwealth's funding system results in proportionately less funding per child to school districts with high proportions of nonwhite students than to school districts with high proportions of white students. They argue that the effect of less funding per student is larger class sizes, higher pupil per teacher ratios, reduced curricula, fewer programs, and less textbooks, equipment, supplies, and technology per student than received by school districts with proportionately more white students. While it may ultimately be more difficult to prove the impact, and consequently the disparate impact, on the school children because the funding is directed to the school districts, that potential difficulty does not justify denying plaintiffs the opportunity to prove the effect alleged.

* * *

As we have stated earlier, we take no position on the merits of the allegations of the complaint. It is indeed a serious matter for plaintiffs to charge that the practices of the Commonwealth of Pennsylvania in funding public schools have a racially disparate effect. But if the charge is serious, so are the inevitable effects if the charge turns out to have merit. We need no long list of citations to note the widespread recognition of the importance of a good public school education for all of our young people—rich and poor, black and white. Horace Mann, the great educator, wrote "Education, . . . beyond all other devices of human origin, is the great equalizer of the conditions of men,—the balance-wheel of the social machinery."

We will reverse the order of the District Court dismissing the complaint, and remand for further proceedings consistent with this opinion.

NOTES AND QUESTIONS

1. Private Right of Action

The defendants in *Powell v. Ridge* also argued that Title VI regulations do not provide a private right of action. The Third Circuit disagreed, noting that Supreme Court precedent, citing *Guardians Ass'n v. Civil Service Comm'n*, 463 U.S. 582, 103 S.Ct. 3221, 77 L.Ed.2d 866 (1983), gives rise to an implied right of action, at least for injunctive relief. The court cited cases from the Eleventh, Tenth, Second, and Ninth Circuits to the same effect. However, the Supreme Court has recently held, in a five-to-four decision, that Title VI regulations do not create a private right of action. *Alexander v. Sandoval*, ___ U.S. ___, 121 S. Ct. 1511, 149 L.Ed.2d 517 2001). Enforcement would have to be by the U.S. Department of Education, and not private plaintiffs.

2. Title VI Challenges to Resource Equity

Other cases have also addressed whether a Title VI claim could go forward alleging that the state's method of distributing education funds has a dis-

criminatory impact on minority students. *See Campaign for Fiscal Equity, Inc. v. New York*, 86 N.Y.2d 307, 655 N.E.2d 661 (N.Y. 1995). On remand in that case, the trial court found that New York's funding system had an adverse and disparate impact on minority students in New York City (who constitute 84% of the public school enrollment), and that defendants were unable to show the state system of financing education was justified by "educational necessity." 187 Misc.2d 1, 719 N.Y.S.2d 475, 2001 N.Y. Slip Op. 21051 (N.Y.Sup. Jan. 9, 2001). Two cases brought in federal court alleging violation of the Title VI disparate impact regulation resulting from the state's distribution of educational resources have survived motions to dismiss. *Robinson v. Kansas*, 117 F.Supp.2d 1124 (D. Kan. 2000); *Ceaser v. Pataki*, 98 Civ.8532(LLM), 2000 WL 1154318 (S.D.N.Y. Aug. 14, 2000). As a result of the Supreme Court's decision in *Alexander v. Sandoval*, *supra*, however, these claims are likely to be dismissed.

What is the linkage, if any, between a state's obligation under its constitution and its duty under Title VI, if any? What is the state's obligation if resource disparities are attributable not to inequitable distribution of state revenues among districts within the state, but to the fact that the local district contribution is less per pupil than other districts in the state due to the effect of municipal overburden on the tax effort for education? Is the Title VI disparate impact regulation violated when the state's financing scheme provides equal resources to predominantly minority school districts and other districts, but the educational needs of predominantly minority districts are greater?

What must the percentage of minority students be within a school district to trigger a Title VI disparate impact claim for resource inequities? Inasmuch as a state's school funding scheme provides money to school districts, not to individual students, how can plaintiffs demonstrate that the adverse impact falls on individual students rather than the school district? How might plaintiffs prove that the state's school financing scheme *caused* the disparate impact?

EIGHT

Educational Governance and the Law

I. INTRODUCTION

All of the issues discussed in the preceding chapters—compulsory education, school socialization, the dilemma of difference, and school finance—are inextricably tied to the question of how public education is and should be governed. Although Gutmann's discussion of democratic education in chapter 1 treats the state as a monolithic entity, it is actually a complex system of decision making. As a consequence, underlying the dilemmas of what should be taught and to whom are basic considerations of who should decide such matters. The question of who governs is vital to the legitimacy of the entire public education enterprise. A legitimate educational system must be founded upon some notions of public control of educational decision making. To be sure, expertise and professionalism have their place, but ultimately there should be an ongoing process of consultation and consent that renders the exercise of expertise and professionalism acceptable. This does not assume that the majority embraces every educational decision or even that there is an informed and articulate citizenry that presses its leaders at every turn. What is at stake is the ability of citizens to assert control over educational institutions through elections and other political and economic means. As Robert Dahl and Charles Lindblom have noted, the question of whether the citizenry has this "last word" is a matter of degree, for there are no absolute criteria. *See* R. Dahl and C. Lindblom, *Politics, Economics, and Welfare* 278 (1953).

Democratic legitimacy is important with respect to all of the institutions, bureaucracies, and functions of the modern welfare state, but it is critical in the realm of public education because public schools are the primary public institution (as opposed to family and church in the private sector, for example) for socializing the young and bringing them into the larger culture. In a sense, public schools are responsible for inculcating the rules by which democracy survives and thrives. If this task is performed well, students learn to appreciate the ways of democracy while retaining the flexibility and critical judgment necessary to engage in a continuing process of reevaluating its premises, values, and practices. The individual's capacity for autonomous choice is increased. *See* I. Berlin, *Four Essays on Liberty* (1969). But this introduces a serious problem of circularity. Public schools are charged with communicating an understanding of the very processes by which public schools are held accountable. In this fashion, there is a mutually affecting relationship between educational governance and the socialization functions of the public schools described in chapters 1 through 3.

The structure and processes of educational governance are also linked to the quality of education and to equality of educational opportunity, the subject of chapters 4 through 6. As in the case of any enterprise that produces goods and services for the public, the nature of the mechanisms for controlling organizational and individual behavior will determine the types and quality of the goods and services produced. This is a particularly knotty problem in the case of public schooling because market forces, the preferences of consumers as expressed through voluntary economic transactions, traditionally have played a marginal role in the allocation of free (and compulsory) education services. Public school systems can be looked upon as institutional devices to insulate to a large extent the distribution of school services from market forces, to provide educational opportunities irrespective of student or parental preferences or wealth. Indeed, the challenges of school finance reform analyzed in chapter 7 demonstrate the difficulties of determining an equitable distribution of public education. In economic jargon, education has been treated as a merit good, a good to which everyone is entitled and which one may not sell or transfer. In part, this reflects the notion that education (or educational opportunity) should be distributed equally. This further complicates the problem of educational governance. Concerns about equality are superimposed on concerns about quality and democratic accountability. Satisfaction of these concerns can overlap, but then again it may not. If people act in their own best interest (narrowly conceived), this suggests that the approximation of some criterion of equality may be a function of who governs (and to whom they feel beholden or accountable). If, for example, racial minorities are excluded from the governing processes of education (say by disenfranchisement), then one could reasonably predict that minority students will suffer for this in the distribution of educational services. This, in turn, can have profound consequences for socialization of all students to democratic norms.

This brings us to the politics of education. The tendency is to think exclusively in terms of electoral constraints on public school systems. These constraints are clearly essential, and they are discussed below. But, as Charles Lindblom notes in *Politics and Markets* (1977), there are in reality a great number of components to the "social machinery for control of authority." This chapter is devoted to exploring these different control components or mechanisms in the public education context. *See generally* J. Chubb and T. Moe, *Politics, Markets, and America's Schools* (1990). School organizations can be controlled and receive direction through rules and regulations, intergovernmental constraints (some hierarchical, some not), inducements, institutional restructuring, capacity-building, interest-group pressures, professionalism, bureaucracy, and so on. *See generally* L. McDonnell and R. Elmore, *Alternative Policy Instruments* (1987). To this array,

we have added recent proposals and experiments that reintroduce market systems into education as a method of improving the performance of schools.

This chapter is organized around three key dynamics in educational governance: (1) the allocation of decision-making authority among federal, state, and local policymakers; (2) the division of responsibility for overseeing schools that develops among elected officials, career professionals, and courts; and (3) the respective roles of public officials and private enterprise in delivering educational services. The first part of the chapter explores the waxing and waning of national influence in setting educational policy. Although federal influence has declined in recent years, Congress continues to play a role by emphasizing national standards in education. The second part focuses on the renewed importance of elected officials, particularly state legislatures, in charting the direction of educational reform. At the same time, state courts have emerged as critical forces in school reform. Meanwhile, teachers struggle to preserve a sense of professionalism, while federal courts and agencies have retreated from active intervention in the schools. The final section addresses the demands for increased privatization of educational service delivery. The push for market-style remedies has led to a wide array of reform initiatives with mixed evidence of success.

What this chapter demonstrates is that educational governance has become a lively focus of reform initiatives. These initiatives implicate many of the fundamental concerns addressed in earlier chapters. Should state and local governments continue to be the primary source of educational policy, even as the United States faces the prospect of competing in a global economy? If the focus shifts to high standards and accountability, how can policymakers ensure that no child is unfairly neglected and left behind? Does a focus on output measures, like test scores, distract the public from shortcomings in input measures, including teacher pay and training; funding for school construction, books, and materials; hours of instruction; and teacher-student ratios? Does the rhetoric of privatization, with its analogies to the marketplace, divert attention from the public obligation to distribute education fairly, regardless of ability to pay? As you explore the current controversies regarding school governance, consider how reform initiatives make fundamental value judgments sometimes in the guise of neutral principles of process.

II. FEDERAL, STATE, AND LOCAL AUTHORITY OVER EDUCATIONAL DECISION MAKING

A. The Changing Federal Role

Traditionally, state and local educational agencies have assumed principal responsibility for delivering educational services. As chapter 1 showed, when confronted with industrialization and immigration in the 1800s and early 1900s, state legislatures and local school districts took the lead in making school attendance compulsory and establishing a curriculum for the common school. The federal government's role in these developments was quite limited. Federal courts made the most important contribution by establishing constitutional protections for parents who preferred to enroll their children in alternative educational programs in private schools.

After World War II, the federal government became more active in shaping the direction of educational policy. Some of its efforts were targeted at improving national competitiveness in areas like mathematics and science instruction. The most notable efforts, however, focused on improving educational access for the disadvantaged. At first, much of the push for educational equity was generated by federal court decisions, particularly in the field of desegregation. These cases are discussed at length in chapter 4.

Beginning with the passage of the 1964 Civil Rights Act, the legislative and executive branches of the federal government assumed a more activist role in defining and legislating educational rights. Aggrieved groups, that in the recent past had gone to court, obtained through legislation much of—and in some instances more than—what they sought through litigation. The claims of racial minorities and women, as well as those of children with disabilities, the limited-English-proficient, Native Americans, migrants, and the educationally disadvantaged, have to some extent been honored by the federal government. The creation, in 1979, of a Department of Education was meant at the time to signal a more aggressive federal role. Courts have played a part in this process, but it is a secondary role that involves delineating and enforcing rights created by other branches of government.

This federal activism on behalf of the disadvantaged was substantially slowed with the 1980 election of Ronald Reagan. *See* Meyer, "Social Programs and Social Policy," in J. Palmer, ed., *Perspectives on*

the Reagan Years 88 (1986). President Reagan broke with policy set by every President since Truman when he proposed to decentralize education and reduce federal involvement. *See* T. Bell, *The Thirteenth Man: A Reagan Cabinet Memoir* (1988); Pincus, "From Equity to Excellence: The Rebirth of Educational Conservatism," *Social Policy* 50 (Winter 1984); Verstegen and Clark, "The Diminution in Federal Expenditures for Education During the Reagan Administration," 70 *Phi Delta Kappan* 134 (Oct. 1988); Birman and Ginsburg, "The Federal Role in Elementary and Secondary Education: New Directions and Continuing Concerns," 14 *Urban Lawyer* 471 (Summer 1982). Numbers tell part of the story. Between 1980 and 1988, federal outlays for the Department of Education decreased as a percentage of the gross national product from 0.6 percent to 0.4 percent; funding for the department as a percentage of the federal budget declined from 2.5 percent to 1.8 percent. And the federal share of all primary and secondary educational expenditures dropped from 8.7 percent to 6.2 percent.

Key equal opportunity programs for children with disabilities, the limited-English-proficient, and the educationally disadvantaged remained intact. They avoided the 1981 consolidation of forty-three separate programs—among them, the grants under the Emergency School Aid Act for problems of desegregation—into a single block grant. But these programs suffered cuts, ranging from 6 percent to 54 percent, between 1980 and 1988. The block grant, which was meant to support state and local school improvement efforts, was cut 76 percent. And these budget levels were substantially higher than those proposed by President Reagan.

President Reagan's successors, George Bush and Bill Clinton, both were more receptive to a role for the federal government in influencing educational policy. During a 1989 educational summit, George Bush acknowledged that the federal government has a key—if unspecified—role in financing educational programs that help poor children, minorities, and the handicapped. Bill Clinton wanted to be remembered as the education president. Still, these professed commitments to education have led to relatively modest efforts to promote equal educational opportunity. In 1996, the federal government contributed 6.6 percent of the cost of public elementary and secondary education, only a slight increase over its 6.2 percent share at the end of the 1980s. National Center for Education Statistics, *Digest of Education Statistics,*

1999 at 45 (May 2000) (http://nces.ed.gov.). The substantive focus of educational policy has shifted since 1980, with quality and accountability replacing equal opportunity on the agenda. For the present, what merits mention is that excellence, unlike equal opportunity, is a concept inherently resistant to legalization. It does not readily translate into rights, but instead reflects a "morality of aspiration." *See* L. Fuller, *The Morality of Law* (1962).

1. The Rise of Federal Activism. The rise in federal influence after World War II reflected a number of significant social pressures. The United States, as the self-proclaimed leader of the free world, faced new demands for educational excellence and equity. Schooling became a matter of national interest.

"ESEA: The Office of Education Administers a Law"

S. Bailey and E. Mosher, *ESEA: The Office of Education Administers a Law* 1–36 (1968).

I. The Historical Setting

In America, government interest in education dates back at least to the "old deluder Satan" law in the colony of Massachusetts in 1642. Intermittently at first, but with increasing consistency in the nineteenth and twentieth centuries, public education came to be considered a matter of government interest and concern. However, for most of American history, the view prevailed that education was primarily a function of local authority and control—even though both State governments and the Federal government had a substantial impact upon the course and direction of American educational development. Until the twentieth century, the Federal government's main impact was through land grants for educational purposes. The influence of State governments came to be felt increasingly during the nineteenth century in the standardization of minimal educational requirements and services. The fact remains, however, that up to the end of World War II, local educational programs were financed and determined in large part by local school systems.

* * *

In the scant period of 13 years (1954–1967), however, a sea change has occurred. The Federal government's interest in stimulating change and improving quality in public education at the pre-collegiate level has been increasingly visible in four fields: (1) desegregation; (2) education related to defense and to vocations; (3) aid to research; and (4) education of the economically and culturally disadvantaged, and of the handicapped. Federal activity—judicial, legislative, and executive—in these four areas has unquestionably affected the traditional, decentralized autonomies of American education. This is especially true when one adds the fact that Federal aid to parochial school children was an important corollary, even a precondition, of many of these new Federal thrusts, and that Supreme Court decisions on the place of religion in the schools had widespread impact. Quality and equality of opportunity in education have become matters of national concern. All levels of government, and a variety of branches and agencies at each level, are now deeply involved in a complex and uneasy partnership whose collective aims are transforming educational priorities and methods. Education, like so many other governmental services, has now become involved in a "marble cake," not a "layer cake," of federalism.

* * *

The New Educational Demands

The postwar years in the United States were marked by a series of demands upon the educational system that were unprecedented in scope and magnitude. Any one of the new demands would have produced disquiet and concern. Together they constituted an explosive admixture.

The Postwar Explosion in the Learning Force. An unanticipated increase in the birth rate, and an equally unanticipated growth in school attendance through high school and beyond, placed unprecedented strains on the staff and facilities of American education.

* * *

How were these additional students to be housed? Who would teach them? Who would pay for the facilities and staff needed to serve them? If no other educational demands had existed in the postwar years, the sheer volume of responsibility for teaching millions of additional children would by itself have produced extraordinary claims upon the educational system.

The Knowledge Explosion. Concomitant to the school population explosion was an intellectual and technological explosion. The postwar rate of technological invention and economic growth; break-throughs in electronic communications, and in the speed and ease of publishing and disseminating information; the heightened mobility of people and ideas; the intractability and unprecedented responsibilities of the cold war; the vast outpouring of research findings in the social and behavioral sciences; and the rising expectations of the dispossessed at home and abroad—all combined to challenge the adequacy of the American educational system. How could it produce the skills needed to understand, and ultimately manage, these new forces? . . .

Other scholars and intellectual brokers brought other points of view to America's educational problems. Economists . . . began to point out that education was a nation's most important investment in sustaining and promoting a viable economy in a highly technological culture. . . .

This vast increase in concern and analysis led reformers to wonder whether anything short of substantial Federal infusions of money could move the educational system off its traditional dead center. Were pupils being educated well enough and fast enough to adapt to a world in massive flux? Could new knowledge be controlled by a new wisdom?

The notion that demands for substantial help from the Federal treasury might well be feasible grew as the fiscal performance of the Federal tax system showed increasing resiliency—especially in the early 1960's. . . .

Segregation. A major catalyst to the educational ferment of the 1950's and early 1960's, and a source of new demands on the educational system, was the Supreme Court's historic decision of 1954 on school segregation. . . .

In terms of the dynamics of national educational policy, *Brown v. Board of Education* . . . made visible the condition of Negro education in America and thereby highlighted the social and economic costs and consequences of prejudice, cultural deprivation, and poverty. These costs and consequences were being felt increasingly outside of the American South. During the 1950's, approximately a quarter of a million Negroes a year moved from rural southern farms to northern and western industrial cities. By and large miserably educated, they found themselves relegated to welfare rolls, forced by prejudice and income to live in segregated slum housing, and unrelated to existing job markets. Negro children constituted the largest percentage of "drop-outs" from the schools. Too fre-

quently their unutilized energies and their frustrations led to delinquency and crime. Altogether, Negroes constituted the most intractable element in hard-core poverty across the land.

Although the impact of the Negro migration was uneven, hundreds of school districts—particularly in large cities—found themselves facing the postwar years with an influx of pupils from a tragic sub-culture largely unrelated to the middle-class orientation of urban education. The educational demands prompted by this in-migration were insistent and almost cruelly complex, especially since it was accompanied by a flight of middle-class whites to the suburbs.

Poverty and Cultural Deprivation. Closely tied to the segregation issue was the question of the relationship of education to the nation's economic health. By the early 1960's, two issues had become particularly prominent. First, although over-all national productivity had been steadily increasing since the end of World War II, marked disparities in income and in employment opportunities persisted. Large pockets of unemployment and poverty remained, especially in the large cities and in dispersed rural slums. These disparities came to be viewed not only as a deterrent to regional prosperity and a violation of the individual's right to the dignity of gainful employment, but as a blot on America's international reputation as a humane democracy.

The second issue related particularly to young people. Although their numbers were increasing in proportion to the total population, they accounted for a disproportionately high percentage of the unemployed. As noted earlier, problems such as school drop-outs and juvenile delinquency were all parts of the same picture. It was becoming more obvious that ignorance, unemployment, and dependency were interrelated and self-perpetuating. High incidence of unemployment and dependency invariably correlated with low educational achievement. Traditional educational programs appeared to be both unable to hold such young people for a sufficient training period, and unable to train effectively those who did stay aboard.

During the mid-50's, the superintendents and board members of the country's largest cities formed a Great Cities Program for School Improvement to study the special problems of urban areas. One of their basic concerns was the needs of educationally disadvantaged children, especially Negroes. It was becoming obvious that conventional educational designs were inadequate to meet the learning problems of the culturally deprived, and it seemed that desegregation alone was not the answer. . . .

Parochial Schools. . . . [A]fter the war, inflation, the explosion in the learning force (which affected parochial schools quite as much as public schools), and a shortage of teaching staff placed an enormous financial burden upon parochial schools. Increasingly, church fathers went to public sources to find funds for supplementary services like transportation and school health. The justification was that such services were for the benefit of the child and did not support religious instruction. The Supreme Court upheld this position in *Everson v. Board of Education*. . . .

*   *   *

Two other Supreme Court cases on the church-state issue followed in 1948 and 1952. In *McCollum v. Board of Education*, the Court ruled that children released 30 minutes a week for religious instruction could not receive such instruction in public school facilities. Four years later, in *Zorach v. Clauson*, the Court ruled that "released-time" was permissible if religious instruction took place on private property.

These court decisions were both the cause and effect of increased parochial school demands upon public resources in the post-war years. The demands were often subtle and indirect, but they were persistent and politically powerful. And the fact that many States had strict constitutional prohibitions against direct or indirect aid to parochial schools gave a special impetus to asserting church claims upon Federal largess.

Limited and Inadequate Resources

This congeries of new demands fell upon an educational system woefully shy of institutional, human, and fiscal resources. Some of these inadequacies were long-standing, but some at least were traceable to World War II and its aftermaths, and to the Great Depression which preceded it.

Deferred Investment and Postwar Inflation. A major war inevitably produces massive shifts in any society's allocation of resources. The war machine is a great maw that consumes enormous quantities of human and physical goods and services. The effects of World War II upon the American school system were manifold but one of its most profound effects was to defer capital outlays for schools. This deferment came on top of ten years of depression during which time capital outlay for public elementary and secondary schools had dropped from $370 million in 1929–30 to only $258 million in 1939–40. By the late 1940's, America's school plant was by and large old, dilapidated, and over-crowded. . . .

Heroic measures were taken by State and local governments and local school districts to adjust tax levies and tax assessment policies to help close the inflation gap. . . . But the demands for new buildings, equipment, staff, and services continued to outrun revenues. As local school districts and their property-tax payers came to feel the fiscal pinch, both local and professional educational interests pressured State governments to increase both general and categorical aid to education. But States were also suffering from fiscal rigidities and inadequacies and were forced increasingly to turn toward the Federal government. . . .

Traditionalism and Educational Balkanization. It is conceivable that the American educational system could have weathered the fiscal storms and the winds of change of the postwar period without undue strain, if its own ship had been in order. But it was not. Conservative in outlook and fragmented in structure, the American school system had developed an entrenched neglect of efforts to improve educational productivity. It was both too ponderous and too Balkanized to be regenerative.

Local Autonomy.

*   *   *

The historic Balkanization of the American school system into tens of thousands of districts—most of them of a patently inefficient size—was unlikely to produce talents and economies of a scale relevant to the educational demands of the postwar years. Little scope was afforded for innovative activities, and almost none for project-planning aimed at external sources of aid. . . .

At the State level, not more than a half dozen State educational agencies had either the resources, the leadership, or the quality of staff needed to give spirited direction to grass roots educational improvement for meeting the extraordinary demands of the postwar years.

Fiscal Disparities. The scatteration of local school districts had for generations produced glaring financial, and consequently educational, inequities. As long as schools were almost entirely supported from a local property tax base, the quality of education tended to vary in direct proportion to the availability of local tax revenues. . . .

. . . In the postwar years, the persistence of a large degree of disparity in local economic resources, educational requirements, and tax effort, was another indication of the gap which existed between new educational demands on the one hand and the capacity of the educational system to respond effectively and equitably to them.

* * *

The Old United States Office of Education. Even if the stars had been propitious during the postwar years for a dramatic response of the Federal government to the new educational demands, there would have been a serious question about the administrative capacity of the U.S. Office of Education [USOE] to adjust imaginatively and effectively to its vast new educational responsibilities. USOE had lived most of its life since 1867 as a stepchild of other Federal departments and agencies—notably the Department of the Interior and HEW's forerunner, the Federal Security Agency—dominated by noneducational concerns. Until the late 1950's, limited largely to the collection and dissemination of educational statistics, and to technical consultancies, the Office was almost entirely service-oriented rather than operations-oriented. . . . It had few friends apart from the National Education Association, the American Association of School Administrators and the Council of Chief State School Officers, whose Washington staffs and whose constituencies found the statistical and advisory services of USOE of direct value. There was at least some validity to the widely held assumption that USOE was, in fact, the "kept" Federal agent of these major private educational associations.

Over the decades, Congress had virtually ignored USOE—occasionally criticizing it for "meddling" if it showed initiative; for ineptitude if it did not. Financially it was starved; administratively it was victimized. . . .

. . . [T]he total appropriation for the United States Office of Education did not reach the $1 million mark until the 1930's, and even then three quarters of this amount was specifically awarded for educating Eskimos in Alaska. Even when vast new responsibilities were added to the work of the Office in the 1950's, and its visibility was increased by the word

Education appearing in the title of its new departmental home (HEW [Health, Education and Welfare], 1953), it received inadequate authorizations and appropriations for staff and for effective program management. . . .

* * *

Expediential Responses

The irresistible force of new educational demands was not exactly stopped by the immovable object of limited and inadequate resources—for the latter turned out not to be totally immovable. But the irresistible force was enormously slowed, and in the two decades following World War II the gap between need and response was, if anything, widened. . . .

At the national level, a few developments occurred incrementally in the late 1940's, notably the GI Bill and the creation of the National Science Foundation (hereafter NSF). Although addressed largely to the needs of higher education, these provided spin-offs for elementary and secondary education in terms of teacher training and/or support for curricular revisions—especially in the sciences. And NSF was a harbinger of later Federal programs addressed directly to the support of educational research.

A Federal program was passed in 1950, solidifying World War II legislation that was passed to provide financial aid to school districts impacted by Federal defense plants and other Federal establishments. These plants and establishments were tax exempt, yet they inevitably involved a substantial increase in the local labor force and in the need for schools for the children of federally sponsored workers. . . . Following the dramatic orbiting of Sputnik by the Russians in the fall of 1957, Congress, with presidential backing, passed the National Defense Education Act (NDEA) of 1958. The Act provided for substantial Federal support to secondary-school and higher-education programs to increase the quantity and quality of scientists, engineers, and foreign-language specialists throughout the American educational system. It established fellowships and supported curricula-revision aimed at a major transformation of defense-related aspects of the American educational system. It also provided for student loans, guidance counseling, grants for audio-visual aid and for various additional types of technical assistance. Although NDEA was later criticized for warping the educational curriculum away from the humanities and the social studies, it was nonetheless an important harbinger of the kinds of Federal support for American education that blossomed in the mid-1960's. It was categorical aid; it affected both secondary and higher education; it was substantial in the volume of funding; some of its titles included religious affiliated institutions among NDEA's beneficiaries; and it proclaimed that education was a matter of national concern. But it was still a far cry from general Federal aid for the nation's elementary and secondary schools. And even within its own limited domain, the Act tended to strengthen superior and wealthier secondary schools that had the staff, the equipment, the matching funds, and the students to profit from marginal infusions of Federal money for science, mathematics, and foreign languages. Poorer schools in the countryside and in the urban ghettos were left largely untouched. Like the renewals of impacted area legislation, extensions of NDEA went forward with almost no effect upon the substantive concerns of those seeking some answer to education's general need for massive Federal support.

* * *

Political Inventiveness and Legislative Forerunners

In the field of Federal school aid, the half-decade 1960–64 was filled with political inventiveness and some major breakthroughs in cognate legislative areas; but it was a period of massive frustration in regard to the central target issue.

* * *

The Kennedy Education Bill of 1961. The struggle peaked early. In what the President called "probably the most important piece of domestic legislation of the year," he asked in early 1961 for grants of $2.3 billion over three years to be used by the States primarily for construction of public elementary and high school classrooms and for boosting public teachers' salaries; and an even greater amount over a five-year period for higher education facilities, and for construction loans and student scholarships to both public and private colleges. . . .

But under the Kennedy proposal, aid to private elementary and secondary schools was barred, and the Catholic hierarchy issued a pronouncement that unless the public school bill included private school loans, it should be defeated.

It did not, and it was.

* * *

To the observant, victory could be discerned in the very ashes of defeat. These new ideas and directions that emerged over a four year period can be classified as follows: (1) the shift toward program aid; (2) attempts to improve the quality of education; (3) emphasis on "educationally disadvantaged" children.

Increasingly Categorical Limits on Federal Grants. From 1961 on, there was a gradual shift in Congress from aid proposals for teachers' salaries and school construction under general State administration, to proposals with a specific program emphasis under federally set standards.

* * *

Cognate Developments

While these various shifts in forces [support from teachers' organizations for targeted, not just general aid; efforts to resolve the church-state issue] were occurring in the field of school aid, other domestic legislation was being developed and passed in the areas of civil rights and poverty, and precedents were being set for liberalizing Federal aid to church-related institutions. These cognate developments were important antecedents to the emergence of the Elementary and Secondary Education Act of 1965.

Civil Rights.

* * *

. . . By outlawing discrimination in all federally-aided programs, the Civil Rights Act of 1964 added full presidential and congressional authority to the Supreme Court's school desegregation mandate of 1954. . . . Hopefully, the mobilization of the legal, fiscal, and administrative resources of the Federal government under the 1964 Act would be more effective and quicker than litigation alone. The Attorney General was given authority to intervene in school desegregation suits or to initiate such suits. And a threat of withdrawal of funds from States with discriminatory practices was a powerful weapon—a weapon that became even more powerful as Federal aid to education increased.

One of the most important aspects of the Civil Rights Act of 1964 was the fact that . . . the race issue was removed from the political calculus of those supporting or attacking increased Federal aid to education. . . . [T]he passage of ESEA in 1965 was testament to the fact that the civil rights issue vis-a-vis education had been at least temporarily blunted by the previous passage of the Civil Rights Act of 1964.

Poverty Legislation.

* * *

. . . [The] Economic Opportunity Act of 1964 (hereafter EOA) created a number of programs such as the Job Corps, the Neighborhood Youth Corps, and Adult Basic Education. Some of these programs were logical extensions of past Federal experiments. Conceptually, however, the Act leapt beyond the goals of vocational education. Its overriding purpose was to mobilize "the human and financial resources of the Nation to combat poverty by opening to everyone opportunity for education and training and opportunity to work."

The Economic Opportunity Act presaged the Elementary and Secondary Education Act of 1965 in at least two respects: its stress upon the importance of variety and innovation; and its acknowledgement of the special needs of educationally disadvantaged children. And, of course, both acts reflected in turn the influence of scholarly evidence that the handicaps of poverty are translated into educational disadvantage at a very early age, and that those who come to adulthood without adequate schooling will have at best a future of uncertain, unskilled employment and low income. It should also be noted that "the church-state settlement" in Title II of the Economic Opportunity Act provided a strategic precedent for ESEA.

Church-State Relations. The judicial tight-rope walking that marked church-state relations in the post-war years was accompanied by legislative actions and pressure-group détentes that had the effect of liberalizing traditional concepts of appropriate public assistance to church-related institutions. The GI Bill, the National Defense Education Act, the National Science Foundation Act, college housing loans, the National School Lunch Act, and the Hill-Burton Hospital Construction Act all involved Federal assistance to sectarian institutions. And an increasing number of people came to argue that the very fact of tax exemption for religious property, including parochial schools, was a tacit acceptance of the notion that certain kinds of public assistance for parochial schools, had in fact been accepted for generations as within the legitimate sanctions of the

Constitution. Furthermore, in the postwar years, a number of State legislatures and local school systems had authorized the practice of "shared-time"— allowing parochial school children to attend public school classes during certain hours on certain days each week. . . . More than any other single issue, the church-state controversy precluded the formation of a workable coalition to pass the Kennedy general-aid-to-education bills in 1961 and 1963.

From the ashes of these two defeats there emerged two realities which were to have important effects upon the future of Federal aid: first, a new grasp of political realities on the part of both Catholic and professional public educational associations, and a recognition that intransigencies on both sides had in fact denied children the benefit of extensive Federal resources for education; and second, the realization on the part of key policy makers in Washington that if substantial Federal aid to elementary and secondary education were to emerge, compromises . . . would have to be reached. . . .

* * *

Overview

These were the forces and developments that led to the passage of the Elementary and Secondary Education Act of 1965. Explosive postwar demands; inadequate institutional, human, and financial resources at all levels of government; a series of expediential, if sometimes heroic, responses; and political inventions born of frustration—all of these had combined to set the stage for a new legislative breakthrough. But the breakthrough would be a far cry from the general aid bills, for school construction and teachers' salaries for public schools only, that had dominated the congressional educational agenda during the postwar years.

---

2. From Equity to Excellence: Standards and Accountability. After the ESEA was passed in 1965, Congress continued to play a vigorous role in educational policymaking until the 1980s. With the rise of the "new federalism," education was considered primarily a state and local matter. Federal funding, always a relatively small part of the education budget, dropped during this period. Doyle and Finn, "American Schools and the Future of Local Control," 77 *Pub.Int.* 77, 79–80 (1984). In the 1990s, however, federal policymakers once again began to exert their influence over education issues. This time, the focus was on high educational standards to prod failing schools. In 1983, the National Commission on Excellence chronicled the shortcomings of education in a widely publicized report entitled *A Nation at Risk: The Imperative for Educational Reform*. In response to the report's findings, parents, educators, foundations, and public officials clamored for change. *See* D. Massell and S. Fuhrman, *Ten Years of State Education Reform, 1983–1993: Overview with Four Case Studies* (1994). In 1989, President George Bush held an education summit with the nation's governors to draw up a blueprint for transforming America's schools. *The National Education Goals: A Report to the Nation's Governors* (1990) (setting forth the results of the education summit). Five years after the summit, Congress enacted Goals 2000, Pub.L.No. 103-227, 108 Stat. 125 (1994). The legislation represented a new phase in the federalization of education policy.

"Goals 2000: Educate America Act: The Federalization and Legalization of Educational Policy"

M. Heise, 63 *Fordham L.Rev.* 345, 356–361, 363, 368–372 (1994).

* * *

Goals 2000 recognizes the overall failure of past, incremental educational reform efforts and embraces a new approach: systemic reform. Systemic reform, as construed by the Act's drafters, involves establishing ambitious educational goals, and then comparing content standards, instructional goals, and periodic assessments of student performance with those goals. Rather than casting aside past state reform efforts, Congress hopes to build on existing state efforts and to incorporate them into a broader, coherent, and comprehensive educational reform effort. Of course, the systemic approach to educational reform includes an enlarged policymaking role for the federal government.

Uniformity and efficiency underlie the Congressional approach to educational reform. According to Congress, the next step for the federal government is to "support efforts that will improve education across the board for all students." Goals 2000 "encourages States and local school districts to recognize the importance of linkages among the different aspects of their educational systems—especially the connections between curriculum and instructional materials, assessment practices, and professional development."

Congress gave several reasons for such a dramatic expansion of the federal government's role. First, Congress noted that career work for high-school graduates with general skills had become obsolete. An increasingly technology-driven workplace required students to "acquire higher order thinking and workforce related skills." Second, Congress argued that an emerging consensus dictated the need for comprehensive reform involving the entire educational system. In addition, Congress argued that the federal government can enable states and local school boards to reduce redundant school reform activities. Specifically, Congress asserted that the federal government can more efficiently assemble and disseminate information to states and local school boards about their counterparts' reform activities than if they continued to collect such information independently.

Goals 2000 adopts the principles that emerged from the 1989 Education Summit by amending and codifying the governors' educational goals. Title I of the Act sets eight broad "national educational goals." In addition, Goals 2000 encourages state and local educational agencies to develop content and opportunity-to-learn standards and to submit them to the federal government for certification. By delineating "Voluntary National Content Standards," Congress attempts to structure a uniform national curriculum, developed and approved by bipartisan groups consisting of members of Congress and state legislatures, professional educators, academics, representatives of business, industry, labor, universities, low-income and minority groups, and other civic leaders.

Whereas content standards focus on students, "Voluntary National Opportunity-To-Learn Standards" focus on evaluating school conditions necessary to establish a successful working environment for students. Stated another way, "[W]hen students are not learning at desired levels, opportunity to learn standards can help communities identify where the child is failing school or the school is failing the child."

Goals 2000 establishes the National Education Standards and Improvement Council ("NESIC"), a committee of nineteen members appointed by the president. NESIC is charged with overseeing the development of national educational standards by identifying areas in which sets of standards need to be developed, establishing criteria to assess those standards, and certifying content and opportunity-to-learn standards submitted by states or other entities.

In developing the criteria it will use to certify standards voluntarily submitted by states and local agencies, NESIC will consider appropriate international standards, cognitive and pedagogical research, and the openness of the processes by which the standards were developed.

The National Education Goals Panel ("NEGP") is an independent agency created in 1989. Goals 2000 delegates to NEGP the task of building a national consensus for educational improvement, reporting on the nation's progress in meeting the National Education Goals set out above, and reviewing and commenting on certification criteria and standards developed by the National Education Standards and Improvement Council.

Goals 2000 also provides grants for states that develop "state improvement plans" to meet the National Educational Goals by developing their own content standards, assessments, curriculum development, teacher training, and instructional materials. In addition, the Act reauthorizes state allotments under the Elementary and Secondary Education Act of 1965. Title IV of Goals 2000 awards grants to nonprofit organizations that provide training and support to parents of students. Title IV endeavors "to increase parents' knowledge of and confidence in child-rearing activities . . . and strengthen partnerships between parents and professionals in meeting the educational needs of children." Title V establishes a "National Skill Standards Board" to encourage the development of a national system of skill standards. Such skills standards are intended to ensure that the workforce is qualified enough to maintain the competitiveness of American industry in an increasingly globalized, high-technology economy.

Further, Goals 2000 establishes an international educational program to study the educational systems in foreign countries, exchange ideas with educators abroad, and engage in joint research. Title VII of the Act endeavors to purge schools of drugs and violence. Title VIII, the "Minority-Focused Civics Education Act of 1994," attempts to improve instruction for minorities and Native Americans in American government and civics.

Goals 2000 indeed is comprehensive. Accordingly, it will produce far-reaching results and significantly alter American educational policymaking in at least two notable ways. First, NESIC's role as the certifier of content and opportunity-to-learn standards will further federalize educational policymaking. Increased federalization of educational policymaking will centralize and homogenize educational policies designed to serve an increasingly heterogenous student population. Second, state and local agencies enticed into developing and implementing content and opportunity-to-learn standards will face an increase in litigation as those standards are transformed into legal entitlements. Increased legalization of educational policymaking will further inject the judiciary into the development and implementation of educational policies. Empirical evidence on the efficacy of such judicial involvement is mixed, at best. Yet, the likelihood that the Act will achieve its primary desired benefit — improved student academic achievement — is dubious, particularly in light of these expected costs. Essentially, Goals 2000 focuses on shifting the allocation of educational policymaking authority rather than on any particular substantive reform. Because it is the most significant and comprehensive Congressional effort to reform American education in the past few decades, the Act will certainly command significant public attention. Unfortunately, it may also deter efforts fundamentally to restructure the delivery of educational services.

* * *

Traditionally, state and local governments, particularly local school boards, developed and implemented educational policies. After all, state and local governments bear the constitutional duty to educate their citizens; they provide most of the school funding, and presumably, state and local governments know more than Congress does about the specific needs of the students that they serve. One reason that local — and to a lesser extent state — educational officials know more about their specific educational needs is their proximity to students. During the 1992 school year, more than forty-two million students attended public elementary and secondary schools in the United States. As Professors Doyle and Finn note, many school principals find it difficult enough to have more than a passing acquaintance with individual students and to know what actually transpires in individual teachers' classrooms. It is demonstrably more difficult for school district superintendents and board of education members to do so. Thus, as one moves progressively further away from classrooms, schools, and communities, and toward Congress and federal officials, familiarity with students and specific educational conditions and circumstances decreases exponentially. Even the Supreme Court has endorsed local control of public schools.

* * *

Although the 1980s witnessed a dramatic increase in state educational reform initiatives, state leadership in educational policy waned in the 1990s. Several factors account for the relative decline in state educational policy initiatives. First, budget constraints have limited educational reforms in the 1990s; today's state coffers are no longer as flush as they were in the early and mid-1980s. Second, changes to the makeup of state legislatures reduced state educational reform activity. Many of the state politicians who provided crucial leadership on educational reform matters no longer serve or have moved off of education-related committees. The third reason relates to earlier legislative work at the state level. Prior work on state educational statutes established a capacity to incorporate new reforms without substantial changes to state laws. As a result, standard-based reform, including many of the systemic reforms proposed in Goals 2000, can be accommodated without the need for legislative change. Yet, state legislators often distrust state departments of education, viewing them as creatures of the "educational establishment." "This distrust, as well as the fact that political benefit comes from placing scarce dollars in local schools rather than in state agencies, has led to a vicious cycle of underfunding [of state educational agencies] and failure to keep up with reform demands."[150]

* * *

The enormous and persistent difficulties that confront America's school systems and the unsatisfactory results from a significant public investment led to a realignment of educational policymaking responsibilities. Although perhaps inevitable, the increased federalization of educational policy is not without risks. The precise extent to which Goals 2000 will realign the existing balance among the federal, state, and local governments and increase federal influence over educational policy remains unclear. Unlike previous formal and informal federal educational reform initiatives, however, Goals 2000 is a mechanism and framework that enables the federal government to influence every public school student and every public school.

* * *

One risk posed by Goals 2000 is that its top-down orientation and centralizing tendencies conflict with two discrete trends initiated during the 1980s, both involving the location of educational policymaking authority. One trend is the consolidation of educational policymaking authority by state governments. Financial concerns partially account for this trend. While the percentage of the state contribution to school districts varies, during the past decade state contributions to local school budgets increased in both relative and absolute terms. Moreover, "the velocity of change was often dramatic." One legacy of the 1980s is that states are regarded as the senior partners in educational financing and policymaking, rather than as supplements to predominately local structures. At the same time that states were asserting educational policymaking authority, many school districts began decentralizing educational policymaking authority. For more than ten years, school districts across the country have developed and implemented various educational policies designed to shift decisionmaking authority from centralized bureaucracies to local schools and school-based management structures. Large urban school districts encumbered with substantial bureaucracies and facing difficult educational problems have been particularly partial to school decentralization policies. On the heels of reallocation of educational policymaking at the state and local school levels, Goals 2000 proposes to reallocate significant policymaking authority to the federal government. Such reallocation is consistent with neither school decentralization efforts nor consolidation at the state level. It is ironic that, as states and localities seek to further localize educational policymaking, the federal government's educational reform initiative seeks the opposite.

Second, Goals 2000, through NESIC, now the nation's educational standards certifier, threatens to homogenize the development of educational standards. NESIC's potential to increase the federal government's influence over educational reform efforts cannot be easily overstated. As the certifier of content and opportunity-to-learn standards, NESIC will influence the educational reform efforts of all states that choose to engage in Goals 2000 reform activities. Though nothing in the Act requires the establishment of a "one best system" of standards, criticized by some commentators, a centralized, federal certification council exerts pressure toward uniform content and opportunity-to-learn standards. Of course, state and local agencies willing to participate in Goals 2000 activities also will be eager to receive NESIC certification for their educational standards.

---

[150]*Id.* [D. Massell and S. Fuhrman, *Ten Years of State Education Reform, 1983–1993: Overview with Four Case Studies* (1994)] at 21.

The initial sets of content and opportunity-to-learn standards to receive formal NESIC certification will influence the development of later standards. States and local school boards developing educational standards and desirous of NESIC approval may look first to those that have already received NESIC approval for guidance rather than to the particular educational needs of their schools and students. By inducing local school authorities to focus on NESIC approval as well as local educational needs, Goals 2000 encourages the development of homogenous content and opportunity-to-learn standards. The resulting homogeneity erodes the array of benefits produced by more than 15,000 local school boards' "laboratories of democracy." While it is painfully clear that existing educational policies, largely the product of the nation's local school boards, have not improved student achievement, it is equally clear that NESIC and its activities will not adequately address the array of educational problems facing the nation. As a single, centralized certifier of standards submitted by states and local school boards, NESIC will instead chill imaginative thinking about much-needed educational reforms.

A third risk presented by Goals 2000 is that it will divert educational reform attention away from state and local school boards and toward the federal government. By dramatically increasing the federal government's educational policymaking role, Goals 2000 implicitly assumes that certain educational reform functions—notably, though not exclusively, certification of content and opportunity-to-learn standards—are best administered by the federal government. Not only do the assumptions implicit in Goals 2000 lack support in comparative institutional analysis, but such a shifting of focus to the federal government will only allow states and localities to avoid accountability for shortcomings in their educational systems.

Fourth, though the federal government is able to offer technical expertise and disseminate educational reform information to states and local school boards, individual states and even local agencies are also capable of performing such tasks. A great deal of self-generated educational reform information is available to state and local agencies, and it is in their self-interest to accumulate and distribute relevant information. State and local governmental units deliver and pay for most educational services so they have incentives to duplicate successful educational policies and avoid unsuccessful and costly ones.

Indeed, a few elements of the Act will certainly give states pause and perhaps deter some from participating. Participation in the development of Goals 2000 content or opportunity-to-learn standards is voluntary, which mitigates NESIC's immediate impact on American educational policy.

Financial concerns will deter states. The standards development processes, outlined in Title III of the Act, are cumbersome, lengthy, and potentially expensive. It is not clear from the text of the Act whether the federal funds allocated for participating state and local agencies will cover all the costs associated with standards development.

States also will have federalism concerns. Traditionally, states and local school boards have resisted ceding too much authority to the federal government. Those states and local school boards that decide to participate in Goals 2000 activities, develop educational standards, and seek certification for those standards, will need to submit those standards to NESIC for review and approval.

Despite these deterrents, the Act will likely attract state participation, thereby increasing federal influence over educational policy. Like other federal educational programs, states have financial incentives to participate in the Act. For the 1994 fiscal year alone, Congress appropriated $105 million for Goals 2000. Federal funds targeted to such efforts will ensure some level of participation even if these funds do not entirely cover the costs associated with Goals 2000 activities.

States currently engaged in similar reform efforts will be even more amenable to participation. Such states may only need to tailor existing, ongoing educational reform efforts to meet the Act's requirements. Also, political and public pressure to engage in a major educational reform will encourage additional participation. As one study explains, one of the most significant functions of the federal government is its ability to provide a "bully pulpit" on matters of federal interest.

Yet, increased federal activity will not provide any long-term solutions to the pressing problems confronting America's schools. Notwithstanding Goals 2000, constitutional and legal authority to provide education remains firmly rooted at the state and local government levels. Also, despite creating new federal educational funds, Goals 2000 will not significantly alter the relative financial contributions from governments to school districts . . . [T]he primary source of revenue for elementary and secondary education is state and local taxes. Nothing contained in Goals 2000 upsets this balance. Through Goals 2000, the federal government shapes educational policy, and the states and localities fund the federal educational policy goals.

* *

NOTES AND QUESTIONS

1. Funding and Standards

Is it appropriate for Congress to adopt educational standards if it contributes only a small share of the cost of schooling America's children? Do the standards become nothing more than unfunded mandates? Is standard-setting appropriately left to state and local officials? Why or why not?

2. Federal and State Responsibility for Standards Testing

In 1999, President Clinton promoted an Education Accountability Act that would condition schools' receipt of federal funds on ending social promotion, adopting higher standards, holding school districts and teachers accountable for poor student achievement, and informing parents about school quality. Congress responded by prohibiting the use of the Department of Education's general appropriations to construct and administer a national examination. Elul, "Making the Grade, Public Education Reform: The Use of Standardized Testing to Retain Students and Deny Diplomas," 30 *Colum.Human Rights L.Rev.* 495, 495–96, 500 (1999). His efforts to put a national curriculum in place were also defeated. Kelly, "Yearning for Lake Wobegon: The Quest for the Best Test at the Expense of the Best Education," 7 *S.Cal.Interdis.L.J.* 41, 49–50 (1998). Instead, Congress continued to pursue arrangements in which states assume primary responsibility for devising their own educational standards, testing procedures, and systems of accountability. As a result, for example, state participation in the National Assessment of Educational Progress is entirely voluntary. How the objectives set forth in Goals 2000 are achieved is a matter left to the states, and states must determine how to formulate challenging standards for children in schools eligible for federal aid based on the disadvantaged status of their student populations. *Id.* at 50–54. To further promote state and local innovation, Congress authorized

waivers from some federal educational regulations. Education Flexibility Partnership Act, Pub.L.No. 25, 106th Cong., 1st Sess. (1999). Still, efforts to impose national standards persist. *See, e.g.*, Student Achievement Act, S. 853, 106th Cong., 1st Sess. (1999). George W. Bush has announced his intention to offer states greater flexibility in using federal funds so long as they demonstrate their accountability through annual testing. Brownstein, "For a Start, Education Reform Offers Bush a Policy Path of Least Resistance," *L.A.Times*, Dec. 18, 2000, at pt. A, pt. 1, p. 5.

3. High-Stakes Testing and Fairness

Although states have been granted considerable leeway to implement standards testing, the federal courts have played an important role in ensuring that testing is done fairly. The courts have focused most closely on challenges to high-stakes tests, which deny children who fail them promotion to the next grade, a high school diploma, or access to college. Very often, students of color, low-income students, and students with disabilities have disproportionate failure rates. Concerns have arisen about whether the tests are discriminatory and whether they punish vulnerable children instead of the schools that fail them. As discussed in chapter 4, some state tests have been challenged in federal court based on claims that they violate equal protection, due process, and Title VI. To address these concerns, Congress and the Clinton Administration commissioned the National Research Council to report on legal and pedagogical problems with the tests. National Research Council, *High Stakes: Testing for Tracking, Promotion, and Graduation* (1999). After the Council's report was released, the Office for Civil Rights (OCR) in the Department of Education issued draft guidelines on high-stakes testing. In response to charges that guidelines circulated in May 1999 were "anti-test" and an assault on merit-based standards, OCR revised and reissued the draft provisions in December 1999. Healy, "Education Department Softens Its Tone in Latest Draft of Guide to Using Test Scores in Admissions," *Chronicle of Higher Education*, Dec. 13, 1999. In December 2000, OCR issued the final version of a guidebook on the appropriate use of standardized tests in admissions and other placement decisions. U.S. Department of Education, Office for Civil Rights, *The Use of Tests When Making High-Stakes Decisions for Students: A Guide for Educators and Policy-Makers* (Dec. 2000) (http://www.ed.gov/offices/OCR/testing).

B. State Authority and Local Control

1. The Formal Allocation of Power. As a legal and practical matter, state and local governments are the primary providers of educational services. States are almost always vested with responsibility for schooling, but they typically delegate the task of implementing broad directives to local school districts. The result is a complex set of legal and administrative relationships between state and local policymakers.

"The Legal Foundation of Public Education"

M. McCarthy and N. Cambron-McCabe, *Public School Law, Teacher and Student Rights* 2–7 (1992). Copyright © 1992 by Allyn & Bacon. Reprinted by permission.

All state constitutions specifically address the legislative responsibility for establishing public schools. For example, the Arizona Constitution stipulates: "The legislature shall . . . provide for the establishment and maintenance of a general and uniform public school system. . . ." The state legislature has plenary, or absolute, power to make laws governing education. . . .

Courts have recognized the state legislature's authority to raise revenue and distribute educational funds, control teacher certification, prescribe curricular offerings, establish pupil performance standards, and regulate other specific aspects of public school operations. Legislatures are empowered to create, reorganize, consolidate, and abolish school districts, even over the objections of affected residents. . . .

* * *

Although the state legislature cannot relinquish its law-making powers, it can delegate to subordinate agencies the authority to make rules and regulations necessary to implement laws. These administrative functions must be carried out within the guidelines established by the legislature. Some states are quite liberal in delegating administrative authority, whereas other states prescribe detailed standards that must be followed by subordinate agencies. It is a widely held perception that local school boards control public education within this nation, but local boards have only those powers conferred by the state. Courts consistently have reiterated that the authority for public education is not a local one, but rather is a central power residing in the state legislature. School buildings are considered state property, local school board members are state officials, and teachers are state employees. Public school funds, regardless of where collected, are state funds.

* * *

Since it has been neither feasible nor desirable to include in statutes every minor detail governing public schools, all states have established some type of state board of education. This board typically supplies the structural details necessary to implement broad legislative mandates. In most states, members of the state board of education are elected by the citizenry or appointed by the governor, and the board usually functions immediately below the legislature in the hierarchy of educational governance.

Licensure is an important tool used by state boards to compel local school districts to abide by their directives. School districts often must satisfy state licensure or accreditation requirements as a condition of receiving state funds. Though licensure models vary among states, the most common approach involves the establishment of minimum standards in areas such as curriculum, teacher qualifications, instructional materials, and facilities. In some states, different grades of school accreditation exist, with financial incentives to encourage local schools to attain the highest licensure level.

* * *

In addition to the state board, generally considered a policy-making body, all states have designated a chief state school officer (often known as the superintendent of public instruction or commissioner of education) to function in an executive capacity. Traditionally, the duties of the chief state school officer (CSSO) have been regulatory in nature. However, other activities, such as research and long-range planning, have been added to this role. In some states, the CSSO is charged with adjudicating educational controversies, and citizens cannot invoke judicial remedies for a grievance pertaining to internal school operations until such administrative appeals have been exhausted. When considering an appeal of a CSSO's decision, courts will not judge the wisdom of the decision or overrule such a decision unless it is clearly arbitrary or against the preponderance of evidence.

Each state also has established a state department of education, consisting of educational specialists who provide consultation to the state board, chief state school officer, and local school boards. State department personnel often collect data from school districts to ensure that legislative enactments and state board policies are properly implemented. Most state departments also engage in research and development activities to improve educational practices within the state.*

* * *

See generally Murphy, "The Paradox of State Government Reform," 64 *The Public Interest* 124 (1981).

Although public education is state controlled in our nation, it is for the most part locally administered. All states except Hawaii have created local school boards in addition to state education agencies and have delegated certain administrative authority over schools to these local boards. Nationwide, there are approximately 15,700 school districts, ranging from a few students to several hundred thousand. Some states, particularly those with a large number of small school districts, have established intermediate or regional administrative units that perform regulatory or service functions for several local districts.

As with the delegation of authority to state agencies, delegation of powers to local school boards is handled very differently across states. Some states with a deeply rooted tradition of local control over education (e.g., Colorado), give local boards a great deal of latitude in making operational decisions about schools. In other states that tend toward centralized control of education (e.g., Florida), local boards must function within the framework of detailed legislative directives. . . .

Local school board members usually are elected by the citizenry within the school district. The Supreme Court has recognized that the equal protection clause requires each qualified voter to be given an opportunity to participate in the election of board members, with each vote given the same weight as far as practicable. When board members are elected from geographical districts, such districts must be established to protect voting rights under the "one man, one vote" principle. If "at-large" elections result in a dilution of the minority vote, an abridgment of the federal Voting Rights Act may be found.

The state legislature can specify the qualifications, method of selection, and terms and conditions of local school board membership. Board members are considered public school officers with sovereign power, in contrast to school employees, who are hired to implement directives. Public officers cannot hold two offices if one is subordinate to the other, cannot have an interest in contracts made by their agencies, and in some states cannot occupy more than one office for which they receive pay. Generally, statutes stipulate procedures that must be followed in removing public officers from their positions. Typical causes for removal include neglect of duty, illegal performance of duty, breach of good faith, negligence, and incapacity.

A local board must act as a body; individual board members are not empowered to make policies or perform official acts on behalf of the board. . . .

School board meetings and records must be open to the public. Most states have enacted "sunshine" or "open meeting" laws,* acknowledging that the public has a right to be fully informed regarding the actions of public agencies. What constitutes a meeting is sometimes defined by statute, and certain exceptions to open meeting requirements are usually specified. For example, in many states, school boards can meet in executive session to discuss matters that threaten public safety or pertain to pending or current litigation, personnel matters, collective bargaining, or the disposition of real property. While discussion of these matters may take place in closed meetings, statutes usually stipulate that formal action must take place in open meetings.

Local school boards hold powers specified or implied in state law and other powers considered necessary to achieve the purposes of the express powers. These delegated powers generally encompass the authority to determine the specifics of the curriculum offered within the school district, raise revenue to build and maintain schools, select personnel, and enact other policies necessary to implement the educational program pursuant to law. Courts have recognized that without specific enabling legislation local boards have discretionary authority to establish and support secondary schools, kindergartens, nongraded schools, and various school-related programs; alter school attendance zones; and close schools.

* * *

Local school boards cannot delegate their decision-making authority to other agencies or associations. In an illustrative case, a New Jersey court ruled that a school board could not relinquish to the teachers' association responsibility for determining courses of study or settling classroom controversies. Also, the Iowa Supreme Court held that a school board could not delegate its rule-making authority to a state high school athletic association.

Local boards are authorized to perform discretionary duties (i.e., involving judgment), while school employees, such as superintendents, principals, and teachers, can perform only ministerial duties necessary to carry out policies. Hence, a superintendent can recommend personnel to be hired and propose a budget to the board, but the board

---

*See, e.g., Cox Enterprises v. Board of Trustees, 706 S.W.2d 956 (Tex. 1986); Braswell v. Roche, 299 S.C. 181 (1989).

must make the actual decisions. Although it might appear that educators at the building level retain little decision-making authority, administrators as well as classroom teachers can enact rules and regulations, consistent with board policy and law, to ensure the efficient operation of the school or class under their supervision.

2. State Regulation and the Quest for Excellence. The formal allocation of authority establishes the parameters of state and local governance of the schools. The exercise of this authority often depends on political trends and pressures. In recent years, for example, highly publicized school failures have prompted state legislatures to take an aggressive role in promoting educational excellence. Part of the states' quest for excellence has turned on standards testing and accountability measures to ensure that students master basic skills. So far, federal efforts to set national standards have been stymied by political in-fighting. *See* "Fixing Education: Makeover of Kentucky Schools Reflects Challenges Hill Faces in Setting Goals," 56(9) *Congressional Quarterly Weekly Report* 491, 493 (Feb. 28, 1998). Each state therefore has been left to decide whether to adopt standards testing and how to use the test results in reforming education.

In two states, Kentucky and Texas, standards testing has been part of a comprehensive reform package. The Kentucky legislature adopted wide-ranging reforms in 1990 after the Kentucky Supreme Court declared the entire public school system unconstitutional because of inequities and inadequacies in financing it. *Rose v. Council for Better Education, Inc.,* 790 S.W.2d 186 (Ky. 1989). *See also* Alexander, "The Common School Ideal and the Limits of Legislative Authority: The Kentucky Case," 28 *Harv.J. on Legis.* 341 (1991); Combs, "Creative Constitutional Law: The Kentucky School Reform Law," 28 *Harv.J.on Legis.* 367 (1991); Dove, "Acorns in a Mountain Pool: The Role of Litigation, Law and Lawyers in Kentucky Education Reform," 17 *J.Educ.Fin.* 83 (1991); Thro, "The Third Wave: The Impact of the Montana, Kentucky, and Texas Decisions on the Future of Public School Finance Reform Litigation," 19 *J.L. & Educ.* 219 (1990). The Kentucky Education Reform Act of 1990, Ch. 476, 1990 Ky. Acts 1208, covers curriculum, school governance, and school finance. Russo, "School-Based Decision Making in Kentucky: Dawn of a New Era

or Nothing New Under the Sun?" 83 *Ky.L.J.* 123, 125 (1994–1995); "Systemic Reform: The Kentucky Example," 3(2) *ERIC Review,* 5, 5–6 (Fall 1994); Adams, "School Finance Reform and Systemic School Change: Reconstituting Kentucky's Public Schools," 18 *J.Educ.Fin.* 318 (1993). Under the 1990 Kentucky law, standards have been established for all students, schools are held accountable for meeting the standards based on performance testing, and school-based decision making can be usurped if student scores remain unacceptably low.

"Achieving Equity and Excellence in Kentucky Education"
C. Trimble and A. Forsaith, 28 (3) *U.Mich.J.L.Ref.* 599, 613–622, 653 (1995).

* * *

II. Kera's Implementation

The distinguishing feature of *Council for Better Education* is not only that it mandates that all students achieve an adequate level of skills, but also that it requires the performance level of the entire system to shift toward higher performance standards. Accomplishing this goal requires the state to confront three important questions. First, what constitutes high performance and how will the schools convert the broad "capacities" provided by the Supreme Court of Kentucky into the everyday curriculum? Second, how will the state know when it has achieved these goals? Third, how will the state ensure that every school achieves these goals, and what will the state do if they do not?

Kentucky's response to these questions may be measured by examining the development and implementation of the new statewide assessment system. KERA [the Kentucky Education Reform Act] is a comprehensive package of accountability, governance, and instructional reform. The central mechanism driving the system, however, is assessment. Assessment establishes goals for the system and keeps it on track toward those goals. It communicates instructions to parties at the ground level and determines whether those instructions have been followed. Because it is so central, assessment provides the means for understanding the obstacles to be overcome and the decisions to be made in building a high performance educational system.

A. The Assessment Program

KERA created a statewide, performance-based assessment program. Originally, KERA established that students in grades four, eight, and twelve were to be tested each year in each major content area: reading, mathematics, science, social studies, and writing. Based on their performance, students are rated according to four levels of achievement: novice, apprentice, proficient, and distinguished. Ultimately, assessment will consider a combination of portfolios, small-group exercises, and open-ended essay questions.

KERA requires the establishment of an interim assessment program similar to the National Assessment of Educational Progress (NAEP). The interim assessment program must measure reading, math, science, social studies, and writing. This program must also provide statewide and national comparative data. The most critical component of the assessment program, however, is the requirement that the State Board for Elementary and Secondary Education establish a primarily performance-based program no later than the 1995–1996 school year and as early as the 1994–1995 school year.

B. Goals and Curriculum

The principal goal of the Kentucky assessment program is to measure whether students are receiving an adequate education as defined by the Supreme Court of Kentucky in *Council for Better Education*. In this case, the court articulated seven capacities that broadly describe what students must know and be able to do. [The capacities are related to: (1) sufficient skills to communicate orally and in writing in a complex society; (2) sufficient knowledge about economic, social, and political systems to make informed choices; (3) sufficient awareness of government processes to understand issues that affect a student's community, state, and nation; (4) sufficient self-knowledge and knowledge of a student's own mental and physical well-being; (5) sufficient grounding in the arts to appreciate the student's own cultural and historical heritage; (6) sufficient training for advanced work in academic or vocational fields for a student to choose and pursue a career intelligently; and (7) sufficient levels of academic or vocational skills to compete favorably with students in surrounding states.]

The statute directed specific student outcomes by setting six statewide goals for student achievement:

a) Schools shall expect a high level of achievement of all students.

b) Schools shall develop their students' ability to:
   1) Use basic communication and mathematics skills for purposes and situations they will encounter throughout their lives;
   2) Apply core concepts and principles from mathematics, the sciences, the arts, the humanities, social studies, and practical living studies to situations they will encounter through their lives;
   3) Become a self-sufficient individual;
   4) Become responsible members of a family, work group or community, including demonstrating effectiveness in community service;
   5) Think and solve problems in school situations and in a variety of situations they will encounter in life; and
   6) Connect and integrate experiences and new knowledge from all subject matter fields with what they have previously learned and build on past learning experiences to acquire new information through various media sources.

c) Schools shall increase their students' rate of school attendance.

d) Schools shall reduce their students' dropout and retention rates.

e) Schools shall reduce physical and mental health barriers to learning.

f) Schools shall be measured on the proportion of students who make a successful transition to work, post-secondary education, and the military.

Along with developing specific goals from which success may be assessed, it also is important for the state to communicate the curriculum to teachers. This communication may be accomplished in the following ways:

a. State curriculum frameworks;

b. State textbook adoption through a State Textbook Commission;

c. Expanded professional development opportunities for teachers; and

d. Education Professional Standards Board to oversee teacher certification and training.

C. Measuring Student Achievement

The purpose of an assessment in a high-stakes accountability system, however, is not merely to monitor school effectiveness; it is also a key component in affecting change. Because consequences for the district are tied to student performance on the assessment, instruction and learning will conform to the content and method of the assessment. Thus, the assessment is a powerful tool for raising student achievement through improving instruction. At the same time, any assessment program should be designed very carefully so that teachers employ the best instructional practices and students learn what they should learn.

1. Kentucky's Reliance on Performance-Based Assessments — To accomplish these goals, Kentucky has implemented performance-based assessments. Performance-based assessments differ from traditional multiple-choice tests in that their items are designed to probe students' understanding more deeply and to resemble more closely exercises that students might perform everyday in the classroom. In mathematics, for example, instead of choosing among four or five possible answers, students solve the problems on paper and include a written explanation of their answers. Performance assessments include writing and mathematics portfolios, which are collections of the students' best work.

The trade-offs of the two forms of assessment are quite straightforward and have been understood among teachers for many years. While a multiple-choice test can survey a student's level of specific knowledge, a single open-ended item in a performance-based assessment can measure a student's ability to organize knowledge on a particular matter and to communicate, usually in written form, a level of understanding. The two forms of assessment may in fact require similar kinds of background knowledge, but the method of applying this knowledge may be very different. Teachers often acknowledge this difference when they construct their own classroom tests. Teacher-designed classroom tests may award, for example, one point of credit for a multiple-choice item and five to ten points for an essay question.

2. Measuring Content Validity — Performance assessments and traditional multiple-choice tests are equally useful in achieving content-related validity, i.e., in assuring the right skills are assessed. Content validity typically is accomplished by using juries of content area experts to review the assessments for the purpose of certifying, for example, that a set of mathematical items measures the content intended to be measured. The state used this process in developing

the Kentucky Instructional Results Information System (KIRIS) performance assessments. Committees of teachers from across the state were brought together for the purpose of advising the test development process.

Achieving content validity for the Kentucky assessments, however, will differ in an important way from the traditional task of achieving content validity, because Kentucky assessments are designed to raise learning above current levels. In traditional test development environments, the content validity review process would direct the content area experts to consider a survey of what is being taught within a discipline and to determine whether the proposed items actually measure the curriculum currently in place. This process is well-defined because the function of assessment prior to the reform movement was to understand the curriculum as it was being offered and to measure that curriculum. In contrast, the aim of the new Kentucky assessments is to test students against "world-class" standards, rather than against the curriculum existing before the reform. Therefore, Kentucky's content experts must evaluate assessments against the newer and higher expectations.

3. Measuring Consequential Validity — The great advantage of performance-based assessments is that they can achieve the proper consequential validity. They encourage instructional practices that will challenge students to apply a broad range of knowledge and skills to real and complex problems. Consequential validity will result because teachers prepare students to perform well on the tests used to evaluate themselves and their schools. Therefore, in planning assessment design, Kentucky's educators must consider the means by which they want teachers to teach students routinely. If the assessment employs open-ended essays, then teachers likely will use open-ended essays routinely.

Traditional multiple-choice assessments cannot encourage the kind of instructional practices KERA aims to implement, because they typically test only a sample of skills within a curriculum and do not measure application in a realistic way. Because tests are used for high-stakes accountability measures, such as public listings of school data, instructional programs must adjust to the specific tests used and, just as importantly, to the method of assessment. When accountability measures are based solely on multiple-choice items, schools will devote resources, both financial and human, to instructional activities that teach students to view a problem as having several alternatives, one of which is a best response. If this instructional model were preferred, then the traditional modes of assessment and accountability probably were sufficient. While real statistical data is scarce, it was not uncommon to hear of instructional programs in which teachers focused their curriculum on assessment content, which, by design, was to have been a sample of the total curriculum. Consequently, Kentucky's curriculum narrowed and its instructional program concentrated on strategies for taking multiple-choice tests.

In the same manner, Kentucky should encourage better instructional practices by basing assessment and accountability on performance-based components such as open-response items. For these items, students organize and produce written responses to particular problems, participate in group activities to gather data and understand problems before producing written responses, and produce relatively lengthy responses that are entered into a portfolio of best work. Responses by teachers and students indicate that a positive change in instruction has been taking place since the adoption of the new Kentucky assessments. In more and more classes, students must demonstrate their comprehension through open-response items, instead of simply recalling enough specific information to answer multiple-choice questions. From these developments, it is reasonable to predict that future instructional processes will focus less on helping students to select a correct response from a set of possible answers and more on discovering an answer and communicating it in a meaningful way.

4. Accountability—While some might argue that one system cannot achieve both instructional leadership and school accountability, the Kentucky model demonstrates that if both leadership and accountability are needed, they must be guided by the same assessment, or at least by assessments that are parallel in structure, content, and format. Teachers cannot be asked to produce students who demonstrate, through written products and other modes of communication, their ability to apply knowledge to complex problems and, at the same time, be held accountable for student performance on traditional tests that do not require them to apply such knowledge. The kinds of routine instruction necessary to prepare students for success on traditional and performance-based assessments are not necessarily mutually exclusive, but rather are different in their emphasis and in the time devoted to different teaching strategies.

5. Teachers' and Parents' Anxiety Over Performance-Based Assessment—When a new assessment that is oriented toward what should be taught and the way it should be taught is introduced, teachers undertake a new type of responsibility which may cause them significant anxiety. Traditionally, accountability pressures have encouraged or forced educators to design their assessment to mirror the instruction they offer. Such traditional assessment allows the instructors to know from past experience the content that they will be responsible for teaching. Textbooks and content guidelines typically have defined this content. When the assessment is designed to lead instruction, however, or build a test worth teaching to, in the initial phases, teachers will likely feel that they are not fully aware of how they should teach students in order to ensure achievement according to the new assessment design. While Kentucky hopes that daily classroom experience and the content and format of assessment will become congruent over time, it is unlikely that this vision will be immediately obvious to classroom teachers or immediately implemented in the classroom. The system should allow time for such consistency to evolve. Although teachers may not demand a traditional scope and sequence of what is to be taught, they will demand an explanation of the assessment and a compatible curriculum designed to achieve the desired results.

Performance-based assessments may produce anxiety among parents as well. Parents, at times, become concerned because they believe traditional multiple-choice assessments are more objective. Both parents and teachers may be concerned that the new assessment and the instructional reforms that accompany it may not prepare their children to do well on the traditional college entrance exams. Studies show a positive correlation between performance on the American College Testing Program admissions test (ACT) and KIRIS, at least in the areas of reading, mathematics and science. Still others are concerned about what values the teachers apply when scoring the open-ended responses and, therefore, what values will be promoted at school. This concern has caused some parents to withhold their children from the new assessment. This is not a trivial matter, because the Kentucky accountability model holds the school accountable for the performance of all students enrolled in public education. The state assigns students who have not taken the assessment to the novice level of performance for purposes of accountability.

* * *

High-stakes accountability has imposed new pressures and responsibilities on both the assessment and instructional process. Within this environment, student assessment cannot be designed and implemented without confronting the impact that these assessments will have on the daily instruction and on the educational experiences of students. Instruction and assessment can no longer be designed independently of each other. A statistically well-designed assessment conceived to run efficiently in terms of time and financial costs still may be indefensible and too expensive if it causes the instructional process to narrow its curriculum inappropriately. Such an assessment may be too expensive if it results in an instructional program that does not cause teachers to challenge all students to reach for high levels of performance or to apply and communicate their academic achievements. In the end, any assessment and accountability system that puts at risk our ability to produce the quality students we seek is a system that is too expensive.

In Texas, the legislature undertook comprehensive school reform in 1995. Again, these actions were related to a longstanding judicial review of the constitutionality of Texas' school finance system. The Texas Supreme Court finally held that the system was constitutional after years of litigation in *Edgewood Indep. Sch. Dist. v. Meno*, 893 S.W. 2d 450 (Tex. 1995). As a result, the legislature, with strong support from Governor George W. Bush, was able to turn its attention to other educational concerns. Williams, "Annual Survey of Texas Law—Education," 49 *SMU L.Rev.* 901, 903–904 (May–June 1996). Like Kentucky, Texas decentralized school decision making and used standards testing to promote accountability. The reforms, though relatively recent, already have won rave reviews from some commentators, particularly conservatives who believe public schools need a drastic overhaul.

"The Gold Star State"

T. Palmaffy, 88 *Policy Rev.* 30, 33–38, (Mar. 1, 1998).

* * *

Led by Charles Duncan, an investment banker from Houston, TBEC [the Texas Business and Education Coalition] in the early 1980s pulled together powerful CEOs and educators interested in reform. Throughout the 1980s, in his role as head of TBEC

and as an appointed member of the Texas school board, Duncan continued to jawbone educators into focusing on student performance.

In the late 1980s, court rulings forced Texas to narrow the gap in funding between wealthy and poor school districts. In the course of overhauling the finance system, lawmakers wanted to ensure that redistributed funds would be spent well. Thus the legislature established the Educational Economic Policy Center, a quasi-governmental body charged with developing an accountability system. Chaired by Charles Miller, another Houston-based money manager and a founder of TBEC, the center presented its report in 1993. With strong support from the Texas legislature, most of Miller's recommendations became law, including the rating system and testing in most grades.

Many educators were not pleased about business meddling in their bailiwick. One superintendent called the system "despicable." Nancy McClaran, the executive director of the Texas Association for Supervision and Curriculum Development, wrote in the *Houston Chronicle* that Miller's report "contradicts every major, reputable piece of research on student testing that has been done in our nation in recent years. . . . If implemented, the recommendations would mean the dismantling of the public schools."

Despite such resistance, the Texas Education Code was rewritten in 1995 to further decentralize authority from the Texas Education Agency to local districts, giving schools even more autonomy to find solutions while holding them accountable for the results.

"The new Code put a major emphasis on performance and deleted references to telling districts how to teach," says Criss Cloudt, an associate commissioner at the TEA [Texas Education Agency]. Unlike rating systems such as Kentucky's that credit schools for simply making progress each year, Texas schools must reach a set of absolute benchmarks to improve their standing. In a school seeking an "exemplary" rating, for instance, 90 percent of the students must pass the TAAS [Texas Assessment of Academic Skills] in reading, writing, and math, the dropout rate must not exceed 1 percent, and the attendance rate must surpass 94 percent. In short, an "exemplary" school in the poverty-stricken barrios of El Paso must meet the same standards as an "exemplary" school in the cozy Bellaire section of Houston.

The TEA is sensitive to a school's socioeconomic or racial makeup, but only to hold it equally responsible for the performance of its most vulnerable students. A school striving to earn a "recognized" ranking this year must achieve not only a TAAS passage rate of at least 80 percent of all students, but at least 80 percent of each of three special racial and economic subgroups as well. If any one subgroup, such as black students, should fall below 80 percent or fail one of the other measures, the school would receive a lower ranking.

That's why affluent Bellaire High School in Houston was labeled "low performing" last year. Its overall scores were typical of a school that sends its top 50 students to the Ivy League, but its Hispanic dropout rate was too high. Average scores at Royal Middle School in rural Pattison were good enough for an "acceptable" rating in 1996, but only 28 percent of its black students had passed the TAAS math test. Because that fell below the 30 percent cutoff for "acceptable" schools (which has since been raised), Royal was also branded "low performing."

Royal Middle's plight illustrates the slow pace of improvement at most schools. In the end, the "low performing" rating had its desired effect: Midway through the 1996–97 school year, the district replaced the ineffective principal with Patsy Ann Parker, who initiated two-hour afternoon tutoring sessions, cracked down on truancy by hauling parents into court, and began offering 7 A.M. breakfasts to lure struggling students to before-school tutoring sessions. Her efforts earned the school an "acceptable" rating in 1997.

The school, though, still occupies a precarious position between "low performing" and "acceptable." According to Parker, parental involvement is low, in part because the truck stops along Interstate 10 bring a steady flow of drugs into the community. To encourage parents to care about academic results, Parker requires teachers to call each student's home once a week. She is also using computer programs in reading and math to track students' progress; from now on, 80 percent of the children who advance to the next grade must have skills at or above grade level. Where gang fights once were routine at Royal, "now we have quiet halls and productive classrooms," Parker proudly says. She also brings drug-sniffing dogs into the school regularly. Still, Parker says, it will take three to five years to turn the school around.

If Royal is typical, Isaacs Elementary is extraordinary. One-hundred percent of the school's students qualify for Title I funds, yet they scored higher than the statewide average on the TAAS in 1995, when Isaacs received an "acceptable" rating. Even so, principal Leon Pettis was determined to raise scores. To him, "acceptable" was unacceptable.

He adopted the Saxon reading and math programs known widely for their adherence to traditional methods such as phonics-based instruction. He also began to monitor his teachers' instructional habits by requiring them to give him portfolios of students' work each week. Teachers in turn were expected to act on the feedback Pettis delivered. "He would tell the teachers, 'If your students aren't performing, you as a teacher are lacking something,' " says Fredye Hemanes, the school's Title I coordinator. He also required students who had failed or nearly failed the TAAS to attend after-school tutoring sessions four days a week.

Two years later, 95 percent of the Isaacs kids who sat for the TAAS tests in reading, math, and writing passed all three tests, compared to just 66 percent in 1995 and 73 percent statewide. The reward came when Isaacs was named an elite "exemplary" school in 1997, a distinction it shared with just 10 percent of Texas schools.

The Lessons

The successes of school districts all over Texas yield many lessons about accountability:

First, decentralization is critical. The TEA gave districts wide discretion in running their school systems. In turn, the most effective superintendents have decentralized even further, allowing individual schools to make most curriculum and training decisions. "Site-based management" has become the new catch phrase in Texas education. Superintendents see the district office as less a regulatory overseer than as a source of instructional expertise, information, and targeted spending. In Corpus Christi, where the percentage of kids passing the TAAS in reading rose from 66 percent in 1994 to 82 percent in 1997, superintendent Abelardo Saavedra managed the creation of tough district-wide standards and gave his schools broad freedoms to meet them.

"We expect all our schools to be on track towards 'exemplary,' " says Saavedra, "and we look at the central office as their support system as opposed to the autocratic system we used to operate under."

The Houston school district, the largest in Texas, once mandated instructional methods like "whole language." Now superintendent Rod Paige routinely grants exemptions to principals who believe that district mandates are hampering their efforts. Houston was also the first district in Texas to permit public charter schools, which are liberated from most regulations in return for meeting rigorous performance standards. "We have turned the schools loose," says Paige. "We tell them that they're going to be responsible for the pie, so we're not going to give them the recipe." Paige's district boasted 25 "exemplary" schools in 1997, up from none in 1993, when the standards were easier to meet.

Second, student testing, used properly, helps schools to identify weaknesses among students and teachers. One key to Houston's resurgence has been its innovative use of the test data provided by the accountability system. The district office breaks apart the data to ensure that principals know how their schools, their students, and their individual teachers are doing. "We're able with this kind of data to go back down to the classroom, to the teacher," says Paige. "That makes the teacher's performance visible. It can be used to provide staff training and, in some cases, to make changes."

It's hard to overestimate the importance of test data in evaluating teachers *and* students. Teachers, says Saavedra, would like to improve but often don't know where their weaknesses lie. They often have no measure of their students' weaknesses either. Test scores provide the information they need. "When we do poorly in reading, we know specifically what part of reading we're not doing well in," says Saavedra. "There's no excuse for a classroom teacher not to be able to identify where she is weak. Scores should help guide the teacher."

Third, test data can also illuminate good practices. With schools' scores and demographic makeup in hand, educators can identify high-performing schools that are succeeding despite their obstacles. Without its TAAS scores, how else would Texans be able to identify a gem like Isaacs? "We've shown," says Darvin Winick, now an advisor to Texas governor George W. Bush's business council, "that you can't get credit for doing well without accountability." Then places like Isaacs become models for reform. According to Paige, more and more Houston schools are adopting programs such as Direct Instruction, Success for All, and Saxon reading and math because they have found that other successful schools are using them. "Schools are trying to find proven solutions because they're accountable for the results," says Paige.

Sonny Donaldson, superintendent of the nearby Aldine district, sent a team of curriculum and in-structional specialists to the North Forest and Brazosport districts three years ago to divine their secrets. Both districts are famous for educating children who live, like those in Aldine, on the troubled outskirts of Houston, and Donaldson wanted to find strategies that would work for his students.

He found that these districts were closely analyzing individual students' test scores in order to tailor instructional programs to their needs. So he hired a consultant to write a computer program that would break down his own district's scores in a fashion helpful to teachers. He also sent curriculum specialists to any school rated below "recognized" to work with teachers in the field. With these reforms in place, 13 of the 26 schools that had been rated "acceptable" in 1995 rose to the "recognized" level in 1997. The district as a whole improved from "acceptable" to "recognized" in just two years. "We set out to be a 'recognized' school district," says Donaldson. "Now our goal is to be 'exemplary.' If 85 percent of a campus's kids are passing the TAAS, and they set a goal of maintaining that, we reject that. We want them to set more challenging goals."

Educators can use the test data to scour the state for proven instructional programs. At Stephens Elementary in Aldine, principal Ruth Dimmick used the Success for All reading program developed at Johns Hopkins University to raise her school from "acceptable" in 1995 to "exemplary" in 1997—the only school in the district to do so. Don Hancock, the superintendent of the Connally school district near Waco, dispatched his math teachers to travel the state for the best program and they returned with Saxon math in hand. As a result, his district rose from "acceptable" in 1995 to "recognized" in 1997. Taft High School near Corpus Christi brought in Saxon math in 1996 and shot from "low performing" to "recognized" in one year. These programs are spreading throughout Texas as educators search for what works.

Fourth, in the most troubled schools, principals say, parental involvement is indispensable to reform. The principal at Brandon Elementary, a school north of Houston that went from "low performing" in 1996 to "acceptable" in 1997, now requires his teachers to call home whenever a student's performance falters. This is supposed to prompt parents to monitor their child's study habits or at least, in the worst of cases, just make sure their child comes to school regularly. Stephens Elementary in Aldine offers parents of its mostly Hispanic student population free English lessons. Hambrick Middle School in the same district offered parents gang-awareness workshops conducted by police officers, and exempts students from homework if they bring their parents to school. Hambrick parents now volunteer more hours than parents at any other school in the district. Frazier Elementary in Dallas, which jumped from a "low performing" rating in 1994 to "exemplary" in 1997, gives away donated furniture, pots and pans, and clothing to entice low-income parents to teacher conferences.

Lastly, the success of any reform depends on the deeply held conviction that any child can learn, even in the most challenging of circumstances. "I will not accept low student performance or excuses that students can't learn," says superintendent Gerald Anderson of the Brazosport school district. "We have a basic philosophy in this district that if one teacher can do it, then all teachers can do it. The same goes for school campuses and districts." Houston's Rod Paige adds, "We don't accept the conventional wisdom that some kids won't be able to handle the content and that we should lower the standards for them. There are schools in Houston loaded with low-income kids who perform. We believe that the school itself can make a difference."

Building Accountability

Texas is one of a handful of states fulfilling the model of an accountability system for educators. Such a system, says researcher Heidi Glidden of the American Federation of Teachers union (AFT), must have four prongs:

A set of standards describing the knowledge and skills students are expected to learn at each grade level. Teachers and principals in Texas know what they need to cover each year because the state gives them clear guideposts. The magazine *Education Week* and the AFT both gave Texas high marks for its academic standards.

A set of tests that are closely aligned with the state's standards. That way, the schools, the state, and the public know whether children are learning the skills needed to succeed in each grade. "Norm-referenced" tests such as the Stanford Achievement Test only measure where their students are relative to all the students who take the test. "Criterion-referenced" tests such as the TAAS and the NAEP [National Assessment of Educational Progress] tell them how much knowledge a student has acquired. The TAAS is easier than the NAEP, but it is much tougher than most states' assessments.

A system of rewards and sanctions for schools and students based on student test scores and other criteria such as dropout rates. Sanctions in Texas include the shame of a "low-performing" rating and the public hearing that accompanies it, the threat of a state takeover, and, for students who don't pass the 10th-grade TAAS exam, failure to graduate high school. But these are merely stopgap measures, used only when the state is confronted with massive failure. For the average school or district, the surreptitious ways in which educators base their promotion decisions on performance have much more influence over achievement.

A system of aid to failing schools. Without extra help, says Chris Pipho, a senior fellow at the Denver-based Education Commission of the States, giving a "low performing" rating would be like "giving an 'F' in an algebra class and saying the student is going to improve because he got an 'F.'" Many schools could use the instructional expertise of top-flight teachers as well as an infusion of funds to purchase textbooks or to give teachers merit bonuses. Last fall, TEA commissioner Mike Moses visited the Dallas school district to scold the school board for public infighting. The district, in turn, provided $25,000 and a team of specialists to each of its two "low-performing" schools.

Standards and tests are clearly an important piece in the accountability puzzle, but what is most important—and what is lost in the debate over national testing—is what you do with the results. Key to Texas's reforms is how public and how understandable the ratings are. The TEA holds an annual press conference to announce the rankings, after which big city newspapers such as the *Houston Chronicle* and the *Dallas Morning News* splash the names of "low performing" and "exemplary" schools across their front pages. In addition, every school's ranking and vital statistics are readily available on the Internet, a key tool in the accountability movement.

"We're finding more and more that when people come from other cities and states, they've already done a lot of legwork over the Internet," says Diane Craig, a real-estate agent in San Antonio. Homeowners and businessmen take a keener interest in the local schools when their quality affects property values.

Subterfuge and Solutions

Texas's system is by no means perfect. For one thing, the benchmark for earning an "acceptable" rating is still rather low. In fact, just four years ago a school could see 80 percent of its students fail the TAAS and still avoid the "low performing" stigma. But the threshold to qualify as "acceptable" rises each year by 5 percentage points. By the year 2000, a school will need a TAAS passage rate of 50 percent to earn an "acceptable" rating. "The standards aren't where we want them to be," says Chris Cloudt of the TEA. "But that's a pretty fast pace to be increasing them." The standard for a "recognized" rating has also ratcheted up, from 60 percent in 1994 to 80 percent this year.

Another major weakness in the system is the loophole that overlooks the performance of special-ed and LEP students. The TEA already reports the scores of Hispanic students who take the TAAS in Spanish, and those scores will soon influence the rankings. A test for special-ed students is in the works. "There's a dual emphasis on raising standards and including the maximum number of students," says Cloudt of the TEA.

A more troubling issue is the sheer number of children labeled special education and LEP in the first place. Statewide, 10 percent of students are exempted from the TAAS, and another 6 percent or so take the test, yet are not included in the rating system because of their special-ed status. At some schools, those numbers are alarmingly higher. In 1997, the Houston school district only used the test scores of 39 percent of Brock Elementary students in determining the school's accountability rating because the school had labeled 40 percent of its students special ed and another 18 percent LEP. "The number of kids who are special ed ought to be 5 percent, max," says John Cole of the TFT [Texas Federation of Teachers] union. Superintendent Thomas Tocco of the Fort Worth school district recently ordered an investigation of its special-education programs after discovering that one-third of all Fort Worth elementary schools had exempted at least 20 percent of their kids for special ed.

What is happening here is a cloudy and controversial issue. Some observers claim that principals are finding ways to hide struggling students because the accountability system carries such high stakes. "We told lawmakers that if they didn't make the exemptions very tight, schools would test only the kids who do well," says Gayle Fallon, the president of the Houston Federation of Teachers, the largest local arm of the TFT. "And that's precisely what happened." Houston superintendent Rod Paige denies such charges, saying that schools have strict guidelines for placing children into special education classes. Just last year, the TEA set up a special unit to investigate such claims.

Equally important is the question of how often students should be tested. Many teachers say the state tests students too often, and some say they are spending too much time teaching to the test, but others disagree. "If you're sure you have a strong link between the curriculum and the test, then you're testing what you want the children to learn," says Cloudt of the TEA. And there is strong support among business leaders and policy analysts for expanding testing to the first and second grades and to grades nine through 11. "When you last test kids at the 10th-grade level, you have not told them whether they are qualified to move past high school," says John Stevens, the executive director of TBEC.

Stevens's point is punctuated by the prevalence of high schools among the ranks of the "low performing." While many elementary-school pupils, with their fresh minds and pre-adolescent innocence, have little trouble climbing to a higher rating, high schools and, to a lesser degree, middle schools, have proven more intransigent.

The story that unfolded at Fox Technical High School in San Antonio illustrates the difficulty. After two straight years as a "low-performing" school, in 1995 auditors from the TEA deemed the problems plaguing Fox Technical High School too intractable for minor tinkering. Citing divisions among the staff and low morale, the team of auditors recommended a rare measure called "reconstitution"—essentially, starting from scratch. A new principal with a reputation for reform was brought in and the entire staff had to reapply to the school. Every principal's dream became a reality for Joanne Cockrell: She was able to hand-pick her entire staff, only a third of whom were holdovers from the preconstitution days. "We thought that it would be ludicrous to keep the same teachers and expect different results," says Cockrell.

Two years later, Cockrell unexpectedly found herself having to explain to TEA commissioner Mike Moses why the results had hardly improved. Despite higher reading scores and a declining dropout rate, in 1997 Fox Tech was saddled with the "low-performing" stigma for the fourth straight year because the proportion of its students passing the TAAS in math remained below 35 percent, the benchmark for an "acceptable" rating. The improvements were strong enough to justify some faith in Cockrell and her staff, but the TEA's monitoring of Fox Tech continues.

The Coming Years

The Texas accountability system must continue to prove itself. The gains of eighth-graders on the 1996 NAEP math tests were not as impressive as those of fourth-graders, perhaps because they had already received five years of Texas schooling by the time reforms began in 1993. It will be interesting to see what happens in the coming years, as kids who began their schooling during the reform era start to enter middle school. (Likewise, the benefits of reforms would not have shown up on the last NAEP reading assessment in 1994. On that assessment, Texas's fourth-graders performed at the national average.)

In the meantime, the reforms continue to spark some opposition. In October, the Mexican American Legal Defense and Education Fund (MALDEF) filed suit against the TAAS. The suit charges that the TAAS's 10th-grade test, which students must pass to graduate, discriminates against minorities. This accords with MALDEF's long history of opposition to student testing in general and to testing as a graduation requirement in particular. Fortunately, the U.S. Department of Education ruled against a similar complaint filed by the NAACP last summer, and few observers expect the outcome to change.

These groups are finding themselves on the wrong side of public opinion in Texas, even among educators. "Now the system is just a part of Texas," says Catherine Clark, director of the Texas Center for Educational Research. "It's not a subject of debate." Of the educators I have spoken with, the ones who did criticize the system argued that it wasn't tough enough.

Meanwhile, reforms continue apace. Governor Bush has proposed ending social promotion—the practice of graduating children to the next grade regardless of their skill level—statewide, and Rod Paige is in the process of drafting a plan for his district. A nascent program, the Public Education Grant, now allows students to leave any school receiving a "low-performing" rating within the past three years as long as another school or district will take them. Texas lawmakers are looking to provide incentives for districts to open their doors.

While many educational reform efforts quickly buckle to union pressure or public discontent, Texas's system has only become more rigorous over time. If this trend continues, Texas, one of the nation's poorest states, may soon become the best place to get an education.

* * *

NOTES AND QUESTIONS

1. Legal Challenges to the TAAS Test

Despite this optimistic view of the TAAS test, community organizations and black and Latino schoolchildren filed suit alleging that the test's use as a high school exit requirement violated equal protection, Title VI, the Equal Educational Opportunity Act, and due process. A federal district court found that there was insufficient evidence to establish discriminatory intent in the adoption or construction of the test. Although the TAAS test did lead to disproportionate failure rates among black and Latino students, the court held that this adverse impact was justified by educational necessity. There was no alternative that could accomplish the state's goal of ensuring that students mastered basic skills before receiving a diploma because less stringent measures would sacrifice the motivational benefits of a high-stakes test. Students had adequate notice of the requirement, and the state offered sufficient evidence that students had an adequate opportunity to prepare for it both through the standard curriculum and remediation. *GI Forum v. Texas Education Agency*, 87 F.Supp.2d 667 (W.D.Tex. 2000). The plaintiffs chose not to appeal the decision. Stutz, "Ruling Rejecting Bias on TAAS Won't Be Appealed; Fear of Setting Bad Precedent Led Group to Drop Issue, Lawyer Says," *Dallas Morning News*, Feb. 9, 2000, at 19A; Walt, "Minorities Give Up High School Exit-Exam Fight," *Houston Chronicle*, Feb. 8, 2000, at A22; Balli, "MALDEF Won't Appeal Ruling; Group Will Eye Texas' New Test," *San Antonio Express-News*, Feb. 8, 2000, at 1B.

2. Scholarly Critiques of the TAAS Test

In addition to legal challenges, the TAAS test has prompted intense debate in the academic community. In October 2000, researchers at RAND Corporation released a report that concluded that the "Texas miracle" of improving TAAS scores and narrowing the gap in white and nonwhite achievement was misleading. Texas students did not show comparable gains on the National Assessment of Educational Progress. The authors concluded that TAAS scores were inflated by teaching to the test and narrowing the curriculum. Klein et al., *What Do Test Scores in Texas Tell Us?* (2000) (http://www.rand.org/publications/IP/IP202/). Other researchers have raised similar concerns about the

TAAS test. *See, e.g.,* Carnoy, Loeb, and Smith, *Do Higher State Test Scores in Texas Make for Better High School Outcomes?* (2000) (Paper presented at the Annual Meeting of the American Educational Research Association in New Orleans); McNeil and Valenzuela, *The Harmful Impact of the TAAS System of Testing in Texas: Beneath the Accountability Rhetoric* (2000) (Harvard Civil Rights Project). For a general discussion of some of the problems with high-stakes testing, see Moran, "Sorting and Reforming: High-Stakes Testing in the Public Schools," 34 *Akron L. Rev.* 107 (2000).

3. Kentucky and Texas Compared

Although both Kentucky and Texas adopted comprehensive educational reform bills in response to problems in their school finance systems, the two states relied on very different approaches to measuring achievement and enforcing accountability. What are the strengths and weaknesses of each approach? Which do you prefer and why? Is there some other approach that would be preferable to either system of accountability? What would it look like?

4. Centralized Standards and Local Variability

Despite their differences, both Kentucky and Texas have relied heavily on centralized control to cure ailing public schools. Some critics have charged that these initiatives are simplistic and ineffective at best and destructive and intrusive at worst:

> The tension between increased state regulation and the need to maintain local flexibility poses a fundamental dilemma in the effort to encourage excellence in the schools. It is a problem rooted in the nature of excellence itself. Excellence cannot be coerced or mandated. Rather, it is a condition to which individuals may aspire. Aspirations to excellence generally arise from subtle and pervasive qualities: a love of learning, a sense of history, a command of analytical skills, an appreciation of humanistic values, and the like. For teachers and administrators, excellence means caring about students; being sympathetic to the needs of students with diverse educational and, often, personal problems; demonstrating a commitment to learning. It also includes a host of other attitudes, such as excitement about one's subject matter and a commitment to the domain of the intellect. This commitment entails a dedication to a way of life that is rooted in a historical tradition of cultural enlightenment.
>
> Thus, aspirations to excellence cannot be achieved by regulation. Rules simply cannot compel teachers to be more caring toward students or require that administrators be fair. Such regulations would clearly be unenforceable and would probably violate due process norms as well. Consequently, reformers tend to focus on that which can be measured, quantified, and, therefore, enforced. Regulations, such as those concerning the length of the school day, participation in sports, curriculum, and teacher promotion and evaluation, become rough proxies for excellence. The danger is that, as Schrag has noted, it becomes very easy to "systematically confuse rigor with 'basics,' success with test scores, standards with hours spent in the classroom or doing homework. None of that would necessarily be objectionable if it were understood that there is a real difference between kinds of homework, that makework is self-defeating, and that longer classroom exposure to a teacher contemptuous of literature or history or mathematics is worse than no exposure."

* * *

Stripped to its essence, the goal of the current educational reform is to change the behavior of individuals and institutions so that they conform to the goals of the excellence agenda. If one accepts the assumption that those who staff the nation's schools are to blame for the present condition of the nation's educational system, transforming mediocrity into excellence means altering the interaction between student and teacher. If students are inattentive, uninterested, and unmotivated by school, they must be made attentive, interested, and motivated. And if teachers are operating under the well-known institutional ethic of "doing just enough to get by," excellence would demand adoption of a new work ethic consonant with much higher standards. Such a view underestimates the complexity of the problem of educational mediocrity and overestimates the capacity of policymakers to solve it. As psychologists, parole officers, social workers, doctors, and others who work with people eventually discover, behavior is not easily manipulated. Public policymakers have been forced to confront the often unhappy truth that when the successful implementation of policy depends upon changing behavior, failure can often be anticipated.

Altering institutional behavior may prove to be even harder than changing individual behavior. Schools in the United States are highly durable organizations: they have been able to respond to and accommodate almost any change or any demand that has been made of them. School reform movements have occurred about every decade, without altering schools fundamentally. If accommodation is the practiced and well-learned response to demands for change, why should the latest round of reforms prompt a different response?

* * *

Excellence is a difficult product for educational policymakers to deliver. High academic standards may require some individuals—students, teachers, parents, administrators—to change their attitudes about schooling. One of the underlying assumptions, for example, is

that students can be made to value education intrinsically. An appreciation of education for its own sake, it is thought, can be fostered with some clever policy engineering. Making class periods longer, requiring more school days each year, promoting enrollment in academic courses, creating a curriculum that emphasizes basics, and curtailing students' extracurricular activities are generally thought to be ways of redressing mediocrity.

Many policymakers, however, overlook the fact that students go to school for a variety of reasons. Some are there because they want to go on to college and have careers, others because their friends are there. Still others attend because they like art or shop classes or enjoy extracurricular activities. And then there are those who attend simply because a state law requires them to. For high school students, in particular, school may be competing with other interests—and losing out. . . .

Another dimension of reform, improving the teaching profession, also relies in good measure on strategies to alter entrenched patterns of behavior that lie beyond the bounds of policy manipulation. Incentive-based pay schemes, for example, may have marginal effects, and competency tests may eliminate the bottom 10 percent of teachers—those who cannot read, write, or compute—but those strategies cannot turn "a frog into a prince."[14] Raising the salaries of beginning teachers . . . and raising average annual salaries . . . may encourage highly motivated and intelligent individuals to enter the teaching profession and to stay there. But are higher salaries enough? How well do such salary incentives compete with working conditions in attracting and retaining teachers? Consider the working environment in some urban schools where plaster falls from the ceiling, "street people" and irate parents roam the halls, old *Readers Digests* are the closest and only approximations to textbooks, where there are consistently no toilet paper, towels, or soap in the teachers' restrooms, where midterm exams have to be canceled for lack of paper, and teachers face threats of transfer and layoff throughout the school year.[*] Those schools that face the most adversity need committed and qualified teachers most, but they are also the least likely to get them. It is doubtful that pay incentives to both currently employed and prospective teachers can outweigh the adverse working conditions in many schools.

* * *

A wide range of behaviors, attitudes, and incentives lies beyond the purview of state policy. The effects of schooling are mitigated by various factors. As education

researchers have found, poor children who come from what are euphemistically called "disadvantaged homes"—a sanitized policy term that masks the hardship and poverty of life in the inner city—and who live in slum neighborhoods with all their usual attributes, will find it more difficult to benefit from the current excellence reform efforts than their counterparts who live in affluent suburban environments. Although they may be quite interested in their children's education, many parents with children in inner-city schools often lack the time and resources that more affluent parents possess to devote to their children's educational success. In short, the excellence movement may strike a responsive chord in the parents of inner-city school children but it may prove to be ephemeral as a plan of action. Some schools clearly are more successful than others in teaching poor inner-city children, but it is not easy to create educational policy from a handful of success stories. Government lacks resources to change people's life styles, health habits, and associations. . . .

Timar and Kirp, "Educational Reform and Institutional Competence," 57 *Harv.Educ.Rev.* 308, 309–24, 328 (1987).

Timar and Kirp suggest that state initiatives to standardize education are doomed to fail because of the complexity of local conditions. Others have expressed concern about the impact of comprehensive statewide regulations on local control and innovation.

"Is Local Control of the Schools Still a Viable Option?"
C. Faber, 14 *Harv.J.L. & Pub.Pol'y* 447 (Spring, 1991).

* * *

B. The Growth of State Control

A brief historical review of legislation in the area of education provides convincing evidence of the trend toward increased state control. All states have had compulsory school attendance laws throughout most of the Twentieth Century. Pupil admission standards, including age, residence, and immunization requirements, are established directly by statute in most states. In all states, the local district must offer a curriculum approved by the state. States differ in the degree of control exercised, but even in states

---

[14]Cuban, "Transforming the Frog," pp. 131–32 [Cuban, "Transforming the Frog into a Prince: Effective Schools Research, Policy and Practice at the District Level," 54 *Harv. Educ. Rev.* (1974)]; *see also* Cuban's "School Reform by Remote Control: SB 813 in California," 66 *Phi Delta Kappan*, 213–15 (1984).

[*]*See* S. Johnson, *Teachers at Work* (1990).

where local districts retain some discretion, course offerings must meet state guidelines. Most states permit local school districts to select their own textbooks, but these districts usually must choose books from state approved lists. Virtually every state requires certification of public school teachers. Most states have teacher tenure statutes and laws that govern the employment, transfer, dismissal, and demotion of teachers. State laws authorizing or requiring collective negotiations proliferated during the 1960s and early 1970s. The first such law was enacted in Wisconsin in 1959; by 1975, a majority of the states had enacted negotiation statutes.

Except for negotiation legislation, state control in the areas of compulsory attendance, curriculum, certification, and employment did not increase greatly at the expense of local control during the decades immediately preceding 1980. The decade of the 1980s, however, witnessed a surge in state control of education under the banner of reform. During the years 1982 to 1986, eleven states passed omnibus reform laws. Most of these acts imposed more rigorous academic standards for students and higher standards for teachers. Between 1980 and 1986, forty-five states altered their requirements for earning a standard high school diploma. These alterations have almost invariably entailed increases in required courses. Since 1980, the age span of compulsory school attendance has been increased in fifteen states, and since 1983, eleven states have increased the length of the school year. Although the length of the school day has not been changed significantly as a result of new state mandates, some states have reinterpreted existing regulations to ban certain nonacademic activities during the school day. Restrictions on students' athletic participation ("no pass, no play") have been imposed in fourteen states, and restrictions on students' driving privileges have been imposed in five states, usually in the form of revoking driver's licenses of school dropouts.

In the realm of stiffening teacher requirements, the most usual course of states has been to require prospective teachers to pass a state-mandated competency examination prior to initial certification. Between 1975 and 1986, legislation mandating teacher testing was enacted in thirty-three states. By 1989, passing a competency examination was required in forty-five states. Career ladder plans have not been nearly so pervasive.

Two states, Florida and Tennessee, have such plans in place, and several other states have enacted legislation or field-tested such plans.

Perhaps the most intrusive state intervention in local school district affairs arises in the context of "academic bankruptcy," or situations in which schools are performing poorly. Nine states now have provisions for state intervention in the operation of school districts that are performing poorly. New Jersey's law is probably the best known; it permits state officials to take complete control of a district and to dismiss school board members and top administrators. The state's takeover of the Jersey City school district was widely publicized.

Similarly, Kentucky's statute permits the state superintendent to intervene in the operation of local school districts and to limit the authority of the local superintendent and local board when identified deficiencies are not corrected. The state's use of this authority to intervene in the Whitley County, Kentucky system, however, was invalidated because the implementing regulations were vague and were applied in an arbitrary manner.

Recent court cases challenging the constitutionality of state school aid formulas have also led to some diminution of local control. Beginning with the 1971 California decision, *Serrano v. Priest*,[25] formulas have been challenged across the country under equal protection, "uniform system," or "thorough and efficient system" clauses of state constitutions. In at least eight states, constitutional violations requiring remedial legislative action have been found. In some cases, courts have required states to enact legislation to prohibit local districts from raising more than a given amount of local revenue for their schools, even if the local citizenry wants to levy more taxes. Local control is not always denigrated by such court rulings, however; providing additional funding at the state level for poor districts increases the programming options such districts can afford and, for them, enhances local control, assuming the increased funds are made available without strings attached.

A far-reaching decision in the area of school reform was the Supreme Court of Kentucky's 1989 declaration that not merely the finance plan but the entire school system of Kentucky was constitutionally deficient because it did not meet the mandate of an efficient system of common schools

---

[25] 5 Cal. 3d 584, 487 P.2d 1241, 96 Cal.Rptr. 601 (1971) (holding that the California public school financing system, based primarily on local property taxes, violates the Equal Protection Clause of the Fourteenth Amendment).

throughout the state. The court was outspoken and adamant:

> The sole responsibility for providing the system of common schools is that of our General Assembly. . . . The General Assembly must not only establish the system, but it must monitor it on a continuing basis so that it will always be maintained in a constitutional manner. The General Assembly must carefully supervise it, so there is no waste, no duplication, no mismanagement, at any level.

The court went on to state that the obligation to provide an adequate education to every child in the Commonwealth "cannot be shifted to local counties and local school districts."

* * *

State Educational Reform Strategies

In the fervor for educational reform following the publication of A Nation at Risk, most states were unwilling to wait for individual schools to become effective on their own. Instead, almost all states have engaged in some type of statewide reform effort. States have used approaches ranging from giving aid and encouragement to local districts with no usurpation of local control to transferring most decisionmaking from the local to the state level. Does research reveal anything about the most desirable approach for states to take in the reform of local schools?

Professor Timar has studied three possible strategies to manage the substance and process of education reform, as those strategies were implemented in Texas, California, and South Carolina.[62] He identified the Texas approach [before the changes made in 1995 that are discussed in the Palmaffy excerpt] as rational planning, based on the assumption that there are single, best policy solutions that can be discovered through rational planning. This strategy relies on top-down mandates, centralized authority and decisionmaking, and standardization and uniformity in substance and process. Obviously, this approach removes much autonomy from local districts and increases state control. Because increased state regulation and rational planning are insensitive to the complexities of schools as social and political organizations, they are crude policy instruments for effecting change.

California, on the other hand, has employed a market incentive strategy that concentrates policy development at the state level, but allows implementation to be determined at the local level. Although rules and regulations are proclaimed by the state, adherence is a matter of local choice. Timar observed that organizationally competent schools in California may take advantage of the state's proposed reforms, but organizationally weak schools do not have the capability to integrate them into their own programs. His research on the implementation of the California reform measure led him to conclude that "it is difficult to point to changes in the structure and organization of schooling that will substantially improve the quality of the state's educational system." Centralized policy formulation combined with a laissez-faire implementation strategy, it appears, may lead nowhere.

The third approach identified by Timar is the political interaction model, exemplified by South Carolina. In contrast to the other strategies studied, this approach shifts the policy perspective from reliance on formal control and regulation by a central authority to informal devices that rely on delegation, discretion, and dispersal of authority. The interactive model of decisionmaking establishes a process for problem-solving instead of proposing single, best solutions. The state mandates certain programs, but permits the local schools to determine the best way to organize those programs. Although the state does not allow the local districts to decide whether to adopt specified reforms, it does allow them to determine how to adopt them. Timar's research shows that this reform strategy has been more successful than the other two approaches studied. He concluded that the interactive model works not because it relies on local control or state control, but because it recognizes the need for balance between accountability to the state and local autonomy. This finding suggests that authority and responsibility for education are best distributed among the various levels of government.

* * *

Given that South Carolina has been successful in securing adoption of the reform package, what difference has it made? Are South Carolina's schools more effective than before? Are South Carolina's students learning more? Are goals for schooling in South Carolina being met to a greater degree?

---

[62]See T. Timar, Educational Reform: The Need to Redefine State-Local Governance of Schools 17 (1989).

A review of studies of South Carolina's education reform shows mixed results.[65] The State of South Carolina's own analysis of the effects of the reform legislation indicates that achievement test scores have improved; services for preschool, remedial, gifted and talented, and vocational students are better; and salaries for teachers are higher.[66] Although a national study reported that teachers throughout the nation are frustrated with much of the recent reform effort, teachers in South Carolina were less dissatisfied than others. Even so, forty-three percent of South Carolina teachers stated that morale had declined as a result of reform, while only forty percent indicated that morale had improved.[67] Scholars at the South Carolina Educational Policy Center concluded that "many teachers and principals feel overwhelmed by the sheer volume of the mandates. . . . Despite their support for the reform initiatives, these educators are crying out for changes in education policies."[68]

Even though districts are allowed wide latitude in determining how to implement reforms, many South Carolina educators perceive the spirit of the reforms as too prescriptive. This point has been recognized by the state's leading policymakers, including the governor and state superintendent, both of whom have called for looser state regulation of certain districts.

Although surveys show that South Carolina educators support the concept of reform, its implementation troubles many of them. This conclusion is derived from two studies authorized by the South Carolina Educational Policy Center. The first study, an assessment of the state's Principal Evaluation Program, found solid support for the concept of evaluating principals.[71] The principals were quite dissatisfied, however, partly because they felt that the program's application of preset criteria in evaluating principals' performance does not adequately account for situational factors, contingencies, or context. The second study focused on working conditions of teachers, teacher burnout, and the impact of reform in South Carolina. The results of this study reinforced the concerns raised in the Carnegie study, which concluded: "We are troubled that the nation's

teachers remain so skeptical. Why is it that teachers, of all people, are demoralized and largely unimpressed by the reform actions taken?"[74]

The findings of these South Carolina studies are indeed discouraging. More than sixty percent of the teachers believe morale is worse as a result of reform, nearly eighty-five percent find the burden of paperwork greater, nearly seventy percent said that they must handle things differently than they believe is appropriate, and over two-thirds said that they must work on unnecessary tasks. Moreover, a scale used to measure teacher burnout yielded emotional exhaustion scores for South Carolina teachers about fifty percent higher than the national average.

Individual interviews with teachers indicate that some of them feel degraded by the collective impact of curriculum mandates, testing, paperwork, and evaluation—all aspects of the reform legislation. Consider some quotations from individual teachers:

> "We teach to the test now, but there are so many things we are leaving out."
> "It seems like we don't care about children anymore."
> "We just want passing scores. . . . The tests make a lot of teachers lie."
> "I am being made into a machine, and my students are being made into machines."

Obviously, a great deal of frustration exists among South Carolina teachers. Is this important? The purpose of public schools is not to provide easy, pleasant employment for teachers. If teacher dissatisfaction reflects normal resistance to change, an unwillingness to work harder, or rejection of accountability, should policymakers be concerned about teachers' feelings? Although South Carolina has made a great deal of progress as a result of its reform movement, is teacher dissatisfaction too high a price to pay? Do negative reactions by teachers and principals mean that reform is not working? Ginsberg and Berry assert that improvements, based on such indicators as test scores, have begun to level off in South Carolina.[79] They posit that the initial momentum of the reform movement may be beginning to decline and suggest that perhaps the teachers' feelings of frustration may

---

[65]See Ginsberg & Berry, "*Experiencing School Reform: The View from South Carolina,*" 71 *Phi Delta Kappan* 549 (1990).

[66]See *id.* at 549 (citing South Carolina State Bd. of Educ., *What Is the Penny Buying for South Carolina?* (1988)).

[67]See *id.* (citing Carnegie Foundation for the Advancement of Teaching, *Report Card on School Reform: The Teachers Speak* (1988)).

[68]*Id.* at 549–50.

[71]See *id.* [*supra* note 65] at 550–51.

[74]*Id.* [*supra* note 65 at 551] (quoting Carnegie Foundation for the Advancement of Teaching, *Report Card on School Reform: The Teachers Speak* 10 (1988)).

[79]See *id.* [*supra* note 65 at 552].

be beginning to take their toll. If this is true—if the reforms in fact become counterproductive—teacher frustration may indeed be too high a price to pay.

By contrast, Professors Timar and Kirp, who analyzed the reform movement in several states, give South Carolina high marks for its approach. They state: "The most important conclusion we can draw from state reform efforts is that a major shift in policy needs to occur. Policymakers must focus their attention on making schools better places in which to work and generally more satisfying places for those who are associated with them."[81]

Judged by this criterion, however, the South Carolina reform effort can hardly be deemed a success. Professors Ginsberg and Berry found that South Carolina teachers are tired, frustrated, and unhappy, and feel that much of the joy of teaching is gone. Teachers complain that the reforms have made schools in South Carolina much more rigid and demanding places in which to work. Consequently, Ginsberg and Berry raise the question: "Can emotionally exhausted teachers and principals provide the energy, wisdom, and spirit needed to continue with the reforms and develop organizationally mature schools?"

If Ginsberg and Berry are correct in their assessment of the atmosphere of South Carolina schools, the reform effort has not established the positive school climate identified by the South Carolina Department of Education as one of the components of effective schools. Consequently, the state may be undermining its own reform efforts by failing to deal with the concerns of teachers and principals.

The South Carolina experience serves as a reminder of the difficulty of achieving improvement by top-down mandates. Policymakers and leaders who impose change cannot ignore the people most vitally affected by reform efforts.

Public Support for Local Control

There appears to be no real possibility that the local school district will disappear completely from the American educational scene within the foreseeable future. It is too entrenched by tradition and too well accepted by American culture. A 1986 study by the Institute for Educational Leadership concluded that strong support exists for maintaining the institutional role and structure of the school board.[86] If schools are to maintain public and political support, however, they must remain responsive at the local level. To achieve this responsiveness, local school boards must continue to serve as effective mechanisms of representative democracy.

Local school districts will remain intact even in Kentucky, where the entire system of common schools was ruled unconstitutional in 1989. As part of the process of restructuring the Kentucky state system of public schools, the governor and legislature appointed a Task Force on Education Reform, consisting of committees to address governance, curriculum, and finance issues. The consultants to the committee on governance presented six preliminary models for the committee's consideration. Among the models proposed were radical departures from present practice, such as adopting a unitary district plan (one school district for the entire state), creating larger operating districts, and combining educational services with other types of human services into districts of "well-being." Ultimately, the committee preferred the "Fine Tuning the Present System" model, which called for only minimal adjustments from the status quo and proposed no changes in the number or classifications of school districts.

The committee did recommend restructuring educational governance at the state level, creating regional service centers, and restricting the power of local school boards. Furthermore, the committee recommended modifications of the process for declaring a district educationally deficient, an action that became necessary in light of the decision in *Whitley County Board of Education v. Brock*.[93] Other committee recommendations addressed perceived problems relating to lack of accountability, undue political influence in personnel decisions, and nepotism. After a brief but spirited debate, the General Assembly adopted all of these recommendations in the Kentucky Education Reform Act of 1990.

In summary, research on effective schools and reform management indicates that leadership is more effective than regulation in achieving improvements in practice. Yet, swept up in the fervor of the reform movement, states have mandated changes from the top down, sometimes with counterproductive results, because they have lost faith in the will or capacity of local districts to improve by themselves without state direction. Nevertheless, local school districts will not

---

[81]Timar & Kirp, *"Education Reform in the 1980s: Lessons from the States,"* 70 *Phi Delta Kappan* 504, 510 (1989).

[86]*See* Inst. for Educ. Leadership, *School Boards: Strengthening Grass Roots Leadership* 10 (1986).

[93]No. 89-CI-0302 (Franklin Cir. Ct., Div. II Jan. 5, 1990).

disappear, because they are too firmly entrenched and too well accepted by American culture.

* * *

3. Local Reform Initiatives. If local control is here to stay, questions arise about how that control should be exercised. Because of dissatisfaction with centralized mandates, some reformers have turned to decentralization as a strategy for improving schools, particularly in urban areas. These initiatives emphasize the importance of returning power to individual schools, both to enhance efficiency and ensure responsiveness to local community needs. Just as there is debate about the utility of centralized mandates, there are also serious concerns about the workability of decentralized decision making.

a. Decentralization and School Reform.

"The Politics of School Restructuring"

T. Timar, *Politics of Education Association Yearbook* 55, 55–60, 71–72 (1989).

A current of the educational reform movement that is attracting increased policy attention is school "restructuring." Theodore Sizer's Coalition of Essential Schools and the "Carnegie Plan," which began as a loose confederation of schools, are moving onto legislative policy agendas. Various states, including Massachusetts, Arkansas, and Washington, as well as school districts such as Dade County, Florida, Rochester, New York, and Santa Fe, New Mexico, have adopted some form of school restructuring as major components of reform. On a national level, the Education Commission of the States, the National Governors' Association, the American Federation of Teachers and the National Education Association are promoting some form of school restructuring among their members. . . .

* * *

Bureaucratic decentralization, which is at the heart of restructuring—whether in the form of school site management, "choice," or some variation on privatization—swims against a thirty-year current of educational policy reform that relied on centralization and regulation to achieve specific policy goals. Indeed, many state-level school reform strategies

adopted since 1983 perpetuate and elaborate the regulatory orientation to school improvement. Teacher and student testing, adoption of state-wide curriculum standards and state-mandated homework, class size, and teacher salary policies are among the most obvious efforts to tighten the reins of local decision makers. Consequently, understanding where the Sizer Coalition and kindred efforts fit into this policy stream is an important issue for school reformers.

* * *

As a school reform strategy, restructuring has its roots in various sources. In large measure, it repudiates central elements in the reform movement of the early 1980s. Without challenging the importance of recent state-initiated reforms, restructuring advocates have reacted to the heavy hand used to effect them. The unprecedented flood of state policies that swept schools in the 1980s aimed at changing them through mandates and regulations. . . .* Critics of these state reform efforts argue that schools as institutions, not students, teachers or curricula must be the target of reform. Tightening curriculum standards, changing teacher certification requirements, or extending the school year, for example, will have negligible effects if schools lack the organizational will and competence to implement them. Furthermore, piecemeal reform policies do not necessarily change the fundamental relationship between teaching and learning. Fundamentally, the critics insist, high quality education is the product of *robust organizational cultures*, not disparate programs. Instead of improving them, state reform strategies relying on regulations and mandates for new programs tended to overwhelm schools with additional baggage or mire them in a regulatory swamp. . . . Historians, like Diane Ravitch, argue that school reform trends and policies of the 1960s and 1970s had—in spite of their social necessity—seriously undermined the institutional competence of schools. . . .**

A further impediment to centralized school reform is the fact that state-level policymakers have a limited repertoire of policy options from which to draw. They can manage macro-policy—funding, teacher certification, textbook adoption, curriculum standards and equity and the like—but have limited control over daily school operations. State policy cannot change what it cannot control. The fact that

---

See T. Timar and D. Kirp, *Managing Educational Excellence* (1988).

**D. Ravitch, *The Troubled Crusade* (1985).

the most significant locus of educational interaction—student/teacher nexus—is largely embedded within the interstices of institutional life poses a fundamental dilemma for state-level policymakers.

Criticism of the first wave of state reform drew its power from the Effective Schools literature . . . and from several critical works on the American High School. . . .* These lines of research were largely ignored by policymakers in their initial haste to reform schools. Effective Schools studies underscored the importance of organizational culture and its attendant manifestations. Teacher collegiality, shared decision-making, common goals and clear priorities were essential to forging the disparate experiences and expectations of teachers, administrators, students and parents into coherent organizational cultures. Broader high school studies, e.g., A Place Called School . . ., Horace's Compromise . . . and The Shopping Mall High School . . ., pointed to normative models for school improvement. But they also showed how far short most schools fell of those models. Reality consisted of schools that were characterized by a rampant lack of direction; intellectual incoherence, blandness and sterility; diffuse authority and accountability; and bureaucratic calcification. Even in schools that appeared to work well, a complex set of treaties between teachers and students tend to circumvent intellectual give-and-take and replace genuine efforts to shape the minds and souls of students.

Nationally, various reform reports, including A Nation Prepared from the Carnegie Forum on Education and the Economy (1986), Time for Results from the National Governors' Association (1986), and Investing in Our Children from the Committee for Economic Development (1985), called for fundamental changes in school structure and organization. The Carnegie Forum responded to the perceived need to attract and retain highly qualified individuals to the teaching profession by encouraging schools to develop innovative organization and management systems aimed at giving teachers greater control over their work environment. The Carnegie Forum underscores the need for restructuring by calling for management systems that provide autonomy and discretion at the school site level and encourage innovative organizational strategies to enhance student learning. . . .

. . . While restructuring is a commonly proposed strategy to fix what ails the schools, intentions differ. Kearns' notion of restructuring is anchored in organizational efficiency. The Carnegie Forum and Albert Shanker regard restructuring as the means to empower teachers and thereby improving school effectiveness. Sizer aims to change the fundamental interaction between teacher and child not only in terms of how teaching occurs, but also in terms of what is taught, changing the whole character and mission of the schools. At the heart of Sizer's call for change is the need to examine the cultural norms and ideas that inform school structure. Structural changes are secondary to the ideas that inform them. . . .

The Coalition of Essential Schools is anchored in a set of common principles that aim to reverse the bureaucratic engine responsible for the incoherence and organizational rigidity of public schools. The Coalition's principles focus attention on some common features of schooling: the school's purpose is to help students use their minds well; learning should focus on student mastery of a limited number of skills and areas of knowledge; the academic and social goals of the school should apply to all students; teaching and learning should be personalized; the student is a worker and the teacher is a coach; diplomas should be awarded on the basis of demonstrated competence, not seat time; the school's norms should emphasize trust, decency, and unanxious expectation; faculties should view themselves as generalists, not specialists; and the budget should permit pupil-teacher ratios of no more than 1:80, while allowing staff salaries to become competitive and total school expenditures not to increase by more than 10%. . . .

Other school reformers, like Goodlad, advocate restructuring as a way of improving working conditions for teachers by encouraging greater professional discretion, providing teachers with opportunities to define and administer school policy through school site management—the devolution of greater authority over curriculum, instructional strategies, and resource allocation to the school level. . . .**

One useful conceptual framework for understanding the bureaucratic organization of schools is Aaron Wildavsky and Mary Douglas' . . . models of four cultures.# Within that framework, contemporary schools

---

*See A. Powell, E. Farrar, and D. Cohen, The Shopping Mall High School: Winners and Losers in the Educational Marketplace (1985); E. Boyer, High School: A Report on Secondary Education in America (1985); T. Sizer, Horace's Compromise: The Dilemma of the American High School (1984).

**Hawley, "Missing Pieces of the Educational Reform Agenda: Or, Why the First and Second Waves May Miss the Boat," 24 Educ. Admin.Q. 416 (1988). See also Metz, "Some Missing Elements in the School Reform Movement," 24 Educ. Admin.Q. 446 (1988).

#Wildavsky, "Choosing Preferences by Constructing Institutions: A Cultural Theory of Preference Formation," 81 Amer.Pol.Sci.Rev. 3 (1987).

can be described as hierarchical cultures which are "strong groups with numerous prescriptions that vary with social roles." The hierarchical culture of schools is clearly evident by the high degree of role differentiation and specialization within them. The duties and responsibilities of principals, assistant principals, counselors, school psychologists and teachers are functionally differentiated; and teachers, particularly in high schools, rarely have contact with one another outside of their immediate areas or departments. Students, curriculum and instruction are similarly sorted and differentiated according to bureaucratic norms, which define the school's order. Students, teachers and administrators are passive subjects whose professional judgment is often subordinated for the sake of bureaucratic convenience.

Clearly, bureaucratic cultures are organizationally incompatible with schools based on the Coalition principles which subordinate bureaucratic norms to organizational competence. The institutional culture consonant with the goals of the Coalition is Wildavsky's competitive-individualist model. The social ideal of individualistic cultures is described as "self-regulation." Such cultures "favor bidding and bargaining to reduce the need for authority." The long term effect of such a culture is to build into the organization a dynamic of change—the expectation that the organization will modify itself to respond flexibly to new problems and new demands. For schools, this means that organizational needs are subordinate to the intellectual and spiritual development of students. It is based upon a system of institutional ordering that places its own competence as its highest priority.

By contrast, hierarchical cultures measure themselves by activities and focus on service delivery. Such cultures measure their success quantitatively. For schools, such measures include the number of hours spent in class, the number of credits completed, and the like. Furthermore, considerable organizational energy is spent on the care and feeding of status and role differentiation. Teachers, administrators, counselors, and coaches, for example, spend a good deal of time protecting their turf. Departments within schools similarly guard against encroachment on their areas of expertise.

An organizational metaphor of competitive-individualism is a baseball team. In order to win games and to be competitive against other teams, a team's manager puts together what he believes will be a winning combination of players; and the manager is free to substitute players throughout the game. While players are assigned functional roles, the manager is free to assign players to those roles as situations warrant. He can choose among pitchers, pinch-hitters, utility outfielders, and relief pitchers, as the need arises. During the game, players cover each other's positions as necessary. Playing (and ultimately winning and losing) is a shared responsibility. Everyone has to hit; sometimes the pitcher has to cover first base or home plate. A baseball team exemplifies a dynamic organizational culture which reconfigures itself to be competitive in new situations. Finally, whether a team has a winning or losing season does not depend upon any one player, but the team as a whole. Individual performance is important; but so is a team's "chemistry." The manager has much to do with that chemistry. He has to train rookies and keep veterans from becoming burned out.

In contrast to a baseball team, bureaucratic schools resemble factories. As in factories, jobs are differentiated and rigidly defined. Production line workers, supervisors, quality control engineers, and the like have separate duties and responsibilities that are clearly specified. Accountability is based on performance of the specified tasks. The person who puts wheels on cars in an automobile assembly line, for example, is not responsible for the installation of the seats. Once a person becomes a foreman, he no longer works on the production line. Once a teacher becomes a principal, she no longer teaches. The point is not to suggest that schools are strict analogues of baseball teams or factories, but to illustrate the polar extremes of two organizational models. Today's schools are more accustomed to norms that evoke factory rather than baseball images.

Creating an organizational model of competitive-individualism is complicated by the fact that schools must change not only their own micro-cultures, but also district and state policy—the macro-culture in which they are embedded. Schools are parts of complex district bureaucracies. A district's organization, like the school's, is hierarchical, with rigidly assigned roles, responsibilities, and accountability. Personnel and budgetary decisions, two critical elements of organizational autonomy, are generally made at the district level. The start and end of the school day are also decided by the district, especially when bus schedules are a factor. And, with the advent of district-wide collective bargaining, schools must live with contractual provisions entered into by district negotiators.

* * *

There is increasing evidence that schools are products of state and district political cultures. . . . An atomized state policy and political culture will reproduce similar policy cultures at local levels. Hence, the integrated response to restructuring at the school level is unlikely to occur in politically balkanized and programmatically fragmented districts and states. Since a school's political culture is derivative, it cannot create coherence in an environment where there is none.

* * *

Contemporary issues of school governance are further complicated by present patterns of control. The emergence of policy spheres and issue politics over the past 20 years signals new configurations of power and control. The delineation of control along political and jurisdictional lines is incomplete. Competing centers of power have stalemated one another. In urban districts, for example, neither the union nor the board controls schools. Instead, groups compete over issues. Unions generally want to control issues like staff development, merit pay, and career ladders. Administrators want to control finance, resource allocation, and personnel decisions. Other groups control special education issues; yet others bilingual, compensatory education, or gifted and talented. Schools, like the fragmented world of public management in the United States generally, have become more balkanized over the past two decades. While state legislative power has grown, it has also become more widely dispersed. Interest groups, particularly single-interest groups, have proliferated while formal patterns of authority have waned. The "iron triangles" of educational politics—schools of education, state education departments, and affiliates of the National Education Association—that prevailed until the mid-1960s have given way to more porous systems. Finding the center of control over schools in order to create a more hospitable policy environment for restructuring is like "nailing Jello to a wall."

Furthermore, the evidence is not systematic, the state policy trend of the early 1980s toward increased regulation and compliance does not appear to be shifting. States continue to embrace student testing, school accreditation, and teacher certification requirements in efforts to regulate and control schools. . . .

This conclusion does not augur well for states that have the Carnegie model (or some variation of it) to encourage school restructuring or for the Coalition of Essential Schools. As more and more decisions formerly left to local discretion become embodied in state policy, the potential for policy proliferation and fragmentation increases. With few exceptions, states have responded to political pressure by "giving a little something to everybody." While such a strategy may have political benefits, it is doubtful whether it can produce good policy. The same factions that contend over policies at the state level have the power to reproduce fractious conflicts at the local level. Consequently, programmatic and procedural responses to restructuring efforts are inevitable.

* * *

Over the past 50 years, the response of schools to external demands has been to multiply programs and regulations. The absence of a broad consensus about the purpose of schooling has created a patchwork of programs to meet various, and often competing, demands. The major threat to restructuring is that it succumbs to that trend. Restructuring must fundamentally alter the way schools do business. That will not happen if it becomes another piece of baggage that schools drag around with them.

* * *

The metaphor of the school as a baseball team evokes an organizational ethos of community of *Gemeinschaft*. It is based on its capacity to achieve unanimity in its goals. Whether its orientation is to produce a winning season or to produce a crop of students who have mastered a set of fundamental skills, its focus of action is organizational competence. Whether restructuring, in its various manifestations, takes root as an effective reform strategy depends on the willingness and capacity of schools to reassess their mission and their strategies for carrying it out. If restructuring is limited to an accumulation of new programs and practices, reform is unlikely. Instead, restructuring will be an exercise in renegotiating existing treaties.

---

b. Urban Schools and Community Control. One example of this type of renegotiation of power relations was the community control movement that arose in the late 1960s. Although there were many variations, the basic idea was to subdivide large urban districts into smaller districts, with lay community-based school boards that possessed the authority to make personnel, budgetary, and other decisions. This movement was quite controversial and often met with resistance from school teachers and administrators. The most famous confrontation arose when New York City experimented with community-controlled districts in Brooklyn and Harlem using funding from the Ford Foundation. The New York schools had been widely criticized for their bureaucratic red tape, inertia, and inefficiency. *See generally* D. Rogers, *110 Livingston Street* (1968). Ultimately the New York City schools were decentralized over the vigorous objections of teachers and administrators. *See* F. Wirt and M. Kirst, *Political and Social Foundations of Education* 87–92 (1975); M. Zimet, *Decentralization and School Effectiveness* (1973); M. Fantini, M. Gittell, and R. Magat, *Community Control and the Urban School* (1970); H. Levin, ed., *Community Control of Schools* (1970); M. Berube and M. Gittell, *Confrontation at Ocean Hill-Brownsville* (1969).

For more than fifteen years after the adoption of community control in New York City, little attention was paid to the question by policymakers—albeit some scholars continued to advance such proposals. *See, e.g.*, S. Lightfoot, *Worlds Apart: Relationships Between Families and Schools* (1978); Bell, "Book Review," 92 *Harv.L.Rev.* 1826 (1979); Bell, "Wait-ing on the Promise of Brown," 39 *Law & Contemp.Probs.* 341 (1978). However, the impact of decentralization on school performance remained uncertain and contested. *See, e.g.*, Fainstein and Fainstein, "The Future of Community Control," 70 *Am.Pol.Sci.Rev.* 905 (1976); Cohen, "The Price of Community Control," 48 *Commentary* 23 (July 1969). Despite limited evidence of success, community control appeared on the agenda in a number of large cities, including Los Angeles and Chicago, in the 1980s. The Chicago school reform legislation was enacted in July 1988. The product of a contentious political process, the law was designed to empower parents by giving Local School Councils (LSCs) increased authority over hiring, the development of annual budgets and school improvement plans (SIPs), and school policies and programs affecting students and instruction. At the same time, and perhaps somewhat inconsistently, the legislation sought to convert principals into chief executives who were entrepreneurial, educational leaders. Principals had to demonstrate these qualities while subject to four-year performance reviews. At the same time that the roles for parents and principals were expanded, the autonomy of teachers was undercut as they lost district-wide protections and faced removal from the classroom by LSCs and the principals who answered to them. Wong and Rollow, "A Case Study of the Recent Chicago School Reform," (pts. 1 and 2) 34 *Administrator's Notebook* 5 (1990); G. Hess, *Restructur-*

ing Urban Schools: A Chicago Perspective 37–46 (1995). The school restructuring plan created dangers of conflict as well as the promise of cooperation. Here is what happened at some reform-minded Chicago elementary schools in the wake of the legislation.

"Charting Chicago School Reform: Democratic Localism as a Lever for Change"

* * *

An Active and Supportive Local School Council

The passage of PA 85-1418 was widely heralded as a radical plan of parent and community empowerment over local schools. Some critics . . . worried about the likely chaos and confusion that would ensue as uneducated parents, many of whom had been victimized by this very system, would now take control. They feared what might happen when parents and community members started telling the professionals what to do.

For the most part, these concerns proved unfounded. . . . [M]ost LSCs did not become the adversarial local community boards of education that some had envisioned. To the contrary, principals, teachers, and LSC and PPAC [Professional Personnel Advisory Committee] chairs generally reported that the LSC was a positive addition to their school community.

For many this was a surprise. This sentiment was well captured by a teacher we interviewed at Hefferan:

> I am so impressed with this LSC . . . because I had heard all the rumors about "these parents." "These parents" don't know anything. They don't have any educational background. They can't . . . not here. This is one of the most impressive LSCs that I have seen in the city.

Even though Hefferan is a very disadvantaged school in a very poor neighborhood, this teacher went on to note that there was some expertise in the parents and local community which the first LSC was able to draw upon:

> Experience and expertise is definitely here. One LSC member is a vice president of a local corporation, another is a manager for Rush Presbyterian-St. Luke's

Hospital, and another works in the criminal court system. So you see people with a strong business and educational background within the Local School Council.... What I also like about the LSC is that their total attention is on what is best for the children. They don't have a lot of hidden agendas to promote themselves or maybe get a job for a relative. Instead it is what is best for the children at Hefferan.

Selecting a School Leader

The single most important responsibility exercised by an LSC was its evaluation of the school principal and decision to award (or not award) a four-year performance contract. In each of the six EARS schools [schools chosen for the study because of their strong commitment to implementing the reforms], the LSC endorsed a person committed to the students and parents in their particular community. At one school, Bass, this meant retaining a principal who had already initiated significant improvement efforts prior to reform. In a second, Ebinger, it meant holding onto a relatively new principal who had started a lot very quickly. At Hoyne, the principalship was vacant, and the LSC set out with deliberateness to fill this position. At Field, Hefferan, and Spry, the LSC went through a process that eventually denied a contract to the original principal and chose a new person instead. In 1990, Field, like Spry, was among the most conflictual school communities in the city. Our observations, three years later, offer testimony to how new leadership can help to move a school beyond adversarial politics and catalyze major organizational change in a very short period of time.

Although we do not know all of the details of these principal selection processes, since they occurred two or three years prior to our inquiry, we can distinguish some general features. Of perhaps most significance, at least some council members in each EARS school had expertise to bring to this critical task. In the more advantaged schools, such as Hoyne and Ebinger, parents and community members on the LSC brought considerable professional expertise from their own work. In some of the more disadvantaged schools, the teacher representatives played a particularly important role. At both Spry and Field, for example, the faculty members on the LSC helped to organize council opposition to the pre-reform principal. They joined with parents and community members who were also actively seeking advice from a variety of sources

(including citywide advocacy groups, community-based organizations, staff from the Chicago Board of Education, and local colleges and universities). Some of these parent and community members brought relevant experiences with community organizing and political campaigning to the process. Thus, in contrast to schools with consolidated principal power, there was a broad base of human resources in these councils.

Even so, the task of evaluating principals appeared daunting and frightening. No one had ever done this before, and there was not much official guidance on how councils should go about the process. As one teacher representative on an LSC stated:

> When I became a council member, I had never been in another school. So it was difficult to compare how things were here.... When reform started, we became exposed to other people in other schools [through a program at Roosevelt University] and began to learn about these wonderful things and exciting innovations and couldn't understand why we weren't doing that. The level of enthusiasm and motivation that we saw in our instructors [who were CPS principals]; we just knew something wasn't right here. I felt our students deserved the best we could possibly give them.... In January and February of '90 there was a lot of fear, and the terrible thing about fear is that it stretches the truth and people were afraid of change.... I think a lot of people couldn't believe that parents and teachers could possibly know what to do.

In spite of these fears, these LSCs were able to work through the process. Although the final decision was not always unanimous, the councils were able to move on. For example, at Spry one former LSC member noted:

> We had certain members who wanted to keep the principal. That was OK. We weren't alienating them. We respected their opinions and we just tried to figure out how we're going through this journey together. In the end, even the members that had voted to keep him after a couple of months realized that we had made the right decision.

Thus, even in the cases where the decision-making process was conflictual, councils were able to maintain a focus on "making the school a better place for kids." This stands in sharp contrast to LSCs, . . . where sustained adversarial politics played out among local community interests and individual personalities. Although participants argued vehemently at times, a base of social support for school change was maintained in EARS schools.

The LSC-Principal Dynamic

Once a principal was selected (or retained, as at Bass and Ebinger), the LSCs saw their primary role as supporting their new leaders. They entrusted these principals to help them realize their collective aspirations for their schools. These principals, in turn, enjoyed a mandate to promote change. Good, close working relations characterized this dynamic. EARS principals were quite active at their council meetings, often sharing power with LSC chairs. Frequent informal communication, especially between the principal and LSC chair, was the norm outside of meetings.

Strong LSC support for school staff to promote change is evident throughout our field interviews. Nelda Hobbs put it this way:

> Many things that have gone on [in the past here] with good intention have been misinterpreted by people in the community. But now the LSC trusts me, and they come and we talk. They understand what we are trying to do. So now they have become my "soldiers." Instead of me having to dispel rumors, they go and dispel them, and that makes a big difference. . . . We have a great working relationship . . . we work as a family.

And a Field LSC member agreed:

> There isn't a week that goes by that [the principal] doesn't grab me in the hallway and tell me, "This problematic event has occurred. What am I going to do?" We just say, "You do what you have to do! And we will approve whatever you need!" The LSC has backed her entirely. We believe in what she is doing.

We heard similar comments at other schools. For example, an LSC member at Bass said:

> See, my job [as LSC member] stops at Mrs. Gillie's [the principal]. I say, "Mrs. Gillie, what do you think we are doing wrong? What do you think we are doing right? What do you think we need to help the children with? What can we do? What do the teachers say about this?" This is the kind of thing that we [the LSC] talk about. We will talk to the kids, and they know we are involved. The teachers know that they are not out there by themselves . . . We hope there aren't many fences [between people]. We want to get close to each other, the kind of closeness that ensures integrity within our school environment.

Likewise at Hoyne, an LSC member commented:

> Our efforts here are certainly to bring more parents into the process . . . extending the school home relationship and linking them because teachers can only do so much. Once that child leaves the classroom and goes home, teachers have no control. . . . Our role is certainly one of support here. As you know, the principal is always

the point person in terms of where ideas are coming from. When these proposals are brought to the table, we always look at them carefully and give them serious thought. . . . The point is to keep the morale of teachers high. When they have to worry, those feelings can be reflected in the classroom and ultimately in the student. So we always want to keep our teaching staff happy.

Much of the responsibility for the functioning of the LSC devolved to the principal, who saw this as a new part of his or her job. While these principals valued the strengthened ties to parents and community and appreciated the personal support of council members, working with an LSC was a major new undertaking for which they had received no formal preparation prior to the onset of reform. Among other things, this meant a major increase in principals' work load. The initiating activities—getting a council organized, developing bylaws, making sure they understood their basic responsibilities and functioned effectively as a group—were especially daunting. In reminiscing about the early days of reform, Nelda Hobbs said:

> It is another layer of responsibility. . . . This whole legislation is a bit complicated for the average person who is really trying to do it by the law. I just know what I have—a commitment to kids, and I know where I am trying to go with the kids, and I figure that if I am doing that I'm not going to break the law, knowingly. I don't think you can expect anyone to do all of that stuff on their own.

In general, LSCs have neither a budget nor a staff. As a result, most councils remain dependent on their principals for support and guidance. Since EARS principals saw their councils as valuable new local resources providing service to their schools, keeping councils vital was an important added dimension to their work.

Focus of LSC Initiatives

LSCs in the EARS sites took active roles in efforts to improve parent and community involvement in the schools, to encourage parents to support children's learning at home, to enhance and maintain the physical plants, and to improve order and safety both inside and outside of schools. For example, at Bass school, an LSC member talked about her work in the community:

> I work out in the community a lot. We try to make ourselves available for those parents that view the school as the power structure and unapproachable. So as we walk down the street, we have become the persons who are approachable. They can talk to us. . . . There are a lot of ways that we can get the message across that this is a place where you need to be.

Similarly, a parent LSC member at Spry told us:

> We have a safety committee. We work with the police department. The police send different people here [to Spry school] to work with us on different problems in the community and then they come back the next month to report on what they did on those problems. . . . [We tell them], "they are selling drugs in this house" and the police come back to tell us what they have done about it. And we work with the Boys and Girls Club. The Club donated the property; so we put up the playground for the school next door, and we work with St. Ludmilla's [the nearby Catholic Church].

Such institutional collaboration at the community level is an important consequence of Chicago's reform that can make a significant difference in the quality of students' lives. For example, a parent at Spry told us:

> [Gang members] really scared the children because they used to just go around doing things to people. But my son has not been bothered anymore. I consider this school a real safe haven, because they don't put up with this stuff now. If something happens, they take care of it, even if it is on a holiday or weekend. A child's coat was stolen out on the playground on a weekend. [Someone at the school] recognized the boy and they called the police and they got the boy's coat back.

Similarly at Hefferan, an LSC member spoke about how they provided security for the children:

> We [the LSC members and other parents] are here in the morning. We watch the people coming in. We watch the children being dismissed in the afternoon. What is so important is that our [adult] male population is a part of this. The[y] don't stand up with their hands crossed upon their chest. They are out talking to children, directing them, offering them suggestions, what did you do and so forth, so that they can model while they monitor the building. I think this is the essence of what should happen in education. . . . They are out here and they don't have badges on or anything. They are just with the children, walking the playground, looking to see.

In general, LSCs have heightened the attention of school staff and other community professionals to local needs. On some occasions, such as the collaboration between Spry and the neighborhood Boys Club to create a playground, LSCs have found creative and efficient solutions to local needs. With both fiscal resources and authority to act, the LSC solved this problem on their own. Putting this in perspective, it is hard to imagine how the Chicago Board of Education could have worked out such a cost-effective resolution.

In fact, LSCs can lead to a real expansion of resources for children. As an LSC member at Hefferan commented, for example:

> [We are] really looking at identifying people who can help us to obtain resources beyond what comes through government money and the Board of Ed. So if we want to do something special for children, we still have opportunities to do that because we will write proposals, we will seek outside resources, we will go and speak on behalf of what is going on here. Anytime, anyplace.

Professional Initiative for Instructional Improvement

Shifting our focus to specific school activities aimed at instructional improvement, we found, not surprisingly, that it was the principal and teacher leaders who created these initiatives rather than the LSC. The comments of the Hoyne LSC members, offered earlier, certainly reflected this. Similarly, an LSC member at Ebinger noted: "The development here has been largely principal-driven as opposed to being LSC driven." It is noteworthy that these comments came from the two most advantaged schools in the EARS sample. The reliance on the judgments of local professionals is even stronger in the more disadvantaged sites. For example, an LSC member at Hefferan commented:

> We have confidence in our educational leader. I don't think any of us at any time have questioned Pat Harvey's [the principal] decisions. We understood very early on that our first goal is to support our educational leader. . . . We look to our principal to make those decisions and to keep us informed about what is going on. We trust her judgment. . . . All of the teachers are respected, and the school staff too. That includes the people who work in the lunchroom and the engineers. We try to make everyone feel important. Everybody contributes to the education of children.

To be sure, there were many conversations in the LSC about the need for instructional improvement. And these were real discussions; the LSC was not just a puppet being controlled by the principal or teacher leaders. Rather, professional staff actively discussed with parents and community members their concerns in these areas, and really worked at building a common understanding about the school's needs. For example, the principal at Ebinger linked each LSC member with a particular class for a whole day in order to give them a better sense of the teachers' work:

They started out on the playground, brought the children into class, did the lunch count, did attendance, and started class. They were in each class for 40 minutes. The council was learning about what teachers had to go through. That it is not just "open up a book and discuss world events." It is dealing with wet pants and scraped knees. A child's not here, and somebody is crying, and it's a lot of other things besides learning. They [LSC members] are less apt to just say now "Well we need the best books, and we need this or that program." They are more likely now to pay attention to what is in place here and what we are trying to do.

In short, while the direction for instructional improvements typically started with the professional staff, considerable effort focused on keeping parents and community members involved.

Our Analysis

The councils in EARS schools were vital institutions. They each played a central role in catalyzing the organizational change efforts underway at their school. They selected principals to lead them, and then they supported these individuals as they challenged the status quo and began moving their schools forward. The LSCs were an important context for ongoing discussions about the improvement of the school community. They helped out wherever they could, but they certainly did not "tell the professionals what to do." With only three school staff members out of eleven on each LSC, this result was especially noteworthy.

In most general terms, an effective partnership emerged within these actively restructuring schools among local professionals, parents, and the community. At base here is a subtle blending of individual respect and mutual trust. This key social dynamic, which is a significant problem in many urban schools, had been transformed into a resource with positive impacts on students and teachers alike. With parents backing the efforts of the school staff, a more consistent and supportive learning environment resulted for students. Similarly, with professionals taking an interest in the needs and concerns of parents, they were more likely to receive support back. This in turn helps teachers feel (and be) more efficacious in their work. In the context of the longstanding, widespread distrust and hostility between parents and local professionals prior to reform in Chicago, this was a remarkable turn of events.

* * *

Despite some success in schools committed to reform, the momentous changes in educational governance in Chicago did not last long. As Professor David Kirp has noted, "What happened in Chicago was hailed by historian Michael Katz as 'the most radical structural reform of an American urban school system since the mid-19th century.' But it also turned out to be among the most short-lived structural reforms." Kirp, "Book Review," 107 *Am.J.Educ.* 178 (1999). In 1995, only seven years after the experiment with Chicago school decentralization had begun, the Illinois legislature passed the Chicago School Reform Amendatory Act, Ill.Rev.Stat., ch. 105, art. 34 (2000). This Act recentralized authority in the mayor, although the LSCs continued to wield considerable influence. The legislation was a response to concerns about fiscal mismanagement and low academic performance in the Chicago schools.

"Transforming Urban School Systems: Integrated Governance in Chicago and Birmingham (UK)"

K. Wong, *Report for a Working Conference on School Reform in Chicago and Birmingham,* University of Chicago Gleacher Center, May 11–12, 1998.

* * *

Reducing Institutional and Policy Fragmentation

While the 1995 legislation left intact some features of the previous arrangements, it reduced competing institutional authority and recentralized administrative authority. The law decreased the size of the fifteen member board [i.e., Board of Education] to five and put the mayor in charge of appointing board members, the board president, and the Chief Executive Officer [CEO] in charge of the schools. Since the board appoints the top administrative officers, these changes facilitate an effective link between the mayor's office and the central office. Under this arrangement, education becomes a part of the mayor's policy agenda and gives the mayor the option to decide the amount of political capital he is willing to invest in improving the schools.

The new administration acted swiftly to demonstrate a commitment to efficient management by adopting a business management model. . . .

By strengthening the centralized authority of the school system, the 1995 legislation shifted the balance of power between the central office and the Local School Councils [LSCs]. Prior to 1995, the central office competed with the Local School

Councils for authority over the educational agenda. The LSCs had broad authority, but there was little direct accountability or oversight. For example, state Chapter 1 funds went directly to the schools, but the board remained accountable if the money was misused. Selection of principals by the LSC was often influenced by the constituencies of the particular neighborhood.

The new administration has signaled that LSCs can no longer operate with complete independence and have incorporated the LSCs into the overall system by defining standards and responsibilities they must adhere to. This policy establishes fifteen criteria covering the actions of the principal, staff, local school council, and local school council members. Under the new board policy, the board declared that an "educational crisis" existed at Prosser Preparatory Center and Nathan Hale School. At each school, the board disbanded the LSC. The LSC at Prosser was declared nonfunctional in part because of its failure to approve the School Improvement Plan or evaluate the principal. At Hale, the LSC was suspended after LSC members were found to have intruded in the day-to-day operations of the school, entered classrooms unannounced and uninvited, and failed "to follow the law regarding their powers and responsibilities," among other violations. The board has also requested that the state legislature tighten guidelines on the use of Chapter 1 funds currently controlled by LSCs. This request stems from a controversy in which LSC members at Roberto Clemente High School allegedly used Chapter 1 funds to send parents to Puerto Rico and to support the Puerto Rican independence movement. After a preliminary investigation, the board found the politicized climate at Clemente to be counterproductive to student learning and appointed a new principal without the LSC's consent. A special legislative committee and the Cook County State's Attorney are currently investigating the use of Chapter 1 funds by Clemente's LSC.

Improving Financial Management and Upgrading the Physical Infrastructure

The 1995 governance redesign enhanced the ability of the central administration to perform financial and management functions efficiently. The 1995 law suspended the budget oversight authority of the SFA, removed the balanced budget requirement, and placed the Inspector General under the authority of the board. In addition, the board was granted new authorities that expanded their financial powers. A number of funded programs (for example, K–6 reading improvement, Substance Abuse Prevention, Hispanic Programs, Gifted Education, among others) and categorical funds were collapsed into a general education block grant and an educational services block grant, respectively. Although total revenues available to the board declined by 8% in FY 1996 from the previous year, revenues going into the General Funds increased by about 2% (or $28.5 million). Additionally, the board acquired greater flexibility over the use of pension funds and Chapter 1 funds not allocated to the schools. Finally, there were no longer separate tax levies earmarked for specific purposes.

These changes increased board discretion over school revenues, allowing the board to prepare a four year balanced budget and negotiate a four year contract, including a raise, with the Chicago Teachers Union. The four year teachers' contract brought both financial and labor stability to the system. Indeed, by March 1996, Standard and Poor's raised the CPS bond rating from a BBB- to BBB, and Moody's from a Ba to Baa, allowing the board to issue bonds for the construction of new buildings under lower interest rates than before. By the summer of 1997 the CPS bond ratings were A minus from Standard and Poor's and Baa 1 from Moody's.

Enjoying its much improved standing in the bond market, the Chicago Public Schools launched a major capital improvement campaign for the first time in decades. . . .

Pressuring and Supporting Low Performing Schools

The 1995 law incorporated a focus on accountability and academic achievement that compelled the administration to target the lowest performing schools within the system for intervention. Declaring that an "educational crisis" existed in Chicago, the 1995 legislation directed the Board of Trustees and the CEO to increase the quality of educational services within the system. It enhanced the powers of the CEO to identify poorly performing schools and place these schools on remediation, probation, intervention, or reconstitution. Prior to 1995, the subdistrict superintendent, not the school board, had the primary responsibility to monitor the performance of the schools and identify non-performing schools. In the past, to place a school on remediation or probation required the approval of the subdistrict council, which was made up of parent or community members from each Local School Council within the subdistrict.

With the new legislation, the board and central office focused on the lowest performing schools within the system. In January 1996, the CEO placed twenty-one schools on remediation for failing to meet state standards on the Illinois Goals Assessment Program (IGAP), for three consecutive years. Only six schools were placed on remediation by the previous administration. At the same time, the board removed two elementary school principals because the schools failed to improve after a year on remediation. In September 1996, the CEO placed 20% of the district's schools on probation.

Probation

In 1996, the district placed 109 of the 550 Chicago Public Schools on academic probation because 15% or less of their students scored at grade level on nationally normed tests. These schools are being held accountable to their School Improvement Plans as well as to improvements in test scores. Since this initiative began, nine schools have been removed from the list, 15 have been added, and seven have been reconstituted. In addition, 36 principals have been removed.

* * *

While the district holds the probation schools accountable for improving student performance on standardized tests, it also provides several types of support. Each school must select from a list of board-approved external partners. The external partners are teams of support personnel from local universities and national reform groups who are charged with improving instruction in probation schools. The district paid for the external partners in full the first year of probation. Schools are expected to pick up one quarter of the cost each year of probation. The district also provides schools with probation managers who oversee the school improvement plan and assist the principal in all areas of school operations. Finally, the district provides the schools with business managers to oversee the school budget and financial operations. All of these supports are intended to enable the principal to become an effective instructional leader.

Our preliminary analysis of the probation policy in our case study high schools suggests that the policy has created new incentives for schools to examine how they allocate resources, in particular, time,

teachers and students. Schools have responded to probation by devoting more class time to test-practice. In addition, schools have altered the ways in which they assign teachers to classrooms. Our detailed comparative case studies of four high schools indicates that the schools under probation tend to assign the most experienced teachers with the best reputations to students who are testing close to the national norms. Some schools have developed new basic skills math and reading scores to assist low-performing students.

Reconstitution

Seven schools have been reconstituted based on continual low performance of students' test scores (none of the reconstituted schools had more than 7% of their students reading at or above grade level according to test scores). Five of the seven schools had their principals replaced, and 188 of 675 teachers, or 29%, were not rehired. These schools will have to improve their test scores or risk being shut down.

* * *

The seven reconstituted schools are located in the most racially and economically isolated wards of the city. The mobility rates reflect conditions of extreme poverty. . . . [S]upport as well as pressure is needed to assist both the schools which operate in these conditions and the young people they serve. Pressure alone will not be sufficient given the severe challenges both face. Our case studies suggest that principals and teachers in reconstituted schools feel enormous amounts of pressure to increase test scores. This has led to an increasing standardization of instruction and even more attention being paid to test-taking practice and drill than in probation schools. A reconstituted school in our study has informally tracked students in order to provide those students near the national average access to [a] more effective learning environment. The school has also been affected by the district's academic promotion policy. Due to the failure of eighth graders from the feeder schools to score at the district benchmark on the Iowa Test of Basic Skills (ITBS), ninth grade enrollment dropped significantly. Because of this drop, the percentage of special education students in ninth grade classrooms has increased. To date, teachers feel that they have been provided inadequate support to deal with this situation. This suggests the need to examine how student promotion policies interact with school accountability policies, and to consider ways to link elementary and secondary schools together more effectively.

Reorganizing the Office of Accountability to Support Schools

The board and top administration reorganized the central office to reflect the focus on accountability and established the improvement of standardized test scores as the primary objective of the system. While other departments within the central office were eliminated or significantly downsized, the administration created the Office of Accountability, which has grown from a staff of fifty in September 1995 to almost eighty in this year. This office monitors the performance of the schools, and identifies and intervenes in low performing schools. One administrator said that the mission of the department is "to fix schools . . . so they won't fall below a safety net."

The Office of Accountability not only pressures schools to improve but it also provides professional support. . . .

Few principals and teachers in our case study schools on probation and reconstitution report satisfaction with the contracted external partners the board financed. Teachers feel that the external partners, which the district requires schools on probation to hire, offer little meaningful assistance. Teachers resent planning time being controlled by the external partners and resist attempts by the external partners to evaluate instruction. Teachers in one school actually locked their doors to prevent the external partners from entering. Similarly, principals feel that the external partners lack a focused plan for school improvement, particularly in the area of instruction. While many principals report satisfaction with the probation managers, they feel that the external partners have not been cost effective. Overall, the variation in terms of support provided to schools by external partners poses a serious challenge to the district. The district has delegated responsibility for improving teaching and learning in low-performing schools to external partners. Our case studies suggest that the district needs to monitor the quality of the services provided by the external partners more closely and to consider whether or not these contracted services could be provided by district personnel . . ., thereby building the district's instructional support capacity for long term improvement.

Pressuring and Supporting Low-Performing Students

The End of Social Promotion

In an expanded program from the summer of 1996, third-, sixth-, eighth-, and ninth-grade students who did not meet set levels on one of two nationally normed tests (the Iowa Test of Basic Skills or the Test of Achievement and Proficiency) were required to participate in a system-sponsored summer school called the Summer Bridge Program during 1997. The pressure is particularly great for the eighth graders as those who failed the spring tests cannot attend graduation ceremonies. In 1997, 22% of the eighth graders failed to meet the cutoff point in spring and were placed in Summer Bridge. Sixty-two percent of eighth-graders who participated in the program met the promotion requirements after the seven weeks. In other words, by the end of the summer, 92% of the 27,800 eighth-graders had met the school system's new promotion standards. The district provided teachers in the program with day-by-day lesson plans. Students were promoted to the next grade if they brought their scores to the established cut-off point. If they did not, they were required to repeat their grade. Repeating students returned to their original schools, unless they were older eighth-graders. Half of the repeating eighth-graders (about 4% of the total cohort), who will be fifteen by December 1st, are attending one of thirteen transition centers which feature a basic skills curriculum.

Seeing the Summer Bridge as providing an opportunity for social and academic development for many inner-city children, the school board decided to expand it to the first and second grades beginning in the summer of 1998. From a broader institutional perspective, the expanded Summer Bridge for students across six different grade levels constitutes only a part of the district's overall summer initiatives that involve the Chicago Public Library, the Chicago Park District, and the Mayor's Office of Employment and Training. The system is expected to spend a total of $65 million to provide a variety of learning, social, and job experience to 175,000 children, or about 40% of the CPS enrollment, this summer. As Mayor Daley envisions the longer term impacts of these collaborative programs, "By providing safe and productive ways for our young people to spend their summer vacation, we help keep them away from the dangerous influences of gangs, guns and drugs."

Political Will and a Broadened Base of Political Support

The link between the mayor's office and the board can facilitate political support for the school system. With the redesign of the governance system, Mayor Richard Daley has been more willing to invest his political capital in the Chicago schools. To restore public confidence, the new administration has projected an image of efficient, responsive, and "clean" government. The administration has also taken a number of steps to strengthen the support of the business community for the public schools. This support becomes crucial when appealing to the Illinois legislature because the business community can lobby in favor of the board's legislative agenda, thereby lending the board credibility.

* * *

An Ambitious Agenda for Systemwide Restructuring

As integrated governance operates at the end of its third year, the CEO and the school board has broadened the reform agenda. Designed to improve the quality of schools throughout the system, these new initiatives include the following:

- The system has designed and disseminated their own standards (Chicago Academic Standards) in the areas of English Language Arts, mathematics, biological and physical sciences, and social sciences. Benchmark exams for selected cut-off grades are being developed and piloted this June. These standards and assessments may mark a new phase of outcome-based accountability in the district. Results of the district exams may provide additional information concerning probation and reconstitution. Thus, while these standards and assessments may provide an educational vision by which to guide teaching and learning district wide, they may also serve as a tool by which to develop further sanctions on low-performing students and schools.
- All high schools have established Junior Academies for 9th and 10th graders and are moving towards creating Senior Academies for all 11th and 12th graders. The academy structure creates teams of teachers who are responsible for a group of students over the course of their high school careers. Teachers move through the grades with their students.
- The structure is intended to provide students with academic and personal support as well as providing for teacher collaboration. Teachers are expected to participate in professional development that is supportive and consistent with their school's action plan.
- Local School Council elections were held on report-card-pickup days in order to improve parental participation. Between 1988 and 1993, voter turnout for these elections declined by 68%. This is consistent with a sharp decline in the number of people seeking LSC seats. In 1989, over 17,000 candidates ran for LSC seats. In 1991, that number declined to 8,398 and by 1996, only 7,288 candidates ran. This year 84 schools, or slightly more than 15% of the system, slated fewer than the six parents needed. Clearly, attracting widespread parental support and involvement in the LSCs remains a challenge.

Under integrated governance, the Chicago Public Schools has undertaken an impressive effort to improve the operations of the system and the performance of its schools and students. The district administration has brought financial stability to the system, and in conjunction with the mayor, has regained public and political confidence in the schools. While the administration has addressed a number of functions, including teacher recruitment, principal standards, and facilities improvement, its most visible efforts have been those policies which place pressure on poorly performing schools and students. Probation and reconstitution have served as wake-up calls for schools, teachers and students alike. Yet, without adequate technical support such policies will not insure improvement. The district has yet to develop an instructional and organizational model which provides schools and teachers with a vision to guide their improvement efforts. The new curricular frameworks and exams the district has begun to implement may provide the base for such a vision. The district has made tremendous strides in several key areas. The challenge of developing an educational vision which provides the support as well as pressure for improved performance lays ahead.

NOTES AND QUESTIONS

1. The Lessons of the Chicago Experiment

Does the Chicago experiment with community control suggest that this strategy is doomed to fail because some degree of centralized administration is necessary? Is Chicago's experience unique because of the troubled nature of many of its schools? Did community control lead to problems because the legislature responded to political pressures rather than pedagogical imperatives? How was the original reform effort affected by the attempt to merge community control with business efficiency?

2. Community Control and Social Capital

In his book *Bowling Alone*, Robert D. Putnam argues that social capital contributes to students' academic success. R. Putnam, *Bowling Alone* 296–306 (2000). He defines social capital as the value that arises from social networks. In his view, parental and community involvement in schools can contribute to a positive learning environment, and this involvement may be especially critical in poor, urban districts in which social cohesion has markedly deteriorated. How can the checkered history of community control and decentralization initiatives be squared with Putnam's account?

III. THE BALANCE OF POWER: ELECTED OFFICIALS, CAREER PROFESSIONALS, AND COURTS

Just as educational authority is allocated among federal, state, and local government, it is also shared by elected officials, teachers and administrators, and judges. This separation of powers is designed to prevent overreaching by any one policymaking authority. That is, each branch of government serves as a check on excesses by the other branches. This method of curbing official abuses of power does have a price: It can lead to conflict and uncertainty in a fragmented educational policymaking process.

A. Ballots and Board Elections

One way that citizens exercise control over the schools is through the electoral process. The use of popular elections to hold school officials accountable is in tension with images of the schools as nonpartisan institutions that should transcend politics to offer universal access and equity. Moreover, letting voters decide educational matters undercuts the claim that teachers and administrators should control the operation of the schools in light of their expertise and professionalism. Because of these value conflicts, local school board elections are often structured in ways that defeat the participatory goals of the democratic process.

"Schools in Conflict"

From Frederick M. Wirt and Michael Kirst, Schools in Conflict: The Politics of Education. Copyright 1989 by McCutran Publishing Corporation, Richmond, California, 94806. Used by permission of the publisher.

Popular participation in school policymaking has traditionally taken two forms—election of officials and referendums on issues. . . . *Local* school elections operate independently of political parties. Contrary to popular impression, political parties at the *national* level have sought unsuccessfully to serve as a link between citizens and school policy. For almost a century of national party platforms, education has been among "the predominant forces in operation during election years."

Yet schools have not escaped citizen control by avoiding the clutches of national parties, for direct and indirect popular control still exists. Directly, there is the widespread practice of electing school boards at the local level and boards and superintendents at the state level. Indirectly, control exists in the election of state legislators, executives, and judges, whose broad responsibilities include authority over many aspects of public education. . . .

* * *

. . . Eighty-five percent of local school boards in this country are elective. . . . We know that these officials, five to seven on a board, almost always seek their three- or four-year terms on a nonpartisan ballot. We also know that the board appoints a superintendent, usually professionally trained, who operates under its general policy guides and who may also be removed by it. The exception to this pattern is the appointment method often used in our biggest cities. In the usual community, the theory of democratic control makes the board member a pivot between community demands and school operations. . . .

* * *

School board elections have little voter turnout, even less than that for other government offices. The reasons for this are not clear. Is it because of the nonpartisan myth of school politics or because school board elections are held in off years and at primary dates when turnout is low for all contests? . . . It is clear, though, that campaigning in school contests is limited, candidate visibility low, and the contest rarely based on specific policies. . . .

* * *

When the Progressive reforms of nonpartisanship in school matters finally settled into place across the nation, the large working-class membership had almost disappeared from school boards, and white middle-class members dominated everywhere. Moreover, most of these members were male, married with children in the public schools, and active in the community. From the landmark study by Counts in 1924[#] to a replication by the National School Boards Association almost fifty years later, all the research substantiates this finding. A test of the link between representation and the possession of resources appears with blacks. Their representation on 168 big-city boards was smaller than their resources (i.e., numbers, money, organization); at-large systems effectively widened the gap between resources and board seats.

High social status alone does not give entry to the school board, but community activity—whether civic, business, political, or educational—joined with high social status provides training for office that few of the well-off actually use. . . .

* * *

Time and again what emerges from studies of board elections is that they are little-used channels to the political system. Like arroyos in the Southwest, only rarely does intense turmoil surge through these channels. Certain occasions can, however, have the effect of flash floods through desert courses—enormous conflict followed by altered features in the immediate environment. Much more often, however, these election campaigns offer only slight variations in ideology or policy orientation. And, as noted earlier, the structure of voting, dominated by nonpartisanship, depresses turnout. These conditions make the democratic model of informed choice between significant policy options by a sizable electorate more a pleasant fiction than a hard fact. . . .

* * *

In short, political scientists have found that what applies to nonpartisanship in other aspects of the local political scene holds true for school politics. Such reforms increase the cost of citizen participation, make the bridge between representative and citizen more tenuous, and consequently muffle expression of the full range of political interests within a community. Those constrained citizens tend to be of lower socioeconomic status, so governing structures are not value free. Rather, these reforms actually encourage the access and satisfaction of another group, middle-class and higher-status people. The rhetoric of Progressivism proclaimed the expansion of democracy—"the cure for

the evils of democracy is more democracy" was their standard. The reality has been otherwise, deflecting those who cannot use the cue of political party to decide among complicated public issues, including those of schooling. Such reforms ensure that—until recently at any rate—the game of school politics was played by few, and mostly by those whom fortune favored.

* * *

. . . School boards are faced with extramural pressures they cannot control that determine what they can do. Thus, changes in the shape of the national economy—a time of boom or a bust—can drastically affect the local school budget. The oil crisis after 1973 seriously redirected school budgets away from strictly educational purposes to cover rising energy costs. In the boom time for the Sunbelt states in the 1980s, school programs expanded under the pressure of greater resources. . . . Perhaps an even greater outside influence stemmed from the state itself, as it expanded its constitutional powers under political pressures. The rise of strong teacher organizations also represents a local sign of what is in essence a national development. This group's influence in one big city's schools has led an analyst to label it "union rule in Chicago." If the state continues to extend its control and take up its share of local costs into the 1990s, teacher groups may well escalate their pressure on state legislatures to reach decisions that are binding on local districts. We know how teachers, under fiscal stress, favor instructional and personnel costs or resist merit pay schemes suddenly popular in the 1980s.

* * *

The result of all this has been an increase in the number of groups seeking to influence local school governance, in the issues that get on the school agenda, and in the resources brought to bear upon the school board. . . .

* * *

. . . One finding seems consistent: Relatively few citizens use the channels available to them to register their educational needs. Popular participation is episodic at best, providing spasms rather than a flow of demands. When finally aroused, these demands do not focus on broad policies but rather on specifics. Of late, this involvement has taken the form of an increasing failure to pass local school levies, from almost two-thirds passing in the mid-1960s to only one-third by 1980. Alongside this flood of dissatisfaction with public schools by an apathetic

[#]G. Counts, *The Social Composition of Boards of Education* (1927).

public are occasional waves of protest generated by a sex education course, a too-liberal textbook, student dress regulations, or some other specific causes.

Interest groups may thus be the most common form of participation, but few citizens belong to them; the difficulties PTAs have in getting members enrolled and turned out are well known. Even groups seeking wide popular authority over local schools through "community control" programs have found it hard to get "the community" to participate. And board elections are rarely enticing enough to attract more than a small minority; they are dominated by the success of incumbents in getting reelected, and the competition is negligible. The potential exists for sweeping the "school rascals" out of office and replacing them with members who have different ideas. Elections certainly can operate in this fashion—but usually they do not.

Yet to say that relatively few participate is not to say that this frees the school authorities to do whatever they wish. The power of one parent with a complaint raised against a perceived injustice is enough to agitate administrators and can, if not met, escalate into a flood of community energy. . . . While the day-to-day life of school officials or teachers is filled with simply administering past directives from the public and profession, the potential exists for new waves of citizen inputs. At any moment, the schools can be caught between the forces of popular participation and bureaucratization. . . . Over time, the latter prevails, but also through time the influence of citizen participation becomes a zone of tolerance within which school authorities must act. This does not mean that they live in ongoing hypersensitivity to community and group demands—far from it, if one accepts the continuous criticism of school bureaucracy. Nor does this mean that the authorities are so inert that they cannot change their course—the history of educational reform belies that charge.

* * *

Why is there more concern about the effectiveness of school boards at this time in our history? One major reason is the lack of attention to school boards in virtually all the major national and state reports on education from 1983–86. For example, rather than not discussing school boards, the reform reports could have said that the school board is the crucial agent for school improvement and that state reforms should be directed at strengthening the local school board's capacity to bring about and monitor change. Instead, the unstated implication of many reports is that school boards are part of the problem and have not exercised leadership and their authority to improve education. This message further implies that boards need to be circumvented, if not through direct state regulation, then certainly through vastly increased state prescriptions and monitoring. . . .

This suspicion about the inability of school boards to provide academic leadership was exacerbated by the predominant research emphasis of these reports, which was on effective schools (in contrast to effective school districts). It was the school site that was the crucial focus for improvement, and the principal was the key catalyst. . . .

* * *

The apathy and ignorance about school boards is made worse by another finding. Local boards and board members interact with general government only occasionally and seem to be isolated (in boards' and civic leaders' perceptions) from mainstream community political structures. Very little systematic communication takes place between school boards and general government, despite the fact that ever more students have learning problems associated with nonschool factors such as poor housing, lack of family support and resources, and drug dependencies. When such interaction does exist on a regular basis, it often is only through the superintendent. . . .

NOTES AND QUESTIONS

1. Further Readings

The literature on the politics of education is quite extensive. For those interested in pursuing the subject further, the following books should be considered: J. Chubb and T. Moe, *Politics, Markets and America's Schools* (1990); M. Engel, *The Struggle for Control of Public Education: Market Ideology vs. Democratic Values* (2000); B. Fuller and R. Elmore with G. Orfield, *Who Chooses? Who Loses?: Culture, Institutions, and the Unequal Effects of School Choice* (1996); J. Kahne, *Reframing Educational Policy: Democracy, Community, and the Individual* (1996); F. Lutz, *The Politics of School/Community Relations* (1992); S. Sarason, *Political Leadership and Educational Failure* (1998); J. Spring, *Conflict of Interests: The Politics of American Education* (3d ed. 1998); D. Tyack and L. Cuban, *Tinkering toward Utopia: A Century of Public School Reform* (1995); F. Wirt and M. Kirst, *The Political Dynamics of American Education* (1997); L. McDonnell,

P. Timpane, and R. Benjamin, eds., *Rediscovering the Democratic Purposes of Education* (2000).

2. Elections and Public Accountability

Are Professors Wirt and Kirst suggesting that the election of members of the local school board is an ineffective way for citizens to exercise control over public education? Why is this? Is it because such elections usually are nonpartisan? Because the public, most often, is apathetic? Because of the nature of educational services? Is it because nonelected officials are not subordinate to elected leaders, or because different groups have unequal influence in the electoral process—even if all votes are equally weighted? *See generally* D. Rogers, *110 Livingston Street: Politics and Bureaucracy in the New York City School System* (1968); R. Dahl and C. Lindblom, *Politics, Economics, and Welfare* 277–78 (1953).

Does the problem lurk in the structure of school board elections? Government establishes qualifications for voting, procedures for establishing voter qualifications, candidate eligibility requirements, lines for district boundaries, rules on campaign financing, single- and multi-member districts, and the like, and this structure presumably has a powerful influence on electoral outcomes. *See generally* "Developments in the Law—Elections," 88 *Harv.L.Rev.* 1111 (1975). But are not all elections marked by such structural constraints? Would it be better for school board members to be appointed by other governmental bodies? Would an appointive system be more or less protective than an elective system of the interests of racial and other minorities? *See generally Irby v. Virginia State Board of Elections*, 889 F.2d 1352 (4th Cir. 1989).

Do school boards play a greater role in legitimizing school policies than in setting and implementing them? *See generally* Kerr, "The School Board as an Agency of Legitimation," 38 *Soc.of Educ.* 35 (1964).

3. Direct Democracy and the Initiative Process

In addition to local board elections, some states have an initiative process, which allows voters statewide to enact statutes and constitutional amendments at the polls. Not surprisingly, some of these initiatives have been directed at educational policy. For example, as discussed in chapter 6, immigrant students' access to education in California was shaped by ballot propositions that addressed undocumented immigration and bilingual education. Chapter 7 described how another California initiative to cap property taxes substantially weakened funding for public education. The trend to use initiatives to make school pol-

icy continues. In 2000, there were eleven such ballot propositions pending, over twice as many as the record five initiatives in 1998. The initiatives deal with topics as disparate as school choice, teacher salaries, school funding, and bans on bilingual education and instruction that endorses homosexuality. Cooper, "Ballot Initiatives Turning to Schools; Citizen Interest, Powerful Sponsors Generate Record Number of State Measures," *Washington Post*, Aug. 28, 2000, at A8.

4. The Scope of Representative Democracy in Education

The structure of school board elections suggests that voters should act primarily as citizens in pursuit of the common good, rather than as consumers of public educational services. At times, however, the gap between the citizen and consumer can become painfully wide. For instance, children are ineligible to vote, although their very future is at stake when school policy is set. Admittedly, their parents can vote in school board elections, but they cast ballots only in their own right and do not receive additional proxies on behalf of their school-age children. *See* Bennett, "Should Parents Be Given Extra Votes on Account of Their Children? Toward a Conversational Understanding of American Democracy," 94 *NW.U.L.Rev.* 503 (2000). In some instances, even the students' parents are ineligible to vote. In some cities like Los Angeles, immigrant parents cannot participate in school board elections, even though their children make up a substantial part of the public school population. In other urban school systems like New York and Chicago, noncitizens can vote for board members. Raskin, "Legal Aliens, Local Citizens: The Historical, Constitutional and Theoretical Meanings of Alien Suffrage," 141 *Univ.of Penn.L.Rev.* 1391 (1993).

The unrepresentativeness of school boards has led one author to conclude that the role of school boards is largely mythical and that they should be abolished:

"Parental Involvement and the Political Principle"

S. Sarason, *Parental Involvement and the Political Principle: Why the Existing Governance Structure of Schools Should be Abolished* 99–100, 103–107, 108 (1995). Copyright © 1995 Jossey-Bass, Inc. Reprinted by permission of Jossey-Bass, Inc., a subsidiary of John Wiley & Sons, Inc.

Boards of education, elected or appointed, represent the community, and represent means taking the community's interests, attitudes, and desires into account; insuring that state rules and regulations are met; developing, approving, and defending the school system's budget; approving policies that will sustain or improve educational practice and outcomes. Even though these boards oversee schools that are creations and instruments of state government, they nevertheless potentially have powers to change schools in myriads of ways.[1] Hiring and firing, approving or rejecting a curriculum, setting salary schedules, the construction or renovation of schools—these are only a few of the ways the policies and decisions of boards impact on schools. Members of the board are involved in schools in order to represent and protect the welfare of the community. A board member may or may not have (or had) a child in the public schools; a board member may or may not have any experiential credentials in regard to a school or school system. What a board is expected to possess is the time, energy, motivation, and maturity dispassionately to learn what schools are about and why, and to use that learning to maintain and improve schools in ways satisfying to the community. A board member is expected to be involved, to be active, to become knowledgeable, to be the opposite of passive in representing the interests of the community and the needs of students. To be elected or to accept appointment to a board of education signifies that the person has the qualities and ability to learn the game and the score.

I had trouble writing that paragraph because so much of it is myth; where it is not myth it is misleading, and where it is not misleading it is of trivial significance . . . .

* * *

The first point is that ignorance of the substance of the arena of problems for which a board member has responsibility may not be lethal but it is certainly not inherently virtuous. It could be argued that such a board member has less to *unlearn*. If you so argue, you are suggesting that it is the responsibility of that person to *learn* what is going on and why, and, I assume, by learning you mean active learning: making and exploiting opportunities to gain first-hand knowledge of how life is perceived and experienced by all groups in the school. That kind of learning is not "in-trusive" as long as several criteria are met: that kind of learning is acknowledged as a responsibility of the board member; it is not for the purpose of on-the-spot decision making; whatever information is obtained is inevitably incomplete or misinterpretable in some way and, therefore, has to be judged by other sources of information presented and discussed in other forums; the board member is an openly acknowledged sounding board, not conducting a witch hunt, not undercutting the day-to-day responsibility and authority of others; the board member is in a listening, learning, question-asking role. However you state the criteria, they should reflect the board member's responsibility to the community to have a feel for "what is going on," a basis for raising questions and ultimately for voting on policy issues. I am quite aware that this responsibility is an onerous one requiring time and tact, and not one that is free of problems, but let us not forget that board members are not elected or appointed to be as ignorant of what is going on at the end of their term as they were at the beginning, to cast their votes on the basis of what other people say, not on any direct experience.

In my experience I have never known a board member, however bright, motivated, and well intentioned, who sought actively truly to acquire knowledge about the substance of the important educational issues. And by important I mean organizational climate, job satisfaction of staff, *chronic* problems, classroom atmospheres, and the quality and level of student interest, motivation, activity, and curiosity, to name but a few of the factors that determine educational outcomes. How can a board member vote on anything that affects schools without *some* firsthand experience *in* schools with the different groups upon whom that vote impacts? Apparently, they can and do. . . .

What board members know or learn is what superintendents (and some of their assistants) want them to learn and know. I do not say that with malice or as an accusation of insincerity. The superintendents are agents of their boards, but it is not infrequent that, psychologically speaking, superintendents regard the boards as *their* agent, in which case the board is getting a particular view of issues and problems. That is not inherently bad as long as

---

[1]When I use the term *governance structure*, I mean not only boards of education but the state department of education as well. The two, of course, are in relation to each other and very frequently in ways that make innovation and school change difficult, aside from ensuring that the paper manufacturers will show a handsome profit. Although there is a literature on boards of education, there is hardly one on state departments of education, a fact I find puzzling, as if their role is of no practical significance, a conclusion that no member of a state department would think of accepting. As presently constituted, boards and state departments of education are part of the problem and not of the solution.

it is recognized that it is a particular view that may or may not be justified, in whole or in part. What boards do not confront is that the superintendent and his or her top administrative staff have one thing in common with the board: *what they say are the realities of the school system is not based on firsthand experience in schools; what boards and superintendents know and learn are derived from reports or other forms of communication from lower-level administrators where direct experience in schools is frequently minuscule. . . .*

Several objections will be raised to what I have said. The first is the "intrusive" or "meddling" argument: to encourage board members to gain direct experiences in schools and classrooms can only undercut the authority and responsibility of administrators and teachers alike, and this by a group with no credentials for comprehending educational issues. This argument is in principle identical to that against parent involvement in decision making, although this objection overlooks the fact that boards are *legally* empowered and morally obligated to be *involved*, to know what is going on, to seek understanding, to be proactive and not passively reactive, to be other than a rubber stamp, an ignorant voter. In its most blatant form it is an argument that education is too important and complex an affair to let nonprofessionals meaningfully enter the scene. If these kinds of arguments overlook the legal and moral responsibilities of boards, they also deny that educators have contributed anything to the inadequacies of our schools, inadequacies that only educators presumably can correct. That denial is not only wrong, it is inexcusable. There is a saying that "war is too important to be left to the generals," and that is true for education, medicine, law, and more.

A second argument is one I have gotten from board members with whom I have discussed these issues. It goes like this: "You seem to be vastly underestimating how much time we have to spend in reading reports on all kinds of matters, committee meetings of one kind or another, the regular board meeting that can go on for hours and that averages more than one a month, interviewing candidates for top positions, and then there are budgetary issues and the preparation of the budget that involve mind-boggling details like should we repair this school rather than that school. And if there is a new school to be built, or one that should be closed, or it is a year in which new union contracts have to be negotiated, there go our evenings and even some of our days.

Most board members have jobs—they also have families—and there is only a limited amount of time you can expect a board member to give, which is why some of them don't want another term. They paid their dues. We have no alternative to depending on the superintendent and his staff to provide us with the information we need. Even if the criticisms you are making have merit, and I don't think they do, they are unreasonable and unrealistic." . . .

The third argument is an implicit one in that it accepts the traditional board-administrative-school structure and relationships but explains the plethora of problems by the deficiencies of people, be they on the board, in administrative positions, or in the classroom, or in political positions outside of the school system. Change people and you will desirably change schools. Employ better personnel selection procedures, develop better and more stringent criteria for job performance, mandate more continuing education credits, make it less a life career to fire an inadequate but tenured teacher, improve the quality of preparatory programs for educators, and choose board members who have independent minds and are not beholden to or captives of political figures or a racial or religious group or a "one agenda" group. It is hard to quarrel with any of these suggestions. Alone or in combination these suggestions completely bypass the problem of how the present structure and its undergirding rationale, indeed its ideology about relationships within and among different groups in the hierarchy, set drastic limits on the consequences of "people" changers. More specifically, the structure and rationale have given us a school culture devoid of forums that serve the purpose of ensuring that the ideas, attitudes, and proposals of the different groups can be voiced and discussed instead of going underground (or nowhere) or being, as it now is, a limitless supply of fodder for a rumor mill. . . .

* * *

Boards of education are an anachronism with an ancestry going back to the one-room schoolhouse. Whatever virtues they may have had no longer are evident or even possible. They are now part of the problem, not of the solution. That is a conclusion that many people, in and out of schools, have voiced in the post–World War II era.

* * *

Do you agree that school boards are an anachronism? Does the structure of board elections presume that schools serve small, tight-knit communities that are relatively homogeneous? Does the nature of school board membership assume that decisions are relatively simple and straightforward so that no special expertise is required? Could an alternative form of representation work? Or would it simply create new problems of democratic access and fairness? Would any alternative system likely succumb to value conflicts and competing interests in heterogeneous communities?

5. *Civic Virtue and School Board Elections*

Another difficulty with an electoral model that depends on civic virtue is that parents may not see schooling as primarily a way to promote the common good. Rather, parents may believe that they must pursue their special interests (or their child's) in a competitive race for scarce resources. Those parents with the most clout may use the political process to win even more advantages for their children, while educational opportunities for other children remain scarce.

"Only for My Kid: How Privileged Parents Undermine School Reform"

A. Kohn, 79 *Phi Delta Kappan* 568, 570–574 (April 1, 1998). Copyright 1998 by Alfie Kohn. Reprinted from Phi Delta Kappan with the author's permission.

* * *

There is no national organization called Rich Parents Against School Reform, in part because there doesn't have to be. But with unaffiliated individuals working on different issues in different parts of the country, the pattern is generally missed and the story is rarely told. Take a step back, however, and you begin to grasp the import of what is happening from Amherst, Massachusetts, where highly educated white parents have fought to preserve a tracking system that keeps virtually every child of color out of advanced classes, to Palo Alto, California, where a similarly elite constituency demands a return to a "skill and drill" math curriculum and fiercely opposes the more conceptual learning outlined in the National Council of Teachers of Mathematics (NCTM) standards; from an affluent suburb of Buffalo, where parents of honors students quashed an attempt to replace letter grades with standards-based progress reports, to San Diego, where a program to provide underachieving students with support that will help them succeed in higher-level courses has run "head-on into vigorous opposition from some of the community's more outspoken, influential members—the predominantly white, middle-class parents of high-achieving students."

Jeannie Oakes, author of *Keeping Track*, calls them "Volvo vigilantes," but that isn't quite accurate—first, because they work within, and skillfully use, the law; and second, because many of them drive Jeeps. They may be pro-choice and avid recyclers, with nothing good to say about the likes of Pat Robertson and Rush Limbaugh; yet on educational issues they are, perhaps unwittingly, making common cause with, and furthering the agenda of, the Far Right.

The controversies in which these parents involve themselves fall into three clusters, the first of which concerns the type of instruction that is offered. Here we find a tension between, on the one hand, traditional methods and practices, geared toward a classroom that is construed as a collection of discrete individuals, each of whom is supposed to absorb a body of knowledge and basic skills, and, on the other hand, an approach distinguished by active discovery and problem solving by a community of learners.

Second, there is the question of placement, or which students get what. This category includes debates over such issues as tracking, ability grouping, gifted-and-talented programs, and honors courses—as distinguished from efforts to create more heterogeneous and inclusive classrooms.

Finally, there are the practices that take place after (but undeniably affect) the instruction, in which the emphasis is on selecting and sorting students so only a few are recognized: awards, letter grades, weighted grades (which give an additional advantage to those in the selective courses), honor rolls, and class ranks—as opposed to the absence of these practices and, sometimes, the presence of an assessment system geared more to enhancing learning than to distinguishing one student from another. It is the difference between a bumper sticker that says, "My Child Is an Honors Student at . . ." (with the understood postscript: "And Yours Isn't") and one that says, "Every Child Is an Honored Student at. . . ."

All affluent parents, of course, do not necessarily line up on the same side of every dispute. With respect to the type of instruction, anecdotal reports suggest that highly educated, middle-class parents sometimes support—or even demand—an emphasis on higher-order thinking, a literature-based approach to teaching reading, and the use of cooperative learning—at least within homogeneous groups. (After all, as Syracuse University's Mara Sapon-Shevin observes wryly, some parents figure, "My kid will have to learn to negotiate with the other Fortune 500 companies.") But just because most parents who support these innovations are middle-class doesn't mean that most middle-class parents support these innovations—just as the fact that a disproportionate number of truly progressive schools are private doesn't mean that a disproportionate number of private schools are progressive. The parents who prefer worksheets and lectures can use their clout to reverse or forestall a move to more learner-centered classrooms. Moreover, a tolerance for whole language or cooperative learning often does not extend to the newer approaches to teaching math, as reformers in Palo Alto and other California communities are discovering.

By the same token, resistance to the elimination of letter grades and awards assemblies is not confined to those who live in large houses. Parents in some working-class neighborhoods have been particularly outraged by these proposals, banding together under such names as PURGE: Parents United to Restore Graded Evaluations. Still, the experience of some educators matches that of Bob Gallagher, a staff development coordinator in the Buffalo area, who reports that the "parents of kids who were struggling" were pleased by a shift to rubrics and narrative assessments, while the parents of honors students "absolutely went crazy" at the prospect of losing traditional letter grades. Perhaps the reaction can more accurately be predicted by the status of the student than by the income level of the parent—although the significant correlation between these two is itself cause for concern.

If the position of a certain group of parents is not always clear-cut with respect to teaching and assessing, the battle lines are sharply drawn when it comes to placement and allocation issues, and the "gifted parents," as some observers like to call them, know what they want and how to get it. Sometimes their success is a function of being able to choose not only classes but schools—specifically, selective independent schools or well-funded public schools in affluent suburbs. American education is so segregated and stratified today that the elite mingle mostly with one another. Annette Lareau of Temple University wanted to study a school in Philadelphia whose student population cut across lines of race and class; she was unable to find a single example. "Who are the middle-class parents arguing against?" she asks. "I think that's why you don't see more of these conflicts. Poor kids are generally not in the same schools."

Pitched battles are more common in integrated schools, but even here they happen rarely because, in large measure, the affluent white parents have already won. The plum classes and programs for their children already exist, as do the letter grades and awards to distinguish them from those other children. The system serves these parents well, and their influences is such—or the fear that they will yank their children out is sufficient—that few superintendents (and even fewer school boards) dare to rock this boat on which first-class cabins are so clearly delineated from steerage. The reformers eventually get tired—or fired.

As Amy Stuart Wells of UCLA sees it, even many liberal white parents may say, in effect, "We like the fact that our kids are in desegregated schools, but the fact that the white kids are in the top classes and the black kids are in the bottom is someone else's problem." Last fall, *US. News and World Report* published an article documenting how many "schools that appear integrated from the outside are highly segregated within . . . Honors classes are dominated by whites, regular classes by blacks." In response, a liberal *New Republic* columnist readily agreed that the honors program in his own daughter's school in Montgomery County, Maryland, amounted to a "school within a school" for the white and Asian students—and then announced that if this program were eliminated, he would pull his daughter out of that school "in a nanosecond."

What is interesting about this exchange is that the *US. News* reporter had pretty much taken for granted the existence of tracking and seemed concerned only about the racial make-up of each track; the possibility of heterogeneous classrooms was not even raised until the very end of the article, and then it was immediately dismissed. Yet the liberal columnist served notice in a national magazine that any attempt to create a fairer system would be an invitation to white flight, something in which he would unapologetically participate. Most affluent parents send this message more quietly and locally, of course, but it reverberates through the offices of administrators and effectively discourages meaningful change.

Or consider two essays published independently in 1996. The first, in the *American Educational Research Journal*, describes a series of interviews with "educated, middle-class mothers, perceived by others as well as themselves as liberals who believe in integrated and inclusive education." In the course of conversation, these women pronounced themselves committed to equity and tolerance but then proceeded (under questioning) to become far more passionate in dismissing these very ideals when it came to the advantages they thought their own children should receive. The self-described liberals tended to "support segregated and stratified school structures that mainly benefit stsudents of the middle class," the researchers discovered.

The second article, published in the *Harvard Educational Review*, contains a very serious charge leveled by Wells and her colleague Irene Senna: tracking, advanced placement (AP) courses, and gifted programs do not provide differential instruction for legitimate pedagogical reasons–or allow for a system based on merit–so much as they represent a naked grab for artificially scarce benefits by those who have the power to get them.

Think scientifically for a moment about how this disturbing hypothesis might be tested. If it were accurate, the beneficiaries of these educational advantages would "be more concerned about the labels placed on their children than about what actually goes on in the classroom." And indeed, there is reason to think that this is frequently true. To begin with, AP classes at the high school level are usually difficult but often poorly taught, with an emphasis on short-term memorization of facts presented in lectures and textbooks–in effect, one long test-prep session. Yet many parents seem to care a lot more about who is in these classes (namely, their own children and a few others who look like them) than about how they are taught.

Granted, it is hard to deny the superiority of the instruction in gifted-and-talented programs and some other honors or hightrack classes, what with hands-on learning, student-designed projects, computers, field trips, and other enrichments. But research generally shows that it is precisely those enrichments that produce better results rather than the fact that they are accorded to only to a select few. What happens in those classes is more decisive than the fact that they are homogeneous. So if parents of those students were concerned about the quality of learning, they would have no reason to object to extending those benefits to everyone.

But object they do. Wells and Oakes have been studying the experience of 10 schools across the country that are trying to ease away from tracking. Many of these schools have taken the advice of Anne Wheelock, who urged educators to help parents of top-tracked students understand that "inclusive schooling offers all students the type of education usually reserved for gifted and talented students." The detracking in these 10 schools was carefully planned to bring other students up to a high level, but not to take anything away from the priviledged children. Yet the reaction from the parents of the latter students has been powerfully negative–often fatal for the reform efforts. These parents have pressured educators "to maintain separate and unequal classes for their children, . . . [demanding] to know what their children will 'get' that other students will not have access to.

This is essentially what happened in San Diego, where an attempt to give a leg up to lower-tracked students was, as Elizabeth Cohen of Stanford University puts it, "the kind of project that you'd think wouldn't bother upper-status parents at all. Wrong! They said, 'What are you going to do special for my kids?'" This posture, she adds, goes beyond a simple and commendable desire to do everything possible for one's own children. "When parents tell me they're terribly anxious about their kids getting ahead, I'm sympathetic. Everyone wants the best for their kids. But when it extends to sabotaging programs that are designed to help people, I have to draw the line."

Notice what is going on here. It isn't just that these parents are ignoring everyone else's children, focusing their efforts solely on giving their own children the most desirable education. Rather, they are in effect sacrificing other children to their own. It's not about success but victory, not about responding to a competitive environment but creating one. As Harvey Daniels of National Louis University sees it, "The psychology of those parents is that it's not enough for their kids to win: others must lose — and they must lose conspicuously."

This explains much of the frustration experienced by educators who insist that narratives or portfolios are far more informative about students' learning than letter grades are, or who cite evidence to show that focusing students' attention on getting A's tends to reduce their interest in the learning itself. These arguments will only persuade someone who is looking for more information about his or her child's improvement or someone who is concerned about sustaining the child's interest. If, however, the point is not for assessment to be authentic but for it to serve as a sorting device, to show not how well the student is doing but how much better he or she is doing than others, then A's will always be necessary — and it will always be necessary for some people's children not to get them. It will be necessary not only to rate children but to rank them, to give out not only report cards but trophies and plaques and certificates and membership in elite societies, all of which are made artificially scarce.

This agenda is arguably anti-child, but should that surprise us? We live in a culture that is remarkably unfriendly toward children in general; a "good" child is one who doesn't cause us any trouble. Even when politicians and businesspeople demand "world-class" schools, they usually mean those that produce high test scores, and their reasons evidently don't have much to do with meeting the children's own needs. As for material possessions, it is true that some parents—those who have enough income— spend lavishly on their children, generating the notion that we are a child-centered society. But public spending for children is often meager and always surrounded by contention, and it embodies the peculiar conception that children are not valuable as persons in their own right but only for the adults they will grow up to be. . . . The saccharine myth [that] . . . children are [America's] most precious natural resources has in practice been falsified by our hostility to other people's children and our unwillingness to support them.[15]

The problem does not rest solely with our attitude toward children, however, but also with our attenuated sense of community. Our culture is distinguished by an ethic of individualism as well as a tendency to collapse all human interaction and most matters of public policy into economic laws. Vouchers and school choice plans effectively say to parents, "Never mind about what's best for kids; just shop for the school that's best for your kids." It's not a community; it's a market—so why would we expect things to be any different inside the school? How much commitment to inclusive education can we expect in an exclusive society? Sadly, when parents (and, shamefully, some educators) go to great lengths to erect walls between the "gifted" and the ordinary, another generation is raised without a commitment to the values of community, and the vicious circle closes in.

Beyond attitudes toward children and community, there is the question of how we view education itself. In a new book titled *How to Succeed in School Without Really Learning*, David Labaree of Michigan State University argues that schooling these days is not seen as a way to create democratic citizens or even capable workers, but serves more as a credentialing mechanism. "The purpose of education from

this angle is not what it can do for democracy or the economy but what it can do for me," and this shift turns our school systems into "a vast public subsidy for private ambition." One implication of such a transformation is that education becomes "an arena for zero-sum competition filled with self-interested actors seeking opportunities or gaining educational distinctions at the expense of each other"—precisely what we've seen affluent parents doing so relentlessly and so well.

Labaree incisively demonstrates another implication of viewing education this way, which is that the quality of learning itself is likely to decline. "We have credentialism to thank for the aversion to learning that, to a great extent, lies at the heart of our educational system," he observes. While the pages of journals like this one [*Phi Delta Kappan*] are brimming with suggestions for how to make schools more effective, the impact of these ideas is perforce limited if making schools more effective is really beside the point for most Americans. The point is not to get an education but to get ahead—and therefore, from the student/consumer's point of view, "to gain the highest grade with the minimum amount of learning." In fact, efforts to help all students succeed, or to place more emphasis on teaching and less on sorting, would be not merely irrelevant but utterly contrary to the individualistic, competitive credentialing model of school—and so such efforts would be bitterly contested by those with the best chances of getting the shiniest credentials.

> It is elite parents [who] see the most to gain from the special distinctions offered by a stratified educational system, and they are therefore the ones who play the game of academic one-upmanship most aggressively. . . . They vigorously resist when educators (pursuing a more egalitarian vision) propose to eliminate some form of within-school distinction or another—by promoting multiability reading groups, for example, ending curriculum tracking, or dropping a program for the gifted.[17]

No wonder a somewhat disillusioned Anne Wheelock now muses that "all the research in the world" about the positive effects of detracking or abolishing letter grades "doesn't persuade these folks." No wonder such parents are more likely to

---

[15]W. Norton Grubb and Martin Lazerson, *Broken Promises: How Americans Fail Their Children* (New York: Basic, 1982), pp. 56, 85.

[17]*See* David F. Labaree, *How to Succeed in School Without Really Learning: The Credentials Race in American Education* (New Haven: Yale University Press, 1997). The first chapter, which contains the heart of the argument, was also published as "Public Goods, Private Goods: The American Struggle over Educational Goals," *American Educational Research Journal*, vol. 34, 1997, pp. 39–81. The quotations used here are taken from pages 30, 32, 258, and 259 of the book and, in one case, from Labaree's article "Are Students 'Consumers'?: The Rise of Public Education as a Private Good," *Education Week*, 17 September 1997, pp. 48, 38.

ask, "How is my child doing compared to everyone else?" than to inquire about how effectively that child is learning. To paraphrase a popular song, What's learning got to do with it?

* * *

This trade-off raises the intriguing possibility that the exertions of the moms and dads of top students may exact a price not only from other children but also from their own. Consider those parents who essentially mortgage their children's present to the future, sacrificing what might bring meaning or enjoyment—or even produce higher-quality learning—in a ceaseless effort to prepare the children for Harvard (a process I have come to call "Preparation H"). This bottom line is never far from the minds of such parents, who weigh every decision about what their children do in school, or even after school, against the yardstick of what it might contribute to future success. They are not raising a child so much as a living resume. As repellent as we might find the corporate groups and politicians who regard education—and even children themselves—as little more than an "investment," these parents are doing the dirty work implied by this reductive world view, and they are doing it to their own children.

Before long, the children internalize this quest and come to see their childhood as one long period of getting ready: they sign up for activities that might impress an admissions committee, ignoring (perhaps eventually losing sight of) what they personally find interesting in the here and now. They ask teachers, "Do we need to know this?" and grimly try to squeeze out another few points to bolster their grade point averages (GPAs) or SAT scores. What they don't know, for their parents surely will not tell them, is that this straining toward the future, this poisonous assumption that the value of everything is solely a function of its contribution to something that might come later, will continue right through college, right through professional school, right through the early stages of a career, until at last they wake up in a tastefully appointed bedroom to discover that their lives are mostly gone.

And those are just the successful students. The parents, then, could be described as having sacrificed other children to their own, and also their own children's present to the imagined future. But there is a third sacrifice, too, and, like the second, it does

their own children no favor: moral, social, artistic, emotional, and other forms of development are often jettisoned in favor of a narrow academic agenda. (Academics, of course, may simply be a stand-in for the ultimate goal of material success.) By ruling out a heterogeneous classroom on the grounds that it might slow down their precocious child's race to acquire more advanced math or reading skills, they ignore what he or she loses in other respects. By insisting that students be graded and then ranked against one another—or forced to compete for various awards—they deprive their children of the richer rewards to be gained from attending a school that feels like a caring community.

* * *

———————

Are stratification and sorting inevitable features of the educational process? If schools prepare students for both citizenship and employment, do the demands of the economy require that skills be identified and ranked? Is it possible for schools to reward mastery of certain tasks without making interpersonal comparisons that affect a child's sense of self-worth? How can a single school undertake such efforts without running into parental resistance? Are parents right to fear that such experiments may leave their children less able to compete with children in traditional schools based on grades and awards?

B. Teachers and Administrators: An Ethic of Professionalism

Because the electoral process can succumb to voter apathy on the one hand and destructive and divisive politics on the other, those who have committed themselves to a career in education often seek a voice in school governance. In their view, professionalism can provide an important check on the passions and prejudices of the public. Teachers and administrators believe that their expertise can bring stability and sound pedagogy to the schools.

1. Administrators: Superintendents and Principals. Public school systems are large-scale organizations that require professional management. School administrators must be responsive to a number of constituencies: parents, students, teachers, community members, and other elected officials. In negotiating among these constituencies, superintendents and principals must reconcile politics and professionalism.

"Schools in Conflict"

From Frederick M. Wirt and Michael Kirst, Schools in Conflict: The Politics of Education. Copyright 1989 by McCutran Publishing Corporation, Richmond, California, 94806. Used by permission of the publisher.

If the community is only occasionally active and the board has strong limitations, school professionals should retain a greater influence on policy issues. Professional educators have their resources, too. They define choices, produce research, provide specific recommendations, and shape the formal agenda. Using these resources, professionals generate pressures and information that can affect, if not determine, the board's deliberations and decisions. In Easton's framework, the school superintendent and staff provide inputs to the school board and the bureaucracy. Many specific policy issues, however, may never reach the school board if the superintendent and staff act under broad discretion from the school board. Consequently, both board and superintendent are authorities seeking to gain support from the community through the use of appropriate outputs in the form of budget, curriculum, teacher selection, and so on.

The professional staff does operate under certain constraints, however. They must anticipate reactions of board members to their actions because the board does have the basic power to fire them. They also know that the ultimate power of a provoked electorate is to remove them by changing the board, as noted earlier. It is also likely that the superintendent would act in keeping with the school board's wishes on many issues even without the threat of job loss. It is natural to assume that board members would hire a person whose values were similar to their own. An example of this is the low rate of turnover in smaller districts, which tend to be more homogeneous in their values. In effect, the board's impact on specific decisions may be more indirect than direct, but it is nevertheless real. The superintendent operates with considerable latitude as long as he or she stays within the board's ideological zone of tolerance.

A major research question during the 1970s was whether superintendents molded school boards into suppliant agents by professional control of policy-making. One way this was thought to occur was the socialization of the new board member to professional values. . . .

The question about who controlled whom received much national attention among educational administrators with the publication of the Zeigler and Jennings study of eighty-eight school districts.[4] The authors focused on whether democratic principles were being served in the interaction between board and superintendent; their answer was an emphatic "No," although numerous qualifying conditions were given. . . . Ironically, . . . Zeigler and Jennings found that effective opposition to professional influence by the board occurred in small districts with their limited political conflict and consensual elite board. Urban boards, on the other hand, were more contentious but had only limited effect against professional power.

* * *

But an immediate and powerful critique of this finding of superintendent dominance arose. Boyd pointed out that administrator control over the board was highly contingent on other matters.[6] It varied with the kind of policy at issue and with the size and homogeneity of the district. . . .

In all this, Boyd noted, one factor of the board-administrator relation not tapped in research is the force of what political scientists term the "law of anticipated reaction." This is the capacity of the administrator to estimate the limits within which she or he could act without board concern—the "zone of tolerance" in organizational theory. In other words, superintendents inhibit their own behavior based on knowing the controls these boards may exert. Subtle and hard to measure, this influence is still a reality that superintendents will detail in endless anecdotes. . . .

When school decentralization initiatives have been undertaken, policymakers often have argued that principals should be given strong leadership roles to promote parent involvement, teacher morale, and educational innovation. In the following excerpt, however, John Chubb and Terry Moe argue that the path to becoming a principal is not one that produces bold leaders.

[4]L. Harmon Zeigler and M. Kent Jennings, *Governing American Schools* (North Scituate, Mass.: Duxbury, 1974), pp. 39–42, Pt. III.

[6]William L. Boyd, "The Public, the Professionals, and Educational Policy-Making: Who Governs?" *Teachers College Record* 77 (1976): 556–58.

"Politics, Markets, and America's Schools"

J. Chubb and T. Moe, *Politics, Markets & America's Schools*
156–60 (1990).

It may be better to think of the public school principal as a lower-level manager than as a leader. In the public sector, the principal is a bureaucrat with supervisory responsibility for a public agency. Most of the important decisions about policy have been taken by higher authorities: they set the goals and the principal is expected to administer them. Many of the important structural decisions are also taken by higher authorities: the principal is bound by all sorts of formal rules and regulations that dictate aspects of internal structure. And many of the important personnel decisions are imposed from above as well: the principal is unlikely to have much control over the choice of teachers or the incentives that motivate them. The real leaders of the public school are the authorities, not the principal.

Most of the high-level rhetoric about the importance of the principal's leadership role is essentially just that. The fact is that those who succeed in exercising public authority want principals to behave more like bureaucrats than leaders. Authorities want principals to ensure that formal hierarchical directives are put into effect; they do not want principals to exercise real discretion. The public system is set up accordingly. The position of principal is a bureaucratic office in a recognized hierarchy of offices. People who desire advancement within the educational system begin as teachers—the lowliest of bureaucrats—then advance up the ladder to assistant principal, then principal, then into the district office as assistant superintendent, and so on. They are on a career track, and the principalship is one step along the way. Doing a good job as principal qualifies one for advancement.

The nature of the job and its career path inevitably generate a process of selective attraction. People who like administrative work and who desire advancement in an administrative hierarchy tend to be attracted to the job, while people who want to be genuine leaders tend to be turned off. Once in the job, moreover, the incentives promote behavior that is classically bureaucratic. Doing a good job, and thus doing what is necessary to get ahead, requires playing by the rules, implementing them as faithfully and effectively as possible—and staying out of trouble. The easiest way to get into trouble is to launch bold, aggressive, innovative moves: discretionary acts of leadership that are

bound to be threatening to the interests of someone, somewhere, in a position of political power.

* * *

In the public sector, the whole thrust of democratic politics is to formalize and constrain educational practice. As public authority is captured and put to use by various interests over time, the discretionary exercise of professional judgment is systematically curtailed, and the practice of education is transformed into an exercise in administration. Because technical concerns remain important to those who make political decisions, all discretion is not eliminated. Moreover, because so much technical and operational knowledge is concentrated at the lower reaches of the organization, in people whose professional sensibilities are violated by formal constraint, hierarchical control is inevitably imperfect: teachers will subtly be able to evade some of the rules without detection or punishment.

Nonetheless, the public world of educational practice is a world of rules imposed on the schools by local, state, and federal authorities. Some of these specify what teachers are to do and how they are to do it—rules about curriculum, about instructional methods, about the design of special programs, about textbooks, about time spent on various activities, about what can and cannot be discussed. In addition, there are all sorts of rules—monitoring and reporting rules—designed to ensure that teachers are doing these things and not evading hierarchical control. Thus teachers are doubly constrained in their efforts to perform their educational tasks as they see fit. First, they are required to follow rules that cause them to depart from what they might otherwise do, and thus to behave in ways that contradict or fail to take advantage of their professional expertise and judgment. Second, they are required to spend time and effort documenting, usually through formal paperwork, that they have in fact followed these rules. The combination may leave little room for them to do the kind of teaching they think they ought to be doing.

The most formal aspects of educational practice are often imposed by federal and state authorities, who are far from the scene and thus particularly vulnerable to discretionary departures from the objectives they want schools to pursue. But local politics is an important source of formalization as well—collective bargaining agreements, for instance, may specify in detail who is to do what, when, and how. Even in the absence of formalization, moreover, local politics still puts an indelible stamp on how education gets carried out.

Consider, for instance, local practices having to do with such things as homework, academic tracking, or discipline. Districts may abstain from imposing formal rules on these scores, but this does not mean schools are truly free to adopt practices that, on professional grounds, seem most conducive to effective education. The fact is that school practices can easily become politicized when one or more groups become disgruntled and pressure the authorities for action. Were teachers to decide that most students should be academically tracked, assigned significantly more homework, and held to strict academic standards in order to pass, the size and heterogeneity of the democratic constituency virtually guarantees a fearsome political response. Similarly, were schools unable to control violence and drugs on their campuses, the political authorities would inevitably come under pressure to "do something" by imposing disciplinary policies from without.

If schools do not anticipate and defuse these political problems through their choice of practices, then, the district is likely to exercise its authority to adopt formal rules on homework, tracking, discipline, and any other school practices that excite constituents—the result of which is still more formalization and still less discretion for schools. Conversely, the absence of formal rules does not mean the schools are using their apparent discretion to adopt practices that are considered best on professional grounds. It means that they have settled practices that are politically acceptable, and thus safe from formal reprisal by the authorities.

* * *

NOTES AND QUESTIONS

1. Bureaucratic Constraints and School-Level Innovation

Do you agree that principals are constrained by the bureaucratic imperatives of their own advancement and the political pressures of special-interest groups? Do you think that these pressures make school-level reform unlikely? Are other educational decision makers in any better position to innovate than principals? Why or why not?

2. Further Readings

For additional reading on the role of the principal in school reform, *see* Geisert, "Principal Leadership in American School Reform," 13 *Gov.Union Rev.* 1 (1992); "Strengthening School Leadership and School-Level Accountability: Rethinking Principals' Rights and Responsibilities After Governance Reform," 54 *Record of the Association of the Bar of the City of New York* 33 (1999).

2. Teachers and an Ethic of Professionalism. It is a truism that teachers are critical to the success of schools. Yet, many people have in mind the individual talent and dedication that teachers bring to their jobs. While the image of the hard-working public servant is extremely popular, teachers' efforts to act collectively for change are far more controversial. Teachers' unions that claim to cement the professional standing of teachers are often criticized as nothing but self-interested organizations. *See* M. Lieberman, *The Teachers Unions: How the NEA and AFT Sabotage Reform and Hold Students, Parents, Teachers, and Taxpayers Hostage to Bureaucracy* (1997); M. Lieberman, *Public Education: An Autopsy* 45–66 (1993). On the other hand, some claim that educational reform is not possible without the support of teachers and the unions that afford them a collective voice. *See* C. Kerchner, J. Koppich, and J. Weeres, *United Mind Workers: Unions and Teaching in the Knowledge Society* (1997); C. Kerchner and D. Mitchell, *The Changing Idea of a Teachers' Union* (1988). Charting a middle course, Susan Moore Johnson and Susan M. Kardos have argued that the role of unions changes as the vision of public education is transformed. When the Efficiency Movement of the 1920s prized standardization of schools, particularly in urban areas, unions operated on a factory model that focused on improving work conditions for teachers through adversarial bargaining. In the mid-1980s, however, unions began to engage in reform bargaining in response to a professional model of education. The professional model emphasizes responsiveness to individual students and local needs. Because teachers need autonomy and flexibility to be responsive, reform bargaining relies on collaborative relations between unions and administrators to develop a climate for innovative and improved teaching:

"Reform Bargaining and Its Promise for School Improvement"

S. Johnson and S. Kardos, in T. Loveless, ed. *Conflicting Missions: Teachers Unions and Educational Reform* 19–30 (2000).

* * *

During the first decade of bargaining, researchers who analyzed contracts predicted that unions would make steady gains until, eventually, all contracts would look alike. Like the general public, these researchers assumed that all local teachers unions had the same goals in negotiations, that districts across the country bargained about the same set of issues, and that eventually they would adopt essentially the same contract provisions. In short, negotiated agreements would become ever stronger and more alike. In 1979 McDonnell and Pascal analyzed the 1970 and 1975 contracts from a national sample of 151 districts and reported that there was a "convergence of collective bargaining outcomes over time. As more and more school systems follow the lead of flagship districts, there is less variation among individual contracts." In 1984 Goldschmidt and Stuart analyzed eighty local contracts and compared them with contracts studied by McDonnell and Pascal ten years earlier. Based on these comparisons, they concluded that the extent of bargaining over noncompensation items increased over time. Perry was the only researcher who before 1980 noted the slackened pace of union gains. Returning to nine of the twenty-four districts he and Wildman had studied in 1970, Perry found that, although class size was bargained about in all of them, the unions had "made relatively little concrete progress in achieving definite, enforceable limits on class size or in reducing those limits where they exist."[21]

The predicted convergence, in fact, never happened. Subsequent analyses of union contracts revealed that, with the exception of layoff and transfer provisions, collective bargaining did little from 1975 to 1985 to reduce teachers' obligations, further standardize practice, or extend job protections. When McDonnell and Pascal returned to their original sample of districts and analyzed agreements through 1985, they discovered that "[w]ith relatively few exceptions, the improvements in working conditions unions had

attained by 1975 were not enhanced in the 1980 and 1985 contracts." Their study showed "quite conclusively that there are real limits on what teachers can obtain through the traditional collective bargaining process. Not only did the rate of gain for our sample slow in the 1980s as compared with the previous decade, but a majority of unions still cannot obtain key provisions such as strong class size limits, curbs on teachers having to teach outside their fields, and clear criteria for involuntary transfers." Similarly Jessup's longitudinal analysis of three small districts revealed that the "strongest" contract of the group was "essentially the same" in 1979 as in 1973. Further, Johnson, Nelson, and Potter, who studied a national sample of 155 contracts in 1985, concluded that "collective bargaining agreements are neither as comprehensive nor prescriptive as some might believe. Many do not address key staffing issues. [And] although many contract provisions are intended to advance teacher interests, the contracts reviewed were not simply lists of union privileges. Much contract language about staffing specifies the prerogatives of management." Empirical research does not support the conventional belief that collective bargaining produces ever "stronger" union privileges and protections for teachers.[22]

There is, therefore, convincing evidence that what seemed to be a steady pace of union gains came to a virtual halt by the end of the 1970s, yet there is only speculation about why this occurred. One explanation is that management, who had been unprepared for early bargaining and often made unwise concessions to union demands, started to encounter the consequences of careless negotiation and resisted further union gains. Another related explanation is that declining enrollments and budget cuts in the 1970s led to much more cautious, conservative negotiations by administrators and school boards. Jessup explains how hard times strengthened the hand of management in the districts she studied:

> At first, union leaders believed they could simply postpone negotiations on the unacceptable issues into future years, regarding collective bargaining as a long-term process in which each contract would represent a step forward. As the 1970s progressed, however, this possibility receded. The atmosphere of economic crisis, heightened

---

[21]McDonnell and Pascal [L. McDonnell and A. Pascal, *Organized Teachers in American Schools* (1979)], p. 31; Goldschmidt and Stuart [S. Goldschmidt and L. Stuart, "The Extent of Educational Policy Bargaining and its Impacts on School System Adaptability," Center for Educational Policy and Management (1984)]; Perry [C. Perry, "Teacher Bargaining: The Experience in Nine Systems," 33 *Industrial and Labor Relations Review* 3 (1979)], p. 13.

[22]McDonnell and Pascal [*id.*], pp. vi, 52; Jessup [D. Jessup, *Teachers, Unions, and Change: A Comparative Study* (1985)]; Johnson, Nelson, and Potter [S. Johnson, N. Nelson, and J. Potter, *Teacher Unions, School Staffing, and Reform* (1985)], p. i.

by local tax revolts and declining student enrollments, led boards not to be more expansive, but to cut back on school financing. The atmosphere of public criticism and distrust led them to try to tighten, not loosen, controls over teachers. These situations pressed all three unions into far more defensive positions during the 1970s so that protection of existing staff positions and the contract took priority.

During this period in many districts, deadlocked negotiations and subsequent union "give-backs" were common.

In addition to these two explanations of the slowed pace of union gains, a third deserves attention. There is evidence that teachers, themselves, started to see the limits of industrial bargaining and to resent the inflexibility it sometimes imposed on them and their schools. There can be no doubt that teachers appreciated their union's success in winning better wages, defining reasonable boundaries on their in-school responsibilities, and gaining assurances of fair treatment. Yet teachers also recognized that the realities of their schools were different from the realities of the factories. Children were not undifferentiated raw materials, and good schooling should not be an impersonal process of mass production. Despite having similar credentials, all teachers were not the same, and seniority was not an invariably sound criterion for deciding who would teach where. In the view of many teachers, individual schools needed to retain (or regain) the capacity to make important decisions for themselves about how best to organize instruction and use the resources they had (time, money, and expertise) to support that instruction.

School Reform Brings New Approaches to Bargaining

With the publication of *A Nation at Risk*, the political context of both public education and collective bargaining abruptly changed.[25] Schools and teachers, widely ignored by the public, suddenly were surveyed and found to be lacking. Critics predicted that the shortcomings of schools would compromise the country's economic security, and teachers became easy targets of blame. Many state legislatures took the lead in responding to this report's disturbing alarm.

State-Initiated Reforms

During the so-called first wave of reform (1983–86), which came as a response to *A Nation at Risk*, individual states set out to change teachers by monitoring and assessing their practices or offering state money to fund local programs that would identify and reward meritorious teachers and schools. Since these state reforms would affect some teachers' wages and working conditions, they were subject to local negotiation, and as local districts bargained about their impact, the scope of negotiations gradually increased to include explicit discussion of instructional policy, long assumed to be the exclusive province of management. For example, a plan to implement performance-based pay typically involved discussions of curriculum and testing. Over the next few years the state-initiated reforms changed the substance of what labor and management saw to be appropriate topics for negotiation. In some districts the prospect of getting more money or protecting the district from outside meddlers fostered a collaborative spirit among many who had always assumed that the people on the other side of the bargaining table were their enemies.

McDonnell and Pascal studied the role of teachers unions in such reforms and found that between 1983 and 1986 local union officials and their teachers sought to gain "material benefits (i.e., higher salaries, restrictions on class size, etc.)" rather than pursue "strategies aimed at enhancing teacher professionalism (e.g., performance-based compensation, increased teacher participation in school-site decisionmaking)." And when local union leaders advocated professional reforms, "many rank-and-file teachers reacted with skepticism and even hostility." McDonnell and Pascal found that California's Mentor Teacher Program "was implemented in most districts as a classic pork barrel, with benefits allocated as broadly as possible and on criteria other than strict merit." In Pennsylvania unions sought to "accommodate" the state's reforms and "mitigate" the perceived negative effects on teachers of local curricular reforms triggered by state legislation.

Similarly, Johnson, Potter, and Nelson found that major state initiatives in California and Florida had redirected local bargaining in the two districts under study. The local union in California initially resisted

---

[25]National Commission on Excellence in Education [*A Nation at Risk: The Imperative for Educational Reform* (1983)].

merit pay but eventually acceded to a carefully fashioned plan that would sidestep the very initiatives that California legislators had hoped to achieve. One local union official explained, "We wanted input into the policy and the selection process. We wanted to help manage the process of the program. We wanted to protect our members." Pitner and Goldschmidt, who analyzed contracts and documents regarding California's Mentor Teacher Program in the state's eleven largest districts, also found that the program had been "shaped through bargaining to reflect more closely the teachers union goals of deference to seniority."

In Florida, where legislators passed a merit program intended to promote healthy competition by rewarding outstanding schools, the union and management of a large county district devised plans to secure state funds without imposing competition that might divide the staff or pit schools against each other. Many in the district thought that these state-sponsored programs would eventually disappear because of limited funding or faulty implementation. In the meantime, union leaders and school officials tried to garner the funds while protecting their schools from adverse effects. They did not see themselves as participants in school reform. As the union's executive director explained: "What we're doing here is a whole lot of damage control."[26]

Although the rhetoric of the day was reform, local teachers widely saw the reforming legislators as ignorant outsiders offering money in exchange for ill-advised concessions. Often unions undermined the state policies during implementation, complying superficially while continuing business as usual. Yet there were far-reaching, unexpected effects. Labor and management, accustomed to highlighting their disagreements, discovered new reasons to cooperate as they explored how best to secure state funds without undermining their current programs. Inadvertently, through their new reform agenda, state officials reshaped both the scope and tenor of local bargaining practices.

Home-Grown Reform

While most local districts' attention was captured by the agendas of state legislators, key leaders in a few local districts began to review their own policies and practices, undistracted by the demands of state mandates or the lure of state money. These reformers began to acknowledge publicly what many had privately understood: teachers' interests and management's interests were not necessarily at odds. Often the process of adversarial bargaining, pitting teachers against administrators in ritualized dissembling and bullying, undermined the possibility of collaborative work once the contract was signed. The dissension and disappointment caused by public blame and militant job actions damaged working relationships and dimmed the public's view of local educators. Some who had experienced the cost of such combat began to moderate its effects. In some places union and school officials recognized that they would have to experiment with new approaches in order to find their way to better schools. In 1981 negotiators in Toledo signed a contract that "pledged the parties to begin a program of teacher evaluation"; that program eventually would engage teachers in assessing their peers, a practice that most unions vehemently opposed. After publication of A Nation at Risk in 1983, the teachers union president and superintendent in Miami-Dade County, Florida, met regularly about reform. In Rochester, superintendent Peter McWalters and union president Adam Urbanski recognized that industrial bargaining had mixed effects on their schools, and they began to search for a better approach to unionism and schooling. Urbanski said, "It was clear we needed a change in kind, not just a change in degree. We had reached the point where not taking risks was a greater risk than taking risks."[27]

In a large urban district dubbed East Port by Johnson, Nelson, and Potter, labor and management agreed in 1982 to modify several contract provisions

---

[26]McDonnell and Pascal [L. McDonnell and A. Pascal, "Teacher Unions and Educational Reform," Center for Policy Research in Education (1988)], pp. viii, 42, 45; Johnson, Potter, and Nelson [supra note 22]; Pitner and Goldschmidt [N. Pitner and S. Goldschmidt, "Bargaining over School Reform: California Teacher Mentor Program," Paper presented at the annual meeting of the American Educational Research Association, Washington, D.C., April 1987], pp. 5, 58.

[27]Gallagher [D. Gallagher, "Teacher Bargaining and School District Expenditures," 17 Industrial Relations 231 (1977)], p. 158; Phillips [L. Phillips, "Miami: After the Hype," in C. Kerchner and J. Koppich, eds., A Union of Professionals: Labor Relations and Educational Reform (1993)], p. 120; Koppich [J. Koppich, "Rochester: The Rocky Road to Reform," in C. Kerchner and J. Koppich, eds., A Union of Professionals: Labor Relations and Educational Reform (1993)], p. 141.

that had excessively favored teachers and short-changed children. Relying on conventional bargaining practices, East Port's negotiators reached a settlement that included union concessions "most would never have anticipated three years before." They eliminated sequential bumping, prohibited assigning teachers to program areas where they had not recently demonstrated competence, added an "excellent" rating category to recognize exemplary teachers, extended the school year, required that teachers attend extra meetings, and granted principals the right to choose from among the three most senior applicants for voluntary and involuntary transfers. Despite the many give-backs in this settlement, the union president called it "fair," and a district official said it was "a giant step toward professionalism in the teaching ranks. There's no way that one could perceive this as a management-imposed agreement." Yet the participants recognized that conventional bargaining practices could take them no further. The superintendent spoke about the need for a new relationship—"We're in the same leaky lifeboat together"—while the union president asserted publicly: "The animosity which characterized labor/management relations last summer and fall must give way to a spirit of professional cooperation. To improve the quality of education, to restore public confidence in the school system, and to secure adequate funding for public education, such cooperation is not only desirable, it is vital." A union representative observed that the "union is attempting to change its approach to unionism. I think we realize that unionism, as we have known it in the sixties and seventies, is gone by the boards."[28]

When negotiators entertained new possibilities and experimented with practices unprecedented in educational bargaining, collaboration often emerged. McDonnell and Pascal point out that such risk taking was possible only because teachers had already attained "traditional bread-and-butter items that regulate teachers' basic working conditions (e.g., length of working day, class size)." These researchers conclude that such basic guarantees serve as "enabling conditions that unions must attain before they can move on to questions of professional autonomy and full participation." In their view, industrial unionism had been a necessary precursor to the professional unionism that some districts subsequently undertook.[29]

This attention to locally initiated change was augmented in 1986 when two influential publications, *A Nation Prepared* and *Tomorrow's Teachers*, started what would come to be called the "second wave" of school reform. The authors of these reports proposed approaches to reform that were fundamentally different from those the states had feverishly introduced just a few years before. Teachers, they argued, should be the agents rather than the objects of school reform. *A Nation Prepared* called for a "profession of well-educated teachers prepared to assume new powers and responsibilities to redesign schools for the future." *Tomorrow's Teachers* warned against continuing "to attempt educational reform by telling teachers what to do rather than empowering them to do what is necessary."[30]

Suddenly local districts that had been exploring new labor-management approaches quietly found they had a special license to empower teachers. In Miami-Dade County, the superintendent and union president "talked about the whole professionalization movement that came out of Carnegie" and agreed to add to the contract a task force on the professionalization of teaching. Later that year at the convention of the American Federation of Teachers (AFT), president Albert Shanker urged local union leaders to experiment with reforms at the local level, and many seized the opportunity to do so. Cincinnati union president Tom Mooney, who had already introduced in his district a union campaign called "Bargaining for Better Schools," explained that Shanker's authorization enabled him to promote his reform agenda among the rank-and-file: "The AFT gave us the sanction internally. That makes the stuff easier to sell."[31]

[28]Johnson, Nelson, and Potter [*supra* note 22], pp. 65, 66, 67, 68.

[29]McDonnell and Pascal [*supra* note 26], p. ix.

[30]Carnegie Forum on Education and the Economy [*A Nation Prepared: Teachers for the 21st Century* (1986)], p. 2; Holmes Group [*Tomorrow's Teachers* (1986)], p. 61.

[31]Provenzo [E. Provenzo, "School-Based Management and Shared Decision Making in the Dade County Public Schools," in J. Rosow and R. Zager, eds., *Allies in Educational Reform: How Teachers, Unions, and Administration Can Join Forces for Better Schools* (1989)], pp. 150–51; Johnson [S. Johnson, "Bargaining for Better Schools: Reshaping Education in the Cincinnati Public Schools," in J. Rosow and R. Zager, eds., *Allies in Educational Reform: How Teachers, Unions, and Administration Can Join Forces for Better Schools* (1989)], p. 128.

Collaborative Approaches to Bargaining. In devising new reforms, local districts found that they first had to invent new approaches to negotiation. Conventional bargaining, with its dissembling, distrust, and deceit, could never create conditions that would inspire teachers and administrators to work on hard problems together. Moreover, the split-the-difference settlements that typically emerge from bartering were hardly the kind of creative solutions that schools needed. Therefore, the parties in these flagship districts began to experiment with collaborative bargaining practices, variously called "win-win negotiations" or "principled bargaining."[32] Rather than exchanging demands and counteroffers across the table, negotiators sat side-by-side in labor-management task forces, seeking solutions to challenging problems. Since union leaders and administrators in districts such as Miami and Rochester were long-time professional colleagues who had committed themselves to working together, their new experiments were further supported by personal candor, a readiness to try new things, and an underlying trust in each other's good intentions.

The detailed accounts of these districts' efforts, the difficulties they encountered, and the reforms they devised are instructive, even inspiring, although perhaps overly optimistic about the outcomes.[33] What is certain, however, is that the scope of bargaining, still technically restricted in many states to issues of wages, hours, and working conditions, had in practice greatly expanded beyond those formal limits. Local negotiators dealt with a wide range of issues, including teachers' role and responsibilities, professional accountability, curriculum reform, staff development, administrative practice, and parental involvement. Educational policy was at the center, rather than the margins, of their attention.

In some local districts, this shift from industrial unionism to "professional unionism" led to contract provisions that directly challenged the three tenets of industrial unionism: adversarial labor-management relations, standardized practice, and generic roles for employees. . . . Examples of these new approaches will be discussed briefly.

Joint Committees Promote Labor-Management Co-operation. Recognizing that the challenges of reform could not be met simply by negotiating and signing a contract, many districts instituted joint labor-management committees to promote ongoing, collaborative problem solving. Kerchner and Koppich report that such committees were "universal [among these reforming districts], although their configuration and mission var[ied] markedly." In Cincinnati, where there were at least thirty-seven such committees, administrators joined union-appointed teachers in equal numbers to "address a variety of issues, including curriculum reform, textbook selection, staff development, Chapter I . . . planning, and the school calendar." One of the most successful of these joint committees in Cincinnati, the Teacher Allocation Committee, monitored enrollments and then assigned teachers from a surplus pool in order to reduce class size in overcrowded grades and schools. "The district agreed to leave decisions solely in the hands of this joint labor-management committee. The union agreed not to grieve the committee's decisions." In the past, class size would have been bargained contentiously and then enforced class-by-class and school-by-school, seldom solving the class-size problem and rarely using resources creatively or efficiently. By creating a joint committee that would assess ever-changing needs and carefully assign surplus teachers, labor and management acknowledged and acted on their shared interest in staffing the schools as wisely as possible. They also recognized the need to continue their collaboration long after the contract was signed.[35]

Peer Review and Career Ladders Challenge Teachers' Generic Roles. Industrial bargaining reinforces the generic definition of teachers' roles. Although some teachers have earned more academic degrees than their peers and may be paid better salaries as a result of that education, their jobs, in fact, are much the same from the first day of employment to the last. There were two reforms introduced by several of these flagship districts that fundamentally changed that uniform conception of teachers' roles. Peer review, first developed in Toledo, identifies a small

---

[32]Fisher and Ury [R. Fisher and W. Ury, *Getting to Yes: Reaching Agreement without Giving In* (1981)].

[33]Kerchner and Koppich [C. Kerchner and J. Koppich, *A Union of Professionals: Labor Relations and Educational Reform* (1993)]; Rosow and Zager [J. Rosow and R. Zager, eds., *Allies in Educational Reform: How Teachers, Unions, and Administration Can Join Forces for Better Schools* (1989)].

[35]Kerchner and Koppich [*supra* note 33], p. 11. For Cincinnati *see* King [B. King, "Cincinnati: Betting on an Unfinished Season," in Kerchner and Koppich, *supra* note 33], p. 73.

number of accomplished teachers who advise and assess both beginning teachers and experienced teachers judged to be in need of assistance. Peer review typically is overseen by a joint labor-management committee that selects the consulting teachers and weighs their recommendations for reappointment or dismissal. In Toledo, Cincinnati, and Rochester, this approach has won support among teachers because the peer reviewers bring expertise to the task and make a genuine effort to help. Remarkably, the process has led to considerably more dismissals of incompetent teachers than administrators accomplished before the program began.

Several of these districts also introduced the basic elements of a career ladder with promotional steps that signaled individuals' increasing skill and rewarded them for assuming new responsibilities. Rochester's Career in Teaching Program created a four-step ladder that included new intern teachers, provisional resident teachers, tenured professional teachers, and competitively selected lead teachers. Lead teachers take on roles as mentors, peer reviewers, staff developers, curriculum designers, or adjunct instructors at local colleges or universities. Similarly, Cincinnati introduced a Career in Teaching Program that was inspired, union president Mooney reports, by ideas from *A Nation Prepared*. In Cincinnati, as in Rochester, a joint committee was "formed to oversee the assessment process, credential lead teachers, and recommend additional roles and responsibilities for lead teachers."[36] In these districts, therefore, teachers were recognized and compensated for having attained different levels of competence and for exercising different kinds of responsibilities.

Decentralization and School-Based Management Moderate Standardization. Many reforming districts instituted some form of school-based management after 1986. Where in the past the policies of the district office and union contract applied equally to all schools, this decentralized approach to governance was designed to empower local schools to hire staff, allocate the budget, select their instructional programs, and seek waivers from union or district requirements. The point of this reform was to ensure that local schools could adapt their practices to meet the needs of their students.

Educators in Miami-Dade County had been working on these ideas since 1973, even though school-based management was not approved as a pilot program until 1986. The next year thirty-two schools participated in this experiment, and most had requested and received waivers from particular provisions of the contract. Provenzo observes that "despite all the hoopla" about innovation in Miami-Dade, "one does get the sense that a number of very important changes are taking place—ones that have the potential to be not only long lasting but of national importance." According to Phillips, by 1993 school-based management had been instituted in more than 160 schools and had served as a model for similar initiatives across the country. Every school that successfully won control of its budget or gained the right to regulate class size despite contract language stood as a challenge to union and bureaucratic pursuit of standardized practice.[37]

* * *

In addressing the changing nature of teachers' roles within the educational process, some commentators have argued that collaborative approaches should supplement but not supplant collective bargaining agreements. When governance decisions are delegated to individual schools through site-based management reforms, there is great promise for teacher participation but a continuing need for teacher protection. In the excerpt that follows, the author discusses how binding arbitration and educational trust agreements could promote collaboration without displacing collective bargaining agreements.

"Forging New Partnerships: Teacher Unions and Educational Reform in the 90s"
D. S. Doty, 1994 *B.Y.U.Educ. & L.J.* 117, 118–134 (Spring, 1994).

* * *

Over the past forty years, there has been a dramatic increase in both state and national control of public schools, with a corresponding decrease in local control. The surge in state control has been especially strong due to public pressure for reform and the "new federalism" policies of the Reagan and Bush administrations. However, in an attempt to

---

[36]For Rochester *see* Koppich [*supra* note 27], pp. 144, 145; for Cincinnati *see* King [*supra* note 35], pp. 71, 72.
[37]Provenzo [*supra* note 31], pp. 156–57; Phillips [*supra* note 27], p. 122.

make schools more responsive to communities and improve the educational process, many school districts are beginning to transfer authority to local schools under a system called site-based or school-based management.

The reasoning behind this trend is that the complex problems facing schools are "best handled where and when instruction occurs." In addition, proponents of site-based management view it as a concrete way to improve the terms and conditions of teachers' employment. The idea is that as teachers come to be treated as "professional partners" instead of hired servants, they will be more satisfied with their jobs and be more productive. Teacher unions, however, have been reluctant to endorse employee involvement initiatives for the following reasons.

A. Participatory Management as a Token Gesture

While active employee participation can result in a variety of positive outcomes, the inclusion of employees in decision making does not automatically improve the success of an enterprise. Participatory schemes often fail when employees are given the trappings of authority but not the power to set their own agenda and act conclusively thereon.

Failed participatory schemes have been common in public education. Several studies have concluded that teachers often feel that participation is nothing more than a "manipulative tool" devoid of any real meaning. According to one national survey, teachers felt that "previous participation afforded them little real influence and hence increased their skepticism. Nonetheless, they thought they should be more involved in school and district decision making, especially with respect to issues directly affecting their immediate teaching responsibilities."

A good example of this dilemma is the use of quality circles in public schools. Designed to give teachers the opportunity to have meaningful input into the decisions affecting their workplace, quality circles have not met with overwhelming approval. First, teachers have protested that circle proposals are not taken seriously and administrators often delay implementation of the proposals. Second, teachers complain that quality circles "lack an explicit and ongoing purpose," and that the circles do not represent a legitimate long-term solution to the lack of

teacher decision making. Finally, because they are usually imposed by management, quality circles are often perceived by teachers as only one more token gesture by management meant to appease, not actively involve, them.

B. The Down Side of Administration

A second reason that site-based management programs have met with resistance from unions is that while it is plausible to view teachers as managers, the reality is that many teachers do not want to be managers, at least as managers are traditionally defined. Even the most reform-minded teachers have expressed doubt with respect to the benefits of becoming quasi- administrators. Teachers do not want to waste time performing administrative tasks, particularly when such tasks are viewed as unproductive. For example, consider the following description of teachers at Central Park East Secondary School in New York City, the site of a groundbreaking reform effort:

> [T]hey did not want the same kind of information and control over budget and resources that [the principals] had, because they did not want to take the time to deal with the complexities, the politics, and the work. They clearly did want to continue their role in policy making, but not with the same detailed responsibility for implementation that the principal had.[22]

C. Egalitarian Norms of Teachers and the Collective Bargaining Agreement

Finally, unions have opposed giving teachers more administrative responsibilities because of the threat such a shift poses to egalitarian values held by teachers as a group and to the protections embodied in collective bargaining agreements. On one hand, unions recognize that without proper incentives, site-based management initiatives will flounder because teachers will not assume more work for the same pay. On the other hand, unions have largely rejected attempts to pay individual teachers more for assuming managerial responsibilities on grounds that providing "managerial teachers" higher salaries violates egalitarian norms held by teachers as a community. From the unions' perspective, even partial movement out of the classroom to take on administrative duties as a reward

---

[22]Rosow & Zager, *supra* note 8 [J. Rosow and R. Zager, *Allies in Educational Reform* (1989)], at 239.

for good teaching is intolerable. Therefore, unions argue that all teachers should be given the opportunity to share in school governance, not just a select group of quasi-administrators.

One way that unions assert the participation rights of all teachers is through collective bargaining. While critics argue that teacher unions are interested only in prescribing narrow rules governing the workplace, in truth, the underlying purpose of collective bargaining is to secure fair treatment for all teachers. Therefore, unions are wary of site-based management programs because of the possibility that these programs will undermine collective bargaining processes. Unions are worried that school-based management programs will fracture the bargaining unit and replace collective bargaining with a new form of labor-management relations unable to adequately protect teachers.

III. The Relationship Between Collective Bargaining and "Collaborative" Alternatives

The role of collective bargaining in education has been sharply criticized in recent years as being antagonistic to constructive school reform. This criticism has focused on two elements. First, the charge is made that collective bargaining creates an adversarial relationship between school boards, administrators, and teachers that discourages the cooperation necessary to improve schools' performance. Second, it is claimed that teacher unions use collective bargaining for narrow and self-serving interests which impede the development of innovative educational policies. Although collective bargaining still retains a critical role in the educational setting, teacher unions should explore alternative methods of bargaining. Union willingness to depart, at least initially, from formal negotiations may increase the success of traditional bargaining and secure more direct participation by teachers in the decision making process.

A. Two Potential Alternatives to Positional Bargaining

While several avenues exist whereby unions might deal with management in a less formal and less confrontational manner than traditional collective bargaining, two of the most promising for teachers will be examined in the following discussion.

1. Binding Arbitration. Teacher unions have been largely unsuccessful in their efforts to improve the workplace for teachers through conventional collective bargaining. Consequently, they have vigorously petitioned state legislatures to recognize the right to strike or to codify the right to binding arbitration. Unfortunately, as with the right to strike, binding arbitration has met with substantial political opposition. Most of the resistance to arbitration is centered on the perception that arbitrators will hasten the loss of local control that is alleged to already have occurred under collective bargaining. Yet the reality is that binding arbitration could have exactly the opposite effect.

First, arbitration can resolve conflict in a much less hostile and disruptive manner than a strike. By channelling labor disagreements into a process designed to encourage "best offers" and settlement, binding arbitration forces both teachers and management to be realistic in their demands. It also provides incentives for collaboration; both sides must compromise or risk having a decision imposed on them by an "outsider." Ideally, an arbitrator is rarely employed; binding arbitration actually encourages voluntary settlement of localized disputes by creating the threat of outside intervention.

Second, there is evidence that arbitration can have an inflationary impact on teacher salary levels. If teacher salaries were to increase through arbitration at least to the point where they were comparable to other salaries in the labor market, teachers would perhaps be more willing to assume additional responsibilities in local site-based management initiatives. By raising teachers' pay, binding arbitration could facilitate teachers' active endorsement of the reforms many argue are necessary to increase teacher professionalism.

Finally, binding arbitration has the potential to increase the success of the most local of procedures, i.e., collective bargaining itself. The procedure of submitting disputes to a neutral third party for his or her independent judgment on the merits not only promotes peaceful settlement but also establishes precedent. Knowing that this precedent will weigh heavily in the outcome of future disputes, a party can exert significant bargaining leverage by threatening to invoke arbitration when a conflict arises. Consequently, "the outcomes of arbitration proceedings can have dramatic effect on non-arbitrated outcomes."[46] The specter of

---

[46]*Id.* [M. Finch & T. Nagel, "Collective Bargaining in the Public Schools: Reassessing Labor Policy in an Era of Reform," *1984 Wis.L.Rev.* 1630 (1984)].

arbitration could play a large role in reducing the intransigent positions and deadlocks that often arise in public school collective bargaining.

2. Educational Policy Trust Agreements. A second alternative to conventional bargaining that has the potential both to enhance collective bargaining and to increase the direct participation of teachers in school decision making is the Educational Policy Trust Agreement. In one interesting study, two researchers found that "in virtually every case in which unions and management had explicitly and intentionally tried to solve educational problems they did so outside of the contract." Therefore, they designed a new form of agreement that would build upon, not replace, negotiated teacher contracts, and that would "allow labor and management to negotiate and reach accord on organizational goals and policies."[48] The procedures involved in reaching the agreement are relatively simple and the end product is a written compact between the school district and its teachers that gives teachers extensive authority over school policy matters.

Trust agreements work to the benefit of individual teachers and collective bargaining procedures in a number of ways. With respect to teachers, the primary advantage trust agreements present is that they provide teachers with an opportunity to participate directly in educational policy making without the negative effects of conventional employee involvement (EI) programs. It is argued that teacher unions adhering to industrial-union principles are now incompatible with public education, particularly because they focus bargaining on narrow rules of employment rather than on educational policies that have the most significant long-term impact on the workplace of teachers. Indeed, scholars recognize that while industrial-mode collective bargaining has accomplished much good for employees in all settings, "it has given workers only a very limited voice in the operation of the firm."[53] Stating that it is time for a change, one author has noted:

> [I]t is clear that more and more American workers want something beyond just a package of rights and benefits in return for agreeing to do what they are told. Employees also want the chance to exercise their own judgment

about the work they are doing; they want to face the challenge of making a difference in the quality of their services and the success of the enterprise.[54]

Trust agreements address this concept for teachers, enabling them to design and implement such central educational policies as "curriculum development, instructional goals, the assignment of students or teachers, the substance of evaluation, and the bases for discipline and discharge of unprofessional teachers."[55] Interestingly, whereas conventional EI initiatives automatically assume that management will implement their terms, a properly designed trust agreement would empower teachers themselves to carry out its provisions. Thus, trust agreements would go a long way in resolving the tension "between the goal of enlarging workers' influence over what happens to them in their daily lives on the job and the delegation of the representation role to a large external union organization, in which the individual member or local unit has only limited influence."

With respect to collective bargaining, trust agreements are needed supplements, because they help to establish a solid relationship of trust between labor and management. While trust agreements may not be legally binding in the same fashion as collective bargaining agreements, they have the capacity to influence formal negotiations that do result in legally enforceable documents. Certainly if an atmosphere of creative risk-sharing and problem-solving is developed through trust agreement processes, both teachers and management will be more willing to make binding commitments on educational policy issues in collective bargaining agreements.

B. The Continued Importance of Strong Teacher Unions and Traditional Collective Bargaining

Collaboration between teachers and management outside the formal bargaining process appears to play a critical role both in promoting more individual participation by teachers in school policy decisions and in encouraging better labor/management relations. However, the essential role of collective bargaining itself in school reform efforts should not be overlooked by either side, for it is bargaining that validates and solidifies the changes being sought.

---

[48]*Id.* [C. Kerchner & D. Mitchell, *The Changing Idea of a Teachers' Union* 247 (1988)].

[53]Weiler, *supra* note 51 [P. Weiler, *Governing the Workplace* (1990)], at 219.
[54]*Id.*

[55]Kerchner & Mitchell, *supra* note 47 [C. Kerchner & D. Mitchell, *The Changing Idea of a Teachers' Union* (1988)], at 250.

There are certainly compelling arguments to be made for changing the conventional bargaining tactics used by educators. In fact, several scholars advocate a complete overhaul of teacher union methods that would move away from "industrial" unionism in favor of more cooperative strategies.[66] Yet "tough" unionism and "hard" bargaining still have a legitimate place in education; it is arguable that without such an aggressive approach by teacher unions, teacher protections will be eroded and meaningful participation will drown under the tidal wave of reform initiatives. It is necessary for unions to maintain at least some degree of spirited self-interest and firmness in order for teachers to be true agents for change in educational policy making.

1. Confrontational Bargaining Is Essential to Reform.
Many policymakers and educators are of the opinion that teacher unions are inherently adversarial and necessarily opposed to any efforts made to improve the performance and participation of teachers. Such opinion may influence, at least indirectly, the behavior of unions; if unions act in conformity with expectations, they may adamantly oppose change and innovation with respect to school policy. Yet it would be a myth to assume that current efforts to increase teacher participation through a new regime of "collaborative" bargaining will result in labor-management relations that are particularly cooperative and nonconfrontational. At the same time, it would be inaccurate to claim that a surge of "new bargaining," based on informal, cooperative rendezvous between teachers and management, will automatically bring about substantial school reform.

A better view is that collective bargaining does not generate conflict, but rather reveals it in a forum specially suited for securing its resolution. As one scholar has explained, "[o]ne of the most distinctive features of collective bargaining is that it combines elements of conflict and cooperation, providing incentives for the parties to cooperate by posing conflict as an alternative."[72] Differences between teachers and management, both as to priorities and policies, should not be discouraged, but encouraged through the collective bargaining process. Not only does collective bargaining validate the existence of teachers' perspective and expertise, but by juxtaposing differences it provides an avenue whereby these differences may become the "source of interdependence and accommodation."[74] This interdependence, in turn, is highly consistent with notions of local control that are behind school-based management programs.

2. Collective Bargaining Fosters Democracy and Professionalism.
Besides fostering cooperation through conflict, collective bargaining also plays a direct role in providing individual employees with an opportunity to be active participants in the management of an enterprise. Critics have argued that participatory norms valued by employees are effectively quashed by the process of collective bargaining as it now exists. In reality, however, unionized employees are often very involved in the decisions affecting their workplace. As teachers learn to be participants within the bargaining process itself, there is hope that they will be accepted much more readily into the arena of school policy making, long the sole prerogative of management.

Moreover, collective bargaining is consistent with notions of teacher "professionalism." Certainly the push by teacher unions for things such as higher salaries and reduced work loads demonstrates a substantial degree of professional self-interest. However, these professional goals of teachers are not antithetical to the goals of education reform. In fact, the goals of teachers and the goals of the educational system are often parallel, if not closely connected.

3. Collective Bargaining Legitimizes "Employee Involvement Programs" and Fosters a "Team" Approach.
There are undoubtedly several advantages to "collaborative" negotiations outside formal collective bargaining processes. In addition to those already mentioned, the National Education

---

[66]See Weiler, *supra* note 51 [P. Weiler, *Governing the Workplace* (1990)], at 218–223 (advocating a move away from traditional industrial unionism toward "enterprise unionism": "it is undeniably characteristic of [industrial-style] union representation that although the process may well be achieving many good things for workers, it is not doing so through the workers"); Kerchner & Mitchell, *supra* note 47 [C. Kerchner & D. Mitchell, *The Changing Idea of a Teachers' Union* (1988)], at 232 (proposing a shift from industrial unionism to "professional unionism," which would "give first priority to formulating appropriate teacher job definitions and supporting the development of a productive work culture").

[72]*Id.* [S. Bacharach et al., "School Management and Teacher Unions: The Capacity for Cooperation in an Age of Reform," 91 *Teachers College Record* (1989), at 98].

[74]*Id.*

Association (NEA) has noted that potential benefits of collaborative bargaining include: (1) its support of the use of collective bargaining as a vehicle for education reform, (2) its potential to improve public confidence in the system, (3) its potential to improve local associations' relationships with districts, (4) its encouragement of creative solutions to difficult problems, and (5) its role in the development of long-term vision. Yet "collaborative" methods also pose at least three significant problems for teachers, all of which can be minimized by conventional collective bargaining.

First, a primary danger of collaborative, participatory approaches is that they can lead to the failure of the union to appropriately deal with member interests. This failure results from the fact that teacher participation schemes, like the Educational Policy Trust Agreement, tend to stray beyond the bounds of policy making and enter into areas covered by the collective bargaining agreement. When conflicts arise between the trust agreement and the contract, both sides may negotiate a change in the contract or waive individual contract provisions, resulting in the loss of contractual teacher protections. If by doing so, unions compromise important terms and conditions of teachers' employment such as compensation and seniority, teachers may feel deserted. When teachers view the collective bargaining agreement as nothing but an empty shell, their faith in the system will be destroyed and they will be unwilling to participate in any form of school-based management.

Second, teacher participatory management schemes have the potential to fracture the bargaining unit and create serious hostility in the workplace. Practical reality dictates that when union facilitators in charge of school-based management programs continually have to lobby the administration for financial support, and when most training is conducted by the administration, the union facilitators themselves will often begin to think and act like administrators. This development causes division between union members integrally involved in site-based management and union members concerned with implementing the contract and handling grievances. Collective bargaining, on the other hand, emphasizes team building and recognizes the unique roles belonging to each educator in the system. By properly and clearly separating the roles of teachers

and managers, collective bargaining can structure site-based management in a way that allows active teacher participation in policy making but that leaves true administrative duties with administrators. In short, collective bargaining fosters confidence and trust among all parties in a site-based management program. As a Transportation Communications Union official, speaking on Quality of Work Life programs, stated:

> Through the use of the collective bargaining tool, we feel we can set the stage for success in the use of Quality of Work Life programs. We want to help and to participate, but only if we can know and trust our partners. Again, this means coming to an agreement through the bargaining process. Agreements that clearly spell out the formation of such committees, their purpose, their duration, methods of evaluation, and if successful, how the rewards of that success will be shared by the parties involved.[93]

Third and most importantly, because of their nonbinding status, participatory management programs may not represent meaningful, permanent solutions to the lack of teacher decision-making involvement. Even though the creators of the Educational Policy Trust Agreement concept envision a type of binding compact, the fact is that trust agreements differ from collective bargaining in that they are morally, but not legally binding. Therefore, even if teachers are empowered through the agreement to help make school policies, implementation of their proposals may be frustrated if a revenue short-fall or other unexpected problem arises. Collective bargaining by an independent union is necessary to secure the contractual right to teacher participation and to secure the implementation of agreements reached by means of such participation.

4. Independent Unions Provide Stability. Finally, with respect to radical reform efforts, teacher unions may represent the only stability school districts have. With the public outcry for change in education, many people are proposing drastic overhauls that could not only seriously undermine important terms and conditions of teachers' employment, but that also represent ineffective "quick-fix" schemes. Commenting on this situation, one author has noted:

> Teachers . . . have been accused of sacrificing the betterment of schools to their own narrow, selfish ends, such as better pay and benefits. Other evidence exists

[93]*Employee Participation Programs, supra* note 7 [National Education Association, *Employee Participation Programs: Considerations for the School Site* (1988)], at 21.

that unions are perhaps the only major hope for children, since the "producers" of education are among the few large, powerful, organized forces that fight regularly for more resources and better working conditions in education. Parents, the consumers of education, are becoming more active in "choice" schemes for selecting a school for their children but are limited by their short-lived interest in education and their lack of organized power.[100]

Consequently, teacher unions are capable not only of providing the impetus for reform, but also of providing the staying power necessary for effective reform measures to succeed.

* * *

NOTES AND QUESTIONS

1. Adversarialism and Cooperation: An Uneasy Coexistence?

Can collaborative arrangements exist alongside an adversarial bargaining process? How would this compartmentalization of teachers' roles take place? Would teachers use adversarial methods to secure economic benefits while pursuing cooperative approaches to promote educational reform? Can such distinctions in goals and methods endure over the long run? See also Bacharach, Shedd, and Conley, "School Management and Teacher Unions: The Capacity for Cooperation in an Age of Reform," 91 Teachers College Report 97 (1989).

2. Teacher Training and Professional Collaboration

Clearly, teachers are grappling with their role in a shifting educational landscape. Most experts see professional collaboration and collective action as critical to educational reform, but they disagree about how such efforts can be implemented in a public educational system that is often faced with stringent demands and scarce resources. Limited financial resources translate into low teacher salaries and a shortage of qualified staff. Wise, "Teacher Professionalism: The Movement Has Begun," 3 ERIC Rev. 12 (1995). If the nation is seriously committed to teacher preparation and participation in policy making, new models for training and development will be an essential component. Little, "Teachers' Professional Development in a Climate of Educa-

tional Reform," 15 Educational Evaluation and Policy Analysis 130–139 (Summer 1993); Disworth and Inig, "Professional Teacher Development," 3 ERIC Rev. 5, 8–10 (1995).

C. The Courts, Institutional Reform, and Student Rights

In addition to elected officials and career professionals, state and federal judges have played a significant role in shaping educational policy. Judicial oversight is supposed to be the exception rather than the rule. Courts interpret education laws and regulations, but they are generally not involved in the day-to-day business of overseeing the schools. Only when judges find that invasions of students' rights are serious enough to constitute an abuse of discretion do courts assume a direct role in monitoring educational governance.

1. Institutional Reform Litigation. The courts began to play a critically important role in school governance in the 1950s when the United States Supreme Court declared legally-mandated segregation in public schools unconstitutional. Brown v. Board of Education, 347 U.S. 483 (1954). The federal courts remained extremely active in this area throughout the 1960s and 1970s, as discussed in chapter 4. As a result, leading scholars began to speculate that an entirely new model of judicial decision making was in the making. In his seminal work, Abram Chayes laid out the key features of this new kind of litigation.

"The Role of the Judge in Public Law Litigation"
A. Chayes, 89 (7) Harv.L.Rev. 1281, 1282–1284 (May 1976).
Copyright © 1976 by the Harvard Law Review Association.

* * *

In our received tradition, the lawsuit is a vehicle for settling disputes between private parties about private rights. The defining features of this conception of civil adjudication are:

(1) The lawsuit is bipolar. Litigation is organized as a contest between two individuals or at least two unitary interests, diametrically opposed, to be decided on a winner-takes-all basis.

---

[100]Labor Relations in Education 333 (B. Cooper ed., 1992).

(2) Litigation is *retrospective.* The controversy is about an identified set of completed events: whether they occurred, and if so, with what consequences for the legal relations of the parties.

(3) *Right and remedy are interdependent.* The scope of the relief is derived more or less logically from the substantive violation under the general theory that the plaintiff will get compensation measured by the harm caused by the defendant's breach of duty—in contract by giving plaintiff the money he would have had absent the breach; in tort by paying the value of the damage caused.

(4) The lawsuit is a *self-contained* episode. The impact of the judgment is confined to the parties. If plaintiff prevails there is a simple compensatory transfer, usually of money, but occasionally the return of a thing or the performance of a definite act. If defendant prevails, a loss lies where it has fallen. In either case, entry of judgment ends the court's involvement.

(5) The process is *party-initiated* and *party-controlled.* The case is organized and the issues defined by exchanges between the parties. Responsibility for fact development is theirs. The trial judge is a neutral arbiter of their interactions who decides questions of law only if they are put in issue by an appropriate move of a party.

This capsule description of what I have called the traditional conception of adjudication is no doubt overdrawn. It was not often, if ever, expressed so severely; indeed, because it was so thoroughly taken for granted, there was little occasion to do so. Although I do not contend that the traditional conception ever conformed fully to what judges were doing in fact, I believe it has been central to our understanding and our analysis of the legal system.

Whatever its historical validity, the traditional model is clearly invalid as a description of much current civil litigation in the federal district courts. Perhaps the dominating characteristic of modern federal litigation is that lawsuits do not arise out of disputes between private parties about private rights. Instead, the object of litigation is the vindication of constitutional or statutory policies. The shift in the legal basis of the lawsuit explains many, but not all, facets of what is going on "in fact" in federal trial courts. For this reason, although the label is not wholly satisfactory, I shall call the emerging model "public law litigation."

The characteristic features of the public law model are very different from those of the traditional model.

The party structure is sprawling and amorphous, subject to change over the course of the litigation. The traditional adversary relationship is suffused and intermixed with negotiating and mediating processes at every point. The judge is the dominant figure in organizing and guiding the case, and he draws for support not only on the parties and their counsel, but on a wide range of outsiders—masters, experts, and oversight personnel. Most important, the trial judge has increasingly become the creator and manager of complex forms of ongoing relief, which have widespread effects on persons not before the court and require the judge's continuing involvement in administration and implementation. School desegregation . . . cases come readily to mind as avatars of this new form of litigation.

* * *

As Professor Chayes indicates, desegregation lawsuits epitomized public law litigation. In the decades that followed, other groups used the same model to challenge school policies related to gender, language and culture, disability, and poverty, as discussed in chapters 5 and 6. The proliferation of institutional reform litigation prompted deep concern about the legitimacy of far-ranging judicial activism. Building on Chayes' work, Owen Fiss defended structural reform by courts as the vindication of public values.

"The Forms of Justice"

O. Fiss, 93 *Harv.L.Rev.* 1, 9–17 (1979). Copyright © 1979 by the Harvard Law Review Association.

* * *

The values that lie at the heart of most structural litigation today—equality, due process, liberty, security of the person, no cruel and unusual punishment—are not embodied in textually-specific prohibitions; the equal protection clause—no state shall deny any person equal protection of the laws is as specific as the free speech clause—Congress shall pass no law abridging the freedom of speech—but neither is very specific. They simply contain public values that must be given concrete meaning and harmonized with the general structure of the Constitution. The same is probably true of all the other provisions of the Constitution (*e.g.,* the commerce clause) that have been central to constitutional litigation for almost two centuries. The absence of textual specificity does not make the values any less real, nor any less important. The values embodied in such non-textually-specific prohibitions as the equal protection and due process clauses are central to our constitutional order. They give our society an identity and inner coherence—its distinctive public morality. The absence of a textually-specific prohibition does not deny the importance of these values, but only makes the meaning-giving enterprise more arduous: less reliance can be placed on text.

Of course, the further one moves from text, the greater the risk of abuse; it is easier for judges, even unwittingly, to enact into law their own preferences in the name of having discovered the true meaning, say, of equality or liberty. . . . The judges of *Brown* [*v. Board of Education*, which struck down state-mandated segregation in public schools] may have, as the critics of the Right and Left keep reminding us, enacted into law their own preferences, peculiarly reflecting their privileged social position; but it is also possible, indeed, I would say, it is eminently probable, that these judges had given a true account of the constitutional value of equality. . . .

This conception of the judicial function, which sees the judge as trying to give meaning to our constitutional values, expects a lot from judges—maybe too much. The expectation is not founded on a belief in their moral expertise, or on a denial of their humanity. Judges are most assuredly people. They are lawyers, but in terms of personal characteristics they are no different from successful businessmen or politicians. Their capacity to make a special contribution to our social life derives not from any personal traits or knowledge, but from the definition of the office in which they find themselves and through which they exercise power. That office is structured by both ideological and institutional factors that enable and perhaps even force the judge to be objective—not to express his preferences or personal beliefs, or those of the citizenry, as to what is right or just, but constantly to strive for the true meaning of the constitutional value. Two aspects of the judicial office give it this special cast: one is the judge's obligation to participate in a dialogue, and the second is his independence.

The judge is entitled to exercise power only after he has participated in a dialogue about the meaning of the public values. It is a dialogue with very special qualities: (a) Judges are not in control of their agenda, but are compelled to confront grievances or claims they would otherwise prefer to ignore. (b) Judges do not have full control over whom they must listen to. They are bound by rules requir-

ing them to listen to a broad range of persons or spokesmen. (c) Judges are compelled to speak back, to respond to the grievance or the claim, and to assume individual responsibility for that response. (d) Judges must also justify their decisions.

The obligation to justify a decision has given rise to never-ending debates as to the proper sources of judicial decisions—text, intentions of the Framers, general structure of the Constitution, ethics, the good of the nation, etc. For the notion of justification, as opposed to explanation, implies that the reasons supporting a decision be "good" reasons, and this in turn requires norms or rules for determining what counts as a "good" reason. My intention is not to participate in the debate about the rules for justification, but to stress two facts that all seem to agree on as to what might count as a "good" reason. The first is that the reason cannot consist of a preference, be it a preference of the contestants, of the body politic, or of the judge. The statement "I prefer" or "we prefer" in the context of a judicial, rather than a legislative decision, merely constitutes an explanation, not a justification. Second, the reason must somehow transcend the personal, transient beliefs of the judge or the body politic as to what is right or just or what should be done. Something more is required to transform these personal beliefs into values that are worthy of the status "constitutional" and all that it implies—binding on society as a whole, entitled to endure, not forever but long enough to give our public morality an inner coherence, and largely to be enforced by courts.

The judge is required to listen and to speak, and to speak in certain ways. He is also required to be independent. This means, for one thing, that he not identify with or in any way be connected to the particular contestants. He must be impartial, distant, and detached from the contestants, thereby increasing the likelihood that his decision will not be an expression of the self-interest (or preferences) of the contestants, which is the antithesis of the right or just decision. The norm of impartiality also requires that the judge be independent from politics, in this instance understood as the process of expressing the preferences of the people. The judge must not view his job as one of registering those preferences. Independence is clearly the norm in the federal system with its promise of life tenure, but is present also in those state systems in which judges are elected. The judge might be vulnerable to the body politic when he stands for election, but that does not determine how he should define his job, or how the body politic should use its power.

The task of a judge, then, should be seen as giving meaning to our public values and adjudication as the process through which that meaning is revealed or elaborated. The question still remains of determining the relationship between the courts and the other agencies of government, for structural reform places the courts in the position of issuing directives to other agencies of government. The judiciary's essential function is to give meaning to our constitutional values, but many of these other agencies can perform that function in addition to that of registering the preferences of the people. The legislature or the school board . . . is entitled to express the preferences of the citizenry, a function not entrusted to the courts, but these agencies can also strive to give meaning to equality, or to work out the complicated relationship between liberty and equality. . . . The existing practices in and of themselves cannot be taken as a reflection of the considered judgment of another branch of government on the meaning of a constitutional value, particularly since we are dealing with bureaucracies, in which policy is often determined by internal power plays and default. On the other hand, there can be genuine conflicts. Situations—school desegregation is probably a good example—will arise where the courts and other agencies of government will come to the opposite conclusion as to the meaning of a constitutional value, and the need will arise to work out the relationship between the branches.

To simply postulate the supremacy of the more majoritarian branches, the legislative or the executive . . . is no answer, for, as we saw, the people's preferences are not the standard, and there is no discernible connection between majoritarianism and the meaning of a constitutional value. Courts may have their difficulties in giving a constitutional value its correct meaning, but so would the other branches. History is as filled with legislative and executive mistakes as it is filled with judicial ones. Admittedly, adjudication will have its class and professional biases, because so much power is entrusted to lawyers, but the legislative and executive processes will have their own biases—wealth, dynasty, charisma. It is not clear which set of biases will cause the greatest departure from the truth.

* * *

The theory of structural reform, no more than any other form of constitutional litigation, does not require that courts have the *only* word or even the *last*

word, but that they be allowed to speak and to do so with some authority. Process is the measure of that authority. The right of the judge to speak, and the obligation of others to listen, depends not on the judge's personal attributes, nor even on the content of his message, but on the quality of his process—on his ability to be distant and detached from the immediate contestants and from the body politic, yet fully attentive to grievances, and responsive in terms that transcend preferences and that are sufficient to support a judgment deemed "constitutional." There may be other processes or methods for giving meaning to constitutional values, though what they might be is not clear to me, but the process I have just described—the core of adjudication—is the only one open to the judge. This process is a limitation on his legitimacy, and even more importantly, it has a close conceptual connection—not just a contingent or instrumental one—to the very act of giving meaning to a constitutional value. We impute function largely on the basis of process and at the same time function shapes process. Others may search for the true meaning of our constitutional values, but when they do, they will have to mimic—if they can—the process of the judge.

In the 1960's, the courts played a central role in our social life because they saw that the ideal of equality was inconsistent with the caste system implied by Jim Crow laws. In the decade that followed, they struggled to give meaning to a broader range of constitutional values, and perceived the threat to those values in a wide variety of contexts—the barbarisms of total institutions, the abuses of the police, the indignities of welfare systems. Today we have doubts about the role of courts and, just as we are rediscovering the market, we are quickly resurrecting . . . the claim of legislative supremacy. This development cannot be wholly explained in terms of increasing doubts as to the competency of courts; for without a belief in the conceptual connection between function and process, without a belief in the capacity of courts to give meaning to our constitutional values, [there is no way] to explain the judicial function in cases of legislative failure or why the void left by legislative failure should be filled by the courts. In my judgment, the resurgence of [legislative supremacy] does not stem from doubts about the special capacity of courts and their processes to move us closer to a correct understanding of our constitutional values, but from the frail quality of our substantive vision. We have lost our confidence in the existence of the values that underlie the litigation of the 1960's, or, for that matter, in the existence of any public values.

All is preference. That seems to be the crucial issue, not the issue of relative institutional competence. Only once we reassert our belief in the existence of public values, that values such as equality, liberty, due process, no cruel and unusual punishment, security of the person, or free speech can have a true and important meaning, that must be articulated and implemented—yes, discovered—will the role of the courts in our political system become meaningful, or for that matter even intelligible.

* * *

Despite defenses like those offered by Professor Fiss, judicial activism has come under increasing attack, and courts have retreated from the oversight of large-scale bureaucracies. As chapter 4 has shown, for example, federal courts were terminating desegregation cases throughout the 1980s and 1990s with the Supreme Court's support. As a result, scholars have come to question not just the legitimacy but also the efficacy of judicial intervention.

"The Hollow Hope: Can Courts Bring About Social Change?"

G. Rosenberg, *The Hollow Hope: Can Courts Bring About Social Change?* 10–16 (1991). Copyright © 1991, The University of Chicago Press.

* * *

The Limited Nature of Rights

The Constitution, and the set of beliefs that surround it, is not unbounded. Certain rights are enshrined in it and others are rejected. In economic terms, private control over the allocation and distribution of resources, the use of property, is protected. "Rights" to certain minimums, or equal shares of basic goods, are not. Further, judicial discretion is bound by the norms and expectations of the legal culture. These two parameters . . . present a problem for litigators pressing the courts for significant social reform because most such litigation is based on constitutional claims that rights are being denied. An individual or group comes into a court claiming it is being denied some benefit, or protection from arbitrary and discriminatory action, and that it is *entitled*

to this benefit or that protection. . . . [T]his has four important consequences for social reformers.

First, . . . it limits the sorts of claims that can be made, for not all social reform goals can be plausibly presented in the name of constitutional rights. For example, there are no constitutional rights to decent housing, adequate levels of welfare, or clean air, while there are constitutional rights to minimal governmental interference in the use of one's property. This may mean that "practically significant but legally irrelevant policy matters may remain beyond the purview of the court."* Further, as Gordon** suggests, "the legal forms we use set limits on what we can imagine as practical outcomes." Thus, the nature of rights in the U.S. legal system, embedded in the Constitution, may constrain the courts in producing significant social reform by preventing them from hearing many claims.

A second consequence . . . is that, even where claims can be made, social reformers must often argue for the establishment of a new right, or the extension of a generally accepted right to a new situation. In welfare rights litigation, for example, the Court was asked to find a constitutional right to welfare. This need to push the courts to read the Constitution in an expansive or "liberal" way creates two main difficulties. Underlying these difficulties is judicial awareness of the need for predictability in the law and the politically exposed nature of judges whose decisions go beyond the positions of electorally accountable officials. First, the Constitution, lawyers, judges, and legal academics form a dominant legal culture that at any given time accepts some rights and not others and sets limits on the interpretation and expansion of rights. Judicial discretion is bound by the beliefs and norms of this legal culture, and decisions that stray too far from them are likely to be reversed and severely criticized. Put simply, courts, and the judges that compose them, even if sympathetic to social reform plaintiffs, may be unwilling to risk crossing this nebulous yet real boundary. Second, and perhaps more important, is the role of precedent and what Justice Traynor calls the "continuity scripts of the law." Traynor, a justice of the California Supreme Court for twenty-five years, Chief Justice from 1964 to 1970, and known as a judge open to new ideas, wrote of the "very caution of the judicial process." Arguing that "a judge must plod rather than soar," Traynor saw that the "greatest judges" proceed "at the pace of a tortoise that steadily makes advances though it carries the

---

*Note, "Implementation Problems in Institutional Reform Litigation," 91 *Harv.L.Rev.* 428, 436 (1977).

**R. Gordon, "Critical Legal Histories," 36 *Stan.L.Rev.* 57, 111 (1984).

past on its back." Constrained by precedent and the beliefs of the dominant legal culture, judges . . . are not likely to act as crusaders.

Third, . . . as Scheingold*** points out, that to claim a right in court is to accept the procedures and obligations of the legal system. These procedures are designed, in part, to make it difficult for courts to hear certain kinds of cases. As the Council for Public Interest Law (CPIL) puts it, doctrines of standing and of class actions, the so-called political question doctrine, the need to have a live controversy, and other technical doctrines can "deter courts from deciding cases on the merits" and can result in social reform groups being unable to present their best arguments, or even have their day in court. Once in court, however, the legal process tends to dissipate significant social reform by making appropriate remedies unlikely. This can occur, McCann# points out, because policy-based litigation aimed at significant social reform is usually "disaggregate[d] . . . into discrete conflicts among limited actors over specific individual entitlements." Remedial decrees, it has been noted, "must not confuse what is socially or judicially desirable with what is legally required." Thus, litigation seldom deals with "underlying issues and problems" and is "directed more toward symptoms than causes."

Finally, it has long been argued that framing issues in legally sound ways robs them of "political and purposive appeal." In the narrow sense, the technical nature of legal argument can denude issues of emotional, widespread appeal. More broadly, there is the danger that litigation by the few will replace political action by the many and reduce the democratic nature of the American polity. James Bradley Thayer, writing in 1901, was concerned that reliance on litigation would sap the democratic process of its vitality. He warned that the "tendency of a common and easy resort" to the courts, especially in asking them to invalidate acts of the democratically accountable branches, would "dwarf the political capacity of the people."% This view was echoed more recently by McCann, who found that litigation-prone activists' "legal rights approach to expanding democracy has significantly narrowed their conception of political action itself."@ Expanding the point, McCann argued that "legal tactics not only absorb scarce resources that could be used for popular mobilization . . . [but also] make it difficult to develop broadly based, multiissue grassroots associations of sustained citizen allegiance."& . . .

Limits on Judicial Independence — The Institutional Factor

. . . [R]eformers have often turned to courts when opposition to significant social reform in the other branches has prevented them from acting. Thus, much significant social reform litigation takes place in the context of stalemate within, or opposition from, the other branches. For courts to be effective in such situations, they must, logically, be independent of those other branches. . . . [A] broad array of evidence . . . suggests the founders did not thoroughly insulate courts or provide them with unfailing independence.

To start, the appointment process, of course, limits judicial independence. Judges do not select themselves. Rather, they are chosen by politicians, the president and the Senate at the federal level. Presidents, while not clairvoyant, tend to nominate judges who they think will represent their judicial philosophies. Clearly, changing court personnel can bring court decisions into line with prevailing political opinion (and dampen support for significant social reform). Thus, . . . the appointment process . . . limit[s] judicial independence.

Judicial independence requires that court decisions, in comparison to legislation, do not invariably reflect public opinion. . . . [H]owever, . . . Supreme Court decisions, historically, have seldom strayed far from what was politically acceptable. Rather than suggesting independence, this judicial unwillingness to often blaze its own trail perhaps suggests, in the words of Finley Peter Dunne's Mr. Dooley, that "th' supreme coort follows th' iliction returns."

In at least two important ways, . . . Congress may constrain court actions. First, in the statutory area, Congress can override decisions, telling the courts they misinterpreted the intent of the law. That is, Congress may rewrite a provision to meet court objections or simply state more clearly what it meant so that the

---

*** S. Scheingold, *The Politics of Rights: Lawyers, Public Policy, and Political Change* (1974).

M. McCann, *Taking Reform Seriously: Perspectives on Public Interest Liberalism* 200 (1986).

% J. Thayer, *John Marshall* 107 (1901).

@ M. McCann, *Taking Reform Seriously: Perspectives on Public Interest Liberalism* 26 (1986).
& *Id.* at 200 (1986).

courts' reading of the law is repudiated. Second, although Congress cannot directly reverse decisions based on constitutional interpretations, presumably untouchable by the democratic process, it may be able to constrain them by threatening certain changes in the legal structure. A large part of the reason, of course, is the appointment process. But even without the power of appointment, the Court may be susceptible to credible threats against it. Historical review of the relations of the Court to the other branches of the federal government suggests that the Court cannot for long stand alone against such pressure. From the "Court-packing" plan of FDR [Franklin Delano Roosevelt] to recent bills proposing to remove federal court jurisdiction over certain issues, court-curbing proposals may allow Congress to constrain courts as producers of significant social reform.

American courts . . . are particularly deferential to the positions of the federal government. On the Supreme Court level, the solicitor general is accorded a special role. The office has unusual access to the Court and is often asked by the Court to intervene in cases and present the government's position. When the solicitor general petitions the Court to enter a case, the Court almost invariably grants the request, regardless of the position of the parties. The government is also unusually successful in convincing the Court to hear cases it appeals and to not hear those it opposes. The solicitor general's access to the Court carries over to the winning of cases. Historically, the solicitor general (or the side the government is supporting when it enters a case as *amicus*) wins about 70 percent of the time. It appears that the federal government has both extraordinary access to and persuasive abilities with the Court. That does not comport with notions of independence and a judicial system able to defy legislative and political majorities. . . .

Implementation and Institutional Relations

For courts, or any other institution, to effectively produce significant social reform, they must have the ability to develop appropriate policies and the power to implement them. This, in turn, requires a host of tools that courts . . . lack. In particular, successful implementation requires enforcement powers. Court decisions, requiring people to act, are not self-executing. But as Hamilton pointed out two centuries ago in *The Federalist Papers* (1787–88), courts lack such powers. Indeed, it is for this reason more than any other that Hamilton emphasized the courts'

character as the least dangerous branch. Assuaging fears that the federal courts would be a political threat, Hamilton argued in *Federalist* 78 that the judiciary "has no influence over either the sword or the purse; no direction either of the strength or of the wealth of the society; and can take no active resolution whatever. It may truly be said to have neither FORCE nor WILL, but merely judgment; and must ultimately depend upon the aid of the executive arm even for the efficacy of its judgments." Unlike Congress and the executive branch, Hamilton argued, the federal courts were utterly dependent on the support of the other branches and elite actors. In other words, for Court orders to be carried out, political elites, electorally accountable, must support them and act to implement them. . . . [T]his structural "fact" of American political life [was recognized] by early Chief Justices John Jay and John Marshall, both of whom were acutely aware of the Court's limits. President Jackson recognized these limits, too, when he reputedly remarked about a decision with which he did not agree, "John Marshall has made his decision, now let him enforce it." More recently, the unwillingness of state authorities to follow court orders, and the need to send federal troops to Little Rock, Arkansas, to carry them out, makes the same point. Without elite support (the federal government in this case), the Court's orders would have been frustrated. While it is clear that courts can stymie change, though ultimately not prevent it, the Constitution . . . appears to leave the courts few tools to insure that their decisions are carried out.

If the separation of powers, and the placing of the power to enforce court decisions in the executive branch, leaves courts practically powerless to insure that their decisions are supported by elected and administrative officials, then they are heavily dependent on popular support to implement their decisions. If American citizens are aware of Court decisions, and feel duty-bound to carry them out, then Court orders will be implemented. However, . . . survey data suggest that the American public is consistently uninformed of even major Supreme Court decisions and thus not in a position to support them. If the public or political elites are not ready or willing to make changes, the most elegant legal reasoning will be for nought.

This constraint may be particularly powerful with issues of significant social reform. It is likely that as courts deal with issues involving contested values, as issues of significant social reform do almost by definition, they will generate opposition. In turn, opposition may induce a withdrawal of the elite and public support crucial for implementation. Thus, . . . the contested nature of issues of significant social reform makes it unlikely that the popular support necessary for implementation will be forthcoming.

* * *

NOTES AND QUESTIONS

1. Activism and Constraint

Are judges suited to the role of enunciating public values and implementing institutional reform? Do Professor Fiss and Professor Rosenberg reach different conclusions because one focuses on adjudicating fundamental values while the other focuses on the practical barriers to implementing change? How should unique judicial competencies and limitations be weighed in evaluating whether courts should undertake reform?

2. Courts Compared to Other Forums for Reform

Can courts promote values in traditional, bipolar lawsuits? Does the adversarial process permit value disputes to be fully explored, even in a multipolar litigation? Can legislatures or administrative agencies engage in fact finding superior to that which courts can undertake? Is agenda-setting a proper role for the courts? Are other government actors likely to undertake institutional reform without judicial prodding? For a discussion of how the New Jersey court's decisions on school finance forced the legislature to confront the need for reform, see R. Lehne, The Quest for Justice (1978).

2. Educational Malpractice. The debate over institutional reform litigation has captured the imagination of scholars, but courts can play other roles in the educational process. For example, they can harken back to a more traditional model of dispute resolution in which an individual student alleges that a particular school district has failed to meet its obligation to deliver an adequate education. Yet, as educational malpractice litigation shows, courts have been reluctant to intervene in these disputes for fear of becoming a "super school board." Despite this judicial reluctance, some commentators have contended that school districts should be directly accountable to students for the educational harms that they inflict on them. See, e.g., Ratner, "A New Legal Duty for Ur-

ban Public Schools: Effective Education in Basic Skills," 63 Tex.L.Rev. 777 (1985); Loscalzo, "Liability for Malpractice in Education," 14 J.of Law & Educ. 595 (1985); Elson, "A Common Law Remedy for the Educational Harms Caused by Incompetent or Careless Teaching," 73 Nw.U.L.Rev. 641 (1978); Note, "Educational Malpractice: Can the Judiciary Remedy the Growing Problem of Functional Illiteracy?" 13 Suffolk U.L.Rev. 27 (1979). But see Yudof, "Effective Schools and Federal and State Constitutions: A Variety of Opinions," 63 Tex.L.Rev. 865 (1985); Comment, "Educational Malpractice," 64 U.Det.L.Rev. 717 (1987).

Just as lawyers and physicians, in appropriate circumstances, may be held liable under common law tort principles for professional incompetence, so too, they argue, educators should be held to professional standards. See Foster, "Educational Malpractice: A Tort for the Untaught?" 19 U.B.C.L.Rev. 161 (1985). The theory is that the prospect of large monetary recoveries constitutes a form of accountability, deterring negligent educational practices and the retention of incompetent teachers and compensating the victims for their losses. See Note, "Educational Malpractice," 124 U.Pa.L.Rev. 755 (1976). See generally Foster, supra. The courts have not been receptive to educational malpractice claims. The first and most famous educational malpractice suit is Peter W. v. San Francisco Unified School District, a California case brought in the 1970s.

Peter W. v. San Francisco Unified School District
60 Cal.App.3d 814, 131 Cal.Rptr. 854 (1976).

Rattigan, Associate Justice.

The novel—and troublesome—question on this appeal is whether a person who claims to have been inadequately educated, while a student in a public school system, may state a cause of action in tort against the public authorities who operate and administer the system. We hold that he may not.

* * *

On plaintiff's appeal, which is from the judgment, the question is whether a cause of action is stated against defendants in any of the complaint's seven counts. . . .

The first count, which is the prototype of the others (each of which incorporates all of its allegations by reference), sounds in negligence. Its opening allegations may be summarized, and quoted in part, as follows:

Defendant district is "a unified school district . . . existing under the laws of the State of California" and functioning under the direction of its governing board and superintendent of schools. Plaintiff is an 18-year-old male who was recently graduated from a high school operated by the district. He had theretofore been enrolled in its schools, and had attended them, for a period of twelve years. Allegations explicitly charging negligence next appear as follows:

"XI. Defendant school district, its agents and employees, negligently and carelessly failed to provide plaintiff with adequate instruction, guidance, counseling and/or supervision in basic academic skills such as reading and writing, although said school district had the authority, responsibility and ability . . . [to do so]. . . . Defendant school district, its agents and employees, negligently failed to use reasonable care in the discharge of its duties to provide plaintiff with adequate instruction . . . in basic academic skills and failed to exercise that degree of professional skill required of an ordinary prudent educator under the same circumstances [,] as exemplified, but not limited to [,] the following acts:"

In five enumerated subsections which follow in the same paragraph ("XI."), plaintiff alleges that the school district and its agents and employees, "negligently and carelessly" in each instance, (1) failed to apprehend his reading disabilities, (2) assigned him to classes in which he could not read "the books and other materials," (3) allowed him "to pass and advance from a course or grade level" with knowledge that he had not achieved either its completion or the skills "necessary for him to succeed or benefit from subsequent courses," (4) assigned him to classes in which the instructors were unqualified or which were not "geared" to his reading level, and (5) permitted him to graduate from high school although he was "unable to read above the eighth grade level, as required by Education Code section 8573, . . . thereby depriving him of additional instruction in reading and other academic skills."

The first count continues with allegations of proximate cause and injury: "XII. . . . [A]s a direct and proximate result of the negligent acts and omissions by the defendant school district, its agents and employees, plaintiff graduated from high school with a reading ability of only the fifth grade [sic]. As a further proximate result . . . [thereof] . . ., plaintiff has suffered a loss of earning capacity by his limited ability to read and write and is unqualified for any employment other than . . . labor which requires little or no ability to read or write. . . ."

In the closing paragraphs of the first count, plaintiff alleges general damages based upon his "permanent disability and inability to gain meaningful employment"; special damages incurred as the cost of compensatory tutoring allegedly required by reason of the "negligence, acts and omissions of defendants"; that he had presented to the school district an appropriate and timely claim for such damages; and that the claim had been rejected in its entirety.

* * *

A public entity may be held vicariously liable for the conduct of its employee, under Government Code section 815.2, subdivision (a)[1] . . . only if it established that the employee would be personally liable for the conduct upon some "acceptable theory of liability." . . .

According to the familiar California formula, the allegations requisite to a cause of action for negligence are (1) facts showing a duty of care in the defendant, (2) negligence constituting a breach of the duty, and (3) injury to the plaintiff as a proximate result. . . . The present parties do not debate the adequacy of plaintiff's first count with respect to the elements of negligence, proximate cause, and injury; they focus exclusively upon the issue (which we find dispositive, as will appear) of whether it alleges facts sufficient to show that defendants owed him a "duty of care."

The facts which it shows in this respect—or not—appear in its allegations that he had been a student undergoing academic instruction in the public school system operated and administered by defendants. He argues that these facts alone show the requisite "duty of care" upon three judicially recognized theories, for which he cites authorities, pertaining to the public schools.

According to the first theory, "[a]ssumption of the function of instruction of students imposes the duty to exercise reasonable care in its discharge." (Summarizing this and the other two theories advanced by plaintiff, we quote the pertinent captions of his opening brief.) The decisions he cites for his first theory have no application here; in each, the question was whether a public employee's discharge of a function, the performance of which he had "assumed" in the exercise of his discretion, was reached by statutes which granted him immunity from tort liability for the results of his discretionary actions.

---

[1]"815.2. (a) A public entity is liable for injury proximately caused by an act or omission of an employee of the public entity within the scope of his employment if the act or omission would, apart from this section, have given rise to a cause of action against that employee or his personal representative."

Plaintiff's second theory is that "[t]here is a special relationship between students and teachers which supports [the teachers'] duty to exercise reasonable care." He cites for this theory a wide-ranged array of decisions which enforced or addressed various "rights," "opportunities," or privileges of public school students (particularly in equal protection contexts), but none of which involved the question whether the school authorities owed them a "duty of care" in the process of their academic education. (*See, e.g., Lau v. Nichols* (1973) 414 U.S. 563, 564–68 . . .; *Ward v. Flood* (1874) 48 Cal. 36, 50–51; *Serrano v. Priest* (1971) 5 Cal.3d 584, 606–07, 96 Cal.Rptr. 601, 487 P.2d 1241; *Governing Board v. Metcalf* (1974) 36 Cal.App.3d 546, 550, 111 Cal.Rptr. 724.) The third theory is that the "[d]uty of teachers to exercise reasonable care in instruction and supervision of students is recognized in California." The decisions cited here are inapplicable because they establish only that public school authorities have a duty to exercise reasonable care for the *physical safety* of students under their supervision. (*See, e.g., Dailey v. Los Angeles Unified Sch. Dist.* (1970) 2 Cal.3d 741, 745–47, 87 Cal.Rptr. 376, 470 P.2d 360.)

For want of relevant authority in each instance, plaintiff's allegations of his enrollment and attendance at defendants' schools do not plead the requisite "duty of care," relative to his academic instruction, upon any of the three theories he invokes. Of course, no reasonable observer would be heard to say that these facts did not impose upon defendants a "duty of care" within any common meaning of the term; given the commanding importance of public education in society, we state a truism in remarking that the public authorities who are dutybound to educate are also bound to do it with "care." But the truism does not answer the present inquiry, in which "duty of care" is not a term of common parlance; it is instead a legalistic concept of "duty" which will sustain liability for negligence in its breach, and it must be analyzed in that light.

* * *

["Duty of care" is] . . . an essential factor in any assessment of liability for negligence. . . . [W]hether a defendant owes the requisite "duty of care," in a given factual situation, presents a question of law which is to be determined by the courts alone. . . . [J]udicial recognition of such duty in the defendant, with the consequence of his liability in negligence for its breach . . . [may be] dictated or precluded by considerations of public policy. . . .[3]

* * *

On occasions when the Supreme Court [of California] has opened or sanctioned new areas of tort liability, it has noted that the wrongs and injuries involved were both comprehensible and assessable within the existing judicial framework. . . . This is simply not true of wrongful conduct and injuries allegedly involved in educational malfeasance. Unlike the activity of the highway or the marketplace, classroom methodology affords no readily acceptable standards of care, or cause, or injury. The science of pedagogy itself is fraught with different and conflicting theories of how or what a child should be taught, and any layman might—and commonly does—have his own emphatic views on the subject. The "injury" claimed here is plaintiff's inability to read and write. Substantial professional authority attests that the achievement of literacy in the schools, or its failure, are influenced by a host of factors which affect the pupil subjectively, from outside the formal teaching process, and beyond the control of its ministers. They may be physical, neurological, emotional, cultural, environmental; they may be present but not perceived, recognized but not identified.

We find in this situation no conceivable "workability of a rule of care" against which defendants' alleged conduct may be measured . . ., no reasonable "degree of certainty that . . . plaintiff suffered injury" within the meaning of the law of negligence . . ., and no such perceptible "connection between the defendant's conduct and the injury suffered," as alleged, which would establish a causal link between them within the same meaning. . . .

These recognized policy considerations alone negate an actionable "duty of care" in persons and agencies who administer the academic phases of the public educational process. Others, which are even more important in practical terms, command the same result. Few of our institutions, if any, have aroused the controversies, or incurred the public dissatisfaction, which have attended the operation of the public schools during the last few decades.

---

[3]"Protection" of the plaintiff is the initial element in the Restatement formula defining the requisites of a cause of action for negligence. The formula's essentials include negligence, causation, and injury (the "invasion of an interest" of the plaintiff) but, unlike the California formula, the first element is not a "duty of care" in the defendant: it is the condition that the *"interest invaded is protected."* (Res.2d Torts, § 281 [*emphasis* added]).

Rightly or wrongly, but widely, they are charged with outright failure in the achievement of their educational objectives; according to some critics, they bear responsibility for many of the social and moral problems of our society at large. Their public plight in these respects is attested in the daily media, in bitter governing board elections, in wholesale rejections of school bond proposals, and in survey upon survey. To hold them to an actionable "duty of care" in the discharge of their academic functions, would expose them to the tort claims—real or imagined—of disaffected students and parents in countless numbers. They are already beset by social and financial problems which have gone to major litigation, but for which no permanent solution has yet appeared. (*See, e.g., Crawford v. Board of Education* (1976) 17 Cal.3d 280, 130 Cal.Rptr. 724, 551 P.2d 28; *Serrano v. Priest, supra,* 5 Cal.3d 584, 96 Cal.Rptr. 601, 487 P.2d 1241.) The ultimate consequences, in terms of public time and money, would burden them—and society—beyond calculation.

* * *

In each of his last five counts . . . plaintiff repleads all the allegations of the first one. He further alleges, in each, that he had incurred "the damages alleged herein" "as a direct and proximate result" of a specified violation, by one or more of the defendants and as to him, of a respectively described "duty" (or "mandatory duty") allegedly imposed upon them by an express provision of law.[5] The theory of each count is that it states a cause of action for breach of a "mandatory duty" under Government Code section 815.6.[6]

If it be assumed that each of these counts effectively pleads the district's failure to have exercised "reasonable diligence to discharge the duty" respectively alleged, as mentioned in the statute . . . none states a cause of action. This is because the statute imposes liability for failure to discharge only such "mandatory duty" as is "imposed by an enactment that is designed to protect against the risk of a particular kind of injury." . . . The various "enactments" cited in these counts (*see* fn. 5 *ante*) are not so "designed." We have already seen that the failure of educational achievement may not be characterized as an "injury" within the meaning of tort law. It further appears that the several "enactments" have been conceived as provisions directed to the attainment of optimum educational results, but not as safeguards against "injury" of any kind: i.e., as administrative but not protective. Their violation accordingly imposes no liability under Government Code section 815.6.

Plaintiff's second count requires separate treatment because the theory of liability invoked in it is materially different from those reflected in the others. After incorporating into it all the allegations of the first count, he further alleges as follows:

"Defendant school district, its agents and employees, falsely and fraudulently represented to plaintiff's mother and natural guardian that plaintiff was performing at or near grade level in basic academic skills such as reading and writing. . . ." The representations were false. The charged defendants knew that they were false, or had no basis for believing them to be true. "As a direct and proximate result of the intentional or negligent misrepresentation made . . ., plaintiff suffered the damages set forth herein."

For the public policy reasons heretofore stated with respect to plaintiff's first count, we hold that this one states no cause of action for *negligence* in the form of the "misrepresentation" alleged. The possibility of its stating a cause of action for *intentional* misrepresentation, to which it expressly refers in the alternative, is assisted by judicial limitations placed upon the scope of the governmental immunity which is granted, as to liability for "misrepresentation," by Government Code section 818.8. . . .

---

[5] The third count thus refers to the district's and the governing board's having violated their "mandatory duty," allegedly imposed upon them by Education Code section 10759 and Title V of the California Administrative Code, "of keeping the parents and natural guardians of minor school children advised as to their accurate educational progress and achievements." The fourth count alleges a violation, by the district, of its "duty of instructing plaintiff, and other students, in the basic skills of reading and writing" as imposed "under the Constitution and laws of the State of California." The fifth count refers to the district's having graduated plaintiff from high school as a violation of a "mandatory duty not to graduate students from high school without demonstration of proficiency in basic skills" as allegedly imposed by Education Code section 8573 et seq. The sixth count speaks to a violation, by the governing board, of its "mandatory duty" to inspect and evaluate the district's educational program pursuant to Education Code sections 1053 and 8002; the seventh, to the district's violation of its "mandatory duty," allegedly imposed by Education Code section 8505, "to design the course of instruction offered in the public schools to meet the needs of the pupils for which the course of study is prescribed."

[6] "815.6. Where a public entity is under a mandatory duty imposed by an enactment that is designed to protect against the risk of a particular kind of injury, the public entity is liable for an injury of that kind proximately caused by its failure to discharge the duty unless the public entity establishes that it exercised reasonable diligence to discharge the duty."

The second count nevertheless does not state a cause of action, for intentional misrepresentation, because it alleges no facts showing the requisite element of *reliance* upon the "misrepresentation" it asserts. . . .

The judgment of dismissal is affirmed.

Caldecott, P. J., and Christian, J., concur.

_____

NOTES AND QUESTIONS

1. Other Education Malpractice Suits

In *Donohue v. Copiague Union Free School District*, 47 N.Y.2d 440, 418 N.Y.S.2d 375, 391 N.E.2d 1352 (1979), the New York Court of Appeals (the highest court in New York) reached a result in an education malpractice suit that was essentially similar to that reached in *Peter W.* The court, however, admitted that education malpractice suits might well fit within traditional negligence notions, including the duty of care, citing Elson, "A Common Law Remedy for Educational Harms Caused by Incompetent or Careless Teaching," 73 *Nw.L.Rev.* 641, 693–744 (1978). It opined, however, that such claims should not be entertained as a matter of public policy:

> To entertain a cause of action for "educational malpractice" would require the courts not merely to make judgments as to the validity of broad educational policies . . . but, more importantly, to sit in review of the day-to-day implementation of these policies. . . . [This] . . . would constitute blatant interference with the responsibility for the administration of the public school system lodged by Constitution and statute in school administrative agencies.

418 N.Y.S.2d at 378, 391 N.E.2d at 1354. *See also Page v. Klein Tools, Inc.*, 461 Mich. 703, 610 N.W.2d 900 (2000); *Nogel v. Maimonides Academy of Western Connecticut*, 58 Conn.App. 624, 754 A.2d 824 (2000); *Brantley v. District of Columbia*, 640 A.2d 181 (D.C.App. 1994); *Tolman v. CenCor Career Colleges, Inc.*, 851 P.2d 203 (Colo. 1992); *Rich v. Kentucky Country Day, Inc.*, 793 S.W.2d 832 (Ky. 1990); *Torres v. Little Flower Children's Services*, 64 N.Y.2d 119, 485 N.Y.S.2d 15, 474 N.E.2d 223 (1984); *D.S.W. v. Fairbanks North Star Borough School Dist.*, 628 P.2d 554 (Alaska 1981).

Is this essentially the same reasoning the *Peter W.* court adopted in analyzing the duty of care? Is it a recognition that courts are relatively poor monitors

for accountability purposes? *But see* Elson, *supra.* In this respect, how, if at all, does education malpractice differ from school segregation (chapter 4) or restraints on student liberties (chapter 2)? Is the court's confidence in the accountability functions of administrative agencies well placed?

For results similar to *Peter W.* and *Donohue, see Trustees of Columbia University v. Jacobsen*, 53 N.J.Super. 574, 148 A.2d 63 (App.Div.), *aff'd* 31 N.J. 221, 156 A.2d 251, *cert. denied*, 363 U.S. 808, 80 S.Ct. 1243, 4 L.Ed.2d 1150 (1960); *McNeil v. Board of Education*, No. L-17297 (Super.Ct.Law Div. N.J., 1978).

In *Hoffman v. Board of Education*, 64 A.D.2d 369, 410 N.Y.S.2d 99 (S.Ct., App.Div., 1978), a New York appellate court upheld a substantial judgment against a school district, reducing a $750,000 jury verdict to $500,000. In that case, plaintiff had been placed in classes for children with retarded mental development for eleven years, based upon a certified psychologist's determination that the plaintiff had an IQ of 74 (75 was the cutoff point for assignment to such classes). Thirteen years later, it was determined that plaintiff was not retarded. No effort had been made to ascertain the "social history" of the plaintiff, the mother was not informed that plaintiff was classified as retarded by only one IQ point, and plaintiff's intelligence was never retested despite high scores on a "reading readiness" examination. Plaintiff apparently suffered from some "severe speech problem," which may have had an impact on his IQ score. A neurologist and psychiatrist testified at trial that

> [P]laintiff has a marked stutter, that his articulation was not clear and that he had difficulty in making himself understood. On neurological testing he found him to be normal in all respects and he ruled out any brain damage. . . . His opinion was that plaintiff was not mentally retarded, but that he had a "defective self-image and feelings of inadequacy." This was because plaintiff had been placed in a class of mentally retarded children and "this result[ed] in an alteration in his concept of himself, particularly because he is intelligent enough to appreciate the position in which he is placed." . . . He testified the plaintiff was still trainable and that he could be helped with special education and psycho-therapeutic support, but even that could not "correct all the damage of ten years or more of deprivation educationally and characterization as a mentally retarded person."

Id. at 105.

Given these facts, is the *Hoffman* case distinguishable from *Donohue* and *Peter W.? See also In re Peter*

H., 66 Misc.2d 1097, 323 N.Y.S.2d 302 (Fam.Ct. 1971) (defendant school district ordered to pay one year tuition for a private education). On appeal in the *Hoffman* case, the New York Court of Appeals reversed the lower court, relying on its reasoning in *Donohue.* 49 N.Y.2d 121, 424 N.Y.S.2d 376, 400 N.E.2d 317 (1979). *See also Brosnan v. Livonia Public Schools*, 123 Mich.App. 377, 333 N.W.2d 288 (1983); *Tubell v. Dade County Public Schools*, 419 So.2d 388 (Fla.App. 1982).

2. *The Aftermath of* Peter W.

The *Peter W.* case did not prompt widespread reliance on negligence actions to reform failing schools. Is the nature of education so complex, comprehensive, and contingent that education malpractice suits are generally not appropriate under negligence theories? *But see* Ratner, "A New Legal Duty for Urban Public Schools: Effective Education in Basic Skills," 63 *Tex.L.Rev.* 777 (1985); Elson, *supra*; Martinez, "Educational Malpractice: California School District Held Not Liable for Negligence in Instruction in Academic Subjects," 22 *Inequality in Education* 132 (1977); Note, "Educational Malpractice: Can the Judiciary Remedy the Growing Problem of Functional Illiteracy?" 13 *Suffolk U.L.Rev.* 27 (1979) [hereinafter "Functional Illiteracy"]. *See generally* Abel, "Can a Student Sue the Schools for Educational Malpractice?" 44 *Harv.Educ.Rev.* 416 (1974); Comment, "Educational Negligence: A Student's Cause of Action for Incompetent Academic Instruction," 58 *N.C.L.Rev.* 561 (1980). Is it responsive to argue that we may justifiably suspect incompetence when a child of normal intelligence has not gained basic skills? *See* Ratner, *supra*; Sugarman, "Accountability Through the Courts," 82 *Sch.Rev.* 233, 250 (1974). Would it be responsive to argue that other children with similar IQs perform better in similar schools in similar communities with similar programs? *See* Ratner, *supra*; "Educational Malpractice" at 791. If so, would this be a form of strict liability, i.e., liability without proof of negligence? *But see* Ratner, *supra* at 857–59.

3. *Rights and Duties Created by Competency-Based Requirements*

Might the existence of state-mandated minimum competency tests that purport to test essential skills and competencies that students should have learned at various stages in their school career establish a duty on the part of the state to provide remedial education adequate to enable students to pass these tests? *See* Liebman, "Implementing *Brown* in the 90's: Political Reconstruction, Liberal Recollection, and Litigatively Enforced Legislative Reform," 76 *Va.L.Rev.* 3439 (1990), in which Professor Liebman argues that competency-based or educational performance standards mandated by the state could establish a judicially enforceable right to a minimally adequate education.

4. *Contract Actions*

A number of courts have been willing to entertain contract actions brought by students against private schools, alleging that the private school did not live up to its contractual obligations contained in catalogs or other documents. *See, e.g., Russell v. Salve Regina College*, 890 F.2d 484 (1st Cir. 1989); *Warren v. Drake University*, 886 F.2d 200 (8th Cir. 1989); *Doherty v. Southern College of Optometry*, 862 F.2d 570 (6th Cir. 1988); *Dr. Franklin Perkins School v. Freeman*, 741 F.2d 1503 (7th Cir. 1984); *Corso v. Creighton University*, 731 F.2d 529 (8th Cir. 1984); *VanLoock v. Curran*, 489 So.2d 525 (Ala. 1986); *King v. American Academy of Dramatic Arts*, 102 Misc.2d 1111, 425 N.Y.S.2d 505 (1980); *Basch v. George Washington University*, 370 A.2d 1364 (D.C.Ct.App., 1977) (language of bulletin expressed an expectancy and not an enforceable promise); *Behrend v. State*, 55 Ohio App.2d 135, 379 N.E.2d 617 (1977) (plaintiffs stated a cause of action under an implied contract). *See generally* "Functional Illiteracy" *supra* at 30–31; Semas, "Students Filing 'Consumer' Suits," 11 *Chronicle of Higher Education*, Nov. 24, 1975, at 1; Comment, "Consumer Protection and Higher Education: Student Suits Against Schools," 37 *Ohio St.L.J.* 608 (1976); Note, "Educational Malpractice," 124 *U.Pa.L.Rev.* 755, 785–86 (1976).

Given the analysis of educational malpractice suits, should contract claims against private education institutions be entertained? Should they be entertained against public institutions? What would constitute proof of a contractual undertaking? How would a contract recovery differ in theory or effect from a recovery based upon misrepresentation? *See generally* Ray, "Toward Contractual Rights for College Students," 10 *J.of Law & Educ.* 163 (1981).

---

*The text refers to the concept of allocative efficiency in which the dollar gains and losses by everyone affected are considered, and for present purposes, allocative efficiency is equated with maximizing utility. If dollars do not adequately describe overall utility—for example, if the dollars were worth more to the poor than to the rich and the policy favored the rich—then an allocatively efficient policy would not necessarily maximize satisfaction.

Can a private educational institution alter the terms of the "contract" at will, for example, by changing graduation requirements? *See Mahavongsanan v. Hall*, 529 F.2d 448 (5th Cir. 1976); *Slaughter v. Brigham Young University*, 514 F.2d 622 (10th Cir. 1975).

Can education malpractice be premised on an implied or express contract or estoppel theory? *See* Jerry, "Recovery in Tort in Educational Malpractice: Problems of Theory and Policy," 29 *Kan.L.Rev.* 195 (1981); "Educational Malpractice" *supra* at 784–89.

Professor Dodd has urged that contract theories are conceptually and legally inappropriate to define the relationship between students and schools:

> There is little in the student-university relationship, particularly as it has been viewed by the courts, that reflects principles and policies that are associated with theories of contract. To the limited extent that the law of contract now in strained use and tort theory are readily separable, and they are not, contracts center around promises. Contract liability is imposed by the law for the protection of a single, limited interest, that of having the promises of others performed. Indeed, many would further limit that definition to include primarily promises in the "commercial realm." Further, "[c]ontract obligations are created to enforce promises which are manifestations not only of a present intention to do or not to do something, but also of a commitment to the future. They are, therefore, obligations based on the manifested intention of the parties to a bargaining transaction." This article has delineated the lack of a true bargaining and promise orientation in the student-university context, and hence, the intrinsically noncontractual nature of that relationship. Indeed, the myriad of individual student problems that can arise in a university situation would defy an attempt to embody in fair, written terms all of the "promises" inherent in such a situation.
>
> The student-university relationship instead seems to fall more naturally into the realm of tort analysis. Tort liability generally is "based upon the relations of persons with others; and those relations may arise generally, with large groups or classes of persons, or singly, with an individual. The wrongs or injuries described in this article flow from the relationship between student and university. Although this relationship is created by a contract of sorts, through the payment of tuition, its survival extends beyond notions of contract. At least historically, too, one of the closest analogues to the student-university rela-

tionship has been the familial relationship. Perhaps that similarity helped to prevent the development of tort theory in education cases; the recognition of intra-familial tort liability is relatively recent.

Dodd, "The Non-Contractual Nature of the Student-University Contractual Relationship," 33 *Kan.L.Rev.* 701, 730–31 (1985).

Do you agree with her conclusions?

5. *Intentional Infliction of Emotional Distress*

May a student who is suspended or expelled from a private educational institution recover for intentional infliction of emotional distress? *See Russell v. Salve Regina College*, 890 F.2d 484 (1st Cir. 1989), *rev'd and remanded on other grounds*, 499 U.S. 225 (1991), *modified and reinstated*, 938 F.2d 315 (1st Cir. 1991) (college's conduct in asking overweight nursing student to withdraw may be unprofessional but not sufficiently outrageous to constitute a tort).

IV. SCHOOLS AND MARKETS

This chapter so far has treated education as a public good, one that government should provide. In fact, though, there have been longstanding pressures to break the state's near-monopoly on education and to rely on the competition and accountability that come with market principles to reform the schools. The school choice movement is fueled by a variety of objectives. Many proponents consider that public schools are a failing monopoly and can only be reformed by competition with alternative schools (the market-driven objective). Other reasons given for school choice are that because there are differences in children's learning styles, different options must be available; that parents should be able to choose schools that cater to their particular values, including their religious values; or that notions of equity require opportunities for the poor as well as the rich to bail out of the perceived failing public system. *See generally* Raywid, "Choice Orientations, Discussions, and Prospects," in P. Cookson, ed., *The Choice Controversy* 1 (1992). In this section, several types of market initiatives will be examined: voucher plans, charter schools, contracts for private corporations to provide educational services, and commercial marketing arrangements to generate resources for cash-strapped public schools.

---

*This argument is not critical to the Tiebout model. A consumer may consider the community's package of public services and other characteristics in order to reach an overall decision that maximizes satisfaction.

**This argument disregards possible economies of scale.

A. Consumer-Voters in the Public Sector: Selecting a School District

Although choice initiatives have been touted as a radical innovation, parents always have had the power to "vote with their feet" by removing a child from public school and placing the child in another school district or a private institution. When citizens move to an affluent school district or one with a heady reputation, or they seek to escape urban schools, they are expressing educational preferences. They leave one community, where apparently a majority does not or cannot agree with their educational preferences, and seek out a community that offers, in their eyes, a superior educational opportunity. Such voters no longer seek to influence political decisions about education within their present district but rather refuse to pay taxes to that district, exit it, and move on to a more compatible school district. *See generally* A. Hirschman, *Exit, Voice, and Loyalty* (1970).

In an ideal society, every member would pay an amount (user fee or tax) for an education equaling exactly what it was worth to him or her. The value of the education to the society would be the sum of the indirect benefits to each individual—for example, higher lifetime earnings or preferred lifestyle—and of the direct benefits to all, for example, stimulating conversation and lower crime rates. Parents presumably would make such utilitarian calculations for children too immature to estimate the benefits for themselves. The educational system in that ideal society would allocate fiscal, material, and human resources so expertly that no other combination of information generation and distribution of resources would produce more total benefit among the citizenry.

The achievement of the ideal society is staggering. The prices paid for education by the members would purchase a package of services that, of all other imaginable packages, was best for each member.* It would also be the best imaginable way for society to have spent that portion of its educational resources. What is best for one is best for the many. The sum of all these perfectly efficient transactions by millions of consumers of education would equal the actual production of the most dollar-stretching educational expenditures imaginable for the society. This is true so long as there are not so many packages chosen and

available that the society cannot take advantage of economies of scale which would reduce the average minimum cost to a point that would allow for efficient production of the packages. Putting aside questions of the influence of inequalities in wealth distribution, the gap between the real world of conflicting interests and the ideal is caused by a lack of information (and perhaps also by an inability to know or calculate benefits). With respect to public services, the means we use to transform our needs into educational outputs are insufficiently sensitive to transmit the necessary information to the producers. Charles Tiebout has described this problem:

> If all consumer-voters could somehow be forced to reveal their true preferences for public goods, then the amount of such goods to be produced and the appropriate benefits tax could be determined. As things now stand, there is no mechanism to force the consumer-voter to state his true preferences; and in fact, the "rational" consumer will understate his preferences and hope to enjoy the goods while avoiding the tax.

Tiebout, "A Pure Theory of Local Expenditures," 64 *J.of Pol.Econ.* 416, 417 (1956).

Economists have long known what conditions are sufficient to achieve the ideal, an ideal in which "each individual . . . would be led by an Invisible Hand to the grand solution of the social maximum position." *Id.* at 422. Those conditions compose the marketplace that has come to be the standard by which to measure real methods of resource allocation. The public sector is often thought to suffer by comparison with the private sector because of its relatively greater distance from those conditions. Tax burdens and education outputs are determined by collective political action through voting and otherwise, and the ideal allocation for each individual and for the collectivity is not achieved. Professor Tiebout, however, suggests in his classic 1956 article that local government may represent "a sector where the allocation of public goods (and the reflection of the preferences of the population) need not take a back seat to the private sector." *Id.* at 424.

Tiebout suggests that in choosing where to live, consumers effectively vote with their feet. They pick among communities as they would among products in a private market, looking for the combination of community services—for example, education, police

---

*This assumes that technological inefficiency may be equated with allocative inefficiency. Considering the other factors that go into a relocation decision, this need not necessarily be the case.

protection, and recreational facilities—that most closely approximates their needs. What variables influence a consumer-voter's decision?

> If he has children, a high level of expenditures on schools may be important. Another person may prefer a community with a municipal golf course. The availability and quality of such facilities and services as beaches, parks, police protection, roads, and parking facilities will enter into the decision-making process. . . . The consumer-voter may be viewed as picking that community which best satisfies his preference for public goods.

Id. at 418. *See also* Inman and Rubinfeld, "The Judicial Pursuit of Local Fiscal Equity," 92 *Harv.L.Rev.* 1662 (1979).

To illustrate the market characteristics of the public sector, Tiebout constructed a marketplace model of local governments that requires certain conditions parallel to those which must prevail in the private marketplace for efficient transactions to take place.

1. Each consumer must know his or her real needs and how to satisfy them best among the competing communities' packages of public goods. If a parent erroneously believes that his or her child would be better off as a musician rather than as an automobile mechanic, the mistaken belief that the child would be better off as a musician creates waste. The parent's tax dollars could have brought more value had they been spent another way, that is, on training the child to be an automobile mechanic. And if the parent chooses to live in School District A rather than School District B because A has a superior music program while B has a superior vocational education program, his or her mistaken preference distorts the market by causing the music program to be overpurchased in relation to the vocational education program.

2. Each consumer is fully mobile and will move to the community where he or she can find the best mesh of community services and needs. There are no significant transaction costs (for example, moving expenses) to relocating. The mobility assumption also screens out distortions caused by factors other than community expenditure patterns. Communities will differ in job opportunities, and some cities will have better and closer shopping centers. Population density, aesthetic appeal, and ambiance may be allocated unequally among communities. But none of these

factors will affect the consumer's decision to move in the Tiebout model. Consumers react only to community expenditure patterns and will costlessly move wherever they find the best package of public services.* Nor does the mobile consumer attempt to persuade the community to change its spending pattern, any more than the community attempts to accommodate itself to the consumer's special needs. The consumer can only stay or leave, and the community notes only whether someone is there.

3. Consumer-voters must have a large number of local communities with differing bundles of public goods from which to choose. This condition ensures that some community will meet each consumer's needs. Ideally, there will be at least one community, even if it has but one citizen, for every consumer preference bundle.** (The bundle is of course limited. It represents the best possible expenditure for the consumer of the dollars he or she is willing or perhaps able to spend on education.) At the state and national level, relatively little opportunity is available to pick and choose among public expenditure patterns. Unless the consumer's preference pattern matches up perfectly with the nation's expenditure pattern, the consumer's preferences are not produced. Under such circumstances, the consumer may seek to influence politically the composition of the national bundle of public services or he or she may move to another nation. *See generally* A. Hirschman, *supra* [*Exit, Voice, and Loyalty* (1970)]. At the state level, American consumer-voters have fifty choices. Local governments, including school districts, provide considerably greater latitude. Morton Grodzins noted in 1966 that the United States contains 18,000 general purpose municipalities, 3,000 counties, and 92,000 tax-levy governments (including special purpose districts). *See* M. Grodzins, *The American System* 3 (1966). Competition among communities vying for the consumer's presence insures efficient production of services and sensitivity to his or her needs. If the competition is sufficiently intense, the price to the consumer will be the cheapest possible cost to the community for the services provided. This is so because if a community falters, consumers will leave and produce the collapse and dissolution of the government or the subsequent reconstitution of the government, with the succession of new elected officials with a new community expenditure pattern. *But see* M. Schiesl, *The Politics of Efficiency* (1977). An

---

*This again raises the question of allocative efficiency versus utility. Given the costs of moving, it may not be allocatively efficient to offer the package of services that the poor want. Such a package, however, might maximize overall utility.

important caveat is that if laws prevent a community from keeping people out or charging user fees, no community may opt for a high price package. This is because the majority and its elected leaders may resist wealth transfers to those who cannot afford the expensive package. This may be reinforced by the inability to control the mobility of capital and labor. *See* P. Peterson, *City Limits* (1981). So too, local districts may be more constrained by fiscal capacity than differences in willingness to tax. *See* chapter 7. *See generally* Stein, "Market Maximization of Individual Preferences and Metropolitan Service Responsibility," 25 *Urban Aff.Q.* 86 (1989).

4. Every pattern of community services will have an optimal community size associated with it that represents the point at which neither more nor fewer people could be served without increasing the average cost to those served. To carry the idea to a meticulous extreme, assume that the optimal size of a particular class is twenty students and that the most effective way to teach the materials is to send the whole class to the blackboards. The addition of one student will introduce waste.* If the classroom has five blackboards holding four students each, the teacher must ask the school district either to buy a new blackboard, or she must reduce the effectiveness of her teaching by changing her methods. Buying a new blackboard will be wasteful because the price paid will be for four places at the blackboard, but three places will go unused. Even buying just one small blackboard will be wasteful. The per pupil cost of one large blackboard for four students will be below the price of four small blackboards. Thus the school must pay more for the last child than it did for the first twenty. Waste will also result if class size falls even one student below the optimum. The school district will expend resources that could educate twenty children to educate nineteen, resulting in a higher average cost for each than at the optimum. Thus, deviation in either direction from the optimum will create resource misallocation. If four students and one blackboard are added to the class, this may dilute the teacher's ability to supervise the class's work.

5. Community executives will be rational persons who know what the optimal size is for their bundle of services and try to reach or remain there:

> [C]ommunities below the optimum size, through chambers of commerce or other agencies, seek to attract new residents. . . . The case of the city that is too large and tries to get rid of residents is more difficult to imagine. . . . Nevertheless, economic forces are at work to push people out of it. Every resident who moves to the

suburbs to find better schools, more parks, and so forth, is reacting, in part, against the pattern the city has to offer. The community which is at the optimum size and tries to remain so is not hard to visualize. . . . [P]roper zoning laws, implicit agreements among realtors, and the like are sufficient to keep the population stable.

6. Finally, the community's production of services and the consumer-voter's consumption of them can have no effects—positive or negative—on any other community and its consumers. This insures that every citizen and his or her community "pay for all the resources their decisions prevent from being used in alternative economically productive ways. . . ." Markovits, "A Basic Structure for Microeconomic Policy Analysis in Our Worst than Second-Best World: A Proposal and Related Critique of the Chicago Approach to the Study of Law and Economics," 1975 *Wis.L.Rev.* 950, 962. If, for example, Centreville builds its high school football stadium in neighboring Jonesville so its own streets will not be clogged by traffic, it is imposing external costs on Jonesville that are not reflected in the price that Centreville residents pay for the privilege of having a stadium. The real value of Centreville's expenditure is the benefit to its citizens minus the harm to the citizens of Jonesville. External benefits can also be conveyed by a community's expenditure pattern, producing a free ride or reduced cost for its neighbors. When outsiders are welcomed at the free park performance of a city-subsidized orchestra, they receive a free ride. When they pay for the $10 ticket at the paid performance, they get a reduced rate because they did not contribute to the subsidy. The real value of the symphony to society is its value to Centreville residents plus its value to the outsiders. As a result, the fact that the outsiders' community is at its optimum size does not necessarily mean that its consumer-voters approve of its bundle of services. It may mean that some people in that community want a free ride and would prefer to use services they do not have to pay for. When a service costs less than it is worth, it will be overproduced, and some other services may be underproduced. On the other hand, if the cost to the community producing the service is greater than it is worth, it may be underproduced in relation to other services.

Important consequences flow from understanding how and why the theoretical model works. Most traditional economists believe that the closer we approach each of the optimal conditions, the closer we approach the most allocatively efficient distribution of public resources. Others argue that real-world imperfections can be manipulated instrumentally to offset each other. In some cases, they say, two distortions will be closer to the social maximum position than one distortion. Consider, for example, the Centreville stadium hypothetical example. If Jonesville taxes Centreville at a rate that exactly compensates it for the harm Centreville's stadium imposes, the harm is wiped out. Taxes automatically distort markets. If X is willing to spend only fifty-one cents on a magazine priced at its cost of fifty cents, a tax raising its total cost to him to fifty-five cents keeps it out of his hands or causes a four-cent misallocation. In the stadium example, however, the tax just canceled the harm. Two wrongs make a right. To state the point differently, once both distortions are in place and offsetting each other, the removal of one—thus reducing the total number of distortions—will move us farther from the optimum position.

Although the possibility of choosing among school districts, no doubt, creates some increment of consumer choice, the divergencies between the real world and the Tiebout model are numerous. Consider the fact that education is a merit good—that is, a good of such importance that a certain amount of it is allocated to each person regardless of ability to pay and personal preferences. This may reflect a group decision as to what is allocatively efficient or as to what is an equitable allocation of education services. This is the economic meaning of universal and compulsory elementary and secondary education. One notion is that parents, if left to their own devices, may systematically underinvest in education, and this will have adverse consequences for the child and for the entire community. Another is that children from different socioeconomic and other groupings should have an equal education opportunity. For example, a poorly educated child may not grow up to be economically self-sufficient, and there may be increased welfare, public housing, and police protection costs as a result. Equally as fundamental, education is not simply an investment; it is also a consumption good. Education can enrich the individual irrespective of its allocative efficiency. Thus, minimum education services are offered in every community, and this distorts the public sector market model.

The mobility assumption is subject to challenge on any number of grounds. The poor may not be able to afford to move to the community that offers the package of education services they prefer.* The

very fact that a district is perceived as offering a superior educational opportunity can itself raise housing prices. There may be a community bias toward the retention of wealthier residents and fears of an in-migration of low-income families. *See* Buchanan, "Principles of Urban Fiscal Structures," 4 *Pub. Choice* 1 (1971). Thus, zoning restrictions and other growth control devices may be used to create barriers to mobility. An urban area may consist of only one countywide or metropolitan school district, thereby denying parents the ability to choose among a variety of district education packages except by moving great distances.

Consider the choice of an education package, for example, as compared to the choice of a retirement community by a senior citizen planning to move to some retirement community. First, the senior citizen chooses where to live in the light of his or her preferred package of services. The child's choices must be filtered through the expressed preferences of his or her parents. One decision may be best for the adults, and another for the children. The parents will consider the welfare of the entire family and usually attach great importance to keeping the family together. Even if the child's interests are treated as paramount to those of the family, different children in the same family may have different educational needs. Second, the community developer may go bankrupt unless he or she offers an attractive retirement community package of services at a competitive price. A compulsory education system, financed through compulsory taxes, is not nearly so threatened by such dire consequences if it is not responsive to consumer tastes. Third, the senior citizen is already planning to change communities, whereas the parents still must be persuaded of the desirability of moving. Fourth, and most important, the retirement community will offer nearly the entire package of services that the senior citizen prefers—ambiance, shopping, recreation, restaurants, health care, and so on. The parents must consider many factors beyond the control of the school system: employment opportunities, distance to work, availability of public transportation, minimum housing space requirements for the whole family, and so forth. In other words, there are more components to the choice of a place to live for the working family with school-age children than there are for the retired senior citizen seeking a relatively well-defined retirement environment. The Tiebout

---

*A. Hirschman, *Exit, Voice and Loyalty* (1970).

model works best if the consumer-voter seeks to maximize his or her satisfaction with respect to a relatively few public and private goods than with respect to a large number. The number of variables may psychologically confuse the consumer and hence render the choice less rational.

Finally, maximizing rational consumer choice with respect to education, a very special public good, presents its own set of problems. If the parents are uneducated, this may mean that they do not know what they or their children need in the way of educational services. This is presumably one of the things one means by describing a person as uneducated. Even if the consumer-voter has a good idea as to his or her educational preferences, the flow of information may not be sufficient to allow rational choice. Accurate information as to the quality of educational services is difficult to come by. Parents could depend on unreliable sources; they may not visit schools; they may not know what to look for if they do visit schools. And unlike goods in the private sector, the cost of the education may not be a reliable guide to its quality. Additional infusions of funds for schools may purchase additional inputs, but once a minimum threshold level of expenditure is reached, additional monies may not yield superior outcomes (achievement, self-fulfillment, and so on). *See* chapter 7.

Parents can seek out a school system with a particular racial or socioeconomic student population or a school system that is perceived as providing a physically safe environment, but beyond such factors (which may or may not be determined correctly), parents may not be able to evaluate educational quality because of the lack of knowledge about what constitutes a quality education. The process by which educational inputs are translated into educational outputs remains mysterious. *See* chapters 4 and 7. And this task is further complicated by the fact that parents must not only seek to satisfy the present educational needs of their children but also to project those needs into the future.

The obvious difficulties with respect to exercising consumer choice in education through location decisions have led to efforts to reform public education so that consumers can vote with dollars and not with their feet. The idea is to give all parents the same types of options that the affluent have, with their ability to choose and pay for a private education. The dilemma is how to do this in a world of unequal wealth distribution, a world in which there is widespread commitment to public schooling and equal educational opportunity. In this section, we turn to the various proposals that have been made, their strengths and weaknesses, and to evaluations of the limited experiences with such market proposals.

B. Voucher Plans, Accountability, and Educational Quality

In 1955, the free-market economist Milton Friedman offered a plan to use vouchers that would empower parents to exercise choices about which schools their children would attend. Friedman, "The Role of Government in Education," in R. Solo, ed., *Economics and the Public Interest* (1955). The idea did not catch on politically because the public was generally satisfied with the school system. Moreover, "freedom of choice" plans were tainted by their association with Southern efforts to resist desegregation. As described in chapter 4, white parents used the plans to transfer their children from schools that blacks would be attending. The Supreme Court eventually declared these evasive policies unconstitutional. *Green v. County School Board*, 391 U.S. 430 (1968). In the early 1970s, the Office of Economic Opportunity sponsored a modest experiment with vouchers, but the experiment did not lead to any broad-ranging policy reform. *See* Bulman and Kirp, "From Vouchers to Charters: The Shifting Politics of School Choice," in S. Sugarman and F. Kemerer, eds., *School Choice and Social Controversy: Politics, Policy and Law* (1999). For descriptions of this experiment, *see* E. Levinson, *The Alum Rock Voucher Demonstration: Three Years of Implementation* (1976); J. Mecklenburger and R. Hostrop, *Education Vouchers: From Theory to Alum Rock* (1972); S. Grovinsky, *Final Report: Alum Rock Union Elementary School District Voucher Feasibility Study* (1971). Despite these setbacks, some academics continued to press for voucher plans. Two Berkeley law professors, John Coons and Stephen Sugarman, tried without success to convert theory into practice by putting an initiative to create a school choice program on the California ballot. J. Coons and S. Sugarman, *Education by Choice: The Case for Family Control* (1978); J. Catterall, *Education Vouchers* (1984).

In the 1980s, calls for voucher reform by academics coincided with a push to deregulate government, including education, under Presidents Ronald Reagan and George Bush. The work of John Chubb and Terry Moe was particularly influential.

"Politics, Markets, and the Organization of Schools"

J. Chubb and T. Moe, 82 *Amer.Pol.Sci.Rev.* 1065, 1067–70, 1084–85 (1988).

Public schools are controlled by democratic authority and administration. The specifics vary from district to district and state to state, but the basic framework is remarkably uniform throughout the country. The private sector might seem to lack any comparable uniformity. Most private schools are affiliated with a church; some are elite preparatory schools; some are military academies; and there are other types as well. . . . But they all have two important institutional features in common: society does not control them directly through democratic politics, and society does control them—indirectly—through the marketplace. Rather than marvel at diversity, we find it useful to think about schools in terms of these alternative institutions of social control. As a shorthand, we will refer to them as politics and markets.

* * *

Popular myth lauds the role of local citizens and their elected school boards in governing the public schools. But the fact is that the schools are not locally controlled and are not supposed to be. The state and federal governments have legitimate roles to play in financing schools, setting standards, and otherwise imposing their own policies. This means that U.S. citizens everywhere, whether or not they have children in school and whether or not they live in the district or even the state, have a legitimate hand in governing each school. . . .

The proper constituency of even a single public school is a huge and heterogeneous one whose interests are variously represented by formally prescribed agents—politicians and administrators—at all levels of government. Parents and students, therefore, are but a small part of the legitimate constituency of "their own" schools. The schools are not meant to be theirs to control and are literally not supposed to provide the kind of education they might want. Public education is shaped by larger social purposes as defined by larger constituencies.

Private schools determine their own goals, standards, and methods. These may reflect the values of owners or patrons, or perhaps a collective such as a diocese. But the market imposes a fundamental constraint. Private schools provide services in exchange for payment, and unless heavily subsidized from the outside, they must please their consumers—students and parents—if they are to prosper. Whatever the constituency of the private school, therefore, it will surely be much smaller and more homogeneous than the democratic constituency of the public school, and students and parents will occupy a much more central position within it.

In the private marketplace, educational choice is founded on what has come to be called, following Hirschman . . .*, the *exit* option. If parents and students do not like the services they are being provided, they can exit and find another school whose offerings are more congruent with their needs. This process of selection promotes a match between what educational consumers want and what their schools supply. Matching is reinforced by the population effects . . . of selection: schools that fail to satisfy a sufficiently large clientele will be weeded out (or, if subsidized, become an increasing burden).

Selection also forges a strong bond between consumer satisfaction and organizational well-being. This gives schools incentives to please their clientele, as well as to set up voice mechanisms—committees, associations—that build a capacity for responsiveness into organizational structure. These incentives, too, promote a match—but they are not necessary for success. A school might rigidly adhere to purist doctrine yet succeed because that is what enough consumers happen to want. Either way, the result tends to be the same: a match.

In the public sector, popular control is built around voice. Exit plays a minimal role. The public school is usually a local monopoly, in the sense that all children living in a given area are assigned to a particular school. This does not eliminate choice, since parents can take account of school quality in deciding where to live. But residential decisions involve many factors in addition to education, and once they are made, sunk costs are high. Low or declining quality need not keep parents from moving into an area, and it is even less likely to prompt existing residents to pick up and leave.

It might prompt them to consider a private school. But here they confront a major disincentive: public schools are free, private schools are

---

*D. Tyack, *The One Best System* (1974).

not. Due to this cost differential, the perceived value of private schools must far outweigh that of public schools if they are to win students. To put it the other way around, public schools, because they are relatively inexpensive, can attract students without seeming to be particularly good at educating them.

Lacking a real exit option, many parents and students will choose a public school despite dissatisfaction with its goals, methods, or personnel. Having done so, they have a right to voice their preferences through the democratic control structure—but everyone else has the same rights, and many are well armed and organized. Voice cannot remedy the mismatch between what parents and students want and what schools provide. Conflict and disharmony are built into the system.

In the private sector, the exit option not only promotes harmony and responsiveness, it also promotes school autonomy. This is true even for schools that are part of a hierarchy, as the Catholic schools are. The reason is that most of the technology and resources needed to please clients are inherently present at the bottom of the hierarchy—in the school—since educational services are based on personal relationships and interactions, on continual feedback, and on the knowledge, skills, and experience of teachers. The school is thus in the best position to know how to enhance its own organizational well-being. Hierarchical control, or any external imposition, tends to be inefficient and counterproductive.

* * *

In the public sector the institutional forces work in the opposite direction. The *raison d'etre* of democratic control is to impose higher-order values on schools and thus limit their autonomy. Exit is an obstacle to control: when the governance structure imposes a policy on parents and students who disagree, exit allows them to avoid compliance by "voting with their feet," thus defeating the purpose of the policy. But public officials do not have to take exit as a given. They can simply pass laws restricting its availability. While private decision makers value autonomy because it helps them cope with problems of exit, public officials eliminate exit in order to facilitate their imposition of higher-order values.

The drive to restrict autonomy is built into the incentive structures of politicians and bureaucrats. Politicians seek political support by responding to various constituency groups, particularly those that are well organized and active. These include teachers' unions and associations of administrators, but also a vast array of groups representing more specialized interests—those of minorities, the handicapped, bilingual education, drivers' education, schools of education, book publishers, and accrediting and testing organizations, among others. These groups typically have financial or occupational stakes in existing educational arrangements, and their policy positions reflect as much. They all want a share of the public's educational resources. They want to influence educational programs. They want to have a say in how the schools are organized and operated. And politicians are only too happy to oblige—this is the path to political popularity. . . .

Bureaucrats play both sides of the governmental fence. Their power rests on the fact that bureaucracy is essential to direct democratic control. The imposition of higher-order values is hardly automatic, particularly given the built-in dissatisfaction of parents and students and the inevitable pressures from teachers and principals for autonomy. Control requires rules and regulations, monitoring, incentive structures, and other means of ensuring that those engaged in the educational process behave as they are supposed to behave. It requires bureaucracy—and bureaucrats.

As public officials they have incentives to expand their budgets, programs, and administrative controls. These are the basics of bureaucratic well-being, and their pursuit is an integral part of the job. But bureaucrats also belong to important interest groups—of administrators, of professionals—that lobby government from the outside (ostensibly) as well. Although traditionally they have portrayed themselves as nonpolitical experts pursuing the greater good, they are in fact a powerful special interest—an interest dedicated to hierarchical control. . . .

The system, in short, is inherently destructive of autonomy. Politicians have the authority to shape the schools through public policy, and, precisely because they have the authority, they are consistently under pressure from interest groups to exercise it. It is in their own best interests to impose choices on the schools. The same is true of bureaucrats, who have occupational and professional stakes in control: a world of autonomous schools would be a world without educational bureaucrats. Thus, while principals and teachers may praise the virtues of autonomy, the "one best system"* is organized against it. Politicians, bureaucrats, and virtually the full spectrum of interest groups tend to see autonomy for what it is: a transfer of power and threat to their interests.

* * *

Are private schools also likely to be better than public schools? In an important sense, the answer is yes. Parents and students who choose a private school are revealing their judgment of quality: the private school is not only better, it is better by an amount that exceeds the cost differential. Since there is clearly an objective basis for their judgment—they directly experience private education and are free to return to the public sector at any time—we have good reason to believe that private schools are in fact more effective at providing the types of educational services their clients care about.

But are they better at the important things schools ought to be doing? This question cannot be answered without substituting our value judgments for those parents and students. A church school that attracts students on the basis of religious and moral training almost surely outperforms the local public school on this dimension. But this says nothing about their relative effectiveness in transmitting democratic values or an appreciation of cultural diversity. Performance is only desirable if the goals are desirable.

This, of course, is the justification for democratic control. In principle, our institutions are set up to articulate important social goals and to ensure that schools act effectively on them. If private schools do a better job of providing certain services or of pleasing parents and students, this does not mean that society must therefore prefer private to public education. Any evaluation has to depend on a more fundamental judgment about what the schools ought to be doing.

In objective terms the two institutional systems are simply very different, and they give rise to schools that reflect these differences—providing different services in different ways to please different constituencies.

* * *

[Our study] provides the first opportunity to document public-private differences by means of a large, representative sample of schools, and its findings dovetail nicely with major lines of argument in the education literature. If it is true, as Coleman, Hoffer, and Kilgore . . .[+] and Coleman and Hoffer . . .[**] have claimed, that private schools outperform public schools on academic grounds, and if the effective schools research is basically correct in the characteristics it tends to associate with effectiveness, then we should find that private schools disproportionately possess these characteristics.

That is just what we find. Private schools have simpler, less constraining environments of administrators, school boards, and parents. They are more autonomous and strongly led. They have clearer goals and stricter requirements, and they put greater stress on academic excellence. Relations between principals and teachers and among teachers themselves are more harmonious, interactive, and focused on teaching. Teachers are more involved in policy decisions, have greater control over their work, and are more satisfied with their jobs.

* * *

Private schools are controlled by society too, but not through politics or bureaucracy. They make their own decisions about policy, organization, and personnel subject to market forces that signal how they can best pursue their own interests. Given their substantial autonomy—and given the incentives for autonomy that are built into the system—it is not surprising to find that principals are stronger leaders; that principals have greater control over hiring and firing; that principals and the teachers they choose have greater respect for, and interaction with, one another; and that teachers—without conflict or formal requirement—are more integrally involved in policy making. These sorts of characteristics are bound up with one another, and they jointly arise from the institutional environment. Different institutions promote different organizational syndromes.

If this is essentially correct, the standard proposals for reforming public schools are misconceived. It is easy to say, for instance, that schools should have greater autonomy or that principals should be stronger leaders. But these sorts of reforms are incompatible with the "one best system" and cannot succeed. Politicians and bureaucrats have little incentive to move forcefully in these directions. Their careers are tied to their own control over the schools, and they are unavoidably responsive to well-

---

[+] J. Coleman, T. Hoffer, and S. Kilgore, *High School Achievement* (1982).

[**] J. Coleman and T. Hoffer, *Public and Private Schools* (1987).

organized interests that have stakes in the system's capacity to impose higher-order values on the local schools. Restricting autonomy is what democratic control is all about.

* * *

This does not mean that the public schools must be freed from all democratic governance. But it is instructive that the private schools, which are products of an institutional system that decentralizes power to the producers and immediate consumers of educational services, tend to develop precisely the sorts of organizational characteristics reformers want the public schools to have. Some sort of voucher system, combining broad democratic guidance with a radical decentralization of resources and choice, is at least a reasonable alternative to direct control—one that might transform the public schools into different, more effective organizations, while still leaving them truly public.

* * *

Two years after publication of this article, Chubb and Moe released a book that made the case for school choice. J. Chubb and T. Moe, *Politics, Markets and America's Schools* (1990). Their work was well timed to attract attention in the policy arena in the late 1980s and the early 1990s. The findings launched new efforts to promote school choice. Still, voucher proponents faced an uphill battle, and significant compromise would be necessary to use market principles to enhance educational offerings.

"From Vouchers to Charters: The Shifting Politics of School Choice"

R. Bulman and D. Kirp, in S. Sugarman and F. Kemerer, eds., *School Choice and Social Controversy: Politics, Policy and Law* 36, 45–50 (1999).

* * *

Chubb and Moe were able to capitalize on a moment when choice was the mantra; they also drew upon empirically-based analysis to support their policy preferences. Friedman had applied a classic welfare economics model to education. Chubb and Moe added a data-driven defense, deploying interpretations of national test scores to buttress their contention that students from similar socioeconomic backgrounds do better in schools organized by the

market rather than the state. It mattered little to political partisans in the choice debate that these claims were contested by other scholars who pointed out flaws in Chubb and Moe's methodology that called into question their anti–public school conclusions.[52] In a policy world captivated by the seeming neutrality of regression analyses, *Politics, Markets, and America's Schools* offered valuable cover for what otherwise could be dismissed as an ideologically-rooted preference for the market.

At a time when other efforts to reform public education were being criticized as too little and too late, Chubb and Moe's more sweeping critique found a receptive audience. A growing number of policymakers, impatient with costly public school reform that seemed incapable of producing dramatic results, preferred radical surgery. They wanted to invent a new system—to construct the educational counterpart to the interstate highway system. Chubb and Moe obligingly, and explicitly, promised that choice represented the sought-after panacea.

The Failure of Market-Based Vouchers in California

Intellectual excitement did not necessarily translate into political triumph. Despite this renewed attention, efforts to pass voucher legislation failed in Oregon in 1990 and Colorado in 1992. A 1993 California initiative, Proposition 174, provided for a voucher, worth about half the average per-pupil public school expenditure in California, available to all families with children in private schools. That measure failed for politically instructive reasons. Initial drafts of the initiative drew heavily on an equity-based voucher plan developed by Berkeley professors Coons and Sugarman in *Scholarships for Children.* As consultants to the sponsoring organization, Excellence for Choice in Education League, they proposed a plan that primarily benefited poor students. But EXCEL's financial backers opted instead for a market-based plan more philosophically attuned to Milton Friedman's nostrums.

After failing to qualify for the 1992 ballot, the proposition appeared on a special election ballot one year later. The campaign pitted the wealthy and conservative Southern Californians of EXCEL against the teachers' unions. The California Teachers Association

---

[52]*Id.* [Ted Kolderie, *Beyond Choice to New Public Schools: Withdrawing the Exclusive Francise in Public Education,* Washington, D.C.: Progressive Policy Institute, 1990.]

vowed to do "whatever it took" to defeat the proposition. The union's passion and dollars prevailed. Opponents outspent proponents by a 10–1 margin, with the CTA alone spending an unprecedented $13 million. "The business community wimped out," complained Ken Kachigian, the campaign manager for Proposition 174, by not delivering comparable sums to the effort, but money was not the only reason for the outcome of the campaign. Political support was also lacking. Pro-initiative forces were startled when, shortly before the election, Governor Wilson announced his opposition to the measure, ostensibly because of concerns about its fiscal impact.

Some commentators argued that the measure failed because suburbanites were satisfied with their schools and did not want public money drained from them to support private education. But a poll taken two months prior to the election suggests otherwise: the real problem resided in the particulars of the voucher plan, not the attitudes of the citizenry. Hefty majorities—62 percent of urban residents and 64 percent of suburban residents; 64 percent of blacks and 60 percent of whites—were for vouchers in principle. Californians were suspicious of Proposition 174 in particular, not vouchers in general. Widely aired fears that this plan would mainly benefit the wealthy, drain public schools of needed funds, and publicly support bizarre private schools—a witches' coven school became the favorite non-hypothetical example—killed the measure.

Concerns about inequities and the lack of meaningful state regulation led to the defeat of market-based voucher plans such as California's. By contrast, carefully regulated equity-based plans were considerably more successful.

The Modest Success of Equity-Based Voucher Plans

By the 1990s, the social and political climate had sufficiently changed that private school vouchers, which could muster almost no political support a generation earlier, became a political reality in two heavily African American cities, Milwaukee and Cleveland. The equity and regulatory components built into those reforms made the difference.

An Odd Alliance in Milwaukee

The Milwaukee Parental Choice Program, launched in 1990, was the first to provide public funds for private schooling, offering poor inner-city students an opportunity to attend private schools at public expense. Its success marks a significant shift in racial politics and shows a greater willingness of conservative groups to support equity-based school choice.

The political history of vouchers in Milwaukee has its start in the long struggle over desegregation. A lawsuit alleging deliberate segregation by the city's schools was filed in 1965; eleven years and countless hearings later, the district was required fully to desegregate. In an effort to encourage the transfer of white students from suburban to city schools, and black students from Milwaukee to suburban schools, Wisconsin implemented a voluntary desegregation program. As a result of enrollment shifts, several public schools in Milwaukee's black neighborhoods were either closed or converted to magnet schools, but the plan neither fully integrated the schools nor significantly boosted the achievement of black students. By 1991, slightly over one-quarter of the 99,000 students in the Milwaukee public schools were white and nearly 60 percent were black. Only 4000 African American pupils (7 percent of the entire black student population) took advantage of the opportunity to transfer to suburban schools. Just 873 students, about 3 percent of the total white student body in Milwaukee, transferred into city schools.

Black parents who had earlier backed the desegregation lawsuit became angry that their local public schools had closed, their children bore the primary burden of busing, the suburban districts had creamed off the best students, and the educational performance of their children had not improved. Their frustration prompted them to search for new answers. Among the possibilities were all-black schools, locally controlled schools, and parental choice. Annette "Polly" Williams, an African American Wisconsin state representative, summarized the feelings of many black Milwaukee parents:

> The only kids who are benefactors of this whole system [desegregation] are the White students. . . . We don't want this desegregation. Desegregation in the city of Milwaukee is terrible, and I'd like to see it abolished and go back to educating our children in our neighborhoods regardless of color. And it doesn't matter if they're all Black schools. I think Black kids can learn in an all-Black situation.

Unhappy with the public schools, many African American families who could afford to do so enrolled their children in private schools. Some of these schools were formerly Catholic schools that had been transformed into nonsectarian community schools mainly serving black and Latino students. These schools had long been engaged in a struggle for public funds. Initially, they hoped to affiliate with the Milwaukee school district, receiving public funding while maintaining administrative autonomy, but when these efforts failed the community schools urged that their students receive vouchers. Although the district opposed the idea, it had in effect set a precedent by having contracted with these very schools to educate a small number of at-risk students. Meanwhile, African American activists led by Polly Williams proposed the creation of an autonomous district in a nearly all-black part of the city. Within this new district, teachers and administrators would have control over the schools and parents would have the freedom to choose among them. The teachers' union, the school board, and the NAACP were arrayed in opposition.

The Republican Governor of Wisconsin, Tommy Thompson, took no position on this proposal. Thompson was a national pioneer in efforts to reduce government provision of social services generally. He had promoted welfare reform and, twice previously, in 1988 and 1989, had put forward private school voucher schemes. Williams had supported Thompson's voucher plans, but her priority was the creation of the inner-city district. Although the legislature approved neither the new school district nor Governor Thompson's voucher scheme, some change in school governance looked to be imminent. These pressures prompted Milwaukee to suggest a controlled public school choice plan, then to propose expanding the at-risk voucher plan. But Williams regarded this latter idea as a strategy for dumping problem youngsters on private schools.

Together with other community activists, Williams made a counterproposal. The state, not the school district, would administer the voucher plan; and poor families generally, not just those with at-risk children, would be eligible to participate. The black community in Milwaukee rallied behind Williams' plan; Governor Thompson embraced it as a way to advance the cause of school vouchers; and soon this local controversy became a topic of national interest. President Bush supported the proposal, and so did other influential conservatives, including Michael Joyce, President of the Milwaukee-based Bradley Foundation. The Catholic Church in Milwaukee gave its blessing to a plan that it regarded as a step toward public financial support for the schools it ran.

The Milwaukee voucher plan was promoted by an unusual political coalition that included both liberal black Democrats and conservative white Republicans. While the state's education department and the teachers' unions maintained their historic posture of resistance, the liberal-labor political coalition that had traditionally opposed school vouchers was fatally split.

The Milwaukee parental choice plan became law in 1990. It gives vouchers to children of families whose incomes do not exceed 1.75 times the poverty level. Participating schools cannot charge more than the voucher; if oversubscribed, those schools must use a lottery to admit students. Initially, no more than 1.5 percent of the Milwaukee student population could participate in the voucher program and no more than 65 percent of the students in any private school could receive vouchers. The program survived a series of court challenges, with the Bradley Foundation, a frequent supporter of conservative causes, paying the bulk of the legal costs.

In 1995, the Wisconsin State Legislature, newly controlled by Republicans, broadened the Milwaukee voucher plan. The new law expanded eligibility to include students already attending private schools; increased the number of students allowed to participate to 15,000; and allowed all students in a private school to receive vouchers. Most significantly, it authorized religious schools to participate—a provision upheld in a landmark 1998 Wisconsin Supreme Court ruling. These changes troubled some members of the coalition whose backing had been vital to winning passage of the earlier voucher statute. Polly Williams was interested in strengthening the equity-based elements of the choice program, not expanding it to parochial schools. "Right now," Williams says, "I'm one of the only ones talking about preserving the Milwaukee public schools system. Things like choice always used to be about improving the public schools." This split illustrates a deeper division among the provoucher forces. To many market-oriented conservatives, equity-based choice is a politically expedient way to promote broader, market-based choice. To the black activists who embraced vouchers, choice itself is essentially a means to an end—promoting equity. The future of school choice, in Wisconsin and elsewhere, will depend on the strength and character of the political coalition that is able to promote it.

* * *

NOTES AND QUESTIONS

1. Publicly Funded Voucher Plans in the Courts: Church and State Issues

As the Kirp and Bulman excerpt shows, courts until recently have not stood in the way of legislatively created voucher initiatives. Two of the most prominent recent experiments with vouchers have taken place in Milwaukee, Wisconsin; and Cleveland, Ohio. Both programs were challenged in the courts. The Wisconsin Supreme Court upheld the constitutionality of an expanded voucher plan that includes religious schools, and the United States Supreme Court declined to review the decision. *Jackson v. Benson*, 218 Wis.2d 835, 578 N.W.2d 602 (1998), *cert. denied*, 525 U.S. 997 (1998). The Wisconsin Supreme Court concluded that the Milwaukee Parental Choice Program did not violate the Establishment Clause, although the state sent tuition payments directly to participating private schools, including sectarian ones. According to the *Jackson* decision, the checks had to be endorsed by parents for the school, so funds flowed only as a result of independent, private choices. *Id.* at 853–75, 578 N.W.2d at 610–20. In two later decisions, however, high courts in Maine and Vermont rejected this reasoning and found that direct payments of tuition to religious schools constituted an impermissible establishment of religion. *Bagley v. Raymond School Department*, 728 A.2d 127 (Me. 1999), *cert. denied,*528 U.S.947, 145 L.Ed.2d 285, 120 S.Ct. 364 (1999); *Chittenden Town School District v. Department of Education*, 738 A.2d 539 (Vt. 1999), *cert. denied sub nom. Andrews v. Vermont Dept. of Educ.* 528U.S.1066, 145 L.Ed.2d 518, 120 S.Ct. 626 (1999). However, the Arizona Supreme Court upheld a tuition tax credit for parents who sent their children to private schools, including sectarian institutions. *Kotterman v. Killian*, 193 Ariz. 273, 972 P.2d 606 (1999), *cert. denied sub nom. Rhodes v. Killian*, 528 U.S.810, 145 L.Ed.2d 38, 120 S.Ct. 42 (1999), and *Kotterman v. Killian*, 528 U.S.921, 145 L.Ed.2d 237, 120 S.Ct. 283 (1999). So far, the United States Supreme Court has declined to resolve these conflicts. For a fuller discussion of the questions of separation of church and state raised by these cases, see chapter 1.

2. Other Legal Challenges to Publicly Funded Vouchers

Some courts have invalidated voucher programs on grounds unrelated to the Establishment Clause. The Ohio Supreme Court's decision in *Simmons-Harris v. Goff*, 86 Ohio St.3d 1, 711 N.E.2d 203 (1999), struck down the Cleveland voucher plan because it violated the state constitutional mandate that a bill deal with a single subject. The court stayed enforcement of the decision so that the legislature could properly reenact the program. Although the Ohio legislature did so and the governor signed the bill into law, a federal district court issued a preliminary injunction staying implementation of the Cleveland plan based on concerns that it would violate the Establishment Clause. *Simmons-Harris v. Zelman*, 54 F.Supp.2d 725 (N.D. Ohio 1999). The United States Supreme Court subsequently modified the order to allow students already in the program to continue participating. *Zelman v. Simmons-Harris*, __U.S. __, 120 S.Ct. 443, 145 L.Ed.2d 346 (1999). One month after the United States Supreme Court stayed the preliminary injunction in its entirety, the district court judge found the Cleveland voucher program unconstitutional. The court's order enjoining the program was stayed pending appeal. *Simmons-Harris v. Zelman*, 72 F.Supp.2d 834 (N.D.Ohio 1999). Recently, the Sixth Circuit affirmed the district court's decision. *Simmons-Harris v. Zelman*, 2000 U.S. App. LEXIS 31367 (6th Cir. 2000). State officials have vowed to seek en banc and Supreme Court review. Bradshaw, "Voucher Case Edges Closer to High Court," *Columbus Dispatch*, Dec. 26, 2000, at 4D. Note: The official Fed. Rep. cite is not yet available,.The Westlaw cite is 2000 WL 1816079 (6th Cir. 2000). *See also* Rees, "School Choice 2000 Annual Report," *Heritage Foundation Reports*, Mar. 30, 2000. A Florida trial judge recently declared a proposed statewide voucher plan unconstitutional because it ran afoul of the state's obligation to provide "an efficient, safe, secure and high-quality system of public schools" by diverting tax revenues to private schools. The decision is being appealed. *Id.*; Bockhorn, "A Pyrrhic Victory for Voucher Foes," *Weekly Standard*, Apr. 3, 2000, at 18; "Poor Children Lose Again," *Providence Journal-Bulletin*, Mar. 31, 2000, at 6B; "Governor Appeals Court's Ruling Against Vouchers," *Orlando Sentinel*, Mar. 22, 2000, at D3.

3. *Vouchers and Educational Equity*

In addition to legal concerns, voucher plans can raise questions about educational equity. Although some programs are targeted at low-income, minority children, general voucher plans could potentially reinforce stratification by race and class. Levin, "Race and School Choice," in S. Sugarman and F. Kemerer, eds., *School Choice and Social Controversy: Politics, Policy, and Law* 266 (1999); Biegel, "School Choice Policy and Title VI: Maximizing Equal Access for K–12 Students in a Substantially Deregulated Educational Environment," 46 *Hastings L.J.* 1533 (1995). In addition, vouchers trigger doubts about the impact on students with special educational needs that are expensive to meet. Some fear that students with disabilities will be disproportionately excluded from choice alternatives and left behind in failing public schools. Rothstein, "School Choice and Students with Disabilities," in S. Sugarman and F. Kemerer, eds., *School Choice and Social Controversy: Politics, Policy, and Law* 332 (1999).

Just as contentious is the question whether voucher plans actually are beneficial for the students they serve. In Milwaukee, for instance, researchers have been drawn into intense debate about whether vouchers have improved academic performance in the city. Indeed, the attacks and counterattacks by two prominent scholars led to a front-page *Wall Street Journal* article describing the "class warfare."

"Class Warfare: Dueling Professors Have Milwaukee Dazed Over School Vouchers"

B. Davis, *The Wall Street Journal*, October 11, 1996, at A1.

This city is the front line in the battle over school vouchers.

Since 1990, the families of several thousand low-income Milwaukee students have used state-funded vouchers to pull their children out of public schools and enroll them in private ones. Have the vouchers helped poor kids academically? Education scholars were hoping the Milwaukee experiment would finally settle the question.

Fat chance.

The Milwaukee voucher plan has become entangled in a brawl between two leading political scientists with clashing egos, ambitions and analyses. They look at the same student data and reach opposite conclusions. No matter. Their allies wield the dueling studies as weapons in fights over voucher programs nationwide. "Findings are irrelevant unless they make headlines," says George Mitchell, an educational consultant and a voucher proponent in Milwaukee. "Headlines and spin are everything."

On one side is the University of Wisconsin's John Witte, brash and combative, who was appointed by the state to track student progress. His finding: Voucher students don't advance faster academically than their public-school classmates.

On the other is Harvard University's Paul Peterson, a deceptively easygoing scholar who has dogged Mr. Witte for four years. Slicing the Milwaukee data differently, he concludes that voucher students make significant gains in their third and fourth years in the program.

The two men have come to despise each other, with Mr. Witte at the Milwaukee university calling his foe a "snake" and Mr. Peterson shooting back that Mr. Witte's work is "lousy."

"It's escalated to the point where I don't trust him enough to talk to him on the telephone," Mr. Witte says. "He'd be recording the conversation, and so would I."

The brawl reaches well beyond academic conferences and journals. For years, Milwaukee had the nation's only large-scale voucher program, so its results have become influential in education battles elsewhere. Teacher unions and their allies have used the Witte findings to defeat voucher initiatives in Washington, D.C., California and Texas. But the fight continues.

* * *

Supporters say vouchers give poor kids a chance to get ahead by letting their parents send them to successful private schools. A dose of competition would also improve the public schools, they add. But opponents object that voucher plans would skim off the brightest students and most involved parents, especially in inner-city neighborhoods, further undermining public schools.

Mr. Witte was asked by the state in 1990 to try to settle the debate by conducting annual evaluations comparing voucher students with those who remained in public school. His work took him to places such as Urban Day School, a private elementary school in a gritty African-American neighborhood of tiny homes and poor families. There, stories like those of Delores Andrews, a part-time bus driver, are common.

Disgusted that her third-grade son, Ronald, was falling behind in math at a Milwaukee public school, Ms. Andrews used a voucher to enroll him at Urban Day. Last year, Ronald was held back in third grade while he polished his math skills. This year he moved up to fourth grade, where Ms. Andrews believes he is getting much stronger in math. "It took him that long to get adjusted," she says.

Urban Day requires big adjustments from parents, too. They must sign an agreement to volunteer 20 hours a year at the school, attend teacher conferences and check that homework is done. If they don't live up to the deal, their children can be expelled—although very few are. Public schools can't make the same demands or threats. "It's easy to fall in love with these [private] schools," Mr. Witte says. "People there are devoting their lives to these enterprises, and they're not getting paid much for it."

But in evaluating vouchers, the 50-year-old Wisconsin scholar had to be hardnosed. Were students like Ronald really improving academically? Or were their parents just observing better behavior as students dressed in school uniforms and conformed to the requirements of whisper-quiet classrooms?

Each year, from 1991 to 1995, Mr. Witte surveyed Milwaukee parents to see whether they were pleased with their children's schools and also analyzed the reading and math scores of Milwaukee students. Each year, he released a report. And each year he drew the same seemingly contradictory conclusions: Parents loved the voucher schools and said they were more involved with their children's education. But the voucher children didn't improve any faster, as measured by standardized reading and math tests, than Milwaukee students generally.

In other words, if the voucher kids had remained in their old schools, they would probably be doing just about as well academically. He recommended that the legislature continue the voucher experiment but not expand it to Catholic schools, which could handle many times the 1,613 students currently enrolled in the program. Wisconsin this school year is paying private schools $4,373 for each voucher student, about $7 million in total.

Voucher proponents were outraged and took aim at Mr. Witte, who proved to be an inviting target. The grandson of the scholar who designed the Social Security system, Mr. Witte has a pro boxer's love of confrontation and theater. Once, after being ribbed for predicting that the 1986 tax-reform act would never become law, he printed out his prediction, folded it into a wad at a meeting of political scientists and literally ate his words.

For years, he balked at releasing the voucher data he collected. He argued that he deserved extra time to write academic articles, but conservatives charged a cover-up.

Mr. Witte says he relented only after a dozen state officials lectured him before Thanksgiving in 1992 about the requirements of Wisconsin's open-records laws. Nevertheless, he didn't post the full set of Milwaukee data on the Internet until February of this year. Before that, he released information piecemeal, which Mr. Peterson found so confusing that he threatened to sue the state for more complete disclosure. Mr. Witte acknowledges that he released the data "grudgingly," although he accuses Mr. Peterson of failing to use information that was already available.

Mr. Peterson is Mr. Witte's most formidable opponent. The 56-year-old political scientist is best known for his welfare studies and for his stiletto-sharp writing style. "There are three Wittes," Mr. Peterson wrote in a 1995 critique circulated to the Wisconsin legislature. The real Mr. Witte, "the unabashed critic" of vouchers, hides behind the facades of an objective social scientist and a friend of voucher schools, Mr. Peterson charged.

Mr. Witte stacks the deck against voucher students, Mr. Peterson says, by comparing them with Milwaukee students generally. The latter students are whiter, wealthier and more frequently live in two-parent families than voucher students—and thus are more likely to perform better on standardized tests. Mr. Witte's efforts to make adjustments for the different groups are doomed, Mr. Peterson says, because they are too dissimilar. The statistical controls that Mr. Witte used can't turn middle-income white students into lower-income blacks, the Harvard researcher says. "It ain't gonna happen."

Mr. Peterson followed with a second broadside this summer. He reanalyzed the Milwaukee data, finally posted on the Internet, and says Mr. Witte missed an obvious experiment. Four private elementary schools had more applicants than they had space for, and they used a lottery to choose which voucher students to admit. The children who were admitted to private schools and those who were turned away came from similar families and had similar test scores. Rather than comparing voucher students with Milwaukee students generally, Mr. Peterson proposed, why not compare them with those who missed out on the lottery?

After running the data, he found a stunning result: After three years, voucher students pulled far ahead of the randomly rejected students. Standardized test scores are ranked by "percentiles"—meaning how well an individual test-taker performs compared with test-takers nationally. According to Mr. Peterson's data, voucher students scored between three and 12 percentile points higher in math and reading scores than their public-school counterparts after three or four years in private school.

The private schools are so different from Milwaukee's public schools, he says, that the students need time to adapt. "It's like growing a garden," Mr. Peterson says. "First year you plant, you see nothing. Second year, a little bit. Third year, boom."

In response, Mr. Witte branded Mr. Peterson's findings "insane" and suggested the Harvard researcher was part of a conspiracy to attack him.

* * *

But Mr. Peterson's study is hardly the last word in the voucher debate. Critics say it may have a flaw as deep as any in the Witte reports. Each year, roughly one-fourth of the students at the voucher schools don't return. Mostly, that reflects the rootlessness of life for poor urban kids, whose families break up and move far more frequently than middle-class families. But what if a large number of the children don't come back because they are doing poorly at the voucher schools? Then the students remaining after three years would be the voucher program's elite, whose higher test scores would simply reflect a more select group of test takers.

Mr. Peterson rejects that theory, saying that third-year voucher students had "essentially the same" test scores before they entered the program as those who weren't selected. But Mr. Witte thinks there is bias in Mr. Peterson's study. During their second year in the program, Mr. Witte says, voucher schools "got rid of some kids" who weren't keeping up and encouraged them to return to Milwaukee public schools that had counseling programs. Don Rubin, a Harvard statistician who consulted with Mr. Peterson, says "it's a little early to have a great deal of confidence" in the Peterson results.

Mr. Peterson also undermined his credibility with some by being loose with his claims. Some of his results don't pass a rigorous bar known as "statistical significance"—which attests that results aren't produced by chance. Instead of stating that up front, Mr. Peterson used a looser standard, "substantively signif-

icant," to describe his work—without explaining the differences in meaning. Mr. Peterson defends his choice of language, but his co-author, University of Houston political scientist Jay Greene, says that using the different terms synonymously "misled people."

So after four years of charge and countercharge, the results of the Milwaukee experiment remain ambiguous. Mr. Witte doesn't plan to lead a new voucher-research project. "The payoffs are too low, and the dangers too high," he says.

And no one else will get fresh data soon from Milwaukee: The acrimony over the voucher fight has been so intense that the Wisconsin legislature called off new evaluations until the year 2000.

This *Wall Street Journal* article portrays the battle, but it remains unclear who should win the war. To allow you to evaluate Witte's and Peterson's claims for yourself, their research on the Milwaukee choice plan is set forth here:

"The Milwaukee Voucher Experiment"

J. Witte, 20 *Educational Evaluation and Policy Analysis* 229, 231–38, 240–46, 248–49 (Winter 1998).

* * *

The Milwaukee Voucher Program

The Milwaukee Parental Choice Program (its statutory title) can be categorized as a limited and targeted voucher program. In contrast with more or less open-ended voucher proposals, such as those proposed and defeated in referendums in Colorado and California, the Milwaukee program was initially designed to create an experimental program to provide an opportunity for some poor children to attend private schools. The program was enacted at the initiative of Republican Governor Tommy Thompson and Democratic Assemblywoman Annette (Polly) Williams. There are a number of detailed specifications that are relevant for understanding what happened in the program.

The Initial Program

The Milwaukee Parental Choice Program allows students living in Milwaukee and meeting specific criteria to attend private, *nonsectarian* schools located in the city. For each Choice student, in lieu of tuition and fees, schools receive a payment from public funds equivalent to the Milwaukee Public Schools (MPS) per-member state aid ($2,500 in 1990–91; $4,373 in 1996–97). Students must come from families with incomes not exceeding 1.75 times the national poverty line. New Choice students initially could not have been in private schools in the prior year or in public schools in districts other than MPS. The total number of Choice students in any year was limited to 1% of the MPS membership in the first four years, but was increased to 1.5% beginning with the 1994–95 school year.

Schools initially had to limit Choice students to 49% of their total enrollment. The legislature increased that to 65% beginning in 1994–95. Schools must admit choice students without discrimination based on race, ethnicity, or prior school performance (as specified in Section 118.13, Wisconsin Statutes). Both the statute and administrative rules specify that pupils must be "accepted on a random basis." This has been interpreted to mean that if a school were oversubscribed in a grade, random selection is required in that grade. However, a 1990 court ruling exempted the private schools from having to enroll all types of disabled students. In addition, in situations in which one child from a family attended the school, a sibling was exempt from random selection even if random selection was required in the child's grade.

The New Program

The legislation was amended as part of the biennial state budget in June 1995. The changes were dramatic. The principal changes were (a) to allow religious schools to enter the program; (b) to allow students in grades kindergarten through grade three, who were already attending private schools, to be eligible for the program; (c) to increase the number of students allowed in the program over three years to a maximum of 15,000 students (from approximately 1,500 allowed prior to 1995); (d) to allow 100% of students in a school to be Choice students; and (e) to eliminate all data collection and evaluations, specifying instead that the Wisconsin Legislative Audit Bureau file a report in the year 2000. Because of court challenges to the new program, parochial schools were not allowed in the program until the Wisconsin Supreme Court ruled 4–2 in favor of the new, expanded program in June 1998. Voucher-receiving students attended parochial and nonsectarian private schools for the first time in the fall of 1998.

The evidence reported in this article is based on the initial program, with modifications in 1993.

Thus, this policy experiment is far from a test of a universal voucher program. And neither the positive nor negative findings should be generalized to programs without income limits on families and to wider sets of schools that may also be unconstrained in their ability to select students.

* * *

Findings
Enrollment in Choice

Because most people assume that private schools provide superior education to public schools, it is usually assumed that demand for vouchers would exceed supply and that the issue would be the generation of new schools. However, evidence from the Milwaukee Choice Program indicates that this assumption is too simplistic. The program has not included religious private schools, which have always been the mainstay of private education in the United States. Without religiously affiliated schools being eligible for vouchers, there appear to be both supply and demand problems.

Supply and Demand in the Choice Program. . . . Enrollment in the program increased steadily but slowly, never reaching the maximum number of students allowed by the law. September enrollments were 341, 521, 620, 742, and 830 from 1990–91 to 1994–95. The number of schools participating was: 7 in 1990–91, 6 in 1991–92, 11 in 1992–93, and 12 from fall 1993 to 1995. The number of applications also increased, with again the largest increase in 1992–93. In the last two years, however, applications leveled off at a little over 1,000 per year. Applications exceeded the number of available seats (as determined by the private schools) by 171, 143, 307, 238, and 64 from 1990–91 through 1994–95. Some of these students eventually filled seats of students who were accepted but did not actually enroll.

The number of potential schools in the program was an obvious limitation. Only 22–23 secular private schools existed in Milwaukee during this period. That compared to close to 100 religious private schools. Of the secular schools, more than half chose not to participate in the Choice Program. We contacted those schools in the third year of the program. The reason for nonparticipation varied. Several schools concluded it was too costly for the school (the voucher would not match tuition); others were devoted "contract" schools with MPS; others were wary that this program was established by African Americans—primarily for African Americans.

However, the limited supply was not much of a constraining factor because applications were far from the avalanche that Choice supporters often tout. The number of seats available consistently exceeded the number of students enrolled, but primarily because not enough seats were available in the most desirable schools. It is difficult to determine how many more applications would have been made if more schools participated and more seats were available. In 1992–93, when the number of participating schools increased from 6 to 11, applications rose by 45%. From fall 1993 to 1995, however, seats available increased by 22% and 21%, but applications increased by only 5% in 1993–94 and declined in the last year.

During the Choice experiment, there was a parallel privately funded "scholarship" program that clearly affected the demand for vouchers—and possibly the supply of schools as well. This program, Partners Advancing Values in Education (PAVE), provided half of the tuition (up to $1,000) for free-lunch-eligible students and allowed them to attend any private school. Nearly all of the PAVE scholarship students attended parochial schools. The draw of religious schools was clear in that almost three times the number of students applied for PAVE scholarships as applied for vouchers, yet families were required to come up with half of the tuition for PAVE schools. Because many parochial schools had vacancies, the program also probably deterred new private schools from opening.

Who Applied for Vouchers? Vouchers raise concerns about both equal opportunity and equality of results. The opportunity concerns surrounding voucher programs can be broken down into two separate issues: (a) Without any program limits or eligibility requirements, who would use vouchers to attend private schools? And (b) can a targeted voucher program be created that will increase opportunities for students currently unable to attend private schools? The Milwaukee voucher program provides little evidence on the former question, but considerable evidence on the latter. However, given the political inclination to move this program from a targeted to an open-ended voucher program, the former issue is of ultimate importance and will be addressed in the conclusion of the article.

Based on survey responses sent to parents of Choice applicants, the picture of parents applying to the targeted Milwaukee Program is very clear. Five years of survey data, for five separate family cohorts, are extremely consistent. . . .

The demographic profile was quite consistent over each of the five years. Both applicants, and students who ultimately enrolled in Choice, were from very-low-income families, considerably below the average MPS family and about $500 per year below the low-income (free-lunch-eligible) MPS family. Blacks and Hispanics were the primary applicants to the program, both being overrepresented compared with the MPS control groups. Asian students essentially did not apply, and White students were considerably underrepresented. Also, Choice students were considerably less likely to come from a household in which parents were married (25%) than their counterparts in MPS (35% for low-income and 51% for all MPS families).

In contrast, however, Choice mothers reported considerably more education than did mothers in MPS. Fifty-two percent of applicant parents and 55% of enrollees reported some college. This contrasted with 30% and 40% for the two MPS samples. Finally, there is also evidence that Choice families were small, averaging about 2.5 children in contrast with 3.24 and 2.95 for the MPS samples.

. . . . For all forms of parental involvement—contacts with schools, organizational involvement, or home involvement—Choice parents reported considerably greater involvement than MPS parents.

Finally, there was evidence that Choice parents were very dissatisfied with their former (MPS) schools; there may have been good reasons for it, as indicated by test scores taken in MPS prior to students enrolling in Choice. In terms of attitudes, the judgment of Choice parents of their child's prior public school was especially harsh in contrast with the MPS control groups.

* * *

Choice applicants were also asked why they applied to the Choice Program. "Educational quality" led the list, eliciting an 89% "very important" response. That was followed by "teaching approach and style," 86%; "discipline," 75%; "general educational atmosphere," 74%; and "classroom size," 72%. Although this list is not surprising, it is relevant that several of the top categories—"educational quality" and "discipline"—were also the most alienating issues in Choice parents' assessment of their prior public schools.

The portrait of Choice students and families is thus complex and not simple to interpret. On one hand, the program clearly demonstrated that a program could successfully be targeted on poor families who have had bad experiences in their prior public schools. Thus, the program created the type of equalizing opportunity that was intended. On the other hand, one could also argue that the program is depriving the public schools of families who have more educated parents and who are actively involved in their children's education—in short, the type of parents who could potentially aid in reform efforts.

Outcomes: Effects on Families and Students

Outcomes are broken down simply into effects on families and students and then on schools. In each set of results, there are outcomes that most people would interpret positively and negatively. Given the complex normative issues surrounding vouchers, as outlined above, I let the reader reach his or her own judgment. I count among the positive results positive parental attitudes toward Choice schools (in contrast to prior public schools), positive attitudes toward the program, increased parental involvement, and some benefits for most of the private schools. More critical results, certainly as interpreted by foes of vouchers, include similar test score gains for Choice and MPS students, seemingly high attrition from the program, and the collapse of three private schools in mid-year.

Attitudes and Parental Involvement. Too often, outcomes of experiments in education are reduced to their effects on "achievement." Although any sensible conceptualization of "achievement" would extend well beyond standardized test scores, the vast majority of evaluations of educational programs focus, often exclusively, on test score results. That is not the case in this study. Parents of Choice students were surveyed as they applied to the program and at the end of each subsequent year. Thus, we are able to ascertain their attitudes toward their prior schools and compare them to their attitudes toward the Choice private schools. And all of those attitude comparisons are extremely positive.

Satisfaction of Choice parents with private schools was just as dramatic as dissatisfaction was with prior public schools. As noted in the last section, Choice parents were much less satisfied with their public schools than either the average MPS parent or the low-income group. Exactly the reverse occurs when parents respond to the same questions for private schools. . . .

The results were a dramatic reversal—high levels of dissatisfaction with prior public schools, but considerable satisfaction with private schools. There were eight questions in the school satisfaction scale. . . . [M]ost parents were from very to somewhat satisfied on all measures. Interestingly, the two measures on which parents were least satisfied in the public schools—"educational environment" and "discipline"—were the areas of greatest satisfaction in the private schools.

* * *

There was also, in each year, overwhelming support among participants that the Choice program should continue. The positive responses averaged 98%, even in the first year, when a school went bankrupt and almost 90 students ended their year in MPS schools. Those parents overwhelmingly supported the program.

Finally, parental involvement, which was clearly very high for Choice parents before they enrolled in the program, increased while their children were in private schools. . . . [C]omparing the prior involvement of parents of students who enrolled in Choice (fall) to private school involvement, parental involvement increased on all dimensions. The differences were statistically significant . . . on school contacts and organizations, but not on involvement at home. Part of the reason for this increase may have been that some of the private schools required participation and made parents sign parental involvement agreements. However, these were involved parents from the beginning, and at best, the contracts would have been a marginal incentive.

Achievement Test Scores. Extensive analysis of achievement results, with all the glorified technicalities, are presented elsewhere. . . . The general conclusion is that there is no substantial difference over the life of the program between the Choice and MPS students, especially the low-income MPS students. On a positive note, estimates for the overall samples, while always below national norms, do not substantially decline as the students enter higher grades. This is not the normal pattern in that usually inner-city student average scores decline relative to national norms in higher grades. That these students held their own is a positive result for the city as [a] whole.

* * *

. . . . Policymakers certainly would be interested in understanding the overall effect of a program intervention. However, they might also be interested in the trend in the program. Does it show variance from year to year, or are the results stable over time? Finally, we would also be interested in a learning curve or trend effect for individual students. It could be that students need time to become acclimated to the different approaches applied in the private schools, and thus achievement gains might be delayed. It could also be that as initial enthusiasm with a new school wears off or a student fails to adjust to a different educational style, achievement could drop.

The basic results mirror the descriptive statistics. With some complexities, which will be described, the general conclusion is that there were no consistent differences between Choice and MPS students in value-added achievement scores using any of these modeling approaches.

* * *

The trend over time in student performance has been a very controversial aspect of the Choice Program. Several other authors have claimed a trend effect favoring Choice students. Specifically, they argue, using rejected Choice students as a control, that third- and especially fourth-year Choice students make remarkable gains in math, but (with little explanation) no statistically significant gains in reading. . . .

* * *

Why does this analysis not include the reject students? As noted above, Greene et al.,* relying exclusively on the Choice/reject comparison, claimed a large and significant difference favoring Choice students in math scores for students remaining in the Choice Program for three or four years. I question the Choice/reject math results based on two major problems: (a) The rejects who remained in the experiment were not a random sample of rejected students, and (b) small sample sizes and outlier effects produced the large result in math.

In subsequent research, I looked at selection and samples size problems in two ways. First I analyzed the differences between all students who applied and were not selected and those on whom we had subsequent test data. That test data had to come from MPS. Therefore, rejected students who did not enroll in MPS or were not tested essentially dropped

out of the experiment. Because most rejects were very young, there was little prior test data on them. However, all applicants were sent surveys, so information exists on both those who later returned to MPS and those who did not. When we initially compared *all* rejects with Choice enrollees, we found few differences among the groups. The most notable were that rejected students were more likely to be Black and their parents had lower educational expectations for their children than parents of selected students. Those differences may, of course, indicate selection biases for all rejects, and they would likely bias reject scores downward.

However, the major problem was with those rejects who, in effect, left the experiment. Both descriptive statistics and a logistic regression indicated that the rejected students who remained in the study were (a) poorer, (b) in higher grades, and (c) from families whose parents were likely to be less educated and were less involved in their children's education than students who disappeared from the program. This makes sense. Rejects were looking to leave MPS in the first place. If not selected for Choice and if they had the means (and especially if their children were young), they left for private schools, either on their own or with the help of privately funded vouchers, or they went to another public school district. Thus the reject "control group" that remained behind in MPS was hardly a random sample of those who applied and were rejected. And all indications suggest those remaining in the experiment were likely to be an educationally weak representation of the initial group.

Small samples were a second problem with the Choice/reject comparison, especially when the results focus on one or two years. In such a situation, the scores of a few students could influence the general results. And that is exactly what happened. My prior research more or less reproduced the third- and fourth-year effects (in math only) that favored Choice students and were so widely circulated in the unpublished paper by Greene, Peterson, and Du. However, I then analyzed more carefully the scores of the two sets of students. As one might anticipate from the selection problems outlined above, low reject scores created the difference. For the most significant fourth-year effect, there were only 27 reject students who tried to

---

*J. Greene, P. Peterson, and J. Du, "The effectiveness of school choice in Milwaukee: A secondary analysis of data from the program's evaluation," paper presented at the American Political Science Association's Annual Meeting, San Francisco 1996.

enter the Milwaukee Parental Choice Program in 1990 for whom there were test scores four years later. Of those rejects, 5 students (18.5 %) received a score of 1 on the math test. A 1 NCE [normal curve equivalent] is the lowest recorded score on the Iowa Test of Basic Skills. It often results from a student *simply not filling in the dots* on the test form. There were no similar 1 scores in the Choice schools. The lowest Choice score (of 85 in the fourth year) was 4.

* * *

Thus, unfortunately, the natural experiment, which would have controlled for selection bias, was hopelessly contaminated by systematic attrition from the reject group, and the results were dramatically affected by outlier cases because of small samples.

Attrition from the Program. A final concern, as both an outcome measure and as a methodological issue, is the level of attrition from the program. For whatever reasons, the attrition rates from the Choice schools were quite high, although they declined over time. . . . Attrition is defined as leaving a school before a terminal grade is reached. Because students only had to submit to lottery conditions once, subsequent leaving was the result of either family or school choice. Because the program did not require schools to list nonreadmitted students (and they do not have to readmit Choice students), we cannot distinguish between these reasons. For whichever reason, the numbers are, in one sense, substantial.

Annual attrition averaged 33.4% for all Choice schools, and 30.2% if we exclude alternative schools in the Choice Program. The numbers are substantial in the sense that if the Choice Program is to have a major impact for a number of students, those students would have to remain in the Choice schools—and few do. For example, of the initial class of 341 in 1990, four years later, in spring 1994, there were only 57 students left—and very few "had graduated."

Is attrition itself a measure of Choice school failures? The answer is probably no. Although the numbers appear high, they seem to be in line with the attrition rates in the public schools for the elementary grades. Given data reporting problems on who is in what school in the first month of school, the range of attrition for K[kindergarten] to eighth graders was estimated at 22% to 28%, which is close to that in the Choice Program. Thus, attrition appears to be a common problem in inner-city school districts, regardless of the type of school.

Who was likely to leave and for what reasons? The characteristics of leavers varied from year to year, but the four-year profile is interesting and suggestive. . . . The general characteristics of continuing compared to leaving students indicate that Whites and Blacks were somewhat more likely to leave than Hispanics, and boys more likely to leave than girls. Also, students living farther away were more likely to leave.

Perhaps more important, however, it appears that leavers were underachievers in every sense: lower prior scores, lower post scores, and lower change scores. This was reflected in a considerably lower opinion of the private school among leaving parents than those who stayed. This latter difference is as large as the differences were between Choice applicants and MPS parents in appraising their prior public schools. The combination of results makes sense to either explain family choices to not return—the hoped-for educational improvement did not occur—or schools not readmitting lower achieving and nonimproving students.

* * *

These attrition levels suggest several other methodological cautions. First, the small sample sizes among Choice students allow for unique selective actions—such as one or two schools changing readmission decisions—to have quite dramatic effects. Second, the overall attrition of Choice students indicates that if a similar attrition did not occur among the Milwaukee sample, the achievement test results could be biased in favor of Choice students. Clearly, over the four-year period, lower achieving students left the Choice Program. A subsequent analysis, correcting for attrition from both samples, indicated that reading differences (which favored MPS) were probably not significant. But the general lesson is that program attrition is a major problem both in terms of policy conclusions and in terms of subsequent evaluations of similar programs.

Several final questions concerning attrition are: Why did students not return? And where did they go? The characteristics of leavers described above indicate that they were not doing as well as students who continued and were much less satisfied with Choice schools. Follow-up survey data tend to confirm that conclusion, although it is far from perfect data. Because those who left were not known until the September following the close of school in June, it was extremely hard to track down nonreturning families. The response rates to mailed and phone surveys were only 38%. We must assume that the largest bias in these responses was missing families who moved out of the Milwaukee area. Telephone searches were impossible for that group.

Parents were asked two open-ended questions: Why did your child leave the Choice Program school? And where is he/she going to school now? Of the reasons parents gave for leaving, only 15% of the responses (and they could give more than one) indicated child- or family-specific reasons—including moving. This category is clearly underestimated, however. Almost all of the remaining responses were critical of some aspect of the Choice Program or the private schools. The leading problems with the program were the lack of religious training, school transportation problems, and difficulties in reapplying to the program (including references to not being readmitted). Within-school problems most often cited were unhappiness with the staff—usually teachers—dissatisfaction with the general quality of education, and perceptions that discipline was too strict. The lack of special programs, which might have been available elsewhere, was also cited in 6% of the responses.

Thus, survey responses fit in with the factors that seem to distinguish attrition students from those who remain—distance and transportation problems, less achievement success, and resulting dissatisfaction with the private schools.

Finally, where did the students go? Survey data were very consistent with later efforts by the Wisconsin Legislative Audit Bureau to track leaving students back to MPS. Survey data indicated that approximately half of the students who left after the second and third year (57%) enrolled in MPS schools, 26% in other private schools in the area (often for religious reasons), with the remaining 16% going to MPS contract schools, home schooling, or schools outside Milwaukee. The Legislative Audit Bureau confirmed that 51.5% of the students had enrolled in MPS.

Outcomes: Effects on Schools

Effects on Public Schools. Ideally, an analysis of a voucher program would include a study of the impact of vouchers on both private and public schools. Choice supporters argue that competition will improve all schools, including those in the public sector. There are, unfortunately, several research problems that make such a study difficult if not impossible in the Milwaukee case and possibly for a much larger and less targeted voucher program as well. First, in the case of Milwaukee (and now Cleveland), the program was simply too small to

have discernible direct effects on the school system. There was no doubt that with the hundreds of media presentations about Milwaukee, usually prefaced by anguished examples of failures of the public schools, the program provided a bully pulpit for public school critics. This may have had indirect effects on MPS. However, given that the number of students enrolled barely reached 1% of the MPS enrollment, direct competition for students was not likely.

The problems of determining the effects of vouchers on public schools are not only a question of size, however. Large inner-city school districts are constantly reforming, experimenting, and reorganizing their schools and systems. The effect is that change is ongoing, and trying to causally distinguish "routine" changes from those specifically tied to the onset of a voucher program will be very difficult if not impossible.

Effects on Private Schools. Some would argue that publicly subsidizing the improvement of private schools is far from a positive outcome. Others may believe that maintaining and improving all options makes sense in what everyone agrees is a difficult educational environment. Whatever normative spin the reader wants to assume, improvement in many of the surviving Choice schools did occur.

Of the initial seven schools in the Choice Program in 1990, one was a very small, highly regarded, upper-class Montessori school that enrolled only several Choice students. One was a school for extremely-at-risk students (on the verge of dropping out), and the other five were kindergarten-through-eighth-grade schools. Of those, one, Juanita Virgil Academy, with initially 90 students, went bankrupt and closed abruptly in February 1991. The other six survived and remained in the program for the entire five years of this study.

However, two of the surviving schools were on the verge of bankruptcy when the program began. One had declared its intention to close when the program was enacted, and another was in an extremely difficult financial position. It went through three principals in the first year and probably only survived because of an infusion of money and support from a powerful neighborhood community center. These two schools today enroll over 700 children. . . .

The other schools, while their stories are not as dramatic, also improved their facilities, expanded their programs (one adding an additional preschool site), and improved turnover and diversity in their faculty. . . . [T]urnover and new personnel rates declined substantially over the life of the program.

Undoubtedly, this was due to increasing teacher salaries and benefits, but precise data were unavailable. Certification figures are less clear because of the types of certifications available, but the number of teachers with no certification clearly declined.

Correlated with the decline in turnover, the seniority levels of teachers also increased, although they remain well behind average seniority in public schools. . . .

Finally, with 1990–91 as the base year (the teaching force was more or less set before the program was finally enacted), over the course of the program, there was racial and gender diversification among teachers in the schools. Although these schools were primarily minority schools (with one exception), the teaching force was not. One of the reasons for this was that MPS had an aggressive affirmative action program, and minority teachers could easily find much higher paying jobs in the public schools. Over the life of the program, while the trend is not uniform, there was a decline in White teachers from 75 to 62%. This was approximately matched by an increase in males from 11% to 24%.

Finally, continual visits to the schools also confirmed the positive impact of the Choice Program among the major schools. From the beginning, the voucher amount was considerably higher than tuition (more than double) for the three largest schools (accounting for over 80% of the students). These schools fought hard to keep the program going and lobbied extensively for the first round of program expansions. Teachers and principals went out of their way to express their gratitude to influential politicians and were consistently positive in hundreds of media contacts.

Private School Failures. A full understanding of the impact of the Choice Program would be incomplete without mention of three Choice schools that went out of existence in mid-year. The first occurred in the first year; the last two in 1995–96. The first case, which was the only one researched for this study, was a case of bankruptcy preceded by very inadequate instruction and administration. By the time the school actually went bankrupt in February 1991, more than half of the students had already quit and returned to MPS. The later failures were of one school that was in the program for two and one half years and one school that began in 1995. In both cases, the founders, who were also the directors, are under various criminal charges, including but not limited to mishandling and embezzlement of public funds. Three hundred fifty-six students were in these schools, and the state lost an estimated $390,000 in funds that were paid for education that never occurred.

Thus, as with the effects on students and families, school effects of the Milwaukee voucher experiment are mixed. For most schools, the program was a welcome source of support. In a minority of schools, not only were public moneys wasted, but also precious months of children's education. To assume that vouchers will not be subject to some corruption and abuse and that simply pumping money into private schools will automatically enhance education and create great schools is hopelessly naive. But these problems are offset by the enhanced opportunities provided for families who otherwise could not afford a private school alternative.

Conclusions

Although somewhat frustrating, the mixed results of the Milwaukee voucher program are what we might anticipate from a very controversial program applied to an inner-city educational system. Controversy exists for a reason. Studies comparing public and private school achievement have reached varying conclusions. And claims favoring private schools were often questioned because of the problem of unmeasured selection bias. So why, in a program that required random assignment, would one assume that the private schools would work miracles that the public schools could not? And given that vouchers were provided to schools with no requirements other than being registered private schools, why would one assume that the quality of these schools would be uniformly high? More realistic assumptions would be that educational results and the quality of schools would vary, and that is what our research found.

One final point must be addressed. This study is of a targeted and limited voucher program. But the Milwaukee program also exemplifies the tendency to expand vouchers to a much wider population. The 1995 expansion, which has just been approved by the Wisconsin Supreme Court, expanded the program to include religious schools, many more students, and students already in private schools. If that becomes law after an appeal to the U.S. Supreme Court [which declined to review the case] and later just a few more words were removed from the statute, the result would be an open-ended voucher program. The mayor of Milwaukee, John Norquist, has already proposed removing all income limits on the program. In that case, the outcomes presented here might look very different.

The strongest argument for vouchers in this article is equal opportunity. The program clearly provided an opportunity for some poor families, whose children were not doing well in public schools, to obtain an alternative education that it is unlikely they could have afforded on their own. Would an open-ended voucher program produce the same results? We do not know. However, we can be quite confident that at least in the short term the students likely to benefit from vouchers would differ considerably from those who received them in the Milwaukee Parental Choice Program. Without income constraints or random selection, and given that most students attend private schools for religious purposes, it is reasonable to assume that the current private school population would be a good guide to those who will benefit under an open-ended voucher program. And they are not poor, minority families. In Milwaukee, based on 1990 census data, they are quite the opposite. The average private school family made over $42,000 a year compared to $25,000 for the average public school family. In terms of race, 84% of private school children in Milwaukee were White, whereas only 33% of the public school children were White. To open this program up to everyone, which certainly is the direction of change, would undoubtedly produce a very different program with very different consequences.

See also J. Witte, T. Sterr, and C. Thorn, *Fifth-Year Report: Milwaukee Parental Choice Program* (1995) (available at http://dpls.dacc.wisc.edu/choice/choice_rep95.html); J. Witte, *et al.*, *Fourth-Year Report: Milwaukee Parental Choice Program* (1994); J. Witte, *et al.*, *Third-Year Report: Milwaukee Parental Choice Program* (1993); J. Witte, *et al.*, *Second-Year Report: Milwaukee Parental Choice Program* (1991).

Now consider Peterson's critique of Witte's evaluation of the Milwaukee program:

"School Choice in Milwaukee"

P. Peterson, J. Greene, and C. Noyes, 125 *Pub.Int.* 38, 41–47, 49, 50–56 (Fall 1996).

* * *

The Milwaukee choice plan, as finally approved by the Wisconsin state legislature in 1990, provides ap-

proximately one thousand children from low-income families with a voucher that can be used to attend a private school. Though but a "modest proposal," in concept it has posed a major challenge to defenders of the educational status quo, for it is the first publicly funded program offering central-city families the option of choosing between government-run and privately operated schools. As one early proponent put it, "It was to be the tail that wags the dog—the entire Milwaukee public school system."

So worried were choice critics about the potential national impact of the Milwaukee experiment that they have rushed to judge its worth. The Carnegie Foundation for the Advancement of Teaching claims that "Milwaukee's plan has failed to demonstrate that vouchers can . . . spark school improvement." Albert Shanker, president of the American Federation of Teachers, declares that the "private schools [in the Milwaukee choice plan] are not outperforming public schools." The Texas State Teachers Association, an NEA affiliate, avows that "the results [in Milwaukee] have been dismal—test scores have actually declined." The head of Wisconsin's leading teacher organization echoes these sentiments. "The bottom line ought to be whether kids learn more . . . and if you gauge it by that, it doesn't measure up."

All of these critiques depend upon an evaluation prepared by John Witte, which was widely circulated in unpublished reports and is now available in the collection, *Who Chooses? Who Loses?: Culture, Institutions and the Unequal Effects of School Choice,* edited by Harvard School of Education professors Richard Elmore, Bruce Fuller, and Gary Orfield. Witte makes two types of claims. First, he argues that "the Milwaukee program offers a long-term laboratory for empirically assessing" the claims of choice proponents. But, as we will show, this is hardly the case, for the Milwaukee program hardly provided any choice.

Second, he argues that the laboratory test provides evidence of failure. "This school experiment . . . [has] not yet led to more effective schools. . . . Choice creates enormous enthusiasm among parents . . . but student achievement fails to rise." After penning these words, Witte, in early 1996, released to the social-science research community the data upon which his findings are based. After analyzing these data, we found that the evidence supports parental enthusiasm rather than Witte's skepticism. The reading scores of choice students in their third and fourth years were, on average, 3 and 5 percentile points higher, respectively, than those of comparable public-school students. Math scores, on average, were 5 and 12 percentile points higher for the third and fourth years, respectively. These differences are substantively significant. If similar success could be achieved for all minority students nationwide, it could close the gap separating white and minority test scores by somewhere between one-third and more than one-half.

Compromised Legislation

These gains were achieved despite the highly compromised nature of the program. Far from providing "liberal choice conditions," as Witte would have it, the legislature so restricted the program that it seemed destined to fail. The voucher bill was voted out of the House Urban Education Committee by a single vote, the decisive vote cast by a liberal Democrat, who was paying her niece's private-school tuition. A vote on the House floor to strip all funding for the program also failed by a single vote. Only the governor's item veto saved the program from a provision requiring reauthorization by the legislature after five years. Even more important compromises had been struck before the committee deliberations had been made. Written by a legislature controlled by Democrats, the bill gave only enough choice to satisfy [Polly] Williams's most urgent demands.

Choice is, of course, an extraordinarily elastic term. It can refer to choice among curricula within a school, choice among public schools, choice more or less hampered by rules and regulations, and choice that does or does not include religious schools. But, if choice is to stimulate innovation, diversity, and responsiveness in American education, it must have certain basic characteristics: families must be given a large enough voucher so that they, especially the poorest, can afford quality education; existing schools must be invited to participate and new ones encouraged to form; religious liberty must not be constrained; and regulations must not be overburdensome.

Milwaukee's choice program fell short of these requirements, in large measure because WEAC [the Wisconsin Educational Association Committee] forced legislative compromises that restricted the choice made available. The result nearly insured a stillborn birth. Limiting participation to low-income families was only the least, and most justifiable, of the numerous restrictions imposed.

In the candid words of one participant, the program did not "amount . . . to a good-sized flea on the tail of a dog."

Limited size. The legislature limited the size of the choice program to 1 percent of the city's public-school enrollment (with an increase to 1.5 percent in 1994). The action was taken because "we didn't want [the public schools] to take a significant financial loss." In other words, the plan was designed explicitly to avoid the competition between public and private schools which choice theory requires.

No new schools. If choice is to enhance educational quality, it must do so in part by encouraging the creation of new schools with new technologies, new approaches, and new systems of management. As those establishing charter schools are discovering, the formation of a new school is a challenging task. At a minimum, it involves obtaining financing, finding a location, assembling a staff, and recruiting students.

In Milwaukee, the legislature required any new choice school to do all this and also to fund one-third to one-half of its student body from some other source than the state voucher. The Milwaukee school-choice legislation was thus much more restrictive than charter-school legislation recently passed by many state legislatures. Though charter-school laws have restrictions of their own, none require that one-third or more of charter-school students pay their own tuition. Because of the severity of this restriction, not a single new school was formed in Milwaukee.

No students from private schools. The Milwaukee choice plan excludes from participation all students currently enrolled in private schools. One cannot receive a voucher unless one had been attending a public school or been young enough not to be of school age. One parent tried to get around the rule by enrolling his child in a public school for the last two weeks of the public-school year (after the choice school's academic year had come to an end). The ruse did not work.

The rule did have the effect of minimizing initial costs to the state. Had students already enrolled in private schools been entitled to a voucher, immediate costs would have been much higher. As it was, the state aid simply followed students from public to choice schools. But the restriction denied participation in the program to those families most likely to be interested. Some of the people who had worked the hardest to secure passage of the legislation were the very ones specifically denied the right to benefit from its provisions. The restrictive impact of this rule decayed with time, however; every low-income family with a child yet to attend school may now receive a voucher.

Half-funded. Williams originally proposed $3,100 vouchers. But the state senate cut the funding level to $2,500 so the plan would be "revenue neutral." Though the amount would adjust annually to keep pace with increases in public-school funding. The voucher still amounted to less than half the per-pupil cost of Milwaukee's public schools.

Several schools found the tuition voucher too small to participate. One private-school administrator said that it would have admitted as many as half of its students under the choice program, if the voucher had been more generous. Another said that his school "would participate further if we did not lose so much money per student accepted."

No parental contributions. Milwaukee public schools supplement state aid with their own local tax revenue. But voucher schools cannot ask parents to top off the voucher with additional tuition money. The ostensible purpose of this ban was to keep school choice from becoming elitist, a goal that was already assured by the rule limiting participation to low-income families. But the restriction on parental contributions, coupled with the small size of the tuition voucher, guaranteed that most choice students would attend fiscally constrained institutions with limited facilities and poorly paid teachers. It also made more difficult the establishment of a financial link between home and school which many private-school officials think is key to educational success.

No religious schools. In 1994, nearly 20,000 students (or nearly 18 percent of all Milwaukee students) attended one of over 100 schools with a religious affiliation—most of them Catholic, but many Lutheran, as well as a Jewish Yeshiva, a Muslim school, and two Christian Pentecostal schools. Most of the religious schools were ready and eager to enroll more students. In 1995, when the choice program was waiting for court permission to expand to include religious schools, approximately 100 schools indicated that they wished to participate, and places for over 6,200 more students were found. By denying parents the opportunity to choose a school with a religious affiliation, the Wisconsin state legislature denied families access to 90 percent of the private-school capacity available in Milwaukee.

A Hostile Bureaucracy

Wisconsin's Superintendent of Public Instruction is responsible for the administration of the Milwaukee choice plan. The superintendent is elected for a four-year term in low-visibility elections held in odd-numbered years. With light voter interest, WEAC is in a strong position to dominate the outcome. Herbert Grover, a five-term Democratic state assemblyman, was first elected state school superintendent with the support of WEAC in 1981. In return, Grover "assumed the position of point man in the battle against vouchers," says Daniel McGroarty in his new book, *Break These Chains: The Battle for School Choice.*

Legal challenge. Calling the program "fundamentally flawed and very possibly unconstitutional," Grover invited citizens to file law suits to prevent its implementation. The NAACP [National Association for the Advancement of Colored People], with the backing of WEAC and other public-school groups, accepted Grover's invitation. Though the program's constitutionality was upheld in the trial court, and again by the Wisconsin state supreme court, the prolonged legal wrangle cast a shadow over the plan well into its second year.

Minimal publicity. The agency Grover headed, the Department of Public Instruction (DPI), did nothing to implement the program beyond the legal minimum. Though required by law to "ensure" that Milwaukee parents were adequately informed about the availability of school choice, Grover chose to wait until May 29 to issue a press release telling schools that, in order to participate, they had to apply within two weeks. Given the time constraints, only seven schools expressed interest. In mid June, DPI gave parents two weeks to apply. Only 577 applied; space was available for 341.

Excessive regulation. In what McGroarty calls the "red-tape war," Grover also threatened the choice schools with a host of regulatory burdens, which they managed to avoid only by securing a court order invalidating them.

Defining secular. Grover then moved to keep virtually all high-school students out of the choice program. Messmer High, a private high school serving a largely African-American, inner-city population, submitted an application. The school had once been a Catholic parochial school, but, in 1985, the archdiocese decided it could no longer afford to keep the school in operation. Under the leadership of Brother

Bob Smith, a Franciscan, it re-created itself as a community school. It purchased the building from the archdiocese, raised funds from alumna, and appealed to local foundations and the business community. Only a minority of students were Catholic. Given its independence from the archdiocese, school officials felt their educational program was not so "pervasively religious" to require exclusion from the choice plan.

Yet the school did not altogether deny its Catholic heritage. Students were still expected to take classes in religion, though these were said to be educational, rather than proselytizing, in nature. Smith wore a clerical collar, and a sharp observer could occasionally spy a cross or religious portrait when walking the corridors. When the Milwaukee newspapers cried foul, Grover hastened to investigate. . . .

. . . DPI concluded that the school was, indeed, pervasively religious and that it could not participate in the choice program. With this decision, Grover eliminated all access to a sound high-school education via the choice program. To which one parent responded: "Do you think the biggest thing we've got to worry about in school is our kids coming in contact with religion?"

* * *

Surprising Success

If programs can overcome initial challenges, an experiment may succeed, provided its basic premises are sound. Uncertainties are gradually reduced, obvious weaknesses eliminated, routines established, appropriate personnel recruited, and acceptance finally achieved. Sometimes even programs designed to fail can succeed.

The number of students participating in the choice program more than doubled over the first five years of the program. The number of participating schools increased from seven to 12, giving parents somewhat greater choice.

* * *

So, despite hardships, the Milwaukee experiment still provided evidence that school choice can lead to more effective schools. Parents were pleased, retention rates increased, test scores rose. As a result, Milwaukee's choice program has become an institutionalized component of the city's educational system. The program has even prospered to the point that the Wisconsin state legislature felt confident enough in the spring of 1995 to strip the program of many of

its restrictions. Although the expanded version still must survive constitutional scrutiny by the Wisconsin judiciary, the very fact that choice continues to move toward the center of the state's educational agenda suggests that the Milwaukee experiment might still "wag the dog."

The Politics of Evaluation

But what about the Witte evaluation? Did it not find that the choice students learn no more than public-school students? Can parental satisfaction and anecdotal evidence substitute for the knowledge generated by high-powered academic research? Given the politically biased origins of the Witte evaluation, the answer is yes.

The legislature gave the responsibility for overseeing the evaluation to Superintendent Grover, who picked his evaluator on September 9, 1990, just days after the first choice students began going to school. A choice critic like Grover had good reason to move expeditiously. The early years are times when experimental programs are most fragile, most prone to error. Nothing can pose as great a danger to an innovative governmental program as an immediate, apparently rigorous evaluation of its effects. But Grover's eagerness to move quickly jeopardized his ability to obtain a high-quality evaluation. Reliable evaluations are complicated undertakings in which a number of major research organizations have specialized, including such well-known entities as Abt Associates, Mathematica, NORC, RAND, and the Manpower Development Research Corporation. If Grover had followed standard practice, he would have asked for bids from these research organizations to undertake the evaluation. Instead, he gave the assignment to John Witte, a political-science professor with minimal experience with large-scale evaluations.

Moreover, Witte was hardly disinterested. In fact, he had written a paper, well received in teacher-union circles, which criticized studies finding private schools outperforming public schools. Witte would later become a public opponent of the expansion of the Milwaukee choice program in 1995.

Witte quite frankly reports that choice-school parents were much happier with their new school than with their prior public school. Seventy-five percent of choice parents gave their child's school a grade of either "A" or "B," 10 percentage points higher than the grades given public schools. Choice parents expressed substantially greater satisfaction than public-school parents with every aspect of their child's education: the amount their child learned, the teacher's performance, the program of instruction, the discipline in the school, the opportunities for parental involvement, the textbooks, and the location of the school.

If Witte's handling of parental satisfaction is quite straightforward, the same cannot be said about his discussions of the ability of the program to retain its students. When assessing "benefits to students," he concludes that "attrition from the program is . . . high, which means that few students are remaining in the schools over a period of years," a conclusion constantly trumpeted by teacher unions and other critics of the program. But, as McGroarty points out in his book, Witte's conclusion is contradicted by his own data. Student retention within any one school is an extraordinary problem in Milwaukee, in good part because of the residential mobility of low-income, welfare-dependent populations. For central-city, female-headed households with children between the ages of six and 17 (which constitutes 77 percent of the choice-student population), the annual residential mobility rate is 30 percent for African Americans and 35 percent for Latinos. Not every change in residence dictates a change in school attendance. But, in Milwaukee's public elementary schools, nearly 20 percent leave even before the end of the school year in June. Come the following fall, 35 percent of the students are no longer in attendance at the same public elementary school that they were the year before.

The choice schools substantially reduced this migration from one school setting to another. All but 23 percent of the choice students returned to the same elementary school the following fall (as compared to 35 percent in Milwaukee's low-income public schools). Within the school year itself, the percentage leaving choice elementary schools was as little as 4 percent in 1993 and just 6 percent in 1994 (much lower than the near 20 percent changing from one low-income public elementary school to another). It is thus wrong for Witte to say that these percentages are high. They instead constitute a substantial improvement on the turnover rates within the Milwaukee public schools.

Flawed Evaluation Methodology

Witte's claim that the choice program has "not yet led to more effective schools" relies upon three types of comparisons with Milwaukee public schools: (1) comparison of test scores of cohorts of choice students with those of both all and low-income public-school students; (2) comparison of the changes from year to year in the individual test scores of choice students with those of both all and low-income public-school students; and (3) analysis of the effect of choice by means of a multiple regression analysis of all changes in test scores. None provide useful information about choice-school effectiveness.

When comparing the test scores of cohorts of choice students with those of public-school students, Witte finds no stable, significant difference between them. But, even if he had, the finding would have been meaningless. Before entering the program, the soon-to-become choice students scored well below the average of a cross section of Milwaukee public-school (MPS) students. Only 23 percent of the first-year choice students scored above the national average on the reading test, and only 31 percent attained that score on the math test. For the so-called MPS control group, the scores were 35 percent and 43 percent, respectively. Since students had decidedly lower scores before entering choice schools, it is misleading simply to compare scores from before and after the students entered choice schools. Since even Witte admits that this is not a "way to accurately measure achievement gains and losses," one can only wonder why the comparison is reported.

Witte next compares annual changes in achievement scores by choice and public-school students. Annual gains for 1991, 1992, and 1993 are compared. In two of the six comparisons, the choice schools do better; in the other four, the public schools do better.

This kind of comparison also does not control for the family background of students. Yet choice students and those attending Milwaukee public schools differed in the following ways: Seventy-four percent of the choice students were African American; only 59 percent of the "control group" were. Twenty-one percent of the choice students were Latino; only 11 percent of the "control group" were. Choice parents reported their family income to be about one-half that of the family income reported by the average Milwaukee public-school parent. Only 24 percent of choice families reported a two-parent household; 47 percent of Milwaukee public-school parents did.

Witte's third method regresses scores on their prior-year scores as well as on the pupil's gender, ethnicity, family income, and whether the student participated in a choice program. He finds choice students do better in only one-half the comparisons. There are many problems with this approach, three worthy of special mention.

First, Witte "stacks" his data, a practice that combines all year-to-year changes into one analysis. The unit of analysis is no longer the student but something known as the "student-year." Some students are counted once, some twice. In unpublished reports, Witte counts the same student as many as four times. Data stacking makes the improbable assumption that students learn at uniform rates throughout the length of the program.

Second, Witte's measure of family income—namely, whether the student receives free or reduced-price school lunches—is, to say the least, woefully inadequate. The measure is inaccurate because not all those eligible for free lunch apply, parental income is misreported to the schools, and errors are made by teachers and administrators. The measure is only weakly correlated with the parents' reports of their own income in a confidential survey. More than 16 percent of Milwaukee public-school families who reported incomes over $42,500 are designated as receiving subsidized lunch. Meanwhile, 26 percent of choice students with family income below $17,500 did not receive free lunch, compared to 14 percent of public-school students.

Third, improbable assumptions must be made when using regressions comparing a test group to a much more heterogeneous control group (wider range of educational performance, greater ethnic diversity, wider range of incomes, etc.). Regression analysis must assume that relationships among these variables are identical over their entire range; but this is unlikely to be the case. Moreover, choice students can be expected to differ from public-school students in many respects other than the few factors (race, gender, and income) which Witte tries to take into account. In short, Witte's three attempts to find out whether choice schools are effective prove nothing.

A Better Measure of Choice

Witte fails to exploit a fourth research strategy—the comparison of choice students with a randomly selected control group—which Witte himself originally promised to carry out. The choice legislation required that choice schools accept students at random. For research purposes, those rejected for lack of space constituted an ideal comparison group, because they would presumably be similar to choice students in all respects (eligibility, desire to participate, informed about the availability of the program,

etc.), except for the fact that their number did not come up in the selection process.

When Witte proposed to conduct the evaluation, he emphasized the unique research opportunity this random acceptance requirement presented to him. But he reports no such comparison in the Fuller et al. volume. (In an unpublished paper he has a brief, inadequate discussion of these data.) In the absence of an appropriate analysis of these data by Witte, two of the authors of this article, with the aid of others, conducted an analysis of our own. The results supercede the findings generated by Witte's approaches.

Since students were randomly assigned to test and control groups, their demographic and educational characteristics, upon entering the choice program, should be similar. This in fact proved to be the case. As Witte himself says: "In terms of demographic characteristics, non-selected . . . students came from very similar homes as choice" students did. Upon entering the choice program, the selected students scored, on average, at the 39th percentile of the math test; those not selected scored at the 40th. On the reading test, the selected scored at the 38th; the non-selected scored at the 39th. The income of the selected families was $11,250, the non-selected $11,500. However, the selected students had slightly better-educated mothers (but when this difference was controlled for, the results remained essentially the same).

Enrollment in a choice school did not affect student performance on standardized tests during their first two years in the program. But, in year three and four, choice students made substantial gains. On the math test, choice students scored, on average, 5 percentile points higher than non-selected students in year three and over 11 points higher in year four. On the reading test, choice students scored, on average, 3 percentile points higher after three years than those not selected into the program. After four years, they scored nearly 5 percentile points higher. Statistical tests suggest that one can have confidence in these results. Substantively, the findings are impressive. If duplicated nationwide, they could reduce by somewhere between one-third and more than one-half the current difference between white and minority test score performance.

That the improved performance does not appear until the third and fourth years is quite consistent with a common-sense understanding of the educational process. Choice schools are not magic bullets that transform children overnight. It takes time to adjust to a new teaching and learning environment. The disruption of switching schools and adjusting to new routines and expectations may hinder improvement in test scores in the first year or two of being in a choice school. Educational benefits accumulate and multiply with the passage of time.

Some may think the strong results in years three and four were due to the retention in the choice schools of the better-performing students. But, at the end of the second year, the test performance of students who remained in choice schools did not differ significantly from all second-year students. Others may claim that the results were affected by the distress experienced by families who applied to the choice schools but were not admitted. But if that were the case, the differential success rate should have been the greatest in the first year, when no differences between the two groups were observed.

Because test scores were not available for all students, one cannot draw conclusions with complete certainty. But an appropriate statistical analysis of data from a natural randomized experiment indicates that the Milwaukee choice program, for all the compromises and problems it endured, has proven successful after all.

On August 15, 1996, after this essay was drafted, the findings reported here were presented before a Wisconsin state judge, Paul Higgenbotham, who was asked to lift an injunction preventing the expansion of the choice program. Higgenbotham left intact the injunction against attendance at a religious school until the case could be considered on its merits, but, after referring to the success of choice students in their third and fourth years, he allowed the secular choice program to expand to 15,000 students, and he no longer kept in place the limits on the percentage of students in a school who had tuition vouchers. The worst fears of teacher organizations were coming true: Even a highly compromised choice plan was proving so effective it could not be contained.

NOTES AND QUESTIONS

1. Empirical Uncertainty and Policy Judgments

Who has the better part of the argument in this academic debate over the efficacy of choice plans? How should legislators deal with these conflicting claims? With a moratorium on further research evaluations until the year 2000, how will policy judgments about

the Milwaukee plan be made? How is the situation in Wisconsin likely to affect voucher experiments in other states, if at all?

2. Subsequent Developments in the Dispute Over Vouchers

Since their widely publicized dispute, Witte and Peterson have continued to assess the impact of voucher plans. Witte has softened his position by finding that vouchers may help selected student populations, particularly low-income children in inner-city schools. J. Witte, *The Market Approach to Education: An Analysis of America's First Voucher Program* (2000). Peterson has studied the publicly funded Cleveland program as well as a privately funded program in San Antonio, Texas. He has concluded that the Cleveland plan led to improved parental satisfaction and the San Antonio plan neither "creamed" the best students nor produced a damaging mass exodus from the public schools. *See* John F. Kennedy School of Government web site at http://www.ksg.harvard.edu/ksgpress/ksg_news/press_releases/press_santoniovoucher.htm.

3. Further Reading

For more analysis of the Milwaukee voucher experiment, *see* J. Greene, *et al.*, *Effectiveness of School Choice: The Milwaukee Experiment* (Occasional Paper 97-1/March, 1997) (available at http://data.fas.harvard.edu/pepg/op/mil.htm); J. Greene, *et al.*, *The Effectiveness of School Choice in Milwaukee: A Secondary Analysis of Data from the Program's Evaluation* (Aug. 14, 1996) (available at http://hdc-www.harvard.edu/pepg/op/evaluate.htm). Professor Peterson and his fellow researchers also have arrived at positive conclusions regarding voucher programs in Cleveland and Dayton, Ohio; New York City; San Antonio, Texas; and Washington, D.C. W. Howell, *et al.*, *Test-Score Effects of School Vouchers in Dayton, Ohio, New York City, and Washington, D.C.: Evidence from Randomized Field Trials* (Aug. 2000) (available at http://data.fas.harvard.edu/pepg.papers.htm) (reporting positive results for African American students in choice plans); P. Peterson, *et al.*, *An Evaluation of the Horizon Scholarship Program in the Edgewood Independent School District, San Antonio, Texas: The First Year* (Sept. 1999) (available at http://data.fas.harvard.edu/pepg.papers.htm) (parents of choice students reported lower levels of fighting and more time spent on homework than those with children in the public schools); P. Peterson, *et al.*, *An Evaluation of the Cleveland Voucher Program After Two Years* (June

1999) (available at http://data.fas.harvard.edu/pepg. papers.htm) (reporting high levels of parental satisfaction with choice schools, though test scores did not improve appreciably).

C. Charter Schools: A Hybrid Model

Although voucher plans have yet to play a major role in the field of education, the school choice movement has prompted other innovations in the delivery of instructional services. One of its most visible offspring has been the charter school movement, which seeks to foster choice and experimentation within the public education system.

"From Vouchers to Charters: The Shifting Politics of School Choice"

R. Bulman and D. Kirp, in S. Sugarman and F. Kemerer, eds., *School Choice and Social Controversy: Politics, Policy, and Law* 36, 52–62 (1999).

* * *

Unlike vouchers, there was no grand theory to support charter schools; no Milton Friedman or Christopher Jencks to give them intellectual respectability; no shift in the rhetorical ground to accompany their emergence; and no empirically-based discussion, on the order of *Politics, Markets and America's Schools,* to justify them. But if charter schools have less dramatic origins than vouchers, they have also had a much greater impact on education.

The beginnings of the charter school movement date to a 1988 conference on public school reform, held in Minneapolis, which drew together many of the key participants in the Minnesota public school choice movement. Albert Shanker, head of the American Federation of Teachers, who fifteen years earlier had embraced the concept of Christopher Jencks' voucher model, delivered the key speech. Shanker praised a concept—charter schools—that he had come across in *Education by Charter: Restructuring School Districts,* a report drafted by a former schoolteacher and administrator named Ray Budde. The AFT President took this obscure report and gave it air-time, not only at the Minneapolis conference but also in a speech at the National Press Club and in his weekly *New York Times* advertisement *cum* opinion piece. While Shanker and Budde had in mind a reform that would enable teachers, with the approval of their union, to develop new programs within existing schools—some-

thing not so different from the Alum Rock experiment [an early choice experiment that permitted students to select among various "schools within a school"]—the concept and the term "charter school" were now available for policy entrepreneurs to tinker with.

Tinker they did. Two tireless advocates, Joe Nathan, a former school teacher and now a researcher at the Hubert Humphrey Public Policy Institute at the University of Minnesota, and Ted Kolderie, the former executive director of Citizens' League, played key roles in shaping the charter school concept, first in Minnesota and then elsewhere. They drew for inspiration upon   Shanker's remarks as well as on a variety of existing initiatives, including alternative public schools, site-based management and British grant-maintained schools.

The choice-promoting measures that Minnesota had recently implemented were themselves an inspiration for charter schools. As Kolderie noted in a widely-circulated report, while those earlier reforms formally opened up choice to parents, they did nothing to create any additional *school* choices. Charter legislation encouraged the creation of new schools—not schools within schools, as Shanker envisioned, but "new public schools" that exist outside the "exclusive franchise" of the public school district to meet the new demand.

A 1988 Citizens' League report, *Chartered Schools = Choices for Educators + Quality for All Students,* drew together the many strands of the charter concept. Enabling legislation was introduced by the same state senator who had carried the public school choice bill and, three years later, the first charter schools in the nation were authorized.

The concept has proved astonishingly popular. Since Minnesota acted, in 1991, thirty-three states and the District of Columbia have authorized this new kind of institution, and with each legislative term that number grows. The Clinton administration, which initially limited its involvement with charter schools to providing modest subsidies for new schools and supporting a national evaluation, is contemplating a substantial increase in direct federal aid.

As with vouchers, where Milton Friedman–inspired market plans vie with Christopher Jencks–influenced equity plans, charter schools have come to mean very different things in different states. Indeed, charter regimes are as different from one another as vouchers in Alum Rock and Milwaukee.

Those differences reflect distinct philosophies underlying the legislation. In some states, charter schools have been promoted as a way to manage discontent by offering an outlet for students unhappy with the public schools. Elsewhere, they are regarded as a way of educating the hardest-to-educate, those "at-risk" students on whom the Milwaukee voucher plan initially focused. Charter schools are sometimes viewed as incubators for new ideas that can be adapted by the public schools. In other places, they are seen as the entering wedge in a war on publicly-run schools, a way to demonstrate that the market can replace the bureaucracy.

The history of charter school legislation in two states, California and Arizona, suggests how these variations play out in the field.

Charter Schools in California

California was the second state to adopt charter school legislation. As in Minnesota, the 1992 law had bipartisan support in the legislature and the backing of a Republican governor. There, however, the political similarities end.

The political history of charter schools in California is intertwined with the politics of vouchers. Democrats supported charter schools in hopes that this variant of choice would diminish support for Proposition 174, the voucher measure that was about to be put to the voters. The author of the legislation, Democratic state senator Gary Hart, sought a way to achieve greater choice that, while responsive to the frustrations of voucher supporters, was less threatening to the public schools. That balancing act was critical to securing the support, or at least not arousing the potent opposition, of the teachers' unions. As Hart later observed:

> [I]t seemed possible to us to craft a legislative proposal that did not sacrifice the attractive features of the voucher movement—namely, choice of schools, local control, and responsiveness to clients—while still preserving the basic principles of public education: that it be free, nonsectarian, and nondiscriminatory.

The 1992 California law reflected this mix of hopes and suspicions. It permitted the creation of no more than 100 charter schools. At least 10 percent of the teachers in a district, or half of the teachers in any one school, were required to endorse the proposed school.

Six years later, California significantly liberalized its charter school law. The legislation expands the number of charter schools, to 250, and authorizes an additional 100 charter schools in each subsequent year. It also makes obtaining a charter much easier.

The reason for this legislative shift has less to do with pedagogy than with politics, especially teacher union politics. When the possibility of liberalizing the charter school regime was first broached, in 1997, the California Teachers' Association, which had demonstrated its political muscle in the voucher wars, was opposed. The union was prompted to reconsider its position, though, when a group of Silicon Valley businessmen, hostile to the public system, gathered enough signatures to demonstrate that it could place an even more open-ended charter school initiative on the November 1998 ballot. That initiative allowed an unlimited number of charter schools, removed the proviso that teachers approve the conversion of a public school to a charter school, and eliminated the requirement that charter school teachers be certified.

This was bad news from the union's perspective, but another measure that had already qualified for the June 1998 ballot posed a far greater threat. Proposition 226, widely regarded as payback for the teacher union's earlier anti-voucher campaigns, was designed to prevent unions from spending their members' dues on political activities without the written consent of each member. Had this measure passed, it would effectively have killed unions as a political force in the state. In the spring of 1998, as the legislative deal on charters was being negotiated, polls showed that Proposition 226 was likely to pass. The CTA, which spent more than $20 million in the ultimately successful effort to defeat it, lacked the resources to mount a second costly campaign. For that reason, the union agreed to work with the legislature on a new charter law if the sponsors of the initiative would agree, as they did, to withdraw their ballot measure.

In the ensuing negotiations, both sides gave ground. The new law permits a substantial increase in charter schools and loosens the system of public regulatory controls. For example, a school district cannot turn down a charter application unless it is prepared to show that the proposed venture is educationally unsound, a very hard burden to meet. But the CTA's influence is felt in provisions that fix a limit on the total number of charter schools, require that charter school teachers have some form of state certification and mandate that half of all permanent teachers in a public school approve its conversion to a charter school.

This new legislation confirms a fact on the ground: charter schools in California are a significant presence. As one exultant charter advocate proclaimed: "These schools are the ram's horn of Joshua that will one day bring the walls of Jericho tumbling down."[88]

A Market of Charters in Arizona

While charter schools in California have been touted as alternatives to vouchers, elsewhere they have taken on the complexion of vouchers, for the state has effectively abdicated its regulatory role. Charter schools in Arizona exemplify this possibility.

Arizona's charter school law, passed in 1994 and liberalized in 1996, is without question the broadest, most charter-promoting statute in the nation. It establishes multiple routes for the granting of charters and, unlike almost all other states, does not limit the total number of charters that may be granted. There is no requirement that teachers be certified by the state and, with the exception of auditing standards, participation in a statewide testing regime and anti-discrimination requirements, the regulations that govern public schools are waived.

Thus, once a charter is granted in Arizona—for a period of fifteen years, by far the longest in the nation—a school is effectively subject only to the discipline of the market. "Charters have already closed their doors; that is the genius of this plan," says the Republican speaker of the House, one of its initial backers. Schools are left to sink or swim in an educational environment characterized by ever-increasing competition, not only from other charter schools but also from private schools and newly market-conscious public school districts.

In Arizona as in California, charter schools were initially regarded as a way to forestall vouchers. In the early 1990s a statewide task force of business and education leaders proposed an array of public school reforms, including statewide open enrollment, site-based management, and school "report cards." The task force also urged stronger statewide academic standards as well as the development of a test that would assess students' ability to meet those standards.

Many Arizona conservatives, including then-Governor Fife Symington, regarded such reforms as inadequate. The replacement of bureaucratic accountability with outcome accountability, as the task force was urging, was insufficient; the surest form of accountability, they argued, was market accountability. In their view, the real problem lay with public

education itself, which needed to be subjected to competition, not simply mended.

Partly taking their cues from the Goldwater Institute, a conservative local think tank, Governor Symington and others, among them House Education Committee chair Lisa Graham, framed their arguments for more fundamental change not in educationese but in the language of welfare economics. Public schools, like other monopolies, were naturally unresponsive to consumer (i.e., parent) demand; only the introduction of choice would pry open this market, enabling parents to obtain an education for their children that they regarded as responsive to their needs.

The preferred strategy for introducing competition into the Arizona education market was vouchers. Over a three year period beginning in 1992, voucher legislation passed the state House of Representatives, only to be bottled up in the Senate. In 1994, with the election of a GOP Senate majority coupled with strong gubernatorial support, voucher advocates were confident that they would finally prevail. Leading conservative figures, among them William Bennett, Pat Robertson and Jack Kemp, were flown into the state to stump for vouchers (by many accounts, the tactic backfired, as the outsiders' perceived arrogance turned off the lawmakers). And while earlier voucher statutes were sweeping in scope, the 1995 measure, modeled on Wisconsin's legislation, provided vouchers to 10,000 low income children from the primarily black South Phoenix area. That bill was regarded by its proponents as a first step toward a statewide voucher plan.

After passing the House, the bill was put to a vote in the Senate, where it came tantalizingly close. Backers hoped that a deal could be cut with one or two conservative Democrats; opponents feared that the bill might squeak through. Confronted with this perceived deadlock, as well as mounting public demands that the state do something about the issue, Lisa Graham and Beverly Harmon, the respective chairs of the Senate and House education committees opted for compromise, and some Democrats went along.

In a special legislative session called to address this single issue, the voucher bill was shelved and in its place a charter school law was approved. Passage came swiftly, with broad bipartisan support and almost no debate. The teachers' association (teachers' unions are not permitted in Arizona) and school

---

[88]Alan Bonsteel, "The Proposition 174 Story," in Alan Bonsteel and Carlos Bonilla, eds., *A Choice for Our Children* (1997).

boards association, natural opponents of the measure, had little input.

Most Arizona lawmakers ignored the details, concentrating instead on the concept, but those details have proved crucial. Not only has this measure led to a proliferation of charter schools—more than anyplace else in the nation—it has also changed the nature of political debate over public education in the state.

Charter supporters were determined that these new schools have an immediate and visible presence. In a matter of months, the state gave charters to scores of schools. As one legislator observed, "anyone who could stand up and breathe got a charter." In order to protect the charter school concept from the local school boards and state Board of Education, both regarded as hostile to the innovation, the legislation created a new entity, the Charter School Board, whose sole mission was issuing charters and promoting charter schools, authorizing the Board to issue up to twenty-five charters each year. Thus, if school districts turned down charters and the state Board of Education balked, a significant number of new schools would still be launched. In addition, school districts were authorized to issue charters to schools anywhere in the state and, as a consequence, a market for charters has sprung up, with districts charging upwards of $20,000 to would-be school operators.

Charter schools have become a fixture in Arizona's educational landscape. In 1998, 266 such schools operated under 166 charters granted by state and local educational agencies; they serve some 35,000 students, nearly three percent of the school-age population. These schools are freed from most of the nearly 800 pages of regulations that govern public schools. Back-to-basic schools, often with strong religious ties, have flourished in the suburbs, while in Phoenix, new schools have sprung up for hard-to-educate youngsters and school dropouts. Some are "chain" schools, which package the same educational approach in several sites. For-profit educational organizations regard Arizona as a promising new market.

Charter schools, not vouchers, are the vehicle for educational choice in the state. Since the passage of the charter school law, there has been little pressure to revisit the voucher issue, a result that was not anticipated when the charter school law was passed. Nor is this the only unanticipated development. Instead of the state providing vouchers for 15,000 poor children—the measure that failed because of liberals' qualms—Arizona underwrites the education of a potentially unlimited number of youngsters in essentially unregulated schools. Conservatives are as surprised as liberals by these developments, and what they suggest about the pent-up demand for choice. "The charter school movement took off far more rapidly than any of us imagined," says the head of the Goldwater Institute, which earlier had been unsuccessful in pushing the concept of market-oriented vouchers.

In theory, public accountability—that is, the satisfaction of public values as well as family preferences—distinguishes charter schools from vouchers, where accountability is supposed to flow entirely from family sovereignty. In practice, however, the two choice models blur the boundary between accountability and sovereignty. The laws governing the Milwaukee and Cleveland voucher plans prohibit use of such admission criteria as prior academic achievement; require that the voucher cover all regular school costs; and determine who is eligible, based on their family income. In these respects, the voucher schemes are more attentive to equity concerns than the Arizona charter school law.

The philosophy of regulation that prevails in Arizona is that parents are the real "regulators," and that the state's role should essentially be limited to financial oversight. Schools that are chartered by districts hundreds of miles away are even less subject to monitoring, since the chartering districts lack the resources, the personnel and the inclination to do so.

Thus, while oversight is in theory a way to assure public accountability, the practice in Arizona is otherwise. The Department of Education acknowledges state Superintendent of Public Instruction Lisa Graham Keegan (formerly Lisa Graham: the pro-voucher legislator was elected state superintendent in 1995) is advocate, licenser and reviewer for charter schools. "There is no separation of powers." Nor is there any interest on the state's part in closing bad schools. "These are small businesses, which live or die by the market," says the bureaucrat with responsibility for regulating them. Superintendent Keegan is entirely unapologetic. "In Arizona, charter schools are effectively group vouchers."

In Arizona as in California, there is widespread popular acceptance of charter schools. Even among those who were initially resistant, there is growing acknowledgment that, because of their small size and focused curricula, these institutions can help students who would likely fare badly in more impersonal public institutions. The Arizona Education Association, the statewide teachers' group, is designing its own charter school plan, and even the state School Boards Association, the most vehement opponent, concedes that charter schools have become a fixture.

Superintendent Keegan, borrowing President Clinton's welfare rhetoric, wants to "change the face of public education as we know it." In 1998 Keegan introduced a school financing plan that could do just that, in the process further blurring the line between ordinary public schools, charter schools and vouchers. Arizona currently provides school districts with per pupil allocations. Dollars follow a student across district lines: thus, pupils who take advantage of open enrollment to attend schools outside their community of residence bring their allocation to their new districts. Charter school funds, by contrast, are given directly to the school. In effect, each school is its own school district.

It is this model that Keegan wants to apply to public education. If her proposal becomes law, dollars would be distributed not to school districts but directly to individual public schools, thus giving real teeth to the concept of site-based management. A public school, like a charter school, would depend for its survival on the number of students it attracted. It would be free, within the broad constraints of state law, to shape its own curriculum; it would be free, as well, to draw students from outside its historic attendance boundaries. If this plan passes, the typical Arizona public school would look not so very different from the "public school conversion" charter schools that elsewhere in the nation represent a substantial proportion of all charter schools.

Conclusion: The Transformed Politics of School Choice

Political support for school choice has mushroomed in a quarter of a century. In 1972 the federally-sponsored Alum Rock voucher experiment had to drop private schools from its design; even its public school choice plan was initially controversial and ultimately insignificant. By 1998 two voucher programs were operating in urban school districts and more were being considered; public school choice was commonplace across the country; and most states had launched a new public-private hybrid, charter schools.

The growing importance of choice in educational policy is partly explained by the ways advocates have been able to characterize their ideas, creating a more

sympathetic picture by shifting the conversation away from an emphasis on market-based, and toward equity-based, choice. This transformation set the stage for charter schools, equity-based voucher programs and public school choice plans; and these in turn have kept less regulated, market-based plans under consideration.

But the primacy of choice is attributable to more than a new political vocabulary. In Cleveland and East Harlem, Phoenix and Milwaukee, diverse coalitions of special interest groups have struggled to shape and implement a variety of school choice plans. The details of those plans, hammered out through bargaining, have proved at least as important as the concept and the rhetoric. Altered political contexts have opened up new windows of opportunity to implement school choice policies, and able entrepreneurs have taken advantage of these situations.

The federal government's efforts to launch a federal voucher experiment in the 1970s failed because of a hesitancy to alienate the teachers' unions, concerns about undermining school desegregation efforts, the reluctance of private schools to subject themselves to state regulation—and, vitally, the lack of grassroots political support. By the early 1990s, however, public school choice had become commonplace and educational and racial politics had begun to shift. Vouchers, in turn, became a viable political possibility. In Milwaukee and Cleveland, anger at failed desegregation policies and poor performing public schools led some blacks to split from the traditional liberal-labor coalition that had previously blocked any voucher plan. The cultivation of private schools eager for public funding added an element that had been missing from the Alum Rock equation. Renewed efforts among conservative politicians and foundations to support school voucher reforms, including support for equity-based plans, produced much needed funding as well as ideological support. But vouchers have yet to take off, for reasons suggested in the New Jersey story: the traditional anti-voucher coalition—teachers' unions, civil rights organizations, civil libertarians—has generally stayed united and potent in its opposition.

While only two cities have implemented voucher plans to date, the voucher wars boosted the fledgling charter school movement. Opponents of vouchers pin their hopes on charter schools as the public alternative to private school aid, even as voucher advocates support charters as a foot-in-the-door of the public school monopoly.

What is the political future of school choice? The historic capacity of public school bureaucracies and their political supporters to resist the best efforts of reformers suggests that the safest prediction is that little will ultimately happen—that choice will remain a marginal phenomenon in education, functioning as a regulated safety valve for unhappy parents, students and professionals. But among the structural reforms currently receiving serious attention, systemic change of public schooling notable among them, choice seems the likeliest to survive. It has become institutionalized in recent years through open enrollment, alternative schools and especially charter schools, and this makes it hard to dislodge from the system. Each new site where choice exists brings new constituents into the movement.

New equity-based voucher plans are most likely to emerge in urban school districts where black activists and conservative politicians and foundations forge an alliance that contests the traditional liberal-labor coalition. Whether vouchers will eventually have wider appeal, though, remains uncertain. Insisting on an equity component in a voucher plan risks losing the support of middle class parents and existing private schools, who may well find the new charter school regime a better bet. On the other hand, market-based plans are unlikely to get very far. The absence of equity strings and accountability-promoting regulation makes them threatening, not only to the politically powerful teachers' unions and civil rights groups but also to the majority of families who report that they are happy with their local public schools and don't want public dollars siphoned to private schools. For these groups as well, charter schools may well be more attractive precisely because of their public-private character.

The wild card in these political projections is the judiciary. If the U.S. Supreme Court reverses nearly forty years of precedent and permits the expenditure of public funds for parochial school tuition, the political fortunes for vouchers will dramatically improve. The Catholic Church will renew its push for vouchers. Parents who send their children to parochial schools, including a sizable number of non-Catholic, inner-city parents, will support that effort as well, thus further splintering the old anti-voucher coalition. The fastest growing segment of the private school sector, fundamentalist Christian schools, will also back vouchers as long as restrictions on admissions and curriculum are not perceived as undermining their mission.

Whether the new political dynamic set in motion by a changed constitutional standard actually leads to voucher legislation may turn on whether support can be generated in suburban districts, where support for vouchers has so far been weakest and charter schools are beginning to be a presence. If the next generation of voucher proposals includes religious schools as an option, if voucher-supported private schools can peacefully co-exist with a system of quasi-private charter schools, and if elements of equity and regulation are included in the design—that is, if these proposals resemble the original Alum Rock proposal outlined nearly three decades ago by Christopher Jencks—then once again the politics of choice will shift dramatically.

* * *

Charter schools have largely escaped serious judicial challenge. Courts have upheld the state's ability to restructure the delivery of educational services through the grant of charters. *Villanueva v. Carere*, 85 F.3d 481 (10th Cir. 1996) (closing two neighborhood schools and opening a new charter school was not racially discriminatory); *Council of Organizations and Others for Education About Parochiaid, Inc. v. Engler*, 455 Mich. 557 (1997) (charter school legislation did not contravene a state constitutional requirement that public education be under the "exclusive control" of Michigan officials). *See generally* Huffman, "Charter Schools, Equal Protection Litigation, and the New School Reform Movement," 73 *N.Y.U.L.Rev.* 1290 (1988) (reviewing the rise of the charter school movement, various state legislative approaches, and possible legal challenges).

This permissive legal environment has not led to consensus among educators about the prospects for charter schools. Some believe that these schools can improve educational achievement, enhance parental involvement, stimulate teacher innovation, and promote accountability. Others are doubtful that there can be any "quick fix" for the public school system's problems. *See* Minow, "Reforming School Reform," 68 *Fordham L.Rev.* 257, 285–88 (1999) (questioning exaggerated claims made for school reform but concluding that charter schools offer a more promising avenue for change than vouchers).

"The Promise of Charter Schools"

L. Bierlein and L. Mulholland, 52 *Educational Leadership* 34, 34, 38–40 (Sept. 1994).

Charter schools are not for the faint of heart. Their creation, governance, and day-to-day operation require a large investment of time and energy, and a high tolerance for ambiguity. Significant education reform undertakings are, after all, uncharted waters.

Yet, perhaps more than most reforms, charter schools force educators to question the wisdom of conventional practices and may create the dynamics that will foster change within the entire school system. Such potential exists because charter schools integrate various reform ideas that, by themselves, have not produced desired systemic changes. Charter schools hold a key to:

- cresolving the school autonomy struggle in a way that traditional site-based decision making has not;
- creating additional "real" choices within the public school arena for students, parents, and teachers;
- offering new professional opportunities for teachers;
- enabling local school boards to overcome micro-management tendencies and become true policy boards;
- eliminating many real and perceived barriers to innovation through blanket waivers of most state laws and local policies; and
- focusing educational energies on outcomes, not inputs.

While charter schools hold great promise, as with any reform, they present formidable challenges.

* * *

New Challenges and Opportunities

Educators have long operated under a system of rules and regulations that have not rewarded deep change. Thus, any serious move from the status quo is difficult. There are, however, a few leadership challenges that are particularly germane to charter schools.

- *Charter schools require new relationships between school boards and schools.* School boards have historically been the sole providers of, and primary decision makers for, public education in their communities. Many charge that such boards try to micro-manage

events, rather than set broad policy direction. Under charter school legislation, local boards and district offices may find their roles and responsibilities greatly altered. For example, some states limit board authority over charter schools to contract oversight, while other states eliminate board authority completely if the school's sponsor is not the local board. To date, school board associations have resisted legislation that either allows sponsorship by authorities other than local boards or declares charter schools legally and financially autonomous.

Some school board members, however, see a brighter side to the charter school picture, especially as an alternative to private school vouchers. Randy Quinn, executive director of the Colorado Association of School Boards, writes that charter schools represent

> . . . a dramatic, very fundamental difference, one that forces the school board to reexamine its role. Rather than serving as provider, the board has an opportunity to become the purchaser of education services on behalf of the citizens of the community served by the board.

He further suggests that boards may want to aggressively solicit charter proposals to create a diversity of schools within their district.

Paul Hill, a senior social scientist at RAND, takes Quinn's concept one step further.* He suggests that *every* public school (especially within a large city setting) should be under contract to a local school board. Such contracting, Hill believes, would provide necessary market incentives for teachers and administrators, while maintaining enough "public" oversight by local boards to preserve the ideals of the common school.

- *Charter schools utilize true site-based decision making.* Despite frequent lip service paid to site-based decision making practices in many districts, most current school-based decisions focus on curriculum and involve only a small amount of discretionary funding. This is true, in part, because school boards remain legally responsible for decisions. Further, except for salary negotiations, many school staff members prefer not to become involved in personnel and other major decisions.

Charter schools address decentralization and empowerment issues in a way that current site-based management may not. Ideally, charter schools are legally and financially autonomous. However, even if the local board remains legally liable, charter school per-

---

*P. Hill, "Reinventing Urban Public Education," 75 *Phi Delta Kappan* 396–401 (1994).

sonnel gain substantial budgetary control, thus realizing greater control over their professional lives and the education of their students.

Expanded decision-making authority, however, presents a serious leadership concern even for those eager to assume such responsibility. Are school personnel adequately prepared to manage what is, essentially, a small business? Perhaps not. Most principals currently focus their energies on instructional activities, not financial and management matters; and most teachers are justifiably hesitant to make personnel or budgetary decisions for which they have no training and that take time away from the classroom.

There is no easy solution to this concern. Without proper training and outside technical support, principals and teachers will find it difficult to envision their schools, and their roles in those schools, in ways that are radically different from the present. Unfortunately, few state legislatures have appropriated funding for support activities (though some state departments and private organizations have risen to the challenge). For this and other reasons, the choice (or voluntary) aspect of charter schools must be preserved because many educators may never want to participate in such an endeavor and should not be forced to do so.

• *Charter schools provide new roles for teachers.* Charter schools offer teachers a chance to work in autonomous and innovative schools, with many attempting to use new philosophical approaches, teaching methods, and assessment tools. Teachers also have the opportunity to become directly involved in all phases of school operations, from curriculum planning to management. That may be as far as many teachers want to go in expanding their roles. Some, however, may want to go further.

Charter schools could open the door for teachers to become school "owners," rather than employees, with an owner's chance to earn profits or build equity. Kolderie notes that groups of teachers in a cooperative or partnership arrangement could either contract with a sponsor or subcontract with a charter school management team to organize and run an instructional program at a charter school. As a professional group, these teachers would control curriculum, personnel, and financial decisions. Kolderie suggests that this arrangement would give teacher-owners a strong incentive to use innovative instructional methods and technologies and to modify existing patterns of expenditures. And, because these teachers would be their own employer, bargaining issues would be minimized or eliminated. Although this concept runs counter to

current practice, growing support for charter or contract services makes it plausible.

Such empowerment of individual schools and teachers, while hailed by many educators, introduces some perceived threats to teacher unions. An issue brief prepared by the National Education Association states that only *"under the right conditions,* [italics added] charter schools could become change agents promoting new and creative ways of teaching and learning. . . ." Two of these conditions are that all teachers be licensed practitioners and that district collective bargaining provisions remain applicable. In an ideal charter school situation, the organizers may desire these two conditions and make them a part of the charter, but they would not be mandated by statute.

Teacher unions are also concerned that charter school provisions could become a "back door" for private school vouchers. Stuart notes that one reason the Minnesota Federation of Teachers lobbied against that state's charter school legislation is that it allowed private, nonsectarian schools to become public charter schools. These issues and the concern over the loss of collective bargaining power have caused unions to lobby against charter school legislation in many states.

Lessons from Charter Schools

What can we learn from those already working in charter schools? Start-up is one of the most time-consuming tasks, according to organizers and staff in several states. Many problems are similar to those that confront any new small business owner. First, organizers and staff must be prepared to translate their vision of the school into reality. This entails securing additional start-up funding (foundation grants or other contributions) and developing community contacts to help create the educational environment they envision and obtain appropriate facilities. Finally, they must constantly reevaluate their process and results, making adjustments as necessary. Activities such as these are challenging and result in longer-than-normal teacher and administrator workdays. The bottom line is that, while some may view these new tasks as stimulating, others may find implementing charter schools overwhelming. In short, charter schools are not for everyone.

However, even in the early stages, the charter school participants we interviewed made the following point clear: Those who believe in the charter school concept and can meet the challenging workload will reap rewards not possible in other schools. The tremendous emphasis on collaboration, alone, is welcome change to many. In the words of Milo Cutter at the City Academy charter school in St. Paul, a charter school is "the best opportunity for teamwork. It's a natural outlet for diversity and inclusion."

Nevertheless, many questions remain: Will charter schools become just another fad, or will they successfully integrate a number of promising reform ideas? And if charter schools do succeed, will they dramatically change learning environments for a great number of students and teachers, or will they affect only those within their halls? It is too early to tell, but many educators, policymakers, and community members believe that charter schools represent a bold reform attempt that holds great promise.

See also Nathan "Early Lessons of the Charter School Movement," 54 *Educ.Leadership* 16 (1996); Manno, *et al.*, "Charter Schools: Accomplishments and Dilemmas," 99 *Teachers College Record* 537 (1998).

While some believe that charter schools are a promising path to innovation, other commentators fear that charter schools are nothing but a diversion from the need for systematic educational reform and improved funding.

"Charter Schools: The Smiling Face of Disinvestment"

A. Molnar, 54 *Educ.Leadership*, 9, 12–14, 15 (October 1996).

* * *

Free-Market Accountability

As yet, no national evaluation of the effectiveness of charter schools has been completed. The Pew Charitable Trusts have funded a study to be conducted by Chester Finn and Louann Bierlein at the Hudson Institute. And the U.S. Department of Education has commissioned a study that should begin to provide some data in the next two or three years.

In the meantime there are a few clues about the impact of the reform. A 1995 report issued by the Indiana Policy Center, "Charter Schools: Legislation and Results After Four Years," found little in the way of systematic evidence that charter schools increased student achievement.

In December 1994, the Minnesota legislature released a report on charter schools in Minnesota. The authors did not try to judge the success or failure of the charter experiment; they felt it was too early for that.

They did, however, highlight a number of problems that threw into question the idea that charter schools would provide a model for public school reform.

Because Minnesota charter schools were free of all legal requirements placed on public schools, except those clearly spelled out in their charters, the charter schools didn't necessarily have to operate in open meetings or otherwise be open to public scrutiny. That made it difficult for the public to hold them accountable for proper and efficient conduct of their activities. Accountability was further complicated by a finding that some school boards granting charters were unwilling or unable to adequately evaluate charter school outcomes or student success.

One of the biggest problems Minnesota charter schools faced was financing. Thus, in order to reduce class size and afford other reforms, the schools relied on experienced teachers to accept low salaries and take on administrative and other responsibilities. The schools also had difficulty finding facilities and paying for even the most basic equipment—books and desks—without additional income from private sources that could not be relied upon for continuing, long-term support.

These problems are not unique. In a recent survey of charter schools around the country, financial support and the lack of start-up funds were the most frequently mentioned problems. The authors of the Minnesota legislative report concluded that without increased support, "it is not clear that charter schools will be able to function as anything but educational reformers 'on the margin.'"

Despite the report's perfectly reasonable conclusion, most charter school supporters would be the last ones to admit publicly that they are backing a reform that has neither a logical nor a demonstrated relationship to increased academic achievement and that will cost someone lots of money to get off the ground and keep afloat. Most would rather claim that the market will somehow provide.

For this reason, charter school advocates often prefer to frame the issue of accountability the way voucher supporters do. Real accountability, they say, is imposed by competition in the marketplace. Parents who "know what they like" and who are "empowered" to choose the school their children attend will send their kids to a charter school if they think its program is good; and if they don't, they won't. This view assumes parents know an effective school program when they see one and that they could not possibly be satisfied with an ineffective school.

Undeniably, this position has populist appeal. In practice, however, parents' decisions about where to send their children are much more complex than a simple judgment about a school's academic program. Considerations such as proximity to the school, work schedules, availability of after-school care, and extracurricular activities get thrown into the mix. Also, the ability of parents to choose the best school for their children requires more than the freedom to walk away from schools they don't like: they also must be able to get their children into schools they like better.

The chance of a market creating a multitude of options for all parents, especially those in the most impoverished urban areas, is so small as to be nonexistent. Obviously that is why no one has yet explained in practical terms how to create the surplus educational capacity needed to give parents such an opportunity. Should a dissatisfied parent decide to switch schools, who pays to keep a vast network of partially filled schools at the ready? In the real world, financing limits parents' choices. Charter schools do nothing to change that basic fact.

Real-World Money Problems

If the popularity of charter schools demonstrates anything, it is America's enduring faith that major educational reforms can be accomplished on the cheap. Charter school reformers in Massachusetts and elsewhere have sold the idea that charter schools won't cost anyone anything—a real win-win reform. This fiscal miracle is accomplished by a budgetary sleight of hand in which the money to educate charter school students is, for the most part, taken out of state aid to the district in which the student lives. In the case of hard-pressed urban school systems such as Boston's, such financing further undermines the district's ability to serve the children attending its schools.

Raising the necessary money is one problem; keeping track of it after it has been raised is another. Few of the institutions legally empowered to grant charters are likely to have the expertise or the resources to monitor and enforce those charters. If educational performance contracting during the Nixon administration and the more recent contract problems between Education Alternatives Inc. and the Baltimore and Hartford school systems are any indication, we will soon be reading stories of mismanagement and educational short-sheeting at charter schools.

In fact, in 1994, one California charter school, Edutrain, went belly up with more than $1 million in public money unaccounted for. Apparently the school administration had been spending money to help pay the principal's rent, lease the principal a sports car, hire a bodyguard, and fund a $7,000 staff retreat in Carmel—this while teachers lacked textbooks and supplies.

To some charter school supporters the failure of Edutrain was an example of the educational market imposing its discipline. The problem with their logic is this: An educational "market" does not punish the people who set up a school the way a financial market punishes investors in stocks and bonds when share prices plummet or a bond issuer defaults. In the Edutrain fiasco, the people punished were the students who had their education disrupted and the taxpayers and students in the Los Angeles Unified School District who were out of education money and received nothing in return. In the charter school market, the financial risks are socialized, while the financial gains are privatized.

Demonizing Teachers

The lack of a common educational vision helps assure that the argument for charter schools is dominated by economic, not educational, ideas. Central to the logic of charter schools is the idea that competition will force public schools, which now have a monopoly in providing educational services, to improve or perish as parents choose to send their children to better schools. Unfortunately, *how* competition will result in better teaching and more learning is never specified.

The assumptions are that educators have grown fat and complacent in the warm embrace of a government monopoly and that a threat to their now-secure futures will force them to figure out how to do better. In this scenario, teachers unions are considered self-interested culprits responsible for driving up the cost of education without accepting accountability for student achievement.

Neoconservative charter school zealots, such as Chester Finn and the Center for Educational Reform's Jeanne Allen, ridicule the idea that schools (particularly those in poor, urban districts) might need more money to improve. Any increase in funding would, from their perspective, be throwing good money after bad. In what has become the conventional wisdom in the charter school movement, the enemies of school improvement are rigid union contracts; bloated, unresponsive bureaucracies; and over-regulation, not fiscal constraints.

Hostility toward teachers unions and the teacher certification requirements they have achieved is built into some so-called "strong" charter school laws, including those in Arizona, California, Colorado, and Massachusetts. Under those laws, virtually any adult with "qualifications" is allowed to teach in a charter school, or administer one for that matter, without the need for certification. It's an approach that is in some ways analogous to trying to solve the problem of access to health care by allowing anyone who can attract patients to practice medicine.

* * *

The Public Debate vs. the Real One

Free-market zealots are likely to continue to claim vindication or argue that their reactionary ideas need more time to work. Supporters of public education will call the experiment a costly failure and marvel at the willingness to spend large sums on unproven alternatives while cutting resources for the public system that serves most children. With an absence of uniform standards, the war of educational anecdotes and misleading statistics will remain "subject to interpretation."

All the while, the desperation of America's poorest children and their families will grow. No state's charter schools, under laws strong or weak, will make an appreciable difference for most of these children. They are failing in public schools. They are failing in Catholic schools. They are going under. That is not because they cannot succeed, but because they have been abandoned in a political and economic debate that masks selfish interests with educational rhetoric.

No amount of entrepreneurial zeal will make up for a lack of sufficient resources to provide for them. Indeed, it is the market that has destroyed their neighborhoods and the livelihoods of the adults they rely on. Unleashing the market on the public schools will only compound the harm.

Charter schools, like private school vouchers and for-profit schools, are built on the illusion that our society can be held together solely by the self-interested pursuit of our individual purposes. Considered in this light, the charter school movement represents a radical rejection not only of the possibility of the common school, but of common purposes outside the school as well. The struggle is not between market-based reforms and the educational status quo. It is about whether the democratic ideal of the common good can survive the onslaught of a market mentality that threatens to turn every human relationship into a commercial transaction.

———————

See also Hill, "The Supply Side of School Choice," in S. Sugarman and F. Kemerer, eds., *School Choice and Social Controversy: Politics, Policy, and Law* 140 (1999). For the views of teachers and administrators who have become involved in a charter school initiative, *see* Kass, "Boston's City on a Hill," 125 *Pub.Int.* 27 (Fall 1996); Page with Levine, "The Pitfalls and Triumphs of Launching a Charter School," 54 *Educ.Leadership* 26 (1996).

D. Other Privatization Initiatives

Vouchers have generated high-profile controversy, while charter schools' potential to prompt meaningful reform remains contested and uncertain. Even more volatile debate has resulted from other privatization initiatives. These initiatives fall into two basic categories: (1) local boards contract out the management of schools to private corporations; and (2) corporations offer goods and services to schools in exchange for the opportunity to market products to the student body.

1. For-Profit Management of Public Schools. Although there was some interest in contracting out education to for-profit firms in the 1970s, there was a renaissance of interest in the idea in the late 1980s and 1990s. Several private education service providers, including Education Alternatives, Inc. and the Edison Project, sprang up to offer their management services, particularly to districts with failing schools. Solomon, "The Role of For-Profit Corporations in Revitalizing Public Education: A Legal and Policy Analysis," 24 *U.Toledo L.Rev.* 883 (1993). These entrepreneurial efforts have received mixed reviews, as the following account of a high-profile experiment in the Baltimore school system makes clear.

———————————————————

"Privatization in Baltimore, 1992–95"
C. Ascher, N. Fruchter, and R. Berne, *Hard Lessons: Public Schools and Privatization*, 43–59 (1996).

* * *

In a sentence, we either dramatically improve student performance without spending more money or our contract is canceled. That's what I call accountability!

John Golle, chairman and CEO, Education Alternatives., Inc.

Baltimore, a former steel town, faces many of the challenges typical of American cities—a declining economic base, constrained public sector revenues, and widespread poverty. The 183 schools in the Baltimore City Public Schools system (BCPS) serve 130,000 students, of whom 82 percent receive a free or reduced-price lunch. According to a recent Government Accounting Office report, the average Baltimore student "is a poor, African American child living in a female-headed, single-parent household." Even with large numbers of students involved in compensatory education programs, BCPS's test scores have ranked among the lowest in the state, and the dropout rate has hovered around 14 percent, compared to a statewide average of 5 percent.

Despite comparatively low administrative outlays, the Baltimore City Public Schools have ranked at the bottom of Maryland's twenty-four school districts in spending for regular instruction. In 1991, a study of inequalities in the Maryland system found that to bring the Baltimore City Public Schools up to the average per-pupil expenditures in the state would require an additional $26,250 per classroom.

Education innovation is not new in Baltimore. In the late 1980s, with strong backing from its mayor, Kurt L. Schmoke, Baltimore began a variety of innovative educational experiments. The public school system was the site for Robert Slavin's Success for All program, the first attempt to use Chapter 1 funds schoolwide to improve learning in the early grades. When Maryland initiated a statewide Challenge Schools program for schools with low attendance and performance, twelve of the twenty-seven designated targets were Baltimore middle schools. Two other programs, TIPS (Teachers Involve Parents in Schoolwork) and the Family-School Partnership, backed by Baltimore's Fund for Educational Excellence, were investigating new ways to improve teaching effectiveness and parent-teacher relations. Several public schools were also experimenting with BERRI, a computer-driven curriculum. With support from the Abell Foundation, the BCPS was developing a reputation as a "laboratory for incorporating a number of private-sector resources and public/private collaboratives into its operations."

In 1991, Dr. Walter G. Amprey became the new district superintendent. Given Baltimore's financial problems, as well as its inclination toward experimentation, it seemed a logical development when, in June 1992, the Baltimore City Public Schools hired Education Alternatives, Inc. (EAI), a for-profit

corporation based in Minneapolis, to run nine of its schools: one primary school (prekindergarten through second grade), seven elementary schools (prekindergarten through fifth grade), and a middle school (sixth–eighth grade).

The Introduction of Education Alternatives, Inc.

Both supporters and opponents of privatization in Baltimore would agree that the experience was controversial. Moreover, controversy appears to have characterized the efforts of Education Alternatives, Inc., long before its Baltimore enterprise. In 1986, in the course of its transformation from a subsidiary of Control Data Corporation to an independent corporation, questions were raised about its designation as a minority-owned firm. EAI's initial contracts were in Eagan, Minnesota, and Paradise Valley, Arizona, where its early successes were used as a basis for its public stock offering in 1991. However, in 1993, analysts raised questions about EAI's reported revenues and stock sales by executives.

In fall 1991, Education Alternatives raised more than $2 million to showcase its instructional approach, "The Tesseract Way," in a third venture at South Pointe Elementary School in the Miami-Dade County public school district. An enthusiastic review from South Pointe described EAI's Tesseract method as involving the latest in educational thinking. The teacher had become "a coach, facilitator, model, guide, and mediator" who was granted unprecedented professional autonomy in exchange for being charged with accountability for student performance. Students were reportedly becoming "self-regulated" learners, who puzzled over problems alone or worked in cooperative groups. Through authentic (non-multiple-choice) testing and tasks built on "real life experiences," critical thinking was being developed. And parents were allowed to help develop the educational goals for their children during quarterly parent-teacher conferences.

To expand the company's capacity for involvement in public education, in December 1991 Education Alternatives, Inc., formed an alliance of four firms known as the Educational Alliance. While EAI itself was responsible for running the instructional program according to the Tesseract model, Johnson Controls, the largest janitorial service in the United States, was to provide maintenance; KPMG Peat Marwick, an accounting colossus, was to initiate computerized accounting; and the Computer Curriculum Company (CCC) would offer SuccessMaker, an instructional technology system.

Baltimore City Public Schools' contract gave EAI approximately $27 million a year, calculated according to average per-pupil expenditures in the district, including Chapter 1 and special education funds. The contract was to run for five years, beginning with the 1992–93 school year. Although many support personnel would work directly for EAI, the Baltimore public schools had a strong American Federation of Teachers (AFT) local of 8,500 members; thus, the contract stipulated that administrative and teaching personnel would remain employees of the Baltimore City Public Schools, with provisions negotiated by the union left intact. This was to be EAI's first major venture. Using Tesseract and computerized instructional programs and its expanded capacity to improve operational efficiency, the firm promised immediate and dramatic improvements in student achievement in its nine schools.

Although publicized as a performance contract, Baltimore's deal with EAI did not set forth performance standards for the four companies in the alliance. As Norman J. Walsh, then an associate superintendent in Baltimore, has since written, "Unfortunately, none of the procedures that the school system and the city have historically taken to safeguard the public interest when awarding contracts for public services was given the slightest heed." Calling the contract process with EAI "extremely odd," Judson Porter, the school district's finance officer at the time, remarked, "You don't put out a bid, you don't negotiate the best price you can possibly get, and quite frankly, [Amprey has] operated as an advocate of the company since."

Difficulties were encountered during the early stages of implementation in the fall of 1992. EAI began by training teachers in the new programs and by making improvements in physical facilities at the nine schools, including floor and locker repairs, repainting, and furniture and plumbing restoration. But the SuccessMaker instructional technology was not ready until several months after the start of the school year.

Early in the contract period, conflicts arose with the Baltimore Teachers Union (BTU), beginning with a dispute over EAI's replacement of seasoned, neighborhood paraprofessionals, who had been earning $10,000–$20,000 annually, with recent college graduates, who, as interns, were paid $6,000–$9,000 annually and suffered extremely high turnover rates.

Compromise was reached by allowing those paraprofessionals who had college degrees to remain. EAI also transferred all counselors and specialists, including teachers of art, music, physical education, and special education, out of the Tesseract schools, eliminating nearly one hundred instructional positions in the eight primary/elementary schools. In addition, the company cut costs by offering teachers less than their standard training rates for attending Tesseract training and by cutting teacher planning time. Salaries for custodians in EAI schools were cut from an average of $11.00 per hour to $8.75.

EAI's cost cutting in special education and compensatory education programs was no less controversial. In any urban district, a good deal of the money spent on education comes from state and federal money for low-income, low-achieving students who need extra help (Chapter 1, Compensatory Education, now called Title I) or for students who have been diagnosed as having particular disabilities (Special Education). While compensatory education has traditionally been carried out in "pull-out programs," special education has been accomplished through a range of programming, but particularly through special classes. Over the past several years, an "inclusion" movement has resulted in Title I money being available for schoolwide improvement in poverty-stricken areas, as well as in efforts to bring special education students into regular classes whenever possible. However, both policy shifts have been accompanied by clear rules that guarantee a continuing, high level of programming and services. In EAI schools, by contrast, both compensatory education and special education students were simply brought into regular classes, and the omission of specialized personnel and small-group instruction were supposed to be made up for by spending more time on computers.

A first-year analysis of EAI's budget by the BCPS Department of Research and Evaluation showed that while EAI spent 62.5 percent of its Baltimore budget on regular instruction, the BCPS spent 72.3 percent. EAI also spent 5.6 percent of its budget on special education, compared to 11.2 percent by the BCPS. Conversely, during its first year EAI lavished more than double the amount provided by the BCPS for facilities (18.5 percent vs. 9.2 percent) and three times the amount for security (1.4 percent vs. 0.5 percent).

The "Early Implementation" report by the Baltimore City Public Schools' Department of Research and Evaluation, issued in January 1994, was very measured. The report complimented the company for the "dramatic improvements in school facilities." It also described the implementation difficulties EAI had experienced during the first year, including delays in the installation of the Computer Curriculum Corporation's SuccessMaker and problems with hiring the interns. Interviews conducted by the BCPS with teachers in the Tesseract schools showed 11 percent very satisfied, 42 percent fairly satisfied, 28 percent somewhat satisfied, and 18 percent not satisfied. The report, however, criticized increased demands on teachers, insufficient training in the Tesseract method, and poor use and high turnover of interns.

"The Private Management of Public Schools: An Analysis of the EAI Experience in Baltimore," released by the American Federation of Teachers in May 1994, took a more aggressive stance than the district's report. The AFT document, which covered the first year and a half of the EAI contract, cited more absenteeism and declines in student test scores in EAI elementary schools, whereas attendance and performance in non-EAI schools had shown modest gains. It also raised questions about financial accounting, special education, cuts in teaching staff, increased class size, and instability in classrooms. In addition, the AFT noted that although instructional spending in EAI schools was lower than in other BCPS schools, EAI had initially received as much as $500 per student more.

Although there were plans to expand EAI's role in Baltimore, continuing controversy prevented this. Moreover, the conflict with the union continued into 1993–94, when the BTU filed suit against the school district, charging that the delegation of school management to private enterprises violated the city charter and denied local citizens their right to decide how public schools should be run. Threats of layoffs, calls for the superintendent's resignation, and low teacher morale all appeared to be by-products of the privatization initiative.

Special education was a particularly troubling area in the EAI schools, in part because Baltimore's special education program had been under scrutiny since the 1980s. Baltimore was already engaged in a decade-old legal battle resulting from its failure to comply with federal law on the length of time handicapped students had to wait for formal evaluations and services such as physical therapy and psychological counseling.

EAI's waiver from the state of Maryland allowed it to move a majority of elementary students with special needs from self-contained classrooms to regular classrooms under three conditions: that the children's parents approved; that the Individual Education Plan required by law for all children in special education was incorporated in the personalized education plan that EAI students were supposed to receive; and that a formal review of the new placements would be held within ninety days.

The AFT, which had been monitoring EAI's special education program, asked the U.S. Department of Education to investigate whether EAI had violated federal law. The Department of Education in turn requested that the Maryland Education Department investigate. Among the state's findings were that, of the 396 special education students that EAI had placed in regular classes, only in 16 cases had parents given their consent; that teachers in the EAI schools had not participated sufficiently in student placement decisions, and many remained unaware of students' disabilities; and that the mainstream classes failed to meet the disabled students' requirements.

According to the state's report, violations at the Tesseract middle school exceeded the total number of violations at all other Baltimore public schools. The Maryland Department of Education directed the city to craft a plan to correct violations by August 1. The U.S. Department of Education meanwhile charged the state of Maryland with "poor supervision of special-education programs in EAI schools," and a federal judge ruled that in the future a court-appointed team would have to monitor key staffing decisions in the BCPS.

As a result of the investigation, Maryland awarded special education students at the Tesseract middle school with 136,893 compensatory hours of education. EAI's plan was to enable the three hundred students to make up 120 hours in a summer session run by three teachers, three interns, and three college students. The AFT called this a "questionable practice," and a contempt hearing was brought by the BTU. In the agreement eventually reached, the Baltimore City Public Schools admitted that the system was in substantial noncompliance with the Maryland consent decree.

The controversial nature of the privatization initiative carried on into its third year, 1994–95. The city school system admitted that achievement gains reported in the previous spring were overstated, prompting charges by city council members and countercharges by EAI. Superintendent Amprey's closeness to EAI was also called into question, and the mayor warned that EAI's fate in Baltimore would depend both on improving student achievement and on the results of an independent evaluation, commissioned by the BCPS, being conducted by the University of Maryland. The effects were felt well beyond Baltimore, as the price of EAI stock dropped sharply.

Criticisms of EAI by the union, and of the union by EAI, continued. With an upcoming reelection campaign in mind, Mayor Schmoke proposed a renegotiated contract with EAI, this time with explicit performance criteria. By April 1995, the Baltimore city council's EAI Financial Oversight Committee, created after a lengthy hearing the previous December, had compiled a five-page list of unanswered questions concerning Education Alternatives' financial activities. Although the committee identified few new concerns, it showed the major issues left unclassified in the BCPS-EAI contract: problems with contract implementation, failure to provide budget and financial information about Title I spending, attorney, special education, subcontractor finances, and EAI's corporate financial activities. By August 1995 some resolution appeared to be in sight. But the situation changed when, on September 1, the University of Maryland–Baltimore County issued an independent three-year evaluation report showing only modest improvement in achievement in EAI schools. Once again, whatever understanding EAI had with the district was in jeopardy.

The University of Maryland Evaluation Report

Given the heated atmosphere that surrounded the privatization initiative in Baltimore, an unbiased evaluation report took on particular importance. Since any educational initiative like the EAI contract in Baltimore is complex and multidimensional, any sophisticated evaluation of the effects is likely to be subject to diverse interpretations. Moreover, the UMBC evaluation was not a classic scientific experiment, or even an experimental evaluation of a social program: the real world impinged on the research in ways that complicated the interpretation of the results. For example, the Tesseract schools were evaluated by comparison with an equal number of control schools; however, after EAI exerted pressure, several of the specific control schools were changed by the Baltimore City Public School evaluation unit in 1994. The Department of Research and Evaluation substituted for the original control group three schools whose students had been somewhat lower-achieving in the year prior to implementation of the contract with EAI than students in the EAI schools. This is a complication with unknown effects. The UMBC evaluation report notes, "Changing comparison schools once they were named was irregular. . . . It is important to point out that, in contrast to the statement, 'EAI was handed the worst schools in Baltimore City,' the schools designated as Tesseract schools, while including many schools that were among the most challenging schools in Baltimore City, represented a mix of student achievement levels."

This section of the report uses the five criteria set out earlier—educational outcomes; cost; parental voice; accountability; and equity—to review and interpret the University of Maryland–Baltimore County (UMBC) report. Before turning to the specific findings in these areas, however, it is worth presenting the general assessment from the evaluation report:

> The accomplishments of Educational [sic] Alternatives, Inc. in the management of seven elementary schools in Baltimore City are considerable, particularly in the area of change in classroom instructional practices toward varied activities, flexible grouping and a focus on the individual student. The initial test score decline [from 1991–92 to the first year of the contract, 1992–93] was substantial, with the lost ground recovered only by the end of the third year, and early implementation problems were accentuated by the opposition of the Baltimore Teachers Union. However, EAI would not be faulted for the level of change already accomplished in Tesseract schools were it not for the public's expectation of immediate and substantial change, and the symbolism of a "really different education" implied by the Tesseract name. Nevertheless, the early problems have been largely resolved and the infrastructure for program management is now in place. Change takes time and there has been an investment in the first three years that can be recouped by continuation. Should the Tesseract program continue through the last two years of the contract, EAI has an obligation to effect real improvement in the schools that they have been managing and to demonstrate an excellent urban education program. In turn, it is important that Baltimore City have an appropriate monitoring mechanism of the EAI contract and its components.

One other fact is important to state at the outset: the per-pupil costs in the Tesseract schools were 11.2 percent higher than in the comparison schools. Thus, this was not a case of equal spending.

Outcomes

The UMBC evaluation report noted that too much instructional time was being devoted to testing, and particularly to test preparation, in all Baltimore City schools. However, the preoccupation with test scores, and the concomitant use of instructional time for examination and preparation, was particularly evident at Tesseract schools, where, instead of moving toward less testing, EAI had added a fall test. As for test scores, the UMBC evaluation report used several tests to compare the Tesseract schools over several years against the control schools. In general, during the three years of the initiative, the Tesseract schools first declined, then improved, so that they ended the period studied in a similar position to the comparison schools, with neither group making significant gains. . . .

* * *

. . . . Clearly, if privatization was expected to produce large differences, the results were disappointing.

Two other categories were examined: attendance and special education enrollment. In terms of attendance, there were similarly modest improvements in the Tesseract schools, the comparison schools, and the Baltimore City schools altogether. The area of special education enrollment showed a large difference between the Tesseract and comparison schools. In 1991–92, the preimplementation year, 8 percent of enrollment in what would become the Tesseract schools, the comparison schools, and in all the schools throughout Baltimore were eligible for Level IV special education services. While this percentage dropped to 7.5 percent in the comparison schools and 5.6 percent in all Baltimore City schools in 1994–95, it fell precipitously to 2.7 percent in the Tesseract schools. When students who are eligible for special education Levels II, III, and IV are combined, the changes from 1991–92 to 1994–95 were 15.4 to 14.2 percent in the comparison schools, 15.0 to 12.0 percent in all Baltimore City schools, and 15.1 to 7.9 percent in the Tesseract schools.

Although these changes are dramatic, the UMBC evaluation report did not investigate whether the services that these pupils received, or the results that they posted, were better or worse in the Tesseract schools than in the comparison schools. This may be because the courts had already awarded compensation to students who had not received all services due them. On the current assumption that inclusion programs can improve outcomes for special education students, the Maryland evaluators commended EAI

> for its success in cutting the number of students eligible for Level IV special education services, its mission to educate otherwise-segregated students in the regular classroom, and its efforts to eliminate the fragmentation of "pull-out" instruction through a full inclusion program

for students needing special services. This aspect of the Tesseract program, if eventually judged successful, may be EAI's shining contribution to urban education.

However, the program was said to be in need of careful evaluation "to determine whether the students who would otherwise have been eligible for Level IV special education services have been well-served." This was particularly true since EAI had cut the number of students eligible for all special education services, which suggested that "students who should be receiving services are not."

One side effect of the inclusion of Level IV special education services for the Tesseract schools should be noted: owing to the lower percentage of children eligible for Level IV services, a higher percentage of pupils' scores are reported for inclusion in the test result analysis.

Thus, with the exception of the proportion of pupils who are eligible for special education services, the overall similarity between the Tesseract and comparison schools is the most salient finding with respect to outcomes detailed in the evaluation report.

Costs

The assessment of cost information is important for the overall interpretation of the findings from Baltimore. According to the evaluation report, EAI received $6,056 for each pupil in the Tesseract schools. It was permitted to use 7.5 percent of that amount, or $454, for "nonschool costs." Thus, the report indicates that EAI spent $5,602 per pupil at the school level, against an average of $4,973.50 for school-level costs in the comparison schools, a difference of 11.2 percent. Note that it is possible that EAI used some of the school-level funding for central-office-type services. Unfortunately, the nonschool costs of the Baltimore City public schools are not reported in the evaluation.

These data indicate that EAI had more resources to work with in the Tesseract schools than did the comparison schools. As stated in the evaluation,

> The promise that EAI could improve instruction without spending more than Baltimore City was spending on schools has been discredited. The exact level of difference between Tesseract and comparison schools in spending for the school-basic costs has yet to be determined, although the difference between Tesseract and comparison schools for school-based costs will be 11.2 percent in 1995–96. Understandably, there is an expectation of visible and significant results for an increase in expenditure.

If the company made some headway, then "11 percent more than the comparison schools is not an excessive price differential for significant school improvement efforts in a school system with a per-pupil spending level that is considerably lower than the average per-pupil spending in Maryland school systems."

Although it is not possible to determine precisely where the additional resources were spent in the Tesseract schools, EAI used interns in its classrooms more than control schools used paraprofessionals or other adults. Observations indicate that an intern was present in Tesseract schools 84 percent of the time, while an assisting adult was present in the control-group schools 23 percent of the time.

Finally, there are important cost-related issues not addressed in the evaluation report. Nothing indicates how much of the money received by EAI actually went into the schools and how much went to profit, a contentious issue in the privatization debate. Since only 1 page out of a 118-page report devoted to costs clearly detailed cost analysis, that was not part of this investigation. However, a recent report by the Government Accounting Office notes that, for the first two years of the contract, EAI reported gross profits of $1.9 million and $3.3 million respectively.

Parental Voice

Choice was not one of the features of the EAI initiative. However, Tesseract's stated commitment was to parent involvement, and while six Tesseract schools had full-time parent liaison staff in 1994–95, only three comparison schools did. The evaluation report developed a scale for assessing parental involvement that included thirteen categories and scored the schools based on interviews. The scale ranges from 0 (no activity) to 4 (fully functional activity), and each school's score was an average across the thirteen areas of parent involvement. Based on this research the evaluators concluded, "Despite the introduction of four new parent involvement activities into Tesseract schools, there appears to be little difference between parent involvement in Tesseract and comparison schools. . . ." Even with parent liaison staff, EAI's program seemed to make little difference.

Accountability

One of the effects of the privatization debate is that attention to school performance appears to increase

in districts involved in experimentation. Clearly this has been the case in Baltimore, where local debates and press coverage of the EAI contract have reached a national audience.

A key claim of privatizers is that firms that undertake initiatives such as EAI's in Baltimore are willing to submit themselves to a direct test of their effectiveness that is not present in the typical public school arrangement: a contract is entered into with the express understanding that it will not be renewed if performance is unsatisfactory. If the UMBC evaluation report shows one thing, though, it is that even with a professional research approach, it is not simple to determine the beneficial or harmful effects of privatization initiatives. (For example, though the report found too much preparation for testing in all Baltimore schools, it is not clear whether being in the limelight had anything to do with this.) At a different level, the very fact that the school district must evaluate whether the privatization initiative has "worked" can lead to an increase in accountability; a detailed report such as the one prepared by UMBC, which provides information on all public schools in Baltimore, may not have been produced without the need to evaluate EAI.

There is another lesson in accountability derived from the EAI experience that was not appreciated sufficiently in the era of performance contracting. Education has multiple outcomes, and if an organization such as EAI is going to be judged on one or more of those in particular, then there will be strong incentives to effect change in that area more forcefully than in others, in order to present information that supports a continuation of the contract. For EAI, as well as for the Baltimore schools in general, test score changes have become paramount, eclipsing other teaching.

Another accountability issue is how money is spent. While UMBC researchers and Baltimore public school officials were able to track decreases in staffing as well as increases in computers in the Tesseract schools, EAI used its legal rights as a private firm to keep its financial books closed to scrutiny. The GAO reports that when they asked the company for documentation on expenses, EAI refused to provide it. Public institutions are often wracked by scandals about unwise or even illegal spending, but this is because their finances are open to public view. When private firms enter the world of services traditionally provided by government, the public loses out in terms of accountability.

Equity

Of its nine schools, the EAI initiative involved seven elementary schools, representative of Baltimore public elementary schools generally, and thus there are no macro-level equity issues involving school selection. For example, 85 percent of the students in the Tesseract schools qualified for free or reduced-price lunch compared to 86 percent of the pupils in the comparison schools. Moreover, because the EAI initiative did not turn over the entire district's management to a private company, and because it did not involve choice, there do not appear to be equity issues at stake.

One equity-related concern with privatization initiatives that include rewards based on test scores is that the contractor will concentrate on students near a particular cutoff score, where more apparent progress can be achieved. Assistance for students who are far below the cutoff, which would require greater efforts, might well be deemphasized as a consequence of the difficulty of raising their scores above the contractor's performance threshold. The independent evaluation does not discuss the issue of poorly performing students and does not present a special analysis of this subgroup.

Beyond this, it is important to recall that per-pupil spending for the Baltimore City Public Schools does not approach the levels common to surrounding suburban districts; in those districts, ample funding enables students to have both computers and high ratios of teachers to students. The narrow range of data comparing Tesseract with other Baltimore schools suggests that EAI's profits, garnered largely through substituting computers for teachers, did not harm (or help) Tesseract students. However, the most serious equity issue—that privatization may have exacerbated the differences between the urban and suburban schools—remained outside the study.

Concluding Findings on Baltimore

The UMBC evaluation report is useful reading for anyone interested in recent privatization initiatives and the intricacies of educational evaluation. Many of the evaluators' observations point out the similarities between the Tesseract and comparison schools rather than the differences. BCPS's broader reform efforts may well have affected all schools, rather than just the Tesseract schools. Or perhaps the Tesseract effort, which was seen as a radical alternative, spurred the entire system to action. But in most cases, the evaluator's positive findings reflected approaches to school revitalization in evidence wherever there is a genuine commitment to public school reform.

* * *

Thus, in Baltimore, after three years of private sector management, the overall results more closely resembled the outcomes of other efforts at public school reform than they did some profoundly new conception of education. Moreover, a number of conclusions at least call into question the far-reaching claims of the outspoken privatization cheerleaders. For example:

> To date, the "management expertise" that the private sector should be able to bring to bear on a public enterprise has not been sufficient for the expected level of transformation of the Tesseract schools in Baltimore City. The evaluation team inferred inadequate strategic planning processes in a number of areas. . . . Computer-assisted instruction was sufficiently implemented in the Tesseract schools so that the . . . reading and integrated learning system was given a fair test of its effectiveness in raising test scores. After two full years, the CTBS reading scores were not sufficiently improved to establish the success of the reading integrated learning system.

The Denouement

Even though it found positive points to make, the evaluation by the University of Maryland research team presented serious criticisms of privatization in Baltimore. At the same time as the report came out, the city of Baltimore was experiencing a financial shortfall that would necessitate cuts in school funding, and thus in payments to EAI.

By the first two weeks of November 1995, negotiations between the city and the company were intense but shaky, with Mayor Schmoke threatening to end the EAI contract. A vociferous public meeting was held at city hall on November 20. In the next few days, a tentative agreement was reached, which would have saved the city $7 million. But the agreement apparently left many details unresolved, and perhaps unresolvable.

On November 22, Mayor Schmoke and members of the Baltimore school board announced jointly that the EAI contract would be terminated. "We think we led the nation going into this," Superintendent Amprey said in an interview. "We can now probably give some lessons on how you sever from it."

John Golle, EAI's chief executive, claimed to be "proud" of what the company had done. He also warned that the district would have to take over the $4–6 million leasing costs of EAI computers and other equipment "unless you want us to back up the truck and haul it away."

Conclusion

In December 1995, the Maryland School Performance Assessment Program, which had tested grades 3, 5, and 8 statewide in the fall, released test results showing that, despite slight yearly gains (including EAI schools), scores in Baltimore City schools were lowest in the state.

Does the EAI experience in Baltimore prove that a private company cannot produce educational results? Obviously not. Yet a number of complications contributed to the problematic nature of the EAI experience in Baltimore. While some can be avoided by other cities seeking to privatize, others appear inherent in the privatization process and thus more difficult to counteract.

First, the EAI contract, which was entered into with surprising haste, did not specify exactly how much test scores, attendance, or other educational outcomes were to improve with each year of the contract. Although both BCPS and the city were pleased with the physical changes in the Tesseract schools, there were no criteria for evaluating EAI in these and other areas, like accounting. Thus, no one—not EAI, nor the union, nor BCPS personnel, nor city officials, nor the evaluators—had clear benchmarks to assess progress and contract compliance.

Clearly, both Education Alternatives and districts throughout the country have learned from this difficult experience. However, while future contracts can be made more clear about performance criteria, such contracts will not resolve underlying issues of what is to be evaluated, and how to make more useful and accurate the evaluation of a company's effectiveness without inducing a narrowing of the objectives of the instruction offered merely to raising student test scores. EAI defined its Tesseract Way as a program stressing many of the most progressive ideas in education, from using hands-on activities and real life experiences as a basis for learning to encouraging group work through cooperative education and fostering students' different learning styles. However, all the student testing on which the company's effective-

ness was judged was traditional in nature. Student portfolios and other forms of "authentic" assessment were never mentioned. There appears to be nothing in the EAI evaluation plan to encourage the development of these progressive educational methods in the Tesseract schools.

Second, EAI's cost-cutting measures focused on personnel. This has been the privatizers' key method of trimming budgets, and some school districts have clearly hoped that privatizers would wield a stronger arm against unions than they themselves have been able to. In Baltimore, EAI focused on two areas. It eliminated teaching and counseling positions. It also replaced classroom paraprofessionals with interns. Beyond the issue of apparent illegalities involved in the practice, EAI's method of mainstreaming special education students escaped rigorous evaluation. These methods could feed teachers' and parents' worst fears about what can happen to such students without appropriate supports and training of instructors.

EAI's attempts to remove all paraprofessionals in the classrooms, many of whom had years of experience and lived in the same neighborhoods as their students, may have alienated community constituencies as well as members of the Baltimore Teachers Union. Throughout the contract period, there was high turnover among the intern replacements, raising the question of whether the interns adequately filled the role of providing a second adult in the classroom.

Like other privatizers, Education Alternatives, Inc., has sold its programming as yielding better results for lower costs than the public sector. In Baltimore, rather than saving money, EAI cost the city in excess of 11 percent more on the Tesseract schools than it spent on other BCPS schools. This is a significant difference in a city as financially strapped as Baltimore, particularly given the negligible improvement in academic performance.

If trimming the fat from urban school district budgets means spending on corporate travel, lawyers, and public relations consultants while cutting teachers and paraprofessionals and increasing class size, then even with the addition of computers it is unlikely that private companies can improve student achievement. Unions have fought for working conditions that have not always enhanced the education of students, but privatization aimed at union busting may offer neither instructional benefits nor financial savings to public education.

Finally, it is important to stress that EAI sought to make a profit in a district whose per-pupil spending was already at the bottom of its state's rankings. [There are] somewhat different stories, among them the Hartford experience, where EAI sought to improve education in a high-spending district.

———————

Despite these real-world shortcomings, some market-oriented scholars continue to insist that private business can do a better job than public bureaucracies. *See* P. Hill, *Reinventing Public Education* (1995). Others insist that the simple invocation of "free enterprise" cannot cure larger social problems that ail failing schools. *See* A. Molnar, *Giving Kids the Business: The Commercialization of America's Schools* (1996); Note, "The Hazards of Making Public Schooling a Private Business," 112 *Harv.L.Rev.* 695 (1999). As with vouchers, the merits of contracting arrangements remain contested and uncertain with the controversy driven as much by ideology as by the evidence. Once again, the debate over how best to manage the schools seems likely to continue. *See generally* J. Murphy, *The Privatization of Schooling Problems and Possibilities* (1996).

2. Commercials in the Classroom: The Case of Channel One. In addition to contracting out the provision of educational services to private, for-profit corporations, some schools have entered into marketing agreements with businesses. In exchange for much needed corporate support, public educators agree to let a business market products to students on school premises. The most prominent effort is Channel One, the brainchild of Chris Whittle of Whittle Communications. The Knoxville, Tennessee–based company has created Channel One, which consists of ten minutes of current events programming and two minutes of commercials that are broadcast daily in public school classrooms. Schools can obtain expensive technical equipment free of charge if they agree to show Channel One. Created in 1990, Channel One is now broadcast in approximately 12,000 middle and high schools nationwide. A. Molnar, *Sponsored Schools and Commercialized Classrooms: Schoolhouse Commercializing Trends in the 1990's* (August 1998) (available at http://www.uwm.edu/Dept/CACE/). Because Channel One is directed at a captive student audience, it has generated legal challenges and legislative action. In California, a state court of appeals concluded that Channel One could be shown so long as students could opt out from watching it.

———————

Dawson v. East Side Union High School District
28 Cal.App.4th 998, 34 Cal.Rptr.2d 108 (1994)

* * *

Intervener Whittle Communications, L.P., a limited partnership, characterizes itself as a developer and publisher, for profit, of informational material including video programs. Beginning in 1987 Whittle developed a concept of short current-events video programs for teenaged students. Whittle determined that middle schools and high schools would want to use such programs but would find it difficult to pay for the programs or for video equipment to display the programs. Whittle concluded that it could provide both programs and equipment without direct cost to the schools, and could nevertheless realize an adequate profit, by selling commercial advertising time in its video programs to advertisers interested in penetrating the teenage market. The upshot was "Channel One," a daily 12-minute video program which integrates 10 minutes of fast-paced current events coverage designed to appeal to teenaged students with slots for a total of 2 minutes of advertising in a format indistinguishable from ordinary television commercials.

Although Whittle expresses pride in the quality of its current-events coverage, it has made clear from the outset that its motivation is the profit to be made, and that its profit depends on Whittle's ability to persuade advertisers that "Channel One" is a viable advertising medium: That "Channel One" will effectively convey the advertisers' sales solicitations to a significant segment of the target market of teenaged consumers.

To develop a market sufficient to attract the advertisers who would ultimately provide its profit, Whittle has packaged "Channel One" with other educational programming which does not contain commercials and has offered to furnish the package, known as the Whittle Educational Network, together with television sets, a satellite receiver, cabling, and other electronic equipment to be installed by Whittle, to school districts "without any charge or fee." Whittle makes quite clear that its willingness to provide this package will be conditioned in each instance on the likelihood that Whittle will thus significantly add to the market it can offer to its advertisers. Whittle acknowledges that it is "free not to contract if viewership is too small. . . ." Whittle's printed form "district agreement" is made subject to a number of terms, conditions, and "responsibilities of the School" many of which are patently intended to provide assurances to advertisers and in other ways to serve Whittle's profit motive. For example:

(1) "The School agrees to provide to Whittle once a year upon request the annual schoolwide daily attendance figures and change of enrollment information." Whittle may terminate the agreement if enrollment declines more than 25 percent from enrollment at the beginning of the three-year agreement term; implicitly Whittle could decline to enter into an agreement with a district in which it considered enrollment insufficient. Also, although a school could elect not to have television sets installed in certain of its classrooms, "[t]he number of television sets to be installed must be mutually agreeable to Whittle and the School."

(2) Although a school can use Whittle's equipment for purposes other than to broadcast Whittle Educational Network materials, "written approval by Whittle is required should the School desire to show any other news program specifically designed for viewing by teenagers in schools and which contains advertising." Nor may the school use Whittle's wiring without Whittle's prior written consent, even after termination of the agreement, "to service equipment provided by another entity to show its programs designed for a teenage audience and containing advertisements."

(3) "The School agrees . . . to either show the entire daily ["Channel One"] newscast on all installed television sets or not show it at all. . . . *Channel One* must be shown when students are present in a homeroom or classroom. . . . The only penalty to the School for not showing *Channel One* is that Whittle may terminate this agreement and remove the Equipment."

(4) "If the School does not consistently show *Channel One* (i.e., on at least 90% of the days the School is in session and *Channel One* is transmitted), then Whittle may terminate this agreement."

On the other hand Whittle's form agreement specifies that its twelve-minute "Channel One" newscasts "will include not more than two minutes of commercial content" and that the commercial content "will be limited to materials suitable for teenagers" in accordance with detailed written "standards and guidelines" attached to the agreement. The agreement also explicitly takes account of the possibility that individual students may elect not to watch "Channel One": "This agreement does not require that all teachers use *Channel One* or that all students or any particular student view *Channel One*. The School may at its discretion develop ap-propriate procedures to accommodate students who do not wish to view *Channel One* or whose parents do not wish them to view *Channel One*."

Beginning with pilot tests in 1988, Whittle has achieved remarkable success in persuading school districts nationwide to agree to accept Whittle Educational Network programming and equipment. The record includes videotapes of several "Channel One" segments, all of which skillfully present current events material written to be interesting and comprehensible to teenaged viewers. Advertisements for products such as fast foods, candy bars and snacks, soft drinks, and deodorants are smoothly integrated into the presentation but readily identifiable as commercial rather than editorial content. In some instances public service announcements—for example, warnings against drug abuse or drunk driving—are substituted for advertisements: The record reflects that Whittle uses such announcements to fill slots allocated to, but for which it has been unable to sell, advertising. The overall impression is of a television-like presentation of uniformly high quality, broadly comparable to current events programs on commercial television channels, but tailored to appeal to teenaged viewers.

In August 1989 California's Superintendent of Public Instruction, in a letter addressed to county and district school superintendents, took a strong position against use of "Channel One" in California public schools. He concluded "that participation by public schools in proposals such as 'Channel One' is not permitted by state law and the California Constitution. Based on California Education Code section 46000, I cannot pay schools to have their students watch commercials. Therefore, I will not certify as 'instructional minutes' any time spent watching advertisements in any broadcast similar to that proposed by 'Channel One.'" Presumably the Superintendent of Public Instruction was referring to his statutory power to certify average daily attendance for the purpose of apportioning state funds to local school districts. (Cf. Ed. Code, §§14000 et seq., 46000 et seq.) He suggested that Whittle's proposal, "even if it were legal, should be resisted for ethical and educational reasons. Parents entrust their children to our public schools. We have no right legally or morally to sell access to our students even if schools receive some benefit in return." The Superintendent of Public Instruction developed on these and similar arguments in considerable detail, characterizing "the crux of the issue" as "the illegal and unethical use of schools' unique access to an extremely valuable commercial audience which Whittle Communications wants to monopolize."

At the time the Superintendent of Public Instruction sent his letter, defendant and respondent East Side Union High School District had been considering "Channel One" and other elements of the Whittle Educational Network for installation and use at Overfelt High School for several months. The record supports the school district's statement that Overfelt "has an extremely high proportion of minority students . . .; few students have the habit of news viewing or reading at home . . .; most students are from low socioeconomic backgrounds . . .; and a high percentage of students is considered 'at-risk' in terms of dropping out of school, drug abuse or teen pregnancy. . . . Further, the school's ability to deal with such problems is handicapped by the grim financial plight of both the State and the District itself, which make it difficult to fund even basic educational programs, much less special efforts to address specific local needs." After comparison to other similar video programs (which they found to be costly and not as well adapted to the district's needs) and extensive consultation with district teachers and parents (a substantial majority of whom approved of the "Channel One" concept) the school district administrators decided, subject to the approval of the district Board of Trustees, to contract with Whittle to receive the Whittle Educational Network.

In a letter to the chair of the Board of Trustees, in May 1990, the Superintendent of Public Instruction reiterated that, "I am unalterably opposed to public schools contracting for commercial television programs in the classroom during the school day." Notwithstanding the position taken by the Superintendent of Public Instruction, the Board of Trustees voted to approve a contract with Whittle, and Whittle's equipment was installed at Overfelt during the spring of 1990. No written contract was signed between the school district and Whittle, but apparently both the school district and Whittle have proceeded in accordance with the terms of Whittle's form agreement. Among other things, the record reflects that Whittle and the school district agreed orally that "the District would not require students to watch Channel One but would instead make this an optional student activity," and that from the outset parents were advised "that students could opt out of viewing Channel One with parental permission."

It appears that "Channel One" has been regularly shown to students in Overfelt classrooms since no later than the fall of 1990. The video is displayed at the same time every day, during a 20-minute time period variously characterized in the record as "the communication period" and as "a period . . . exclusively to promote critical thinking and awareness of current events and important issues of concern to the students . . .," and formerly used for "Sustained Silent Reading." In declarations in the record several teachers express strong support for the educational value of "Channel One." Some teachers use the advertisements themselves as instructional materials, asking students to evaluate the effectiveness and impact of various commercial presentations upon consumers; no party has criticized this use of the "Channel One" advertisements.

In October 1990 California's State Board of Education adopted a resolution, headed "Use of Commercial Television Advertising in the Classroom," which stated the Board's belief that "decisions concerning the use of commercial products and services are within the decision making authority of the local governing boards, consistent with state law." The resolution encouraged local governing boards to use care in considering and auditing use of electronic media in the classroom. The Superintendent of Public Instruction forwarded this resolution to local school officials with a cover letter in which he stated that the resolution "has been characterized as supporting the use of . . . 'Channel One' " and that "I disagree with [the] resolution," and briefly reviewed his August 1989 arguments against "Channel One." The president of the State Board of Education then wrote to the same officials, stating that "the State Board of Education neither supports nor opposes the use of Channel One in the classroom. . . . Our resolution simply states that the decision concerning the use of commercial products and services [is] the domain of local governing boards, consistent with state law."

In December 1991 the Superintendent of Public Instruction, joined by the California Congress of Parents, Teachers, and Students, Inc., and by two teachers at Overfelt, sued the school district for preliminary and permanent injunctions against contracting for or using "Channel One," for a declaration that the school district's use of "Channel One" was illegal in various respects, and for ancillary relief. Whittle was granted leave to intervene in the lawsuit.

* * *

[The trial court held that the school district could broadcast Channel One, but it had to ensure that viewing was strictly voluntary by providing students with the means to opt out of watching the segments. The court reserved the right to appoint a monitor to ensure compliance with its order. The plaintiffs, school district, and Whittle all appealed.] The essence of the plaintiffs' position in this court, supported by amicus curiae California Teachers Association, is that it is unlawful in any circumstances for a public school district to contract for use in its classrooms of video programming which contains commercial advertising.

Whittle endorses the trial court's rejection of the plaintiffs' position, but challenges the court's determination that student viewing of the "Channel One" commercials must be strictly voluntary and the court's orders requiring specified opt-out procedures and reserving jurisdiction to appoint a monitor.

The school district has abandoned its appeal, but supports Whittle's arguments.

* * *

The plaintiffs have conceded that the current events programming (as distinct from the classroom video advertising) of "Channel One" may be found to have legitimate educational value. The school district's implicit determination that "Channel One's" current events programming served a valid educational purpose is supported by the record and was well within the sound discretion of the school district.

On the other hand, Whittle has conceded that "[n]o one contends that the ["Channel One"] advertising is educational." Viewed, in isolation, as a commercial marketing vehicle, classroom video advertising has nothing whatsoever to do with the broad educational goal specified by the California Constitution. Neither Whittle nor anyone else suggests that the school district could properly have given Whittle carte blanche to display classroom video advertising without limitation as to content or duration. Whittle concedes that the district " 'cannot enter the advertising business.' "

As thus framed by the parties, the primary issue before us is whether the concededly noncurricular "Channel One" advertising could be deemed incidental to the valid educational purpose of the current events programming.

Addressing this issue on a factual level, the trial court determined that the classroom video advertising would be illegal "if the material . . . has such great quantitative or qualitative impact upon the educational process that it cannot reasonably be considered

to be incidental." We agree with the trial court's premises as we understand them: That particular classroom video advertising might be found to be either so inconsistent with, or otherwise disruptive of, orthodox curriculum in terms of content, or so disproportionately invasive of instructional time in terms of length, as to require a judicial conclusion that the classroom video advertising could not be deemed incidental, and that to permit the classroom video advertising in such circumstances would be an abuse of the school district's broad discretion notwithstanding the existence of a valid educational purpose.

Whittle and the school district argued to the trial court that when the two minutes of classroom video advertising, limited and subject to faculty veto as to content, were evaluated in light of the students' known right to opt out and were compared to the 10 minutes of current events programming and to the substantially more than 240 minutes of instruction provided by the school district each school day, the classroom video advertising should be deemed incidental to the valid educational purpose to be served by the current events programming.

The trial court found, in essence, that "Channel One's" classroom video advertising had not been shown to be more than incidental to a valid educational purpose. . . .

Reading the trial court's finding as a conclusion that the district had not abused its discretion, on the record before us we would agree with the trial court. We should point out, however, that our concurrence does not and cannot extend beyond the precise circumstances of record in this case: In another case, a showing of more intrusive commercial content, or of less effective editorial content, might warrant a conclusion that it would be an abuse of discretion for a school district to enter into such a contract. Nor should we be understood to suggest that it would have been a clear abuse of discretion for this (or another) school district to have *declined* to enter into the Whittle contract, either because it concluded that the classroom video advertising was not incidental or because it found that the editorial content of "Channel One" did not serve a valid educational purpose: We must emphasize once again that a local school district's discretion to make such determinations is broad and must be judicially respected as such.

* * *

[The court of appeals then rejected various state constitutional and statutory challenges to the Channel One contract.]

* * *

c. "Core Values"

Finally, the plaintiffs assert that "[w]hile this case presents novel and difficult issues, it must ultimately be resolved by reliance upon our core values regarding 'public education.' "

(1) Commercial Advertising

The crux of the plaintiffs' core values argument appears to be their perception that the motives and methods of commercial advertising are simply and irreconcilably antithetical to the ideals of public education.

The plaintiffs acknowledge that "[i]n our view, the case rises or falls on the characterization of the transaction itself" and that "[w]e believe, as matter more of principle than of absolute fact, that selling the minds of public school students to commercial advertisers is simply inappropriate and an invitation to compromise the integrity of the entire public school system." In the plaintiffs' view, "we are dealing with a commercial advertising scheme that uses student attendance and attention as saleable property. That scheme cannot reasonably be characterized as educational. It does not matter that the television equipment and nonadvertising portion of 'Channel One' serve educational purposes. It is the advertising scheme itself that is the problem, not the educational resources purchased with the revenue from the advertising. . . . In our view, [the school district] has entered into a three-way advertising partnership with Whittle and its commercial advertisers. Each party is selling something and receiving something valuable in return: [the school district] sells the students' attention; Whittle sells advertising opportunities; and [the advertiser] sells candy bars. If 'Channel One' is a legitimate way for school districts to raise money, then eventually the entire public school system will be one big market opportunity with the children available to the highest bidder."

Amicus curiae suggests that "[p]resumably all parties would agree that had the District contracted with the Mars Candy Company to show students daily ads for Mars candy bars, this would be in conflict with the purposes for which the District was established, whether or not the District used the income from the advertising campaign to purchase curricular materials or classroom technology. The only question here, then, is whether this result can be escaped when, rather than being paid with money which is then used to buy curriculum or technology, the District is paid directly with curriculum and technology."

The plaintiffs generalize, broadly, that "[t]he children are inherently vulnerable; they deserve our extraordinary protection from indoctrination in all of its forms," and that they "are grossly offended by the very idea of television advertising as a regular part of a child's school day," but they identify no specific harm to students, or to their educational experience, to be anticipated from commercial advertising in the classroom. Nor do the plaintiffs appear to address the specific facts of this case, and in particular, the strict limits as to content and length applicable to "Channel One" advertising. Nor is the argument supported by citation to the record or to any source of legal precedent of which this court may take cognizance. The gist of the argument, from factual premises the plaintiffs perhaps assume would be subject to judicial notice, is that sellers of goods and services cannot be allowed to use video to market their wares in the classroom, and that school districts cannot become parties to the sellers' attempts to do so. The argument appears to focus on the financial motives of the sellers and of the school districts with which the sellers might contract, and primarily to express the plaintiffs' aversion to such motives.

The misdirection of the plaintiffs' argument is illustrated by the plaintiffs' assertion that "[i]f the ads were 'incidental,' Whittle could not sell them at a rate that would support the investment." The argument misses the point that, to meet what we perceive to be the applicable standard, the noncurricular material need only be incidental in relation to a *valid educational purpose*. That Whittle stands to make a great deal of money from "Channel One" has nothing whatsoever to do with whether, from the educational standpoint of the school district and its students, the "Channel One" advertisements were incidental to a valid educational purpose.

The record before us contains no evidence to suggest that the school district was motivated by anything other than a wish to obtain "Channel One," other Whittle video programming, and video equipment for educational purposes. Whittle, on the other hand, has already conceded and could hardly deny that its motivation is (as the plaintiffs assert) to make a profit by selling advertising opportunities. But in our view Whittle's concession (if relevant at all to the question whether classroom video advertising must inevitably be "in conflict with the purposes for which school districts are established") supports a negative rather than an affirmative answer to the question: To sell advertising opportunities, Whittle must be able to persuade advertisers that it can deliver the market. To deliver the market, by obtaining school district contracts for "Channel One," Whittle must produce a current events program of educational quality sufficient to attract the interest of teachers and at the same time to pass muster with school boards and educational administrators under California's educational standards. If the current events product is not well done and attractive it will not be accepted; if it does not serve valid educational purposes it cannot be used in the classroom; in either event advertisers will not buy Whittle's advertising time and Whittle will not realize the profit it seeks.

The plaintiffs' argument also glosses over the public education system's longstanding tolerance for many other forms of commercial encroachment on the public schools.

The record reflects, and the plaintiffs do not deny, that student exposure to many forms of advertising, often directly associated with overt commercial ventures, has long been tolerated, if not encouraged, within the school district: Vending machines containing a wide variety of brand-marked snacks, commercial logos on computer equipment and sports scoreboards, printed advertisements in library periodicals and in assigned reading materials from magazines or newspapers as well as in school yearbooks, direct promotion of school-authorized class photographers, brand-name identification of food service products, sale of school rings and jackets, commercial announcements on the public address system, and even commercials in programs students are assigned to watch on commercial television channels.

The plaintiffs undertake to distinguish these forms of commercialism (which they characterize as "less intrusive") from "the invasive and pervasive nature of the televised program known as 'Channel One'" which, in the plaintiffs' view, "clearly crosses the line of appropriateness and changes 'school' from an educational to a commercial experience." Amicus curiae argues that none of these other commercial advertisements "involve classroom time that is taken up by the video showing of commercial advertisements. These other commercial advertising presences . . . can appropriately be deemed passive presences, i.e., ones that need not take any of a student's time." Amicus curiae adds that "[t]he issue in this case is not whether any commercial advertising in the school is appropriate. The issue is whether the use of designated classroom time to show video commercial advertisements constitutes an abuse of school district discretion." The

plaintiffs' position on this point is clear: "[A]s a matter of law, advertising as powerful as that found in 'Channel One' *should be prohibited per se.*"

The record in the case before us would not appear to warrant these arguments. The absolutism of the positions taken by the plaintiffs—"one second" of classroom video advertising would be too much—and amicus curiae—"[t]here is simply no way to draw a line between one minute a day of commercials, five minutes a day of commercials, and an hour a day of commercials"—strongly suggests that both the plaintiffs and amicus curiae are troubled not so much by this case as by where this case might lead. Both in their briefs and at oral argument the plaintiffs have essentially acknowledged their concern that this case might be simply the entry point for unlimited commercial advertising in the classroom. As they put it in their reply brief: "Given the shortage of funds for public education, it is easy to reach for Whittle's 'quick fix.' The implications of television advertising, however, present a dire future for public education. If 'Channel 1' is legal, then all manner of commercial, profit-making schemes will gradually seep into the school day. If two minutes per day of advertising is harmless, why not ten minutes or twenty? What if entire class periods are devoted to commercial indoctrination and the sponsors offer to give out free soda and candy to students who attend? How much of the school day—that is supposed to be dedicated to learning—can be diverted into an active advertising campaign before the public education system ceases to be either public or educational? This is a case for line-drawing."

We are more optimistic of the abilities of school districts, administrators, and teachers, and (in an extreme case) of trial courts, to draw any lines that need be drawn on a case-by-case basis. Neither the plaintiffs nor amicus curiae have given us a judicially cognizable basis for a declaration that classroom video advertising can never be deemed incidental to a valid educational purpose, or that on any other basis such advertising must invariably be declared unlawful.

(2) *Separation of Powers*

In any event an abstract appeal to "core values" of public education is not within our purview.

"The powers of state government are legislative, executive, and judicial. Persons charged with the exercise of one power may not exercise either of the others except as permitted by this Constitution." (Cal. Const., art. III, § 3.)

"[C]ourts are not school boards or legislatures . . . ." (*Wisconsin v. Yoder* (1972) 406 U.S. 205, 235 [32 L.Ed.2d 15, 36–37, 92 S.Ct. 1526].) Abstract assessment of "core values" is beyond the scope of our judicial function. Our own perceptions of "core values regarding 'public education'" would be essentially irrelevant: As judges we can be neither makers of educational policy nor arbiters of the philosophical propriety of educational policies developed, in accordance with our system of government, by the Legislature and by state and local school officials. The plaintiffs must address their argument to local school districts, to the Legislature, and ultimately to the people, in whom the power to develop public educational policy properly resides. . . .

2. Must Student Viewing Be Voluntary?

The trial court also made clear that in its view student exposure to "Channel One" should be "strictly voluntary." It would have found particular classroom video advertising illegal "if students are coerced directly or indirectly into viewing commercial material . . . ." The trial court found no evidence of *direct* coercion but concluded that the plaintiffs had "raised a legitimate concern about the possibility of indirect coercion" upon teachers to use, and students to watch, "Channel One." On this basis the trial court ultimately required that the school district, as a condition to continued use of "Channel One," take specified steps to assure that students were aware of their options not to use, or not to watch, "Channel One," and that the school district require "a regular, structured, supervised alternative to 'Channel One'" for students who wished to opt out.

In support of its own appeal in this court, Whittle argues that students can be compelled to watch classroom video advertising.

The crux of Whittle's argument is that if (as Whittle has consistently asserted) the trial court was correct in its determination that the commercial advertising in "Channel One" was necessary and incidental to a legitimate educational purpose, then *by virtue of that determination* any arguable coercion upon students to watch the commercial advertising must be deemed incidental as well. Whittle argues that "[s]chools *require* students to do things"—implicitly, things more integral to orthodox public education than video commercials—"all the time . . .," and that compulsory noneducational activities are not illegal if incidental to a valid educational purpose.

Whittle's argument is superficially attractive. If the impact of "Channel One's" commercial solicitation

upon the educational process is in fact so slight as to warrant a finding that it is incidental, then at least as a practical matter the significance of a requirement that students submit to the solicitation might be similarly discounted. This is not, after all, a case of asserted state-sponsored religious (cf., e.g., *Abington School Dist. v. Schempp* (1963) 374 U.S. 203, 226 [10 L.Ed.2d 844, 860–861, 83 S.Ct. 1560]) or ideological (cf., e.g., *Board of Education v. Barnette* (1943) 319 U.S. 624, 637, 642 [87 L.Ed. 1628, 1637, 1639–1640, 63 S.Ct. 1178, 147 A.L.R. 674]) indoctrination but simply another manifestation of a commercial ethic to which all of us have been increasingly exposed, but which, despite its proliferation, has not yet been authoritatively characterized as indoctrination in any constitutionally significant sense.

But amicus curiae California Teachers Association suggests a plausible reason, of constitutional provenance if not of constitutional dimension, why students cannot be compelled to listen to commercial speech in the public school classroom during *mandatory instructional time.* As we perceive it, the argument is that mandatory school attendance laws such as California's (Ed. Code, § 48200 et seq.) effectively confine students during the school day, that students share with all other citizens a constitutional right not to be confined without compelling reason (cf., e.g., *Parham v. J.R.* (1979) 442 U.S. 584, 600 [61 L.Ed.2d 101, 117, 99 S.Ct. 2493] [commitment of children to mental hospital]), and that although mandatory attendance laws have been constitutionally validated for orthodox educational purposes "where nothing more than the general interest of the parent in the nurture and education of his children is involved" (*Wisconsin v. Yoder, supra,* 406 U.S. 205, 233 [32 L.Ed.2d 15, 35]; cf. also *Meyer v. Nebraska* (1923) 262 U.S. 390, 402 [67 L.Ed. 1042, 1046, 43 S.Ct. 625, 29 A.L.R. 1446]; *Pierce v. Society of Sisters* (1925) 268 U.S. 510, 534 [69 L.Ed. 1070, 1077–1078, 45 S.Ct. 571, 39 A.L.R. 468]), the power to decree universal compulsory education "is by no means absolute . . ." (*Wisconsin v. Yoder, supra,* 406 U.S. at p. 215 [32 L.Ed.2d at p. 25]). Amicus curiae argues that "[t]he justification for depriving the liberty of juveniles by compelling their attendance at school simply does not apply" to classroom video advertising. "In [such a] situation, the fundamental educational purpose that justifies compelled school attendance is missing. The constitutional violation inherent in compelling student attendance to view commercial advertisements can be overcome only if the viewing is purely voluntary."

Having previously acknowledged that the "Channel One" commercials cannot be deemed educational, Whittle relies, in response to amicus curiae, entirely on its argument that the commercials have been found to be, and in fact are, incidental.

We agree with the trial court, on the basis of amicus curiae's argument, that public school students *cannot be compelled* to watch classroom video advertising. The fact that the concededly noneducational classroom video advertising is incidental to a valid educational purpose or purposes does not alter the fact that the advertising is noneducational. Whittle's proffered examples of assertedly noneducational activities which *can* be required of students do not support its position: "Passing time" between classes can properly be regarded as integral to the educational process; certainly students can be required to move, in accordance with a reasonable timetable, from one class to the next. Recesses, even if not dedicated to other education-related activities such as passing between classes and opportunities for meals, may reasonably be regarded as periods of respite essential to effective classroom performance by both students and teachers. Printed advertisements adjacent to assigned reading materials in commercial magazines and newspapers presumably have no educational value in and of themselves, but students are not compelled to read the advertisements. The essence of amicus curiae's plausible argument is that students should no more be compelled to watch classroom video advertising than they are compelled to read printed advertisements adjacent to assigned reading materials. And because the commercial video advertising is seamlessly integrated into "Channel One's" current events programming, we perceive no practical way to permit students to opt out of only the classroom video advertising: to assure that student viewing of the advertisements is voluntary, the students must be allowed to opt out of "Channel One" altogether.

Patently the conclusion we reach offends neither Whittle's asserted constitutional right to transmit commercial speech to students nor the students' constitutional right (asserted by Whittle in their behalf) to receive it (cf. *Va. Pharmacy Bd.* v. *Va. Consumer Council, supra,* 425 U.S. at pp. 756–757 [48 L.Ed.2d at pp. 334–355]): Whittle remains free to transmit, and the students to receive, as much commercial speech (within the constraints of Whittle's contract with the school district) as the students are freely willing to hear. Nor can Whittle assert that our conclusion would frustrate its reasonable expectations under its contract with the school district: Whittle's own contract form permits the school district to "accommodate" students who wish to opt out.

* * *

NOTES AND QUESTIONS

1. *Judicial and Legislative Responses to Channel One*

Channel One has survived legal challenges in New Jersey, North Carolina, and Tennessee. *New Jersey Education Ass'n v. Bd. of Educ. of Trenton,* 139 N.J. L84 (1994); *Wallace v. Knox County Bd. of Educ.,* 1 F.3d 1243, reported in full, 1993 U.S. App. LEXIS 20477, at *1 (6th Cir. 1993); *State v. Whittle Communications,* 328 N.C., 456, *rehearing denied* 328 N.C. 735 (1991).

Although Channel One weathered individual challenges, New York and Rhode Island have banned the program from their public classrooms. N.Y.Educ.Law 23.1–23.2 (McKinney 1997); R.I.Gen.Laws 16-38-6 (Michie 1996).

2. *The Pedagogical Value of Channel One*

Commercial advertising is now a pervasive feature of children's lives. Does the commonplace nature of advertising strengthen or weaken arguments about the impropriety of commercials in the classroom? Is the issue whether Channel One, commercials and all, is pedagogically valuable? If so, who should make the determination: courts, legislatures, state educational agencies, or local educational officials?

3. *Opt Out Provisions and Voluntary Viewing*

Once the decision is made to broadcast Channel One, why should children ever have a special right to opt out of this portion of the curriculum and not others? Is the ability to opt out a necessary safeguard to ensure that children are not a captive audience of advertisers? Are the opt out provisions meaningful here because the students are teenagers? Would the right to opt out be sufficient protection if Whittle tried to introduce similar programming in elementary schools?

---

*"When Chips Are Down, Nabisco Offers Lesson That Kids Eat Up," *Selling to Kids,* 15 October 1997.

3. Other Forms of Classroom Commercialization.

Channel One has earned the greatest notoriety in educational reform circles, but it is far from the only commercial intrusion into the classroom. Two rapidly growing areas of business activity in public schools involve sponsorship of programs and activities and use of exclusive agreements.

"Sponsored Schools and Commercialized Classrooms: Schoolhouse Commercializing Trends in the 1990s"

A. Molnar, Report for Center for the Analysis of Commercialism in Education (CACE), August 1998.

* * *

Sponsorship of Programs and Activities

* * *

Sponsorship of athletic events [in public schools] opened the door. In 1984, for example, the Idaho High School Activities Association negotiated an agreement with the United Dairymen of Idaho that provided $37,000 for the travel expenses of students participating in boys and girls basketball tournaments. By 1988 *Newsday* was accurately predicting that it was only a matter of time before ". . . we see something like the 'Reebok/New York State High School Basketball Tournament,' the 'Nike/New York Scholastic Wrestling Championship,' or the 'Coca-Cola/New York Public School Track Meet.' "

It is now common for marketing firms to negotiate a wide variety of sports-related sponsorship agreements that funnel money to schools. The work of one such firm, School Properties, Inc., was described in a 1991 *Forbes* magazine article. The firm, based in Yorba Linda, Calif., was founded in 1987 to seek exclusive rights to sell sponsorships for regional and state championships in all sports. School Properties gets 35 percent of the take the first year and 25 percent thereafter. In 1991 the firm negotiated a $2.8 million multi-year contract between Reebok and California Interscholastic Federation (CIF). The deal guaranteed that all California state play-off competitions and title events would be called the "CIF/Reebok Championships." According to the *Sacramento Bee*, by 1993, 27 percent of CIF's 500-school Southern Section's $1.1 million budget came from corporate sponsorship, creating financial de-

pendency and leaving the organization vulnerable to corporate decisions made on the basis of corporate, not school, priorities. CIF thus faced a financial crisis when Reebok announced in 1993 that it would not renew its contract because it wanted to focus on product-driven advertising.

During the nineties, School Properties, Inc., has also signed up Hardee's and First Security Bank for a sponsorship agreement in Utah, and Kraft, General Foods, and Burger King for one in Alaska. In the words of the *Forbes* article ". . . you can thank [School Properties founder] Don Baird for bringing together big-time advertising and boondock jocks."

Some educators such as Pinellas County Florida athletic director Bob Hosack are concerned. Hosack commented to the *St. Petersburg Times*, "It's a shame we have to do these things to raise money. But it's getting to a point where costs are so high, schools throughout the state and county are raising their own money. Just about anything they can think of that's legal is fair game."

Despite such misgivings, in the 1990's sponsorship activities have moved well beyond athletics. They touch on almost every aspect of school life. School districts and professional education organizations actively solicit sponsorships and sometimes form consortia to do so. In the early nineties, for example, five Illinois education associations (Illinois Association of School Administrators, Illinois Association of School Boards, Illinois Association of School Business Officials, Illinois Principals Association, Illinois High School Association) formed a school licensing cooperative. In 1994 the *Chicago Tribune* reported that the group had decided to hire School Properties, Inc., to oversee the marketing of Illinois schools. According to Walt Warfield, the executive director of the Illinois Association of School Administrators, "We understand the power of a company being able to say, for example, 'We're the official soft drink of the Illinois schools.' We want to capitalize on that." David Turner, executive director of the Illinois Principals Association acknowledged that idea was commercial. He commented, "Sure it's commercial. Of course, it's commercial. But money's tight. We're looking for ways to augment school financing. What's for sale is a relationship with Illinois schools." The Illinois organization is not just interested in negotiating exclusive agreements with soft drink companies. The cooperative gets ¾ of one percent of the cost of purchases made by participating Illinois residents who use its affinity credit card.

The Jefferson County Colorado School District and US West Communications Group have signed a ten-year $2 million agreement that makes the phone company the school district's "strategic supplier." Under the terms of the deal US West will have naming rights to a planned high school sports stadium. The company will also offer school groups phone cards with the school district logo that they can sell for a commission to raise money for schools.

The Denver school district created a Community Sponsorship of the Curriculum program through which it has invited local and national companies to support the district's education programs in return for advertising rights throughout the district. Sunkist, for example, sponsored . . . Denver's Comprehensive Health Initiative. In return the company was given space for its "Just One—A Whole Day's Vitamin C" advertising campaign on school buses, scoreboards, and print material sent home with students.

Other sponsorship activities reported during 1997 included a Chips Ahoy! contest in which students were asked to verify that there were indeed 1,000 chips in every bag of Chips Ahoy! cookies. Contestants then sent in essays or videos that demonstrated ingenious ways of counting the chips. Three finalists competed for the top prize of $25,000 in scholarships.

The Chips Ahoy! contest was launched by Nabisco after the company received 130 letters from an elementary school in Wadesboro, N.C. Students complained that they had been able to locate only 600 of the promised chips and accused the company of false advertising and lying. According to *Selling to Kids,** by launching the contest in response to its 600 chip problem, Nabisco not only got extensive press coverage they gained "access to schools and kids nationwide."

In Maryland, AT&T signed on with the Family Education Network to launch an initiative to connect parents to their children's schools via the Internet. In return for its $500,000, AT&T got corporate banners on each school web site and the rights to sell AT&T long distance and Internet access. Maryland AT&T customers could also earn "Learning Points" that schools could redeem for Internet accounts and computer equipment.

The Mars candy company created a half-finished Halloween commercial for students to complete. The ad was broadcast on Channel One, a twelve-minute current events program containing two minutes of commercials broadcast into approximately 12,000 middle and high schools. Students then got to vote on one of three endings. By casting their vote, via a toll-free telephone call, students were entered in a sweepstakes with two $5,000 first prizes and 100 second prizes of 24 compact discs.

Explaining the Trend Toward Corporate Sponsorships of School Activities

The justification for the sponsorship agreements most often used by educators is the need for money. Money also drives the corporate side of the equation. It is estimated that children between the ages of 4–12 purchase or influence the purchase of goods and services worth nearly $500 billion a year. David Siegel, general manager of Small Talk, a division of Sive/Young & Rubicam, notes that advertising directed at children has increased twenty-fold in the past decade to $2 billion. Small wonder marketing professor James McNeal describes children as "the brightest star in the consumer constellation." According to McNeal, "Virtually every consumer-goods industry, from airlines to zinnia-seed sellers, targets kids."

With school districts short of cash and the consumer power of children growing, it is not surprising that the commercial pressure on schools is increasing steadily. Ira Mayer, publisher of *Youth Markets Alert,* a newsletter that tracks developments in marketing to children, believes that it is the purchasing power of kids that has led to an increase in both the sophistication and the magnitude of the advertising directed at them. And, according to *Youth Markets Alert* associate editor Gene Newman, "In the past, there was maybe more of a feeling that shameless promotion in school wasn't right, that you should keep education separate. I think in today's business climate, that is definitely beginning to change."

Exclusive Agreements

* * *

The trend toward exclusive contracts especially with bottlers and athletic apparel companies may reflect corporate recognition that, as James McNeal has found, school-age children spend about a third of their money on food and beverages and that apparel spending is the fastest growing category of the children's market.

Soft Drink Bottlers and the School Market

From Colorado, to Texas, to Ohio, exclusive "pouring rights" agreements between soft drink companies and school districts provide a good illustration of how schools chronically short of money are attempting to turn access to their students into cash. As Pepsico spokesman Larry Jabbonsky told *The New York Times,* "Schools are serving up exclusivity as a carrot. They need to generate funds. At the same time we are constantly looking for new ways to broaden our exposure among young people. It's a pretty natural interdependent fit."

In 1998 the Oakland, Calif[ornia]–based Center for Commercial-Free Public Education identified 24 exclusive contracts between bottlers and school districts with another 25 under consideration. The volume of press reports on the topic suggests that these figures may understate the prevalence of the practice. DD Marketing, based in Pueblo, Colo., for example, negotiates sponsorships and exclusive agreements for 240 high schools. The typical exclusive contract with a soft drink bottler gives a school or district a percentage of the sales derived from soft drink purchases. In some cases there are additional incentives such as score boards, coolers, and free products for special events.

In 1997 one of the more unusual exclusive agreements was announced by Dr Pepper and the Grapevine-Colleyville school district in the Dallas–Fort Worth area. As part of its 10-year, $4 million exclusive agreement with Dr Pepper, the district allowed the company to paint its logo atop the high school building. The school's roof was of interest to Dr Pepper officials because it can be seen from planes taking off and landing at Dallas–Fort Worth International Airport. Grapevine-Colleyville deputy superintendent, Larry Groppel told *The Houston Chronicle,* "If it weren't for the acute need for funds we would never have entered into anything like this. . . . It's totally driven by need."

The Madison, Wis[consin], school district signed a more conventional three-year contract that could potentially net the district $1.5 million over three years. In addition, the district received a $100,000 "signing bonus," $5,000 annual teacher-of-the-year scholarships, $5,000 to support students in annual marketing competitions, two $5-an-hour internships for students handling Coke promotional activities, a summer internship, and a post-graduation position with Coke for one student.

Athletic Apparel Companies and the School Market

Having saturated the college market, manufacturers of athletic apparel, primarily Nike and Reebok, have been turning increasing attention to high school athletics, described by the *Sacramento Bee* as "one of the last untapped markets for corporations looking to tie themselves to a wholesome and marketable activity." According to Bill Paterson, author of the *Bee* article, another probable factor in Nike's decision to associate itself with high school athletics is the company's need to overcome the negative publicity associated with minority hiring, exploitation of foreign workers, and victimization of poor African-American children through its advertising practices.

Athletic apparel agreements are an opportunity that at least some educators seem to welcome. Randy Quinn, executive director of the Colorado Association of School Boards told *The Denver Post:* "It started on the university level. Nobody blinks an eye when Nike arranges for a contract with university football teams, or someone sponsors a scoreboard in university stadiums. The next logical progression in that movement would be the public schools. . . . Given the reality of economics and the scramble for dollars, it just seems to reflect reality."

In 1996 the Financial Network, a service of CNN, reported on the trend and described the competition between sportswear companies to represent high school basketball programs as a war, suggesting that it was only a matter of time before the battle lines ran through elementary schools. The Nike strategy seems to be to go after the best teams in the biggest markets. Reebok has tended to favor more broadly based agreements. According to CNN, Nike pays an undisclosed number of high school teams $20,000 to wear Nike gear. Mike Levine, director of marketing at Athletes and Artists, described Nike as a company with little shame in promoting its products. According to Levine, "This is the latest surge in that—I don't want to call it arrogance. I will call it pride in what they are doing."

Many school districts don't seem to be interested in Nike's or any other corporation's pride—they want the money. As Ron Lynch, athletic director of the Alvin, Texas, school district told *The Houston Chronicle:* "With budgets being tight in school districts, it's hard to get uniforms. . . . Because money is tight we're doing everything we can to try and find ways in which to help."

Schools accepting money and equipment from athletic apparel companies run the risk, however, of creating conflicts of interest potentially harmful to students and the integrity of their programs, a danger that has officials at the college level worried. Bill Friday, former president of the University of North Carolina, told *Newsweek* in 1996: "They [Nike] influence the coaches' salary, they influence who wears what, and prescribe what logo is worn. I think they've gone too far."

Occasional Controversy

Sponsorships and exclusive agreements are becoming more and more common; they are, however, sometimes a source of controversy. Seattle superintendent John Stanford proposed in 1996 that, as a way of reducing a projected $35 million budget shortfall, the Seattle School Board allow him to solicit major national firms to enter into advertising agreements with the district. The idea was so controversial that after a series of public meetings at which he was roundly criticized for attempting to sell the district's children to advertisers, the superintendent was forced to back away from his plan.

In early 1998, Milwaukee Public School Superintendent Alan Brown announced that he would recommend that the Milwaukee Board of School Directors enter into a contract with Pepsico that would give the soft drink bottler the exclusive right to market its products in Milwaukee's public schools. Superintendent Brown estimated that the three-year agreement would net the school district $5.2 million. Brown's recommendation immediately came under fire from high school principals who had already cut deals with other bottlers and from community members who opposed the idea of offering any firm an exclusive agreement. In addition, the city attorney found that the way the agreement was negotiated and its potential violation of the school district's advertising guidelines might make it illegal. As a result, Brown was forced to withdraw from the proposed deal.

The Seattle and Milwaukee cases appear, however, to be exceptions. In Palmyra, Wis[consin], for example, high school principal Jeff Tortomasi explained "we played one [bottling firm] off the other" to get what school officials felt was the best deal. Greendale, Wis[consin], athletic director Jim Andrus told the *Milwaukee Journal Sentinel,* "The way money is with the revenue caps, for us to look away and say, 'We don't want to get into that,' it's kind of stupid." Asked by the *Dallas Morning News* how much money was in corporate agreements, Dave Fry, executive director of the Illinois High School Association, replied, "Who knows? There's got to be millions of dollars. Let your mind go. The imagination is the limit."

The Motives of Marketers

The imagination is the limit for advertisers. And the stakes are high, as corporations try to "brand" children early. Asked by *The Pittsburgh Business Times* why sports firms are interested in sponsorship agreements with schools, Ted Black, an attorney with the Pittsburgh firm Katarincic & Salmon, commented that "The number-one reason is to build brand loyalty and to build it as early as possible." Kevin Popovic, a marketing specialist with The St. George Group, noted that "Once you have a loyal customer, you really have to do something to lose him. Companies are making the investment and buying that market early."

Apparently the strategy is a success. According [to] James McNeal, about ninety percent of the product requests made by children to their parents are by brand name. He argues that "Customers cultivated as children may be critical of changes in products, both those they love and hate. But they will probably be less resistant to price increases and size reductions." George Carey, the president of Just Kid, Inc., a Stamford, Conn., marketing company, reported that his firm's research found that when his company "asked kids to draw something cool, they overwhelmingly drew a brand." *Technos* magazine reports that market research shows that ". . . brand names are important to kids, because they help young consumers forge and express their identities. If marketers can capitalize on that need for self-expression, if they can woo and win the child, they're likely to enjoy his or her loyalty for the next 70 years." Thus, the message to marketers is clear: Establish product loyalty as soon as possible. Schools represent an attractive venue for advertisers because, to paraphrase Willy Sutton, that's where the children are, and because they represent one of the least ad-saturated environments available.

The Financial Payout and Potential Trade-Offs Involved When Schools Sign On with Marketers

Despite the promise of millions of dollars in new revenue for schools, it is by no means clear that the fiscal benefits are as great as supporters of sponsorship programs and other commercializing activities suggest. In 1993, Colorado Springs School District 11 was the first in the nation to launch a comprehensive campaign to offer advertisers a chance to rent space in its hallways, on its buses, and at other locations on its property. *Marketing News* reports that between 1993 and 1997 the district received $338,680 from advertisers. With approximately 36,000 students, that works out to about $2.50 per student per year over the four-year period, hardly an amount that seems destined to make much of an impact on the district's finances. It is possible that the real financial winners in the trend toward sponsorship and exclusive sales agreements are not schools but the firms that broker the deals. In a 1997 editorial, the *Dallas Business Journal* pointed out that marketing firms that help negotiate agreements between school districts and corporations can take up to 40 percent of corporate payout.

In 1997, Colorado Springs District 11 signed a 10-year exclusive agreement with Coca-Cola that the district projects is worth about $8.1 million, a figure that represents less than 1 percent of the district's budget. If the district meets "sales incentive thresholds," the contract could be worth up to $11.1 million according to district officials. The existence of "sales incentives" underlines the kind of conflict of interest that critics argue is inherent in exclusive sales agreements. The Colorado Springs school district will not only profit from the sale of a particular brand of soft drink, it now has a financial incentive to promote the greatest possible consumption of that soft drink as well. Such a situation potentially places the Colorado Springs school district in the position of implicitly asking students to ignore the health and nutrition advice they are likely getting in the district's curriculum in order to benefit the district financially by drinking as much of Coke's soft drink products as possible.

* * *

As these readings demonstrate, the term "privatization" covers a wide array of market initiatives in public education. Some, like vouchers, are designed to promote systemic reform, while others, like sponsorships and exclusive marketing agreements, provide a badly needed infusion of funds on an ad hoc basis. The most popular of the current efforts appears to be the charter school movement, which blends choice into a traditional public school system.

In general, educational governance trends in recent years suggest that there is an ongoing interest in decentralization of educational policymaking, a shift of authority back to legislators and administrators and away from courts, and a willingness to experiment with private alternatives to public education. Because educational reform is often cyclical, these trends are worth watching, but there is no guarantee that they will persist in the new millennium.

United States Constitution

Preamble

We the People of the United States, in Order to form a more perfect Union, establish Justice, insure domestic Tranquility, provide for the common defence, promote the general Welfare, and secure the Blessings of Liberty to ourselves and our Posterity, do ordain and establish this Constitution for the United States of America.

Article I

Section 1. All legislative Powers herein granted shall be vested in a Congress of the United States, which shall consist of a Senate and House of Representatives.

Section 2. The House of Representatives shall be composed of Members chosen every second Year by the People of the several States, and the Electors in each State shall have the Qualifications requisite for Electors of the most numerous Branch of the State Legislature.

No Person shall be a Representative who shall not have attained to the Age of twenty five Years, and been seven Years a Citizen of the United States, and who shall not, when elected, be an Inhabitant of that State in which he shall be chosen.

Representatives and direct Taxes shall be apportioned among the several States which may be included within this Union, according to their respective Numbers, which shall be determined by adding to the whole Number of free Persons, including those bound to Service for a Term of Years, and ex-cluding Indians not taxed, three fifths of all other Persons. The actual Enumeration shall be made within three Years after the first Meeting of the Congress of the United States, and within every subsequent Term of ten Years, in such Manner as they shall by Law direct. The Number of Representatives shall not exceed one for every thirty Thousand, but each State shall have at Least one Representative; and until such enumeration shall be made, the State of New Hampshire shall be entitled to chuse three, Massachusetts eight, Rhode Island and Providence Plantations one, Connecticut five, New York six, New Jersey four, Pennsylvania eight, Delaware one, Maryland six, Virginia ten, North Carolina five, South Carolina five, and Georgia three.

When vacancies happen in the Representation from any State, the Executive Authority thereof shall issue Writs of Election to fill such Vacancies.

The House of Representatives shall chuse their Speaker and other Officers; and shall have the sole Power of Impeachment.

Section 3. The Senate of the United States shall be composed of two Senators from each State, chosen by the Legislature thereof, for six Years; and each Senator shall have one Vote.

Immediately after they shall be assembled in Consequence of the first Election, they shall be divided as equally as may be into three Classes. The Seats of the Senators of the first Class shall be vacated at the Expiration of the second Year, of the second Class at the Expiration of the fourth Year, and of the third Class at the Expiration of the sixth Year, so that one third may be chosen every second

Year; and if Vacancies happen by Resignation, or otherwise, during the Recess of the Legislature of any State, the Executive thereof may make temporary Appointments until the next Meeting of the Legislature, which shall then fill such Vacancies.

No Person shall be a Senator who shall not have attained to the Age of thirty Years, and been nine Years a Citizen of the United States, and who shall not, when elected, be an Inhabitant of that State for which he shall be chosen.

The Vice President of the United States shall be President of the Senate, but shall have no Vote, unless they be equally divided.

The Senate shall chuse their other Officers, and also a President pro tempore, in the Absence of the Vice President, or when he shall exercise the Office of President of the United States.

The Senate shall have the sole Power to try all Impeachments. When sitting for that Purpose, they shall be on Oath or Affirmation. When the President of the United States is tried, the Chief Justice shall preside: And no Person shall be convicted without the Concurrence of two thirds of the Members present.

Judgment in Cases of Impeachment shall not extend further than to removal from Office, and disqualification to hold and enjoy any Office of honor, Trust or Profit under the United States: but the Party convicted shall nevertheless be liable and subject to Indictment, Trial, Judgment and Punishment, according to Law.

Section 4.   The Times, Places and Manner of holding Elections for Senators and Representatives, shall be prescribed in each State by the Legislature thereof; but the Congress may at any time by Law make or alter such Regulations, except as to the Places of chusing Senators.

The Congress shall assemble at least once in every Year, and such Meeting shall be on the first Monday in December, unless they shall by Law appoint a different Day.

Section 5.   Each House shall be the Judge of the Elections, Returns and Qualifications of its own Members, and a Majority of each shall constitute a Quorum to do Business; but a smaller Number may adjourn from day to day, and may be authorized to compel the Attendance of absent Members, in such Manner, and under such Penalties as each House may provide.

Each House may determine the Rules of its Proceedings, punish its Members for disorderly Behav-

iour, and, with the Concurrence of two thirds, expel a Member.

Each House shall keep a Journal of its Proceedings, and from time to time publish the same, excepting such Parts as may in their Judgment require Secrecy; and the Yeas and Nays of the Members of either House on any question shall, at the Desire of one fifth of those Present, be entered on the Journal.

Neither House, during the Session of Congress, shall, without the Consent of the other, adjourn for more than three days, nor to any other Place than that in which the two Houses shall be sitting.

Section 6.   The Senators and Representatives shall receive a Compensation for their Services, to be ascertained by Law, and paid out of the Treasury of the United States. They shall in all Cases, except Treason, Felony and Breach of the Peace, be privileged from Arrest during their Attendance at the Session of their respective Houses, and in going to and returning from the same; and for any Speech or Debate in either House, they shall not be questioned in any other Place.

No Senator or Representative shall, during the Time for which he was elected, be appointed to any civil Office under the Authority of the United States, which shall have been created, or the Emoluments whereof shall have been encreased during such time; and no Person holding any Office under the United States, shall be a Member of either House during his Continuance in Office.

Section 7.   All Bills for raising Revenue shall originate in the House of Representatives; but the Senate may propose or concur with Amendments as on other Bills.

Every Bill which shall have passed the House of Representatives and the Senate, shall, before it become a Law, be presented to the President of the United States: If he approve he shall sign it, but if not he shall return it, with his Objections to that House in which it shall have originated, who shall enter the Objections at large on their Journal, and proceed to reconsider it. If after such Reconsideration two thirds of that House shall agree to pass the Bill, it shall be sent, together with the Objections, to the other House, by which it shall likewise be reconsidered, and if approved by two thirds of that House, it shall become a Law. But in all such Cases the Votes of both Houses shall be determined by Yeas and Nays, and the Names of the Persons voting for and against the Bill shall be entered on the Journal of each House respectively. If any Bill shall not be returned by the President within ten Days (Sundays excepted) after it shall have been presented to him, the Same shall be a Law, in like Manner as if he had signed it, unless the Congress by their Adjournment prevent its Return, in which Case it shall not be a Law.

Every Order, Resolution, or Vote, to which the Concurrence of the Senate and House of Representatives may be necessary (except on a question of Adjournment) shall be presented to the President of the United States; and before the Same shall take Effect, shall be approved by him, or being disapproved by him, shall be repassed by two thirds of the Senate and House of Representatives, according to the Rules and Limitations prescribed in the Case of a Bill.

Section 8.   The Congress shall have Power To lay and collect Taxes, Duties, Imposts and Excises, to pay the Debts and provide for the common Defence and general Welfare of the United States; but all Duties, Imposts and Excises shall be uniform throughout the United States;

To borrow Money on the credit of the United States;

To regulate Commerce with foreign Nations, and among the several States, and with the Indian Tribes;

To establish an uniform Rule of Naturalization, and uniform Laws on the subject of Bankruptcies throughout the United States;

To coin Money, regulate the Value thereof, and of foreign Coin, and fix the Standard of Weights and Measures;

To provide for the Punishment of counterfeiting the Securities and current Coin of the United States;

To establish Post Offices and post Roads;

To promote the Progress of Science and useful Arts, by securing for limited Times to Authors and Inventors the exclusive Right to their respective Writings and Discoveries;

To constitute Tribunals inferior to the supreme Court;

To define and punish Piracies and Felonies committed on the high Seas, and Offenses against the Law of Nations;

To declare War, grant Letters of Marque and Reprisal, and make Rules concerning Captures on Land and Water;

To raise and support Armies, but no Appropriation of Money to that Use shall be for a longer Term than two Years;

To provide and maintain a Navy;

To make Rules for the Government and Regulation of the land and naval Forces;

To provide for calling forth the Militia to execute the Laws of the Union, suppress Insurrections and repel Invasions;

To provide for organizing, arming, and disciplining, the Militia, and for governing such Part of them as may be employed in the Service of the United States, reserving to the States respectively, the Appointment of the Officers, and the Authority of training the Militia according to the discipline prescribed by Congress;

To exercise exclusive Legislation in all Cases whatsoever, over such District (not exceeding ten Miles square) as may, by Cession of particular States, and the Acceptance of Congress, become the Seat of the Government of the United States, and to exercise like Authority over all Places purchased by the Consent of the Legislature of the State in which the Same shall be, for the Erection of Forts, Magazines, Arsenals, dock-Yards, and other needful Buildings;—And

To make all Laws which shall be necessary and proper for carrying into Execution the foregoing Powers, and all other Powers vested by this Constitution in the Government of the United States, or in any Department or Officer thereof.

Section 9.   The Migration or Importation of such Persons as any of the States now existing shall think proper to admit, shall not be prohibited by the Congress prior to the Year one thousand eight hundred and eight, but a Tax or duty may be imposed on such Importation, not exceeding ten dollars for each Person.

The Privilege of the Writ of Habeas Corpus shall not be suspended, unless when in Cases of Rebellion or Invasion the public Safety may require it.

No Bill of Attainder or ex post facto Law shall be passed.

No Capitation, or other direct, Tax shall be laid, unless in Proportion to the Census or Enumeration herein before directed to be taken.

No Tax or Duty shall be laid on Articles exported from any State.

No Preference shall be given by any Regulation of Commerce or Revenue to the Ports of one State over those of another: nor shall Vessels bound to, or from, one State, be obliged to enter, clear, or pay Duties in another.

No Money shall be drawn from the Treasury, but in Consequence of Appropriations made by Law; and a regular Statement and Account of the Receipts and Expenditures of all public Money shall be published from time to time.

No Title of Nobility shall be granted by the United States: And no Person holding any Office of Profit or Trust under them, shall, without the Consent of the Congress, accept of any present, Emolument, Office, or Title, of any kind whatever, from any King, Prince, or foreign State.

Section 10.   No State shall enter into any Treaty, Alliance, or Confederation; grant Letters of Marque and Reprisal; coin Money; emit Bills of Credit; make any Thing but gold and silver Coin a Tender in Payment of Debts; pass any Bill of Attainder, ex post facto Law, or Law impairing the Obligation of Contracts, or grant any Title of Nobility.

No State shall, without the Consent of the Congress, lay any Imposts or Duties on Imports or Exports, except what may be absolutely necessary for executing it's inspection Laws: and the net Produce of all Duties and Imposts, laid by any State on Imports or Exports, shall be for the Use of the Treasury of the United States; and all such Laws shall be subject to the Revision and Controul of the Congress.

No State shall, without the Consent of Congress, lay any Duty of Tonnage, keep Troops, or Ships of War in time of Peace, enter into any Agreement or Compact with another State, or with a foreign Power, or engage in War, unless actually invaded, or in such imminent Danger as will not admit of delay.

Article II

Section 1.   The executive Power shall be vested in a President of the United States of America. He shall hold his Office during the Term of four Years, and, together with the Vice President, chosen for the same Term, be elected, as follows:

Each State shall appoint, in such Manner as the Legislature thereof may direct, a Number of Electors, equal to the whole Number of Senators and Representatives to which the State may be entitled in the Congress: but no Senator or Representative, or Person holding an Office of Trust or Profit under the United States, shall be appointed an Elector.

The Electors shall meet in their respective States, and vote by Ballot for two Persons, of whom one at least shall not be an Inhabitant of the same State with themselves. And they shall make a List of all the Persons voted for, and of the Number of Votes for each; which List they shall sign and certify, and transmit sealed to the Seat of the Government of the United States, directed to the President of the Senate. The President of the Senate shall, in the Presence of the Senate and House of Representatives, open all the Certificates, and the Votes shall then be counted. The Person having the greatest Number of Votes shall be the President, if such Number be a Majority of the whole Number of Electors appointed; and if there be more than one who have such Majority, and have an equal Number of Votes, then the House of Representatives shall immediately chuse by Ballot one of them for President; and if no Person have a Majority, then from the five highest on the List the said House shall in like Manner chuse the President. But in chusing the President, the Votes shall be taken by States, the Representation from each State having one Vote; A quorum for this Purpose shall consist of a Member or Members from two thirds of the States, and a Majority of all the States shall be necessary to a Choice. In every Case, after the Choice of the President, the Person having the greatest Number of Votes of the Electors shall be the Vice President. But if there should remain two or more who have equal Votes, the Senate shall chuse from them by Ballot the Vice President.

The Congress may determine the Time of chusing the Electors, and the Day on which they shall give their Votes; which Day shall be the same throughout the United States.

No person except a natural born Citizen, or a Citizen of the United States, at the time of the Adoption of this Constitution, shall be eligible to the Office of President; neither shall any person be eligible to that Office who shall not have attained to the Age of thirty five Years, and been fourteen Years a Resident within the United States.

In Case of the Removal of the President from Office, or of his Death, Resignation, or Inability to discharge the Powers and Duties of the said Office, the same shall devolve on the Vice President, and the Congress may be Law provide for the Case of Removal, Death, Resignation or Inability, both of the President and Vice President, declaring what Officer shall then act as President, and such Officer shall act accordingly, until the Disability be removed, or a President shall be elected.

The President shall, at stated Times, receive for his Services, a Compensation, which shall neither be increased nor diminished during the Period for which he shall have been elected, and he shall not receive within that Period any other Emolument from the United States, or any of them.

Before he enter on the Execution of his Office, he shall take the following Oath or Affirmation: "I do solemnly swear (or affirm) that I will faithfully execute the Office of President of the United States, and will to the best of my Ability, preserve, protect and defend the Constitution of the United States."

Section 2.   The President shall be Commander in Chief of the Army and Navy of the United States, and of the Militia of the several States, when called into the actual Service of the United States; he may require the Opinion, in writing, of the principal Officer in each of the executive Departments, upon any Subject relating to the Duties of their respective Offices, and he shall have Power to grant Reprieves and Pardons for Offenses against the United States, except in Cases of Impeachment.

He shall have Power, by and with the Advice and Consent of the Senate to make Treaties, provided two thirds of the Senators present concur; and he shall nominate, and by and with the Advice and Consent of the Senate, shall appoint Ambassadors, other public Ministers and Consuls, Judges of the Supreme Court, and all other Officers of the United States, whose Appointments are not herein otherwise provided for, and which shall be established by Law: but the Congress may be Law vest the Appointment of such inferior Officers, as they think proper, in the President alone, in the Courts of Law, or in the Heads of Departments.

The President shall have Power to fill up all Vacancies that may happen during the Recess of the Senate, by granting Commissions which shall expire at the End of their next Session.

Section 3.   He shall from time to time give to the Congress Information of the State of the Union, and recommend to their Consideration such Measures as he shall judge necessary and expedient; he may, on extraordinary Occasions, convene both Houses, or either of them, and in Case of Disagreement between them, with Respect to the Time of Adjournment, he may adjourn them to such Time as he shall think proper; he shall receive Ambassadors and other public Ministers; he shall take Care that the Laws be faithfully executed, and shall Commission all the Officers of the United States.

Section 4.   The President, Vice President and all civil Officers of the United States, shall be removed from Office on Impeachment for, and Conviction of, Treason, Bribery, or other high Crimes and Misdemeanors.

Article III

Section 1.   The judicial Power of the United States, shall be vested in one supreme Court, and in such inferior Courts as the Congress may from time to time ordain and establish. The Judges, both of the supreme and inferior Courts, shall hold their Offices during good Behaviour, and shall, at stated Times, receive for their Services, a Compensation, which shall not be diminished during their Continuance in Office.

Section 2.   The judicial Power shall extend to all Cases, in Law and Equity, arising under this Constitution, the Laws of the United States, and Treaties made, or which shall be made, under their Authority;—to all Cases affecting Ambassadors, other public Ministers and Consuls;—to all Cases of admiralty and maritime Jurisdiction;—to Controversies to which the United States shall be a Party;—to Controversies between two or more States;—between a State and Citizens of another State;—between Citizens of different States;—between Citizens of the same State claiming Lands under Grants of different States, and between a State, or the Citizens thereof, and foreign States, Citizens or Subjects.

In all Cases affecting Ambassadors, other public Ministers and Consuls, and those in which a State shall be a Party, the supreme Court shall have original Jurisdiction. In all the other Cases before mentioned, the supreme Court shall have appellate Jurisdiction, both as to Law and Fact, with such Exceptions, and under such Regulations as the Congress shall make.

The Trial of all Crimes, except in Cases of Impeachment, shall be by Jury; and such Trial shall be held in the State where the said Crimes shall have been committed; but when not committed within any State, the Trial shall be at such Place or Places as the Congress may by Law have directed.

Section 3.   Treason against the United States, shall consist only in levying War against them, or in adhering to their Enemies, giving them Aid and Comfort. No Person shall be convicted of Treason unless on the Testimony of two Witnesses to the same overt Act, or on Confession in open Court.

The Congress shall have Power to declare the Punishment of Treason, but no Attainder of Treason shall work Corruption of Blood, or Forfeiture except during the Life of the Person attainted.

Article IV

Section 1.   Full Faith and Credit shall be given in each State to the public Acts, Records, and judicial Proceedings of every other State. And the Congress may by general Laws prescribe the Manner in which such Acts, Records and Proceedings shall be proved, and the Effect thereof.

Section 2.   The Citizens of each State shall be entitled to all Privileges and Immunities of Citizens in the several States.

A Person charged in any State with Treason, Felony, or other Crime, who shall flee from Justice, and be found in another State, shall on Demand of the executive Authority of the State from which he fled, be delivered up, to be removed to the State having Jurisdiction of the Crime.

No Person held to Service or Labour in one State, under the Laws thereof, escaping into another, shall, in Consequence of any Law or Regulation therein, be discharged from such Service or Labour, but shall be delivered up on Claim of the Party to whom such Service or Labour may be due.

Section 3.   New States may be admitted by the Congress into this Union; but no new State shall be formed or erected within the Jurisdiction of any other State; nor any State be formed by the Junction of two or more States, or Parts of States, without the Consent of the Legislatures of the States concerned as well as of the Congress.

The Congress shall have Power to dispose of and make all needful Rules and Regulations respecting the Territory or other Property belonging to the United States; and nothing in this Constitution shall be so construed as to Prejudice any Claims of the United States, or of any particular State.

Section 4.   The United States shall guarantee to every State in this Union a Republican Form of Government, and shall protect each of them against Invasion; and on Application of the Legislature, or of the Executive (when the Legislature cannot be convened) against domestic Violence.

Article V

The Congress, whenever two thirds of both Houses shall deem it necessary, shall propose Amendments to this Constitution, or, on the Application of the Legislatures of two thirds of the several States, shall call a Convention for proposing Amendments, which, in either Case, shall be valid to all Intents and Purposes, as part of this Constitution, when ratified by the Legislatures of three fourths of the several States, or by Conventions in three fourths thereof, as the one or the other Mode of Ratification may be proposed by the Congress; Provided that no Amendment which may be made prior to the Year One thousand eight hundred and eight shall in any Manner affect the first and fourth Clauses in the Ninth Section of the first Article; and that no State, without its Consent, shall be deprived of its equal Suffrage in the Senate.

Article VI

All Debts contracted and Engagements entered into, before the Adoption of this Constitution, shall be as valid against the United States under this Constitution, as under the Confederation.

This Constitution, and the Laws of the United States which shall be made in Pursuance thereof; and all Treaties made, or which shall be made, under the Authority of the United States, shall be the supreme Law of the Land; and the Judges in every State shall be bound thereby, any Thing in the Constitution or Laws of any State to the Contrary notwithstanding.

The Senators and Representatives before mentioned, and the Members of the several State Legislatures, and all executive and judicial Officers, both of the United States and of the several States, shall be bound by Oath or Affirmation, to support this Constitution; but no religious Test shall ever be required as a Qualification to any Office or public Trust under the United States.

Article VII

The Ratification of the Conventions of nine States shall be sufficient for the Establishment of this Constitution between the States so ratifying the same.

Articles in addition to, and amendment of, the Constitution of the United States of America, proposed by Congress, and ratified by the several States, pursuant to the fifth Article of the original Constitution.

Amendment I [1791]

Congress shall make no law respecting an establishment of religion, or prohibiting the free exercise thereof; or abridging the freedom of speech, or of the press; or the right of the people peaceably to assembly, and to petition the Government for a redress of grievances.

Amendment II [1791]

A well regulated Militia, being necessary to the security of a free State, the right of the people to keep and bear Arms, shall not be infringed.

Amendment III [1791]

No Soldier shall, in time of peace be quartered in any house, without the consent of the Owner, nor in time of war, but in a manner to be prescribed by law.

Amendment IV [1791]

The right of the people to be secure in their persons, houses, papers, and effects, against unreasonable searches and seizures, shall not be violated, and no Warrants shall issue, but upon probable cause, supported by Oath or affirmation, and particularly describing the place to be searched, and the persons or things to be seized.

Amendment V [1791]

No person shall be held to answer for a capital, or otherwise infamous crime, unless on a presentment or indictment of a Grand Jury, except in cases arising in the land or naval forces, or in the Militia, when in actual service in time of War or public danger; nor shall any person be subject for the same offence to be twice put in jeopardy of life or limb; nor shall be compelled in any criminal case to be a witness against himself, nor be deprived of life, liberty, or property, without due process of law; nor shall private property be taken for public use, without just compensation.

Amendment VI [1791]

In all criminal prosecutions, the accused shall enjoy the right to a speedy and public trial, by an impartial jury of the State and district wherein the crime shall have been committed, which district shall have been previously ascertained by law, and to be informed of the nature and cause of the accusation; to be confronted with the witnesses against him; to

have compulsory process for obtaining witnesses in his favor, and to have the Assistance of Counsel for his defence.

Amendment VII [1791]

In Suits at common law, where the value in controversy shall exceed twenty dollars, the right of trial by jury shall be preserved, and no fact tried by jury, shall be otherwise re-examined in any Court of the United States, than according to the rules of the common law.

Amendment VIII [1791]

Excessive bail shall not be required, nor excessive fines imposed, nor cruel and unusual punishments inflicted.

Amendment IX [1791]

The enumeration in the Constitution, of certain rights, shall not be construed to deny or disparage others retained by the people.

Amendment X [1791]

The powers not delegated to the United States by the Constitution, nor prohibited by it to the States, are reserved to the States respectively, or to the people.

Amendment XI [1798]

The Judicial power of the United States shall not be construed to extend to any suit in law or equity, commenced or prosecuted against one of the United States by Citizens of another State, or by Citizens or Subjects of any Foreign State.

Amendment XII [1804]

The Electors shall meet in their respective states and vote by ballot for President and Vice-President, one of whom, at least, shall not be an inhabitant of the same state with themselves; they shall name in their ballots the person voted for as President, and in distinct ballots the person voted for as Vice-President, and they shall make distinct lists of all persons voted for as President, and of all persons voted for as Vice-President, and of the number of votes for each, which lists they shall sign and certify, and transmit sealed to the seat of the government of the United States, directed to the President of the Senate; — The President of the Senate shall, in the presence of the Senate and House of Representatives, open all the certificates and the votes shall then be counted; — The person having the greatest Number of votes for President, shall be the President, if such number be a majority of the whole number of Electors appointed; and if no person have such majority, then from the persons having the highest numbers not exceeding three on the list of those voted for as President, the House of Representatives shall choose immediately, by ballot, the President. But in choosing the President, the votes shall be taken by states, the representation from each state having one vote; a quorum for this purpose shall consist of a member or members from two-thirds of the states, and a majority of all states shall be necessary to a choice. And if the House of Representatives shall not choose a President whenever the right of choice shall devolve upon them, before the fourth day of March next following, then the Vice-President shall act as President, as in the case of the death or other constitutional disability of the President — The person having the greatest number of votes as Vice-President, shall be the Vice-President, if such number be a majority of the whole number of Electors appointed, and if no person have a majority, then from the two highest numbers on the list, the Senate shall choose the Vice-President; a quorum for the purpose shall consist of two-thirds of the whole number of Senators, and a majority of the whole number shall be necessary to a choice. But no person constitutionally ineligible to the office of President shall be eligible to that of Vice-President of the United States.

Amendment XIII [1865]

Section 1.   Neither slavery nor involuntary servitude, except as a punishment for crime whereof the party shall have been duly convicted, shall exist within the United States, or any place subject to their jurisdiction.

Section 2.   Congress shall have power to enforce this article by appropriate legislation.

Amendment XIV [1868]

Section 1.   All persons born or naturalized in the United States and subject to the jurisdiction thereof, are citizens of the United States and of the State wherein they reside. No State shall make or enforce any law which shall abridge the privileges or immunities of citizens of the United States; nor shall any State deprive any person of life, liberty, or property, without due process of law; nor deny to any person within its jurisdiction the equal protection of the laws.

Section 2.   Representatives shall be apportioned among the several States according to their respective numbers, counting the whole number of persons in each State, excluding Indians not taxed. But when the right to vote at any election for the choice of electors for President and Vice President of the United States, Representatives in Congress, the Executive and Judicial officers of a State, or the members of the Legislature thereof, is denied to any of the male inhabitants of such State, being twenty-one years of age, and citizens of the United States, or in any way abridged, except for participation in rebellion, or other crime, the basis of representation therein shall be reduced in the proportion which the number of such male citizens shall bear to the whole number of male citizens twenty-one years of age in such State.

Section 3.   No person shall be a Senator or Representative in Congress, or elector of President and Vice President, or hold any office, civil or military, under the United States, or under any State, who, having previously taken an oath, as a member of Congress, or as an officer of the United States, or as a member of any State legislature, or as an executive or judicial officer of any State, to support the Constitution of the United States, shall have engaged in insurrection or rebellion against the same, or given aid or comfort to the enemies thereof. But Congress may by a vote of two-thirds of each House, remove such disability.

Section 4.   The validity of the public debt of the United States, authorized by law, including debts incurred for payment of pensions and bounties for services in suppressing insurrection or rebellion, shall not be questioned. But neither the United States nor any State shall assume or pay any debt or obligation incurred in aid of insurrection or rebellion against the United States, or any claim for the loss or emancipation of any slave; but all such debts, obligations and claims shall be held illegal and void.

Section 5.   The Congress shall have power to enforce, by appropriate legislation, the provisions of this article.

Amendment XV [1870]

Section 1. The right of citizens of the United States to vote shall not be denied or abridged by the United States or by any State on account of race, color, or previous condition of servitude.

Section 2. The Congress shall have power to enforce this article by appropriate legislation.

Amendment XVI [1913]

The Congress shall have power to lay and collect taxes on incomes, from whatever source derived, without apportionment among the several States, and without regard to any census or enumeration.

Amendment XVII [1913]

The Senate of the United States shall be composed of two Senators from each State, elected by the people thereof, for six years; and each Senator shall have one vote. The electors in each State shall have the qualifications requisite for electors of the most numerous branch of the State legislatures.

When vacancies happen in the representation of any State in the Senate, the executive authority of such State shall issue writs of election to fill such vacancies: *Provided,* That the legislature of any State may empower the executive thereof to make temporary appointments until the people fill the vacancies by election as the legislature may direct.

This amendment shall not be so construed as to affect the election or term of any Senator chosen before it becomes valid as part of the Constitution.

Amendment XVIII [1919]

Section 1. After one year from the ratification of this article the manufacture, sale, or transportation of intoxicating liquors within, the importation thereof into, or the exportation thereof from the United States and all territory subject to the jurisdiction thereof for beverage purposes is hereby prohibited.

Section 2. The Congress and the several States shall have concurrent power to enforce this article by appropriate legislation.

Section 3. This article shall be inoperative unless it shall have been ratified as an amendment to the Constitution by the legislatures of the several States, as provided in the Constitution, within seven

years from the date of the submission hereof to the States by the Congress.

Amendment XIX [1920]

The right of citizens of the United States to vote shall not be denied or abridged by the United States or by any State on account of sex.

Congress shall have power to enforce this article by appropriate legislation.

Amendment XX [1933]

Section 1. The terms of the President and Vice President shall end at noon on the 20th day of January, and the terms of Senators and Representatives at noon on the 3d day of January, of the years in which such terms would have ended if this article had not been ratified; and the terms of their successors shall then begin.

Section 2. The Congress shall assemble at least once in every year, and such meeting shall begin at noon on the 3d day of January, unless they shall by law appoint a different day.

Section 3. If, at the time fixed for the beginning of the term of the President, the President elect shall have died, the Vice President elect shall become President. If a President shall not have been chosen before the time fixed for the beginning of his term, or if the President elect shall have failed to qualify, then the Vice President elect shall act as President until a President shall have qualified; and the Congress may by law provide for the case wherein neither a President elect nor a Vice President elect shall have qualified, declaring who shall then act as President, or the manner in which one who is to act shall be selected, and such person shall act accordingly until a President or Vice President shall have qualified.

Section 4. The Congress may by law provide for the case of the death of any of the persons from whom the House of Representatives may choose a president whenever the right of choice shall have devolved upon them, and for the case of the death of any of the persons from whom the Senate may choose a Vice President whenever the right of choice shall have devolved upon them.

Section 5. Sections 1 and 2 shall take effect on the 15th day of October following the ratification of this article.

Section 6. This article shall be inoperative unless it shall have been ratified as an amendment to the Constitution by the legislatures of three-fourths of the several States within seven years from the date of its submission.

Amendment XXI [1933]

Section 1.   The eighteenth article of amendment to the Constitution of the United States is hereby repealed.

Section 2.   The transportation or importation into any State, Territory, or possession of the United States for delivery or use therein of intoxicating liquors, in violation of the laws thereof, is hereby prohibited.

Section 3.   This article shall be inoperative unless it shall have been ratified as an amendment to the Constitution by conventions in the several States, as provided in the Constitution, within seven years from the date of the submission hereof to the States by the Congress.

Amendment XXII [1951]

Section 1.   No person shall be elected to the office of the President more than twice, and no person who has held the office of President, or acted as President, for more than two years of a term to which some other person was elected President shall be elected to the office of President more than once. But this Article shall not apply to any person holding the office of President, when this Article was proposed by the Congress, and shall not prevent any person who may be holding the office of President, or acting as President, during the term within which this Article becomes operative from holding the office of President or acting as President during the remainder of such term.

Section 2.   This article shall be inoperative unless it shall have been ratified as an amendment to the Constitution by the legislatures of three-fourths of the several States within seven years from the date of its submission to the States by the Congress.

Amendment XXIII [1961]

Section 1.   The District constituting the seat of Government of the United States shall appoint in such manner as the Congress may direct:

A number of electors of President and Vice President equal to the whole number of Senators and Representatives in Congress to which the District

would be entitled if it were a State, but in no event more than the least populous State; they shall be in addition to those appointed by the States, but they shall be considered, for the purposes of the election of President and Vice President, to be electors appointed by a State; and they shall meet in the District and perform such duties as provided by the twelfth article of amendment.

Section 2.   The Congress shall have power to enforce this article by appropriate legislation.

Amendment XXIV [1964]

Section 1.   The right of citizens of the United States to vote in any primary or other election for President or Vice President, for electors for President or Vice President, or for Senator or Representative in Congress, shall not be denied or abridged by the United States or any State by reason of failure to pay any poll tax or other tax.

Section 2.   The Congress shall have power to enforce this article by appropriate legislation.

Amendment XXV [1967]

Section 1.   In case of the removal of the President from office or of his death or resignation, the Vice President shall become President.

Section 2.   Whenever there is a vacancy in the office of the Vice President, the President shall nominate a Vice President who shall take office upon confirmation by a majority vote of both Houses of Congress.

Section 3.   Whenever the President transmits to the President pro tempore of the Senate and the Speaker of the House of Representatives his written declaration that he is unable to discharge the powers and duties of his office, and until he transmits to them a written declaration to the contrary, such powers and duties shall be discharged by the Vice President as Acting President.

Section 4.   Whenever the Vice President and a majority of either the principal officers of the executive departments or of such other body as Congress may by law provide, transmit to the President pro tempore of the Senate and the Speaker of the House of Representatives their written declaration that the President is unable to discharge the powers and duties of his office, the Vice President shall immediately assume the powers and duties of the office as Acting President.

Thereafter, when the President transmits to the President pro tempore of the Senate and the Speaker of the House of Representatives his written declaration that no inability exists, he shall resume the powers and duties of his office unless the Vice President and a majority of either the principal officers of the executive department or of such other body as Congress may by law provide, transmit within four days to the President pro tempore of the Senate and the Speaker of the House of Representatives their written declaration that the President is unable to discharge the powers and duties of his office. Thereupon Congress shall decide the issue, assembling within forty-eight hours for that purpose if not in session. If the Congress, within twenty-one days after receipt of the latter written declaration, or, if Congress is not in session, within twenty-one days after Congress is required to assemble, determines by two-thirds vote of both Houses that the President is unable to discharge the powers and duties of his office, the Vice President shall continue to discharge the same as Acting President; otherwise, the President shall resume the powers and duties of his office.

Amendment XXVI [1971]

Section 1.   The right of citizens of the United States, who are eighteen years of age or older, to vote shall not be denied or abridged by the United States or by any State on account of age.

Section 2.   The Congress shall have power to enforce this article by appropriate legislation.

Index of Authors

Subject Index